D MAP PAGES

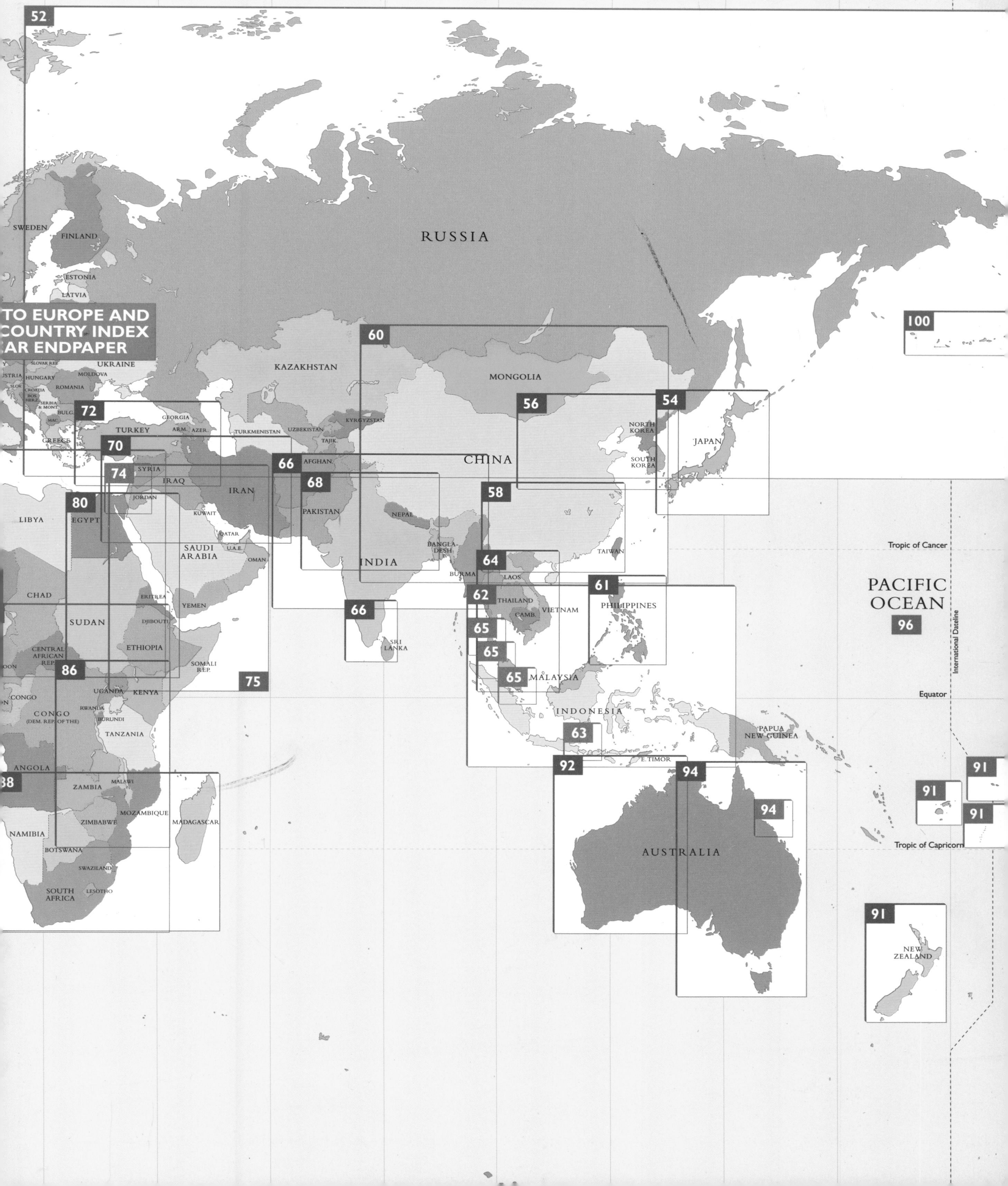

52
SWEDEN
FINLAND
RUSSIA
ESTONIA
LATVIA
TO EUROPE AND
COUNTRY INDEX
AR ENDPAPER
UKRAINE
SLOVAK REP.
MOLDOVA
HUNGARY
ROMANIA
CROATIA
BOS. HERZ.
SERBIA & MONT.
BULG.
MAC.
GREECE
KAZAKHSTAN
MONGOLIA
100
60
56
54
72
GEORGIA
ARM.
AZER.
TURKEY
TURKMENISTAN
UZBEKISTAN
KYRGYZSTAN
TAJIK.
70
NORTH KOREA
SOUTH KOREA
JAPAN
CHINA
74
SYRIA
IRAQ
66
AFGHAN.
68
IRAN
JORDAN
58
80
LIBYA
EGYPT
KUWAIT
PAKISTAN
NEPAL
QATAR
U.A.E.
SAUDI ARABIA
OMAN
BANGLA-DESH
INDIA
TAIWAN
Tropic of Cancer
64
BURMA
LAOS
PACIFIC OCEAN
96
CHAD
ERITREA
YEMEN
62
THAILAND
CAMB.
VIETNAM
61
PHILIPPINES
SUDAN
DJIBOUTI
66
65
SRI LANKA
ETHIOPIA
65
International Dateline
CENTRAL AFRICAN REP.
SOMALI REP.
86
65
MALAYSIA
75
UGANDA
KENYA
CONGO
Equator
RWANDA
CONGO (DEM. REP. OF THE)
BURUNDI
INDONESIA
TANZANIA
63
PAPUA NEW GUINEA
ANGOLA
92
E. TIMOR
94
91
MALAWI
ZAMBIA
91
94
91
MOZAMBIQUE
ZIMBABWE
MADAGASCAR
NAMIBIA
Tropic of Capricorn
BOTSWANA
AUSTRALIA
SWAZILAND
SOUTH AFRICA
LESOTHO
91
NEW ZEALAND

OXFORD

NEW CONCISE
WORLD
ATLAS

OXFORD

NEW CONCISE WORLD ATLAS

THE EARTH IN SPACE
Cartography by Philip's

Text
Keith Lye

Illustrations
Stefan Chabluk

Star Charts
Wil Tirion

PICTURE ACKNOWLEDGEMENTS
Corbis */Ed Eckstein* 42, */Colin Garratt; Milepost 92 1/2* 44, */Wolfgang Kaehler* 21, */Gunter Marx Photography* 45, */Galen Rowell* 46, */Royalty-Free* 31, */Peter Turnley* 35
Corbis Saba */Shepard Sherbell* 40
Corbis Sygma */Thorne Anderson* 47
Akira Fujii/David Malin Images 11
Getty Images/The Image Bank */Peter Hendrie* 20, */Pete Turner* 39
Getty Images/Stone */James Balog* 16, */Simeone Huber* 33, */Gary John Norman* 36, */Frank Oberle* 25 top, */Dennis Oda* 17, */Donovan Reese* 18–19, */Hugh Sitton* 32, */Michael Townsend* 29, */World Perspectives* 10
Robert Harding Picture Library */Bill Ross* 41, */Adam Woolfitt* 43
Images Colour Library Limited 15
NASA */Hubble Heritage Team (STScI/AURA)/R.G. French (Wellesley College)/ J. Cuzzi and J. Lissauer (NASA/Ames Research Center)/L. Dones (SwRI)* 9 bottom left, */JPL* 8 centre left, 8 bottom, 9 centre right, */JPL/Caltech* 9 top, */JPL/Univ. Arizona* 9 centre left, */JPL/USGS* 8 centre right, */A. Stern (SwRI), M. Buie (Lowell Observatory)/ESA* 9 bottom right, */R. Williams (STScI)/the Hubble Deep Field Team* 2
NPA Group, Edenbridge, UK 12, 13, 48
Chris Rayner 19 top
Rex Features */Sipa* 34
Science Photo Library */Martin Bond* 14, */CNES, 1992 Distribution SPOT Image* 27 top, */Luke Dodd* 3, 6, */Earth Satellite Corporation* 25 bottom, */ESA/PLI* 8 top, */Simon Fraser* 38, */NASA* 22, 23, 24, */David Parker* 26, */Peter Ryan* 27 bottom, */Jerry Schad* 4
Still Pictures */François Pierrel* 28
Tony Stone Images */Neil Beer* 30, */Nigel Press* 37

Philip's,
a division of Octopus Publishing Group Limited,
2–4 Heron Quays, London E14 4JP

Cartography by Philip's

Published in North America by
Oxford University Press, Inc.
198 Madison Avenue,
New York, NY 10016

www.oup.com/us

OXFORD UNIVERSITY PRESS Oxford is a registered trademark of Oxford University Press

Library of Congress Cataloging-in-Publication Data
The new concise atlas of the world.
p. cm.
Prev. ed.: Philip's concise world atlas / George Philip & Son. 2000.
Includes index.
ISBN 0-19-521983-X
1. Atlases. 2. World maps. I. George Philip & Son. Philip's atlas of the world. II. Oxford University Press.

G1021.N54 2003
912--dc22

2003057201

ISBN 0–19–521983–X

Printing (last digit): 9 8 7 6 5 4 3 2

Printed in Hong Kong

User Guide

The reference maps which form the main body of this atlas have been prepared in accordance with the highest standards of international cartography to provide an accurate and detailed representation of the Earth. The scales and projections used have been carefully chosen to give balanced coverage of the world, while emphasizing the most densely populated and economically significant regions. A hallmark of Philip's mapping is the use of hill shading and relief coloring to create a graphic impression of landforms: this makes the maps exceptionally easy to read. However, knowledge of the key features employed in the construction and presentation of the maps will enable the reader to derive the fullest benefit from the atlas.

MAP SEQUENCE

The atlas covers the Earth continent by continent: first Europe; then its land neighbor Asia (mapped north before south, in a clockwise sequence), then Africa, Australia and Oceania, North America, and South America. This is the classic arrangement adopted by most cartographers since the 16th century. For each continent, there are maps at a variety of scales. First, physical relief and political maps

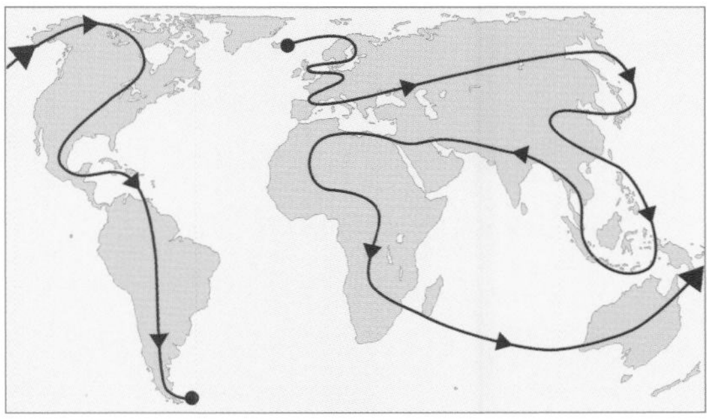

of the whole continent; then a series of larger-scale maps of the regions within the continent, each followed, where required, by still larger-scale maps of the most important or densely populated areas. The governing principle is that by turning the pages of the atlas, the reader moves steadily from north to south through each continent, with each map overlapping its neighbors.

MAP PRESENTATION

With very few exceptions (e.g. for the Arctic and Antarctica), the maps are drawn with north at the top, regardless of whether they are presented upright or sideways on the page. In the borders will be found the map title; a locator diagram showing the area covered; continuation arrows showing the page numbers for maps of adjacent areas; the scale; the projection used; the degrees of latitude and longitude; and the letters and figures used in the index for locating place names and geographical features. Physical relief maps also have a height reference panel identifying the colors used for each layer of contouring.

MAP SYMBOLS

Each map contains a vast amount of detail which can only be conveyed clearly and accurately by the use of symbols. Points and circles of varying sizes locate and identify the relative importance of towns and cities; different styles of type are employed for administrative, geographical and regional place names to aid identification. A variety of pictorial symbols denote landscape features such as glaciers, marshes, and coral reefs, and man-made structures including roads, railroads, airports, canals, and dams. International borders are shown by red lines. Where neighboring countries are in dispute, for example in parts of the Middle East, the maps show the *de facto* boundary between nations, regardless of the legal or historical situation. The symbols are explained on the first page of the *World Maps* section of the atlas.

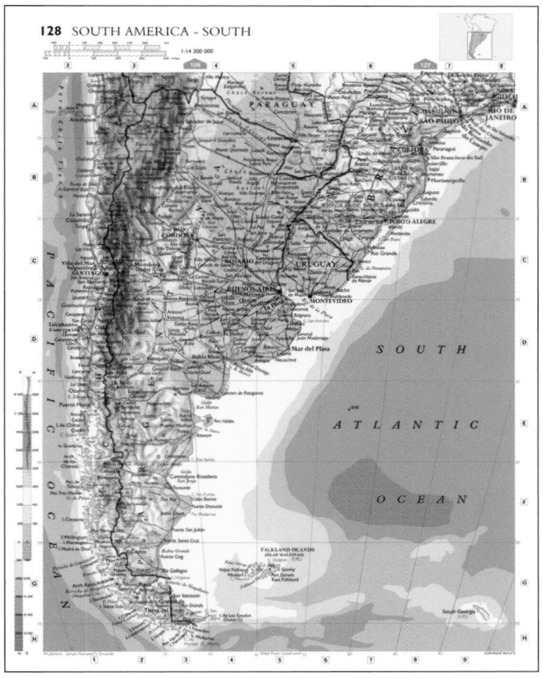

MAP SCALES

1:16 000 000
1 inch = 252 statute miles

The scale of each map is given in the numerical form known as the "representative fraction." The first figure is always one, signifying one unit of distance on the map; the second figure, usually in millions, is the number by which the map unit must be multiplied to give the equivalent distance on the Earth's surface. Calculations can easily be made in centimeters and kilometers, by dividing the Earth units figure by 100 000 (i.e. deleting the last five 0s). Thus 1:1 000 000 means 1 cm = 10 km. The calculation for inches and miles is more laborious, but 1 000 000 divided by 63 360 (the number of inches in a mile) shows that 1:1 000 000 means approximately 1 inch = 16 miles. The table below provides distance equivalents for scales down to 1:50 000 000.

LARGE SCALE		
1:1 000 000	1 cm = 10 km	1 inch = 16 miles
1:2 500 000	1 cm = 25 km	1 inch = 39.5 miles
1:5 000 000	1 cm = 50 km	1 inch = 79 miles
1:6 000 000	1 cm = 60 km	1 inch = 95 miles
1:8 000 000	1 cm = 80 km	1 inch = 126 miles
1:10 000 000	1 cm = 100 km	1 inch = 158 miles
1:15 000 000	1 cm = 150 km	1 inch = 237 miles
1:20 000 000	1 cm = 200 km	1 inch = 316 miles
1:50 000 000	1 cm = 500 km	1 inch = 790 miles
SMALL SCALE		

MEASURING DISTANCES

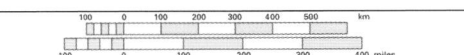

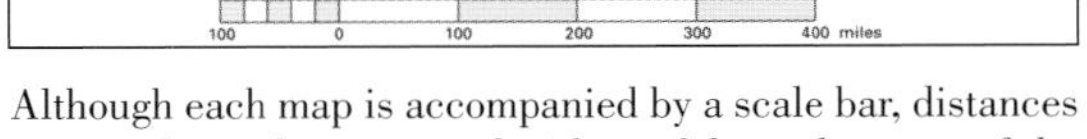

Although each map is accompanied by a scale bar, distances cannot always be measured with confidence because of the distortions involved in portraying the curved surface of the Earth on a flat page. As a general rule, the larger the map scale (i.e. the lower the number of Earth units in the representative fraction), the more accurate and reliable will be the distance measured. On small-scale maps such as those of the world and of entire continents, measurement may only be accurate along the "standard parallels," or central axes, and should not be attempted without considering the map projection.

MAP PROJECTIONS

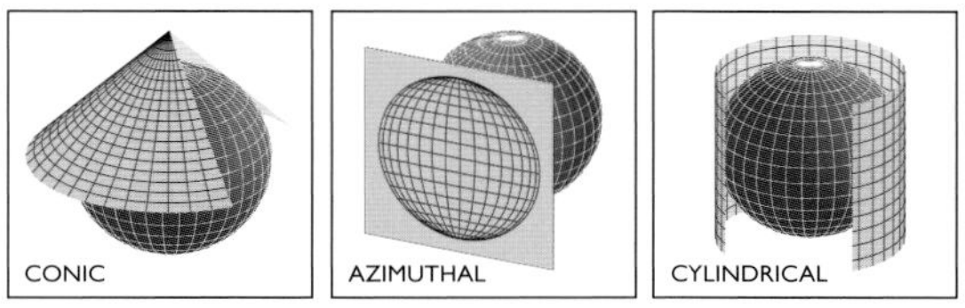

Unlike a globe, no flat map can give a true scale representation of the world in terms of area, shape, and position of every region. Each of the numerous systems that have been devised for projecting the curved surface of the Earth on to a flat page involves the sacrifice of accuracy in one or more of these elements. The variations in shape and position of land masses such as Alaska, Greenland, and Australia, for example, can be quite dramatic when different projections are compared.

For this atlas, the guiding principle has been to select projections that involve the least distortion of size and distance. The projection used for each map is noted in the border. Most fall into one of three categories – conic, azimuthal, or cylindrical – whose basic concepts are shown above. Each involves plotting the forms of the Earth's surface on a grid of latitude and longitude lines, which may be shown as parallels, curves, or radiating spokes.

LATITUDE AND LONGITUDE

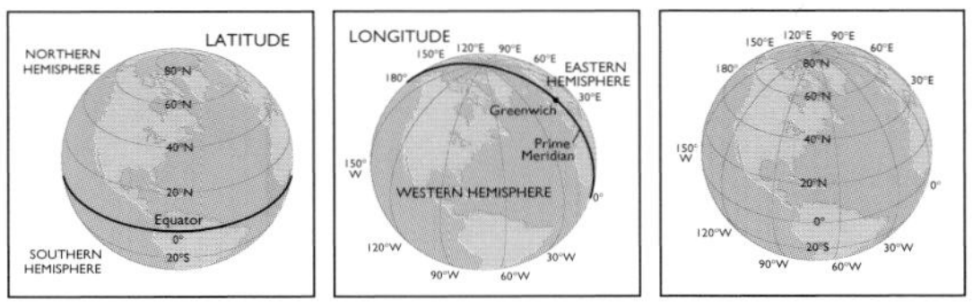

Accurate positioning of individual points on the Earth's surface is made possible by reference to the geometrical system of latitude and longitude. Latitude *parallels* are drawn west–east around the Earth and numbered by degrees north and south of the Equator, which is designated 0° of latitude. Longitude *meridians* are drawn north–south and numbered by degrees east and west of the *prime meridian*, 0° of longitude, which passes through Greenwich in England. By referring to these coordinates and their subdivisions of minutes (1/60th of a degree) and seconds (1/60th of a minute), any place on Earth can be located to within a few hundred yards. Latitude and longitude are indicated by blue lines on the maps; they are straight or curved according to the projection employed. Reference to these lines is the easiest way of determining the relative positions of places on different maps, and for plotting compass directions.

NAME FORMS

For ease of reference, both English and local name forms appear in the atlas. Oceans, seas, and countries are shown in English throughout the atlas; country names may be abbreviated to their commonly accepted form (e.g. Germany, not The Federal Republic of Germany). Conventional English forms are also used for place names on the smaller-scale maps of the continents. However, local name forms are used on all large-scale and regional maps, with the English form given in brackets only for important cities – the large-scale map of Russia and Central Asia thus shows Moskva (Moscow). For countries which do not use a Roman script, place names have been transcribed according to the systems adopted by the British and US Geographic Names Authorities. For China, the Pin Yin system has been used, with some more widely known forms appearing in brackets, as with Beijing (Peking). Both English and local names appear in the index, the English form being cross-referenced to the local form.

Contents

World Statistics

Countries	x
Cities	xi
Climate	xii–xiii
Physical Dimensions	xiv–xv
Regions in the News	xvi

The Earth In Space

The Universe	2–3
Star Charts and Constellations	4–7
The Solar System	8–9
The Earth: Time and Motion	10–11
The Earth from Space	12–13
The Dynamic Earth	14–15
Earthquakes and Volcanoes	16–17
Forces of Nature	18–19
Oceans and Ice	20–21
The Earth's Atmosphere	22–23
Climate and Weather	24–25
Water and Land Use	26–27
The Natural World	28–29
The Human World	30–31
Languages and Religions	32–33
International Organizations	34–35
Agriculture	36–37
Energy and Minerals	38–39
World Economies	40–41
Trade and Commerce	42–43
Travel and Communications	44–45
The World Today	46–47

World Maps

Map Symbols 1

The World: Political
1:71 100 000 **2–3**

Arctic Ocean
1:31 100 000 **4**

Antarctica
1:31 100 000 **5**

Europe

Europe: Physical
1:17 800 000 **6**

Europe: Political
1:17 800 000 **7**

Scandinavia
1:4 400 000
Iceland 1:4 400 000

8–9

Denmark and Southern Sweden
1:2 200 000

10–11

Ireland
1:1 800 000

12

Scotland
1:1 800 000

13

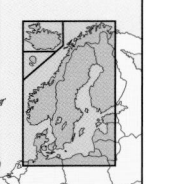

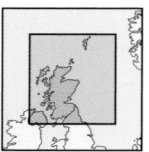

England and Wales
1:1 800 000

14–15

British Isles
1:4 400 000

16

Netherlands, Belgium and Luxembourg
1:2 200 000

17

Northern France
1:2 200 000

18–19

Southern France
1:2 200 000

20–21

Central Europe
1:4 400 000

22–23

Germany
1:2 200 000

24–25

Austria, Czech Republic and Slovak Republic
1:2 200 000

26–27

Hungary, Romania and the Lower Danube
1:2 200 000

28–29

Poland and the Southern Baltic
1:2 200 000

30–31

Baltic States, Belarus and Ukraine
1:4 400 000

32–33

The Volga Basin and the Caucasus
1:4 400 000

34–35

Western Spain and Portugal
1:2 200 000

36–37

Eastern Spain
1:2 200 000

38–39

Northern Italy, Slovenia and Croatia
1:2 200 000

40–41

Southern Italy
1:2 200 000

42–43

Serbia and Montenegro, Bulgaria and Northern Greece
1:2 200 000

44–45

Southern Greece and Western Turkey
1:2 200 000

46–47

The Balearics, the Canaries and Madeira
1:900 000 / 1:1 800 000

48

Malta, Crete, Corfu, Rhodes and Cyprus
1:900 000 / 1:1 200 000

49

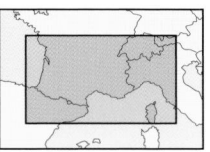

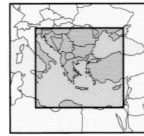

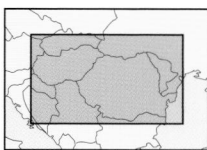

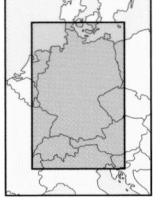

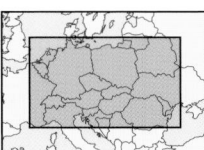

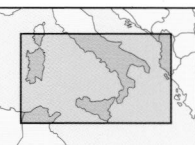

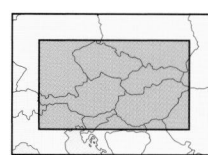

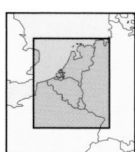

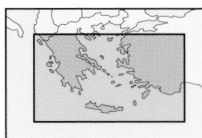

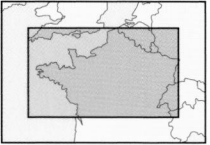

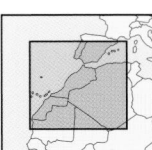

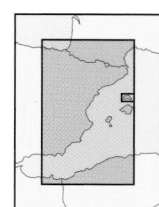

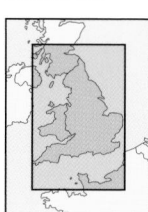

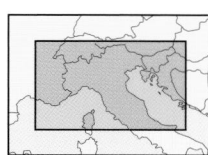

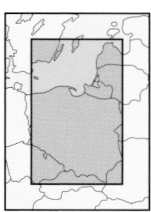

Asia

Asia: Physical 50
1:44 400 000

Asia: Political 51
1:44 400 000

Russia and Central Asia 52–53
1:17 800 000

Japan 54–55
1:4 400 000

Northern China and Korea 56–57
1:5 300 000

Southern China 58–59
1:5 300 000

China 60
1:17 800 000

The Philippines 61
1:6 700 000

Indonesia and the Philippines 62–63
1:11 100 000
Java and Madura 1:6 700 000
Bali 1:1 800 000

Mainland South-east Asia 64–65
1:5 300 000
Ko Phuket 1:900 000
Ko Samui 1:900 000
Pinang 1:900 000
Singapore 1:900 000

South Asia 66–67
1:8 900 000

Northern India and Nepal 68–69
1:5 300 000
Jammu and Kashmir 1:5 300 000

The Middle East 70–71
1:6 200 000

Turkey and Transcaucasia 72–73
1:4 400 000

The Near East 74
1:2 200 000

Arabia and the Horn of Africa 75
1:13 300 000

Africa

Africa: Physical 76
1:37 300 000

Africa: Political 77
1: 37 300 000

Northern Africa 78–79
1:13 300 000

The Nile Valley 80–81
1:7 100 000
The Nile Delta 1:3 600 000

West Africa 82–83
1:7 100 000

Central and Southern Africa 84–85
1:13 300 000

East Africa 86–87
1:7 100 000

Southern Africa 88–89
1:7 100 000
Madagascar 1:7 100 000

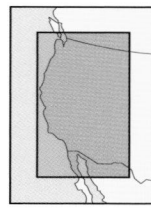

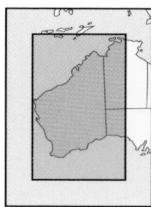

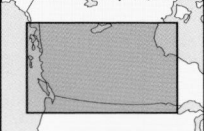

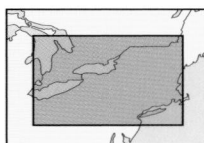

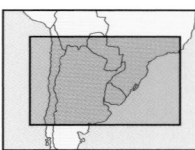

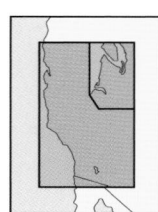

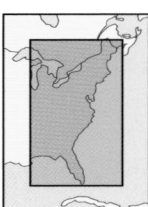

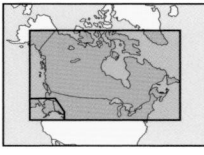

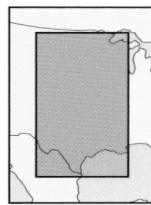

Australia and Oceania

Australia and Oceania: Physical and Political
1:44 400 000 — **90**

New Zealand
1:5 300 000
Samoan Islands 1:10 700 000
Fiji and Tonga 1:10 700 000

91

Western Australia
1:7 100 000

92–93

Eastern Australia
1:7 100 000
Whitsunday Islands 1:2 200 000

94–95

Pacific Ocean
1:48 000 000 — **96–97**

North America

North America: Physical
1:31 100 000 — **98**

North America: Political
1:31 100 000 — **99**

Canada
1:13 300 000
Alaska 1:26 700 000

100–101

Western Canada
1:6 200 000

102–103

Eastern Canada
1:6 200 000

104–105

United States
1:10 700 000
Hawaii 1:8 900 000

106–107

Western United States
1:5 300 000

108–109

Central and Southern California and Western Washington
1:2 200 000

110–111

Middle United States
1:5 300 000

112–113

Eastern United States
1:5 300 000

114–115

Northeastern United States
1:2 200 000

116–117

Mexico
1:7 100 000

118–119

Central America and the West Indies
1:7 100 000
Jamaica 1:2 700 000
Guadeloupe 1:1 800 000
Martinique 1:1 800 000
Puerto Rico 1:2 700 000
Virgin Islands 1:1 800 000
St Lucia 1:890 000
Barbados 1:890 000

120–121

South America

South America: Physical
1:31 100 000 — **122**

South America: Political
1:31 100 000 — **123**

South America – North
1:14 200 000
Trinidad and Tobago 1:2 200 000

124–125

Central South America
1:7 100 000

126–127

South America – South
1:14 200 000

128

Index to World Maps

129–224

World Statistics: Countries

This alphabetical list includes the principal countries and territories of the world. If a territory is not completely independent, the country it is associated with is named. The area figures give the total area of land, inland water, and ice. The population figures are 2003 estimates where available. The annual income is the Gross Domestic Product per capita† in US dollars. The figures are the latest available, usually 2002 estimates.

Country/Territory	Area km^2 Thousands	Area miles^2 Thousands	Population Thousands	Capital	Annual Income US $
Afghanistan	652	252	28,717	Kabul	700
Albania	28.7	11.1	3,582	Tirana	4,400
Algeria	2,382	920	32,819	Algiers	5,400
American Samoa (US)	0.20	0.08	70	Pago Pago	8,000
Andorra	0.47	0.18	69	Andorra La Vella	19,000
Angola	1,247	481	10,766	Luanda	1,700
Anguilla (UK)	0.10	0.04	13	The Valley	8,600
Antigua & Barbuda	0.44	0.17	68	St John's	11,000
Argentina	2,780	1,074	38,741	Buenos Aires	10,500
Armenia	29.8	11.5	3,326	Yerevan	3,600
Aruba (Netherlands)	0.19	0.07	71	Oranjestad	28,000
Australia	7,741	2,989	19,732	Canberra	26,900
Austria	83.9	32.4	8,188	Vienna	27,900
Azerbaijan	86.6	33.4	7,831	Baku	3,700
Azores (Portugal)	2.2	0.86	236	Ponta Delgada	15,000
Bahamas	13.9	5.4	297	Nassau	15,300
Bahrain	0.69	0.27	667	Manama	15,100
Bangladesh	144	55.6	138,448	Dhaka	1,800
Barbados	0.43	0.17	277	Bridgetown	15,000
Belarus	208	80.2	10,322	Minsk	8,700
Belgium	30.5	11.8	10,289	Brussels	29,200
Belize	23.0	8.9	266	Belmopan	4,900
Benin	113	43.5	7,041	Porto-Novo	1,100
Bermuda (UK)	0.05	0.02	64	Hamilton	35,200
Bhutan	47.0	18.1	2,140	Thimphu	1,300
Bolivia	1,099	424	8,586	La Paz/Sucre	2,500
Bosnia-Herzegovina	51.2	19.8	3,989	Sarajevo	1,900
Botswana	582	225	1,573	Gaborone	8,500
Brazil	8,514	3,287	182,033	Brasília	7,600
Brunei	5.8	2.2	358	Bandar Seri Begawan	18,600
Bulgaria	111	42.8	7,538	Sofia	6,500
Burkina Faso	274	106	13,228	Ouagadougou	1,100
Burma (= Myanmar)	677	261	42,511	Rangoon	1,700
Burundi	27.8	10.7	6,096	Bujumbura	500
Cambodia	181	69.9	13,125	Phnom Penh	1,600
Cameroon	475	184	15,746	Yaoundé	1,700
Canada	9,971	3,850	32,207	Ottawa	29,300
Canary Is. (Spain)	7.2	2.8	1,682	Las Palmas/Santa Cruz	19,900
Cape Verde Is.	4.0	1.6	412	Praia	1,400
Cayman Is. (UK)	0.26	0.10	42	George Town	35,000
Central African Republic	623	241	3,684	Bangui	1,200
Chad	1,284	496	9,253	Ndjaména	1,000
Chile	757	292	15,665	Santiago	10,100
China	9,597	3,705	1,286,975	Beijing	4,700
Colombia	1,139	440	41,662	Bogotá	6,100
Comoros	2.2	0.86	633	Moroni	700
Congo	342	132	2,954	Brazzaville	900
Congo (Dem. Rep. of the)	2,345	905	56,625	Kinshasa	600
Cook Is. (NZ)	0.24	0.09	21	Avarua	5,000
Costa Rica	51.1	19.7	3,896	San José	8,300
Croatia	56.5	21.8	4,422	Zagreb	9,800
Cuba	111	42.8	11,263	Havana	2,700
Cyprus	9.3	3.6	772	Nicosia	13,200
Czech Republic	78.9	30.5	10,249	Prague	15,300
Denmark	43.1	16.6	5,384	Copenhagen	28,900
Djibouti	23.2	9.0	457	Djibouti	1,300
Dominica	0.75	0.29	70	Roseau	5,400
Dominican Republic	48.5	18.7	8,716	Santo Domingo	6,300
East Timor	14.9	5.7	998	Dili	500
Ecuador	284	109	13,710	Quito	3,200
Egypt	1,001	387	74,719	Cairo	4,000
El Salvador	21.0	8.1	6,470	San Salvador	4,600
Equatorial Guinea	28.1	10.8	510	Malabo	2,700
Eritrea	118	45.4	4,362	Asmara	700
Estonia	45.1	17.4	1,409	Tallinn	11,000
Ethiopia	1,104	426	66,558	Addis Ababa	700
Faroe Is. (Denmark)	1.4	0.54	46	Tórshavn	22,000
Fiji	18.3	7.1	869	Suva	5,600
Finland	338	131	5,191	Helsinki	25,800
France	552	213	60,181	Paris	26,000
French Guiana (France)	90.0	34.7	187	Cayenne	14,400
French Polynesia (France)	4.0	1.5	262	Papeete	5,000
Gabon	268	103	1,322	Libreville	6,500
Gambia, The	11.3	4.4	1,501	Banjul	1,800
Gaza Strip (OPT)*	0.36	0.14	1,275	–	600
Georgia	69.7	26.9	4,934	Tbilisi	3,200
Germany	357	138	82,398	Berlin	26,200
Ghana	239	92.1	20,468	Accra	2,000
Gibraltar (UK)	0.006	0.002	28	Gibraltar Town	17,500
Greece	132	50.9	10,666	Athens	19,100
Greenland (Denmark)	2,176	840	56	Nuuk (Godthåb)	20,000
Grenada	0.34	0.13	89	St George's	5,000
Guadeloupe (France)	1.7	0.66	440	Basse-Terre	9,000
Guam (US)	0.55	0.21	164	Agana	21,000
Guatemala	109	42.0	13,909	Guatemala City	3,900
Guinea	246	94.9	9,030	Conakry	2,100
Guinea-Bissau	36.1	13.9	1,361	Bissau	700
Guyana	215	83.0	702	Georgetown	3,800
Haiti	27.8	10.7	7,528	Port-au-Prince	1,400
Honduras	112	43.3	6,670	Tegucigalpa	2,500
Hong Kong (China)	1.1	0.42	7,394	–	27,200
Hungary	93.0	35.9	10,045	Budapest	13,300
Iceland	103	39.8	281	Reykjavik	30,200
India	3,287	1,269	1,049,700	New Delhi	2,600
Indonesia	1,905	735	234,893	Jakarta	3,100
Iran	1,648	636	68,279	Tehran	6,800
Iraq	438	169	24,683	Baghdad	2,400
Ireland	70.3	27.1	3,924	Dublin	29,300
Israel	20.6	8.0	6,117	Jerusalem	19,500
Italy	301	116	57,998	Rome	25,100
Ivory Coast (= Côte d'Ivoire)	322	125	16,962	Yamoussoukro	1,400
Jamaica	11.0	4.2	2,696	Kingston	3,800
Japan	378	146	127,214	Tokyo	28,700
Jordan	89.3	34.5	5,460	Amman	4,300
Kazakhstan	2,725	1,052	16,764	Astana	7,200
Kenya	580	224	31,639	Nairobi	1,100
Kiribati	0.73	0.28	99	Tarawa	800
Korea, North	121	46.5	22,466	Pyŏngyang	1,000
Korea, South	99.3	38.3	48,289	Seoul	19,600
Kuwait	17.8	6.9	2,183	Kuwait City	17,500
Kyrgyzstan	200	77.2	4,893	Bishkek	2,900
Laos	237	91.4	5,922	Vientiane	1,800
Latvia	64.6	24.9	2,349	Riga	8,900

*OPT = Occupied Palestinian Territory N/A = Not available

Country/Territory	Area km^2 Thousands	Area miles^2 Thousands	Population Thousands	Capital	Annual Income US $
Lebanon	10.4	4.0	3,728	Beirut	4,800
Lesotho	30.4	11.7	1,862	Maseru	2,700
Liberia	111	43.0	3,317	Monrovia	1,000
Libya	1,760	679	5,499	Tripoli	6,200
Liechtenstein	0.16	0.06	33	Vaduz	25,000
Lithuania	65.2	25.2	3,593	Vilnius	8,400
Luxembourg	2.6	1.0	454	Luxembourg	48,900
Macau (China)	0.02	0.007	470	–	18,500
Macedonia (FYROM)	25.7	9.9	2,063	Skopje	5,100
Madagascar	587	227	16,980	Antananarivo	800
Madeira (Portugal)	0.78	0.30	241	Funchal	22,700
Malawi	118	45.7	11,651	Lilongwe	600
Malaysia	330	127	23,093	Kuala Lumpur/Putrajaya	8,800
Maldives	0.30	0.12	330	Malé	3,900
Mali	1,240	479	11,626	Bamako	900
Malta	0.32	0.12	400	Valletta	17,200
Marshall Is.	0.18	0.07	56	Majuro	1,600
Martinique (France)	1.1	0.43	426	Fort-de-France	10,700
Mauritania	1,026	396	2,913	Nouakchott	1,700
Mauritius	2.0	0.79	1,210	Port Louis	10,100
Mayotte (France)	0.37	0.14	178	Mamoundzou	600
Mexico	1,958	756	104,908	Mexico City	8,900
Micronesia, Fed. States of	0.70	0.27	108	Palikir	2,000
Moldova	33.9	13.1	4,440	Chişinău	2,600
Monaco	0.001	0.0004	32	Monaco	27,000
Mongolia	1,567	605	2,712	Ulan Bator	1,900
Montserrat (UK)	0.10	0.04	9	Plymouth	3,400
Morocco	447	172	31,689	Rabat	3,900
Mozambique	802	309	17,479	Maputo	1,100
Namibia	824	318	1,927	Windhoek	6,900
Nauru	0.02	0.008	13	Yaren District	5,000
Nepal	147	56.8	26,470	Katmandu	1,400
Netherlands	41.5	16.0	16,151	Amsterdam/The Hague	27,200
Netherlands Antilles (Neths)	0.80	0.31	216	Willemstad	11,400
New Caledonia (France)	18.6	7.2	211	Nouméa	14,000
New Zealand	271	104	3,951	Wellington	20,100
Nicaragua	130	50.2	5,129	Managua	2,200
Niger	1,267	489	11,059	Niamey	800
Nigeria	924	357	133,882	Abuja	900
Northern Mariana Is. (US)	0.46	0.18	80	Saipan	12,500
Norway	324	125	4,546	Oslo	33,000
Oman	310	119	2,807	Muscat	8,300
Pakistan	796	307	150,695	Islamabad	2,000
Palau	0.46	0.18	20	Koror	9,000
Panama	75.5	29.2	2,961	Panamá	6,200
Papua New Guinea	463	179	5,296	Port Moresby	2,100
Paraguay	407	157	6,037	Asunción	4,300
Peru	1,285	496	28,410	Lima	5,000
Philippines	300	116	84,620	Manila	4,600
Poland	323	125	38,623	Warsaw	9,700
Portugal	88.8	34.3	10,102	Lisbon	19,400
Puerto Rico (US)	8.9	3.4	3,886	San Juan	11,100
Qatar	11.0	4.2	817	Doha	20,100
Réunion (France)	2.5	0.97	755	St-Denis	5,600
Romania	238	92.0	22,272	Bucharest	7,600
Russia	17,075	6,593	144,526	Moscow	9,700
Rwanda	26.3	10.2	7,810	Kigali	1,200
St Kitts & Nevis	0.26	0.10	39	Basseterre	8,800
St Lucia	0.54	0.21	162	Castries	5,400
St Vincent & Grenadines	0.39	0.15	117	Kingstown	2,900
Samoa	2.8	1.1	178	Apia	5,600
San Marino	0.06	0.02	28	San Marino	34,600
São Tomé & Príncipe	0.96	0.37	176	São Tomé	1,200
Saudi Arabia	2,150	830	24,294	Riyadh	11,400
Senegal	197	76.0	10,580	Dakar	1,500
Serbia & Montenegro	102	39.4	10,656	Belgrade	2,200
Seychelles	0.46	0.18	80	Victoria	7,800
Sierra Leone	71.7	27.7	5,733	Freetown	500
Singapore	0.68	0.26	4,609	Singapore	25,200
Slovak Republic	49.0	18.9	5,430	Bratislava	12,400
Slovenia	20.3	7.8	1,936	Ljubljana	19,200
Solomon Is.	28.9	11.2	509	Honiara	1,700
Somalia	638	246	8,025	Mogadishu	600
South Africa	1,221	471	42,769	C. Town/Pretoria/Bloem.	10,000
Spain	498	192	40,217	Madrid	21,200
Sri Lanka	65.6	25.3	19,742	Colombo	3,700
Sudan	2,506	967	38,114	Khartoum	1,400
Suriname	163	63.0	435	Paramaribo	3,400
Swaziland	17.4	6.7	1,161	Mbabane	4,800
Sweden	450	174	8,878	Stockholm	26,000
Switzerland	41.3	15.9	7,319	Bern	32,000
Syria	185	71.5	17,586	Damascus	3,700
Taiwan	36.0	13.9	22,603	Taipei	18,000
Tajikistan	143	55.3	6,864	Dushanbe	1,300
Tanzania	945	365	35,922	Dodoma	600
Thailand	513	198	64,265	Bangkok	7,000
Togo	56.8	21.9	5,429	Lomé	1,400
Tonga	0.65	0.25	108	Nuku'alofa	2,200
Trinidad & Tobago	5.1	2.0	1,104	Port of Spain	10,000
Tunisia	164	63.2	9,925	Tunis	6,800
Turkey	775	299	68,109	Ankara	7,300
Turkmenistan	488	188	4,776	Ashkhabad	6,700
Turks & Caicos Is. (UK)	0.43	0.17	19	Cockburn Town	9,600
Tuvalu	0.03	0.01	11	Fongafale	1,100
Uganda	241	93.1	25,633	Kampala	1,200
Ukraine	604	233	48,055	Kiev	4,500
United Arab Emirates	83.6	32.3	2,485	Abu Dhabi	22,100
United Kingdom	242	93.4	60,095	London	25,500
United States of America	9,629	3,718	290,343	Washington, DC	36,300
Uruguay	175	67.6	3,413	Montevideo	7,900
Uzbekistan	447	173	25,982	Tashkent	2,600
Vanuatu	12.2	4.7	199	Port-Vila	2,900
Vatican City	0.0004	0.0002	1	Vatican City	N/A
Venezuela	912	352	24,655	Caracas	5,400
Vietnam	332	128	81,625	Hanoi	2,300
Virgin Is. (UK)	0.15	0.06	22	Road Town	16,000
Virgin Is. (US)	0.35	0.13	125	Charlotte Amalie	19,000
Wallis & Futuna Is. (France)	0.20	0.08	16	Mata-Utu	2,000
West Bank (OPT)*	5.9	2.3	2,237	–	800
Western Sahara	266	103	262	El Aaiún	N/A
Yemen	528	204	19,350	Sana	800
Zambia	753	291	10,307	Lusaka	800
Zimbabwe	391	151	12,577	Harare	2,100

† Gross Domestic Product per capita has been measured using the purchasing power parity method. This enables comparisons to be made between countries through their purchasing power (in US dollars), showing real price levels of goods and services rather than using currency exchange rates.

World Statistics: Cities

This list shows the principal cities with more than 500,000 inhabitants (only cities with more than 1 million inhabitants are included for Brazil, China, India, Indonesia, Japan, and Russia). The figures are taken from the most recent census or estimate available, and as far as possible are the population of the metropolitan area, e.g. greater New York, Mexico, or Paris. All the figures are in thousands. Local name forms have been used for the smaller cities (e.g. Kraków).

AFGHANISTAN	
Kabul	1,565
ALGERIA	
Algiers	1,722
Oran	664
ANGOLA	
Luanda	2,250
ARGENTINA	
Buenos Aires	10,990
Córdoba	1,198
Rosario	1,096
Mendoza	775
La Plata	640
San Miguel de Tucumán	622
Mar del Plata	520
ARMENIA	
Yerevan	1,256
AUSTRALIA	
Sydney	4,041
Melbourne	3,417
Brisbane	1,601
Perth	1,364
Adelaide	1,093
AUSTRIA	
Vienna	1,560
AZERBAIJAN	
Baku	1,713
BANGLADESH	
Dhaka	7,832
Chittagong	2,041
Khulna	877
Rajshahi	517
BELARUS	
Minsk	1,717
Homyel	502
BELGIUM	
Brussels	948
BENIN	
Cotonou	537
BOLIVIA	
La Paz	1,126
Santa Cruz	767
BOSNIA-HERZEGOVINA	
Sarajevo	526
BRAZIL	
São Paulo	10,434
Rio de Janeiro	5,858
Salvador	2,443
Belo Horizonte	2,239
Fortaleza	2,141
Brasília	2,051
Curitiba	1,587
Recife	1,423
Manaus	1,406
Pôrto Alegre	1,361
Belém	1,281
Goiânia	1,093
Guarulhos	1,073
BULGARIA	
Sofia	1,139
BURKINA FASO	
Ouagadougou	690
BURMA (MYANMAR)	
Rangoon	2,513
Mandalay	533
CAMBODIA	
Phnom Penh	570
CAMEROON	
Douala	1,200
Yaoundé	800
CANADA	
Toronto	4,881
Montréal	3,511
Vancouver	2,079
Ottawa–Hull	1,107
Calgary	972
Edmonton	957
Québec	693
Winnipeg	685
Hamilton	681
CENTRAL AFRICAN REPUBLIC	
Bangui	553
CHAD	
Ndjaména	530
CHILE	
Santiago	4,691
CHINA	
Shanghai	15,082
Beijing	12,362
Tianjin	10,687
Hong Kong (SAR)*	6,502
Chongqing	3,870
Shenyang	3,762
Wuhan	3,520
Guangzhou	3,114
Harbin	2,505
Nanjing	2,211
Xi'an	2,115
Chengdu	1,933
Dalian	1,855
Changchun	1,810
Jinan	1,660
Taiyuan	1,642
Qingdao	1,584
Zibo	1,346
Zhengzhou	1,324
Lanzhou	1,296
Anshan	1,252
Fushun	1,246
Kunming	1,242
Changsha	1,198
Hangzhou	1,185
Nanchang	1,169
Shijiazhuang	1,159
Guiyang	1,131
Ürümqi	1,130
Jilin	1,118
Tangshan	1,110
Qiqihar	1,104
Baotou	1,033
COLOMBIA	
Bogotá	6,005
Cali	1,986
Medellín	1,971
Barranquilla	1,158
Cartagena	813
Cúcuta	589
Bucaramanga	508
CONGO	
Brazzaville	938
Pointe-Noire	576
CONGO (DEM. REP.)	
Kinshasa	2,664
Lubumbashi	565
CROATIA	
Zagreb	868
CUBA	
Havana	2,204
CZECH REPUBLIC	
Prague	1,203
DENMARK	
Copenhagen	1,362
DOMINICAN REPUBLIC	
Santo Domingo	2,135
Stgo. de los Caballeros	691
ECUADOR	
Guayaquil	2,070
Quito	1,574
EGYPT	
Cairo	6,800
Alexandria	3,339
El Gîza	2,222
Shubra el Kheima	871
EL SALVADOR	
San Salvador	1,522
ETHIOPIA	
Addis Ababa	2,316
FINLAND	
Helsinki	532
FRANCE	
Paris	11,175
Lyons	1,648
Marseilles	1,516
Lille	1,143
Toulouse	965
Nice	933
Bordeaux	925
Nantes	711
Strasbourg	612
Toulon	565
Douai	553
Rennes	521
Rouen	518
Grenoble	515
GEORGIA	
Tbilisi	1,253
GERMANY	
Berlin	3,426
Hamburg	1,705
Munich	1,206
Cologne	964
Frankfurt	644
Essen	609
Dortmund	595
Stuttgart	585
Düsseldorf	571
Bremen	547
Duisburg	529
Hanover	521
GHANA	
Accra	1,781
GREECE	
Athens	3,097
GUATEMALA	
Guatemala	1,167
GUINEA	
Conakry	1,508
HAITI	
Port-au-Prince	885
HONDURAS	
Tegucigalpa	814
HUNGARY	
Budapest	1,885
INDIA	
Mumbai (Bombay)	16,368
Kolkata (Calcutta)	13,217
Delhi	12,791
Chennai (Madras)	6,425
Bangalore	5,687
Hyderabad	5,534
Ahmadabad	4,519
Pune	3,756
Surat	2,811
Kanpur	2,690
Jaipur	2,324
Lucknow	2,267
Nagpur	2,123
Patna	1,707
Indore	1,639
Vadodara	1,492
Bhopal	1,455
Coimbatore	1,446
Ludhiana	1,395
Cochin	1,355
Vishakhapatnam	1,329
Agra	1,321
Varanasi	1,212
Madurai	1,195
Meerut	1,167
Nasik	1,152
Jabalpur	1,117
Jamshedpur	1,102
Asansol	1,090
Faridabad	1,055
Allahabad	1,050
Amritsar	1,011
Vijayawada	1,011
Rajkot	1,002
INDONESIA	
Jakarta	11,500
Surabaya	2,701
Bandung	2,368
Medan	1,910
Semarang	1,366
Palembang	1,352
Tangerang	1,198
Ujung Pandang	1,092
IRAN	
Tehran	6,759
Mashhad	1,887
Esfahan	1,266
Tabriz	1,191
Shiraz	1,053
Karaj	941
Ahvaz	805
Qom	778
Bakhtaran	693
IRAQ	
Baghdad	3,841
As Sulaymaniyah	952
Arbil	770
Al Mawsil	664
Al Kazimiyah	521
IRELAND	
Dublin	1,024
ISRAEL	
Tel Aviv-Yafo	1,880
Jerusalem	591
ITALY	
Rome	2,654
Milan	1,306
Naples	1,050
Turin	923
Palermo	689
Genoa	659
IVORY COAST	
Abidjan	2,500
JAMAICA	
Kingston	644
JAPAN	
Tokyo	17,950
Yokohama	3,427
Osaka	2,599
Nagoya	2,171
Sapporo	1,822
Kobe	1,494
Kyoto	1,468
Fukuoka	1,341
Kawasaki	1,250
Hiroshima	1,126
Kitakyushu	1,011
Sendai	1,008
JORDAN	
Amman	1,752
KAZAKHSTAN	
Almaty	1,151
Qaraghandy	574
KENYA	
Nairobi	2,000
Mombasa	600
KOREA, NORTH	
Pyŏngyang	2,741
Hamhung	710
Chŏngjin	583
KOREA, SOUTH	
Seoul	10,231
Pusan	3,814
Taegu	2,449
Inch'on	2,308
Taejŏn	1,272
Kwangju	1,258
Ulsan	967
Sŏngnam	869
Puch'on	779
Suwŏn	756
Anyang	590
Chŏnju	563
Chŏngju	531
Ansan	510
P'ohang	509
KYRGYZSTAN	
Bishkek	589
LAOS	
Vientiane	532
LATVIA	
Riga	811
LEBANON	
Beirut	1,500
Tripoli	500
LIBERIA	
Monrovia	962
LIBYA	
Tripoli	960
LITHUANIA	
Vilnius	580
MACEDONIA	
Skopje	541
MADAGASCAR	
Antananarivo	1,053
MALAYSIA	
Kuala Lumpur	1,145
MALI	
Bamako	810
MAURITANIA	
Nouakchott	735
MEXICO	
Mexico City	15,643
Guadalajara	2,847
Monterrey	2,522
Puebla	1,055
León	872
Ciudad Juárez	798
Tijuana	743
Culiacán	602
Mexicali	602
Acapulco	592
Mérida	557
Chihuahua	530
San Luis Potosí	526
Aguascalientés	506
MOLDOVA	
Chişinău	658
MONGOLIA	
Ulan Bator	673
MOROCCO	
Casablanca	2,943
Rabat-Salé	1,220
Marrakesh	602
Fès	564
MOZAMBIQUE	
Maputo	2,000
NEPAL	
Katmandu	535
NETHERLANDS	
Amsterdam	1,115
Rotterdam	1,086
The Hague	700
Utrecht	557
NEW ZEALAND	
Auckland	1,090
NICARAGUA	
Managua	864
NIGERIA	
Lagos	10,287
Ibadan	1,432
Ogbomosho	730
Kano	674
NORWAY	
Oslo	502
PAKISTAN	
Karachi	9,269
Lahore	5,064
Faisalabad	1,977
Rawalpindi	1,406
Multan	1,182
Hyderabad	1,151
Gujranwala	1,125
Peshawar	988
Quetta	560
Islamabad	525
PARAGUAY	
Asunción	945
PERU	
Lima	6,601
Arequipa	620
Trujillo	509
PHILIPPINES	
Manila	8,594
Quezon City	1,989
Caloocan	1,023
Davao	1,009
Cebu	662
Zamboanga	511
POLAND	
Warsaw	1,626
Lódz	815
Kraków	740
Wroclaw	641
Poznań	580
PORTUGAL	
Lisbon	2,561
Oporto	1,174
ROMANIA	
Bucharest	2,028
RUSSIA	
Moscow	8,405
St Petersburg	4,216
Nizhniy Novgorod	1,371
Novosibirsk	1,367
Yekaterinburg	1,275
Samara	1,170
Omsk	1,158
Kazan	1,085
Chelyabinsk	1,084
Ufa	1,082
Perm	1,025
Rostov	1,023
Volgograd	1,005
SAUDI ARABIA	
Riyadh	1,800
Jedda	1,500
Mecca	630
SENEGAL	
Dakar	1,905
SERBIA & MONTENEGRO	
Belgrade	1,598
SIERRA LEONE	
Freetown	505
SINGAPORE	
Singapore	3,866
SOMALIA	
Mogadishu	997
SOUTH AFRICA	
Cape Town	2,350
Johannesburg	1,196
Durban	1,137
Pretoria	1,080
Port Elizabeth	853
Vanderbijlpark–Vereeniging	774
Soweto	597
Sasolburg	540
SPAIN	
Madrid	3,030
Barcelona	1,615
Valencia	763
Sevilla	720
Zaragoza	608
Málaga	532
SRI LANKA	
Colombo	1,863
SUDAN	
Omdurman	1,271
Khartoum	925
Khartoum North	701
SWEDEN	
Stockholm	727
SWITZERLAND	
Zürich	733
SYRIA	
Aleppo	1,813
Damascus	1,394
Homs	659
TAIWAN	
T'aipei	2,596
Kaohsiung	1,435
T'aichung	858
T'ainan	708
Panch'iao	539
TAJIKISTAN	
Dushanbe	524
TANZANIA	
Dar-es-Salaam	1,361
THAILAND	
Bangkok	7,507
TOGO	
Lomé	590
TUNISIA	
Tunis	1,827
TURKEY	
Istanbul	8,506
Ankara	3,294
Izmir	2,554
Bursa	1,485
Adana	1,273
Konya	1,140
Mersin (Içel)	956
Gaziantep	867
Antalya	867
Kayseri	862
Diyarbakir	833
Urfa	785
Manisa	696
Kocaeli	629
Antalya	591
Samsun	590
Kahramanmaras	551
Balikesir	538
Eskisehir	519
Erzurum	512
Malatya	510
TURKMENISTAN	
Ashkhabad	536
UGANDA	
Kampala	954
UKRAINE	
Kiev	2,621
Kharkov	1,521
Dnepropetrovsk	1,122
Donetsk	1,065
Odessa	1,027
Zaporizhzhya	863
Lviv	794
Kryvyy Rih	720
Mykolayiv	518
Mariupol	500
UNITED ARAB EMIRATES	
Abu Dhabi	928
Dubai	674
UNITED KINGDOM	
London	8,089
Birmingham	2,373
Manchester	2,353
Liverpool	852
Glasgow	832
Sheffield	661
Nottingham	649
Newcastle	617
Bristol	552
Leeds	529
UNITED STATES	
New York	21,200
Los Angeles	16,374
Chicago–Gary	9,158
Washington–Baltimore	7,608
San Francisco–San Jose	7,039
Philadelphia–Atlantic City	6,188
Boston–Worcester	5,819
Detroit–Flint	5,456
Dallas–Fort Worth	5,222
Houston–Galveston	4,670
Atlanta	4,112
Miami–Fort Lauderdale	3,876
Seattle–Tacoma	3,554
Phoenix–Mesa	3,252
Minneapolis–St Paul	2,969
Cleveland–Akron	2,946
San Diego	2,814
St Louis	2,604
Denver–Boulder	2,582
San Juan	2,450
Tampa–Saint Petersburg	2,396
Pittsburgh	2,359
Portland–Salem	2,265
Cincinnati–Hamilton	1,979
Sacramento–Yolo	1,797
Kansas City	1,776
Milwaukee–Racine	1,690
Orlando	1,645
Indianapolis	1,607
San Antonio	1,592
Norfolk–Virginia Beach–Newport News	1,570
Las Vegas	1,563
Columbus, OH	1,540
Charlotte–Gastonia	1,499
New Orleans	1,338
Salt Lake City	1,334
Greensboro–Winston Salem–High Point	1,252
Austin–San Marcos	1,250
Nashville	1,231
Providence–Fall River	1,189
Raleigh–Durham	1,188
Hartford	1,183
Buffalo–Niagara Falls	1,170
Memphis	1,136
West Palm Beach	1,131
Jacksonville, FL	1,100
Rochester	1,098
Grand Rapids	1,089
Oklahoma City	1,083
Louisville	1,026
Richmond–Petersburg	997
Greenville	962
Dayton–Springfield	951
Fresno	923
Birmingham	921
Honolulu	876
Albany–Schenectady	876
Tucson	844
Tulsa	803
Syracuse	732
Omaha	717
Albuquerque	713
Knoxville	687
El Paso	680
Bakersfield	662
Allentown	638
Harrisburg	629
Scranton	625
Toledo	618
Baton Rouge	603
Youngstown–Warren	595
Springfield, MA	592
Sarasota	590
Little Rock	584
McAllen	569
Stockton–Lodi	564
Charleston	549
Wichita	545
Mobile	540
Columbia, SC	537
Colorado Springs	517
Fort Wayne	502
URUGUAY	
Montevideo	1,379
UZBEKISTAN	
Tashkent	2,118
VENEZUELA	
Caracas	1,975
Maracaibo	1,706
Valencia	1,263
Barquisimeto	811
Ciudad Guayana	642
VIETNAM	
Ho Chi Minh City	4,322
Hanoi	3,056
Haiphong	783
YEMEN	
Sana'	972
Aden	562
ZAMBIA	
Lusaka	982
ZIMBABWE	
Harare	1,189
Bulawayo	622

* SAR = Special Administrative Region of China

World Statistics: Climate

Rainfall and temperature figures are provided for more than 70 cities around the world. As climate is affected by altitude, the height of each city is shown in meters beneath its name. For each location, the top row of figures shows the total rainfall or snow in millimeters, and the bottom row the average temperature in degrees Celsius; the average annual temperature and total annual rainfall are at the end of the rows. The map opposite shows the city locations.

CITY	JAN.	FEB.	MAR.	APR.	MAY	JUNE	JULY	AUG.	SEPT.	OCT.	NOV.	DEC.	YEAR
EUROPE													
Athens, Greece	62	37	37	23	23	14	6	7	15	51	56	71	402
107 m	10	10	12	16	20	25	28	28	24	20	15	11	18
Berlin, Germany	46	40	33	42	49	65	73	69	48	49	46	43	603
55 m	–1	0	4	9	14	17	19	18	15	9	5	1	9
Istanbul, Turkey	109	92	72	46	38	34	34	30	58	81	103	119	816
14 m	5	6	7	11	16	20	23	23	20	16	12	8	14
Lisbon, Portugal	111	76	109	54	44	16	3	4	33	62	93	103	708
77 m	11	12	14	16	17	20	22	23	21	18	14	12	17
London, UK	54	40	37	37	46	45	57	59	49	57	64	48	593
5 m	4	5	7	9	12	16	18	17	15	11	8	5	11
Málaga, Spain	61	51	62	46	26	5	1	3	29	64	64	62	474
33 m	12	13	16	17	19	29	25	26	23	20	16	13	18
Moscow, Russia	39	38	36	37	53	58	88	71	58	45	47	54	624
156 m	–13	–10	–4	6	13	16	18	17	12	6	–1	–7	4
Odesa, Ukraine	57	62	30	21	34	34	42	37	37	13	35	71	473
64 m	–3	–1	2	9	15	20	22	22	18	12	9	1	10
Paris, France	56	46	35	42	57	54	59	64	55	50	51	50	619
75 m	3	4	8	11	15	18	20	19	17	12	7	4	12
Rome, Italy	71	62	57	51	46	37	15	21	63	99	129	93	744
17 m	8	9	11	14	18	22	25	25	22	17	13	10	16
Shannon, Ireland	94	67	56	53	61	57	77	79	86	86	96	117	929
2 m	5	5	7	9	12	14	16	16	14	11	8	6	10
Stockholm, Sweden	43	30	25	31	34	45	61	76	60	48	53	48	554
44 m	–3	–3	–1	5	10	15	18	17	12	7	3	0	7
ASIA													
Bahrain	8	18	13	8	<3	0	0	0	0	0	18	18	81
5 m	17	18	21	25	29	32	33	34	31	28	24	19	26
Bangkok, Thailand	8	20	36	58	198	160	160	175	305	206	66	5	1,397
2 m	26	28	29	30	29	29	28	28	28	28	26	25	28
Beirut, Lebanon	191	158	94	53	18	3	<3	<3	5	51	132	185	892
34 m	14	14	16	18	22	24	27	28	26	24	19	16	21
Colombo, Sri Lanka	89	69	147	231	371	224	135	109	160	348	315	147	2,365
7 m	26	26	27	28	28	27	27	27	27	27	26	26	27
Harbin, China	6	5	10	23	43	94	112	104	46	33	8	5	488
160 m	–18	–15	–5	6	13	19	22	21	14	4	–6	–16	3
Ho Chi Minh, Vietnam	15	3	13	43	221	330	315	269	335	269	114	56	1,984
9 m	26	27	29	30	29	28	28	28	27	27	27	26	28
Hong Kong, China	33	46	74	137	292	394	381	361	257	114	43	31	2,162
33 m	16	15	18	22	26	28	28	28	27	25	21	18	23

CITY	JAN.	FEB.	MAR.	APR.	MAY	JUNE	JULY	AUG.	SEPT.	OCT.	NOV.	DEC.	YEAR
ASIA (continued)													
Jakarta, Indonesia	300	300	211	147	114	97	64	43	66	112	142	203	1,798
8 m	26	26	27	27	27	27	27	27	27	27	27	26	27
Kabul, Afghanistan	31	36	94	102	20	5	3	3	<3	15	20	10	338
1,815 m	–3	–1	6	13	18	22	25	24	20	14	7	3	12
Karachi, Pakistan	13	10	8	3	3	18	81	41	13	<3	3	5	196
4 m	19	20	24	28	30	31	30	29	28	28	24	20	26
Kazalinsk, Kazakhstan	10	10	13	13	15	5	5	8	8	10	13	15	125
63 m	–12	–11	–3	6	18	23	25	23	16	8	–1	–7	7
Kolkata (Calcutta), India	10	31	36	43	140	297	325	328	252	114	20	5	1,600
6 m	20	22	27	30	30	30	29	29	29	28	23	19	26
Mumbai (Bombay), India	3	3	3	<3	18	485	617	340	264	64	13	3	1,809
11 m	24	24	26	28	30	29	27	27	27	28	27	26	27
New Delhi, India	23	18	13	8	13	74	180	172	117	10	3	10	640
218 m	14	17	23	28	33	34	31	30	29	26	20	15	25
Omsk, Russia	15	8	8	13	31	51	51	51	28	25	18	20	318
85 m	–22	–19	–12	–1	10	16	18	16	10	1	–11	–18	–1
Shanghai, China	48	58	84	94	94	180	147	142	130	71	51	36	1,135
7 m	4	5	9	14	20	24	28	28	23	19	12	7	16
Singapore	252	173	193	188	173	173	170	196	178	208	254	257	2,413
10 m	26	27	28	28	28	28	28	27	27	27	27	27	27
Tehran, Iran	46	38	46	36	13	3	3	3	3	8	20	31	246
1,220 m	2	5	9	16	21	26	30	29	25	18	12	6	17
Tokyo, Japan	48	74	107	135	147	165	142	152	234	208	97	56	1,565
6 m	3	4	7	13	17	21	25	26	23	17	11	6	14
Ulan Bator, Mongolia	<3	<3	3	5	10	28	76	51	23	5	5	3	208
1,325 m	–26	–21	–13	–1	6	14	16	14	8	–1	–13	–22	–3
Verkhoyansk, Russia	5	5	3	5	8	23	28	25	13	8	8	5	134
100 m	–50	–45	–32	–15	0	12	14	9	2	–15	–38	–48	–17
AFRICA													
Addis Ababa, Ethiopia	<3	3	25	135	213	201	206	239	102	28	<3	0	1,151
2,450 m	19	20	20	20	19	18	18	19	21	22	21	20	20
Antananarivo, Madag.	300	279	178	53	18	8	8	10	18	61	135	287	1,356
1,372 m	21	21	21	19	18	15	14	15	17	19	21	21	19
Cairo, Egypt	5	5	5	3	3	<3	0	0	<3	<3	3	5	28
116 m	13	15	18	21	25	28	28	28	26	24	20	15	22
Cape Town, S. Africa	15	8	18	48	79	84	89	66	43	31	18	10	508
17 m	21	21	20	17	14	13	12	13	14	16	18	19	17
Jo'burg, S. Africa	114	109	89	38	25	8	8	8	23	56	107	125	709
1,665 m	20	20	18	16	13	10	11	13	16	18	19	20	16

CITY	JAN.	FEB.	MAR.	APR.	MAY	JUNE	JULY	AUG.	SEPT.	OCT.	NOV.	DEC.	YEAR
AFRICA (continued)													
Khartoum, Sudan	<3	<3	<3	<3	3	8	53	71	18	5	<3	0	158
390 m	24	25	28	31	33	34	32	31	32	32	28	25	29
Kinshasa, Congo (D.R.)	135	145	196	196	158	8	3	3	31	119	221	142	1,354
325 m	26	26	27	27	26	24	23	24	25	26	26	26	25
Lagos, Nigeria	28	46	102	150	269	460	279	64	140	206	69	25	1,836
3 m	27	28	29	28	28	26	26	25	26	26	28	28	27
Lusaka, Zambia	231	191	142	18	3	<3	<3	0	<3	10	91	150	836
1,277 m	21	22	21	21	19	16	16	18	22	24	23	22	21
Monrovia, Liberia	31	56	97	216	516	973	996	373	744	772	236	130	5,138
23 m	26	26	27	27	26	25	24	25	25	25	26	26	26
Nairobi, Kenya	38	64	125	211	158	46	15	23	31	53	109	86	958
820 m	19	19	19	19	18	16	16	16	18	19	18	18	18
Timbuktu, Mali	<3	<3	3	<3	5	23	79	81	38	3	<3	<3	231
301 m	22	24	28	32	34	35	32	30	32	31	28	23	29
Tunis, Tunisia	64	51	41	36	18	8	3	8	33	51	48	61	419
66 m	10	11	13	16	19	23	26	27	25	20	16	11	18
Walvis Bay, Namibia	<3	5	8	3	3	<3	<3	3	<3	<3	<3	<3	23
7 m	19	19	19	18	17	16	15	14	14	15	17	18	18
AUSTRALIA, NEW ZEALAND AND ANTARCTICA													
Alice Springs, Aust.	43	33	28	10	15	13	8	8	8	18	31	38	252
579 m	29	28	25	20	15	12	12	14	18	23	26	28	21
Christchurch, N.Z.	56	43	48	48	66	66	69	48	46	43	48	56	638
10 m	16	16	14	12	9	6	6	7	9	12	14	16	11
Darwin, Australia	386	312	254	97	15	3	<3	3	13	51	119	239	1,491
30 m	29	29	29	29	28	26	25	26	28	29	30	29	28
Mawson, Antarctica	11	30	20	10	44	180	4	40	3	20	0	0	362
14 m	0	–5	–10	–14	–15	–16	–18	–18	–19	–13	–5	–1	–11
Perth, Australia	8	10	20	43	130	180	170	149	86	56	20	13	881
60 m	23	23	22	19	16	14	13	13	15	16	19	22	18
Sydney, Australia	89	102	127	135	127	117	117	76	73	71	73	73	1,181
42 m	22	22	21	18	15	13	12	13	15	18	19	21	17
NORTH AMERICA													
Anchorage, USA	20	18	15	10	13	18	41	66	66	56	25	23	371
40 m	–11	–8	–5	2	7	12	14	13	9	2	–5	–11	2
Chicago, USA	51	51	66	71	86	89	84	81	79	66	61	51	836
251 m	–4	–3	2	9	14	20	23	22	19	12	5	–1	10
Churchill, Canada	15	13	18	23	32	44	46	58	51	43	39	21	402
13 m	–28	–26	–20	–10	–2	6	12	11	5	–2	–12	–22	–7
Edmonton, Canada	25	19	19	22	43	77	89	78	39	17	16	25	466
676 m	–15	–10	–5	4	11	15	17	16	11	6	–4	–10	3
Honolulu, USA	104	66	79	48	25	18	23	28	36	48	64	104	643
12 m	23	18	19	20	22	24	25	26	26	24	22	19	22
Houston, USA	89	76	84	91	119	117	99	99	104	94	89	109	1,171
12 m	12	13	17	21	24	27	28	29	26	22	16	12	21

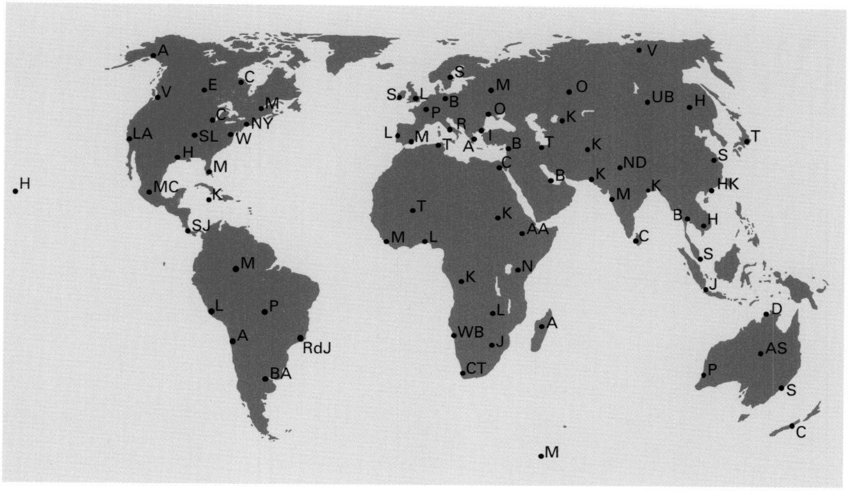

CITY	JAN.	FEB.	MAR.	APR.	MAY	JUNE	JULY	AUG.	SEPT.	OCT.	NOV.	DEC.	YEAR
NORTH AMERICA (continued)													
Kingston, Jamaica	23	15	23	31	102	89	38	91	99	180	74	36	800
34 m	25	25	25	26	26	28	28	28	27	27	26	26	26
Los Angeles, USA	79	76	71	25	10	3	<3	<3	5	15	31	66	381
95 m	13	14	14	16	17	19	21	22	21	18	16	14	17
Mexico City, Mexico	13	5	10	20	53	119	170	152	130	51	18	8	747
2,309 m	12	13	16	18	19	19	17	18	18	16	14	13	16
Miami, USA	71	53	64	81	173	178	155	160	203	234	71	51	1,516
8 m	20	20	22	23	25	27	28	28	27	25	22	21	24
Montréal, Canada	72	65	74	74	66	82	90	92	88	76	81	87	946
57 m	–10	–9	–3	–6	13	18	21	20	15	9	2	–7	6
New York City, USA	94	97	91	81	81	84	107	109	86	89	76	91	1,092
96 m	–1	–1	3	10	16	20	23	23	21	15	7	2	11
St Louis, USA	58	64	89	97	114	114	89	86	81	74	71	64	1,001
173 m	0	1	7	13	19	24	26	26	22	15	8	2	14
San José, Costa Rica	15	5	20	46	229	241	211	241	305	300	145	41	1,798
1,146 m	19	19	21	21	22	21	21	21	21	20	20	19	20
Vancouver, Canada	154	115	101	60	52	45	32	41	67	114	150	182	1,113
14 m	3	5	6	9	12	15	17	17	14	10	6	4	10
Washington, DC, USA	86	76	91	84	94	99	112	109	94	74	66	79	1,064
22 m	1	2	7	12	18	23	25	24	20	14	8	3	13
SOUTH AMERICA													
Antofagasta, Chile	0	0	0	<3	<3	3	5	3	<3	3	<3	0	13
94 m	21	21	20	18	16	15	14	14	15	16	18	19	17
Buenos Aires, Arg.	79	71	109	89	76	61	56	61	79	86	84	99	950
27 m	23	23	21	17	13	9	10	11	13	15	19	22	16
Lima, Peru	3	<3	<3	<3	5	5	8	8	8	3	3	<3	41
120 m	23	24	24	22	19	17	17	16	17	18	19	21	20
Manaus, Brazil	249	231	262	221	170	84	58	38	46	107	142	203	1,811
44 m	28	28	28	27	28	28	28	28	29	29	29	28	28
Paraná, Brazil	287	236	239	102	13	<3	3	5	28	127	231	310	1,582
260 m	23	23	23	23	23	21	21	22	24	24	24	23	23
Rio de Janeiro, Brazil	125	122	130	107	79	53	41	43	66	79	104	137	1,082
61 m	26	26	25	24	22	21	21	21	21	22	23	25	23

World Statistics: Physical Dimensions

Each topic list is divided into continents and within a continent the items are listed in order of size. The bottom part of many of the lists is selective in order to give examples from as many different countries as possible. The order of the continents is as in the atlas, Europe through to South America. The world top ten are shown in square brackets; in the case of mountains this has not been done because the world top 30 are all in Asia. The figures are rounded as appropriate.

WORLD, CONTINENTS, OCEANS

THE WORLD	km²	miles²	%
The World	509,450,000	196,672,000	–
Land	149,450,000	57,688,000	29.3
Water	360,000,000	138,984,000	70.7
Asia	44,500,000	17,177,000	29.8
Africa	30,302,000	11,697,000	20.3
North America	24,241,000	9,357,000	16.2
South America	17,793,000	6,868,000	11.9
Antarctica	14,100,000	5,443,000	9.4
Europe	9,957,000	3,843,000	6.7
Australia & Oceania	8,557,000	3,303,000	5.7
Pacific Ocean	179,679,000	69,356,000	49.9
Atlantic Ocean	92,373,000	35,657,000	25.7
Indian Ocean	73,917,000	28,532,000	20.5
Arctic Ocean	14,090,000	5,439,000	3.9

SEAS

PACIFIC	km²	miles²
South China Sea	2,974,600	1,148,500
Bering Sea	2,268,000	875,000
Sea of Okhotsk	1,528,000	590,000
East China & Yellow	1,249,000	482,000
Sea of Japan	1,008,000	389,000
Gulf of California	162,000	62,500
Bass Strait	75,000	29,000

ATLANTIC	km²	miles²
Caribbean Sea	2,766,000	1,068,000
Mediterranean Sea	2,516,000	971,000
Gulf of Mexico	1,543,000	596,000
Hudson Bay	1,232,000	476,000
North Sea	575,000	223,000
Black Sea	462,000	178,000
Baltic Sea	422,170	163,000
Gulf of St Lawrence	238,000	92,000

INDIAN	km²	miles²
Red Sea	438,000	169,000
The Gulf	239,000	92,000

MOUNTAINS

EUROPE		m	ft
Elbrus	Russia	5,642	18,510
Mont Blanc	France/Italy	4,807	15,771
Monte Rosa	Italy/Switzerland	4,634	15,203
Dom	Switzerland	4,545	14,911
Liskamm	Switzerland	4,527	14,852
Weisshorn	Switzerland	4,505	14,780
Taschorn	Switzerland	4,490	14,730
Matterhorn/Cervino	Italy/Switz.	4,478	14,691
Mont Maudit	France/Italy	4,465	14,649
Dent Blanche	Switzerland	4,356	14,291
Nadelhorn	Switzerland	4,327	14,196
Grandes Jorasses	France/Italy	4,208	13,806
Jungfrau	Switzerland	4,158	13,642
Barre des Ecrins	France	4,103	13,461
Gran Paradiso	Italy	4,061	13,323
Piz Bernina	Italy/Switzerland	4,049	13,284
Eiger	Switzerland	3,970	13,025
Monte Viso	Italy	3,841	12,602
Grossglockner	Austria	3,797	12,457
Wildspitze	Austria	3,772	12,382
Monte Disgrazia	Italy	3,678	12,066
Mulhacén	Spain	3,478	11,411
Pico de Aneto	Spain	3,404	11,168
Marmolada	Italy	3,342	10,964
Etna	Italy	3,340	10,958
Zugspitze	Germany	2,962	9,718
Musala	Bulgaria	2,925	9,596
Olympus	Greece	2,917	9,570
Triglav	Slovenia	2,863	9,393
Monte Cinto	France (Corsica)	2,710	8,891
Galdhöpiggen	Norway	2,468	8,100
Ben Nevis	UK	1,343	4,406

ASIA		m	ft
Everest	China/Nepal	8,850	29,035
K2 (Godwin Austen)	China/Kashmir	8,611	28,251
Kanchenjunga	India/Nepal	8,598	28,208
Lhotse	China/Nepal	8,516	27,939
Makalu	China/Nepal	8,481	27,824
Cho Oyu	China/Nepal	8,201	26,906
Dhaulagiri	Nepal	8,172	26,811
Manaslu	Nepal	8,156	26,758
Nanga Parbat	Kashmir	8,126	26,660
Annapurna	Nepal	8,078	26,502
Gasherbrum	China/Kashmir	8,068	26,469
Broad Peak	China/Kashmir	8,051	26,414
Xixabangma	China	8,012	26,286
Kangbachen	India/Nepal	7,902	25,925
Jannu	India/Nepal	7,902	25,925
Gayachung Kang	Nepal	7,897	25,909
Himalchuli	Nepal	7,893	25,896
Disteghil Sar	Kashmir	7,885	25,869
Nuptse	Nepal	7,879	25,849
Khunyang Chhish	Kashmir	7,852	25,761
Masherbrum	Kashmir	7,821	25,659
Nanda Devi	India	7,817	25,646
Rakaposhi	Kashmir	7,788	25,551
Batura	Kashmir	7,785	25,541
Namche Barwa	China	7,756	25,446
Kamet	India	7,756	25,446
Soltoro Kangri	Kashmir	7,742	25,400
Gurla Mandhata	China	7,728	25,354
Trivor	Pakistan	7,720	25,328
Kongur Shan	China	7,719	25,324
Tirich Mir	Pakistan	7,690	25,229
K'ula Shan	Bhutan/China	7,543	24,747
Pik Kommunizma	Tajikistan	7,495	24,590
Demavend	Iran	5,604	18,386
Ararat	Turkey	5,165	16,945
Gunong Kinabalu	Malaysia (Borneo)	4,101	13,455
Yu Shan	Taiwan	3,997	13,113
Fuji-San	Japan	3,776	12,388

AFRICA		m	ft
Kilimanjaro	Tanzania	5,895	19,340
Mt Kenya	Kenya	5,199	17,057
Ruwenzori (Margherita)	Uganda/Congo (D.R.)	5,109	16,762
Ras Dashan	Ethiopia	4,620	15,157
Meru	Tanzania	4,565	14,977
Karisimbi	Rwanda/Congo (D.R.)	4,507	14,787
Mt Elgon	Kenya/Uganda	4,321	14,176
Batu	Ethiopia	4,307	14,130
Guna	Ethiopia	4,231	13,882
Toubkal	Morocco	4,165	13,665
Irhil Mgoun	Morocco	4,071	13,356
Mt Cameroon	Cameroon	4,070	13,353
Amba Ferit	Ethiopia	3,875	13,042
Pico del Teide	Spain (Tenerife)	3,718	12,198
Thabana Ntlenyana	Lesotho	3,482	11,424
Emi Koussi	Chad	3,415	11,204
Mt aux Sources	Lesotho/S. Africa	3,282	10,768
Mt Piton	Réunion	3,069	10,069

OCEANIA		m	ft
Puncak Jaya	Indonesia	5,029	16,499
Puncak Trikora	Indonesia	4,750	15,584
Puncak Mandala	Indonesia	4,702	15,427
Mt Wilhelm	Papua NG	4,508	14,790
Mauna Kea	USA (Hawaii)	4,205	13,796
Mauna Loa	USA (Hawaii)	4,169	13,681
Mt Cook (Aoraki)	New Zealand	3,753	12,313
Mt Balbi	Solomon Is.	2,439	8,002
Orohena	Tahiti	2,241	7,352
Mt Kosciuszko	Australia	2,230	7,316

NORTH AMERICA		m	ft
Mt McKinley (Denali)	USA (Alaska)	6,194	20,321
Mt Logan	Canada	5,959	19,551
Pico de Orizaba	Mexico	5,610	18,405
Mt St Elias	USA/Canada	5,489	18,008
Popocatepetl	Mexico	5,452	17,887
Mt Foraker	USA (Alaska)	5,304	17,401
Ixtaccihuatl	Mexico	5,286	17,342
Lucania	Canada	5,227	17,149
Mt Steele	Canada	5,073	16,644
Mt Bona	USA (Alaska)	5,005	16,420
Mt Blackburn	USA (Alaska)	4,996	16,391
Mt Sanford	USA (Alaska)	4,940	16,207
Mt Wood	Canada	4,848	15,905
Nevado de Toluca	Mexico	4,670	15,321
Mt Fairweather	USA (Alaska)	4,663	15,298
Mt Hunter	USA (Alaska)	4,442	14,573
Mt Whitney	USA	4,418	14,495
Mt Elbert	USA	4,399	14,432
Mt Harvard	USA	4,395	14,419
Mt Rainier	USA	4,392	14,409
Blanca Peak	USA	4,372	14,344
Longs Peak	USA	4,345	14,255
Tajumulco	Guatemala	4,220	13,845
Grand Teton	USA	4,197	13,770
Mt Waddington	Canada	3,994	13,104
Mt Robson	Canada	3,954	12,972
Chirripó Grande	Costa Rica	3,837	12,589
Pico Duarte	Dominican Rep.	3,175	10,417

SOUTH AMERICA		m	ft
Aconcagua	Argentina	6,962	22,841
Bonete	Argentina	6,872	22,546
Ojos del Salado	Argentina/Chile	6,863	22,516
Pissis	Argentina	6,779	22,241
Mercedario	Argentina/Chile	6,770	22,211
Huascaran	Peru	6,768	22,204
Llullaillaco	Argentina/Chile	6,723	22,057
Nudo de Cachi	Argentina	6,720	22,047
Yerupaja	Peru	6,632	21,758
N. de Tres Cruces	Argentina/Chile	6,620	21,719
Incahuasi	Argentina/Chile	6,601	21,654
Cerro Galan	Argentina	6,600	21,654
Tupungato	Argentina/Chile	6,570	21,555
Sajama	Bolivia	6,542	21,463
Illimani	Bolivia	6,485	21,276
Coropuna	Peru	6,425	21,079
Ausangate	Peru	6,384	20,945
Cerro del Toro	Argentina	6,380	20,932
Siula Grande	Peru	6,356	20,853
Chimborazo	Ecuador	6,267	20,561
Alpamayo	Peru	5,947	19,511
Cotapaxi	Ecuador	5,896	19,344
Pico Colon	Colombia	5,800	19,029
Pico Bolivar	Venezuela	5,007	16,427

ANTARCTICA		m	ft
Vinson Massif		4,897	16,066
Mt Kirkpatrick		4,528	14,855
Mt Markham		4,349	14,268

OCEAN DEPTHS

ATLANTIC OCEAN	m	ft	
Puerto Rico (Milwaukee) Deep	9,220	30,249	[7]
Cayman Trench	7,680	25,197	[10]
Gulf of Mexico	5,203	17,070	
Mediterranean Sea	5,121	16,801	
Black Sea	2,211	7,254	
North Sea	660	2,165	
Baltic Sea	463	1,519	
Hudson Bay	258	846	

INDIAN OCEAN	m	ft
Java Trench	7,450	24,442
Red Sea	2,635	8,454
Persian Gulf	73	239

PACIFIC OCEAN	m	ft	
Mariana Trench	11,022	36,161	[1]
Tonga Trench	10,882	35,702	[2]
Japan Trench	10,554	34,626	[3]
Kuril Trench	10,542	34,587	[4]
Mindanao Trench	10,497	34,439	[5]
Kermadec Trench	10,047	32,962	[6]

PACIFIC OCEAN (continued)	m	ft	
Peru–Chile Trench	8,050	26,410	[8]
Aleutian Trench	7,822	25,662	[9]

ARCTIC OCEAN	m	ft
Molloy Deep	5,608	18,399

LAND LOWS

		m	ft
Caspian Sea	Europe	–28	–92
Dead Sea	Asia	–411	–1,348
Lake Assal	Africa	–156	–512
Lake Eyre North	Oceania	–16	–52
Death Valley	N. America	–86	–282
Valdés Peninsula	S. America	–40	–131

RIVERS

EUROPE		km	miles
Volga	Caspian Sea	3,700	2,300
Danube	Black Sea	2,850	1,770
Ural	Caspian Sea	2,535	1,575
Dnepr (Dnipro)	Black Sea	2,285	1,420
Kama	Volga	2,030	1,260
Don	Black Sea	1,990	1,240
Petchora	Arctic Ocean	1,790	1,110
Oka	Volga	1,480	920
Belaya	Kama	1,420	880
Dnister (Dniester)	Black Sea	1,400	870
Vyatka	Kama	1,370	850
Rhine	North Sea	1,320	820
N. Dvina	Arctic Ocean	1,290	800
Desna	Dnepr (Dnipro)	1,190	740
Elbe	North Sea	1,145	710
Wisla	Baltic Sea	1,090	675
Loire	Atlantic Ocean	1,020	635

ASIA		km	miles	
Yangtze	Pacific Ocean	6,380	3,960	[3]
Yenisey–Angara	Arctic Ocean	5,550	3,445	[5]
Huang He	Pacific Ocean	5,464	3,395	[6]
Ob–Irtysh	Arctic Ocean	5,410	3,360	[7]
Mekong	Pacific Ocean	4,500	2,795	[9]
Amur	Pacific Ocean	4,400	2,730	[10]
Lena	Arctic Ocean	4,400	2,730	
Irtysh	Ob	4,250	2,640	
Yenisey	Arctic Ocean	4,090	2,540	
Ob	Arctic Ocean	3,680	2,285	
Indus	Indian Ocean	3,100	1,925	
Brahmaputra	Indian Ocean	2,900	1,800	
Syrdarya	Aral Sea	2,860	1,775	
Salween	Indian Ocean	2,800	1,740	
Euphrates	Indian Ocean	2,700	1,675	
Vilyuy	Lena	2,650	1,645	
Kolyma	Arctic Ocean	2,600	1,615	
Amudarya	Aral Sea	2,540	1,575	
Ural	Caspian Sea	2,535	1,575	
Ganges	Indian Ocean	2,510	1,560	
Si Kiang	Pacific Ocean	2,100	1,305	
Irrawaddy	Indian Ocean	2,010	1,250	
Tarim–Yarkand	Lop Nor	2,000	1,240	
Tigris	Indian Ocean	1,900	1,180	

AFRICA		km	miles	
Nile	Mediterranean	6,670	4,140	[1]
Congo	Atlantic Ocean	4,670	2,900	[8]
Niger	Atlantic Ocean	4,180	2,595	
Zambezi	Indian Ocean	3,540	2,200	
Oubangi/Uele	Congo (D.R.)	2,250	1,400	
Kasai	Congo (D.R.)	1,950	1,210	
Shaballe	Indian Ocean	1,930	1,200	
Orange	Atlantic Ocean	1,860	1,155	
Cubango	Okavango Delta	1,800	1,120	
Limpopo	Indian Ocean	1,600	995	
Senegal	Atlantic Ocean	1,600	995	
Volta	Atlantic Ocean	1,500	930	

AUSTRALIA		km	miles
Murray–Darling	Southern Ocean	3,750	2,330
Darling	Murray	3,070	1,905
Murray	Southern Ocean	2,575	1,600
Murrumbidgee	Murray	1,690	1,050

NORTH AMERICA		km	miles	
Mississippi–Missouri	Gulf of Mexico	6,020	3,740	[4]
Mackenzie	Arctic Ocean	4,240	2,630	
Mississippi	Gulf of Mexico	3,780	2,350	
Missouri	Mississippi	3,780	2,350	
Yukon	Pacific Ocean	3,185	1,980	
Rio Grande	Gulf of Mexico	3,030	1,880	

NORTH AMERICA (continued)		km	miles
Arkansas	Mississippi	2,340	1,450
Colorado	Pacific Ocean	2,330	1,445
Red	Mississippi	2,040	1,270
Columbia	Pacific Ocean	1,950	1,210
Saskatchewan	Lake Winnipeg	1,940	1,205
Snake	Columbia	1,670	1,040
Churchill	Hudson Bay	1,600	990
Ohio	Mississippi	1,580	980
Brazos	Gulf of Mexico	1,400	870
St Lawrence	Atlantic Ocean	1,170	730

SOUTH AMERICA		km	miles	
Amazon	Atlantic Ocean	6,450	4,010	[2]
Paraná–Plate	Atlantic Ocean	4,500	2,800	
Purus	Amazon	3,350	2,080	
Madeira	Amazon	3,200	1,990	
São Francisco	Atlantic Ocean	2,900	1,800	
Paraná	Plate	2,800	1,740	
Tocantins	Atlantic Ocean	2,750	1,710	
Paraguay	Paraná	2,550	1,580	
Orinoco	Atlantic Ocean	2,500	1,550	
Pilcomayo	Paraná	2,500	1,550	
Araguaia	Tocantins	2,250	1,400	
Juruá	Amazon	2,000	1,240	
Xingu	Amazon	1,980	1,230	
Ucayali	Amazon	1,900	1,180	
Maranón	Amazon	1,600	990	
Uruguay	Plate	1,600	990	

LAKES

EUROPE		km²	miles²
Lake Ladoga	Russia	17,700	6,800
Lake Onega	Russia	9,700	3,700
Saimaa system	Finland	8,000	3,100
Vänern	Sweden	5,500	2,100
Rybinskoye Res.	Russia	4,700	1,800

ASIA		km²	miles²	
Caspian Sea	Asia	371,800	143,550	[1]
Lake Baykal	Russia	30,500	11,780	[8]
Aral Sea	Kazakhstan/Uzbekistan	28,687	11,086	[10]
Tonlé Sap	Cambodia	20,000	7,700	
Lake Balqash	Kazakhstan	18,500	7,100	
Lake Dongting	China	12,000	4,600	
Lake Ysyk	Kyrgyzstan	6,200	2,400	
Lake Orumiyeh	Iran	5,900	2,300	
Lake Koko	China	5,700	2,200	
Lake Poyang	China	5,000	1,900	
Lake Khanka	China/Russia	4,400	1,700	
Lake Van	Turkey	3,500	1,400	

AFRICA		km²	miles²	
Lake Victoria	E. Africa	68,000	26,000	[3]
Lake Tanganyika	C. Africa	33,000	13,000	[6]
Lake Malawi/Nyasa	E. Africa	29,600	11,430	[9]
Lake Chad	C. Africa	25,000	9,700	
Lake Turkana	Ethiopia/Kenya	8,500	3,300	
Lake Volta	Ghana	8,500	3,300	
Lake Bangweulu	Zambia	8,000	3,100	
Lake Rukwa	Tanzania	7,000	2,700	
Lake Mai-Ndombe	Congo (D.R.)	6,500	2,500	
Lake Kariba	Zambia/Zimbabwe	5,300	2,000	
Lake Albert	Uganda/Congo (D.R.)	5,300	2,000	
Lake Nasser	Egypt/Sudan	5,200	2,000	
Lake Mweru	Zambia/Congo (D.R.)	4,900	1,900	
Lake Cabora Bassa	Mozambique	4,500	1,700	
Lake Kyoga	Uganda	4,400	1,700	
Lake Tana	Ethiopia	3,630	1,400	

AUSTRALIA		km²	miles²
Lake Eyre	Australia	8,900	3,400
Lake Torrens	Australia	5,800	2,200
Lake Gairdner	Australia	4,800	1,900

NORTH AMERICA		km²	miles²	
Lake Superior	Canada/USA	82,350	31,800	[2]
Lake Huron	Canada/USA	59,600	23,010	[4]
Lake Michigan	USA	58,000	22,400	[5]
Great Bear Lake	Canada	31,800	12,280	[7]
Great Slave Lake	Canada	28,500	11,000	
Lake Erie	Canada/USA	25,700	9,900	
Lake Winnipeg	Canada	24,400	9,400	
Lake Ontario	Canada/USA	19,500	7,500	
Lake Nicaragua	Nicaragua	8,200	3,200	
Lake Athabasca	Canada	8,100	3,100	
Smallwood Reservoir	Canada	6,530	2,520	
Reindeer Lake	Canada	6,400	2,500	
Nettilling Lake	Canada	5,500	2,100	
Lake Winnipegosis	Canada	5,400	2,100	

SOUTH AMERICA		km²	miles²
Lake Titicaca	Bolivia/Peru	8,300	3,200
Lake Poopo	Bolivia	2,800	1,100

ISLANDS

EUROPE		km²	miles²	
Great Britain	UK	229,880	88,700	[8]
Iceland	Atlantic Ocean	103,000	39,800	
Ireland	Ireland/UK	84,400	32,600	
Novaya Zemlya (N.)	Russia	48,200	18,600	
W. Spitzbergen	Norway	39,000	15,100	
Novaya Zemlya (S.)	Russia	33,200	12,800	
Sicily	Italy	25,500	9,800	
Sardinia	Italy	24,000	9,300	
N.E. Spitzbergen	Norway	15,000	5,600	
Corsica	France	8,700	3,400	
Crete	Greece	8,350	3,200	
Zealand	Denmark	6,850	2,600	

ASIA		km²	miles²	
Borneo	S. E. Asia	744,360	287,400	[3]
Sumatra	Indonesia	473,600	182,860	[6]
Honshu	Japan	230,500	88,980	[7]
Sulawesi (Celebes)	Indonesia	189,000	73,000	
Java	Indonesia	126,700	48,900	
Luzon	Philippines	104,700	40,400	
Mindanao	Philippines	101,500	39,200	
Hokkaido	Japan	78,400	30,300	
Sakhalin	Russia	74,060	28,600	
Sri Lanka	Indian Ocean	65,600	25,300	
Taiwan	Pacific Ocean	36,000	13,900	
Kyushu	Japan	35,700	13,800	
Hainan	China	34,000	13,100	
Timor	Indonesia	33,600	13,000	
Shikoku	Japan	18,800	7,300	
Halmahera	Indonesia	18,000	6,900	
Ceram	Indonesia	17,150	6,600	
Sumbawa	Indonesia	15,450	6,000	
Flores	Indonesia	15,200	5,900	
Samar	Philippines	13,100	5,100	
Negros	Philippines	12,700	4,900	
Bangka	Indonesia	12,000	4,600	
Palawan	Philippines	12,000	4,600	
Panay	Philippines	11,500	4,400	
Sumba	Indonesia	11,100	4,300	
Mindoro	Philippines	9,750	3,800	

AFRICA		km²	miles²	
Madagascar	Indian Ocean	587,040	226,660	[4]
Socotra	Indian Ocean	3,600	1,400	
Réunion	Indian Ocean	2,500	965	
Tenerife	Atlantic Ocean	2,350	900	
Mauritius	Indian Ocean	1,865	720	

OCEANIA		km²	miles²	
New Guinea	Indon./Papua NG	821,030	317,000	[2]
New Zealand (S.)	Pacific Ocean	150,500	58,100	
New Zealand (N.)	Pacific Ocean	114,700	44,300	
Tasmania	Australia	67,800	26,200	
New Britain	Papua NG	37,800	14,600	
New Caledonia	Pacific Ocean	19,100	7,400	
Viti Levu	Fiji	10,500	4,100	
Hawaii	Pacific Ocean	10,450	4,000	
Bougainville	Papua NG	9,600	3,700	
Guadalcanal	Solomon Is.	6,500	2,500	
Vanua Levu	Fiji	5,550	2,100	
New Ireland	Papua NG	3,200	1,200	

NORTH AMERICA		km²	miles²	
Greenland	Atlantic Ocean	2,175,600	839,800	[1]
Baffin Is.	Canada	508,000	196,100	[5]
Victoria Is.	Canada	212,200	81,900	[9]
Ellesmere Is.	Canada	212,000	81,800	[10]
Cuba	Caribbean Sea	110,860	42,800	
Newfoundland	Canada	110,680	42,700	
Hispaniola	Dom. Rep./Haiti	76,200	29,400	
Banks Is.	Canada	67,000	25,900	
Devon Is.	Canada	54,500	21,000	
Melville Is.	Canada	42,400	16,400	
Vancouver Is.	Canada	32,150	12,400	
Somerset Is.	Canada	24,300	9,400	
Jamaica	Caribbean Sea	11,400	4,400	
Puerto Rico	Atlantic Ocean	8,900	3,400	
Cape Breton Is.	Canada	4,000	1,500	

SOUTH AMERICA		km²	miles²
Tierra del Fuego	Argentina/Chile	47,000	18,100
Falkland Is. (East)	Atlantic Ocean	6,800	2,600
South Georgia	Atlantic Ocean	4,200	1,600
Galapagos (Isabela)	Pacific Ocean	2,250	870

World: Regions in the News

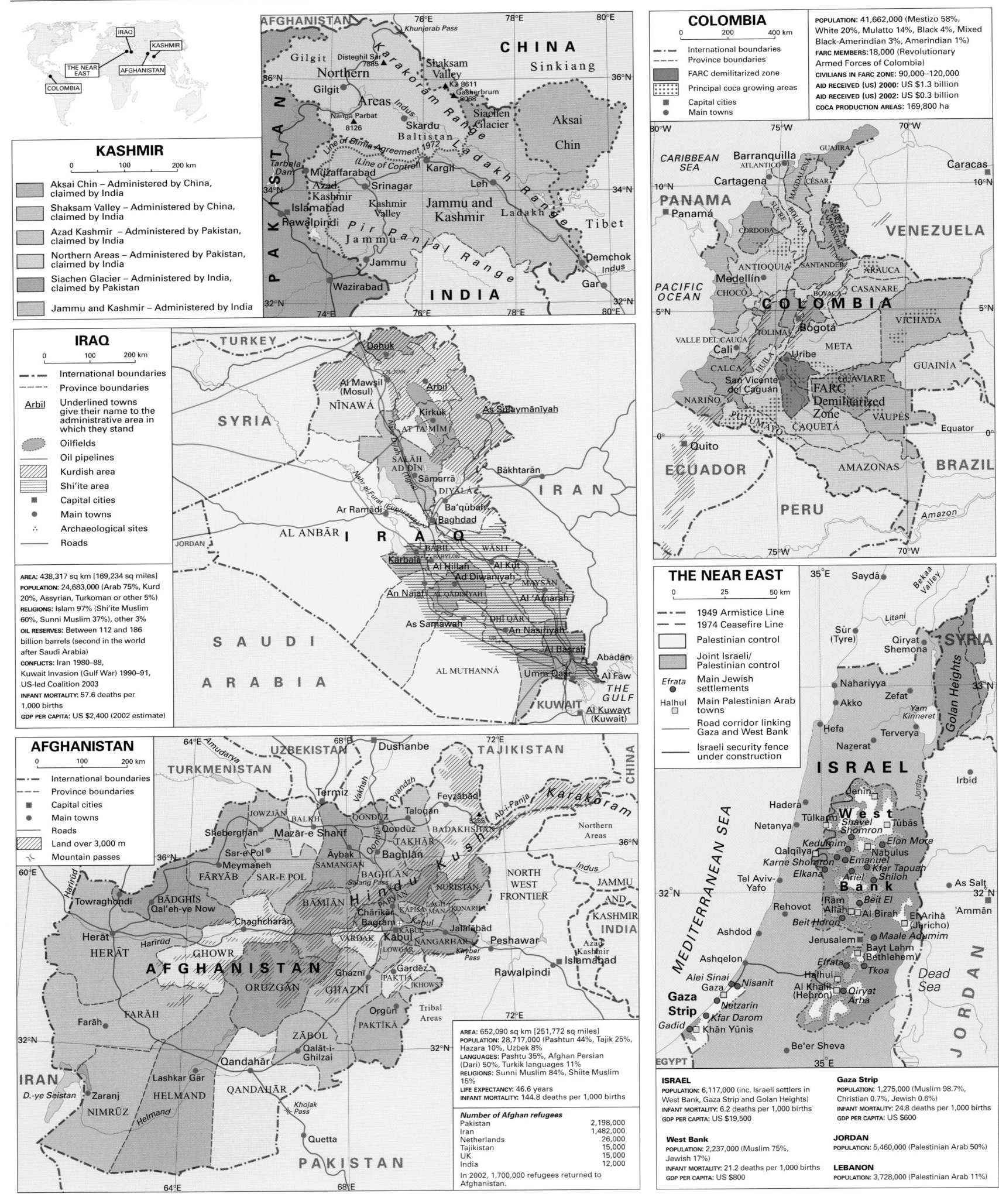

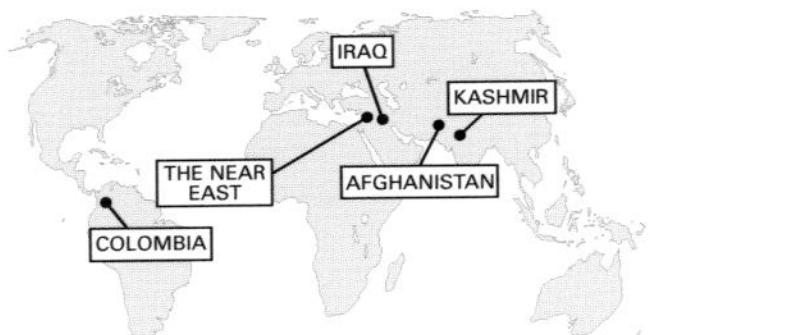

KASHMIR

0 100 200 km

- Aksai Chin – Administered by China, claimed by India
- Shaksam Valley – Administered by China, claimed by India
- Azad Kashmir – Administered by Pakistan, claimed by India
- Northern Areas – Administered by Pakistan, claimed by India
- Siachen Glacier – Administered by India, claimed by Pakistan
- Jammu and Kashmir – Administered by India

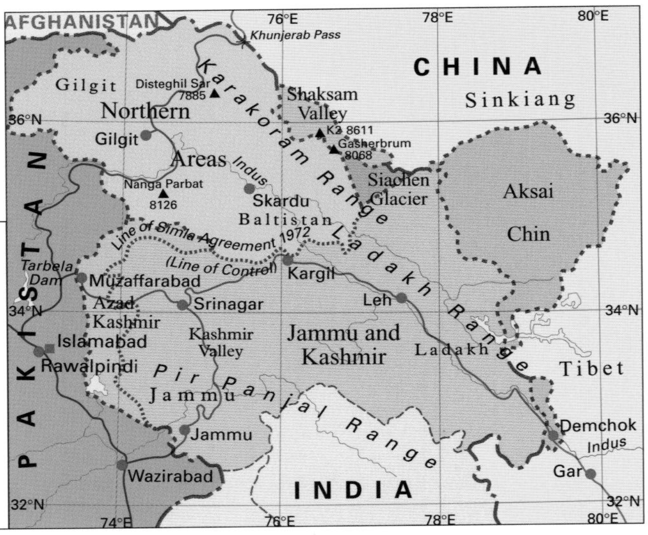

IRAQ

0 100 200 km

- International boundaries
- Province boundaries
- Arbil — Underlined towns give their name to the administrative area in which they stand
- Oilfields
- Oil pipelines
- Kurdish area
- Shi'ite area
- Capital cities
- Main towns
- Archaeological sites
- Roads

AREA: 438,317 sq km [169,234 sq miles]
POPULATION: 24,683,000 (Arab 75%, Kurd 20%, Assyrian, Turkoman or other 5%)
RELIGIONS: Islam 97% (Shi'ite Muslim 60%, Sunni Muslim 37%), other 3%
OIL RESERVES: Between 112 and 186 billion barrels (second in the world after Saudi Arabia)
CONFLICTS: Iran 1980–88, Kuwait Invasion (Gulf War) 1990–91, US-led Coalition 2003
INFANT MORTALITY: 57.6 deaths per 1,000 births
GDP PER CAPITA: US $2,400 (2002 estimate)

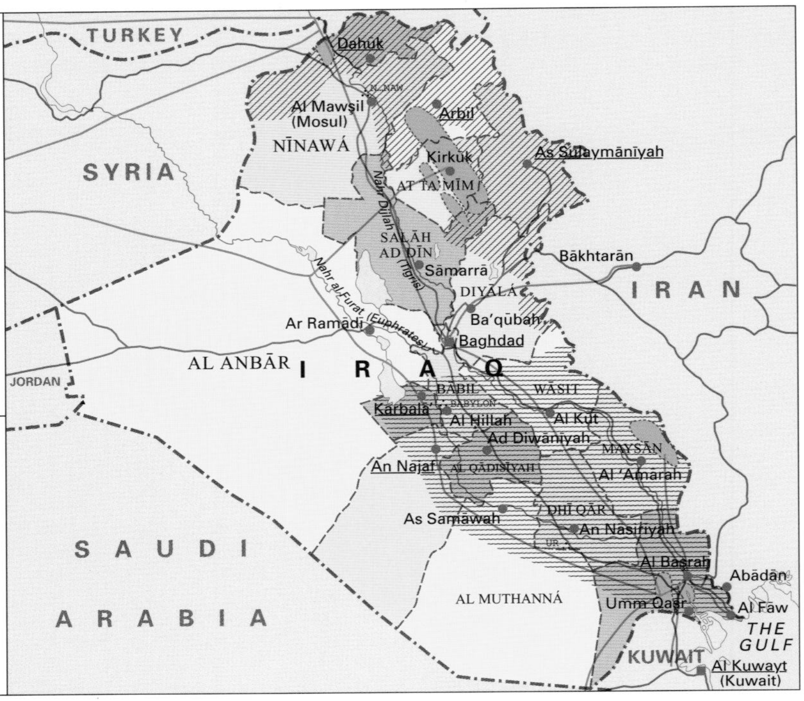

AFGHANISTAN

0 100 200 km

- International boundaries
- Province boundaries
- Capital cities
- Main towns
- Roads
- Land over 3,000 m
- Mountain passes

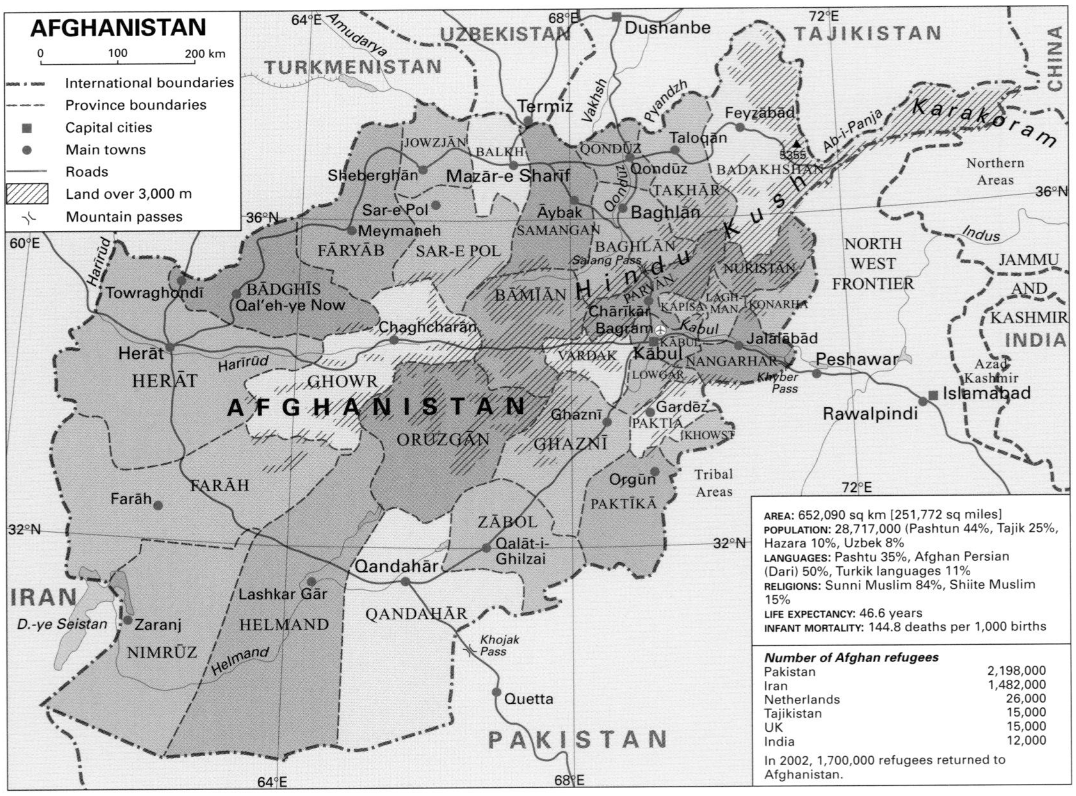

AREA: 652,090 sq km [251,772 sq miles]
POPULATION: 28,717,000 (Pashtun 44%, Tajik 25%, Hazara 10%, Uzbek 8%
LANGUAGES: Pashtu 35%, Afghan Persian (Dari) 50%, Turkik languages 11%
RELIGIONS: Sunni Muslim 84%, Shiite Muslim 15%
LIFE EXPECTANCY: 46.6 years
INFANT MORTALITY: 144.8 deaths per 1,000 births

Number of Afghan refugees

Pakistan	2,198,000
Iran	1,482,000
Netherlands	26,000
Tajikistan	15,000
UK	15,000
India	12,000

In 2002, 1,700,000 refugees returned to Afghanistan.

COLOMBIA

0 200 400 km

- International boundaries
- Province boundaries
- FARC demilitarized zone
- Principal coca growing areas
- Capital cities
- Main towns

POPULATION: 41,662,000 (Mestizo 58%, White 20%, Mulatto 14%, Black 4%, Mixed Black-Amerindian 3%, Amerindian 1%)
FARC MEMBERS: 18,000 (Revolutionary Armed Forces of Colombia)
CIVILIANS IN FARC ZONE: 90,000–120,000
AID RECEIVED (US) 2000: US $1.3 billion
AID RECEIVED (US) 2002: US $0.3 billion
COCA PRODUCTION AREAS: 169,800 ha

THE NEAR EAST

0 25 50 km

- 1949 Armistice Line
- 1974 Ceasefire Line
- Palestinian control
- Joint Israeli/Palestinian control
- Efrata — Main Jewish settlements
- Halhul — Main Palestinian Arab towns
- Road corridor linking Gaza and West Bank
- Israeli security fence under construction

ISRAEL
POPULATION: 6,117,000 (inc. Israeli settlers in West Bank, Gaza Strip and Golan Heights)
INFANT MORTALITY: 6.2 deaths per 1,000 births
GDP PER CAPITA: US $19,500

West Bank
POPULATION: 2,237,000 (Muslim 75%, Jewish 17%)
INFANT MORTALITY: 21.2 deaths per 1,000 births
GDP PER CAPITA: US $800

Gaza Strip
POPULATION: 1,275,000 (Muslim 98.7%, Christian 0.7%, Jewish 0.6%)
INFANT MORTALITY: 24.8 deaths per 1,000 births
GDP PER CAPITA: US $600

JORDAN
POPULATION: 5,460,000 (Palestinian Arab 50%)

LEBANON
POPULATION: 3,728,000 (Palestinian Arab 11%)

THE EARTH IN SPACE

The Universe 2

Star Charts and Constellations 4

The Solar System 8

The Earth: Time and Motion 10

The Earth from Space 12

The Dynamic Earth 14

Earthquakes and Volcanoes 16

Forces of Nature 18

Oceans and Ice 20

The Earth's Atmosphere 22

Climate and Weather 24

Water and Land Use 26

The Natural World 28

The Human World 30

Languages and Religions 32

International Organizations 34

Agriculture 36

Energy and Minerals 38

World Economies 40

Trade and Commerce 42

Travel and Communications 44

The World Today 46

The Universe

The depths of the Universe

This photograph shows some of the 1,500 or more galaxies that were recorded in the montage of photographs taken by the Hubble Space Telescope in 1995–6.

THE NEAREST STARS

The 20 nearest stars, excluding the Sun, with their distance from the Earth in light-years.*

Proxima Centauri	4.2
Alpha Centauri A	4.3
Alpha Centauri B	4.3
Barnard's Star	6.0
Wolf 359	7.8
Lalande 21185	8.3
Sirius A	8.7
Sirius B	8.7
UV Ceti A	8.7
UV Ceti B	8.7
Ross 154	9.4
Ross 248	10.3
Epsilon Eridani	10.7
Ross 128	10.9
61 Cygni A	11.1
61 Cygni B	11.1
Epsilon Indi	11.2
Groombridge 34 A	11.2
Groombridge 34 B	11.2
L789-6	11.2

** A light-year equals approximately 5,900 billion miles [9,500 billion km].*

In early 2003, NASA scientists produced an image of the Universe as it was about 380,000 years after its creation. The image was produced by an American satellite called the Wilkinson Microwave Anisotropy Probe (WMAP), which has been supplying data since its launch in June 2001.

The probe measures small variations in the cosmic wave radiation (CMB). By measuring the size of hot and cold spots in the CMB, scientists have calculated how far away they are, and this data has enabled them to calculate the age of the Universe. It has also established the proportions of its three ingredients, namely 4% ordinary matter (made up of atoms), 23% of "cold dark matter," whose nature is unknown, and 73% of the mysterious "dark energy," which seems to be accelerating the expansion of space.

Armed with the new data, scientists have established that our Universe was created, or "time" began, about 13.7 billion years ago (disproving earlier estimates that ranged from 8 billion to 24 billion years), that it is flat, and that the first stars did not appear until it was 200 million years old.

The Big Bang

Most scientists agree that the Universe was formed by a colossal explosion, called the "Big Bang." In the first millionth of a second after the Big Bang, the Universe expanded from a dimensionless point of infinite mass and

The end of the Universe

The diagram shows two theories concerning the fate of the Universe. One theory, top, suggests that the Universe will expand indefinitely, moving into an immense dark graveyard. Another theory, bottom, suggests that the galaxies will fall back until everything is again concentrated in one point in a so-called "Big Crunch." This might then be followed by a new "Big Bang."

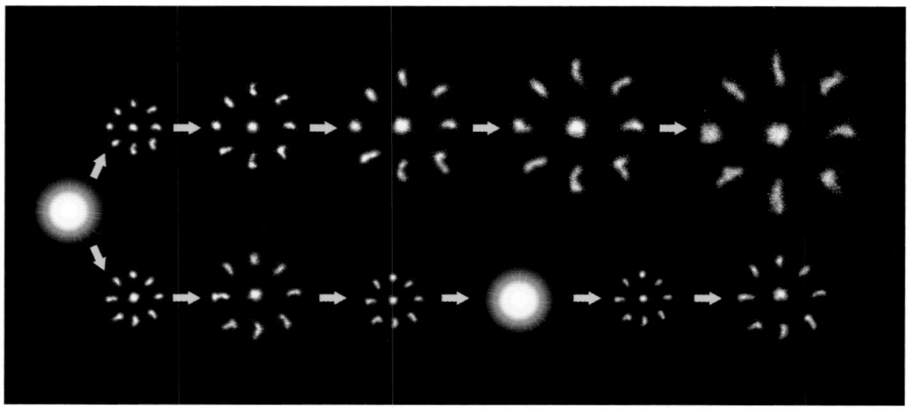

density into a fireball about 19 billion miles [30 billion km] across. The Universe has been expanding ever since, as demonstrated in the 1920s by Edwin Hubble, the American astronomer after whom the Hubble Space Telescope, which has also been shedding light on the origins of the Universe, was named.

The temperature at the end of the first second was perhaps 10 billion degrees – far too hot for composite atomic nuclei to exist. As a result, the fireball consisted mainly of radiation mixed with microscopic particles of matter. Almost a million years passed before the Universe was cool enough for atoms to form.

The Home Galaxy

This schematic plan shows that our Solar System is located in one of the spiral arms of the Milky Way galaxy, a little less than 30,000 light-years from its center. The center of the Milky Way galaxy is not visible from Earth. Instead, it is masked by light-absorbing clouds of interstellar dust.

In regions where matter was relatively dense, atoms began, under the influence of gravity, to move together to form protogalaxies – masses of gas separated by empty space. The protogalaxies were dark, because the Universe had cooled. But 200 million years after its creation, stars began to form within the protogalaxies as particles were drawn together. The internal pressure produced as matter condensed created the high temperatures required to cause nuclear fusion. Stars were born and later destroyed. Each generation of stars fed on the debris of extinct ones. Each generation produced larger atoms, increasing the number of different chemical elements.

The Galaxies

At least a billion galaxies are scattered through the Universe, though the discoveries made by the Hubble Space Telescope suggest that there may be far more than once thought, and some estimates are as high as 100 billion. The largest galaxies contain trillions of stars, while small ones contain less than a billion.

Galaxies tend to occur in groups or clusters, while some clusters appear to be grouped in vast superclusters. Our Local Cluster includes the spiral Milky Way galaxy, whose diameter is about 100,000 light-years; one light-year, the distance that light travels in one year, measures about 5,900 billion miles [9,500 billion km]. The Milky Way is a huge galaxy, shaped like a disk with a bulge at the center. It is larger, brighter and more massive than many other known galaxies. It contains about 100 billion stars which rotate around the center of the galaxy in the same direction as the Sun does.

One medium-sized star in the Milky Way galaxy is the Sun. After its formation, about 5 billion years ago, there was enough leftover matter around it to create the planets, asteroids, moons, and other bodies that together form our Solar System. The Solar System rotates around the center of the Milky Way galaxy approximately every 225 million years.

The Milky Way

This section of the Milky Way is dominated by Sirius, the Dog Star, top center, in the constellation of Canis Major. Sirius is the brightest star in the sky.

Stars similar to our Sun are known to have planets orbiting around them. By the start of 2003, 100 or so extrasolar planets had been reported, and evidence from the Hubble Space Telescope suggests that the raw materials from which planets are formed is common in dusty disks around many stars. This provokes one of the most intriguing questions that has ever faced humanity. If other planets exist in the Universe, then are they home to living organisms?

Before the time of Galileo, people thought that the Earth lay at the center of the Universe. But we now know that our Solar System and even the Milky Way galaxy are tiny specks in the Universe as a whole. Perhaps our planet is also not unique in being the only one to support intelligent life.

Star Charts and Constellations

The Big Dipper

The Big Dipper, or Plough, above glowing yellow clouds lit by city lights. It is part of a larger group called Ursa Major, one of the best-known constellations of the northern hemisphere. The two bright stars to the lower right of the photograph (Merak and Dubhe) are known as the Pointers because they show the way to the Pole Star.

THE BRIGHTEST STARS

The 15 brightest stars visible from northern Europe and similar latitudes. Magnitudes are given to the nearest tenth.

Sirius	−1.5
Arcturus	0.0
Vega	0.0
Capella	0.1
Rigel	0.1
Procyon	0.4
Betelgeuse	0.4
Altair	0.8
Aldebaran	0.8
Antares	1.0
Spica	1.0
Pollux	1.1
Fomalhaut	1.2
Deneb	1.2
Regulus	1.3

On a clear night, under the best conditions and far away from the glare of city lights, a person in northern Europe or North America can look up and see about 2,500 stars. In a town, however, light pollution can reduce visibility to 200 stars or less. Over the whole celestial sphere it is possible to see about 8,500 stars with the naked eye and it is only when you look through a telescope that you begin to realize that the number of stars is countless.

Small and Large Stars

Stars come in several sizes. Some, called neutron stars, are compact, with the same mass as the Sun but with diameters of only about 12 miles [20 km]. Larger than neutron stars are the small white dwarfs. Our Sun is a medium-sized star, but many visible stars in the night sky are giants with diameters between 10 and 100 times that of the Sun, or supergiants with diameters over 100 times that of the Sun.

Two bright stars in the constellation Orion are Betelgeuse (also known as Alpha Orionis) and Rigel (or Beta Orionis). Betelgeuse is an orange-red supergiant, whose diameter is about 400 times that of the Sun. Rigel is also a supergiant. Its diameter is about 50 times that of the Sun, but its luminosity is estimated to be over 100,000 times that of the Sun.

The stars we see in the night sky all belong to our home galaxy, the Milky Way. This name is also used for the faint, silvery band that arches across the sky. This band, a slice through our

THE CONSTELLATIONS

The constellations and their English names. Constellations visible from both hemispheres are listed.

Andromeda	Andromeda	Delphinus	Dolphin	Perseus	Perseus
Antlia	Air Pump	Dorado	Swordfish	Phoenix	Phoenix
Apus	Bird of Paradise	Draco	Dragon	Pictor	Easel
Aquarius	Water Carrier	Equuleus	Little Horse	Pisces	Fishes
Aquila	Eagle	Eridanus	River Eridanus	Piscis Austrinus	Southern Fish
Ara	Altar	Fornax	Furnace	Puppis	Ship's Stern
Aries	Ram	Gemini	Twins	Pyxis	Mariner's Compass
Auriga	Charioteer	Grus	Crane	Reticulum	Net
Boötes	Herdsman	Hercules	Hercules	Sagitta	Arrow
Caelum	Chisel	Horologium	Clock	Sagittarius	Archer
Camelopardalis	Giraffe	Hydra	Water Snake	Scorpius	Scorpion
Cancer	Crab	Hydrus	Sea Serpent	Sculptor	Sculptor
Canes Venatici	Hunting Dogs	Indus	Indian	Scutum	Shield
Canis Major	Great Dog	Lacerta	Lizard	Serpens*	Serpent
Canis Minor	Little Dog	Leo	Lion	Sextans	Sextant
Capricornus	Sea Goat	Leo Minor	Little Lion	Taurus	Bull
Carina	Ship's Keel	Lepus	Hare	Telescopium	Telescope
Cassiopeia	Cassiopeia	Libra	Scales	Triangulum	Triangle
Centaurus	Centaur	Lupus	Wolf	Triangulum Australe	Southern Triangle
Cepheus	Cepheus	Lynx	Lynx	Tucana	Toucan
Cetus	Whale	Lyra	Lyre	Ursa Major	Great Bear
Chamaeleon	Chameleon	Mensa	Table	Ursa Minor	Little Bear
Circinus	Compasses	Microscopium	Microscope	Vela	Ship's Sails
Columba	Dove	Monoceros	Unicorn	Virgo	Virgin
Coma Berenices	Berenice's Hair	Musca	Fly	Volans	Flying Fish
Corona Australis	Southern Crown	Norma	Level	Vulpecula	Fox
Corona Borealis	Northern Crown	Octans	Octant		
Corvus	Crow	Ophiuchus	Serpent Bearer		
Crater	Cup	Orion	Hunter		
Crux	Southern Cross	Pavo	Peacock		
Cygnus	Swan	Pegasus	Winged Horse		

** In two halves: Serpens Caput, the head, and Serpens Cauda, the tail.*

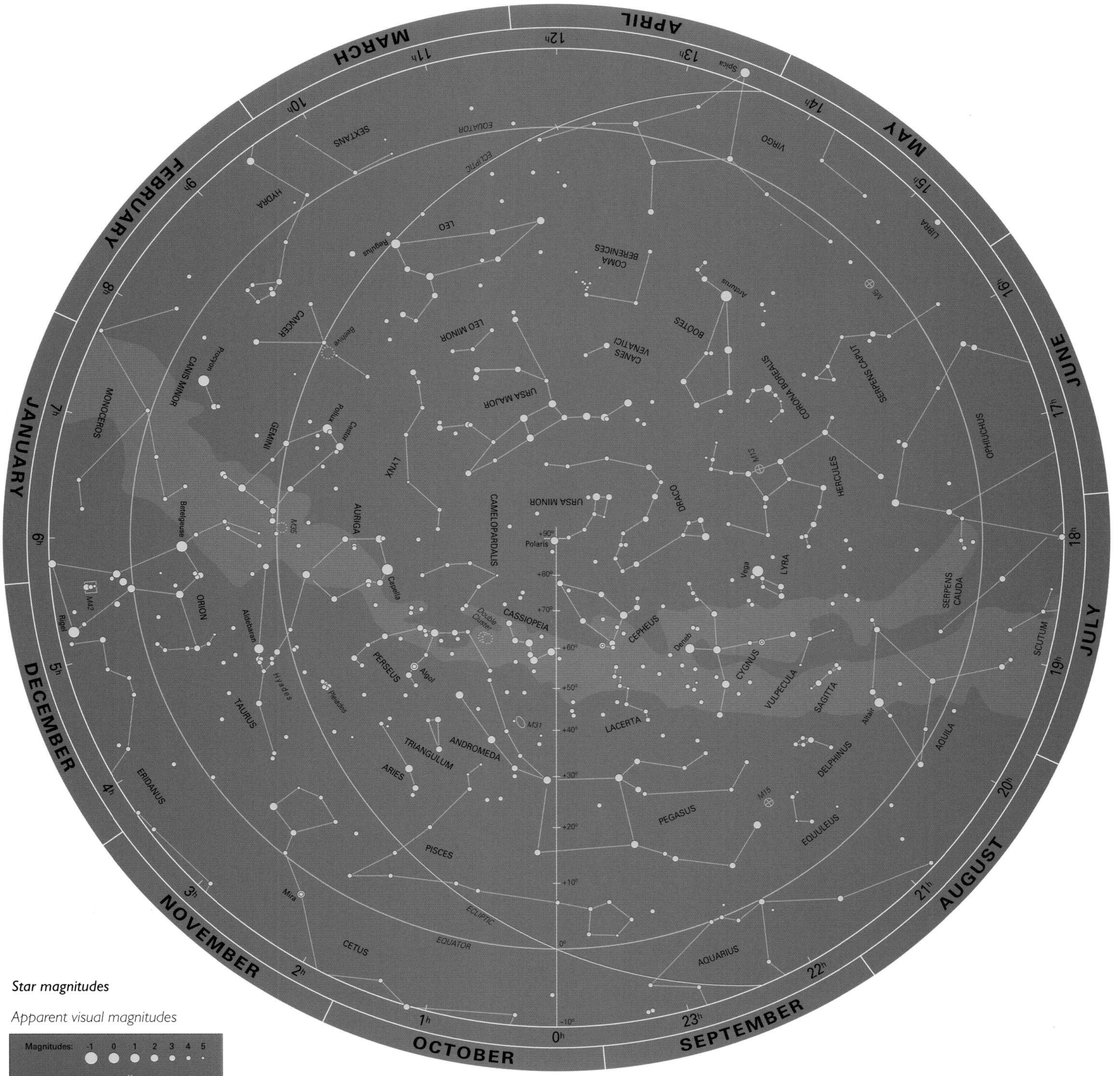

Star magnitudes

Apparent visual magnitudes

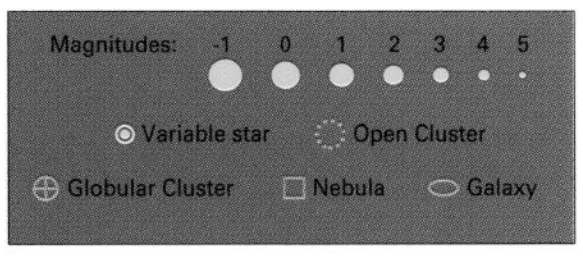

The Milky Way is shown in light blue on the above chart.

Star chart of the northern hemisphere

When you look into the sky, the stars seem to be on the inside of a huge dome. This gives astronomers a way of mapping them. This chart shows the sky as it would appear from the North Pole. To use the star chart above, an observer in the northern hemisphere should face south and turn the chart so that the current month appears at the bottom. The chart will then show the constellations on view at approximately 11 p.m. Greenwich Mean Time. The map should be rotated clockwise 15° for each hour before 11 p.m. and counterclockwise for each hour after 11 p.m.

galaxy, contains an enormous number of stars. The nucleus of the Milky Way galaxy cannot be seen from Earth. Lying in the direction of the constellation Sagittarius in the southern hemisphere, it is masked by clouds of dust.

The Brightness of Stars

Astronomers use a scale of magnitudes to measure the brightness of stars. The brightest visible to the naked eye were originally known as first-magnitude stars, ones not so bright were second-magnitude, down to the faintest visible, which were rated as sixth-magnitude. The brighter the star, the lower the magnitude. With the advent of telescopes and the development of accurate instruments for measuring brightnesses, the magnitude scale has been refined and extended. Very bright bodies such as Sirius, Venus, and the Sun have negative magnitudes. The nearest star is Proxima Centauri, part of a multiple star system, which is 4.2 light-years away. Proxima Centauri is very faint and has a magnitude of 11.3. Alpha Centauri A, one of the two brighter members of the system, is the nearest visible star to Earth. It has a magnitude of 1.7.

These magnitudes are known as apparent magnitudes – measures of the brightnesses of the stars as they appear to us. These are the magnitudes shown on the charts on these pages. But the stars are at very different distances. The star Deneb, in the constellation Cygnus, for example, is over 1,200 light-years away. So astronomers also use absolute magnitudes – measures of how bright the stars really are. A star's absolute magnitude is the apparent magnitude it would have if it could be placed 32.6 light-years away. So Deneb, with an apparent magnitude of 1.2, has an absolute magnitude of –7.2.

The brightest star in the night sky is Sirius, the Dog Star, with a magnitude of –1.5. This medium-sized star is 8.64 light-years distant but it gives out about 20 times as much light as the Sun. After the Sun and the Moon, the brightest objects in the sky are the planets Venus, Mars, and Jupiter. For example, Venus has a magnitude of up to –4. The planets have no light of their own, however, and shine only because they reflect the Sun's rays. But whilst stars have fixed positions, the planets shift nightly in relation to the constellations, following a path called the Ecliptic (shown on the star charts). As they follow their orbits around the Sun, their distances from the Earth vary, and therefore so also do their magnitudes.

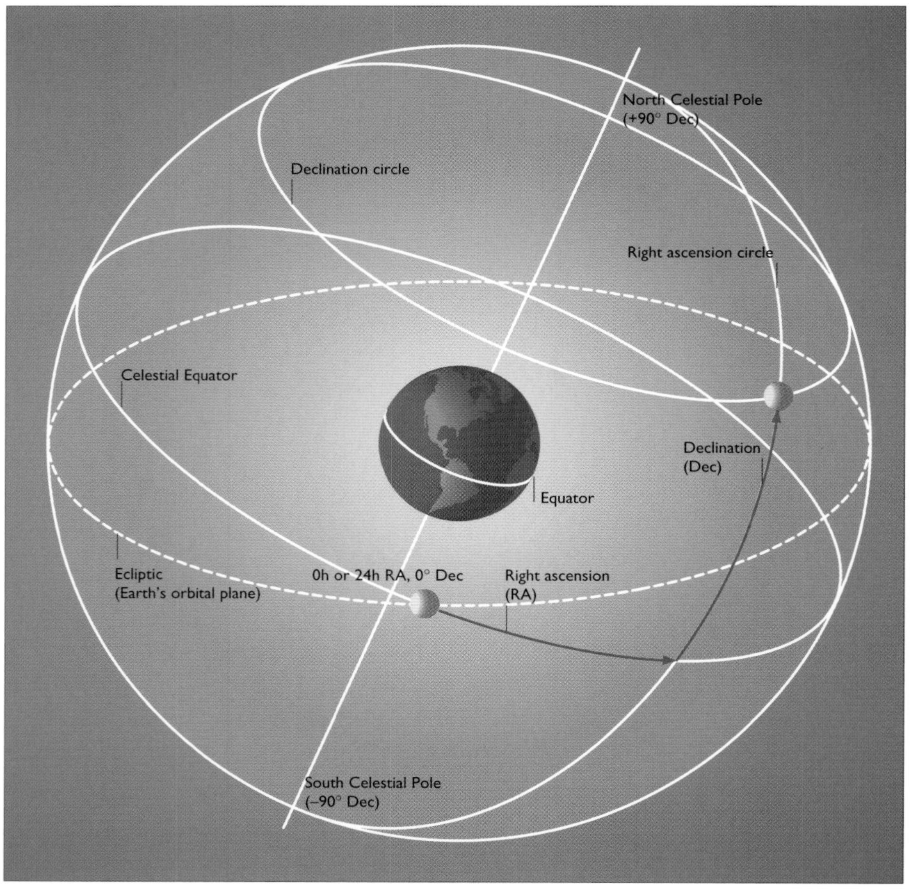

Celestial sphere
The diagram shows the imaginary surface on which astronomical positions are measured. The celestial sphere appears to rotate about the celestial poles, as though an extension of the Earth's own axis. The Earth's axis points toward the celestial poles.

While atlas maps record the details of the Earth's surface, star charts are a guide to the heavens. An observer at the Equator can see the entire sky at some time during the year, but an observer at the poles can see only the stars in a single hemisphere. As a result, star charts of both hemispheres are produced. The northern hemisphere chart is centered on the North Celestial Pole, while the southern hemisphere chart is centered on the South Celestial Pole.

In the northern hemisphere, the North Pole is marked by the star Polaris, or North Star. Polaris lies within a degree of the point where an extension of the Earth's axis meets the sky. Polaris appears to be stationary and navigators throughout history have used it as a guide. Unfortunately, the South Pole has no convenient reference point.

Star charts of the two hemispheres are bounded by the Celestial Equator, an imaginary line in the sky directly above the terrestrial Equator. Astronomical coordinates, which give the location of stars, are normally stated in terms of right ascension (the equivalent of longitude) and declination (the equivalent of latitude). Because the stars appear to rotate around the Earth every 24 hours, right ascension is measured eastward in hours and minutes. Declination is measured in degrees north or south of the Celestial Equator.

The Southern Cross
The Southern Cross, or Crux, in the southern hemisphere, was classified as a constellation in the 17th century. It is as familiar to Australians and New Zealanders as the Big Dipper (or Plough) is to people in the northern hemisphere. The vertical axis of the Southern Cross points toward the South Celestial Pole.

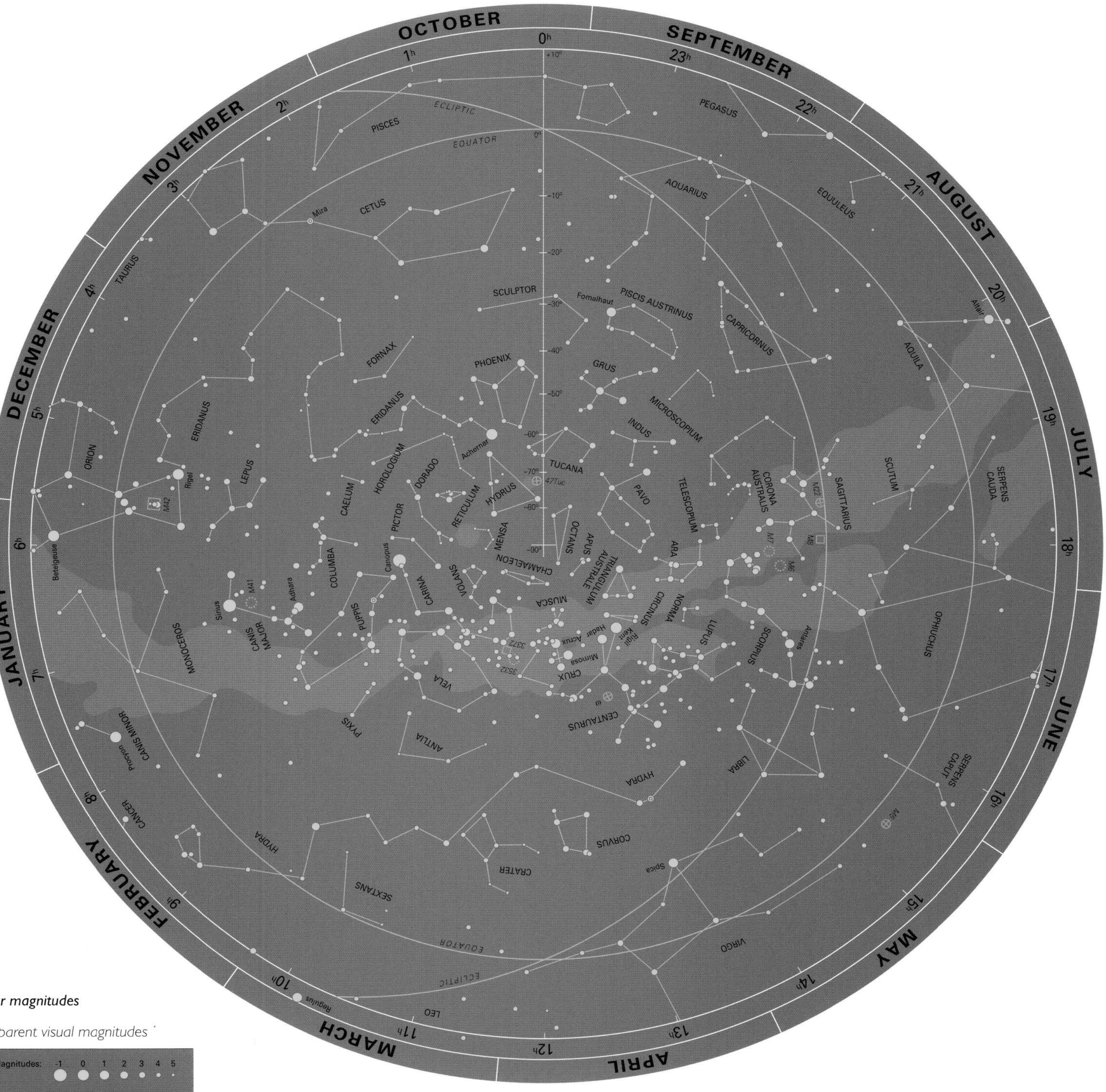

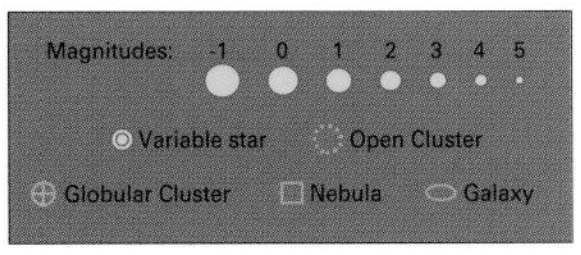

Star magnitudes

Apparent visual magnitudes

The Milky Way is shown in light blue on the above chart.

Star chart of the southern hemisphere

Many constellations in the southern hemisphere were named not by the ancients but by later astronomers. Some, including Antila (Air Pump) and Microscopium (Microscope), have modern names. The Large and Small Magellanic Clouds (LMC, SMC) are small "satellite" galaxies of the Milky Way. To use the chart, an observer in the southern hemisphere should face north and turn the chart so that the current month appears at the bottom. The map will then show the constellations on view at approximately 11 p.m. Greenwich Mean Time. The chart should be rotated clockwise 15° for each hour before 11 p.m. and counterclockwise for each hour after 11 p.m.

Constellations

Every star is identifiable as a member of a constellation. The night sky contains 88 constellations, many of which were named by the ancient Greeks, Romans, and other early peoples after animals and mythological characters, such as Orion and Perseus. More recently, astronomers invented names for constellations seen in the southern hemisphere, in areas not visible around the Mediterranean Sea.

Some groups of easily recognizable stars form parts of a constellation. For example, seven stars form the shape of the Big Dipper, or Plough, within the constellation Ursa Major. Such groups are called asterisms.

The stars in constellations lie in the same direction in space, but normally at vastly different distances. Hence, there is no real connection between them. The positions of stars seem fixed, but in fact the shapes of the constellations are changing slowly over very long periods of time. This is because the stars have their own "proper motions," which because of the huge distances involved are imperceptible to the naked eye.

The Solar System

Although the origins of the Solar System are still a matter of debate, many scientists believe that it was formed from a cloud of gas and dust, the debris from some long-lost, exploded star. Around 5 billion years ago, material was drawn towards the hub of the rotating disk of gas and dust, where it was compressed to thermonuclear fusion temperatures. A new star, the Sun, was born, containing 99.8% of the mass of the Solar System. The remaining material was later drawn together to form the planets and the other bodies in the Solar System. Spacecraft, manned and unmanned, have greatly increased our knowledge of the Solar System since the start of the Space Age in 1957, when the Soviet Union launched the satellite Sputnik I.

The Planets

Mercury is the closest planet to the Sun and the fastest moving. Space probes have revealed that its surface is covered by craters, and looks much like our Moon. Mercury is a hostile place, with no significant atmosphere and temperatures ranging between 750°F [400°C] by day and –275°F [–170°C] by night. It seems unlikely that anyone will ever want to visit this planet.

Venus is much the same size as Earth, but it is the hottest of the planets, with temperatures reaching 885°F [475°C], even at night. The reason for this scorching heat is the atmosphere, which consists mainly of carbon dioxide, a gas that traps heat thus creating a greenhouse effect. The density of the atmosphere is about 90 times that of Earth and dense clouds permanently mask the surface. Active volcanic regions discharging sulfur dioxide may account for the haze of sulfuric acid droplets in the upper atmosphere.

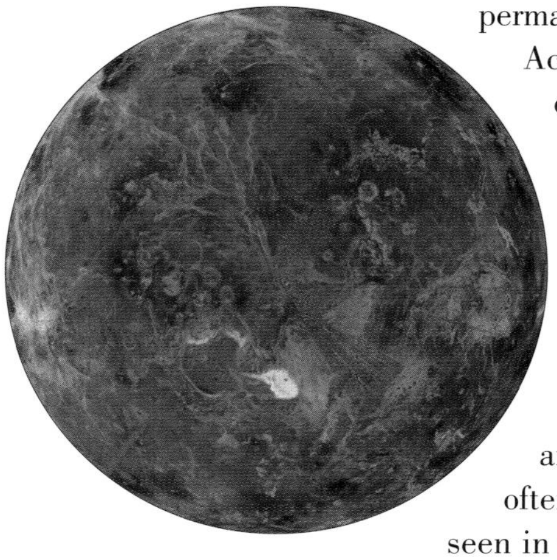

From planet Earth, Venus is brighter than any other star or planet and is easy to spot. It is often the first object to be seen in the evening sky and the last to be seen in the morning sky. It can even be seen in daylight.

Earth, seen from space, looks blue (because of the oceans which cover more than 70% of the planet) and white (a result of clouds in the atmosphere). The atmosphere and water make Earth the only planet known to support life. The Earth's hard outer layers, including the crust and the top of the mantle, are divided into rigid plates. Forces inside the Earth move the plates, modifying the landscape, and causing earthquakes and volcanic activity. Weathering and erosion also change the surface.

Mars has many features in common with Earth, including an atmosphere with clouds and polar caps that partly melt in summer. Scientists once considered that it was the most likely planet on which other life might exist, but the two Viking space probes that went there in the 1970s found only a barren rocky surface with no trace of water. But in 2004, two NASA Mars rovers, Spirit and Opportunity, sent back evidence that Mars was once wet and potentially habitable, at least by simple microbes.

PLANETARY DATA

Planet	Mean distance from Sun (million miles)	Mass (Earth=1)	Period of orbit (Earth days/yrs)	Period of rotation (Earth days)	Equatorial diameter (miles)	Average density (water=1)	Surface gravity (Earth=1)	Number of known satellites
Sun	–	*332,946*	–	*25.4*	*865,000*	*1.41*	*27.9*	–
Mercury	36.0	0.055	87.97d	58.67	3,031	5.44	0.38	0
Venus	67.2	0.815	224.7d	243.00	7,521	5.25	0.90	0
Earth	93.0	1.0	365.3d	1.00	7,926	5.52	1.00	1
Mars	141.6	0.11	687.0d	1.028	4,222	3.94	0.38	2
Jupiter	483.4	317.9	11.86y	0.411	89,405	1.33	2.64	63
Saturn	886.7	95.2	29.46y	0.427	74,898	0.71	1.16	31
Uranus	1,783.3	14.6	84.01y	0.748	31,763	1.27	0.79	27
Neptune	2,794.3	17.2	164.8y	0.710	31,403	1.77	0.98	13
Pluto	3,666.1	0.002	247.7y	6.39	1,444	2.02	0.06	1

Asteroids are small, rocky bodies. Most of them orbit the Sun between Mars and Jupiter, but some small ones can approach the Earth. The largest is Ceres, 567 miles [913 km] in diameter. There may be around a million asteroids bigger than 0.6 miles [1 km].

Jupiter, the giant planet, lies beyond Mars and the asteroid belt. Its mass is almost three times as much as all the other planets combined and, because of its size, it shines more brightly than any other planet apart from Venus and, occasionally, Mars. The four largest moons of Jupiter were discovered by Galileo. Jupiter is made up mostly of hydrogen and helium, covered by a layer of clouds. Its Great Red Spot is a high-pressure storm. Jupiter made headline news when it was struck by fragments of Comet Shoemaker–Levy 9 in July 1994. This was the greatest collision ever seen by scientists between a planet and another heavenly body. The fragments of the comet that crashed into Jupiter created huge fireballs that caused scars on the planet that remained visible for months after the event.

Saturn is structurally similar to Jupiter but it is best known for its rings. The rings measure about 170,000 miles [270,000 km] across, yet they are no more than a few hundred yards thick. Seen from Earth, the rings seem divided into three main bands of varying brightness, but photographs sent back by the Voyager space probes in 1980 and 1981 showed that they are broken up into thousands of thin ringlets composed of ice particles ranging in size from a snowball to an iceberg. The origin of the rings is still a matter of debate.

Uranus was discovered in 1781 by William Herschel, who first thought it was a comet. It is broadly similar to Jupiter and Saturn in composition, though its distance from the Sun makes its surface even colder. Uranus is circled by thin rings which were discovered in 1977. Unlike the rings of Saturn, the rings of Uranus are black, which explains why they cannot be seen from Earth.

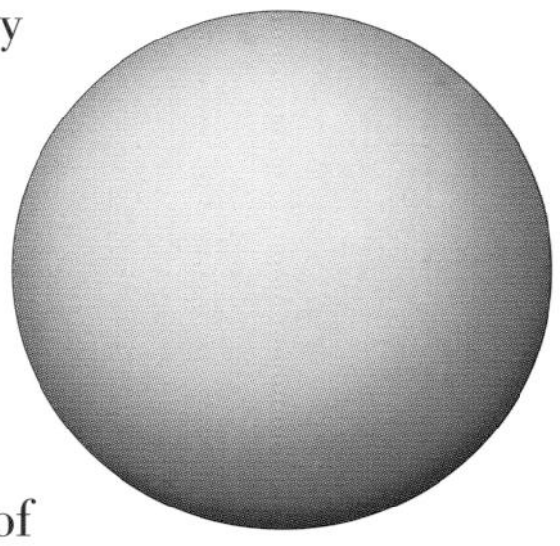

Neptune, named after the mythological sea god, was discovered in 1846 as the result of mathematical predictions made by astronomers to explain irregularities in the orbit of Uranus, its near twin. Little was known about this distant body until Voyager 2 came close to it in 1989. Neptune has thin rings, like those of Uranus. Among its blue-green clouds is a prominent dark spot, which rotates counterclockwise every 18 hours or so.

Pluto is the smallest planet in the Solar System, even smaller than our Moon. The American astronomer Clyde Tombaugh discovered Pluto in 1930. Its orbit is odd and it sometimes comes closer to the Sun than Neptune. Beyond Pluto are many small asteroid-like bodies. In 2004, astronomers announced that the Solar System's most distant object, which they named Sedna after an Inuit goddess, was a planetoid rather than a tenth planet.

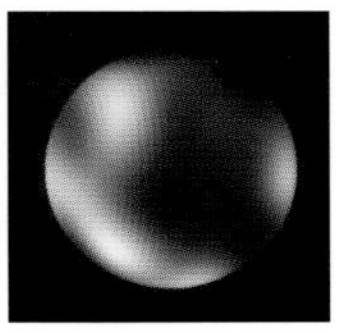

Comets are small icy bodies that orbit the Sun in highly elliptical orbits. When a comet swings in toward the Sun some of its ice evaporates, and the comet brightens and may become visible from Earth. The best known is Halley's Comet, which takes 76 years to orbit the Sun.

The Earth: Time and Motion

The Earth is constantly moving through space like a huge, self-sufficient spaceship. First, with the rest of the Solar System, it moves around the center of the Milky Way galaxy. Second, it rotates around the Sun at a speed of more than 60,000 mph [more than 100,000 km/h], covering a distance of nearly 600 million miles [1,000 million km] in a little over 365 days. The Earth also spins on its axis, an imaginary line joining the North and South Poles, via the center of the Earth, completing one turn in a day. The Earth's movements around the Sun determine our calendar, though accurate observations of the stars made by astronomers help to keep our clocks in step with the rotation of the Earth around the Sun.

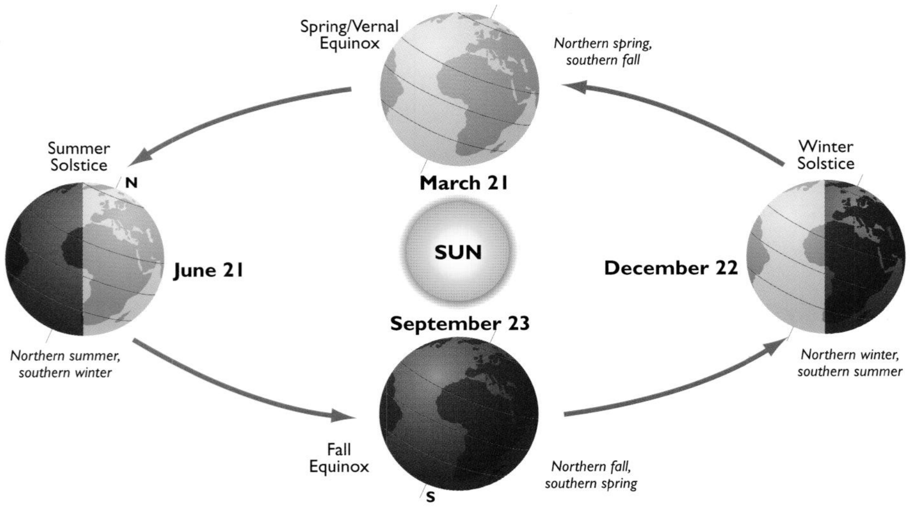

The Seasons
The 23½° tilt of the Earth's axis remains constant as the Earth orbits around the Sun. As a result, first the northern and then the southern hemispheres lean toward the Sun. Annual variations in the amount of sunlight received in turn by each hemisphere are responsible for the four seasons experienced in the middle latitudes.

The Earth from the Moon
In 1969, Neil Armstrong and Edwin "Buzz" Aldrin, Junior, were the first people to set foot on the Moon. The photographs forming this composite view of the Earth and Moon were taken by the crew of Apollo 11.

The Changing Year

The Earth takes 365 days, 6 hours, 9 minutes, and 9.54 seconds to complete one orbit around the Sun. We have a calendar year of 365 days, so allowance has to be made for the extra time over and above the 365 days. This is allowed for by introducing leap years of 366 days. Leap years are generally those, such as 1992 and 1996, which are divisible by four. Century years, however, are not leap years unless they are divisible by 400. Hence, 1700, 1800, and 1900 were not leap years, but the year 2000 was one. Leap years help to make the calendar conform with the solar year.

Because the Earth's axis is tilted by 23½°, the middle latitudes enjoy four distinct seasons. On March 21, the vernal or spring equinox in the northern hemisphere, the Sun is directly overhead at the Equator and everywhere on Earth has about 12 hours of daylight and 12 hours of darkness. But as the Earth continues on its journey around the Sun, the northern hemisphere tilts more and more toward the Sun. Finally, on June 21, the Sun is overhead at the Tropic of Cancer (latitude 23½° North). This is

Tides
The daily rises and falls of the ocean's waters are caused by the gravitational pull of the Moon and the Sun. The effect is greatest on the hemisphere facing the Moon, causing a "tidal bulge." The diagram below shows that the Sun, Moon, and Earth are in line when the spring tides occur. This causes the greatest tidal ranges. On the other hand, the neap tides occur when the pull of the Moon and the Sun are opposed. Neap tides, when tidal ranges are at their lowest, occur near the Moon's first and third quarters.

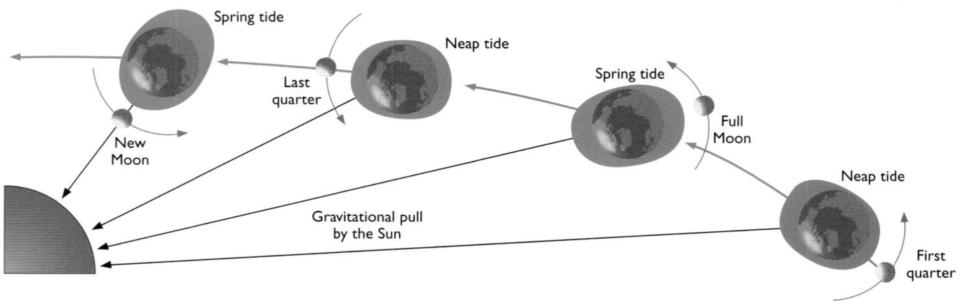

SUN DATA	
DIAMETER	865,000 miles
VOLUME (EARTH=1)	1.303×10^6
MASS	1.989×10^{30} kg
MASS (EARTH=1)	3.329×10^6
MEAN DENSITY (WATER=1)	1.409
ROTATION PERIOD	
AT EQUATOR	25.4 days
AT POLES	about 35 days
SURFACE GRAVITY (EARTH=1)	28
MAGNITUDE	
APPARENT	–26.9
ABSOLUTE	+4.71
TEMPERATURE	
AT SURFACE	5,400°C [5,700 K]
AT CORE	15×10^6 K

MOON DATA	
DIAMETER	2,160 miles
MASS (EARTH=1)	0.0123
DENSITY (WATER=1)	3.34
MEAN DISTANCE FROM EARTH	238,828 miles
MAXIMUM DISTANCE (APOGEE)	252,681 miles
MINIMUM DISTANCE (PERIGEE)	221,438 miles
SIDEREAL ROTATION AND REVOLUTION PERIOD	27.322 days
SYNODIC MONTH (NEW MOON TO NEW MOON)	29.531 days
SURFACE GRAVITY (EARTH=1)	0.165
MAXIMUM SURFACE TEMPERATURE	+130°C [403 K]
MINIMUM SURFACE TEMPERATURE	–158°C [115 K]

the summer solstice in the northern hemisphere.

The overhead Sun then moves south again until on September 23, the fall equinox in the northern hemisphere, the Sun is again overhead at the Equator. The overhead Sun then moves south until, on around December 22, it is overhead at the Tropic of Capricorn. This is the winter solstice in the northern hemisphere, and the summer solstice in the southern, where the seasons are reversed.

At the poles, there are two seasons. During half of the year, one of the poles leans toward the Sun and has continuous sunlight. For the other six months, the pole leans away from the Sun and is in continuous darkness.

Regions around the Equator do not have marked seasons. Because the Sun is high in the sky throughout the year, it is always hot or warm. When people talk of seasons in the tropics, they are usually referring to other factors, such as rainy and dry periods.

Day, Night and Tides

As the Earth rotates on its axis every 24 hours, first one side of the planet and then the other faces the Sun and enjoys daylight, while the opposite side is in darkness.

The length of daylight varies throughout the year. The longest day in the northern hemisphere falls on the summer solstice, June 21, while the longest day in the southern hemisphere is on December 22. At 40° latitude, the length of daylight on the longest day is 14 hours, 30 minutes. At 60° latitude, daylight on that day lasts 18 hours, 30 minutes. On the shortest day, December 22 in the northern hemisphere and June 21 in the southern, daylight hours at 40° latitude total 9 hours and 9 minutes. At latitude 60°, daylight lasts only 5 hours, 30 minutes in the 24-hour period.

Tides are caused by the gravitational pull of the Moon and, to a lesser extent, the Sun on the waters in the world's oceans. Tides occur twice every 24 hours, 50 minutes – one complete orbit of the Moon around the Earth.

The highest tides, the spring tides, occur when the Earth, Moon, and Sun are in a straight line, so that the gravitational pulls of the Moon and Sun are combined. The lowest, or neap, tides occur when the Moon, Earth, and Sun form a right angle. The gravitational pull of the Moon is then opposed by the gravitational pull of the Sun. The greatest tidal ranges occur in the Bay of Fundy in North America. The greatest mean spring range is 47.5 ft [14.5 m].

The speed at which the Earth is spinning on its axis is gradually slowing down, because of the movement of tides. As a result, experts have calculated that, in about 200 million years, the day will be 25 hours long.

Total eclipse of the Sun
A total eclipse is caused when the Moon passes between the Sun and the Earth. With the Sun's bright disk completely obscured, the Sun's corona, or outer atmosphere, can be viewed.

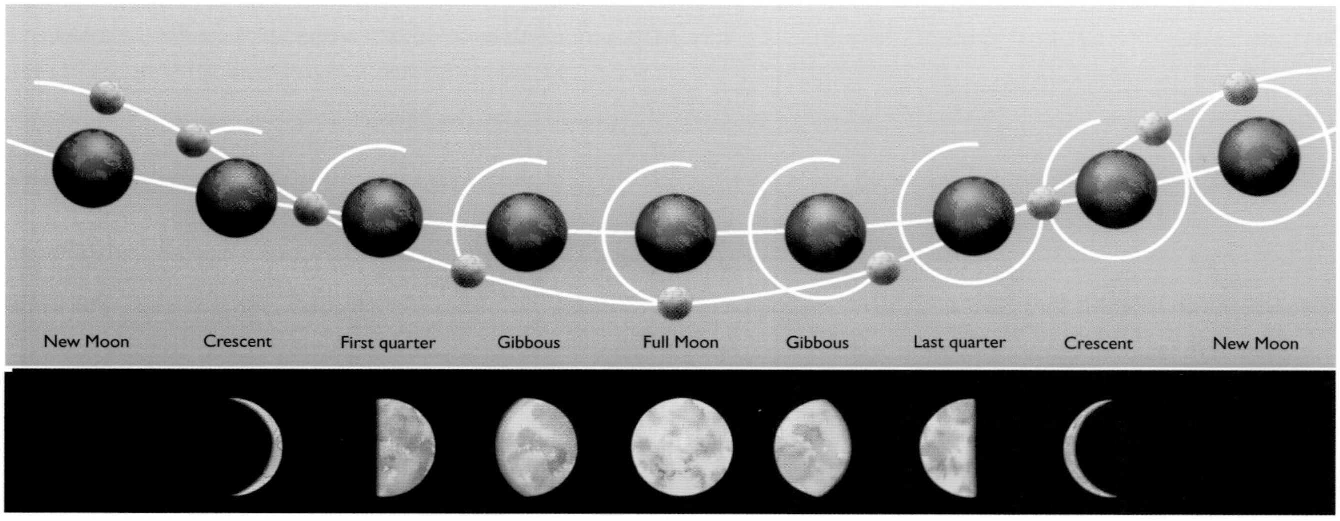

Phases of the Moon
The Moon rotates more slowly than the Earth, making one complete turn on its axis in just over 27 days. This corresponds to its period of revolution around the Earth and, hence, the same hemisphere always faces us. The interval between one full Moon and the next (and also between new Moons) is about 29½ days, or one lunar month. The apparent changes in the appearance of the Moon are caused by its changing position in relation to Earth. Like the planets, the Moon produces no light of its own. It shines by reflecting the Sun's rays, varying from a slim crescent to a full circle and back again.

The Earth from Space

Any last doubts about whether the Earth was round or flat were finally resolved by the appearance of the first photographs of our planet taken at the start of the Space Age. Satellite images also confirmed that map- and globe-makers had correctly worked out the shapes of the continents and the oceans.

More importantly, images of our beautiful, blue, white, and brown planet from space impressed on many people that the Earth and its resources are finite. They made people realize that if we allow our planet to be damaged by such factors as overpopulation, pollution, and irresponsible over-use of resources, then its future and the survival of all the living things upon it may be threatened.

Views from Above

The first aerial photographs were taken from balloons in the mid-19th century and their importance in military reconnaissance was recognized as early as the 1860s during the American Civil War.

Vesuvius and the Bay of Naples

Space photographs have given us a new perspective on planet Earth. They vividly convey the dramatic quality of landforms, such as Vesuvius, the volcanic craters that lie just west of Naples, and the isle of Capri to the south.

Since the end of World War II, photographs taken by aircraft have been widely used in map-making. The use of air photographs has greatly speeded up the laborious process of mapping land details and they have enabled cartographers to produce maps of the most remote parts of the world.

Aerial photographs have also proved useful because they reveal features that are not visible at ground level. For example, circles that appear on many air photographs do not correspond to visible features on the ground. Many of these mysterious shapes have turned out to be the sites of ancient settlements previously unknown to archaeologists.

Images from Space

Space probes equipped with cameras and a variety of remote-sensing instruments have sent back images of distant planets and moons. From these images, detailed maps have been produced, rapidly expanding our knowledge of the Solar System.

Photographs from space are also proving invaluable in the study of the Earth. One of the best known uses of space imagery is the study of the atmosphere. Polar-orbiting weather satellites that circle the Earth, together with geostationary satellites, whose motion is synchronized with the Earth's rotation, now regularly transmit images showing the changing patterns of weather systems from above. Forecasters use these images to track the development and the paths taken by hurricanes, enabling them to issue storm warnings to endangered areas, saving lives, and reducing damage to property.

Remote-sensing devices are now monitoring changes in temperatures over the land and sea, while photographs indicate the melting of ice sheets. Such evidence is vital in the study of global warming. Other devices reveal polluted areas, patterns of vegetation growth, and areas suffering deforestation.

In recent years, remote-sensing devices have been used to monitor the damage being done to the ozone layer in the stratosphere, which prevents most of the Sun's harmful ultraviolet radiation from reaching the surface. The discovery of "ozone holes," where the protective layer of ozone is being thinned by chlorofluorocarbons (CFCs), chemicals used in the manufacture of such things as air conditioners and refrigerators, has enabled governments to take concerted action to save our planet from imminent danger.

Earth Data

MAXIMUM DISTANCE FROM SUN (APHELION)
94,452,780 miles

MINIMUM DISTANCE FROM SUN (PERIHELION)
91,342,080 miles

LENGTH OF YEAR – SOLAR TROPICAL (EQUINOX TO EQUINOX)
365.24 days

LENGTH OF YEAR – SIDEREAL (FIXED STAR TO FIXED STAR)
365.26 days

LENGTH OF DAY – MEAN SOLAR DAY
24 hours, 03 minutes, 56 seconds

LENGTH OF DAY – MEAN SIDEREAL DAY
23 hours, 56 minutes, 4 seconds

SUPERFICIAL AREA
197,000,000 sq miles

LAND SURFACE
57,500,000 sq miles (29.2%)

WATER SURFACE
139,500,000 sq miles (70.8%)

EQUATORIAL CIRCUMFERENCE
24,903 miles

POLAR CIRCUMFERENCE
24,860 miles

EQUATORIAL DIAMETER
7,926 miles

POLAR DIAMETER
7,900 miles

EQUATORIAL RADIUS
3,963.4 miles

POLAR RADIUS
3,950 miles

VOLUME OF THE EARTH
260,000 x 10^6 cu miles

MASS OF THE EARTH
6.5 x 10^{21} tons

Satellite image of San Francisco Bay
Unmanned scientific satellites called ERTS (Earth Resources Technology Satellites), *or* Landsats, *were designed to collect information about the Earth's resources. The satellites transmitted images of the land using different wavelengths of light in order to identify, in false colors, such subtle features as areas that contain valuable minerals or areas covered with growing crops, that are not identifiable on simple photographs using the visible range of the spectrum. They were also equipped to monitor conditions in the atmosphere and oceans, and also to detect pollution levels. This* Landsat *image of San Francisco Bay covers an area of great interest to geologists because it lies in an earthquake zone in the path of the San Andreas fault.*

The Dynamic Earth

The Earth was formed about 4.6 billion years [4,600 million years] ago from the ring of gas and dust left over after the formation of the Sun. As the Earth took shape, lighter elements, such as silicon, rose to the surface, while heavy elements, notably iron, sank toward the center.

Gradually, the outer layers cooled to form a hard crust. The crust enclosed the dense mantle which, in turn, surrounded the even denser liquid outer and solid inner core. Around the Earth was an atmosphere, which contained abundant water

Lulworth Cove, southern England

When undisturbed by earth movements, sedimentary rock strata are generally horizontal. But lateral pressure has squeezed the Jurassic strata at Lulworth Cove into complex folds.

vapor. When the surface cooled, rainwater began to fill hollows, forming the first lakes and seas. Since that time, our planet has been subject to constant change – the result of powerful internal and external forces that still operate today.

The History of the Earth

From their study of rocks, geologists have pieced together the history of our planet and the life forms that evolved upon it. They have dated the oldest known crystals, composed of the mineral zircon, at 4.2 billion years. But the oldest rocks are younger, less than 4 billion years old. This is because older rocks have been recycled or weathered away by natural processes.

The oldest rocks that contain fossils, which are evidence of once-living organisms, are around 3.5 billion years old. But fossils are rare in rocks formed in the first 4 billion years of Earth history. This vast expanse of time is called the Precambrian. This is because it precedes the Cambrian period, at the start of which, about 590 million years ago, life was abundant in the seas.

The Cambrian is the first period in the Paleozoic (or ancient life) era. The Paleozoic era is followed by the Mesozoic (middle life) era, which witnessed the spectacular rise and fall of the dinosaurs, and the Cenozoic (recent life) era, which was dominated by the evolution of mammals. Each of the eras is divided into periods, and the periods in the Cenozoic era, covering the last 65 million years, are further divided into epochs.

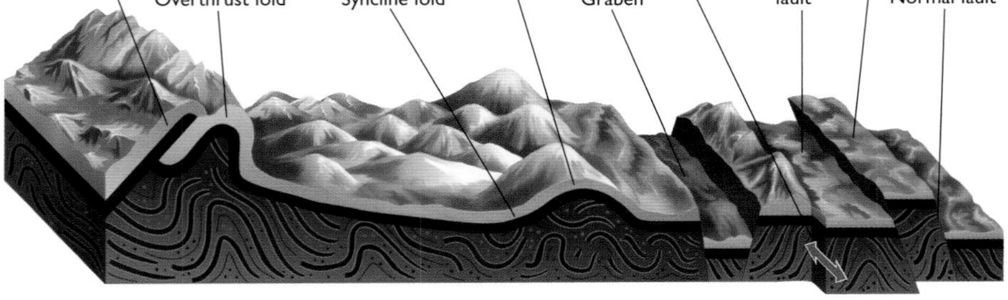

Mountain building

Lateral pressure, which occurs when plates collide, squeezes and compresses rocks into folds. Simple symmetrical upfolds are called anticlines, while downfolds are synclines. As the pressure builds up, strata become asymmetrical and they may be tilted over to form recumbent folds. The rocks often crack under the intense pressure and the folds are sheared away and pushed forward over other rocks. These features are called overthrust folds or nappes. Plate movements also create faults along which rocks move upward, downward, and sideways. The diagram shows a downfaulted graben, or rift valley, and an uplifted horst, or block mountain.

The Earth's Changing Face

While life was gradually evolving, the face of the Earth was constantly changing. By piecing together evidence of rock structures and fossils, geologists have demonstrated that around 250 million years ago, all the world's land areas were grouped together in one huge land mass called Pangaea. Around 180 million years ago, the supercontinent Pangaea, began to break up. New oceans opened up as the continents began to move toward their present positions.

Evidence of how continents drift came from studies of the ocean floor in the 1950s and 1960s. Scientists discovered that the oceans are young features. By contrast with the continents, no part of the ocean floor is more than 200 million years old. The floors of oceans older than 200 million years have completely vanished.

Studies of long undersea ranges, called ocean ridges, revealed that the youngest rocks occur along their centers, which are the edges of huge plates – rigid blocks of the Earth's lithosphere, which is made up of the crust and the solid upper layer of the mantle. The Earth's lithosphere is split into six large and several smaller

The Himalayas seen from Nepal
The Himalayas are a young fold mountain range formed by a collision between two plates. The earthquakes felt in the region testify that the plate movements are still continuing.

plates. The ocean ridges are "constructive" plate margins, because new crustal rock is being formed there from magma that wells up from the mantle as the plates gradually move apart. By contrast, the deep ocean trenches are "destructive" plate edges. Here, two plates are pushing against each other and one plate is descending beneath the other into the mantle where it is melted and destroyed. Geologists call these areas subduction zones.

A third type of plate edge is called a transform fault. Here two plates are moving alongside each other. The best known of these plate edges is the San Andreas fault in California, which separates the Pacific plate from the North American plate.

Slow-moving currents in the partly molten asthenosphere, which underlies the solid lithosphere, are responsible for moving the plates, a process called plate tectonics.

Geological time scale
The geological time scale was first constructed by a study of the stratigraphic, or relative, ages of layers of rock. But the absolute ages of rock strata could not be fixed until the discovery of radioactivity in the early 20th century. Some names of periods, such as Cambrian (Latin for Wales), come from places where the rocks were first studied. Others, such as Carboniferous, refer to the nature of the rocks formed during the period. For example, coal seams (containing carbon) were formed from decayed plant matter during the Carboniferous period.

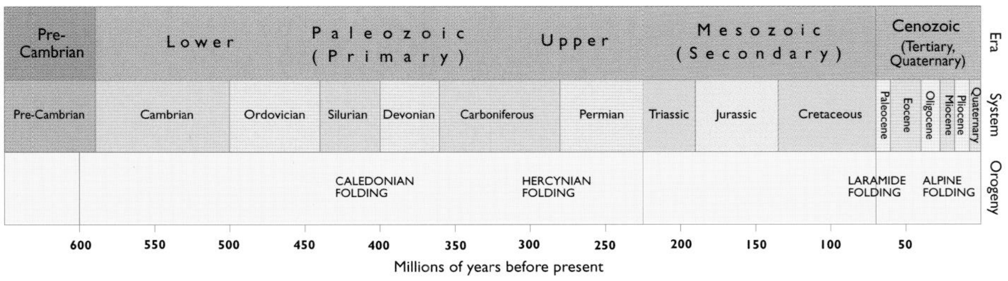
Pre-Cambrian
Lower
Paleozoic (Primary)
Upper
Mesozoic (Secondary)
Cenozoic (Tertiary, Quaternary)
Era
Pre-Cambrian
Cambrian
Ordovician
Silurian
Devonian
Carboniferous
Permian
Triassic
Jurassic
Cretaceous
Paleocene
Eocene
Oligocene
Miocene
Pliocene
Quaternary
System
CALEDONIAN FOLDING
HERCYNIAN FOLDING
LARAMIDE FOLDING
ALPINE FOLDING
Orogeny
600
550
500
450
400
350
300
250
200
150
100
50
Millions of years before present

MOUNTAIN BUILDING

The study of plate tectonics has helped geologists to understand the mechanisms that are responsible for the creation of mountains. Many of the world's greatest ranges were created by the collision of two plates and the bending of the intervening strata into huge loops, or folds. For example, the Himalayas began to rise around 50 million years ago, when a plate supporting India collided with the huge Eurasian plate. Rocks on the floor of the intervening and long-vanished Tethys Sea were squeezed up to form the Himalayan Mountain Range.

Plate movements also create tension that cracks rocks, producing long faults along which rocks move upward, downward, or sideways. Block mountains are formed when blocks of rock are pushed upward along faults. Steep-sided rift valleys are formed when blocks of land sink down between faults. For example, the basin and range region of the southwestern United States has both block mountains and downfaulted basins, such as Death Valley.

Earthquakes and Volcanoes

On December 26, 2003, a powerful earthquake measuring 6.7 on the Richter scale devastated the city of Bam in southeastern Iran. The earthquake struck before dawn when most people were asleep and the official death toll was 26,271. About 80% of the buildings in Bam and the surrounding area collapsed, and much of the huge medieval fortress outside Bam, a major tourist attraction, was also destroyed.

The Restless Earth

Earthquakes can occur anywhere, whenever rocks move along faults. But the most severe and most numerous earthquakes occur near the edges of the plates that make up the Earth's lithosphere. Japan, for example, lies in a particularly unstable region above subduction zones, where plates are descending into the Earth's mantle. It lies in a zone encircling the Pacific Ocean, called the "Pacific ring of fire."

Plates do not move smoothly. Their edges are jagged and for most of the time they are locked together. However, pressure gradually builds up until the rocks break and the plates lurch forward, setting off vibrations ranging from slight tremors to terrifying earthquakes. The greater the pressure released, the more destructive the earthquake.

Earthquakes are also common along the ocean trenches where plates are moving apart, but they mostly occur so far from land that they do little damage. Far more destructive are the earthquakes that occur where plates are moving alongside each other. For example, the earthquakes that periodically rock southwestern California are caused by movements along the San Andreas Fault.

The spot where an earthquake originates is called the focus, while the point on the Earth's surface directly above the focus is called the epicenter. Two kinds of waves, P-waves or compressional waves and S-waves or shear waves, travel from the focus to the surface where they make the ground shake. P-waves travel faster than S-waves and the time difference between their arrival at recording stations enables scientists to calculate the distance from a station to the epicenter.

Earthquakes are measured on the Richter scale, which indicates the magnitude of the shock. The most destructive earthquakes are shallow-focus, that is, the focus is within 37 miles [60 km] of the surface. A magnitude of 7.0 is a major earthquake, but earthquakes with a somewhat lower magnitude can cause tremendous damage if their epicenters are on or close to densely populated areas.

San Andreas Fault, United States
Geologists call the San Andreas fault in southwestern California a transform, or strike-slip, fault. Sudden movements along it cause earthquakes. In 1906, shifts of about 15 ft [4.5 m] occurred near San Francisco, causing a massive earthquake.

NOTABLE EARTHQUAKES
(since 1900)

Year	Location	Mag.
1906	San Francisco, USA	8.3
1906	Valparaiso, Chile	8.6
1908	Messina, Italy	7.5
1915	Avezzano, Italy	7.5
1920	Gansu, China	8.6
1923	Yokohama, Japan	8.3
1927	Nan Shan, China	8.3
1932	Gansu, China	7.6
1934	Bihar, India/Nepal	8.4
1935	Quetta, India†	7.5
1939	Chillan, Chile	8.3
1939	Erzincan, Turkey	7.9
1964	Anchorage, Alaska	8.4
1968	N. E. Iran	7.4
1970	N. Peru	7.7
1976	Guatemala	7.5
1976	Tangshan, China	8.2
1978	Tabas, Iran	7.7
1980	El Asnam, Algeria	7.3
1980	S. Italy	7.2
1985	Mexico City, Mexico	8.1
1988	N. W. Armenia	6.8
1990	N. Iran	7.7
1993	Maharashtra, India	6.4
1994	Los Angeles, USA	6.6
1995	Kobe, Japan	7.2
1995	Sakhalin Is., Russia	7.5
1996	Yunnan, China	7.0
1997	N. E. Iran	7.1
1998	N. Afghanistan	6.1
1998	N. E. Afghanistan	7.0
1999	Izmit, Turkey	7.4
1999	Taipei, Taiwan	7.6
2001	El Salvador	7.7
2001	Gujarat, India	7.7
2002	Afyon, Turkey	6.0
2002	Baghlan, Afghanistan	6.1
2003	Mexico	7.8
2003	Bam, Iran	6.7
2004	N. Morocco	6.5

† *now Pakistan*

Earthquakes in subduction zones
Along subduction zones, one plate is descending beneath another. The plates are locked together until the rocks break and the descending plate lurches forward. From the point where the plate moves – the origin – seismic waves spread through the lithosphere, making the ground shake. The earthquake in Mexico City in 1985 occurred in this way.

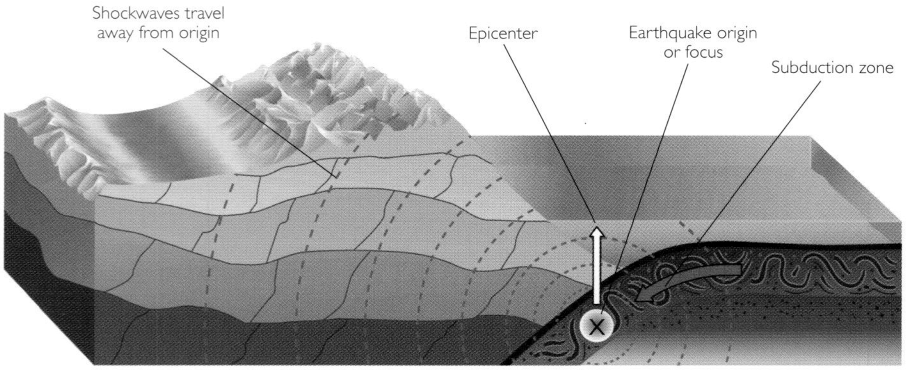

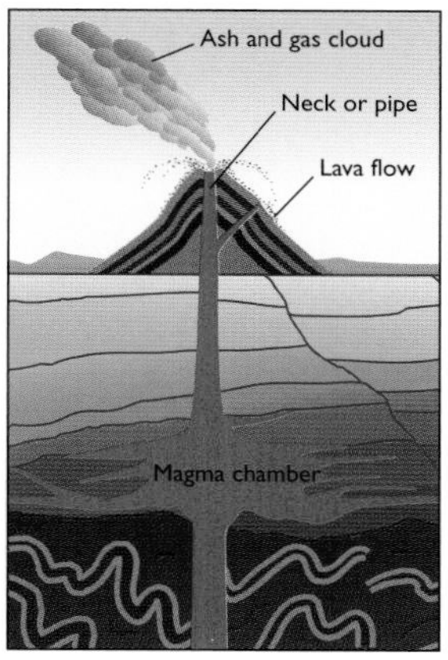

Cross-section of a volcano
Volcanoes are vents in the ground, through which magma reaches the surface. The term volcano is also used for the mountains formed from volcanic rocks. Beneath volcanoes are pockets of magma derived from the semi-molten asthenosphere in the mantle. The magma rises under pressure through the overlying rocks until it reaches the surface. There it emerges through vents as pyroclasts, ranging in size from large lumps of magma, called volcanic bombs, to fine volcanic ash and dust. In quiet eruptions, streams of liquid lava run down the side of the mountain. Side vents sometimes appear on the flanks of existing volcanoes.

Scientists have been working for years to find effective ways of forecasting earthquakes but with limited success. But in the early 2000s, some scientists claimed that they had successfully forecast eruptions by identifying tremors, called "long-period events." They believe these relatively minor but long-lasting tremors are caused when magma surges up underground passages but fails to reach the surface.

Volcanic Eruptions

Most active volcanoes also occur on or near plate edges. Many undersea volcanoes along the ocean ridges are formed from magma that wells up from the asthenosphere to fill the gaps created as the plates, on the opposite sides of the ridges, move apart. Some of these volcanoes reach the surface to form islands. Iceland is a country which straddles the Mid-Atlantic Ocean Ridge. It is gradually becoming wider as magma rises to the surface through faults and vents. Other volcanoes lie alongside subduction zones. The magma that fuels them comes from the melted edges of the descending plates.

A few volcanoes lie far from plate edges. For example, Mauna Loa and Kilauea on Hawaii are situated near the center of the huge Pacific plate. The molten magma that reaches the surface is created by a source of heat, called a "hot spot," in the Earth's mantle.

Magma is molten rock at temperatures of about 2,012°F to 2,192°F [1,100°C to 1,200°C]. It contains gases and superheated steam. The chemical composition of magma varies. Viscous magma is rich in silica and superheated steam, while runny magma contains less silica and steam. The chemical composition of the magma affects the nature of volcanic eruptions.

Explosive volcanoes contain thick, viscous magma. When they erupt, they usually hurl clouds of ash (shattered fragments of cooled magma) into the air. By contrast, quiet volcanoes emit long streams of runny magma, or lava. However, many volcanoes are intermediate in type, sometimes erupting explosively and sometimes emitting streams of fluid lava. Explosive and intermediate volcanoes usually have a conical shape, while quiet volcanoes are flattened, resembling upturned saucers. They are often called shield volcanoes.

One dangerous type of eruption is called a *nuée ardente*, or "glowing cloud." It occurs when a cloud of intensely hot volcanic gases and dust particles and superheated steam are exploded from a volcano. They move rapidly downhill, burning everything in their path and choking animals and people. The blast that creates the *nuée ardente* may release the pressure inside the volcano, resulting in a tremendous explosion that hurls tall columns of ash into the air.

Kilauea Volcano, Hawaii
The volcanic Hawaiian islands in the North Pacific Ocean were formed as the Pacific plate moved over a "hot spot" in the Earth's mantle. Kilauea on Hawaii emits blazing streams of liquid lava.

Forces of Nature

When the volcano Mount Pinatubo erupted in the Philippines in 1991, loose ash covered large areas around the mountain. During the 1990s and early 2000s, rainwater mixed with the ash on sloping land, creating *lahars*, or mudflows, which swept down river valleys burying many areas. Such incidents are not only reminders of the great forces that operate inside our planet but also of those natural forces operating on the surface, which can have dramatic effects on the land.

The chief forces acting on the surface of the Earth are weathering, running water, ice and winds. The forces of erosion seem to act slowly. One estimate suggests that an average of only 1.4 inches [3.5 cm] of land is removed by natural processes every 1,000 years. This may not sound much, but over millions of years, it can reduce mountains to almost flat surfaces.

Weathering

Weathering occurs in all parts of the world, but the most effective type of weathering in any area depends on the climate and the nature of the rocks. For example, in cold mountain areas, when water freezes in cracks in rocks, the ice occupies 9% more space than the water. This exerts a force which, when repeated over and over again, can split boulders apart. By contrast, in hot deserts, intense heating by day and cooling by night causes the outer layers of rocks to expand and contract until they break up and peel away like layers of an onion. These are examples of what is called mechanical weathering.

Other kinds of weathering include chemical reactions usually involving water. Rainwater containing carbon dioxide dissolved from the air or the soil is a weak acid which reacts with limestone, wearing out pits, tunnels and networks of caves in layers of limestone rock. Water also combines with some minerals, such as the feldspars in granite, to create kaolin, a white

RATES OF EROSION

	SLOW ← WEATHERING RATE		→ FAST
Mineral solubility	low (e.g. quartz)	moderate (e.g. feldspar)	high (e.g. calcite)
Rainfall	low	moderate	heavy
Temperature	cold	temperate	hot
Vegetation	sparse	moderate	lush
Soil cover	bare rock	thin to moderate soil	thick soil

Weathering is the breakdown and decay of rocks in situ. It may be mechanical (physical), chemical, or biological.

Rates of erosion
The chart shows that the rates at which weathering takes place depend on the chemistry and hardness of rocks, climatic factors, especially rainfall and temperature, the vegetation, and the nature of the soil cover in any area. The effects of weathering are increased by human action, particularly the removal of vegetation and the exposure of soils to the rain and wind.

Grand Canyon, Arizona, at dusk
The Grand Canyon in the United States is one of the world's natural wonders. Eroded by the Colorado River and its tributaries, it is up to 1 mile [1.6 km] deep and 18 miles [29 km] wide.

clay. These are examples of chemical weathering which constantly wears away rock.

Running Water, Ice and Wind

In moist regions, rivers are effective in shaping the land. They transport material worn away by weathering and erode the land. They wear out V-shaped valleys in upland regions, while vigorous meanders widen their middle courses. The work of rivers is at its most spectacular when earth movements lift up flat areas and rejuvenate the rivers, giving them a new erosive power capable of wearing out such features as the Grand Canyon. Rivers also have a constructive role. Some of the world's most fertile regions are deltas and flood plains composed of sediments periodically dumped there by such rivers as the Ganges, Mississippi, and Nile.

Glaciers

During Ice Ages, ice spreads over large areas but, during warm periods, the ice retreats. The chart shows that the volume of ice in many glaciers is decreasing, possibly as a result of global warming. Experts estimate that, between 1850 and the early 21st century, more than half of the ice in Alpine glaciers has melted.

ANNUAL FLUCTUATIONS FOR SELECTED GLACIERS

Glacier name and location	Changes in the annual mass balance †		
	1970–1	1990–1	2000–2001
Alfotbreen, Norway	+940	+790	–50
Careser, Italy	–650	–1,730	–1,860
Djankuat, Russia	–230	–310	–1,760
Grasubreen, Norway	+470	–520	–30
Gries, Switzerland	–970	–1,480	–902
Hintereisferner, Austria	–600	–1,325	–806
Place, Canada	–343	–990	–690
Sarennes, France	–1,100	–1,360	–1,160
Storglaciaren, Sweden	–190	+170	–115
Ürümqi, China	+102	–706	–1,170
Wolverine, USA	+770	–410	–480

† *The annual mass balance is defined as the difference between glacier accumulation and ablation (melting) averaged over the whole glacier. Balances are expressed as water equivalent in millimeters. A plus indicates an increase in the depth or length of the glacier; a minus indicates a reduction.*

Juneau Glacier, Alaska

Like huge conveyor belts, glaciers transport weathered debris from mountain regions. Rocks frozen in the ice give the glaciers teeth, enabling them to wear out typical glaciated land features.

Running water in the form of sea waves and currents shapes coastlines, wearing out caves, natural arches, and stacks. The sea also transports and deposits worn material to form such features as spits and bars.

Glaciers in cold mountain regions flow downhill, gradually deepening valleys and shaping dramatic landscapes. They erode steep-sided U-shaped valleys, into which rivers often plunge in large waterfalls. Other features include cirques, armchair-shaped basins bounded by knife-edged ridges called *arêtes*. When several glacial cirques erode to form radial *arêtes*, pyramidal peaks like the Matterhorn are created. Deposits of moraine, rock material dumped by the glacier, are further evidence that ice once covered large areas. The work of glaciers, like other agents of erosion, varies with the climate. In recent years, global warming has been making glaciers retreat in many areas, while several of the ice shelves in Antarctica have been breaking up.

Many land features in deserts were formed by running water at a time when the climate was much rainier than it is today. Water erosion also occurs when flash floods are caused by rare thunderstorms. But the chief agent of erosion in dry areas is wind-blown sand, which can strip the paint from cars, and undercut boulders to create mushroom-shaped rocks.

Oceans and Ice

Since the 1970s, oceanographers have found numerous hot vents on the ocean ridges. Called black smokers, the vents emit dark, mineral-rich water reaching 662°F [350°C]. Around the vents are chimney-like structures formed from minerals deposited from the hot water. The discovery of black smokers did not surprise scientists who already knew that the ridges were plate edges, where new crustal rock was being formed as molten magma welled up to the surface. But what was astonishing was that the hot water contained vast numbers of bacteria, which provided the base of a food chain that included many strange creatures, such as giant worms, eyeless shrimps, and white clams. Many species were unknown to science.

Little was known about the dark world beneath the waves until about 50 years ago. But through the use of modern technology such as echo-sounders, magnetometers, research ships equipped with huge drills, submersibles that can carry scientists down to the ocean floor, and satellites, the secrets of the oceans have been gradually revealed.

The study of the ocean floor led to the discovery that the oceans are geologically young features – no more than 200 million years old. It also revealed evidence as to how oceans form and continents drift because of the action of plate tectonics.

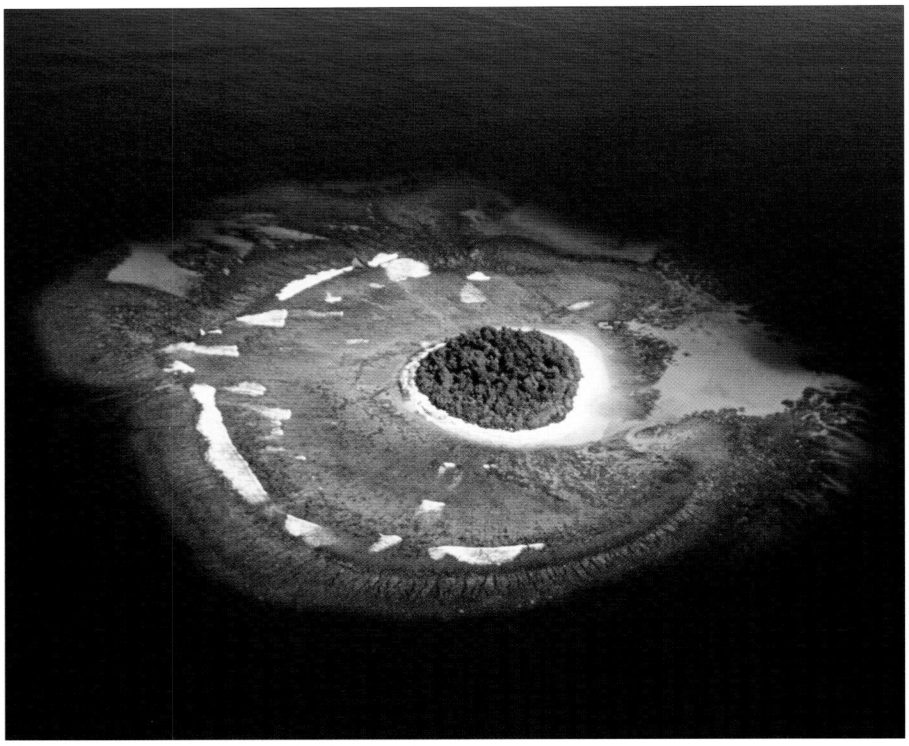

Vava'u Island, Tonga
This small coral atoll in northern Tonga consists of a central island covered by rain forest. Low coral reefs washed by the waves surround a shallow central lagoon.

The Blue Planet

Water covers almost 71% of the Earth, which makes it look blue when viewed from space. Although the oceans are interconnected, geographers divide them into four main areas: the Pacific, Atlantic, Indian, and Arctic oceans. The average depth of the oceans is 12,238 ft [3,370 m], but they are divided into several zones.

Around most continents are gently sloping continental shelves, which are flooded parts of the continents. The shelves end at the continental slope, at a depth of about 656 ft [200 m]. This slope leads steeply down to the abyss. The deepest parts of the oceans are the trenches, which reach a maximum depth of 36,161 ft [11,022 m] in the Mariana Trench in the western Pacific.

Most marine life is found in the top 656 ft [200 m], where there is sufficient sunlight for plants, called phytoplankton, to grow. Below this zone, life becomes more and more scarce, though no part of the ocean, even at the bottom of the deepest trenches, is completely without living things.

Continental islands, such as the British Isles, are high parts of the continental shelves. For example, until about 7,500 years ago, when the ice sheets formed during the Ice Ages were melting, raising the sea level and filling the North Sea and the Strait of Dover, Britain was linked to mainland Europe.

By contrast, oceanic islands, such as the Hawaiian chain in the North Pacific Ocean, rise from the ocean floor. All oceanic islands are of volcanic origin, although many of them in warm parts of the oceans have sunk and are capped by layers of coral to form ring- or horseshoe-shaped atolls and coral reefs.

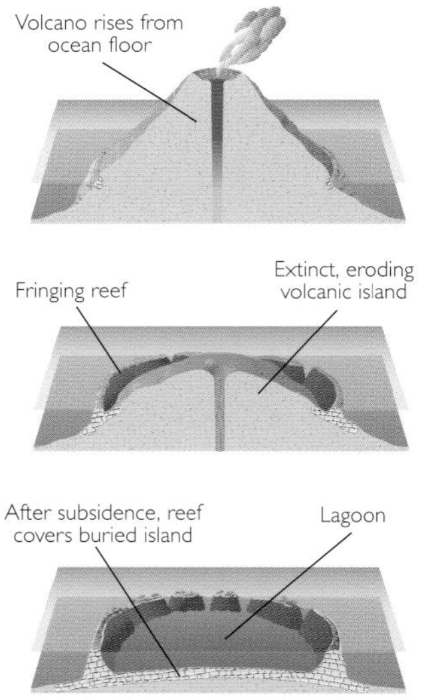

Development of an atoll
Some of the volcanoes that rise from the ocean floor reach the surface to form islands. Some of these islands subside and become submerged. As an island sinks, coral starts to grow around the rim of the volcano, building up layer upon layer of limestone deposits to form fringing reefs. Sometimes coral grows on the tip of a central cone to form an island in the middle of the atoll.

Ocean Water

The oceans contain about 97% of the world's water. Seawater contains more than 70 dissolved elements, but chloride and sodium make up 85% of the total. Sodium chloride is common salt and it makes seawater salty. The salinity of the oceans is mostly between 3.3–3.7%. Ocean water fed by icebergs or large rivers is less saline than shallow seas in the tropics, where the evaporation rate is high. Seawater is a source of salt but the water is useless for agriculture or drinking unless it is desalinated. However, land

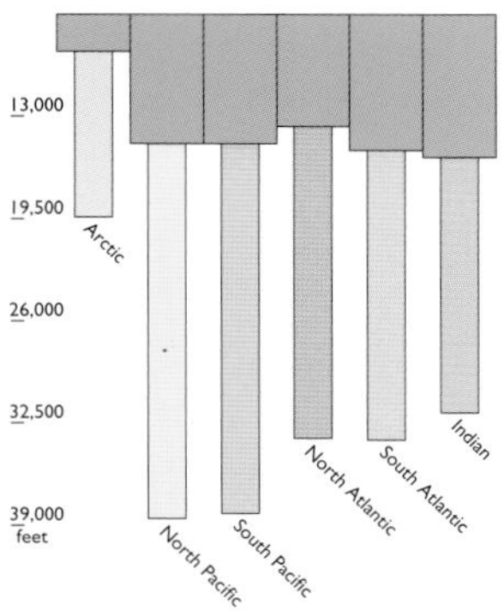

The ocean depths

The diagram shows the average depths (in dark blue) and the greatest depths in the four oceans. The North Pacific Ocean contains the world's deepest trenches, including the Mariana Trench, where the deepest manned descent was made by the bathyscaphe Trieste *in 1960. It reached a depth of 35,813 ft [10,916 m].*

Relative sizes of the world's oceans:

PACIFIC	49%	ATLANTIC	26%
INDIAN	21%	ARCTIC	4%

Some geographers distinguish a fifth ocean, the Southern or Antarctic Ocean, but others regard these waters as the southern extension of the Pacific, Atlantic, and Indian oceans.

areas get a regular supply of fresh water through the hydrological cycle (see page 26).

The density of seawater depends on its salinity and temperature. Temperatures vary from 28°F [–2°C], the freezing point of seawater at the poles, to around 86°F [30°C] in parts of the tropics. Density differences help to maintain the circulation of the world's oceans, especially deep-sea currents. But the main cause of currents within 1,148 ft [350 m] of the surface is the wind. Because of the Earth's rotation, currents are deflected, creating huge circular motions of surface water – clockwise in the northern hemisphere and counterclockwise in the southern hemisphere.

Ocean currents transport heat from the tropics to the polar regions and thus form part of the heat engine that drives the Earth's climates. Ocean currents have an especially marked effect on coastal climates, such as northwestern Europe. In the mid-1990s, scientists warned that global warming may be weakening currents, including the warm Gulf Stream which is responsible for the mild winters experienced in northwestern Europe.

Ice Sheets, Ice Caps and Glaciers

Of the world's two ice sheets, the largest, covering most of Antarctica, has maximum depths of 15,748 ft [4,800 m]. Its volume is about nine times greater than the Greenland ice sheet. The ice sheets, together with smaller ice caps and glaciers together account for about 2% of the world's water. However, in many parts of the world, the ice is melting and many scientists think the cause is global warming. In March 2002, the vast Larsen ice shelf bordering the Antarctic peninsula collapsed and broke up into icebergs. Some scientists thought this was evidence of global warming, though some attributed the event to local factors.

Only about 11,000 years ago, during the final phase of the Pleistocene Ice Age, ice covered much of the northern hemisphere. The Ice Age, which began about 1.8 million years ago, was not a continuous period of cold. Instead, it consisted of glacial periods when the ice advanced and warmer interglacial periods when temperatures rose and the ice retreated.

Some scientists believe that we are now living in an interglacial period, and that glacial conditions will recur in the future. Others fear that global warming, caused mainly by pollution, may melt the world's ice, raising sea levels by up to 180 ft [55 m]. Many fertile and densely populated coastal plains, islands and cities would vanish from the map.

Weddell Sea, Antarctica

Antarctica contains two huge bays, occupied by the Ross and Weddell seas. Ice shelves extend from the ice sheet across parts of these seas. Researchers fear that warmer weather is melting Antarctica's ice sheets at a dangerous rate, after large chunks of the Larsen ice shelf and the Ronne ice shelf broke away in 1997 and 1998 respectively. This was followed in March 2002 by the disintegration of the Larsen B ice shelf.

The Earth's Atmosphere

Since the discovery in 1985 of a thinning of the ozone layer, creating a so-called "ozone hole," over Antarctica, many governments have worked to reduce the emissions of ozone-eating substances, notably the chlorofluorocarbons (CFCs) used in aerosols, refrigeration, air conditioning, and dry cleaning.

Following forecasts that the ozone layer would rapidly repair itself as a result of controls on these emissions, scientists were surprised in early 1996 when a marked thinning of the ozone layer occurred over the Arctic, northern Europe, Russia, and Canada. Again, in 2003, scientists were concerned that the thinning of the ozone layer over Antarctica was as serious as in the record year of 2000. Many predicted that it might take more than the originally estimated 50 years before the ozone layer made a full recovery.

The ozone layer in the stratosphere blocks out most of the dangerous ultraviolet B radiation in the Sun's rays. This radiation causes skin cancer and cataracts, as well as harming plants on the land and plankton in the oceans. The ozone layer is only one way in which the atmosphere protects life on Earth. The atmosphere also provides the air we breathe and the carbon dioxide required by plants. It is also a shield against meteors and it acts as a blanket to prevent heat radiated from the Earth escaping into space.

Layers of Air

The atmosphere is divided into four main layers. The troposphere at the bottom contains about 85% of the atmosphere's total mass, where most weather conditions occur. The troposphere is about 9 miles [15 km] thick over the Equator and 5 miles [8 km] thick at the poles. Temperatures decrease with height by approximately 2°F [1°C] for every 328 ft [100 m]. At the top of the troposphere is a level called the tropopause where temperatures are stable at around –67°F [–55°C]. Above the tropopause is the stratosphere, which contains the ozone layer. Here, at about 30 miles [50 km] above the Earth's surface, temperatures rise to about 32°F [0°C].

The ionosphere extends from the stratopause to about 373 miles [600 km] above the surface. Here temperatures fall up to about 50 miles

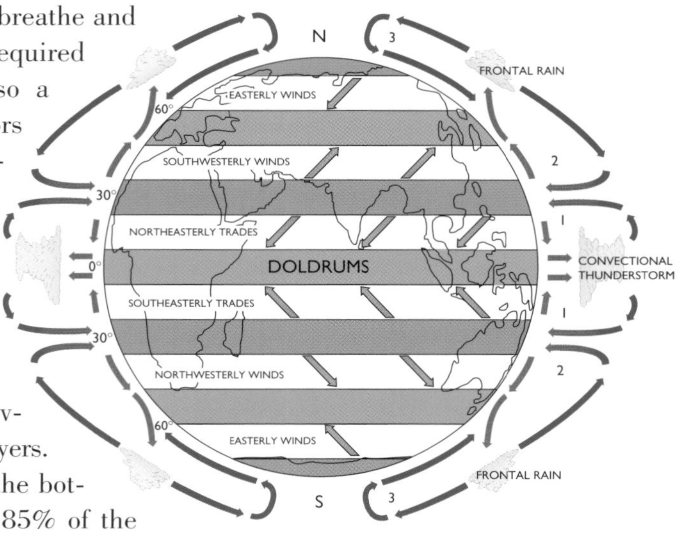

The circulation of the atmosphere can be divided into three rotating but interconnected air systems, or cells. The Hadley cell (figure 1 on the above stylized diagram) is in the tropics; the Ferrel cell (2) lies between the subtropics and the mid-latitudes; and the Polar cell (3) is in the high latitudes.

Moonrise seen from orbit

This photograph taken by an orbiting Shuttle shows the crescent of the Moon. Silhouetted at the horizon is a dense cloud layer. The reddish-brown band is the tropopause, which separates the blue-white stratosphere from the yellow troposphere.

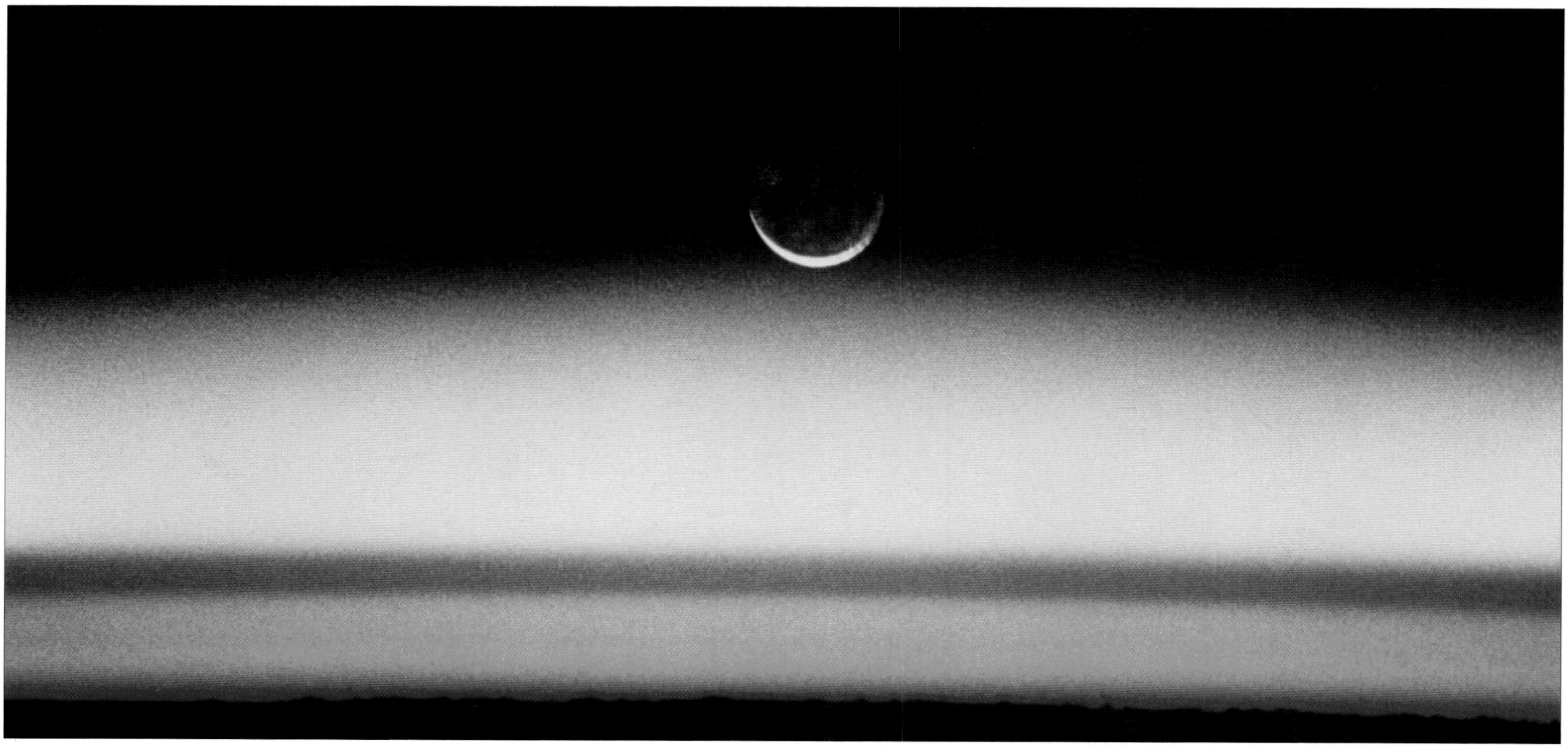

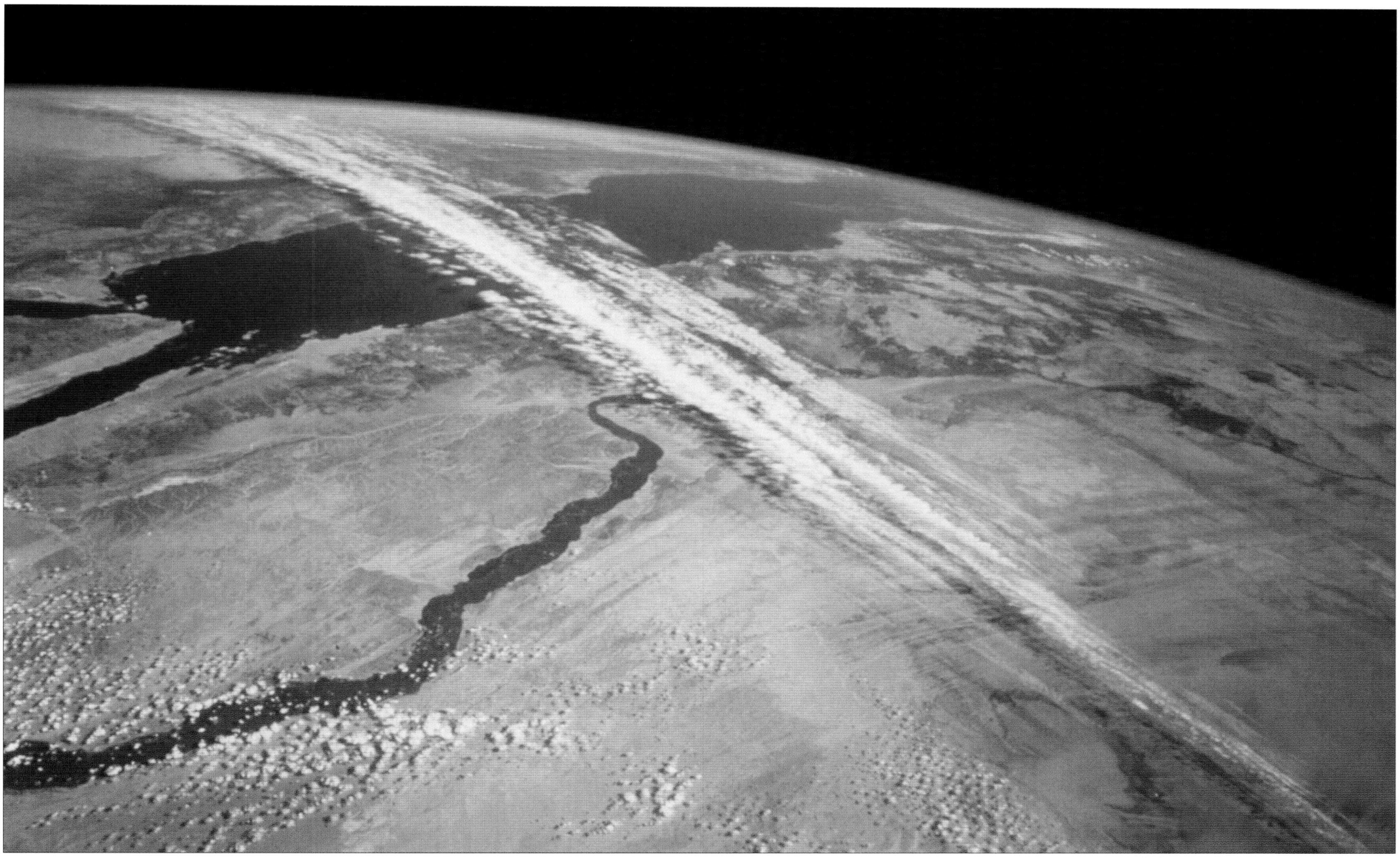

Jetstream from space

Jetstreams are strong winds that normally blow near the tropopause. Cirrus clouds mark the route of the jet stream in this photograph, which shows the Red Sea, North Africa, and the Nile valley, which appears as a dark band crossing the desert.

[80 km], but then rise. The aurorae, which occur in the ionosphere when charged particles from the Sun interact with the Earth's magnetic field, are strongest near the poles. In the exosphere, the outermost layer, the atmosphere merges into space.

Circulation of the Atmosphere

The heating of the Earth is most intense around the Equator where the Sun is high in the sky. Here warm, moist air rises in strong currents, creating a zone of low air pressure: the doldrums. The rising air eventually cools and spreads out north and south until it sinks back to the ground around latitudes 30° North and 30° South. This forms two zones of high air pressure called the horse latitudes.

From the horse latitudes, trade winds blow back across the surface toward the Equator, while westerly winds blow toward the poles. The warm westerlies finally meet the polar easterlies (cold dense air flowing from the poles). The line along which the warm and cold air streams meet is called the polar front. Depressions (or cyclones) are low air pressure frontal systems that form along the polar front.

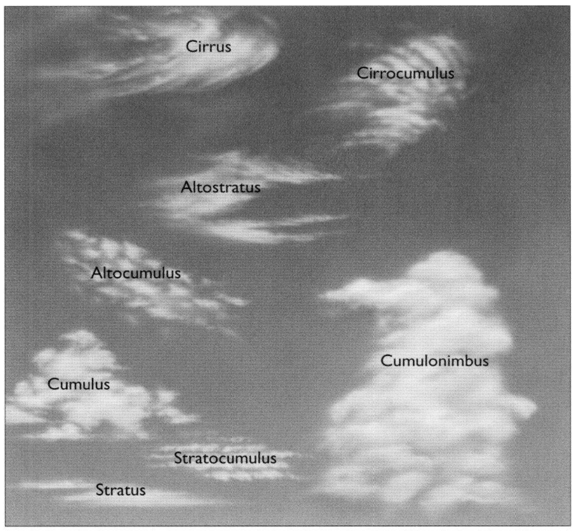

Classification of clouds

Clouds are classified broadly into cumuliform, or "heap" clouds, and stratiform, or "layer" clouds. Both types occur at all levels. The highest clouds, composed of ice crystals, are cirrus, cirrostratus, and cirrocumulus. Medium-height clouds include altostratus, a gray cloud that often indicates the approach of a depression, and altocumulus, a thicker and fluffier version of cirrocumulus. Low clouds include stratus, which forms dull, overcast skies; nimbostratus, a dark gray layer cloud which brings almost continuous rain and snow; cumulus, a brilliant white heap cloud; and stratocumulus, a layer cloud arranged in globular masses or rolls. Cumulonimbus, a cloud associated with thunderstorms, lightning, and heavy rain, often extends from low to medium altitudes. It has a flat base, a fluffy outline, and often an anvil-shaped top.

Composition of the Atmosphere

The air in the troposphere is made up mainly of nitrogen (78%) and oxygen (21%). Argon makes up more than 0.9% and there are also minute amounts of carbon dioxide, helium, hydrogen, krypton, methane, ozone, and xenon. The atmosphere also contains water vapor, the gaseous form of water, which, when it condenses around minute specks of dust and salt, forms tiny water droplets or ice crystals. Large masses of water droplets or ice crystals form clouds.

Climate and Weather

In 1992, Hurricane Andrew struck the Bahamas, Florida and Louisiana, causing record damage estimated at $30 billion. In September 1998, following heavy monsoon rains, floods submerged two-thirds of Bangladesh. The same month, in Central America, more than 7,000 people died in floods and mudslides caused by Hurricane Mitch. In September 2003, Hurricane Isabel hit North Carolina, causing extensive flooding in the Chesapeake Bay area. The storm led to about 40 deaths, while nearly 60 million people lost power.

Every year, exceptional weather conditions cause disasters around the world. Modern forecasting techniques now give people warning of advancing storms, but the toll of human deaths continues as people are powerless in the face of the awesome forces of nature.

Weather is the day-to-day condition of the atmosphere. In some places, the weather is normally stable, but in other areas, especially the middle latitudes, it is highly variable, changing with the passing of a depression. By contrast, climate is the average weather of a place, based on data obtained over a long period.

Hurricane Elena, 1985

Hurricanes form over warm oceans north and south of the Equator. Their movements are tracked by satellites, enabling forecasters to issue storm warnings as they approach land. In North America, forecasters identify them with boys' and girls' names.

Climatic Factors

Climate depends basically on the unequal heating of the Sun between the Equator and the poles. But ocean currents and terrain also affect climate. For example, despite their northerly positions, Norway's ports remain ice-free in winter. This is because of the warming effect of the North Atlantic Drift, an extension of the Gulf Stream which flows across the Atlantic Ocean from the Gulf of Mexico.

By contrast, the cold Benguela current which flows up the coast of southwestern Africa cools the coast and causes arid conditions. This is because the cold onshore winds are warmed as they pass over the land. The warm air can hold more water vapor than cold air, giving the winds a drying effect.

The terrain affects climate in several ways. Because temperatures fall with altitude, highlands are cooler than lowlands in the same

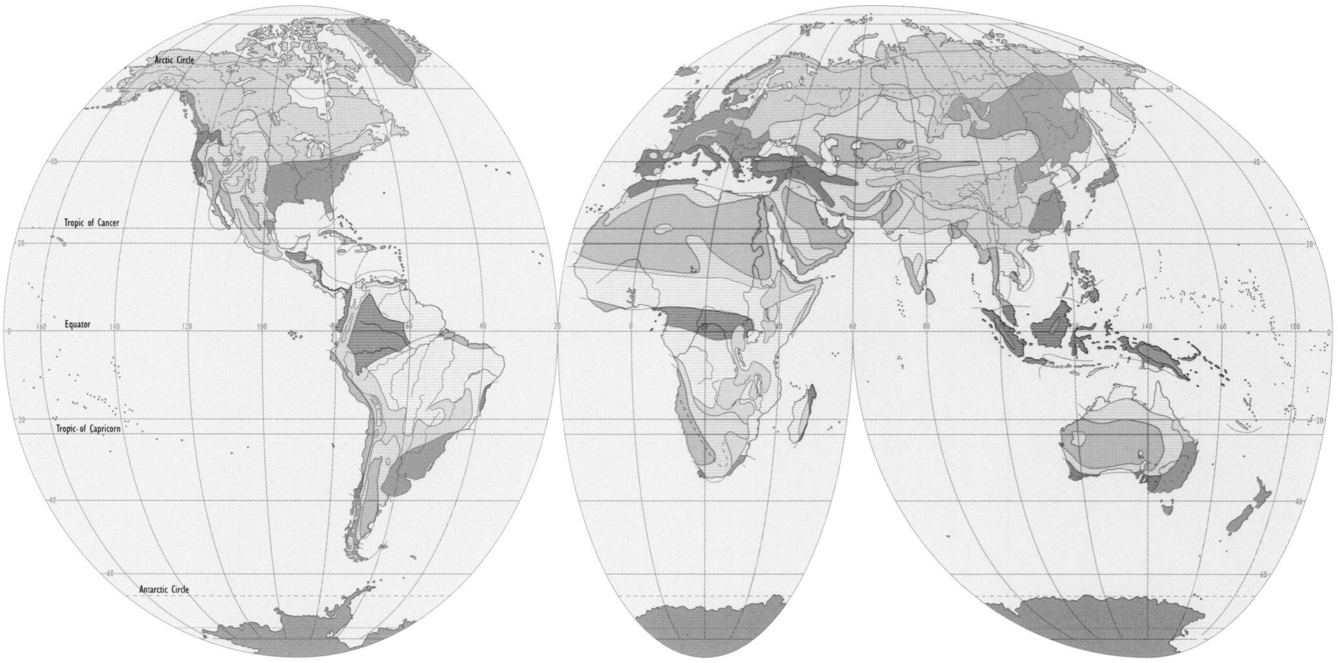

CLIMATIC REGIONS

Tropical rainy climates
All mean monthly temperatures above 64°F [18°C].

- RAIN FOREST CLIMATE
- MONSOON CLIMATE
- SAVANNA CLIMATE

Dry climates
Low rainfall combined with a wide range of temperatures.

- STEPPE CLIMATE
- DESERT CLIMATE

Warm temperate rainy climates
The mean temperature is below 64°F [18°C] but above 26°F [–3°C], and that of the warmest month is over 50°F [10°C].

- DRY WINTER CLIMATE
- DRY SUMMER CLIMATE
- CLIMATE WITH NO DRY SEASON

Cold temperate rainy climates
The mean temperature of the coldest month is below 37°F [3°C] but the warmest month is over 50°F [10°C].

- DRY WINTER CLIMATE
- CLIMATE WITH NO DRY SEASON

Polar climates
The temperature of the warmest month is below 50°F [10°C], giving permanently frozen subsoil.

- TUNDRA CLIMATE
- POLAR CLIMATE

Flood damage in the United States
In June and July 1993, the Mississippi River basin suffered record floods. The photograph shows a sunken church in Illinois. The flooding along the Mississippi, Missouri, and other rivers caused great damage, amounting to about $12 billion. At least 48 people died in the floods.

Floods in St Louis, United States
The satellite image, right, shows the extent of the floods at St Louis at the confluence of the Mississippi and the Missouri rivers in June and July 1993. The floods occurred when very heavy rainfall raised river levels by up to 46 ft [14 m]. The floods reached their greatest extent between Minneapolis in the north and a point approximately 93 miles [150 km] south of St Louis. In places, the width of the Mississippi increased to nearly 7 miles [11 km], while the Missouri reached widths of 20 miles [32 km]. In all, more than 10,800 sq miles [28,000 sq km] were inundated and hundreds of towns and cities were flooded. Damage to crops was estimated at $8 billion. The USA was hit again by flooding in early 1997, when heavy rainfall in North Dakota and Minnesota caused the Red River to flood. The flooding had a catastrophic effect on the city of Grand Forks, which was inundated for months.

latitude. Terrain also affects rainfall. When moist onshore winds pass over mountain ranges, they are chilled as they are forced to rise and the water vapor they contain condenses to form clouds which bring rain and snow. After the winds have crossed the mountains, the air descends and is warmed. These warm, dry winds create rain shadow (arid) regions on the lee side of the mountains.

Climatic Regions

The two major factors that affect climate are temperature and precipitation, including rain and snow. In addition, seasonal variations and other climatic features are also taken into account. Climatic classifications vary because of the weighting given to various features. Yet most classifications are based on five main climatic types: tropical rainy climates; dry climates; warm temperate rainy climates; cold temperate rainy climates; and very cold polar climates. Some classifications also allow for the effect of altitude. The main climatic regions are subdivided according to seasonal variations and also to the kind of vegetation associated with the climatic conditions. Thus, the rain forest climate, with rain throughout the year, differs from monsoon and savanna climates, which have marked dry seasons. Similarly, parched desert climates differ from steppe climates which have enough moisture for grasses to grow.

Water and Land Use

All life on land depends on fresh water. Yet about 80 countries now face acute water shortages. The world demand for fresh water is increasing by about 2.3% a year and this demand will double every 21 years. About a billion people, mainly in developing countries, do not have access to clean drinking water and around 10 million die every year from drinking dirty water. This problem is made worse in many countries by the pollution of rivers and lakes.

UN experts predict that water is becoming the most pressing environmental and development issue facing the world. By 2003, heavily populated regions in 26 countries were suffering serious water shortages. In 20 years, this number will probably rise to 65. As resources dwindle, conflicts over water are becoming more common. They are likely to increase.

However, experts stress that while individual countries face water crises, there is no global crisis. The chief global problems are the uneven distribution of water and its inefficient and wasteful use.

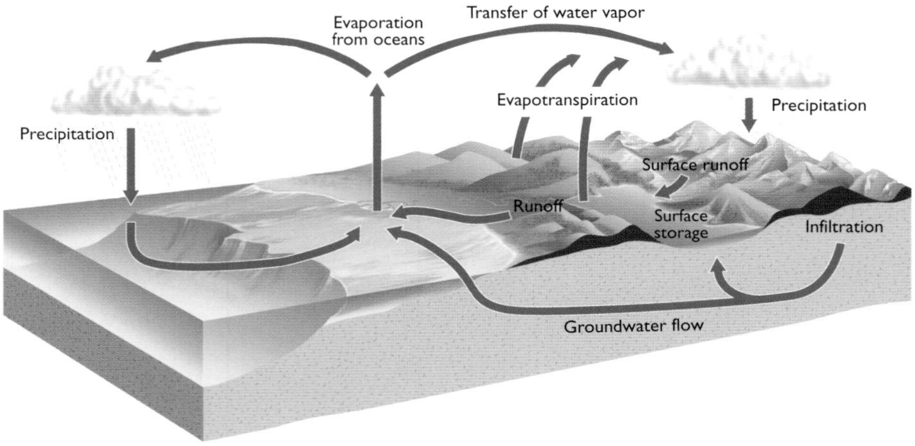

The hydrological cycle

The hydrological cycle is responsible for the continuous circulation of water around the planet. Water vapor contains and transports latent heat, or latent energy. When the water vapor condenses back into water (and falls as rain, hail, or snow), the heat is released. When condensation takes place on cold nights, the cooling effect associated with nightfall is offset by the liberation of latent heat.

The World's Water Supply

Of the world's total water supply, 99.4% is in the oceans or frozen in bodies of ice. Most of the rest circulates through the rocks beneath our feet as groundwater. Water in rivers and lakes, in the soil and in the atmosphere together make up only 0.013% of the world's water.

The freshwater supply on land is dependent on the hydrological, or water cycle which is driven by the Sun's heat. Water is evaporated from the oceans and carried into the air as invisible water vapor. Although this vapor averages less than 2% of the total mass of the atmosphere, it is the chief component from the standpoint of weather.

When air rises, water vapor condenses into visible water droplets or ice crystals, which eventually fall to earth as rain, snow, sleet, hail, or frost. Some of the precipitation that reaches the ground returns directly to the atmosphere through evaporation or transpiration via plants. Much of the rest of the water flows into the rocks to become groundwater, or across the surface into rivers and, eventually, back to the oceans, so completing the hydrological cycle.

Water and Agriculture

Only about a third of the world's land area is used for growing crops, while another third

WATER DISTRIBUTION

The distribution of planetary water, by percentage.

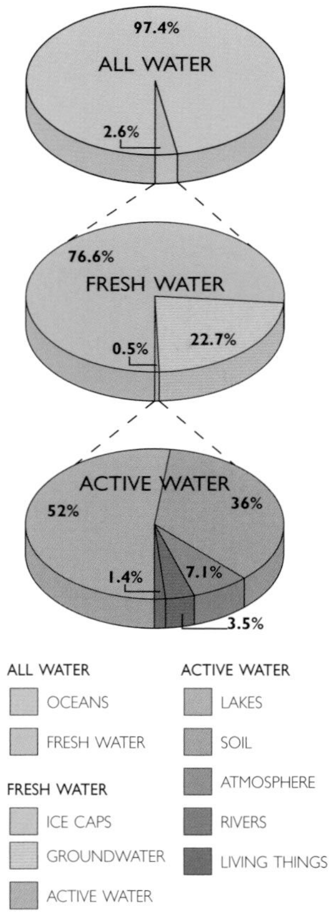

Hoover Dam, United States

The Hoover Dam in Arizona controls the Colorado River's flood waters. Its reservoir supplies domestic and irrigation water to the southwest, while a hydroelectric plant produces electricity.

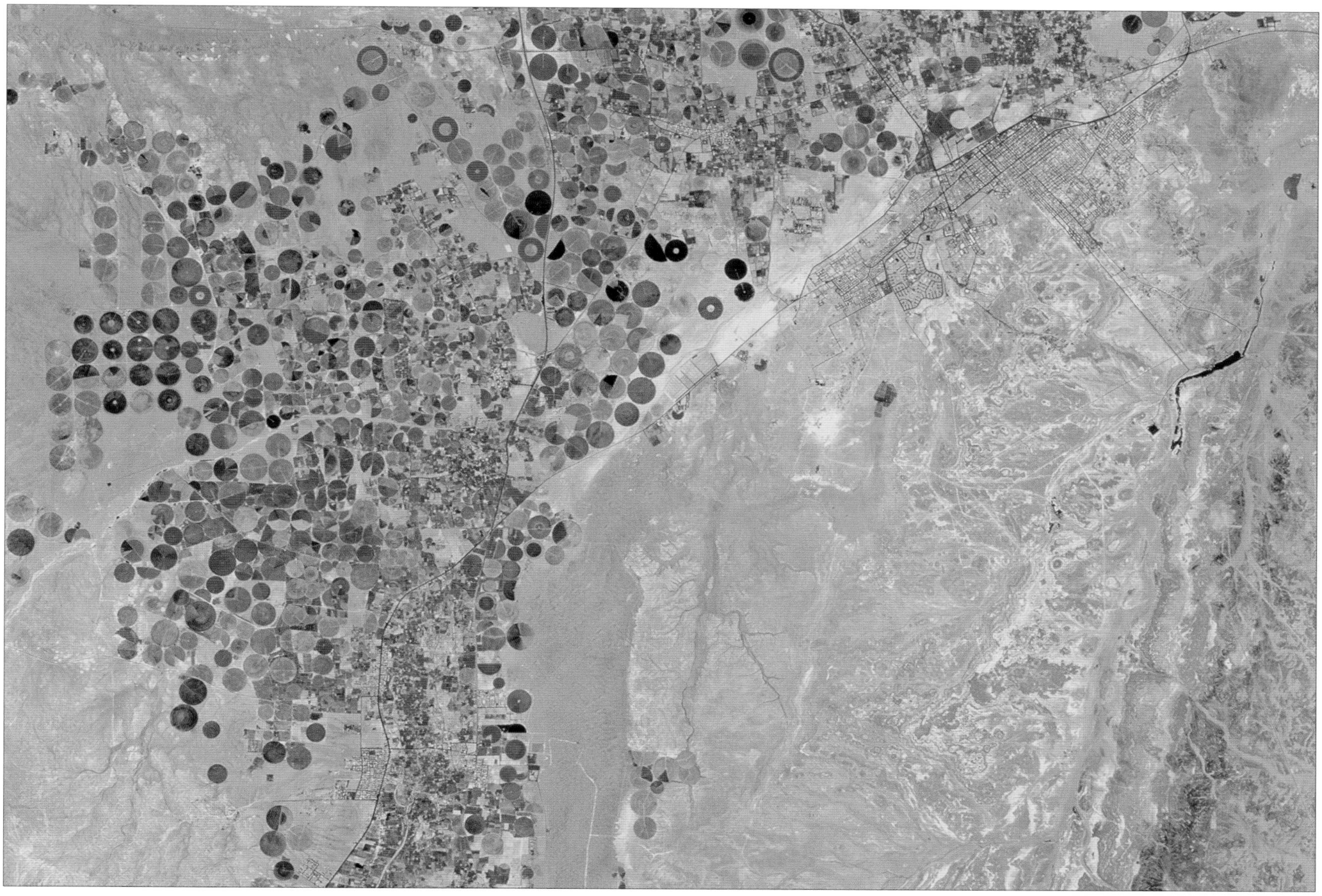

Irrigation boom
The photograph shows a pivotal irrigation boom used to sprinkle water over a wheat field in Saudi Arabia. Irrigation in hot countries often takes place at night so that water loss through evaporation is reduced. Irrigation techniques vary from place to place. In monsoon areas with abundant water, the fields are often flooded, or the water is led to the crops along straight furrows. Sprinkler irrigation has become important since the 1940s. In other types of irrigation, the water is led through pipes which are on or under the ground. Underground pipes supply water directly to the plant roots and, as a result, water loss through evaporation is minimized.

consists of meadows and pasture. The rest of the world is unsuitable for farming, being too dry, too cold, too mountainous, or covered by dense forests. Although the demand for food increases every year, problems arise when attempts are made to increase the existing area of farmland. For example, the soils and climates of tropical forest and semiarid regions of Africa and South America are not ideal for farming. Attempts to work such areas usually end in failure. To increase the world's food supply, scientists now concentrate on making existing farmland more productive rather than farming marginal land.

To grow crops, farmers need fertile, workable land, an equable climate, including a frost-free growing period, and an adequate supply of fresh water. In some areas, the water falls directly as rain. But many other regions depend on irrigation.

Irrigation involves water conservation through the building of dams which hold back storage reservoirs. In some areas, irrigation water comes from underground aquifers, layers of permeable and porous rocks through which groundwater percolates. But in many cases, the water in the aquifers has been there for thousands of years, having accumulated at a time when the rainfall was much greater than it is today. As a result, these aquifers are not being renewed and will, one day, dry up.

Other sources of irrigation water are desalination plants, which remove salt from seawater and pump it to farms. This is a highly expensive process and is employed in areas where water supplies are extremely low, such as the island of Malta, or in the oil-rich desert countries around the Gulf, which can afford to build huge desalination plants.

Irrigation in Saudi Arabia
Saudi Arabia is a desert country which gets its water from oases, which tap groundwater supplies, and desalination plants. The sale of oil has enabled the arid countries of southwestern Asia to develop their agriculture. In the above satellite image, vegetation appears brown and red.

LAND USE BY CONTINENT (2000)

	Forest	Permanent pasture	Permanent crops	Arable	Non-productive
N. & C. America	25.7%	17.2%	0.4%	12.1%	44.6%
S. America	50.5%	28.7%	1.1%	5.5%	14.2%
Europe	46.0%	8.0%	0.7%	12.8%	32.5%
Africa	21.8%	30.2%	0.9%	6.1%	41.0%
Asia	17.8%	35.8%	1.9%	15.7%	28.8%
Oceania	23.3%	49.3%	0.4%	6.2%	20.8%

The Natural World

In 2003, a report by the International Union for the Conservation of Nature released its Red List of more than 12,250 plant and animal species threatened with extinction – more than 1,000 species than in 2002. Human activities, ranging from habitat destruction to the introduction of alien species from one area to another, are the main causes of this devastating reduction of our planet's biodiversity, which might lead to the loss of unique combinations of genes that could be vital in improving food yields on farms or in the production of drugs to combat disease.

Extinctions of species have occurred throughout Earth history, but today the extinction rate is estimated to be about 10,000 times the natural average. Some scientists have even compared it with the mass extinction that wiped out the dinosaurs 65 million years ago. However, the main cause of today's high extinction rate is not some natural disaster, such as the impact of an asteroid a few miles across, but it is the result of human actions, most notably the destruction of natural habitats for farming and other purposes. In some densely populated areas, such as Western Europe, the natural habitats were destroyed long ago. Today, the greatest damage is occurring in tropical rain forests, which contain more than half of the world's known species.

Modern technology has enabled people to live comfortably almost anywhere on Earth. But most plants and many animals are adapted to particular climatic conditions, and they live in association with and dependent on each other. Plant and animal communities that cover large areas are called biomes.

The World's Biomes

The world's biomes are defined mainly by climate and vegetation. They range from the tundra, in polar regions and high mountain regions, to the lush equatorial rain forests.

The Arctic tundra covers large areas in the polar regions of the northern hemisphere. Snow covers the land for more than half of the year and the subsoil, called permafrost, is permanently frozen. Comparatively few species can survive in this harsh, treeless environment. The main plants are hardy mosses, lichens, grasses, sedges, and low shrubs. However, in summer, the tundra plays an important part in world animal geography, when its growing plants and swarms of insects provide food for migrating animals and birds that arrive from the south.

The tundra of the northern hemisphere merges in the south into a vast region of needleleaf evergreen forest, called the boreal forest or taiga. Such trees as fir, larch, pine, and spruce are adapted to survive the long, bitterly cold winters of this region, but the number of plant and animal species is again small. South of the boreal forests is a zone of mixed needleleaf evergreens and broadleaf deciduous trees, which

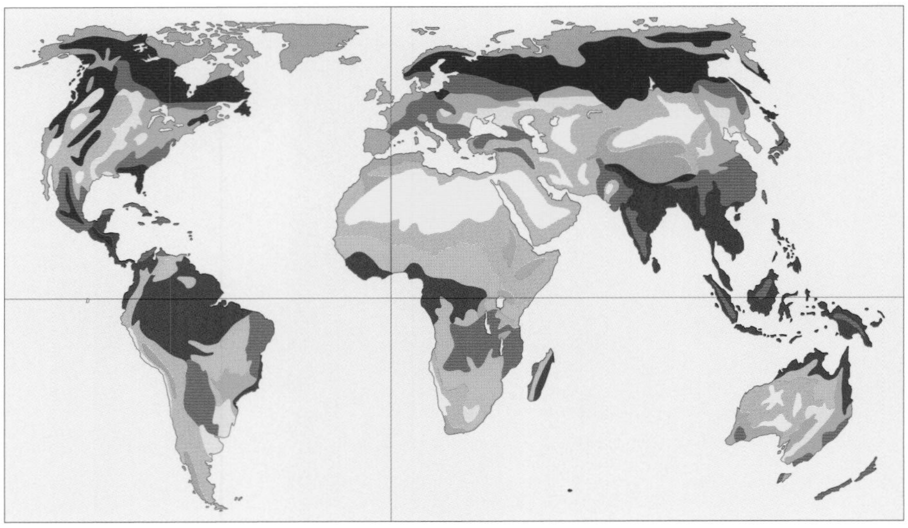

NATURAL VEGETATION

- TUNDRA & MOUNTAIN VEGETATION
- NEEDLELEAF EVERGREEN FOREST
- MIXED NEEDLELEAF EVERGREEN & BROADLEAF DECIDUOUS TREES
- BROADLEAF DECIDUOUS WOODLAND
- MID-LATITUDE GRASSLAND
- EVERGREEN BROADLEAF & DECIDUOUS TREES & SHRUBS
- SEMIDESERT SCRUB
- DESERT
- TROPICAL GRASSLAND (SAVANNA)
- TROPICAL BROADLEAF RAIN FOREST & MONSOON FOREST
- SUBTROPICAL BROADLEAF & NEEDLELEAF FOREST

The map shows the world's main biomes. The classification is based on the natural "climax" vegetation of regions, a result of the climate and the terrain. But human activities have greatly modified this basic division. For example, the original deciduous forests of Western Europe and the eastern United States have largely disappeared. In recent times, human development of some semiarid areas has turned former dry grasslands into barren desert.

Rain forest in Rwanda

Rain forests are the most threatened of the world's biomes. Effective conservation policies must demonstrate to poor local people that they can benefit from the survival of the forests.

Tundra in subarctic Alaska

The Denali National Park, Alaska, contains magnificent mountain scenery and tundra vegetation which flourishes during the brief summer. The park is open between June 1 and September 15.

shed their leaves in winter. In warmer areas, this mixed forest merges into broadleaf deciduous forest, where the number and diversity of plant species is much greater.

Deciduous forests are adapted to temperate, humid regions. Evergreen broadleaf and deciduous trees grow in Mediterranean regions, with their hot, dry summers. But much of the original deciduous forest has been cut down and has given way to scrub and heathland. Grasslands occupy large areas in the middle latitudes, where the rainfall is insufficient to support forest growth. The moister grasslands are often called prairies, while drier areas are called steppe.

The tropics also contain vast dry areas of semidesert scrub which merges into desert, as well as large areas of savanna, which is grassland with scattered trees. Savanna regions, with their marked dry season, support a wide range of mammals.

Tropical and subtropical regions contain three types of forest biomes. The tropical rain forest, the world's richest biome measured by its plant and animal species, experiences rain and high temperatures throughout the year. Similar forests occur in monsoon regions, which have a season of very heavy rainfall. They, too, are rich in plant species, though less so than the tropical rain forest. A third type of forest is the subtropical broadleaf and needleleaf forest, found in such places as southeastern China, south-central Africa, and eastern Brazil.

NET PRIMARY PRODUCTION OF EIGHT MAJOR BIOMES

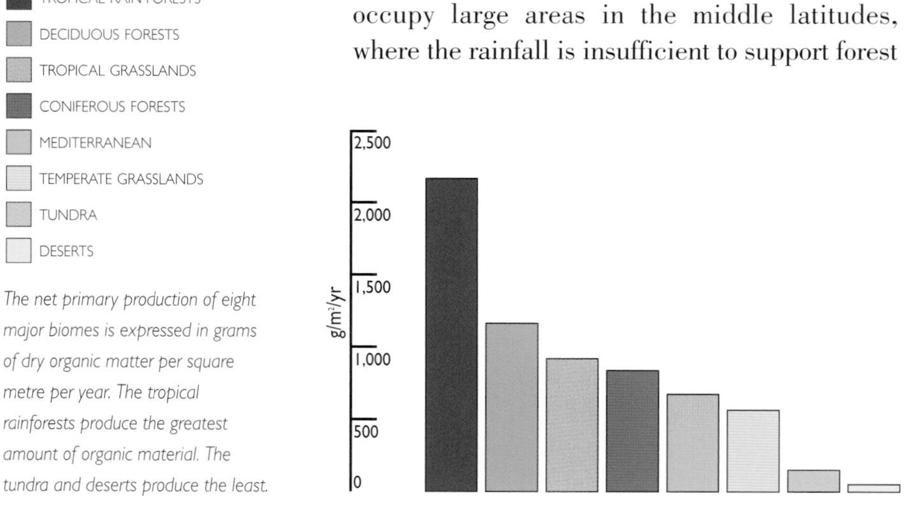

The net primary production of eight major biomes is expressed in grams of dry organic matter per square metre per year. The tropical rainforests produce the greatest amount of organic material. The tundra and deserts produce the least.

The Human World

Every minute, the world's population increases by around 140. Predictions of future growth vary. In 1999, UN demographers stated that the population, which passed the 6 billion mark in October 1999, would reach 8.9 million by 2050. It would level out after 2200 when it would peak at 11 million. But, in 2003, UN demographers predicted that the world's population would peak at 9 billion in 2050 and then could start to decline. But while some European countries are concerned about declining birth rates, all experts agree that the fastest rates of population increase will occur in developing countries – the places least able to afford the high costs arising from a rapidly growing population.

Average world population growth rates are expected to decline from 1.6% per year in 1975–2001 to 1.1% in 2001–15. This is partly due to a decline in fertility rates – that is, the number of births to the number of women of child-bearing age – especially in developed countries where, as income has risen, the average size of families has fallen.

Declining fertility rates were also evident in many developing countries. Even Africa shows signs of such change, though its population is expected to triple before it begins to fall. Population growth is also dependent on death rates, which are affected by such factors as famine, disease, and the quality of medical care.

Elevated view of Ki Lung Street, Hong Kong
Urban areas of Hong Kong, a Special Administrative Region on the southern coast of China, contain busy streets overlooked by crowded apartments.

The Population Explosion

The world's population has grown steadily throughout most of human history, though certain events triggered periods of population growth. The invention of agriculture, around 10,000 years ago, led to great changes in human society. Before then, most people had obtained food by hunting animals and gathering plants. Average life expectancies were probably no more than 20 years and life was hard. However, when farmers began to produce food surpluses, people began to live settled lives. This major milestone in human history led to the development of the first cities and early civilizations.

From an estimated 8 million in 8000 BC, the world population rose to about 300 million by AD 1000. Between 1000 and 1750, the rate of world population increase was around 0.1% per year, but another period of major economic and social change – the Industrial Revolution – began in the late 18th century. The Industrial Revolution led to improvements in farm technology and increases in food production. The world population began to increase quickly as industrialization spread across Europe and into North America. By 1850, it had reached 1.2 billion. The 2 billion mark was passed in the 1920s, and then the population rapidly doubled to 4 billion by the 1970s.

Population Features

Population growth affects the structure of societies. In developing countries with high annual rates of population increase, the large majority of the people are young and soon to become parents themselves. For example, in Kenya, which had until recently an annual rate of population growth of around 4%, about 42%

Largest Cities

Within 10 years, for the first time ever, the majority of the world's population will live in urban areas. Almost all the urban growth will be in developing countries. Below is a list of cities with their estimated populations in the year 2015, in millions.

1	Tokyo	28.7
2	Mumbai (Bombay)	27.4
3	Lagos	24.1
4	Shanghai	23.2
5	Jakarta	21.5
6	São Paulo	21.0
7	Karachi	20.6
8	Beijing	19.6
9	Dhaka	19.2
10	Mexico City	19.1
11	Kolkata (Calcutta)	17.6
12	Delhi	17.5
13	New York City	17.4
14	Tianjin	17.1
15	Metro Manila	14.9
16	Cairo	14.7
17	Los Angeles	14.5
18	Seoul	13.1
19	Buenos Aires	12.5
20	Istanbul	12.1

These city populations are based on figures for urban agglomerations rather than actual city limits.

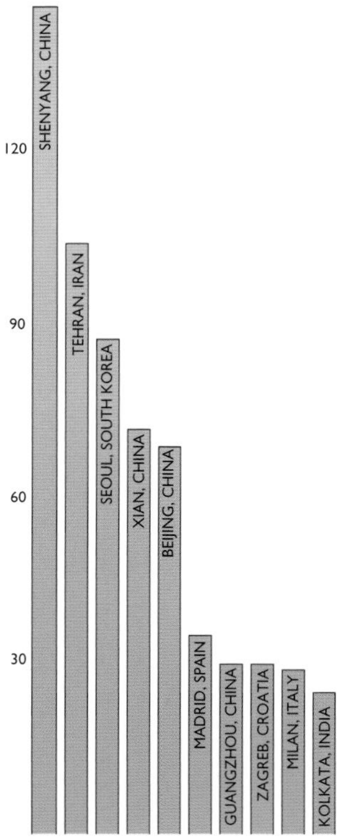

Urban air pollution
This diagram of the world's most polluted cities indicates the number of days per year when sulfur dioxide levels exceed the WHO threshhold of 150 micrograms per cubic meter.

Hong Kong's business district

By contrast with the picturesque old streets of Hong Kong, the business district of Hong Kong City, on the northern shore of Hong Kong Island, is a cluster of modern high-rise buildings. The glittering skyscrapers reflect the success of this tiny region, which has one of the strongest economies in Asia.

of the population is under 15 years of age, as compared with 21% in the United States. Most developed countries have a fairly even spread across the age groups.

Such differences are reflected in average life expectancies. In a rich country, such as the USA, the average life expectancy in 2001 was 77 years (74 for men and 80 for women; women live longer, on average, than men). As a result, an increasing proportion of the people are elderly and retired. The reverse applies in many poor countries, where average life expectancies are below 60 years. In the early 21st century, life expectancies were falling in parts of southern Africa because of the spread of HIV and AIDS. However, overall, the world population is aging. In 2003, demographers predicted that the average age of the world's people will rise from 28 to 40 years.

Paralleling the population explosion has been a rapid growth in the number and size of cities and towns, which contained nearly half of the world's people by the 1990s. This proportion is expected to rise to nearly two-thirds by 2025.

Urbanization occurred first in areas undergoing the industrialization of their economies, but today it is also a feature of the developing world. In developing countries, people are leaving impoverished rural areas hoping to gain access to the education, health, and other services available in cities. But many cities cannot provide the facilities necessitated by rapid population growth. Slums develop and pollution, crime, and disease become features of everyday life.

The population explosion poses another problem for the entire world. No one knows how many people the world can support or how consumer demand will damage the fragile environments on our planet. The British economist Thomas Malthus argued in the late 18th century that overpopulation would lead to famine and war. But an increase in farm technology in the 19th and 20th centuries, combined with a green revolution, in which scientists developed high-yield crop varieties, has greatly increased food production since Malthus' time.

However, some modern scientists argue that overpopulation may become a problem in the 21st century. They argue that food shortages leading to disastrous famines will result unless population growth can be halted. Such people argue in favor of birth control programs. China, one of the two countries with more than a billion people, introduced a one-child family policy. Its action has slowed the growth of China's huge population.

POPULATION CHANGE 1990–2000

The population change for the years 1990–2000.

- OVER 40% POPULATION GAIN
- 20–40% POPULATION GAIN
- 10–20% POPULATION GAIN
- 0–10% POPULATION GAIN
- LOSS OR NO CHANGE
- NO DATA

TOP 5 COUNTRIES	
Kuwait	+75.9%
Namibia	+69.4%
Afghanistan	+60.1%
Mali	+55.5%
Tanzania	+54.6%

BOTTOM 5 COUNTRIES	
Belgium	–0.1%
Hungary	–0.2%
Grenada	–2.4%
Tonga	–3.2%
Germany	–3.2%

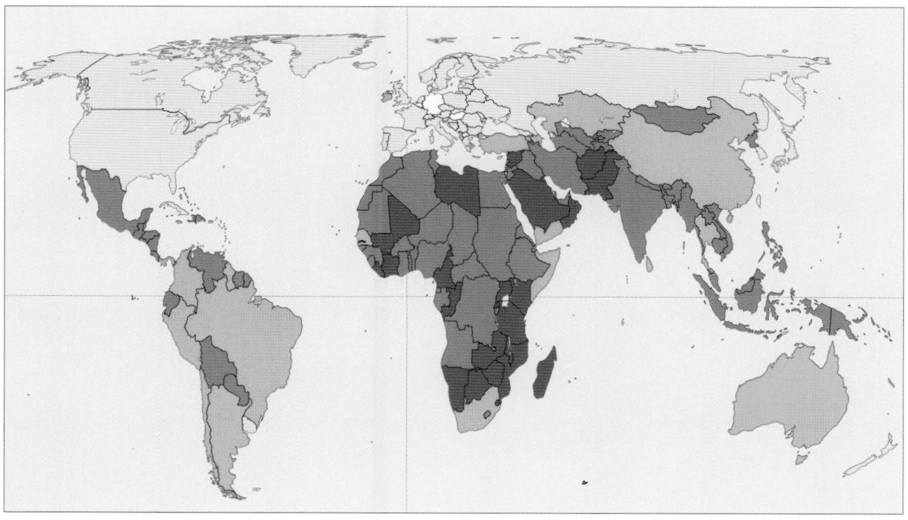

Languages and Religions

In 1995, 90-year-old Edna Guerro died in northern California. She was the last person able to speak Northern Pomo, one of about 50 Native American languages spoken in the state. Her death marked the extinction of one of the world's languages.

This event is not an isolated incident. Language experts regularly report the disappearance of languages and some of them predict that up to 90% of the world's languages will no longer exist by the end of the 21st century. Improved transport and communications are partly to blame, because they bring people from various cultures into closer and closer contact. Many children no longer speak the language of their parents, preferring instead to learn the language used at their schools. The pressures on children to speak dominant rather than minority languages are often great. In the first part of the 20th century, Native American children were punished if they spoke their native language.

The disappearance of a language represents the extinction of a way of thinking, a unique expression of the experiences and knowledge of a group of people. Language and religion together give people an identity and a sense of belonging. However, there are others who argue that the disappearance of minority languages is a step toward international understanding and economic efficiency.

The World's Languages

Definitions of what is a language or a dialect vary and, hence, estimates of the number of languages spoken around the world range from about 3,000 to 6,000. But whatever the figure, it is clear that the number of languages far exceeds the number of countries.

RELIGIOUS ADHERENTS

Number of adherents to the world's major religions, in millions (2003).

Christianity	**2,070**
Roman Catholic	1,093
Protestant	364
Orthodox	217
Anglican	80
Independent	406
Others	110
Islam	**1,254**
Sunni	1,041
Shi'ite	201
Others	12
Secular/Atheist/Agnostic/ Non-religious	**933**
Hinduism	**837**
Chinese folk	**398**
Buddhism	**362**
Ethnic religions	**373**
New religions	**105**
Sikhism	**24**
Judaism	**14**
Spiritism	**13**
Baha'i	**7**
Confucianism	**7**
Jainism	**3**
Shintoism	**3**

Buddhist monks in Katmandu, Nepal

Hinduism is Nepal's official religion, but the Nepalese observe the festivals of both Hinduism and Buddhism. They also regard Buddhist shrines and Hindu temples as equally sacred.

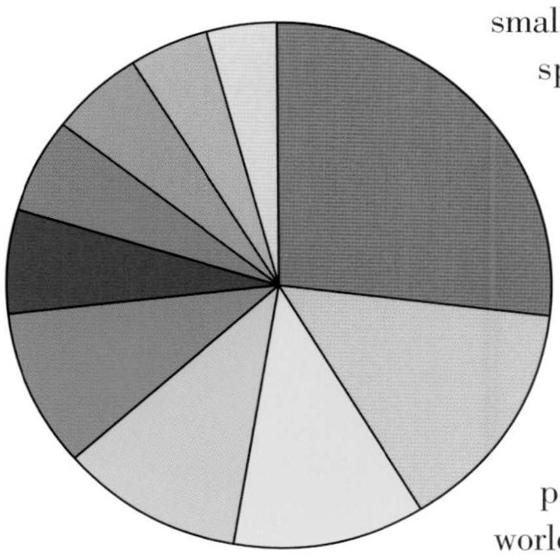

MOTHER TONGUES
First-language speakers of the major languages, in millions (1999).

- MANDARIN CHINESE 885M
- SPANISH 332M
- ENGLISH 322M
- BENGALI 189M
- HINDI 182M
- PORTUGUESE 170M
- RUSSIAN 170M
- JAPANESE 125M
- GERMAN 98M
- WU CHINESE 77M

Countries with only one language tend to be small. For example, in Liechtenstein, everyone speaks German. By contrast, more than 860 languages have been identified in Papua New Guinea, whose population is only about 5.3 million people. Hence, many of its languages are spoken by only small groups of people. In fact, scientists have estimated that about a third of the world's languages are now spoken by less than 1,000 people. By contrast, more than half of the world's population speak just seven languages.

The world's languages are grouped into families. The Indo-European family consists of languages spoken between Europe and the Indian subcontinent. The growth of European empires over the last 300 years led several Indo-European languages, most notably English, French, Portuguese, and Spanish, to spread throughout much of North and South America, Africa, Australia, and New Zealand.

English has become the official language in many countries which together contain more than a quarter of the world's population. It is now a major international language, surpassing in importance Mandarin Chinese, a member of the Sino-Tibetan family, which is the world's leading first language. Without a knowledge of English, businessmen face many problems when conducting international trade, especially with the United States or other English-speaking countries. But proposals that English, French, Russian, or some other language should become a world language seem unlikely to be acceptable to a majority of the world's peoples.

World Religions

Religion is another fundamental aspect of human culture. It has inspired much of the world's finest architecture, literature, music, and painting. It has also helped to shape human cultures since prehistoric times and is responsible for the codes of ethics by which most people live.

The world's major religions were all founded in Asia. Judaism, one of the first faiths to teach that there is only one god, is one of the world's oldest. Founded in southwestern Asia, it influenced the more recent Christianity and Islam, two other monotheistic religions which now have the greatest number of followers. Hinduism, the third leading faith in terms of the numbers of followers, originated in the Indian subcontinent and most Hindus are now found in India. Another major religion, Buddhism, was founded in the subcontinent partly as a reaction to certain aspects of Hinduism. But unlike Hinduism, it has spread from India throughout much of eastern Asia.

Religion and language are powerful creative forces. They are also essential features of nationalism, which gives people a sense of belonging and pride. But nationalism is often also a cause of rivalry and tension. Cultural differences have led to racial hatred, the persecution of minorities, and to war between national groups.

The Church of San Giovanni, Dolomites, Italy
Christianity has done much to shape Western civilization. Christian churches were built as places of worship, but many of them are among the finest achievements of world architecture.

OFFICIAL LANGUAGES: % OF WORLD POPULATION	
English	27.0%
Chinese	19.0%
Hindi	13.5%
Spanish	5.4%
Russian	5.2%
French	4.2%
Arabic	3.3%
Portuguese	3.0%
Malay	3.0%
Bengali	2.9%
Japanese	2.3%

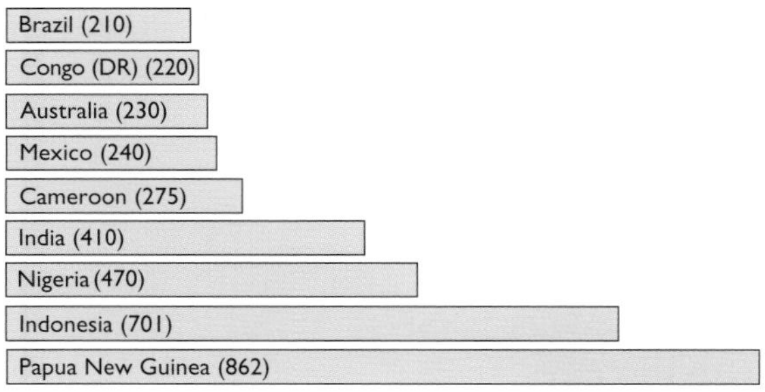

Polyglot nations
The graph, right, shows countries of the world with more than 200 languages. Although it has only about 5.3 million people, Papua New Guinea holds the record for the number of languages spoken.

International Organizations

Twelve days before the surrender of Germany and four months before the final end of World War II, representatives of 50 nations met in San Francisco to create a plan to set up a peace-keeping organization, the United Nations. Since its birth on October 24, 1945, its membership has grown from 51 to 191 in 2003.

Its first 50 years have been marked by failures as well as successes. While it has helped to prevent some disputes from flaring up into full-scale wars, the Blue Berets, as the UN troops are called, have been forced, because of their policy of neutrality, to stand by when atrocities are committed by rival warring groups.

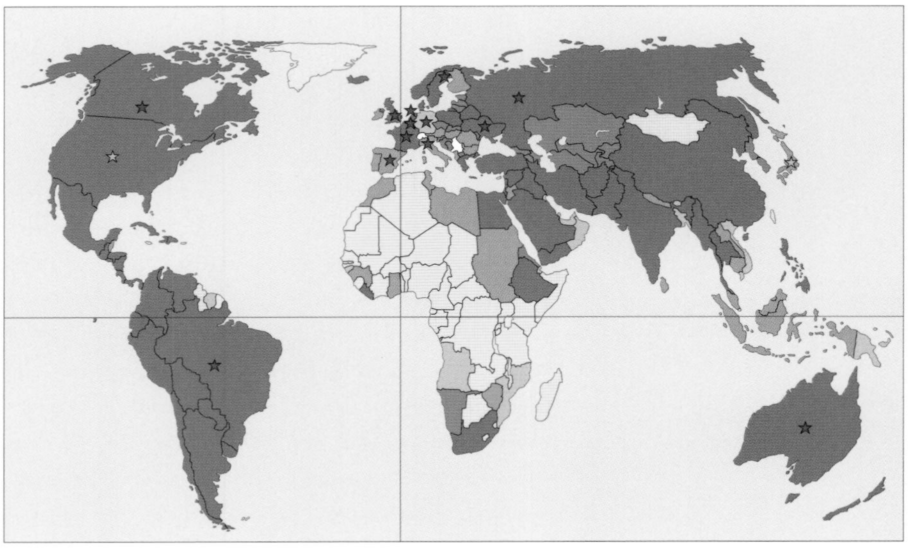

MEMBERS OF THE UN
Year of joining.

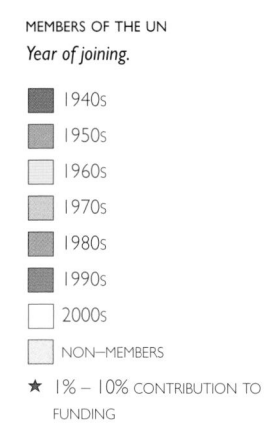

- 1940s
- 1950s
- 1960s
- 1970s
- 1980s
- 1990s
- 2000s
- NON–MEMBERS
- ★ 1% – 10% CONTRIBUTION TO FUNDING
- ☆ OVER 10% CONTRIBUTION TO FUNDING

The Work of the UN

The United Nations has six main organs. They include the General Assembly, where member states meet to discuss issues concerned with peace, security and development. The Security Council, containing 15 members, is concerned with maintaining world peace. The Secretariat, under the Secretary-General, helps the other organs to do their jobs effectively, while the Economic and Social Council works with specialized agencies to implement policies concerned with such matters as development, education, and health. The International Court of Justice, or World Court, helps to settle disputes between member nations. The sixth organ of the UN, the Trusteeship Council, was designed to bring 11 UN trust territories to independence. Its task has now been completed.

The specialized agencies do much important work. For example, UNICEF (United Nations International Children's Fund) has provided health care and aid for children in many parts of the world. The ILO (International Labor Organization) has improved working conditions in many areas, while the FAO (Food and Agricultural Organization) has worked to improve the production and distribution of food. Among the other agencies are organizations to help refugees, to further human rights, and to control the environment. The latest agency, set up in 1995, is the WTO (World Trade Organization), which took over the work of GATT (General Agreement on Tariffs and Trade).

Other Organizations

In a world in which nations have become increasingly interdependent, many other organizations have been set up to deal with a variety of problems. Some, such as NATO (the North Atlantic Treaty Organization), are defense alliances. In the early 1990s, the end of the Cold War suggested that NATO's role might be finished, but the civil war in the former Yugoslavia showed that it still has a role in maintaining peace and security.

Other organizations encourage social and economic cooperation in various regions. Some are NGOs (non-governmental organizations), such as the Red Cross and its Muslim equivalent, the Red Crescent. Other NGOs raise funds to provide aid to countries facing major crises, such as famine.

Some major international organizations aim at economic cooperation and the removal of trade barriers. For example, in 2003, the European Union had 15 members, of which 12 had adopted a single currency, the euro, on January 1, 2001.

UN peace-keeping missions

In the 1990s, a UN peace-keeping mission worked to restore peace to Bosnia-Herzegovina, following the Dayton Peace Accord of 1995. By 2003, hopes of long-term stability were high and refugees were returning home in large numbers.

INTERNATIONAL AID AND GNP
Aid provided as a percentage of GNP, with total aid in brackets (latest available year).

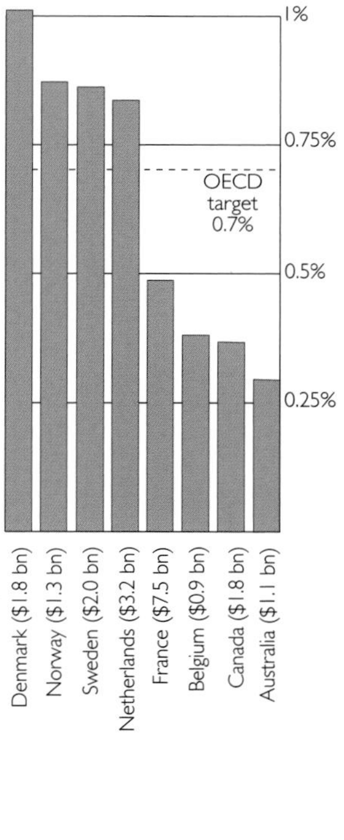

Refugee camp, Sudan

In the late 20th and early 21st centuries, many people in the Horn of Africa and Sudan were displaced by war. Here, and in other parts of the world, refugees from war depended largely on aid from international organizations and NGOs.

On May 1, 2004, another ten countries in eastern and southern Europe joined the EU, bringing the total membership to 25. Further expansion is anticipated in the next decade.

Other groupings include ASEAN (the Association of Southeast Asian Nations) which aims to reduce trade barriers between its members (Brunei, Burma [Myanmar], Cambodia, Indonesia, Laos, Malaysia, the Philippines, Singapore, Thailand, and Vietnam). APEC (the Asia-Pacific Cooperation Group), founded in 1989, aims to create a free trade zone between the countries of eastern Asia, North America, Australia, and New Zealand by 2020. Meanwhile, Canada, Mexico, and the United States have formed NAFTA (the North American Free Trade Agreement), while other economic groupings link most of the countries in Latin America. Another grouping with a more limited but important objective is OPEC (the Organization of Oil-Exporting Countries). OPEC works to unify policies concerning trade in oil on the world markets.

Some organizations exist to discuss matters of common interest between groups of nations. The Commonwealth of Nations, for example, grew out of links created by the British Empire. In North and South America, the OAS (Organization of American States) aims to increase understanding in the Western hemisphere. The African Union, which replaced the Organization of African Unity in 2002, has a similar role in Africa, while the Arab League represents the Arab nations.

COUNTRIES OF THE EUROPEAN UNION

Country	Total land area (sq miles)	Total population (2003 est.)	Year of accession to the EU
Austria	32,378	8,188,000	1995
Belgium	11,787	10,289,000	1958
Cyprus	3,572	772,000	2004
Czech Republic	30,450	10,249,000	2004
Denmark	16,639	5,384,000	1973
Estonia	17,413	1,409,000	2004
Finland	130,558	5,191,000	1995
France	212,934	60,181,000	1958
Germany	137,846	82,398,000	1958
Greece	50,949	10,666,000	1981
Hungary	35,920	10,045,000	2004
Ireland	27,132	3,924,000	1973
Italy	116,339	57,998,000	1958
Latvia	24,942	2,349,000	2004
Lithuania	25,174	3,593,000	2004
Luxembourg	998	454,000	1958
Malta	122	400,000	2004
Netherlands	16,033	16,151,000	1958
Poland	124,807	38,623,000	2004
Portugal	34,285	10,102,000	1986
Slovak Republic	18,924	5,430,000	2004
Slovenia	7,821	1,936,000	2004
Spain	192,103	40,217,000	1986
Sweden	173,731	8,878,000	1995
United Kingdom	93,381	60,095,000	1973

Agriculture

In the 1990s, partly as a result of the breakup of the former Soviet Union in 1991, the increase in world food production was less than the rise in the world's population, creating a small per capita fall in food production. Downward trends in world food production reopened an old debate – whether food production will be able to keep pace with the predicted rapid rises in the world population in the 21st century.

Some experts predicted a period of relative scarcity of food. But others pointed to the "green revolution" which, through the use of new crop varieties, irrigation, and the extensive use of fertilizers and pesticides, revolutionized food production from the 1950s. For example, the "green revolution" made India, once a food importer, self-sufficient in food.

In the early 2000s, many people placed hopes in the use of genetically modified crops. Supporters argued that GM crops could be one of the greatest advances ever in farming. But critics of GM crops voiced serious environmental and health concerns. The lack of conclusive scientific evidence led to strong consumer resistance in some parts of the world, notably in western Europe. Even some developing countries were doubtful. For example, in 2004, Angola, a country badly in need of food aid, joined several other southern African countries in rejecting offers of GM foods.

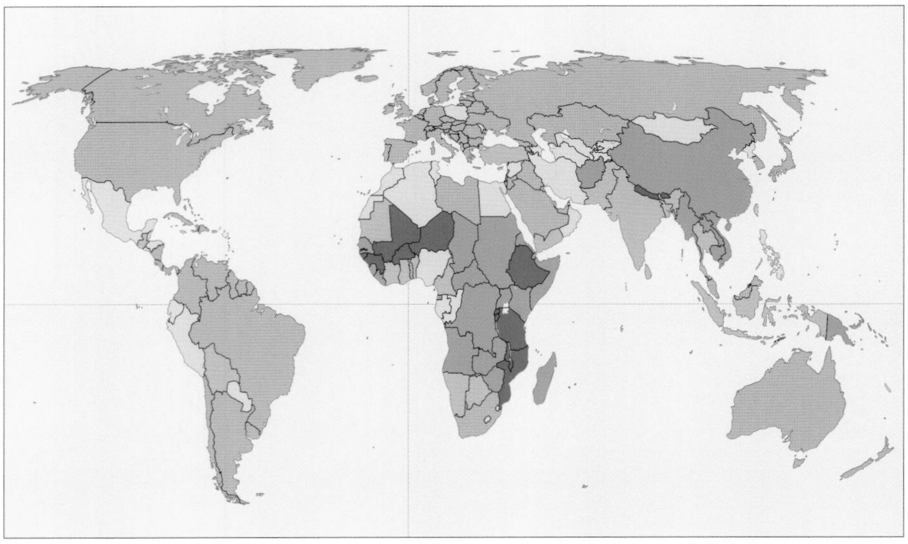

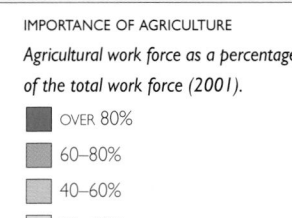

IMPORTANCE OF AGRICULTURE
Agricultural work force as a percentage of the total work force (2001).
OVER 80%
60–80%
40–60%
20–40%
UNDER 20%
NO DATA

Rice harvest, Bali, Indonesia
More than half of the world's people eat rice as their basic food. Rice grows well in tropical and subtropical regions, such as in Indonesia, India and southeastern China.

Food Production

Agriculture, which supplies most of our food, together with materials to make clothes and other products, is the world's most important economic activity. But its relative importance has declined in comparison with manufacturing and service industries. As a result, the end of the 20th century marked the first time for 10,000 years when the vast majority of the people no longer had to depend for their living on growing crops and herding animals.

However, agriculture remains the dominant economic activity in many developing countries in Africa and Asia. For example, in the early 21st century, 80% or more of the people of Bhutan, Burundi, Nepal, and Rwanda depended on farming for their living.

Many people in developing countries eke out the barest of livings by nomadic herding or shifting cultivation, combined with hunting, fishing, and gathering plant foods. A large proportion of farmers live at subsistence level, producing little more than they require to provide the basic needs of their families.

The world's largest food producer and exporter is the United States, although agriculture employs

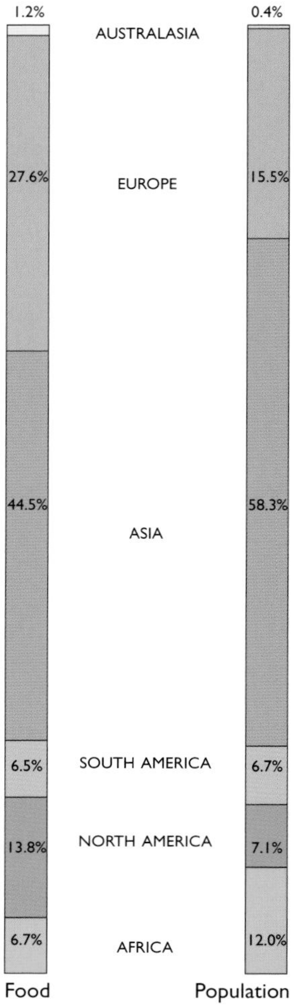

A comparison of world food production and population by continent.

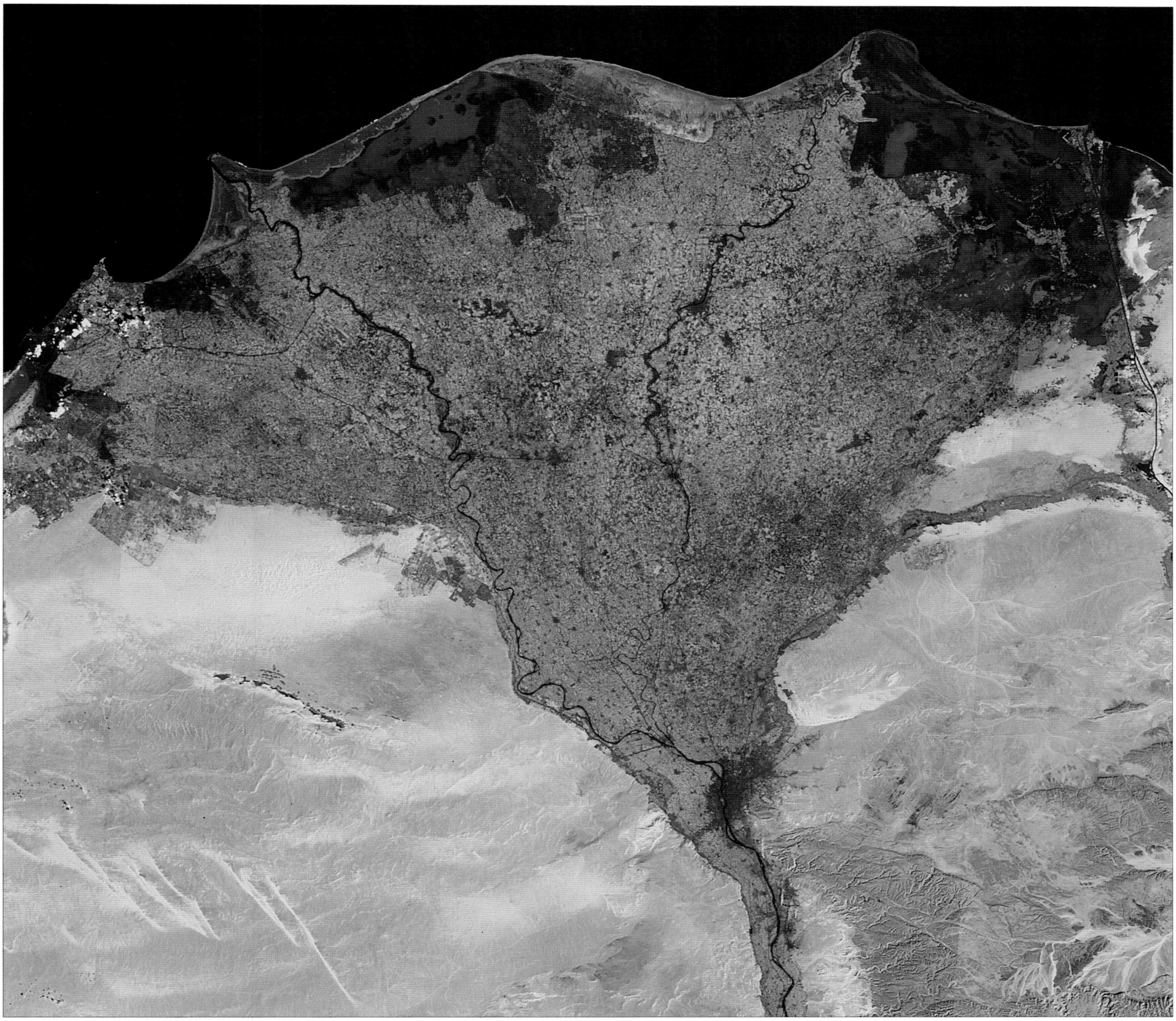

Landsat *image of the Nile delta, Egypt*

Most Egyptians live in the Nile valley and on its delta. Because much of the silt carried by the Nile now ends up on the floor of Lake Nasser, upstream of the Aswan Dam, the delta is now retreating and seawater is seeping inland. This eventuality was not foreseen when the Aswan High Dam was built in the 1960s.

WHEAT

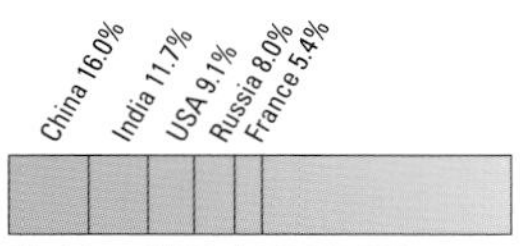

World total (2001): 582,692,000 tons

RICE

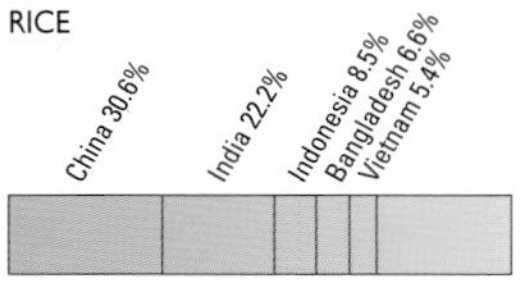

World total (2001): 592,831,000 tons

CASSAVA

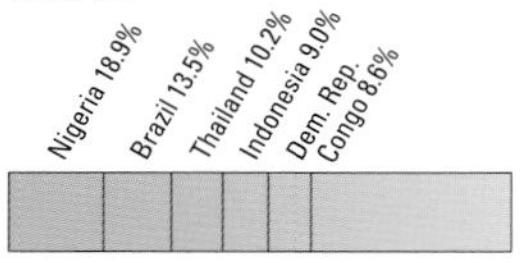

World total (2001): 178,868,000 tons

around 1.4% of its total work force. The high production of the United States is explained by its use of scientific methods and mechanization, which are features of agriculture throughout the developed world.

Intensive or Organic Farming

In the early 21st century, some people were beginning to question the dependence of farmers on chemical fertilizers and pesticides. Many people became concerned that the widespread use of chemicals was seriously polluting and damaging the environment.

Others objected to the intensive farming of animals to raise production and lower prices. For example, the suggestion in Britain in 1996 that BSE, or "mad cow disease," might be passed on to people causing CJD (Creuzfeldt-Jakob Disease) caused widespread alarm. Such factors, combined with the debate about the safety issues surrounding GM foods, have caused much concern.

Some farmers have returned to organic farming, which is based on animal-welfare principles and the banning of chemical fertilizers and pesticides. Organic foods are more expensive to produce than those produced by intensive farming, but an increasing number of consumers are demanding them.

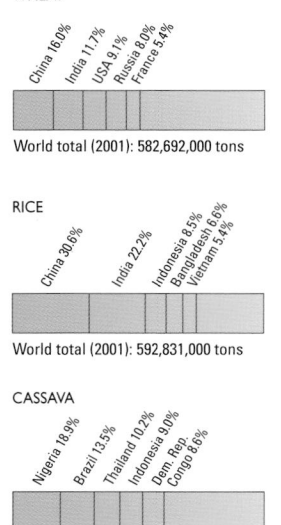

Energy and Minerals

In September 2000, Japan experienced its worst nuclear accident, when more than 400 people were exposed to harmful levels of radiation. This was the worst nuclear incident since the explosion at the Chernobyl nuclear power station, in Ukraine, in 1986. Nuclear power provides around 17% of the world's electricity and experts once thought that it would generate much of the world's energy supply. But concerns about safety and worries about the high costs make this seem unlikely. By 2002, five European countries were committed to abandoning nuclear energy.

Fossil Fuels

Huge amounts of energy are needed for heating, generating electricity, and for transport. In the early years of the Industrial Revolution, coal, formed from organic matter buried beneath the Earth's surface, was the leading source of energy. It remains important as a raw material in the manufacture of drugs and other products, and also as a fuel, despite the fact that burning coal causes air pollution and gives off carbon dioxide, an important greenhouse gas.

However, oil and natural gas, which came into wide use in the 20th century, are cheaper to produce and easier to handle than coal, while, kilogram for kilogram, they give out more heat. Oil is especially important in moving transport, supplying about 97% of the fuel required.

In the 1990s, proven reserves of oil were sufficient to supply the world, at current rates of production, for 43 years, while supplies of natural gas stood at about 66 years. Coal reserves are more abundant and known reserves would last 200 years at present rates of use. Although these figures must be regarded with caution, because they do not allow for future discoveries, it is clear that fossil fuel reserves will one day run out.

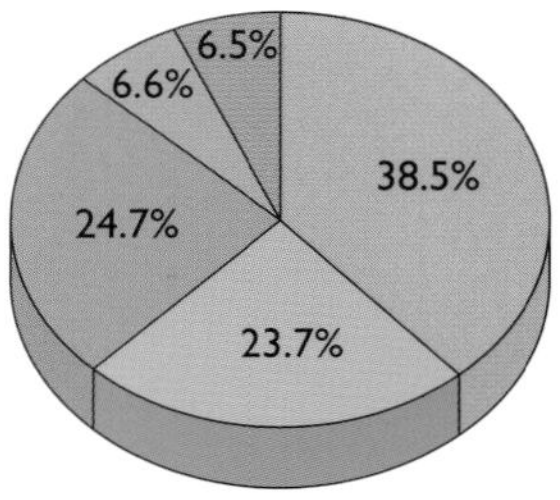

The diagram shows the proportion of world energy consumption in 2001 by form. Total energy consumption was 9,124.8 million tons of oil equivalent. Such fuels as wood, peat, and animal wastes, together with renewable forms of energy, such as wind and geothermal power, are not included, although they are important in some areas.

Wind farms in California, United States

Wind farms using giant turbines can produce electricity at a lower cost than conventional power stations. But in many areas, winds are too light or too strong for wind farms to be effective.

SELECTED MINERAL PRODUCTION STATISTICS (2000)

Bauxite		Diamonds	
Australia	39.9%	Australia	22.7%
Guinea	11.1%	Botswana	21.4%
Brazil	10.4%	Russia	19.7%
Jamaica	8.2%	Congo (D.R.)	15.0%
China	6.7%	S. Africa	9.2%
Gold		**Iron ore**	
S. Africa	16.9%	China	21.1%
USA	13.8%	Brazil	18.4%
Australia	11.6%	Australia	15.8%
China	7.1%	Russia	8.2%
Canada	6.0%	India	7.1%
Manganese		**Zinc**	
Ukraine	32.1%	China	19.6%
China	18.8%	Australia	16.3%
S. Africa	14.4%	Canada	10.7%
Gabon	10.9%	Peru	10.4%
Brazil	7.7%	USA	9.5%

Potash mines in Utah, United States

Potash is a mineral used mainly to make fertilizers. Much of it comes from mines where deposits formed when ancient seas dried up are exploited. Potash is also extracted from salt lakes.

ALTERNATIVE ENERGY

Other sources of energy are therefore required. Besides nuclear energy, the main alternative to fossil fuels is water power. The costs of building dams and hydroelectric power stations is high, though hydroelectric production is comparatively cheap and it does not cause pollution. But the creation of reservoirs uproots people and, in tropical rain forests, it destroys natural habitats. Hydroelectricity is also suitable only in areas with plenty of rivers and steep slopes, such as Norway, while it is unsuitable in flat areas, such as the Netherlands.

In Brazil, alcohol made from sugar has been used to fuel cars. Initially, this government-backed policy met with success. However, it proved to be expensive and the production of ethanol-fuelled cars was halted until Brazil struck a deal with Germany in the early 2000s. Battery-run electric cars have been developed in the United States, but regular and time-consuming recharging is a major drawback.

Other forms of energy, which are renewable and cleaner than fossil fuels, are winds, sea waves, the rise and fall of tides, and geothermal power. In many Western countries seeking to reduce carbon dioxide emissions, these forms of energy seem to have a bright future.

MINERALS FOR INDUSTRY

In addition to energy, manufacturing industries need raw materials, including minerals, and these natural resources, like fossil fuels, are being used in such huge quantities that some experts have predicted shortages of some of them before long.

Manufacturers depend on supplies of about 80 minerals. Some, such as bauxite (aluminum ore) and iron, are abundant, but others are scarce or are found only in deposits that are uneconomical to mine. Many experts advocate a policy of recycling scrap metal, including aluminum, chromium, copper, lead, nickel, and zinc. This practice would reduce pollution and conserve the energy required for extracting and refining mineral ores.

MINERAL DISTRIBUTION

The map shows the richest sources of the most important minerals. Major mineral locations are named. Undersea deposits, most of which are considered inaccessible, are not shown.

- GOLD
- SILVER
- DIAMONDS
- TUNGSTEN
- IRON ORE
- NICKEL
- CHROME
- MANGANESE
- COBALT
- MOLYBDENUM
- COPPER
- LEAD
- BAUXITE
- TIN
- ZINC
- MERCURY

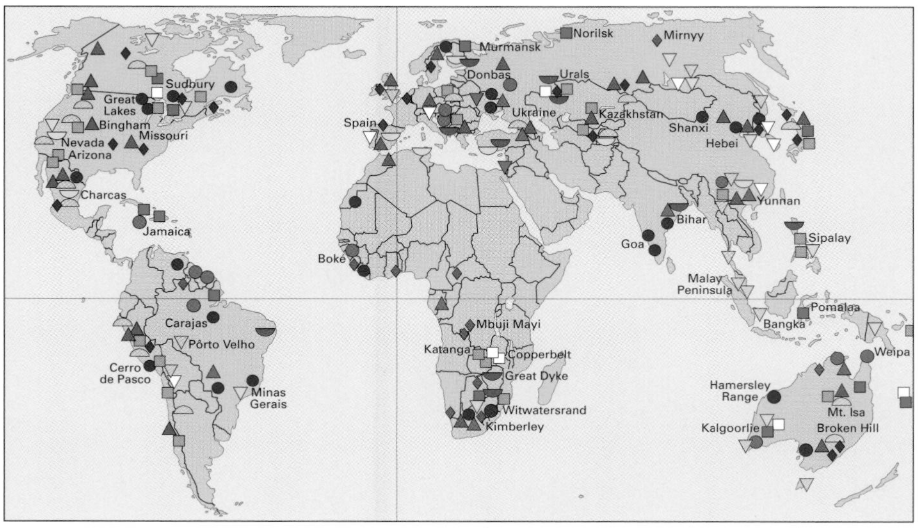

World Economies

In 2001, Tanzania had a per capita GNI (Gross National Income) of US$270, as compared with Switzerland, whose per capita GNI stood at $38,330. These figures indicate the vast gap between the economies and standards of living of the two countries.

The GNI includes the GDP (Gross Domestic Product), which consists of the total output of goods and services in a country in a given year, plus net exports – that is, the value of goods and services sold abroad less the value of foreign goods and services used in the country in the same year. The GNI divided by the population gives a country's GNI per capita. In low-income developing countries, agriculture makes a high contribution to the GNI. For example, in Tanzania, 40% of the GDP in 1999 came from agriculture. On the other hand, manufacturing was small scale and contributed only 6.6% of the GDP. By comparison, in high-income economies, the percentage contribution of manufacturing far exceeds that of agriculture.

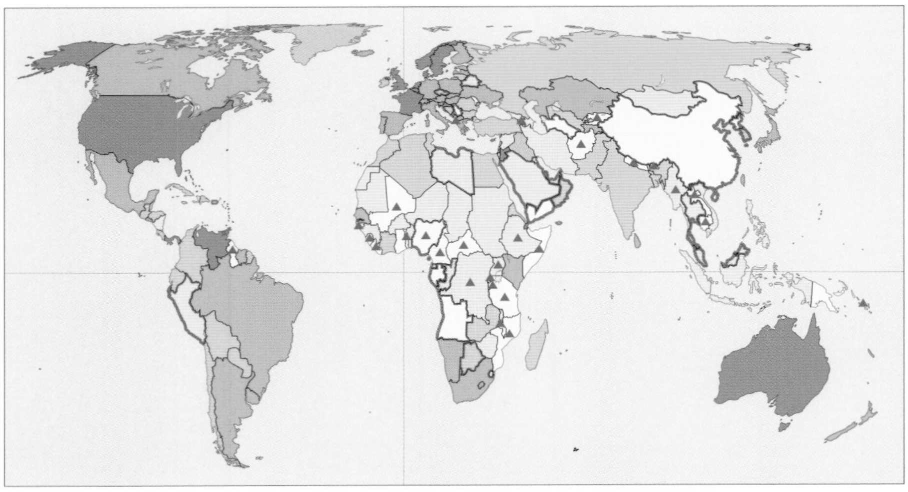

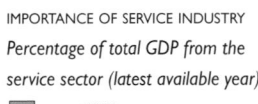

IMPORTANCE OF SERVICE INDUSTRY
Percentage of total GDP from the service sector (latest available year).

- OVER 70%
- 60–70%
- 50–60%
- 40–50%
- UNDER 40%
- NO DATA
- OVER 40% OF TOTAL GDP FROM INDUSTRIAL SECTOR
- OVER 40% OF TOTAL GDP FROM AGRICULTURAL SECTOR

Industrialization

The Industrial Revolution began in Britain in the late 18th century. Before that time, most people worked on farms. But with the Industrial Revolution came factories, using machines that could manufacture goods much faster and more cheaply than those made by cottage industries which already existed.

The Industrial Revolution soon spread to several countries in mainland Europe and the United States and, by the late 19th century, it had reached Canada, Japan, and Russia. At first,

Hard-disk assembly factory
The manufacture of computers and computer software is a fairly new industrial phenomenon. In Asia, high-tech industries have developed quickly, helping relatively poor developing countries to achieve rapid economic growth.

GROSS NATIONAL INCOME PER CAPITA, US$ (2001)

1	Luxembourg	39,840
2	Switzerland	38,330
3	Norway	35,630
4	Japan	35,610
5	United States	34,280
6	Denmark	30,600
7	Iceland	28,910
8	Sweden	26,400
9	United Kingdom	25,120
10	Netherlands	24,330
11	Austria	23,940
12	Belgium	23,850
13	Finland	23,780
14	Germany	23,560
15	Ireland	22,850
16	France	22,730
17	Canada	21,930
18	Singapore	21,500
19	Australia	19,900
20	Italy	19,390

New cars awaiting transportation, Los Angeles, United States
Cars are the most important single manufactured item in world trade, followed by vehicle parts and engines. The world's leading car producers are Japan, the United States, Germany, and France.

industrial development was based on such areas as coalfields or ironfields. But in the 20th century, the use of oil, which is easy to transport along pipelines, made it possible for industries to be set up anywhere.

Some nations, such as Switzerland, became industrialized even though they lacked natural resources. They depended instead on the specialized skills of their workers. This same pattern applies today. Some countries with rich natural resources, such as Mexico (with a per capita GNI in 2001 of US$5,530), lag far behind Japan ($35,610) and Cyprus ($12,320), which lack resources and have to import many of the materials they need to sustain their manufacturing industries.

Service Industries

Experts often refer to high-income countries as industrial economies. But manufacturing employs only one in six workers in the United States, one in five in Britain, and one in three in Germany and Japan.

In most developed economies, the percentage of manufacturing jobs has fallen in recent years, while jobs in service industries have risen. For example, in Britain, the proportion of jobs in manufacturing fell from 37% in 1970 to 12.8% in 2003, while jobs in the service sector rose from just under 50% to 78.6%. While change in Britain was especially rapid, similar changes were taking place in most industrial economies. By the late 1990s, service industries accounted for well over half the jobs in the generally prosperous countries that made up the OECD (Organization for Economic Cooperation and Development). Instead of being called the "industrial" economies, these countries might be better named the "service" economies.

Service industries offer a wide range of jobs and many of them require high educational qualifications. These include finance, insurance, and high-tech industries, such as computer programing, entertainment and telecommunications. Service industries also include marketing and advertising, which are essential if the cars and television sets made by manufacturers are to be sold. Another valuable service industry is tourism; in some countries, such as the Gambia, it is the major foreign exchange earner. Trade in services plays a crucial part in world economics. The share of services in world trade rose from 17% in 1980 to 22% in the 1990s.

THE WORK FORCE
Percentage of men and women over 15 years old in employment, selected countries (2001).

MEN
WOMEN

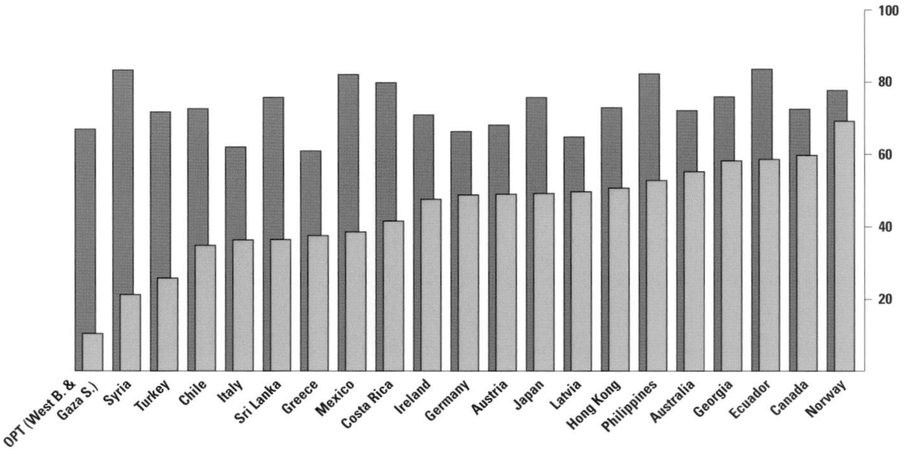

Trade and Commerce

The establishment of the WTO (World Trade Organization) on January 1, 1995, was the latest step in the long history of world trade. The WTO was set up by the eighth round of negotiations, popularly called the "Uruguay round," conducted by the General Agreement on Tariffs and Trade (GATT). This treaty was signed by representatives of 125 governments in April 1994. By mid-2003, the WTO had 146 members.

GATT was first established in 1948. Its initial aim was to produce a charter to create a body called the International Trade Organization. This body never came into being. Instead, GATT, acting as an *ad hoc* agency, pioneered a series of agreements aimed at liberalizing world trade by reducing tariffs on imports and other obstacles to free trade.

GATT's objectives were based on the belief that international trade creates wealth. Trade occurs because the world's resources are not distributed evenly between countries, and, in theory, free trade means that every country should concentrate on what it can do best and purchase from others goods and services that they can supply more cheaply. In practice, however, free trade may cause unemployment when imported goods are cheaper than those produced within the country.

Trade is sometimes an important factor in world politics, especially when trade sanctions are applied against countries whose actions incur the disapproval of the international community. For example, in the 1990s, worldwide trade sanctions were imposed on Serbia because of its involvement in the civil war in Bosnia-Herzegovina.

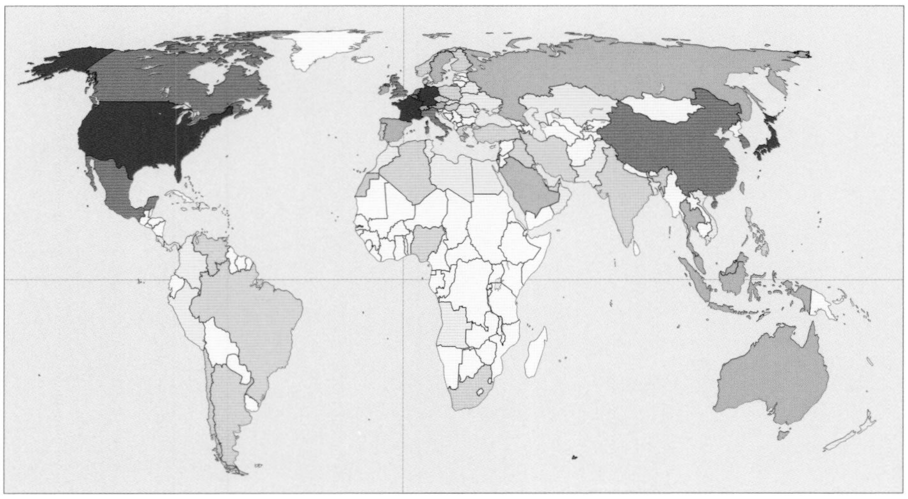

WORLD TRADE

Percentage share of total world exports by value (2000).

- OVER 5%
- 2.5–5%
- 1–2.5%
- 0.25–1%
- 0.1–0.25%
- UNDER 0.1%
- NO DATA

The world's leading trading nations, according to the combined value of their exports and imports, are the United States, Germany, Japan, France, and the United Kingdom.

New York City Stock Exchange, United States

Stock exchanges, where stocks and shares are sold and bought, are important in channeling savings and investments to companies and governments. The world's largest stock exchange is in Tokyo, Japan.

Changing Trade Patterns

The early 16th century, when Europeans began to divide the world into huge empires, opened up a new era in international trade. By the 19th century, the colonial powers, who were among the first industrial powers, promoted trade with their colonies, from which they obtained unprocessed raw materials, such as food, natural fibers, minerals, and timber. In return, they shipped clothes, shoes, and other cheap items to the colonies.

From the late 19th century until the early 1950s, primary products dominated world trade, with oil becoming the leading item in the later part of this period. Many developing countries still depend heavily on the export of one or two primary products, such as coffee or iron ore, but overall the proportion of primary products in world trade has fallen since the 1950s. Today the most important elements in world trade are

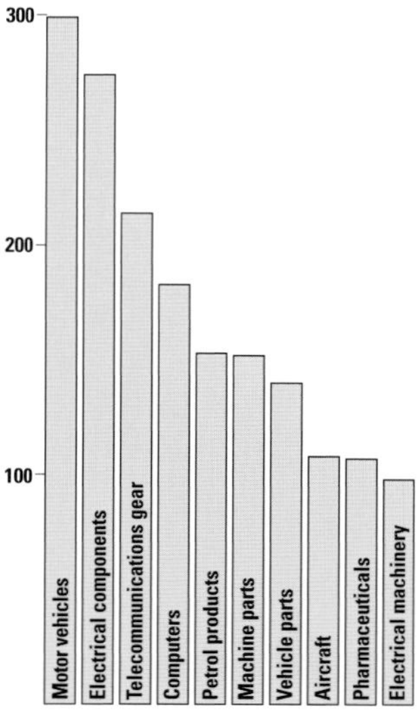

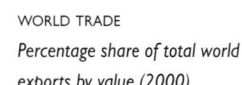

Traded products

Major manufactures traded by value in billions of US$ (2000).

Rotterdam, Netherlands

World trade depends on transport. Rotterdam, the world's largest port, serves not only the Netherlands, but also industrial areas in parts of Germany, France, and Switzerland.

DEPENDENCE ON TRADE

Value of exports as a percentage of GDP (latest available year).

- OVER 50% GDP FROM EXPORTS
- 40–50% GDP FROM EXPORTS
- 30–40% GDP FROM EXPORTS
- 20–30% GDP FROM EXPORTS
- 10–20% GDP FROM EXPORTS
- UNDER 10% GDP FROM EXPORTS
- MOST DEPENDENT ON INDUSTRIAL EXPORTS (OVER 75% OF TOTAL)
- MOST DEPENDENT ON FUEL EXPORTS (OVER 75% OF TOTAL)
- MOST DEPENDENT ON METAL & MINERAL EXPORTS (OVER 75% OF TOTAL)

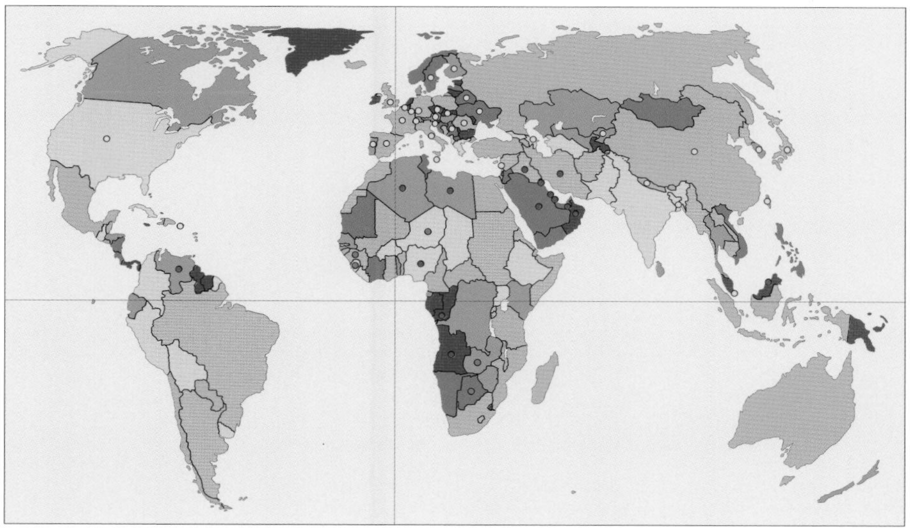

manufactures and semimanufactures, exchanged mainly between the industrialized nations.

The World's Markets

Private companies conduct most of world trade, but government policies affect it. Governments which believe that certain industries are strategic, or essential for the country's future, may impose tariffs on imports, or import quotas to limit the volume of imports, if they are thought to be undercutting the domestic industries.

For example, the United States has argued that Japan has greater access to its markets than the United States has to Japan's. This might have led the United States to resort to protectionism, but instead the United States remains committed to free trade despite occasional disputes.

Other problems in international trade occur when governments give subsidies to its producers, who can then export products at low prices. Another difficulty, called "dumping," occurs when products are sold at below the market price in order to gain a market share. One of the aims of the newly-created WTO is the phasing out of government subsidies for agricultural products, though the world's poorest countries will be exempt from many of the WTO's most severe regulations.

Governments are also concerned about the volume of imports and exports and most countries keep records of international transactions. When the total value of goods and services imported exceeds the value of goods and services exported, then the country has a deficit in its balance of payments. Large deficits can weaken a country's economy.

Travel and Communications

By the early 21st century, millions of people were linked to an "information superhighway" called the Internet. Equipped with a personal computer, an electricity supply, a telephone and a modem, people are able to communicate with others all over the world. People can now send messages by e-mail (electronic mail), they can engage in electronic discussions, contacting people with similar interests, and engage in "chat lines," which are the latest equivalent of telephone conferences.

These new developments are likely to affect the working lives of people everywhere, enabling them to work at home whilst having many of the facilities that are available in an office. The Internet is part of an ongoing and astonishingly rapid evolution in the fields of communications and transport.

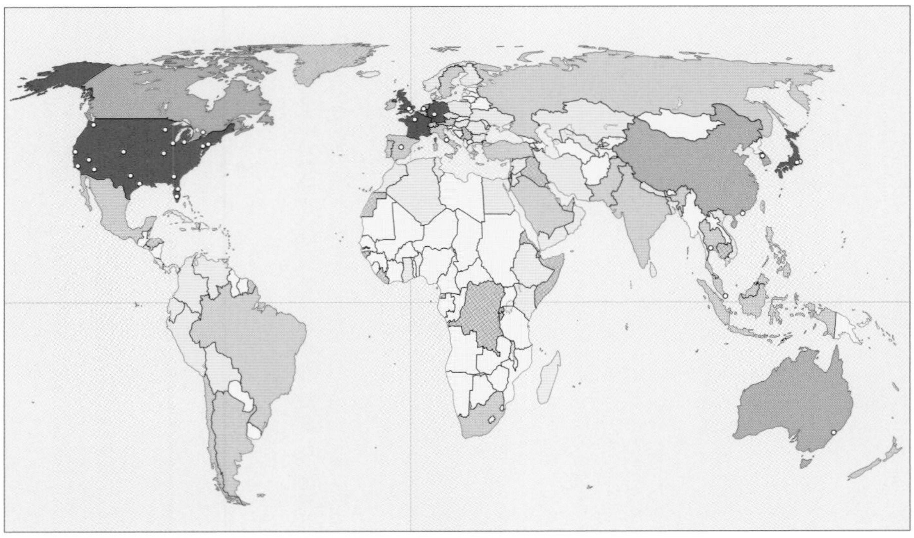

** Passenger kilometers are the number of passengers (both international and domestic) multiplied by the distance flown by each passenger from the airport of origin.*

Transport

Around 200 years ago, most people never travelled far from their birthplace, but today we are much more mobile. Cars and buses now provide convenient forms of transport for many millions of people, huge ships transport massive cargoes around the world, and jet airliners, some traveling faster than the speed of sound, can transport high-value goods as well as vacationers to almost any part of the world.

Land transport of freight has developed greatly since the start of the Industrial Revolution. Canals, which became important in the 18th century, could not compete with rail transport in the 19th century. Rail transport remains important, but, during the 20th century, it suffered from competition with road transport, which is cheaper and has the advantage of carrying materials and goods from door to door.

Road transport causes pollution and the burning of fuels creates greenhouse gases that contribute to global warming. Yet privately owned cars are now the leading form of passenger traffic in developed nations, especially for journeys of less than around 250 miles [400 km]. Car owners do not have to suffer the inconvenience of waiting for public transport, such as buses, though they often have to endure traffic jams at peak travel times.

Ocean passenger traffic is now modest, but ships carry the bulk of international trade. Huge oil tankers and bulk grain carriers now ply the oceans with their cargoes, while container ships carry mixed cargoes. Containers are boxes built

Eurostar travel

High-speed Eurostar services connect London to Paris and Brussels via the $15 billion Channel Tunnel, linking the UK to mainland Europe. Only eight years after the tunnel opened in 1994, Eurostar carried about 6.6 million passengers.

SELECTED NEWSPAPER CIRCULATION FIGURES (2002)

France	
Le Monde	389,200
Le Figaro	352,700
Germany	
Bild	4,100,000
Süddeutsche Zeitung	427,000
India	
The Times of India	2,145,000
The Hindustan Times	1,857,000
Italy	
Corriere della Sera	690,000
La Repubblica	624,000
La Stampa	398,000
Japan	
Yomiuri Shimbun	14,500,000
Asahi Shimbun	12,600,000
Russia	
Argumenty i Fakty	2,900,000
Pravda	674,000
Izvestia	218,000
Spain	
El Pais	578,000
United Kingdom	
The Sun	3,541,000
Daily Mail	2,343,000
Daily Mirror	2,148,000
The Daily Telegraph	924,000
Daily Express	916,000
United States	
USA Today	2,100,000
The Wall Street Journal	1,801,000
The New York Times	1,113,000
Los Angeles Times	966,000

JAL Airways Boeing-747, Vancouver Airport, Canada
Air travel has transformed world tourism. However, the terrorist attacks on the United States in September 2001 and the spread of the SARS (Severe Acute Respiratory Syndrome) virus in 2003 led to large falls in passenger numbers.

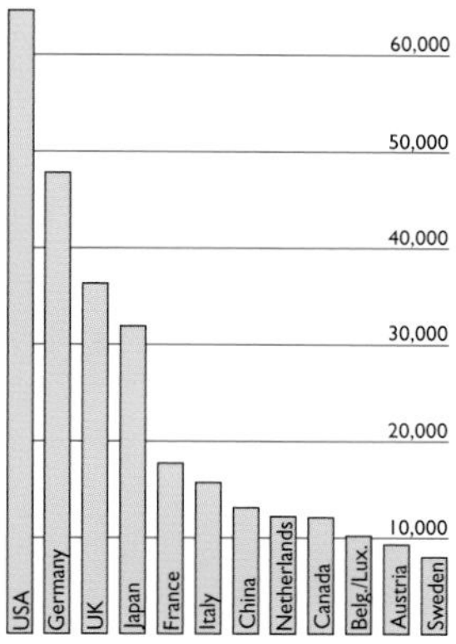

Spending on tourism
Countries spending the most on overseas tourism, US$ million (2000).

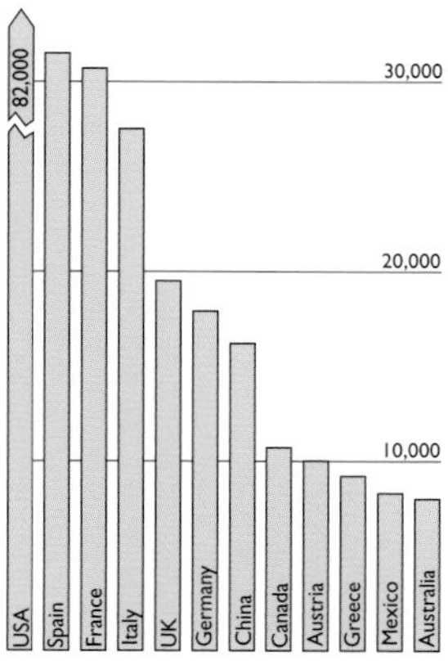

Receipts from tourism
Countries receiving the most from overseas tourism, US$ million (2000).

to international standards that contain cargo. Containers are easy to handle, and so they reduce shipping costs, speed up deliveries, and cut losses caused by breakages. Most large ports now have the facilities to handle containers.

Air transport is suitable for carrying goods that are expensive, light and compact, or perishable. However, because of the high costs of air freight, it is most suitable for carrying passengers along long-distance routes around the world. Through air travel, international tourism, with people sometimes flying considerable distances, has become a major and rapidly expanding industry.

Communications

After humans first began to communicate by using the spoken word, the next great stage in the development of communications was the invention of writing around 5,500 years ago.

The invention of movable type in the mid 15th century led to the mass production of books and, in the early 17th century, the first newspapers. Newspapers now play an important part in the mass communication of information, although today radio and, even more important, television have led to a decline in the circulation of newspapers in many parts of the world.

The most recent developments have occurred in the field of electronics. Artificial communications satellites now circle the planet, relaying radio, television, telegraph, and telephone signals. This enables people to watch events on the far side of the globe as they are happening. Electronic equipment is also used in many other ways, such as in navigation systems used in air, sea, and space, and also in modern weaponry, as shown vividly in the television coverage of such military action as that in Iraq in 2003–4.

The Age of Computers

One of the most remarkable applications of electronics is in the field of computers. Computers are now making a huge contribution to communications. They are able to process data at incredibly high speeds and can store vast quantities of information. For example, the work of weather forecasters has been greatly improved now that computers can process the enormous amount of data required for a single weather forecast. They also have many other applications in such fields as business, government, science, and medicine.

Through the Internet, computers provide a free interchange of news and views around the world. But the dangers of misuse, such as the exchange of pornographic images, have led to calls for censorship. Censorship, however, is a blunt weapon, which can be used by authoritarian governments to suppress the free exchange of information that the new information superhighway makes possible.

The World Today

The early years of the 20th century witnessed the exploration of Antarctica, the last uncharted continent. Today, less than 100 years later, tourists are able to take cruises to the icy southern continent, while almost no part of the globe is inaccessible to the determined traveler. Improved transport and images from space have made our world seem smaller.

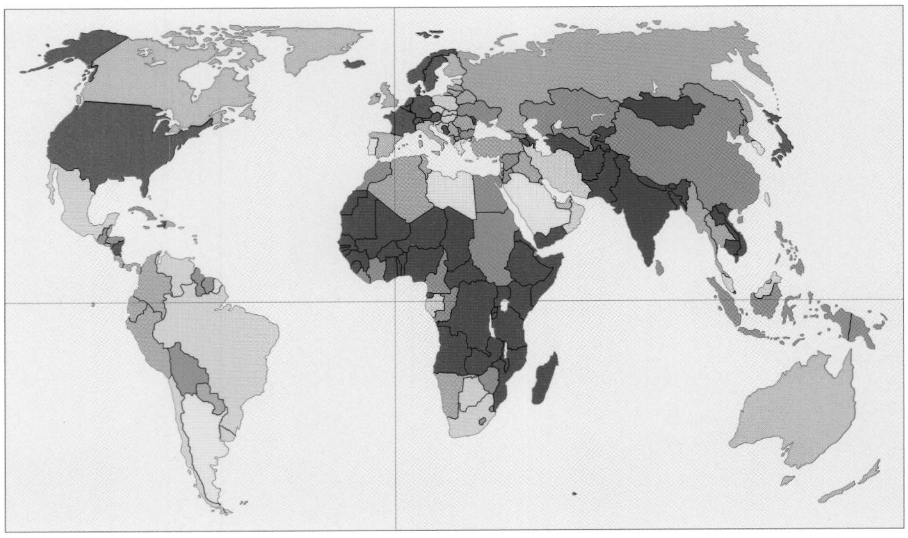

GROSS NATIONAL PRODUCT PER CAPITA

The value of total production divided by the population (latest available year).

- OVER 400% OF WORLD AVERAGE
- 200–400% OF WORLD AVERAGE
- 100–200% OF WORLD AVERAGE

[WORLD AVERAGE WEALTH PER PERSON US$6,316]

- 50–100% OF WORLD AVERAGE
- 25–50% OF WORLD AVERAGE
- 10–25% OF WORLD AVERAGE
- UNDER 10% OF WORLD AVERAGE

RICHEST COUNTRIES

Luxembourg	$39,840
Switzerland	$38,330
Norway	$35,630
Japan	$35,610
United States	$34,280

POOREST COUNTRIES

Congo (Dem. Rep.)	$80
Ethiopia	$100
Burundi	$100
Sierra Leone	$140
Liberia	$140

A Divided World

Between the end of World War II in 1945 and the late 1980s, the world was divided, politically and economically, into three main groups: the developed countries or Western democracies, with their free enterprise or mixed economies; the centrally planned or Communist countries; and the developing countries or Third World.

This division became obsolete when the former Soviet Union and its old European allies, together with the "special economic zones" in eastern China, began the transition from centrally planned to free enterprise economies. This left the world divided into two broad camps: the prosperous developed countries and the poorer developing countries. The simplest way of distinguishing between the groups is with reference to their per capita Gross National Products (per capita GNPs).

The World Bank divides the developing countries into three main groups. At the bottom are the low-income economies, which include China, India, and most of sub-Saharan Africa. In 2001, this group contained about 41% of the world's population, but its average per capita GNP was only US$430. The other two groups are the lower-middle-income economies, with an average per capita GNP of $1,230, and the upper-middle-income economies with an average per capita GNP of $4,550. By contrast, the high-income economies, also called the developed countries, contained only 15.6% of the world's population, but have the high (and rising) average per capita GNP of $26,510.

Economic and Social Contrasts

Economic differences are coupled with other factors, such as rates of population growth. For example, around the turn of the century, the low- and middle-income economies had a high population growth rate of 1.7%, while the growth rate in high-income economies was about 0.1%. In high-income economies, youths made up only 18% of the population and people over 65, 14%.

Stark contrasts exist worldwide in the quality

East African tourism

Improved transport, including the use of four-wheel drive vehicles, has led to a boom in tourism in many developing regions, such as East Africa. But terrorist incidents may slow down the development of tourism in some areas.

Operation Enduring Freedom, Afghanistan
A joint patrol of US Marines and Army soldiers is seen here patrolling through the village of Cem, Afghanistan, some 6 miles [10 km] from the airport near Kandahar, in January 2002.

of life. Generally, the people in Western Europe and North America are better fed, healthier, and have more cars and better homes than the people in low- and middle-income economies.

In 2001, the average life expectancy at birth in sub-Saharan Africa was 46 years. By contrast, the average life expectancy in the United States was 78 years. Illiteracy in low-income economies for people aged 15 and above was 46.7% in 2001. But for women aged 15 and above, the percentage of those who could not read or write was 56.2%. Illiteracy is relatively rare for both sexes in developed countries.

Future Development

In the last 50 years, despite all the aid supplied to developing countries, much of the world still suffers from poverty and economic backwardness. Some countries are even poorer now than they were a generation ago while others have become substantially richer.

However, several factors suggest that poor countries may find progress easier in the 21st century. For example, technology is now more readily transferable between countries, while improved transport and communications make it easier for countries to take part in the world economy. But industrial development could lead to an increase in global pollution. Hence, any strategy for global economic expansion must also take account of environmental factors.

Years of life expectancy at birth, selected countries (2001).
The chart shows the contrasting range of average life expectancies at birth for a range of countries, including both low-income and high-income economies. Generally, improved health services are raising life expectancies. On average, women live longer than men, even in the poorer developing countries.

A World In Conflict

The end of the Cold War held out hopes of a new world order. But ethnic, religious and other rivalries have subsequently led to appalling violence in places as diverse as the Balkan peninsula, Israel and the Palestinian territories, and Rwanda–Burundi. Then, on September 11, 2001, the attack on those symbols of the economic and military might of the United States – the World Trade Center and the Pentagon Building – demonstrated that nowhere on Earth is safe from attack by extremists prepared to sacrifice their lives in pursuit of their aims.

The danger posed by terrorist groups, such as al Qaida, or by rogue states, possibly in possession of nuclear or biological weapons, has forced many countries into new alliances to combat the terrorists and the governments that give them shelter. Many people also recognize a pressing need to understand and correct the wrongs, real or perceived, that lead people to acts of martyrdom or murderous destruction.

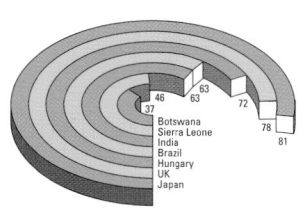

WESTERN CAPE, SOUTH AFRICA

WORLD
MAPS

SETTLEMENTS

■ **PARIS**   ◉ Rotterdam   ◉ Livorno   ◎ Brugge   ◉ Exeter   ◦ *Torremolinos*   ◦ *Oberammergau*   ◦ *Thira*

Settlement symbols and type styles vary according to the scale of each map and indicate the importance of towns on the map rather than specific population figures

◦ *Vaduz*   Capital cities have red infills   ∴   Ruins or archaeological sites

⬠   Urban agglomerations   Wells in desert

ADMINISTRATION

——— International boundaries

– – – – International boundaries (undefined or disputed)

············· Internal boundaries

⬠ National parks

PERU   Country names

KENT   Administrative area names

International boundaries show the *de facto* situation where there are rival claims to territory

COMMUNICATIONS

——— Motorways, freeways and expressways

——— Principal roads

——— Other roads

+---+ Road tunnels

——— Principal railways

– – – Railways under construction

——— Other railways

+---+ Railway tunnels

LHR ✈ Principal airports

✈ Other airports

············· Principal canals

⤨ Passes

PHYSICAL FEATURES

〰 Perennial streams

– – – Intermittent streams

◯ Perennial lakes

◯ Intermittent lakes

Swamps and marshes

Permanent ice and glaciers

▲ 8850 Elevations in metres

▼ 8500 Sea depths in metres

1134 Height of lake surface above sea level in metres

ELEVATION AND DEPTH TINTS

Height of land above sea level

Land below sea level

Depth of sea

in metres   6000 4000 3000 2000 1500 1000 400 200   0

in feet   18 000 12 000 9000 6000 4500 3000 1200 600

6000 12 000 15 000 18 000 24 000   in feet

0   200   2000 4000 5000 6000 8000   in metres

Some of the maps have different contours to highlight and clarify the principal relief features

 Equatorial Scale 1:84 000 000

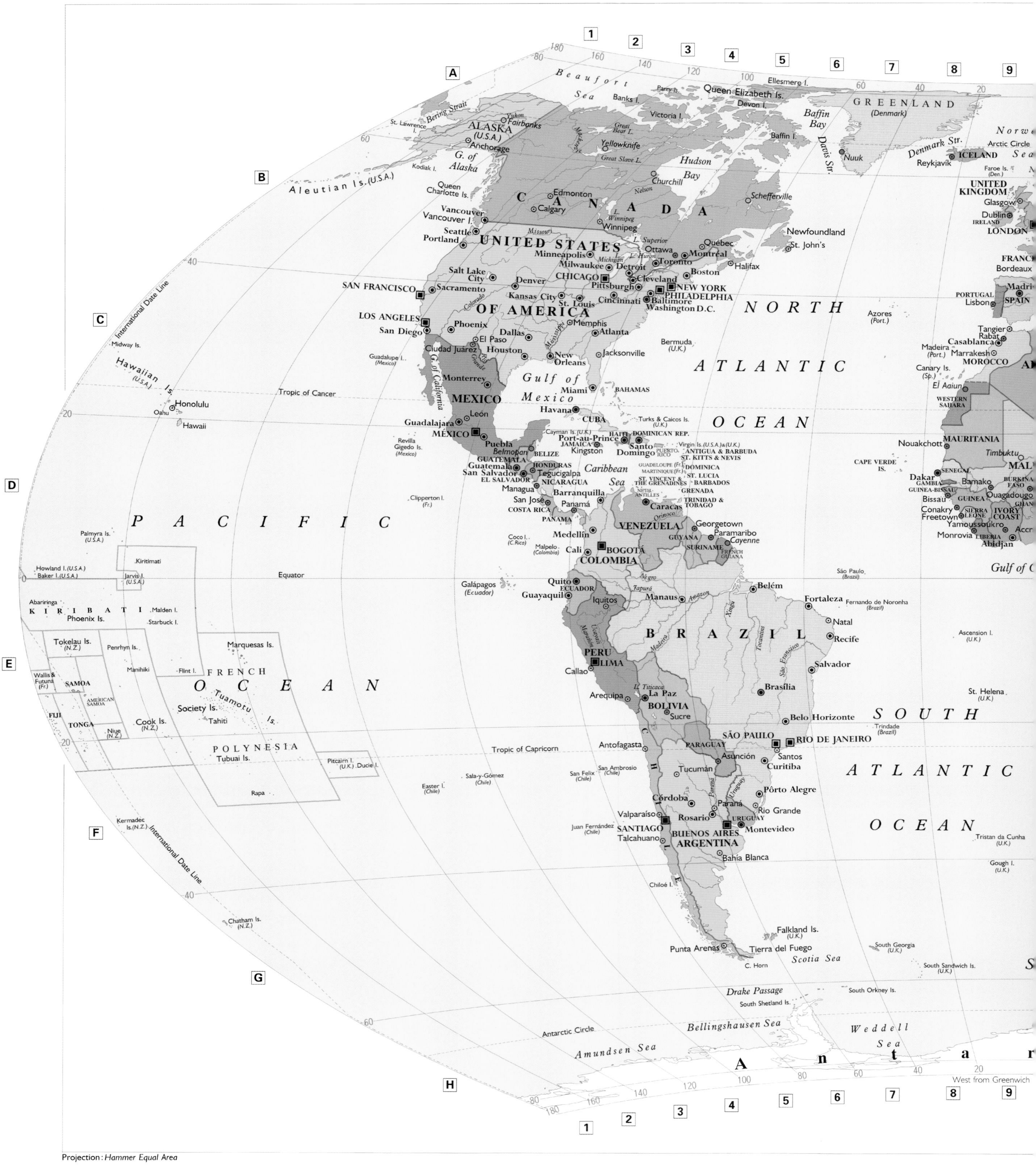

Projection: *Hammer Equal Area*

Hanoi ◉ Capital Cities

4 ARCTIC OCEAN

100 0 200 400 600 800 1000 1200 1400 km

1:31 100 000

100 0 200 400 600 800 1000 miles

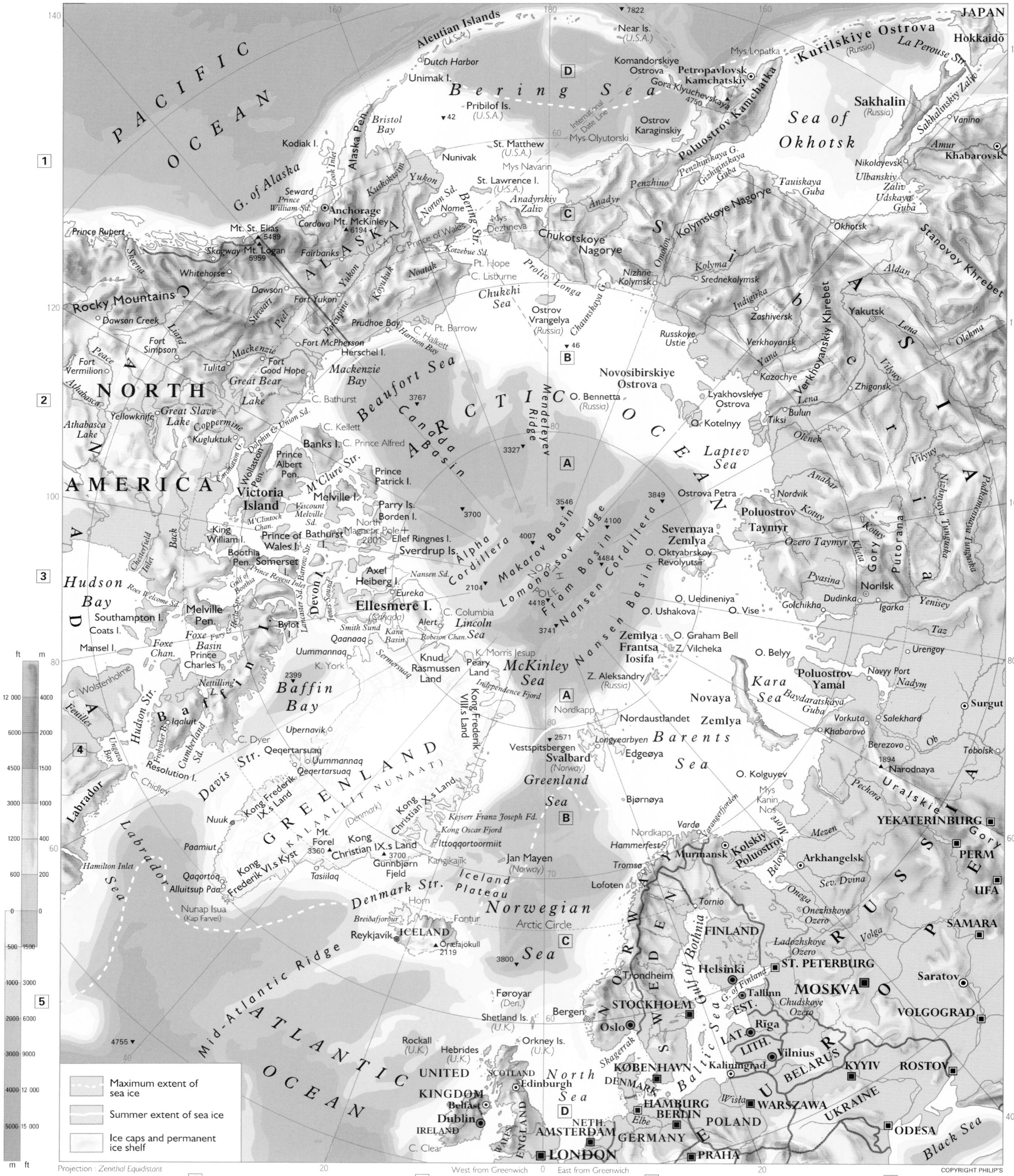

Projection : Zenithal Equidistant

1:31 100 000

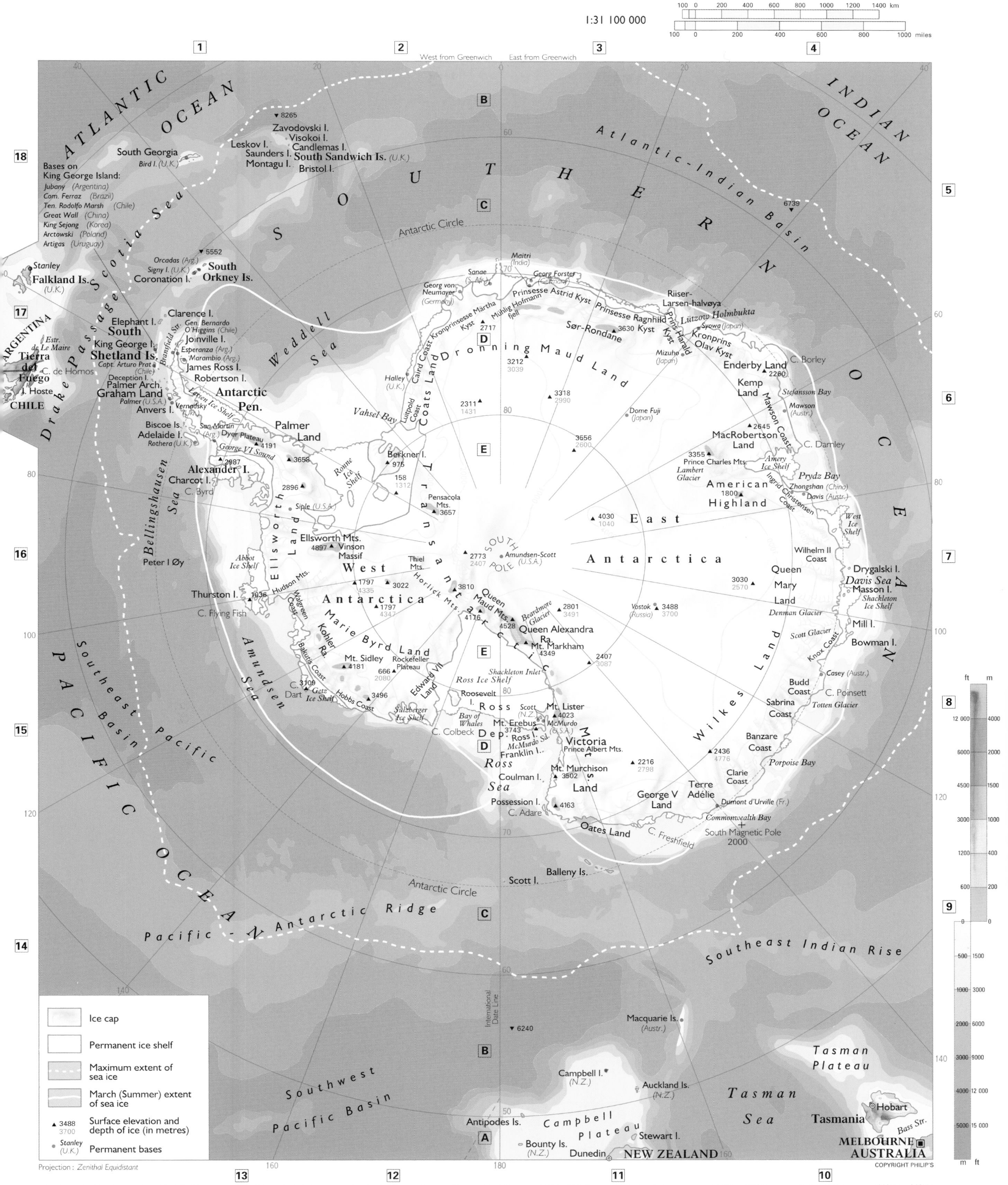

The Antarctic Treaty was signed in Washington in 1959 so that scientific and technical research could continue unhampered by international politics.

All territorial claims covering land areas south of latitude 60°S have been suspended. Those claims were:

Norwegian claim (Dronning Maud Land)	45°E - 20°W
Australian claims	45°E - 136°E 142°E - 160°E
French claim (Terre Adélie)	136°E - 142°E
New Zealand claim (Ross Dependency)	160°E - 150°W
British claim	80°W - 20°W
Argentine claim	74°W - 53°W
Chilean claim	90°W - 53°W

100 0 100 200 300 400 500 600 700 800 km

100 0 100 200 300 400 500 miles

1:17 800 000

1:17 800 000

100 0 100 200 300 400 500 600 700 800 km

100 0 100 200 300 400 500 miles

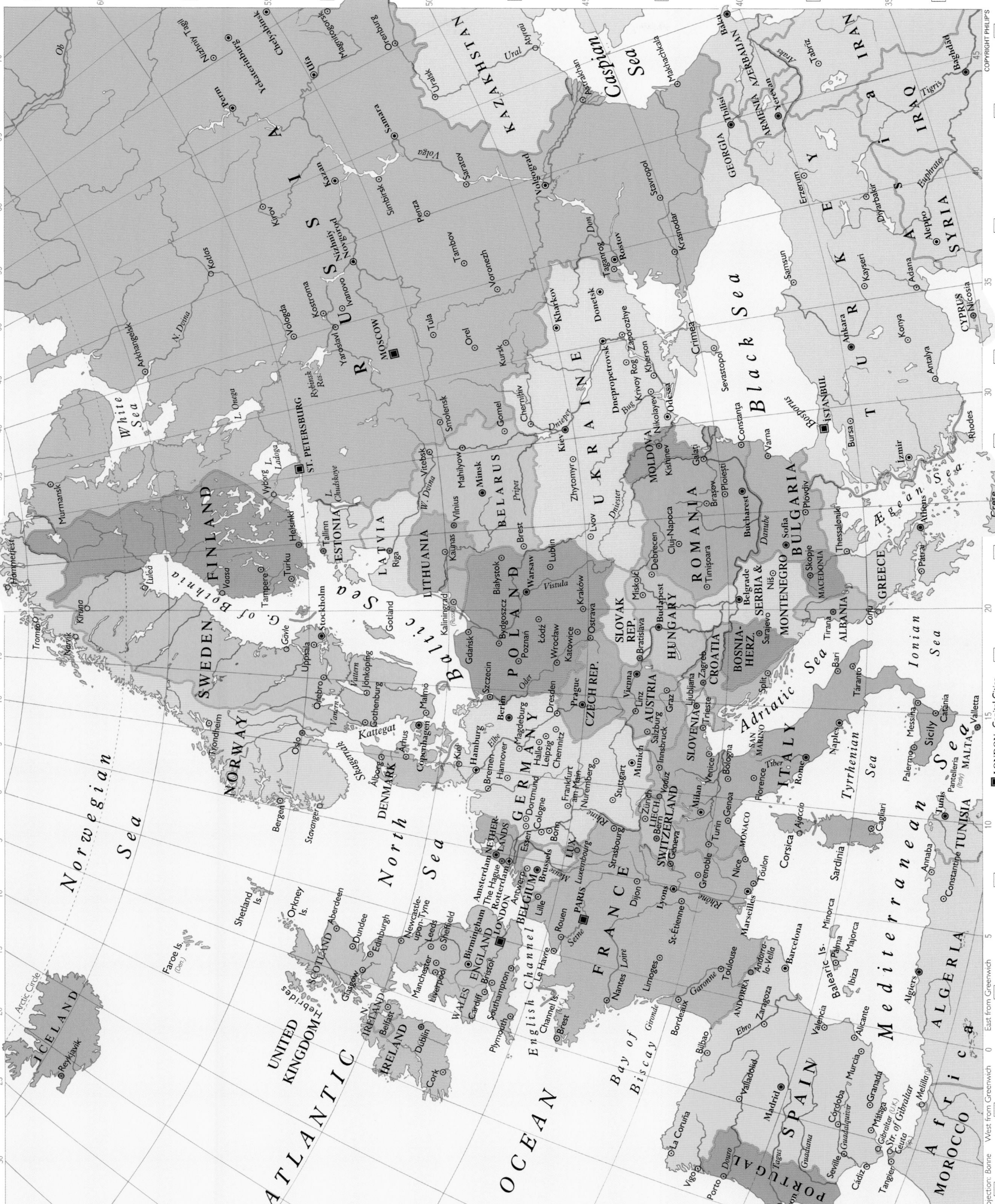

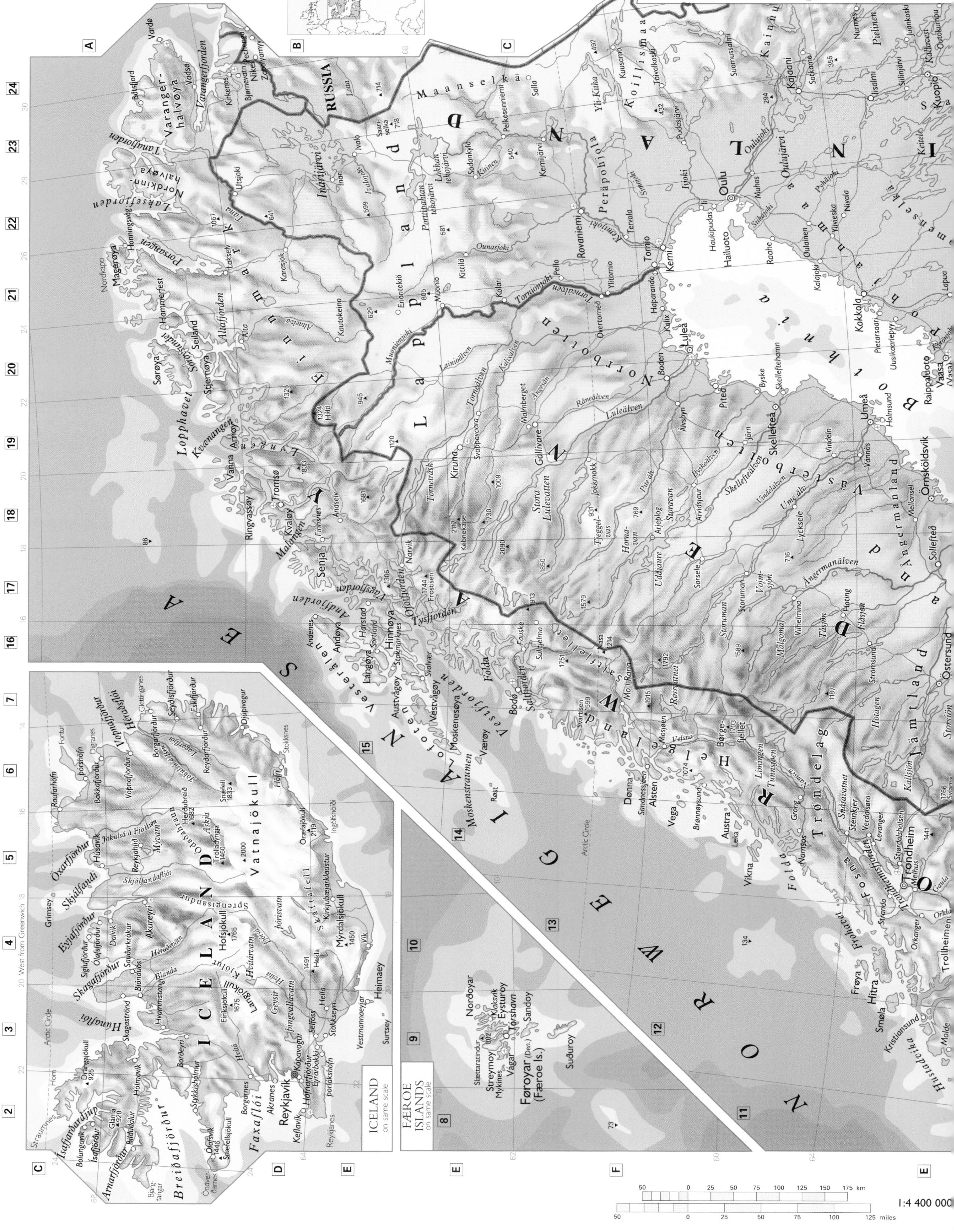

RUSSIA
Lappland
Finnmark
Norrbotten
Västerbotten
Ångermanland
Jämtland
Trøndelag
Helgeland
Lofoten
Vesterålen
Vestfjorden
Vatnajökull
Hofsjökull
Langjökull
Mýrdalsjökull
Reykjavík
Akureyri
Húsavík
Ísafjörður
Keflavík
Heimaey
Surtsey
Faxaflói
Breiðafjörður
Tórshavn
Streymoy
Suðuroy
Sandoy
Eysturoy
Norðoyar
Vágar
Oulu
Kemi
Tornio
Rovaniemi
Kajaani
Kokkola
Luleå
Boden
Piteå
Skellefteå
Umeå
Örnsköldsvik
Östersund
Kiruna
Gällivare
Narvik
Tromsø
Hammerfest
Vardø
Vadsø
Kirkenes
Bodø
Harstad
Trondheim
Namsos
Kristiansund
Alta
Kautokeino
Karasjok
Inari
Ivalo
Mo i Rana
Mosjøen
Arctic Circle
ICELAND
on same scale
FÆROE ISLANDS
on same scale
1:4 400 000
km
miles

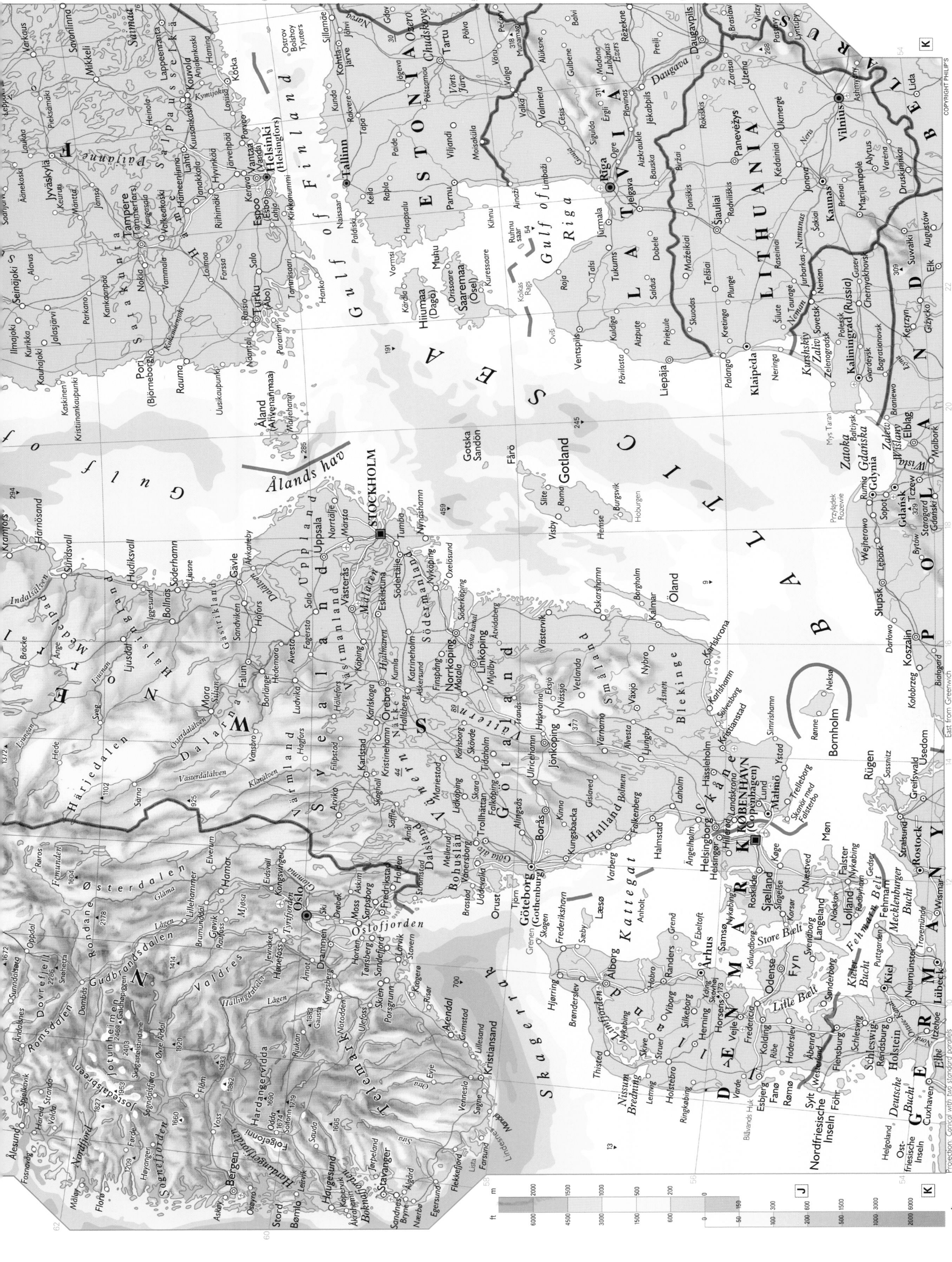
NORWAY
SWEDEN
FINLAND
ESTONIA
LATVIA
LITHUANIA
POLAND
GERMANY
DENMARK
BELARUS
BALTIC SEA
Gulf of Finland
Gulf of Bothnia
Gulf of Riga
Skagerrak
Kattegat
Ålands hav
STOCKHOLM
Oslo
Helsinki (Helsingfors)
Tallinn
Riga
Vilnius
KØBENHAVN (Copenhagen)
Gotland
Öland
Bornholm
Saaremaa (Ösel)
Hiiumaa (Dagö)
Åland (Ahvenanmaa)
Sjælland
Fyn
Jotunheimen
Hardangervidda
Telemark
Dalarna
Småland
Götaland
Svealand
Norrland
Projection: Conical with two standard parallels
East from Greenwich
COPYRIGHT PHILIP'S

10 0 10 20 30 40 50 60 70 80 90 km

10 0 10 20 30 40 50 60 miles

1:2 200 000

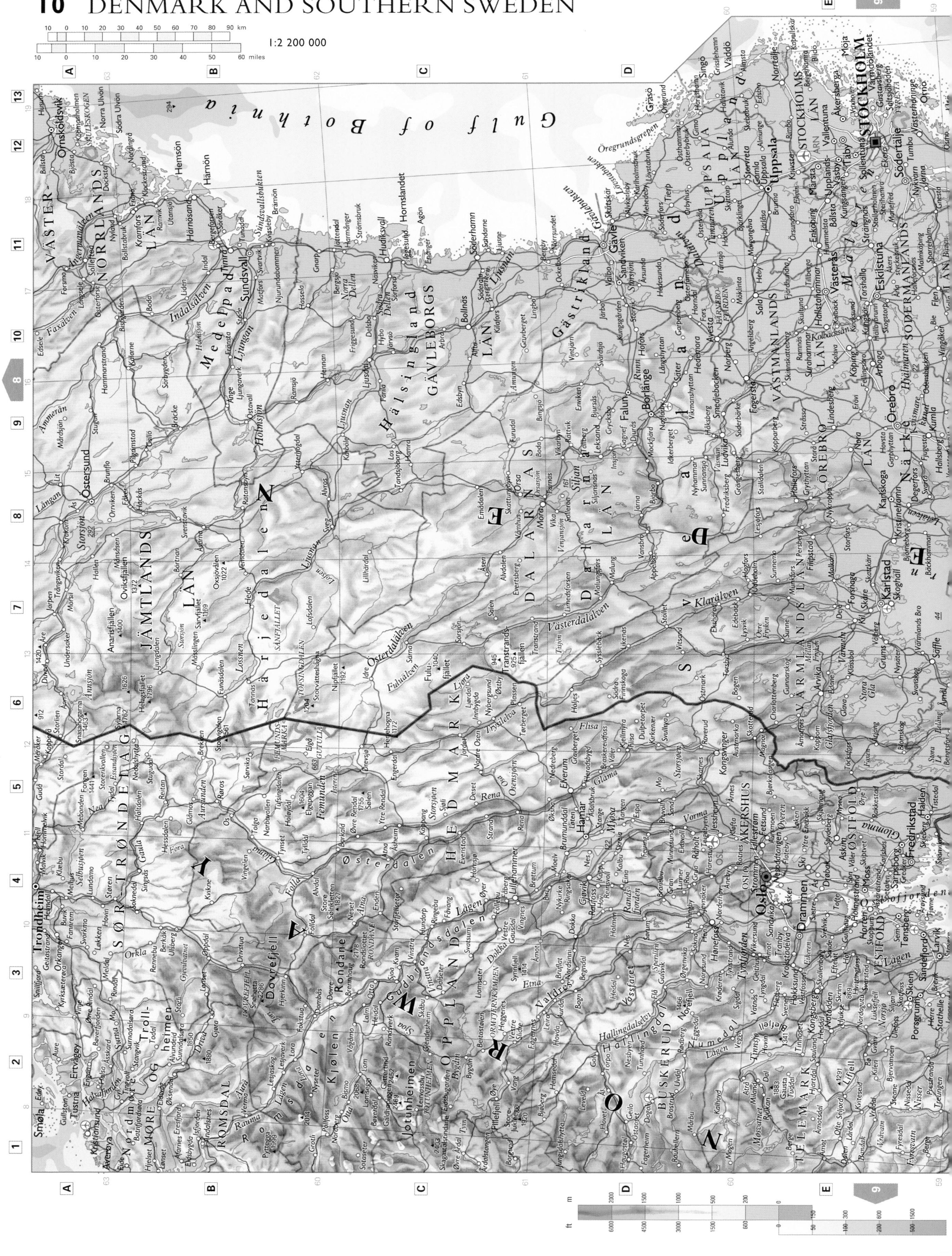

National Parks

10 0 10 20 30 40 50 60 70 80 km

10 0 10 20 30 40 50 miles

1:1 800 000

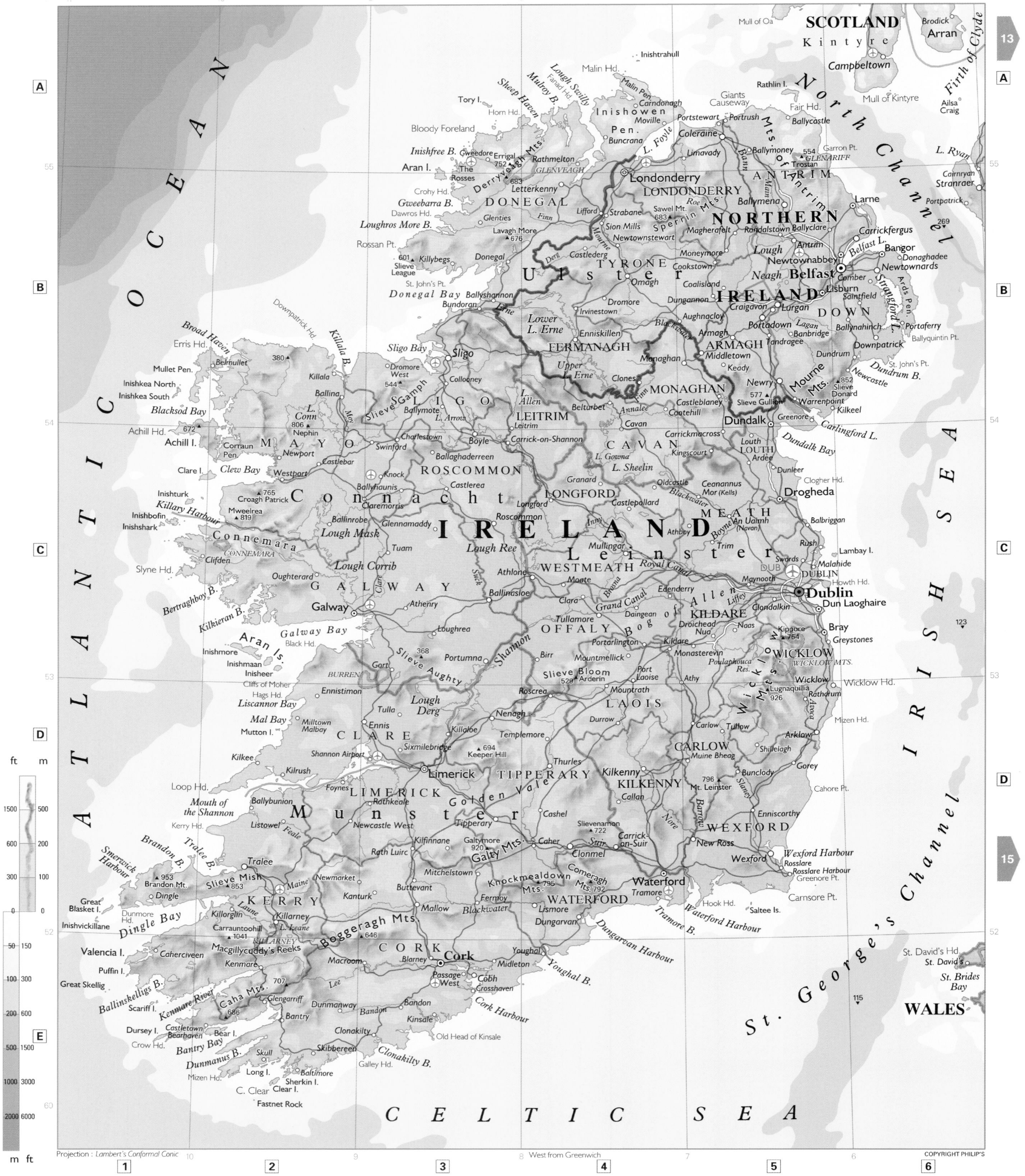

Projection : Lambert's Conformal Conic

West from Greenwich

National Parks

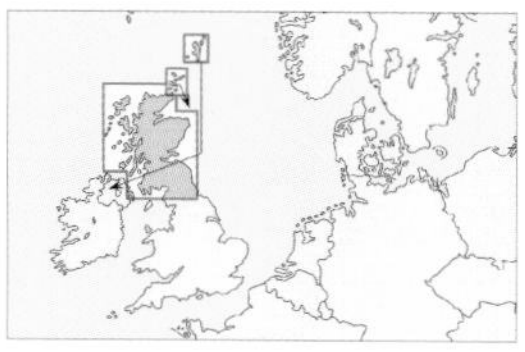

1:1 800 000

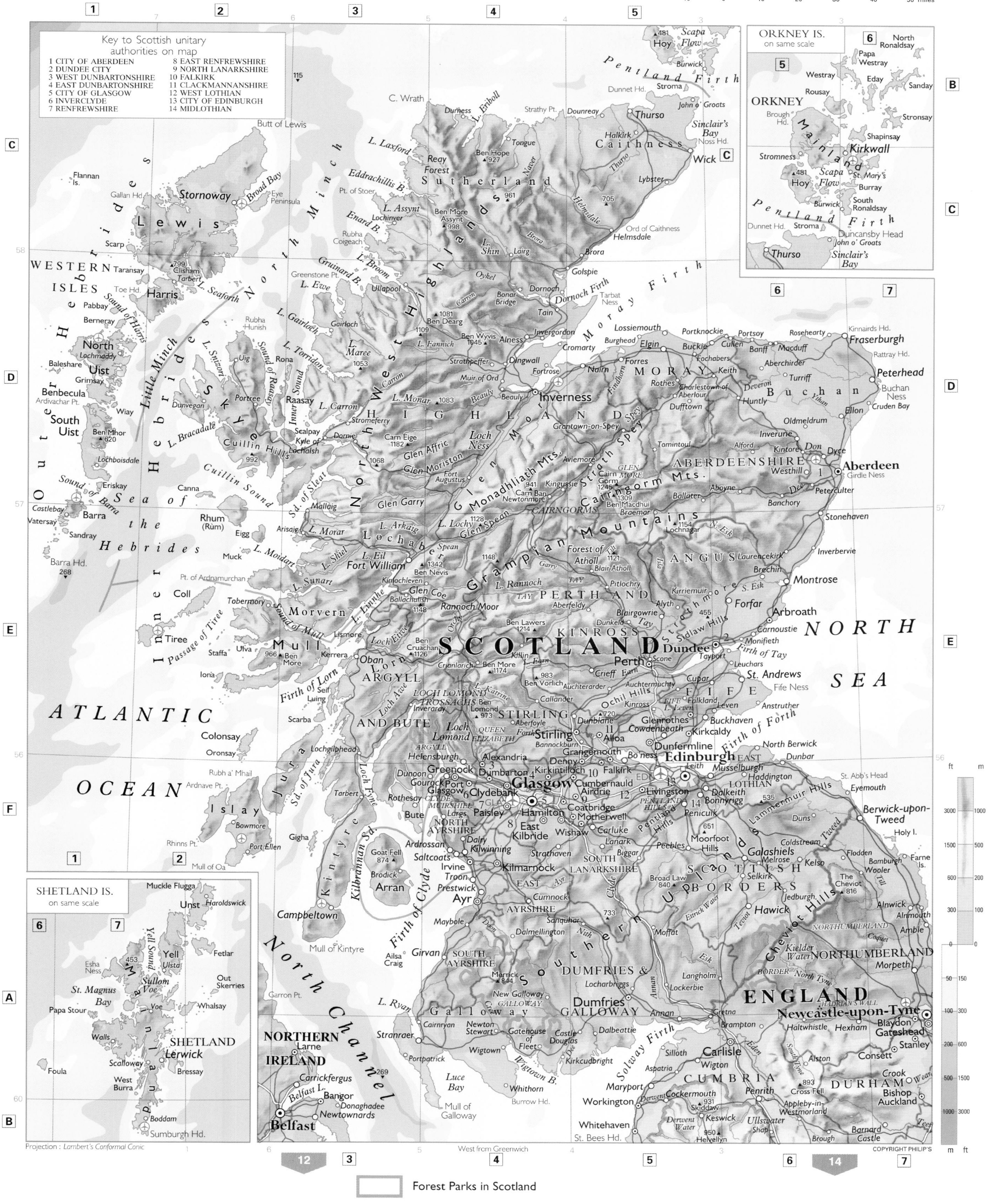
Key to Scottish unitary authorities on map
1 CITY OF ABERDEEN
2 DUNDEE CITY
3 WEST DUNBARTONSHIRE
4 EAST DUNBARTONSHIRE
5 CITY OF GLASGOW
6 INVERCLYDE
7 RENFREWSHIRE
8 EAST RENFREWSHIRE
9 NORTH LANARKSHIRE
10 FALKIRK
11 CLACKMANNANSHIRE
12 WEST LOTHIAN
13 CITY OF EDINBURGH
14 MIDLOTHIAN
ORKNEY IS. on same scale
SHETLAND IS. on same scale
SCOTLAND
ATLANTIC OCEAN
NORTH SEA
North Channel
Pentland Firth
Moray Firth
Firth of Forth
Firth of Clyde
Firth of Lorn
Solway Firth
The Minch
Little Minch
Sea of the Hebrides
Outer Hebrides
Inner Hebrides
WESTERN ISLES
Lewis
Harris
North Uist
Benbecula
South Uist
Barra
Skye
Mull
Islay
Jura
Arran
Tiree
Coll
Stornoway
Thurso
Wick
Inverness
Aberdeen
Dundee
Perth
Stirling
Edinburgh
Glasgow
Fort William
Oban
Ayr
Dumfries
Kirkwall
Lerwick
Grampian Mountains
Cairngorm Mts.
Monadhliath Mts.
Southern Uplands
Cheviot Hills
North West Highlands
Sutherland
Caithness
HIGHLAND
MORAY
ABERDEENSHIRE
ANGUS
PERTH AND KINROSS
FIFE
ARGYLL AND BUTE
STIRLING
EAST LOTHIAN
SCOTTISH BORDERS
DUMFRIES & GALLOWAY
SOUTH AYRSHIRE
EAST AYRSHIRE
NORTH AYRSHIRE
SOUTH LANARKSHIRE
ORKNEY
SHETLAND
NORTHERN IRELAND
Belfast
ENGLAND
Newcastle-upon-Tyne
Carlisle
NORTHUMBERLAND
CUMBRIA
DURHAM
Ben Nevis 1342
Ben Macdhui 1309
Projection : Lambert's Conformal Conic
West from Greenwich
COPYRIGHT PHILIP'S
Forest Parks in Scotland

ENGLAND AND WALES

1:1 800 000

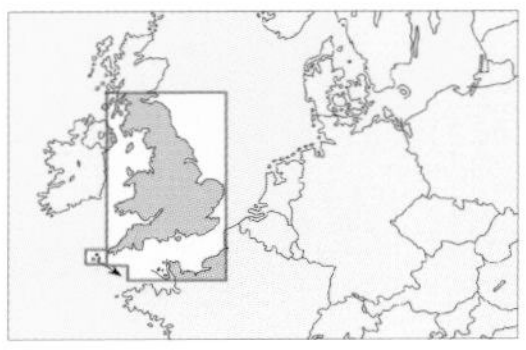

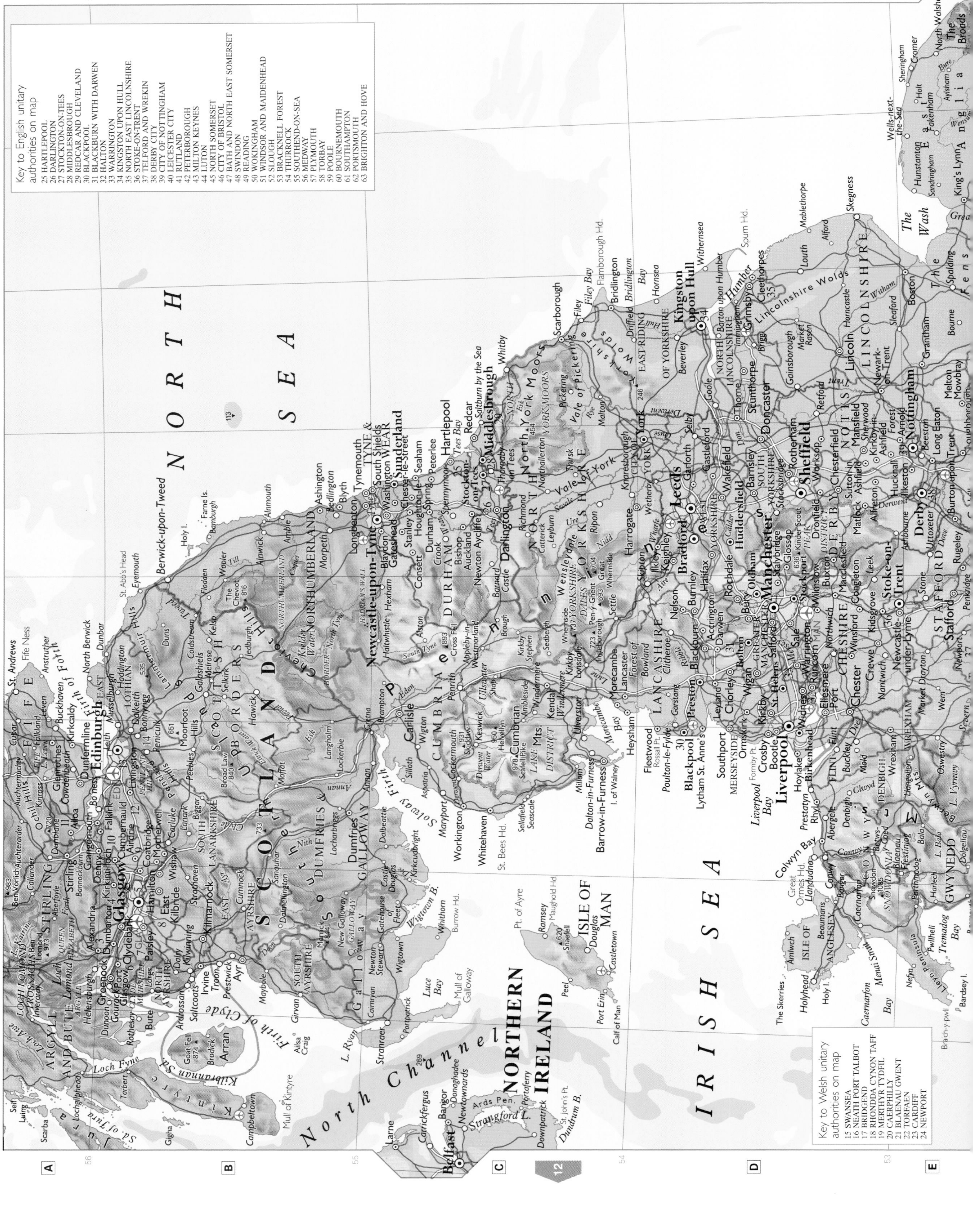

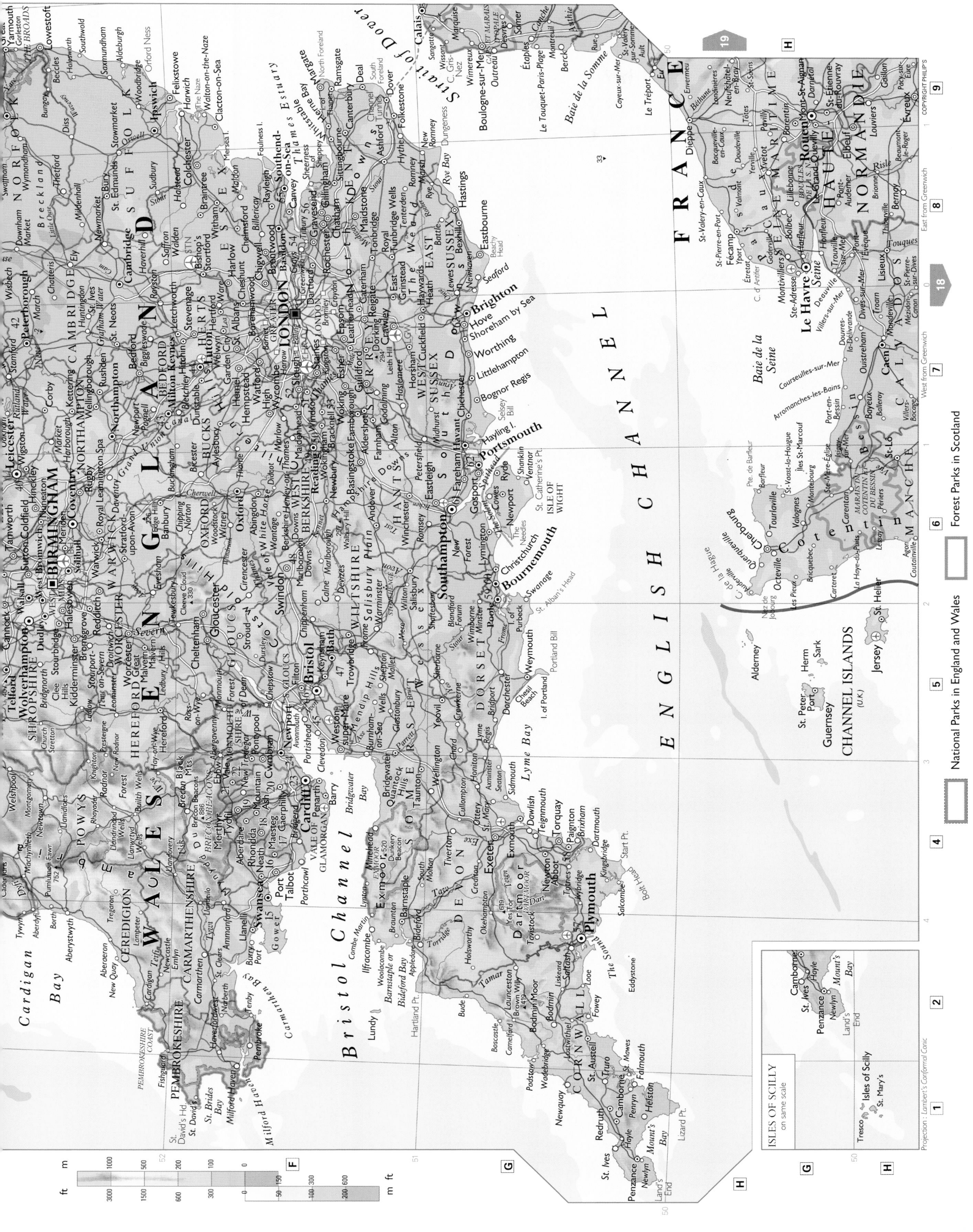
ENGLAND
WALES
FRANCE
ENGLISH CHANNEL
Bristol Channel
Cardigan Bay
Strait of Dover
Thames Estuary
Lyme Bay
Baie de la Seine
Baie de la Somme
CHANNEL ISLANDS (U.K.)
Guernsey
Jersey
Alderney
Sark
Herm
ISLE OF WIGHT
ISLES OF SCILLY on same scale
LONDON
BIRMINGHAM
Bristol
Cardiff
Southampton
Portsmouth
Brighton
Bournemouth
Plymouth
Exeter
Swansea
Newport
Oxford
Cambridge
Ipswich
Norwich
Leicester
Coventry
Northampton
Bedford
Luton
Reading
Gloucester
Cheltenham
Worcester
Hereford
Dover
Calais
Boulogne-sur-Mer
Dieppe
Le Havre
Rouen
Caen
Cherbourg
CORNWALL
DEVON
DORSET
SOMERSET
WILTSHIRE
HAMPSHIRE
WEST SUSSEX
EAST SUSSEX
SURREY
KENT
ESSEX
SUFFOLK
NORFOLK
CAMBRIDGESHIRE
NORTHAMPTON
OXFORDSHIRE
BERKSHIRE
BUCKS
HERTS
BEDFORD
WARWICK
WORCESTER
HEREFORDSHIRE
GLOUCS
POWYS
CEREDIGION
CARMARTHENSHIRE
PEMBROKESHIRE
SHROPSHIRE
HAUTE-NORMANDIE
SEINE-MARITIME
CALVADOS
MANCHE
Dartmoor
Exmoor
National Parks in England and Wales
Forest Parks in Scotland
Projection: Lambert's Conformal Conic
COPYRIGHT PHILIP'S
West from Greenwich
East from Greenwich
ft m
3000 1000
1500 500
600 200
300 100
0 0
m ft
50 150
100 300
200 600

1:4 400 000
50 0 25 50 75 100 125 150 175 km
50 0 25 50 75 100 125 miles
Projection: Conical with two standard parallels
East from Greenwich
West from Greenwich
COPYRIGHT PHILIP'S
ATLANTIC OCEAN
NORTH SEA
CELTIC SEA
IRISH SEA
English Channel
Bristol Channel
St. George's Channel
North Channel
Firth of Clyde
Moray Firth
Pentland Firth
North Minch
Sea of the Hebrides
Cardigan Bay
The Wash
Str. of Dover
UNITED KINGDOM
SCOTLAND
ENGLAND
WALES
NORTHERN IRELAND
IRELAND
FRANCE
BELGIUM
NETHERLANDS
NORWAY
Shetland Is.
Unst
Yell
Fetlar
Mainland
Lerwick
Foula
Fair Isle
Orkney Is.
Westray
Sanday
Stronsay
Mainland
Kirkwall
Hoy
South Ronaldsay
Outer Hebrides
Inner Hebrides
Lewis
Stornoway
Harris
St. Kilda
North Uist
Benbecula
South Uist
Barra
Skye
Portree
Rhum
Eigg
Coll
Tiree
Mull
Tobermory
Colonsay
Jura
Islay
Arran
C. Wrath
Thurso
Wick
Helmsdale
Lairg
Golspie
Ullapool
Tain
Invergordon
Dingwall
North West Highlands
Buckie
Banff
Fraserburgh
Peterhead
Nairn
Elgin
Inverness
Huntly
Inverurie
Aberdeen
L. Ness
Spey
Don
Aviemore
Glen More
Grampian Mts.
Dee
Ballater
Stonehaven
Mallaig
Ben Nevis
Fort William
Forfar
Montrose
Arbroath
Dundee
St. Andrews
Perth
Tay
Oban
L. Awe
L. Lomond
Glenrothes
Kirkcaldy
Stirling
Dunfermline
Dunbar
L. Fyne
Dumbarton
Greenock
Glasgow
Edinburgh
Paisley
Motherwell
East Kilbride
Hamilton
Clyde
Irvine
Kilmarnock
Campbeltown
Ayr
Southern Uplands
Galashiels
Jedburgh
Hawick
Berwick-upon-Tweed
Cheviot Hills
Alnwick
Girvan
Dumfries
Stranraer
Kirkcudbright
Annan
Carlisle
Hexham
Newcastle-upon-Tyne
South Shields
Sunderland
Gateshead
Durham
Hartlepool
Redcar
Middlesbrough
Stockton-on-Tees
Darlington
Pennines
Workington
Whitehaven
Cumbrian Mts.
Barrow-in-Furness
Lancaster
Scarborough
Bridlington
Harrogate
York
Keighley
Leeds
Bradford
Burnley
Blackpool
Preston
Blackburn
Bolton
Halifax
Huddersfield
Barnsley
Beverley
Kingston upon Hull
Scunthorpe
Humber
Grimsby
Doncaster
Manchester
Oldham
Rotherham
Liverpool
Warrington
Stockport
Sheffield
Lincoln
Louth
Skegness
Chesterfield
Chester
Crewe
Derby
Nottingham
Boston
Mansfield
Stoke on Trent
Stafford
Grantham
Trent
King's Lynn
Norwich
Cromer
Great Yarmouth
Lowestoft
Shrewsbury
Telford
Leicester
Peterborough
Welshpool
Wolverhampton
Nuneaton
Corby
Thetford
BIRMINGHAM
Coventry
Rugby
Bury St. Edmunds
Redditch
Northampton
Ely
Worcester
Royal Leamington Spa
Bedford
Cambridge
Ipswich
Hereford
Milton Keynes
Felixstowe
Stevenage
Harwich
Cheltenham
Luton
Harlow
Colchester
Gloucester
Cotswold Hills
Oxford
Hemel Hempstead
Chelmsford
Cwmbran
High Wycombe
Watford
Basildon
Newport
Southend-on-Sea
Cardiff
Bristol
Swindon
Slough
Thames
Margate
Barry
Bath
Newbury
Reading
LONDON
Chatham
Canterbury
Basingstoke
Reigate
Maidstone
Dover
Guildford
Ashford
Folkestone
Crawley
Winchester
Salisbury
Southampton
Hastings
Fareham
Havant
Eastbourne
Brighton
Worthing
Portsmouth
Isle of Wight
Newport
Bournemouth
Poole
Weymouth
Weston-super-Mare
Yeovil
Taunton
Exmoor
Barnstaple
Bude
Exeter
Exmouth
Dartmoor
Torbay
Plymouth
Newquay
Truro
St. Austell
Falmouth
Penzance
Land's End
Isles of Scilly
Anglesey
Holyhead
Bangor
Colwyn Bay
Snowdon
Wrexham
Pwllheli
Cambrian Mts.
Aberystwyth
Fishguard
Carmarthen
Brecon
Haverfordwest
Milford Haven
Pembroke
Merthyr Tydfil
Neath
Llanelli
Swansea
Port Talbot
Rhondda
I. of Man
Douglas
Mull of Galloway
Malin Hd.
Buncrana
Letterkenny
Aran I.
Coleraine
Londonderry
Ballymena
Larne
Lifford
Ulster
Donegal
Lough Neagh
Antrim
Bangor
Belfast
Bundoran
Lower L. Erne
Omagh
Portadown
Lisburn
Lurgan
Enniskillen
Armagh
Newry
Clones
Ballina
Sligo
Castleblaney
Achill I.
L. Conn
Leitrim
Cavan
Castlebar
Dundalk
Westport
Connacht
Roscommon
Longford
Ceanannus Mor
Drogheda
Lough Mask
Boyne
Lough Corrib
Lough Ree
Mullingar
Connemara
Athlone
Ballinasloe
Tullamore
Liffey
Dublin
Dun Laoghaire
Galway
Galway B.
Aran Is.
Birr
Bray
Lough Derg
Port Laoise
Athy
Leinster
Wicklow Mts.
Ennis
Nenagh
Carlow
Arklow
Kilrush
Limerick
Thurles
Kilkenny
Shannon
Listowel
Tipperary
Munster
Tralee
Clonmel
Carrick-on-Suir
Wexford
Dingle
Mallow
Waterford
Rosslare
Carrauntoohill
Killarney
Blackwater
Macgillycuddy's Reeks
Valencia I.
Dungarvan
Cork
Youghal
Cobh
Bantry
Bandon
Kinsale
C. Clear
Bergen
Askøy
Osøyro
Stord
Bømlo
Leirvik
Haugesund
Kopervik
Åkrahamn
Boknafjord
Stavanger
Sandnes
Bryne
Nærbø
Texel
Den Helder
Alkmaar
Haarlem
's-Gravenhage (Den Haag)
Hoek van Holland
ROTTERDAM
Dordrecht
Vlissingen
Zeebrugge
Oostende
Brugge
Antwerpen
Gent
Mechelen
Brussel (Bruxelles)
Dunkerque
Calais
Flandre
C. Gris Nez
Tourcoing
Lille
Tournai
Boulogne-sur-Mer
Béthune
Villeneuve-d'Ascq
Le Touquet-Paris-Plage
Artois
Bruay-la-Buissière
Lens
Valenciennes
Cambrai
Abbeville
Le Tréport
Picardie
Somme
St.-Quentin
Dieppe
Amiens
Laon
Fécamp
Pays de Caux
Rouen
Le Havre
Bolbec
Seine
Elbeuf
Trouville-sur-Mer
Lisieux
Bayeux
Caen
Cherbourg
Valognes
Cotentin
C. de la Hague
Pte. de Barfleur
Alderney
Guernsey
St. Peter Port
Sark
Channel Is. (U.K.)
Jersey
St. Helier
1224
316
789
1182
1311
1342
1214
973
840
816
893
978
636
1085
926
886
953
1041
618
238
99
36
33
16

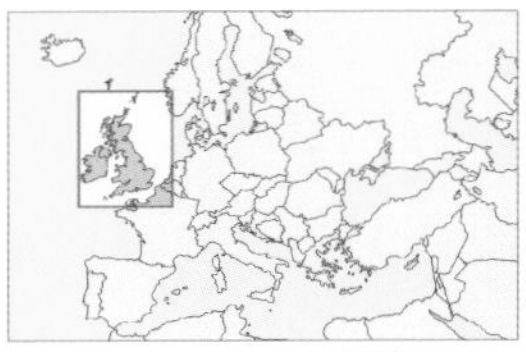

1:2 200 000

10 0 10 20 30 40 50 60 70 80 90 km

10 0 10 20 30 40 50 60 miles

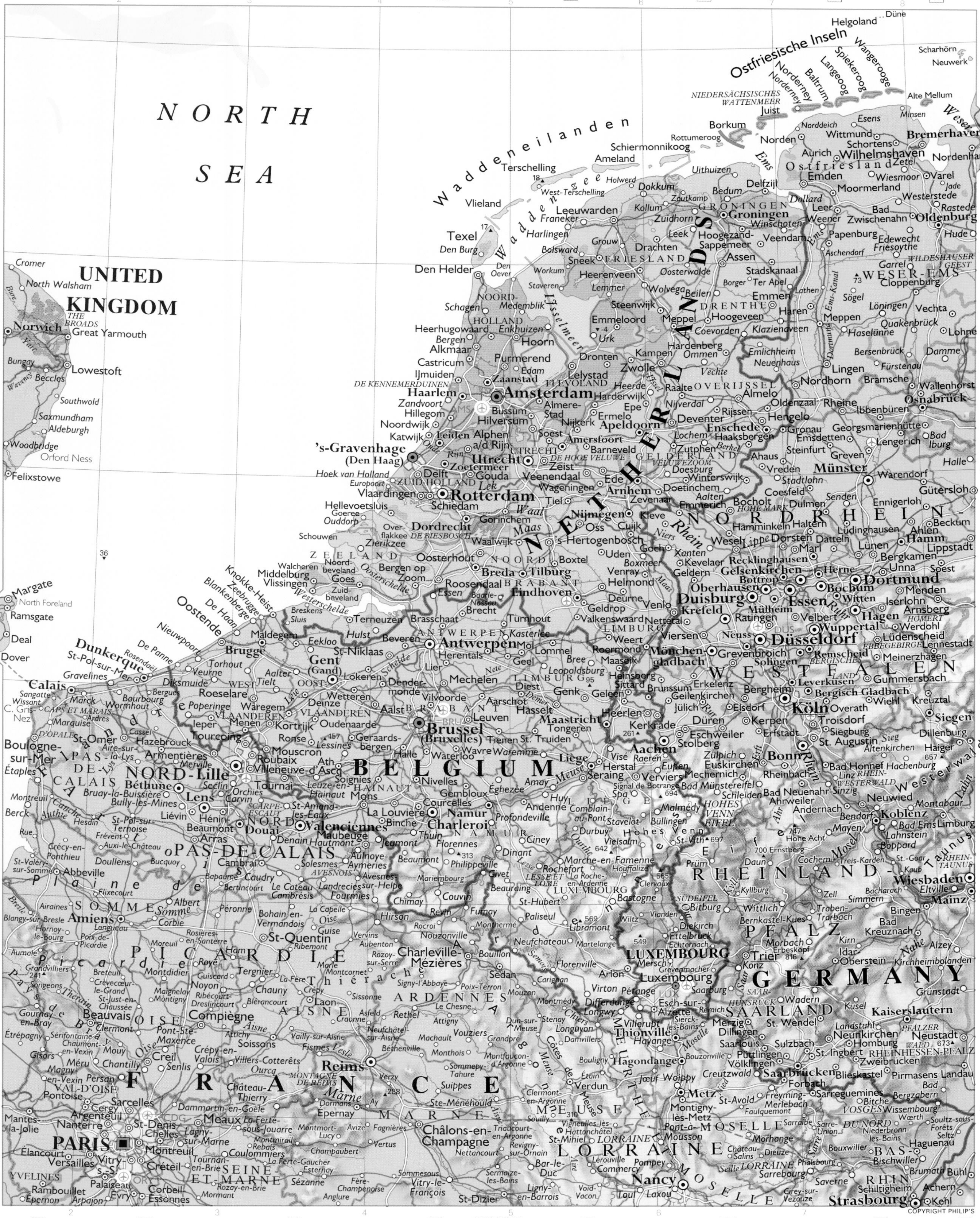

15
24
19

National Parks

Underlined towns give their name to the administrative area in which they stand.

18 NORTHERN FRANCE

DÉPARTEMENTS IN THE PARIS AREA

1 Ville de Paris
2 Seine-St-Denis
3 Val-de-Marne
4 Hauts-de-Seine

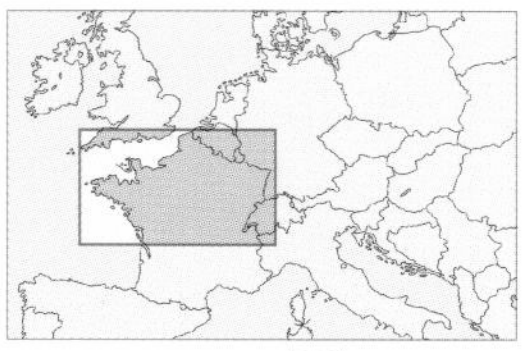

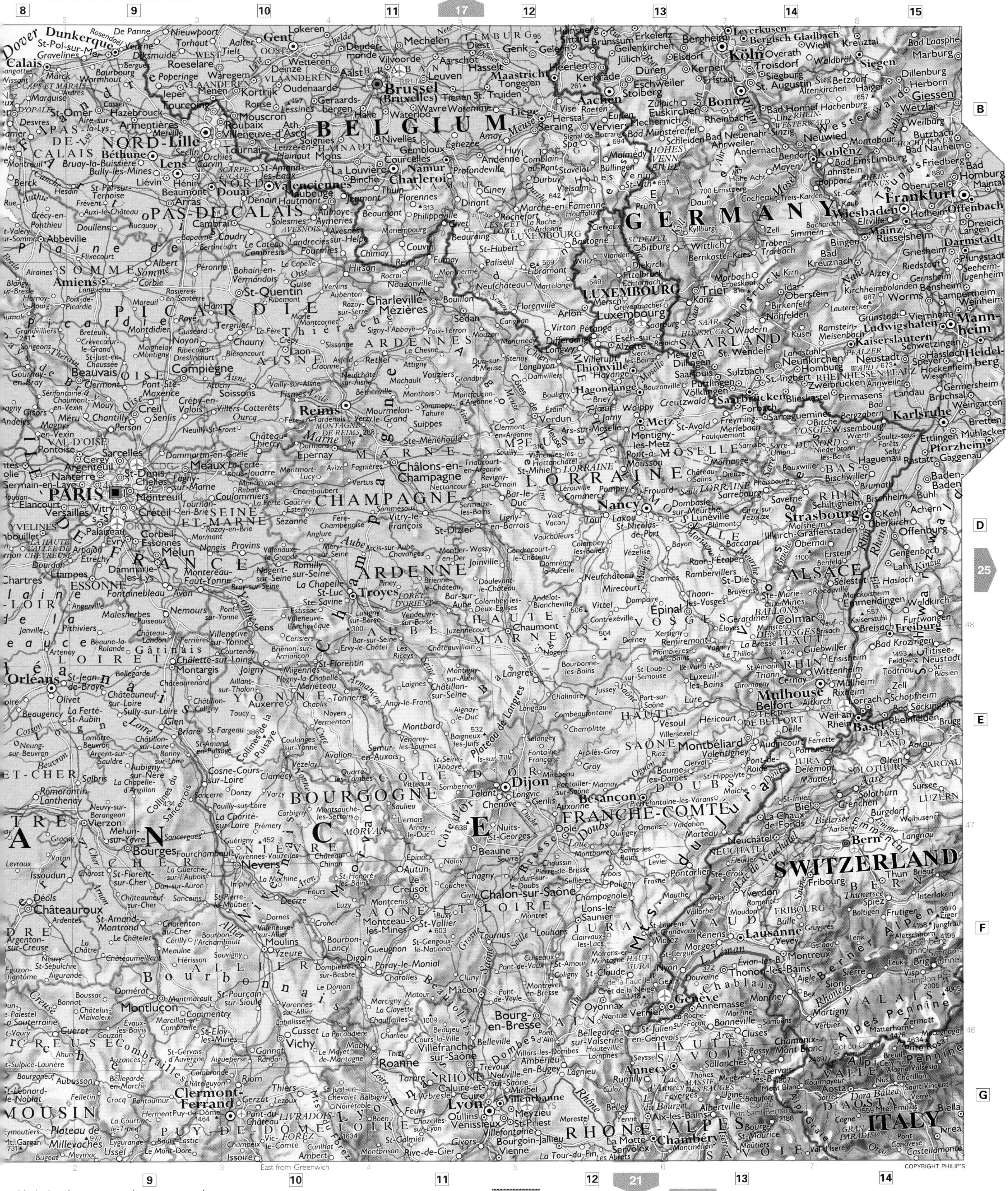

Underlined towns give their name to the administrative area in which they stand.

National Parks

Regional Nature Parks in France

1:2 200 000

10 0 10 20 30 40 50 60 70 80 90 km
10 0 10 20 30 40 50 60 miles
ATLANTIC OCEAN
Golfe de Gascogne
Golfe du Lion
Costa Brava
F R A N C E
S P A I N
ANDORRA
POITOU-CHARENTES
AQUITAINE
LIMOUSIN
AUVERGNE
MIDI-PYRÉNÉES
LANGUEDOC-ROUSSILLON
PYRÉNÉES-ATLANTIQUES
HAUTES-PYRÉNÉES
PYRÉNÉES-ORIENTALES
NAVARRA
HUESCA
LLEIDA
GIRONA
ZARAGOZA
CATALUÑA
BARCELONA
Massif Central
Landes de Gascogne
Bordeaux
Toulouse
Limoges
Poitiers
La Rochelle
Angoulême
Périgueux
Agen
Pau
Bayonne
Montauban
Albi
Rodez
Clermont-Ferrand
Montpellier
Béziers
Narbonne
Carcassonne
Perpignan
Andorra la Vella
Pamplona
Donostia-San Sebastián
Zaragoza
Huesca
Lleida
Girona
Tudela
Figueres
Cholet
Bourges
Nevers
Châteauroux
Montluçon
Vichy
Moulins
Niort
Île d'Yeu
Île de Ré
Île d'Oléron
Projection : Lambert's Conformal Conic
West from Greenwich
East from Greenwich

National Parks

Regional Nature Parks in France

1:4 400 000
km
miles
NORTH SEA
BALTIC SEA
ADRIATIC SEA
UNITED KINGDOM
NETHERLANDS
BELGIUM
LUXEMBOURG
DENMARK
GERMANY
FRANCE
SWITZERLAND
LIECHTENSTEIN
AUSTRIA
CZECH R.
SLOVENIA
ITALY
MONACO
SAN MARINO
AMSTERDAM
's-Gravenhage (Den Haag)
ROTTERDAM
Brussel (Bruxelles)
LUXEMBOURG
PARIS
BERLIN
HAMBURG
PRAHA (Prague)
MÜNCHEN (Munich)
MILANO
TORINO (Turin)
LYON
MARSEILLE
Bern
Zagreb
Ljubljana
Golfo di Venézia
Golfo di Génova
Projection: Conical with two standard parallels

LITHUANIA
BELARUS
POLAND
UKRAINE
SLOVAK REP.
HUNGARY
ROMANIA
MOLDOVA
SERBIA AND MONTENEGRO
BOSNIA-HERZEGOVINA
BULGARIA
Vilnius
Kaliningrad (Russia)
MINSK
WARSZAWA (Warsaw)
Gdańsk
Gdynia
Elbląg
Olsztyn
Białystok
Hrodna
Brest
Pinsk
Homyel
Mahilyow
Babruysk
Baranavichy
Bydgoszcz
Toruń
Włocławek
Płock
Łódź
Radom
Lublin
Kielce
Częstochowa
Wrocław
Opole
Katowice
Kraków
Tarnów
Rzeszów
Przemyśl
Lviv (Lvov)
Lutsk
Rivne
Ternopil
Khmelnytskyy
Vinnytsya
Zhytomyr
KYYIV (Kiev)
Bila Tserkva
Ivano-Frankivsk
Chernivtsi
Uzhhorod
Košice
Prešov
Žilina
Bratislava
Miskolc
Debrecen
Nyíregyháza
BUDAPEST
Győr
Szeged
Pécs
Oradea
Cluj-Napoca
Satu Mare
Baia Mare
Suceava
Iaşi
Chişinău (Kishinev)
Tiraspol
Bacău
Braşov
Sibiu
Timişoara
Arad
Craiova
Ploieşti
Galaţi
Brăila
Constanţa
BUCUREŞTI (Bucharest)
Ruse
Varna
Dobrich
BEOGRAD (Belgrade)
Novi Sad
Subotica
Osijek
Sarajevo
Tuzla
Banja Luka
Kragujevac
Transilvania
Carpaţii Meridionali
Vojvodina
Dunărea (Danube)
Dnister
Pripet Marshes
COPYRIGHT PHILIP'S
East from Greenwich

10 0 10 20 30 40 50 60 70 80 90 km

10 0 10 20 30 40 50 60 miles

1:2 200 000

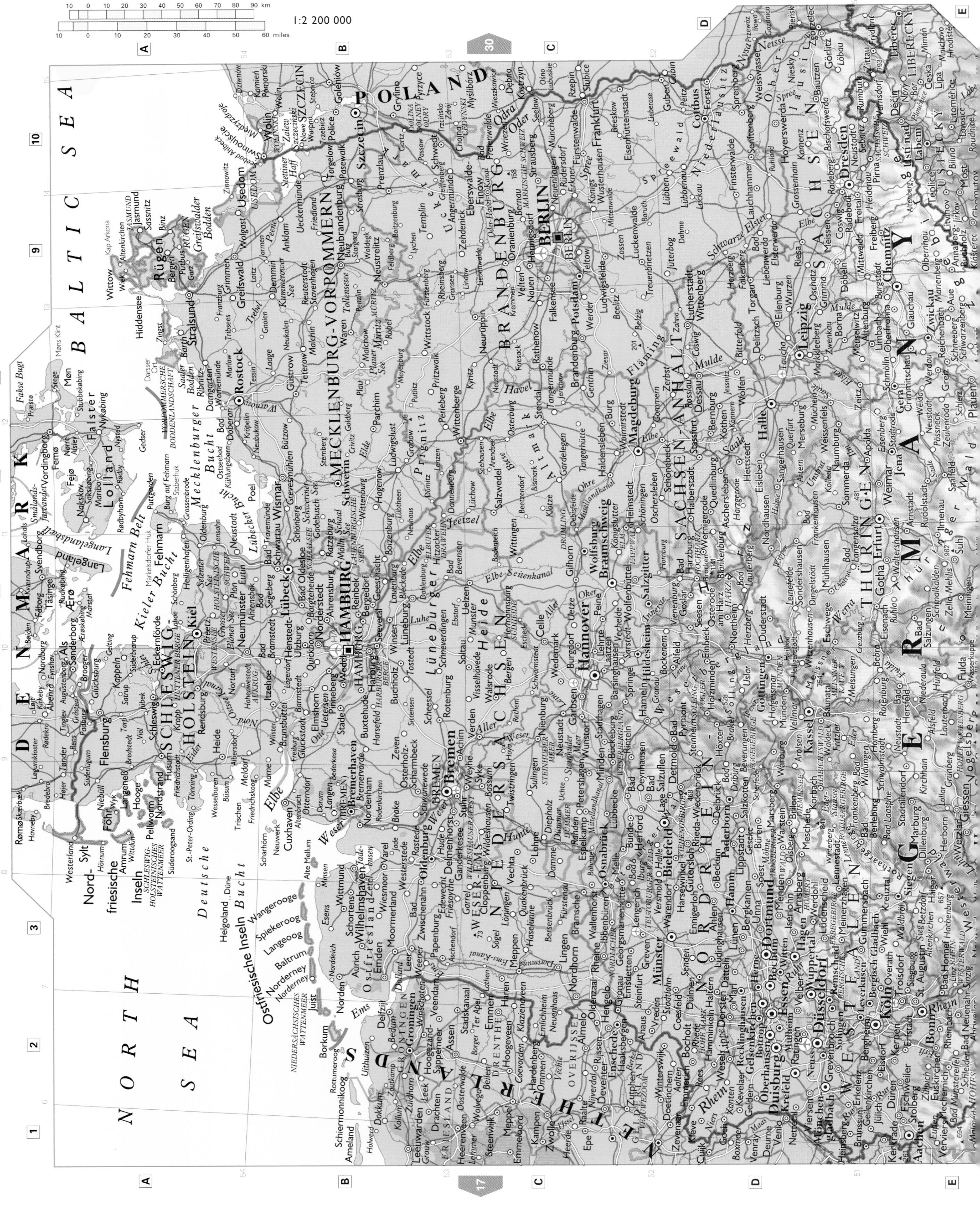

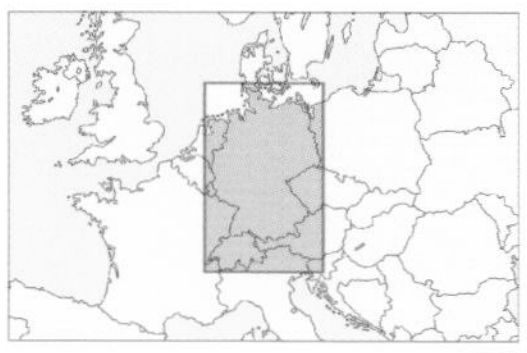

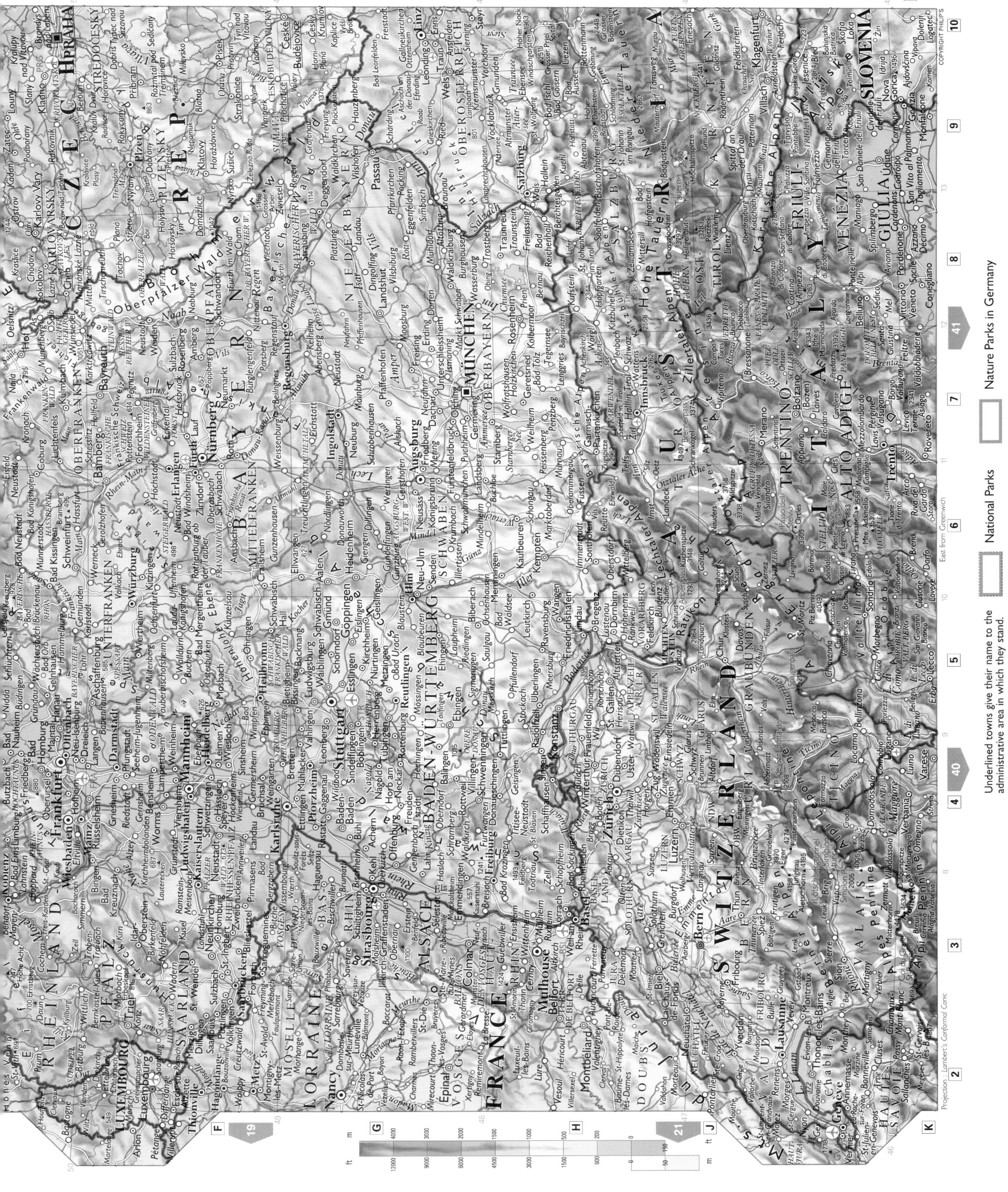

Underlined towns give their name to the administrative area in which they stand.
National Parks
Nature Parks in Germany
Projection: Lambert's Conformal Conic
East from Greenwich
COPYRIGHT PHILIP'S
CZECH REP.
GERMANY
FRANCE
SWITZERLAND
AUSTRIA
ITALY
SLOVENIA
LUXEMBOURG
BAYERN
BADEN-WÜRTTEMBERG
RHEINLAND-PFALZ
SAARLAND
ALSACE
LORRAINE
TRENTINO-ALTO ADIGE
FRIULI-VENEZIA GIULIA
HPRAHA
MÜNCHEN
Stuttgart
Frankfurt
Nürnberg
Innsbruck
Salzburg
Strasbourg
Basel
Zürich
Bern
Genève
Lausanne
26
40
41
19
21

1:2 200 000

24
25
40
41

National Parks

Underlined towns give their name to the administrative area in which they stand.

10 0 10 20 30 40 50 60 70 80 90 km

1:2 200 000

10 0 10 20 30 40 50 60 miles

Administrative divisions in Croatia:
1 Brodsko-Posavska
2 Koprivničko-Križevačka
4 Međimurska
5 Osječko-Baranjska
6 Požeško-Slavonska
8 Virovitičko-Podravska
9 Vukovarsko-Srijemska

Inter-entity boundaries as agreed at the 1995 Dayton Peace Agreement

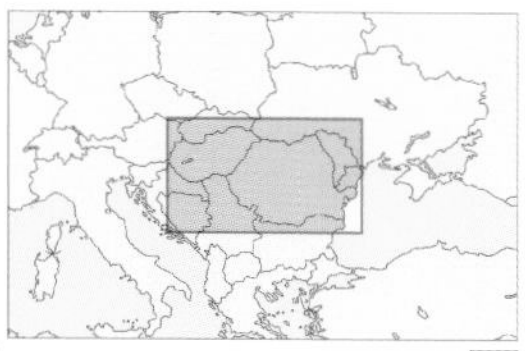

UKRAINE
ROMANIA
MOLDOVA
BULGARIA
BLACK SEA
Ivano-Frankivsk
IVANO-FRANKIVSKA
ZAKARPATSKA
CHERNIVETSKA
VINNYTSKA
ODESKA
Chernivtsi
Kamyanets-Podilskyy
Kolomyya
Mohyliv-Podilskyy
Bălți
Chișinău (Kishinev)
Tiraspol
Tighina
STINGA NISTRULUI
GAGAUZIA
Comrat
Cahul
Izmayil
Kiliya
Iași
Botoșani
Suceava
Piatra Neamț
Bacău
Vaslui
Bârlad
Focșani
Galați
Brăila
Tulcea
Constanța
Cluj-Napoca
Baia Mare
Târgu Mureș
Sibiu
Brașov
Ploiești
Pitești
Buzău
Craiova
Slobozia
Călărași
Târgoviște
BUCUREȘTI (Bucharest)
Ruse
Pleven
Dobrich
Silistra
Giurgiu
Alexandria
Dunărea
Dunay
Prut
Nistru
Siret
Olt
Argeș
Ialomița
Munții Carpați
Munții Făgăraș
Munții Rodnei
DELTA DUNĂREA
Lacul Razim
National Parks
COPYRIGHT PHILIP'S

30 POLAND AND THE SOUTHERN BALTIC

10 0 10 20 30 40 50 60 70 80 90 km

10 0 10 20 30 40 50 60 miles

1:2 200 000

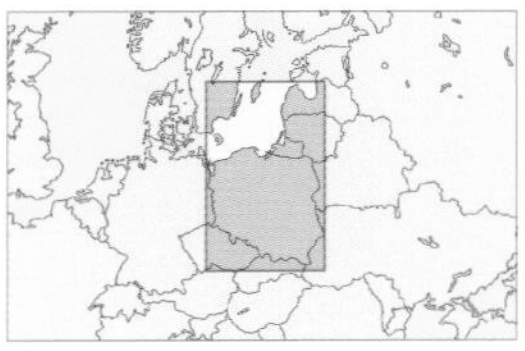

National Parks

Underlined towns give their name to the administrative area in which they stand.

50 0 25 50 75 100 125 150 175 km

1:4 400 000

50 0 25 50 75 100 125 miles

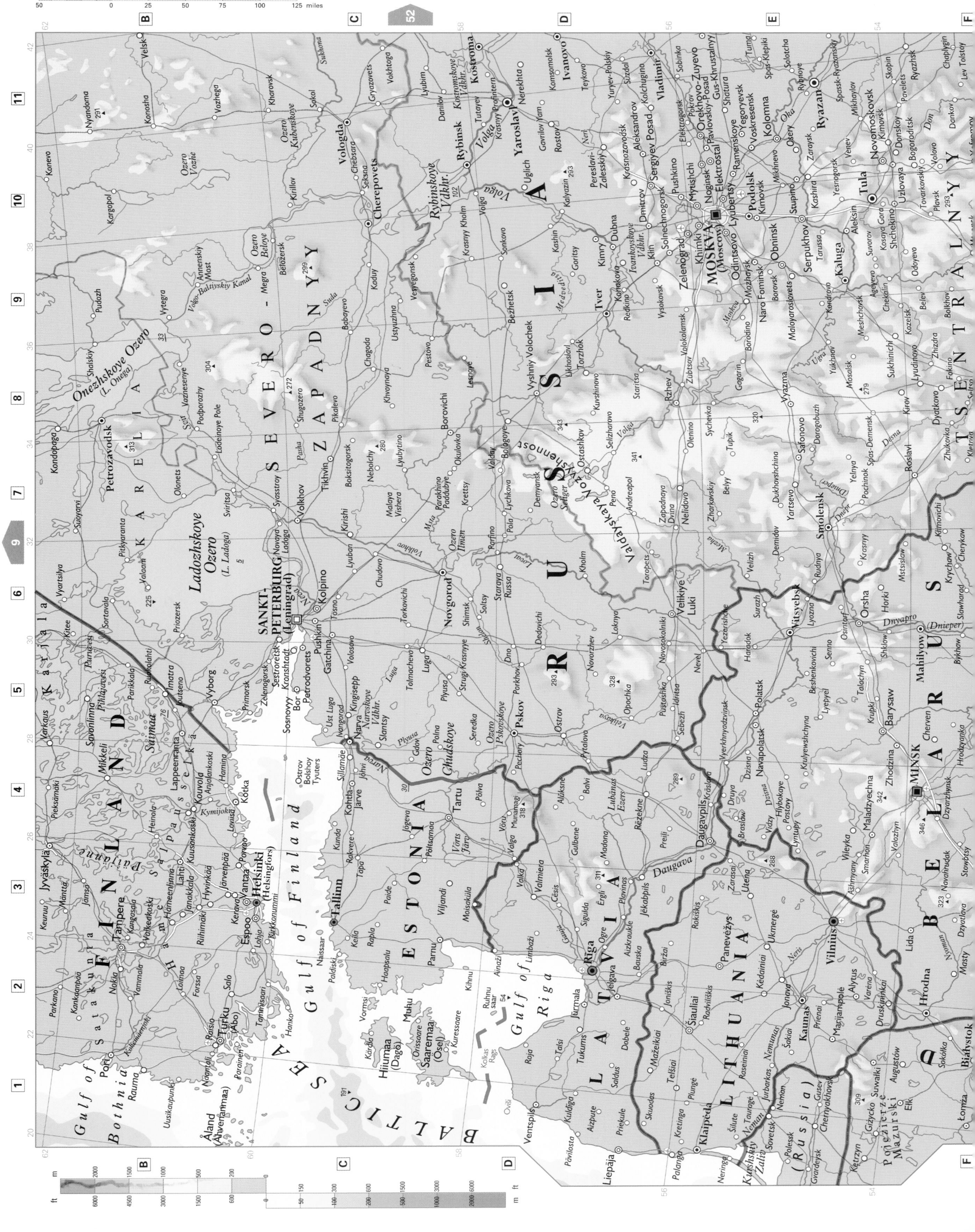

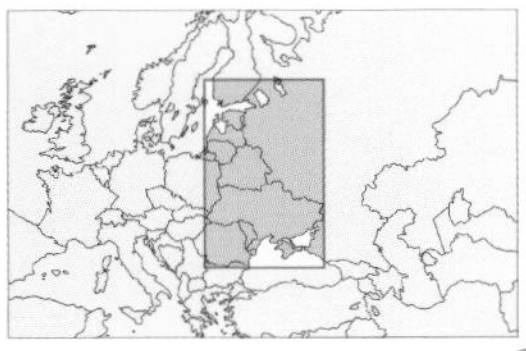

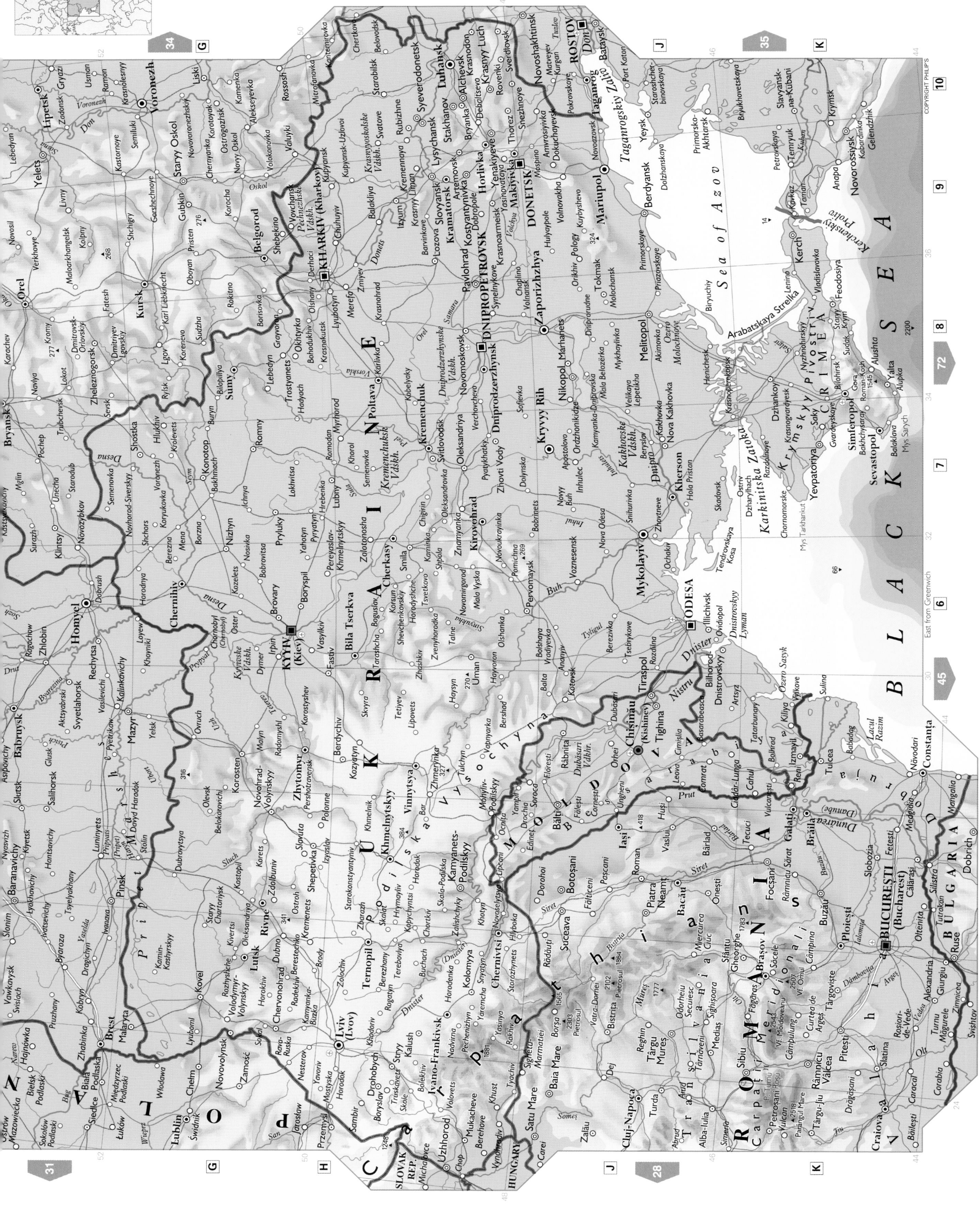
UKRAINE
ROMANIA
MOLDOVA
BULGARIA
POLAND
HUNGARY
SLOVAK REP.
BLACK SEA
Sea of Azov
CRIMEA
Karkinitska Zatoka
Kerchenskiy Proliv
Taganrogskiy Zaliv
KYYIV (Kiev)
BUCUREŞTI (Bucharest)
CHIŞINĂU (Kishinev)
ODESA
KHARKIV (Kharkov)
DNIPROPETROVSK
DONETSK
ROSTOV
Lviv (Lvov)
Zaporizhzhya
Kryvyy Rih
Mykolayiv
Kherson
Simferopol
Sevastopol
Mariupol
Luhansk
Voronezh
Kursk
Belgorod
Orel
Bryansk
Homyel
Brest
Pinsk
Mazyr
Chernihiv
Zhytomyr
Vinnytsya
Rivne
Lutsk
Ternopil
Chernivtsi
Khmelnytskyy
Poltava
Sumy
Cherkasy
Kirovohrad
Kremenchuk
Lipetsk
Constanţa
Galaţi
Brăila
Iaşi
Cluj-Napoca
Braşov
Ploieşti
Dnister
Dunărea (Danube)
Pripet Marshes
Podilska Vysochyna
Carpaţii Meridionali
Transilvania
Desna
Dobruja
Kerch
East from Greenwich
Projection: Conical with two standard parallels
COPYRIGHT PHILIP'S

50 0 25 50 75 100 125 150 175 km

1:4 400 000

50 0 25 50 75 100 125 miles

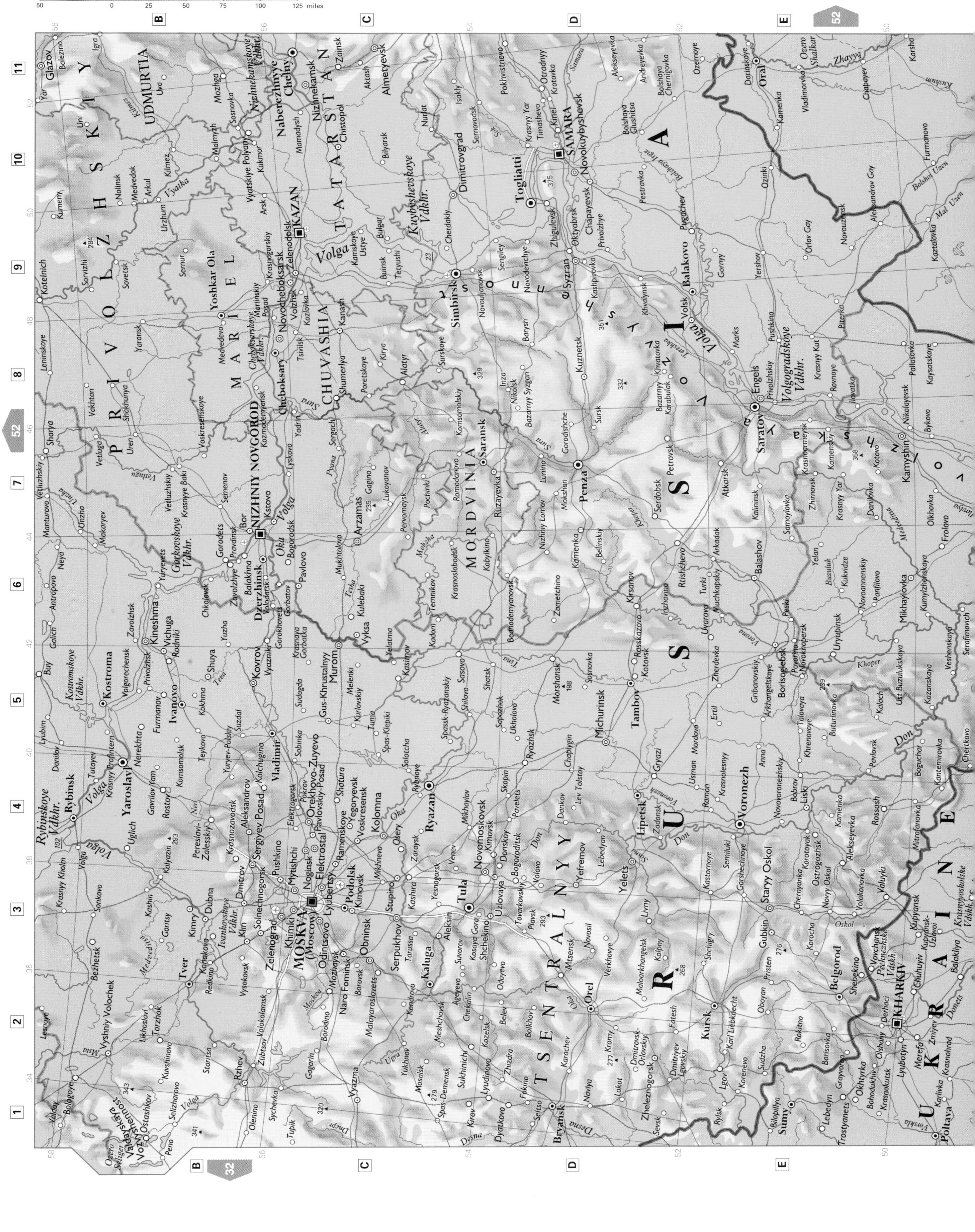

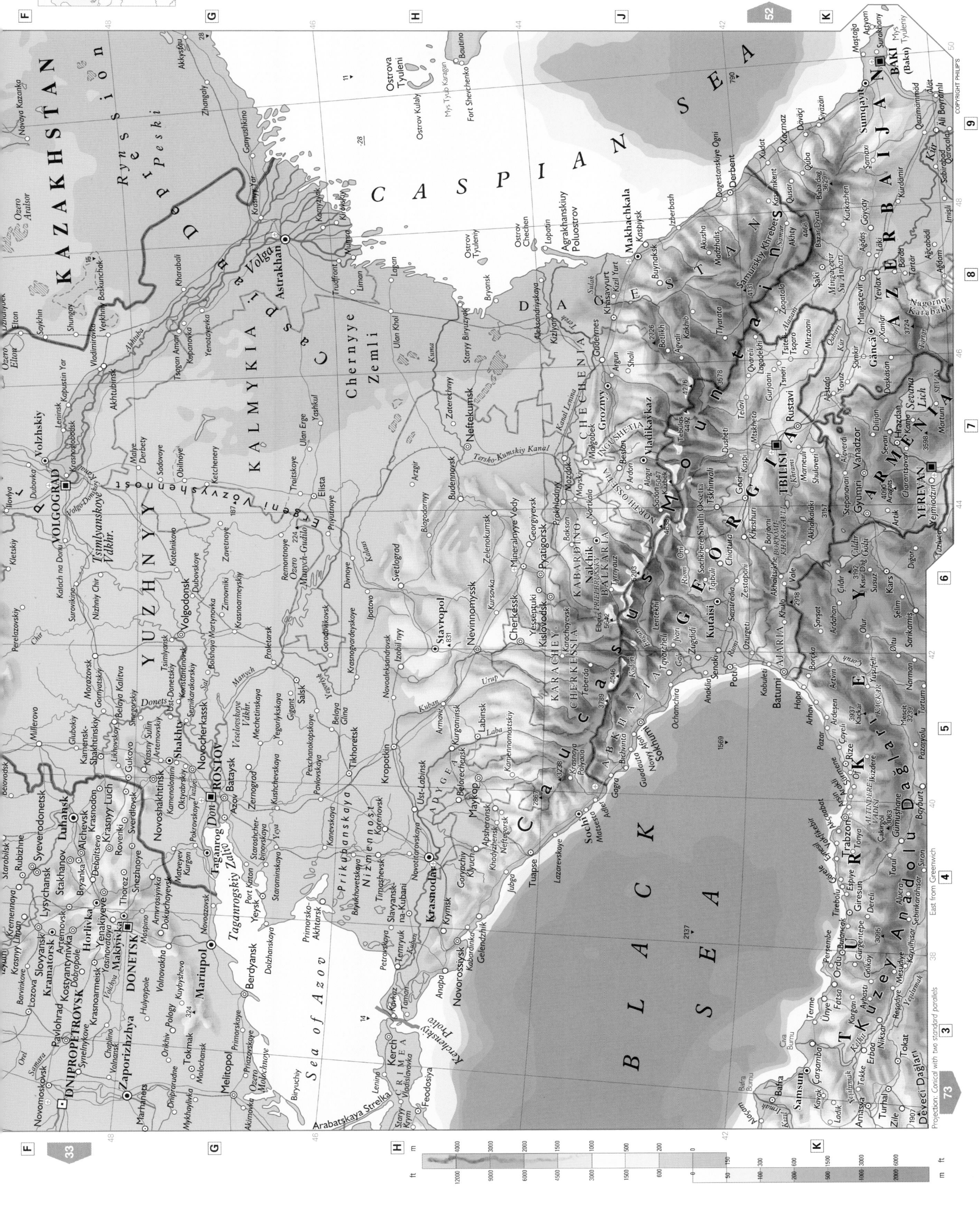
KAZAKHSTAN
CASPIAN SEA
BLACK SEA
Sea of Azov
KALMYKIA
DAGESTAN
CHECHENIA
INGUSHETIA
NORTH OSSETIA
KABARDINO-BALKARIA
KARACHAY-CHERKESSIA
ADYGEA
CRIMEA
GEORGIA
ARMENIA
AZERBAIJAN
TURKEY
ABKHAZIA
AJARIA
Nagorno-Karabakh
Caucasus Mountains
Prikubanskaya Nizmennost
Chernyye Zemli
Yergeni
Ryn Peski
VOLGOGRAD
ROSTOV
DONETSK
DNIPROPETROVSK
Zaporizhzhya
Mariupol
Luhansk
Taganrog
Krasnodar
Stavropol
Elista
Astrakhan
Makhachkala
Groznyy
Vladikavkaz
Nalchik
Sochi
Novorossiysk
Kerch
TBILISI
YEREVAN
BAKI (Baku)
Sumqayit
Gäncä
Kutaisi
Batumi
Trabzon
Samsun
Derbent
Volga
Don
Kuban
Kür
Manych
Tsimlyanskoye Vdkhr.
Taganrogskiy Zaliv
Kerchenskiy Proliv
Arabatskaya Strelka
Elbrus 5642
Kazbek 5047
Ostrova Tyuleni
Poluostrov Agrakhanskiy
Projection: Conical with two standard parallels
East from Greenwich
COPYRIGHT PHILIP'S
m 4000 3000 2000 1500 1000 500 200 0
ft 12000 9000 6000 4500 3000 1500 600 0
50 150 300 600 1500 3000 6000
150 300 600 1500 3000 6000 ft
33
52
73

10 0 10 20 30 40 50 60 70 80 90 km

1:2 200 000

10 0 10 20 30 40 50 60 miles

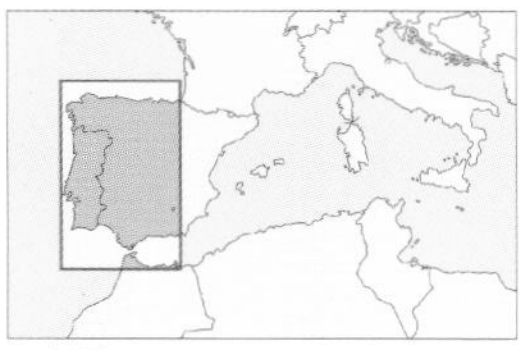

ATLANTIC OCEAN
MEDITERRANEAN SEA
Golfo de Cádiz
Costa de la Luz
Costa del Sol
Strait of Gibraltar
EXTREMADURA
CASTILLA-LA MANCHA
ANDALUCÍA
PORTUGAL
MOROCCO
Lisboa
Setúbal
Évora
Beja
Faro
Huelva
Sevilla
Cádiz
Jerez de la Frontera
Córdoba
Jaén
Granada
Málaga
Almería
Badajoz
Cáceres
Mérida
Ciudad Real
Algeciras
Gibraltar (U.K.)
Ceuta (Sp.)
Tanger (Tangier)
Tétouan
Melilla (Sp.)
Nador
Larache
Marbella
Guadalquivir
Guadiana
National Parks
Nature Parks in Spain and Portugal
Projection : Lambert's Conformal Conic
COPYRIGHT PHILIP'S
West from Greenwich
m
ft

10 0 10 20 30 40 50 60 70 80 90 km

1:2 200 000

10 0 10 20 30 40 50 60 miles

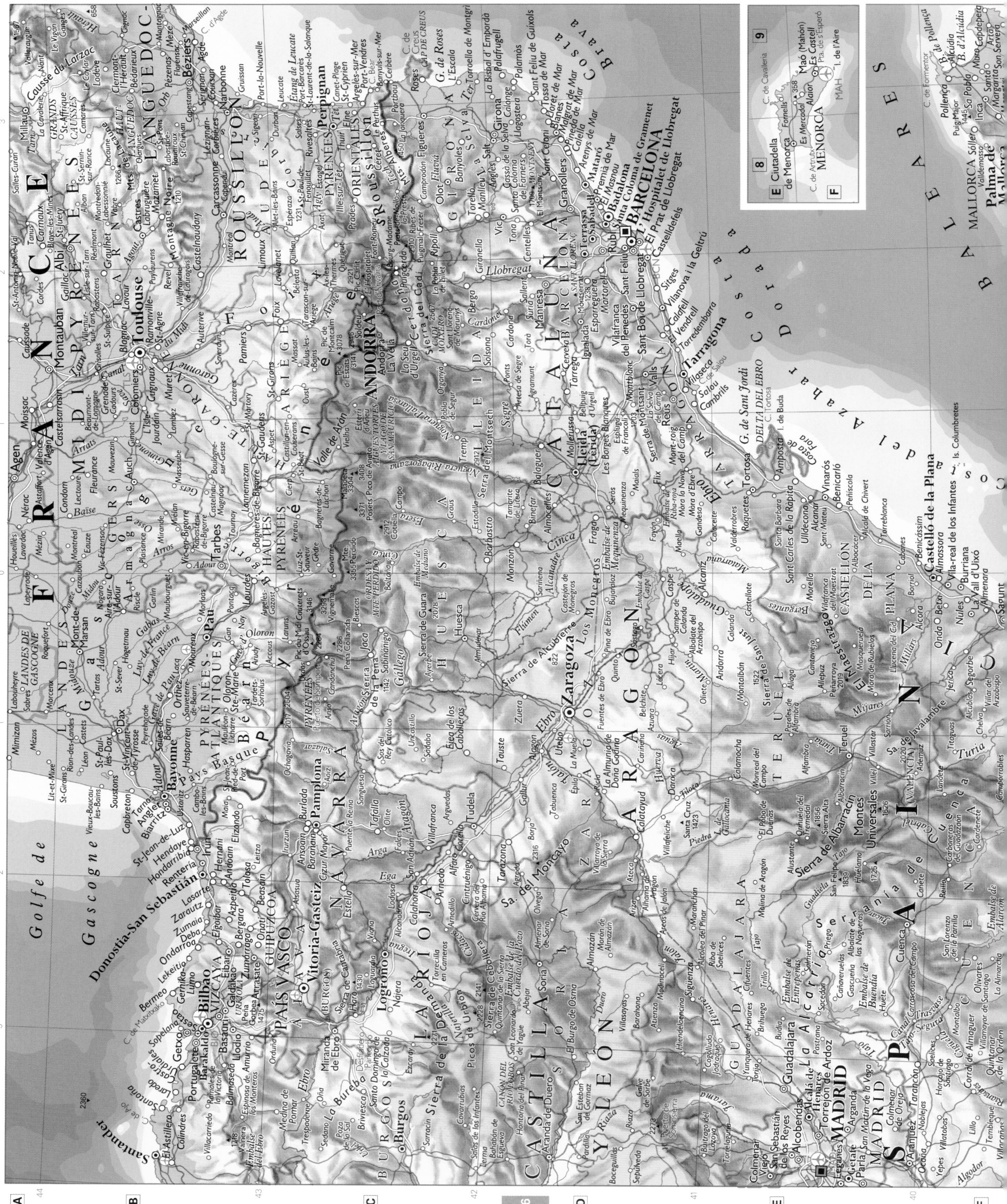

20
36

MEDITERRANEAN SEA
CASTILLA-LA MANCHA
VALENCIA
MURCIA
ALGERIA
CIUDAD REAL
ALBACETE
ALICANTE
GRANADA
ALMERÍA
JAÉN
Golfo de Valencia
ISLAS
Costa Blanca
Costa del Sol
Valencia
Alicante
Elche
Murcia
Cartagena
Albacete
Granada
Almería
Lorca
Linares
Eivissa (Ibiza)
Formentera
Palma
Cabrera
ALGER (Algiers)
Oran (Ouahran)
Mostaganem
Sidi-bel-Abbès
Blida
Médéa
Ech Cheliff
Tiaret
Melilla (Sp.)
Nador
Alborán (Sp.)
Islas Chafarinas (Sp.)
Sierra Nevada
Sierra de los Filabres
Sierra de Segura
Sierra de Alcaraz
Mar Menor
G. de Almería
G. de Mazarrón
Golfe d'Arzew
RELIZANE
TISSEMSILT
MASCARA
TIARET
AÏN DEFLA
MOSTAGANEM
ECH CHELIFF
TIPASA
AÏN TÉMOUCHENT
DJELFA
National Parks
Nature Parks in Spain
Projection : Lambert's Conformal Conic
East from Greenwich
West from Greenwich
COPYRIGHT PHILIP'S

1:2 200 000

Projection : Lambert's Conformal Conic

East from Greenwich

National Parks

Underlined towns give their name to the administrative area in which they stand.

25
21
42

26
28
43
44

Administrative divisions in Croatia:

Brodsko-Posavska
Koprivničko-Križevačka
Krapinsko-Zagorska
4 Međimurska
6 Požeško-Slavonska
7 Varaždinska
8 Virovitičko-Podravska
10 Zagreba čka

Nature Parks in Italy

Inter-entity boundaries as agreed at the 1995 Dayton Peace Agreement

1:2 200 000

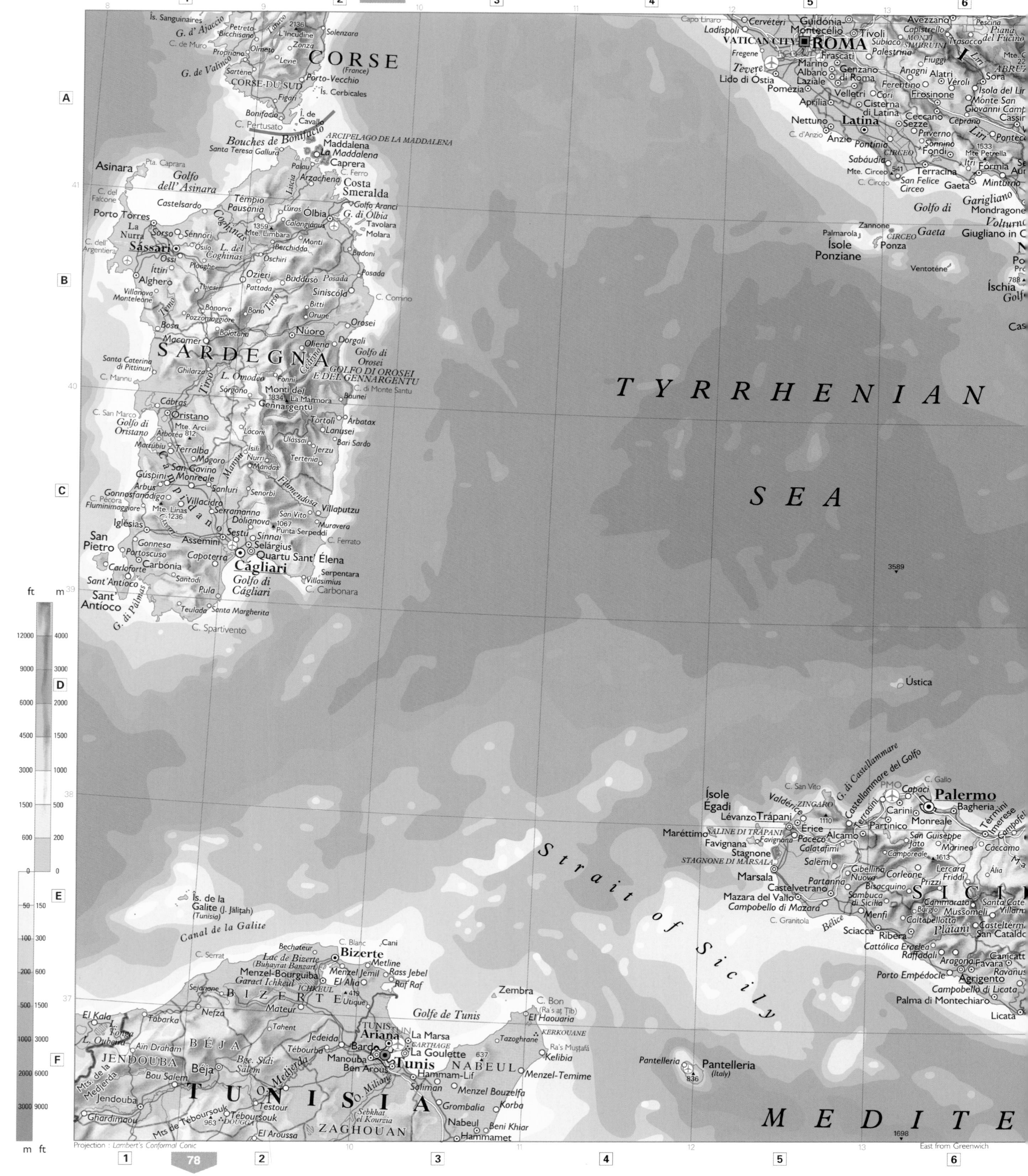
CORSE
(France)
SARDEGNA
TYRRHENIAN SEA
Strait of Sicily
MEDITE
TUNISIA
Cágliari
Sássari
Oristano
Nùoro
Olbia
ROMA
VATICAN CITY
Latina
Palermo
Trapani
Marsala
Ústica
Pantelleria
(Italy)
Tunis
Bizerte
Ariana
Golfe de Tunis
Ìsole Ponziane
Ìsole Ègadi
Projection : Lambert's Conformal Conic
East from Greenwich
40
78

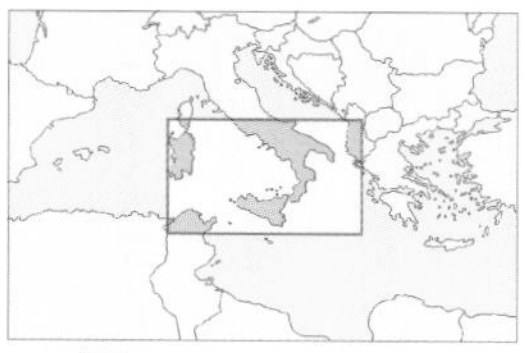

Nature Parks in Italy

National Parks

Underlined towns give their name to the administrative area in which they stand.

1:2 200 000
km
miles
28
41
43
46
SERBIA
&
MONTENEGRO
BOSNIA-
HERZEGOVINA
CROATIA
ALBANIA
MACEDONIA
ITALY
VOJVODINA
KOSOVO
BEOGRAD
(Belgrade)
SOFIYA
Skopje
Tiranë
Sarajevo
Podgorica
Thessaloníki
(Salonica)
Priština
Niš
Novi Sad
Kragujevac
ADRIATIC
SEA
Strait of Otranto
Thermaïkós
Kólpos
KENTRIKÍ
MAKEDHONÍA
DYTIKÍ
MAKEDHONÍA
Dunav
Dunărea
Projection : Lambert's Conformal Conic
East from Greenwich
Inter-entity boundaries as agreed
at the 1995 Dayton Peace Agreement

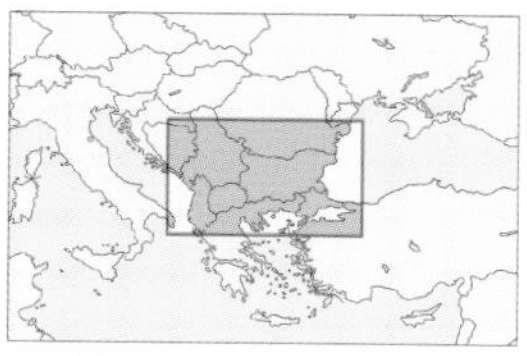

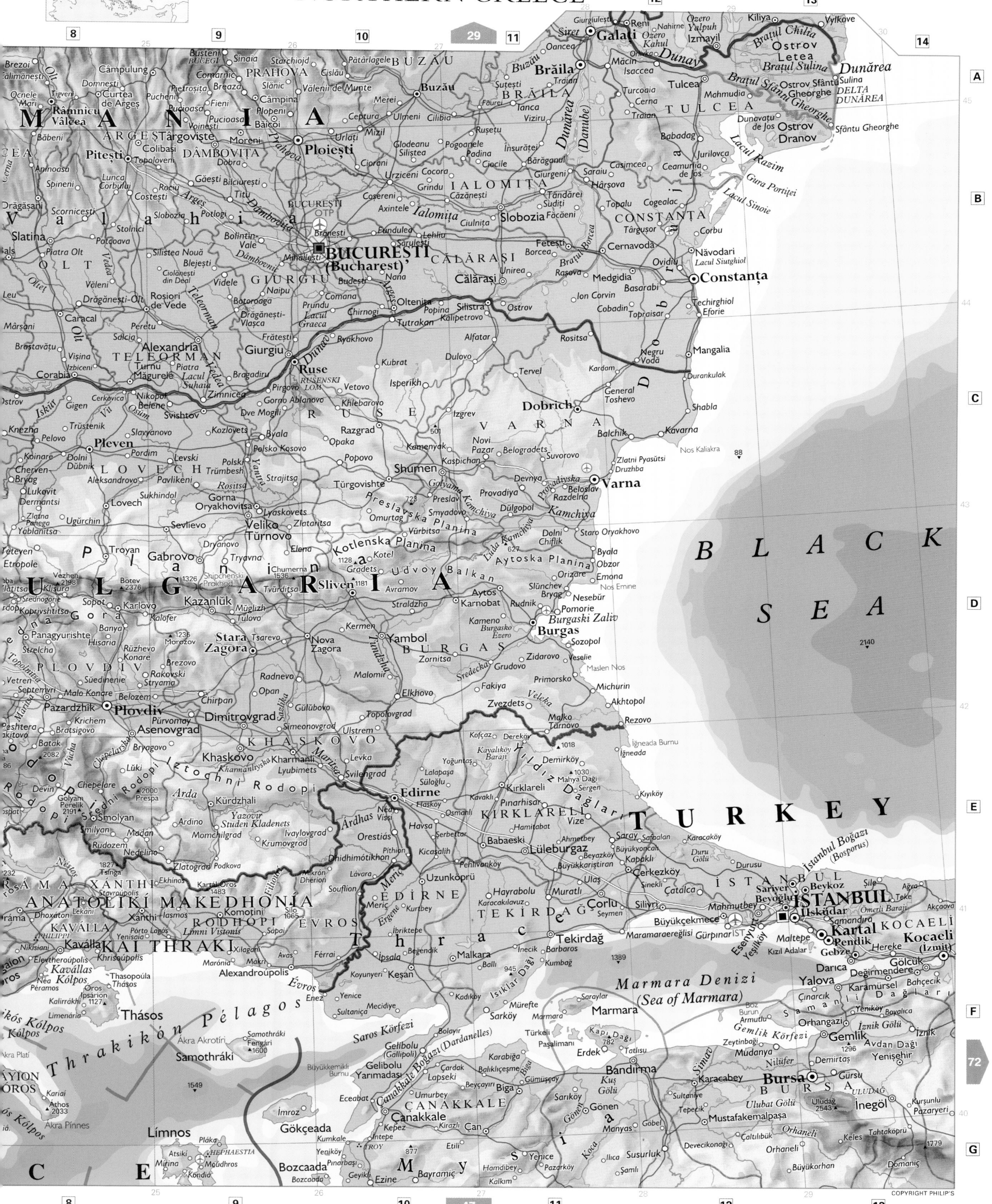

National Parks

Underlined towns give their name to the administrative area in which they stand.

29 11 12 13 14 72 47

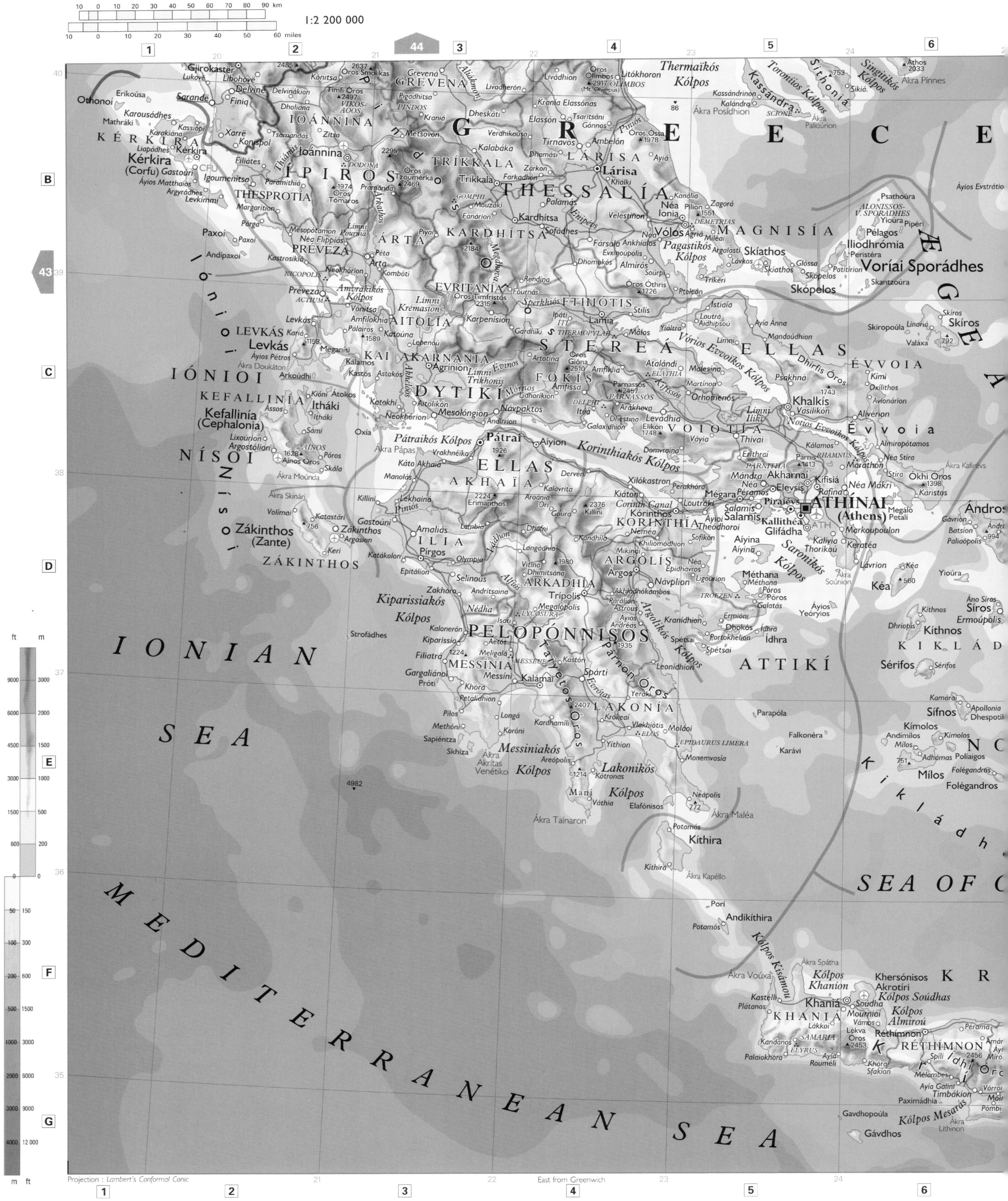
1:2 200 000
km
miles
44
43
GREECE
Thermaïkós Kólpos
Toronaíos Kólpos
Singitikós Kólpos
Kassándra
Sithonía
Áthos
Ákra Pínnes
Gjirokastër
Sarandë
Delvinë
Othonoí
Erikoúsa
Mathráki
KÉRKIRA
Kérkira
(Corfu)
Ioánnina
IOÁNNINA
GREVENÁ
Grevená
ÍPIROS
THESPROTÍA
Igoumenítsa
Paxoí
Antípaxoi
PRÉVEZA
Préveza
ÁRTA
Árta
Amvrakikós Kólpos
TRÍKKALA
Tríkkala
Kalabáka
THESSALÍA
Lárisa
LÁRISA
KARDHÍTSA
Kardhítsa
MAGNISÍA
Vólos
Pagastikós Kólpos
Skíathos
Skópelos
Vóriai Sporádhes
Alónnisos
Iliodhrómia
Pélagos
Psathoúra
Áyios Evstrátios
Óros Ólimbos
Óros Óssa
EVRITANÍA
Karpenísion
FTHIÓTIS
Lamía
STERÉA ELLAS
AITOLÍA KAI AKARNANÍA
Agrínion
Mesolóngion
Návpaktos
FOKÍS
Ámfissa
VOIOTÍA
Thívai
ÉVVOIA
Khalkís
Évvoia
Skíros
Skíropoúla
LEVKÁS
Levkás
IÓNIOI NÍSOI
KEFALLINÍA
Kefallinía
(Cephalonia)
Itháki
Argostólion
Zákinthos
(Zante)
ZÁKINTHOS
Strofádhes
Pátrai
Patraïkós Kólpos
Korinthiakós Kólpos
AKHAÏA
ACHAÏA
ILÍA
Pírgos
KORINTHÍA
Kórinthos
ARGOLÍS
Árgos
Návplion
ARKADHÍA
Trípolis
PELOPÓNNISOS
MESSINÍA
Kalámai
Kiparissiakós Kólpos
Messiniakós Kólpos
LAKONÍA
Spárti
Lakonikós Kólpos
Ákra Taínaron
Ákra Maléa
Kíthira
Andikíthira
ATTIKÍ
ATHÍNAI
(Athens)
Piraiévs
Salamís
Elevsís
Mégara
Saronikós Kólpos
Aíyina
Ídhra
Méthana
Póros
Kéa
Kíthnos
Sérifos
Sífnos
Mílos
Kímolos
Folégandros
Síros
Ándros
KIKLÁDHES
SEA OF CRETE
Kólpos Kísamou
Kólpos Khaníon
Khaniá
KHANIÁ
Kólpos Soúdhas
Réthimnon
RÉTHIMNON
Kólpos Mesarás
Gávdhos
Gavdhopoúla
IONIAN SEA
MEDITERRANEAN SEA
Projection : Lambert's Conformal Conic
East from Greenwich

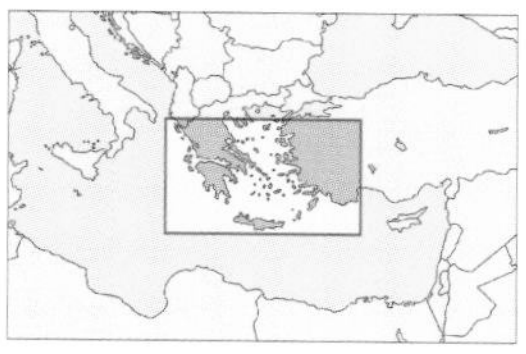

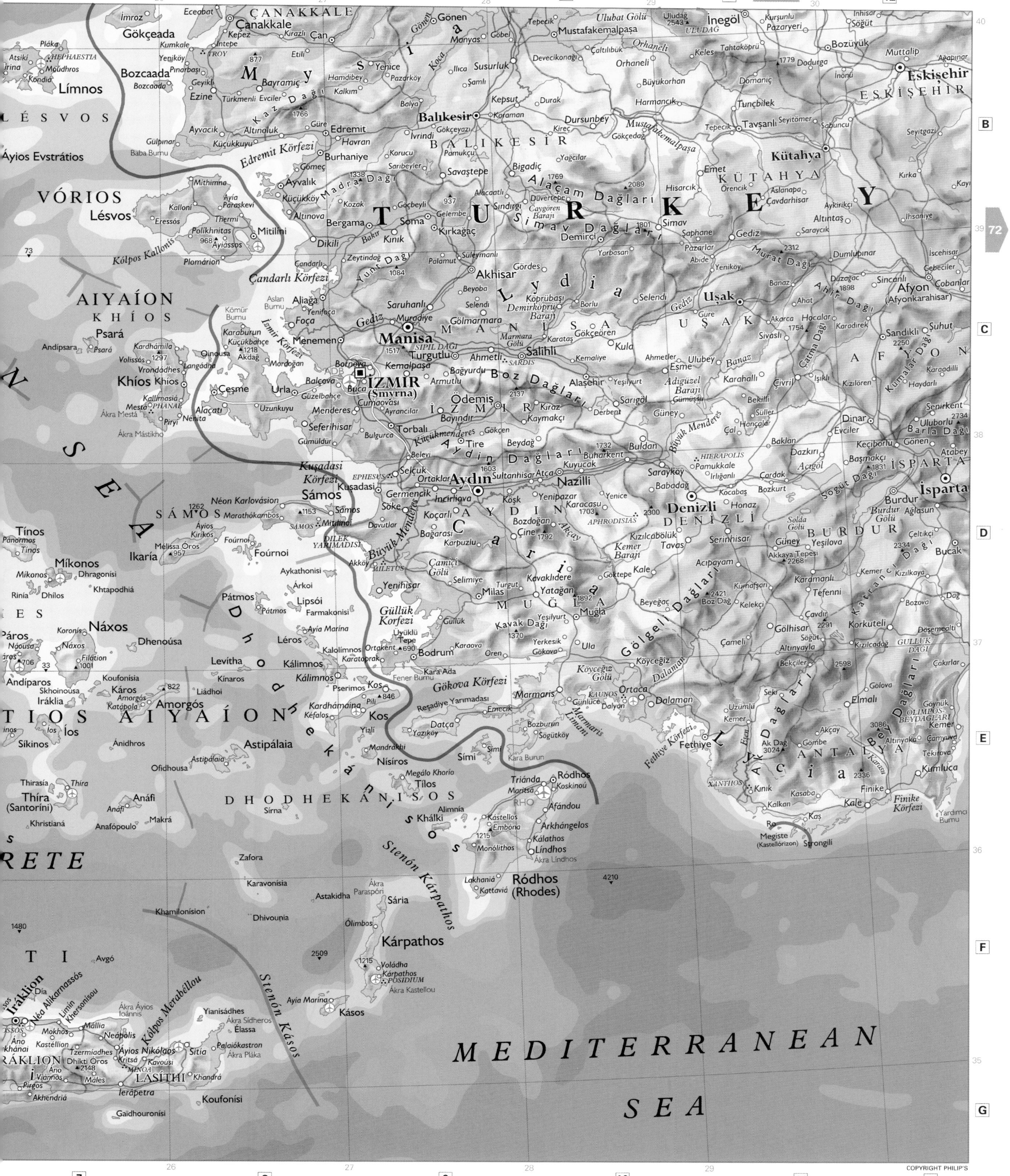

National Parks

Madeira
Balearic Islands
Canary Islands

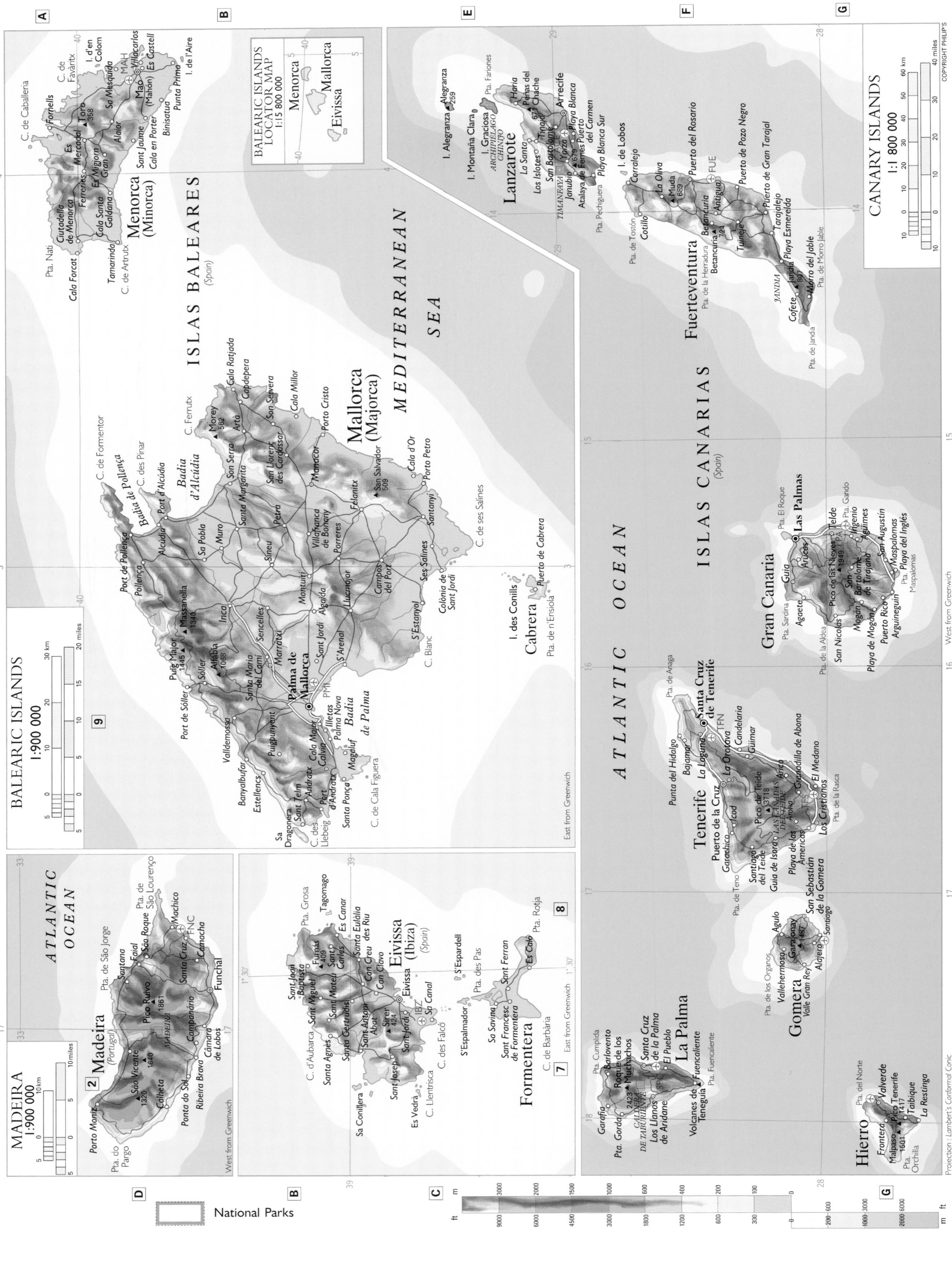
BALEARIC ISLANDS
1:900 000
BALEARIC ISLANDS LOCATOR MAP
1:15 800 000
ISLAS BALEARES
(Spain)
MEDITERRANEAN SEA
Mallorca
(Majorca)
Menorca
(Minorca)
Eivissa
(Ibiza)
Formentera
Cabrera
Palma de Mallorca
Badia de Palma
Badia d'Alcúdia
Badia de Pollença
Mao (Mahón)
Ciutadella de Menorca
MADEIRA
1:900 000
Madeira
(Portugal)
ATLANTIC OCEAN
Funchal
Pico Ruivo
CANARY ISLANDS
1:1 800 000
ISLAS CANARIAS
(Spain)
ATLANTIC OCEAN
Lanzarote
Fuerteventura
Gran Canaria
Tenerife
La Palma
Gomera
Hierro
Las Palmas
Santa Cruz de Tenerife
Pico de Teide
Arrecife
West from Greenwich
East from Greenwich
Projection : Lambert's Conformal Conic
COPYRIGHT PHILIP'S
National Parks

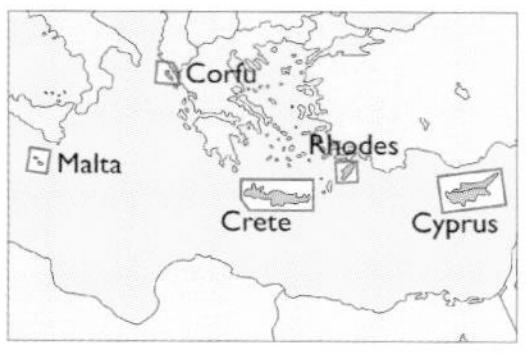
Corfu
Malta
Rhodes
Crete
Cyprus

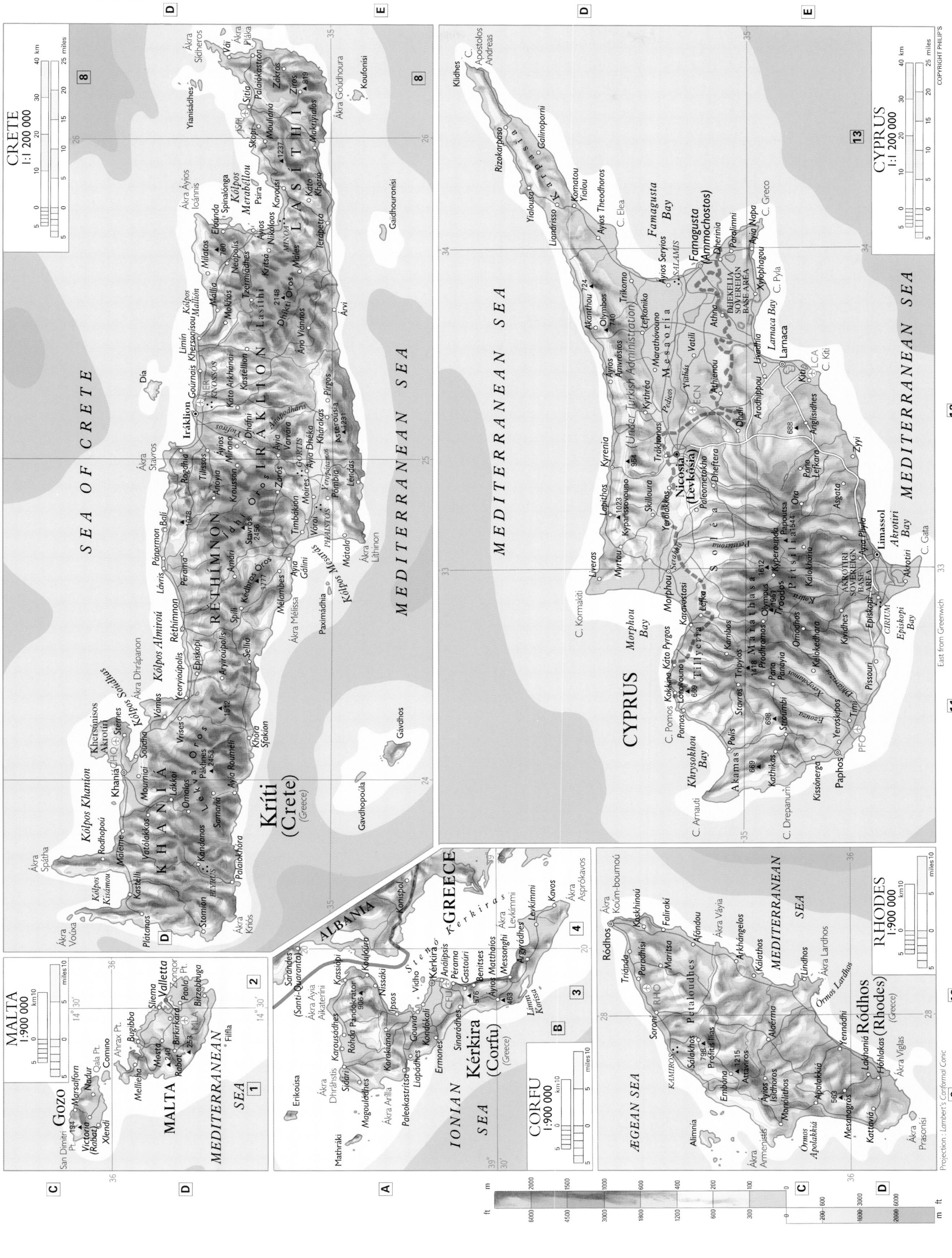
CRETE
1:1 200 000
SEA OF CRETE
MEDITERRANEAN SEA
Kríti
(Crete)
(Greece)
CYPRUS
1:1 200 000
CYPRUS
MEDITERRANEAN SEA
Famagusta Bay
Morphou Bay
Larnaca Bay
Akrotiri Bay
Episkopi Bay
Khrysokhou Bay
Nicosia (Levkosía)
Famagusta (Ammokhostos)
Larnaca
Limassol
Paphos
(Under Turkish Administration)
MALTA
1:900 000
Gozo
MALTA
MEDITERRANEAN SEA
Valletta
CORFU
1:900 000
Kérkira (Corfu)
(Greece)
IONIAN SEA
ALBANIA
GREECE
RHODES
1:900 000
Ródhos (Rhodes)
(Greece)
ÆGEAN SEA
MEDITERRANEAN SEA
East from Greenwich
Projection : Lambert's Conformal Conic
COPYRIGHT PHILIP'S

1:44 400 000

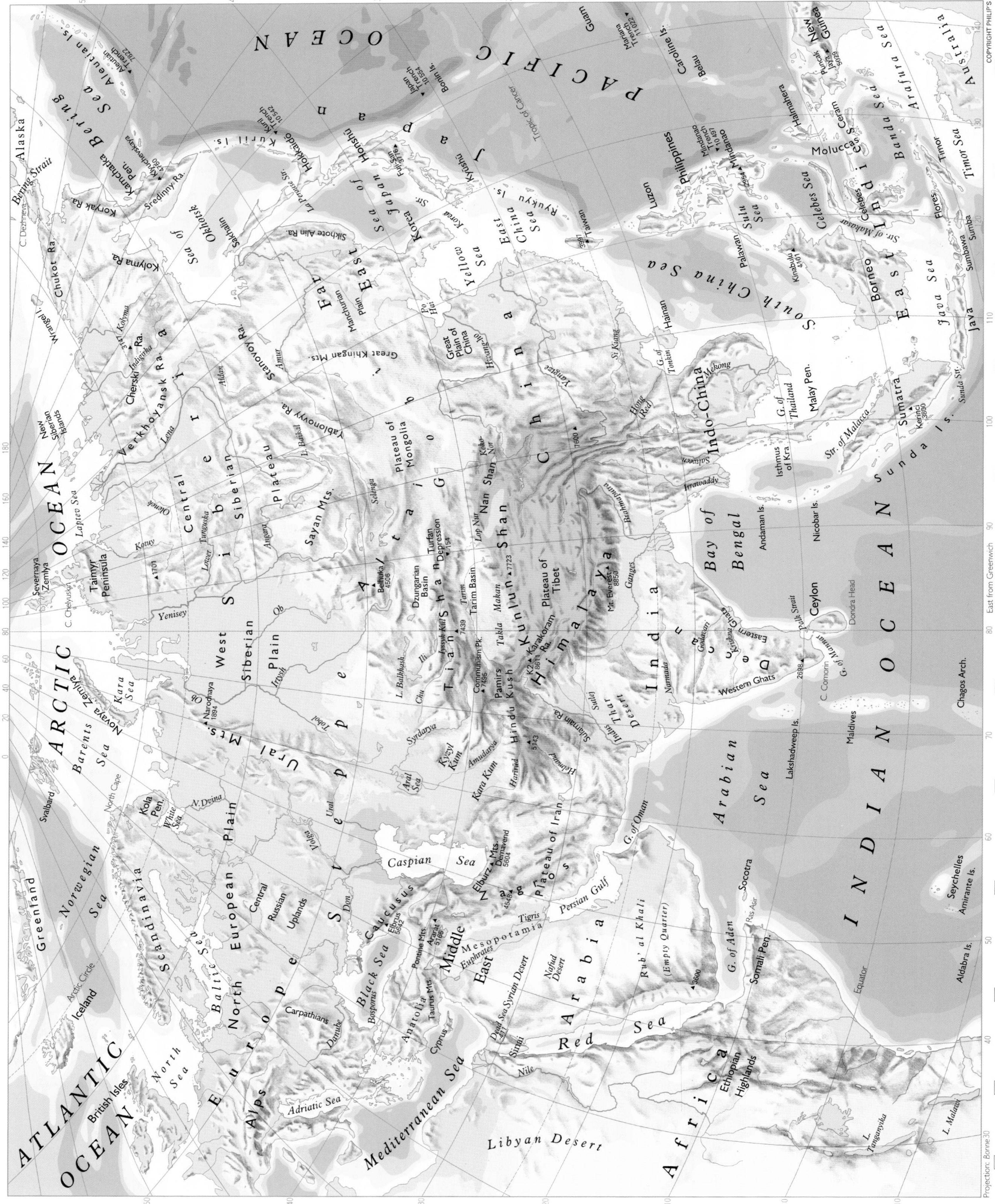

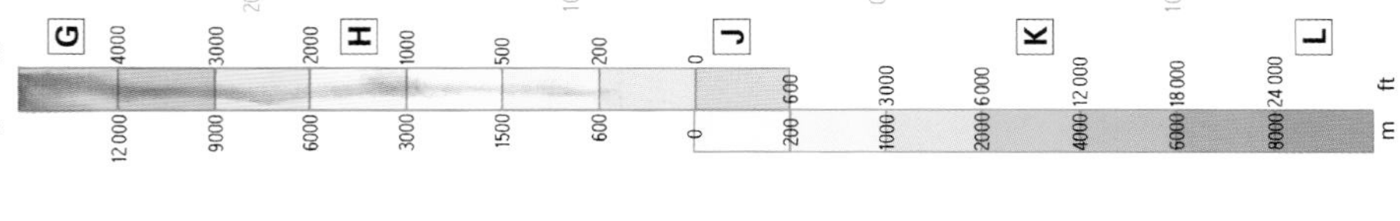

Projection: Bonne 30

East from Greenwich

1:44 400 000

500	0	250	500	750	1000	1250	1500	1750 km
500	0	250	500	750	1000	1250 miles		

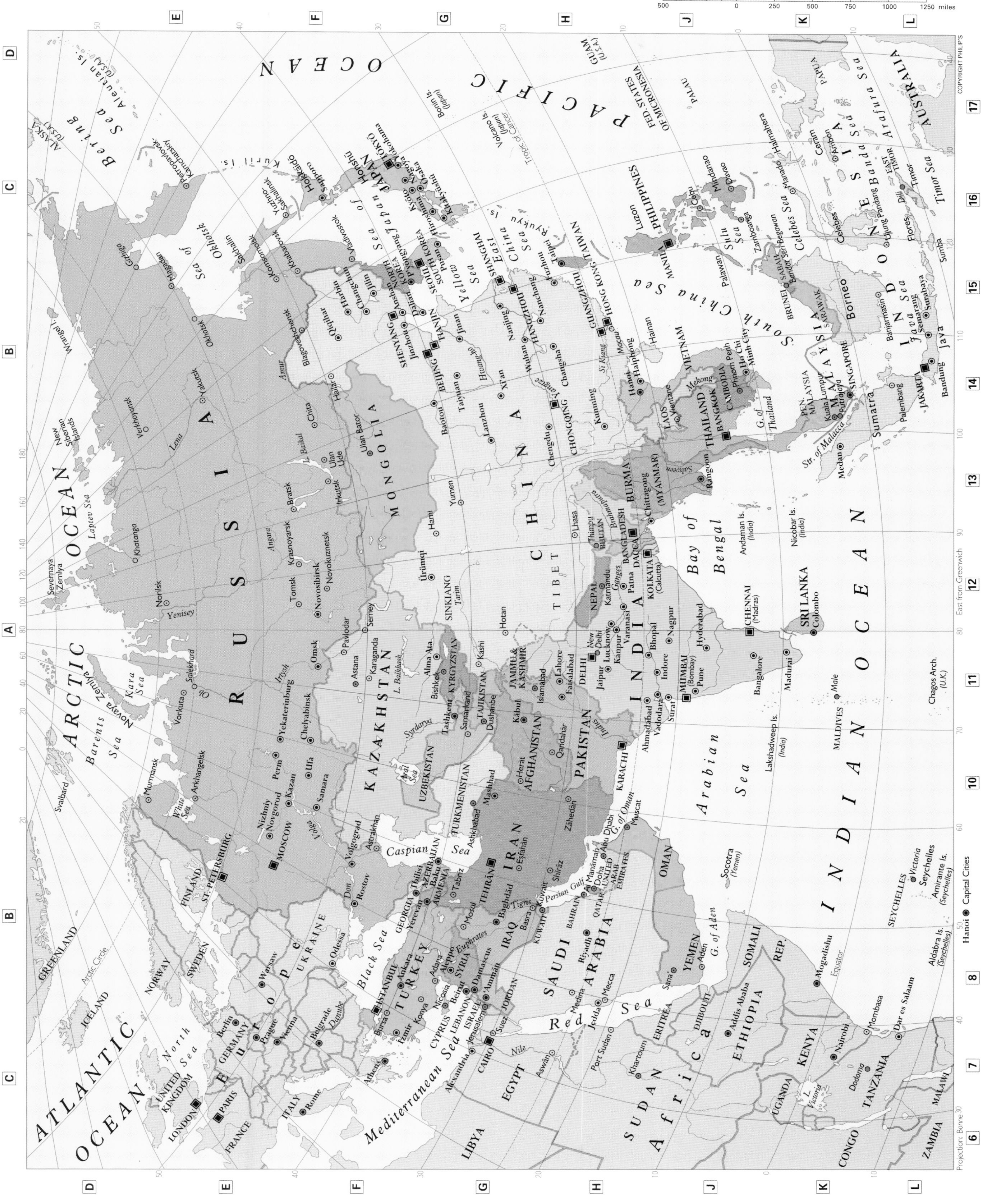

100 0 100 200 300 400 500 600 700 800 km

1:17 800 000

100 0 100 200 300 400 500 miles

D C B

E

ft m

12 000 4000

9000 3000

6000 2000

3000 1000

1200 400

600 200

0 0

200 600

2000 6000

4000 12 000

m ft

F

G

6 7 8 9

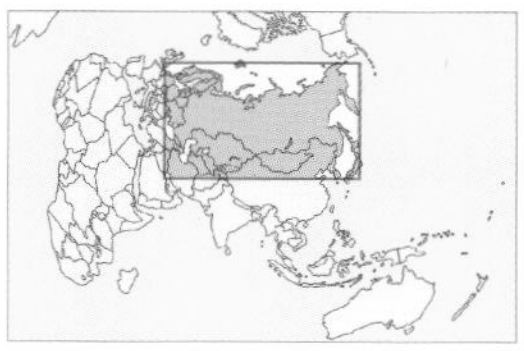

A
B
C
D
E
F
8
9
10
11
12
13
14
15
16
17
18
19
Mys Dezhneva (East C.)
Uelen
Chukchi Sea
St. Lawrence I. (U.S.A.)
Provideniya
Anadyrskiy Zaliv
Beringovskiy
Ostrov Vrangelya
East Siberian Sea
Ostrov Genriyetty
Ostrov Zhannetty
Ostrova Delonga
Ostrov Zhokhova
Ostrov Bennetta
Novosibirskiye Ostrova
Ostrov Faddeyevskiy
Ostrov Novaya Sibir
Ostrov Malyy Lyakhovskiy
Ostrov Bolshoy Lyakhovskiy
Lyakhovskiye Ostrova
Proliv Dmitriya Lapteva
Ostrov Belkovskiy
Ostrov Kotelnyy
Ostrov Stolbovoy
Laptev Sea
OCEAN
3800
Mys Arkticheskiy
Ostrov Shmidta
Ostrov Komsomolets
Ostrov Oktyabrskoy Revolyutsii
Ostrov Pioner
965
Ostrov Bolshevik
Severnaya Zemlya
Proliv Vilkitskogo
Mys Chelyuskin
374
Poluostrov Taymyr
Gory Byrranga
1146
Oz. Taymyr
Ostrov Bolshoy Begichev
Nordvik
Mys Buorkhaya
Ust Olenek
Tiksi
Tit-Ary
Olenek
Kazachye
Ust Kuyga
Chokurdakh
Indigirka
Novorybnoye
Khatanga
Saskylakh
Bulun
Kyusyur
Deputatskiy
Druzhina
Srednekolymsk
Nizhne Kolymsk
Cherskiy
Ambarchik
Ostrova Medvezhi
Ostrov Ayon
Pevek
Ust Chaun
Chukotskoye Nagorye
1843
Vankarem
Egvekinot
1853
Bilibino
Bolshoy Anyuy
Oloy
Omolon
1752
Anadyr
Yeropol
Markovo
Penzhino
Kamenskoye
Koryakskoye Nagorye
2562
Khatyrka
Bering Sea
Tilichiki
Korf
Kolymskoye Nagorye
Volochanka
Kheta
Khernaya
Dudinka
Norilsk
Gory Putorana
1701
Kotuy
Anabar
Zhilinda
Olenek
Yessey
Moyero
962
Arctic Circle
Kystotyam
Zhigansk
Verkhoyansk
Batagai
2389
Verkhoyanskiy Khrebet
Gora Chen 2682
Khonuu
Zyryanka
Kolyma
Pobeda 3147
Ust-Nera
Khrebet Cherskogo
Taskan
Omsukchan
Orotukan
Yagodnoye
Oymyakon
2959
Susuman
Ust-Omchug
Atka
Palatka
Magadan
Evensk
Nayakhan
Gizhiga
Paren
Penzhinskaya Guba
Gizhiginskaya Guba
Zaliv Shelikhova
Palana
Tigil
Sredinnyy Khrebet
Ossora
Ostrov Karaginskiy
Uka
Ust-Kamchatsk
Komandorskiye Ostrova
Nikolskoye
Poluostrov Kamchatka
Klyuchevskaya Sopka 4750
3621
3456
Petropavlovsk-Kamchatskiy
Ust Khayryuzovo
Kirovskiy
Ust-Bolsheretsk
Severo-Kurilsk
Ostrov Paramushir
Ostrov Onekotan
Kurilskiye Ostrova
Ostrov Simushir
Ostrov Urup
Ostrov Iturup
Kurilsk
Ostrov Kunashir
Sea of Okhotsk
1780
DALNEVOSTOCHNY
Turukhansk
Vilyuy
Sangar
Lena
Batamay
Borogontsy
Khandyga
Okhotskiy Perevoz
Ytyk-Kyuyel
Okhotsk
Arka
Ulya
Vilyuysk
Verkhnevilyuysk
Namtsy
Yakutsk
Mayya
Amga
Ust Maya
Aldan
Noginsk
Nizhnyaya Tunguska
Tura
Nyurba
Suntar
Pokrovsk
Sinsk
Ust-Mil
Aim
Maya
Nelkan
Khrebet Dzhugdzur
Yukta
Chernyshevskiy
Mirnyy
Chagda
Ayan
Olekminsk
Tommot
Uchur
Yerbogachen
Lensk
Aldan
2246
Ostrov Bolshoy Shantar
Sakhalinskiy Zaliv
Okha
Sakhalin
Kuyumba
Mutoray
Podkamennaya Tunguska
Vanavara
Vitim
Yenyuka
Olekma
Neryungri
Nikolayevsk-na-Amur
Aleksandrovsk-Sakhalinskiy
Gora Lopatina 1609
Yartsevo
Severo-Yeniseyskiy
1104
Kezhma
Korshunovo
Mama
Bodaybo
2999
Chara
Nagornyy
Stanovoy Khrebet
2246
Chumikan
Tugur
Uda
Amgun
Poronaysk
Uglegorsk
Yeniseysk
Boguchany
Ust-Ilimsk
Kirensk
Karalon
Ust-Nyukzha
Tynda
Zeya
Selemdzha
Bureya
Amur
Khrebet Sikhote Alin
Vanino
Yuzhno-Sakhalinsk
Strelka
Angara
Kondratyevo
Makarovo
Ust-Kut
Kalakan
Skovorodino
Zeya
Ushumun
Norsk
2640
Komsomolsk
Amursk
2078
Kholmsk
Korsakov
Chuna
Zheleznogorsk-Ilimskiy
Magistralnyy
Nizhneangarsk
Dzhalinda
Achinsk
Kansk
Ilanskiy
Bratsk
Bagdarin
Mogocha
Khrebet
Gulian
Shimanovsk
Svobodnyy
Belogorsk
Chegdomyn
Zavitinsk
Raychikhinsk
Obluchye
Birobidzhan
Smidovich
Khabarovsk
Wakkanai
Abashiri
2290
Kushiro
Krasnoyarsk
Tayshet
2840
Barguzin
Vitim
Bukachacha
Sretensk
Argun
1054
Blagoveshchensk
Poyarkovo
Vyazemskiy
Bikin
Amgu
Terney
Rumoi
Obihiro
SAPPORO
Hokkaidō
Artemovsk
Nizhneudinsk
Tulun
Zima
Chita
Shilka
Nerchinsk
Da Hinggan Ling
Chernogorsk
Minusinsk
Abakan
Vostochnyy Sayan
Cheremkhovo
Usolye Sibirskoye
Angarsk
1620
Ulan Ude
Yablonovyy Khrebet
Aginskoye
Baykal
456
Hegang
Jiamusi
Lesozavodsk
Dalnegorsk
3669
Otaru
Hakodate
Zapadnyy Sayan
Turan
Toora-Khem
Munku-Sardyk 3491
Irkutsk
Khilok
Petrovsk-Zabaykalskiy
Olovyannaya
Zabaykalsk
Nenjiang
QIQIHAR
Songhua Jiang
Dalnerechensk
Spassk Dalniy
Olga
Kyzyl
Chadan
TUVA
Slyudyanka
Hövsgöl Nuur
Gusinoozersk
Kyakhta
Borzya
Khapcheranga
Manzhouli
Hailar
HARBIN
Ussuriysk
Artem
Vladivostok
Nakhodka
Aomori
Hachinohe
Tannu Ola
Samagaltay
Hatgal
Zakamensk
Darhan
Hulun Nur
Ang'angxi
Nen Jiang
Dongbei
Mudanjiang
Khanka
Uvs Nuur
Erzin
Onon
Choybalsan
Kraskino
Akita
Hentiyn Nuruu
2800
Tamsagbulag
Taonan
JILIN
Yanji
Chŏngjin
Honshū
Har Us Nuur
Hyargas Nuur
Hangayn Nuruu
Ulaanbaatar
Lün
Öndörhaan
CHANGCHUN
Siping
Songhua Hu
2744
Sea of Japan (East Sea)
Niigata
Dörgön Nuur
Uliastay
Tsetserleg
Hovd
4362
MONGOLIA
1949
Linxi
FUSHUN
Tonghua
Altay
Saynshand
Xilinhot
Chifeng
SHENYANG
ANSHAN
NORTH KOREA
Dandong
Wŏnsan
Kansŏng
Kanazawa
Fuji-San 3776
3957
Gobi
Erenhot
Chengde
Yingkou
PYONGYANG
Nampo
SOUL (Seoul)
INCH'ON
JAPAN
4266
Dalandzadgad
CHINA
Hami
Zhangjiakou
BEIJING
DALIAN
SOUTH KOREA
TAEJON
TAEGU
PUSAN
Gaxun Nur
Baotou
Hohhot
OSAKA
60
50
40
70
80
90
100
110
120
130
140
150
170

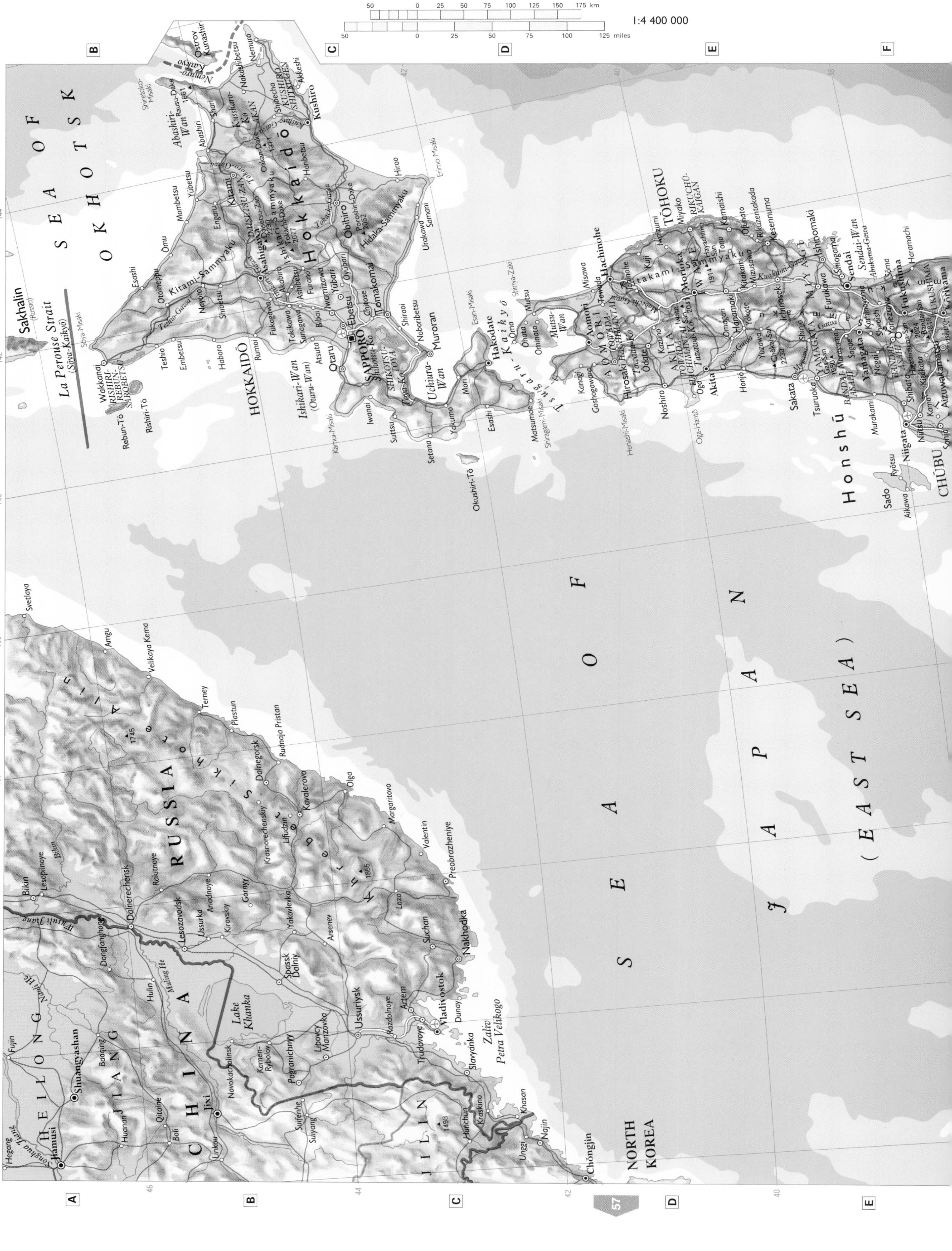
1:4 400 000
50 0 25 50 75 100 125 150 175 km
50 0 25 50 75 100 125 miles
SEA OF OKHOTSK
Sakhalin
(Russia)
La Perouse Strait
(Sōya-Kaikyō)
HOKKAIDŌ
Hokkaidō
SAPPORO
Otaru
Asahikawa
Kitami
Abashiri
Kushiro
Nemuro
Obihiro
Tomakomai
Muroran
Hakodate
Wakkanai
Rishiri-Tō
Rebun-Tō
Ishikari-Wan
(Otaru-Wan)
Uchiura-Wan
Tsugaru-Kaikyō
Okushiri-Tō
Ostrov Kunashir
TŌHOKU
Aomori
Hachinohe
Morioka
Akita
Sendai
Sendai-Wan
Yamagata
Fukushima
Sakata
Niigata
Sado
Honshū
CHŪBU
SEA OF JAPAN
(EAST SEA)
RUSSIA
CHINA
HEILONGJIANG
JILIN
NORTH KOREA
Vladivostok
Nakhodka
Ussuriysk
Lake Khanka
Zaliv Petra Velikogo
Chŏngjin
Jixi
Shuangyashan
Dalnerechensk
Terney
Olga
Svetlaya
Amgu
Preobrazheniye
Bikin
Hunchun
Khasan
Najin
Suifenhe
Wusuli Jiang
53
57
A
B
C
D
E
F
5
6
7
8
9
10
11
12

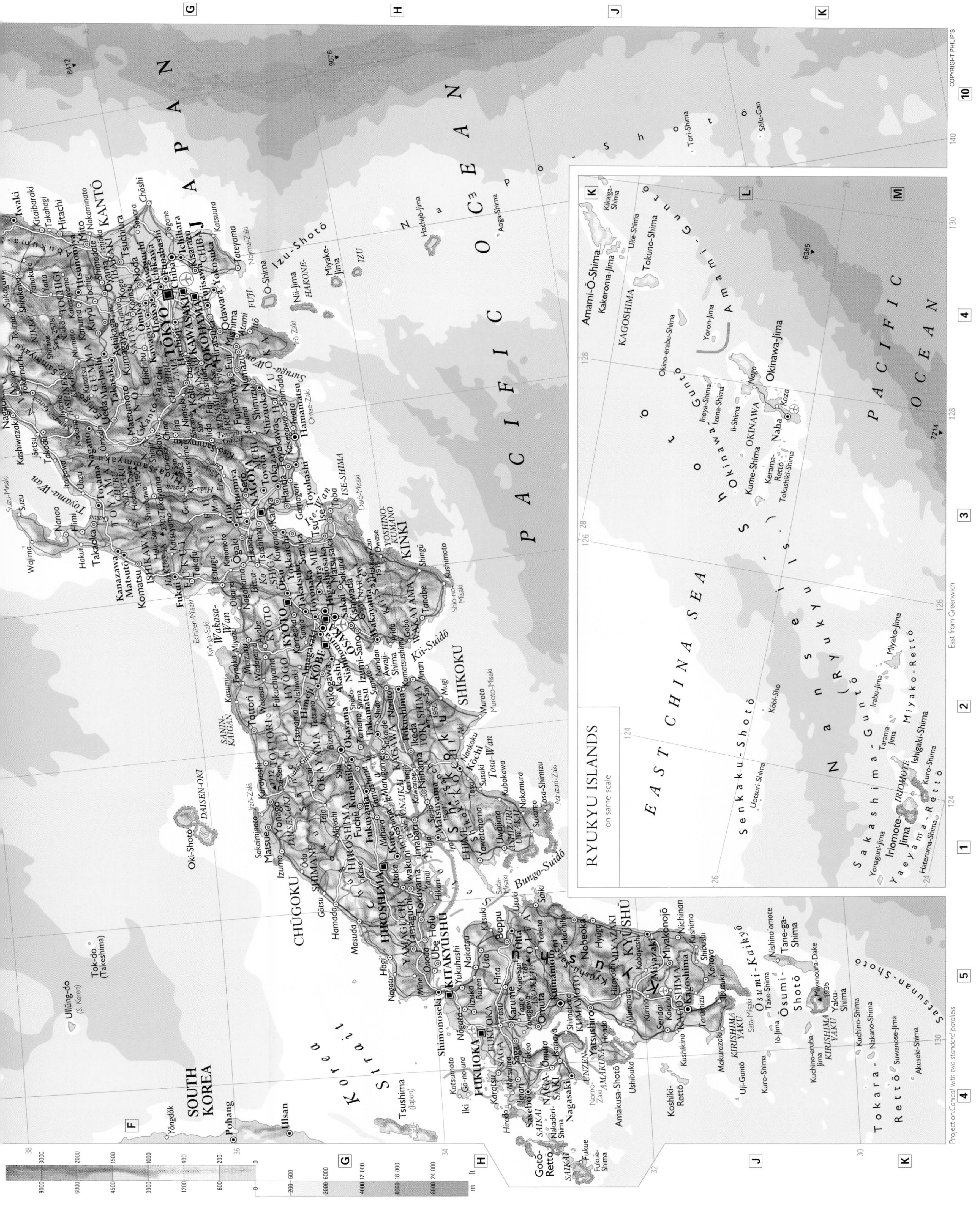
PACIFIC OCEAN
SEA OF JAPAN
EAST CHINA SEA
Korea Strait
SOUTH KOREA
RYUKYU ISLANDS
on same scale
Nansei-shotō (Ryukyu Is.)
Okinawa-Guntō
Amami-Guntō
Sakishima-Guntō
Yaeyama-Rettō
Miyako-Rettō
Senkaku-Shotō
Izu-Shotō
Satsunan-Shotō
Tokara-Rettō
Ōsumi-Shotō
Gotō-Rettō
Oki-Shotō
TOKYO
YOKOHAMA
KAWASAKI
Chiba
NAGOYA
KYŌTO
ŌSAKA
KŌBE
HIROSHIMA
KITAKYUSHU
FUKUOKA
Kagoshima
Nagasaki
Kumamoto
Okayama
Shizuoka
Hamamatsu
Kanazawa
Toyama
Naha
SHIKOKU
KYŪSHŪ
CHŪGOKU
KINKI
KANTŌ
Tsushima (Japan)
Ullŭng-do (S. Korea)
Tok-do (Takeshima)
Pohang
Ulsan
Projection: Conical with two standard parallels
East from Greenwich
COPYRIGHT PHILIP'S

1:5 300 000

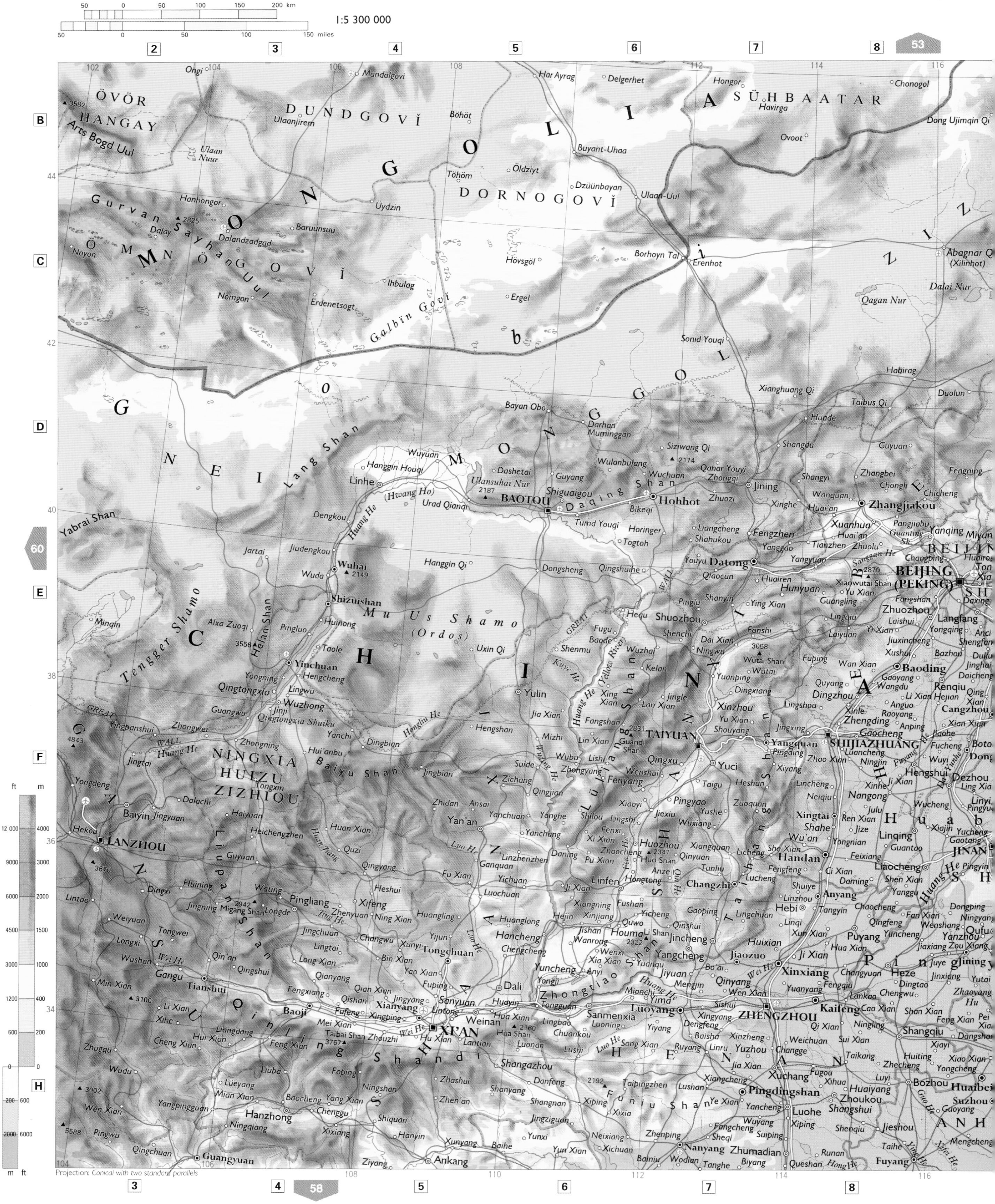

50 0 50 100 150 200 km
50 0 50 100 150 miles
2 3 4 5 6 7 8
53
60
58
Projection: Conical with two standard parallels
MONGOLIA
ÖVÖR HANGAY
DUNDGOVĬ
DORNOGOVĬ
SÜHBAATAR
ÖMNÖGOVĬ
Arts Bogd Uul
Gurvan Sayhan Uul
Galbin Govĭ
Gobi
Mandalgovi
Ongi
Har Ayrag
Delgerhet
Hongor
Chonogol
Havirga
Dong Ujimqin Qi
Ovoot
Ulaanjirem
Böhöt
Ulaan Nuur
Buyant-Uhaa
Töhöm
Öldziyt
Dzüünbayan
Ulaan-Uul
Hanhongor
Üydzin
Dalay
Dalandzadgad
Baruunsuu
Noyon
Hövsgöl
Borhoyn Tal
Erenhot
Abagnar Qi (Xilinhot)
Dalai Nur
Qagan Nur
Ihbulag
Nomgon
Erdenetsogt
Ergel
Sonid Youqi
NEI MONGOL
Habirag
Duolun
Xianghuang Qi
Taibus Qi
Bayan Obo
Darhan Muminggan
Huade
Shangdu
Guyuan
Sizwang Qi
Wuyuan
Hanggin Houqi
Dashetai
Ulansuhai Nur
Wulanbulang
Qahar Youyi Zhongqi
Guyang
Wuchuan
Shangyi
Zhangbei
Chongli
Fengning
Linhe
Shiguaigou
Daqing Shan
Hohhot
Jining
Zhuozi
Wanquan
Chicheng
BAOTOU
Urad Qianqi
Bikeqi
Xinghe
Huai'an
Zhangjiakou
Dengkou
Huang He
Tumd Youqi
Horinger
Liangcheng
Shahukou
Fengzhen
Xuanhua
Pangjiabu
Guanting Sk.
Yanqing
Miyun
Jartai
Jiudengkou
Togtoh
Yanggao
Tianzhen
Zhuolu
Wuhai
Hanggin Qi
Dongsheng
Qingshuihe
Youyu
Datong
Yangyuan
BEIJING (PEKING)
Wuda
Qiaocun
Huairen
Hunyuan
Xiaowutai Shan
Yu Xian
Guangling
Fangshan
Daxing
Shizuishan
Mu Us Shamo (Ordos)
Pinglu
Shanyin
Ying Xian
Zhuozhou
Langfang
Alxa Zuoqi
Huinong
Pingluo
Hequ
Shuozhou
Lingqiu
Laishui
Yongqing
Minqin
Tengger Shamo
Helan Shan
Taole
Fugu
Baode
Shenchi
Fanshi
Laiyuan
Yi Xian
Jiuxincheng
Shenmu
Wuzhai
Dai Xian
Ningwu
Wutai Shan
Wutai
Xushui
Bazhou
Uxin Qi
Yinchuan
Kelan
Fuping
Wan Xian
Baoding
Yongning
Hengcheng
Yulin
Yuanping
Dingxiang
Quyang
Gaoyang
Wangdu
Renqiu
Qingtongxia
Lingwu
Jingle
Lan Xian
Xinzhou
Dingzhou
Li Xian
Hejian
Guangwu
Wuzhong
Jinji
Qingtongxia Shuiku
Jia Xian
Xing Xian
Yu Xian
Shouyang
Lingshou
Xinle
Zhengding
Raoyang
Cangzhou
Yingpanshui
Zhongwei
Hengshan
Fangshan
TAIYUAN
Jingxing
Gaocheng
Anping
Xian Xian
Zhongning
Yanchi
Dingbian
Mizhi
Lin Xian
Guandi Shan
Yangquan
Pingding
SHIJIAZHUANG
Luancheng
Fucheng
Jingtai
NINGXIA HUIZU ZIZHIQU
Hui'anbu
Baiyu Shan
Suide
Wubu
Lishi
Zhongyang
Qingxu
Yuci
Zhao Xian
Ningjin
Hengshui
Dezhou
Yongdeng
Tongxin
Jingbian
Zichang
Qingjian
Fenyang
Wenshui
Taigu
Heshun
Lincheng
Jixian
Ling Xian
Dalachi
Zhidan
Ansai
Xiaoyi
Pingyao
Zuoquan
Neiqiu
Nangong
Baiyin
Jingyuan
Haiyuan
Yan'an
Yanchuan
Yonghe
Shilou
Lingshi
Jiexiu
Yushe
Xingtai
Ren Xian
Wucheng
Hekou
LANZHOU
Heichengzhen
Huan Xian
Yanchang
Fenxi
Wuxiang
Shahe
Jize
Linqing
Xiajin
Gaotang
Quzi
Xi Xian
Huozhou
Wu'an
Yongnian
Qinyuan
Licheng
She Xian
Handan
Feixiang
Guantao
JINAN
Guyuan
Qingyang
Daning
Pu Xian
Zhaocheng
Huo Shan
Anze
Tunliu
Fengfeng
Ci Xian
Liaocheng
Ganquan
Linzhenzhen
Fu Xian
Ji Xian
Linfen
Hongtong
Changzhi
Lucheng
Shuiye
Anyang
Daming
Shen Xian
Yanggu
Huining
Dingxi
Wating
Pingliang
Xifeng
Heshui
Yichuan
Luochuan
Xiangning
Fushan
Gaoping
Linzhou
Hebi
Lintao
Jingning
Migang Shan
Longde
Zhenyuan
Ning Xian
Huanglong
Hejin
Xinjiang
Yicheng
Qinshui
Lingchuan
Tangyin
Chaocheng
Dongping
Weiyuan
Tongwei
Jingchuan
Changwu
Huangling
Hancheng
Houma
Jishan
Wanrong
Quwo
Jincheng
Linqi
Puyang
Qingfeng
Yuncheng
Fan Xian
Wenshang
Ningyang
Longxi
Lingtai
Xunyi
Yijun
Tongchuan
Chengcheng
Wenxi
Xia Xian
Yangcheng
Jiaozuo
Huixian
Xun Xian
Ji Xian
Hua Xian
Juye
Jining
Yanzhou
Qufu
Zou Xian
Wushan
Qin'an
Qingshui
Long Xian
Bin Xian
Yao Xian
Yuncheng
Anyi
Yuanqu
Jiyuan
Bo'ai
Wuzhi
Xinxiang
Changyuan
Heze
Jiaxiang
Gangu
Tianshui
Qianyang
Qian Xian
Fuping
Dali
Yongji
Zhongtiao Shan
Mianchi
Mengjin
Qinyang
Yimd
Wen Xian
Fengqiu
Dingtao
Jinxiang
Zhaoyang
Yutai
Min Xian
Fengxiang
Qishan
Jingyang
Xianyang
Sanyuan
Lintong
Huayin
Tongguan
Luoyang
Sishui
ZHENGZHOU
Kaifeng
Lankao
Chengwu
Yuanyang
Baoji
Fufeng
Xingping
XI'AN
Weinan
Hua Xian
Sanmenxia
Lingbao
Luoning
Yiyang
Xingyang
Dengfeng
Xinzheng
Cao Xian
Shan Xian
Feng Xian
Pei Xian
Li Xian
Xihe
Liangdang
Hui Xian
Mei Xian
Taibai Shan
Zhouzhi
Hu Xian
Lantian
Hua Shan
Chuankou
Lushi
Song Xian
Ruyang
Linru
Baisha
Qi Xian
Ningling
Shangqiu
Dangshan
Cheng Xian
Feng Xian
Qinling Shandi
Luonan
Yuzhou
Weichuan
Sui Xian
Xiayi
Zhugqu
Shangzhou
Luanchuan
Jia Xian
Changge
Taikang
Zhecheng
Huiting
Xiao Xian
Wudu
Liuba
Foping
Zhashui
Danfeng
Lushan
Xuchang
Fugou
Luyi
Yongcheng
Lueyang
Mian Xian
Ningshan
Shanyang
Xixia
Funiu Shan
Ye Xian
Pingdingshan
Xihua
Bozhou
Huaibei
Wen Xian
Yangpingguan
Baocheng
Chenggu
Yang Xian
Zhen'an
Shangnan
Xiping
Yancheng
Huaiyang
Zhoukou
Suzhou
Pingwu
Hanzhong
Ningqiang
Xixiang
Shiquan
Hanyin
Jingziguan
Neixiang
Zhenping
Wuyang
Sheqi
Shangshui
Guoyang
Jieshou
Mengcheng
Qingchuan
Guangyuan
Ziyang
Ankang
Xunyang
Baihe
Yunxi
Yun Xian
Xichuan
Nanyang
Zhumadian
Suiping
Taihe
Runan
Bainiu
Wodian
Tanghe
Biyang
Queshan
Fuyang
GANSU
SHAANXI
SHANXI
HENAN
HEBEI
SHANDONG
ANHUI
Huabei Pingyuan
Great Wall
Luliang Shan
Taihang Shan
Wei He
Luo He
Huang He (Yellow River)
ft m
12 000 4000
9000 3000
6000 2000
4500 1500
3000 1000
1200 400
600 200
0 0
200 600
2000 6000
m ft

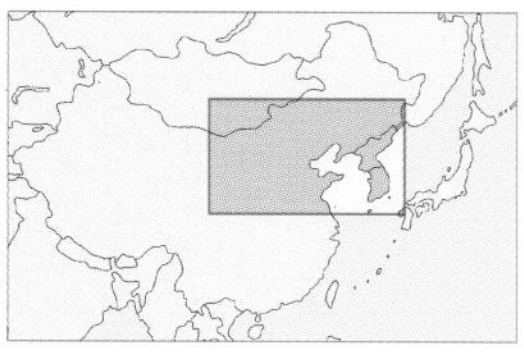

HARBIN
Bin Xian
Acheng
Shuangcheng
Zhaoyuan
Maoxing
Da'an
Baicheng
Zhenlai
Horqin Youyi Qianqi
(Ulanhot)
Taonan
Tuquan
Hulingol
Anguang
Qagan Nur
Qian Gorlos
Qian'an
Shenjingzi
Changchunling
Fuyu
Beitaolaizhao
Sanchahe
Yushu
Wuchang
Shanhetun
Shangzhi
Yanshou
Linkou
Jixi
Turiy Rog
Lake Khanka
Yimianpo
Lalin
Hengdaohezi
Mudanjiang
Muling
Maqiaohe
Xiachengzi
Pogranichnyy
Suifenhe
Suiyang
Hailin
Ning'an
Zhangguangcai Ling
1690
Kaoshan
Nong'an
Dehui
Shulan
Tongyu
Jarud Qi
Zhanyu
Beizhengzhen
Fulongquan
Jiutai
Gangyao
Wulajie
Changling
Horqin Zuoyi Zhongqi
Maolin
CHANGCHUN
Huaidezhen
JILIN
Jiaohe
Xinzhan
Emu
Huangsongdian
Jingpo Hu
Chunyang
Dongjingcheng
Luozigou
Dongning
Golenki
Ussuriysk
Razdolnoye
Artem
Tavrichanka
Vladivostok
Slavyanka
Posyet
Kraskino
Hunchun
Shixian
Wangqing
Daxinggou
Dunhua
Tumen
Yanji
Longjing
Namyang
Helong
Mingyuegue
Songhua Hu
Fanjiatun
Gongzhuling
Shuangyang
Yitong
Siping
Lishu
Shuangliao
Tongliao
Kailu
Xiliao He
Bairin Zuoqi
Bairin Youqi
Linxi
2029
Hexigten Qi
Xar Moron He
Ongniud Qi
Jargalang
Bamiancheng
Liaoyuan
Panshi
Huadian
Huinan
Baishan
Dongfeng
Xifeng
Zhangwu
Kangping
Wutonghaolai
Hure Qi
Xiawa
2020
Kaiyuan
Meihekou
Tiefa
Faku
Tieling
Shanchengzhen
Liuhe
Jingyu
Fusong
Antu
Baihe
1677
Changbai Shan
Hoeryong
Musan
Unggi
Sosura
Najin
Puryong
Pugodong
Chifeng
Fuxin
Zhangwu
Xinlitun
Xinmin
Qingyuan
SHENYANG
FUSHUN
Xinbin
Hunjiang
Linjiang
Chunggang-up
Paektu-san
2744
Hyesan
Changbai
Nanam
Chongjin
Kyongsong
Chuuronjang
2541
Hachon
Ondaejin
Irhyangdong
Heishui
Beipiao
Qinghemen
Weichang
1885
Ningcheng
Chaoyang
Heishan
Liaozhong
Benxi
Qinghecheng
Tonghua
Inpundong
Huch'ang
Kasan-dong
Hapsu
Kapsan
Simpungdong
Kilchu
Musudan
Beizhen
Goubangzi
Yi Xian
Liaoyang
Anping
Tianshifu
Huanren
1845
Manp'o
Ji'an
Kanggye
P'ungsan
Chiai-bong
2522
Kosongni
Kimch'aek
(Songjin)
Tanch'on
Longhua
Chengde
Luanne
Luanping
Lingyuan
Pingquan
Jinzhou
Panjin
ANSHAN
Lianshanguan
Kuup-tong
Ch'osan
Usi
Pyoktong
Kwangdaeri
Changhungni
Pukch'ong
Sinch'ang
Liugou
Shangbancheng
Kuancheng
Jianchang
Jinxi
Tianzhuangtai
Niuzhuang
Haicheng
Huludao
Yingkou
Dashiqiao
Kuandian
Supung
Koin-dong
Changjin
Sinhung
Sinp'o
Sohori
Miyun
Xinglong
Shuangshanzi
Xingcheng
Gaizhou
Fengcheng
Sakchu
Taegwan
NORTH
Pukchin
Oro
Hamhung
Hungnam
Hongwon
Suizhong
Jianchangying
Xiongyuecheng
Wafu
1131
Xiuyan
Dandong
Sinuiju
Uiju
Kusong
Kujang
Yongamp'o
Chongju
Pakch'on
Tokch'on
KOREA
Tongjoson Man
Tongch'on-ni
Zunhua
Fengrun
Lulong
Funing
Qinhuangdao
Liaodong Wan
Buyun Shan
Gushan
Donggou
Sonch'on
Anju
Sunch'on
Yonghung
Kowon
Munch'on
Wonsan
Anbyon
Kojo
Tangshan
Luan Xian
Yutian
Baodi
TANGSHAN
TIANJIN SHI
Changli
Leting
Wafangdian
Zhuanghe
Sukch'on
Sinchang-ni
Songch'on
Kangdong
Tongyang
Singosan
Hoeyang
Kosong
Wuqing
Hangu
TIANJIN
Tanggu
Dagu
Pulandian
Pikou
Jin Xian
Lushun
DALIAN
Korea Bay
P'YONGYANG
Sunan
Chunghwa
Nampo
Songnim
Koksan
Sepo-ri
1638
Changdo-ri
Kansong
Sokch'o
Yangyang
SEA OF JAPAN
(EAST SEA)
Oikou
Bo Hai
Miaodao
Qundao
Cho-do
Sariwon
Chaeryong
Sinmak
Nam-ch'on
Kumhwa
Hwach'on-chosuji
1578
Chumunjin
Huanghua
Changyon
Sinch'on
Kumch'on
Haeju
Kaesong
Panmunjom
Uijongbu
Ch'unch'on
Kangnung
Hongch'on
Tonghae
Samch'ok
Yanshan
Paengnyong-do
(S. Korea)
Ongjin
Yonan
Kanghwa
SOUL
Puch'on
INCH'ON
Songnam
Wonju
Ullung-do
Longkou
Penglai
Daxindian
Yantai
Weihai
Wudi
Zhanhua
Huang He
Huimin
Laizhou Wan
Huang Xian
Fushan
Muping
Wendeng
Chengshan Jiao
Rongcheng
Ansan
Anyang
Suwon
Ich'on
Yoju
Osan
Ch'ungju
Chech'on
Yongju
Ulchin
Deping
Shanghe
Kenli
Binzhou
Dongying
Zhaoyuan
Qixia
923
Qingcheng
Gaoyuan
Laizhou
Shandong Bandao
Rushan
P'yongt'aek
Ch'onan
SOUTH
Chongju
Yech'on
Andong
Yongdok
Guangrao
Shouguang
Huantai
Linzi
Laiyang
Haiyang
Nanhuang
Shidao
Sosan
Hongsong
Yesan
KOREA
Kongju
Sangju
Sonsan
Uisong
Chongha
P'ohang
Zhoucun
ZIBO
Yidu
Weifang
Changyi
Pingdu
Laixi
Anmyon-do
Taechon-ni
Nonsan
TAEJON
Yongdong
Kimch'on
Kumi
Yongch'on
Kyongju
Changgi-Ap
Tai Shan
1524
Boshan
Linqu
Anqiu
Gaomi
Fangzi
Jimo
Langun
Chengyang
Jiaozhou
1108
Laiwu
Tai'an
Zhucheng
QINGDAO
Jiaozhou Wan
Kunsan
Kanggyong
Iri
Chonju
Waegwan
TAEGU
Kimje
Puan
Chongup
Kochang
Koryong
Miryang
Ch'ongdo
Ulsan
Xintai
Mengyin
Yishui
Wulian
Sishui
YELLOW SEA
(Huang Hai)
Namwon
Chii-san
Tamyang
1915
Chinju
Masan
Kimhae
Tongnae
PUSAN
Pingyi
Ju Xian
Liangcheng
Rizhao
Yi He
Tangtou
Shijiusuo
Andongwei
Fei Xian
Tengzhou
Linyi
Sago-ri
Songjong-ni
KWANGJU
Hadong
Naju
Ch'angwon
Samch'onp'o
Ch'ungmu
Sunch'on
Mokp'o
Posong
Polgyo-ri
Yosu
Korea Strait
Tsushima
Izuhara
Teng Xian
Zaozhuang
Gangyu
Haizhou Wan
Lianyungang
Weishan
Hanzhuang
Jiawang
Pizhou
Tancheng
Haizhou
Weishan Hu
Xuzhou
Xinyi
Guanyun
Chenjiagang
Changhung
Haenam
Chindo
Huksan-chedo
(S. Korea)
Iki
Xiangshui
Yaowan
Guannan
Shuanggou
Suqian
Shuyang
Binhai
JIANGSU
Suining
Da Yunhe
Lianshui
Funing
Sheyang
Cheju
Cheju-do (S. Korea)
Onpyong-ni
Hallim
Taejong
Halla-san
1950
Mosulpo
Sogwipo
Karatsu
Imari
JAPAN
Sasebo
Kashima
Omura
Isahaya
Nagasaki
Kuchinotsu
Nakadori-Shima
Fukue-Shima
Lingbi
Sixian
Hongze Hu
Huaiyin
Huai'an
Grand Canal
Yancheng
Baoying
Liuzhuang
Guzhen
Wuhe
Huaiyuan
Bengbu
Fengyang
Gaoyou Hu
Xinghua
Dongtai
Shuiku
Sanhe
HEILONG JIANG
RUSSIA
JILIN
LIAONING
HEBEI
SHANDONG
Dongbei (Manchuria)
Liaodong Bandao
THE WILLOW WALL
Liao He
Songhua Jiang
Nen Jiang
Tao'er He
Hulin He
Xinkai He
Dongliao He
Laoha He
Daling He
Hun Jiang
Yalu Jiang
Luan He
Tumen Jiang
Erdao Jiang
Huifa He
Mudan Jiang
1949
118
120
122
124
126
128
130
132
44
42
40
38
36
34
9
10
11
12
13
14
15
16
B
C
D
E
F
G
H
East from Greenwich
55
59

1:5 300 000

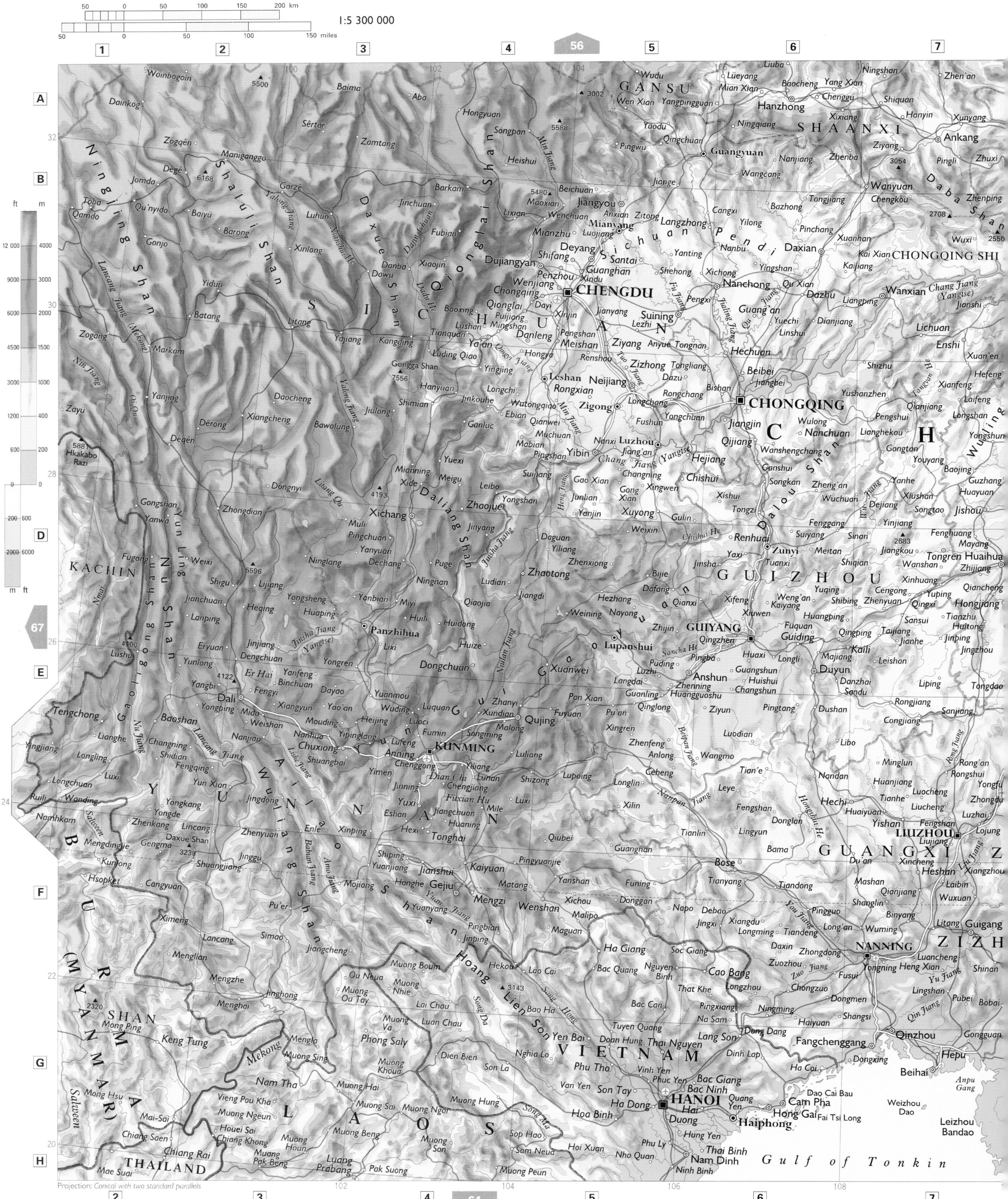
GANSU
SHAANXI
SICHUAN
Sichuan Pendi
CHONGQING SHI
CHENGDU
CHONGQING
GUIZHOU
GUIYANG
YUNNAN
KUNMING
GUANGXI
NANNING
LIUZHOU
KACHIN
SHAN
BURMA (MYANMAR)
LAOS
VIETNAM
HANOI
THAILAND
Gulf of Tonkin
Daba Shan
Ningjing Shan
Shaluli Shan
Daxue Shan
Qionglai Shan
Daliang Shan
Dalou Shan
Wuliang Shan
Ailao Shan
Gaoligong Shan
Nu Shan
Yun Ling
Hoang Lien Son
Gongga Shan
Hkakabo Razi
Chang Jiang (Yangtze)
Jinsha Jiang (Yangtze)
Lancang Jiang (Mekong)
Mekong
Salween
Nu Jiang
Yalong Jiang
Min Jiang
Jialing Jiang
Wu Jiang
Nanpan Jiang
Hongshui He
You Jiang
Zuo Jiang
Yu Jiang
Qin Jiang
Song Da
Song Hong
Song Ma
Er Hai
Dian Chi
Fuxian Hu
Lanzhou
Panzhihua
Xichang
Leshan
Zigong
Yibin
Luzhou
Neijiang
Mianyang
Deyang
Nanchong
Guangyuan
Hanzhong
Ankang
Dazhou
Wanxian
Zunyi
Anshun
Lupanshui
Duyun
Kaili
Qujing
Dali
Baoshan
Tengchong
Yuxi
Gejiu
Kaiyuan
Wenshan
Bose
Qinzhou
Beihai
Hepu
Fangchenggang
Lao Cai
Cao Bang
Haiphong
Nam Dinh
Hong Gai
Cam Pha
Dien Bien
Phong Saly
Luang Prabang
Chiang Rai
Chiang Saen
Keng Tung
Weizhou Dao
Leizhou Bandao
Projection: Conical with two standard parallels

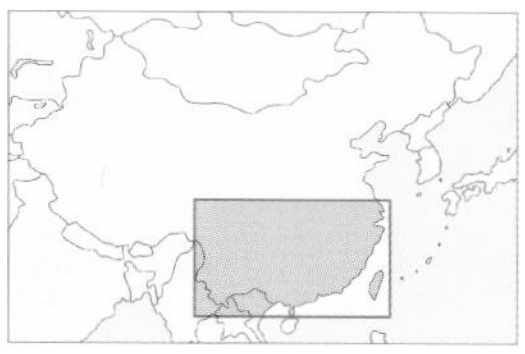

57
61
8
9
10
11
12
13
14
A
B
C
D
E
F
G
H
HENAN
HUBEI
ANHUI
JIANGSU
ZHEJIANG
JIANGXI
HUNAN
FUJIAN
GUANGDONG
GUANGXI ZHUANGZU
TAIWAN
SHANGHAI SHI
NANJING
SHANGHAI
WUHAN
HANGZHOU
NANCHANG
CHANGSHA
GUANGZHOU
HONG KONG (XIANGGANG)
T'AIPEI
KAOHSIUNG
Hefei
Fuzhou
Xiamen
Shantou
Shenzhen
Kowloon
Macau
Zhuhai
Ningbo
Wenzhou
Suzhou
Wuxi
Changzhou
Zhenjiang
Yangzhou
Huainan
Bengbu
Anqing
Jiujiang
Yichang
Shashi
Yueyang
Xiangtan
Zhuzhou
Hengyang
Shaoguan
Ganzhou
Meizhou
Zhanjiang
Maoming
Wuzhou
Guilin
Quanzhou
Zhangzhou
T'aichung
T'ainan
Chilung
Hsinchu
Hualien
T'aitung
Dabie Shan
Wuyi Shan
Nan Ling
Luoxiao Shan
Jiuling Shan
Mufu Shan
Wugong Shan
Yunkai Dashan
Chungyang Shanmo
Dongting Hu
Poyang Hu
Tai Hu
Hongze Hu
Chang Jiang (Yangtse)
Han Shui
Gan Jiang
Xiang Jiang
Xi Jiang
Min Jiang
Bei Jiang
Dong Jiang
Zhu Jiang
Three Gorges Dam
Taiwan Strait
Luzon Strait
SOUTH CHINA SEA
Tropic of Cancer
Matsu Tao (Taiwan)
Chinmen (Quemoy)
Chinmen Tao (Taiwan)
P'enghu Ch'üntou (Pescadores) (Taiwan)
Dongsha Dao (Pratas I.) (China)
Haitan Dao
Nanri Dao
Zhoushan
Daishan
Shangchuan Dao
Xiachuan Dao
Hailing Dao
Donghai Dao
Naozhou Dao
Leizhou Wan
Dangan Liedao
Gaolan Dao
Honghai Wan
Hangzhou Wan
Lü-Tao
Hungt'ou Hsü
3931
3997
1725
2120
1836
1834
1810
1794
1596
1474
1510
2164
1629
1636
1963
2393
1703
112
114
116
118
120
122
20
22
24
26
28
30
32
East from Greenwich
COPYRIGHT PHILIP'S

100 0 100 200 300 400 500 600 700 800 km

1:17 800 000

100 0 100 200 300 400 500 miles

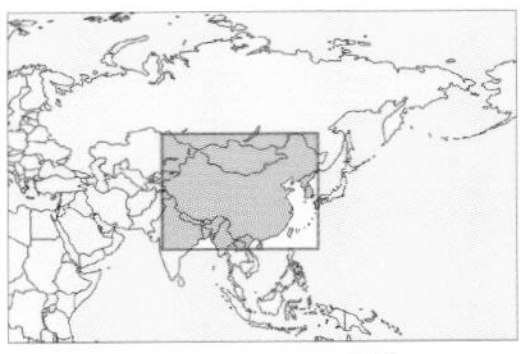

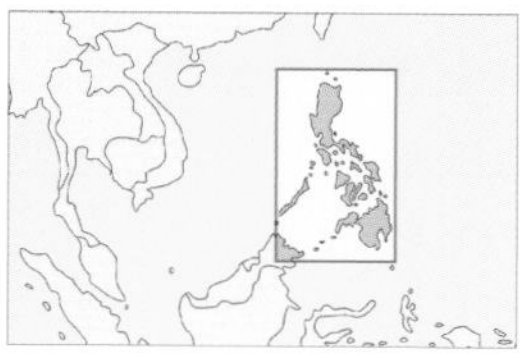

1:6 700 000

50 0 100 150 200 250 300 km
50 0 50 100 150 200 miles

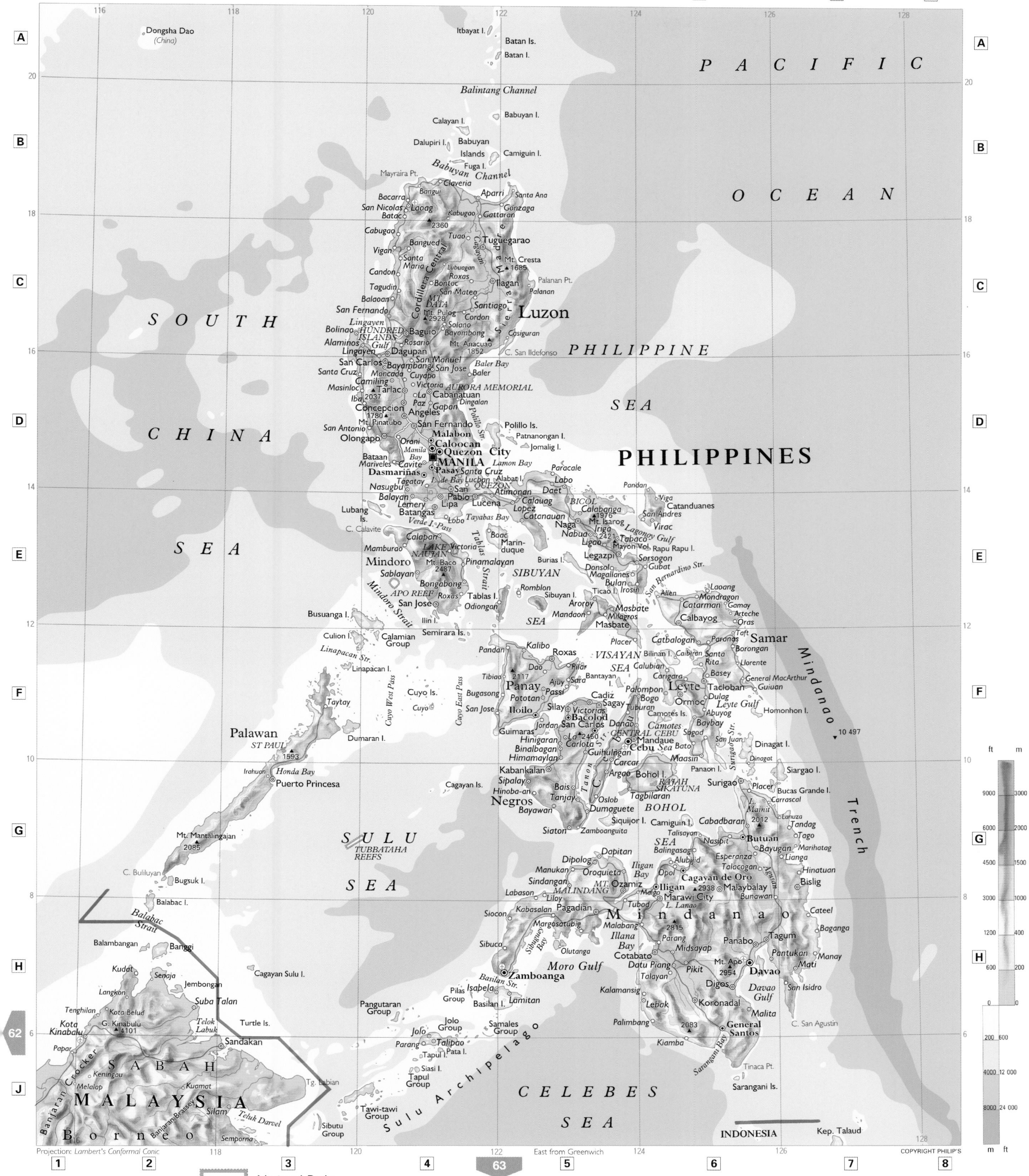

Projection: Lambert's Conformal Conic

National Parks

100 0 100 200 300 400 500 km

1:11 100 000

100 0 50 100 150 200 250 300 350 miles

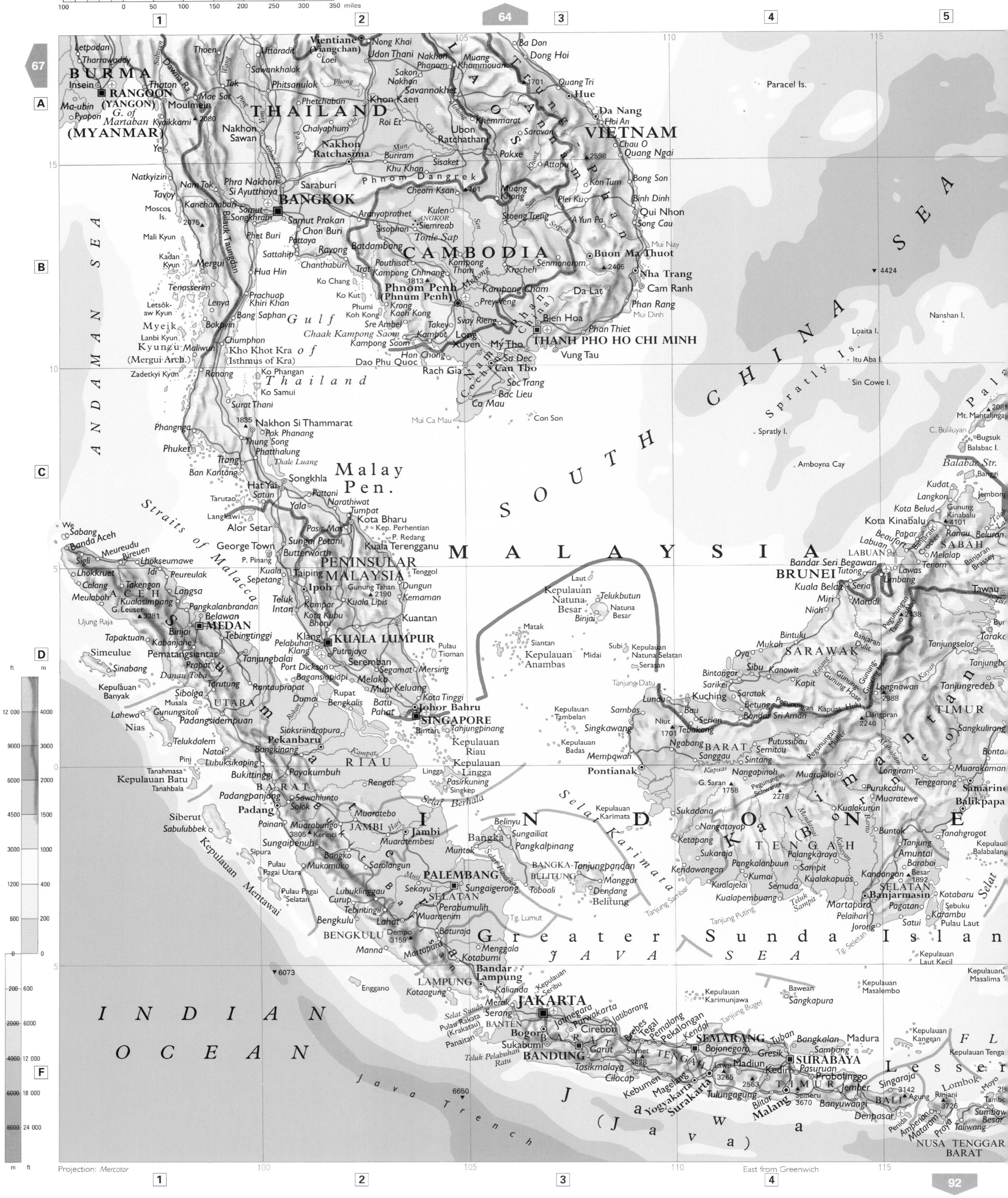

Projection: Mercator

East from Greenwich

92

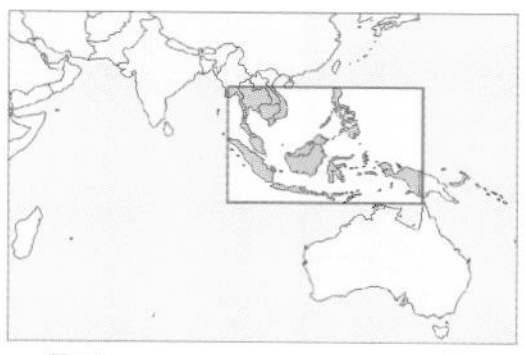

JAVA AND MADURA
1:6 700 000
BALI
1:1 800 000
PHILIPPINES
SULU SEA
CELEBES SEA
PACIFIC OCEAN
INDIAN OCEAN
MOLUCCA SEA
BANDA SEA
FLORES SEA
ARAFURA SEA
Luzon
MANILA
Quezon City
Mindanao
Davao
Zamboanga
Cebu
JAKARTA
BANDUNG
SEMARANG
SURABAYA
Yogyakarta
Surakarta
Malang
Madura
Bali
Denpasar
Lombok
Mataram
Jawa
Sulawesi (Celebes)
Manado
Ujung Pandang
Halmahera
Seram
Ambon
Buru
Flores
Sumba
Timor
EAST TIMOR
Dili
Kupang
NUSA TENGGARA TIMUR
Sunda Is.
Jazirah Doberai
PAPUA
Pegunungan Maoke
Puncak Jaya
Jayapura
Merauke
PAPUA NEW GUINEA
Kepulauan Aru
Kepulauan Tanimbar
Kepulauan Kai
MALUKU
Equator
COPYRIGHT PHILIP'S

50 0 50 100 150 200 km

1:5 300 000

50 0 50 100 150 miles

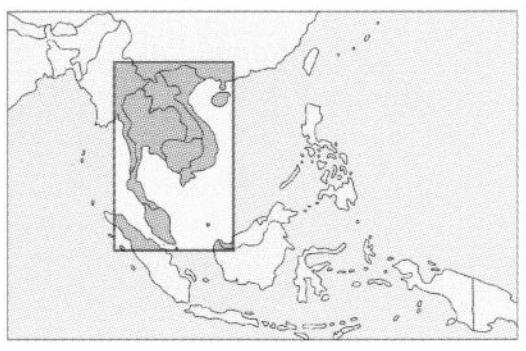

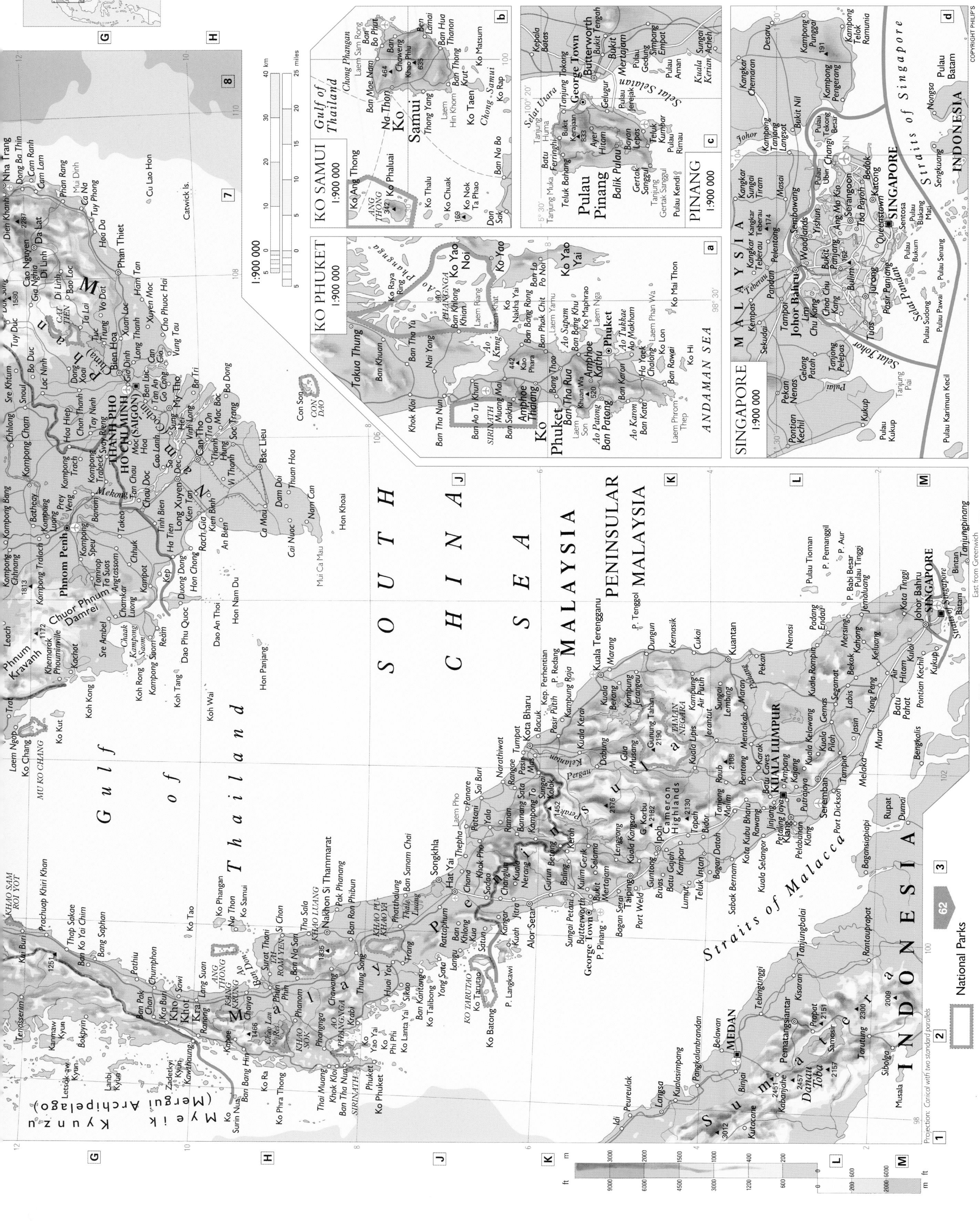

Myeik Kyunzu (Mergui Archipelago)
Gulf of Thailand
SOUTH CHINA SEA
MALAYSIA
PENINSULAR MALAYSIA
INDONESIA
Straits of Malacca
Phnom Penh
HO CHI MINH (SAIGON)
THANH PHO HO CHI MINH
KUALA LUMPUR
SINGAPORE
MEDAN
KO PHUKET 1:900 000
KO SAMUI 1:900 000
PINANG 1:900 000
SINGAPORE 1:900 000
ANDAMAN SEA
Straits of Singapore
Projection: Conical with two standard parallels
East from Greenwich
National Parks
1:900 000

1:8 900 000

0 50 100 200 300 400 km
0 50 100 150 200 250 miles

71
50

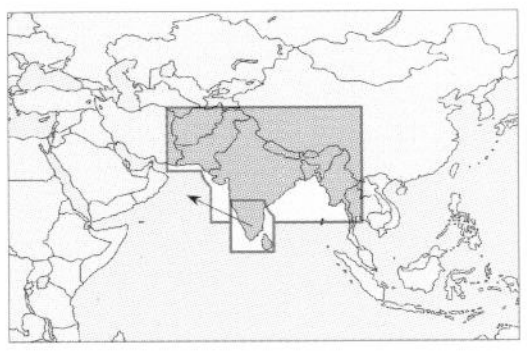

12
13
14
60
15
16
17
18
19
20
21
22
B
C
D
E
F
G
H
J
K
L
M
64
65
East from Greenwich
82
84
86
88
90
92
94
96
98
100
102
34
32
30
28
26
24
22
20
18
16
14
CHINA
XIZANG
(TIBET)
QINGHAI
SICHUAN
YUNNAN
Huh Xil Shan
Bayan Har Shan
Tanggula (Dangla) Shan
Nyainqentanglha Shan
Gangdisê Shan
Kunlun Shan
Tanggula Shankou
Lhasa
Nagqu
Qamdo
Garzê
Yushu
Dainkog
Nangqen
Baiyü
Xinlong
Litang
Yidun
Yajiang
Ningjing
Zhaxizê
Lhorong
Gongbo'gyamda
Lhari
Lhünzub
Xigazê
Gyangzê
Saga
Zhongba
Coqên
Xainza
Ombu
Siling Co
Nam Co
Gyaring Hu
Ngoring Hu
Dogai Coring
Yarlung Zangbo Jiang
Maquan He (Tsangpo)
Nu Jiang (Salween)
Lancang Jiang (Mekong)
NEPAL
Katmandu
Bhaktapur
Mt. Everest 8850
Kanchenjunga 8598
Annapurna 8078
Dhaulagiri 8172
Siwalik Range
SIKKIM
Gangtok
BHUTAN
Thimphu
Punakha
ARUNACHAL PRADESH
ASSAM
Guwahati
Shillong
MEGHALAYA
NAGALAND
Kohima
MANIPUR
Imphal
MIZORAM
TRIPURA
Agartala
BANGLADESH
DHAKA
Chittagong
Khulna
Rajshahi
Rangpur
Mymensingh
Comilla
Jessore
Barisal
Dinajpur
Brahmaputra
Ganga
Mouths of the Ganges
The Sundarbans
INDIA
BIHAR
Patna
JHARKHAND
Ranchi
Jamshedpur
Dhanbad
Asansol
WEST BENGAL
KOLKATA (CALCUTTA)
Haora
ORISSA
Cuttack
Bhubaneshwar
Puri
Brahmapur
CHHATTISGARH
Raipur
Durg
UTTAR PRADESH
Lucknow
Varanasi
Allahabad
Kanpur
Gorakhpur
Faizabad
Vishakhapatnam
Vizianagaram
Kakinada
Rajahmundry
Vijayawada
Machilipatnam
Northern Circars
Eastern Ghats
BAY OF BENGAL
INDIAN OCEAN
BURMA (MYANMAR)
RANGOON
Mandalay
Sittwe (Akyab)
Moulmein
Bassein
Pegu
Monywa
Taunggyi
Myitkyina
Bhamo
Lashio
Meiktila
KACHIN
SAGAING
CHIN
MAGWE
ARAKAN
KAYAH
SHAN
MON
IRRAWADDY
PEGU
Arakan Yoma
Pegu Yoma
Chin Hills
Arakan Coast
Irrawaddy
Chindwin
Mouths of the Irrawaddy
G. of Martaban
Cheduba I.
Ramree I.
Preparis North Channel
Preparis South Channel
Paripart Kyun (Burma)
Coco Kyunzu (Burma)
Moscos Is.
THAILAND
Chiang Mai
Chiang Rai
Tropic of Cancer
COPYRIGHT PHILIP'S

1:5 300 000

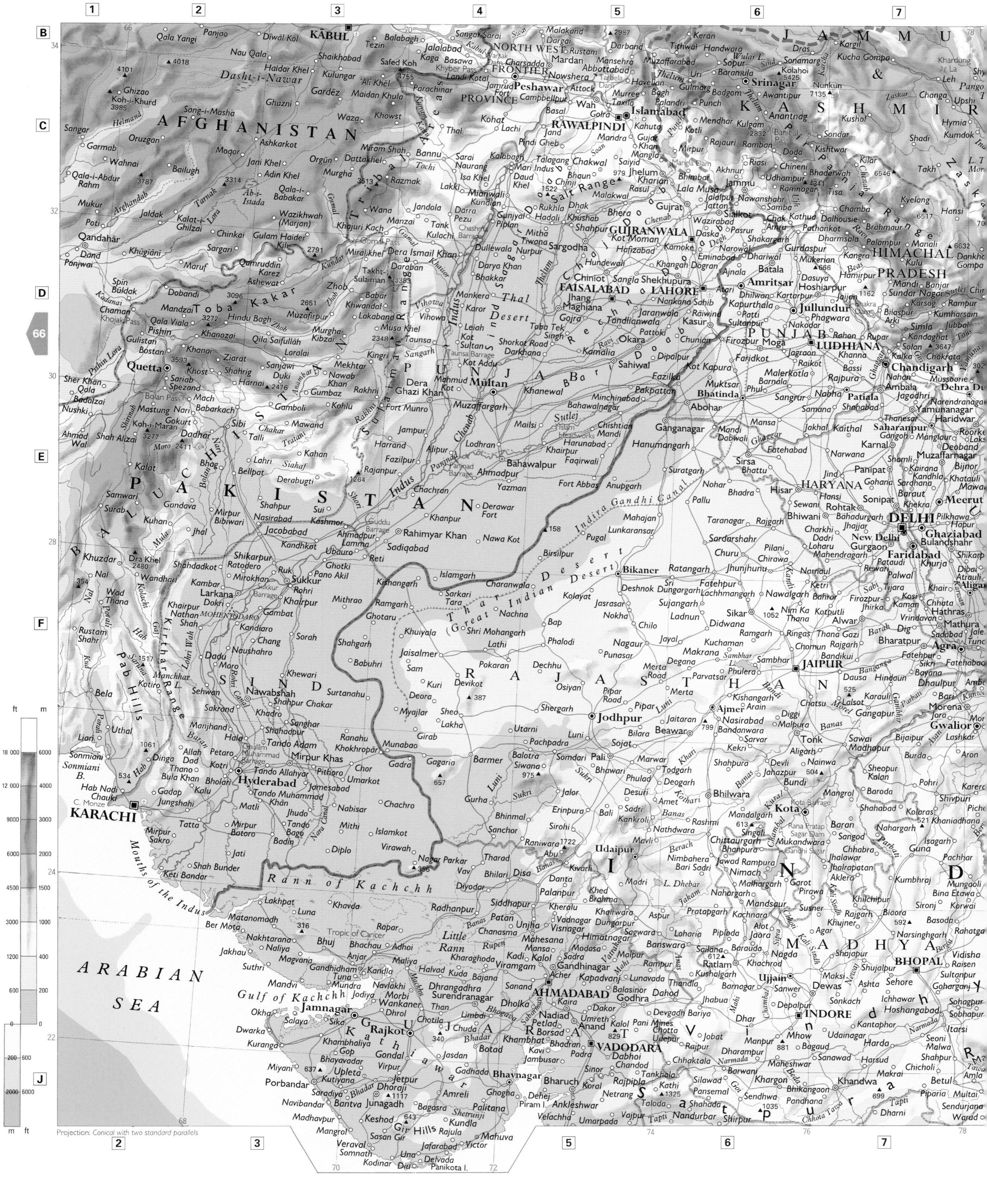
AFGHANISTAN
PAKISTAN
BALUCHISTAN
SIND
PUNJAB
RAJASTHAN
HARYANA
HIMACHAL PRADESH
JAMMU & KASHMIR
MADHYA PRADESH
NORTH WEST FRONTIER PROVINCE
ARABIAN SEA
Gulf of Kachchh
Rann of Kachchh
Thar Desert (Great Indian Desert)
Thal Desert
Mouths of the Indus
Tropic of Cancer
KĀBUL
Peshawar
RAWALPINDI
Islamabad
Srinagar
Quetta
Multan
FAISALABAD
LAHORE
GUJRANWALA
Amritsar
LUDHIANA
Chandigarh
DELHI
New Delhi
JAIPUR
Jodhpur
Bikaner
KARACHI
Hyderabad
AHMADABAD
VADODARA
INDORE
BHOPAL
Projection: Conical with two standard parallels

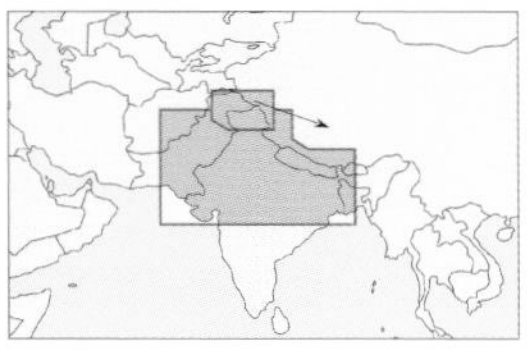

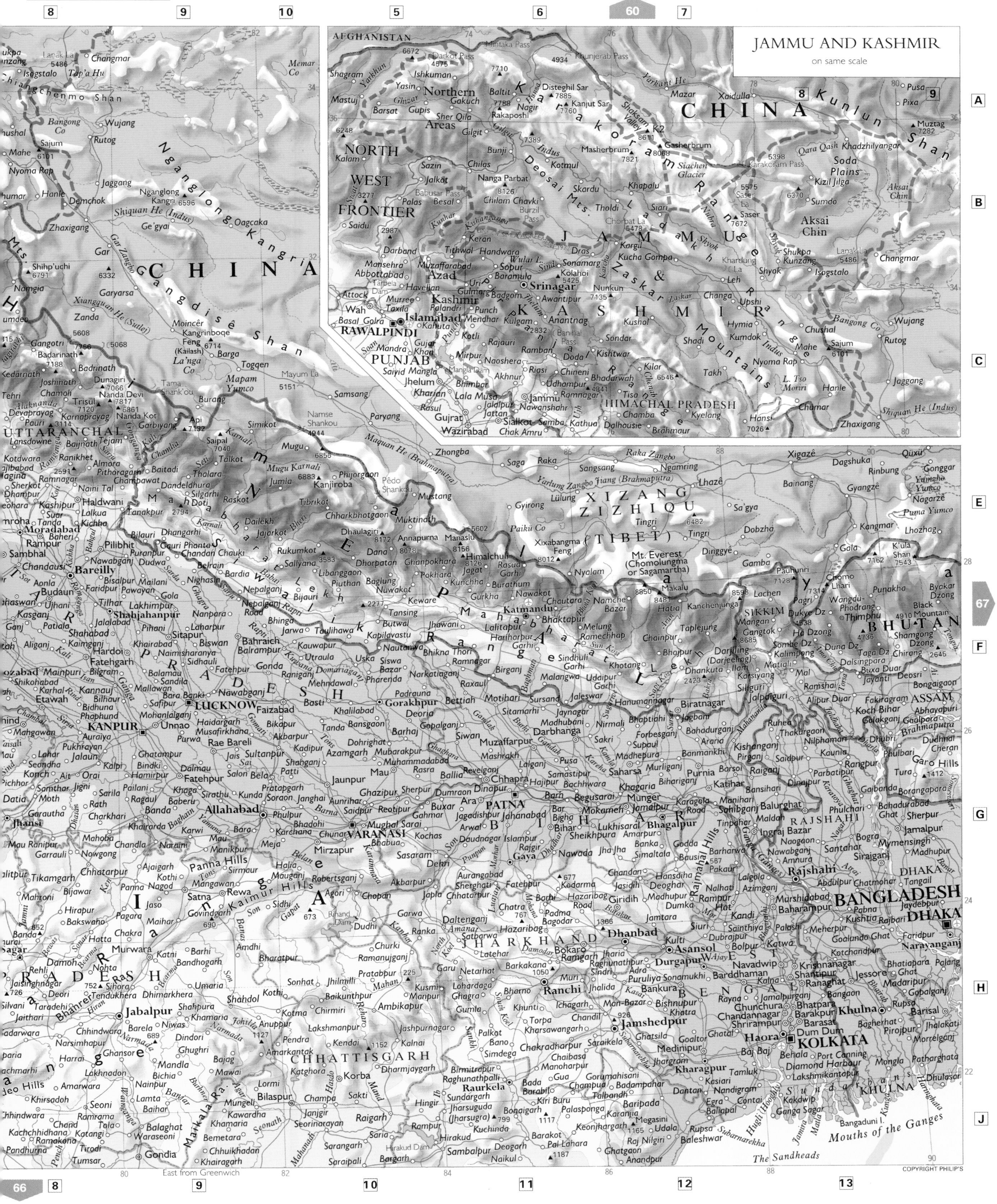
JAMMU AND KASHMIR
on same scale
AFGHANISTAN
CHINA
NORTH WEST FRONTIER
Northern Areas
Azad Kashmir
PUNJAB
RAWALPINDI
Islamabad
Srinagar
JAMMU & KASHMIR
HIMACHAL PRADESH
Karakoram Range
Ladakh Range
Zaskar Mountains
Deosai Mts.
Kunlun Shan
Aksai Chin
K2
Gasherbrum
Nanga Parbat
CHINA
Nganglong Kangri
Gangdisê Shan
UTTARANCHAL
NEPAL
Mahabharat Lekh
Siwalik Range
XIZANG ZIZHIQU (TIBET)
Yarlung Zangbo Jiang (Brahmaputra)
Mt. Everest (Chomolungma or Sagamartha)
Katmandu
SIKKIM
BHUTAN
Thimphu
ASSAM
UTTAR PRADESH
LUCKNOW
KANPUR
Allahabad
VARANASI
PATNA
BIHAR
JHARKHAND
WEST BENGAL
KOLKATA
BANGLADESH
DHAKA
Rajshahi
RAJSHAHI
Khulna
KHULNA
MADHYA PRADESH
CHHATTISGARH
Jabalpur
Ranchi
Jamshedpur
Dhanbad
Mouths of the Ganges
The Sandheads
East from Greenwich
COPYRIGHT PHILIP'S
60
66
67

1:6 200 000

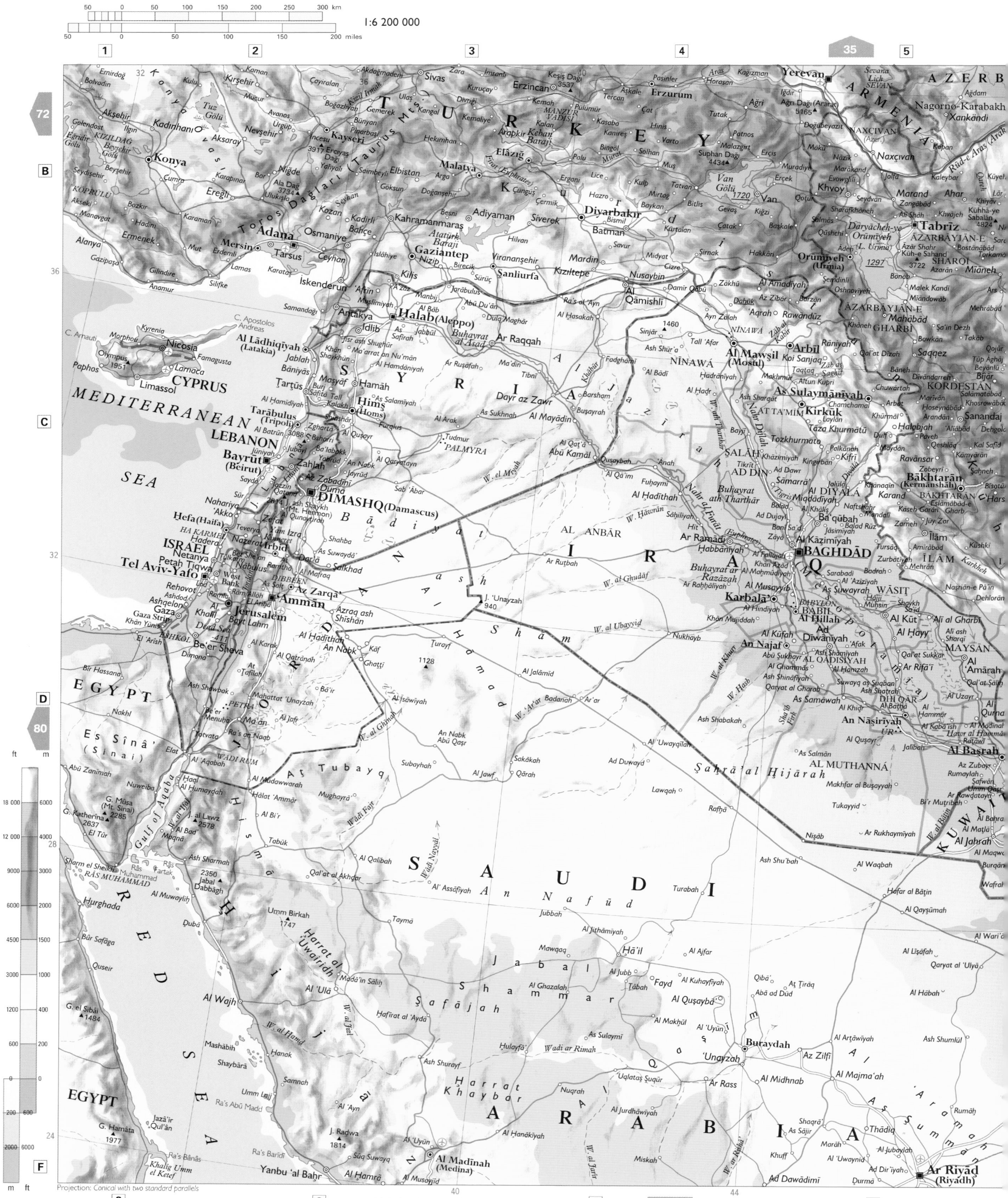

Projection: Conical with two standard parallels

Underlined towns in Iraq give their name to the administrative area in which they stand

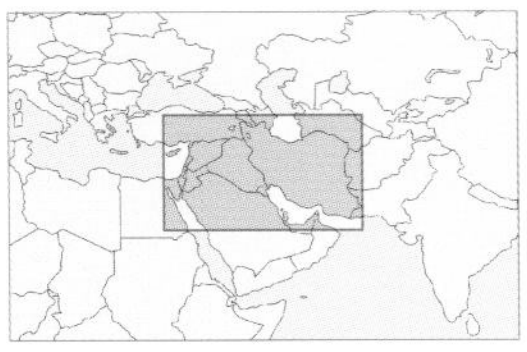

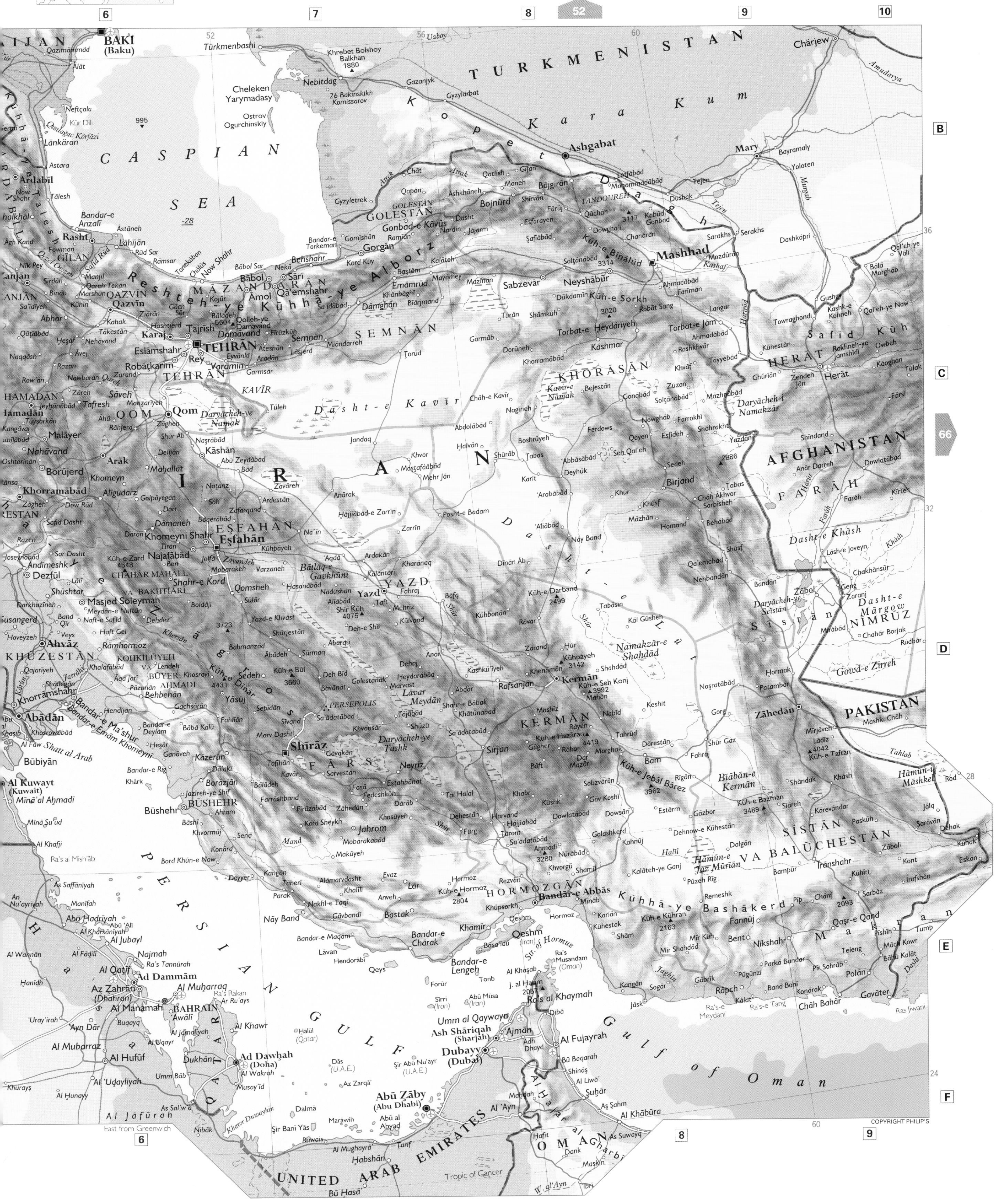

6
7
8
52
9
10
TURKMENISTAN
Kara Kum
Kopet Dagh
CASPIAN SEA
BAKI (Baku)
Türkmenbashi
Cheleken Yarymadasy
Ostrov Ogurchinskiy
Khrebet Bolshoy Balkhan 1880
Nebitdag
Gazanjyk
Gyzylarbat
Ashgabat
Mary
Bayramaly
Yoloten
Chärjew
Amudarya
Tejen
Serakhs
Dashköpri
Uzboy
Neftçala
Kür Dili
Qızılağac Körfäzi
Länkäran
Astara
Ardabil
Tälesh
Bandar-e Anzali
Rasht
GILAN
Lahijan
Qazvin
Abhar
Karaj
Tajrish
TEHRĀN
Eslāmshahr
Rey
Varāmin
Robātkarim
Damāvand
Semnān
SEMNĀN
Dāmghān
Shāhrūd
Mazandaran
Bābol
Sāri
Āmol
Behshahr
Gorgān
GOLESTĀN
Gonbad-e Kāvūs
Bandar-e Torkeman
Bojnūrd
Shirvān
Qūchān
Mashhad
Kūh-e Binālūd
Neyshābūr
Sabzevār
Kūh-e Sorkh
Torbat-e Heydārīyeh
Torbat-e Jām
Kāshmar
KHORĀSĀN
Reshteh-ye Kūhhā-ye Alborz
Dasht-e Kavīr
Kavīr
Daryācheh-ye Namak
Qom
QOM
Kāshān
Sāveh
Arāk
Malāyer
Hamadān
HAMADĀN
Borūjerd
Khorramābād
Ahvāz
Dezfūl
Shūshtar
KHUZESTĀN
Khorramshahr
Ābādān
Bandar-e Ma'shur
Bandar-e Emām Khomeynī
Shatt al Arab
Būbiyān
Al Kuwayt (Kuwait)
Mīnā' al Aḥmadī
Eşfahān
EŞFAHĀN
Najafābād
Khomeynī Shahr
Shahr-e Kord
Kūh-e Zard 4548
CHAHĀR MAHALL VA BAKHTĪARI
Zāgros
Kūh-e Dīnār 4431
KOHKĪLŪYEH VA BŪYER AHMADI
Yāsūj
Behbahān
Bandar-e Deylam
Bandar-e Rig
Būshehr
BŪSHEHR
Kāzerūn
Shīrāz
FĀRS
PERSEPOLIS
Daryācheh-ye Tashk
Neyrīz
Jahrom
Lār
Yazd
YAZD
Shīr Kūh 4075
Kermān
KERMĀN
Rafsanjān
Sīrjān
Bam
Kūh-e Hazārān 4419
Kūh-e Jebāl Bārez 3962
Dasht-e Lūt
Namakzār-e Shahdād
Bīābān-e Kermān
Zāhedān
Zābol
SĪSTĀN VA BALŪCHESTĀN
Kūh-e Taftān 4042
Īrānshahr
Chāh Bahār
Jāsk
Makran
Kūhhā-ye Bashākerd
Bandar-e Abbās
HORMOZGĀN
Qeshm
Str. of Hormuz
Bandar-e Lengeh
Kish
PERSIAN GULF
Gulf of Oman
IRAN
AFGHANISTAN
PAKISTAN
Herāt
HERĀT
Safīd Kūh
Farāh
FARĀH
NĪMRŪZ
Daryācheh-ye Sīstān
Gowd-e Zirreh
Dasht-e Khāsh
Hāmūn-i Māshkel
BAHRAIN
Al Manāmah
Ad Dawḥah (Doha)
QATAR
Al Qaţīf
Ad Dammām
Al Jubayl
Aẓ Ẓahrān (Dhahran)
Al Hufūf
Al Mubarraz
Al Jāfūrah
Abū Ẓaby (Abu Dhabi)
Dubayy (Dubai)
Ash Shāriqah (Sharjah)
Ra's al Khaymah
Al Fujayrah
Al 'Ayn
UNITED ARAB EMIRATES
OMAN
Tropic of Cancer
Ra's Musandam (Oman)
Şuḥār
Al Khābūra
East from Greenwich
COPYRIGHT PHILIP'S
B
C
D
E
F
66

50 0 25 50 75 100 125 150 175 km

50 0 25 50 75 100 125 miles

1: 4 400 000

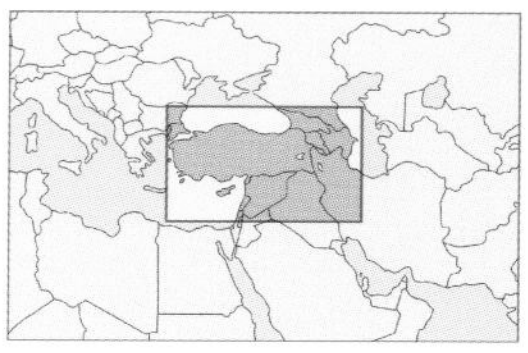

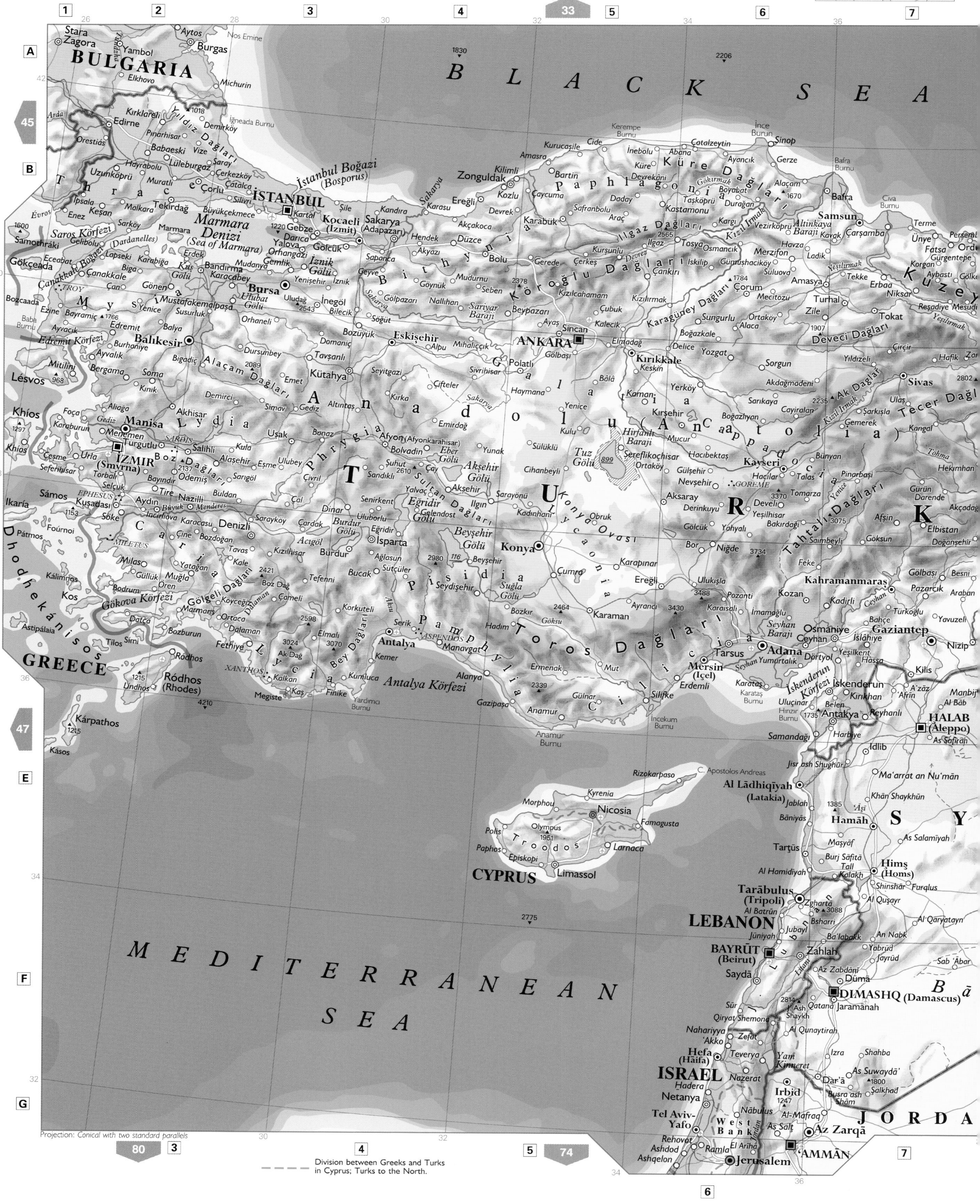

Division between Greeks and Turks in Cyprus; Turks to the North.

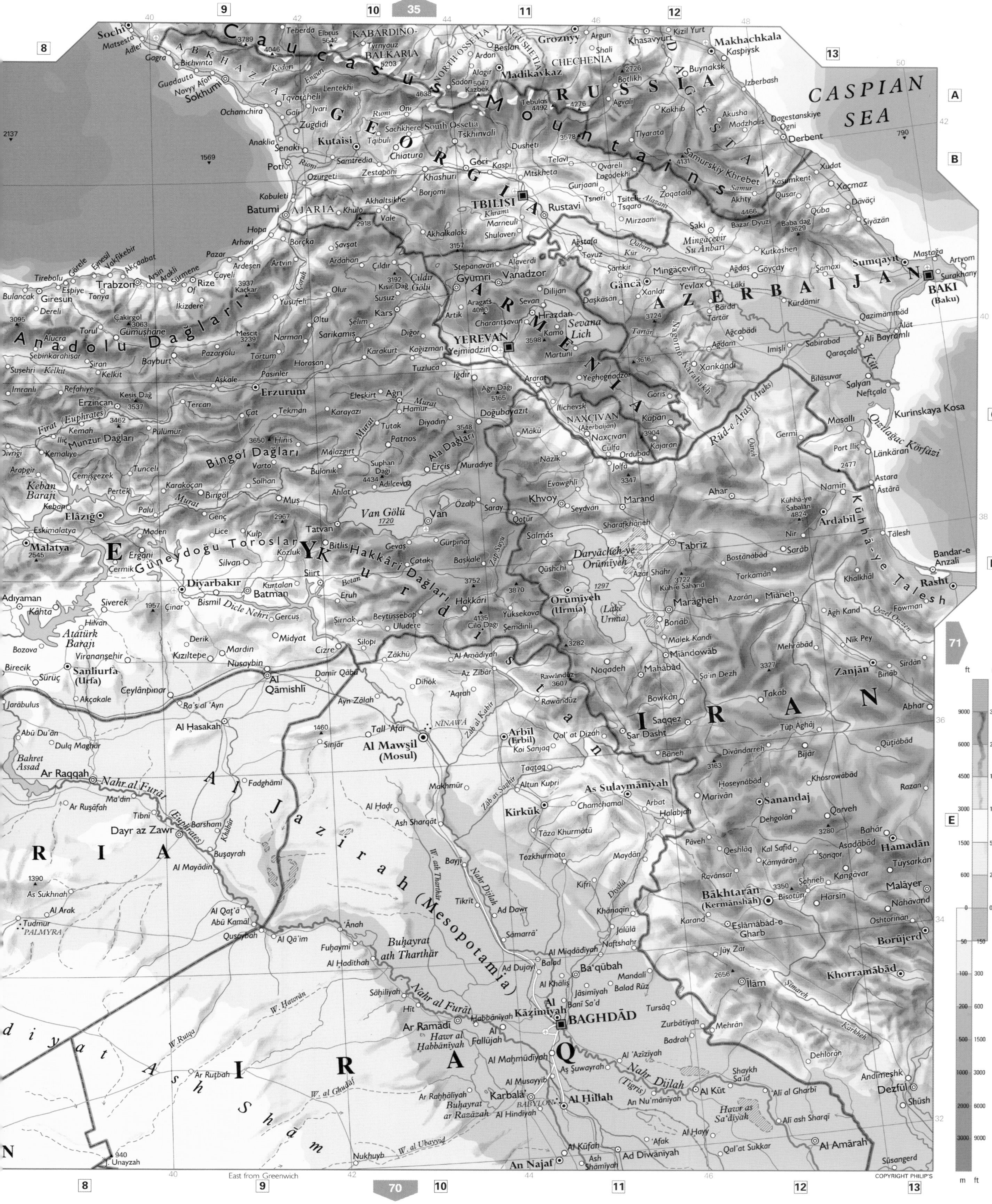
CASPIAN SEA
Caucasus Mountains
GEORGIA
ARMENIA
AZERBAIJAN
RUSSIA
DAGESTAN
CHECHENIA
INGUSHETIA
NORTH OSSETIA
KABARDINO-BALKARIA
ABKHAZIA
AJARIA
South Ossetia
TBILISI
YEREVAN
BAKI (Baku)
Sochi
Sokhumi
Batumi
Kutaisi
Gori
Rustavi
Gumri
Vanadzor
Gäncä
Mingäçevir
Sumqayit
Grozny
Makhachkala
Derbent
Vladikavkaz
Trabzon
Rize
Giresun
Erzurum
Erzincan
Kars
Ağri
Elâzığ
Malatya
Diyarbakır
Batman
Siirt
Van
Van Gölü
Bitlis
Muş
Hakkâri
Mardin
Şanlıurfa (Urfa)
Anadolu Dağları
Munzur Dağları
Bingöl Dağları
Güneydoğu Toroslar
Hakkâri Dağları
Ala Dağları
Kurdistan
Atatürk Barajı
Keban Barajı
NAXÇIVAN (Azerbaijan)
Nagorno-Karabakh
Sevana Lich
Ağri Dağı 5165
Tabriz
Orūmīyeh (Urmia)
Daryācheh-ye Orūmīyeh (Lake Urmia)
Ardabīl
Rasht
Zanjān
Hamadān
Sanandaj
Bākhtarān (Kermānshāh)
Khorramābād
Borūjerd
Dezfūl
Kūhhā-ye Tālesh
IRAN
IRAQ
Al Mawşil (Mosul)
Arbīl (Erbil)
Kirkūk
As Sulaymānīyah
BAGHDĀD
Al Ḩillah
Karbalā'
An Najaf
Al Kūt
Al 'Amārah
Ar Ramādī
Al Fallūjah
Sāmarrā'
Tikrīt
Al Jazīrah (Mesopotamia)
Nahr al Furāt (Euphrates)
Nahr Dijlah (Tigris)
Buḩayrat ath Tharthār
Dayr az Zawr
Ar Raqqah
Al Ḩasakah
Al Qāmishlī
SYRIA
Bādiyat ash Shām
Tudmur PALMYRA
Ar Ruţbah
Qizilağac Körfäzi
Kurinskaya Kosa
Mount Elbrus 5642
Kazbek 5047
East from Greenwich
COPYRIGHT PHILIP'S

10 0 10 20 30 40 50 60 70 80 100 km

1:2 200 000

10 0 10 20 30 40 50 60 miles

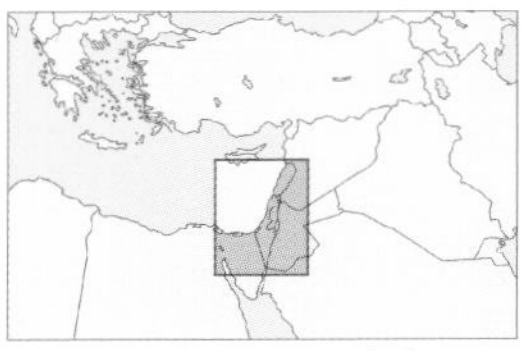

1974 Cease Fire Lines

National Parks

72 70 80 80

1:13 300 000

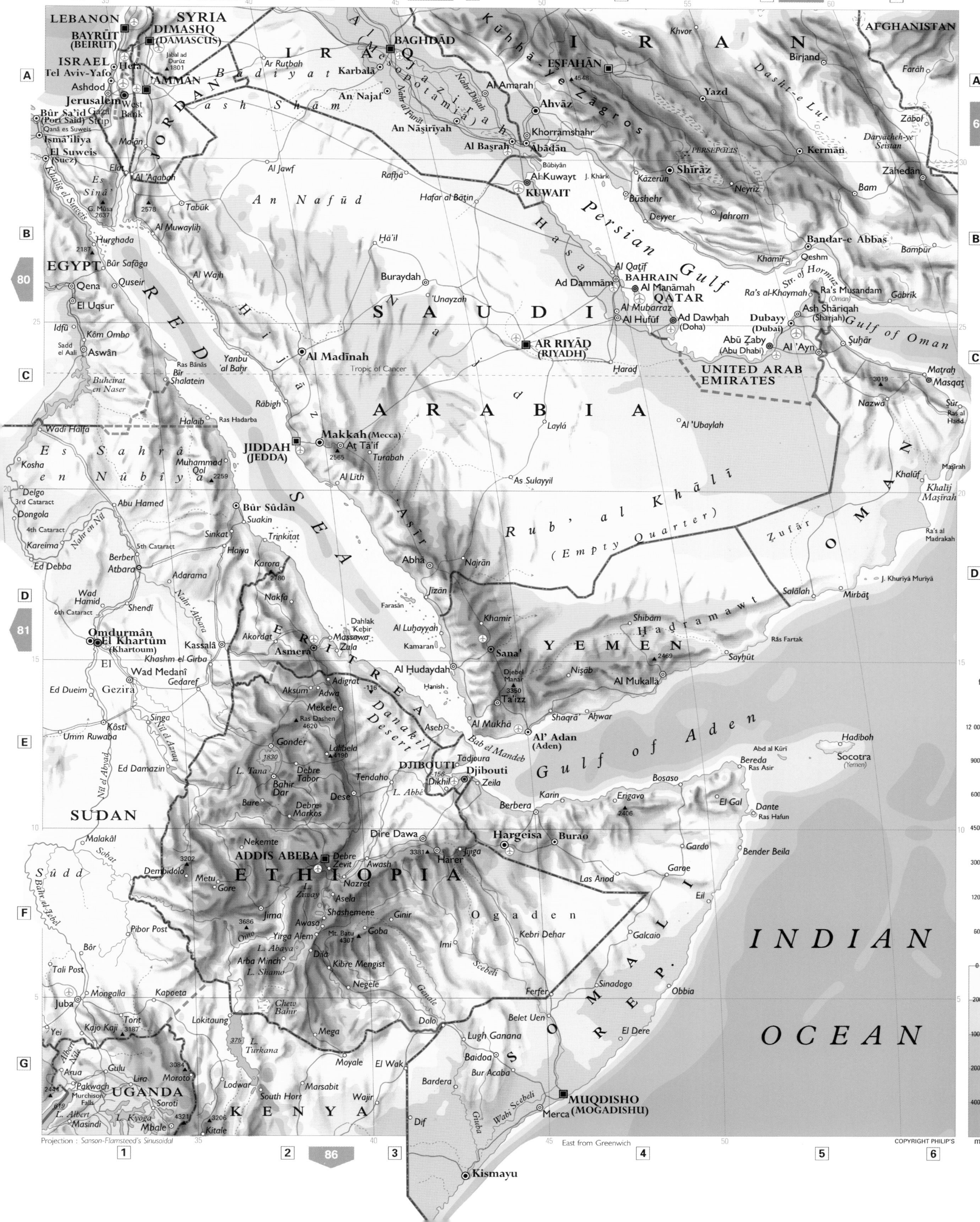

Projection : Sanson-Flamsteed's Sinusoidal

East from Greenwich

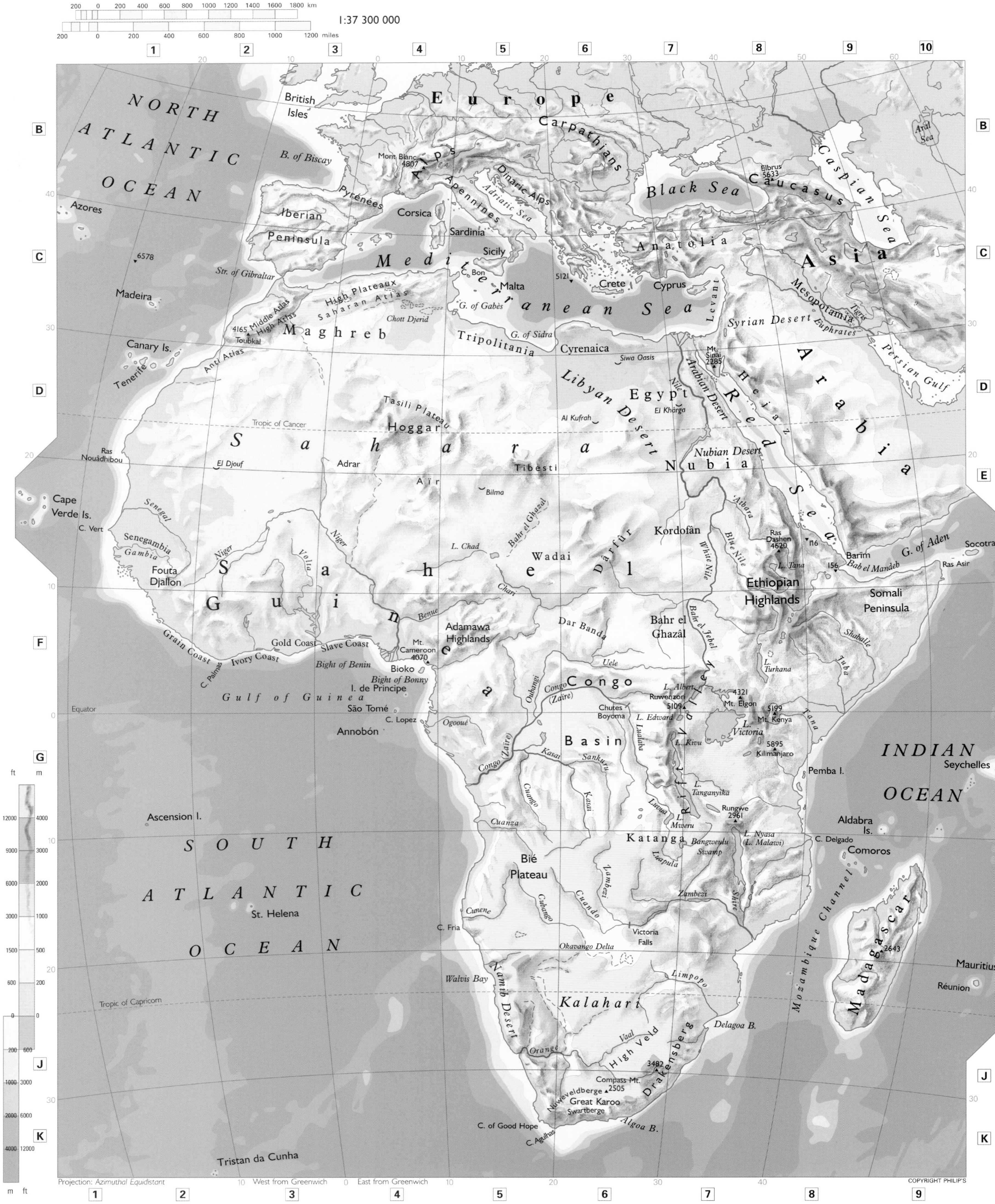
200 0 200 400 600 800 1000 1200 1400 1600 1800 km
200 0 200 400 600 800 1000 1200 miles
1:37 300 000
NORTH ATLANTIC OCEAN
Azores
Madeira
Canary Is.
Tenerife
Cape Verde Is.
C. Vert
British Isles
B. of Biscay
Pyrénées
Iberian Peninsula
Str. of Gibraltar
Europe
Carpathians
Mont Blanc 4807
Alps
Apennines
Adriatic Sea
Dinaric Alps
Corsica
Sardinia
Sicily
Black Sea
Elbrus 5633
Caucasus
Caspian Sea
Aral Sea
Anatolia
Asia
Mediterranean Sea
C. Bon
Malta
Crete
Cyprus
5121
Levant
Mesopotamia
Tigris
Euphrates
Syrian Desert
Persian Gulf
Arabia
High Plateaux
Saharan Atlas
Middle Atlas
High Atlas
4165 Toubkal
Anti Atlas
Maghreb
Chott Djerid
G. of Gabès
G. of Sidra
Tripolitania
Cyrenaica
Siwa Oasis
Mt. Sinai 2285
Hejaz
Red Sea
Arabian Desert
Nile
Libyan Desert
Egypt
El Kharga
Al Kufrah
Tasili Plateau
Hoggar
Tropic of Cancer
Sahara
Ras Nouâdhibou
El Djouf
Adrar
Aïr
Tibesti
Bilma
Nubian Desert
Nubia
Atbara
Senegal
Senegambia
Gambia
Fouta Djallon
Niger
Volta
Sahel
L. Chad
Bahr el Ghazal
Wadai
Darfur
Kordofân
White Nile
Blue Nile
Ras Dashen 4620
L. Tana
Ethiopian Highlands
Barim
Bab el Mandeb
G. of Aden
Socotra
Ras Asir
Somali Peninsula
Chari
Benue
Guinea
Grain Coast
Ivory Coast
Gold Coast
Slave Coast
C. Palmas
Bight of Benin
Bight of Bonny
Mt. Cameroon 4070
Adamawa Highlands
Bioko
I. de Principe
São Tomé
Gulf of Guinea
Equator
C. Lopez
Annobón
Dar Banda
Bahr el Ghazâl
Bahr el Jebel
Shabale
Juba
L. Turkana
Uele
Oubangi
Congo (Zaïre)
Congo Basin
Chutes Boyoma
L. Albert
Ruwenzori 5109
4321 Mt. Elgon
5199 Mt. Kenya
L. Edward
L. Victoria
L. Kivu
5895 Kilimanjaro
Tana
Rift Valley
Ogooué
Kasai
Sankuru
Lualaba
Cuango
Lukuga
L. Tanganyika
Rungwe 2961
INDIAN OCEAN
Seychelles
Pemba I.
Cuanza
L. Mweru
Katanga
Bangweulu Swamp
Luapula
L. Nyasa (L. Malawi)
Aldabra Is.
C. Delgado
Comoros
Bié Plateau
Zambezi
Cuando
Cubango
Cunene
Shire
Mozambique Channel
Madagascar
2643
C. Fria
Victoria Falls
Okavango Delta
Walvis Bay
Namib Desert
Kalahari
Limpopo
Mauritius
Réunion
Delagoa B.
Tropic of Capricorn
Vaal
High Veld
Orange
Drakensberg
3482
Compass Mt. 2505
Nuweveldberge
Great Karoo
Swartberge
C. of Good Hope
C. Agulhas
Algoa B.
Ascension I.
SOUTH ATLANTIC OCEAN
St. Helena
Tristan da Cunha
Projection: Azimuthal Equidistant
West from Greenwich
East from Greenwich
COPYRIGHT PHILIP'S
ft m
12000 4000
9000 3000
6000 2000
3000 1000
1500 500
600 200
0 0
200 600
1000 3000
2000 6000
4000 12000
m ft

1:37 300 000
200 0 200 400 600 800 1000 1200 1400 1600 1800 km
200 0 200 400 600 800 1000 1200 miles
NORTH ATLANTIC OCEAN
SOUTH ATLANTIC OCEAN
INDIAN OCEAN
Mediterranean Sea
Black Sea
Caspian Sea
Red Sea
Persian Gulf
Gulf of Guinea
Bight of Benin
B. of Biscay
G. of Aden
Mozambique Channel
Sahara
Tropic of Cancer
Tropic of Capricorn
Equator
MOROCCO
ALGERIA
TUNISIA
LIBYA
EGYPT
WESTERN SAHARA
MAURITANIA
MALI
NIGER
CHAD
SUDAN
SENEGAL
GAMBIA
GUINEA-BISSAU
GUINEA
SIERRA LEONE
LIBERIA
IVORY COAST
BURKINA FASO
GHANA
TOGO
BENIN
NIGERIA
CAMEROON
CENTRAL AFRICAN REP.
EQUATORIAL GUINEA
SÃO TOMÉ & PRINCIPE
GABON
CONGO
CONGO (DEM. REP. OF THE)
CABINDA (Angola)
ERITREA
DJIBOUTI
ETHIOPIA
SOMALI REP.
UGANDA
KENYA
RWANDA
BURUNDI
TANZANIA
ANGOLA
ZAMBIA
MALAWI
MOZAMBIQUE
ZIMBABWE
NAMIBIA
BOTSWANA
SOUTH AFRICA
LESOTHO
SWAZ.
MADAGASCAR
COMOROS
Mayotte (Fr.)
SEYCHELLES
MAURITIUS
Réunion (Fr.)
Aldabra Is.
CAPE VERDE IS.
Canary Is. (Sp.)
Madeira (Port.)
Azores (Port.)
Ascension I. (U.K.)
St. Helena (U.K.)
Tristan da Cunha (U.K.)
Annobón
Socotra (Yemen)
UNITED KINGDOM
NETH.
BELG.
GERMANY
POLAND
FRANCE
SWITZ.
AUSTRIA
CZECH REP.
SLOVAK REP.
HUNGARY
ROMANIA
CROATIA
BOS.-HERZ.
SERBIA & MONT.
BULGARIA
MAC.
ALB.
ITALY
GREECE
SPAIN
PORTUGAL
RUSSIA
UKRAINE
KAZAKHSTAN
GEORGIA
ARM.
AZER.
TURKMEN.
TURKEY
CYPRUS
SYRIA
LEB.
ISRAEL
JORDAN
IRAQ
IRAN
KUWAIT
BAHRAIN
QATAR
SAUDI ARABIA
YEMEN
Syrian Desert
LONDON
PARIS
Madrid
Lisbon
Rome
Warsaw
Prague
Vienna
Kiev
Odessa
Volgograd
Ankara
Athens
TEHRĀN
Baghdād
Damascus
Riyadh
CAIRO
Algiers
Tunis
Tripoli
Rabat
Dakar
Bamako
Niamey
Ouagadougou
Abuja
Ndjamena
Khartoum
Addis Ababa
Nairobi
Kinshasa
Luanda
Lusaka
Harare
Pretoria
Maputo
Cape Town
Antananarivo
Mogadishu
Dar es Salaam
Capital Cities
Projection: Azimuthal Equidistant
West from Greenwich
East from Greenwich
COPYRIGHT PHILIP'S

1:13 300 000

km 100 0 100 200 300 400 500 600
miles 100 0 100 200 300 400
ATLANTIC OCEAN
Azores (Port.)
Madeira (Port.)
Funchal
Porto Santo
Islas Canarias (Sp.)
SPAIN
Málaga
Almería
Cádiz
Gibraltar (U.K.)
Str. of Gibraltar
Tanger
Ceuta (Sp.)
Melilla (Sp.)
MOROCCO
Rabat
CASABLANCA
Marrakech
Fès
Meknès
Agadir
Haut Atlas
Moyen Atlas
Anti Atlas
ALGER (ALGIERS)
Oran
ALGERIA
Grand Erg Occidental
Grand Erg Oriental
Plateau du Tademaït
Tassili n Ajjer
Ahaggar
Tamanrasset
WESTERN SAHARA
El Aaiún
Dakhla
Tropic of Cancer
MAURITANIA
Nouakchott
Nouâdhibou
Adrar
Aoukâr
El Djouf
Erg Chech
Tanezrouft
Adrar des Iforas
MALI
Bamako
Tombouctou
Gao
NIGER
Niamey
Agadez
Aïr
Ténéré
SENEGAL
DAKAR
St. Louis
GAMBIA
Banjul
GUINEA BISSAU
Bissau
GUINEA
Conakry
Fouta Djallon
SIERRA LEONE
Freetown
LIBERIA
Monrovia
IVORY COAST
ABIDJAN
Yamoussoukro
BURKINA FASO
Ouagadougou
GHANA
Accra
Kumasi
TOGO
Lomé
BENIN
Porto-Novo
Cotonou
NIGERIA
LAGOS
IBADAN
Kano
Abuja
Grain Coast
Ivory Coast
Gold Coast
Slave Coast
Bight of Benin
Bioko
Projection : Sanson-Flamsteed's Sinusoidal
West from Greenwich 0 East from Greenwich

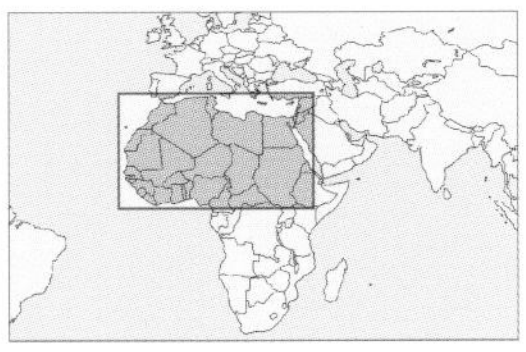

MEDITERRANEAN SEA
RED SEA
LIBYA
EGYPT
SUDAN
CHAD
CENTRAL AFRICAN REPUBLIC
ETHIOPIA
ERITREA
SAUDI ARABIA
SYRIA
LEBANON
ISRAEL
JORDAN
IRAQ
TURKEY
GREECE
CYPRUS
MALTA
TUNISIA
Niger
Sicilia
Kriti
Rodhos
TUNIS
Tarābulus (Tripoli)
Banghāzī
EL ISKANDARÎYA (ALEXANDRIA)
EL QÂHIRA (CAIRO)
EL GÎZA
BAYRŪT (BEIRUT)
DIMASHQ (DAMASCUS)
'AMMĀN
Jerusalem
HALAB
ADANA
Antalya
Nicosia
Valletta
Sahrâ' Lîbîya
Es Sahrâ en Nûbîya
Cyrenaica
Tripolitania
Fezzan
Tibesti
Borkou
Ennedi
Dârfûr
Kordofân
Sudd
Bahr el Ghazâl
El Istiwa'iya
Aozou Strip
Grand Erg du Bilma
Erg du Djourab
Dépression du Mourdi
Lac Tchad
Ndjamena
Omdurmân
El Khartûm (Khartoum)
Port Sudan
Bangui
Yaoundé
Nahr en Nil
Nil el Abyad
Nil el Azraq
Buheirat en Naser
Aswân
Asyût
Sabhah
Al Kufrah
Abéché
El Fasher
El Obeid
Juba
Maiduguri
Garoua
Emi Koussi 3415
Djebel Mara 3088

75
84
86

1:7 100 000

50 0 50 100 150 200 250 300 km
50 0 50 100 150 200 miles
74
75
79
THE NILE DELTA
1:3 600 000
MEDITERRANEAN SEA
Rashîd (Rosetta)
EL ISKANDARÎYA (Alexandria)
Damanhûr
El Dilingat
Shibîn el Kôm
Tanta
El Mahalla el Kubra
Dumyât (Damietta)
Bûr Sa'îd (Port Said)
El Mansûra
Zagazig
Ismâ'ilîya
Shubrâ el Kheima
Imbâbah
El Gîza
EL QÂHIRA (Cairo)
Heliopolis
El Suweis (Suez)
El Faiyûm
Beni Suef
Helwân
East from Greenwich
Tropic of Cancer
MEDITERRANEAN SEA
Es Sahrâ el Gharbîya
(Western Desert)
Munkhafed el Qattâra (Qattâra Depression)
Ed-Déffa (Libyan Plateau)
Marsa Matrûh
Siwa
El Wâhât el Bahariya
El Wâhât el-Farâfra
El Wâhât el-Dakhla
El Wâhât el-Khârga
El Minya
Asyût
Sohâg
Qena
El Uqsur (Luxor)
Aswân
Buheirat en Naser (Lake Nasser)
Wadi Halfa
Es Sahrâ en Nûbîya (Nubian Desert)
Es Sahrâ esh Sharqîya
Khalig el Suweis
Es Sînâ'
G. of Aqaba
Tel Aviv-Yafo
Jerusalem (Al Quds)
'Ammân
ISRAEL
JORDAN
Al 'Aqabah
SAUDI ARABIA
Al Madinah (Medina)
Yanbu 'al Bahr
Jiddah (Jedda)
Makkah (Mecca)
At Tâ'if
Al Qunfudhah
Abha
BAHR EL AHMAR
Bûr Sûdân (Port Sudan)
Suakin
Berber
Atbara
Ed Damer
Dongola
Merowe
Karima
Third Cataract
Fourth Cataract
Fifth Cataract
Gilf el Kebir
Hadabat el Gilf el Kebir
ESH SHAMÂLIYA
Sahrâ
A
B
C
D
2
3
4
6
7
8
20
25
30
32
35

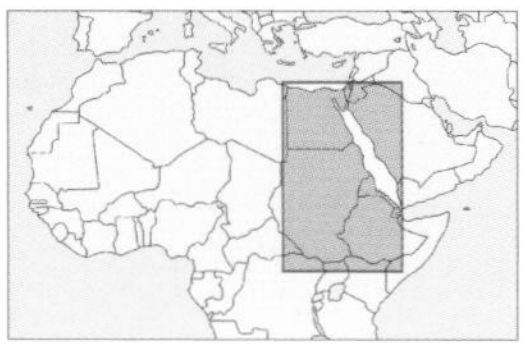

National Parks

Nature Reserves and Game Reserves

∴ UNESCO World Heritage Sites

1:7 100 000

S A H A
MAURITANIA
Nouakchott
Akjoujt
Ouject
Bennichchab
Nouâmghâr
Râs Timirist
Et Tidra
BANC D'ARGUIN
Bou Rjeimât
Sebkhet Te-n-Dghâmcha
Rachid
Tidjikja
Tagânt
Tîchît
Akreijit
Aratâne
Aoukâr
El Mreyyé
Moudjeria
Boutilimit
Magta Lahjar
Boûmdeid
Tâmchekket
Tagourâret
Oualâta
Mederdra
Aleg
Mâl
Bogué
Kiffa
'Ayoûn el 'Atroûs
Néma
Timbedgha
Kobenni
Boulouli
Rosso
Dagana
Podor
Kaédi
Mbout
Kankossa
Massif de l'Assaba
Sélibabi
Nioro du Sahel
Araouane
Bou Djébéha
Tombouctou (Timbuktu)
Goundam
Diré
Niafounké
L. Faguibine
Râs el Mâ
Bassikounou
Nampala
Douentza
Mopti
Djenné
Tenenkou
Macina
Ségou
Niono
Sansanding
Bamako
Koulikoro
Kati
Kita
Kayes
Bafoulabé
Sikasso
Koutiala
San
Bobo-Dioulasso
Banfora
Orodara
SENEGAL
St. Louis
Louga
Linguère
Vallée du Ferlo
Thiès
DAKAR
Rufisque
Diourbel
Mbour
Fatick
Kaolack
Kaffrine
Tambacounda
Kédougou
Kolda
Ziguinchor
Sédhiou
GAMBIA
Banjul
Brikama
Casamance
C. Vert
GUINEA-BISSAU
Bissau
Bolama
Arquipélago dos Bijagós
Bafatá
Gabú
GUINEA
Fouta Djallon
Labé
Kindia
Conakry
Îles de Los
Kankan
Faranah
Kissidougou
Guékédou
Macenta
Nzérékoré
Siguiri
Kouroussa
Dabola
Boké
Mamou
SIERRA LEONE
Freetown
Makeni
Bo
Kenema
Sherbro I.
LIBERIA
Monrovia
Buchanan
Greenville
Harper
Gbarnga
Robertsport
IVORY COAST
Yamoussoukro
ABIDJAN
Bouaké
Korhogo
Daloa
Man
Odienné
Séguéla
Gagnoa
Divo
Sassandra
San Pédro
Grand Bassam
Ferkessédougou
Katiola
Dimbokro
ATLANTIC OCEAN
Grain Coast
Ivory Coast
GULF
Projection: Lambert's Equivalent Azimuthal
West from Greenw

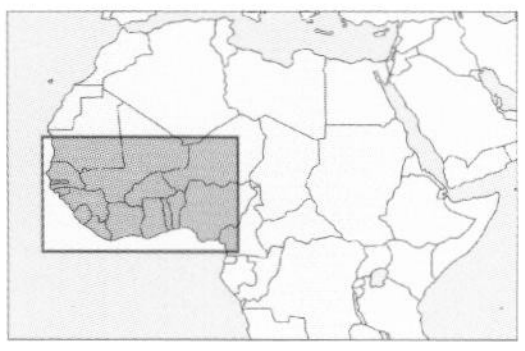

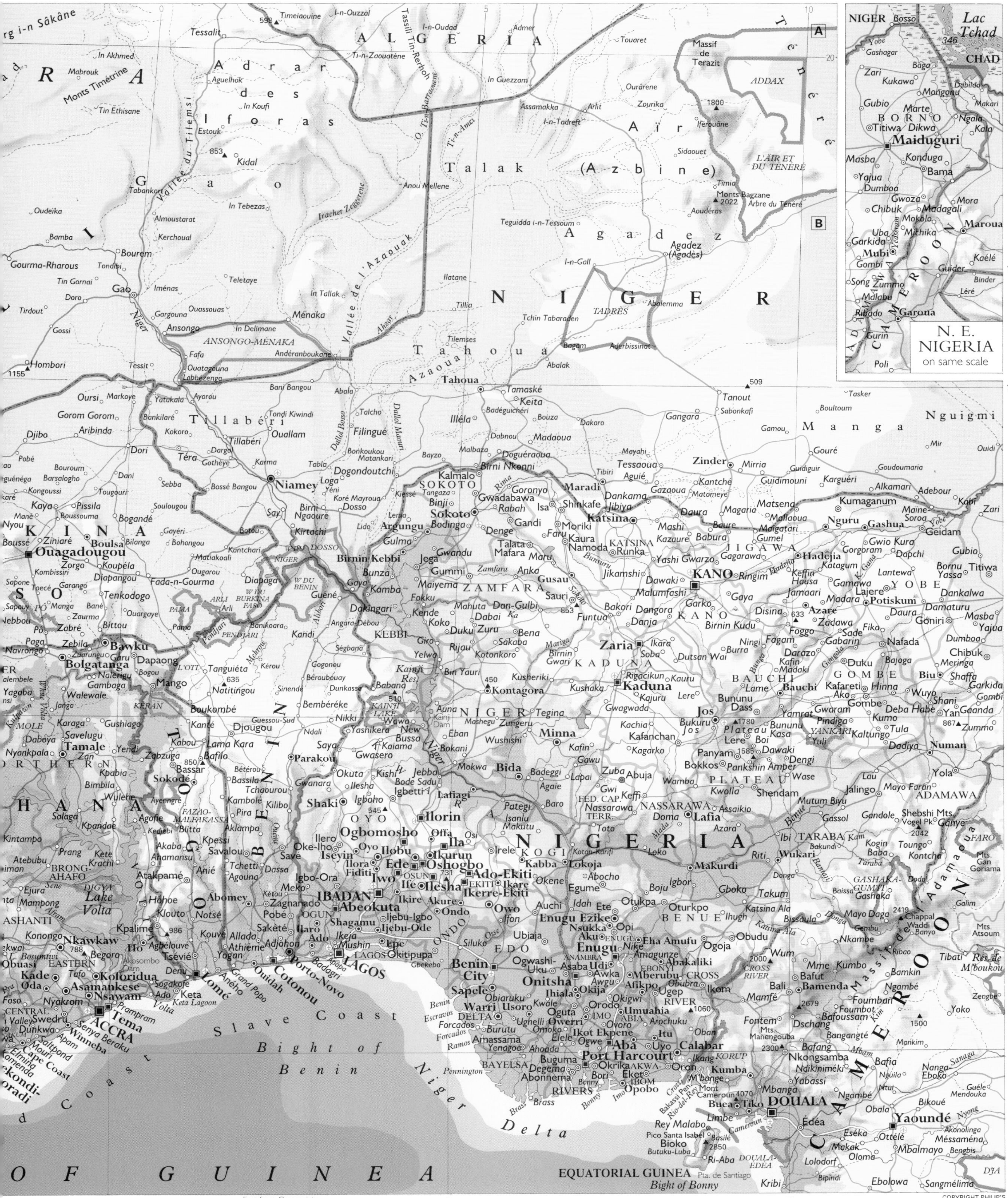

National Parks

Nature Reserves and Game Reserves

∴ UNESCO World Heritage Sites

1:13 300 000

100 0 100 200 300 400 500 600 km

100 0 100 200 300 400 miles

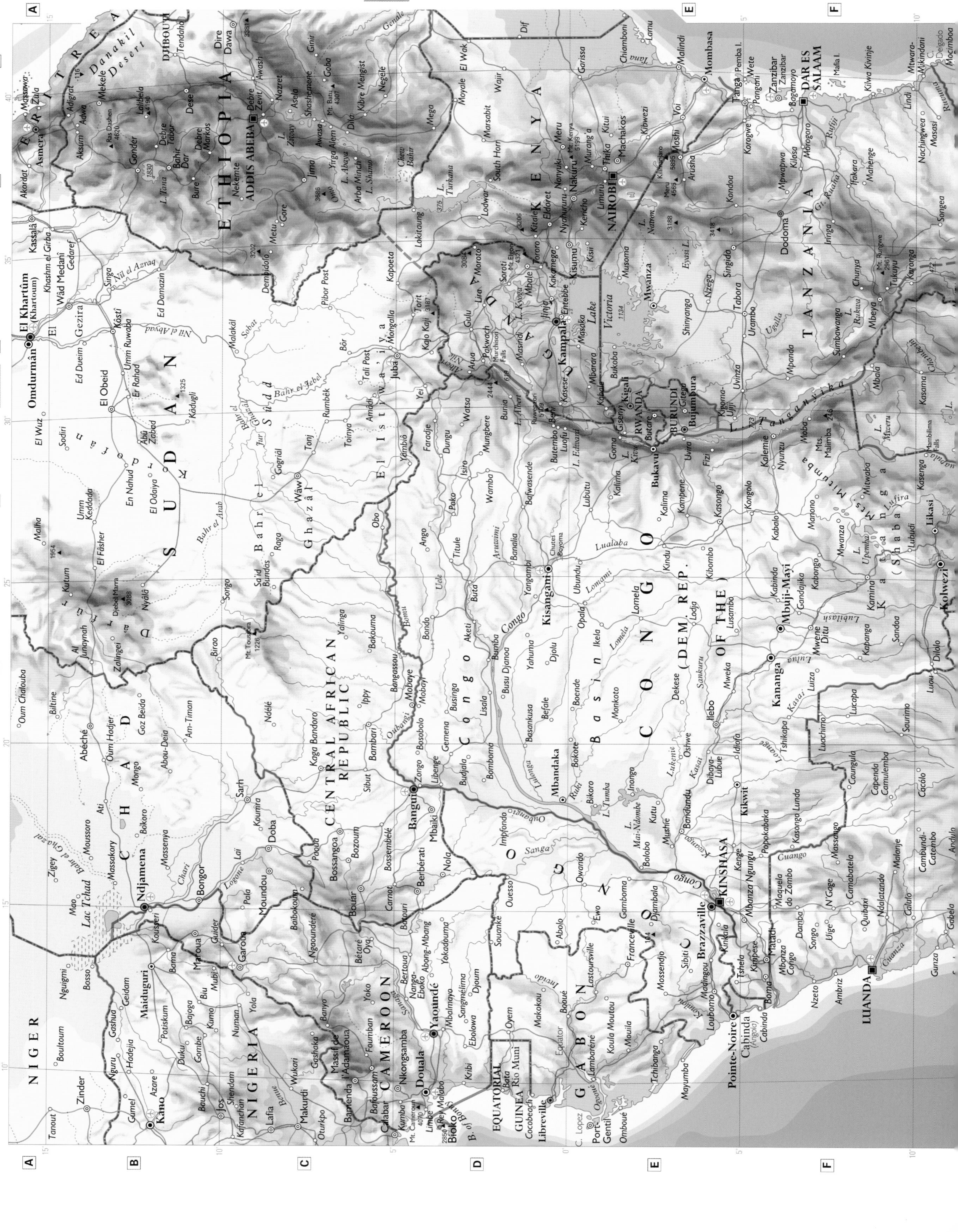

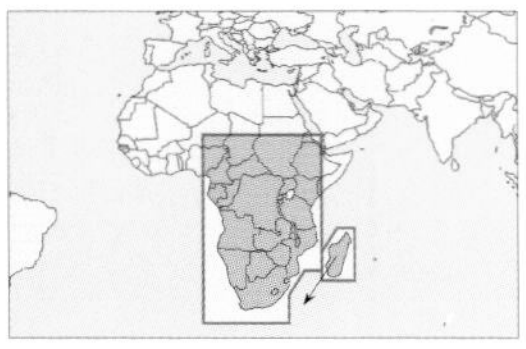

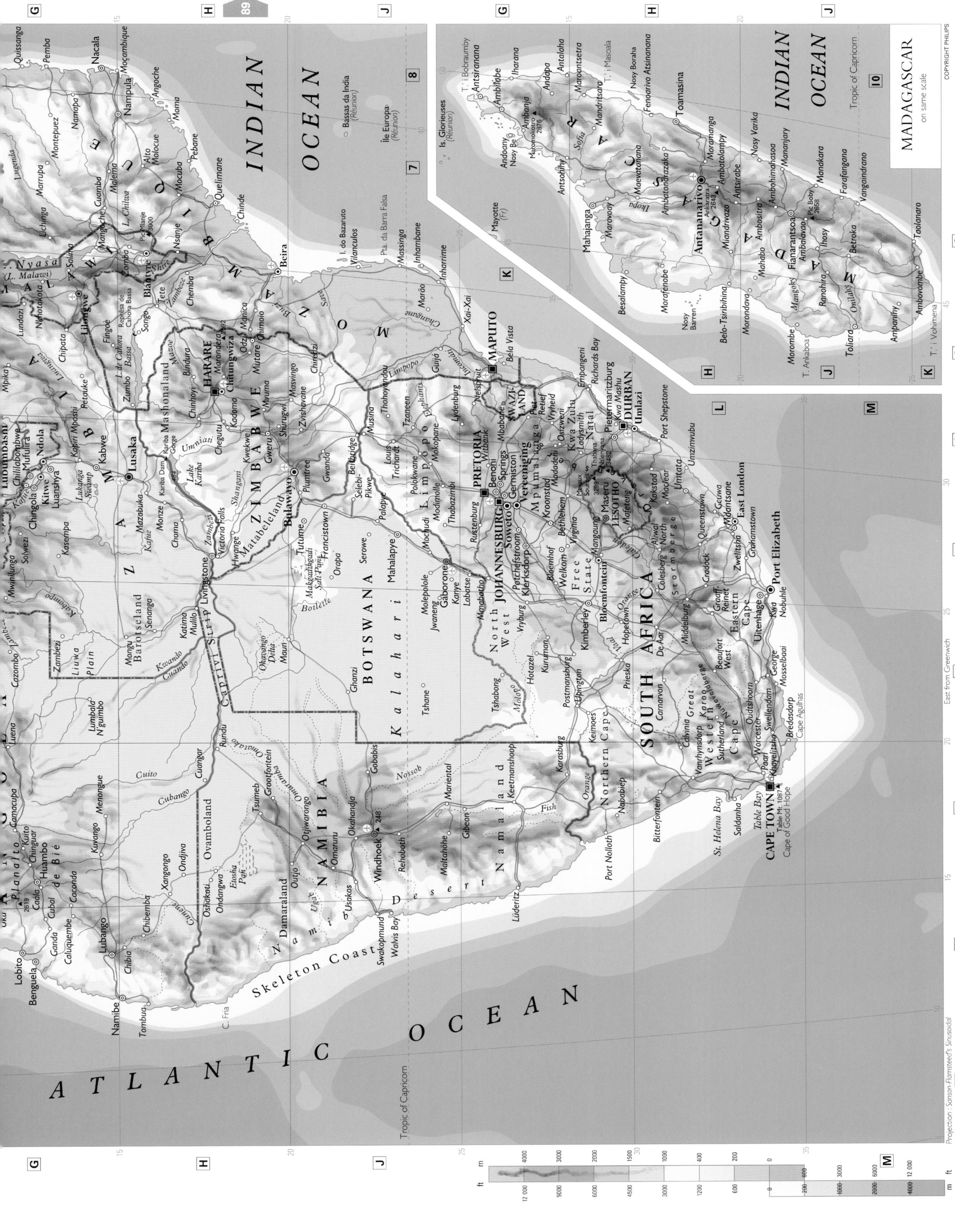

ATLANTIC OCEAN
INDIAN OCEAN
NAMIBIA
BOTSWANA
SOUTH AFRICA
ZIMBABWE
ZAMBIA
MOZAMBIQUE
LESOTHO
SWAZILAND
MADAGASCAR
on same scale
Kalahari
Namib Desert
Skeleton Coast
Tropic of Capricorn
CAPE TOWN
PRETORIA
JOHANNESBURG
HARARE
MAPUTO
Lusaka
DURBAN
Windhoek
Bulawayo
Gaborone
Bloemfontein
Port Elizabeth
East London
Maseru
Beira
Antananarivo
Toamasina
Cape of Good Hope
Cape Agulhas
Projection : Sanson-Flamsteed's Sinusoidal
East from Greenwich
COPYRIGHT PHILIPS

50 0 50 100 150 200 250 300 km

50 0 50 100 150 200 miles

1:7 100 000

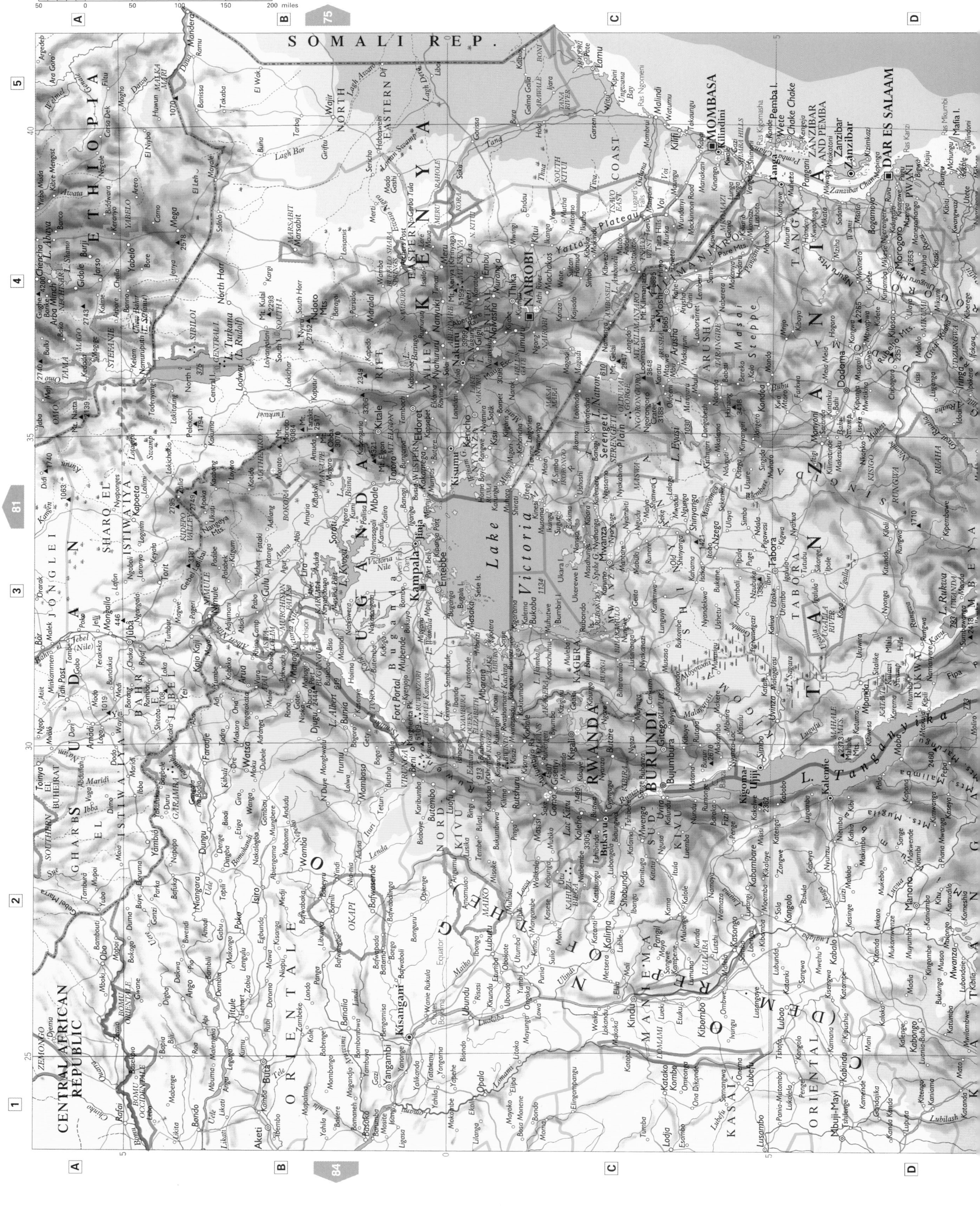

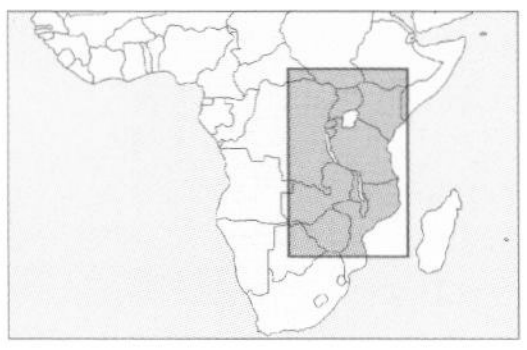

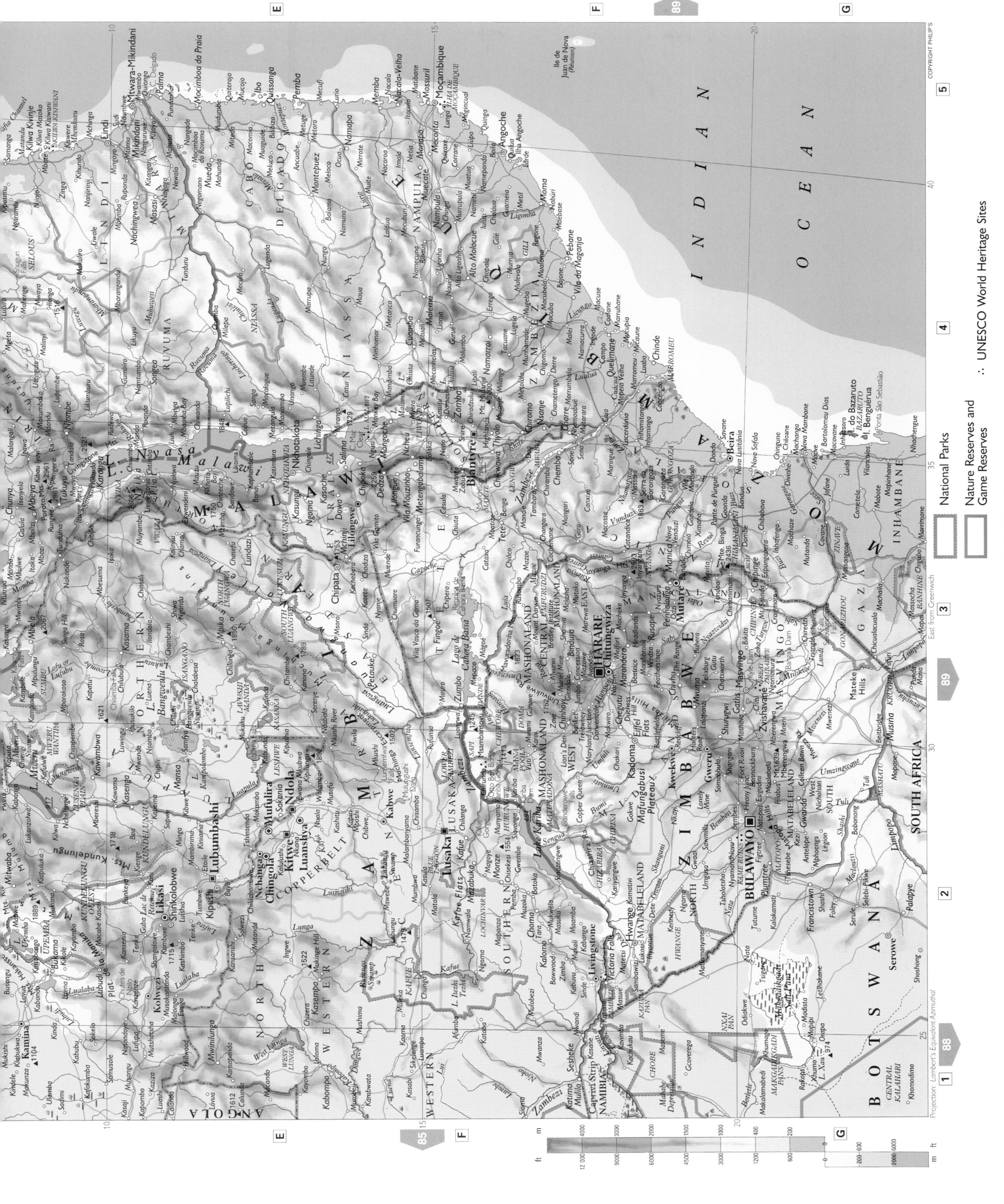

INDIAN OCEAN
ZAMBIA
ZIMBABWE
MALAWI
MOZAMBIQUE
BOTSWANA
SOUTH AFRICA
NAMIBIA
ANGOLA
LUSAKA
HARARE
BULAWAYO
Lilongwe
Blantyre
Beira
Lusaka
Ndola
Kitwe
Mutare
Gweru
Kwekwe
Livingstone
Victoria Falls
Lake Kariba
L. Nyasa
L. Malawi
L. Mweru
Zambezi
Limpopo
Nampula
Moçambique
Pemba
Lindi
Mtwara-Mikindani
Ile de Juan de Nova (Réunion)
National Parks
Nature Reserves and Game Reserves
UNESCO World Heritage Sites
Projection: Lambert's Equivalent Azimuthal
East from Greenwich
COPYRIGHT PHILIP'S
85
88
89

50 0 50 100 150 200 250 300 km

50 0 50 100 150 200 miles

1:7 100 000

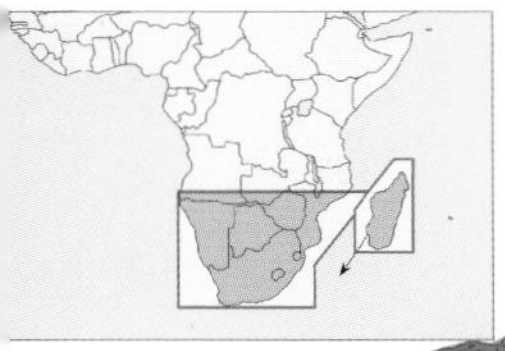

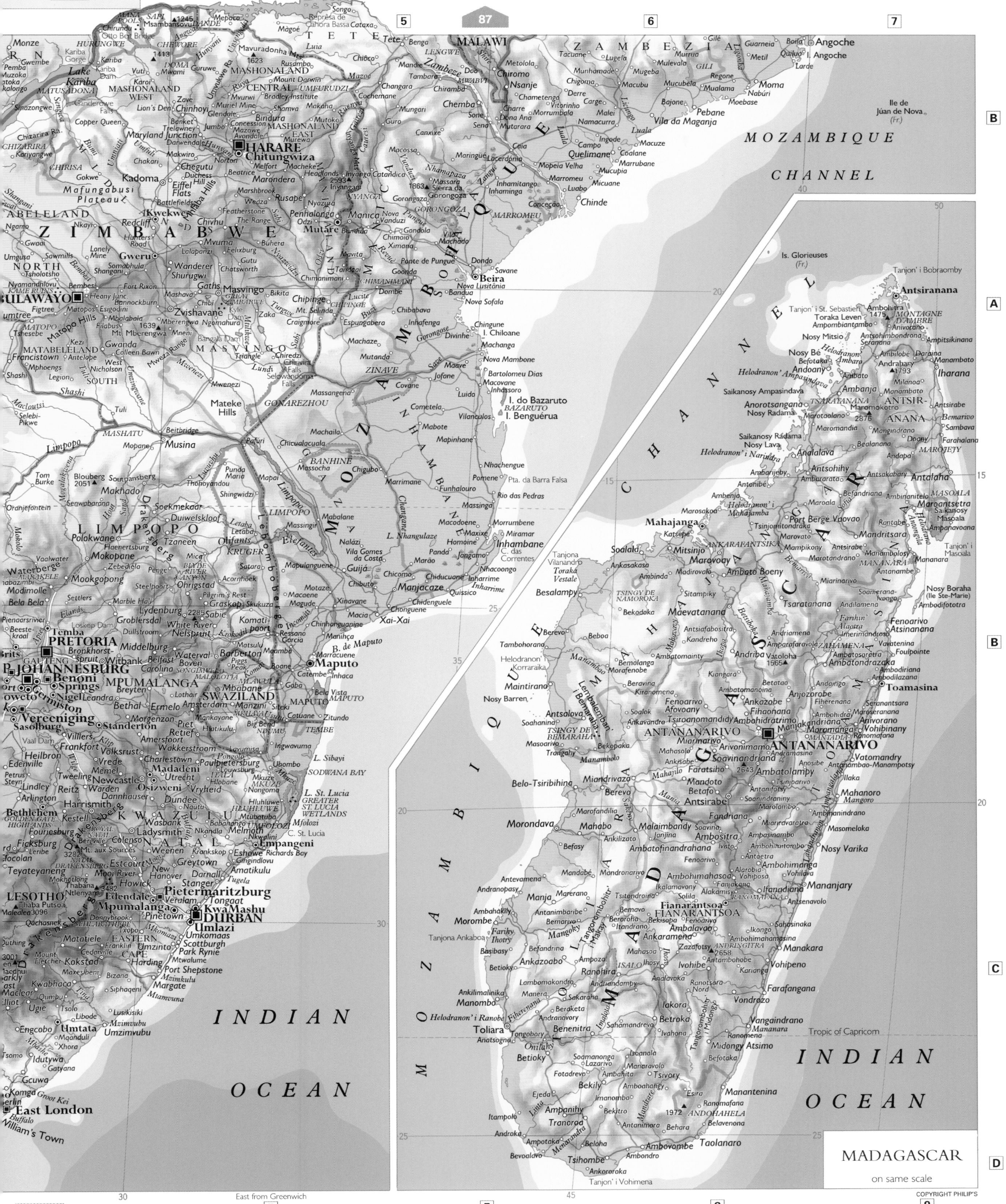

National Parks

Nature Reserves and Game Reserves

∴ UNESCO World Heritage Sites

500 0 250 500 750 1000 1250 1500 1750 km
500 0 250 500 750 1000 1250 miles
1:44 400 000

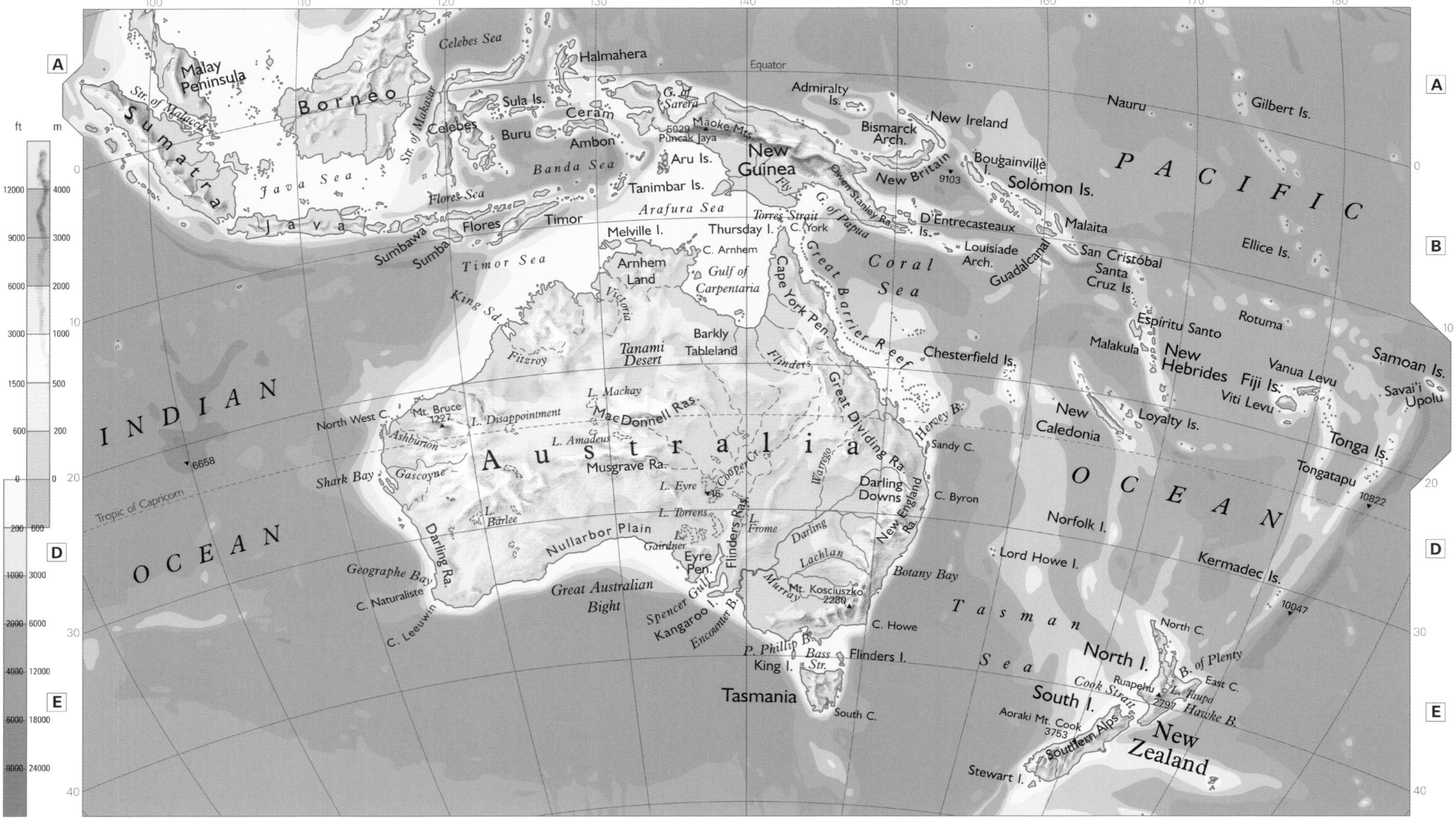

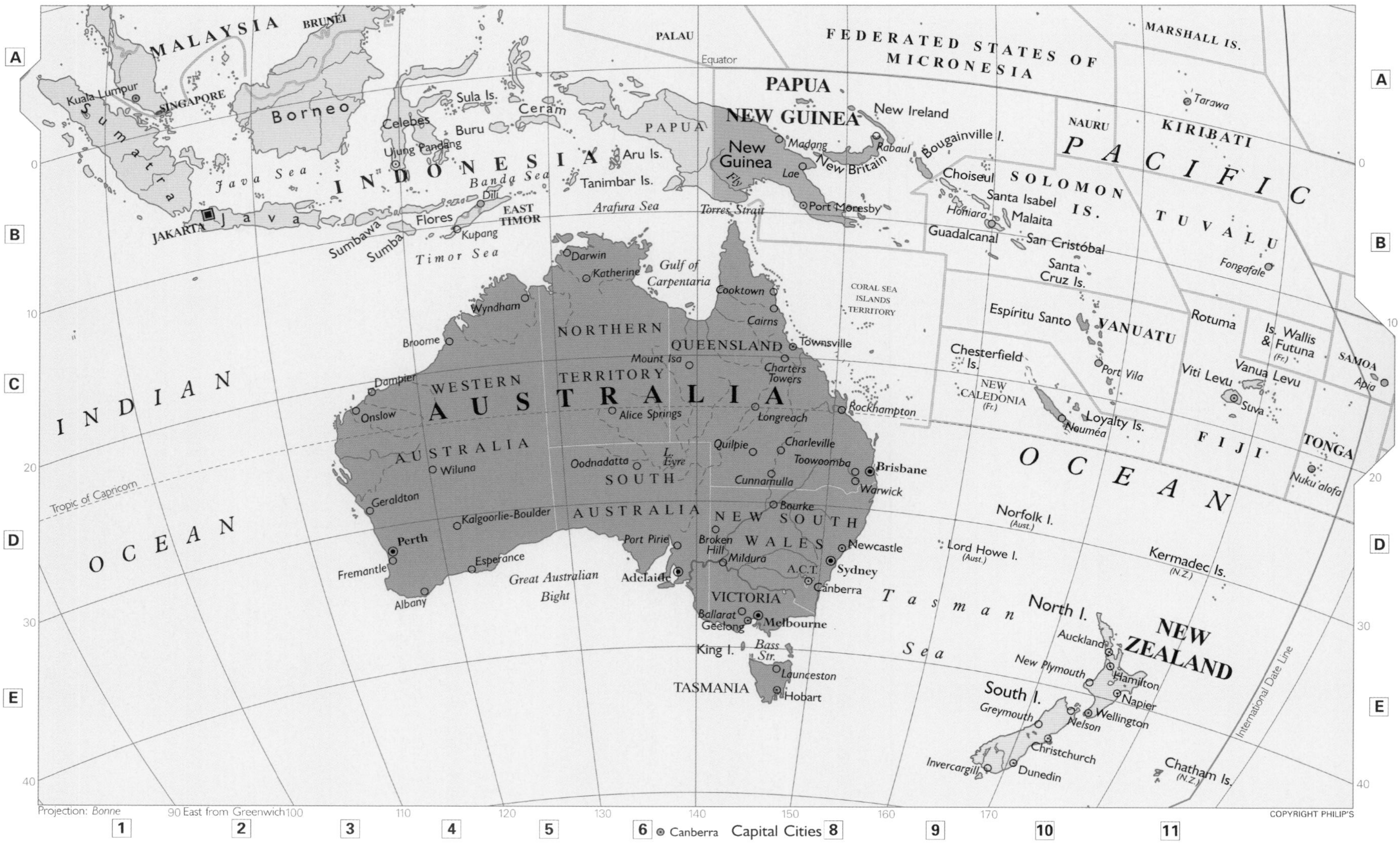

Projection: Bonne   90 East from Greenwich 100 110 120 130 140 150 160 170

⊙ Canberra Capital Cities

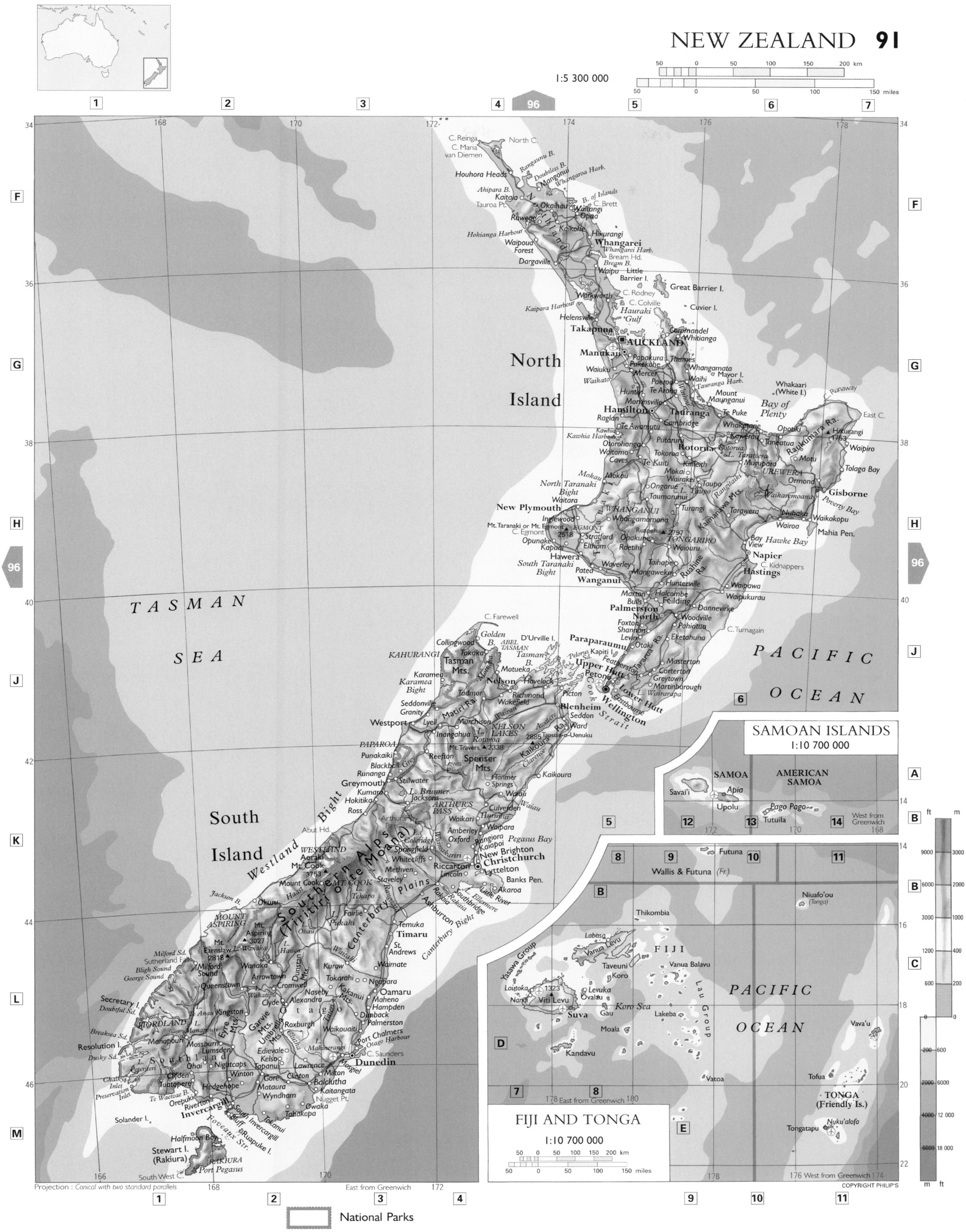
1:5 300 000
North Island
South Island
TASMAN SEA
PACIFIC OCEAN
C. Reinga
C. Maria van Diemen
North C.
Houhora Heads
Kaitaia
Whangarei
Dargaville
Great Barrier I.
Cuvier I.
Hauraki Gulf
Takapuna
AUCKLAND
Manukau
Coromandel
Thames
Hamilton
Tauranga
Bay of Plenty
Whakaari (White I.)
Rotorua
Taupo
L. Taupo
East C.
Hikurangi 1753
Gisborne
Mahia Pen.
Hawke Bay
Napier
Hastings
C. Kidnappers
New Plymouth
Mt. Taranaki or Mt. Egmont 2518
EGMONT
TONGARIRO
Ruapehu 2797
WHANGANUI
Wanganui
Palmerston North
Masterton
Paraparaumu
Upper Hutt
Lower Hutt
Wellington
Cook Strait
C. Turnagain
C. Farewell
D'Urville I.
KAHURANGI
ABEL TASMAN
Tasman B.
Nelson
Blenheim
NELSON LAKES
Kaikoura
Westport
PAPAROA
Greymouth
Hokitika
ARTHUR'S PASS
Westland Bight
WESTLAND
Aoraki Mt. Cook 3753
MT. COOK
Southern Alps (Tiritiri o te Moana)
Christchurch
Lyttelton
Banks Pen.
Pegasus Bay
Canterbury Plains
Canterbury Bight
Ashburton
Timaru
Oamaru
MOUNT ASPIRING
Mt. Aspiring 3027
Mt. Earnslaw 2818
Milford Sd.
Queenstown
Wanaka
FIORDLAND
Dunedin
Invercargill
Bluff
Foveaux Str.
Stewart I. (Rakiura)
RAKIURA
Solander I.
South West C.
Projection : Conical with two standard parallels
East from Greenwich
SAMOAN ISLANDS
1:10 700 000
SAMOA
AMERICAN SAMOA
Savai'i
Apia
Upolu
Pago Pago
Tutuila
West from Greenwich
Wallis & Futuna (Fr.)
Futuna
Niuafo'ou (Tonga)
FIJI
Vanua Levu
Viti Levu
Suva
Lautoka
Koro Sea
Lau Group
Yasawa Group
Kandavu
Vava'u
TONGA (Friendly Is.)
Tongatapu
Nuku'alofa
FIJI AND TONGA
1:10 700 000
COPYRIGHT PHILIP'S
National Parks

50 0 50 100 150 200 250 300 km

1:7 100 000

50 0 50 100 150 200 miles

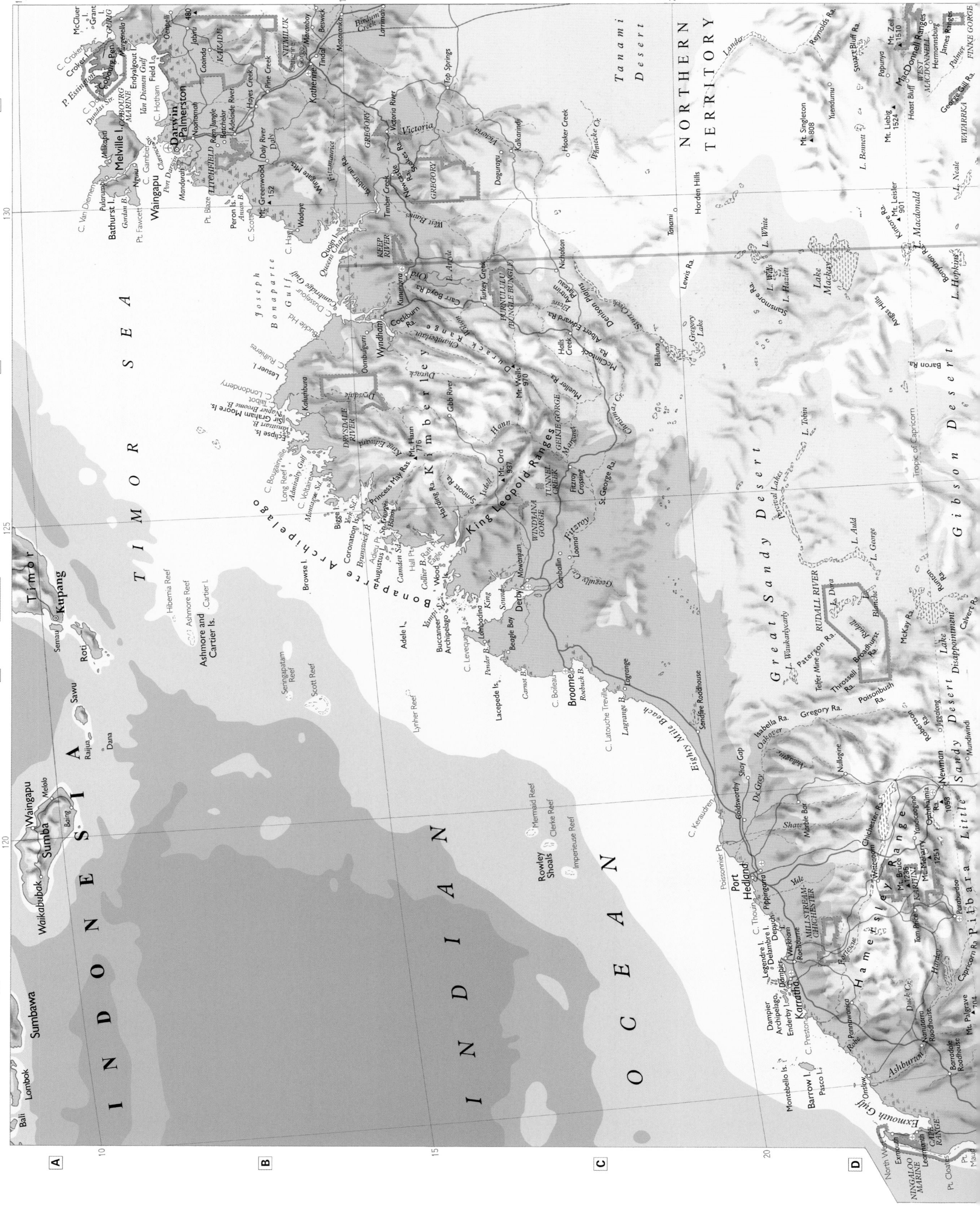

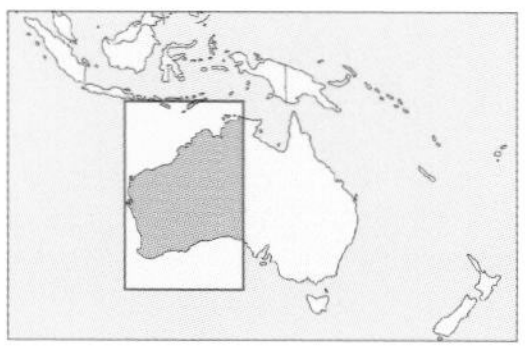

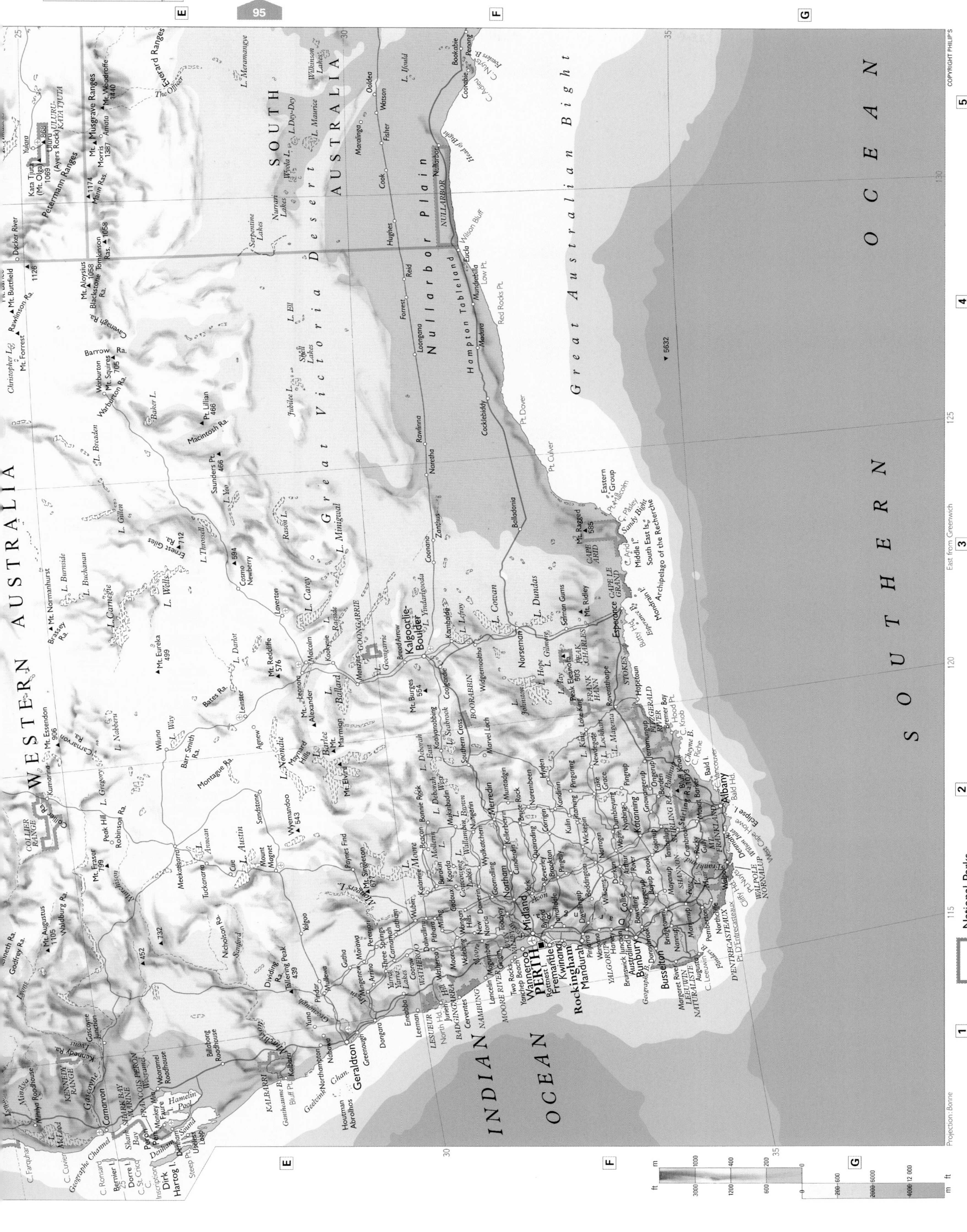
95
WESTERN AUSTRALIA
SOUTH AUSTRALIA
INDIAN OCEAN
SOUTHERN OCEAN
Great Australian Bight
Great Victoria Desert
Nullarbor Plain
Hampton Tableland
Gibson Desert
PERTH
Fremantle
Rockingham
Mandurah
Bunbury
Busselton
Albany
Esperance
Geraldton
Carnarvon
Kalgoorlie-Boulder
Coolgardie
Norseman
Merredin
Northam
Midland
Wanneroo
Kwinana
Collie
Katanning
Narrogin
Southern Cross
Meekatharra
Wiluna
Leonora
Laverton
Menzies
Kalbarri
Northampton
Eucla
Nullarbor
Ceduna
Penong
Hopetoun
Ravensthorpe
Denham
Shark Bay
Houtman Abrolhos
Rottnest I.
Archipelago of the Recherche
C. Leeuwin
C. Naturaliste
C. Arid
C. Pasley
Lake Carnegie
L. Wells
L. Barlee
L. Moore
L. Cowan
L. Dundas
L. Lefroy
L. Carey
L. Throssell
L. Minigwal
Kata Tjuta (Mt. Olga) 1069
Uluru (Ayers Rock)
Petermann Ranges
Musgrave Ranges
Everard Ranges
Mt. Woodroffe 1440
Stirling Ra. Bluff Knoll 1073
5632
National Parks
Projection: Bonne
East from Greenwich
COPYRIGHT PHILIP'S
m
ft
3000
1000
1200
400
600
200
0
200
600
2000
6000
4000
12 000
115
120
125
130
25
30
35
1
2
3
4
5
E
F
G

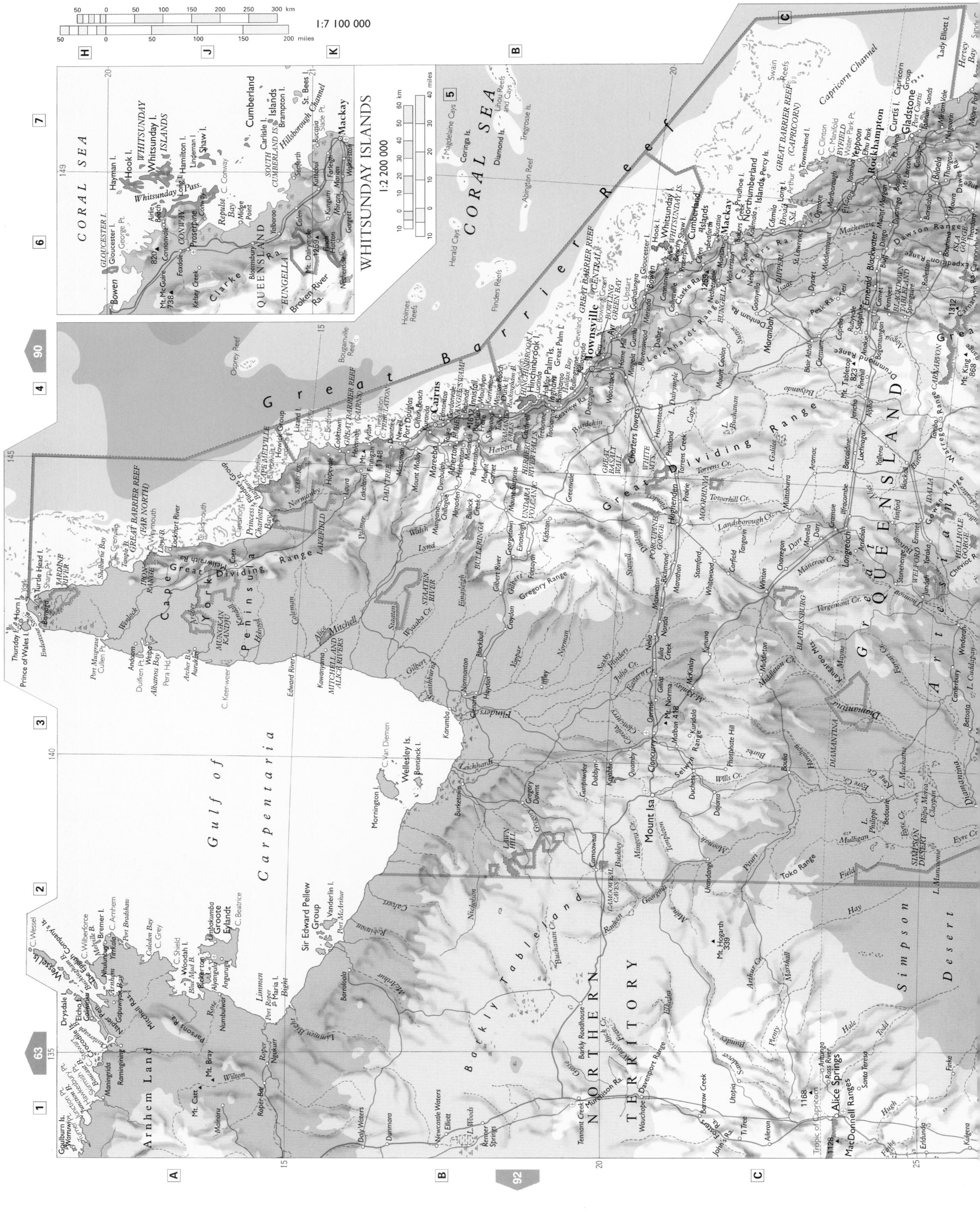
1:7 100 000
0 50 100 150 200 250 300 km
0 50 100 150 200 miles
WHITSUNDAY ISLANDS
1:2 200 000
CORAL SEA
Whitsunday I.
Hook I.
Hayman I.
Proserpine
Bowen
Mackay
Cumberland Islands
Great Barrier Reef
Gulf of Carpentaria
Cape York Peninsula
Great Dividing Range
Arnhem Land
Barkly Tableland
Simpson Desert
NORTHERN TERRITORY
QUEENSLAND
Cairns
Townsville
Rockhampton
Gladstone
Mount Isa
Alice Springs
Longreach
Charters Towers
Cloncurry
Hughenden
Emerald
Cooktown
Weipa
Normanton
Tennant Creek
Mornington I.
Wellesley Is.
Groote Eylandt
Sir Edward Pellew Group
Wessel Is.
Capricorn Channel
Tropic of Capricorn
MacDonnell Ranges

TASMAN SEA
NEW SOUTH WALES
SOUTH AUSTRALIA
TASMANIA
Bass Strait
National Parks
on same scale
East from Greenwich
Projection: Bonne
COPYRIGHT PHILIP'S

 Equatorial Scale 1:48 000 000

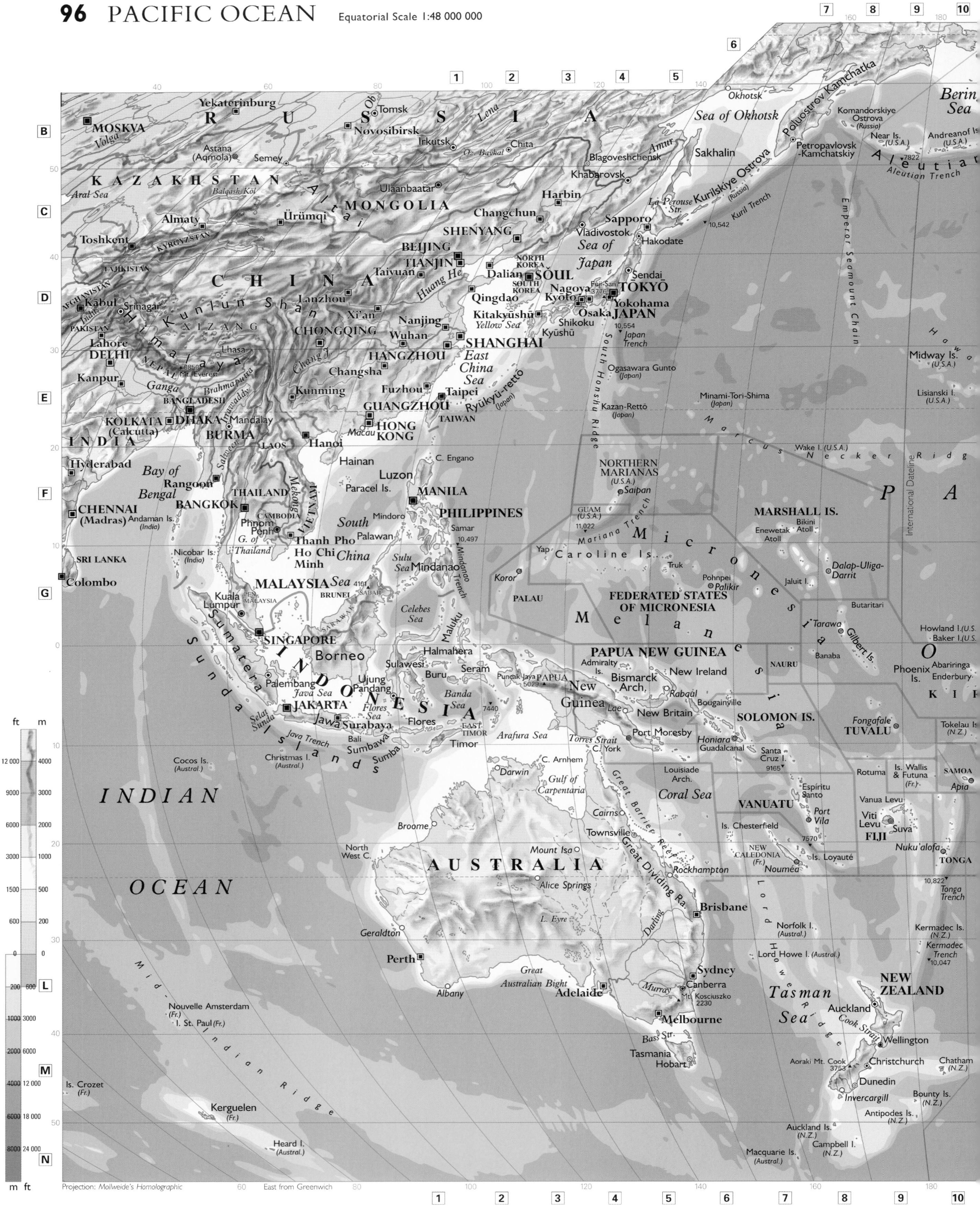

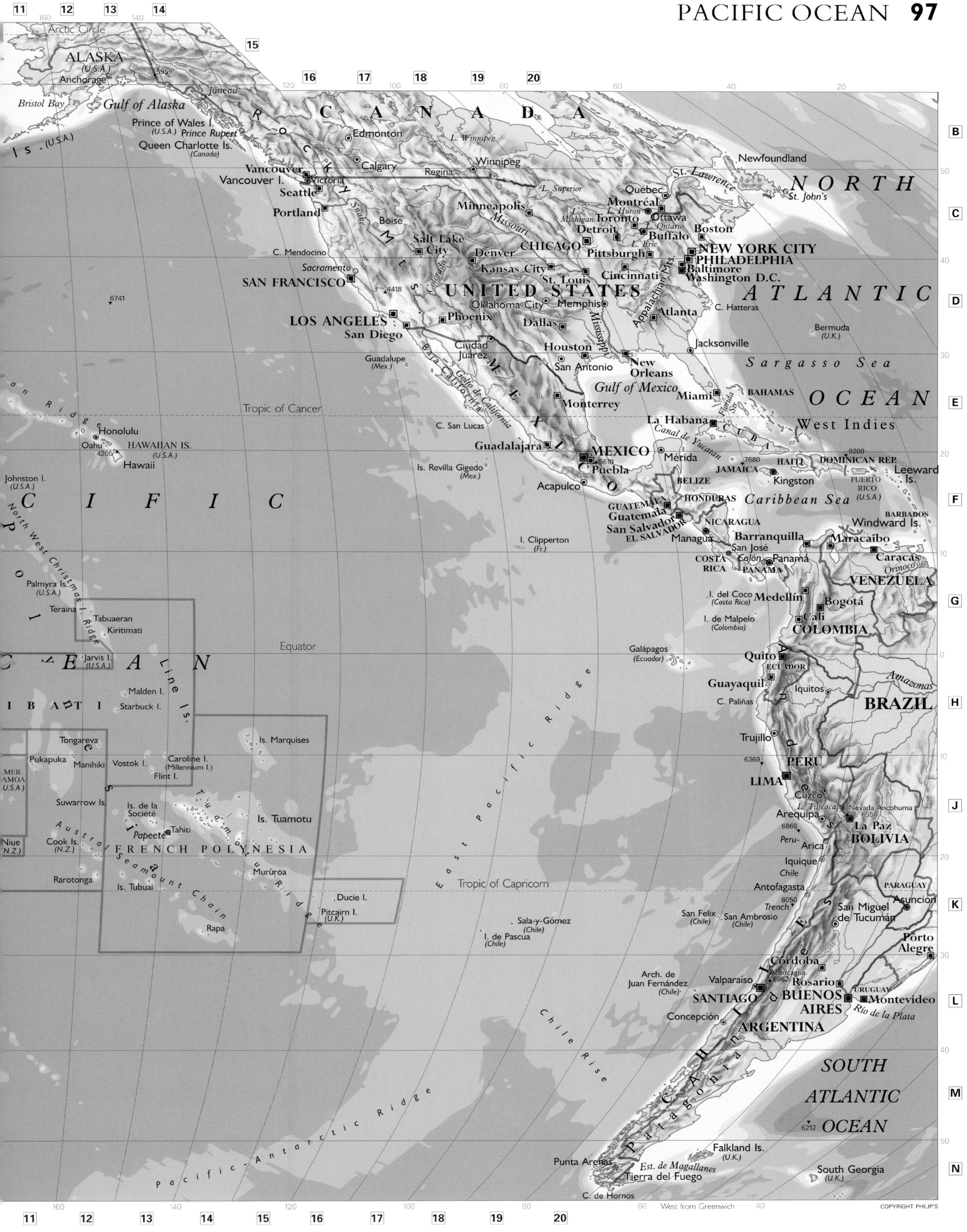
Arctic Circle
ALASKA
(U.S.A.)
Anchorage
5959
Bristol Bay
Gulf of Alaska
Juneau
Prince of Wales I.
(U.S.A.)
Prince Rupert
Queen Charlotte Is.
(Canada)
Vancouver
Victoria
Vancouver I.
Seattle
Portland
CANADA
ROCKY MTS.
Edmonton
Calgary
Regina
Winnipeg
L. Winnipeg
L. Superior
Newfoundland
St. Lawrence
St. John's
NORTH ATLANTIC OCEAN
Québec
Montréal
Ottawa
L. Huron
L. Michigan
Toronto
Ontario
Detroit
L. Erie
Buffalo
Boston
NEW YORK CITY
PHILADELPHIA
Baltimore
Washington D.C.
Pittsburgh
Cincinnati
Appalachian Mts.
Minneapolis
Missouri
Snake
Boise
Salt Lake City
CHICAGO
Denver
Kansas City
St. Louis
Colorado
C. Mendocino
Sacramento
SAN FRANCISCO
4418
UNITED STATES
Oklahoma City
Memphis
Mississippi
Atlanta
C. Hatteras
Bermuda
(U.K.)
Phoenix
Dallas
LOS ANGELES
San Diego
Ciudad Juárez
Houston
San Antonio
New Orleans
Jacksonville
Sargasso Sea
Guadalupe
(Mex.)
Baja California
Golfo de California
MEXICO
Gulf of Mexico
Miami
Florida Str.
BAHAMAS
Monterrey
Tropic of Cancer
C. San Lucas
La Habana
CUBA
West Indies
Canal de Yucatan
Guadalajara
MEXICO
5610
Puebla
Mérida
7680
JAMAICA
HAITI
Kingston
9200
DOMINICAN REP.
PUERTO RICO
(U.S.A.)
Leeward Is.
Is. Revilla Gigedo
(Mex.)
Acapulco
BELIZE
GUATEMALA
Guatemala
HONDURAS
Caribbean Sea
San Salvador
EL SALVADOR
NICARAGUA
Managua
BARBADOS
Windward Is.
I. Clipperton
(Fr.)
Barranquilla
Maracaibo
Caracas
Orinoco
San José
COSTA RICA
Colón
Panamá
PANAMA
VENEZUELA
I. del Coco
(Costa Rica)
Medellín
Bogotá
I. de Malpelo
(Colombia)
Cali
COLOMBIA
Equator
Galápagos
(Ecuador)
Quito
ECUADOR
Guayaquil
Iquitos
Amazonas
BRAZIL
C. Paliñas
Trujillo
ANDES
6369
PERU
LIMA
Cuzco
L. Titicaca
Nevada Ancohuma
6550
Arequipa
La Paz
BOLIVIA
6866
Peru-Chile Trench
Arica
Iquique
Antofagasta
8050
PARAGUAY
Asunción
San Miguel de Tucumán
San Felix
(Chile)
San Ambrosio
(Chile)
Sala-y-Gómez
(Chile)
I. de Pascua
(Chile)
Tropic of Capricorn
East Pacific Ridge
Porto Alegre
Córdoba
Aconcagua
6962
Rosario
Arch. de Juan Fernández
(Chile)
Valparaíso
SANTIAGO
BUENOS AIRES
URUGUAY
Montevideo
Río de la Plata
Concepción
ARGENTINA
Chile Rise
SOUTH ATLANTIC OCEAN
6212
PATAGONIA
Falkland Is.
(U.K.)
Punta Arenas
Est. de Magallanes
Tierra del Fuego
South Georgia
(U.K.)
C. de Hornos
West from Greenwich
Pacific-Antarctic Ridge
Honolulu
Oahu
4205
HAWAIIAN IS.
(U.S.A.)
Hawaii
6741
Johnston I.
(U.S.A.)
PACIFIC OCEAN
North West Christmas I. Ridge
Palmyra Is.
(U.S.A.)
Teraina
Tabuaeran
Kiritimati
Jarvis I.
(U.S.A.)
Line Is.
Malden I.
Starbuck I.
POLYNESIA
Tongareva
Pukapuka
Manihiki
Vostok I.
Caroline I.
(Millennium I.)
Flint I.
Is. Marquises
AMER. SAMOA
(U.S.A.)
Suwarrow Is.
Is. de la Société
Tahiti
Papeete
Is. Tuamotu
Tuamotu Ridge
Niue
(N.Z.)
Cook Is.
(N.Z.)
Austral Seamount Chain
FRENCH POLYNESIA
Mururoa
Rarotonga
Is. Tubuai
Ducie I.
Pitcairn I.
(U.K.)
Rapa
COPYRIGHT PHILIP'S

1:31 100 000

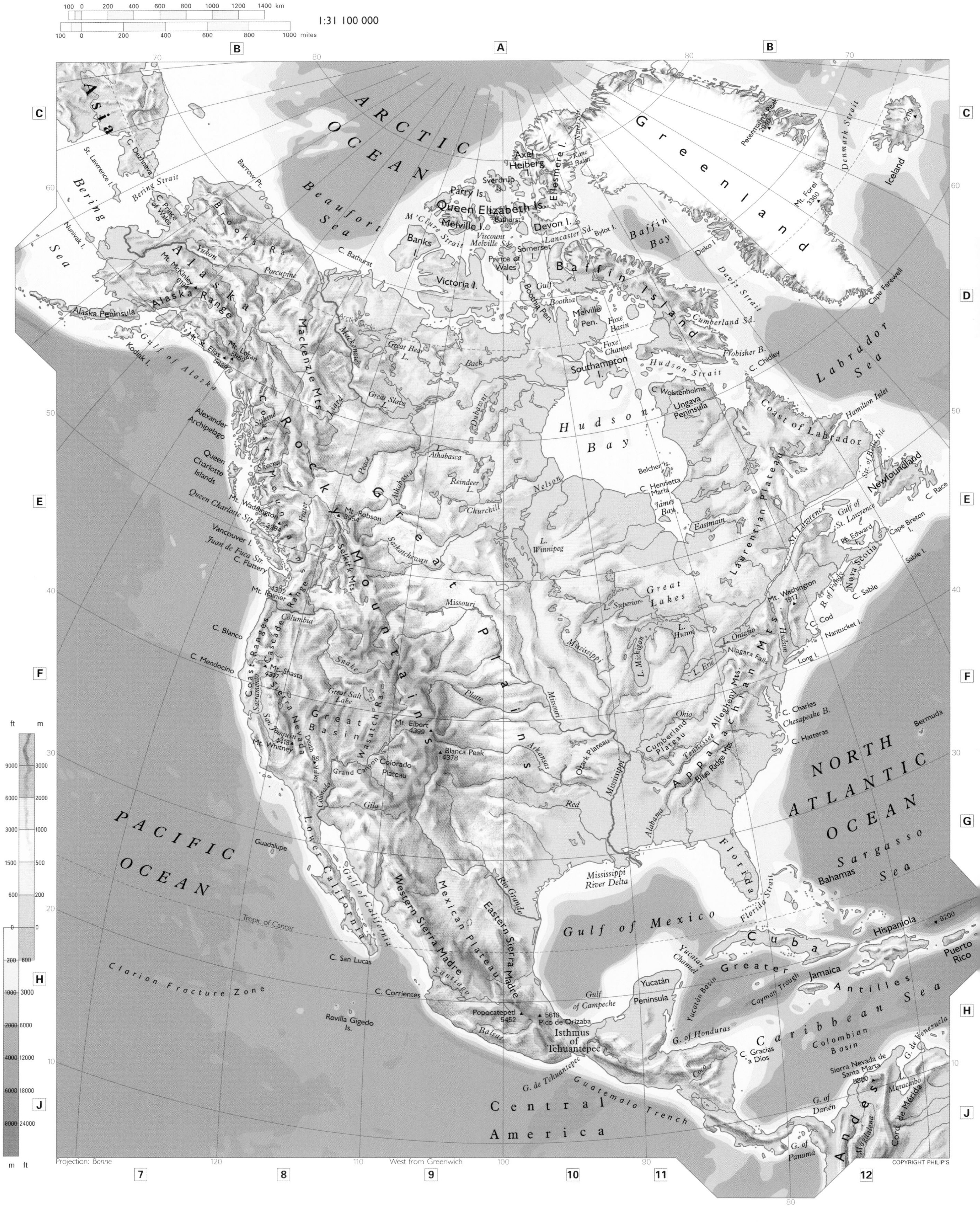
ARCTIC OCEAN
Beaufort Sea
Asia
C. Dezhneva
St. Lawrence I.
Bering Strait
Bering Sea
Nunivak I.
Barrow Pt.
C. Prince of Wales
Brooks Ra.
Yukon
Porcupine
Mt. McKinley 6194
Alaska
Alaska Range
Alaska Peninsula
Gulf of Alaska
Kodiak I.
Mt. St. Elias 5489
Mt. Logan 5959
Mackenzie Mts.
Mackenzie
Arctic Circle
Great Bear L.
Great Slave L.
Liard
Back
Dubawnt
Greenland
Petermanns Peak 2940
Mt. Forel 3360
Denmark Strait
Iceland
2119
Axel Heiberg I.
Ellesmere I.
Kane Basin
Sverdrup Is.
Parry Is.
Queen Elizabeth Is.
Bathurst I.
Devon I.
Melville I.
M'Clure Strait
Viscount Melville Sd.
Lancaster Sd.
Bylot I.
Baffin Bay
Banks I.
C. Bathurst
Prince of Wales I.
Somerset I.
Baffin Island
Disko I.
Davis Strait
Victoria I.
Gulf of Boothia
Boothia Pen.
Melville Pen.
Foxe Basin
Foxe Channel
Cumberland Sd.
Cape Farewell
Frobisher B.
C. Chidley
Hudson Strait
Southampton I.
Labrador Sea
Hamilton Inlet
C. Wolstenholme
Ungava Peninsula
Coast of Labrador
Hudson Bay
Alexander Archipelago
Queen Charlotte Islands
Stikine
Skeena
Coast Mountains
Rocky Mountains
Athabasca
L. Athabasca
Peace
Reindeer L.
Churchill
Nelson
Belcher Is.
C. Henrietta Maria
James Bay
Eastmain
Laurentian Plateau
Str. of Belle Isle
Newfoundland
C. Race
Gulf of St. Lawrence
St. Lawrence
Pr. Edward I.
Cape Breton I.
Nova Scotia
Sable I.
Queen Charlotte Str.
Mt. Waddington 3994
Fraser
Mt. Robson 3954
Vancouver I.
Juan de Fuca Str.
C. Flattery
Great Plains
Saskatchewan
Selkirk Mts.
L. Winnipeg
Mt. Rainier 4392
Cascade Range
Columbia
Missouri
L. Superior
Great Lakes
Mt. Washington 1917
B. of Fundy
C. Sable
C. Cod
Nantucket I.
C. Blanco
C. Mendocino
Snake
Mississippi
L. Michigan
L. Huron
L. Ontario
Niagara Falls
L. Erie
Hudson
Long I.
Mt. Shasta 4317
Coast Ranges
Sacramento
Sierra Nevada
Great Salt Lake
Wasatch Ra.
Great Basin
Platte
Allegheny Mts.
Appalachian Mts.
Ohio
C. Charles
Chesapeake B.
Bermuda
San Joaquin
Mt. Whitney 4418
Death Valley -86
Mt. Elbert 4399
Blanca Peak 4378
Arkansas
Ozark Plateau
Cumberland Plateau
Tennessee
Blue Ridge Mts.
C. Hatteras
Colorado
Grand Canyon
Colorado Plateau
NORTH ATLANTIC OCEAN
Gila
Red
Alabama
Florida
PACIFIC OCEAN
Guadalupe
Lower California
Gulf of California
Rio Grande
Mississippi River Delta
Sargasso Sea
Bahamas
Tropic of Cancer
Western Sierra Madre
Mexican Plateau
Eastern Sierra Madre
Florida Strait
Gulf of Mexico
Cuba
Hispaniola
9200
Puerto Rico
C. San Lucas
Santiago
Yucatan Channel
Greater Antilles
Jamaica
Cayman Trough
Yucatán Basin
Clarion Fracture Zone
C. Corrientes
Gulf of Campeche
Yucatán Peninsula
Caribbean Sea
Revilla Gigedo Is.
Popocatepetl 5452
5610 Pico de Orizaba
Isthmus of Tehuantepec
Balsas
G. of Honduras
C. Gracias a Dios
Colombian Basin
G. de Venezuela
Coco
Sierra Nevada de Santa Marta 5800
L. Maracaibo
G. de Tehuantepec
Guatemala Trench
Central America
G. of Darién
Andes
Magdalena
Cord. de Mérida
G. of Panamá
Projection: Bonne
West from Greenwich
COPYRIGHT PHILIP'S

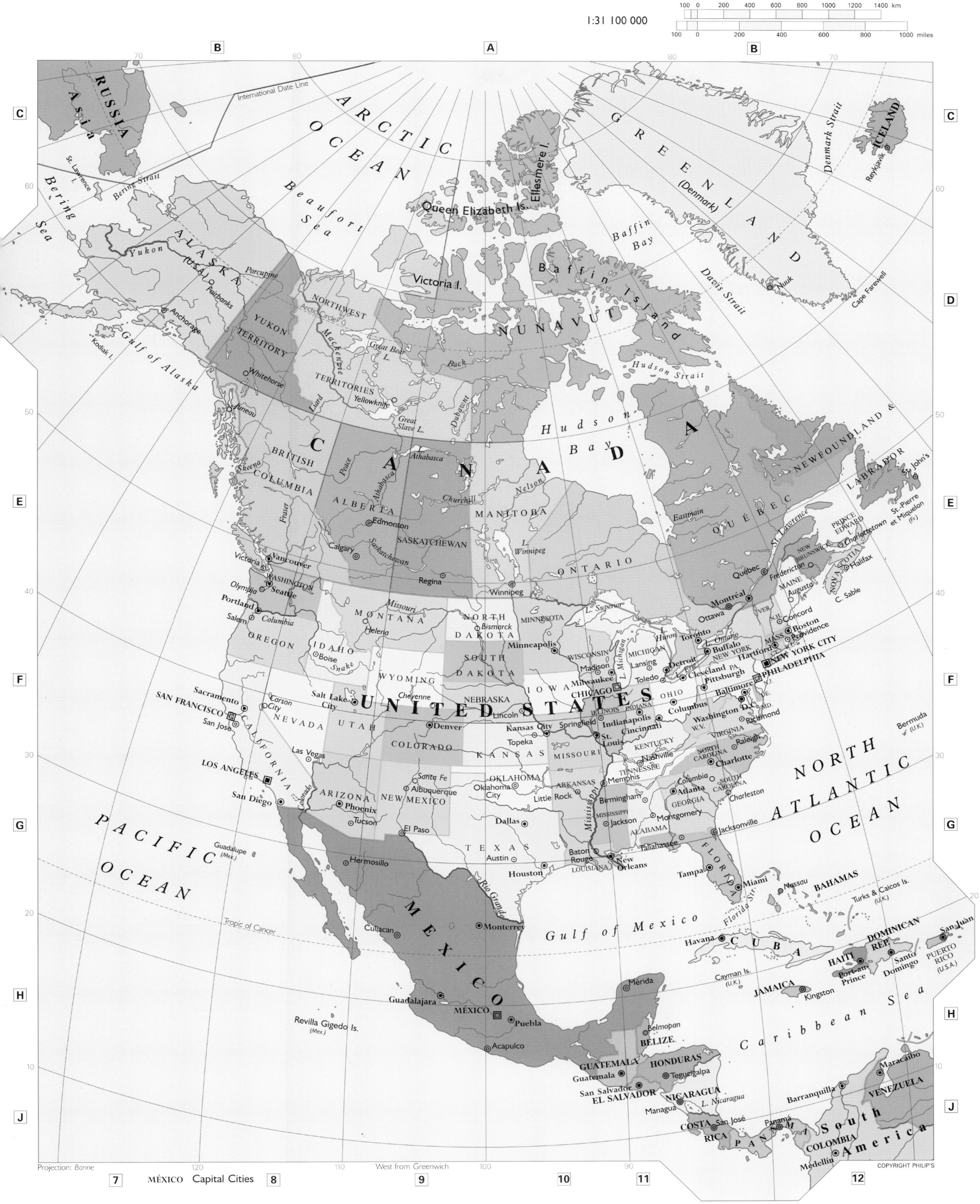
1:31 100 000
100 0 200 400 600 800 1000 1200 1400 km
100 0 200 400 600 800 1000 miles
B
A
B
C
D
E
F
G
H
J
RUSSIA
Asia
International Date Line
ARCTIC OCEAN
St. Lawrence I.
Bering Strait
Bering Sea
Beaufort Sea
Queen Elizabeth Is.
Ellesmere I.
GREENLAND (Denmark)
Denmark Strait
ICELAND
Reykjavik
Baffin Bay
Davis Strait
Nuuk
Cape Farewell
Yukon
ALASKA (U.S.A.)
Porcupine
Fairbanks
Anchorage
Kodiak I.
Gulf of Alaska
Victoria I.
Baffin Island
NORTHWEST TERRITORIES
Arctic Circle
Mackenzie
Great Bear L.
NUNAVUT
Back
YUKON TERRITORY
Whitehorse
Juneau
Yellowknife
Great Slave L.
Dubawnt
Hudson Strait
Hudson Bay
CANADA
BRITISH COLUMBIA
Skeena
Peace
Athabasca
Churchill
Nelson
ALBERTA
Edmonton
Fraser
Calgary
Saskatchewan
SASKATCHEWAN
MANITOBA
L. Winnipeg
Regina
Winnipeg
ONTARIO
Eastmain
QUÉBEC
NEWFOUNDLAND & LABRADOR
St. John's
St. Lawrence
PRINCE EDWARD I.
Charlottetown
St.-Pierre et Miquelon (Fr.)
NEW BRUNSWICK
Fredericton
NOVA SCOTIA
Halifax
C. Sable
Québec
Montréal
Ottawa
Victoria
Vancouver
WASHINGTON
Olympia
Seattle
Portland
Salem
Columbia
OREGON
Missouri
MONTANA
Helena
NORTH DAKOTA
Bismarck
MINNESOTA
L. Superior
MAINE
Augusta
VER.
N.H.
Concord
MASS.
Boston
Providence
IDAHO
Boise
Snake
SOUTH DAKOTA
Minneapolis
WISCONSIN
MICHIGAN
L. Michigan
L. Huron
Toronto
L. Ontario
Buffalo
NEW YORK
Hartford
NEW YORK CITY
PHILADELPHIA
WYOMING
Madison
Lansing
Detroit
L. Erie
Cleveland
PA.
Pittsburgh
Milwaukee
Toledo
N.J.
Sacramento
SAN FRANCISCO
San Jose
Carson City
NEVADA
Salt Lake City
Cheyenne
UNITED STATES
NEBRASKA
IOWA
CHICAGO
OHIO
Baltimore
DE.
MD.
Lincoln
ILLINOIS
INDIANA
Columbus
Washington D.C.
Richmond
Bermuda (U.K.)
UTAH
Denver
Kansas City
Springfield
Indianapolis
Cincinnati
W.V.
VIRGINIA
CALIFORNIA
COLORADO
Topeka
KANSAS
St. Louis
KENTUCKY
MISSOURI
Nashville
NORTH CAROLINA
Raleigh
Charlotte
Las Vegas
LOS ANGELES
San Diego
Colorado
Santa Fe
Albuquerque
OKLAHOMA
Oklahoma City
TENNESSEE
Memphis
ARKANSAS
Little Rock
Columbia
SOUTH CAROLINA
Atlanta
GEORGIA
Charleston
Birmingham
ARIZONA
Phoenix
Tucson
NEW MEXICO
El Paso
Dallas
Mississippi
MISSISSIPPI
Jackson
ALABAMA
Montgomery
Jacksonville
NORTH ATLANTIC OCEAN
PACIFIC OCEAN
Guadalupe (Mex.)
TEXAS
Austin
Houston
Baton Rouge
LOUISIANA
New Orleans
Tallahassee
FLORIDA
Tampa
Miami
Hermosillo
Rio Grande
Nassau
BAHAMAS
Turks & Caicos Is. (U.K.)
Florida Str.
Tropic of Cancer
MEXICO
Monterrey
Culiacán
Gulf of Mexico
Havana
CUBA
DOMINICAN REP.
San Juan
HAITI
Port-au-Prince
Santo Domingo
PUERTO RICO (U.S.A.)
Cayman Is. (U.K.)
JAMAICA
Kingston
Mérida
Guadalajara
MÉXICO
Puebla
Revilla Gigedo Is. (Mex.)
Belmopan
BELIZE
Caribbean Sea
Acapulco
GUATEMALA
Guatemala
HONDURAS
Tegucigalpa
San Salvador
EL SALVADOR
NICARAGUA
L. Nicaragua
Managua
COSTA RICA
San José
PANAMA
Panamá
Barranquilla
Maracaibo
VENEZUELA
COLOMBIA
Medellín
South America
Projection: Bonne
West from Greenwich
COPYRIGHT PHILIP'S
7
MÉXICO Capital Cities
8
9
10
11
12

1:13 300 000

100 0 100 200 300 400 500 600 km

100 0 100 200 300 400 miles

4 5 6 7 8 9 4 10

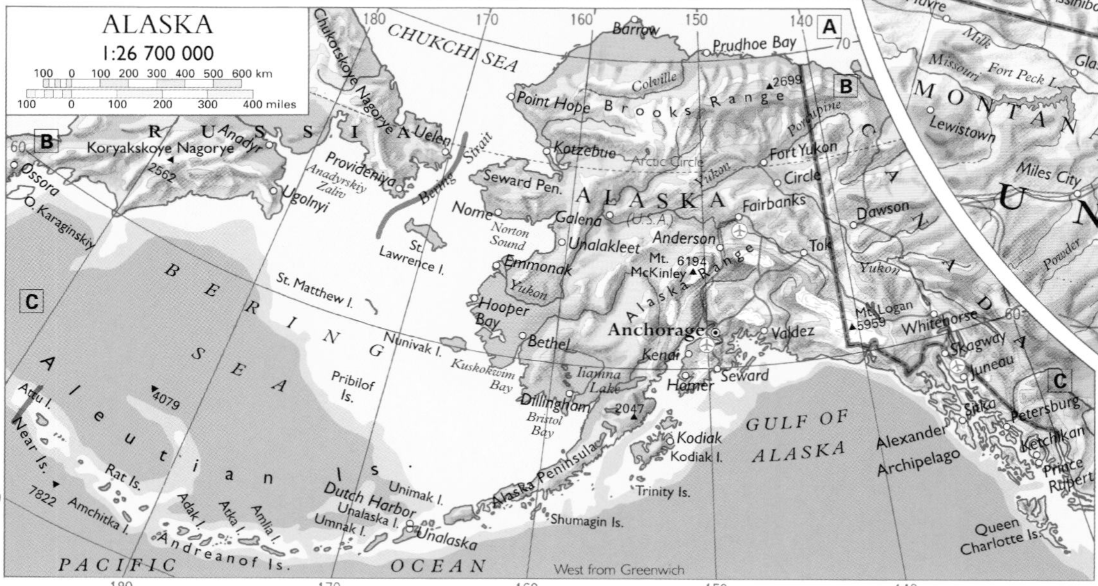

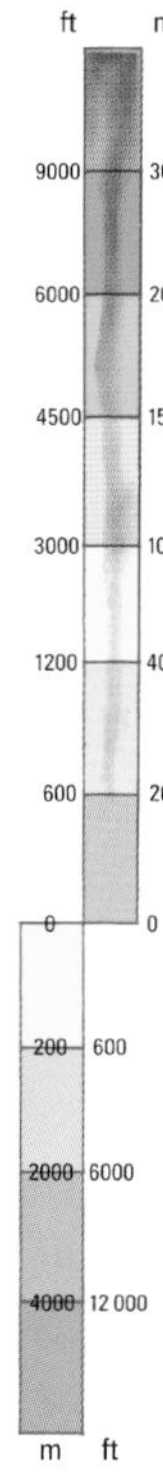

1 2 3 4 5 6 9 106 10

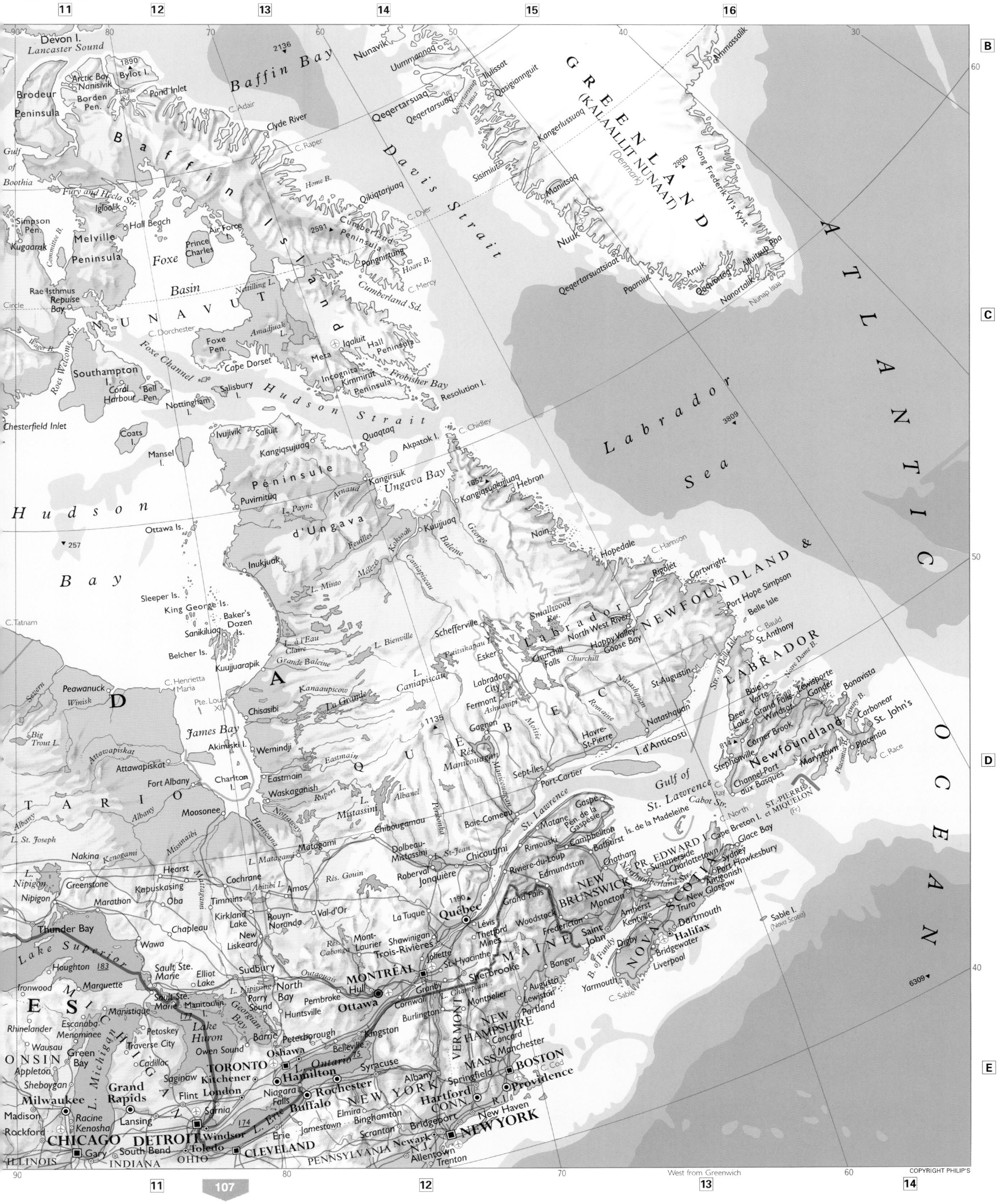

11
12
13
14
15
16
B
C
D
E
Devon I.
Lancaster Sound
Bylot I.
Arctic Bay
Nanisivik
Pond Inlet
Borden Pen.
Brodeur Peninsula
Gulf of Boothia
Baffin Bay
Baffin Island
Clyde River
C. Raper
C. Adair
Home B.
Qikiqtarjuaq
C. Dyer
Cumberland Peninsula
Pangnirtung
Hoare B.
C. Mercy
Cumberland Sd.
Fury and Hecla Str.
Igloolik
Hall Beach
Simpson Pen.
Kugaaruk
Committee B.
Melville Peninsula
Air Force I.
Prince Charles I.
Foxe Basin
Nettilling L.
Rae Isthmus
Repulse Bay
Circle
NUNAVUT
C. Dorchester
Amadjuak L.
Foxe Pen.
Cape Dorset
Iqaluit
Hall Peninsula
Meta Incognita Peninsula
Kimmirut
Frobisher Bay
Resolution I.
Wager B.
Roes Welcome Sd.
Foxe Channel
Southampton I.
Coral Harbour
Bell Pen.
Salisbury I.
Nottingham I.
Hudson Strait
Chesterfield Inlet
Coats I.
Mansel I.
Ivujivik
Salluit
Kangiqsujuaq
Quaqtaq
Akpatok I.
C. Chidley
Péninsule d'Ungava
Puvirnituq
Kangirsuk
Ungava Bay
Arnaud
L. Payne
Kangiqsualujjuaq
Hebron
Hudson Bay
Ottawa Is.
Feuilles
Koksoak
Kuujjuaq
George
Baleine
Nain
Inukjuak
Mélèzes
Caniapiscau
L. Minto
Sleeper Is.
King George Is.
Baker's Dozen Is.
Sanikiluaq
C. Tatnam
Belcher Is.
Kuujjuarapik
L. à l'Eau Claire
Grande Baleine
L. Bienville
Schefferville
Smallwood Res.
Labrador
North West River
Happy Valley-Goose Bay
Churchill Falls
Churchill
Esker
Hopedale
C. Harrison
Rigolet
Cartwright
NEWFOUNDLAND & LABRADOR
Port Hope Simpson
Belle Isle
C. Bauld
St. Anthony
Peawanuck
Winisk
Severn
C. Henrietta Maria
Pte. Louis XIV
Chisasibi
L. Caniapiscau
Kanaaupscow
La Grande
Labrador City
Fermont
Ashuanipi
Natashquan
Romaine
St-Augustin
Str. of Belle Isle
Notre Dame B.
James Bay
Akimiski I.
Wemindji
QUÉBEC
Gagnon
Rés. Manicouagan
Moisie
Havre-St-Pierre
Î. d'Anticosti
Natashquan
Deer Lake
Baie Verte
Grand Falls-Windsor
Lewisporte
Gander
Bonavista
Trinity B.
Carbonear
St. John's
Corner Brook
Newfoundland
Stephenville
Marystown
Placentia
Placentia B.
C. Race
Channel-Port aux Basques
Big Trout L.
Attawapiskat
Fort Albany
Charlton I.
Eastmain
Waskaganish
Rupert
L. Mistassini
L. Albanel
Sept-Îles
Port-Cartier
Gulf of St. Lawrence
Cabot Str.
ST-PIERRE ET MIQUELON (Fr.)
ONTARIO
Albany
Moosonee
Nottaway
Harricana
Missinaibi
L. St. Joseph
Chibougamau
Péribonka
Manicouagan
Baie-Comeau
Matane
Gaspé
Pén. de la Gaspésie
Îs. de la Madeleine
C. North
Cape Breton I.
Glace Bay
Sydney
Port Hawkesbury
Antigonish
Nakina
Kenogami
L. Matagami
Matagami
Dolbeau-Mistassini
L. St-Jean
Chicoutimi
Rimouski
Campbellton
Bathurst
Chatham
PR. EDWARD I.
Summerside
Charlottetown
Northumberland Str.
Hearst
Cochrane
Abitibi
Amos
Rés. Gouin
Roberval
Jonquière
Rivière-du-Loup
Edmundston
NEW BRUNSWICK
Moncton
Amherst
NOVA SCOTIA
Truro
New Glasgow
L. Nipigon
Nipigon
Greenstone
Kapuskasing
Oba
Marathon
Timmins
Kirkland Lake
Rouyn-Noranda
Val-d'Or
La Tuque
Québec
Lévis
Thetford Mines
Grand Falls
Woodstock
Fredericton
Saint John
Kentville
Dartmouth
Halifax
Sable I. (Nova Scotia)
Thunder Bay
Chapleau
Wawa
New Liskeard
Rés. Cabonga
Mont-Laurier
Shawinigan
Trois-Rivières
Joliette
St-Hyacinthe
MAINE
Bangor
Digby
Bridgewater
Liverpool
B. of Fundy
Lake Superior
Houghton
Sault Ste. Marie
Elliot Lake
Sudbury
Outaouais
MONTRÉAL
Granby
Sherbrooke
Augusta
Lewiston
Yarmouth
C. Sable
Ironwood
Marquette
MICHIGAN
Manitoulin I.
L. Nipissing
North Bay
Parry Sound
Georgian Bay
Pembroke
Hull
Ottawa
Huntsville
Cornwall
Burlington
L. Champlain
Montpelier
NEW HAMPSHIRE
Portland
WISCONSIN
Manistique
Escanaba
Menominee
Rhinelander
Wausau
Lake Huron
Petoskey
Traverse City
Barrie
Owen Sound
Peterborough
Kingston
Belleville
Oshawa
VERMONT
Concord
Manchester
Green Bay
Appleton
Sheboygan
Cadillac
TORONTO
L. Ontario
Syracuse
MASS.
BOSTON
C. Cod
L. Michigan
Grand Rapids
Saginaw
Kitchener
Hamilton
Rochester
Albany
Springfield
Providence
Milwaukee
Flint
London
Niagara Falls
Buffalo
NEW YORK
Hartford
CONN.
R.I.
Madison
Racine
Kenosha
Lansing
Sarnia
L. Erie
Elmira
Binghamton
New Haven
Bridgeport
Rockford
CHICAGO
DETROIT
Windsor
Erie
Jamestown
Scranton
Newark
NEW YORK
Gary
South Bend
Toledo
CLEVELAND
PENNSYLVANIA
N.J.
Allentown
Trenton
ILLINOIS
INDIANA
OHIO
GREENLAND (KALAALLIT NUNAAT) (Denmark)
Nunavik
Uummannaq
Ilulissat
Qasigiannguit
Qeqertarsuaq
Kangerlussuaq
Sisimiut
Maniitsoq
Nuuk
Paamiut
Arsuk
Qaqortoq
Nanortalik
Alluitsup Paa
Nunap Isua
Qeqertarsuatsiaat
Kong Frederik VI's Kyst
Ammassalik
Davis Strait
Labrador Sea
ATLANTIC OCEAN
2136
1890
2591
2850
3809
1652
257
1135
814
1190
183
177
174
6309
90
80
70
60
50
40
30
West from Greenwich
COPYRIGHT PHILIP'S

107

50 0 50 100 150 200 250 300 km

1:6 200 000

50 0 50 100 150 200 miles

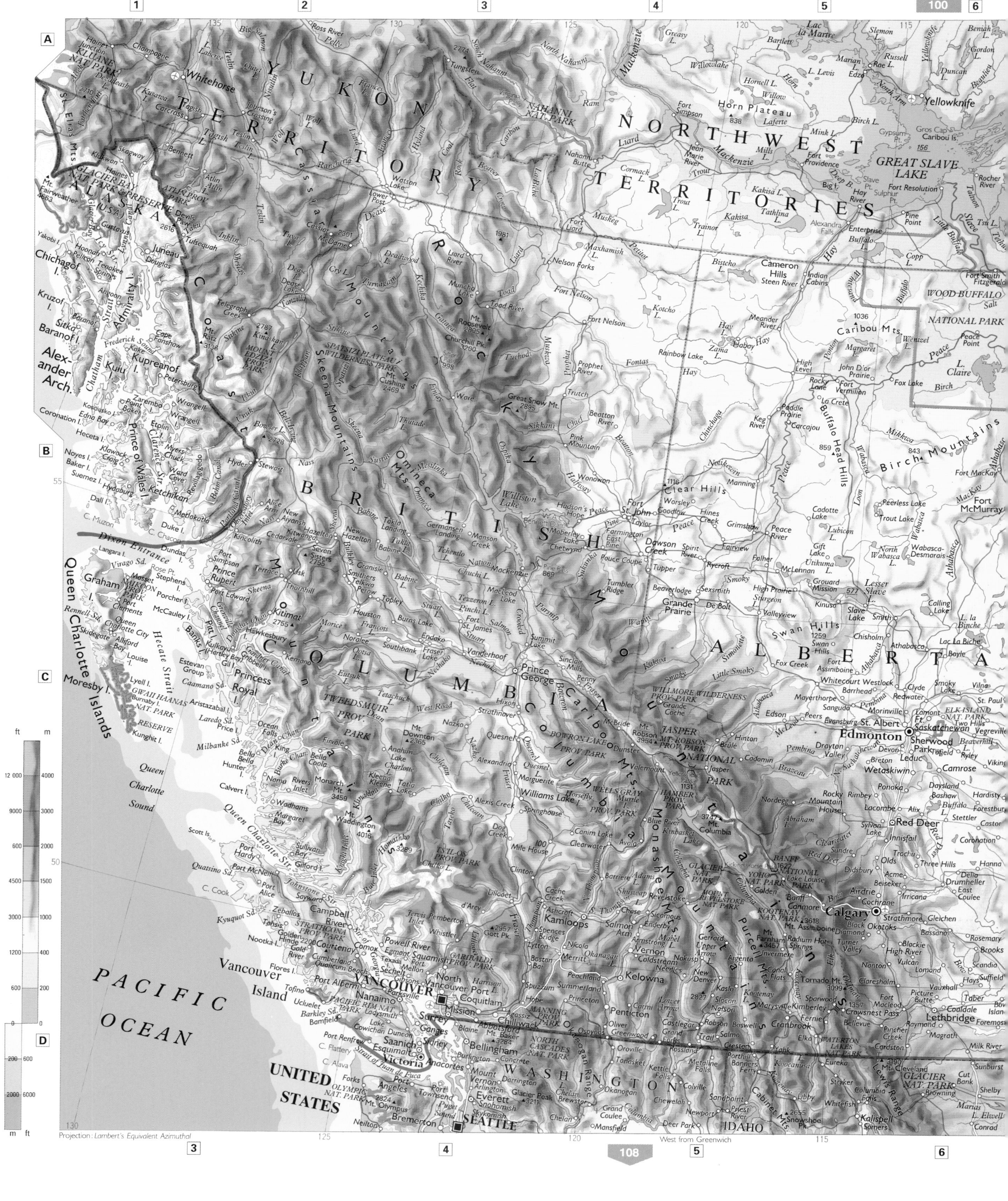

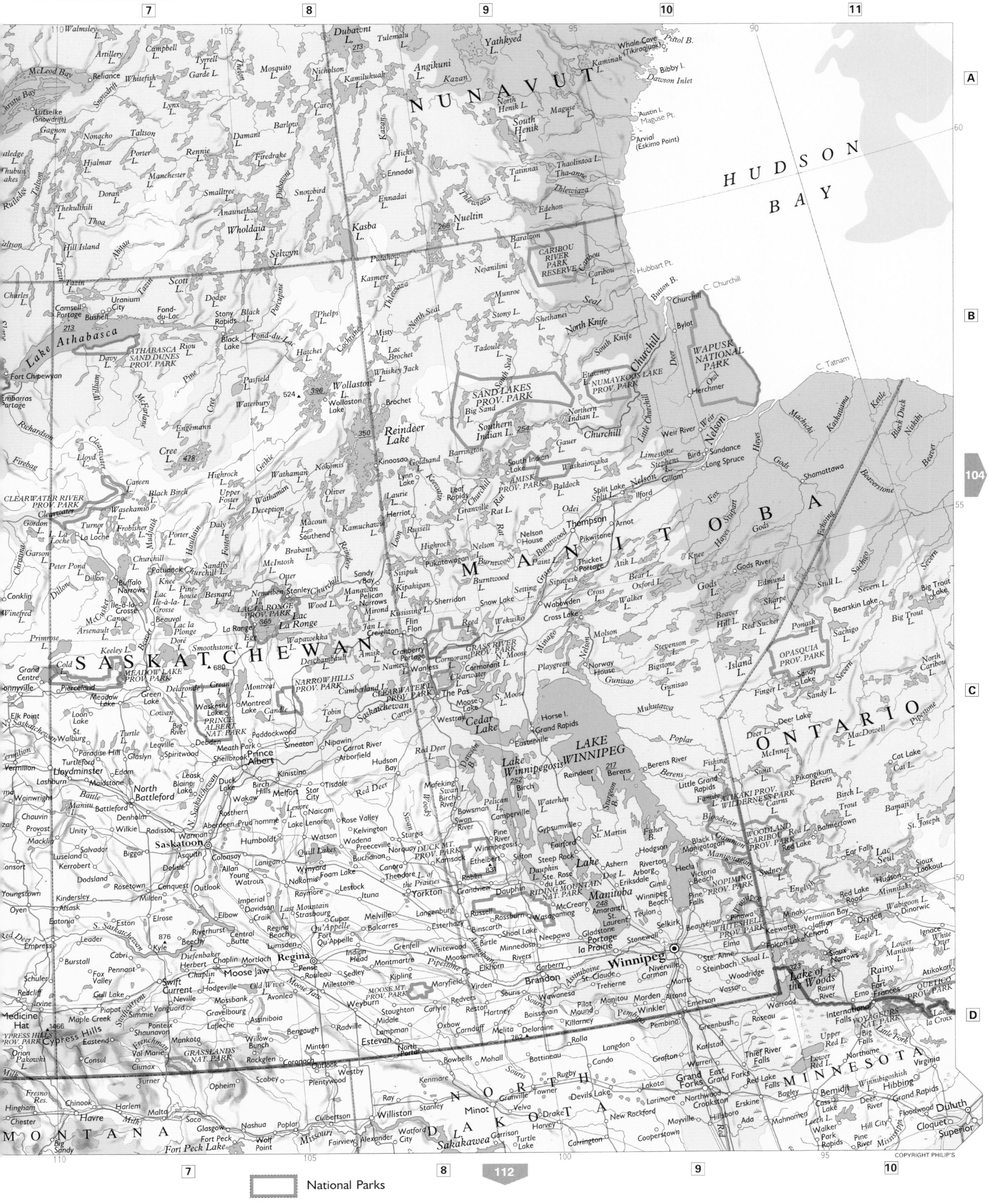
7
8
9
10
11
A
B
C
D
104
NUNAVUT
HUDSON BAY
MANITOBA
SASKATCHEWAN
ONTARIO
MINNESOTA
NORTH DAKOTA
MONTANA
LAKE WINNIPEG
Lake Winnipegosis
Lake Manitoba
Lake Athabasca
Reindeer Lake
Wollaston L.
Cedar Lake
Lake of the Woods
WAPUSK NATIONAL PARK
PRINCE ALBERT NAT. PARK
RIDING MOUNTAIN NAT. PARK
GRASSLANDS NAT. PARK
Winnipeg
Regina
Saskatoon
Brandon
Moose Jaw
Prince Albert
Thompson
Churchill
Flin Flon
The Pas
Yorkton
Swift Current
North Battleford
Lloydminster
Medicine Hat
Kenora
Fort Frances
Grand Forks
Minot
Duluth
112
National Parks
COPYRIGHT PHILIP'S

1:6 200 000

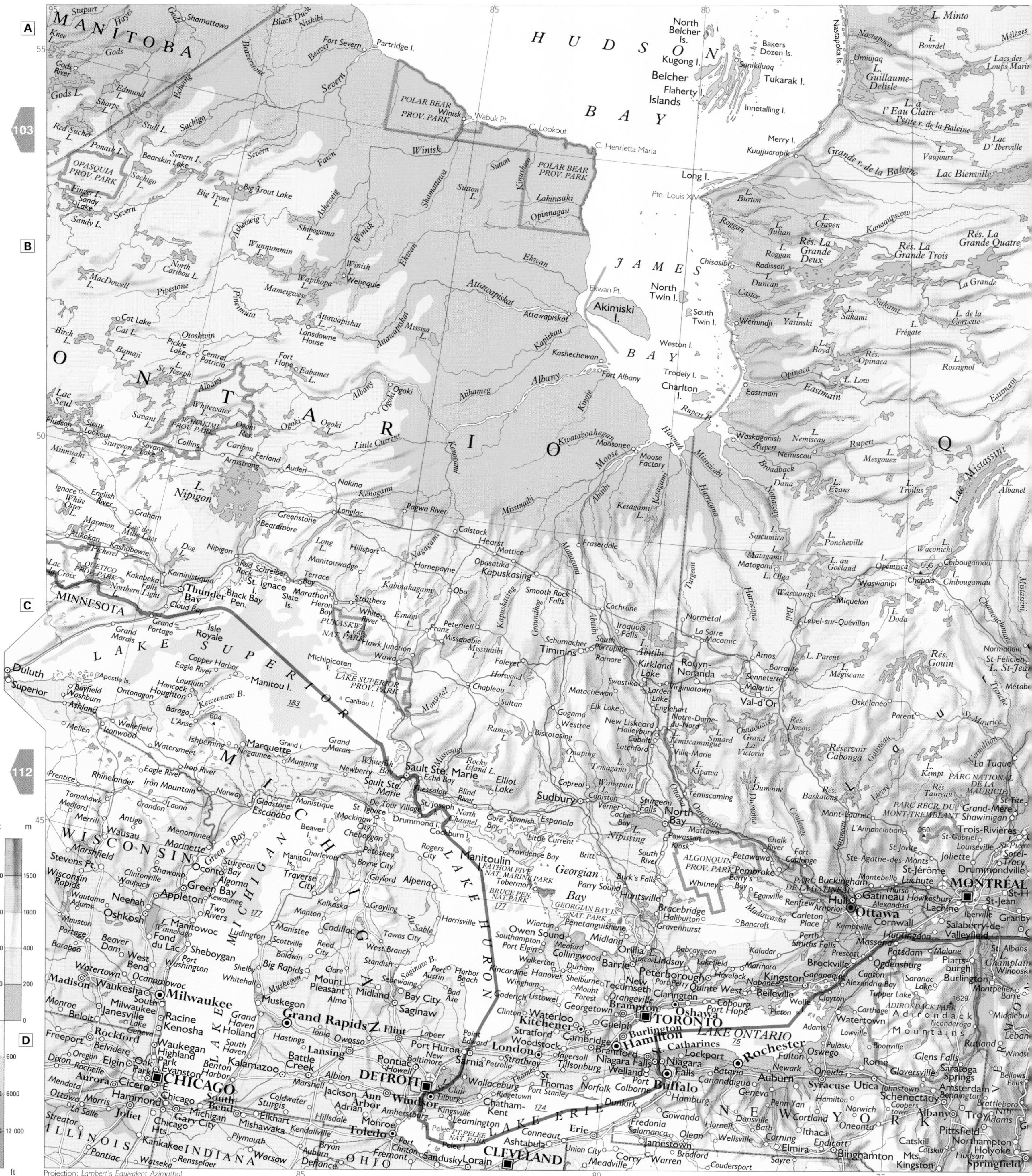

Projection: Lambert's Equivalent Azimuthal

National Parks

LABRADOR SEA
NEWFOUNDLAND & LABRADOR
Labrador
Newfoundland
QUÉBEC
NEW BRUNSWICK
NOVA SCOTIA
PRINCE EDWARD ISLAND
MAINE
UNITED STATES
ATLANTIC OCEAN
GULF OF ST. LAWRENCE
St. Lawrence
Î. d'Anticosti
Cabot Strait
Str. of Belle Isle
Bay of Fundy
Cape Breton Island
ST-PIERRE et MIQUELON (France)
Smallwood Reservoir
Mealy Mts.
Long Range Mts.
Pén. de la Gaspésie
Mts. Chic-Chocs
Québec
Halifax
Fredericton
Charlottetown
St. John's
BOSTON
Sable I. (Nova Scotia)
West from Greenwich
COPYRIGHT PHILIP'S

101

1:10 700 000

100 0 100 200 300 400 500 km

100 0 50 100 150 200 250 300 350 miles

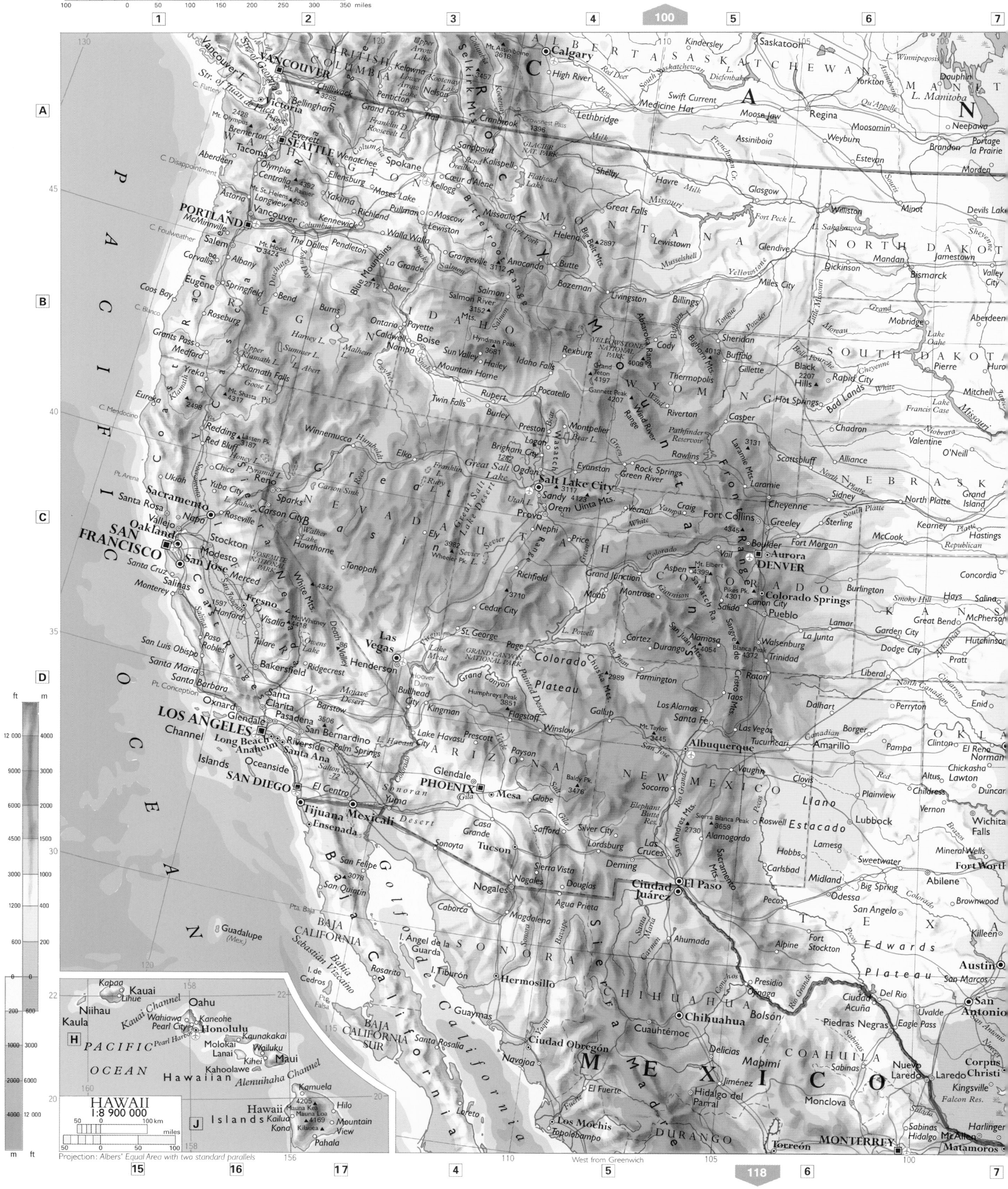

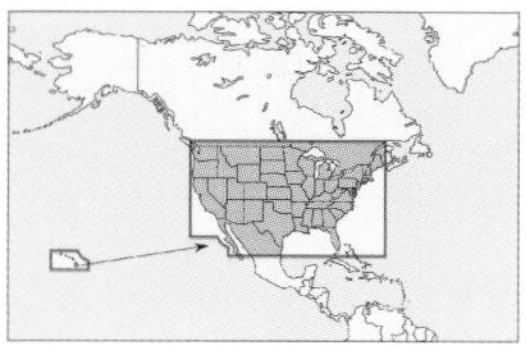

8
9
10
11
12
101
13
A
B
C
D
E
F
C A N A D A
Lake Winnipeg
Winnipeg
Lake of the Woods
Lake Nipigon
Thunder Bay
Lake Superior
Sault Ste. Marie
Lake Michigan
Lake Huron
Lake Erie
Lake Ontario
Québec
MONTRÉAL
Ottawa
TORONTO
Hamilton
Buffalo
DETROIT
CLEVELAND
CHICAGO
Milwaukee
Minneapolis
St. Paul
MINNESOTA
WISCONSIN
MICHIGAN
IOWA
ILLINOIS
INDIANA
OHIO
PENNSYLVANIA
NEW YORK
VERMONT
NEW HAMPSHIRE
MAINE
New England
BOSTON
Providence
Hartford
PHILADELPHIA
PITTSBURGH
BALTIMORE
WASHINGTON D.C.
WEST VIRGINIA
Midwest
Indianapolis
Columbus
Cincinnati
Louisville
KENTUCKY
TENNESSEE
Nashville
Memphis
ST. LOUIS
Kansas City
MISSOURI
Ozark Plateau
ARKANSAS
Little Rock
Oklahoma City
Tulsa
Wichita
DALLAS
HOUSTON
LOUISIANA
New Orleans
Baton Rouge
MISSISSIPPI
Jackson
ALABAMA
Birmingham
GEORGIA
ATLANTA
SOUTH CAROLINA
NORTH CAROLINA
Charlotte
VIRGINIA
Richmond
Norfolk
Virginia Beach
Jacksonville
FLORIDA
Orlando
TAMPA
MIAMI
Straits of Florida
BAHAMAS
GULF OF MEXICO
ATLANTIC OCEAN
95
90
85
80
75
70
65
45
40
35
30
25
119
8
9
10
11
120
12

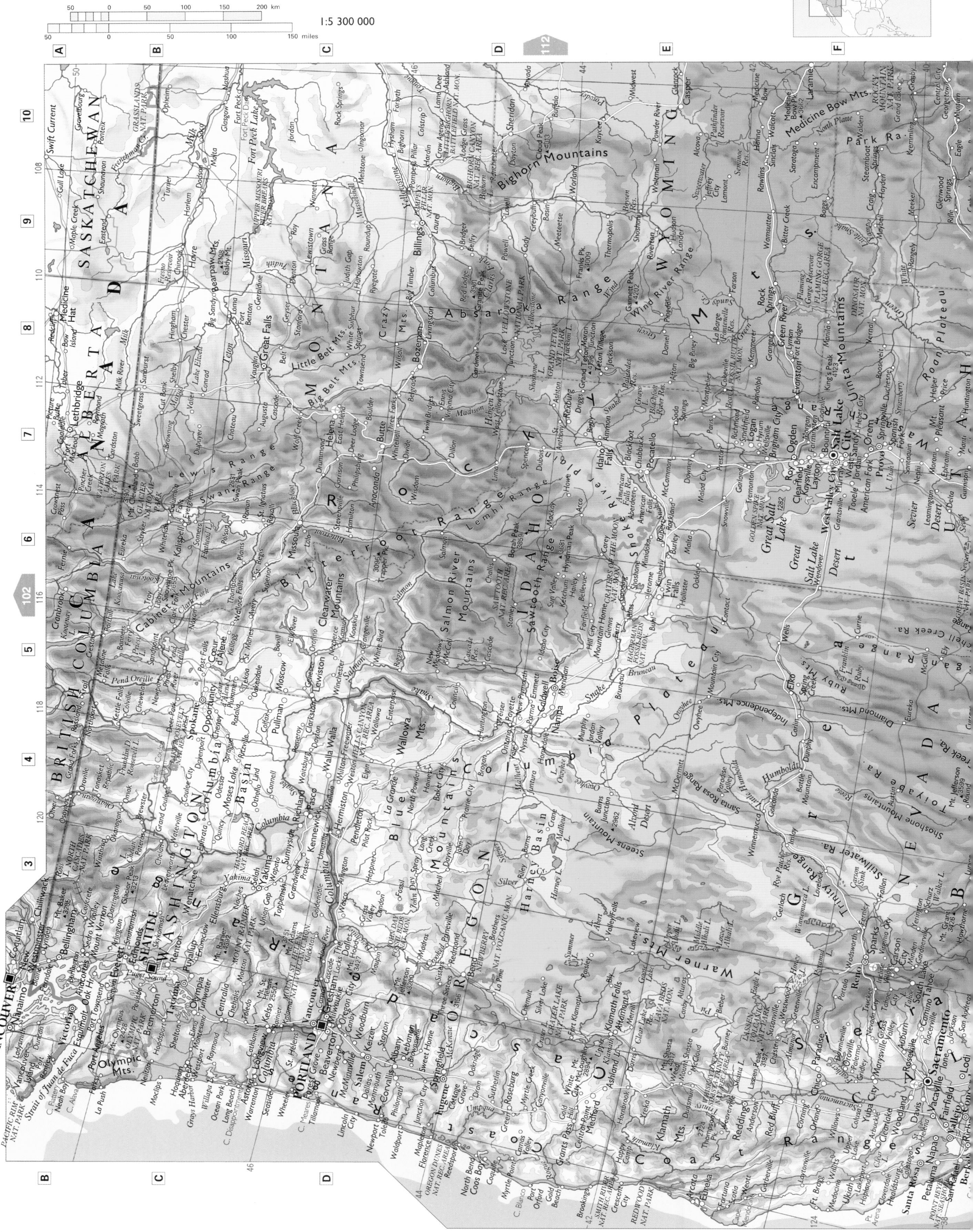

1:5 300 000
km
miles
BRITISH COLUMBIA
ALBERTA
SASKATCHEWAN
CANADA
WASHINGTON
OREGON
IDAHO
MONTANA
WYOMING
NEVADA
UTAH
VANCOUVER
SEATTLE
PORTLAND
Salt Lake City
Sacramento
Spokane
Boise
Reno
Great Falls
Billings
Helena
Missoula
Cascade Range
Coast Ranges
Blue Mountains
Bitterroot Range
Salmon River Mountains
Bighorn Mountains
Wind River Range
Absaroka Range
Uinta Mountains
Great Salt Lake
Great Salt Lake Desert
Snake River Plain
Columbia Basin
Harney Basin
Warner Mts.
Sierra Nevada
Olympic Mts.
Klamath Mts.
102
112

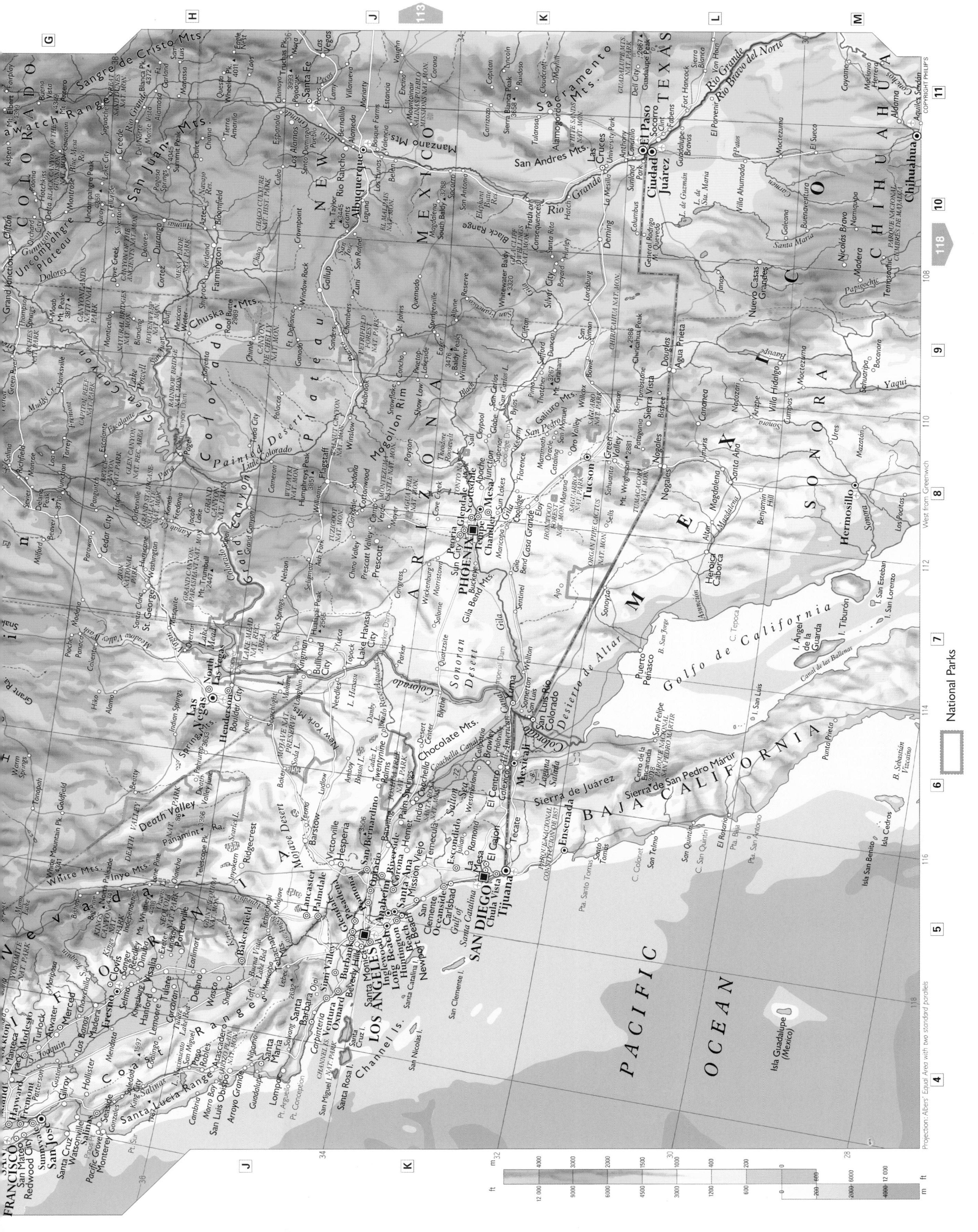
COLORADO
NEW MEXICO
ARIZONA
TEXAS
CHIHUAHUA
SONORA
MEXICO
BAJA CALIFORNIA
PACIFIC OCEAN
Golfo de California
Colorado Plateau
Sangre de Cristo Mts.
San Juan Mts.
Sacramento Mts.
Mojave Desert
Sonoran Desert
Desierto de Altar
Painted Desert
Mogollon Rim
Death Valley
Channel Is.
Sierra de San Pedro Mártir
Sierra de Juárez
Santa Lucia Range
LOS ANGELES
SAN DIEGO
PHOENIX
Santa Fe
Albuquerque
El Paso
Ciudad Juárez
Chihuahua
Hermosillo
Tucson
Las Vegas
Tijuana
Mexicali
Ensenada
Flagstaff
Bakersfield
Fresno
San Bernardino
Isla Guadalupe (Mexico)
Isla Cedros
I. Tiburón
I. Ángel de la Guarda
Río Grande
Río Bravo del Norte
Grand Canyon
National Parks
West from Greenwich
Projection: Albers' Equal Area with two standard parallels
COPYRIGHT PHILIP'S
113
118

10 0 10 20 30 40 50 60 70 80 90 km

10 0 10 20 30 40 50 60 miles

1:2 200 000

CENTRAL AND SOUTHERN CALIFORNIA AND WESTERN WASHINGTON

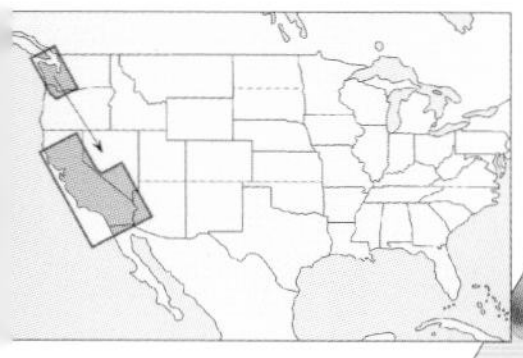

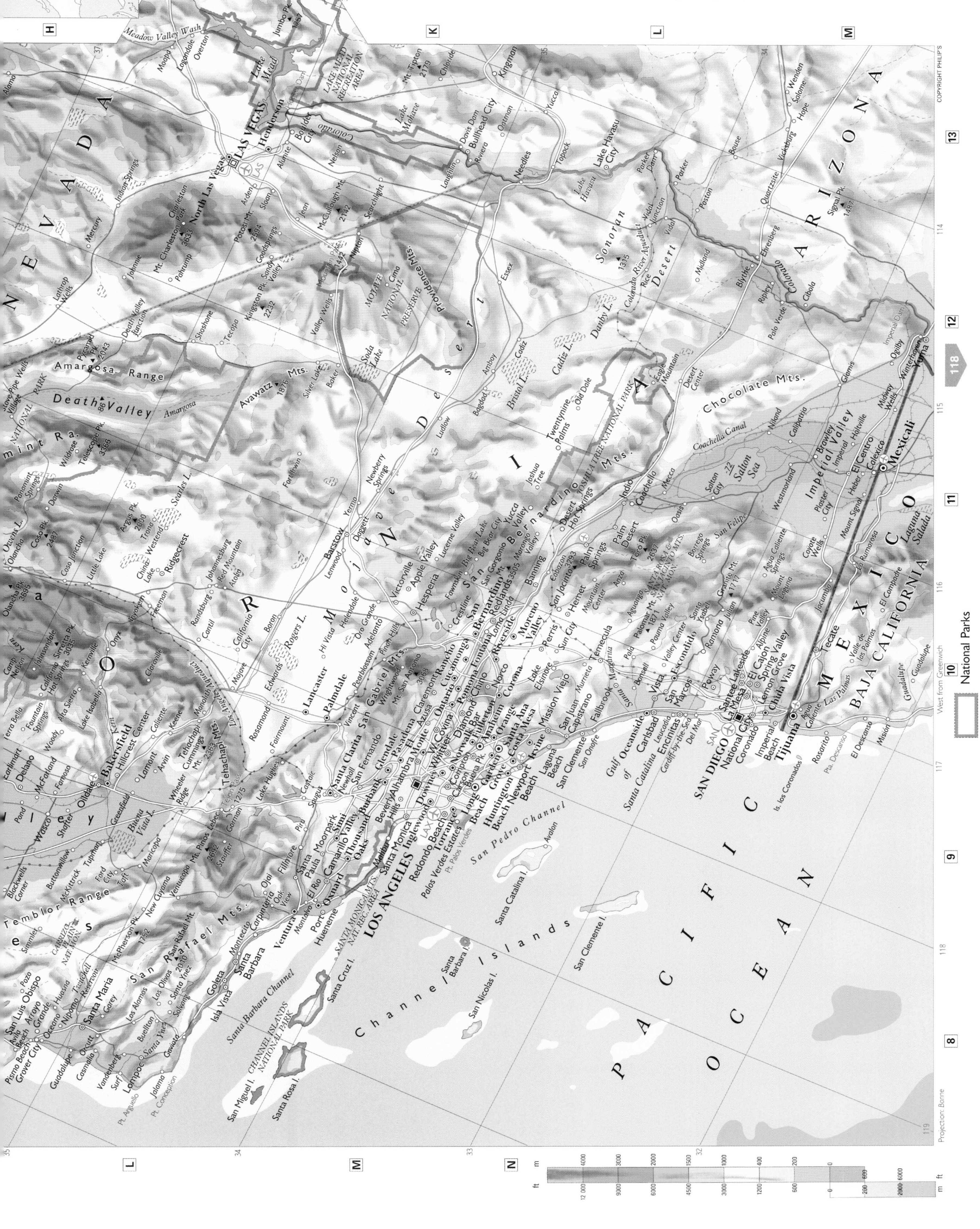

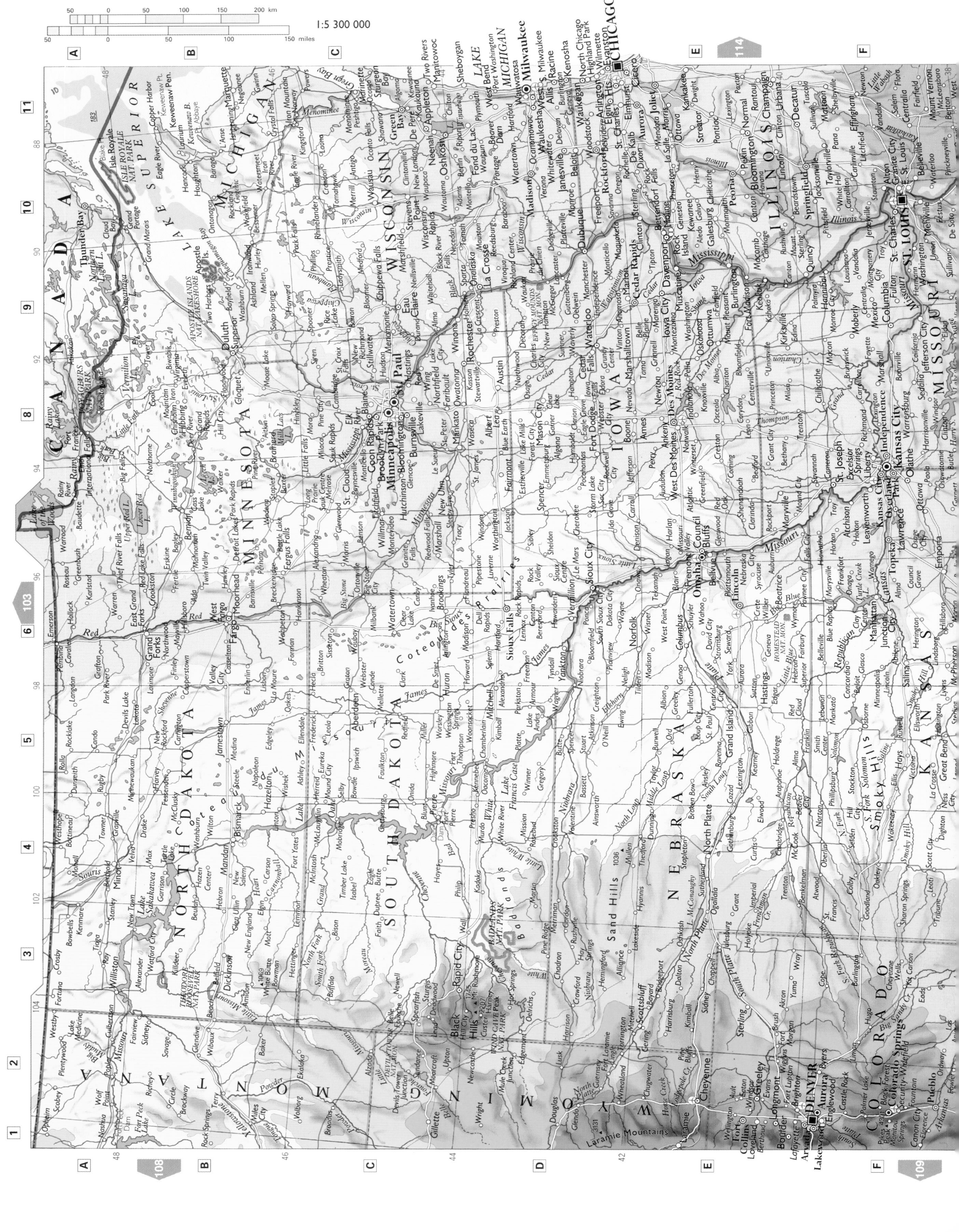

50 0 50 100 150 200 km
1:5 300 000
50 0 50 100 150 miles
CANADA
MINNESOTA
WISCONSIN
MICHIGAN
IOWA
ILLINOIS
MISSOURI
NORTH DAKOTA
SOUTH DAKOTA
NEBRASKA
KANSAS
COLORADO
WYOMING
MONTANA
LAKE SUPERIOR
LAKE MICHIGAN
CHICAGO
Milwaukee
Minneapolis
St Paul
ST. LOUIS
Kansas City
Omaha
DENVER
Des Moines
Sioux Falls
Fargo
Bismarck
Duluth
Rapid City
Sand Hills
Badlands
Smoky Hills
Laramie Mountains
Black Hills
Mississippi
Missouri
103
108
109
114

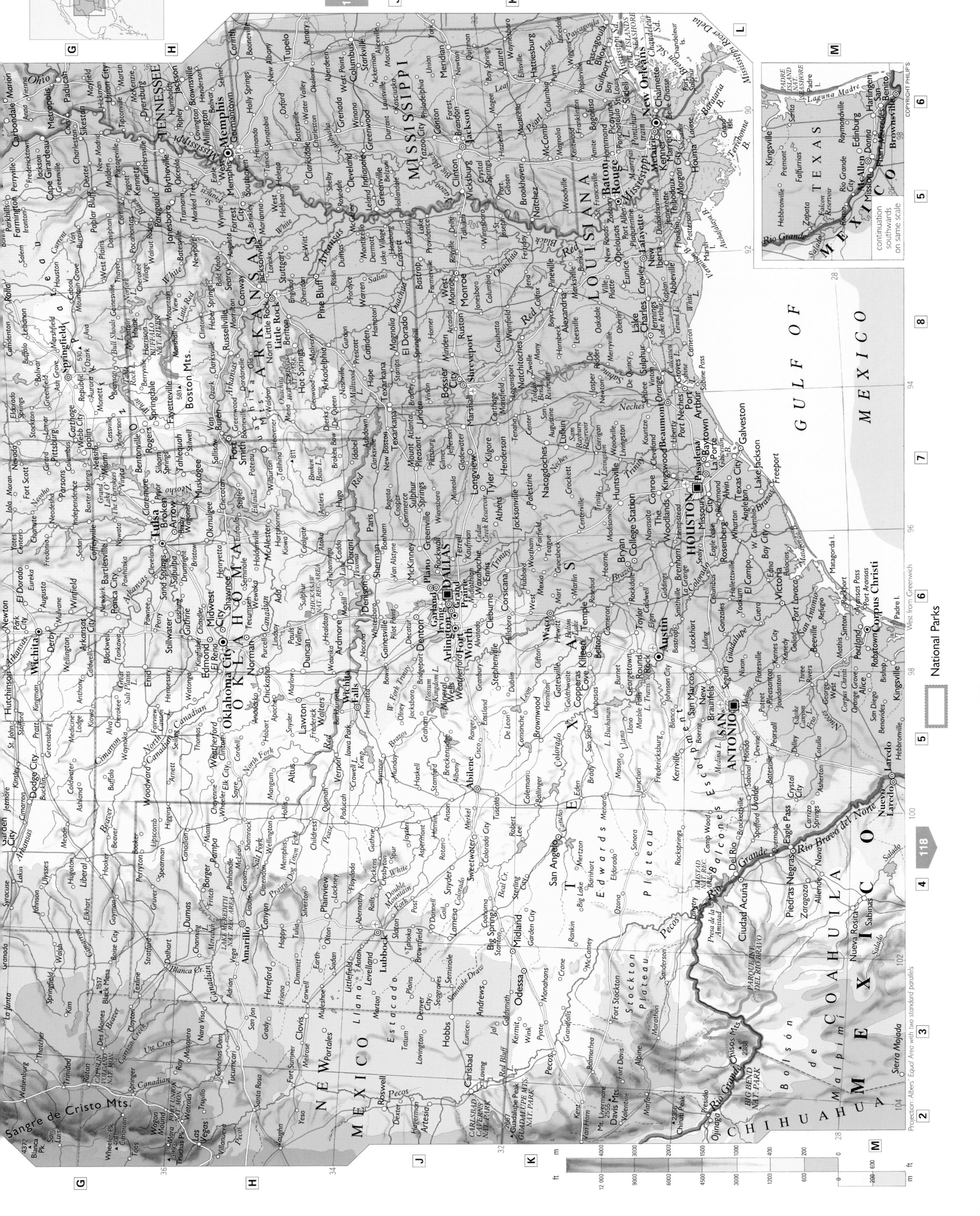

GULF OF MEXICO
TEXAS
OKLAHOMA
ARKANSAS
LOUISIANA
MISSISSIPPI
TENNESSEE
NEW MEXICO
MEXICO
COAHUILA
CHIHUAHUA
Dallas
Fort Worth
Houston
San Antonio
Austin
New Orleans
Memphis
Oklahoma City
Tulsa
Little Rock
Jackson
Shreveport
Baton Rouge
Lubbock
Amarillo
Wichita
Corpus Christi
Sangre de Cristo Mts.
Llano Estacado
Edwards Plateau
Stockton Plateau
Balcones Escarpment
Bolsón de Mapimí
BIG BEND NAT. PARK
continuation southwards on same scale
National Parks
West from Greenwich
Projection: Albers' Equal Area with two standard parallels
COPYRIGHT PHILIP'S

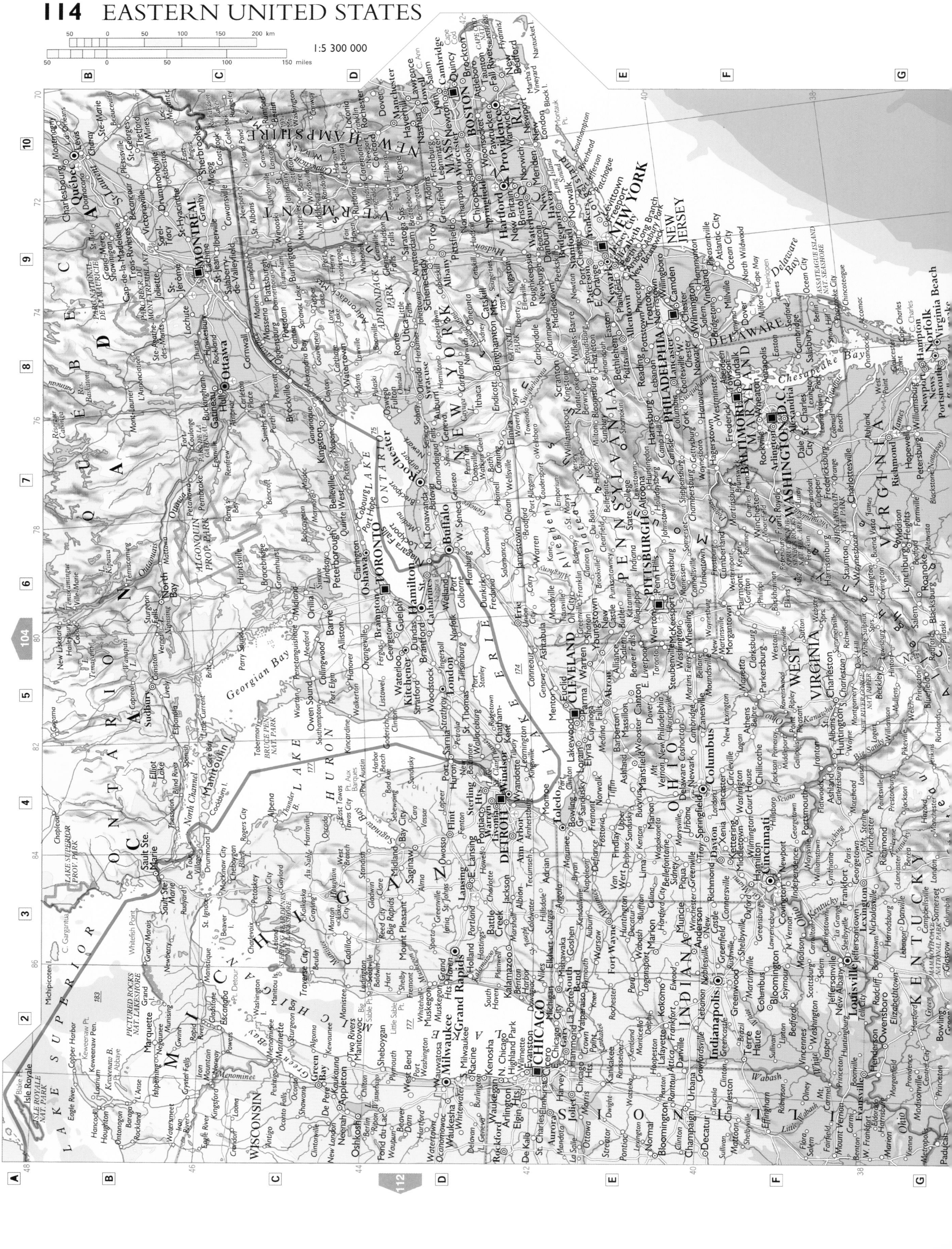

50 0 50 100 150 200 km
1:5 300 000
50 0 50 100 150 miles
B C D E F G
10 9 8 7 6 5 4 3 2 1
A B C D E F G
104
112
QUÉBEC
ONTARIO
NEW YORK
PENNSYLVANIA
NEW JERSEY
MARYLAND
DELAWARE
WEST VIRGINIA
VIRGINIA
OHIO
INDIANA
KENTUCKY
MICHIGAN
WISCONSIN
ILLINOIS
NEW HAMPSHIRE
VERMONT
MASS.
R.I.
LAKE SUPERIOR
LAKE HURON
LAKE ERIE
LAKE ONTARIO
Georgian Bay
Chesapeake Bay
Delaware Bay
MONTRÉAL
Ottawa
TORONTO
BOSTON
Providence
Hartford
NEW YORK
PHILADELPHIA
BALTIMORE
WASHINGTON D.C.
PITTSBURGH
CLEVELAND
DETROIT
Windsor
Columbus
Cincinnati
Indianapolis
CHICAGO
Milwaukee
Grand Rapids
Buffalo
Rochester
Hamilton
Québec
Louisville
Toledo

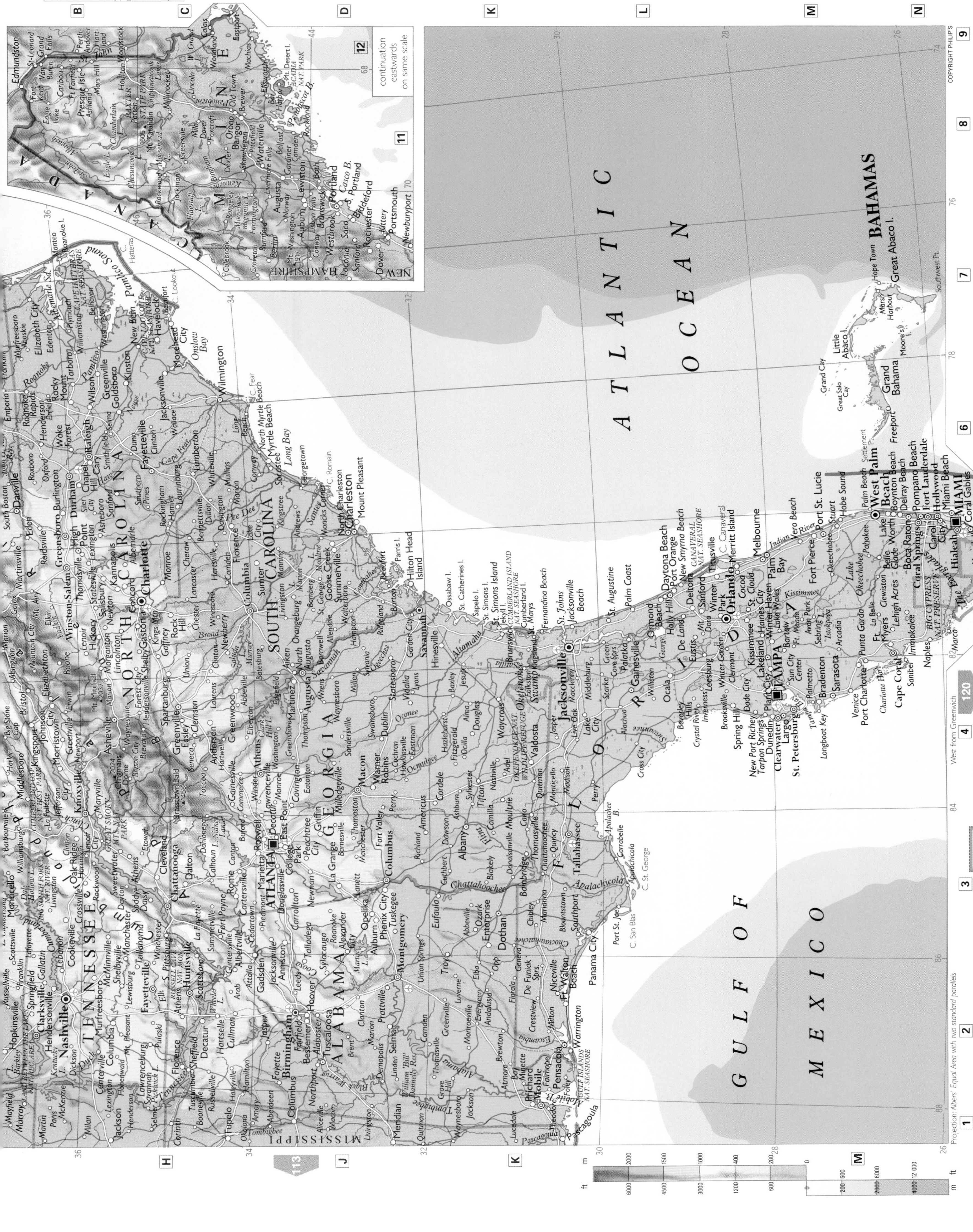
ATLANTIC OCEAN
GULF OF MEXICO
BAHAMAS
TENNESSEE
NORTH CAROLINA
SOUTH CAROLINA
GEORGIA
ALABAMA
FLORIDA
MISSISSIPPI
MAINE
NEW HAMPSHIRE
CANADA
Nashville
Atlanta
Charlotte
Jacksonville
Orlando
Tampa
Miami
Savannah
Charleston
Birmingham
Montgomery
Tallahassee
Knoxville
Chattanooga
Raleigh
Durham
Wilmington
Mobile
Pensacola
Portland
Bangor
Augusta
continuation eastwards on same scale
National Parks
Projection: Albers' Equal Area with two standard parallels
West from Greenwich
COPYRIGHT PHILIP'S
113
120

1:2 200 000

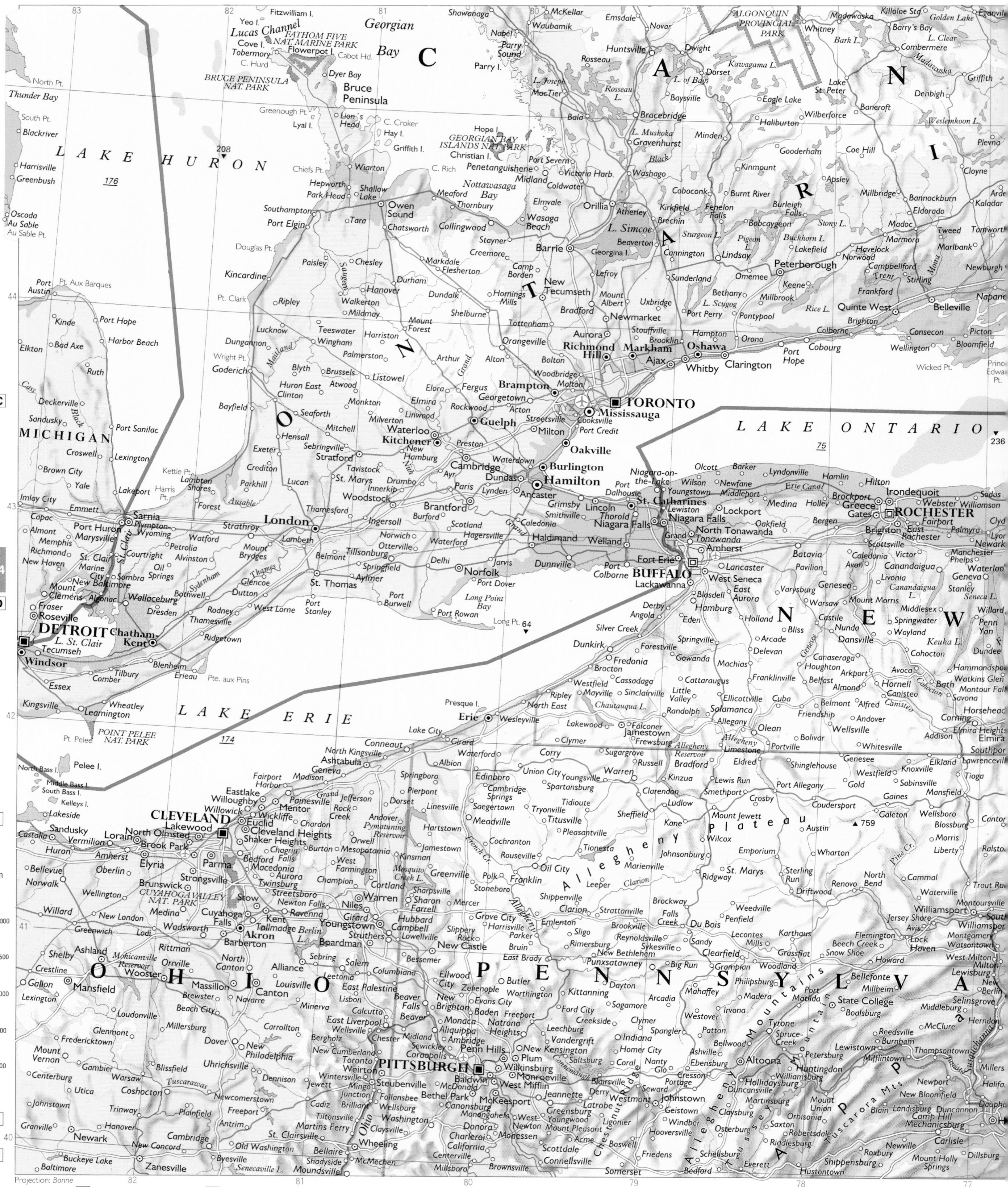

National Parks

104
114
114

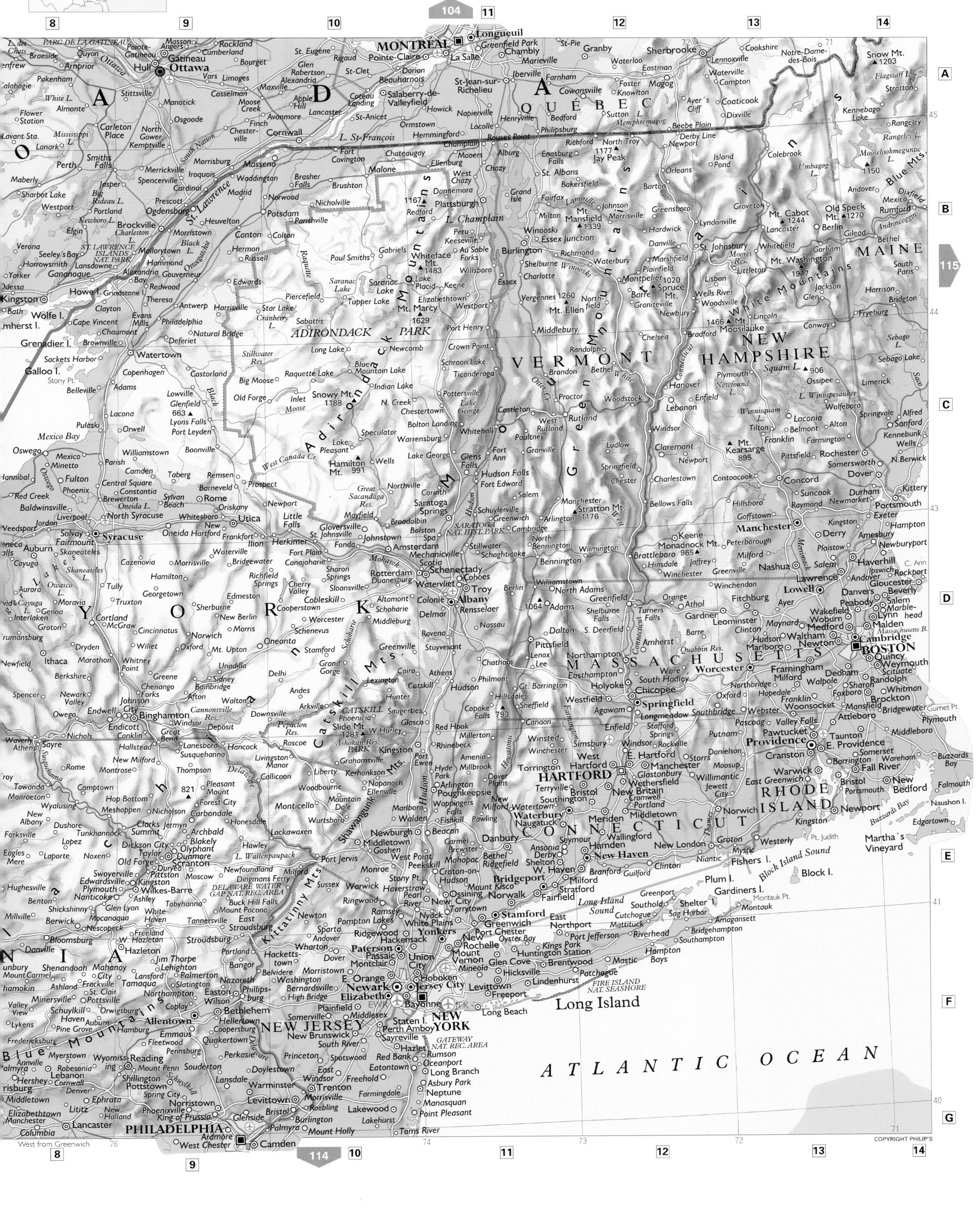
104
115
114
8
9
10
11
12
13
14
A
B
C
D
E
F
G
MONTREAL
Longueuil
Ottawa
Gatineau
Hull
Q U É B E C
Sherbrooke
Granby
Cornwall
L. St-François
Kingston
Wolfe I.
Amherst I.
Galloo I.
Watertown
Ogdensburg
Brockville
St. Lawrence
ST. LAWRENCE ISLANDS NAT. PARK
Massena
Malone
Plattsburgh
L. Champlain
Burlington
Montpelier
Mt. Mansfield 1339
Jay Peak
Mt. Marcy 1629
ADIRONDACK PARK
Adirondack Mountains
Whiteface Mt. 1483
Lake Placid
Saranac Lake
Tupper Lake
Long Lake
Blue Mountain Lake
Snowy Mt. 1188
Lake George
Glens Falls
Saratoga Springs
Great Sacandaga Res.
Oswego
Syracuse
Utica
Rome
Herkimer
Amsterdam
Schenectady
Albany
Troy
Rensselaer
Mohawk
V E R M O N T
Green Mountains
Rutland
Stratton Mt. 1176
Bennington
Brattleboro
White Mountains
Mt. Washington 1917
N E W H A M P S H I R E
Concord
Manchester
Nashua
Portsmouth
L. Winnipesaukee
M A I N E
Lowell
Lawrence
Haverhill
BOSTON
Cambridge
Quincy
Worcester
Springfield
Pittsfield
M A S S A C H U S E T T S
Quabbin Res.
Mt. Monadnock 965
Providence
R H O D E I S L A N D
Newport
Fall River
New Bedford
Cape Cod Bay
Buzzards Bay
Martha's Vineyard
Block I.
Block Island Sound
Fishers I.
Montauk Pt.
HARTFORD
New Haven
Bridgeport
Stamford
Waterbury
C O N N E C T I C U T
Long Island Sound
Long Island
FIRE ISLAND NAT. SEASHORE
NEW YORK
Yonkers
Jersey City
Newark
Elizabeth
Paterson
Staten I.
GATEWAY NAT. REC. AREA
NEW JERSEY
Trenton
PHILADELPHIA
Camden
Allentown
Bethlehem
Reading
Scranton
Wilkes-Barre
Binghamton
Ithaca
Cortland
Y O R K
Catskill Mts.
Slide Mt. 1281
Kingston
Poughkeepsie
Newburgh
Hudson
Delaware
DELAWARE WATER GAP NAT. REC. AREA
Kittatinny Mts.
Blue Mountains
L. Wallenpaupack
A T L A N T I C   O C E A N
West from Greenwich
COPYRIGHT PHILIP'S

50 0 50 100 150 200 250 300 km

50 0 50 100 150 200 miles

1:7 100 000

109

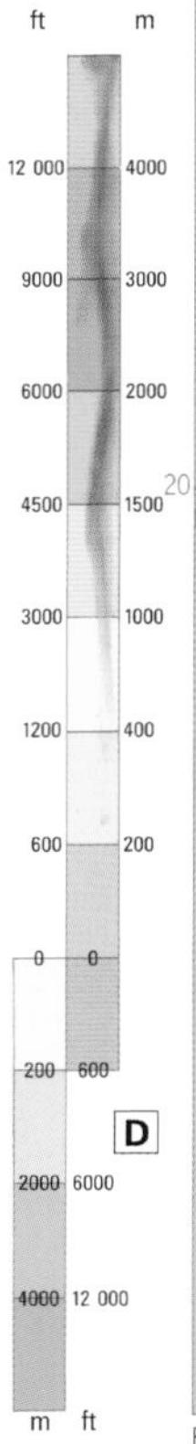

Projection: *Bi-polar oblique Conical Orthomorphic*

West from Greenwich

2 3 4

National Parks

State names in Central Mexico

1 DISTRITO FEDERAL	5 MÉXICO
2 AGUASCALIENTES	6 MORELOS
3 GUANAJUATO	7 QUERÉTARO
4 HIDALGO	8 TLAXCALA

5
6
113
7
8
A
B
C
D
E
120
UNITED STATES
ARKANSAS
MISSISSIPPI
ALABAMA
GEORGIA
LOUISIANA
TEXAS
FLORIDA
Wichita Falls
Denison
Sherman
Paris
Hope
Camden
Texarkana
El Dorado
Greenville
Tuscaloosa
Opelika
Columbus
McRae
Denton
Greenville
Phenix City
Selma
Montgomery
Americus
Cordele
FORT WORTH
DALLAS
Marshall
Monroe
Vicksburg
Meridian
Troy
Albany
Tifton
Possum Kingdom Res.
Ranger
Abilene
Longview
Tyler
Shreveport
Tallulah
Jackson
Waycross
Cleburne
Hillsboro
Corsicana
Palestine
Toledo Bend Res.
Nacogdoches
Natchez
Laurel
Hattiesburg
Dothan
Jim Woodruff Res.
Valdosta
Chattahoochee
Tallahassee
Brownwood
Waco
Jewett
Lufkin
Sam Rayburn Reservoir
Alexandria
McComb
Flomaton
MOBILE
Pensacola
Panama City
Lake City
Temple
Baton Rouge
Hammond
Bogalusa
Biloxi
Gulfport
Huntsville
Bryan
College Station
Navasota
Lake Charles
Lafayette
L. Pontchartrain
NEW ORLEANS
Mobile Bay
C. San Blas
Apalachee Bay
Suwannee
Austin
Beaumont
Port Arthur
HOUSTON
Breton Sd.
Rosenberg
Galveston
Atchafalaya Bay
Terrebonne Bay
Mississippi River Delta
Clearwater
SAN ANTONIO
Victoria
Dilley
Nueces
Alice
Corpus Christi
Laredo
Kingsville
Nuevo Laredo
PADRE ISLAND NAT. SEASHORE
Zapata
Laguna Madre
Presa Falcón
Nuevo Guerrero
Camargo
McAllen
Harlingen
Brownsville
General Treviño
Presa M. R. Gomez
Reynosa
Matamoros
China
Cadereyta
Montemorelos
Valle Hermoso
Santa Teresa
Mendez
Laguna Madre
Linares
San Fernando
Villagrán
Hidalgo
Santander Jiménez
Zaragoza
La Pesca
Soto la Marina
Ciudad Victoria
Sierra de Tamaulipas
Llera
Tula
Aldama
Pta. Jerez
Ocampo
Ciudad Mante
Altamira
Ciudad Madero
Tampico
Ciudad Valles
Cárdenas
Pánuco
Ozuluama
L. de Tamiahua
Tempoal
C. Rojo
Tantoyuca
Tamazunchale
Chicontepec
Tuxpan
Zimapán
Zacualtipán
Poza Rica
San Juan del Río
Huichapan
Papantla
Nautla
Pachuca
Huauchinango
Tulancingo
Misantla
Teziutlán
Tula
El Oro
TEOTIHUACAN
MÉXICO
Tlaxcala
Apizaco
COFRE DE PEROTE
ZEMPOALA
Xalapa
Coatepec
Veracruz
Toluca
Amecameca
PUEBLA
Pico de Orizaba
Tenancingo
Popocatépetl
Alvarado
Tlacotalpan
Córdoba
Orizaba
Cuernavaca
Cosamaloapan
San Andrés Tuxtla
Coatzacoalcos
Comalcalco
Paraíso
Frontera
Ciudad del Carmen
L. de Términos
Campeche
Champotón
Chenkán
Tehuacán
Tierra Blanca
Tres Valles
Minatitlán
Cárdenas
Villahermosa
Palizada
Balancán
TABASCO
Taxco
Izúcar de Matamoros
Chilac
Iguala
Chiautla
Acatlán
Huautla de Jiménez
Presa Miguel Alemán
Túxtepec
Acayucan
Teloloapan
Balsas
Chilapa
Huajuapan de León
Asunción Nochixtlán
San Juan Bautista Valle Nacional
Jesús Carranza
Istmo de Tehuantepec
Presa Malpaso
Raudales de Malpaso
Macuspana
Teapa
Tenosique
Chilpancingo
Tierra Colorada
Tlaxiaco
Oaxaca
Tlacolula
MONTE ALBÁN
Matías Romero
Tuxtla Gutiérrez
Chiapa de Corzo
San Cristóbal de las Casas
Ocosingo
Simojovel
La Independencia
Comitán
Coyuca de Benítez
Ayutla
Ometepec
Ocotlán
Ejutla
San Jerónimo Taviche
Ixtepec
Juchitán
Tehuantepec
Salina Cruz
Arriaga
Tonalá
La Concordia
Acapulco
Pinotepa Nacional
Jamiltepec
Miahuatlán
Tututepec
Pochutla
Bahías de Huatulco
Puerto Arista
Pijijiapan
Mapastepec
Motozintla
Puerto Ángel
Puerto Escondido
Golfo de Tehuantepec
Huixtla
Tapachula
Puerto Madero
Punta Maldonado
Papagayo
OAXACA
CHIAPAS
GUERRERO
Sierra Madre del Sur
Sierra Madre de Chiapas
GULF OF MEXICO
Golfo de Campeche
Tropic of Cancer
I. Desterrada
I. Pérez (Mexico)
Canal de Yucatán
C. San Antonio
C. Corrientes
La Esperanza
CUBA
Guane
La Fé
C. Catoche
Pta. Yalkubul
Río Lagartos
Isla Mujeres
Cancún
El Cuyo
Dzilam de Bravo
Tizimín
Progreso
Motul
Temax
Izamal
Espita
Puerto Morelos
DZIBILCHALTÚN
Mérida
YUCATÁN
CHICHÉN ITZÁ
Valladolid
COBA
Cozumel
Isla Cozumel
Maxcanú
MAYAPÁN
Sotuta
TULUM
UXMAL
Ticul
Peto
Tekax
Tenabo
Bolonchenticul
Vigía Chico
B. de la Ascensión
SIAN KA'AN
B. del Espíritu Santo
Hopelchén
Felipe Carrillo Puerto
EDZNÁ
XOCHOB
QUINTANA ROO
Banco Chinchorro
Bacalar
Chetumal
B. de Chetumal
Escárcega
BECÁN
Corozal
Ambergris Cay
CAMPECHE
CALAKMUL
Orange Walk
San Pedro
Hondo
Belize City
Turneffe Is.
BELIZE
Belmopan
Dangriga
MIRADOR-RÍO AZUL
LAGUNA DEL TIGRE
SIERRA DE LACANDÓN
Uaxactún
TIKAL
San Ignacio
BLUE HOLE
Benque Viejo
L. Petén Itzá
Flores
La Libertad
Maya Mts.
Golfo de Honduras
Is. de la Bahía
Roatán
Puerto Castilla
Trujillo
Balfate
La Ceiba
Iriona
Monkey River
San Antonio
San Luis
Punta Gorda
Livingston
Puerto Barrios
Puerto Cortés
Tela
PICO BONITO
Sava
Olanchito
RÍO PLÁTANO
Sebol
L. de Izabal
RÍO DULCE
San Pedro Sula
El Progreso
Arenal
Yoro
HONDURAS
GUATEMALA
Cuchumatanes
Cobán
Huehuetenango
Sierra de las Minas
Gualán
Santa Barbara
Juticalpa
Catacamas
San Marcos
Totonicapán
Sololá
Zacapa
Chiquimula
Santa Rosa de Copán
Comayagua
PATUCA
Tegucigalpa
Coatepeque
ATITLÁN
Antigua
GUATEMALA
Jalapa
La Esperanza
La Paz
Danlí
Yuscarán
Retalhuleu
Mazatenango
Amatitlán
COPÁN
95
90
85
100
30
25
20
15

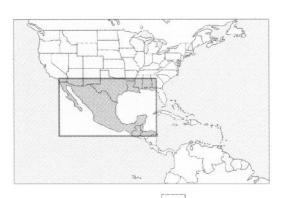

1:7 100 000

Projection: *Conical with two standard parallels*

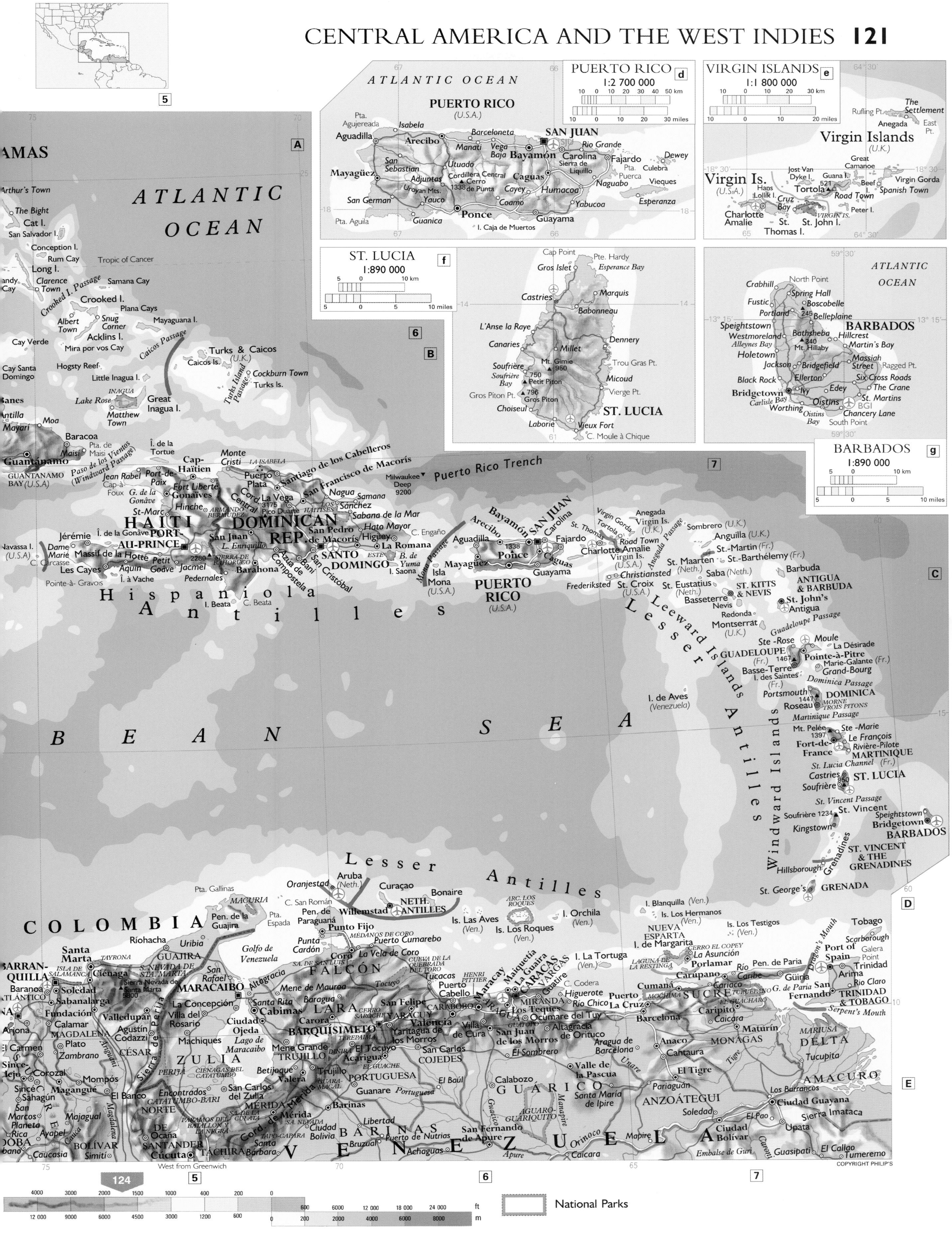
PUERTO RICO d
1:2 700 000
ATLANTIC OCEAN
PUERTO RICO (U.S.A.)
Pta. Agujereada
Isabela
Aguadilla
Arecibo
Barceloneta
SAN JUAN
Rio Grande
Manatí
Vega Baja
Bayamón
Carolina
Sierra de Luquillo
Fajardo
Dewey
Pta. Puerca
Culebra
Vieques
Mayagüez
San Sebastian
Utuado
Cordillera Central
Cerro de Punta 1338
Adjuntas
Caguas
Humacao
Naguabo
Uroyan Mts.
Yauco
Cayey
Coamo
Yabucoa
Esperanza
San German
Pta. Aguila
Guanica
Ponce
Guayama
I. Caja de Muertos
VIRGIN ISLANDS e
1:1 800 000
The Settlement
Rufling Pt.
Anegada
East Pt.
Virgin Islands (U.K.)
Great Camanoe
Virgin Is. (U.S.A.)
Jost Van Dyke I.
Guana I.
Tortola
Beef I.
Virgin Gorda
Spanish Town
Hans Lollik I.
Road Town
Cruz Bay
Peter I.
Charlotte Amalie
St. Thomas I.
St. John I.
VIRGIN IS.
ST. LUCIA f
1:890 000
Cap Point
Pte. Hardy
Gros Islet
Esperance Bay
Castries
Marquis
Babonneau
L'Anse la Raye
Canaries
Dennery
Millet
Mt. Gimie 950
Trou Gras Pt.
Soufrière
Soufrière Bay
Petit Piton 750
Micoud
Gros Piton Pt.
Gros Piton 796
Vierge Pt.
Choiseul
ST. LUCIA
Laborie
Vieux Fort
C. Moule à Chique
ATLANTIC OCEAN
Crabhill
North Point
Spring Hall
Fustic
Boscobelle
Portland
Belleplaine
Speightstown
BARBADOS
Westmoreland
Bathsheba
Hillcrest
Alleynes Bay
Mt. Hillaby 340
Martin's Bay
Holetown
Massiah Street
Ragged Pt.
Jackson
Bridgefield
Black Rock
Ellerton
Six Cross Roads
Bridgetown
Ivy
Edey
The Crane
Carlisle Bay
St. Martins
Worthing
Oistins
Oistins Bay
BGI
Chancery Lane
South Point
BARBADOS g
1:890 000
AMAS
Arthur's Town
ATLANTIC OCEAN
The Bight
Cat I.
San Salvador I.
Conception I.
Rum Cay
Tropic of Cancer
Long I.
Clarence Town
Samana Cay
Crooked I. Passage
Crooked I.
Plana Cays
Albert Town
Snug Corner
Mayaguana I.
Acklins I.
Caicos Passage
Cay Verde
Mira por vos Cay
Turks & Caicos (U.K.)
Caicos Is.
Cay Santa Domingo
Hogsty Reef
Cockburn Town
Turks Is.
Little Inagua I.
Turks Island Passage
INAGUA
Lake Rose
Great Inagua I.
Matthew Town
Moa
Mayarí
Baracoa
Pta. de Maisi
Maisí
Guantánamo
GUANTANAMO BAY (U.S.A.)
Paso de los Vientos (Windward Passage)
Î. de la Tortue
Monte Cristi
Cap-Haïtien
Puerto Plata
Santiago de los Cabelleros
San Francisco de Macorís
Puerto Rico Trench
Milwaukee Deep 9200
Jean Rabel
Port-de-Paix
Cap-à-Foux
Fort Liberté
G. de la Gonâve
Gonaïves
Cord. Central
La Vega
Nagua
Samana
Sánchez
Hinche
Pico Duarte 3175
St-Marc
HAITI
DOMINICAN REP.
Sabana de la Mar
Hato Mayor
Jérémie
Î. de la Gonâve
PORT-AU-PRINCE
San Juan
San Pedro de Macorís
Higüey
C. Engaño
La Romana
L. Enriquillo
Navassa I. (U.S.A.)
Dame Marie
Massif de la Hotte
SANTO DOMINGO
B. de Yuma
Les Cayes
Aquin
Petit Goâve
Jacmel
Barahona
Azua de Compostela
Baní
San Cristóbal
I. Saona
Pointe-à-Gravois
Î. à Vache
Pedernales
Hispaniola
I. Beata
C. Beata
Greater Antilles
Mona Passage
Isla Mona (U.S.A.)
Aguadilla
Arecibo
Bayamón
SAN JUAN
Carolina
Fajardo
Mayagüez
Ponce
Caguas
Guayama
PUERTO RICO (U.S.A.)
Virgin Gorda
Tortola
St. Thomas
Anegada
Virgin Is. (U.K.)
Road Town
Charlotte Amalie
Virgin Is. (U.S.A.)
Anegada Passage
Christiansted
Frederiksted
St. Croix (U.S.A.)
Sombrero (U.K.)
Anguilla (U.K.)
St.-Martin (Fr.)
St. Maarten (Neth.)
St.-Barthélemy (Fr.)
Saba (Neth.)
Barbuda
St. Eustatius (Neth.)
ST. KITTS & NEVIS
ANTIGUA & BARBUDA
Basseterre
Nevis
St. John's
Antigua
Redonda
Montserrat (U.K.)
Guadeloupe Passage
Leeward Islands
Lesser Antilles
Ste -Rose
Moule
La Désirade
GUADELOUPE (Fr.)
Pointe-à-Pitre
Basse-Terre
Marie-Galante (Fr.)
Grand-Bourg
I. des Saintes (Fr.)
Dominica Passage
Portsmouth
DOMINICA
Roseau
MORNE TROIS PITONS
I. de Aves (Venezuela)
Martinique Passage
Mt. Pelée 1397
Ste -Marie
Le François
Fort-de-France
Rivière-Pilote
MARTINIQUE (Fr.)
St. Lucia Channel
Castries
ST. LUCIA
Soufrière
St. Vincent Passage
Soufrière 1234
St. Vincent
Speightstown
Bridgetown
Kingstown
BARBADOS
Windward Islands
Grenadines
ST. VINCENT & THE GRENADINES
Hillsborough
St. George's
GRENADA
CARIBBEAN SEA
Lesser Antilles
Oranjestad
Aruba (Neth.)
Curaçao
Bonaire
Willemstad
NETH. ANTILLES
Pta. Gallinas
MACURIA
C. San Román
Pen. de Paraguaná
Pta. Espada
Punto Fijo
Pen. de la Guajira
COLOMBIA
I. Blanquilla (Ven.)
Is. Los Hermanos (Ven.)
Is. Las Aves (Ven.)
Is. Los Roques (Ven.)
I. Orchila (Ven.)
Is. Los Testigos (Ven.)
NUEVA ESPARTA
I. de Margarita
La Asunción
Porlamar
Tobago
Scarborough
Dragon's Mouth
Port of Spain
Galera Point
Trinidad
Arima
Rio Claro
TRINIDAD & TOBAGO
San Fernando
Serpent's Mouth
Ríohacha
Uribia
GUAJIRA
Golfo de Venezuela
Punta Cardón
MÉDANOS DE CORO
Puerto Cumarebo
Coro
La Vela de Coro
FALCÓN
Santa Marta
TAYRONA
BARRANQUILLA
Ciénaga
Sierra Nevada de Santa Marta 5800
San Rafael
MARACAIBO
Altagracia
Tucacas
Puerto Cabello
Maracay
Maiquetía
La Guaira
CARACAS
VARGAS
Guatire
I. La Tortuga (Ven.)
C. Codera
Higuerote
Puerto La Cruz
Cumaná
Carupano
Pen. de Paria
Río Caribe
Güiria
G. de Paria
Baranoa
Soledad
Sabanalarga
La Concepción
Mene de Mauroa
Santa Rita
Cabimas
Baragua
LARA
San Felipe
CARABOBO
MIRANDA
Los Teques
Ocumare del Tuy
Barcelona
SUCRE
Caripito
Caicara
Maturín
Fundación
Valledupar
Villa del Rosario
Ciudad Ojeda
Carora
BARQUISIMETO
YARACUY
Valencia
Villa de Cura
San Juan de los Morros
Altagracia de Orituco
Aragua de Barcelona
Anaco
MONAGAS
DELTA
Tucupita
MAGDALENA
Agustín Codazzi
Machiques
Lago de Maracaibo
Mene Grande
TRUJILLO
El Tocuyo
Acarigua
San Carlos
COJEDES
El Sombrero
Cantaura
El Tigre
Plato
CÉSAR
ZULIA
Betijoque
Trujillo
Valera
PORTUGUESA
Guanare
El Baúl
Calabozo
GUÁRICO
Valle de la Pascua
Pariaguán
ANZOÁTEGUI
AMACURO
Los Barrancos
Ciudad Guayana
Sierra Imataca
Zambrano
Corozal
Sincé
Magangué
Mompós
Sahagún
El Banco
Encontrados
San Carlos del Zulia
MÉRIDA
Mérida
Barinas
Santa María de Ipire
Soledad
El Pao
Upata
San Marcos
Majagual
NORTE DE SANTANDER
Ocaña
Cúcuta
TÁCHIRA
Santa Bárbara
Bolívia
BARINAS
Libertad
Puerto de Nutrias
San Fernando de Apure
VENEZUELA
Orinoco
Mapire
Ciudad Bolívar
Embalse de Guri
Guasipati
El Callao
Tumeremo
BOLÍVAR
Simití
Caucasia
Apure
Caicara
West from Greenwich
COPYRIGHT PHILIP'S
National Parks

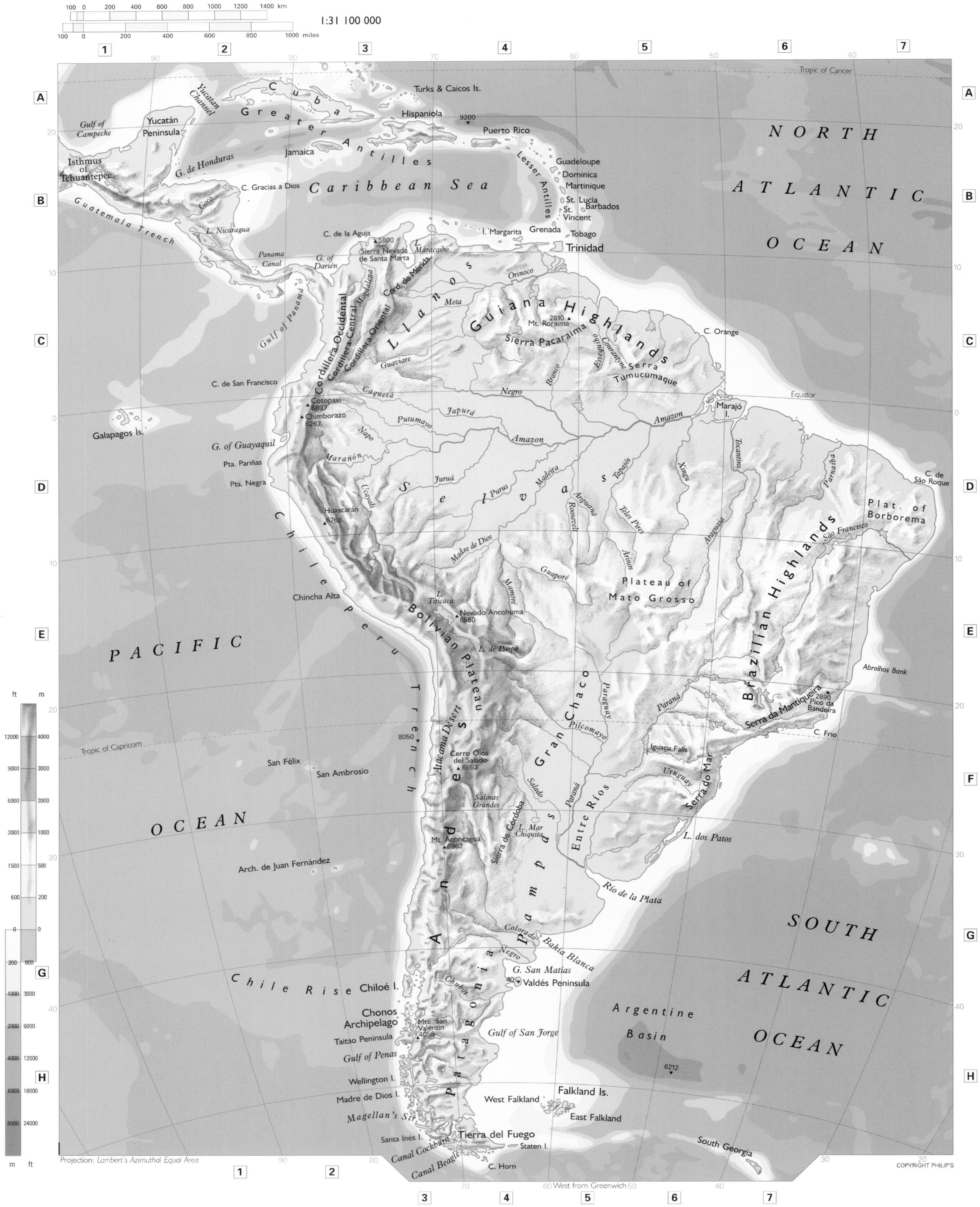
1:31 100 000
Turks & Caicos Is.
Cuba
Greater Antilles
Yucatan Channel
Gulf of Campeche
Yucatán Peninsula
Isthmus of Tehuantepec
G. de Honduras
Hispaniola
Puerto Rico
Jamaica
Caribbean Sea
C. Gracias a Dios
Guatemala Trench
L. Nicaragua
Coco
Lesser Antilles
Guadeloupe
Dominica
Martinique
St. Lucia
Barbados
St. Vincent
Grenada
Tobago
Trinidad
I. Margarita
C. de la Aguja
Sierra Nevada de Santa Marta
5800
L. Maracaibo
Panama Canal
G. of Darién
Gulf of Panamá
Cordillera Occidental
Cordillera Central
Cordillera Oriental
Magdalena
Cord. de Mérida
Llanos
Orinoco
Meta
Guiana Highlands
Mt. Roraima
2810
Sierra Pacaraima
Essequibo
Courantyne
Serra Tumucumaque
C. Orange
Guaviare
Branco
Negro
Caquetá
C. de San Francisco
Cotopaxi
5897
Chimborazo
6267
Galapagos Is.
Japurá
Putumayo
Napo
Amazon
Marajó I.
Equator
G. of Guayaquil
Pta. Pariñas
Pta. Negra
Marañón
Juruá
Ucayali
Selvas
Purus
Madeira
Tapajós
Xingu
Tocantins
Parnaíba
C. de São Roque
Aripuanã
Roosevelt
Teles Pires
Araguaia
Plat. of Borborema
São Francisco
Huascarán
6768
Madre de Dios
Arinos
Guaporé
Mamoré
Plateau of Mato Grosso
Brazilian Highlands
Chincha Alta
L. Titicaca
Nevado Ancohuma
6550
L. de Poopó
Bolivian Plateau
Peru Chile Trench
PACIFIC OCEAN
Abrolhos Bank
Gran Chaco
Paraguay
Paraná
Pilcomayo
Serra da Mantiqueira
2890
Pico da Bandeira
C. Frio
Tropic of Capricorn
8050
Atacama Desert
Cerro Ojos del Salado
6863
San Félix
San Ambrosio
Iguaçu Falls
Uruguay
Serra do Mar
Salado
Entre Ríos
Salinas Grandes
Sierra de Córdoba
L. Mar Chiquita
Mt. Aconcagua
6962
Andes
L. dos Patos
Arch. de Juan Fernández
Pampas
Río de la Plata
SOUTH ATLANTIC OCEAN
Colorado
Bahía Blanca
Negro
G. San Matías
Valdés Peninsula
40
Chile Rise
Chiloé I.
Chubut
Patagonia
Chonos Archipelago
Mte. San Valentín
4058
Taitao Peninsula
Gulf of San Jorge
Argentine Basin
Gulf of Penas
6212
Wellington I.
Madre de Dios I.
West Falkland
Falkland Is.
East Falkland
Magellan's Str.
Tierra del Fuego
Santa Inés I.
Canal Cockburn
Staten I.
Canal Beagle
C. Horn
South Georgia
NORTH ATLANTIC OCEAN
Tropic of Cancer
West from Greenwich
Projection: Lambert's Azimuthal Equal Area
COPYRIGHT PHILIP'S

1:31 100 000
100 0 200 400 600 800 1000 1200 1400 km
100 0 200 400 600 800 1000 miles
Tropic of Cancer
Havana
CUBA
BAHAMAS
Turks & Caicos Is. (U.K.)
MEXICO
BELIZE
GUATEMALA
Guatemala
HONDURAS
Tegucigalpa
San Salvador
EL SALVADOR
NICARAGUA
Managua
COSTA RICA
San José
PANAMA
Panamá
JAMAICA
Kingston
HAITI
Port-au-Prince
DOMINICAN REP.
San Juan
PUERTO RICO (U.S.A.)
Virgin Is. (U.K.)
ANTIGUA & BARBUDA
ST. KITTS & NEVIS
Basse-Terre
GUADELOUPE (Fr.)
DOMINICA
Fort-de-France
MARTINIQUE (Fr.)
Castries
ST. LUCIA
ST. VINCENT
Kingstown
BARBADOS
Bridgetown
GRENADA
St. George's
Port of Spain
TRINIDAD & TOBAGO
Caribbean Sea
NORTH ATLANTIC OCEAN
Aruba
Curaçao
C. de la Aguja
Barranquilla
Cartagena
G. of Darién
Maracaibo
Barquisimeto
Caracas
Valencia
Cúcuta
San Cristóbal
Orinoco
Ciudad Guayana
Medellín
Bucaramanga
VENEZUELA
Georgetown
Paramaribo
Cayenne
C. Orange
GUYANA
SURINAME
FRENCH GUIANA
Bogotá
Cali
Gulf of Panamá
Magdalena
COLOMBIA
RORAIMA
Branco
Essequibo
AMAPÁ
Equator
Galapagos Is. (Ecuador)
Quito
ECUADOR
Guayaquil
G. of Guayaquil
Napo
Putumayo
Japurá
Marajó I.
Belém
Amazon
Manaus
Santarém
Iquitos
Marañón
São Luís
AMAZONAS
PARÁ
Tapajós
Xingu
Tocantins
Fortaleza
Juruá
Madeira
Purus
MARANHÃO
Teresina
C. de São Roque
CEARÁ
RIO G. DO NORTE
Natal
Chiclayo
Ucayali
ACRE
Parnaíba
PIAUÍ
PARAÍBA
Campina Grande
Trujillo
Chimbote
Pôrto Velho
PERNAMBUCO
Recife
ALAGOAS
Maceió
PERU
RONDÔNIA
Madre de Dios
Araguaia
TOCANTINS
SERGIPE
Aracaju
BRAZIL
Callao
LIMA
Cuzco
Mamoré
MATO GROSSO
BAHÍA
Salvador
L. Titicaca
GOIÁS
Cuiabá
Arequipa
La Paz
BOLIVIA
DIS. FED.
Brasília
São Francisco
Cochabamba
Santa Cruz
Goiânia
PACIFIC OCEAN
Sucre
Paraguay
MINAS GERAIS
MATO GROSSO DO SUL
Belo Horizonte
Iquique
ESPIRITO SANTO
Ribeirão Prêto
Vitória
Paraná
Juiz de Fora
SÃO PAULO
Campos
PARAGUAY
Campinas
R. DE J.
Niterói
Antofagasta
Pilcomayo
SÃO PAULO
RIO DE JANEIRO
Salta
Asunción
PARANÁ
Tropic of Capricorn
Curitiba
San Félix (Chile)
San Ambrosio (Chile)
San Miguel de Tucumán
Resistencia
Corrientes
SANTA CATARINA
Salado
Uruguay
RIO GRANDE DO SUL
Córdoba
Santa Fe
Pôrto Alegre
San Juan
Paraná
Pelotas
Viña del Mar
Mendoza
Rosario
URUGUAY
Valparaíso
SANTIAGO
Arch. de Juan Fernández (Chile)
BUENOS AIRES
Montevideo
La Plata
Río de la Plata
Talca
Concepción
CHILE
ARGENTINA
Bahía Blanca
Mar del Plata
Colorado
SOUTH ATLANTIC OCEAN
Valdivia
Negro
Viedma
Puerto Montt
Chubut
Comodoro Rivadavia
Gulf of San Jorge
Gulf of Penas
West Falkland
FALKLAND IS. (U.K.)
Stanley
East Falkland
Magellan's Str.
Punta Arenas
Tierra del Fuego
South Georgia (U.K.)
C. Horn
West from Greenwich
Projection: Lambert's Azimuthal Equal Area
COPYRIGHT PHILIP'S
LIMA Capital Cities

1:14 200 000
km
miles
120
121
126
NICARAGUA
Managua
Granada
L. de Nicaragua
Bluefields
San Juan del Norte
COSTA RICA
San José
Limón
Panama Canal
Colón
Panamá
PANAMA
G. de Panamá
I. de Coiba
BARRANQUILLA
Cartagena
Santa Marta
Montería
MEDELLÍN
BOGOTÁ
CALI
Popayán
Cúcuta
Bucaramanga
Villavicencio
COLOMBIA
MARACAIBO
Barquisimeto
VALENCIA
CARACAS
Barcelona
Cumaná
Ciudad Guayana
Ciudad Bolívar
VENEZUELA
Orinoco
TRINIDAD & TOBAGO
Port of Spain
Georgetown
GUYANA
Mt. Roraima
Sierra Pacaraima
Boa Vista
RORAIMA
QUITO
GUAYAQUIL
Cuenca
ECUADOR
Equator
Iquitos
Leticia
MANAUS
AMAZONAS
Solimões (Amazonas)
Porto Velho
Rio Branco
ACRE
RONDÔNIA
Trujillo
Chimbote
Callao
LIMA
Huancayo
Cuzco
Arequipa
PERU
L. Titicaca
LA PAZ
Cochabamba
Santa Cruz
Sucre
Potosí
Oruro
BOLIVIA
Arica
Iquique
Antofagasta
CHILE
ARGENTINA
PARAGUAY
Peru-Chile Trench
PACIFIC OCEAN
Projection: Sanson-Flamsteed's Sinusoidal
West from Greenwich

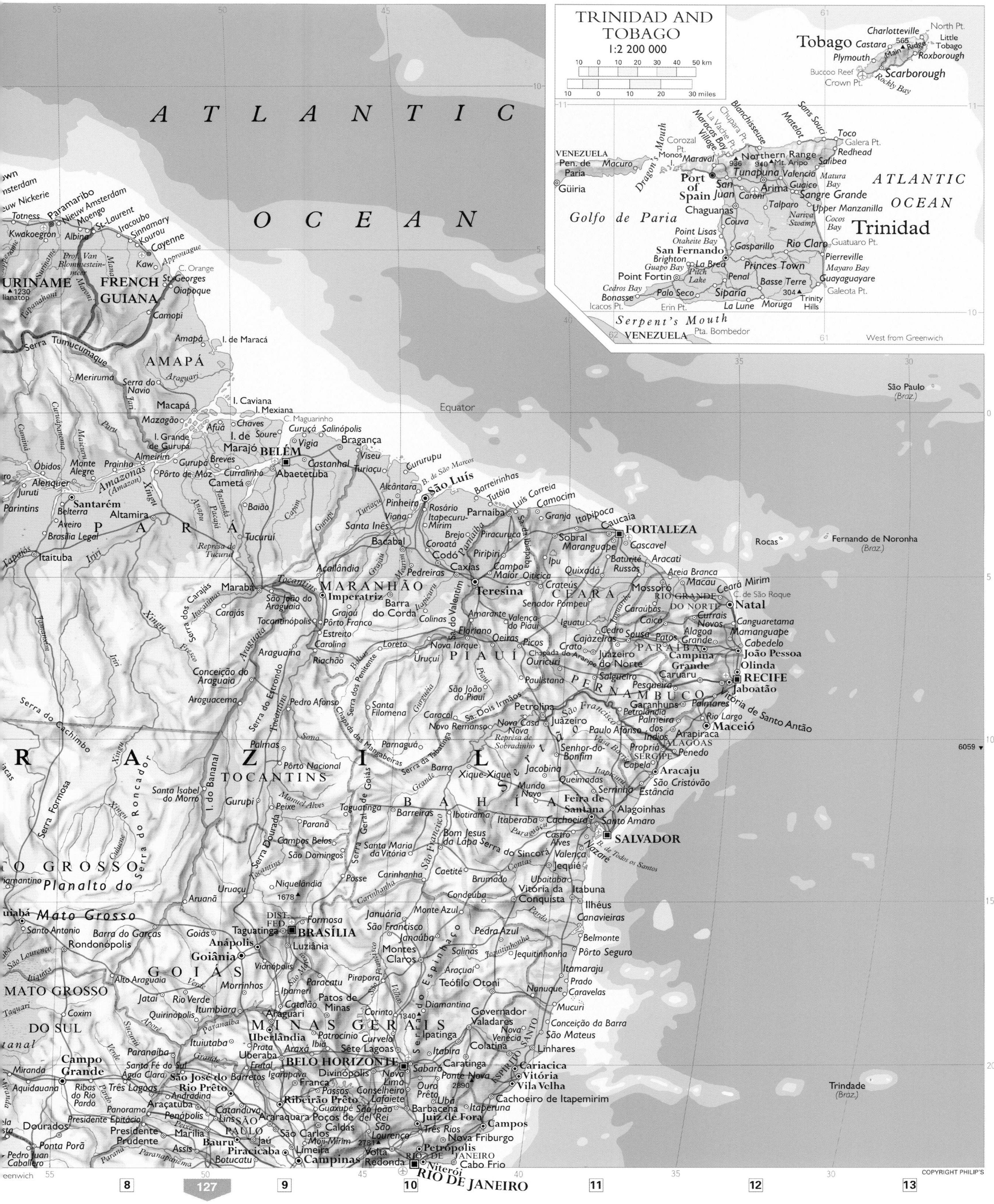

8
9
10
14
15
16
J
K
L
D
E
F
G
H
ATLANTIC OCEAN
TRINIDAD AND TOBAGO
1:2 200 000
10 0 10 20 30 40 50 km
10 0 10 20 30 miles
Tobago
Charlotteville
North Pt.
Little Tobago
Castara
Main Ridge
565
Roxborough
Plymouth
Buccoo Reef
Crown Pt.
Scarborough
Rockly Bay
Blanchisseuse
Chupara Pt.
La Vache Pt.
Maracas Bay Village
Sans Souci
Matelot
Toco
Galera Pt.
Redhead
Salibea
Corozal Pt.
Monos I.
Dragon's Mouth
VENEZUELA
Pen. de Paria
Macuro
Güiria
Maraval
Northern Range
936
940 Mt. Aripo
Port of Spain
Tunapuna
Valencia
Matura Bay
San Juan
Caroni
Arima
Guaico
Sangre Grande
Golfo de Paria
Chaguanas
Talparo
Upper Manzanilla
Nariva Swamp
Cocos Bay
Couva
Trinidad
Point Lisas
Otaheite Bay
Gasparillo
Rio Claro
Guatuaro Pt.
San Fernando
Brighton
Guapo Bay
La Brea
Pitch Lake
Princes Town
Pierreville
Mayaro Bay
Point Fortin
Penal
Basse Terre
Guayaguayare
Cedros Bay
Bonasse
Palo Seco
Siparia
304
Galeota Pt.
Trinity Hills
Icacos Pt.
Erin Pt.
La Lune
Moruga
Serpent's Mouth
Pta. Bombedor
VENEZUELA
West from Greenwich
São Paulo (Braz.)
Equator
Rocas
Fernando de Noronha (Braz.)
6059
Trindade (Braz.)
SURINAME
Paramaribo
Nieuw Amsterdam
Nieuw Nickerie
Totness
Moengo
Albina
St.-Laurent
Kwakoegron
Iracoubo
Sinnamary
Kourou
Cayenne
FRENCH GUIANA
Approuague
Kaw
C. Orange
St-Georges
Oiapoque
Camopi
Amapá
I. de Maracá
AMAPÁ
Serra Tumucumaque
Meriruma
Serra do Navio
Macapá
I. Caviana
I. Mexiana
C. Maguarinho
Mazagão
Chaves
Afuá
I. de Marajó
Soure
Curuçá
Salinópolis
Vigia
Bragança
BELÉM
Castanhal
Viseu
Gurupá
Breves
Almeirim
Monte Alegre
Prainha
Óbidos
Alenquer
Juruti
Parintins
Santarém
Belterra
Amazonas (Amazon)
Pôrto de Móz
Curralinho
Abaetetuba
Cametá
Baião
Altamira
Aveiro
Brasília Legal
PARÁ
Tucuruí
Represa de Tucuruí
Itaituba
Cururupu
Turiaçu
Alcântara
São Luís
Barreirinhas
Tutóia
Luís Correia
Camocim
Pinheiro
Rosário
Itapecuru-Mirim
Viana
Parnaíba
Granja
Itapipoca
Caucaia
FORTALEZA
Santa Inês
Bacabal
Brejo
Piracuruca
Sobral
Maranguape
Cascavel
Coroatá
Codó
Piripiri
Ipu
Baturité
Aracati
Açailândia
Pedreiras
Caxias
Campo Maior
Quixadá
Russas
Areia Branca
Marabá
MARANHÃO
Imperatriz
Teresina
Crateús
Macau
Mossoró
Ceará Mirim
C. de São Roque
Natal
São João do Araguaia
Barra do Corda
CEARÁ
Senador Pompeu
RIO GRANDE DO NORTE
Carajás
Grajaú
Tocantinópolis
Pôrto Franco
Estreito
Carolina
Colinas
Amarante
Valença do Piauí
Floriano
Oeiras
Picos
Iguatu
Caraúbas
Caicó
Currais Novos
Canguaretama
Mamanguape
Cajazeiras
Cedro
Sousa
Patos
Alagoa Grande
Cabedelo
João Pessoa
PARAÍBA
Campina Grande
Olinda
Araguaína
Loreto
Nova Iorque
Uruçuí
PIAUÍ
Crato
Juazeiro do Norte
Ouricuri
Chapada do Araripe
Salgueiro
Caruaru
Pesqueira
RECIFE
Jaboatão
Conceição do Araguaia
Riachão
Paulistana
PERNAMBUCO
Vitória de Santo Antão
Araguacema
Pedro Afonso
Santa Filomena
São João do Piauí
Petrolina
Garanhuns
Palmares
Caracol
Juazeiro
Petrolândia
Rio Largo
Maceió
Novo Remanso
Nova Casa Nova
Paulo Afonso
Palmeira dos Índios
Arapiraca
ALAGOAS
Represa de Sobradinho
Senhor-do-Bonfim
Propriá
Penedo
SERGIPE
Capela
Aracaju
São Cristóvão
Estância
Serra do Cachimbo
Palmas
Parnaguá
Serra da Tabatinga
Chapada das Mangabeiras
Barra
Xique-Xique
Jacobina
Queimadas
Serrinha
Pôrto Nacional
TOCANTINS
I. do Bananal
BRAZIL
Serra do Roncador
Serra Formosa
Santa Isabel do Morro
Gurupi
Peixe
Taguatinga
Barreiras
Ibotirama
Mundo Novo
BAHIA
Feira de Santana
Alagoinhas
Itaberaba
Cachoeira
Santo Amaro
SALVADOR
Castro Alves
Valença
Nazaré
B. de Todos os Santos
Paranã
Campos Belos
São Domingos
Serra Geral de Goiás
Santa Maria da Vitória
Bom Jesus da Lapa
Serra do Sincorá
Jequié
MATO GROSSO
Planalto do Mato Grosso
Diamantino
Serra Dourada
Posse
Carinhanha
Caetité
Brumado
Ubaitaba
Vitória da Conquista
Itabuna
Ilhéus
Uruaçu
Niquelândia
1678
Aruanã
Condeúba
Canavieiras
Cuiabá
Santo Antonio
Barra do Garças
Rondonópolis
DIST. FED.
Formosa
Taguatinga
BRASÍLIA
Januária
São Francisco
Monte Azul
Pedra Azul
Belmonte
Goiás
Anápolis
Luziânia
Janaúba
Salinas
Jequitinhonha
Pôrto Seguro
Goiânia
Montes Claros
Vianópolis
GOIÁS
Araçuaí
Itamaraju
Alto Araguaia
Morrinhos
Paracatu
Pirapora
Teófilo Otoni
Prado
Caravelas
Nanuque
MATO GROSSO DO SUL
Coxim
Jataí
Rio Verde
Quirinópolis
Itumbiara
Ipameri
Catalão
Patos de Minas
Araguari
Corinto
1340
Diamantina
Mucuri
Governador Valadares
Conceição da Barra
MINAS GERAIS
Uberlândia
Patrocínio
Curvelo
Ipatinga
Nova Venécia
São Mateus
ESPÍRITO SANTO
Paranaíba
Ituiutaba
Prata
Araxá
Ibiá
Sete Lagoas
Itabira
Colatina
Linhares
Campo Grande
Uberaba
Frutal
Santa Fé do Sul
BELO HORIZONTE
Sabará
Caratinga
Cariacica
Vitória
Vila Velha
Miranda
Aquidauana
Água Clara
São José do Barretos
Igarapava
Divinópolis
Nova Lima
Ponte Nova
Ouro Prêto
2890
Ribas do Rio Pardo
Três Lagoas
Rio Prêto
Andradina
Franca
Passos
Conselheiro Lafaiete
Ubá
Cachoeiro de Itapemirim
Araçatuba
Ribeirão Prêto
Guaxupé
São João del Rei
Barbacena
Itaperuna
Panorama
Presidente Epitácio
Penápolis
Catanduva
Lins
SÃO PAULO
Araraquara
Poços de Caldas
Juiz de Fora
Campos
Dourados
Presidente Prudente
Marília
Jaú
São Carlos
Três Rios
São Lourenço
Nova Friburgo
Ponta Porã
Pedro Juan Caballero
Assis
Bauru
Piracicaba
Limeira
Moji-Mirim
2787
Volta Redonda
Petrópolis
Botucatu
Campinas
RIO DE JANEIRO
Niterói
Cabo Frio
Greenwich
55
50
45
40
35
30
0
5
10
15
20
11
12
13

1:7 100 000

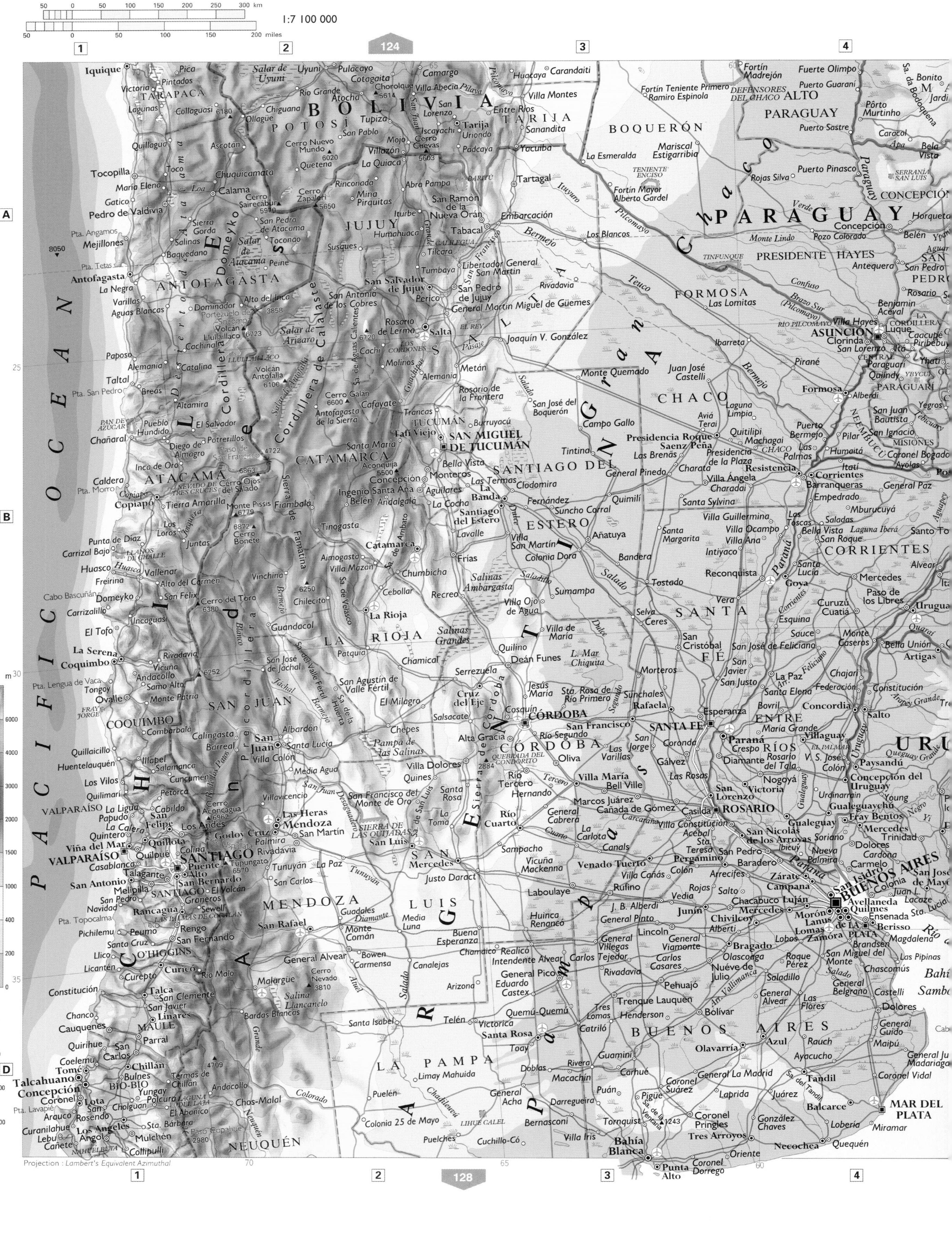
50 0 50 100 150 200 250 300 km
50 0 50 100 150 200 miles
124
128
PACIFIC OCEAN
BOLIVIA
PARAGUAY
CHILE
ARGENTINA
Gran Chaco
Cordillera de los Andes
Cordillera Domeyko
Desierto de Atacama
Precordillera
Sierras de Córdoba
Pampas
ANTOFAGASTA
ATACAMA
COQUIMBO
VALPARAÍSO
SANTIAGO
O'HIGGINS
MAULE
BIO-BIO
TARAPACA
POTOSÍ
TARIJA
BOQUERÓN
ALTO PARAGUAY
PRESIDENTE HAYES
JUJUY
SALTA
FORMOSA
CHACO
TUCUMÁN
CATAMARCA
SANTIAGO DEL ESTERO
CORRIENTES
SANTA FÉ
ENTRE RÍOS
LA RIOJA
SAN JUAN
CÓRDOBA
SAN LUIS
MENDOZA
LA PAMPA
BUENOS AIRES
NEUQUÉN
ASUNCIÓN
SANTIAGO
BUENOS AIRES
Antofagasta
Iquique
Salta
SAN MIGUEL DE TUCUMÁN
CÓRDOBA
ROSARIO
Mendoza
MAR DEL PLATA
Bahía Blanca
Concepción
Valparaíso
8050
Projection : Lambert's Equivalent Azimuthal
ft m
18 000 6000
12 000 4000
9000 3000
6000 2000
4500 1500
3000 1000
1200 400
600 200
35
0 0
200 600
2000 6000
4000 12 000
6000 18 000
m ft

National Parks

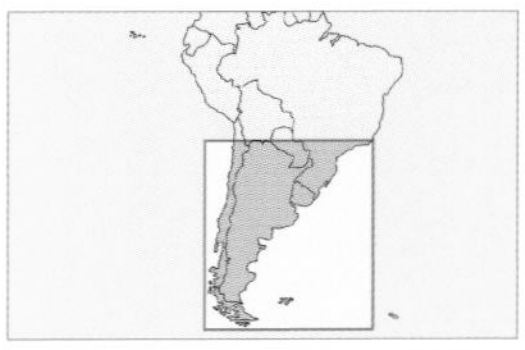

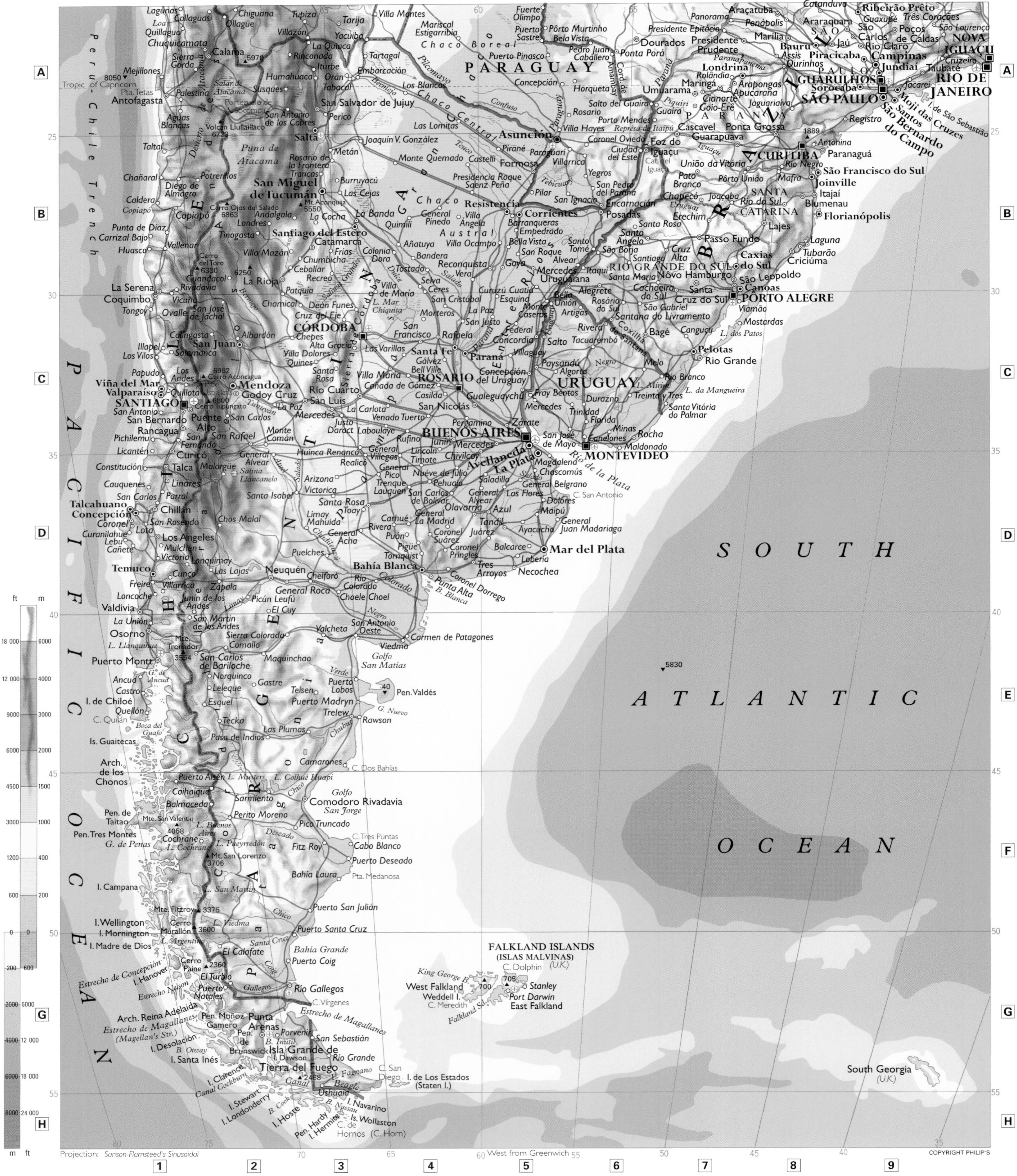

km 100 0 100 200 300 400 500
100 0 100 200 300 400 miles
1:14 200 000
126
127
1 2 3 4 5 6 7 8 9
A B C D E F G H
PARAGUAY
URUGUAY
BRAZIL
ARGENTINA
CHILE
SOUTH ATLANTIC OCEAN
PACIFIC OCEAN
Peru - Chile Trench
Tropic of Capricorn
Chaco Boreal
Chaco Central
Chaco Austral
Gran Chaco
PATAGONIA
Puna de Atacama
Desierto de Atacama
Salar de Atacama
Pampas
Sierras de Córdoba
Lagunas
Collaguasi
Quillagua
Chuquicamata
Calama
Mejillones
Antofagasta
Taltal
Chañaral
Caldera
Copiapó
Vallenar
Huasco
La Serena
Coquimbo
Ovalle
Illapel
Los Vilos
Viña del Mar
Valparaíso
SANTIAGO
San Antonio
Rancagua
Curicó
Talca
Linares
Chillán
Talcahuano
Concepción
Los Angeles
Temuco
Valdivia
Osorno
Puerto Montt
I. de Chiloé
Castro
Quellón
Is. Guaitecas
Arch. de los Chonos
Puerto Aisén
Coihaique
Pen. de Taitao
G. de Penas
I. Campana
I. Wellington
I. Madre de Dios
Puerto Natales
Arch. Reina Adelaida
Estrecho de Magallanes
(Magellan's Str.)
I. Desolación
I. Santa Inés
Punta Arenas
Pen. Brunswick
Isla Grande de Tierra del Fuego
Porvenir
San Sebastián
Río Grande
Ushuaia
Canal Beagle
I. Navarino
I. Hoste
Is. Wollaston
C. de Hornos (C. Horn)
I. de Los Estados (Staten I.)
Ojos del Salado 6863
Cerro Aconcagua 6962
Volcán Llullaillaco 6723
Cerro Tupungato 6800
Mt. San Valentín 4058
Mte. Fitzroy 3375
Mt. San Lorenzo 3706
Salta
San Salvador de Jujuy
San Miguel de Tucumán
Santiago del Estero
Catamarca
La Rioja
San Juan
Mendoza
San Luis
San Rafael
CÓRDOBA
Río Cuarto
ROSARIO
Santa Fe
Paraná
Resistencia
Corrientes
Posadas
Formosa
BUENOS AIRES
La Plata
Mar del Plata
Bahía Blanca
Santa Rosa
Neuquén
Viedma
Puerto Madryn
Rawson
Trelew
Pen. Valdés
Golfo San Matías
Golfo San Jorge
Comodoro Rivadavia
Puerto Deseado
Puerto San Julián
Puerto Santa Cruz
Río Gallegos
San Carlos de Bariloche
Esquel
Asunción
Encarnación
Concepción
MONTEVIDEO
Río de la Plata
Salto
Paysandú
Rivera
Melo
Maldonado
PÔRTO ALEGRE
Pelotas
Rio Grande
Lagoa dos Patos
L. Mirim
CURITIBA
SÃO PAULO
RIO DE JANEIRO
NOVA IGUAÇU
GUARULHOS
Campinas
Santos
Londrina
Maringá
Florianópolis
Joinville
Blumenau
Foz do Iguaçu
RIO GRANDE DO SUL
SANTA CATARINA
PARANÁ
SÃO PAULO
FALKLAND ISLANDS (ISLAS MALVINAS) (U.K.)
West Falkland
East Falkland
Stanley
South Georgia (U.K.)
5830
ft m
18 000 6000
12 000 4000
9000 3000
6000 2000
4500 1500
3000 1000
1200 400
600 200
0 0
200 600
2000 6000
4000 12 000
6000 18 000
8000 24 000
m ft
Projection: Sanson-Flamsteed's Sinusoidal
West from Greenwich
COPYRIGHT PHILIP'S

INDEX TO WORLD MAPS

How to use the index

The index contains the names of all the principal places and features shown on the World Maps. Each name is followed by an additional entry in italics giving the country or region within which it is located. The alphabetical order of names composed of two or more words is governed primarily by the first word and then by the second. This is an example of the rule:

Mīr Kūh, *Iran* **71 E8**
Mīr Shahdād, *Iran* **71 E8**
Mira, *Italy* **41 C9**
Mira por vos Cay, *Bahamas* .. **121 B5**
Miraj, *India* **66 F2**

Physical features composed of a proper name (Erie) and a description (Lake) are positioned alphabetically by the proper name. The description is positioned after the proper name and is usually abbreviated:

Erie, L., *N. Amer.* **116 D4**

Where a description forms part of a settlement or administrative name however, it is always written in full and put in its true alphabetic position:

Mount Morris, *U.S.A.* **116 D7**

Names beginning with M' and Mc are indexed as if they were spelled Mac. Names beginning St. are alphabetised under Saint, but Sankt, Sint, Sant', Santa and San are all spelt in full and are alphabetised accordingly. If the same place name occurs two or more times in the index and all are in the same country, each is followed by the name of the administrative subdivision in which it is located. For example:

Jackson, Ky., *U.S.A.* **114 G4**
Jackson, Mich., *U.S.A.* **114 D3**
Jackson, Minn., *U.S.A.* **112 D7**

The number in bold type which follows each name in the index refers to the number of the map page where that feature or place will be found. This is usually the largest scale at which the place or feature appears.

The letter and figure which are in bold type immediately after the page number give the grid square on the map page, within which the feature is situated. The letter represents the latitude and the figure the longitude. A lower case letter immediately after the page number refers to an inset map on that page.

In some cases the feature itself may fall within the specified square, while the name is outside. This is usually the case only with features which are larger than a grid square.

Rivers are indexed to their mouths or confluences, and carry the symbol → after their names. The following symbols are also used in the index: ■ country, ⊠ overseas territory or dependency, □ first order administrative area, △ national park, ⌓ other park (provincial park, nature reserve or game reserve), ✈ (LHR) principal airport (and location identifier).

How to pronounce place names

English-speaking people usually have no difficulty in reading and pronouncing correctly English place names. However, foreign place name pronunciations may present many problems. Such problems can be minimised by following some simple rules. However, these rules cannot be applied to all situations, and there will be many exceptions.

1. In general, stress each syllable equally, unless your experience suggests otherwise.
2. Pronounce the letter 'a' as a broad 'a' as in 'arm'.
3. Pronounce the letter 'e' as a short 'e' as in 'elm'.
4. Pronounce the letter 'i' as a cross between a short 'i' and long 'e', as the two 'i's in 'California'.
5. Pronounce the letter 'o' as an intermediate 'o' as in 'soft'.
6. Pronounce the letter 'u' as an intermediate 'u' as in 'sure'.
7. Pronounce consonants hard, except in the Romance-language areas where 'g's are likely to be pronounced softly like 'j' in 'jam'; 'j' itself may be pronounced as 'y'; and 'x's may be pronounced as 'h'.
8. For names in mainland China, pronounce 'q' like the 'ch' in 'chin', 'x' like the 'sh' in 'she', 'zh' like the 'j' in 'jam', and 'z' as if it were spelled 'dz'. In general pronounce 'a' as in 'father', 'e' as in 'but', 'i' as in 'keep', 'o' as in 'or', and 'u' as in 'rule'.

Moreover, English has no diacritical marks (accent and pronunciation signs), although some languages do. The following is a brief and general guide to the pronunciation of those most frequently used in the principal Western European languages.

		Pronunciation as in
French	é	day and shows that the e is to be pronounced; e.g. Orléans.
	è	mare
	î	used over any vowel and does not affect pronunciation; shows contraction of the name, usually omission of 's' following a vowel.
	ç	's' before 'a', 'o' and 'u'.
	ë, ï, ü	over 'e', 'i' and 'u' when they are used with another vowel and shows that each is to be pronounced.
German	ä	fate
	ö	fur
	ü	no English equivalent; like French 'tu'
Italian	à, é	over vowels and indicates stress.
Portuguese	ã, õ	vowels pronounced nasally.
	ç	boss
	á	shows stress
	ô	shows that a vowel has an 'i' or 'u' sound combined with it.
Spanish	ñ	canyon
	ü	pronounced as w and separately from adjoining vowels.
	á	usually indicates that this is a stressed vowel.

Abbreviations

A.C.T. – Australian Capital Territory
A.R. – Autonomous Region
Afghan. – Afghanistan
Afr. – Africa
Ala. – Alabama
Alta. – Alberta
Amer. – America(n)
Arch. – Archipelago
Ariz. – Arizona
Ark. – Arkansas
Atl. Oc. – Atlantic Ocean
B. – Baie, Bahía, Bay, Bucht, Bugt
B.C. – British Columbia
Bangla. – Bangladesh
Barr. – Barrage
Bos.-H. – Bosnia-Herzegovina
C. – Cabo, Cap, Cape, Coast
C.A.R. – Central African Republic
C. Prov. – Cape Province
Calif. – California
Cat. – Catarata
Cent. – Central
Chan. – Channel
Colo. – Colorado
Conn. – Connecticut
Cord. – Cordillera
Cr. – Creek
Czech. – Czech Republic
D.C. – District of Columbia
Del. – Delaware
Dem. – Democratic
Dep. – Dependency
Des. – Desert
Dét. – Détroit
Dist. – District
Dj. – Djebel
Domin. – Dominica
Dom. Rep. – Dominican Republic
E. – East
E. Salv. – El Salvador
Eq. Guin. – Equatorial Guinea
Est. – Estrecho
Falk. Is. – Falkland Is.
Fd. – Fjord
Fla. – Florida
Fr. – French
G. – Golfe, Golfo, Gulf, Guba, Gebel
Ga. – Georgia
Gt. – Great, Greater
Guinea-Biss. – Guinea-Bissau
H.K. – Hong Kong
H.P. – Himachal Pradesh
Hants. – Hampshire
Harb. – Harbor, Harbour
Hd. – Head
Hts. – Heights
I.(s). – Île, Ilha, Insel, Isla, Island, Isle
Ill. – Illinois
Ind. – Indiana
Ind. Oc. – Indian Ocean
Ivory C. – Ivory Coast
J. – Jabal, Jebel
Jaz. – Jazīrah
Junc. – Junction
K. – Kap, Kapp
Kans. – Kansas
Kep. – Kepulauan
Ky. – Kentucky
L. – Lac, Lacul, Lago, Lagoa, Lake, Limni, Loch, Lough
La. – Louisiana
Ld. – Land
Liech. – Liechtenstein
Lux. – Luxembourg
Mad. P. – Madhya Pradesh
Madag. – Madagascar
Man. – Manitoba
Mass. – Massachusetts
Md. – Maryland
Me. – Maine
Medit. S. – Mediterranean Sea
Mich. – Michigan
Minn. – Minnesota
Miss. – Mississippi
Mo. – Missouri
Mont. – Montana
Mozam. – Mozambique
Mt.(s) – Mont, Montaña, Mountain
Mte. – Monte
Mti. – Monti
N. – Nord, Norte, North, Northern, Nouveau
N.B. – New Brunswick
N.C. – North Carolina
N. Cal. – New Caledonia
N. Dak. – North Dakota
N.H. – New Hampshire
N.I. – North Island
N.J. – New Jersey
N. Mex. – New Mexico
N.S. – Nova Scotia
N.S.W. – New South Wales
N.W.T. – North West Territory
N.Y. – New York
N.Z. – New Zealand
Nac. – Nacional
Nat. – National
Nebr. – Nebraska
Neths. – Netherlands
Nev. – Nevada
Nfld. & L. – Newfoundland and Labrador
Nic. – Nicaragua
O. – Oued, Ouadi
Occ. – Occidentale
Okla. – Oklahoma
Ont. – Ontario
Or. – Orientale
Oreg. – Oregon
Os. – Ostrov
Oz. – Ozero
P. – Pass, Passo, Pasul, Pulau
P.E.I. – Prince Edward Island
Pa. – Pennsylvania
Pac. Oc. – Pacific Ocean
Papua N.G. – Papua New Guinea
Pass. – Passage
Peg. – Pegunungan
Pen. – Peninsula, Péninsule
Phil. – Philippines
Pk. – Peak
Plat. – Plateau
Prov. – Province, Provincial
Pt. – Point
Pta. – Ponta, Punta
Pte. – Pointe
Qué. – Québec
Queens. – Queensland
R. – Rio, River
R.I. – Rhode Island
Ra. – Range
Raj. – Rajasthan
Recr. – Recreational, Récréatif
Reg. – Region
Rep. – Republic
Res. – Reserve, Reservoir
Rhld-Pfz. – Rheinland-Pfalz
S. – South, Southern, Sur
Si. Arabia – Saudi Arabia
S.C. – South Carolina
S. Dak. – South Dakota
S.I. – South Island
S. Leone – Sierra Leone
Sa. – Serra, Sierra
Sask. – Saskatchewan
Scot. – Scotland
Sd. – Sound
Serbia & M.. – Serbia & Montenegro
Sev. – Severnaya
Sib. – Siberia
Sprs. – Springs
St. – Saint
Sta. – Santa
Ste. – Sainte
Sto. – Santo
Str. – Strait, Stretto
Switz. – Switzerland
Tas. – Tasmania
Tenn. – Tennessee
Terr. – Territory, Territoire
Tex. – Texas
Tg. – Tanjung
Trin. & Tob. – Trinidad & Tobago
U.A.E. – United Arab Emirates
U.K. – United Kingdom
U.S.A. – United States of America
Ut. P. – Uttar Pradesh
Va. – Virginia
Vdkhr. – Vodokhranilishche
Vdskh. – Vodoskhovyshche
Vf. – Vírful
Vic. – Victoria
Vol. – Volcano
Vt. – Vermont
W. – Wadi, West
W. Va. – West Virginia
Wall. & F. Is. – Wallis and Futuna Is.
Wash. – Washington
Wis. – Wisconsin
Wlkp. – Wielkopolski
Wyo. – Wyoming
Yorks. – Yorkshire

A

A 'Âli an Nîl □, *Sudan* 81 F3
A Baña, *Spain* 36 C2
A Cañiza, *Spain* 36 C2
A Coruña, *Spain* 36 B2
A Estrada, *Spain* 36 C2
A Fonsagrada, *Spain* 36 B3
A Guarda, *Spain* 36 D2
A Gudiña, *Spain* 36 C3
A Rúa, *Spain* 36 C3
Aachen, *Germany* 24 E2
Aalborg = Ålborg, *Denmark* 11 G3
Aalen, *Germany* 25 G6
Aalst, *Belgium* 17 D4
Aalten, *Neths.* 17 C6
Aalter, *Belgium* 17 C3
Äänekoski, *Finland* 9 E21
Aarau, *Switz.* 25 H4
Aarberg, *Switz.* 25 H3
Aare ➛, *Switz.* 25 H4
Aargau □, *Switz.* 25 H4
Aarhus = Århus, *Denmark* 11 H4
Aarschot, *Belgium* 17 D4
Aba, *China* 58 A3
Aba, *Dem. Rep. of the Congo* 86 B3
Aba, *Nigeria* 83 D6
Âbâ, Jazîrat, *Sudan* 81 E3
Abaco I., *Bahamas* 120 A4
Abadab, J., *Sudan* 80 D4
Ābādān, *Iran* 71 D6
Abade, *Ethiopia* 81 F4
Ābādeh, *Iran* 71 D7
Abadin, *Spain* 36 B3
Abadla, *Algeria* 78 B5
Abaetetuba, *Brazil* 125 D9
Abagnar Qi, *China* 56 C9
Abah, Tanjung, *Indonesia* 63 K18
Abai, *Paraguay* 127 B4
Abak, *Nigeria* 83 E6
Abakaliki, *Nigeria* 83 D6
Abakan, *Russia* 53 D10
Abala, *Niger* 83 C5
Abalak, *Niger* 83 B6
Abalemma, *Niger* 83 B6
Abana, *Turkey* 72 B6
Abancay, *Peru* 124 F4
Abano Terme, *Italy* 41 C8
Abarán, *Spain* 39 G3
Abariringa, *Kiribati* 96 H10
Abarqū, *Iran* 71 D7
Abashiri, *Japan* 54 B12
Abashiri-Wan, *Japan* 54 C12
Abaújszántó, *Hungary* 28 B6
Abava ➛, *Latvia* 30 A8
Ābay = Nîl el Azraq ➛, *Sudan* 81 D3
Abay, *Kazakhstan* 52 E8
Abaya, L., *Ethiopia* 81 F4
Abayita-Shala Lakes △, *Ethiopia* 81 F4
Abaza, *Russia* 52 D9
Abbadia di Fiastra ⌓, *Italy* 41 E10
Abbadia San Salvatore, *Italy* 41 F8
'Abbāsābād, *Iran* 71 C8
Abbay = Nîl el Azraq ➛, *Sudan* 81 D3
Abbaye, Pt., *U.S.A.* 114 B1
Abbé, L., *Ethiopia* 81 E5
Abbeville, *France* 19 B8
Abbeville, *Ala., U.S.A.* 115 K3
Abbeville, *La., U.S.A.* 113 L8
Abbeville, *S.C., U.S.A.* 115 H4
Abbiategrasso, *Italy* 40 C5
Abbot Ice Shelf, *Antarctica* 5 D16
Abbottabad, *Pakistan* 68 B5
Abd al Kūrī, *Yemen* 75 E5
Ābdar, *Iran* 71 D7
'Abdolābād, *Iran* 71 C8
Abdulpur, *Bangla.* 69 G13
Abéché, *Chad* 79 F10
Abejar, *Spain* 38 D2
Abekr, *Sudan* 81 E2
Abel Tasman △, *N.Z.* 91 J4
Abengourou, *Ivory C.* 82 D4
Abenójar, *Spain* 37 G6
Åbenrå, *Denmark* 11 J3
Abensberg, *Germany* 25 G7
Abeokuta, *Nigeria* 83 D5
Aber, *Uganda* 86 B3
Aberaeron, *U.K.* 15 E3
Aberayron = Aberaeron, *U.K.* 15 E3
Aberchirder, *U.K.* 13 D6
Abercorn, *Australia* 95 D5
Aberdare, *U.K.* 15 F4
Aberdare △, *Kenya* 86 C4
Aberdare Ra., *Kenya* 86 C4
Aberdeen, *Australia* 95 E5
Aberdeen, *Canada* 103 C7
Aberdeen, *S. Africa* 88 E3
Aberdeen, *U.K.* 13 D6
Aberdeen, *Ala., U.S.A.* 115 J1
Aberdeen, *Idaho, U.S.A.* 108 E7
Aberdeen, *Md., U.S.A.* 114 F7
Aberdeen, *S. Dak., U.S.A.* 112 C5
Aberdeen, *Wash., U.S.A.* 110 D3
Aberdeen, City of □, *U.K.* 13 D6
Aberdeenshire □, *U.K.* 13 D6
Aberdovey = Aberdyfi, *U.K.* 15 E3
Aberdyfi, *U.K.* 15 E3
Aberfeldy, *U.K.* 13 E5
Aberfoyle, *U.K.* 13 E4
Abergavenny, *U.K.* 15 F4
Abergele, *U.K.* 14 D4
Abernathy, *U.S.A.* 113 J4
Abert, L., *U.S.A.* 108 E3
Aberystwyth, *U.K.* 15 E3
Abhā, *Si. Arabia* 75 D3
Abhar, *Iran* 71 B6
Abhayapuri, *India* 69 F14
Abia □, *Nigeria* 83 D6
Abide, *Turkey* 47 C11
Abidiya, *Sudan* 80 D3
Abidjan, *Ivory C.* 82 D4
Abilene, *Kans., U.S.A.* 112 F6
Abilene, *Tex., U.S.A.* 113 J5
Abingdon, *U.K.* 15 F6
Abingdon, *U.S.A.* 115 G5
Abington Reef, *Australia* 94 B4
Abitau ➛, *Canada* 103 B7
Abitibi ➛, *Canada* 104 B3
Abitibi, L., *Canada* 104 C4
Abiy Adi, *Ethiopia* 81 E4
Abkhaz Republic = Abkhazia □, *Georgia* 35 J5
Abkhazia □, *Georgia* 35 J5
Abminga, *Australia* 95 D1
Abnūb, *Egypt* 80 B3
Åbo = Turku, *Finland* 9 F20
Abocho, *Nigeria* 83 D6
Abohar, *India* 68 D6
Aboisso, *Ivory C.* 82 D4
Abomey, *Benin* 83 D5
Abong-Mbang, *Cameroon* 84 D2
Abonnema, *Nigeria* 83 E6
Abony, *Hungary* 28 C5
Aboso, *Ghana* 82 D4
Abou-Deïa, *Chad* 79 F9
Aboyne, *U.K.* 13 D6
Abra Pampa, *Argentina* 126 A2
Abraham L., *Canada* 102 C5
Abrantes, *Portugal* 37 F2
Abreojos, Pta., *Mexico* 118 B2
Abri, *Esh Shamâliya, Sudan* 80 C3
Abri, *Janub Kordofân, Sudan* 81 E3
Abrolhos, Banka, *Brazil* 122 E7
Abrud, *Romania* 28 D8
Abruzzo □, *Italy* 41 F10
Absaroka Range, *U.S.A.* 108 D9
Abtenau, *Austria* 26 D6
Abu, *India* 68 G5
Abū al Abyad, *U.A.E.* 71 E7
Abū al Khaşīb, *Iraq* 71 D6
Abū 'Alī, *Si. Arabia* 71 E6
Abū 'Alī ➛, *Lebanon* 74 A4
Abu Ballas, *Egypt* 80 C2
Abu Deleiq, *Sudan* 81 D3
Abu Dhabi = Abū Z̧āby, *U.A.E.* 71 E7
Abu Dis, *Sudan* 80 D3
Abu Dom, *Sudan* 81 D3
Abū Du'ān, *Syria* 70 B3
Abu el Gairi, W. ➛, *Egypt* 74 F2
Abu Fatma, Ras, *Sudan* 80 C4
Abu Gabra, *Sudan* 81 E2
Abu Ga'da, W. ➛, *Egypt* 74 F1
Abu Gelba, *Sudan* 81 E3
Abu Gubeiha, *Sudan* 81 E3
Abu Habl, Khawr ➛, *Sudan* 81 E3
Abū Ḩadrīyah, *Si. Arabia* 71 E6
Abu Hamed, *Sudan* 80 D3
Abu Haraz, *An Nîl el Azraq, Sudan* 80 D3
Abu Haraz, *El Gezira, Sudan* 81 E3
Abu Haraz, *Esh Shamâliya, Sudan* 80 D3
Abu Higar, *Sudan* 81 E3
Abū Kamāl, *Syria* 70 C4
Abu Kuleiwat, *Sudan* 81 E2
Abū Madd, Ra's, *Si. Arabia* 70 E3
Abu Matariq, *Sudan* 81 E2
Abu Mendi, *Ethiopia* 81 E4
Abū Mūsā, *U.A.E.* 71 E7
Abū Qaşr, *Si. Arabia* 70 D3
Abu Qir, *Egypt* 80 H7
Abu Qireiya, *Egypt* 80 C4
Abu Qurqâs, *Egypt* 80 B3
Abu Shagara, Ras, *Sudan* 80 C4
Abu Shanab, *Sudan* 81 E2
Abu Simbel, *Egypt* 80 C3
Abū Şukhayr, *Iraq* 70 D5
Abu Şultân, *Egypt* 80 H8
Abu Tabari, *Sudan* 80 D2
Abu Tig, *Egypt* 80 B3
Abu Tiga, *Sudan* 81 E3
Abu Tineitin, *Sudan* 81 E3
Abu Uruq, *Sudan* 81 D3
Abu Zabad, *Sudan* 81 E2
Abū Z̧āby, *U.A.E.* 71 E7
Abū Zeydābād, *Iran* 71 C6
Abuja, *Nigeria* 83 D6
Abukuma-Gawa ➛, *Japan* 54 E10
Abukuma-Sammyaku, *Japan* 54 F10
Abunã, *Brazil* 124 E5
Abunã ➛, *Brazil* 124 E5
Abune Yosef, *Ethiopia* 81 E4
Aburo, *Dem. Rep. of the Congo* 86 B3
Abut Hd., *N.Z.* 91 K3
Abuye Meda, *Ethiopia* 81 E4
Abwong, *Sudan* 81 F3
Åby, *Sweden* 11 F10
Aby, Lagune, *Ivory C.* 82 D4
Abyad, *Sudan* 81 E2
Åbybro, *Denmark* 11 G3
Acadia △, *U.S.A.* 115 C11
Açailândia, *Brazil* 125 D9
Acajutla, *El Salv.* 120 D2
Acámbaro, *Mexico* 118 D4
Acanthus, *Greece* 44 F7
Acaponeta, *Mexico* 118 C3
Acapulco, *Mexico* 119 D5
Acarai, Serra, *Brazil* 124 C7
Acarigua, *Venezuela* 124 B5
Acatlán, *Mexico* 119 D5
Acayucan, *Mexico* 119 D6
Accéglio, *Italy* 40 D4
Accomac, *U.S.A.* 114 G8
Accous, *France* 20 E3
Accra, *Ghana* 83 D4
Accrington, *U.K.* 14 D5
Acebal, *Argentina* 126 C3
Aceh □, *Indonesia* 62 D1
Acerra, *Italy* 43 B7
Aceuchal, *Spain* 37 G4
Achalpur, *India* 66 J10
Acheng, *China* 57 B14
Achenkirch, *Austria* 26 D4
Achensee, *Austria* 26 D4
Acher, *India* 68 H5
Achern, *Germany* 25 G4
Achill Hd., *Ireland* 12 C1
Achill I., *Ireland* 12 C1
Achim, *Germany* 24 B5
Achinsk, *Russia* 53 D10
Acıgöl, *Turkey* 47 D11
Acıpayam, *Turkey* 47 D11
Acireale, *Italy* 43 E8
Ackerman, *U.S.A.* 113 J10
Acklins I., *Bahamas* 121 B5
Acme, *Canada* 102 C6
Acme, *U.S.A.* 116 F5
Aconcagua, Cerro, *Argentina* 126 C2
Aconquija, Mt., *Argentina* 126 B2
Açores, Is. dos, *Atl. Oc.* 78 A1
Acornhoek, *S. Africa* 89 C5
Acquapendente, *Italy* 41 F8
Acquasanta Terme, *Italy* 41 F10
Acquasparta, *Italy* 41 F9
Acquaviva delle Fonti, *Italy* 43 B9
Ácqui Terme, *Italy* 40 D5
Acraman, L., *Australia* 95 E2
Acre = 'Akko, *Israel* 74 C4
Acre □, *Brazil* 124 E4
Acre ➛, *Brazil* 124 E5
Acri, *Italy* 43 C9
Acs, *Hungary* 28 C3
Actium, *Greece* 46 C2
Acton, *Canada* 116 C4
Acuña, *Mexico* 118 B4
Ad Dammām, *Si. Arabia* 71 E6
Ad Dāmūr, *Lebanon* 74 B4
Ad Dawādimī, *Si. Arabia* 70 E5
Ad Dawḩah, *Qatar* 71 E6
Ad Dawr, *Iraq* 70 C4
Ad Dir'īyah, *Si. Arabia* 70 E5
Ad Dīwānīyah, *Iraq* 70 D5
Ad Dujayl, *Iraq* 70 C5
Ad Duwayd, *Si. Arabia* 70 D4
Ada, *Ghana* 83 D5
Ada, *Serbia & M.* 28 E5
Ada, *Minn., U.S.A.* 112 B6
Ada, *Okla., U.S.A.* 113 H6
Adabiya, *Egypt* 74 F1
Adair, C., *Canada* 101 A12
Adaja ➛, *Spain* 36 D6
Adak I., *U.S.A.* 100 C2
Adamaoua, Massif de l', *Cameroon* 83 D7
Adamawa □, *Nigeria* 83 D7
Adamawa Highlands = Adamaoua, Massif de l', *Cameroon* 83 D7
Adamello ⌓, *Italy* 40 B7
Adamello, Mte., *Italy* 40 B7
Adami Tulu, *Ethiopia* 81 F4
Adaminaby, *Australia* 95 F4
Adams, *Mass., U.S.A.* 117 D11
Adams, *N.Y., U.S.A.* 117 C8
Adams, *Wis., U.S.A.* 112 D10
Adams, Mt., *U.S.A.* 110 D5
Adam's Bridge, *Sri Lanka* 66 Q11
Adams L., *Canada* 102 C5
Adam's Peak, *Sri Lanka* 66 R12
Adamuz, *Spain* 37 G6
Adana, *Turkey* 70 B2
Adanero, *Spain* 36 E6
Adapazarı = Sakarya, *Turkey* 72 B4
Adar Gwagwa, J., *Sudan* 80 C4
Adarama, *Sudan* 81 D3
Adare, C., *Antarctica* 5 D11
Adarte, *Eritrea* 81 E5
Adaut, *Indonesia* 63 F8
Adavale, *Australia* 95 D3
Adda ➛, *Italy* 40 C6
Addis Ababa = Addis Abeba, *Ethiopia* 81 F4
Addis Abeba, *Ethiopia* 81 F4
Addis Alem, *Ethiopia* 81 F4
Addis Zemen, *Ethiopia* 81 E4
Addison, *U.S.A.* 116 D7
Addo, *S. Africa* 88 E4
Addo △, *S. Africa* 88 E4
Adebour, *Niger* 83 C7
Ādeh, *Iran* 70 B5
Adel, *U.S.A.* 115 K4
Adelaide, *Australia* 95 E2
Adelaide, *S. Africa* 88 E4
Adelaide I., *Antarctica* 5 C17
Adelaide Pen., *Canada* 100 B10
Adelaide River, *Australia* 92 B5
Adelaide Village, *Bahamas* 120 A4
Adelanto, *U.S.A.* 111 L9
Adele I., *Australia* 92 C3
Adélie, Terre, *Antarctica* 5 C10
Adélie Land = Adélie, Terre, *Antarctica* 5 C10
Adelsk, *Belarus* 30 E10
Ademuz, *Spain* 38 E3
Aden = Al 'Adan, *Yemen* 75 E4
Aden, G. of, *Asia* 75 E4
Adendorp, *S. Africa* 88 E3
Aderbissinat, *Niger* 83 B6
Adh Dhayd, *U.A.E.* 71 E7
Adhoi, *India* 68 H4
Adi, *Indonesia* 63 E8
Adi Arkai, *Ethiopia* 81 E4
Adi Daro, *Ethiopia* 81 E4
Adi Keyih, *Eritrea* 81 E4
Adi Kwala, *Eritrea* 81 E4
Adi Ugri, *Eritrea* 81 E4
Adieu, C., *Australia* 93 F5
Adieu Pt., *Australia* 92 C3
Adigala, *Ethiopia* 81 E5
Adige ➛, *Italy* 41 C9
Adigrat, *Ethiopia* 81 E4
Adigüzel Barajı, *Turkey* 47 C11
Adilabad, *India* 66 K11
Adilcevaz, *Turkey* 73 C10
Adirondack ⌓, *U.S.A.* 117 C10
Adirondack Mts., *U.S.A.* 117 C10
Adis Abeba = Addis Abeba, *Ethiopia* 81 F4
Adıyaman, *Turkey* 73 D8
Adjohon, *Benin* 83 D5
Adjud, *Romania* 29 D12
Adjumani, *Uganda* 86 B3
Adjuntas, *Puerto Rico* 121 d
Adlavik Is., *Canada* 105 B8
Adler, *Russia* 35 J4
Admer, *Algeria* 83 A6
Admiralty G., *Australia* 92 B4
Admiralty I., *U.S.A.* 102 B2
Admiralty Is., *Papua N. G.* 96 H6
Adnan Menderes, İzmir ✈ (ADB), *Turkey* 47 C9
Ado, *Nigeria* 83 D5
Ado-Ekiti, *Nigeria* 83 D6
Adok, *Sudan* 81 F3
Adola, *Ethiopia* 81 E5
Adonara, *Indonesia* 63 F6
Adoni, *India* 66 M10
Adony, *Hungary* 28 C3
Adour ➛, *France* 20 E2
Adra, *India* 69 H12
Adra, *Spain* 37 J7
Adrano, *Italy* 43 E7
Adrar, *Mauritania* 78 D3
Adrar des Iforas, *Algeria* 78 C5
Ádria, *Italy* 41 C9
Adrian, *Mich., U.S.A.* 114 E3
Adrian, *Tex., U.S.A.* 113 H3
Adriatic Sea, *Medit. S.* 6 G9
Adua, *Indonesia* 63 E7
Adwa, *Ethiopia* 81 E4
Adygea □, *Russia* 35 H5
Adzhar Republic = Ajaria □, *Georgia* 35 K6
Adzopé, *Ivory C.* 82 D4
Ægean Sea, *Medit. S.* 47 C7
Aerhtai Shan, *Mongolia* 60 B4
Ærø, *Denmark* 11 K4
Ærøskøbing, *Denmark* 11 K4
Aëtós, *Greece* 46 D3
'Afak, *Iraq* 70 C5
Afándou, *Greece* 49 C10
Afar □, *Ethiopia* 81 E5
Afghanistan ■, *Asia* 66 C4
Afikpo, *Nigeria* 83 D6
Aflou, *Algeria* 78 B6
Afragóla, *Italy* 43 B7
Afram ➛, *Ghana* 83 D4
Afrera, *Ethiopia* 81 E5
Africa 76 E6
'Afrīn, *Syria* 70 B3
Afşin, *Turkey* 72 C7
Afton, *N.Y., U.S.A.* 117 D9
Afton, *Wyo., U.S.A.* 108 E8
Afuá, *Brazil* 125 D8
'Afula, *Israel* 74 C4
Afyon, *Turkey* 47 C12
Afyon □, *Turkey* 47 C12
Afyonkarahisar = Afyon, *Turkey* 47 C12
Aga, *Egypt* 80 H7
Agadès = Agadez, *Niger* 83 B6
Agadez, *Niger* 83 B6
Agadir, *Morocco* 78 B4
Agaete, *Canary Is.* 48 F4
Agaie, *Nigeria* 83 D6
Again, *Sudan* 81 F2
Agalega Is., *Mauritius* 3 E12
Ağapınar, *Turkey* 47 B12
Agar, *India* 68 H7
Agaro, *Ethiopia* 81 F4
Agartala, *India* 67 H17
Agăş, *Romania* 29 D11
Agassiz, *Canada* 102 D4
Agats, *Indonesia* 63 F9
Agawam, *U.S.A.* 117 D12
Agbélouvé, *Togo* 83 D5
Agboville, *Ivory C.* 82 D4
Ağcabädi, *Azerbaijan* 35 K8
Ağdam, *Azerbaijan* 35 L8
Ağdaş, *Azerbaijan* 35 K8
Agde, *France* 20 E7
Agde, C. d', *France* 20 E7
Agdzhabedi = Ağcabädi, *Azerbaijan* 35 K8
Agen, *France* 20 D4
Agerbæk, *Denmark* 11 J2
Agersø, *Denmark* 11 J5
Ageyevo, *Russia* 32 E9
Aggteleki △, *Hungary* 28 B5
Āgh Kand, *Iran* 71 B6
Aghireşu, *Romania* 29 D8
Aginskoye, *Russia* 53 D12
Ağlasun, *Turkey* 47 D12
Agly ➛, *France* 20 F7
Agnew, *Australia* 93 E3
Agnibilékrou, *Ivory C.* 82 D4
Agnita, *Romania* 29 E9
Agnone, *Italy* 41 G11
Agofie, *Ghana* 83 D5
Agogna ➛, *Italy* 40 C5
Agogo, *Sudan* 81 F2
Agön, *Sweden* 10 C11
Agon Coutainville, *France* 18 C5
Ágordo, *Italy* 41 B9
Agori, *India* 69 G10
Agouna, *Benin* 83 D5
Agout ➛, *France* 20 E5
Agra, *India* 68 F7
Agrakhanskiy Poluostrov, *Russia* 35 J8
Agramunt, *Spain* 38 D6
Agreda, *Spain* 38 D3
Ağri, *Turkey* 73 C10
Agri ➛, *Italy* 43 B9
Ağrı Dağı, *Turkey* 70 B5
Ağri Karakose = Ağri, *Turkey* 73 C10
Agriá, *Greece* 46 B5
Agrigento, *Italy* 42 E6
Agrínion, *Greece* 46 C3
Agrópoli, *Italy* 43 B7
Ağstafa, *Azerbaijan* 35 K7
Agua Caliente, *Baja Calif., Mexico* 111 N10
Agua Caliente, *Sinaloa, Mexico* 118 B3
Agua Caliente Springs, *U.S.A.* 111 N10
Água Clara, *Brazil* 125 H8
Agua Fria ⌓, *U.S.A.* 109 J8
Agua Hechicero, *Mexico* 111 N10
Agua Prieta, *Mexico* 118 A3
Aguadilla, *Puerto Rico* 121 d
Aguadulce, *Panama* 120 E3
Aguanga, *U.S.A.* 111 M10
Aguanish, *Canada* 105 B7
Aguanus ➛, *Canada* 105 B7
Aguapey ➛, *Argentina* 126 B4
Aguaray Guazú ➛, *Paraguay* 126 A4
Aguarico ➛, *Ecuador* 124 D3
Aguaro-Guariquito △, *Venezuela* 121 E6
Aguas ➛, *Spain* 38 D4
Aguas Blancas, *Chile* 126 A2
Aguas Calientes, Sierra de, *Argentina* 126 B2
Aguascalientes, *Mexico* 118 C4
Aguascalientes □, *Mexico* 118 C4
Agudo, *Spain* 37 G6
Águeda, *Portugal* 36 E2
Agueda ➛, *Spain* 36 D4
Aguelhok, *Mali* 83 B5
Aguié, *Niger* 83 C6
Aguila, Punta, *Puerto Rico* 121 d
Aguilafuente, *Spain* 36 D6
Aguilar, *Spain* 37 H6
Aguilar de Campóo, *Spain* 36 C6
Aguilares, *Argentina* 126 B2
Aguilas, *Spain* 39 H3
Agüimes, *Canary Is.* 48 G4
Aguja, C. de la, *Colombia* 122 B3
Agujereada, Pta., *Puerto Rico* 121 d
Agulaa, *Ethiopia* 81 E4
Agulhas, C., *S. Africa* 88 E3
Agulo, *Canary Is.* 48 F2
Agung, Gunung, *Indonesia* 63 J18
Agur, *Uganda* 86 B3
Agusan ➛, *Phil.* 61 G6
Ağva, *Turkey* 45 E13
Agvali, *Russia* 35 J8
Aha Mts., *Botswana* 88 B3
Ahaggar, *Algeria* 78 D7
Ahamansu, *Ghana* 83 D5
Ahar, *Iran* 70 B5
Ahat, *Turkey* 47 C11
Ahaus, *Germany* 24 C2
Ahipara B., *N.Z.* 91 F4
Ahir Dağı, *Turkey* 47 C12
Ahiri, *India* 66 K12
Ahlat, *Turkey* 73 C10
Ahlen, *Germany* 24 D3
Ahmad Wal, *Pakistan* 68 E1
Ahmadabad, *India* 68 H5
Aḩmadābād, *Khorāsān, Iran* 71 C9
Aḩmadābād, *Khorāsān, Iran* 71 C8
Aḩmadī, *Iran* 71 E8
Ahmadnagar, *India* 66 K9
Ahmadpur, *Pakistan* 68 E4
Ahmadpur Lamma, *Pakistan* 68 E4
Ahmar, *Ethiopia* 81 F5
Ahmedabad = Ahmadabad, *India* 68 H5
Ahmednagar = Ahmadnagar, *India* 66 K9
Ahmetbey, *Turkey* 45 E11
Ahmetler, *Turkey* 47 C11
Ahmetli, *Turkey* 47 C9
Ahoada, *Nigeria* 83 D6
Ahome, *Mexico* 118 B3
Ahoskie, *U.S.A.* 115 G7
Ahr ➛, *Germany* 24 E3
Ahram, *Iran* 71 D6
Ahrax Pt., *Malta* 49 D1
Ahrensbök, *Germany* 24 A6
Ahrensburg, *Germany* 24 B6
Āhū, *Iran* 71 C6
Ahuachapán, *El Salv.* 120 D2
Ahun, *France* 19 F9
Åhus, *Sweden* 11 J8
Ahvāz, *Iran* 71 D6
Ahvenanmaa, *Finland* 9 F19
Aḩwar, *Yemen* 75 E4
Ahzar ➛, *Mali* 83 B5
Ai ➛, *India* 69 F14
Ai-Ais, *Namibia* 88 D2
Ai-Ais and Fish River Canyon △, *Namibia* 88 C2
Aichach, *Germany* 25 G7
Aichi □, *Japan* 55 G8
Aigle, *Switz.* 25 J2
Aignay-le-Duc, *France* 19 E11
Aigoual, Mt., *France* 20 D7
Aigre, *France* 20 C4
Aigua, *Uruguay* 127 C5
Aigueperse, *France* 19 F10
Aigues ➛, *France* 21 D8
Aigues-Mortes, *France* 21 E8
Aigues-Mortes, G. d', *France* 21 E8
Aigües Tortes y Lago San Mauricio △, *Spain* 38 C4
Aiguilles, *France* 21 D10
Aiguillon, *France* 20 D4
Aigurande, *France* 19 F8
Aihui, *China* 60 A7
Aija, *Peru* 124 E3
Aikawa, *Japan* 54 E9
Aiken, *U.S.A.* 115 J5
Ailao Shan, *China* 58 F3
Aileron, *Australia* 94 C1
Aillant-sur-Tholon, *France* 19 E10
Aillik, *Canada* 105 A8
Ailsa Craig, *U.K.* 13 F3
Aim, *Russia* 53 D14
Aimere, *Indonesia* 63 F6

Aimogasta, *Argentina* 126 B2
Ain □, *France* 19 F12
Ain →, *France* 21 C9
Aïn Ben Tili, *Mauritania* 78 C4
Ain Dalla, *Egypt* 80 B2
Ain el Mafki, *Egypt* 80 B2
Ain Girba, *Egypt* 80 B2
Ain Murr, *Sudan* 80 C2
Ain Qeiqab, *Egypt* 80 B1
Aïn Sefra, *Algeria* 78 B5
Ain Sheikh Murzûk, *Egypt* 80 B2
Ain Sudr, *Egypt* 74 F2
Ain Sukhna, *Egypt* 80 J8
Ain Zeitûn, *Egypt* 80 B2
Ainaži, *Latvia* 9 H21
Aínos Óros, *Greece* 46 C2
Ainsworth, *U.S.A.* 112 D5
Aiquile, *Bolivia* 124 G5
Aïr, *Niger* 83 B6
Air Force I., *Canada* 101 B12
Air Hitam, *Malaysia* 65 M4
Airaines, *France* 19 C8
Airdrie, *Canada* 102 C6
Airdrie, *U.K.* 13 F5
Aire →, *France* 19 C11
Aire →, *U.K.* 14 D7
Aire, I. de l', *Spain* 48 B11
Aire-sur-la-Lys, *France* 19 B9
Aire-sur-l'Adour, *France* 20 E3
Airlie Beach, *Australia* 94 J6
Airvault, *France* 18 F6
Aisch →, *Germany* 25 F6
Aisne □, *France* 19 C10
Aisne →, *France* 19 C9
Ait, *India* 69 G8
Aitana, Sierra de, *Spain* 39 G4
Aitkin, *U.S.A.* 112 B8
Aitolía kai Akarnanía □, *Greece* 46 C3
Aitolikón, *Greece* 46 C3
Aiud, *Romania* 29 D8
Aix-en-Provence, *France* 21 E9
Aix-la-Chapelle = Aachen, *Germany* 24 E2
Aix-les-Bains, *France* 21 C9
Aixe-sur-Vienne, *France* 20 C5
Áïyina, *Greece* 46 D5
Aiyínion, *Greece* 44 F6
Aíyion, *Greece* 46 C4
Aizawl, *India* 67 H18
Aizenay, *France* 18 F5
Aizkraukle, *Latvia* 9 H21
Aizpute, *Latvia* 9 H19
Aizuwakamatsu, *Japan* 54 F9
Ajaccio, *France* 21 G12
Ajaccio, G. d', *France* 21 G12
Ajai ⌂, *Uganda* 86 B3
Ajaigarh, *India* 69 G9
Ajalpan, *Mexico* 119 D5
Ajanta Ra., *India* 66 J9
Ajari Rep. = Ajaria □, *Georgia* 35 K6
Ajaria □, *Georgia* 35 K6
Ajax, *Canada* 116 C5
Ajdābiyā, *Libya* 79 B10
Ajdovščina, *Slovenia* 41 C10
Ajibar, *Ethiopia* 81 E4
Ajka, *Hungary* 28 C2
'Ajlūn, *Jordan* 74 C4
'Ajlūn □, *Jordan* 74 C4
'Ajmān, *U.A.E.* 71 E7
Ajmer, *India* 68 F6
Ajnala, *India* 68 D6
Ajo, *U.S.A.* 109 K7
Ajo, C. de, *Spain* 36 B7
Ajok, *Sudan* 81 F2
Ajuy, *Phil.* 61 F5
Ak Dağ, *Turkey* 47 E11
Ak Dağları, *Muğla, Turkey* 47 E11
Ak Dağları, *Sivas, Turkey* 72 C7
Akaba, *Togo* 83 D5
Akabira, *Japan* 54 C11
Akagera △, *Rwanda* 86 C3
Akaki Beseka, *Ethiopia* 81 F4
Akala, *Sudan* 81 D4
Akamas, *Cyprus* 49 D11
Akan △, *Japan* 54 C12
Akanthou, *Cyprus* 49 D12
Akarca, *Turkey* 47 C11
Akaroa, *N.Z.* 91 K4
Akasha, *Sudan* 80 C3
Akashi, *Japan* 55 G7
Akbarpur, *Bihar, India* 69 G10
Akbarpur, *Ut. P., India* 69 F10
Akçaabat, *Turkey* 73 B8
Akçadağ, *Turkey* 72 C7
Akçakale, *Turkey* 73 D8
Akçakoca, *Turkey* 72 B4
Akçaova, *Turkey* 45 E13
Akçay, *Turkey* 47 E11
Akçay →, *Turkey* 47 D10
Akdağ, *Turkey* 47 C8
Akdağmadeni, *Turkey* 72 C6
Akelamo, *Indonesia* 63 D7
Åkers styckebruk, *Sweden* 10 E11
Åkersberga, *Sweden* 10 E12
Aketi, *Dem. Rep. of the Congo* 84 D4
Akhaïa □, *Greece* 46 C3
Akhalkalaki, *Georgia* 35 K6
Akhaltsikhe, *Georgia* 35 K6
Akharnaí, *Greece* 46 C5
Akhelóös →, *Greece* 46 C3
Akhendriá, *Greece* 47 G7
Akhisar, *Turkey* 47 C9
Akhladhókambos, *Greece* 46 D4
Akhmîm, *Egypt* 80 B3
Akhnur, *India* 69 C6
Akhtopol, *Bulgaria* 45 D11
Akhtuba →, *Russia* 35 G8
Akhtubinsk, *Russia* 35 F8
Akhty, *Russia* 35 K8
Akhtyrka = Okhtyrka, *Ukraine* 33 G8
Aki, *Japan* 55 H6
Akimiski I., *Canada* 104 B3
Akimovka, *Ukraine* 33 J8
Åkirkeby, *Denmark* 11 J8
Akita, *Japan* 54 E10
Akita □, *Japan* 54 E10
Akjoujt, *Mauritania* 82 B2
Akka, *Mali* 82 B4
Akkaya Tepesi, *Turkey* 47 D11
Akkeshi, *Japan* 54 C12
'Akko, *Israel* 74 C4
Akköy, *Turkey* 47 D9
Aklampa, *Benin* 83 D5
Aklavik, *Canada* 100 B6
Aklera, *India* 68 G7
Akmenė, *Lithuania* 30 B9
Akmenrags, *Latvia* 30 B8
Akmonte = Almonte, *Spain* 37 H4
Akō, *Japan* 55 G7
Ako, *Nigeria* 83 C7
Akôbô, *Sudan* 81 F3
Akobo →, *Ethiopia* 81 F3
Akola, *India* 66 J10
Akonolinga, *Cameroon* 83 E7
Akor, *Mali* 82 C3
Akordat, *Eritrea* 81 D4
Akosombo Dam, *Ghana* 83 D5
Akot, *Sudan* 81 F3
Akoupé, *Ivory C.* 82 D4
Akpatok I., *Canada* 101 B13
Åkrahamn, *Norway* 9 G11
Akranes, *Iceland* 8 D2
Akreïjit, *Mauritania* 82 B3
Akrítas Venétiko, Ákra, *Greece* 46 E3
Akron, *Colo., U.S.A.* 112 E3
Akron, *Ohio, U.S.A.* 116 E3
Akrotiri, *Cyprus* 49 E11
Akrotíri, Ákra, *Greece* 45 F9
Akrotiri Bay, *Cyprus* 49 E12
Aksai Chin, *China* 69 B8
Aksaray, *Turkey* 70 B2
Aksay, *Kazakhstan* 52 D6
Akşehir, *Turkey* 70 B1
Akşehir Gölü, *Turkey* 72 C4
Akstafa = Ağstafa, *Azerbaijan* 35 K7
Aksu, *China* 60 B3
Aksu →, *Turkey* 72 D4
Aksum, *Ethiopia* 81 E4
Aktash, *Russia* 34 C11
Aktogay, *Kazakhstan* 52 E8
Aktsyabrski, *Belarus* 33 F5
Aktyubinsk = Aqtöbe, *Kazakhstan* 52 D6
Aku, *Nigeria* 83 D6
Akure, *Nigeria* 83 D6
Akureyri, *Iceland* 8 D4
Akuseki-Shima, *Japan* 55 K4
Akusha, *Russia* 35 J8
Akwa-Ibom □, *Nigeria* 83 E6
Akyab = Sittwe, *Burma* 67 J18
Akyazı, *Turkey* 72 B4
Al 'Adan, *Yemen* 75 E4
Al Aḩsā = Hasa □, *Si. Arabia* 71 E6
Al Ajfar, *Si. Arabia* 70 E4
Al Amādīyah, *Iraq* 70 B4
Al 'Amārah, *Iraq* 70 D5
Al 'Aqabah, *Jordan* 74 F4
Al 'Aqabah □, *Jordan* 74 F4
Al Arak, *Syria* 70 C3
Al 'Aramah, *Si. Arabia* 70 E5
Al 'Artāwīyah, *Si. Arabia* 70 E5
Al 'Āşimah = 'Ammān □, *Jordan* 74 D5
Al 'Assāfiyah, *Si. Arabia* 70 D3
Al 'Ayn, *Si. Arabia* 70 E3
Al 'Ayn, *U.A.E.* 71 E7
Al 'Azīzīyah, *Iraq* 70 C5
Al Bāb, *Syria* 70 B3
Al Bad', *Si. Arabia* 70 D2
Al Bādī, *Iraq* 70 C4
Al Baḩrah, *Kuwait* 70 D5
Al Baḩral Mayyit = Dead Sea, *Asia* 74 D4
Al Balqā' □, *Jordan* 74 C4
Al Bārūk, J., *Lebanon* 74 B4
Al Başrah, *Iraq* 70 D5
Al Baţḩā, *Iraq* 70 D5
Al Batrūn, *Lebanon* 74 A4
Al Bayḑā, *Libya* 79 B10
Al Biqā, *Lebanon* 74 A5
Al Bi'r, *Si. Arabia* 70 D3
Al Burayj, *Syria* 74 A5
Al Faḑilī, *Si. Arabia* 71 E6
Al Fallūjah, *Iraq* 70 C4
Al Fāw, *Iraq* 71 D6
Al Fujayrah, *U.A.E.* 71 E8
Al Ghadaf, W. →, *Jordan* 74 D5
Al Ghammās, *Iraq* 70 D5
Al Ghazālah, *Si. Arabia* 70 E4
Al Ḩadīthah, *Iraq* 70 C4
Al Ḩadīthah, *Si. Arabia* 74 D6
Al Ḩaḑr, *Iraq* 70 C4
Al Ḩājānah, *Syria* 74 B5
Al Ḩajar al Gharbī, *Oman* 71 E8
Al Ḩāmad, *Si. Arabia* 70 D3
Al Hamdāniyah, *Syria* 70 C3
Al Ḩamīdīyah, *Syria* 74 A4
Al Ḩammār, *Iraq* 70 D5
Al Ḩamrā', *Si. Arabia* 70 E3
Al Ḩamzah, *Iraq* 70 D5
Al Ḩanākīyah, *Si. Arabia* 70 E4
Al Ḩarīr, W. →, *Syria* 74 C4
Al Ḩasā, W. →, *Jordan* 74 D4
Al Ḩasakah, *Syria* 70 B4
Al Haydān, W. →, *Jordan* 74 D4
Al Ḩayy, *Iraq* 70 C5
Al Ḩijarah, *Asia* 70 D4
Al Ḩillah, *Iraq* 70 C5
Al Ḩillah, *Si. Arabia* 75 B4
Al Hindīyah, *Iraq* 70 C5
Al Hirmil, *Lebanon* 74 A5
Al Hoceïma, *Morocco* 78 A5
Al Ḩudaydah, *Yemen* 75 E3
Al Hufūf, *Si. Arabia* 71 E6
Al Ḩumayḑah, *Si. Arabia* 70 D2
Al Ḩunayy, *Si. Arabia* 71 E6
Al Īsāwīyah, *Si. Arabia* 70 D3
Al Jafr, *Jordan* 74 E5
Al Jāfūrah, *Si. Arabia* 71 E7
Al Jaghbūb, *Libya* 79 C10
Al Jahrah, *Kuwait* 70 D5
Al Jalāmīd, *Si. Arabia* 70 D3
Al Jamalīyah, *Qatar* 71 E6
Al Janūb □, *Lebanon* 74 B4
Al Jawf, *Libya* 79 D10
Al Jawf, *Si. Arabia* 70 D3
Al Jazirah, *Iraq* 70 C5
Al Jithāmīyah, *Si. Arabia* 70 E4
Al Jubayl, *Si. Arabia* 71 E6
Al Jubaylah, *Si. Arabia* 70 E5
Al Jubb, *Si. Arabia* 70 E4
Al Junaynah, *Sudan* 79 F10
Al Kabā'ish, *Iraq* 70 D5
Al Karak, *Jordan* 74 D4
Al Karak □, *Jordan* 74 E5
Al Kāẓimīyah, *Iraq* 70 C5
Al Khābūra, *Oman* 71 F8
Al Khafji, *Si. Arabia* 71 E6
Al Khalīl, *West Bank* 74 D4
Al Khāliş, *Iraq* 70 C5
Al Kharsānīyah, *Si. Arabia* 71 E6
Al Khaşab, *Oman* 71 E8
Al Khawr, *Qatar* 71 E6
Al Khiḑr, *Iraq* 70 D5
Al Khiyām, *Lebanon* 74 B4
Al Khums, *Libya* 79 B8
Al Kiswah, *Syria* 74 B5
Al Kūfah, *Iraq* 70 C5
Al Kufrah, *Libya* 79 D10
Al Kuhayfīyah, *Si. Arabia* 70 E4
Al Kūt, *Iraq* 70 C5
Al Kuwayt, *Kuwait* 70 D5
Al Labwah, *Lebanon* 74 A5
Al Lādhiqīyah, *Syria* 70 C2
Al Līth, *Si. Arabia* 75 C3
Al Liwā', *Oman* 71 E8
Al Luḩayyah, *Yemen* 75 D3
Al Madīnah, *Iraq* 70 D5
Al Madīnah, *Si. Arabia* 70 E3
Al Mafraq, *Jordan* 74 C5
Al Mafraq □, *Jordan* 74 C5
Al Maḩmūdīyah, *Iraq* 70 C5
Al Majma'ah, *Si. Arabia* 70 E5
Al Makhruq, W. →, *Jordan* 74 D6
Al Makḩūl, *Si. Arabia* 70 E4
Al Manāmah, *Bahrain* 71 E6
Al Maqwa', *Kuwait* 70 D5
Al Marj, *Libya* 79 B10
Al Maţlā, *Kuwait* 70 D5
Al Mawjib, W. →, *Jordan* 74 D4
Al Mawşil, *Iraq* 70 B4
Al Mayādin, *Syria* 70 C4
Al Mazār, *Jordan* 74 D4
Al Midhnab, *Si. Arabia* 70 E5
Al Minā', *Lebanon* 74 A4
Al Miqdādīyah, *Iraq* 70 C5
Al Mubarraz, *Si. Arabia* 71 E6
Al Mudawwarah, *Jordan* 74 F5
Al Mughayrā', *U.A.E.* 71 E7
Al Muḩarraq, *Bahrain* 71 E6
Al Mukallā, *Yemen* 75 E4
Al Mukhā, *Yemen* 75 E3
Al Musayjīd, *Si. Arabia* 70 E3
Al Musayyib, *Iraq* 70 C5
Al Muthanná □, *Iraq* 70 D5
Al Muwayh, *Si. Arabia* 80 C5
Al Muwayliḩ, *Si. Arabia* 70 E2
Al Owuho = Otukpa, *Nigeria* 83 D6
Al Qādisīyah □, *Iraq* 70 D5
Al Qā'im, *Iraq* 70 C4
Al Qalībah, *Si. Arabia* 70 D3
Al Qāmishlī, *Syria* 70 B4
Al Qaryatayn, *Syria* 74 A6
Al Qaşīm, *Si. Arabia* 70 E4
Al Qaţ'ā, *Syria* 70 C4
Al Qaţīf, *Si. Arabia* 71 E6
Al Qatrānah, *Jordan* 74 D5
Al Qaţrūn, *Libya* 79 D9
Al Qayşūmah, *Si. Arabia* 70 D5
Al Quds = Jerusalem, *Israel* 74 D4
Al Qunayţirah, *Syria* 74 C4
Al Qunfudhah, *Si. Arabia* 80 D5
Al Qurnah, *Iraq* 70 D5
Al Quşayr, *Iraq* 70 D5
Al Quşayr, *Syria* 74 A5
Al Qutayfah, *Syria* 74 B5
Al 'Ubaylah, *Si. Arabia* 75 C5
Al 'Uḑaylīyah, *Si. Arabia* 71 E6
Al 'Ulā, *Si. Arabia* 70 E3
Al 'Uqayr, *Si. Arabia* 71 E6
Al 'Uwaynid, *Si. Arabia* 70 E5
Al 'Uwayqīlah, *Si. Arabia* 70 D4
Al 'Uyūn, *Ḩijāz, Si. Arabia* 70 E3
Al 'Uyūn, *Najd, Si. Arabia* 70 E4
Al 'Uzayr, *Iraq* 70 D5
Al Wajh, *Si. Arabia* 70 E3
Al Wakrah, *Qatar* 71 E6
Al Waqbah, *Si. Arabia* 70 D5
Al Wari'āh, *Si. Arabia* 71 E6
Ala, *Italy* 40 C8
Ala Dağ, *Turkey* 70 B2
Ala Dağları, *Turkey* 73 C10
Alabama □, *U.S.A.* 115 J2
Alabama →, *U.S.A.* 115 K2
Alabaster, *U.S.A.* 115 J2
Alaca, *Turkey* 72 B6
Alacaatlı, *Turkey* 47 B10
Alaçam, *Turkey* 72 B6
Alaçam Dağları, *Turkey* 47 B10
Alacant = Alicante, *Spain* 39 G4
Alaçatı, *Turkey* 47 C8
Alachua, *U.S.A.* 115 L4
Alaejos, *Spain* 36 D5
Alaérma, *Greece* 49 C9
Alagir, *Russia* 35 J7
Alagna Valsésia, *Italy* 40 C4
Alagoa Grande, *Brazil* 125 E11
Alagoas □, *Brazil* 125 E11
Alagoinhas, *Brazil* 125 F11
Alagón, *Spain* 38 D3
Alagón →, *Spain* 36 F4
Alaior, *Spain* 48 B11
Alajero, *Canary Is.* 48 F2
Alajuela, *Costa Rica* 120 D3
Alakamisy, *Madag.* 89 C8
Alaknanda →, *India* 69 D8
Alakol, Ozero, *Kazakhstan* 60 B3
Alamarvdasht, *Iran* 71 E7
Alamata, *Ethiopia* 81 E4
Alameda, *Calif., U.S.A.* 110 H4
Alameda, *N. Mex., U.S.A.* 109 J10
Alaminos, *Phil.* 61 C3
Alamo, *U.S.A.* 111 J11
Alamo Crossing, *U.S.A.* 111 L13
Alamogordo, *U.S.A.* 109 K11
Alamos, *Mexico* 118 B3
Alamosa, *U.S.A.* 109 H11
Åland = Ahvenanmaa, *Finland* 9 F19
Alandroal, *Portugal* 37 G3
Ålands hav, *Europe* 9 F18
Alange, Embalse d', *Spain* 37 G4
Alania = North Ossetia □, *Russia* 35 J7
Alanís, *Spain* 37 G5
Alanya, *Turkey* 70 B1
Alaotra, Farihin', *Madag.* 89 B8
Alapayevsk, *Russia* 52 D7
Alappuzha = Alleppey, *India* 66 Q10
Alar del Rey, *Spain* 36 C6
Alaraz, *Spain* 36 E5
Alarcón, Embalse de, *Spain* 38 F2
Alarobia-Vohiposa, *Madag.* 89 C8
Alaşehir, *Turkey* 47 C10
Alaska □, *U.S.A.* 100 B5
Alaska, G. of, *Pac. Oc.* 100 C5
Alaska Peninsula, *U.S.A.* 100 C4
Alaska Range, *U.S.A.* 100 B4
Alássio, *Italy* 40 E5
Älät, *Azerbaijan* 35 L9
Alatri, *Italy* 41 G10
Alatyr, *Russia* 34 C8
Alatyr →, *Russia* 34 C8
Alausi, *Ecuador* 124 D3
Álava □, *Spain* 38 C2
Alava, C., *U.S.A.* 108 B1
Alaverdi, *Armenia* 35 K7
Alavo = Alavus, *Finland* 9 E20
Alavus, *Finland* 9 E20
Alawoona, *Australia* 95 E3
'Alayh, *Lebanon* 74 B4
Alazani →, *Azerbaijan* 35 K8
Alba, *Italy* 40 D5
Alba □, *Romania* 29 D8
Alba Adriática, *Italy* 41 F10
Alba de Tormes, *Spain* 36 E5
Alba-Iulia, *Romania* 29 D8
Albac, *Romania* 28 D7
Albacete, *Spain* 39 F3
Albacete □, *Spain* 39 G3
Albacutya, L., *Australia* 95 F3
Ålbæk, *Denmark* 11 G4
Ålbæk Bugt, *Denmark* 11 G4
Albaida, *Spain* 39 G4
Albalate de las Nogueras, *Spain* 38 E2
Albalate del Arzobispo, *Spain* 38 D4
Alban, *France* 20 E6
Albanel, L., *Canada* 104 B5
Albania ■, *Europe* 44 E4
Albano Laziale, *Italy* 41 G9
Albany, *Australia* 93 G2
Albany, *Ga., U.S.A.* 115 K3
Albany, *N.Y., U.S.A.* 117 D11
Albany, *Oreg., U.S.A.* 108 D2
Albany, *Tex., U.S.A.* 113 J5
Albany →, *Canada* 104 B3
Albardón, *Argentina* 126 C2
Albarracín, *Spain* 38 E3
Albarracín, Sierra de, *Spain* 38 E3
Albatera, *Spain* 39 G4
Albatross B., *Australia* 94 A3
Albegna →, *Italy* 41 F8
Albemarle, *U.S.A.* 115 H5
Albemarle Sd., *U.S.A.* 115 H7
Albenga, *Italy* 40 D5
Alberche →, *Spain* 36 F6
Alberdi, *Paraguay* 126 B4
Albères, Mts., *France* 20 F6
Ålberga, *Sweden* 11 F10
Alberga, The →, *Australia* 95 D2
Albersdorf, *Germany* 24 A5
Albert, *France* 19 C9
Albert, L., *Africa* 86 B3
Albert, L., *Australia* 95 F2
Albert Edward Ra., *Australia* 92 C4
Albert Lea, *U.S.A.* 112 D8
Albert Nile →, *Uganda* 86 B3
Albert Town, *Bahamas* 121 B5
Alberta □, *Canada* 102 C6
Alberti, *Argentina* 126 D3
Albertinia, *S. Africa* 88 E3
Albertirsa, *Hungary* 28 C4
Alberton, *Canada* 105 C7
Albertville, *France* 21 C10
Albertville, *U.S.A.* 115 H2
Albi, *France* 20 E6
Albia, *U.S.A.* 112 E8
Albina, *Suriname* 125 B8
Albina, Ponta, *Angola* 88 B1
Albino, *Italy* 40 C6
Albion, *Mich., U.S.A.* 114 D3
Albion, *Nebr., U.S.A.* 112 E6
Albion, *Pa., U.S.A.* 116 E4
Albocácer, *Spain* 38 E5
Albolote, *Spain* 37 H7
Alborán, *Medit. S.* 37 K7
Alborea, *Spain* 39 F3
Ålborg, *Denmark* 11 G3
Ålborg Bugt, *Denmark* 11 H4
Alborz, Reshteh-ye Kūhhā-ye, *Iran* 71 C7
Albox, *Spain* 39 H2
Albufeira, *Portugal* 37 H2
Albula →, *Switz.* 25 J5
Albuñol, *Spain* 37 J7
Albuquerque, *U.S.A.* 109 J10
Albuquerque, Cayos de, *Caribbean* 120 D3
Alburg, *U.S.A.* 117 B11
Alburno, Mte., *Italy* 43 B8
Alburquerque, *Spain* 37 F4
Albury = Albury-Wodonga, *Australia* 95 F4
Albury-Wodonga, *Australia* 95 F4
Alcácer do Sal, *Portugal* 37 G2
Alcáçovas, *Portugal* 37 G2
Alcalá de Chivert, *Spain* 38 E5
Alcalá de Guadaira, *Spain* 37 H5
Alcalá de Henares, *Spain* 36 E7
Alcalá de los Gazules, *Spain* 37 J5
Alcalá del Júcar, *Spain* 39 F3
Alcalá del Río, *Spain* 37 H5
Alcalá del Valle, *Spain* 37 J5
Alcalá la Real, *Spain* 37 H7
Álcamo, *Italy* 42 E5
Alcanadre, *Spain* 38 C2
Alcanadre →, *Spain* 38 D4
Alcanar, *Spain* 38 E5
Alcanede, *Portugal* 37 F2
Alcanena, *Portugal* 37 F2
Alcañices, *Spain* 36 D4
Alcañiz, *Spain* 38 D4
Alcântara, *Brazil* 125 D10
Alcántara, *Spain* 36 F4
Alcántara, Embalse de, *Spain* 36 F4
Alcantarilla, *Spain* 39 H3
Alcaracejos, *Spain* 37 G6
Alcaraz, *Spain* 39 G2
Alcaraz, Sierra de, *Spain* 39 G2
Alcaudete, *Spain* 37 H6
Alcázar de San Juan, *Spain* 37 F7
Alchevsk, *Ukraine* 33 H10
Alcira = Alzira, *Spain* 39 F4
Alcobaça, *Portugal* 37 F2
Alcobendas, *Spain* 36 E7
Alcolea del Pinar, *Spain* 38 D2
Alcora, *Spain* 38 E4
Alcorcón, *Spain* 36 E7
Alcoutim, *Portugal* 37 H3
Alcova, *U.S.A.* 108 E10
Alcoy, *Spain* 39 G4
Alcubierre, Sierra de, *Spain* 38 D4
Alcublas, *Spain* 38 F4
Alcúdia, *Spain* 48 B10
Alcúdia, B. d', *Spain* 48 B10
Alcudia, Sierra de la, *Spain* 37 G6
Aldabra Is., *Seychelles* 77 G8
Aldama, *Mexico* 119 C5
Aldan, *Russia* 53 D13
Aldan →, *Russia* 53 C13
Aldea, Pta. de la, *Canary Is.* 48 G4
Aldeburgh, *U.K.* 15 E9
Alder Pk., *U.S.A.* 110 K5
Alderney, *U.K.* 15 H5
Aldershot, *U.K.* 15 F7
Åled, *Sweden* 11 H6
Aledo, *U.S.A.* 112 E9
Alefa, *Ethiopia* 81 E4
Aleg, *Mauritania* 82 B2
Alegranza, *Canary Is.* 48 E6
Alegranza, I., *Canary Is.* 48 E6
Alegre, *Brazil* 127 A7
Alegrete, *Brazil* 127 B4
Aleisk, *Russia* 52 D9
Aleksandriya = Oleksandriya, *Kirovohrad, Ukraine* 33 H7
Aleksandriya = Oleksandriya, *Rivne, Ukraine* 33 G4
Aleksandriyskaya, *Russia* 35 J8
Aleksandrov, *Russia* 32 D10
Aleksandrov Gay, *Russia* 34 E9
Aleksandrovac, *Serbia & M.* 44 C5
Aleksandrovac, *Serbia & M.* 44 B5
Aleksandrovka = Oleksandrovka, *Ukraine* 33 H7
Aleksandrovo, *Bulgaria* 45 C8
Aleksandrovsk-Sakhalinskiy, *Russia* 53 D15
Aleksandrów Kujawski, *Poland* 31 F5
Aleksandrów Łódźki, *Poland* 31 G6
Aleksandry, Z., *Russia* 4 A10
Alekseyevka, *Samara, Russia* 34 D10
Alekseyevka, *Voronezh, Russia* 33 G10
Aleksin, *Russia* 32 E9
Aleksinac, *Serbia & M.* 44 C5
Além Paraíba, *Brazil* 127 A7
Alemania, *Argentina* 126 B2
Alemania, *Chile* 126 B2
Alençon, *France* 18 D7
Alenquer, *Brazil* 125 D8
Alenuihaha Channel, *U.S.A.* 106 H17
Alépé, *Ivory C.* 82 D4
Aleppo = Ḩalab, *Syria* 70 B3
Aléria, *France* 21 F13
Alert, *Canada* 4 A4
Alès, *France* 21 D8
Aleşd, *Romania* 28 C7
Alessándria, *Italy* 40 D5
Ålestrup, *Denmark* 11 H3
Ålesund, *Norway* 9 E12
Alet-les-Bains, *France* 20 F6
Aletschhorn, *Switz.* 25 J4
Aleutian Is., *Pac. Oc.* 100 C2
Aleutian Trench, *Pac. Oc.* 96 C10
Alexander, *U.S.A.* 112 B3
Alexander, Mt., *Australia* 93 E3
Alexander Arch., *U.S.A.* 100 C6
Alexander Bay, *S. Africa* 88 D2
Alexander City, *U.S.A.* 115 J3
Alexander I., *Antarctica* 5 C17
Alexandra, *Australia* 95 F4
Alexandra, *N.Z.* 91 L2
Alexandra Falls, *Canada* 102 A5

Alexandria = El Iskandarîya, *Egypt* 80 H7
Alexandria, *B.C., Canada* 102 C4
Alexandria, *Ont., Canada* 117 A10
Alexandria, *Romania* 29 G10
Alexandria, *S. Africa* 88 E4
Alexandria, *U.K.* 13 F4
Alexandria, *La., U.S.A.* 113 K8
Alexandria, *Minn., U.S.A.* 112 C7
Alexandria, *S. Dak., U.S.A.* 112 D6
Alexandria, *Va., U.S.A.* 114 F7
Alexandria Bay, *U.S.A.* 117 B9
Alexandrina, L., *Australia* 95 F2
Alexandroúpolis, *Greece* 45 F9
Alexis →, *Canada* 105 B8
Alexis Creek, *Canada* 102 C4
Alfabia, *Spain* 48 B9
Alfambra, *Spain* 38 E3
Alfândega da Fé, *Portugal* 36 D4
Alfaro, *Spain* 38 C3
Alfatar, *Bulgaria* 45 C11
Alfaz del Pi, *Spain* 39 G4
Alfeld, *Germany* 24 D5
Alfenas, *Brazil* 127 A6
Alfiós →, *Greece* 46 D3
Alföld, *Hungary* 28 D5
Alfonsine, *Italy* 41 D9
Alford, *Aberds., U.K.* 13 D6
Alford, *Lincs., U.K.* 14 D8
Alfred, *Maine, U.S.A.* 117 C14
Alfred, *N.Y., U.S.A.* 116 D7
Alfreton, *U.K.* 14 D6
Alfta, *Sweden* 10 C10
Alga, *Kazakhstan* 52 E6
Algaida, *Spain* 48 B9
Algar, *Spain* 37 J5
Ålgård, *Norway* 9 G11
Algarinejo, *Spain* 37 H6
Algarve, *Portugal* 37 J2
Algeciras, *Spain* 37 J5
Algemesí, *Spain* 39 F4
Alger, *Algeria* 78 A6
Alger ✕ (ALG), *Algeria* 39 J8
Algeria ■, *Africa* 78 C6
Alghero, *Italy* 42 B1
Älghult, *Sweden* 11 G9
Algiers = Alger, *Algeria* 78 A6
Algoa B., *S. Africa* 88 E4
Algodonales, *Spain* 37 J5
Algodor →, *Spain* 36 F7
Algoma, *U.S.A.* 114 C2
Algona, *U.S.A.* 112 D7
Algonac, *U.S.A.* 116 D2
Algonquin ⌓, *Canada* 104 C4
Algorta, *Uruguay* 128 C5
Alhama de Almería, *Spain* 37 J8
Alhama de Aragón, *Spain* 38 D3
Alhama de Granada, *Spain* 37 H7
Alhama de Murcia, *Spain* 39 H3
Alhambra, *U.S.A.* 111 L8
Alhaurín el Grande, *Spain* 37 J6
Alhucemas = Al Hoceïma, *Morocco* 78 A5
'Alī al Gharbī, *Iraq* 70 C5
'Alī ash Sharqī, *Iraq* 70 C5
Äli Bayramlı, *Azerbaijan* 35 L9
'Alī Khēl, *Afghan.* 68 C3
Ali Sahîh, *Djibouti* 81 E5
Alī Shāh, *Iran* 70 B5
Ália, *Italy* 42 E6
'Alīābād, *Khorāsān, Iran* 71 C8
'Alīābād, *Kordestān, Iran* 70 C5
'Alīābād, *Yazd, Iran* 71 D7
Aliaga, *Spain* 38 E4
Aliağa, *Turkey* 47 C8
Aliákmon →, *Greece* 44 F6
Alibo, *Ethiopia* 81 F4
Alibori →, *Benin* 83 C5
Alibunar, *Serbia & M.* 28 E5
Alicante, *Spain* 39 G4
Alicante □, *Spain* 39 G4
Alicante ✕ (ALC), *Spain* 39 G4
Alice, *S. Africa* 88 E4
Alice, *U.S.A.* 113 M5
Alice →, *Queens., Australia* 94 C3
Alice →, *Queens., Australia* 94 B3
Alice, Punta, *Italy* 43 C10
Alice Arm, *Canada* 102 B3
Alice Springs, *Australia* 94 C1
Alicedale, *S. Africa* 88 E4
Aliceville, *U.S.A.* 115 J1
Alicudi, *Italy* 43 D7
Aliganj, *India* 69 F8
Aligarh, *Raj., India* 68 G7
Aligarh, *Ut. P., India* 68 F8
Alīgūdarz, *Iran* 71 C6
Alijó, *Portugal* 36 D3
Alimnía, *Greece* 49 C9
Alingsås, *Sweden* 11 G6
Alipur, *Pakistan* 68 E4
Alipur Duar, *India* 67 F16
Aliquippa, *U.S.A.* 116 F4
Alishan, *Taiwan* 59 F13
Aliste →, *Spain* 36 D5
Alitus = Alytus, *Lithuania* 9 J21
Alivérion, *Greece* 46 C6
Aliwal North, *S. Africa* 88 E4
Alix, *Canada* 102 C6
Aljezur, *Portugal* 37 H2
Aljustrel, *Portugal* 37 H2
Alkamari, *Niger* 83 C7
Alkmaar, *Neths.* 17 B4
All American Canal, *U.S.A.* 109 K6
Allada, *Benin* 83 D5
Allagash →, *U.S.A.* 115 B11
Allah Dad, *Pakistan* 68 G2
Allahabad, *India* 69 G9
Allan, *Canada* 103 C7
Allanche, *France* 20 C6
Allanridge, *S. Africa* 88 D4
Allaqi, Wadi →, *Egypt* 80 C3
Allariz, *Spain* 36 C3
Allassac, *France* 20 C5
Ålleberg, *Sweden* 11 F7
Allegany, *U.S.A.* 116 D6
Allegheny →, *U.S.A.* 116 F5
Allegheny Mts., *U.S.A.* 114 G6
Allegheny Reservoir, *U.S.A.* 116 E6
Allègre, *France* 20 C7
Allègre, Pte., *Guadeloupe* 120 b
Allen, Bog of, *Ireland* 12 C5
Allen, L., *Ireland* 12 B3
Allendale, *U.S.A.* 115 J5
Allende, *Mexico* 118 B4
Allentown, *U.S.A.* 117 F9
Allentsteig, *Austria* 26 C8
Alleppey, *India* 66 Q10
Allepuz, *Spain* 38 E4
Aller →, *Germany* 24 C5
Alleynes B., *Barbados* 121 g
Alliance, *Nebr., U.S.A.* 112 D3
Alliance, *Ohio, U.S.A.* 116 F3
Allier □, *France* 19 F9
Allier →, *France* 19 F10
Alliford Bay, *Canada* 102 C2
Alligator Pond, *Jamaica* 120 a
Allinge, *Denmark* 11 J8
Alliston = New Tecumseth, *Canada* 116 B5
Alloa, *U.K.* 13 E5
Allones, *France* 18 D8
Allora, *Australia* 95 D5
Allos, *France* 21 D10
Alluitsup Paa, *Greenland* 101 B15
Alma, *Canada* 105 C5
Alma, *Ga., U.S.A.* 115 K4
Alma, *Kans., U.S.A.* 112 F6
Alma, *Mich., U.S.A.* 114 D3
Alma, *Nebr., U.S.A.* 112 E5
Alma Ata = Almaty, *Kazakhstan* 52 E8
Almacelles, *Spain* 38 D5
Almada, *Portugal* 37 G1
Almaden, *Australia* 94 B3
Almadén, *Spain* 37 G6
Almanor, L., *U.S.A.* 108 F3
Almansa, *Spain* 39 G3
Almanza, *Spain* 36 C5
Almanzor, Pico, *Spain* 36 E5
Almanzora →, *Spain* 39 H3
Almaş, Munţii, *Romania* 28 F7
Almassora, *Spain* 38 F4
Almaty, *Kazakhstan* 52 E8
Almazán, *Spain* 38 D2
Almeirim, *Brazil* 125 D8
Almeirim, *Portugal* 37 F2
Almelo, *Neths.* 17 B6
Almenar de Soria, *Spain* 38 D2
Almenara, *Spain* 38 F4
Almenara, Sierra de la, *Spain* 39 H3
Almendra, Embalse de, *Spain* 36 D4
Almendralejo, *Spain* 37 G4
Almere-Stad, *Neths.* 17 B5
Almería, *Spain* 37 J8
Almería □, *Spain* 39 H2
Almería, G. de, *Spain* 39 J2
Almetyevsk, *Russia* 34 C11
Älmhult, *Sweden* 11 H8
Almirante, *Panama* 120 E3
Almiropótamos, *Greece* 46 C6
Almirós, *Greece* 46 B4
Almiroú, Kólpos, *Greece* 49 D6
Almodôvar, *Portugal* 37 H2
Almodóvar del Campo, *Spain* 37 G6
Almodóvar del Río, *Spain* 37 H5
Almond, *U.S.A.* 116 D7
Almont, *U.S.A.* 116 D1
Almonte, *Canada* 117 A8
Almonte, *Spain* 37 H4
Almora, *India* 69 E8
Almoradí, *Spain* 39 G4
Almorox, *Spain* 36 E6
Almoustarat, *Mali* 83 B5
Älmsta, *Sweden* 10 E12
Almudévar, *Spain* 38 C4
Almuñécar, *Spain* 37 J7
Almunge, *Sweden* 10 E12
Almuradiel, *Spain* 37 G7
Alness, *U.K.* 13 D4
Alnmouth, *U.K.* 14 B6
Alnwick, *U.K.* 14 B6
Aloi, *Uganda* 86 B3
Alon, *Burma* 67 H19
Alonissos-Voríai Sporades △, *Greece* 46 B6
Alor, *Indonesia* 63 F6
Alor Setar, *Malaysia* 65 J3
Álora, *Spain* 37 J6
Alosno, *Spain* 37 H3
Alot, *India* 68 H6
Aloysius, Mt., *Australia* 93 E4
Alpaugh, *U.S.A.* 110 K7
Alpe Apuane ⌓, *Italy* 40 D7
Alpedrinha, *Portugal* 36 E3
Alpena, *U.S.A.* 114 C4
Alpes-de-Haute-Provence □, *France* 21 D10
Alpes-Maritimes □, *France* 21 E11
Alpha, *Australia* 94 C4
Alpha Cordillera, *Arctic* 4 A2
Alphen aan den Rijn, *Neths.* 17 B4
Alpiarça, *Portugal* 37 F2
Alpine, *Ariz., U.S.A.* 109 K9
Alpine, *Calif., U.S.A.* 111 N10
Alpine, *Tex., U.S.A.* 113 K3
Alps, *Europe* 6 F7
Alpu, *Turkey* 72 C4
Alqueta, Barragem do, *Portugal* 37 G3
Alrø, *Denmark* 11 J4
Als, *Denmark* 11 K3
Alsace □, *France* 19 D14
Alsask, *Canada* 103 C7
Alsasua, *Spain* 38 C2
Alsek →, *U.S.A.* 102 B1
Alsfeld, *Germany* 24 E5
Alsten, *Norway* 8 D15
Alstermo, *Sweden* 11 H9
Alston, *U.K.* 14 C5
Alta, *Norway* 8 B20
Alta, Sierra, *Spain* 38 E3
Alta Gracia, *Argentina* 126 C3
Alta Sierra, *U.S.A.* 111 K8
Altaelva →, *Norway* 8 B20
Altafjorden, *Norway* 8 A20
Altai = Aerhtai Shan, *Mongolia* 60 B4
Altamaha →, *U.S.A.* 115 K5
Altamira, *Brazil* 125 D8
Altamira, *Chile* 126 B2
Altamira, *Mexico* 119 C5
Altamira, Cuevas de, *Spain* 36 B6
Altamont, *U.S.A.* 117 D10
Altamura, *Italy* 43 B9
Altanbulag, *Mongolia* 60 A5
Altar, *Mexico* 118 A2
Altar, Desierto de, *Mexico* 118 B2
Altata, *Mexico* 118 C3
Altavista, *U.S.A.* 114 G6
Altay, *China* 60 B3
Altdorf, *Switz.* 25 J4
Alte Mellum, *Germany* 24 B4
Altea, *Spain* 39 G4
Altenberg, *Germany* 24 E9
Altenbruch, *Germany* 24 B4
Altenburg, *Germany* 24 E8
Altenkirchen, *Mecklenburg-Vorpommern, Germany* 24 A9
Altenkirchen, *Rhld-Pfz., Germany* 24 E3
Altenmarkt, *Austria* 26 D7
Alter do Chão, *Portugal* 37 F3
Altınoluk, *Turkey* 47 B8
Altınova, *Turkey* 47 B8
Altıntaş, *Turkey* 47 B12
Altınyaka, *Turkey* 47 E12
Altınyayla, *Turkey* 47 D11
Altiplano, *Bolivia* 122 E4
Altkirch, *France* 19 E14
Altmark, *Germany* 24 C7
Altmühl →, *Germany* 25 G7
Altmühltal ⌓, *Germany* 25 G7
Altmunster, *Austria* 26 D6
Alto Adige = Trentino-Alto Adige □, *Italy* 41 B8
Alto Araguaia, *Brazil* 125 G8
Alto Cuchumatanes = Cuchumatanes, Sierra de los, *Guatemala* 120 C1
Alto del Carmen, *Chile* 126 B1
Alto del Inca, *Chile* 126 A2
Alto Garda Bresciano ⌓, *Italy* 40 C7
Alto Ligonha, *Mozam.* 87 F4
Alto Molocue, *Mozam.* 87 F4
Alto Paraguay □, *Paraguay* 126 A4
Alto Paraná □, *Paraguay* 127 B5
Alton, *Canada* 116 C4
Alton, *U.K.* 15 F7
Alton, *Ill., U.S.A.* 112 F9
Alton, *N.H., U.S.A.* 117 C13
Altona, *Canada* 103 D9
Altoona, *U.S.A.* 116 F6
Altötting, *Germany* 25 G8
Altstätten, *Switz.* 25 H5
Altun Kupri, *Iraq* 70 C5
Altun Shan, *China* 60 C3
Alturas, *U.S.A.* 108 F3
Altus, *U.S.A.* 113 H5
Alubijid, *Phil.* 61 G6
Alucra, *Turkey* 73 B8
Aluk, *Sudan* 81 F2
Alūksne, *Latvia* 9 H22
Alunda, *Sweden* 10 D12
Alunite, *U.S.A.* 111 K12
Aluoro →, *Ethiopia* 81 F3
Alupka, *Ukraine* 33 K8
Alushta, *Ukraine* 33 K8
Alusi, *Indonesia* 63 F8
Alustante, *Spain* 38 E3
Alva, *U.S.A.* 113 G5
Alvaiázere, *Portugal* 36 F2
Älvängen, *Sweden* 11 G6
Alvão ⌓, *Portugal* 36 D3
Alvarado, *Mexico* 119 D5
Alvarado, *U.S.A.* 113 J6
Alvaro Obregón, Presa, *Mexico* 118 B3
Älvdalen, *Sweden* 10 C8
Alvear, *Argentina* 126 B4
Alverca, *Portugal* 37 G1
Alvesta, *Sweden* 11 H8
Alvin, *U.S.A.* 113 L7
Alvinston, *Canada* 116 D3
Alvito, *Portugal* 37 G3
Älvkarleby, *Sweden* 10 D11
Alvord Desert, *U.S.A.* 108 E4
Älvros, *Sweden* 10 B8
Älvsbyn, *Sweden* 8 D19
Alwar, *India* 68 F7
Alxa Zuoqi, *China* 56 E3
Alyangula, *Australia* 94 A2
Alyata = Älät, *Azerbaijan* 35 L9
Alyth, *U.K.* 13 E5
Alytus, *Lithuania* 9 J21
Alzada, *U.S.A.* 112 C2
Alzey, *Germany* 25 F4
Alzira, *Spain* 39 F4
Am Timan, *Chad* 79 F10
Amadeus, L., *Australia* 93 D5
Amadi, *Dem. Rep. of the Congo* 86 B2
Amâdi, *Sudan* 81 F3
Amadjuak L., *Canada* 101 B12
Amadora, *Portugal* 37 G1
Amagansett, *U.S.A.* 117 F12
Amagasaki, *Japan* 55 G7
Amager, *Denmark* 11 J6
Amagunze, *Nigeria* 83 D6
Amahai, *Indonesia* 63 E7
Amakusa-Shotō, *Japan* 55 H5
Åmål, *Sweden* 10 E6
Amalfi, *Italy* 43 B7
Amaliás, *Greece* 46 D3
Amalner, *India* 66 J9
Amamapare, *Indonesia* 63 E9
Amambaí, *Brazil* 127 A4
Amambaí →, *Brazil* 127 A5
Amambay □, *Paraguay* 127 A4
Amambay, Cordillera de, *S. Amer.* 127 A4
Amami-Guntō, *Japan* 55 L4
Amami-Ō-Shima, *Japan* 55 L4
Aman, Pulau, *Malaysia* 65 c
Amanã, L., *Brazil* 124 D6
Amanat →, *India* 69 G11
Amanda Park, *U.S.A.* 110 C3
Amangeldy, *Kazakhstan* 52 D7
Amantea, *Italy* 43 C9
Amapá, *Brazil* 125 C8
Amapá □, *Brazil* 125 C8
Amara, *Sudan* 81 E3
Amara □, *Ethiopia* 81 E4
Amarante, *Brazil* 125 E10
Amarante, *Portugal* 36 D2
Amaranth, *Canada* 103 C9
Amareleja, *Portugal* 37 G3
Amargosa →, *U.S.A.* 111 J10
Amargosa Range, *U.S.A.* 111 J10
Amári, *Greece* 49 D6
Amarillo, *U.S.A.* 113 H4
Amarkantak, *India* 69 H9
Amârna, Tell el', *Sudan* 80 B3
Amaro, Mte., *Italy* 41 F11
Amarpur, *India* 69 G12
Amarti, *Eritrea* 81 E5
Amarwara, *India* 69 H8
Amasra, *Turkey* 72 B5
Amassama, *Nigeria* 83 D6
Amasya, *Turkey* 72 B6
Amata, *Australia* 93 E5
Amatikulu, *S. Africa* 89 D5
Amatitlán, *Guatemala* 120 D1
Amatrice, *Italy* 41 F10
Amay, *Belgium* 17 D5
Amazon = Amazonas →, *S. Amer.* 125 D9
Amazonas □, *Brazil* 124 E6
Amazonas →, *S. Amer.* 125 D9
Amba Ferit, *Ethiopia* 81 E4
Ambah, *India* 68 F8
Ambahakily, *Madag.* 89 C7
Ambahita, *Madag.* 89 C8
Ambala, *India* 68 D7
Ambalavao, *Madag.* 89 C8
Ambanja, *Madag.* 89 A8
Ambararata, *Madag.* 89 B8
Ambarchik, *Russia* 53 C17
Ambarijeby, *Madag.* 89 A8
Ambaro, Helodranon', *Madag.* 89 A8
Ambato, *Ecuador* 124 D3
Ambato, *Madag.* 89 A8
Ambato, Sierra de, *Argentina* 126 B2
Ambato Boeny, *Madag.* 89 B8
Ambatofinandrahana, *Madag.* 89 C8
Ambatolampy, *Madag.* 89 B8
Ambatomainty, *Madag.* 89 B8
Ambatomanoina, *Madag.* 89 B8
Ambatondrazaka, *Madag.* 89 B8
Ambatosoratra, *Madag.* 89 B8
Ambelón, *Greece* 46 B4
Ambenja, *Madag.* 89 B8
Amberg, *Germany* 25 F7
Ambergris Cay, *Belize* 119 D7
Ambérieu-en-Bugey, *France* 21 C9
Amberley, *N.Z.* 91 K4
Ambert, *France* 20 C7
Ambidédi, *Mali* 82 C2
Ambikapur, *India* 69 H10
Ambikol, *Sudan* 80 C3
Ambilobé, *Madag.* 89 A8
Ambinanindrano, *Madag.* 89 C8
Ambinanitelo, *Madag.* 89 B8
Ambinda, *Madag.* 89 B8
Amble, *U.K.* 14 B6
Ambleside, *U.K.* 14 C5
Ambo, *Peru* 124 F3
Amboahangy, *Madag.* 89 C8
Ambodifototra, *Madag.* 89 B8
Ambodilazana, *Madag.* 89 B8
Ambodiriana, *Madag.* 89 B8
Ambohidratrimo, *Madag.* 89 B8
Ambohidray, *Madag.* 89 B8
Ambohimahamasina, *Madag.* 89 C8
Ambohimahasoa, *Madag.* 89 C8
Ambohimanga, *Madag.* 89 C8
Ambohimitombo, *Madag.* 89 C8
Ambohitra, *Madag.* 89 A8
Amboise, *France* 18 E8
Ambon, *Indonesia* 63 E7
Ambondro, *Madag.* 89 D8
Amboseli △, *Kenya* 86 C4
Amboseli, L., *Kenya* 86 C4
Ambositra, *Madag.* 89 C8
Ambovombe, *Madag.* 89 D8
Amboy, *U.S.A.* 111 L11
Amboyna Cay, *S. China Sea* 62 C4
Ambridge, *U.S.A.* 116 F4
Ambriz, *Angola* 84 F2
Amchitka I., *U.S.A.* 100 C1
Amderma, *Russia* 52 C7
Amdhi, *India* 69 H9
Ameca, *Mexico* 118 C4
Ameca →, *Mexico* 118 C3
Amecameca, *Mexico* 119 D5
Ameland, *Neths.* 17 A5
Amélia, *Italy* 41 F9
Amendolara, *Italy* 43 C9
Amenia, *U.S.A.* 117 E11
American Falls, *U.S.A.* 108 E7
American Falls Reservoir, *U.S.A.* 108 E7
American Fork, *U.S.A.* 108 F8
American Highland, *Antarctica* 5 D6
American Samoa ☑, *Pac. Oc.* 91 B13
Americana, *Brazil* 127 A6
Americus, *U.S.A.* 115 K3
Amerigo Vespucci, Firenze ✕ (FLR), *Italy* 40 E8
Amersfoort, *Neths.* 17 B5
Amersfoort, *S. Africa* 89 D4
Amery Ice Shelf, *Antarctica* 5 C6
Ames, *Spain* 36 C2
Ames, *U.S.A.* 112 E8
Amesbury, *U.S.A.* 117 D14
Amet, *India* 68 G5
Amfíklia, *Greece* 46 C4
Amfilokhía, *Greece* 46 C3
Amfípolis, *Greece* 44 F7
Ámfissa, *Greece* 46 C4
Amga, *Russia* 53 C14
Amga →, *Russia* 53 C14
Amgu, *Russia* 53 E14
Amgun →, *Russia* 53 D14
Amherst, *Canada* 105 C7
Amherst, *Mass., U.S.A.* 117 D12
Amherst, *N.Y., U.S.A.* 116 D6
Amherst, *Ohio, U.S.A.* 116 E2
Amherst I., *Canada* 117 B8
Amherstburg, *Canada* 104 D3
Amiata, Mte., *Italy* 41 F8
Amidon, *U.S.A.* 112 B3
Amiens, *France* 19 C9
Amindaion, *Greece* 44 F5
Åminne, *Sweden* 11 G7
Amino, *Ethiopia* 81 G5
Aminuis, *Namibia* 88 C2
Amīrābād, *Iran* 70 C5
Amirante Is., *Seychelles* 50 K9
Amisk ⌓, *Canada* 103 B9
Amisk L., *Canada* 103 C8
Amistad ⌓, *U.S.A.* 113 L4
Amistad, Presa de la, *Mexico* 118 B4
Amite, *U.S.A.* 113 K9
Amla, *India* 68 J8
Amlapura = Karangasem, *Indonesia* 63 J18
Amlia I., *U.S.A.* 100 C2
Amlwch, *U.K.* 14 D3
Amm Adam, *Sudan* 81 D4
'Ammān, *Jordan* 74 D4
'Ammān □, *Jordan* 74 D5
'Ammān ✕ (AMM), *Jordan* 74 D5
Ammanford, *U.K.* 15 F4
Ammassalik = Tasiilaq, *Greenland* 4 C6
Ammerån →, *Sweden* 10 A10
Ammersee, *Germany* 25 G7
Ammochostos = Famagusta, *Cyprus* 49 D12
Ammon, *U.S.A.* 108 E8
Amnat Charoen, *Thailand* 64 E5
Amnura, *Bangla.* 69 G13
Amo Jiang →, *China* 58 F3
Āmol, *Iran* 71 B7
Amorgós, *Greece* 47 E7
Amory, *U.S.A.* 115 J1
Amos, *Canada* 104 C4
Åmot, *Norway* 9 G13
Åmotfors, *Sweden* 10 E6
Amoy = Xiamen, *China* 59 E12
Ampanavoana, *Madag.* 89 B9
Ampang, *Malaysia* 65 L3
Ampangalana, Lakandranon', *Madag.* 89 C8
Ampanihy, *Madag.* 89 C7
Amparafaravola, *Madag.* 89 B8
Ampasinambo, *Madag.* 89 C8
Ampasindava, Helodranon', *Madag.* 89 A8
Ampasindava, Saikanosy, *Madag.* 89 A8
Ampenan, *Indonesia* 63 K18
Amper, *Nigeria* 83 D6
Amper →, *Germany* 25 G7
Ampezzo, *Italy* 41 B9
Amphoe Kathu, *Thailand* 65 a
Amphoe Thalang, *Thailand* 65 a
Ampitsikinana, *Réunion* 89 A8
Ampombiantambo, *Madag.* 89 A8
Amposta, *Spain* 38 E5
Ampotaka, *Madag.* 89 D7
Ampoza, *Madag.* 89 C7
Amqui, *Canada* 105 C6
Amravati, *India* 66 J10
Amreli, *India* 68 J4
Amritsar, *India* 68 D6
Amroha, *India* 69 E8
Amrum, *Germany* 24 A4
Amsterdam, *Neths.* 17 B4
Amsterdam, *U.S.A.* 117 D10
Amsterdam ✕ (AMS), *Neths.* 17 B4
Amsterdam, I. = Nouvelle-Amsterdam, Î., *Ind. Oc.* 3 F13
Amstetten, *Austria* 26 C7
Amudarya →, *Uzbekistan* 52 E6
Amundsen Gulf, *Canada* 100 A7
Amundsen-Scott, *Antarctica* 5 E
Amundsen Sea, *Antarctica* 5 D15
Amungen, *Sweden* 10 C9
Amuntai, *Indonesia* 62 E5
Amur →, *Russia* 53 D15
Amur, W. →, *Sudan* 80 D3
Amurang, *Indonesia* 63 D6
Amurrio, *Spain* 38 B1
Amursk, *Russia* 53 D14
Amusco, *Spain* 36 C6
Amvrakikós Kólpos, *Greece* 46 C2
Amvrosiyivka, *Ukraine* 33 J10
Amyderya = Amudarya →, *Uzbekistan* 52 E6
An Anbār □, *Iraq* 70 C4
An Bien, *Vietnam* 65 H5
An Hoa, *Vietnam* 64 E7
An Nabatīyah at Tahta, *Lebanon* 74 B4
An Nabk, *Si. Arabia* 70 D3
An Nabk, *Syria* 74 A5

An Nafūd, *Si. Arabia* 70 D4
An Najaf, *Iraq* 70 C5
An Nāṣirīyah, *Iraq* 70 D5
An Nhon, *Vietnam* 64 F7
An Nîl □, *Sudan* 80 D3
An Nîl el Abyad □, *Sudan* 81 E3
An Nîl el Azraq □, *Sudan* 81 E3
An Nu'ayrīyah, *Si. Arabia* 71 E6
An Nu'mānīyah, *Iraq* 73 F11
An Nuwayb'ī, W. →, *Si. Arabia* 74 F3
An Thoi, Dao, *Vietnam* 65 H4
An Uaimh, *Ireland* 12 C5
Anabar →, *Russia* 53 B12
'Anabtā, *West Bank* 74 C4
Anaconda, *U.S.A.* 108 C7
Anacortes, *U.S.A.* 110 B4
Anacuao, Mt., *Phil.* 61 C4
Anadarko, *U.S.A.* 113 H5
Anadia, *Portugal* 36 E2
Anadolu, *Turkey* 72 C5
Anadyr, *Russia* 53 C18
Anadyr →, *Russia* 53 C18
Anadyrskiy Zaliv, *Russia* 53 C19
Anáfi, *Greece* 47 E7
Anafópoulo, *Greece* 47 E7
Anaga, Pta. de, *Canary Is.* 48 F3
Anagni, *Italy* 41 G10
'Ānah, *Iraq* 70 C4
Anaheim, *U.S.A.* 111 M9
Anahim Lake, *Canada* 102 C3
Anáhuac, *Mexico* 118 B4
Anakapalle, *India* 67 L13
Anakie, *Australia* 94 C4
Anaklia, *Georgia* 35 J5
Analalava, *Madag.* 89 A8
Analavoka, *Madag.* 89 C8
Análipsis, *Greece* 49 A3
Anambar →, *Pakistan* 68 D3
Anambas, Kepulauan, *Indonesia* 62 D3
Anambas Is. = Anambas, Kepulauan, *Indonesia* 62 D3
Anambra □, *Nigeria* 83 D6
Anamosa, *U.S.A.* 112 D9
Anamur, *Turkey* 70 B2
Anamur Burnu, *Turkey* 72 D5
Anan, *Japan* 55 H7
Anand, *India* 68 H5
Anánes, *Greece* 46 E6
Anantapur, *India* 66 M10
Anantnag, *India* 69 C6
Ananyiv, *Ukraine* 29 C14
Anapa, *Russia* 33 K9
Anapodháris →, *Greece* 49 E7
Anápolis, *Brazil* 125 G9
Anapu →, *Brazil* 125 D8
Anār, *Iran* 71 D7
Anārak, *Iran* 71 C7
Anarisfjällen, *Sweden* 10 A7
Anas →, *India* 68 H5
Anatolia = Anadolu, *Turkey* 72 C5
Anatsogno, *Madag.* 89 C7
Añatuya, *Argentina* 126 B3
Anaunethad L., *Canada* 103 A8
Anbyŏn, *N. Korea* 57 E14
Ancares ⌂, *Spain* 36 C4
Ancares, Sierra de, *Spain* 36 C4
Ancaster, *Canada* 116 C5
Ancenis, *France* 18 E5
Anchor Bay, *U.S.A.* 110 G3
Anchorage, *U.S.A.* 100 B5
Anci, *China* 56 E9
Ancohuma, Nevado, *Bolivia* 124 G5
Ancón, *Peru* 124 F3
Ancona, *Italy* 41 E10
Ancud, *Chile* 128 E2
Ancud, G. de, *Chile* 128 E2
Ancy-le-Franc, *France* 19 E11
Andacollo, *Argentina* 126 D1
Andacollo, *Chile* 126 C1
Andaingo, *Madag.* 89 B8
Andalgalá, *Argentina* 126 B2
Åndalsnes, *Norway* 9 E12
Andalucía □, *Spain* 37 H6
Andalusia = Andalucía □, *Spain* 37 H6
Andalusia, *U.S.A.* 115 K2
Andaman Is., *Ind. Oc.* 50 H13
Andaman Sea, *Ind. Oc.* 62 B1
Andamooka Opal Fields, *Australia* 95 E2
Andapa, *Madag.* 89 A8
Andara, *Namibia* 88 B3
Andelot-Blancheville, *France* 19 D12
Andenes, *Norway* 8 B17
Andenne, *Belgium* 17 D5
Andéranboukane, *Mali* 83 B5
Andermatt, *Switz.* 25 J4
Andernach, *Germany* 24 E3
Andernos-les-Bains, *France* 20 D2
Anderslöv, *Sweden* 11 J7
Anderson, *Alaska, U.S.A.* 100 B5
Anderson, *Calif., U.S.A.* 108 F2
Anderson, *Ind., U.S.A.* 114 E3
Anderson, *Mo., U.S.A.* 113 G7
Anderson, *S.C., U.S.A.* 115 H4
Anderson →, *Canada* 100 B7
Anderstorp, *Sweden* 11 G7
Andes, *U.S.A.* 117 D10
Andes, Cord. de los, *S. Amer.* 124 H5
Andfjorden, *Norway* 8 B17
Andhra Pradesh □, *India* 66 L11
Andijon, *Uzbekistan* 52 E8
Andikíthira, *Greece* 46 F5
Andilamena, *Madag.* 89 B8
Andīmeshk, *Iran* 71 C6
Andímilos, *Greece* 46 E6
Andíparos, *Greece* 47 D7
Andípaxoi, *Greece* 46 B2
Andípsara, *Greece* 47 C7
Andírrion, *Greece* 46 C3
Andizhan = Andijon, *Uzbekistan* 52 E8
Andoain, *Spain* 38 B2
Andoany, *Madag.* 89 A8
Andohahela ⌂, *Madag.* 89 C8
Andong, *S. Korea* 57 F15
Andongwei, *China* 57 G10
Andoom, *Australia* 94 A3
Andorra, *Spain* 38 E4
Andorra ■, *Europe* 20 F5
Andorra La Vella, *Andorra* 20 F5
Andover, *U.K.* 15 F6
Andover, *Maine, U.S.A.* 117 B14
Andover, *Mass., U.S.A.* 117 D13
Andover, *N.J., U.S.A.* 117 F10
Andover, *N.Y., U.S.A.* 116 D7
Andover, *Ohio, U.S.A.* 116 E4
Andøya, *Norway* 8 B16
Andradina, *Brazil* 125 H8
Andrahary, Mt., *Madag.* 89 A8
Andramasina, *Madag.* 89 B8
Andranopasy, *Madag.* 89 C7
Andranovory, *Madag.* 89 C7
Andratx, *Spain* 48 B9
Andreanof Is., *U.S.A.* 100 C2
Andreapol, *Russia* 32 D7
Andrews, *S.C., U.S.A.* 115 J6
Andrews, *Tex., U.S.A.* 113 J3
Andreyevka, *Russia* 34 D10
Ándria, *Italy* 43 A9
Andriamena, *Madag.* 89 B8
Andriandampy, *Madag.* 89 C8
Andriba, *Madag.* 89 B8
Andrijevica, *Serbia & M.* 44 D3
Andringitra ⌂, *Madag.* 89 C8
Andrítsaina, *Greece* 46 D3
Androka, *Madag.* 89 C7
Ándros, *Greece* 46 D6
Andros I., *Bahamas* 120 B4
Andros Town, *Bahamas* 120 B4
Androscoggin →, *U.S.A.* 117 C14
Andrychów, *Poland* 31 J6
Andselv, *Norway* 8 B18
Andújar, *Spain* 37 G6
Andulo, *Angola* 84 G3
Aneby, *Sweden* 11 G8
Anegada, *Br. Virgin Is.* 121 e
Anegada Passage, *W. Indies* 121 C7
Anécho, *Togo* 83 D5
Anenni-Noi, *Moldova* 29 D14
Aneto, Pico de, *Spain* 38 C5
Anfu, *China* 59 D10
Ang Mo Kio, *Singapore* 65 d
Ang Thong, *Thailand* 64 E3
Ang Thong △, *Thailand* 65 H2
Ang Thong, Ko, *Thailand* 65 b
Angamos, Punta, *Chile* 126 A1
Angara →, *Russia* 53 D10
Angara-Débou, *Benin* 83 C5
Angarab, *Ethiopia* 81 E4
Angarbaka, *Sudan* 81 F1
Angarsk, *Russia* 53 D11
Angas Hills, *Australia* 92 D4
Angaston, *Australia* 95 E2
Ånge, *Sweden* 10 B9
Ángel, Salto = Angel Falls, *Venezuela* 124 B6
Ángel de la Guarda, I., *Mexico* 118 B2
Angel Falls, *Venezuela* 124 B6
Angeles, *Phil.* 61 D4
Ängelholm, *Sweden* 11 H6
Angels Camp, *U.S.A.* 110 G6
Ängelsberg, *Sweden* 10 E10
Anger →, *Ethiopia* 81 F4
Angereb →, *Ethiopia* 81 E4
Ångermanälven →, *Sweden* 10 B11
Ångermanland, *Sweden* 8 E18
Angermünde, *Germany* 24 B9
Angers, *Canada* 117 A9
Angers, *France* 18 E6
Angerville, *France* 19 D9
Ängesån →, *Sweden* 8 C20
Angikuni L., *Canada* 103 A9
Angkor, *Cambodia* 64 F4
Anglès, *Spain* 38 D7
Anglesey, Isle of □, *U.K.* 14 D3
Anglet, *France* 20 E2
Angleton, *U.S.A.* 113 L7
Anglin →, *France* 20 B4
Anglisidhes, *Cyprus* 49 E12
Anglure, *France* 19 D10
Angmagssalik = Tasiilaq, *Greenland* 4 C6
Ango, *Dem. Rep. of the Congo* 86 B2
Angoche, *Mozam.* 87 F4
Angoche, I., *Mozam.* 87 F4
Angol, *Chile* 126 D1
Angola, *Ind., U.S.A.* 114 E3
Angola, *N.Y., U.S.A.* 116 D5
Angola ■, *Africa* 85 G3
Angoulême, *France* 20 C4
Angoumois, *France* 20 C4
Angra dos Reis, *Brazil* 127 A7
Angrapa →, *Russia* 30 D8
Angren, *Uzbekistan* 52 E8
Angtassom, *Cambodia* 65 G5
Angu, *Dem. Rep. of the Congo* 86 B1
Anguang, *China* 57 B12
Anguilla ⧄, *W. Indies* 121 C7
Anguo, *China* 56 E8
Angurugu, *Australia* 94 A2
Angus □, *U.K.* 13 E6
Angwa →, *Zimbabwe* 89 B5
Anhanduí →, *Brazil* 127 A5
Anholt, *Denmark* 11 H5
Anhua, *China* 59 C8
Anhui □, *China* 59 B11
Anhwei = Anhui □, *China* 59 B11
Anichab, *Namibia* 88 C1
Ánidhros, *Greece* 47 E7
Anié, *Togo* 83 D5
Animas →, *U.S.A.* 109 H9
Anina, *Romania* 28 E6
Aninoasa, *Romania* 29 F9
Anivorano, *Madag.* 89 B8
Anjalankoski, *Finland* 9 F22
Anjar, *India* 68 H4
Anji, *China* 59 B12
Anjou, *France* 18 E6
Anjozorobe, *Madag.* 89 B8
Anju, *N. Korea* 57 E13
Anka, *Nigeria* 83 C6
Ankaboa, Tanjona, *Madag.* 89 C7
Ankang, *China* 56 H5
Ankara, *Turkey* 72 C5
Ankarafantsika ⌂, *Madag.* 89 B8
Ankaramena, *Madag.* 89 C8
Ankaratra, *Madag.* 85 H9
Ankarsrum, *Sweden* 11 G10
Ankasakasa, *Madag.* 89 B7
Ankavandra, *Madag.* 89 B8
Ankazoabo, *Madag.* 89 C7
Ankazobe, *Madag.* 89 B8
Ankeny, *U.S.A.* 112 E8
Ankilimalinika, *Madag.* 89 C7
Ankilizato, *Madag.* 89 C8
Ankisabe, *Madag.* 89 B8
Anklam, *Germany* 24 B9
Ankober, *Ethiopia* 81 F4
Ankoro, *Dem. Rep. of the Congo* 86 D2
Ankororoka, *Madag.* 89 D8
Anlong, *China* 58 E5
Anlu, *China* 59 B9
Anmyŏn-do, *S. Korea* 57 F14
Ånn, *Sweden* 10 A6
Ann, C., *U.S.A.* 117 D14
Ann Arbor, *U.S.A.* 114 D4
Anna, *Russia* 34 E5
Anna, *U.S.A.* 113 G10
Annaba, *Algeria* 78 A7
Annaberg-Buchholz, *Germany* 24 E9
Annalee →, *Ireland* 12 B4
Annam, *Vietnam* 64 E7
Annamitique, Chaîne, *Asia* 64 D6
Annan, *U.K.* 13 G5
Annan →, *U.K.* 13 G5
Annapolis, *U.S.A.* 114 F7
Annapolis Royal, *Canada* 105 D6
Annapurna, *Nepal* 69 E10
Annean, L., *Australia* 93 E2
Anneberg, *Sweden* 11 G8
Annecy, *France* 21 C10
Annecy, Lac d', *France* 21 C10
Annemasse, *France* 19 F13
Annenskiy Most, *Russia* 32 B9
Anning, *China* 58 E4
Anniston, *U.S.A.* 115 J3
Annobón, *Atl. Oc.* 77 G4
Annonay, *France* 21 C8
Annot, *France* 21 E10
Annotto B., *Jamaica* 120 a
Ånnsjön, *Sweden* 10 A6
Annville, *U.S.A.* 117 F8
Annweiler, *Germany* 25 F3
Áno Arkhánai, *Greece* 47 F7
Áno Porróia, *Greece* 44 E7
Áno Síros, *Greece* 46 D6
Áno Viánnos, *Greece* 49 D7
Anorotsangana, *Madag.* 89 A8
Anosibe, *Madag.* 89 B8
Anou Mellene, *Mali* 83 B5
Anoumaba, *Ivory C.* 82 D4
Anóyia, *Greece* 49 D6
Anping, *Hebei, China* 56 E8
Anping, *Liaoning, China* 57 D12
Anpu Gang, *China* 58 G7
Anqing, *China* 59 B11
Anqiu, *China* 57 F10
Anren, *China* 59 D9
Ansager, *Denmark* 11 J2
Ansai, *China* 56 F5
Ansbach, *Germany* 25 F6
Anse la Raye, *St. Lucia* 121 f
Anseba →, *Eritrea* 81 D4
Ansfelden, *Austria* 26 C7
Anshan, *China* 57 D12
Anshun, *China* 58 D5
Ansião, *Portugal* 36 F2
Ansley, *U.S.A.* 112 E5
Ansó, *Spain* 38 C4
Ansoain, *Spain* 38 C3
Anson, *U.S.A.* 113 J5
Anson B., *Australia* 92 B5
Ansongo, *Mali* 83 B5
Ansongo-Ménaka ⌂, *Mali* 83 B5
Ansonia, *U.S.A.* 117 E11
Anstruther, *U.K.* 13 E6
Ansudu, *Indonesia* 63 E9
Antabamba, *Peru* 124 F4
Antakya, *Turkey* 70 B3
Antalaha, *Madag.* 89 A9
Antalya, *Turkey* 72 D4
Antalya □, *Turkey* 47 E12
Antalya Körfezi, *Turkey* 72 D4
Antambohobe, *Madag.* 89 C8
Antanambao-Manampotsy, *Madag.* 89 B8
Antanambe, *Madag.* 89 B8
Antananarivo, *Madag.* 89 B8
Antananarivo □, *Madag.* 89 B8
Antanifotsy, *Madag.* 89 B8
Antanimbaribe, *Madag.* 89 C7
Antanimora, *Madag.* 89 C8
Antarctic Pen., *Antarctica* 5 C18
Antarctica 5 E3
Antelope, *Zimbabwe* 87 G2
Antequera, *Paraguay* 126 A4
Antequera, *Spain* 37 H6
Antero, Mt., *U.S.A.* 109 G10
Antevamena, *Madag.* 89 C7
Anthemoús, *Greece* 44 F7
Anthony, *Kans., U.S.A.* 113 G5
Anthony, *N. Mex., U.S.A.* 109 K10
Anti Atlas, *Morocco* 78 C4
Anti-Lebanon = Ash Sharqi, Al Jabal, *Lebanon* 74 B5
Antibes, *France* 21 E11
Antibes, C. d', *France* 21 E11
Anticosti, Î. d', *Canada* 105 C7
Antifer, C. d', *France* 18 C7
Antigo, *U.S.A.* 112 C10
Antigonish, *Canada* 105 C7
Antigua, *Canary Is.* 48 F5
Antigua, *Guatemala* 120 D1
Antigua, *W. Indies* 121 C7
Antigua & Barbuda ■, *W. Indies* 121 C7
Antilla, *Cuba* 120 B4
Antilles = West Indies, *Cent. Amer.* 121 D7
Antioch, *U.S.A.* 110 G5
Antioche, Pertuis d', *France* 20 B2
Antioquia, *Colombia* 124 B3
Antipodes Is., *Pac. Oc.* 96 M9
Antlers, *U.S.A.* 113 H7
Antoetra, *Madag.* 89 C8
Antofagasta, *Chile* 126 A1
Antofagasta □, *Chile* 126 A2
Antofagasta de la Sierra, *Argentina* 126 B2
Antofalla, *Argentina* 126 B2
Antofalla, Salar de, *Argentina* 126 B2
Anton, *U.S.A.* 113 J3
Antongila, Helodrano, *Madag.* 89 B8
Antonibé, *Madag.* 89 B8
Antonibé, Presqu'île d', *Madag.* 89 A8
Antonina, *Brazil* 127 B6
Antrain, *France* 18 D5
Antrim, *U.K.* 12 B5
Antrim, *U.S.A.* 116 F3
Antrim □, *U.K.* 12 B5
Antrim, Mts. of, *U.K.* 12 A5
Antrim Plateau, *Australia* 92 C4
Antrodoco, *Italy* 41 F10
Antropovo, *Russia* 34 A6
Antsakabary, *Madag.* 89 B8
Antsalova, *Madag.* 89 B7
Antsenavolo, *Madag.* 89 C8
Antsiafabositra, *Madag.* 89 B8
Antsirabe, *Antananarivo, Madag.* 89 B8
Antsirabe, *Antsiranana, Madag.* 89 A8
Antsirabe, *Mahajanga, Madag.* 89 B8
Antsiranana, *Madag.* 89 A8
Antsiranana □, *Madag.* 89 A8
Antsohihy, *Madag.* 89 A8
Antsohimbondrona Seranana, *Madag.* 89 A8
Antu, *China* 57 C15
Antwerp = Antwerpen, *Belgium* 17 C4
Antwerp, *U.S.A.* 117 B9
Antwerpen, *Belgium* 17 C4
Antwerpen □, *Belgium* 17 C4
Anupgarh, *India* 68 E5
Anuppur, *India* 69 H9
Anuradhapura, *Sri Lanka* 66 Q12
Anveh, *Iran* 71 E7
Anvers = Antwerpen, *Belgium* 17 C4
Anvers I., *Antarctica* 5 C17
Anwen, *China* 59 C13
Anxi, *Fujian, China* 59 E12
Anxi, *Gansu, China* 60 B4
Anxian, *China* 58 B5
Anxiang, *China* 59 C9
Anxious B., *Australia* 95 E1
Anyama, *Ivory C.* 82 D4
Anyang, *China* 56 F8
Anyer-Kidul, *Indonesia* 63 G11
Anyi, *Jiangxi, China* 59 C10
Anyi, *Shanxi, China* 56 G6
Anyuan, *China* 59 E10
Anyue, *China* 58 B5
Anza, *U.S.A.* 111 M10
Anze, *China* 56 F7
Anzhero-Sudzhensk, *Russia* 52 D9
Ánzio, *Italy* 42 A5
Ao Makham, *Thailand* 65 a
Ao Phangnga △, *Thailand* 65 a
Aoga-Shima, *Japan* 55 H9
Aoiz, *Spain* 38 C3
Aomen = Macau, *China* 59 F9
Aomori, *Japan* 54 D10
Aomori □, *Japan* 54 D10
Aonla, *India* 69 E8
Aoraki Mount Cook, *N.Z.* 91 K3
Aosta, *Italy* 40 C4
Aotearoa = New Zealand ■, *Oceania* 91 J6
Aoudéras, *Niger* 83 B6
Aoukâr, *Mauritania* 82 B3
Aozou, Couloir d', *Chad* 79 D9
Apa →, *S. Amer.* 126 A4
Apache, *U.S.A.* 113 H5
Apache Junction, *U.S.A.* 109 K8
Apalachee B., *U.S.A.* 115 L4
Apalachicola, *U.S.A.* 115 L3
Apalachicola →, *U.S.A.* 115 L3
Apam, *Ghana* 83 D4
Apapa, *Nigeria* 83 D5
Apaporis →, *Colombia* 124 D5
Aparados da Serra △, *Brazil* 127 B5
Aparri, *Phil.* 61 B4
Apateu, *Romania* 28 D6
Apatin, *Serbia & M.* 28 E4
Apatity, *Russia* 52 C4
Apatzingán, *Mexico* 118 D4
Apeldoorn, *Neths.* 17 B5
Apen, *Germany* 24 B3
Apennines = Appennini, *Italy* 40 D7
Aphrodisias, *Turkey* 47 D10
Apia, *Samoa* 91 A13
Apiacás, Serra dos, *Brazil* 124 E7
Apies →, *S. Africa* 89 D4
Apizaco, *Mexico* 119 D5
Aplao, *Peru* 124 G4
Apo, Mt., *Phil.* 63 C7
Apolakkiá, *Greece* 49 C9
Apolakkiá, Órmos, *Greece* 49 C9
Apolda, *Germany* 24 D7
Apollonia, *Greece* 46 E6
Apolo, *Bolivia* 124 F5
Aporé →, *Brazil* 125 G8
Apostle Is., *U.S.A.* 112 B9
Apostle Islands ⌂, *U.S.A.* 112 B9
Apóstoles, *Argentina* 127 B4
Apostolos Andreas, C., *Cyprus* 49 D13
Apostolovo, *Ukraine* 33 J7
Apoteri, *Guyana* 124 C7
Appalachian Mts., *U.S.A.* 114 G6
Äppelbo, *Sweden* 10 D8
Appennini, *Italy* 40 D7
Appennino Ligure, *Italy* 40 D6
Appenzell-Ausser Rhoden □, *Switz.* 25 H5
Appenzell-Inner Rhoden □, *Switz.* 25 H5
Appiano, *Italy* 41 B8
Apple Hill, *Canada* 117 A10
Apple Valley, *U.S.A.* 111 L9
Appleby-in-Westmorland, *U.K.* 14 C5
Appledore, *U.K.* 15 F3
Appleton, *U.S.A.* 114 C1
Approuague →, *Fr. Guiana* 125 C8
Apricena, *Italy* 41 G12
Aprília, *Italy* 42 A5
Apsheronsk, *Russia* 35 H4
Apsley, *Canada* 116 B6
Apt, *France* 21 E9
Apuane, Alpi, *Italy* 40 D7
Apucarana, *Brazil* 127 A5
Apulia = Púglia □, *Italy* 43 A9
Apure →, *Venezuela* 124 B5
Apurimac →, *Peru* 124 F4
Apuseni, Munţii, *Romania* 28 D7
Āqā Jarī, *Iran* 71 D6
Aqaba = Al 'Aqabah, *Jordan* 74 F4
Aqaba, G. of, *Red Sea* 70 D2
'Aqabah, Khalīj al = Aqaba, G. of, *Red Sea* 70 D2
'Aqdā, *Iran* 71 C7
Aqīq, *Sudan* 80 D4
Aqîq, Khalîg, *Sudan* 80 D4
'Aqrah, *Iraq* 70 B4
Aqtaū, *Kazakhstan* 52 E6
Aqtöbe, *Kazakhstan* 52 D6
Aquidauana, *Brazil* 125 H7
Aquiles Serdán, *Mexico* 118 B3
Aquin, *Haiti* 121 C5
Aquitaine □, *France* 20 D3
Ar Rachidiya = Er Rachidia, *Morocco* 78 B5
Ar Rafīd, *Syria* 74 C4
Ar Raḥḥālīyah, *Iraq* 70 C4
Ar Ramādī, *Iraq* 70 C4
Ar Ramthā, *Jordan* 74 C5
Ar Raqqah, *Syria* 70 C3
Ar Rass, *Si. Arabia* 70 E4
Ar Rawshān, *Si. Arabia* 80 C5
Ar Rifā'ī, *Iraq* 70 D5
Ar Riyāḍ, *Si. Arabia* 70 E5
Ar Ru'ays, *Qatar* 71 E6
Ar Rukhaymīyah, *Iraq* 70 D5
Ar Ruṣāfah, *Syria* 70 C3
Ar Ruṭbah, *Iraq* 70 C4
Ara, *India* 69 G11
Ara Goro, *Ethiopia* 81 F5
Ara Tera, *Ethiopia* 81 F5
Arab, *U.S.A.* 115 H2
'Arab, Bahr el →, *Sudan* 81 F2
Arab, Khalîg el, *Egypt* 80 A2
Arab, Shatt al →, *Asia* 71 D6
'Araba, W. →, *Egypt* 80 J8
'Arabābād, *Iran* 71 C8
Araban, *Turkey* 72 D7
Arabatskaya Strelka, *Ukraine* 33 K8
Arabba, *Italy* 41 B8
Arabia, *Asia* 50 G8
Arabian Desert = Es Sahrâ' Esh Sharqîya, *Egypt* 80 B3
Arabian Gulf = Persian Gulf, *Asia* 71 E6
Arabian Sea, *Ind. Oc.* 50 H10
Araç, *Turkey* 72 B5
Aracaju, *Brazil* 125 F11
Aracati, *Brazil* 125 D11
Araçatuba, *Brazil* 127 A5
Aracena, *Spain* 37 H4
Aracena, Sierra de, *Spain* 37 H4
Aračinovo, *Macedonia* 44 D5
Araçuaí, *Brazil* 125 G10
'Arad, *Israel* 74 D4
Arad, *Romania* 28 D6
Arad □, *Romania* 28 D6
Arādān, *Iran* 71 C7
Aradhippou, *Cyprus* 49 E12
Arafura Sea, *E. Indies* 96 H5
Aragats, *Armenia* 35 K7
Aragón □, *Spain* 38 D4
Aragón →, *Spain* 38 C3
Aragona, *Italy* 42 E6
Araguacema, *Brazil* 125 E9
Araguaia →, *Brazil* 125 E9
Araguaína, *Brazil* 125 E9
Araguari, *Brazil* 125 G9
Araguari →, *Brazil* 125 C9
Arain, *India* 68 F6
Arak, *Algeria* 78 C6
Arāk, *Iran* 71 C6
Araka, *Sudan* 81 G3
Arakan Coast, *Burma* 67 K19
Arakan Yoma, *Burma* 67 K19
Arákhova, *Greece* 46 C4
Arakli, *Turkey* 73 B8
Araks = Aras, Rūd-e →, *Asia* 35 K9
Aral, *Kazakhstan* 52 E7
Aral Sea, *Asia* 52 E7
Aral Tengizi = Aral Sea, *Asia* 52 E7
Aralsk = Aral, *Kazakhstan* 52 E7
Aralskoye More = Aral Sea, *Asia* 52 E7
Aralsor, Ozero, *Kazakhstan* 35 F9
Aramac, *Australia* 94 C4
Aran I., *Ireland* 12 A3
Aran Is., *Ireland* 12 C2
Aranda de Duero, *Spain* 36 D7
Arandān, *Iran* 70 C5

Aranđelovac, *Serbia & M.* 44 **B4**
Aranjuez, *Spain* 36 **E7**
Aranos, *Namibia* 88 **C2**
Aransas Pass, *U.S.A.* 113 **M6**
Aranyaprathet, *Thailand* 64 **F4**
Araouane, *Mali* 82 **B4**
Arapahoe, *U.S.A.* 112 **E5**
Arapey Grande →, *Uruguay* 126 **C4**
Arapgir, *Turkey* 70 **B3**
Arapiraca, *Brazil* 125 **E11**
Arapongas, *Brazil* 127 **A5**
Ar'ar, *Si. Arabia* 70 **D4**
Araranguá, *Brazil* 127 **B6**
Araraquara, *Brazil* 125 **H9**
Ararás, Serra das, *Brazil* 127 **B5**
Ararat, *Armenia* 73 **C11**
Ararat, *Australia* 95 **F3**
Ararat, Mt. = Ağrı Dağı, *Turkey* 70 **B5**
Araria, *India* 69 **F12**
Araripe, Chapada do, *Brazil* 125 **E11**
Araruama, L. de, *Brazil* 127 **A7**
Aras, Rūd-e →, *Asia* 35 **K9**
Aratâne, *Mauritania* 82 **B3**
Arauca, *Colombia* 124 **B4**
Arauca →, *Venezuela* 124 **B5**
Arauco, *Chile* 126 **D1**
Arawa, *Ethiopia* 81 **F5**
Arawale ⌓, *Kenya* 86 **C5**
Araxá, *Brazil* 125 **G9**
Araya, Pen. de, *Venezuela* 124 **A6**
Arba Gugu, *Ethiopia* 81 **F5**
Arba Minch, *Ethiopia* 81 **F4**
Arbat, *Iraq* 70 **C5**
Árbatax, *Italy* 42 **C2**
Arbi, *Ethiopia* 81 **F4**
Arbīl, *Iraq* 70 **B5**
Arboga, *Sweden* 10 **E9**
Arbois, *France* 19 **F12**
Arbore, *Ethiopia* 81 **F4**
Arboréa, *Italy* 42 **C1**
Arborfield, *Canada* 103 **C8**
Arborg, *Canada* 103 **C9**
Arbre du Ténéré, *Niger* 83 **B7**
Arbroath, *U.K.* 13 **E6**
Arbuckle, *U.S.A.* 110 **F4**
Arbus, *Italy* 42 **C1**
Arc →, *France* 21 **C10**
Arc-lès-Gray, *France* 19 **E12**
Arcachon, *France* 20 **D2**
Arcachon, Bassin d', *France* 20 **D2**
Arcade, *Calif., U.S.A.* 111 **L8**
Arcade, *N.Y., U.S.A.* 116 **D6**
Arcadia, *Fla., U.S.A.* 115 **M5**
Arcadia, *La., U.S.A.* 113 **J8**
Arcadia, *Pa., U.S.A.* 116 **F6**
Arcata, *U.S.A.* 108 **F1**
Arcévia, *Italy* 41 **E9**
Archangel = Arkhangelsk, *Russia* 52 **C5**
Archar, *Bulgaria* 44 **C6**
Archbald, *U.S.A.* 117 **E9**
Archena, *Spain* 39 **G3**
Archer →, *Australia* 94 **A3**
Archer B., *Australia* 94 **A3**
Archer Bend = Mungkan Kandju △, *Australia* 94 **A3**
Archers Post, *Kenya* 86 **B4**
Arches △, *U.S.A.* 109 **G9**
Archidona, *Spain* 37 **H6**
Archipel-de-Mingan △, *Canada* 105 **B7**
Archipiélago Chinijo △, *Canary Is.* 48 **E6**
Archipiélago Los Roques △, *Venezuela* 121 **D6**
Arci, Mte., *Italy* 42 **C1**
Arcidosso, *Italy* 41 **F8**
Arcipelago de la Maddalena △, *Italy* 42 **A2**
Arcipelago Toscano △, *Italy* 40 **F7**
Arcis-sur-Aube, *France* 19 **D11**
Arckaringa Cr. →, *Australia* 95 **D2**
Arco, *Italy* 40 **C7**
Arco, *U.S.A.* 108 **E7**
Arcos de Jalón, *Spain* 38 **D2**
Arcos de la Frontera, *Spain* 37 **J5**
Arcos de Valdevez, *Portugal* 36 **D2**
Arcot, *India* 66 **N11**
Arcozelo, *Portugal* 36 **E3**
Arctic Bay, *Canada* 101 **A11**
Arctic Ocean, *Arctic* 4 **B18**
Arctic Red River = Tsiigehtchic, *Canada* 100 **B6**
Arctowski, *Antarctica* 5 **C18**
Arda →, *Bulgaria* 45 **E10**
Arda →, *Italy* 40 **C7**
Ardabīl, *Iran* 71 **B6**
Ardabīl □, *Iran* 71 **B6**
Ardahan, *Turkey* 73 **B10**
Ardakān = Sepīdān, *Iran* 71 **D7**
Ardakān, *Iran* 71 **C7**
Ardala, *Sweden* 11 **F7**
Ardales, *Spain* 37 **J6**
Ardèche □, *France* 21 **D8**
Ardèche →, *France* 21 **D8**
Ardee, *Ireland* 12 **C5**
Arden, *Canada* 116 **B8**
Arden, *Denmark* 11 **H3**
Arden, *Calif., U.S.A.* 110 **G5**
Arden, *Nev., U.S.A.* 111 **J11**
Ardenne, *Belgium* 17 **E5**
Ardennes = Ardenne, *Belgium* 17 **E5**
Ardennes □, *France* 19 **C11**
Ardentes, *France* 19 **F8**
Arderin, *Ireland* 12 **C4**
Ardeşen, *Turkey* 73 **B9**
Ardestān, *Iran* 71 **C7**
Árdhas →, *Greece* 45 **E10**
Ardhéa, *Greece* 44 **F6**
Ardila →, *Portugal* 37 **G3**
Ardino, *Bulgaria* 45 **E9**
Ardivachar Pt., *U.K.* 13 **D1**
Ardlethan, *Australia* 95 **E4**
Ardmore, *Okla., U.S.A.* 113 **H6**
Ardmore, *Pa., U.S.A.* 117 **G9**
Ardnamurchan, Pt. of, *U.K.* 13 **E2**
Ardnave Pt., *U.K.* 13 **F2**
Ardon, *Russia* 35 **J7**
Ardore, *Italy* 43 **D9**
Ardres, *France* 19 **B8**
Ardrossan, *Australia* 95 **E2**
Ardrossan, *U.K.* 13 **F4**
Ards Pen., *U.K.* 12 **B6**
Arduan, *Sudan* 80 **D3**
Ardud, *Romania* 28 **C7**
Åre, *Sweden* 10 **A7**
Arecibo, *Puerto Rico* 121 **d**
Areia Branca, *Brazil* 125 **E11**
Arena, Pt., *U.S.A.* 110 **G3**
Arenal, *Honduras* 120 **C2**
Arenas = Las Arenas, *Spain* 36 **B6**
Arenas de San Pedro, *Spain* 36 **E5**
Arendal, *Norway* 9 **G13**
Arendsee, *Germany* 24 **C7**
Arenys de Mar, *Spain* 38 **D7**
Arenzano, *Italy* 40 **D5**
Areópolis, *Greece* 46 **E4**
Arequipa, *Peru* 124 **G4**
Arero, *Ethiopia* 81 **G4**
Arès, *France* 20 **D2**
Arévalo, *Spain* 36 **D6**
Arezzo, *Italy* 41 **E8**
Arga, *Turkey* 70 **B3**
Arga →, *Spain* 38 **C3**
Argalastí, *Greece* 46 **B5**
Argamasilla de Alba, *Spain* 37 **F7**
Argamasilla de Calatrava, *Spain* 37 **G6**
Arganda, *Spain* 36 **E7**
Arganil, *Portugal* 36 **E2**
Argedeb, *Ethiopia* 81 **F5**
Argelès-Gazost, *France* 20 **E3**
Argelès-sur-Mer, *France* 20 **F7**
Argens →, *France* 21 **E10**
Argent-sur-Sauldre, *France* 19 **E9**
Argenta, *Canada* 102 **C5**
Argenta, *Italy* 41 **D8**
Argentan, *France* 18 **D6**
Argentário, Mte., *Italy* 41 **F8**
Argentat, *France* 20 **C5**
Argentera, *Italy* 40 **D4**
Argenteuil, *France* 19 **D9**
Argentia, *Canada* 105 **C9**
Argentiera, C. dell', *Italy* 42 **B1**
Argentina ■, *S. Amer.* 128 **D3**
Argentine Basin, *S. Amer.* 122 **H5**
Argentino, L., *Argentina* 128 **G2**
Argenton-Château, *France* 18 **F6**
Argenton-sur-Creuse, *France* 19 **F8**
Argeş □, *Romania* 29 **F9**
Argeş →, *Romania* 29 **F11**
Arghandab →, *Afghan.* 68 **D1**
Argheile, *Ethiopia* 81 **F5**
Argo, *Sudan* 80 **D3**
Argolikós Kólpos, *Greece* 46 **D4**
Argolís □, *Greece* 46 **D4**
Argonne, *France* 19 **C12**
Árgos, *Greece* 46 **D4**
Árgos Orestikón, *Greece* 44 **F5**
Argostólion, *Greece* 46 **C2**
Arguedas, *Spain* 38 **C3**
Arguello, Pt., *U.S.A.* 111 **L6**
Arguineguín, *Canary Is.* 48 **G4**
Argun, *Russia* 35 **J7**
Argun →, *Russia* 53 **D13**
Argungu, *Nigeria* 83 **C5**
Argus Pk., *U.S.A.* 111 **K9**
Argyle, L., *Australia* 92 **C4**
Argyll ⌓, *U.K.* 13 **E4**
Argyll & Bute □, *U.K.* 13 **E3**
Arhavi, *Turkey* 73 **B9**
Århus, *Denmark* 11 **H4**
Århus Amtskommune □, *Denmark* 11 **H4**
Ariadnoye, *Russia* 54 **B7**
Ariamsvlei, *Namibia* 88 **D2**
Ariano Irpino, *Italy* 43 **A8**
Aribinda, *Burkina Faso* 83 **C4**
Arica, *Chile* 124 **G4**
Arica, *Colombia* 124 **D4**
Arico, *Canary Is.* 48 **F3**
Arid, C., *Australia* 93 **F3**
Arida, *Japan* 55 **G7**
Ariège □, *France* 20 **F5**
Ariège →, *France* 20 **E5**
Arieş →, *Romania* 29 **D8**
Arihā, *Israel* 80 **A4**
Arilje, *Serbia & M.* 44 **C4**
Aríllа, Ákra, *Greece* 49 **A3**
Arima, *Trin. & Tob.* 121 **D7**
Arinos →, *Brazil* 124 **F7**
Ario de Rosales, *Mexico* 118 **D4**
Ariogala, *Lithuania* 30 **C10**
Aripo, Mt., *Trin. & Tob.* 125 **K15**
Aripuanã, *Brazil* 124 **E6**
Aripuanã →, *Brazil* 124 **E6**
Ariquemes, *Brazil* 124 **E6**
Arisaig, *U.K.* 13 **E3**
Arîsh, W. el →, *Egypt* 80 **A3**
Arissa, *Ethiopia* 81 **E5**
Aristazabal I., *Canada* 102 **C3**
Arivonimamo, *Madag.* 89 **B8**
Ariza, *Spain* 38 **D2**
Arizaro, Salar de, *Argentina* 126 **A2**
Arizona, *Argentina* 126 **D2**
Arizona □, *U.S.A.* 109 **J8**
Arizpe, *Mexico* 118 **A2**
Årjäng, *Sweden* 10 **E6**
Arjeplog, *Sweden* 8 **D18**
Arjepluovve = Arjeplog, *Sweden* 8 **D18**
Arjona, *Colombia* 124 **A3**
Arjona, *Spain* 37 **H6**
Arjuna, *Indonesia* 63 **G15**
Arka, *Russia* 53 **C15**
Arkadak, *Russia* 34 **E6**
Arkadelphia, *U.S.A.* 113 **H8**
Arkadhía □, *Greece* 46 **D4**
Arkaig, L., *U.K.* 13 **E3**
Arkalyk = Arqalyk, *Kazakhstan* 52 **D7**
Arkansas □, *U.S.A.* 113 **H8**
Arkansas →, *U.S.A.* 113 **J9**
Arkansas City, *U.S.A.* 113 **G6**
Arkaroola, *Australia* 95 **E2**
Árkathos →, *Greece* 46 **B3**
Arkhángelos, *Greece* 49 **C10**
Arkhangelsk, *Russia* 52 **C5**
Arkhangelskoye, *Russia* 34 **E5**
Arki, *India* 68 **D7**
Arkiko, *Eritrea* 81 **D4**
Arklow, *Ireland* 12 **D5**
Árkoi, *Greece* 47 **D8**
Arkona, Kap, *Germany* 24 **A9**
Arkösund, *Sweden* 11 **F10**
Arkoúdhi Nisís, *Greece* 46 **C2**
Arkport, *U.S.A.* 116 **D7**
Arkticheskiy, Mys, *Russia* 53 **A10**
Arkul, *Russia* 34 **B10**
Arkville, *U.S.A.* 117 **D10**
Årla, *Sweden* 10 **E10**
Arlanda, Stockholm ✕ (ARN), *Sweden* 10 **E11**
Arlanza →, *Spain* 36 **C6**
Arlanzón →, *Spain* 36 **C6**
Arlbergpass, *Austria* 26 **D3**
Arles, *France* 21 **E8**
Arli, *Burkina Faso* 83 **C5**
Arli △, *Burkina Faso* 83 **C5**
Arlington, *S. Africa* 89 **D4**
Arlington, *N.Y., U.S.A.* 117 **E11**
Arlington, *Oreg., U.S.A.* 108 **D3**
Arlington, *S. Dak., U.S.A.* 112 **C6**
Arlington, *Tex., U.S.A.* 113 **J6**
Arlington, *Va., U.S.A.* 114 **F7**
Arlington, *Vt., U.S.A.* 117 **C11**
Arlington, *Wash., U.S.A.* 110 **B4**
Arlington Heights, *U.S.A.* 114 **D2**
Arlit, *Niger* 78 **E7**
Arlon, *Belgium* 17 **E5**
Arltunga, *Australia* 94 **C1**
Armagh, *U.K.* 12 **B5**
Armagh □, *U.K.* 12 **B5**
Armagnac, *France* 20 **E4**
Armançon →, *France* 19 **E10**
Armando Bermudez △, *Dom. Rep.* 121 **C5**
Armavir, *Russia* 35 **H5**
Armenia, *Colombia* 124 **C3**
Armenia ■, *Asia* 35 **K7**
Armeniş, *Romania* 28 **E7**
Armenistís, Ákra, *Greece* 49 **C9**
Armentières, *France* 19 **B9**
Armidale, *Australia* 95 **E5**
Armilla, *Spain* 37 **H7**
Armorique ⌓, *France* 18 **D3**
Armour, *U.S.A.* 112 **D5**
Armstrong, *B.C., Canada* 102 **C5**
Armstrong, *Ont., Canada* 104 **B2**
Armutlu, *Bursa, Turkey* 45 **F12**
Armutlu, *Izmir, Turkey* 47 **C9**
Arnaía, *Greece* 44 **F7**
Arnarfjörður, *Iceland* 8 **D2**
Arnaud →, *Canada* 101 **B12**
Arnauti, C., *Cyprus* 49 **D11**
Arnay-le-Duc, *France* 19 **E11**
Arnedillo, *Spain* 38 **C2**
Arnedo, *Spain* 38 **C2**
Arnett, *U.S.A.* 113 **G5**
Arnhem, *Neths.* 17 **C5**
Arnhem, C., *Australia* 94 **A2**
Arnhem B., *Australia* 94 **A2**
Arnhem Land, *Australia* 94 **A1**
Árnissa, *Greece* 44 **F5**
Arno →, *Italy* 40 **E7**
Arno Bay, *Australia* 95 **E2**
Arnold, *U.K.* 14 **D6**
Arnold, *U.S.A.* 110 **G6**
Arnoldstein, *Austria* 26 **E6**
Arnon →, *France* 19 **E9**
Arnot, *Canada* 103 **B9**
Arnøy, *Norway* 8 **A19**
Arnprior, *Canada* 117 **A8**
Arnsberg, *Germany* 24 **D4**
Arnsberger Wald ⌓, *Germany* 24 **D4**
Arnstadt, *Germany* 24 **E6**
Aroab, *Namibia* 88 **D2**
Aroánia Óri, *Greece* 46 **D4**
Aroche, *Spain* 37 **H4**
Arochuku, *Nigeria* 83 **D6**
Arolsen, *Germany* 24 **D5**
Aron, *India* 68 **G6**
Aron →, *France* 19 **F10**
Arona, *Canary Is.* 48 **F3**
Arona, *Italy* 40 **C5**
Aroroy, *Phil.* 61 **E5**
Arosa, Ría de, *Spain* 36 **C2**
Arpajon, *France* 19 **D9**
Arpajon-sur-Cère, *France* 20 **D6**
Arpaşu de Jos, *Romania* 29 **E9**
Arqalyk, *Kazakhstan* 52 **D7**
Arrah = Ara, *India* 69 **G11**
Arrah, *Ivory C.* 82 **D4**
Arraiolos, *Portugal* 37 **G3**
Arran, *U.K.* 13 **F3**
Arras, *France* 19 **B9**
Arrasate, *Spain* 38 **B2**
Arrats →, *France* 20 **D4**
Arreau, *France* 20 **F4**
Arrecife, *Canary Is.* 48 **F6**
Arrecifes, *Argentina* 126 **C3**
Arrée, Mts. d', *France* 18 **D3**
Arresø, *Denmark* 11 **J6**
Arriaga, *Chiapas, Mexico* 119 **D6**
Arriaga, *San Luis Potosí, Mexico* 118 **C4**
Arribes del Duero ⌓, *Spain* 36 **D4**
Arrilalah, *Australia* 94 **C3**
Arrino, *Australia* 93 **E2**
Arriondas, *Spain* 36 **B5**
Arromanches-les-Bains, *France* 18 **C6**
Arronches, *Portugal* 37 **F3**
Arros →, *France* 20 **E3**
Arrow, L., *Ireland* 12 **B3**
Arrowhead, L., *U.S.A.* 111 **L9**
Arrowtown, *N.Z.* 91 **L2**
Arroyo de la Luz, *Spain* 37 **F4**
Arroyo Grande, *U.S.A.* 111 **K6**
Års, *Denmark* 11 **H3**
Ars, *Iran* 70 **B5**
Ars-sur-Moselle, *France* 19 **C13**
Arsenault L., *Canada* 103 **B7**
Arsenev, *Russia* 54 **B6**
Arsi, *Ethiopia* 81 **F4**
Arsiero, *Italy* 41 **C8**
Arsin, *Turkey* 73 **B8**
Arsk, *Russia* 34 **B9**
Årsunda, *Sweden* 10 **D10**
Árta, *Greece* 46 **B3**
Artà, *Spain* 48 **B10**
Árta □, *Greece* 46 **B3**
Arteaga, *Mexico* 118 **D4**
Arteche, *Phil.* 61 **E6**
Arteijo = Arteixo, *Spain* 36 **B2**
Arteixo, *Spain* 36 **B2**
Artem = Artyom, *Azerbaijan* 35 **K10**
Artem, *Russia* 54 **C6**
Artemovsk, *Russia* 53 **D10**
Artemovsk, *Ukraine* 33 **H9**
Artemovskiy, *Russia* 35 **G5**
Artenay, *France* 19 **D8**
Artern, *Germany* 24 **D7**
Artesa de Segre, *Spain* 38 **D6**
Artesia = Mosomane, *Botswana* 88 **C4**
Artesia, *U.S.A.* 113 **J2**
Arthington, *Liberia* 82 **D2**
Arthur, *Canada* 116 **C4**
Arthur →, *Australia* 95 **G3**
Arthur Cr. →, *Australia* 94 **C2**
Arthur Pt., *Australia* 94 **C5**
Arthur River, *Australia* 93 **F2**
Arthur's Pass, *N.Z.* 91 **K3**
Arthur's Pass △, *N.Z.* 91 **K3**
Arthur's Town, *Bahamas* 121 **B4**
Artigas, *Antarctica* 5 **C18**
Artigas, *Uruguay* 126 **C4**
Artik, *Armenia* 35 **K6**
Artillery L., *Canada* 103 **A7**
Artois, *France* 19 **B9**
Artotína, *Greece* 46 **C4**
Artrutx, C. de, *Spain* 48 **B10**
Artsyz, *Ukraine* 29 **D14**
Artvin, *Turkey* 73 **B9**
Artyom, *Azerbaijan* 35 **K10**
Aru, Kepulauan, *Indonesia* 63 **F8**
Aru Is. = Aru, Kepulauan, *Indonesia* 63 **F8**
Arua, *Uganda* 86 **B3**
Aruanã, *Brazil* 125 **F8**
Aruba ☒, *W. Indies* 121 **D6**
Arucas, *Canary Is.* 48 **F4**
Arudy, *France* 20 **E3**
Arun →, *Nepal* 69 **F12**
Arun →, *U.K.* 15 **G7**
Arunachal Pradesh □, *India* 67 **F19**
Arusha, *Tanzania* 86 **C4**
Arusha □, *Tanzania* 86 **C4**
Arusha △, *Tanzania* 86 **C4**
Arusha Chini, *Tanzania* 86 **C4**
Aruwimi →, *Dem. Rep. of the Congo* 86 **B1**
Arvada, *Colo., U.S.A.* 112 **F2**
Arvada, *Wyo., U.S.A.* 108 **D10**
Arve →, *France* 19 **F13**
Árvi, *Greece* 49 **E7**
Arviat, *Canada* 103 **A10**
Arvidsjaur, *Sweden* 8 **D18**
Arvika, *Sweden* 10 **E6**
Arvin, *U.S.A.* 111 **K8**
Arwal, *India* 69 **G11**
Arxan, *China* 60 **B6**
Åryd, *Sweden* 11 **H8**
Aryirádhes, *Greece* 49 **B3**
Aryiroúpolis, *Greece* 49 **D6**
Arys, *Kazakhstan* 52 **E7**
Arzachena, *Italy* 42 **A2**
Arzamas, *Russia* 34 **C6**
Arzgir, *Russia* 35 **H7**
Arzignano, *Italy* 41 **C8**
Arzúa, *Spain* 36 **C2**
Aš, *Czech Rep.* 26 **A5**
Ås, *Sweden* 10 **A8**
As Pontes de García Rodríguez, *Spain* 36 **B3**
Aş Şafā, *Syria* 74 **B6**
As Saffānīyah, *Si. Arabia* 71 **E6**
As Safīrah, *Syria* 70 **B3**
Aş Şahm, *Oman* 71 **E8**
As Sājir, *Si. Arabia* 70 **E5**
As Salamīyah, *Syria* 70 **C3**
As Salmān, *Iraq* 70 **D5**
As Salṭ, *Jordan* 74 **C4**
As Sal'w'a, *Qatar* 71 **E6**
As Samāwah, *Iraq* 70 **D5**
As Sanamayn, *Syria* 74 **B5**
As Sohar = Şuḩār, *Oman* 71 **E8**
As Sukhnah, *Syria* 70 **C3**
As Sulaymānīyah, *Iraq* 70 **C5**
As Sulaymī, *Si. Arabia* 70 **E4**
As Sulayyil, *Si. Arabia* 75 **C4**
As Summān, *Si. Arabia* 70 **E5**
As Suwaydā', *Syria* 74 **C5**
As Suwaydā' □, *Syria* 74 **C5**
As Suwayq, *Oman* 71 **F8**
Aş Şuwayrah, *Iraq* 70 **C5**
Åsa, *Sweden* 11 **G6**
Asab, *Namibia* 88 **D2**
Asaba, *Nigeria* 83 **D6**
Asad, Buḩayrat al, *Syria* 70 **C3**
Asadābād, *Iran* 73 **E13**
Asafo, *Ghana* 82 **D4**
Asahi-Gawa →, *Japan* 55 **G6**
Asahigawa, *Japan* 54 **C11**
Asale, L., *Ethiopia* 81 **E5**
Asamankese, *Ghana* 83 **D4**
Asan →, *India* 69 **F8**
Asansol, *India* 69 **H12**
Åsarna, *Sweden* 10 **B8**
Asayita, *Ethiopia* 81 **E5**
Asbe Teferi, *Ethiopia* 81 **F5**
Asbesberge, *S. Africa* 88 **D3**
Asbestos, *Canada* 105 **C5**
Asbury Park, *U.S.A.* 117 **F10**
Ascea, *Italy* 43 **B8**
Ascensión, *Mexico* 118 **A3**
Ascensión, B. de la, *Mexico* 119 **D7**
Ascension I., *Atl. Oc.* 77 **G2**
Aschach an der Donau, *Austria* 26 **C7**
Aschaffenburg, *Germany* 25 **F5**
Aschendorf, *Germany* 24 **B3**
Aschersleben, *Germany* 24 **D7**
Asciano, *Italy* 41 **E8**
Áscoli Piceno, *Italy* 41 **F10**
Áscoli Satriano, *Italy* 43 **A8**
Ascope, *Peru* 124 **E3**
Ascotán, *Chile* 126 **A2**
Aseb, *Eritrea* 81 **E5**
Åseda, *Sweden* 11 **G9**
Asela, *Ethiopia* 81 **F4**
Åsen, *Sweden* 10 **C7**
Asenovgrad, *Bulgaria* 45 **D8**
Aserradero, *Mexico* 118 **C3**
Asfeld, *France* 19 **C11**
Asfûn el Matâ'na, *Egypt* 80 **B3**
Asgata, *Cyprus* 49 **E12**
Ash Fork, *U.S.A.* 109 **J7**
Ash Grove, *U.S.A.* 113 **G8**
Ash Shabakah, *Iraq* 70 **D4**
Ash Shamāl □, *Lebanon* 74 **A5**
Ash Shāmīyah, *Iraq* 70 **D5**
Ash Shāriqah, *U.A.E.* 71 **E7**
Ash Sharmah, *Si. Arabia* 70 **D2**
Ash Sharqāt, *Iraq* 70 **C4**
Ash Sharqi, Al Jabal, *Lebanon* 74 **B5**
Ash Shaṭrah, *Iraq* 70 **D5**
Ash Shawbak, *Jordan* 70 **D2**
Ash Shawmari, J., *Jordan* 74 **E5**
Ash Shināfīyah, *Iraq* 70 **D5**
Ash Shu'bah, *Si. Arabia* 70 **D5**
Ash Shumlūl, *Si. Arabia* 70 **E5**
Ash Shūr'a, *Iraq* 70 **C4**
Ash Shurayf, *Si. Arabia* 70 **E3**
Ash Shuwayfāt, *Lebanon* 74 **B4**
Ashanti □, *Ghana* 83 **D4**
Ashau, *Vietnam* 64 **D6**
Ashbourne, *U.K.* 14 **D6**
Ashburn, *U.S.A.* 115 **K4**
Ashburton, *N.Z.* 91 **K3**
Ashburton →, *Australia* 92 **D1**
Ashcroft, *Canada* 102 **C4**
Ashdod, *Israel* 74 **D3**
Ashdown, *U.S.A.* 113 **J7**
Asheboro, *U.S.A.* 115 **H6**
Ashern, *Canada* 103 **C9**
Asherton, *U.S.A.* 113 **L5**
Asheville, *U.S.A.* 115 **H4**
Ashewat, *Pakistan* 68 **D3**
Asheweig →, *Canada* 104 **B2**
Ashford, *Australia* 95 **D5**
Ashford, *U.K.* 15 **F8**
Ashgabat, *Turkmenistan* 52 **F6**
Ashibetsu, *Japan* 54 **C11**
Ashikaga, *Japan* 55 **F9**
Ashington, *U.K.* 14 **B6**
Ashizuri-Uwakai △, *Japan* 55 **H6**
Ashizuri-Zaki, *Japan* 55 **H6**
Ashkarkot, *Afghan.* 68 **C2**
Ashkhabad = Ashgabat, *Turkmenistan* 52 **F6**
Āshkhāneh, *Iran* 71 **B8**
Ashland, *Kans., U.S.A.* 113 **G5**
Ashland, *Ky., U.S.A.* 114 **F4**
Ashland, *Mont., U.S.A.* 108 **D10**
Ashland, *Ohio, U.S.A.* 116 **F2**
Ashland, *Oreg., U.S.A.* 108 **E2**
Ashland, *Pa., U.S.A.* 117 **F8**
Ashland, *Va., U.S.A.* 114 **G7**
Ashland, *Wis., U.S.A.* 112 **B9**
Ashley, *N. Dak., U.S.A.* 112 **B5**
Ashley, *Pa., U.S.A.* 117 **E9**
Ashmore and Cartier Is., *Ind. Oc.* 92 **B3**
Ashmore Reef, *Australia* 92 **B3**
Ashmûn, *Egypt* 80 **H7**
Ashmyany, *Belarus* 9 **J21**
Ashokan Reservoir, *U.S.A.* 117 **E10**
Ashqelon, *Israel* 74 **D3**
Ashta, *India* 68 **H7**
Ashtabula, *U.S.A.* 116 **E4**
Ashton, *S. Africa* 88 **E3**
Ashton, *U.S.A.* 108 **D8**
Ashuanipi, L., *Canada* 105 **B6**
Ashuapmushuan →, *Canada* 104 **C5**
Ashville, *U.S.A.* 116 **F6**
'Āşī →, *Asia* 72 **D6**
Asia 50 **E11**
Asia, Kepulauan, *Indonesia* 63 **D8**
Asiago, *Italy* 41 **C8**
Asifabad, *India* 66 **K11**
Asinara, *Italy* 42 **A1**
Asinara, G. dell', *Italy* 42 **A1**
Asino, *Russia* 52 **D9**
Asipovichy, *Belarus* 32 **F5**
'Asīr □, *Si. Arabia* 75 **D3**
Asir, Ras, *Somali Rep.* 75 **E5**
Aşkale, *Turkey* 73 **C9**
Askersund, *Sweden* 11 **F8**
Askham, *S. Africa* 88 **D3**
Askim, *Norway* 9 **G14**
Askja, *Iceland* 8 **D5**
Askøy, *Norway* 9 **F11**
Asl, *Egypt* 80 **B3**
Aslan Burnu, *Turkey* 47 **C8**
Aslanapa, *Turkey* 47 **B11**
Asmara = Asmera, *Eritrea* 81 **D4**
Asmera, *Eritrea* 81 **D4**
Asnæs, *Denmark* 11 **J4**

Åsnen, *Sweden* 11 H8
Aso Kuju △, *Japan* 55 H5
Àsola, *Italy* 40 C7
Asosa, *Ethiopia* 81 E3
Asoteriba, Jebel, *Sudan* 80 C4
Aspatria, *U.K.* 14 C4
Aspe, *Spain* 39 G4
Aspen, *U.S.A.* 109 G10
Aspendos, *Turkey* 72 D4
Aspermont, *U.S.A.* 113 J4
Aspet, *France* 20 E4
Aspiring, Mt., *N.Z.* 91 L2
Aspres-sur-Buëch, *France* 21 D9
Asprókavos, Ákra, *Greece* 49 B4
Aspromonte △, *Italy* 43 D8
Aspur, *India* 68 H6
Asquith, *Canada* 103 C7
Assab = Aseb, *Eritrea* 81 E5
Assâba, Massif de l', *Mauritania* 82 B2
Assagny △, *Ivory C.* 82 D4
Assaikio, *Nigeria* 83 D6
Assal, L., *Djibouti* 81 E5
Assam □, *India* 67 G18
Assamakka, *Niger* 83 B6
Assateague Island ⌓, *U.S.A.* 114 F8
Asse, *Belgium* 17 D4
Assémini, *Italy* 42 C1
Assen, *Neths.* 17 A6
Assens, *Denmark* 11 J3
Assini, *Ivory C.* 82 D4
Assiniboia, *Canada* 103 D7
Assiniboine →, *Canada* 103 D9
Assiniboine, Mt., *Canada* 102 C5
Assis, *Brazil* 127 A5
Assisi, *Italy* 41 E9
Ássos, *Greece* 46 C2
Assynt, L., *U.K.* 13 C3
Astaffort, *France* 20 D4
Astakidha, *Greece* 47 F8
Astakós, *Greece* 46 C3
Astana, *Kazakhstan* 52 D8
Āstāneh, *Iran* 71 B6
Astara, *Azerbaijan* 71 B6
Āstārā, *Iran* 73 C13
Asteroúsia, *Greece* 49 E7
Asti, *Italy* 40 D5
Astipálaia, *Greece* 47 E8
Astorga, *Spain* 36 C4
Astoria, *U.S.A.* 110 D3
Åstorp, *Sweden* 11 H6
Astrakhan, *Russia* 35 G9
Astudillo, *Spain* 36 C6
Asturias □, *Spain* 36 B5
Asturias ✕ (OVD), *Spain* 36 B4
Asunción, *Paraguay* 126 B4
Asunción Nochixtlán, *Mexico* 119 D5
Åsunden, *Sweden* 11 F9
Asutri, *Sudan* 81 D4
Aswa →, *Uganda* 86 B3
Aswa-Lolim ⌓, *Uganda* 86 B3
Aswad, Ra's al, *Si. Arabia* 80 C4
Aswân, *Egypt* 80 C3
Aswan Dam = Sadd el Aali, *Egypt* 80 C3
Asyût, *Egypt* 80 B3
Asyûti, Wadi →, *Egypt* 80 B3
Aszód, *Hungary* 28 C4
At Ţafīlah, *Jordan* 74 E4
At Ţafīlah □, *Jordan* 74 E4
Aţ Tā'if, *Si. Arabia* 75 C3
At Ta'mīm □, *Iraq* 70 C5
Aţ Ţirāq, *Si. Arabia* 70 E5
Aţ Tubayq, *Si. Arabia* 70 D3
Atabey, *Turkey* 47 D12
Atacama □, *Chile* 126 B2
Atacama, Desierto de, *Chile* 126 A2
Atacama, Salar de, *Chile* 126 A2
Atakpamé, *Togo* 83 D5
Atalándi, *Greece* 46 C4
Atalaya, *Peru* 124 F4
Atalaya de Femes, *Canary Is.* 48 F6
Atami, *Japan* 55 G9
Atapupu, *E. Timor* 63 F6
Atâr, *Mauritania* 78 D3
Atarfe, *Spain* 37 H7
Atari, *Pakistan* 68 D6
Atascadero, *U.S.A.* 110 K6
Atasu, *Kazakhstan* 52 E8
Ataturk, Istanbul ✕ (IST), *Turkey* 45 F12
Atatürk Barajı, *Turkey* 73 D8
Atauro, *E. Timor* 63 F7
'Atbara, *Sudan* 80 D3
'Atbara, Nahr →, *Sudan* 80 D3
Atbasar, *Kazakhstan* 52 D7
Atça, *Turkey* 47 D10
Atchafalaya B., *U.S.A.* 113 L9
Atchison, *U.S.A.* 112 F7
Atebubu, *Ghana* 83 D4
Ateca, *Spain* 38 D3
Aterno →, *Italy* 41 F10
Āteshān, *Iran* 71 C7
Atesine, Alpi, *Italy* 41 B8
Atessa, *Italy* 41 F11
Atfîh, *Egypt* 80 J7
Ath, *Belgium* 17 D3
Athabasca, *Canada* 102 C6
Athabasca →, *Canada* 103 B6
Athabasca, L., *Canada* 103 B7
Athabasca Sand Dunes ⌓, *Canada* 103 B7
Athboy, *Ireland* 12 C5
Athenry, *Ireland* 12 C3
Athens = Athínai, *Greece* 46 D5
Athens, *Ala., U.S.A.* 115 H2
Athens, *Ga., U.S.A.* 115 J4
Athens, *N.Y., U.S.A.* 117 D11
Athens, *Ohio, U.S.A.* 114 F4
Athens, *Pa., U.S.A.* 117 E8
Athens, *Tenn., U.S.A.* 115 H3
Athens, *Tex., U.S.A.* 113 J7
Atherley, *Canada* 116 B5
Atherton, *Australia* 94 B4
Athiéme, *Benin* 83 D5
Athienou, *Cyprus* 49 D12
Athínai, *Greece* 46 D5
Athínai ✕ (ATH), *Greece* 46 D5
Athlone, *Ireland* 12 C4
Athna, *Cyprus* 49 D12
Athol, *U.S.A.* 117 D12
Atholl, Forest of, *U.K.* 13 E5
Atholville, *Canada* 105 C6
Áthos, *Greece* 45 F8
Athy, *Ireland* 12 C5
Ati, *Chad* 79 F9
Ati, *Sudan* 81 E2
Atiak, *Uganda* 86 B3
Atienza, *Spain* 38 D2
Atiit, *Sudan* 81 F3
Atik L., *Canada* 103 B9
Atikaki ⌓, *Canada* 103 C9
Atikameg →, *Canada* 104 B3
Atikokan, *Canada* 104 C1
Atikonak L., *Canada* 105 B7
Atimonan, *Phil.* 61 E4
Atitlán △, *Cent. Amer.* 119 E6
Atka, *Russia* 53 C16
Atka I., *U.S.A.* 100 C2
Atkarsk, *Russia* 34 E7
Atkinson, *U.S.A.* 112 D5
Atlanta, *Ga., U.S.A.* 115 J3
Atlanta, *Tex., U.S.A.* 113 J7
Atlantic, *U.S.A.* 112 E7
Atlantic City, *U.S.A.* 114 F8
Atlantic-Indian Basin, *Antarctica* 5 B4
Atlantic-Indian Ridge, *Atl. Oc.* 5 B3
Atlantic Ocean 2 E9
Atlas Mts. = Haut Atlas, *Morocco* 78 B4
Atlin, *Canada* 102 B2
Atlin ⌓, *Canada* 102 B2
Atlin, L., *Canada* 102 B2
Atmore, *U.S.A.* 115 K2
Atoka, *U.S.A.* 113 H6
Átokos Nisís, *Greece* 46 C2
Atolia, *U.S.A.* 111 K9
Atrai →, *Bangla.* 69 G13
Atrak = Atrek →, *Turkmenistan* 71 B8
Ätran, *Sweden* 11 G6
Ätran →, *Sweden* 11 H6
Atrauli, *India* 68 E8
Atrek →, *Turkmenistan* 71 B8
Atri, *Italy* 41 F10
Atsikí, *Greece* 47 B7
Atsoum, Mts., *Cameroon* 83 D7
Atsuta, *Japan* 54 C10
Attalla, *U.S.A.* 115 H2
Attapu, *Laos* 64 E6
Attáviros, *Greece* 49 C9
Attawapiskat, *Canada* 104 B3
Attawapiskat →, *Canada* 104 B3
Attawapiskat L., *Canada* 104 B2
Attersee, *Austria* 26 D6
Attica, *Ind., U.S.A.* 114 E2
Attica, *Ohio, U.S.A.* 116 E2
Attichy, *France* 19 C10
Attigny, *France* 19 C11
Attika = Attikí □, *Greece* 46 D5
Attikamagen L., *Canada* 105 B6
Attikí □, *Greece* 46 D5
Attleboro, *U.S.A.* 117 E13
Attock, *Pakistan* 68 C5
Attopeu = Attapu, *Laos* 64 E6
Attu I., *U.S.A.* 100 C1
Attur, *India* 66 P11
Atuel →, *Argentina* 126 D2
Åtvidaberg, *Sweden* 11 F10
Atwater, *U.S.A.* 110 H6
Atwood, *Canada* 116 C3
Atwood, *U.S.A.* 112 F4
Atyraū, *Kazakhstan* 52 E6
Au Sable, *U.S.A.* 116 B1
Au Sable →, *U.S.A.* 114 C4
Au Sable Forks, *U.S.A.* 117 B11
Au Sable Pt., *U.S.A.* 116 B1
Aubagne, *France* 21 E9
Aubarca, C. d', *Spain* 48 B7
Aube □, *France* 19 D11
Aube →, *France* 19 D10
Aubenas, *France* 21 D8
Aubenton, *France* 19 C11
Auberry, *U.S.A.* 110 H7
Aubigny-sur-Nère, *France* 19 E9
Aubin, *France* 20 D6
Aubrac, Mts. d', *France* 20 D7
Auburn, *Ala., U.S.A.* 115 J3
Auburn, *Calif., U.S.A.* 110 G5
Auburn, *Ind., U.S.A.* 114 E3
Auburn, *Maine, U.S.A.* 115 C10
Auburn, *N.Y., U.S.A.* 117 D8
Auburn, *Nebr., U.S.A.* 112 E7
Auburn, *Pa., U.S.A.* 117 F8
Auburn, *Wash., U.S.A.* 110 C4
Auburn Ra., *Australia* 95 D5
Auburndale, *U.S.A.* 115 L5
Aubusson, *France* 20 C6
Auce, *Latvia* 30 B9
Auch, *France* 20 E4
Auchi, *Nigeria* 83 D6
Auchterarder, *U.K.* 13 E5
Auchtermuchty, *U.K.* 13 E5
Auckland, *N.Z.* 91 G5
Auckland Is., *Pac. Oc.* 96 N8
Aude □, *France* 20 E6
Aude →, *France* 20 E7
Auden, *Canada* 104 B2
Auderville, *France* 18 C5
Audierne, *France* 18 D2
Audincourt, *France* 19 E13
Audo Ra., *Ethiopia* 81 F5
Audubon, *U.S.A.* 112 E7
Aue, *Germany* 24 E8
Auerbach, *Germany* 24 E8
Augathella, *Australia* 95 D4
Aughnacloy, *U.K.* 12 B5
Augrabies Falls, *S. Africa* 88 D3
Augrabies Falls △, *S. Africa* 88 D3
Augsburg, *Germany* 25 G6
Augsburg-Westliche Wälder ⌓, *Germany* 25 G6
Augusta, *Australia* 93 F2
Augusta, *Italy* 43 E8
Augusta, *Ark., U.S.A.* 113 H9
Augusta, *Ga., U.S.A.* 115 J5
Augusta, *Kans., U.S.A.* 113 G6
Augusta, *Maine, U.S.A.* 101 D13
Augusta, *Mont., U.S.A.* 108 C7
Augustenborg, *Denmark* 11 K3
Augustów, *Poland* 30 E9
Augustus, Mt., *Australia* 93 D2
Augustus I., *Australia* 92 C3
Aukan, *Eritrea* 81 D5
Aukrug ⌓, *Germany* 24 A5
Aukum, *U.S.A.* 110 G6
Auld, L., *Australia* 92 D3
Aulla, *Italy* 40 D6
Aulnay, *France* 20 B3
Aulne →, *France* 18 D2
Aulnoye-Aymeries, *France* 19 B10
Ault, *France* 18 B8
Ault, *U.S.A.* 112 E2
Aulus-les-Bains, *France* 20 F5
Aumale, *France* 19 C8
Aumont-Aubrac, *France* 20 D7
Auna, *Nigeria* 83 C5
Auning, *Denmark* 11 H4
Aunis, *France* 20 B3
Auponhia, *Indonesia* 63 E7
Aups, *France* 21 E10
Aur, Pulau, *Malaysia* 65 L5
Auraiya, *India* 69 F8
Aurangabad, *Bihar, India* 69 G11
Aurangabad, *Maharashtra, India* 66 K9
Auray, *France* 18 E4
Aurich, *Germany* 24 B3
Aurillac, *France* 20 D6
Auronzo di Cadore, *Italy* 41 B9
Aurora, *Canada* 116 C5
Aurora, *S. Africa* 88 E2
Aurora, *Colo., U.S.A.* 112 F2
Aurora, *Ill., U.S.A.* 114 E1
Aurora, *Mo., U.S.A.* 113 G8
Aurora, *N.Y., U.S.A.* 117 D8
Aurora, *Nebr., U.S.A.* 112 E6
Aurora, *Ohio, U.S.A.* 116 E3
Aurukun, *Australia* 94 A3
Aus, *Namibia* 88 D2
Ausable →, *Canada* 116 C3
Auschwitz = Oświęcim, *Poland* 31 H6
Austerlitz = Slavkov u Brna, *Czech Rep.* 27 B9
Austin, *Minn., U.S.A.* 112 D8
Austin, *Nev., U.S.A.* 108 G5
Austin, *Pa., U.S.A.* 116 E6
Austin, *Tex., U.S.A.* 113 K6
Austin, L., *Australia* 93 E2
Austin I., *Canada* 103 A10
Austra, *Norway* 8 D14
Austral Is. = Tubuai Is., *French Polynesia* 97 K13
Austral Seamount Chain, *Pac. Oc.* 97 K13
Australia ■, *Oceania* 96 K5
Australian Capital Territory □, *Australia* 95 F4
Australind, *Australia* 93 F2
Austria ■, *Europe* 26 E7
Austvågøy, *Norway* 8 B16
Auterive, *France* 20 E5
Authie →, *France* 19 B8
Authon-du-Perche, *France* 18 D7
Autlán, *Mexico* 118 D4
Autun, *France* 19 F11
Auvergne □, *France* 20 C7
Auvergne, Mts. d', *France* 20 C6
Auvézère →, *France* 20 C4
Auxerre, *France* 19 E10
Auxi-le-Château, *France* 19 B9
Auxonne, *France* 19 E12
Auzances, *France* 19 F9
Ava, *U.S.A.* 113 G8
Avallon, *France* 19 E10
Avalon, *U.S.A.* 111 M8
Avalon Pen., *Canada* 105 C9
Avanos, *Turkey* 70 B2
Avaré, *Brazil* 127 A6
Ávas, *Greece* 45 F9
Avawatz Mts., *U.S.A.* 111 K10
Avdan Dağı, *Turkey* 45 F13
Aveiro, *Brazil* 125 D7
Aveiro, *Portugal* 36 E2
Aveiro □, *Portugal* 36 E2
Āvej, *Iran* 71 C6
Avellaneda, *Argentina* 126 C4
Avellino, *Italy* 43 B7
Avenal, *U.S.A.* 110 K6
Aversa, *Italy* 43 B7
Avery, *U.S.A.* 108 C6
Aves, I. de, *W. Indies* 121 C7
Aves, Is. las, *Venezuela* 121 D6
Avesnes-sur-Helpe, *France* 19 B10
Avesnois ⌓, *France* 19 B10
Avesta, *Sweden* 10 D10
Aveyron □, *France* 20 D6
Aveyron →, *France* 20 D5
Avezzano, *Italy* 41 F10
Avgó, *Greece* 47 F7
Aviá Terai, *Argentina* 126 B3
Aviano, *Italy* 41 B9
Aviemore, *U.K.* 13 D5
Avigliana, *Italy* 40 C4
Avigliano, *Italy* 43 B8
Avignon, *France* 21 E8
Ávila, *Spain* 36 E6
Ávila □, *Spain* 36 E6
Ávila, Sierra de, *Spain* 36 E5
Avila Beach, *U.S.A.* 111 K6
Avilés, *Spain* 36 B5
Avintes, *Portugal* 36 D2
Avionárion, *Greece* 46 C6
Avis, *Portugal* 37 F3
Avis, *U.S.A.* 116 E7
Avísio →, *Italy* 40 B8
Aviz = Avis, *Portugal* 37 F3
Avize, *France* 19 D11
Avlum, *Denmark* 11 H2
Avoca, *U.S.A.* 116 D7
Avoca →, *Australia* 95 F3
Avoca →, *Ireland* 12 D5
Avola, *Canada* 102 C5
Avola, *Italy* 43 F8
Avon, *U.S.A.* 116 D7
Avon →, *Australia* 93 F2
Avon →, *Bristol, U.K.* 15 F5
Avon →, *Dorset, U.K.* 15 G6
Avon →, *Warks., U.K.* 15 E5
Avon Park, *U.S.A.* 115 M5
Avondale, *Zimbabwe* 87 F3
Avonlea, *Canada* 103 D8
Avonmore, *Canada* 117 A10
Avonmouth, *U.K.* 15 F5
Avramov, *Bulgaria* 45 D10
Avranches, *France* 18 D5
Avre →, *France* 18 D8
Avrig, *Romania* 29 E9
Avrillé, *France* 18 E6
Avtovac, *Bos.-H.* 44 C2
Awag el Baqar, *Sudan* 81 E3
A'waj →, *Syria* 74 B5
Awaji-Shima, *Japan* 55 G7
'Awālī, *Bahrain* 71 E6
Awantipur, *India* 69 C6
Awasa, *Ethiopia* 81 F4
Awasa, L., *Ethiopia* 81 F4
Awash, *Ethiopia* 81 F5
Awash △, *Ethiopia* 81 F5
Awash →, *Ethiopia* 81 E5
Awaso, *Ghana* 82 D4
Awatere →, *N.Z.* 91 J5
Awbārī, *Libya* 79 C8
Awbārī, Idehan, *Libya* 79 C8
Awe, L., *U.K.* 13 E3
Aweil, *Sudan* 81 F2
Awgu, *Nigeria* 83 D6
Awjilah, *Libya* 79 C10
Awka, *Nigeria* 83 D6
Ax-les-Thermes, *France* 20 F5
Axat, *France* 20 F6
Axe →, *U.K.* 15 F5
Axel Heiberg I., *Canada* 98 A10
Axim, *Ghana* 82 E4
Axintele, *Romania* 29 F11
Axiós →, *Greece* 44 F6
Axminster, *U.K.* 15 G4
Axvall, *Sweden* 11 F7
Ay, *France* 19 C11
Ayabaca, *Peru* 124 D3
Ayabe, *Japan* 55 G7
Ayacucho, *Argentina* 126 D4
Ayacucho, *Peru* 124 F4
Ayaguz, *Kazakhstan* 52 E9
Ayamé, *Ivory C.* 82 D4
Ayamonte, *Spain* 37 H3
Ayan, *Russia* 53 D14
Ayancık, *Turkey* 72 B6
Ayas, *Turkey* 72 B5
Ayaviri, *Peru* 124 F4
Aybastı, *Turkey* 72 B7
Aydın, *Turkey* 72 D2
Aydin □, *Turkey* 47 D9
Aydin Dağları, *Turkey* 47 D10
Ayelu, *Ethiopia* 81 E5
Ayenngré, *Togo* 83 D5
Ayer, *U.S.A.* 117 D13
Ayer Hitam, *Malaysia* 65 c
Ayerbe, *Spain* 38 C4
Ayer's Cliff, *Canada* 117 A12
Ayers Rock, *Australia* 93 E5
Ayiá, *Greece* 46 B4
Ayia Aikateríni, Ákra, *Greece* 49 A3
Ayía Ánna, *Greece* 46 C5
Ayía Dhéka, *Greece* 49 D6
Ayía Gálini, *Greece* 49 D6
Ayía Marína, *Kásos, Greece* 47 F8
Ayía Marína, *Léros, Greece* 47 D8
Áyia Napa, *Cyprus* 49 E13
Ayía Paraskeví, *Greece* 47 B8
Áyia Phyla, *Cyprus* 49 E12
Ayía Rouméli, *Greece* 46 F5
Ayía Varvára, *Greece* 49 D7
Ayiássos, *Greece* 47 B8
Áyioi Theódhoroi, *Greece* 46 D5
Áyion Óros □, *Greece* 45 F8
Áyios Amvrósios, *Cyprus* 49 D12
Áyios Andréas, *Greece* 46 D4
Áyios Evstrátios, *Greece* 46 B6
Áyios Ioánnis, Ákra, *Greece* 49 D7
Áyios Isidhoros, *Greece* 49 C9
Áyios Kiríkos, *Greece* 47 D8
Áyios Matthaíos, *Greece* 49 B3
Áyios Mírono, *Greece* 49 D7
Áyios Nikólaos, *Greece* 49 D7
Áyios Pétros, *Greece* 46 C2
Áyios Seryios, *Cyprus* 49 D12
Áyios Theodhoros, *Cyprus* 49 D13
Áyios Yeóryios, *Greece* 46 D5
Aykathonisi, *Greece* 47 D8
Aykirikçi, *Turkey* 47 B12
Aylesbury, *U.K.* 15 F7
Aylmer, *Canada* 116 D4
Aylmer, L., *Canada* 100 B8
'Ayn, Wādī al, *Oman* 71 F7
Ayn Dār, *Si. Arabia* 71 E7
Ayn Zālah, *Iraq* 70 B4
Ayna, *Spain* 39 G2
Ayod, *Sudan* 81 F3
Ayolas, *Paraguay* 126 B4
Ayom, *Sudan* 81 F2
Ayon, Ostrov, *Russia* 53 C17
Ayora, *Spain* 39 F3
Ayorou, *Niger* 83 C5
'Ayoûn el 'Atroûs, *Mauritania* 82 B3
Ayr, *Australia* 94 B4
Ayr, *Canada* 116 C4
Ayr, *U.K.* 13 F4
Ayr →, *U.K.* 13 F4
Ayrancı, *Turkey* 72 D5
Ayrancılar, *Turkey* 47 C9
Ayre, Pt. of, *I. of Man* 14 C3
Aysha, *Ethiopia* 81 E5
Ayton, *Australia* 94 B4
Aytos, *Bulgaria* 45 D11
Aytoska Planina, *Bulgaria* 45 D11
Ayu, Kepulauan, *Indonesia* 63 D8
Ayutla, *Guatemala* 120 D1
Ayutla, *Mexico* 119 D5
Ayvacık, *Turkey* 72 C2
Ayvalık, *Turkey* 47 B8
Az Zabadānī, *Syria* 74 B5
Az Ẓāhirīyah, *West Bank* 74 D3
Az Ẓahrān, *Si. Arabia* 71 E6
Az Zarqā, *Jordan* 74 C5
Az Zarqā', *U.A.E.* 71 E7
Az Zarqā □, *Jordan* 74 C5
Az Zāwiyah, *Libya* 79 B8
Az Zībār, *Iraq* 70 B5
Az Zilfī, *Si. Arabia* 70 E5
Az Zubayr, *Iraq* 70 D5
Az Zuqur, *Yemen* 81 E5
Azad Kashmir □, *Pakistan* 69 C5
Azambuja, *Portugal* 37 F2
Azamgarh, *India* 69 F10
Azangaro, *Peru* 124 F4
Azaoua, *Niger* 83 B5
Azaouad, *Mali* 82 B4
Azaouak, Vallée de l', *Mali* 83 B5
Āzār Shahr, *Iran* 70 B5
Azara, *Nigeria* 83 D6
Azarān, *Iran* 70 B5
Azärbayjan = Azerbaijan ■, *Asia* 35 K9
Āzarbāyjān-e Gharbī □, *Iran* 70 B5
Āzarbāyjān-e Sharqī □, *Iran* 70 B5
Azare, *Nigeria* 83 C7
Azay-le-Rideau, *France* 18 E7
A'zāz, *Syria* 70 B3
Azbine = Aïr, *Niger* 83 B6
Azerbaijan ■, *Asia* 35 K9
Azerbaijchan = Azerbaijan ■, *Asia* 35 K9
Azezo, *Ethiopia* 81 E4
Azimganj, *India* 69 G13
Aznalcóllar, *Spain* 37 H4
Azogues, *Ecuador* 124 D3
Azores = Açores, Is. dos, *Atl. Oc.* 78 A1
Azov, *Russia* 35 G4
Azov, Sea of, *Europe* 33 J9
Azovskoye More = Azov, Sea of, *Europe* 33 J9
Azpeitia, *Spain* 38 B2
Azraq ash Shīshān, *Jordan* 74 D5
Aztec, *U.S.A.* 109 H10
Azúa de Compostela, *Dom. Rep.* 121 C5
Azuaga, *Spain* 37 G5
Azuara, *Spain* 38 D4
Azuer →, *Spain* 37 F7
Azuero, Pen. de, *Panama* 120 E3
Azuga, *Romania* 29 E10
Azul, *Argentina* 126 D4
Azusa, *U.S.A.* 111 L9
Azzano Décimo, *Italy* 41 C9

B

Ba Be △, *Vietnam* 64 A5
Ba Don, *Vietnam* 64 D6
Ba Dong, *Vietnam* 65 H6
Ba Ngoi = Cam Lam, *Vietnam* 65 G7
Ba Tri, *Vietnam* 65 G6
Ba Vi △, *Vietnam* 64 B5
Ba Xian = Bazhou, *China* 56 E9
Baa, *Indonesia* 63 F6
Baamonde, *Spain* 36 B3
Baardeere = Bardera, *Somali Rep.* 75 G3
Baarle-Nassau, *Belgium* 17 C4
Bab el Mandeb, *Red Sea* 75 E3
Baba, *Bulgaria* 44 D7
Bābā, Koh-i-, *Afghan.* 66 B5
Baba Burnu, *Turkey* 47 B8
Baba dag, *Azerbaijan* 35 K9
Bābā Kalū, *Iran* 71 D6
Babadag, *Romania* 29 F13
Babadağ, *Turkey* 47 D10
Babaeski, *Turkey* 45 E11
Babahoyo, *Ecuador* 124 D3
Babai = Sarju →, *India* 69 F9
Babana, *Nigeria* 83 C5
Babanusa, *Sudan* 81 E2
Babar, *Indonesia* 63 F7
Babar, *Pakistan* 68 D3
Babarkach, *Pakistan* 68 E3
Babayevo, *Russia* 32 C8
Babb, *U.S.A.* 108 B7
Babenhausen, *Germany* 25 F4
Băbeni, *Romania* 29 F9
Baberu, *India* 69 G9
Babi Besar, Pulau, *Malaysia* 65 L4
Babia Gora, *Europe* 31 J6
Babian Jiang →, *China* 58 F3
Babīl □, *Iraq* 70 C5
Babile, *Ethiopia* 81 F5
Babimost, *Poland* 31 F2
Babinda, *Australia* 94 B4
Babine, *Canada* 102 B3
Babine →, *Canada* 102 B3
Babine L., *Canada* 102 C3
Babiogórski △, *Poland* 31 J6
Babo, *Indonesia* 63 E8
Babócsa, *Hungary* 28 D2
Bābol, *Iran* 71 B7
Bābol Sar, *Iran* 71 B7

Baborów, *Poland* 31 H5
Babruysk, *Belarus* 33 F5
Babuhri, *India* 68 F3
Babuna, *Macedonia* 44 E5
Babura, *Nigeria* 83 C6
Babusar Pass, *Pakistan* 69 B5
Babushkin, *Russia* 60 A5
Babušnica, *Serbia & M.* 44 C6
Babuyan Chan., *Phil.* 61 B4
Babylon, *Iraq* 70 C5
Bač, *Serbia & M.* 28 E4
Bâc →, *Moldova* 29 D14
Bac Can, *Vietnam* 58 F5
Bac Giang, *Vietnam* 58 G6
Bac Lieu, *Vietnam* 65 H5
Bac Ninh, *Vietnam* 58 G6
Bac Phan, *Vietnam* 64 B5
Bac Quang, *Vietnam* 58 F5
Bacabal, *Brazil* 125 D10
Bacalar, *Mexico* 119 D7
Bacan, Kepulauan, *Indonesia* 63 E7
Bacarra, *Phil.* 61 B4
Bacău, *Romania* 29 D11
Bacău □, *Romania* 29 D11
Baccarat, *France* 19 D13
Bacerac, *Mexico* 118 A3
Băceşti, *Romania* 29 D12
Bach Long Vi, Dao, *Vietnam* 64 B6
Bach Ma △, *Vietnam* 64 D6
Bacharach, *Germany* 25 E3
Bachhwara, *India* 69 G11
Bachuma, *Ethiopia* 81 F4
Bačina, *Serbia & M.* 44 C5
Back →, *Canada* 100 B9
Bačka Palanka, *Serbia & M.* 28 E4
Bačka Topola, *Serbia & M.* 28 E4
Bäckebo, *Sweden* 11 H10
Bäckefors, *Sweden* 11 F6
Bäckhammar, *Sweden* 10 E8
Bački Petrovac, *Serbia & M.* 28 E4
Backnang, *Germany* 25 G5
Baco, Mt., *Phil.* 61 E4
Bacolod, *Phil.* 61 F5
Bacqueville-en-Caux, *France* 18 C8
Bács-Kiskun □, *Hungary* 28 D4
Bácsalmás, *Hungary* 28 D4
Bacuag = Placer, *Phil.* 61 G6
Bacuk, *Malaysia* 65 J4
Bād, *Iran* 71 C7
Bad →, *U.S.A.* 112 C4
Bad Aussee, *Austria* 26 D6
Bad Axe, *U.S.A.* 116 C2
Bad Bergzabern, *Germany* 25 F3
Bad Berleburg, *Germany* 24 D4
Bad Bevensen, *Germany* 24 B6
Bad Bramstedt, *Germany* 24 B5
Bad Brückenau, *Germany* 25 E5
Bad Doberan, *Germany* 24 A7
Bad Driburg, *Germany* 24 D5
Bad Ems, *Germany* 25 E3
Bad Frankenhausen, *Germany* 24 D7
Bad Freienwalde, *Germany* 24 C10
Bad Goisern, *Austria* 26 D6
Bad Harzburg, *Germany* 24 D6
Bad Hersfeld, *Germany* 24 E5
Bad Hofgastein, *Austria* 26 D6
Bad Homburg, *Germany* 25 E4
Bad Honnef, *Germany* 24 E3
Bad Iburg, *Germany* 24 C4
Bad Ischl, *Austria* 26 D6
Bad Kissingen, *Germany* 25 E6
Bad Königshofen, *Germany* 25 E6
Bad Kreuznach, *Germany* 25 F3
Bad Krozingen, *Germany* 25 H3
Bad Laasphe, *Germany* 24 E4
Bad Lands, *U.S.A.* 112 D3
Bad Langensalza, *Germany* 24 D6
Bad Lauterberg, *Germany* 24 D6
Bad Leonfelden, *Austria* 26 C7
Bad Liebenwerda, *Germany* 24 D9
Bad Mergentheim, *Germany* 25 F5
Bad Münstereifel, *Germany* 24 E2
Bad Nauheim, *Germany* 25 E4
Bad Neuenahr-Ahrweiler, *Germany* 24 E3
Bad Neustadt, *Germany* 25 E6
Bad Oeynhausen, *Germany* 24 C4
Bad Oldesloe, *Germany* 24 B6
Bad Orb, *Germany* 25 E5
Bad Pyrmont, *Germany* 24 D5
Bad Reichenhall, *Germany* 25 H8
Bad Säckingen, *Germany* 25 H3
Bad Salzuflen, *Germany* 24 C4
Bad Salzungen, *Germany* 24 E6
Bad Schwartau, *Germany* 24 B6
Bad Segeberg, *Germany* 24 B6
Bad St. Leonhard, *Austria* 26 E7
Bad Tölz, *Germany* 25 H7
Bad Urach, *Germany* 25 G5
Bad Vöslau, *Austria* 27 D9
Bad Waldsee, *Germany* 25 H5
Bad Wildungen, *Germany* 24 D5
Bad Wimpfen, *Germany* 25 F5
Bad Windsheim, *Germany* 25 F6
Bad Zwischenahn, *Germany* 24 B4
Bada Barabil, *India* 69 H11
Badagara, *India* 66 P9
Badagri, *Nigeria* 83 D5
Badajós, L., *Brazil* 124 D6
Badajoz, *Spain* 37 G4
Badajoz □, *Spain* 37 G4
Badakhshān □, *Afghan.* 66 A7
Badalona, *Spain* 38 D7
Badalzai, *Afghan.* 68 E1
Badampahar, *India* 67 H15
Badanah, *Si. Arabia* 70 D4
Badarinath, *India* 69 D8
Badas, Kepulauan, *Indonesia* 62 D3
Baddo →, *Pakistan* 66 F4
Bade, *Indonesia* 63 F9
Badeggi, *Nigeria* 83 D6
Badéguichéri, *Niger* 83 C6
Baden, *Austria* 27 C9
Baden, *Switz.* 25 H4
Baden, *U.S.A.* 116 F4
Baden-Baden, *Germany* 25 G4
Baden-Württemberg □, *Germany* 25 G4
Badgastein, *Austria* 26 D6
Badger, *Canada* 105 C8
Badger, *U.S.A.* 110 J7
Bādghīs □, *Afghan.* 66 B3
Badgingarra △, *Australia* 93 F2
Badgom, *India* 69 B6
Badia Polésine, *Italy* 41 C8
Badiar △, *Guinea* 82 C2
Badin, *Pakistan* 68 G3
Badinka ⌓, *Mali* 82 C3
Badlands △, *U.S.A.* 112 D3
Badogo, *Mali* 82 C3
Badoumbé, *Mali* 82 C2
Badrah, *Iraq* 70 C5
Badrinath, *India* 69 D8
Badulla, *Sri Lanka* 66 R12
Badung, Selat, *Indonesia* 63 K18
Baena, *Spain* 37 H6
Baeza, *Spain* 37 H7
Bafang, *Cameroon* 83 D7
Bafatá, *Guinea-Biss.* 82 C2
Baffin B., *Canada* 101 A13
Baffin I., *Canada* 101 B12
Bafia, *Cameroon* 83 E7
Bafilo, *Togo* 83 D5
Bafing △, *Mali* 82 C2
Bafing →, *Mali* 82 C2
Bafliyūn, *Syria* 70 B3
Bafoulabé, *Mali* 82 C2
Bafoussam, *Cameroon* 83 D7
Bāfq, *Iran* 71 D7
Bafra, *Turkey* 72 B6
Bafra Burnu, *Turkey* 72 B7
Bāft, *Iran* 71 D8
Bafut, *Cameroon* 83 D7
Bafwasende, *Dem. Rep. of the Congo* 86 B2
Bagam, *Niger* 83 B6
Bagamoyo, *Tanzania* 86 D4
Bagan Datoh, *Malaysia* 65 L3
Bagan Serai, *Malaysia* 65 K3
Baganga, *Phil.* 61 H7
Bagani, *Namibia* 88 B3
Bagansiapiapi, *Indonesia* 62 D2
Bagasra, *India* 68 J4
Bagaud, *India* 68 H6
Bagawi, *Sudan* 81 E3
Bagbag, *Sudan* 81 D3
Bagdad, *U.S.A.* 111 L11
Bagdarin, *Russia* 53 D12
Bagé, *Brazil* 127 C5
Bagenalstown = Muine Bheag, *Ireland* 12 D5
Baggs, *U.S.A.* 108 F10
Bagh, *Pakistan* 69 C5
Baghain →, *India* 69 G9
Baghdād, *Iraq* 70 C5
Bagheria, *Italy* 42 D6
Baghlān, *Afghan.* 66 A6
Baghlān □, *Afghan.* 66 B6
Bagley, *U.S.A.* 112 B7
Bagnara Cálabra, *Italy* 43 D8
Bagnasco, *Italy* 40 D5
Bagnères-de-Bigorre, *France* 20 E4
Bagnères-de-Luchon, *France* 20 F4
Bagni di Lucca, *Italy* 40 D7
Bagno di Romagna, *Italy* 41 E8
Bagnoles-de-l'Orne, *France* 18 D6
Bagnols-sur-Cèze, *France* 21 D8
Bagnorégio, *Italy* 41 F9
Bago = Pegu, *Burma* 67 L20
Bagodar, *India* 69 G11
Bagrationovsk, *Russia* 9 J19
Bagrdan, *Serbia & M.* 44 B5
Baguio, *Phil.* 61 C4
Bağyurdu, *Turkey* 47 C9
Bagzane, Monts, *Niger* 83 B6
Bah, *India* 69 F8
Bahabón de Esgueva, *Spain* 36 D7
Bahadurganj, *India* 69 F12
Bahadurgarh, *India* 68 E7
Bahama, Canal Viejo de, *W. Indies* 120 B4
Bahamas ■, *N. Amer.* 121 B5
Bahār, *Iran* 73 E13
Baharampur, *India* 69 G13
Baharîya, El Wâhât al, *Egypt* 80 B2
Baharu Pandan = Pandan, *Malaysia* 65 d
Bahawalnagar, *Pakistan* 68 E5
Bahawalpur, *Pakistan* 68 E4
Bahçe, *Turkey* 72 D7
Bahçecik, *Turkey* 45 F13
Baheri, *India* 69 E8
Bahgul →, *India* 69 F8
Bahi, *Tanzania* 86 D4
Bahi Swamp, *Tanzania* 86 D4
Bahía = Salvador, *Brazil* 125 F11
Bahía □, *Brazil* 125 F10
Bahía, Is. de la, *Honduras* 120 C2
Bahía Blanca, *Argentina* 126 D3
Bahía de Caráquez, *Ecuador* 124 D2
Bahía Honda, *Cuba* 120 B3
Bahía Laura, *Argentina* 128 F3
Bahía Negra, *Paraguay* 124 H7
Bahir Dar, *Ethiopia* 81 E4
Bahmanzād, *Iran* 71 D6
Bahr el Ahmar □, *Sudan* 80 D4
Bahr el Ghazâl □, *Sudan* 81 F2
Bahr el Jabal □, *Sudan* 81 G3
Bahraich, *India* 69 F9
Bahrain ■, *Asia* 71 E6
Bahror, *India* 68 F7
Bāhū Kalāt, *Iran* 71 E9
Bai, *Mali* 82 C4
Bai Bung, Mui = Ca Mau, Mui, *Vietnam* 65 H5
Bai Duc, *Vietnam* 64 C5
Bai Thuong, *Vietnam* 64 C5
Baia de Aramă, *Romania* 28 E7
Baia Mare, *Romania* 29 C8
Baia-Sprie, *Romania* 29 C8
Baião, *Brazil* 125 D9
Baïbokoum, *Chad* 79 G9
Baicheng, *China* 57 B12
Băicoi, *Romania* 29 E10
Baidoa, *Somali Rep.* 75 G3
Baie-Comeau, *Canada* 105 C6
Baie-St-Paul, *Canada* 105 C5
Baie-Trinité, *Canada* 105 C6
Baie Verte, *Canada* 105 C8
Baignes-Ste-Radegonde, *France* 20 C3
Baigneux-les-Juifs, *France* 19 E11
Baihar, *India* 69 H9
Baihe, *China* 56 H6
Baijnath, *India* 69 E8
Baikal, L. = Baykal, Oz., *Russia* 53 D11
Baikunthpur, *India* 69 H10
Baile Atha Cliath = Dublin, *Ireland* 12 C5
Băile Govora, *Romania* 29 E9
Băile Herculane, *Romania* 28 F7
Băile Olăneşti, *Romania* 29 E9
Băile Tuşnad, *Romania* 29 D10
Bailén, *Spain* 37 G7
Băileşti, *Romania* 29 F8
Baima, *China* 58 A3
Bain-de-Bretagne, *France* 18 E5
Bainbridge, *Ga., U.S.A.* 115 K3
Bainbridge, *N.Y., U.S.A.* 117 D9
Baing, *Indonesia* 63 F6
Bainiu, *China* 56 H7
Baiona, *Spain* 36 C2
Bā'ir, *Jordan* 74 E5
Bairiki = Tarawa, *Kiribati* 96 G9
Bairin Youqi, *China* 57 C10
Bairin Zuoqi, *China* 57 C10
Bairnsdale, *Australia* 95 F4
Bais, *Phil.* 61 G5
Baisha, *China* 56 G7
Baissa, *Nigeria* 83 D7
Baitadi, *Nepal* 69 E9
Baixa Limia-Sierra do Xurés ⌓, *Spain* 36 D2
Baiyin, *China* 56 F3
Baiyü, *China* 58 B2
Baiyu Shan, *China* 56 F4
Baiyuda, *Sudan* 80 D3
Baj Baj, *India* 69 H13
Baja, *Hungary* 28 D3
Baja, Pta., *Mexico* 118 B1
Baja California, *Mexico* 118 A1
Baja California □, *Mexico* 118 B2
Baja California Sur □, *Mexico* 118 B2
Bajag, *India* 69 H9
Bajamar, *Canary Is.* 48 F3
Bajana, *India* 68 H4
Bajatrejo, *Indonesia* 63 J17
Bajera, *Indonesia* 63 J18
Bājgīrān, *Iran* 71 B8
Bajimba, Mt., *Australia* 95 D5
Bajina Bašta, *Serbia & M.* 44 C3
Bajmok, *Serbia & M.* 28 E4
Bajo Nuevo, *Caribbean* 120 C4
Bajoga, *Nigeria* 83 C7
Bajool, *Australia* 94 C5
Bak, *Hungary* 28 D1
Bakar, *Croatia* 41 C11
Bakasi Pen., *Cameroon* 83 E6
Bakel, *Senegal* 82 C2
Baker, *Calif., U.S.A.* 111 K10
Baker, *Mont., U.S.A.* 112 B2
Baker, L., *Canada* 100 B10
Baker, Mt., *U.S.A.* 108 B3
Baker City, *U.S.A.* 108 D5
Baker I., *Pac. Oc.* 96 G10
Baker I., *U.S.A.* 102 B2
Baker L., *Australia* 93 E4
Baker Lake, *Canada* 100 B10
Bakers Creek, *Australia* 94 C4
Bakers Dozen Is., *Canada* 104 A4
Bakersfield, *Calif., U.S.A.* 111 K8
Bakersfield, *Vt., U.S.A.* 117 B12
Bakhchysaray, *Ukraine* 33 K7
Bakhmach, *Ukraine* 33 G7
Bākhtarān, *Iran* 70 C5
Bākhtarān □, *Iran* 70 C5
Bakı, *Azerbaijan* 35 K9
Bakır →, *Turkey* 47 C9
Bakırdaği, *Turkey* 72 C6
Bakkafjörður, *Iceland* 8 C6
Baklan, *Turkey* 47 C11
Bako, *Ethiopia* 81 F4
Bako, *Ivory C.* 82 D3
Bakony, *Hungary* 28 C2
Bakony Forest = Bakony, *Hungary* 28 C2
Bakori, *Nigeria* 83 C6
Bakouma, *C.A.R.* 84 C4
Baksan, *Russia* 35 J6
Bakswaho, *India* 69 G8
Baku = Bakı, *Azerbaijan* 35 K9
Bakundi, *Nigeria* 83 D7
Bakutis Coast, *Antarctica* 5 D15
Baky = Bakı, *Azerbaijan* 35 K9
Bala, *Canada* 116 A5
Bala, *Senegal* 82 C2
Bâlâ, *Turkey* 72 C5
Bala, *U.K.* 14 E4
Bala, L., *U.K.* 14 E4
Balabac I., *Phil.* 62 C5
Balabac Str., *E. Indies* 62 C5
Balabagh, *Afghan.* 68 B4
Ba'labakk, *Lebanon* 74 B5
Balabalangan, Kepulauan, *Indonesia* 62 E5
Bălăciţa, *Romania* 29 F8
Balad, *Iraq* 70 C5
Balad Rūz, *Iraq* 70 C5
Bālādeh, *Fārs, Iran* 71 D6
Bālādeh, *Māzandaran, Iran* 71 B6
Balaghat, *India* 66 J12
Balaghat Ra., *India* 66 K10
Balaguer, *Spain* 38 D5
Balakhna, *Russia* 34 B6
Balaklava, *Ukraine* 33 K7
Balakliya, *Ukraine* 33 H9
Balakovo, *Russia* 34 D8
Balamau, *India* 69 F9
Bălan, *Romania* 29 D10
Balancán, *Mexico* 119 D6
Balanivka, *Ukraine* 29 B14
Balashov, *Russia* 34 E6
Balasinor, *India* 68 H5
Balasore = Baleshwar, *India* 67 J15
Balassagyarmat, *Hungary* 28 B4
Balât, *Egypt* 80 B2
Balaton, *Hungary* 28 D2
Balaton-Felvidéki △, *Hungary* 28 D2
Balatonboglár, *Hungary* 28 D2
Balatonfüred, *Hungary* 28 D2
Balatonszentgyörgy, *Hungary* 28 D2
Balayan, *Phil.* 61 E4
Balazote, *Spain* 39 G2
Balbieriškis, *Lithuania* 30 D10
Balbigny, *France* 21 C8
Balbina, Reprêsa de, *Brazil* 124 D7
Balboa, *Panama* 120 E4
Balbriggan, *Ireland* 12 C5
Balcarce, *Argentina* 126 D4
Balcarres, *Canada* 103 C8
Bălceşti, *Romania* 29 F8
Balchik, *Bulgaria* 45 C12
Balclutha, *N.Z.* 91 M2
Balcones Escarpment, *U.S.A.* 113 L5
Balçova, *Turkey* 47 C9
Bald Hd., *Australia* 93 G2
Bald I., *Australia* 93 F2
Bald Knob, *U.S.A.* 113 H9
Baldock L., *Canada* 103 B9
Baldwin, *Mich., U.S.A.* 114 D3
Baldwin, *Pa., U.S.A.* 116 F5
Baldwinsville, *U.S.A.* 117 C8
Baldy Mt., *U.S.A.* 108 B9
Baldy Peak, *U.S.A.* 109 K9
Bale, *Croatia* 41 C10
Bale, *Ethiopia* 81 F5
Bale, *Ethiopia* 81 F5
Bale Mts. △, *Ethiopia* 81 F4
Baleares, Is., *Spain* 48 B10
Balearic Is. = Baleares, Is., *Spain* 48 B10
Baleine = Whale →, *Canada* 105 A6
Baleine, Petite R. de la →, *Canada* 104 A4
Băleni, *Romania* 29 E12
Baler, *Phil.* 61 D4
Baler Bay, *Phil.* 61 D4
Baleshare, *U.K.* 13 D1
Baleshwar, *India* 67 J15
Balezino, *Russia* 34 B11
Balfate, *Honduras* 120 C2
Balí, *Cameroon* 83 D7
Balí, *Greece* 49 D6
Bali, *India* 68 G5
Bali, *Indonesia* 63 J18
Bali □, *Indonesia* 63 J18
Bali, Selat, *Indonesia* 63 J17
Bali Sea, *Indonesia* 63 J17
Balia, *S. Leone* 82 D2
Baliapal, *India* 69 J12
Baligród, *Poland* 31 J9
Balik Pulau, *Malaysia* 65 c
Balıkeşir, *Turkey* 47 B9
Balıkeşir □, *Turkey* 47 B9
Balıklıçeşme, *Turkey* 45 F11
Balikpapan, *Indonesia* 62 E5
Balimbing, *Phil.* 63 C5
Baling, *Malaysia* 65 K3
Balingen, *Germany* 25 G4
Balinţ, *Romania* 28 E6
Balintang Channel, *Phil.* 61 B4
Balipara, *India* 67 F18
Balkan Mts. = Stara Planina, *Bulgaria* 44 C7
Balkhash = Balqash, *Kazakhstan* 52 E8
Balkhash, Ozero = Balqash Köl, *Kazakhstan* 52 E8
Balla, *Bangla.* 67 G17
Ballachulish, *U.K.* 13 E3
Balladonia, *Australia* 93 F3
Ballaghaderreen, *Ireland* 12 C3
Ballarat, *Australia* 95 F3
Ballard, L., *Australia* 93 E3
Ballater, *U.K.* 13 D5
Ballé, *Mali* 82 B3
Ballena Gris = Ojo de Liebre ⌓, *Mexico* 118 B2
Ballenas, Canal de, *Mexico* 118 B2
Balleny Is., *Antarctica* 5 C11
Balleroy, *France* 18 C6
Ballerup, *Denmark* 11 J6
Ballı, *Turkey* 45 F11
Ballia, *India* 69 G11
Ballina, *Australia* 95 D5
Ballina, *Ireland* 12 B2
Ballinasloe, *Ireland* 12 C3
Ballinger, *U.S.A.* 113 K5
Ballinrobe, *Ireland* 12 C2
Ballinskelligs B., *Ireland* 12 E1
Ballon, *France* 18 D7
Ballons des Vosges ⌓, *France* 19 E14
Ballsh, *Albania* 44 F3
Ballston Spa, *U.S.A.* 117 D11
Ballybunion, *Ireland* 12 D2
Ballycastle, *U.K.* 12 A5
Ballyclare, *U.K.* 12 B5
Ballyhaunis, *Ireland* 12 C3
Ballymena, *U.K.* 12 B5
Ballymoney, *U.K.* 12 A5
Ballymote, *Ireland* 12 B3
Ballynahinch, *U.K.* 12 B6
Ballyquintin Pt., *U.K.* 12 B6
Ballyshannon, *Ireland* 12 B3
Balmaceda, *Chile* 128 F2
Balmaseda, *Spain* 38 B1
Balmazújváros, *Hungary* 28 C6
Balmertown, *Canada* 103 C10
Balmoral, *Australia* 95 F3
Balmorhea, *U.S.A.* 113 K3
Balochistan = Baluchistan □, *Pakistan* 66 F4
Balonne →, *Australia* 95 D4
Balotra, *India* 68 G5
Balqash, *Kazakhstan* 52 E8
Balqash Köl, *Kazakhstan* 52 E8
Balrampur, *India* 69 F10
Balranald, *Australia* 95 E3
Balş, *Romania* 29 F9
Balsas, *Mexico* 119 D5
Balsas →, *Brazil* 125 E9
Balsas →, *Mexico* 118 D4
Bålsta, *Sweden* 10 E11
Balston Spa, *U.S.A.* 117 D11
Balta, *Romania* 28 F7
Balta, *Ukraine* 29 B14
Baltanás, *Spain* 36 D6
Bălţi, *Moldova* 29 C12
Baltic Sea, *Europe* 9 H18
Baltîm, *Egypt* 80 H7
Baltimore, *Ireland* 12 E2
Baltimore, *Md., U.S.A.* 114 F7
Baltimore, *Ohio, U.S.A.* 116 G2
Baltit, *Pakistan* 69 A6
Baltiysk, *Russia* 9 J18
Baltrum, *Germany* 24 B3
Baluchistan □, *Pakistan* 66 F4
Balurghat, *India* 69 G13
Balvi, *Latvia* 9 H22
Balya, *Turkey* 47 B9
Bam, *Iran* 71 D8
Bama, *China* 58 E6
Bama, *Nigeria* 83 C7
Bamaga, *Australia* 94 A3
Bamaji L., *Canada* 104 B1
Bamako, *Mali* 82 C3
Bamba, *Mali* 83 B4
Bambara Maoundé, *Mali* 82 B4
Bambari, *C.A.R.* 84 C4
Bambaroo, *Australia* 94 B4
Bambaya, *Guinea* 82 D2
Bamberg, *Germany* 25 F6
Bamberg, *U.S.A.* 115 J5
Bambesi, *Ethiopia* 81 F3
Bambey, *Senegal* 82 C1
Bambili, *Dem. Rep. of the Congo* 86 B2
Bamboi, *Ghana* 82 D4
Bamburgh, *U.K.* 14 B6
Bamenda, *Cameroon* 83 D7
Bamfield, *Canada* 102 D3
Bāmīān □, *Afghan.* 66 B5
Bamiancheng, *China* 57 C13
Bamkin, *Cameroon* 83 D7
Bampūr, *Iran* 71 E9
Ban, *Burkina Faso* 82 C4
Ban Ao Tu Khun, *Thailand* 65 a
Ban Ban, *Laos* 64 C4
Ban Bang Hin, *Thailand* 65 H2
Ban Bang Khu, *Thailand* 65 a
Ban Bang Rong, *Thailand* 65 a
Ban Bo Phut, *Thailand* 65 b
Ban Chaweng, *Thailand* 65 b
Ban Chiang Klang, *Thailand* 64 C3
Ban Chik, *Laos* 64 D4
Ban Choho, *Thailand* 64 E4
Ban Dan Lan Hoi, *Thailand* 64 D2
Ban Don = Surat Thani, *Thailand* 65 H2
Ban Don, *Vietnam* 64 F6
Ban Don, Ao →, *Thailand* 65 H2
Ban Dong, *Thailand* 64 C3
Ban Hong, *Thailand* 64 C2
Ban Hua Thanon, *Thailand* 65 b
Ban Kaeng, *Thailand* 64 D3
Ban Kantang, *Thailand* 65 J2
Ban Karon, *Thailand* 65 a
Ban Kata, *Thailand* 65 a
Ban Keun, *Laos* 64 C4
Ban Khai, *Thailand* 64 F3
Ban Kheun, *Laos* 64 B3
Ban Khlong Khian, *Thailand* 65 a
Ban Khlong Kua, *Thailand* 65 J3
Ban Khuan, *Thailand* 65 a
Ban Khuan Mao, *Thailand* 65 J2
Ban Ko Yai Chim, *Thailand* 65 G2
Ban Kok, *Thailand* 64 D4
Ban Laem, *Thailand* 64 F2
Ban Lamai, *Thailand* 65 b
Ban Lao Ngam, *Laos* 64 E6
Ban Le Kathe, *Thailand* 64 E2
Ban Lo Po Noi, *Thailand* 65 a
Ban Mae Chedi, *Thailand* 64 C2
Ban Mae Laeng, *Thailand* 64 B2
Ban Mae Nam, *Thailand* 65 b
Ban Mae Sariang, *Thailand* 64 C1
Ban Mê Thuôt = Buon Ma Thuot, *Vietnam* 64 F7
Ban Mi, *Thailand* 64 E3
Ban Muong Mo, *Laos* 64 C4
Ban Na Bo, *Thailand* 65 b
Ban Na Mo, *Laos* 64 D5
Ban Na San, *Thailand* 65 H2
Ban Na Tong, *Laos* 64 B3
Ban Nam Bac, *Laos* 64 B4
Ban Nam Ma, *Laos* 64 A3
Ban Ngang, *Laos* 64 E6
Ban Nong Bok, *Laos* 64 D5
Ban Nong Boua, *Laos* 64 E6
Ban Nong Pling, *Thailand* 64 E3
Ban Pak Chan, *Thailand* 65 G2
Ban Patong, *Thailand* 65 a
Ban Phai, *Thailand* 64 D4
Ban Phak Chit, *Thailand* 65 a
Ban Pong, *Thailand* 64 F2
Ban Rawai, *Thailand* 65 a

Ban Ron Phibun, *Thailand* 65 H2
Ban Sakhu, *Thailand* 65 a
Ban Sanam Chai, *Thailand* 65 J3
Ban Sangkha, *Thailand* 64 E4
Ban Tak, *Thailand* 64 D2
Ban Tako, *Thailand* 64 E4
Ban Tha Dua, *Thailand* 64 D2
Ban Tha Li, *Thailand* 64 D3
Ban Tha Nun, *Thailand* 65 a
Ban Tha Rua, *Thailand* 65 a
Ban Tha Yu, *Thailand* 65 a
Ban Thahine, *Laos* 64 E5
Ban Thong Krut, *Thailand* 65 b
Ban Xien Kok, *Laos* 64 B3
Ban Yen Nhan, *Vietnam* 64 B6
Banaba, *Kiribati* 96 H8
Banalia, *Dem. Rep. of the Congo* 86 B2
Banam, *Cambodia* 65 G5
Banamba, *Mali* 82 C3
Banana Is., *S. Leone* 82 D2
Bananal, I. do, *Brazil* 125 F8
Banaras = Varanasi, *India* 69 G10
Banas →, *Gujarat, India* 68 H4
Banas →, *Mad. P., India* 69 G9
Bânâs, Ras, *Egypt* 80 C4
Banaz, *Turkey* 47 C11
Banaz →, *Turkey* 47 C11
Banbridge, *U.K.* 12 B5
Banbury, *U.K.* 15 E6
Banchory, *U.K.* 13 D6
Banco, *Ethiopia* 81 F4
Bancroft, *Canada* 116 A7
Band, *Romania* 29 D9
Band Bonī, *Iran* 71 E8
Band Qīr, *Iran* 71 D6
Banda, *Mad. P., India* 69 G8
Banda, *Ut. P., India* 69 G9
Banda, Kepulauan, *Indonesia* 63 E7
Banda Aceh, *Indonesia* 62 C1
Banda Banda, Mt., *Australia* 95 E5
Banda Elat, *Indonesia* 63 F8
Banda Is. = Banda, Kepulauan, *Indonesia* 63 E7
Banda Sea, *Indonesia* 63 F7
Bandai-Asahi △, *Japan* 54 F10
Bandai-San, *Japan* 54 F10
Bandama →, *Ivory C.* 82 D3
Bandama Blanc →, *Ivory C.* 82 D3
Bandama Rouge →, *Ivory C.* 82 D4
Bandān, *Iran* 71 D9
Bandanaira, *Indonesia* 63 E7
Bandanwara, *India* 68 F6
Bandar = Machilipatnam, *India* 67 L12
Bandar-e Abbās, *Iran* 71 E8
Bandar-e Anzalī, *Iran* 71 B6
Bandar-e Bushehr = Būshehr, *Iran* 71 D6
Bandar-e Chārak, *Iran* 71 E7
Bandar-e Deylam, *Iran* 71 D6
Bandar-e Emām Khomeynı, *Iran* 71 D6
Bandar-e Lengeh, *Iran* 71 E7
Bandar-e Maqām, *Iran* 71 E7
Bandar-e Ma'shur, *Iran* 71 D6
Bandar-e Rīg, *Iran* 71 D6
Bandar-e Torkeman, *Iran* 71 B7
Bandar Lampung = Tanjungkarang Telukbetung, *Indonesia* 62 F3
Bandar Maharani = Muar, *Malaysia* 65 L4
Bandar Penggaram = Batu Pahat, *Malaysia* 65 M4
Bandar Seri Begawan, *Brunei* 62 C4
Bandar Sri Aman, *Malaysia* 62 D4
Bandawe, *Malawi* 87 E3
Bande, *Spain* 36 C3
Bandeira, Pico da, *Brazil* 127 A7
Bandera, *Argentina* 126 B3
Banderas, B. de, *Mexico* 118 C3
Bandhogarh, *India* 69 H9
Bandi →, *India* 68 F6
Bandiagara, *Mali* 82 C4
Bandikui, *India* 68 F7
Bandırma, *Turkey* 45 F11
Bandjarmasin = Banjarmasin, *Indonesia* 62 E4
Bandol, *France* 21 E9
Bandon, *Ireland* 12 E3
Bandon →, *Ireland* 12 E3
Bandula, *Mozam.* 87 F3
Bandundu, *Dem. Rep. of the Congo* 84 E3
Bandung, *Indonesia* 63 G12
Bané, *Burkina Faso* 83 C4
Băneasa, *Romania* 29 E12
Bāneh, *Iran* 70 C5
Bañeres, *Spain* 39 G4
Banes, *Cuba* 121 B4
Banff, *Canada* 102 C5
Banff, *U.K.* 13 D6
Banff △, *Canada* 102 C5
Banfora, *Burkina Faso* 82 C4
Bang Fai →, *Laos* 64 D5
Bang Hieng →, *Laos* 64 D5
Bang Krathum, *Thailand* 64 D3
Bang Lamung, *Thailand* 64 F3
Bang Mun Nak, *Thailand* 64 D3
Bang Pa In, *Thailand* 64 E3
Bang Rakam, *Thailand* 64 D3
Bang Saphan, *Thailand* 65 G2
Bang Thao, *Thailand* 65 a
Bangaduni I., *India* 69 J13
Bangala Dam, *Zimbabwe* 87 G3
Bangalore, *India* 66 N10
Banganga →, *India* 68 F6
Bangangté, *Cameroon* 83 D7
Bangaon, *India* 69 H13
Bangassou, *C.A.R.* 84 D4
Banggai, *Indonesia* 63 E6
Banggai, Kepulauan, *Indonesia* 63 E6
Banggai Arch. = Banggai, Kepulauan, *Indonesia* 63 E6
Banggi, *Malaysia* 62 C5
Banghāzī, *Libya* 79 B10
Bangjang, *Sudan* 81 E3
Bangka, *Sulawesi, Indonesia* 63 D7
Bangka, *Sumatera, Indonesia* 62 E3
Bangka, Selat, *Indonesia* 62 E3
Bangka-Belitung □, *Indonesia* 62 E3
Bangkalan, *Indonesia* 63 G15
Bangkinang, *Indonesia* 62 D2
Bangko, *Indonesia* 62 E2
Bangkok, *Thailand* 64 F3
Bangladesh ■, *Asia* 67 H17
Bangli, *Indonesia* 63 J18
Bangolo, *Ivory C.* 82 D3
Bangong Co, *India* 69 B8
Bangor, *Down, U.K.* 12 B6
Bangor, *Gwynedd, U.K.* 14 D3
Bangor, *Maine, U.S.A.* 101 D13
Bangor, *Pa., U.S.A.* 117 F9
Bangued, *Phil.* 61 C4
Bangui, *C.A.R.* 84 D3
Bangui, *Phil.* 61 B4
Banguru, *Dem. Rep. of the Congo* 86 B2
Bangweulu, L., *Zambia* 87 E3
Bangweulu Swamp, *Zambia* 87 E3
Banhine △, *Mozam.* 89 C5
Baní, *Dom. Rep.* 121 C5
Bani →, *Mali* 82 C4
Bani Bangou, *Niger* 83 B5
Banī Sa'd, *Iraq* 70 C5
Bania, *Ivory C.* 82 D4
Banihal Pass, *India* 69 C6
Banikoara, *Benin* 83 C5
Bāniyās, *Syria* 70 C3
Banja Luka, *Bos.-H.* 28 F2
Banjar, *India* 68 D7
Banjar →, *India* 69 H9
Banjarmasin, *Indonesia* 62 E4
Banjul, *Gambia* 82 C1
Banka, *India* 69 G12
Bankas, *Mali* 82 C4
Bankeryd, *Sweden* 11 G8
Banket, *Zimbabwe* 87 F3
Bankilaré, *Niger* 83 C5
Bankipore, *India* 67 G14
Banks I., *B.C., Canada* 102 C3
Banks I., *N.W.T., Canada* 100 A7
Banks Pen., *N.Z.* 91 K4
Banks Str., *Australia* 95 G4
Bankura, *India* 69 H12
Bankya, *Bulgaria* 44 D7
Banmankhi, *India* 69 G12
Bann →, *Arm., U.K.* 12 B5
Bann →, *L'derry., U.K.* 12 A5
Bannalec, *France* 18 E3
Bannang Sata, *Thailand* 65 J3
Banning, *U.S.A.* 111 M10
Banno, *Ethiopia* 81 G4
Bannockburn, *Canada* 116 B7
Bannockburn, *U.K.* 13 E5
Bannockburn, *Zimbabwe* 87 G2
Bannu, *Pakistan* 66 C7
Bano, *India* 69 H11
Bañolas = Banyoles, *Spain* 38 C7
Banon, *France* 21 D9
Baños de la Encina, *Spain* 37 G7
Baños de Molgas, *Spain* 36 C3
Bánovce nad Bebravou, *Slovak Rep.* 27 C11
Banovići, *Bos.-H.* 28 F3
Bansgaon, *India* 69 F10
Banská Bystrica, *Slovak Rep.* 27 C12
Banská Štiavnica, *Slovak Rep.* 27 C11
Bansko, *Bulgaria* 44 E7
Banskobystrický □, *Slovak Rep.* 27 C12
Banswara, *India* 68 H6
Bantaeng, *Indonesia* 63 F5
Bantaji, *Nigeria* 83 D7
Bantayan, *Phil.* 61 F5
Banten □, *Indonesia* 63 G11
Bantry, *Ireland* 12 E2
Bantry B., *Ireland* 12 E2
Bantul, *Indonesia* 63 G14
Bantva, *India* 68 J4
Banya, *Bulgaria* 45 D8
Banyak, Kepulauan, *Indonesia* 62 D1
Banyalbufar, *Spain* 48 B9
Banyo, *Cameroon* 83 D7
Banyoles, *Spain* 38 C7
Banyuls-sur-Mer, *France* 20 F7
Banyumas, *Indonesia* 63 G13
Banyuwangi, *Indonesia* 63 J17
Banzare Coast, *Antarctica* 5 C9
Bao Ha, *Vietnam* 58 F5
Bao Lac, *Vietnam* 64 A5
Bao Loc, *Vietnam* 65 G6
Bao'an = Shenzhen, *China* 59 F10
Baocheng, *China* 56 H4
Baode, *China* 56 E6
Baodi, *China* 57 E9
Baoding, *China* 56 E8
Baoji, *China* 56 G4
Baojing, *China* 58 C7
Baokang, *China* 59 B8
Baoshan, *Shanghai, China* 59 B13
Baoshan, *Yunnan, China* 58 E2
Baotou, *China* 56 D6
Baoxing, *China* 58 B4
Baoying, *China* 57 H10
Bap, *India* 68 F5
Bapatla, *India* 67 M12
Bapaume, *France* 19 B9
Bāqerābād, *Iran* 71 C6
Ba'qūbah, *Iraq* 70 C5
Baquedano, *Chile* 126 A2
Bar, *Serbia & M.* 44 D3
Bar, *Ukraine* 33 H4
Bar Bigha, *India* 69 G11
Bar Harbor, *U.S.A.* 115 C11
Bar-le-Duc, *France* 19 D12
Bar-sur-Aube, *France* 19 D11
Bar-sur-Seine, *France* 19 D11
Bara, *India* 69 G9
Băra, *Romania* 29 C12
Bara Banki, *India* 69 F9
Barabai, *Indonesia* 62 E5
Baraboo, *U.S.A.* 112 D10
Baracoa, *Cuba* 121 B5
Baradā →, *Syria* 74 B5
Baradero, *Argentina* 126 C4
Baraga, *U.S.A.* 112 B10
Bărăganul, *Romania* 29 F12
Barah →, *India* 68 F6
Barahona, *Dom. Rep.* 121 C5
Barahona, *Spain* 38 D2
Barail Range, *India* 67 G18
Barajas, Madrid ✕ (MAD), *Spain* 36 E7
Baraka, *Sudan* 81 E2
Baraka →, *Sudan* 80 D4
Barakaldo, *Spain* 38 B2
Barakar →, *India* 69 G12
Barakhola, *India* 67 G18
Barakot, *India* 69 J11
Barakpur, *India* 69 H13
Baralaba, *Australia* 94 C4
Baralla, *Spain* 36 C3
Baralzon L., *Canada* 103 B9
Barameiya, *Sudan* 80 D4
Baramula, *India* 69 B6
Baran, *India* 68 G7
Baran →, *Pakistan* 68 G3
Barañain, *Spain* 38 C3
Baranavichy, *Belarus* 33 F4
Barani, *Burkina Faso* 82 C4
Baranof, *U.S.A.* 102 B2
Baranof I., *U.S.A.* 100 C6
Baranów Sandomierski, *Poland* 31 H8
Baranya □, *Hungary* 28 E3
Baraolt, *Romania* 29 D10
Barapasi, *Indonesia* 63 E9
Barasat, *India* 69 H13
Barat Daya, Kepulauan, *Indonesia* 63 F7
Barataria B., *U.S.A.* 113 L10
Barauda, *India* 68 H6
Baraut, *India* 68 E7
Barbacena, *Brazil* 127 A7
Barbados ■, *W. Indies* 121 g
Barban, *Croatia* 41 C11
Barbària, C. de, *Spain* 48 C7
Barbaros, *Turkey* 45 F11
Barbastro, *Spain* 38 C5
Barbate de Franco, *Spain* 37 J5
Barberino di Mugello, *Italy* 41 E8
Barberton, *S. Africa* 89 D5
Barberton, *U.S.A.* 116 E3
Barbezieux-St-Hilaire, *France* 20 C3
Barbosa, *Colombia* 124 B4
Barbourville, *U.S.A.* 115 G4
Barbuda, *W. Indies* 121 C7
Bârca, *Romania* 29 G8
Barcaldine, *Australia* 94 C4
Barcarrota, *Spain* 37 G4
Barcellona Pozzo di Gotto, *Italy* 43 D8
Barcelona, *Spain* 38 D7
Barcelona, *Venezuela* 124 A6
Barcelona □, *Spain* 38 D7
Barcelona ✕ (BCN), *Spain* 38 D7
Barceloneta, *Puerto Rico* 121 d
Barcelonette, *France* 21 D10
Barcelos, *Brazil* 124 D6
Barcin, *Poland* 31 F4
Barclayville, *Liberia* 82 E3
Barcoo →, *Australia* 94 D3
Barcs, *Hungary* 28 E2
Barczewo, *Poland* 30 E7
Bärdä, *Azerbaijan* 35 K8
Bardaï, *Chad* 79 D9
Bardas Blancas, *Argentina* 126 D2
Bardawîl, Sabkhet el, *Egypt* 74 D2
Barddhaman, *India* 69 H12
Bardejov, *Slovak Rep.* 27 B14
Bardera, *Somali Rep.* 75 G3
Bardi, *Italy* 40 D6
Bardīyah, *Libya* 79 B10
Bardolino, *Italy* 40 C7
Bardonécchia, *Italy* 40 C3
Bardsey I., *U.K.* 14 E3
Bardstown, *U.S.A.* 114 G3
Bareilly, *India* 69 E8
Barela, *India* 69 H9
Barentin, *France* 18 C7
Barenton, *France* 18 D6
Barents Sea, *Arctic* 50 B7
Barentu, *Eritrea* 81 D4
Barfleur, *France* 18 C5
Barfleur, Pte. de, *France* 18 C5
Barga, *Italy* 40 D7
Bargara, *Australia* 94 C5
Bargas, *Spain* 36 F6
Bârgăului Bistriţa, *Romania* 29 C9
Barge, *Italy* 40 D4
Bargnop, *Sudan* 81 F2
Bargteheide, *Germany* 24 B6
Barguzin, *Russia* 53 D11
Barh, *India* 69 G11
Barhaj, *India* 69 F10
Barharwa, *India* 69 G12
Barhi, *India* 69 G11
Bari, *India* 68 F7
Bari, *Italy* 43 A9
Bari Doab, *Pakistan* 68 D5
Bari Sadri, *India* 68 G6
Bari Sardo, *Italy* 42 C2
Barīdī, Ra's, *Si. Arabia* 70 E3
Barīm, *Yemen* 76 E8
Barinas, *Venezuela* 124 B4
Baring, C., *Canada* 100 B8
Baringo, L., *Kenya* 86 B4
Bârîs, *Egypt* 80 C3
Barisal, *Bangla.* 67 H17
Barisal □, *Bangla.* 67 H17
Barisan, Bukit, *Indonesia* 62 E2
Barito →, *Indonesia* 62 E4
Baritú △, *Argentina* 126 A3
Barjac, *France* 21 D8
Barjols, *France* 21 E10
Bark L., *Canada* 116 A7
Barka = Baraka →, *Sudan* 80 D4
Barkakana, *India* 69 H11
Barkam, *China* 58 B4
Barker, *U.S.A.* 116 C6
Barkley, L., *U.S.A.* 115 G2
Barkley Sound, *Canada* 102 D3
Barkly East, *S. Africa* 88 E4
Barkly Roadhouse, *Australia* 94 B2
Barkly Tableland, *Australia* 94 B2
Barkly West, *S. Africa* 88 D3
Barkol, Wadi →, *Sudan* 80 D3
Barla Dağı, *Turkey* 47 C12
Bârlad, *Romania* 29 D12
Bârlad →, *Romania* 29 E12
Barlee, L., *Australia* 93 E2
Barlee, Mt., *Australia* 93 D4
Barletta, *Italy* 43 A9
Barlinek, *Poland* 31 F2
Barlovento, *Canary Is.* 48 F2
Barlow L., *Canada* 103 A8
Barmedman, *Australia* 95 E4
Barmer, *India* 68 G4
Barmera, *Australia* 95 E3
Barmouth, *U.K.* 14 E3
Barmstedt, *Germany* 24 B5
Barna →, *India* 69 G10
Barnagar, *India* 68 H6
Barnala, *India* 68 D6
Barnard Castle, *U.K.* 14 C6
Barnaul, *Russia* 52 D9
Barnesville, *U.S.A.* 115 J3
Barnet □, *U.K.* 15 F7
Barneveld, *Neths.* 17 B5
Barneveld, *U.S.A.* 117 C9
Barneville-Cartevert, *France* 18 C5
Barnhart, *U.S.A.* 113 K4
Barnsley, *U.K.* 14 D6
Barnstaple, *U.K.* 15 F3
Barnstaple Bay = Bideford Bay, *U.K.* 15 F3
Barnsville, *U.S.A.* 112 B6
Barnwell, *U.S.A.* 115 J5
Baro, *Nigeria* 83 D6
Baro →, *Ethiopia* 81 F3
Baroda = Vadodara, *India* 68 H5
Baroda, *India* 68 G7
Baroe, *S. Africa* 88 E3
Baron Ra., *Australia* 92 D4
Barong, *China* 58 B2
Barotseland, *Zambia* 85 H4
Barouéli, *Mali* 82 C3
Barpeta, *India* 67 F17
Barques, Pt. Aux, *U.S.A.* 116 B2
Barquísimeto, *Venezuela* 124 A5
Barr, Ras el, *Egypt* 80 H7
Barr Smith Range, *Australia* 93 E3
Barra, *Brazil* 125 F10
Barra, *U.K.* 13 E1
Barra, Sd. of, *U.K.* 13 D1
Barra de Navidad, *Mexico* 118 D4
Barra do Corda, *Brazil* 125 E9
Barra do Piraí, *Brazil* 127 A7
Barra Falsa, Pta. da, *Mozam.* 89 C6
Barra Hd., *U.K.* 13 E1
Barra Mansa, *Brazil* 127 A7
Barraba, *Australia* 95 E5
Barrackpur = Barakpur, *India* 69 H13
Barradale Roadhouse, *Australia* 92 D1
Barrafranca, *Italy* 43 E7
Barraigh = Barra, *U.K.* 13 E1
Barranca, *Lima, Peru* 124 F3
Barranca, *Loreto, Peru* 124 D3
Barranca del Cobre ⌓, *Mexico* 118 B3
Barrancabermeja, *Colombia* 124 B4
Barrancas, *Venezuela* 124 B6
Barrancos, *Portugal* 37 G4
Barranqueras, *Argentina* 126 B4
Barranquilla, *Colombia* 124 A4
Barraute, *Canada* 104 C4
Barre, *Mass., U.S.A.* 117 D12
Barre, *Vt., U.S.A.* 117 B12
Barreal, *Argentina* 126 C2
Barreiras, *Brazil* 125 F10
Barreirinhas, *Brazil* 125 D10
Barreiro, *Portugal* 37 G1
Barrême, *France* 21 E10
Barren, Nosy, *Madag.* 89 B7
Barretos, *Brazil* 125 H9
Barrhead, *Canada* 102 C6
Barrie, *Canada* 116 B5
Barrier Ra., *Australia* 95 E3
Barrière, *Canada* 102 C4
Barrington, *U.S.A.* 117 E13
Barrington L., *Canada* 103 B8
Barrington Tops, *Australia* 95 E5
Barringun, *Australia* 95 D4
Barro do Garças, *Brazil* 125 G8
Barron, *U.S.A.* 112 C9
Barrow, *U.S.A.* 100 A4
Barrow →, *Ireland* 12 D5
Barrow Creek, *Australia* 94 C1
Barrow I., *Australia* 92 D2
Barrow-in-Furness, *U.K.* 14 C4
Barrow Pt., *Australia* 94 A3
Barrow Pt., *U.S.A.* 98 B4
Barrow Ra., *Australia* 93 E4
Barrow Str., *Canada* 4 B3
Barruecopardo, *Spain* 36 D4
Barruelo de Santullán, *Spain* 36 C6
Barry, *U.K.* 15 F4
Barry's Bay, *Canada* 116 A7
Barsalogho, *Burkina Faso* 83 C4
Barsat, *Pakistan* 69 A5
Barsham, *Syria* 70 C4
Barsi, *India* 66 K9
Barsinghausen, *Germany* 24 C5
Barsoi, *India* 67 G15
Barstow, *U.S.A.* 111 L9
Barth, *Germany* 24 A8
Barthélemy, Col, *Vietnam* 64 C5
Bartica, *Guyana* 124 B7
Bartin, *Turkey* 72 B5
Bartle Frere, *Australia* 94 B4
Bartlesville, *U.S.A.* 113 G7
Bartlett, *U.S.A.* 110 J8
Bartlett, L., *Canada* 102 A5
Bartolomeu Dias, *Mozam.* 87 G4
Barton, *U.S.A.* 117 B12
Barton upon Humber, *U.K.* 14 D7
Bartoszyce, *Poland* 30 D7
Bartow, *U.S.A.* 115 M5
Barú, Volcan, *Panama* 120 E3
Barumba, *Dem. Rep. of the Congo* 86 B1
Baruth, *Germany* 24 C9
Baruunsuu, *Mongolia* 56 C3
Barvinkove, *Ukraine* 33 H9
Barwani, *India* 68 H6
Barwice, *Poland* 30 E3
Barycz →, *Poland* 31 G3
Barysaw, *Belarus* 32 E5
Barysh, *Russia* 34 D8
Barzān, *Iraq* 70 B5
Bârzava, *Romania* 28 D6
Bas-Rhin □, *France* 19 D14
Bašaid, *Serbia & M.* 28 E5
Bāsa'idū, *Iran* 71 E7
Basal, *Pakistan* 68 C5
Basankusa, *Dem. Rep. of the Congo* 84 D3
Basarabeasca, *Moldova* 29 D13
Basarabi, *Romania* 29 F13
Basarabia = Bessarabiya, *Moldova* 33 J5
Basauri, *Spain* 38 B2
Basawa, *Afghan.* 68 B4
Bascuñán, C., *Chile* 126 B1
Basel, *Switz.* 25 H3
Basel, Euroairport ✕ (BSL), *Europe* 19 E14
Basel-Landschaft □, *Switz.* 25 H3
Basento →, *Italy* 43 B9
Bashākerd, Kūhhā-ye, *Iran* 71 E8
Bashaw, *Canada* 102 C6
Bāshī, *Iran* 71 D6
Bashkir Republic = Bashkortostan □, *Russia* 52 D6
Bashkortostan □, *Russia* 52 D6
Bashtanivka, *Ukraine* 29 E14
Basibasy, *Madag.* 89 C7
Basilan I., *Phil.* 61 H5
Basilan Str., *Phil.* 61 H5
Basildon, *U.K.* 15 F8
Basile, *Eq. Guin.* 83 E6
Basilicata □, *Italy* 43 B9
Basim = Washim, *India* 66 J10
Basin, *U.S.A.* 108 D9
Basingstoke, *U.K.* 15 F6
Baška, *Croatia* 41 D11
Başkale, *Turkey* 73 C10
Baskatong, Rés., *Canada* 104 C4
Basle = Basel, *Switz.* 25 H3
Başmakçı, *Turkey* 47 D12
Basoda, *India* 68 H7
Basoko, *Dem. Rep. of the Congo* 86 B1
Basque, Pays, *France* 20 E2
Basque Provinces = País Vasco □, *Spain* 38 C2
Basra = Al Başrah, *Iraq* 70 D5
Bass Str., *Australia* 95 F4
Bassano, *Canada* 102 C6
Bassano del Grappa, *Italy* 41 C8
Bassar, *Togo* 83 D5
Bassas da India, *Ind. Oc.* 85 J7
Basse-Normandie □, *France* 18 D6
Basse-Pointe, *Martinique* 120 c
Basse Santa-Su, *Gambia* 82 C2
Basse-Terre, *Guadeloupe* 120 b
Basse Terre, *Trin. & Tob.* 125 K15
Bassein, *Burma* 67 L19
Basses, Pte. des, *Guadeloupe* 120 b
Basseterre, *St. Kitts & Nevis* 121 C7
Bassett, *U.S.A.* 112 D5
Bassi, *India* 68 D7
Bassigny, *France* 19 E12
Bassikounou, *Mauritania* 82 B3
Bassila, *Benin* 83 D5
Bassum, *Germany* 24 C4
Båstad, *Sweden* 11 H6
Bastak, *Iran* 71 E7
Baştām, *Iran* 71 B7
Bastar, *India* 67 K12
Bastelica, *France* 21 F13
Basti, *India* 69 F10
Bastia, *France* 21 F13
Bastogne, *Belgium* 17 D5
Bastrop, *La., U.S.A.* 113 J9
Bastrop, *Tex., U.S.A.* 113 K6
Bat Yam, *Israel* 74 C3
Bata, *Eq. Guin.* 84 D1
Bata, *Romania* 28 D7
Bataan □, *Phil.* 61 D4
Batabanó, *Cuba* 120 B3
Batabanó, G. de, *Cuba* 120 B3
Batac, *Phil.* 61 B4
Batagai, *Russia* 53 C14
Batajnica, *Serbia & M.* 44 B4
Batak, *Bulgaria* 45 E8
Batala, *India* 68 D6
Batalha, *Portugal* 36 F2
Batama, *Dem. Rep. of the Congo* 86 B2
Batamay, *Russia* 53 C13
Batang, *China* 58 B2
Batang, *Indonesia* 63 G13
Batangas, *Phil.* 61 E4
Batanta, *Indonesia* 63 E8
Batatais, *Brazil* 127 A6
Batavia, *U.S.A.* 116 D6
Bataysk, *Russia* 33 J10
Batchelor, *Australia* 92 B5
Batdambang, *Cambodia* 64 F4

Batemans B., *Australia* 95 F5
Batemans Bay, *Australia* 95 F5
Bates Ra., *Australia* 93 E3
Batesburg-Leesville, *U.S.A.* 115 J5
Batesville, *Ark., U.S.A.* 113 H9
Batesville, *Miss., U.S.A.* 113 H10
Batesville, *Tex., U.S.A.* 113 L5
Bath, *Canada* 117 B8
Bath, *U.K.* 15 F5
Bath, *Maine, U.S.A.* 115 D11
Bath, *N.Y., U.S.A.* 116 D7
Bath & North East Somerset □, *U.K.* 15 F5
Batheay, *Cambodia* 65 G5
Bathsheba, *Barbados* 121 g
Bathurst, *Australia* 95 E4
Bathurst, *Canada* 105 C6
Bathurst, *S. Africa* 88 E4
Bathurst, C., *Canada* 100 A7
Bathurst B., *Australia* 94 A3
Bathurst Harb., *Australia* 95 G4
Bathurst I., *Australia* 92 B5
Bathurst I., *Canada* 98 B9
Bathurst Inlet, *Canada* 100 B9
Bati, *Ethiopia* 81 E5
Batie, *Burkina Faso* 82 D4
Batlow, *Australia* 95 F4
Batman, *Turkey* 70 B4
Baṭn al Ghūl, *Jordan* 74 F4
Batna, *Algeria* 78 A7
Batobato = San Isidro, *Phil.* 61 H7
Batočina, *Serbia & M.* 44 B5
Batoka, *Zambia* 87 F2
Baton Rouge, *U.S.A.* 113 K9
Batong, Ko, *Thailand* 65 J2
Bátonyterenye, *Hungary* 28 C4
Batopilas, *Mexico* 118 B3
Batouri, *Cameroon* 84 D2
Båtsfjord, *Norway* 8 A23
Battambang = Batdambang, *Cambodia* 64 F4
Batticaloa, *Sri Lanka* 66 R12
Battipáglia, *Italy* 43 B7
Battle, *U.K.* 15 G8
Battle →, *Canada* 103 C7
Battle Creek, *U.S.A.* 114 D3
Battle Ground, *U.S.A.* 110 E4
Battle Harbour, *Canada* 105 B8
Battle Lake, *U.S.A.* 112 B7
Battle Mountain, *U.S.A.* 108 F5
Battlefields, *Zimbabwe* 87 F2
Battleford, *Canada* 103 C7
Battonya, *Hungary* 28 D6
Batu, *Ethiopia* 81 F4
Batu, Kepulauan, *Indonesia* 62 E1
Batu Caves, *Malaysia* 65 L3
Batu Ferringhi, *Malaysia* 65 c
Batu Gajah, *Malaysia* 65 K3
Batu Is. = Batu, Kepulauan, *Indonesia* 62 E1
Batu Pahat, *Malaysia* 65 M4
Batuata, *Indonesia* 63 F6
Batugondang, Tanjung, *Indonesia* 63 J17
Batukau, Gunung, *Indonesia* 63 J18
Batumi, *Georgia* 35 K5
Batur, *Indonesia* 63 J18
Batur, Gunung, *Indonesia* 63 J18
Baturaja, *Indonesia* 62 E2
Baturité, *Brazil* 125 D11
Baturiti, *Indonesia* 63 J18
Bau, *Malaysia* 62 D4
Baubau, *Indonesia* 63 F6
Baucau, *E. Timor* 63 F7
Bauchi, *Nigeria* 83 C6
Bauchi □, *Nigeria* 83 C7
Baud, *France* 18 E3
Baudette, *U.S.A.* 112 A7
Bauer, C., *Australia* 95 E1
Bauhinia, *Australia* 94 C4
Baukau = Baucau, *E. Timor* 63 F7
Bauld, C., *Canada* 101 C14
Baume-les-Dames, *France* 19 E13
Baunatal, *Germany* 24 D5
Baunei, *Italy* 42 B2
Baure, *Nigeria* 83 C6
Bauru, *Brazil* 127 A6
Bausi, *India* 69 G12
Bauska, *Latvia* 9 H21
Bautino, *Kazakhstan* 35 H10
Bautzen, *Germany* 24 D10
Bauya, *S. Leone* 82 D2
Bavānāt, *Iran* 71 D7
Bavanište, *Serbia & M.* 28 F5
Bavaria = Bayern □, *Germany* 25 G7
Båven, *Sweden* 10 E10
Bavispe →, *Mexico* 118 B3
Bawdwin, *Burma* 67 H20
Bawean, *Indonesia* 62 F4
Bawku, *Ghana* 83 C4
Bawlake, *Burma* 67 K20
Bawolung, *China* 58 C3
Baxley, *U.S.A.* 115 K4
Baxoi, *China* 58 B1
Baxter, *U.S.A.* 112 B7
Baxter Springs, *U.S.A.* 113 G7
Baxter State ⌓, *U.S.A.* 115 B11
Bay, L. de, *Phil.* 61 D4
Bay City, *Mich., U.S.A.* 114 D4
Bay City, *Tex., U.S.A.* 113 L7
Bay Minette, *U.S.A.* 115 K2
Bay Roberts, *Canada* 105 C9
Bay St. Louis, *U.S.A.* 113 K10
Bay Springs, *U.S.A.* 113 K10
Bay View, *N.Z.* 91 H6
Baya, *Dem. Rep. of the Congo* 87 E2
Bayamo, *Cuba* 120 B4
Bayamón, *Puerto Rico* 121 d
Bayan Har Shan, *China* 60 C4
Bayan Hot = Alxa Zuoqi, *China* 56 E3
Bayan Lepas, *Malaysia* 65 c
Bayan Obo, *China* 56 D5
Bayan-Ovoo = Erdenetsogt, *Mongolia* 56 C4
Bayana, *India* 68 F7
Bayanaŭyl, *Kazakhstan* 52 D8
Bayandalay, *Mongolia* 56 C2
Bayanhongor, *Mongolia* 60 B5
Bayard, *N. Mex., U.S.A.* 109 K9
Bayard, *Nebr., U.S.A.* 112 E3
Bayawan, *Phil.* 61 G5
Baybay, *Phil.* 61 F6
Bayburt, *Turkey* 73 B9
Baydhabo = Baidoa, *Somali Rep.* 75 G3
Bayelsa □, *Nigeria* 83 E6
Bayerische Alpen, *Germany* 25 H7
Bayerische Rhön ⌓, *Germany* 25 E6
Bayerischer Spessart ⌓, *Germany* 25 F6
Bayerischer Wald, *Germany* 25 G8
Bayern □, *Germany* 25 G7
Bayeux, *France* 18 C6
Bayfield, *Canada* 116 C3
Bayfield, *U.S.A.* 112 B9
Bayındır, *Turkey* 47 C9
Bayjī, *Iraq* 70 C4
Baykal, Oz., *Russia* 53 D11
Baykan, *Turkey* 70 B4
Baykonur = Bayqongyr, *Kazakhstan* 52 E7
Baynes Mts., *Namibia* 88 B1
Bayombong, *Phil.* 61 C4
Bayon, *France* 19 D13
Bayona = Baiona, *Spain* 36 C2
Bayonne, *France* 20 E2
Bayonne, *U.S.A.* 117 F10
Bayovar, *Peru* 124 E2
Bayqongyr, *Kazakhstan* 52 E7
Bayram-Ali = Bayramaly, *Turkmenistan* 52 F7
Bayramaly, *Turkmenistan* 52 F7
Bayramiç, *Turkey* 47 B8
Bayreuth, *Germany* 25 F7
Bayrischzell, *Germany* 25 H8
Bayrūt, *Lebanon* 74 B4
Bays, L. of, *Canada* 116 A5
Baysville, *Canada* 116 A5
Bayt Lahm, *West Bank* 74 D4
Baytown, *U.S.A.* 113 L7
Bayun, *Indonesia* 63 J18
Bayzo, *Niger* 83 C5
Baza, *Spain* 37 H8
Bazar Dyuzi, *Russia* 35 K8
Bazardüzü = Bazar Dyuzi, *Russia* 35 K8
Bazarny Karabulak, *Russia* 34 D8
Bazarnyy Syzgan, *Russia* 34 D8
Bazaruto △, *Mozam.* 89 C6
Bazaruto, I. do, *Mozam.* 89 C6
Bazas, *France* 20 D3
Bazhong, *China* 58 B6
Bazhou, *China* 56 E9
Bazmān, Kūh-e, *Iran* 71 D9
Beach, *U.S.A.* 112 B3
Beach City, *U.S.A.* 116 F3
Beachport, *Australia* 95 F3
Beachy Hd., *U.K.* 15 G8
Beacon, *Australia* 93 F2
Beacon, *U.S.A.* 117 E11
Beaconsfield, *Australia* 95 G4
Beagle, Canal, *S. Amer.* 128 H3
Beagle Bay, *Australia* 92 C3
Bealanana, *Madag.* 89 A8
Beals Cr. →, *U.S.A.* 113 J4
Beamsville, *Canada* 116 C5
Bear →, *Calif., U.S.A.* 110 G5
Bear →, *Utah, U.S.A.* 106 B4
Béar, C., *France* 20 F7
Bear I., *Ireland* 12 E2
Bear L., *Canada* 103 B9
Bear L., *U.S.A.* 108 F8
Beardmore, *Canada* 104 C2
Beardmore Glacier, *Antarctica* 5 E11
Beardstown, *U.S.A.* 112 F9
Bearma →, *India* 69 G8
Béarn, *France* 20 E3
Bearpaw Mts., *U.S.A.* 108 B9
Bearskin Lake, *Canada* 104 B1
Beas →, *India* 68 D6
Beas de Segura, *Spain* 37 G8
Beasain, *Spain* 38 B2
Beata, C., *Dom. Rep.* 121 C5
Beata, I., *Dom. Rep.* 121 C5
Beatrice, *U.S.A.* 112 E6
Beatrice, *Zimbabwe* 87 F3
Beatrice, C., *Australia* 94 A2
Beatton →, *Canada* 102 B4
Beatton River, *Canada* 102 B4
Beatty, *U.S.A.* 110 J10
Beaucaire, *France* 21 E8
Beauce, Plaine de la, *France* 19 D8
Beauceville, *Canada* 105 C5
Beaudesert, *Australia* 95 D5
Beaufort, *France* 21 C10
Beaufort, *Malaysia* 62 C5
Beaufort, *N.C., U.S.A.* 115 H7
Beaufort, *S.C., U.S.A.* 115 J5
Beaufort Sea, *Arctic* 98 B5
Beaufort West, *S. Africa* 88 E3
Beaugency, *France* 19 E8
Beauharnois, *Canada* 117 A11
Beaujeu, *France* 19 F11
Beaujolais, *France* 19 F11
Beaulieu →, *Canada* 102 A6
Beaulieu-sur-Dordogne, *France* 20 D5
Beaulieu-sur-Mer, *France* 21 E11
Beauly, *U.K.* 13 D4
Beauly →, *U.K.* 13 D4
Beaumaris, *U.K.* 14 D3
Beaumont, *Belgium* 17 D4
Beaumont, *France* 20 D4
Beaumont, *U.S.A.* 113 K7
Beaumont-de-Lomagne, *France* 20 E5
Beaumont-le-Roger, *France* 18 C7
Beaumont-sur-Sarthe, *France* 18 D7
Beaune, *France* 19 E11
Beaune-la-Rolande, *France* 19 D9
Beaupré, *Canada* 105 C5
Beaupréau, *France* 18 E6
Beauraing, *Belgium* 17 D4
Beaurepaire, *France* 21 C9
Beausejour, *Canada* 103 C9
Beauvais, *France* 19 C9
Beauval, *Canada* 103 B7
Beauvoir-sur-Mer, *France* 18 F4
Beauvoir-sur-Niort, *France* 20 B3
Beaver, *Okla., U.S.A.* 113 G4
Beaver, *Pa., U.S.A.* 116 F4
Beaver, *Utah, U.S.A.* 109 G7
Beaver →, *B.C., Canada* 102 B4
Beaver →, *Ont., Canada* 104 A2
Beaver →, *Sask., Canada* 103 B7
Beaver →, *U.S.A.* 113 G5
Beaver City, *U.S.A.* 112 E5
Beaver Creek, *Canada* 100 B5
Beaver Dam, *U.S.A.* 112 D10
Beaver Falls, *U.S.A.* 116 F4
Beaver Hill L., *Canada* 103 C10
Beaver I., *U.S.A.* 114 C3
Beaverhill L., *Canada* 102 C6
Beaverlodge, *Canada* 102 B5
Beaverstone →, *Canada* 104 B2
Beaverton, *Canada* 116 B5
Beaverton, *U.S.A.* 110 E4
Beawar, *India* 68 F6
Bebedouro, *Brazil* 127 A6
Bebera, Tanjung, *Indonesia* 63 K18
Beboa, *Madag.* 89 B7
Bebra, *Germany* 24 E5
Becan, *Mexico* 119 D7
Beccles, *U.K.* 15 E9
Bečej, *Serbia & M.* 28 E5
Beceni, *Romania* 29 E11
Becerreá, *Spain* 36 C3
Béchar, *Algeria* 78 B5
Bechyně, *Czech Rep.* 26 B7
Beckley, *U.S.A.* 114 G5
Beckum, *Germany* 24 D4
Beclean, *Romania* 29 C9
Bečov nad Teplou, *Czech Rep.* 26 A5
Bečva →, *Czech Rep.* 27 B10
Bédar, *Spain* 39 H3
Bédarieux, *France* 20 E7
Beddouza, Ras, *Morocco* 78 B4
Bedele, *Ethiopia* 81 F4
Bederkesa, *Germany* 24 B4
Bedeso, *Ethiopia* 81 F5
Bedford, *Canada* 117 A12
Bedford, *S. Africa* 88 E4
Bedford, *U.K.* 15 E7
Bedford, *Ind., U.S.A.* 114 F2
Bedford, *Iowa, U.S.A.* 112 E7
Bedford, *Ohio, U.S.A.* 116 E3
Bedford, *Pa., U.S.A.* 116 F6
Bedford, *Va., U.S.A.* 114 G6
Bedford, C., *Australia* 94 B4
Bedfordshire □, *U.K.* 15 E7
Będków, *Poland* 31 G6
Bednja →, *Croatia* 41 B13
Bednodemyanovsk, *Russia* 34 D6
Bedok, *Singapore* 65 d
Bedónia, *Italy* 40 D6
Bedourie, *Australia* 94 C2
Bedum, *Neths.* 17 A6
Będzin, *Poland* 31 H6
Beebe Plain, *Canada* 117 A12
Beech Creek, *U.S.A.* 116 E7
Beef I., *Br. Virgin Is.* 121 e
Beelitz, *Germany* 24 C8
Beenleigh, *Australia* 95 D5
Be'er Menuha, *Israel* 70 D2
Be'er Sheva, *Israel* 74 D3
Beersheba = Be'er Sheva, *Israel* 74 D3
Beeskow, *Germany* 24 C10
Beestekraal, *S. Africa* 89 D4
Beeston, *U.K.* 14 E6
Beetzendorf, *Germany* 24 C7
Beeville, *U.S.A.* 113 L6
Befale, *Dem. Rep. of the Congo* 84 D4
Befandriana, *Mahajanga, Madag.* 89 B8
Befandriana, *Toliara, Madag.* 89 C7
Befasy, *Madag.* 89 C7
Befotaka, *Antsiranana, Madag.* 89 A8
Befotaka, *Fianarantsoa, Madag.* 89 C8
Bega, *Australia* 95 F4
Bega, Canalul, *Romania* 28 E5
Bégard, *France* 18 D3
Beğendik, *Turkey* 45 F10
Begoro, *Ghana* 83 D4
Begusarai, *India* 69 G12
Behābād, *Iran* 71 C8
Behala, *India* 69 H13
Behara, *Madag.* 89 C8
Behbehān, *Iran* 71 D6
Behm Canal, *U.S.A.* 102 B2
Behshahr, *Iran* 71 B7
Bei Jiang →, *China* 59 F9
Bei'an, *China* 60 B7
Beibei, *China* 58 C6
Beichuan, *China* 58 B5
Beihai, *China* 58 G7
Beijing, *China* 56 E9
Beijing □, *China* 56 E9
Beilen, *Neths.* 17 B6
Beiliu, *China* 59 F8
Beilngries, *Germany* 25 F7
Beilpajah, *Australia* 95 E3
Beilul, *Eritrea* 81 E5
Beinn na Faoghla = Benbecula, *U.K.* 13 D1
Beipan Jiang, *China* 58 E5
Beipiao, *China* 57 D11
Beira, *Mozam.* 87 F3
Beirut = Bayrūt, *Lebanon* 74 B4
Beiseker, *Canada* 102 C6
Beitaolaizhao, *China* 57 B13
Beitbridge, *Zimbabwe* 87 G3
Beiuş, *Romania* 28 D7
Beizhen = Binzhou, *China* 57 F10
Beizhen, *China* 57 D11
Beizhengzhen, *China* 57 B12
Beja, *Portugal* 37 G3
Béja, *Tunisia* 79 A7
Beja □, *Portugal* 37 H3
Bejaïa, *Algeria* 78 A7
Béjar, *Spain* 36 E5
Bejestān, *Iran* 71 C8
Bekaa Valley = Al Biqā, *Lebanon* 74 A5
Bekçiler, *Turkey* 47 E11
Békés, *Hungary* 28 D6
Békés □, *Hungary* 28 D6
Békéscsaba, *Hungary* 28 D6
Bekilli, *Turkey* 47 C11
Bekily, *Madag.* 89 C8
Bekisopa, *Madag.* 89 C8
Bekitro, *Madag.* 89 C8
Bekodoka, *Madag.* 89 B8
Bekoji, *Ethiopia* 81 F4
Bekok, *Malaysia* 65 L4
Bekopaka, *Madag.* 89 B7
Bekuli, *Indonesia* 63 J17
Bekwai, *Ghana* 83 D4
Bela, *India* 69 G10
Bela, *Pakistan* 68 F2
Bela Bela, *S. Africa* 89 C4
Bela Crkva, *Serbia & M.* 28 F6
Bela Palanka, *Serbia & M.* 44 C6
Bela Vista, *Brazil* 126 A4
Bela Vista, *Mozam.* 89 D5
Bélâbre, *France* 20 B5
Belalcázar, *Spain* 37 G5
Belan →, *India* 69 G9
Belanovica, *Serbia & M.* 44 B4
Belarus ■, *Europe* 32 F4
Belau = Palau ■, *Pac. Oc.* 96 G5
Belavenona, *Madag.* 89 C8
Belawan, *Indonesia* 62 D1
Belaya, *Ethiopia* 81 E4
Belaya Glina, *Russia* 35 G5
Belaya Kalitva, *Russia* 35 F5
Belaya Tserkov = Bila Tserkva, *Ukraine* 33 H6
Belceşti, *Romania* 29 C12
Bełchatów, *Poland* 31 G6
Belcher Is., *Canada* 104 A3
Belchite, *Spain* 38 D4
Belden, *U.S.A.* 110 E5
Beled Weyne = Belet Uen, *Somali Rep.* 75 G4
Belém, *Brazil* 125 D9
Belén, *Argentina* 126 B2
Belén, *Paraguay* 126 A4
Belen, *U.S.A.* 109 J10
Belene, *Bulgaria* 45 C9
Beleni, *Turkey* 72 D7
Bélesta, *France* 20 F5
Belet Uen, *Somali Rep.* 75 G4
Belev, *Russia* 32 F9
Belevi, *Turkey* 47 C9
Belfair, *U.S.A.* 110 C4
Belfast, *S. Africa* 89 D5
Belfast, *U.K.* 12 B6
Belfast, *Maine, U.S.A.* 115 C11
Belfast, *N.Y., U.S.A.* 116 D6
Belfast L., *U.K.* 12 B6
Belfield, *U.S.A.* 112 B3
Belfort, *France* 19 E13
Belfort, Territoire de □, *France* 19 E13
Belfry, *U.S.A.* 108 D9
Belgaum, *India* 66 M9
Belgioioso, *Italy* 40 C6
Belgium ■, *Europe* 17 D4
Belgodère, *France* 21 F13
Belgorod, *Russia* 33 G9
Belgorod-Dnestrovskiy = Bilhorod-Dnistrovskyy, *Ukraine* 33 J6
Belgrade = Beograd, *Serbia & M.* 44 B4
Belgrade, *U.S.A.* 108 D8
Belhaven, *U.S.A.* 115 H7
Beli Drim →, *Europe* 44 D4
Beli Manastir, *Croatia* 28 E3
Beli Timok →, *Serbia & M.* 44 C6
Bélice →, *Italy* 42 E5
Belimbing, *Indonesia* 63 J18
Belinskiy, *Russia* 34 D6
Belinyu, *Indonesia* 62 E3
Beliton Is. = Belitung, *Indonesia* 62 E3
Belitung, *Indonesia* 62 E3
Beliu, *Romania* 28 D6
Belize ■, *Cent. Amer.* 119 D7
Belize City, *Belize* 119 D7
Beljakovci, *Macedonia* 44 D5
Beljanica, *Serbia & M.* 44 B5
Belkovskiy, Ostrov, *Russia* 53 B14
Bell →, *Canada* 104 C4
Bell I., *Canada* 105 B8
Bell-Irving →, *Canada* 102 B3
Bell Peninsula, *Canada* 101 B11
Bell Ville, *Argentina* 126 C3
Bella, *Italy* 43 B8
Bella Bella, *Canada* 102 C3
Bella Coola, *Canada* 102 C3
Bella Unión, *Uruguay* 126 C4
Bella Vista, *Corrientes, Argentina* 126 B4
Bella Vista, *Tucuman, Argentina* 126 B2
Bellac, *France* 20 B5
Bellágio, *Italy* 40 C6
Bellaire, *U.S.A.* 116 F4
Bellária, *Italy* 41 D9
Bellary, *India* 66 M10
Bellata, *Australia* 95 D4
Belle-Chasse, *U.S.A.* 113 L10
Belle Fourche, *U.S.A.* 112 C3
Belle Fourche →, *U.S.A.* 112 C3
Belle Glade, *U.S.A.* 115 M5
Belle-Île, *France* 18 E3
Belle Isle, *Canada* 105 B8
Belle Isle, Str. of, *Canada* 105 B8
Belle Plaine, *U.S.A.* 112 E8
Belle Yella, *Liberia* 82 D3
Belledonne, *France* 21 C10
Bellefontaine, *U.S.A.* 114 E4
Bellefonte, *U.S.A.* 116 F7
Bellegarde, *France* 19 E9
Bellegarde-en-Marche, *France* 20 C6
Bellegarde-sur-Valserine, *France* 19 F12
Bellême, *France* 18 D7
Belleoram, *Canada* 105 C8
Belleplaine, *Barbados* 121 g
Belleville, *Canada* 116 B7
Belleville, *France* 19 F11
Belleville, *Ill., U.S.A.* 112 F10
Belleville, *Kans., U.S.A.* 112 F6
Belleville, *N.Y., U.S.A.* 117 C8
Belleville-sur-Vie, *France* 18 F5
Bellevue, *Canada* 102 D6
Bellevue, *Idaho, U.S.A.* 108 E6
Bellevue, *Nebr., U.S.A.* 112 E7
Bellevue, *Ohio, U.S.A.* 116 E2
Bellevue, *Wash., U.S.A.* 110 C4
Belley, *France* 21 C9
Bellin = Kangirsuk, *Canada* 101 B13
Bellinge, *Denmark* 11 J4
Bellingen, *Australia* 95 E5
Bellingham, *U.S.A.* 100 D7
Bellingshausen Sea, *Antarctica* 5 C17
Bellinzona, *Switz.* 25 J5
Bello, *Colombia* 124 B3
Bellows Falls, *U.S.A.* 117 C12
Bellpat, *Pakistan* 68 E3
Bellpuig d'Urgell, *Spain* 38 D6
Belluno, *Italy* 41 B9
Bellwood, *U.S.A.* 116 F6
Bélmez, *Spain* 37 G5
Belmont, *Canada* 116 D3
Belmont, *S. Africa* 88 D3
Belmont, *U.S.A.* 116 D6
Belmonte, *Brazil* 125 G11
Belmonte, *Portugal* 36 E3
Belmonte, *Spain* 39 F2
Belmopan, *Belize* 119 D7
Belmullet, *Ireland* 12 B2
Belo Horizonte, *Brazil* 125 G10
Belo-sur-Mer, *Madag.* 89 C7
Belo-Tsiribihina, *Madag.* 89 B7
Belogorsk = Bilohirsk, *Ukraine* 33 K8
Belogorsk, *Russia* 53 D13
Belogradchik, *Bulgaria* 44 C6
Belogradets, *Bulgaria* 45 C11
Beloha, *Madag.* 89 D8
Beloit, *Kans., U.S.A.* 112 F5
Beloit, *Wis., U.S.A.* 112 D10
Belokorovichi, *Ukraine* 33 G5
Belomorsk, *Russia* 52 C4
Belonia, *India* 67 H17
Belopolye = Bilopillya, *Ukraine* 33 G8
Belorechensk, *Russia* 35 H4
Belorussia = Belarus ■, *Europe* 32 F4
Beloslav, *Bulgaria* 45 C11
Belovo, *Bulgaria* 45 D8
Belovo, *Russia* 52 D9
Belovodsk, *Ukraine* 33 H10
Beloye, Ozero, *Russia* 32 B9
Beloye More, *Russia* 52 C4
Belozem, *Bulgaria* 45 D9
Belozersk, *Russia* 32 B9
Belpasso, *Italy* 43 E7
Belpre, *U.S.A.* 114 F5
Belrain, *India* 69 E9
Belt, *U.S.A.* 108 C8
Beltana, *Australia* 95 E2
Belterra, *Brazil* 125 D8
Beltinci, *Slovenia* 41 B13
Belton, *U.S.A.* 113 K6
Belton L., *U.S.A.* 113 K6
Beltsy = Bălţi, *Moldova* 29 C12
Belturbet, *Ireland* 12 B4
Belukha, *Russia* 52 E9
Beluran, *Malaysia* 62 C5
Beluša, *Slovak Rep.* 27 B11
Belušić, *Serbia & M.* 44 C5
Belvedere Marittimo, *Italy* 43 C8
Belvès, *France* 20 D5
Belvidere, *Ill., U.S.A.* 112 D10
Belvidere, *N.J., U.S.A.* 117 F9
Belvis de la Jara, *Spain* 36 F6
Belyando →, *Australia* 94 C4
Belyy, *Russia* 32 E7
Belyy, Ostrov, *Russia* 52 B8
Belyy Yar, *Russia* 52 D9
Belz, *Ukraine* 31 H11
Bełżec, *Poland* 31 H10
Belzig, *Germany* 24 C8
Belzoni, *U.S.A.* 113 J9
Bełżyce, *Poland* 31 G9
Bemaraha, Lembalemban' i, *Madag.* 89 B7
Bemarivo, *Madag.* 89 C7
Bemarivo →, *Antsiranana, Madag.* 89 A9
Bemarivo →, *Mahajanga, Madag.* 89 B8
Bemavo, *Madag.* 89 C8
Bembéréke, *Benin* 83 C5
Bembesi, *Zimbabwe* 87 G2
Bembesi →, *Zimbabwe* 87 F2
Bembézar →, *Spain* 37 H5
Bembibre, *Spain* 36 C4
Bemetara, *India* 69 J9
Bemidji, *U.S.A.* 112 B7
Bemolanga, *Madag.* 89 B8
Ben, *Iran* 71 C6
Ben Cruachan, *U.K.* 13 E3
Ben Dearg, *U.K.* 13 D4
Ben En △, *Vietnam* 64 C5
Ben Hope, *U.K.* 13 C4
Ben Lawers, *U.K.* 13 E4
Ben Lomond, *N.S.W., Australia* 95 E5
Ben Lomond, *Tas., Australia* 95 G4
Ben Lomond, *U.K.* 13 E4
Ben Lomond △, *Australia* 95 G4
Ben Luc, *Vietnam* 65 G6

Ben Macdhui, *U.K.* 13 D5
Ben Mhor, *U.K.* 13 D1
Ben More, *Arg. & Bute, U.K.* 13 E2
Ben More, *Stirl., U.K.* 13 E4
Ben More Assynt, *U.K.* 13 C4
Ben Nevis, *U.K.* 13 E3
Ben Quang, *Vietnam* 64 D6
Ben Vorlich, *U.K.* 13 E4
Ben Wyvis, *U.K.* 13 D4
Bena, *Nigeria* 83 C6
Benalla, *Australia* 95 F4
Benalmádena, *Spain* 37 J6
Benares = Varanasi, *India* 69 G10
Bénat, C., *France* 21 E10
Benavente, *Portugal* 37 G2
Benavente, *Spain* 36 C5
Benavides, *U.S.A.* 113 M5
Benavides de Órbigo, *Spain* 36 C5
Benbecula, *U.K.* 13 D1
Benbonyathe, *Australia* 95 E2
Bend, *U.S.A.* 108 D3
Bender Beila, *Somali Rep.* 75 F5
Bendery = Tighina, *Moldova* 29 D14
Bendigo, *Australia* 95 F3
Bendorf, *Germany* 24 E3
Benē Beraq, *Israel* 74 C3
Bénéna, *Mali* 82 C4
Benenitra, *Madag.* 89 C8
Benešov, *Czech Rep.* 26 B7
Benevento, *Italy* 43 A7
Benfeld, *France* 19 D14
Benga, *Mozam.* 87 F3
Bengal, Bay of, *Ind. Oc.* 67 M17
Bengalûru = Bangalore, *India* 66 N10
Bengbis, *Cameroon* 83 E7
Bengbu, *China* 57 H9
Benghazi = Banghāzī, *Libya* 79 B10
Bengkalis, *Indonesia* 62 D2
Bengkulu, *Indonesia* 62 E2
Bengkulu □, *Indonesia* 62 E2
Bengough, *Canada* 103 D7
Bengtsfors, *Sweden* 10 E6
Benguela, *Angola* 85 G2
Benguérua, I., *Mozam.* 89 C6
Benha, *Egypt* 80 H7
Beni, *Dem. Rep. of the Congo* 86 B2
Beni →, *Bolivia* 124 F5
Beni Mazâr, *Egypt* 80 B3
Beni Mellal, *Morocco* 78 B4
Beni Suef, *Egypt* 80 J7
Beniah L., *Canada* 102 A6
Benicarló, *Spain* 38 E5
Benicássim, *Spain* 38 E5
Benicia, *U.S.A.* 110 G4
Benidorm, *Spain* 39 G4
Benin ■, *Africa* 83 D5
Benin →, *Nigeria* 83 D6
Benin, Bight of, *W. Afr.* 83 E5
Benin City, *Nigeria* 83 D6
Benisa, *Spain* 39 G5
Benitses, *Greece* 49 A3
Benjamin Aceval, *Paraguay* 126 A4
Benjamin Constant, *Brazil* 124 D4
Benjamin Hill, *Mexico* 118 A2
Benkelman, *U.S.A.* 112 E4
Benkovac, *Croatia* 41 D12
Bennett, *Canada* 102 B2
Bennett, L., *Australia* 92 D5
Bennetta, Ostrov, *Russia* 53 B15
Bennettsville, *U.S.A.* 115 H6
Bennichchāb, *Mauritania* 82 B1
Bennington, *N.H., U.S.A.* 117 D11
Bennington, *Vt., U.S.A.* 117 D11
Bénodet, *France* 18 E2
Benoni, *S. Africa* 89 D4
Benque Viejo del Carmen, *Belize* 119 D7
Bensheim, *Germany* 25 F4
Benson, *Ariz., U.S.A.* 109 L8
Benson, *Minn., U.S.A.* 112 C7
Bent, *Iran* 71 E8
Benteng, *Indonesia* 63 F6
Bentinck I., *Australia* 94 B2
Bentiu, *Sudan* 81 F2
Bento Gonçalves, *Brazil* 127 B5
Benton, *Ark., U.S.A.* 113 H8
Benton, *Calif., U.S.A.* 110 H8
Benton, *Ill., U.S.A.* 112 G10
Benton, *Pa., U.S.A.* 117 E8
Benton Harbor, *U.S.A.* 114 D2
Bentong, *Malaysia* 65 L3
Bentonville, *U.S.A.* 113 G7
Bentu Liben, *Ethiopia* 81 F4
Benue □, *Nigeria* 83 D6
Benue →, *Nigeria* 83 D6
Benxi, *China* 57 D12
Beo, *Indonesia* 63 D7
Beograd, *Serbia & M.* 44 B4
Beograd ✈ (BEG), *Serbia & M.* 44 C4
Beoumi, *Ivory C.* 82 D3
Bepan Jiang →, *China* 58 E6
Beppu, *Japan* 55 H5
Beqaa Valley = Al Biqā, *Lebanon* 74 A5
Ber Mota, *India* 68 H3
Berach →, *India* 68 G6
Beraketa, *Madag.* 89 C7
Berane, *Serbia & M.* 44 D3
Berat, *Albania* 44 F3
Berau, Teluk, *Indonesia* 63 E8
Beravina, *Madag.* 89 B8
Berber, *Sudan* 80 D3
Berbera, *Somali Rep.* 75 E4
Berbérati, *C.A.R.* 84 D3
Berbice →, *Guyana* 124 B7
Berceto, *Italy* 40 D6
Berchidda, *Italy* 42 B2
Berchtesgaden, *Germany* 25 H8
Berchtesgaden △, *Germany* 25 H8
Berck, *France* 19 B8
Berdichev = Berdychiv, *Ukraine* 33 H5
Berdsk, *Russia* 52 D9
Berdyansk, *Ukraine* 33 J9
Berdychiv, *Ukraine* 33 H5
Berea, *U.S.A.* 114 G3
Berebere, *Indonesia* 63 D7
Bereda, *Somali Rep.* 75 E5
Berehomet, *Ukraine* 29 B10
Berehove, *Ukraine* 28 B7
Berekum, *Ghana* 82 D4
Berenice, *Egypt* 80 C4
Berens →, *Canada* 103 C9
Berens I., *Canada* 103 C9
Berens River, *Canada* 103 C9
Beresford, *U.S.A.* 112 D6
Berestechko, *Ukraine* 33 G3
Bereşti, *Romania* 29 D12
Beretău →, *Romania* 28 C6
Berettyó →, *Hungary* 28 D6
Berettyóújfalu, *Hungary* 28 C6
Berevo, *Mahajanga, Madag.* 89 B7
Berevo, *Toliara, Madag.* 89 B7
Bereza = Byaroza, *Belarus* 33 F3
Berezhany, *Ukraine* 33 H3
Berezina = Byarezina →, *Belarus* 33 F6
Berezivka, *Ukraine* 33 J6
Berezna, *Ukraine* 33 G6
Bereznik, *Russia* 52 C5
Berezniki, *Russia* 52 D6
Berezovo, *Russia* 52 C7
Berezyne, *Ukraine* 29 D14
Berga, *Spain* 38 C6
Berga, *Sweden* 11 G10
Bergama, *Turkey* 47 B9
Bérgamo, *Italy* 40 C6
Bergara, *Spain* 38 B2
Bergby, *Sweden* 10 D11
Bergedorf, *Germany* 24 B6
Bergeforsen, *Sweden* 10 B11
Bergen, *Mecklenburg-Vorpommern, Germany* 24 A9
Bergen, *Niedersachsen, Germany* 24 C5
Bergen, *Neths.* 17 B4
Bergen, *Norway* 9 F11
Bergen, *U.S.A.* 116 C7
Bergen op Zoom, *Neths.* 17 C4
Bergerac, *France* 20 D4
Bergheim, *Germany* 24 E2
Bergholz, *U.S.A.* 116 F4
Bergisch Gladbach, *Germany* 17 D7
Bergisches Land ⌓, *Germany* 24 E3
Bergkamen, *Germany* 24 D3
Bergkvara, *Sweden* 11 H10
Bergshamra, *Sweden* 10 E12
Bergsjö, *Sweden* 10 C11
Bergstrasse-Odenwald ⌓, *Germany* 25 F1
Bergues, *France* 19 B9
Bergviken, *Sweden* 10 C10
Bergville, *S. Africa* 89 D4
Berhala, Selat, *Indonesia* 62 E2
Berhampore = Baharampur, *India* 69 G13
Berhampur = Brahmapur, *India* 67 K14
Berheci →, *Romania* 29 E12
Bering Sea, *Pac. Oc.* 100 C1
Bering Strait, *Pac. Oc.* 100 B3
Beringovskiy, *Russia* 53 C18
Berisso, *Argentina* 126 C4
Berja, *Spain* 37 J8
Berkeley, *U.S.A.* 110 H4
Berkner I., *Antarctica* 5 D18
Berkovitsa, *Bulgaria* 44 C7
Berkshire, *U.S.A.* 117 D8
Berkshire Downs, *U.K.* 15 F6
Berlanga, *Spain* 37 G5
Berlenga, I., *Portugal* 37 F1
Berlin, *Germany* 24 C9
Berlin, *Md., U.S.A.* 114 F8
Berlin, *N.H., U.S.A.* 117 B13
Berlin, *N.Y., U.S.A.* 117 D11
Berlin, *Wis., U.S.A.* 114 D1
Berlin □, *Germany* 24 C9
Berlin L., *U.S.A.* 116 E4
Berlin Tegel ✈ (TXL), *Germany* 24 C9
Bermeja, Sierra, *Spain* 37 J5
Bermejo →, *Formosa, Argentina* 126 B4
Bermejo →, *San Juan, Argentina* 126 C2
Bermen, L., *Canada* 105 B6
Bermeo, *Spain* 38 B2
Bermillo de Sayago, *Spain* 36 D4
Bermuda ☒, *Atl. Oc.* 98 F13
Bern, *Switz.* 25 J3
Bern □, *Switz.* 25 J3
Bernalda, *Italy* 43 B9
Bernalillo, *U.S.A.* 109 J10
Bernardo de Irigoyen, *Argentina* 127 B5
Bernardo O'Higgins □, *Chile* 126 C1
Bernardsville, *U.S.A.* 117 F10
Bernasconi, *Argentina* 126 D3
Bernau, *Bayern, Germany* 25 H8
Bernau, *Brandenburg, Germany* 24 C9
Bernay, *France* 18 C7
Bernburg, *Germany* 24 D7
Berndorf, *Austria* 26 D9
Berne = Bern, *Switz.* 25 J3
Berne = Bern □, *Switz.* 25 J3
Berner Alpen, *Switz.* 25 J3
Berneray, *U.K.* 13 D1
Bernier I., *Australia* 93 D1
Bernina, Piz, *Switz.* 25 J5
Bernkastel-Kues, *Germany* 25 F3
Beroroha, *Madag.* 89 C8
Béroubouay, *Benin* 83 C5
Beroun, *Czech Rep.* 26 B7
Berounka →, *Czech Rep.* 26 B7
Berovo, *Macedonia* 44 E6
Berre, Étang de, *France* 21 E9
Berre-l'Étang, *France* 21 E9
Berri, *Australia* 95 E3
Berriane, *Algeria* 78 B6
Berry, *Australia* 95 E5
Berry, *France* 19 F8
Berry Is., *Bahamas* 120 A4
Berryessa L., *U.S.A.* 110 G4
Berryville, *U.S.A.* 113 G8
Berseba, *Namibia* 88 D2
Bersenbrück, *Germany* 24 C3
Bershad, *Ukraine* 29 B14
Berthold, *U.S.A.* 112 A4
Berthoud, *U.S.A.* 112 E2
Bertincourt, *France* 19 B9
Bertoua, *Cameroon* 84 D2
Bertraghboy B., *Ireland* 12 C2
Berwick, *U.S.A.* 117 E8
Berwick-upon-Tweed, *U.K.* 14 B6
Berwyn Mts., *U.K.* 14 E4
Beryslav, *Ukraine* 33 J7
Berzasca, *Romania* 28 F6
Berzence, *Hungary* 28 D2
Besal, *Pakistan* 69 B5
Besalampy, *Madag.* 89 B7
Besançon, *France* 19 E13
Besar, *Indonesia* 62 E5
Beshenkovichi, *Belarus* 32 E5
Beška, *Serbia & M.* 28 E5
Beslan, *Russia* 35 J7
Besna Kobila, *Serbia & M.* 44 D6
Besnard L., *Canada* 103 B7
Besni, *Turkey* 70 B3
Besor, N. →, *Egypt* 74 D3
Bessarabiya, *Moldova* 33 J5
Bessarabka = Basarabeasca, *Moldova* 29 D13
Bessèges, *France* 21 D8
Bessemer, *Ala., U.S.A.* 115 J2
Bessemer, *Mich., U.S.A.* 112 B9
Bessemer, *Pa., U.S.A.* 116 F4
Bessin, *France* 18 C6
Bessines-sur-Gartempe, *France* 20 B5
Beswick, *Australia* 92 B5
Bet She'an, *Israel* 74 C4
Bet Shemesh, *Israel* 74 D4
Betafo, *Madag.* 89 B8
Betancuria, *Canary Is.* 48 F5
Betanzos, *Spain* 36 B2
Bétaré Oya, *Cameroon* 84 C2
Betatao, *Madag.* 89 B8
Bétera, *Spain* 39 F4
Bétérou, *Benin* 83 D5
Bethal, *S. Africa* 89 D4
Bethanien, *Namibia* 88 D2
Bethany, *Canada* 116 B6
Bethany, *U.S.A.* 112 E7
Bethel, *Alaska, U.S.A.* 100 B3
Bethel, *Conn., U.S.A.* 117 E11
Bethel, *Maine, U.S.A.* 117 B14
Bethel, *Vt., U.S.A.* 117 C12
Bethel Park, *U.S.A.* 116 F4
Béthenville, *France* 19 C11
Bethlehem = Bayt Lahm, *West Bank* 74 D4
Bethlehem, *S. Africa* 89 D4
Bethlehem, *U.S.A.* 117 F9
Bethulie, *S. Africa* 88 E4
Béthune, *France* 19 B9
Béthune →, *France* 18 C8
Betioky, *Madag.* 89 C7
Betong, *Thailand* 65 K3
Betoota, *Australia* 94 D3
Betor, *Ethiopia* 81 E4
Betroka, *Madag.* 89 C8
Betsiamites, *Canada* 105 C6
Betsiamites →, *Canada* 105 C6
Betsiboka →, *Madag.* 89 B8
Bettendorf, *U.S.A.* 112 E9
Bettiah, *India* 69 F11
Bettna, *Sweden* 11 F10
Béttola, *Italy* 40 D6
Betul, *India* 66 J10
Betung, *Malaysia* 62 D4
Betws-y-Coed, *U.K.* 14 D4
Betxi, *Spain* 38 F4
Betzdorf, *Germany* 24 E3
Beuil, *France* 21 D10
Beulah, *Mich., U.S.A.* 114 C2
Beulah, *N. Dak., U.S.A.* 112 B4
Beuvron →, *France* 18 E8
Beveren, *Belgium* 17 C4
Beverley, *Australia* 93 F2
Beverley, *U.K.* 14 D7
Beverley Hills, *U.S.A.* 115 L4
Beverly, *U.S.A.* 117 D14
Beverly Hills, *U.S.A.* 111 L8
Beverungen, *Germany* 24 D5
Bevoalavo, *Madag.* 89 D7
Bewas →, *India* 69 H8
Bex, *Switz.* 25 J3
Bexhill, *U.K.* 15 G8
Bey Dağları, *Turkey* 47 E12
Beyānlū, *Iran* 70 C5
Beyazköy, *Turkey* 45 E11
Beyçayırı, *Turkey* 45 F10
Beydağ, *Turkey* 47 C10
Beyeğaç, *Turkey* 47 D10
Beyin, *Ghana* 82 D4
Beykoz, *Turkey* 45 E13
Beyla, *Guinea* 82 D3
Beynat, *France* 20 C5
Beyneu, *Kazakhstan* 52 E6
Beyoba, *Turkey* 47 C9
Beyoğlu, *Turkey* 45 E12
Beypazarı, *Turkey* 72 B4
Beyşehir, *Turkey* 72 D4
Beyşehir Gölü, *Turkey* 70 B1
Beytüşşebap, *Turkey* 73 D10
Bezdan, *Serbia & M.* 28 E3
Bezhetsk, *Russia* 32 D9
Béziers, *France* 20 E7
Bezwada = Vijayawada, *India* 67 L12
Bhabua, *India* 69 G10
Bhachau, *India* 66 H7
Bhadar →, *Gujarat, India* 68 H5
Bhadar →, *Gujarat, India* 68 J3
Bhadarwah, *India* 69 C6
Bhadgaon = Bhaktapur, *Nepal* 69 F11
Bhadohi, *India* 69 G10
Bhadra, *India* 68 E6
Bhadrakh, *India* 67 J15
Bhadran, *India* 68 H5
Bhadravati, *India* 66 N9
Bhag, *Pakistan* 68 E2
Bhagalpur, *India* 69 G12
Bhagirathi →, *Uttaranchal, India* 69 D8
Bhagirathi →, *W. Bengal, India* 69 H13
Bhakkar, *Pakistan* 68 D4
Bhakra Dam, *India* 68 D7
Bhaktapur, *Nepal* 69 F11
Bhamo, *Burma* 67 G20
Bhandara, *India* 66 J11
Bhanpura, *India* 68 G6
Bhanrer Ra., *India* 69 H8
Bhaptiahi, *India* 69 F12
Bharat = India ■, *Asia* 66 K11
Bharatpur, *Chhattisgarh, India* 69 H9
Bharatpur, *Raj., India* 68 F7
Bharno, *India* 69 H11
Bharuch, *India* 66 J8
Bhatinda, *India* 68 D6
Bhatpara, *India* 69 H13
Bhattu, *India* 68 E6
Bhaun, *Pakistan* 68 C5
Bhaunagar = Bhavnagar, *India* 66 J8
Bhavnagar, *India* 66 J8
Bhawari, *India* 68 G5
Bhayavadar, *India* 68 J4
Bhera, *Pakistan* 68 C5
Bhikangaon, *India* 68 J6
Bhilsa = Vidisha, *India* 68 H7
Bhilwara, *India* 68 G6
Bhima →, *India* 66 L10
Bhimbar, *Pakistan* 69 C6
Bhind, *India* 69 F8
Bhinga, *India* 69 F9
Bhinmal, *India* 68 G5
Bhiwandi, *India* 66 K8
Bhiwani, *India* 68 E7
Bhogava →, *India* 68 H5
Bhola, *Bangla.* 67 H17
Bholari, *Pakistan* 68 G3
Bhopal, *India* 68 H7
Bhubaneshwar, *India* 67 J14
Bhuj, *India* 68 H3
Bhumiphol Res., *Thailand* 64 D2
Bhusawal, *India* 66 J9
Bhutan ■, *Asia* 67 F17
Biafra, B. of = Bonny, Bight of, *Africa* 83 E6
Biak, *Indonesia* 63 E9
Biała, *Poland* 31 H4
Biała →, *Poland* 31 H7
Biała Piska, *Poland* 30 E9
Biała Podlaska, *Poland* 31 F10
Biała Rawska, *Poland* 31 G7
Białobrzegi, *Poland* 31 G7
Białogard, *Poland* 30 D2
Białowieski △, *Poland* 31 F10
Białowieża, *Poland* 31 F10
Biały Bór, *Poland* 30 E3
Białystok, *Poland* 31 E10
Biancavilla, *Italy* 43 E7
Bianco, *Italy* 43 D9
Biankouma, *Ivory C.* 82 D3
Biaora, *India* 68 H7
Bīārjmand, *Iran* 71 B7
Biaro, *Indonesia* 63 D7
Biarritz, *France* 20 E2
Bias, *Indonesia* 63 J18
Biasca, *Switz.* 25 J4
Biba, *Egypt* 80 J7
Bibai, *Japan* 54 C10
Bibbiena, *Italy* 41 E8
Bibby I., *Canada* 103 A10
Bibel →, *Spain* 36 C3
Biberach, *Germany* 25 G5
Bibiani, *Ghana* 82 D4
Bibungwa, *Dem. Rep. of the Congo* 86 C2
Bicaj, *Albania* 44 E4
Bicaz, *Romania* 29 D11
Bicazu Ardelean, *Romania* 29 D10
Biccari, *Italy* 43 A8
Bicester, *U.K.* 15 F6
Bichena, *Ethiopia* 81 E4
Bicheno, *Australia* 95 G4
Bichia, *India* 69 H9
Bichvinta, *Georgia* 35 J5
Bickerton I., *Australia* 94 A2
Bicske, *Hungary* 28 C3
Bida, *Nigeria* 83 D6
Bidar, *India* 66 L10
Biddeford, *U.S.A.* 115 D10
Biddwara, *Ethiopia* 81 F4
Bideford, *U.K.* 15 F3
Bideford Bay, *U.K.* 15 F3
Bidhuna, *India* 69 F8
Bidor, *Malaysia* 65 K3
Bie, *Sweden* 10 E10
Bié, Planalto de, *Angola* 85 G3
Bieber, *U.S.A.* 108 F3
Biebrza →, *Poland* 31 E9
Biebrzański △, *Poland* 30 E9
Biecz, *Poland* 31 J8
Biel, *Switz.* 25 H3
Bielawa, *Poland* 31 H3
Bielefeld, *Germany* 24 C4
Bielersee, *Switz.* 25 H3
Biella, *Italy* 40 C5
Bielsk Podlaski, *Poland* 31 F10
Bielsko-Biała, *Poland* 31 J6
Bien Hoa, *Vietnam* 65 G6
Bienne = Biel, *Switz.* 25 H3
Bienvenida, *Spain* 37 G4
Bienville, L., *Canada* 104 A5
Bierné, *France* 18 E6
Bierun, *Poland* 31 H6
Bierutów, *Poland* 31 G4
Biescas, *Spain* 38 C4
Biese →, *Germany* 24 C7
Biesiesfontein, *S. Africa* 88 E2
Bieszczadzki △, *Poland* 31 J9
Bietigheim-Bissingen, *Germany* 25 G5
Bieżuń, *Poland* 31 F6
Biferno →, *Italy* 41 G12
Big →, *Canada* 105 B8
Big B., *Canada* 105 A7
Big Bear City, *U.S.A.* 111 L10
Big Bear Lake, *U.S.A.* 111 L10
Big Belt Mts., *U.S.A.* 108 C8
Big Bend, *Swaziland* 89 D5
Big Bend △, *U.S.A.* 113 L3
Big Black →, *U.S.A.* 113 K9
Big Blue →, *U.S.A.* 112 F6
Big Creek, *U.S.A.* 110 H7
Big Cypress ⌓, *U.S.A.* 115 M5
Big Cypress Swamp, *U.S.A.* 115 M5
Big Falls, *U.S.A.* 112 A8
Big Fork →, *U.S.A.* 112 A8
Big Horn Mts. = Bighorn Mts., *U.S.A.* 108 D10
Big I., *Canada* 102 A5
Big Lake, *U.S.A.* 113 K4
Big Moose, *U.S.A.* 117 C10
Big Muddy Cr. →, *U.S.A.* 112 A2
Big Pine, *U.S.A.* 110 H8
Big Piney, *U.S.A.* 108 E8
Big Rapids, *U.S.A.* 114 D3
Big Rideau L., *Canada* 117 B8
Big River, *Canada* 103 C7
Big Run, *U.S.A.* 116 F6
Big Sable Pt., *U.S.A.* 114 C2
Big Salmon →, *Canada* 102 A2
Big Sand L., *Canada* 103 B9
Big Sandy, *U.S.A.* 108 B8
Big Sandy →, *U.S.A.* 114 F4
Big Sandy Cr. →, *U.S.A.* 112 F3
Big Sioux →, *U.S.A.* 112 D6
Big South Fork △, *U.S.A.* 115 G3
Big Spring, *U.S.A.* 113 J4
Big Stone City, *U.S.A.* 112 C6
Big Stone Gap, *U.S.A.* 115 G4
Big Stone L., *U.S.A.* 112 C6
Big Sur, *U.S.A.* 110 J5
Big Timber, *U.S.A.* 108 D9
Big Trout L., *Canada* 104 B2
Big Trout Lake, *Canada* 104 B2
Biğa, *Turkey* 45 F11
Biga →, *Turkey* 45 F11
Bigadiç, *Turkey* 47 B10
Biganos, *France* 20 D3
Biggar, *Canada* 103 C7
Biggar, *U.K.* 13 F5
Bigge I., *Australia* 92 B4
Biggenden, *Australia* 95 D5
Biggleswade, *U.K.* 15 E7
Biggs, *U.S.A.* 110 F5
Bighorn, *U.S.A.* 108 C10
Bighorn →, *U.S.A.* 108 C10
Bighorn Canyon ⌓, *U.S.A.* 108 D9
Bighorn L., *U.S.A.* 108 D9
Bighorn Mts., *U.S.A.* 108 D10
Bignona, *Senegal* 82 C1
Bigorre, *France* 20 E4
Bigstone L., *Canada* 103 C9
Biguglia, Étang de, *France* 21 F13
Bigwa, *Tanzania* 86 D4
Bihać, *Bos.-H.* 41 D12
Bihar, *India* 69 G11
Bihar □, *India* 69 G12
Biharamulo, *Tanzania* 86 C3
Biharamulo ⌓, *Tanzania* 86 C3
Bihariganj, *India* 69 G12
Biharkeresztes, *Hungary* 28 C6
Bihor □, *Romania* 28 D7
Bihor, Munţii, *Romania* 28 D7
Bijagós, Arquipélago dos, *Guinea-Biss.* 82 C1
Bijaipur, *India* 68 F7
Bijapur, *Chhattisgarh, India* 67 K12
Bijapur, *Karnataka, India* 66 L9
Bījār, *Iran* 70 C5
Bijawar, *India* 69 G8
Bijeljina, *Bos.-H.* 28 F4
Bijelo Polje, *Serbia & M.* 44 C3
Bijie, *China* 58 D5
Bijnor, *India* 68 E8
Bikaner, *India* 68 E5
Bikapur, *India* 69 F10
Bikeqi, *China* 56 D6
Bikfayyā, *Lebanon* 74 B4
Bikin, *Russia* 53 E14
Bikin →, *Russia* 54 A7
Bikini Atoll, *Marshall Is.* 96 F8
Bikita, *Zimbabwe* 89 C5
Bikoué, *Cameroon* 83 E7
Bila Tserkva, *Ukraine* 33 H6
Bilanga, *Burkina Faso* 83 C4
Bilara, *India* 68 F5
Bilaspur, *Chhattisgarh, India* 69 H10
Bilaspur, *Punjab, India* 68 D7
Biläsuvar, *Azerbaijan* 73 C13
Bilauk Taungdan, *Thailand* 64 F2
Bilbao, *Spain* 38 B2
Bilbao ✈ (BIO), *Spain* 36 B8
Bilbeis, *Egypt* 80 H7
Bilbo = Bilbao, *Spain* 38 B2
Bilbor, *Romania* 29 C10
Bilche-Zolote, *Ukraine* 29 B10
Bilciureşti, *Romania* 29 F10
Bíldudalur, *Iceland* 8 D2
Bílé Karpaty, *Europe* 27 B11
Bileća, *Bos.-H.* 44 D2
Bilecik, *Turkey* 72 B4
Biłgoraj, *Poland* 31 H9
Bilgram, *India* 69 F9
Bilhaur, *India* 69 F9
Bilhorod-Dnistrovskyy, *Ukraine* 33 J6
Bilibino, *Russia* 53 C17
Bilibiza, *Mozam.* 87 E5
Bilisht, *Albania* 44 F5
Billabong Roadhouse, *Australia* 93 E2
Billdal, *Sweden* 11 G5

Billiluna, *Australia* 92 C4
Billings, *U.S.A.* 108 D9
Billiton Is. = Belitung, *Indonesia* 62 E3
Billsta, *Sweden* 10 A12
Billund, *Denmark* 11 J3
Bilma, *Niger* 79 E8
Bilo Gora, *Croatia* 28 E2
Biloela, *Australia* 94 C5
Bilohirsk, *Ukraine* 33 K8
Bilopillya, *Ukraine* 33 G8
Biloxi, *U.S.A.* 113 K10
Bilpa Morea Claypan, *Australia* 94 D3
Biltine, *Chad* 79 F10
Bilyarsk, *Russia* 34 C10
Bima, *Indonesia* 63 F5
Bimban, *Egypt* 80 C3
Bimbila, *Ghana* 83 D5
Bimini Is., *Bahamas* 120 A4
Bin Xian, *Heilongjiang, China* 57 B14
Bin Xian, *Shaanxi, China* 56 G5
Bin Yauri, *Nigeria* 83 C5
Bina-Etawah, *India* 68 G8
Bināb, *Iran* 71 B6
Binalbagan, *Phil.* 61 F5
Binalong, *Australia* 95 E4
Bīnālūd, Kūh-e, *Iran* 71 B8
Binatang = Bintangor, *Malaysia* 62 D4
Binche, *Belgium* 17 D4
Binchuan, *China* 58 E3
Binder, *Chad* 83 D7
Bindki, *India* 69 F9
Bindslev, *Denmark* 11 G4
Bindura, *Zimbabwe* 87 F3
Binefar, *Spain* 38 D5
Bingara, *Australia* 95 D5
Bingen, *Germany* 25 F3
Bingerville, *Ivory C.* 82 D4
Bingham, *U.S.A.* 115 C11
Binghamton, *U.S.A.* 117 D9
Bingöl, *Turkey* 70 B4
Bingöl Dağları, *Turkey* 73 C9
Bingsjö, *Sweden* 10 C9
Binh Dinh = An Nhon, *Vietnam* 64 F7
Binh Khe, *Vietnam* 64 F7
Binh Son, *Vietnam* 64 E7
Binhai, *China* 57 G10
Binic, *France* 18 D4
Binisatua, *Spain* 48 B11
Binjai, *Indonesia* 62 D3
Binji, *Nigeria* 83 C5
Binnaway, *Australia* 95 E4
Binongko, *Indonesia* 63 F6
Binscarth, *Canada* 103 C8
Binshangul Gumuz □, *Ethiopia* 81 E4
Bint Goda, *Sudan* 81 E3
Bintan, *Indonesia* 62 D2
Bintangor, *Malaysia* 62 D4
Bintulu, *Malaysia* 62 D4
Bintuni, *Indonesia* 63 E8
Binyang, *China* 58 F7
Binz, *Germany* 24 A9
Binzert = Bizerte, *Tunisia* 79 A7
Binzhou, *China* 57 F10
Bío Bío □, *Chile* 126 D1
Biograd na Moru, *Croatia* 41 E12
Biogradska Gora △, *Serbia & M.* 44 D3
Bioko, *Eq. Guin.* 83 E6
Biokovo, *Croatia* 41 E14
Bipindi, *Cameroon* 83 E7
Bir, *India* 66 K9
Bir, Ras, *Djibouti* 81 E5
Bîr Abu Hashim, *Egypt* 80 C3
Bîr Abu Minqar, *Egypt* 80 B2
Bîr Abu Muḥammad, *Egypt* 74 F3
Bi'r ad Dabbāghāt, *Jordan* 74 E4
Bîr Adal Deib, *Sudan* 80 C4
Bi'r al Butayyihāt, *Jordan* 74 F4
Bi'r al Mārī, *Jordan* 74 E4
Bi'r al Qattār, *Jordan* 74 F4
Bir 'Asal, *Egypt* 80 B3
Bir Atrun, *Sudan* 80 D2
Bîr Beiḍa, *Egypt* 74 E3
Bîr Diqnash, *Egypt* 80 A2
Bîr el 'Abd, *Egypt* 74 D2
Bîr el Basur, *Egypt* 80 B2
Bîr el Biarât, *Egypt* 74 F3
Bîr el Duweidar, *Egypt* 74 E1
Bîr el Garârât, *Egypt* 74 D2
Bîr el Gellaz, *Egypt* 80 A2
Bîr el Heisi, *Egypt* 74 F3
Bîr el Jafir, *Egypt* 74 E1
Bîr el Mâlḥi, *Egypt* 74 E2
Bîr el Shaqqa, *Egypt* 80 A2
Bîr el Thamâda, *Egypt* 74 E2
Bîr Fuad, *Egypt* 80 A2
Bîr Gebeil Ḥiṣn, *Egypt* 74 E2
Bi'r Ghadīr, *Syria* 74 A6
Bîr Haimur, *Egypt* 80 C3
Bîr Ḥasana, *Egypt* 74 E2
Bîr Hōōker, *Egypt* 80 H7
Bîr Kanayis, *Egypt* 80 C3
Bîr Kaseiba, *Egypt* 74 E2
Bîr Kerawein, *Egypt* 80 B2
Bîr Lahfân, *Egypt* 74 E2
Bîr Madkûr, *Egypt* 74 E1
Bîr Maql, *Egypt* 80 C3
Bîr Mîneiga, *Sudan* 80 C4
Bîr Misaha, *Egypt* 80 C2
Bîr Mogreïn, *Mauritania* 78 C3
Bîr Murr, *Egypt* 80 C3
Bi'r Muṭribah, *Kuwait* 70 D5
Bîr Nakheila, *Egypt* 80 C3
Bîr Qaṭia, *Egypt* 74 E1
Bîr Qatrani, *Egypt* 80 A2
Bîr Ranga, *Egypt* 80 C4
Bîr Sahara, *Egypt* 80 C2
Bîr Seiyâla, *Egypt* 80 B3
Bîr Shalatein, *Egypt* 80 C4
Bîr Shebb, *Egypt* 80 C2
Bîr Shût, *Egypt* 80 C4
Bîr Terfawi, *Egypt* 80 C2
Bîr Umm Qubûr, *Egypt* 80 C3
Bîr Ungât, *Egypt* 80 C3
Bîr Za'farâna, *Egypt* 80 J8
Bîr Zeidûn, *Egypt* 80 B3
Biramféro, *Guinea* 82 C3
Biratnagar, *Nepal* 69 F12
Birawa, *Dem. Rep. of the Congo* 86 C2
Birch →, *Canada* 102 B6
Birch Hills, *Canada* 103 C7
Birch I., *Canada* 103 C9
Birch L., *N.W.T., Canada* 102 A5
Birch L., *Ont., Canada* 104 B1
Birch Mts., *Canada* 102 B6
Birch River, *Canada* 103 C8
Birchip, *Australia* 95 F3
Birchiş, *Romania* 28 E7
Bird, *Canada* 103 B10
Bird I. = Aves, I. de, *W. Indies* 121 C7
Bird I., *Antarctica* 5 B1
Birdsville, *Australia* 94 D2
Birdum Cr. →, *Australia* 92 C5
Birecik, *Turkey* 70 B3
Birein, *Israel* 74 E3
Bireuen, *Indonesia* 62 C1
Biri →, *Sudan* 81 F2
Birifo, *Gambia* 82 C2
Birigui, *Brazil* 127 A5
Birjand, *Iran* 71 C8
Birkenfeld, *Germany* 25 F3
Birkenhead, *U.K.* 14 D4
Birkerød, *Denmark* 11 J6
Birket Qârûn, *Egypt* 80 J7
Birkfeld, *Austria* 26 D8
Bîrlad = Bârlad, *Romania* 29 D12
Birmingham, *U.K.* 15 E6
Birmingham, *U.S.A.* 115 J2
Birmingham International ✈ (BHX), *U.K.* 15 E6
Birmitrapur, *India* 67 H14
Birni Ngaouré, *Niger* 83 C5
Birni Nkonni, *Niger* 83 C6
Birnin Gwari, *Nigeria* 83 C6
Birnin Kebbi, *Nigeria* 83 C5
Birnin Kudu, *Nigeria* 83 C6
Birobidzhan, *Russia* 53 E14
Birr, *Ireland* 12 C4
Birrie →, *Australia* 95 D4
Birsilpur, *India* 68 E5
Birsk, *Russia* 52 D6
Birštonas, *Lithuania* 30 D11
Birtle, *Canada* 103 C8
Birur, *India* 66 N9
Biryuchiy, *Ukraine* 33 J8
Biržai, *Lithuania* 9 H21
Birzebbugga, *Malta* 49 D2
Bisa, *Indonesia* 63 E7
Bisáccia, *Italy* 43 A8
Bisacquino, *Italy* 42 E6
Bisalpur, *India* 69 E8
Bisbee, *U.S.A.* 109 L9
Biscarrosse, *France* 20 D2
Biscarrosse et de Parentis, Étang de, *France* 20 D2
Biscay, B. of, *Atl. Oc.* 6 F5
Biscayne B., *U.S.A.* 115 N5
Biscéglie, *Italy* 43 A9
Bischheim, *France* 19 D14
Bischofshofen, *Austria* 26 D6
Bischofswerda, *Germany* 24 D10
Bischwiller, *France* 19 D14
Biscoe Is., *Antarctica* 5 C17
Biscotasing, *Canada* 104 C3
Biševo, *Croatia* 41 F13
Bisha, *Eritrea* 81 D4
Bishah, W. →, *Si. Arabia* 80 C5
Bishan, *China* 58 C6
Bishkek, *Kyrgyzstan* 52 E8
Bishnupur, *India* 69 H12
Bisho, *S. Africa* 89 E4
Bishop, *Calif., U.S.A.* 110 H8
Bishop, *Tex., U.S.A.* 113 M6
Bishop Auckland, *U.K.* 14 C6
Bishop's Falls, *Canada* 105 C8
Bishop's Stortford, *U.K.* 15 F8
Bisignano, *Italy* 43 C9
Bisina, L., *Uganda* 86 B3
Biskra, *Algeria* 78 B7
Biskupiec, *Poland* 30 E7
Bismarck, *U.S.A.* 112 B4
Bismarck Arch., *Papua N. G.* 96 H7
Bismark, *Germany* 24 C7
Bismil, *Turkey* 73 D9
Biso, *Uganda* 86 B3
Bison, *U.S.A.* 112 C3
Bīsotūn, *Iran* 70 C5
Bispgården, *Sweden* 10 A10
Bissagos = Bijagós, Arquipélago dos, *Guinea-Biss.* 82 C1
Bissau, *Guinea-Biss.* 82 C1
Bissaula, *Nigeria* 83 D7
Bissikrima, *Guinea* 82 C2
Bissorã, *Guinea-Biss.* 82 C1
Bistcho L., *Canada* 102 B5
Bistreţ, *Romania* 29 G8
Bistrica = Ilirska-Bistrica, *Slovenia* 41 C11
Bistriţa, *Romania* 29 C9
Bistriţa →, *Romania* 29 D11
Bistriţa Năsăud □, *Romania* 29 C9
Bistriţei, Munţii, *Romania* 29 C10
Biswan, *India* 69 F9
Bisztynek, *Poland* 30 D7
Bitburg, *Germany* 25 F2
Bitche, *France* 19 C14
Bithynia, *Turkey* 72 B4
Bitlis, *Turkey* 70 B4
Bitola, *Macedonia* 44 E5
Bitolj = Bitola, *Macedonia* 44 E5
Bitonto, *Italy* 43 A9
Bitter Creek, *U.S.A.* 108 F9
Bitter L. = Buheirat-Murrat-el-Kubra, *Egypt* 80 H8
Bitterfeld, *Germany* 24 D8
Bitterfontein, *S. Africa* 88 E2
Bitterroot →, *U.S.A.* 108 C6
Bitterroot Range, *U.S.A.* 108 D6
Bitterwater, *U.S.A.* 110 J6
Bitti, *Italy* 42 B2
Bittou, *Burkina Faso* 83 C4
Biu, *Nigeria* 83 C7
Bivolari, *Romania* 29 C12
Bivolu, Vf., *Romania* 29 C10
Biwa-Ko, *Japan* 55 G8
Biwabik, *U.S.A.* 112 B8
Bixad, *Romania* 29 C8
Bixby, *U.S.A.* 113 H7
Biyang, *China* 56 H7
Biysk, *Russia* 52 D9
Bizana, *S. Africa* 89 E4
Bizen, *Japan* 55 G7
Bizerte, *Tunisia* 79 A7
Bjargtangar, *Iceland* 8 D1
Bjärnum, *Sweden* 11 H7
Bjästa, *Sweden* 10 A12
Bjelasica, *Serbia & M.* 44 D3
Bjelašnica, *Bos.-H.* 28 G3
Bjelovar, *Croatia* 41 C13
Bjerringbro, *Denmark* 11 H3
Björbo, *Sweden* 10 D8
Björklinge, *Sweden* 10 D11
Björneborg = Pori, *Finland* 9 F19
Björneborg, *Sweden* 10 E8
Bjørnevatn, *Norway* 8 B23
Bjørnøya, *Arctic* 4 B8
Bjursås, *Sweden* 10 D9
Bjuv, *Sweden* 11 H6
Bla, *Mali* 82 C3
Blace, *Serbia & M.* 44 C5
Blachownia, *Poland* 31 H5
Black = Da →, *Vietnam* 58 G5
Black →, *Canada* 116 B5
Black →, *Ariz., U.S.A.* 109 K8
Black →, *Ark., U.S.A.* 113 H9
Black →, *Mich., U.S.A.* 116 D2
Black →, *N.Y., U.S.A.* 117 C8
Black →, *Wis., U.S.A.* 112 D9
Black Bay Pen., *Canada* 104 C2
Black Birch L., *Canada* 103 B7
Black Canyon of the Gunnison ⌂, *U.S.A.* 109 G10
Black Diamond, *Canada* 102 C6
Black Duck →, *Canada* 104 A2
Black Forest = Schwarzwald, *Germany* 25 G4
Black Forest, *U.S.A.* 112 F2
Black Hd., *Ireland* 12 C2
Black Hills, *U.S.A.* 112 D3
Black I., *Canada* 103 C9
Black L., *Canada* 103 B7
Black L., *Mich., U.S.A.* 114 C3
Black L., *N.Y., U.S.A.* 117 B9
Black Lake, *Canada* 103 B7
Black Mesa, *U.S.A.* 113 G3
Black Mt. = Mynydd Du, *U.K.* 15 F4
Black Mts., *U.K.* 15 F4
Black Range, *U.S.A.* 109 K10
Black River, *Jamaica* 120 a
Black River Falls, *U.S.A.* 112 C9
Black Rock, *Barbados* 121 g
Black Sea, *Eurasia* 6 G12
Black Tickle, *Canada* 105 B8
Black Volta →, *Africa* 82 D4
Black Warrior →, *U.S.A.* 115 J2
Blackall, *Australia* 94 C4
Blackball, *N.Z.* 91 K3
Blackbull, *Australia* 94 B3
Blackburn, *U.K.* 14 D5
Blackburn with Darwen □, *U.K.* 14 D5
Blackdown Tableland △, *Australia* 94 C4
Blackfoot, *U.S.A.* 108 E7
Blackfoot →, *U.S.A.* 108 C7
Blackfoot River Reservoir, *U.S.A.* 108 E8
Blackpool, *U.K.* 14 D4
Blackpool □, *U.K.* 14 D4
Blackriver, *U.S.A.* 116 B1
Blacks Harbour, *Canada* 105 C6
Blacksburg, *U.S.A.* 114 G5
Blacksod B., *Ireland* 12 B1
Blackstone, *U.S.A.* 114 G7
Blackstone Ra., *Australia* 93 E4
Blackwater = West Road →, *Canada* 102 C4
Blackwater, *Australia* 94 C4
Blackwater →, *Meath, Ireland* 12 C4
Blackwater →, *Waterford, Ireland* 12 D4
Blackwater →, *U.K.* 12 B5
Blackwell, *U.S.A.* 113 G6
Blackwells Corner, *U.S.A.* 111 K7
Bladensburg △, *Australia* 94 C3
Blaenau Ffestiniog, *U.K.* 14 E4
Blaenau Gwent □, *U.K.* 15 F4
Blagaj, *Bos.-H.* 44 C1
Blagnac, *France* 20 E5
Blagnac, Toulouse ✈ (TLS), *France* 20 E5
Blagodarnoye = Blagodarnyy, *Russia* 35 H6
Blagodarnyy, *Russia* 35 H6
Blagoevgrad, *Bulgaria* 44 D7
Blagoveshchensk, *Russia* 53 D13
Blahkiuh, *Indonesia* 63 J18
Blain, *France* 18 E5
Blain, *U.S.A.* 116 F7
Blaine, *Minn., U.S.A.* 112 C8
Blaine, *Wash., U.S.A.* 110 B4
Blaine Lake, *Canada* 103 C7
Blair, *U.S.A.* 112 E6
Blair Athol, *Australia* 94 C4
Blair Atholl, *U.K.* 13 E5
Blairgowrie, *U.K.* 13 E5
Blairsden, *U.S.A.* 110 F6
Blairsville, *U.S.A.* 116 F5
Blaj, *Romania* 29 D8
Blakang Mati, Pulau, *Singapore* 65 d
Blake Pt., *U.S.A.* 112 A10
Blakely, *Ga., U.S.A.* 115 K3
Blakely, *Pa., U.S.A.* 117 E9
Blâmont, *France* 19 D13
Blanc, C., *Spain* 48 B9
Blanc, Mont, *Europe* 21 C10
Blanc-Sablon, *Canada* 105 B8
Blanca, B., *Argentina* 128 D4
Blanca Peak, *U.S.A.* 109 H11
Blanche, C., *Australia* 95 E1
Blanche, L., *S. Austral., Australia* 95 D2
Blanche, L., *W. Austral., Australia* 92 D3
Blanchisseuse, *Trin. & Tob.* 125 K15
Blanco, *S. Africa* 88 E3
Blanco, *U.S.A.* 113 K5
Blanco →, *Argentina* 126 C2
Blanco, C., *Costa Rica* 120 E2
Blanco, C., *U.S.A.* 108 E1
Blanda →, *Iceland* 8 D3
Blandford Forum, *U.K.* 15 G5
Blanding, *U.S.A.* 109 H9
Blanes, *Spain* 38 D7
Blangy-sur-Bresle, *France* 19 C8
Blanice →, *Czech Rep.* 26 B7
Blankaholm, *Sweden* 11 G10
Blankenberge, *Belgium* 17 C3
Blankenburg, *Germany* 24 D6
Blanquefort, *France* 20 D3
Blanquillo, *Uruguay* 127 C4
Blansko, *Czech Rep.* 27 B9
Blantyre, *Malawi* 87 F4
Blarney, *Ireland* 12 E3
Blasdell, *U.S.A.* 116 D6
Błaszki, *Poland* 31 G5
Blatná, *Czech Rep.* 26 B6
Blato, *Croatia* 41 F13
Blaubeuren, *Germany* 25 G5
Blaustein, *Germany* 25 G5
Blåvands Huk, *Denmark* 11 J2
Blaydon, *U.K.* 14 C6
Blaye, *France* 20 C3
Blaye-les-Mines, *France* 20 D6
Blayney, *Australia* 95 E4
Blaze, Pt., *Australia* 92 B5
Błażowa, *Poland* 31 J9
Bleckede, *Germany* 24 B6
Bled, *Slovenia* 41 B11
Bleiburg, *Austria* 26 E7
Blejeşti, *Romania* 29 F10
Blekinge, *Sweden* 9 H16
Blekinge län □, *Sweden* 11 H9
Blenheim, *Canada* 116 D3
Blenheim, *N.Z.* 91 J4
Bléone →, *France* 21 D10
Blérancourt, *France* 19 C10
Bletchley, *U.K.* 15 F7
Blida, *Algeria* 78 A6
Blidö, *Sweden* 10 E12
Blidsberg, *Sweden* 11 G7
Blieskastel, *Germany* 25 F3
Bligh Sound, *N.Z.* 91 L1
Blind River, *Canada* 104 C3
Blinisht, *Albania* 44 E3
Bliss, *Idaho, U.S.A.* 108 E6
Bliss, *N.Y., U.S.A.* 116 D6
Blissfield, *U.S.A.* 116 F3
Blitar, *Indonesia* 63 H15
Blitta, *Togo* 83 D5
Block I., *U.S.A.* 117 E13
Block Island Sd., *U.S.A.* 117 E13
Bloemfontein, *S. Africa* 88 D4
Bloemhof, *S. Africa* 88 D4
Blois, *France* 18 E8
Blomskog, *Sweden* 10 E6
Blomstermåla, *Sweden* 11 H10
Blönduós, *Iceland* 8 D3
Blongas, *Indonesia* 63 K19
Blonie, *Poland* 31 F7
Bloodvein →, *Canada* 103 C9
Bloody Foreland, *Ireland* 12 A3
Bloomer, *U.S.A.* 112 C9
Bloomfield, *Canada* 116 C7
Bloomfield, *Iowa, U.S.A.* 112 E8
Bloomfield, *N. Mex., U.S.A.* 109 H10
Bloomfield, *Nebr., U.S.A.* 112 D6
Bloomington, *Ill., U.S.A.* 112 E10
Bloomington, *Ind., U.S.A.* 114 F2
Bloomington, *Minn., U.S.A.* 112 C8
Bloomsburg, *U.S.A.* 117 F8
Bloomsbury, *Australia* 94 J6
Blora, *Indonesia* 63 G14
Blossburg, *U.S.A.* 116 E7
Blouberg, *S. Africa* 89 C4
Blountstown, *U.S.A.* 115 K3
Bludenz, *Austria* 26 D2
Blue Earth, *U.S.A.* 112 D8
Blue Hole △, *Belize* 120 C2
Blue Lagoon △, *Zambia* 87 F2
Blue Mesa Reservoir, *U.S.A.* 109 G10
Blue Mountain Lake, *U.S.A.* 117 C10
Blue Mountain Pk., *Jamaica* 120 a
Blue Mts., *Jamaica* 120 a
Blue Mts., *Maine, U.S.A.* 117 B14
Blue Mts., *Oreg., U.S.A.* 108 D4
Blue Mts., *Pa., U.S.A.* 117 F8
Blue Mud B., *Australia* 94 A2
Blue Nile = Nîl el Azraq →, *Sudan* 81 D3
Blue Rapids, *U.S.A.* 112 F6
Blue Ridge Mts., *U.S.A.* 115 G5
Blue River, *Canada* 102 C5
Bluefield, *U.S.A.* 114 G5
Bluefields, *Nic.* 120 D3
Bluff, *Australia* 94 C4
Bluff, *N.Z.* 91 M2
Bluff, *U.S.A.* 109 H9
Bluff Knoll, *Australia* 93 F2
Bluff Pt., *Australia* 93 E1
Bluffton, *U.S.A.* 114 E3
Blumenau, *Brazil* 127 B6
Blunt, *U.S.A.* 112 C5
Bly, *U.S.A.* 108 E3
Blyde River Canyon ⌂, *S. Africa* 89 C5
Blyth, *Canada* 116 C3
Blyth, *U.K.* 14 B6
Blythe, *U.S.A.* 111 M12
Blytheville, *U.S.A.* 113 H10
Bo, *S. Leone* 82 D2
Bo Duc, *Vietnam* 65 G6
Bo Hai, *China* 57 E10
Bo Xian = Bozhou, *China* 56 H8
Boa Vista, *Brazil* 124 C6
Boac, *Phil.* 61 E4
Boaco, *Nic.* 120 D2
Bo'ai, *China* 56 G7
Boal, *Spain* 36 B4
Boalsburg, *U.S.A.* 116 F7
Boane, *Mozam.* 89 D5
Boardman, *U.S.A.* 116 E4
Bobadah, *Australia* 95 E4
Bobai, *China* 58 F7
Bobbili, *India* 67 K13
Bóbbio, *Italy* 40 D6
Bobcaygeon, *Canada* 116 B6
Böblingen, *Germany* 25 G5
Bobo-Dioulasso, *Burkina Faso* 82 C4
Bobolice, *Poland* 30 E3
Boboshevo, *Bulgaria* 44 D7
Bobov Dol, *Bulgaria* 44 D6
Bóbr →, *Poland* 31 F2
Bobraomby, Tanjon' i, *Madag.* 89 A8
Bobrinets, *Ukraine* 33 H7
Bobrov, *Russia* 34 E5
Bobrovitsa, *Ukraine* 33 G6
Bobruysk = Babruysk, *Belarus* 33 F5
Boby, Pic, *Madag.* 85 J9
Boca de Drago, *Venezuela* 125 K15
Bôca do Acre, *Brazil* 124 E5
Boca Raton, *U.S.A.* 115 M5
Bocanda, *Ivory C.* 82 D4
Bocas del Toro, *Panama* 120 E3
Boceguillas, *Spain* 36 D7
Bochmanivka, *Ukraine* 29 C14
Bochnia, *Poland* 31 J7
Bocholt, *Germany* 24 D2
Bochum, *Germany* 24 D3
Bockenem, *Germany* 24 C6
Boćki, *Poland* 31 F10
Bocognano, *France* 21 F13
Bocoyna, *Mexico* 118 B3
Bocşa, *Romania* 28 E6
Boda, *Dalarna, Sweden* 10 C9
Böda, *Kalmar, Sweden* 11 G11
Boda, *Västernorrland, Sweden* 10 B10
Bodafors, *Sweden* 11 G8
Bodaybo, *Russia* 53 D12
Boddam, *U.K.* 13 B7
Boddington, *Australia* 93 F2
Bode Sadu, *Nigeria* 83 D5
Bodega Bay, *U.S.A.* 110 G3
Boden, *Sweden* 8 D19
Bodensee, *Europe* 25 H5
Bodenteich, *Germany* 24 C6
Bodhan, *India* 66 K10
Bodinga, *Nigeria* 83 C6
Bodmin, *U.K.* 15 G3
Bodmin Moor, *U.K.* 15 G3
Bodø, *Norway* 8 C16
Bodrog →, *Hungary* 28 B6
Bodrum, *Turkey* 47 D9
Bódva →, *Hungary* 28 B5
Boën, *France* 21 C8
Boende, *Dem. Rep. of the Congo* 84 E4
Boerne, *U.S.A.* 113 L5
Boesmans →, *S. Africa* 88 E4
Boffa, *Guinea* 82 C2
Bogalusa, *U.S.A.* 113 K10
Bogan →, *Australia* 95 D4
Bogan Gate, *Australia* 95 E4
Bogandé, *Burkina Faso* 83 C4
Bogantungan, *Australia* 94 C4
Bogata, *U.S.A.* 113 J7
Bogatić, *Serbia & M.* 44 B3
Boğazkale, *Turkey* 72 B6
Boğazlıyan, *Turkey* 72 C6
Bogen, *Sweden* 10 D6
Bogense, *Denmark* 11 J4
Bogetići, *Serbia & M.* 44 D2
Boggabilla, *Australia* 95 D5
Boggabri, *Australia* 95 E5
Boggeragh Mts., *Ireland* 12 D3
Boglan = Solhan, *Turkey* 70 B4
Bognor Regis, *U.K.* 15 G7
Bogo, *Phil.* 61 F6
Bogodukhov = Bohodukhiv, *Ukraine* 33 G8
Bogol Manya, *Ethiopia* 81 G5
Bogong, Mt., *Australia* 95 F4
Bogor, *Indonesia* 63 G12
Bogoroditsk, *Russia* 32 F10
Bogorodsk, *Russia* 34 B6
Bogoso, *Ghana* 82 D4
Bogotá, *Colombia* 124 C4
Bogotol, *Russia* 52 D9
Bogou, *Togo* 83 C5
Bogra, *Bangla.* 67 G16
Boguchany, *Russia* 53 D10
Boguchar, *Russia* 34 F5
Bogué, *Mauritania* 82 B2
Boguslav, *Ukraine* 33 H6
Boguszów-Gorce, *Poland* 31 H3
Bohain-en-Vermandois, *France* 19 C10
Bohdan, *Ukraine* 29 B9
Bohemian Forest = Böhmerwald, *Germany* 25 F9
Bohinjska Bistrica, *Slovenia* 41 B11
Böhmerwald, *Germany* 25 F9
Bohmte, *Germany* 24 C4
Bohodukhiv, *Ukraine* 33 G8
Bohol □, *Phil.* 61 G6
Bohol Sea, *Phil.* 63 C6
Bohongou, *Burkina Faso* 83 C5
Böhönye, *Hungary* 28 D2
Bohorodchany, *Ukraine* 29 B9

Bohuslän, *Sweden* 11 F5
Boi, *Nigeria* 83 D6
Boi, Pta. de, *Brazil* 127 A6
Boiaçu, *Brazil* 124 D6
Boileau, C., *Australia* 92 C3
Boing'o, *Sudan* 81 F3
Boiro, *Spain* 36 C2
Boise, *U.S.A.* 108 E5
Boise City, *U.S.A.* 113 G3
Boissevain, *Canada* 103 D8
Bóite →, *Italy* 41 B9
Boitzenburg, *Germany* 24 B9
Boizenburg, *Germany* 24 B6
Bojador, C., *W. Sahara* 78 C3
Bojana →, *Albania* 44 E3
Bojano, *Italy* 43 A7
Bojanowo, *Poland* 31 G3
Bøjden, *Denmark* 11 J4
Bojnūrd, *Iran* 71 B8
Bojonegoro, *Indonesia* 63 G14
Boju, *Nigeria* 83 D6
Boka, *Serbia & M.* 28 E5
Boka Kotorska, *Serbia & M.* 44 D2
Bokala, *Ivory C.* 82 D4
Bokani, *Nigeria* 83 D6
Bokaro, *India* 69 H11
Boké, *Guinea* 82 C2
Bokhara →, *Australia* 95 D4
Bokkos, *Nigeria* 83 D6
Boknafjorden, *Norway* 9 G11
Bokora ⌓, *Uganda* 86 B3
Bokoro, *Chad* 79 F9
Bokpyin, *Burma* 65 G2
Boksitogorsk, *Russia* 32 C7
Bol, *Croatia* 41 E13
Bolama, *Guinea-Biss.* 82 C1
Bolan →, *Pakistan* 68 E2
Bolan Pass, *Pakistan* 66 E5
Bolaños →, *Mexico* 118 C4
Bolaños de Calatrava, *Spain* 37 G7
Bolayır, *Turkey* 45 F10
Bolbec, *France* 18 C7
Boldājī, *Iran* 71 D6
Boldeşti-Scăeni, *Romania* 29 E11
Bole, *China* 60 B3
Bole, *Ethiopia* 81 F4
Bole, *Ghana* 82 D4
Bolekhiv, *Ukraine* 33 H2
Bolesławiec, *Poland* 31 G2
Bolgatanga, *Ghana* 83 C4
Bolgrad = Bolhrad, *Ukraine* 29 E13
Bolhrad, *Ukraine* 29 E13
Bolinao, *Phil.* 61 C3
Bolintin-Vale, *Romania* 29 F10
Bolívar, *Argentina* 126 D3
Bolivar, *Mo., U.S.A.* 113 G8
Bolivar, *N.Y., U.S.A.* 116 D6
Bolivar, *Tenn., U.S.A.* 113 H10
Bolivia ■, *S. Amer.* 124 G6
Bolivian Plateau = Altiplano, *Bolivia* 122 E4
Boljevac, *Serbia & M.* 44 C5
Bolkhov, *Russia* 32 F9
Bolków, *Poland* 31 H3
Bollebygd, *Sweden* 11 G6
Bollène, *France* 21 D8
Bollnäs, *Sweden* 10 C10
Bollon, *Australia* 95 D4
Bollstabruk, *Sweden* 10 B11
Bolmen, *Sweden* 11 H7
Bolobo, *Dem. Rep. of the Congo* 84 E3
Bologna, *Italy* 41 D8
Bologna ✗ (BLQ), *Italy* 41 D8
Bologoye, *Russia* 32 D8
Bolon, Ozero, *Russia* 60 B8
Bolonchenticul, *Mexico* 119 D7
Bolótana, *Italy* 42 B1
Boloven, Cao Nguyen, *Laos* 64 E6
Bolpur, *India* 69 H12
Bolsena, *Italy* 41 F8
Bolsena, L. di, *Italy* 41 F8
Bolshakovo, *Russia* 30 D8
Bolshaya Chernigovka, *Russia* 34 D10
Bolshaya Glushitsa, *Russia* 34 D10
Bolshaya Martynovka, *Russia* 35 G5
Bolshaya Vradiyevka, *Ukraine* 33 J6
Bolshevik, Ostrov, *Russia* 53 B11
Bolshoy Anyuy →, *Russia* 53 C17
Bolshoy Begichev, Ostrov, *Russia* 53 B12
Bolshoy Kavkas = Caucasus Mountains, *Eurasia* 35 J7
Bolshoy Lyakhovskiy, Ostrov, *Russia* 53 B15
Bolshoy Tyuters, Ostrov, *Russia* 9 G22
Bolsward, *Neths.* 17 A5
Bolt Head, *U.K.* 15 G4
Boltaña, *Spain* 38 C5
Boltigen, *Switz.* 25 J3
Bolton, *Canada* 116 C5
Bolton, *U.K.* 14 D5
Bolton Landing, *U.S.A.* 117 C11
Bolu, *Turkey* 72 B4
Bolungavík, *Iceland* 8 C2
Boluo, *China* 59 F10
Bolvadin, *Turkey* 70 B1
Bolzano, *Italy* 41 B8
Bom Jesus da Lapa, *Brazil* 125 F10
Boma, *Dem. Rep. of the Congo* 84 F2
Bombala, *Australia* 95 F4
Bombarral, *Portugal* 37 F1
Bombay = Mumbai, *India* 66 K8
Bombedor, Pta., *Venezuela* 125 L15
Bomboma, *Dem. Rep. of the Congo* 84 D3
Bombombwa, *Dem. Rep. of the Congo* 86 B2
Bomi Hills, *Liberia* 82 D2
Bomili, *Dem. Rep. of the Congo* 86 B2
Bømlo, *Norway* 9 G11
Bomokandi →, *Dem. Rep. of the Congo* 86 B2
Bomu →, *C.A.R.* 84 D4
Bon, C., *Tunisia* 76 C5
Bon Sar Pa, *Vietnam* 64 F6
Bonāb, *Iran* 73 D12
Bonaigarh, *India* 69 J11
Bonaire, *Neth. Ant.* 121 D6
Bonampak, *Mexico* 119 D6
Bonang, *Australia* 95 F4
Bonanza, *Nic.* 120 D3
Bonaparte Arch., *Australia* 92 B3
Boñar, *Spain* 36 C5
Bonar Bridge, *U.K.* 13 D4
Bonasse, *Trin. & Tob.* 125 K15
Bonaventure, *Canada* 105 C6
Bonavista, *Canada* 105 C9
Bonavista, C., *Canada* 105 C9
Bonavista B., *Canada* 105 C9
Bondeno, *Italy* 41 D8
Bondo, *Dem. Rep. of the Congo* 86 B1
Bondoukou, *Ivory C.* 82 D4
Bondowoso, *Indonesia* 63 G15
Bone, Teluk, *Indonesia* 63 E6
Bonerate, *Indonesia* 63 F6
Bonerate, Kepulauan, *Indonesia* 63 F6
Bo'ness, *U.K.* 13 E5
Bonete, Cerro, *Argentina* 126 B2
Bong Son = Hoai Nhon, *Vietnam* 64 E7
Bonga, *Ethiopia* 81 F4
Bongabong, *Phil.* 61 E4
Bongor, *Chad* 79 F9
Bongouanou, *Ivory C.* 82 D4
Bonham, *U.S.A.* 113 J6
Boni, *Mali* 82 B4
Boni ⌓, *Kenya* 86 C5
Bonifacio, *France* 21 G13
Bonifacio, Bouches de, *Medit. S.* 42 A2
Bonin Is. = Ogasawara Gunto, *Pac. Oc.* 96 E6
Bonke, *Ethiopia* 81 F4
Bonkoukou, *Niger* 83 C5
Bonn, *Germany* 24 E3
Bonnat, *France* 19 F8
Bonne Terre, *U.S.A.* 113 G9
Bonners Ferry, *U.S.A.* 108 B5
Bonnétable, *France* 18 D7
Bonneval, *France* 21 C11
Bonneval-sur-Arc, *France* 18 D8
Bonneville, *France* 19 F13
Bonney, L., *Australia* 95 F3
Bonnie Rock, *Australia* 93 F2
Bonny, *Nigeria* 83 E6
Bonny →, *Nigeria* 83 E6
Bonny, Bight of, *Africa* 83 E6
Bonny-sur-Loire, *France* 19 E9
Bonnyrigg, *U.K.* 13 F5
Bonnyville, *Canada* 103 C6
Bono, *Italy* 42 B2
Bonoi, *Indonesia* 63 E9
Bonorva, *Italy* 42 B1
Bonsall, *U.S.A.* 111 M9
Bontang, *Indonesia* 62 D5
Bontebok △, *S. Africa* 88 E3
Bonthe, *S. Leone* 82 D2
Bontoc, *Phil.* 61 C4
Bonyeri, *Ghana* 82 D4
Bonyhád, *Hungary* 28 D3
Bonython Ra., *Australia* 92 D4
Boobakie, *Australia* 93 F5
Booker, *U.S.A.* 113 G4
Boola, *Guinea* 82 D3
Booligal, *Australia* 95 E3
Boonah, *Australia* 95 D5
Boone, *Iowa, U.S.A.* 112 D8
Boone, *N.C., U.S.A.* 115 G5
Booneville, *Ark., U.S.A.* 113 H8
Booneville, *Miss., U.S.A.* 115 H1
Boonville, *Calif., U.S.A.* 110 F3
Boonville, *Ind., U.S.A.* 114 F2
Boonville, *Mo., U.S.A.* 112 F8
Boonville, *N.Y., U.S.A.* 117 C9
Boorabbin △, *Australia* 93 F4
Boorindal, *Australia* 95 E4
Boorowa, *Australia* 95 E4
Boosaaso = Bosaso, *Somali Rep.* 75 E4
Boothia, Gulf of, *Canada* 101 A11
Boothia Pen., *Canada* 100 A10
Bootle, *U.K.* 14 D4
Booué, *Gabon* 84 E2
Boppard, *Germany* 25 E3
Boquete, *Panama* 120 E3
Boquilla, Presa de la, *Mexico* 118 B3
Boquillas del Carmen, *Mexico* 118 B4
Bor, *Czech Rep.* 26 B5
Bor, *Russia* 34 B7
Bor, *Serbia & M.* 44 B6
Bôr, *Sudan* 81 F3
Bor, *Sweden* 11 G8
Bor, *Turkey* 72 D6
Bor Mashash, *Israel* 74 D3
Borah Peak, *U.S.A.* 108 D7
Borang, *Sudan* 81 G3
Borås, *Sweden* 11 G6
Borāzjān, *Iran* 71 D6
Borba, *Brazil* 124 D7
Borba, *Portugal* 37 G3
Borborema, Planalto da, *Brazil* 122 D7
Borcea, *Romania* 29 F12
Borçka, *Turkey* 73 B9
Bord Khūn-e Now, *Iran* 71 D6
Borda, C., *Australia* 95 F2
Bordeaux, *France* 20 D3
Bordeaux ✗ (BOD), *France* 20 D3
Borden, *Australia* 93 F2
Borden-Carleton, *Canada* 105 C7
Borden I., *Canada* 4 B2
Borden Pen., *Canada* 101 A11
Border Ranges △, *Australia* 95 D5
Borders = Scottish Borders □, *U.K.* 13 F6
Bordertown, *Australia* 95 F3
Borðeyri, *Iceland* 8 D3
Bordighera, *Italy* 40 E4
Bordj Fly Ste. Marie, *Algeria* 78 C5
Bordj-in-Eker, *Algeria* 78 D7
Bordj Omar Driss, *Algeria* 78 C7
Bore, *Ethiopia* 81 G4
Borehamwood, *U.K.* 15 F7
Borek Wielkopolski, *Poland* 31 G4
Borensberg, *Sweden* 11 F9
Borgå = Porvoo, *Finland* 9 F21
Borgarfjörður, *Iceland* 8 D7
Borgarnes, *Iceland* 8 D3
Børgefjellet, *Norway* 8 D15
Borger, *Neths.* 17 B6
Borger, *U.S.A.* 113 H4
Borgholm, *Sweden* 11 H10
Bórgia, *Italy* 43 D9
Borgo San Dalmazzo, *Italy* 40 D4
Borgo San Lorenzo, *Italy* 41 E8
Borgo Val di Taro, *Italy* 40 D6
Borgo Valsugana, *Italy* 41 B8
Borgomanero, *Italy* 40 C5
Borgorose, *Italy* 41 F10
Borgosésia, *Italy* 40 C5
Borhoyn Tal, *Mongolia* 56 C6
Bori, *Nigeria* 83 E6
Borikhane, *Laos* 64 C4
Borisoglebsk, *Russia* 34 E6
Borisov = Barysaw, *Belarus* 32 E5
Borisovka, *Russia* 33 G9
Borja, *Peru* 124 D3
Borja, *Spain* 38 D3
Borjas Blancas = Les Borges Blanques, *Spain* 38 D5
Borjomi, *Georgia* 35 K6
Børkop, *Denmark* 11 J3
Borkou, *Chad* 79 E9
Borkum, *Germany* 24 B2
Borlänge, *Sweden* 10 D9
Borley, C., *Antarctica* 5 C5
Borlu, *Turkey* 47 C10
Bormida →, *Italy* 40 D5
Bórmio, *Italy* 40 B7
Borna, *Germany* 24 D8
Borne Sulinowo, *Poland* 30 E3
Borneo, *E. Indies* 62 D5
Bornholm, *Denmark* 11 J8
Bornholms Amtskommune □, *Denmark* 11 J8
Bornholmsgattet, *Europe* 11 J8
Borno □, *Nigeria* 83 C7
Bornos, *Spain* 37 J5
Bornova, *Turkey* 47 C9
Bornu Yassa, *Nigeria* 83 C7
Boro →, *Sudan* 81 F2
Borodino, *Russia* 32 E8
Borodino, *Ukraine* 29 D14
Borogontsy, *Russia* 53 C14
Boromo, *Burkina Faso* 82 C4
Boron, *U.S.A.* 111 L9
Borongan, *Phil.* 61 F6
Borotangba Mts., *C.A.R.* 81 F2
Borotou, *Ivory C.* 82 D3
Borovan, *Bulgaria* 44 C7
Borovichi, *Russia* 32 C7
Borovsk, *Russia* 32 E9
Borrby, *Sweden* 11 J8
Borrego Springs, *U.S.A.* 111 M10
Borriol, *Spain* 38 E4
Borroloola, *Australia* 94 B2
Borşa, *Cluj, Romania* 29 D8
Borşa, *Maramureş, Romania* 29 C9
Borsad, *India* 68 H5
Borsec, *Romania* 29 D10
Borshchiv, *Ukraine* 29 B11
Borsod-Abaúj-Zemplén □, *Hungary* 28 B6
Bort-les-Orgues, *France* 20 C6
Borth, *U.K.* 15 E3
Börtnan, *Sweden* 10 B7
Borūjerd, *Iran* 71 C6
Borynya, *Ukraine* 31 J10
Boryslav, *Ukraine* 31 J10
Boryspil, *Ukraine* 33 G6
Borzhomi = Borjomi, *Georgia* 35 K6
Borzna, *Ukraine* 33 G7
Borzya, *Russia* 53 D12
Bosa, *Italy* 42 B1
Bosanska Dubica, *Bos.-H.* 41 C13
Bosanska Gradiška, *Bos.-H.* 28 E2
Bosanska Kostajnica, *Bos.-H.* 41 C13
Bosanska Krupa, *Bos.-H.* 41 D13
Bosanski Brod, *Bos.-H.* 28 E2
Bosanski Novi, *Bos.-H.* 41 C13
Bosanski Petrovac, *Bos.-H.* 41 D13
Bosanski Šamac, *Bos.-H.* 28 E3
Bosansko Grahovo, *Bos.-H.* 41 D13
Bosaso, *Somali Rep.* 75 E4
Boscastle, *U.K.* 15 G3
Boscobelle, *Barbados* 121 g
Bose, *China* 58 F6
Boshan, *China* 57 F9
Boshof, *S. Africa* 88 D4
Boshrūyeh, *Iran* 71 C8
Bosilegrad, *Serbia & M.* 44 D6
Boskovice, *Czech Rep.* 27 B9
Bosna →, *Bos.-H.* 28 E3
Bosna i Hercegovina = Bosnia-Herzegovina ■, *Europe* 28 G2
Bosnia-Herzegovina ■, *Europe* 28 G2
Bosnik, *Indonesia* 63 E9
Bosobolo, *Dem. Rep. of the Congo* 84 D3
Bosporus = İstanbul Boğazı, *Turkey* 45 E13
Bosque Farms, *U.S.A.* 109 J10
Bossangoa, *C.A.R.* 84 C3
Bossé Bangou, *Niger* 83 C5
Bossier City, *U.S.A.* 113 J8
Bosso, *Niger* 83 C7
Bosso, Dallol →, *Niger* 83 C5
Bostan, *Pakistan* 68 D2
Bostānābād, *Iran* 70 B5
Bosten Hu, *China* 60 B3
Boston, *U.K.* 14 E7
Boston, *U.S.A.* 117 D13
Boston Bar, *Canada* 102 D4
Boston Mts., *U.S.A.* 113 H8
Bosumtwi, L., *Ghana* 83 D4
Bosut →, *Croatia* 28 E3
Boswell, *Canada* 102 D5
Boswell, *U.S.A.* 116 F5
Botad, *India* 68 H4
Botan →, *Turkey* 73 D10
Botene, *Laos* 64 D3
Botev, *Bulgaria* 45 D8
Botevgrad, *Bulgaria* 44 D7
Bothaville, *S. Africa* 88 D4
Bothnia, G. of, *Europe* 8 E19
Bothwell, *Australia* 95 G4
Bothwell, *Canada* 116 D3
Boticas, *Portugal* 36 D3
Botletle →, *Botswana* 88 C3
Botlikh, *Russia* 35 J8
Botna →, *Moldova* 29 D14
Botoroaga, *Romania* 29 F10
Botoşani, *Romania* 29 C11
Botoşani □, *Romania* 29 C11
Botou, *Burkina Faso* 83 C5
Botricello, *Italy* 43 D9
Botro, *Ivory C.* 82 D3
Botswana ■, *Africa* 88 C3
Bottineau, *U.S.A.* 112 A4
Bottnaryd, *Sweden* 11 G7
Bottrop, *Germany* 17 C6
Botucatu, *Brazil* 127 A6
Botwood, *Canada* 105 C8
Bou Djébéha, *Mali* 82 B4
Boû Rjeïmât, *Mauritania* 82 B1
Bouaflé, *Ivory C.* 82 D3
Bouaké, *Ivory C.* 82 D3
Bouar, *C.A.R.* 84 C3
Bouârfa, *Morocco* 78 B5
Boucaut B., *Australia* 94 A1
Bouches-du-Rhône □, *France* 21 E9
Boucle de Baoulé △, *Mali* 82 C3
Boucles de la Seine Normande ⌓, *France* 18 C7
Bouctouche, *Canada* 105 C7
Bougainville, C., *Australia* 92 B4
Bougainville I., *Papua N. G.* 96 H7
Bougainville Reef, *Australia* 94 B4
Bougie = Bejaïa, *Algeria* 78 A7
Bougouni, *Mali* 82 C3
Bouillon, *Belgium* 17 E5
Boukombé, *Benin* 83 C5
Boulal, *Mali* 82 B3
Boulazac, *France* 20 C4
Boulder, *Colo., U.S.A.* 112 E2
Boulder, *Mont., U.S.A.* 108 C7
Boulder City, *U.S.A.* 111 K12
Boulder Creek, *U.S.A.* 110 H4
Boulder Dam = Hoover Dam, *U.S.A.* 111 K12
Bouli, *Mauritania* 82 B2
Boulia, *Australia* 94 C2
Bouligny, *France* 19 C12
Boulogne →, *France* 18 E5
Boulogne-sur-Gesse, *France* 20 E4
Boulogne-sur-Mer, *France* 19 B8
Bouloire, *France* 18 E7
Boulouli, *Mali* 82 B3
Boulsa, *Burkina Faso* 83 C4
Boultoum, *Niger* 83 C7
Boûmdeïd, *Mauritania* 82 B2
Boun Neua, *Laos* 64 B3
Boun Tai, *Laos* 64 B3
Bouna, *Ivory C.* 82 D4
Boundary Peak, *U.S.A.* 110 H8
Boundiali, *Ivory C.* 82 D3
Bountiful, *U.S.A.* 108 F8
Bounty Is., *Pac. Oc.* 96 M9
Boura, *Mali* 82 C4
Bourbon-Lancy, *France* 19 F10
Bourbon-l'Archambault, *France* 19 F10
Bourbonnais, *France* 19 F10
Bourbonne-les-Bains, *France* 19 E12
Bourbourg, *France* 19 B9
Bourdel L., *Canada* 104 A5
Bourem, *Mali* 83 B4
Bourg, *France* 20 C3
Bourg-Argental, *France* 21 C8
Bourg-de-Péage, *France* 21 C9
Bourg-en-Bresse, *France* 19 F12
Bourg-Lastic, *France* 20 C6
Bourg-Madame, *France* 20 F5
Bourg-St-Andéol, *France* 21 D8
Bourg-St-Maurice, *France* 21 C10
Bourganeuf, *France* 20 C5
Bourges, *France* 19 E9
Bourget, *Canada* 117 A9
Bourget, Lac du, *France* 21 C9
Bourgneuf, B. de, *France* 18 E4
Bourgneuf-en-Retz, *France* 18 E5
Bourgogne □, *France* 19 F11
Bourgoin-Jallieu, *France* 21 C9
Bourgueil, *France* 18 E7
Bourke, *Australia* 95 E4
Bourne, *U.K.* 14 E7
Bournemouth, *U.K.* 15 G6
Bournemouth □, *U.K.* 15 G6
Bouroum, *Burkina Faso* 83 C4
Bouse, *U.S.A.* 111 M13
Boussac, *France* 19 F9
Boussé, *Burkina Faso* 83 C4
Boussouma, *Burkina Faso* 83 C4
Boutilimit, *Mauritania* 82 B2
Boutonne →, *France* 20 C3
Bouvet I. = Bouvetøya, *Antarctica* 3 G10
Bouvetøya, *Antarctica* 3 G10
Bouxwiller, *France* 19 D14
Bouza, *Niger* 83 C6
Bouzonville, *France* 19 C13
Bova Marina, *Italy* 43 E8
Bovalino Marina, *Italy* 43 D9
Bovec, *Slovenia* 41 B10
Bovill, *U.S.A.* 108 C5
Bovino, *Italy* 43 A8
Bovril, *Argentina* 126 C4
Bow →, *Canada* 102 C6
Bow Island, *Canada* 102 D6
Bowbells, *U.S.A.* 112 A3
Bowdle, *U.S.A.* 112 C5
Bowelling, *Australia* 93 F2
Bowen, *Argentina* 126 D2
Bowen, *Australia* 94 J6
Bowen Mts., *Australia* 95 F4
Bowie, *Ariz., U.S.A.* 109 K9
Bowie, *Tex., U.S.A.* 113 J6
Bowkān, *Iran* 70 B5
Bowland, Forest of, *U.K.* 14 D5
Bowling Green, *Ky., U.S.A.* 114 G2
Bowling Green, *Ohio, U.S.A.* 114 E4
Bowling Green, C., *Australia* 94 B4
Bowling Green Bay △, *Australia* 94 B4
Bowman, *U.S.A.* 112 B3
Bowman I., *Antarctica* 5 C8
Bowmanville = Clarington, *Canada* 116 C6
Bowmore, *U.K.* 13 F2
Bowral, *Australia* 95 E5
Bowraville, *Australia* 95 E5
Bowron →, *Canada* 102 C4
Bowron Lake ⌓, *Canada* 102 C4
Bowser L., *Canada* 102 B3
Bowsman, *Canada* 103 C8
Bowwood, *Zambia* 87 F2
Box Cr. →, *Australia* 95 E3
Boxholm, *Sweden* 11 F9
Boxmeer, *Neths.* 17 C5
Boxtel, *Neths.* 17 C5
Boyabat, *Turkey* 72 B6
Boyalıca, *Turkey* 45 F13
Boyang, *China* 59 C11
Boyany, *Ukraine* 29 B11
Boyce, *U.S.A.* 113 K8
Boyd L., *Canada* 104 B4
Boyle, *Canada* 102 C6
Boyle, *Ireland* 12 C3
Boyne →, *Ireland* 12 C5
Boyne City, *U.S.A.* 114 C3
Boynitsa, *Bulgaria* 44 C6
Boynton Beach, *U.S.A.* 115 M5
Boyolali, *Indonesia* 63 G14
Boyoma, Chutes, *Dem. Rep. of the Congo* 86 B2
Boysen Reservoir, *U.S.A.* 108 E9
Boyuibe, *Bolivia* 124 G6
Boyup Brook, *Australia* 93 F2
Boz Burun, *Turkey* 45 F12
Boz Dağ, *Turkey* 47 D11
Boz Dağları, *Turkey* 47 C10
Bozburun, *Turkey* 47 E10
Bozcaada, *Turkey* 72 C2
Bozdoğan, *Turkey* 47 D10
Bozeman, *U.S.A.* 108 D8
Bozen = Bolzano, *Italy* 41 B8
Boževac, *Serbia & M.* 44 B5
Bozhou, *China* 56 H8
Bozkır, *Turkey* 72 D5
Bozkurt, *Turkey* 47 D11
Bozouls, *France* 20 D6
Bozoum, *C.A.R.* 84 C3
Bozova, *Antalya, Turkey* 47 D12
Bozova, *Sanliurfa, Turkey* 73 D8
Bozovici, *Romania* 28 F7
Bozüyük, *Turkey* 47 B12
Bra, *Italy* 40 D4
Braås, *Sweden* 11 G9
Brabant □, *Belgium* 17 D4
Brabant L., *Canada* 103 B8
Brabrand, *Denmark* 11 H4
Brač, *Croatia* 41 E13
Bracadale, L., *U.K.* 13 D2
Bracciano, *Italy* 41 F9
Bracciano, L. di, *Italy* 41 F9
Bracebridge, *Canada* 116 A5
Brach, *Libya* 79 C8
Bracieux, *France* 18 E8
Bräcke, *Sweden* 10 B9
Brackettville, *U.S.A.* 113 L4
Brački Kanal, *Croatia* 41 E13
Bracknell, *U.K.* 15 F7
Bracknell Forest □, *U.K.* 15 F7
Brad, *Romania* 28 D7
Brádano →, *Italy* 43 B9
Bradenton, *U.S.A.* 115 M4
Bradford, *Canada* 116 B5
Bradford, *U.K.* 14 D6
Bradford, *Pa., U.S.A.* 116 E6
Bradford, *Vt., U.S.A.* 117 C12
Bradley, *Ark., U.S.A.* 113 J8
Bradley, *Calif., U.S.A.* 110 K6
Bradley Institute, *Zimbabwe* 87 F3
Brady, *U.S.A.* 113 K5
Brædstrup, *Denmark* 11 J3
Braeside, *Canada* 117 A8
Braga, *Portugal* 36 D2
Braga □, *Portugal* 36 D2
Bragadiru, *Romania* 29 G10
Bragado, *Argentina* 126 D3
Bragança, *Brazil* 125 D9
Bragança, *Portugal* 36 D4
Bragança □, *Portugal* 36 D4
Bragança Paulista, *Brazil* 127 A6
Brahestad = Raahe, *Finland* 8 D21
Brahmanbaria, *Bangla.* 67 H17
Brahmani →, *India* 67 J15
Brahmapur, *India* 67 K14
Brahmaputra →, *Asia* 69 H13
Braich-y-pwll, *U.K.* 14 E3
Braidwood, *Australia* 95 F4
Brăila, *Romania* 29 E12
Brăila □, *Romania* 29 E12
Brainerd, *U.S.A.* 112 B7
Braintree, *U.K.* 15 F8
Braintree, *U.S.A.* 117 D14
Brak →, *S. Africa* 88 D3
Brake, *Germany* 24 B4

Brakel, *Germany* 24 D5
Bräkne-Hoby, *Sweden* 11 H9
Brakwater, *Namibia* 88 C2
Brålanda, *Sweden* 11 F6
Bramberg, *Germany* 25 E6
Bramdrupdam, *Denmark* 11 J3
Bramming, *Denmark* 11 J2
Brämön, *Sweden* 10 B11
Brampton, *Canada* 116 C5
Brampton, *U.K.* 14 C5
Bramsche, *Germany* 24 C3
Bramton I., *Australia* 94 J7
Branco →, *Brazil* 124 D6
Brandberg, *Namibia* 88 C1
Brandberg ⌂, *Namibia* 88 C1
Brande, *Denmark* 11 J3
Brandenburg = Neubrandenburg, *Germany* 24 B9
Brandenburg, *Germany* 24 C8
Brandenburg □, *Germany* 24 C9
Brandfort, *S. Africa* 88 D4
Brando, *France* 21 F13
Brandon, *Canada* 103 D9
Brandon, *U.S.A.* 117 C11
Brandon B., *Ireland* 12 D1
Brandon Mt., *Ireland* 12 D1
Brandsen, *Argentina* 126 D4
Brandvlei, *S. Africa* 88 E3
Brandýs nad Labem, *Czech Rep.* 26 A7
Brăneşti, *Romania* 29 F11
Branford, *U.S.A.* 117 E12
Braniewo, *Poland* 30 D6
Bransfield Str., *Antarctica* 5 C18
Brańsk, *Poland* 31 F9
Branson, *U.S.A.* 113 G8
Brantford, *Canada* 116 C4
Brantôme, *France* 20 C4
Branzi, *Italy* 40 B6
Bras d'Or L., *Canada* 105 C7
Brasher Falls, *U.S.A.* 117 B10
Brasil, Planalto, *Brazil* 122 E6
Brasiléia, *Brazil* 124 F5
Brasília, *Brazil* 125 G9
Brasília Legal, *Brazil* 125 D7
Braslaw, *Belarus* 9 J22
Braslovče, *Slovenia* 41 B12
Braşov, *Romania* 29 E10
Braşov □, *Romania* 29 E10
Brass, *Nigeria* 83 E6
Brass →, *Nigeria* 83 E6
Brassac-les-Mines, *France* 20 C7
Brasschaat, *Belgium* 17 C4
Brassey, Banjaran, *Malaysia* 62 D5
Brassey Ra., *Australia* 93 E3
Brasstown Bald, *U.S.A.* 115 H4
Brastad, *Sweden* 11 F5
Brastavățu, *Romania* 29 G9
Bratan = Morozov, *Bulgaria* 45 D9
Brateş, *Romania* 29 E11
Bratislava, *Slovak Rep.* 27 C10
Bratislava M.R. Stefanik ✕ (BTS), *Slovak Rep.* 27 C10
Bratislavský □, *Slovak Rep.* 27 C10
Bratsigovo, *Bulgaria* 45 D8
Bratsk, *Russia* 53 D11
Brattleboro, *U.S.A.* 117 D12
Bratunac, *Bos.-H.* 28 F4
Braunau, *Austria* 26 C6
Braunschweig, *Germany* 24 C6
Braunton, *U.K.* 15 F3
Bravicea, *Moldova* 29 C13
Bråviken, *Sweden* 11 F10
Bravo del Norte, Rio = Grande, Rio →, *U.S.A.* 113 N6
Brawley, *U.S.A.* 111 N11
Bray, *Ireland* 12 C5
Bray, Mt., *Australia* 94 A1
Bray-sur-Seine, *France* 19 D10
Brazeau →, *Canada* 102 C5
Brazil, *U.S.A.* 114 F2
Brazil ■, *S. Amer.* 125 F9
Brazilian Highlands = Brasil, Planalto, *Brazil* 122 E6
Brazo Sur →, *S. Amer.* 126 B4
Brazos →, *U.S.A.* 113 L7
Brazzaville, *Congo* 84 E3
Brčko, *Bos.-H.* 28 F3
Brda →, *Poland* 31 E5
Brdy, *Czech Rep.* 26 B6
Breaden, L., *Australia* 93 E4
Breaksea Sd., *N.Z.* 91 L1
Bream B., *N.Z.* 91 F5
Bream Hd., *N.Z.* 91 F5
Breas, *Chile* 126 B1
Breaza, *Romania* 29 E10
Brebes, *Indonesia* 63 G13
Brechin, *Canada* 116 B5
Brechin, *U.K.* 13 E6
Brecht, *Belgium* 17 C4
Breckenridge, *Colo., U.S.A.* 108 G10
Breckenridge, *Minn., U.S.A.* 112 B6
Breckenridge, *Tex., U.S.A.* 113 J5
Breckland, *U.K.* 15 E8
Břeclav, *Czech Rep.* 27 C9
Brecon, *U.K.* 15 F4
Brecon Beacons, *U.K.* 15 F4
Brecon Beacons △, *U.K.* 15 F4
Breda, *Neths.* 17 C4
Bredaryd, *Sweden* 11 G7
Bredasdorp, *S. Africa* 88 E3
Bredebro, *Denmark* 11 J2
Bredstedt, *Germany* 24 A4
Bree, *Belgium* 17 C5
Bregalnica →, *Macedonia* 44 E6
Bregenz, *Austria* 26 D2
Bregovo, *Bulgaria* 44 B6
Bréhal, *France* 18 D5
Bréhat, Î. de, *France* 18 D4
Breiðafjörður, *Iceland* 8 D2
Breil-sur-Roya, *France* 21 E11
Breisach, *Germany* 25 G3
Brejo, *Brazil* 125 D10
Bremen, *Germany* 24 B4
Bremen □, *Germany* 24 B4
Bremer Bay, *Australia* 93 F2
Bremer I., *Australia* 94 A2
Bremerhaven, *Germany* 24 B4
Bremerton, *U.S.A.* 110 C4
Bremervörde, *Germany* 24 B5
Brenes, *Spain* 37 H5
Brenham, *U.S.A.* 113 K6
Brenne, *France* 20 B5
Brenne ⌂, *France* 20 B5
Brennerpass, *Austria* 26 D4
Breno, *Italy* 40 C7
Brent, *U.S.A.* 115 J2
Brenta →, *Italy* 41 C9
Brentwood, *U.K.* 15 F8
Brentwood, *Calif., U.S.A.* 110 H5
Brentwood, *N.Y., U.S.A.* 117 F11
Bréscia, *Italy* 40 C7
Breskens, *Neths.* 17 C3
Breslau = Wrocław, *Poland* 31 G4
Bresle →, *France* 18 B8
Bressanone, *Italy* 41 B8
Bressay, *U.K.* 13 A7
Bresse, *France* 19 F12
Bressuire, *France* 18 F6
Brest, *Belarus* 33 F2
Brest, *France* 18 D2
Brest-Litovsk = Brest, *Belarus* 33 F2
Bretagne □, *France* 18 D3
Bretçu, *Romania* 29 D11
Bretenoux, *France* 20 D5
Breteuil, *Eure, France* 18 D7
Breteuil, *Oise, France* 19 C9
Breton, *Canada* 102 C6
Breton, Pertuis, *France* 20 B2
Breton Sd., *U.S.A.* 113 L10
Brett, C., *N.Z.* 91 F5
Bretten, *Germany* 25 F4
Breuil-Cervínia, *Italy* 40 C4
Brevard, *U.S.A.* 115 H4
Breves, *Brazil* 125 D8
Brewarrina, *Australia* 95 E4
Brewer, *U.S.A.* 115 C11
Brewer, Mt., *U.S.A.* 110 J8
Brewerville, *Liberia* 82 D2
Brewster, *N.Y., U.S.A.* 117 E11
Brewster, *Ohio, U.S.A.* 116 F3
Brewster, *Wash., U.S.A.* 108 B4
Brewster, Kap = Kangikajik, *Greenland* 4 B6
Brewton, *U.S.A.* 115 K2
Breyten, *S. Africa* 89 D5
Breza, *Bos.-H.* 28 F3
Brežice, *Slovenia* 41 C12
Březnice, *Czech Rep.* 26 B6
Breznik, *Bulgaria* 44 D6
Brezno, *Slovak Rep.* 27 C12
Brezoi, *Romania* 29 E9
Brezovica, *Serbia & M.* 44 D5
Brezovo, *Bulgaria* 45 D9
Briançon, *France* 21 D10
Briare, *France* 19 E9
Briático, *Italy* 43 D9
Bribie I., *Australia* 95 D5
Bribri, *Costa Rica* 120 E3
Briceni, *Moldova* 29 B12
Bricquebec, *France* 18 C5
Bridgefield, *Barbados* 121 g
Bridgehampton, *U.S.A.* 117 F12
Bridgend, *U.K.* 15 F4
Bridgend □, *U.K.* 15 F4
Bridgeport, *Calif., U.S.A.* 110 G7
Bridgeport, *Conn., U.S.A.* 117 E11
Bridgeport, *Nebr., U.S.A.* 112 E3
Bridgeport, *Tex., U.S.A.* 113 J6
Bridger, *U.S.A.* 108 D9
Bridgeton, *U.S.A.* 114 F8
Bridgetown, *Australia* 93 F2
Bridgetown, *Barbados* 121 g
Bridgetown, *Canada* 105 D6
Bridgewater, *Canada* 105 D7
Bridgewater, *Mass., U.S.A.* 117 E14
Bridgewater, *N.Y., U.S.A.* 117 D9
Bridgewater, C., *Australia* 95 F3
Bridgewater-Gagebrook, *Australia* 95 G4
Bridgnorth, *U.K.* 15 E5
Bridgton, *U.S.A.* 117 B14
Bridgwater, *U.K.* 15 F5
Bridgwater B., *U.K.* 15 F4
Bridlington, *U.K.* 14 C7
Bridlington B., *U.K.* 14 C7
Bridport, *Australia* 95 G4
Bridport, *U.K.* 15 G5
Briec, *France* 18 D2
Brienne-le-Château, *France* 19 D11
Brienon-sur-Armançon, *France* 19 E10
Brienz, *Switz.* 25 J4
Brienzersee, *Switz.* 25 J3
Brière ⌂, *France* 18 E4
Brig, *Switz.* 25 J3
Brigg, *U.K.* 14 D7
Brigham City, *U.S.A.* 108 F7
Bright, *Australia* 95 F4
Brighton, *Australia* 95 F2
Brighton, *Canada* 116 B7
Brighton, *Trin. & Tob.* 125 K15
Brighton, *U.K.* 15 G7
Brighton, *Colo., U.S.A.* 112 F2
Brighton, *N.Y., U.S.A.* 116 C7
Brignogan-Plage, *France* 18 D2
Brignoles, *France* 21 E10
Brihuega, *Spain* 38 E2
Brikama, *Gambia* 82 C1
Brilliant, *U.S.A.* 116 F4
Brilon, *Germany* 24 D4
Bríndisi, *Italy* 43 B10
Brinje, *Croatia* 41 D12
Brinkley, *U.S.A.* 113 H9
Brinnon, *U.S.A.* 110 C4
Brion, Î., *Canada* 105 C7
Brionne, *France* 18 C7
Brionski, *Croatia* 41 D10
Brioude, *France* 20 C7
Briouze, *France* 18 D6
Brisbane, *Australia* 95 D5
Brisbane →, *Australia* 95 D5
Brisighella, *Italy* 41 D8
Bristol, *U.K.* 15 F5
Bristol, *Conn., U.S.A.* 117 E12
Bristol, *Pa., U.S.A.* 117 F10
Bristol, *R.I., U.S.A.* 117 E13
Bristol, *Tenn., U.S.A.* 115 G4
Bristol, City of □, *U.K.* 15 F5
Bristol B., *U.S.A.* 100 C4
Bristol Channel, *U.K.* 15 F3
Bristol I., *Antarctica* 5 B1
Bristol L., *U.S.A.* 109 J5
Bristow, *U.S.A.* 113 H6
Britain = Great Britain, *Europe* 6 E5
British Columbia □, *Canada* 102 C3
British Indian Ocean Terr. = Chagos Arch. ◩, *Ind. Oc.* 50 K11
British Isles, *Europe* 6 D4
British Virgin Is. ◩, *W. Indies* 121 e
Brits, *S. Africa* 89 D4
Britstown, *S. Africa* 88 E3
Britt, *Canada* 104 C3
Brittany = Bretagne □, *France* 18 D3
Britton, *U.S.A.* 112 C6
Brive-la-Gaillarde, *France* 20 C5
Briviesca, *Spain* 36 C7
Brixen = Bressanone, *Italy* 41 B8
Brixham, *U.K.* 15 G4
Brnaze, *Croatia* 41 E13
Brnenský □, *Czech Rep.* 27 B9
Brno, *Czech Rep.* 27 B9
Broach = Bharuch, *India* 66 J8
Broad →, *U.S.A.* 115 J5
Broad Arrow, *Australia* 93 F3
Broad B., *U.K.* 13 C2
Broad Haven, *Ireland* 12 B2
Broad Law, *U.K.* 13 F5
Broad Sd., *Australia* 94 C4
Broadalbin, *U.S.A.* 117 C10
Broadback →, *Canada* 104 B4
Broadhurst Ra., *Australia* 92 D3
Broads △, *U.K.* 15 E9
Broads, The, *U.K.* 14 E9
Broadus, *U.S.A.* 112 C2
Broager, *Denmark* 11 K3
Broby, *Sweden* 11 H8
Broceni, *Latvia* 30 B9
Brochet, *Canada* 103 B8
Brochet, L., *Canada* 103 B8
Brocken, *Germany* 24 D6
Brockport, *U.S.A.* 116 C7
Brockton, *U.S.A.* 117 D13
Brockville, *Canada* 117 B9
Brockway, *Mont., U.S.A.* 112 B2
Brockway, *Pa., U.S.A.* 116 E6
Brocton, *U.S.A.* 116 D5
Brod, *Macedonia* 44 E5
Brodarevo, *Serbia & M.* 44 C3
Brodeur Pen., *Canada* 101 A11
Brodhead, Mt., *U.S.A.* 116 E7
Brodick, *U.K.* 13 F3
Brodnica, *Poland* 31 E6
Brody, *Ukraine* 33 G3
Brogan, *U.S.A.* 108 D5
Broglie, *France* 18 C7
Brok, *Poland* 31 F8
Broken Arrow, *U.S.A.* 113 G7
Broken Bow, *Nebr., U.S.A.* 112 E5
Broken Bow, *Okla., U.S.A.* 113 H7
Broken Bow Lake, *U.S.A.* 113 H7
Broken Hill, *Australia* 95 E3
Broken River Ra., *Australia* 94 K6
Brokind, *Sweden* 11 F9
Bromley □, *U.K.* 15 F8
Bromo, *Indonesia* 63 G15
Bromölla, *Sweden* 11 H8
Bromsgrove, *U.K.* 15 E5
Brønderslev, *Denmark* 11 G3
Brong-Ahafo □, *Ghana* 82 D4
Broni, *Italy* 40 C6
Bronkhorstspruit, *S. Africa* 89 D4
Brønnøysund, *Norway* 8 D15
Bronte, *Italy* 43 E7
Brook Park, *U.S.A.* 116 E4
Brookhaven, *U.S.A.* 113 K9
Brookings, *Oreg., U.S.A.* 108 E1
Brookings, *S. Dak., U.S.A.* 112 C6
Brooklin, *Canada* 116 C6
Brooklyn Park, *U.S.A.* 112 C8
Brooks, *Canada* 102 C6
Brooks Range, *U.S.A.* 100 B5
Brooksville, *U.S.A.* 115 L4
Brookton, *Australia* 93 F2
Brookville, *U.S.A.* 116 E5
Broom, L., *U.K.* 13 D3
Broome, *Australia* 92 C3
Broons, *France* 18 D4
Brora, *U.K.* 13 C5
Brora →, *U.K.* 13 C5
Brørup, *Denmark* 11 J2
Brösarp, *Sweden* 11 J8
Brosna →, *Ireland* 12 C4
Broşteni, *Mehedinți, Romania* 28 F7
Broşteni, *Suceava, Romania* 29 C10
Brothers, *U.S.A.* 108 E3
Brou, *France* 18 D8
Brouage, *France* 20 C2
Brough, *U.K.* 14 C5
Brough Hd., *U.K.* 13 B5
Broughton Island = Qikiqtarjuaq, *Canada* 101 B13
Broumov, *Czech Rep.* 27 A9
Brovary, *Ukraine* 33 G6
Brovst, *Denmark* 11 G3
Brown, L., *Australia* 93 F2
Brown, Pt., *Australia* 95 E1
Brown City, *U.S.A.* 116 C2
Brown Willy, *U.K.* 15 G3
Brownfield, *U.S.A.* 113 J3
Browning, *U.S.A.* 108 B7
Brownsville, *Oreg., U.S.A.* 108 D2
Brownsville, *Pa., U.S.A.* 116 F5
Brownsville, *Tenn., U.S.A.* 113 H10
Brownsville, *Tex., U.S.A.* 113 N6
Brownville, *U.S.A.* 117 C9
Brownwood, *U.S.A.* 113 K5
Browse I., *Australia* 92 B3
Bruas, *Malaysia* 65 K3
Bruay-la-Buissière, *France* 19 B9
Bruce, Mt., *Australia* 92 D2
Bruce Pen., *Canada* 116 B3
Bruce Peninsula △, *Canada* 116 A3
Bruce Rock, *Australia* 93 F2
Bruche →, *France* 19 D14
Bruchsal, *Germany* 25 F4
Bruck an der Leitha, *Austria* 27 C9
Bruck an der Mur, *Austria* 26 D8
Brue →, *U.K.* 15 F5
Bruges = Brugge, *Belgium* 17 C3
Brugg, *Switz.* 25 H4
Brugge, *Belgium* 17 C3
Bruin, *U.S.A.* 116 E5
Brûlé, *Canada* 102 C5
Brûlon, *France* 18 E6
Brumado, *Brazil* 125 F10
Brumath, *France* 19 D14
Brumunddal, *Norway* 9 F14
Bruneau, *U.S.A.* 108 E6
Bruneau →, *U.S.A.* 108 E6
Bruneck = Brunico, *Italy* 41 B8
Brunei = Bandar Seri Begawan, *Brunei* 62 C4
Brunei ■, *Asia* 62 D4
Brunflo, *Sweden* 10 A8
Brunico, *Italy* 41 B8
Brunna, *Sweden* 10 E11
Brunnen, *Switz.* 25 J4
Brunner, L., *N.Z.* 91 K3
Brunsbüttel, *Germany* 24 B5
Brunssum, *Neths.* 17 D5
Brunswick = Braunschweig, *Germany* 24 C6
Brunswick, *Ga., U.S.A.* 115 K5
Brunswick, *Maine, U.S.A.* 115 D11
Brunswick, *Md., U.S.A.* 114 F7
Brunswick, *Mo., U.S.A.* 112 F8
Brunswick, *Ohio, U.S.A.* 116 E3
Brunswick, Pen. de, *Chile* 128 G2
Brunswick B., *Australia* 92 C3
Brunswick Junction, *Australia* 93 F2
Bruntál, *Czech Rep.* 27 B10
Bruny I., *Australia* 95 G4
Brus Laguna, *Honduras* 120 C3
Brusartsi, *Bulgaria* 44 C7
Brush, *U.S.A.* 112 E3
Brushton, *U.S.A.* 117 B10
Brusio, *Switz.* 25 J6
Brusque, *Brazil* 127 B6
Brussel, *Belgium* 17 D4
Brussel ✕ (BRU), *Belgium* 17 D5
Brussels = Brussel, *Belgium* 17 D4
Brussels, *Canada* 116 C3
Brusy, *Poland* 30 E4
Bruthen, *Australia* 95 F4
Bruxelles = Brussel, *Belgium* 17 D4
Bruyères, *France* 19 D13
Bruz, *France* 18 D5
Brwinów, *Poland* 31 F7
Bryagovo, *Bulgaria* 45 E9
Bryan, *Ohio, U.S.A.* 114 E3
Bryan, *Tex., U.S.A.* 113 K6
Bryan, Mt., *Australia* 95 E2
Bryanka, *Ukraine* 33 H10
Bryansk, *Bryansk, Russia* 33 F8
Bryansk, *Dagestan, Russia* 35 H8
Bryanskoye = Bryansk, *Russia* 35 H8
Bryce Canyon △, *U.S.A.* 109 H7
Bryne, *Norway* 9 G11
Bryson City, *U.S.A.* 115 H4
Bryukhovetskaya, *Russia* 33 K10
Brza Palanka, *Serbia & M.* 44 B6
Brzeg, *Poland* 31 H4
Brzeg Dolny, *Poland* 31 G3
Brześć Kujawski, *Poland* 31 F5
Brzesko, *Poland* 31 J7
Brzeziny, *Poland* 31 G6
Brzozów, *Poland* 31 J9
Bsharri, *Lebanon* 74 A5
Bū Baqarah, *U.A.E.* 71 E8
Bu Craa, *W. Sahara* 78 C3
Bū Ḩasā, *U.A.E.* 71 F7
Bua, *Sweden* 11 G6
Bua Yai, *Thailand* 64 E4
Buapinang, *Indonesia* 63 E6
Buba, *Guinea-Biss.* 82 C2
Bubanza, *Burundi* 86 C2
Bubaque, *Guinea-Biss.* 82 C1
Bube, *Ethiopia* 81 F4
Būbiyān, *Kuwait* 71 D6
Buca, *Turkey* 47 C9
Bucak, *Turkey* 47 D12
Bucaramanga, *Colombia* 124 B4
Bucas Grande I., *Phil.* 61 G6
Bucasia, *Australia* 94 K7
Buccaneer Arch., *Australia* 92 C3
Buccino, *Italy* 43 B8
Buccoo Reef, *Trin. & Tob.* 125 J16
Bucecea, *Romania* 29 C11
Bucegi △, *Romania* 29 E10
Buchach, *Ukraine* 33 H3
Buchan, *U.K.* 13 D6
Buchan Ness, *U.K.* 13 D7
Buchanan, *Canada* 103 C8
Buchanan, *Liberia* 82 D2
Buchanan, L., *Queens., Australia* 94 C4
Buchanan, L., *W. Austral., Australia* 93 E3
Buchanan, L., *U.S.A.* 113 K5
Buchanan Cr. →, *Australia* 94 B2
Buchans, *Canada* 105 C8
Bucharest = Bucureşti, *Romania* 29 F11
Buchen, *Germany* 25 F5
Buchholz, *Germany* 24 B5
Buchloe, *Germany* 25 G6
Buchon, Pt., *U.S.A.* 110 K6
Buciumi, *Romania* 28 C8
Buck Hill Falls, *U.S.A.* 117 E9
Bückeburg, *Germany* 24 C5
Buckeye, *U.S.A.* 109 K7
Buckeye Lake, *U.S.A.* 116 G2
Buckhannon, *U.S.A.* 114 F5
Buckhaven, *U.K.* 13 E5
Buckhorn L., *Canada* 116 B6
Buckie, *U.K.* 13 D6
Buckingham, *Canada* 104 C4
Buckingham, *U.K.* 15 F7
Buckingham B., *Australia* 94 A2
Buckinghamshire □, *U.K.* 15 F7
Buckle Hd., *Australia* 92 B4
Buckleboo, *Australia* 95 E2
Buckley, *U.K.* 14 D4
Buckley →, *Australia* 94 C2
Bucklin, *U.S.A.* 113 G5
Bucks L., *U.S.A.* 110 F5
Bucquoy, *France* 19 B9
Bucureşti, *Romania* 29 F11
Bucureşti Otopeni ✕ (OTP), *Romania* 45 B10
Bucyrus, *U.S.A.* 114 E4
Budacu, Vf., *Romania* 29 C10
Budalin, *Burma* 67 H19
Budaörs, *Hungary* 28 C3
Budapest, *Hungary* 28 C4
Budapest □, *Hungary* 28 C4
Budapest ✕ (BUD), *Hungary* 28 C4
Budaun, *India* 69 E8
Budd Coast, *Antarctica* 5 C8
Buddusò, *Italy* 42 B2
Bude, *U.K.* 15 G3
Budennovsk, *Russia* 35 H7
Budeşti, *Romania* 29 F11
Budeyi, *Ukraine* 29 B14
Budge Budge = Baj Baj, *India* 69 H13
Budgewoi, *Australia* 95 E5
Budia, *Spain* 38 E2
Büdingen, *Germany* 25 E5
Budjala, *Dem. Rep. of the Congo* 84 D3
Budoni, *Italy* 42 B2
Búdrio, *Italy* 41 D8
Budva, *Serbia & M.* 44 D2
Budzyń, *Poland* 31 F3
Buea, *Cameroon* 83 E6
Buellton, *U.S.A.* 111 L6
Buena Esperanza, *Argentina* 126 C2
Buena Park, *U.S.A.* 111 M9
Buena Vista, *Colo., U.S.A.* 109 G10
Buena Vista, *Va., U.S.A.* 114 G6
Buena Vista Lake Bed, *U.S.A.* 111 K7
Buenaventura, *Colombia* 124 C3
Buenaventura, *Mexico* 118 B3
Buendía, Embalse de, *Spain* 38 E2
Buenos Aires, *Argentina* 126 C4
Buenos Aires, *Costa Rica* 120 E3
Buenos Aires □, *Argentina* 126 D4
Buenos Aires, L., *Chile* 128 F2
Buffalo, *Mo., U.S.A.* 113 G8
Buffalo, *N.Y., U.S.A.* 116 D6
Buffalo, *Okla., U.S.A.* 113 G5
Buffalo, *S. Dak., U.S.A.* 112 C3
Buffalo, *Wyo., U.S.A.* 108 D10
Buffalo △, *U.S.A.* 113 G8
Buffalo →, *Canada* 102 A5
Buffalo →, *S. Africa* 89 D5
Buffalo Head Hills, *Canada* 102 B5
Buffalo L., *Alta., Canada* 102 C6
Buffalo L., *N.W.T., Canada* 102 A5
Buffalo Narrows, *Canada* 103 B7
Buffalo Springs ⌂, *Kenya* 86 B4
Buffels →, *S. Africa* 88 D2
Buford, *U.S.A.* 115 H4
Bug = Buh →, *Ukraine* 33 J6
Bug →, *Poland* 31 F8
Buga, *Colombia* 124 C3
Bugala I., *Uganda* 86 C3
Buganda, *Uganda* 86 C3
Buganga, *Uganda* 86 C3
Bugasong, *Phil.* 61 F5
Bugeat, *France* 20 C5
Bugel, Tanjung, *Indonesia* 63 G14
Bugibba, *Malta* 49 D1
Bugojno, *Bos.-H.* 28 F2
Bugsuk, *Phil.* 62 C5
Buguma, *Nigeria* 83 E6
Bugun Shara, *Mongolia* 60 B5
Bugungu ⌂, *Uganda* 86 B3
Buguruslan, *Russia* 52 D6
Buh →, *Ukraine* 33 J6
Buharkent, *Turkey* 47 D10
Buheirat-Murrat-el-Kubra, *Egypt* 80 H8
Buhera, *Zimbabwe* 89 B5
Bühl, *Germany* 25 G4
Buhl, *U.S.A.* 108 E6
Buhuşi, *Romania* 29 D11
Bui △, *Ghana* 82 D4
Builth Wells, *U.K.* 15 E4
Buinsk, *Russia* 34 C9
Buir Nur, *Mongolia* 60 B6
Buis-les-Baronnies, *France* 21 D9
Buitrago del Lozoya, *Spain* 36 E7
Bujalance, *Spain* 37 H6
Bujanovac, *Serbia & M.* 44 D5
Bujaraloz, *Spain* 38 D4
Buje, *Croatia* 41 C10
Bujumbura, *Burundi* 86 C2
Bük, *Hungary* 28 C1
Buk, *Poland* 31 F3
Bukachacha, *Russia* 53 D12
Bukama, *Dem. Rep. of the Congo* 87 D2
Bukavu, *Dem. Rep. of the Congo* 86 C2
Bukene, *Tanzania* 86 C3
Bukhara = Bukhoro, *Uzbekistan* 52 F7

Bukhoro, *Uzbekistan* 52 F7
Bukima, *Tanzania* 86 C3
Bukit Badung, *Indonesia* 63 K18
Bukit Kerajaan, *Malaysia* 65 c
Bukit Mertajam, *Malaysia* 65 c
Bukit Ni, *Malaysia* 65 d
Bukit Panjang, *Singapore* 65 d
Bukit Tengah, *Malaysia* 65 c
Bukittinggi, *Indonesia* 62 E2
Bükk, *Hungary* 28 B5
Bükki △, *Hungary* 28 B5
Bukoba, *Tanzania* 86 C3
Bukum, Pulau, *Singapore* 65 d
Bukuru, *Nigeria* 83 D6
Bukuya, *Uganda* 86 B3
Būl, Kuh-e, *Iran* 71 D7
Bula, *Guinea-Biss.* 82 C1
Bula, *Indonesia* 63 E8
Bülach, *Switz.* 25 H4
Bulahdelah, *Australia* 95 E5
Bulan, *Phil.* 61 E5
Bulancak, *Turkey* 73 B8
Bulandshahr, *India* 68 E7
Bulanık, *Turkey* 73 C10
Bûlâq, *Egypt* 80 B3
Bulawayo, *Zimbabwe* 87 G2
Buldan, *Turkey* 47 C10
Bulgar, *Russia* 34 C9
Bulgaria ■, *Europe* 45 D9
Bulgheria, Monte, *Italy* 43 B8
Bulgurca, *Turkey* 47 C9
Buli, Teluk, *Indonesia* 63 D7
Buliluyan, C., *Phil.* 61 G2
Bulim, *Singapore* 65 d
Bulki, *Ethiopia* 81 F4
Bulkley →, *Canada* 102 B3
Bull Shoals L., *U.S.A.* 113 G8
Bullaque →, *Spain* 37 G6
Bullas, *Spain* 39 G3
Bulle, *Switz.* 25 J3
Bulleringa △, *Australia* 94 B3
Bullhead City, *U.S.A.* 111 K12
Büllingen, *Belgium* 17 D6
Bullock Creek, *Australia* 94 B3
Bulloo →, *Australia* 95 D3
Bulloo L., *Australia* 95 D3
Bulls, *N.Z.* 91 J5
Bully-les-Mines, *France* 19 B9
Bulnes, *Chile* 126 D1
Bulqizë, *Albania* 44 E4
Bulsar = Valsad, *India* 66 J8
Bultfontein, *S. Africa* 88 D4
Bulukumba, *Indonesia* 63 F6
Bulun, *Russia* 53 B13
Bumba, *Dem. Rep. of the Congo* 84 D4
Bumbeşti-Jiu, *Romania* 29 E8
Bumbiri I., *Tanzania* 86 C3
Bumbuna, *S. Leone* 82 D2
Bumhpa Bum, *Burma* 67 F20
Bumi →, *Zimbabwe* 87 F2
Buna, *Kenya* 86 B4
Bunawan, *Phil.* 61 G6
Bunazi, *Tanzania* 86 C3
Bunbury, *Australia* 93 F2
Bunclody, *Ireland* 12 D5
Buncrana, *Ireland* 12 A4
Bundaberg, *Australia* 95 C5
Bünde, *Germany* 24 C4
Bundey →, *Australia* 94 C2
Bundi, *India* 68 G6
Bundjalung △, *Australia* 95 D5
Bundoran, *Ireland* 12 B3
Bundukia, *Sudan* 81 F3
Bung Kan, *Thailand* 64 C4
Bunga →, *Nigeria* 83 C6
Bungay, *U.K.* 15 E9
Bungil Cr. →, *Australia* 95 D4
Bungle Bungle = Purnululu △, *Australia* 92 C4
Bungo-Suidō, *Japan* 55 H6
Bungoma, *Kenya* 86 B3
Bungotakada, *Japan* 55 H5
Bungu, *Tanzania* 86 D4
Bunia, *Dem. Rep. of the Congo* 86 B3
Bunji, *Pakistan* 69 B6
Bunkie, *U.S.A.* 113 K8
Bunnell, *U.S.A.* 115 L5
Buñol, *Spain* 39 F4
Bunsuru, *Nigeria* 83 C5
Buntok, *Indonesia* 62 E4
Bununu Dass, *Nigeria* 83 C6
Bununu Kasa, *Nigeria* 83 D6
Bunya Mts. △, *Australia* 95 D5
Bünyan, *Turkey* 72 C6
Bunyu, *Indonesia* 62 D5
Bunza, *Nigeria* 83 C5
Buol, *Indonesia* 63 D6
Buon Brieng, *Vietnam* 64 F7
Buon Ma Thuot, *Vietnam* 64 F7
Buong Long, *Cambodia* 64 F6
Buorkhaya, Mys, *Russia* 53 B14
Buqayq, *Si. Arabia* 71 E6
Buqbuq, *Egypt* 80 A2
Bur Acaba, *Somali Rep.* 75 G3
Bûr Fuad, *Egypt* 80 H8
Bûr Safâga, *Egypt* 70 E2
Bûr Sa'îd, *Egypt* 80 H8
Bûr Sûdân, *Sudan* 80 D4
Bûr Taufiq, *Egypt* 80 J8
Bura, *Kenya* 86 C4
Burakin, *Australia* 93 F2
Buram, *Sudan* 81 E2
Burao, *Somali Rep.* 75 F4
Burāq, *Syria* 74 B5
Buraydah, *Si. Arabia* 70 E4
Burbank, *U.S.A.* 111 L8
Burda, *India* 68 G6
Burdekin →, *Australia* 94 B4
Burdur, *Turkey* 47 D12
Burdur □, *Turkey* 47 D12
Burdur Gölü, *Turkey* 47 D12
Burdwan = Barddhaman, *India* 69 H12
Bure, *Gojam, Ethiopia* 81 E4
Bure, *Ilubabor, Ethiopia* 81 F4
Bure →, *U.K.* 14 E9
Büren, *Germany* 24 D4
Bureya →, *Russia* 53 E13
Burford, *Canada* 116 C4
Burg, *Germany* 24 C7
Burg auf Fehmarn, *Germany* 24 A7
Burg el Arab, *Egypt* 80 H6
Burg et Tuyur, *Sudan* 80 C2
Burg Stargard, *Germany* 24 B9
Burgas, *Bulgaria* 45 D11
Burgas □, *Bulgaria* 45 D10
Burgaski Zaliv, *Bulgaria* 45 D11
Burgdorf, *Germany* 24 C6
Burgdorf, *Switz.* 25 H3
Burgenland □, *Austria* 27 D9
Burgeo, *Canada* 105 C8
Burgersdorp, *S. Africa* 88 E4
Burges, Mt., *Australia* 93 F3
Burghausen, *Germany* 25 G8
Burghead, *U.K.* 13 D5
Búrgio, *Italy* 42 E6
Burglengenfeld, *Germany* 25 F8
Burgohondo, *Spain* 36 E6
Burgos, *Spain* 36 C7
Burgos □, *Spain* 36 C7
Burgstädt, *Germany* 24 E8
Burgsvik, *Sweden* 11 G12
Burguillos del Cerro, *Spain* 37 G4
Burgundy = Bourgogne □, *France* 19 F11
Burhaniye, *Turkey* 47 B8
Burhanpur, *India* 66 J10
Burhi Gandak →, *India* 69 G12
Burhner →, *India* 69 H9
Buri Pen., *Eritrea* 81 D4
Burias I., *Phil.* 61 E5
Burica, Pta., *Costa Rica* 120 E3
Burien, *U.S.A.* 110 C4
Burigi ⌓, *Tanzania* 86 C3
Burigi, L., *Tanzania* 86 C3
Burin, *Canada* 105 C8
Buriram, *Thailand* 64 E4
Burj Sāfitā, *Syria* 70 C3
Burji, *Ethiopia* 81 F4
Burkburnett, *U.S.A.* 113 H5
Burke →, *Australia* 94 C2
Burke Chan., *Canada* 102 C3
Burketown, *Australia* 94 B2
Burkina Faso ■, *Africa* 82 C4
Burk's Falls, *Canada* 104 C4
Burlada, *Spain* 38 C3
Burleigh Falls, *Canada* 116 B6
Burley, *U.S.A.* 108 E7
Burlingame, *U.S.A.* 110 H4
Burlington, *Canada* 116 C5
Burlington, *Colo., U.S.A.* 112 F3
Burlington, *Iowa, U.S.A.* 112 E9
Burlington, *Kans., U.S.A.* 112 F7
Burlington, *N.C., U.S.A.* 115 G6
Burlington, *N.J., U.S.A.* 117 F10
Burlington, *Vt., U.S.A.* 117 B11
Burlington, *Wash., U.S.A.* 110 B4
Burlington, *Wis., U.S.A.* 114 D1
Burlyu-Tyube, *Kazakhstan* 52 E8
Burma ■, *Asia* 67 J20
Burnaby I., *Canada* 102 C2
Burnet, *U.S.A.* 113 K5
Burney, *U.S.A.* 108 F3
Burnham, *U.S.A.* 116 F7
Burnham-on-Sea, *U.K.* 15 F5
Burnie, *Australia* 95 G4
Burnley, *U.K.* 14 D5
Burns, *U.S.A.* 108 E4
Burns Lake, *Canada* 102 C3
Burnside →, *Canada* 100 B9
Burnside, L., *Australia* 93 E3
Burnsville, *U.S.A.* 112 C8
Burnt, L., *Canada* 105 B7
Burnt River, *Canada* 116 B6
Burntwood →, *Canada* 103 B9
Burntwood L., *Canada* 103 B8
Burqān, *Kuwait* 70 D5
Burra, *Australia* 95 E2
Burra, *Nigeria* 83 C6
Burray, *U.K.* 13 C6
Burrel, *Albania* 44 E4
Burren △, *Ireland* 12 C3
Burren Junction, *Australia* 95 E4
Burriana, *Spain* 38 F4
Burrinjuck Res., *Australia* 95 F4
Burro, Serranías del, *Mexico* 118 B4
Burrow Hd., *U.K.* 13 G4
Burrum Coast △, *Australia* 95 D5
Burruyacú, *Argentina* 126 B3
Burry Port, *U.K.* 15 F3
Bursa, *Turkey* 45 F13
Burseryd, *Sweden* 11 G7
Burstall, *Canada* 103 C7
Burton, *Ohio, U.S.A.* 116 E3
Burton, *S.C., U.S.A.* 115 J5
Burton, L., *Canada* 104 B4
Burton upon Trent, *U.K.* 14 E6
Buru, *Indonesia* 63 E7
Burullus, Bahra el, *Egypt* 80 H7
Burûn, Râs, *Egypt* 74 D2
Burundi ■, *Africa* 86 C3
Bururi, *Burundi* 86 C2
Burutu, *Nigeria* 83 D6
Burwell, *U.S.A.* 112 E5
Burwick, *U.K.* 13 C5
Bury, *U.K.* 14 D5
Bury St. Edmunds, *U.K.* 15 E8
Buryatia □, *Russia* 53 D11
Buryn, *Ukraine* 33 G7
Burzenin, *Poland* 31 G5
Busalla, *Italy* 40 D5
Busan = Pusan, *S. Korea* 57 G15
Busango Swamp, *Zambia* 87 E2
Buşayrah, *Syria* 70 C4
Busca, *Italy* 40 D4
Bushat, *Albania* 44 E3
Būshehr, *Iran* 71 D6
Būshehr □, *Iran* 71 D6
Bushell, *Canada* 103 B7
Bushenyi, *Uganda* 86 C3
Bushire = Būshehr, *Iran* 71 D6
Bushtyna, *Ukraine* 29 B8
Busie, *Ghana* 82 C4
Businga, *Dem. Rep. of the Congo* 84 D4
Busko-Zdrój, *Poland* 31 H7
Busovača, *Bos.-H.* 28 F2
Buşra ash Shām, *Syria* 74 C5
Busselton, *Australia* 93 F2
Busseri →, *Sudan* 81 F2
Busseto, *Italy* 40 D7
Bussière-Badil, *France* 20 C4
Bussolengo, *Italy* 40 C7
Bussum, *Neths.* 17 B5
Buşteni, *Romania* 29 E10
Busto, C., *Spain* 36 B4
Busto Arsízio, *Italy* 40 C5
Busu Djanoa, *Dem. Rep. of the Congo* 84 D4
Busuanga I., *Phil.* 61 E3
Büsum, *Germany* 24 A4
Busungbiu, *Indonesia* 63 J17
Buta, *Dem. Rep. of the Congo* 86 B1
Butare, *Rwanda* 86 C2
Butaritari, *Kiribati* 96 G9
Bute, *U.K.* 13 F3
Bute Inlet, *Canada* 102 C4
Butemba, *Uganda* 86 B3
Butembo, *Dem. Rep. of the Congo* 86 B2
Buteni, *Romania* 28 D7
Butera, *Italy* 43 E7
Butha Qi, *China* 60 B7
Butiaba, *Uganda* 86 B3
Butler, *Mo., U.S.A.* 112 F7
Butler, *Pa., U.S.A.* 116 F5
Buton, *Indonesia* 63 E6
Butte, *Mont., U.S.A.* 108 C7
Butte, *Nebr., U.S.A.* 112 D5
Butte Creek →, *U.S.A.* 110 F5
Butterworth = Gcuwa, *S. Africa* 89 E4
Butterworth, *Malaysia* 65 c
Buttevant, *Ireland* 12 D3
Buttfield, Mt., *Australia* 93 D4
Button B., *Canada* 103 B10
Buttonwillow, *U.S.A.* 111 K7
Butty Hd., *Australia* 93 F3
Butuan, *Phil.* 61 G6
Butuku-Luba, *Eq. Guin.* 83 E6
Butung = Buton, *Indonesia* 63 E6
Buturlinovka, *Russia* 34 E5
Butzbach, *Germany* 25 E4
Bützow, *Germany* 24 B7
Buur Hakaba = Bur Acaba, *Somali Rep.* 75 G3
Buxa Duar, *India* 69 F13
Buxar, *India* 69 G10
Buxtehude, *Germany* 24 B5
Buxton, *U.K.* 14 D6
Buxy, *France* 19 F11
Buy, *Russia* 34 A5
Buynaksk, *Russia* 35 J8
Buyo, *Ivory C.* 82 D3
Buyo, L. de, *Ivory C.* 82 D3
Büyük Menderes →, *Turkey* 47 D9
Büyükçekmece, *Turkey* 45 E12
Büyükkariştiran, *Turkey* 45 E11
Büyükkemikli Burnu, *Turkey* 45 F10
Büyükorhan, *Turkey* 47 B10
Büyükyoncalı, *Turkey* 45 E11
Buzançais, *France* 18 F8
Buzău, *Romania* 29 E11
Buzău □, *Romania* 29 E11
Buzău →, *Romania* 29 E12
Buzău, Pasul, *Romania* 29 E11
Buzen, *Japan* 55 H5
Buzet, *Croatia* 41 C10
Buzi →, *Mozam.* 87 F3
Buziaş, *Romania* 28 E6
Buzuluk, *Russia* 52 D6
Buzuluk →, *Russia* 34 E6
Buzzards B., *U.S.A.* 117 E14
Buzzards Bay, *U.S.A.* 117 E14
Bwana Mkubwe, *Dem. Rep. of the Congo* 87 E2
Bwindi △, *Uganda* 86 C2
Byala, *Ruse, Bulgaria* 45 C9
Byala, *Varna, Bulgaria* 45 D11
Byala Slatina, *Bulgaria* 44 C7
Byarezina →, *Belarus* 33 F6
Byaroza, *Belarus* 33 F3
Bychawa, *Poland* 31 G9
Byczyna, *Poland* 31 G5
Bydgoszcz, *Poland* 31 E5
Byelarus = Belarus ■, *Europe* 32 F4
Byelorussia = Belarus ■, *Europe* 32 F4
Byers, *U.S.A.* 112 F2
Byesville, *U.S.A.* 116 G3
Byfield △, *Australia* 94 C5
Byford, *Australia* 93 F2
Bykhaw, *Belarus* 32 F6
Bykhov = Bykhaw, *Belarus* 32 F6
Bykovo, *Russia* 34 F7
Bylas, *U.S.A.* 109 K8
Bylot, *Canada* 103 B10
Bylot I., *Canada* 101 A12
Byrd, C., *Antarctica* 5 C17
Byrock, *Australia* 95 E4
Byron, C., *Australia* 95 D5
Byron Bay, *Australia* 95 D5
Byrranga, Gory, *Russia* 53 B11
Byrranga Mts. = Byrranga, Gory, *Russia* 53 B11
Byrum, *Denmark* 11 G5
Byske, *Sweden* 8 D19
Byskeälven →, *Sweden* 8 D19
Bystrytsya, *Ukraine* 29 B9
Bystrzyca →, *Dolnośląskie, Poland* 31 G3
Bystrzyca →, *Lubelskie, Poland* 31 G9
Bystrzyca Kłodzka, *Poland* 31 H3
Bytča, *Slovak Rep.* 27 B11
Bytkiv, *Ukraine* 29 B9
Bytom, *Poland* 31 H5
Bytom Odrzański, *Poland* 31 G2
Bytów, *Poland* 30 D4
Byumba, *Rwanda* 86 C3
Bzenec, *Czech Rep.* 27 C10
Bzura →, *Poland* 31 F7

C

Ca →, *Vietnam* 64 C5
Ca Mau, *Vietnam* 65 H5
Ca Mau, Mui, *Vietnam* 65 H5
Ca Na, *Vietnam* 65 G7
Caacupé, *Paraguay* 126 B4
Caaguazú △, *Paraguay* 127 B4
Caála, *Angola* 85 G3
Caamaño Sd., *Canada* 102 C3
Caazapá, *Paraguay* 126 B4
Caazapá □, *Paraguay* 127 B4
Cabadbaran, *Phil.* 61 G6
Cabalian = San Juan, *Phil.* 61 F6
Caballeria, C. de, *Spain* 48 A11
Cabana, *Spain* 36 B2
Cabañaquinta, *Spain* 36 B5
Cabanatuan, *Phil.* 61 D4
Cabañeros ⌓, *Spain* 37 F6
Cabanes, *Spain* 38 E5
Cabano, *Canada* 105 C6
Čabar, *Croatia* 41 C11
Cabazon, *U.S.A.* 111 M10
Cabedelo, *Brazil* 125 E12
Cabeza del Buey, *Spain* 37 G5
Cabezón de la Sal, *Spain* 36 B6
Cabildo, *Chile* 126 C1
Cabimas, *Venezuela* 124 A4
Cabinda, *Angola* 84 F2
Cabinda □, *Angola* 84 F2
Cabinet Mts., *U.S.A.* 108 C6
Cabo Blanco, *Argentina* 128 F3
Cabo de Gata-Níjar ⌓, *Spain* 39 J2
Cabo Frio, *Brazil* 127 A7
Cabo Pantoja, *Peru* 124 D3
Cabonga, Réservoir, *Canada* 104 C4
Cabool, *U.S.A.* 113 G8
Caboolture, *Australia* 95 D5
Cabora Bassa Dam = Cahora Bassa, Reprêsa de, *Mozam.* 87 F3
Caborca, *Mexico* 118 A2
Cabot, Mt., *U.S.A.* 117 B13
Cabot Hd., *Canada* 116 A3
Cabot Str., *Canada* 105 C8
Cabra, *Spain* 37 H6
Cabra del Santo Cristo, *Spain* 37 H7
Cábras, *Italy* 42 C1
Cabrera, *Spain* 48 B9
Cabrera △, *Spain* 39 F7
Cabrera, Sierra, *Spain* 36 C4
Cabri, *Canada* 103 C7
Cabriel →, *Spain* 39 F3
Cabugao, *Phil.* 61 C4
Cacabelos, *Spain* 36 C4
Caçador, *Brazil* 127 B5
Čačak, *Serbia & M.* 44 C4
Caçapava do Sul, *Brazil* 127 C5
Cáccamo, *Italy* 42 E6
Cacém, *Portugal* 37 G1
Cáceres, *Brazil* 124 G7
Cáceres, *Spain* 37 F4
Cáceres □, *Spain* 36 F5
Cache Bay, *Canada* 104 C4
Cache Cr. →, *U.S.A.* 110 G5
Cache Creek, *Canada* 102 C4
Cacheu, *Guinea-Biss.* 82 C1
Cachi, *Argentina* 126 B2
Cachimbo, Serra do, *Brazil* 125 E7
Cachinal de la Sierra, *Chile* 126 A2
Cachoeira, *Brazil* 125 F11
Cachoeira do Sul, *Brazil* 127 C5
Cachoeiro de Itapemirim, *Brazil* 127 A7
Cachopo, *Portugal* 37 H3
Cacine, *Guinea-Biss.* 82 C1
Cacoal, *Brazil* 124 F6
Cacólo, *Angola* 84 G3
Caconda, *Angola* 85 G3
Čadca, *Slovak Rep.* 27 B11
Caddo, *U.S.A.* 113 H6
Cader Idris, *U.K.* 15 E4
Cadereyta, *Mexico* 118 B5
Cadí, Sierra del, *Spain* 38 C6
Cadí-Moixeró ⌓, *Spain* 38 C3
Cadibarrawirracanna, L., *Australia* 95 D2
Cadillac, *France* 20 D3
Cadillac, *U.S.A.* 114 C3
Cadiz, *Phil.* 61 F5
Cádiz, *Spain* 37 J4
Cadiz, *Calif., U.S.A.* 111 L11
Cadiz, *Ohio, U.S.A.* 116 F4
Cádiz □, *Spain* 37 J5
Cádiz, G. de, *Spain* 37 J3
Cadiz L., *U.S.A.* 109 J6
Cadney Park, *Australia* 95 D1
Cadomin, *Canada* 102 C5
Cadotte Lake, *Canada* 102 B5
Cadours, *France* 20 E5
Cadoux, *Australia* 93 F2
Caen, *France* 18 C6
Caernarfon, *U.K.* 14 D3
Caernarfon B., *U.K.* 14 D3
Caernarvon = Caernarfon, *U.K.* 14 D3
Caerphilly, *U.K.* 15 F4
Caerphilly □, *U.K.* 15 F4
Caesarea, *Israel* 74 C3
Caetité, *Brazil* 125 F10
Cafayate, *Argentina* 126 B2
Cafu, *Angola* 88 B2
Cagayan →, *Phil.* 61 B4
Cagayan de Oro, *Phil.* 61 G6
Cagayan Is., *Phil.* 61 G4
Cagayan Sulu I., *Phil.* 61 H3
Cagli, *Italy* 41 E9
Cágliari, *Italy* 42 C2
Cágliari, G. di, *Italy* 42 C2
Cagnano Varano, *Italy* 41 G12
Cagnes-sur-Mer, *France* 21 E11
Caguán →, *Colombia* 124 D4
Caguas, *Puerto Rico* 121 d
Caha Mts., *Ireland* 12 E2
Cahama, *Angola* 88 B1
Caher, *Ireland* 12 D4
Caherciveen, *Ireland* 12 E1
Cahora Bassa, L. de, *Mozam.* 87 F3
Cahora Bassa, Reprêsa de, *Mozam.* 87 F3
Cahore Pt., *Ireland* 12 D5
Cahors, *France* 20 D5
Cahul, *Moldova* 29 E13
Cai Bau, Dao, *Vietnam* 58 G6
Cai Nuoc, *Vietnam* 65 H5
Caia, *Mozam.* 87 F4
Caianda, *Angola* 87 E1
Caibarién, *Cuba* 120 B4
Caibiran, *Phil.* 61 F6
Caicara, *Venezuela* 124 B5
Caicó, *Brazil* 125 E11
Caicos Is., *Turks & Caicos* 121 B5
Caicos Passage, *W. Indies* 121 B5
Caidian, *China* 59 B10
Căinari, *Moldova* 29 D14
Caird Coast, *Antarctica* 5 D1
Cairn Gorm, *U.K.* 13 D5
Cairngorm Mts., *U.K.* 13 D5
Cairngorms △, *U.K.* 13 D5
Cairnryan, *U.K.* 13 G3
Cairns, *Australia* 94 B4
Cairns L., *Canada* 103 C10
Cairo = El Qâhira, *Egypt* 80 H7
Cairo, *Ga., U.S.A.* 115 K3
Cairo, *Ill., U.S.A.* 113 G10
Cairo, *N.Y., U.S.A.* 117 D11
Cairo Montenotte, *Italy* 40 D5
Caithness, *U.K.* 13 C5
Caithness, Ord of, *U.K.* 13 C5
Caja de Muertos, I., *Puerto Rico* 121 d
Cajamarca, *Peru* 124 E3
Cajarc, *France* 20 D5
Cajàzeiras, *Brazil* 125 E11
Čajetina, *Serbia & M.* 44 C3
Çakirgol, *Turkey* 73 B8
Çakırlar, *Turkey* 47 E12
Čakovec, *Croatia* 41 B13
Çal, *Turkey* 47 C11
Cala, *Spain* 37 H4
Cala →, *Spain* 37 H4
Cala Cadolar, Punta de = Rotja, Pta., *Spain* 39 G6
Cala d'Or, *Spain* 48 B10
Cala en Porter, *Spain* 48 B11
Cala Figuera, C. de, *Spain* 48 B9
Cala Forcat, *Spain* 48 B10
Cala Major, *Spain* 48 B9
Cala Mezquida = Sa Mesquida, *Spain* 48 B11
Cala Millor, *Spain* 48 B10
Cala Ratjada, *Spain* 48 B10
Cala Santa Galdana, *Spain* 48 B10
Calabanga, *Phil.* 61 E5
Calabar, *Nigeria* 83 E6
Calabogie, *Canada* 117 A8
Calabozo, *Venezuela* 124 B5
Calábria □, *Italy* 43 C9
Calábria △, *Italy* 43 C9
Calaburras, Pta. de, *Spain* 37 J6
Calaceite, *Spain* 38 D5
Calacuccia, *France* 21 F13
Calafat, *Romania* 28 G7
Calafate, *Argentina* 128 G2
Calafell, *Spain* 38 D6
Calahorra, *Spain* 38 C3
Calais, *France* 19 B8
Calais, *U.S.A.* 115 C12
Calakmul ⌓, *Mexico* 119 D7
Calalaste, Cord. de, *Argentina* 126 B2
Calama, *Brazil* 124 E6
Calama, *Chile* 126 A2
Calamar, *Colombia* 124 A4
Calamian Group, *Phil.* 61 F3
Calamocha, *Spain* 38 E3
Calamonte, *Spain* 37 G4
Călan, *Romania* 28 E7
Calañas, *Spain* 37 H4
Calanda, *Spain* 38 E4
Calang, *Indonesia* 62 D1
Calangiánus, *Italy* 42 B2
Calapan, *Phil.* 61 E4
Călăraşi, *Moldova* 29 C13
Călăraşi, *Romania* 29 F12
Călăraşi □, *Romania* 29 F12
Calasparra, *Spain* 39 G3
Calatafimi, *Italy* 42 E5
Calatayud, *Spain* 38 D3
Călăţele, *Romania* 28 D8
Calato = Kálathos, *Greece* 47 E10
Calauag, *Phil.* 61 E5
Calavà, C., *Italy* 43 D7
Calavite, C., *Phil.* 61 E4
Calayan, *Phil.* 61 B4
Calbayog, *Phil.* 61 E6
Calca, *Peru* 124 F4
Calcasieu L., *U.S.A.* 113 L8
Calcutta = Kolkata, *India* 69 H13
Calcutta, *U.S.A.* 116 F4
Caldaro, *Italy* 41 B8
Caldas da Rainha, *Portugal* 37 F1
Caldas de Reis, *Spain* 36 C2
Calder →, *U.K.* 14 D6
Caldera, *Chile* 126 B1

Caldera de Taburiente △, *Canary Is.* 48 F2
Caldwell, *Idaho, U.S.A.* 108 E5
Caldwell, *Kans., U.S.A.* 113 G6
Caldwell, *Tex., U.S.A.* 113 K6
Caledon, *S. Africa* 88 E2
Caledon →, *S. Africa* 88 E4
Caledon B., *Australia* 94 A2
Caledonia, *Canada* 116 C5
Caledonia, *U.S.A.* 116 D7
Calella, *Spain* 38 D7
Calemba, *Angola* 88 B2
Calen, *Australia* 94 J6
Calenzana, *France* 21 F12
Caletones, *Chile* 126 C1
Calexico, *U.S.A.* 111 N11
Calf of Man, *I. of Man* 14 C3
Calgary, *Canada* 102 C6
Calheta, *Madeira* 48 D2
Calhoun, *U.S.A.* 115 H3
Cali, *Colombia* 124 C3
Calicut, *India* 66 P9
Caliente, *U.S.A.* 109 H6
California, *Mo., U.S.A.* 112 F8
California, *Pa., U.S.A.* 116 F5
California □, *U.S.A.* 110 H7
California, Baja, *Mexico* 118 A1
California, Baja, T.N. = Baja California □, *Mexico* 118 B2
California, Baja, T.S. = Baja California Sur □, *Mexico* 118 B2
California, G. de, *Mexico* 118 B2
California City, *U.S.A.* 111 K9
California Hot Springs, *U.S.A.* 111 K8
Calilegua △, *Argentina* 126 B3
Călimăneşti, *Romania* 29 E9
Călimani, Munţii, *Romania* 29 C10
Calingasta, *Argentina* 126 C2
Calipatria, *U.S.A.* 111 M11
Calistoga, *U.S.A.* 110 G4
Calitri, *Italy* 43 B8
Calitzdorp, *S. Africa* 88 E3
Callabonna, L., *Australia* 95 D3
Callac, *France* 18 D3
Callan, *Ireland* 12 D4
Callander, *U.K.* 13 E4
Callao, *Peru* 124 F3
Calles, *Mexico* 119 C5
Callicoon, *U.S.A.* 117 E9
Calling Lake, *Canada* 102 B6
Calliope, *Australia* 94 C5
Callosa de Ensarriá, *Spain* 39 G4
Callosa de Segura, *Spain* 39 G4
Calne, *U.K.* 15 F6
Calola, *Angola* 88 B2
Calolbon = San Andres, *Phil.* 61 E6
Calonge, *Spain* 38 D8
Caloocan, *Phil.* 61 D4
Calore →, *Italy* 43 A7
Caloundra, *Australia* 95 D5
Calpe, *Spain* 39 G5
Calpella, *U.S.A.* 110 F3
Calpine, *U.S.A.* 110 F6
Calstock, *Canada* 104 C3
Caltabellotta, *Italy* 42 E6
Caltagirone, *Italy* 43 E7
Caltanissetta, *Italy* 43 E7
Çaltılıbük, *Turkey* 45 G12
Caluire-et-Cuire, *France* 19 G11
Calulo, *Angola* 84 G2
Caluso, *Italy* 40 C4
Calvados □, *France* 18 C6
Calvert →, *Australia* 94 B2
Calvert I., *Canada* 102 C3
Calvert Ra., *Australia* 92 D3
Calvi, *France* 21 F12
Calvià, *Spain* 39 F7
Calvillo, *Mexico* 118 C4
Calvinia, *S. Africa* 88 E2
Calvo, Mte., *Italy* 41 G12
Calwa, *U.S.A.* 110 J7
Calzada Almuradiel = Almuradiel, *Spain* 37 G7
Calzada de Calatrava, *Spain* 37 G7
Cam →, *U.K.* 15 E8
Cam Lam, *Vietnam* 65 G7
Cam Pha, *Vietnam* 58 G6
Cam Ranh, *Vietnam* 65 G7
Cam Xuyen, *Vietnam* 64 C6
Camabatela, *Angola* 84 F3
Camacha, *Madeira* 48 D3
Camacho, *Mexico* 118 C4
Camacupa, *Angola* 85 G3
Camagüey, *Cuba* 120 B4
Camaiore, *Italy* 40 E7
Camaná, *Peru* 124 G4
Camanche Reservoir, *U.S.A.* 110 G6
Camaquã, *Brazil* 127 C5
Camaquã →, *Brazil* 127 C5
Câmara de Lobos, *Madeira* 48 D3
Camarat, C., *France* 21 E10
Camarès, *France* 20 E6
Camaret-sur-Mer, *France* 18 D2
Camargo, *Mexico* 119 B5
Camargue, *France* 21 E8
Camargue ⌓, *France* 21 E8
Camarillo, *U.S.A.* 111 L7
Camariñas, *Spain* 36 B1
Camarón, C., *Honduras* 120 C2
Camarones, *Argentina* 128 E3
Camas, *Spain* 37 H4
Camas, *U.S.A.* 110 E4
Camas Valley, *U.S.A.* 108 E2
Camballin, *Australia* 92 C3
Cambará, *Brazil* 127 A5
Cambay = Khambhat, *India* 68 H5
Cambay, G. of = Khambhat, G. of, *India* 66 J8
Cambil, *Spain* 37 H7
Cambo-les-Bains, *France* 20 E2
Cambodia ■, *Asia* 64 F5
Camborne, *U.K.* 15 G2
Cambrai, *France* 19 B10
Cambre, *Spain* 36 B2
Cambria, *U.S.A.* 110 K5
Cambrian Mts., *U.K.* 15 E4
Cambridge, *Canada* 116 C4
Cambridge, *Jamaica* 120 a
Cambridge, *N.Z.* 91 G5
Cambridge, *U.K.* 15 E8
Cambridge, *Mass., U.S.A.* 117 D13
Cambridge, *Minn., U.S.A.* 112 C8
Cambridge, *N.Y., U.S.A.* 117 C11
Cambridge, *Nebr., U.S.A.* 112 E4
Cambridge, *Ohio, U.S.A.* 116 F3
Cambridge Bay = Ikaluktutiak, *Canada* 100 B9
Cambridge G., *Australia* 92 B4
Cambridge Springs, *U.S.A.* 116 E4
Cambridgeshire □, *U.K.* 15 E7
Cambrils, *Spain* 38 D6
Cambuci, *Brazil* 127 A7
Cambundi-Catembo, *Angola* 84 G3
Camden, *Ala., U.S.A.* 115 K2
Camden, *Ark., U.S.A.* 113 J8
Camden, *Maine, U.S.A.* 115 C11
Camden, *N.J., U.S.A.* 117 G9
Camden, *N.Y., U.S.A.* 117 C9
Camden, *S.C., U.S.A.* 115 H5
Camden Sd., *Australia* 92 C3
Camdenton, *U.S.A.* 113 F8
Camelford, *U.K.* 15 G3
Çameli, *Turkey* 47 D11
Camenca, *Moldova* 29 B13
Camerino, *Italy* 41 E10
Cameron, *Ariz., U.S.A.* 109 J8
Cameron, *La., U.S.A.* 113 L8
Cameron, *Mo., U.S.A.* 112 F7
Cameron, *Tex., U.S.A.* 113 K6
Cameron Highlands, *Malaysia* 65 K3
Cameron Hills, *Canada* 102 B5
Cameroon ■, *Africa* 79 G7
Camerota, *Italy* 43 B8
Cameroun →, *Cameroon* 83 E6
Cameroun, Mt., *Cameroon* 83 E6
Cametá, *Brazil* 125 D9
Çamiçi Gölü, *Turkey* 47 D9
Camiguin □, *Phil.* 61 G6
Camiguin I., *Phil.* 61 B4
Camiling, *Phil.* 61 D4
Camilla, *U.S.A.* 115 K3
Caminha, *Portugal* 36 D2
Camino, *U.S.A.* 110 G6
Camira Creek, *Australia* 95 D5
Cammal, *U.S.A.* 116 E7
Cammarata, *Italy* 42 E6
Camocim, *Brazil* 125 D10
Camooweal, *Australia* 94 B2
Camooweal Caves △, *Australia* 94 C2
Camopi, *Fr. Guiana* 125 C8
Camotes Is., *Phil.* 61 F6
Camotes Sea, *Phil.* 61 F6
Camp Borden, *Canada* 116 B5
Camp Hill, *U.S.A.* 116 F8
Camp Nelson, *U.S.A.* 111 J8
Camp Pendleton, *U.S.A.* 111 M9
Camp Verde, *U.S.A.* 109 J8
Camp Wood, *U.S.A.* 113 L5
Campagna, *Italy* 43 B8
Campana, *Argentina* 126 C4
Campana, I., *Chile* 128 F1
Campanário, *Madeira* 48 D2
Campanario, *Spain* 37 G5
Campània □, *Italy* 43 B7
Campbell, *S. Africa* 88 D3
Campbell, *Calif., U.S.A.* 110 H5
Campbell, *Ohio, U.S.A.* 116 E4
Campbell I., *Pac. Oc.* 96 N8
Campbell L., *Canada* 103 A7
Campbell River, *Canada* 102 C3
Campbell Town, *Australia* 95 G4
Campbellford, *Canada* 116 B7
Campbellpur, *Pakistan* 68 C5
Campbellsville, *U.S.A.* 114 G3
Campbellton, *Canada* 105 C6
Campbelltown, *Australia* 95 E5
Campbeltown, *U.K.* 13 F3
Campeche, *Mexico* 119 D6
Campeche □, *Mexico* 119 D6
Campeche, Golfo de, *Mexico* 119 D6
Campello, *Spain* 39 G4
Câmpeni, *Romania* 28 D8
Camperdown, *Australia* 95 F3
Camperville, *Canada* 103 C8
Campi Salentina, *Italy* 43 B11
Câmpia Turzii, *Romania* 29 D8
Campidano, *Italy* 42 C1
Campíglia Maríttima, *Italy* 40 E7
Campillo de Altobuey, *Spain* 39 F3
Campillos, *Spain* 37 H6
Câmpina, *Romania* 29 E10
Campina Grande, *Brazil* 125 E11
Campinas, *Brazil* 127 A6
Campli, *Italy* 41 F10
Campo, *Spain* 38 C5
Campo de Criptana, *Spain* 37 F7
Campo de Gibraltar, *Spain* 37 J5
Campo Grande, *Brazil* 125 H8
Campo Maior, *Brazil* 125 D10
Campo Maior, *Portugal* 37 F3
Campo Mourão, *Brazil* 127 A5
Campo Túres, *Italy* 41 B8
Campobasso, *Italy* 43 A7
Campobello di Licata, *Italy* 42 E6
Campobello di Mazara, *Italy* 42 E5
Campofelice di Roccella, *Italy* 42 E6
Campomarino, *Italy* 41 G12
Camporeale, *Italy* 42 E6
Camporrobles, *Spain* 38 F3
Campos, *Brazil* 127 A7
Campos Belos, *Brazil* 125 F9
Campos del Port, *Spain* 48 B10
Campos Novos, *Brazil* 127 B5
Camprodón, *Spain* 38 C7
Camptonville, *U.S.A.* 110 F5
Camptown, *U.S.A.* 117 E8
Câmpulung, *Argeş, Romania* 29 E10
Câmpulung, *Suceava, Romania* 29 C10
Câmpuri, *Romania* 29 D11
Camrose, *Canada* 102 C6
Camsell Portage, *Canada* 103 B7
Çamyuva, *Turkey* 47 E12
Çan, *Turkey* 45 F11
Can Clavo, *Spain* 48 C7
Can Creu, *Spain* 48 C7
Can Gio, *Vietnam* 65 G6
Can Tho, *Vietnam* 65 G5
Canaan, *U.S.A.* 117 D11
Canada ■, *N. Amer.* 100 C10
Canada Basin, *Arctic* 4 B18
Cañada de Gómez, *Argentina* 126 C3
Canadian, *U.S.A.* 113 H4
Canadian →, *U.S.A.* 113 H7
Canajoharie, *U.S.A.* 117 D10
Çanakkale, *Turkey* 45 F10
Çanakkale □, *Turkey* 45 F10
Çanakkale Boğazı, *Turkey* 45 F10
Canal Flats, *Canada* 102 C5
Canalejas, *Argentina* 126 D2
Canals, *Argentina* 126 C3
Canals, *Spain* 39 G4
Canandaigua, *U.S.A.* 116 D7
Canandaigua L., *U.S.A.* 116 D7
Cananea, *Mexico* 118 A2
Canarias, Is., *Atl. Oc.* 48 F4
Canaries, *St. Lucia* 121 f
Canarreos, Arch. de los, *Cuba* 120 B3
Canary Is. = Canarias, Is., *Atl. Oc.* 48 F4
Canaseraga, *U.S.A.* 116 D7
Canatlán, *Mexico* 118 C4
Canaveral ⌓, *U.S.A.* 115 L5
Canaveral, C., *U.S.A.* 115 L5
Cañaveruelas, *Spain* 38 E2
Canavieiras, *Brazil* 125 G11
Canberra, *Australia* 95 F4
Canby, *Calif., U.S.A.* 108 F3
Canby, *Minn., U.S.A.* 112 C6
Canby, *Oreg., U.S.A.* 110 E4
Cancale, *France* 18 D5
Canche →, *France* 19 B8
Cancún, *Mexico* 119 C7
Candanchu, *Spain* 38 C4
Çandarlı, *Turkey* 47 C8
Çandarlı Körfezi, *Turkey* 47 C8
Candas, *Spain* 36 B5
Candé, *France* 18 E5
Candela, *Italy* 43 A8
Candelaria, *Argentina* 127 B4
Candelaria, *Canary Is.* 48 F3
Candelario ⌓, *Spain* 36 E5
Candeleda, *Spain* 36 E5
Candelo, *Australia* 95 F4
Candi Dasa, *Indonesia* 63 J18
Candia = Iráklion, *Greece* 49 D7
Candia, Sea of = Crete, Sea of, *Greece* 47 E7
Candle L., *Canada* 103 C7
Candlemas I., *Antarctica* 5 B1
Cando, *U.S.A.* 112 A5
Candon, *Phil.* 61 C4
Canea = Khaniá, *Greece* 49 D6
Canelli, *Italy* 40 D5
Canelones, *Uruguay* 127 C4
Canet-Plage, *France* 20 F7
Cañete, *Chile* 126 D1
Cañete, *Peru* 124 F3
Cañete, *Spain* 38 E3
Cañete de las Torres, *Spain* 37 H6
Cangas, *Spain* 36 C2
Cangas de Narcea, *Spain* 36 B4
Cangas de Onís, *Spain* 36 B5
Cangnan, *China* 59 D13
Canguaretama, *Brazil* 125 E11
Canguçu, *Brazil* 127 C5
Canguçu, Serra do, *Brazil* 127 C5
Cangwu, *China* 59 F8
Cangxi, *China* 58 B5
Cangyuan, *China* 58 F2
Cangzhou, *China* 56 E9
Caniapiscau →, *Canada* 105 A6
Caniapiscau, L. de, *Canada* 105 B6
Canicattì, *Italy* 42 E6
Canicattini Bagni, *Italy* 43 E8
Caniles, *Spain* 37 H8
Canim Lake, *Canada* 102 C4
Canindeyu □, *Paraguay* 127 A5
Canino, *Italy* 41 F8
Canisteo, *U.S.A.* 116 D7
Canisteo →, *U.S.A.* 116 D7
Cañitas, *Mexico* 118 C4
Cañizal, *Spain* 36 D5
Canjáyar, *Spain* 37 H8
Çankırı, *Turkey* 72 B5
Cankuzo, *Burundi* 86 C3
Canmore, *Canada* 102 C5
Cann River, *Australia* 95 F4
Canna, *U.K.* 13 D2
Cannanore, *India* 66 P9
Cannes, *France* 21 E11
Canning Town = Port Canning, *India* 69 H13
Cannington, *Canada* 116 B5
Cannóbio, *Italy* 40 B5
Cannock, *U.K.* 15 E5
Cannon Ball →, *U.S.A.* 112 B4
Cannondale Mt., *Australia* 94 D4
Cannonsville Reservoir, *U.S.A.* 117 D9
Cannonvale, *Australia* 94 J6
Canoas, *Brazil* 127 B5
Canoe L., *Canada* 103 B7
Canon City, *U.S.A.* 112 F2
Cañón de Río Blanco △, *Mexico* 119 D5
Cañón del Río Lobos ⌓, *Spain* 36 D7
Cañón del Sumidero △, *Mexico* 119 D5
Canora, *Canada* 103 C8
Canosa di Púglia, *Italy* 43 A9
Canowindra, *Australia* 95 E4
Canso, *Canada* 105 C7
Cantabria □, *Spain* 36 B7
Cantabria, Sierra de, *Spain* 38 C2
Cantabrian Mts. = Cantábrica, Cordillera, *Spain* 36 C5
Cantábrica, Cordillera, *Spain* 36 C5
Cantal □, *France* 20 C6
Cantal, Plomb du, *France* 20 C6
Cantanhede, *Portugal* 36 E2
Cantavieja, *Spain* 38 E4
Čantavir, *Serbia & M.* 28 E4
Cantemir, *Moldova* 29 D13
Canterbury, *Australia* 94 D3
Canterbury, *U.K.* 15 F9
Canterbury Bight, *N.Z.* 91 L3
Canterbury Plains, *N.Z.* 91 K3
Cantil, *U.S.A.* 111 K9
Cantillana, *Spain* 37 H5
Canton = Guangzhou, *China* 59 F9
Canton, *Ga., U.S.A.* 115 H3
Canton, *Ill., U.S.A.* 112 E9
Canton, *Miss., U.S.A.* 113 J9
Canton, *Mo., U.S.A.* 112 E9
Canton, *N.Y., U.S.A.* 117 B9
Canton, *Ohio, U.S.A.* 116 F3
Canton, *Pa., U.S.A.* 116 E8
Canton, *S. Dak., U.S.A.* 112 D6
Canton L., *U.S.A.* 113 G5
Cantù, *Italy* 40 C6
Canudos, *Brazil* 124 E7
Canumã →, *Brazil* 124 D7
Canutama, *Brazil* 124 E6
Canutillo, *U.S.A.* 109 L10
Canvey, *U.K.* 15 F8
Canyon, *U.S.A.* 113 H4
Canyon De Chelly ⌓, *U.S.A.* 109 H9
Canyon of the Ancients ⌓, *U.S.A.* 109 H9
Canyonlands △, *U.S.A.* 109 G9
Canyonville, *U.S.A.* 108 E2
Cao Bang, *Vietnam* 58 F6
Cao He →, *China* 57 D13
Cao Lanh, *Vietnam* 65 G5
Cao Xian, *China* 56 G8
Cáorle, *Italy* 41 C9
Cap-aux-Meules, *Canada* 105 C7
Cap-Chat, *Canada* 105 C6
Cap-de-la-Madeleine, *Canada* 104 C5
Cap-Haïtien, *Haiti* 121 C5
Cap Pt., *St. Lucia* 121 f
Capac, *U.S.A.* 116 C2
Capáccio, *Italy* 43 B8
Capaci, *Italy* 42 D6
Capanaparo →, *Venezuela* 124 B5
Capánnori, *Italy* 40 E7
Capbreton, *France* 20 E2
Capdenac, *France* 20 D6
Capdepera, *Spain* 38 F8
Cape →, *Australia* 94 C4
Cape Arid △, *Australia* 93 F3
Cape Barren I., *Australia* 95 G4
Cape Breton Highlands △, *Canada* 105 C7
Cape Breton I., *Canada* 105 C7
Cape Charles, *U.S.A.* 114 G8
Cape Coast, *Ghana* 83 D4
Cape Cod ⌓, *U.S.A.* 114 E10
Cape Coral, *U.S.A.* 115 M5
Cape Dorset, *Canada* 101 B12
Cape Fear →, *U.S.A.* 115 H6
Cape Girardeau, *U.S.A.* 113 G10
Cape Hatteras ⌓, *U.S.A.* 115 H8
Cape Lee △, *Australia* 93 F3
Cape Lookout ⌓, *U.S.A.* 115 H7
Cape May, *U.S.A.* 114 F8
Cape May Point, *U.S.A.* 114 F8
Cape Melville △, *Australia* 94 A3
Cape Mount △, *Liberia* 82 D2
Cape Peninsula △, *S. Africa* 88 E2
Cape Range △, *Australia* 92 D1
Cape Tormentine, *Canada* 105 C7
Cape Town, *S. Africa* 88 E2
Cape Tribulation △, *Australia* 94 B4
Cape Verde Is. ■, *Atl. Oc.* 77 E1
Cape Vincent, *U.S.A.* 117 B8
Cape York Peninsula, *Australia* 94 A3
Capela, *Brazil* 125 F11
Capella, *Australia* 94 C4
Capendu, *France* 20 E6
Capestang, *France* 20 E7
Capesterre-Belle-Eau, *Guadeloupe* 120 b
Capesterre-de-Marie-Galante, *Guadeloupe* 120 b
Capim →, *Brazil* 125 D9
Capistrello, *Italy* 41 G10
Capitan, *U.S.A.* 109 K11
Capitán Arturo Prat, *Antarctica* 5 C17
Capitol Reef △, *U.S.A.* 109 G8
Capitola, *U.S.A.* 110 J5
Capizzi, *Italy* 43 E7
Capoche →, *Mozam.* 87 F3
Capodichino, Nápoli ✕ (NAP), *Italy* 43 B7
Capoterra, *Italy* 42 C1
Cappadocia, *Turkey* 72 C6
Capraia, *Italy* 40 E6
Caprara, Pta., *Italy* 42 A1
Caprarola, *Italy* 41 F9
Capreol, *Canada* 104 C3
Caprera, *Italy* 42 A2
Capri, *Italy* 43 B7
Capricorn Group, *Australia* 94 C5
Capricorn Ra., *Australia* 92 D2
Caprino Veronese, *Italy* 40 C7
Caprivi Game ⌓, *Namibia* 88 B3
Caprivi Strip, *Namibia* 88 B3
Caps et Marais d'Opale ⌓, *France* 19 B9
Captain's Flat, *Australia* 95 F4
Captieux, *France* 20 D3
Capulin Volcano ⌓, *U.S.A.* 113 G3
Caquetá →, *Colombia* 124 D5
Caracal, *Romania* 29 F9
Caracas, *Venezuela* 124 A5
Caracol, *Mato Grosso do Sul, Brazil* 126 A4
Caracol, *Piauí, Brazil* 125 E10
Caráglio, *Italy* 40 D4
Carajas, *Brazil* 125 E8
Carajás, Serra dos, *Brazil* 125 E8
Carangola, *Brazil* 127 A7
Caransebeş, *Romania* 28 E7
Carantec, *France* 18 D3
Caraquet, *Canada* 105 C6
Caras, *Peru* 124 E3
Caraş Severin □, *Romania* 28 E7
Caraşova, *Romania* 28 E6
Caratasca, L., *Honduras* 120 C3
Caratinga, *Brazil* 125 G10
Caraúbas, *Brazil* 125 E11
Caravaca de la Cruz, *Spain* 39 G3
Caravággio, *Italy* 40 C6
Caravela, *Guinea-Biss.* 82 C1
Caravelas, *Brazil* 125 G11
Caraveli, *Peru* 124 G4
Caravelle, Presqu'île de la, *Martinique* 120 c
Caràzinho, *Brazil* 127 B5
Carballino = O Carballiño, *Spain* 36 C2
Carballo, *Spain* 36 B2
Carberry, *Canada* 103 D9
Carbó, *Mexico* 118 B2
Carbonara, C., *Italy* 42 C2
Carbondale, *Colo., U.S.A.* 108 G10
Carbondale, *Ill., U.S.A.* 113 G10
Carbondale, *Pa., U.S.A.* 117 E9
Carbonear, *Canada* 105 C9
Carboneras, *Spain* 39 J3
Carboneras de Guadazaón, *Spain* 38 F3
Carbónia, *Italy* 42 C1
Carcabuey, *Spain* 37 H6
Carcagente = Carcaixent, *Spain* 39 F4
Carcaixent, *Spain* 39 F4
Carcajou, *Canada* 102 B5
Carcar, *Phil.* 61 F5
Carcarana →, *Argentina* 126 C3
Carcasse, C., *Haiti* 121 C5
Carcassonne, *France* 20 E6
Carcross, *Canada* 102 A2
Çardak, *Çanakkale, Turkey* 45 F10
Çardak, *Denizli, Turkey* 47 D11
Cardamon Hills, *India* 66 Q10
Cardeña, *Spain* 37 G6
Cárdenas, *Cuba* 120 B3
Cárdenas, *San Luis Potosí, Mexico* 119 C5
Cárdenas, *Tabasco, Mexico* 119 D6
Cardenete, *Spain* 38 F3
Cardiff, *U.K.* 15 F4
Cardiff □, *U.K.* 15 F4
Cardiff-by-the-Sea, *U.S.A.* 111 M9
Cardigan, *U.K.* 15 E3
Cardigan B., *U.K.* 15 E3
Cardinal, *Canada* 117 B9
Cardona, *Spain* 38 D6
Cardona, *Uruguay* 126 C4
Cardoner →, *Spain* 38 D6
Cardoso, Ilha do, *Brazil* 127 B5
Cardston, *Canada* 102 D6
Cardwell, *Australia* 94 B4
Careen L., *Canada* 103 B7
Carei, *Romania* 28 C7
Careme = Ciremay, *Indonesia* 63 G13
Carentan, *France* 18 C5
Carey, *U.S.A.* 108 E7
Carey, L., *Australia* 93 E3
Carey L., *Canada* 103 A8
Careysburg, *Liberia* 82 D2
Cargèse, *France* 21 F12
Carhaix-Plouguer, *France* 18 D3
Carhué, *Argentina* 126 D3
Caria, *Turkey* 47 D10
Cariacica, *Brazil* 125 H10
Cariati, *Italy* 43 C9
Caribbean Sea, *W. Indies* 121 D5
Cariboo Mts., *Canada* 102 C4
Caribou, *U.S.A.* 115 B12
Caribou →, *Man., Canada* 103 B10
Caribou →, *N.W.T., Canada* 102 A3
Caribou I., *Canada* 104 C2
Caribou Is., *Canada* 102 A6
Caribou L., *Man., Canada* 103 B9
Caribou L., *Ont., Canada* 104 B2
Caribou Mts., *Canada* 102 B5
Caribou River ⌓, *Canada* 103 B9
Caribrod = Dimitrovgrad, *Serbia & M.* 44 C6
Carichic, *Mexico* 118 B3
Carigara, *Phil.* 61 F6
Carignan, *France* 19 C12
Carignano, *Italy* 40 D4
Carillo, *Mexico* 118 B4
Carinda, *Australia* 95 E4
Cariñena, *Spain* 38 D3
Carinhanha, *Brazil* 125 F10
Carinhanha →, *Brazil* 125 F10
Carini, *Italy* 42 D6
Cariño, *Spain* 36 B3
Carínola, *Italy* 42 A6
Carinthia = Kärnten □, *Austria* 26 E6
Caripito, *Venezuela* 124 A6
Carlet, *Spain* 39 F4
Carleton, Mt., *Canada* 105 C6
Carleton Place, *Canada* 117 A8
Carletonville, *S. Africa* 88 D4
Cărlibaba, *Romania* 29 C10
Carlin, *U.S.A.* 108 F5
Carlingford L., *U.K.* 12 B5
Carlinville, *U.S.A.* 112 F10
Carlisle, *U.K.* 14 C5
Carlisle, *U.S.A.* 116 F7
Carlisle B., *Barbados* 121 g
Carlisle I., *Australia* 94 J7
Carlit, Pic, *France* 20 F5

Carloforte, *Italy* 42 C1
Carlos Casares, *Argentina* 126 D3
Carlos Tejedor, *Argentina* 126 D3
Carlow, *Ireland* 12 D5
Carlow □, *Ireland* 12 D5
Carlsbad, *Calif., U.S.A.* 111 M9
Carlsbad, *N. Mex., U.S.A.* 113 J2
Carlsbad Caverns △, *U.S.A.* 113 J2
Carluke, *U.K.* 13 F5
Carlyle, *Canada* 103 D8
Carmacks, *Canada* 100 B6
Carmagnola, *Italy* 40 D4
Carman, *Canada* 103 D9
Carmarthen, *U.K.* 15 F3
Carmarthen B., *U.K.* 15 F3
Carmarthenshire □, *U.K.* 15 F3
Carmaux, *France* 20 D6
Carmel, *U.S.A.* 117 E11
Carmel-by-the-Sea, *U.S.A.* 110 J5
Carmel Valley, *U.S.A.* 110 J5
Carmelo, *Uruguay* 126 C4
Carmen, *Colombia* 124 B3
Carmen, *Paraguay* 127 B4
Carmen →, *Mexico* 118 A3
Carmen, I., *Mexico* 118 B2
Carmen de Patagones, *Argentina* 128 E4
Cármenes, *Spain* 36 C5
Carmensa, *Argentina* 126 D2
Carmi, *Canada* 102 D5
Carmi, *U.S.A.* 114 F1
Carmichael, *U.S.A.* 110 G5
Carmila, *Australia* 94 C4
Carmona, *Costa Rica* 120 E2
Carmona, *Spain* 37 H5
Carn Ban, *U.K.* 13 D4
Carn Eige, *U.K.* 13 D3
Carnamah, *Australia* 93 E2
Carnarvon, *Australia* 93 D1
Carnarvon, *S. Africa* 88 E3
Carnarvon △, *Australia* 94 C4
Carnarvon Ra., *Queens., Australia* 94 D4
Carnarvon Ra., *W. Austral., Australia* 93 E3
Carnation, *U.S.A.* 110 C5
Carndonagh, *Ireland* 12 A4
Carnduff, *Canada* 103 D8
Carnegie, *U.S.A.* 116 F4
Carnegie, L., *Australia* 93 E3
Carnic Alps = Karnische Alpen, *Europe* 26 E6
Carniche Alpi = Karnische Alpen, *Europe* 26 E6
Carnot, *C.A.R.* 84 D3
Carnot, C., *Australia* 95 E2
Carnot B., *Australia* 92 C3
Carnoustie, *U.K.* 13 E6
Carnsore Pt., *Ireland* 12 D5
Caro, *U.S.A.* 114 D4
Carol City, *U.S.A.* 115 N5
Carolina, *Brazil* 125 E9
Carolina, *Puerto Rico* 121 d
Carolina, *S. Africa* 89 D5
Caroline I., *Kiribati* 97 H12
Caroline Is., *Micronesia* 96 G7
Caroni, *Trin. & Tob.* 125 K15
Caroni →, *Venezuela* 124 B6
Caroníe = Nébrodi, Monti, *Italy* 43 E7
Caroona, *Australia* 95 E5
Carpathians, *Europe* 6 F10
Carpaţii Meridionali, *Romania* 29 E9
Carpentaria, G. of, *Australia* 94 A2
Carpentras, *France* 21 D9
Carpi, *Italy* 40 D7
Cărpineni, *Moldova* 29 D13
Carpinteria, *U.S.A.* 111 L7
Carpio, *Spain* 36 D5
Carr Boyd Ra., *Australia* 92 C4
Carrabelle, *U.S.A.* 115 L3
Carral, *Spain* 36 B2
Carranza, Presa V., *Mexico* 118 B4
Carrara, *Italy* 40 D7
Carrascal, *Phil.* 61 G6
Carrascosa del Campo, *Spain* 38 E2
Carrauntoohill, *Ireland* 12 D2
Carrick-on-Shannon, *Ireland* 12 C3
Carrick-on-Suir, *Ireland* 12 D4
Carrickfergus, *U.K.* 12 B6
Carrickmacross, *Ireland* 12 C5
Carrieton, *Australia* 95 E2
Carrington, *U.S.A.* 112 B5
Carrión →, *Spain* 36 D6
Carrión de los Condes, *Spain* 36 C6
Carrizal Bajo, *Chile* 126 B1
Carrizalillo, *Chile* 126 B1
Carrizo Cr. →, *U.S.A.* 113 G3
Carrizo Plain ⌂, *U.S.A.* 110 K7
Carrizo Springs, *U.S.A.* 113 L5
Carrizozo, *U.S.A.* 109 K11
Carroll, *U.S.A.* 112 D7
Carrollton, *Ga., U.S.A.* 115 J3
Carrollton, *Ill., U.S.A.* 112 F9
Carrollton, *Ky., U.S.A.* 114 F3
Carrollton, *Mo., U.S.A.* 112 F8
Carrollton, *Ohio, U.S.A.* 116 F3
Carron →, *U.K.* 13 D4
Carron, L., *U.K.* 13 D3
Carrot →, *Canada* 103 C8
Carrot River, *Canada* 103 C8
Carrouges, *France* 18 D6
Carrù, *Italy* 40 D4
Carruthers, *Canada* 103 C7
Carsa Dek, *Ethiopia* 81 F4
Çarşamba, *Turkey* 72 B7
Carsóli, *Italy* 41 F10
Carson, *Calif., U.S.A.* 111 M8
Carson, *N. Dak., U.S.A.* 112 B4
Carson →, *U.S.A.* 110 F8
Carson City, *U.S.A.* 110 F7
Carson Sink, *U.S.A.* 108 G4
Cartagena, *Colombia* 124 A3
Cartagena, *Spain* 39 H4
Cartago, *Colombia* 124 C3
Cartago, *Costa Rica* 120 E3
Cártama, *Spain* 37 J6
Cartaxo, *Portugal* 37 F2
Cartaya, *Spain* 37 H3
Cartersville, *U.S.A.* 115 H3
Carterton, *N.Z.* 91 J5
Carthage, *Tunisia* 42 F3
Carthage, *Ill., U.S.A.* 112 E9
Carthage, *Mo., U.S.A.* 113 G7
Carthage, *N.Y., U.S.A.* 114 D8
Carthage, *Tex., U.S.A.* 113 J7
Cartier I., *Australia* 92 B3
Cartwright, *Canada* 105 B8
Caruaru, *Brazil* 125 E11
Carúpano, *Venezuela* 124 A6
Caruthersville, *U.S.A.* 113 G10
Carvin, *France* 19 B9
Carvoeiro, *Brazil* 124 D6
Carvoeiro, C., *Portugal* 37 F1
Cary, *U.S.A.* 115 H6
Casa, Pas de la = Envalira, Port d', *Europe* 38 C6
Casa Branca, *Portugal* 37 G2
Casa Grande, *U.S.A.* 109 K8
Casablanca, *Chile* 126 C1
Casablanca, *Morocco* 78 B4
Casacalenda, *Italy* 41 G11
Casalbordino, *Italy* 41 F11
Casale Monferrato, *Italy* 40 C5
Casalmaggiore, *Italy* 40 D7
Casalpusterlengo, *Italy* 40 C6
Casamance →, *Senegal* 82 C1
Casarano, *Italy* 43 B11
Casares, *Spain* 37 J5
Casas Ibáñez, *Spain* 39 F3
Casasimarro, *Spain* 39 F2
Casatejada, *Spain* 36 F5
Casavieja, *Spain* 36 E6
Cascada de Basaseachic △, *Mexico* 118 B3
Cascade, *Idaho, U.S.A.* 108 D5
Cascade, *Mont., U.S.A.* 108 C8
Cascade Locks, *U.S.A.* 110 E5
Cascade Ra., *U.S.A.* 110 D5
Cascade Reservoir, *U.S.A.* 108 D5
Cascais, *Portugal* 37 G1
Cascavel, *Brazil* 127 A5
Cáscina, *Italy* 40 E7
Casco B., *U.S.A.* 115 D10
Caselle Torinese, *Italy* 40 C4
Caserta, *Italy* 43 A7
Casey, *Antarctica* 5 C8
Caseyr, Raas = Asir, Ras, *Somali Rep.* 75 E5
Cashel, *Ireland* 12 D4
Casiguran, *Phil.* 61 C5
Casilda, *Argentina* 126 C3
Casimcea, *Romania* 29 F13
Casino, *Australia* 95 D5
Casiquiare →, *Venezuela* 124 C5
Čáslav, *Czech Rep.* 26 B8
Casma, *Peru* 124 E3
Casmalia, *U.S.A.* 111 L6
Cásola Valsénio, *Italy* 41 D8
Cásoli, *Italy* 41 F11
Caspe, *Spain* 38 D4
Casper, *U.S.A.* 108 E10
Caspian Depression, *Eurasia* 35 G9
Caspian Sea, *Eurasia* 52 E6
Cass Lake, *U.S.A.* 112 B7
Cassà de la Selva, *Spain* 38 D7
Cassadaga, *U.S.A.* 116 D5
Cassano allo Iónio, *Italy* 43 C9
Cassel, *France* 19 B9
Casselman, *Canada* 117 A9
Casselton, *U.S.A.* 112 B6
Cassiar, *Canada* 102 B3
Cassiar Mts., *Canada* 102 B2
Cassino, *Italy* 42 A6
Cassis, *France* 21 E9
Cassville, *U.S.A.* 113 G8
Castagneto Carducci, *Italy* 40 E7
Castaic, *U.S.A.* 111 L8
Castalia, *U.S.A.* 116 E2
Castanhal, *Brazil* 125 D9
Castara, *Trin. & Tob.* 125 J16
Castéggio, *Italy* 40 C6
Castejón de Monegros, *Spain* 38 D4
Castèl di Sangro, *Italy* 41 G11
Castèl San Giovanni, *Italy* 40 C6
Castèl San Pietro Terme, *Italy* 41 D8
Castelbuono, *Italy* 43 E7
Castelfidardo, *Italy* 41 E10
Castelfiorentino, *Italy* 40 E7
Castelfranco Emília, *Italy* 40 D8
Castelfranco Véneto, *Italy* 41 C8
Casteljaloux, *France* 20 D4
Castellabate, *Italy* 43 B7
Castellammare, G. di, *Italy* 42 D5
Castellammare del Golfo, *Italy* 42 D5
Castellammare di Stábia, *Italy* 43 B7
Castellamonte, *Italy* 40 C4
Castellane, *France* 21 E10
Castellaneta, *Italy* 43 B9
Castelli, *Argentina* 126 D4
Castelló de la Plana, *Spain* 38 F4
Castellón de la Plana □, *Spain* 38 E4
Castellote, *Spain* 38 E4
Castelmáuro, *Italy* 41 G11
Castelnau-de-Médoc, *France* 20 C3
Castelnau-Magnoac, *France* 20 E4
Castelnaudary, *France* 20 E5
Castelnovo ne' Monti, *Italy* 40 D7
Castelnuovo di Val di Cécina, *Italy* 40 E7
Castelo, *Brazil* 127 A7
Castelo Branco, *Portugal* 36 F3
Castelo Branco □, *Portugal* 36 F3
Castelo de Paiva, *Portugal* 36 D2
Castelo de Vide, *Portugal* 37 F3
Castelsardo, *Italy* 42 B1
Castelsarrasin, *France* 20 D5
Casteltérmini, *Italy* 42 E6
Castelvetrano, *Italy* 42 E5
Casterton, *Australia* 95 F3
Castets, *France* 20 E2
Castiglion Fiorentino, *Italy* 41 E8
Castiglione del Lago, *Italy* 41 E9
Castiglione della Pescáia, *Italy* 40 F7
Castiglione delle Stiviere, *Italy* 40 C7
Castilblanco, *Spain* 37 F5
Castile, *U.S.A.* 116 D6
Castilla, Playa de, *Spain* 37 J4
Castilla-La Mancha □, *Spain* 6 H5
Castilla y Leon □, *Spain* 36 D6
Castillo de Locubín, *Spain* 37 H7
Castillon-en-Couserans, *France* 20 F5
Castillonès, *France* 20 D4
Castillos, *Uruguay* 127 C5
Castle Dale, *U.S.A.* 108 G8
Castle Douglas, *U.K.* 13 G5
Castle Rock, *Colo., U.S.A.* 112 F2
Castle Rock, *Wash., U.S.A.* 110 D4
Castlebar, *Ireland* 12 C2
Castlebay, *U.K.* 13 E1
Castleblaney, *Ireland* 12 B5
Castlederg, *U.K.* 12 B4
Castleford, *U.K.* 14 D6
Castlegar, *Canada* 102 D5
Castlemaine, *Australia* 95 F3
Castlepollard, *Ireland* 12 C4
Castlerea, *Ireland* 12 C3
Castlereagh →, *Australia* 95 E4
Castlereagh B., *Australia* 94 A2
Castleton, *U.S.A.* 117 C11
Castletown, *I. of Man* 14 C3
Castletown Bearhaven, *Ireland* 12 E2
Castor, *Canada* 102 C6
Castor →, *Canada* 104 B4
Castorland, *U.S.A.* 117 C9
Castres, *France* 20 E6
Castricum, *Neths.* 17 B4
Castries, *St. Lucia* 121 f
Castril, *Spain* 37 H8
Castro, *Brazil* 127 A6
Castro, *Chile* 128 E2
Castro Alves, *Brazil* 125 F11
Castro del Río, *Spain* 37 H6
Castro-Urdiales, *Spain* 36 B7
Castro Verde, *Portugal* 37 H2
Castrojeriz, *Spain* 36 C6
Castropol, *Spain* 36 B3
Castroreale, *Italy* 43 D8
Castrovíllari, *Italy* 43 C9
Castroville, *U.S.A.* 110 J5
Castuera, *Spain* 37 G5
Çat, *Turkey* 73 C9
Cat Ba △, *Vietnam* 64 B6
Cat Ba, Dao, *Vietnam* 64 B6
Cat I., *Bahamas* 121 B4
Cat L., *Canada* 104 B1
Cat Lake, *Canada* 104 B1
Cat Tien △, *Vietnam* 65 G6
Čata, *Slovak Rep.* 27 D11
Catacamas, *Honduras* 120 D2
Cataguases, *Brazil* 127 A7
Çatak, *Turkey* 73 C10
Catalão, *Brazil* 125 G9
Çatalca, *Turkey* 45 E12
Catalina, *Canada* 105 C9
Catalina, *Chile* 126 B2
Catalina, *U.S.A.* 109 K8
Catalonia = Cataluña □, *Spain* 38 D6
Cataluña □, *Spain* 38 D6
Çatalzeytin, *Turkey* 72 B6
Catamarca, *Argentina* 126 B2
Catamarca □, *Argentina* 126 B2
Catanauan, *Phil.* 61 E5
Catanduanes □, *Phil.* 61 E6
Catanduva, *Brazil* 127 A6
Catánia, *Italy* 43 E8
Catánia, G. di, *Italy* 43 E8
Catanzaro, *Italy* 43 D9
Catarman, *Phil.* 61 E6
Catatumbo-Bari △, *Colombia* 121 E5
Catbalogan, *Phil.* 61 F6
Cateel, *Phil.* 61 H7
Catembe, *Mozam.* 89 D5
Caterham, *U.K.* 15 F7
Cathcart, *S. Africa* 88 E4
Cathlamet, *U.S.A.* 110 D3
Catio, *Guinea-Biss.* 82 C1
Catlettsburg, *U.S.A.* 114 F4
Çatma Dağı, *Turkey* 47 C11
Catoche, C., *Mexico* 119 C7
Cátria, Mte., *Italy* 41 E9
Catriló, *Argentina* 126 D3
Catrimani, *Brazil* 124 C6
Catrimani →, *Brazil* 124 C6
Catskill, *U.S.A.* 117 D11
Catskill ⌂, *U.S.A.* 117 D10
Catskill Mts., *U.S.A.* 117 D10
Catt, Mt., *Australia* 94 A1
Cattaraugus, *U.S.A.* 116 D6
Catterick, *U.K.* 14 C6
Cattólica, *Italy* 41 E9
Cattólica Eraclea, *Italy* 42 E6
Catuala, *Angola* 88 B2
Catuane, *Mozam.* 89 D5
Catur, *Mozam.* 87 E4
Catwick Is., *Vietnam* 65 G7
Cauca →, *Colombia* 124 B4
Caucaia, *Brazil* 125 D11
Caucasus Mountains, *Eurasia* 35 J7
Caudete, *Spain* 39 G3
Caudry, *France* 19 B10
Caulnes, *France* 18 D4
Caulónia, *Italy* 43 D9
Caungula, *Angola* 84 F3
Cauquenes, *Chile* 126 D1
Caura →, *Venezuela* 124 B6
Cauresi →, *Mozam.* 87 F3
Căuşani, *Moldova* 29 D14
Causapscal, *Canada* 105 C6
Caussade, *France* 20 D5
Causse-Méjean, *France* 20 D7
Causses du Quercy ⌂, *France* 20 D5
Cauterets, *France* 20 F3
Cauvery →, *India* 66 P11
Caux, Pays de, *France* 18 C7
Cava de' Tirreni, *Italy* 43 B7
Cávado →, *Portugal* 36 D2
Cavagrande del Cassibile ⌂, *Italy* 43 F8
Cavaillon, *France* 21 E9
Cavalaire-sur-Mer, *France* 21 E10
Cavalese, *Italy* 41 B8
Cavalier, *U.S.A.* 112 A6
Cavalla = Cavally →, *Africa* 82 E3
Cavallo, Î. de, *France* 21 G13
Cavally →, *Africa* 82 E3
Cavan, *Ireland* 12 B4
Cavan □, *Ireland* 12 C4
Cavárzere, *Italy* 41 C9
Çavdarhisar, *Turkey* 47 B11
Çavdır, *Turkey* 47 D11
Cave Creek, *U.S.A.* 109 K7
Cavenagh Ra., *Australia* 93 E4
Cavendish, *Australia* 95 F3
Caviana, I., *Brazil* 125 C8
Cavite, *Phil.* 61 D4
Cavnic, *Romania* 29 C8
Cavour, *Italy* 40 D4
Cavtat, *Croatia* 44 D2
Cawndilla L., *Australia* 95 E3
Cawnpore = Kanpur, *India* 69 F9
Caxias, *Brazil* 125 D10
Caxias do Sul, *Brazil* 127 B5
Çay, *Turkey* 72 C4
Cay Sal Bank, *Bahamas* 120 B4
Cayambe, *Ecuador* 124 C3
Çaycuma, *Turkey* 72 B5
Çayeli, *Turkey* 73 B9
Cayenne, *Fr. Guiana* 125 B8
Cayey, *Puerto Rico* 121 d
Caygören Barajı, *Turkey* 47 B10
Cayiralan, *Turkey* 72 C6
Caylus, *France* 20 D5
Cayman Brac, *Cayman Is.* 120 C4
Cayman Is. ☑, *W. Indies* 120 C3
Cayman Trough, *Caribbean* 98 H11
Cayres, *France* 20 D7
Cayuga, *U.S.A.* 117 D8
Cayuga L., *U.S.A.* 117 D8
Cazalla de la Sierra, *Spain* 37 H5
Căzăneşti, *Romania* 29 F12
Cazaubon, *France* 20 E3
Cazaux et de Sanguinet, Étang de, *France* 20 D2
Cazenovia, *U.S.A.* 117 D9
Cazères, *France* 20 E5
Cazin, *Bos.-H.* 41 D12
Čazma, *Croatia* 41 C13
Cazombo, *Angola* 85 G4
Cazorla, *Spain* 37 H7
Cazorla, Sierra de, *Spain* 37 G8
Cea →, *Spain* 36 C5
Ceamurlia de Jos, *Romania* 29 F13
Ceanannus Mor, *Ireland* 12 C5
Ceará = Fortaleza, *Brazil* 125 D11
Ceará □, *Brazil* 125 E11
Ceará Mirim, *Brazil* 125 E11
Ceauru, L., *Romania* 29 F8
Cebaco, I. de, *Panama* 120 E3
Cebollar, *Argentina* 126 B2
Cebollera, Sierra de, *Spain* 38 D2
Cebreros, *Spain* 36 E6
Cebu, *Phil.* 61 F5
Čečava, *Bos.-H.* 28 F2
Ceccano, *Italy* 42 A6
Cece, *Hungary* 28 D3
Cechi, *Ivory C.* 82 D4
Cecil Plains, *Australia* 95 D5
Cécina, *Italy* 40 E7
Cécina →, *Italy* 40 E7
Ceclavín, *Spain* 36 F4
Cedar →, *U.S.A.* 112 E9
Cedar City, *U.S.A.* 109 H7
Cedar Creek Reservoir, *U.S.A.* 113 J6
Cedar Falls, *Iowa, U.S.A.* 112 D8
Cedar Falls, *Wash., U.S.A.* 110 C5
Cedar Key, *U.S.A.* 115 L4
Cedar L., *Canada* 103 C9
Cedar Rapids, *U.S.A.* 112 E9
Cedartown, *U.S.A.* 115 H3
Cedarvale, *Canada* 102 B3
Cedarville, *S. Africa* 89 E4
Cedeira, *Spain* 36 B2
Cedral, *Mexico* 118 C4
Cedrino →, *Italy* 42 B2
Cedro, *Brazil* 125 E11
Cedros, I. de, *Mexico* 118 B1
Cedros B., *Trin. & Tob.* 125 K15
Ceduna, *Australia* 95 E1
Cedynia, *Poland* 31 F1
Cée, *Spain* 36 C1
Ceerigaabo = Erigavo, *Somali Rep.* 75 E4
Cefalù, *Italy* 43 D7
Cega →, *Spain* 36 D6
Cegléd, *Hungary* 28 C4
Céglie Messápico, *Italy* 43 B10
Cehegín, *Spain* 39 G3
Ceheng, *China* 58 E5
Cehu-Silvaniei, *Romania* 29 C8
Ceica, *Romania* 28 D7
Ceira →, *Portugal* 36 E2
Çekik, *Indonesia* 63 J17
Čelákovice, *Czech Rep.* 26 A7
Celano, *Italy* 41 F10
Celanova, *Spain* 36 C3
Celaque △, *Honduras* 120 D2
Celaya, *Mexico* 118 C4
Celebes = Sulawesi, *Indonesia* 63 E6
Celebes Sea, *Indonesia* 63 D6
Čelić, *Bos.-H.* 28 F3
Celina, *U.S.A.* 114 E3
Celinac, *Bos.-H.* 28 F2
Celje, *Slovenia* 41 B12
Celldömölk, *Hungary* 28 C2
Celle, *Germany* 24 C6
Celorico da Beira, *Portugal* 36 E3
Celtic Sea, *Atl. Oc.* 6 E4
Çeltikçi, *Turkey* 47 D12
Çemişgezek, *Turkey* 73 C8
Cenderwasih, Teluk, *Indonesia* 63 E9
Cengong, *China* 58 D7
Ceno →, *Italy* 40 D7
Centallo, *Italy* 40 D4
Centelles, *Spain* 38 D7
Center, *N. Dak., U.S.A.* 112 B4
Center, *Tex., U.S.A.* 113 K7
Centerburg, *U.S.A.* 116 F2
Centerville, *Calif., U.S.A.* 110 J7
Centerville, *Iowa, U.S.A.* 112 E8
Centerville, *Pa., U.S.A.* 116 F5
Centerville, *Tenn., U.S.A.* 115 H2
Centerville, *Tex., U.S.A.* 113 K7
Cento, *Italy* 41 D8
Central = Tsentralnyy □, *Russia* 34 D4
Central □, *Ghana* 83 D4
Central □, *Kenya* 86 C4
Central □, *Malawi* 87 E3
Central □, *Zambia* 87 E2
Central, Cordillera, *Colombia* 124 C4
Central, Cordillera, *Costa Rica* 120 D3
Central, Cordillera, *Dom. Rep.* 121 C5
Central, Cordillera, *Phil.* 61 C4
Central, Cordillera, *Puerto Rico* 121 d
Central African Rep. ■, *Africa* 79 G9
Central America, *America* 98 H11
Central Butte, *Canada* 103 C7
Central City, *Colo., U.S.A.* 108 G11
Central City, *Ky., U.S.A.* 114 G2
Central City, *Nebr., U.S.A.* 112 E6
Central I., *Kenya* 86 B4
Central Island △, *Kenya* 86 B4
Central Kalahari ⌂, *Botswana* 88 C3
Central Makran Range, *Pakistan* 66 F4
Central Patricia, *Canada* 104 B1
Central Point, *U.S.A.* 108 E2
Central Russian Uplands, *Europe* 6 E13
Central Siberian Plateau, *Russia* 50 C14
Central Square, *U.S.A.* 117 C8
Centralia, *Ill., U.S.A.* 112 F10
Centralia, *Mo., U.S.A.* 112 F8
Centralia, *Wash., U.S.A.* 110 D4
Cenxi, *China* 59 F8
Čeotina →, *Bos.-H.* 44 C2
Cephalonia = Kefallinía, *Greece* 46 C2
Čepin, *Croatia* 28 E3
Ceprano, *Italy* 42 A6
Ceptura, *Romania* 29 E11
Cepu, *Indonesia* 63 G14
Ceram = Seram, *Indonesia* 63 E7
Ceram Sea = Seram Sea, *Indonesia* 63 E7
Cerbère, *France* 20 F7
Cerbicales, Îs., *France* 21 G13
Cercal, *Portugal* 37 H2
Cerdaña, *Spain* 38 C6
Cère →, *France* 20 D5
Cerea, *Italy* 41 C8
Ceredigion □, *U.K.* 15 E3
Ceres, *Argentina* 126 B3
Ceres, *S. Africa* 88 E2
Ceres, *U.S.A.* 110 H6
Céret, *France* 20 F6
Cergy, *France* 19 C9
Cerignola, *Italy* 43 A8
Cerigo = Kíthira, *Greece* 46 E5
Cérilly, *France* 19 F9
Cerisiers, *France* 19 D10
Cerizay, *France* 18 F6
Çerkeş, *Turkey* 72 B5
Çerkezköy, *Turkey* 45 E12
Cerknica, *Slovenia* 41 C11
Cerkovica, *Bulgaria* 45 C8
Cermerno, *Serbia & M.* 44 C4
Çermik, *Turkey* 73 C8
Cerna, *Romania* 29 E13
Cerna →, *Romania* 29 F8
Cernavodă, *Romania* 29 F13
Cernay, *France* 19 E14
Cernik, *Croatia* 28 E2
Cerralvo, I., *Mexico* 118 C3
Cërrik, *Albania* 44 E3
Cerritos, *Mexico* 118 C4
Cerro Chato, *Uruguay* 127 C4
Cerro Corá △, *Paraguay* 127 A4
Cerro el Copey △, *Venezuela* 121 D7
Cerro Hoya △, *Panama* 120 E3
Cerro Saroche △, *Venezuela* 121 D6
Certaldo, *Italy* 40 E8
Cervaro →, *Italy* 43 A8
Cervati, Monte, *Italy* 43 B8
Cerventes, *Australia* 93 F2
Cervera, *Spain* 38 D6
Cervera de Pisuerga, *Spain* 36 C6
Cervera del Río Alhama, *Spain* 38 C3
Cervéteri, *Italy* 41 F9
Cérvia, *Italy* 41 D9
Cervignano del Friuli, *Italy* 41 C10
Cervinara, *Italy* 43 A7
Cervione, *France* 21 F13
Cervo, *Spain* 36 B3
Cesarò, *Italy* 43 E7
Cesena, *Italy* 41 D9
Cesenático, *Italy* 41 D9
Cēsis, *Latvia* 9 H21
Česká Lípa, *Czech Rep.* 26 A7
Česká Třebová, *Czech Rep.* 27 B9
České Budějovice, *Czech Rep.* 26 C7
České Velenice, *Czech Rep.* 26 C7
Českobudějovický □, *Czech Rep.* 26 B7
Českomoravská Vrchovina, *Czech Rep.* 26 B8
Český Brod, *Czech Rep.* 26 A7
Český Krumlov, *Czech Rep.* 26 C7

Český Těšín, Czech Rep. 27 B11
Česma →, Croatia 41 C13
Çeşme, Turkey 47 C8
Cessnock, Australia 95 E5
Cesson-Sévigné, France 18 D5
Cestas, France 20 D3
Cestos →, Liberia 82 D3
Cestos Sehnkwehn △, Liberia 82 D3
Cetate, Romania 28 F8
Cetin Grad, Croatia 41 C12
Cetina →, Croatia 41 E13
Cetinje, Serbia & M. 44 D2
Cetraro, Italy 43 C8
Ceuta, N. Afr. 78 A4
Ceva, Italy 40 D5
Cévennes, France 20 D7
Cévennes △, France 20 D7
Ceyhan, Turkey 70 B2
Ceyhan →, Turkey 72 D6
Ceylânpınar, Turkey 73 D9
Ceylon = Sri Lanka ■, Asia 66 R12
Cèze →, France 21 D8
Cha-am, Thailand 64 F2
Cha Pa, Vietnam 64 A4
Chabanais, France 20 C4
Chabeuil, France 21 D9
Chablais, France 19 F13
Chablis, France 19 E10
Chacabuco, Argentina 126 C3
Chachapoyas, Peru 124 E3
Chachoengsao, Thailand 64 F3
Chachran, Pakistan 66 E7
Chachro, Pakistan 68 G4
Chaco △, Argentina 126 B4
Chaco □, Argentina 126 B3
Chaco □, Paraguay 126 B4
Chaco →, U.S.A. 109 H9
Chaco Austral, S. Amer. 128 B4
Chaco Boreal, S. Amer. 124 H6
Chaco Central, S. Amer. 128 A4
Chaco Culture △, U.S.A. 109 H10
Chacon, C., U.S.A. 102 C2
Chad ■, Africa 79 F8
Chad, L. = Tchad, L., Chad 79 F8
Chadan, Russia 53 D10
Chadileuvú →, Argentina 126 D2
Chadiza, Zambia 87 E3
Chadron, U.S.A. 112 D3
Chadyr-Lunga = Ciadâr-Lunga, Moldova 29 D13
Chae Hom, Thailand 64 C2
Chae Son △, Thailand 64 C2
Chaem →, Thailand 64 C2
Chaeryŏng, N. Korea 57 E13
Chagai Hills = Chāh Gay Hills, Afghan. 66 E3
Chagda, Russia 53 D14
Chaghcharān, Afghan. 66 B4
Chagny, France 19 F11
Chagoda, Russia 32 C8
Chagos Arch. ☒, Ind. Oc. 50 K11
Chagres △, Panama 120 E4
Chagrin Falls, U.S.A. 116 E3
Chaguanas, Trin. & Tob. 125 K15
Chāh Ākhvor, Iran 71 C8
Chāh Bahar, Iran 71 E9
Chāh-e Kavīr, Iran 71 C8
Chāh Gay Hills, Afghan. 66 E3
Chahar Burjak, Afghan. 66 D3
Chahār Mahāll va Bakhtīarī □, Iran 71 C6
Chaibasa, India 67 H14
Chaillé-les-Marais, France 20 B2
Chainat, Thailand 64 E3
Chaiya, Thailand 65 H2
Chaiyaphum, Thailand 64 E4
Chaj Doab, Pakistan 68 C5
Chajari, Argentina 126 C4
Chak Amru, Pakistan 68 C6
Chaka, Sudan 81 G3
Chakar →, Pakistan 68 E3
Chakari, Zimbabwe 89 B4
Chake Chake, Tanzania 86 D4
Chakhānsūr, Afghan. 66 D3
Chakonipau, L., Canada 105 A6
Chakradharpur, India 69 H11
Chakrata, India 68 D7
Chakwal, Pakistan 68 C5
Chala, Peru 124 G4
Chalais, France 20 C4
Chalchihuites, Mexico 118 C4
Chalcis = Khalkís, Greece 46 C5
Châlette-sur-Loing, France 19 D9
Chaleur B., Canada 105 C6
Chalfant, U.S.A. 110 H8
Chalhuanca, Peru 124 F4
Chalindrey, France 19 E12
Chaling, China 59 D9
Chalisgaon, India 66 J9
Chalk River, Canada 104 C4
Chalky Inlet, N.Z. 91 M1
Challans, France 18 F5
Challapata, Bolivia 124 G5
Challis, U.S.A. 108 D6
Chalmette, U.S.A. 113 L10
Chalon-sur-Saône, France 19 F11
Chalonnes-sur-Loire, France 18 E6
Châlons-en-Champagne, France 19 D11
Châlus, France 20 C4
Chālūs, Iran 71 B6
Cham, Germany 25 F8
Cham, Cu Lao, Vietnam 64 E7
Chama, U.S.A. 109 H10
Chamaicó, Argentina 126 D3
Chaman, Pakistan 66 D5
Chamba, India 68 C7
Chamba, Tanzania 87 E4
Chambal →, India 69 F8
Chamberlain, U.S.A. 112 D5
Chamberlain →, Australia 92 C4
Chamberlain L., U.S.A. 115 B11
Chambers, U.S.A. 109 J9
Chambersburg, U.S.A. 114 F7
Chambéry, France 21 C9
Chambeshi →, Zambia 84 G6
Chambly, Canada 117 A11
Chambord, Canada 105 C5
Chamboulive, France 20 C5
Chamchamal, Iraq 70 C5
Chamela, Mexico 118 D3
Chamical, Argentina 126 C2
Chamkar Luong, Cambodia 65 G4
Chamoli, India 69 D8
Chamonix-Mont Blanc, France 21 C10
Champa, India 69 H10
Champagne, Canada 102 A1
Champagne, France 19 D11
Champagnole, France 19 F12
Champaign, U.S.A. 114 E1
Champassak, Laos 64 E5
Champaubert, France 19 D10
Champawat, India 69 E9
Champdeniers-St-Denis, France 20 B3
Champdoré, L., Canada 105 A6
Champeix, France 20 C7
Champion, U.S.A. 116 E4
Champlain, U.S.A. 117 B11
Champlain, L., U.S.A. 117 B11
Champlitte, France 19 E12
Champotón, Mexico 119 D6
Champua, India 69 H11
Chamusca, Portugal 37 F2
Chana, Thailand 65 J3
Chañaral, Chile 126 B1
Chanārān, Iran 71 B8
Chanasma, India 68 H5
Chancery Lane, Barbados 121 g
Chanco, Chile 126 D1
Chand, India 69 J8
Chandan, India 69 G12
Chandan Chauki, India 69 E9
Chandannagar, India 69 H13
Chandausi, India 69 E8
Chandeleur Is., U.S.A. 113 L10
Chandeleur Sd., U.S.A. 113 L10
Chandigarh, India 68 D7
Chandil, India 69 H12
Chandler, Australia 95 D1
Chandler, Canada 105 C7
Chandler, Ariz., U.S.A. 109 K8
Chandler, Okla., U.S.A. 113 H6
Chandod, India 68 J5
Chandpur, Bangla. 67 H17
Chandrapur, India 66 K11
Chānf, Iran 71 E9
Chang, Pakistan 68 F3
Chang, Ko, Thailand 65 F4
Ch'ang Chiang = Chang Jiang →, China 59 B13
Chang Jiang →, China 59 B13
Changa, India 69 C7
Changanacheri, India 66 Q10
Changane →, Mozam. 89 C5
Changbai, China 57 D15
Changbai Shan, China 57 C15
Changchiak'ou = Zhangjiakou, China 56 D8
Ch'angchou = Changzhou, China 59 B12
Changchun, China 57 C13
Changchunling, China 57 B13
Changde, China 59 C8
Changdo-ri, N. Korea 57 E14
Changfeng, China 59 A11
Changhai = Shanghai, China 59 B13
Changhua, China 59 B12
Changhua, Taiwan 59 E13
Changhŭng, S. Korea 57 G14
Changhŭngni, N. Korea 57 D15
Changi, Singapore 65 d
Changi, Singapore ✈ (SIN), Singapore 65 M4
Changjiang, China 64 C7
Changjin, N. Korea 57 D14
Changjin-chŏsuji, N. Korea 57 D14
Changle, China 59 E12
Changli, China 57 E10
Changling, China 57 B12
Changlun, Malaysia 65 J3
Changning, Hunan, China 59 D9
Changning, Sichuan, China 58 C5
Changning, Yunnan, China 58 E2
Changping, China 56 D9
Changsha, China 59 C9
Changshan, China 59 C12
Changshu, China 59 B13
Changshun, China 58 D6
Changtai, China 59 E11
Changting, China 59 E11
Changwu, China 56 G4
Changxing, China 59 B12
Changyang, China 59 B8
Changyi, China 57 F10
Changyŏn, N. Korea 57 E13
Changyuan, China 56 G8
Changzhi, China 56 F7
Changzhou, China 59 B12
Chanhanga, Angola 88 B1
Chania = Khaniá, Greece 49 D6
Chanlar = Xanlar, Azerbaijan 35 K8
Channapatna, India 66 N10
Channel Is., U.K. 15 H5
Channel Is., U.S.A. 111 M7
Channel Islands △, U.S.A. 111 L7
Channel-Port aux Basques, Canada 105 C8
Channel Tunnel, Europe 15 F9
Channing, U.S.A. 113 H3
Chantada, Spain 36 C3
Chanthaburi, Thailand 64 F4
Chantilly, France 19 C9
Chantonnay, France 18 F5
Chantrey Inlet, Canada 100 B10
Chanute, U.S.A. 113 G7
Chanza →, Spain 37 H3
Chao Hu, China 59 B11
Chao Phraya →, Thailand 64 F3
Chao Phraya Lowlands, Thailand 64 E3
Chaocheng, China 56 F8
Chaohu, China 59 B11
Chaoyang, Guangdong, China 59 F11
Chaoyang, Liaoning, China 57 D11
Chaozhou, China 59 F11
Chapais, Canada 104 C5
Chapala, Mozam. 87 F4
Chapala, L. de, Mexico 118 C4
Chapayev, Kazakhstan 34 E10
Chapayevsk, Russia 34 D9
Chapecó, Brazil 127 B5
Chapel Hill, U.S.A. 115 H6
Chapleau, Canada 104 C3
Chaplin, Canada 103 C7
Chaplin L., Canada 103 C7
Chaplino, Ukraine 33 H9
Chaplygin, Russia 32 F11
Chappell, U.S.A. 112 E3
Chapra = Chhapra, India 69 G11
Chara, Russia 53 D12
Charadai, Argentina 126 B4
Charagua, Bolivia 124 G6
Charambirá, Punta, Colombia 124 C3
Charaña, Bolivia 124 G5
Charantsavan, Armenia 35 K7
Charanwala, India 68 F5
Charata, Argentina 126 B3
Charcas, Mexico 118 C4
Charcot I., Antarctica 5 C17
Chard, U.K. 15 G5
Chardon, U.S.A. 116 E3
Chardzhou = Chärjew, Turkmenistan 52 F7
Charente □, France 20 C4
Charente →, France 20 C2
Charente-Maritime □, France 20 C3
Charenton-du-Cher, France 19 F9
Chari →, Chad 79 F8
Chārīkār, Afghan. 66 B6
Chariton →, U.S.A. 112 F8
Chärjew, Turkmenistan 52 F7
Charkhari, India 69 G8
Charkhi Dadri, India 68 E7
Charleroi, Belgium 17 D4
Charleroi, U.S.A. 116 F5
Charles, C., U.S.A. 114 G8
Charles City, U.S.A. 112 D8
Charles de Gaulle, Paris ✈ (CDG), France 19 D9
Charles L., Canada 103 B6
Charles Town, U.S.A. 114 F7
Charleston, Ill., U.S.A. 114 F1
Charleston, Miss., U.S.A. 113 H9
Charleston, Mo., U.S.A. 113 G10
Charleston, S.C., U.S.A. 115 J6
Charleston, W. Va., U.S.A. 114 F5
Charleston L., Canada 117 B9
Charleston Peak, U.S.A. 111 J11
Charlestown, Ireland 12 C3
Charlestown, S. Africa 89 D4
Charlestown, Ind., U.S.A. 114 F3
Charlestown, N.H., U.S.A. 117 C12
Charlestown of Aberlour, U.K. 13 D5
Charleville = Rath Luirc, Ireland 12 D3
Charleville, Australia 95 D4
Charleville-Mézières, France 19 C11
Charlevoix, U.S.A. 114 C3
Charlieu, France 19 F11
Charlotte, Mich., U.S.A. 114 D3
Charlotte, N.C., U.S.A. 115 H5
Charlotte, Vt., U.S.A. 117 B11
Charlotte Amalie, U.S. Virgin Is. 121 e
Charlotte Harbor, U.S.A. 115 M4
Charlotte L., Canada 102 C3
Charlottenberg, Sweden 10 E6
Charlottesville, U.S.A. 114 F6
Charlottetown, Nfld. & L., Canada 105 B8
Charlottetown, P.E.I., Canada 105 C7
Charlotteville, Trin. & Tob. 125 J16
Charlton, Australia 95 F3
Charlton, U.S.A. 112 E8
Charlton I., Canada 104 B4
Charmes, France 19 D13
Charny, Canada 105 C5
Charnyany, Belarus 31 G11
Charolles, France 19 F11
Chârost, France 19 F9
Charre, Mozam. 87 F4
Charroux, France 20 B4
Charsadda, Pakistan 68 B4
Charters Towers, Australia 94 C4
Chartres, France 18 D8
Chartreuse ⌓, France 21 C9
Chascomús, Argentina 126 D4
Chasefu, Zambia 87 E3
Chashma Barrage, Pakistan 68 C4
Chasseneuil-sur-Bonnieure, France 20 C4
Chât, Iran 71 B7
Chatal Balkan = Udvoy Balkan, Bulgaria 45 D10
Château-Arnoux-St-Auban, France 21 D10
Château-Chinon, France 19 E10
Château-d'Olonne, France 20 B2
Château-du-Loir, France 18 E7
Château-Gontier, France 18 E6
Château-la-Vallière, France 18 E7
Château-Landon, France 19 D9
Château-Renard, France 19 E9
Château-Renault, France 18 E7
Château-Salins, France 19 D13
Château-Thierry, France 19 C10
Châteaubourg, France 18 D5
Châteaubriant, France 18 E5
Châteaudun, France 18 D8
Chateaugay, U.S.A. 117 B10
Châteaugiron, France 18 D5
Châteauguay, L., Canada 105 A5
Châteaulin, France 18 D2
Châteaumeillant, France 19 F9
Châteauneuf-du-Faou, France 18 D3
Châteauneuf-sur-Charente, France 20 C3
Châteauneuf-sur-Cher, France 19 F9
Châteauneuf-sur-Loire, France 19 E9
Châteaurenard, France 21 E8
Châteauroux, France 19 F8
Châteauvillain, France 19 D11
Châteaux, Pte. des, Guadeloupe 120 b
Châtelaillon-Plage, France 20 B2
Châtelguyon, France 20 C7
Châtellerault, France 18 F7
Châtelus-Malvaleix, France 19 F9
Chatham = Chatham-Kent, Canada 116 D2
Chatham = Miramichi, Canada 105 C6
Chatham, U.K. 15 F8
Chatham, U.S.A. 117 D11
Chatham Is., Pac. Oc. 96 M10
Chatham-Kent, Canada 116 D2
Châtillon, Italy 40 C4
Châtillon-Coligny, France 19 E9
Châtillon-en-Diois, France 21 D9
Châtillon-sur-Indre, France 18 F8
Châtillon-sur-Loire, France 19 E9
Châtillon-sur-Seine, France 19 E11
Chatmohar, Bangla. 69 G13
Chatra, India 69 G11
Chatrapur, India 67 K14
Chats, L. des, Canada 117 A8
Chatsu, India 68 F6
Chatsworth, Canada 116 B4
Chatsworth, Zimbabwe 87 F3
Chāttagām = Chittagong, Bangla. 67 H17
Chattahoochee, U.S.A. 115 K3
Chattahoochee →, U.S.A. 115 K3
Chattanooga, U.S.A. 115 H3
Chatteris, U.K. 15 E8
Chaturat, Thailand 64 E3
Chau Doc, Vietnam 65 G5
Chaudes-Aigues, France 20 D7
Chauffailles, France 19 F11
Chaukan Pass, Burma 67 F20
Chaumont, France 19 D12
Chaumont, U.S.A. 117 B8
Chaumont-en-Vexin, France 19 C8
Chaumont-sur-Loire, France 18 E8
Chaunay, France 20 B4
Chaunskaya G., Russia 4 C16
Chauny, France 19 C10
Chausey, Îs., France 18 D5
Chaussin, France 19 F12
Chautauqua L., U.S.A. 116 D5
Chauvigny, France 18 F7
Chauvin, Canada 103 C6
Chavanges, France 19 D11
Chaves, Brazil 125 D9
Chaves, Portugal 36 D3
Chawang, Thailand 65 H2
Chazelles-sur-Lyon, France 21 C8
Chazy, U.S.A. 117 B11
Cheb, Czech Rep. 26 A5
Cheboksarskoye Vdkhr., Russia 34 B8
Cheboksary, Russia 34 B8
Cheboygan, U.S.A. 114 C3
Chebsara, Russia 32 C10
Chech, Erg, Africa 78 D5
Chechelnyk, Ukraine 29 B14
Chechen, Ostrov, Russia 35 H8
Chechenia □, Russia 35 J7
Checheno-Ingush Republic = Chechenia □, Russia 35 J7
Chechnya = Chechenia □, Russia 35 J7
Chech'ŏn, S. Korea 57 F15
Chęciny, Poland 31 H7
Checotah, U.S.A. 113 H7
Chedabucto B., Canada 105 C7
Cheduba I., Burma 67 K18
Cheepie, Australia 95 D4
Chef-Boutonne, France 20 B3
Chegdomyn, Russia 53 D14
Chegga, Mauritania 78 C4
Chegutu, Zimbabwe 87 F3
Chehalis, U.S.A. 110 D4
Chehalis →, U.S.A. 110 D3
Cheile Nerei-Beusnita △, Romania 28 F6
Cheiron, Mt., France 21 E10
Cheju do, S. Korea 57 H14
Chekalin, Russia 32 E9
Chekhovo, Russia 30 D7
Chekiang = Zhejiang □, China 59 C13
Chel = Kuru, Bahr el →, Sudan 81 F2
Chela, Sa. da, Angola 88 B1
Chelan, U.S.A. 108 C4
Chelan, L., U.S.A. 108 B3
Cheleken, Turkmenistan 52 F6
Cheleken Yarymadasy, Turkmenistan 71 B7
Chelforó, Argentina 128 D3
Chelkar = Shalqar, Kazakhstan 52 E6
Chelkar Tengiz, Solonchak, Kazakhstan 52 E7
Chella, Ethiopia 81 F4
Chelles, France 19 D9
Chełm, Poland 31 G10
Chełmno, Poland 31 E5
Chelmsford, U.K. 15 F8
Chełmża, Poland 31 E5
Chelsea, U.S.A. 117 C12
Cheltenham, U.K. 15 F5
Chelva, Spain 38 F4
Chelyabinsk, Russia 52 D7
Chelyuskin, C. = Chelyuskin, Mys, Russia 53 B11
Chelyuskin, Mys, Russia 53 B11
Chemainus, Canada 110 B3
Chemba, Mozam. 85 H6
Chembar = Belinskiy, Russia 34 D6
Chemillé, France 18 E6
Chemnitz, Germany 24 E8
Chemult, U.S.A. 108 E3
Chen, Gora, Russia 53 C15
Chenab →, Pakistan 68 D4
Chenango Forks, U.S.A. 117 D9
Chencha, Ethiopia 81 F4
Chenchiang = Zhenjiang, China 59 A12
Cheney, U.S.A. 108 C5
Cheng Xian, China 56 H3
Chengbu, China 59 D8
Chengcheng, China 56 G5
Chengchou = Zhengzhou, China 56 G7
Chengde, China 57 D9
Chengdong Hu, China 59 A11
Chengdu, China 58 B5
Chenggong, China 58 E4
Chenggu, China 56 H4
Chenghai, China 59 F11
Chengjiang, China 58 E4
Chengkou, China 58 B7
Ch'engmai, China 64 C7
Ch'engtu = Chengdu, China 58 B5
Chengwu, China 56 G8
Chengxi Hu, China 59 A11
Chengyang, China 57 F11
Chenjiagang, China 57 G10
Chenkán, Mexico 119 D6
Chennai, India 66 N12
Chenôve, France 19 E12
Chenxi, China 59 C8
Chenzhou, China 59 E9
Cheo Reo, Vietnam 62 B3
Cheom Ksan, Cambodia 64 E5
Chepelare, Bulgaria 45 E8
Chepén, Peru 124 E3
Chepes, Argentina 126 C2
Chepo, Panama 120 E4
Chepstow, U.K. 15 F5
Chequamegon B., U.S.A. 112 B9
Cher □, France 19 E9
Cher →, France 18 E7
Chéradi, Italy 43 B10
Cherasco, Italy 40 D4
Cheraw, U.S.A. 115 H6
Cherbourg, France 18 C5
Cherdakly, Russia 34 C9
Cherdyn, Russia 52 C6
Cheremkhovo, Russia 53 D11
Cherepanovo, Russia 52 D9
Cherepovets, Russia 32 C9
Chergui, Chott ech, Algeria 78 B6
Cherikov = Cherykaw, Belarus 32 F6
Cherkasy, Ukraine 33 H7
Cherkessk, Russia 35 H6
Cherlak, Russia 52 D8
Chernaya, Russia 53 B9
Chernelytsya, Ukraine 29 B10
Cherni, Bulgaria 44 D7
Chernigov = Chernihiv, Ukraine 33 G6
Chernihiv, Ukraine 33 G6
Chernivetska □, Ukraine 29 B10
Chernivtsi, Ukraine 29 B13
Chernivtsi, Ukraine 29 B10
Chernobyl = Chornobyl, Ukraine 33 G6
Chernogorsk, Russia 53 D10
Chernomorskoye = Chornomorske, Ukraine 33 K7
Chernovtsy = Chernivtsi, Ukraine 29 B10
Chernyakhovsk, Russia 9 J19
Chernyanka, Russia 33 G9
Chernysheyskiy, Russia 53 C12
Chernyye Zemli, Russia 35 H8
Cherokee, Iowa, U.S.A. 112 D7
Cherokee, Okla., U.S.A. 113 G5
Cherokee Village, U.S.A. 113 G9
Cherokees, Grand Lake O' The, U.S.A. 113 G7
Cherrapunji, India 67 G17
Cherry Valley, Calif., U.S.A. 111 M10
Cherry Valley, N.Y., U.S.A. 117 D10
Cherskiy, Russia 53 C17
Cherskogo Khrebet, Russia 53 C15
Chertkovo, Russia 33 H11
Cherven, Belarus 32 F5
Cherven-Bryag, Bulgaria 45 C8
Chervonoarmiyske, Ukraine 29 E13
Chervonohrad, Ukraine 33 G3
Cherwell →, U.K. 15 F6
Cherykaw, Belarus 32 F6
Chesapeake, U.S.A. 114 G7
Chesapeake B., U.S.A. 114 G7
Cheshire □, U.K. 14 D5
Cheshskaya Guba, Russia 52 C5
Cheshunt, U.K. 15 F7
Chesil Beach, U.K. 15 G5
Chesley, Canada 116 B3
Cheste, Spain 39 F4
Chester, U.K. 14 D5
Chester, Calif., U.S.A. 108 F3
Chester, Ill., U.S.A. 113 G10
Chester, Mont., U.S.A. 108 B8
Chester, Pa., U.S.A. 114 F8
Chester, S.C., U.S.A. 115 H5
Chester, Vt., U.S.A. 117 C12
Chester, W. Va., U.S.A. 116 F4
Chester-le-Street, U.K. 14 C6
Chesterfield, U.K. 14 D6
Chesterfield, Is., N. Cal. 96 J7
Chesterfield Inlet, Canada 100 B10
Chesterton Ra., Australia 95 D4
Chesterton Range △, Australia 95 D4
Chestertown, U.S.A. 117 C11
Chesterville, Canada 117 A9
Chestnut Ridge, U.S.A. 116 F5
Chesuncook L., U.S.A. 115 C11
Chéticamp, Canada 105 C7
Chetrosu, Moldova 29 B12
Chetumal, Mexico 119 D7
Chetumal, B. de, Mexico 119 D7
Chetwynd, Canada 102 B4
Chevanceaux, France 20 C3

Cheviot, The, U.K. 14 B5
Cheviot Hills, U.K. 14 B5
Cheviot Ra., Australia 94 D3
Chew Bahir, Ethiopia 81 G4
Chewelah, U.S.A. 108 B5
Chewore ⌓, Zimbabwe 87 F2
Cheyenne, Okla., U.S.A. 113 H5
Cheyenne, Wyo., U.S.A. 112 E2
Cheyenne →, U.S.A. 112 C4
Cheyenne Wells, U.S.A. 112 F3
Cheyne B., Australia 93 F2
Chhabra, India 68 G7
Chhaktala, India 68 H6
Chhapra, India 69 G11
Chhata, India 68 F7
Chhatarpur, Jharkhand, India 69 G11
Chhatarpur, Mad. P., India 69 G8
Chhattisgarh □, India 69 J10
Chhep, Cambodia 64 F5
Chhindwara, Mad. P., India 69 H8
Chhindwara, Mad. P., India 69 H8
Chhlong, Cambodia 65 F5
Chhota Tawa →, India 68 H7
Chhoti Kali Sindh →, India 68 G6
Chhuikhadan, India 69 J9
Chhuk, Cambodia 65 G5
Chi →, Thailand 64 E5
Chiai, Taiwan 59 F13
Chiali, Taiwan 59 F13
Chiamboni, Somali Rep. 84 E8
Chianciano Terme, Italy 41 E8
Chiang Dao, Thailand 64 C2
Chiang Kham, Thailand 64 C3
Chiang Khan, Thailand 64 D3
Chiang Khong, Thailand 58 G3
Chiang Mai, Thailand 64 C2
Chiang Rai, Thailand 58 H2
Chiang Saen, Thailand 58 G3
Chianti, Italy 41 E8
Chiapa →, Mexico 119 D6
Chiapa de Corzo, Mexico 119 D6
Chiapas □, Mexico 119 D6
Chiaramonte Gulfi, Italy 43 E7
Chiaravalle, Italy 41 E10
Chiaravalle Centrale, Italy 43 D9
Chiari, Italy 40 C6
Chiatura, Georgia 35 J6
Chiautla, Mexico 119 D5
Chiávari, Italy 40 D6
Chiavenna, Italy 40 B6
Chiba, Japan 55 G10
Chiba □, Japan 55 G10
Chibabava, Mozam. 89 C5
Chibemba, Cunene, Angola 85 H2
Chibemba, Huila, Angola 88 B2
Chibi, Zimbabwe 89 C5
Chibia, Angola 85 H2
Chibougamau, Canada 104 C5
Chibougamau, L., Canada 104 C5
Chibuk, Nigeria 83 C7
Chibuto, Mozam. 89 C5
Chic-Chocs, Mts., Canada 105 C6
Chicacole = Srikakulam, India 67 K13
Chicago, U.S.A. 114 E2
Chicago Heights, U.S.A. 114 E2
Chichagof I., U.S.A. 100 C6
Chichén-Itzá, Mexico 119 C7
Chicheng, China 56 D8
Chichester, U.K. 15 G7
Chichester Ra., Australia 92 D2
Chichibu, Japan 55 F9
Chichibu-Tama △, Japan 55 G9
Ch'ich'ihaerh = Qiqihar, China 53 E13
Chicholi, India 68 H8
Chickasaw ⌓, U.S.A. 113 H6
Chickasha, U.S.A. 113 H6
Chiclana de la Frontera, Spain 37 J4
Chiclayo, Peru 124 E3
Chico, U.S.A. 110 F5
Chico →, Chubut, Argentina 128 E3
Chico →, Santa Cruz, Argentina 128 G3
Chicomo, Mozam. 89 C5
Chicomostoc, Mexico 118 C4
Chicontepec, Mexico 119 C5
Chicopee, U.S.A. 117 D12
Chicoutimi, Canada 105 C5
Chicualacuala, Mozam. 89 C5
Chidambaram, India 66 P11
Chidenguele, Mozam. 89 C5
Chidley, C., Canada 101 B13
Chiducuane, Mozam. 89 C5
Chiede, Angola 88 B2
Chiefs Pt., Canada 116 B3
Chiem Hoa, Vietnam 64 A5
Chiemsee, Germany 25 H8
Chiengi, Zambia 87 D2
Chiengmai = Chiang Mai, Thailand 64 C2
Chienti →, Italy 41 E10
Chieri, Italy 40 C4
Chiers →, France 19 C11
Chiesa in Valmalenco, Italy 40 B6
Chiese →, Italy 40 C7
Chieti, Italy 41 F11
Chifeng, China 57 C10
Chigirin, Ukraine 33 H7
Chignecto B., Canada 105 C7
Chiguana, Bolivia 126 A2
Chigwell, U.K. 15 F8
Chiha-ri, N. Korea 57 E14
Chihli, G. of = Bo Hai, China 57 E10
Chihuahua, Mexico 118 B3
Chihuahua □, Mexico 118 B3
Chiili = Shīeli, Kazakhstan 52 E7
Chik Bollapur, India 66 N10
Chikmagalur, India 66 N9
Chikwawa, Malawi 87 F3
Chilac, Mexico 119 D5
Chilam Chavki, Pakistan 69 B6
Chilanga, Zambia 87 F2
Chilapa, Mexico 119 D5
Chilas, Pakistan 69 B6
Chilaw, Sri Lanka 66 R11
Chilcotin →, Canada 102 C4
Childers, Australia 95 D5
Childress, U.S.A. 113 H4
Chile ■, S. Amer. 128 D2
Chile Rise, Pac. Oc. 97 L18
Chilecito, Argentina 126 B2
Chilete, Peru 124 E3
Chilia, Braţul →, Romania 29 E14
Chililabombwe, Zambia 87 E2
Chilin = Jilin, China 57 C14
Chilka L., India 67 K14
Chilko →, Canada 102 C4
Chilko L., Canada 102 C4
Chillagoe, Australia 94 B3
Chillán, Chile 126 D1
Chillicothe, Ill., U.S.A. 112 E10
Chillicothe, Mo., U.S.A. 112 F8
Chillicothe, Ohio, U.S.A. 114 F4
Chilliwack, Canada 102 D4
Chilo, India 68 F5
Chiloane, I., Mozam. 89 C5
Chiloé, I. de, Chile 128 E2
Chilpancingo, Mexico 119 D5
Chiltern Hills, U.K. 15 F7
Chilton, U.S.A. 114 C1
Chilubi, Zambia 87 E2
Chilubula, Zambia 87 E3
Chilumba, Malawi 87 E3
Chilung, Taiwan 59 E13
Chilwa, L., Malawi 87 F4
Chimaltitán, Mexico 118 C4
Chimán, Panama 120 E4
Chimanimani, Zimbabwe 89 B5
Chimanimani △, Zimbabwe 87 F3
Chimay, Belgium 17 D4
Chimayo, U.S.A. 109 H11
Chimbay, Uzbekistan 52 E6
Chimborazo, Ecuador 124 D3
Chimbote, Peru 124 E3
Chimkent = Shymkent, Kazakhstan 52 E7
Chimoio, Mozam. 87 F3
Chimpembe, Zambia 87 D2
Chin □, Burma 67 J18
Chin Ling Shan = Qinling Shandi, China 56 H5
China, Mexico 119 B5
China ■, Asia 60 D6
China, Great Plain of, Asia 50 F15
China Lake, U.S.A. 111 K9
Chinan = Jinan, China 56 F9
Chinandega, Nic. 120 D2
Chinati Peak, U.S.A. 113 L2
Chincha Alta, Peru 124 F3
Chinchaga →, Canada 102 B5
Chinchilla, Australia 95 D5
Chinchilla de Monte Aragón, Spain 39 G3
Chinchorro, Banco, Mexico 119 D7
Chinchou = Jinzhou, China 57 D11
Chincoteague, U.S.A. 114 G8
Chinde, Mozam. 87 F4
Chindo, S. Korea 57 G14
Chindwin →, Burma 67 J19
Chineni, India 69 C6
Chinga, Mozam. 87 F4
Chingola, Zambia 87 E2
Chingole, Malawi 87 E3
Ch'ingtao = Qingdao, China 57 F11
Chinguetti, Mauritania 78 D3
Chingune, Mozam. 89 C5
Chinhae, S. Korea 57 G15
Chinhanguanine, Mozam. 89 D5
Chinhoyi, Zimbabwe 87 F3
Chini, India 68 D8
Chiniot, Pakistan 68 D5
Chínipas, Mexico 118 B3
Chinji, Pakistan 68 C5
Chinju, S. Korea 57 G15
Chinle, U.S.A. 109 H9
Chinmen, Taiwan 59 E13
Chinmen Tao, Taiwan 59 E12
Chinnampo = Namp'o, N. Korea 57 E13
Chino, Japan 55 G9
Chino, U.S.A. 111 L9
Chino Valley, U.S.A. 109 J7
Chinon, France 18 E7
Chinook, U.S.A. 108 B9
Chinsali, Zambia 87 E3
Chióggia, Italy 41 C9
Chíos = Khíos, Greece 47 C8
Chipata, Zambia 87 E3
Chiperceni, Moldova 29 C13
Chipinge, Zimbabwe 87 G3
Chipinge ⌓, Zimbabwe 87 G3
Chipiona, Spain 37 J4
Chipley, U.S.A. 115 K3
Chipman, Canada 105 C6
Chipoka, Malawi 87 E3
Chippenham, U.K. 15 F5
Chippewa →, U.S.A. 112 C8
Chippewa Falls, U.S.A. 112 C9
Chipping Norton, U.K. 15 F6
Chiprovtsi, Bulgaria 44 C6
Chiputneticook Lakes, U.S.A. 115 C11
Chiquián, Peru 124 F3
Chiquibul △, Belize 120 C2
Chiquimula, Guatemala 120 D2
Chiquinquira, Colombia 124 B4
Chir →, Russia 35 F6
Chirala, India 66 M12
Chiramba, Mozam. 87 F3
Chirawa, India 68 E6
Chirchiq, Uzbekistan 52 E7
Chiredzi, Zimbabwe 89 C5
Chiricahua ⌓, U.S.A. 109 K9
Chiricahua Peak, U.S.A. 109 L9
Chiriquí, G. de, Panama 120 E3
Chiriquí, L. de, Panama 120 E3
Chirisa ⌓, Zimbabwe 87 F2
Chirivira Falls, Zimbabwe 87 G3
Chirmiri, India 67 H13
Chirnogi, Romania 29 F11
Chirpan, Bulgaria 45 D9
Chirripó Grande, Cerro, Costa Rica 120 E3
Chirundu, Zimbabwe 89 B4
Chisamba, Zambia 87 E2
Chisapani Garhi, Nepal 67 F14
Chisasibi, Canada 104 B4
Ch'ishan, Taiwan 59 F13
Chisholm, Canada 102 C6
Chisholm, U.S.A. 112 B8
Chishtian Mandi, Pakistan 68 E5
Chishui, China 58 C5
Chishui He →, China 58 C5
Chisimaio, Somali Rep. 77 G8
Chisimba Falls, Zambia 87 E3
Chişinău, Moldova 29 C13
Chişinaŭ ✕ (KIV), Moldova 29 C13
Chişineu Criş, Romania 28 D6
Chisone →, Italy 40 D4
Chisos Mts., U.S.A. 113 L3
Chistopol, Russia 34 C10
Chita, Russia 53 D12
Chitipa, Malawi 87 D3
Chitose, Japan 54 C10
Chitral, Pakistan 66 B7
Chitré, Panama 120 E3
Chittagong, Bangla. 67 H17
Chittagong □, Bangla. 67 G17
Chittaurgarh, India 68 G6
Chittoor, India 66 N11
Chitungwiza, Zimbabwe 87 F3
Chiusi, Italy 41 E8
Chiva, Spain 39 F4
Chivasso, Italy 40 C4
Chivhu, Zimbabwe 87 F3
Chivilcoy, Argentina 126 C4
Chiwanda, Tanzania 87 E3
Chixi, China 59 G9
Chizarira, Zimbabwe 87 F2
Chizarira △, Zimbabwe 87 F2
Chizera, Zambia 87 E2
Chkalov = Orenburg, Russia 52 D6
Chkolovsk, Russia 34 B6
Chloride, U.S.A. 111 K12
Chlumec nad Cidlinou, Czech Rep. 26 A8
Chmielnik, Poland 31 H7
Cho Bo, Vietnam 58 G5
Cho-do, N. Korea 57 E13
Cho Phuoc Hai, Vietnam 65 G6
Choa Chu Kang, Singapore 65 d
Choba, Kenya 86 B4
Chobe △, Botswana 88 B4
Choch'iwŏn, S. Korea 57 F14
Chocianów, Poland 31 G2
Chociwel, Poland 30 E2
Chocolate Mts., U.S.A. 111 M11
Choctawhatchee →, U.S.A. 115 K3
Chodecz, Poland 31 F6
Chodov, Czech Rep. 26 A5
Chodziez, Poland 31 F3
Choele Choel, Argentina 128 D3
Choiseul, St. Lucia 121 f
Choix, Mexico 118 B3
Chojna, Poland 31 F1
Chojnice, Poland 30 E4
Chojnów, Poland 31 G2
Chŏkai-San, Japan 54 E10
Choke Canyon L., U.S.A. 113 L5
Choke Mts., Ethiopia 81 E4
Chokurdakh, Russia 53 B15
Cholame, U.S.A. 110 K6
Cholet, France 18 E6
Cholguan, Chile 126 D1
Choluteca, Honduras 120 D2
Choluteca →, Honduras 120 D2
Chom Bung, Thailand 64 F2
Chom Thong, Thailand 64 C2
Choma, Zambia 87 F2
Chomolungma = Everest, Mt., Nepal 69 E12
Chomun, India 68 F6
Chomutov, Czech Rep. 26 A6
Chon Buri, Thailand 64 F3
Chon Thanh, Vietnam 65 G6
Ch'onan, S. Korea 57 F14
Chone, Ecuador 124 D3
Chong Kai, Cambodia 64 F4
Chong Mek, Thailand 64 E5
Chong Phangan, Thailand 65 b
Chong Samui, Thailand 65 b
Chongde, China 59 B13
Chŏngdo, S. Korea 57 G15
Chŏngha, S. Korea 57 F15
Chŏngjin, N. Korea 57 D15
Chŏngjiu, S. Korea 57 F14
Chŏngju, N. Korea 57 E13
Chongli, China 56 D8
Chongming, China 59 B13
Chongming Dao, China 59 B13
Chongqing, Chongqing, China 58 C6
Chongqing, Sichuan, China 58 B4
Chongqing Shi □, China 58 C6
Chongren, China 59 D11
Chonguene, Mozam. 89 C5
Chŏngŭp, S. Korea 57 G14
Chongyi, China 59 E10
Chongzuo, China 58 F6
Chŏnju, S. Korea 57 G14
Chonos, Arch. de los, Chile 128 F2
Chop, Ukraine 28 B7
Chopim →, Brazil 127 B5
Chor, Pakistan 68 G3
Chorbat La, India 69 B7
Chorley, U.K. 14 D5
Chorna, Ukraine 29 C14
Chornobyl, Ukraine 33 G6
Chornomorske, Ukraine 33 K7
Chorolque, Cerro, Bolivia 126 A2
Choroszcz, Poland 31 E9
Chorregon, Australia 94 C3
Chorro el Indio △, Venezuela 121 E5
Chortkiv, Ukraine 33 H3
Ch'ŏrwon, S. Korea 57 E14
Chorzele, Poland 31 E7
Chorzów, Poland 31 H5
Chos-Malal, Argentina 126 D1
Ch'osan, N. Korea 57 D13
Choszczno, Poland 31 E2
Choteau, U.S.A. 108 C7
Chotěboř, Czech Rep. 26 B8
Chotila, India 68 H4
Chotta Udepur, India 68 H6
Chowchilla, U.S.A. 110 H6
Choybalsan, Mongolia 60 B6
Christchurch, N.Z. 91 K4
Christchurch, U.K. 15 G6
Christian I., Canada 116 B4
Christiana, S. Africa 88 D4
Christiansfeld, Denmark 11 J3
Christiansted, U.S. Virgin Is. 121 C7
Christie B., Canada 103 A6
Christina →, Canada 103 B6
Christmas Cr. →, Australia 92 C4
Christmas I. = Kiritimati, Kiribati 97 G12
Christmas I., Ind. Oc. 96 J2
Christopher L., Australia 93 D4
Chrudim, Czech Rep. 26 B8
Chrzanów, Poland 31 H6
Chtimba, Malawi 87 E3
Chū = Shū, Kazakhstan 52 E8
Chū = Shū →, Kazakhstan 50 E10
Chu →, Vietnam 64 C5
Chu Lai, Vietnam 64 E7
Chuak, Ko, Thailand 65 b
Ch'uanchou = Quanzhou, China 59 E12
Chuankou, China 56 G6
Chubbuck, U.S.A. 108 E7
Chūbu □, Japan 55 F8
Chubu-Sangaku △, Japan 55 F8
Chubut →, Argentina 128 E3
Chuchi L., Canada 102 B4
Chuda, India 68 H4
Chudovo, Russia 32 C6
Chudskoye, Ozero, Russia 9 G22
Chūgoku □, Japan 55 G6
Chūgoku-Sanchi, Japan 55 G6
Chuguyev = Chuhuyiv, Ukraine 33 H9
Chugwater, U.S.A. 112 E2
Chuhuyiv, Ukraine 33 H9
Chukchi Sea, Russia 53 C19
Chukotskoye Nagorye, Russia 53 C18
Chula Vista, U.S.A. 111 N9
Chulucanas, Peru 124 E2
Chulym →, Russia 52 D9
Chum Phae, Thailand 64 D4
Chum Saeng, Thailand 64 E3
Chumar, India 69 C8
Chumbicha, Argentina 126 B2
Chumerna, Bulgaria 45 D9
Chumikan, Russia 53 D14
Chumphon, Thailand 65 G2
Chumuare, Mozam. 87 E3
Chumunjin, S. Korea 57 F15
Chuna →, Russia 53 D10
Chun'an, China 59 C12
Ch'unch'ŏn, S. Korea 57 F14
Chunchura, India 69 H13
Chunga, Zambia 87 F2
Chunggang-ŭp, N. Korea 57 D14
Chunghwa, N. Korea 57 E13
Ch'ungju, S. Korea 57 F14
Chungking = Chongqing, China 58 C6
Chungli, Taiwan 59 E13
Ch'ungmu, S. Korea 57 G15
Chungt'iaoshan = Zhongtiao Shan, China 56 G6
Chungyang Shanmo, Taiwan 59 F13
Chunian, Pakistan 68 D6
Chunya, Tanzania 87 D3
Chunyang, China 57 C15
Chupara Pt., Trin. & Tob. 125 K15
Chuquibamba, Peru 124 G4
Chuquicamata, Chile 126 A2
Chur, Switz. 25 J5
Churachandpur, India 67 G18
Church Stretton, U.K. 15 E5
Churchill, Canada 103 B10
Churchill →, Man., Canada 103 B10
Churchill →, Nfld. & L., Canada 105 B7
Churchill, C., Canada 103 B10
Churchill Falls, Canada 105 B7
Churchill L., Canada 103 B7
Churchill Pk., Canada 102 B3
Churki, India 69 H10
Churu, India 68 E6
Churún Merú = Angel Falls, Venezuela 124 B6
Chushal, India 69 C8
Chuska Mts., U.S.A. 109 H9
Chusovoy, Russia 52 D6
Chute-aux-Outardes, Canada 105 C6
Chuuronjang, N. Korea 57 D15
Chuvash Republic = Chuvashia □, Russia 34 C8
Chuvashia □, Russia 34 C8
Chuwārtah, Iraq 70 C5
Chuxiong, China 58 E3
Chuy, Uruguay 127 C5
Chuzhou, China 59 A12
Chynadiyeve, Ukraine 28 B7
Ci Xian, China 56 F8
Ciacova, Romania 28 E6
Ciadâr-Lunga, Moldova 29 D13
Ciamis, Indonesia 63 G13
Cianjur, Indonesia 63 G12
Cianorte, Brazil 127 A5
Cibola, U.S.A. 111 M12
Cicero, U.S.A. 114 E2
Cidacos →, Spain 38 C3
Cide, Turkey 72 B5
Ciéagas del Cataumbo △, Venezuela 121 E5
Ciechanów, Poland 31 F7
Ciechanowiec, Poland 31 F9
Ciechocinek, Poland 31 F5
Ciego de Avila, Cuba 120 B4
Ciénaga, Colombia 124 A4
Cienfuegos, Cuba 120 B3
Cierp-Gaud, France 20 F4
Cíes, Is., Spain 36 C2
Cieszanów, Poland 31 H10
Cieszyn, Poland 31 J5
Cieza, Spain 39 G3
Çifteler, Turkey 72 C4
Cifuentes, Spain 38 E2
Cihanbeyli, Turkey 72 C5
Cihuatlán, Mexico 118 D4
Cijara ⌓, Spain 37 F6
Cijara, Embalse de, Spain 37 F6
Cijulang, Indonesia 63 G13
Cilacap, Indonesia 63 G13
Çıldır, Turkey 73 B10
Çıldır Gölü, Turkey 73 B10
Cilento e Vallo di Diano △, Italy 43 B8
Cili, China 59 C8
Cilibia, Romania 29 E12
Cilicia, Turkey 72 D5
Cill Chainnigh = Kilkenny, Ireland 12 D4
Cilo Dağı, Turkey 73 D10
Cima, U.S.A. 111 K11
Cimarron, Kans., U.S.A. 113 G4
Cimarron, N. Mex., U.S.A. 113 G2
Cimarron →, U.S.A. 113 G6
Cimişlia, Moldova 29 D13
Cimone, Mte., Italy 40 D7
Çinar, Turkey 73 D9
Çınarcık, Turkey 45 F13
Cinca →, Spain 38 D5
Cincar, Bos.-H. 28 G2
Cincinnati, U.S.A. 114 F3
Cincinnatus, U.S.A. 117 D9
Çine, Turkey 47 D10
Ciney, Belgium 17 D5
Cíngoli, Italy 41 E10
Cinigiano, Italy 41 F8
Cinto, Mte., France 21 F12
Cintruénigo, Spain 38 C3
Ciocile, Romania 29 F12
Ciolăneşti din Deal, Romania 29 F10
Ciorani, Romania 29 F11
Čiovo, Croatia 41 E13
Circeo, Mte., Italy 42 A6
Çirçir, Turkey 72 C7
Circle, Alaska, U.S.A. 100 B5
Circle, Mont., U.S.A. 112 B2
Circleville, U.S.A. 114 F4
Cirebon, Indonesia 63 G13
Ciremay, Indonesia 63 G13
Cirencester, U.K. 15 F6
Cireşu, Romania 28 F7
Cirey-sur-Vezouze, France 19 D13
Ciriè, Italy 40 C4
Cirium, Cyprus 49 E11
Cirò, Italy 43 C10
Cirò Marina, Italy 43 C10
Ciron →, France 20 D3
Cisco, U.S.A. 113 J5
Cislău, Romania 29 E11
Cisna, Poland 31 J9
Cisnădie, Romania 29 E9
Cisterna di Latina, Italy 42 A5
Cisternino, Italy 43 B10
Cistierna, Spain 36 C5
Citeli-Ckaro = Tsiteli-Tsqaro, Georgia 35 K8
Citlaltépetl = Orizaba, Pico de, Mexico 119 D5
Citrus Heights, U.S.A. 110 G5
Citrusdal, S. Africa 88 E2
Città della Pieve, Italy 41 F9
Città di Castello, Italy 41 E9
Città Sant' Angelo, Italy 41 F11
Cittadella, Italy 41 C8
Cittaducale, Italy 41 F9
Cittanova, Italy 43 D9
Ciuc, Munţii, Romania 29 D11
Ciucaş, Vf., Romania 29 E10
Ciucea, Romania 28 D7
Ciuciulea, Moldova 29 C12
Ciuciuleni, Moldova 29 C13
Ciudad Altamirano, Mexico 118 D4
Ciudad Bolívar, Venezuela 124 B6
Ciudad Camargo, Mexico 118 B3
Ciudad de Valles, Mexico 119 C5
Ciudad del Carmen, Mexico 119 D6
Ciudad del Este, Paraguay 127 B5
Ciudad Delicias = Delicias, Mexico 118 B3
Ciudad Guayana, Venezuela 124 B6
Ciudad Guerrero, Mexico 118 B3
Ciudad Guzmán, Mexico 118 D4
Ciudad Juárez, Mexico 118 A3
Ciudad Madero, Mexico 119 C5
Ciudad Mante, Mexico 119 C5
Ciudad Obregón, Mexico 118 B3
Ciudad Real, Spain 37 G7
Ciudad Real □, Spain 37 G7
Ciudad Rodrigo, Spain 36 E4
Ciudad Victoria, Mexico 119 C5
Ciudadela, Spain 48 B10
Ciulniţa, Romania 29 F12
Ciumeghiu, Romania 28 D6
Ciuperceni, Romania 28 F8
Civa Burnu, Turkey 72 B7
Cividale del Friuli, Italy 41 B10
Civita Castellana, Italy 41 F9
Civitanova Marche, Italy 41 E10
Civitavécchia, Italy 41 F8
Civray, France 20 B4
Çivril, Turkey 47 C11
Cixerri →, Italy 42 C1

Cixi, *China* **59 B13**
Cizre, *Turkey* **70 B4**
Cizur Mayor, *Spain* **38 C3**
Clackmannanshire □, *U.K.* **13 E5**
Clacton-on-Sea, *U.K.* **15 F9**
Clain →, *France* **18 F7**
Claire, L., *Canada* **102 B6**
Clairton, *U.S.A.* **116 F5**
Clairvaux-les-Lacs, *France* **19 F12**
Claise →, *France* **20 B5**
Clallam Bay, *U.S.A.* **110 B2**
Clamecy, *France* **19 E10**
Clanton, *U.S.A.* **115 J2**
Clanwilliam, *S. Africa* **88 E2**
Clara, *Ireland* **12 C4**
Claraville, *U.S.A.* **111 K8**
Clare, *Australia* **95 E2**
Clare, *U.S.A.* **114 D3**
Clare □, *Ireland* **12 D3**
Clare →, *Ireland* **12 C2**
Clare I., *Ireland* **12 C1**
Claremont, *Calif., U.S.A.* **111 L9**
Claremont, *N.H., U.S.A.* **117 C12**
Claremont Pt., *Australia* **94 A3**
Claremore, *U.S.A.* **113 G7**
Claremorris, *Ireland* **12 C3**
Clarence →, *Australia* **95 D5**
Clarence →, *N.Z.* **91 K4**
Clarence, I., *Chile* **128 G2**
Clarence I., *Antarctica* **5 C18**
Clarence Str., *Australia* **92 B5**
Clarence Town, *Bahamas* **121 B5**
Clarendon, *Pa., U.S.A.* **116 E5**
Clarendon, *Tex., U.S.A.* **113 H4**
Clarenville-Shoal Harbour, *Canada* **105 C9**
Claresholm, *Canada* **102 D6**
Clarie Coast, *Antarctica* **5 C9**
Clarinda, *U.S.A.* **112 E7**
Clarington, *Canada* **116 C6**
Clarion, *Iowa, U.S.A.* **112 D8**
Clarion, *Pa., U.S.A.* **116 E5**
Clarion →, *U.S.A.* **116 E5**
Clarion Fracture Zone, *Pac. Oc.* **98 H7**
Clark, *U.S.A.* **112 C6**
Clark, Pt., *Canada* **116 B3**
Clark Fork, *U.S.A.* **108 B5**
Clark Fork →, *U.S.A.* **108 B5**
Clarkdale, *U.S.A.* **109 J7**
Clarke City, *Canada* **105 B6**
Clarke I., *Australia* **95 G4**
Clarke Ra., *Australia* **94 J6**
Clark's Fork →, *U.S.A.* **108 D9**
Clark's Harbour, *Canada* **105 D6**
Clarks Hill L., *U.S.A.* **115 J4**
Clarks Summit, *U.S.A.* **117 E9**
Clarksburg, *U.S.A.* **114 F5**
Clarksdale, *U.S.A.* **113 H9**
Clarksville, *Ark., U.S.A.* **113 H8**
Clarksville, *Tenn., U.S.A.* **115 G2**
Clarksville, *Tex., U.S.A.* **113 J7**
Clatskanie, *U.S.A.* **110 D3**
Claude, *U.S.A.* **113 H4**
Claveria, *Phil.* **61 B4**
Clay, *U.S.A.* **110 G5**
Clay Center, *U.S.A.* **112 F6**
Claypool, *U.S.A.* **109 K8**
Claysburg, *U.S.A.* **116 F6**
Claysville, *U.S.A.* **116 F4**
Clayton, *N. Mex., U.S.A.* **113 G3**
Clayton, *N.Y., U.S.A.* **117 B8**
Clear, C., *Ireland* **12 E2**
Clear, L., *Canada* **116 A7**
Clear Hills, *Canada* **102 B5**
Clear I., *Ireland* **12 E2**
Clear L., *U.S.A.* **110 F4**
Clear Lake, *Iowa, U.S.A.* **112 D8**
Clear Lake, *S. Dak., U.S.A.* **112 C6**
Clear Lake Reservoir, *U.S.A.* **108 F3**
Clearfield, *Pa., U.S.A.* **116 E6**
Clearfield, *Utah, U.S.A.* **108 F8**
Clearlake, *U.S.A.* **108 G2**
Clearlake Highlands, *U.S.A.* **110 G4**
Clearwater, *Canada* **102 C4**
Clearwater, *U.S.A.* **115 M4**
Clearwater →, *Alta., Canada* **102 C6**
Clearwater →, *Alta., Canada* **103 B6**
Clearwater L., *Canada* **103 C9**
Clearwater Lake ⌓, *Canada* **103 C8**
Clearwater Mts., *U.S.A.* **108 C6**
Clearwater River ⌓, *Canada* **103 B7**
Cleburne, *U.S.A.* **113 J6**
Clee Hills, *U.K.* **15 E5**
Cleethorpes, *U.K.* **14 D7**
Cleeve Cloud, *U.K.* **15 F6**
Clelles, *France* **21 D9**
Clemson, *U.S.A.* **115 H4**
Clerke Reef, *Australia* **92 C2**
Clermont, *Australia* **94 C4**
Clermont, *France* **19 C9**
Clermont, *U.S.A.* **115 L5**
Clermont-en-Argonne, *France* **19 C12**
Clermont-Ferrand, *France* **20 C7**
Clermont-l'Hérault, *France* **20 E7**
Clerval, *France* **19 E13**
Clervaux, *Lux.* **17 D6**
Cles, *Italy* **40 B8**
Clevedon, *U.K.* **15 F5**
Cleveland, *Miss., U.S.A.* **113 J9**
Cleveland, *Ohio, U.S.A.* **116 E3**
Cleveland, *Okla., U.S.A.* **113 G6**
Cleveland, *Tenn., U.S.A.* **115 H3**
Cleveland, *Tex., U.S.A.* **113 K7**
Cleveland, C., *Australia* **94 B4**
Cleveland, Mt., *U.S.A.* **108 B7**
Cleveland Heights, *U.S.A.* **116 E3**
Clevelândia, *Brazil* **127 B5**
Clew B., *Ireland* **12 C2**
Clewiston, *U.S.A.* **115 M5**
Clifden, *Ireland* **12 C1**
Clifden, *N.Z.* **91 M1**
Cliffdell, *U.S.A.* **110 D5**
Cliffy Hd., *Australia* **93 G2**
Clifton, *Australia* **95 D5**
Clifton, *Ariz., U.S.A.* **109 K9**
Clifton, *Colo., U.S.A.* **109 G9**
Clifton, *Tex., U.S.A.* **113 K6**
Clifton Beach, *Australia* **94 B4**
Climax, *Canada* **103 D7**
Clinch →, *U.S.A.* **115 H3**
Clingmans Dome, *U.S.A.* **115 H4**
Clint, *U.S.A.* **109 L10**
Clinton, *B.C., Canada* **102 C4**
Clinton, *Ont., Canada* **116 C3**
Clinton, *N.Z.* **91 M2**
Clinton, *Ark., U.S.A.* **113 H8**
Clinton, *Conn., U.S.A.* **117 E12**
Clinton, *Ill., U.S.A.* **112 E10**
Clinton, *Ind., U.S.A.* **114 F2**
Clinton, *Iowa, U.S.A.* **112 E9**
Clinton, *Mass., U.S.A.* **117 D13**
Clinton, *Miss., U.S.A.* **113 J9**
Clinton, *Mo., U.S.A.* **112 F8**
Clinton, *N.C., U.S.A.* **115 H6**
Clinton, *Okla., U.S.A.* **113 H5**
Clinton, *S.C., U.S.A.* **115 H5**
Clinton, *Tenn., U.S.A.* **115 G3**
Clinton, *Wash., U.S.A.* **110 C4**
Clinton C., *Australia* **94 C5**
Clinton Colden L., *Canada* **100 B9**
Clintonville, *U.S.A.* **112 C10**
Clipperton, I., *Pac. Oc.* **97 F17**
Clisham, *U.K.* **13 D2**
Clisson, *France* **18 E5**
Clitheroe, *U.K.* **14 D5**
Clo-oose, *Canada* **110 B2**
Cloates, Pt., *Australia* **92 D1**
Clocolan, *S. Africa* **89 D4**
Clodomira, *Argentina* **126 B3**
Clogher Hd., *Ireland* **12 C5**
Clonakilty, *Ireland* **12 E3**
Clonakilty B., *Ireland* **12 E3**
Cloncurry, *Australia* **94 C3**
Cloncurry →, *Australia* **94 B3**
Clondalkin, *Ireland* **12 C5**
Clones, *Ireland* **12 B4**
Clonmel, *Ireland* **12 D4**
Cloppenburg, *Germany* **24 C4**
Cloquet, *U.S.A.* **112 B8**
Clorinda, *Argentina* **126 B4**
Cloud Bay, *Canada* **104 C2**
Cloud Peak, *U.S.A.* **108 D10**
Cloudcroft, *U.S.A.* **109 K11**
Cloverdale, *U.S.A.* **110 G4**
Clovis, *Calif., U.S.A.* **110 J7**
Clovis, *N. Mex., U.S.A.* **113 H3**
Cloyes-sur-le-Loir, *France* **18 E8**
Cloyne, *Canada* **116 B7**
Cluj □, *Romania* **29 D8**
Cluj-Napoca, *Romania* **29 D8**
Clunes, *Australia* **95 F3**
Cluny, *France* **19 F11**
Cluses, *France* **19 F13**
Clusone, *Italy* **40 C6**
Clutha →, *N.Z.* **91 M2**
Clwyd →, *U.K.* **14 D4**
Clyde, *Canada* **102 C6**
Clyde, *N.Z.* **91 L2**
Clyde, *U.S.A.* **116 C8**
Clyde →, *U.K.* **13 F4**
Clyde, Firth of, *U.K.* **13 F3**
Clyde Muirshiel ⌓, *U.K.* **13 F4**
Clyde River, *Canada* **101 A13**
Clydebank, *U.K.* **13 F4**
Clymer, *N.Y., U.S.A.* **116 D5**
Clymer, *Pa., U.S.A.* **116 D5**
Ćmielów, *Poland* **31 H8**
Côa →, *Portugal* **36 D3**
Coachella, *U.S.A.* **111 M10**
Coachella Canal, *U.S.A.* **111 N12**
Coahoma, *U.S.A.* **113 J4**
Coahuayana →, *Mexico* **118 D4**
Coahuila □, *Mexico* **118 B4**
Coal →, *Canada* **102 B3**
Coalane, *Mozam.* **87 F4**
Coalcomán, *Mexico* **118 D4**
Coaldale, *Canada* **102 D6**
Coalgate, *U.S.A.* **113 H6**
Coalinga, *U.S.A.* **110 J6**
Coalisland, *U.K.* **12 B5**
Coalville, *U.K.* **14 E6**
Coalville, *U.S.A.* **108 F8**
Coamo, *Puerto Rico* **121 d**
Coari, *Brazil* **124 D6**
Coast □, *Kenya* **86 C4**
Coast Mts., *Canada* **102 C3**
Coast Ranges, *U.S.A.* **110 G4**
Coatbridge, *U.K.* **13 F4**
Coatepec, *Mexico* **119 D5**
Coatepeque, *Guatemala* **120 D1**
Coatesville, *U.S.A.* **114 F8**
Coaticook, *Canada* **117 A13**
Coats I., *Canada* **101 B11**
Coats Land, *Antarctica* **5 D1**
Coatzacoalcos, *Mexico* **119 D6**
Coba, *Mexico* **119 C7**
Cobadin, *Romania* **29 F13**
Cobalt, *Canada* **104 C4**
Cobán, *Guatemala* **120 C1**
Çobanlar, *Turkey* **47 C12**
Cobar, *Australia* **95 E4**
Cóbh, *Ireland* **12 E3**
Cobija, *Bolivia* **124 F5**
Cobleskill, *U.S.A.* **117 D10**
Coboconk, *Canada* **116 B6**
Cobourg, *Canada* **116 C6**
Cobourg ⌓, *Australia* **92 B5**
Cobourg Pen., *Australia* **92 B5**
Cobram, *Australia* **95 F4**
Cóbué, *Mozam.* **87 E3**
Coburg, *Germany* **25 E6**
Coca, *Spain* **36 D6**
Cocanada = Kakinada, *India* **67 L13**
Cocentaina, *Spain* **39 G4**
Cochabamba, *Bolivia* **124 G5**
Cochem, *Germany* **25 E3**
Cochemane, *Mozam.* **87 F3**
Cochin, *India* **66 Q10**
Cochin China = Nam-Phan, *Vietnam* **65 G6**
Cochran, *U.S.A.* **115 J4**
Cochrane, *Alta., Canada* **102 C6**
Cochrane, *Ont., Canada* **104 C3**
Cochrane, *Chile* **128 F2**
Cochrane →, *Canada* **103 B8**
Cochrane, L., *Chile* **128 F2**
Cochranton, *U.S.A.* **116 E4**
Cockburn, *Australia* **95 E3**
Cockburn, Canal, *Chile* **128 G2**
Cockburn I., *Canada* **104 C3**
Cockburn Ra., *Australia* **92 C4**
Cockermouth, *U.K.* **14 C4**
Cocklebiddy, *Australia* **93 F4**
Cockpit Country, The, *Jamaica* **120 a**
Coco →, *Cent. Amer.* **120 D3**
Coco, I. del, *Pac. Oc.* **97 G19**
Cocoa, *U.S.A.* **115 L5**
Cocobeach, *Gabon* **84 D1**
Cocora, *Romania* **29 F12**
Cocos B., *Trin. & Tob.* **125 K15**
Cocos Is., *Ind. Oc.* **96 J1**
Cod, C., *U.S.A.* **114 D10**
Codajás, *Brazil* **124 D6**
Codigoro, *Italy* **41 D9**
Codlea, *Romania* **29 E10**
Codó, *Brazil* **125 D10**
Codogno, *Italy* **40 C6**
Codróipo, *Italy* **41 C10**
Codru, Munţii, *Romania* **28 D7**
Cody, *U.S.A.* **108 D9**
Coe Hill, *Canada* **116 B7**
Coelemu, *Chile* **126 D1**
Coen, *Australia* **94 A3**
Coesfeld, *Germany* **24 D3**
Cœur d'Alene, *U.S.A.* **108 C5**
Cœur d'Alene L., *U.S.A.* **108 C5**
Coevorden, *Neths.* **17 B6**
Cofete, *Canary Is.* **48 F5**
Coffeyville, *U.S.A.* **113 G7**
Coffin B., *Australia* **95 E2**
Coffin Bay, *Australia* **95 E2**
Coffin Bay △, *Australia* **95 E2**
Coffin Bay Peninsula, *Australia* **95 E2**
Coffs Harbour, *Australia* **95 E5**
Cofre de Perote △, *Mexico* **119 D5**
Cofrentes, *Spain* **39 F3**
Cogalnic →, *Moldova* **29 E14**
Cogealac, *Romania* **29 F13**
Coghinas →, *Italy* **42 B1**
Coghinas, L. del, *Italy* **42 B2**
Cognac, *France* **20 C3**
Cogne, *Italy* **40 C4**
Cogolin, *France* **21 E10**
Cogolludo, *Spain* **38 E1**
Cohocton, *U.S.A.* **116 D7**
Cohocton →, *U.S.A.* **116 D7**
Cohoes, *U.S.A.* **117 D11**
Cohuna, *Australia* **95 F3**
Coiba, I., *Panama* **120 E3**
Coig →, *Argentina* **128 G3**
Coigeach, Rubha, *U.K.* **13 C3**
Coihaique, *Chile* **128 F2**
Coimbatore, *India* **66 P10**
Coimbra, *Brazil* **124 G7**
Coimbra, *Portugal* **36 E2**
Coimbra □, *Portugal* **36 E2**
Coín, *Spain* **37 J6**
Coipasa, Salar de, *Bolivia* **124 G5**
Cojimies, *Ecuador* **124 C3**
Cojocna, *Romania* **29 D8**
Cojutepeque, *El Salv.* **120 D2**
Čoka, *Serbia & M.* **28 E5**
Cokeville, *U.S.A.* **108 E8**
Colac, *Australia* **95 F3**
Colatina, *Brazil* **125 G10**
Colbeck, C., *Antarctica* **5 D13**
Colborne, *Canada* **116 C7**
Colby, *U.S.A.* **112 F4**
Colchester, *U.K.* **15 F8**
Cold L., *Canada* **103 C7**
Coldstream, *Canada* **102 C5**
Coldstream, *U.K.* **13 F6**
Coldwater, *Canada* **116 B5**
Coldwater, *Kans., U.S.A.* **113 G5**
Coldwater, *Mich., U.S.A.* **114 E3**
Colebrook, *U.S.A.* **117 B13**
Coleman, *U.S.A.* **113 K5**
Coleman →, *Australia* **94 B3**
Colenso, *S. Africa* **89 D4**
Coleraine, *Australia* **95 F3**
Coleraine, *U.K.* **12 A5**
Coleridge, L., *N.Z.* **91 K3**
Colesberg, *S. Africa* **88 E4**
Coleville, *U.S.A.* **110 G7**
Colfax, *Calif., U.S.A.* **110 F6**
Colfax, *La., U.S.A.* **113 K8**
Colfax, *Wash., U.S.A.* **108 C5**
Colhué Huapi, L., *Argentina* **128 F3**
Colibaşi, *Moldova* **29 E13**
Colibaşi, *Romania* **29 F9**
Cólico, *Italy* **40 B6**
Coligny, *France* **19 F12**
Coligny, *S. Africa* **89 D4**
Colima, *Mexico* **118 D4**
Colima □, *Mexico* **118 D4**
Colima, Nevado de, *Mexico* **118 D4**
Colina, *Chile* **126 C1**
Colina do Norte, *Guinea-Biss.* **82 C2**
Colinas, *Brazil* **125 E10**
Colindres, *Spain* **36 B7**
Coll, *U.K.* **13 E2**
Collaguasi, *Chile* **126 A2**
Collarada, Peña, *Spain* **38 C4**
Collarenebri, *Australia* **95 D4**
Colle di Val d'Elsa, *Italy* **40 E8**
Collécchio, *Italy* **40 D7**
Colleen Bawn, *Zimbabwe* **87 G2**
College Park, *U.S.A.* **115 J3**
College Station, *U.S.A.* **113 K6**
Collesalvetti, *Italy* **40 E7**
Colli Euganei ⌓, *Italy* **41 C8**
Collie, *Australia* **93 F2**
Collier B., *Australia* **92 C3**
Collier Ra., *Australia* **93 D2**
Collier Range △, *Australia* **93 D2**
Collina, Passo di, *Italy* **40 D7**
Collingwood, *Canada* **116 B4**
Collingwood, *N.Z.* **91 J4**
Collins, *Canada* **104 B2**
Collinsville, *Australia* **94 C4**
Collipulli, *Chile* **126 D1**
Collooney, *Ireland* **12 B3**
Colmar, *France* **19 D14**
Colmars, *France* **21 D10**
Colmenar, *Spain* **37 J6**
Colmenar de Oreja, *Spain* **36 E7**
Colmenar Viejo, *Spain* **36 E7**
Colo →, *Australia* **95 E5**
Cologne = Köln, *Germany* **24 E2**
Colom, I. d'en, *Spain* **48 B11**
Coloma, *U.S.A.* **110 G6**
Colomb-Béchar = Béchar, *Algeria* **78 B5**
Colombey-les-Belles, *France* **19 D12**
Colombey-les-Deux-Églises, *France* **19 D11**
Colombia ■, *S. Amer.* **124 C4**
Colombian Basin, *S. Amer.* **98 H12**
Colombo, *Sri Lanka* **66 R11**
Colomiers, *France* **20 E5**
Colón, *Buenos Aires, Argentina* **126 C3**
Colón, *Entre Ríos, Argentina* **126 C4**
Colón, *Cuba* **120 B3**
Colón, *Panama* **120 E4**
Colón, Arch. de, *Ecuador* **97 H18**
Colònia de Sant Jordi, *Spain* **48 B9**
Colonia del Sacramento, *Uruguay* **126 C4**
Colonia Dora, *Argentina* **126 B3**
Colonial Beach, *U.S.A.* **114 F7**
Colonie, *U.S.A.* **117 D11**
Colonna, C., *Italy* **43 C10**
Colonsay, *Canada* **103 C7**
Colonsay, *U.K.* **13 E2**
Colorado □, *U.S.A.* **109 G10**
Colorado →, *Argentina* **128 D4**
Colorado →, *N. Amer.* **109 L6**
Colorado →, *U.S.A.* **113 L7**
Colorado City, *U.S.A.* **113 J4**
Colorado Plateau, *U.S.A.* **109 H8**
Colorado River Aqueduct, *U.S.A.* **111 L12**
Colorado Springs, *U.S.A.* **112 F2**
Colorno, *Italy* **40 D7**
Colotlán, *Mexico* **118 C4**
Colstrip, *U.S.A.* **108 D10**
Colton, *U.S.A.* **117 B10**
Columbia, *Ky., U.S.A.* **114 G3**
Columbia, *La., U.S.A.* **113 J8**
Columbia, *Miss., U.S.A.* **113 K10**
Columbia, *Mo., U.S.A.* **112 F8**
Columbia, *Pa., U.S.A.* **117 F8**
Columbia, *S.C., U.S.A.* **115 J5**
Columbia, *Tenn., U.S.A.* **115 H2**
Columbia →, *N. Amer.* **110 D2**
Columbia, C., *Canada* **4 A4**
Columbia, District of □, *U.S.A.* **114 F7**
Columbia, Mt., *Canada* **102 C5**
Columbia Basin, *U.S.A.* **108 C4**
Columbia Falls, *U.S.A.* **108 B6**
Columbia Mts., *Canada* **102 C5**
Columbia Plateau, *U.S.A.* **108 D5**
Columbiana, *U.S.A.* **116 F4**
Columbretes, Is., *Spain* **38 F5**
Columbus, *Ga., U.S.A.* **115 J3**
Columbus, *Ind., U.S.A.* **114 F3**
Columbus, *Kans., U.S.A.* **113 G7**
Columbus, *Miss., U.S.A.* **115 J1**
Columbus, *Mont., U.S.A.* **108 D9**
Columbus, *N. Mex., U.S.A.* **109 L10**
Columbus, *Nebr., U.S.A.* **112 E6**
Columbus, *Ohio, U.S.A.* **114 F4**
Columbus, *Tex., U.S.A.* **113 L6**
Colunga, *Spain* **36 B5**
Colusa, *U.S.A.* **110 F4**
Colville, *U.S.A.* **108 B5**
Colville →, *U.S.A.* **100 A4**
Colville, C., *N.Z.* **91 G5**
Colwood, *Canada* **110 B3**
Colwyn Bay, *U.K.* **14 D4**
Coma, *Ethiopia* **81 F4**
Comácchio, *Italy* **41 D9**
Comalcalco, *Mexico* **119 D6**
Comallo, *Argentina* **128 E2**
Comana, *Romania* **29 F11**
Comanche, *U.S.A.* **113 K5**
Comandante Ferraz, *Antarctica* **5 C18**
Comăneşti, *Romania* **29 D11**
Comarnic, *Romania* **29 E10**
Comayagua, *Honduras* **120 D2**
Combahee →, *U.S.A.* **115 J5**
Combarbalá, *Chile* **126 C1**
Combe Martin, *U.K.* **15 F3**
Combeaufontaine, *France* **19 E12**
Comber, *Canada* **116 D2**
Comber, *U.K.* **12 B6**
Combermere, *Canada* **116 A7**
Comblain-au-Pont, *Belgium* **17 D5**
Combourg, *France* **18 D5**
Combrailles, *France* **19 F9**
Combronde, *France* **20 C7**
Comeragh Mts., *Ireland* **12 D4**
Comet, *Australia* **94 C4**
Comilla, *Bangla.* **67 H17**
Comino, *Malta* **49 C1**
Comino, C., *Italy* **42 B2**
Cómiso, *Italy* **43 F7**
Comitán, *Mexico* **119 D6**
Commentry, *France* **19 F9**
Commerce, *Ga., U.S.A.* **115 H4**
Commerce, *Tex., U.S.A.* **113 J7**
Commercy, *France* **19 D12**
Committee B., *Canada* **101 B11**
Commonwealth B., *Antarctica* **5 C10**
Commoron Cr. →, *Australia* **95 D5**
Communism Pk. = Kommunizma, Pik, *Tajikistan* **52 F8**
Como, *Italy* **40 C6**
Como, Lago di, *Italy* **40 B6**
Comodoro Rivadavia, *Argentina* **128 F3**
Comoé △, *Ivory C.* **82 D4**
Comorâşte, *Romania* **28 E6**
Comorin, C., *India* **66 Q10**
Comoro Is. = Comoros ■, *Ind. Oc.* **77 H8**
Comoros ■, *Ind. Oc.* **77 H8**
Comox, *Canada* **102 D4**
Compiègne, *France* **19 C9**
Comporta, *Portugal* **37 G2**
Compostela, *Mexico* **118 C4**
Comprida, I., *Brazil* **127 A6**
Compton, *Canada* **117 A13**
Compton, *U.S.A.* **111 M8**
Comrat, *Moldova* **29 D13**
Con Cuong, *Vietnam* **64 C5**
Con Dao △, *Vietnam* **65 H6**
Con Son, *Vietnam* **65 H6**
Conakry, *Guinea* **82 D2**
Conara, *Australia* **95 G4**
Concarneau, *France* **18 E3**
Conceição, *Mozam.* **87 F4**
Conceição da Barra, *Brazil* **125 G11**
Conceição do Araguaia, *Brazil* **125 E9**
Concepción, *Argentina* **126 B2**
Concepción, *Bolivia* **124 G6**
Concepción, *Chile* **126 D1**
Concepción, *Mexico* **119 D6**
Concepción, *Paraguay* **126 A4**
Concepción □, *Chile* **126 D1**
Concepción →, *Mexico* **118 A2**
Concepción, Est. de, *Chile* **128 G2**
Concepción, L., *Bolivia* **124 G6**
Concepción, Punta, *Mexico* **118 B2**
Concepción del Oro, *Mexico* **118 C4**
Concepción del Uruguay, *Argentina* **126 C4**
Conception, Pt., *U.S.A.* **111 L6**
Conception B., *Canada* **105 C9**
Conception B., *Namibia* **88 C1**
Conception I., *Bahamas* **121 B4**
Concession, *Zimbabwe* **87 F3**
Conchas Dam, *U.S.A.* **113 H2**
Conches-en-Ouche, *France* **18 D7**
Concho, *U.S.A.* **109 J9**
Concho →, *U.S.A.* **113 K5**
Conchos →, *Chihuahua, Mexico* **118 B4**
Conchos →, *Tamaulipas, Mexico* **119 B5**
Concord, *Calif., U.S.A.* **110 H4**
Concord, *N.C., U.S.A.* **115 H5**
Concord, *N.H., U.S.A.* **117 C13**
Concordia, *Argentina* **126 C4**
Concórdia, *Brazil* **124 D5**
Concordia, *Mexico* **118 C3**
Concordia, *U.S.A.* **112 F6**
Concrete, *U.S.A.* **108 B3**
Condamine, *Australia* **95 D5**
Condat, *France* **20 C6**
Conde, *U.S.A.* **112 C5**
Condé-sur-Noireau, *France* **18 D6**
Condeúba, *Brazil* **125 F10**
Condobolin, *Australia* **95 E4**
Condom, *France* **20 E4**
Condon, *U.S.A.* **108 D3**
Conegliano, *Italy* **41 C9**
Conejera, I. = Conills, I. des, *Spain* **48 B9**
Conejos, *Mexico* **118 B4**
Conemaugh →, *U.S.A.* **116 F5**
Conero ⌓, *Italy* **41 E10**
Confolens, *France* **20 B4**
Confuso →, *Paraguay* **126 B4**
Congaz, *Moldova* **29 D13**
Conghua, *China* **59 F9**
Congjiang, *China* **58 E7**
Congleton, *U.K.* **14 D5**
Congo (Kinshasa) = Congo, Dem. Rep. of the ■, *Africa* **84 E4**
Congo ■, *Africa* **84 E3**
Congo →, *Africa* **84 F2**
Congo, Dem. Rep. of the ■, *Africa* **84 E4**
Congo Basin, *Africa* **84 E4**
Congonhas, *Brazil* **127 A7**
Congress, *U.S.A.* **109 J7**
Conil de la Frontera, *Spain* **37 J4**
Conills, I. des, *Spain* **48 B9**
Coniston, *Canada* **104 C3**
Conjeeveram = Kanchipuram, *India* **66 N11**
Conklin, *Canada* **103 B6**
Conklin, *U.S.A.* **117 D9**
Conn, L., *Ireland* **12 B2**
Connacht □, *Ireland* **12 C2**
Conneaut, *U.S.A.* **116 E4**
Connecticut □, *U.S.A.* **117 E12**
Connecticut →, *U.S.A.* **117 E12**
Connell, *U.S.A.* **108 C4**
Connellsville, *U.S.A.* **116 F5**
Connemara, *Ireland* **12 C2**
Connemara △, *Ireland* **12 C2**
Connerré, *France* **18 D7**
Connersville, *U.S.A.* **114 F3**
Connors Ra., *Australia* **94 C4**
Conques, *France* **20 D6**
Conquest, *Canada* **103 C7**
Conrad, *U.S.A.* **108 B8**
Conran, C., *Australia* **95 F4**
Conroe, *U.S.A.* **113 K7**
Consecon, *Canada* **116 C7**
Conselheiro Lafaiete, *Brazil* **127 A7**
Conselve, *Italy* **41 C8**
Consett, *U.K.* **14 C6**
Consort, *Canada* **103 C6**

Constance = Konstanz, *Germany* 25 H5
Constance, L. = Bodensee, *Europe* 25 H5
Constanţa, *Romania* 29 F13
Constanţa □, *Romania* 29 F13
Constantia, *U.S.A.* 117 C8
Constantina, *Spain* 37 H5
Constantine, *Algeria* 78 A7
Constitución, *Chile* 126 D1
Constitución, *Uruguay* 126 C4
Constitucion de 1857 △, *Mexico* 118 A1
Consuegra, *Spain* 37 F7
Consul, *Canada* 103 D7
Contact, *U.S.A.* 108 F6
Contai, *India* 69 J12
Contamana, *Peru* 124 E4
Contarina, *Italy* 41 C9
Contas →, *Brazil* 125 F11
Contes, *France* 21 E11
Contoocook, *U.S.A.* 117 C13
Contra Costa, *Mozam.* 89 D5
Contres, *France* 18 E8
Contrexéville, *France* 19 D12
Contwoyto L., *Canada* 100 B8
Conversano, *Italy* 43 B10
Conway = Conwy, *U.K.* 14 D4
Conway = Conwy →, *U.K.* 14 D4
Conway, *Australia* 94 J6
Conway, *Ark., U.S.A.* 113 H8
Conway, *N.H., U.S.A.* 117 C13
Conway, *S.C., U.S.A.* 115 J6
Conway, C., *Australia* 94 J6
Conway, L., *Australia* 95 D2
Conwy, *U.K.* 14 D4
Conwy □, *U.K.* 14 D4
Conwy →, *U.K.* 14 D4
Coober Pedy, *Australia* 95 D1
Cooch Behar = Koch Bihar, *India* 67 F16
Cooinda, *Australia* 92 B5
Cook, *Australia* 93 F5
Cook, *U.S.A.* 112 B8
Cook, B., *Chile* 128 H3
Cook, C., *Canada* 102 C3
Cook, Mt. = Aoraki Mount Cook, *N.Z.* 91 K3
Cook Inlet, *U.S.A.* 100 C4
Cook Is., *Pac. Oc.* 97 J12
Cook Strait, *N.Z.* 91 J5
Cookeville, *U.S.A.* 115 G3
Cookhouse, *S. Africa* 88 E4
Cookshire, *Canada* 117 A13
Cookstown, *U.K.* 12 B5
Cooksville, *Canada* 116 C5
Cooktown, *Australia* 94 B4
Coolabah, *Australia* 95 E4
Cooladdi, *Australia* 95 D4
Coolah, *Australia* 95 E4
Coolamon, *Australia* 95 E4
Coolgardie, *Australia* 93 F3
Coolidge, *U.S.A.* 109 K8
Coolidge Dam, *U.S.A.* 109 K8
Cooloola △, *Australia* 95 D5
Cooma, *Australia* 95 F4
Coon Rapids, *U.S.A.* 112 C8
Coonabarabran, *Australia* 95 E4
Coonamble, *Australia* 95 E4
Coonana, *Australia* 93 F3
Coondapoor, *India* 66 N9
Cooninie, L., *Australia* 95 D2
Cooper, *U.S.A.* 113 J7
Cooper Cr. →, *Australia* 95 D2
Cooperstown, *N. Dak., U.S.A.* 112 B5
Cooperstown, *N.Y., U.S.A.* 117 D10
Coorabie, *Australia* 93 F5
Coorong, The, *Australia* 95 F2
Coorow, *Australia* 93 E2
Cooroy, *Australia* 95 D5
Coos Bay, *U.S.A.* 108 E1
Coosa →, *U.S.A.* 115 J2
Cootamundra, *Australia* 95 E4
Cootehill, *Ireland* 12 B4
Copahue Paso, *Argentina* 126 D1
Copainalá, *Mexico* 119 D6
Copake Falls, *U.S.A.* 117 D11
Copalnic Mănăştur, *Romania* 29 C8
Copán, *Honduras* 120 D2
Cope, *U.S.A.* 112 F3
Cope, C., *Spain* 39 H3
Copenhagen = København, *Denmark* 11 J6
Copenhagen, *U.S.A.* 117 C9
Copertino, *Italy* 43 B11
Copiapó, *Chile* 126 B1
Copiapó →, *Chile* 126 B1
Coplay, *U.S.A.* 117 F9
Copp L., *Canada* 102 A6
Copparo, *Italy* 41 D8
Coppename →, *Suriname* 125 B7
Copper Harbor, *U.S.A.* 114 B2
Copper Queen, *Zimbabwe* 87 F2
Copperas Cove, *U.S.A.* 113 K6
Copperbelt □, *Zambia* 87 E2
Coppermine = Kugluktuk, *Canada* 100 B8
Coppermine →, *Canada* 100 B8
Copperopolis, *U.S.A.* 110 H6
Copşa Mică, *Romania* 29 D9
Coquet →, *U.K.* 14 B6
Coquille, *U.S.A.* 108 E1
Coquimbo, *Chile* 126 C1
Coquimbo □, *Chile* 126 C1
Corabia, *Romania* 29 G9
Coracora, *Peru* 124 G4
Coraki, *Australia* 95 D5
Coral, *U.S.A.* 116 F5
Coral Gables, *U.S.A.* 115 N5
Coral Harbour, *Canada* 101 B11
Coral Sea, *Pac. Oc.* 96 J7
Coral Springs, *U.S.A.* 115 M5
Coraopolis, *U.S.A.* 116 F4
Corato, *Italy* 43 A9
Corbeil-Essonnes, *France* 19 D9
Corbie, *France* 19 C9
Corbières, *France* 20 F6
Corbigny, *France* 19 E10
Corbin, *U.S.A.* 114 G3
Corbones →, *Spain* 37 H5
Corbu, *Romania* 29 F13
Corby, *U.K.* 15 E7
Corcaigh = Cork, *Ireland* 12 E3
Corcoran, *U.S.A.* 110 J7
Corcovado △, *Costa Rica* 120 E3
Cordele, *U.S.A.* 115 K4
Cordell, *U.S.A.* 113 H5
Cordenòns, *Italy* 41 C9
Cordes-sur-Ciel, *France* 20 D5
Córdoba, *Argentina* 126 C3
Córdoba, *Mexico* 119 D5
Córdoba, *Spain* 37 H6
Córdoba □, *Argentina* 126 C3
Córdoba □, *Spain* 37 G6
Córdoba, Sierra de, *Argentina* 126 C3
Cordon, *Phil.* 61 C4
Cordova, *U.S.A.* 100 B5
Corella, *Spain* 38 C3
Corella →, *Australia* 94 B3
Corfield, *Australia* 94 C3
Corfu = Kérkira, *Greece* 49 A3
Corfu ✈ (CFU), *Greece* 46 B1
Corfu, Str. of, *Greece* 49 A4
Corgo = O Corgo, *Spain* 36 C3
Cori, *Italy* 42 A5
Coria, *Spain* 36 F4
Coria del Río, *Spain* 37 H4
Corigliano Cálabro, *Italy* 43 C9
Coringa Is., *Australia* 94 B4
Corinth = Kórinthos, *Greece* 46 D4
Corinth, *Miss., U.S.A.* 115 H1
Corinth, *N.Y., U.S.A.* 117 C11
Corinth, G. of = Korinthiakós Kólpos, *Greece* 46 C4
Corinth Canal, *Greece* 46 D4
Corinto, *Brazil* 125 G10
Corinto, *Nic.* 120 D2
Cork, *Ireland* 12 E3
Cork □, *Ireland* 12 E3
Cork Harbour, *Ireland* 12 E3
Corlay, *France* 18 D3
Corleone, *Italy* 42 E6
Corleto Perticara, *Italy* 43 B9
Çorlu, *Turkey* 45 E11
Cormack L., *Canada* 102 A4
Cormòns, *Italy* 41 C10
Cormorant, *Canada* 103 C8
Cormorant L., *Canada* 103 C8
Corn Is. = Maiz, Is. del, *Nic.* 120 D3
Cornalvo ⌓, *Spain* 37 F4
Cornélio Procópio, *Brazil* 127 A5
Corner Brook, *Canada* 105 C8
Corneşti, *Moldova* 29 C13
Corníglio, *Italy* 40 D7
Corning, *Ark., U.S.A.* 113 G9
Corning, *Calif., U.S.A.* 108 G2
Corning, *Iowa, U.S.A.* 112 E7
Corning, *N.Y., U.S.A.* 116 D7
Corno Grande, *Italy* 41 F10
Cornwall, *Canada* 117 A10
Cornwall, *U.S.A.* 117 F8
Cornwall □, *U.K.* 15 G3
Corny Pt., *Australia* 95 E2
Coro, *Venezuela* 124 A5
Coroatá, *Brazil* 125 D10
Corocoro, *Bolivia* 124 G5
Coroico, *Bolivia* 124 G5
Coromandel, *N.Z.* 91 G5
Coromandel Coast, *India* 66 N12
Corona, *Calif., U.S.A.* 111 M9
Corona, *N. Mex., U.S.A.* 109 J11
Coronach, *Canada* 103 D7
Coronado, *U.S.A.* 111 N9
Coronado, B. de, *Costa Rica* 120 E3
Coronados, Is. los, *U.S.A.* 111 N9
Coronation, *Canada* 102 C6
Coronation Gulf, *Canada* 100 B8
Coronation I., *Antarctica* 5 C18
Coronation Is., *Australia* 92 B3
Coronda, *Argentina* 126 C3
Coronel, *Chile* 126 D1
Coronel Bogado, *Paraguay* 126 B4
Coronel Dorrego, *Argentina* 126 D3
Coronel Oviedo, *Paraguay* 126 B4
Coronel Pringles, *Argentina* 126 D3
Coronel Suárez, *Argentina* 126 D3
Coronel Vidal, *Argentina* 126 D4
Coropuna, Nevado, *Peru* 124 G4
Çorovodë, *Albania* 44 F4
Corowa, *Australia* 95 F4
Corozal □, *Belize* 119 D7
Corozal Pt., *Trin. & Tob.* 125 K15
Corps, *France* 21 D9
Corpus, *Argentina* 127 B4
Corpus Christi, *U.S.A.* 113 M6
Corpus Christi, L., *U.S.A.* 113 L6
Corral de Almaguer, *Spain* 36 F7
Corralejo, *Canary Is.* 48 F6
Corraun Pen., *Ireland* 12 C2
Corréggio, *Italy* 40 D7
Correntes, C. das, *Mozam.* 89 C6
Corrèze □, *France* 20 C5
Corrèze →, *France* 20 C5
Corrib, L., *Ireland* 12 C2
Corridónia, *Italy* 41 E10
Corrientes, *Argentina* 126 B4
Corrientes □, *Argentina* 126 B4
Corrientes →, *Argentina* 126 C4
Corrientes →, *Peru* 124 D4
Corrientes, C., *Colombia* 124 B3
Corrientes, C., *Cuba* 120 B3
Corrientes, C., *Mexico* 118 C3
Corrigan, *U.S.A.* 113 K7
Corrigin, *Australia* 93 F2
Corry, *U.S.A.* 116 E5
Corse ⌓, *France* 21 F13
Corse □, *France* 21 G13
Corse, C., *France* 21 E13
Corse-du-Sud □, *France* 21 G13
Corsica = Corse □, *France* 21 G13
Corsicana, *U.S.A.* 113 J6
Corte, *France* 21 F13
Corte Pinto, *Portugal* 37 H3
Cortegana, *Spain* 37 H4
Cortés, Mar de = California, G. de, *Mexico* 118 B2
Cortez, *U.S.A.* 109 H9
Cortina d'Ampezzo, *Italy* 41 B9
Cortland, *N.Y., U.S.A.* 117 D8
Cortland, *Ohio, U.S.A.* 116 E4
Cortona, *Italy* 41 E8
Corubal →, *Guinea-Biss.* 82 C2
Coruche, *Portugal* 37 G2
Çoruh →, *Turkey* 35 K5
Çorum, *Turkey* 72 B6
Corumbá, *Brazil* 124 G7
Corund, *Romania* 29 D10
Corunna = A Coruña, *Spain* 36 B2
Corvallis, *U.S.A.* 108 D2
Corvette, L. de la, *Canada* 104 B5
Corydon, *U.S.A.* 112 E8
Cosalá, *Mexico* 118 C3
Cosamaloapan, *Mexico* 119 D5
Cosenza, *Italy* 43 C9
Coşereni, *Romania* 29 F11
Coshocton, *U.S.A.* 116 F3
Cosmo Newberry, *Australia* 93 E3
Cosne-Cours-sur-Loire, *France* 19 E9
Coso Junction, *U.S.A.* 111 J9
Coso Pk., *U.S.A.* 111 J9
Cospeito, *Spain* 36 B3
Cosquín, *Argentina* 126 C3
Cossato, *Italy* 40 C5
Cossé-le-Vivien, *France* 18 E6
Cosson →, *France* 18 E8
Costa Blanca, *Spain* 39 G4
Costa Brava, *Spain* 38 D8
Costa del Sol, *Spain* 37 J6
Costa Dorada, *Spain* 38 D6
Costa Mesa, *U.S.A.* 111 M9
Costa Rica ■, *Cent. Amer.* 120 E3
Costa Smeralda, *Italy* 42 A2
Costeşti, *Romania* 29 F9
Costigliole d'Asti, *Italy* 40 D5
Cosumnes →, *U.S.A.* 110 G5
Coswig, *Sachsen, Germany* 24 D9
Coswig, *Sachsen-Anhalt, Germany* 24 D8
Cotabato, *Phil.* 61 H6
Cotagaita, *Bolivia* 126 A2
Côte d'Azur, *France* 21 E11
Côte-d'Ivoire = Ivory Coast ■, *Africa* 82 D4
Côte d'Or, *France* 19 E11
Côte-d'Or □, *France* 19 E11
Coteau des Prairies, *U.S.A.* 112 C6
Coteau du Missouri, *U.S.A.* 112 B4
Cotentin, *France* 18 C5
Côtes-d'Armor □, *France* 18 D4
Côtes de Meuse, *France* 19 C12
Côtes-du-Nord = Côtes-d'Armor □, *France* 18 D4
Cotiella, *Spain* 38 C5
Cotillo, *Canary Is.* 48 F5
Cotiujeni, *Moldova* 29 C13
Cotonou, *Benin* 83 D5
Cotopaxi, *Ecuador* 124 D3
Cotronei, *Italy* 43 C9
Cotswold Hills, *U.K.* 15 F5
Cottage Grove, *U.S.A.* 108 E2
Cottbus, *Germany* 24 D10
Cottonwood, *U.S.A.* 109 J7
Cotulla, *U.S.A.* 113 L5
Coubre, Pte. de la, *France* 20 C2
Couches, *France* 19 F11
Couço, *Portugal* 37 G2
Coudersport, *U.S.A.* 116 E6
Couedic, C. du, *Australia* 95 F2
Couëron, *France* 18 E5
Couesnon →, *France* 18 D5
Couhé, *France* 20 B4
Coulanges-sur-Yonne, *France* 19 E10
Coulee City, *U.S.A.* 108 C4
Coulman I., *Antarctica* 5 D11
Coulommiers, *France* 19 D10
Coulon →, *France* 21 E9
Coulonge →, *Canada* 104 C4
Coulonges-sur-l'Autize, *France* 20 B3
Coulounieix-Chamiers, *France* 20 C4
Coulterville, *U.S.A.* 110 H6
Council, *U.S.A.* 108 D5
Council Bluffs, *U.S.A.* 112 E7
Council Grove, *U.S.A.* 112 F6
Coupeville, *U.S.A.* 110 B4
Courantyne →, *S. Amer.* 124 B7
Courcelles, *Belgium* 17 D4
Courchevel, *France* 21 C10
Courçon, *France* 20 B3
Courmayeur, *Italy* 40 C3
Couronne, C., *France* 21 E9
Cours-la-Ville, *France* 19 F11
Coursan, *France* 20 E7
Courseulles-sur-Mer, *France* 18 C6
Courtenay, *Canada* 102 D4
Courtenay, *France* 19 D10
Courtland, *U.S.A.* 110 G5
Courtrai = Kortrijk, *Belgium* 17 D3
Courtright, *Canada* 116 D2
Coushatta, *U.S.A.* 113 J8
Coutances, *France* 18 C5
Coutras, *France* 20 C3
Coutts Crossing, *Australia* 95 D5
Couva, *Trin. & Tob.* 125 K15
Couvin, *Belgium* 17 D4
Covarrubias, *Spain* 36 C7
Covasna, *Romania* 29 E11
Covasna □, *Romania* 29 E10
Cove I., *Canada* 116 A3
Coventry, *U.K.* 15 E6
Covilhã, *Portugal* 36 E3
Covington, *Ga., U.S.A.* 115 J4
Covington, *Ky., U.S.A.* 114 F3
Covington, *Okla., U.S.A.* 113 G6
Covington, *Tenn., U.S.A.* 113 H10
Covington, *Va., U.S.A.* 114 G5
Cowal, L., *Australia* 95 E4
Cowan, L., *Australia* 93 F3
Cowan L., *Canada* 103 C7
Cowangie, *Australia* 95 F3
Cowansville, *Canada* 117 A12
Coward Springs, *Australia* 95 D2
Cowcowing Lakes, *Australia* 93 F2
Cowdenbeath, *U.K.* 13 E5
Cowell, *Australia* 95 E2
Cowes, *U.K.* 15 G6
Cowichan L., *Canada* 110 B2
Cowlitz →, *U.S.A.* 110 D4
Cowra, *Australia* 95 E4
Cox, *Spain* 39 G4
Coxilha Grande, *Brazil* 127 B5
Coxim, *Brazil* 125 G8
Cox's Bazar, *Bangla.* 67 J17
Coyote Wells, *U.S.A.* 111 N11
Coyuca de Benítez, *Mexico* 119 D4
Coyuca de Catalan, *Mexico* 118 D4
Cozad, *U.S.A.* 112 E5
Cozes, *France* 20 C3
Cozumel, *Mexico* 119 C7
Cozumel, Isla, *Mexico* 119 C7
Crab Hill, *Barbados* 121 g
Cracow = Kraków, *Poland* 31 H6
Cracow, *Australia* 95 D5
Cradle Mt.-Lake St. Clair △, *Australia* 95 G4
Cradock, *Australia* 95 E2
Cradock, *S. Africa* 88 E4
Craig, *U.S.A.* 108 F10
Craigavon, *U.K.* 12 B5
Craigmore, *Zimbabwe* 87 G3
Craik, *Canada* 103 C7
Crailsheim, *Germany* 25 F6
Craiova, *Romania* 29 F8
Cramsie, *Australia* 94 C3
Cranberry L., *U.S.A.* 117 B10
Cranberry Portage, *Canada* 103 C8
Cranbrook, *Australia* 93 F2
Cranbrook, *Canada* 102 D5
Crandon, *U.S.A.* 112 C10
Crane, *Oreg., U.S.A.* 108 E4
Crane, *Tex., U.S.A.* 113 K3
Cranston, *U.S.A.* 117 E13
Craon, *France* 18 E6
Craonne, *France* 19 C10
Craponne-sur-Arzon, *France* 20 C7
Crasna, *Romania* 29 D12
Crasna →, *Romania* 28 C7
Crasnei, Munţii, *Romania* 29 C8
Crater L., *U.S.A.* 108 E2
Crater Lake △, *U.S.A.* 108 E2
Craters of the Moon △, *U.S.A.* 108 E7
Crateús, *Brazil* 125 E10
Crati →, *Italy* 43 C9
Crato, *Brazil* 125 E11
Crato, *Portugal* 37 F3
Craven, L., *Canada* 104 B4
Crawford, *U.S.A.* 112 D3
Crawfordsville, *U.S.A.* 114 E2
Crawley, *U.K.* 15 F7
Crazy Mts., *U.S.A.* 108 C8
Crean L., *Canada* 103 C7
Crécy-en-Ponthieu, *France* 19 B8
Crediton, *Canada* 116 C3
Crediton, *U.K.* 15 G4
Cree →, *Canada* 103 B7
Cree →, *U.K.* 13 G4
Cree L., *Canada* 103 B7
Creede, *U.S.A.* 109 H10
Creekside, *U.S.A.* 116 F5
Creel, *Mexico* 118 B3
Creemore, *Canada* 116 B4
Creighton, *Canada* 103 C8
Creighton, *U.S.A.* 112 D6
Creil, *France* 19 C9
Crema, *Italy* 40 C6
Cremona, *Italy* 40 C7
Crepaja, *Serbia & M.* 28 E5
Crépy, *France* 19 C10
Crépy-en-Valois, *France* 19 C9
Cres, *Croatia* 41 D11
Crescent City, *U.S.A.* 108 F1
Crescentino, *Italy* 40 C5
Crespo, *Argentina* 126 C3
Cresson, *U.S.A.* 116 F6
Crest, *France* 21 D9
Cresta, Mt., *Phil.* 61 C5
Crestline, *Calif., U.S.A.* 111 L9
Crestline, *Ohio, U.S.A.* 116 F2
Creston, *Canada* 102 D5
Creston, *Calif., U.S.A.* 110 K6
Creston, *Iowa, U.S.A.* 112 E7
Crestview, *Calif., U.S.A.* 110 H8
Crestview, *Fla., U.S.A.* 115 K2
Crêt de la Neige, *France* 19 F12
Crete = Kríti, *Greece* 49 D7
Crete, *U.S.A.* 112 E6
Crete, Sea of, *Greece* 47 E7
Créteil, *France* 19 D9
Creus, C. de, *Spain* 38 C8
Creuse □, *France* 19 F9
Creuse →, *France* 20 B4
Creutzwald, *France* 19 C13
Creuzburg, *Germany* 24 D6
Crèvecœur-le-Grand, *France* 19 C9
Crevillente, *Spain* 39 G4
Crewe, *U.K.* 14 D5
Crewkerne, *U.K.* 15 G5
Crianlarich, *U.K.* 13 E4
Criciúma, *Brazil* 127 B6
Cricova, *Moldova* 29 C13
Crieff, *U.K.* 13 E5
Crikvenica, *Croatia* 41 C11
Crimea □, *Ukraine* 33 K8
Crimean Pen. = Krymskyy Pivostriv, *Ukraine* 33 K8
Crimmitschau, *Germany* 24 E8
Cristuru Secuiesc, *Romania* 29 D10
Crişul Alb →, *Romania* 28 D6
Crişul Negru →, *Romania* 28 D6
Crişul Repede →, *Romania* 28 D5
Criuleni, *Moldova* 29 C14
Crivitz, *Germany* 24 B7
Crna →, *Macedonia* 44 E5
Crna Gora = Montenegro □, *Serbia & M.* 44 D3
Crna Gora, *Macedonia* 44 D5
Crna Reka = Crna →, *Macedonia* 44 E5
Crna Trava, *Serbia & M.* 44 D6
Crni Drim →, *Macedonia* 44 E4
Crni Timok →, *Serbia & M.* 44 C6
Crnoljeva Planina, *Serbia & M.* 44 D5
Črnomelj, *Slovenia* 41 C12
Croagh Patrick, *Ireland* 12 C2
Croatia ■, *Europe* 41 C13
Crocker, Banjaran, *Malaysia* 62 C5
Crockett, *U.S.A.* 113 K7
Crocodile = Krokodil →, *Mozam.* 89 D5
Crocodile Is., *Australia* 94 A1
Crocq, *France* 20 C6
Crodo, *Italy* 40 B5
Crohy Hd., *Ireland* 12 B3
Croisette, C., *France* 21 E9
Croisic, Pte. du, *France* 18 E4
Croix, L. La, *Canada* 104 C1
Croker, C., *Australia* 92 B5
Croker, C., *Canada* 116 B4
Croker I., *Australia* 92 B5
Cromarty, *U.K.* 13 D4
Cromer, *U.K.* 14 E9
Cromwell, *N.Z.* 91 L2
Cromwell, *U.S.A.* 117 E12
Cronat, *France* 19 F10
Crook, *U.K.* 14 C6
Crooked →, *Canada* 102 C4
Crooked →, *U.S.A.* 108 D3
Crooked I., *Bahamas* 121 B5
Crooked Island Passage, *Bahamas* 121 B5
Crookston, *Minn., U.S.A.* 112 B6
Crookston, *Nebr., U.S.A.* 112 D4
Crookwell, *Australia* 95 E4
Cropane-Micone ⌓, *Italy* 43 D9
Crosby, *U.K.* 14 D4
Crosby, *N. Dak., U.S.A.* 112 A3
Crosby, *Pa., U.S.A.* 116 E6
Crosbyton, *U.S.A.* 113 J4
Crosía, *Italy* 43 C9
Cross →, *Nigeria* 83 E6
Cross City, *U.S.A.* 115 L4
Cross Fell, *U.K.* 14 C5
Cross L., *Canada* 103 C9
Cross Lake, *Canada* 103 C9
Cross River □, *Nigeria* 83 D6
Cross River △, *Nigeria* 83 D6
Cross Sound, *U.S.A.* 100 C6
Crossett, *U.S.A.* 113 J9
Crosshaven, *Ireland* 12 E3
Crossville, *U.S.A.* 115 G3
Croswell, *U.S.A.* 116 C2
Croton-on-Hudson, *U.S.A.* 117 E11
Crotone, *Italy* 43 C10
Crow →, *Canada* 102 B4
Crow Agency, *U.S.A.* 108 D10
Crow Hd., *Ireland* 12 E1
Crowell, *U.S.A.* 113 J5
Crowley, *U.S.A.* 113 K8
Crowley, L., *U.S.A.* 110 H8
Crown Point, *Ind., U.S.A.* 114 E2
Crown Point, *N.Y., U.S.A.* 117 C11
Crown Pt., *Trin. & Tob.* 125 J16
Crownpoint, *U.S.A.* 109 J9
Crows Landing, *U.S.A.* 110 H5
Crows Nest, *Australia* 95 D5
Crowsnest Pass, *Canada* 102 D6
Croydon, *Australia* 94 B3
Croydon □, *U.K.* 15 F7
Crozet, Is., *Ind. Oc.* 3 G12
Crozon, *France* 18 D2
Cruz, C., *Cuba* 120 C4
Cruz Alta, *Brazil* 127 B5
Cruz Bay, *U.S. Virgin Is.* 121 e
Cruz de Incio, *Spain* 36 C3
Cruz del Eje, *Argentina* 126 C3
Cruzeiro, *Brazil* 127 A7
Cruzeiro do Oeste, *Brazil* 127 A5
Cruzeiro do Sul, *Brazil* 124 E4
Cry L., *Canada* 102 B3
Crystal Bay, *U.S.A.* 110 F7
Crystal Brook, *Australia* 95 E2
Crystal City, *U.S.A.* 113 L5
Crystal Falls, *U.S.A.* 114 B1
Crystal River, *U.S.A.* 115 L4
Crystal Springs, *U.S.A.* 113 K9
Csenger, *Hungary* 28 C7
Csongrád, *Hungary* 28 D5
Csongrád □, *Hungary* 28 D5
Csorna, *Hungary* 28 C2
Csurgo, *Hungary* 28 D2
Cu Lao Hon, *Vietnam* 65 G7
Cua Rao, *Vietnam* 64 C5
Cuácua →, *Mozam.* 87 F4
Cuamato, *Angola* 88 B2
Cuamba, *Mozam.* 87 E4
Cuando →, *Angola* 85 H4
Cuando Cubango □, *Angola* 88 B3
Cuangar, *Angola* 88 B2
Cuango = Kwango →, *Dem. Rep. of the Congo* 84 E3
Cuanza →, *Angola* 84 F2
Cuarto →, *Argentina* 126 C3
Cuatrociénegas, *Mexico* 118 B4
Cuauhtémoc, *Mexico* 118 B3
Cuba, *Portugal* 37 G3
Cuba, *N. Mex., U.S.A.* 109 J10
Cuba, *N.Y., U.S.A.* 116 D6
Cuba ■, *W. Indies* 120 B4

Cubango →, *Africa* 88 B3
Çubuk, *Turkey* 72 B5
Cuc Phuong △, *Vietnam* 64 B5
Cuchumatanes, Sierra de los, *Guatemala* 120 C1
Cuckfield, *U.K.* 15 F7
Cucuí, *Brazil* 124 C5
Cucurpe, *Mexico* 118 A2
Cúcuta, *Colombia* 124 B4
Cudalbi, *Romania* 29 E12
Cuddalore, *India* 66 P11
Cuddapah, *India* 66 M11
Cuddapan, L., *Australia* 94 D3
Cudillero, *Spain* 36 B4
Cue, *Australia* 93 E2
Cuéllar, *Spain* 36 D6
Cuenca, *Ecuador* 124 D3
Cuenca, *Spain* 38 E2
Cuenca □, *Spain* 38 F3
Cuenca, Serranía de, *Spain* 38 F3
Cuenca Alta del Manzanares ⌓, *Spain* 36 E7
Cuerdo del Pozo, Embalse de la, *Spain* 38 D2
Cuernavaca, *Mexico* 119 D5
Cuero, *U.S.A.* 113 L6
Cuers, *France* 21 E10
Cueva de la Quebrada del Toro △, *Venezuela* 121 D6
Cuevas del Almanzora, *Spain* 39 H3
Cuevo, *Bolivia* 124 H6
Cugir, *Romania* 29 E8
Cugnaux, *France* 20 E5
Cuhai-Bakony →, *Hungary* 28 C2
Cuiabá, *Brazil* 125 G7
Cuiabá →, *Brazil* 125 G7
Cuijk, *Neths.* 17 C5
Cuilco, *Guatemala* 120 C1
Cuillin Hills, *U.K.* 13 D2
Cuillin Sd., *U.K.* 13 D2
Cuiseaux, *France* 19 F12
Cuito →, *Angola* 88 B3
Cuitzeo, L. de, *Mexico* 118 D4
Cujmir, *Romania* 28 F7
Cukai, *Malaysia* 65 K4
Culbertson, *U.S.A.* 112 A2
Culcairn, *Australia* 95 F4
Culebra, Isla de, *Puerto Rico* 121 d
Culebra, Sierra de la, *Spain* 36 D4
Culfa, *Azerbaijan* 73 C11
Culgoa →, *Australia* 95 D4
Culgoa Flood Plain △, *Australia* 95 D4
Culiacán, *Mexico* 118 C3
Culiacán →, *Mexico* 118 C3
Culik, *Indonesia* 63 J18
Culion, *Phil.* 61 F4
Cúllar, *Spain* 37 H8
Cullarin Ra., *Australia* 95 E4
Cullen, *U.K.* 13 D6
Cullen Pt., *Australia* 94 A3
Cullera, *Spain* 39 F4
Cullman, *U.S.A.* 115 H2
Cullompton, *U.K.* 15 G4
Culoz, *France* 21 C9
Culpeper, *U.S.A.* 114 F7
Culuene →, *Brazil* 125 F8
Culver, Pt., *Australia* 93 F3
Culverden, *N.Z.* 91 K4
Cumaná, *Venezuela* 124 A6
Cumaovası, *Turkey* 47 C9
Cumberland, *B.C., Canada* 102 D4
Cumberland, *Ont., Canada* 117 A9
Cumberland, *U.S.A.* 114 F6
Cumberland →, *U.S.A.* 115 G2
Cumberland, L., *U.S.A.* 115 G3
Cumberland Gap △, *U.S.A.* 115 G4
Cumberland I., *U.S.A.* 115 K5
Cumberland Is., *Australia* 94 J7
Cumberland Island ⌓, *U.S.A.* 115 K5
Cumberland L., *Canada* 103 C8
Cumberland Pen., *Canada* 101 B13
Cumberland Plateau, *U.S.A.* 115 H3
Cumberland Sd., *Canada* 101 B13
Cumbernauld, *U.K.* 13 F5
Cumborah, *Australia* 95 D4
Cumbres de Majalca △, *Mexico* 118 B3
Cumbres de Monterrey △, *Mexico* 118 B4
Cumbres Mayores, *Spain* 37 G4
Cumbria □, *U.K.* 14 C5
Cumbrian Mts., *U.K.* 14 C5
Cumbum, *India* 66 M11
Cuminá →, *Brazil* 125 D7
Cummings Mt., *U.S.A.* 111 K8
Cummins, *Australia* 95 E2
Cumnock, *Australia* 95 E4
Cumnock, *U.K.* 13 F4
Cumpas, *Mexico* 118 B3
Cumplida, Pta., *Canary Is.* 48 F2
Çumra, *Turkey* 72 D5
Cunco, *Chile* 128 D2
Cuncumén, *Chile* 126 C1
Cunderdin, *Australia* 93 F2
Cunene →, *Angola* 88 B1
Cúneo, *Italy* 40 D4
Çüngüş, *Turkey* 70 B3
Cunillera, I. = Sa Conillera, *Spain* 48 C7
Cunlhat, *France* 20 C7
Cunnamulla, *Australia* 95 D4
Cuorgnè, *Italy* 40 C4
Cupar, *Canada* 103 C8
Cupar, *U.K.* 13 E5
Cupcini, *Moldova* 29 B12
Cupica, G. de, *Colombia* 124 B3
Ćuprija, *Serbia & M.* 44 C5
Curaçao, *Neth. Ant.* 121 D6
Curanilahue, *Chile* 126 D1
Curaray →, *Peru* 124 D4
Cure →, *France* 19 E10
Curepto, *Chile* 126 D1
Curiapo, *Venezuela* 124 B6
Curicó, *Chile* 126 C1
Curinga, *Italy* 43 D9
Curitiba, *Brazil* 127 B6
Curitibanos, *Brazil* 127 B5
Currabubula, *Australia* 95 E5
Currais Novos, *Brazil* 125 E11
Curralinho, *Brazil* 125 D9
Currant, *U.S.A.* 108 G6
Currawinya △, *Australia* 95 D3
Current →, *U.S.A.* 113 G9
Currie, *Australia* 95 F3
Currie, *U.S.A.* 108 F6
Curtea de Argeş, *Romania* 29 E9
Curtici, *Romania* 28 D6
Curtis, *U.S.A.* 112 E4
Curtis Group, *Australia* 95 F4
Curtis I., *Australia* 94 C5
Curuápanema →, *Brazil* 125 D7
Curuçá, *Brazil* 125 D9
Curuguaty, *Paraguay* 127 A4
Curup, *Indonesia* 62 E2
Cururupu, *Brazil* 125 D10
Curuzú Cuatiá, *Argentina* 126 B4
Curvelo, *Brazil* 125 G10
Cushing, *U.S.A.* 113 H6
Cushing, Mt., *Canada* 102 B3
Cusihuiriáchic, *Mexico* 118 B3
Cusna, Mte., *Italy* 40 D7
Cusset, *France* 19 F10
Custer, *U.S.A.* 112 D3
Cut Bank, *U.S.A.* 108 B7
Cuthbert, *U.S.A.* 115 K3
Cuthogue, *U.S.A.* 117 E12
Cutler, *U.S.A.* 110 J7
Cutro, *Italy* 43 C9
Cuttaburra →, *Australia* 95 D3
Cuttack, *India* 67 J14
Cuvier, C., *Australia* 93 D1
Cuvier I., *N.Z.* 91 G5
Cuxhaven, *Germany* 24 B4
Cuyahoga Falls, *U.S.A.* 116 E3
Cuyahoga Valley △, *U.S.A.* 116 E3
Cuyapo, *Phil.* 61 D4
Cuyo, *Phil.* 61 F4
Cuyo East Pass, *Phil.* 61 F4
Cuyo West Pass, *Phil.* 61 F4
Cuyuni →, *Guyana* 124 B7
Cuzco, *Bolivia* 124 H5
Cuzco, *Peru* 124 F4
Čvrsnica, *Bos.-H.* 28 G2
Cwmbran, *U.K.* 15 F4
Cyangugu, *Rwanda* 86 C2
Cybinka, *Poland* 31 F1
Cyclades = Kikládhes, *Greece* 46 E6
Cygnet, *Australia* 95 G4
Cynthiana, *U.S.A.* 114 F3
Cypress Hills, *Canada* 103 D7
Cypress Hills ⌓, *Canada* 103 D7
Cyprus ■, *Asia* 49 E12
Cyrenaica, *Libya* 79 C10
Czaplinek, *Poland* 30 E3
Czar, *Canada* 103 C6
Czarna →, *Łódzkie, Poland* 31 G6
Czarna →, *Świętokrzyskie, Poland* 31 H8
Czarna Białostocka, *Poland* 31 E10
Czarna Woda, *Poland* 30 E5
Czarne, *Poland* 30 E3
Czarnków, *Poland* 31 F3
Czech Rep. ■, *Europe* 26 B8
Czechowice-Dziedzice, *Poland* 31 J5
Czempiń, *Poland* 31 F3
Czeremcha, *Poland* 31 F10
Czerniejewo, *Poland* 31 F4
Czersk, *Poland* 30 E4
Czerwieńsk, *Poland* 31 F2
Czerwionka-Leszczyny, *Poland* 31 H5
Częstochowa, *Poland* 31 H6
Człopa, *Poland* 31 E3
Człuchów, *Poland* 30 E4
Czyżew-Osada, *Poland* 31 F9

D

Da →, *Vietnam* 58 G5
Da Hinggan Ling, *China* 60 B7
Da Lat, *Vietnam* 65 G7
Da Nang, *Vietnam* 64 D7
Da Qaidam, *China* 60 C4
Da Yunhe →, *China* 57 G11
Da'an, *China* 57 B13
Daan Viljoen ⌓, *Namibia* 88 C2
Dab'a, Ras el, *Egypt* 80 H6
Daba Shan, *China* 58 B7
Dabai, *Nigeria* 83 C6
Dabakala, *Ivory C.* 82 D4
Dabas, *Hungary* 28 C4
Dabat, *Ethiopia* 81 E4
Dabbagh, Jabal, *Si. Arabia* 70 E2
Dabhoi, *India* 68 H5
Dąbie, *Poland* 31 F5
Dabie Shan, *China* 59 B10
Dabilda, *Cameroon* 83 C7
Dabnou, *Niger* 83 C6
Dabo = Pasirkuning, *Indonesia* 62 E2
Dabola, *Guinea* 82 C2
Dabou, *Ivory C.* 82 D4
Daboya, *Ghana* 83 D4
Dabravolya, *Belarus* 31 F10
Dąbrowa Białostocka, *Poland* 30 E10
Dąbrowa Górnicza, *Poland* 31 H6
Dąbrowa Tarnowska, *Poland* 31 H7
Dabu, *China* 59 E11
Dabung, *Malaysia* 65 K4
Dabus →, *Ethiopia* 81 E4
Dacato →, *Ethiopia* 81 F5
Dacca = Dhaka, *Bangla.* 69 H14
Dacca = Dhaka □, *Bangla.* 69 G14
Dachau, *Germany* 25 G7
Dachstein, Hoher, *Austria* 26 D6
Dačice, *Czech Rep.* 26 B8
Dadanawa, *Guyana* 124 C7
Daday, *Turkey* 72 B5
Dade City, *U.S.A.* 115 L4
Dadhar, *Pakistan* 68 E2
Dadiya, *Nigeria* 83 D7
Dadra & Nagar Haveli □, *India* 66 J8
Dadri = Charkhi Dadri, *India* 68 E7
Dadu, *Pakistan* 68 F2
Dadu He →, *China* 58 C4
Daet, *Phil.* 61 D5
Dafang, *China* 58 D5
Dağ, *Turkey* 47 D12
Dagana, *Senegal* 82 B1
Dagash, *Sudan* 80 D3
Dagestan □, *Russia* 35 J8
Dagestanskiye Ogni, *Russia* 35 J9
Daggett, *U.S.A.* 111 L10
Daghestan Republic = Dagestan □, *Russia* 35 J8
Daghfeli, *Sudan* 80 D3
Dağlıq Qarabağ = Nagorno-Karabakh □, *Azerbaijan* 70 B5
Dagö = Hiiumaa, *Estonia* 9 G20
Dagu, *China* 57 E9
Daguan, *China* 58 D4
Dagupan, *Phil.* 61 C4
Daguragu, *Australia* 92 C5
Dahab, *Egypt* 80 B3
Dahlak △, *Eritrea* 81 D5
Dahlak Kebir, *Eritrea* 81 D5
Dahlenburg, *Germany* 24 B6
Dahlonega, *U.S.A.* 115 H4
Dahme, *Germany* 24 D9
Dahod, *India* 68 H6
Dahong Shan, *China* 59 B9
Dahra, *Senegal* 82 B1
Dahshûr, *Egypt* 80 J7
Dahūk, *Iraq* 70 B3
Dai Hao, *Vietnam* 64 C6
Dai-Sen, *Japan* 55 G6
Dai Shan, *China* 59 B14
Dai Xian, *China* 56 E7
Daicheng, *China* 56 E9
Daimiel, *Spain* 37 F7
Daingean, *Ireland* 12 C4
Dainkog, *China* 58 A1
Daintree, *Australia* 94 B4
Daintree △, *Australia* 94 B4
Daiō-Misaki, *Japan* 55 G8
Dair, J. ed, *Sudan* 81 E3
Dairût, *Egypt* 80 B3
Daisen-Oki △, *Japan* 55 G6
Daisetsu-Zan, *Japan* 54 C11
Daisetsu-Zan △, *Japan* 54 C11
Dajarra, *Australia* 94 C2
Dajin Chuan →, *China* 58 B3
Dak Dam, *Cambodia* 64 F6
Dak Nhe, *Vietnam* 64 E6
Dak Pek, *Vietnam* 64 E6
Dak Song, *Vietnam* 65 F6
Dak Sui, *Vietnam* 64 E6
Dakar, *Senegal* 82 C1
Dakhla, *W. Sahara* 78 D2
Dakhla, El Wâhât el-, *Egypt* 80 B2
Dakingari, *Nigeria* 83 C5
Dakor, *India* 68 H5
Dakoro, *Niger* 83 C6
Dakota City, *U.S.A.* 112 D6
Đakovica, *Serbia & M.* 44 D4
Đakovo, *Croatia* 28 E3
Dalaba, *Guinea* 82 C2
Dalachi, *China* 56 F3
Dalai Nur, *China* 56 C9
Dālakī, *Iran* 71 D6
Dalälven →, *Sweden* 10 D10
Dalaman, *Turkey* 47 E10
Dalaman →, *Turkey* 47 E10
Dalandzadgad, *Mongolia* 56 C3
Dalap-Uliga-Darrit, *Marshall Is.* 96 G9
Dalarna, *Sweden* 10 D8
Dalarnas län □, *Sweden* 10 C8
Dālbandīn, *Pakistan* 66 E4
Dalbeattie, *U.K.* 13 G5
Dalbeg, *Australia* 94 C4
Dalbosjön, *Sweden* 11 F6
Dalby, *Australia* 95 D5
Dalby, *Sweden* 11 J7
Dalby Söderskog △, *Sweden* 11 J7
Dale City, *U.S.A.* 114 F7
Dale Hollow L., *U.S.A.* 115 G3
Dalga, *Egypt* 80 B3
Dalgān, *Iran* 71 E8
Dalhart, *U.S.A.* 113 G3
Dalhousie, *Canada* 105 C6
Dalhousie, *India* 68 C6
Dali, *Shaanxi, China* 56 G5
Dali, *Yunnan, China* 58 E3
Dalian, *China* 57 E11
Daliang Shan, *China* 58 D4
Daling He →, *China* 57 D11
Dāliyat el Karmel, *Israel* 74 C4
Dalj, *Croatia* 28 E3
Dalkeith, *U.K.* 13 F5
Dallas, *Oreg., U.S.A.* 108 D2
Dallas, *Tex., U.S.A.* 113 J6
Dallol, *Ethiopia* 81 E5
Dalmā, *U.A.E.* 71 E7
Dalmacija, *Croatia* 41 E13
Dalmas, L., *Canada* 105 B5
Dalmatia = Dalmacija, *Croatia* 41 E13
Dalmau, *India* 69 F9
Dalmellington, *U.K.* 13 F4
Dalnegorsk, *Russia* 53 E14
Dalnerechensk, *Russia* 53 E14
Dalnevostochnyy □, *Russia* 53 C14
Daloa, *Ivory C.* 82 D3
Dalou Shan, *China* 58 C6
Dalry, *U.K.* 13 F4
Dalrymple, L., *Australia* 94 C4
Dalrymple, Mt., *Australia* 94 K6
Dals Långed, *Sweden* 11 F6
Dalsjöfors, *Sweden* 11 G7
Dalsland, *Sweden* 11 F6
Daltenganj, *India* 69 H11
Dalton, *Ga., U.S.A.* 115 H3
Dalton, *Mass., U.S.A.* 117 D11
Dalton, *Nebr., U.S.A.* 112 E3
Dalton-in-Furness, *U.K.* 14 C4
Dalupiri I., *Phil.* 61 B4
Dalvík, *Iceland* 8 D4
Dálvvadis = Jokkmokk, *Sweden* 8 C18
Dalwallinu, *Australia* 93 F2
Daly →, *Australia* 92 B5
Daly City, *U.S.A.* 110 H4
Daly L., *Canada* 103 B7
Daly River, *Australia* 92 B5
Daly Waters, *Australia* 94 B1
Dalyan, *Turkey* 47 E10
Dam Doi, *Vietnam* 65 H5
Dam Ha, *Vietnam* 64 B6
Damachova, *Belarus* 31 G10
Daman, *India* 66 J8
Dāmaneh, *Iran* 71 C6
Damanhûr, *Egypt* 80 H7
Damant L., *Canada* 103 A7
Damanzhuang, *China* 56 E9
Damar, *Indonesia* 63 F7
Damaraland, *Namibia* 88 C2
Damascus = Dimashq, *Syria* 74 B5
Damaturu, *Nigeria* 83 C7
Damāvand, *Iran* 71 C7
Damāvand, Qolleh-ye, *Iran* 71 C7
Damba, *Angola* 84 F3
Dâmboviţa □, *Romania* 29 F10
Dâmboviţa →, *Romania* 29 F11
Dâmbovnic →, *Romania* 29 F10
Dame Marie, *Haiti* 121 C5
Dāmghān, *Iran* 71 B7
Dămienesti, *Romania* 29 D11
Damietta = Dumyât, *Egypt* 80 H7
Daming, *China* 56 F8
Damīr Qābū, *Syria* 70 B4
Dammam = Ad Dammām, *Si. Arabia* 71 E6
Dammarie-les-Lys, *France* 19 D9
Dammartin-en-Goële, *France* 19 C9
Damme, *Germany* 24 C4
Damodar →, *India* 69 H12
Damoh, *India* 69 H8
Dampier, *Australia* 92 D2
Dampier, Selat, *Indonesia* 63 E8
Dampier Arch., *Australia* 92 D2
Damrei, Chuor Phnum, *Cambodia* 65 G4
Damvillers, *France* 19 C12
Dan-Gulbi, *Nigeria* 83 C6
Dan Xian, *China* 64 C7
Dana, *Indonesia* 63 F6
Dana, L., *Canada* 104 B4
Dana, Mt., *U.S.A.* 110 H7
Danakil Desert, *Ethiopia* 81 E5
Danané, *Ivory C.* 82 D3
Danao, *Phil.* 61 F6
Danau Poso, *Indonesia* 63 E6
Danba, *China* 58 B3
Danbury, *U.S.A.* 117 E11
Danby L., *U.S.A.* 109 J6
Dand, *Afghan.* 68 D1
Dande →, *Zimbabwe* 87 F3
Dandeldhura, *Nepal* 69 E9
Dandeli, *India* 66 M9
Dandenong, *Australia* 95 F4
Dandīl, *Egypt* 80 J7
Dandong, *China* 57 D13
Danfeng, *China* 56 H6
Dangan Liedao, *China* 59 F10
Dangé-St-Romain, *France* 20 B4
Dângeni, *Romania* 29 C11
Danger Is. = Pukapuka, *Cook Is.* 97 J11
Danger Pt., *S. Africa* 88 E2
Danginpuri, *Indonesia* 63 K18
Dangla, *Ethiopia* 81 E4
Dangla Shan = Tanggula Shan, *China* 60 C4
Dangora, *Nigeria* 83 C6
Dangouadougou, *Burkina Faso* 82 D4
Dangrek, Phnom, *Thailand* 64 E5
Dangriga, *Belize* 119 D7
Dangshan, *China* 56 G9
Dangtu, *China* 59 B12
Dangyang, *China* 59 B8
Dani, *Burkina Faso* 83 C4
Daniel, *U.S.A.* 108 E8
Daniel's Harbour, *Canada* 105 B8
Danielskuil, *S. Africa* 88 D3
Danielson, *U.S.A.* 117 E13
Danilov, *Russia* 32 C11
Danilovgrad, *Serbia & M.* 44 D3
Danilovka, *Russia* 34 E7
Daning, *China* 56 F6
Danja, *Nigeria* 83 C6
Danjiangkou, *China* 59 A8
Danjiangkou Shuiku, *China* 59 A8
Dank, *Oman* 71 F8
Dankalwa, *Nigeria* 83 C7
Dankama, *Nigeria* 83 C6
Dankhar Gompa, *India* 66 C11
Dankov, *Russia* 32 F10
Danleng, *China* 58 B4
Danlí, *Honduras* 120 D2
Dannemora, *U.S.A.* 117 B11
Dannenberg, *Germany* 24 B7
Dannevirke, *N.Z.* 91 J6
Dannhauser, *S. Africa* 89 D5
Dansville, *U.S.A.* 116 D7
Danta, *India* 68 G5
Dantan, *India* 69 J12
Danube = Dunărea →, *Europe* 29 E14
Danvers, *U.S.A.* 117 D14
Danville, *Ill., U.S.A.* 114 E2
Danville, *Ky., U.S.A.* 114 G3
Danville, *Pa., U.S.A.* 117 F8
Danville, *Va., U.S.A.* 115 G6
Danville, *Vt., U.S.A.* 117 B12
Danyang, *China* 59 B12
Danzhai, *China* 58 D6
Danzig = Gdańsk, *Poland* 30 D5
Dão →, *Portugal* 36 E2
Dao Xian, *China* 59 E8
Daocheng, *China* 58 C3
Daoukro, *Ivory C.* 82 D4
Dapaong, *Togo* 83 C5
Dapchi, *Nigeria* 83 C7
Dapitan, *Phil.* 61 G5
Daqing Shan, *China* 56 D6
Daqu Shan, *China* 59 B14
Dar Banda, *Africa* 76 F6
Dar el Beida = Casablanca, *Morocco* 78 B4
Dar es Salaam, *Tanzania* 86 D4
Dar Mazār, *Iran* 71 D8
Dar'ā, *Syria* 74 C5
Dar'ā □, *Syria* 74 C5
Dārāb, *Iran* 71 D7
Daraban, *Pakistan* 68 D4
Darabani, *Romania* 29 B11
Daraina, *Madag.* 89 A8
Daraj, *Libya* 79 B8
Dārān, *Iran* 71 C6
Daravica, *Serbia & M.* 44 D4
Darawa, *Egypt* 80 C3
Dārayyā, *Syria* 74 B5
Darazo, *Nigeria* 83 C7
Darband, *Pakistan* 68 B5
Darband, Kūh-e, *Iran* 71 D8
Darbhanga, *India* 69 F11
D'Arcy, *Canada* 102 C4
Darda, *Croatia* 28 E3
Dardanelle, *Ark., U.S.A.* 113 H8
Dardanelle, *Calif., U.S.A.* 110 G7
Dardanelles = Çanakkale Boğazı, *Turkey* 45 F10
Dare →, *Ethiopia* 81 F5
Darende, *Turkey* 72 C7
Dārestān, *Iran* 71 D8
Darfo, *Italy* 40 C7
Dârfûr, *Sudan* 79 F10
Dargai, *Pakistan* 68 B4
Dargan Ata, *Turkmenistan* 52 E7
Dargaville, *N.Z.* 91 F4
Dargol, *Niger* 83 C5
Darhan, *Mongolia* 60 B5
Darhan Muminggan Lianheqi, *China* 56 D6
Dari, *Sudan* 81 F3
Darıca, *Turkey* 72 B3
Darién △, *Panama* 120 E4
Darién, G. del, *Colombia* 124 B3
Dariganga = Ovoot, *Mongolia* 56 B7
Darinskoye, *Kazakhstan* 34 E10
Darjeeling = Darjiling, *India* 69 F13
Darjiling, *India* 69 F13
Darkan, *Australia* 93 F2
Darkhana, *Pakistan* 68 D5
Darkhazīneh, *Iran* 71 D6
Darkot Pass, *Pakistan* 69 A5
Darling →, *Australia* 95 E3
Darling Downs, *Australia* 95 D5
Darling Ra., *Australia* 93 F2
Darlington, *U.K.* 14 C6
Darlington, *U.S.A.* 115 H6
Darlington □, *U.K.* 14 C6
Darlington, L., *S. Africa* 88 E4
Darlot, L., *Australia* 93 E3
Darłowo, *Poland* 30 D3
Dărmăneşti, *Bacău, Romania* 29 D11
Dărmăneşti, *Suceava, Romania* 29 C11
Darmstadt, *Germany* 25 F4
Darnah, *Libya* 79 B10
Darnall, *S. Africa* 89 D5
Darney, *France* 19 D13
Darnley, C., *Antarctica* 5 C6
Darnley B., *Canada* 100 B7
Daroca, *Spain* 38 D3
Darou-Mousti, *Senegal* 82 B1
Darr →, *Australia* 94 C3
Darra Pezu, *Pakistan* 68 C4
Darrequeira, *Argentina* 126 D3
Darrington, *U.S.A.* 108 B3
Darsser Ort, *Germany* 24 A8
Dart →, *U.K.* 15 G4
Dart, C., *Antarctica* 5 D14
Dartford, *U.K.* 15 F8
Dartmoor, *U.K.* 15 G4
Dartmoor △, *U.K.* 15 G4
Dartmouth, *Canada* 105 D7
Dartmouth, *U.K.* 15 G4
Dartmouth Res., *Australia* 95 D4
Dartuch, C. = Artrutx, C. de, *Spain* 48 B10
Daruvar, *Croatia* 28 E2
Darvaza, *Turkmenistan* 52 E6
Darvel, Teluk = Lahad Datu, Teluk, *Malaysia* 63 D5
Darwen, *U.K.* 14 D5
Darwendale, *Zimbabwe* 89 B5
Darwha, *India* 66 J10
Darwin, *Australia* 92 B5
Darwin, *U.S.A.* 111 J9
Darya Khan, *Pakistan* 68 D4
Daryoi Amu = Amudarya →, *Uzbekistan* 52 E6
Dās, *U.A.E.* 71 E7
Dashen, Ras, *Ethiopia* 81 E4
Dashetai, *China* 56 D5
Dashhowuz, *Turkmenistan* 52 E6
Dashkesan = Daşkäsän, *Azerbaijan* 35 K7
Dashköpri, *Turkmenistan* 71 B9
Dasht, *Iran* 71 B8
Dasht →, *Pakistan* 66 G2
Daska, *Pakistan* 68 C6
Daşkäsän, *Azerbaijan* 35 K7
Dassa, *Benin* 83 D5
Dasuya, *India* 68 D6

Datça, *Turkey* **47 E9**
Datia, *India* **69 G8**
Datian, *China* **59 E11**
Datong, *Anhui, China* **59 B11**
Datong, *Shanxi, China* **56 D7**
Dattakhel, *Pakistan* **68 C3**
Datteln, *Germany* **24 D3**
Datu, Tanjung, *Indonesia* **62 D3**
Datu Piang, *Phil.* **61 H6**
Datuk, Tanjong = Datu, Tanjung, *Indonesia* **62 D3**
Daua = Dawa →, *Africa* **81 G5**
Daud Khel, *Pakistan* **68 C4**
Daudnagar, *India* **69 G11**
Daugava →, *Latvia* **9 H21**
Daugavpils, *Latvia* **9 J22**
Daulpur, *India* **68 F7**
Daun, *Germany* **25 E2**
Dauphin, *Canada* **103 C8**
Dauphin, *U.S.A.* **116 F8**
Dauphin L., *Canada* **103 C9**
Dauphiné, *France* **21 C9**
Daura, *Borno, Nigeria* **83 C7**
Daura, *Katsina, Nigeria* **83 C6**
Dausa, *India* **68 F7**
Däväçi, *Azerbaijan* **35 K9**
Davangere, *India* **66 M9**
Davao, *Phil.* **61 H6**
Davao G., *Phil.* **61 H6**
Dāvar Panāh = Sarāvān, *Iran* **71 E9**
Davenport, *Calif., U.S.A.* **110 H4**
Davenport, *Iowa, U.S.A.* **112 E9**
Davenport, *Wash., U.S.A.* **108 C4**
Davenport Ra., *Australia* **94 C1**
Daventry, *U.K.* **15 E6**
David, *Panama* **120 E3**
David City, *U.S.A.* **112 E6**
David Gorodok = Davyd Haradok, *Belarus* **33 F4**
Davidson, *Canada* **103 C7**
Davis, *Antarctica* **5 C6**
Davis, *U.S.A.* **110 G5**
Davis Dam, *U.S.A.* **111 K12**
Davis Inlet, *Canada* **105 A7**
Davis Mts., *U.S.A.* **113 K2**
Davis Sea, *Antarctica* **5 C7**
Davis Str., *N. Amer.* **101 B14**
Davo →, *Ivory C.* **82 D3**
Davos, *Switz.* **25 J5**
Davutlar, *Turkey* **47 D9**
Davy L., *Canada* **103 B7**
Davyd Haradok, *Belarus* **33 F4**
Dawa →, *Africa* **81 G5**
Dawaki, *Bauchi, Nigeria* **83 D6**
Dawaki, *Kano, Nigeria* **83 C6**
Dawei = Tavoy, *Burma* **64 E2**
Dawes Ra., *Australia* **94 C5**
Dawlish, *U.K.* **15 G4**
Dawna Ra., *Burma* **64 D2**
Dawros Hd., *Ireland* **12 B3**
Dawson, *Canada* **100 B6**
Dawson, *U.S.A.* **115 K3**
Dawson, I., *Chile* **128 G2**
Dawson B., *Canada* **103 C8**
Dawson Creek, *Canada* **102 B4**
Dawson Inlet, *Canada* **103 A10**
Dawson Ra., *Australia* **94 C4**
Dawu, *Hubei, China* **59 B9**
Dawu, *Sichuan, China* **58 B3**
Dax, *France* **20 E2**
Daxian, *China* **58 B6**
Daxin, *China* **58 F6**
Daxindian, *China* **57 F11**
Daxinggou, *China* **57 C15**
Daxue Shan, *Sichuan, China* **58 B3**
Daxue Shan, *Yunnan, China* **58 F2**
Dayao, *China* **58 E3**
Daye, *China* **59 B10**
Dayet en Naharat, *Mali* **82 B4**
Dayi, *China* **58 B4**
Daylesford, *Australia* **95 F3**
Dayong, *China* **59 C8**
Dayr az Zawr, *Syria* **70 C4**
Daysland, *Canada* **102 C6**
Dayton, *Nev., U.S.A.* **110 F7**
Dayton, *Ohio, U.S.A.* **114 F3**
Dayton, *Pa., U.S.A.* **116 F5**
Dayton, *Tenn., U.S.A.* **115 H3**
Dayton, *Wash., U.S.A.* **108 C4**
Dayton, *Wyo., U.S.A.* **108 D10**
Daytona Beach, *U.S.A.* **115 L5**
Dayu, *China* **59 E10**
Dayville, *U.S.A.* **108 D4**
Dazhu, *China* **58 B6**
Dazkırı, *Turkey* **47 D11**
Dazu, *China* **58 C5**
De Aar, *S. Africa* **88 E3**
De Biesbosch △, *Neths.* **17 C4**
De Funiak Springs, *U.S.A.* **115 K2**
De Grey →, *Australia* **92 D2**
De Haan, *Belgium* **17 C3**
De Hoge Veluwe △, *Neths.* **17 B5**
De Hoop ⌓, *S. Africa* **88 E3**
De Kalb, *U.S.A.* **112 E10**
De Kennemerduinen △, *Neths.* **17 B4**
De Land, *U.S.A.* **115 L5**
De Leon, *U.S.A.* **113 J5**
De Panne, *Belgium* **17 C2**
De Pere, *U.S.A.* **114 C1**
De Queen, *U.S.A.* **113 H7**
De Quincy, *U.S.A.* **113 K8**
De Ridder, *U.S.A.* **113 K8**
De Smet, *U.S.A.* **112 C6**
De Soto, *U.S.A.* **112 F9**
De Tour Village, *U.S.A.* **114 C4**
De Witt, *U.S.A.* **113 H9**
Dead Sea, *Asia* **74 D4**
Deadwood, *U.S.A.* **112 C3**
Deadwood L., *Canada* **102 B3**
Deal, *U.K.* **15 F9**
Deal I., *Australia* **95 F4**
Dealesville, *S. Africa* **88 D4**
De'an, *China* **59 C10**
Dean →, *Canada* **102 C3**
Dean, Forest of, *U.K.* **15 F5**
Dean Chan., *Canada* **102 C3**
Deán Funes, *Argentina* **126 C3**
Dease →, *Canada* **102 B3**
Dease L., *Canada* **102 B2**
Dease Lake, *Canada* **102 B2**
Death Valley, *U.S.A.* **111 J10**
Death Valley △, *U.S.A.* **111 J10**
Death Valley Junction, *U.S.A.* **111 J10**
Deauville, *France* **18 C7**
Deba, *Spain* **38 B2**
Deba Habe, *Nigeria* **83 C7**
Debaltsevo, *Ukraine* **33 H10**
Debao, *China* **58 F6**
Debar, *Macedonia* **44 E4**
Debark, *Ethiopia* **81 E4**
Debden, *Canada* **103 C7**
Dębica, *Poland* **31 H8**
Dęblin, *Poland* **31 G8**
Dębno, *Poland* **31 F1**
Débo, L., *Mali* **82 B4**
DeBolt, *Canada* **102 B5**
Deborah East, L., *Australia* **93 F2**
Deborah West, L., *Australia* **93 F2**
Debrc, *Serbia & M.* **44 B3**
Debre Birhan, *Ethiopia* **81 F4**
Debre Markos, *Ethiopia* **81 E4**
Debre May, *Ethiopia* **81 E4**
Debre Sina, *Ethiopia* **81 F4**
Debre Tabor, *Ethiopia* **81 E4**
Debre Zebit, *Ethiopia* **81 E4**
Debre Zevit, *Ethiopia* **81 F4**
Debrecen, *Hungary* **28 C6**
Debrzno, *Poland* **30 E4**
Dečani, *Serbia & M.* **44 D4**
Decatur, *Ala., U.S.A.* **115 H2**
Decatur, *Ga., U.S.A.* **115 J3**
Decatur, *Ill., U.S.A.* **112 F10**
Decatur, *Ind., U.S.A.* **114 E3**
Decatur, *Tex., U.S.A.* **113 J6**
Decazeville, *France* **20 D6**
Deccan, *India* **66 L11**
Deception Bay, *Australia* **95 D5**
Deception I., *Antarctica* **5 C17**
Deception L., *Canada* **103 B8**
Dechang, *China* **58 D4**
Dechhu, *India* **68 F5**
Děčín, *Czech Rep.* **26 A7**
Decize, *France* **19 F10**
Deckerville, *U.S.A.* **116 C2**
Decollatura, *Italy* **43 C9**
Decorah, *U.S.A.* **112 D9**
Deda, *Romania* **29 D9**
Dedéagach = Alexandroúpolis, *Greece* **45 F9**
Deder, *Ethiopia* **81 F5**
Dedham, *U.S.A.* **117 D13**
Dédougou, *Burkina Faso* **82 C4**
Dedovichi, *Russia* **32 D5**
Dedza, *Malawi* **87 E3**
Dee →, *Aberds., U.K.* **13 D6**
Dee →, *Dumf. & Gall., U.K.* **13 G4**
Dee →, *Wales, U.K.* **14 D4**
Deep B., *Canada* **102 A5**
Deepwater, *Australia* **95 D5**
Deer →, *Canada* **103 B10**
Deer L., *Canada* **103 C10**
Deer Lake, *Nfld. & L., Canada* **105 C8**
Deer Lake, *Ont., Canada* **103 C10**
Deer Lodge, *U.S.A.* **108 C7**
Deer Park, *U.S.A.* **108 C5**
Deer River, *U.S.A.* **112 B8**
Deeragun, *Australia* **94 B4**
Deerdepoort, *S. Africa* **88 C4**
Deferiet, *U.S.A.* **117 B9**
Defiance, *U.S.A.* **114 E3**
Degana, *India* **68 F6**
Dêgê, *China* **58 B2**
Degebe →, *Portugal* **37 G3**
Degeberga, *Sweden* **11 J8**
Dégelis, *Canada* **105 C6**
Degema, *Nigeria* **83 E6**
Degerfors, *Sweden* **10 E8**
Degerhamn, *Sweden* **11 H10**
Deggendorf, *Germany* **25 G8**
Degh →, *Pakistan* **68 D5**
Değirmendere, *Turkey* **45 F13**
Deh Bīd, *Iran* **71 D7**
Deh-e Shīr, *Iran* **71 D7**
Dehaj, *Iran* **71 D7**
Dehak, *Iran* **71 E9**
Dehdez, *Iran* **71 D6**
Dehej, *India* **68 J5**
Dehestān, *Iran* **71 D7**
Dehgolān, *Iran* **70 C5**
Dehibat, *Tunisia* **79 B8**
Dehlorān, *Iran* **70 C5**
Dehnow-e Kūhestān, *Iran* **71 E8**
Dehra Dun, *India* **68 D8**
Dehri, *India* **69 G11**
Dehua, *China* **59 E12**
Dehui, *China* **57 B13**
Deim Zubeir, *Sudan* **81 F2**
Deinze, *Belgium* **17 D3**
Dej, *Romania* **29 C8**
Deje, *Sweden* **10 E7**
Dejiang, *China* **58 C7**
Deka →, *Zimbabwe* **88 B4**
Dekemhare, *Eritrea* **81 D4**
Dekese, *Dem. Rep. of the Congo* **84 E4**
Del Mar, *U.S.A.* **111 N9**
Del Norte, *U.S.A.* **109 H10**
Del Rio, *U.S.A.* **113 L4**
Delai, *Sudan* **80 D4**
Delambre I., *Australia* **92 D2**
Delami, *Sudan* **81 E3**
Delano, *U.S.A.* **111 K7**
Delano Peak, *U.S.A.* **109 G7**
Delareyville, *S. Africa* **88 D4**
Delaronde L., *Canada* **103 C7**
Delavan, *U.S.A.* **112 D10**
Delaware, *U.S.A.* **114 E4**
Delaware □, *U.S.A.* **114 F8**
Delaware →, *U.S.A.* **117 G9**
Delaware B., *U.S.A.* **114 F8**
Delaware Water Gap ⌓, *U.S.A.* **117 E10**
Delay →, *Canada* **105 A5**
Delbrück, *Germany* **24 D4**
Delčevo, *Macedonia* **44 E6**
Delegate, *Australia* **95 F4**
Delémont, *Switz.* **25 H3**
Delevan, *U.S.A.* **116 D6**
Delft, *Neths.* **17 B4**
Delfzijl, *Neths.* **17 A6**
Delgado, C., *Mozam.* **87 E5**
Delgerhet, *Mongolia* **56 B6**
Delgo, *Sudan* **80 C3**
Delhi, *Canada* **116 D4**
Delhi, *India* **68 E7**
Delhi, *La., U.S.A.* **113 J9**
Delhi, *N.Y., U.S.A.* **117 D10**
Deli Jovan, *Serbia & M.* **44 B6**
Delia, *Canada* **102 C6**
Delice, *Turkey* **72 C6**
Delicias, *Mexico* **118 B3**
Delījān, *Iran* **71 C6**
Déline, *Canada* **100 B7**
Delisle, *Canada* **103 C7**
Delitzsch, *Germany* **24 D8**
Dell City, *U.S.A.* **109 L11**
Dell Rapids, *U.S.A.* **112 D6**
Delle, *France* **19 E14**
Delmar, *U.S.A.* **117 D11**
Delmenhorst, *Germany* **24 B4**
Delnice, *Croatia* **41 C11**
Delonga, Ostrova, *Russia* **53 B15**
Deloraine, *Australia* **95 G4**
Deloraine, *Canada* **103 D8**
Delphi, *Greece* **46 C4**
Delphi, *U.S.A.* **114 E2**
Delphos, *U.S.A.* **114 E3**
Delportshoop, *S. Africa* **88 D3**
Delray Beach, *U.S.A.* **115 M5**
Delsbo, *Sweden* **10 C10**
Delta, *Colo., U.S.A.* **109 G9**
Delta, *Utah, U.S.A.* **108 G7**
Delta □, *Nigeria* **83 D6**
Delta del Ebro ⌓, *Spain* **38 E5**
Delta del Po ⌓, *Italy* **41 D9**
Delta du Saloum △, *Senegal* **82 C1**
Delta Dunărea ⌓, *Romania* **29 E14**
Delta Junction, *U.S.A.* **100 B5**
Deltona, *U.S.A.* **115 L5**
Delungra, *Australia* **95 D5**
Delvada, *India* **68 J4**
Delvinákion, *Greece* **46 B2**
Delvinë, *Albania* **44 G4**
Delyatyn, *Ukraine* **29 B9**
Demak, *Indonesia* **63 G14**
Demanda, Sierra de la, *Spain* **38 C2**
Demavend = Damāvand, Qolleh-ye, *Iran* **71 C7**
Dembecha, *Ethiopia* **81 E4**
Dembi, *Ethiopia* **81 F4**
Dembia, *Dem. Rep. of the Congo* **86 B2**
Dembidolo, *Ethiopia* **81 F3**
Demchok, *India* **69 C8**
Demer →, *Belgium* **17 D4**
Demetrias, *Greece* **46 B5**
Demidov, *Russia* **32 E6**
Deming, *N. Mex., U.S.A.* **109 K10**
Deming, *Wash., U.S.A.* **110 B4**
Demini →, *Brazil* **124 D6**
Demirci, *Turkey* **47 B10**
Demirköprü Barajı, *Turkey* **47 C10**
Demirköy, *Turkey* **45 E11**
Demmin, *Germany* **24 B9**
Demonte, *Italy* **40 D4**
Demopolis, *U.S.A.* **115 J2**
Dempo, *Indonesia* **62 E2**
Demyansk, *Russia* **32 D7**
Den Burg, *Neths.* **17 A4**
Den Chai, *Thailand* **64 D3**
Den Haag = 's-Gravenhage, *Neths.* **17 B4**
Den Helder, *Neths.* **17 B4**
Den Oever, *Neths.* **17 B5**
Denain, *France* **19 B10**
Denair, *U.S.A.* **110 H6**
Denau, *Uzbekistan* **52 F7**
Denbigh, *Canada* **116 A7**
Denbigh, *U.K.* **14 D4**
Denbighshire □, *U.K.* **14 D4**
Dendang, *Indonesia* **62 E3**
Dendermonde, *Belgium* **17 C4**
Deneba, *Ethiopia* **81 F4**
Dengchuan, *China* **58 E3**
Denge, *Nigeria* **83 C6**
Dengfeng, *China* **56 G7**
Dengi, *Nigeria* **83 D6**
Dengkou, *China* **56 D4**
Dengzhou, *China* **59 A9**
Denham, *Australia* **93 E1**
Denham, Mt., *Jamaica* **120 a**
Denham Ra., *Australia* **94 C4**
Denham Sd., *Australia* **93 E1**
Denholm, *Canada* **103 C7**
Denia, *Spain* **39 G5**
Denial B., *Australia* **95 E1**
Deniliquin, *Australia* **95 F3**
Denison, *Iowa, U.S.A.* **112 E7**
Denison, *Tex., U.S.A.* **113 J6**
Denison Plains, *Australia* **92 C4**
Denizli, *Turkey* **47 D11**
Denizli □, *Turkey* **47 D11**
Denman Glacier, *Antarctica* **5 C7**
Denmark, *Australia* **93 F2**
Denmark ■, *Europe* **11 J3**
Denmark Str., *Atl. Oc.* **4 C6**
Dennery, *St. Lucia* **121 f**
Dennison, *U.S.A.* **116 F3**
Denny, *U.K.* **13 E5**
Denpasar, *Indonesia* **63 K18**
Denpasar ✕ (DPS), *Indonesia* **63 K18**
Denton, *Mont., U.S.A.* **108 C9**
Denton, *Tex., U.S.A.* **113 J6**
D'Entrecasteaux △, *Australia* **93 F2**
D'Entrecasteaux, Pt., *Australia* **93 F2**
Denu, *Ghana* **83 D5**
Denver, *Colo., U.S.A.* **112 F2**
Denver, *Pa., U.S.A.* **117 F8**
Denver City, *U.S.A.* **113 J3**
Deoband, *India* **68 E7**
Deogarh, *India* **68 G5**
Deoghar, *India* **69 G12**
Deolali, *India* **66 K8**
Deoli = Devli, *India* **68 G6**
Déols, *France* **19 F8**
Deora, *India* **68 F4**
Deori, *India* **69 H8**
Deoria, *India* **69 F10**
Deosai Mts., *Pakistan* **69 B6**
Deosri, *India* **69 F14**
Depalpur, *India* **68 H6**
Deping, *China* **57 F9**
Deposit, *U.S.A.* **117 D9**
Depuch I., *Australia* **92 D2**
Deputatskiy, *Russia* **53 C14**
Dêqên, *China* **58 C2**
Deqing, *China* **59 F8**
Dera Ghazi Khan, *Pakistan* **68 D4**
Dera Ismail Khan, *Pakistan* **68 D4**
Derabugti, *Pakistan* **68 E3**
Derawar Fort, *Pakistan* **68 E4**
Derbent, *Russia* **35 J9**
Derbent, *Turkey* **47 C10**
Derby, *Australia* **92 C3**
Derby, *U.K.* **14 E6**
Derby, *Conn., U.S.A.* **117 E11**
Derby, *Kans., U.S.A.* **113 G6**
Derby, *N.Y., U.S.A.* **116 D6**
Derby City □, *U.K.* **14 E6**
Derby Line, *U.S.A.* **117 B12**
Derbyshire □, *U.K.* **14 D6**
Đerdap △, *Serbia & M.* **44 B6**
Derdepoort, *S. Africa* **88 C4**
Derecske, *Hungary* **28 C6**
Dereham, *U.K.* **15 E8**
Dereköy, *Turkey* **45 E11**
Dereli, *Turkey* **73 B8**
Derg →, *U.K.* **12 B4**
Derg, L., *Ireland* **12 D3**
Dergachi = Derhaci, *Ukraine* **33 G9**
Dergaon, *India* **67 F19**
Derhaci, *Ukraine* **33 G9**
Derik, *Turkey* **73 D9**
Derinkuyu, *Turkey* **72 C6**
Dermantsi, *Bulgaria* **45 C8**
Dermott, *U.S.A.* **113 J9**
Dêrong, *China* **58 C2**
Derry = Londonderry, *U.K.* **12 B4**
Derry = Londonderry □, *U.K.* **12 B4**
Derry, *N.H., U.S.A.* **117 D13**
Derry, *Pa., U.S.A.* **116 F5**
Derryveagh Mts., *Ireland* **12 B3**
Derudub, *Sudan* **80 D4**
Derval, *France* **18 E5**
Dervéni, *Greece* **46 C4**
Derventa, *Bos.-H.* **28 F2**
Derwent →, *Cumb., U.K.* **14 C4**
Derwent →, *Derby, U.K.* **14 E6**
Derwent →, *N. Yorks., U.K.* **14 D7**
Derwent Water, *U.K.* **14 C4**
Des Moines, *Iowa, U.S.A.* **112 E8**
Des Moines, *N. Mex., U.S.A.* **113 G3**
Des Moines →, *U.S.A.* **112 E9**
Desa, *Romania* **28 G8**
Desaguadero →, *Argentina* **126 C2**
Desaguadero →, *Bolivia* **124 G5**
Desantne, *Ukraine* **29 E14**
Desar, *Malaysia* **65 d**
Descanso, Pta., *Mexico* **111 N9**
Descartes, *France* **20 B4**
Deschaillons-sur-St-Laurent, *Canada* **105 C5**
Deschambault L., *Canada* **103 C8**
Deschutes →, *U.S.A.* **108 D3**
Dese, *Ethiopia* **81 E4**
Deseado →, *Argentina* **128 F3**
Desenzano del Garda, *Italy* **40 C7**
Desert Center, *U.S.A.* **111 M11**
Desert Hot Springs, *U.S.A.* **111 M10**
Deshnok, *India* **68 F5**
Desierto Central de Baja California ⌓, *Mexico* **118 B2**
Desna →, *Ukraine* **33 G6**
Desnătui →, *Romania* **29 G8**
Desolación, I., *Chile* **128 G2**
Despeñaperros ⌓, *Spain* **37 G7**
Despeñaperros, Paso, *Spain* **37 G7**
Despotovac, *Serbia & M.* **44 B5**
Dessau, *Germany* **24 D8**
Dessye = Dese, *Ethiopia* **81 E4**
D'Estrees B., *Australia* **95 F2**
Desuri, *India* **68 G5**
Desvres, *France* **19 B8**
Det Udom, *Thailand* **64 E5**
Deta, *Romania* **28 E6**
Dete, *Zimbabwe* **88 B4**
Đetinja →, *Serbia & M.* **44 C4**
Detmold, *Germany* **24 D4**
Detour, Pt., *U.S.A.* **114 C2**
Detroit, *U.S.A.* **116 D1**
Detroit Lakes, *U.S.A.* **112 B7**
Detva, *Slovak Rep.* **27 C12**
Deurne, *Neths.* **17 C5**
Deutsch-Luxemburgischer ⌓, *Germany* **25 F2**
Deutsche Bucht, *Germany* **24 A4**
Deutschlandsberg, *Austria* **26 E8**
Deux-Sèvres □, *France* **18 F6**
Deva, *Romania* **28 E7**
Devakottai, *India* **66 Q11**
Devaprayag, *India* **69 D8**
Dévaványa, *Hungary* **28 C5**
Deveci Dağları, *Turkey* **72 B7**
Devecikonağı, *Turkey* **45 G12**
Devecser, *Hungary* **28 C2**
Develi, *Turkey* **72 C6**
Deventer, *Neths.* **17 B6**
Deveron →, *U.K.* **13 D6**
Devesel, *Romania* **28 F7**
Devgadh Bariya, *India* **68 H5**
Devikot, *India* **68 F4**
Devils Den, *U.S.A.* **110 K7**
Devils Lake, *U.S.A.* **112 A5**
Devils Paw, *Canada* **102 B2**
Devils Postpile ⌓, *U.S.A.* **110 H7**
Devils Tower ⌓, *U.S.A.* **112 C2**
Devils Tower Junction, *U.S.A.* **112 C2**
Devin, *Bulgaria* **45 E8**
Devine, *U.S.A.* **113 L5**
Devizes, *U.K.* **15 F6**
Devli, *India* **68 G6**
Devnya, *Bulgaria* **45 C11**
Devoll →, *Albania* **44 F4**
Devon, *Canada* **102 C6**
Devon □, *U.K.* **15 G4**
Devon I., *Canada* **98 B11**
Devonport, *Australia* **95 G4**
Devonport, *N.Z.* **91 G5**
Devrek, *Turkey* **72 B4**
Devrekâni, *Turkey* **72 B5**
Devrez →, *Turkey* **72 B6**
Dewas, *India* **68 H7**
Dewetsdorp, *S. Africa* **88 D4**
Dewey, *Puerto Rico* **121 d**
Dexing, *China* **59 C11**
Dexter, *Maine, U.S.A.* **115 C11**
Dexter, *Mo., U.S.A.* **113 G10**
Dexter, *N. Mex., U.S.A.* **113 J2**
Dey-Dey, L., *Australia* **93 E5**
Deyang, *China* **58 B5**
Deyhūk, *Iran* **71 C8**
Deyyer, *Iran* **71 E6**
Dezadeash L., *Canada* **102 A1**
Dezfūl, *Iran* **71 C6**
Dezhneva, Mys, *Russia* **53 C19**
Dezhou, *China* **56 F9**
Dhadhar →, *India* **69 G11**
Dháfni, *Kríti, Greece* **49 D7**
Dháfni, *Pelóponnisos, Greece* **46 D4**
Dhahabān, *Si. Arabia* **80 C4**
Dhahiriya = Az̧ Z̧āhirīyah, *West Bank* **74 D3**
Dhahran = Az̧ Z̧ahrān, *Si. Arabia* **71 E6**
Dhak, *Pakistan* **68 C5**
Dhaka, *Bangla.* **69 H14**
Dhaka □, *Bangla.* **69 G14**
Dhali, *Cyprus* **49 D12**
Dhamási, *Greece* **46 B4**
Dhampur, *India* **69 E8**
Dhamtari, *India* **67 J12**
Dhanbad, *India* **69 H12**
Dhangarhi, *Nepal* **67 E12**
Dhankuta, *Nepal* **69 F12**
Dhar, *India* **68 H6**
Dharampur, *India* **68 H6**
Dharamsala = Dharmsala, *India* **68 C7**
Dhariwal, *India* **68 D6**
Dharla →, *Bangla.* **69 G13**
Dharmapuri, *India* **66 N11**
Dharmjaygarh, *India* **69 H10**
Dharmsala, *India* **68 C7**
Dharni, *India* **68 J7**
Dharwad, *India* **66 M9**
Dhasan →, *India* **69 G8**
Dhaulagiri, *Nepal* **69 E10**
Dhebar, L., *India* **68 G6**
Dheftera, *Cyprus* **49 D12**
Dhenkanal, *India* **67 J14**
Dhenoúsa, *Greece* **47 D7**
Dherinia, *Cyprus* **49 D12**
Dheskáti, *Greece* **44 G5**
Dhespotikó, *Greece* **46 E6**
Dhestina, *Greece* **46 C4**
Dhī Qār □, *Iraq* **70 D5**
Dhiarrizos →, *Cyprus* **49 E11**
Dhībān, *Jordan* **74 D4**
Dhidhimótikhon, *Greece* **45 E10**
Dhíkti Óros, *Greece* **49 D7**
Dhilianáta, *Greece* **46 C2**
Dhílos, *Greece* **47 D7**
Dhilwan, *India* **68 D6**
Dhimarkhera, *India* **69 H9**
Dhimitsána, *Greece* **46 D4**
Dhírfis Óros, *Greece* **46 C5**
Dhodhekánisos, *Greece* **47 E8**
Dhodhekánisos □, *Greece* **47 E8**
Dhokós, *Greece* **46 D5**
Dholiana, *Greece* **46 B2**
Dholka, *India* **68 H5**
Dhomokós, *Greece* **46 B4**
Dhoraji, *India* **68 J4**
Dhoxáton, *Greece* **45 E8**
Dhragonísi, *Greece* **47 D7**
Dhráhstis, Ákra, *Greece* **49 A3**
Dhrangadhra, *India* **68 H4**
Dhrápanon, Ákra, *Greece* **49 D6**
Dhriopís, *Greece* **46 D6**
Dhrol, *India* **68 H4**
Dhuburi, *India* **67 F16**
Dhule, *India* **66 J9**
Di-ib, W. →, *Sudan* **80 C4**
Di Linh, *Vietnam* **65 G7**
Di Linh, Cao Nguyen, *Vietnam* **65 G7**
Día, *Greece* **49 D7**
Diabakania, *Guinea* **82 C2**
Diablo, Mt., *U.S.A.* **110 H5**
Diablo Range, *U.S.A.* **110 J5**
Diafarabé, *Mali* **82 C4**
Diala, *Mali* **82 C3**
Dialakoro, *Mali* **82 C3**
Dialakoto, *Senegal* **82 C2**
Diallassagou, *Mali* **82 C4**
Diamante, *Argentina* **126 C3**

Diamante, *Italy* 43 C8
Diamante →, *Argentina* 126 C2
Diamantina, *Brazil* 125 G10
Diamantina △, *Australia* 94 C3
Diamantina →, *Australia* 95 D2
Diamantino, *Brazil* 125 F7
Diamond Bar, *U.S.A.* 111 L9
Diamond Harbour, *India* 69 H13
Diamond Is., *Australia* 94 B5
Diamond Mts., *U.S.A.* 108 G6
Diamond Springs, *U.S.A.* 110 G6
Dian Chi, *China* 58 E4
Dianalund, *Denmark* 11 J5
Dianbai, *China* 59 G8
Diancheng, *China* 59 G8
Dianjiang, *China* 58 B6
Diano Marina, *Italy* 40 E5
Dianra, *Ivory C.* 82 D3
Diapaga, *Burkina Faso* 83 C5
Diapangou, *Burkina Faso* 83 C5
Diariguila, *Guinea* 82 C2
Dībā, *U.A.E.* 71 E8
Dibai, *India* 68 E8
Dibaya-Lubue, *Dem. Rep. of the Congo* 84 E3
Dibbeen △, *Jordan* 74 C4
Dibete, *Botswana* 88 C4
Dibrugarh, *India* 67 F19
Dickens, *U.S.A.* 113 J4
Dickinson, *U.S.A.* 112 B3
Dickson, *U.S.A.* 115 G2
Dickson City, *U.S.A.* 117 E9
Dicle Nehri →, *Turkey* 73 D9
Dicomano, *Italy* 41 E8
Didesa, W. →, *Ethiopia* 81 E4
Didi, *Sudan* 81 F3
Didiéni, *Mali* 82 C3
Didsbury, *Canada* 102 C6
Didwana, *India* 68 F6
Die, *France* 21 D9
Diébougou, *Burkina Faso* 82 C4
Diecke, *Guinea* 82 D3
Diefenbaker, L., *Canada* 103 C7
Diego de Almagro, *Chile* 126 B1
Diego Garcia, *Ind. Oc.* 3 E13
Diekirch, *Lux.* 17 E6
Diéma, *Mali* 82 C3
Diembéring, *Senegal* 82 C1
Diemelsee ⌂, *Germany* 24 D4
Dien Ban, *Vietnam* 64 E7
Dien Bien, *Vietnam* 58 G4
Dien Khanh, *Vietnam* 65 F7
Diepholz, *Germany* 24 C4
Dieppe, *France* 18 C8
Dierks, *U.S.A.* 113 H8
Diest, *Belgium* 17 D5
Dietikon, *Switz.* 25 H4
Dieulefit, *France* 21 D9
Dieuze, *France* 19 D13
Dif, *Somali Rep.* 75 G3
Differdange, *Lux.* 17 E5
Dig, *India* 68 F7
Digba, *Dem. Rep. of the Congo* 86 B2
Digby, *Canada* 105 D6
Diggi, *India* 68 F6
Dighinala, *Bangla.* 67 H18
Dighton, *U.S.A.* 112 F4
Digna, *Mali* 82 C3
Digne-les-Bains, *France* 21 D10
Digoin, *France* 19 F11
Digor, *Turkey* 73 B10
Digos, *Phil.* 61 H6
Digranes, *Iceland* 8 C6
Digul →, *Indonesia* 63 F9
Digya △, *Ghana* 83 D5
Dihang = Brahmaputra →, *Asia* 69 H13
Dijlah, Nahr →, *Asia* 70 D5
Dijon, *France* 19 E12
Dikhil, *Djibouti* 81 E5
Dikili, *Turkey* 47 B8
Dikirnis, *Egypt* 80 H7
Dikkil = Dikhil, *Djibouti* 81 E5
Dikodougou, *Ivory C.* 82 D3
Diksmuide, *Belgium* 17 C2
Dikson, *Russia* 52 B9
Dikwa, *Nigeria* 83 C7
Dila, *Ethiopia* 81 F4
Dilek Yarimadisi △, *Turkey* 47 D9
Dili, *E. Timor* 63 F7
Dilijan, *Armenia* 35 K7
Dilizhan = Dilijan, *Armenia* 35 K7
Dilj, *Croatia* 28 E3
Dillenburg, *Germany* 24 E4
Dilley, *U.S.A.* 113 L5
Dilli = Delhi, *India* 68 E7
Dilling, *Sudan* 81 E2
Dillingen, *Bayern, Germany* 25 G6
Dillingen, *Saarland, Germany* 25 F2
Dillingham, *U.S.A.* 100 C4
Dillon, *Canada* 103 B7
Dillon, *Mont., U.S.A.* 108 D7
Dillon, *S.C., U.S.A.* 115 H6
Dillon →, *Canada* 103 B7
Dillsburg, *U.S.A.* 116 F7
Dilly, *Mali* 82 C3
Dilolo, *Dem. Rep. of the Congo* 84 G4
Dilove, *Ukraine* 29 C9
Dimas, *Mexico* 118 C3
Dimashq, *Syria* 74 B5
Dimashq □, *Syria* 74 B5
Dimbaza, *S. Africa* 89 E4
Dimbokro, *Ivory C.* 82 D4
Dimboola, *Australia* 95 F3
Dîmboviţa = Dâmboviţa →, *Romania* 29 F11
Dimbulah, *Australia* 94 B4
Dimitrovgrad, *Bulgaria* 45 D9
Dimitrovgrad, *Russia* 34 C9
Dimitrovgrad, *Serbia & M.* 44 C6
Dimitrovo = Pernik, *Bulgaria* 44 D7
Dimmitt, *U.S.A.* 113 H3
Dimo, *Sudan* 81 F2
Dimona, *Israel* 74 D4
Dimovo, *Bulgaria* 44 C6
Dinagat, *Phil.* 61 F6
Dinajpur, *Bangla.* 67 G16
Dinan, *France* 18 D4
Dīnān Āb, *Iran* 71 C8
Dinant, *Belgium* 17 D4
Dinapur, *India* 69 G11
Dinar, *Turkey* 47 C12
Dīnār, Kūh-e, *Iran* 71 D6
Dinara Planina, *Croatia* 41 D13
Dinard, *France* 18 D4
Dinaric Alps = Dinara Planina, *Croatia* 41 D13
Dindanko, *Mali* 82 C3
Dinder △, *Sudan* 81 E4
Dinder, Nahr ed →, *Sudan* 81 E3
Dindigul, *India* 66 P11
Dindori, *India* 69 H9
Ding Xian = Dingzhou, *China* 56 E8
Dinga, *Pakistan* 68 G2
Dingalan, *Phil.* 61 D4
Dingbian, *China* 56 F4
Dingelstädt, *Germany* 24 D6
Dingle, *Ireland* 12 D1
Dingle, *Sweden* 11 F5
Dingle B., *Ireland* 12 D1
Dingmans Ferry, *U.S.A.* 117 E10
Dingnan, *China* 59 E10
Dingo, *Australia* 94 C4
Dingolfing, *Germany* 25 G8
Dingtao, *China* 56 G8
Dinguira, *Mali* 82 C2
Dinguiraye, *Guinea* 82 C2
Dingwall, *U.K.* 13 D4
Dingxi, *China* 56 G3
Dingxiang, *China* 56 E7
Dingyuan, *China* 59 A11
Dingzhou, *China* 56 E8
Dinh, Mui, *Vietnam* 65 G7
Dinh Lap, *Vietnam* 58 G6
Dinira △, *Venezuela* 121 E6
Dinokwe, *Botswana* 88 C4
Dinorwic, *Canada* 103 D10
Dinosaur ⌂, *Canada* 102 C6
Dinosaur ⌂, *U.S.A.* 108 F9
Dinuba, *U.S.A.* 110 J7
Diö, *Sweden* 11 H8
Dioïla, *Mali* 82 C3
Dioka, *Mali* 82 C2
Diongoï, *Mali* 82 C3
Diósgyör, *Hungary* 28 B5
Diosig, *Romania* 28 C7
Diougani, *Mali* 82 C4
Diouloulou, *Senegal* 82 C1
Dioura, *Mali* 82 C3
Diourbel, *Senegal* 82 C1
Dipalpur, *Pakistan* 68 D5
Diplo, *Pakistan* 68 G3
Dipolog, *Phil.* 61 G5
Dipperu △, *Australia* 94 C4
Dir, *Pakistan* 66 B7
Diré, *Mali* 82 B4
Dire Dawa, *Ethiopia* 81 F5
Diriamba, *Nic.* 120 D2
Dirk Hartog I., *Australia* 93 E1
Dirranbandi, *Australia* 95 D4
Disa, *India* 68 G5
Disa, *Sudan* 81 E3
Disappointment, C., *U.S.A.* 108 C2
Disappointment, L., *Australia* 92 D3
Disaster B., *Australia* 95 F4
Discovery B., *Australia* 95 F3
Disentis Muster, *Switz.* 25 J4
Dishna, *Egypt* 80 B3
Disina, *Nigeria* 83 C6
Disko = Qeqertarsuaq, *Greenland* 101 B5
Disna = Dzisna →, *Belarus* 32 E5
Diss, *U.K.* 15 E9
Disteghil Sar, *Pakistan* 69 A6
Distrito Federal □, *Brazil* 125 G9
Distrito Federal □, *Mexico* 119 D5
Disûq, *Egypt* 80 H7
Diu, *India* 68 J4
Dīvāndarreh, *Iran* 70 C5
Dives →, *France* 18 C6
Dives-sur-Mer, *France* 18 C6
Divichi = Däväçi, *Azerbaijan* 35 K9
Divide, *U.S.A.* 108 D7
Dividing Ra., *Australia* 93 E2
Divinópolis, *Brazil* 125 H10
Divjake, *Albania* 44 F3
Divnoye, *Russia* 35 H6
Divo, *Ivory C.* 82 D3
Divriği, *Turkey* 73 C8
Dīwāl Kol, *Afghan.* 68 B2
Dixie Mt., *U.S.A.* 110 F6
Dixon, *Calif., U.S.A.* 110 G5
Dixon, *Ill., U.S.A.* 112 E10
Dixon Entrance, *U.S.A.* 100 C6
Dixville, *Canada* 117 A13
Diyadin, *Turkey* 73 C10
Diyālā □, *Iraq* 70 C5
Diyālā →, *Iraq* 70 C5
Diyarbakır, *Turkey* 70 B4
Diyodar, *India* 68 G4
Djakarta = Jakarta, *Indonesia* 63 G12
Djamba, *Angola* 88 B1
Djambala, *Congo* 84 E2
Djanet, *Algeria* 78 D7
Djawa = Jawa, *Indonesia* 62 F3
Djelfa, *Algeria* 78 B6
Djema, *C.A.R.* 86 A2
Djenné, *Mali* 82 C4
Djerba, I. de, *Tunisia* 79 B8
Djerid, Chott, *Tunisia* 78 B7
Djibo, *Burkina Faso* 83 C4
Djibouti, *Djibouti* 81 E5
Djibouti ■, *Africa* 81 E5
Djolu, *Dem. Rep. of the Congo* 84 D4
Djougou, *Benin* 83 D5
Djoum, *Cameroon* 84 D2
Djourab, Erg du, *Chad* 79 E9
Djugu, *Dem. Rep. of the Congo* 86 B3
Djúpivogur, *Iceland* 8 D6
Djurås, *Sweden* 10 D9
Djurö △, *Sweden* 11 F7
Djursland, *Denmark* 11 H4
Dmitriya Lapteva, Proliv, *Russia* 53 B15
Dmitriyev Lgovskiy, *Russia* 33 F8
Dmitrov, *Russia* 32 D9
Dmitrovsk-Orlovskiy, *Russia* 33 F8
Dnepr = Dnipro →, *Ukraine* 33 J7
Dneprodzerzhinsk = Dniprodzerzhynsk, *Ukraine* 33 H8
Dneprodzerzhinskoye Vdkhr. = Dniprodzerzhynske Vdskh., *Ukraine* 33 H8
Dnepropetrovsk = Dnipropetrovsk, *Ukraine* 33 H8
Dneprorudnoye = Dniprorudne, *Ukraine* 33 J8
Dnestr = Dnister →, *Europe* 33 J6
Dnieper = Dnipro →, *Ukraine* 33 J7
Dniester = Dnister →, *Europe* 33 J6
Dnipro →, *Ukraine* 33 J7
Dniprodzerzhynsk, *Ukraine* 33 H8
Dniprodzerzhynske Vdskh., *Ukraine* 33 H8
Dnipropetrovsk, *Ukraine* 33 H8
Dniprorudne, *Ukraine* 33 J8
Dnister →, *Europe* 33 J6
Dnistrovskyy Lyman, *Ukraine* 33 J6
Dno, *Russia* 32 D5
Dnyapro = Dnipro →, *Ukraine* 33 J7
Doaktown, *Canada* 105 C6
Doan Hung, *Vietnam* 58 G5
Doany, *Madag.* 89 A8
Doba, *Chad* 79 G9
Dobandi, *Pakistan* 68 D2
Dobbiaco, *Italy* 41 B9
Dobbyn, *Australia* 94 B3
Dobczyce, *Poland* 31 J7
Dobele, *Latvia* 9 H20
Dobele □, *Latvia* 30 B10
Döbeln, *Germany* 24 D9
Doberai, Jazirah, *Indonesia* 63 E8
Dobiegniew, *Poland* 31 F2
Doblas, *Argentina* 126 D3
Dobo, *Indonesia* 63 F8
Doboj, *Bos.-H.* 28 F3
Dobra, *Wielkopolskie, Poland* 31 G5
Dobra, *Zachodnio-Pomorskie, Poland* 30 E2
Dobra, *Dâmbovita, Romania* 29 F10
Dobra, *Hunedoara, Romania* 28 E7
Dobre Miasto, *Poland* 30 E7
Dobreşti, *Romania* 28 D7
Dobrich, *Bulgaria* 45 C11
Dobrinishta, *Bulgaria* 44 E7
Dobříš, *Czech Rep.* 26 B7
Dobrodzień, *Poland* 31 H5
Dobromyl, *Ukraine* 31 J9
Dobron, *Ukraine* 28 B7
Dobropole, *Ukraine* 33 H9
Dobrovolsk, *Russia* 30 D9
Dobruja, *Europe* 29 F13
Dobrush, *Belarus* 33 F6
Dobrzany, *Poland* 30 E2
Dobrzyń nad Wisłą, *Poland* 31 F6
Doc, Mui, *Vietnam* 64 D6
Docker River, *Australia* 93 D4
Docksta, *Sweden* 10 A12
Doctor Arroyo, *Mexico* 118 C4
Doda, *India* 69 C6
Doda, L., *Canada* 104 C4
Dodecanese = Dhodhekánisos, *Greece* 47 E8
Dodge City, *U.S.A.* 113 G5
Dodge L., *Canada* 103 B7
Dodgeville, *U.S.A.* 112 D9
Dodo, *Cameroon* 83 D7
Dodo, *Sudan* 81 F2
Dodola, *Ethiopia* 81 F4
Dodoma, *Tanzania* 86 D4
Dodoma □, *Tanzania* 86 D4
Dodona, *Greece* 46 B2
Dodori ⌂, *Kenya* 86 C5
Dodsland, *Canada* 103 C7
Dodson, *U.S.A.* 108 B9
Dodurga, *Turkey* 47 B11
Doesburg, *Neths.* 17 B6
Doetinchem, *Neths.* 17 C6
Dog Creek, *Canada* 102 C4
Dog L., *Man., Canada* 103 C9
Dog L., *Ont., Canada* 104 C2
Doğanşehir, *Turkey* 72 C7
Dogliani, *Italy* 40 D4
Dogondoutchi, *Niger* 83 C5
Dogran, *Pakistan* 68 D5
Doğubayazıt, *Turkey* 70 B5
Doguéraoua, *Niger* 83 C6
Doha = Ad Dawḩah, *Qatar* 71 E6
Dohazari, *Bangla.* 67 H18
Dohrighat, *India* 69 F10
Doi, *Indonesia* 63 D7
Doi Inthanon △, *Thailand* 64 C2
Doi Khuntan △, *Thailand* 64 C2
Doi Luang, *Thailand* 64 C3
Doi Luang △, *Thailand* 64 C2
Doi Saket, *Thailand* 64 C2
Doi Suthep △, *Thailand* 64 C2
Dois Irmãos, Sa., *Brazil* 125 E10
Dojransko Jezero, *Macedonia* 44 E6
Dokkum, *Neths.* 17 A5
Dokri, *Pakistan* 68 F3
Dokuchayevsk, *Ukraine* 33 J9
Dol-de-Bretagne, *France* 18 D5
Dolac, *Serbia & M.* 44 D4
Dolak, Pulau, *Indonesia* 63 F9
Dolbeau-Mistassini, *Canada* 105 C5
Dole, *France* 19 E12
Doleib, Wadi →, *Sudan* 81 E3
Dolenji Logatec, *Slovenia* 41 C11
Dolgellau, *U.K.* 14 E4
Dolgelley = Dolgellau, *U.K.* 14 E4
Dolhasca, *Romania* 29 C11
Dolianova, *Italy* 42 C2
Dolinskaya = Dolynska, *Ukraine* 33 H7
Dolj □, *Romania* 29 F8
Dollard, *Neths.* 17 A7
Dolna Banya, *Bulgaria* 44 D7
Dolni Chiflik, *Bulgaria* 45 D11
Dolni Dŭbnik, *Bulgaria* 45 C8
Dolnośląskie □, *Poland* 31 G3
Dolný Kubín, *Slovak Rep.* 27 B12
Dolo, *Ethiopia* 81 G5
Dolo, *Italy* 41 C9
Dolomites = Dolomiti, *Italy* 41 B8
Dolomiti, *Italy* 41 B8
Dolomiti Bellunesi △, *Italy* 41 B9
Dolores, *Argentina* 126 D4
Dolores, *Uruguay* 126 C4
Dolores, *U.S.A.* 109 H9
Dolores →, *U.S.A.* 109 G9
Dolovo, *Serbia & M.* 28 F5
Dolphin, C., *Falk. Is.* 128 G5
Dolphin and Union Str., *Canada* 100 B8
Dolsk, *Poland* 31 G4
Dolyna, *Ukraine* 29 B9
Dolynska, *Ukraine* 33 H7
Dolynske, *Ukraine* 29 C14
Dolzhanskaya, *Russia* 33 J9
Dom Pedrito, *Brazil* 127 C5
Doma, *Nigeria* 83 D6
Doma ⌂, *Zimbabwe* 87 F3
Domaniç, *Turkey* 47 B11
Domariaganj →, *India* 69 F10
Domasi, *Malawi* 87 F4
Domažlice, *Czech Rep.* 26 B5
Dombarovskiy, *Russia* 52 D6
Dombås, *Norway* 9 E13
Dombasle-sur-Meurthe, *France* 19 D13
Dombes, *France* 21 C9
Dombóvár, *Hungary* 28 D3
Dombrád, *Hungary* 28 B6
Domel I. = Letsôk-aw Kyun, *Burma* 65 G2
Domérat, *France* 19 F9
Domeyko, *Chile* 126 B1
Domeyko, Cordillera, *Chile* 126 A2
Domfront, *France* 18 D6
Dominador, *Chile* 126 A2
Dominica ■, *W. Indies* 121 C7
Dominica Passage, *W. Indies* 121 C7
Dominican Rep. ■, *W. Indies* 121 C5
Dömitz, *Germany* 24 B7
Domme, *France* 20 D5
Domneşti, *Romania* 29 E9
Domodóssola, *Italy* 40 B5
Domogled-Valea Cernei △, *Romania* 28 F7
Dompaire, *France* 19 D13
Dompierre-sur-Besbre, *France* 19 F10
Dompim, *Ghana* 82 D4
Domrémy-la-Pucelle, *France* 19 D12
Domville, Mt., *Australia* 95 D5
Domvraína, *Greece* 46 C4
Domžale, *Slovenia* 41 B11
Don →, *Russia* 33 J10
Don →, *Aberds., U.K.* 13 D6
Don →, *S. Yorks., U.K.* 14 D7
Don, C., *Australia* 92 B5
Don Benito, *Spain* 37 G5
Don Figuerero Mts., *Jamaica* 120 a
Don Sak, *Thailand* 65 b
Dona Ana = Nhamaabué, *Mozam.* 87 F4
Doña Mencía, *Spain* 37 H6
Donaghadee, *U.K.* 12 B6
Donald, *Australia* 95 F3
Donaldsonville, *U.S.A.* 113 K9
Donalsonville, *U.S.A.* 115 K3
Doñana △, *Spain* 37 J4
Donau = Dunărea →, *Europe* 29 E14
Donau →, *Austria* 27 C10
Donau Auen △, *Austria* 27 C9
Donaueschingen, *Germany* 25 H4
Donauwörth, *Germany* 25 G6
Doncaster, *U.K.* 14 D6
Dondo, *Mozam.* 87 F3
Dondo, Teluk, *Indonesia* 63 D6
Dondra Head, *Sri Lanka* 66 S12
Donduşeni, *Moldova* 29 B12
Donegal, *Ireland* 12 B3
Donegal □, *Ireland* 12 B4
Donegal B., *Ireland* 12 B3
Donets →, *Russia* 35 G5
Donets Basin, *Ukraine* 6 F13
Donetsk, *Ukraine* 33 J9
Dong Ba Thin, *Vietnam* 65 F7
Dong Dang, *Vietnam* 58 G6
Dong Giam, *Vietnam* 64 C5
Dong Ha, *Vietnam* 64 D6
Dong Hene, *Laos* 64 D5
Dong Hoi, *Vietnam* 64 D6
Dong Jiang →, *China* 59 F10
Dong Khe, *Vietnam* 64 A6
Dong Ujimqin Qi, *China* 56 B9
Dong Van, *Vietnam* 64 A5
Dong Xoai, *Vietnam* 65 G6
Donga, *Nigeria* 83 D7
Donga →, *Nigeria* 83 D7
Dong'an, *China* 59 D8
Dongara, *Australia* 93 E1
Dongbei, *China* 53 E13
Dongchuan, *China* 58 D4
Donges, *France* 18 E4
Dongfang, *China* 64 C7
Dongfeng, *China* 57 C13
Donggala, *Indonesia* 63 E5
Donggan, *China* 58 F5
Donggou, *China* 57 E13
Dongguan, *China* 59 F9
Dongguang, *China* 56 F9
Donghai Dao, *China* 59 G8
Dongjingcheng, *China* 57 B15
Dongkou, *China* 59 D8
Donglan, *China* 58 E6
Dongliu, *China* 59 B11
Dongmen, *China* 58 F6
Dongning, *China* 57 B16
Dongnyi, *China* 58 C3
Dongola, *Sudan* 80 D3
Dongping, *China* 56 G9
Dongsha Dao, *China* 59 G11
Dongshan, *China* 59 F11
Dongsheng, *China* 56 E6
Dongtai, *China* 57 H11
Dongting Hu, *China* 59 C9
Dongtou, *China* 59 D13
Dongxiang, *China* 59 C11
Dongxing, *China* 58 G7
Dongyang, *China* 59 C13
Dongzhi, *China* 59 B11
Donington, C., *Australia* 95 E2
Doniphan, *U.S.A.* 113 G9
Donja Stubica, *Croatia* 41 C12
Donji Dušnik, *Serbia & M.* 44 C6
Donji Miholjac, *Croatia* 28 E3
Donji Milanovac, *Serbia & M.* 44 B6
Donji Vakuf, *Bos.-H.* 28 F2
Dønna, *Norway* 8 C15
Donna, *U.S.A.* 113 M5
Donnacona, *Canada* 105 C5
Donnelly's Crossing, *N.Z.* 91 F4
Donnybrook, *Australia* 93 F2
Donnybrook, *S. Africa* 89 D4
Donora, *U.S.A.* 116 F5
Donostia = Donostia-San Sebastián, *Spain* 38 B3
Donostia-San Sebastián, *Spain* 38 B3
Donskoy, *Russia* 32 F10
Donsol, *Phil.* 61 E5
Donzère, *France* 21 D8
Donzy, *France* 19 E10
Doon →, *U.K.* 13 F4
Dora, L., *Australia* 92 D3
Dora Báltea →, *Italy* 40 C5
Dora Ripária →, *Italy* 40 C4
Doran L., *Canada* 103 A7
Dorchester, *U.K.* 15 G5
Dorchester, C., *Canada* 101 B12
Dordabis, *Namibia* 88 C2
Dordogne □, *France* 20 C4
Dordogne →, *France* 20 C3
Dordrecht, *Neths.* 17 C4
Dordrecht, *S. Africa* 88 E4
Dore →, *France* 20 C7
Dore, Mts., *France* 20 C6
Doré L., *Canada* 103 C7
Doré Lake, *Canada* 103 C7
Dorfen, *Germany* 25 G8
Dorgali, *Italy* 42 B2
Dori, *Burkina Faso* 83 C4
Doring →, *S. Africa* 88 E2
Doringbos, *S. Africa* 88 E2
Dorking, *U.K.* 15 F7
Dormaa-Ahenkro, *Ghana* 82 D4
Dormans, *France* 19 C10
Dormo, Ras, *Eritrea* 81 E5
Dornbirn, *Austria* 26 D2
Dornes, *France* 19 F10
Dorneşti, *Romania* 29 C11
Dornie, *U.K.* 13 D3
Dornoch, *U.K.* 13 D4
Dornoch Firth, *U.K.* 13 D4
Dornogovĭ □, *Mongolia* 56 C6
Doro, *Mali* 83 B4
Dorog, *Hungary* 28 C3
Dorogobuzh, *Russia* 32 E7
Dorohoi, *Romania* 29 C11
Döröö Nuur, *Mongolia* 60 B4
Dorr, *Iran* 71 C6
Dorre I., *Australia* 93 E1
Dorrigo, *Australia* 95 E5
Dorris, *U.S.A.* 108 F3
Dorset, *Canada* 116 A6
Dorset, *U.S.A.* 116 E4
Dorset □, *U.K.* 15 G5
Dorsten, *Germany* 24 D2
Dortmund, *Germany* 24 D3
Dortmund-Ems-Kanal →, *Germany* 24 D3
Dörtyol, *Turkey* 72 D7
Dorum, *Germany* 24 B4
Doruma, *Dem. Rep. of the Congo* 86 B2
Dorūneh, *Iran* 71 C8
Dos Bahías, C., *Argentina* 128 E3
Dos Hermanas, *Spain* 37 H5
Dos Palos, *U.S.A.* 110 J6
Döşemealtı, *Turkey* 47 D12
Dosso, *Niger* 83 C5
Dosso ⌂, *Niger* 83 C5
Dothan, *U.S.A.* 115 K3
Doty, *U.S.A.* 110 D3
Douai, *France* 19 B10
Douako, *Guinea* 82 D2
Douala, *Cameroon* 83 E6
Douarnenez, *France* 18 D2
Doubabougou, *Mali* 82 C3
Double Island Pt., *Australia* 95 D5
Double Mountain Fork →, *U.S.A.* 113 J4
Doubrava →, *Czech Rep.* 26 A8
Doubs □, *France* 19 E13
Doubs →, *France* 19 F12
Doubtful Sd., *N.Z.* 91 L1
Doubtless B., *N.Z.* 91 F4
Doudeville, *France* 18 C7
Doué-la-Fontaine, *France* 18 E6
Douentza, *Mali* 82 C4
Douentza ⌂, *Mali* 82 B4
Douglas, *I. of Man* 14 C3
Douglas, *S. Africa* 88 D3
Douglas, *Ariz., U.S.A.* 109 L9
Douglas, *Ga., U.S.A.* 115 K4

Douglas, *Wyo., U.S.A.* 112 D2
Douglas Apsley △, *Australia* 95 G4
Douglas Chan., *Canada* 102 C3
Douglas Pt., *Canada* 116 B3
Douglasville, *U.S.A.* 115 J3
Doukáton, Ákra, *Greece* 46 C2
Doulevant-le-Château, *France* 19 D11
Doullens, *France* 19 B9
Doumen, *China* 59 F9
Douna, *Mali* 82 C3
Dounreay, *U.K.* 13 C5
Dourada, Serra, *Brazil* 125 F9
Dourados, *Brazil* 127 A5
Dourados →, *Brazil* 127 A5
Dourados, Serra dos, *Brazil* 127 A5
Dourdan, *France* 19 D9
Douro →, *Europe* 36 D2
Douvaine, *France* 19 F13
Douvres-la-Délivrande, *France* 18 C6
Douze →, *France* 20 E3
Dove →, *U.K.* 14 E6
Dove Creek, *U.S.A.* 109 H9
Dover, *Australia* 95 G4
Dover, *U.K.* 15 F9
Dover, *Del., U.S.A.* 114 F8
Dover, *N.H., U.S.A.* 117 C14
Dover, *N.J., U.S.A.* 117 F10
Dover, *Ohio, U.S.A.* 116 F3
Dover, Pt., *Australia* 93 F4
Dover, Str. of, *Europe* 15 G9
Dover-Foxcroft, *U.S.A.* 115 C11
Dover Plains, *U.S.A.* 117 E11
Dovey = Dyfi →, *U.K.* 15 E3
Dovhe, *Ukraine* 29 B8
Dovrefjell, *Norway* 9 E13
Dow Rūd, *Iran* 71 C6
Dowa, *Malawi* 87 E3
Dowagiac, *U.S.A.* 114 E2
Dowerin, *Australia* 93 F2
Dowgha'i, *Iran* 71 B8
Dowlatābād, *Iran* 71 D8
Down □, *U.K.* 12 B5
Downey, *Calif., U.S.A.* 111 M8
Downey, *Idaho, U.S.A.* 108 E7
Downham Market, *U.K.* 15 E8
Downieville, *U.S.A.* 110 F6
Downpatrick, *U.K.* 12 B6
Downpatrick Hd., *Ireland* 12 B2
Downsville, *U.S.A.* 117 D10
Downton, Mt., *Canada* 102 C4
Dowsārī, *Iran* 71 D8
Doyle, *U.S.A.* 110 E6
Doylestown, *U.S.A.* 117 F9
Dozois, Rés., *Canada* 104 C4
Dra Khel, *Pakistan* 68 F2
Drac →, *France* 21 C9
Dračevo, *Macedonia* 44 E5
Drachten, *Neths.* 17 A6
Drăgăneşti, *Moldova* 29 C13
Drăgăneşti-Olt, *Romania* 29 F9
Drăgăneşti-Vlaşca, *Romania* 29 F10
Dragaš, *Serbia & M.* 44 D4
Drăgăşani, *Romania* 29 F9
Dragichyn, *Belarus* 33 F3
Dragocvet, *Serbia & M.* 44 C5
Dragon's Mouth = Boca de Drago, *Venezuela* 125 K15
Dragovishtitsa, *Bulgaria* 44 D6
Draguignan, *France* 21 E10
Drahove, *Ukraine* 29 B8
Drain, *U.S.A.* 108 E2
Drake, *U.S.A.* 112 B4
Drake Passage, *S. Ocean* 5 B17
Drakensberg, *S. Africa* 89 D4
Dráma, *Greece* 45 E8
Dráma □, *Greece* 45 E8
Drammen, *Norway* 9 G14
Drangajökull, *Iceland* 8 C2
Dranov, Ostrov, *Romania* 29 F14
Dras, *India* 69 B6
Drau = Drava →, *Croatia* 28 E3
Drava →, *Croatia* 28 E3
Dravograd, *Slovenia* 41 B12
Drawa →, *Poland* 31 F2
Drawieński △, *Poland* 31 E2
Drawno, *Poland* 31 E2
Drawsko Pomorskie, *Poland* 30 E2
Drayton Valley, *Canada* 102 C6
Dreieich, *Germany* 25 E4
Dren, *Serbia & M.* 44 C4
Drenthe □, *Neths.* 17 B6
Drepanum, C., *Cyprus* 49 E11
Dresden, *Canada* 116 D2
Dresden, *Germany* 24 D9
Dreux, *France* 18 D8
Drezdenko, *Poland* 31 F2
Driffield, *U.K.* 14 C7
Driftwood, *U.S.A.* 116 E6
Driggs, *U.S.A.* 108 E8
Drin →, *Albania* 44 D3
Drin i Zi →, *Albania* 44 E4
Drina →, *Bos.-H.* 44 B3
Drincea →, *Romania* 28 F7
Drinjača →, *Bos.-H.* 28 F4
Drissa = Vyerkhnyadzvinsk, *Belarus* 32 E4
Drniš, *Croatia* 41 E13
Drøbak, *Norway* 9 G14
Drobeta-Turnu Severin, *Romania* 28 F7
Drobin, *Poland* 31 F6
Drochia, *Moldova* 29 B12
Drogheda, *Ireland* 12 C5
Drogichin = Dragichyn, *Belarus* 33 F3
Drogobych = Drohobych, *Ukraine* 31 J10
Drohiczyn, *Poland* 31 F9
Drohobych, *Ukraine* 31 J10
Droichead Atha = Drogheda, *Ireland* 12 C5
Droichead Nua, *Ireland* 12 C5
Droitwich, *U.K.* 15 E5
Drôme □, *France* 21 D9
Drôme →, *France* 21 D8
Dromedary, C., *Australia* 95 F5
Drömling ⌓, *Germany* 24 C7
Dromore, *U.K.* 12 B4
Dromore West, *Ireland* 12 B3
Dronero, *Italy* 40 D4
Dronfield, *U.K.* 14 D6
Dronne →, *France* 20 C3
Dronning Maud Land, *Antarctica* 5 D3
Dronninglund, *Denmark* 11 G4
Dronten, *Neths.* 17 B5
Dropt →, *France* 20 D3
Drosendorf, *Austria* 26 C8
Droué, *France* 18 D8
Drumbo, *Canada* 116 C4
Drumheller, *Canada* 102 C6
Drummond, *U.S.A.* 108 C7
Drummond I., *U.S.A.* 114 C4
Drummond Pt., *Australia* 95 E2
Drummond Ra., *Australia* 94 C4
Drummondville, *Canada* 104 C5
Drumright, *U.S.A.* 113 H6
Druskininkai, *Lithuania* 9 J20
Drut →, *Belarus* 33 F6
Druya, *Belarus* 32 E4
Druzhba, *Bulgaria* 45 C12
Druzhina, *Russia* 53 C15
Drvar, *Bos.-H.* 41 D13
Drvenik, *Croatia* 41 E13
Drwęca →, *Poland* 31 E5
Dry Harbour Mts., *Jamaica* 120 a
Dry Tortugas, *U.S.A.* 120 B3
Dryanovo, *Bulgaria* 45 D9
Dryden, *Canada* 103 D10
Dryden, *U.S.A.* 117 D8
Drygalski I., *Antarctica* 5 C7
Drysdale →, *Australia* 92 B4
Drysdale I., *Australia* 94 A2
Drysdale River △, *Australia* 92 B4
Drzewica, *Poland* 31 G7
Drzewiczka →, *Poland* 31 G7
Dschang, *Cameroon* 83 D7
Du Bois, *U.S.A.* 116 E6
Du Gué →, *Canada* 104 A5
Du He, *China* 59 A8
Du Quoin, *U.S.A.* 112 G10
Du'an, *China* 58 F7
Duanesburg, *U.S.A.* 117 D10
Duaringa, *Australia* 94 C4
Duarte, Pico, *Dom. Rep.* 121 D5
Ḍubā, *Si. Arabia* 70 E2
Dubai = Dubayy, *U.A.E.* 71 E7
Dubăsari, *Moldova* 29 C14
Dubăsari Vdkhr., *Moldova* 29 C13
Dubawnt →, *Canada* 103 A8
Dubawnt L., *Canada* 103 A8
Dubayy, *U.A.E.* 71 E7
Dubbo, *Australia* 95 E4
Dubele, *Dem. Rep. of the Congo* 86 B2
Dübendorf, *Switz.* 25 H4
Dubica, *Croatia* 41 C13
Dublin, *Ireland* 12 C5
Dublin, *Ga., U.S.A.* 115 J4
Dublin, *Tex., U.S.A.* 113 J5
Dublin □, *Ireland* 12 C5
Dublin ✕ (DUB), *Ireland* 12 C5
Dubna, *Russia* 32 D9
Dubnica nad Váhom, *Slovak Rep.* 27 C11
Dubno, *Ukraine* 33 G3
Dubois, *U.S.A.* 108 D7
Dubossary = Dubăsari, *Moldova* 29 C14
Dubossary Vdkhr. = Dubăsari Vdkhr., *Moldova* 29 C13
Dubove, *Ukraine* 29 B8
Dubovka, *Russia* 35 F7
Dubovskoye, *Russia* 35 G6
Dubrajpur, *India* 69 H12
Dubréka, *Guinea* 82 D2
Dubrovitsa = Dubrovytsya, *Ukraine* 33 G4
Dubrovnik, *Croatia* 44 D2
Dubrovytsya, *Ukraine* 33 G4
Dubuque, *U.S.A.* 112 D9
Dubysa →, *Lithuania* 30 C10
Duchang, *China* 59 C11
Duchesne, *U.S.A.* 108 F8
Duchess, *Australia* 94 C2
Ducie I., *Pac. Oc.* 97 K15
Duck →, *U.S.A.* 115 G2
Duck Cr. →, *Australia* 92 D2
Duck Lake, *Canada* 103 C7
Duck Mountain ⌓, *Canada* 103 C8
Duckwall, Mt., *U.S.A.* 110 H6
Duderstadt, *Germany* 24 D6
Dudhi, *India* 67 G13
Dudinka, *Russia* 53 C9
Dudley, *U.K.* 15 E5
Dudwa, *India* 69 E9
Duékoué, *Ivory C.* 82 D3
Dueñas, *Spain* 36 D6
Duero = Douro →, *Europe* 36 D2
Dufftown, *U.K.* 13 D5
Dufourspitz, *Switz.* 25 K3
Dūghī Kalā, *Afghan.* 66 C3
Dugi Otok, *Croatia* 41 D11
Dugo Selo, *Croatia* 41 C13
Duifken Pt., *Australia* 94 A3
Duisburg, *Germany* 24 D2
Duiwelskloof, *S. Africa* 89 C5
Dujiangyan, *China* 58 B4
Duk Fadiat, *Sudan* 81 F3
Duk Faiwil, *Sudan* 81 F3
Dukat, *Albania* 44 F3
Dūkdamīn, *Iran* 71 C8
Dukelský Průsmyk, *Slovak Rep.* 27 B14
Dukhān, *Qatar* 71 E6
Dukhovshchina, *Russia* 32 E7
Duki, *Pakistan* 66 D6
Dukla, *Poland* 31 J8
Duku, *Bauchi, Nigeria* 83 C7
Duku, *Sokoto, Nigeria* 83 C5
Dulag, *Phil.* 61 F6
Dulce, *U.S.A.* 109 H10
Dulce →, *Argentina* 126 C3
Dulce, G., *Costa Rica* 120 E3
Dulf, *Iraq* 70 C5
Dŭlgopol, *Bulgaria* 45 C11
Dulit, Banjaran, *Malaysia* 62 D4
Duliu, *China* 56 E9
Dullewala, *Pakistan* 68 D4
Dullstroom, *S. Africa* 89 D5
Dülmen, *Germany* 24 D3
Dulovo, *Bulgaria* 45 C11
Dulq Maghār, *Syria* 70 B3
Duluth, *U.S.A.* 112 B8
Dum Dum, *India* 69 H13
Dum Duma, *India* 67 F19
Dūmā, *Syria* 74 B5
Dumaguete, *Phil.* 61 G5
Dumai, *Indonesia* 62 D2
Dumaran, *Phil.* 61 F3
Dumas, *Ark., U.S.A.* 113 J9
Dumas, *Tex., U.S.A.* 113 H4
Ḍumayr, *Syria* 74 B5
Dumbarton, *U.K.* 13 F4
Ďumbier, *Slovak Rep.* 27 C12
Dumbleyung, *Australia* 93 F2
Dumboa, *Nigeria* 83 C7
Dumbrăveni, *Romania* 29 D9
Dumfries, *U.K.* 13 F5
Dumfries & Galloway □, *U.K.* 13 F5
Dumitreşti, *Romania* 29 E11
Dumka, *India* 69 G12
Dumlupınar, *Turkey* 47 C12
Dümmer, *Germany* 24 C4
Dümmer ⌓, *Germany* 24 C4
Dumoine →, *Canada* 104 C4
Dumoine, L., *Canada* 104 C4
Dumont d'Urville, *Antarctica* 5 C10
Dumraon, *India* 69 G11
Dumyât, *Egypt* 80 H7
Dumyât, Masabb, *Egypt* 80 H7
Dún Dealgan = Dundalk, *Ireland* 12 B5
Dún Laoghaire, *Ireland* 12 C5
Dun-le-Palestel, *France* 19 F8
Dun-sur-Auron, *France* 19 F9
Dun-sur-Meuse, *France* 19 C12
Duna = Dunărea →, *Europe* 29 E14
Duna →, *Hungary* 28 E3
Duna-Drava △, *Hungary* 28 D3
Duna-völgyi-főcsatorna, *Hungary* 28 D4
Dunaföldvár, *Hungary* 28 D3
Dunagiri, *India* 69 D8
Dunaj = Dunărea →, *Europe* 29 E14
Dunaj →, *Slovak Rep.* 27 D11
Dunajec →, *Poland* 31 H7
Dunajská Streda, *Slovak Rep.* 27 C10
Dunakeszi, *Hungary* 28 C4
Dunapataj, *Hungary* 28 D4
Dunărea →, *Europe* 29 E14
Dunaszekcső, *Hungary* 28 D3
Dunaújváros, *Hungary* 28 D3
Dunav = Dunărea →, *Europe* 29 E14
Dunavaţu de Jos, *Romania* 29 F14
Dunavtsi, *Bulgaria* 44 C6
Dunay, *Russia* 54 C6
Dunayivtsi, *Ukraine* 29 B11
Dunback, *N.Z.* 91 L3
Dunbar, *U.K.* 13 E6
Dunblane, *U.K.* 13 E5
Duncan, *Canada* 102 D4
Duncan, *Ariz., U.S.A.* 109 K9
Duncan, *Okla., U.S.A.* 113 H6
Duncan, L., *Canada* 104 B4
Duncan L., *Canada* 102 A6
Duncan Town, *Bahamas* 120 B4
Duncannon, *U.S.A.* 116 F7
Duncansby Head, *U.K.* 13 C5
Duncansville, *U.S.A.* 116 F6
Dundaga, *Latvia* 30 A9
Dundalk, *Canada* 116 B4
Dundalk, *Ireland* 12 B5
Dundalk, *U.S.A.* 114 F7
Dundalk Bay, *Ireland* 12 C5
Dundas = Uummannaq, *Greenland* 4 B4
Dundas = Uummannaq, *Greenland* 4 B5
Dundas, *Canada* 116 C5
Dundas, L., *Australia* 93 F3
Dundas I., *Canada* 102 C2
Dundas Str., *Australia* 92 B5
Dundee, *S. Africa* 89 D5
Dundee, *U.K.* 13 E6
Dundee, *U.S.A.* 116 D8
Dundee City □, *U.K.* 13 E6
Dundgovĭ □, *Mongolia* 56 B4
Dundrum, *U.K.* 12 B6
Dundrum B., *U.K.* 12 B6
Dunedin, *N.Z.* 91 L3
Dunedin, *U.S.A.* 115 L4
Dunfermline, *U.K.* 13 E5
Dungannon, *Canada* 116 C3
Dungannon, *U.K.* 12 B5
Dungarpur, *India* 68 H5
Dungarvan, *Ireland* 12 D4
Dungarvan Harbour, *Ireland* 12 D4
Dungeness, *U.K.* 15 G8
Dungo, L. do, *Angola* 88 B2
Dungog, *Australia* 95 E5
Dungu, *Dem. Rep. of the Congo* 86 B2
Dungun, *Malaysia* 65 K4
Dungunâb, *Sudan* 80 C4
Dungunâb, Khalîg, *Sudan* 80 C4
Dunhua, *China* 57 C15
Dunhuang, *China* 60 B4
Dunk I., *Australia* 94 B4
Dunkassa, *Benin* 83 C5
Dunkeld, *Australia* 95 E4
Dunkeld, *U.K.* 13 E5
Dunkerque, *France* 19 A9
Dunkery Beacon, *U.K.* 15 F4
Dunkirk = Dunkerque, *France* 19 A9
Dunkirk, *U.S.A.* 116 D5
Dunkuj, *Sudan* 81 E3
Dunkwa, *Central, Ghana* 82 D4
Dunkwa, *Central, Ghana* 83 D4
Dúnleary = Dún Laoghaire, *Ireland* 12 C5
Dunleer, *Ireland* 12 C5
Dunmanus B., *Ireland* 12 E2
Dunmanway, *Ireland* 12 E2
Dunmara, *Australia* 94 B1
Dunmore, *U.S.A.* 117 E9
Dunmore Hd., *Ireland* 12 D1
Dunmore Town, *Bahamas* 120 A4
Dunn, *U.S.A.* 115 H6
Dunnellon, *U.S.A.* 115 L4
Dunnet Hd., *U.K.* 13 C5
Dunning, *U.S.A.* 112 E4
Dunnville, *Canada* 116 D5
Dunolly, *Australia* 95 F3
Dunoon, *U.K.* 13 F4
Dunphy, *U.S.A.* 108 F5
Dunqul, *Egypt* 80 C3
Duns, *U.K.* 13 F6
Dunseith, *U.S.A.* 112 A4
Dunsmuir, *U.S.A.* 108 F2
Dunstable, *U.K.* 15 F7
Dunstan Mts., *N.Z.* 91 L2
Dunster, *Canada* 102 C5
Dunvegan, *U.K.* 13 D2
Dunvegan L., *Canada* 103 A7
Duolun, *China* 56 C9
Duong Dong, *Vietnam* 65 G4
Dupree, *U.S.A.* 112 C4
Dupuyer, *U.S.A.* 108 B7
Duque de Caxias, *Brazil* 127 A7
Durack →, *Australia* 92 C4
Durack Ra., *Australia* 92 C4
Durağan, *Turkey* 72 B6
Durak, *Turkey* 47 B10
Đurakovac, *Serbia & M.* 44 D4
Durance →, *France* 21 E8
Durand, *U.S.A.* 112 C9
Durango, *Mexico* 118 C4
Durango, *Spain* 38 B2
Durango, *U.S.A.* 109 H10
Durango □, *Mexico* 118 C4
Durankulak, *Bulgaria* 45 C12
Durant, *Miss., U.S.A.* 113 J10
Durant, *Okla., U.S.A.* 113 J6
Duratón →, *Spain* 36 D6
Durazno, *Uruguay* 126 C4
Durazzo = Durrës, *Albania* 44 E3
Durban, *France* 20 F6
Durban, *S. Africa* 89 D5
Durbuy, *Belgium* 17 D5
Dúrcal, *Spain* 37 J7
Đurđevac, *Croatia* 28 D2
Düren, *Germany* 24 E2
Durg, *India* 67 J12
Durgapur, *India* 69 H12
Durham, *Canada* 116 B4
Durham, *U.K.* 14 C6
Durham, *Calif., U.S.A.* 110 F5
Durham, *N.C., U.S.A.* 115 H6
Durham, *N.H., U.S.A.* 117 C14
Durham □, *U.K.* 14 C6
Durleşti, *Moldova* 29 C13
Ḍurmā, *Si. Arabia* 70 E5
Durmitor, *Serbia & M.* 44 C2
Durmitor △, *Serbia & M.* 44 C3
Durness, *U.K.* 13 C4
Durrës, *Albania* 44 E3
Durrow, *Ireland* 12 D4
Dursey I., *Ireland* 12 E1
Dursley, *U.K.* 15 F5
Dursunbey, *Turkey* 47 B10
Durtal, *France* 18 E6
Duru, *Dem. Rep. of the Congo* 86 B2
Duru Gölü, *Turkey* 45 E12
Durusu, *Turkey* 45 E12
Durūz, Jabal ad, *Jordan* 74 C5
D'Urville, Tanjung, *Indonesia* 63 E9
D'Urville I., *N.Z.* 91 J4
Duryea, *U.S.A.* 117 E9
Dûsh, *Egypt* 80 C3
Dushak, *Turkmenistan* 52 F7
Dushan, *China* 58 E6
Dushanbe, *Tajikistan* 52 F7
Dusheti, *Georgia* 35 J7
Dushore, *U.S.A.* 117 E8
Dusky Sd., *N.Z.* 91 L1
Dussejour, C., *Australia* 92 B4
Düsseldorf, *Germany* 24 D2
Düsseldorf Rhein-Ruhr ✕ (DUS), *Germany* 24 D2
Duszniki-Zdrój, *Poland* 31 H3
Dutch Harbor, *U.S.A.* 100 C3
Dutlwe, *Botswana* 88 C3
Dutsan Wai, *Nigeria* 83 C6
Dutton, *Canada* 116 D3
Dutton →, *Australia* 94 C3
Duved, *Sweden* 10 A6
Düvertepe, *Turkey* 47 B10
Duwayhin, Khawr, *U.A.E.* 71 E6
Duyun, *China* 58 D6
Düzağaç, *Turkey* 47 C12
Düzce, *Turkey* 72 B4
Dve Mogili, *Bulgaria* 45 C9
Dvina, Severnaya →, *Russia* 52 C5
Dvinsk = Daugavpils, *Latvia* 9 J22
Dvor, *Croatia* 41 C13
Dvůr Králové nad Labem, *Czech Rep.* 26 A8
Dwarka, *India* 68 H3
Dwellingup, *Australia* 93 F2
Dwight, *Canada* 116 A5
Dwight, *U.S.A.* 114 E1
Dyakove, *Ukraine* 28 B7
Dyatkovo, *Russia* 32 F8
Dyatlovo = Dzyatlava, *Belarus* 32 F3
Dyce, *U.K.* 13 D6
Dyer, C., *Canada* 101 B13
Dyer Bay, *Canada* 116 A3
Dyer Plateau, *Antarctica* 5 D17
Dyersburg, *U.S.A.* 113 G10
Dyfi →, *U.K.* 15 E3
Dyje →, *Czech Rep.* 27 C9
Dymer, *Ukraine* 33 G6
Dynów, *Poland* 31 J9
Dysart, *Australia* 94 C4
Dyviziya 29 E14
Dzerzhinsk, *Russia* 34 B6
Dzhalinda, *Russia* 53 D13
Dzhambul = Taraz, *Kazakhstan* 52 E8
Dzhankoy, *Ukraine* 33 K8
Dzhanybek, *Kazakhstan* 34 F8
Dzharylhach, Ostriv, *Ukraine* 33 J7
Dzhezkazgan = Zhezqazghan, *Kazakhstan* 52 E7
Dzhizak = Jizzakh, *Uzbekistan* 52 E7
Dzhugdzur, Khrebet, *Russia* 53 D14
Dzhulynk, *Ukraine* 29 B14
Dzhuryn, *Ukraine* 29 B13
Dzhvari = Jvari, *Georgia* 35 J6
Działdowo, *Poland* 31 E7
Działoszyce, *Poland* 31 H7
Działoszyn, *Poland* 31 G5
Dzibilchaltún, *Mexico* 119 C7
Dzibilchaltun, *Yucatán, Mexico* 119 C7
Dzierzgoń, *Poland* 30 E6
Dzierżoniów, *Poland* 31 H3
Dzilam de Bravo, *Mexico* 119 C7
Dzisna, *Belarus* 32 E5
Dzisna →, *Belarus* 32 E5
Dziwnów, *Poland* 30 D1
Dzungaria = Junggar Pendi, *China* 60 B3
Dzungarian Basin = Junggar Pendi, *China* 60 B3
Dzuumod, *Mongolia* 60 B5
Dzyarzhynsk, *Belarus* 32 F4
Dzyatlava, *Belarus* 32 F3

E

E.C. Manning ⌓, *Canada* 102 D4
Eabamet L., *Canada* 104 B2
Eads, *U.S.A.* 112 F3
Eagar, *U.S.A.* 109 J9
Eagle, *Alaska, U.S.A.* 100 B5
Eagle, *Colo., U.S.A.* 108 G10
Eagle →, *Canada* 105 B8
Eagle Butte, *U.S.A.* 112 C4
Eagle Grove, *U.S.A.* 112 D8
Eagle L., *Canada* 103 D10
Eagle L., *Calif., U.S.A.* 108 F3
Eagle L., *Maine, U.S.A.* 115 B11
Eagle Lake, *Canada* 116 A6
Eagle Lake, *Maine, U.S.A.* 115 B11
Eagle Lake, *Tex., U.S.A.* 113 L6
Eagle Mountain, *U.S.A.* 111 M11
Eagle Nest, *U.S.A.* 109 H11
Eagle Pass, *U.S.A.* 113 L4
Eagle Pk., *U.S.A.* 110 G7
Eagle Pt., *Australia* 92 C3
Eagle River, *Mich., U.S.A.* 114 B1
Eagle River, *Wis., U.S.A.* 112 C10
Eaglehawk, *Australia* 95 F3
Eagles Mere, *U.S.A.* 117 E8
Ealing □, *U.K.* 15 F7
Ear Falls, *Canada* 103 C10
Earle, *U.S.A.* 113 H9
Earlimart, *U.S.A.* 111 K7
Earn →, *U.K.* 13 E5
Earn, L., *U.K.* 13 E4
Earnslaw, Mt., *N.Z.* 91 L2
Earth, *U.S.A.* 113 H3
Easley, *U.S.A.* 115 H4
East Anglia, *U.K.* 14 E9
East Angus, *Canada* 105 C5
East Antarctica, *Antarctica* 5 D7
East Aurora, *U.S.A.* 116 D6
East Ayrshire □, *U.K.* 13 F4
East Bengal, *Bangla.* 67 H17
East Beskids = Vychodné Beskydy, *Europe* 27 B15
East Brady, *U.S.A.* 116 F5
East C., *N.Z.* 91 G7
East Chicago, *U.S.A.* 114 E2
East China Sea, *Asia* 60 C7
East Coulee, *Canada* 102 C6
East Dereham = Dereham, *U.K.* 15 E8
East Dunbartonshire □, *U.K.* 13 F4
East Falkland, *Falk. Is.* 128 G5
East Grand Forks, *U.S.A.* 112 B6
East Greenwich, *U.S.A.* 117 E13
East Grinstead, *U.K.* 15 F8
East Hartford, *U.S.A.* 117 E12
East Helena, *U.S.A.* 108 C8
East Indies, *Asia* 50 K15
East Kilbride, *U.K.* 13 F4
East Lansing, *U.S.A.* 114 D3
East Liverpool, *U.S.A.* 116 F4
East London, *S. Africa* 89 E4
East Lothian □, *U.K.* 13 F6
East Main = Eastmain, *Canada* 104 B4
East Northport, *U.S.A.* 117 F11
East Orange, *U.S.A.* 117 F10
East Pacific Ridge, *Pac. Oc.* 97 J17
East Palestine, *U.S.A.* 116 F4
East Pine, *Canada* 102 B4
East Point, *U.S.A.* 115 J3
East Providence, *U.S.A.* 117 E13
East Pt., *Br. Virgin Is.* 121 e
East Pt., *Canada* 105 C7
East Renfrewshire □, *U.K.* 13 F4
East Retford = Retford, *U.K.* 14 D7
East Riding of Yorkshire □, *U.K.* 14 D7
East Rochester, *U.S.A.* 116 C7
East St. Louis, *U.S.A.* 112 F9
East Schelde = Oosterschelde →, *Neths.* 17 C4
East Sea = Japan, Sea of, *Asia* 54 E7
East Siberian Sea, *Russia* 53 B17

East Stroudsburg, *U.S.A.* 117 E9
East Sussex □, *U.K.* 15 G8
East Tawas, *U.S.A.* 114 C4
East Timor ■, *Asia* 63 F7
East Toorale, *Australia* 95 E4
East Walker →, *U.S.A.* 110 G7
East Windsor, *U.S.A.* 117 F10
Eastbourne, *N.Z.* 91 J5
Eastbourne, *U.K.* 15 G8
Eastend, *Canada* 103 D7
Easter I. = Pascua, I. de, *Chile* 97 K17
Eastern □, *Ghana* 83 D4
Eastern □, *Kenya* 86 C4
Eastern □, *S. Leone* 82 D2
Eastern Cape □, *S. Africa* 88 E4
Eastern Cr. →, *Australia* 94 C3
Eastern Ghats, *India* 66 N11
Eastern Group = Lau Group, *Fiji* 91 C9
Eastern Group, *Australia* 93 F3
Eastern Transvaal = Mpumalanga □, *S. Africa* 89 D5
Easterville, *Canada* 103 C9
Easthampton, *U.S.A.* 117 D12
Eastlake, *U.S.A.* 116 E3
Eastland, *U.S.A.* 113 J5
Eastleigh, *U.K.* 15 G6
Eastmain, *Canada* 104 B4
Eastmain →, *Canada* 104 B4
Eastman, *Canada* 117 A12
Eastman, *U.S.A.* 115 J4
Easton, *Md., U.S.A.* 114 F7
Easton, *Pa., U.S.A.* 117 F9
Easton, *Wash., U.S.A.* 110 C5
Eastpointe, *U.S.A.* 116 D2
Eastport, *U.S.A.* 115 C12
Eastsound, *U.S.A.* 110 B4
Eaton, *U.S.A.* 112 E2
Eatonia, *Canada* 103 C7
Eatonton, *U.S.A.* 115 J4
Eatontown, *U.S.A.* 117 F10
Eatonville, *U.S.A.* 110 D4
Eau Claire, *U.S.A.* 112 C9
Eau Claire, L. à l', *Canada* 104 A5
Eauze, *France* 20 E4
Eban, *Nigeria* 83 D5
Ebbegebirge ⌓, *Germany* 24 D3
Ebbw Vale, *U.K.* 15 F4
Ebeltoft, *Denmark* 11 H4
Ebeltoft Vig, *Denmark* 11 H4
Ebensburg, *U.S.A.* 116 F6
Ebensee, *Austria* 26 D6
Eber Gölü, *Turkey* 72 C4
Eberbach, *Germany* 25 F4
Eberswalde-Finow, *Germany* 24 C9
Ebetsu, *Japan* 54 C10
Ebey's Landing ⌓, *U.S.A.* 110 B4
Ebian, *China* 58 C4
Ebingen, *Germany* 25 G5
Éboli, *Italy* 43 B8
Ebolowa, *Cameroon* 83 E7
Ebonyi □, *Nigeria* 83 D6
Ebrach, *Germany* 25 F6
Ébrié, Lagune, *Ivory C.* 82 D4
Ebro →, *Spain* 38 E5
Ebro, Embalse del, *Spain* 36 C7
Ebstorf, *Germany* 24 B6
Eceabat, *Turkey* 45 F10
Ech Chéliff, *Algeria* 78 A6
Echigo-Sammyaku, *Japan* 55 F9
Échirolles, *France* 21 C9
Echizen-Misaki, *Japan* 55 G7
Echmiadzin = Yejmiadzin, *Armenia* 35 K7
Echo Bay, *N.W.T., Canada* 100 B8
Echo Bay, *Ont., Canada* 104 C3
Echoing →, *Canada* 104 B1
Echterdingen, Stuttgart ✕ (STR), *Germany* 25 G5
Echternach, *Lux.* 17 E6
Echuca, *Australia* 95 F3
Ecija, *Spain* 37 H5
Eckental, *Germany* 25 F7
Eckernförde, *Germany* 24 A5
Eclipse I., *Australia* 93 G2
Eclipse Is., *Australia* 92 B4
Eclipse Sd., *Canada* 101 A11
Écommoy, *France* 18 E7
Écouché, *France* 18 D6
Ecrins △, *France* 21 D10
Ecuador ■, *S. Amer.* 124 D3
Écueillé, *France* 18 E8
Ed, *Sweden* 11 F5
Ed Dabbura, *Sudan* 80 D3
Ed Da'ein, *Sudan* 81 E2
Ed Damazin, *Sudan* 79 F12
Ed Dâmer, *Sudan* 80 D3
Ed Dar el Beida = Casablanca, *Morocco* 78 B4
Ed Debba, *Sudan* 80 D3
Ed-Déffa, *Egypt* 80 A2
Ed Deim, *Sudan* 81 E2
Ed Dueim, *Sudan* 81 E3
Edam, *Canada* 103 C7
Edam, *Neths.* 17 B5
Edane, *Sweden* 10 E6
Eday, *U.K.* 13 B6
Edd, *Eritrea* 81 E5
Eddrachillis B., *U.K.* 13 C3
Eddystone, *U.K.* 15 G3
Eddystone Pt., *Australia* 95 G4
Ede, *Neths.* 17 B5
Ede, *Nigeria* 83 D5
Édéa, *Cameroon* 83 E7
Edebäck, *Sweden* 10 D7
Edehon L., *Canada* 103 A9
Edelény, *Hungary* 28 B5
Eden, *Australia* 95 F4
Eden, *N.C., U.S.A.* 115 G6
Eden, *N.Y., U.S.A.* 116 D6
Eden, *Tex., U.S.A.* 113 K5
Eden →, *U.K.* 14 C4
Edenburg, *S. Africa* 88 D4
Edendale, *S. Africa* 89 D5
Edenderry, *Ireland* 12 C4
Edenton, *U.S.A.* 115 G7
Edenville, *S. Africa* 89 D4
Eder →, *Germany* 24 D5
Eder-Stausee, *Germany* 24 D4
Edewecht, *Germany* 24 B3
Edgar, *U.S.A.* 112 E6
Edgartown, *U.S.A.* 117 E14
Edge Hill, *U.K.* 15 E6
Edgefield, *U.S.A.* 115 J5
Edgeley, *U.S.A.* 112 B5
Edgemont, *U.S.A.* 112 D3
Edgeøya, *Svalbard* 4 B9
Édhessa, *Greece* 44 F6
Edievale, *N.Z.* 91 L2
Edina, *Liberia* 82 D2
Edina, *U.S.A.* 112 E8
Edinboro, *U.S.A.* 116 E4
Edinburg, *U.S.A.* 113 M5
Edinburgh, *U.K.* 13 F5
Edinburgh ✕ (EDI), *U.K.* 13 F5
Edinburgh, City of □, *U.K.* 13 F5
Edineţ, *Moldova* 29 B12
Edirne, *Turkey* 45 E10
Edirne □, *Turkey* 45 E10
Edison, *U.S.A.* 110 B4
Edithburgh, *Australia* 95 F2
Edmeston, *U.S.A.* 117 D9
Edmond, *U.S.A.* 113 H6
Edmonds, *U.S.A.* 110 C4
Edmonton, *Australia* 94 B4
Edmonton, *Canada* 102 C6
Edmund L., *Canada* 104 B1
Edmundston, *Canada* 105 C6
Edna, *U.S.A.* 113 L6
Edo □, *Nigeria* 83 D6
Edolo, *Italy* 40 B7
Edremit, *Turkey* 47 B9
Edremit Körfezi, *Turkey* 47 B8
Edsbro, *Sweden* 10 E12
Edsbyn, *Sweden* 10 C9
Edson, *Canada* 102 C5
Eduardo Castex, *Argentina* 126 D3
Edward →, *Australia* 95 F3
Edward, L., *Africa* 86 C2
Edward River, *Australia* 94 A3
Edward VII Land, *Antarctica* 5 E13
Edwards, *Calif., U.S.A.* 111 L9
Edwards, *N.Y., U.S.A.* 117 B9
Edwards Air Force Base, *U.S.A.* 111 L9
Edwards Plateau, *U.S.A.* 113 K4
Edwardsville, *U.S.A.* 117 E9
Edxná, *Mexico* 119 D6
Edzo, *Canada* 102 A5
Eeklo, *Belgium* 17 C3
Eferding, *Austria* 26 C7
Effigy Mounds ⌓, *U.S.A.* 112 D9
Effingham, *U.S.A.* 114 F1
Eforie, *Romania* 29 F13
Ega →, *Spain* 38 C3
Égadi, Ísole, *Italy* 42 E5
Egan Range, *U.S.A.* 108 G6
Eganville, *Canada* 116 A7
Eger = Cheb, *Czech Rep.* 26 A5
Eger, *Hungary* 28 C5
Eger →, *Hungary* 28 C5
Egersund, *Norway* 9 G12
Egg L., *Canada* 103 B7
Eggegebirge Südlicher Teutoburger Wald ⌓, *Germany* 24 D4
Eggenburg, *Austria* 26 C8
Eggenfelden, *Germany* 25 G8
Éghezée, *Belgium* 17 D4
Égletons, *France* 20 C6
Egmont, *Canada* 102 D4
Egmont △, *N.Z.* 91 H5
Egmont, C., *N.Z.* 91 H4
Egmont, Mt. = Taranaki, Mt., *N.Z.* 91 H5
Egra, *India* 69 J12
Eğridir, *Turkey* 72 D4
Eğridir Gölü, *Turkey* 70 B1
Egtved, *Denmark* 11 J3
Egume, *Nigeria* 83 D6
Éguzon-Chantôme, *France* 19 F8
Egvekinot, *Russia* 53 C19
Egyek, *Hungary* 28 C5
Egypt ■, *Africa* 80 B3
Eha Amufu, *Nigeria* 83 D6
Ehime □, *Japan* 55 H6
Ehingen, *Germany* 25 G5
Ehrenberg, *U.S.A.* 111 M12
Ehrwald, *Austria* 26 D3
Eibar, *Spain* 38 B2
Eichstätt, *Germany* 25 G7
Eider →, *Germany* 24 A4
Eidsvold, *Australia* 95 D5
Eidsvoll, *Norway* 9 F14
Eifel, *Germany* 25 E2
Eiffel Flats, *Zimbabwe* 87 F3
Eiger, *Switz.* 40 B5
Eigg, *U.K.* 13 E2
Eighty Mile Beach, *Australia* 92 C3
Eil, *Somali Rep.* 75 F4
Eil, L., *U.K.* 13 E3
Eildon, L., *Australia* 95 F4
Eilenburg, *Germany* 24 D8
Ein el Luweiqa, *Sudan* 81 E3
Einasleigh, *Australia* 94 B3
Einasleigh →, *Australia* 94 B3
Einbeck, *Germany* 24 D5
Eindhoven, *Neths.* 17 C5
Einsiedeln, *Switz.* 25 H4
Eire = Ireland ■, *Europe* 12 C4
Eiríksjökull, *Iceland* 8 D3
Eirunepé, *Brazil* 124 E5
Eiseb →, *Namibia* 88 C2
Eisenach, *Germany* 24 E6
Eisenberg, *Germany* 24 E7
Eisenerz, *Austria* 26 D7
Eisenhüttenstadt, *Germany* 24 C10
Eisenkappel, *Austria* 26 E7
Eisenstadt, *Austria* 27 D9
Eisfeld, *Germany* 25 E6
Eisleben, *Germany* 24 D7
Eislingen, *Germany* 25 G5
Eivissa, *Spain* 48 C7
Eixe, Serra do, *Spain* 36 C4
Ejea de los Caballeros, *Spain* 38 C3
Ejeda, *Madag.* 89 C7
Ejura, *Ghana* 83 D4
Ejutla, *Mexico* 119 D5
Ekalaka, *U.S.A.* 112 C2
Ekenäs = Tammisaari, *Finland* 9 F20
Ekenässjön, *Sweden* 11 G9
Ekerö, *Sweden* 10 E11
Eket, *Nigeria* 83 E6
Eketahuna, *N.Z.* 91 J5
Ekhínos, *Greece* 45 E9
Ekibastuz, *Kazakhstan* 52 D8
Ekiti □, *Nigeria* 83 D6
Ekoli, *Dem. Rep. of the Congo* 86 C1
Ekoln, *Sweden* 10 E11
Ekshärad, *Sweden* 10 D7
Eksjö, *Sweden* 11 G8
Ekuma →, *Namibia* 88 B2
Ekwan →, *Canada* 104 B3
Ekwan Pt., *Canada* 104 B3
El Aaiún, *W. Sahara* 78 C3
El Abanico, *Chile* 126 D1
El Abbasiya, *Sudan* 81 E3
El 'Agrûd, *Egypt* 74 E3
El Ait, *Sudan* 81 E2
El 'Aiyat, *Egypt* 80 J7
El 'Alamein, *Egypt* 80 A2
El 'Aqaba, W. →, *Egypt* 74 E2
El 'Arag, *Egypt* 80 B2
El Arahal, *Spain* 37 H5
El Arīḩā, *West Bank* 74 D4
El 'Arîsh, *Egypt* 74 D2
El 'Arîsh, W. →, *Egypt* 74 D2
El Asnam = Ech Chéliff, *Algeria* 78 A6
El Astillero, *Spain* 36 B7
El Badâri, *Egypt* 80 B3
El Bahrein, *Egypt* 80 B2
El Ballâs, *Egypt* 80 B3
El Balyana, *Egypt* 80 B3
El Baqeir, *Sudan* 80 D3
El Barco de Ávila, *Spain* 36 E5
El Barco de Valdeorras = O Barco, *Spain* 36 C4
El Bauga, *Sudan* 80 D3
El Bawiti, *Egypt* 80 B2
El Bayadh, *Algeria* 78 B6
El Bierzo, *Spain* 36 C4
El Bluff, *Nic.* 120 D3
El Bonillo, *Spain* 39 G2
El Brûk, W. →, *Egypt* 74 E2
El Buheirat □, *Sudan* 81 F3
El Burgo de Osma, *Spain* 38 D1
El Cajon, *U.S.A.* 111 N10
El Campo, *U.S.A.* 113 L6
El Centro, *U.S.A.* 111 N11
El Cerro, *Bolivia* 124 G6
El Cerro de Andévalo, *Spain* 37 H4
El Compadre, *Mexico* 111 N10
El Coronil, *Spain* 37 H5
El Cuy, *Argentina* 128 D3
El Cuyo, *Mexico* 119 C7
El Dab'a, *Egypt* 80 H6
El Daheir, *Egypt* 74 D3
El Dátil, *Mexico* 118 B2
El Deir, *Egypt* 80 B3
El Dere, *Somali Rep.* 75 G4
El Descanso, *Mexico* 111 N10
El Desemboque, *Mexico* 118 A2
El Dilingat, *Egypt* 80 H7
El Diviso, *Colombia* 124 C3
El Djouf, *Mauritania* 78 D4
El Dorado, *Ark., U.S.A.* 113 J8
El Dorado, *Kans., U.S.A.* 113 G6
El Dorado, *Venezuela* 124 B6
El 'Ein, *Sudan* 81 D2
El Ejido, *Spain* 37 J8
El Escorial, *Spain* 36 E6
El Espinar, *Spain* 36 D6
El Faiyûm, *Egypt* 80 J7
El Fâsher, *Sudan* 81 E2
El Fashn, *Egypt* 80 J7
El Ferrol = Ferrol, *Spain* 36 B2
El Fifi, *Sudan* 81 E2
El Fuerte, *Mexico* 118 B3
El Ga'a, *Sudan* 81 E2
El Gal, *Somali Rep.* 75 E5
El Garef, *Sudan* 81 E3
El Gebir, *Sudan* 81 E2
El Gedida, *Egypt* 80 B2
El Geneina = Al Junaynah, *Sudan* 79 F10
El Geteina, *Sudan* 81 E3
El Gezira □, *Sudan* 81 E3
El Gir, *Sudan* 80 D2
El Gîza, *Egypt* 80 J7
El Gogorron △, *Mexico* 118 C4
El Goléa, *Algeria* 78 B6
El Grau, *Spain* 39 G4
El Guácharo △, *Venezuela* 121 D7
El Guache △, *Venezuela* 121 E6
El Hagiz, *Sudan* 81 D4
El Hâi, *Egypt* 80 J7
El Hammam, *Egypt* 80 A2
El Hawata, *Sudan* 81 E3
El Heiz, *Egypt* 80 B2
El Hideib, *Sudan* 81 E3
El Hilla, *Sudan* 81 E2
El 'Idisât, *Egypt* 80 B3
El Iskandarîya, *Egypt* 80 H7
El Istiwa'iya, *Sudan* 79 G11
El Jadida, *Morocco* 78 B4
El Jardal, *Honduras* 120 D2
El Jebelein, *Sudan* 81 E3
El Kab, *Sudan* 80 D3
El Kabrît, G., *Egypt* 74 F2
El Kafr el Sharqi, *Egypt* 80 H7
El Kamlin, *Sudan* 81 D3
El Karaba, *Sudan* 80 D3
El Kere, *Ethiopia* 81 F5
El Khandaq, *Sudan* 80 D3
El Khârga, *Egypt* 80 B3
El Khartûm, *Sudan* 81 D3
El Khartûm □, *Sudan* 81 D3
El Khartûm Bahrî, *Sudan* 81 D3
El Kuntilla, *Egypt* 74 E3
El Laqâwa, *Sudan* 81 E2
El Leh, *Ethiopia* 81 G4
El Leiya, *Sudan* 81 D4
El Maestrazgo, *Spain* 38 E4
El Mafâza, *Sudan* 81 E3
El Maghra, *Egypt* 80 A2
El Mahalla el Kubra, *Egypt* 80 H7
El Mahârîq, *Egypt* 80 B3
El Maîmûn, *Egypt* 80 J7
El Maks el Bahari, *Egypt* 80 C3
El Malpais ⌓, *U.S.A.* 109 J10
El Manshâh, *Egypt* 80 B3
El Mansûra, *Egypt* 80 H7
El Manzala, *Egypt* 80 H7
El Marâgha, *Egypt* 80 B3
El Masid, *Sudan* 81 D3
El Masnou, *Spain* 38 D7
El Matariya, *Egypt* 80 H8
El Meda, *Ethiopia* 81 F5
El Medano, *Canary Is.* 48 F3
El Metemma, *Sudan* 81 D3
El Milagro, *Argentina* 126 C2
El Minyâ, *Egypt* 80 B3
El Monte, *U.S.A.* 111 L8
El Montseny, *Spain* 38 D7
El Mreyye, *Mauritania* 82 B3
El Niybo, *Ethiopia* 81 G4
El Obeid, *Sudan* 81 E3
El Odaiya, *Sudan* 81 E2
El Oro, *Mexico* 119 D4
El Oued, *Algeria* 78 B7
El Palmar △, *Argentina* 126 C4
El Palmito, Presa, *Mexico* 118 B3
El Paso, *U.S.A.* 109 L10
El Paso Robles, *U.S.A.* 110 K6
El Pedernoso, *Spain* 39 F2
El Pedroso, *Spain* 37 H5
El Pinacate y Gran Desierto de Altar = Gran Desierto del Pinacate ⌓, *Mexico* 118 A2
El Pobo de Dueñas, *Spain* 38 E3
El Portal, *U.S.A.* 110 H7
El Porvenir, *Mexico* 118 A3
El Prat de Llobregat, *Spain* 38 D7
El Progreso, *Honduras* 120 C2
El Pueblito, *Mexico* 118 B3
El Pueblo, *Canary Is.* 48 F2
El Puente del Arzobispo, *Spain* 36 F5
El Puerto de Santa María, *Spain* 37 J4
El Qâhira, *Egypt* 80 H7
El Qantara, *Egypt* 74 E1
El Qasr, *Egypt* 80 B2
El Qubâbât, *Egypt* 80 J7
El Quseima, *Egypt* 74 E3
El Qusîya, *Egypt* 80 B3
El Râshda, *Egypt* 80 B2
El Real, *Panama* 124 B3
El Reno, *U.S.A.* 113 H6
El Rey △, *Argentina* 126 A3
El Rîdisiya, *Egypt* 80 C3
El Rio, *U.S.A.* 111 L7
El Ronquillo, *Spain* 37 H4
El Roque, Pta., *Canary Is.* 48 F4
El Rosarito, *Mexico* 118 B2
El Rubio, *Spain* 37 H5
El Saff, *Egypt* 80 J7
El Saheira, W. →, *Egypt* 74 E2
El Salto, *Mexico* 118 C3
El Salvador ■, *Cent. Amer.* 120 D2
El Sauce, *Nic.* 120 D2
El Saucejo, *Spain* 37 H5
El Shallal, *Egypt* 80 C3
El Simbillawein, *Egypt* 80 H7
El Sueco, *Mexico* 118 B3
El Suweis, *Egypt* 80 J8
El Tabbîn, *Egypt* 80 J7
El Tamarâni, W. →, *Egypt* 74 E3
El Thamad, *Egypt* 74 F3
El Tigre, *Venezuela* 124 B6
El Tîh, Gebal, *Egypt* 74 F2
El Tîna, *Egypt* 80 H8
El Tîna, Khalîg, *Egypt* 74 D1
El Tofo, *Chile* 126 B1
El Tránsito, *Chile* 126 B1
El Tûr, *Egypt* 70 D2
El Turbio, *Argentina* 128 G2
El Uqsur, *Egypt* 80 B3
El Valle ⌓, *Spain* 39 H3
El Venado, *Mexico* 118 C4
El Vendrell, *Spain* 38 D6
El Vergel, *Mexico* 118 B3
El Vigía, *Venezuela* 124 B4
El Viso del Alcor, *Spain* 37 H5
El Wabeira, *Egypt* 74 F2
El Wak, *Kenya* 86 B5
El Waqf, *Egypt* 80 B3
El Weguet, *Ethiopia* 81 F5
El Wuz, *Sudan* 81 D3
Elafónisos, *Greece* 46 E4
Élancourt, *France* 19 D8
Élassa, *Greece* 47 F8
Elassón, *Greece* 46 B4
Elat, *Israel* 74 F3
Eláthia, *Greece* 46 C4
Elâzığ, *Turkey* 70 B3
Elba, *Italy* 40 F7
Elba, *U.S.A.* 115 K2
Elbasan, *Albania* 44 E4
Elbe, *U.S.A.* 110 D4
Elbe →, *Europe* 24 B4
Elbe-Seitenkanal, *Germany* 24 C6
Elbert, Mt., *U.S.A.* 109 G10
Elberton, *U.S.A.* 115 H4
Elbeuf, *France* 18 C8
Elbidtan, *Turkey* 70 B3
Elbing = Elbląg, *Poland* 30 D6
Elbistan, *Turkey* 72 C7
Elbląg, *Poland* 30 D6
Elbow, *Canada* 103 C7
Elbrus, *Asia* 35 J6
Elbufer-Drawehn ⌓, *Germany* 24 B6
Elburz Mts. = Alborz, Reshteh-ye Kūhhā-ye, *Iran* 71 C7
Elche, *Spain* 39 G4
Elche de la Sierra, *Spain* 39 G2
Elcho I., *Australia* 94 A2
Elda, *Spain* 39 G4
Elde →, *Germany* 24 B7
Eldon, *Mo., U.S.A.* 112 F8
Eldon, *Wash., U.S.A.* 110 C3
Eldora, *U.S.A.* 112 D8
Eldorado, *Argentina* 127 B5
Eldorado, *Canada* 116 B7
Eldorado, *Mexico* 118 C3
Eldorado, *Ill., U.S.A.* 114 G1
Eldorado, *Tex., U.S.A.* 113 K4
Eldorado Springs, *U.S.A.* 113 G8
Eldoret, *Kenya* 86 B4
Eldred, *U.S.A.* 116 E6
Elea, C., *Cyprus* 49 D13
Eleanora, Pk., *Australia* 93 F3
Elefantes →, *Africa* 89 C5
Elektrogorsk, *Russia* 32 E10
Elektrostal, *Russia* 32 E10
Elele, *Nigeria* 83 D6
Elena, *Bulgaria* 45 D9
Elephant Butte Reservoir, *U.S.A.* 109 K10
Elephant I., *Antarctica* 5 C18
Eleshnitsa, *Bulgaria* 44 E7
Eleşkirt, *Turkey* 73 C10
Eleuthera, *Bahamas* 120 B4
Elevsís, *Greece* 46 C5
Elevtheroúpolis, *Greece* 45 F8
Elgin, *Canada* 117 B8
Elgin, *U.K.* 13 D5
Elgin, *Ill., U.S.A.* 114 D1
Elgin, *N. Dak., U.S.A.* 112 B4
Elgin, *Oreg., U.S.A.* 108 D5
Elgin, *Tex., U.S.A.* 113 K6
Elgoibar, *Spain* 38 B2
Elgon, Mt., *Africa* 86 B3
Eliase, *Indonesia* 63 F8
Elikón, *Greece* 46 C4
Elim, *Namibia* 88 B2
Elim, *S. Africa* 88 E2
Elin Pelin, *Bulgaria* 44 D7
Elista, *Russia* 35 G7
Elizabeth, *Australia* 95 E2
Elizabeth, *U.S.A.* 117 F10
Elizabeth City, *U.S.A.* 115 G7
Elizabethton, *U.S.A.* 115 G4
Elizabethtown, *Ky., U.S.A.* 114 G3
Elizabethtown, *N.Y., U.S.A.* 117 B11
Elizabethtown, *Pa., U.S.A.* 117 F8
Elizondo, *Spain* 38 B3
Ełk, *Poland* 30 E9
Elk →, *Canada* 102 C5
Ełk →, *Poland* 30 E9
Elk →, *U.S.A.* 115 H2
Elk City, *U.S.A.* 113 H5
Elk Creek, *U.S.A.* 110 F4
Elk Grove, *U.S.A.* 110 G5
Elk Island △, *Canada* 102 C6
Elk Lake, *Canada* 104 C3
Elk Point, *Canada* 103 C6
Elk River, *Idaho, U.S.A.* 108 C5
Elk River, *Minn., U.S.A.* 112 C8
Elkedra →, *Australia* 94 C2
Elkhart, *Ind., U.S.A.* 114 E3
Elkhart, *Kans., U.S.A.* 113 G4
Elkhorn, *Canada* 103 D8
Elkhorn →, *U.S.A.* 112 E6
Elkhovo, *Bulgaria* 45 D10
Elkin, *U.S.A.* 115 G5
Elkins, *U.S.A.* 114 F6
Elkland, *U.S.A.* 116 E7
Elko, *Canada* 102 D5
Elko, *U.S.A.* 108 F6
Elkton, *U.S.A.* 116 C1
Ell, L., *Australia* 93 E4
Ellef Ringnes I., *Canada* 4 B2
Ellen, Mt., *U.S.A.* 117 B12
Ellenburg, *U.S.A.* 117 B11
Ellendale, *U.S.A.* 112 B5
Ellensburg, *U.S.A.* 108 C3
Ellenville, *U.S.A.* 117 E10
Ellerton, *Barbados* 121 g
Ellery, Mt., *Australia* 95 F4
Ellesmere, L., *N.Z.* 91 M4
Ellesmere I., *Canada* 98 B11
Ellesmere Port, *U.K.* 14 D5
Ellice Is. = Tuvalu ■, *Pac. Oc.* 96 H9
Ellicottville, *U.S.A.* 116 D6
Ellinikón, Athínai ✕ (ATH), *Greece* 46 D5
Elliot, *Australia* 94 B1
Elliot, *S. Africa* 89 E4
Elliot Lake, *Canada* 104 C3
Elliotdale = Xhora, *S. Africa* 89 E4
Ellis, *U.S.A.* 112 F5
Elliston, *Australia* 95 E1
Ellisville, *U.S.A.* 113 K10
Ellon, *U.K.* 13 D6
Ellore = Eluru, *India* 67 L12
Ellsworth, *Kans., U.S.A.* 112 F5
Ellsworth, *Maine, U.S.A.* 115 C11
Ellsworth Land, *Antarctica* 5 D16
Ellsworth Mts., *Antarctica* 5 D16
Ellwangen, *Germany* 25 G6
Ellwood City, *U.S.A.* 116 F4
Elm, *Switz.* 25 J5
Elm-Lappwald ⌓, *Germany* 24 C6
Elma, *Canada* 103 D9
Elma, *U.S.A.* 110 D3
Elmadağ, *Turkey* 72 C5

Elmalı, *Turkey* 47 E11
Elmhurst, *U.S.A.* 114 E2
Elmina, *Ghana* 83 D4
Elmira, *Canada* 116 C4
Elmira, *U.S.A.* 116 D8
Elmira Heights, *U.S.A.* 116 D8
Elmore, *Australia* 95 F3
Elmore, *U.S.A.* 111 M11
Elmshorn, *Germany* 24 B5
Elmvale, *Canada* 116 B5
Elne, *France* 20 F6
Elora, *Canada* 116 C4
Elos, *Greece* 46 E4
Eloúnda, *Greece* 49 D7
Eloy, *U.S.A.* 109 K8
Éloyes, *France* 19 D13
Elrose, *Canada* 103 C7
Elsdorf, *Germany* 24 E2
Elsie, *U.S.A.* 110 E3
Elsinore = Helsingør, *Denmark* 11 H6
Elster →, *Germany* 24 D7
Elsterwerda, *Germany* 24 D9
Eltham, *N.Z.* 91 H5
Elton, *Russia* 35 F8
Elton, Ozero, *Russia* 35 F8
Eltville, *Germany* 25 E4
Eluru, *India* 67 L12
Elvas, *Portugal* 37 G3
Elven, *France* 18 E4
Elverum, *Norway* 9 F14
Elvire →, *Australia* 92 C4
Elvire, Mt., *Australia* 93 E2
Elvo →, *Italy* 40 C5
Elwell, L., *U.S.A.* 108 B8
Elwood, *Ind., U.S.A.* 114 E3
Elwood, *Nebr., U.S.A.* 112 E5
Elx = Elche, *Spain* 39 G4
Ely, *U.K.* 15 E8
Ely, *Minn., U.S.A.* 112 B9
Ely, *Nev., U.S.A.* 108 G6
Elyria, *U.S.A.* 116 E2
Elyrus, *Greece* 46 F5
Elz →, *Germany* 25 G3
Emådalen, *Sweden* 10 C8
Emāmrūd, *Iran* 71 B7
Emån →, *Sweden* 11 G10
Emba, *Kazakhstan* 52 E6
Emba →, *Kazakhstan* 52 E6
Embarcación, *Argentina* 126 A3
Embarras Portage, *Canada* 103 B6
Embetsu, *Japan* 54 B10
Embi = Emba, *Kazakhstan* 52 E6
Embi = Emba →, *Kazakhstan* 52 E6
Embóna, *Greece* 49 C9
Embrun, *France* 21 D10
Embu, *Kenya* 86 C4
Emden, *Germany* 24 B3
Emecik, *Turkey* 47 E9
Emerald, *Australia* 94 C4
Emerson, *Canada* 103 D9
Emet, *Turkey* 47 B11
Emi Koussi, *Chad* 79 E9
Emília-Romagna □, *Italy* 40 D8
Emilius, Mte., *Italy* 40 C4
Eminabad, *Pakistan* 68 C6
Emine, Nos, *Bulgaria* 45 D11
Emirdağ, *Turkey* 72 C4
Emissi, Tarso, *Chad* 79 D9
Emlenton, *U.S.A.* 116 E5
Emlichheim, *Germany* 24 C2
Emmaboda, *Sweden* 11 H9
Emmaus, *S. Africa* 88 D4
Emmaus, *U.S.A.* 117 F9
Emme →, *Switz.* 25 H3
Emmeloord, *Neths.* 17 B5
Emmen, *Neths.* 17 B6
Emmen, *Switz.* 25 H4
Emmendingen, *Germany* 25 G3
Emmental, *Switz.* 25 J3
Emmerich, *Germany* 24 D2
Emmet, *Australia* 94 C3
Emmetsburg, *U.S.A.* 112 D7
Emmett, *Idaho, U.S.A.* 108 E5
Emmett, *Mich., U.S.A.* 116 D2
Emmonak, *U.S.A.* 100 B3
Emo, *Canada* 103 D10
Emőd, *Hungary* 28 C5
Emona, *Bulgaria* 45 D11
Empalme, *Mexico* 118 B2
Empangeni, *S. Africa* 89 D5
Empedrado, *Argentina* 126 B4
Emperor Seamount Chain, *Pac. Oc.* 96 D9
Empoli, *Italy* 40 E7
Emporia, *Kans., U.S.A.* 112 F6
Emporia, *Va., U.S.A.* 115 G7
Emporium, *U.S.A.* 116 E6
Empress, *Canada* 103 C7
Empty Quarter = Rub' al Khālī, *Si. Arabia* 75 D4
Ems →, *Germany* 24 B3
Emsdale, *Canada* 116 A5
Emsdetten, *Germany* 24 C3
Emu, *China* 57 C15
Emu Park, *Australia* 94 C5
'En 'Avrona, *Israel* 74 F4
En Nahud, *Sudan* 81 E2
En Nofalab, *Sudan* 81 D3
Ena, *Japan* 55 G8
Enana, *Namibia* 88 B2
Enånger, *Sweden* 10 C11
Enard B., *U.K.* 13 C3
Enare = Inarijärvi, *Finland* 8 B22
Enarotali, *Indonesia* 63 E9
Encampment, *U.S.A.* 108 F10
Encantadas, Serra, *Brazil* 127 C5
Encarnación, *Paraguay* 127 B4
Encarnación de Diaz, *Mexico* 118 C4
Enchi, *Ghana* 82 D4
Encinitas, *U.S.A.* 111 M9
Encino, *U.S.A.* 109 J11
Encounter B., *Australia* 95 F2
Encs, *Hungary* 28 B6
Endako, *Canada* 102 C3
Ende, *Indonesia* 63 F6
Endeavour Str., *Australia* 94 A3
Endelave, *Denmark* 11 J4
Enderbury I., *Kiribati* 96 H10
Enderby, *Canada* 102 C5
Enderby I., *Australia* 92 D2
Enderby Land, *Antarctica* 5 C5
Enderlin, *U.S.A.* 112 B6
Endicott, *U.S.A.* 117 D8
Endwell, *U.S.A.* 117 D8
Endyalgout I., *Australia* 92 B5
Eneabba, *Australia* 93 E2
Enewetak Atoll, *Marshall Is.* 96 F8
Enez, *Turkey* 45 F10
Enfer, Pte. d', *Martinique* 120 c
Enfield, *Canada* 105 D7
Enfield, *Conn., U.S.A.* 117 E12
Enfield, *N.H., U.S.A.* 117 C12
Engadin, *Switz.* 25 J6
Engaño, C., *Dom. Rep.* 121 C6
Engaño, C., *Phil.* 63 A6
Engaru, *Japan* 54 B11
Engcobo, *S. Africa* 89 E4
Engelberg, *Switz.* 25 J4
Engels, *Russia* 34 E8
Engemann L., *Canada* 103 B7
Engershatu, *Eritrea* 81 D4
Enggano, *Indonesia* 62 F2
England, *U.S.A.* 113 H9
England □, *U.K.* 15 E5
Englee, *Canada* 105 B8
Englehart, *Canada* 104 C4
Englewood, *U.S.A.* 112 F2
English →, *Canada* 103 C10
English Bazar = Ingraj Bazar, *India* 69 G13
English Channel, *Europe* 15 G6
English Company's Is., The, *Australia* 94 A2
English River, *Canada* 104 C1
Engures ezers, *Latvia* 30 A10
Enguri →, *Georgia* 35 J5
Enid, *U.S.A.* 113 G6
Enipévs →, *Greece* 46 B4
Enkhuizen, *Neths.* 17 B5
Enköping, *Sweden* 10 E11
Enle, *China* 58 F3
Enna, *Italy* 43 E7
Ennadai, *Canada* 103 A8
Ennadai L., *Canada* 103 A8
Ennedi, *Chad* 79 E10
Engonia, *Australia* 95 D4
Ennigerloh, *Germany* 24 D4
Ennis, *Ireland* 12 D3
Ennis, *Mont., U.S.A.* 108 D8
Ennis, *Tex., U.S.A.* 113 J6
Enniscorthy, *Ireland* 12 D5
Enniskillen, *U.K.* 12 B4
Ennistimon, *Ireland* 12 D2
Enns, *Austria* 26 C7
Enns →, *Austria* 26 C7
Enontekiö, *Finland* 8 B20
Enosburg Falls, *U.S.A.* 117 B12
Enping, *China* 59 F9
Enriquillo, L., *Dom. Rep.* 121 C5
Enschede, *Neths.* 17 B6
Ensenada, *Argentina* 126 C4
Ensenada, *Mexico* 118 A1
Ensenada de los Muertos, *Mexico* 118 C2
Enshi, *China* 58 B7
Ensiola, Pta. de n', *Spain* 48 B9
Ensisheim, *France* 19 E14
Entebbe, *Uganda* 86 B3
Enterprise, *Canada* 102 A5
Enterprise, *Ala., U.S.A.* 115 K3
Enterprise, *Oreg., U.S.A.* 108 D5
Entorno de Doñana ⌂, *Spain* 37 J4
Entraygues-sur-Truyère, *France* 20 D6
Entre Ríos, *Bolivia* 126 A3
Entre Ríos □, *Argentina* 126 C4
Entrepeñas, Embalse de, *Spain* 38 E2
Entroncamento, *Portugal* 37 F2
Enugu, *Nigeria* 83 D6
Enugu □, *Nigeria* 83 D6
Enugu Ezike, *Nigeria* 83 D6
Enumclaw, *U.S.A.* 110 C5
Envalira, Port d', *Europe* 38 C6
Envermeu, *France* 18 C8
Enviken, *Sweden* 10 D9
Enying, *Hungary* 28 D3
Enza →, *Italy* 40 D7
Éolie, Ís., *Italy* 43 D7
Epanomí, *Greece* 44 F6
Epe, *Neths.* 17 B5
Epe, *Nigeria* 83 D5
Épernay, *France* 19 C10
Épernon, *France* 19 D8
Ephesus, *Turkey* 47 D9
Ephraim, *U.S.A.* 108 G8
Ephrata, *Pa., U.S.A.* 117 F8
Ephrata, *Wash., U.S.A.* 108 C4
Epidaurus Limera, *Greece* 46 E5
Épila, *Spain* 38 D3
Épinac, *France* 19 F11
Épinal, *France* 19 D13
Episkopi, *Cyprus* 49 E11
Episkopí, *Greece* 49 D6
Episkopi Bay, *Cyprus* 49 E11
Epitálion, *Greece* 46 D3
Eppan = Appiano, *Italy* 41 B8
Eppingen, *Germany* 25 F4
Epsom, *U.K.* 15 F7
Epukiro, *Namibia* 88 C2
Equatoria = El Istiwa'iya, *Sudan* 79 G11
Equatorial Guinea ■, *Africa* 84 D1
Er Hai, *China* 58 E3
Er Rachidia, *Morocco* 78 B5
Er Rahad, *Sudan* 81 E3
Er Rif, *Morocco* 78 A5
Er Rogel, *Sudan* 80 D4
Er Roseires, *Sudan* 81 E3
Er Rua'at, *Sudan* 81 E3
Eraclea, *Italy* 41 C9
Erāwadī Myit = Irrawaddy →, *Burma* 67 M19
Erāwadī Myitwanya = Irrawaddy, Mouths of the, *Burma* 67 M19
Erba, *Italy* 40 C6
Erba, *Sudan* 80 D4
Erba, J., *Sudan* 80 C4
Erbaa, *Turkey* 72 B7
Erbeskopf, *Germany* 25 F3
Erbil = Arbīl, *Iraq* 70 B5
Erbu, *Ethiopia* 81 E3
Erçek, *Turkey* 70 B4
Erçiş, *Turkey* 73 C10
Erciyaş Dağı, *Turkey* 70 B2
Érd, *Hungary* 28 C3
Erdao Jiang →, *China* 57 C14
Erdek, *Turkey* 45 F11
Erdemli, *Turkey* 72 D6
Erdene = Ulaan-Uul, *Mongolia* 56 B6
Erdenetsogt, *Mongolia* 56 C4
Erding, *Germany* 25 G7
Erdre →, *France* 18 E5
Erebus, Mt., *Antarctica* 5 D11
Erechim, *Brazil* 127 B5
Ereğli, *Konya, Turkey* 70 B2
Ereğli, *Zonguldak, Turkey* 72 B4
Erei, Monti, *Italy* 43 E7
Erenhot, *China* 56 C7
Eresma →, *Spain* 36 D6
Eressós, *Greece* 47 B7
Erfenisdam, *S. Africa* 88 D4
Erfstadt, *Germany* 24 E2
Erft →, *Germany* 24 D2
Erfurt, *Germany* 24 E7
Ergani, *Turkey* 70 B3
Ergel, *Mongolia* 56 C5
Ergene →, *Turkey* 45 E10
Ergeni Vozvyshennost, *Russia* 35 G7
Ērgli, *Latvia* 9 H21
Erhlin, *Taiwan* 59 F13
Eria →, *Spain* 36 C5
Eriba, *Sudan* 81 D4
Eriboll, L., *U.K.* 13 C4
Érice, *Italy* 42 D5
Erie, *U.S.A.* 116 D4
Erie, L., *N. Amer.* 116 D4
Erie Canal, *U.S.A.* 116 C7
Erieau, *Canada* 116 D3
Erigavo, *Somali Rep.* 75 E4
Erikoúsa, *Greece* 49 A3
Eriksdale, *Canada* 103 C9
Erímanthos, *Greece* 46 D3
Erimo-misaki, *Japan* 54 D11
Erin Pt., *Trin. & Tob.* 125 K15
Erinpura, *India* 68 G5
Eriskay, *U.K.* 13 D1
Erithraí, *Greece* 46 C5
Eritrea ■, *Africa* 81 E4
Erjas →, *Portugal* 36 F3
Erkelenz, *Germany* 24 D2
Erkner, *Germany* 24 C9
Erlangen, *Germany* 25 F6
Erldunda, *Australia* 94 D1
Ermelo, *Neths.* 17 B5
Ermelo, *S. Africa* 89 D4
Ermenek, *Turkey* 70 B2
Ermil, *Sudan* 81 E2
Ermióni, *Greece* 46 D5
Ermones, *Greece* 49 A3
Ernakulam, *India* 66 Q10
Erne →, *Ireland* 12 B3
Erne, Lower L., *U.K.* 12 B4
Erne, Upper L., *U.K.* 12 B4
Ernée, *France* 18 D6
Ernest Giles Ra., *Australia* 93 E3
Ernstberg, *Germany* 25 E2
Erode, *India* 66 P10
Eromanga, *Australia* 95 D3
Erongo, *Namibia* 88 C2
Erquy, *France* 18 D4
Erramala Hills, *India* 66 M11
Errer →, *Ethiopia* 81 F5
Errigal, *Ireland* 12 A3
Erris Hd., *Ireland* 12 B1
Ersekë, *Albania* 44 F4
Erskine, *U.S.A.* 112 B7
Erstein, *France* 19 D14
Ertholmene, *Denmark* 11 J9
Ertil, *Russia* 34 E5
Ertis = Irtysh →, *Russia* 52 C7
Eruh, *Turkey* 73 D10
Eruwa, *Nigeria* 83 D5
Ervy-le-Châtel, *France* 19 D10
Erwin, *U.S.A.* 115 G4
Eryuan, *China* 58 D2
Erzgebirge, *Germany* 24 E8
Erzin, *Russia* 53 D10
Erzincan, *Turkey* 70 B3
Erzurum, *Turkey* 70 B4
Es Caló, *Spain* 48 C8
Es Canar, *Spain* 48 B8
Es Mercadal, *Spain* 48 B11
Es Migjorn Gran, *Spain* 48 B11
Es Safiya, *Sudan* 81 D3
Es Sahrâ' Esh Sharqîya, *Egypt* 80 B3
Es Sînâ', *Egypt* 74 F3
Es Sûkî, *Sudan* 81 E3
Es Vedrà, *Spain* 48 C7
Esambo, *Dem. Rep. of the Congo* 86 C1
Esan-Misaki, *Japan* 54 D10
Esashi, *Hokkaidō, Japan* 54 B11
Esashi, *Hokkaidō, Japan* 54 D10
Esbjerg, *Denmark* 11 J2
Esbo = Espoo, *Finland* 9 F21
Escalante, *U.S.A.* 109 H8
Escalante →, *U.S.A.* 109 H8
Escalón, *Mexico* 118 B4
Escambia →, *U.S.A.* 115 K2
Escanaba, *U.S.A.* 114 C2
Esch-sur-Alzette, *Lux.* 17 E6
Eschede, *Germany* 24 C6
Eschwege, *Germany* 24 D6
Eschweiler, *Germany* 24 E2
Escondido, *U.S.A.* 111 M9
Escravos →, *Nigeria* 83 D6
Escuinapa, *Mexico* 118 C3
Escuintla, *Guatemala* 120 D1
Eséka, *Cameroon* 83 E7
Eşen →, *Turkey* 47 E11
Esenguly, *Turkmenistan* 52 F6
Esens, *Germany* 24 B3
Esenyurt, *Turkey* 45 E12
Esera →, *Spain* 38 C5
Eşfahān, *Iran* 71 C6
Eşfahān □, *Iran* 71 C6
Esfarāyen, *Iran* 71 B8
Esfideh, *Iran* 71 C8
Esgueva →, *Spain* 36 D6
Esh Sham = Dimashq, *Syria* 74 B5
Esh Shamâlîya □, *Sudan* 80 D2
Esha Ness, *U.K.* 13 A7
Eshan, *China* 58 E4
Esher, *U.K.* 15 F7
Eshkol △, *Israel* 74 D3
Eshowe, *S. Africa* 89 D5
Esiama, *Ghana* 82 E4
Esigodini, *Zimbabwe* 89 C4
Esil = Ishim →, *Russia* 52 D8
Esino →, *Italy* 41 E10
Esira, *Madag.* 89 C8
Esk →, *Cumb., U.K.* 13 G5
Esk →, *N. Yorks., U.K.* 14 C7
Eskān, *Iran* 71 E9
Esker, *Canada* 105 B6
Eskifjörður, *Iceland* 8 D7
Eskilsäter, *Sweden* 11 F7
Eskilstuna, *Sweden* 10 E10
Eskimalatya, *Turkey* 73 C8
Eskimo Point = Arviat, *Canada* 103 A10
Eskişehir, *Turkey* 47 B12
Eskişehir □, *Turkey* 47 B12
Esla →, *Spain* 36 D4
Eslāmābād-e Gharb, *Iran* 70 C5
Eslāmshahr, *Iran* 71 C6
Eslöv, *Sweden* 11 J7
Eşme, *Turkey* 47 C10
Esmeraldas, *Ecuador* 124 C3
Esnagi L., *Canada* 104 C3
Espalion, *France* 20 D6
Espanola, *Canada* 104 C3
Espanola, *U.S.A.* 109 H10
Esparreguera, *Spain* 38 D6
Esparta, *Costa Rica* 120 E3
Espelkamp, *Germany* 24 C4
Esperance, *Australia* 93 F3
Esperance B., *Australia* 93 F3
Esperance Harbour, *St. Lucia* 121 f
Esperanza, *Antarctica* 5 C18
Esperanza, *Argentina* 126 C3
Esperanza, *Phil.* 61 G6
Esperanza, *Puerto Rico* 121 d
Espéraza, *France* 20 F6
Espichel, C., *Portugal* 37 G1
Espiel, *Spain* 37 G5
Espigão, Serra do, *Brazil* 127 B5
Espinazo, Sierra del = Espinhaço, Serra do, *Brazil* 125 G10
Espinhaço, Serra do, *Brazil* 125 G10
Espinho, *Portugal* 36 D2
Espinilho, Serra do, *Brazil* 127 B5
Espinosa de los Monteros, *Spain* 36 B7
Espírito Santo □, *Brazil* 125 H10
Espíritu Santo, *Vanuatu* 96 J8
Espíritu Santo, B. del, *Mexico* 119 D7
Espíritu Santo, I., *Mexico* 118 C2
Espita, *Mexico* 119 C7
Espiye, *Turkey* 73 B8
Espluga de Francolí, *Spain* 38 D6
Espoo, *Finland* 9 F21
Espuña, Sierra de, *Spain* 39 H3
Espungabera, *Mozam.* 89 C5
Esquel, *Argentina* 128 E2
Esquimalt, *Canada* 102 D4
Esquina, *Argentina* 126 C4
Essaouira, *Morocco* 78 B4
Essebie, *Dem. Rep. of the Congo* 86 B3
Essen, *Belgium* 17 C4
Essen, *Germany* 24 D3
Essendon, Mt., *Australia* 93 E3
Essequibo →, *Guyana* 124 B7
Essex, *Canada* 116 D2
Essex, *Calif., U.S.A.* 111 L11
Essex, *N.Y., U.S.A.* 117 B11
Essex □, *U.K.* 15 F8
Essex Junction, *U.S.A.* 117 B11
Esslingen, *Germany* 25 G5
Essonne □, *France* 19 D9
Estaca de Bares, C. de, *Spain* 36 B3
Estadilla, *Spain* 38 C5
Estados, I. de Los, *Argentina* 128 G4
Estagel, *France* 20 F6
Eşţahbānāt, *Iran* 71 D7
Estância, *Brazil* 125 F11
Estancia, *U.S.A.* 109 J10
Estārm, *Iran* 71 D8
Estarreja, *Portugal* 36 E2
Estats, Pic d', *Spain* 38 C6
Estcourt, *S. Africa* 89 D4
Este, *Italy* 41 C8
Este △, *Dom. Rep.* 121 C6
Estelí, *Nic.* 120 D2
Estella, *Spain* 38 C2
Estellencs, *Spain* 48 B9
Estena →, *Spain* 37 F6
Estepa, *Spain* 37 H6
Estepona, *Spain* 37 J5
Esterhazy, *Canada* 103 C8
Esternay, *France* 19 D10
Esterri d'Aneu, *Spain* 38 C6
Estevan, *Canada* 103 D8
Estevan Group, *Canada* 102 C3
Estherville, *U.S.A.* 112 D7
Estissac, *France* 19 D10
Eston, *Canada* 103 C7
Estonia ■, *Europe* 9 G21
Estoril, *Portugal* 37 G1
Estouk, *Mali* 83 B5
Estreito, *Brazil* 125 E9
Estrela, Serra da, *Portugal* 36 E3
Estrella, *Spain* 37 G7
Estremoz, *Portugal* 37 G3
Estrondo, Serra do, *Brazil* 125 E9
Esztergom, *Hungary* 28 C3
Et Tîdra, *Mauritania* 82 B1
Etah, *India* 69 F8
Étain, *France* 19 C12
Étampes, *France* 19 D9
Etanga, *Namibia* 88 B1
Étaples, *France* 19 B8
Etawah, *India* 69 F8
Etawney L., *Canada* 103 B9
Ete, *Nigeria* 83 D6
Ethel, *U.S.A.* 110 D4
Ethelbert, *Canada* 103 C8
Ethiopia ■, *Africa* 75 F3
Ethiopian Highlands, *Ethiopia* 50 J7
Etili, *Turkey* 45 G10
Etive, L., *U.K.* 13 E3
Etna, *Italy* 43 E7
Etoile, *Dem. Rep. of the Congo* 87 E2
Etosha △, *Namibia* 88 B2
Etosha Pan, *Namibia* 88 B2
Etowah, *U.S.A.* 115 H3
Étréchy, *France* 19 D9
Étrépagny, *France* 19 C8
Étretat, *France* 18 C7
Etropole, *Bulgaria* 45 D8
Ettelbruck, *Lux.* 17 E6
Ettlingen, *Germany* 25 G4
Ettrick Water →, *U.K.* 13 F6
Etuku, *Dem. Rep. of the Congo* 86 C2
Etulia, *Moldova* 29 E13
Etzatlán, *Mexico* 118 C4
Etzná, *Mexico* 119 D6
Etzná-Tixmucuy = Edxná, *Mexico* 119 D6
Eu, *France* 18 B8
Eubenangee Swamp △, *Australia* 94 B4
Euboea = Évvoia, *Greece* 46 C6
Eucla, *Australia* 93 F4
Euclid, *U.S.A.* 116 E3
Eucumbene, L., *Australia* 95 F4
Eudora, *U.S.A.* 113 J9
Eufaula, *Ala., U.S.A.* 115 K3
Eufaula, *Okla., U.S.A.* 113 H7
Eufaula L., *U.S.A.* 113 H7
Eugene, *U.S.A.* 108 E2
Eugowra, *Australia* 95 E4
Eulo, *Australia* 95 D4
Eungella △, *Australia* 94 C4
Eunice, *La., U.S.A.* 113 K8
Eunice, *N. Mex., U.S.A.* 113 J3
Eupen, *Belgium* 17 D6
Euphrates = Furāt, Nahr al →, *Asia* 70 D5
Eure □, *France* 18 C8
Eure →, *France* 18 C8
Eure-et-Loir □, *France* 18 D8
Eureka, *Canada* 4 B3
Eureka, *Calif., U.S.A.* 108 F1
Eureka, *Kans., U.S.A.* 113 G6
Eureka, *Mont., U.S.A.* 108 B6
Eureka, *Nev., U.S.A.* 108 G5
Eureka, *S. Dak., U.S.A.* 112 C5
Eureka, Mt., *Australia* 93 E3
Euroa, *Australia* 95 F4
Europa, Île, *Ind. Oc.* 85 J8
Europa, Picos de, *Spain* 36 B6
Europa, Pta. de, *Gib.* 37 J5
Europe 6 E10
Europoort, *Neths.* 17 C4
Euskirchen, *Germany* 24 E2
Eustis, *U.S.A.* 115 L5
Eutin, *Germany* 24 A6
Eutsuk L., *Canada* 102 C3
Evale, *Angola* 88 B2
Evans, *U.S.A.* 112 E2
Evans, L., *Canada* 104 B4
Evans City, *U.S.A.* 116 F4
Evans Head, *Australia* 95 D5
Evans Mills, *U.S.A.* 117 B9
Evansburg, *Canada* 102 C5
Evanston, *Ill., U.S.A.* 114 E2
Evanston, *Wyo., U.S.A.* 108 F8
Evansville, *U.S.A.* 114 G2
Évaux-les-Bains, *France* 19 F9
Evaz, *Iran* 71 E7
Evciler, *Afyon, Turkey* 47 C11
Evciler, *Çanakkale, Turkey* 47 B8
Eveleth, *U.S.A.* 112 B8
Evensk, *Russia* 53 C16
Everard, L., *Australia* 95 E2
Everard Ranges, *Australia* 93 E5
Everest, Mt., *Nepal* 69 E12
Everett, *Pa., U.S.A.* 116 F6
Everett, *Wash., U.S.A.* 110 C4
Everglades △, *U.S.A.* 115 N5
Everglades, The, *U.S.A.* 115 N5
Everglades City, *U.S.A.* 115 N5
Evergreen, *Ala., U.S.A.* 115 K2
Evergreen, *Mont., U.S.A.* 108 B6
Everöd, *Sweden* 11 J8
Evertsberg, *Sweden* 10 C7
Evesham, *U.K.* 15 E6
Évian-les-Bains, *France* 19 F13
Évinos →, *Greece* 46 C3
Évisa, *France* 21 F12
Evje, *Norway* 9 G12
Évora, *Portugal* 37 G3
Évora □, *Portugal* 37 G3
Evowghlī, *Iran* 70 B5
Évreux, *France* 18 C8
Evritanía □, *Greece* 46 B3
Évron, *France* 18 D6

Évros □, *Greece* 45 E10
Évros ➛, *Greece* 72 B2
Evrótas ➛, *Greece* 46 E4
Évry, *France* 19 D9
Évvoia, *Greece* 46 C6
Évvoia □, *Greece* 46 C5
Evxinoúpolis, *Greece* 46 B4
Ewe, L., *U.K.* 13 D3
Ewing, *U.S.A.* 112 D5
Ewo, *Congo* 84 E2
Exaltación, *Bolivia* 124 F5
Excelsior Springs, *U.S.A.* 112 F7
Excideuil, *France* 20 C5
Exe ➛, *U.K.* 15 G4
Exeter, *Canada* 116 C3
Exeter, *U.K.* 15 G4
Exeter, *Calif., U.S.A.* 110 J7
Exeter, *N.H., U.S.A.* 117 D14
Exmoor, *U.K.* 15 F4
Exmoor △, *U.K.* 15 F4
Exmouth, *Australia* 92 D1
Exmouth, *U.K.* 15 G4
Exmouth G., *Australia* 92 D1
Expedition △, *Australia* 95 D4
Expedition Ra., *Australia* 94 C4
Extremadura □, *Spain* 37 F4
Exuma Sound, *Bahamas* 120 B4
Eyasi, L., *Tanzania* 86 C4
Eye Pen., *U.K.* 13 C2
Eyemouth, *U.K.* 13 F6
Eygues = Aigues ➛, *France* 21 D8
Eygurande, *France* 19 G9
Eyjafjörður, *Iceland* 8 C4
Eymet, *France* 20 D4
Eymoutiers, *France* 20 C5
Eynesil, *Turkey* 73 B8
Eyre (North), L., *Australia* 95 D2
Eyre (South), L., *Australia* 95 D2
Eyre Mts., *N.Z.* 91 L2
Eyre Pen., *Australia* 95 E2
Eysturoy, *Færoe Is.* 8 E9
Eyvānkī, *Iran* 71 C6
Ez Zeidab, *Sudan* 80 D3
Ezcaray, *Spain* 38 C1
Ežerėlis, *Lithuania* 30 D10
Ezhou, *China* 59 B10
Ezine, *Turkey* 47 B8
Ezouza ➛, *Cyprus* 49 E11

F

F.Y.R.O.M. = Macedonia ■, *Europe* 44 E5
Fabala, *Guinea* 82 D3
Fabens, *U.S.A.* 109 L10
Fabero, *Spain* 36 C4
Fåborg, *Denmark* 11 J4
Fabriano, *Italy* 41 E9
Făcăeni, *Romania* 29 F12
Fachi, *Niger* 79 E8
Fada, *Chad* 79 E10
Fada-n-Gourma, *Burkina Faso* 83 C5
Fadd, *Hungary* 28 D3
Faddeyevskiy, Ostrov, *Russia* 53 B15
Faddor, *Sudan* 81 F3
Fadghāmī, *Syria* 70 C4
Fadlab, *Sudan* 80 D3
Faenza, *Italy* 41 D8
Færoe Is. = Føroyar, *Atl. Oc.* 8 F9
Fafa, *Mali* 83 B5
Fafe, *Portugal* 36 D2
Fagam, *Nigeria* 83 C7
Făgăras, *Romania* 29 E9
Făgăras, Munţii, *Romania* 29 E9
Fågelmara, *Sweden* 11 H9
Fagerhult, *Sweden* 11 G9
Fagersta, *Sweden* 10 D9
Făget, *Romania* 28 E7
Făget, Munţii, *Romania* 29 C8
Fagnano, L., *Argentina* 128 G3
Fagnières, *France* 19 D11
Faguibine, L., *Mali* 82 B4
Fahlīān, *Iran* 71 D6
Fahraj, *Kermān, Iran* 71 D8
Fahraj, *Yazd, Iran* 71 D7
Fai Tsi Long, *Vietnam* 58 G6
Faial, *Madeira* 48 D3
Fair Haven, *U.S.A.* 114 D9
Fair Hd., *U.K.* 12 A5
Fair Oaks, *U.S.A.* 110 G5
Fairbanks, *U.S.A.* 100 B5
Fairbury, *U.S.A.* 112 E6
Fairfax, *U.S.A.* 117 B11
Fairfield, *Ala., U.S.A.* 115 J2
Fairfield, *Calif., U.S.A.* 110 G4
Fairfield, *Conn., U.S.A.* 117 E11
Fairfield, *Idaho, U.S.A.* 108 E6
Fairfield, *Ill., U.S.A.* 114 F1
Fairfield, *Iowa, U.S.A.* 112 E9
Fairfield, *Tex., U.S.A.* 113 K7
Fairford, *Canada* 103 C9
Fairhope, *U.S.A.* 115 K2
Fairlie, *N.Z.* 91 L3
Fairmead, *U.S.A.* 110 H6
Fairmont, *Minn., U.S.A.* 112 D7
Fairmont, *W. Va., U.S.A.* 114 F5
Fairmount, *Calif., U.S.A.* 111 L8
Fairmount, *N.Y., U.S.A.* 117 C8
Fairplay, *U.S.A.* 109 G11
Fairport, *U.S.A.* 116 C7
Fairport Harbor, *U.S.A.* 116 E3
Fairview, *Canada* 102 B5
Fairview, *Mont., U.S.A.* 112 B2
Fairview, *Okla., U.S.A.* 113 G5
Fairweather, Mt., *U.S.A.* 102 B1
Faisalabad, *Pakistan* 68 D5
Faith, *U.S.A.* 112 C3
Faizabad, *India* 69 F10
Fajardo, *Puerto Rico* 121 d
Fajr, W. ➛, *Si. Arabia* 70 D3
Fakenham, *U.K.* 14 E8
Fåker, *Sweden* 10 A8
Fakfak, *Indonesia* 63 E8
Fakiya, *Bulgaria* 45 D11
Fakobli, *Ivory C.* 82 D3
Fakse, *Denmark* 11 J6
Fakse Bugt, *Denmark* 11 J6
Fakse Ladeplads, *Denmark* 11 J6
Faku, *China* 57 C12
Falaba, *S. Leone* 82 D2
Falaise, *France* 18 D6
Falaise, Mui, *Vietnam* 64 C5
Falakrón Óros, *Greece* 44 E7
Falam, *Burma* 67 H18
Falces, *Spain* 38 C3
Fălciu, *Romania* 29 D13
Falcó, C. des, *Spain* 48 C7
Falcón, Presa, *Mexico* 119 B5
Falcon Lake, *Canada* 103 D9
Falcon Reservoir, *U.S.A.* 113 M5
Falconara Marítima, *Italy* 41 E10
Falcone, C. del, *Italy* 42 B1
Falconer, *U.S.A.* 116 D5
Faléa, *Mali* 82 C2
Falémé ➛, *Senegal* 82 C2
Falerum, *Sweden* 11 F10
Faleshty = Făleşti, *Moldova* 29 C12
Făleşti, *Moldova* 29 C12
Falfurrias, *U.S.A.* 113 M5
Falher, *Canada* 102 B5
Falirakí, *Greece* 49 C10
Falkenberg, *Germany* 24 D9
Falkenberg, *Sweden* 11 H6
Falkensee, *Germany* 24 C9
Falkirk, *U.K.* 13 F5
Falkirk □, *U.K.* 13 F5
Falkland, *U.K.* 13 E5
Falkland Is. ⊠, *Atl. Oc.* 128 G5
Falkland Sd., *Falk. Is.* 128 G5
Falkonéra, *Greece* 46 E5
Falköping, *Sweden* 11 F7
Fall River, *U.S.A.* 117 E13
Fallbrook, *U.S.A.* 111 M9
Fallon, *U.S.A.* 108 G4
Falls City, *U.S.A.* 112 E7
Falls Creek, *U.S.A.* 116 E6
Falmouth, *Jamaica* 120 a
Falmouth, *U.K.* 15 G2
Falmouth, *U.S.A.* 117 E14
Falsa, Pta., *Mexico* 118 B1
False B., *S. Africa* 88 E2
Falso, C., *Honduras* 120 C3
Falster, *Denmark* 11 K5
Falsterbo, *Sweden* 9 J15
Fălticeni, *Romania* 29 C11
Falun, *Sweden* 10 D9
Famagusta, *Cyprus* 49 D12
Famagusta Bay, *Cyprus* 49 D13
Famalé, *Niger* 78 F6
Famatina, Sierra de, *Argentina* 126 B2
Family L., *Canada* 103 C9
Famoso, *U.S.A.* 111 K7
Fan Xian, *China* 56 G8
Fana, *Mali* 82 C3
Fanad Hd., *Ireland* 12 A4
Fanárion, *Greece* 46 B3
Fandriana, *Madag.* 89 C8
Fánes-Sénnes e Braies ⌓, *Italy* 41 B9
Fang, *Thailand* 58 H2
Fang Xian, *China* 59 A8
Fangaga, *Sudan* 80 D4
Fangak, *Sudan* 81 F3
Fangchang, *China* 59 B12
Fangcheng, *China* 56 H7
Fangchenggang, *China* 58 G7
Fangliao, *Taiwan* 59 F13
Fangshan, *China* 56 E6
Fangzi, *China* 57 F10
Fani i Madh ➛, *Albania* 44 E4
Fanjakana, *Madag.* 89 C8
Fanjiatun, *China* 57 C13
Fannich, L., *U.K.* 13 D4
Fannūj, *Iran* 71 E8
Fanø, *Denmark* 11 J2
Fano, *Italy* 41 E10
Fanshi, *China* 56 E7
Fao = Al Fāw, *Iraq* 71 D6
Faqirwali, *Pakistan* 68 E5
Fâqûs, *Egypt* 80 H7
Far East = Dalnevostochnyy □, *Russia* 53 C14
Far East, *Asia* 50 E16
Fara in Sabina, *Italy* 41 F9
Faradje, *Dem. Rep. of the Congo* 86 B2
Farafangana, *Madag.* 89 C8
Farâfra, El Wâhât el-, *Egypt* 80 B2
Farāh, *Afghan.* 66 C3
Farāh □, *Afghan.* 66 C3
Farahalana, *Madag.* 89 A9
Faraid, Gebel, *Egypt* 80 C4
Farako, *Ivory C.* 82 D4
Faramana, *Burkina Faso* 82 C4
Faranah, *Guinea* 82 C2
Farasān, Jazā'ir, *Si. Arabia* 75 D3
Farasan Is. = Farasān, Jazā'ir, *Si. Arabia* 75 D3
Faratsiho, *Madag.* 89 B8
Fardes ➛, *Spain* 37 H7
Fareham, *U.K.* 15 G6
Farewell, C., *N.Z.* 91 J4
Farewell C. = Nunap Isua, *Greenland* 101 C15
Färgelanda, *Sweden* 11 F5
Farghona, *Uzbekistan* 52 E8
Fargo, *U.S.A.* 112 B6
Fār'iah, W. al ➛, *West Bank* 74 C4
Faribault, *U.S.A.* 112 C8
Faridabad, *India* 68 E6
Faridkot, *India* 68 D6
Faridpur, *Bangla.* 69 H13
Faridpur, *India* 69 E8
Färila, *Sweden* 10 C9
Farim, *Guinea-Biss.* 82 C1
Farīmān, *Iran* 71 C8
Farina, *Australia* 95 E2
Fariones, Pta., *Canary Is.* 48 E6
Fâriskûr, *Egypt* 80 H7
Färjestaden, *Sweden* 11 H10
Farkadhón, *Greece* 46 B4
Farleigh, *Australia* 94 K7
Farmakonisi, *Greece* 47 D9
Farmerville, *U.S.A.* 113 J8
Farmingdale, *U.S.A.* 117 F10
Farmington, *Canada* 102 B4
Farmington, *Calif., U.S.A.* 110 H6
Farmington, *Maine, U.S.A.* 115 C10
Farmington, *Mo., U.S.A.* 113 G9
Farmington, *N.H., U.S.A.* 117 C13
Farmington, *N. Mex., U.S.A.* 109 H9
Farmington, *Utah, U.S.A.* 108 F8
Farmington ➛, *U.S.A.* 117 E12
Farmville, *U.S.A.* 114 G6
Färnäs, *Sweden* 10 D8
Farne Is., *U.K.* 14 B6
Färnebofjärden △, *Sweden* 10 D10
Farnham, *Canada* 117 A12
Farnham, Mt., *Canada* 102 C5
Faro, *Brazil* 125 D7
Faro, *Canada* 100 B6
Faro, *Portugal* 37 H3
Fårö, *Sweden* 9 H18
Faro □, *Portugal* 37 H2
Faro ✈ (FAO), *Portugal* 37 H3
Fårösund, *Sweden* 11 G13
Farquhar, C., *Australia* 93 D1
Farrars Cr. ➛, *Australia* 94 D3
Farrāshband, *Iran* 71 D7
Farrell, *U.S.A.* 116 E4
Farrokhī, *Iran* 71 C8
Farruch, C. = Ferrutx, C., *Spain* 48 B10
Fārs □, *Iran* 71 D7
Fársala, *Greece* 46 B4
Farsø, *Denmark* 11 H3
Farson, *U.S.A.* 108 E9
Farsund, *Norway* 9 G12
Fartak, Râs, *Si. Arabia* 70 D2
Fartak, Ra's, *Yemen* 75 D5
Fârtăneşti, *Romania* 29 E12
Fartura, Serra da, *Brazil* 127 B5
Faru, *Nigeria* 83 C6
Fārūj, *Iran* 71 B8
Fårup, *Denmark* 11 H3
Farvel, Kap = Nunap Isua, *Greenland* 101 C15
Farwell, *U.S.A.* 113 H3
Fāryāb □, *Afghan.* 66 B4
Fasā, *Iran* 71 D7
Fasano, *Italy* 43 B10
Fashoda, *Sudan* 81 F3
Fassa, *Mali* 82 C3
Fastiv, *Ukraine* 33 G5
Fastnet Rock, *Ireland* 12 E2
Fastov = Fastiv, *Ukraine* 33 G5
Fatagar, Tanjung, *Indonesia* 63 E8
Fatehabad, *Haryana, India* 68 E6
Fatehabad, *Ut. P., India* 68 F8
Fatehgarh, *India* 69 F8
Fatehpur, *Bihar, India* 69 G11
Fatehpur, *Raj., India* 68 F6
Fatehpur, *Ut. P., India* 69 G9
Fatehpur, *Ut. P., India* 69 F9
Fatehpur Sikri, *India* 68 F6
Fatesh, *Russia* 33 F8
Fathai, *Sudan* 81 F3
Fathom Five ⌓, *Canada* 116 A3
Fatick, *Senegal* 82 C1
Fatima, *Canada* 105 C7
Fátima, *Portugal* 37 F2
Fatoya, *Guinea* 82 C3
Fatsa, *Turkey* 72 B7
Faucille, Col de la, *France* 19 F13
Faulkton, *U.S.A.* 112 C5
Faulquemont, *France* 19 C13
Faure I., *Australia* 93 E1
Făurei, *Romania* 29 E12
Fauresmith, *S. Africa* 88 D4
Fauske, *Norway* 8 C16
Favara, *Italy* 42 E6
Faváritx, C. de, *Spain* 48 B11
Faverges, *France* 21 C10
Favignana, *Italy* 42 E5
Favignana, I., *Italy* 42 E5
Fawcett, Pt., *Australia* 92 B5
Fawn ➛, *Canada* 104 A2
Fawnskin, *U.S.A.* 111 L10
Faxaflói, *Iceland* 8 D2
Faxälven ➛, *Sweden* 10 A10
Faya-Largeau, *Chad* 79 E9
Fayd, *Si. Arabia* 70 E4
Fayence, *France* 21 E10
Fayette, *Ala., U.S.A.* 115 J2
Fayette, *Mo., U.S.A.* 112 F8
Fayetteville, *Ark., U.S.A.* 113 G7
Fayetteville, *N.C., U.S.A.* 115 H6
Fayetteville, *Tenn., U.S.A.* 115 H2
Fayied, *Egypt* 80 H8
Fayón, *Spain* 38 D5
Fazao-Malfakassa △, *Togo* 83 D5
Fazilka, *India* 68 D6
Fazilpur, *Pakistan* 68 E4
Fdérik, *Mauritania* 78 D3
Feale ➛, *Ireland* 12 D2
Fear, C., *U.S.A.* 115 J7
Feather ➛, *U.S.A.* 108 G3
Feather Falls, *U.S.A.* 110 F5
Featherston, *N.Z.* 91 J5
Featherstone, *Zimbabwe* 87 F3
Fécamp, *France* 18 C7
Fedala = Mohammedia, *Morocco* 78 B4
Federación, *Argentina* 126 C4
Féderal, *Argentina* 128 C5
Federal Capital Terr. □, *Nigeria* 83 D6
Federal Way, *U.S.A.* 110 C4
Fedeshkūh, *Iran* 71 D7
Fehérgyarmat, *Hungary* 28 C7
Fehmarn, *Germany* 24 A7
Fehmarn Bælt, *Europe* 11 K5
Fehmarn Belt = Fehmarn Bælt, *Europe* 11 K5
Fei Xian, *China* 57 G9
Feijó, *Brazil* 124 E4
Feilding, *N.Z.* 91 J5
Feira de Santana, *Brazil* 125 F11
Feixi, *China* 59 B11
Feixiang, *China* 56 F8
Fejér □, *Hungary* 28 C3
Fejø, *Denmark* 11 K5
Feke, *Turkey* 72 D6
Fekete ➛, *Hungary* 28 E3
Felanitx, *Spain* 48 B10
Feldbach, *Austria* 26 E8
Feldberg, *Baden-W., Germany* 25 H3
Feldberg, *Mecklenburg-Vorpommern, Germany* 24 B9
Feldkirch, *Austria* 26 D2
Feldkirchen, *Austria* 26 E7
Felipe Carrillo Puerto, *Mexico* 119 D7
Felixburg, *Zimbabwe* 89 B5
Felixstowe, *U.K.* 15 F9
Felletin, *France* 20 C6
Fellingsbro, *Sweden* 10 E9
Felton, *U.S.A.* 110 H4
Feltre, *Italy* 41 B8
Femer Bælt = Fehmarn Bælt, *Europe* 11 K5
Femø, *Denmark* 11 K5
Femunden, *Norway* 9 E14
Fen He ➛, *China* 56 G6
Fene, *Spain* 36 B2
Fenelon Falls, *Canada* 116 B6
Fener Burnu, *Turkey* 47 E9
Feneroa, *Ethiopia* 81 E4
Feng Xian, *Jiangsu, China* 56 G9
Feng Xian, *Shaanxi, China* 56 H4
Fengári, *Greece* 45 F9
Fengcheng, *Jiangxi, China* 59 C10
Fengcheng, *Liaoning, China* 57 D13
Fengfeng, *China* 56 F8
Fenggang, *China* 58 D6
Fenghua, *China* 59 C13
Fenghuang, *China* 58 D7
Fengkai, *China* 59 F8
Fengkang, *Taiwan* 59 F13
Fengle, *China* 59 B9
Fenglin, *Taiwan* 59 F13
Fengning, *China* 56 D9
Fengqing, *China* 58 E2
Fengqiu, *China* 56 G8
Fengrun, *China* 57 E10
Fengshan, *Guangxi Zhuangzu, China* 58 E7
Fengshan, *Guangxi Zhuangzu, China* 58 E6
Fengshan, *Taiwan* 59 F13
Fengshun, *China* 59 F11
Fengtai, *Anhui, China* 59 A11
Fengtai, *Beijing, China* 56 E9
Fengxian, *China* 59 B13
Fengxiang, *China* 56 G4
Fengxin, *China* 59 C10
Fengyang, *China* 57 H9
Fengyi, *China* 58 E3
Fengyüan, *Taiwan* 59 E13
Fengzhen, *China* 56 D7
Feno, C. de, *France* 21 G12
Fenoarivo, *Fianarantsoa, Madag.* 89 C8
Fenoarivo, *Fianarantsoa, Madag.* 89 C8
Fenoarivo Afovoany, *Madag.* 89 B8
Fenoarivo Atsinanana, *Madag.* 89 B8
Fens, The, *U.K.* 14 E7
Fensmark, *Denmark* 11 J5
Fenton, *U.S.A.* 114 D4
Fenxi, *China* 56 F6
Fenyang, *China* 56 F6
Fenyi, *China* 59 D10
Feodosiya, *Ukraine* 33 K8
Ferdows, *Iran* 71 C8
Fère-Champenoise, *France* 19 D10
Fère-en-Tardenois, *France* 19 C10
Ferentino, *Italy* 41 G10
Ferfer, *Somali Rep.* 75 F4
Fergana = Farghona, *Uzbekistan* 52 E8
Fergus, *Canada* 116 C4
Fergus Falls, *U.S.A.* 112 B6
Feričanci, *Croatia* 28 E2
Ferihegy, Budapest ✈ (BUD), *Hungary* 28 C4
Ferkéssédougou, *Ivory C.* 82 D3
Ferlach, *Austria* 26 E7
Ferland, *Canada* 104 B2
Ferlo, Vallée du, *Senegal* 82 B2
Ferlo-Nord ⌓, *Senegal* 82 B2
Ferlo-Sud ⌓, *Senegal* 82 B2
Fermanagh □, *U.K.* 12 B4
Fermo, *Italy* 41 E10
Fermont, *Canada* 105 B6
Fermoselle, *Spain* 36 D4
Fermoy, *Ireland* 12 D3
Fernán Nuñez, *Spain* 37 H6
Fernández, *Argentina* 126 B3
Fernandina Beach, *U.S.A.* 115 K5
Fernando de Noronha, *Brazil* 125 D12
Fernando Póo = Bioko, *Eq. Guin.* 83 E6
Ferndale, *U.S.A.* 110 B4
Fernie, *Canada* 102 D5
Fernlees, *Australia* 94 C4
Fernley, *U.S.A.* 108 G4
Ferozepore = Firozpur, *India* 68 D6
Férrai, *Greece* 45 F10
Ferrandina, *Italy* 43 B9
Ferrara, *Italy* 41 D8
Ferrato, C., *Italy* 42 C2
Ferreira do Alentejo, *Portugal* 37 G2
Ferreñafe, *Peru* 124 E3
Ferrerías, *Spain* 48 B11
Ferret, C., *France* 20 D2
Ferrette, *France* 19 E14
Ferriday, *U.S.A.* 113 K9
Ferriere, *Italy* 40 D6
Ferrières, *France* 19 D9
Ferro, Capo, *Italy* 42 A2
Ferrol, *Spain* 36 B2
Ferron, *U.S.A.* 109 G8
Ferrutx, C., *Spain* 48 B10
Ferryland, *Canada* 105 C9
Fertile, *U.S.A.* 112 B6
Fertőszentmiklós, *Hungary* 28 C1
Fertotavi △, *Hungary* 28 C1
Fès, *Morocco* 78 B5
Fessenden, *U.S.A.* 112 B5
Festus, *U.S.A.* 112 F9
Feté Bowé, *Senegal* 82 C2
Feteşti, *Romania* 29 F12
Fethiye, *Turkey* 47 E11
Fethiye Körfezi, *Turkey* 47 E10
Fetlar, *U.K.* 13 A8
Feuilles ➛, *Canada* 101 C12
Feurs, *France* 21 C8
Fez = Fès, *Morocco* 78 B5
Fezzan, *Libya* 79 C8
Fiambalá, *Argentina* 126 B2
Fianarantsoa, *Madag.* 89 C8
Fianarantsoa □, *Madag.* 89 B8
Fiche, *Ethiopia* 81 F4
Fichtelgebirge, *Germany* 25 E7
Fichtelgebirge ⌓, *Germany* 25 E8
Ficksburg, *S. Africa* 89 D4
Fidenza, *Italy* 40 D7
Fiditi, *Nigeria* 83 D5
Field ➛, *Australia* 94 C2
Field I., *Australia* 92 B5
Fieni, *Romania* 29 E10
Fier, *Albania* 44 F3
Fierzë, *Albania* 44 D4
Fife ⌓, *U.K.* 13 E5
Fife □, *U.K.* 13 E5
Fife Ness, *U.K.* 13 E6
Fifth Cataract, *Sudan* 80 D3
Figari, *France* 21 G13
Figeac, *France* 20 D6
Figeholm, *Sweden* 11 G10
Figline Valdarno, *Italy* 41 E8
Figtree, *Zimbabwe* 87 G2
Figueira Castelo Rodrigo, *Portugal* 36 E4
Figueira da Foz, *Portugal* 36 E2
Figueiró dos Vinhos, *Portugal* 36 F2
Figueres, *Spain* 38 C7
Figuig, *Morocco* 78 B5
Fihaonana, *Madag.* 89 B8
Fiherenana, *Madag.* 89 B8
Fiherenana ➛, *Madag.* 89 C7
Fiji ■, *Pac. Oc.* 91 C8
Fik, *Ethiopia* 81 F5
Fika, *Nigeria* 83 C7
Filabres, Sierra de los, *Spain* 37 H8
Filabusi, *Zimbabwe* 89 C4
Filadélfia, *Italy* 43 D9
Fil'akovo, *Slovak Rep.* 27 C12
Filey, *U.K.* 14 C7
Filey B., *U.K.* 14 C7
Filfla, *Malta* 49 D1
Filiaşi, *Romania* 29 F8
Filiátes, *Greece* 46 B2
Filiatrá, *Greece* 46 D3
Filicudi, *Italy* 43 D7
Filingué, *Niger* 83 C5
Filiourí ➛, *Greece* 45 E9
Filipstad, *Sweden* 10 E8
Filisur, *Switz.* 25 J5
Fillmore, *Calif., U.S.A.* 111 L8
Fillmore, *Utah, U.S.A.* 109 G7
Filótion, *Greece* 47 D7
Filottrano, *Italy* 41 E10
Filtu, *Ethiopia* 81 F5
Fina ⌓, *Mali* 82 C3
Finale Emília, *Italy* 41 D8
Finale Lígure, *Italy* 40 D5
Fiñana, *Spain* 37 H8
Finch, *Canada* 117 A9
Finch Hatton, *Australia* 94 K6
Findhorn ➛, *U.K.* 13 D5
Findlay, *U.S.A.* 114 E4
Finger L., *Canada* 104 B1
Finger Lakes, *U.S.A.* 117 D8
Fíngoè, *Mozam.* 87 E3
Finike, *Turkey* 47 E12
Finike Körfezi, *Turkey* 47 E12
Finiq, *Albania* 44 G4
Finistère □, *France* 18 D3
Finisterre = Fisterra, *Spain* 36 C1
Finisterre, C. = Fisterra, C., *Spain* 36 C1
Finke, *Australia* 94 D1
Finke Gorge △, *Australia* 92 D5
Finland ■, *Europe* 8 E22
Finland, G. of, *Europe* 9 G21
Finlay ➛, *Canada* 102 B3
Finley, *Australia* 95 F4
Finley, *U.S.A.* 112 B6
Finn ➛, *Ireland* 12 B4
Finnerödja, *Sweden* 11 F8
Finnigan, Mt., *Australia* 94 B4
Finniss, C., *Australia* 95 E1
Finnmark, *Norway* 8 B20
Finnsnes, *Norway* 8 B18
Finspång, *Sweden* 11 F9
Finsteraarhorn, *Switz.* 25 J4
Finsterwalde, *Germany* 24 D9
Fiora ➛, *Italy* 41 F8
Fiordland △, *N.Z.* 91 L1
Fiorenzuola d'Arda, *Italy* 40 D6
Fīq, *Syria* 74 C4

Firat = Furāt, Nahr al →, *Asia* 70 **D5**
Fire Island ◠, *U.S.A.* 117 **F11**
Firebag →, *Canada* 103 **B6**
Firebaugh, *U.S.A.* 110 **J6**
Firedrake L., *Canada* 103 **A8**
Firenze, *Italy* 41 **E8**
Firenze Amerigo Vespucci ✈ (FLR), *Italy* 40 **E8**
Firenze Pisa ✈ (PSA), *Italy* 40 **E7**
Firenzuola, *Italy* 41 **D8**
Firk, Sha'ib →, *Iraq* 70 **D5**
Firmi, *France* 20 **D6**
Firminy, *France* 21 **C8**
Firozabad, *India* 69 **F8**
Firozpur, *India* 68 **D6**
Firozpur-Jhirka, *India* 68 **F7**
Fīrūzābād, *Iran* 71 **D7**
Fīrūzkūh, *Iran* 71 **C7**
Firvale, *Canada* 102 **C3**
Fish →, *Namibia* 88 **D2**
Fish →, *S. Africa* 88 **E3**
Fish River Canyon, *Namibia* 88 **D2**
Fisher, *Australia* 93 **F5**
Fisher B., *Canada* 103 **C9**
Fishers I., *U.S.A.* 117 **E13**
Fishguard, *U.K.* 15 **E3**
Fishing L., *Canada* 103 **C9**
Fishkill, *U.S.A.* 117 **E11**
Fismes, *France* 19 **C10**
Fisterra, *Spain* 36 **C1**
Fisterra, C., *Spain* 36 **C1**
Fitchburg, *U.S.A.* 117 **D13**
Fitz Roy, *Argentina* 128 **F3**
Fitzgerald, *Canada* 102 **B6**
Fitzgerald, *U.S.A.* 115 **K4**
Fitzgerald River △, *Australia* 93 **F3**
Fitzmaurice →, *Australia* 92 **B5**
Fitzroy →, *Queens., Australia* 94 **C5**
Fitzroy →, *W. Austral., Australia* 92 **C3**
Fitzroy, Mte., *Argentina* 128 **F2**
Fitzroy Crossing, *Australia* 92 **C4**
Fitzwilliam I., *Canada* 116 **A3**
Fiuggi, *Italy* 41 **G10**
Fiume = Rijeka, *Croatia* 41 **C11**
Fiumicino, Roma ✈ (FCO), *Italy* 41 **G9**
Five Points, *U.S.A.* 110 **J6**
Fivizzano, *Italy* 40 **D7**
Fizi, *Dem. Rep. of the Congo* 86 **C2**
Fjällbacka, *Sweden* 11 **F5**
Fjärdhundra, *Sweden* 10 **E10**
Fjellerup, *Denmark* 11 **H4**
Fjerritslev, *Denmark* 11 **G3**
Fjugesta, *Sweden* 10 **E8**
Flagstaff, *U.S.A.* 109 **J8**
Flagstaff L., *U.S.A.* 115 **C10**
Flaherty I., *Canada* 104 **A4**
Flåm, *Norway* 9 **F12**
Flambeau →, *U.S.A.* 112 **C9**
Flamborough Hd., *U.K.* 14 **C7**
Fläming, *Germany* 24 **C8**
Flaming Gorge ◠, *U.S.A.* 108 **F9**
Flaming Gorge Reservoir, *U.S.A.* 108 **F9**
Flamingo, Teluk, *Indonesia* 63 **F9**
Flanders = Flandre, *Europe* 19 **B9**
Flandre, *Europe* 19 **B9**
Flandre-Occidentale = West-Vlaanderen □, *Belgium* 17 **D2**
Flandre-Orientale = Oost-Vlaanderen □, *Belgium* 17 **C3**
Flandreau, *U.S.A.* 112 **C6**
Flanigan, *U.S.A.* 110 **E7**
Flannan Is., *U.K.* 13 **C1**
Flåsjön, *Sweden* 8 **D16**
Flat →, *Canada* 102 **A3**
Flathead L., *U.S.A.* 108 **C7**
Flattery, C., *Australia* 94 **A4**
Flattery, C., *U.S.A.* 110 **B2**
Flatwoods, *U.S.A.* 114 **F4**
Fleetwood, *U.K.* 14 **D4**
Fleetwood, *U.S.A.* 117 **F9**
Flekkefjord, *Norway* 9 **G12**
Flemington, *U.S.A.* 116 **E7**
Flen, *Sweden* 10 **E10**
Flensburg, *Germany* 24 **A5**
Flers, *France* 18 **D6**
Flesherton, *Canada* 116 **B4**
Flesko, Tanjung, *Indonesia* 63 **D6**
Fleurance, *France* 20 **E4**
Fleurier, *Switz.* 25 **J2**
Fleurieu Pen., *Australia* 95 **F2**
Flevoland □, *Neths.* 17 **B5**
Flin Flon, *Canada* 103 **C8**
Flinders →, *Australia* 94 **B3**
Flinders B., *Australia* 93 **F2**
Flinders Group, *Australia* 94 **A3**
Flinders I., *S. Austral., Australia* 95 **E1**
Flinders I., *Tas., Australia* 95 **G4**
Flinders Ranges, *Australia* 95 **E2**
Flinders Reefs, *Australia* 94 **B4**
Flint, *U.K.* 14 **D4**
Flint, *U.S.A.* 114 **D4**
Flint →, *U.S.A.* 115 **K3**
Flint I., *Kiribati* 97 **J12**
Flintshire □, *U.K.* 14 **D4**
Fliseryd, *Sweden* 11 **G10**
Flix, *Spain* 38 **D5**
Flixecourt, *France* 19 **B9**
Floby, *Sweden* 11 **F7**
Floda, *Sweden* 11 **G6**
Flodden, *U.K.* 14 **B5**
Flogny-la-Chapelle, *France* 19 **E10**
Floodwood, *U.S.A.* 112 **B8**
Flora, *U.S.A.* 114 **F1**
Florac, *France* 20 **D7**
Florala, *U.S.A.* 115 **K2**
Florence = Firenze, *Italy* 41 **E8**
Florence, *Ala., U.S.A.* 115 **H2**
Florence, *Ariz., U.S.A.* 109 **K8**
Florence, *Colo., U.S.A.* 112 **F2**
Florence, *Oreg., U.S.A.* 108 **E1**
Florence, *S.C., U.S.A.* 115 **H6**
Florence, L., *Australia* 95 **D2**
Florencia, *Colombia* 124 **C3**
Florennes, *Belgium* 17 **D4**
Florensac, *France* 20 **E7**
Florenville, *Belgium* 17 **E5**
Flores, *Guatemala* 120 **C2**
Flores, *Indonesia* 63 **F6**
Flores I., *Canada* 102 **D3**
Flores Sea, *Indonesia* 63 **F6**
Floreşti, *Moldova* 29 **C13**
Floresville, *U.S.A.* 113 **L5**
Floriano, *Brazil* 125 **E10**
Florianópolis, *Brazil* 127 **B6**
Florida, *Cuba* 120 **B4**
Florida, *Uruguay* 127 **C4**
Florida □, *U.S.A.* 115 **L5**
Florida, Straits of, *U.S.A.* 120 **B4**
Florida B., *U.S.A.* 120 **B3**
Florida Keys, *U.S.A.* 115 **N5**
Florídia, *Italy* 43 **E8**
Flórina, *Greece* 44 **F5**
Flórina □, *Greece* 44 **F5**
Florø, *Norway* 9 **F11**
Flower Station, *Canada* 117 **A8**
Flowerpot I., *Canada* 116 **A3**
Floydada, *U.S.A.* 113 **J4**
Fluk, *Indonesia* 63 **E7**
Flúmen →, *Spain* 38 **D4**
Flumendosa →, *Italy* 42 **C2**
Fluminimaggiore, *Italy* 42 **C1**
Flushing = Vlissingen, *Neths.* 17 **C3**
Fluviá →, *Spain* 38 **C8**
Flying Fish, C., *Antarctica* 5 **D15**
Foam Lake, *Canada* 103 **C8**
Foča, *Bos.-H.* 44 **C2**
Foça, *Turkey* 47 **C8**
Fochabers, *U.K.* 13 **D5**
Focşani, *Romania* 29 **E12**
Fodécontéa, *Guinea* 82 **C2**
Fogang, *China* 59 **F9**
Fóggia, *Italy* 43 **A8**
Foggo, *Nigeria* 83 **C6**
Foglia →, *Italy* 41 **E9**
Fogo, *Canada* 105 **C9**
Fogo I., *Canada* 105 **C9**
Fohnsdorf, *Austria* 26 **D7**
Föhr, *Germany* 24 **A4**
Foia, *Portugal* 37 **H2**
Foix, *France* 20 **F5**
Fojnica, *Bos.-H.* 28 **G2**
Fokino, *Russia* 32 **F8**
Fokís □, *Greece* 46 **C4**
Fokku, *Nigeria* 83 **C5**
Folda, *Nord-Trøndelag, Norway* 8 **D14**
Folda, *Nordland, Norway* 8 **C16**
Földeák, *Hungary* 28 **D5**
Folégandros, *Greece* 46 **E6**
Foley, *Botswana* 88 **C4**
Foley, *U.S.A.* 115 **K2**
Foleyet, *Canada* 104 **C3**
Folgefonni, *Norway* 9 **F12**
Foligno, *Italy* 41 **F9**
Folkestone, *U.K.* 15 **F9**
Folkston, *U.S.A.* 115 **K5**
Follansbee, *U.S.A.* 116 **F4**
Follónica, *Italy* 40 **F7**
Follónica, G. di, *Italy* 40 **F7**
Folsom L., *U.S.A.* 110 **G5**
Folteşti, *Romania* 29 **E13**
Fond-du-Lac, *Canada* 103 **B7**
Fond du Lac, *U.S.A.* 112 **D10**
Fond-du-Lac →, *Canada* 103 **B7**
Fonda, *U.S.A.* 117 **D10**
Fondi, *Italy* 42 **A6**
Fonfría, *Spain* 36 **D4**
Fongafale, *Tuvalu* 96 **H9**
Fonni, *Italy* 42 **B2**
Fonsagrada = A Fonsagrada, *Spain* 36 **B3**
Fonseca, G. de, *Cent. Amer.* 120 **D2**
Font-Romeu-Odeillo-Via, *France* 20 **F5**
Fontaine-Française, *France* 19 **E12**
Fontainebleau, *France* 19 **D9**
Fontana, *U.S.A.* 111 **L9**
Fontas →, *Canada* 102 **B4**
Fonte Boa, *Brazil* 124 **D5**
Fontem, *Cameroon* 83 **D6**
Fontenay-le-Comte, *France* 20 **B3**
Fontenelle Reservoir, *U.S.A.* 108 **E8**
Fontur, *Iceland* 8 **C6**
Fonyód, *Hungary* 28 **D2**
Foochow = Fuzhou, *China* 59 **D12**
Foping, *China* 56 **H5**
Forbach, *France* 19 **C13**
Forbes, *Australia* 95 **E4**
Forbesganj, *India* 69 **F12**
Forcados, *Nigeria* 83 **D6**
Forcados →, *Nigeria* 83 **D6**
Forcalquier, *France* 21 **E9**
Forchheim, *Germany* 25 **F7**
Ford City, *Calif., U.S.A.* 111 **K7**
Ford City, *Pa., U.S.A.* 116 **F5**
Førde, *Norway* 9 **F11**
Ford's Bridge, *Australia* 95 **D4**
Fordyce, *U.S.A.* 113 **J8**
Forécariah, *Guinea* 82 **D2**
Forel, Mt., *Greenland* 98 **C16**
Foremost, *Canada* 102 **D6**
Forest, *Canada* 116 **C3**
Forest, *U.S.A.* 113 **J10**
Forest City, *Iowa, U.S.A.* 112 **D8**
Forest City, *N.C., U.S.A.* 115 **H5**
Forest City, *Pa., U.S.A.* 117 **E9**
Forest Grove, *U.S.A.* 110 **E3**
Forestburg, *Canada* 102 **C6**
Foreste Casentinesi-Monte Falterona-Campigna △, *Italy* 41 **E8**
Foresthill, *U.S.A.* 110 **F6**
Forestier Pen., *Australia* 95 **G4**
Forestville, *Canada* 105 **C6**
Forestville, *Calif., U.S.A.* 110 **G4**
Forestville, *N.Y., U.S.A.* 116 **D5**
Forêt d'Orient ◠, *France* 19 **D11**
Forez, Mts. du, *France* 20 **C7**
Forfar, *U.K.* 13 **E6**
Forillon △, *Canada* 105 **C7**
Forks, *U.S.A.* 110 **C2**
Forksville, *U.S.A.* 117 **E8**
Forlì, *Italy* 41 **D9**
Forman, *U.S.A.* 112 **B6**
Formazza, *Italy* 40 **B5**
Formby Pt., *U.K.* 14 **D4**
Formentera, *Spain* 48 **C7**
Formentor, C. de, *Spain* 48 **B10**
Former Yugoslav Republic of Macedonia = Macedonia ■, *Europe* 44 **E5**
Fórmia, *Italy* 42 **A6**
Formígine, *Italy* 40 **D7**
Formosa = Taiwan ■, *Asia* 59 **F13**
Formosa, *Argentina* 126 **B4**
Formosa, *Brazil* 125 **G9**
Formosa □, *Argentina* 126 **B4**
Formosa, Serra, *Brazil* 125 **F8**
Formosa B. = Ungwana B., *Kenya* 86 **C5**
Fornells, *Spain* 48 **A11**
Fornos de Algodres, *Portugal* 36 **E3**
Fornovo di Taro, *Italy* 40 **D7**
Føroyar, *Atl. Oc.* 8 **F9**
Forres, *U.K.* 13 **D5**
Forrest, *Australia* 93 **F4**
Forrest, Mt., *Australia* 93 **D4**
Forrest City, *U.S.A.* 113 **H9**
Fors, *Sweden* 10 **D10**
Forsayth, *Australia* 94 **B3**
Forshaga, *Sweden* 10 **E7**
Förslöv, *Sweden* 11 **H6**
Forsmo, *Sweden* 10 **A11**
Forssa, *Finland* 9 **F20**
Forst, *Germany* 24 **D10**
Forsvik, *Sweden* 11 **F8**
Forsyth, *U.S.A.* 108 **C10**
Fort Abbas, *Pakistan* 68 **E5**
Fort Albany, *Canada* 104 **B3**
Fort Ann, *U.S.A.* 117 **C11**
Fort Assiniboine, *Canada* 102 **C6**
Fort Augustus, *U.K.* 13 **D4**
Fort Beaufort, *S. Africa* 88 **E4**
Fort Benton, *U.S.A.* 108 **C8**
Fort Bragg, *U.S.A.* 108 **G2**
Fort Bridger, *U.S.A.* 108 **F8**
Fort Chipewyan, *Canada* 103 **B6**
Fort Clatsop ◠, *U.S.A.* 110 **D3**
Fort Collins, *U.S.A.* 112 **E2**
Fort-Coulonge, *Canada* 104 **C4**
Fort Covington, *U.S.A.* 117 **B10**
Fort Davis, *U.S.A.* 113 **K3**
Fort-de-France, *Martinique* 120 **c**
Fort Defiance, *U.S.A.* 109 **J9**
Fort Dodge, *U.S.A.* 112 **D7**
Fort Edward, *U.S.A.* 117 **C11**
Fort Erie, *Canada* 116 **D6**
Fort Fairfield, *U.S.A.* 115 **B12**
Fort Frances, *Canada* 103 **D10**
Fort Franklin = Déline, *Canada* 100 **B7**
Fort Garland, *U.S.A.* 109 **H11**
Fort George = Chisasibi, *Canada* 104 **B4**
Fort Good Hope, *Canada* 100 **B7**
Fort Hancock, *U.S.A.* 109 **L11**
Fort Hope, *Canada* 104 **B2**
Fort Irwin, *U.S.A.* 111 **K10**
Fort Kent, *U.S.A.* 115 **B11**
Fort Klamath, *U.S.A.* 108 **E3**
Fort Laramie, *U.S.A.* 112 **D2**
Fort Lauderdale, *U.S.A.* 115 **M5**
Fort Liard, *Canada* 102 **A4**
Fort Liberté, *Haiti* 121 **C5**
Fort Lupton, *U.S.A.* 112 **E2**
Fort MacKay, *Canada* 102 **B6**
Fort Macleod, *Canada* 102 **D6**
Fort McMurray, *Canada* 102 **B6**
Fort McPherson, *Canada* 100 **B6**
Fort Madison, *U.S.A.* 112 **E9**
Fort Meade, *U.S.A.* 115 **M5**
Fort Morgan, *U.S.A.* 112 **E3**
Fort Myers, *U.S.A.* 115 **M5**
Fort Nelson, *Canada* 102 **B4**
Fort Nelson →, *Canada* 102 **B4**
Fort Norman = Tulita, *Canada* 100 **B7**
Fort Payne, *U.S.A.* 115 **H3**
Fort Peck, *U.S.A.* 108 **B10**
Fort Peck Dam, *U.S.A.* 108 **C10**
Fort Peck L., *U.S.A.* 108 **C10**
Fort Pierce, *U.S.A.* 115 **M5**
Fort Pierre, *U.S.A.* 112 **C4**
Fort Plain, *U.S.A.* 117 **D10**
Fort Portal, *Uganda* 86 **B3**
Fort Providence, *Canada* 102 **A5**
Fort Qu'Appelle, *Canada* 103 **C8**
Fort Resolution, *Canada* 102 **A6**
Fort Rixon, *Zimbabwe* 87 **G2**
Fort Ross, *U.S.A.* 110 **G3**
Fort Rupert = Waskaganish, *Canada* 104 **B4**
Fort St. James, *Canada* 102 **C4**
Fort St. John, *Canada* 102 **B4**
Fort Saskatchewan, *Canada* 102 **C6**
Fort Scott, *U.S.A.* 113 **G7**
Fort Severn, *Canada* 104 **A2**
Fort Shevchenko, *Kazakhstan* 35 **H10**
Fort Simpson, *Canada* 102 **A4**
Fort Smith, *Canada* 102 **B6**
Fort Smith, *U.S.A.* 113 **H7**
Fort Stockton, *U.S.A.* 113 **K3**
Fort Sumner, *U.S.A.* 113 **H2**
Fort Thompson, *U.S.A.* 112 **C5**
Fort Union ◠, *U.S.A.* 113 **H2**
Fort Valley, *U.S.A.* 115 **J4**
Fort Vermilion, *Canada* 102 **B5**
Fort Walton Beach, *U.S.A.* 115 **K2**
Fort Wayne, *U.S.A.* 114 **E3**
Fort William, *U.K.* 13 **E3**
Fort Worth, *U.S.A.* 113 **J6**
Fort Yates, *U.S.A.* 112 **B4**
Fort Yukon, *U.S.A.* 100 **B5**
Fortaleza, *Brazil* 125 **D11**
Forteau, *Canada* 105 **B8**
Fortescue →, *Australia* 92 **D2**
Forth →, *U.K.* 13 **E5**
Forth, Firth of, *U.K.* 13 **E6**
Fortore →, *Italy* 41 **G12**
Fortrose, *U.K.* 13 **D4**
Fortuna, *Spain* 39 **G3**
Fortuna, *Calif., U.S.A.* 108 **F1**
Fortuna, *N. Dak., U.S.A.* 112 **A3**
Fortune, *Canada* 105 **C8**
Fortune B., *Canada* 105 **C8**
Forūr, *Iran* 71 **E7**
Fos-sur-Mer, *France* 21 **E8**
Foshan, *China* 59 **F9**
Fosna, *Norway* 8 **E14**
Fosnavåg, *Norway* 9 **E11**
Foso, *Ghana* 83 **D4**
Fossano, *Italy* 40 **D4**
Fossil, *U.S.A.* 108 **D3**
Fossil Butte ◠, *U.S.A.* 108 **F8**
Fossombrone, *Italy* 41 **E9**
Foster, *Canada* 117 **A12**
Foster →, *Canada* 103 **B7**
Fosters Ra., *Australia* 94 **C1**
Fostoria, *U.S.A.* 114 **E4**
Fotadrevo, *Madag.* 89 **C8**
Fouesnant, *France* 18 **E2**
Fougères, *France* 18 **D5**
Foul Pt., *Sri Lanka* 66 **Q12**
Foula, *U.K.* 13 **A6**
Foulalaba, *Mali* 82 **C3**
Foulness I., *U.K.* 15 **F8**
Foulpointe, *Madag.* 89 **B8**
Foulweather, C., *U.S.A.* 106 **B2**
Foumban, *Cameroon* 83 **D7**
Foumbot, *Cameroon* 83 **D7**
Foundiougne, *Senegal* 82 **C1**
Fountain, *U.S.A.* 112 **F2**
Fountain Springs, *U.S.A.* 111 **K8**
Fourchambault, *France* 19 **E10**
Fouriesburg, *S. Africa* 88 **D4**
Fourmies, *France* 19 **B11**
Fournás, *Greece* 46 **B3**
Foúrnoi, *Greece* 47 **D8**
Fours, *France* 19 **F10**
Fourth Cataract, *Sudan* 80 **D3**
Fouta Djallon, *Guinea* 82 **C2**
Foux, Cap-à-, *Haiti* 121 **C5**
Foveaux Str., *N.Z.* 91 **M2**
Fowey, *U.K.* 15 **G3**
Fowler, *Calif., U.S.A.* 110 **J7**
Fowler, *Colo., U.S.A.* 112 **F3**
Fowlers B., *Australia* 93 **F5**
Fowman, *Iran* 71 **B6**
Fox →, *Canada* 103 **B10**
Fox Creek, *Canada* 102 **C5**
Fox Lake, *Canada* 102 **B6**
Fox Valley, *Canada* 103 **C7**
Foxboro, *U.S.A.* 117 **D13**
Foxdale, *Australia* 94 **J6**
Foxe Basin, *Canada* 101 **B12**
Foxe Chan., *Canada* 101 **B11**
Foxe Pen., *Canada* 101 **B12**
Foxen, *Sweden* 10 **E5**
Foxton, *N.Z.* 91 **J5**
Foyle, Lough, *U.K.* 12 **A4**
Foynes, *Ireland* 12 **D2**
Foz, *Spain* 36 **B3**
Foz do Cunene, *Angola* 88 **B1**
Foz do Iguaçu, *Brazil* 127 **B5**
Frackville, *U.S.A.* 117 **F8**
Fraga, *Spain* 38 **D5**
Fraile Muerto, *Uruguay* 127 **C5**
Fram Basin, *Arctic* 4 **A**
Framingham, *U.S.A.* 117 **D13**
Frampol, *Poland* 31 **H9**
Franca, *Brazil* 125 **H9**
Francavilla al Mare, *Italy* 41 **F11**
Francavilla Fontana, *Italy* 43 **B10**
France ■, *Europe* 7 **F6**
Frances, *Australia* 95 **F3**
Frances →, *Canada* 102 **A3**
Frances L., *Canada* 102 **A3**
Franceville, *Gabon* 84 **E2**
Franche-Comté □, *France* 19 **F12**
Francis Case, L., *U.S.A.* 112 **D5**
Francisco Beltrão, *Brazil* 127 **B5**
Francisco I. Madero, *Coahuila, Mexico* 118 **B4**
Francisco I. Madero, *Durango, Mexico* 118 **C4**
Francistown, *Botswana* 89 **C4**
Francofonte, *Italy* 43 **E7**
François, *Canada* 105 **C8**
François L., *Canada* 102 **C3**
Francois Peron △, *Australia* 93 **E1**
Franeker, *Neths.* 17 **A5**
Frank Hann △, *Australia* 93 **F3**
Frankado, *Djibouti* 81 **E5**
Frankenberg, *Germany* 24 **D4**
Frankenhöhe ◠, *Germany* 25 **F6**
Frankenwald, *Germany* 25 **E7**
Frankenwald ◠, *Germany* 25 **E7**
Frankford, *Canada* 116 **B7**
Frankfort, *S. Africa* 89 **D4**
Frankfort, *Ind., U.S.A.* 114 **E2**
Frankfort, *Kans., U.S.A.* 112 **F6**
Frankfort, *Ky., U.S.A.* 114 **F3**
Frankfort, *N.Y., U.S.A.* 117 **C9**
Frankfurt, *Brandenburg, Germany* 24 **C10**
Frankfurt, *Hessen, Germany* 25 **E4**
Frankfurt ✈ (FRA), *Germany* 25 **E4**
Fränkische Alb, *Germany* 25 **F7**
Fränkische Rezat →, *Germany* 25 **F7**
Fränkische Saale →, *Germany* 25 **E5**
Fränkische Schweiz, *Germany* 25 **F7**
Fränkische Schweiz-Veldensteiner Forst ◠, *Germany* 25 **F7**
Frankland →, *Australia* 93 **G2**
Franklin, *Ky., U.S.A.* 115 **G2**
Franklin, *La., U.S.A.* 113 **L9**
Franklin, *Mass., U.S.A.* 117 **D13**
Franklin, *N.H., U.S.A.* 117 **C13**
Franklin, *Nebr., U.S.A.* 112 **E5**
Franklin, *Pa., U.S.A.* 116 **E5**
Franklin, *Va., U.S.A.* 115 **G7**
Franklin, *W. Va., U.S.A.* 114 **F6**
Franklin B., *Canada* 100 **B7**
Franklin D. Roosevelt L., *U.S.A.* 108 **B4**
Franklin-Gordon Wild Rivers △, *Australia* 95 **G4**
Franklin I., *Antarctica* 5 **D11**
Franklin L., *U.S.A.* 108 **F6**
Franklin Mts., *Canada* 100 **B7**
Franklin Str., *Canada* 100 **A10**
Franklinton, *U.S.A.* 113 **K9**
Franklinville, *U.S.A.* 116 **D6**
Franks Pk., *U.S.A.* 108 **E9**
Frankston, *Australia* 95 **F4**
Frånö, *Sweden* 10 **B11**
Fransfontein, *Namibia* 88 **C2**
Frånsta, *Sweden* 10 **B10**
Frantsa Iosifa, Zemlya, *Russia* 52 **A6**
Franz, *Canada* 104 **C3**
Franz Josef Land = Frantsa Iosifa, Zemlya, *Russia* 52 **A6**
Franz Josef Strauss, München ✈ (MUC), *Germany* 25 **G7**
Franzburg, *Germany* 24 **A8**
Frascati, *Italy* 41 **G9**
Fraser, *U.S.A.* 116 **D2**
Fraser →, *B.C., Canada* 102 **D4**
Fraser →, *Nfld. & L., Canada* 105 **A7**
Fraser, Mt., *Australia* 93 **E2**
Fraser I., *Australia* 95 **D5**
Fraser Lake, *Canada* 102 **C4**
Fraserburg, *S. Africa* 88 **E3**
Fraserburgh, *U.K.* 13 **D6**
Fraserdale, *Canada* 104 **C3**
Frashër, *Albania* 44 **F4**
Frasne, *France* 19 **F13**
Frăteşti, *Romania* 29 **G10**
Frauenfeld, *Switz.* 25 **H4**
Fray Bentos, *Uruguay* 126 **C4**
Fray Jorge △, *Chile* 126 **C1**
Frechilla, *Spain* 36 **C6**
Fredericia, *Denmark* 11 **J3**
Frederick, *Md., U.S.A.* 114 **F7**
Frederick, *Okla., U.S.A.* 113 **H5**
Frederick, *S. Dak., U.S.A.* 112 **C5**
Fredericksburg, *Pa., U.S.A.* 117 **F8**
Fredericksburg, *Tex., U.S.A.* 113 **K5**
Fredericksburg, *Va., U.S.A.* 114 **F7**
Fredericktown, *Mo., U.S.A.* 113 **G9**
Fredericktown, *Ohio, U.S.A.* 116 **F2**
Frederico I. Madero, Presa, *Mexico* 118 **B3**
Frederico Westphalen, *Brazil* 127 **B5**
Fredericton, *Canada* 105 **C6**
Fredericton Junction, *Canada* 105 **C6**
Frederiksborg Amtskommune □, *Denmark* 11 **J6**
Frederikshåb = Paamiut, *Greenland* 101 **B15**
Frederikshamn = Hamina, *Finland* 9 **F22**
Frederikshavn, *Denmark* 11 **G4**
Frederikssund, *Denmark* 11 **J6**
Frederiksted, *U.S. Virgin Is.* 121 **C7**
Frederiksværk, *Denmark* 11 **J6**
Fredonia, *Ariz., U.S.A.* 109 **H7**
Fredonia, *Kans., U.S.A.* 113 **G7**
Fredonia, *N.Y., U.S.A.* 116 **D5**
Fredriksberg, *Sweden* 10 **D8**
Fredrikstad, *Norway* 9 **G14**
Free State □, *S. Africa* 88 **D4**
Freehold, *U.S.A.* 117 **F10**
Freel Peak, *U.S.A.* 110 **G7**
Freeland, *U.S.A.* 117 **E9**
Freels, C., *Canada* 105 **C9**
Freeman, *Calif., U.S.A.* 111 **K9**
Freeman, *S. Dak., U.S.A.* 112 **D6**
Freeport, *Bahamas* 120 **A4**
Freeport, *Ill., U.S.A.* 112 **D10**
Freeport, *N.Y., U.S.A.* 117 **F11**
Freeport, *Ohio, U.S.A.* 116 **F3**
Freeport, *Pa., U.S.A.* 116 **F5**
Freeport, *Tex., U.S.A.* 113 **L7**
Freetown, *S. Leone* 82 **D2**
Frégate, L. de la, *Canada* 104 **B5**
Fregenal de la Sierra, *Spain* 37 **G4**
Fregene, *Italy* 41 **G9**
Fréhel, C., *France* 18 **D4**
Freiberg, *Germany* 24 **E9**
Freibourg = Fribourg, *Switz.* 25 **J3**
Freiburg, *Baden-W., Germany* 25 **H3**
Freiburg, *Niedersachsen, Germany* 24 **B5**
Freilassing, *Germany* 25 **H8**
Freire, *Chile* 128 **D2**
Freirina, *Chile* 126 **B1**
Freising, *Germany* 25 **G7**
Freistadt, *Austria* 26 **C7**
Freital, *Germany* 24 **D9**
Fréjus, *France* 21 **E10**
Fremantle, *Australia* 93 **F2**
Fremont, *Calif., U.S.A.* 110 **H4**
Fremont, *Mich., U.S.A.* 114 **D3**
Fremont, *Nebr., U.S.A.* 112 **E6**
Fremont, *Ohio, U.S.A.* 114 **E4**
Fremont →, *U.S.A.* 109 **G8**
French Camp, *U.S.A.* 110 **H5**
French Cays = Plana Cays, *Bahamas* 121 **B5**
French Creek →, *U.S.A.* 116 **E5**
French Guiana ☒, *S. Amer.* 125 **C8**

French Polynesia ◪, *Pac. Oc.* 97 K13
Frenchman Cr. →, *N. Amer.* 108 B10
Frenchman Cr. →, *U.S.A.* 112 E4
Frenštát pod Radhoštěm, *Czech Rep.* 27 B11
Fresco, *Ivory C.* 82 D3
Fresco →, *Brazil* 125 E8
Freshfield, C., *Antarctica* 5 C10
Fresnay-sur-Sarthe, *France* 18 D7
Fresnillo, *Mexico* 118 C4
Fresno, *U.S.A.* 110 J7
Fresno Alhandiga, *Spain* 36 E5
Fresno Reservoir, *U.S.A.* 108 B9
Freudenstadt, *Germany* 25 G4
Frévent, *France* 19 B9
Frew →, *Australia* 94 C2
Frewsburg, *U.S.A.* 116 D5
Freycinet △, *Australia* 95 G4
Freycinet Pen., *Australia* 95 G4
Freyming-Merlebach, *France* 19 C13
Freyung, *Germany* 25 G9
Fria, *Guinea* 82 C2
Fria, C., *Namibia* 88 B1
Friant, *U.S.A.* 110 J7
Frías, *Argentina* 126 B2
Fribourg, *Switz.* 25 J3
Fribourg □, *Switz.* 25 J3
Fridafors, *Sweden* 11 H8
Friday Harbor, *U.S.A.* 110 B3
Friedberg, *Bayern, Germany* 25 G6
Friedberg, *Hessen, Germany* 25 E4
Friedens, *U.S.A.* 116 F6
Friedland, *Germany* 24 B9
Friedrichshafen, *Germany* 25 H5
Friedrichskoog, *Germany* 24 A4
Friedrichstadt, *Germany* 24 A5
Friendship, *U.S.A.* 116 D6
Friesach, *Austria* 26 E7
Friesack, *Germany* 24 C8
Friesland □, *Neths.* 17 A5
Friesoythe, *Germany* 24 B3
Friggesund, *Sweden* 10 C10
Frillesås, *Sweden* 11 G6
Frinnaryd, *Sweden* 11 G8
Frio →, *U.S.A.* 113 L5
Frio, C., *Brazil* 122 F6
Friol, *Spain* 36 B3
Friona, *U.S.A.* 113 H3
Fristad, *Sweden* 11 G6
Fritch, *U.S.A.* 113 H4
Fritsla, *Sweden* 11 G6
Fritzlar, *Germany* 24 D5
Friuli-Venézia Giulia □, *Italy* 41 B9
Frobisher B., *Canada* 101 B13
Frobisher Bay = Iqaluit, *Canada* 101 B13
Frobisher L., *Canada* 103 B7
Frohavet, *Norway* 8 E13
Frohnleiten, *Austria* 26 D8
Frolovo, *Russia* 34 F6
Frombork, *Poland* 30 D6
Frome, *U.K.* 15 F5
Frome →, *U.K.* 15 G5
Frome, L., *Australia* 95 E2
Frome, The →, *Australia* 95 D2
Frómista, *Spain* 36 C6
Front Range, *U.S.A.* 106 C5
Front Royal, *U.S.A.* 114 F6
Fronteira, *Portugal* 37 F3
Frontera, *Canary Is.* 48 G2
Frontera, *Mexico* 119 D6
Fronteras, *Mexico* 118 A3
Frontignan, *France* 20 E7
Frosinone, *Italy* 42 A6
Frostburg, *U.S.A.* 114 F6
Frostisen, *Norway* 8 B17
Frouard, *France* 19 D13
Frövi, *Sweden* 10 E9
Frøya, *Norway* 8 E13
Frumoasa, *Romania* 29 D10
Frunze = Bishkek, *Kyrgyzstan* 52 E8
Frunzivka, *Ukraine* 29 C14
Fruška Gora, *Serbia & M.* 28 E4
Fruška Gora △, *Serbia & M.* 44 A3
Frutal, *Brazil* 125 H9
Frutigen, *Switz.* 25 J3
Frýdek-Místek, *Czech Rep.* 27 B11
Frýdlant, *Czech Rep.* 26 A8
Fryeburg, *U.S.A.* 117 B14
Fryvaldov = Jeseník, *Czech Rep.* 27 A10
Fthiótis □, *Greece* 46 C4
Fu Jiang →, *China* 58 C6
Fu Xian = Wafangdian, *China* 57 E11
Fu Xian, *China* 56 G5
Fu'an, *China* 59 D12
Fubian, *China* 58 B4
Fucécchio, *Italy* 40 E7
Fucheng, *China* 56 F9
Fuchou = Fuzhou, *China* 59 D12
Fuchū, *Japan* 55 G6
Fuchuan, *China* 59 E8
Fuchun Jiang →, *China* 59 B13
Fúcino, Piana del, *Italy* 41 F10
Fuding, *China* 59 D13
Fuencaliente, *Canary Is.* 48 F2
Fuencaliente, *Spain* 37 G6
Fuencaliente, Pta., *Canary Is.* 48 F2
Fuengirola, *Spain* 37 J6
Fuenlabrada, *Spain* 36 E7
Fuensalida, *Spain* 36 E6
Fuente-Álamo, *Spain* 39 G3
Fuente-Álamo de Murcia, *Spain* 39 H3
Fuente de Cantos, *Spain* 37 G4
Fuente del Maestre, *Spain* 37 G4
Fuente el Fresno, *Spain* 37 F7
Fuente Obejuna, *Spain* 37 G5
Fuente Palmera, *Spain* 37 H5
Fuentes de Andalucía, *Spain* 37 H5
Fuentes de Ebro, *Spain* 38 D4
Fuentes de León, *Spain* 37 G4
Fuentes de Oñoro, *Spain* 36 E4
Fuentesaúco, *Spain* 36 D5
Fuerte →, *Mexico* 118 B3
Fuerte Olimpo, *Paraguay* 126 A4
Fuerteventura, *Canary Is.* 48 F6
Fuerteventura ✕ (FUE), *Canary Is.* 48 F6
Fufeng, *China* 56 G5
Fuga I., *Phil.* 61 B4
Fugong, *China* 58 D2
Fugou, *China* 56 G8
Fugu, *China* 56 E6
Fuhai, *China* 60 B3
Fuḩaymī, *Iraq* 70 C4
Fuhlsbüttel, Hamburg ✕ (HAM), *Germany* 24 B5
Fuji, *Japan* 55 G9
Fuji-Hakone-Izu △, *Japan* 55 G9
Fuji-San, *Japan* 55 G9
Fuji-Yoshida, *Japan* 55 G9
Fujian □, *China* 59 E12
Fujinomiya, *Japan* 55 G9
Fujisawa, *Japan* 55 G9
Fujiyama, Mt. = Fuji-San, *Japan* 55 G9
Fukagawa, *Japan* 54 C11
Fukien = Fujian □, *China* 59 E12
Fukuchiyama, *Japan* 55 G7
Fukue-Shima, *Japan* 55 H4
Fukui, *Japan* 55 F8
Fukui □, *Japan* 55 G8
Fukuoka, *Japan* 55 H5
Fukuoka □, *Japan* 55 H5
Fukushima, *Japan* 54 F10
Fukushima □, *Japan* 54 F10
Fukuyama, *Japan* 55 G6
Fulacunda, *Guinea-Biss.* 82 C1
Fulda, *Germany* 24 E5
Fulda →, *Germany* 24 D5
Fulford Harbour, *Canada* 110 B3
Fuliang, *China* 59 C11
Fullerton, *Calif., U.S.A.* 111 M9
Fullerton, *Nebr., U.S.A.* 112 E6
Fulongquan, *China* 57 B13
Fülöpszállás, *Hungary* 28 D4
Fulton, *Mo., U.S.A.* 112 F9
Fulton, *N.Y., U.S.A.* 117 C8
Fuluälven →, *Sweden* 10 C7
Fulufjället, *Sweden* 10 C6
Fumay, *France* 19 C11
Fumel, *France* 20 D4
Fumin, *China* 58 E4
Funabashi, *Japan* 55 G10
Funafuti = Fongafale, *Tuvalu* 96 H9
Funäsdalen, *Sweden* 10 B6
Funchal, *Madeira* 48 D3
Funchal ✕ (FNC), *Madeira* 48 D3
Fundación, *Colombia* 124 A4
Fundão, *Portugal* 36 E3
Fundu Moldovei, *Romania* 29 C10
Fundulea, *Romania* 29 F11
Fundy △, *Canada* 105 C6
Fundy, B. of, *Canada* 105 D6
Funhalouro, *Mozam.* 89 C5
Funing, *Hebei, China* 57 E10
Funing, *Jiangsu, China* 57 H10
Funing, *Yunnan, China* 58 F5
Funiu Shan, *China* 56 H7
Funsi, *Ghana* 82 C4
Funtua, *Nigeria* 83 C6
Fuping, *Hebei, China* 56 E8
Fuping, *Shaanxi, China* 56 G5
Fuqing, *China* 59 E12
Fuquan, *China* 58 D6
Furano, *Japan* 54 C11
Furāt, Nahr al →, *Asia* 70 D5
Fūrg, *Iran* 71 D7
Furmanov, *Russia* 34 B5
Furmanovo, *Kazakhstan* 34 F9
Furnás, *Spain* 48 B8
Furnas, Represa de, *Brazil* 127 A6
Furneaux Group, *Australia* 95 G4
Furqlus, *Syria* 74 A6
Fürstenau, *Germany* 24 C3
Fürstenberg, *Germany* 24 B9
Fürstenfeld, *Austria* 26 D9
Fürstenfeldbruck, *Germany* 25 G7
Fürstenwalde, *Germany* 24 C10
Fürth, *Germany* 25 F6
Furth im Wald, *Germany* 25 F8
Furtwangen, *Germany* 25 G4
Furudal, *Sweden* 10 C9
Furukawa, *Japan* 54 E10
Furulund, *Sweden* 11 J7
Fury and Hecla Str., *Canada* 101 B11
Fusagasuga, *Colombia* 124 C4
Fuscaldo, *Italy* 43 C9
Fushan, *Shandong, China* 57 F11
Fushan, *Shanxi, China* 56 G6
Fushë Arrëz, *Albania* 44 D4
Fushë Krujë, *Albania* 44 E3
Fushun, *Liaoning, China* 57 D12
Fushun, *Sichuan, China* 58 C5
Fusong, *China* 57 C14
Füssen, *Germany* 25 H6
Fustic, *Barbados* 121 g
Fusui, *China* 58 F6
Futog, *Serbia & M.* 28 E4
Futuna, *Wall. & F. Is.* 91 B8
Fuwa, *Egypt* 80 H7
Fuxian Hu, *China* 58 E4
Fuxin, *China* 57 C11
Fuyang, *Anhui, China* 56 H8
Fuyang, *Zhejiang, China* 59 B12
Fuyang He →, *China* 56 E9
Fuying Dao, *China* 59 D13
Fuyu, *China* 57 B13
Fuyuan, *China* 58 E5
Füzesgyarmat, *Hungary* 28 C6
Fuzhou, *China* 59 D12
Fylde, *U.K.* 14 D5
Fyn, *Denmark* 11 J4
Fyne, L., *U.K.* 13 F3
Fyns Amtskommune □, *Denmark* 11 J4
Fynshav, *Denmark* 11 K3

G

Ga, *Ghana* 82 D4
Gaanda, *Nigeria* 83 C7
Gabarin, *Nigeria* 83 C7
Gabas →, *France* 20 E3
Gabela, *Angola* 84 G2
Gabès, *Tunisia* 79 B8
Gabès, G. de, *Tunisia* 79 B8
Gabgaba, W. →, *Egypt* 80 C3
Gąbin, *Poland* 31 F6
Gabon ■, *Africa* 84 E2
Gaborone, *Botswana* 88 C4
Gabriels, *U.S.A.* 117 B10
Gābrīk, *Iran* 71 E8
Gabrovo, *Bulgaria* 45 D9
Gacé, *France* 18 D7
Gāch Sār, *Iran* 71 B6
Gachsārān, *Iran* 71 D6
Gacko, *Bos.-H.* 44 C2
Gadag, *India* 66 M9
Gadamai, *Sudan* 81 D4
Gadap, *Pakistan* 68 G2
Gadarwara, *India* 69 H8
Gadebusch, *Germany* 24 B7
Gadein, *Sudan* 81 F2
Gadhada, *India* 68 J4
Gádor, Sierra de, *Spain* 37 J8
Gadra, *Pakistan* 68 G4
Gadsden, *U.S.A.* 115 H3
Gadwal, *India* 66 L10
Gadyach = Hadyach, *Ukraine* 33 G8
Găeşti, *Romania* 29 F10
Gaeta, *Italy* 42 A6
Gaeta, G. di, *Italy* 42 A6
Gaffney, *U.S.A.* 115 H5
Gafsa, *Tunisia* 78 B7
Gagarawa, *Nigeria* 83 C6
Gagaria, *India* 68 G4
Gagarin, *Russia* 32 E8
Găgăuzia □, *Moldova* 29 D13
Gaggenau, *Germany* 25 G4
Gaghamni, *Sudan* 81 E2
Gagino, *Russia* 34 C7
Gagliano del Capo, *Italy* 43 C11
Gagnef, *Sweden* 10 D9
Gagnoa, *Ivory C.* 82 D3
Gagnon, *Canada* 105 B6
Gagnon, L., *Canada* 103 A6
Gagra, *Georgia* 35 J5
Gahini, *Rwanda* 86 C3
Gahmar, *India* 69 G10
Gai Xian = Gaizhou, *China* 57 D12
Gaïdhouronísi, *Greece* 49 E7
Gail, *U.S.A.* 113 J4
Gail →, *Austria* 26 E6
Gaillac, *France* 20 E5
Gaillimh = Galway, *Ireland* 12 C2
Gaillon, *France* 18 C8
Gaines, *U.S.A.* 116 E7
Gainesville, *Fla., U.S.A.* 115 L4
Gainesville, *Ga., U.S.A.* 115 H4
Gainesville, *Mo., U.S.A.* 113 G8
Gainesville, *Tex., U.S.A.* 113 J6
Gainsborough, *U.K.* 14 D7
Gairdner, L., *Australia* 95 E2
Gairloch, *U.K.* 13 D3
Gairloch, L., *U.K.* 13 D3
Gaizhou, *China* 57 D12
Gaj, *Croatia* 28 E2
Gaj →, *Pakistan* 68 F2
Gakuch, *Pakistan* 69 A5
Galala, Gebel el, *Egypt* 80 J8
Galán, Cerro, *Argentina* 126 B2
Galana →, *Kenya* 86 C5
Galanta, *Slovak Rep.* 27 C10
Galapagar, *Spain* 36 E7
Galápagos = Colón, Arch. de, *Ecuador* 97 H18
Galashiels, *U.K.* 13 F6
Galatás, *Greece* 46 D5
Galaţi, *Romania* 29 E13
Galaţi □, *Romania* 29 E12
Galatia, *Turkey* 72 C5
Galatina, *Italy* 43 B11
Galátone, *Italy* 43 B11
Galax, *U.S.A.* 115 G5
Galaxídhion, *Greece* 46 C4
Galcaio, *Somali Rep.* 75 F4
Galdhøpiggen, *Norway* 9 F12
Galeana, *Chihuahua, Mexico* 118 A3
Galeana, *Nuevo León, Mexico* 118 A3
Galegu, *Sudan* 81 E4
Galela, *Indonesia* 63 D7
Galena, *U.S.A.* 100 B4
Galeota Pt., *Trin. & Tob.* 125 K16
Galera, *Spain* 39 H2
Galera Pt., *Trin. & Tob.* 121 D7
Galesburg, *U.S.A.* 112 E9
Galeton, *U.S.A.* 116 E7
Galga, *Ethiopia* 81 F4
Gali, *Georgia* 35 J5
Galicea Mare, *Romania* 29 F8
Galich, *Russia* 34 A6
Galiche, *Bulgaria* 44 C7
Galicia □, *Spain* 36 C3
Galičica △, *Macedonia* 44 E4
Galilee = Hagalil, *Israel* 74 C4
Galilee, L., *Australia* 94 C4
Galilee, Sea of = Yam Kinneret, *Israel* 74 C4
Galim, *Cameroon* 83 D7
Galina Pt., *Jamaica* 120 a
Galinoporni, *Cyprus* 49 D13
Galion, *U.S.A.* 116 F2
Galiuro Mts., *U.S.A.* 109 K8
Galiwinku, *Australia* 94 A2
Gallabat, *Sudan* 81 E4
Gallan Hd., *U.K.* 13 C1
Gallarate, *Italy* 40 C5
Gallatin, *U.S.A.* 115 G2
Galle, *Sri Lanka* 66 R12
Gállego →, *Spain* 38 D4
Gallegos →, *Argentina* 128 G3
Galletti →, *Ethiopia* 81 F5
Galley Hd., *Ireland* 12 E3
Galliate, *Italy* 40 C5
Gallinas, Pta., *Colombia* 124 A4
Gallipoli = Gelibolu, *Turkey* 45 F10
Gallípoli, *Italy* 43 B10
Gallipolis, *U.S.A.* 114 F4
Gällivare, *Sweden* 8 C19
Gallneukirchen, *Austria* 26 C7
Gällö, *Sweden* 10 B9
Gallo, C., *Italy* 42 D6
Gallocanta, L. de, *Spain* 38 E3
Galloo I., *U.S.A.* 117 C8
Galloway, *U.K.* 13 F4
Galloway ⌓, *U.K.* 13 F4
Galloway, Mull of, *U.K.* 13 G4
Gallup, *U.S.A.* 109 J9
Gallur, *Spain* 38 D3
Galoya, *Sri Lanka* 66 Q12
Galt, *U.S.A.* 110 G5
Galten, *Denmark* 11 H3
Galtür, *Austria* 26 E3
Galty Mts., *Ireland* 12 D3
Galtymore, *Ireland* 12 D3
Galva, *U.S.A.* 112 E9
Galve de Sorbe, *Spain* 38 D1
Galveston, *U.S.A.* 113 L7
Galveston B., *U.S.A.* 113 L7
Gálvez, *Argentina* 126 C3
Galway, *Ireland* 12 C2
Galway □, *Ireland* 12 C2
Galway B., *Ireland* 12 C2
Gam →, *Vietnam* 64 B5
Gamagōri, *Japan* 55 G8
Gamari, L., *Ethiopia* 81 E5
Gamawa, *Nigeria* 83 C7
Gamay, *Phil.* 61 E6
Gambaga, *Ghana* 83 C4
Gambat, *Pakistan* 68 F3
Gambela, *Ethiopia* 81 F3
Gambela △, *Ethiopia* 81 F3
Gambela-Hizboch □, *Ethiopia* 81 F3
Gambhir →, *India* 68 F6
Gambia ■, *W. Afr.* 82 C1
Gambia →, *W. Afr.* 82 C1
Gambier, *U.S.A.* 116 F2
Gambier, C., *Australia* 92 B5
Gambier Is., *Australia* 95 F2
Gambo, *Canada* 105 C9
Gamboli, *Pakistan* 68 E3
Gamboma, *Congo* 84 E3
Gamka →, *S. Africa* 88 E3
Gamkab →, *Namibia* 88 D2
Gamla Uppsala, *Sweden* 10 E11
Gamlakarleby = Kokkola, *Finland* 8 E20
Gamleby, *Sweden* 11 G10
Gammon →, *Canada* 103 C9
Gammon Ranges △, *Australia* 95 E2
Gamo-Gofa, *Ethiopia* 81 F4
Gamou, *Niger* 83 C6
Gamtoos →, *S. Africa* 88 E4
Gan, *France* 20 E3
Gan Goriama, Mts., *Cameroon* 83 D7
Gan Jiang →, *China* 59 C11
Ganado, *U.S.A.* 109 J9
Gananita, *Sudan* 80 D3
Gananoque, *Canada* 117 B8
Ganāveh, *Iran* 71 D6
Gäncä, *Azerbaijan* 35 K8
Gancheng, *China* 64 C7
Gand = Gent, *Belgium* 17 C3
Ganda, *Angola* 85 G2
Gandajika, *Dem. Rep. of the Congo* 84 F4
Gandak →, *India* 69 G11
Gandava, *Pakistan* 68 E2
Gander, *Canada* 105 C9
Gander L., *Canada* 105 C9
Ganderkesee, *Germany* 24 B4
Ganderowe Falls, *Zimbabwe* 87 F2
Gandesa, *Spain* 38 D5
Gandhi Sagar, *India* 68 G6
Gandhinagar, *India* 68 H5
Gandi, *Nigeria* 83 C6
Gandía, *Spain* 39 G4
Gandino, *Italy* 40 C6
Gando, Pta., *Canary Is.* 48 G4
Gandole, *Nigeria* 83 D7
Gâneb, *Mauritania* 82 B2
Ganedidalem = Gani, *Indonesia* 63 E7
Ganetti, *Sudan* 80 D3
Ganga →, *India* 69 H14
Ganga Sagar, *India* 69 J13
Gangafani, *Mali* 82 C4
Gangan →, *India* 69 E8
Ganganagar, *India* 68 E5
Gangapur, *India* 68 F7
Gangara, *Niger* 83 C6
Gangaw, *Burma* 67 H19
Gangdisê Shan, *China* 67 D12
Ganges = Ganga →, *India* 69 H14
Ganges, *Canada* 102 D4
Ganges, *France* 20 E7
Ganges, Mouths of the, *India* 69 J14
Gånghester, *Sweden* 11 G7
Gangi, *Italy* 43 E7
Gângiova, *Romania* 29 G8
Gangoh, *India* 68 E7
Gangotri, *India* 69 D8
Gangtok, *India* 67 F16
Gangu, *China* 56 G3
Gangyao, *China* 57 B14
Gani, *Indonesia* 63 E7
Ganj, *India* 69 F8
Ganluc, *China* 58 C4
Gannat, *France* 19 F10
Gannett Peak, *U.S.A.* 108 E9
Ganquan, *China* 56 F5
Gänserdorf, *Austria* 27 C9
Ganshui, *China* 58 C6
Gansu □, *China* 56 G3
Ganta, *Liberia* 82 D3
Gantheaume, C., *Australia* 95 F2
Gantheaume B., *Australia* 93 E1
Gantsevichi = Hantsavichy, *Belarus* 33 F4
Ganye, *Nigeria* 83 D7
Ganyem = Genyem, *Indonesia* 63 E10
Ganyu, *China* 57 G10
Ganyushkino, *Kazakhstan* 35 G9
Ganzhou, *China* 59 E10
Gao, *Mali* 83 B4
Gao Xian, *China* 58 C5
Gao'an, *China* 59 C10
Gaochun, *China* 59 B12
Gaohe, *China* 59 F9
Gaohebu, *China* 59 B11
Gaokeng, *China* 59 D9
Gaolan Dao, *China* 59 G9
Gaoligong Shan, *China* 58 E2
Gaomi, *China* 57 F10
Gaoming, *China* 59 F9
Gaoping, *China* 56 G7
Gaotang, *China* 56 F9
Gaoua, *Burkina Faso* 82 C4
Gaoual, *Guinea* 82 C2
Gaoxiong = Kaohsiung, *Taiwan* 59 F13
Gaoyang, *China* 56 E8
Gaoyao, *China* 59 F9
Gaoyou, *China* 59 A12
Gaoyou Hu, *China* 57 H10
Gaoyuan, *China* 57 F9
Gaozhou, *China* 59 G8
Gap, *France* 21 D10
Gapan, *Phil.* 61 D4
Gapat →, *India* 69 G10
Gapuwiyak, *Australia* 94 A2
Gar, *China* 60 C2
Garabogazköl Aylagy, *Turkmenistan* 52 E6
Garachico, *Canary Is.* 48 F3
Garachiné, *Panama* 120 E4
Garafia, *Canary Is.* 48 F2
Garah, *Australia* 95 D4
Garajonay, *Canary Is.* 48 F2
Garamba △, *Dem. Rep. of the Congo* 86 B2
Garango, *Burkina Faso* 83 C4
Garanhuns, *Brazil* 125 E11
Garautha, *India* 69 G8
Garawe, *Liberia* 82 E3
Garba Tula, *Kenya* 86 B4
Garberville, *U.S.A.* 108 F2
Garbiyang, *India* 69 D9
Garbsen, *Germany* 24 C5
Gard □, *France* 21 D8
Gard →, *France* 21 E8
Garda, L. di, *Italy* 40 C7
Gardanne, *France* 21 E9
Gårdby, *Sweden* 11 H10
Garde L., *Canada* 103 A7
Gardelegen, *Germany* 24 C7
Garden City, *Ga., U.S.A.* 115 J5
Garden City, *Kans., U.S.A.* 113 G4
Garden City, *Tex., U.S.A.* 113 K4
Garden Grove, *U.S.A.* 111 M9
Gardēz, *Afghan.* 68 C3
Gardhíki, *Greece* 46 C3
Gardiner, *Maine, U.S.A.* 115 C11
Gardiner, *Mont., U.S.A.* 108 D8
Gardiners I., *U.S.A.* 117 E12
Gardner, *U.S.A.* 117 D13
Gardner Canal, *Canada* 102 C3
Gardnerville, *U.S.A.* 110 G7
Gardno, Jezioro, *Poland* 30 D4
Gardo, *Somali Rep.* 75 F4
Gardone Val Trómpia, *Italy* 40 C7
Gárdony, *Hungary* 28 C3
Garešnica, *Croatia* 41 C13
Garéssio, *Italy* 40 D5
Garey, *U.S.A.* 111 L6
Garfield, *U.S.A.* 108 C5
Garforth, *U.K.* 14 D6
Gargaliánoi, *Greece* 46 D3
Gargan, Mt., *France* 20 C5
Gargano △, *Italy* 41 G12
Gargett, *Australia* 94 K6
Gargouna, *Mali* 83 B5
Gargždai, *Lithuania* 30 C8
Garibaldi ⌓, *Canada* 102 D4
Gariep, L., *S. Africa* 88 E4
Garies, *S. Africa* 88 E2
Garigliano →, *Italy* 42 A6
Garissa, *Kenya* 86 C4
Garkida, *Nigeria* 83 C7
Garko, *Nigeria* 83 C6
Garland, *Tex., U.S.A.* 113 J6
Garland, *Utah, U.S.A.* 108 F7
Garlasco, *Italy* 40 C5
Garliava, *Lithuania* 30 D10
Garlin, *France* 20 E3
Garm, *Tajikistan* 52 F8
Garmāb, *Iran* 71 C8
Garmisch-Partenkirchen, *Germany* 25 H7
Garmo, Qullai = Kommunizma, Pik, *Tajikistan* 52 F8
Garmsār, *Iran* 71 C7
Garner, *U.S.A.* 112 D8
Garnett, *U.S.A.* 112 F7
Garo Hills, *India* 69 G14
Garoe, *Somali Rep.* 75 F4
Garonne →, *France* 20 C3
Garonne, Canal Latéral à la, *France* 20 D4
Garoowe = Garoe, *Somali Rep.* 75 F4
Garot, *India* 68 G6
Garoua, *Cameroon* 83 D7
Garpenberg, *Sweden* 10 D10
Garphyttan, *Sweden* 10 E8

Garrauli, *India* 69 G8
Garrel, *Germany* 24 C4
Garrigues, *France* 20 E7
Garrison, *Mont., U.S.A.* 108 C7
Garrison, *N. Dak., U.S.A.* 112 B4
Garrison Res. = Sakakawea, L., *U.S.A.* 112 B4
Garron Pt., *U.K.* 12 A6
Garrovillas, *Spain* 37 F4
Garrucha, *Spain* 39 H3
Garry →, *U.K.* 13 E5
Garry, L., *Canada* 100 B9
Garsen, *Kenya* 86 C5
Gärsnäs, *Sweden* 11 J8
Garson L., *Canada* 103 B6
Garstang, *U.K.* 14 D5
Gartempe →, *France* 20 B4
Gartz, *Germany* 24 B10
Garu, *Ghana* 83 C4
Garu, *India* 69 H11
Garub, *Namibia* 88 D2
Garut, *Indonesia* 63 G12
Garvão, *Portugal* 37 H2
Garvie Mts., *N.Z.* 91 L2
Garwa = Garoua, *Cameroon* 83 D7
Garwa, *India* 69 G10
Garwolin, *Poland* 31 G8
Gary, *U.S.A.* 114 E2
Garz, *Germany* 24 A9
Garzê, *China* 58 B3
Garzón, *Colombia* 124 C3
Gas-San, *Japan* 54 E10
Gasan Kuli = Esenguly, *Turkmenistan* 52 F6
Gascogne, *France* 20 E4
Gascogne, G. de, *Europe* 20 E2
Gascony = Gascogne, *France* 20 E4
Gascoyne →, *Australia* 93 D1
Gascoyne Junction, *Australia* 93 E2
Gascueña, *Spain* 38 E2
Gash, Wadi →, *Ethiopia* 81 D4
Gash-Setit ⌂, *Eritrea* 81 D4
Gashagar, *Nigeria* 83 C7
Gashaka, *Nigeria* 83 D7
Gashaka-Gumti △, *Nigeria* 83 D7
Gasherbrum, *Pakistan* 69 B7
Gashua, *Nigeria* 83 C7
Gasparillo, *Trin. & Tob.* 125 K15
Gaspé, *Canada* 105 C7
Gaspé, C., *Canada* 105 C7
Gaspé Pen. = Gaspésie, Pén. de la, *Canada* 105 C6
Gaspésie ⌂, *Canada* 105 C6
Gaspésie, Pén. de la, *Canada* 105 C6
Gassan, *Burkina Faso* 82 C4
Gassol, *Nigeria* 83 D7
Gasteiz = Vitoria-Gasteiz, *Spain* 38 C2
Gastonia, *U.S.A.* 115 H5
Gastoúni, *Greece* 46 D3
Gastoúri, *Greece* 46 B1
Gastre, *Argentina* 128 E3
Gästrikland, *Sweden* 10 D10
Gata, C., *Cyprus* 49 E12
Gata, C. de, *Spain* 39 J2
Gata, Sierra de, *Spain* 36 E4
Gataga →, *Canada* 102 B3
Gătaia, *Romania* 28 E6
Gatchina, *Russia* 32 C6
Gatehouse of Fleet, *U.K.* 13 G4
Gates, *U.S.A.* 116 C7
Gateshead, *U.K.* 14 C6
Gatesville, *U.S.A.* 113 K6
Gateway ⌂, *U.S.A.* 117 F11
Gaths, *Zimbabwe* 87 G3
Gatico, *Chile* 126 A1
Gâtinais, *France* 19 D9
Gâtine, Hauteurs de, *France* 20 B3
Gatineau, *Canada* 117 A9
Gatineau △, *Canada* 104 C4
Gatineau →, *Canada* 104 C4
Gattaran, *Phil.* 61 B4
Gattinara, *Italy* 40 C5
Gatton, *Australia* 95 D5
Gatun, L., *Panama* 120 E4
Gatwick, London ✈ (LGW), *U.K.* 15 F7
Gatyana, *S. Africa* 89 E4
Gau, *Fiji* 91 D8
Gaucín, *Spain* 37 J5
Gauer L., *Canada* 103 B9
Gauhati = Guwahati, *India* 67 F17
Gauja →, *Latvia* 9 H21
Gaula →, *Norway* 8 E14
Gauri Phanta, *India* 69 E9
Gausta, *Norway* 9 G13
Gauteng □, *S. Africa* 89 D4
Gāv Koshī, *Iran* 71 D8
Gāvakān, *Iran* 71 D7
Gavallai △, *Liberia* 82 D3
Gavarnie, *France* 20 F3
Gavāter, *Iran* 71 E9
Gāvbandī, *Iran* 71 E7
Gavdhopoúla, *Greece* 49 E6
Gávdhos, *Greece* 49 E6
Gavi, *Italy* 40 D5
Gavião, *Portugal* 37 F3
Gaviota, *U.S.A.* 111 L6
Gāvkhūnī, Bāţlāq-e, *Iran* 71 C7
Gävle, *Sweden* 10 D11
Gävleborgs län □, *Sweden* 10 C10
Gävlebukten, *Sweden* 10 D11
Gavorrano, *Italy* 40 F7
Gavray, *France* 18 D5
Gavrilov Yam, *Russia* 32 D10
Gávrion, *Greece* 46 D6
Gawachab, *Namibia* 88 D2
Gawilgarh Hills, *India* 66 J10
Gawler, *Australia* 95 E2
Gawu, *Nigeria* 83 D6
Gaxun Nur, *China* 60 B5
Gaya, *India* 69 G11
Gaya, *Niger* 83 C5
Gaya, *Nigeria* 83 C6
Gayéri, *Burkina Faso* 83 C5
Gaylord, *U.S.A.* 114 C3
Gayndah, *Australia* 95 D5
Gaysin = Haysyn, *Ukraine* 29 B14
Gayvoron = Hayvoron, *Ukraine* 29 B14
Gaza, *Gaza Strip* 74 D3
Gaza □, *Mozam.* 89 C5
Gaza Strip ⧄, *Asia* 74 D3
Gazanjyk, *Turkmenistan* 71 B7
Gazaoua, *Niger* 83 C6
Gāzbor, *Iran* 71 D8
Gazi, *Dem. Rep. of the Congo* 86 B1
Gaziantep, *Turkey* 70 B3
Gazimağosa = Famagusta, *Cyprus* 49 D12
Gazipaşa, *Turkey* 72 D5
Gbarnga, *Liberia* 82 D3
Gbekebo, *Nigeria* 83 D5
Gboko, *Nigeria* 83 D6
Gbongan, *Nigeria* 83 D5
Gcoverega, *Botswana* 88 B3
Gcuwa, *S. Africa* 89 E4
Gdańsk, *Poland* 30 D5
Gdansk ✈ (GDN), *Poland* 30 D5
Gdańska, Zatoka, *Poland* 30 D6
Gdov, *Russia* 9 G22
Gdynia, *Poland* 30 D5
Geba →, *Guinea-Biss.* 82 C1
Gebe, *Indonesia* 63 D7
Gebeciler, *Turkey* 47 C12
Gebeit Mine, *Sudan* 80 C4
Gebel Abyad, *Sudan* 80 D2
Gebel Iweibid, *Egypt* 80 H8
Gebze, *Turkey* 45 F13
Gecha, *Ethiopia* 81 F4
Gedaref, *Sudan* 81 E4
Gedaref □, *Sudan* 81 E4
Gediz, *Turkey* 47 B11
Gediz →, *Turkey* 47 C8
Gedo, *Ethiopia* 81 F4
Gèdre, *France* 20 F4
Gedser, *Denmark* 11 K5
Gedung, Pulau, *Malaysia* 65 c
Geegully Cr. →, *Australia* 92 C3
Geel, *Belgium* 17 C4
Geelong, *Australia* 95 F3
Geelvink B. = Cenderwasih, Teluk, *Indonesia* 63 E9
Geelvink Chan., *Australia* 93 E1
Geesthacht, *Germany* 24 B6
Geidam, *Nigeria* 83 C7
Geikie →, *Canada* 103 B8
Geikie Gorge △, *Australia* 92 C4
Geilenkirchen, *Germany* 24 E2
Geili, *Sudan* 81 D3
Geisingen, *Germany* 25 H4
Geislingen, *Germany* 25 G5
Geistown, *U.S.A.* 116 F6
Geita, *Tanzania* 86 C3
Gejiu, *China* 58 F4
Gel →, *Sudan* 81 F2
Gel, Meydān-e, *Iran* 71 D7
Gel River, *Sudan* 81 F2
Gela, *Italy* 43 E7
Gela, G. di, *Italy* 43 F7
Gelahun, *Liberia* 82 D2
Gelang Patah, *Malaysia* 65 d
Gelderland □, *Neths.* 17 B6
Geldern, *Germany* 24 D2
Geldrop, *Neths.* 17 C5
Geleen, *Neths.* 17 D5
Gelehun, *S. Leone* 82 D2
Gelembe, *Turkey* 47 B9
Gelemso, *Ethiopia* 81 F5
Gelendost, *Turkey* 72 C4
Gelendzhik, *Russia* 33 K10
Gelibolu, *Turkey* 45 F10
Gelibolu Yarımadası, *Turkey* 45 F10
Gelidonya Burnu, *Turkey* 72 D4
Gelnhausen, *Germany* 25 E5
Gelnica, *Slovak Rep.* 27 C13
Gelsenkirchen, *Germany* 24 D3
Gelting, *Germany* 24 A5
Gelugur, *Malaysia* 65 c
Gemas, *Malaysia* 65 L4
Gembloux, *Belgium* 17 D4
Gembu, *Nigeria* 83 D7
Gemena, *Dem. Rep. of the Congo* 84 D3
Gemerek, *Turkey* 70 B3
Gemla, *Sweden* 11 H8
Gemlik, *Turkey* 45 F13
Gemlik Körfezi, *Turkey* 45 F12
Gemona del Friuli, *Italy* 41 B10
Gemsa, *Egypt* 80 B3
Gemsbok △, *Botswana* 88 D3
Gemünden, *Germany* 25 E5
Genale →, *Ethiopia* 81 F4
Genç, *Turkey* 73 C9
Gençay, *France* 20 B4
Geneina, Gebel, *Egypt* 80 B3
General Acha, *Argentina* 126 D3
General Alvear, *Buenos Aires, Argentina* 126 D4
General Alvear, *Mendoza, Argentina* 126 D2
General Artigas, *Paraguay* 126 B4
General Belgrano, *Argentina* 126 D4
General Bernardo O'Higgins, *Antarctica* 5 C18
General Cabrera, *Argentina* 126 C3
General Cepeda, *Mexico* 118 B4
General Guido, *Argentina* 126 D4
General Juan Madariaga, *Argentina* 126 D4
General La Madrid, *Argentina* 126 D3
General MacArthur, *Phil.* 61 F6
General Martin Miguel de Güemes, *Argentina* 126 A3
General Paz, *Argentina* 126 B4
General Pico, *Argentina* 126 D3
General Pinedo, *Argentina* 126 B3
General Pinto, *Argentina* 126 C3
General Roca, *Argentina* 128 D3
General Santos, *Phil.* 61 H6
General Toshevo, *Bulgaria* 45 C12
General Trevino, *Mexico* 119 B5
General Trías, *Mexico* 118 B3
General Viamonte, *Argentina* 126 D3
General Villegas, *Argentina* 126 D3
Genesee, *Idaho, U.S.A.* 108 C5
Genesee, *Pa., U.S.A.* 116 E7
Genesee →, *U.S.A.* 116 C7
Geneseo, *Ill., U.S.A.* 112 E9
Geneseo, *N.Y., U.S.A.* 116 D7
Geneva = Genève, *Switz.* 25 J2
Geneva, *Ala., U.S.A.* 115 K3
Geneva, *N.Y., U.S.A.* 116 D8
Geneva, *Nebr., U.S.A.* 112 E6
Geneva, *Ohio, U.S.A.* 116 E4
Geneva, L. = Léman, L., *Europe* 19 F13
Geneva, L., *U.S.A.* 114 D1
Genève, *Switz.* 25 J2
Gengenbach, *Germany* 25 G4
Gengma, *China* 58 F2
Genichesk = Henichesk, *Ukraine* 33 J8
Genil →, *Spain* 37 H5
Genk, *Belgium* 17 D5
Genlis, *France* 19 E12
Gennargentu, Mti. del, *Italy* 42 B2
Gennes, *France* 18 E6
Genoa = Génova, *Italy* 40 D5
Genoa, *Australia* 95 F4
Genoa, *N.Y., U.S.A.* 117 D8
Genoa, *Nebr., U.S.A.* 112 E6
Genoa, *Nev., U.S.A.* 110 F7
Génova, *Italy* 40 D5
Genova ✈ (GOA), *Italy* 40 D5
Génova, G. di, *Italy* 40 E6
Genriyetty, Ostrov, *Russia* 53 B16
Gent, *Belgium* 17 C3
Genteng, *Bali, Indonesia* 63 J17
Genteng, *Jawa, Indonesia* 63 G12
Genthin, *Germany* 24 C8
Genyem, *Indonesia* 63 E10
Genzano di Lucánia, *Italy* 43 B9
Genzano di Roma, *Italy* 41 G9
Geoagiu, *Romania* 29 E8
Geographe B., *Australia* 93 F2
Geographe Chan., *Australia* 93 D1
Geokchay = Göyçay, *Azerbaijan* 35 K8
Georg Forster, *Antarctica* 5 D3
Georg von Neumayer, *Antarctica* 5 D17
Georga, Zemlya, *Russia* 52 A5
George, *S. Africa* 88 E3
George →, *Canada* 105 A6
George, L., *N.S.W., Australia* 95 F4
George, L., *S. Austral., Australia* 95 F3
George, L., *W. Austral., Australia* 92 D3
George, L., *Uganda* 86 B3
George, L., *Fla., U.S.A.* 115 L5
George, L., *N.Y., U.S.A.* 117 C11
George Gill Ra., *Australia* 92 D5
George Pt., *Australia* 94 J6
George River = Kangiqsualujjuaq, *Canada* 101 C13
George Sound, *N.Z.* 91 L1
George Town, *Australia* 95 G4
George Town, *Bahamas* 120 B4
George Town, *Cayman Is.* 120 C3
George Town, *Malaysia* 65 c
George V Land, *Antarctica* 5 C10
George VI Sound, *Antarctica* 5 D17
George West, *U.S.A.* 113 L5
Georgetown = Janjanbureh, *Gambia* 82 C2
Georgetown, *Australia* 94 B3
Georgetown, *Ont., Canada* 116 C5
Georgetown, *P.E.I., Canada* 105 C7
Georgetown, *Guyana* 124 B7
Georgetown, *Calif., U.S.A.* 110 G6
Georgetown, *Colo., U.S.A.* 108 G11
Georgetown, *Ky., U.S.A.* 114 F3
Georgetown, *N.Y., U.S.A.* 117 D9
Georgetown, *Ohio, U.S.A.* 114 F4
Georgetown, *S.C., U.S.A.* 115 J6
Georgetown, *Tex., U.S.A.* 113 K6
Georgia □, *U.S.A.* 115 K5
Georgia ■, *Asia* 35 J6
Georgia, Str. of, *Canada* 102 D4
Georgian B., *Canada* 116 A4
Georgian Bay Islands △, *Canada* 116 B5
Georgina →, *Australia* 94 C2
Georgina I., *Canada* 116 B5
Georgiyevsk, *Russia* 35 H6
Georgsmarienhütte, *Germany* 24 C4
Gera, *Germany* 24 E8
Geraardsbergen, *Belgium* 17 D3
Geral, Serra, *Brazil* 127 B6
Geral de Goiás, Serra, *Brazil* 125 F9
Geraldine, *U.S.A.* 108 C8
Geraldton, *Australia* 93 E1
Geraldton, *Canada* 104 C2
Gérardmer, *France* 19 D13
Gercüş, *Turkey* 73 D9
Gerede, *Turkey* 72 B5
Gerês, Sierra do, *Portugal* 36 D3
Gereshk, *Afghan.* 66 D4
Geretsried, *Germany* 25 H7
Gérgal, *Spain* 39 H2
Gerik, *Malaysia* 65 K3
Gering, *U.S.A.* 112 E3
Gerlach, *U.S.A.* 108 F4
Gerlachovský štit, *Slovak Rep.* 27 B13
German Planina, *Macedonia* 44 D6
Germansen Landing, *Canada* 102 B4
Germantown, *U.S.A.* 113 M10
Germany ■, *Europe* 24 E6
Germencik, *Turkey* 47 D9
Germering, *Germany* 25 G7
Germersheim, *Germany* 25 F4
Germī, *Iran* 71 B6
Germiston, *S. Africa* 89 D4
Gernika-Lumo, *Spain* 38 B2
Gernsheim, *Germany* 25 F4
Gero, *Japan* 55 G8
Gerokgak, *Indonesia* 63 J17
Gerolzhofen, *Germany* 25 F6
Gerona = Girona, *Spain* 38 D7
Gerrard, *Canada* 102 C5
Gers □, *France* 20 E4
Gers →, *France* 20 D4
Gersfeld, *Germany* 24 E5
Gersthofen, *Germany* 25 G6
Gertak Sanggul, *Malaysia* 65 c
Gertak Sanggul, Tanjung, *Malaysia* 65 c
Gerung, *Indonesia* 63 K19
Gerzat, *France* 20 C7
Gerze, *Turkey* 72 B6
Geseke, *Germany* 24 D4
Geser, *Indonesia* 63 E8
Gesso →, *Italy* 40 D4
Gestro, Wabi →, *Ethiopia* 81 G5
Getafe, *Spain* 36 E7
Getinge, *Sweden* 11 H6
Gettysburg, *Pa., U.S.A.* 114 F7
Gettysburg, *S. Dak., U.S.A.* 112 C5
Getxo, *Spain* 38 B2
Getz Ice Shelf, *Antarctica* 5 D14
Gevaş, *Turkey* 73 C10
Gévaudan, *France* 20 D7
Gevgelija, *Macedonia* 44 E6
Gévora →, *Spain* 37 G4
Gewani, *Ethiopia* 81 E5
Gex, *France* 19 F13
Geyikli, *Turkey* 47 B8
Geyser, *U.S.A.* 108 C8
Geyserville, *U.S.A.* 110 G4
Geyve, *Turkey* 72 B4
Ghâbat el Arab = Wang Kai, *Sudan* 81 F2
Ghabeish, *Sudan* 81 E2
Ghaggar →, *India* 68 E6
Ghaghara →, *India* 69 G11
Ghaghat →, *Bangla.* 69 G13
Ghagra, *India* 69 H11
Ghagra →, *India* 69 F9
Ghalla, Wadi el →, *Sudan* 81 E2
Ghana ■, *W. Afr.* 83 D4
Ghansor, *India* 69 H9
Ghanzi, *Botswana* 88 C3
Gharb el Istiwa'iya □, *Sudan* 81 G3
Gharb Kordofân □, *Sudan* 81 E2
Gharbîya, Es Sahrâ el, *Egypt* 80 B2
Ghardaïa, *Algeria* 78 B6
Ghârib, G., *Egypt* 80 B3
Gharig, *Sudan* 81 E2
Gharyān, *Libya* 79 B8
Ghat, *Libya* 79 D8
Ghatal, *India* 69 H12
Ghatampur, *India* 69 F9
Ghats, Eastern, *India* 66 N11
Ghats, Western, *India* 66 N9
Ghatsila, *India* 69 H12
Ghaţţī, *Si. Arabia* 70 D3
Ghawdex = Gozo, *Malta* 49 C1
Ghazal, Bahr el →, *Chad* 79 F9
Ghazâl, Bahr el →, *Sudan* 81 F3
Ghaziabad, *India* 68 E7
Ghazipur, *India* 69 G10
Ghaznī, *Afghan.* 68 C3
Ghaznī □, *Afghan.* 66 C6
Ghedi, *Italy* 40 C7
Ghelari, *Romania* 28 E7
Ghent = Gent, *Belgium* 17 C3
Gheorghe Gheorghiu-Dej = Oneşti, *Romania* 29 D11
Gheorgheni, *Romania* 29 D10
Gherla, *Romania* 29 C8
Ghidigeni, *Romania* 29 D12
Ghilarza, *Italy* 42 B1
Ghimeş-Făget, *Romania* 29 D11
Ghīnah, Wādī al →, *Si. Arabia* 70 D3
Ghisonaccia, *France* 21 F13
Ghisoni, *France* 21 F13
Ghizao, *Afghan.* 68 C1
Ghizar →, *Pakistan* 69 A5
Ghot Ogrein, *Egypt* 80 A2
Ghotaru, *India* 68 F4
Ghotki, *Pakistan* 68 E3
Ghowr □, *Afghan.* 66 C4
Ghudāf, W. al →, *Iraq* 70 C4
Ghudāmis, *Libya* 77 C4
Ghudāmis □, *Libya* 79 B8
Ghughri, *India* 69 H9
Ghugus, *India* 66 K11
Ghulam Mohammad Barrage, *Pakistan* 68 G3
Ghūriān, *Afghan.* 66 B2
Gia Dinh, *Vietnam* 65 G6
Gia Lai = Plei Ku, *Vietnam* 64 F7
Gia Nghia, *Vietnam* 65 G6
Gia Ngoc, *Vietnam* 64 E7
Gia Vuc, *Vietnam* 64 E7
Giannutri, *Italy* 40 F8
Giant Forest, *U.S.A.* 110 J8
Giant Mts. = Krkonoše, *Czech Rep.* 26 A8
Giant Sequoia ⌂, *U.S.A.* 110 K8
Giants Causeway, *U.K.* 12 A5
Gianyar, *Indonesia* 63 K18
Giarabub = Al Jaghbūb, *Libya* 79 C10
Giarre, *Italy* 43 E8
Giaveno, *Italy* 40 C4
Gibara, *Cuba* 120 B4
Gibb River, *Australia* 92 C4
Gibbon, *U.S.A.* 112 E5
Gibe →, *Ethiopia* 81 F4
Gibellina Nuova, *Italy* 42 E5
Gibeon, *Namibia* 88 D2
Gibraleón, *Spain* 37 H4
Gibraltar ⧄, *Europe* 37 J5
Gibraltar, Str. of, *Medit. S.* 37 K5
Gibraltar Range △, *Australia* 95 D5
Gibson Desert, *Australia* 92 D4
Gibsons, *Canada* 102 D4
Gibsonville, *U.S.A.* 110 F6
Giddings, *U.S.A.* 113 K6
Gidole, *Ethiopia* 81 F4
Giebnegáisi = Kebnekaise, *Sweden* 8 C18
Gien, *France* 19 E9
Giengen, *Germany* 25 G6
Giessen, *Germany* 24 E4
Gīfān, *Iran* 71 B8
Gifatin, Geziret, *Egypt* 80 B3
Gifhorn, *Germany* 24 C6
Gift Lake, *Canada* 102 B5
Gifu, *Japan* 55 G8
Gifu □, *Japan* 55 G8
Gigant, *Russia* 35 G5
Giganta, Sa. de la, *Mexico* 118 B2
Gigen, *Bulgaria* 45 C8
Gigha, *U.K.* 13 F3
Gíglio, *Italy* 40 F7
Gignac, *France* 20 E7
Gigüela →, *Spain* 37 F7
Gijón, *Spain* 36 B5
Gil I., *Canada* 102 C3
Gila →, *U.S.A.* 109 K6
Gila Bend, *U.S.A.* 109 K7
Gila Bend Mts., *U.S.A.* 109 K7
Gila Cliff Dwellings ⌂, *U.S.A.* 109 K9
Gīlān □, *Iran* 71 B6
Gilău, *Romania* 29 D8
Gilbert →, *Australia* 94 B3
Gilbert Is., *Kiribati* 96 G9
Gilbert River, *Australia* 94 B3
Gilead, *U.S.A.* 117 B14
Gilf el Kebîr, Hadabat el, *Egypt* 80 C2
Gilford I., *Canada* 102 C3
Gilgandra, *Australia* 95 E4
Gilgil, *Kenya* 86 C4
Gilgit, *India* 69 B6
Gilgit →, *Pakistan* 69 B6
Gili ⌂, *Mozam.* 87 F4
Gilimanuk, *Indonesia* 63 J17
Giljeva Planina, *Serbia & M.* 44 C3
Gillam, *Canada* 103 B10
Gilleleje, *Denmark* 11 H6
Gillen, L., *Australia* 93 E3
Gilles, L., *Australia* 95 E2
Gillette, *U.S.A.* 112 C2
Gilliat, *Australia* 94 C3
Gillingham, *U.K.* 15 F8
Gilmer, *U.S.A.* 113 J7
Gilmore, L., *Australia* 93 F3
Gilo →, *Ethiopia* 81 F3
Gilort →, *Romania* 29 F8
Gilroy, *U.S.A.* 110 H5
Gimbi, *Ethiopia* 81 F4
Gimie, Mt, *St. Lucia* 121 f
Gimli, *Canada* 103 C9
Gimo, *Sweden* 10 D12
Gimone →, *France* 20 E5
Gimont, *France* 20 E4
Gin Gin, *Australia* 95 D5
Ginâh, *Egypt* 80 B3
Gineifa, *Egypt* 80 H8
Gingin, *Australia* 93 F2
Gingindlovu, *S. Africa* 89 D5
Ginir, *Ethiopia* 81 F5
Ginosa, *Italy* 43 B9
Ginzo de Limia = Xinzo de Limia, *Spain* 36 C3
Gióia, G. di, *Italy* 43 D8
Gióia del Colle, *Italy* 43 B9
Gióia Táuro, *Italy* 43 D8
Gioiosa Iónica, *Italy* 43 D9
Gioiosa Marea, *Italy* 43 D7
Gióna, Óros, *Greece* 46 C4
Giovi, Passo dei, *Italy* 40 D5
Giovinazzo, *Italy* 43 A9
Gir Hills, *India* 68 J4
Girab, *India* 68 F4
Girâfi, W. →, *Egypt* 74 F3
Giraltovce, *Slovak Rep.* 27 B14
Girard, *Kans., U.S.A.* 113 G7
Girard, *Ohio, U.S.A.* 116 E4
Girard, *Pa., U.S.A.* 116 E4
Girdle Ness, *U.K.* 13 D6
Giresun, *Turkey* 73 B8
Girga, *Egypt* 80 B3
Giri →, *India* 68 D7
Giridih, *India* 69 G12
Girifalco, *Italy* 43 D9
Girne = Kyrenia, *Cyprus* 49 D12
Giro, *Nigeria* 83 C5
Giromagny, *France* 19 E13
Giron = Kiruna, *Sweden* 8 C19
Girona, *Spain* 38 D7
Girona □, *Spain* 38 C7
Gironde □, *France* 20 D3
Gironde →, *France* 20 C2
Gironella, *Spain* 38 C6
Girraween △, *Australia* 95 D5
Giru, *Australia* 94 B4
Girvan, *U.K.* 13 F4
Gisborne, *N.Z.* 91 H7
Gisenyi, *Rwanda* 86 C2
Gislaved, *Sweden* 11 G7
Gisors, *France* 19 C8
Gitega, *Burundi* 86 C2
Giuba →, *Somali Rep.* 75 G3
Giugliano in Campania, *Italy* 43 B7
Giulianova, *Italy* 41 F10
Giurgeni, *Romania* 29 F12
Giurgiu, *Romania* 29 G10
Giurgiu □, *Romania* 29 F10
Giurgiuleşti, *Moldova* 29 E13
Give, *Denmark* 11 J3
Givet, *France* 19 B11
Givors, *France* 21 C8
Givry, *France* 19 F11
Giyon, *Ethiopia* 81 F4
Giza = El Gîza, *Egypt* 80 J7
Gizhiga, *Russia* 53 C17
Gizhiginskaya Guba, *Russia* 53 C16
Giżycko, *Poland* 30 D8

Gizzeria, *Italy* 43 D9
Gjalicë e Lumës, Mal., *Albania* 44 D4
Gjegjan, *Albania* 44 E4
Gjirokastër, *Albania* 44 F4
Gjoa Haven, *Canada* 100 B10
Gjøvik, *Norway* 9 F14
Gjuhës, Kep i, *Albania* 44 F3
Glace Bay, *Canada* 105 C8
Glacier △, *Canada* 102 C5
Glacier △, *U.S.A.* 108 B7
Glacier Bay △, *U.S.A.* 102 B1
Glacier Peak, *U.S.A.* 108 B3
Gladewater, *U.S.A.* 113 J7
Gladstone, *Queens., Australia* 94 C5
Gladstone, *S. Austral., Australia* 95 E2
Gladstone, *Canada* 103 C9
Gladstone, *U.S.A.* 114 C2
Gladwin, *U.S.A.* 114 D3
Glafsfjorden, *Sweden* 10 E6
Glagah, *Indonesia* 63 J17
Głagów Małapolski, *Poland* 31 H8
Glåma = Glomma ➛, *Norway* 9 G14
Gláma, *Iceland* 8 D2
Glamis, *U.S.A.* 111 N11
Glamoč, *Bos.-H.* 41 D13
Glamorgan, Vale of □, *U.K.* 15 F4
Glamsbjerg, *Denmark* 11 J4
Glarus, *Switz.* 25 H5
Glarus □, *Switz.* 25 J5
Glasco, *Kans., U.S.A.* 112 F6
Glasco, *N.Y., U.S.A.* 117 D11
Glasgow, *U.K.* 13 F4
Glasgow, *Ky., U.S.A.* 114 G3
Glasgow, *Mont., U.S.A.* 108 B10
Glasgow, City of □, *U.K.* 13 F4
Glasgow International ✈ (GLA), *U.K.* 13 F4
Glaslyn, *Canada* 103 C7
Glastonbury, *U.K.* 15 F5
Glastonbury, *U.S.A.* 117 E12
Glauchau, *Germany* 24 E8
Glava, *Sweden* 10 E6
Glavice, *Croatia* 41 E13
Glazov, *Russia* 34 A11
Gleichen, *Canada* 102 C6
Gleisdorf, *Austria* 26 D8
Gleiwitz = Gliwice, *Poland* 31 H5
Glen, *U.S.A.* 117 B13
Glen Affric, *U.K.* 13 D3
Glen Canyon, *U.S.A.* 109 H8
Glen Canyon ⌂, *U.S.A.* 109 H8
Glen Canyon Dam, *U.S.A.* 109 H8
Glen Coe, *U.K.* 13 E3
Glen Cove, *U.S.A.* 117 F11
Glen Garry, *U.K.* 13 D3
Glen Innes, *Australia* 95 D5
Glen Lyon, *U.S.A.* 117 E8
Glen Mor, *U.K.* 13 D4
Glen More ⌂, *U.K.* 13 D5
Glen Moriston, *U.K.* 13 D4
Glen Robertson, *Canada* 117 A10
Glen Spean, *U.K.* 13 E4
Glen Ullin, *U.S.A.* 112 B4
Glénan, Îs. de, *France* 18 E3
Glenariff △, *Ireland* 12 A5
Glencoe, *Canada* 116 D3
Glencoe, *S. Africa* 89 D5
Glencoe, *U.S.A.* 112 C7
Glendale, *Ariz., U.S.A.* 109 K7
Glendale, *Calif., U.S.A.* 111 L8
Glendale, *Zimbabwe* 87 F3
Glendive, *U.S.A.* 112 B2
Glendo, *U.S.A.* 112 D2
Glenelg ➛, *Australia* 95 F3
Glenfield, *U.S.A.* 117 C9
Glengarriff, *Ireland* 12 E2
Glenmont, *U.S.A.* 116 F2
Glenmorgan, *Australia* 95 D4
Glenn, *U.S.A.* 110 F4
Glennallen, *U.S.A.* 100 B5
Glennamaddy, *Ireland* 12 C3
Glenns Ferry, *U.S.A.* 108 E6
Glenore, *Australia* 94 B3
Glenreagh, *Australia* 95 E5
Glenrock, *U.S.A.* 108 E11
Glenrothes, *U.K.* 13 E5
Glens Falls, *U.S.A.* 117 C11
Glenside, *U.S.A.* 117 F9
Glenties, *Ireland* 12 B3
Glenveagh △, *Ireland* 12 A3
Glenville, *U.S.A.* 114 F5
Glenwood, *Canada* 105 C9
Glenwood, *Ark., U.S.A.* 113 H8
Glenwood, *Iowa, U.S.A.* 112 E7
Glenwood, *Minn., U.S.A.* 112 C7
Glenwood, *Wash., U.S.A.* 110 D5
Glenwood Springs, *U.S.A.* 108 G10
Glettinganes, *Iceland* 8 D7
Glifádha, *Greece* 46 D5
Glimåkra, *Sweden* 11 H8
Glina, *Croatia* 41 C13
Glinojeck, *Poland* 31 F7
Gliwice, *Poland* 31 H5
Globe, *U.S.A.* 109 K8
Glodeanu Siliştea, *Romania* 29 F11
Glodeni, *Moldova* 29 C12
Glödnitz, *Austria* 26 E7
Gloggnitz, *Austria* 26 D8
Głogów, *Poland* 31 G3
Głogówek, *Poland* 31 H4
Glomma ➛, *Norway* 9 G14
Glorieuses, Is., *Ind. Oc.* 89 A8
Glóssa, *Greece* 46 B5
Glossop, *U.K.* 14 D6
Gloucester, *Australia* 95 E5
Gloucester, *U.K.* 15 F5
Gloucester, *U.S.A.* 117 D14
Gloucester I., *Australia* 94 J6
Gloucester Island △, *Australia* 94 J6
Gloucester Point, *U.S.A.* 114 G7
Gloucestershire □, *U.K.* 15 F5
Gloversville, *U.S.A.* 117 C10
Glovertown, *Canada* 105 C9
Głowno, *Poland* 31 G6
Głubczyce, *Poland* 31 H4
Glubokiy, *Russia* 35 F5
Glubokoye = Hlybokaye, *Belarus* 32 E4
Głuchołazy, *Poland* 31 H4
Glücksburg, *Germany* 24 A5
Glückstadt, *Germany* 24 B5
Glukhov = Hlukhiv, *Ukraine* 33 G7
Glusk, *Belarus* 33 F5
Głuszyca, *Poland* 31 H3
Glyngøre, *Denmark* 11 H2
Gmünd, *Kärnten, Austria* 26 E6
Gmünd, *Niederösterreich, Austria* 26 C8
Gmunden, *Austria* 26 D6
Gnarp, *Sweden* 10 B11
Gnesta, *Sweden* 10 E11
Gniew, *Poland* 30 E5
Gniewkowo, *Poland* 31 F5
Gniezno, *Poland* 31 F4
Gnjilane, *Serbia & M.* 44 D5
Gnoien, *Germany* 24 B8
Gnosjö, *Sweden* 11 G7
Gnowangerup, *Australia* 93 F2
Go Cong, *Vietnam* 65 G6
Gō-no-ura, *Japan* 55 H4
Goa, *India* 66 M8
Goa □, *India* 66 M8
Goalen Hd., *Australia* 95 F5
Goalpara, *India* 67 F17
Goaltor, *India* 69 H12
Goalundo Ghat, *Bangla.* 69 H13
Goaso, *Ghana* 82 D4
Goat Fell, *U.K.* 13 F3
Goba, *Ethiopia* 81 F4
Goba, *Mozam.* 89 D5
Gobabis, *Namibia* 88 C2
Göbel, *Turkey* 45 F12
Gobi, *Asia* 56 C6
Gobō, *Japan* 55 H7
Gobo, *Sudan* 81 F3
Göçbeyli, *Turkey* 47 B9
Goch, *Germany* 24 D2
Gochas, *Namibia* 88 C2
Godalming, *U.K.* 15 F7
Godavari ➛, *India* 67 L13
Godavari Pt., *India* 67 L13
Godbout, *Canada* 105 C6
Godda, *India* 69 G12
Godech, *Bulgaria* 44 C7
Goderich, *Canada* 116 C3
Goderville, *France* 18 C7
Godfrey Ra., *Australia* 93 D2
Godhavn = Qeqertarsuaq, *Greenland* 101 B14
Godhra, *India* 68 H5
Gödöllő, *Hungary* 28 C4
Godoy Cruz, *Argentina* 126 C2
Gods ➛, *Canada* 104 A1
Gods L., *Canada* 104 B1
Gods River, *Canada* 103 C10
Godthåb = Nuuk, *Greenland* 101 B14
Goeie Hoop, Kaap die = Good Hope, C. of, *S. Africa* 88 E2
Goéland, L. au, *Canada* 104 C4
Goélands, L. aux, *Canada* 105 A7
Goeree, *Neths.* 17 C3
Goes, *Neths.* 17 C3
Goffstown, *U.S.A.* 117 C13
Gogama, *Canada* 104 C3
Gogebic, L., *U.S.A.* 112 B10
Goggetti, *Ethiopia* 81 F4
Gogolin, *Poland* 31 H5
Gogonou, *Benin* 83 C5
Gogra = Ghaghara ➛, *India* 69 G11
Gogriāl, *Sudan* 81 F2
Gogti, *Ethiopia* 81 E5
Gohana, *India* 68 E7
Goharganj, *India* 68 H7
Goi ➛, *India* 68 H6
Goiânia, *Brazil* 125 G9
Goiás, *Brazil* 125 G8
Goiás □, *Brazil* 125 F9
Goio-Erê, *Brazil* 127 A5
Góis, *Portugal* 36 E2
Gojam, *Ethiopia* 81 E4
Gojeb, Wabi ➛, *Ethiopia* 81 F4
Gojō, *Japan* 55 G7
Gojra, *Pakistan* 68 D5
Gökçeada, *Turkey* 45 F9
Gökçedağ, *Turkey* 47 B10
Gökçen, *Turkey* 47 C9
Gökçeören, *Turkey* 47 C10
Gökçeyazı, *Turkey* 47 B9
Gökırmak ➛, *Turkey* 72 B6
Gökova, *Turkey* 47 D10
Gökova Körfezi, *Turkey* 47 E9
Göksu ➛, *Turkey* 72 D6
Göksun, *Turkey* 72 C7
Gokteik, *Burma* 67 H20
Göktepe, *Turkey* 47 D10
Gokurt, *Pakistan* 68 E2
Gokwe, *Zimbabwe* 89 B4
Gola, *India* 69 E9
Golakganj, *India* 69 F13
Golan Heights = Hagolan, *Syria* 74 C4
Gołańcz, *Poland* 31 F4
Golāshkerd, *Iran* 71 E8
Golaya Pristen = Hola Pristan, *Ukraine* 33 J7
Gölbaşı, *Adiyaman, Turkey* 72 D7
Gölbaşı, *Ankara, Turkey* 72 C5
Golchikha, *Russia* 4 B12
Golconda, *U.S.A.* 108 F5
Gölcük, *Kocaeli, Turkey* 45 F13
Gölcük, *Niğde, Turkey* 72 C6
Gold, *U.S.A.* 116 E7
Gold Beach, *U.S.A.* 108 E1
Gold Coast, *W. Afr.* 83 E4
Gold Hill, *U.S.A.* 108 E2
Gold River, *Canada* 102 D3
Gołdap, *Poland* 30 D9
Goldberg, *Germany* 24 B8
Golden, *Canada* 102 C5
Golden B., *N.Z.* 91 J4
Golden Gate, *U.S.A.* 108 H2
Golden Gate Highlands △, *S. Africa* 89 D4
Golden Hinde, *Canada* 102 D3
Golden Lake, *Canada* 116 A7
Golden Spike ⌂, *U.S.A.* 108 F7
Golden Vale, *Ireland* 12 D3
Goldendale, *U.S.A.* 108 D3
Goldfield, *U.S.A.* 109 H5
Goldsand L., *Canada* 103 B8
Goldsboro, *U.S.A.* 115 H7
Goldsmith, *U.S.A.* 113 K3
Goldsworthy, *Australia* 92 D2
Goldthwaite, *U.S.A.* 113 K5
Golegã, *Portugal* 37 F2
Goleniów, *Poland* 30 E1
Golestān □, *Iran* 71 B7
Golestānak, *Iran* 71 D7
Goleta, *U.S.A.* 111 L7
Golfito, *Costa Rica* 120 E3
Golfo Aranci, *Italy* 42 B2
Golfo di Orosei e del Gennargentu △, *Italy* 42 B2
Gölgeli Dağları, *Turkey* 47 D10
Gölhisar, *Turkey* 47 D11
Goliad, *U.S.A.* 113 L6
Golija, *Serbia & M.* 44 C2
Golija, *Serbia & M.* 44 C4
Golina, *Poland* 31 F5
Gölköy, *Turkey* 72 B7
Göllersdorf, *Austria* 26 C9
Gölmarmara, *Turkey* 47 C9
Golo ➛, *France* 21 F13
Gölova, *Turkey* 47 E12
Golpāyegān, *Iran* 71 C6
Gölpazarı, *Turkey* 72 B4
Golra, *Pakistan* 68 C5
Golspie, *U.K.* 13 D5
Golub-Dobrzyń, *Poland* 31 E6
Golubac, *Serbia & M.* 44 B5
Golyam Perelik, *Bulgaria* 45 E8
Golyama Kamchiya ➛, *Bulgaria* 45 C11
Goma, *Dem. Rep. of the Congo* 86 C2
Gomal Pass, *Pakistan* 68 D3
Gomati ➛, *India* 69 G10
Gombari, *Dem. Rep. of the Congo* 86 B2
Gombe, *Nigeria* 83 C7
Gömbe, *Turkey* 47 E11
Gombe □, *Nigeria* 83 C7
Gombe ➛, *Tanzania* 86 C3
Gombi, *Nigeria* 83 C7
Gomel = Homyel, *Belarus* 33 F6
Gomera, *Canary Is.* 48 F2
Gómez Palacio, *Mexico* 118 B4
Gomīshān, *Iran* 71 B7
Gommern, *Germany* 24 C7
Gomogomo, *Indonesia* 63 F8
Gomoh, *India* 67 H15
Gomotartsi, *Bulgaria* 44 B6
Gompa = Ganta, *Liberia* 82 D3
Gomphi, *Greece* 46 B3
Gonābād, *Iran* 71 C8
Gonaïves, *Haiti* 121 C5
Gonarezhou △, *Zimbabwe* 87 G3
Gonâve, G. de la, *Haiti* 121 C5
Gonâve, Île de la, *Haiti* 121 C5
Gonbad-e Kāvūs, *Iran* 71 B7
Gönc, *Hungary* 28 B6
Gonda, *India* 69 F9
Gondal, *India* 68 J4
Gonder, *Ethiopia* 81 E4
Gondia, *India* 66 J12
Gondola, *Mozam.* 87 F3
Gondomar, *Portugal* 36 D2
Gondrecourt-le-Château, *France* 19 D12
Gönen, *Balıkesir, Turkey* 45 F11
Gönen, *Isparta, Turkey* 47 D12
Gönen ➛, *Turkey* 45 F11
Gong Xian, *China* 58 C5
Gong'an, *China* 59 B9
Gongcheng, *China* 59 E8
Gongga Shan, *China* 58 C3
Gongguan, *China* 58 G7
Gonghe, *China* 60 C5
Gongola ➛, *Nigeria* 83 D7
Gongolgon, *Australia* 95 E4
Gongshan, *China* 58 D2
Gongtan, *China* 58 C7
Gongzhuling, *China* 57 C13
Goniadz, *Poland* 30 E9
Goniri, *Nigeria* 83 C7
Gonjo, *China* 58 B2
Gonnesa, *Italy* 42 C1
Gónnos, *Greece* 46 B4
Gonnosfanádiga, *Italy* 42 C1
Gonzaga, *Phil.* 61 B5
Gonzales, *Calif., U.S.A.* 110 J5
Gonzales, *Tex., U.S.A.* 113 L6
González Chaves, *Argentina* 126 D3
Good Hope, C. of, *S. Africa* 88 E2
Gooderham, *Canada* 116 B6
Goodhouse, *S. Africa* 88 D2
Gooding, *U.S.A.* 108 E6
Goodland, *U.S.A.* 112 F4
Goodlow, *Canada* 102 B4
Goodooga, *Australia* 95 D4
Goodsprings, *U.S.A.* 111 K11
Goole, *U.K.* 14 D7
Goolgowi, *Australia* 95 E4
Goomalling, *Australia* 93 F2
Goomeri, *Australia* 95 D5
Goonda, *Mozam.* 87 F3
Goondiwindi, *Australia* 95 D5
Goongarrie △, *Australia* 93 F3
Goongarrie, L., *Australia* 93 F3
Goonyella, *Australia* 94 C4
Goose ➛, *Canada* 105 B7
Goose Creek, *U.S.A.* 115 J5
Goose L., *U.S.A.* 108 F3
Gop, *India* 66 H6
Gopalganj, *India* 69 F11
Göppingen, *Germany* 25 G5
Gor, *Spain* 37 H8
Góra, *Dolnośląskie, Poland* 31 G3
Góra, *Mazowieckie, Poland* 31 F7
Góra Kalwaria, *Poland* 31 G8
Gorakhpur, *India* 69 F10
Goražde, *Bos.-H.* 28 G3
Gorbatov, *Russia* 34 B6
Gorbea, Peña, *Spain* 38 B2
Gorczański △, *Poland* 31 J7
Gorda, *U.S.A.* 110 K5
Gorda, Pta., *Canary Is.* 48 F2
Gorda, Pta., *Nic.* 120 D3
Gordan B., *Australia* 92 B5
Gördes, *Turkey* 47 C10
Gordon, *U.S.A.* 112 D3
Gordon ➛, *Australia* 95 G4
Gordon L., *Alta., Canada* 103 B6
Gordon L., *N.W.T., Canada* 102 A6
Gordonvale, *Australia* 94 B4
Gore, *Ethiopia* 81 F4
Gore, *N.Z.* 91 M2
Gore Bay, *Canada* 104 C3
Görele, *Turkey* 73 B8
Goreme, *Turkey* 72 C6
Gorey, *Ireland* 12 D5
Gorg, *Iran* 71 D8
Gorgān, *Iran* 71 B7
Gorgona, *Italy* 40 E6
Gorgona, I., *Colombia* 124 C3
Gorgora, *Ethiopia* 81 E4
Gorgoram, *Nigeria* 83 C7
Gorham, *U.S.A.* 117 B13
Gori, *Georgia* 35 J7
Goriganga ➛, *India* 69 E9
Gorinchem, *Neths.* 17 C4
Goris, *Armenia* 73 C12
Goritsy, *Russia* 32 D9
Gorízia, *Italy* 41 C10
Gorj □, *Romania* 29 E8
Gorki = Horki, *Belarus* 32 E6
Gorki = Nizhniy Novgorod, *Russia* 34 B7
Gorkiy = Nizhniy Novgorod, *Russia* 34 B7
Gorkovskoye Vdkhr., *Russia* 34 B6
Gorleston, *U.K.* 15 E9
Gorlice, *Poland* 31 J8
Görlitz, *Germany* 24 D10
Gorlovka = Horlivka, *Ukraine* 33 H10
Gorman, *U.S.A.* 111 L8
Gorna Dzhumayo = Blagoevgrad, *Bulgaria* 44 D7
Gorna Oryakhovitsa, *Bulgaria* 45 C9
Gornja Radgona, *Slovenia* 41 B13
Gornja Tuzla, *Bos.-H.* 28 F3
Gornji Grad, *Slovenia* 41 B11
Gornji Milanovac, *Serbia & M.* 44 B4
Gornji Vakuf, *Bos.-H.* 28 G2
Gorno Ablanovo, *Bulgaria* 45 C9
Gorno-Altay □, *Russia* 52 D9
Gorno-Altaysk, *Russia* 52 D9
Gornyatskiy, *Russia* 35 F5
Gornyy, *Saratov, Russia* 34 E9
Gornyy, *Sib., Russia* 54 B6
Gorodenka = Horodenka, *Ukraine* 29 B10
Gorodets, *Russia* 34 B6
Gorodishche = Horodyshche, *Ukraine* 33 H6
Gorodishche, *Russia* 34 D7
Gorodnya = Horodnya, *Ukraine* 33 G6
Gorodok = Haradok, *Belarus* 32 E6
Gorodok = Horodok, *Ukraine* 33 H2
Gorodovikovsk, *Russia* 35 G5
Gorokhov = Horokhiv, *Ukraine* 33 G3
Gorokhovets, *Russia* 34 B6
Gorom Gorom, *Burkina Faso* 83 C4
Goromonzi, *Zimbabwe* 87 F3
Gorong, Kepulauan, *Indonesia* 63 E8
Gorongosa △, *Mozam.* 89 B5
Gorongose ➛, *Mozam.* 89 C5
Gorongoza, *Mozam.* 87 F3
Gorongoza, Sa. da, *Mozam.* 87 F3
Gorontalo, *Indonesia* 63 D6
Gorontalo □, *Indonesia* 63 D6
Goronyo, *Nigeria* 83 C6
Górowo Iławeckie, *Poland* 30 D7
Gorron, *France* 18 D6
Gorshechnoye, *Russia* 33 G10
Gort, *Ireland* 12 C3
Gortis, *Greece* 49 D6
Góry Bystrzyckie, *Poland* 31 H3
Goryachiy Klyuch, *Russia* 35 H4
Gorzkowice, *Poland* 31 G6
Górzno, *Poland* 31 E6
Gorzów Śląski, *Poland* 31 G5
Gorzów Wielkopolski, *Poland* 31 F2
Gosford, *Australia* 95 E5
Goshen, *Calif., U.S.A.* 110 J7
Goshen, *Ind., U.S.A.* 114 E3
Goshen, *N.Y., U.S.A.* 117 E10
Goshogawara, *Japan* 54 D10
Goslar, *Germany* 24 D6
Gospič, *Croatia* 41 D12
Gosport, *U.K.* 15 G6
Gossas, *Senegal* 82 C1
Gosse ➛, *Australia* 94 B1
Gossi, *Mali* 83 B4
Gossinga, *Sudan* 81 F2
Gostivar, *Macedonia* 44 E4
Gostyń, *Poland* 31 G4
Gostynin, *Poland* 31 F6
Göta älv ➛, *Sweden* 11 G5
Göta kanal, *Sweden* 11 F9
Götaland, *Sweden* 11 G8
Göteborg, *Sweden* 11 G5
Götene, *Sweden* 11 F7
Goteşti, *Moldova* 29 D13
Gotha, *Germany* 24 E6
Gothenburg = Göteborg, *Sweden* 11 G5
Gothenburg, *U.S.A.* 112 E4
Gothèye, *Niger* 83 C5
Gotland, *Sweden* 11 G12
Gotlands län □, *Sweden* 11 G12
Gotō-Rettō, *Japan* 55 H4
Gotse Delchev, *Bulgaria* 44 E7
Gotska Sandön, *Sweden* 9 G18
Gōtsu, *Japan* 55 G6
Gott Pk., *Canada* 102 C4
Góttero, Monte, *Italy* 40 D6
Göttingen, *Germany* 24 D5
Gottwald = Zmiyev, *Ukraine* 33 H9
Gottwaldov = Zlín, *Czech Rep.* 27 B10
Goubangzi, *China* 57 D11
Gouda, *Neths.* 17 B4
Goúdhoura, Ákra, *Greece* 49 E8
Goudiry, *Senegal* 82 C2
Goudoumaria, *Niger* 83 C7
Gouéké, *Guinea* 82 D3
Gough I., *Atl. Oc.* 2 G9
Gouin, Rés., *Canada* 104 C5
Gouitafla, *Ivory C.* 82 D3
Goulburn, *Australia* 95 E4
Goulburn Is., *Australia* 94 A1
Goulia, *Ivory C.* 82 C3
Goulimine, *Morocco* 78 C3
Goumbou, *Mali* 82 B3
Gouménissa, *Greece* 44 F6
Goundam, *Mali* 82 B4
Goúra, *Greece* 46 D4
Gourbassi, *Mali* 82 C2
Gourdon, *France* 20 D5
Gouré, *Niger* 83 C7
Gourin, *France* 18 D3
Gourits ➛, *S. Africa* 88 E3
Gourma-Rharous, *Mali* 83 B4
Goúrnais, *Greece* 49 D7
Gournay-en-Bray, *France* 19 C8
Gourock, *U.K.* 13 F4
Goursi, *Burkina Faso* 82 C4
Gouverneur, *U.S.A.* 117 B9
Gouviá, *Greece* 49 A3
Gouzon, *France* 19 F9
Governador Valadares, *Brazil* 125 G10
Governor's Harbour, *Bahamas* 120 A4
Govindgarh, *India* 69 G9
Gowan Ra., *Australia* 94 D4
Gowanda, *U.S.A.* 116 D6
Gower, *U.K.* 15 F3
Gowna, L., *Ireland* 12 C4
Goya, *Argentina* 126 B4
Göyçay, *Azerbaijan* 35 K8
Goyder Lagoon, *Australia* 95 D2
Goyllarisquisga, *Peru* 124 F3
Göynük, *Antalya, Turkey* 47 E12
Göynük, *Bolu, Turkey* 72 B4
Goz Beïda, *Chad* 79 F10
Goz Regeb, *Sudan* 81 D4
Gozdnica, *Poland* 31 G2
Gozo, *Malta* 49 C1
Graaff-Reinet, *S. Africa* 88 E3
Grabo, *Ivory C.* 82 D3
Grabow, *Germany* 24 B7
Grabów nad Prosną, *Poland* 31 G5
Gračac, *Croatia* 41 D12
Gračanica, *Bos.-H.* 28 F3
Graçay, *France* 19 E8
Gracias a Dios, C., *Honduras* 120 D3
Graciosa, I., *Canary Is.* 48 E6
Grad Sofiya □, *Bulgaria* 44 D7
Gradac, *Serbia & M.* 44 C3
Gradačac, *Bos.-H.* 28 F3
Gradeška Planina, *Macedonia* 44 E6
Gradets, *Bulgaria* 45 D10
Gradišče, *Slovenia* 41 B12
Grădiştea de Munte, *Romania* 29 E8
Grado, *Italy* 41 C10
Grado, *Spain* 36 B4
Grady, *U.S.A.* 113 H3
Graeca, Lacul, *Romania* 29 F11
Grafenau, *Germany* 25 G9
Gräfenberg, *Germany* 25 F7
Grafham Water, *U.K.* 15 E7
Grafton, *Australia* 95 D5
Grafton, *N. Dak., U.S.A.* 112 A6
Grafton, *W. Va., U.S.A.* 114 F5
Graham, *Canada* 104 C1
Graham, *U.S.A.* 113 J5
Graham, Mt., *U.S.A.* 109 K9
Graham Bell, Ostrov = Greem-Bell, Ostrov, *Russia* 52 A7
Graham I., *Canada* 102 C2
Graham Land, *Antarctica* 5 C17
Grahamstown, *S. Africa* 88 E4
Grahamsville, *U.S.A.* 117 E10
Grahovo, *Serbia & M.* 44 D2
Graie, Alpi, *Europe* 21 C11
Grain Coast, *W. Afr.* 82 E3
Grajagan, *Indonesia* 63 K17
Grajagan, Teluk, *Indonesia* 63 K17
Grajaú, *Brazil* 125 E9
Grajaú ➛, *Brazil* 125 D10
Grajewo, *Poland* 30 E9
Gramada, *Bulgaria* 44 C6
Gramat, *France* 20 D5
Grammichele, *Italy* 43 E7
Grámmos, Óros, *Greece* 44 F4
Grampian, *U.S.A.* 116 F6
Grampian Highlands = Grampian Mts., *U.K.* 13 E5
Grampian Mts., *U.K.* 13 E5
Grampians, The, *Australia* 95 F3
Gramsh, *Albania* 44 F4
Gran Canaria, *Canary Is.* 48 G4
Gran Chaco, *S. Amer.* 126 B3
Gran Desierto del Pinacate ⌂, *Mexico* 118 A2
Gran Paradiso, *Italy* 40 C4
Gran Sasso d'Itália, *Italy* 41 F10
Gran Sasso e Monti Della Laga △, *Italy* 41 F10

Granada, *Nic.* 120 D2
Granada, *Spain* 37 H7
Granada, *U.S.A.* 113 F3
Granada □, *Spain* 37 H7
Granadilla de Abona, *Canary Is.* 48 F3
Granard, *Ireland* 12 C4
Granbury, *U.S.A.* 113 J6
Granby, *Canada* 117 A12
Granby, *U.S.A.* 108 F11
Grand →, *Canada* 116 D5
Grand →, *Mo., U.S.A.* 112 F8
Grand →, *S. Dak., U.S.A.* 112 C4
Grand Bahama I., *Bahamas* 120 A4
Grand Bank, *Canada* 105 C8
Grand Bassam, *Ivory C.* 82 D4
Grand Béréby, *Ivory C.* 82 E3
Grand-Bourg, *Guadeloupe* 120 b
Grand Canal = Yun Ho →, *China* 57 E9
Grand Canyon, *U.S.A.* 109 H7
Grand Canyon △, *U.S.A.* 109 H7
Grand Canyon-Parashant ⌂, *U.S.A.* 109 H7
Grand Cayman, *Cayman Is.* 120 C3
Grand Centre, *Canada* 103 C6
Grand Cess, *Liberia* 82 E3
Grand Coulee, *U.S.A.* 108 C4
Grand Coulee Dam, *U.S.A.* 108 C4
Grand Falls, *Canada* 105 C6
Grand Falls-Windsor, *Canada* 105 C8
Grand Forks, *Canada* 102 D5
Grand Forks, *U.S.A.* 112 B6
Grand Gorge, *U.S.A.* 117 D10
Grand Haven, *U.S.A.* 114 D2
Grand I., *Mich., U.S.A.* 114 B2
Grand I., *N.Y., U.S.A.* 116 D6
Grand Island, *U.S.A.* 112 E5
Grand Isle, *La., U.S.A.* 113 L9
Grand Isle, *Vt., U.S.A.* 117 B11
Grand Junction, *U.S.A.* 109 G9
Grand L., *N.B., Canada* 105 C6
Grand L., *Nfld. & L., Canada* 105 C8
Grand L., *Nfld. & L., Canada* 105 B7
Grand L., *U.S.A.* 113 L8
Grand Lahou, *Ivory C.* 82 D3
Grand Lake, *U.S.A.* 108 F11
Grand-Lieu, L. de, *France* 18 E5
Grand Manan I., *Canada* 105 D6
Grand Marais, *Canada* 112 B9
Grand Marais, *U.S.A.* 114 B3
Grand-Mère, *Canada* 104 C5
Grand Popo, *Benin* 83 D5
Grand Portage, *U.S.A.* 112 B10
Grand Prairie, *U.S.A.* 113 J6
Grand Rapids, *Canada* 103 C9
Grand Rapids, *Mich., U.S.A.* 114 D2
Grand Rapids, *Minn., U.S.A.* 112 B8
Grand St-Bernard, Col du, *Europe* 25 K3
Grand Staircase-Escalante ⌂, *U.S.A.* 109 H8
Grand Teton, *U.S.A.* 108 E8
Grand Teton △, *U.S.A.* 108 D8
Grand Union Canal, *U.K.* 15 E7
Grand-Vigie, Pte. de la, *Guadeloupe* 120 b
Grandas de Salime, *Spain* 36 B4
Grande →, *Jujuy, Argentina* 126 A2
Grande →, *Mendoza, Argentina* 126 D2
Grande →, *Bolivia* 124 G6
Grande →, *Bahia, Brazil* 125 F10
Grande →, *Minas Gerais, Brazil* 125 H8
Grande, B., *Argentina* 128 G3
Grande, Rio →, *U.S.A.* 113 N6
Grande Baleine, R. de la →, *Canada* 104 A4
Grande Cache, *Canada* 102 C5
Grande Casse, Pte. de la, *France* 21 C10
Grande-Entrée, *Canada* 105 C7
Grande Prairie, *Canada* 102 B5
Grande-Rivière, *Canada* 105 C7
Grande-Terre, *Guadeloupe* 120 b
Grande-Vallée, *Canada* 105 C6
Grandfalls, *U.S.A.* 113 K3
Grândola, *Portugal* 37 G2
Grandpré, *France* 19 C11
Grands Causses ⌂, *France* 20 D6
Grands-Jardins ⌂, *Canada* 105 C5
Grandview, *Canada* 103 C8
Grandview, *U.S.A.* 108 C4
Grandvilliers, *France* 19 C8
Graneros, *Chile* 126 C1
Grangemouth, *U.K.* 13 E5
Granger, *U.S.A.* 108 F9
Grängesberg, *Sweden* 10 D9
Grangeville, *U.S.A.* 108 D5
Granisle, *Canada* 102 C3
Granite City, *U.S.A.* 112 F9
Granite Falls, *U.S.A.* 112 C7
Granite L., *Canada* 105 C8
Granite Mt., *U.S.A.* 111 M10
Granite Pk., *U.S.A.* 108 D9
Graniteville, *U.S.A.* 117 B12
Granitola, C., *Italy* 42 E5
Granity, *N.Z.* 91 J3
Granja, *Brazil* 125 D10
Granja de Moreruela, *Spain* 36 D5
Granja de Torrehermosa, *Spain* 37 G5
Gränna, *Sweden* 11 F8
Granollers, *Spain* 38 D7
Gransee, *Germany* 24 B9
Grant, *U.S.A.* 112 E4
Grant, Mt., *U.S.A.* 108 G4
Grant City, *U.S.A.* 112 E7
Grant I., *Australia* 92 B5
Grant Range, *U.S.A.* 109 G6
Grantham, *U.K.* 14 E7
Grantown-on-Spey, *U.K.* 13 D5
Grants, *U.S.A.* 109 J10
Grants Pass, *U.S.A.* 108 E2
Grantsville, *U.S.A.* 108 F7
Granville, *France* 18 D5
Granville, *N. Dak., U.S.A.* 112 A4
Granville, *N.Y., U.S.A.* 117 C11
Granville, *Ohio, U.S.A.* 116 F2
Granville L., *Canada* 103 B8
Graskop, *S. Africa* 89 C5
Gräsö, *Sweden* 10 D12
Grass →, *Canada* 103 B9
Grass Range, *U.S.A.* 108 C9
Grass River ⌂, *Canada* 103 C8
Grass Valley, *Calif., U.S.A.* 110 F6
Grass Valley, *Oreg., U.S.A.* 108 D3
Grassano, *Italy* 43 B9
Grasse, *France* 21 E10
Grassflat, *U.S.A.* 116 F6
Grasslands △, *Canada* 103 D7
Grassy, *Australia* 95 G3
Gråsten, *Denmark* 11 K3
Grästorp, *Sweden* 11 F6
Gratkorn, *Austria* 26 D8
Graubünden □, *Switz.* 25 J5
Graulhet, *France* 20 E5
Graus, *Spain* 38 C5
Grave, Pte. de, *France* 20 C2
Gravelbourg, *Canada* 103 D7
Gravelines, *France* 19 A9
's-Gravenhage, *Neths.* 17 B4
Gravenhurst, *Canada* 116 B5
Gravesend, *Australia* 95 D5
Gravesend, *U.K.* 15 F8
Gravina in Púglia, *Italy* 43 B9
Gravois, Pointe-à-, *Haiti* 121 C5
Gravone →, *France* 21 G12
Gray, *France* 19 E12
Grayling, *U.S.A.* 114 C3
Grays, *U.K.* 15 F8
Grays Harbor, *U.S.A.* 108 C1
Grays L., *U.S.A.* 108 E8
Grays River, *U.S.A.* 110 D3
Grayvoron, *Russia* 33 G8
Graz, *Austria* 26 D8
Grdelica, *Serbia & M.* 44 D6
Greasy L., *Canada* 102 A4
Great Abaco I. = Abaco I., *Bahamas* 120 A4
Great Artesian Basin, *Australia* 94 C3
Great Australian Bight, *Australia* 93 F5
Great Bahama Bank, *Bahamas* 120 B4
Great Barrier I., *N.Z.* 91 G5
Great Barrier Reef, *Australia* 94 B4
Great Barrier Reef ⌂, *Australia* 94 B4
Great Barrington, *U.S.A.* 117 D11
Great Basalt Wall △, *Australia* 94 B4
Great Basin, *U.S.A.* 108 G5
Great Basin △, *U.S.A.* 108 G6
Great Bear →, *Canada* 100 B7
Great Bear L., *Canada* 100 B7
Great Belt = Store Bælt, *Denmark* 11 J4
Great Bend, *Kans., U.S.A.* 112 F5
Great Bend, *Pa., U.S.A.* 117 E9
Great Blasket I., *Ireland* 12 D1
Great Britain, *Europe* 6 E5
Great Camanoe, *Br. Virgin Is.* 121 e
Great Codroy, *Canada* 105 C8
Great Dividing Ra., *Australia* 94 C4
Great Driffield = Driffield, *U.K.* 14 C7
Great Exuma I., *Bahamas* 120 B4
Great Falls, *U.S.A.* 108 C8
Great Fish = Groot Vis →, *S. Africa* 88 E4
Great Guana Cay, *Bahamas* 120 B4
Great Inagua I., *Bahamas* 121 B5
Great Indian Desert = Thar Desert, *India* 68 F5
Great Karoo, *S. Africa* 88 E3
Great Khingan Mts. = Da Hinggan Ling, *China* 60 B7
Great Lake, *Australia* 95 G4
Great Lakes, *N. Amer.* 98 E11
Great Malvern, *U.K.* 15 E5
Great Miami →, *U.S.A.* 114 F3
Great Ormes Head, *U.K.* 14 D4
Great Ouse →, *U.K.* 14 E8
Great Palm I., *Australia* 94 B4
Great Pedro Bluff, *Jamaica* 120 a
Great Plains, *N. Amer.* 98 E9
Great Ruaha →, *Tanzania* 86 D4
Great Sacandaga L., *U.S.A.* 117 C10
Great Saint Bernard Pass = Grand St-Bernard, Col du, *Europe* 25 K3
Great Salt L., *U.S.A.* 108 F7
Great Salt Lake Desert, *U.S.A.* 108 F7
Great Salt Plains L., *U.S.A.* 113 G5
Great Sand Dunes ⌂, *U.S.A.* 109 H11
Great Sandy △, *Australia* 95 D5
Great Sandy Desert, *Australia* 92 D3
Great Sangi = Sangihe, Pulau, *Indonesia* 63 D7
Great Scarcies →, *S. Leone* 82 D2
Great Skellig, *Ireland* 12 E1
Great Slave L., *Canada* 102 A5
Great Smoky Mts. △, *U.S.A.* 115 H4
Great Snow Mt., *Canada* 102 B4
Great Stour = Stour →, *U.K.* 15 F9
Great Victoria Desert, *Australia* 93 E4
Great Wall, *Antarctica* 5 C18
Great Wall, *China* 56 E5
Great Whernside, *U.K.* 14 C6
Great Yarmouth, *U.K.* 15 E9
Great Zab = Zāb al Kabīr →, *Iraq* 70 C4
Great Zimbabwe, *Zimbabwe* 87 G3
Greater Antilles, *W. Indies* 121 C5
Greater London □, *U.K.* 15 F7
Greater Manchester □, *U.K.* 14 D5
Greater St. Lucia Wetlands ⌂, *S. Africa* 89 D5
Greater Sudbury = Sudbury, *Canada* 104 C3
Greater Sunda Is., *Indonesia* 62 F4
Grebbestad, *Sweden* 11 F5
Grebenka = Hrebenka, *Ukraine* 33 G7
Greco, C., *Cyprus* 49 E13
Greco, Mte., *Italy* 41 G10
Gredos, Sierra de, *Spain* 36 E6
Greece, *U.S.A.* 116 C7
Greece ■, *Europe* 46 B3
Greeley, *Colo., U.S.A.* 112 E2
Greeley, *Nebr., U.S.A.* 112 E5
Greem-Bell, Ostrov, *Russia* 52 A7
Green, *U.S.A.* 108 E2
Green →, *Ky., U.S.A.* 114 G2
Green →, *Utah, U.S.A.* 109 G9
Green B., *U.S.A.* 114 C2
Green Bay, *U.S.A.* 114 C2
Green C., *Australia* 95 F5
Green Cove Springs, *U.S.A.* 115 L5
Green Lake, *Canada* 103 C7
Green Mts., *U.S.A.* 117 C12
Green River, *Utah, U.S.A.* 109 G8
Green River, *Wyo., U.S.A.* 108 F9
Green Valley, *U.S.A.* 109 L8
Greenbank, *U.S.A.* 110 B4
Greenbush, *Mich., U.S.A.* 116 B1
Greenbush, *Minn., U.S.A.* 112 A6
Greencastle, *U.S.A.* 114 F2
Greene, *U.S.A.* 117 D9
Greenfield, *Calif., U.S.A.* 110 J5
Greenfield, *Calif., U.S.A.* 111 K8
Greenfield, *Ind., U.S.A.* 114 F3
Greenfield, *Iowa, U.S.A.* 112 E7
Greenfield, *Mass., U.S.A.* 117 D12
Greenfield, *Mo., U.S.A.* 113 G8
Greenfield Park, *Canada* 117 A11
Greenland ☒, *N. Amer.* 4 C5
Greenland Sea, *Arctic* 4 B7
Greenock, *U.K.* 13 F4
Greenore, *Ireland* 12 B5
Greenore Pt., *Ireland* 12 D5
Greenough, *Australia* 93 E1
Greenough →, *Australia* 93 E1
Greenough Pt., *Canada* 116 B3
Greenport, *U.S.A.* 117 E12
Greensboro, *Ga., U.S.A.* 115 J4
Greensboro, *N.C., U.S.A.* 115 G6
Greensboro, *Vt., U.S.A.* 117 B12
Greensburg, *Ind., U.S.A.* 114 F3
Greensburg, *Kans., U.S.A.* 113 G5
Greensburg, *Pa., U.S.A.* 116 F5
Greenstone Pt., *U.K.* 13 D3
Greenvale, *Australia* 94 B4
Greenville, *Liberia* 82 D3
Greenville, *Ala., U.S.A.* 115 K2
Greenville, *Calif., U.S.A.* 110 E6
Greenville, *Maine, U.S.A.* 115 C11
Greenville, *Mich., U.S.A.* 114 D3
Greenville, *Miss., U.S.A.* 113 J9
Greenville, *Mo., U.S.A.* 113 G9
Greenville, *N.C., U.S.A.* 115 H7
Greenville, *N.H., U.S.A.* 117 D13
Greenville, *N.Y., U.S.A.* 117 D10
Greenville, *Ohio, U.S.A.* 114 E3
Greenville, *Pa., U.S.A.* 116 E4
Greenville, *S.C., U.S.A.* 115 H4
Greenville, *Tenn., U.S.A.* 115 G4
Greenville, *Tex., U.S.A.* 113 J6
Greenwater Lake ⌂, *Canada* 103 C8
Greenwich, *Conn., U.S.A.* 117 E11
Greenwich, *N.Y., U.S.A.* 117 C11
Greenwich, *Ohio, U.S.A.* 116 E2
Greenwich □, *U.K.* 15 F8
Greenwood, *Canada* 102 D5
Greenwood, *Ark., U.S.A.* 113 H7
Greenwood, *Ind., U.S.A.* 114 F2
Greenwood, *Miss., U.S.A.* 113 J9
Greenwood, *S.C., U.S.A.* 115 H4
Greenwood, Mt., *Australia* 92 B5
Gregbe, *Ivory C.* 82 D3
Gregory, *U.S.A.* 112 D5
Gregory △, *Australia* 92 C5
Gregory →, *Australia* 94 B2
Gregory, L., *S. Austral., Australia* 95 D2
Gregory, L., *W. Austral., Australia* 92 E2
Gregory Downs, *Australia* 94 B2
Gregory L., *Australia* 92 D4
Gregory Ra., *Queens., Australia* 94 B3
Gregory Ra., *W. Austral., Australia* 92 D3
Greiffenberg, *Germany* 24 B9
Greifswald, *Germany* 24 A9
Greifswalder Bodden, *Germany* 24 A9
Grein, *Austria* 26 C7
Greiz, *Germany* 24 E8
Gremikha, *Russia* 52 C4
Grenå, *Denmark* 11 H4
Grenada, *U.S.A.* 113 J10
Grenada ■, *W. Indies* 121 D7
Grenade, *France* 20 E5
Grenadier I., *U.S.A.* 117 B8
Grenadines, The, *St. Vincent* 121 D7
Grenchen, *Switz.* 25 H3
Grenen, *Denmark* 11 G4
Grenfell, *Australia* 95 E4
Grenfell, *Canada* 103 C8
Grenoble, *France* 21 C9
Grenville, C., *Australia* 94 A3
Grenville Chan., *Canada* 102 C3
Gréoux-les-Bains, *France* 21 E9
Gresham, *U.S.A.* 110 E4
Gresik, *Indonesia* 63 G15
Gretna, *U.K.* 13 F5
Greven, *Germany* 24 C3
Grevená, *Greece* 44 F5
Grevená □, *Greece* 44 F5
Grevenbroich, *Germany* 24 D2
Grevenmacher, *Lux.* 17 E6
Grevesmühlen, *Germany* 24 B7
Grevestrand, *Denmark* 11 J6
Grey →, *Canada* 105 C8
Grey →, *N.Z.* 91 K3
Grey, C., *Australia* 94 A2
Grey Ra., *Australia* 95 D3
Greybull, *U.S.A.* 108 D9
Greymouth, *N.Z.* 91 K3
Greystones, *Ireland* 12 C5
Greytown, *N.Z.* 91 J5
Greytown, *S. Africa* 89 D5
Gribanovskiy, *Russia* 34 E5
Gribbell I., *Canada* 102 C3
Gribës, Mal i, *Albania* 44 F3
Gridley, *U.S.A.* 110 F5
Griekwastad, *S. Africa* 88 D3
Griesheim, *Germany* 25 F4
Grieskirchen, *Austria* 26 C6
Griffin, *U.S.A.* 115 J3
Griffith, *Australia* 95 E4
Griffith, *Canada* 116 A7
Griffith I., *Canada* 116 B4
Grignols, *France* 20 D3
Grigoriopol, *Moldova* 29 C14
Grimaylov = Hrymayliv, *Ukraine* 33 H4
Grimes, *U.S.A.* 110 F5
Grimma, *Germany* 24 D8
Grimmen, *Germany* 24 A9
Grimsay, *U.K.* 13 D1
Grimsby, *Canada* 116 C5
Grimsby, *U.K.* 14 D7
Grímsey, *Iceland* 8 C5
Grimshaw, *Canada* 102 B5
Grimslöv, *Sweden* 11 H8
Grimstad, *Norway* 9 G13
Grindelwald, *Switz.* 25 J4
Grindsted, *Denmark* 11 J2
Grindstone I., *Canada* 117 B8
Grindu, *Romania* 29 F11
Grinnell, *U.S.A.* 112 E8
Grintavec, *Slovenia* 41 B11
Gris-Nez, C., *France* 19 B8
Grisolles, *France* 20 E5
Grisons = Graubünden □, *Switz.* 25 J5
Grisslehamn, *Sweden* 10 D12
Grmeč Planina, *Bos.-H.* 41 D13
Groais I., *Canada* 105 B8
Grobiņa, *Latvia* 30 B8
Groblersdal, *S. Africa* 89 D4
Grobming, *Austria* 26 D6
Grocka, *Serbia & M.* 44 B4
Gródek, *Poland* 31 E10
Grodków, *Poland* 31 H4
Grodno = Hrodna, *Belarus* 30 E10
Grodzisk Mazowiecki, *Poland* 31 F7
Grodzisk Wielkopolski, *Poland* 31 F3
Grodzyanka = Hrodzyanka, *Belarus* 32 F5
Groesbeck, *U.S.A.* 113 K6
Groix, *France* 18 E3
Groix, Î. de, *France* 18 E3
Grójec, *Poland* 31 G7
Gronau, *Niedersachsen, Germany* 24 C5
Gronau, *Nordrhein-Westfalen, Germany* 24 C3
Grong, *Norway* 8 D15
Grönhögen, *Sweden* 11 H10
Groningen, *Neths.* 17 A6
Groningen □, *Neths.* 17 A6
Groom, *U.S.A.* 113 H4
Groot →, *S. Africa* 88 E3
Groot Berg →, *S. Africa* 88 E2
Groot-Brakrivier, *S. Africa* 88 E3
Groot Karasberge, *Namibia* 88 D2
Groot-Kei →, *S. Africa* 89 E4
Groot Vis →, *S. Africa* 88 E4
Grootdrink, *S. Africa* 88 D3
Groote Eylandt, *Australia* 94 A2
Grootfontein, *Namibia* 88 B2
Grootlaagte →, *Africa* 88 C3
Grootvloer →, *S. Africa* 88 E3
Gros C., *Canada* 102 A6
Gros Islet, *St. Lucia* 121 f
Gros Morne △, *Canada* 105 C8
Gros Piton, *St. Lucia* 121 f
Gros Piton Pt., *St. Lucia* 121 f
Grósio, *Italy* 40 B7
Grosne →, *France* 19 F11
Grossa, Pta., *Spain* 48 B8
Grossenbrode, *Germany* 24 A7
Grossenhain, *Germany* 24 D9
Grosser Arber, *Germany* 25 F9
Grosser Plöner See, *Germany* 24 A6
Grosseto, *Italy* 41 F8
Grossgerungs, *Austria* 26 C7
Grossglockner, *Austria* 26 D5
Groswater B., *Canada* 105 B8
Groton, *Conn., U.S.A.* 117 E12
Groton, *N.Y., U.S.A.* 117 D8
Groton, *S. Dak., U.S.A.* 112 C5
Grottáglie, *Italy* 43 B10
Grottaminarda, *Italy* 43 A8
Grottammare, *Italy* 41 F10
Grouard Mission, *Canada* 102 B5
Grouin, Pte. du, *France* 18 D5
Groundhog →, *Canada* 104 C3
Grouw, *Neths.* 17 A5
Grove City, *U.S.A.* 116 E4
Grove Hill, *U.S.A.* 115 K2
Groveland, *U.S.A.* 110 H6
Grover City, *U.S.A.* 111 K6
Groves, *U.S.A.* 113 L8
Groveton, *U.S.A.* 117 B13
Grožnjan, *Croatia* 41 C10
Groznyy, *Russia* 35 J7
Grubišno Polje, *Croatia* 28 E2
Grudovo, *Bulgaria* 45 D11
Grudusk, *Poland* 31 E7
Grudziądz, *Poland* 30 E5
Gruinard B., *U.K.* 13 D3
Gruissan, *France* 20 E7
Grumo Áppula, *Italy* 43 A9
Grums, *Sweden* 10 E7
Grünberg, *Germany* 24 E4
Gründau, *Germany* 25 E5
Grundy Center, *U.S.A.* 112 D8
Grünstadt, *Germany* 25 F4
Gruppo di Tessa ⌂, *Italy* 40 B8
Gruvberget, *Sweden* 10 C10
Gruver, *U.S.A.* 113 G4
Gruyères, *Switz.* 25 J3
Gruža, *Serbia & M.* 44 C4
Gryazi, *Russia* 33 F10
Gryazovets, *Russia* 32 C11
Grybów, *Poland* 31 J7
Grycksbo, *Sweden* 10 D9
Gryfice, *Poland* 30 E2
Gryfino, *Poland* 31 E1
Gryfów Śląski, *Poland* 31 G2
Grythyttan, *Sweden* 10 E8
Gstaad, *Switz.* 25 J3
Gua, *India* 67 H14
Gua Musang, *Malaysia* 65 K3
Guacanayabo, G. de, *Cuba* 120 B4
Guachípas →, *Argentina* 126 B2
Guadajoz →, *Spain* 37 H6
Guadalajara, *Mexico* 118 C4
Guadalajara, *Spain* 38 E1
Guadalajara □, *Spain* 38 E2
Guadalcanal, *Solomon Is.* 96 H8
Guadalcanal, *Spain* 37 G5
Guadalén →, *Spain* 37 G7
Guadales, *Argentina* 126 C2
Guadalete →, *Spain* 37 J4
Guadalimar →, *Spain* 37 G7
Guadalmena →, *Spain* 37 G8
Guadalmez →, *Spain* 37 G5
Guadalope →, *Spain* 38 D4
Guadalquivir →, *Spain* 37 J4
Guadalupe = Guadeloupe ☒, *W. Indies* 120 b
Guadalupe, *Mexico* 111 N10
Guadalupe, *Spain* 37 F5
Guadalupe, *U.S.A.* 111 L6
Guadalupe →, *Mexico* 111 N10
Guadalupe →, *U.S.A.* 113 L6
Guadalupe, Sierra de, *Spain* 37 F5
Guadalupe Bravos, *Mexico* 118 A3
Guadalupe I., *Pac. Oc.* 98 G8
Guadalupe Mts. △, *U.S.A.* 113 K2
Guadalupe Peak, *U.S.A.* 113 K2
Guadalupe y Calvo, *Mexico* 118 B3
Guadarrama, Sierra de, *Spain* 36 E7
Guadauta, *Georgia* 35 J5
Guadeloupe △, *Guadeloupe* 120 b
Guadeloupe ☒, *W. Indies* 120 b
Guadeloupe Passage, *W. Indies* 121 C7
Guadiamar →, *Spain* 37 J4
Guadiana →, *Portugal* 37 H3
Guadiana Menor →, *Spain* 37 H7
Guadiaro →, *Spain* 37 J5
Guadiato →, *Spain* 37 H5
Guadiela →, *Spain* 38 E2
Guadix, *Spain* 37 H7
Guafo, Boca del, *Chile* 128 E2
Guaico, *Trin. & Tob.* 125 K15
Guainía →, *Colombia* 124 C5
Guaíra, *Brazil* 127 A5
Guaíra □, *Paraguay* 126 B4
Guaitecas, Is., *Chile* 128 E2
Guajará-Mirim, *Brazil* 124 F5
Guajira, Pen. de la, *Colombia* 124 A4
Gualán, *Guatemala* 120 C2
Gualdo Tadino, *Italy* 41 E9
Gualeguay, *Argentina* 126 C4
Gualeguaychú, *Argentina* 126 C4
Gualequay →, *Argentina* 126 C4
Guam ☒, *Pac. Oc.* 96 F6
Guaminí, *Argentina* 126 D3
Guamúchil, *Mexico* 118 B3
Guana I., *Br. Virgin Is.* 121 e
Guanabacoa, *Cuba* 120 B3
Guanacaste △, *Costa Rica* 120 D2
Guanacaste, Cordillera del, *Costa Rica* 120 D2
Guanaceví, *Mexico* 118 B3
Guanahani = San Salvador I., *Bahamas* 121 B5
Guanajay, *Cuba* 120 B3
Guanajuato, *Mexico* 118 C4
Guanajuato □, *Mexico* 118 C4
Guandacol, *Argentina* 126 B2
Guane, *Cuba* 120 B3
Guang'an, *China* 58 B6
Guangchang, *China* 59 D11
Guangde, *China* 59 B12
Guangdong □, *China* 59 F9
Guangfeng, *China* 59 C12
Guanghan, *China* 58 B5
Guangling, *China* 56 E8
Guangnan, *China* 58 E5
Guangning, *China* 59 F9
Guangrao, *China* 57 F10
Guangshui, *China* 59 B9
Guangshun, *China* 58 D6
Guangwu, *China* 56 F3
Guangxi Zhuangzu Zizhiqu □, *China* 58 F7
Guangyuan, *China* 58 A5
Guangze, *China* 59 D11
Guangzhou, *China* 59 F9
Guánica, *Puerto Rico* 121 d
Guanipa →, *Venezuela* 124 B6
Guanling, *China* 58 E5
Guannan, *China* 57 G10
Guantánamo, *Cuba* 121 B4
Guantánamo B., *Cuba* 121 C4
Guantao, *China* 56 F8
Guanyang, *China* 59 E8
Guanyun, *China* 57 G10
Guápiles, *Costa Rica* 120 D3
Guapo B., *Trin. & Tob.* 125 K15
Guaporé, *Brazil* 127 B5
Guaporé →, *Brazil* 124 F5
Guaqui, *Bolivia* 124 G5
Guara, Sierra de, *Spain* 38 C4
Guaramacal △, *Venezuela* 121 E5
Guarapari, *Brazil* 127 A7
Guarapuava, *Brazil* 127 B5
Guaratinguetá, *Brazil* 127 A6
Guaratuba, *Brazil* 127 B6
Guarda, *Portugal* 36 E3
Guarda □, *Portugal* 36 E3

Guardafui, C. = Asir, Ras, *Somali Rep.* 75 E5
Guardamar del Segura, *Spain* 39 G4
Guardavalle, *Italy* 43 D9
Guárdia Sanframondi, *Italy* 43 A7
Guardiagrele, *Italy* 41 F11
Guardo, *Spain* 36 C6
Guareña, *Spain* 37 G4
Guareña →, *Spain* 36 D5
Guárico □, *Venezuela* 124 B5
Guarujá, *Brazil* 127 A6
Guarulhos, *Brazil* 127 A6
Guarus, *Brazil* 127 A7
Guasave, *Mexico* 118 B3
Guasdualito, *Venezuela* 124 B4
Guastalla, *Italy* 40 D7
Guatemala, *Guatemala* 120 D1
Guatemala ■, *Cent. Amer.* 120 C1
Guatemala Trench, *Pac. Oc.* 98 H10
Guatopo △, *Venezuela* 121 D6
Guatuaro Pt., *Trin. & Tob.* 125 K16
Guaviare →, *Colombia* 124 C5
Guaxupé, *Brazil* 127 A6
Guayaguayare, *Trin. & Tob.* 125 K15
Guayama, *Puerto Rico* 121 d
Guayaquil, *Ecuador* 124 D3
Guayaquil, G. de, *Ecuador* 124 D2
Guaymas, *Mexico* 118 B2
Guba, *Dem. Rep. of the Congo* 87 E2
Guba, *Ethiopia* 81 E4
Gûbâl, Madîq, *Egypt* 80 B3
Gubat, *Phil.* 61 E6
Gúbbio, *Italy* 41 E9
Guben, *Germany* 24 D10
Gubin, *Poland* 31 G1
Gubio, *Nigeria* 83 C7
Gubkin, *Russia* 33 G9
Guča, *Serbia & M.* 44 C4
Gucheng, *China* 59 A8
Gudata = Guadauta, *Georgia* 35 J5
Gudbrandsdalen, *Norway* 9 F14
Guddu Barrage, *Pakistan* 66 E6
Gudenå →, *Denmark* 11 H4
Gudermes, *Russia* 35 J8
Gudhjem, *Denmark* 11 J8
Gudur, *India* 66 M11
Guebwiller, *France* 19 E14
Guecho = Getxo, *Spain* 38 B2
Guékédou, *Guinea* 82 D2
Guéle Mendouka, *Cameroon* 83 E7
Guelmine = Goulimine, *Morocco* 78 C3
Guelph, *Canada* 116 C4
Guéméné-Penfao, *France* 18 E5
Guéméné-sur-Scorff, *France* 18 D3
Guéné, *Benin* 83 C5
Guer, *France* 18 E4
Guérande, *France* 18 E4
Guéret, *France* 19 F8
Guérigny, *France* 19 E10
Guerneville, *U.S.A.* 110 G4
Guernica = Gernika-Lumo, *Spain* 38 B2
Guernsey, *U.K.* 15 H5
Guernsey, *U.S.A.* 112 D2
Guerrero □, *Mexico* 119 D5
Guessou-Sud, *Benin* 83 C5
Gueugnon, *France* 19 F11
Guéyo, *Ivory C.* 82 D3
Gughe, *Ethiopia* 81 F4
Gügher, *Iran* 71 D8
Guglionesi, *Italy* 41 G11
Guhakolak, Tanjung, *Indonesia* 63 G11
Gui Jiang →, *China* 59 F8
Guia, *Canary Is.* 48 F4
Guia de Isora, *Canary Is.* 48 F3
Guia Lopes da Laguna, *Brazil* 127 A4
Guiana Highlands, *S. Amer.* 122 C4
Guibéroua, *Ivory C.* 82 D3
Guichi, *China* 59 B11
Guider, *Cameroon* 83 D7
Guidiguir, *Niger* 83 C6
Guidimouni, *Niger* 83 C6
Guiding, *China* 58 D6
Guidong, *China* 59 D9
Guidónia-Montecélio, *Italy* 41 F9
Guiers, L. de, *Senegal* 82 B1
Guigang, *China* 58 F7
Guiglo, *Ivory C.* 82 D3
Guihulñgan, *Phil.* 61 F5
Guijá, *Mozam.* 89 C5
Guijuelo, *Spain* 36 E5
Guildford, *U.K.* 15 F7
Guilford, *U.S.A.* 117 E12
Guilin, *China* 59 E8
Guillaume-Delisle, L., *Canada* 104 A4
Guillaumes, *France* 21 D10
Guillestre, *France* 21 D10
Guilvinec, *France* 18 E2
Güimar, *Canary Is.* 48 F3
Guimarães, *Portugal* 36 D2
Guimaras □, *Phil.* 61 F5
Guinda, *U.S.A.* 110 G4
Guinea, *Africa* 76 F4
Guinea ■, *W. Afr.* 82 C2
Guinea, Gulf of, *Atl. Oc.* 83 E5
Guinea-Bissau ■, *Africa* 82 C2
Güines, *Cuba* 120 B3
Guingamp, *France* 18 D3
Guinguinéo, *Senegal* 82 C1
Guipavas, *France* 18 D2
Guiping, *China* 59 F8
Guipúzcoa □, *Spain* 38 B2
Guir, *Mali* 82 B4
Guirel, *Mauritania* 82 B3
Güiria, *Venezuela* 124 A6
Guiscard, *France* 19 C10
Guise, *France* 19 C10
Guitiriz, *Spain* 36 B3
Guitri, *Ivory C.* 82 D3
Guiuan, *Phil.* 61 F6
Guixi, *China* 59 C11
Guiyang, *Guizhou, China* 58 D6
Guiyang, *Hunan, China* 59 E9
Guizhou □, *China* 58 D6
Gujan-Mestras, *France* 20 D2
Gujar Khan, *Pakistan* 68 C5
Gujarat □, *India* 68 H4
Gujiang, *China* 59 D10
Gujranwala, *Pakistan* 68 C6
Gujrat, *Pakistan* 68 C6
Gukovo, *Russia* 35 F5
Gulbarga, *India* 66 L10
Gulbene, *Latvia* 9 H22
Gulf, The = Persian Gulf, *Asia* 71 E6
Gulf Islands ⌓, *U.S.A.* 115 E2
Gulfport, *U.S.A.* 113 K10
Gulgong, *Australia* 95 E4
Gulin, *China* 58 C5
Gulistan, *Pakistan* 68 D2
Gull Lake, *Canada* 103 C7
Gullbrandstorp, *Sweden* 11 H6
Gullspång, *Sweden* 11 F8
Güllük, *Turkey* 47 D9
Güllük Daği △, *Turkey* 47 E12
Güllük Korfezi, *Turkey* 47 D9
Gulma, *Nigeria* 83 C5
Gulmarg, *India* 69 B6
Gülnar, *Turkey* 72 D5
Gülpınar, *Turkey* 47 B8
Gülşehir, *Turkey* 72 C6
Gulshad, *Kazakhstan* 52 E8
Gulu, *Uganda* 86 B3
Gŭlŭbovo, *Bulgaria* 45 D9
Gulud, J., *Sudan* 81 E2
Gulwe, *Tanzania* 86 D4
Gulyaypole = Hulyaypole, *Ukraine* 33 J9
Gumal →, *Pakistan* 68 D4
Gumbaz, *Pakistan* 68 D3
Gumel, *Nigeria* 83 C6
Gumiel de Hizán, *Spain* 36 D7
Gumla, *India* 69 H11
Gumlu, *Australia* 94 B4
Gumma □, *Japan* 55 F9
Gummersbach, *Germany* 24 D3
Gummi, *Nigeria* 83 C6
Gümüldür, *Turkey* 47 C9
Gümüşçay, *Turkey* 45 F11
Gümüşhaciköy, *Turkey* 72 B6
Gümüşhane, *Turkey* 73 B8
Gümüşsu, *Turkey* 47 C11
Gumzai, *Indonesia* 63 F8
Guna, *Ethiopia* 81 F4
Guna, *India* 68 G7
Gundelfingen, *Germany* 25 G6
Güney, *Burdur, Turkey* 47 D11
Güney, *Denizli, Turkey* 47 C11
Güneydoğu Toroslar, *Turkey* 73 C9
Gunisao →, *Canada* 103 C9
Gunisao L., *Canada* 103 C9
Gunjyal, *Pakistan* 68 C4
Günlüce, *Turkey* 47 E10
Gunnarskog, *Sweden* 10 E6
Gunnbjørn Fjeld, *Greenland* 4 C6
Gunnebo, *Sweden* 11 G10
Gunnedah, *Australia* 95 E5
Gunnewin, *Australia* 95 D4
Gunningbar Cr. →, *Australia* 95 E4
Gunnison, *Colo., U.S.A.* 109 G10
Gunnison, *Utah, U.S.A.* 108 G8
Gunnison →, *U.S.A.* 109 G9
Gunpowder, *Australia* 94 B2
Guntakal, *India* 66 M10
Guntersville, *U.S.A.* 115 H2
Guntong, *Malaysia* 65 K3
Guntur, *India* 67 L12
Gunungapi, *Indonesia* 63 F7
Gunungsitoli, *Indonesia* 62 D1
Günz →, *Germany* 25 G6
Gunza, *Angola* 84 G2
Günzburg, *Germany* 25 G6
Gunzenhausen, *Germany* 25 F6
Guo He →, *China* 57 H9
Guoyang, *China* 56 H9
Gupis, *Pakistan* 69 A5
Gura Humorului, *Romania* 29 C10
Gura-Teghii, *Romania* 29 E11
Gurag, *Ethiopia* 81 F4
Gurahonţ, *Romania* 28 D7
Gurdaspur, *India* 68 C6
Gurdon, *U.S.A.* 113 J8
Güre, *Balıkesir, Turkey* 47 B8
Güre, *Uşak, Turkey* 47 C11
Gurgaon, *India* 68 E7
Gürgentepe, *Turkey* 72 B7
Gurghiu, Munţii, *Romania* 29 D10
Gurgueia →, *Brazil* 125 E10
Gurha, *India* 68 G4
Guri, Embalse de, *Venezuela* 124 B6
Gurig △, *Australia* 92 B5
Gurin, *Nigeria* 83 D7
Gurjaani, *Georgia* 35 K7
Gurk →, *Austria* 26 E7
Gurkha, *Nepal* 69 E11
Gurley, *Australia* 95 D4
Gurnet Point, *U.S.A.* 117 D14
Guro, *Mozam.* 87 F3
Gürpınar, *İst., Turkey* 45 F12
Gürpınar, *Van, Turkey* 73 C10
Gürsu, *Turkey* 45 F13
Gurué, *Mozam.* 87 F4
Gurun, *Malaysia* 65 K3
Gürün, *Turkey* 72 C7
Gurupá, *Brazil* 125 D8
Gurupá, I. Grande de, *Brazil* 125 D8
Gurupi, *Brazil* 125 F9
Gurupi →, *Brazil* 125 D9
Guruwe, *Zimbabwe* 89 B5
Guryev = Atyraū, *Kazakhstan* 52 E6
Guryevsk, *Russia* 30 D7
Gus-Khrustalnyy, *Russia* 34 C5
Gusau, *Nigeria* 83 C6
Gusev, *Russia* 9 J20
Gushan, *China* 57 E12
Gushgy, *Turkmenistan* 52 F7
Gushi, *China* 59 A10
Gushiago, *Ghana* 83 D4
Gusinje, *Serbia & M.* 44 D3
Gusinoozersk, *Russia* 53 D11
Gúspini, *Italy* 42 C1
Güssing, *Austria* 27 D9
Gustavsberg, *Sweden* 10 E12
Gustavus, *U.S.A.* 102 B1
Gustine, *U.S.A.* 110 H6
Güstrow, *Germany* 24 B8
Gusum, *Sweden* 11 F10
Guta = Kolárovo, *Slovak Rep.* 27 D10
Gütersloh, *Germany* 24 D4
Gutha, *Australia* 93 E2
Guthalungra, *Australia* 94 B4
Guthrie, *Okla., U.S.A.* 113 H6
Guthrie, *Tex., U.S.A.* 113 J4
Gutian, *China* 59 D12
Guttenberg, *U.S.A.* 112 D9
Gutu, *Zimbabwe* 89 B5
Guwahati, *India* 67 F17
Guy Fawkes River △, *Australia* 95 D5
Guyana ■, *S. Amer.* 124 C7
Guyane française = French Guiana ☑, *S. Amer.* 125 C8
Guyang, *China* 56 D6
Guyenne, *France* 20 D4
Guymon, *U.S.A.* 113 G4
Guyra, *Australia* 95 E5
Guyuan, *Hebei, China* 56 D8
Guyuan, *Ningxia Huizu, China* 56 G4
Güzelbahçe, *Turkey* 47 C8
Güzelyurt = Morphou, *Cyprus* 49 D11
Guzhang, *China* 58 C7
Guzhen, *China* 57 H9
Guzmán, L. de, *Mexico* 118 A3
Gvardeysk, *Russia* 9 J19
Gvardeyskoye, *Ukraine* 33 K8
Gwa, *Burma* 67 L19
Gwaai, *Zimbabwe* 87 F2
Gwaai →, *Zimbabwe* 87 F2
Gwabegar, *Australia* 95 E4
Gwadabawa, *Nigeria* 83 C6
Gwādar, *Pakistan* 66 G3
Gwagwada, *Nigeria* 83 C6
Gwaii Haanas △, *Canada* 102 C2
Gwalior, *India* 68 F8
Gwanara, *Nigeria* 83 D5
Gwanda, *Zimbabwe* 87 G2
Gwandu, *Nigeria* 83 C5
Gwane, *Dem. Rep. of the Congo* 86 B2
Gwaram, *Nigeria* 83 C7
Gwarzo, *Nigeria* 83 C6
Gwasero, *Nigeria* 83 D5
Gwda →, *Poland* 31 E3
Gweebarra B., *Ireland* 12 B3
Gweedore, *Ireland* 12 A3
Gweru, *Zimbabwe* 87 F2
Gwi, *Nigeria* 83 D6
Gwinn, *U.S.A.* 114 B2
Gwio Kura, *Nigeria* 83 C7
Gwoza, *Nigeria* 83 C7
Gwydir →, *Australia* 95 D4
Gwynedd □, *U.K.* 14 E3
Gyandzha = Gäncä, *Azerbaijan* 35 K8
Gyaring Hu, *China* 60 C4
Gydanskiy Poluostrov, *Russia* 52 C8
Gympie, *Australia* 95 D5
Gyomaendrőd, *Hungary* 28 D5
Gyöngyös, *Hungary* 28 C4
Győr, *Hungary* 28 C2
Győr-Moson-Sopron □, *Hungary* 28 C2
Gypsum Pt., *Canada* 102 A6
Gypsumville, *Canada* 103 C9
Gyueshevo, *Bulgaria* 44 D6
Gyula, *Hungary* 28 D6
Gyumri, *Armenia* 35 K6
Gyzylarbat, *Turkmenistan* 52 F6
Gyzyletrek, *Turkmenistan* 71 B7
Gzhatsk = Gagarin, *Russia* 32 E8

H

Ha 'Arava →, *Israel* 74 E4
Ha Coi, *Vietnam* 58 G6
Ha Dong, *Vietnam* 58 G5
Ha Giang, *Vietnam* 58 F5
Ha Karmel △, *Israel* 74 C4
Ha Tien, *Vietnam* 65 G5
Ha Tinh, *Vietnam* 64 C5
Ha Trung, *Vietnam* 64 C5
Ha Yaek Chalong, *Thailand* 65 a
Haaksbergen, *Neths.* 17 B6
Haapsalu, *Estonia* 9 G20
Haarlem, *Neths.* 17 B4
Haast →, *N.Z.* 91 K2
Haast Bluff, *Australia* 92 D5
Hab →, *Pakistan* 68 G3
Hab Nadi Chauki, *Pakistan* 68 G2
Habahe, *China* 60 B3
Habaswein, *Kenya* 86 B4
Habay, *Canada* 102 B5
Ḩabbānīyah, *Iraq* 70 C4
Ḩabbānīyah, Hawr al, *Iraq* 73 F10
Habichtswald ⌓, *Germany* 24 D5
Habo, *Sweden* 11 G8
Haboro, *Japan* 54 B10
Ḩabshān, *U.A.E.* 71 F7
Hachenburg, *Germany* 24 E3
Hachijō-Jima, *Japan* 55 H9
Hachinohe, *Japan* 54 D10
Hachiōji, *Japan* 55 G9
Hachŏn, *N. Korea* 57 D15
Hacıbektaş, *Turkey* 72 C6
Hacılar, *Turkey* 72 C6
Hackås, *Sweden* 10 B8
Hackensack, *U.S.A.* 117 F10
Hackettstown, *U.S.A.* 117 F10
Hadali, *Pakistan* 68 C5
Hadarba, Ras, *Sudan* 80 C4
Hadarom □, *Israel* 74 E4
Ḩadd, Ra's al, *Oman* 75 C6
Haddington, *U.K.* 13 F6
Hadejia, *Nigeria* 83 C7
Hadejia →, *Nigeria* 83 C7
Ḩadera, *Israel* 74 C3
Ḩadera, N. →, *Israel* 74 C3
Haderslev, *Denmark* 11 J3
Hadhramaut = Ḩaḑramawt, *Yemen* 75 D4
Hadiboh, *Yemen* 75 E5
Hadım, *Turkey* 72 D5
Hadong, *S. Korea* 57 G14
Ḩaḑramawt, *Yemen* 75 D4
Ḩadrānīyah, *Iraq* 70 C4
Hadrian's Wall, *U.K.* 14 B5
Hadsten, *Denmark* 11 H4
Hadsund, *Denmark* 11 H4
Hadyach, *Ukraine* 33 G8
Haeju, *N. Korea* 57 E13
Haenam, *S. Korea* 57 G14
Haenertsburg, *S. Africa* 89 C4
Haerhpin = Harbin, *China* 57 B14
Hafar al Bāţin, *Si. Arabia* 70 D5
Hafik, *Turkey* 72 C7
Ḩafīrat al 'Aydā, *Si. Arabia* 70 E3
Ḩafit, *Oman* 71 F7
Hafizabad, *Pakistan* 68 C5
Haflong, *India* 67 G18
Hafnarfjörður, *Iceland* 8 D3
Haft Gel, *Iran* 71 D6
Hafun, Ras, *Somali Rep.* 75 E5
Hagalil, *Israel* 74 C4
Hagby, *Sweden* 11 H10
Hagen, *Germany* 24 D3
Hagenow, *Germany* 24 B7
Hagerman, *U.S.A.* 113 J2
Hagerman Fossil Beds ⌓, *U.S.A.* 108 E6
Hagerstown, *U.S.A.* 114 F7
Hagersville, *Canada* 116 D4
Hagetmau, *France* 20 E3
Hagfors, *Sweden* 10 D7
Hagi, *Japan* 55 G5
Hagolan, *Syria* 74 C4
Hagondange, *France* 19 C13
Hags Hd., *Ireland* 12 D2
Hague, C. de la, *France* 18 C5
Hague, The = 's-Gravenhage, *Neths.* 17 B4
Haguenau, *France* 19 D14
Hai Duong, *Vietnam* 58 G6
Hai'an, *Guangdong, China* 59 G8
Hai'an, *Jiangsu, China* 59 A13
Haicheng, *Fujian, China* 59 E11
Haicheng, *Liaoning, China* 57 D12
Haidar Khel, *Afghan.* 68 C3
Haidarâbâd = Hyderabad, *India* 66 L11
Haidargarh, *India* 69 F9
Haifa = Ḩefa, *Israel* 74 C4
Haifeng, *China* 59 F10
Haiger, *Germany* 24 E4
Haikou, *China* 60 D6
Ḩā'il, *Si. Arabia* 70 E4
Hailar, *China* 60 B6
Hailey, *U.S.A.* 108 E6
Haileybury, *Canada* 104 C4
Hailin, *China* 57 B15
Hailing Dao, *China* 59 G8
Hailong, *China* 57 C13
Hailuoto, *Finland* 8 D21
Haimen, *Guangdong, China* 59 F11
Haimen, *Jiangsu, China* 59 B13
Hainan □, *China* 60 E5
Hainaut □, *Belgium* 17 D4
Hainburg, *Austria* 27 C9
Haines, *Alaska, U.S.A.* 102 B1
Haines, *Oreg., U.S.A.* 108 D5
Haines City, *U.S.A.* 115 L5
Haines Junction, *Canada* 102 A1
Hainfeld, *Austria* 26 C8
Haining, *China* 59 B13
Haiphong, *Vietnam* 58 G6
Haitan Dao, *China* 59 E12
Haiti ■, *W. Indies* 121 C5
Haiya, *Sudan* 80 D4
Haiyan, *China* 59 B13
Haiyang, *China* 57 F11
Haiyuan, *Guangxi Zhuangzu, China* 58 F6
Haiyuan, *Ningxia Huizu, China* 56 F3
Haizhou, *China* 57 G10
Haizhou Wan, *China* 57 G10
Hajdú-Bihar □, *Hungary* 28 C6
Hajdúböszörmény, *Hungary* 28 C6
Hajdúdorog, *Hungary* 28 C6
Hajdúhadház, *Hungary* 28 C6
Hajdúnánás, *Hungary* 28 C6
Hajdúsámson, *Hungary* 28 C6
Hajdúszoboszló, *Hungary* 28 C6
Hajipur, *India* 69 G11
Ḩājjī Muḩsin, *Iraq* 70 C5
Ḩājjīābād, *Iran* 71 D7
Ḩājjīābād-e Zarrīn, *Iran* 71 C7
Hajnówka, *Poland* 31 F10
Hakansson, Mts., *Dem. Rep. of the Congo* 87 D2
Hakkâri, *Turkey* 70 B4
Hakkâri Dağları, *Turkey* 73 C10
Hakken-Zan, *Japan* 55 G7
Hakodate, *Japan* 54 D10
Hakos, *Namibia* 88 C2
Håksberg, *Sweden* 10 D9
Haku-San, *Japan* 55 F8
Haku-San △, *Japan* 55 F8
Hakui, *Japan* 55 F8
Hala, *Pakistan* 66 G6
Ḩalab, *Syria* 70 B3
Ḩalabjah, *Iraq* 70 C5
Halaib, *Sudan* 80 C4
Halasa, *Sudan* 81 E3
Hālat 'Ammār, *Si. Arabia* 70 D3
Halbā, *Lebanon* 74 A5
Halberstadt, *Germany* 24 D7
Halcombe, *N.Z.* 91 J5
Halcon, *Phil.* 63 B6
Halde Fjäll = Haltiatunturi, *Finland* 8 B19
Halden, *Norway* 9 G14
Haldensleben, *Germany* 24 C7
Haldia, *India* 67 H16
Haldimand, *Canada* 116 D5
Haldwani, *India* 69 E8
Hale →, *Australia* 94 C2
Halesowen, *U.K.* 15 E5
Halesworth, *U.K.* 15 E9
Haleyville, *U.S.A.* 115 H2
Half Assini, *Ghana* 82 D4
Halfmoon Bay, *N.Z.* 91 M2
Halfway →, *Canada* 102 B4
Halia, *India* 69 G10
Haliburton, *Canada* 116 A6
Halifax, *Australia* 94 B4
Halifax, *Canada* 105 D7
Halifax, *U.K.* 14 D6
Halifax, *U.S.A.* 116 F8
Halifax B., *Australia* 94 B4
Halifax I., *Namibia* 88 D2
Halīl →, *Iran* 71 E8
Halkirk, *U.K.* 13 C5
Hall Beach = Sanirajak, *Canada* 101 B11
Hall in Tirol, *Austria* 26 D4
Hall Pen., *Canada* 101 B13
Hall Pt., *Australia* 92 C3
Hallabro, *Sweden* 11 H9
Halland, *Sweden* 9 H15
Hallands län □, *Sweden* 11 H6
Hallands Väderö, *Sweden* 11 H6
Hallandsås, *Sweden* 11 H7
Hällbybrunn, *Sweden* 10 E10
Halle, *Belgium* 17 D4
Halle, *Nordrhein-Westfalen, Germany* 24 C4
Halle, *Sachsen-Anhalt, Germany* 24 D7
Hällefors, *Sweden* 10 E8
Hälleforsnäs, *Sweden* 10 E10
Hallein, *Austria* 26 D6
Hällekis, *Sweden* 11 F7
Hallen, *Sweden* 10 A8
Hallett, *Australia* 95 E2
Hallettsville, *U.S.A.* 113 L6
Hallim, *S. Korea* 57 H14
Hallingdalselvi →, *Norway* 9 F13
Hallock, *U.S.A.* 112 A6
Halls Creek, *Australia* 92 C4
Hallsberg, *Sweden* 10 E9
Hallstahammar, *Sweden* 10 E10
Hallstatt, *Austria* 26 D6
Hallstavik, *Sweden* 10 D12
Hallstead, *U.S.A.* 117 E9
Halmahera, *Indonesia* 63 D7
Halmeu, *Romania* 28 C8
Halmstad, *Sweden* 11 H6
Hals, *Denmark* 11 H4
Hälsingborg = Helsingborg, *Sweden* 11 H6
Hälsingland, *Sweden* 10 C10
Halstead, *U.K.* 15 F8
Haltern, *Germany* 24 D3
Haltiatunturi, *Finland* 8 B19
Halton □, *U.K.* 14 D5
Haltwhistle, *U.K.* 14 C5
Ḩālūl, *Qatar* 71 E7
Halvad, *India* 68 H4
Ḩalvān, *Iran* 71 C8
Ham, *France* 19 C10
Ham Tan, *Vietnam* 65 G6
Ham Yen, *Vietnam* 64 A5
Hamab, *Namibia* 88 D2
Hamad, *Sudan* 81 D3
Hamada, *Japan* 55 G6
Hamadān, *Iran* 71 C6
Hamadān □, *Iran* 71 C6
Hamāh, *Syria* 70 C3
Hamamatsu, *Japan* 55 G8
Hamar, *Norway* 9 F14
Hamâta, Gebel, *Egypt* 70 E2
Hambantota, *Sri Lanka* 66 R12
Hamber ⌓, *Canada* 102 C5
Hamburg, *Germany* 24 B5
Hamburg, *Ark., U.S.A.* 113 J9
Hamburg, *N.Y., U.S.A.* 116 D6
Hamburg, *Pa., U.S.A.* 117 F9
Hamburg □, *Germany* 24 B5
Hamburg Fuhlsbüttel ✕ (HAM), *Germany* 24 B5
Ḩamḑ, W. al →, *Si. Arabia* 70 E3
Hamden, *U.S.A.* 117 E12
Hamdibey, *Turkey* 47 B9
Häme, *Finland* 9 F20
Hämeenlinna, *Finland* 9 F21
Hamélé, *Ghana* 82 C4
Hamelin Pool, *Australia* 93 E1
Hameln, *Germany* 24 C5
Hamerkaz □, *Israel* 74 C3
Hamersley Ra., *Australia* 92 D2
Hamhung, *N. Korea* 57 E14
Hami, *China* 60 B4
Hamilton, *Australia* 95 F3
Hamilton, *Canada* 116 C5
Hamilton, *N.Z.* 91 G5
Hamilton, *U.K.* 13 F4
Hamilton, *Ala., U.S.A.* 115 H1
Hamilton, *Mont., U.S.A.* 108 C6
Hamilton, *N.Y., U.S.A.* 117 D9
Hamilton, *Ohio, U.S.A.* 114 F3
Hamilton, *Tex., U.S.A.* 113 K5
Hamilton →, *Australia* 94 C2
Hamilton, The →, *Australia* 95 D2
Hamilton City, *U.S.A.* 110 F4
Hamilton I., *Australia* 94 J6
Hamilton Inlet, *Canada* 105 B8
Hamilton Mt., *U.S.A.* 117 C10

Hamina, *Finland* 9 F22
Hamirpur, *H.P., India* 68 D7
Hamirpur, *Ut. P., India* 69 G9
Hamitabat, *Turkey* 45 E11
Hamlet, *U.S.A.* 115 H6
Hamley Bridge, *Australia* 95 E2
Hamlin = Hameln, *Germany* 24 C5
Hamlin, *N.Y., U.S.A.* 116 C7
Hamlin, *Tex., U.S.A.* 113 J4
Hamm, *Germany* 24 D3
Ḩammār, Hawr al, *Iraq* 70 D5
Hammarstrand, *Sweden* 10 A10
Hammelburg, *Germany* 25 E5
Hammeren, *Denmark* 11 J8
Hammerfest, *Norway* 8 A20
Hammerum, *Denmark* 11 H3
Hamminkeln, *Germany* 24 D2
Hammond, *Ind., U.S.A.* 114 E2
Hammond, *La., U.S.A.* 113 K9
Hammond, *N.Y., U.S.A.* 117 B9
Hammondsport, *U.S.A.* 116 D7
Hammonton, *U.S.A.* 114 F8
Hamneda, *Sweden* 11 H7
Hamoyet, Jebel, *Sudan* 80 D4
Hampden, *N.Z.* 91 L3
Hampshire □, *U.K.* 15 F6
Hampshire Downs, *U.K.* 15 F6
Hampton, *N.B., Canada* 105 C6
Hampton, *Ont., Canada* 116 C6
Hampton, *Ark., U.S.A.* 113 J8
Hampton, *Iowa, U.S.A.* 112 D8
Hampton, *N.H., U.S.A.* 117 D14
Hampton, *S.C., U.S.A.* 115 J5
Hampton, *Va., U.S.A.* 114 G7
Hampton Bays, *U.S.A.* 117 F12
Hampton Tableland, *Australia* 93 F4
Hamra, *Sweden* 10 C8
Hamrat esh Sheykh, *Sudan* 81 E2
Hamur, *Turkey* 73 C10
Hamyang, *S. Korea* 57 G14
Han Jiang →, *China* 59 F11
Han Shui, *China* 58 A7
Han Shui →, *China* 59 B10
Hanak, *Si. Arabia* 70 E3
Hanamaki, *Japan* 54 E10
Hanang, *Tanzania* 86 C4
Hanau, *Germany* 25 E4
Hanbogd = Ihbulag, *Mongolia* 56 C4
Hançalar, *Turkey* 47 C11
Hânceşti, *Moldova* 29 D13
Hancheng, *China* 56 G6
Hanchuan, *China* 59 B9
Hancock, *Mich., U.S.A.* 112 B10
Hancock, *N.Y., U.S.A.* 117 E9
Handa, *Japan* 55 G8
Handan, *China* 56 F8
Handeni, *Tanzania* 86 D4
Handlová, *Slovak Rep.* 27 C11
Handub, *Sudan* 80 D4
Handwara, *India* 69 B6
Hanegev, *Israel* 74 E4
Hanford, *U.S.A.* 110 J7
Hanford Reach ⌂, *U.S.A.* 108 C4
Hang Chat, *Thailand* 64 C2
Hang Dong, *Thailand* 64 C2
Hangang →, *S. Korea* 57 F14
Hangayn Nuruu, *Mongolia* 60 B4
Hangchou = Hangzhou, *China* 59 B13
Hanggin Houqi, *China* 56 D4
Hanggin Qi, *China* 56 E5
Hangu, *China* 57 E9
Hangzhou, *China* 59 B13
Hangzhou Wan, *China* 59 B13
Hanhongor, *Mongolia* 56 C3
Ḩanīdh, *Si. Arabia* 71 E6
Ḩanīsh, *Yemen* 75 E3
Haniska, *Slovak Rep.* 27 C14
Hanjiang, *China* 59 E12
Hankinson, *U.S.A.* 112 B6
Hankö, *Finland* 9 G20
Hankou, *China* 59 B10
Hanksville, *U.S.A.* 109 G8
Hanle, *India* 69 C8
Hanmer Springs, *N.Z.* 91 K4
Hann →, *Australia* 92 C4
Hann, Mt., *Australia* 92 C4
Hanna, *Canada* 102 C6
Hanna, *U.S.A.* 108 F10
Hannah B., *Canada* 104 B4
Hannibal, *Mo., U.S.A.* 112 F9
Hannibal, *N.Y., U.S.A.* 117 C8
Hannik, *Sudan* 80 D3
Hannover, *Germany* 24 C5
Hanö, *Sweden* 11 H8
Hanöbukten, *Sweden* 11 J8
Hanoi, *Vietnam* 58 G5
Hanover = Hannover, *Germany* 24 C5
Hanover, *Canada* 116 B3
Hanover, *S. Africa* 88 E3
Hanover, *N.H., U.S.A.* 117 C12
Hanover, *Ohio, U.S.A.* 116 F2
Hanover, *Pa., U.S.A.* 114 F7
Hanover, I., *Chile* 128 G2
Hans Lollik I., *U.S. Virgin Is.* 121 e
Hansdiha, *India* 69 G12
Hanshou, *China* 59 C8
Hansi, *India* 68 E6
Hanson, L., *Australia* 95 E2
Hanstholm, *Denmark* 11 G2
Hantsavichy, *Belarus* 33 F4
Hanumangarh, *India* 68 E6
Hanyin, *China* 58 A7
Hanyuan, *China* 58 C4
Hanzhong, *China* 56 H4
Hanzhuang, *China* 57 G9
Haora, *India* 69 H13
Haoxue, *China* 59 B9
Haparanda, *Sweden* 8 D21
Happy, *U.S.A.* 113 H4
Happy Camp, *U.S.A.* 108 F2
Happy Valley-Goose Bay, *Canada* 105 B7
Hapsu, *N. Korea* 57 D15
Hapur, *India* 68 E7
Ḩaql, *Si. Arabia* 74 F3
Har, *Indonesia* 63 F8
Har-Ayrag, *Mongolia* 56 B5
Har Hu, *China* 60 C4
Har Us Nuur, *Mongolia* 60 B4
Har Yehuda, *Israel* 74 D3
Ḩaraḑ, *Si. Arabia* 75 C4
Haradok, *Belarus* 32 E6
Häradsbäck, *Sweden* 11 H8
Haranomachi, *Japan* 54 F10
Harare, *Zimbabwe* 87 F3
Harat, *Eritrea* 81 D4
Harbin, *China* 57 B14
Harbiye, *Turkey* 72 D7
Harbo, *Sweden* 10 D11
Harboør, *Denmark* 11 H2
Harbor Beach, *U.S.A.* 116 C2
Harbour Breton, *Canada* 105 C8
Harbour Deep, *Canada* 105 B8
Harburg, *Germany* 24 B5
Harburger Berge ⌂, *Germany* 24 B5
Hårby, *Denmark* 11 J4
Harda, *India* 68 H7
Hardangerfjorden, *Norway* 9 F12
Hardangervidda, *Norway* 9 F12
Hardap ⌂, *Namibia* 88 C2
Hardap Dam, *Namibia* 88 C2
Hardenberg, *Neths.* 17 B6
Harderwijk, *Neths.* 17 B5
Hardey →, *Australia* 92 D2
Hardin, *U.S.A.* 108 D10
Harding, *S. Africa* 89 E4
Harding Ra., *Australia* 92 C3
Hardisty, *Canada* 102 C6
Hardoi, *India* 69 F9
Hardwar = Haridwar, *India* 68 E8
Hardwick, *U.S.A.* 117 B12
Hardy, Pen., *Chile* 128 H3
Hardy, Pte., *St. Lucia* 121 f
Hare B., *Canada* 105 B8
Hareid, *Norway* 9 E12
Haren, *Germany* 24 C3
Harer, *Ethiopia* 81 F5
Harerge, *Ethiopia* 81 F5
Hareto, *Ethiopia* 81 F4
Harfleur, *France* 18 C7
Hargeisa, *Somali Rep.* 75 F3
Harghita □, *Romania* 29 D10
Harghita, Munţii, *Romania* 29 D10
Hargshamn, *Sweden* 10 D12
Hari →, *Indonesia* 62 E2
Haria, *Canary Is.* 48 E6
Haridwar, *India* 68 E8
Harim, Jabal al, *Oman* 71 E8
Haringhata →, *Bangla.* 67 J16
Harīrūd →, *Asia* 66 A2
Härjedalen, *Sweden* 10 B7
Harlan, *Iowa, U.S.A.* 112 E7
Harlan, *Ky., U.S.A.* 115 G4
Hârlău, *Romania* 29 C11
Harlech, *U.K.* 14 E3
Harlem, *U.S.A.* 108 B9
Hårlev, *Denmark* 11 J6
Harlingen, *Neths.* 17 A5
Harlingen, *U.S.A.* 113 M6
Harlow, *U.K.* 15 F8
Harlowton, *U.S.A.* 108 C9
Harmancık, *Turkey* 47 B11
Harmånger, *Sweden* 10 C11
Harmil, *Eritrea* 81 D5
Harnai, *Pakistan* 68 D2
Harney Basin, *U.S.A.* 108 E4
Harney L., *U.S.A.* 108 E4
Harney Peak, *U.S.A.* 112 D3
Härnön, *Sweden* 10 B12
Härnösand, *Sweden* 10 B11
Haro, *Spain* 38 C2
Haroldswick, *U.K.* 13 A8
Harp L., *Canada* 105 A7
Harper, *Liberia* 82 E3
Harplinge, *Sweden* 11 H6
Harr, *Mauritania* 82 B2
Harrai, *India* 69 H8
Harrand, *Pakistan* 68 E4
Ḩarrat Khaybar, *Si. Arabia* 80 B5
Ḩarrat Nawāşīf, *Si. Arabia* 80 C5
Harricana →, *Canada* 104 B4
Harriman, *U.S.A.* 115 H3
Harrington Harbour, *Canada* 105 B8
Harris, *U.K.* 13 D2
Harris, L., *Australia* 95 E2
Harris, Sd. of, *U.K.* 13 D1
Harris Pt., *Canada* 116 C2
Harrisburg, *Ill., U.S.A.* 113 G10
Harrisburg, *Nebr., U.S.A.* 112 E3
Harrisburg, *Pa., U.S.A.* 116 F8
Harrismith, *S. Africa* 89 D4
Harrison, *Ark., U.S.A.* 113 G8
Harrison, *Maine, U.S.A.* 117 B14
Harrison, *Nebr., U.S.A.* 112 D3
Harrison, C., *Canada* 105 B8
Harrison L., *Canada* 102 D4
Harrisonburg, *U.S.A.* 114 F6
Harrisonville, *U.S.A.* 112 F7
Harriston, *Canada* 116 C4
Harrisville, *Mich., U.S.A.* 116 B1
Harrisville, *N.Y., U.S.A.* 117 B9
Harrisville, *Pa., U.S.A.* 116 E5
Harrodsburg, *U.S.A.* 114 G3
Harrogate, *U.K.* 14 C6
Harrow □, *U.K.* 15 F7
Harrowsmith, *Canada* 117 B8
Harry S. Truman Reservoir, *U.S.A.* 112 F7
Harsefeld, *Germany* 24 B5
Harsewinkel, *Germany* 24 D4
Harsīn, *Iran* 70 C5
Hârşova, *Romania* 29 F12
Harstad, *Norway* 8 B17
Harsud, *India* 68 H7
Hart, *U.S.A.* 114 D2
Hart, L., *Australia* 95 E2
Hartbees →, *S. Africa* 88 D3
Hartberg, *Austria* 26 D8
Hartford, *Conn., U.S.A.* 117 E12
Hartford, *Ky., U.S.A.* 114 G2
Hartford, *S. Dak., U.S.A.* 112 D6
Hartford, *Wis., U.S.A.* 112 D10
Hartford City, *U.S.A.* 114 E3
Hartland, *Canada* 105 C6
Hartland Pt., *U.K.* 15 F3
Hartlepool, *U.K.* 14 C6
Hartlepool □, *U.K.* 14 C6
Hartley Bay, *Canada* 102 C3
Hartmannberge, *Namibia* 88 B1
Hartney, *Canada* 103 D8
Hârtop, *Moldova* 29 D13
Harts →, *S. Africa* 88 D3
Hartselle, *U.S.A.* 115 H2
Hartshorne, *U.S.A.* 113 H7
Hartstown, *U.S.A.* 116 E4
Hartsville, *U.S.A.* 115 H5
Hartswater, *S. Africa* 88 D3
Hartwell, *U.S.A.* 115 H4
Harunabad, *Pakistan* 68 E5
Harvand, *Iran* 71 D7
Harvey, *Australia* 93 F2
Harvey, *Ill., U.S.A.* 114 E2
Harvey, *N. Dak., U.S.A.* 112 B5
Harwich, *U.K.* 15 F9
Haryana □, *India* 68 E7
Haryn →, *Belarus* 33 F4
Harz, *Germany* 24 D6
Harz △, *Germany* 24 D6
Harzgerode, *Germany* 24 D7
Hasa □, *Si. Arabia* 71 E6
Hasaheisa, *Sudan* 81 E3
Ḩasanābād, *Iran* 71 C7
Ḩasb, W. →, *Iraq* 70 D5
Hasdo →, *India* 69 J10
Haselünne, *Germany* 24 C3
Hashimoto, *Japan* 55 G7
Hashtjerd, *Iran* 71 C6
Haskell, *U.S.A.* 113 J5
Hasköy, *Turkey* 45 E10
Haslach, *Germany* 25 G4
Hasle, *Denmark* 11 J8
Haslemere, *U.K.* 15 F7
Haslev, *Denmark* 11 J5
Hasparren, *France* 20 E2
Hassa, *Turkey* 72 D7
Hassberge ⌂, *Germany* 25 E6
Hassela, *Sweden* 10 B10
Hasselt, *Belgium* 17 D5
Hassfurt, *Germany* 25 E6
Hassi Messaoud, *Algeria* 78 B7
Hässleholm, *Sweden* 11 H7
Hassloch, *Germany* 25 F4
Hästholmen, *Sweden* 11 F8
Hastings, *N.Z.* 91 H6
Hastings, *U.K.* 15 G8
Hastings, *Mich., U.S.A.* 114 D3
Hastings, *Minn., U.S.A.* 112 C8
Hastings, *Nebr., U.S.A.* 112 E5
Hastings Ra., *Australia* 95 E5
Hästveda, *Sweden* 11 H7
Hat, *Ukraine* 28 B7
Hat Yai, *Thailand* 65 J3
Hatanbulag = Ergel, *Mongolia* 56 C5
Hatay = Antalya, *Turkey* 72 D4
Hatch, *U.S.A.* 109 K10
Hatchet L., *Canada* 103 B8
Haţeg, *Romania* 28 E7
Hateruma-Shima, *Japan* 55 M1
Hatfield P.O., *Australia* 95 E3
Hatgal, *Mongolia* 60 A5
Hathras, *India* 68 F8
Hatia, *Bangla.* 67 H17
Ḩāţibah, Ra's, *Si. Arabia* 80 C4
Hato Mayor, *Dom. Rep.* 121 C6
Hatta, *India* 69 G8
Hattah, *Australia* 95 E3
Hatteras, C., *U.S.A.* 115 H8
Hattiesburg, *U.S.A.* 113 K10
Hatvan, *Hungary* 28 C4
Hau Bon = Cheo Reo, *Vietnam* 62 B3
Hau Duc, *Vietnam* 64 E7
Haugesund, *Norway* 9 G11
Haukipudas, *Finland* 8 D21
Haultain →, *Canada* 103 B7
Hauraki G., *N.Z.* 91 G5
Hausruck, *Austria* 26 C6
Haut Atlas, *Morocco* 78 B4
Haut-Jura ⌂, *France* 19 F9
Haut-Languedoc ⌂, *France* 20 E6
Haut Niger △, *Guinea* 82 C2
Haut-Rhin □, *France* 19 E14
Haute-Corse □, *France* 21 F13
Haute-Garonne □, *France* 20 E5
Haute-Loire □, *France* 20 C7
Haute-Marne □, *France* 19 D12
Haute-Normandie □, *France* 18 C7
Haute-Saône □, *France* 19 E13
Haute-Savoie □, *France* 21 C10
Haute-Vienne □, *France* 20 C5
Hautes-Alpes □, *France* 21 D10
Hautes Fagnes = Hohe Venn, *Belgium* 17 D6
Hautes Fagnes = Hohes Venn-Eifel ⌂, *Europe* 24 E2
Hautes-Pyrénées □, *France* 20 F4
Hauteville-Lompnès, *France* 21 C9
Hautmont, *France* 19 B10
Hauts-de-Seine □, *France* 19 D9
Hauts Plateaux, *Algeria* 76 C4
Hauzenberg, *Germany* 25 G9
Havana = La Habana, *Cuba* 120 B3
Havana, *U.S.A.* 112 E9
Havant, *U.K.* 15 G7
Havârna, *Romania* 29 B11
Havasor = Kığzı, *Turkey* 70 B4
Havasu, L., *U.S.A.* 111 L12
Havdhem, *Sweden* 11 G12
Havel →, *Germany* 24 C8
Havelian, *Pakistan* 68 B5
Havelock, *Canada* 116 B7
Havelock, *N.Z.* 91 J4
Havelock, *U.S.A.* 115 H7
Haverfordwest, *U.K.* 15 F3
Haverhill, *U.K.* 15 E8
Haverhill, *U.S.A.* 117 D13
Haverstraw, *U.S.A.* 117 E11
Håverud, *Sweden* 11 F6
Havirga, *Mongolia* 56 B7
Havířov, *Czech Rep.* 27 B11
Havlíčkův Brod, *Czech Rep.* 26 B8
Havneby, *Denmark* 11 J2
Havran, *Turkey* 47 B9
Havre, *U.S.A.* 108 B9
Havre-Aubert, *Canada* 105 C7
Havre-St.-Pierre, *Canada* 105 B7
Havsa, *Turkey* 45 E10
Havza, *Turkey* 72 B6
Haw →, *U.S.A.* 115 H6
Hawaii □, *U.S.A.* 106 H16
Hawaii I., *Pac. Oc.* 106 J17
Hawaiian Is., *Pac. Oc.* 106 H17
Hawaiian Ridge, *Pac. Oc.* 97 E11
Hawarden, *U.S.A.* 112 D6
Hawea, L., *N.Z.* 91 L2
Hawera, *N.Z.* 91 H5
Hawick, *U.K.* 13 F6
Hawk Junction, *Canada* 104 C3
Hawke B., *N.Z.* 91 H6
Hawker, *Australia* 95 E2
Hawkesbury, *Canada* 104 C5
Hawkesbury I., *Canada* 102 C3
Hawkesbury Pt., *Australia* 94 A1
Hawkinsville, *U.S.A.* 115 J4
Hawley, *Minn., U.S.A.* 112 B6
Hawley, *Pa., U.S.A.* 117 E9
Ḩawrān, W. →, *Iraq* 70 C4
Hawsh Mūssá, *Lebanon* 74 B4
Hawthorne, *U.S.A.* 108 G4
Hay, *Australia* 95 E3
Hay →, *Australia* 94 C2
Hay →, *Canada* 102 A5
Hay, C., *Australia* 92 B4
Hay I., *Canada* 116 B4
Hay L., *Canada* 102 B5
Hay-on-Wye, *U.K.* 15 E4
Hay River, *Canada* 102 A5
Hay Springs, *U.S.A.* 112 D3
Haya = Tehoru, *Indonesia* 63 E7
Hayachine-San, *Japan* 54 E10
Hayange, *France* 19 C13
Haydarlı, *Turkey* 47 C12
Hayden, *U.S.A.* 108 F10
Haydon, *Australia* 94 B3
Hayes, *U.S.A.* 112 C4
Hayes →, *Canada* 104 A1
Hayes Creek, *Australia* 92 B5
Hayle, *U.K.* 15 G2
Hayling I., *U.K.* 15 G7
Haymana, *Turkey* 72 C5
Haymen I., *Australia* 94 J6
Hayrabolu, *Turkey* 45 E11
Hays, *Canada* 102 C6
Hays, *U.S.A.* 112 F5
Haysyn, *Ukraine* 29 B14
Hayvoron, *Ukraine* 29 B14
Hayward, *Calif., U.S.A.* 110 H4
Hayward, *Wis., U.S.A.* 112 B9
Haywards Heath, *U.K.* 15 G7
Hazafon □, *Israel* 74 C4
Hazārān, Kūh-e, *Iran* 71 D8
Hazard, *U.S.A.* 114 G4
Hazaribag, *India* 69 H11
Hazaribag Road, *India* 69 G11
Hazebrouck, *France* 19 B9
Hazelton, *Canada* 102 B3
Hazelton, *U.S.A.* 112 B4
Hazen, *U.S.A.* 112 B4
Hazlehurst, *Ga., U.S.A.* 115 K4
Hazlehurst, *Miss., U.S.A.* 113 K9
Hazlet, *U.S.A.* 117 F10
Hazleton, *U.S.A.* 117 F9
Hazlett, L., *Australia* 92 D4
Hazro, *Turkey* 70 B4
He Xian, *Anhui, China* 59 B12
He Xian, *Guangxi Zhuangzu, China* 59 E8
Head of Bight, *Australia* 93 F5
Headlands, *Zimbabwe* 87 F3
Healdsburg, *U.S.A.* 110 G4
Healdton, *U.S.A.* 113 H6
Healesville, *Australia* 95 F4
Heany Junction, *Zimbabwe* 89 C4
Heard I., *Ind. Oc.* 3 G13
Hearne, *U.S.A.* 113 K6
Hearst, *Canada* 104 C3
Heart →, *U.S.A.* 112 B4
Heart's Content, *Canada* 105 C9
Heath, Pte., *Canada* 105 C7
Heathrow, London ✕ (LHR), *U.K.* 15 F7
Heavener, *U.S.A.* 113 H7
Hebbronville, *U.S.A.* 113 M5
Hebei □, *China* 56 E9
Hebel, *Australia* 95 D4
Heber, *U.S.A.* 111 N11
Heber City, *U.S.A.* 108 F8
Heber Springs, *U.S.A.* 113 H9
Hebert, *Canada* 103 C7
Hebgen L., *U.S.A.* 108 D8
Hebi, *China* 56 G8
Hebrides, *U.K.* 6 D4
Hebrides, Sea of the, *U.K.* 13 D2
Hebron = Al Khalīl, *West Bank* 74 D4
Hebron, *Canada* 101 C13
Hebron, *N. Dak., U.S.A.* 112 B3
Hebron, *Nebr., U.S.A.* 112 E6
Heby, *Sweden* 10 E10
Hecate Str., *Canada* 102 C2
Heceta I., *U.S.A.* 102 B2
Hechi, *China* 58 E7
Hechingen, *Germany* 25 G4
Hechuan, *China* 58 B6
Hecla, *U.S.A.* 112 C5
Hecla I., *Canada* 103 C9
Hédé, *France* 18 D5
Hede, *Sweden* 10 B7
Hedemora, *Sweden* 10 D9
Hedensted, *Denmark* 11 J3
Hedesunda, *Sweden* 10 D10
Heerde, *Neths.* 17 B6
Heerenveen, *Neths.* 17 B5
Heerhugowaard, *Neths.* 17 B4
Heerlen, *Neths.* 17 D5
Ḩefa, *Israel* 74 C4
Ḩefa □, *Israel* 74 C4
Hefei, *China* 59 B11
Hefeng, *China* 59 C8
Hegalig, *Sudan* 81 E3
Hegang, *China* 60 B8
Heiban, *Sudan* 81 E3
Heichengzhen, *China* 56 F4
Heide, *Germany* 24 A5
Heidelberg, *Germany* 25 F4
Heidelberg, *S. Africa* 88 E3
Heidenau, *Germany* 24 E9
Heidenheim, *Germany* 25 G6
Heijing, *China* 58 E3
Heilbad Heiligenstadt, *Germany* 24 D6
Heilbron, *S. Africa* 89 D4
Heilbronn, *Germany* 25 F5
Heiligenblut, *Austria* 26 D5
Heiligenhafen, *Germany* 24 A6
Heilongjiang □, *China* 60 B7
Heilunkiang = Heilongjiang □, *China* 60 B7
Heimaey, *Iceland* 8 E3
Heinola, *Finland* 9 F22
Heinsberg, *Germany* 24 D2
Heinze Kyun, *Burma* 64 E1
Heishan, *China* 57 D12
Heishui, *Liaoning, China* 57 C10
Heishui, *Sichuan, China* 58 A4
Hejaz = Ḩijāz □, *Si. Arabia* 70 E3
Hejian, *China* 56 E9
Hejiang, *China* 58 C5
Hejin, *China* 56 G6
Hekımhan, *Turkey* 70 B3
Hekla, *Iceland* 8 E4
Hekou, *Guangdong, China* 59 F9
Hekou, *Yunnan, China* 58 F4
Hel, *Poland* 30 D5
Helagsfjället, *Sweden* 10 B6
Helan Shan, *China* 56 E3
Helechosa, *Spain* 37 F6
Helen Atoll, *Pac. Oc.* 63 D8
Helena, *Ark., U.S.A.* 113 H9
Helena, *Mont., U.S.A.* 108 C7
Helendale, *U.S.A.* 111 L9
Helensburgh, *U.K.* 13 E4
Helensville, *N.Z.* 91 G5
Helenvale, *Australia* 94 B4
Helgasjön, *Sweden* 11 H8
Helgeland, *Norway* 8 C15
Helgoland, *Germany* 24 A3
Heligoland = Helgoland, *Germany* 24 A3
Heligoland B. = Deutsche Bucht, *Germany* 24 A4
Heliopolis, *Egypt* 80 H7
Hella, *Iceland* 8 E3
Hellertown, *U.S.A.* 117 F9
Hellespont = Çanakkale Boğazı, *Turkey* 45 F10
Hellevoetsluis, *Neths.* 17 C4
Hellhole Gorge △, *Australia* 94 D3
Hellín, *Spain* 39 G3
Hells Canyon ⌂, *U.S.A.* 108 D5
Hell's Gate △, *Kenya* 86 C4
Helmand □, *Afghan.* 66 D4
Helmand →, *Afghan.* 66 D2
Helme →, *Germany* 24 D7
Helmeringhausen, *Namibia* 88 D2
Helmond, *Neths.* 17 C5
Helmsdale, *U.K.* 13 C5
Helmsdale →, *U.K.* 13 C5
Helmstedt, *Germany* 24 C7
Helong, *China* 57 C15
Helper, *U.S.A.* 108 G8
Helsingborg, *Sweden* 11 H6
Helsinge, *Denmark* 11 H6
Helsingfors = Helsinki, *Finland* 9 F21
Helsingør, *Denmark* 11 H6
Helsinki, *Finland* 9 F21
Helska, Mierzeja, *Poland* 30 D5
Helston, *U.K.* 15 G2
Helvellyn, *U.K.* 14 C4
Helwân, *Egypt* 80 J7
Hemel Hempstead, *U.K.* 15 F7
Hemet, *U.S.A.* 111 M10
Hemingford, *U.S.A.* 112 D3
Hemmingford, *Canada* 117 A11
Hempstead, *U.S.A.* 113 K6
Hemse, *Sweden* 11 G12
Hemsön, *Sweden* 10 B12
Henån, *Sweden* 11 F5
Henan □, *China* 56 H8
Henares →, *Spain* 36 E7
Henashi-Misaki, *Japan* 54 D9
Hendaye, *France* 20 E2
Hendek, *Turkey* 72 B4
Henderson, *Argentina* 126 D3
Henderson, *Ky., U.S.A.* 114 G2
Henderson, *N.C., U.S.A.* 115 G6
Henderson, *Nev., U.S.A.* 111 J12
Henderson, *Tenn., U.S.A.* 115 H1
Henderson, *Tex., U.S.A.* 113 J7
Hendersonville, *N.C., U.S.A.* 115 H4
Hendersonville, *Tenn., U.S.A.* 115 G2
Hendījān, *Iran* 71 D6

Hendorābī, *Iran* 71 E7
Heng Jiang, *China* 58 C5
Heng Xian, *China* 58 F7
Hengcheng, *China* 56 E4
Hëngchun, *Taiwan* 59 F13
Hengdaohezi, *China* 57 B15
Hengelo, *Neths.* 17 B6
Hengfeng, *China* 59 C10
Hengshan, *Hunan, China* 59 D9
Hengshan, *Shaanxi, China* 56 F5
Hengshui, *China* 56 F8
Hengyang, *China* 59 D9
Henichesk, *Ukraine* 33 J8
Hénin-Beaumont, *France* 19 B9
Henley-on-Thames, *U.K.* 15 F7
Henlopen, C., *U.S.A.* 114 F8
Hennan, *Sweden* 10 B9
Hennebont, *France* 18 E3
Hennenman, *S. Africa* 88 D4
Hennessey, *U.S.A.* 113 G6
Hennigsdorf, *Germany* 24 C9
Henri Pittier △, *Venezuela* 121 D6
Henrietta, *U.S.A.* 113 J5
Henrietta, Ostrov = Genriyetty, Ostrov, *Russia* 53 B16
Henrietta Maria, C., *Canada* 104 A3
Henry, *U.S.A.* 112 E10
Henryetta, *U.S.A.* 113 H7
Henryville, *Canada* 117 A11
Hensall, *Canada* 116 C3
Henstedt-Ulzburg, *Germany* 24 B6
Hentiesbaai, *Namibia* 88 C1
Hentiyn Nuruu, *Mongolia* 60 B5
Henty, *Australia* 95 F4
Henzada, *Burma* 67 L19
Hephaestia, *Greece* 47 B7
Heping, *China* 59 E10
Heppner, *U.S.A.* 108 D4
Hepu, *China* 58 G7
Hepworth, *Canada* 116 B3
Heqing, *China* 58 D3
Hequ, *China* 56 E6
Héraðsflói, *Iceland* 8 D6
Héraðsvötn →, *Iceland* 8 D4
Heraklion = Iráklion, *Greece* 49 D7
Herald Cays, *Australia* 94 B4
Herāt, *Afghan.* 66 B3
Herāt □, *Afghan.* 66 B3
Hérault □, *France* 20 E7
Hérault →, *France* 20 E7
Herbault, *France* 18 E8
Herbert →, *Australia* 94 B4
Herbert River Falls △, *Australia* 94 B4
Herberton, *Australia* 94 B4
Herbertsdale, *S. Africa* 88 E3
Herbignac, *France* 18 E4
Herborn, *Germany* 24 E4
Herby, *Poland* 31 H5
Herceg-Novi, *Serbia & M.* 44 D2
Herchmer, *Canada* 103 B10
Herðubreið, *Iceland* 8 D5
Hereford, *U.K.* 15 E5
Hereford, *U.S.A.* 113 H3
Herefordshire □, *U.K.* 15 E5
Hereke, *Turkey* 45 F13
Herencia, *Spain* 37 F7
Herentals, *Belgium* 17 C4
Herford, *Germany* 24 C4
Héricourt, *France* 19 E13
Herington, *U.S.A.* 112 F6
Herisau, *Switz.* 25 H5
Hérisson, *France* 19 F9
Herkimer, *U.S.A.* 117 D10
Herlong, *U.S.A.* 110 E6
Herm, *U.K.* 15 H5
Hermakivka, *Ukraine* 29 B11
Hermann, *U.S.A.* 112 F9
Hermannsburg, *Australia* 92 D5
Hermannsburg, *Germany* 24 C6
Hermanus, *S. Africa* 88 E2
Herment, *France* 20 C6
Hermidale, *Australia* 95 E4
Hermiston, *U.S.A.* 108 D4
Hermite, I., *Chile* 128 H3
Hermon, *U.S.A.* 117 B9
Hermon, Mt. = Shaykh, J. ash, *Lebanon* 74 B4
Hermosillo, *Mexico* 118 B2
Hernád →, *Hungary* 28 C6
Hernandarias, *Paraguay* 127 B5
Hernandez, *U.S.A.* 110 J6
Hernando, *Argentina* 126 C3
Hernando, *U.S.A.* 113 H10
Hernani, *Spain* 38 B3
Herndon, *U.S.A.* 116 F8
Herne, *Germany* 17 C7
Herne Bay, *U.K.* 15 F9
Herning, *Denmark* 11 H2
Heroica = Caborca, *Mexico* 118 A2
Heroica Nogales = Nogales, *Mexico* 118 A2
Heron Bay, *Canada* 104 C2
Herradura, Pta. de la, *Canary Is.* 48 F5
Herreid, *U.S.A.* 112 C4
Herrenberg, *Germany* 25 G4
Herrera, *Spain* 37 H6
Herrera de Alcántara, *Spain* 37 F3
Herrera de Pisuerga, *Spain* 36 C6
Herrera del Duque, *Spain* 37 F5
Herrestad, *Sweden* 11 F5
Herrin, *U.S.A.* 113 G10
Herriot, *Canada* 103 B8
Herrljunga, *Sweden* 11 F7
Hersbruck, *Germany* 25 F7
Herschel I., *Canada* 4 C1
Hershey, *U.S.A.* 117 F8
Hersonissos, *Greece* 49 D7
Herstal, *Belgium* 17 D5
Hertford, *U.K.* 15 F7
Hertfordshire □, *U.K.* 15 F7
's-Hertogenbosch, *Neths.* 17 C5
Hertsa, *Ukraine* 29 B11
Hertzogville, *S. Africa* 88 D4
Hervás, *Spain* 36 E5
Hervey B., *Australia* 94 C5
Herzberg, *Brandenburg, Germany* 24 D9
Herzberg, *Niedersachsen, Germany* 24 D6
Herzliyya, *Israel* 74 C3
Herzogenburg, *Austria* 26 C8
Ḩeşār, *Fārs, Iran* 71 D6
Ḩeşār, *Markazī, Iran* 71 C6
Hesdin, *France* 19 B9
Heshan, *China* 58 F7
Heshui, *China* 56 G5
Heshun, *China* 56 F7
Hesperia, *U.S.A.* 111 L9
Hesse = Hessen □, *Germany* 24 E4
Hessen □, *Germany* 24 E4
Hessenreuther und Manteler Wald ⌓, *Germany* 25 F8
Hestra, *Sweden* 11 G7
Hetch Hetchy Aqueduct, *U.S.A.* 110 H5
Hettinger, *U.S.A.* 112 C3
Hettstedt, *Germany* 24 D7
Heuvelton, *U.S.A.* 117 B9
Heves, *Hungary* 28 C5
Heves □, *Hungary* 28 C5
Hewitt, *U.S.A.* 113 K6
Hexham, *U.K.* 14 C5
Hexi, *Yunnan, China* 58 E4
Hexi, *Zhejiang, China* 59 D12
Hexigten Qi, *China* 57 C9
Ḩeydarābād, *Iran* 71 D7
Heysham, *U.K.* 14 C5
Heyuan, *China* 59 F10
Heywood, *Australia* 95 F3
Heze, *China* 56 G8
Hezhang, *China* 58 D5
Hi, Ko, *Thailand* 65 a
Hi Vista, *U.S.A.* 111 L9
Hialeah, *U.S.A.* 115 N5
Hiawatha, *U.S.A.* 112 F7
Hibbing, *U.S.A.* 112 B8
Hibbs B., *Australia* 95 G4
Hibernia Reef, *Australia* 92 B3
Hickman, *U.S.A.* 113 G10
Hickory, *U.S.A.* 115 H5
Hicks, Pt., *Australia* 95 F4
Hicks L., *Canada* 103 A9
Hicksville, *U.S.A.* 117 F11
Hida, *Romania* 29 C8
Hida-Gawa →, *Japan* 55 G8
Hida-Sammyaku, *Japan* 55 F8
Hidaka-Sammyaku, *Japan* 54 C11
Hidalgo, *Mexico* 119 C5
Hidalgo □, *Mexico* 119 C5
Hidalgo, Presa M., *Mexico* 118 B3
Hidalgo del Parral, *Mexico* 118 B3
Hiddensee, *Germany* 24 A9
Hieflau, *Austria* 26 D7
Hiendelaencina, *Spain* 38 D2
Hierro, *Canary Is.* 48 G1
Higashiajima-San, *Japan* 54 F10
Higashiōsaka, *Japan* 55 G7
Higgins, *U.S.A.* 113 G4
Higgins Corner, *U.S.A.* 110 F5
High Bridge, *U.S.A.* 117 F10
High Level, *Canada* 102 B5
High Point, *U.S.A.* 115 H6
High Prairie, *Canada* 102 B5
High River, *Canada* 102 C6
High Tatra = Tatry, *Slovak Rep.* 27 B13
High Veld, *Africa* 76 J6
High Wycombe, *U.K.* 15 F7
Highland □, *U.K.* 13 D4
Highland Park, *U.S.A.* 114 D2
Highmore, *U.S.A.* 112 C5
Highrock L., *Man., Canada* 103 B8
Highrock L., *Sask., Canada* 103 B7
Higüey, *Dom. Rep.* 121 C6
Hihya, *Egypt* 80 H7
Hiiumaa, *Estonia* 9 G20
Híjar, *Spain* 38 D4
Ḩijāz □, *Si. Arabia* 70 E3
Hijo = Tagum, *Phil.* 61 H6
Hikari, *Japan* 55 H5
Hikmak, Ras el, *Egypt* 80 A2
Hiko, *U.S.A.* 110 H11
Hikone, *Japan* 55 G8
Hikurangi, *Gisborne, N.Z.* 91 H6
Hikurangi, *Northland, N.Z.* 91 F5
Hildburghausen, *Germany* 24 E6
Hildesheim, *Germany* 24 C5
Hill →, *Australia* 93 F2
Hill City, *Idaho, U.S.A.* 108 E6
Hill City, *Kans., U.S.A.* 112 F5
Hill City, *S. Dak., U.S.A.* 112 D3
Hill Island L., *Canada* 103 A7
Hillaby, Mt., *Barbados* 121 g
Hillared, *Sweden* 11 G7
Hillcrest, *Barbados* 121 g
Hillcrest Center, *U.S.A.* 111 K8
Hillegom, *Neths.* 17 B4
Hillerød, *Denmark* 11 J6
Hillerstorp, *Sweden* 11 G7
Hillsboro, *Kans., U.S.A.* 112 F6
Hillsboro, *N. Dak., U.S.A.* 112 B6
Hillsboro, *Ohio, U.S.A.* 114 F4
Hillsboro, *Oreg., U.S.A.* 110 E4
Hillsboro, *Tex., U.S.A.* 113 J6
Hillsborough, *Grenada* 121 D7
Hillsborough, *U.S.A.* 117 C13
Hillsborough Channel, *Australia* 94 J7
Hillsdale, *Mich., U.S.A.* 114 E3
Hillsdale, *N.Y., U.S.A.* 117 D11
Hillsport, *Canada* 104 C2
Hillston, *Australia* 95 E4
Hilo, *U.S.A.* 106 J17
Hilton, *U.S.A.* 116 C7
Hilton Head Island, *U.S.A.* 115 J5
Hilvan, *Turkey* 73 D8
Hilversum, *Neths.* 17 B5
Himachal Pradesh □, *India* 68 D7
Himalaya, *Asia* 69 E11
Himamaylan, *Phil.* 61 F5
Himarë, *Albania* 44 F3
Himatnagar, *India* 66 H8
Himeji, *Japan* 55 G7
Himi, *Japan* 55 F8
Himmerland, *Denmark* 11 H3
Ḩimş, *Syria* 74 A5
Ḩimş □, *Syria* 74 A6
Hinche, *Haiti* 121 C5
Hinchinbrook I., *Australia* 94 B4
Hinchinbrook Island △, *Australia* 94 B4
Hinckley, *U.K.* 15 E6
Hinckley, *U.S.A.* 112 B8
Hindaun, *India* 68 F7
Hindmarsh, L., *Australia* 95 F3
Hindsholm, *Denmark* 11 J4
Hindu Bagh, *Pakistan* 68 D2
Hindu Kush, *Asia* 66 B7
Hindupur, *India* 66 N10
Hines Creek, *Canada* 102 B5
Hinesville, *U.S.A.* 115 K5
Hinganghat, *India* 66 J11
Hingham, *U.S.A.* 108 B8
Hingir, *India* 69 J10
Hingoli, *India* 66 K10
Hinigaran, *Phil.* 61 F5
Hinis, *Turkey* 73 C9
Hinna = Imi, *Ethiopia* 81 F5
Hinna, *Nigeria* 83 C7
Hinnerup, *Denmark* 11 H4
Hinnøya, *Norway* 8 B16
Hinojosa del Duque, *Spain* 37 G5
Hinsdale, *U.S.A.* 117 D12
Hinterrhein →, *Switz.* 25 J5
Hinton, *Canada* 102 C5
Hinton, *U.S.A.* 114 G5
Hınzır Burnu, *Turkey* 72 D6
Hirado, *Japan* 55 H4
Hirakud Dam, *India* 67 J13
Hiran →, *India* 69 H8
Hirapur, *India* 69 G8
Hiratsuka, *Japan* 55 G9
Hirfanlı Barajı, *Turkey* 72 C5
Hiroo, *Japan* 54 C11
Hirosaki, *Japan* 54 D10
Hiroshima, *Japan* 55 G6
Hiroshima □, *Japan* 55 G6
Hirson, *France* 19 C11
Hirtshals, *Denmark* 11 G3
Hisar, *India* 68 E6
Hisarcık, *Turkey* 47 B11
Hisaria, *Bulgaria* 45 D8
Hisb, Sha'ib = Ḩasb, W. →, *Iraq* 70 D5
Ḩismá, *Si. Arabia* 70 D3
Hispaniola, *W. Indies* 121 C5
Hīt, *Iraq* 70 C4
Hita, *Japan* 55 H5
Hitachi, *Japan* 55 F10
Hitchin, *U.K.* 15 F7
Hitoyoshi, *Japan* 55 H5
Hitra, *Norway* 8 E13
Hitzacker, *Germany* 24 B7
Hixon, *Canada* 102 C4
Hiyyon, N. →, *Israel* 74 E4
Hjalmar L., *Canada* 103 A7
Hjälmaren, *Sweden* 10 E9
Hjältevad, *Sweden* 11 G9
Hjo, *Sweden* 11 F8
Hjørring, *Denmark* 11 G3
Hjortkvarn, *Sweden* 11 F9
Hkakabo Razi, *Burma* 67 E20
Hlinsko, *Czech Rep.* 26 B8
Hlobane, *S. Africa* 89 D5
Hlohovec, *Slovak Rep.* 27 C10
Hlučín, *Czech Rep.* 27 B11
Hluhluwe, *S. Africa* 89 D5
Hluhluwe ⌓, *S. Africa* 89 C5
Hlukhiv, *Ukraine* 33 G7
Hlyboka, *Ukraine* 29 B10
Hlybokaye, *Belarus* 32 E4
Hnúšt'a, *Slovak Rep.* 27 C12
Ho, *Ghana* 83 D5
Ho Chi Minh City = Thanh Pho Ho Chi Minh, *Vietnam* 65 G6
Ho Thuong, *Vietnam* 64 C5
Hoa Binh, *Vietnam* 58 G5
Hoa Da, *Vietnam* 65 G7
Hoa Hiep, *Vietnam* 65 G5
Hoai Nhon, *Vietnam* 64 E7
Hoang Lien Son, *Vietnam* 58 F4
Hoanib →, *Namibia* 88 B2
Hoare B., *Canada* 101 B13
Hoarusib →, *Namibia* 88 B2
Hobart, *Australia* 95 G4
Hobart, *U.S.A.* 113 H5
Hobbs, *U.S.A.* 113 J3
Hobbs Coast, *Antarctica* 5 D14
Hobe Sound, *U.S.A.* 115 M5
Hoboken, *U.S.A.* 117 F10
Hobro, *Denmark* 11 H3
Hoburgen, *Sweden* 11 H12
Hocalar, *Turkey* 47 C11
Hochfeld, *Namibia* 88 C2
Hochharz △, *Germany* 24 D6
Hochschwab, *Austria* 26 D8
Höchstadt, *Germany* 25 F6
Hochtaunus ⌓, *Germany* 25 E4
Hockenheim, *Germany* 25 F4
Hodaka-Dake, *Japan* 55 F8
Hodeida = Al Ḩudaydah, *Yemen* 75 E3
Hodgeville, *Canada* 103 C7
Hodgson, *Canada* 103 C9
Hódmezővásárhely, *Hungary* 28 D5
Hodna, Chott el, *Algeria* 78 A6
Hodonín, *Czech Rep.* 27 C10
Hoeamdong, *N. Korea* 57 C16
Hœdic, Î. de, *France* 18 E4
Hoek van Holland, *Neths.* 17 C4
Hoengsŏng, *S. Korea* 57 F14
Hoeryong, *N. Korea* 57 C15
Hoeyang, *N. Korea* 57 E14
Hof, *Germany* 25 E7
Hofgeismar, *Germany* 24 D5
Hofheim, *Germany* 25 E4
Hofmeyr, *S. Africa* 88 E4
Höfn, *Iceland* 8 D6
Hofors, *Sweden* 10 D10
Hofsjökull, *Iceland* 8 D4
Hōfu, *Japan* 55 G5
Hogan Group, *Australia* 95 F4
Höganäs, *Sweden* 11 H6
Hogarth, Mt., *Australia* 94 C2
Hoggar = Ahaggar, *Algeria* 78 D7
Högsäter, *Sweden* 11 F6
Högsby, *Sweden* 11 G10
Högsjö, *Sweden* 10 E9
Hogsty Reef, *Bahamas* 121 B5
Hoh →, *U.S.A.* 110 C2
Hohe Acht, *Germany* 25 E3
Hohe Tauern, *Austria* 26 D5
Hohe Tauern △, *Austria* 26 D5
Hohe Venn, *Belgium* 17 D6
Hohenau, *Austria* 27 C9
Hohenems, *Austria* 26 D2
Hohenloher Ebene, *Germany* 25 F5
Hohenwald, *U.S.A.* 115 H2
Hohenwestedt, *Germany* 24 A5
Hoher Rhön = Rhön, *Germany* 24 E5
Hoher Vogelsberg ⌓, *Germany* 24 D5
Hohes Venn-Eifel ⌓, *Europe* 24 E2
Hohhot, *China* 56 D6
Hóhlakas, *Greece* 49 D9
Hohoe, *Ghana* 83 D5
Hoi An, *Vietnam* 64 E7
Hoi Xuan, *Vietnam* 58 G5
Hoisington, *U.S.A.* 112 F5
Højer, *Denmark* 11 K2
Hōjō, *Japan* 55 H6
Hok, *Sweden* 11 G8
Hökensås, *Sweden* 11 G8
Hökerum, *Sweden* 11 G7
Hokianga Harbour, *N.Z.* 91 F4
Hokitika, *N.Z.* 91 K3
Hokkaidō □, *Japan* 54 C11
Hol-Hol, *Djibouti* 81 E5
Hola Pristan, *Ukraine* 33 J7
Holbæk, *Denmark* 11 J5
Holbrook, *Australia* 95 F4
Holbrook, *U.S.A.* 109 J8
Holden, *U.S.A.* 108 G7
Holdenville, *U.S.A.* 113 H6
Holdrege, *U.S.A.* 112 E5
Holešov, *Czech Rep.* 27 B10
Holetown, *Barbados* 121 g
Holguín, *Cuba* 120 B4
Holíč, *Slovak Rep.* 27 C10
Holice, *Czech Rep.* 26 A8
Höljes, *Sweden* 10 D6
Hollabrunn, *Austria* 26 C9
Hollams Bird I., *Namibia* 88 C1
Holland, *Mich., U.S.A.* 114 D2
Holland, *N.Y., U.S.A.* 116 D6
Hollandale, *U.S.A.* 113 J9
Holley, *U.S.A.* 116 C6
Hollfeld, *Germany* 25 F7
Hollidaysburg, *U.S.A.* 116 F6
Hollis, *U.S.A.* 113 H5
Hollister, *Calif., U.S.A.* 110 J5
Hollister, *Idaho, U.S.A.* 108 E6
Höllviken = Höllviksnäs, *Sweden* 11 J6
Höllviksnäs, *Sweden* 11 J6
Holly Hill, *U.S.A.* 115 L5
Holly Springs, *U.S.A.* 113 H10
Hollywood, *U.S.A.* 115 N5
Holman, *Canada* 100 A8
Hólmavík, *Iceland* 8 D3
Holmen, *U.S.A.* 112 D9
Holmes Reefs, *Australia* 94 B4
Holmsjö, *Sweden* 11 H9
Holmsjön, *Västernorrland, Sweden* 10 B10
Holmsjön, *Västernorrland, Sweden* 10 B9
Holmsland Klit, *Denmark* 11 J2
Holmsund, *Sweden* 8 E19
Holod, *Romania* 28 D7
Holovne, *Ukraine* 31 G11
Holozubyntsi, *Ukraine* 29 B11
Holroyd →, *Australia* 94 A3
Holstebro, *Denmark* 11 H2
Holsteinische Schweiz ⌓, *Germany* 24 A6
Holsworthy, *U.K.* 15 G3
Holton, *Canada* 105 B8
Holton, *U.S.A.* 112 F7
Holtville, *U.S.A.* 111 N11
Holwerd, *Neths.* 17 A5
Holy I., *Angl., U.K.* 14 D3
Holy I., *Northumberland, U.K.* 14 B6
Holyhead, *U.K.* 14 D3
Holyoke, *Colo., U.S.A.* 112 E3
Holyoke, *Mass., U.S.A.* 117 D12
Holyrood, *Canada* 105 C9
Holzkirchen, *Germany* 25 H7
Holzminden, *Germany* 24 D5
Homa Bay, *Kenya* 86 C3
Homalin, *Burma* 67 G19
Homand, *Iran* 71 C8
Homathko →, *Canada* 102 C4
Homberg, *Germany* 24 D5
Hombori, *Mali* 83 B4
Homburg, *Germany* 25 F3
Home B., *Canada* 101 B13
Home Hill, *Australia* 94 B4
Homedale, *U.S.A.* 108 E5
Homer, *Alaska, U.S.A.* 100 C4
Homer, *La., U.S.A.* 113 J8
Homer City, *U.S.A.* 116 F5
Homert ⌓, *Germany* 24 D4
Homestead, *Australia* 94 C4
Homestead, *U.S.A.* 115 N5
Homestead ⌓, *U.S.A.* 112 E6
Homewood, *U.S.A.* 110 F6
Homoine, *Mozam.* 89 C6
Homoljske Planina, *Serbia & M.* 44 B5
Homorod, *Romania* 29 D10
Homs = Ḩimş, *Syria* 74 A5
Homyel, *Belarus* 33 F6
Hon Chong, *Vietnam* 65 G5
Hon Me, *Vietnam* 64 C5
Honan = Henan □, *China* 56 H8
Honaz, *Turkey* 47 D11
Honbetsu, *Japan* 54 C11
Honcut, *U.S.A.* 110 F5
Honda Bay, *Phil.* 61 G3
Hondarribia, *Spain* 38 B3
Hondeklipbaai, *S. Africa* 88 E2
Hondo, *Japan* 55 H5
Hondo, *U.S.A.* 113 L5
Hondo, Rio →, *Belize* 119 D7
Honduras ■, *Cent. Amer.* 120 D2
Honduras, G. de, *Caribbean* 120 C2
Hønefoss, *Norway* 9 F14
Honesdale, *U.S.A.* 117 E9
Honey L., *U.S.A.* 110 E6
Honfleur, *France* 18 C7
Høng, *Denmark* 11 J5
Hong →, *Vietnam* 58 F5
Hong Gai, *Vietnam* 58 G6
Hong He →, *China* 56 H8
Hong Hu, *China* 59 C9
Hong Kong □, *China* 59 F10
Hong'an, *China* 59 B10
Hongch'ŏn, *S. Korea* 57 F14
Honghai Wan, *China* 59 F10
Honghe, *China* 58 F4
Honghu, *China* 59 C9
Hongjiang, *China* 58 D7
Hongliu He →, *China* 56 F5
Hongor, *Mongolia* 56 B7
Hongsa, *Laos* 64 C3
Hongshui He →, *China* 58 F7
Hongsŏng, *S. Korea* 57 F14
Hongtong, *China* 56 F6
Honguedo, Détroit d', *Canada* 105 C7
Hongwon, *N. Korea* 57 E14
Hongya, *China* 58 C4
Hongyuan, *China* 58 A4
Hongze Hu, *China* 57 H10
Honiara, *Solomon Is.* 96 H7
Honiton, *U.K.* 15 G4
Honjō, *Japan* 54 E10
Honkorâb, Ras, *Egypt* 80 C4
Honningsvåg, *Norway* 8 A21
Hönö, *Sweden* 11 G5
Honolulu, *U.S.A.* 106 H16
Hontoria del Pinar, *Spain* 38 D1
Hood, Mt., *U.S.A.* 108 D3
Hood, Pt., *Australia* 93 F2
Hood River, *U.S.A.* 108 D3
Hoodsport, *U.S.A.* 110 C3
Hooge, *Germany* 24 A4
Hoogeveen, *Neths.* 17 B6
Hoogezand-Sappemeer, *Neths.* 17 A6
Hooghly = Hugli →, *India* 69 J13
Hooghly-Chinsura = Chunchura, *India* 69 H13
Hook Hd., *Ireland* 12 D5
Hook I., *Australia* 94 J6
Hook of Holland = Hoek van Holland, *Neths.* 17 C4
Hooker, *U.S.A.* 113 G4
Hooker Creek, *Australia* 92 C5
Hoonah, *U.S.A.* 102 B1
Hooper Bay, *U.S.A.* 100 B3
Hoopeston, *U.S.A.* 114 E2
Hoopstad, *S. Africa* 88 D4
Höör, *Sweden* 11 J7
Hoorn, *Neths.* 17 B5
Hoover, *U.S.A.* 115 J2
Hoover Dam, *U.S.A.* 111 K12
Hooversville, *U.S.A.* 116 F6
Hop Bottom, *U.S.A.* 117 E9
Hopa, *Turkey* 73 B9
Hope, *Canada* 102 D4
Hope, *Ariz., U.S.A.* 111 M13
Hope, *Ark., U.S.A.* 113 J8
Hope, L., *S. Austral., Australia* 95 D2
Hope, L., *W. Austral., Australia* 93 F3
Hope, Pt., *U.S.A.* 4 C17
Hope I., *Canada* 116 B4
Hope Town, *Bahamas* 120 A4
Hopedale, *Canada* 105 A7
Hopedale, *U.S.A.* 117 D13
Hopefield, *S. Africa* 88 E2
Hopei = Hebei □, *China* 56 E9
Hopelchén, *Mexico* 119 D7
Hopetoun, *Vic., Australia* 95 F3
Hopetoun, *W. Austral., Australia* 93 F3
Hopetown, *S. Africa* 88 D3
Hopevale, *Australia* 94 B4
Hopewell, *U.S.A.* 114 G7
Hopfgarten, *Austria* 26 D5
Hopkins, L., *Australia* 92 D4
Hopkinsville, *U.S.A.* 115 G2
Hopland, *U.S.A.* 110 G3
Hoquiam, *U.S.A.* 110 D3
Hora Hoverla, *Ukraine* 29 B9
Horasan, *Turkey* 73 B10
Horažďovice, *Czech Rep.* 26 B6
Horb, *Germany* 25 G4
Hörby, *Sweden* 11 J7
Horcajo de Santiago, *Spain* 38 F1
Horden Hills, *Australia* 92 D5
Horezu, *Romania* 29 E8
Horgen, *Switz.* 25 H4
Horgoš, *Serbia & M.* 28 D4
Hořice, *Czech Rep.* 26 A8
Horinchove, *Ukraine* 29 B8
Horinger, *China* 56 D6

Horki, *Belarus* 32 E6
Horlick Mts., *Antarctica* 5 E15
Horlivka, *Ukraine* 33 H10
Hormak, *Iran* 71 D9
Hormoz, *Iran* 71 E7
Hormoz, Jaz.-ye, *Iran* 71 E8
Hormozgān □, *Iran* 71 E8
Hormuz, Kūh-e, *Iran* 71 E7
Hormuz, Str. of, *The Gulf* 71 E8
Horn, *Austria* 26 C8
Horn, *Iceland* 8 C2
Horn, *Sweden* 11 G9
Horn →, *Canada* 102 A5
Horn, Cape = Hornos, C. de, *Chile* 128 H3
Horn Head, *Ireland* 12 A3
Horn I., *Australia* 94 A3
Horn Plateau, *Canada* 102 A5
Hornachuelos, *Spain* 37 H5
Hornavan, *Sweden* 8 C17
Hornbeck, *U.S.A.* 113 K8
Hornbrook, *U.S.A.* 108 F2
Hornburg, *Germany* 24 C6
Horncastle, *U.K.* 14 D7
Horndal, *Sweden* 10 D10
Hornell, *U.S.A.* 116 D7
Hornell L., *Canada* 102 A5
Hornepayne, *Canada* 104 C3
Horní Planá, *Czech Rep.* 26 C7
Hornings Mills, *Canada* 116 B4
Hornitos, *U.S.A.* 110 H6
Hornos, C. de, *Chile* 128 H3
Hornoy-le-Bourg, *France* 19 C8
Hornsea, *U.K.* 14 D7
Hornslandet, *Sweden* 10 C11
Hörnum, *Germany* 24 A4
Horobetsu = Noboribetsu, *Japan* 54 C10
Horodenka, *Ukraine* 29 B10
Horodnya, *Ukraine* 33 G6
Horodok, *Khmelnytskyy, Ukraine* 33 H4
Horodok, *Lviv, Ukraine* 33 H2
Horodyshche, *Ukraine* 33 H6
Horokhiv, *Ukraine* 33 G3
Horovice, *Czech Rep.* 26 B6
Horqin Youyi Qianqi, *China* 57 A12
Horqueta, *Paraguay* 126 A4
Horred, *Sweden* 11 G6
Horse Creek, *U.S.A.* 112 E3
Horse I., *Canada* 103 C9
Horse Is., *Canada* 105 B8
Horsefly L., *Canada* 102 C4
Horseheads, *U.S.A.* 116 D8
Horsens, *Denmark* 11 J3
Horsham, *Australia* 95 F3
Horsham, *U.K.* 15 F7
Horšovský Týn, *Czech Rep.* 26 B5
Horten, *Norway* 9 G14
Hortobágy →, *Hungary* 28 C6
Hortobágyi △, *Hungary* 28 C6
Horton, *U.S.A.* 112 F7
Horton →, *Canada* 100 B7
Horwood L., *Canada* 104 C3
Hosaina, *Ethiopia* 81 F4
Hose, Gunung-Gunung, *Malaysia* 62 D4
Ḩoseynābād, *Khuzestān, Iran* 71 C6
Ḩoseynābād, *Kordestān, Iran* 70 C5
Hoshangabad, *India* 68 H7
Hoshiarpur, *India* 68 D6
Hospet, *India* 66 M10
Hoste, I., *Chile* 128 H3
Hostens, *France* 20 D3
Hot, *Thailand* 64 C2
Hot Creek Range, *U.S.A.* 108 G6
Hot Springs, *Ark., U.S.A.* 113 H8
Hot Springs, *S. Dak., U.S.A.* 112 D3
Hot Springs △, *U.S.A.* 113 H8
Hotagen, *Sweden* 8 E16
Hotan, *China* 60 C2
Hotazel, *S. Africa* 88 D3
Hotchkiss, *U.S.A.* 109 G10
Hotham, C., *Australia* 92 B5
Hoting, *Sweden* 8 D17
Hotolisht, *Albania* 44 E4
Hotte, Massif de la, *Haiti* 121 C5
Hottentotsbaai, *Namibia* 88 D1
Houat, Î. de, *France* 18 E4
Houdan, *France* 19 D8
Houei Sai, *Laos* 58 G3
Houeillès, *France* 20 D4
Houffalize, *Belgium* 17 D5
Houghton, *Mich., U.S.A.* 112 B10
Houghton, *N.Y., U.S.A.* 116 D6
Houghton L., *U.S.A.* 114 C3
Houghton-le-Spring, *U.K.* 14 C6
Houhora Heads, *N.Z.* 91 F4
Houlton, *U.S.A.* 115 B12
Houma, *U.S.A.* 113 L9
Houndé, *Burkina Faso* 82 C4
Hourtin, *France* 20 C2
Hourtin-Carcans, Étang d', *France* 20 C2
Housatonic →, *U.S.A.* 117 E11
Houston, *Canada* 102 C3
Houston, *Mo., U.S.A.* 113 G9
Houston, *Tex., U.S.A.* 113 L7
Hout →, *S. Africa* 89 C4
Houtkraal, *S. Africa* 88 E3
Houtman Abrolhos, *Australia* 93 E1
Hovd, *Mongolia* 60 B4
Hove, *U.K.* 15 G7
Hovenweep ⌓, *U.S.A.* 109 H9
Hoveyzeh, *Iran* 71 D6
Hovmantorp, *Sweden* 11 H9
Hövsgöl, *Mongolia* 56 C5
Hövsgöl Nuur, *Mongolia* 60 A5
Hovsta, *Sweden* 10 E9
Howakil, *Eritrea* 81 D5
Howar, Wadi →, *Sudan* 81 D2
Howard, *Australia* 95 D5
Howard, *Pa., U.S.A.* 116 F7
Howard, *S. Dak., U.S.A.* 112 C6
Howe, *U.S.A.* 108 E7
Howe, C., *Australia* 95 F5
Howe I., *Canada* 117 B8
Howell, *U.S.A.* 114 D4
Howick, *Canada* 117 A11
Howick, *S. Africa* 89 D5
Howick Group, *Australia* 94 A4
Howitt, L., *Australia* 95 D2
Howland I., *Pac. Oc.* 96 G10
Howrah = Haora, *India* 69 H13
Howth Hd., *Ireland* 12 C5
Höxter, *Germany* 24 D5
Hoy, *U.K.* 13 C5
Hoya, *Germany* 24 C5
Høyanger, *Norway* 9 F12
Hoyerswerda, *Germany* 24 D10
Hoylake, *U.K.* 14 D4
Hoyos, *Spain* 36 E4
Hpa-an = Pa-an, *Burma* 67 L20
Hpungan Pass, *Burma* 67 F20
Hradec Králové, *Czech Rep.* 26 A8
Hrádek, *Czech Rep.* 27 C9
Hranice, *Czech Rep.* 27 B10
Hrazdan, *Armenia* 35 K7
Hrebenka, *Ukraine* 33 G7
Hrodna, *Belarus* 30 E10
Hrodzyanka, *Belarus* 32 F5
Hron →, *Slovak Rep.* 27 D11
Hrubieszów, *Poland* 31 H10
Hrubý Jeseník, *Czech Rep.* 27 A10
Hrvatska = Croatia ■, *Europe* 41 C13
Hrymayliv, *Ukraine* 33 H4
Hrynyava, *Ukraine* 29 C9
Hsenwi, *Burma* 67 H20
Hsiamen = Xiamen, *China* 59 E12
Hsian = Xi'an, *China* 56 G5
Hsinchu, *Taiwan* 59 E13
Hsinhailien = Lianyungang, *China* 57 G10
Hsinying, *Taiwan* 59 F13
Hsopket, *Burma* 58 F2
Hsüchou = Xuzhou, *China* 57 G9
Hu Xian, *China* 56 G5
Hua Hin, *Thailand* 64 F2
Hua Xian, *Henan, China* 56 G8
Hua Xian, *Shaanxi, China* 56 G5
Hua'an, *China* 59 E11
Huab →, *Namibia* 88 B2
Huacheng, *China* 59 E10
Huachinera, *Mexico* 118 A3
Huacho, *Peru* 124 F3
Huade, *China* 56 D7
Huadian, *China* 57 C14
Huadu, *China* 59 F9
Huai Had △, *Thailand* 64 D5
Huai He →, *China* 59 A12
Huai Nam Dang △, *Thailand* 64 C2
Huai Yot, *Thailand* 65 J2
Huai'an, *Hebei, China* 56 D8
Huai'an, *Jiangsu, China* 57 H10
Huaibei, *China* 56 G9
Huaibin, *China* 59 A10
Huaide = Gongzhuling, *China* 57 C13
Huaidezhen, *China* 57 C13
Huaihua, *China* 58 D7
Huaiji, *China* 59 F9
Huainan, *China* 59 A11
Huaining, *China* 59 B11
Huairen, *China* 56 E7
Huairou, *China* 56 D9
Huaiyang, *China* 56 H8
Huaiyin, *China* 57 H10
Huaiyuan, *Anhui, China* 57 H9
Huaiyuan, *Guangxi Zhuangzu, China* 58 E7
Huajianzi, *China* 57 D13
Huajuapan de Leon, *Mexico* 119 D5
Hualapai Peak, *U.S.A.* 109 J7
Hualien, *Taiwan* 59 E13
Huallaga →, *Peru* 124 E3
Huambo, *Angola* 85 G3
Huan Jiang →, *China* 56 G5
Huan Xian, *China* 56 F4
Huancabamba, *Peru* 124 E3
Huancane, *Peru* 124 G5
Huancavelica, *Peru* 124 F3
Huancayo, *Peru* 124 F3
Huanchaca, *Bolivia* 124 H5
Huang Hai = Yellow Sea, *China* 57 G12
Huang He →, *China* 57 F10
Huang Xian, *China* 57 F11
Huangchuan, *China* 59 A10
Huanggang, *China* 59 B10
Huangguoshu, *China* 58 E5
Huangling, *China* 56 G5
Huanglong, *China* 56 G5
Huanglongtan, *China* 59 A8
Huangmei, *China* 59 B10
Huangpi, *China* 59 B10
Huangping, *China* 58 D6
Huangshan, *China* 59 C12
Huangshi, *China* 59 B10
Huangsongdian, *China* 57 C14
Huangyan, *China* 59 C13
Huangyangsi, *China* 59 D8
Huaning, *China* 58 E4
Huanjiang, *China* 58 E7
Huantai, *China* 57 F9
Huánuco, *Peru* 124 E3
Huaping, *China* 58 D3
Huaraz, *Peru* 124 E3
Huarmey, *Peru* 124 F3
Huarong, *China* 59 C9
Huascarán, *Peru* 124 E3
Huasco, *Chile* 126 B1
Huasco →, *Chile* 126 B1
Huasna, *U.S.A.* 111 K6
Huatabampo, *Mexico* 118 B3
Huauchinango, *Mexico* 119 C5
Huautla de Jiménez, *Mexico* 119 D5
Huaxi, *China* 58 D6
Huay Namota, *Mexico* 118 C4
Huayin, *China* 56 G6
Huayuan, *China* 58 C7
Huayun, *China* 58 B6
Huazhou, *China* 59 G8
Hubbard, *Ohio, U.S.A.* 116 E4
Hubbard, *Tex., U.S.A.* 113 K6
Hubbart Pt., *Canada* 103 B10
Hubei □, *China* 59 B9
Hubli, *India* 66 M9
Huch'ang, *N. Korea* 57 D14
Hucknall, *U.K.* 14 D6
Huddersfield, *U.K.* 14 D6
Hude, *Germany* 24 B4
Hudi, *Sudan* 80 D3
Hudiksvall, *Sweden* 10 C11
Hudson, *Canada* 104 B1
Hudson, *Mass., U.S.A.* 117 D13
Hudson, *N.Y., U.S.A.* 117 D11
Hudson, *Wis., U.S.A.* 112 C8
Hudson, *Wyo., U.S.A.* 108 E9
Hudson →, *U.S.A.* 117 F10
Hudson Bay, *Nunavut, Canada* 101 C11
Hudson Bay, *Sask., Canada* 103 C8
Hudson Falls, *U.S.A.* 117 C11
Hudson Mts., *Antarctica* 5 D16
Hudson Str., *Canada* 101 B13
Hudson's Hope, *Canada* 102 B4
Hue, *Vietnam* 64 D6
Huebra →, *Spain* 36 D4
Huedin, *Romania* 28 D8
Huehuetenango, *Guatemala* 120 C1
Huejúcar, *Mexico* 118 C4
Huélamo, *Spain* 38 E3
Huelgoat, *France* 18 D3
Huelma, *Spain* 37 H7
Huelva, *Spain* 37 H4
Huelva □, *Spain* 37 H4
Huelva →, *Spain* 37 H5
Huentelauquén, *Chile* 126 C1
Huércal-Overa, *Spain* 39 H3
Huerta, Sa. de la, *Argentina* 126 C2
Huertas, C. de las, *Spain* 39 G4
Huerva →, *Spain* 38 D4
Huesca, *Spain* 38 C4
Huesca □, *Spain* 38 C5
Huéscar, *Spain* 39 H2
Huetamo, *Mexico* 118 D4
Huete, *Spain* 38 E2
Hugh →, *Australia* 94 D1
Hughenden, *Australia* 94 C3
Hughes, *Australia* 93 F4
Hughesville, *U.S.A.* 117 E8
Hugli →, *India* 69 J13
Hugo, *Colo., U.S.A.* 112 F3
Hugo, *Okla., U.S.A.* 113 H7
Hugoton, *U.S.A.* 113 G4
Hui Xian = Huixian, *China* 56 G7
Hui Xian, *China* 56 H4
Hui'an, *China* 59 E12
Hui'anbu, *China* 56 F4
Huichang, *China* 59 E10
Huichapán, *Mexico* 119 C5
Huidong, *Guangdong, China* 59 F10
Huidong, *Sichuan, China* 58 D4
Huifa He →, *China* 57 C14
Huila, Nevado del, *Colombia* 124 C3
Huilai, *China* 59 F11
Huili, *China* 58 D4
Huimin, *China* 57 F9
Huinan, *China* 57 C14
Huinca Renancó, *Argentina* 126 C3
Huining, *China* 56 G3
Huinong, *China* 56 E4
Huisache, *Mexico* 118 C4
Huishui, *China* 58 D6
Huisne →, *France* 18 E7
Huiting, *China* 56 G9
Huitong, *China* 58 D7
Huixian, *China* 56 G7
Huixtla, *Mexico* 119 D6
Huize, *China* 58 D4
Huizhou, *China* 59 F10
Hukawng Valley, *Burma* 67 F20
Hukou, *China* 59 C11
Hŭksan-chedo, *S. Korea* 57 G13
Hukuntsi, *Botswana* 88 C3
Ḩulayfā', *Si. Arabia* 70 E4
Hulin He →, *China* 57 B12
Hull = Kingston upon Hull, *U.K.* 14 D7
Hull, *Canada* 117 A9
Hull →, *U.K.* 14 D7
Hulst, *Neths.* 17 C4
Hultsfred, *Sweden* 11 G9
Hulun Nur, *China* 60 B6
Hulyaypole, *Ukraine* 33 J9
Huma, Tanjung, *Malaysia* 65 c
Humacao, *Puerto Rico* 121 d
Humahuaca, *Argentina* 126 A2
Humaitá, *Brazil* 124 E6
Humaitá, *Paraguay* 126 B4
Humansdorp, *S. Africa* 88 E3
Humara, J., *Sudan* 81 D3
Humbe, *Angola* 88 B1
Humber →, *U.K.* 14 D7
Humboldt, *Canada* 103 C7
Humboldt, *Iowa, U.S.A.* 112 D7
Humboldt, *Tenn., U.S.A.* 113 H10
Humboldt →, *U.S.A.* 108 F4
Humboldt Gletscher = Sermersuaq, *Greenland* 4 B4
Hume, *U.S.A.* 110 J8
Hume, L., *Australia* 95 F4
Humenné, *Slovak Rep.* 27 C14
Hummelsta, *Sweden* 10 E10
Humphreys, Mt., *U.S.A.* 110 H8
Humphreys Peak, *U.S.A.* 109 J8
Humpolec, *Czech Rep.* 26 B8
Humptulips, *U.S.A.* 110 C3
Hūn, *Libya* 79 C9
Hun Jiang →, *China* 57 D13
Húnaflói, *Iceland* 8 D3
Hunan □, *China* 59 D9
Hunchun, *China* 57 C16
Hundested, *Denmark* 11 J5
Hundewali, *Pakistan* 68 D5
Hundred Mile House, *Canada* 102 C4
Hunedoara, *Romania* 28 E7
Hunedoara □, *Romania* 28 E7
Hünfeld, *Germany* 24 E5
Hung Yen, *Vietnam* 58 G6
Hungary ■, *Europe* 27 D12
Hungary, Plain of, *Europe* 6 F10
Hungerford, *Australia* 95 D3
Hŭngnam, *N. Korea* 57 E14
Hungt'ou Hsü, *Taiwan* 59 G13
Huni Valley, *Ghana* 82 D4
Hunneberg, *Sweden* 11 F6
Hunnebostrand, *Sweden* 11 F5
Hunsberge, *Namibia* 88 D2
Hunsrück, *Germany* 25 F3
Hunstanton, *U.K.* 14 E8
Hunte →, *Germany* 24 B4
Hunter, *U.S.A.* 117 D10
Hunter I., *Australia* 95 G3
Hunter I., *Canada* 102 C3
Hunter Ra., *Australia* 95 E5
Hunters Road, *Zimbabwe* 87 F2
Hunterville, *N.Z.* 91 H5
Huntingburg, *U.S.A.* 114 F2
Huntingdon, *Canada* 104 C5
Huntingdon, *U.K.* 15 E7
Huntingdon, *U.S.A.* 116 F6
Huntington, *Ind., U.S.A.* 114 E3
Huntington, *N.Y., U.S.A.* 117 F11
Huntington, *Oreg., U.S.A.* 108 D5
Huntington, *Utah, U.S.A.* 108 G8
Huntington, *W. Va., U.S.A.* 114 F4
Huntington Beach, *U.S.A.* 111 M9
Huntly, *N.Z.* 91 G5
Huntly, *U.K.* 13 D6
Huntsville, *Canada* 116 A5
Huntsville, *Ala., U.S.A.* 115 H2
Huntsville, *Tex., U.S.A.* 113 K7
Hunyani →, *Zimbabwe* 87 F3
Hunyuan, *China* 56 E7
Hunza →, *India* 69 B6
Huo Xian = Huozhou, *China* 56 F6
Huong Khe, *Vietnam* 64 C5
Huonville, *Australia* 95 G4
Huoqiu, *China* 59 A11
Huoshan, *Anhui, China* 59 A12
Huoshan, *Anhui, China* 59 B11
Huoshao Dao = Lü-Tao, *Taiwan* 59 F13
Huozhou, *China* 56 F6
Hupeh = Hubei □, *China* 59 B9
Ḩūr, *Iran* 71 D8
Hurbanovo, *Slovak Rep.* 27 D11
Hurd, C., *Canada* 116 A3
Hure Qi, *China* 57 C11
Hurezani, *Romania* 29 F8
Hurghada, *Egypt* 80 B3
Hurley, *N. Mex., U.S.A.* 109 K9
Hurley, *Wis., U.S.A.* 112 B9
Huron, *Calif., U.S.A.* 110 J6
Huron, *Ohio, U.S.A.* 116 E2
Huron, *S. Dak., U.S.A.* 112 C5
Huron, L., *U.S.A.* 116 B2
Huron East, *Canada* 116 C3
Hurricane, *U.S.A.* 109 H7
Hurso, *Ethiopia* 81 F5
Hurungwe ⌓, *Zimbabwe* 87 F2
Hurunui →, *N.Z.* 91 K4
Hurup, *Denmark* 11 H2
Húsavík, *Iceland* 8 C5
Huşi, *Romania* 29 D13
Huskvarna, *Sweden* 11 G8
Hustadvika, *Norway* 8 E12
Hustontown, *U.S.A.* 116 F6
Hustopeče, *Czech Rep.* 27 C9
Husum, *Germany* 24 A5
Husum, *Sweden* 10 A13
Hutchinson, *Kans., U.S.A.* 113 F6
Hutchinson, *Minn., U.S.A.* 112 C7
Hutte Sauvage, L. de la, *Canada* 105 A7
Hüttenberg, *Austria* 26 E7
Hüttener Berge ⌓, *Germany* 24 A5
Hutton, Mt., *Australia* 95 D4
Huwun, *Ethiopia* 81 G5
Huy, *Belgium* 17 D5
Huzhou, *China* 59 B13
Hvalpsund, *Denmark* 11 H3
Hvammstangi, *Iceland* 8 D3
Hvar, *Croatia* 41 E13
Hvarski Kanal, *Croatia* 41 E13
Hvítá →, *Iceland* 8 D3
Hvizdets, *Ukraine* 29 B10
Hwachŏn-chŏsuji, *S. Korea* 57 E14
Hwang Ho = Huang He →, *China* 57 F10
Hwange, *Zimbabwe* 87 F2
Hwange △, *Zimbabwe* 88 B4
Hyannis, *Mass., U.S.A.* 114 E10
Hyannis, *Nebr., U.S.A.* 112 E4
Hyargas Nuur, *Mongolia* 60 B4
Hybo, *Sweden* 10 C10
Hydaburg, *U.S.A.* 102 B2
Hyde Park, *U.S.A.* 117 E11
Hyden, *Australia* 93 F2
Hyder, *U.S.A.* 102 B2
Hyderabad, *India* 66 L11
Hyderabad, *Pakistan* 68 G3
Hyères, *France* 21 E10
Hyères, Îs. d', *France* 21 F10
Hyesan, *N. Korea* 57 D15
Hyland →, *Canada* 102 B3
Hyltebruk, *Sweden* 11 H7
Hymia, *India* 69 C8
Hyndman Peak, *U.S.A.* 108 E6
Hyōgo □, *Japan* 55 G7
Hyrum, *U.S.A.* 108 F8
Hysham, *U.S.A.* 108 C10
Hythe, *U.K.* 15 F9
Hyūga, *Japan* 55 H5
Hyvinge = Hyvinkää, *Finland* 9 F21
Hyvinkää, *Finland* 9 F21

I

I-n-Gall, *Niger* 83 B6
I-n-Oudad, *Algeria* 83 A5
I-n-Ouzzal, *Algeria* 83 A5
I-n-Tadreft, *Niger* 83 B6
Iablaniţa, *Romania* 28 F7
Iaco →, *Brazil* 124 E5
Iacobeni, *Romania* 29 C10
Iakora, *Madag.* 89 C8
Ialomiţa □, *Romania* 29 F12
Ialomiţa →, *Romania* 29 F12
Ialoveni, *Moldova* 29 D13
Ialpug →, *Moldova* 29 E13
Ianca, *Romania* 29 E12
Iara, *Romania* 29 D8
Iarda, *Ethiopia* 81 E4
Iargara, *Moldova* 29 D13
Iaşi, *Romania* 29 C12
Iaşi □, *Romania* 29 C12
Íasmos, *Greece* 45 E9
Ib →, *India* 69 J10
Iba, *Phil.* 61 D3
Ibadan, *Nigeria* 83 D5
Ibagué, *Colombia* 124 C3
Iballë, *Albania* 44 D4
Ibăneşti, *Botoşani, Romania* 29 B11
Ibăneşti, *Mureş, Romania* 29 D9
Ibar →, *Serbia & M.* 44 C4
Ibaraki □, *Japan* 55 F10
Ibarra, *Ecuador* 124 C3
Ibba, *Sudan* 81 G2
Ibba, Bahr el →, *Sudan* 81 F2
Ibbenbüren, *Germany* 24 C3
Ibembo, *Dem. Rep. of the Congo* 86 B1
Ibera, L., *Argentina* 126 B4
Iberian Peninsula, *Europe* 6 H5
Iberville, *Canada* 117 A11
Iberville, Lac d', *Canada* 104 A5
Ibi, *Nigeria* 83 D6
Ibi, *Spain* 39 G4
Ibiá, *Brazil* 125 G9
Ibiapaba, Sa. da, *Brazil* 125 D10
Ibicuí →, *Brazil* 127 B4
Ibicuy, *Argentina* 126 C4
Ibiza = Eivissa, *Spain* 48 C7
Ibiza ✕ (IBZ), *Spain* 39 G6
Íblei, Monti, *Italy* 43 E7
Ibo, *Mozam.* 87 E5
Ibonma, *Indonesia* 63 E8
Ibotirama, *Brazil* 125 F10
Ibrāhīm →, *Lebanon* 74 A4
'Ibrī, *Oman* 71 F8
Ibriktepe, *Turkey* 45 E10
Ibshawâi, *Egypt* 80 J7
Ibu, *Indonesia* 63 D7
Ibusuki, *Japan* 55 J5
Ica, *Peru* 124 F3
Iça →, *Brazil* 124 D5
Icacos Pt., *Trin. & Tob.* 125 K15
Içana, *Brazil* 124 C5
Içana →, *Brazil* 124 C5
İçel = Mersin, *Turkey* 70 B2
Iceland ■, *Europe* 8 D4
Iceland Plateau, *Arctic* 4 C7
Ich'ang = Yichang, *China* 59 B8
Ichchapuram, *India* 67 K14
Ichhawar, *India* 68 H7
Ichihara, *Japan* 55 G10
Ichikawa, *Japan* 55 G9
Ichilo →, *Bolivia* 124 G6
Ichinohe, *Japan* 54 D10
Ichinomiya, *Japan* 55 G8
Ichinoseki, *Japan* 54 E10
Ichnya, *Ukraine* 33 G7
Icod, *Canary Is.* 48 F3
Ida Grove, *U.S.A.* 112 D7
Idabel, *U.S.A.* 113 J7
Idaga Hamus, *Ethiopia* 81 E4
Idah, *Nigeria* 83 D6
Idaho □, *U.S.A.* 108 D7
Idaho City, *U.S.A.* 108 E6
Idaho Falls, *U.S.A.* 108 E7
Idalia △, *Australia* 94 C3
Idanha-a-Nova, *Portugal* 36 F3
Idar-Oberstein, *Germany* 25 F3
Idensalmi = Iisalmi, *Finland* 8 E22
Idfû, *Egypt* 80 C3
Ídhi Óros, *Greece* 49 D6
Ídhra, *Greece* 46 D5
Idi, *Indonesia* 62 C1
Idiofa, *Dem. Rep. of the Congo* 84 E3
Idkerberget, *Sweden* 10 D9
Idku, Bahra el, *Egypt* 80 H7
Idlib, *Syria* 70 C3
Idre, *Sweden* 10 C6
Idria, *U.S.A.* 110 J6
Idrija, *Slovenia* 41 C11
Idritsa, *Russia* 32 D5
Idutywa, *S. Africa* 89 E4
Ieper, *Belgium* 17 D2
Ierápetra, *Greece* 49 E7
Ierissós, *Greece* 44 F7
Ierissóu Kólpos, *Greece* 44 F7
Iernut, *Romania* 29 D9
Iesi, *Italy* 41 E10
Iésolo, *Italy* 41 C9
Ifach, Peñón de, *Spain* 39 G5
Ifakara, *Tanzania* 84 F7
'Ifāl, W. al →, *Si. Arabia* 70 D2
Ifanadiana, *Madag.* 89 C8
Ife, *Nigeria* 83 D5
Iférouâne, *Niger* 83 B6
Iffley, *Australia* 94 B3
Ifon, *Nigeria* 83 D6
Iforas, Adrar des, *Africa* 83 B5
Ifould, L., *Australia* 93 F5
Iganga, *Uganda* 86 B3
Igarapava, *Brazil* 125 H9
Igarka, *Russia* 52 C9

Igatimi, *Paraguay* **127 A4**
Igbetti, *Nigeria* **83 D5**
Igbo-Ora, *Nigeria* **83 D5**
Igboho, *Nigeria* **83 D5**
Igbor, *Nigeria* **83 D6**
Iğdır, *Turkey* **73 C11**
Igelfors, *Sweden* **11 F9**
Iggesund, *Sweden* **10 C11**
Iglésias, *Italy* **42 C1**
Igloolik, *Canada* **101 B11**
Igluligaarjuk = Chesterfield Inlet, *Canada* **100 B10**
Iglulik = Igloolik, *Canada* **101 B11**
'Igma, Gebel el, *Egypt* **80 B3**
Ignace, *Canada* **104 C1**
İğneada, *Turkey* **45 E11**
İğneada Burnu, *Turkey* **45 E12**
Igoumenítsa, *Greece* **46 B2**
Igra, *Russia* **34 B11**
Iguaçu △, *Brazil* **127 B5**
Iguaçu →, *Brazil* **127 B5**
Iguaçu, Cat. del, *Brazil* **127 B5**
Iguaçu Falls = Iguaçu, Cat. del, *Brazil* **127 B5**
Iguala, *Mexico* **119 D5**
Igualada, *Spain* **38 D6**
Iguassu = Iguaçu →, *Brazil* **127 B5**
Iguatu, *Brazil* **125 E11**
Iguazú △, *Argentina* **127 B5**
Iguidi, Erg, *Africa* **78 C4**
Iharana, *Madag.* **89 A9**
Ihbulag, *Mongolia* **56 C4**
Iheya-Shima, *Japan* **55 L3**
Ihiala, *Nigeria* **83 D6**
Ihosy, *Madag.* **89 C8**
Ihotry, Farihy, *Madag.* **89 C7**
Ihugh, *Nigeria* **83 D6**
Ii, *Finland* **8 D21**
Ii-Shima, *Japan* **55 L3**
Iida, *Japan* **55 G8**
Iijoki →, *Finland* **8 D21**
Iisalmi, *Finland* **8 E22**
Iiyama, *Japan* **55 F9**
Iizuka, *Japan* **55 H5**
Ijebu-Igbo, *Nigeria* **83 D5**
Ijebu-Ode, *Nigeria* **83 D5**
IJmuiden, *Neths.* **17 B4**
Ijo älv = Iijoki →, *Finland* **8 D21**
IJssel →, *Neths.* **17 B5**
IJsselmeer, *Neths.* **17 B5**
Ijuí, *Brazil* **127 B5**
Ijuí →, *Brazil* **127 B4**
Ikalamavony, *Madag.* **89 C8**
Ikale, *Nigeria* **83 D6**
Ikaluktutiak, *Canada* **100 B9**
Ikang, *Nigeria* **83 E6**
Ikara, *Nigeria* **83 C6**
Ikare, *Nigeria* **83 D6**
Ikaría, *Greece* **47 D8**
Ikast, *Denmark* **11 H3**
Ikeda, *Japan* **55 G6**
Ikeja, *Nigeria* **83 D5**
Ikela, *Dem. Rep. of the Congo* **84 E4**
Ikerre-Ekiti, *Nigeria* **83 D6**
Ikhtiman, *Bulgaria* **44 D7**
Iki, *Japan* **55 H4**
Ikimba L., *Tanzania* **86 C3**
Ikire, *Nigeria* **83 D5**
Ikizdere, *Turkey* **73 B9**
Ikom, *Nigeria* **83 D6**
Ikongo, *Madag.* **89 C8**
Ikopa →, *Madag.* **89 B8**
Ikorongo ⌓, *Tanzania* **86 C3**
Ikot Ekpene, *Nigeria* **83 D6**
Ikparjuk = Arctic Bay, *Canada* **101 A11**
Ikungu, *Tanzania* **86 C3**
Ikurun, *Nigeria* **83 D5**
Ila, *Nigeria* **83 D5**
Ilagan, *Phil.* **61 C4**
Ilaka, *Madag.* **89 B8**
Īlām, *Iran* **70 C5**
Ilam, *Nepal* **69 F12**
Īlām □, *Iran* **70 C5**
Ilan, *Taiwan* **59 E13**
Ilanskiy, *Russia* **53 D10**
Ilaro, *Nigeria* **83 D5**
Ilatane, *Niger* **83 B5**
Iława, *Poland* **30 E6**
Ile →, *Kazakhstan* **52 E8**
Île-à-la-Crosse, *Canada* **103 B7**
Île-à-la-Crosse, Lac, *Canada* **103 B7**
Île-de-France □, *France* **19 D9**
Ileanda, *Romania* **29 C8**
Ilebo, *Dem. Rep. of the Congo* **84 E4**
Ilek, *Russia* **52 D6**
Ilero, *Nigeria* **83 D5**
Ilesha, *Kwara, Nigeria* **83 D5**
Ilesha, *Oyo, Nigeria* **83 D5**
Ilford, *Canada* **103 B9**
Ilfracombe, *Australia* **94 C3**
Ilfracombe, *U.K.* **15 F3**
Ilgaz, *Turkey* **72 B5**
Ilgaz Dağları, *Turkey* **72 B5**
Ilgın, *Turkey* **72 C4**
Ilha de Moçambique, *Mozam.* **87 F5**
Ílhavo, *Portugal* **36 E2**
Ilhéus, *Brazil* **125 F11**
Ili = Ile →, *Kazakhstan* **52 E8**
Ilia, *Romania* **28 E7**
Ilia □, *Greece* **46 D3**
Iliamna L., *U.S.A.* **100 C4**
Iliç, *Turkey* **73 C8**
Ilica, *Turkey* **47 B9**
Ilichevsk, *Azerbaijan* **73 C11**
Iligan, *Phil.* **61 G6**
Iligan Bay, *Phil.* **61 G6**
Ilikí, L., *Greece* **46 C5**
Ilin I., *Phil.* **61 E4**
Iliodhrómia, *Greece* **46 B5**
Ilion, *U.S.A.* **117 D9**
Ilirska-Bistrica, *Slovenia* **41 C11**
Ilkeston, *U.K.* **14 E6**
Ilkley, *U.K.* **14 D6**
Illampu = Ancohuma, Nevado, *Bolivia* **124 G5**
Illana B., *Phil.* **61 H5**
Illapel, *Chile* **126 C1**
Ille-et-Vilaine □, *France* **18 D5**
Ille-sur-Têt, *France* **20 F6**
Illéla, *Niger* **83 C6**
Iller →, *Germany* **25 G5**
Illertissen, *Germany* **25 G6**
Illescas, *Spain* **36 E7**
Illetas, *Spain* **48 B9**
Illichivsk, *Ukraine* **33 J6**
Illiers-Combray, *France* **18 D8**
Illimani, Nevado, *Bolivia* **124 G5**
Illinois □, *U.S.A.* **112 E10**
Illinois →, *U.S.A.* **112 F9**
Illizi, *Algeria* **78 C7**
Illkirch-Graffenstaden, *France* **19 D14**
Íllora, *Spain* **37 H7**
Ilm →, *Germany* **24 D7**
Ilmajoki, *Finland* **9 E20**
Ilmen, Ozero, *Russia* **32 C6**
Ilmenau, *Germany* **24 E6**
Ilnytsya, *Ukraine* **28 B8**
Ilo, *Peru* **124 G4**
Ilobu, *Nigeria* **83 D5**
Iloilo, *Phil.* **61 F5**
Ilora, *Nigeria* **83 D5**
Ilorin, *Nigeria* **83 D5**
Ilovatka, *Russia* **34 E7**
Ilovlya, *Russia* **35 F7**
Ilovlya →, *Russia* **35 F7**
Iłowa, *Poland* **31 G2**
Ilubabor, *Ethiopia* **81 F4**
Ilva Mică, *Romania* **29 C9**
Ilwaco, *U.S.A.* **110 D2**
Ilwaki, *Indonesia* **63 F7**
Ilyichevsk = Illichivsk, *Ukraine* **33 J6**
Iłża, *Poland* **31 G8**
Iłżanka →, *Poland* **31 G8**
Imabari, *Japan* **55 G6**
Imaloto →, *Madag.* **89 C8**
İmamoğlu, *Turkey* **72 D6**
Imandra, Ozero, *Russia* **52 C4**
Imanombo, *Madag.* **89 C8**
Imari, *Japan* **55 H4**
Imasa, *Sudan* **80 D4**
Imathía □, *Greece* **44 F6**
Imatra, *Finland* **32 B5**
Iménas, *Mali* **83 B5**
imeni 26 Bakinskikh Komissarov = Neftçala, *Azerbaijan* **71 B6**
imeni 26 Bakinskikh Komissarov, *Turkmenistan* **71 B7**
Imeri, Serra, *Brazil* **124 C5**
Imerimandroso, *Madag.* **89 B8**
Imi, *Ethiopia* **81 F5**
Imishly = İmişli, *Azerbaijan* **35 L9**
İmişli, *Azerbaijan* **35 L9**
Imlay, *U.S.A.* **108 F4**
Imlay City, *U.S.A.* **116 D1**
Immaseri, *Sudan* **81 D2**
Immenstadt, *Germany* **25 H6**
Immingham, *U.K.* **14 D7**
Immokalee, *U.S.A.* **115 M5**
Imo □, *Nigeria* **83 D6**
Imo →, *Nigeria* **83 E6**
Ímola, *Italy* **41 D8**
Imotski, *Croatia* **41 E14**
Imperatriz, *Brazil* **125 E9**
Impéria, *Italy* **40 E5**
Imperial, *Canada* **103 C7**
Imperial, *Calif., U.S.A.* **111 N11**
Imperial, *Nebr., U.S.A.* **112 E4**
Imperial Beach, *U.S.A.* **111 N9**
Imperial Dam, *U.S.A.* **111 N12**
Imperial Reservoir, *U.S.A.* **111 N12**
Imperial Valley, *U.S.A.* **111 N11**
Imperieuse Reef, *Australia* **92 C2**
Impfondo, *Congo* **84 D3**
Imphal, *India* **67 G18**
Imphy, *France* **19 F10**
İmranlı, *Turkey* **73 C8**
İmroz = Gökçeada, *Turkey* **45 F9**
İmroz, *Turkey* **45 F9**
Imst, *Austria* **26 D3**
Imuris, *Mexico* **118 A2**
Imuruan B., *Phil.* **63 B5**
In Akhmed, *Mali* **83 B4**
In Aleï, *Mali* **82 B4**
In Delimane, *Mali* **83 B5**
In Guezzam, *Algeria* **83 B6**
In Koufi, *Mali* **83 B5**
In Salah, *Algeria* **78 C6**
In Tallak, *Mali* **83 B5**
In Tebezas, *Mali* **83 B5**
Ina, *Japan* **55 G8**
Inagua △, *Bahamas* **121 B5**
Inangahua, *N.Z.* **91 J3**
Inanwatan, *Indonesia* **63 E8**
Iñapari, *Peru* **124 F5**
Inari, *Finland* **8 B22**
Inarijärvi, *Finland* **8 B22**
Inawashiro-Ko, *Japan* **54 F10**
Inca, *Spain* **48 B9**
Inca de Oro, *Chile* **126 B2**
Incaguasi, *Chile* **126 B1**
İnce Burun, *Turkey* **72 A6**
İncekum Burnu, *Turkey* **72 D5**
İncesu, *Turkey* **70 B2**
Inch'ŏn, *S. Korea* **57 F14**
Incio = Cruz de Incio, *Spain* **36 C3**
İncirliova, *Turkey* **47 D9**
Incline Village, *U.S.A.* **108 G4**
Incomáti →, *Mozam.* **89 D5**
Incudine, Mte., *France* **21 G13**
Inda Silase, *Ethiopia* **81 E4**
Indal, *Sweden* **10 B11**
Indalsälven →, *Sweden* **10 B11**
Indaw, *Burma* **67 G20**
Indbir, *Ethiopia* **81 F4**
Independence, *Calif., U.S.A.* **110 J8**
Independence, *Iowa, U.S.A.* **112 D9**
Independence, *Kans., U.S.A.* **113 G7**
Independence, *Ky., U.S.A.* **114 F3**
Independence, *Mo., U.S.A.* **112 F7**
Independence Fjord, *Greenland* **4 A6**
Independence Mts., *U.S.A.* **108 F5**
Independenţa, *Romania* **29 E12**
Index, *U.S.A.* **110 C5**
India ■, *Asia* **66 K11**
Indian →, *U.S.A.* **115 M5**
Indian Cabins, *Canada* **102 B5**
Indian Harbour, *Canada* **105 B8**
Indian Head, *Canada* **103 C8**
Indian Lake, *U.S.A.* **117 C10**
Indian Ocean **50 K11**
Indian Springs, *U.S.A.* **111 J11**
Indiana, *U.S.A.* **116 F5**
Indiana □, *U.S.A.* **114 F3**
Indianapolis, *U.S.A.* **114 F2**
Indianola, *Iowa, U.S.A.* **112 E8**
Indianola, *Miss., U.S.A.* **113 J9**
Indigirka →, *Russia* **53 B15**
Inđija, *Serbia & M.* **28 E5**
Indio, *U.S.A.* **111 M10**
Indira Gandhi Canal, *India* **68 F5**
Indo-China, *Asia* **50 H14**
Indonesia ■, *Asia* **62 F5**
Indore, *India* **68 H6**
Indramayu, *Indonesia* **63 G13**
Indravati →, *India* **67 K12**
Indre □, *France* **19 F8**
Indre →, *France* **18 E7**
Indre-et-Loire □, *France* **18 E7**
Indulkana, *Australia* **95 D1**
Indura, *Belarus* **30 E10**
Indus →, *Pakistan* **68 G2**
Indus, Mouths of the, *Pakistan* **68 H3**
Inebolu, *Turkey* **72 B5**
İnecik, *Turkey* **45 F11**
İnegöl, *Turkey* **45 F13**
Ineu, *Romania* **28 D6**
Infantes = Villanueva de los Infantes, *Spain* **37 G7**
Infiernillo, Presa del, *Mexico* **118 D4**
Infiesto, *Spain* **36 B5**
Ingelstad, *Sweden* **11 H8**
Ingenio, *Canary Is.* **48 G4**
Ingenio Santa Ana, *Argentina* **126 B2**
Ingersoll, *Canada* **116 C4**
Ingham, *Australia* **94 B4**
Ingleborough, *U.K.* **14 C5**
Inglewood, *Queens., Australia* **95 D5**
Inglewood, *Vic., Australia* **95 F3**
Inglewood, *N.Z.* **91 H5**
Inglewood, *U.S.A.* **111 M8**
Ingólfshöfði, *Iceland* **8 E5**
Ingolstadt, *Germany* **25 G7**
Ingomar, *U.S.A.* **108 C10**
Ingonish, *Canada* **105 C7**
Ingore, *Guinea-Biss.* **82 C1**
Ingraj Bazar, *India* **69 G13**
Ingrid Christensen Coast, *Antarctica* **5 C6**
Ingul = Inhul →, *Ukraine* **33 J7**
Ingulec = Inhulec, *Ukraine* **33 J7**
Ingulets = Inhulets →, *Ukraine* **33 J7**
Inguri = Enguri →, *Georgia* **35 J5**
Ingushetia □, *Russia* **35 J7**
Ingwavuma, *S. Africa* **89 D5**
Inhaca, *Mozam.* **89 D5**
Inhafenga, *Mozam.* **89 C5**
Inhambane, *Mozam.* **89 C6**
Inhambane □, *Mozam.* **89 C5**
Inhaminga, *Mozam.* **87 F4**
Inharrime, *Mozam.* **89 C6**
Inharrime →, *Mozam.* **89 C6**
Inhisar, *Turkey* **47 A12**
Inhul →, *Ukraine* **33 J7**
Inhulec, *Ukraine* **33 J7**
Inhulets →, *Ukraine* **33 J7**
Iniesta, *Spain* **39 F3**
Ining = Yining, *China* **52 E9**
Inírida →, *Colombia* **124 C5**
Inishbofin, *Ireland* **12 C1**
Inisheer, *Ireland* **12 C2**
Inishfree B., *Ireland* **12 A3**
Inishkea North, *Ireland* **12 B1**
Inishkea South, *Ireland* **12 B1**
Inishmaan, *Ireland* **12 C2**
Inishmore, *Ireland* **12 C2**
Inishowen Pen., *Ireland* **12 A4**
Inishshark, *Ireland* **12 C1**
Inishturk, *Ireland* **12 C1**
Inishvickillane, *Ireland* **12 D1**
Injibara, *Ethiopia* **81 E4**
Injune, *Australia* **95 D4**
Inklin →, *Canada* **102 B2**
Inland Kaikoura Ra., *N.Z.* **91 J4**
Inland Sea = Setonaikai, *Japan* **55 G6**
Inle L., *Burma* **67 J20**
Inlet, *U.S.A.* **117 C10**
Inn →, *Austria* **26 C6**
Innamincka, *Australia* **95 D3**
Inner Hebrides, *U.K.* **13 E2**
Inner Mongolia = Nei Monggol Zizhiqu □, *China* **56 D7**
Inner Sound, *U.K.* **13 D3**
Innerkip, *Canada* **116 C4**
Innetalling I., *Canada* **104 A4**
Innisfail, *Australia* **94 B4**
Innisfail, *Canada* **102 C6**
In'noshima, *Japan* **55 G6**
Innsbruck, *Austria* **26 D4**
Innviertel, *Austria* **26 C6**
Inny →, *Ireland* **12 C4**
Inongo, *Dem. Rep. of the Congo* **84 E3**
İnönü, *Turkey* **47 B12**
Inoucdjouac = Inukjuak, *Canada* **101 C12**
Inowrocław, *Poland* **31 F5**
Inpundong, *N. Korea* **57 D14**
Inscription, C., *Australia* **93 E1**
Insein, *Burma* **67 L20**
Insjön, *Sweden* **10 D9**
Ińsko, *Poland* **30 E2**
Însurăţei, *Romania* **29 F12**
Inta, *Russia* **52 C6**
Intendente Alvear, *Argentina* **126 D3**
İntepe, *Turkey* **47 A8**
Interlaken, *Switz.* **25 J3**
Interlaken, *U.S.A.* **117 D8**
International Falls, *U.S.A.* **112 A8**
Intiyaco, *Argentina* **126 B3**
Întorsura Buzăului, *Romania* **29 E11**
Inukjuak, *Canada* **101 C12**
Inútil, B., *Chile* **128 G2**
Inuvik, *Canada* **100 B6**
Inveraray, *U.K.* **13 E3**
Inverbervie, *U.K.* **13 E6**
Invercargill, *N.Z.* **91 M2**
Inverclyde □, *U.K.* **13 F4**
Inverell, *Australia* **95 D5**
Invergordon, *U.K.* **13 D4**
Inverloch, *Australia* **95 F4**
Invermere, *Canada* **102 C5**
Inverness, *Canada* **105 C7**
Inverness, *U.K.* **13 D4**
Inverness, *U.S.A.* **115 L4**
Inverurie, *U.K.* **13 D6**
Investigator Group, *Australia* **95 E1**
Investigator Str., *Australia* **95 F2**
Inya, *Russia* **52 D9**
Inyanga, *Zimbabwe* **87 F3**
Inyangani, *Zimbabwe* **87 F3**
Inyantue, *Zimbabwe* **88 B4**
Inyo Mts., *U.S.A.* **110 J9**
Inyokern, *U.S.A.* **111 K9**
Inza, *Russia* **34 D8**
Inzhavino, *Russia* **34 D6**
Iō-Jima, *Japan* **55 J5**
Ioánnina, *Greece* **46 B2**
Ioánnina □, *Greece* **46 B2**
Iola, *U.S.A.* **113 G7**
Ion Corvin, *Romania* **29 F12**
Iona, *U.K.* **13 E2**
Ione, *U.S.A.* **110 G6**
Ionia, *U.S.A.* **114 D3**
Ionian Is. = Iónioi Nísoi, *Greece* **46 C2**
Ionian Sea, *Medit. S.* **6 H9**
Iónioi Nísoi, *Greece* **46 C2**
Iónioi Nísoi □, *Greece* **46 C2**
Íos, *Greece* **47 E7**
Iowa □, *U.S.A.* **112 D8**
Iowa →, *U.S.A.* **112 E9**
Iowa City, *U.S.A.* **112 E9**
Iowa Falls, *U.S.A.* **112 D8**
Iowa Park, *U.S.A.* **113 J5**
Ipala, *Tanzania* **86 C3**
Ipameri, *Brazil* **125 G9**
Ipáti, *Greece* **46 C4**
Ipatinga, *Brazil* **125 G10**
Ipatovo, *Russia* **35 H6**
Ipel' →, *Europe* **27 D11**
Ipiales, *Colombia* **124 C3**
Ipin = Yibin, *China* **58 C5**
Ípiros □, *Greece* **46 B2**
Ipixuna, *Brazil* **124 E4**
Ipoh, *Malaysia* **65 K3**
Ippy, *C.A.R.* **84 C4**
Ipsala, *Turkey* **45 F10**
Ipsárion, Óros, *Greece* **45 F8**
Ipswich, *Australia* **95 D5**
Ipswich, *U.K.* **15 E9**
Ipswich, *Mass., U.S.A.* **117 D14**
Ipswich, *S. Dak., U.S.A.* **112 C5**
Ipu, *Brazil* **125 D10**
Iqaluit, *Canada* **101 B13**
Iquique, *Chile* **124 H4**
Iquitos, *Peru* **124 D4**
Irabu-Jima, *Japan* **55 M2**
Iracoubo, *Fr. Guiana* **125 B8**
Irafshān, *Iran* **71 E9**
Irahuan, *Phil.* **61 G3**
Iráklia, *Kikládhes, Greece* **47 E7**
Iráklia, *Sérrai, Greece* **44 E7**
Iráklion, *Greece* **49 D7**
Iráklion □, *Greece* **49 D7**
Irala, *Paraguay* **127 B5**
Iran ■, *Asia* **71 C7**
Iran, Gunung-Gunung, *Malaysia* **62 D4**
Iran, Plateau of, *Asia* **50 F9**
Iran Ra. = Iran, Gunung-Gunung, *Malaysia* **62 D4**
Īrānshahr, *Iran* **71 E9**
Irapuato, *Mexico* **118 C4**
Iraq ■, *Asia* **70 C5**
Irati, *Brazil* **127 B5**
Irbes saurums, *Latvia* **30 A9**
Irbid, *Jordan* **74 C4**
Irbid □, *Jordan* **74 C5**
Iregua →, *Spain* **38 C7**
Ireland ■, *Europe* **12 C4**
Irele, *Nigeria* **83 D6**
Irgiz, Bolshaya →, *Russia* **34 D9**
Irhyangdong, *N. Korea* **57 D15**
Iri, *S. Korea* **57 G14**
Irian Jaya = Papua □, *Indonesia* **63 E9**
Irié, *Guinea* **82 D3**
Iriga, *Phil.* **61 E5**
Iringa, *Tanzania* **86 D4**
Iringa □, *Tanzania* **86 D4**
Iriomote △, *Japan* **55 M1**
Iriomote-Jima, *Japan* **55 M1**
Iriona, *Honduras* **120 C2**
Iriri →, *Brazil* **125 D8**
Irish Republic ■, *Europe* **12 C4**
Irish Sea, *Europe* **14 D3**
Irkutsk, *Russia* **53 D11**
Irlığanlı, *Turkey* **47 D11**
Irma, *Canada* **103 C6**
Irō-Zaki, *Japan* **55 G9**
Iroise, Mer d', *France* **18 D2**
Iron Baron, *Australia* **95 E2**
Iron Gate = Portile de Fier, *Europe* **28 F7**
Iron Knob, *Australia* **95 E2**
Iron Mountain, *U.S.A.* **114 C1**
Iron Range △, *Australia* **94 A3**
Iron River, *U.S.A.* **112 B10**
Irondequoit, *U.S.A.* **116 C7**
Ironton, *Mo., U.S.A.* **113 G9**
Ironton, *Ohio, U.S.A.* **114 F4**
Ironwood, *U.S.A.* **112 B9**
Ironwood Forest ⌓, *U.S.A.* **109 K8**
Iroquois, *Canada* **117 B9**
Iroquois Falls, *Canada* **104 C3**
Irosin, *Phil.* **61 E6**
Irpin, *Ukraine* **33 G6**
Irrara Cr. →, *Australia* **95 D4**
Irrawaddy □, *Burma* **67 L19**
Irrawaddy →, *Burma* **67 M19**
Irrawaddy, Mouths of the, *Burma* **67 M19**
Irricana, *Canada* **102 C6**
Irshava, *Ukraine* **28 B8**
Irsina, *Italy* **43 B9**
Irtysh →, *Russia* **52 C7**
Irumu, *Dem. Rep. of the Congo* **86 B2**
Irún, *Spain* **38 B3**
Irunea = Pamplona, *Spain* **38 C3**
Irurzun, *Spain* **38 C3**
Irvine, *U.K.* **13 F4**
Irvine, *Calif., U.S.A.* **111 M9**
Irvine, *Ky., U.S.A.* **114 G4**
Irvinestown, *U.K.* **12 B4**
Irving, *U.S.A.* **113 J6**
Irvona, *U.S.A.* **116 F6**
Irwin →, *Australia* **93 E1**
Irymple, *Australia* **95 E3**
Is, Jebel, *Sudan* **80 C4**
Is-sur-Tille, *France* **19 E12**
Isa, *Nigeria* **83 C6**
Isa Khel, *Pakistan* **68 C4**
Isaac →, *Australia* **94 C4**
Isabel, *U.S.A.* **112 C4**
Isabela, *Phil.* **61 H5**
Isabela, *Puerto Rico* **121 d**
Isabela, I., *Mexico* **118 C3**
Isabelia, Cord., *Nic.* **120 D2**
Isabella Ra., *Australia* **92 D3**
Isaccea, *Romania* **29 E13**
Ísafjarðardjúp, *Iceland* **8 C2**
Ísafjörður, *Iceland* **8 C2**
Isagarh, *India* **68 G7**
Isahaya, *Japan* **55 H5**
Isaka, *Tanzania* **86 C3**
Işalniţa, *Romania* **29 F8**
Isalo △, *Madag.* **89 C8**
Isan →, *India* **69 F9**
Isana = Içana →, *Brazil* **124 C5**
Isangano △, *Zambia* **87 E3**
Isanlu Makutu, *Nigeria* **83 D6**
Isar →, *Germany* **25 G8**
Isarco →, *Italy* **41 B8**
Ísari, *Greece* **46 D3**
Íscar, *Spain* **36 D6**
İscehisar, *Turkey* **47 C12**
Íschia, *Italy* **42 B6**
Isdell →, *Australia* **92 C3**
Ise, *Japan* **55 G8**
Ise-Shima △, *Japan* **55 G8**
Ise-Wan, *Japan* **55 G8**
Isefjord, *Denmark* **11 J5**
Isel →, *Austria* **26 E5**
Iseo, *Italy* **40 C7**
Iseo, L. d', *Italy* **40 C7**
Iseramagazi, *Tanzania* **86 C3**
Isère □, *France* **21 C9**
Isère →, *France* **21 D8**
Iserlohn, *Germany* **24 D3**
Isérnia, *Italy* **43 A7**
Iseyin, *Nigeria* **83 D5**
Isfahan = Eşfahān, *Iran* **71 C6**
Ishëm, *Albania* **44 E3**
Ishigaki-Shima, *Japan* **55 M2**
Ishikari-Gawa →, *Japan* **54 C10**
Ishikari-Sammyaku, *Japan* **54 C11**
Ishikari-Wan, *Japan* **54 C10**
Ishikawa □, *Japan* **55 F8**
Ishim, *Russia* **52 D7**
Ishim →, *Russia* **52 D8**
Ishinomaki, *Japan* **54 E10**
Ishioka, *Japan* **55 F10**
Ishkuman, *Pakistan* **69 A5**
Ishpeming, *U.S.A.* **114 B2**
Isigny-sur-Mer, *France* **18 C5**
Işıklar Dağı, *Turkey* **45 F11**
Işıklı, *Turkey* **47 C11**
Isil Kul, *Russia* **52 D8**
Ísili, *Italy* **42 C2**
Isiolo, *Kenya* **86 B4**
Isiro, *Dem. Rep. of the Congo* **86 B2**
Isisford, *Australia* **94 C3**
İskenderun, *Turkey* **70 B3**
İskenderun Körfezi, *Turkey* **72 D6**
İskilip, *Turkey* **72 B6**
Iskŭr →, *Bulgaria* **45 C8**
Iskŭr, Yazovir, *Bulgaria* **44 D7**
Iskut →, *Canada* **102 B2**
Isla →, *U.K.* **13 E5**
Isla Coiba △, *Panama* **120 E3**
Isla Cristina, *Spain* **37 H3**
Isla de Salamanca △, *Colombia* **121 D5**
Isla Gorge △, *Australia* **94 D4**
Isla Tiburón y San Esteban ⌓, *Mexico* **118 B2**
Isla Vista, *U.S.A.* **111 L7**
Islâhiye, *Turkey* **72 D7**
Islam Headworks, *Pakistan* **68 E5**
Islamabad, *Pakistan* **68 C5**
Islamgarh, *Pakistan* **68 F4**
Islamkot, *Pakistan* **68 G4**
Islampur, *India* **69 G11**
Island L., *Canada* **103 C10**
Island Lagoon, *Australia* **95 E2**
Island Pond, *U.S.A.* **117 B13**

Islands, B. of, *Canada* . . . 105 **C8**
Islands, B. of, *N.Z.* . . . 91 **F5**
Islay, *U.K.* . . . 13 **F2**
Isle →, *France* . . . 20 **D3**
Isle aux Morts, *Canada* . . . 105 **C8**
Isle of Wight □, *U.K.* . . . 15 **G6**
Isle Royale △, *U.S.A.* . . . 114 **B1**
Isleton, *U.S.A.* . . . 110 **G5**
Ismail = Izmayil, *Ukraine* . . . 29 **E13**
Ismâ'ilîya, *Egypt* . . . 80 **H8**
Ismaning, *Germany* . . . 25 **G7**
Isna, *Egypt* . . . 80 **B3**
Isoanala, *Madag.* . . . 89 **C8**
Isogstalo, *India* . . . 69 **B8**
Ísola del Liri, *Italy* . . . 41 **G10**
Ísola della Scala, *Italy* . . . 40 **C7**
Ísola di Capo Rizzuto, *Italy* . . . 43 **D10**
İsparta, *Turkey* . . . 47 **D12**
Isperikh, *Bulgaria* . . . 45 **C10**
Íspica, *Italy* . . . 43 **F7**
Israel ■, *Asia* . . . 74 **D3**
Isratu, *Eritrea* . . . 81 **D4**
Issakly, *Russia* . . . 34 **C10**
Issia, *Ivory C.* . . . 82 **D3**
Issoire, *France* . . . 20 **C7**
Issoudun, *France* . . . 19 **F8**
Issyk-Kul, Ozero = Ysyk-Köl, *Kyrgyzstan* . . . 52 **E8**
Ist, *Croatia* . . . 41 **D11**
Istállós-kő, *Hungary* . . . 28 **B5**
İstanbul, *Turkey* . . . 45 **E12**
İstanbul □, *Turkey* . . . 45 **E12**
İstanbul ✕ (IST), *Turkey* . . . 45 **F12**
İstanbul Boğazı, *Turkey* . . . 45 **E13**
Istiaía, *Greece* . . . 46 **C5**
Istok, *Serbia & M.* . . . 44 **D4**
Istokpoga, L., *U.S.A.* . . . 115 **M5**
Istra, *Croatia* . . . 41 **C10**
Istres, *France* . . . 21 **E8**
Istria = Istra, *Croatia* . . . 41 **C10**
Itá, *Paraguay* . . . 126 **B4**
Itaberaba, *Brazil* . . . 125 **F10**
Itabira, *Brazil* . . . 125 **G10**
Itabirito, *Brazil* . . . 127 **A7**
Itabuna, *Brazil* . . . 125 **F11**
Itacaunas →, *Brazil* . . . 125 **E9**
Itacoatiara, *Brazil* . . . 124 **D7**
Itaipú, Represa de, *Brazil* . . . 127 **B5**
Itaituba, *Brazil* . . . 125 **D7**
Itajaí, *Brazil* . . . 127 **B6**
Itajubá, *Brazil* . . . 127 **A6**
Itaka, *Tanzania* . . . 87 **D3**
Itala ⌓, *S. Africa* . . . 89 **D5**
Italy ■, *Europe* . . . 7 **G8**
Itamaraju, *Brazil* . . . 125 **G11**
Itampolo, *Madag.* . . . 89 **C7**
Itandrano, *Madag.* . . . 89 **C8**
Itapecuru-Mirim, *Brazil* . . . 125 **D10**
Itaperuna, *Brazil* . . . 127 **A7**
Itapetininga, *Brazil* . . . 127 **A6**
Itapeva, *Brazil* . . . 127 **A6**
Itapicuru →, *Bahia, Brazil* . . . 125 **F11**
Itapicuru →, *Maranhão, Brazil* . . . 125 **D10**
Itapipoca, *Brazil* . . . 125 **D11**
Itapuá □, *Paraguay* . . . 127 **B4**
Itaquari, *Brazil* . . . 127 **A7**
Itaquí, *Brazil* . . . 126 **B4**
Itararé, *Brazil* . . . 127 **A6**
Itarsi, *India* . . . 68 **H7**
Itatí, *Argentina* . . . 126 **B4**
Itatiaia △, *Brazil* . . . 127 **A7**
Itbayat, *Phil.* . . . 61 **A4**
Itchen →, *U.K.* . . . 15 **G6**
Itéa, *Greece* . . . 46 **C4**
Itezhi Tezhi, L., *Zambia* . . . 87 **F2**
Ithaca = Itháki, *Greece* . . . 46 **C2**
Ithaca, *U.S.A.* . . . 117 **D8**
Itháki, *Greece* . . . 46 **C2**
Íti △, *Greece* . . . 46 **C4**
Itiquira →, *Brazil* . . . 125 **G7**
Itō, *Japan* . . . 55 **G9**
Itoigawa, *Japan* . . . 55 **F8**
Iton →, *France* . . . 18 **C8**
Itonamas →, *Bolivia* . . . 124 **F6**
Itri, *Italy* . . . 42 **A6**
Itsa, *Egypt* . . . 80 **J7**
Íttiri, *Italy* . . . 42 **B1**
Ittoqqortoormiit, *Greenland* . . . 4 **B6**
Itu, *Brazil* . . . 127 **A6**
Itu, *Nigeria* . . . 83 **D6**
Itu Aba I., *S. China Sea* . . . 62 **B4**
Ituiutaba, *Brazil* . . . 125 **G9**
Itumbiara, *Brazil* . . . 125 **G9**
Ituna, *Canada* . . . 103 **C8**
Itunge Port, *Tanzania* . . . 87 **D3**
Iturbe, *Argentina* . . . 126 **A2**
Ituri →, *Dem. Rep. of the Congo* . . . 86 **B2**
Iturup, Ostrov, *Russia* . . . 53 **E15**
Ituxi →, *Brazil* . . . 124 **E6**
Ituyuro →, *Argentina* . . . 126 **A3**
Itzehoe, *Germany* . . . 24 **B5**
Ivahona, *Madag.* . . . 89 **C8**
Ivaí →, *Brazil* . . . 127 **A5**
Ivalo, *Finland* . . . 8 **B22**
Ivalojoki →, *Finland* . . . 8 **B22**
Ivanava, *Belarus* . . . 33 **F3**
Ivančice, *Czech Rep.* . . . 27 **B9**
Ivane-Puste, *Ukraine* . . . 29 **B11**
Ivănești, *Romania* . . . 29 **D12**
Ivangorod, *Russia* . . . 32 **C5**
Ivanhoe, *Australia* . . . 95 **E3**
Ivanhoe, *Calif., U.S.A.* . . . 110 **J7**
Ivanhoe, *Minn., U.S.A.* . . . 112 **C6**
Ivanhorod, *Ukraine* . . . 29 **B14**
Ivanić Grad, *Croatia* . . . 41 **C13**
Ivanjica, *Serbia & M.* . . . 44 **C4**
Ivanjska, *Bos.-H.* . . . 28 **F2**
Ivankoyskoye Vdkhr., *Russia* . . . 32 **D9**
Ivano-Frankivsk, *Ukraine* . . . 29 **B9**
Ivano-Frankivska □, *Ukraine* . . . 29 **B9**
Ivanovo = Ivanava, *Belarus* . . . 33 **F3**
Ivanovo, *Russia* . . . 32 **D11**
Ivanšćica, *Croatia* . . . 41 **B13**
Ivato, *Madag.* . . . 89 **C8**
Ivatsevichy, *Belarus* . . . 33 **F3**
Ivaylovgrad, *Bulgaria* . . . 45 **E10**
Ivinheima →, *Brazil* . . . 127 **A5**
Ivinhema, *Brazil* . . . 127 **A5**
Ivohibe, *Madag.* . . . 89 **C8**
Ivory Coast, *W. Afr.* . . . 82 **E4**
Ivory Coast ■, *Africa* . . . 82 **D4**
Ivösjön, *Sweden* . . . 11 **H8**
Ivrea, *Italy* . . . 40 **C4**
Ivrindi, *Turkey* . . . 47 **B9**
Ivujivik, *Canada* . . . 101 **B12**
Ivybridge, *U.K.* . . . 15 **G4**
Iwaizumi, *Japan* . . . 54 **E10**
Iwaki, *Japan* . . . 55 **F10**
Iwakuni, *Japan* . . . 55 **G6**
Iwamizawa, *Japan* . . . 54 **C10**
Iwanai, *Japan* . . . 54 **C10**
Iwata, *Japan* . . . 55 **G8**
Iwate □, *Japan* . . . 54 **E10**
Iwate-San, *Japan* . . . 54 **E10**
Iwo, *Nigeria* . . . 83 **D5**
Iwonicz-Zdrój, *Poland* . . . 31 **J8**
Ixiamas, *Bolivia* . . . 124 **F5**
Ixopo, *S. Africa* . . . 89 **E5**
Ixtepec, *Mexico* . . . 119 **D5**
Ixtlán del Río, *Mexico* . . . 118 **C4**
Iyal Bakhit, *Sudan* . . . 81 **E2**
Iyo, *Japan* . . . 55 **H6**
Izabal, L. de, *Guatemala* . . . 120 **C2**
Izamal, *Mexico* . . . 119 **C7**
Izberbash, *Russia* . . . 35 **J8**
Izbica, *Poland* . . . 31 **H10**
Izbica Kujawska, *Poland* . . . 31 **F5**
Izbiceni, *Romania* . . . 29 **G9**
Izena-Shima, *Japan* . . . 55 **L3**
Izgrev, *Bulgaria* . . . 45 **C10**
Izhevsk, *Russia* . . . 52 **D6**
Izmayil, *Ukraine* . . . 29 **E13**
İzmir, *Turkey* . . . 47 **C9**
İzmir □, *Turkey* . . . 47 **C9**
İzmir Adnan Menderes ✕ (ADB), *Turkey* . . . 47 **C9**
İzmir Körfezi, *Turkey* . . . 47 **C8**
İzmit = Kocaeli, *Turkey* . . . 45 **F13**
Iznájar, *Spain* . . . 37 **H6**
Iznalloz, *Spain* . . . 37 **H7**
İznik, *Turkey* . . . 72 **B3**
İznik Gölü, *Turkey* . . . 45 **F13**
Izobil'nyy, *Russia* . . . 35 **H5**
Izola, *Slovenia* . . . 41 **C10**
Izra, *Syria* . . . 74 **C5**
Iztochni Rodopi, *Bulgaria* . . . 45 **E9**
Izu-Shotō, *Japan* . . . 55 **G10**
Izúcar de Matamoros, *Mexico* . . . 119 **D5**
Izumi-Sano, *Japan* . . . 55 **G7**
Izumo, *Japan* . . . 55 **G6**
Izyaslav, *Ukraine* . . . 33 **G4**
Izyum, *Ukraine* . . . 33 **H9**

J

Jaba, *Ethiopia* . . . 81 **F4**
Jabal at Tā'ir, *Red Sea* . . . 81 **D5**
Jabalón →, *Spain* . . . 37 **G6**
Jabalpur, *India* . . . 69 **H8**
Jabbūl, *Syria* . . . 70 **B3**
Jabiru, *Australia* . . . 92 **B5**
Jablah, *Syria* . . . 70 **C3**
Jablanac, *Croatia* . . . 41 **D11**
Jablanica, *Bos.-H.* . . . 28 **G2**
Jablonec nad Nisou, *Czech Rep.* . . . 26 **A8**
Jablonica, *Slovak Rep.* . . . 27 **C10**
Jabłonowo Pomorskie, *Poland* . . . 30 **E6**
Jablunkov, *Czech Rep.* . . . 27 **B11**
Jaboatão, *Brazil* . . . 125 **E11**
Jaboticabal, *Brazil* . . . 127 **A6**
Jabukovac, *Serbia & M.* . . . 44 **B6**
Jaca, *Spain* . . . 38 **C4**
Jacareí, *Brazil* . . . 127 **A6**
Jacarèzinho, *Brazil* . . . 127 **A6**
Jackman, *U.S.A.* . . . 115 **C10**
Jacksboro, *U.S.A.* . . . 113 **J5**
Jackson, *Barbados* . . . 121 **g**
Jackson, *Ala., U.S.A.* . . . 115 **K2**
Jackson, *Calif., U.S.A.* . . . 110 **G6**
Jackson, *Ky., U.S.A.* . . . 114 **G4**
Jackson, *Mich., U.S.A.* . . . 114 **D3**
Jackson, *Minn., U.S.A.* . . . 112 **D7**
Jackson, *Miss., U.S.A.* . . . 113 **J9**
Jackson, *Mo., U.S.A.* . . . 113 **G10**
Jackson, *N.H., U.S.A.* . . . 117 **B13**
Jackson, *Ohio, U.S.A.* . . . 114 **F4**
Jackson, *Tenn., U.S.A.* . . . 115 **H1**
Jackson, *Wyo., U.S.A.* . . . 108 **E8**
Jackson B., *N.Z.* . . . 91 **K2**
Jackson L., *U.S.A.* . . . 108 **E8**
Jacksons, *N.Z.* . . . 91 **K3**
Jackson's Arm, *Canada* . . . 105 **C8**
Jacksonville, *Ala., U.S.A.* . . . 115 **J3**
Jacksonville, *Ark., U.S.A.* . . . 113 **H8**
Jacksonville, *Calif., U.S.A.* . . . 110 **H6**
Jacksonville, *Fla., U.S.A.* . . . 115 **K5**
Jacksonville, *Ill., U.S.A.* . . . 112 **F9**
Jacksonville, *N.C., U.S.A.* . . . 115 **H7**
Jacksonville, *Tex., U.S.A.* . . . 113 **K7**
Jacksonville Beach, *U.S.A.* . . . 115 **K5**
Jacmel, *Haiti* . . . 121 **C5**
Jacob Lake, *U.S.A.* . . . 109 **H7**
Jacobabad, *Pakistan* . . . 68 **E3**
Jacobina, *Brazil* . . . 125 **F10**
Jacques-Cartier ⌓, *Canada* . . . 105 **C5**
Jacques-Cartier, Dét. de, *Canada* . . . 105 **C7**
Jacques-Cartier, Mt., *Canada* . . . 105 **C6**
Jacqueville, *Ivory C.* . . . 82 **D4**
Jacuí →, *Brazil* . . . 127 **C5**
Jacumba, *U.S.A.* . . . 111 **N10**
Jacundá →, *Brazil* . . . 125 **D8**
Jade, *Germany* . . . 24 **B4**
Jadebusen, *Germany* . . . 24 **B4**
Jadovnik, *Serbia & M.* . . . 44 **C3**
Jadraque, *Spain* . . . 38 **E2**
Jaén, *Peru* . . . 124 **E3**
Jaén, *Spain* . . . 37 **H7**
Jaén □, *Spain* . . . 37 **H7**
Jafarabad, *India* . . . 68 **J4**
Jaffa = Tel Aviv-Yafo, *Israel* . . . 74 **C3**
Jaffa, C., *Australia* . . . 95 **F2**
Jaffna, *Sri Lanka* . . . 66 **Q12**
Jaffray, *Canada* . . . 103 **D10**
Jaffrey, *U.S.A.* . . . 117 **D12**
Jagadhri, *India* . . . 68 **D7**
Jagadishpur, *India* . . . 69 **G11**
Jagdalpur, *India* . . . 67 **K13**
Jagersfontein, *S. Africa* . . . 88 **D4**
Jaghīn →, *Iran* . . . 71 **E8**
Jagodina, *Serbia & M.* . . . 44 **B5**
Jagraon, *India* . . . 66 **D9**
Jagst →, *Germany* . . . 25 **F5**
Jagtial, *India* . . . 66 **K11**
Jaguariaíva, *Brazil* . . . 127 **A6**
Jaguaribe →, *Brazil* . . . 125 **D11**
Jagüey Grande, *Cuba* . . . 120 **B3**
Jahanabad, *India* . . . 69 **G11**
Jahazpur, *India* . . . 68 **G6**
Jahrom, *Iran* . . . 71 **D7**
Jaijon, *India* . . . 68 **D7**
Jailolo, *Indonesia* . . . 63 **D7**
Jailolo, Selat, *Indonesia* . . . 63 **D7**
Jaipur, *India* . . . 68 **F6**
Jais, *India* . . . 69 **F9**
Jaisalmer, *India* . . . 68 **F4**
Jaisinghnagar, *India* . . . 69 **H8**
Jaitaran, *India* . . . 68 **F5**
Jaithari, *India* . . . 69 **H8**
Jājarm, *Iran* . . . 71 **B8**
Jajce, *Bos.-H.* . . . 28 **F2**
Jakam →, *India* . . . 68 **H6**
Jakarta, *Indonesia* . . . 63 **G12**
Jakhal, *India* . . . 68 **E6**
Jakhau, *India* . . . 68 **H3**
Jakobstad = Pietarsaari, *Finland* . . . 8 **E20**
Jakupica, *Macedonia* . . . 44 **E5**
Jal, *U.S.A.* . . . 113 **J3**
Jalālābād, *Afghan.* . . . 68 **B4**
Jalalabad, *India* . . . 69 **F8**
Jalalpur Jattan, *Pakistan* . . . 68 **C6**
Jalama, *U.S.A.* . . . 111 **L6**
Jalapa, *Guatemala* . . . 120 **D2**
Jalapa Enríquez = Xalapa, *Mexico* . . . 119 **D5**
Jalasjärvi, *Finland* . . . 9 **E20**
Jalaun, *India* . . . 69 **F8**
Jaldhaka →, *Bangla.* . . . 69 **F13**
Jalesar, *India* . . . 68 **F8**
Jaleswar, *Nepal* . . . 69 **F11**
Jalgaon, *India* . . . 66 **J9**
Jalībah, *Iraq* . . . 70 **D5**
Jalingo, *Nigeria* . . . 83 **D7**
Jalisco □, *Mexico* . . . 118 **D4**
Jalkot, *Pakistan* . . . 69 **B5**
Jallas →, *Spain* . . . 36 **C1**
Jalna, *India* . . . 66 **K9**
Jalón →, *Spain* . . . 38 **D3**
Jalor, *India* . . . 68 **G5**
Jalpa, *Mexico* . . . 118 **C4**
Jalpaiguri, *India* . . . 67 **F16**
Jaluit I., *Marshall Is.* . . . 96 **G8**
Jalūlā, *Iraq* . . . 70 **C5**
Jamaari, *Nigeria* . . . 83 **C6**
Jamaica ■, *W. Indies* . . . 120 **a**
Jamalpur, *Bangla.* . . . 67 **G16**
Jamalpur, *India* . . . 69 **G12**
Jamalpurganj, *India* . . . 69 **H13**
Jamanxim →, *Brazil* . . . 125 **D7**
Jambewangi, *Indonesia* . . . 63 **J17**
Jambi, *Indonesia* . . . 62 **E2**
Jambi □, *Indonesia* . . . 62 **E2**
Jambusar, *India* . . . 68 **H5**
James →, *S. Dak., U.S.A.* . . . 112 **D6**
James →, *Va., U.S.A.* . . . 114 **G7**
James B., *Canada* . . . 104 **B3**
James Ranges, *Australia* . . . 92 **D5**
James Ross I., *Antarctica* . . . 5 **C18**
Jamesabad, *Pakistan* . . . 68 **G3**
Jamestown, *Australia* . . . 95 **E2**
Jamestown, *S. Africa* . . . 88 **E4**
Jamestown, *N. Dak., U.S.A.* . . . 112 **B5**
Jamestown, *N.Y., U.S.A.* . . . 116 **D5**
Jamestown, *Pa., U.S.A.* . . . 116 **E4**
Jamīlābād, *Iran* . . . 71 **C6**
Jamiltepec, *Mexico* . . . 119 **D5**
Jamira →, *India* . . . 69 **J13**
Jämjö, *Sweden* . . . 11 **H9**
Jamkhandi, *India* . . . 66 **L9**
Jammerbugt, *Denmark* . . . 11 **G3**
Jammu, *India* . . . 68 **C6**
Jammu & Kashmir □, *India* . . . 69 **B7**
Jamnagar, *India* . . . 68 **H4**
Jamni →, *India* . . . 69 **G8**
Jampur, *Pakistan* . . . 68 **E4**
Jamrud, *Pakistan* . . . 68 **C4**
Jämsä, *Finland* . . . 9 **F21**
Jamshedpur, *India* . . . 69 **H12**
Jamtara, *India* . . . 69 **H12**
Jämtland, *Sweden* . . . 8 **E15**
Jämtlands län □, *Sweden* . . . 10 **B7**
Jan L., *Canada* . . . 103 **C8**
Jan Mayen, *Arctic* . . . 4 **B7**
Janakkala, *Finland* . . . 9 **F21**
Janaúba, *Brazil* . . . 125 **G10**
Jand, *Pakistan* . . . 68 **C5**
Jandaq, *Iran* . . . 71 **C7**
Jandía, *Canary Is.* . . . 48 **F5**
Jandía △, *Canary Is.* . . . 48 **F5**
Jandía, Pta. de, *Canary Is.* . . . 48 **F5**
Jandola, *Pakistan* . . . 68 **C4**
Jandowae, *Australia* . . . 95 **D5**
Jándula →, *Spain* . . . 37 **G6**
Janesville, *U.S.A.* . . . 112 **D10**
Janga, *Ghana* . . . 83 **C4**
Jangamo, *Mozam.* . . . 89 **C6**
Janghai, *India* . . . 69 **G10**
Janikowo, *Poland* . . . 31 **F5**
Janinà = Ioánnina □, *Greece* . . . 46 **B2**
Janja, *Bos.-H.* . . . 28 **F4**
Janjanbureh, *Gambia* . . . 82 **C2**
Janjevo, *Serbia & M.* . . . 44 **D5**
Janjgir, *India* . . . 69 **J10**
Janjina, *Croatia* . . . 41 **F14**
Janjina, *Madag.* . . . 89 **C8**
Janos, *Mexico* . . . 118 **A3**
Jánoshalma, *Hungary* . . . 28 **D4**
Jánosháza, *Hungary* . . . 28 **C2**
Jánossomorja, *Hungary* . . . 28 **C2**
Janów, *Poland* . . . 31 **H6**
Janów Lubelski, *Poland* . . . 31 **H9**
Janów Podlaski, *Poland* . . . 31 **F10**
Janowiec Wielkopolski, *Poland* . . . 31 **F4**
Januária, *Brazil* . . . 125 **G10**
Janub △, *Sudan* . . . 81 **F2**
Janub Dârfûr □, *Sudan* . . . 81 **E2**
Janub Kordofân □, *Sudan* . . . 81 **E3**
Janûb Sînî □, *Egypt* . . . 74 **F2**
Janubio, *Canary Is.* . . . 48 **F6**
Janville, *France* . . . 19 **D8**
Janzé, *France* . . . 18 **E5**
Jaora, *India* . . . 68 **H6**
Japan ■, *Asia* . . . 55 **G8**
Japan, Sea of, *Asia* . . . 54 **E7**
Japan Trench, *Pac. Oc.* . . . 96 **D6**
Japen = Yapen, *Indonesia* . . . 63 **E9**
Japla, *India* . . . 69 **G11**
Japurá →, *Brazil* . . . 124 **D5**
Jaquarão, *Brazil* . . . 127 **C5**
Jaqué, *Panama* . . . 120 **E4**
Jarābulus, *Syria* . . . 70 **B3**
Jaraicejo, *Spain* . . . 37 **F5**
Jaraíz de la Vera, *Spain* . . . 36 **E5**
Jarama →, *Spain* . . . 36 **E7**
Jaramānah, *Syria* . . . 72 **F7**
Jarandilla, *Spain* . . . 36 **E5**
Jaranwala, *Pakistan* . . . 68 **D5**
Jarash, *Jordan* . . . 74 **C4**
Jarash □, *Jordan* . . . 74 **C4**
Järbo, *Sweden* . . . 10 **D10**
Jardim, *Brazil* . . . 126 **A4**
Jardín →, *Spain* . . . 39 **G2**
Jardine River △, *Australia* . . . 94 **A3**
Jardines de la Reina, Arch. de los, *Cuba* . . . 120 **B4**
Jargalang, *China* . . . 57 **C12**
Jari →, *Brazil* . . . 125 **D8**
Jarīr, W. al →, *Si. Arabia* . . . 70 **E4**
Järlåsa, *Sweden* . . . 10 **E11**
Jarmen, *Germany* . . . 24 **B9**
Järna, *Dalarna, Sweden* . . . 10 **D8**
Järna, *Stockholm, Sweden* . . . 10 **E11**
Jarnac, *France* . . . 20 **C3**
Jarny, *France* . . . 19 **C12**
Jarocin, *Poland* . . . 31 **G4**
Jaroměř, *Czech Rep.* . . . 26 **A8**
Jarosław, *Poland* . . . 31 **H9**
Järpås, *Sweden* . . . 11 **F6**
Järpen, *Sweden* . . . 10 **A7**
Jarrahdale, *Australia* . . . 93 **F2**
Jarrahi →, *Iran* . . . 71 **D6**
Jarres, Plaine des, *Laos* . . . 64 **C4**
Jarso, *Ethiopia* . . . 81 **F4**
Jartai, *China* . . . 56 **E3**
Jarud Qi, *China* . . . 57 **B11**
Järvenpää, *Finland* . . . 9 **F21**
Jarvis, *Canada* . . . 116 **D4**
Jarvis I., *Pac. Oc.* . . . 97 **H12**
Jarvorník, *Czech Rep.* . . . 27 **A10**
Järvsö, *Sweden* . . . 10 **C10**
Jarwa, *India* . . . 69 **F10**
Jaša Tomić, *Serbia & M.* . . . 28 **E5**
Jasdan, *India* . . . 68 **H4**
Jashpurnagar, *India* . . . 69 **H11**
Jasidih, *India* . . . 69 **G12**
Jasień, *Poland* . . . 31 **G2**
Jāsimīyah, *Iraq* . . . 70 **C5**
Jasin, *Malaysia* . . . 65 **L4**
Jāsk, *Iran* . . . 71 **E8**
Jasło, *Poland* . . . 31 **J8**
Jasmund, *Germany* . . . 24 **A9**
Jasmund △, *Germany* . . . 24 **A9**
Jaso, *India* . . . 69 **G9**
Jasper, *Alta., Canada* . . . 102 **C5**
Jasper, *Ont., Canada* . . . 117 **B9**
Jasper, *Ala., U.S.A.* . . . 115 **J2**
Jasper, *Fla., U.S.A.* . . . 115 **K4**
Jasper, *Ind., U.S.A.* . . . 114 **F2**
Jasper, *Tex., U.S.A.* . . . 113 **K8**
Jasper △, *Canada* . . . 102 **C5**
Jasrasar, *India* . . . 68 **F5**
Jastarnia, *Poland* . . . 30 **D5**
Jastrebarsko, *Croatia* . . . 41 **C12**
Jastrowie, *Poland* . . . 30 **E3**
Jastrzębie Zdrój, *Poland* . . . 31 **J5**
Jász-Nagykun-Szolnok □, *Hungary* . . . 28 **C5**
Jászapáti, *Hungary* . . . 28 **C5**
Jászárokszállás, *Hungary* . . . 28 **C4**
Jászberény, *Hungary* . . . 28 **C4**
Jászkisér, *Hungary* . . . 28 **C5**
Jászladány, *Hungary* . . . 28 **C5**
Jataí, *Brazil* . . . 125 **G8**
Jati, *Pakistan* . . . 68 **G3**
Jatibarang, *Indonesia* . . . 63 **G13**
Jatiluwih, *Indonesia* . . . 63 **J18**
Jatinegara, *Indonesia* . . . 63 **G12**
Játiva = Xátiva, *Spain* . . . 39 **G4**
Jättendal, *Sweden* . . . 10 **C11**
Jaú, *Brazil* . . . 127 **A6**
Jauja, *Peru* . . . 124 **F3**
Jaunpur, *India* . . . 69 **G10**
Java = Jawa, *Indonesia* . . . 62 **F3**
Java Sea, *Indonesia* . . . 62 **E3**
Java Trench, *Ind. Oc.* . . . 62 **F3**
Javalambre, Sa. de, *Spain* . . . 38 **E4**
Jávea, *Spain* . . . 39 **G5**
Jawa, *Indonesia* . . . 62 **F3**
Jawa Barat □, *Indonesia* . . . 63 **G12**
Jawa Tengah □, *Indonesia* . . . 63 **G14**
Jawa Timur □, *Indonesia* . . . 63 **G15**
Jawad, *India* . . . 68 **G6**
Jawor, *Poland* . . . 31 **G3**
Jaworzno, *Poland* . . . 31 **H6**
Jaworzyna Śląska, *Poland* . . . 31 **H3**
Jay Peak, *U.S.A.* . . . 117 **B12**
Jaya, Puncak, *Indonesia* . . . 63 **E9**
Jayanti, *India* . . . 67 **F16**
Jayapura, *Indonesia* . . . 63 **E10**
Jayawijaya, Pegunungan, *Indonesia* . . . 63 **E9**
Jaynagar, *India* . . . 67 **F15**
Jayrūd, *Syria* . . . 70 **C3**
Jayton, *U.S.A.* . . . 113 **J4**
Jāz Mūrīān, Hāmūn-e, *Iran* . . . 71 **E8**
Jazīreh-ye Shīf, *Iran* . . . 71 **D6**
Jazminal, *Mexico* . . . 118 **C4**
Jazzīn, *Lebanon* . . . 74 **B4**
Jean, *U.S.A.* . . . 111 **K11**
Jean Marie River, *Canada* . . . 102 **A4**
Jean-Rabel, *Haiti* . . . 121 **C5**
Jeanerette, *U.S.A.* . . . 113 **L9**
Jeanette, Ostrov = Zhannetty, Ostrov, *Russia* . . . 53 **B16**
Jeannette, *U.S.A.* . . . 116 **F5**
Jebāl Bārez, Kūh-e, *Iran* . . . 71 **D8**
Jebba, *Nigeria* . . . 83 **D5**
Jebel, Bahr el →, *Sudan* . . . 81 **F3**
Jebel Dud, *Sudan* . . . 81 **E3**
Jebel Qerri, *Sudan* . . . 81 **D3**
Jedburgh, *U.K.* . . . 13 **F6**
Jedda = Jiddah, *Si. Arabia* . . . 75 **C2**
Jeddore L., *Canada* . . . 105 **C8**
Jedlicze, *Poland* . . . 31 **J8**
Jędrzejów, *Poland* . . . 31 **H7**
Jedwabne, *Poland* . . . 31 **E9**
Jeetzel →, *Germany* . . . 24 **B7**
Jefferson, *Iowa, U.S.A.* . . . 112 **D7**
Jefferson, *Ohio, U.S.A.* . . . 116 **E4**
Jefferson, *Tex., U.S.A.* . . . 113 **J7**
Jefferson, Mt., *Nev., U.S.A.* . . . 108 **G5**
Jefferson, Mt., *Oreg., U.S.A.* . . . 108 **D3**
Jefferson City, *Mo., U.S.A.* . . . 112 **F8**
Jefferson City, *Tenn., U.S.A.* . . . 115 **G4**
Jeffersontown, *U.S.A.* . . . 114 **F3**
Jeffersonville, *U.S.A.* . . . 114 **F3**
Jeffrey City, *U.S.A.* . . . 108 **E10**
Jega, *Nigeria* . . . 83 **C5**
Jeju = Cheju do, *S. Korea* . . . 57 **H14**
Jēkabpils, *Latvia* . . . 9 **H21**
Jekyll I., *U.S.A.* . . . 115 **K5**
Jelcz-Laskowice, *Poland* . . . 31 **G4**
Jelenia Góra, *Poland* . . . 31 **H2**
Jelgava, *Latvia* . . . 9 **H20**
Jelgava □, *Latvia* . . . 30 **B10**
Jelica, *Serbia & M.* . . . 44 **C4**
Jelli, *Sudan* . . . 81 **F3**
Jelšava, *Slovak Rep.* . . . 27 **C13**
Jemaja, *Indonesia* . . . 65 **L5**
Jemaluang, *Malaysia* . . . 65 **L4**
Jember, *Indonesia* . . . 63 **H15**
Jembongan, *Malaysia* . . . 62 **C5**
Jena, *Germany* . . . 24 **E7**
Jena, *U.S.A.* . . . 113 **K8**
Jenbach, *Austria* . . . 26 **D4**
Jenīn, *West Bank* . . . 74 **C4**
Jenkins, *U.S.A.* . . . 114 **G4**
Jenner, *U.S.A.* . . . 110 **G3**
Jennings, *U.S.A.* . . . 113 **K8**
Jepara, *Indonesia* . . . 63 **G14**
Jeparit, *Australia* . . . 95 **F3**
Jequié, *Brazil* . . . 125 **F10**
Jequitinhonha, *Brazil* . . . 125 **G10**
Jequitinhonha →, *Brazil* . . . 125 **G11**
Jerantut, *Malaysia* . . . 65 **L4**
Jerejak, Pulau, *Malaysia* . . . 65 **c**
Jérémie, *Haiti* . . . 121 **C5**
Jerez, Punta, *Mexico* . . . 119 **C5**
Jerez de García Salinas, *Mexico* . . . 118 **C4**
Jerez de la Frontera, *Spain* . . . 37 **J4**
Jerez de los Caballeros, *Spain* . . . 37 **G4**
Jericho = El Arīḥā, *West Bank* . . . 74 **D4**
Jericho, *Australia* . . . 94 **C4**
Jerichow, *Germany* . . . 24 **C8**
Jerid, Chott el = Djerid, Chott, *Tunisia* . . . 78 **B7**
Jerilderie, *Australia* . . . 95 **F4**
Jermyn, *U.S.A.* . . . 117 **E9**
Jerome, *U.S.A.* . . . 108 **E6**
Jerramungup, *Australia* . . . 93 **F2**
Jersey, *U.K.* . . . 15 **H5**
Jersey City, *U.S.A.* . . . 117 **F10**
Jersey Shore, *U.S.A.* . . . 116 **E7**
Jerseyville, *U.S.A.* . . . 112 **F9**
Jerusalem, *Israel* . . . 74 **D4**
Jervis B., *Australia* . . . 95 **F5**
Jervis Inlet, *Canada* . . . 102 **C4**
Jerzu, *Italy* . . . 42 **C2**
Jesenice, *Slovenia* . . . 41 **B11**
Jeseník, *Czech Rep.* . . . 27 **A10**
Jesenké, *Slovak Rep.* . . . 27 **C13**
Jesi = Iesi, *Italy* . . . 41 **E10**
Jessnitz, *Germany* . . . 24 **D8**
Jessore, *Bangla.* . . . 67 **H16**
Jesup, *U.S.A.* . . . 115 **K5**
Jesús Carranza, *Mexico* . . . 119 **D5**
Jesús María, *Argentina* . . . 126 **C3**
Jetmore, *U.S.A.* . . . 113 **F5**
Jetpur, *India* . . . 68 **J4**
Jeumont, *France* . . . 19 **B11**
Jevnaker, *Norway* . . . 9 **F14**
Jewett, *U.S.A.* . . . 116 **F3**
Jewett City, *U.S.A.* . . . 117 **E13**
Jeyḫūnābād, *Iran* . . . 71 **C6**
Jeypore, *India* . . . 67 **K13**
Jeziorak, Jezioro, *Poland* . . . 30 **E6**
Jeziorany, *Poland* . . . 30 **E7**
Jeziorka →, *Poland* . . . 31 **F8**

Jha Jha, *India* 69 G12
Jhaarkand = Jharkhand □, *India* 69 H11
Jhabua, *India* 68 H6
Jhajjar, *India* 68 E7
Jhal, *Pakistan* 68 E2
Jhal Jhao, *Pakistan* 66 F4
Jhalawar, *India* 68 G7
Jhalida, *India* 69 H11
Jhalrapatan, *India* 68 G7
Jhang Maghiana, *Pakistan* 68 D5
Jhansi, *India* 69 G8
Jhargram, *India* 69 H12
Jharia, *India* 69 H12
Jharkhand □, *India* 69 H11
Jharsuguda, *India* 67 J14
Jhelum, *Pakistan* 68 C5
Jhelum →, *Pakistan* 68 D5
Jhilmilli, *India* 69 H10
Jhudo, *Pakistan* 68 G3
Jhunjhunu, *India* 68 E6
Ji-Paraná, *Brazil* 124 F6
Ji Xian, *Hebei, China* 56 F8
Ji Xian, *Henan, China* 56 G8
Ji Xian, *Shanxi, China* 56 F6
Jia Xian, *Henan, China* 56 H7
Jia Xian, *Shaanxi, China* 56 E6
Jiading, *China* 59 B13
Jiahe, *China* 59 E9
Jialing Jiang →, *China* 58 C6
Jiamusi, *China* 60 B8
Ji'an, *Jiangxi, China* 59 D10
Ji'an, *Jilin, China* 57 D14
Jianchang, *China* 57 D11
Jianchangying, *China* 57 D10
Jianchuan, *China* 58 D2
Jiande, *China* 59 C12
Jiang'an, *China* 58 C5
Jiangbei, *China* 58 C6
Jiangcheng, *China* 58 F3
Jiangchuan, *China* 58 E4
Jiangdi, *China* 58 D4
Jiangdu, *China* 59 A12
Jiange, *China* 58 A5
Jianghua, *China* 59 E8
Jiangjin, *China* 58 C6
Jiangkou, *China* 58 D7
Jiangle, *China* 59 D11
Jiangling, *China* 59 B9
Jiangmen, *China* 59 F9
Jiangning, *China* 59 B12
Jiangshan, *China* 59 C12
Jiangsu □, *China* 57 H11
Jiangxi □, *China* 59 D11
Jiangyan, *China* 59 A13
Jiangyin, *China* 59 B13
Jiangyong, *China* 59 E8
Jiangyou, *China* 58 B5
Jianhe, *China* 58 D7
Jianli, *China* 59 C9
Jianning, *China* 59 D11
Jian'ou, *China* 59 D12
Jianshi, *China* 58 B7
Jianshui, *China* 58 F4
Jianyang, *Fujian, China* 59 D12
Jianyang, *Sichuan, China* 58 B5
Jiao Xian = Jiaozhou, *China* 57 F11
Jiaohe, *Hebei, China* 56 E9
Jiaohe, *Jilin, China* 57 C14
Jiaojiang, *China* 59 C13
Jiaoling, *China* 59 E11
Jiaozhou, *China* 57 F11
Jiaozhou Wan, *China* 57 F11
Jiaozuo, *China* 56 G7
Jiashan, *China* 59 B13
Jiawang, *China* 57 G9
Jiaxiang, *China* 56 G9
Jiaxing, *China* 59 B13
Jiayi = Chiai, *Taiwan* 59 F13
Jiayu, *China* 59 C9
Jibiya, *Nigeria* 83 C6
Jibou, *Romania* 29 C8
Jibuti = Djibouti ■, *Africa* 81 E5
Jicarón, I., *Panama* 120 E3
Jičín, *Czech Rep.* 26 A8
Jiddah, *Si. Arabia* 75 C2
Jido, *India* 67 E19
Jieshou, *China* 56 H8
Jiexiu, *China* 56 F6
Jieyang, *China* 59 F11
Jigawa □, *Nigeria* 83 C6
Jiggalong, *Australia* 92 D3
Jigni, *India* 69 G8
Jihlava, *Czech Rep.* 26 B8
Jihlava →, *Czech Rep.* 27 C9
Jihlavský □, *Czech Rep.* 26 B8
Jihočeský □, *Czech Rep.* 26 B7
Jihomoravský □, *Czech Rep.* 27 B9
Jijiga, *Ethiopia* 75 F3
Jikamshi, *Nigeria* 83 C6
Jikau, *Sudan* 81 F3
Jilin, *China* 57 C14
Jilin □, *China* 57 C14
Jiloca →, *Spain* 38 D3
Jilong = Chilung, *Taiwan* 59 E13
Jim Thorpe, *U.S.A.* 117 F9
Jima, *Ethiopia* 81 F4
Jimbaran, Teluk, *Indonesia* 63 K18
Jimbolia, *Romania* 28 E5
Jimena de la Frontera, *Spain* 37 J5
Jiménez, *Mexico* 118 B4
Jimo, *China* 57 F11
Jin Jiang →, *China* 59 C10
Jin Xian = Jinzhou, *China* 56 E8
Jin Xian, *China* 57 E11
Jinan, *China* 56 F9
Jinchang, *China* 60 C5
Jincheng, *China* 56 G7
Jinchuan, *China* 58 B4
Jind, *India* 68 E7
Jindabyne, *Australia* 95 F4
Jindřichův Hradec, *Czech Rep.* 26 B8
Jing He →, *China* 56 G5
Jing Shan, *China* 59 B8
Jing Xian, *China* 59 B12
Jing'an, *China* 59 C10
Jingbian, *China* 56 F5
Jingchuan, *China* 56 G4
Jingde, *China* 59 B12
Jingdezhen, *China* 59 C11
Jingdong, *China* 58 E3
Jinggangshan, *China* 59 D10
Jinggu, *China* 58 F3
Jinghai, *China* 56 E9
Jinghong, *China* 58 G3
Jingjiang, *China* 59 A13
Jingle, *China* 56 E6
Jingmen, *China* 59 B9
Jingning, *China* 56 G3
Jingpo Hu, *China* 57 C15
Jingshan, *China* 59 B9
Jingtai, *China* 56 F3
Jingxi, *China* 58 F6
Jingxing, *China* 56 E8
Jingyang, *China* 56 G5
Jingyu, *China* 57 C14
Jingyuan, *China* 56 F3
Jingzhou, *China* 58 D7
Jingziguan, *China* 56 H6
Jinhua, *China* 59 C12
Jining, *Nei Monggol Zizhiqu, China* 56 D7
Jining, *Shandong, China* 56 G9
Jinja, *Uganda* 86 B3
Jinjang, *Malaysia* 65 L3
Jinji, *China* 56 F4
Jinjiang, *Fujian, China* 59 E12
Jinjiang, *Yunnan, China* 58 D3
Jinjini, *Ghana* 82 D4
Jinkou, *China* 59 B10
Jinkouhe, *China* 58 C4
Jinmen Dao, *China* 59 E12
Jinnah Barrage, *Pakistan* 66 C7
Jinning, *China* 58 E4
Jinotega, *Nic.* 120 D2
Jinotepe, *Nic.* 120 D2
Jinping, *Guizhou, China* 58 D7
Jinping, *Yunnan, China* 58 F4
Jinsha, *China* 58 D6
Jinsha Jiang →, *China* 58 C5
Jinshan, *China* 59 B13
Jinshi, *China* 59 C8
Jintan, *China* 59 B12
Jinxi, *Jiangxi, China* 59 D11
Jinxi, *Liaoning, China* 57 D11
Jinxian, *China* 59 C11
Jinxiang, *China* 56 G9
Jinyang, *China* 58 D4
Jinyun, *China* 59 C13
Jinzhai, *China* 59 B10
Jinzhou, *Hebei, China* 56 E8
Jinzhou, *Liaoning, China* 57 D11
Jiparaná →, *Brazil* 124 E6
Jipijapa, *Ecuador* 124 D2
Jiquilpan, *Mexico* 118 D4
Jishan, *China* 56 G6
Jishou, *China* 58 C7
Jishui, *China* 59 D10
Jisr ash Shughūr, *Syria* 70 C3
Jitarning, *Australia* 93 F2
Jitra, *Malaysia* 65 J3
Jiu →, *Romania* 29 G8
Jiudengkou, *China* 56 E4
Jiujiang, *Guangdong, China* 59 F9
Jiujiang, *Jiangxi, China* 59 C10
Jiuling Shan, *China* 59 C10
Jiulong = Kowloon, *China* 59 F10
Jiulong, *China* 58 C3
Jiutai, *China* 57 B13
Jiuxincheng, *China* 56 E8
Jiuyuhang, *China* 59 B12
Jixi, *Anhui, China* 59 B12
Jixi, *Heilongjiang, China* 57 B16
Jiyang, *China* 57 F9
Jiyuan, *China* 56 G7
Jīzān, *Si. Arabia* 75 D3
Jize, *China* 56 F8
Jizera →, *Czech Rep.* 26 A7
Jizl, Wādī al →, *Si. Arabia* 70 E3
Jizō-Zaki, *Japan* 55 G6
Jizzakh, *Uzbekistan* 52 E7
Joaçaba, *Brazil* 127 B5
Joal Fadiout, *Senegal* 82 C1
João Pessoa, *Brazil* 125 E12
Joaquín V. González, *Argentina* 126 B3
Jobat, *India* 68 H6
Jobourg, Nez de, *France* 18 C5
Jódar, *Spain* 37 H7
Jodhpur, *India* 68 F5
Jodiya, *India* 68 H4
Jōetsu, *Japan* 55 F9
Jœuf, *France* 19 C12
Jofane, *Mozam.* 89 C5
Jogbani, *India* 69 F12
Jõgeva, *Estonia* 9 G22
Jogjakarta = Yogyakarta, *Indonesia* 63 G14
Johannesburg, *S. Africa* 89 D4
Johannesburg, *U.S.A.* 111 K9
Johansfors, *Sweden* 11 H9
Johilla →, *India* 69 H9
John Crow Mts., *Jamaica* 120 a
John Day, *U.S.A.* 108 D4
John Day →, *U.S.A.* 108 D3
John Day Fossil Beds ⌓, *U.S.A.* 108 D4
John D'Or Prairie, *Canada* 102 B5
John F. Kennedy International, New York ✈ (JFK), *U.S.A.* 117 F11
John H. Kerr Reservoir, *U.S.A.* 115 G6
John o' Groats, *U.K.* 13 C5
Johnnie, *U.S.A.* 111 J10
John's Ra., *Australia* 94 C1
Johnson, *Kans., U.S.A.* 113 G4
Johnson, *Vt., U.S.A.* 117 B12
Johnson City, *N.Y., U.S.A.* 117 D9
Johnson City, *Tenn., U.S.A.* 115 G4
Johnson City, *Tex., U.S.A.* 113 K5
Johnsonburg, *U.S.A.* 116 E6
Johnsondale, *U.S.A.* 111 K8
Johnsons Crossing, *Canada* 102 A2
Johnston, L., *Australia* 93 F3
Johnston Falls = Mambilima Falls, *Zambia* 87 E2
Johnston I., *Pac. Oc.* 97 F11
Johnstone Str., *Canada* 102 C3
Johnstown, *N.Y., U.S.A.* 117 C10
Johnstown, *Ohio, U.S.A.* 116 F2
Johnstown, *Pa., U.S.A.* 116 F6
Johor, Selat, *Asia* 65 d
Johor Bahru, *Malaysia* 65 d
Jōhvi, *Estonia* 9 G22
Joigny, *France* 19 E10
Joinville, *Brazil* 127 B6
Joinville, *France* 19 D12
Joinville I., *Antarctica* 5 C18
Jojutla, *Mexico* 119 D5
Jokkmokk, *Sweden* 8 C18
Jökulsá á Bru →, *Iceland* 8 D6
Jökulsá á Fjöllum →, *Iceland* 8 C5
Jolfā, *Āzarbājān-e Sharqī, Iran* 70 B5
Jolfā, *Eşfahan, Iran* 71 C6
Joliet, *U.S.A.* 114 E1
Joliette, *Canada* 104 C5
Jolo, *Phil.* 61 J4
Jolon, *U.S.A.* 110 K5
Jomalig I., *Phil.* 61 D5
Jombang, *Indonesia* 63 G15
Jomda, *China* 58 B2
Jonava, *Lithuania* 9 J21
Jones Sound, *Canada* 4 B3
Jonesboro, *Ark., U.S.A.* 113 H9
Jonesboro, *La., U.S.A.* 113 J8
Jong →, *S. Leone* 82 D2
Jonglei, *Sudan* 81 F3
Jonglei □, *Sudan* 81 F3
Joniškis, *Lithuania* 9 H20
Jönköping, *Sweden* 11 G8
Jönköpings län □, *Sweden* 11 G8
Jonquière, *Canada* 105 C5
Jonsered, *Sweden* 11 G6
Jonzac, *France* 20 C3
Joplin, *U.S.A.* 113 G7
Jora, *India* 68 F6
Jordan, *Mont., U.S.A.* 108 C10
Jordan, *N.Y., U.S.A.* 117 C8
Jordan ■, *Asia* 74 E5
Jordan →, *Asia* 74 D4
Jordan Valley, *U.S.A.* 108 E5
Jordanów, *Poland* 31 J6
Jorhat, *India* 67 F19
Jörn, *Sweden* 8 D19
Jorong, *Indonesia* 62 E4
Jørpeland, *Norway* 9 G11
Jorquera →, *Chile* 126 B2
Jos, *Nigeria* 83 D6
Jos Plateau, *Nigeria* 83 D6
Jošanička Banja, *Serbia & M.* 44 C4
José Batlle y Ordóñez, *Uruguay* 127 C4
Joseni, *Romania* 29 D10
Joseph, L., *Nfld. & L., Canada* 105 B6
Joseph, L., *Ont., Canada* 116 A5
Joseph Bonaparte G., *Australia* 92 B4
Joshinath, *India* 69 D8
Joshinetsu-Kōgen △, *Japan* 55 F9
Joshua Tree, *U.S.A.* 111 L10
Joshua Tree △, *U.S.A.* 111 M10
Josselin, *France* 18 E4
Jost Van Dyke, *Br. Virgin Is.* 121 e
Jostedalsbreen, *Norway* 9 F12
Jotunheimen, *Norway* 9 F13
Joubertberge, *Namibia* 88 B1
Joué-lès-Tours, *France* 18 E7
Jourdanton, *U.S.A.* 113 L5
Joutseno, *Finland* 32 B5
Jovellanos, *Cuba* 120 B3
Joyeuse, *France* 21 D8
Józefów, *Lubelskie, Poland* 31 H10
Józefów, *Mazowieckie, Poland* 31 F8
Ju Xian, *China* 57 F10
Juan Aldama, *Mexico* 118 C4
Juan Bautista Alberdi, *Argentina* 126 C3
Juan de Fuca Str., *Canada* 110 B3
Juan de Nova, *Ind. Oc.* 89 B7
Juan Fernández, Arch. de, *Pac. Oc.* 97 L20
Juan José Castelli, *Argentina* 126 B3
Juan L. Lacaze, *Uruguay* 126 C4
Juankoski, *Finland* 8 E23
Juárez, *Argentina* 126 D4
Juárez, *Mexico* 111 N11
Juárez, Sierra de, *Mexico* 118 A1
Juàzeiro, *Brazil* 125 E10
Juàzeiro do Norte, *Brazil* 125 E11
Juba = Giuba →, *Somali Rep.* 75 G3
Juba, *Sudan* 81 G3
Jubany, *Antarctica* 5 C18
Jubayl, *Lebanon* 74 A4
Jubbah, *Si. Arabia* 70 D4
Jubbal, *India* 68 D7
Jubbulpore = Jabalpur, *India* 69 H8
Jübek, *Germany* 24 A5
Jubga, *Russia* 35 H4
Jubilee L., *Australia* 93 E4
Juby, C., *Morocco* 78 C3
Júcar = Xúquer →, *Spain* 39 F4
Júcaro, *Cuba* 120 B4
Juchitán, *Mexico* 119 D5
Judaea = Har Yehuda, *Israel* 74 D3
Judenburg, *Austria* 26 D7
Judith →, *U.S.A.* 108 C9
Judith, Pt., *U.S.A.* 117 E13
Judith Gap, *U.S.A.* 108 C9
Juelsminde, *Denmark* 11 J4
Jugoslavia = Serbia & Montenegro ■, *Europe* 44 C4
Juigalpa, *Nic.* 120 D2
Juillac, *France* 20 C5
Juist, *Germany* 24 B2
Juiz de Fora, *Brazil* 127 A7
Jujuy □, *Argentina* 126 A2
Julesburg, *U.S.A.* 112 E3
Juli, *Peru* 124 G5
Julia Cr. →, *Australia* 94 C3
Julia Creek, *Australia* 94 C3
Juliaca, *Peru* 124 G4
Julian, *U.S.A.* 111 M10
Julian, L., *Canada* 104 B4
Julian Alps = Julijske Alpe, *Slovenia* 41 B11
Julianatop, *Suriname* 125 C7
Julianehåb = Qaqortoq, *Greenland* 101 B6
Jülich, *Germany* 24 E2
Julijske Alpe, *Slovenia* 41 B11
Julimes, *Mexico* 118 B3
Jullundur, *India* 68 D6
Julu, *China* 56 F8
Jumbo, *Zimbabwe* 87 F3
Jumbo Pk., *U.S.A.* 111 J12
Jumentos Cays, *Bahamas* 120 B4
Jumilla, *Spain* 39 G3
Jumla, *Nepal* 69 E10
Jumna = Yamuna →, *India* 69 G9
Junagadh, *India* 68 J4
Junction, *Tex., U.S.A.* 113 K5
Junction, *Utah, U.S.A.* 109 G7
Junction B., *Australia* 94 A1
Junction City, *Kans., U.S.A.* 112 F6
Junction City, *Oreg., U.S.A.* 108 D2
Junction Pt., *Australia* 94 A1
Jundah, *Australia* 94 C3
Jundiaí, *Brazil* 127 A6
Juneau, *U.S.A.* 102 B2
Junee, *Australia* 95 E4
Jungfrau, *Switz.* 25 J3
Junggar Pendi, *China* 60 B3
Jungshahi, *Pakistan* 68 G2
Juniata →, *U.S.A.* 116 F7
Junín, *Argentina* 126 C3
Junín de los Andes, *Argentina* 128 D2
Jūniyah, *Lebanon* 74 B4
Junlian, *China* 58 C5
Juntas, *Chile* 126 B2
Juntura, *U.S.A.* 108 E4
Jur, Nahr el →, *Sudan* 81 F2
Jura = Jura, Mts. du, *Europe* 19 F13
Jura = Schwäbische Alb, *Germany* 25 G5
Jura, *U.K.* 13 F3
Jura □, *France* 19 F12
Jura □, *Switz.* 25 H3
Jūra →, *Lithuania* 30 C9
Jura, Mts. du, *Europe* 19 F13
Jura, Sd. of, *U.K.* 13 F3
Jurbarkas, *Lithuania* 9 J20
Jurien, *Australia* 93 F2
Jurilovca, *Romania* 29 F13
Jūrmala, *Latvia* 9 H20
Jurong, *China* 59 B12
Jurong, *Singapore* 65 d
Juruá →, *Brazil* 124 D5
Juruena, *Brazil* 124 F7
Juruena →, *Brazil* 124 E7
Juruti, *Brazil* 125 D7
Jussey, *France* 19 E12
Justo Daract, *Argentina* 126 C2
Jutaí →, *Brazil* 124 D5
Jüterbog, *Germany* 24 D9
Juticalpa, *Honduras* 120 D2
Jutland = Jylland, *Denmark* 11 H3
Juventud, I. de la, *Cuba* 120 B3
Juvigny-sous-Andaine, *France* 18 D6
Jūy Zar, *Iran* 70 C5
Juye, *China* 56 G9
Juzennecourt, *France* 19 D11
Jvari, *Georgia* 35 J6
Jwaneng, *Botswana* 85 J4
Jyderup, *Denmark* 11 J5
Jylland, *Denmark* 11 H3
Jyväskylä, *Finland* 9 E21

K

K2, *Pakistan* 69 B7
Ka →, *Nigeria* 83 C5
Kaap Plateau, *S. Africa* 88 D3
Kaapkruis, *Namibia* 88 C1
Kaapstad = Cape Town, *S. Africa* 88 E2
Kaba, *Guinea* 82 C2
Kabaena, *Indonesia* 63 F6
Kabala, *S. Leone* 82 D2
Kabale, *Uganda* 86 C3
Kabalo, *Dem. Rep. of the Congo* 86 D2
Kabambare, *Dem. Rep. of the Congo* 86 C2
Kabango, *Dem. Rep. of the Congo* 87 D2
Kabanjahe, *Indonesia* 62 D1
Kabankalan, *Phil.* 61 G5
Kabara, *Mali* 82 B4
Kabardinka, *Russia* 33 K10
Kabardino-Balkar Republic = Kabardino-Balkaria □, *Russia* 35 J6
Kabardino-Balkaria □, *Russia* 35 J6
Kabarega Falls = Murchison Falls, *Uganda* 86 B3
Kabasalan, *Phil.* 61 H5
Kabat, *Indonesia* 63 J17
Kabba, *Nigeria* 83 D6
Kabetogama, *U.S.A.* 112 A8
Kabi, *Niger* 83 C7
Kabin Buri, *Thailand* 64 F3
Kabinakagami L., *Canada* 104 C3
Kabinda, *Dem. Rep. of the Congo* 84 F4
Kabna, *Sudan* 80 D3
Kabompo, *Zambia* 87 E1
Kabompo →, *Zambia* 85 G4
Kabondo, *Dem. Rep. of the Congo* 87 D2
Kabongo, *Dem. Rep. of the Congo* 86 D2
Kabot, *Guinea* 82 C2
Kabou, *Togo* 83 D5
Kabr, *Sudan* 81 E2
Kabrousse, *Senegal* 82 C1
Kabūd Gonbad, *Iran* 71 B8
Kabugao, *Phil.* 61 B4
Kābul, *Afghan.* 68 B3
Kābul □, *Afghan.* 66 B6
Kābul →, *Pakistan* 68 C5
Kabunga, *Dem. Rep. of the Congo* 86 C2
Kaburuang, *Indonesia* 63 D7
Kabushiya, *Sudan* 81 D3
Kabwe, *Zambia* 87 E2
Kačanik, *Serbia & M.* 44 D5
Kačerginė, *Lithuania* 30 D10
Kachchh, Gulf of, *India* 68 H3
Kachchh, Rann of, *India* 68 H4
Kachchhidhana, *India* 69 J8
Kachebera, *Zambia* 87 E3
Kachia, *Nigeria* 83 D6
Kachikau, *Botswana* 88 B3
Kachin □, *Burma* 58 D1
Kachira, L., *Uganda* 86 C3
Kachiry, *Kazakhstan* 52 D8
Kachisi, *Ethiopia* 81 F4
Kachnara, *India* 68 H6
Kachot, *Cambodia* 65 G4
Kaçkar, *Turkey* 73 B9
Kadan, *Czech Rep.* 26 A6
Kadan Kyun, *Burma* 64 F2
Kadanai →, *Afghan.* 68 D1
Kadarkút, *Hungary* 28 D2
Kadavu, *Fiji* 91 D8
Kade, *Ghana* 83 D4
Kadhimain = Al Kāẓimīyah, *Iraq* 70 C5
Kadi, *India* 68 H5
Kadina, *Australia* 95 E2
Kadınhanı, *Turkey* 72 C5
Kadiolo, *Mali* 82 C3
Kadipur, *India* 69 F10
Kadirli, *Turkey* 70 B3
Kadiyevka = Stakhanov, *Ukraine* 33 H10
Kadodo, *Sudan* 81 E2
Kadoka, *U.S.A.* 112 D4
Kadom, *Russia* 34 C6
Kadoma, *Zimbabwe* 87 F2
Kâdugli, *Sudan* 81 E2
Kaduna, *Nigeria* 83 C6
Kaduna □, *Nigeria* 83 C6
Kaduy, *Russia* 32 C9
Kaédi, *Mauritania* 82 B2
Kaélé, *Cameroon* 83 C7
Kaeng Khoï, *Thailand* 64 E3
Kaeng Kra Chan △, *Thailand* 64 F2
Kaeng Tana △, *Thailand* 64 E5
Kaesŏng, *N. Korea* 57 F14
Kāf, *Si. Arabia* 70 D3
Kafan = Kapan, *Armenia* 70 B5
Kafanchan, *Nigeria* 83 D6
Kafareti, *Nigeria* 83 C7
Kaffrine, *Senegal* 82 C1
Kafin, *Nigeria* 83 D6
Kafin Madaki, *Nigeria* 83 C6
Kafinda, *Zambia* 87 E3
Kafirévs, Ákra, *Greece* 46 C6
Kafr el Battikh, *Egypt* 80 H7
Kafr el Dauwâr, *Egypt* 80 H7
Kafr el Sheikh, *Egypt* 80 H7
Kafue, *Zambia* 87 F2
Kafue △, *Zambia* 87 F2
Kafue →, *Zambia* 85 H5
Kafue Flats, *Zambia* 87 F2
Kafulwe, *Zambia* 87 D2
Kaga, *Afghan.* 68 B4
Kaga Bandoro, *C.A.R.* 84 C3
Kagan, *Uzbekistan* 52 F7
Kagarko, *Nigeria* 83 D6
Kagawa □, *Japan* 55 G7
Kagera □, *Tanzania* 86 C3
Kagera →, *Uganda* 86 C3
Kağızman, *Turkey* 70 B4
Kagmar, *Sudan* 81 E3
Kagoshima, *Japan* 55 J5
Kagoshima □, *Japan* 55 J5
Kagul = Cahul, *Moldova* 29 E13
Kahak, *Iran* 71 B6
Kahama, *Tanzania* 86 C3
Kahan, *Pakistan* 68 E3
Kahang, *Malaysia* 65 L4
Kahayan →, *Indonesia* 62 E4
Kahe, *Tanzania* 86 C4
Kahnūj, *Iran* 71 E8
Kahoka, *U.S.A.* 112 E9
Kahoolawe, *U.S.A.* 106 H16
Kahramanmaraş, *Turkey* 70 B3
Kâhta, *Turkey* 73 D8
Kahul, Ozero, *Ukraine* 29 E13
Kahurangi △, *N.Z.* 91 J4
Kahuta, *Pakistan* 68 C5
Kahuzi-Biega △, *Dem. Rep. of the Congo* 86 C2
Kai, Kepulauan, *Indonesia* 63 F8
Kai Besar, *Indonesia* 63 F8
Kai Is. = Kai, Kepulauan, *Indonesia* 63 F8
Kai Kecil, *Indonesia* 63 F8
Kai Xian, *China* 58 B7
Kaiama, *Nigeria* 83 D5
Kaiapoi, *N.Z.* 91 K4
Kaieteur Falls, *Guyana* 124 B7
Kaifeng, *China* 56 G8
Kaihua, *China* 59 C12
Kaijiang, *China* 58 B6
Kaikohe, *N.Z.* 91 F4
Kaikoura, *N.Z.* 91 K4
Kailahun, *S. Leone* 82 D2
Kailash = Kangrinboqe Feng, *China* 69 D9
Kaili, *China* 58 D6
Kailu, *China* 57 C11

Kailua Kona, *U.S.A.* 106 J17
Kaimana, *Indonesia* 63 E8
Kaimanawa Mts., *N.Z.* 91 H5
Kaimganj, *India* 69 F8
Kaimur Hills, *India* 69 G10
Kainab →, *Namibia* 88 D2
Kainji Dam, *Nigeria* 83 D5
Kainji Lake △, *Nigeria* 83 C5
Kainji Res., *Nigeria* 83 C5
Kainuu, *Finland* 8 D23
Kaipara Harbour, *N.Z.* 91 G5
Kaiping, *China* 59 F9
Kaipokok B., *Canada* 105 B8
Kaira, *India* 68 H5
Kairana, *India* 68 E7
Kaironi, *Indonesia* 63 E8
Kairouan, *Tunisia* 79 A8
Kaiserslautern, *Germany* 25 F3
Kaiserstuhl, *Germany* 25 G3
Kaitaia, *N.Z.* 91 F4
Kaitangata, *N.Z.* 91 M2
Kaithal, *India* 68 E7
Kaitu →, *Pakistan* 68 C4
Kaiyang, *China* 58 D6
Kaiyuan, *Liaoning, China* 57 C13
Kaiyuan, *Yunnan, China* 58 F4
Kajaani, *Finland* 8 D22
Kajabbi, *Australia* 94 C3
Kajana = Kajaani, *Finland* 8 D22
Kajang, *Malaysia* 65 L3
Kajaran, *Armenia* 73 C12
Kajiado, *Kenya* 86 C4
Kajo Kaji, *Sudan* 81 G3
Kajuru, *Nigeria* 83 C6
Kaka, *Sudan* 81 E3
Kakabeka Falls, *Canada* 104 C2
Kakadu △, *Australia* 92 B5
Kakamas, *S. Africa* 88 D3
Kakamega, *Kenya* 86 B3
Kakanj, *Bos.-H.* 28 F3
Kakanui Mts., *N.Z.* 91 L3
Kakata, *Liberia* 82 D2
Kakdwip, *India* 69 J13
Kake, *Japan* 55 G6
Kake, *U.S.A.* 102 B2
Kakegawa, *Japan* 55 G9
Kakeroma-Jima, *Japan* 55 K4
Kakhib, *Russia* 35 J8
Kakhovka, *Ukraine* 33 J7
Kakhovske Vdskh., *Ukraine* 33 J7
Kakinada, *India* 67 L13
Kakisa →, *Canada* 102 A5
Kakisa L., *Canada* 102 A5
Kakogawa, *Japan* 55 G7
Kakum △, *Ghana* 83 D4
Kakwa →, *Canada* 102 C5
Kāl Gūsheh, *Iran* 71 D8
Kal Safīd, *Iran* 70 C5
Kala, *Nigeria* 83 C7
Kalaallit Nunaat = Greenland ☑, *N. Amer.* 4 C5
Kalabagh, *Pakistan* 68 C4
Kalabahi, *Indonesia* 63 F6
Kalabáka, *Greece* 46 B3
Kalabana, *Mali* 82 C3
Kalach, *Russia* 34 E5
Kalach na Donu, *Russia* 35 F6
Kaladan →, *Burma* 67 J18
Kaladar, *Canada* 116 B7
Kalahari, *Africa* 88 C3
Kalahari Gemsbok △, *S. Africa* 88 D3
Kalajoki, *Finland* 8 D20
Kalakamati, *Botswana* 89 C4
Kalakan, *Russia* 53 D12
K'alak'unlun Shank'ou = Karakoram Pass, *Asia* 69 B7
Kalam, *Pakistan* 69 B5
Kalama, *Dem. Rep. of the Congo* 86 C2
Kalama, *U.S.A.* 110 E4
Kalámai, *Greece* 46 D4
Kalamariá, *Greece* 44 F6
Kalamazoo, *U.S.A.* 114 D3
Kalamazoo →, *U.S.A.* 114 D2
Kalambo Falls, *Tanzania* 87 D3
Kálamos, *Greece* 46 C5
Kálamos Nisís, *Greece* 46 C2
Kalan, *Turkey* 70 B3
Kalankalan, *Guinea* 82 C3
Kalannie, *Australia* 93 F2
Kalāntarī, *Iran* 71 C7
Kalao, *Indonesia* 63 F6
Kalaotoa, *Indonesia* 63 F6
Kälarne, *Sweden* 10 B10
Kalasin, *Thailand* 64 D4
Kālat, *Iran* 71 E8
Kalat, *Pakistan* 66 E5
Kalāteh, *Iran* 71 B7
Kalāteh-ye Ganj, *Iran* 71 E8
Kálathos, *Greece* 47 E10
Kalaus →, *Russia* 35 H7
Kalávrita, *Greece* 46 C4
Kalbarri, *Australia* 93 E1
Kalbarri △, *Australia* 93 E1
Kale, *Antalya, Turkey* 47 E12
Kale, *Denizli, Turkey* 47 D10
Kalecik, *Turkey* 72 B5
Kalegauk Kyun, *Burma* 67 M20
Kalehe, *Dem. Rep. of the Congo* 86 C2
Kalema, *Tanzania* 86 C3
Kalemie, *Dem. Rep. of the Congo* 86 D2
Kalety, *Poland* 31 H5
Kalewa, *Burma* 67 H19
Kaleybar, *Iran* 70 B5
Kalgoorlie-Boulder, *Australia* 93 F3
Kali →, *India* 69 F8
Kali Sindh →, *India* 68 G6
Kaliakra, Nos, *Bulgaria* 45 C12
Kalianda, *Indonesia* 62 F3
Kalibo, *Phil.* 61 F5
Kalima, *Dem. Rep. of the Congo* 86 C2
Kalimantan, *Indonesia* 62 E4
Kalimantan Barat □, *Indonesia* 62 E4
Kalimantan Selatan □, *Indonesia* 62 E5
Kalimantan Tengah □, *Indonesia* 62 E4
Kalimantan Timur □, *Indonesia* 62 D5
Kálimnos, *Greece* 47 D8
Kalimpong, *India* 69 F13
Kaliningrad, *Russia* 9 J19
Kaliningrad ✕ (KGD), *Russia* 30 D7
Kalininsk, *Russia* 34 E7
Kalinkavichy, *Belarus* 33 F5
Kalinkovichi = Kalinkavichy, *Belarus* 33 F5
Kalinovik, *Bos.-H.* 44 C2
Kalipetrovo, *Bulgaria* 45 B11
Kaliro, *Uganda* 86 B3
Kalirrákhi, *Greece* 45 F8
Kalispell, *U.S.A.* 108 B6
Kalisz, *Poland* 31 G5
Kalisz Pomorski, *Poland* 31 E2
Kaliua, *Tanzania* 86 D3
Kalívia Thorikoú, *Greece* 46 D5
Kalix = Kalixälven →, *Sweden* 8 D20
Kalix, *Sweden* 8 D20
Kalixälven →, *Sweden* 8 D20
Kalka, *India* 68 D7
Kalkan, *Turkey* 47 E11
Kalkarindji, *Australia* 92 C5
Kalkaska, *U.S.A.* 114 C3
Kalkfeld, *Namibia* 88 C2
Kalkfontein, *Botswana* 88 C3
Kalkım, *Turkey* 47 B9
Kalkrand, *Namibia* 88 C2
Kållandsö, *Sweden* 11 F7
Kallavesi, *Finland* 8 E22
Källby, *Sweden* 11 F7
Källered, *Sweden* 11 G6
Kallimasiá, *Greece* 47 C8
Kallinge, *Sweden* 11 H9
Kallithéa, *Greece* 46 D5
Kallmet, *Albania* 44 E3
Kalloní, *Greece* 47 B8
Kallonís, Kólpos, *Greece* 47 B8
Kallsjön, *Sweden* 8 E15
Kalmalo, *Nigeria* 83 C6
Kalmar, *Sweden* 11 H10
Kalmar län □, *Sweden* 11 G10
Kalmar sund, *Sweden* 11 H10
Kalmyk Republic = Kalmykia □, *Russia* 35 G8
Kalmykia □, *Russia* 35 G8
Kalmykovo, *Kazakhstan* 52 E6
Kalna, *India* 69 H13
Kalnai, *India* 69 H10
Kalocsa, *Hungary* 28 D4
Kalofer, *Bulgaria* 45 D8
Kalokhorio, *Cyprus* 49 E12
Kaloko, *Dem. Rep. of the Congo* 86 D2
Kalol, *Gujarat, India* 68 H5
Kalol, *Gujarat, India* 68 H5
Kalolímnos, *Greece* 47 D9
Kalomo, *Zambia* 87 F2
Kalonerón, *Greece* 46 D3
Kalpi, *India* 69 F8
Kaltern = Caldaro, *Italy* 41 B8
Kaltungo, *Nigeria* 83 D7
Kalu, *Pakistan* 68 G2
Kaluga, *Russia* 32 E9
Kalulushi, *Zambia* 87 E2
Kalundborg, *Denmark* 11 J5
Kalush, *Ukraine* 33 H3
Kałuszyn, *Poland* 31 F8
Kalutara, *Sri Lanka* 66 R12
Kalvarija, *Lithuania* 30 D10
Kalyan, *India* 66 K8
Kalyazin, *Russia* 32 D9
Kam, *Albania* 44 D4
Kam →, *Nigeria* 83 D7
Kama, *Dem. Rep. of the Congo* 86 C2
Kama →, *Russia* 6 D16
Kamachumu, *Tanzania* 86 C3
Kamaishi, *Japan* 54 E10
Kamalia, *Pakistan* 68 D5
Kaman, *India* 68 F6
Kaman, *Turkey* 72 C5
Kamanjab, *Namibia* 88 B2
Kamapanda, *Zambia* 87 E1
Kamarān, *Yemen* 75 D3
Kamativi, *Zimbabwe* 88 B4
Kamba, *Nigeria* 83 C5
Kambalda, *Australia* 93 F3
Kambar, *Pakistan* 68 F3
Kambia, *S. Leone* 82 D2
Kambolé, *Togo* 83 D5
Kambolé, *Zambia* 87 D3
Kambos, *Cyprus* 49 D11
Kambove, *Dem. Rep. of the Congo* 87 E2
Kamchatka, Poluostrov, *Russia* 53 D16
Kamchatka Pen. = Kamchatka, Poluostrov, *Russia* 53 D16
Kamchiya →, *Bulgaria* 45 C11
Kame Ruins, *Zimbabwe* 87 G2
Kamen, *Russia* 52 D9
Kamen-Rybolov, *Russia* 54 B6
Kamenica, *Serbia & M.* 44 C6
Kamenica, *Serbia & M.* 44 B3
Kamenice nad Lipou, *Czech Rep.* 26 B8
Kamenjak, Rt, *Croatia* 41 D10
Kamenka = Kaminka, *Ukraine* 33 H7
Kamenka, *Kazakhstan* 34 E10
Kamenka, *Penza, Russia* 34 D6
Kamenka, *Voronezh, Russia* 33 G10
Kamenka Bugskaya = Kamyanka-Buzka, *Ukraine* 33 G3
Kamenka Dneprovskaya = Kamyanka-Dniprovska, *Ukraine* 33 J8
Kamennomostskiy, *Russia* 35 H5
Kameno, *Bulgaria* 45 D11
Kamenolomini, *Russia* 35 G5
Kamensk-Shakhtinskiy, *Russia* 35 F5
Kamensk Uralskiy, *Russia* 52 D7
Kamenskiy, *Russia* 34 E7
Kamenskoye, *Russia* 53 C17
Kamenyak, *Bulgaria* 45 C10
Kamenz, *Germany* 24 D10
Kameoka, *Japan* 55 G7
Kamiah, *U.S.A.* 108 C5
Kamień Krajeński, *Poland* 30 E4
Kamień Pomorski, *Poland* 30 E1
Kamienna →, *Poland* 31 G8
Kamienna Góra, *Poland* 31 H3
Kamieńsk, *Poland* 31 G6
Kamieskroon, *S. Africa* 88 E2
Kamilukuak L., *Canada* 103 A8
Kamin-Kashyrskyy, *Ukraine* 33 G3
Kamina, *Dem. Rep. of the Congo* 87 D2
Kaminak L., *Canada* 103 A10
Kaministiquia, *Canada* 104 C1
Kaminka, *Ukraine* 33 H7
Kaminoyama, *Japan* 54 E10
Kamiros, *Greece* 49 C9
Kamituga, *Dem. Rep. of the Congo* 86 C2
Kamla →, *India* 69 G12
Kamloops, *Canada* 102 C4
Kamnik, *Slovenia* 41 B11
Kamo, *Armenia* 35 K7
Kamo, *Japan* 54 F9
Kamoke, *Pakistan* 68 C6
Kamp →, *Austria* 26 C8
Kampala, *Uganda* 86 B3
Kampar, *Malaysia* 65 K3
Kampar →, *Indonesia* 62 D2
Kampen, *Neths.* 17 B5
Kampene, *Dem. Rep. of the Congo* 84 E5
Kamphaeng Phet, *Thailand* 64 D2
Kampinoski △, *Poland* 31 F7
Kampolombo, L., *Zambia* 87 E2
Kampong Chhnang, *Cambodia* 65 F5
Kampong Pengerang, *Malaysia* 65 d
Kampong Punggai, *Malaysia* 65 d
Kampong Saom, *Cambodia* 65 G4
Kampong Saom, Chaak, *Cambodia* 65 G4
Kampong Tanjong Langsat, *Malaysia* 65 d
Kampong Telok Ramunia, *Malaysia* 65 d
Kampong To, *Thailand* 65 J3
Kampot, *Cambodia* 65 G5
Kampti, *Burkina Faso* 82 C4
Kampuchea = Cambodia ■, *Asia* 64 F5
Kampung Air Putih, *Malaysia* 65 K4
Kampung Jerangau, *Malaysia* 65 K4
Kampung Raja, *Malaysia* 65 K4
Kampungbaru = Tolitoli, *Indonesia* 63 D6
Kamrau, Teluk, *Indonesia* 63 E8
Kamsack, *Canada* 103 C8
Kamsai, *Guinea* 82 C2
Kamskoye Ustye, *Russia* 34 C9
Kamuchawie L., *Canada* 103 B8
Kamui-Misaki, *Japan* 54 C10
Kamyanets-Podilskyy, *Ukraine* 29 B11
Kamyanka-Buzka, *Ukraine* 33 G3
Kamyanka-Dniprovska, *Ukraine* 33 J8
Kamyanyets, *Belarus* 31 F10
Kamyanyuki, *Belarus* 31 F10
Kāmyārān, *Iran* 70 C5
Kamyshin, *Russia* 34 E7
Kamyzyak, *Russia* 35 G9
Kan, *Sudan* 81 F3
Kanaaupscow, *Canada* 101 C12
Kanaaupscow →, *Canada* 104 B4
Kanab, *U.S.A.* 109 H7
Kanab →, *U.S.A.* 109 H7
Kanagi, *Japan* 54 D10
Kanairiktok →, *Canada* 105 A7
Kanália, *Greece* 46 B4
Kananga, *Dem. Rep. of the Congo* 84 F4
Kanash, *Russia* 34 C8
Kanaskat, *U.S.A.* 110 C5
Kanastraíon, Ákra = Palioúrion, Ákra, *Greece* 44 G7
Kanawha →, *U.S.A.* 114 F4
Kanazawa, *Japan* 55 F8
Kanchanaburi, *Thailand* 64 E2
Kanchenjunga, *Nepal* 69 F13
Kanchipuram, *India* 66 N11
Kańczuga, *Poland* 31 J9
Kandaghat, *India* 68 D7
Kandahar = Qandahār, *Afghan.* 66 D4
Kandalaksha, *Russia* 52 C4
Kandangan, *Indonesia* 62 E5
Kandanghaur, *Indonesia* 63 G13
Kandanos, *Greece* 49 D5
Kandava, *Latvia* 30 A9
Kandavu = Kadavu, *Fiji* 91 D8
Kandhíla, *Greece* 46 D4
Kandhkot, *Pakistan* 68 E3
Kandhla, *India* 68 E7
Kandi, *Benin* 83 C5
Kandi, *India* 69 H13
Kandiaro, *Pakistan* 68 F3
Kandıra, *Turkey* 72 B4
Kandla, *India* 68 H4
Kandos, *Australia* 95 E4
Kandreho, *Madag.* 89 B8
Kandy, *Sri Lanka* 66 R12
Kane, *U.S.A.* 116 E6
Kane Basin, *Greenland* 98 B12
Kanel, *Senegal* 82 B2
Kaneohe, *U.S.A.* 106 H16
Kanevskaya, *Russia* 35 G4
Kanfanar, *Croatia* 41 C10
Kang, *Botswana* 88 C3
Kang Krung △, *Thailand* 65 H2
Kangaba, *Mali* 82 C3
Kangal, *Turkey* 72 C7
Kangān, *Fārs, Iran* 71 E7
Kangān, *Hormozgān, Iran* 71 E8
Kangar, *Malaysia* 65 J3
Kangaré, *Mali* 82 C3
Kangaroo I., *Australia* 95 F2
Kangaroo Mts., *Australia* 94 C3
Kangasala, *Finland* 9 F21
Kangāvar, *Iran* 71 C6
Kangding, *China* 58 B3
Kangdong, *N. Korea* 57 E14
Kangean, Kepulauan, *Indonesia* 62 F5
Kangean Is. = Kangean, Kepulauan, *Indonesia* 62 F5
Kangen →, *Sudan* 81 F3
Kanggye, *N. Korea* 57 D14
Kanggyŏng, *S. Korea* 57 F14
Kanghwa, *S. Korea* 57 F14
Kangikajik, *Greenland* 4 B6
Kangiqliniq = Rankin Inlet, *Canada* 100 B10
Kangiqsualujjuaq, *Canada* 101 C13
Kangiqsujuaq, *Canada* 101 B12
Kangiqtugaapik = Clyde River, *Canada* 101 A13
Kangirsuk, *Canada* 101 B13
Kangkar Chemaran, *Malaysia* 65 d
Kangkar Sungai Tiram, *Malaysia* 65 d
Kangkar Teberau, *Malaysia* 65 d
Kangnŭng, *S. Korea* 57 F15
Kangping, *China* 57 C12
Kangra, *India* 68 C7
Kangrinboqe Feng, *China* 69 D9
Kangto, *India* 67 F18
Kanhar →, *India* 69 G10
Kani, *Ivory C.* 82 D3
Kaniama, *Dem. Rep. of the Congo* 86 D1
Kaniapiskau = Caniapiscau →, *Canada* 105 A6
Kaniapiskau, L. = Caniapiscau, L. de, *Canada* 105 B6
Kanin, Poluostrov, *Russia* 52 C5
Kanin Nos, Mys, *Russia* 52 C5
Kanin Pen. = Kanin, Poluostrov, *Russia* 52 C5
Kaninë, *Albania* 44 F3
Kaniva, *Australia* 95 F3
Kanjiža, *Serbia & M.* 28 D5
Kanjut Sar, *Pakistan* 69 A6
Kankaanpää, *Finland* 9 F20
Kankakee, *U.S.A.* 114 E2
Kankakee →, *U.S.A.* 114 E1
Kankan, *Guinea* 82 C3
Kankendy = Xankändi, *Azerbaijan* 70 B5
Kanker, *India* 67 J12
Kankossa, *Mauritania* 82 B2
Kankroli, *India* 68 G5
Kannapolis, *U.S.A.* 115 H5
Kannauj, *India* 69 F8
Kannod, *India* 66 H10
Kano, *Nigeria* 83 C6
Kano □, *Nigeria* 83 C6
Kan'onji, *Japan* 55 G6
Kanoroba, *Ivory C.* 82 D3
Kanowit, *Malaysia* 62 D4
Kanoya, *Japan* 55 J5
Kanpetlet, *Burma* 67 J18
Kanpur, *India* 69 F9
Kansas □, *U.S.A.* 112 F6
Kansas →, *U.S.A.* 112 F7
Kansas City, *Kans., U.S.A.* 112 F7
Kansas City, *Mo., U.S.A.* 112 F7
Kansenia, *Dem. Rep. of the Congo* 87 E2
Kansk, *Russia* 53 D10
Kansŏng, *S. Korea* 57 E15
Kansu = Gansu □, *China* 56 G3
Kantaphor, *India* 68 H7
Kantchari, *Burkina Faso* 83 C5
Kantché, *Niger* 83 C6
Kanté, *Togo* 83 D5
Kantemirovka, *Russia* 33 H10
Kantharalak, *Thailand* 64 E5
Kantli →, *India* 68 E6
Kantō □, *Japan* 55 F9
Kantō-Sanchi, *Japan* 55 G9
Kanturk, *Ireland* 12 D3
Kanuma, *Japan* 55 F9
Kanus, *Namibia* 88 D2
Kanye, *Botswana* 88 C4
Kanzenze, *Dem. Rep. of the Congo* 87 E2
Kanzi, Ras, *Tanzania* 86 D4
Kao Phara, *Thailand* 65 a
Kaohsiung, *Taiwan* 59 F13
Kaokoveld, *Namibia* 88 B1
Kaolack, *Senegal* 82 C1
Kaoshan, *China* 57 B13
Kapaa, *U.S.A.* 106 G15
Kapadvanj, *India* 68 H5
Kapaklı, *Turkey* 45 E11
Kapan, *Armenia* 70 B5
Kapanga, *Dem. Rep. of the Congo* 84 F4
Kapchagai = Qapshaghay, *Kazakhstan* 52 E8
Kapela = Velika Kapela, *Croatia* 41 C12
Kapéllo, Ákra, *Greece* 46 E5
Kapema, *Dem. Rep. of the Congo* 87 E2
Kapfenberg, *Austria* 26 D8
Kapı Dağı, *Turkey* 45 F11
Kapiri Mposhi, *Zambia* 87 E2
Kāpīsā □, *Afghan.* 66 B6
Kapiskau →, *Canada* 104 B3
Kapit, *Malaysia* 62 D4
Kapiti I., *N.Z.* 91 J5
Kaplan, *U.S.A.* 113 K8
Kaplice, *Czech Rep.* 26 C7
Kapoe, *Thailand* 65 H2
Kapoeta, *Sudan* 81 G3
Kápolnásnyék, *Hungary* 28 C3
Kapos →, *Hungary* 28 D3
Kaposvár, *Hungary* 28 D2
Kapowsin, *U.S.A.* 110 D4
Kappeln, *Germany* 24 A5
Kappelshamn, *Sweden* 11 G12
Kapps, *Namibia* 88 C2
Kaprije, *Croatia* 41 E12
Kapsan, *N. Korea* 57 D15
Kapsukas = Marijampolė, *Lithuania* 9 J20
Kaptai L., *Bangla.* 67 H18
Kapuas →, *Indonesia* 62 E3
Kapuas Hulu, Pegunungan, *Malaysia* 62 D4
Kapuas Hulu Ra. = Kapuas Hulu, Pegunungan, *Malaysia* 62 D4
Kapulo, *Dem. Rep. of the Congo* 87 D2
Kapunda, *Australia* 95 E2
Kapuni, *N.Z.* 91 H5
Kapurthala, *India* 68 D6
Kapuskasing, *Canada* 104 C3
Kapuskasing →, *Canada* 104 C3
Kapustin Yar, *Russia* 35 F7
Kaputar, *Australia* 95 E5
Kaputir, *Kenya* 86 B4
Kapuvár, *Hungary* 28 C2
Kara, *Russia* 52 C7
Karā, W. →, *Si. Arabia* 80 C5
Kara Ada, *Turkey* 47 E9
Kara Bogaz Gol, Zaliv = Garabogazköl Aylagy, *Turkmenistan* 52 E6
Kara Burun, *Turkey* 47 E9
Kara Kalpak Republic = Qoraqalpoghistan □, *Uzbekistan* 52 E6
Kara Kum, *Turkmenistan* 52 F6
Kara Sea, *Russia* 52 B7
Karaadilli, *Turkey* 47 C12
Karabiğa, *Turkey* 45 F11
Karabük, *Turkey* 72 B5
Karaburun, *Albania* 44 F3
Karaburun, *Turkey* 47 C8
Karabutak = Qarabutaq, *Kazakhstan* 52 E7
Karacabey, *Turkey* 45 F12
Karacakılavuz, *Turkey* 45 E11
Karacaköy, *Turkey* 45 E12
Karacasu, *Turkey* 47 D10
Karachala = Qaraçala, *Azerbaijan* 35 L9
Karachayevsk, *Russia* 35 J5
Karachev, *Russia* 33 F8
Karachey-Cherkessia □, *Russia* 35 J5
Karachi, *Pakistan* 68 G2
Karad, *India* 66 L9
Karadirek, *Turkey* 47 C12
Karaga, *Ghana* 83 D4
Karaganda = Qaraghandy, *Kazakhstan* 52 E8
Karagayly = Qaraghayly, *Kazakhstan* 52 E8
Karaginskiy, Ostrov, *Russia* 53 D17
Karagola Road, *India* 69 G12
Karagüney Dağları, *Turkey* 72 B6
Karahallı, *Turkey* 47 C11
Karaikal, *India* 66 P11
Karaikkudi, *India* 66 P11
Karaisali, *Turkey* 72 D6
Karaj, *Iran* 71 C6
Karak, *Malaysia* 65 L4
Karakalpakstan = Qoraqalpoghistan □, *Uzbekistan* 52 E6
Karakelong, *Indonesia* 63 D7
Karakitang, *Indonesia* 63 D7
Karakoçan, *Turkey* 73 C9
Karakol, *Kyrgyzstan* 52 E8
Karakoram Pass, *Asia* 69 B7
Karakoram Ra., *Pakistan* 69 B7
Karakurt, *Turkey* 73 B10
Karakuwisa, *Namibia* 88 B2
Karalon, *Russia* 53 D12
Karama, *Jordan* 74 D4
Karaman, *Balıkesir, Turkey* 47 B9
Karaman, *Konya, Turkey* 70 B2
Karamanlı, *Turkey* 47 D11
Karamay, *China* 60 B3
Karambu, *Indonesia* 62 E5
Karamea Bight, *N.Z.* 91 J3
Karamnasa →, *India* 69 G10
Karamürsel, *Turkey* 45 F13
Karand, *Iran* 70 C5
Karangana, *Mali* 82 C3
Karanganyar, *Indonesia* 63 G13
Karangasem, *Indonesia* 63 J18
Karanjia, *India* 69 J11
Karankasso, *Burkina Faso* 82 C4
Karaova, *Turkey* 47 D9
Karapınar, *Turkey* 72 D5
Karasburg, *Namibia* 88 D2
Karasino, *Russia* 52 C9
Karasjok, *Norway* 8 B21
Karasu, *Turkey* 72 B4
Karasu →, *Turkey* 47 E12
Karasuk, *Russia* 52 D8
Karasuyama, *Japan* 55 F10
Karataş, *Adana, Turkey* 72 D6
Karataş, *Manisa, Turkey* 47 C10
Karataş Burnu, *Turkey* 72 D6
Karatau, Khrebet = Qarataū, *Kazakhstan* 52 E7
Karatoprak, *Turkey* 47 D9
Karatsu, *Japan* 55 H5
Karaul, *Russia* 52 B9
Karauli, *India* 68 F7
Karavastasë, L. e, *Albania* 44 F3
Karávi, *Greece* 46 E5
Karavostasi, *Cyprus* 49 D11
Karawang, *Indonesia* 63 G12
Karawanken, *Europe* 26 E7
Karayazı, *Turkey* 73 C10
Karazhal, *Kazakhstan* 52 E8
Karbalā', *Iraq* 70 C5
Kårböle, *Sweden* 10 C9
Karcag, *Hungary* 28 C5
Karcha →, *Pakistan* 69 B7
Karchana, *India* 69 G9
Karczew, *Poland* 31 F8
Kardam, *Bulgaria* 45 C12

Kardeljovo = Ploče, *Croatia* 41 E14
Kardhámila, *Greece* 47 C8
Kardhamíli, *Greece* 46 E4
Kardhítsa, *Greece* 46 B3
Kardhítsa □, *Greece* 46 B3
Kärdla, *Estonia* 9 G20
Kareeberge, *S. Africa* 88 E3
Kareha →, *India* 69 G12
Kareima, *Sudan* 80 D3
Karelia □, *Russia* 52 C4
Karelian Republic = Karelia □, *Russia* 52 C4
Karera, *India* 68 G8
Kārevāndar, *Iran* 71 E9
Kargasok, *Russia* 52 D9
Kargat, *Russia* 52 D9
Kargı, *Turkey* 72 B6
Kargil, *India* 69 B7
Kargopol, *Russia* 32 B10
Kargowa, *Poland* 31 F2
Karguéri, *Niger* 83 C7
Karhal, *India* 69 F8
Kariá, *Greece* 46 C2
Kariaí, *Greece* 45 F8
Karīān, *Iran* 71 E8
Karianga, *Madag.* 89 C8
Kariba, *Zimbabwe* 87 F2
Kariba, L., *Zimbabwe* 87 F2
Kariba Dam, *Zimbabwe* 87 F2
Kariba Gorge, *Zambia* 87 F2
Karibib, *Namibia* 88 C2
Karijini △, *Australia* 92 D2
Karimata, Kepulauan, *Indonesia* 62 E3
Karimata, Selat, *Indonesia* 62 E3
Karimata Is. = Karimata, Kepulauan, *Indonesia* 62 E3
Karimnagar, *India* 66 K11
Karimun Kecil, Pulau, *Indonesia* 65 d
Karimunjawa, Kepulauan, *Indonesia* 62 F4
Karin, *Somali Rep.* 75 E4
Káristos, *Greece* 46 C6
Karīt, *Iran* 71 C8
Kariya, *Japan* 55 G8
Kariyangwe, *Zimbabwe* 89 B4
Karjala, *Finland* 32 A5
Karkaralinsk = Qarqaraly, *Kazakhstan* 52 E8
Karkheh →, *Iran* 70 D5
Karkinitska Zatoka, *Ukraine* 33 K7
Karkinitskiy Zaliv = Karkinitska Zatoka, *Ukraine* 33 K7
Karkuk = Kirkūk, *Iraq* 70 C5
Karkur Tohl, *Egypt* 80 C2
Karl Liebknecht, *Russia* 33 G8
Karleby = Kokkola, *Finland* 8 E20
Karlholmsbruk, *Sweden* 10 D11
Karlino, *Poland* 30 D2
Karlivka, *Ukraine* 33 H8
Karlobag, *Croatia* 41 D12
Karlovac, *Croatia* 41 C12
Karlovarský □, *Czech Rep.* 26 A5
Karlovka = Karlivka, *Ukraine* 33 H8
Karlovo, *Bulgaria* 45 D8
Karlovy Vary, *Czech Rep.* 26 A5
Karlsbad = Karlovy Vary, *Czech Rep.* 26 A5
Karlsborg, *Sweden* 11 F8
Karlshamn, *Sweden* 11 H8
Karlskoga, *Sweden* 10 E8
Karlskrona, *Sweden* 11 H9
Karlsruhe, *Germany* 25 F4
Karlstad, *Sweden* 10 E7
Karlstad, *U.S.A.* 112 A6
Karlstadt, *Germany* 25 F5
Karma, *Niger* 83 C5
Karmėlava, *Lithuania* 30 D11
Karmi'el, *Israel* 74 C4
Karnak, *Egypt* 80 B3
Karnal, *India* 68 E7
Karnali →, *Nepal* 69 E9
Karnaphuli Res. = Kaptai L., *Bangla.* 67 H18
Karnaprayag, *India* 69 D8
Karnataka □, *India* 66 N10
Karnes City, *U.S.A.* 113 L6
Karnische Alpen, *Europe* 26 E6
Karnobat, *Bulgaria* 45 D10
Kärnten □, *Austria* 26 E6
Karo, *Mali* 82 C4
Karoi, *Zimbabwe* 87 F2
Karon, Ao, *Thailand* 65 a
Karonga, *Malawi* 87 D3
Karoo △, *S. Africa* 88 E3
Karoonda, *Australia* 95 F2
Karor, *Pakistan* 68 D4
Karora, *Sudan* 80 D4
Káros, *Greece* 47 E7
Karounga, *Mali* 82 B3
Karousádhes, *Greece* 46 B1
Karpacz, *Poland* 31 H2
Karpasia, *Cyprus* 49 D13
Kárpathos, *Greece* 47 F9
Kárpathos, Stenón, *Greece* 47 F9
Karpatsky △, *Ukraine* 29 B9
Karpenísion, *Greece* 46 C3
Karpuz Burnu = Apostolos Andreas, C., *Cyprus* 49 D13
Karpuzlu, *Turkey* 47 D9
Karratha, *Australia* 92 D2
Kars, *Turkey* 73 B10
Karsakpay, *Kazakhstan* 52 E7
Karsha, *Kazakhstan* 34 F10
Karshi = Qarshi, *Uzbekistan* 52 F7
Karsiyang, *India* 69 F13
Karsog, *India* 68 D7
Karst = Kras, *Croatia* 41 C10
Kartal, *Turkey* 45 F13
Kartál Óros, *Greece* 45 E9
Kartaly, *Russia* 52 D7
Kartapur, *India* 68 D6
Karthaus, *U.S.A.* 116 E6
Kartuzy, *Poland* 30 D5
Karufa, *Indonesia* 63 E8
Karuma ⌓, *Uganda* 86 B3
Karumba, *Australia* 94 B3
Karumo, *Tanzania* 86 C3
Karumwa, *Tanzania* 86 C3
Kārūn →, *Iran* 71 D6
Karungu, *Kenya* 86 C3
Karup, *Denmark* 11 H3
Karviná, *Czech Rep.* 27 B11
Karwan →, *India* 68 F8
Karwar, *India* 66 M9
Karwendel ⌓, *Austria* 26 D4
Karwi, *India* 69 G9
Kaş, *Turkey* 47 E11
Kasaba, *Turkey* 47 E11
Kasache, *Malawi* 87 E3
Kasai →, *Dem. Rep. of the Congo* 84 E3
Kasai-Oriental □, *Dem. Rep. of the Congo* 86 D1
Kasaji, *Dem. Rep. of the Congo* 87 E1
Kasama, *Zambia* 87 E3
Kasan-dong, *N. Korea* 57 D14
Kasane, *Namibia* 88 B3
Kasanga, *Tanzania* 87 D3
Kasanka △, *Zambia* 87 E3
Kasar, Ras, *Sudan* 80 D4
Kasaragod, *India* 66 N9
Kasba L., *Canada* 103 A8
Kāseh Garān, *Iran* 70 C5
Kasempa, *Zambia* 87 E2
Kasenga, *Dem. Rep. of the Congo* 87 E2
Kasese, *Uganda* 86 B3
Kasewa, *Zambia* 87 E2
Kasganj, *India* 69 F8
Kashabowie, *Canada* 104 C1
Kashaf, *Iran* 71 C9
Kāshān, *Iran* 71 C6
Kashechewan, *Canada* 104 B3
Kashgar = Kashi, *China* 60 C2
Kashi, *China* 60 C2
Kashimbo, *Dem. Rep. of the Congo* 87 E2
Kashin, *Russia* 32 D9
Kashipur, *India* 69 E8
Kashira, *Russia* 32 E10
Kashiwazaki, *Japan* 55 F9
Kashk-e Kohneh, *Afghan.* 66 B3
Kashkū'īyeh, *Iran* 71 D7
Kāshmar, *Iran* 71 C8
Kashmir, *Asia* 69 C7
Kashmor, *Pakistan* 68 E3
Kashpirovka, *Russia* 34 D9
Kashun Noerh = Gaxun Nur, *China* 60 B5
Kasiari, *India* 69 H12
Kasimov, *Russia* 34 C5
Kasinge, *Dem. Rep. of the Congo* 86 D2
Kasiruta, *Indonesia* 63 E7
Kaskaskia →, *U.S.A.* 112 G10
Kaskattama →, *Canada* 103 B10
Kaskinen, *Finland* 9 E19
Kaskö = Kaskinen, *Finland* 9 E19
Kaslo, *Canada* 102 D5
Kasmere L., *Canada* 103 B8
Kasongo, *Dem. Rep. of the Congo* 86 C2
Kasongo Lunda, *Dem. Rep. of the Congo* 84 F3
Kásos, *Greece* 47 F8
Kásos, Stenón, *Greece* 47 F8
Kaspi, *Georgia* 35 K7
Kaspichan, *Bulgaria* 45 C11
Kaspiysk, *Russia* 35 J8
Kaspiyskiy, *Russia* 35 H8
Kassab ed Doleib, *Sudan* 81 E3
Kassaba, *Egypt* 80 C2
Kassalâ, *Sudan* 81 D4
Kassalâ □, *Sudan* 81 D4
Kassándra, *Greece* 44 F7
Kassándrinon, *Greece* 44 F7
Kassel, *Germany* 24 D5
Kassinger, *Sudan* 80 D3
Kassiópi, *Greece* 49 A3
Kasson, *U.S.A.* 112 C8
Kastamonu, *Turkey* 72 B5
Kastav, *Croatia* 41 C11
Kastélli, *Greece* 49 D5
Kastéllion, *Greece* 49 D7
Kastellórizon = Megiste, *Greece* 47 E11
Kástellos, *Greece* 47 E9
Kastellou, Ákra, *Greece* 47 F9
Kasterlee, *Belgium* 17 C4
Kastlösa, *Sweden* 11 H10
Kastóri, *Greece* 46 D4
Kastoría, *Greece* 44 F5
Kastoría □, *Greece* 44 F5
Kastorías, Límni, *Greece* 44 F5
Kastornoye, *Russia* 33 G10
Kastós Nisís, *Greece* 46 C2
Kastrosikiá, *Greece* 46 B2
Kastrup, København ✈ (CPH), *Denmark* 11 J6
Kastsyukovichy, *Belarus* 32 F7
Kasulu, *Tanzania* 86 C3
Kasumi, *Japan* 55 G7
Kasumkent, *Russia* 35 K9
Kasungu, *Malawi* 87 E3
Kasungu △, *Malawi* 87 E3
Kasur, *Pakistan* 68 D6
Kata Tjuta = Olga, Mt., *Australia* 93 E5
Kataba, *Zambia* 87 F2
Katagum, *Nigeria* 83 C7
Katahdin, Mt., *U.S.A.* 115 C11
Katako Kombe, *Dem. Rep. of the Congo* 86 C1
Katákolon, *Greece* 46 D3
Katale, *Tanzania* 86 C3
Katanda, *Katanga, Dem. Rep. of the Congo* 86 D1
Katanda, *Nord-Kivu, Dem. Rep. of the Congo* 86 C2
Katanga □, *Dem. Rep. of the Congo* 86 D2
Katangi, *India* 66 J11
Katanning, *Australia* 93 F2
Katastári, *Greece* 46 D2
Katavi △, *Tanzania* 86 D3
Katavi Swamp, *Tanzania* 86 D3
Kateríni, *Greece* 44 F6
Katghora, *India* 69 H10
Katha, *Burma* 67 G20
Katherîna, Gebel, *Egypt* 70 D2
Katherine, *Australia* 92 B5
Katherine Gorge, *Australia* 92 B5
Kathi, *India* 68 J6
Kathiawar, *India* 68 H4
Kathikas, *Cyprus* 49 E11
Kathmandu = Katmandu, *Nepal* 69 F11
Kathua, *India* 68 C6
Kati, *Mali* 82 C3
Katihar, *India* 69 G12
Katima Mulilo, *Zambia* 88 B3
Katimbira, *Malawi* 87 E3
Katingan = Mendawai →, *Indonesia* 62 E4
Katiola, *Ivory C.* 82 D3
Katlabukh, Ozero, *Ukraine* 29 E14
Katlanovo, *Macedonia* 44 E5
Katmandu, *Nepal* 69 F11
Katni, *India* 69 H9
Káto Akhaïa, *Greece* 46 C3
Káto Arkhánai, *Greece* 49 D7
Káto Khorió, *Greece* 49 D7
Káto Pyrgos, *Cyprus* 49 D11
Káto Stavros, *Greece* 44 F7
Katokhí, *Greece* 46 C3
Katompe, *Dem. Rep. of the Congo* 86 D2
Katong, *Singapore* 65 d
Katonga →, *Uganda* 86 B3
Katoomba, *Australia* 95 E5
Katoúna, *Greece* 46 C3
Katowice, *Poland* 31 H6
Katrancı Dağı, *Turkey* 47 D12
Katrine, L., *U.K.* 13 E4
Katrineholm, *Sweden* 10 E10
Katsepe, *Madag.* 89 B8
Katsina, *Nigeria* 83 C6
Katsina □, *Nigeria* 83 C6
Katsina Ala, *Nigeria* 83 D6
Katsina Ala →, *Nigeria* 83 D6
Katsumoto, *Japan* 55 H4
Katsuura, *Japan* 55 G10
Katsuyama, *Japan* 55 F8
Kattaviá, *Greece* 49 D9
Kattegat, *Denmark* 11 H5
Katthammarsvik, *Sweden* 11 G12
Katul, J., *Sudan* 81 E2
Katumba, *Dem. Rep. of the Congo* 86 D2
Katwa, *India* 69 H13
Katwijk, *Neths.* 17 B4
Kąty Wrocławskie, *Poland* 31 G3
Kauai, *U.S.A.* 106 H15
Kauai Channel, *U.S.A.* 106 H15
Kaub, *Germany* 25 E3
Kaudom ⌓, *Namibia* 88 B3
Kaufbeuren, *Germany* 25 H6
Kaufman, *U.S.A.* 113 J6
Kauhajoki, *Finland* 9 E20
Kaukauna, *U.S.A.* 114 C1
Kaukauveld, *Namibia* 88 C3
Kaunakakai, *U.S.A.* 106 H16
Kaunas, *Lithuania* 9 J20
Kaunas ✈ (KUN), *Lithuania* 30 D11
Kaunia, *Bangla.* 69 G13
Kaunos, *Turkey* 47 E10
Kaura Namoda, *Nigeria* 83 C6
Kauru, *Nigeria* 83 C6
Kautokeino, *Norway* 8 B20
Kauwapur, *India* 69 F10
Kavacha, *Russia* 53 C17
Kavadarci, *Macedonia* 44 E6
Kavajë, *Albania* 44 E3
Kavak, *Turkey* 72 B7
Kavak Dağı, *Turkey* 47 D10
Kavaklı, *Turkey* 45 E11
Kavaklıdere, *Turkey* 47 D10
Kavalerovo, *Russia* 54 B7
Kavali, *India* 66 M12
Kavála, *Greece* 45 F8
Kavála □, *Greece* 45 E8
Kavála Kólpos, *Greece* 45 F8
Kavār, *Iran* 71 D7
Kavarna, *Bulgaria* 45 C12
Kavi, *India* 68 H5
Kavimba, *Botswana* 88 B3
Kavīr, Dasht-e, *Iran* 71 C7
Kavkaz, *Russia* 33 K9
Kävlinge, *Sweden* 11 J7
Kavos, *Greece* 49 B4
Kavoúsi, *Greece* 47 F7
Kaw, *Fr. Guiana* 125 C8
Kawa, *Sudan* 81 E3
Kawagama L., *Canada* 116 A6
Kawagoe, *Japan* 55 G9
Kawaguchi, *Japan* 55 G9
Kawambwa, *Zambia* 87 D2
Kawanoe, *Japan* 55 G6
Kawardha, *India* 69 J9
Kawasaki, *Japan* 55 G9
Kawasi, *Indonesia* 63 E7
Kawerau, *N.Z.* 91 H6
Kawhia, *N.Z.* 91 H5
Kawhia Harbour, *N.Z.* 91 H5
Kawio, Kepulauan, *Indonesia* 63 D7
Kawnro, *Burma* 67 H21
Kawthaung, *Burma* 65 H2
Kawthoolei = Kayin □, *Burma* 67 L20
Kawthule = Kayin □, *Burma* 67 L20
Kaxholmen, *Sweden* 11 G8
Kaya, *Burkina Faso* 83 C4
Kayah □, *Burma* 67 K20
Kayalıköy Barajı, *Turkey* 45 E11
Kayan →, *Indonesia* 62 D5
Kaycee, *U.S.A.* 108 E10
Kayeli, *Indonesia* 63 E7
Kayenta, *U.S.A.* 109 H8
Kayes, *Mali* 82 C2
Kayı, *Turkey* 47 B12
Kayima, *S. Leone* 82 D2
Kayin □, *Burma* 67 L20
Kaymakçı, *Turkey* 47 C10
Kayoa, *Indonesia* 63 D7
Kayomba, *Zambia* 87 E1
Kaysatskoye, *Russia* 34 F8
Kayseri, *Turkey* 70 B2
Kaysville, *U.S.A.* 108 F8
Kaz Dağı, *Turkey* 47 B8
Kazachye, *Russia* 53 B14
Kazakhstan ■, *Asia* 52 E7
Kazan, *Russia* 34 C9
Kazan →, *Canada* 103 A9
Kazan-Rettō, *Pac. Oc.* 96 E6
Kazanlŭk, *Bulgaria* 45 D9
Kazanskaya, *Russia* 34 F5
Kazatin = Kozyatyn, *Ukraine* 33 H5
Kazaure, *Nigeria* 83 C6
Kazbek, *Russia* 35 J7
Kāzerūn, *Iran* 71 D6
Kazi Magomed = Qazimämmäd, *Azerbaijan* 35 K9
Kazimierz Dolny, *Poland* 31 G8
Kazimierza Wielka, *Poland* 31 H7
Kazincbarcika, *Hungary* 28 B5
Kazlų Rūda, *Lithuania* 30 D10
Kaztalovka, *Kazakhstan* 34 F9
Kazuma Pan △, *Zimbabwe* 87 F2
Kazuno, *Japan* 54 D10
Kazym →, *Russia* 52 C7
Kcynia, *Poland* 31 F4
Ké-Macina, *Mali* 82 C3
Kéa, *Greece* 46 D6
Keady, *U.K.* 12 B5
Kearney, *U.S.A.* 112 E5
Kearny, *U.S.A.* 109 K8
Kearsarge, Mt., *U.S.A.* 117 C13
Keban, *Turkey* 73 C8
Keban Barajı, *Turkey* 70 B3
Kebbi □, *Nigeria* 83 C5
Kébi, *Ivory C.* 82 D3
Kebnekaise, *Sweden* 8 C18
Kebri Dehar, *Ethiopia* 75 F3
Kebumen, *Indonesia* 63 G13
Kecel, *Hungary* 28 D4
Kechika →, *Canada* 102 B3
Keçiborlu, *Turkey* 47 D12
Kecskemét, *Hungary* 28 D4
Kedada, *Ethiopia* 81 F4
Kėdainiai, *Lithuania* 9 J21
Kedarnath, *India* 69 D8
Kedgwick, *Canada* 105 C6
Kédhros Óros, *Greece* 49 D6
Kediri, *Indonesia* 63 G15
Kedjebi, *Ghana* 83 D5
Kédougou, *Senegal* 82 C2
Kędzierzyn-Koźle, *Poland* 31 H5
Keeler, *U.S.A.* 110 J9
Keeley L., *Canada* 103 C7
Keeling Is. = Cocos Is., *Ind. Oc.* 96 J1
Keelung = Chilung, *Taiwan* 59 E13
Keene, *Canada* 116 B6
Keene, *Calif., U.S.A.* 111 K8
Keene, *N.H., U.S.A.* 117 D12
Keene, *N.Y., U.S.A.* 117 B11
Keep River △, *Australia* 92 C4
Keeper Hill, *Ireland* 12 D3
Keer-Weer, C., *Australia* 94 A3
Keeseville, *U.S.A.* 117 B11
Keetmanshoop, *Namibia* 88 D2
Keewatin, *Canada* 103 D10
Keewatin →, *Canada* 103 B8
Kefa, *Ethiopia* 81 F4
Kefallinía, *Greece* 46 C2
Kefallinía □, *Greece* 46 C2
Kéfalos, *Greece* 47 E8
Kefamenanu, *Indonesia* 63 F6
Kefar Sava, *Israel* 74 C3
Keffi, *Nigeria* 83 D6
Keffin Hausa, *Nigeria* 83 C6
Keflavík, *Iceland* 8 D2
Keftya, *Ethiopia* 81 E4
Keg River, *Canada* 102 B5
Kegaska, *Canada* 105 B7
Keheili, *Sudan* 80 D3
Kehl, *Germany* 25 G3
Keighley, *U.K.* 14 D6
Keila, *Estonia* 9 G21
Keimoes, *S. Africa* 88 D3
Keita, *Niger* 83 C6
Keitele, *Finland* 8 E22
Keith, *Australia* 95 F3
Keith, *U.K.* 13 D6
Keizer, *U.S.A.* 108 D2
Kejimkujik △, *Canada* 105 D6
Kejserr Franz Joseph Fd., *Greenland* 4 B6
Kekri, *India* 68 G6
Kelam, *Ethiopia* 81 G4
Kelamet, *Eritrea* 81 D4
Kelan, *China* 56 E6
Kelang = Klang, *Malaysia* 65 L3
Kelantan →, *Malaysia* 65 J4
Këlcyrë, *Albania* 44 F4
Kelekçi, *Turkey* 47 D11
Keles, *Turkey* 45 G13
Keleti-főcsatorna, *Hungary* 28 C6
Kelheim, *Germany* 25 G7
Kelkit, *Turkey* 73 B8
Kelkit →, *Turkey* 72 B7
Kellerberrin, *Australia* 93 F2
Kellett, C., *Canada* 4 B1
Kelleys I., *U.S.A.* 116 E2
Kellogg, *U.S.A.* 108 C5
Kells = Ceanannus Mor, *Ireland* 12 C5
Kelmė, *Lithuania* 30 C9
Kelmentsi, *Ukraine* 29 B11
Kelokedhara, *Cyprus* 49 E11
Kelowna, *Canada* 102 D5
Kelsey Creek, *Australia* 94 J6
Kelseyville, *U.S.A.* 110 G4
Kelso, *N.Z.* 91 L2
Kelso, *U.K.* 13 F6
Kelso, *U.S.A.* 110 D4
Keluang, *Malaysia* 65 L4
Kelvington, *Canada* 103 C8
Kem, *Russia* 52 C4
Kema, *Indonesia* 63 D7
Kemah, *Turkey* 70 B3
Kemaliye, *Erzincan, Turkey* 73 C8
Kemaliye, *Manisa, Turkey* 47 C10
Kemalpaşa, *Turkey* 47 C9
Kemaman, *Malaysia* 62 D2
Kemano, *Canada* 102 C3
Kemasik, *Malaysia* 65 K4
Kembolcha, *Ethiopia* 81 E4
Kemer, *Antalya, Turkey* 47 E12
Kemer, *Burdur, Turkey* 47 D12
Kemer, *Muğla, Turkey* 47 E11
Kemer Barajı, *Turkey* 47 D10
Kemerovo, *Russia* 52 D9
Ķemeru △, *Latvia* 30 B10
Kemi, *Finland* 8 D21
Kemi älv = Kemijoki →, *Finland* 8 D21
Kemi träsk = Kemijärvi, *Finland* 8 C22
Kemijärvi, *Finland* 8 C22
Kemijoki →, *Finland* 8 D21
Kemmerer, *U.S.A.* 108 F8
Kemmuna = Comino, *Malta* 49 C1
Kemp, L., *U.S.A.* 113 J5
Kemp Land, *Antarctica* 5 C5
Kempas, *Malaysia* 65 d
Kempsey, *Australia* 95 E5
Kempt, L., *Canada* 104 C5
Kempten, *Germany* 25 H6
Kempton, *Australia* 95 G4
Kemptville, *Canada* 117 B9
Ken →, *India* 69 G9
Kenai, *U.S.A.* 100 B4
Kendai, *India* 69 H10
Kendal, *Indonesia* 63 G14
Kendal, *U.K.* 14 C5
Kendall, *Australia* 95 E5
Kendall, *U.S.A.* 115 N5
Kendall →, *Australia* 94 A3
Kendallville, *U.S.A.* 114 E3
Kendari, *Indonesia* 63 E6
Kendawangan, *Indonesia* 62 E4
Kende, *Nigeria* 83 C5
Kendi, Pulau, *Malaysia* 65 c
Kendrapara, *India* 67 J15
Këndrevicës, Maja e, *Albania* 44 F3
Kendrew, *S. Africa* 88 E3
Kene Thao, *Laos* 64 D3
Kenedy, *U.S.A.* 113 L6
Kenema, *S. Leone* 82 D2
Keng Kok, *Laos* 64 D5
Keng Tawng, *Burma* 67 J21
Keng Tung, *Burma* 58 G2
Kengeja, *Tanzania* 86 D4
Kenhardt, *S. Africa* 88 D3
Kéniéba, *Mali* 82 C2
Kenitra, *Morocco* 78 B4
Kenli, *China* 57 F10
Kenmare, *Ireland* 12 E2
Kenmare, *U.S.A.* 112 A3
Kenmare River, *Ireland* 12 E2
Kennebago Lake, *U.S.A.* 117 A14
Kennebec, *U.S.A.* 112 D5
Kennebec →, *U.S.A.* 115 D11
Kennebunk, *U.S.A.* 117 C14
Kennedy, *Zimbabwe* 88 B4
Kennedy Ra., *Australia* 93 D2
Kennedy Range △, *Australia* 93 D2
Kenner, *U.S.A.* 113 L9
Kennet →, *U.K.* 15 F7
Kenneth Ra., *Australia* 93 D2
Kennett, *U.S.A.* 113 G9
Kennewick, *U.S.A.* 108 C4
Kenogami →, *Canada* 104 B3
Kenora, *Canada* 103 D10
Kenosha, *U.S.A.* 114 D2
Kensington, *Canada* 105 C7
Kent, *Ohio, U.S.A.* 116 E3
Kent, *Tex., U.S.A.* 113 K2
Kent, *Wash., U.S.A.* 110 C4
Kent □, *U.K.* 15 F8
Kent Group, *Australia* 95 F4
Kent Pen., *Canada* 100 B9
Kentaū, *Kazakhstan* 52 E7
Kentland, *U.S.A.* 114 E2
Kenton, *U.S.A.* 114 E4
Kentucky □, *U.S.A.* 114 G3
Kentucky →, *U.S.A.* 114 F3
Kentucky L., *U.S.A.* 115 G2
Kentville, *Canada* 105 C7
Kentwood, *U.S.A.* 113 K9
Kenya ■, *Africa* 86 B4
Kenya, Mt., *Kenya* 86 C4
Keo Neua, Deo, *Vietnam* 64 C5
Keokuk, *U.S.A.* 112 E9
Keonjhargarh, *India* 69 J11
Kep, *Cambodia* 65 G5
Kep, *Vietnam* 64 B6
Kepala Batas, *Malaysia* 65 c
Kepez, *Turkey* 45 F10
Kepi, *Indonesia* 63 F9
Kępice, *Poland* 30 D3
Kępno, *Poland* 31 G4
Kepsut, *Turkey* 47 B10
Kerala □, *India* 66 P10
Kerama-Rettō, *Japan* 55 L3
Keran, *Pakistan* 69 B5
Keran △, *Togo* 83 C5
Kerang, *Australia* 95 F3
Keranyo, *Ethiopia* 81 F4
Kerao →, *Sudan* 81 E3
Keratéa, *Greece* 46 D5
Keraudren, C., *Australia* 92 C2

Kerava, *Finland* 9 F21
Kerch, *Ukraine* 33 K9
Kerchenskiy Proliv, *Black Sea* 33 K9
Kerchoual, *Mali* 83 B5
Kerempe Burnu, *Turkey* 72 A5
Keren, *Eritrea* 81 D4
Kerewan, *Gambia* 82 C1
Kerguelen, *Ind. Oc.* 3 G13
Keri, *Greece* 46 D2
Keri Kera, *Sudan* 81 E3
Kericho, *Kenya* 86 C4
Kerinci, *Indonesia* 62 E2
Kerki, *Turkmenistan* 52 F7
Kerkinítis, Límni, *Greece* 44 E7
Kérkira, *Greece* 49 A3
Kérkira □, *Greece* 46 B1
Kérkira ✕ (CFU), *Greece* 46 B1
Kerkouane, *Tunisia* 42 F4
Kerkrade, *Neths.* 17 D6
Kerma, *Sudan* 80 D3
Kermadec Is., *Pac. Oc.* 96 L10
Kermadec Trench, *Pac. Oc.* 96 L10
Kermān, *Iran* 71 D8
Kerman, *U.S.A.* 110 J6
Kermān □, *Iran* 71 D8
Kermān, Bīābān-e, *Iran* 71 D8
Kermānshāh = Bākhtarān, *Iran* 70 C5
Kermen, *Bulgaria* 45 D10
Kermit, *U.S.A.* 113 K3
Kern →, *U.S.A.* 111 K7
Kernhof, *Austria* 26 D8
Kernow = Cornwall □, *U.K.* 15 G3
Kernville, *U.S.A.* 111 K8
Keroh, *Malaysia* 65 K3
Kérou, *Benin* 83 C5
Kérouane, *Guinea* 82 D3
Kerpen, *Germany* 24 E2
Kerrera, *U.K.* 13 E3
Kerrobert, *Canada* 103 C7
Kerrville, *U.S.A.* 113 K5
Kerry □, *Ireland* 12 D2
Kerry Hd., *Ireland* 12 D2
Kersa, *Ethiopia* 81 F5
Kerulen →, *Asia* 60 B6
Kervo = Kerava, *Finland* 9 F21
Kerzaz, *Algeria* 78 C5
Kesagami →, *Canada* 104 B4
Kesagami L., *Canada* 104 B3
Keşan, *Turkey* 45 F10
Kesennuma, *Japan* 54 E10
Keshit, *Iran* 71 D8
Keşiş Dağ, *Turkey* 73 C8
Keskin, *Turkey* 72 C5
Kestell, *S. Africa* 89 D4
Kestenga, *Russia* 52 C4
Keswick, *U.K.* 14 C4
Keszthely, *Hungary* 28 D2
Ket →, *Russia* 52 D9
Keta, *Ghana* 83 D5
Keta Lagoon, *Ghana* 83 D5
Ketapang, *Bali, Indonesia* 63 J17
Ketapang, *Kalimantan, Indonesia* 62 E4
Ketchenery, *Russia* 35 G7
Ketchikan, *U.S.A.* 102 B2
Ketchum, *U.S.A.* 108 E6
Kete Krachi, *Ghana* 83 D4
Ketef, Khalîg Umm el, *Egypt* 70 F2
Keti Bandar, *Pakistan* 68 G2
Kétou, *Benin* 83 D5
Ketri, *India* 68 E6
Kętrzyn, *Poland* 30 D8
Kettering, *U.K.* 15 E7
Kettering, *U.S.A.* 114 F3
Kettle →, *Canada* 103 B11
Kettle Falls, *U.S.A.* 108 B4
Kettle Pt., *Canada* 116 C2
Kettleman City, *U.S.A.* 110 J7
Kęty, *Poland* 31 J6
Keuka L., *U.S.A.* 116 D7
Keuruu, *Finland* 9 E21
Kevelaer, *Germany* 24 D2
Kewanee, *U.S.A.* 112 E10
Kewaunee, *U.S.A.* 114 C2
Keweenaw B., *U.S.A.* 114 B1
Keweenaw Pen., *U.S.A.* 114 B2
Keweenaw Pt., *U.S.A.* 114 B2
Key Largo, *U.S.A.* 115 N5
Key West, *U.S.A.* 107 F10
Keyala, *Sudan* 81 G3
Keynsham, *U.K.* 15 F5
Keyser, *U.S.A.* 114 F6
Kezhma, *Russia* 53 D11
Kezi, *Zimbabwe* 89 C4
Kežmarok, *Slovak Rep.* 27 B13
Kgalagadi Transfrontier ⌓, *Africa* 88 D3
Khabarovsk, *Russia* 53 E14
Khabr, *Iran* 71 D8
Khābūr →, *Syria* 70 C4
Khachmas = Xaçmaz, *Azerbaijan* 35 K9
Khachrod, *India* 68 H6
Khadari, W. el →, *Sudan* 81 E2
Khadro, *Pakistan* 68 F3
Khadyzhensk, *Russia* 35 H4
Khadzhilyangar, *China* 69 B8
Khaga, *India* 69 G9
Khagaria, *India* 69 G12
Khaipur, *Pakistan* 68 E5
Khair, *India* 68 F7
Khairabad, *India* 69 F9
Khairagarh, *India* 69 J9
Khairpur, *Pakistan* 68 F3
Khairpur Nathan Shah, *Pakistan* 68 F2
Khairwara, *India* 68 H5
Khaisor →, *Pakistan* 68 D3
Khajuri Kach, *Pakistan* 68 C3
Khakassia □, *Russia* 52 D9
Khakhea, *Botswana* 88 C3
Khalafābād, *Iran* 71 D6
Khalilabad, *India* 69 F10
Khalīlī, *Iran* 71 E7
Khalkhāl, *Iran* 71 B6
Khálki, *Dhodhekánisos, Greece* 47 E9
Khálki, *Thessalía, Greece* 46 B4
Khalkidhikí □, *Greece* 44 F7
Khalkís, *Greece* 46 C5
Khalmer Yu, *Russia* 52 C7
Khalūf, *Oman* 75 C6
Kham Keut, *Laos* 64 C5
Khamaria, *India* 69 H9
Khambhaliya, *India* 68 H3
Khambhat, *India* 68 H5
Khambhat, G. of, *India* 66 J8
Khamilonísion, *Greece* 47 F8
Khamīr, *Iran* 71 E7
Khamir, *Yemen* 75 D3
Khamsa, *Egypt* 74 E1
Khan →, *Namibia* 88 C2
Khān Abū Shāmat, *Syria* 74 B5
Khān Azād, *Iraq* 70 C5
Khān Mujiddah, *Iraq* 70 C4
Khān Shaykhūn, *Syria* 70 C3
Khān Yūnis, *Gaza Strip* 74 D3
Khanai, *Pakistan* 68 D2
Khānaqīn, *Iraq* 70 C5
Khānbāghī, *Iran* 71 B7
Khandrá, *Greece* 47 F8
Khandwa, *India* 66 J10
Khandyga, *Russia* 53 C14
Khāneh, *Iran* 70 B5
Khanewal, *Pakistan* 68 D4
Khangah Dogran, *Pakistan* 68 D5
Khanh Duong, *Vietnam* 64 F7
Khaniá, *Greece* 49 D6
Khaniá □, *Greece* 49 D6
Khaniadhana, *India* 68 G8
Khaníon, Kólpos, *Greece* 49 D5
Khanka, L., *Asia* 53 E14
Khankendy = Xankändi, *Azerbaijan* 70 B5
Khanna, *India* 68 D7
Khanozai, *Pakistan* 68 D2
Khanpur, *Pakistan* 68 E4
Khanty-Mansiysk, *Russia* 52 C7
Khao Laem △, *Thailand* 64 E2
Khao Laem Res., *Thailand* 64 E2
Khao Luang △, *Thailand* 65 H2
Khao Phlu, *Thailand* 65 b
Khao Pu-Khao Ya △, *Thailand* 65 J2
Khao Sam Roi Yot △, *Thailand* 65 F2
Khao Sok △, *Thailand* 65 H2
Khao Yai △, *Thailand* 64 E3
Khaoen Si Nakarin △, *Thailand* 64 E2
Khapalu, *Pakistan* 69 B7
Khapcheranga, *Russia* 53 E12
Kharabali, *Russia* 35 G8
Kharaghoda, *India* 68 H4
Kharagpur, *India* 69 H12
Khárakas, *Greece* 49 D7
Kharan Kalat, *Pakistan* 66 E4
Kharānaq, *Iran* 71 C7
Kharda, *India* 66 K9
Khardung La, *India* 69 B7
Kharg = Khārk, Jazīreh-ye, *Iran* 71 D6
Khârga, El Wâhât-el, *Egypt* 80 B3
Khargon, *India* 66 J9
Khari →, *India* 68 G6
Kharian, *Pakistan* 68 C5
Kharit, Wadi el →, *Egypt* 80 C3
Khārk, Jazīreh-ye, *Iran* 71 D6
Kharkiv, *Ukraine* 33 H9
Kharkov = Kharkiv, *Ukraine* 33 H9
Kharmanli, *Bulgaria* 45 E9
Kharovsk, *Russia* 32 C11
Kharsawangarh, *India* 69 H11
Kharta, *Turkey* 72 B3
Khartoum = El Khartûm, *Sudan* 81 D3
Khasan, *Russia* 54 C5
Khasavyurt, *Russia* 35 J8
Khāsh, *Iran* 66 E2
Khashm el Girba, *Sudan* 81 E4
Khashum, *Sudan* 81 E2
Khashuri, *Georgia* 35 J6
Khaskovo, *Bulgaria* 45 E9
Khaskovo □, *Bulgaria* 45 E9
Khatanga, *Russia* 53 B11
Khatanga →, *Russia* 53 B11
Khatauli, *India* 68 E7
Khatra, *India* 69 H12
Khātūnābād, *Iran* 71 D7
Khatyrka, *Russia* 53 C18
Khavda, *India* 68 H3
Khaybar, Ḥarrat, *Si. Arabia* 70 E4
Khayelitsha, *S. Africa* 85 L3
Khāzimiyah, *Iraq* 70 C4
Khazzān Jabal al Awliyā, *Sudan* 81 D3
Khe Bo, *Vietnam* 64 C5
Khe Long, *Vietnam* 64 B5
Khe Sanh, *Vietnam* 64 D6
Khed Brahma, *India* 66 G8
Khekra, *India* 68 E7
Khemarak Phouminville, *Cambodia* 65 G4
Khemisset, *Morocco* 78 B4
Khemmarat, *Thailand* 64 D5
Khenāmān, *Iran* 71 D8
Khenchela, *Algeria* 78 A7
Khersān →, *Iran* 71 D6
Khérson, *Greece* 44 E6
Kherson, *Ukraine* 33 J7
Khersónisos Akrotíri, *Greece* 49 D6
Kheta →, *Russia* 53 B11
Khewari, *Pakistan* 68 F3
Khilchipur, *India* 68 G7
Khiliomódhion, *Greece* 46 D4
Khilok, *Russia* 53 D12
Khimki, *Russia* 32 E9
Khíos, *Greece* 47 C8
Khíos □, *Greece* 47 C8
Khirsadoh, *India* 69 H8
Khiuma = Hiiumaa, *Estonia* 9 G20
Khiva, *Uzbekistan* 52 E7
Khīyāv, *Iran* 70 B5
Khlebarovo, *Bulgaria* 45 C10
Khlong Khlung, *Thailand* 64 D2
Khmelnik, *Ukraine* 33 H4
Khmelnitskiy = Khmelnytskyy, *Ukraine* 33 H4
Khmelnytskyy, *Ukraine* 33 H4
Khmer Rep. = Cambodia ■, *Asia* 64 F5
Khoai, Hon, *Vietnam* 65 H5
Khodoriv, *Ukraine* 33 H3
Khodzent = Khŭjand, *Tajikistan* 52 E7
Khojak Pass, *Afghan.* 68 D2
Khok Kloi, *Thailand* 65 a
Khok Pho, *Thailand* 65 J3
Kholm, *Russia* 32 D6
Kholmsk, *Russia* 53 E15
Khomas Hochland, *Namibia* 88 C2
Khombole, *Senegal* 82 C1
Khomeyn, *Iran* 71 C6
Khomeynī Shahr, *Iran* 71 C6
Khomodino, *Botswana* 88 C3
Khon Kaen, *Thailand* 64 D4
Khong →, *Cambodia* 64 F5
Khong Sedone, *Laos* 64 E5
Khonuu, *Russia* 53 C15
Khoper →, *Russia* 34 F6
Khor el 'Atash, *Sudan* 81 E3
Khóra, *Greece* 46 D3
Khóra Sfakíon, *Greece* 49 D6
Khorāsān □, *Iran* 71 C8
Khorat = Nakhon Ratchasima, *Thailand* 64 E4
Khorat, Cao Nguyen, *Thailand* 64 E4
Khorixas, *Namibia* 88 C1
Khorol, *Ukraine* 33 H7
Khorramābād, *Khorāsān, Iran* 71 C8
Khorramābād, *Lorestān, Iran* 71 C6
Khorrāmshahr, *Iran* 71 D6
Khorugh, *Tajikistan* 52 F8
Khosravī, *Iran* 71 D6
Khosrowābād, *Khuzestān, Iran* 71 D6
Khosrowābād, *Kordestān, Iran* 70 C5
Khost, *Pakistan* 68 D2
Khosūyeh, *Iran* 71 D7
Khotyn, *Ukraine* 29 B11
Khouribga, *Morocco* 78 B4
Khowst, *Afghan.* 68 C3
Khowst □, *Afghan.* 66 C6
Khoyniki, *Belarus* 33 G5
Khrami →, *Georgia* 35 K7
Khrenovoye, *Russia* 34 E5
Khrisoúpolis, *Greece* 45 F8
Khristianá, *Greece* 47 E7
Khrysokhou B., *Cyprus* 49 D11
Khtapodhiá, *Greece* 47 D7
Khu Khan, *Thailand* 64 E5
Khuan Wa, *Thailand* 65 a
Khudzhand = Khŭjand, *Tajikistan* 52 E7
Khuff, *Si. Arabia* 70 E5
Khūgīānī, *Afghan.* 68 D2
Khuis, *Botswana* 88 D3
Khuiyala, *India* 68 F4
Khŭjand, *Tajikistan* 52 E7
Khujner, *India* 68 H7
Khulna, *Bangla.* 67 H16
Khulna □, *Bangla.* 67 H16
Khulo, *Georgia* 35 K6
Khumago, *Botswana* 88 C3
Khūnsorkh, *Iran* 71 E8
Khunti, *India* 69 H11
Khūr, *Iran* 71 C8
Khurai, *India* 68 G8
Khurayş, *Si. Arabia* 71 E6
Khureit, *Sudan* 81 E2
Khurīyā Murīyā, Jazā'ir, *Oman* 75 D6
Khurja, *India* 68 E7
Khūrmāl, *Iraq* 70 C5
Khurr, Wādī al, *Iraq* 70 C4
Khūsf, *Iran* 71 C8
Khush, *Afghan.* 66 C3
Khushab, *Pakistan* 68 C5
Khust, *Ukraine* 29 B8
Khutse ⌓, *Botswana* 88 C3
Khuzdar, *Pakistan* 68 F2
Khūzestān □, *Iran* 71 D6
Khvāf, *Iran* 71 C9
Khvājeh, *Iran* 70 B5
Khvalynsk, *Russia* 34 D9
Khvānsār, *Iran* 71 D7
Khvatovka, *Russia* 34 D8
Khvor, *Iran* 71 C7
Khvorgū, *Iran* 71 E8
Khvormūj, *Iran* 71 D6
Khvoy, *Iran* 70 B5
Khvoynaya, *Russia* 32 C8
Khyber Pass, *Afghan.* 68 B4
Khyriv, *Ukraine* 28
Kiabukwa, *Dem. Rep. of the Congo* 87 D1
Kiama, *Australia* 95 E5
Kiamba, *Phil.* 61 H6
Kiambi, *Dem. Rep. of the Congo* 86 D2
Kiambu, *Kenya* 86 C4
Kiang West △, *Gambia* 82 C1
Kiangara, *Madag.* 89 B8
Kiangsi = Jiangxi □, *China* 59 D11
Kiangsu = Jiangsu □, *China* 57 H11
Kiáton, *Greece* 46 C4
Kibæk, *Denmark* 11 H2
Kibale △, *Uganda* 86 B3
Kibanga Port, *Uganda* 86 B3
Kibara, *Tanzania* 86 C3
Kibare, Mts., *Dem. Rep. of the Congo* 86 D2
Kibira △, *Burundi* 86 C3
Kibombo, *Dem. Rep. of the Congo* 86 C2
Kibondo, *Tanzania* 86 C3
Kibre Mengist, *Ethiopia* 81 F4
Kibumbu, *Burundi* 86 C2
Kibungo, *Rwanda* 86 C3
Kibuye, *Burundi* 86 C2
Kibuye, *Rwanda* 86 C2
Kibwesa, *Tanzania* 86 D2
Kibwezi, *Kenya* 86 C4
Kicasalih, *Turkey* 45 E10
Kičevo, *Macedonia* 44 E4
Kichha, *India* 69 E8
Kichha →, *India* 69 E8
Kicking Horse Pass, *Canada* 102 C5
Kidal, *Mali* 83 B5
Kidderminster, *U.K.* 15 E5
Kidepo Valley △, *Uganda* 86 B3
Kidete, *Tanzania* 86 D4
Kidira, *Senegal* 82 C2
Kidnappers, C., *N.Z.* 91 H6
Kidsgrove, *U.K.* 14 D5
Kidston, *Australia* 94 B3
Kidugallo, *Tanzania* 86 D4
Kiel, *Germany* 24 A6
Kiel Canal = Nord-Ostsee-Kanal, *Germany* 24 A5
Kielce, *Poland* 31 H7
Kielder Water, *U.K.* 14 B5
Kieler Bucht, *Germany* 24 A6
Kiembara, *Burkina Faso* 82 C4
Kien Binh, *Vietnam* 65 H5
Kien Tan, *Vietnam* 65 G5
Kienge, *Dem. Rep. of the Congo* 87 E2
Kiessé, *Niger* 83 C5
Kiev = Kyyiv, *Ukraine* 33 G6
Kifaya, *Guinea* 82 C2
Kiffa, *Mauritania* 82 B2
Kifisiá, *Greece* 46 C5
Kifissós →, *Greece* 46 C5
Kifrī, *Iraq* 70 C5
Kigali, *Rwanda* 86 C3
Kigarama, *Tanzania* 86 C3
Kigelle, *Sudan* 81 F3
Kigezi ⌓, *Uganda* 86 C2
Kigoma □, *Tanzania* 86 D3
Kigoma-Ujiji, *Tanzania* 86 C2
Kigomasha, Ras, *Tanzania* 86 C4
Kığzı, *Turkey* 70 B4
Kihei, *U.S.A.* 106 H16
Kihnu, *Estonia* 9 G21
Kii-Sanchi, *Japan* 55 G8
Kii-Suidō, *Japan* 55 H7
Kikaiga-Shima, *Japan* 55 K4
Kikinda, *Serbia & M.* 28 E5
Kikládhes, *Greece* 46 E6
Kikládhes □, *Greece* 46 D6
Kikwit, *Dem. Rep. of the Congo* 84 E3
Kil, *Sweden* 10 E7
Kilafors, *Sweden* 10 C10
Kilar, *India* 68 C7
Kilauea Crater, *U.S.A.* 106 J17
Kilbrannan Sd., *U.K.* 13 F3
Kilchu, *N. Korea* 57 D15
Kilcoy, *Australia* 95 D5
Kildare, *Ireland* 12 C5
Kildare □, *Ireland* 12 C5
Kileikli, *Sudan* 81 E2
Kilfinnane, *Ireland* 12 D3
Kilgore, *U.S.A.* 113 J7
Kilibo, *Benin* 83 D5
Kilifi, *Kenya* 86 C4
Kilimanjaro, *Tanzania* 86 C4
Kilimanjaro □, *Tanzania* 86 C4
Kilimli, *Turkey* 72 B4
Kilindini, *Kenya* 86 C4
Kilis, *Turkey* 70 B3
Kiliya, *Ukraine* 29 E14
Kilkee, *Ireland* 12 D2
Kilkeel, *U.K.* 12 B5
Kilkenny, *Ireland* 12 D4
Kilkenny □, *Ireland* 12 D4
Kilkieran B., *Ireland* 12 C2
Kilkís, *Greece* 44 F6
Kilkís □, *Greece* 44 E6
Killala, *Ireland* 12 B2
Killala B., *Ireland* 12 B2
Killaloe, *Canada* 116 A7
Killaloe, *Ireland* 12 D3
Killarney, *Australia* 95 D5
Killarney, *Canada* 103 D9
Killarney, *Ireland* 12 D2
Killarney △, *Ireland* 12 D2
Killary Harbour, *Ireland* 12 C2
Killdeer, *U.S.A.* 112 B3
Killeberg, *Sweden* 11 H8
Killeen, *U.S.A.* 113 K6
Killin, *U.K.* 13 E4
Killíni, *Ilía, Greece* 46 D3
Killíni, *Korinthía, Greece* 46 D4
Killorglin, *Ireland* 12 D2
Killybegs, *Ireland* 12 B3
Kilmarnock, *U.K.* 13 F4
Kilmez, *Russia* 34 B10
Kilmez →, *Russia* 34 B10
Kilmore, *Australia* 95 F3
Kilondo, *Tanzania* 87 D3
Kilosa, *Tanzania* 86 D4
Kilrush, *Ireland* 12 D2
Kilwa Kisiwani, *Tanzania* 87 D4
Kilwa Kivinje, *Tanzania* 87 D4
Kilwa Masoko, *Tanzania* 87 D4
Kilwinning, *U.K.* 13 F4
Kim, *U.S.A.* 113 G3
Kim →, *Cameroon* 83 D7
Kimaam, *Indonesia* 63 F9
Kimamba, *Tanzania* 86 D4
Kimba, *Australia* 95 E2
Kimball, *Nebr., U.S.A.* 112 E3
Kimball, *S. Dak., U.S.A.* 112 D5
Kimberley, *Australia* 92 C4
Kimberley, *Canada* 102 D5
Kimberley, *S. Africa* 88 D3
Kimberly, *U.S.A.* 108 E6
Kimch'aek, *N. Korea* 57 D15
Kimch'ŏn, *S. Korea* 57 F15
Kími, *Greece* 46 C6
Kimje, *S. Korea* 57 G14
Kimmirut, *Canada* 101 B13
Kímolos, *Greece* 46 E6
Kimovsk, *Moskva, Russia* 32 E9
Kimovsk, *Tula, Russia* 32 E10
Kimparana, *Mali* 82 C4
Kimpese, *Dem. Rep. of the Congo* 84 F2
Kimry, *Russia* 32 D9
Kimstad, *Sweden* 11 F9
Kinabalu, Gunung, *Malaysia* 62 C5
Kínaros, *Greece* 47 E8
Kinaskan L., *Canada* 102 B2
Kinbasket L., *Canada* 102 C5
Kincardine, *Canada* 116 B3
Kincolith, *Canada* 102 C3
Kinda, *Dem. Rep. of the Congo* 87 D2
Kindberg, *Austria* 26 D8
Kinde, *U.S.A.* 116 C2
Kinder Scout, *U.K.* 14 D6
Kindersley, *Canada* 103 C7
Kindia, *Guinea* 82 D2
Kindu, *Dem. Rep. of the Congo* 86 C2
Kinel, *Russia* 34 D10
Kineshma, *Russia* 34 B6
Kinesi, *Tanzania* 86 C3
King, L., *Australia* 93 F2
King, Mt., *Australia* 94 D4
King City, *U.S.A.* 110 J5
King Cr. →, *Australia* 94 C2
King Edward →, *Australia* 92 B4
King Frederick VI Land = Kong Frederik VI Kyst, *Greenland* 101 B15
King George B., *Falk. Is.* 128 G4
King George I., *Antarctica* 5 C18
King George Is., *Canada* 101 C11
King I. = Kadan Kyun, *Burma* 64 F2
King I., *Australia* 95 F3
King I., *Canada* 102 C3
King Leopold Ranges, *Australia* 92 C4
King of Prussia, *U.S.A.* 117 F9
King Sd., *Australia* 92 C3
King Sejong, *Antarctica* 5 C18
King William I., *Canada* 100 B10
King William's Town, *S. Africa* 88 E4
Kingait = Cape Dorset, *Canada* 101 B12
Kingaok = Bathurst Inlet, *Canada* 100 B9
Kingaroy, *Australia* 95 D5
Kingfisher, *U.S.A.* 113 H6
Kingirbān, *Iraq* 70 C5
Kingisepp = Kuressaare, *Estonia* 9 G20
Kingisepp, *Russia* 32 C5
Kingman, *Ariz., U.S.A.* 111 K12
Kingman, *Kans., U.S.A.* 113 G5
Kingoonya, *Australia* 95 E2
Kingri, *Pakistan* 68 D3
Kings →, *U.S.A.* 110 J7
Kings Canyon △, *U.S.A.* 110 J8
King's Lynn, *U.K.* 14 E8
Kings Mountain, *U.S.A.* 115 H5
Kings Park, *U.S.A.* 117 F11
King's Peak, *U.S.A.* 108 F8
Kingsbridge, *U.K.* 15 G4
Kingsburg, *U.S.A.* 110 J7
Kingscote, *Australia* 95 F2
Kingscourt, *Ireland* 12 C5
Kingsford, *U.S.A.* 114 C1
Kingsland, *U.S.A.* 115 K5
Kingsley, *U.S.A.* 112 D7
Kingsport, *U.S.A.* 115 G4
Kingston, *Canada* 117 B8
Kingston, *Jamaica* 120 a
Kingston, *N.Z.* 91 L2
Kingston, *N.H., U.S.A.* 117 D13
Kingston, *N.Y., U.S.A.* 117 E11
Kingston, *Pa., U.S.A.* 117 E9
Kingston, *R.I., U.S.A.* 117 E13
Kingston Pk., *U.S.A.* 111 K11
Kingston South East, *Australia* 95 F2
Kingston upon Hull, *U.K.* 14 D7
Kingston upon Hull □, *U.K.* 14 D7
Kingston-upon-Thames □, *U.K.* 15 F7
Kingstown, *St. Vincent* 121 D7
Kingstree, *U.S.A.* 115 J6
Kingsville, *Canada* 116 D2
Kingsville, *U.S.A.* 113 M6
Kingussie, *U.K.* 13 D4
Kingwood, *U.S.A.* 113 K7
Kınık, *Antalya, Turkey* 47 E11
Kınık, *İzmir, Turkey* 47 B9
Kinistino, *Canada* 103 C7
Kinkala, *Congo* 84 E2
Kinki □, *Japan* 55 H8
Kinleith, *N.Z.* 91 H5
Kinlochleven, *U.K.* 13 E4
Kinmount, *Canada* 116 B6
Kinna, *Sweden* 11 G6
Kinnairds Hd., *U.K.* 13 D6
Kinnared, *Sweden* 11 G7
Kinnarp, *Sweden* 11 F7
Kinneviken, *Sweden* 11 F7
Kino, *Mexico* 118 B2
Kinoje →, *Canada* 104 B3
Kinomoto, *Japan* 55 G8
Kinoni, *Uganda* 86 C3
Kinoosao, *Canada* 103 B8
Kinross, *U.K.* 13 E5
Kinsale, *Ireland* 12 E3
Kinsale, Old Hd. of, *Ireland* 12 E3
Kinsha = Chang Jiang →, *China* 59 B13
Kinshasa, *Dem. Rep. of the Congo* 84 E3
Kinsley, *U.S.A.* 113 G5
Kinsman, *U.S.A.* 116 E4
Kinston, *U.S.A.* 115 H7
Kintamani, *Indonesia* 63 J18
Kintampo, *Ghana* 83 D4
Kintore, *U.K.* 13 D6
Kintore Ra., *Australia* 92 D4
Kintyre, *U.K.* 13 F3
Kintyre, Mull of, *U.K.* 13 F3
Kinushseo →, *Canada* 104 A3
Kinuso, *Canada* 102 B5
Kinyangiri, *Tanzania* 86 C3
Kinyeti, *Sudan* 81 G3
Kinzig →, *Germany* 25 G3
Kinzua, *U.S.A.* 116 E6
Kinzua Dam, *U.S.A.* 116 E6
Kióni, *Greece* 46 C2

Kiosk, Canada 104 C4
Kiowa, Kans., U.S.A. 113 G5
Kiowa, Okla., U.S.A. 113 H7
Kipahigan L., Canada 103 B8
Kipanga, Tanzania 86 D4
Kiparissía, Greece 46 D3
Kiparissiakós Kólpos, Greece 46 D3
Kipawa, L., Canada 104 C4
Kipembawe, Tanzania 86 D3
Kipengere Ra., Tanzania 87 D3
Kipili, Tanzania 86 D3
Kipini, Kenya 86 C5
Kipling, Canada 103 C8
Kippure, Ireland 12 C5
Kipushi, Dem. Rep. of the Congo 87 E2
Kirane, Mali 82 B2
Kiranomena, Madag. 89 B8
Kiraz, Turkey 47 C10
Kirazlı, Turkey 45 F10
Kirchhain, Germany 24 E4
Kirchheim, Germany 25 G5
Kirchheimbolanden, Germany 25 F3
Kirchschlag, Austria 27 D9
Kireç, Turkey 47 B10
Kirensk, Russia 53 D11
Kirghizia = Kyrgyzstan ■, Asia 52 E8
Kirghizstan = Kyrgyzstan ■, Asia 52 E8
Kiribati ■, Pac. Oc. 96 H10
Kırıkhan, Turkey 72 D7
Kırıkkale, Turkey 72 C5
Kirillov, Russia 32 C10
Kirin = Jilin, China 57 C14
Kirinyaga = Kenya, Mt., Kenya 86 C4
Kirishi, Russia 32 C7
Kirishima Yaku △, Japan 55 J5
Kiritimati, Kiribati 97 G12
Kırka, Turkey 47 B12
Kırkağaç, Turkey 47 B9
Kirkby, U.K. 14 D5
Kirkby-in-Ashfield, U.K. 14 D6
Kirkby Lonsdale, U.K. 14 C5
Kirkby Stephen, U.K. 14 C5
Kirkcaldy, U.K. 13 E5
Kirkcudbright, U.K. 13 G4
Kirkee, India 66 K8
Kirkenes, Norway 8 B23
Kirkfield, Canada 116 B6
Kirkintilloch, U.K. 13 F4
Kirkjubæjarklaustur, Iceland 8 E4
Kirkkonummi, Finland 9 F21
Kirkland Lake, Canada 104 C3
Kırklareli, Turkey 45 E11
Kırklareli □, Turkey 45 E11
Kirksville, U.S.A. 112 E8
Kirkūk, Iraq 70 C5
Kirkwall, U.K. 13 C6
Kirkwood, S. Africa 88 E4
Kirn, Germany 25 F3
Kirov, Kaluga, Russia 32 E8
Kirov, Kirov, Russia 52 D5
Kirovabad = Gäncä, Azerbaijan 35 K8
Kirovograd = Kirovohrad, Ukraine 33 H7
Kirovohrad, Ukraine 33 H7
Kirovskiy, Astrakhan, Russia 35 H9
Kirovskiy, Kamchatka, Russia 53 D16
Kirovskiy, Primorsk, Russia 54 B6
Kirriemuir, U.K. 13 E5
Kirsanov, Russia 34 D6
Kırşehir, Turkey 70 B2
Kirtachi, Niger 83 C5
Kirthar Range, Pakistan 68 F2
Kirtland, U.S.A. 109 H9
Kiruna, Sweden 8 C19
Kirundu, Dem. Rep. of the Congo 86 C2
Kirya, Russia 34 C8
Kiryū, Japan 55 F9
Kisa, Sweden 11 G9
Kisaga, Tanzania 86 C3
Kisalaya, Nic. 120 D3
Kisalföld, Hungary 28 C2
Kisámou, Kólpos, Greece 49 D5
Kisanga, Dem. Rep. of the Congo 86 B2
Kisangani, Dem. Rep. of the Congo 86 B2
Kisar, Indonesia 63 F7
Kisarawe, Tanzania 86 D4
Kisarazu, Japan 55 G9
Kisbér, Hungary 28 C3
Kishanganga →, Pakistan 69 B5
Kishanganj, India 69 F13
Kishangarh, Raj., India 68 F6
Kishangarh, Raj., India 68 F4
Kishi, Nigeria 83 D5
Kishinev = Chişinău, Moldova 29 C13
Kishiwada, Japan 55 G7
Kishtwar, India 69 C6
Kisielice, Poland 30 E6
Kisigo ⌂, Tanzania 86 D3
Kisii, Kenya 86 C3
Kisiju, Tanzania 86 D4
Kisir, Turkey 73 B10
Kisizi, Uganda 86 C2
Kiskomárom = Zalakomár, Hungary 28 D2
Kiskörei-víztároló, Hungary 28 C5
Kiskőrös, Hungary 28 D4
Kiskundorozsma, Hungary 28 D5
Kiskunfélegyháza, Hungary 28 D4
Kiskunhalas, Hungary 28 D4
Kiskunmajsa, Hungary 28 D4
Kiskunsági △, Hungary 28 D4
Kislovodsk, Russia 35 J6
Kismayu = Chisimaio, Somali Rep. 77 G8
Kiso-Gawa →, Japan 55 G8
Kiso-Sammyaku, Japan 55 G8
Kisofukushima, Japan 55 G8
Kisoro, Uganda 86 C2
Kissidougou, Guinea 82 D2
Kissimmee, U.S.A. 115 L5
Kissimmee →, U.S.A. 115 M5
Kississing L., Canada 103 B8
Kissónerga, Cyprus 49 E11
Kissu, J., Sudan 80 C2
Kistanje, Croatia 41 E12
Kisújszállás, Hungary 28 C5
Kisumu, Kenya 86 C3
Kisvárda, Hungary 28 B7
Kiswani, Tanzania 86 C4
Kiswere, Tanzania 87 D4
Kit Carson, U.S.A. 112 F3
Kita, Mali 82 C3
Kitaibaraki, Japan 55 F10
Kitakami, Japan 54 E10
Kitakami-Gawa →, Japan 54 E10
Kitakami-Sammyaku, Japan 54 E10
Kitakata, Japan 54 F9
Kitakyūshū, Japan 55 H5
Kitale, Kenya 86 B4
Kitami, Japan 54 C11
Kitami-Sammyaku, Japan 54 B11
Kitangiri, L., Tanzania 86 C3
Kitaya, Tanzania 87 E5
Kitchener, Canada 116 C4
Kitee, Finland 32 A6
Kitega = Gitega, Burundi 86 C2
Kitengo, Dem. Rep. of the Congo 86 D1
Kitgum, Uganda 86 B3
Kíthira, Greece 46 E5
Kíthnos, Greece 46 D6
Kiti, Cyprus 49 E12
Kiti, C., Cyprus 49 E12
Kitimat, Canada 102 C3
Kitinen →, Finland 8 C22
Kitiyab, Sudan 81 D3
Kítros, Greece 44 F6
Kitsman, Ukraine 29 B10
Kitsuki, Japan 55 H5
Kittakittaooloo, L., Australia 95 D2
Kittanning, U.S.A. 116 F5
Kittatinny Mts., U.S.A. 117 F10
Kittery, U.S.A. 115 D10
Kittilä, Finland 8 C21
Kitui, Kenya 86 C4
Kitwanga, Canada 102 B3
Kitwe, Zambia 87 E2
Kitzbühel, Austria 26 D5
Kitzbühler Alpen, Austria 26 D5
Kitzingen, Germany 25 F6
Kivarli, India 68 G5
Kivertsi, Ukraine 33 G3
Kividhes, Cyprus 49 E11
Kivik, Sweden 11 J8
Kivotós, Greece 44 F5
Kivu, L., Dem. Rep. of the Congo 86 C2
Kiyev = Kyyiv, Ukraine 33 G6
Kiyevskoye Vdkhr. = Kyyivske Vdskh., Ukraine 33 G6
Kıyıköy, Turkey 45 E12
Kiziguru, Rwanda 86 C3
Kızıl Adalar, Turkey 45 F13
Kızıl Irmak →, Turkey 72 B6
Kizil Jilga, China 69 B8
Kizil Yurt, Russia 35 J8
Kızılcabölük, Turkey 47 D11
Kızılcadağ, Turkey 47 D11
Kızılcahamam, Turkey 72 B5
Kızılhisar, Turkey 72 D3
Kızılırmak, Turkey 72 B5
Kızılkaya, Turkey 47 D12
Kızılören, Turkey 47 C12
Kızıltepe, Turkey 70 B4
Kizimkazi, Tanzania 86 D4
Kizlyar, Russia 35 J8
Kizyl-Arvat = Gyzylarbat, Turkmenistan 52 F6
Kjellerup, Denmark 11 H3
Kjölur, Iceland 8 D4
Kladanj, Bos.-H. 28 F3
Kladnica, Serbia & M. 44 C4
Kladno, Czech Rep. 26 A7
Kladovo, Serbia & M. 44 B6
Klaeng, Thailand 64 F3
Klagenfurt, Austria 26 E7
Klaipėda, Lithuania 9 J19
Klaipėda □, Lithuania 30 C8
Klaksvík, Færoe Is. 8 E9
Klamath →, U.S.A. 108 F1
Klamath Falls, U.S.A. 108 E3
Klamath Mts., U.S.A. 108 F2
Klamono, Indonesia 63 E8
Klang, Malaysia 65 L3
Klanjec, Croatia 41 B12
Klappan →, Canada 102 B3
Klarälven →, Sweden 10 E7
Klässbol, Sweden 10 E6
Klatovy, Czech Rep. 26 B6
Klawer, S. Africa 88 E2
Klazienaveen, Neths. 17 B6
Klé, Mali 82 C3
Kłecko, Poland 31 F4
Kleczew, Poland 31 F5
Kleena Kleene, Canada 102 C4
Klein-Karas, Namibia 88 D2
Klekovača, Bos.-H. 41 D13
Klembivka, Ukraine 29 B13
Klenoec, Macedonia 44 E4
Klenovec, Slovak Rep. 27 C12
Klerksdorp, S. Africa 88 D4
Kleszczele, Poland 31 F10
Kletnya, Russia 32 F7
Kletsk = Klyetsk, Belarus 33 F4
Kletskiy, Russia 35 F6
Kleve, Germany 24 D2
Klickitat, U.S.A. 108 D3
Klickitat →, U.S.A. 110 E5
Klidhes, Cyprus 49 D13
Klimovichi, Belarus 32 F6
Klin, Russia 32 D9
Klina, Serbia & M. 44 D4
Klinaklini →, Canada 102 C3
Klintehamn, Sweden 11 G12
Klintsy, Russia 33 F7
Klip →, S. Africa 89 D4
Klipdale, S. Africa 88 E2
Klippan, Sweden 11 H7
Klipplaat, S. Africa 88 E3
Klishkivtsi, Ukraine 29 B11
Klisura, Bulgaria 45 D8
Kljajićevo, Serbia & M. 28 E4
Ključ, Bos.-H. 41 D13
Kłobuck, Poland 31 H5
Klockestrand, Sweden 10 B11
Kłodawa, Poland 31 F5
Kłodzko, Poland 31 H3
Klong Wang Chao △, Thailand 64 D2
Klos, Albania 44 E4
Klosterneuburg, Austria 27 C9
Klosters, Switz. 25 J5
Klötze, Germany 24 C7
Klouto, Togo 83 D5
Kluane △, Canada 102 A1
Kluane L., Canada 100 B6
Kluczbork, Poland 31 H5
Klukwan, U.S.A. 102 B1
Klungkung, Indonesia 63 K18
Klyetsk, Belarus 33 F4
Klyuchevskaya, Gora, Russia 53 D17
Knäred, Sweden 11 H7
Knaresborough, U.K. 14 C6
Knee L., Man., Canada 104 A1
Knee L., Sask., Canada 103 B7
Knezha, Bulgaria 45 C8
Knight Inlet, Canada 102 C3
Knighton, U.K. 15 E4
Knights Ferry, U.S.A. 110 H6
Knights Landing, U.S.A. 110 G5
Knin, Croatia 41 D13
Knislinge, Sweden 11 H8
Knittelfeld, Austria 26 D7
Knivsta, Sweden 10 E11
Knjaževac, Serbia & M. 44 C6
Knob, C., Australia 93 F2
Knock, Ireland 12 C3
Knockmealdown Mts., Ireland 12 D4
Knokke-Heist, Belgium 17 C3
Knossós, Greece 49 D7
Knowlton, Canada 117 A12
Knox, U.S.A. 114 E2
Knox Coast, Antarctica 5 C8
Knoxville, Iowa, U.S.A. 112 E8
Knoxville, Pa., U.S.A. 116 E7
Knoxville, Tenn., U.S.A. 115 H4
Knud Rasmussen Land, Greenland 4 A5
Knysna, S. Africa 88 E3
Knyszyn, Poland 30 E9
Ko Kha, Thailand 64 C2
Ko Tarutao △, Thailand 65 J2
Ko Yao, Thailand 65 a
Koartac = Quaqtaq, Canada 101 B13
Koba, Indonesia 63 F8
Kobarid, Slovenia 41 B10
Kobayashi, Japan 55 J5
Kōbe, Japan 55 G7
Kobelyaky, Ukraine 33 H8
København, Denmark 11 J6
København ✈ (CPH), Denmark 11 J6
Københavns Amtskommune □, Denmark 11 J6
Kobenni, Mauritania 82 B3
Kōbi-Sho, Japan 55 M1
Koblenz, Germany 25 E3
Kobo, Ethiopia 81 E4
Kobryn, Belarus 33 F3
Kobuleti, Georgia 35 K5
Kobyletska Polyana, Ukraine 29 B9
Kobylin, Poland 31 G4
Kobyłka, Poland 31 F8
Kobylkino, Russia 34 C6
Koca →, Turkey 45 F11
Kocabaş, Turkey 47 D11
Kocaeli, Turkey 45 F13
Kocaeli □, Turkey 45 F13
Kočane, Serbia & M. 44 C5
Kočani, Macedonia 44 E6
Koçarlı, Turkey 47 D9
Koceljevo, Serbia & M. 44 B3
Kočevje, Slovenia 41 C11
Koch Bihar, India 67 F16
Kochang, S. Korea 57 G14
Kochas, India 69 G10
Kocher →, Germany 25 F5
Kochi = Cochin, India 66 Q10
Kōchi, Japan 55 H6
Kōchi □, Japan 55 H6
Kochiu = Gejiu, China 58 F4
Kock, Poland 31 G9
Kodarma, India 69 G11
Kode, Sweden 11 G5
Kodiak, U.S.A. 100 C4
Kodiak I., U.S.A. 100 C4
Kodinar, India 68 J4
Kodok, Sudan 81 F3
Kodori →, Georgia 35 J5
Kodyma, Ukraine 29 B14
Koedoesberge, S. Africa 88 E3
Koes, Namibia 88 D2
Kofçaz, Turkey 45 E11
Koffiefontein, S. Africa 88 D4
Kofiau, Indonesia 63 E7
Köflach, Austria 26 D8
Koforidua, Ghana 83 D4
Kōfu, Japan 55 G9
Koga, Japan 55 F9
Kogaluc →, Canada 105 A7
Køge, Denmark 11 J6
Køge Bugt, Denmark 11 J6
Kogi □, Nigeria 83 D6
Kogin Baba, Nigeria 83 D7
Koh-i-Khurd, Afghan. 68 C1
Koh-i-Maran, Pakistan 68 E2
Kohat, Pakistan 68 C4
Kohima, India 67 G19
Kohkīlūyeh va Būyer Aḩmadi □, Iran 71 D6
Kohler Ra., Antarctica 5 D15
Kohlu, Pakistan 68 E3
Kohtla-Järve, Estonia 9 G22
Kohylnyk →, Ukraine 29 E14
Koi Sanjaq, Iraq 70 B5
Koillismaa, Finland 8 D23
Koin-dong, N. Korea 57 D14
Koinare, Bulgaria 45 C8
Koindu, S. Leone 82 D2
Kojetín, Czech Rep. 27 B10
Kojŏ, N. Korea 57 E14
Kojonup, Australia 93 F2
Kojūr, Iran 71 B6
Koka, Sudan 80 C3
Kokand = Qŭqon, Uzbekistan 52 E8
Kokas, Indonesia 63 E8
Kokava, Slovak Rep. 27 C12
Kokchetav = Kökshetaū, Kazakhstan 52 D7
Kokemäenjoki →, Finland 9 F19
Kokhma, Russia 34 B5
Koki, Senegal 82 B1
Kokkola, Finland 8 E20
Koko, Nigeria 83 C5
Koko Kyunzu, Burma 67 M18
Kokolopozo, Ivory C. 82 D3
Kokomo, U.S.A. 114 E2
Kokoro, Niger 83 C5
Koksan, N. Korea 57 E14
Kökshetaū, Kazakhstan 52 D7
Koksoak →, Canada 101 C13
Kokstad, S. Africa 89 E4
Kokubu, Japan 55 J5
Kola, Indonesia 63 F8
Kola Pen. = Kolskiy Poluostrov, Russia 52 C4
Kolachi →, Pakistan 68 F2
Kolahoi, India 69 B6
Kolahun, Liberia 82 D2
Kolaka, Indonesia 63 E6
Kolar, India 66 N11
Kolar Gold Fields, India 66 N11
Kolaras, India 68 G6
Kolari, Finland 8 C20
Kolárovo, Slovak Rep. 27 D10
Kolašin, Serbia & M. 44 D3
Kolayat, India 66 F8
Kolbäck, Sweden 10 E10
Kolbäcksån →, Sweden 10 E10
Kolbermoor, Germany 25 H8
Kolbuszowa, Poland 31 H8
Kolchugino, Russia 32 D10
Kolda, Senegal 82 C2
Koldegi, Sudan 81 E3
Kolding, Denmark 11 J3
Kolepom = Dolak, Pulau, Indonesia 63 F9
Kolguyev, Ostrov, Russia 52 C5
Kolhapur, India 66 L9
Kolia, Ivory C. 82 D3
Kolín, Czech Rep. 26 A8
Kolind, Denmark 11 H4
Kolkas rags, Latvia 9 H20
Kolkata, India 69 H13
Kollam = Quilon, India 66 Q10
Kölleda, Germany 24 D7
Kollum, Neths. 17 A6
Kolmanskop, Namibia 88 D2
Köln, Germany 24 E2
Kolno, Poland 30 E8
Koło, Poland 31 F5
Kołobrzeg, Poland 30 D2
Kolochava, Ukraine 29 B8
Kolokani, Mali 82 C3
Koloko, Burkina Faso 82 C3
Kololo, Ethiopia 81 F5
Kolomna, Russia 32 E10
Kolomyya, Ukraine 29 B10
Kolondiéba, Mali 82 C3
Kolonodale, Indonesia 63 E6
Kolonowskie, Poland 31 H5
Kolosib, India 67 G18
Kolpashevo, Russia 52 D9
Kolpino, Russia 32 C6
Kolpny, Russia 33 F9
Kolskiy Poluostrov, Russia 52 C4
Kolsva, Sweden 10 E9
Kolubara →, Serbia & M. 44 B4
Koluszki, Poland 31 G6
Kolwezi, Dem. Rep. of the Congo 87 E2
Kolyma →, Russia 53 C17
Kolymskoye Nagorye, Russia 53 C16
Kôm Hamâda, Egypt 80 H7
Kôm Ombo, Egypt 80 C3
Komadugu Gana →, Nigeria 83 C7
Komandorskiye Is. = Komandorskiye Ostrova, Russia 53 D17
Komandorskiye Ostrova, Russia 53 D17
Komárno, Slovak Rep. 27 D11
Komarnyky, Ukraine 28 B8
Komárom, Hungary 28 C3
Komárom-Esztergom □, Hungary 28 C3
Komatipoort, S. Africa 89 D5
Komatou Yialou, Cyprus 49 D13
Komatsu, Japan 55 F8
Komatsushima, Japan 55 H7
Kombissiri, Burkina Faso 83 C4
Kombori, Burkina Faso 82 C4
Kombóti, Greece 46 B3
Komen, Slovenia 41 C10
Komenda, Ghana 83 D4
Komi □, Russia 52 C6
Komiža, Croatia 41 E13
Komló, Hungary 28 D3
Kommunarsk = Alchevsk, Ukraine 33 H10
Kommunizma, Pik, Tajikistan 52 F8
Komodo, Indonesia 63 F5
Komoé →, Ivory C. 82 D4
Komoran, Pulau, Indonesia 63 F9
Komoro, Japan 55 F9
Komotini, Greece 45 E9
Komovi, Serbia & M. 44 D3
Kompasberg, S. Africa 88 E3
Kompong Bang, Cambodia 65 F5
Kompong Cham, Cambodia 65 F5
Kompong Chhnang = Kampong Chhnang, Cambodia 65 F5
Kompong Chikreng, Cambodia 64 F5
Kompong Kleang, Cambodia 64 F5
Kompong Luong, Cambodia 65 G5
Kompong Pranak, Cambodia 64 F5
Kompong Som = Kampong Saom, Cambodia 65 G4
Kompong Som, Chhung = Kampong Saom, Chaak, Cambodia 65 G4
Kompong Speu, Cambodia 65 G5
Kompong Sralau, Cambodia 64 E5
Kompong Thom, Cambodia 64 F5
Kompong Trabeck, Cambodia 64 F5
Kompong Trabeck, Cambodia 65 G5
Kompong Trach, Cambodia 65 G5
Kompong Tralach, Cambodia 65 G5
Komrat = Comrat, Moldova 29 D13
Komsberg, S. Africa 88 E3
Komsomolets, Ostrov, Russia 53 A10
Komsomolsk, Amur, Russia 53 D14
Komsomolsk, Ivanovo, Russia 32 D11
Komsomolskiy, Russia 34 C7
Kömür Burnu, Turkey 47 C8
Kon Tum, Vietnam 64 E7
Kon Tum, Plateau du, Vietnam 64 E7
Kona, Mali 82 C4
Konakovo, Russia 32 D9
Konarhā □, Afghan. 66 B7
Konārī, Iran 71 D6
Konch, India 69 G8
Konde, Tanzania 86 C4
Kondiá, Greece 47 B7
Kondinin, Australia 93 F2
Kondoa, Tanzania 86 C4
Kondókali, Greece 49 A3
Kondopaga, Russia 32 A8
Kondratyevo, Russia 53 D10
Kondrovo, Russia 32 E8
Konduga, Nigeria 83 C7
Köneürgench, Turkmenistan 52 E6
Konevo, Russia 32 A10
Kong = Khong →, Cambodia 64 F5
Kong, Ivory C. 82 D4
Kong, Koh, Cambodia 65 G4
Kong Christian IX Land, Greenland 4 C6
Kong Christian X Land, Greenland 4 B6
Kong Frederik IX Land, Greenland 4 C5
Kong Frederik VI Kyst, Greenland 101 B15
Kong Frederik VIII Land, Greenland 4 B6
Kong Oscar Fjord, Greenland 4 B6
Kongeå →, Denmark 11 J2
Kongerslev, Denmark 11 H4
Kongju, S. Korea 57 F14
Konglu, Burma 67 F20
Kongola, Namibia 88 B3
Kongolo, Kasai-Or., Dem. Rep. of the Congo 86 D1
Kongolo, Katanga, Dem. Rep. of the Congo 86 D2
Kongor, Sudan 81 F3
Kongoussi, Burkina Faso 83 C4
Kongsberg, Norway 9 G13
Kongsvinger, Norway 9 F15
Kongwa, Tanzania 86 D4
Koni, Dem. Rep. of the Congo 87 E2
Koni, Mts., Dem. Rep. of the Congo 87 E2
Koniakari, Mali 82 C2
Koniecpol, Poland 31 H6
Königs Wusterhausen, Germany 24 C9
Königsbrunn, Germany 25 G6
Königslutter, Germany 24 C6
Konin, Poland 31 F5
Konispol, Albania 44 G4
Kónitsa, Greece 46 A2
Konjic, Bos.-H. 28 G2
Konkiep, Namibia 88 D2
Konkouré →, Guinea 82 D2
Könnern, Germany 24 D7
Kono, S. Leone 82 D2
Konongo, Ghana 83 D4
Konosha, Russia 32 B11
Kōnosu, Japan 55 F9
Konotop, Ukraine 33 G7
Konsankoro, Guinea 82 D3
Końskie, Poland 31 G7
Konstancin-Jeziorna, Poland 31 F8
Konstantinovka = Kostyantynivka, Ukraine 33 H9
Konstantinovsk, Russia 35 G5
Konstantynów Łódźki, Poland 31 G6
Konstanz, Germany 25 H5
Kont, Iran 71 E9
Kontagora, Nigeria 83 C6
Kontcha, Cameroon 83 D7
Konya, Turkey 70 B2
Konya Ovası, Turkey 72 C5
Konz, Germany 25 F2
Konza, Kenya 86 C4
Koocanusa, L., Canada 108 B6
Kookynie, Australia 93 E3
Koolyanobbing, Australia 93 F2
Koonibba, Australia 95 E1
Koorawatha, Australia 95 E4
Koorda, Australia 93 F2
Kooskia, U.S.A. 108 C6
Kootenay △, Canada 102 C5
Kootenay →, U.S.A. 102 D5

Kootenay L., *Canada* 102 D5
Kootjieskolk, *S. Africa* 88 E3
Kopanovka, *Russia* 35 G8
Kopaonik, *Serbia & M.* 44 C4
Kopaonik △, *Serbia & M.* 44 C4
Kópavogur, *Iceland* 8 D3
Kopayhorod, *Ukraine* 29 B12
Koper, *Slovenia* 41 C10
Kopervik, *Norway* 9 G11
Kopet Dagh, *Asia* 71 B8
Kopi, *Australia* 95 E2
Köping, *Sweden* 10 E10
Köpingsvik, *Sweden* 11 H10
Kopište, *Croatia* 41 F13
Koplik, *Albania* 44 D3
Köpmanholmen, *Sweden* 10 A12
Kopparberg, *Sweden* 10 E9
Koppeh Dāgh = Kopet Dagh, *Asia* 71 B8
Koppies, *S. Africa* 89 D4
Koppom, *Sweden* 10 E6
Koprivlen, *Bulgaria* 44 E7
Koprivnica, *Croatia* 41 B13
Kopřivnice, *Czech Rep.* 27 B11
Koprivshtitsa, *Bulgaria* 45 D8
Köprübaşı, *Turkey* 47 C10
Kopychyntsi, *Ukraine* 33 H3
Kora △, *Kenya* 86 C4
Korab, *Macedonia* 44 E4
Korakiána, *Greece* 49 A3
Koral, *India* 68 J5
Korarou, L., *Mali* 82 B4
Korba, *India* 69 H10
Korbach, *Germany* 24 D4
Korbu, G., *Malaysia* 65 K3
Korçë, *Albania* 44 F4
Korčula, *Croatia* 41 F13
Korčulanski Kanal, *Croatia* 41 E13
Kord Kūy, *Iran* 71 B7
Kord Sheykh, *Iran* 71 D7
Kordestan = Kurdistan, *Asia* 73 D10
Kordestān □, *Iran* 70 C5
Kordofân, *Sudan* 79 F11
Koré Mayroua, *Niger* 83 C5
Korea, North ■, *Asia* 57 E14
Korea, South ■, *Asia* 57 G15
Korea Bay, *Korea* 57 E13
Korea Strait, *Asia* 57 H15
Korem, *Ethiopia* 81 E4
Korenevo, *Russia* 33 G8
Korenovsk, *Russia* 35 H4
Korets, *Ukraine* 33 G4
Korfantów, *Poland* 31 H4
Korgan, *Turkey* 72 B7
Korgus, *Sudan* 80 D3
Korhogo, *Ivory C.* 82 D3
Koribundu, *S. Leone* 82 D2
Korienzé, *Mali* 82 B4
Korinthía □, *Greece* 46 D4
Korinthiakós Kólpos, *Greece* 46 C4
Kórinthos, *Greece* 46 D4
Korioumé, *Mali* 82 B4
Koríssa, Límni, *Greece* 49 B3
Kōriyama, *Japan* 54 F10
Korkuteli, *Turkey* 47 D12
Kormakiti, C., *Cyprus* 49 D11
Körmend, *Hungary* 28 C1
Kornat, *Croatia* 41 E12
Kornat △, *Croatia* 41 E12
Korneshty = Corneşti, *Moldova* 29 C13
Korneuburg, *Austria* 27 C9
Kórnik, *Poland* 31 F4
Koro, *Fiji* 91 C8
Koro, *Ivory C.* 82 D3
Koro, *Mali* 82 C4
Koro Sea, *Fiji* 91 C9
Korocha, *Russia* 33 G9
Köroğlu Dağları, *Turkey* 72 B5
Korogwe, *Tanzania* 86 D4
Koroleve, *Ukraine* 29 B8
Koronadal, *Phil.* 61 H6
Koróni, *Greece* 46 E3
Koronía, Límni, *Greece* 44 F7
Koronís, *Greece* 47 D7
Koronowo, *Poland* 31 E4
Koropets, *Ukraine* 29 B10
Koror, *Palau* 96 G5
Körös →, *Hungary* 28 D5
Körös Maros △, *Hungary* 28 C5
Körösstarcsa, *Hungary* 28 D6
Korosten, *Ukraine* 33 G5
Korostyshev, *Ukraine* 33 G5
Korotoyak, *Russia* 33 G10
Korraraika, Helodranon' i, *Madag.* 89 B7
Korsakov, *Russia* 53 E15
Korsberga, *Sweden* 11 G9
Korshiv, *Ukraine* 29 B10
Korshunovo, *Russia* 53 D12
Korsør, *Denmark* 11 J5
Korsun Shevchenkovskiy, *Ukraine* 33 H6
Korsze, *Poland* 30 D8
Korti, *Sudan* 80 D3
Kortrijk, *Belgium* 17 D3
Korucu, *Turkey* 47 B9
Korwai, *India* 68 G8
Koryakskoye Nagorye, *Russia* 53 C18
Koryŏng, *S. Korea* 57 G15
Koryukovka, *Ukraine* 33 G7
Kos, *Greece* 47 E9
Kosa, *Ethiopia* 81 F4
Kosaya Gora, *Russia* 32 E9
Kościan, *Poland* 31 F3
Kościerzyna, *Poland* 30 D4
Kosciusko, *U.S.A.* 113 J10
Kosciuszko, Mt., *Australia* 95 F4
Kőszeg →, *Hungary* 28 C6
Kosha, *Sudan* 80 C3
Koshava, *Bulgaria* 44 B7
K'oshih = Kashi, *China* 60 C2
Koshiki-Rettō, *Japan* 55 J4
Kosi, *India* 68 F7
Kosi →, *India* 69 E8
Košice, *Slovak Rep.* 27 C14
Košický □, *Slovak Rep.* 27 C14
Kosiv, *Ukraine* 29 B10
Kosjerić, *Serbia & M.* 44 B3
Köşk, *Turkey* 47 D10
Koskinoú, *Greece* 49 C10
Koslan, *Russia* 52 C5
Kosmach, *Ukraine* 29 B9
Kosŏng, *N. Korea* 57 E15
Kosovo □, *Serbia & M.* 44 D4
Kosovo Polje, *Serbia & M.* 44 D5
Kosovska Kamenica, *Serbia & M.* 44 D5
Kosovska Mitrovica, *Serbia & M.* 44 D4
Kossou, L. de, *Ivory C.* 82 D3
Kosta, *Sweden* 11 H9
Kostajnica, *Croatia* 41 C13
Kostanjevica, *Slovenia* 41 C12
Kostenets, *Bulgaria* 44 D7
Koster, *S. Africa* 88 D4
Kôstî, *Sudan* 81 E3
Kostinbrod, *Bulgaria* 44 D7
Kostolac, *Serbia & M.* 44 B5
Kostopil, *Ukraine* 33 G4
Kostroma, *Russia* 32 D11
Kostromskoye Vdkhr., *Russia* 32 D11
Kostryzhivka, *Ukraine* 29 B10
Kostrzyn, *Lubuskie, Poland* 31 F1
Kostrzyn, *Wielkopolskie, Poland* 31 F4
Kostyantynivka, *Ukraine* 33 H9
Kostyukovichi = Kastsyukovichy, *Belarus* 32 F7
Koszalin, *Poland* 30 D3
Kőszeg, *Hungary* 28 C1
Kot Addu, *Pakistan* 68 D4
Kot Kapura, *India* 68 D6
Kot Moman, *Pakistan* 68 C5
Kot Sultan, *Pakistan* 68 D4
Kota, *India* 68 G6
Kota Barrage, *India* 68 G6
Kota Belud, *Malaysia* 62 C5
Kota Bharu, *Malaysia* 65 J4
Kota Kinabalu, *Malaysia* 62 C5
Kota Kubu Bharu, *Malaysia* 65 L3
Kota Tinggi, *Malaysia* 65 M4
Kotaagung, *Indonesia* 62 F2
Kotabaru, *Indonesia* 62 E5
Kotabumi, *Indonesia* 62 E2
Kotamobagu, *Indonesia* 63 D6
Kotcho L., *Canada* 102 B4
Kotdwara, *India* 69 E8
Kotel, *Bulgaria* 45 D10
Kotelnich, *Russia* 34 A9
Kotelnikovo, *Russia* 35 G6
Kotelnyy, Ostrov, *Russia* 53 B14
Kothari →, *India* 68 G6
Köthen, *Germany* 24 D7
Kothi, *Chhattisgarh, India* 69 H10
Kothi, *Mad. P., India* 69 G9
Kotiro, *Pakistan* 68 F2
Kotka, *Finland* 9 F22
Kotlas, *Russia* 52 C5
Kotlenska Planina, *Bulgaria* 45 D10
Kotli, *Pakistan* 68 C5
Kotma, *India* 69 H9
Kotmul, *Pakistan* 69 B6
Koton-Karifi, *Nigeria* 83 D6
Kotonkoro, *Nigeria* 83 C6
Kotor, *Serbia & M.* 44 D2
Kotor Varoš, *Bos.-H.* 28 F2
Kotoriba, *Croatia* 41 B13
Kotovo, *Russia* 34 E7
Kotovsk, *Russia* 34 D5
Kotovsk, *Ukraine* 33 J5
Kotputli, *India* 68 F7
Kotri, *Pakistan* 68 G3
Kótronas, *Greece* 46 E4
Kötschach-Mauthen, *Austria* 26 E6
Kotturu, *India* 66 M10
Kotuy →, *Russia* 53 B11
Kotyuzhany, *Ukraine* 29 B12
Kotzebue, *U.S.A.* 100 B3
Kouchibouguac △, *Canada* 105 C6
Koudougou, *Burkina Faso* 82 C4
Koufonísi, *Greece* 49 E8
Koufonísia, *Greece* 47 E7
Kougaberge, *S. Africa* 88 E3
Kouibli, *Ivory C.* 82 D3
Kouilou →, *Congo* 84 E2
Koula Moutou, *Gabon* 84 E2
Koulen = Kulen, *Cambodia* 64 F5
Koulikoro, *Mali* 82 C3
Kouloúra, *Greece* 49 A3
Koúm-bournoú, Ákra, *Greece* 49 C10
Koumala, *Australia* 94 C4
Koumankou, *Mali* 82 C3
Koumbia, *Burkina Faso* 82 C4
Koumbia, *Guinea* 82 C2
Koumboum, *Guinea* 82 C2
Koumpenntoum, *Senegal* 82 C2
Koumra, *Chad* 79 G9
Koun-Fao, *Ivory C.* 82 D4
Koundara, *Guinea* 82 C2
Koundian, *Guinea* 82 C3
Koungheul, *Senegal* 82 C2
Kounradskiy, *Kazakhstan* 52 E8
Kountze, *U.S.A.* 113 K7
Koupéla, *Burkina Faso* 83 C4
Kourémalé, *Mali* 82 C3
Kouris →, *Cyprus* 49 E11
Kourou, *Fr. Guiana* 125 B8
Kourouba, *Mali* 82 C2
Kouroukoto, *Mali* 82 C2
Kourouma, *Burkina Faso* 82 C4
Kourouninkoto, *Mali* 82 C3
Kouroussa, *Guinea* 82 C3
Koussanar, *Senegal* 82 C2
Koussané, *Mali* 82 C2
Koussane, *Senegal* 82 C2
Kousseri, *Cameroon* 79 F8
Koutiala, *Mali* 82 C3
Kouto, *Ivory C.* 82 D3
Kouvé, *Togo* 83 D5
Kouvola, *Finland* 9 F22
Kovačica, *Serbia & M.* 28 E5
Kovel, *Ukraine* 33 G3
Kovin, *Serbia & M.* 28 F5
Kovrov, *Russia* 34 B5
Kowal, *Poland* 31 F6
Kowalewo Pomorskie, *Poland* 31 E5
Kowanyama, *Australia* 94 B3
Kowloon, *China* 59 F10
Kowŏn, *N. Korea* 57 E14
Koyampattur = Coimbatore, *India* 66 P10
Köyceğiz, *Turkey* 47 E10
Köyceğız Gölü, *Turkey* 47 E10
Koyulhisar, *Turkey* 72 B7
Koyunyeri, *Turkey* 45 F10
Koza, *Japan* 55 L3
Kozak, *Turkey* 47 B9
Kozan, *Turkey* 70 B2
Kozáni, *Greece* 44 F5
Kozáni □, *Greece* 44 F5
Kozara, *Bos.-H.* 41 D14
Kozara △, *Bos.-H.* 28 F2
Kozarac, *Bos.-H.* 41 D13
Kozelets, *Ukraine* 33 G6
Kozelsk, *Russia* 32 E8
Kozhikode = Calicut, *India* 66 P9
Koziegłowy, *Poland* 31 H6
Kozienice, *Poland* 31 G8
Kozje, *Slovenia* 41 B12
Kozloduy, *Bulgaria* 44 C7
Kozlovets, *Bulgaria* 45 C9
Kozlovka, *Russia* 34 C9
Kozlu, *Turkey* 72 B4
Kozluk, *Turkey* 73 C9
Koźmin, *Poland* 31 G4
Kozmodemyansk, *Russia* 34 B8
Kożuchów, *Poland* 31 G2
Kozyatyn, *Ukraine* 33 H5
Kpabia, *Ghana* 83 D4
Kpalimé, *Togo* 83 D5
Kpandae, *Ghana* 83 D4
Kpessi, *Togo* 83 D5
Kra, Isthmus of = Kra, Kho Khot, *Thailand* 65 G2
Kra, Kho Khot, *Thailand* 65 G2
Kra Buri, *Thailand* 65 G2
Kraai →, *S. Africa* 88 E4
Krabi, *Thailand* 65 H2
Kracheh, *Cambodia* 64 F6
Kragan, *Indonesia* 63 G14
Kragerø, *Norway* 9 G13
Kragujevac, *Serbia & M.* 44 B4
Krajenka, *Poland* 31 E3
Krakatau = Rakata, Pulau, *Indonesia* 62 F3
Krakatoa = Rakata, Pulau, *Indonesia* 62 F3
Krakor, *Cambodia* 64 F5
Kraków, *Poland* 31 H6
Kraków ✕ (KRK), *Poland* 31 H6
Kralanh, *Cambodia* 64 F4
Králíky, *Czech Rep.* 27 A9
Kraljevo, *Serbia & M.* 44 C4
Královéhradecký □, *Czech Rep.* 26 A8
Královský Chlmec, *Slovak Rep.* 27 C14
Kralupy nad Vltavou, *Czech Rep.* 26 A7
Kramatorsk, *Ukraine* 33 H9
Kramfors, *Sweden* 10 B11
Kraniá, *Greece* 44 G5
Kranía Elassónas, *Greece* 46 B4
Kranídhion, *Greece* 46 D5
Kranj, *Slovenia* 41 B11
Kranjska Gora, *Slovenia* 41 B10
Krankskop, *S. Africa* 89 D5
Krapina, *Croatia* 41 B12
Krapina →, *Croatia* 41 C12
Krapkowice, *Poland* 31 H4
Kras, *Croatia* 41 C10
Kraskino, *Russia* 53 E14
Krāslava, *Latvia* 32 E4
Kraslice, *Czech Rep.* 26 A5
Krasnaya Gorbatka, *Russia* 34 C5
Krasnaya Polyana, *Russia* 35 J5
Krasne, *Ukraine* 29 D14
Krasni Okny, *Ukraine* 29 C14
Kraśnik, *Poland* 31 H9
Krasnoarmeisk, *Ukraine* 33 H9
Krasnoarmeysk, *Russia* 34 E7
Krasnoarmeyskiy, *Russia* 35 G6
Krasnobrod, *Poland* 31 H10
Krasnodar, *Russia* 35 H4
Krasnodon, *Ukraine* 33 H10
Krasnogorskiy, *Russia* 34 B9
Krasnograd = Krasnohrad, *Ukraine* 33 H8
Krasnogvardeysk, *Ukraine* 33 K8
Krasnogvardeyskoye, *Russia* 35 H5
Krasnohrad, *Ukraine* 33 H8
Krasnokutsk, *Ukraine* 33 G8
Krasnolesnyy, *Russia* 33 G10
Krasnoperekopsk, *Ukraine* 33 J7
Krasnorechenskiy, *Russia* 54 B7
Krasnoselkup, *Russia* 52 C9
Krasnoslobodsk, *Mordvinia, Russia* 34 C6
Krasnoslobodsk, *Volgograd, Russia* 35 F7
Krasnoturinsk, *Russia* 52 D7
Krasnoufimsk, *Russia* 52 D6
Krasnouralsk, *Russia* 52 D7
Krasnovishersk, *Russia* 52 C6
Krasnovodsk = Türkmenbashi, *Turkmenistan* 52 E6
Krasnoyarsk, *Russia* 53 D10
Krasnoyarskoye, *Russia* 30 D8
Krasnoye = Krasnyy, *Russia* 32 E6
Krasnoyilsk, *Ukraine* 29 C10
Krasnozavodsk, *Russia* 32 D10
Krasnoznamensk, *Russia* 30 D9
Krasny Sulin, *Russia* 33 J11
Krasnystaw, *Poland* 31 H10
Krasnyy, *Russia* 32 E6
Krasnyy Kholm, *Russia* 32 C9
Krasnyy Kut, *Russia* 34 E8
Krasnyy Liman, *Ukraine* 33 H9
Krasnyy Luch, *Ukraine* 33 H10
Krasnyy Profintern, *Russia* 32 D11
Krasnyy Yar, *Astrakhan, Russia* 35 G9
Krasnyy Yar, *Samara, Russia* 34 D10
Krasnyy Yar, *Volgograd, Russia* 34 E7
Krasnyye Baki, *Russia* 34 B7
Krasnyyoskolske Vdskh., *Ukraine* 33 H9
Kraszna →, *Hungary* 28 B7
Kratie = Kracheh, *Cambodia* 64 F6
Kratovo, *Macedonia* 44 D6
Krau, *Indonesia* 63 E10
Kravanh, Chuor Phnum, *Cambodia* 65 G4
Krefeld, *Germany* 24 D2
Krémaston, Límni, *Greece* 46 C3
Kremen, *Croatia* 41 D12
Kremenchuk, *Ukraine* 33 H7
Kremenchuksk Vdskh., *Ukraine* 33 H7
Kremenets, *Ukraine* 33 G3
Kremennaya, *Ukraine* 33 H10
Kremges = Svitlovodsk, *Ukraine* 33 H7
Kremmen, *Germany* 24 C9
Kremmling, *U.S.A.* 108 F10
Kremnica, *Slovak Rep.* 27 C11
Krems, *Austria* 26 C8
Kremsmünster, *Austria* 26 C7
Kretinga, *Lithuania* 9 J19
Krettsy, *Russia* 32 C7
Kreuzberg, *Germany* 25 E5
Kreuztal, *Germany* 24 E4
Kría Vrísi, *Greece* 44 F6
Kribi, *Cameroon* 83 E6
Krichem, *Bulgaria* 45 D8
Krichev = Krychaw, *Belarus* 32 F6
Krim, *Slovenia* 41 C11
Kriós, Ákra, *Greece* 49 D5
Krishna →, *India* 67 M12
Krishnanagar, *India* 69 H13
Kristdala, *Sweden* 11 G10
Kristiansand, *Norway* 9 G13
Kristianstad, *Sweden* 11 H8
Kristiansund, *Norway* 8 E12
Kristiinankaupunki, *Finland* 9 E19
Kristinehamn, *Sweden* 10 E8
Kristinestad = Kristiinankaupunki, *Finland* 9 E19
Kríti, *Greece* 49 D7
Kritsá, *Greece* 49 D7
Kriva →, *Macedonia* 44 D5
Kriva Palanka, *Macedonia* 44 D6
Krivaja →, *Bos.-H.* 28 F3
Krivelj, *Serbia & M.* 44 B6
Křivoklátsko ⌂, *Czech Rep.* 26 A6
Krivoy Rog = Kryvyy Rih, *Ukraine* 33 J7
Križevci, *Croatia* 41 B13
Krk, *Croatia* 41 C11
Krka △, *Croatia* 41 E12
Krka →, *Slovenia* 41 C12
Krkonoše, *Czech Rep.* 26 A8
Krkonoše △, *Czech Rep.* 26 A8
Krnov, *Czech Rep.* 27 A10
Krobia, *Poland* 31 G3
Krokeaí, *Greece* 46 E4
Krokek, *Sweden* 11 F10
Krokodil →, *Mozam.* 89 D5
Krokom, *Sweden* 10 A8
Krokowa, *Poland* 30 D5
Krolevets, *Ukraine* 33 G7
Kroměříž, *Czech Rep.* 27 B10
Krompachy, *Slovak Rep.* 27 C13
Kromy, *Russia* 33 F8
Kronach, *Germany* 25 E7
Krong Kaoh Kong, *Cambodia* 62 B2
Kronobergs län □, *Sweden* 11 H8
Kronprins Olav Kyst, *Antarctica* 5 C5
Kronprinsesse Märtha Kyst, *Antarctica* 5 D2
Kronshtadt, *Russia* 32 C5
Kroonstad, *S. Africa* 88 D4
Kröpelin, *Germany* 24 A7
Kropotkin, *Russia* 35 H5
Kropp, *Germany* 24 A5
Krosna, *Lithuania* 30 D10
Krośniewice, *Poland* 31 F6
Krosno, *Poland* 31 J8
Krosno Odrzańskie, *Poland* 31 F2
Krotoszyn, *Poland* 31 G4
Krotovka, *Russia* 34 D10
Kroussón, *Greece* 49 D6
Krrabë, *Albania* 44 E3
Krško, *Slovenia* 41 C12
Krstača, *Serbia & M.* 44 D4
Kruger △, *S. Africa* 89 C5
Krugersdorp, *S. Africa* 89 D4
Kruisfontein, *S. Africa* 88 E3
Krujë, *Albania* 44 E3
Krulevshchina = Krulyewshchyna, *Belarus* 32 E4
Krulyewshchyna, *Belarus* 32 E4
Krumbach, *Germany* 25 G6
Krumë, *Albania* 44 D4
Krumovgrad, *Bulgaria* 45 E9
Krung Thep = Bangkok, *Thailand* 64 F3
Krupanj, *Serbia & M.* 44 B3
Krupina, *Slovak Rep.* 27 C12
Krupinica →, *Slovak Rep.* 27 C11
Krupki, *Belarus* 32 E5
Kruševac, *Serbia & M.* 44 C5
Kruševo, *Macedonia* 44 E5
Krushelnyksya, *Ukraine* 31 J10
Kruszwica, *Poland* 31 F5
Krychaw, *Belarus* 32 F6
Krymsk, *Russia* 33 K10
Krymskiy Poluostrov = Krymskyy Pivostriv, *Ukraine* 33 K8
Krymskyy Pivostriv, *Ukraine* 33 K8
Krynica, *Poland* 31 J7
Krynica Morska, *Poland* 30 D6
Krynki, *Poland* 31 E10
Krynychne, *Ukraine* 29 E13
Kryvyy Rih, *Ukraine* 33 J7
Kryzhopil, *Ukraine* 29 B13
Krzepice, *Poland* 31 H5
Krzeszów, *Poland* 31 H9
Krzna →, *Poland* 31 F10
Krzywiń, *Poland* 31 G3
Krzyż Wielkopolski, *Poland* 31 F2
Ksar el Kebir, *Morocco* 78 B4
Ksar es Souk = Er Rachidia, *Morocco* 78 B5
Książ Wielkopolski, *Poland* 31 F4
Kstovo, *Russia* 34 B7
Ku, W. el →, *Sudan* 81 E2
Kuah, *Malaysia* 65 J2
Kuala Belait, *Malaysia* 62 D4
Kuala Berang, *Malaysia* 65 K4
Kuala Dungun = Dungun, *Malaysia* 65 K4
Kuala Kangsar, *Malaysia* 65 K3
Kuala Kelawang, *Malaysia* 65 L4
Kuala Kerai, *Malaysia* 65 K4
Kuala Kerian, *Malaysia* 65 c
Kuala Lipis, *Malaysia* 65 K4
Kuala Lumpur, *Malaysia* 65 L3
Kuala Nerang, *Malaysia* 65 J3
Kuala Pilah, *Malaysia* 65 L4
Kuala Rompin, *Malaysia* 65 L4
Kuala Selangor, *Malaysia* 65 L3
Kuala Sepetang, *Malaysia* 65 K3
Kuala Terengganu, *Malaysia* 65 K4
Kualajelai, *Indonesia* 62 E4
Kualakapuas, *Indonesia* 62 E4
Kualakurun, *Indonesia* 62 E4
Kualapembuang, *Indonesia* 62 E4
Kualasimpang, *Indonesia* 62 D1
Kuancheng, *China* 57 D10
Kuandang, *Indonesia* 63 D6
Kuandian, *China* 57 D13
Kuangchou = Guangzhou, *China* 59 F9
Kuanshan, *Taiwan* 59 F13
Kuantan, *Malaysia* 65 L4
Kuba = Quba, *Azerbaijan* 35 K9
Kuban →, *Russia* 33 K9
Kuban Depression = Prikubanskaya Nizmennost, *Russia* 35 H4
Kubenskoye, Ozero, *Russia* 32 C10
Kubokawa, *Japan* 55 H6
Kubrat, *Bulgaria* 45 C10
Kubu, *Indonesia* 63 J18
Kubutambahan, *Indonesia* 63 J18
Kucar, Tanjung, *Indonesia* 63 K18
Kučevo, *Serbia & M.* 44 B5
Kucha Gompa, *India* 69 B7
Kuchaman, *India* 68 F6
Kuchenspitze, *Austria* 26 D3
Kuchinda, *India* 69 J11
Kuching, *Malaysia* 62 D4
Kuchino-eruba-Jima, *Japan* 55 J5
Kuchino-Shima, *Japan* 55 K4
Kuchinotsu, *Japan* 55 H5
Kuchl, *Austria* 26 D6
Kuchurhan →, *Ukraine* 29 D14
Kucing = Kuching, *Malaysia* 62 D4
Kuçovë, *Albania* 44 F3
Küçükbahçe, *Turkey* 47 C8
Küçükköy, *Turkey* 47 B8
Küçükkuyu, *Turkey* 47 B8
Küçükmenderes →, *Turkey* 47 D9
Kud →, *Pakistan* 68 F2
Kuda, *India* 66 H7
Kudat, *Malaysia* 62 C5
Kudirkos Naumiestis, *Lithuania* 30 D9
Kudowa-Zdrój, *Poland* 31 H3
Kudus, *Indonesia* 63 G14
Kudymkar, *Russia* 52 D6
Kueiyang = Guiyang, *China* 58 D6
Kufra Oasis = Al Kufrah, *Libya* 79 D10
Kufstein, *Austria* 26 D5
Kugaaruk = Pelly Bay, *Canada* 101 B11
Kugluktuk, *Canada* 100 B8
Kugong I., *Canada* 104 A4
Kūhak, *Iran* 66 F3
Kuhan, *Pakistan* 68 E2
Kūhbonān, *Iran* 71 D8
Kūhestak, *Iran* 71 E8
Kuhin, *Iran* 71 B6
Kūhīrī, *Iran* 71 E9
Kuhnsdorf, *Austria* 26 E7
Kūhpāyeh, *Eşfahan, Iran* 71 C7
Kūhpāyeh, *Kermān, Iran* 71 D8
Kūhrān, Kūh-e, *Iran* 71 E8
Kui Buri, *Thailand* 65 F2
Kuiseb →, *Namibia* 88 C1
Kuito, *Angola* 85 G3
Kuiu I., *U.S.A.* 102 B2
Kujang, *N. Korea* 57 E14
Kujawsko-Pomorskie □, *Poland* 30 E5
Kuji, *Japan* 54 D10
Kujū-San, *Japan* 55 H5
Kukava, *Ukraine* 29 B12
Kukavica, *Serbia & M.* 44 D5
Kukawa, *Nigeria* 83 C7
Kukës, *Albania* 44 D4
Kukmor, *Russia* 34 B10
Kukup, *Malaysia* 65 d
Kukup, Pulau, *Malaysia* 65 d
Kukvidze, *Russia* 34 E6
Kula, *Bulgaria* 44 C6
Kula, *Serbia & M.* 28 E4
Kula, *Turkey* 47 C10
Kulachi, *Pakistan* 68 D4
Kulai, *Malaysia* 65 M4
Kulaly, Ostrov, *Kazakhstan* 35 H10
Kulasekarappattinam, *India* 66 Q11
Kulautuva, *Lithuania* 30 D10
Kuldīga, *Latvia* 9 H19
Kuldīga □, *Latvia* 30 B8
Kuldu, *Sudan* 81 E2
Kulebaki, *Russia* 34 C6
Kulen, *Cambodia* 64 F5
Kulen Vakuf, *Bos.-H.* 41 D13
Kulgam, *India* 69 C6

Kulgera, *Australia* 94 D1
Kulim, *Malaysia* 65 K3
Kulin, *Australia* 93 F2
Kulkayu = Hartley Bay, *Canada* 102 C3
Kullen, *Sweden* 11 H6
Kulmbach, *Germany* 25 E7
Kŭlob, *Tajikistan* 52 F7
Kulp, *Turkey* 73 C9
Kulpawn →, *Ghana* 83 D4
Kulsary, *Kazakhstan* 52 E6
Kulti, *India* 69 H12
Kulu, *India* 68 D7
Kulu, *Turkey* 72 C5
Kulumbura, *Australia* 92 B4
Kulunda, *Russia* 52 D8
Kulungar, *Afghan.* 68 C3
Kūlvand, *Iran* 71 D7
Kulwin, *Australia* 95 F3
Kulyab = Kŭlob, *Tajikistan* 52 F7
Kuma →, *Russia* 35 H8
Kumafşarı, *Turkey* 47 D11
Kumaganum, *Nigeria* 83 C7
Kumagaya, *Japan* 55 F9
Kumai, *Indonesia* 62 E4
Kumalar Dağı, *Turkey* 47 C12
Kumamba, Kepulauan, *Indonesia* 63 E9
Kumamoto, *Japan* 55 H5
Kumamoto □, *Japan* 55 H5
Kumanovo, *Macedonia* 44 D5
Kumara, *N.Z.* 91 K3
Kumarina, *Australia* 93 D2
Kumasi, *Ghana* 82 D4
Kumba, *Cameroon* 83 E6
Kumbağ, *Turkey* 45 F11
Kumbakonam, *India* 66 P11
Kumbarilla, *Australia* 95 D5
Kumbhraj, *India* 68 G7
Kumbia, *Australia* 95 D5
Kumbo, *Cameroon* 83 D7
Kŭmch'ŏn, *N. Korea* 57 E14
Kumdok, *India* 69 C8
Kume-Shima, *Japan* 55 L3
Kumeny, *Russia* 34 A9
Kumharsain, *India* 68 D7
Kŭmhwa, *S. Korea* 57 E14
Kumi, *Uganda* 86 B3
Kumkale, *Turkey* 45 G10
Kumla, *Sweden* 10 E9
Kumluca, *Turkey* 47 E12
Kummerower See, *Germany* 24 B8
Kumo, *Nigeria* 83 C7
Kumo älv = Kokemäenjoki →, *Finland* 9 F19
Kumon Bum, *Burma* 67 F20
Kumylzhenskaya, *Russia* 34 F6
Kunágota, *Hungary* 28 D6
Kunashir, Ostrov, *Russia* 53 E15
Kunda, *Estonia* 9 G22
Kunda, *India* 69 G9
Kundar →, *Pakistan* 68 D3
Kundelungu △, *Dem. Rep. of the Congo* 87 E2
Kundelungu Ouest △, *Dem. Rep. of the Congo* 87 D2
Kundian, *Pakistan* 68 C4
Kundla, *India* 68 J4
Kung, Ao, *Thailand* 65 a
Kunga →, *Bangla.* 69 J13
Kungälv, *Sweden* 11 G5
Kunghit I., *Canada* 102 C2
Kungrad = Qŭnghirot, *Uzbekistan* 52 E6
Kungsängen, *Sweden* 10 E11
Kungsbacka, *Sweden* 11 G6
Kungsgården, *Sweden* 10 D10
Kungshamn, *Sweden* 11 F5
Kungsör, *Sweden* 10 E10
Kungur, *Russia* 52 D6
Kungurri, *Australia* 94 K6
Kunhar →, *Pakistan* 69 B5
Kunhegyes, *Hungary* 28 C5
Kuningan, *Indonesia* 63 G13
Kunlong, *Burma* 58 F2
Kunlun Shan, *Asia* 60 C3
Kunmadaras, *Hungary* 28 C5
Kunming, *China* 58 E4
Kunów, *Poland* 31 H8
Kunsan, *S. Korea* 57 G14
Kunshan, *China* 59 B13
Kunszentmárton, *Hungary* 28 D5
Kunszentmiklós, *Hungary* 28 C4
Kuntaur, *Senegal* 82 C2
Kununurra, *Australia* 92 C4
Kunwari →, *India* 69 F8
Kunya-Urgench = Köneürgench, *Turkmenistan* 52 E6
Künzelsau, *Germany* 25 F5
Kuopio, *Finland* 8 E22
Kupa →, *Croatia* 41 C13
Kupang, *Indonesia* 63 F6
Kupreanof I., *U.S.A.* 102 B2
Kupres, *Bos.-H.* 28 G2
Kupyansk, *Ukraine* 33 H9
Kupyansk-Uzlovoi, *Ukraine* 33 H9
Kuqa, *China* 60 B3
Kür →, *Azerbaijan* 73 C13
Kür Dili, *Azerbaijan* 71 B6
Kura = Kür →, *Azerbaijan* 73 C13
Kuranda, *Australia* 94 B4
Kuranga, *India* 68 H3
Kurashiki, *Japan* 55 G6
Kurayoshi, *Japan* 55 G6
Kürdämir, *Azerbaijan* 35 K9
Kurdistan, *Asia* 73 D10
Kŭrdzhali, *Bulgaria* 45 E9
Kure, *Japan* 55 G6
Küre, *Turkey* 72 B5
Küre Dağları, *Turkey* 72 B6
Kuressaare, *Estonia* 9 G20
Kurgan, *Russia* 52 D7
Kurganinsk, *Russia* 35 H5
Kurgannaya = Kurganinsk, *Russia* 35 H5
Kuri, *India* 68 F4
Kuria Maria Is. = Khurīyā Murīyā, Jazā'ir, *Oman* 75 D6
Kuridala, *Australia* 94 C3
Kurigram, *Bangla.* 67 G16
Kurikka, *Finland* 9 E20
Kuril Is. = Kurilskiye Ostrova, *Russia* 53 E15
Kuril Trench, *Pac. Oc.* 96 C7
Kurilsk, *Russia* 53 E15
Kurilskiye Ostrova, *Russia* 53 E15
Kurino, *Japan* 55 J5
Kurinskaya Kosa = Kür Dili, *Azerbaijan* 71 B6
Kurkur, *Egypt* 80 C3
Kurlovskiy, *Russia* 34 C5
Kurmuk, *Sudan* 81 E3
Kurnool, *India* 66 M11
Kuro-Shima, *Kagoshima, Japan* 55 J4
Kuro-Shima, *Okinawa, Japan* 55 M2
Kuror, J., *Sudan* 80 C3
Kurow, *N.Z.* 91 L3
Kurów, *Poland* 31 G9
Kurram →, *Pakistan* 68 C4
Kurri Kurri, *Australia* 95 E5
Kurrimine, *Australia* 94 B4
Kursavka, *Russia* 35 H6
Kurshskaya Kosa ⌓, *Russia* 30 C7
Kurshskiy Zaliv, *Russia* 9 J19
Kuršių Nerijos △, *Lithuania* 30 C8
Kursk, *Russia* 33 G9
Kuršumlija, *Serbia & M.* 44 C5
Kuršumlijska Banja, *Serbia & M.* 44 C5
Kurşunlu, *Bursa, Turkey* 45 F13
Kurşunlu, *Çankırı, Turkey* 72 B5
Kurtalan, *Turkey* 73 D9
Kurtbey, *Turkey* 45 E10
Kuru, *Sudan* 81 F2
Kuru, Bahr el →, *Sudan* 81 F2
Kurucaşile, *Turkey* 72 B5
Kuruçay, *Turkey* 70 B3
Kuruktag, *China* 60 B3
Kuruman, *S. Africa* 88 D3
Kuruman →, *S. Africa* 88 D3
Kurume, *Japan* 55 H5
Kurun →, *Sudan* 81 F3
Kurunegala, *Sri Lanka* 66 R12
Kurya, *Russia* 52 C6
Kus Gölü, *Turkey* 45 F11
Kuşadası, *Turkey* 72 D2
Kuşadası Körfezı, *Turkey* 47 D8
Kusamba, *Indonesia* 63 K18
Kusatsu, *Japan* 55 F9
Kusawa L., *Canada* 102 A1
Kusel, *Germany* 25 F3
Kushaka, *Nigeria* 83 C6
Kushalgarh, *India* 68 H6
Kushchevskaya, *Russia* 35 G4
Kusheriki, *Nigeria* 83 C6
Kushikino, *Japan* 55 J5
Kushima, *Japan* 55 J5
Kushimoto, *Japan* 55 H7
Kushiro, *Japan* 54 C12
Kushiro-Gawa →, *Japan* 54 C12
Kushiro Shitsugen △, *Japan* 54 C12
Kūshk, *Iran* 71 D8
Kushka = Gushgy, *Turkmenistan* 52 F7
Kūshkī, *Iran* 70 C5
Kushnytsya, *Ukraine* 29 B8
Kushol, *India* 69 C7
Kushtia, *Bangla.* 67 H16
Kushum →, *Kazakhstan* 34 F10
Kuskokwim B., *U.S.A.* 100 C3
Kusmi, *India* 69 H10
Kussharo-Ko, *Japan* 54 C12
Kustanay = Qostanay, *Kazakhstan* 52 D7
Kut, Ko, *Thailand* 65 G4
Kuta, *Indonesia* 63 K18
Kütahya, *Turkey* 47 B12
Kütahya □, *Turkey* 47 B11
Kutaisi, *Georgia* 35 J6
Kutaraja = Banda Aceh, *Indonesia* 62 C1
Kutch, Gulf of = Kachchh, Gulf of, *India* 68 H3
Kutch, Rann of = Kachchh, Rann of, *India* 68 H4
Kutina, *Croatia* 41 C13
Kutiyana, *India* 68 J4
Kutjevo, *Croatia* 28 E2
Kutkashen, *Azerbaijan* 35 K8
Kutná Hora, *Czech Rep.* 26 B8
Kutno, *Poland* 31 F6
Kutse, *Botswana* 88 C3
Kuttabul, *Australia* 94 K6
Kutu, *Dem. Rep. of the Congo* 84 E3
Kutum, *Sudan* 81 E1
Kúty, *Slovak Rep.* 27 C10
Kuty, *Ukraine* 29 B10
Kuujjuaq, *Canada* 101 C13
Kuujjuarapik, *Canada* 104 A4
Kuŭp-tong, *N. Korea* 57 D14
Kuusamo, *Finland* 8 D23
Kuusankoski, *Finland* 9 F22
Kuvshinovo, *Russia* 32 D8
Kuwait = Al Kuwayt, *Kuwait* 70 D5
Kuwait ■, *Asia* 70 D5
Kuwana, *Japan* 55 G8
Kuwana →, *India* 69 F10
Kuybyshev = Samara, *Russia* 34 D10
Kuybyshev, *Russia* 52 D8
Kuybyshevo, *Ukraine* 33 J9
Kuybyshevskoye Vdkhr., *Russia* 34 C9
Kuye He →, *China* 56 E6
Kūyeh, *Iran* 70 B5
Kuyucak, *Turkey* 47 D10
Kuyumba, *Russia* 53 C10
Kuzey Anadolu Dağları, *Turkey* 72 B7
Kuzmin, *Serbia & M.* 28 E4
Kuznetsk, *Russia* 34 D8
Kuzomen, *Russia* 52 C4
Kvænangen, *Norway* 8 A19
Kværndrup, *Denmark* 11 J4
Kvaløy, *Norway* 8 B18
Kvänum, *Sweden* 11 F7
Kvareli = Qvareli, *Georgia* 35 K7
Kvarner, *Croatia* 41 D11
Kvarnerič, *Croatia* 41 D11
Kvicksund, *Sweden* 10 E10
Kvillsfors, *Sweden* 11 G9
Kvismare kanal, *Sweden* 10 E9
Kvissleby, *Sweden* 10 B11
Kwa-Nobuhle, *S. Africa* 85 L5
Kwabhaca, *S. Africa* 89 E4
Kwakhanai, *Botswana* 88 C3
Kwakoegron, *Suriname* 125 B7
Kwale, *Kenya* 86 C4
Kwale, *Nigeria* 83 D6
KwaMashu, *S. Africa* 89 D5
Kwando →, *Africa* 88 B3
Kwangchow = Guangzhou, *China* 59 F9
Kwangdaeri, *N. Korea* 57 D14
Kwangju, *S. Korea* 57 G14
Kwango →, *Dem. Rep. of the Congo* 84 E3
Kwangsi-Chuang = Guangxi Zhuangzu Zizhiqu □, *China* 58 F7
Kwangtung = Guangdong □, *China* 59 F9
Kwara □, *Nigeria* 83 D6
Kwataboahegan →, *Canada* 104 B3
Kwatisore, *Indonesia* 63 E8
KwaZulu Natal □, *S. Africa* 89 D5
Kweichow = Guizhou □, *China* 58 D6
Kwekwe, *Zimbabwe* 87 F2
Kwidzyn, *Poland* 30 E5
Kwiha, *Ethiopia* 81 E4
Kwinana New Town, *Australia* 93 F2
Kwisa →, *Poland* 31 G2
Kwoka, *Indonesia* 63 E8
Kwolla, *Nigeria* 83 D6
Kyabra Cr. →, *Australia* 95 D3
Kyabram, *Australia* 95 F4
Kyaikto, *Burma* 64 D1
Kyakhta, *Russia* 53 D11
Kyambura ⌓, *Uganda* 86 C3
Kyancutta, *Australia* 95 E2
Kyaukpadaung, *Burma* 67 J19
Kyaukpyu, *Burma* 67 K18
Kyaukse, *Burma* 67 J20
Kybartai, *Lithuania* 30 D9
Kyburz, *U.S.A.* 110 G6
Kyelang, *India* 68 C7
Kyenjojo, *Uganda* 86 B3
Kyjov, *Czech Rep.* 27 B10
Kyle, *Canada* 103 C7
Kyle Dam, *Zimbabwe* 87 G3
Kyle of Lochalsh, *U.K.* 13 D3
Kyll →, *Germany* 25 F2
Kyllburg, *Germany* 25 E2
Kymijoki →, *Finland* 9 F22
Kymmene älv = Kymijoki →, *Finland* 9 F22
Kyneton, *Australia* 95 F3
Kynuna, *Australia* 94 C3
Kyō-ga-Saki, *Japan* 55 G7
Kyoga, L., *Uganda* 86 B3
Kyogle, *Australia* 95 D5
Kyom →, *Sudan* 81 F2
Kyongju, *S. Korea* 57 G15
Kyongpyaw, *Burma* 67 L19
Kyŏngsŏng, *N. Korea* 57 D15
Kyōto, *Japan* 55 G7
Kyōto □, *Japan* 55 G7
Kyparissovouno, *Cyprus* 49 D12
Kyperounda, *Cyprus* 49 E11
Kyrenia, *Cyprus* 49 D12
Kyrgyzstan ■, *Asia* 52 E8
Kyritz, *Germany* 24 C8
Kyrkhult, *Sweden* 11 H8
Kyrnasivka, *Ukraine* 29 B13
Kyrnychky, *Ukraine* 29 E14
Kyro älv = Kyrönjoki →, *Finland* 8 E19
Kyrönjoki →, *Finland* 8 E19
Kystatyam, *Russia* 53 C13
Kysucké Nové Mesto, *Slovak Rep.* 27 B11
Kytay, Ozero, *Ukraine* 29 E14
Kythréa, *Cyprus* 49 D12
Kyunhla, *Burma* 67 H19
Kyuquot Sound, *Canada* 102 D3
Kyurdamir = Kürdämir, *Azerbaijan* 35 K9
Kyūshū, *Japan* 55 H5
Kyūshū □, *Japan* 55 H5
Kyūshū-Sanchi, *Japan* 55 H5
Kyustendil, *Bulgaria* 44 D6
Kyusyur, *Russia* 53 B13
Kyyiv, *Ukraine* 33 G6
Kyyivske Vdskh., *Ukraine* 33 G6
Kyzyl, *Russia* 53 D10
Kyzyl Kum, *Uzbekistan* 52 E7
Kyzyl-Kyya, *Kyrgyzstan* 52 E8
Kyzyl-Orda = Qyzylorda, *Kazakhstan* 52 E7

L

La Albuera, *Spain* 37 G4
La Alcarria, *Spain* 38 E2
La Almarcha, *Spain* 38 F2
La Almunia de Doña Godina, *Spain* 38 D3
La Amistad △, *Cent. Amer.* 120 E3
La Asunción, *Venezuela* 124 A6
La Baie, *Canada* 105 C5
La Banda, *Argentina* 126 B3
La Bañeza, *Spain* 36 C5
La Barca, *Mexico* 118 C4
La Barge, *U.S.A.* 108 E8
La Bastide-Puylaurent, *France* 20 D7
La Baule, *France* 18 E4
La Belle, *U.S.A.* 115 M5
La Biche →, *Canada* 102 B4
La Biche, L., *Canada* 102 C6
La Bisbal d'Empordà, *Spain* 38 D8
La Blanquilla, *Venezuela* 121 D7
La Bomba, *Mexico* 118 A1
La Brea, *Trin. & Tob.* 125 K15
La Brède, *France* 20 D3
La Bresse, *France* 19 D13
La Bureba, *Spain* 36 C7
La Calera, *Chile* 126 C1
La Campana △, *Chile* 126 C1
La Campiña, *Spain* 37 H6
La Canal = Sa Canal, *Spain* 48 C7
La Cañiza = A Cañiza, *Spain* 36 C2
La Canourgue, *France* 20 D7
La Capelle, *France* 19 C10
La Carlota, *Argentina* 126 C3
La Carlota, *Phil.* 61 F5
La Carlota, *Spain* 37 H6
La Carolina, *Spain* 37 G7
La Cavalerie, *France* 20 D7
La Ceiba, *Honduras* 120 C2
La Chaise-Dieu, *France* 20 C7
La Chapelle d'Angillon, *France* 19 E9
La Chapelle-St-Luc, *France* 19 D11
La Chapelle-sur-Erdre, *France* 18 E5
La Charité-sur-Loire, *France* 19 E10
La Chartre-sur-le-Loir, *France* 18 E7
La Châtaigneraie, *France* 20 B3
La Châtre, *France* 19 F9
La Chaux-de-Fonds, *Switz.* 25 H2
La Chorrera, *Panama* 120 E4
La Ciotat, *France* 21 E9
La Clayette, *France* 19 F11
La Cocha, *Argentina* 126 B2
La Concepción, *Panama* 120 E3
La Concordia, *Mexico* 119 D6
La Coruña = A Coruña, *Spain* 36 B2
La Coruña □, *Spain* 36 B2
La Côte-St-André, *France* 21 C9
La Courtine, *France* 20 C6
La Crau, *Bouches-du-Rhône, France* 21 E8
La Crau, *Var, France* 21 E10
La Crescent, *U.S.A.* 112 D9
La Crete, *Canada* 102 B5
La Crosse, *Kans., U.S.A.* 112 F5
La Crosse, *Wis., U.S.A.* 112 D9
La Cruz, *Costa Rica* 120 D2
La Cruz, *Mexico* 118 C3
La Désirade, *Guadeloupe* 120 b
La Escondida, *Mexico* 118 C5
La Esmeralda, *Paraguay* 126 A3
La Esperanza, *Cuba* 120 B3
La Esperanza, *Honduras* 120 D2
La Estrada = A Estrada, *Spain* 36 C2
La Faouët, *France* 18 D3
La Fayette, *U.S.A.* 115 H3
La Fé, *Cuba* 120 B3
La Fère, *France* 19 C10
La Ferté-Bernard, *France* 18 D7
La Ferté-Gaucher, *France* 19 D10
La Ferté-Macé, *France* 18 D6
La Ferté-St-Aubin, *France* 19 E8
La Ferté-sous-Jouarre, *France* 19 D10
La Ferté-Vidame, *France* 18 D7
La Flèche, *France* 18 E6
La Follette, *U.S.A.* 115 G3
La Fregeneda, *Spain* 36 E4
La Fuente de San Esteban, *Spain* 36 E4
La Gacilly, *France* 18 E4
La Gineta, *Spain* 39 F2
La Grand'Combe, *France* 21 D8
La Grande, *U.S.A.* 108 D4
La Grande →, *Canada* 104 B5
La Grande Deux, Rés., *Canada* 104 B4
La Grande-Motte, *France* 21 E8
La Grande Quatre, Rés., *Canada* 104 B5
La Grande Trois, Rés., *Canada* 104 B4
La Grange, *Calif., U.S.A.* 110 H6
La Grange, *Ga., U.S.A.* 115 J3
La Grange, *Ky., U.S.A.* 114 F3
La Grange, *Tex., U.S.A.* 113 L6
La Grave, *France* 21 C10
La Guaira, *Venezuela* 124 A5
La Guardia = A Guarda, *Spain* 36 D2
La Gudiña = A Gudiña, *Spain* 36 C3
La Guerche-de-Bretagne, *France* 18 E5
La Guerche-sur-l'Aubois, *France* 19 F9
La Habana, *Cuba* 120 B3
La Haute Vallée de Chevreuse ⌓, *France* 19 D8
La Haye-du-Puits, *France* 18 C5
La Horra, *Spain* 36 D7
La Independencia, *Mexico* 119 D6
La Isabela, *Dom. Rep.* 121 C5
La Jonquera, *Spain* 38 C7
La Junta, *U.S.A.* 113 F3
La Laguna, *Canary Is.* 48 F3
La Libertad, *Guatemala* 120 C1
La Libertad, *Mexico* 118 B2
La Ligua, *Chile* 126 C1
La Línea de la Concepción, *Spain* 37 J5
La Loche, *Canada* 103 B7
La Londe-les-Maures, *France* 21 E10
La Lora, *Spain* 36 C7
La Loupe, *France* 18 D8
La Louvière, *Belgium* 17 D4
La Lune, *Trin. & Tob.* 125 K15
La Machine, *France* 19 F10
La Maddalena, *Italy* 42 A2
La Malbaie, *Canada* 105 C5
La Malinche △, *Mexico* 119 D5
La Mancha, *Spain* 39 F2
La Mariña, *Spain* 36 B3
La Martre, L., *Canada* 102 A5
La Mesa, *U.S.A.* 111 N9
La Misión, *Mexico* 118 A1
La Mothe-Achard, *France* 18 F5
La Motte-Chalançon, *France* 21 D9
La Motte-du-Caire, *France* 21 D10
La Motte-Servolex, *France* 21 C9
La Moure, *U.S.A.* 112 B5
La Muela, *Spain* 38 D3
La Mure, *France* 21 D9
La Negra, *Chile* 126 A1
La Oliva, *Canary Is.* 48 F6
La Orotava, *Canary Is.* 48 F3
La Oroya, *Peru* 124 F3
La Pacaudière, *France* 19 F10
La Palma, *Canary Is.* 48 F2
La Palma, *Panama* 120 E4
La Palma del Condado, *Spain* 37 H4
La Paloma, *Chile* 126 C1
La Pampa □, *Argentina* 126 D2
La Paragua, *Venezuela* 124 B6
La Paz, *Entre Ríos, Argentina* 126 C4
La Paz, *San Luis, Argentina* 126 C2
La Paz, *Bolivia* 124 G5
La Paz, *Honduras* 120 D2
La Paz, *Mexico* 118 C2
La Paz, *Phil.* 61 D4
La Paz Centro, *Nic.* 120 D2
La Pedrera, *Colombia* 124 D5
La Pérade, *Canada* 105 C5
La Perouse Str., *Asia* 54 B11
La Pesca, *Mexico* 119 C5
La Piedad, *Mexico* 118 C4
La Pine, *U.S.A.* 108 E3
La Plata, *Argentina* 126 D4
La Pobla de Lillet, *Spain* 38 C6
La Pocatière, *Canada* 105 C5
La Pola de Gordón, *Spain* 36 C5
La Porta, *France* 21 F13
La Porte, *Ind., U.S.A.* 114 E2
La Porte, *Tex., U.S.A.* 113 L7
La Presanella, *Italy* 40 B7
La Puebla = Sa Pobla, *Spain* 38 F8
La Puebla de Cazalla, *Spain* 37 H5
La Puebla de los Infantes, *Spain* 37 H5
La Puebla de Montalbán, *Spain* 36 F6
La Puebla del Río, *Spain* 37 H4
La Puerta de Segura, *Spain* 37 G8
La Purísima, *Mexico* 118 B2
La Push, *U.S.A.* 110 C2
La Quiaca, *Argentina* 126 A2
La Réole, *France* 20 D3
La Restinga, *Canary Is.* 48 G2
La Rioja, *Argentina* 126 B2
La Rioja □, *Argentina* 126 B2
La Rioja □, *Spain* 38 C2
La Robla, *Spain* 36 C5
La Roche-Bernard, *France* 18 E4
La Roche-Canillac, *France* 20 C5
La Roche-en-Ardenne, *Belgium* 17 D5
La Roche-sur-Foron, *France* 19 F13
La Roche-sur-Yon, *France* 18 F5
La Rochefoucauld, *France* 20 C4
La Rochelle, *France* 20 B2
La Roda, *Spain* 39 F2
La Roda de Andalucía, *Spain* 37 H6
La Romana, *Dom. Rep.* 121 C6
La Ronge, *Canada* 103 B7
La Rumorosa, *Mexico* 111 N10
La Sabina = Sa Savina, *Spain* 48 C7
La Sagra, *Spain* 39 H2
La Salle, *U.S.A.* 112 E10
La Sanabria, *Spain* 36 C4
La Santa, *Canary Is.* 48 E6
La Sarre, *Canada* 104 C4
La Scie, *Canada* 105 C8
La Selva, *Spain* 38 C7
La Selva Beach, *U.S.A.* 110 J5
La Selva del Camp, *Spain* 38 D6
La Serena, *Chile* 126 B1
La Serena, *Spain* 37 G5
La Seu d'Urgell, *Spain* 38 C6
La Seyne-sur-Mer, *France* 21 E9
La Sila, *Italy* 43 C9
La Solana, *Spain* 37 G7
La Soufrière, *St. Vincent* 121 D7
La Souterraine, *France* 19 F8
La Spézia, *Italy* 40 D6
La Suze-sur-Sarthe, *France* 18 E7
La Tagua, *Colombia* 124 C4
La Teste-de-Buch, *France* 20 D2
La Tortuga, *Venezuela* 121 D6
La Tour-du-Pin, *France* 21 C9
La Tranche-sur-Mer, *France* 18 F5
La Tremblade, *France* 20 C2
La Trinité, *Martinique* 120 c
La Tuque, *Canada* 104 C5
La Unión, *Chile* 128 E2
La Unión, *El Salv.* 120 D2
La Unión, *Mexico* 118 D4
La Unión, *Spain* 39 H4
La Urbana, *Venezuela* 124 B5
La Vache Pt., *Trin. & Tob.* 125 K15
La Vall d'Uixó, *Spain* 38 F4
La Vecilla de Curveño, *Spain* 36 C5
La Vega, *Dom. Rep.* 121 C5
La Vela de Coro, *Venezuela* 124 A5
La Veleta, *Spain* 37 H7
La Venta, *Mexico* 119 D6
La Ventura, *Mexico* 118 C4
La Voulte-sur-Rhône, *France* 21 D8
Laa an der Thaya, *Austria* 27 C9
Laaber, Grosse →, *Germany* 25 G8
Laage, *Germany* 24 B8
Laas Caanood = Las Anod, *Somali Rep.* 75 F4
Laatzen, *Germany* 24 C5
Laba →, *Russia* 35 H4
Labasa, *Fiji* 91 C8
Labason, *Phil.* 61 G5
Labastide-Murat, *France* 20 D5
Labastide-Rouairoux, *France* 20 E6
Labbézenga, *Mali* 83 B5
Labe = Elbe →, *Europe* 24 B4
Labé, *Guinea* 82 C2
Laberge, L., *Canada* 102 A1
Labin, *Croatia* 41 C11

Labinsk, *Russia* 35 H5
Labis, *Malaysia* 65 L4
Łabiszyn, *Poland* 31 F4
Labo, *Phil.* 61 D5
Laboe, *Germany* 24 A6
Laborec →, *Slovak Rep.* 27 C14
Laborie, *St. Lucia* 121 f
Labouheyre, *France* 20 D3
Laboulaye, *Argentina* 126 C3
Labrador, *Canada* 105 B7
Labrador City, *Canada* 105 B6
Labrador Sea, *Atl. Oc.* 101 C14
Lábrea, *Brazil* 124 E6
Labruguière, *France* 20 E6
Labuan, *Malaysia* 62 C5
Labuan, Pulau, *Malaysia* 62 C5
Labuha, *Indonesia* 63 E7
Labuhan, *Indonesia* 63 G11
Labuhanbajo, *Indonesia* 63 F6
Labuk, Telok, *Malaysia* 62 C5
Labyrinth, L., *Australia* 95 E2
Labytnangi, *Russia* 52 C7
Laç, *Albania* 44 E3
Lac-Bouchette, *Canada* 105 C5
Lac Édouard, *Canada* 104 C5
Lac La Biche, *Canada* 102 C6
Lac la Martre = Wha Ti, *Canada* 100 B8
Lac La Ronge ⌓, *Canada* 103 B7
Lac-Mégantic, *Canada* 105 C5
Lac Thien, *Vietnam* 64 F7
Lacanau, *France* 20 D2
Lacanau, Étang de, *France* 20 D2
Lacantúm →, *Mexico* 119 D6
Lacara →, *Spain* 37 G4
Lacaune, *France* 20 E6
Lacaune, Mts. de, *France* 20 E6
Laccadive Is. = Lakshadweep Is., *India* 50 H11
Lacepede B., *Australia* 95 F2
Lacepede Is., *Australia* 92 C3
Lacerdónia, *Mozam.* 87 F4
Lacey, *U.S.A.* 110 C4
Lachhmangarh, *India* 68 F6
Lachi, *Pakistan* 68 C4
Lachine, *Canada* 104 C5
Lachlan →, *Australia* 95 E3
Lachute, *Canada* 104 C5
Lackawanna, *U.S.A.* 116 D6
Lackawaxen, *U.S.A.* 117 E10
Lacolle, *Canada* 117 A11
Lacombe, *Canada* 102 C6
Lacona, *U.S.A.* 117 C8
Láconi, *Italy* 42 C2
Laconia, *U.S.A.* 117 C13
Lacq, *France* 20 E3
Ladakh Ra., *India* 69 C8
Lądek-Zdrój, *Poland* 31 H3
Ládhon →, *Greece* 46 D3
Ladik, *Turkey* 72 B6
Ladismith, *S. Africa* 88 E3
Ladíspoli, *Italy* 41 G9
Lādīz, *Iran* 71 D9
Ladnun, *India* 68 F6
Ladoga, L. = Ladozhskoye Ozero, *Russia* 32 B6
Ladozhskoye Ozero, *Russia* 32 B6
Ladushkin, *Russia* 30 D7
Lady Elliott I., *Australia* 94 C5
Lady Grey, *S. Africa* 88 E4
Ladybrand, *S. Africa* 88 D4
Ladysmith, *Canada* 102 D4
Ladysmith, *S. Africa* 89 D4
Ladysmith, *U.S.A.* 112 C9
Ladyzhyn, *Ukraine* 29 B14
Lae, *Papua N. G.* 96 H6
Laem Hin Khom, *Thailand* 65 b
Laem Khat, *Thailand* 65 a
Laem Nga, *Thailand* 65 a
Laem Ngop, *Thailand* 65 F4
Laem Phan Wa, *Thailand* 65 a
Laem Pho, *Thailand* 65 J3
Laem Phrom Thep, *Thailand* 65 a
Laem Riang, *Thailand* 65 a
Laem Sam Rong, *Thailand* 65 b
Laem Son, *Thailand* 65 a
Laem Yamu, *Thailand* 65 a
Læsø, *Denmark* 11 G5
Læsø Rende, *Denmark* 11 G4
Lafayette, *Colo., U.S.A.* 112 F2
Lafayette, *Ind., U.S.A.* 114 E2
Lafayette, *La., U.S.A.* 113 K9
Lafayette, *Tenn., U.S.A.* 115 G2
Laferte →, *Canada* 102 A5
Lafia, *Nigeria* 83 D6
Lafiagi, *Nigeria* 83 D6
Lafleche, *Canada* 103 D7
Lafon, *Sudan* 81 F3
Lagan, *Sweden* 11 H7
Lagan →, *Sweden* 11 H6
Lagan →, *U.K.* 12 B6
Lagarfljót →, *Iceland* 8 D6
Lage, *Germany* 24 D4
Lågen →, *Oppland, Norway* 9 F14
Lågen →, *Vestfold, Norway* 9 G14
Lägerdorf, *Germany* 24 B5
Laghouat, *Algeria* 78 B6
Lagnieu, *France* 21 C9
Lagny-sur-Marne, *France* 19 D9
Lago, *Italy* 43 C9
Lago de Sanabria y Entorno ⌓, *Spain* 36 C4
Lagôa, *Portugal* 37 H2
Lagoa do Peixe △, *Brazil* 127 C5
Lagoa Vermelha, *Brazil* 127 B5
Lagoaça, *Portugal* 36 D4
Lagodekhi, *Georgia* 35 K8
Lagónegro, *Italy* 43 B8
Lagonoy G., *Phil.* 61 E5
Lagos, *Nigeria* 83 D5
Lagos, *Portugal* 37 H2
Lagos □, *Nigeria* 83 D5
Lagos de Moreno, *Mexico* 118 C4
Lagrange, *Australia* 92 C3
Lagrange B., *Australia* 92 C3
Laguardia, *Spain* 38 C2
Laguépie, *France* 20 D5
Laguna, *Brazil* 127 B6
Laguna, *U.S.A.* 109 J10
Laguna Beach, *U.S.A.* 111 M9
Laguna de Duera, *Spain* 36 D6
Laguna de la Restinga △, *Venezuela* 121 D6
Laguna del Laja △, *Chile* 126 D1
Laguna del Tigre △, *Guatemala* 120 C1
Laguna Limpia, *Argentina* 126 B4
Lagunas, *Chile* 126 A2
Lagunas, *Peru* 124 E3
Lagunas de Chacahua △, *Mexico* 119 D5
Lagunas de Montebello △, *Mexico* 119 D6
Lagunas de Ruidera ⌓, *Spain* 39 G2
Lahad Datu, *Malaysia* 63 C5
Lahad Datu, Teluk, *Malaysia* 63 D5
Lahan Sai, *Thailand* 64 E4
Lahanam, *Laos* 64 D5
Lahar, *India* 69 F8
Laharpur, *India* 69 F9
Lahat, *Indonesia* 62 E2
Lahewa, *Indonesia* 62 D1
Lāhījān, *Iran* 71 B6
Lahn →, *Germany* 25 E3
Lahnstein, *Germany* 25 E3
Laholm, *Sweden* 11 H7
Laholmsbukten, *Sweden* 11 H6
Lahore, *Pakistan* 68 D6
Lahr, *Germany* 25 G3
Lahri, *Pakistan* 68 E3
Lahti, *Finland* 9 F21
Lahtis = Lahti, *Finland* 9 F21
Laï, *Chad* 79 G9
Lai Chau, *Vietnam* 58 F4
Lai'an, *China* 59 A12
Laibin, *China* 58 F7
Laifeng, *China* 58 C7
L'Aigle, *France* 18 D7
Laignes, *France* 19 E11
L'Aiguillon-sur-Mer, *France* 20 B2
Laila = Layla, *Si. Arabia* 75 C4
Laingsburg, *S. Africa* 88 E3
Lainioälven →, *Sweden* 8 C20
Lairg, *U.K.* 13 C4
Laishui, *China* 56 E8
Laissac, *France* 20 D6
Láives, *Italy* 41 B8
Laiwu, *China* 57 F9
Laixi, *China* 57 F11
Laiyang, *China* 57 F11
Laiyuan, *China* 56 E8
Laizhou, *China* 57 F10
Laizhou Wan, *China* 57 F10
Laja →, *Mexico* 118 C4
Lajere, *Nigeria* 83 C7
Lajes, *Brazil* 127 B5
Lajkovac, *Serbia & M.* 44 B4
Lajosmizse, *Hungary* 28 C4
Lak Sao, *Laos* 64 C5
Lakaband, *Pakistan* 68 D3
Lakamané, *Mali* 82 C3
Lake Alpine, *U.S.A.* 110 G7
Lake Andes, *U.S.A.* 112 D5
Lake Arthur, *U.S.A.* 113 K8
Lake Bindegolly △, *Australia* 95 D3
Lake Cargelligo, *Australia* 95 E4
Lake Charles, *U.S.A.* 113 K8
Lake City, *Colo., U.S.A.* 109 G10
Lake City, *Fla., U.S.A.* 115 K4
Lake City, *Mich., U.S.A.* 114 C3
Lake City, *Minn., U.S.A.* 112 C8
Lake City, *Pa., U.S.A.* 116 D4
Lake City, *S.C., U.S.A.* 115 J6
Lake Cowichan, *Canada* 102 D4
Lake District △, *U.K.* 14 C4
Lake Elsinore, *U.S.A.* 111 M9
Lake Eyre △, *Australia* 95 D2
Lake Gairdner △, *Australia* 95 E2
Lake George, *U.S.A.* 117 C11
Lake Grace, *Australia* 93 F2
Lake Harbour = Kimmirut, *Canada* 101 B13
Lake Havasu City, *U.S.A.* 111 L12
Lake Hughes, *U.S.A.* 111 L8
Lake Isabella, *U.S.A.* 111 K8
Lake Jackson, *U.S.A.* 113 L7
Lake Junction, *U.S.A.* 108 D8
Lake King, *Australia* 93 F2
Lake Lenore, *Canada* 103 C8
Lake Louise, *Canada* 102 C5
Lake Malawi △, *Malawi* 87 E3
Lake Mburo △, *Uganda* 86 C3
Lake Mead ⌓, *U.S.A.* 111 K12
Lake Meredith ⌓, *U.S.A.* 113 H4
Lake Mills, *U.S.A.* 112 D8
Lake Nakura △, *Kenya* 86 C4
Lake Placid, *U.S.A.* 117 B11
Lake Pleasant, *U.S.A.* 117 C10
Lake Providence, *U.S.A.* 113 J9
Lake Roosevelt ⌓, *U.S.A.* 108 C4
Lake St. Peter, *Canada* 116 A6
Lake Superior ⌓, *Canada* 104 C3
Lake Torrens △, *Australia* 95 E2
Lake Village, *U.S.A.* 113 J9
Lake Wales, *U.S.A.* 115 M5
Lake Worth, *U.S.A.* 115 M5
Lakeba, *Fiji* 91 D9
Lakefield, *Canada* 116 B6
Lakefield △, *Australia* 94 B3
Lakehurst, *U.S.A.* 117 F10
Lakeland, *Australia* 94 B3
Lakeland, *U.S.A.* 115 M5
Lakemba = Lakeba, *Fiji* 91 D9
Lakeport, *Calif., U.S.A.* 110 F4
Lakeport, *Mich., U.S.A.* 116 C2
Lakes Entrance, *Australia* 95 F4
Lakeside, *Ariz., U.S.A.* 109 J9
Lakeside, *Calif., U.S.A.* 111 N10
Lakeside, *Nebr., U.S.A.* 112 D3
Lakeside, *Ohio, U.S.A.* 116 E2
Lakeview, *U.S.A.* 108 E3
Lakeville, *U.S.A.* 112 C8
Lakewood, *Colo., U.S.A.* 112 F2
Lakewood, *N.J., U.S.A.* 117 F10
Lakewood, *N.Y., U.S.A.* 116 D5
Lakewood, *Ohio, U.S.A.* 116 E3
Lakewood, *Wash., U.S.A.* 110 C4
Lakha, *India* 68 F4
Lakhaniá, *Greece* 49 D9
Lakhimpur, *India* 69 F9
Lakhnadon, *India* 69 H8
Lakhnau = Lucknow, *India* 69 F9
Lakhonpheng, *Laos* 64 E5
Lakhpat, *India* 68 H3
Läki, *Azerbaijan* 35 K8
Lakin, *U.S.A.* 113 G4
Lakitusaki →, *Canada* 104 B3
Lakki, *Pakistan* 68 C4
Lákkoi, *Greece* 49 D5
Lakonía □, *Greece* 46 E4
Lakonikós Kólpos, *Greece* 46 E4
Lakor, *Indonesia* 63 F7
Lakota, *Ivory C.* 82 D3
Lakota, *U.S.A.* 112 A5
Laksar, *India* 68 E8
Laksefjorden, *Norway* 8 A22
Lakselv, *Norway* 8 A21
Lakshadweep Is., *India* 50 H11
Lakshmanpur, *India* 69 H10
Lakshmikantapur, *India* 69 H13
Lala Musa, *Pakistan* 68 C5
Lalaghat, *India* 67 G18
Lalago, *Tanzania* 86 C3
Lalapanzi, *Zimbabwe* 87 F3
Lalapaşa, *Turkey* 45 E10
Lalbenque, *France* 20 D5
L'Albufera, *Spain* 39 F4
Lalganj, *India* 69 G11
Lalgola, *India* 69 G13
Lālī, *Iran* 71 C6
Lalibela, *Ethiopia* 81 E4
Lalin, *China* 57 B14
Lalín, *Spain* 36 C2
Lalin He →, *China* 57 B13
Lalinde, *France* 20 D4
Lalitapur, *Nepal* 69 F11
Lalitpur, *India* 69 G8
Lalkua, *India* 69 E8
Lalsot, *India* 68 F7
Lam, *Vietnam* 64 B6
Lam Pao Res., *Thailand* 64 D4
Lama Kara, *Togo* 83 D5
Lamaing, *Burma* 67 M20
Lamar, *Colo., U.S.A.* 112 F3
Lamar, *Mo., U.S.A.* 113 G7
Lamas, *Peru* 124 E3
Lamastre, *France* 21 D8
Lambach, *Austria* 26 C6
Lamballe, *France* 18 D4
Lambaréné, *Gabon* 84 E2
Lambasa = Labasa, *Fiji* 91 C8
Lambay I., *Ireland* 12 C5
Lambert Glacier, *Antarctica* 5 D6
Lambert's Bay, *S. Africa* 88 E2
Lambesc, *France* 21 E9
Lambeth, *Canada* 116 D3
Lámbia, *Greece* 46 D3
Lambomakondro, *Madag.* 89 C7
Lambro →, *Italy* 40 C6
Lambton Shores, *Canada* 116 C3
Lame, *Nigeria* 83 C6
Lame Deer, *U.S.A.* 108 D10
Lamego, *Portugal* 36 D3
Lamèque, *Canada* 105 C7
Lameroo, *Australia* 95 F3
Lamesa, *U.S.A.* 113 J4
Lamía, *Greece* 46 C4
Lamington △, *Australia* 95 D5
Lamitan, *Phil.* 61 H5
Lammermuir Hills, *U.K.* 13 F6
Lammhult, *Sweden* 11 G8
Lamoille →, *U.S.A.* 117 B11
Lamon B., *Phil.* 61 D5
Lamont, *Canada* 102 C6
Lamont, *Calif., U.S.A.* 111 K8
Lamont, *Wyo., U.S.A.* 108 E10
Lamotte-Beuvron, *France* 19 E9
Lampa, *Peru* 124 G4
Lampang, *Thailand* 64 C2
Lampasas, *U.S.A.* 113 K5
Lampazos de Naranjo, *Mexico* 118 B4
Lampertheim, *Germany* 25 F4
Lampeter, *U.K.* 15 E3
Lampman, *Canada* 103 D8
Lamprechtshausen, *Austria* 26 D5
Lampung □, *Indonesia* 62 F2
Lamta, *India* 69 H9
Lamu, *Kenya* 86 C5
Lamy, *U.S.A.* 109 J11
Lan Xian, *China* 56 E6
Lan Yu = Hungt'ou Hsü, *Taiwan* 59 G13
Lanak La, *China* 69 B8
Lanak'o Shank'ou = Lanak La, *China* 69 B8
Lanao, L., *Phil.* 61 H6
Lanark, *Canada* 117 A8
Lanark, *U.K.* 13 F5
Lanbi Kyun, *Burma* 65 G2
Lancang, *China* 58 F2
Lancang Jiang →, *China* 58 G3
Lancashire □, *U.K.* 14 D5
Lancaster, *Canada* 117 A10
Lancaster, *U.K.* 14 C5
Lancaster, *Calif., U.S.A.* 111 L8
Lancaster, *Ky., U.S.A.* 114 G3
Lancaster, *N.H., U.S.A.* 117 B13
Lancaster, *N.Y., U.S.A.* 116 D6
Lancaster, *Ohio, U.S.A.* 114 F4
Lancaster, *Pa., U.S.A.* 117 F8
Lancaster, *S.C., U.S.A.* 115 H5
Lancaster, *Wis., U.S.A.* 112 D9
Lancaster Sd., *Canada* 101 A11
Lancelin, *Australia* 93 F2
Lanchow = Lanzhou, *China* 56 F2
Lanchyn, *Ukraine* 29 B9
Lanciano, *Italy* 41 F11
Lancun, *China* 57 F11
Łańcut, *Poland* 31 H9
Land Between the Lakes ⌓, *U.S.A.* 115 G1
Landau, *Bayern, Germany* 25 G8
Landau, *Rhld-Pfz., Germany* 25 F4
Landeck, *Austria* 26 D3
Lander, *U.S.A.* 108 E9
Lander →, *Australia* 92 D5
Landerneau, *France* 18 D2
Landeryd, *Sweden* 11 G7
Landes, *France* 20 D2
Landes □, *France* 20 E3
Landes de Gascogne ⌓, *France* 20 D3
Landete, *Spain* 38 F3
Landi Kotal, *Pakistan* 68 B4
Landisburg, *U.S.A.* 116 F7
Landivisiau, *France* 18 D2
Landquart, *Switz.* 25 J5
Landrecies, *France* 19 B10
Land's End, *U.K.* 15 G2
Landsberg, *Germany* 25 G6
Landsborough Cr. →, *Australia* 94 C3
Landsbro, *Sweden* 11 G8
Landshut, *Germany* 25 G8
Landskrona, *Sweden* 11 J6
Landstuhl, *Germany* 25 F3
Landvetter, *Sweden* 11 G6
Lanesboro, *U.S.A.* 117 E9
Lanester, *France* 18 E3
Lanett, *U.S.A.* 115 J3
Lang Qua, *Vietnam* 64 A5
Lang Shan, *China* 56 D4
Lang Son, *Vietnam* 58 G6
Lang Suan, *Thailand* 65 H2
Langå, *Denmark* 11 H3
La'nga Co, *China* 67 D12
Lángadhás, *Greece* 44 F7
Langádhia, *Greece* 46 D4
Långan →, *Sweden* 10 A8
Langano, L., *Ethiopia* 81 F4
Langar, *Iran* 71 C9
Langara I., *Canada* 102 C2
Långås, *Sweden* 11 H6
Langdai, *China* 58 D5
Langdon, *U.S.A.* 112 A5
Långe Jan = Ölands södra udde, *Sweden* 11 H10
Langeac, *France* 20 C7
Langeais, *France* 18 E7
Langeb Baraka →, *Sudan* 80 D4
Langeberg, *S. Africa* 88 E3
Langeberge, *S. Africa* 88 D3
Langeland, *Denmark* 11 K4
Langelands Bælt, *Denmark* 11 K4
Langen, *Hessen, Germany* 25 F4
Langen, *Niedersachsen, Germany* 24 B4
Langenburg, *Canada* 103 C8
Langeneß, *Germany* 24 A4
Langenlois, *Austria* 26 C8
Langeoog, *Germany* 24 B3
Langeskov, *Denmark* 11 J4
Långhem, *Sweden* 11 G7
Langhirano, *Italy* 40 D7
Langholm, *U.K.* 13 F5
Langjökull, *Iceland* 8 D3
Langkawi, Pulau, *Malaysia* 65 J2
Langklip, *S. Africa* 88 D3
Langkon, *Malaysia* 62 C5
Langlade, *St-P. & M.* 105 C8
Langley, *Canada* 110 A4
Langnau, *Switz.* 25 J3
Langogne, *France* 20 D7
Langon, *France* 20 D3
Langøya, *Norway* 8 B16
Langreo, *Spain* 36 B5
Langres, *France* 19 E12
Langres, Plateau de, *France* 19 E12
Langsa, *Indonesia* 62 D1
Långsele, *Sweden* 10 A11
Långshyttan, *Sweden* 10 D10
Langtry, *U.S.A.* 113 L4
Langu, *Thailand* 65 J2
Langue de Barbarie △, *Senegal* 82 C1
Languedoc, *France* 20 E7
Languedoc-Roussillon □, *France* 20 E6
Langxi, *China* 59 B12
Langxiangzhen, *China* 56 E9
Langzhong, *China* 58 B5
Lanigan, *Canada* 103 C7
Lankao, *China* 56 G8
Länkäran, *Azerbaijan* 71 B6
Lanmeur, *France* 18 D3
Lannemezan, *France* 20 E4
Lannilis, *France* 18 D2
Lannion, *France* 18 D3
L'Annonciation, *Canada* 104 C5
Lanouaille, *France* 20 C5
Lanping, *China* 58 D2
Lansdale, *U.S.A.* 117 F9
Lansdowne, *Australia* 95 E5
Lansdowne, *Canada* 117 B8
Lansdowne, *India* 69 E8
Lansdowne House, *Canada* 104 B2
L'Anse, *U.S.A.* 114 B1
L'Anse au Loup, *Canada* 105 B8
L'Anse aux Meadows, *Canada* 105 B8
Lansford, *U.S.A.* 117 F9
Lanshan, *China* 59 E9
Lansing, *U.S.A.* 114 D3
Lanslebourg-Mont-Cenis, *France* 21 C10
Lanta Yai, Ko, *Thailand* 65 J2
Lantewa, *Nigeria* 83 C7
Lantian, *China* 56 G5
Lanus, *Argentina* 126 C4
Lanusei, *Italy* 42 C2
Lanuza, *Phil.* 61 G7
Lanxi, *China* 59 C12
Lanzarote, *Canary Is.* 48 F6
Lanzarote ✕ (ACE), *Canary Is.* 48 F6
Lanzhou, *China* 56 F2
Lanzo Torinese, *Italy* 40 C4
Lao →, *Italy* 43 C8
Lao Bao, *Laos* 64 D6
Lao Cai, *Vietnam* 58 F4
Laoag, *Phil.* 61 B4
Laoang, *Phil.* 61 E6
Laoha He →, *China* 57 C11
Laohekou, *China* 59 A8
Laois □, *Ireland* 12 D4
Laon, *France* 19 C10
Laona, *U.S.A.* 114 C1
Laos ■, *Asia* 64 D5
Lapa, *Brazil* 127 B6
Lapai, *Nigeria* 83 D6
Lapalisse, *France* 19 F10
Lapeer, *U.S.A.* 114 D4
Lapeyrade, *France* 20 D3
Lapithos, *Cyprus* 49 D12
Lapland = Lappland, *Europe* 8 B21
Laporte, *U.S.A.* 117 E8
Lapovo, *Serbia & M.* 44 B5
Lappeenranta, *Finland* 9 F23
Lappland, *Europe* 8 B21
Lappo = Lapua, *Finland* 8 E20
Laprida, *Argentina* 126 D3
Lapseki, *Turkey* 45 F10
Laptev Sea, *Russia* 53 B13
Lapua, *Finland* 8 E20
Lăpuş →, *Romania* 29 C8
Lapuş, Munţii, *Romania* 29 C8
Lăpuşna, *Moldova* 29 D13
Łapy, *Poland* 31 F9
Laqiya Arba'in, *Sudan* 80 C2
Laqiya Umran, *Sudan* 80 D2
L'Áquila, *Italy* 41 F10
Lār, *Āzarbājān-e Sharqī, Iran* 70 B5
Lār, *Fārs, Iran* 71 E7
Larabanga, *Ghana* 82 D4
Laragne-Montéglin, *France* 21 D9
Laramie, *U.S.A.* 112 E2
Laramie →, *U.S.A.* 108 F11
Laramie Mts., *U.S.A.* 112 E2
Laranjeiras do Sul, *Brazil* 127 B5
Larantuka, *Indonesia* 63 F6
Larat, *Indonesia* 63 F8
L'Arbresle, *France* 21 C8
Lärbro, *Sweden* 11 G12
Larde, *Mozam.* 87 F4
Larder Lake, *Canada* 104 C4
Lardhos, Ákra = Líndhos, Ákra, *Greece* 49 C10
Lardhos, Órmos, *Greece* 49 C10
Laredo, *Spain* 36 B7
Laredo, *U.S.A.* 113 M5
Laredo Sd., *Canada* 102 C3
Largentière, *France* 21 D8
L'Argentière-la-Bessée, *France* 21 D10
Largo, *U.S.A.* 115 M4
Largs, *U.K.* 13 F4
Lari, *Italy* 40 E7
Lariang, *Indonesia* 63 E5
Larimore, *U.S.A.* 112 B6
Larino, *Italy* 41 G11
Lárisa, *Greece* 46 B4
Lárisa □, *Greece* 46 B4
Larkana, *Pakistan* 68 F3
Larnaca, *Cyprus* 49 E12
Larnaca Bay, *Cyprus* 49 E12
Larne, *U.K.* 12 B6
Larned, *U.S.A.* 112 F5
Laroquebrou, *France* 20 D6
Larose, *U.S.A.* 113 L9
Larrimah, *Australia* 92 C5
Larsen Ice Shelf, *Antarctica* 5 C17
Laruns, *France* 20 F3
Larvik, *Norway* 9 G14
Larzac, Causse du, *France* 20 E7
Las Alpujarras, *Spain* 39 J1
Las Animas, *U.S.A.* 112 F3
Las Anod, *Somali Rep.* 75 F4
Las Arenas, *Spain* 36 B6
Las Batuecas ⌓, *Spain* 36 E4
Las Brenãs, *Argentina* 126 B3
Las Cabezas de San Juan, *Spain* 37 J5
Las Cañadas del Teide △, *Canary Is.* 48 F3
Las Cejas, *Argentina* 128 B4
Las Chimeneas, *Mexico* 111 N10
Las Cruces, *U.S.A.* 109 K10
Las Flores, *Argentina* 126 D4
Las Heras, *Argentina* 126 C2
Las Lajas, *Argentina* 128 D2
Las Lomitas, *Argentina* 126 A3
Las Marismas, *Spain* 37 H4
Las Minas, *Spain* 39 G3
Las Navas de la Concepción, *Spain* 37 H5
Las Navas del Marqués, *Spain* 36 E6
Las Palmas, *Argentina* 126 B4
Las Palmas, *Canary Is.* 48 F4
Las Palmas →, *Mexico* 111 N10
Las Palmas ✕ (LPA), *Canary Is.* 48 G4
Las Palmas de Cocalán △, *Chile* 126 C1
Las Pedroñas, *Spain* 39 F2
Las Piedras, *Uruguay* 127 C4
Las Pipinas, *Argentina* 126 D4
Las Plumas, *Argentina* 128 E3
Las Rosas, *Argentina* 126 C3
Las Rozas, *Spain* 36 E7
Las Tablas, *Panama* 120 E3
Las Termas, *Argentina* 126 B3
Las Toscas, *Argentina* 126 B4
Las Truchas, *Mexico* 118 D4
Las Varillas, *Argentina* 126 C3
Las Vegas, *N. Mex., U.S.A.* 109 J11
Las Vegas, *Nev., U.S.A.* 111 J11

Las Vegas McCarran International ✈ (LAS), *U.S.A.* 111 J11
Lasarte, *Spain* 38 B2
Lascano, *Uruguay* 127 C5
Lash-e Joveyn, *Afghan.* 66 D2
Lashburn, *Canada* 103 C7
Lashio, *Burma* 67 H20
Lashkar, *India* 68 F8
Łasin, *Poland* 30 E6
Lasíthi, *Greece* 49 D7
Lasíthi □, *Greece* 49 D7
Lāsjerd, *Iran* 71 C7
Lask, *Poland* 31 G6
Łaskarzew, *Poland* 31 G8
Laško, *Slovenia* 41 B12
Lassay-les-Châteaux, *France* 18 D6
Lassen Pk., *U.S.A.* 108 F3
Lassen Volcanic △, *U.S.A.* 108 F3
Last Mountain L., *Canada* 103 C7
Lastchance Cr. →, *U.S.A.* 110 E5
Lastoursville, *Gabon* 84 E2
Lastovo, *Croatia* 41 F13
Lastovski Kanal, *Croatia* 41 F14
Lat Yao, *Thailand* 64 E2
Latacunga, *Ecuador* 124 D3
Latakia = Al Lādhiqīyah, *Syria* 70 C2
Latchford, *Canada* 104 C4
Latehar, *India* 69 H11
Laterza, *Italy* 43 B9
Latham, *Australia* 93 E2
Lathen, *Germany* 24 C3
Lathi, *India* 68 F4
Lathrop Wells, *U.S.A.* 111 J10
Latiano, *Italy* 43 B10
Latina, *Italy* 42 A5
Latisana, *Italy* 41 C10
Latium = Lazio □, *Italy* 41 F9
Laton, *U.S.A.* 110 J7
Latorytsya →, *Slovak Rep.* 27 C14
Latouche Treville, C., *Australia* 92 C3
Latrobe, *Australia* 95 G4
Latrobe, *U.S.A.* 116 F5
Latrónico, *Italy* 43 B9
Latvia ■, *Europe* 9 H20
Lau, *Nigeria* 83 D7
Lau Group, *Fiji* 91 C9
Lauchhammer, *Germany* 24 D9
Lauda-Königshofen, *Germany* 25 F5
Lauenburg, *Germany* 24 B6
Lauenburgische Seen ⌓, *Germany* 24 B6
Lauf, *Germany* 25 F7
Laughlin, *U.S.A.* 109 J6
Laujar de Andarax, *Spain* 39 H2
Laukaa, *Finland* 9 E21
Launceston, *Australia* 95 G4
Launceston, *U.K.* 15 G3
Laune →, *Ireland* 12 D2
Launglon Bok, *Burma* 64 F1
Laupheim, *Germany* 25 G5
Laura, *Australia* 94 B3
Laureana di Borrello, *Italy* 43 D9
Laurel, *Miss., U.S.A.* 113 K10
Laurel, *Mont., U.S.A.* 108 D9
Laurencekirk, *U.K.* 13 E6
Laurens, *U.S.A.* 115 H4
Laurentian Plateau, *Canada* 105 B6
Lauria, *Italy* 43 B8
Laurie L., *Canada* 103 B8
Laurinburg, *U.S.A.* 115 H6
Laurium, *U.S.A.* 114 B1
Lausanne, *Switz.* 25 J2
Laut, *Indonesia* 62 D3
Laut, Pulau, *Indonesia* 62 E5
Laut Kecil, Kepulauan, *Indonesia* 62 E5
Lauterbach, *Germany* 24 E5
Lauterecken, *Germany* 25 F3
Lautoka, *Fiji* 91 C7
Lauzès, *France* 20 D5
Lava →, *Russia* 30 D8
Lava Beds ⌓, *U.S.A.* 108 F3
Lavagh More, *Ireland* 12 B3
Lavagna, *Italy* 40 D6
Laval, *France* 18 D6
Lavalle, *Argentina* 126 B2
Lavant Station, *Canada* 117 A8
Lāvar Meydān, *Iran* 71 D7
Lávara, *Greece* 45 E10
Lavardac, *France* 20 D4
Lavaur, *France* 20 E5
Lavelanet, *France* 20 F5
Lavello, *Italy* 43 A8
Laverton, *Australia* 93 E3
Lavis, *Italy* 40 B8
Lávkos, *Greece* 46 B5
Lavos, *Portugal* 36 E2
Lavradio, *Portugal* 37 G1
Lavras, *Brazil* 127 A7
Lavre, *Portugal* 37 G2
Lávrion, *Greece* 46 D6
Lávris, *Greece* 49 D6
Lavumisa, *Swaziland* 89 D5
Lavushi Manda △, *Zambia* 87 E3
Lawas, *Malaysia* 62 D5
Lawele, *Indonesia* 63 F6
Lawn Hill △, *Australia* 94 B2
Lawng Pit, *Burma* 67 G20
Lawqah, *Si. Arabia* 70 D4
Lawra, *Ghana* 82 C4
Lawrence, *N.Z.* 91 L2
Lawrence, *Kans., U.S.A.* 112 F7
Lawrence, *Mass., U.S.A.* 117 D13
Lawrenceburg, *Ind., U.S.A.* 114 F3
Lawrenceburg, *Tenn., U.S.A.* 115 H2
Lawrenceville, *Ga., U.S.A.* 115 J4
Lawrenceville, *Pa., U.S.A.* 116 E7
Laws, *U.S.A.* 110 H8
Lawton, *U.S.A.* 113 H5
Lawu, *Indonesia* 63 G14
Lawz, J. al, *Si. Arabia* 80 B4
Laxå, *Sweden* 11 F8
Laxford, L., *U.K.* 13 C3
Laxou, *France* 19 D13
Lay →, *France* 20 B2
Layla, *Si. Arabia* 75 C4
Laylān, *Iraq* 70 C5
Layon →, *France* 18 E6
Layton, *U.S.A.* 108 F7
Laytonville, *U.S.A.* 108 G2
Lazarevac, *Serbia & M.* 44 B4
Lazarevskoye, *Russia* 35 J4
Lazarivo, *Madag.* 89 C8
Lazdijai, *Lithuania* 30 D10
Lazio □, *Italy* 41 F9
Lazo, *Moldova* 29 C13
Lazo, *Russia* 54 C6
Le Beausset, *France* 21 E9
Le Bic, *Canada* 105 C6
Le Blanc, *France* 20 B5
Le Bleymard, *France* 20 D7
Le Bourgneuf-la-Fôret, *France* 18 D6
Le Bugue, *France* 20 D4
Le Cateau Cambrésis, *France* 19 B10
Le Caylar, *France* 20 E7
Le Chambon-Feugerolles, *France* 21 C8
Le Châtelet, *France* 19 F9
Le Chesne, *France* 19 C11
Le Cheylard, *France* 21 D8
Le Conquet, *France* 18 D2
Le Creusot, *France* 19 F11
Le Croisic, *France* 18 E4
Le Donjon, *France* 19 F10
Le Dorat, *France* 20 B5
Le François, *Martinique* 120 c
Le Gosier, *Guadeloupe* 120 b
Le Grand-Lucé, *France* 18 E7
Le Grand-Pressigny, *France* 18 F7
Le Grand-Quevilly, *France* 18 C8
Le Havre, *France* 18 C7
Le Lamentin, *Martinique* 120 c
Le Lavandou, *France* 21 E10
Le Lion-d'Angers, *France* 18 E6
Le Louroux-Béconnais, *France* 18 E6
Le Luc, *France* 21 E10
Le Lude, *France* 18 E7
Le Mans, *France* 18 E7
Le Marin, *Martinique* 120 c
Le Mars, *U.S.A.* 112 D6
Le Mayet-de-Montagne, *France* 19 F10
Le Mêle-sur-Sarthe, *France* 18 D7
Le Monastier-sur-Gazeille, *France* 20 D7
Le Monêtier-les-Bains, *France* 21 D10
Le Mont-Dore, *France* 20 C6
Le Mont-St-Michel, *France* 18 D5
Le Moule, *Guadeloupe* 120 b
Le Muy, *France* 21 E10
Le Palais, *France* 18 E3
Le Perthus, *France* 20 F6
Le Prêcheur, *Martinique* 120 c
Le Puy-en-Velay, *France* 20 C7
Le Robert, *Martinique* 120 c
Le St-Esprit, *Martinique* 120 c
Le Sueur, *U.S.A.* 112 C8
Le Teil, *France* 21 D8
Le Teilleul, *France* 18 D6
Le Theil, *France* 18 D7
Le Thillot, *France* 19 E13
Le Thuy, *Vietnam* 64 D6
Le Touquet-Paris-Plage, *France* 19 B8
Le Tréport, *France* 18 B8
Le Val-d'Ajol, *France* 19 E13
Le Verdon-sur-Mer, *France* 20 C2
Le Vigan, *France* 20 E7
Lea →, *U.K.* 15 F8
Leach, *Cambodia* 65 F4
Lead, *U.S.A.* 112 C3
Leader, *Canada* 103 C7
Leadville, *U.S.A.* 109 G10
Leaf →, *U.S.A.* 113 K10
Leaf Rapids, *Canada* 103 B9
Leamington, *Canada* 116 D2
Leamington, *U.S.A.* 108 G7
Leamington Spa = Royal Leamington Spa, *U.K.* 15 E6
Le'an, *China* 59 D10
Leandro Norte Alem, *Argentina* 127 B4
Leane, L., *Ireland* 12 D2
Learmonth, *Australia* 92 D1
Leask, *Canada* 103 C7
Leatherhead, *U.K.* 15 F7
Leavenworth, *Kans., U.S.A.* 112 F7
Leavenworth, *Wash., U.S.A.* 108 C3
Łeba, *Poland* 30 D4
Łeba →, *Poland* 30 D4
Lebach, *Germany* 25 F2
Lebak, *Phil.* 61 H6
Lebam, *U.S.A.* 110 D3
Lebane, *Serbia & M.* 44 D5
Lebanon, *Ind., U.S.A.* 114 E2
Lebanon, *Kans., U.S.A.* 112 F5
Lebanon, *Ky., U.S.A.* 114 G3
Lebanon, *Mo., U.S.A.* 113 G8
Lebanon, *N.H., U.S.A.* 117 C12
Lebanon, *Oreg., U.S.A.* 108 D2
Lebanon, *Pa., U.S.A.* 117 F8
Lebanon, *Tenn., U.S.A.* 115 G2
Lebanon ■, *Asia* 74 B5
Lebec, *U.S.A.* 111 L8
Lebedyan, *Russia* 33 F10
Lebedyn, *Ukraine* 33 G8
Lebel-sur-Quévillon, *Canada* 104 C4
Lebomboberge, *S. Africa* 89 C5
Lębork, *Poland* 30 D4
Lebrija, *Spain* 37 J4
Łebsko, Jezioro, *Poland* 30 D4
Lebu, *Chile* 126 D1
Leca da Palmeira, *Portugal* 36 D2
Lecce, *Italy* 43 B11
Lecco, *Italy* 40 C6
Lecco, L. di, *Italy* 40 C6
Lécera, *Spain* 38 D4
Lech, *Austria* 26 D3
Lech →, *Germany* 25 G6
Lechang, *China* 59 E9
Lechtaler Alpen, *Austria* 26 D3
Lecontes Mills, *U.S.A.* 116 E6
Lectoure, *France* 20 E4
Łęczna, *Poland* 31 G9
Łęczyca, *Poland* 31 F6
Ledesma, *Spain* 36 D5
Ledong, *China* 64 C7
Leduc, *Canada* 102 C6
Lee, *U.S.A.* 117 D11
Lee →, *Ireland* 12 E3
Lee Vining, *U.S.A.* 110 H7
Leech L., *U.S.A.* 112 B7
Leechburg, *U.S.A.* 116 F5
Leeds, *U.K.* 14 D6
Leeds, *U.S.A.* 115 J2
Leek, *Neths.* 17 A6
Leek, *U.K.* 14 D5
Leeman, *Australia* 93 E1
Leeper, *U.S.A.* 116 E5
Leer, *Germany* 24 B3
Leesburg, *U.S.A.* 115 L5
Leesville, *U.S.A.* 113 K8
Leeton, *Australia* 95 E4
Leetonia, *U.S.A.* 116 F4
Leeu Gamka, *S. Africa* 88 E3
Leeuwarden, *Neths.* 17 A5
Leeuwin, C., *Australia* 93 F2
Leeuwin Naturaliste △, *Australia* 93 F2
Leeward Is., *Atl. Oc.* 121 C7
Lefka, *Cyprus* 49 D11
Lefkoniko, *Cyprus* 49 D12
Lefroy, *Canada* 116 B5
Lefroy, L., *Australia* 93 F3
Łeg →, *Poland* 31 H8
Leganés, *Spain* 36 E7
Legazpi, *Phil.* 61 E5
Lège-Cap-Ferret, *France* 20 D2
Lege Hida, *Ethiopia* 81 F5
Legendre I., *Australia* 92 D2
Leghorn = Livorno, *Italy* 40 E7
Legionowo, *Poland* 31 F7
Legnago, *Italy* 41 C8
Legnano, *Italy* 40 C5
Legnica, *Poland* 31 G3
Legrad, *Croatia* 41 B13
Leh, *India* 69 B7
Lehigh Acres, *U.S.A.* 115 M5
Lehighton, *U.S.A.* 117 F9
Lehliu, *Romania* 29 F11
Leho, *Sudan* 81 F3
Lehrte, *Germany* 24 C5
Lehututu, *Botswana* 88 C3
Lei Shui →, *China* 59 D9
Leiah, *Pakistan* 68 D4
Leibnitz, *Austria* 26 E8
Leibo, *China* 58 C4
Leicester, *U.K.* 15 E6
Leicester City □, *U.K.* 15 E6
Leicestershire □, *U.K.* 15 E6
Leichhardt →, *Australia* 94 B2
Leichhardt Ra., *Australia* 94 C4
Leiden, *Neths.* 17 B4
Leie →, *Belgium* 17 C3
Leifers = Láives, *Italy* 41 B8
Leimen, *Germany* 25 F4
Leine →, *Germany* 24 C5
Leinefelde, *Germany* 24 D6
Leinster, *Australia* 93 E3
Leinster □, *Ireland* 12 C4
Leinster, Mt., *Ireland* 12 D5
Leipalingis, *Lithuania* 30 D10
Leipzig, *Germany* 24 D8
Leiria, *Portugal* 36 F2
Leiria □, *Portugal* 36 F2
Leirvik, *Norway* 9 G11
Leishan, *China* 58 D7
Leisler, Mt., *Australia* 92 D4
Leith, *U.K.* 13 F5
Leith Hill, *U.K.* 15 F7
Leitha →, *Europe* 27 D10
Leitrim, *Ireland* 12 B3
Leitrim □, *Ireland* 12 B4
Leitza, *Spain* 38 B3
Leiyang, *China* 59 D9
Leizhou, *China* 59 G8
Leizhou Bandao, *China* 58 G7
Leizhou Wan, *China* 59 G8
Lek →, *Neths.* 17 C4
Leka, *Norway* 8 D14
Lekáni, *Greece* 45 E8
Lekbibaj, *Albania* 44 D3
Lekeitio, *Spain* 38 B2
Lekhainá, *Greece* 46 D3
Lekoui, *Burkina Faso* 82 C4
Leksand, *Sweden* 10 D9
Lékva Óros, *Greece* 49 D6
Leland, *Mich., U.S.A.* 114 C3
Leland, *Miss., U.S.A.* 113 J9
Lelång, *Sweden* 10 E6
Leleque, *Argentina* 128 E2
Lelystad, *Neths.* 17 B5
Lem, *Denmark* 11 H2
Lema, *Nigeria* 83 C5
Lema Shilindi, *Ethiopia* 81 G5
Léman, L., *Europe* 19 F13
Lembar, *Indonesia* 63 K19
Lembuak, *Indonesia* 63 K19
Lemera, *Dem. Rep. of the Congo* 86 C2
Lemery, *Phil.* 61 E4
Lemhi Ra., *U.S.A.* 108 D7
Lemmer, *Neths.* 17 B5
Lemmon, *U.S.A.* 112 C3
Lemon Grove, *U.S.A.* 111 N9
Lemoore, *U.S.A.* 110 J7
Lempdes, *France* 20 C7
Lemvig, *Denmark* 11 H2
Lena →, *Russia* 53 B13
Lenart, *Slovenia* 41 B12
Lenartovce, *Slovak Rep.* 27 C13
Lencloître, *France* 18 F7
Léndas, *Greece* 49 E6
Lendava, *Slovenia* 41 B13
Lendeh, *Iran* 71 D6
Lendinara, *Italy* 41 C8
Lengerich, *Germany* 24 C3
Lenggong, *Malaysia* 65 K3
Lenggries, *Germany* 25 H7
Lengshuijiang, *China* 59 D8
Lengshuitan, *China* 59 D8
Lengua de Vaca, Pta., *Chile* 126 C1
Lengwe △, *Malawi* 87 F3
Lengyeltóti, *Hungary* 28 D2
Lenhovda, *Sweden* 11 G9
Lenina, Kanal →, *Russia* 35 J7
Lenino, *Ukraine* 33 K8
Leninogorsk, *Kazakhstan* 52 D9
Leninsk, *Russia* 35 F7
Leninsk-Kuznetskiy, *Russia* 52 D9
Leninskoye, *Russia* 34 A8
Lenk, *Switz.* 25 J3
Lenkoran = Länkäran, *Azerbaijan* 71 B6
Lenmalu, *Indonesia* 63 E8
Lenne →, *Germany* 24 D3
Lennestadt, *Germany* 24 D4
Lennox, *U.S.A.* 112 D6
Lennoxville, *Canada* 117 A13
Leno, *Italy* 40 C7
Lenoir, *U.S.A.* 115 H5
Lenoir City, *U.S.A.* 115 H3
Lenore L., *Canada* 103 C8
Lenox, *U.S.A.* 117 D11
Lens, *France* 19 B9
Lensahn, *Germany* 24 A6
Lensk, *Russia* 53 C12
Lentekhi, *Georgia* 35 J6
Lenti, *Hungary* 28 D1
Lentini, *Italy* 43 E8
Lenwood, *U.S.A.* 111 L9
Lenya, *Burma* 62 B1
Lenzen, *Germany* 24 B7
Léo, *Burkina Faso* 82 C4
Leoben, *Austria* 26 D8
Leodhas = Lewis, *U.K.* 13 C2
Leola, *U.S.A.* 112 C5
Leominster, *U.K.* 15 E5
Leominster, *U.S.A.* 117 D13
Léon, *France* 20 E2
León, *Mexico* 118 C4
León, *Nic.* 120 D2
León, *Spain* 36 C5
Leon, *U.S.A.* 112 E8
León □, *Spain* 36 C5
Leon →, *U.S.A.* 113 K6
León, Montes de, *Spain* 36 C4
Leonardo da Vinci, Roma ✈ (FCO), *Italy* 41 G9
Leonardtown, *U.S.A.* 114 F7
Leonardville, *Namibia* 88 C2
Leonberg, *Germany* 25 G5
Leonding, *Austria* 26 C7
Leonessa, *Italy* 41 F9
Leonforte, *Italy* 43 E7
Leongatha, *Australia* 95 F4
Leonídhion, *Greece* 46 D4
Leonora, *Australia* 93 E3
Leopoldina, *Brazil* 127 A7
Leopoldsburg, *Belgium* 17 C5
Leoti, *U.S.A.* 112 F4
Leova, *Moldova* 29 D13
Leoville, *Canada* 103 C7
Lepe, *Spain* 37 H3
Lepel = Lyepyel, *Belarus* 32 E5
Lepenoú, *Greece* 46 C3
Leping, *China* 59 C11
Lépo, L. do, *Angola* 88 B2
Lepontine, Alpi, *Italy* 40 B5
Leppävirta, *Finland* 9 E22
Lepsény, *Hungary* 28 D3
Lequeitio = Lekeitio, *Spain* 38 B2
Lercara Friddi, *Italy* 42 E6
Lerdo, *Mexico* 118 B4
Léré, *Chad* 83 D7
Léré, *Mali* 82 B4
Lere, *Bauchi, Nigeria* 83 D6
Lere, *Kaduna, Nigeria* 83 C6
Leribe, *Lesotho* 89 D4
Lérici, *Italy* 40 D6
Lérida = Lleida, *Spain* 38 D5
Lérins, Îs. de, *France* 21 E11
Lerma, *Spain* 36 C7
Léros, *Greece* 47 D8
Lérouville, *France* 19 D12
Lerum, *Sweden* 11 G6
Lerwick, *U.K.* 13 A7
Leş, *Romania* 28 D6
Les Abrets, *France* 21 C9
Les Andelys, *France* 18 C8
Les Borges Blanques, *Spain* 38 D5
Les Cayes, *Haiti* 121 C5
Les Coteaux, *Canada* 117 A10
Les Essarts, *France* 18 F5
Les Herbiers, *France* 18 F5
Les Minquiers, Plateau des, *Chan. Is.* 18 D4
Les Pieux, *France* 18 C5
Les Ponts-de-Cé, *France* 18 E6
Les Riceys, *France* 19 E11
Les Sables-d'Olonne, *France* 20 B2
Les Vans, *France* 21 D8
Lesbos = Lésvos, *Greece* 47 B8
L'Escala, *Spain* 38 C8
Leshan, *China* 58 C4
Leshwe ⌓, *Dem. Rep. of the Congo* 87 E2
Lésina, *Italy* 41 G12
Lésina, L. di, *Italy* 41 G12
Lesjöfors, *Sweden* 10 E8
Lesko, *Poland* 31 J9
Leskov I., *Antarctica* 5 B1
Leskovac, *Serbia & M.* 44 C5
Leskovik, *Albania* 44 F4
Leśna, *Poland* 31 G2
Lesneven, *France* 18 D2
Leśnica, *Poland* 31 H5
Lešnica, *Serbia & M.* 44 B3
Lesnoye, *Russia* 32 C8
Lesopilnoye, *Russia* 54 A7
Lesotho ■, *Africa* 89 D4
Lesozavodsk, *Russia* 53 E14
Lesparre-Médoc, *France* 20 C3
Lessay, *France* 18 C5
Lesse →, *Belgium* 17 D4
Lesse et Lomme ⌓, *Belgium* 17 D5
Lessebo, *Sweden* 11 H9
Lesser Antilles, *W. Indies* 121 D7
Lesser Slave L., *Canada* 102 B5
Lesser Sunda Is., *Indonesia* 63 F6
Lessines, *Belgium* 17 D3
Lester, *U.S.A.* 110 C5
Lester B. Pearson International, Toronto ✈ (YYZ), *Canada* 116 C5
Lestock, *Canada* 103 C8
Lesuer I., *Australia* 92 B4
Lesueur △, *Australia* 93 F2
Lésvos, *Greece* 47 B8
Leszno, *Poland* 31 G3
Letaba, *S. Africa* 89 C5
Letälven, *Sweden* 10 E8
Létavértes, *Hungary* 28 C6
Letchworth, *U.K.* 15 F7
Letea, Ostrov, *Romania* 29 E14
Lethbridge, *Canada* 102 D6
Lethem, *Guyana* 124 C7
Leti, Kepulauan, *Indonesia* 63 F7
Leti Is. = Leti, Kepulauan, *Indonesia* 63 F7
Letiahau →, *Botswana* 88 C3
Leticia, *Colombia* 124 D5
Leting, *China* 57 E10
Letjiesbos, *S. Africa* 88 E3
Letlhakane, *Botswana* 88 C4
Letlhakeng, *Botswana* 88 C3
Letong, *Indonesia* 62 D3
Letpadan, *Burma* 67 L19
Letpan, *Burma* 67 K19
Letsôk-aw Kyun, *Burma* 65 G2
Letterkenny, *Ireland* 12 B4
Leu, *Romania* 29 F9
Leucadia, *U.S.A.* 111 M9
Leucate, *France* 20 F7
Leucate, Étang de, *France* 20 F7
Leuchars, *U.K.* 13 E6
Leuk, *Switz.* 25 J3
Leuşeni, *Moldova* 29 D13
Leuser, G., *Indonesia* 62 D1
Leutkirch, *Germany* 25 H6
Leuven, *Belgium* 17 D4
Leuze-en-Hainaut, *Belgium* 17 D3
Lev Tolstoy, *Russia* 32 F10
Levádhia, *Greece* 46 C4
Levan, *Albania* 44 F3
Levanger, *Norway* 8 E14
Levant, Î. du, *France* 21 E10
Lévanto, *Italy* 40 D6
Lévanzo, *Italy* 42 D5
Levelland, *U.S.A.* 113 J3
Leven, *U.K.* 13 E6
Leven, L., *U.K.* 13 E5
Leven, Toraka, *Madag.* 89 A8
Leveque C., *Australia* 92 C3
Leverano, *Italy* 43 B10
Leverkusen, *Germany* 24 D3
Levice, *Slovak Rep.* 27 C11
Lévico Terme, *Italy* 41 C8
Levie, *France* 21 G13
Levier, *France* 19 F13
Levin, *N.Z.* 91 J5
Lévis, *Canada* 105 C5
Lévis, L., *Canada* 102 A5
Levítha, *Greece* 47 D8
Levittown, *N.Y., U.S.A.* 117 F11
Levittown, *Pa., U.S.A.* 117 F10
Levka, *Bulgaria* 45 E10
Levkás, *Greece* 46 C2
Levkás □, *Greece* 46 C2
Levkímmi, *Greece* 49 B4
Levkímmi, Ákra, *Greece* 49 B4
Levkôsia = Nicosia, *Cyprus* 49 D12
Levoča, *Slovak Rep.* 27 B13
Levroux, *France* 19 F8
Levski, *Bulgaria* 45 C9
Levskigrad = Karlovo, *Bulgaria* 45 D8
Lewes, *U.K.* 15 G8
Lewes, *U.S.A.* 114 F8
Lewin Brzeski, *Poland* 31 H4
Lewis, *U.K.* 13 C2
Lewis →, *U.S.A.* 110 E4
Lewis, Butt of, *U.K.* 13 C2
Lewis Ra., *Australia* 92 D4
Lewis Range, *U.S.A.* 108 C7
Lewis Run, *U.S.A.* 116 E6
Lewisburg, *Pa., U.S.A.* 116 F8
Lewisburg, *Tenn., U.S.A.* 115 H2
Lewisburg, *W. Va., U.S.A.* 114 G5
Lewisporte, *Canada* 105 C8
Lewiston, *Idaho, U.S.A.* 108 C5
Lewiston, *Maine, U.S.A.* 115 C11
Lewiston, *N.Y., U.S.A.* 116 C5
Lewistown, *Mont., U.S.A.* 108 C9
Lewistown, *Pa., U.S.A.* 116 F7
Lexington, *Ill., U.S.A.* 112 E10
Lexington, *Ky., U.S.A.* 114 F3
Lexington, *Mich., U.S.A.* 116 C2
Lexington, *Mo., U.S.A.* 112 F8
Lexington, *N.C., U.S.A.* 115 H5
Lexington, *N.Y., U.S.A.* 117 D10
Lexington, *Nebr., U.S.A.* 112 E5
Lexington, *Ohio, U.S.A.* 116 F2
Lexington, *Tenn., U.S.A.* 115 H1
Lexington, *Va., U.S.A.* 114 G6
Lexington Park, *U.S.A.* 114 F7
Leyburn, *U.K.* 14 C6
Leye, *China* 58 E6
Leyland, *U.K.* 14 D5
Leyre →, *France* 20 D2
Leyte □, *Phil.* 61 F6
Leyte Gulf, *Phil.* 61 F6

Leżajsk, *Poland* 31 H9
Lezay, *France* 20 B3
Lezhë, *Albania* 44 E3
Lezhi, *China* 58 B5
Lézignan-Corbières, *France* 20 E6
Lezoux, *France* 20 C7
Lgov, *Russia* 33 G8
Lhasa, *China* 60 D4
Lhazê, *China* 60 D3
Lhokkruet, *Indonesia* 62 D1
Lhokseumawe, *Indonesia* 62 C1
L'Hospitalet de Llobregat, *Spain* 38 D7
Li, *Thailand* 64 D2
Li Shui →, *China* 59 C9
Li Xian, *Gansu, China* 56 G3
Li Xian, *Hebei, China* 56 E8
Li Xian, *Hunan, China* 59 C8
Liádhoi, *Greece* 47 E8
Liancheng, *China* 59 E11
Liancourt Rocks = Tok-do, *Asia* 55 F5
Lianga, *Phil.* 61 G7
Liangcheng, *Nei Monggol Zizhiqu, China* 56 D7
Liangcheng, *Shandong, China* 57 G10
Liangdang, *China* 56 H4
Lianghe, *China* 58 E2
Lianghekou, *China* 58 C7
Liangping, *China* 58 B6
Liangpran, *Indonesia* 62 D4
Lianhua, *China* 59 D9
Lianjiang, *Fujian, China* 59 D12
Lianjiang, *Guangdong, China* 59 G8
Lianping, *China* 59 E10
Lianshan, *China* 59 E9
Lianshanguan, *China* 57 D12
Lianshui, *China* 57 H10
Lianyuan, *China* 59 D8
Lianyungang, *China* 57 G10
Lianzhou, *China* 59 E9
Liao He →, *China* 57 D11
Liaocheng, *China* 56 F8
Liaodong Bandao, *China* 57 E12
Liaodong Wan, *China* 57 D11
Liaoning □, *China* 57 D12
Liaotung, G. of = Liaodong Wan, *China* 57 D11
Liaoyang, *China* 57 D12
Liaoyuan, *China* 57 C13
Liaozhong, *China* 57 D12
Liapádhes, *Greece* 46 B1
Liard →, *Canada* 102 A4
Liard River, *Canada* 102 B3
Liari, *Pakistan* 68 G2
Libau = Liepāja, *Latvia* 9 H19
Libby, *U.S.A.* 108 B6
Libenge, *Dem. Rep. of the Congo* 84 D3
Liberal, *U.S.A.* 113 G4
Liberec, *Czech Rep.* 26 A8
Liberecký □, *Czech Rep.* 26 A8
Liberia, *Costa Rica* 120 D2
Liberia ■, *W. Afr.* 82 D3
Liberty, *Mo., U.S.A.* 112 F7
Liberty, *N.Y., U.S.A.* 117 E10
Liberty, *Pa., U.S.A.* 116 E7
Liberty, *Tex., U.S.A.* 113 K7
Libiąż, *Poland* 31 H6
Lîbîya, Sahrâ', *Africa* 79 C10
Libo, *China* 58 E6
Libobo, Tanjung, *Indonesia* 63 E7
Libode, *S. Africa* 89 E4
Libohovë, *Albania* 44 F4
Libourne, *France* 20 D3
Libramont, *Belgium* 17 E5
Librazhd, *Albania* 44 E4
Libreville, *Gabon* 84 D1
Libya ■, *N. Afr.* 79 C9
Libyan Desert = Lîbîya, Sahrâ', *Africa* 79 C10
Libyan Plateau = Ed-Déffa, *Egypt* 80 A2
Licantén, *Chile* 126 D1
Licata, *Italy* 42 E6
Lice, *Turkey* 73 C9
Licheng, *China* 56 F7
Lichfield, *U.K.* 15 E6
Lichinga, *Mozam.* 87 E4
Lichtenburg, *S. Africa* 88 D4
Lichtenfels, *Germany* 25 E7
Lichuan, *Hubei, China* 58 B7
Lichuan, *Jiangxi, China* 59 D11
Licking →, *U.S.A.* 114 F3
Licosa, Punta, *Italy* 43 B7
Licungo →, *Mozam.* 87 F4
Lida, *Belarus* 9 K21
Liden, *Sweden* 10 B10
Lidhoríkion, *Greece* 46 C4
Lidhult, *Sweden* 11 H7
Lidköping, *Sweden* 11 F7
Lido, *Italy* 41 C9
Lido, *Niger* 83 C5
Lido di Roma = Óstia, Lido di, *Italy* 41 G9
Lidzbark, *Poland* 31 E6
Lidzbark Warmiński, *Poland* 30 D7
Liebenwalde, *Germany* 24 C9
Lieberose, *Germany* 24 D10
Liebig, Mt., *Australia* 92 D5
Liebling, *Romania* 28 E6
Liechtenstein ■, *Europe* 25 H5
Liège, *Belgium* 17 D5
Liège □, *Belgium* 17 D5
Liegnitz = Legnica, *Poland* 31 G3
Lienart, *Dem. Rep. of the Congo* 86 B2
Lienyünchiangshih = Lianyungang, *China* 57 G10
Lienz, *Austria* 26 E5
Liepāja, *Latvia* 9 H19
Liepāja □, *Latvia* 30 B8
Liepājas ezers, *Latvia* 30 B8
Lier, *Belgium* 17 C4
Liernais, *France* 19 E11
Liești, *Romania* 29 E12
Liévin, *France* 19 B9
Lièvre →, *Canada* 104 C4
Liezen, *Austria* 26 D7
Liffey →, *Ireland* 12 C5
Lifford, *Ireland* 12 B4
Liffré, *France* 18 D5
Lifudzin, *Russia* 54 B7
Ligao, *Phil.* 61 E5
Lightning Ridge, *Australia* 95 D4
Lignano Sabbiadoro, *Italy* 41 C10
Ligny-en-Barrois, *France* 19 D12
Ligonha →, *Mozam.* 87 F4
Ligonier, *U.S.A.* 116 F5
Ligoúrion, *Greece* 46 D5
Ligueil, *France* 18 E7
Liguria □, *Italy* 40 D5
Ligurian Sea, *Medit. S.* 6 G7
Lihou Reefs and Cays, *Australia* 94 B5
Lihue, *U.S.A.* 106 H15
Lihué Calel △, *Argentina* 126 D2
Lijiang, *China* 58 D3
Likasi, *Dem. Rep. of the Congo* 87 E2
Likenäs, *Sweden* 10 D7
Likhoslavl, *Russia* 32 D8
Likhovskoy, *Russia* 33 H11
Likoma I., *Malawi* 87 E3
Likumburu, *Tanzania* 87 D4
L'Île-Bouchard, *France* 18 E7
L'Île-Rousse, *France* 21 F12
Liling, *China* 59 D9
Lilla Edet, *Sweden* 11 F6
Lille, *France* 19 B10
Lille Bælt, *Denmark* 11 J3
Lillebonne, *France* 18 C7
Lillehammer, *Norway* 9 F14
Lillesand, *Norway* 9 G13
Lillhärdal, *Sweden* 10 C8
Lillian Pt., *Australia* 93 E4
Lillo, *Spain* 36 F7
Lillooet, *Canada* 102 C4
Lillooet →, *Canada* 102 D4
Lilongwe, *Malawi* 87 E3
Liloy, *Phil.* 63 C6
Lim →, *Bos.-H.* 44 C3
Lim Chu Kang, *Singapore* 65 d
Lima, *Indonesia* 63 E7
Lima, *Peru* 124 F3
Lima, *Mont., U.S.A.* 108 D7
Lima, *Ohio, U.S.A.* 114 E3
Lima →, *Portugal* 36 D2
Liman, *Indonesia* 63 G14
Liman, *Russia* 35 H8
Limanowa, *Poland* 31 J7
Limassol, *Cyprus* 49 E12
Limavady, *U.K.* 12 A5
Limay →, *Argentina* 128 D3
Limay Mahuida, *Argentina* 126 D2
Limbach-Oberfrohna, *Germany* 24 E8
Limbang, *Brunei* 62 D5
Limbara, Mte., *Italy* 42 B2
Limbaži, *Latvia* 9 H21
Limbdi, *India* 68 H4
Limbe, *Cameroon* 83 E6
Limburg, *Germany* 25 E4
Limburg □, *Belgium* 17 C5
Limburg □, *Neths.* 17 C5
Limedsforsen, *Sweden* 10 D7
Limeira, *Brazil* 127 A6
Limenária, *Greece* 45 F8
Limerick, *Ireland* 12 D3
Limerick, *U.S.A.* 117 C14
Limerick □, *Ireland* 12 D3
Limestone, *U.S.A.* 116 D6
Limestone →, *Canada* 103 B10
Limfjorden, *Denmark* 11 H3
Limia = Lima →, *Portugal* 36 D2
Limín Khersonísou, *Greece* 47 F7
Limingen, *Norway* 8 D15
Limmared, *Sweden* 11 G7
Limmen Bight, *Australia* 94 A2
Limmen Bight →, *Australia* 94 B2
Límni, *Greece* 46 C5
Límnos, *Greece* 47 B7
Limoges, *Canada* 117 A9
Limoges, *France* 20 C5
Limón, *Costa Rica* 120 E3
Limon, *U.S.A.* 112 F3
Limone Piemonte, *Italy* 40 D4
Limousin □, *France* 20 C5
Limousin, Plateaux du, *France* 20 C5
Limoux, *France* 20 E6
Limpopo □, *S. Africa* 89 C4
Limpopo →, *Africa* 89 D5
Limuru, *Kenya* 86 C4
Lin Xian, *China* 56 F6
Lin'an, *China* 59 B12
Linapacan I., *Phil.* 61 F3
Linapacan Str., *Phil.* 61 F3
Linares, *Chile* 126 D1
Linares, *Mexico* 119 C5
Linares, *Spain* 37 G7
Linaro, Capo, *Italy* 41 F8
Línas Mte., *Italy* 42 C1
Linate, Milano ✕ (LIN), *Italy* 40 C6
Lincang, *China* 58 F3
Lincheng, *China* 56 F8
Linchuan, *China* 59 D11
Lincoln = Beamsville, *Canada* 116 C5
Lincoln, *Argentina* 126 C3
Lincoln, *N.Z.* 91 K4
Lincoln, *U.K.* 14 D7
Lincoln, *Calif., U.S.A.* 110 G5
Lincoln, *Ill., U.S.A.* 112 E10
Lincoln, *Kans., U.S.A.* 112 F5
Lincoln, *Maine, U.S.A.* 115 C11
Lincoln, *N.H., U.S.A.* 117 B13
Lincoln, *N. Mex., U.S.A.* 109 K11
Lincoln, *Nebr., U.S.A.* 112 E6
Lincoln City, *U.S.A.* 108 D1
Lincoln Hav = Lincoln Sea, *Arctic* 4 A5
Lincoln Sea, *Arctic* 4 A5
Lincolnshire □, *U.K.* 14 D7
Lincolnshire Wolds, *U.K.* 14 D7
Lincolnton, *U.S.A.* 115 H5
Lind, *U.S.A.* 108 C4
Linda, *U.S.A.* 110 F5
Lindau, *Germany* 25 H5
Lindeman I., *Australia* 94 J7
Linden, *Guyana* 124 B7
Linden, *Ala., U.S.A.* 115 J2
Linden, *Calif., U.S.A.* 110 G5
Linden, *Tex., U.S.A.* 113 J7
Lindenhurst, *U.S.A.* 117 F11
Lindesberg, *Sweden* 10 E9
Lindesnes, *Norway* 9 H12
Líndhos, *Greece* 49 C10
Líndhos, Ákra, *Greece* 49 C10
Lindi, *Tanzania* 87 D4
Lindi □, *Tanzania* 87 D4
Lindi →, *Dem. Rep. of the Congo* 86 B2
Lindö, *Sweden* 11 F10
Lindome, *Sweden* 11 G6
Lindoso, *Portugal* 36 D2
Lindow, *Germany* 24 C8
Lindsay, *Canada* 116 B6
Lindsay, *Calif., U.S.A.* 110 J7
Lindsay, *Okla., U.S.A.* 113 H6
Lindsborg, *U.S.A.* 112 F6
Lindsdal, *Sweden* 11 H10
Line Islands, *Pac. Oc.* 97 H12
Linesville, *U.S.A.* 116 E4
Linfen, *China* 56 F6
Ling Xian, *Hunan, China* 59 D9
Ling Xian, *Shandong, China* 56 F9
Lingao, *China* 64 C7
Lingayen, *Phil.* 63 A6
Lingayen G., *Phil.* 61 C4
Lingbi, *China* 57 H9
Lingbo, *Sweden* 10 C10
Lingchuan, *Guangxi Zhuangzu, China* 59 E8
Lingchuan, *Shanxi, China* 56 G7
Lingen, *Germany* 24 C3
Lingga, *Indonesia* 62 E2
Lingga, Kepulauan, *Indonesia* 62 E2
Lingga Arch. = Lingga, Kepulauan, *Indonesia* 62 E2
Linghem, *Sweden* 11 F9
Lingle, *U.S.A.* 112 D2
Lingqiu, *China* 56 E8
Lingshan, *China* 58 F7
Lingshi, *China* 56 F6
Lingshou, *China* 56 E8
Lingshui, *China* 64 C8
Lingtai, *China* 56 G4
Linguère, *Senegal* 82 B1
Lingui, *China* 59 E8
Lingwu, *China* 56 E4
Lingyuan, *China* 57 D10
Lingyun, *China* 58 E6
Linhai, *China* 59 C13
Linhares, *Brazil* 125 G10
Linhe, *China* 56 D4
Linjiang, *China* 57 D14
Linköping, *Sweden* 11 F9
Linkou, *China* 57 B16
Linli, *China* 59 C8
Linnhe, L., *U.K.* 13 E3
Linqi, *China* 56 G7
Linqing, *China* 56 F8
Linqu, *China* 57 F10
Linru, *China* 56 G7
Lins, *Brazil* 127 A6
Linshui, *China* 58 B6
Linstead, *Jamaica* 120 a
Linta →, *Madag.* 89 D7
Linth →, *Switz.* 25 H5
Linthal, *Switz.* 25 J5
Linton, *Ind., U.S.A.* 114 F2
Linton, *N. Dak., U.S.A.* 112 B4
Lintong, *China* 56 G5
Linwood, *Canada* 116 C4
Linwu, *China* 59 E9
Linxi, *China* 57 C10
Linxia, *China* 60 C5
Linxiang, *China* 59 C9
Linyanti →, *Africa* 88 B4
Linyi, *China* 57 G10
Linz, *Austria* 26 C7
Linz, *Germany* 24 E3
Linzhenzhen, *China* 56 F5
Linzi, *China* 57 F10
Lion, G. du, *France* 20 E7
Lionárisso, *Cyprus* 49 D13
Lioni, *Italy* 43 B8
Lions, G. of = Lion, G. du, *France* 20 E7
Lion's Den, *Zimbabwe* 87 F3
Lion's Head, *Canada* 116 B3
Liozno = Lyozna, *Belarus* 32 E6
Lipa, *Phil.* 61 E4
Lipali, *Mozam.* 87 F4
Lipany, *Slovak Rep.* 27 B13
Lípari, *Italy* 43 D7
Lípari, I., *Italy* 43 D7
Lípari, Is. = Eólie, Ís., *Italy* 43 D7
Lipcani, *Moldova* 29 B11
Lipetsk, *Russia* 33 F10
Lipiany, *Poland* 31 E1
Liping, *China* 58 D7
Lipkany = Lipcani, *Moldova* 29 B11
Lipljan, *Serbia & M.* 44 D5
Lipník nad Bečvou, *Czech Rep.* 27 B10
Lipno, *Poland* 31 F6
Lipova, *Romania* 28 D6
Lipovcy Manzovka, *Russia* 54 B5
Lipovets, *Ukraine* 33 H5
Lippe →, *Germany* 24 D2
Lippstadt, *Germany* 24 D4
Lipscomb, *U.S.A.* 113 G4
Lipsk, *Poland* 30 E10
Lipsko, *Poland* 31 G8
Lipsói, *Greece* 47 D8
Liptovský Hrádok, *Slovak Rep.* 27 B12
Liptovský Mikuláš, *Slovak Rep.* 27 B12
Liptrap, C., *Australia* 95 F4
Lipu, *China* 59 E8
Liquillo, Sierra de, *Puerto Rico* 121 d
Lira, *Uganda* 86 B3
Liri →, *Italy* 42 A6
Liria = Llíria, *Spain* 39 F4
Lisala, *Dem. Rep. of the Congo* 84 D4
Lisboa, *Portugal* 37 G1
Lisboa □, *Portugal* 37 F1
Lisboa ✕ (LIS), *Portugal* 37 G1
Lisbon = Lisboa, *Portugal* 37 G1
Lisbon, *N. Dak., U.S.A.* 112 B6
Lisbon, *N.H., U.S.A.* 117 B13
Lisbon, *Ohio, U.S.A.* 116 F4
Lisbon Falls, *U.S.A.* 115 D10
Lisburn, *U.K.* 12 B5
Lisburne, C., *U.S.A.* 4 C17
Liscannor B., *Ireland* 12 D2
Liscia →, *Italy* 42 A2
Lishe Jiang →, *China* 58 E3
Lishi, *China* 56 F6
Lishu, *China* 57 C13
Lishui, *Jiangsu, China* 59 B12
Lishui, *Zhejiang, China* 59 C12
Lisianski I., *Pac. Oc.* 96 E10
Lisichansk = Lysychansk, *Ukraine* 33 H10
Lisieux, *France* 18 C7
Liski, *Russia* 33 G10
L'Isle-Jourdain, *Gers, France* 20 E5
L'Isle-Jourdain, *Vienne, France* 20 B4
L'Isle-sur-la-Sorgue, *France* 21 E9
Lisle-sur-Tarn, *France* 20 E5
Lismore, *Australia* 95 D5
Lismore, *Ireland* 12 D4
Lista, *Norway* 9 G12
Lister, Mt., *Antarctica* 5 D11
Liston, *Australia* 95 D5
Listowel, *Canada* 116 C4
Listowel, *Ireland* 12 D2
Lit, *Sweden* 10 A8
Lit-et-Mixe, *France* 20 D2
Litang, *Guangxi Zhuangzu, China* 58 F7
Litang, *Sichuan, China* 58 B3
Litang Qu →, *China* 58 C3
Litani →, *Lebanon* 74 B4
Litchfield, *Calif., U.S.A.* 110 E6
Litchfield, *Conn., U.S.A.* 117 E11
Litchfield, *Ill., U.S.A.* 112 F10
Litchfield, *Minn., U.S.A.* 112 C7
Litchfield △, *Australia* 92 B5
Liteni, *Romania* 29 C11
Lithgow, *Australia* 95 E5
Líthinon, Ákra, *Greece* 49 E6
Lithuania ■, *Europe* 9 J20
Litija, *Slovenia* 41 B11
Lititz, *U.S.A.* 117 F8
Litókhoron, *Greece* 44 F6
Litoměřice, *Czech Rep.* 26 A7
Litomyšl, *Czech Rep.* 27 B9
Litschau, *Austria* 26 C8
Little Abaco, *Bahamas* 120 A4
Little Barrier I., *N.Z.* 91 G5
Little Belt Mts., *U.S.A.* 108 C8
Little Bighorn Battlefield ⌂, *U.S.A.* 108 D10
Little Blue →, *U.S.A.* 112 F6
Little Buffalo →, *Canada* 102 A6
Little Cayman, *Cayman Is.* 120 C3
Little Churchill →, *Canada* 103 B9
Little Colorado →, *U.S.A.* 109 H8
Little Current, *Canada* 104 C3
Little Current →, *Canada* 104 B3
Little Falls, *Minn., U.S.A.* 112 C7
Little Falls, *N.Y., U.S.A.* 117 C10
Little Fork →, *U.S.A.* 112 A8
Little Grand Rapids, *Canada* 103 C9
Little Humboldt →, *U.S.A.* 108 F5
Little Inagua I., *Bahamas* 121 B5
Little Karoo, *S. Africa* 88 E3
Little Khingan Mts. = Xiao Hinggan Ling, *China* 60 B7
Little Lake, *U.S.A.* 111 K9
Little Laut Is. = Laut Kecil, Kepulauan, *Indonesia* 62 E5
Little Mecatina = Petit-Mécatina →, *Canada* 105 B8
Little Minch, *U.K.* 13 D2
Little Missouri →, *U.S.A.* 112 B3
Little Ouse →, *U.K.* 15 E9
Little Rann, *India* 68 H4
Little Red →, *U.S.A.* 113 H9
Little River, *N.Z.* 91 K4
Little Rock, *U.S.A.* 113 H8
Little Ruaha →, *Tanzania* 86 D4
Little Sable Pt., *U.S.A.* 114 D2
Little Scarcies →, *S. Leone* 82 D2
Little Sioux →, *U.S.A.* 112 E6
Little Smoky →, *Canada* 102 C5
Little Snake →, *U.S.A.* 108 F9
Little Tobago, *Trin. & Tob.* 125 J16
Little Valley, *U.S.A.* 116 D6
Little Wabash →, *U.S.A.* 114 G1
Little White →, *U.S.A.* 112 D4
Little Zab = Zāb aş Şaghīr →, *Iraq* 70 C4
Littlefield, *U.S.A.* 113 J3
Littlehampton, *U.K.* 15 G7
Littleton, *U.S.A.* 117 B13
Litvinov, *Czech Rep.* 26 A6
Liu He →, *China* 57 D11
Liu Jiang →, *China* 58 F7
Liuba, *China* 56 H4
Liucheng, *China* 58 E7
Liugou, *China* 57 D10
Liuhe, *China* 57 C13
Liuheng Dao, *China* 59 C14
Liujiang, *China* 58 E7
Liukang Tenggaja = Sabalana, Kepulauan, *Indonesia* 63 F5
Liuli, *Tanzania* 87 E3
Liuwa Plain, *Zambia* 85 G4
Liuyang, *China* 59 C9
Liuzhou, *China* 58 E7
Liuzhuang, *China* 57 H11
Livada, *Romania* 28 C8
Livadherón, *Greece* 44 F5
Livadhia, *Cyprus* 49 E12
Livádhion, *Greece* 46 A4
Livarot, *France* 18 D7
Live Oak, *Calif., U.S.A.* 110 F5
Live Oak, *Fla., U.S.A.* 115 K4
Liveras, *Cyprus* 49 D11
Livermore, *U.S.A.* 110 H5
Livermore, Mt., *U.S.A.* 113 K2
Livermore Falls, *U.S.A.* 115 C11
Liverpool, *Canada* 105 D7
Liverpool, *U.K.* 14 D4
Liverpool, *U.S.A.* 117 C8
Liverpool Bay, *U.K.* 14 D4
Liverpool Ra., *Australia* 95 E5
Livigno, *Italy* 40 B7
Livingston, *Guatemala* 120 C2
Livingston, *U.K.* 13 F5
Livingston, *Ala., U.S.A.* 115 J1
Livingston, *Calif., U.S.A.* 110 H6
Livingston, *Mont., U.S.A.* 108 D8
Livingston, *S.C., U.S.A.* 115 J5
Livingston, *Tenn., U.S.A.* 115 G3
Livingston, *Tex., U.S.A.* 113 K7
Livingston, L., *U.S.A.* 113 K7
Livingston Manor, *U.S.A.* 117 E10
Livingstone, *Zambia* 87 F2
Livingstone Mts., *Tanzania* 87 D3
Livingstonia, *Malawi* 87 E3
Livno, *Bos.-H.* 28 G2
Livny, *Russia* 33 F9
Livonia, *Mich., U.S.A.* 114 D4
Livonia, *N.Y., U.S.A.* 116 D7
Livorno, *Italy* 40 E7
Livradois-Forez ⌂, *France* 20 E7
Livramento, *Brazil* 127 C4
Livron-sur-Drôme, *France* 21 D8
Livyntsi, *Ukraine* 29 B11
Liwale, *Tanzania* 87 D4
Liwiec →, *Poland* 31 F8
Liwonde △, *Malawi* 87 E4
Lixi, *China* 58 D3
Lixian, *China* 58 B4
Lixoúrion, *Greece* 46 C2
Liyang, *China* 59 B12
Lizard I., *Australia* 94 A4
Lizard Pt., *U.K.* 15 H2
Lizzano, *Italy* 43 B10
Ljig, *Serbia & M.* 44 B4
Ljubija, *Bos.-H.* 41 D13
Ljubinje, *Bos.-H.* 44 D2
Ljubljana, *Slovenia* 41 B11
Ljubljana ✕ (LJU), *Slovenia* 41 B11
Ljubno, *Slovenia* 41 B11
Ljubovija, *Serbia & M.* 44 B3
Ljugarn, *Sweden* 11 G12
Ljung, *Sweden* 11 G7
Ljungan →, *Sweden* 10 B11
Ljungaverk, *Sweden* 10 B10
Ljungby, *Sweden* 11 H7
Ljungbyholm, *Sweden* 11 H10
Ljungdalen, *Sweden* 10 B6
Ljungsbro, *Sweden* 11 F9
Ljungskile, *Sweden* 11 F5
Ljusdal, *Sweden* 10 C10
Ljusfallshammar, *Sweden* 11 F9
Ljusnan →, *Sweden* 10 C11
Ljusne, *Sweden* 10 C11
Ljutomer, *Slovenia* 41 B13
Llagostera, *Spain* 38 D7
Llancanelo, Salina, *Argentina* 126 D2
Llandeilo, *U.K.* 15 F4
Llandovery, *U.K.* 15 F4
Llandrindod Wells, *U.K.* 15 E4
Llandudno, *U.K.* 14 D4
Llanelli, *U.K.* 15 F3
Llanes, *Spain* 36 B6
Llangollen, *U.K.* 14 E4
Llanidloes, *U.K.* 15 E4
Llano, *U.S.A.* 113 K5
Llano →, *U.S.A.* 113 K5
Llano Estacado, *U.S.A.* 113 J3
Llanos, *S. Amer.* 124 C4
Llanos de Challe △, *Chile* 126 B1
Llanquihue, L., *Chile* 128 E1
Llanwrtyd Wells, *U.K.* 15 E4
Llebeig, C. des, *Spain* 48 B9
Lleida, *Spain* 38 D5
Lleida □, *Spain* 38 C6
Llentrisca, C., *Spain* 48 C7
Llera, *Mexico* 119 C5
Llerena, *Spain* 37 G5
Lleyn Peninsula, *U.K.* 14 E3
Llico, *Chile* 126 C1
Llíria, *Spain* 39 F4
Llobregat →, *Spain* 38 D7
Llodio, *Spain* 38 B2
Lloret de Mar, *Spain* 38 D7
Lloyd B., *Australia* 94 A3
Lloyd L., *Canada* 103 B7
Lloydminster, *Canada* 103 C7
Llucena del Cid, *Spain* 38 E4
Llucmajor, *Spain* 48 B9
Llullaillaco △, *Chile* 126 A2
Llullaillaco, Volcán, *S. Amer.* 126 A2
Lo →, *Vietnam* 64 B5
Loa, *U.S.A.* 109 G8
Loa →, *Chile* 126 A1
Loaita I., *S. China Sea* 62 B4
Loange →, *Dem. Rep. of the Congo* 84 E4
Loano, *Italy* 40 D5
Lobatse, *Botswana* 88 D4
Löbau, *Germany* 24 D10
Lobenstein, *Germany* 24 E7
Lobería, *Argentina* 126 D4
Löberöd, *Sweden* 11 J7
Łobez, *Poland* 30 E2
Lobito, *Angola* 85 G2
Lobo →, *Ivory C.* 82 D3

Lobos, *Argentina* 126 D4
Lobos, I., *Mexico* 118 B2
Lobos, I. de, *Canary Is.* 48 F6
Łobżenica, *Poland* 31 E4
Loc Binh, *Vietnam* 64 B6
Loc Ninh, *Vietnam* 65 G6
Locarno, *Switz.* 25 J4
Loch Baghasdail = Lochboisdale, *U.K.* 13 D1
Loch Garman = Wexford, *Ireland* 12 D5
Loch Lomond and the Trossachs △, *U.K.* 13 E4
Loch Nam Madadh = Lochmaddy, *U.K.* 13 D1
Lochaber, *U.K.* 13 E3
Locharbriggs, *U.K.* 13 F5
Lochboisdale, *U.K.* 13 D1
Loche, L. La, *Canada* 103 B7
Lochem, *Neths.* 17 B6
Loches, *France* 18 E7
Lochgilphead, *U.K.* 13 E3
Lochinvar △, *Zambia* 87 F2
Lochinver, *U.K.* 13 C3
Lochmaddy, *U.K.* 13 D1
Lochnagar, *Australia* 94 C4
Lochnagar, *U.K.* 13 E5
Łochów, *Poland* 31 F8
Lochy, L., *U.K.* 13 E4
Lock, *Australia* 95 E2
Lock Haven, *U.S.A.* 116 E7
Lockeford, *U.S.A.* 110 G5
Lockeport, *Canada* 105 D6
Lockerbie, *U.K.* 13 F5
Lockhart, *U.S.A.* 113 L6
Lockhart, L., *Australia* 93 F2
Lockhart River, *Australia* 94 A3
Lockney, *U.S.A.* 113 H4
Lockport, *U.S.A.* 116 C6
Locminé, *France* 18 E4
Locri, *Italy* 43 D9
Locronan, *France* 18 D2
Lod, *Israel* 74 D3
Lodeinoye Pole, *Russia* 32 B7
Lodève, *France* 20 E7
Lodge Bay, *Canada* 105 B8
Lodge Grass, *U.S.A.* 108 D10
Lodgepole Cr. →, *U.S.A.* 112 E2
Lodhran, *Pakistan* 68 E4
Lodi, *Italy* 40 C6
Lodi, *Calif., U.S.A.* 110 G5
Lodi, *Ohio, U.S.A.* 116 E3
Lodja, *Dem. Rep. of the Congo* 86 C1
Lodosa, *Spain* 38 C2
Lödöse, *Sweden* 11 F6
Lodwar, *Kenya* 86 B4
Łódź, *Poland* 31 G6
Łódzkie □, *Poland* 31 G6
Loei, *Thailand* 64 D3
Loengo, *Dem. Rep. of the Congo* 86 C2
Loeriesfontein, *S. Africa* 88 E2
Lofa →, *Liberia* 83 D2
Lofa Mano △, *Liberia* 82 D2
Lofer, *Austria* 26 D5
Lofoten, *Norway* 8 B15
Lofsdalen, *Sweden* 10 B7
Lofsen →, *Sweden* 10 B7
Loftahammar, *Sweden* 11 G10
Loga, *Niger* 83 C5
Logan, *Iowa, U.S.A.* 112 E7
Logan, *Ohio, U.S.A.* 114 F4
Logan, *Utah, U.S.A.* 108 F8
Logan, *W. Va., U.S.A.* 114 G5
Logan, Mt., *Canada* 100 B5
Logandale, *U.S.A.* 111 J12
Logansport, *Ind., U.S.A.* 114 E2
Logansport, *La., U.S.A.* 113 K8
Logirim, *Sudan* 81 G3
Logo, *Sudan* 81 F3
Logone →, *Chad* 79 F9
Logroño, *Spain* 38 C2
Logrosán, *Spain* 37 F5
Løgstør, *Denmark* 11 H3
Løgumkloster, *Denmark* 11 J2
Lohals, *Denmark* 11 J4
Lohardaga, *India* 69 H11
Loharia, *India* 68 H6
Loharu, *India* 68 E6
Lohja, *Finland* 9 F21
Löhne, *Germany* 24 C4
Lohr, *Germany* 25 F5
Lohri Wah →, *Pakistan* 68 F2
Loi-kaw, *Burma* 67 K20
Loimaa, *Finland* 9 F20
Loir →, *France* 18 E6
Loir-et-Cher □, *France* 18 E8
Loire □, *France* 21 C8
Loire →, *France* 18 E4
Loire Anjou Touraine ⌓, *France* 18 E6
Loire-Atlantique □, *France* 18 E5
Loiret □, *France* 19 E9
Loitz, *Germany* 24 B9
Loja, *Ecuador* 124 D3
Loja, *Spain* 37 H6
Loji = Kawasi, *Indonesia* 63 E7
Lojo = Lohja, *Finland* 9 F21
Løjt Kirkeby, *Denmark* 11 J3
Lojung, *China* 58 E7
Loka, *Sudan* 81 G3
Lokandu, *Dem. Rep. of the Congo* 86 C2
Lokeren, *Belgium* 17 C3
Lokgwabe, *Botswana* 88 C3
Lokhvitsa, *Ukraine* 33 G7
Lokichokio, *Kenya* 86 B3
Lokitaung, *Kenya* 86 B4
Lokkan tekojärvi, *Finland* 8 C22
Løkken, *Denmark* 11 G3
Loknya, *Russia* 32 D6
Loko, *Nigeria* 83 D6
Lokoja, *Nigeria* 83 D6
Lokot, *Russia* 33 F8
Lol →, *Sudan* 81 F2
Lola, *Guinea* 82 D3
Lola, Mt., *U.S.A.* 110 F6
Lolibai, Gebel, *Sudan* 81 G3
Lolimi, *Sudan* 81 G3
Loliondo, *Tanzania* 86 C4
Lolland, *Denmark* 11 K5
Lollar, *Germany* 24 E4
Lolo, *U.S.A.* 108 C6
Lolodorf, *Cameroon* 83 E7
Lom, *Bulgaria* 44 C7
Lom →, *Bulgaria* 44 C7
Lom Kao, *Thailand* 64 D3
Lom Sak, *Thailand* 64 D3
Loma, *U.S.A.* 108 C8
Loma Linda, *U.S.A.* 111 L9
Lomami →, *Dem. Rep. of the Congo* 86 B1
Lomas de Zamóra, *Argentina* 126 C4
Lombadina, *Australia* 92 C3
Lombárdia □, *Italy* 40 C6
Lombardy = Lombárdia □, *Italy* 40 C6
Lombez, *France* 20 E4
Lomblen, *Indonesia* 63 F6
Lombok, *Indonesia* 62 F5
Lombok, Selat, *Indonesia* 63 K18
Lomé, *Togo* 83 D5
Lomela, *Dem. Rep. of the Congo* 84 E4
Lomela →, *Dem. Rep. of the Congo* 84 E4
Lomianki, *Poland* 31 F7
Lomma, *Sweden* 11 J7
Lommel, *Belgium* 17 C5
Lomond, *Canada* 102 C6
Lomond, L., *U.K.* 13 E4
Lomonosov Ridge, *Arctic* 4 A
Lomphat, *Cambodia* 64 F6
Lompobatang, *Indonesia* 63 F5
Lompoc, *U.S.A.* 111 L6
Łomża, *Poland* 31 E9
Lon, Ko, *Thailand* 65 a
Loncoche, *Chile* 128 D2
Londa, *India* 66 M9
Londiani, *Kenya* 86 C4
Londinières, *France* 18 C8
London, *Canada* 116 D3
London, *U.K.* 15 F7
London, *Ky., U.S.A.* 114 G3
London, *Ohio, U.S.A.* 114 F4
London, Greater □, *U.K.* 15 F7
London Gatwick ✕ (LGW), *U.K.* 15 F7
London Heathrow ✕ (LHR), *U.K.* 15 F7
London Stansted ✕ (STN), *U.K.* 15 F8
Londonderry, *U.K.* 12 B4
Londonderry □, *U.K.* 12 B4
Londonderry, C., *Australia* 92 B4
Londonderry, I., *Chile* 128 H2
Londres, *Argentina* 128 B3
Londrina, *Brazil* 127 A5
Lone Pine, *U.S.A.* 110 J8
Lonely Mine, *Zimbabwe* 89 B4
Long B., *U.S.A.* 115 J6
Long Beach, *Calif., U.S.A.* 111 M8
Long Beach, *N.Y., U.S.A.* 117 F11
Long Beach, *Wash., U.S.A.* 110 D2
Long Branch, *U.S.A.* 117 F11
Long Creek, *U.S.A.* 108 D4
Long Eaton, *U.K.* 14 E6
Long I., *Australia* 94 J6
Long I., *Bahamas* 121 B4
Long I., *Canada* 104 B4
Long I., *Ireland* 12 E2
Long I., *U.S.A.* 117 F11
Long Island Sd., *U.S.A.* 117 E12
Long L., *Canada* 104 C2
Long Lake, *U.S.A.* 117 C10
Long Point B., *Canada* 116 D4
Long Prairie →, *U.S.A.* 112 C7
Long Pt., *Canada* 116 D4
Long Range Mts., *Canada* 105 C8
Long Reef, *Australia* 92 B4
Long Spruce, *Canada* 103 B10
Long Str. = Longa, Proliv, *Russia* 4 C16
Long Thanh, *Vietnam* 65 G6
Long Xian, *China* 56 G4
Long Xuyen, *Vietnam* 65 G5
Longá, *Greece* 46 E3
Longa, Proliv, *Russia* 4 C16
Long'an, *China* 58 F6
Longarone, *Italy* 41 B9
Longbenton, *U.K.* 14 B6
Longboat Key, *U.S.A.* 115 M4
Longchang, *China* 58 C5
Longchi, *China* 58 C4
Longchuan, *Guangdong, China* 59 E10
Longchuan, *Yunnan, China* 58 E1
Longde, *China* 56 G4
Longeau, *France* 19 E12
Longford, *Australia* 95 G4
Longford, *Ireland* 12 C4
Longford □, *Ireland* 12 C4
Longhai, *China* 59 E11
Longhua, *China* 57 D9
Longhui, *China* 59 D8
Longido, *Tanzania* 86 C4
Longiram, *Indonesia* 62 E5
Longkou, *Jiangxi, China* 59 D10
Longkou, *Shandong, China* 57 F11
Longlac, *Canada* 104 C2
Longli, *China* 58 D6
Longlin, *China* 58 E5
Longling, *China* 58 E2
Longmeadow, *U.S.A.* 117 D12
Longmen, *China* 59 F10
Longming, *China* 58 F6
Longmont, *U.S.A.* 112 E2
Longnan, *China* 59 E10
Longnawan, *Indonesia* 62 D4
Longobucco, *Italy* 43 C9
Longquan, *China* 59 C12
Longreach, *Australia* 94 C3
Longshan, *China* 58 C7
Longsheng, *China* 59 E8
Longué-Jumelles, *France* 18 E6
Longueau, *France* 19 C9
Longueuil, *Canada* 117 A11
Longuyon, *France* 19 C12
Longvic, *France* 19 E12
Longview, *Tex., U.S.A.* 113 J7
Longview, *Wash., U.S.A.* 110 D4
Longwy, *France* 19 C12
Longxi, *China* 56 G3
Longyan, *China* 59 E11
Longyearbyen, *Svalbard* 4 B8
Longyou, *China* 59 C12
Longzhou, *China* 58 F6
Lonigo, *Italy* 41 C8
Löningen, *Germany* 24 C3
Lonja →, *Croatia* 41 C13
Lonoke, *U.S.A.* 113 H9
Lonquimay, *Chile* 128 D2
Lons-le-Saunier, *France* 19 F12
Lönsboda, *Sweden* 11 H8
Looe, *U.K.* 15 G3
Lookout, C., *Canada* 104 A3
Lookout, C., *U.S.A.* 115 H7
Loolmalasin, *Tanzania* 86 C4
Loon →, *Alta., Canada* 102 B5
Loon →, *Man., Canada* 103 B8
Loon Lake, *Canada* 103 C7
Loongana, *Australia* 93 F4
Loop Hd., *Ireland* 12 D2
Lop Buri, *Thailand* 64 E3
Lop Nor = Lop Nur, *China* 60 B4
Lop Nur, *China* 60 B4
Lopare, *Bos.-H.* 28 F3
Lopatin, *Russia* 35 J8
Lopatina, Gora, *Russia* 53 D15
Lopaye, *Sudan* 81 F3
Lopez, *Phil.* 61 E5
Lopez, *U.S.A.* 117 E8
Lopez, C., *Gabon* 84 E1
Lopphavet, *Norway* 8 A19
Lora →, *Afghan.* 66 D4
Lora, Hāmūn-i-, *Pakistan* 66 E4
Lora Cr. →, *Australia* 95 D2
Lora del Río, *Spain* 37 H5
Lorain, *U.S.A.* 116 E2
Loralai, *Pakistan* 68 D3
Lorca, *Spain* 39 H3
Lord Howe I., *Pac. Oc.* 96 L7
Lord Howe Ridge, *Pac. Oc.* 96 L8
Lordsburg, *U.S.A.* 109 K9
Lorestan □, *Iran* 71 C6
Loreto, *Brazil* 125 E9
Loreto, *Italy* 41 E10
Loreto, *Mexico* 118 B2
Lorgues, *France* 21 E10
Lorhosso, *Burkina Faso* 82 C4
Lorient, *France* 18 E3
Lőrinci, *Hungary* 28 C4
Lormi, *India* 69 H9
Lorn, *U.K.* 13 E3
Lorn, Firth of, *U.K.* 13 E3
Lorne, *Australia* 95 F3
Loronyo, *Sudan* 81 G3
Lorovouno, *Cyprus* 49 D11
Lörrach, *Germany* 25 H3
Lorraine ⌓, *France* 19 D12
Lorraine □, *France* 19 D13
Los, *Sweden* 10 C9
Los, Îles de, *Guinea* 82 D2
Los Alamos, *Calif., U.S.A.* 111 L6
Los Alamos, *N. Mex., U.S.A.* 109 J10
Los Alcornocales ⌓, *Spain* 37 J5
Los Altos, *U.S.A.* 110 H4
Los Andes, *Chile* 126 C1
Los Angeles, *Chile* 126 D1
Los Angeles, *U.S.A.* 111 M8
Los Angeles, Bahia de, *Mexico* 118 B2
Los Angeles Aqueduct, *U.S.A.* 111 K9
Los Angeles International ✕ (LAX), *U.S.A.* 111 M8
Los Banos, *U.S.A.* 110 H6
Los Barrios, *Spain* 37 J5
Los Blancos, *Argentina* 126 A3
Los Cardones △, *Argentina* 126 B2
Los Chiles, *Costa Rica* 120 D3
Los Corrales de Buelna, *Spain* 36 B6
Los Cristianos, *Canary Is.* 48 F3
Los Gallardos, *Spain* 39 H3
Los Gatos, *U.S.A.* 110 H5
Los Haïtises △, *Dom. Rep.* 121 C6
Los Hermanos Is., *Venezuela* 121 D7
Los Islotes, *Canary Is.* 48 E6
Los Llanos de Aridane, *Canary Is.* 48 F2
Los Loros, *Chile* 126 B1
Los Lunas, *U.S.A.* 109 J10
Los Mochis, *Mexico* 118 B3
Los Monegros, *Spain* 38 D4
Los Nietos, *Spain* 39 H4
Los Olivos, *U.S.A.* 111 L6
Los Palacios, *Cuba* 120 B3
Los Palacios y Villafranca, *Spain* 37 H5
Los Reyes, *Mexico* 118 D4
Los Roques Is., *Venezuela* 121 D6
Los Santos de Maimona, *Spain* 37 G4
Los Teques, *Venezuela* 124 A5
Los Testigos, Is., *Venezuela* 124 A6
Los Vilos, *Chile* 126 C1
Los Yébenes, *Spain* 37 F7
Łosice, *Poland* 31 F9
Loskop Dam, *S. Africa* 89 D4
Løsning, *Denmark* 11 J3
Lossiemouth, *U.K.* 13 D5
Lossnen △, *Sweden* 10 B6
Lostwithiel, *U.K.* 15 G3
Lot □, *France* 20 D5
Lot →, *France* 20 D4
Lot-et-Garonne □, *France* 20 D4
Lota, *Chile* 126 D1
Lotagipi Swamp, *Sudan* 81 G3
Loṭfābād, *Iran* 71 B8
Lothair, *S. Africa* 89 D5
Lotorp, *Sweden* 11 F9
Lötschbergtunnel, *Switz.* 25 J3
Löttorp, *Sweden* 11 G11
Lotung, *Taiwan* 59 E13
Loubomo, *Congo* 84 E2
Loudéac, *France* 18 D4
Loudi, *China* 59 D8
Loudonville, *U.S.A.* 116 F2
Loudun, *France* 18 E7
Loue →, *France* 19 E12
Louga, *Senegal* 82 B1
Loughborough, *U.K.* 14 E6
Loughrea, *Ireland* 12 C3
Loughros More B., *Ireland* 12 B3
Louhans, *France* 19 F12
Louis Trichardt, *S. Africa* 89 C4
Louis XIV, Pte., *Canada* 104 B4
Louisa, *U.S.A.* 114 F4
Louisbourg, *Canada* 105 C8
Louise I., *Canada* 102 C2
Louiseville, *Canada* 104 C5
Louisiade Arch., *Papua N. G.* 96 J7
Louisiana, *U.S.A.* 112 F9
Louisiana □, *U.S.A.* 113 K9
Louisville, *Ky., U.S.A.* 114 F3
Louisville, *Miss., U.S.A.* 113 J10
Louisville, *Ohio, U.S.A.* 116 F3
Loulay, *France* 20 B3
Loulé, *Portugal* 37 H3
Louny, *Czech Rep.* 26 A6
Loup City, *U.S.A.* 112 E5
Loups Marins, Lacs des, *Canada* 104 A5
Lourdes, *France* 20 E3
Lourinhã, *Portugal* 37 F1
Lousã, *Portugal* 36 E2
Louta, *Burkina Faso* 82 C4
Louth, *Australia* 95 E4
Louth, *Ireland* 12 C5
Louth, *U.K.* 14 D7
Louth □, *Ireland* 12 C5
Loutrá Aidhipsoú, *Greece* 46 C5
Loutráki, *Greece* 46 D4
Louvain = Leuven, *Belgium* 17 D4
Louviers, *France* 18 C8
Louwsburg, *S. Africa* 89 D5
Lovat →, *Russia* 32 C6
Lovćen, *Serbia & M.* 44 D2
Lovćen △, *Serbia & M.* 44 D2
Lovech, *Bulgaria* 45 C8
Lovech □, *Bulgaria* 45 C8
Loveland, *U.S.A.* 112 E2
Lovell, *U.S.A.* 108 D9
Lovelock, *U.S.A.* 108 F4
Lóvere, *Italy* 40 C7
Lövestad, *Sweden* 11 J7
Loviisa, *Finland* 9 F22
Loving, *U.S.A.* 113 J2
Lovington, *U.S.A.* 113 J3
Lovisa = Loviisa, *Finland* 9 F22
Lovosice, *Czech Rep.* 26 A7
Lovran, *Croatia* 41 C11
Lovrin, *Romania* 28 E5
Lövstabruk, *Sweden* 10 D11
Lövstabukten, *Sweden* 10 D11
Low, L., *Canada* 104 B4
Low Pt., *Australia* 93 F4
Low Tatra = Nízké Tatry, *Slovak Rep.* 27 C12
Lowa, *Dem. Rep. of the Congo* 86 C2
Lowa →, *Dem. Rep. of the Congo* 86 C2
Lowell, *U.S.A.* 117 D13
Lowellville, *U.S.A.* 116 E4
Löwen →, *Namibia* 88 D2
Lower Alkali L., *U.S.A.* 108 F3
Lower Arrow L., *Canada* 102 D5
Lower Austria = Niederösterreich □, *Austria* 26 C8
Lower California = Baja California, *Mexico* 118 A1
Lower Hutt, *N.Z.* 91 J5
Lower Lake, *U.S.A.* 110 G4
Lower Manitou L., *Canada* 103 D10
Lower Post, *Canada* 102 B3
Lower Red L., *U.S.A.* 112 B7
Lower Saxony = Niedersachsen □, *Germany* 24 C4
Lower Tunguska = Tunguska, Nizhnyaya →, *Russia* 53 C9
Lower Zambezi △, *Zambia* 87 F2
Lowestoft, *U.K.* 15 E9
Lowgar □, *Afghan.* 66 B6
Łowicz, *Poland* 31 F6
Lowville, *U.S.A.* 117 C9
Loxton, *Australia* 95 E3
Loxton, *S. Africa* 88 E3
Loyalton, *U.S.A.* 110 F6
Loyalty Is. = Loyauté, Îs., *N. Cal.* 96 K8
Loyang = Luoyang, *China* 56 G7
Loyauté, Îs., *N. Cal.* 96 K8
Loyev = Loyew, *Belarus* 33 G6
Loyew, *Belarus* 33 G6
Loyoro, *Uganda* 86 B3
Lož, *Slovenia* 41 C11
Lozère □, *France* 20 D7
Loznica, *Serbia & M.* 44 B3
Lozova, *Ukraine* 33 H9
Lü Shan, *China* 59 C11
Lü-Tao, *Taiwan* 59 F13
Luachimo, *Angola* 84 F4
Luajan →, *India* 69 G11
Lualaba →, *Dem. Rep. of the Congo* 86 B2
Luampa, *Zambia* 87 F1
Lu'an, *China* 59 B11
Luan Chau, *Vietnam* 58 G4
Luan He →, *China* 57 E10
Luan Xian, *China* 57 E10
Luancheng, *Guangxi Zhuangzu, China* 58 F7
Luancheng, *Hebei, China* 56 F8
Luanco, *Spain* 36 B5
Luanda, *Angola* 84 F2
Luang, Thale, *Thailand* 65 J3
Luang Prabang, *Laos* 58 H4
Luangwa, *Zambia* 87 F3
Luangwa →, *Zambia* 87 E3
Luangwa Valley, *Zambia* 87 E3
Luanne, *China* 57 D9
Luanping, *China* 57 D9
Luanshya, *Zambia* 87 E2
Luapula □, *Zambia* 87 E2
Luapula →, *Africa* 87 D2
Luarca, *Spain* 36 B4
Luashi, *Dem. Rep. of the Congo* 87 E1
Luau, *Angola* 84 G4
Lubaczów, *Poland* 31 H10
Lubań, *Poland* 31 G2
Lubana, Ozero = Lubānas Ezers, *Latvia* 9 H22
Lubānas Ezers, *Latvia* 9 H22
Lubang, *Phil.* 61 E4
Lubang Is., *Phil.* 63 B6
Lubango, *Angola* 85 G2
Lubao, *Dem. Rep. of the Congo* 86 D2
Lubartów, *Poland* 31 G9
Lubawa, *Poland* 30 E6
Lübbecke, *Germany* 24 C4
Lübben, *Germany* 24 D9
Lübbenau, *Germany* 24 D9
Lubbock, *U.S.A.* 113 J4
Lübeck, *Germany* 24 B6
Lübecker Bucht, *Germany* 24 A6
Lubefu, *Dem. Rep. of the Congo* 86 C1
Lubefu →, *Dem. Rep. of the Congo* 86 C1
Lubelskie □, *Poland* 31 G9
Lubero = Luofu, *Dem. Rep. of the Congo* 86 C2
Luberon ⌓, *France* 21 E9
Lubersac, *France* 20 C5
Lubicon L., *Canada* 102 B5
Lubień Kujawski, *Poland* 31 F6
Lubilash →, *Dem. Rep. of the Congo* 84 F4
Lubin, *Poland* 31 G3
Lublin, *Poland* 31 G9
Lubliniec, *Poland* 31 H5
Lubnān, Jabal, *Lebanon* 74 B4
Lubniewice, *Poland* 31 F2
Lubny, *Ukraine* 33 G7
Lubomierz, *Poland* 31 G2
Luboń, *Poland* 31 F3
Lubongola, *Dem. Rep. of the Congo* 86 C2
L'ubotín, *Slovak Rep.* 27 B13
Lubraniec, *Poland* 31 F5
Lubsko, *Poland* 31 G1
Lübtheen, *Germany* 24 B7
Lubuagan, *Phil.* 61 C4
Lubudi, *Dem. Rep. of the Congo* 84 F5
Lubudi →, *Dem. Rep. of the Congo* 87 D2
Lubuklinggau, *Indonesia* 62 E2
Lubuksikaping, *Indonesia* 62 D2
Lubumbashi, *Dem. Rep. of the Congo* 87 E2
Lubunda, *Dem. Rep. of the Congo* 86 D2
Lubungu, *Zambia* 87 E2
Lubuskie □, *Poland* 31 F2
Lubutu, *Dem. Rep. of the Congo* 86 C2
Luc An Chau, *Vietnam* 64 A5
Luc-en-Diois, *France* 21 D9
Lucan, *Canada* 116 C3
Lucania, Mt., *Canada* 100 B5
Lucas Channel, *Canada* 116 A3
Lucban, *Phil.* 61 D4
Lucca, *Italy* 40 E7
Lucé, *France* 18 D8
Luce Bay, *U.K.* 13 G4
Lucea, *Jamaica* 120 a
Lucedale, *U.S.A.* 115 K1
Lucena, *Phil.* 61 E4
Lucena, *Spain* 37 H6
Lučenec, *Slovak Rep.* 27 C12
Lucera, *Italy* 43 A8
Lucerne = Luzern, *Switz.* 25 H4
Lucerne, *U.S.A.* 110 F4
Lucerne Valley, *U.S.A.* 111 L10
Lucero, *Mexico* 118 A3
Luchena →, *Spain* 39 H3
Lucheng, *China* 56 F7
Lucheringo →, *Mozam.* 87 E4
Lüchow, *Germany* 24 C7
Luchuan, *China* 59 F8
Lucia, *U.S.A.* 110 J5
Lucinda, *Australia* 94 B4
Luckau, *Germany* 24 D9
Luckenwalde, *Germany* 24 C9
Luckhoff, *S. Africa* 88 D3
Lucknow, *Canada* 116 C3
Lucknow, *India* 69 F9
Luçon, *France* 20 B2
Lüda = Dalian, *China* 57 E11
Luda Kamchiya →, *Bulgaria* 45 C11
Ludbreg, *Croatia* 41 B13
Lüdenscheid, *Germany* 24 D3
Lüderitz, *Namibia* 88 D2
Lüderitzbaai, *Namibia* 88 D2
Ludhiana, *India* 68 D6
Ludian, *China* 58 D4
Luding Qiao, *China* 58 C4
Lüdinghausen, *Germany* 24 D3
Ludington, *U.S.A.* 114 D2
Ludlow, *U.K.* 15 E5
Ludlow, *Calif., U.S.A.* 111 L10
Ludlow, *Pa., U.S.A.* 116 E6
Ludlow, *Vt., U.S.A.* 117 C12
Ludus, *Romania* 29 D9
Ludvika, *Sweden* 10 D9
Ludwigsburg, *Germany* 25 G5
Ludwigsfelde, *Germany* 24 C9
Ludwigshafen, *Germany* 25 F4
Ludwigslust, *Germany* 24 B7
Ludza, *Latvia* 9 H21
Lueki, *Dem. Rep. of the Congo* 86 C2

Luena, *Dem. Rep. of the Congo* 87 D2
Luena, *Zambia* 87 E3
Luenha = Ruenya →, *Africa* 87 F3
Lüeyang, *China* 56 H4
Lufeng, *Guangdong, China* 59 F10
Lufeng, *Yunnan, China* 58 E4
Lufira →, *Dem. Rep. of the Congo* 87 D2
Lufkin, *U.S.A.* 113 K7
Lufupa, *Dem. Rep. of the Congo* 87 E1
Luga, *Russia* 32 C5
Luga →, *Russia* 32 C5
Lugano, *Switz.* 25 J4
Lugano, L. di, *Switz.* 40 C6
Lugansk = Luhansk, *Ukraine* 33 H10
Lugard's Falls, *Kenya* 86 C4
Lugela, *Mozam.* 87 F4
Lugenda →, *Mozam.* 87 E4
Lugh Ganana, *Somali Rep.* 75 G3
Lugnaquillia, *Ireland* 12 D5
Lugo, *Italy* 41 D8
Lugo, *Spain* 36 B3
Lugo □, *Spain* 36 C3
Lugoj, *Romania* 28 E6
Lugovoy = Qulan, *Kazakhstan* 52 E8
Luhansk, *Ukraine* 33 H10
Luhe, *China* 59 A12
Luhe →, *Germany* 24 B6
Luhuo, *China* 58 B3
Luiana, *Angola* 88 B3
Luichow Pen. = Leizhou Bandao, *China* 58 G7
Luimneach = Limerick, *Ireland* 12 D3
Luing, *U.K.* 13 E3
Luino, *Italy* 40 C5
Luís Correia, *Brazil* 125 D10
Luitpold Coast, *Antarctica* 5 D1
Luiza, *Dem. Rep. of the Congo* 84 F4
Luizi, *Dem. Rep. of the Congo* 86 D2
Luján, *Argentina* 126 C4
Lujiang, *China* 59 B11
Lukang, *Taiwan* 59 E13
Lukanga Swamp, *Zambia* 87 E2
Lukavac, *Bos.-H.* 28 F3
Lukenie →, *Dem. Rep. of the Congo* 84 E3
Lukhisaral, *India* 69 G12
Lŭki, *Bulgaria* 45 E8
Lukolela, *Dem. Rep. of the Congo* 86 D1
Lukosi, *Zimbabwe* 87 F2
Lukovë, *Albania* 44 G3
Lukovit, *Bulgaria* 45 C8
Łuków, *Poland* 31 G9
Lukoyanov, *Russia* 34 C7
Lukusuzi △, *Zambia* 87 E3
Luleå, *Sweden* 8 D20
Luleälven →, *Sweden* 8 D19
Lüleburgaz, *Turkey* 45 E11
Luliang, *China* 58 E4
Luling, *U.S.A.* 113 L6
Lulong, *China* 57 E10
Lulonga →, *Dem. Rep. of the Congo* 84 D3
Lulua →, *Dem. Rep. of the Congo* 84 E4
Lumajang, *Indonesia* 63 H15
Lumbala N'guimbo, *Angola* 85 G4
Lumberton, *U.S.A.* 115 H6
Lumsden, *Canada* 103 C8
Lumsden, *N.Z.* 91 L2
Lumut, *Malaysia* 65 K3
Lumut, Tanjung, *Indonesia* 62 E3
Luna, *India* 68 H3
Lunan, *China* 58 E4
Lunavada, *India* 68 H5
Lunca, *Romania* 29 C10
Lunca Corbului, *Romania* 29 F9
Lund, *Sweden* 11 J7
Lundazi, *Zambia* 87 E3
Lunderskov, *Denmark* 11 J3
Lundi →, *Zimbabwe* 87 G3
Lundu, *Malaysia* 62 D3
Lundy, *U.K.* 15 F3
Lune →, *U.K.* 14 C5
Lüneburg, *Germany* 24 B6
Lüneburg Heath = Lüneburger Heide, *Germany* 24 B6
Lüneburger Heide, *Germany* 24 B6
Lunel, *France* 21 E8
Lünen, *Germany* 24 D3
Lunenburg, *Canada* 105 D7
Lunéville, *France* 19 D13
Lunga →, *Zambia* 87 E2
Lungi Airport, *S. Leone* 82 D2
Lunglei, *India* 67 H18
Luni, *India* 68 G5
Luni →, *India* 68 G4
Luninets = Luninyets, *Belarus* 33 F4
Luning, *U.S.A.* 108 G4
Lunino, *Russia* 34 D7
Luninyets, *Belarus* 33 F4
Lunkaransar, *India* 68 E5
Lunsemfwa →, *Zambia* 87 E3
Lunsemfwa Falls, *Zambia* 87 E2
Luo He →, *China* 56 G6
Luocheng, *China* 58 E7
Luochuan, *China* 56 G5
Luoci, *China* 58 E4
Luodian, *China* 58 E6
Luoding, *China* 59 F8
Luofu, *Dem. Rep. of the Congo* 86 C2
Luohe, *China* 56 H8
Luojiang, *China* 58 B5
Luonan, *China* 56 G6
Luoning, *China* 56 G6
Luoshan, *China* 59 A10
Luotian, *China* 59 B10
Luoxiao Shan, *China* 59 D10
Luoyang, *China* 56 G7
Luoyuan, *China* 59 D12
Luozigou, *China* 57 C16
Lupanshui, *China* 58 D5
Lupeni, *Romania* 29 E8
Lupilichi, *Mozam.* 87 E4
Łupków, *Poland* 31 J9
Lupoing, *China* 58 E5
Luquan, *China* 58 E4
Luque, *Paraguay* 126 B4
Lúras, *Italy* 42 B2
Luray, *U.S.A.* 114 F6
Lure, *France* 19 E13
Lurgan, *U.K.* 12 B5
Lusaka, *Zambia* 87 F2
Lusaka □, *Zambia* 87 F2
Lusambo, *Dem. Rep. of the Congo* 86 C1
Lusangaye, *Dem. Rep. of the Congo* 86 C2
Luseland, *Canada* 103 C7
Lusenga Plain △, *Zambia* 87 D2
Lushan, *Henan, China* 56 H7
Lushan, *Sichuan, China* 58 B4
Lushi, *China* 56 G6
Lushnjë, *Albania* 44 F3
Lushoto, *Tanzania* 86 C4
Lushui, *China* 58 E2
Lüshun, *China* 57 E11
Lusignan, *France* 20 B4
Lusigny-sur-Barse, *France* 19 D11
Lusk, *U.S.A.* 112 D2
Lussac-les-Châteaux, *France* 20 B4
Lustenau, *Austria* 26 D2
Lūt, Dasht-e, *Iran* 71 D8
Luta = Dalian, *China* 57 E11
Lutherstadt Wittenberg, *Germany* 24 D8
Luton, *U.K.* 15 F7
Luton □, *U.K.* 15 F7
Łutselk'e, *Canada* 103 A6
Lutsk, *Ukraine* 33 G3
Lützow Holmbukta, *Antarctica* 5 C4
Lutzputs, *S. Africa* 88 D3
Luuq = Lugh Ganana, *Somali Rep.* 75 G3
Luverne, *Ala., U.S.A.* 115 K2
Luverne, *Minn., U.S.A.* 112 D6
Luvua, *Dem. Rep. of the Congo* 87 D2
Luvua →, *Dem. Rep. of the Congo* 86 D2
Luvuvhu →, *S. Africa* 89 C5
Luwegu →, *Tanzania* 87 D4
Luwuk, *Indonesia* 63 E6
Luxembourg, *Lux.* 17 E6
Luxembourg □, *Belgium* 17 E5
Luxembourg ■, *Europe* 7 F7
Luxembourg ✕ (LUX), *Lux.* 17 E6
Luxeuil-les-Bains, *France* 19 E13
Luxi, *Hunan, China* 59 C8
Luxi, *Yunnan, China* 58 E4
Luxi, *Yunnan, China* 58 E2
Luxor = El Uqsur, *Egypt* 80 B3
Luy-de-Béarn →, *France* 20 E3
Luy-de-France →, *France* 20 E3
Luyi, *China* 56 H8
Luz-St-Sauveur, *France* 20 F4
Luzern, *Switz.* 25 H4
Luzern □, *Switz.* 25 H3
Luzhai, *China* 58 E7
Luzhany, *Ukraine* 29 B10
Luzhi, *China* 58 D5
Luzhou, *China* 58 C5
Luziânia, *Brazil* 125 G9
Lužnice →, *Czech Rep.* 26 B7
Luzon, *Phil.* 61 D4
Luzon Strait, *Asia* 59 G13
Luzy, *France* 19 F10
Luzzi, *Italy* 43 C9
Lviv, *Ukraine* 33 H3
Lvov = Lviv, *Ukraine* 33 H3
Lwówek, *Poland* 31 F3
Lwówek Śląski, *Poland* 31 G2
Lyakhavichy, *Belarus* 33 F4
Lyakhovskiye, Ostrova, *Russia* 53 B15
Lyakhvah = Läki, *Azerbaijan* 35 K8
Lyal I., *Canada* 116 B3
Lyaskovets, *Bulgaria* 45 C9
Lyasnaya, *Belarus* 31 F10
Lybster, *U.K.* 13 C5
Lycaonia, *Turkey* 72 D5
Lychen, *Germany* 24 B9
Lychkova, *Russia* 32 D7
Lycia, *Turkey* 47 E11
Lyckebyån →, *Sweden* 11 H9
Lycksele, *Sweden* 8 D18
Lycosura, *Greece* 46 D4
Lydda = Lod, *Israel* 74 D3
Lydenburg, *S. Africa* 89 D5
Lydia, *Turkey* 47 C10
Łydynia →, *Poland* 31 F7
Lyell, *N.Z.* 91 J4
Lyell I., *Canada* 102 C2
Lyepyel, *Belarus* 32 E5
Lygnern, *Sweden* 11 G6
Lykens, *U.S.A.* 117 F8
Lyman, *Ukraine* 29 E14
Lyman, *U.S.A.* 108 F8
Lymanske, *Ukraine* 29 D14
Lyme B., *U.K.* 15 G4
Lyme Regis, *U.K.* 15 G5
Lymington, *U.K.* 15 G6
Łyna →, *Poland* 9 J19
Lynchburg, *U.S.A.* 114 G6
Lynd →, *Australia* 94 B3
Lynd Ra., *Australia* 95 D4
Lynden, *Canada* 116 C4
Lynden, *U.S.A.* 110 B4
Lyndhurst, *Australia* 95 E2
Lyndon →, *Australia* 93 D1
Lyndonville, *N.Y., U.S.A.* 116 C6
Lyndonville, *Vt., U.S.A.* 117 B12
Lyngen, *Norway* 8 B19
Lynher Reef, *Australia* 92 C3
Lynn, *U.S.A.* 117 D14
Lynn Lake, *Canada* 103 B8
Lynnwood, *U.S.A.* 110 C4
Lynton, *U.K.* 15 F4
Lyntupy, *Belarus* 9 J22
Lynx L., *Canada* 103 A7
Lyon, *France* 21 C8
Lyon St-Exupery ✕ (LYS), *France* 21 C9
Lyonnais, *France* 21 C8
Lyons = Lyon, *France* 21 C8
Lyons, *Ga., U.S.A.* 115 J4
Lyons, *Kans., U.S.A.* 112 F5
Lyons, *N.Y., U.S.A.* 116 C8
Lyons →, *Australia* 93 E2
Lyons Falls, *U.S.A.* 117 C9
Lyozna, *Belarus* 32 E6
Lys = Leie →, *Belgium* 17 C3
Lysá nad Labem, *Czech Rep.* 26 A7
Lysekil, *Sweden* 11 F5
Lyskovo, *Russia* 34 B7
Lystrup, *Denmark* 11 H4
Lysvik, *Sweden* 10 D7
Lysychansk, *Ukraine* 33 H10
Lytham St. Anne's, *U.K.* 14 D4
Lyttelton, *N.Z.* 91 K4
Lytton, *Canada* 102 C4
Lyuban, *Russia* 32 C6
Lyubertsy, *Russia* 32 E9
Lyubim, *Russia* 32 C11
Lyubimets, *Bulgaria* 45 E10
Lyuboml, *Ukraine* 31 G11
Lyubotyn, *Ukraine* 33 H8
Lyubytino, *Russia* 32 C7
Lyudinovo, *Russia* 32 F8

M

M.R. Gomez, Presa, *Mexico* 119 B5
M.R. Stefanik, Bratislava ✕ (BTS), *Slovak Rep.* 27 C10
Ma →, *Vietnam* 58 H5
Ma'adaba, *Jordan* 74 E4
Maamba, *Zambia* 88 B4
Ma'ān, *Jordan* 74 E4
Ma'ān □, *Jordan* 74 F5
Maanselkä, *Finland* 8 C23
Ma'anshan, *China* 59 B12
Maarianhamina, *Finland* 9 F18
Ma'arrat an Nu'mān, *Syria* 70 C3
Maas →, *Neths.* 17 C4
Maaseik, *Belgium* 17 C5
Maasin, *Phil.* 63 B6
Maastricht, *Neths.* 17 D5
Maave, *Mozam.* 89 C5
Mababe Depression, *Botswana* 88 B3
Mabalane, *Mozam.* 89 C5
Mabel L., *Canada* 102 C5
Mabenge, *Dem. Rep. of the Congo* 86 B1
Maberly, *Canada* 117 B8
Mabian, *China* 58 C4
Mabil, *Ethiopia* 81 E4
Mablethorpe, *U.K.* 14 D8
Mably, *France* 19 F11
Maboma, *Dem. Rep. of the Congo* 86 B2
Mabonto, *S. Leone* 82 D2
Mabrouk, *Mali* 83 B4
Mabuasehube ⌓, *Botswana* 88 D3
Mac Bac, *Vietnam* 65 H6
Macachín, *Argentina* 126 D3
Macaé, *Brazil* 127 A7
Macael, *Spain* 39 H2
McAlester, *U.S.A.* 113 H7
McAllen, *U.S.A.* 113 M5
MacAlpine L., *Canada* 100 B9
Macamic, *Canada* 104 C4
Macao = Macau, *China* 59 F9
Macão, *Portugal* 37 F3
Macapá, *Brazil* 125 C8
Macarao △, *Venezuela* 121 D6
McArthur →, *Australia* 94 B2
McArthur, Port, *Australia* 94 B2
Macau, *Brazil* 125 E11
Macau, *China* 59 F9
McBride, *Canada* 102 C4
McCall, *U.S.A.* 108 D5
McCamey, *U.S.A.* 113 K3
McCammon, *U.S.A.* 108 E7
McCauley I., *Canada* 102 C2
McCleary, *U.S.A.* 110 C3
Macclenny, *U.S.A.* 115 K4
Macclesfield, *U.K.* 14 D5
M'Clintock Chan., *Canada* 100 A9
McClintock Ra., *Australia* 92 C4
McCloud, *U.S.A.* 108 F2
McCluer I., *Australia* 92 B5
McClure, *U.S.A.* 116 F7
McClure, L., *U.S.A.* 110 H6
M'Clure Str., *Canada* 98 B8
McClusky, *U.S.A.* 112 B4
McComb, *U.S.A.* 113 K9
McConaughy, L., *U.S.A.* 112 E4
McCook, *U.S.A.* 112 E4
McCreary, *Canada* 103 C9
McCullough Mt., *U.S.A.* 111 K11
McCusker →, *Canada* 103 B7
McDame, *Canada* 102 B3
McDermitt, *U.S.A.* 108 F5
McDonald, *U.S.A.* 116 F4
Macdonald, L., *Australia* 92 D4
McDonald Is., *Ind. Oc.* 3 G13
MacDonnell Ranges, *Australia* 92 D5
MacDowell L., *Canada* 104 B1
Macduff, *U.K.* 13 D6
Maceda, *Spain* 36 C3
Macedonia, *U.S.A.* 116 E3
Macedonia ■, *Europe* 44 E5
Maceió, *Brazil* 125 E11
Maceira, *Portugal* 36 F2
Macenta, *Guinea* 82 D3
Macerata, *Italy* 41 E10
McFarland, *U.S.A.* 111 K7
McFarlane →, *Canada* 103 B7
Macfarlane, L., *Australia* 95 E2
McGehee, *U.S.A.* 113 J9
McGill, *U.S.A.* 108 G6
Macgillycuddy's Reeks, *Ireland* 12 E2
McGraw, *U.S.A.* 117 D8
McGregor, *U.S.A.* 112 D9
McGregor Ra., *Australia* 95 D3
McGuire, Mt, *Australia* 94 J6
Mach, *Pakistan* 66 E5
Māch Kowr, *Iran* 71 E9
Machado = Jiparaná →, *Brazil* 124 E6
Machagai, *Argentina* 126 B3
Machakos, *Kenya* 86 C4
Machala, *Ecuador* 124 D3
Machanga, *Mozam.* 89 C6
Machattie, L., *Australia* 94 C2
Machault, *France* 19 C11
Machava, *Mozam.* 89 D5
Machece, *Mozam.* 87 F4
Machecoul, *France* 18 F5
Macheke, *Zimbabwe* 89 B5
Macheng, *China* 59 B10
Machero, *Spain* 37 F6
Machhu →, *India* 68 H4
Machias, *Maine, U.S.A.* 115 C12
Machias, *N.Y., U.S.A.* 116 D6
Machichi →, *Canada* 103 B10
Machico, *Madeira* 48 D3
Machilipatnam, *India* 67 L12
Machiques, *Venezuela* 124 A4
Machupicchu, *Peru* 124 F4
Machynlleth, *U.K.* 15 E4
Macia, *Mozam.* 89 D5
Maciejowice, *Poland* 31 G8
McIlwraith Ra., *Australia* 94 A3
Măcin, *Romania* 29 E13
Macina, *Mali* 82 C4
McInnes L., *Canada* 103 C10
McIntosh, *U.S.A.* 112 C4
McIntosh L., *Canada* 103 B8
Macintosh Ra., *Australia* 93 E4
Macintyre →, *Australia* 95 D5
Macizo Galaico, *Spain* 36 C3
Mackay, *Australia* 94 K7
Mackay, *U.S.A.* 108 E7
MacKay →, *Canada* 102 B6
Mackay, L., *Australia* 92 D4
McKay Ra., *Australia* 92 D3
McKeesport, *U.S.A.* 116 F5
McKellar, *Canada* 116 A5
McKenna, *U.S.A.* 110 D4
Mackenzie, *Canada* 102 B4
McKenzie, *U.S.A.* 115 G1
Mackenzie →, *Australia* 94 C4
Mackenzie →, *Canada* 100 B6
McKenzie →, *U.S.A.* 108 D2
Mackenzie Bay, *Canada* 4 B1
Mackenzie City = Linden, *Guyana* 124 B7
Mackenzie Mts., *Canada* 100 B6
Mackinaw City, *U.S.A.* 114 C3
McKinlay, *Australia* 94 C3
McKinlay →, *Australia* 94 C3
McKinley, Mt., *U.S.A.* 100 B4
McKinley Sea, *Arctic* 4 A7
McKinney, *U.S.A.* 113 J6
Mackinnon Road, *Kenya* 86 C4
McKittrick, *U.S.A.* 111 K7
Macklin, *Canada* 103 C7
Macksville, *Australia* 95 E5
McLaughlin, *U.S.A.* 112 C4
Maclean, *Australia* 95 D5
McLean, *U.S.A.* 113 H4
McLeansboro, *U.S.A.* 112 F10
Maclear, *S. Africa* 89 E4
Maclear, C., *Malawi* 87 E3
Macleay →, *Australia* 95 E5
McLennan, *Canada* 102 B5
McLeod →, *Canada* 102 C5
MacLeod, B., *Canada* 103 A7
McLeod, L., *Australia* 93 D1
MacLeod Lake, *Canada* 102 C4
McLoughlin, Mt., *U.S.A.* 108 E2
McMechen, *U.S.A.* 116 G4
McMinnville, *Oreg., U.S.A.* 108 D2
McMinnville, *Tenn., U.S.A.* 115 H3
McMurdo Sd., *Antarctica* 5 D11
McMurray = Fort McMurray, *Canada* 102 B6
McMurray, *U.S.A.* 110 B4
Macodoene, *Mozam.* 89 C6
Macomb, *U.S.A.* 112 E9
Macomer, *Italy* 42 B1
Mâcon, *France* 19 F11
Macon, *Ga., U.S.A.* 115 J4
Macon, *Miss., U.S.A.* 115 J1
Macon, *Mo., U.S.A.* 112 F8
Macossa, *Mozam.* 87 F3
Macoun L., *Canada* 103 B8
Macovane, *Mozam.* 89 C6
McPherson, *U.S.A.* 112 F6
McPherson Pk., *U.S.A.* 111 L7
McPherson Ra., *Australia* 95 D5
Macquarie →, *Australia* 95 E4
Macquarie Harbour, *Australia* 95 G4
Macquarie Is., *Pac. Oc.* 96 N7
MacRobertson Land, *Antarctica* 5 D6
Macroom, *Ireland* 12 E3
MacTier, *Canada* 116 A5
Macubela, *Mozam.* 87 F4
Macugnaga, *Italy* 40 C4
Macuira △, *Colombia* 121 D5
Macuiza, *Mozam.* 87 F3
Macumba, The →, *Australia* 95 D2
Macuro, *Venezuela* 125 K15
Macusani, *Peru* 124 F4
Macuse, *Mozam.* 87 F4
Macuspana, *Mexico* 119 D6
Macusse, *Angola* 88 B3
Mada →, *Nigeria* 83 D6
Ma'dabā □, *Jordan* 74 D4
Madadeni, *S. Africa* 89 D5
Madagali, *Nigeria* 83 C7
Madagascar ■, *Africa* 89 C8
Madā'in Sālih, *Si. Arabia* 70 E3
Madama, *Niger* 79 D8
Madame, I., *Canada* 105 C7
Madan, *Bulgaria* 45 E8
Madaoua, *Niger* 83 C6
Madara, *Nigeria* 83 C7
Madaripur, *Bangla.* 67 H17
Madauk, *Burma* 67 L20
Madawaska, *Canada* 116 A7
Madawaska →, *Canada* 116 A8
Madaya, *Burma* 67 H20
Madbar, *Sudan* 81 F3
Maddalena, *Italy* 42 A2
Maddaloni, *Italy* 43 A7
Madeira, *Atl. Oc.* 48 D3
Madeira →, *Brazil* 124 D7
Madeleine, Îs. de la, *Canada* 105 C7
Maden, *Turkey* 73 C8
Madera, *Mexico* 118 B3
Madera, *Calif., U.S.A.* 110 J6
Madera, *Pa., U.S.A.* 116 F6
Madha, *India* 66 L9
Madhavpur, *India* 68 J3
Madhepura, *India* 69 F12
Madhubani, *India* 69 F12
Madhupur, *India* 69 G12
Madhya Pradesh □, *India* 68 J8
Madidi →, *Bolivia* 124 F5
Madikeri, *India* 66 N9
Madikwe ⌓, *S. Africa* 89 D5
Madill, *U.S.A.* 113 H6
Madimba, *Dem. Rep. of the Congo* 84 E3
Ma'din, *Syria* 70 C3
Madina, *Mali* 82 C3
Madinani, *Ivory C.* 82 D3
Madingou, *Congo* 84 E2
Madirovalo, *Madag.* 89 B8
Madison, *Calif., U.S.A.* 110 G5
Madison, *Fla., U.S.A.* 115 K4
Madison, *Ind., U.S.A.* 114 F3
Madison, *Nebr., U.S.A.* 112 E6
Madison, *Ohio, U.S.A.* 116 E3
Madison, *S. Dak., U.S.A.* 112 D6
Madison, *Wis., U.S.A.* 112 D10
Madison →, *U.S.A.* 108 D8
Madison Heights, *U.S.A.* 114 G6
Madisonville, *Ky., U.S.A.* 114 G2
Madisonville, *Tex., U.S.A.* 113 K7
Madista, *Botswana* 88 C4
Madiun, *Indonesia* 63 G14
Madoc, *Canada* 116 B7
Madol, *Sudan* 81 F2
Madon →, *France* 19 D13
Madona, *Latvia* 9 H22
Madonie, *Italy* 42 E6
Madonna di Campíglio, *Italy* 40 B7
Madra Dağı, *Turkey* 47 B9
Madrakah, Ra's al, *Oman* 75 D6
Madras = Chennai, *India* 66 N12
Madras = Tamil Nadu □, *India* 66 P10
Madras, *U.S.A.* 108 D3
Madre, Laguna, *U.S.A.* 113 M6
Madre, Sierra, *Phil.* 61 C5
Madre de Dios →, *Bolivia* 124 F5
Madre de Dios, I., *Chile* 128 G1
Madre del Sur, Sierra, *Mexico* 119 D5
Madre Occidental, Sierra, *Mexico* 118 B3
Madre Oriental, Sierra, *Mexico* 118 C5
Madri, *India* 68 G5
Madrid, *Spain* 36 E7
Madrid, *U.S.A.* 117 B9
Madrid □, *Spain* 36 E7
Madrid Barajas ✕ (MAD), *Spain* 36 E7
Madridejos, *Spain* 37 F7
Madrigal de las Altas Torres, *Spain* 36 D6
Madrona, Sierra, *Spain* 37 G6
Madroñera, *Spain* 37 F5
Madu, *Sudan* 81 E2
Madura, *Australia* 93 F4
Madura, *Indonesia* 63 G15
Madura, Selat, *Indonesia* 63 G15
Madurai, *India* 66 Q11
Madurantakam, *India* 66 N11
Madzhalis, *Russia* 35 J8
Mae Chan, *Thailand* 64 B2
Mae Hong Son, *Thailand* 64 C2
Mae Khlong →, *Thailand* 64 F3
Mae Phrik, *Thailand* 64 D2
Mae Ping △, *Thailand* 64 D2
Mae Ramat, *Thailand* 64 D2
Mae Rim, *Thailand* 64 C2
Mae Sot, *Thailand* 64 D2
Mae Suai, *Thailand* 58 H2
Mae Tha, *Thailand* 64 C2
Mae Wong △, *Thailand* 64 E2
Mae Yom △, *Thailand* 64 C3
Maebashi, *Japan* 55 F9
Maella, *Spain* 38 D5
Maesteg, *U.K.* 15 F4
Maestra, Sierra, *Cuba* 120 B4
Maevatanana, *Madag.* 89 B8
Mafeking = Mafikeng, *S. Africa* 88 D4
Mafeking, *Canada* 103 C8
Maféré, *Ivory C.* 82 D4
Mafeteng, *Lesotho* 88 D4
Maffra, *Australia* 95 F4
Mafia I., *Tanzania* 86 D4
Mafikeng, *S. Africa* 88 D4
Mafra, *Brazil* 127 B6
Mafra, *Portugal* 37 G1
Mafungabusi Plateau, *Zimbabwe* 87 F2
Magadan, *Russia* 53 D16
Magadi, *Kenya* 86 C4
Magadi, L., *Kenya* 86 C4
Magaliesburg, *S. Africa* 89 D4
Magallanes, Estrecho de, *Chile* 128 G2
Magaluf, *Spain* 39 F7
Magangué, *Colombia* 124 B4
Magaria, *Niger* 83 C6

Magburaka, *S. Leone* 82 D2
Magdalen Is. = Madeleine, Îs. de la, *Canada* 105 C7
Magdalena, *Argentina* 126 D4
Magdalena, *Bolivia* 124 F6
Magdalena, *Mexico* 118 A2
Magdalena, *U.S.A.* 109 J10
Magdalena →, *Colombia* 124 A4
Magdalena →, *Mexico* 118 A2
Magdalena, B., *Mexico* 118 C2
Magdalena, Llano de la, *Mexico* 118 C2
Magdeburg, *Germany* 24 C7
Magdelaine Cays, *Australia* 94 B5
Magdub, *Sudan* 81 E2
Magee, *U.S.A.* 113 K10
Magelang, *Indonesia* 63 G14
Magellan's Str. = Magallanes, Estrecho de, *Chile* 128 G2
Magenta, *Italy* 40 C5
Magenta, L., *Australia* 93 F2
Magerøya, *Norway* 8 A21
Maggia →, *Switz.* 25 J4
Maggiorasca, Mte., *Italy* 40 D6
Maggiore, Lago, *Italy* 40 B5
Maggotty, *Jamaica* 120 a
Maghâgha, *Egypt* 80 B3
Maghama, *Mauritania* 82 B2
Magherafelt, *U.K.* 12 B5
Maghreb, *N. Afr.* 78 B5
Magione, *Italy* 41 E9
Magistralnyy, *Russia* 53 D11
Maglaj, *Bos.-H.* 28 F3
Magliano in Toscana, *Italy* 41 F8
Máglie, *Italy* 43 B11
Magnac-Laval, *France* 20 B5
Magnetic Pole (North), *Canada* 4 A2
Magnetic Pole (South), *Antarctica* 5 C9
Magnisía □, *Greece* 46 B5
Magnitogorsk, *Russia* 52 D6
Magnolia, *Ark., U.S.A.* 113 J8
Magnolia, *Miss., U.S.A.* 113 K9
Magny-en-Vexin, *France* 19 C8
Mago △, *Ethiopia* 81 F4
Magog, *Canada* 117 A12
Magoro, *Uganda* 86 B3
Magoša = Famagusta, *Cyprus* 49 D12
Magouládhes, *Greece* 49 A3
Magoye, *Zambia* 87 F2
Magozal, *Mexico* 119 C5
Magpie, L., *Canada* 105 B7
Magrath, *Canada* 102 D6
Magre →, *Spain* 39 F4
Magrur, *Sudan* 81 E3
Magrur, Wadi →, *Sudan* 81 D2
Magta Lahjar, *Mauritania* 82 B2
Maguan, *China* 58 F5
Maguarinho, C., *Brazil* 125 D9
Magude, *Mozam.* 89 D5
Magurski △, *Poland* 31 J8
Mağusa = Famagusta, *Cyprus* 49 D12
Maguse L., *Canada* 103 A9
Maguse Pt., *Canada* 103 A10
Magvana, *India* 68 H3
Magwe, *Burma* 67 J19
Magwe, *Sudan* 81 G3
Maha Sarakham, *Thailand* 64 D4
Mahābād, *Iran* 70 B5
Mahabharat Lekh, *Nepal* 69 E10
Mahabo, *Madag.* 89 C7
Mahadeo Hills, *India* 69 H8
Mahaffey, *U.S.A.* 116 F6
Mahagi, *Dem. Rep. of the Congo* 86 B3
Mahajamba →, *Madag.* 89 B8
Mahajamba, Helodranon' i, *Madag.* 89 B8
Mahajan, *India* 68 E5
Mahajanga, *Madag.* 89 B8
Mahajanga □, *Madag.* 89 B8
Mahajilo →, *Madag.* 89 B8
Mahakam →, *Indonesia* 62 E5
Mahalapye, *Botswana* 88 C4
Mahale Mts., *Tanzania* 86 D3
Mahale Mts. △, *Tanzania* 86 D2
Maḥallāt, *Iran* 71 C6
Māhān, *Iran* 71 D8
Mahan →, *India* 69 H10
Mahanadi →, *India* 67 J15
Mahananda →, *India* 69 G12
Mahanoro, *Madag.* 89 B8
Mahanoy City, *U.S.A.* 117 F8
Maharashtra □, *India* 66 J9
Mahasham, W. →, *Egypt* 74 E3
Mahasoa, *Madag.* 89 C8
Mahasolo, *Madag.* 89 B8
Mahattat ash Shīdīyah, *Jordan* 74 F4
Mahattat 'Unayzah, *Jordan* 74 E4
Mahavavy →, *Madag.* 89 B8
Mahaxay, *Laos* 64 D5
Mahbubnagar, *India* 66 L10
Maḥḍah, *Oman* 71 E7
Mahdia, *Tunisia* 79 A8
Mahe, *India* 69 C8
Mahendragarh, *India* 68 E7
Mahenge, *Tanzania* 87 D4
Maheno, *N.Z.* 91 L3
Mahesana, *India* 68 H5
Maheshwar, *India* 68 H6
Mahgawan, *India* 69 F8
Mahi →, *India* 68 H5
Mahia Pen., *N.Z.* 91 H6
Mahilyow, *Belarus* 32 F6
Mahinerangi, L., *N.Z.* 91 L2
Mahmiya, *Sudan* 81 D3
Mahmud Kot, *Pakistan* 68 D4
Mahmudia, *Romania* 29 E14
Mahmudiye, *Turkey* 47 B12
Mahmutbey, *Turkey* 45 E12
Mahnomen, *U.S.A.* 112 B7
Mahoba, *India* 69 G8
Mahón = Maó, *Spain* 48 B11
Mahon, Menorca ✕ (MAH), *Spain* 38 F9
Mahone Bay, *Canada* 105 D7
Mahopac, *U.S.A.* 117 E11
Mahuta, *Nigeria* 83 C5
Mahuva, *India* 68 J4
Mahya Daği, *Turkey* 45 E11
Mai-Ndombe, L., *Dem. Rep. of the Congo* 84 E3
Mai-Sai, *Thailand* 58 G2
Mai Thon, Ko, *Thailand* 65 a
Maia, *Portugal* 36 D2
Maia, *Spain* 38 B3
Maials, *Spain* 38 D5
Maîche, *France* 19 E13
Maicurú →, *Brazil* 125 D8
Máida, *Italy* 43 D9
Maidan Khula, *Afghan.* 68 C3
Maidenhead, *U.K.* 15 F7
Maidstone, *Canada* 103 C7
Maidstone, *U.K.* 15 F8
Maiduguri, *Nigeria* 83 C7
Maiella △, *Italy* 41 F11
Măieruş, *Romania* 29 E10
Maigatari, *Nigeria* 83 C6
Maignelay Montigny, *France* 19 C9
Maigo, *Phil.* 61 G5
Maigudo, *Ethiopia* 81 F4
Maihar, *India* 69 G9
Maijdi, *Bangla.* 67 H17
Maikala Ra., *India* 67 J12
Maiko △, *Dem. Rep. of the Congo* 86 C2
Mailani, *India* 69 E9
Maillezais, *France* 20 B3
Mailsi, *Pakistan* 68 E5
Main →, *Germany* 25 F4
Main →, *U.K.* 12 B5
Main Range △, *Australia* 95 D5
Main Ridge, *Trin. & Tob.* 125 J16
Mainburg, *Germany* 25 G7
Maine, *France* 18 D6
Maine □, *U.S.A.* 115 C11
Maine →, *Ireland* 12 D2
Maine-et-Loire □, *France* 18 E6
Maïne-Soroa, *Niger* 83 C7
Maingkwan, *Burma* 67 F20
Mainit, L., *Phil.* 61 G6
Mainland, *Orkney, U.K.* 13 C5
Mainland, *Shet., U.K.* 13 A7
Mainoru, *Australia* 94 A1
Mainpuri, *India* 69 F8
Maintal, *Germany* 25 E4
Maintenon, *France* 19 D8
Maintirano, *Madag.* 89 B7
Mainz, *Germany* 25 E4
Maipú, *Argentina* 126 D4
Maiquetía, *Venezuela* 124 A5
Máira →, *Italy* 40 D4
Mairabari, *India* 67 F18
Maisí, *Cuba* 121 B5
Maisí, Pta. de, *Cuba* 121 B5
Maitland, *N.S.W., Australia* 95 E5
Maitland, *S. Austral., Australia* 95 E2
Maitland →, *Canada* 116 C3
Maitri, *Antarctica* 5 D3
Maiyema, *Nigeria* 83 C5
Maiyuan, *China* 59 E11
Maiz, Is. del, *Nic.* 120 D3
Maizuru, *Japan* 55 G7
Majalengka, *Indonesia* 63 G13
Majene, *Indonesia* 63 E5
Majete ⌓, *Malawi* 87 F3
Majevica, *Bos.-H.* 28 F3
Maji, *Ethiopia* 81 F4
Majiang, *China* 58 D6
Majorca = Mallorca, *Spain* 48 B10
Maka, *Senegal* 82 C2
Makaha, *Zimbabwe* 89 B5
Makak, *Cameroon* 83 E7
Makalamabedi, *Botswana* 88 C3
Makale, *Indonesia* 63 E5
Makamba, *Burundi* 86 C2
Makari, *Cameroon* 83 C7
Makarikari = Makgadikgadi Salt Pans, *Botswana* 88 C4
Makarov Basin, *Arctic* 4 A
Makarovo, *Russia* 53 D11
Makarska, *Croatia* 41 E14
Makaryev, *Russia* 34 B6
Makasar = Ujung Pandang, *Indonesia* 63 F5
Makasar, Selat, *Indonesia* 63 E5
Makasar, Str. of = Makasar, Selat, *Indonesia* 63 E5
Makat, *Kazakhstan* 52 E6
Makedonija = Macedonia ■, *Europe* 44 E5
Makeni, *S. Leone* 82 D2
Makeyevka = Makiyivka, *Ukraine* 33 H9
Makgadikgadi △, *Botswana* 88 C3
Makgadikgadi Salt Pans, *Botswana* 88 C4
Makhachkala, *Russia* 35 J8
Makhado = Louis Trichardt, *S. Africa* 89 C4
Makharadze = Ozurgeti, *Georgia* 35 K5
Makhfar al Buşayyah, *Iraq* 70 D5
Makhmūr, *Iraq* 70 C4
Makian, *Indonesia* 63 D7
Makindu, *Kenya* 86 C4
Makinsk, *Kazakhstan* 52 D8
Makiv, *Ukraine* 29 B11
Makiyivka, *Ukraine* 33 H9
Makkah, *Si. Arabia* 75 C2
Makkovik, *Canada* 105 A8
Makó, *Hungary* 28 D5
Mako, *Senegal* 82 C2
Makokou, *Gabon* 84 D2
Makongo, *Dem. Rep. of the Congo* 86 B2
Makoro, *Dem. Rep. of the Congo* 86 B2
Maków Mazowiecki, *Poland* 31 F8
Maków Podhalański, *Poland* 31 J6
Makrá, *Greece* 47 E7
Makrai, *India* 66 H10
Makran Coast Range, *Pakistan* 66 G4
Makrana, *India* 68 F6
Makrany, *Belarus* 31 G11
Mákri, *Greece* 45 F9
Makriyialos, *Greece* 49 D7
Mākū, *Iran* 70 B5
Makunda, *Botswana* 88 C3
Makung, *Taiwan* 59 F12
Makurazaki, *Japan* 55 J5
Makurdi, *Nigeria* 83 D6
Makūyeh, *Iran* 71 D7
Makwassie, *S. Africa* 88 D4
Makwiro, *Zimbabwe* 89 B5
Mâl, *Mauritania* 82 B2
Mal B., *Ireland* 12 D2
Mala, Pta., *Panama* 120 E3
Mala Belozërka, *Ukraine* 33 J8
Malá Fatra △, *Slovak Rep.* 27 B12
Mala Kapela, *Croatia* 41 D12
Mała Panew →, *Poland* 31 H4
Mala Vyska, *Ukraine* 33 H6
Malabang, *Phil.* 61 H6
Malabar Coast, *India* 66 P9
Malabon, *Phil.* 61 D4
Malabu, *Nigeria* 83 D7
Malacca, Straits of, *Indonesia* 65 L3
Malacky, *Slovak Rep.* 27 C10
Malad City, *U.S.A.* 108 E7
Maladeta, *Spain* 38 C5
Maladzyechna, *Belarus* 32 E4
Málaga, *Spain* 37 J6
Málaga □, *Spain* 37 J6
Malagarasi, *Tanzania* 86 D3
Malagarasi →, *Tanzania* 86 D2
Malagasy Rep. = Madagascar ■, *Africa* 89 C8
Malagón, *Spain* 37 F7
Malagón →, *Spain* 37 H3
Malahide, *Ireland* 12 C5
Malaimbandy, *Madag.* 89 C8
Malakâl, *Sudan* 81 F3
Malakand, *Pakistan* 68 B4
Malakwal, *Pakistan* 68 C5
Malamala, *Indonesia* 63 E6
Malanda, *Australia* 94 B4
Malang, *Indonesia* 63 G15
Malangen, *Norway* 8 B18
Malanje, *Angola* 84 F3
Mälaren, *Sweden* 10 E11
Malargüe, *Argentina* 126 D2
Malartic, *Canada* 104 C4
Malaryta, *Belarus* 31 G11
Malatya, *Turkey* 70 B3
Malawi ■, *Africa* 87 E3
Malawi, L. = Nyasa, L., *Africa* 87 E3
Malay Pen., *Asia* 65 J3
Malaya Belozërka = Mala Belozërka, *Ukraine* 33 J8
Malaya Vishera, *Russia* 32 C7
Malaya Viska = Mala Vyska, *Ukraine* 33 H6
Malaybalay, *Phil.* 61 G6
Malāyer, *Iran* 71 C6
Malaysia ■, *Asia* 65 K4
Malazgirt, *Turkey* 70 B4
Malbaza, *Niger* 83 C6
Malbon, *Australia* 94 C3
Malbooma, *Australia* 95 E1
Malbork, *Poland* 30 D6
Malcésine, *Italy* 40 C7
Malchin, *Germany* 24 B8
Malchow, *Germany* 24 B8
Malcolm, *Australia* 93 E3
Malcolm, Pt., *Australia* 93 F3
Malczyce, *Poland* 31 G3
Maldah, *India* 69 G13
Maldegem, *Belgium* 17 C3
Malden, *Mass., U.S.A.* 117 D13
Malden, *Mo., U.S.A.* 113 G10
Malden I., *Kiribati* 97 H12
Maldives ■, *Ind. Oc.* 50 J11
Maldon, *U.K.* 15 F8
Maldonado, *Uruguay* 127 C5
Maldonado, Punta, *Mexico* 119 D5
Malè, *Italy* 40 B7
Male, *Maldives* 51 J11
Malé Karpaty, *Slovak Rep.* 27 C10
Maléa, Ákra, *Greece* 46 E5
Malegaon, *India* 66 J9
Malei, *Mozam.* 87 F4
Malek, *Sudan* 81 F3
Malek Kandī, *Iran* 70 B5
Malela, *Dem. Rep. of the Congo* 86 C2
Malema, *Mozam.* 87 E4
Máleme, *Greece* 49 D5
Målerås, *Sweden* 11 H9
Malerkotla, *India* 68 D6
Máles, *Greece* 49 D7
Malesherbes, *France* 19 D9
Maleshevska Planina, *Europe* 44 E7
Malesína, *Greece* 46 C5
Malestroit, *France* 18 E4
Malfa, *Italy* 43 D7
Malgobek, *Russia* 35 J7
Malgomaj, *Sweden* 8 D17
Malgrat de Mar, *Spain* 38 D7
Malha, *Sudan* 81 D2
Malhargarh, *India* 68 G6
Malheur →, *U.S.A.* 108 D5
Malheur L., *U.S.A.* 108 E4
Mali, *Guinea* 82 C2
Mali ■, *Africa* 82 B4
Mali →, *Burma* 67 G20
Mali Kanal, *Serbia & M.* 28 E4
Mali Kyun, *Burma* 64 F2
Malibu, *U.S.A.* 111 L8
Maliku, *Indonesia* 63 E6
Malili, *Indonesia* 63 E6
Målilla, *Sweden* 11 G9
Malimba, Mts., *Dem. Rep. of the Congo* 86 D2
Malin Hd., *Ireland* 12 A4
Malin Pen., *Ireland* 12 A4
Malindi, *Kenya* 86 C5
Malines = Mechelen, *Belgium* 17 C4
Malino, *Indonesia* 63 D6
Malinyi, *Tanzania* 87 D4
Malipo, *China* 58 F5
Maliq, *Albania* 44 F4
Malita, *Phil.* 63 C7
Maliwun, *Burma* 62 B1
Maliya, *India* 68 H4
Maljenik, *Serbia & M.* 44 C5
Malka Mari △, *Kenya* 86 B5
Malkara, *Turkey* 45 F10
Małkinia Górna, *Poland* 31 F9
Malko Tŭrnovo, *Bulgaria* 45 E11
Mallacoota Inlet, *Australia* 95 F4
Mallaig, *U.K.* 13 D3
Mallaoua, *Niger* 83 C6
Mallawan, *India* 69 F9
Mallawi, *Egypt* 80 B3
Mallemort, *France* 21 E9
Mälles Venosta, *Italy* 40 B7
Mállia, *Greece* 49 D7
Mallión, Kólpos, *Greece* 49 D7
Mallorca, *Spain* 48 B10
Mallorytown, *Canada* 117 B9
Mallow, *Ireland* 12 D3
Malmbäck, *Sweden* 11 G8
Malmberget, *Sweden* 8 C19
Malmédy, *Belgium* 17 D6
Malmesbury, *S. Africa* 88 E2
Malmivaara = Malmberget, *Sweden* 8 C19
Malmköping, *Sweden* 10 E10
Malmö, *Sweden* 11 J7
Malmslätt, *Sweden* 11 F9
Malmyzh, *Russia* 34 B10
Malnaş, *Romania* 29 D10
Malo Konare, *Bulgaria* 45 D8
Maloarkhangelsk, *Russia* 33 F9
Malolos, *Phil.* 63 B6
Malolotja ⌓, *Swaziland* 89 D5
Malombe L., *Malawi* 87 E4
Małomice, *Poland* 31 G2
Malomir, *Bulgaria* 45 D10
Malone, *U.S.A.* 117 B10
Malong, *China* 58 E4
Małopolskie □, *Poland* 31 J7
Malorad, *Bulgaria* 44 C7
Måløy, *Norway* 9 F11
Maloyaroslovets, *Russia* 32 E9
Malpartida, *Spain* 37 F4
Malpaso, *Canary Is.* 48 G1
Malpelo, I. de, *Colombia* 124 C2
Malpica de Bergantiños, *Spain* 36 B2
Malpur, *India* 68 H5
Malpura, *India* 68 F6
Mals = Mälles Venosta, *Italy* 40 B7
Malta, *Idaho, U.S.A.* 108 E7
Malta, *Mont., U.S.A.* 108 B10
Malta ■, *Europe* 49 D2
Maltahöhe, *Namibia* 88 C2
Maltepe, *Turkey* 45 F13
Malton, *Canada* 116 C5
Malton, *U.K.* 14 C7
Maluku, *Indonesia* 63 E7
Maluku □, *Indonesia* 63 E7
Maluku Sea = Molucca Sea, *Indonesia* 63 E6
Maluku Utara □, *Indonesia* 63 D7
Malumfashi, *Nigeria* 83 C6
Malung, *Sweden* 10 D7
Malungsfors, *Sweden* 10 D7
Maluwe, *Ghana* 82 D4
Malvan, *India* 66 L8
Malvern, *U.S.A.* 113 H8
Malvern Hills, *U.K.* 15 E5
Malvinas, Is. = Falkland Is. ☑, *Atl. Oc.* 128 G5
Malý Dunaj →, *Slovak Rep.* 27 D11
Malya, *Tanzania* 86 C3
Malye Derbety, *Russia* 35 G7
Malyn, *Ukraine* 33 G5
Malyy Lyakhovskiy, Ostrov, *Russia* 53 B15
Mama, *Russia* 53 D12
Mamadysh, *Russia* 34 C10
Mamanguape, *Brazil* 125 E11
Mamarr Mitlā, *Egypt* 74 E1
Mamasa, *Indonesia* 63 E5
Mambasa, *Dem. Rep. of the Congo* 86 B2
Mamberamo →, *Indonesia* 63 E9
Mambilima Falls, *Zambia* 87 E2
Mambirima, *Dem. Rep. of the Congo* 87 E2
Mambo, *Tanzania* 86 C4
Mambrui, *Kenya* 86 C5
Mamburao, *Phil.* 61 E4
Mameigwess L., *Canada* 104 B2
Mamers, *France* 18 D7
Mamfé, *Cameroon* 83 D6
Mammoth, *U.S.A.* 109 K8
Mammoth Cave △, *U.S.A.* 114 G3
Mamonovo, *Russia* 30 D6
Mamoré →, *Bolivia* 124 F5
Mamou, *Guinea* 82 C2
Mamoudzou, *Mayotte* 77 H8
Mampatá, *Guinea-Biss.* 82 C2
Mampikony, *Madag.* 89 B8
Mampong, *Ghana* 83 D4
Mamry, Jezioro, *Poland* 30 D8
Mamuju, *Indonesia* 63 E5
Mamuno, *Botswana* 88 C3
Mamuras, *Albania* 44 E3
Man, *Ivory C.* 82 D3
Man, I. of, *U.K.* 14 C3
Man-Bazar, *India* 69 H12
Man Na, *Burma* 67 H20
Mana →, *Fr. Guiana* 125 B8
Mana Pools △, *Zimbabwe* 87 F2
Manaar, G. of = Mannar, G. of, *Asia* 66 Q11
Manacapuru, *Brazil* 124 D6
Manacor, *Spain* 48 B10
Manado, *Indonesia* 63 D6
Managua, *Nic.* 120 D2
Managua, L. de, *Nic.* 120 D2
Manakara, *Madag.* 89 C8
Manali, *India* 68 C7
Manama = Al Manāmah, *Bahrain* 71 E6
Manambao →, *Madag.* 89 B7
Manambato, *Madag.* 89 A8
Manambolo →, *Madag.* 89 B7
Manambolosy, *Madag.* 89 B8
Mananara, *Madag.* 89 B8
Mananara ⌓, *Madag.* 89 B8
Mananara →, *Madag.* 89 C8
Mananjary, *Madag.* 89 C8
Manankoro, *Mali* 82 C3
Manantenina, *Madag.* 89 C8
Manaos = Manaus, *Brazil* 124 D7
Manapire →, *Venezuela* 124 B5
Manapouri, *N.Z.* 91 L1
Manapouri, L., *N.Z.* 91 L1
Manaqil, *Sudan* 81 E3
Manār, Jabal, *Yemen* 75 E3
Manaravolo, *Madag.* 89 C8
Manas, *China* 60 B3
Manas →, *India* 67 F17
Manaslu, *Nepal* 69 E11
Manasquan, *U.S.A.* 117 F10
Manassa, *U.S.A.* 109 H11
Manatí, *Puerto Rico* 121 d
Manaung, *Burma* 67 K18
Manaus, *Brazil* 124 D7
Manavgat, *Turkey* 72 D4
Manawan L., *Canada* 103 B8
Manay, *Phil.* 61 H7
Manbij, *Syria* 70 B3
Mancha Real, *Spain* 37 H7
Manche □, *France* 18 C5
Manchegorsk, *Russia* 52 C4
Manchester, *U.K.* 14 D5
Manchester, *Calif., U.S.A.* 110 G3
Manchester, *Conn., U.S.A.* 117 E12
Manchester, *Ga., U.S.A.* 115 J3
Manchester, *Iowa, U.S.A.* 112 D9
Manchester, *Ky., U.S.A.* 114 G4
Manchester, *N.H., U.S.A.* 117 D13
Manchester, *N.Y., U.S.A.* 116 D7
Manchester, *Pa., U.S.A.* 117 F8
Manchester, *Tenn., U.S.A.* 115 H2
Manchester, *Vt., U.S.A.* 117 C11
Manchester International ✕ (MAN), *U.K.* 14 D5
Manchester L., *Canada* 103 A7
Manchhar L., *Pakistan* 68 F2
Manchuria = Dongbei, *China* 53 E13
Manchurian Plain, *China* 50 E16
Manciano, *Italy* 41 F8
Mancifa, *Ethiopia* 81 F5
Mand →, *India* 69 J10
Mand →, *Iran* 71 D7
Manda, *Ludewe, Tanzania* 87 E3
Manda, *Mbeya, Tanzania* 86 D3
Manda, *Mbeya, Tanzania* 87 D3
Mandabé, *Madag.* 89 C7
Mandaguari, *Brazil* 127 A5
Mandah = Töhöm, *Mongolia* 56 B5
Mandal, *Norway* 9 G12
Mandala, Puncak, *Indonesia* 63 E10
Mandalay, *Burma* 67 J20
Mandale = Mandalay, *Burma* 67 J20
Mandalgarh, *India* 68 G6
Mandalgovi, *Mongolia* 56 B4
Mandalī, *Iraq* 70 C5
Mandan, *U.S.A.* 112 B4
Mandaon, *Phil.* 61 E5
Mandar, Teluk, *Indonesia* 63 E5
Mándas, *Italy* 42 C2
Mandaue, *Phil.* 61 F5
Mandelieu-la-Napoule, *France* 21 E10
Mandera, *Kenya* 86 B5
Mandeville, *Jamaica* 120 a
Mandi, *India* 68 D7
Mandi Dabwali, *India* 68 E6
Mandiana, *Guinea* 82 C3
Mandimba, *Mozam.* 87 E4
Mandioli, *Indonesia* 63 E7
Mandla, *India* 69 H9
Mandø, *Denmark* 11 J2
Mandorah, *Australia* 92 B5
Mandoto, *Madag.* 89 B8
Mandoúdhion, *Greece* 46 C5
Mándra, *Greece* 46 C5
Mandra, *Pakistan* 68 C5
Mandrákhi, *Greece* 47 E9
Mandrare →, *Madag.* 89 D8
Mandritsara, *Madag.* 89 B8
Mandronarivo, *Madag.* 89 C8
Mandsaur, *India* 68 G6
Mandurah, *Australia* 93 F2
Mandúria, *Italy* 43 B10
Mandvi, *India* 68 H3
Mandya, *India* 66 N10
Mandzai, *Pakistan* 68 D2
Mané, *Burkina Faso* 83 C4
Maneh, *Iran* 71 B8
Manenggouba, Mts., *Cameroon* 83 E6
Manera, *Madag.* 89 C7
Manérbio, *Italy* 40 C7
Maneroo Cr. →, *Australia* 94 C3
Manfalût, *Egypt* 80 B3
Manfredónia, *Italy* 41 G12
Manfredónia, G. di, *Italy* 41 G13
Manga, *Burkina Faso* 83 C4
Manga, *Niger* 83 C7
Mangabeiras, Chapada das, *Brazil* 125 F9
Mangalia, *Romania* 29 G13
Mangalore, *India* 66 N9
Mangan, *India* 69 F13
Mangaung, *S. Africa* 85 K5

Mangawan, *India* 69 G9
Mangaweka, *N.Z.* 91 H5
Manggar, *Indonesia* 62 E3
Manggawitu, *Indonesia* 63 E8
Manggis, *Indonesia* 63 J18
Mangindrano, *Madag.* 89 A8
Mangkalihat, Tanjung, *Indonesia* 63 D5
Mangla, *Pakistan* 68 C5
Mangla Dam, *Pakistan* 69 C5
Manglaur, *India* 68 E7
Mangnai, *China* 60 C4
Mango, *Togo* 83 C5
Mangoche, *Malawi* 87 E4
Mangoky →, *Madag.* 89 C7
Mangole, *Indonesia* 63 E6
Mangombe, *Dem. Rep. of the Congo* 86 C2
Mangonui, *N.Z.* 91 F4
Mangoro →, *Madag.* 89 B8
Mangrol, *Mad. P., India* 68 J4
Mangrol, *Raj., India* 68 G6
Mangualde, *Portugal* 36 E3
Mangueira, L. da, *Brazil* 127 C5
Mangum, *U.S.A.* 113 H5
Mangyshlak, Poluostrov, *Kazakhstan* 52 E6
Manhattan, *U.S.A.* 112 F6
Manhiça, *Mozam.* 89 D5
Mania →, *Madag.* 89 B8
Maniago, *Italy* 41 B9
Manica, *Mozam.* 89 B5
Manica □, *Mozam.* 89 B5
Manicaland □, *Zimbabwe* 87 F3
Manicoré, *Brazil* 124 E6
Manicouagan →, *Canada* 105 C6
Manicouagan, Rés., *Canada* 105 B6
Maniema □, *Dem. Rep. of the Congo* 86 C2
Manīfah, *Si. Arabia* 71 E6
Manifold, C., *Australia* 94 C5
Maniganggo, *China* 58 B2
Manigotagan, *Canada* 103 C9
Manigotagan →, *Canada* 103 C9
Manihari, *India* 69 G12
Manihiki, *Cook Is.* 97 J11
Manika, Plateau de la, *Dem. Rep. of the Congo* 87 E2
Manikpur, *India* 69 G9
Manila, *Phil.* 61 D4
Manila, *U.S.A.* 108 F9
Manila B., *Phil.* 61 D4
Manilla, *Australia* 95 E5
Manimpé, *Mali* 82 C3
Maningrida, *Australia* 94 A1
Maninian, *Ivory C.* 82 C3
Manipur □, *India* 67 G19
Manipur →, *Burma* 67 H19
Manisa, *Turkey* 47 C9
Manisa □, *Turkey* 47 C9
Manistee, *U.S.A.* 114 C2
Manistee →, *U.S.A.* 114 C2
Manistique, *U.S.A.* 114 C2
Manitoba □, *Canada* 103 B9
Manitoba, L., *Canada* 103 C9
Manitou, *Canada* 103 D9
Manitou, L., *Canada* 105 B6
Manitou Is., *U.S.A.* 114 C3
Manitou L., *Canada* 103 C7
Manitou Springs, *U.S.A.* 112 F2
Manitoulin I., *Canada* 104 C3
Manitouwadge, *Canada* 104 C2
Manitowoc, *U.S.A.* 114 C2
Manizales, *Colombia* 124 B3
Manja, *Madag.* 89 C7
Manjacaze, *Mozam.* 89 C5
Manjakandriana, *Madag.* 89 B8
Manjhand, *Pakistan* 68 G3
Manjil, *Iran* 71 B6
Manjimup, *Australia* 93 F2
Manjra →, *India* 66 K10
Mankato, *Kans., U.S.A.* 112 F5
Mankato, *Minn., U.S.A.* 112 C8
Mankayane, *Swaziland* 89 D5
Mankera, *Pakistan* 68 D4
Mankim, *Cameroon* 83 D7
Mankono, *Ivory C.* 82 D3
Mankota, *Canada* 103 D7
Manlay = Üydzin, *Mongolia* 56 B4
Manlleu, *Spain* 38 C7
Manmad, *India* 66 J9
Mann Ranges, *Australia* 93 E5
Manna, *Indonesia* 62 E2
Mannahill, *Australia* 95 E3
Mannar, *Sri Lanka* 66 Q11
Mannar, G. of, *Asia* 66 Q11
Mannar I., *Sri Lanka* 66 Q11
Mannheim, *Germany* 25 F4
Manning, *Canada* 102 B5
Manning, *Oreg., U.S.A.* 110 E3
Manning, *S.C., U.S.A.* 115 J5
Mannu →, *Italy* 42 C2
Mannu, C., *Italy* 42 B1
Mannum, *Australia* 95 E2
Mano, *S. Leone* 82 D2
Mano →, *Liberia* 82 D2
Mano River, *Liberia* 82 D2
Manoharpur, *India* 69 H11
Manokwari, *Indonesia* 63 E8
Manolás, *Greece* 46 C3
Manombo, *Madag.* 89 C7
Manono, *Dem. Rep. of the Congo* 86 D2
Manoppello, *Italy* 41 F11
Manosque, *France* 21 E9
Manotick, *Canada* 117 A9
Manouane →, *Canada* 105 C5
Manouane, L., *Canada* 105 B5
Manp'o, *N. Korea* 57 D14
Manpojin = Manp'o, *N. Korea* 57 D14
Manpur, *Chhattisgarh, India* 69 H10
Manpur, *Mad. P., India* 68 H6
Manresa, *Spain* 38 D6
Mansa, *Gujarat, India* 68 H5
Mansa, *Punjab, India* 68 E6
Mansa, *Zambia* 87 E2
Månsåsen, *Sweden* 10 A8
Mansehra, *Pakistan* 68 B5
Mansel I., *Canada* 101 B11
Mansfield, *Australia* 95 F4
Mansfield, *U.K.* 14 D6
Mansfield, *La., U.S.A.* 113 J8
Mansfield, *Mass., U.S.A.* 117 D13
Mansfield, *Ohio, U.S.A.* 116 F2
Mansfield, *Pa., U.S.A.* 116 E7
Mansfield, Mt., *U.S.A.* 117 B12
Mansilla de las Mulas, *Spain* 36 C5
Mansle, *France* 20 C4
Mansoa, *Guinea-Biss.* 82 C1
Manson Creek, *Canada* 102 B4
Manta, *Ecuador* 124 D2
Mantadia △, *Madag.* 89 B8
Mantalingajan, Mt., *Phil.* 61 G2
Mantare, *Tanzania* 86 C3
Manteca, *U.S.A.* 110 H5
Manteo, *U.S.A.* 115 H8
Mantes-la-Jolie, *France* 19 D8
Manthani, *India* 66 K11
Manti, *U.S.A.* 108 G8
Mantiqueira, Serra da, *Brazil* 127 A7
Manton, *U.S.A.* 114 C3
Mantorp, *Sweden* 11 F9
Mántova, *Italy* 40 C7
Mänttä, *Finland* 9 E21
Mantua = Mántova, *Italy* 40 C7
Manturovo, *Russia* 34 A7
Manu, *Peru* 124 F4
Manu →, *Peru* 124 F4
Manu'a Is., *Amer. Samoa* 91 B14
Manuel Alves →, *Brazil* 125 F9
Manui, *Indonesia* 63 E6
Manukau, *N.Z.* 91 G5
Manuripi →, *Bolivia* 124 F5
Many, *U.S.A.* 113 K8
Manyara, L., *Tanzania* 86 C4
Manyas, *Turkey* 45 F11
Manyava, *Ukraine* 29 B9
Manych →, *Russia* 35 G5
Manych-Gudilo, Ozero, *Russia* 35 G6
Manyonga →, *Tanzania* 86 C3
Manyoni, *Tanzania* 86 D3
Manzai, *Pakistan* 68 C4
Manzala, Bahra el, *Egypt* 80 H7
Manzanar ⌓, *U.S.A.* 110 J7
Manzanares, *Spain* 37 F7
Manzaneda, *Spain* 36 C3
Manzanillo, *Cuba* 120 B4
Manzanillo, *Mexico* 118 D4
Manzanillo, Pta., *Panama* 120 E4
Manzano Mts., *U.S.A.* 109 J10
Manzarīyeh, *Iran* 71 C6
Manzhouli, *China* 60 B6
Manzini, *Swaziland* 89 D5
Mao, *Chad* 79 F9
Maó, *Spain* 48 B11
Maoke, Pegunungan, *Indonesia* 63 E9
Maolin, *China* 57 C12
Maoming, *China* 59 G8
Maopi T'ou, *China* 59 G13
Maouri, Dallol →, *Niger* 83 C5
Maoxian, *China* 58 B4
Maoxing, *China* 57 B13
Mapam Yumco, *China* 60 C3
Mapastepec, *Mexico* 119 D6
Maphrao, Ko, *Thailand* 65 a
Mapia, Kepulauan, *Indonesia* 63 D8
Mapimí, *Mexico* 118 B4
Mapimí, Bolsón de, *Mexico* 118 B4
Maping, *China* 59 B9
Mapinga, *Tanzania* 86 D4
Mapinhane, *Mozam.* 89 C6
Maple Creek, *Canada* 103 D7
Maple Valley, *U.S.A.* 110 C4
Mapleton, *U.S.A.* 108 D2
Mapuera →, *Brazil* 124 D7
Mapulanguene, *Mozam.* 89 C5
Maputo, *Mozam.* 89 D5
Maputo ⌓, *Mozam.* 89 D5
Maputo □, *Mozam.* 89 D5
Maputo, B. de, *Mozam.* 89 D5
Maqiaohe, *China* 57 B16
Maqnā, *Si. Arabia* 70 D2
Maquan He = Brahmaputra →, *Asia* 69 H13
Maqueda, *Spain* 36 E6
Maquela do Zombo, *Angola* 84 F3
Maquinchao, *Argentina* 128 E3
Maquoketa, *U.S.A.* 112 D9
Mar, Serra do, *Brazil* 127 B6
Mar Chiquita, L., *Argentina* 126 C3
Mar del Plata, *Argentina* 126 D4
Mar Menor, *Spain* 39 H4
Mara, *Tanzania* 86 C3
Mara □, *Tanzania* 86 C3
Maraã, *Brazil* 124 D5
Marabá, *Brazil* 125 E9
Maracá, I. de, *Brazil* 125 C8
Maracaibo, *Venezuela* 124 A4
Maracaibo, L. de, *Venezuela* 124 B4
Maracaju, *Brazil* 127 A4
Maracas Bay Village, *Trin. & Tob.* 125 K15
Maracay, *Venezuela* 124 A5
Maracena, *Spain* 37 H7
Maradi, *Niger* 83 C6
Marāgheh, *Iran* 70 B5
Marāh, *Si. Arabia* 70 E5
Marahoue △, *Ivory C.* 82 D3
Marais du Cotentin et du Bessin ⌓, *France* 18 C5
Marais Poitevin, Val de Sèvre et Vendée ⌓, *France* 20 B3
Marajó, I. de, *Brazil* 125 D9
Marākand, *Iran* 70 B5
Marakele △, *S. Africa* 89 E4
Maralal, *Kenya* 86 B4
Maralinga, *Australia* 93 F5
Maramaraereğlisi, *Turkey* 45 F11
Marambio, *Antarctica* 5 C18
Marampa, *S. Leone* 82 D2
Maramureş □, *Romania* 29 C9
Maran, *Malaysia* 65 L4
Marana, *U.S.A.* 109 K8
Maranboy, *Australia* 92 B5
Maranchón, *Spain* 38 D2
Marand, *Iran* 70 B5
Marang, *Malaysia* 65 K4
Maranguape, *Brazil* 125 D11
Maranhão = São Luís, *Brazil* 125 D10
Maranhão □, *Brazil* 125 E9
Marano, L. di, *Italy* 41 C10
Maranoa →, *Australia* 95 D4
Marañón →, *Peru* 124 D4
Marão, *Mozam.* 89 C5
Maraş = Kahramanmaraş, *Turkey* 70 B3
Mărăşeşti, *Romania* 29 E12
Maratea, *Italy* 43 C8
Marateca, *Portugal* 37 G2
Marathasa, *Cyprus* 49 E11
Marathókambos, *Greece* 47 D8
Marathon, *Australia* 94 C3
Marathon, *Canada* 104 C2
Marathón, *Greece* 46 C5
Marathon, *N.Y., U.S.A.* 117 D8
Marathon, *Tex., U.S.A.* 113 K3
Marathóvouno, *Cyprus* 49 D12
Maratua, *Indonesia* 63 D5
Maraval, *Trin. & Tob.* 125 K15
Maravatío, *Mexico* 118 D4
Marawi City, *Phil.* 61 G6
Marāwih, *U.A.E.* 71 E7
Marazliyivka 29 D15
Marbella, *Spain* 37 J6
Marble Bar, *Australia* 92 D2
Marble Falls, *U.S.A.* 113 K5
Marblehead, *U.S.A.* 117 D14
Marburg, *Germany* 24 E4
Marcal →, *Hungary* 28 C2
Marcali, *Hungary* 28 D2
Marcaria, *Italy* 40 C7
Mărcăuţi, *Moldova* 29 B12
March, *U.K.* 15 E8
Marche, *France* 20 B5
Marche □, *Italy* 41 E10
Marche-en-Famenne, *Belgium* 17 D5
Marchena, *Spain* 37 H5
Marches = Marche □, *Italy* 41 E10
Marchesale ⌓, *Italy* 43 D9
Marciana Marina, *Italy* 40 F7
Marcianise, *Italy* 43 A7
Marcigny, *France* 19 F11
Marcillat-en-Combraille, *France* 19 F9
Marck, *France* 19 B8
Marckolsheim, *France* 19 D14
Marco, *U.S.A.* 115 N5
Marcos Juárez, *Argentina* 126 C3
Mărculeşti, *Moldova* 29 C13
Marcus I. = Minami-Tori-Shima, *Pac. Oc.* 96 E7
Marcus Necker Ridge, *Pac. Oc.* 96 F9
Marcy, Mt., *U.S.A.* 117 B11
Mardan, *Pakistan* 68 B5
Mardarivka, *Ukraine* 29 C14
Mardin, *Turkey* 70 B4
Mårdsjö, *Sweden* 10 A9
Marécchia →, *Italy* 41 D9
Maree, L., *U.K.* 13 D3
Mareeba, *Australia* 94 B4
Mareetsane, *S. Africa* 88 D4
Maremma, *Italy* 41 F8
Maremma ⌓, *Italy* 40 F8
Maréna, *Kayes, Mali* 82 C2
Maréna, *Koulikouro, Mali* 82 C3
Marengo, *U.S.A.* 112 E8
Marennes, *France* 20 C2
Marerano, *Madag.* 89 C7
Marettimo, *Italy* 42 E5
Mareuil, *France* 20 C4
Marfa, *U.S.A.* 113 K2
Marfa Pt., *Malta* 49 D1
Marganets = Marhanets, *Ukraine* 33 J8
Margaret →, *Australia* 92 C4
Margaret Bay, *Canada* 102 C3
Margaret L., *Canada* 102 B5
Margaret River, *Australia* 93 F2
Margarita, I. de, *Venezuela* 124 A6
Margarítion, *Greece* 46 B2
Margaritovo, *Russia* 54 C7
Margate, *S. Africa* 89 E5
Margate, *U.K.* 15 F9
Margeride, Mts. de la, *France* 20 D7
Margherita di Savóia, *Italy* 43 A9
Margherita Pk., *Uganda* 86 B3
Marghita, *Romania* 28 C7
Margonin, *Poland* 31 F4
Margosatubig, *Phil.* 61 H5
Mārgow, Dasht-e, *Afghan.* 66 D3
Marguerite, *Canada* 102 C4
Marhanets, *Ukraine* 33 J8
Mari El □, *Russia* 34 B8
Mari Indus, *Pakistan* 68 C4
Mari Republic = Mari El □, *Russia* 34 B8
María, Sa. de, *Spain* 39 H2
María Elena, *Chile* 126 A2
María Grande, *Argentina* 126 C4
Maria I., *N. Terr., Australia* 94 A2
Maria I., *Tas., Australia* 95 G4
Maria Island △, *Australia* 95 G4
Maria van Diemen, C., *N.Z.* 91 F4
Mariager, *Denmark* 11 H3
Mariager Fjord, *Denmark* 11 H4
Mariakani, *Kenya* 86 C4
Mariala △, *Australia* 95 D4
Marian, *Australia* 94 K6
Marian L., *Canada* 102 A5
Mariana Trench, *Pac. Oc.* 96 F6
Marianao, *Cuba* 120 B3
Marianna, *Ark., U.S.A.* 113 H9
Marianna, *Fla., U.S.A.* 115 K3
Mariannelund, *Sweden* 11 G9
Mariánské Lázně, *Czech Rep.* 26 B5
Marias →, *U.S.A.* 108 C8
Mariato, Punta, *Panama* 120 E3
Mariazell, *Austria* 26 D8
Maribo, *Denmark* 11 K5
Maribor, *Slovenia* 41 B12
Marico →, *Africa* 88 C4
Maricopa, *Ariz., U.S.A.* 109 K7
Maricopa, *Calif., U.S.A.* 111 K7
Marîdî, *Sudan* 81 G2
Marîdî, Wadi →, *Sudan* 81 F2
Marié →, *Brazil* 124 D5
Marie Byrd Land, *Antarctica* 5 D14
Marie-Galante, *Guadeloupe* 120 b
Mariecourt = Kangiqsujuaq, *Canada* 101 B12
Mariefred, *Sweden* 10 E11
Mariehamn = Maarianhamina, *Finland* 9 F18
Marieholm, *Sweden* 11 J7
Mariembourg, *Belgium* 17 D4
Marienbad = Mariánské Lázně, *Czech Rep.* 26 B5
Marienberg, *Germany* 24 E9
Mariental, *Namibia* 88 C2
Marienville, *U.S.A.* 116 E5
Mariestad, *Sweden* 11 F7
Marietta, *Ga., U.S.A.* 115 J3
Marietta, *Ohio, U.S.A.* 114 F5
Marieville, *Canada* 117 A11
Mariga →, *Nigeria* 83 C6
Marignane, *France* 21 E9
Marihatag, *Phil.* 61 G7
Mariinsk, *Russia* 52 D9
Mariinskiy Posad, *Russia* 34 B8
Marijampolė, *Lithuania* 9 J20
Marijampolės □, *Lithuania* 30 D10
Marília, *Brazil* 127 A6
Marín, *Spain* 36 C2
Marina, *U.S.A.* 110 J5
Marinduque, *Phil.* 63 B6
Marine City, *U.S.A.* 116 D2
Marineo, *Italy* 42 E6
Marinette, *U.S.A.* 114 C2
Maringá, *Brazil* 127 A5
Marinha Grande, *Portugal* 36 F2
Marino, *Italy* 41 G9
Marion, *Ala., U.S.A.* 115 J2
Marion, *Ill., U.S.A.* 113 G10
Marion, *Ind., U.S.A.* 114 E3
Marion, *Iowa, U.S.A.* 112 D9
Marion, *Kans., U.S.A.* 112 F6
Marion, *N.C., U.S.A.* 115 H5
Marion, *Ohio, U.S.A.* 114 E4
Marion, *S.C., U.S.A.* 115 H6
Marion, *Va., U.S.A.* 115 G5
Marion, L., *U.S.A.* 115 J5
Mariposa, *U.S.A.* 110 H7
Mariscal Estigarribia, *Paraguay* 126 A3
Maritime Alps = Maritimes, Alpes, *Europe* 21 D11
Maritimes, Alpes, *Europe* 21 D11
Maritsa = Évros →, *Greece* 72 B2
Maritsá, *Greece* 49 C10
Mariupol, *Ukraine* 33 J9
Mariusa △, *Venezuela* 121 E7
Marīvān, *Iran* 70 C5
Marj 'Uyūn, *Lebanon* 74 B4
Marka = Merca, *Somali Rep.* 75 G3
Marka, *Si. Arabia* 80 D5
Markam, *China* 58 C2
Markaryd, *Sweden* 11 H7
Markdale, *Canada* 116 B4
Marked Tree, *U.S.A.* 113 H9
Markelsdorfer Huk, *Germany* 24 A7
Market Drayton, *U.K.* 14 E5
Market Harborough, *U.K.* 15 E7
Market Rasen, *U.K.* 14 D7
Markham, *Canada* 116 C5
Markham, Mt., *Antarctica* 5 E11
Marki, *Poland* 31 F8
Märkische Schweiz ⌓, *Germany* 24 C10
Markkleeberg, *Germany* 24 D8
Markleeville, *U.S.A.* 110 G7
Markoupoulon, *Greece* 46 D5
Markovac, *Serbia & M.* 44 B5
Markovo, *Russia* 53 C17
Markoye, *Burkina Faso* 83 C5
Marks, *Russia* 34 E8
Marksville, *U.S.A.* 113 K8
Markt Schwaben, *Germany* 25 G7
Marktoberdorf, *Germany* 25 H6
Marktredwitz, *Germany* 25 E8
Marl, *Germany* 24 D3
Marla, *Australia* 95 D1
Marlbank, *Canada* 116 B7
Marlboro, *Mass., U.S.A.* 117 D13
Marlboro, *N.Y., U.S.A.* 117 E11
Marlborough, *Australia* 94 C4
Marlborough, *U.K.* 15 F6
Marlborough Downs, *U.K.* 15 F6
Marle, *France* 19 C10
Marlin, *U.S.A.* 113 K6
Marlow, *Germany* 24 A8
Marlow, *U.K.* 15 F7
Marlow, *U.S.A.* 113 H6
Marmagao, *India* 66 M8
Marmande, *France* 20 D4
Marmara, *Turkey* 45 F11
Marmara, Sea of = Marmara Denizi, *Turkey* 45 F12
Marmara Denizi, *Turkey* 45 F12
Marmara Gölü, *Turkey* 47 C10
Marmaris, *Turkey* 47 E10
Marmaris Limanı, *Turkey* 47 E10
Marmion, Mt., *Australia* 93 E2
Marmion L., *Canada* 104 C1
Marmolada, Mte., *Italy* 41 B8
Marmolejo, *Spain* 37 G6
Marmora, *Canada* 116 B7
Mármora, La, *Italy* 42 C2
Marnay, *France* 19 E12
Marne, *Germany* 24 B5
Marne □, *France* 19 D11
Marne →, *France* 19 D9
Marneuli, *Georgia* 35 K7
Maroala, *Madag.* 89 B8
Maroantsetra, *Madag.* 89 B8
Maroelaboom, *Namibia* 88 B2
Marofandilia, *Madag.* 89 C7
Marojejy ⌓, *Madag.* 89 A8
Marolambo, *Madag.* 89 C8
Maromandia, *Madag.* 89 A8
Maromokotro, *Madag.* 89 A8
Marondera, *Zimbabwe* 87 F3
Maroni →, *Fr. Guiana* 125 B8
Marónia, *Greece* 45 F9
Maronne →, *France* 20 C5
Maroochydore, *Australia* 95 D5
Maroona, *Australia* 95 F3
Maros →, *Hungary* 28 D5
Marosakoa, *Madag.* 89 B8
Maroseranana, *Madag.* 89 B8
Maróstica, *Italy* 41 C8
Marotandrano, *Madag.* 89 B8
Marotaolano, *Madag.* 89 A8
Maroua, *Cameroon* 83 C7
Marovato, *Madag.* 89 B8
Marovoay, *Madag.* 89 B8
Marquard, *S. Africa* 88 D4
Marquesas Is. = Marquises, Îs., *French Polynesia* 97 H14
Marquette, *U.S.A.* 114 B2
Marquis, *St. Lucia* 121 f
Marquise, *France* 19 B8
Marquises, Îs., *French Polynesia* 97 H14
Marra, Djebel, *Sudan* 79 F10
Marra, Gebel, *Sudan* 81 F2
Marracuene, *Mozam.* 89 D5
Marradi, *Italy* 41 D8
Marrakech, *Morocco* 78 B4
Marratxi, *Spain* 38 F7
Marrawah, *Australia* 95 G3
Marree, *Australia* 95 D2
Marrero, *U.S.A.* 113 L9
Marrimane, *Mozam.* 89 C5
Marromeu, *Mozam.* 89 B6
Marromeu ⌓, *Mozam.* 89 B6
Marroquí, Punta, *Spain* 37 K5
Marrowie Cr. →, *Australia* 95 E4
Marrubane, *Mozam.* 87 F4
Marrúbiu, *Italy* 42 C1
Marrupa, *Mozam.* 87 E4
Mars Hill, *U.S.A.* 115 B12
Marsá 'Alam, *Egypt* 80 B3
Marsá Matrûh, *Egypt* 80 A2
Marsá Sha'b, *Sudan* 80 C4
Marsabit, *Kenya* 86 B4
Marsabit △, *Kenya* 86 B4
Marsala, *Italy* 42 E5
Marsalforn, *Malta* 49 C1
Mârşani, *Romania* 29 F9
Marsberg, *Germany* 24 D4
Marsciano, *Italy* 41 F9
Marsden, *Australia* 95 E4
Marseillan, *France* 20 E7
Marseille, *France* 21 E9
Marseille ✈ (MRS), *France* 21 E9
Marseilles = Marseille, *France* 21 E9
Marsh I., *U.S.A.* 113 L9
Marshall, *Liberia* 82 D2
Marshall, *Ark., U.S.A.* 113 H8
Marshall, *Mich., U.S.A.* 114 D3
Marshall, *Minn., U.S.A.* 112 C7
Marshall, *Mo., U.S.A.* 112 F8
Marshall, *Tex., U.S.A.* 113 J7
Marshall →, *Australia* 94 C2
Marshall Is. ■, *Pac. Oc.* 96 G9
Marshalltown, *U.S.A.* 112 D8
Marshbrook, *Zimbabwe* 89 B5
Marshfield, *Mo., U.S.A.* 113 G8
Marshfield, *Vt., U.S.A.* 117 B12
Marshfield, *Wis., U.S.A.* 112 C9
Marshūn, *Iran* 71 B6
Mársico Nuovo, *Italy* 43 B8
Märsta, *Sweden* 10 E11
Marstal, *Denmark* 11 K4
Marstrand, *Sweden* 11 G5
Mart, *U.S.A.* 113 K6
Marta →, *Italy* 41 F8
Martaban, *Burma* 67 L20
Martaban, G. of, *Burma* 67 L20
Martano, *Italy* 43 B11
Martapura, *Kalimantan, Indonesia* 62 E4
Martapura, *Sumatera, Indonesia* 62 E2
Marte, *Nigeria* 83 C7
Martel, *France* 20 D5
Martelange, *Belgium* 17 E5
Martellago, *Italy* 41 C9
Martés, Sierra, *Spain* 39 F4
Martfű, *Hungary* 28 C5
Martha's Vineyard, *U.S.A.* 117 E14
Martigné-Ferchaud, *France* 18 E5
Martigny, *Switz.* 25 J3
Martigues, *France* 21 E9
Martin, *Slovak Rep.* 27 B11
Martin, *S. Dak., U.S.A.* 112 D4
Martin, *Tenn., U.S.A.* 113 G10
Martín →, *Spain* 38 D4
Martin, L., *U.S.A.* 115 J3
Martina Franca, *Italy* 43 B10
Martinborough, *N.Z.* 91 J5
Martinez, *Calif., U.S.A.* 110 G4
Martinez, *Ga., U.S.A.* 115 J4
Martinique ☒, *W. Indies* 120 c
Martinique Passage, *W. Indies* 121 C7
Martínon, *Greece* 46 C5
Martinópolis, *Brazil* 127 A5
Martin's Bay, *Barbados* 121 g
Martins Ferry, *U.S.A.* 116 F4
Martinsberg, *Austria* 26 C8

Martinsburg, *Pa., U.S.A.* 116 F6
Martinsburg, *W. Va., U.S.A.* 114 F7
Martinsicuro, *Italy* 41 F10
Martinsville, *Ind., U.S.A.* 114 F2
Martinsville, *Va., U.S.A.* 115 G6
Marton, *N.Z.* 91 J5
Martorell, *Spain* 38 D6
Martos, *Spain* 37 H7
Martuni, *Armenia* 35 K7
Maru, *Nigeria* 83 C6
Marudi, *Malaysia* 62 D4
Maruf, *Afghan.* 66 D5
Marugame, *Japan* 55 G6
Marunga, *Angola* 88 B3
Marungu, Mts., *Dem. Rep. of the Congo* 86 D3
Marv Dasht, *Iran* 71 D7
Marvast, *Iran* 71 D7
Marvejols, *France* 20 D7
Marvel Loch, *Australia* 93 F2
Marwar, *India* 68 G5
Mary, *Turkmenistan* 52 F7
Maryborough = Port Laoise, *Ireland* 12 C4
Maryborough, *Queens., Australia* 95 D5
Maryborough, *Vic., Australia* 95 F3
Maryfield, *Canada* 103 D8
Maryland □, *U.S.A.* 114 F7
Maryland Junction, *Zimbabwe* 87 F3
Maryport, *U.K.* 14 C4
Mary's Harbour, *Canada* 105 B8
Marystown, *Canada* 105 C8
Marysville, *Canada* 102 D5
Marysville, *Calif., U.S.A.* 110 F5
Marysville, *Kans., U.S.A.* 112 F6
Marysville, *Mich., U.S.A.* 116 D2
Marysville, *Ohio, U.S.A.* 114 E4
Marysville, *Wash., U.S.A.* 110 B4
Maryville, *Mo., U.S.A.* 112 E7
Maryville, *Tenn., U.S.A.* 115 H4
Marzūq, *Libya* 79 C8
Masahunga, *Tanzania* 86 C3
Masai, *Malaysia* 65 d
Masai Mara △, *Kenya* 86 C4
Masai Steppe, *Tanzania* 86 C4
Masaka, *Uganda* 86 C3
Masalembo, Kepulauan, *Indonesia* 62 F4
Masalima, Kepulauan, *Indonesia* 62 F5
Masallı, *Azerbaijan* 73 C13
Masamba, *Indonesia* 63 E6
Masan, *S. Korea* 57 G15
Masandam, Ra's, *Oman* 71 E8
Masasi, *Tanzania* 87 E4
Masaya, *Nic.* 120 D2
Masba, *Nigeria* 83 C7
Masbate, *Phil.* 61 E5
Máscali, *Italy* 43 E8
Mascara, *Algeria* 78 A6
Mascota, *Mexico* 118 C4
Masela, *Indonesia* 63 F7
Maseru, *Lesotho* 88 D4
Mashaba, *Zimbabwe* 87 G3
Mashābih, *Si. Arabia* 70 E3
Mashan, *China* 58 F7
Mashar, *Sudan* 81 F2
Mashatu ⌓, *Botswana* 89 C4
Mashegu, *Nigeria* 83 D6
Masherbrum, *Pakistan* 69 B7
Mashhad, *Iran* 71 B8
Mashi, *Nigeria* 83 C6
Mashīz, *Iran* 71 D8
Māshkel, Hāmūn-i-, *Pakistan* 66 E3
Mashki Chāh, *Pakistan* 66 E3
Mashonaland, *Zimbabwe* 85 H6
Mashonaland Central □, *Zimbabwe* 89 B5
Mashonaland East □, *Zimbabwe* 89 B5
Mashonaland West □, *Zimbabwe* 89 B4
Mashrakh, *India* 69 F11
Mashtaga = Maştağa, *Azerbaijan* 35 K10
Masindi, *Uganda* 86 B3
Masindi Port, *Uganda* 86 B3
Maşīrah, *Oman* 75 C6
Maşīrah, Khalīj, *Oman* 75 C6
Masisi, *Dem. Rep. of the Congo* 86 C2
Masjed Soleyman, *Iran* 71 D6
Mask, L., *Ireland* 12 C2
Maskin, *Oman* 71 F8
Maslen Nos, *Bulgaria* 45 D11
Maslinica, *Croatia* 41 E13
Masnou = El Masnou, *Spain* 38 D7
Masoala △, *Madag.* 89 B9
Masoala, Tanjon' i, *Madag.* 89 B9
Masoarivo, *Madag.* 89 B7
Masohi = Amahai, *Indonesia* 63 E7
Masomeloka, *Madag.* 89 C8
Mason, *Nev., U.S.A.* 110 G7
Mason, *Tex., U.S.A.* 113 K5
Mason City, *U.S.A.* 112 D8
Maspalomas, *Canary Is.* 48 G4
Maspalomas, Pta., *Canary Is.* 48 G4
Masqat, *Oman* 75 C6
Massa, *Italy* 40 D7
Massa Maríttima, *Italy* 40 E7
Massachusetts □, *U.S.A.* 117 D13
Massachusetts B., *U.S.A.* 117 D14
Massafra, *Italy* 43 B10
Massakory, *Chad* 79 F9
Massanella, *Spain* 48 B9
Massangena, *Mozam.* 89 C5
Massango, *Angola* 84 F3
Massat, *France* 20 F5
Massawa = Mitsiwa, *Eritrea* 81 D4
Massena, *U.S.A.* 117 B10
Massénya, *Chad* 79 F9
Masset, *Canada* 102 C2
Masseube, *France* 20 E4
Massiac, *France* 20 C7
Massiah Street, *Barbados* 121 g
Massif Central, *France* 20 D7
Massif des Bauges ⌓, *France* 19 G13
Massigui, *Mali* 82 C3
Massillon, *U.S.A.* 116 F3
Massinga, *Mozam.* 89 C6
Massingir, *Mozam.* 89 C5
Masson-Angers, *Canada* 117 A9
Masson I., *Antarctica* 5 C7
Maştağa, *Azerbaijan* 35 K10
Mastanli = Momchilgrad, *Bulgaria* 45 E9
Masterton, *N.Z.* 91 J5
Mastic, *U.S.A.* 117 F12
Mástikho, Ákra, *Greece* 47 C8
Mastuj, *Pakistan* 69 A5
Mastung, *Pakistan* 66 E5
Mastūrah, *Si. Arabia* 80 C4
Masty, *Belarus* 32 F3
Masuda, *Japan* 55 G5
Masvingo, *Zimbabwe* 87 G3
Masvingo □, *Zimbabwe* 87 G3
Maswa ⌓, *Tanzania* 86 C3
Maşyāf, *Syria* 70 C3
Maszewo, *Poland* 30 E2
Mat →, *Albania* 44 E3
Matabeleland, *Zimbabwe* 85 H5
Matabeleland North □, *Zimbabwe* 87 F2
Matabeleland South □, *Zimbabwe* 87 G2
Matachel →, *Spain* 37 G4
Matachewan, *Canada* 104 C3
Matadi, *Dem. Rep. of the Congo* 84 F2
Matagalpa, *Nic.* 120 D2
Matagami, *Canada* 104 C4
Matagami, L., *Canada* 104 C4
Matagorda B., *U.S.A.* 113 L6
Matagorda I., *U.S.A.* 113 L6
Matak, *Indonesia* 62 D3
Mátala, *Greece* 49 E6
Matam, *Senegal* 82 B2
Matameye, *Niger* 83 C6
Matamoros, *Campeche, Mexico* 119 D6
Matamoros, *Coahuila, Mexico* 118 B4
Matamoros, *Tamaulipas, Mexico* 119 B5
Ma'ṭan as Sarra, *Libya* 79 D10
Matandu →, *Tanzania* 87 D3
Matane, *Canada* 105 C6
Matang, *China* 58 F5
Matankari, *Niger* 83 C5
Matanomadh, *India* 68 H3
Matanzas, *Cuba* 120 B3
Matapa, *Botswana* 88 C3
Matapan, C. = Taínaron, Ákra, *Greece* 46 E4
Matapédia, *Canada* 105 C6
Matapo △, *Zimbabwe* 87 G2
Matara, *Sri Lanka* 66 S12
Mataram, *Indonesia* 63 K19
Matarani, *Peru* 124 G4
Mataranka, *Australia* 92 B5
Matarma, Râs, *Egypt* 74 E1
Mataró, *Spain* 38 D7
Matarraña →, *Spain* 38 D5
Mataruška Banja, *Serbia & M.* 44 C4
Matatiele, *S. Africa* 89 E4
Mataura, *N.Z.* 91 M2
Matehuala, *Mexico* 118 C4
Mateke Hills, *Zimbabwe* 87 G3
Matelot, *Trin. & Tob.* 125 K15
Matera, *Italy* 43 B9
Matese ⌓, *Italy* 43 A7
Matese, Monti del, *Italy* 43 A7
Mátészalka, *Hungary* 28 C7
Matetsi, *Zimbabwe* 87 F2
Matfors, *Sweden* 10 B11
Matha, *France* 20 C3
Matheniko ⌓, *Uganda* 86 B3
Mathis, *U.S.A.* 113 L6
Mathráki, *Greece* 49 A3
Mathura, *India* 68 F7
Mati, *Phil.* 61 H7
Matiakoali, *Burkina Faso* 83 C5
Matiali, *India* 69 F13
Matías Romero, *Mexico* 119 D5
Matibane, *Mozam.* 87 E5
Matiri Ra., *N.Z.* 91 J4
Matjiesfontein, *S. Africa* 88 E3
Matla →, *India* 69 J13
Matlamanyane, *Botswana* 88 B4
Matli, *Pakistan* 68 G3
Matlock, *U.K.* 14 D6
Matna, *Sudan* 81 E4
Mato Grosso □, *Brazil* 125 F8
Mato Grosso, Planalto do, *Brazil* 125 G8
Mato Grosso do Sul □, *Brazil* 125 G8
Matobo = Matapo △, *Zimbabwe* 87 G2
Matochkin Shar, *Russia* 52 B6
Matopo Hills, *Zimbabwe* 87 G2
Matopos, *Zimbabwe* 87 G2
Matosinhos, *Portugal* 36 D2
Matour, *France* 19 F11
Matroosberg, *S. Africa* 88 E2
Maṭruḥ, *Oman* 75 C6
Matsena, *Nigeria* 83 C7
Matsesta, *Russia* 35 J4
Matsu Tao, *Taiwan* 59 E13
Matsue, *Japan* 55 G6
Matsum, Ko, *Thailand* 65 b
Matsumae, *Japan* 54 D10
Matsumoto, *Japan* 55 F9
Matsusaka, *Japan* 55 G8
Matsuura, *Japan* 55 H4
Matsuyama, *Japan* 55 H6
Mattagami →, *Canada* 104 B3
Mattancheri, *India* 66 Q10
Mattawa, *Canada* 104 C4
Matterhorn, *Switz.* 25 K3
Mattersburg, *Austria* 27 D9
Matthew Town, *Bahamas* 121 B5
Matthews Ridge, *Guyana* 124 B6
Mattice, *Canada* 104 C3
Mattituck, *U.S.A.* 117 F12
Mattō, *Japan* 55 F8
Mattoon, *U.S.A.* 114 F1
Matuba, *Mozam.* 89 C5
Matucana, *Peru* 124 F3
Matūn = Khowst, *Afghan.* 68 C3
Matura B., *Trin. & Tob.* 125 K15
Maturín, *Venezuela* 124 B6
Matusadona △, *Zimbabwe* 87 F2
Matveyev Kurgan, *Russia* 33 J10
Matxitxako, C., *Spain* 38 B2
Mau, *Mad. P., India* 69 F8
Mau, *Ut. P., India* 69 G10
Mau, *Ut. P., India* 69 G9
Mau Escarpment, *Kenya* 86 C4
Mau Ranipur, *India* 69 G8
Maubeuge, *France* 19 B10
Maubourguet, *France* 20 E4
Maud, Pt., *Australia* 92 D1
Maude, *Australia* 95 E3
Maudin Sun, *Burma* 67 M19
Maués, *Brazil* 124 D7
Mauganj, *India* 67 G12
Maughold Hd., *I. of Man* 14 C3
Mauguio, *France* 20 E7
Maui, *U.S.A.* 106 H16
Maulamyaing = Moulmein, *Burma* 67 L20
Maule □, *Chile* 126 D1
Mauléon-Licharre, *France* 20 E3
Maumee, *U.S.A.* 114 E4
Maumee →, *U.S.A.* 114 E4
Maumere, *Indonesia* 63 F6
Maumusson, Pertuis de, *France* 20 C2
Maun, *Botswana* 88 C3
Mauna Kea, *U.S.A.* 106 J17
Mauna Loa, *U.S.A.* 106 J17
Maungmagan Kyunzu, *Burma* 64 E1
Maupin, *U.S.A.* 108 D3
Maure-de-Bretagne, *France* 18 E5
Maurepas, L., *U.S.A.* 113 K9
Maures, *France* 21 E10
Mauriac, *France* 20 C6
Maurice, L., *Australia* 93 E5
Mauricie △, *Canada* 104 C5
Maurienne, *France* 21 C10
Mauritania ■, *Africa* 78 E3
Mauritius ■, *Ind. Oc.* 77 J9
Mauron, *France* 18 D4
Maurs, *France* 20 D6
Mauston, *U.S.A.* 112 D9
Mauterndorf, *Austria* 26 D6
Mauthen, *Austria* 26 E6
Mauvezin, *France* 20 E4
Mauzé-sur-le-Mignon, *France* 20 B3
Mavli, *India* 68 G5
Mavrovë, *Albania* 44 F3
Mavrovo △, *Macedonia* 44 E4
Mavuradonha Mts., *Zimbabwe* 87 F3
Mawa, *Dem. Rep. of the Congo* 86 B2
Mawai, *India* 69 H9
Mawana, *India* 68 E7
Mawand, *Pakistan* 68 E3
Mawk Mai, *Burma* 67 J20
Mawlaik, *Burma* 67 H19
Mawlamyine = Moulmein, *Burma* 67 L20
Mawqaq, *Si. Arabia* 70 E4
Mawson Base, *Antarctica* 5 C6
Mawson Coast, *Antarctica* 5 C6
Max, *U.S.A.* 112 B4
Maxcanú, *Mexico* 119 C6
Maxesibeni, *S. Africa* 89 E4
Maxhamish L., *Canada* 102 B4
Maxixe, *Mozam.* 89 C6
Maxville, *Canada* 117 A10
Maxwell, *U.S.A.* 110 F4
Maxwelton, *Australia* 94 C3
May, C., *U.S.A.* 114 F8
May Pen, *Jamaica* 120 a
Maya →, *Russia* 53 D14
Maya Mts., *Belize* 119 D7
Mayaguana, *Bahamas* 121 B5
Mayagüez, *Puerto Rico* 121 d
Mayahi, *Niger* 83 C6
Mayaky, *Ukraine* 29 C14
Mayals = Maials, *Spain* 38 D5
Mayāmey, *Iran* 71 B7
Mayang, *China* 58 D7
Mayanup, *Australia* 93 F2
Mayapán, *Mexico* 119 C7
Mayapan, *Yucatán, Mexico* 119 C7
Mayarí, *Cuba* 121 B4
Mayaro B., *Trin. & Tob.* 125 K16
Maybell, *U.S.A.* 108 F9
Maybole, *U.K.* 13 F4
Maychew, *Ethiopia* 81 E4
Maydān, *Iraq* 70 C5
Maydan, *Ukraine* 29 B8
Maydena, *Australia* 95 G4
Mayen, *Germany* 25 E3
Mayenne, *France* 18 D6
Mayenne □, *France* 18 D6
Mayenne →, *France* 18 E6
Mayer, *U.S.A.* 109 J7
Mayerthorpe, *Canada* 102 C5
Mayfield, *Ky., U.S.A.* 115 G1
Mayfield, *N.Y., U.S.A.* 117 C10
Mayhill, *U.S.A.* 109 K11
Maykop, *Russia* 35 H5
Maymyo, *Burma* 64 A1
Maynard, *Mass., U.S.A.* 117 D13
Maynard, *Wash., U.S.A.* 110 C4
Maynard Hills, *Australia* 93 E2
Mayne →, *Australia* 94 C3
Maynooth, *Ireland* 12 C5
Mayo, *Canada* 100 B6
Mayo □, *Ireland* 12 C2
Mayo Daga, *Nigeria* 83 D7
Mayo Faran, *Nigeria* 83 D7
Mayon Volcano, *Phil.* 61 E5
Mayor I., *N.Z.* 91 G6
Mayorga, *Spain* 36 C5
Mayotte ☒, *Ind. Oc.* 85 G9
Mayraira Pt., *Phil.* 61 B4
Maysān □, *Iraq* 70 D5
Mayskiy, *Russia* 35 J7
Maysville, *U.S.A.* 114 F4
Mayu, *Indonesia* 63 D7
Mayville, *N. Dak., U.S.A.* 112 B6
Mayville, *N.Y., U.S.A.* 116 D5
Mayya, *Russia* 53 C14
Mazabuka, *Zambia* 87 F2
Mazagán = El Jadida, *Morocco* 78 B4
Mazagão, *Brazil* 125 D8
Mazamet, *France* 20 E6
Mazán, *Peru* 124 D4
Māzandarān □, *Iran* 71 B7
Mazapil, *Mexico* 118 C4
Mazara del Vallo, *Italy* 42 E5
Mazarrón, *Spain* 39 H3
Mazarrón, G. de, *Spain* 39 H3
Mazaruni →, *Guyana* 124 B7
Mazatán, *Mexico* 118 B2
Mazatenango, *Guatemala* 120 D1
Mazatlán, *Mexico* 118 C3
Mažeikiai, *Lithuania* 9 H20
Māzhān, *Iran* 71 C8
Mazīnān, *Iran* 71 B8
Mazoe, *Mozam.* 87 F3
Mazoe →, *Mozam.* 87 F3
Mazowe, *Zimbabwe* 87 F3
Mazowieckie □, *Poland* 31 F8
Mazrûb, *Sudan* 81 E2
Mazu Dao, *China* 59 D12
Mazurian Lakes = Mazurski, Pojezierze, *Poland* 30 E7
Mazurski, Pojezierze, *Poland* 30 E7
Mazyr, *Belarus* 33 F5
Mbaba, *Senegal* 82 C1
Mbabane, *Swaziland* 89 D5
Mbahiakro, *Ivory C.* 82 D4
M'bahiakro, *Ivory C.* 82 D4
Mbaïki, *C.A.R.* 84 D3
Mbala, *Zambia* 87 D3
Mbalabala, *Zimbabwe* 89 C4
Mbale, *Uganda* 86 B3
Mbalmayo, *Cameroon* 83 E7
Mbam →, *Cameroon* 83 E7
Mbamba Bay, *Tanzania* 87 E3
Mbandaka, *Dem. Rep. of the Congo* 84 D3
Mbanga, *Cameroon* 83 E6
Mbanza Congo, *Angola* 84 F2
Mbanza Ngungu, *Dem. Rep. of the Congo* 84 F2
Mbarangandu, *Tanzania* 87 D4
Mbarara, *Uganda* 86 C3
Mbashe →, *S. Africa* 89 E4
Mbatto, *Ivory C.* 82 D4
Mbenkuru →, *Tanzania* 87 D4
Mberengwa, *Zimbabwe* 87 G2
Mberengwa, Mt., *Zimbabwe* 87 G2
Mberubu, *Nigeria* 83 D6
Mbesuma, *Zambia* 87 E3
Mbeya, *Tanzania* 87 D3
Mbeya □, *Tanzania* 86 D3
M'bili, *Sudan* 81 F2
Mbinga, *Tanzania* 87 E4
Mbini = Río Muni □, *Eq. Guin.* 84 D2
Mboki, *C.A.R.* 81 F2
M'bonge, *Cameroon* 83 E6
Mboro, *Senegal* 82 B1
M'boukou, Rés. de, *Cameroon* 83 D7
Mboune, *Senegal* 82 C2
Mbour, *Senegal* 82 C1
Mbout, *Mauritania* 82 B2
Mbuji-Mayi, *Dem. Rep. of the Congo* 86 D1
Mbulu, *Tanzania* 86 C4
Mburucuyá, *Argentina* 126 B4
McCarran International, Las Vegas ✕ (LAS), *U.S.A.* 111 J11
Mchinja, *Tanzania* 87 D4
Mchinji, *Malawi* 87 E3
McMurdo, *Antarctica* 5 D11
Mdantsane, *S. Africa* 85 L5
Mead, L., *U.S.A.* 111 J12
Meade, *U.S.A.* 113 G4
Meadow Lake, *Canada* 103 C7
Meadow Lake ⌓, *Canada* 103 C7
Meadow Valley Wash →, *U.S.A.* 111 J12
Meadville, *U.S.A.* 116 E4
Meaford, *Canada* 116 B4
Mealhada, *Portugal* 36 E2
Mealy Mts., *Canada* 105 B8
Meander River, *Canada* 102 B5
Meares, C., *U.S.A.* 108 D2
Mearim →, *Brazil* 125 D10
Meath □, *Ireland* 12 C5
Meath Park, *Canada* 103 C7
Meaulne, *France* 19 F9
Meaux, *France* 19 D9
Mebechi-Gawa →, *Japan* 54 D10
Mebulu, Tanjung, *Indonesia* 63 K18
Mecanhelas, *Mozam.* 87 F4
Mecca = Makkah, *Si. Arabia* 75 C2
Mecca, *U.S.A.* 111 M10
Mechanicsburg, *U.S.A.* 116 F8
Mechanicville, *U.S.A.* 117 D11
Mechara, *Ethiopia* 81 F5
Mechelen, *Belgium* 17 C4
Mecheria, *Algeria* 78 B5
Mechernich, *Germany* 24 E2
Mechetinskaya, *Russia* 35 G5
Mecidiye, *Turkey* 45 F10
Mecitözü, *Turkey* 72 B6
Mecklenburg-Vorpommern □, *Germany* 24 B8
Mecklenburger Bucht, *Germany* 24 A7
Meconta, *Mozam.* 87 E4
Mecsek, *Hungary* 28 D3
Meda, *Portugal* 36 E3
Medan, *Indonesia* 62 D1
Médanos de Coro △, *Venezuela* 121 D6
Medanosa, Pta., *Argentina* 128 F3
Mede, *Italy* 40 C5
Médéa, *Algeria* 78 A6
Mededa, *Bos.-H.* 28 G4
Medellín, *Colombia* 124 B3
Medelpad, *Sweden* 10 B10
Medemblik, *Neths.* 17 B5
Mederdra, *Mauritania* 82 B1
Medford, *Mass., U.S.A.* 117 D13
Medford, *Oreg., U.S.A.* 108 E2
Medford, *Wis., U.S.A.* 112 C9
Medgidia, *Romania* 29 F13
Medi, *Sudan* 81 F3
Media Agua, *Argentina* 126 C2
Media Luna, *Argentina* 126 C2
Medianeira, *Brazil* 127 B5
Mediaş, *Romania* 29 D9
Medicina, *Italy* 41 D8
Medicine Bow, *U.S.A.* 108 F10
Medicine Bow Pk., *U.S.A.* 108 F10
Medicine Bow Ra., *U.S.A.* 108 F10
Medicine Hat, *Canada* 103 D6
Medicine Lake, *U.S.A.* 112 A2
Medicine Lodge, *U.S.A.* 113 G5
Medina = Al Madīnah, *Si. Arabia* 70 E3
Medina, *N. Dak., U.S.A.* 112 B5
Medina, *N.Y., U.S.A.* 116 C6
Medina, *Ohio, U.S.A.* 116 E3
Medina →, *U.S.A.* 113 L5
Medina de Pomar, *Spain* 36 C7
Medina de Ríoseco, *Spain* 36 D5
Medina del Campo, *Spain* 36 D6
Medina L., *U.S.A.* 113 L5
Medina Sidonia, *Spain* 37 J5
Medinaceli, *Spain* 38 D2
Medinipur, *India* 69 H12
Mediterranean Sea, *Europe* 6 H7
Médoc, *France* 20 C3
Medulin, *Croatia* 41 D10
Medveđa, *Serbia & M.* 44 D5
Medvedevo, *Russia* 34 B8
Medveditsa →, *Tver, Russia* 32 D9
Medveditsa →, *Volgograd, Russia* 34 F6
Medvedok, *Russia* 34 B10
Medvezhi, Ostrava, *Russia* 53 B17
Medvezhyegorsk, *Russia* 52 C4
Medway □, *U.K.* 15 F8
Medway →, *U.K.* 15 F8
Medzev, *Slovak Rep.* 27 C13
Medzilaborce, *Slovak Rep.* 27 B14
Medžitlija, *Macedonia* 44 F5
Meekatharra, *Australia* 93 E2
Meeker, *U.S.A.* 108 F10
Meelpaeg Res., *Canada* 105 C8
Meersburg, *Germany* 25 H5
Meerut, *India* 68 E7
Meeteetse, *U.S.A.* 108 D9
Mega, *Ethiopia* 81 G4
Megálo Khorío, *Greece* 47 E9
Megálo Petalí, *Greece* 46 D6
Megalópolis, *Greece* 46 D4
Meganísi Nisís, *Greece* 46 C2
Mégara, *Greece* 46 D5
Megasini, *India* 69 J12
Megdhova →, *Greece* 46 B3
Megève, *France* 21 C10
Meghalaya □, *India* 67 G17
Meghezez, *Ethiopia* 81 F4
Meghna →, *Bangla.* 67 H17
Mégiscane, L., *Canada* 104 C4
Megiste, *Greece* 47 E11
Megra, *Russia* 32 B9
Mehadia, *Romania* 28 F7
Meharry, Mt., *Australia* 92 D2
Mehedeby, *Sweden* 10 D11
Mehedinți □, *Romania* 28 F7
Meheisa, *Sudan* 80 D3
Mehlville, *U.S.A.* 112 F9
Mehndawal, *India* 69 F10
Mehr Jān, *Iran* 71 C7
Mehrābād, *Iran* 70 B5
Mehrān, *Iran* 70 C5
Mehrīz, *Iran* 71 D7
Mehun-sur-Yèvre, *France* 19 E9
Mei Jiang →, *China* 59 E11
Mei Xian, *China* 56 G4
Meicheng, *China* 59 C12
Meichengzhen, *China* 59 C8
Meichuan, *China* 59 B10
Meigu, *China* 58 C4
Meiktila, *Burma* 67 J19
Meinerzhagen, *Germany* 24 D3
Meiningen, *Germany* 24 E6
Meira, Serra de, *Spain* 36 B3
Meiringen, *Switz.* 25 J4
Meishan, *China* 58 B4
Meissen, *Germany* 24 D9
Meissner, *Germany* 24 D5
Meissner-Kaufunger Wald ⌓, *Germany* 24 D5
Meitan, *China* 58 D6
Meizhou, *China* 59 E11
Meja, *India* 69 G10
Mejillones, *Chile* 126 A1
Mekdela, *Ethiopia* 81 E4
Mekele, *Ethiopia* 81 E4
Mekhtar, *Pakistan* 66 D6
Meknès, *Morocco* 78 B4
Meko, *Nigeria* 83 D5
Mekong →, *Asia* 65 H6
Mekongga, *Indonesia* 63 E6
Mekrou →, *Benin* 83 C5
Mekvari = Kür →, *Azerbaijan* 73 C13
Mel, *Italy* 41 B9
Melagiri Hills, *India* 66 N10
Melaka, *Malaysia* 65 L4
Melalap, *Malaysia* 62 C5
Mélambes, *Greece* 49 D6
Melanesia, *Pac. Oc.* 96 H7
Melaya, *Indonesia* 63 J17
Melbourne, *Australia* 95 F4
Melbourne, *U.S.A.* 115 L5
Melchor Múzquiz, *Mexico* 118 B4
Melchor Ocampo, *Mexico* 118 C4
Méldola, *Italy* 41 D9

Meldorf, *Germany* 24 A5
Melegnano, *Italy* 40 C6
Melenci, *Serbia & M.* 28 E5
Melenki, *Russia* 34 C5
Mélèzes →, *Canada* 104 A5
Melfi, *Italy* 43 B8
Melfort, *Canada* 103 C8
Melfort, *Zimbabwe* 87 F3
Melgaço, *Portugal* 36 C2
Melgar de Fernamental, *Spain* 36 C6
Melhus, *Norway* 8 E14
Melide, *Spain* 36 C2
Meligalá, *Greece* 46 D3
Melilla, *N. Afr.* 78 A5
Melilli, *Italy* 43 E8
Melipilla, *Chile* 126 C1
Mélissa, Ákra, *Greece* 49 D6
Mélissa Óros, *Greece* 47 D8
Melita, *Canada* 103 D8
Mélito di Porto Salvo, *Italy* 43 E8
Melitopol, *Ukraine* 33 J8
Melk, *Austria* 26 C8
Mellan Fryken, *Sweden* 10 E7
Mellansel, *Sweden* 8 E18
Mellbystrand, *Sweden* 11 H6
Melle, *France* 20 B3
Melle, *Germany* 24 C4
Mellen, *U.S.A.* 112 B9
Mellerud, *Sweden* 11 F6
Mellette, *U.S.A.* 112 C5
Mellid = Melide, *Spain* 36 C2
Mellieha, *Malta* 49 D1
Mellit, *Sudan* 81 E2
Mellrichstadt, *Germany* 24 E6
Melnik, *Bulgaria* 44 E7
Mělník, *Czech Rep.* 26 A7
Melnytsya Podilska, *Ukraine* 29 B11
Melo, *Uruguay* 127 C5
Melolo, *Indonesia* 63 F6
Melouprey, *Cambodia* 64 F5
Melrose, *Australia* 95 E4
Melrose, *U.K.* 13 F6
Melrose, *Minn., U.S.A.* 112 C7
Melrose, *N. Mex., U.S.A.* 113 H3
Melstone, *U.S.A.* 108 C10
Melsungen, *Germany* 24 D5
Melton Mowbray, *U.K.* 14 E7
Melun, *France* 19 D9
Melut, *Sudan* 81 E3
Melville, *Canada* 103 C8
Melville, C., *Australia* 94 A3
Melville, L., *Canada* 105 B8
Melville B., *Australia* 94 A2
Melville I., *Australia* 92 B5
Melville I., *Canada* 98 B8
Melville Pen., *Canada* 101 B11
Mélykút, *Hungary* 28 D4
Memaliaj, *Albania* 44 F3
Memba, *Mozam.* 87 E5
Memboro, *Indonesia* 63 F5
Membrilla, *Spain* 37 G7
Memel = Klaipėda, *Lithuania* 9 J19
Memel, *S. Africa* 89 D4
Memmingen, *Germany* 25 H6
Mempawah, *Indonesia* 62 D3
Memphis, *Egypt* 80 J7
Memphis, *Mich., U.S.A.* 116 D2
Memphis, *Tenn., U.S.A.* 113 H10
Memphis, *Tex., U.S.A.* 113 H4
Memphremagog, L., *U.S.A.* 117 B12
Mena, *Ukraine* 33 G7
Mena, *U.S.A.* 113 H7
Mena →, *Ethiopia* 81 F5
Menai Strait, *U.K.* 14 D3
Ménaka, *Mali* 83 B5
Menan = Chao Phraya →, *Thailand* 64 F3
Menarandra →, *Madag.* 89 D7
Menard, *U.S.A.* 113 K5
Menawashei, *Sudan* 81 E1
Mendawai →, *Indonesia* 62 E4
Mende, *France* 20 D7
Mendebo Mts., *Ethiopia* 81 F4
Mendeleyev Ridge, *Arctic* 4 B17
Menden, *Germany* 24 D3
Menderes, *Turkey* 47 C9
Mendez, *Mexico* 119 B5
Mendhar, *India* 69 C6
Mendi, *Ethiopia* 81 F4
Mendip Hills, *U.K.* 15 F5
Mendocino, *U.S.A.* 108 G2
Mendocino, C., *U.S.A.* 108 F1
Mendota, *Calif., U.S.A.* 110 J6
Mendota, *Ill., U.S.A.* 112 E10
Mendoyo, *Indonesia* 63 J17
Mendoza, *Argentina* 126 C2
Mendoza □, *Argentina* 126 C2
Mene Grande, *Venezuela* 124 B4
Menemen, *Turkey* 47 C9
Menen, *Belgium* 17 D3
Menfi, *Italy* 42 E5
Mengdingjie, *China* 58 F2
Mengeš, *Slovenia* 41 B11
Menggala, *Indonesia* 62 E3
Menghai, *China* 58 G3
Mengíbar, *Spain* 37 H7
Mengjin, *China* 56 G7
Mengla, *China* 58 G3
Menglian, *China* 58 F2
Mengshan, *China* 59 E8
Mengyin, *China* 57 G9
Mengzhe, *China* 58 F3
Mengzi, *China* 58 F4
Menihek, *Canada* 105 B6
Menihek L., *Canada* 105 B6
Menin = Menen, *Belgium* 17 D3
Menindee, *Australia* 95 E3
Menindee L., *Australia* 95 E3
Meningie, *Australia* 95 F2
Menjangan, Pulau, *Indonesia* 63 J17
Menlo Park, *U.S.A.* 110 H4
Menominee, *U.S.A.* 114 C2
Menominee →, *U.S.A.* 114 C2
Menomonie, *U.S.A.* 112 C9
Menongue, *Angola* 85 G3
Menorca, *Spain* 48 B11
Menorca ✕ (MAH), *Spain* 38 F9
Mentakab, *Malaysia* 65 L4
Mentawai, Kepulauan, *Indonesia* 62 E1
Menton, *France* 21 E11
Mentor, *U.S.A.* 116 E3
Menzies, *Australia* 93 E3
Meob B., *Namibia* 88 C1
Me'ona, *Israel* 74 B4
Meoqui, *Mexico* 118 B3
Mepaco, *Mozam.* 87 F3
Meppel, *Neths.* 17 B6
Meppen, *Germany* 24 C3
Mequinenza, *Spain* 38 D5
Mequinenza, Embalse de, *Spain* 38 D5
Mer, *France* 18 E8
Merabéllou, Kólpos, *Greece* 49 D7
Merak, *Indonesia* 63 F12
Meramangye, L., *Australia* 93 E5
Meran = Merano, *Italy* 41 B8
Merano, *Italy* 41 B8
Merate, *Italy* 40 C6
Merauke, *Indonesia* 63 F10
Merbein, *Australia* 95 E3
Merbuk, Gunung, *Indonesia* 63 J17
Merca, *Somali Rep.* 75 G3
Mercantour △, *France* 21 D10
Mercato Saraceno, *Italy* 41 E9
Merced, *U.S.A.* 110 H6
Merced →, *U.S.A.* 110 H6
Merced Pk., *U.S.A.* 110 H7
Mercedes, *Buenos Aires, Argentina* 126 C4
Mercedes, *Corrientes, Argentina* 126 B4
Mercedes, *San Luis, Argentina* 126 C2
Mercedes, *Uruguay* 126 C4
Mercedes, *U.S.A.* 113 M6
Merceditas, *Chile* 126 B1
Mercer, *N.Z.* 91 G5
Mercer, *U.S.A.* 116 E4
Mercer Island, *U.S.A.* 110 C4
Mercury, *U.S.A.* 111 J11
Mercy, C., *Canada* 101 B13
Merdrignac, *France* 18 D4
Mere, *U.K.* 15 F5
Meredith, C., *Falk. Is.* 128 G4
Meredith, L., *U.S.A.* 113 H4
Merefa, *Ukraine* 33 H9
Merei, *Romania* 29 E11
Merga = Nukheila, *Sudan* 80 D2
Mergui, *Burma* 64 F2
Mergui Arch. = Myeik Kyunzu, *Burma* 65 G1
Méribel-les-Allues, *France* 21 C10
Meriç, *Turkey* 45 E10
Meriç →, *Turkey* 45 F10
Mérida, *Mexico* 119 C7
Mérida, *Spain* 37 G4
Mérida, *Venezuela* 124 B4
Mérida, Cord. de, *Venezuela* 124 B4
Meriden, *U.K.* 15 E6
Meriden, *U.S.A.* 117 E12
Meridian, *Calif., U.S.A.* 110 F5
Meridian, *Idaho, U.S.A.* 108 E5
Meridian, *Miss., U.S.A.* 115 J1
Mérignac, *France* 20 D3
Mérinaghène, *Senegal* 82 B1
Merinda, *Australia* 94 C4
Mering, *Germany* 25 G6
Meringa, *Nigeria* 83 C7
Merir, *Pac. Oc.* 63 D8
Merirumã, *Brazil* 125 C8
Merkel, *U.S.A.* 113 J5
Mermaid Reef, *Australia* 92 C2
Merowe, *Sudan* 80 D3
Merredin, *Australia* 93 F2
Merrick, *U.K.* 13 F4
Merrickville, *Canada* 117 B9
Merrill, *Oreg., U.S.A.* 108 E3
Merrill, *Wis., U.S.A.* 112 C10
Merrimack →, *U.S.A.* 117 D14
Merriman, *U.S.A.* 112 D4
Merritt, *Canada* 102 C4
Merritt Island, *U.S.A.* 115 L5
Merriwa, *Australia* 95 E5
Merry I., *Canada* 104 A4
Merryville, *U.S.A.* 113 K8
Mersa Fatma, *Eritrea* 81 E5
Mersch, *Lux.* 17 E6
Merse →, *Italy* 41 E8
Mersea I., *U.K.* 15 F8
Merseburg, *Germany* 24 D7
Mersey →, *U.K.* 14 D4
Merseyside □, *U.K.* 14 D4
Mersin, *Turkey* 70 B2
Mersing, *Malaysia* 65 L4
Merta, *India* 68 F6
Merta Road, *India* 68 F5
Merthyr Tydfil, *U.K.* 15 F4
Merthyr Tydfil □, *U.K.* 15 F4
Mértola, *Portugal* 37 H3
Mertzon, *U.S.A.* 113 K4
Méru, *France* 19 C9
Meru, *Kenya* 86 B4
Meru, *Tanzania* 86 C4
Meru △, *Kenya* 86 B4
Merville, *France* 19 B9
Méry-sur-Seine, *France* 19 D10
Merzifon, *Turkey* 72 B6
Merzig, *Germany* 25 F2
Mesa, *U.S.A.* 109 K8
Mesa Verde △, *U.S.A.* 109 H9
Mesagne, *Italy* 43 B10
Mesanagrós, *Greece* 49 C9
Mesaoría, *Cyprus* 49 D12
Mesarás, Kólpos, *Greece* 49 D6
Meschede, *Germany* 24 D4
Mescit, *Turkey* 73 B9
Mesfinto, *Ethiopia* 81 E4
Mesgouez, L., *Canada* 104 B5
Meshchovsk, *Russia* 32 E8
Meshed = Mashhad, *Iran* 71 B8
Meshoppen, *U.S.A.* 117 E8
Meshra er Req, *Sudan* 81 F2
Mesilinka →, *Canada* 102 B4
Mesilla, *U.S.A.* 109 K10
Meslay-du-Maine, *France* 18 E6
Mesocco, *Switz.* 25 J5
Mesolóngion, *Greece* 46 C3
Mesopotamia = Al Jazirah, *Iraq* 70 C5
Mesopotamia, *U.S.A.* 116 E4
Mesopótamon, *Greece* 46 B2
Mesoraca, *Italy* 43 C9
Mésou Volímais = Volímai, *Greece* 46 D2
Mesquite, *U.S.A.* 109 H6
Messaad, *Algeria* 78 B6
Messac, *France* 18 E5
Messalo →, *Mozam.* 87 E4
Méssaména, *Cameroon* 83 E7
Messeue, *Greece* 46 D3
Messina = Musina, *S. Africa* 89 C5
Messina, *Italy* 43 D8
Messina, Str. di, *Italy* 43 D8
Messíni, *Greece* 46 D4
Messínia □, *Greece* 46 D3
Messiniakós Kólpos, *Greece* 46 E4
Messkirch, *Germany* 25 H5
Messlingen, *Sweden* 10 B6
Messonghi, *Greece* 49 B3
Mesta →, *Bulgaria* 44 E7
Mestá, Ákra, *Greece* 47 C7
Mestanza, *Spain* 37 G6
Mestre, *Italy* 41 C9
Mesudiye, *Turkey* 72 B7
Meta →, *S. Amer.* 124 B5
Meta Incognita Pen., *Canada* 101 B13
Metabetchouan, *Canada* 105 C5
Metairie, *U.S.A.* 113 L9
Metalici, Munţii, *Romania* 28 D7
Metaline Falls, *U.S.A.* 108 B5
Metallifere, Colline, *Italy* 40 E8
Metán, *Argentina* 126 B3
Metangula, *Mozam.* 87 E3
Metauro →, *Italy* 41 E10
Metema, *Ethiopia* 81 E4
Metengobalame, *Mozam.* 87 E3
Méthana, *Greece* 46 D5
Methóni, *Greece* 46 E3
Methven, *N.Z.* 91 K3
Metil, *Mozam.* 87 F4
Metkovets, *Bulgaria* 44 C7
Metković, *Croatia* 41 E14
Metlakatla, *U.S.A.* 100 C6
Metlika, *Slovenia* 41 C12
Metropolis, *U.S.A.* 113 G10
Métsovon, *Greece* 46 B3
Metu, *Ethiopia* 81 F4
Metz, *France* 19 C13
Metzingen, *Germany* 25 G5
Meulaboh, *Indonesia* 62 D1
Meung-sur-Loire, *France* 19 E8
Meureudu, *Indonesia* 62 C1
Meurthe →, *France* 19 D13
Meurthe-et-Moselle □, *France* 19 D13
Meuse □, *France* 19 C12
Meuse →, *Europe* 17 D5
Meuselwitz, *Germany* 24 D8
Mexia, *U.S.A.* 113 K6
Mexiana, I., *Brazil* 125 D9
Mexicali, *Mexico* 111 N11
Mexican Plateau, *Mexico* 98 G9
Mexican Water, *U.S.A.* 109 H9
México, *Mexico* 119 D5
Mexico, *Maine, U.S.A.* 117 B14
Mexico, *Mo., U.S.A.* 112 F9
Mexico, *N.Y., U.S.A.* 117 C8
México □, *Mexico* 119 D5
Mexico ■, *Cent. Amer.* 118 C4
Mexico, G. of, *Cent. Amer.* 119 C7
Mexico B., *U.S.A.* 117 C8
Meydān-e Naftūn, *Iran* 71 D6
Meydani, Ra's-e, *Iran* 71 E8
Meyenburg, *Germany* 24 B8
Meymac, *France* 20 C6
Meymaneh, *Afghan.* 66 B4
Meyrueis, *France* 20 D7
Meyssac, *France* 20 C5
Meyzieu, *France* 21 C8
Mezdra, *Bulgaria* 44 C7
Mèze, *France* 20 E7
Mezen, *Russia* 52 C5
Mezen →, *Russia* 52 C5
Mézenc, Mt., *France* 21 D8
Mezeş, Munţii, *Romania* 28 C8
Mezha →, *Russia* 32 E6
Mezhdurechenskiy, *Russia* 52 D7
Mézidon-Canon, *France* 18 C6
Mézières-en-Brenne, *France* 20 B5
Mézilhac, *France* 21 D8
Mézin, *France* 20 D4
Mezőberény, *Hungary* 28 D6
Mezőfalva, *Hungary* 28 D3
Mezőhegyes, *Hungary* 28 D5
Mezőkövácsháza, *Hungary* 28 D5
Mezőkövesd, *Hungary* 28 C5
Mézos, *France* 20 D2
Mezőtúr, *Hungary* 28 C5
Mezquital, *Mexico* 118 C4
Mezzolombardo, *Italy* 40 B8
Mfolozi →, *S. Africa* 89 D5
Mgeta, *Tanzania* 87 D4
Mglin, *Russia* 33 F7
Mhlaba Hills, *Zimbabwe* 87 F3
Mhow, *India* 68 H6
Miahuatlán, *Mexico* 119 D5
Miajadas, *Spain* 37 F5
Miami, *Fla., U.S.A.* 115 N5
Miami, *Okla., U.S.A.* 113 G7
Miami, *Tex., U.S.A.* 113 H4
Miami Beach, *U.S.A.* 115 N5
Mian Xian, *China* 56 H4
Mianchi, *China* 56 G6
Mīāndarreh, *Iran* 71 C7
Mīāndowāb, *Iran* 70 B5
Miandrivazo, *Madag.* 89 B8
Mīāneh, *Iran* 70 B5
Mianning, *China* 58 C4
Mianwali, *Pakistan* 68 C4
Mianyang, *China* 58 B5
Mianzhu, *China* 58 B5
Miaoli, *Taiwan* 59 E13
Miarinarivo, *Antananarivo, Madag.* 89 B8
Miarinarivo, *Toamasina, Madag.* 89 B8
Miariravaratra, *Madag.* 89 C8
Miass, *Russia* 52 D7
Miasteczko Krajeńskie, *Poland* 31 E4
Miastko, *Poland* 30 E3
Mica, *S. Africa* 89 C5
Micăsasa, *Romania* 29 D9
Michalovce, *Slovak Rep.* 27 C14
Michigan □, *U.S.A.* 114 C3
Michigan, L., *U.S.A.* 114 D2
Michigan City, *U.S.A.* 114 E2
Michika, *Nigeria* 83 C7
Michipicoten I., *Canada* 104 C2
Michoacan □, *Mexico* 118 D4
Michurin, *Bulgaria* 45 D11
Michurinsk, *Russia* 34 D5
Mico, Pta., *Nic.* 120 D3
Micoud, *St. Lucia* 121 f
Micronesia, *Pac. Oc.* 96 G7
Micronesia, Federated States of ■, *Pac. Oc.* 96 G7
Mid-Oceanic Ridge, *Ind. Oc.* 96 M1
Midai, *Indonesia* 62 D3
Midale, *Canada* 103 D8
Middelburg, *Neths.* 17 C3
Middelburg, *Eastern Cape, S. Africa* 88 E4
Middelburg, *Mpumalanga, S. Africa* 89 D4
Middelfart, *Denmark* 11 J3
Middelpos, *S. Africa* 88 E3
Middelwit, *S. Africa* 88 C4
Middle Alkali L., *U.S.A.* 108 F3
Middle Bass I., *U.S.A.* 116 E2
Middle East, *Asia* 50 F7
Middle Fork Feather →, *U.S.A.* 110 F5
Middle I., *Australia* 93 F3
Middle Loup →, *U.S.A.* 112 E5
Middle Sackville, *Canada* 105 D7
Middleboro, *U.S.A.* 117 E14
Middleburg, *Fla., U.S.A.* 115 K5
Middleburg, *Pa., U.S.A.* 116 F7
Middleburgh, *U.S.A.* 117 D10
Middlebury, *U.S.A.* 117 B11
Middlemount, *Australia* 94 C4
Middleport, *N.Y., U.S.A.* 116 C6
Middleport, *Ohio, U.S.A.* 114 F4
Middlesboro, *U.S.A.* 115 G4
Middlesbrough, *U.K.* 14 C6
Middlesbrough □, *U.K.* 14 C6
Middlesex, *Belize* 120 C2
Middlesex, *N.J., U.S.A.* 117 F10
Middlesex, *N.Y., U.S.A.* 116 D7
Middleton, *Australia* 94 C3
Middleton, *Canada* 105 D6
Middleton Cr. →, *Australia* 94 C3
Middletown, *U.K.* 12 B5
Middletown, *Calif., U.S.A.* 110 G4
Middletown, *Conn., U.S.A.* 117 E12
Middletown, *N.Y., U.S.A.* 117 E10
Middletown, *Ohio, U.S.A.* 114 F3
Middletown, *Pa., U.S.A.* 117 F8
Midge Point, *Australia* 94 J6
Midhurst, *U.K.* 15 G7
Mīdī, *Yemen* 81 D5
Midi, Canal du →, *France* 20 E5
Midi d'Ossau, Pic du, *France* 20 F3
Midi-Pyrénées □, *France* 20 E5
Midland, *Australia* 93 F2
Midland, *Canada* 116 B5
Midland, *Calif., U.S.A.* 111 M12
Midland, *Mich., U.S.A.* 114 D3
Midland, *Pa., U.S.A.* 116 F4
Midland, *Tex., U.S.A.* 113 K3
Midlands □, *Zimbabwe* 87 F2
Midleton, *Ireland* 12 E3
Midlothian, *U.S.A.* 113 J6
Midlothian □, *U.K.* 13 F5
Midongy, Tangorombohitr' i, *Madag.* 89 C8
Midongy Atsimo, *Madag.* 89 C8
Midou →, *France* 20 E3
Midouze →, *France* 20 E3
Midsayap, *Phil.* 61 H6
Midu, *China* 58 E3
Midway Is., *Pac. Oc.* 96 E10
Midway Wells, *U.S.A.* 111 N11
Midwest, *U.S.A.* 107 B9
Midwest, *Wyo., U.S.A.* 108 E10
Midwest City, *U.S.A.* 113 H6
Midyat, *Turkey* 70 B4
Midžor, *Bulgaria* 44 C6
Mie □, *Japan* 55 G8
Miechów, *Poland* 31 H7
Miedwie, Jezioro, *Poland* 31 E1
Międzybórz, *Poland* 31 G4
Międzychód, *Poland* 31 F2
Międzylesie, *Poland* 31 H3
Międzyrzec Podlaski, *Poland* 31 G9
Międzyrzecz, *Poland* 31 F2
Międzyzdroje, *Poland* 30 E1
Miejska Górka, *Poland* 31 G3
Miélan, *France* 20 E4
Mielec, *Poland* 31 H8
Mienga, *Angola* 88 B2
Miercurea-Ciuc, *Romania* 29 D10
Miercurea Sibiului, *Romania* 29 E8
Mieres, *Spain* 36 B5
Mieroszów, *Poland* 31 H3
Mieso, *Ethiopia* 81 F5
Mieszkowice, *Poland* 31 F1
Mifflintown, *U.S.A.* 116 F7
Mifraz Ḥefa, *Israel* 74 C4
Migennes, *France* 19 E10
Migliarino, *Italy* 41 D8
Migliarino-San Rossore-Massaciuccoli △, *Italy* 40 E7
Miguel Alemán, Presa, *Mexico* 119 D5
Miguelturra, *Spain* 37 G7
Mihăileni, *Romania* 29 C11
Mihăileşti, *Romania* 29 F10
Mihailovca, *Moldova* 29 D13
Mihalgazi, *Turkey* 47 A12
Mihaliççık, *Turkey* 72 C4
Mihara, *Japan* 55 G6
Miheşu de Cîmpie, *Romania* 29 D9
Mijas, *Spain* 37 J6
Mikese, *Tanzania* 86 D4
Mikha-Tskhakaya = Senaki, *Georgia* 35 J6
Mikhailovka = Mykhaylivka, *Ukraine* 33 J8
Mikhaylov, *Russia* 32 E10
Mikhaylovgrad = Montana, *Bulgaria* 44 C7
Mikhaylovka, *Russia* 34 E6
Mikhnevo, *Russia* 32 E9
Mikínai, *Greece* 46 D4
Mikkeli, *Finland* 9 F22
Mikkwa →, *Canada* 102 B6
Mikniya, *Sudan* 81 D3
Mikołajki, *Poland* 30 E8
Míkonos, *Greece* 47 D7
Mikrí Préspa, Límni, *Greece* 44 F5
Mikrón Dhérion, *Greece* 45 E10
Mikstat, *Poland* 31 G4
Mikulov, *Czech Rep.* 27 C9
Mikumi, *Tanzania* 86 D4
Mikumi △, *Tanzania* 86 D4
Milaca, *U.S.A.* 112 C8
Milagro, *Ecuador* 124 D3
Milagros, *Phil.* 61 E5
Milan = Milano, *Italy* 40 C6
Milan, *Mo., U.S.A.* 112 E8
Milan, *Tenn., U.S.A.* 115 H1
Milange, *Mozam.* 87 F4
Milano, *Italy* 40 C6
Milano Linate ✕ (LIN), *Italy* 40 C6
Milanoa, *Madag.* 89 A8
Milâs, *Turkey* 47 D9
Milatos, *Greece* 49 D7
Milazzo, *Italy* 43 D8
Milbank, *U.S.A.* 112 C6
Milbanke Sd., *Canada* 102 C3
Milden, *Canada* 103 C7
Mildenhall, *U.K.* 15 E8
Mildmay, *Canada* 116 B3
Mildura, *Australia* 95 E3
Mile, *China* 58 E4
Miléai, *Greece* 46 B5
Miles, *Australia* 95 D5
Miles City, *U.S.A.* 112 B2
Mileşti, *Moldova* 29 C13
Milestone, *Canada* 103 D8
Mileto, *Italy* 43 D9
Miletto, Mte., *Italy* 43 A7
Miletus, *Turkey* 47 D9
Milevsko, *Czech Rep.* 26 B7
Milford, *Calif., U.S.A.* 110 E6
Milford, *Conn., U.S.A.* 117 E11
Milford, *Del., U.S.A.* 114 F8
Milford, *Mass., U.S.A.* 117 D13
Milford, *N.H., U.S.A.* 117 D13
Milford, *Pa., U.S.A.* 117 E10
Milford, *Utah, U.S.A.* 109 G7
Milford Haven, *U.K.* 15 F2
Milford Sd., *N.Z.* 91 L1
Milford Sound, *N.Z.* 91 L1
Milḥ, Baḥr al = Razāzah, Buḥayrat ar, *Iraq* 70 C4
Milicz, *Poland* 31 G4
Milikapiti, *Australia* 92 B5
Miling, *Australia* 93 F2
Militello in Val di Catánia, *Italy* 43 E7
Milk →, *U.S.A.* 108 B10
Milk, Wadi el →, *Sudan* 80 D3
Milk River, *Canada* 102 D6
Mill I., *Antarctica* 5 C8
Mill Valley, *U.S.A.* 110 H4
Millárs →, *Spain* 38 F4
Millau, *France* 20 D7
Millbridge, *Canada* 116 B7
Millbrook, *Canada* 116 B6
Millbrook, *U.S.A.* 117 E11
Mille Lacs, L. des, *Canada* 104 C1
Mille Lacs L., *U.S.A.* 112 B8
Milledgeville, *U.S.A.* 115 J4
Millen, *U.S.A.* 115 J5
Millennium I. = Caroline I., *Kiribati* 97 H12
Miller, *U.S.A.* 112 C5
Millerovo, *Russia* 35 F5
Millersburg, *Ohio, U.S.A.* 116 F3
Millersburg, *Pa., U.S.A.* 116 F8
Millerton, *U.S.A.* 117 E11
Millerton L., *U.S.A.* 110 J7
Millet, *St. Lucia* 121 f
Millevaches, Plateau de, *France* 20 C6
Millheim, *U.S.A.* 116 F7
Millicent, *Australia* 95 F3
Millington, *U.S.A.* 113 H10
Millinocket, *U.S.A.* 115 C11
Millmerran, *Australia* 95 D5
Millom, *U.K.* 14 C4
Mills L., *Canada* 102 A5
Millsboro, *U.S.A.* 116 G5
Millstream-Chichester △, *Australia* 92 D2
Milltown Malbay, *Ireland* 12 D2
Millville, *N.J., U.S.A.* 114 F8
Millville, *Pa., U.S.A.* 117 E8

Millwood L., *U.S.A.* 113 J8
Milna, *Croatia* 41 E13
Milne →, *Australia* 94 C2
Milo, *U.S.A.* 115 C11
Mílos, *Greece* 46 E6
Miłosław, *Poland* 31 F4
Milot, *Albania* 44 E3
Milparinka, *Australia* 95 D3
Miltenberg, *Germany* 25 F5
Milton, *N.S., Canada* 105 D7
Milton, *Ont., Canada* 116 C5
Milton, *N.Z.* 91 M2
Milton, *Calif., U.S.A.* 110 G6
Milton, *Fla., U.S.A.* 115 K2
Milton, *Pa., U.S.A.* 116 F8
Milton, *Vt., U.S.A.* 117 B11
Milton-Freewater, *U.S.A.* 108 D4
Milton Keynes, *U.K.* 15 E7
Milton Keynes □, *U.K.* 15 E7
Miluo, *China* 59 C9
Milverton, *Canada* 116 C4
Milwaukee, *U.S.A.* 114 D2
Milwaukee Deep, *Atl. Oc.* 121 C6
Milwaukie, *U.S.A.* 110 E4
Mim, *Ghana* 82 D4
Mimizan, *France* 20 D2
Mimoň, *Czech Rep.* 26 A7
Min Jiang →, *Fujian, China* 59 E12
Min Jiang →, *Sichuan, China* 58 C5
Min Xian, *China* 56 G3
Mina Pirquitas, *Argentina* 126 A2
Mīnā Su'ud, *Si. Arabia* 71 D6
Mīnā'al Aḥmadī, *Kuwait* 71 D6
Minago →, *Canada* 103 C9
Minaki, *Canada* 103 D10
Minamata, *Japan* 55 H5
Minami-Arapusa △, *Japan* 55 G9
Minami-Tori-Shima, *Pac. Oc.* 96 E7
Minas, *Uruguay* 127 C4
Minas, Sierra de las, *Guatemala* 120 C2
Minas Basin, *Canada* 105 C7
Minas de Riotinto, *Spain* 37 H4
Minas Gerais □, *Brazil* 125 G9
Minatitlán, *Mexico* 119 D6
Minbu, *Burma* 67 J19
Minchinabad, *Pakistan* 68 D5
Mincio →, *Italy* 40 C7
Minčol, *Slovak Rep.* 27 B13
Mindanao, *Phil.* 61 H6
Mindanao Sea = Bohol Sea, *Phil.* 63 C6
Mindanao Trench, *Pac. Oc.* 61 F7
Mindel →, *Germany* 25 G6
Mindelheim, *Germany* 25 G6
Minden, *Canada* 116 B6
Minden, *Germany* 24 C4
Minden, *La., U.S.A.* 113 J8
Minden, *Nev., U.S.A.* 110 G7
Mindiptana, *Indonesia* 63 F10
Mindoro, *Phil.* 61 E4
Mindoro Str., *Phil.* 61 E4
Mine, *Japan* 55 G5
Minehead, *U.K.* 15 F4
Mineola, *N.Y., U.S.A.* 117 F11
Mineola, *Tex., U.S.A.* 113 J7
Mineral King, *U.S.A.* 110 J8
Mineral Wells, *U.S.A.* 113 J5
Mineralnyye Vody, *Russia* 35 H6
Minersville, *U.S.A.* 117 F8
Minerva, *U.S.A.* 116 F3
Minervino Murge, *Italy* 43 A9
Minetto, *U.S.A.* 117 C8
Mingäçevir, *Azerbaijan* 35 K8
Mingäçevir Su Anbarı, *Azerbaijan* 35 K8
Mingan, *Canada* 105 B7
Mingechaur = Mingäçevir, *Azerbaijan* 35 K8
Mingechaurskoye Vdkhr. = Mingäçevir Su Anbarı, *Azerbaijan* 35 K8
Mingela, *Australia* 94 B4
Mingenew, *Australia* 93 E2
Mingera Cr. →, *Australia* 94 C2
Minggang, *China* 59 A10
Mingguang, *China* 59 A11
Mingin, *Burma* 67 H19
Mingir, *Moldova* 29 D13
Minglanilla, *Spain* 39 F3
Minglun, *China* 58 E7
Mingo Junction, *U.S.A.* 116 F4
Mingorria, *Spain* 36 E6
Mingshan, *China* 58 B4
Mingteke Daban = Mintaka Pass, *Pakistan* 69 A6
Mingxi, *China* 59 D11
Mingyuegue, *China* 57 C15
Minho = Miño →, *Spain* 36 D2
Minhou, *China* 59 E12
Minićevo, *Serbia & M.* 28 G7
Minidoka, *U.S.A.* 108 E7
Minigwal, L., *Australia* 93 E3
Minilya →, *Australia* 93 D1
Minilya Roadhouse, *Australia* 93 D1
Minipi L., *Canada* 105 B7
Mink L., *Canada* 102 A5
Minkammen, *Sudan* 81 F3
Minna, *Nigeria* 83 D6
Minneapolis, *Kans., U.S.A.* 112 F6
Minneapolis, *Minn., U.S.A.* 112 C8
Minnedosa, *Canada* 103 C9
Minnesota □, *U.S.A.* 112 B8
Minnesota →, *U.S.A.* 112 C8
Minnewaukan, *U.S.A.* 112 A5
Minnipa, *Australia* 95 E2
Minnitaki L., *Canada* 104 C1
Mino, *Japan* 55 G8
Miño, *Spain* 36 B2
Miño →, *Spain* 36 D2
Minoa, *Greece* 47 F7
Minorca = Menorca, *Spain* 48 B11
Minot, *U.S.A.* 112 A4
Minqin, *China* 56 E2
Minqing, *China* 59 D12
Minsen, *Germany* 24 B3
Minsk, *Belarus* 32 F4
Mińsk Mazowiecki, *Poland* 31 F8
Mintabie, *Australia* 95 D1
Mintaka Pass, *Pakistan* 69 A6
Minto, *Canada* 105 C6
Minto, L., *Canada* 104 A5
Minton, *Canada* 103 D8
Minturn, *U.S.A.* 108 G10
Minturno, *Italy* 42 A6
Minûf, *Egypt* 80 H7
Minusinsk, *Russia* 53 D10
Minutang, *India* 67 E20
Minya el Qamh, *Egypt* 80 H7
Minya Konka = Gongga Shan, *China* 58 C3
Mionica, *Bos.-H.* 28 F3
Mionica, *Serbia & M.* 44 B4
Miquelon, *Canada* 104 C4
Miquelon, *St-P. & M.* 105 C8
Mir, *Niger* 83 C7
Mīr Kūh, *Iran* 71 E8
Mīr Shahdād, *Iran* 71 E8
Mira, *Italy* 41 C9
Mira, *Portugal* 36 E2
Mira →, *Portugal* 37 H2
Mira por vos Cay, *Bahamas* 121 B5
Mirabella Eclano, *Italy* 43 A7
Mirador-Río Azul △, *Guatemala* 120 C2
Miraj, *India* 66 L9
Miram Shah, *Pakistan* 68 C4
Miramar, *Argentina* 126 D4
Miramar, *Mozam.* 89 C6
Miramas, *France* 21 E8
Mirambeau, *France* 20 C3
Miramichi, *Canada* 105 C6
Miramichi B., *Canada* 105 C7
Miramont-de-Guyenne, *France* 20 D4
Miranda, *Brazil* 125 H7
Miranda →, *Brazil* 124 G7
Miranda de Ebro, *Spain* 38 C2
Miranda do Corvo, *Portugal* 36 E2
Miranda do Douro, *Portugal* 36 D4
Mirande, *France* 20 E4
Mirandela, *Portugal* 36 D3
Mirándola, *Italy* 40 D8
Mirandópolis, *Brazil* 127 A5
Mirango, *Malawi* 87 E3
Mirani, *Australia* 94 K6
Mirano, *Italy* 41 C9
Miras, *Albania* 44 F4
Mirassol, *Brazil* 127 A6
Mirbāṭ, *Oman* 75 D5
Mirear, *Egypt* 80 C4
Mirebeau, *France* 18 F7
Mirebeau-sur-Bèze, *France* 19 E12
Mirecourt, *France* 19 D13
Mirgorod = Myrhorod, *Ukraine* 33 H7
Miri, *Malaysia* 62 D4
Miriam Vale, *Australia* 94 C5
Miribel, *France* 19 G11
Mirim, L., *S. Amer.* 127 C5
Mirnyy, *Russia* 53 C12
Miroč, *Serbia & M.* 44 B6
Mirokhan, *Pakistan* 68 F3
Mirond L., *Canada* 103 B8
Mirosławiec, *Poland* 30 E3
Mirpur, *Pakistan* 69 C5
Mirpur Batoro, *Pakistan* 68 G3
Mirpur Bibiwari, *Pakistan* 68 E2
Mirpur Khas, *Pakistan* 68 G3
Mirpur Sakro, *Pakistan* 68 G2
Mirria, *Niger* 83 C6
Mirsk, *Poland* 31 H2
Mirtağ, *Turkey* 70 B4
Miryang, *S. Korea* 57 G15
Mirzaani, *Georgia* 35 K8
Mirzapur, *India* 69 G10
Mirzapur-cum-Vindhyachal = Mirzapur, *India* 69 G10
Misantla, *Mexico* 119 D5
Misawa, *Japan* 54 D10
Miscou I., *Canada* 105 C7
Mish'āb, Ra's al, *Si. Arabia* 71 D6
Mishan, *China* 60 B8
Mishawaka, *U.S.A.* 114 E2
Mishbih, Gebel, *Egypt* 80 C3
Mishima, *Japan* 55 G9
Misión, *Mexico* 111 N10
Misiones □, *Argentina* 127 B5
Misiones □, *Paraguay* 126 B4
Miskah, *Si. Arabia* 70 E4
Miskitos, Cayos, *Nic.* 120 D3
Miskolc, *Hungary* 28 B5
Misoke, *Dem. Rep. of the Congo* 86 C2
Misool, *Indonesia* 63 E8
Mişrātah, *Libya* 79 B9
Missanabie, *Canada* 104 C3
Missinaibi →, *Canada* 104 B3
Missinaibi L., *Canada* 104 C3
Mission, *Canada* 102 D4
Mission, *S. Dak., U.S.A.* 112 D4
Mission, *Tex., U.S.A.* 113 M5
Mission Beach, *Australia* 94 B4
Mission Viejo, *U.S.A.* 111 M9
Missirah, *Senegal* 82 C1
Missisa L., *Canada* 104 B2
Missisicabi →, *Canada* 104 B4
Mississagi →, *Canada* 104 C3
Mississauga, *Canada* 116 C5
Mississippi □, *U.S.A.* 113 J10
Mississippi →, *U.S.A.* 113 L10
Mississippi L., *Canada* 117 A8
Mississippi River Delta, *U.S.A.* 113 L9
Mississippi Sd., *U.S.A.* 113 K10
Missoula, *U.S.A.* 108 C7
Missouri □, *U.S.A.* 112 F8
Missouri →, *U.S.A.* 112 F9
Missouri City, *U.S.A.* 113 L7
Missouri Valley, *U.S.A.* 112 E7
Mist, *U.S.A.* 110 E3
Mistassibi →, *Canada* 105 B5
Mistassini →, *Canada* 105 C5
Mistassini, L., *Canada* 104 B5
Mistastin L., *Canada* 105 A7
Mistelbach, *Austria* 27 C9
Misterbianco, *Italy* 43 E8
Mistinibi, L., *Canada* 105 A7
Mistissini, *Canada* 105 C5
Mistretta, *Italy* 43 E7
Misty L., *Canada* 103 B8
Misurata = Mişrātah, *Libya* 79 B9
Mît Ghamr, *Egypt* 80 H7
Mitatib, *Sudan* 81 D4
Mitchell, *Australia* 95 D4
Mitchell, *Canada* 116 C3
Mitchell, *Nebr., U.S.A.* 112 E3
Mitchell, *Oreg., U.S.A.* 108 D3
Mitchell, *S. Dak., U.S.A.* 112 D6
Mitchell →, *Australia* 94 B3
Mitchell, Mt., *U.S.A.* 115 H4
Mitchell and Alice Rivers △, *Australia* 94 B3
Mitchell Ranges, *Australia* 94 A2
Mitchelstown, *Ireland* 12 D3
Mitha Tiwana, *Pakistan* 68 C5
Mithi, *Pakistan* 68 G3
Míthimna, *Greece* 47 B8
Mithrao, *Pakistan* 68 F3
Mitilíni, *Greece* 47 B8
Mitilinoí, *Greece* 47 D8
Mito, *Japan* 55 F10
Mitrofanovka, *Russia* 33 H10
Mitrovica = Kosovska Mitrovica, *Serbia & M.* 44 D4
Mitsinjo, *Madag.* 89 B8
Mitsiwa, *Eritrea* 81 D4
Mitsiwa Channel, *Eritrea* 81 D5
Mitsukaidō, *Japan* 55 F9
Mittagong, *Australia* 95 E5
Mittelberg, *Austria* 26 D3
Mittelfranken □, *Germany* 25 F6
Mittellandkanal →, *Germany* 24 C4
Mittenwalde, *Germany* 24 C9
Mittersill, *Austria* 26 D5
Mitterteich, *Germany* 25 F8
Mittimatalik = Pond Inlet, *Canada* 101 A12
Mittweida, *Germany* 24 E8
Mitú, *Colombia* 124 C4
Mitumba, *Tanzania* 86 D3
Mitumba, Mts., *Dem. Rep. of the Congo* 86 D2
Mitwaba, *Dem. Rep. of the Congo* 87 D2
Mityana, *Uganda* 86 B3
Mixteco →, *Mexico* 119 D5
Miyagi □, *Japan* 54 E10
Miyāh, W. el →, *Egypt* 80 C3
Miyāh, W. el →, *Syria* 70 C3
Miyake-Jima, *Japan* 55 G9
Miyako, *Japan* 54 E10
Miyako-Jima, *Japan* 55 M2
Miyako-Rettō, *Japan* 55 M2
Miyakonojō, *Japan* 55 J5
Miyani, *India* 68 J3
Miyanoura-Dake, *Japan* 55 J5
Miyazaki, *Japan* 55 J5
Miyazaki □, *Japan* 55 H5
Miyazu, *Japan* 55 G7
Miyet, Bahr el = Dead Sea, *Asia* 74 D4
Miyi, *China* 58 D4
Miyoshi, *Japan* 55 G6
Miyun, *China* 56 D9
Miyun Shuiku, *China* 57 D9
Mizan Teferi, *Ethiopia* 81 F4
Mizdah, *Libya* 79 B8
Mizen Hd., *Cork, Ireland* 12 E2
Mizen Hd., *Wicklow, Ireland* 12 D5
Mizhhirya, *Ukraine* 29 B8
Mizhi, *China* 56 F6
Mizil, *Romania* 29 F11
Mizoram □, *India* 67 H18
Mizpe Ramon, *Israel* 74 E3
Mizuho, *Antarctica* 5 D5
Mizusawa, *Japan* 54 E10
Mjällby, *Sweden* 11 H8
Mjöbäck, *Sweden* 11 G6
Mjölby, *Sweden* 11 F9
Mjörn, *Sweden* 11 G6
Mjøsa, *Norway* 9 F14
Mkata, *Tanzania* 86 D4
Mkhaya ⌓, *Swaziland* 89 D5
Mkokotoni, *Tanzania* 86 D4
Mkomazi, *Tanzania* 86 C4
Mkomazi ⌓, *Tanzania* 86 C3
Mkomazi →, *S. Africa* 89 E5
Mkulwe, *Tanzania* 87 D3
Mkumbi, Ras, *Tanzania* 86 D4
Mkushi, *Zambia* 87 E2
Mkushi River, *Zambia* 87 E2
Mkuze, *S. Africa* 89 D5
Mkuze ⌓, *S. Africa* 89 D4
Mladá Boleslav, *Czech Rep.* 26 A7
Mladenovac, *Serbia & M.* 44 B4
Mlala Hills, *Tanzania* 86 D3
Mlange = Mulanje, *Malawi* 87 F4
Mlanje, Pic, *Malawi* 85 H7
Mlava →, *Serbia & M.* 44 B5
Mława, *Poland* 31 E7
Mlawula ⌓, *Swaziland* 89 D5
Mliniště, *Bos.-H.* 41 D13
Mljet, *Croatia* 41 F14
Mljet △, *Croatia* 41 F14
Mljetski Kanal, *Croatia* 41 F14
Młynary, *Poland* 30 D6
Mmabatho, *S. Africa* 88 D4
Mme, *Cameroon* 83 D7
Mnichovo Hradiště, *Czech Rep.* 26 A7
Mo i Rana, *Norway* 8 C16
Moa, *Cuba* 121 B4
Moa, *Indonesia* 63 F7
Moa →, *S. Leone* 82 D2
Moab, *U.S.A.* 109 G9
Moala, *Fiji* 91 D8
Moama, *Australia* 95 F3
Moamba, *Mozam.* 89 D5
Moapa, *U.S.A.* 111 J12
Moate, *Ireland* 12 C4
Moba, *Dem. Rep. of the Congo* 86 D2
Mobārakābād, *Iran* 71 D7
Mobaye, *C.A.R.* 84 D4
Mobayi, *Dem. Rep. of the Congo* 84 D4
Moberley Lake, *Canada* 102 B4
Moberly, *U.S.A.* 112 F8
Mobile, *U.S.A.* 115 K1
Mobile B., *U.S.A.* 115 K2
Mobridge, *U.S.A.* 112 C4
Moc Chau, *Vietnam* 64 B5
Moc Hoa, *Vietnam* 65 G5
Mocabe Kasari, *Dem. Rep. of the Congo* 87 D2
Moçambique, *Mozam.* 87 F5
Mocanaqua, *U.S.A.* 117 E8
Mochima △, *Venezuela* 121 D7
Mochudi, *Botswana* 88 C4
Mocimboa da Praia, *Mozam.* 87 E5
Mociu, *Romania* 29 D9
Möckeln, *Sweden* 11 H8
Mockfjärd, *Sweden* 10 D8
Moclips, *U.S.A.* 110 C2
Mocoa, *Colombia* 124 C3
Mococa, *Brazil* 127 A6
Mocorito, *Mexico* 118 B3
Moctezuma, *Mexico* 118 B3
Moctezuma →, *Mexico* 119 C5
Mocuba, *Mozam.* 87 F4
Mocúzari, Presa, *Mexico* 118 B3
Modane, *France* 21 C10
Modasa, *India* 68 H5
Modder →, *S. Africa* 88 D3
Modderrivier, *S. Africa* 88 D3
Módena, *Italy* 40 D7
Modena, *U.S.A.* 109 H7
Modesto, *U.S.A.* 110 H6
Módica, *Italy* 43 F7
Modimolle, *S. Africa* 89 C4
Mödling, *Austria* 27 C9
Modo, *Sudan* 81 F3
Modra, *Slovak Rep.* 27 C10
Modriča, *Bos.-H.* 28 F3
Moe, *Australia* 95 F4
Moebase, *Mozam.* 87 F4
Moëlan-sur-Mer, *France* 18 E3
Moengo, *Suriname* 125 B8
Moffat, *U.K.* 13 F5
Moga, *India* 68 D6
Mogadishu = Muqdisho, *Somali Rep.* 75 G4
Mogador = Essaouira, *Morocco* 78 B4
Mogadouro, *Portugal* 36 D4
Mogalakwena →, *S. Africa* 89 C4
Mogami-Gawa →, *Japan* 54 E10
Mogán, *Canary Is.* 48 G4
Mogaung, *Burma* 67 G20
Mogente = Moixent, *Spain* 39 G4
Mogho, *Ethiopia* 81 G5
Mogi das Cruzes, *Brazil* 127 A6
Mogi-Guaçu →, *Brazil* 127 A6
Mogi-Mirim, *Brazil* 127 A6
Mogielnica, *Poland* 31 G7
Mogige, *Ethiopia* 81 F4
Mogilev = Mahilyow, *Belarus* 32 F6
Mogilev-Podolskiy = Mohyliv-Podilskyy, *Ukraine* 29 B12
Mogilno, *Poland* 31 F4
Mogincual, *Mozam.* 87 F5
Mogliano Véneto, *Italy* 41 C9
Mogocha, *Russia* 53 D12
Mogok, *Burma* 67 H20
Mogollon Rim, *U.S.A.* 109 J8
Mógoro, *Italy* 42 C1
Mograt, *Sudan* 80 D3
Moguer, *Spain* 37 H4
Mogumber, *Australia* 93 F2
Mohács, *Hungary* 28 E3
Mohales Hoek, *Lesotho* 88 E4
Mohall, *U.S.A.* 112 A4
Moḥammadābād, *Iran* 71 B8
Mohammedia, *Morocco* 78 B4
Mohana →, *India* 69 G11
Mohanlalganj, *India* 69 F9
Mohave, L., *U.S.A.* 111 K12
Mohawk →, *U.S.A.* 117 D11
Moheda, *Sweden* 11 G8
Mohenjodaro, *Pakistan* 68 F3
Moher, Cliffs of, *Ireland* 12 D2
Mohicanville Reservoir, *U.S.A.* 116 F3
Möhne →, *Germany* 24 D3
Mohoro, *Tanzania* 86 D4
Mohyliv-Podilskyy, *Ukraine* 29 B12
Moia, *Sudan* 81 F2
Moidart, L., *U.K.* 13 E3
Moineşti, *Romania* 29 D11
Moira →, *Canada* 116 B7
Moirans, *France* 21 C9
Moirans-en-Montagne, *France* 19 F12
Moíres, *Greece* 49 D6
Moisaküla, *Estonia* 9 G21
Moisie, *Canada* 105 B6
Moisie →, *Canada* 105 B6
Moissac, *France* 20 D5
Moita, *Portugal* 37 G2
Moixent, *Spain* 39 G4
Möja, *Sweden* 10 E12
Mojácar, *Spain* 39 H3
Mojados, *Spain* 36 D6
Mojave, *U.S.A.* 111 K8
Mojave ⌓, *U.S.A.* 111 K11
Mojave Desert, *U.S.A.* 111 L10
Mojiang, *China* 58 F3
Mojjo →, *Ethiopia* 81 F5
Mojkovac, *Serbia & M.* 44 D3
Mojo, *Bolivia* 126 A2
Mojo, *Ethiopia* 81 F4
Mojokerto, *Indonesia* 63 G15
Mokai, *N.Z.* 91 H5
Mokambo, *Dem. Rep. of the Congo* 87 E2
Mokameh, *India* 69 G11
Mokau, *N.Z.* 91 H5
Mokelumne →, *U.S.A.* 110 G5
Mokelumne Hill, *U.S.A.* 110 G6
Mokhós, *Greece* 49 D7
Mokhotlong, *Lesotho* 89 D4
Möklinta, *Sweden* 10 D10
Mokokchung, *India* 67 F19
Mokolo, *Cameroon* 83 C7
Mokolo →, *S. Africa* 89 C4
Mokopane, *S. Africa* 89 C4
Mokp'o, *S. Korea* 57 G14
Mokra Gora, *Serbia & M.* 44 D4
Mokronog, *Slovenia* 41 C12
Moksha →, *Russia* 34 C6
Mokshan, *Russia* 34 D7
Mokwa, *Nigeria* 83 D6
Mol, *Belgium* 17 C5
Mola di Bari, *Italy* 43 A10
Molale, *Ethiopia* 81 E4
Moláoi, *Greece* 46 E4
Molara, *Italy* 42 B2
Molat, *Croatia* 41 D11
Molchanovo, *Russia* 52 D9
Mold, *U.K.* 14 D4
Moldava nad Bodvou, *Slovak Rep.* 27 C14
Moldavia = Moldova ■, *Europe* 29 C13
Moldavia, *Romania* 29 D12
Molde, *Norway* 8 E12
Moldova ■, *Europe* 29 C13
Moldova Nouă, *Romania* 28 F6
Moldoveanu, Vf., *Romania* 29 E9
Moldoviţa, *Romania* 29 C10
Mole △, *Ghana* 83 D4
Mole →, *U.K.* 15 F7
Mole Creek, *Australia* 95 G4
Molepolole, *Botswana* 88 C4
Molfetta, *Italy* 43 A9
Molina de Aragón, *Spain* 38 E3
Molina de Segura, *Spain* 39 G3
Moline, *U.S.A.* 112 E9
Molinella, *Italy* 41 D8
Molinos, *Argentina* 126 B2
Moliro, *Dem. Rep. of the Congo* 86 D3
Moliterno, *Italy* 43 B8
Molkom, *Sweden* 10 E7
Mölle, *Sweden* 11 H6
Molledo, *Spain* 36 B6
Mollendo, *Peru* 124 G4
Mollerin, L., *Australia* 93 F2
Mollerussa, *Spain* 38 D5
Mollina, *Spain* 37 H6
Mölln, *Germany* 24 B6
Mölltorp, *Sweden* 11 F8
Mölnlycke, *Sweden* 11 G6
Molochansk, *Ukraine* 33 J8
Molochnoye, Ozero, *Ukraine* 33 J8
Molodechno = Maladzyechna, *Belarus* 32 E4
Molodove, *Ukraine* 29 D14
Molokai, *U.S.A.* 106 H16
Molong, *Australia* 95 E4
Molopo →, *Africa* 88 D3
Mólos, *Greece* 46 C4
Molsheim, *France* 19 D14
Molson L., *Canada* 103 C9
Molteno, *S. Africa* 88 E4
Molu, *Indonesia* 63 F8
Molucca Sea, *Indonesia* 63 E6
Moluccas = Maluku, *Indonesia* 63 E7
Moma, *Dem. Rep. of the Congo* 86 C1
Moma, *Mozam.* 87 F4
Mombasa, *Kenya* 86 C4
Mombetsu, *Japan* 54 B11
Mombuey, *Spain* 36 C4
Momchilgrad, *Bulgaria* 45 E9
Momi, *Dem. Rep. of the Congo* 86 C2
Mompós, *Colombia* 124 B4
Møn, *Denmark* 11 K6
Mon □, *Burma* 67 L20
Mona, Canal de la = Mona Passage, *W. Indies* 121 C6
Mona, Isla, *Puerto Rico* 121 C6
Mona, Pta., *Costa Rica* 120 E3
Mona Passage, *W. Indies* 121 C6
Monaca, *U.S.A.* 116 F4
Monaco ■, *Europe* 21 E11
Monadhliath Mts., *U.K.* 13 D4
Monadnock, Mt., *U.S.A.* 117 D12
Monaghan, *Ireland* 12 B5
Monaghan □, *Ireland* 12 B5
Monahans, *U.S.A.* 113 K3
Monapo, *Mozam.* 87 E5
Monar, L., *U.K.* 13 D3
Monarch Mt., *Canada* 102 C3
Monashee Mts., *Canada* 102 C5
Monasterevin, *Ireland* 12 C4
Monastir = Bitola, *Macedonia* 44 E5
Moncada, *Phil.* 61 D4
Moncalieri, *Italy* 40 D4
Moncalvo, *Italy* 40 C5
Moncão, *Portugal* 36 C2
Moncarapacho, *Portugal* 37 H3
Moncayo, Sierra del, *Spain* 38 D3
Mönchengladbach, *Germany* 24 D2
Monchique, *Portugal* 37 H2
Moncks Corner, *U.S.A.* 115 J5
Monclova, *Mexico* 118 B4
Moncontour, *France* 18 D4
Moncton, *Canada* 105 C7
Mondariz, *Spain* 36 C2
Mondego →, *Portugal* 36 E2
Mondego, C., *Portugal* 36 E2
Mondeodo, *Indonesia* 63 E6
Mondeville, *France* 18 C6
Mondolfo, *Italy* 41 E10
Mondoñedo, *Spain* 36 B3
Mondovì, *Italy* 40 D4
Mondragon, *Phil.* 61 E6

Mondragone, *Italy* 42 A6
Mondrain I., *Australia* 93 F3
Moneague, *Jamaica* 120 a
Monemvasía, *Greece* 46 E5
Monessen, *U.S.A.* 116 F5
Monesterio, *Spain* 37 G4
Monestier-de-Clermont, *France* 21 D9
Monett, *U.S.A.* 113 G8
Moneymore, *U.K.* 12 B5
Monfalcone, *Italy* 41 C10
Monflanquin, *France* 20 D4
Monforte, *Portugal* 37 F3
Monforte de Lemos, *Spain* 36 C3
Mong Cai, *Vietnam* 64 B6
Mong Hsu, *Burma* 58 G2
Mong Kung, *Burma* 67 J20
Mong Nai, *Burma* 67 J20
Mong Pawk, *Burma* 67 H21
Mong Ping, *Burma* 58 G2
Mong Ton, *Burma* 67 J21
Mong Wa, *Burma* 67 J22
Mong Yai, *Burma* 67 H21
Mongalla, *Sudan* 81 F3
Mongers, L., *Australia* 93 E2
Monghyr = Munger, *India* 69 G12
Mongibello = Etna, *Italy* 43 E7
Mongo, *Chad* 79 F9
Mongo →, *S. Leone* 82 D2
Mongolia ■, *Asia* 53 E10
Mongolia, Plateau of, *Asia* 50 E14
Mongonu, *Nigeria* 83 C7
Mongu, *Zambia* 85 H4
Môngua, *Angola* 88 B2
Monifieth, *U.K.* 13 E6
Monistrol-sur-Loire, *France* 21 C8
Monkey Bay, *Malawi* 87 E4
Monkey Mia, *Australia* 93 E1
Monkey River Town, *Belize* 119 D7
Mońki, *Poland* 30 E9
Monkoto, *Dem. Rep. of the Congo* 84 E4
Monkton, *Canada* 116 C3
Monmouth, *U.K.* 15 F5
Monmouth, *Ill., U.S.A.* 112 E9
Monmouth, *Oreg., U.S.A.* 108 D2
Monmouthshire □, *U.K.* 15 F5
Mono L., *U.S.A.* 110 H7
Monolith, *U.S.A.* 111 K8
Monólithos, *Greece* 49 C9
Monongahela, *U.S.A.* 116 F5
Monópoli, *Italy* 43 B10
Monor, *Hungary* 28 C4
Monos I., *Trin. & Tob.* 125 K15
Monóvar, *Spain* 39 G4
Monreal del Campo, *Spain* 38 E3
Monreale, *Italy* 42 D6
Monroe, *Ga., U.S.A.* 115 J4
Monroe, *La., U.S.A.* 113 J8
Monroe, *Mich., U.S.A.* 114 E4
Monroe, *N.C., U.S.A.* 115 H5
Monroe, *N.Y., U.S.A.* 117 E10
Monroe, *Utah, U.S.A.* 109 G7
Monroe, *Wash., U.S.A.* 110 C5
Monroe, *Wis., U.S.A.* 112 D10
Monroe City, *U.S.A.* 112 F9
Monroeton, *U.S.A.* 117 E8
Monroeville, *Ala., U.S.A.* 115 K2
Monroeville, *Pa., U.S.A.* 116 F5
Monrovia, *Liberia* 82 D2
Mons, *Belgium* 17 D3
Møns Klint, *Denmark* 11 K6
Monsaraz, *Portugal* 37 G3
Monse, *Indonesia* 63 E6
Monségur, *France* 20 D4
Monsélice, *Italy* 41 C8
Mönsterås, *Sweden* 11 G10
Mont Cenis, Col du, *France* 21 C10
Mont-de-Marsan, *France* 20 E3
Mont-Joli, *Canada* 105 C6
Mont-Laurier, *Canada* 104 C4
Mont-Louis, *Canada* 105 C6
Mont Peko △, *Ivory C.* 82 D3
Mont-roig del Camp, *Spain* 38 D5
Mont-St-Michel, Le, *France* 18 D5
Mont Sangbe △, *Ivory C.* 82 D3
Mont-Tremblant ⌓, *Canada* 104 C5
Montabaur, *Germany* 24 E3
Montagnac, *France* 20 E7
Montagnana, *Italy* 41 C8
Montagne d'Ambre △, *Madag.* 89 A8
Montagne de Reims ⌓, *France* 19 C11
Montagu, *S. Africa* 88 E3
Montagu I., *Antarctica* 5 B1
Montague, *Canada* 105 C7
Montague, I., *Mexico* 118 A2
Montague Ra., *Australia* 93 E2
Montague Sd., *Australia* 92 B4
Montaigu, *France* 18 F5
Montalbán, *Spain* 38 E4
Montalbano Iónico, *Italy* 43 B9
Montalbo, *Spain* 38 F2
Montalcino, *Italy* 41 E8
Montalegre, *Portugal* 36 D3
Montalto, *Italy* 43 D8
Montalto di Castro, *Italy* 41 F8
Montalto Uffugo, *Italy* 43 C9
Montalvo, *U.S.A.* 111 L7
Montamarta, *Spain* 36 D5
Montana, *Bulgaria* 44 C7
Montaña, *Peru* 124 E4
Montana □, *Bulgaria* 44 C7
Montana □, *U.S.A.* 108 C9
Montaña Clara, I., *Canary Is.* 48 E6
Montañas de Malaga ⌓, *Spain* 37 J6
Montánchez, *Spain* 37 F4
Montargil, *Portugal* 37 F2
Montargis, *France* 19 E9
Montauban, *France* 20 D5
Montauk, *U.S.A.* 117 E13
Montauk Pt., *U.S.A.* 117 E13
Montbard, *France* 19 E11
Montbarrey, *France* 19 E12
Montbéliard, *France* 19 E13
Montblanc, *Spain* 38 D6
Montbrison, *France* 21 C8
Montcalm, Pic de, *France* 20 F5
Montceau-les-Mines, *France* 19 F11
Montcenis, *France* 21 B8
Montclair, *U.S.A.* 117 F10
Montcornet, *France* 19 C11
Montcuq, *France* 20 D5
Montdidier, *France* 19 C9
Monte Albán, *Mexico* 119 D5
Monte Alegre, *Brazil* 125 D8
Monte Azul, *Brazil* 125 G10
Monte-Carlo, *Monaco* 21 E11
Monte Caseros, *Argentina* 126 C4
Monte Comán, *Argentina* 126 C2
Monte Cristi, *Dom. Rep.* 121 C5
Monte Cucco ⌓, *Italy* 41 E9
Monte Lindo →, *Paraguay* 126 A4
Monte Patria, *Chile* 126 C1
Monte Quemado, *Argentina* 126 B3
Monte Redondo, *Portugal* 36 F2
Monte Rio, *U.S.A.* 110 G4
Monte San Giovanni Campano, *Italy* 42 A6
Monte San Savino, *Italy* 41 E8
Monte Sant' Ángelo, *Italy* 41 G12
Monte Santu, C. di, *Italy* 42 B2
Monte Sibillini △, *Italy* 41 F10
Monte Subasio ⌓, *Italy* 41 E9
Monte Vista, *U.S.A.* 109 H10
Monteagudo, *Argentina* 127 B5
Montealegre del Castillo, *Spain* 39 G3
Montebello, *Canada* 104 C5
Montebello Iónico, *Italy* 43 E8
Montebello Is., *Australia* 92 D2
Montebelluna, *Italy* 41 C9
Montebourg, *France* 18 C5
Montecastrilli, *Italy* 41 F9
Montecatini Terme, *Italy* 40 E7
Montecito, *U.S.A.* 111 L7
Montecristo, *Italy* 40 F7
Montefalco, *Italy* 41 F9
Montefiascone, *Italy* 41 F9
Montefrío, *Spain* 37 H7
Montegiórgio, *Italy* 41 E10
Montego Bay, *Jamaica* 120 a
Montehermoso, *Spain* 36 E4
Montejicar, *Spain* 37 H7
Montélimar, *France* 21 D8
Montella, *Italy* 43 B8
Montellano, *Spain* 37 J5
Montello, *U.S.A.* 112 D10
Montemor-o-Novo, *Portugal* 37 G2
Montemor-o-Velho, *Portugal* 36 E2
Montemorelos, *Mexico* 119 B5
Montendre, *France* 20 C3
Montenegro, *Brazil* 127 B5
Montenegro □, *Serbia & M.* 44 D3
Montenero di Bisáccia, *Italy* 41 G11
Montepuez, *Mozam.* 87 E4
Montepuez →, *Mozam.* 87 E5
Montepulciano, *Italy* 41 E8
Montereale, *Italy* 41 F10
Montereau-Faut-Yonne, *France* 19 D9
Monterey, *U.S.A.* 110 J5
Monterey B., *U.S.A.* 110 J5
Montería, *Colombia* 124 B3
Monteros, *Argentina* 126 B2
Monterotondo, *Italy* 41 F9
Monterrey, *Mexico* 118 B4
Montes Azules ⌓, *Mexico* 119 D6
Montes Claros, *Brazil* 125 G10
Montesano, *U.S.A.* 110 D3
Montesano sulla Marcellana, *Italy* 43 B8
Montesárchio, *Italy* 43 A7
Montescaglioso, *Italy* 43 B9
Montesilvano, *Italy* 41 F11
Montesinho ⌓, *Portugal* 36 D4
Montevarchi, *Italy* 41 E8
Montevideo, *Uruguay* 127 C4
Montevideo, *U.S.A.* 112 C7
Montezuma, *U.S.A.* 112 E8
Montezuma Castle ⌓, *U.S.A.* 109 J8
Montfaucon, *France* 18 E5
Montfaucon-d'Argonne, *France* 19 C12
Montfaucon-en-Velay, *France* 21 C8
Montfort-le-Gesnois, *France* 18 D7
Montfort-sur-Meu, *France* 18 D5
Montfragüe ⌓, *Spain* 36 F5
Montgenèvre, *France* 21 D10
Montgomery, *U.K.* 15 E4
Montgomery, *Ala., U.S.A.* 115 J2
Montgomery, *Pa., U.S.A.* 116 E8
Montgomery, *W. Va., U.S.A.* 114 F5
Montgomery City, *U.S.A.* 112 F9
Montguyon, *France* 20 C3
Monthermé, *France* 19 C11
Monthey, *Switz.* 25 J2
Monthois, *France* 19 C11
Monti, *Italy* 42 B2
Monti Lucrétili ⌓, *Italy* 41 F9
Monti Picentini ⌓, *Italy* 43 B8
Monti Simbruini ⌓, *Italy* 41 G10
Monticelli d'Ongina, *Italy* 40 C6
Monticello, *Ark., U.S.A.* 113 J9
Monticello, *Fla., U.S.A.* 115 K4
Monticello, *Ind., U.S.A.* 114 E2
Monticello, *Iowa, U.S.A.* 112 D9
Monticello, *Ky., U.S.A.* 115 G3
Monticello, *Minn., U.S.A.* 112 C8
Monticello, *Miss., U.S.A.* 113 K9
Monticello, *N.Y., U.S.A.* 117 E10
Monticello, *Utah, U.S.A.* 109 H9
Montichiari, *Italy* 40 C7
Montier-en-Der, *France* 19 D11
Montignac, *France* 20 C5
Montigny-les-Metz, *France* 19 C13
Montigny-sur-Aube, *France* 19 E11
Montijo, *Portugal* 37 G2
Montijo, *Spain* 37 G4
Montilla, *Spain* 37 H6
Montivilliers, *France* 18 C7
Montluçon, *France* 19 F9
Montmagny, *Canada* 105 C5
Montmarault, *France* 19 F9
Montmartre, *Canada* 103 C8
Montmédy, *France* 19 C12
Montmélian, *France* 21 C10
Montmirail, *France* 19 D10
Montmoreau-St-Cybard, *France* 20 C4
Montmorillon, *France* 20 B4
Montmort-Lucy, *France* 19 D10
Monto, *Australia* 94 C5
Montoire-sur-le-Loir, *France* 18 E7
Montongbuwoh, *Indonesia* 63 K19
Montório al Vomano, *Italy* 41 F10
Montoro, *Spain* 37 G6
Montour Falls, *U.S.A.* 116 D8
Montoursville, *U.S.A.* 116 E8
Montpelier, *Idaho, U.S.A.* 108 E8
Montpelier, *Vt., U.S.A.* 117 B12
Montpellier, *France* 20 E7
Montpezat-de-Quercy, *France* 20 D5
Montpon-Ménestérol, *France* 20 D4
Montréal, *Canada* 117 A11
Montréal, *Aude, France* 20 E6
Montréal, *Gers, France* 20 E4
Montreal →, *Canada* 104 C3
Montreal L., *Canada* 103 C7
Montreal Lake, *Canada* 103 C7
Montredon-Labessonnié, *France* 20 E6
Montrésor, *France* 18 E8
Montret, *France* 19 F12
Montreuil, *Pas-de-Calais, France* 19 B8
Montreuil, *Seine-St-Denis, France* 19 D9
Montreuil-Bellay, *France* 18 E6
Montreux, *Switz.* 25 J2
Montrevel-en-Bresse, *France* 19 F12
Montrichard, *France* 18 E8
Montrose, *U.K.* 13 E6
Montrose, *Colo., U.S.A.* 109 G10
Montrose, *Pa., U.S.A.* 117 E9
Monts, Pte. des, *Canada* 105 C6
Montsalvy, *France* 20 D6
Montsant, Serra de, *Spain* 38 D6
Montsauche-les-Settons, *France* 19 E11
Montsec, Serra del, *Spain* 38 C5
Montseny ⌓, *Spain* 38 D2
Montserrat, *Spain* 38 D6
Montserrat ⧄, *W. Indies* 121 C7
Montuenga, *Spain* 36 D6
Montuiri, *Spain* 48 B9
Monywa, *Burma* 67 H19
Monza, *Italy* 40 C6
Monze, *Zambia* 87 F2
Monze, C., *Pakistan* 68 G2
Monzón, *Spain* 38 D5
Mooers, *U.S.A.* 117 B11
Mooi →, *S. Africa* 89 D5
Mooi River, *S. Africa* 89 D4
Moonah →, *Australia* 94 C2
Moonda, L., *Australia* 94 D3
Moonie, *Australia* 95 D5
Moonie →, *Australia* 95 D4
Moonta, *Australia* 95 E2
Moora, *Australia* 93 F2
Moorcroft, *U.S.A.* 112 C2
Moore →, *Australia* 93 F2
Moore, L., *Australia* 93 E2
Moore Park, *Australia* 94 C5
Moore River △, *Australia* 93 F2
Moorefield, *U.S.A.* 114 F6
Moores Res., *U.S.A.* 117 B13
Moorfoot Hills, *U.K.* 13 F5
Moorhead, *U.S.A.* 112 B6
Moormerland, *Germany* 24 B3
Moorpark, *U.S.A.* 111 L8
Moorreesburg, *S. Africa* 88 E2
Moorrinya △, *Australia* 94 C3
Moosburg, *Germany* 25 G7
Moose →, *Canada* 104 B3
Moose →, *U.S.A.* 117 C9
Moose Creek, *Canada* 117 A10
Moose Factory, *Canada* 104 B3
Moose Jaw, *Canada* 103 C7
Moose Jaw →, *Canada* 103 C7
Moose Lake, *U.S.A.* 112 B8
Moose Mountain ⌓, *Canada* 103 D8
Moosehead L., *U.S.A.* 115 C11
Mooselookmeguntic L., *U.S.A.* 115 C10
Moosilauke, Mt., *U.S.A.* 117 B13
Moosomin, *Canada* 103 C8
Moosonee, *Canada* 104 B3
Moosup, *U.S.A.* 117 E13
Mopane, *S. Africa* 89 C4
Mopeia Velha, *Mozam.* 87 F4
Mopipi, *Botswana* 88 C3
Mopoi, *C.A.R.* 86 A2
Mopti, *Mali* 82 C4
Moqatta, *Sudan* 81 E4
Moqor, *Afghan.* 68 C2
Moquegua, *Peru* 124 G4
Mór, *Hungary* 28 C3
Mora, *Cameroon* 83 C7
Móra, *Portugal* 37 G2
Mora, *Spain* 37 F7
Mora, *Sweden* 10 C8
Mora, *Minn., U.S.A.* 112 C8
Mora, *N. Mex., U.S.A.* 109 J11
Mora →, *U.S.A.* 113 H2
Mora de Rubielos, *Spain* 38 E4
Mòra d'Ebre, *Spain* 38 D5
Mòra la Nova, *Spain* 38 D5
Morača →, *Serbia & M.* 44 D3
Moradabad, *India* 69 E8
Morafenobe, *Madag.* 89 B7
Morąg, *Poland* 30 E6
Moral de Calatrava, *Spain* 37 G7
Moraleja, *Spain* 36 E4
Moramanga, *Madag.* 89 B8
Moran, *Kans., U.S.A.* 113 G7
Moran, *Wyo., U.S.A.* 108 E8
Moranbah, *Australia* 94 C4
Morano Cálabro, *Italy* 43 C9
Morant Bay, *Jamaica* 120 a
Morant Cays, *Jamaica* 120 C4
Morant Pt., *Jamaica* 120 a
Morar, *India* 68 F8
Morar, L., *U.K.* 13 E3
Moratalla, *Spain* 39 G3
Moratuwa, *Sri Lanka* 66 R11
Morava →, *Slovak Rep.* 27 C9
Moravia, *U.S.A.* 117 D8
Moravian Hts. = Českomoravská Vrchovina, *Czech Rep.* 26 B8
Moravica →, *Serbia & M.* 44 C4
Moraviţa, *Romania* 28 E6
Moravská Třebová, *Czech Rep.* 27 B9
Moravské Budějovice, *Czech Rep.* 26 B8
Morawa, *Australia* 93 E2
Morawhanna, *Guyana* 124 B7
Moray □, *U.K.* 13 D5
Moray Firth, *U.K.* 13 D5
Morbach, *Germany* 25 F3
Morbegno, *Italy* 40 B6
Morbi, *India* 68 H4
Morbihan □, *France* 18 E4
Mörbylånga, *Sweden* 11 H10
Morcenx, *France* 20 D3
Morcone, *Italy* 43 A7
Mordelles, *France* 18 D5
Morden, *Canada* 103 D9
Mordoğan, *Turkey* 47 C8
Mordovian Republic = Mordvinia □, *Russia* 34 C7
Mordovo, *Russia* 34 D5
Mordvinia □, *Russia* 34 C7
Mordy, *Poland* 31 F9
Morea, *Greece* 6 H10
Moreau →, *U.S.A.* 112 C4
Morecambe, *U.K.* 14 C5
Morecambe B., *U.K.* 14 C5
Moree, *Australia* 95 D4
Morehead, *U.S.A.* 114 F4
Morehead City, *U.S.A.* 115 H7
Morel →, *India* 68 F7
Morelia, *Mexico* 118 D4
Morella, *Australia* 94 C3
Morella, *Spain* 38 E4
Morelos, *Mexico* 118 B3
Morelos □, *Mexico* 119 D5
Moremi △, *Botswana* 88 B3
Morena, *India* 68 F8
Morena, Sierra, *Spain* 37 G7
Moreni, *Romania* 29 F10
Moreno Valley, *U.S.A.* 111 M10
Moresby I., *Canada* 102 C2
Morestel, *France* 21 C9
Moreton I., *Australia* 95 D5
Moreton Island △, *Australia* 95 D5
Moreuil, *France* 19 C9
Morey, *Spain* 48 B10
Morez, *France* 19 F13
Morgan, *U.S.A.* 108 F8
Morgan City, *U.S.A.* 113 L9
Morgan Hill, *U.S.A.* 110 H5
Morganfield, *U.S.A.* 114 G2
Morganton, *U.S.A.* 115 H5
Morgantown, *U.S.A.* 114 F6
Morgenzon, *S. Africa* 89 D4
Morges, *Switz.* 25 J2
Morghak, *Iran* 71 D8
Morgongåva, *Sweden* 10 E10
Morhange, *France* 19 D13
Morhar →, *India* 69 G11
Mori, *Italy* 40 C7
Mori, *Japan* 54 C10
Moriarty, *U.S.A.* 109 J10
Moribaya, *Guinea* 82 D3
Morice L., *Canada* 102 C3
Moriki, *Nigeria* 83 C6
Morinville, *Canada* 102 C6
Morioka, *Japan* 54 E10
Moris, *Mexico* 118 B3
Morlaàs, *France* 20 E3
Morlaix, *France* 18 D3
Mörlunda, *Sweden* 11 G9
Mormanno, *Italy* 43 C8
Mormant, *France* 19 D9
Mornington, *Australia* 95 F4
Mornington, I., *Chile* 128 F1
Mornington I., *Australia* 94 B2
Mórnos →, *Greece* 46 C3
Moro, *Pakistan* 68 F2
Moro, *Sudan* 81 E3
Moro →, *Pakistan* 68 E2
Moro G., *Phil.* 61 H5
Morocco ■, *N. Afr.* 78 B4
Morogoro, *Tanzania* 86 D4
Morogoro □, *Tanzania* 86 D4
Moroleón, *Mexico* 118 C4
Morombe, *Madag.* 89 C7
Moron, *Argentina* 126 C4
Morón, *Cuba* 120 B4
Morón de Almazán, *Spain* 38 D2
Morón de la Frontera, *Spain* 37 H5
Morona →, *Peru* 124 D3
Morondava, *Madag.* 89 C7
Morondo, *Ivory C.* 82 D3
Morongo Valley, *U.S.A.* 111 L10
Moroni, *Comoros Is.* 77 H8
Moroni, *U.S.A.* 108 G8
Moronou, *Ivory C.* 82 D4
Morotai, *Indonesia* 63 D7
Moroto, *Uganda* 86 B3
Moroto, Mt., *Uganda* 86 B3
Morozov, *Bulgaria* 45 D9
Morozovsk, *Russia* 35 F5
Morpeth, *U.K.* 14 B6
Morphou, *Cyprus* 49 D11
Morphou Bay, *Cyprus* 49 D11
Morrilton, *U.S.A.* 113 H8
Morrinhos, *Brazil* 125 G9
Morrinsville, *N.Z.* 91 G5
Morris, *Canada* 103 D9
Morris, *Ill., U.S.A.* 112 E10
Morris, *Minn., U.S.A.* 112 C7
Morris, *N.Y., U.S.A.* 117 D9
Morris, *Pa., U.S.A.* 116 E7
Morris, Mt., *Australia* 93 E5
Morris Jesup, Kap, *Greenland* 4 A5
Morrisburg, *Canada* 117 B9
Morristown, *Ariz., U.S.A.* 109 K7
Morristown, *N.J., U.S.A.* 117 F10
Morristown, *N.Y., U.S.A.* 117 B9
Morristown, *Tenn., U.S.A.* 115 G4
Morrisville, *N.Y., U.S.A.* 117 D9
Morrisville, *Pa., U.S.A.* 117 F10
Morrisville, *Vt., U.S.A.* 117 B12
Morro, Pta., *Chile* 126 B1
Morro Bay, *U.S.A.* 110 K6
Morro del Jable, *Canary Is.* 48 F5
Morro Jable, Pta. de, *Canary Is.* 48 F5
Morrocoy △, *Venezuela* 121 D6
Morrosquillo, G. de, *Colombia* 120 E4
Mörrum, *Sweden* 11 H8
Morrumbene, *Mozam.* 89 C6
Mörrumsån →, *Sweden* 11 H8
Mors, *Denmark* 11 H2
Morshansk, *Russia* 34 D5
Mörsil, *Sweden* 10 A7
Mortagne →, *France* 19 D13
Mortagne-au-Perche, *France* 18 D7
Mortagne-sur-Gironde, *France* 20 C3
Mortagne-sur-Sèvre, *France* 18 F6
Mortain, *France* 18 D6
Mortara, *Italy* 40 C5
Morteau, *France* 19 E13
Morteros, *Argentina* 126 C3
Mortlach, *Canada* 103 C7
Mortlake, *Australia* 95 F3
Morton, *Tex., U.S.A.* 113 J3
Morton, *Wash., U.S.A.* 110 D4
Moruga, *Trin. & Tob.* 125 K15
Morundah, *Australia* 95 E4
Moruya, *Australia* 95 F5
Morvan, *France* 19 E11
Morvan ⌓, *France* 19 E11
Morven, *Australia* 95 D4
Morvern, *U.K.* 13 E3
Morwell, *Australia* 95 F4
Moryń, *Poland* 31 F1
Morzine, *France* 19 F13
Mosalsk, *Russia* 32 E8
Mosbach, *Germany* 25 F5
Mošćenice, *Croatia* 41 C11
Mosciano Sant' Ángelo, *Italy* 41 F10
Moscos Is., *Burma* 64 E1
Moscow = Moskva, *Russia* 32 E9
Moscow, *Idaho, U.S.A.* 108 C5
Moscow, *Pa., U.S.A.* 117 E9
Mosel →, *Europe* 19 B14
Moselle = Mosel →, *Europe* 19 B14
Moselle □, *France* 19 D13
Moses Lake, *U.S.A.* 108 C4
Mosgiel, *N.Z.* 91 L3
Moshaweng →, *S. Africa* 88 D3
Moshi, *Tanzania* 86 C4
Moshupa, *Botswana* 88 C4
Mosina, *Poland* 31 F3
Mosjøen, *Norway* 8 D15
Moskenesøya, *Norway* 8 C15
Moskenstraumen, *Norway* 8 C15
Moskva, *Russia* 32 E9
Moskva →, *Russia* 32 E10
Moslavačka Gora, *Croatia* 41 C13
Mosomane, *Botswana* 88 C4
Mosonmagyaróvár, *Hungary* 28 C2
Mošorin, *Serbia & M.* 28 E5
Mospino, *Ukraine* 33 J9
Mosquera, *Colombia* 124 C3
Mosquero, *U.S.A.* 113 H3
Mosqueruela, *Spain* 38 E4
Mosquitia, *Honduras* 120 C3
Mosquito Coast = Mosquitia, *Honduras* 120 C3
Mosquito Creek L., *U.S.A.* 116 E4
Mosquito L., *Canada* 103 A8
Mosquitos, G. de los, *Panama* 120 E3
Moss, *Norway* 9 G14
Moss Vale, *Australia* 95 E5
Mossbank, *Canada* 103 D7
Mossburn, *N.Z.* 91 L2
Mosselbaai, *S. Africa* 88 E3
Mossendjo, *Congo* 84 E2
Mossgiel, *Australia* 95 E3
Mössingen, *Germany* 25 G5
Mossman, *Australia* 94 B4
Mossoró, *Brazil* 125 E11
Mossuril, *Mozam.* 87 E5
Most, *Czech Rep.* 26 A6
Mosta, *Malta* 49 D1
Mostaganem, *Algeria* 78 A6
Mostar, *Bos.-H.* 28 G2
Mostardas, *Brazil* 127 C5
Mostiska = Mostyska, *Ukraine* 31 J10
Móstoles, *Spain* 36 E7
Mosty = Masty, *Belarus* 32 F3
Mostyska, *Ukraine* 31 J10
Mosul = Al Mawşil, *Iraq* 70 B4
Mosŭlpo, *S. Korea* 57 H14
Mota, *Ethiopia* 81 E4
Mota del Cuervo, *Spain* 39 F2
Mota del Marqués, *Spain* 36 D5
Motagua →, *Guatemala* 120 C2
Motala, *Sweden* 11 F9
Motaze, *Mozam.* 89 C5
Moţca, *Romania* 29 C11
Moth, *India* 69 G8
Motherwell, *U.K.* 13 F5
Motihari, *India* 69 F11
Motilla del Palancar, *Spain* 39 F3
Motnik, *Slovenia* 41 B11
Motovun, *Croatia* 41 C10
Motozintla de Mendoza, *Mexico* 119 D6
Motril, *Spain* 37 J7
Motru, *Romania* 28 F7
Motru →, *Romania* 29 F8

Mott, *U.S.A.* 112 B3
Móttola, *Italy* 43 B10
Motueka, *N.Z.* 91 J4
Motueka →, *N.Z.* 91 J4
Motul, *Mexico* 119 C7
Mouchalagane →, *Canada* 105 B6
Moúdhros, *Greece* 47 B7
Mouding, *China* 58 E3
Moudjeria, *Mauritania* 82 B2
Moudon, *Switz.* 25 J2
Mouila, *Gabon* 84 E2
Moulamein, *Australia* 95 F3
Moule à Chique, C., *St. Lucia* 121 f
Moulianá, *Greece* 49 D7
Moulins, *France* 19 F10
Moulmein, *Burma* 67 L20
Moulouya, O. →, *Morocco* 78 B5
Moultrie, *U.S.A.* 115 K4
Moultrie, L., *U.S.A.* 115 J5
Mound City, *Mo., U.S.A.* 112 E7
Mound City, *S. Dak., U.S.A.* 112 C4
Moúnda, Ákra, *Greece* 46 C2
Moundou, *Chad* 79 G9
Moundsville, *U.S.A.* 116 G4
Moung, *Cambodia* 64 F4
Mount Airy, *U.S.A.* 115 G5
Mount Albert, *Canada* 116 B5
Mount Aspiring △, *N.Z.* 91 L2
Mount Barker, *S. Austral., Australia* 95 F2
Mount Barker, *W. Austral., Australia* 93 F2
Mount Brydges, *Canada* 116 D3
Mount Burr, *Australia* 95 F3
Mount Carmel = Ha Karmel △, *Israel* 74 C4
Mount Carmel, *Ill., U.S.A.* 114 F2
Mount Carmel, *Pa., U.S.A.* 117 F8
Mount Charleston, *U.S.A.* 111 J11
Mount Clemens, *U.S.A.* 116 D2
Mount Coolon, *Australia* 94 C4
Mount Darwin, *Zimbabwe* 87 F3
Mount Desert I., *U.S.A.* 115 C11
Mount Dora, *U.S.A.* 115 L5
Mount Edziza ⌂, *Canada* 102 B2
Mount Elgon △, *E. Afr.* 86 B3
Mount Field △, *Australia* 95 G4
Mount Fletcher, *S. Africa* 89 E4
Mount Forest, *Canada* 116 C4
Mount Gambier, *Australia* 95 F3
Mount Garnet, *Australia* 94 B4
Mount Holly, *U.S.A.* 117 G10
Mount Holly Springs, *U.S.A.* 116 F7
Mount Hope, *N.S.W., Australia* 95 E4
Mount Hope, *S. Austral., Australia* 95 E2
Mount Isa, *Australia* 94 C2
Mount Jewett, *U.S.A.* 116 E6
Mount Kaputar △, *Australia* 95 E5
Mount Kenya △, *Kenya* 86 C4
Mount Kilimanjaro △, *Tanzania* 86 C4
Mount Kisco, *U.S.A.* 117 E11
Mount Laguna, *U.S.A.* 111 N10
Mount Larcom, *Australia* 94 C5
Mount Lofty Ra., *Australia* 95 E2
Mount Magnet, *Australia* 93 E2
Mount Maunganui, *N.Z.* 91 G6
Mount Molloy, *Australia* 94 B4
Mount Morgan, *Australia* 94 C5
Mount Morris, *U.S.A.* 116 D7
Mount Pearl, *Canada* 105 C9
Mount Penn, *U.S.A.* 117 F9
Mount Perry, *Australia* 95 D5
Mount Pleasant, *Iowa, U.S.A.* 112 E9
Mount Pleasant, *Mich., U.S.A.* 114 D3
Mount Pleasant, *Pa., U.S.A.* 116 F5
Mount Pleasant, *S.C., U.S.A.* 115 J6
Mount Pleasant, *Tenn., U.S.A.* 115 H2
Mount Pleasant, *Tex., U.S.A.* 113 J7
Mount Pleasant, *Utah, U.S.A.* 108 G8
Mount Pocono, *U.S.A.* 117 E9
Mount Rainier △, *U.S.A.* 110 D5
Mount Revelstoke △, *Canada* 102 C5
Mount Robson ⌂, *Canada* 102 C5
Mount St. Helens ⌂, *U.S.A.* 110 D4
Mount Selinda, *Zimbabwe* 89 C5
Mount Shasta, *U.S.A.* 108 F2
Mount Signal, *U.S.A.* 111 N11
Mount Sterling, *Ill., U.S.A.* 112 F9
Mount Sterling, *Ky., U.S.A.* 114 F4
Mount Surprise, *Australia* 94 B3
Mount Union, *U.S.A.* 116 F7
Mount Upton, *U.S.A.* 117 D9
Mount Vernon, *Ill., U.S.A.* 114 F1
Mount Vernon, *Ind., U.S.A.* 112 F10
Mount Vernon, *N.Y., U.S.A.* 117 F11
Mount Vernon, *Ohio, U.S.A.* 116 F2
Mount Vernon, *Wash., U.S.A.* 110 B4
Mount William △, *Australia* 95 G4
Mountain Ash, *U.K.* 15 F4
Mountain Center, *U.S.A.* 111 M10
Mountain City, *Nev., U.S.A.* 108 F6
Mountain City, *Tenn., U.S.A.* 115 G5
Mountain Dale, *U.S.A.* 117 E10
Mountain Grove, *U.S.A.* 113 G8
Mountain Home, *Ark., U.S.A.* 113 G8
Mountain Home, *Idaho, U.S.A.* 108 E6
Mountain Iron, *U.S.A.* 112 B8
Mountain Pass, *U.S.A.* 111 K11
Mountain View, *Ark., U.S.A.* 113 H8
Mountain View, *Calif., U.S.A.* 110 H4
Mountain View, *Hawaii, U.S.A.* 106 J17
Mountain Zebra △, *S. Africa* 88 E4
Mountainair, *U.S.A.* 109 J10
Mountlake Terrace, *U.S.A.* 110 C4
Mountmellick, *Ireland* 12 C4
Mountrath, *Ireland* 12 D4
Moura, *Australia* 94 C4
Moura, *Brazil* 124 D6
Moura, *Portugal* 37 G3
Mourão, *Portugal* 37 G3
Mourdi, Dépression du, *Chad* 79 E10
Mourdiah, *Mali* 82 C3
Mourenx, *France* 20 E3
Mouri, *Ghana* 83 D4
Mourilyan, *Australia* 94 B4
Mourmelon-le-Grand, *France* 19 C11
Mourne →, *U.K.* 12 B4
Mourne Mts., *U.K.* 12 B5
Mourniaí, *Greece* 49 D6
Mournies = Mourniaí, *Greece* 49 D6
Mouscron, *Belgium* 17 D3
Moussoro, *Chad* 79 F9
Mouthe, *France* 19 F13
Moutier, *Switz.* 25 H3
Moûtiers, *France* 21 C10
Moutong, *Indonesia* 63 D6
Mouy, *France* 19 C9
Mouzáki, *Greece* 46 B3
Mouzon, *France* 19 C12
Movas, *Mexico* 118 B3
Moville, *Ireland* 12 A4
Mowandjum, *Australia* 92 C3
Moy →, *Ireland* 12 B2
Moyale, *Kenya* 81 G4
Moyamba, *S. Leone* 82 D2
Moyen Atlas, *Morocco* 78 B4
Moyne, L. le, *Canada* 105 A6
Moyo, *Indonesia* 62 F5
Moyobamba, *Peru* 124 E3
Moyyero →, *Russia* 53 C11
Moyynty, *Kazakhstan* 52 E8
Mozambique = Moçambique, *Mozam.* 87 F5
Mozambique ■, *Africa* 87 F4
Mozambique Chan., *Africa* 89 B7
Mozdok, *Russia* 35 J7
Mozdūrān, *Iran* 71 B9
Mozhaysk, *Russia* 32 E9
Mozhga, *Russia* 34 B11
Mozhnābād, *Iran* 71 C9
Mozirje, *Slovenia* 41 B11
Mozyr = Mazyr, *Belarus* 33 F5
Mpanda, *Tanzania* 86 D3
Mpésoba, *Mali* 82 C3
Mphoengs, *Zimbabwe* 89 C4
Mpika, *Zambia* 87 E3
Mpulungu, *Zambia* 87 D3
Mpumalanga, *S. Africa* 89 D5
Mpumalanga □, *S. Africa* 89 D5
Mpwapwa, *Tanzania* 86 D4
Mqanduli, *S. Africa* 89 E4
Mqinvartsveri = Kazbek, *Russia* 35 J7
Mrągowo, *Poland* 30 E8
Mramor, *Serbia & M.* 44 C5
Mrkonjić Grad, *Bos.-H.* 28 F2
Mrkopalj, *Croatia* 41 C11
Mrocza, *Poland* 31 E4
Msambansovu, *Zimbabwe* 87 F3
M'sila →, *Algeria* 78 A6
Msoro, *Zambia* 87 E3
Msta →, *Russia* 32 C6
Mstislavl = Mstsislaw, *Belarus* 32 E6
Mstsislaw, *Belarus* 32 E6
Mszana Dolna, *Poland* 31 J7
Mszczonów, *Poland* 31 G7
Mtama, *Tanzania* 87 E4
Mtamvuna →, *S. Africa* 89 E5
Mtilikwe →, *Zimbabwe* 87 G3
Mtsensk, *Russia* 32 F9
Mtskheta, *Georgia* 35 K7
Mtubatuba, *S. Africa* 89 D5
Mtwalume, *S. Africa* 89 E5
Mtwara-Mikindani, *Tanzania* 87 E5
Mu Gia, Deo, *Vietnam* 64 D5
Mu Ko Chang △, *Thailand* 65 G4
Mu Us Shamo, *China* 56 E5
Muang Chiang Rai = Chiang Rai, *Thailand* 58 H2
Muang Khong, *Laos* 64 E5
Muang Lamphun, *Thailand* 64 C2
Muang Mai, *Thailand* 65 a
Muang Pak Beng, *Laos* 58 H3
Muar, *Malaysia* 65 L4
Muarabungo, *Indonesia* 62 E2
Muaraenim, *Indonesia* 62 E2
Muarajuloi, *Indonesia* 62 E4
Muarakaman, *Indonesia* 62 E5
Muaratebo, *Indonesia* 62 E2
Muaratembesi, *Indonesia* 62 E2
Muaratewe, *Indonesia* 62 E4
Mubarakpur, *India* 69 F10
Mubarraz = Al Mubarraz, *Si. Arabia* 71 E6
Mubende, *Uganda* 86 B3
Mubi, *Nigeria* 83 C7
Mucajaí →, *Brazil* 124 C6
Muchachos, Roque de los, *Canary Is.* 48 F2
Mücheln, *Germany* 24 D7
Muchinga Mts., *Zambia* 87 E3
Muchkapskiy, *Russia* 34 E6
Muchuan, *China* 58 C5
Muck, *U.K.* 13 E2
Muckadilla, *Australia* 95 D4
Muckle Flugga, *U.K.* 13 A8
Mucur, *Turkey* 72 C6
Mucuri, *Brazil* 125 G11
Mucusso, *Angola* 88 B3
Muda, *Canary Is.* 48 F6
Mudanjiang, *China* 57 B15
Mudanya, *Turkey* 45 F12
Muddy Cr. →, *U.S.A.* 109 H8
Mudgee, *Australia* 95 E4
Mudjatik →, *Canada* 103 B7
Mudurnu, *Turkey* 72 B4
Muecate, *Mozam.* 87 E4
Mueda, *Mozam.* 87 E4
Mueller Ra., *Australia* 92 C4
Muende, *Mozam.* 87 E3
Muerto, Mar, *Mexico* 119 D6
Mufu Shan, *China* 59 C10
Mufulira, *Zambia* 87 E2
Mufumbiro Range, *Africa* 86 C2
Mugardos, *Spain* 36 B2
Muge →, *Portugal* 37 F2
Múggia, *Italy* 41 C10
Mughal Sarai, *India* 69 G10
Mughayrā', *Si. Arabia* 70 D3
Mugi, *Japan* 55 H7
Mugia = Muxía, *Spain* 36 B1
Mugila, Mts., *Dem. Rep. of the Congo* 86 D2
Muğla, *Turkey* 47 D10
Muğla □, *Turkey* 47 D10
Muglad, *Sudan* 81 E2
Müglizh, *Bulgaria* 45 D9
Mugu, *Nepal* 69 E10
Muhammad, Râs, *Egypt* 70 E2
Muhammad Qol, *Sudan* 80 C4
Muhammadabad, *India* 69 F10
Muhesi →, *Tanzania* 86 D4
Mühlacker, *Germany* 25 G4
Mühldorf, *Germany* 25 G8
Mühlhausen, *Germany* 24 D6
Mühlig Hofmann fjell, *Antarctica* 5 D3
Mühlviertel, *Austria* 26 C7
Muhos, *Finland* 8 D22
Muhu, *Estonia* 9 G20
Muhutwe, *Tanzania* 86 C3
Muine Bheag, *Ireland* 12 D5
Muir, L., *Australia* 93 F2
Muir of Ord, *U.K.* 13 D4
Mujnak = Muynak, *Uzbekistan* 52 E6
Muka, Tanjung, *Malaysia* 65 c
Mukacheve, *Ukraine* 28 B7
Mukachevo = Mukacheve, *Ukraine* 28 B7
Mukah, *Malaysia* 62 D4
Mukandwara, *India* 68 G6
Mukawwa, Geziret, *Egypt* 80 C4
Mukawwar, *Sudan* 80 C4
Mukdahan, *Thailand* 64 D5
Mukden = Shenyang, *China* 57 D12
Mukerian, *India* 68 D6
Mukhavyets, *Belarus* 31 F10
Mukhtolovo, *Russia* 34 C6
Mukinbudin, *Australia* 93 F2
Mukishi, *Dem. Rep. of the Congo* 87 D1
Mukomuko, *Indonesia* 62 E2
Mukomwenze, *Dem. Rep. of the Congo* 86 D2
Muktsar, *India* 68 D6
Mukur = Moqor, *Afghan.* 68 C2
Mukutawa →, *Canada* 103 C9
Mukwela, *Zambia* 87 F2
Mula, *Spain* 39 G3
Mula →, *Pakistan* 68 F2
Mulange, *Dem. Rep. of the Congo* 86 C2
Mulanje, *Malawi* 87 F4
Mulanje, Mt., *Malawi* 87 F4
Mulchén, *Chile* 126 D1
Mulde →, *Germany* 24 D8
Mule Creek Junction, *U.S.A.* 112 D2
Muleba, *Tanzania* 86 C3
Mulejé, *Mexico* 118 B2
Muleshoe, *U.S.A.* 113 H3
Muletta, Gara, *Ethiopia* 81 F5
Mulgrave, *Canada* 105 C7
Mulhacén, *Spain* 37 H7
Mülheim, *Germany* 24 D2
Mulhouse, *France* 19 E14
Muli, *China* 58 D3
Muling, *China* 57 B16
Mull, *U.K.* 13 E3
Mull, Sound of, *U.K.* 13 E3
Mullaittivu, *Sri Lanka* 66 Q12
Mullen, *U.S.A.* 112 D4
Mullens, *U.S.A.* 114 G5
Muller, Pegunungan, *Indonesia* 62 D4
Mullet Pen., *Ireland* 12 B1
Mullewa, *Australia* 93 E2
Müllheim, *Germany* 25 H3
Mulligan →, *Australia* 94 D2
Mullingar, *Ireland* 12 C4
Mullins, *U.S.A.* 115 H6
Mullsjö, *Sweden* 11 G7
Mullumbimby, *Australia* 95 D5
Mulobezi, *Zambia* 87 F2
Mulroy B., *Ireland* 12 A4
Multan, *Pakistan* 68 D4
Mulumbe, Mts., *Dem. Rep. of the Congo* 87 D2
Mulungushi Dam, *Zambia* 87 E2
Mulvane, *U.S.A.* 113 G6
Mulwad, *Sudan* 80 D3
Mumbai, *India* 66 K8
Mumbwa, *Zambia* 87 F2
Mumra, *Russia* 35 H8
Mun →, *Thailand* 64 E5
Muna, *Indonesia* 63 F6
Munabao, *India* 68 G4
Munamagi, *Estonia* 9 H22
Muncan, *Indonesia* 63 K18
Muncar, *Indonesia* 63 J17
Münchberg, *Germany* 25 E7
Müncheberg, *Germany* 24 C10
München, *Germany* 25 G7
Munchen-Gladbach = Mönchengladbach, *Germany* 24 D2
München International ✈ (MUC), *Germany* 25 G7
Muncho Lake, *Canada* 102 B3
Munch'ŏn, *N. Korea* 57 E14
Muncie, *U.S.A.* 114 E3
Muncoonie, L., *Australia* 94 D2
Mundabbera, *Australia* 95 D5
Munday, *U.S.A.* 113 J5
Münden, *Germany* 24 D5
Münden ⌂, *Germany* 24 D5
Mundiwindi, *Australia* 92 D3
Mundo →, *Spain* 39 G2
Mundo Novo, *Brazil* 125 F10
Mundra, *India* 68 H3
Mundrabilla, *Australia* 93 F4
Munera, *Spain* 39 F2
Mungallala, *Australia* 95 D4
Mungallala Cr. →, *Australia* 95 D4
Mungana, *Australia* 94 B3
Mungaoli, *India* 68 G8
Mungari, *Mozam.* 87 F3
Mungbere, *Dem. Rep. of the Congo* 86 B2
Mungeli, *India* 69 H9
Munger, *India* 69 G12
Mungkan Kandju △, *Australia* 94 A3
Munich = München, *Germany* 25 G7
Munising, *U.S.A.* 114 B2
Munka-Ljungby, *Sweden* 11 H6
Munkebo, *Denmark* 11 J4
Munkedal, *Sweden* 11 F5
Munkfors, *Sweden* 10 E7
Munku-Sardyk, *Russia* 53 D11
Münnerstadt, *Germany* 25 E6
Muñoz Gamero, Pen., *Chile* 128 G2
Munroe L., *Canada* 103 B9
Munsan, *S. Korea* 57 F14
Munster, *France* 19 D14
Münster, *Niedersachsen, Germany* 24 C6
Münster, *Nordrhein-Westfalen, Germany* 24 D3
Munster □, *Ireland* 12 D3
Muntadgin, *Australia* 93 F2
Muntele Mare, Vf., *Romania* 29 D8
Muntok, *Indonesia* 62 E3
Munyama, *Zambia* 87 F2
Munzur Dağları, *Turkey* 73 C8
Muong Beng, *Laos* 58 G3
Muong Boum, *Vietnam* 58 F4
Muong Et, *Laos* 64 B5
Muong Hai, *Laos* 58 G3
Muong Hiem, *Laos* 64 B4
Muong Houn, *Laos* 58 G3
Muong Hung, *Vietnam* 58 G4
Muong Kau, *Laos* 64 E5
Muong Khao, *Laos* 64 C4
Muong Khoua, *Laos* 58 G4
Muong Liep, *Laos* 64 C3
Muong May, *Laos* 64 E6
Muong Ngeun, *Laos* 58 G3
Muong Ngoi, *Laos* 58 G4
Muong Nhie, *Vietnam* 58 F4
Muong Nong, *Laos* 64 D6
Muong Ou Tay, *Laos* 58 F3
Muong Oua, *Laos* 64 C3
Muong Peun, *Laos* 58 G4
Muong Phalane, *Laos* 64 D5
Muong Phieng, *Laos* 64 C3
Muong Phine, *Laos* 64 D6
Muong Sai, *Laos* 58 G3
Muong Saiapoun, *Laos* 64 C3
Muong Sen, *Vietnam* 64 C5
Muong Sing, *Laos* 58 G3
Muong Son, *Laos* 58 G4
Muong Soui, *Laos* 64 C4
Muong Va, *Laos* 58 G4
Muong Xia, *Vietnam* 64 B5
Muonio, *Finland* 8 C20
Muonio älv = Muonionjoki →, *Finland* 8 C20
Muonioälven = Muonionjoki →, *Finland* 8 C20
Muonionjoki →, *Finland* 8 C20
Muping, *China* 57 F11
Mupoi, *Sudan* 81 F2
Muqaddam, Wadi →, *Sudan* 80 D3
Muqdisho, *Somali Rep.* 75 G4
Mur →, *Austria* 27 E9
Mûr-de-Bretagne, *France* 18 D4
Muradiye, *Manisa, Turkey* 47 C9
Muradiye, *Van, Turkey* 73 C10
Murakami, *Japan* 54 E9
Murallón, Cerro, *Chile* 128 F2
Muranda, *Rwanda* 86 C2
Murang'a, *Kenya* 86 C4
Murashi, *Russia* 52 D5
Murat, *France* 20 C6
Murat →, *Turkey* 73 C9
Murat Dağı, *Turkey* 47 C11
Muratlı, *Turkey* 45 E11
Murato, *France* 21 F13
Murau, *Austria* 26 D7
Murava, *Belarus* 31 F11
Muravera, *Italy* 42 C2
Murayama, *Japan* 54 E10
Murça, *Portugal* 36 D3
Murchison →, *Australia* 93 E1
Murchison, Mt., *Antarctica* 5 D11
Murchison Falls, *Uganda* 86 B3
Murchison Falls △, *Uganda* 86 B3
Murchison Ra., *Australia* 94 C1
Murchison Rapids, *Malawi* 87 F3
Murcia, *Spain* 39 G3
Murcia □, *Spain* 39 H3
Murdo, *U.S.A.* 112 D4
Murdoch Pt., *Australia* 94 A3
Mürefte, *Turkey* 45 F11
Mureş □, *Romania* 29 D9
Mureş →, *Romania* 28 D5
Mureşul = Mureş →, *Romania* 28 D5
Muret, *France* 20 E5
Murewa, *Zimbabwe* 89 B5
Murfreesboro, *N.C., U.S.A.* 115 G7
Murfreesboro, *Tenn., U.S.A.* 115 H2
Murgab = Murghob, *Tajikistan* 52 F8
Murgab →, *Turkmenistan* 71 B9
Murgenella, *Australia* 92 B5
Murgeni, *Romania* 29 D13
Murgha Kibzai, *Pakistan* 68 D3
Murghob, *Tajikistan* 52 F8
Murgon, *Australia* 95 D5
Muri, *India* 69 H11
Muria, *Indonesia* 63 G14
Muriaé, *Brazil* 127 A7
Murias de Paredes, *Spain* 36 C4
Muriel Mine, *Zimbabwe* 87 F3
Müritz, *Germany* 24 B8
Müritz △, *Germany* 24 B8
Murliganj, *India* 69 G12
Murmansk, *Russia* 52 C4
Murnau, *Germany* 25 H7
Muro, *France* 21 F12
Muro, *Spain* 48 B10
Muro, C. de, *France* 21 G12
Muro de Alcoy, *Spain* 39 G4
Muro Lucano, *Italy* 43 B8
Murom, *Russia* 34 C6
Muroran, *Japan* 54 C10
Muros, *Spain* 36 C1
Muros y de Noya, Ría de, *Spain* 36 C1
Muroto, *Japan* 55 H7
Muroto-Misaki, *Japan* 55 H7
Murovani Kurylivtsi, *Ukraine* 29 B12
Murowana Goślina, *Poland* 31 F3
Murphy, *U.S.A.* 108 E5
Murphys, *U.S.A.* 110 G6
Murrat, *Sudan* 80 D2
Murrat Wells, *Sudan* 80 C3
Murray, *Ky., U.S.A.* 115 G1
Murray, *Utah, U.S.A.* 108 F8
Murray →, *Australia* 95 F2
Murray, L., *U.S.A.* 115 H5
Murray Bridge, *Australia* 95 F2
Murray Harbour, *Canada* 105 C7
Murray River △, *Australia* 95 E3
Murraysburg, *S. Africa* 88 E3
Murree, *Pakistan* 68 C5
Murrieta, *U.S.A.* 111 M9
Murro di Porco, Capo, *Italy* 43 F8
Murrumbidgee →, *Australia* 95 E3
Murrumburrah, *Australia* 95 E4
Murrurundi, *Australia* 95 E5
Murshid, *Sudan* 80 C3
Murshidabad, *India* 69 G13
Murska Sobota, *Slovenia* 41 B13
Murtle L., *Canada* 102 C5
Murtoa, *Australia* 95 F3
Murtosa, *Portugal* 36 E2
Murungu, *Tanzania* 86 C3
Mururoa, *French Polynesia* 97 K14
Murwara, *India* 69 H9
Murwillumbah, *Australia* 95 D5
Mürz →, *Austria* 26 D8
Mürzzuschlag, *Austria* 26 D8
Muş, *Turkey* 70 B4
Mûsa, Gebel, *Egypt* 70 D2
Musa Khel, *Pakistan* 68 D3
Mūsa Qal'eh, *Afghan.* 66 C4
Musafirkhana, *India* 69 F9
Musala, *Bulgaria* 44 D7
Musala, *Indonesia* 62 D1
Musan, *N. Korea* 57 C15
Musangu, *Dem. Rep. of the Congo* 87 E1
Musasa, *Tanzania* 86 C3
Musay'īd, *Qatar* 71 E6
Muscat = Masqat, *Oman* 75 C6
Muscatine, *U.S.A.* 112 E9
Musengezi = Unsengedsi →, *Zimbabwe* 87 F3
Musgrave Harbour, *Canada* 105 C9
Musgrave Ranges, *Australia* 93 E5
Mushie, *Dem. Rep. of the Congo* 84 E3
Mushin, *Nigeria* 83 D5
Musi →, *Indonesia* 62 E2
Musina, *S. Africa* 89 C5
Muskeg →, *Canada* 102 A4
Muskegon, *U.S.A.* 114 D2
Muskegon →, *U.S.A.* 114 D2
Muskegon Heights, *U.S.A.* 114 D2
Muskogee, *U.S.A.* 113 H7
Muskoka, L., *Canada* 116 B5
Muskwa →, *Canada* 102 B4
Muslīmiyah, *Syria* 70 B3
Musmar, *Sudan* 80 D4
Musofu, *Zambia* 87 E2
Musoma, *Tanzania* 86 C3
Musquaro, L., *Canada* 105 B7
Musquodoboit Harbour, *Canada* 105 D7
Musselburgh, *U.K.* 13 F5
Musselshell →, *U.S.A.* 108 C10
Mussidan, *France* 20 C4
Mussomeli, *Italy* 42 E6
Mussoorie, *India* 68 D8
Mussuco, *Angola* 88 B2
Mustafakemalpaşa, *Turkey* 45 F12
Mustang, *Nepal* 69 E10
Musters, L., *Argentina* 128 F3
Musudan, *N. Korea* 57 D15
Muswellbrook, *Australia* 95 E5
Muszyna, *Poland* 31 J7
Mût, *Egypt* 80 B2
Mut, *Turkey* 70 B2
Mutanda, *Mozam.* 89 C5
Mutanda, *Zambia* 87 E2
Mutare, *Zimbabwe* 87 F3
Muting, *Indonesia* 63 F10
Mutki = Mirtağ, *Turkey* 70 B4
Mutoko, *Zimbabwe* 89 B5
Mutoray, *Russia* 53 C11
Mutshatsha, *Dem. Rep. of the Congo* 87 E1
Mutsu, *Japan* 54 D10
Mutsu-Wan, *Japan* 54 D10
Muttaburra, *Australia* 94 C3
Muttalip, *Turkey* 47 B12
Mutton I., *Ireland* 12 D2
Mutuáli, *Mozam.* 87 E4
Mutum Biyu, *Nigeria* 83 D7
Muweilih, *Egypt* 74 E3
Muxía, *Spain* 36 B1
Muy Muy, *Nic.* 120 D2
Muyinga, *Burundi* 86 C3
Muynak, *Uzbekistan* 52 E6
Muzaffarabad, *Pakistan* 69 B5
Muzaffargarh, *Pakistan* 68 D4
Muzaffarnagar, *India* 68 E7
Muzaffarpur, *India* 69 F11
Muzafirpur, *Pakistan* 68 D3
Muzhi, *Russia* 52 C7
Muzillac, *France* 18 E4

Muzūra, *Egypt* 80 J7
Mvôlô, *Sudan* 81 F2
Mvuma, *Zimbabwe* 87 F3
Mvurwi, *Zimbabwe* 87 F3
Mwabvi ⌓, *Malawi* 87 F3
Mwadui, *Tanzania* 86 C3
Mwambo, *Tanzania* 87 E5
Mwandi, *Zambia* 87 F1
Mwanza, *Dem. Rep. of the Congo* 86 D2
Mwanza, *Tanzania* 86 C3
Mwanza, *Zambia* 87 F1
Mwanza □, *Tanzania* 86 C3
Mwaya, *Tanzania* 87 D3
Mweelrea, *Ireland* 12 C2
Mweka, *Dem. Rep. of the Congo* 84 E4
Mwenezi, *Zimbabwe* 87 G3
Mwenezi →, *Mozam.* 87 G3
Mwenga, *Dem. Rep. of the Congo* 86 C2
Mweru, L., *Zambia* 87 D2
Mweru Wantipa △, *Zambia* 87 D2
Mweza Range, *Zimbabwe* 87 G3
Mwilambwe, *Dem. Rep. of the Congo* 86 D2
Mwimbi, *Tanzania* 87 D3
Mwinilunga, *Zambia* 87 E1
My Tho, *Vietnam* 65 G6
Myajlar, *India* 68 F4
Myanaung, *Burma* 67 K19
Myanmar = Burma ■, *Asia* 67 J20
Myaungmya, *Burma* 67 L19
Myedna, *Belarus* 31 G10
Myeik Kyunzu, *Burma* 65 G1
Myers Chuck, *U.S.A.* 102 B2
Myerstown, *U.S.A.* 117 F8
Myingyan, *Burma* 67 J19
Myitkyina, *Burma* 67 G20
Myjava, *Slovak Rep.* 27 C10
Mykhaylivka, *Ukraine* 33 J8
Mykines, *Færoe Is.* 8 E9
Mykolayiv, *Ukraine* 33 J7
Mymensingh, *Bangla.* 67 G17
Mynydd Du, *U.K.* 15 F4
Mýrdalsjökull, *Iceland* 8 E4
Myrhorod, *Ukraine* 33 H7
Myrtle Beach, *U.S.A.* 115 J6
Myrtle Creek, *U.S.A.* 108 E2
Myrtle Point, *U.S.A.* 108 E1
Myrtou, *Cyprus* 49 D12
Mysia, *Turkey* 45 G11
Myślenice, *Poland* 31 J6
Myślibórz, *Poland* 31 F1
Mysłowice, *Poland* 31 H6
Mysore = Karnataka □, *India* 66 N10
Mysore, *India* 66 N10
Mystic, *U.S.A.* 117 E13
Myszków, *Poland* 31 H6
Myszyniec, *Poland* 30 E8
Mytishchi, *Russia* 32 E9
Mývatn, *Iceland* 8 D5
Mže →, *Czech Rep.* 26 B6
Mzimba, *Malawi* 87 E3
Mzimkulu →, *S. Africa* 89 E5
Mzimvubu →, *S. Africa* 89 E4
Mzuzu, *Malawi* 87 E3

N

Na Hearadh = Harris, *U.K.* 13 D2
Na Noi, *Thailand* 64 C3
Na Phao, *Laos* 64 D5
Na Sam, *Vietnam* 58 F6
Na San, *Vietnam* 64 B5
Na Thon, *Thailand* 65 b
Naab →, *Germany* 25 F8
Na'am, *Sudan* 81 F2
Na'am →, *Sudan* 81 F2
Naantali, *Finland* 9 F19
Naas, *Ireland* 12 C5
Nababeep, *S. Africa* 88 D2
Nabadwip = Navadwip, *India* 69 H13
Nabawa, *Australia* 93 E1
Nabberu, L., *Australia* 93 E3
Nabburg, *Germany* 25 F8
Naberezhnyye Chelny, *Russia* 34 C11
Nabeul, *Tunisia* 79 A8
Nabha, *India* 68 D7
Nabīd, *Iran* 71 D8
Nabire, *Indonesia* 63 E9
Nabisar, *Pakistan* 68 G3
Nabisipi →, *Canada* 105 B7
Nabiswera, *Uganda* 86 B3
Nāblus = Nābulus, *West Bank* 74 C4
Naboomspruit, *S. Africa* 89 C4
Nabou, *Burkina Faso* 82 C4
Nabua, *Phil.* 61 E5
Nābulus, *West Bank* 74 C4
Nacala, *Mozam.* 87 E5
Nacala-Velha, *Mozam.* 87 E5
Nacaome, *Honduras* 120 D2
Nacaroa, *Mozam.* 87 E4
Naches, *U.S.A.* 108 C3
Naches →, *U.S.A.* 110 D6
Nachicapau, L., *Canada* 105 A6
Nachingwea, *Tanzania* 87 E4
Nachna, *India* 68 F4
Náchod, *Czech Rep.* 26 A9
Nacimiento L., *U.S.A.* 110 K6
Naco, *Mexico* 118 A3
Nacogdoches, *U.S.A.* 113 K7
Nácori Chico, *Mexico* 118 B3
Nacozari, *Mexico* 118 A3
Nådendal = Naantali, *Finland* 9 F19
Nadi, *Fiji* 91 C7
Nadi, *Sudan* 80 D3
Nadiad, *India* 68 H5
Nădlac, *Romania* 28 D5
Nador, *Morocco* 78 B5
Nadur, *Malta* 49 C1
Nadūshan, *Iran* 71 C7
Nadvirna, *Ukraine* 29 B9
Nadvornaya = Nadvirna, *Ukraine* 29 B9
Nadym, *Russia* 52 C8
Nadym →, *Russia* 52 C8
Nærbø, *Norway* 9 G11
Næstved, *Denmark* 11 J5
Nafada, *Nigeria* 83 C7
Naft-e Safīd, *Iran* 71 D6
Naftshahr, *Iran* 70 C5
Nafud Desert = An Nafūd, *Si. Arabia* 70 D4
Nag Hammâdi, *Egypt* 80 B3
Naga, *Phil.* 61 E5
Nagahama, *Japan* 55 G8
Nagai, *Japan* 54 E10
Nagaland □, *India* 67 G19
Nagano, *Japan* 55 F9
Nagano □, *Japan* 55 F9
Nagaoka, *Japan* 55 F9
Nagappattinam, *India* 66 P11
Nagar →, *Bangla.* 69 G13
Nagar Parkar, *Pakistan* 68 G4
Nagasaki, *Japan* 55 H4
Nagasaki □, *Japan* 55 H4
Nagato, *Japan* 55 G5
Nagaur, *India* 68 F5
Nagda, *India* 68 H6
Nagercoil, *India* 66 Q10
Nagina, *India* 69 E8
Nagīneh, *Iran* 71 C8
Nagir, *Pakistan* 69 A6
Naglarby, *Sweden* 10 D9
Nagod, *India* 69 G9
Nagold, *Germany* 25 G4
Nagold →, *Germany* 25 G4
Nagoorin, *Australia* 94 C5
Nagorno-Karabakh □, *Azerbaijan* 70 B5
Nagornyy, *Russia* 53 D13
Nagoya, *Japan* 55 G8
Nagpur, *India* 66 J11
Nagua, *Dom. Rep.* 121 C6
Naguabo, *Puerto Rico* 121 d
Nagyatád, *Hungary* 28 D2
Nagyecsed, *Hungary* 28 C7
Nagykálló, *Hungary* 28 C6
Nagykanizsa, *Hungary* 28 D2
Nagykáta, *Hungary* 28 C4
Nagykőrös, *Hungary* 28 C4
Naha, *Japan* 55 L3
Nahan, *India* 68 D7
Nahanni △, *Canada* 102 A4
Nahanni Butte, *Canada* 102 A4
Nahargarh, *Mad. P., India* 68 G6
Nahargarh, *Raj., India* 68 G7
Nahariyya, *Israel* 70 C2
Nahāvand, *Iran* 71 C6
Nahe →, *Germany* 25 F3
Nahirne, *Ukraine* 29 E13
Nahîya, W. →, *Egypt* 80 B3
Nahuelbuta △, *Chile* 126 D1
Nai Yong, *Thailand* 65 a
Naicá, *Mexico* 118 B3
Naicam, *Canada* 103 C8
Naikoon ⌓, *Canada* 102 C2
Naila, *Germany* 25 E7
Naimisharanya, *India* 69 F9
Nain, *Canada* 105 A7
Nā'īn, *Iran* 71 C7
Naini Tal, *India* 69 E8
Nainpur, *India* 66 H12
Naintré, *France* 18 F7
Nainwa, *India* 68 G6
Naipu, *Romania* 29 F10
Nairn, *U.K.* 13 D5
Nairobi, *Kenya* 86 C4
Nairobi △, *Kenya* 86 C4
Naissaar, *Estonia* 9 G21
Naita, Mt., *Ethiopia* 81 F4
Naivasha, *Kenya* 86 C4
Naivasha, L., *Kenya* 86 C4
Najac, *France* 20 D5
Najaf = An Najaf, *Iraq* 70 C5
Najafābād, *Iran* 71 C6
Najd, *Si. Arabia* 75 B3
Nájera, *Spain* 38 C2
Najerilla →, *Spain* 38 C2
Najibabad, *India* 68 E8
Najin, *N. Korea* 57 C16
Najmah, *Si. Arabia* 71 E6
Najrān, *Si. Arabia* 75 D3
Naju, *S. Korea* 57 G14
Nakadōri-Shima, *Japan* 55 H4
Nakalagba, *Dem. Rep. of the Congo* 86 B2
Nakaminato, *Japan* 55 F10
Nakamura, *Japan* 55 H6
Nakano, *Japan* 55 F9
Nakano-Shima, *Japan* 55 K4
Nakashibetsu, *Japan* 54 C12
Nakfa, *Eritrea* 81 D4
Nakfa ⌓, *Eritrea* 81 D4
Nakha Yai, Ko, *Thailand* 65 a
Nakhichevan = Naxçıvan, *Azerbaijan* 70 B5
Nakhichevan Rep. = Naxçıvan □, *Azerbaijan* 52 F5
Nakhl, *Egypt* 74 F2
Nakhl-e Taqī, *Iran* 71 E7
Nakhodka, *Russia* 53 E14
Nakhon Nayok, *Thailand* 64 E3
Nakhon Pathom, *Thailand* 64 F3
Nakhon Phanom, *Thailand* 64 D5
Nakhon Ratchasima, *Thailand* 64 E4
Nakhon Sawan, *Thailand* 64 E3
Nakhon Si Thammarat, *Thailand* 65 H3
Nakhon Thai, *Thailand* 64 D3
Nakhtarana, *India* 68 H3
Nakina, *Canada* 104 B2
Nakło nad Notecią, *Poland* 31 E4
Nako, *Burkina Faso* 82 C4
Nakodar, *India* 68 D6
Nakskov, *Denmark* 11 K5
Naktong →, *S. Korea* 57 G15
Nakuru, *Kenya* 86 C4
Nakuru, L., *Kenya* 86 C4
Nakusp, *Canada* 102 C5
Nal, *Pakistan* 68 F2
Nal →, *Pakistan* 68 G1
Nalázi, *Mozam.* 89 C5
Nalchik, *Russia* 35 J6
Nałęczów, *Poland* 31 G9
Nalerigu, *Ghana* 83 C4
Nalgonda, *India* 66 L11
Nalhati, *India* 69 G12
Naliya, *India* 68 H3
Nallamalai Hills, *India* 66 M11
Nallıhan, *Turkey* 72 B4
Nalón →, *Spain* 36 B4
Nam Can, *Vietnam* 65 H5
Nam-ch'on, *N. Korea* 57 E14
Nam Co, *China* 60 C4
Nam Dinh, *Vietnam* 58 G6
Nam Du, Hon, *Vietnam* 65 H5
Nam Nao △, *Thailand* 64 D3
Nam Ngum Dam, *Laos* 64 C4
Nam-Phan, *Vietnam* 65 G6
Nam Phong, *Thailand* 64 D4
Nam Tha, *Laos* 58 G3
Nam Tok, *Thailand* 64 E2
Namacunde, *Angola* 88 B2
Namacurra, *Mozam.* 89 B6
Namak, Daryācheh-ye, *Iran* 71 C7
Namak, Kavir-e, *Iran* 71 C8
Namakzār, Daryācheh-ye, *Iran* 71 C9
Namaland, *Namibia* 88 C2
Namangan, *Uzbekistan* 52 E8
Namapa, *Mozam.* 87 E4
Namaqualand, *S. Africa* 88 E2
Namasagali, *Uganda* 86 B3
Namber, *Indonesia* 63 E8
Nambour, *Australia* 95 D5
Nambucca Heads, *Australia* 95 E5
Nambung △, *Australia* 93 F2
Namche Bazar, *Nepal* 69 F12
Namchonjŏm = Nam-ch'on, *N. Korea* 57 E14
Namecunda, *Mozam.* 87 E4
Nameponda, *Mozam.* 87 F4
Náměšť nad Oslavou, *Czech Rep.* 27 B9
Námestovo, *Slovak Rep.* 27 B12
Nametil, *Mozam.* 87 F4
Namew L., *Canada* 103 C8
Namgia, *India* 69 D8
Namhkam, *Burma* 58 E1
Namib Desert, *Namibia* 88 C2
Namib-Naukluft ⌓, *Namibia* 88 C2
Namibe, *Angola* 85 H2
Namibe □, *Angola* 88 B1
Namibia ■, *Africa* 88 C2
Namibwoestyn = Namib Desert, *Namibia* 88 C2
Namīn, *Iran* 73 C13
Namlea, *Indonesia* 63 E7
Namoi →, *Australia* 95 E4
Nampa, *U.S.A.* 108 E5
Nampala, *Mali* 82 B3
Namp'o, *N. Korea* 57 E13
Nampō-Shotō, *Japan* 55 J10
Nampula, *Mozam.* 87 F4
Namrole, *Indonesia* 63 E7
Namse Shankou, *China* 67 E13
Namsen →, *Norway* 8 D14
Namsos, *Norway* 8 D14
Namtok Chat Trakan △, *Thailand* 64 D3
Namtok Mae Surin △, *Thailand* 64 C2
Namtsy, *Russia* 53 C13
Namtu, *Burma* 67 H20
Namtumbo, *Tanzania* 87 E4
Namu, *Canada* 102 C3
Namur, *Belgium* 17 D4
Namur □, *Belgium* 17 D4
Namutoni, *Namibia* 88 B2
Namwala, *Zambia* 87 F2
Namwŏn, *S. Korea* 57 G14
Namysłów, *Poland* 31 G4
Nan, *Thailand* 64 C3
Nan →, *Thailand* 64 E3
Nan-ch'ang = Nanchang, *China* 59 C10
Nan Ling, *China* 59 E8
Nan Xian, *China* 59 C9
Nana, *Romania* 29 F11
Nana Kru, *Liberia* 82 E3
Nanaimo, *Canada* 102 D4
Nanam, *N. Korea* 57 D15
Nanan, *China* 59 E12
Nanango, *Australia* 95 D5
Nan'ao, *China* 59 F11
Nanao, *Japan* 55 F8
Nanbu, *China* 58 B6
Nanchang, *Jiangxi, China* 59 C10
Nanchang, *Kiangsi, China* 59 C10
Nancheng, *China* 59 D11
Nanching = Nanjing, *China* 59 A12
Nanchong, *China* 58 B6
Nanchuan, *China* 58 C6
Nancy, *France* 19 D13
Nanda Devi, *India* 69 D8
Nanda Kot, *India* 69 D9
Nandan, *China* 58 E6
Nandan, *Japan* 55 G7
Nanded, *India* 66 K10
Nandewar Ra., *Australia* 95 E5
Nandi = Nadi, *Fiji* 91 C7
Nandigram, *India* 69 H12
Nandurbar, *India* 66 J9
Nandyal, *India* 66 M11
Nanfeng, *Guangdong, China* 59 F8
Nanfeng, *Jiangxi, China* 59 D11
Nanga-Eboko, *Cameroon* 83 E7
Nanga Parbat, *Pakistan* 69 B6
Nangade, *Mozam.* 87 E4
Nangapinoh, *Indonesia* 62 E4
Nangarhār □, *Afghan.* 66 B7
Nangatayap, *Indonesia* 62 E4
Nangeya Mts., *Uganda* 86 B3
Nangis, *France* 19 D10
Nangong, *China* 56 F8
Nanhua, *China* 58 E3
Nanhuang, *China* 57 F11
Nanhui, *China* 59 B13
Nanjeko, *Zambia* 87 F1
Nanji Shan, *China* 59 D13
Nanjian, *China* 58 E3
Nanjiang, *China* 58 A6
Nanjing, *Fujian, China* 59 E11
Nanjing, *Jiangsu, China* 59 A12
Nanjirinji, *Tanzania* 87 D4
Nankana Sahib, *Pakistan* 68 D5
Nankang, *China* 59 E10
Nanking = Nanjing, *China* 59 A12
Nankoku, *Japan* 55 H6
Nanling, *China* 59 B12
Nanning, *China* 58 F7
Nannup, *Australia* 93 F2
Nanpan Jiang →, *China* 58 E6
Nanpara, *India* 69 F9
Nanpi, *China* 56 E9
Nanping, *Fujian, China* 59 D12
Nanping, *Henan, China* 59 C9
Nanri Dao, *China* 59 E12
Nanripe, *Mozam.* 87 E4
Nansei-Shotō = Ryūkyū-rettō, *Japan* 55 M3
Nansen Basin, *Arctic* 4 A10
Nansen Cordillera, *Arctic* 4 A
Nansen Sd., *Canada* 4 A3
Nanshan I., *S. China Sea* 62 B5
Nansio, *Tanzania* 86 C3
Nant, *France* 20 D7
Nanterre, *France* 19 D9
Nantes, *France* 18 E5
Nantiat, *France* 20 B5
Nanticoke, *U.S.A.* 117 E8
Nanton, *Canada* 102 C6
Nantong, *China* 59 A13
Nantou, *Taiwan* 59 F13
Nantua, *France* 19 F12
Nantucket I., *U.S.A.* 114 E10
Nantwich, *U.K.* 14 D5
Nanty Glo, *U.S.A.* 116 F6
Nanuque, *Brazil* 125 G10
Nanusa, Kepulauan, *Indonesia* 63 D7
Nanutarra Roadhouse, *Australia* 92 D2
Nanxi, *China* 58 C5
Nanxiong, *China* 59 E10
Nanyang, *China* 56 H7
Nanyi Hu, *China* 59 B12
Nanyuki, *Kenya* 86 B4
Nanzhang, *China* 59 B8
Nao, C. de la, *Spain* 39 G5
Naococane, L., *Canada* 105 B5
Náousa, *Imathía, Greece* 44 F6
Náousa, *Kikládhes, Greece* 47 D7
Naozhou Dao, *China* 59 G8
Napa, *U.S.A.* 110 G4
Napa →, *U.S.A.* 110 G4
Napanee, *Canada* 116 B8
Napanoch, *U.S.A.* 117 E10
Nape, *Laos* 64 C5
Nape Pass = Keo Neua, Deo, *Vietnam* 64 C5
Napier, *N.Z.* 91 H6
Napier Broome B., *Australia* 92 B4
Napier Pen., *Australia* 94 A2
Napierville, *Canada* 117 A11
Naples = Nápoli, *Italy* 43 B7
Naples, *U.S.A.* 115 M5
Napo, *China* 58 F5
Napo →, *Peru* 124 D4
Napoleon, *N. Dak., U.S.A.* 112 B5
Napoleon, *Ohio, U.S.A.* 114 E3
Nápoli, *Italy* 43 B7
Nápoli, G. di, *Italy* 43 B7
Nápoli Capodichino ✕ (NAP), *Italy* 43 B7
Napopo, *Dem. Rep. of the Congo* 86 B2
Naqâda, *Egypt* 80 B3
Naqadeh, *Iran* 73 D11
Naqb, Ra's an, *Jordan* 74 F4
Naqqāsh, *Iran* 71 C6
Nara, *Japan* 55 G7
Nara, *Mali* 82 B3
Nara □, *Japan* 55 G8
Nara Canal, *Pakistan* 68 G3
Nara Visa, *U.S.A.* 113 H3
Naracoorte, *Australia* 95 F3
Naradhan, *Australia* 95 E4
Naraini, *India* 69 G9
Narasapur, *India* 67 L12
Narathiwat, *Thailand* 65 J3
Narayanganj, *Bangla.* 67 H17
Narayanpet, *India* 66 L10
Narberth, *U.K.* 15 F3
Narbonne, *France* 20 E7
Narcea →, *Spain* 36 B4
Nardīn, *Iran* 71 B7
Nardò, *Italy* 43 B11
Narembeen, *Australia* 93 F2
Narendranagar, *India* 68 D8
Nares Str., *Arctic* 98 A13
Naretha, *Australia* 93 F3
Narew →, *Poland* 31 F7
Nari →, *Pakistan* 68 F2
Narin, *Afghan.* 66 A6
Narindra, Helodranon' i, *Madag.* 89 A8
Narita, *Japan* 55 G10
Nariva Swamp, *Trin. & Tob.* 125 K15
Närke, *Sweden* 10 E8
Narmada →, *India* 68 J5
Narman, *Turkey* 73 B9
Narmland, *Sweden* 9 F15
Narnaul, *India* 68 E7
Narni, *Italy* 41 F9
Naro, *Ghana* 82 C4
Naro Fominsk, *Russia* 32 E9
Narodnaya, *Russia* 6 B17
Narok, *Kenya* 86 C4
Narón, *Spain* 36 B2
Narooma, *Australia* 95 F5
Narowal, *Pakistan* 68 C6
Narrabri, *Australia* 95 E4
Narran →, *Australia* 95 D4
Narrandera, *Australia* 95 E4
Narrogin, *Australia* 93 F2
Narromine, *Australia* 95 E4
Narrow Hills ⌓, *Canada* 103 C8
Narsimhapur, *India* 69 H8
Narsinghgarh, *India* 68 H7
Nartes, L. e, *Albania* 44 F3
Nartkala, *Russia* 35 J6
Naruto, *Japan* 55 G7
Narva, *Estonia* 32 C5
Narva →, *Russia* 9 G22
Narva Bay = Narva Laht, *Estonia* 9 G19
Narva Laht, *Estonia* 9 G19
Narvik, *Norway* 8 B17
Narvskoye Vdkhr., *Russia* 32 C5
Narwana, *India* 68 E7
Narwiański △, *Poland* 31 F9
Naryan-Mar, *Russia* 52 C6
Narym, *Russia* 52 D9
Naryn, *Kyrgyzstan* 52 E8
Nasa, *Norway* 8 C16
Năsăud, *Romania* 29 C9
Naseby, *N.Z.* 91 L3
Naselle, *U.S.A.* 110 D3
Naser, Buheirat en, *Egypt* 80 C3
Nashua, *Mont., U.S.A.* 108 B10
Nashua, *N.H., U.S.A.* 117 D13
Nashville, *Ark., U.S.A.* 113 J8
Nashville, *Ga., U.S.A.* 115 K4
Nashville, *Tenn., U.S.A.* 115 G2
Našice, *Croatia* 28 E3
Nasielsk, *Poland* 31 F7
Nasik, *India* 66 K8
Nasipit, *Phil.* 61 G6
Nasir, *Sudan* 81 F3
Nasirabad, *India* 68 F6
Nasirabad, *Pakistan* 68 E3
Nasiriyah = An Nāşirīyah, *Iraq* 70 D5
Naskaupi →, *Canada* 105 B7
Naso, *Italy* 43 D7
Naşrābād, *Iran* 71 C6
Naşriān-e Pā'īn, *Iran* 70 C5
Nass →, *Canada* 102 C3
Nassarawa, *Nigeria* 83 D6
Nassarawa □, *Nigeria* 83 D6
Nassau, *Bahamas* 120 A4
Nassau, *U.S.A.* 117 D11
Nassau, B., *Chile* 128 H3
Nasser, L. = Naser, Buheirat en, *Egypt* 80 C3
Nassian, *Ivory C.* 82 D4
Nässjö, *Sweden* 11 G8
Nastapoka →, *Canada* 104 A4
Nastapoka, Is., *Canada* 104 A4
Nasugbu, *Phil.* 61 D4
Näsum, *Sweden* 11 H8
Näsviken, *Sweden* 10 C10
Nata, *Botswana* 88 C4
Nata →, *Botswana* 88 C4
Natal, *Brazil* 125 E11
Natal, *Indonesia* 62 D1
Natal, *S. Africa* 85 K6
Natal Drakensberg ⌓, *S. Africa* 89 D4
Natalinci, *Serbia & M.* 28 F5
Naţanz, *Iran* 71 C6
Natashquan, *Canada* 105 B7
Natashquan →, *Canada* 105 B7
Natchez, *U.S.A.* 113 K9
Natchitoches, *U.S.A.* 113 K8
Nathalia, *Australia* 95 F4
Nathdwara, *India* 68 G5
Nati, Pta., *Spain* 48 A10
Natimuk, *Australia* 95 F3
Nation →, *Canada* 102 B4
National City, *U.S.A.* 111 N9
Natitingou, *Benin* 83 C5
Natividad, I., *Mexico* 118 B1
Natkyizin, *Burma* 64 E1
Natron, L., *Tanzania* 86 C4
Natrona Heights, *U.S.A.* 116 F5
Natrûn, W. el →, *Egypt* 80 H7
Nättraby, *Sweden* 11 H9
Natukanaoka Pan, *Namibia* 88 B2
Natuna Besar, Kepulauan, *Indonesia* 62 D3
Natuna Is. = Natuna Besar, Kepulauan, *Indonesia* 62 D3
Natuna Selatan, Kepulauan, *Indonesia* 62 D3
Natural Bridge, *U.S.A.* 117 B9
Natural Bridges ⌓, *U.S.A.* 109 H8
Naturaliste, C., *Australia* 95 G4
Nau Qala, *Afghan.* 68 B3
Naucelle, *France* 20 D6
Nauders, *Austria* 26 E3
Nauen, *Germany* 24 C8
Naugatuck, *U.S.A.* 117 E11
Naujaat = Repulse Bay, *Canada* 101 B11
Naujoji Akmenė, *Lithuania* 30 B9
Naumburg, *Germany* 24 D7
Nā'ūr at Tunayb, *Jordan* 74 D4
Nauru ■, *Pac. Oc.* 96 H8
Naushahra = Nowshera, *Pakistan* 66 C8
Naushahro, *Pakistan* 68 F3
Naushon I., *U.S.A.* 117 E14
Nauta, *Peru* 124 D4
Nautanwa, *India* 67 F13
Naute ⌓, *Namibia* 88 D2
Nautla, *Mexico* 119 C5
Nava, *Mexico* 118 B4
Nava, *Spain* 36 B5
Nava del Rey, *Spain* 36 D5
Navadwip, *India* 69 H13
Navahermosa, *Spain* 37 F6
Navahrudak, *Belarus* 32 F3

Navajo Reservoir, *U.S.A.* **109 H10**
Navalcarnero, *Spain* **36 E6**
Navalmoral de la Mata, *Spain* **36 F5**
Navalvillar de Pela, *Spain* **37 F5**
Navan = An Uaimh, *Ireland* **12 C5**
Navapolatsk, *Belarus* **32 E5**
Navarin, Mys, *Russia* **4 C16**
Navarino, I., *Chile* **128 H3**
Navarra □, *Spain* **38 C3**
Navarre, *U.S.A.* **116 F3**
Navarro →, *U.S.A.* **110 F3**
Navas de San Juan, *Spain* **37 G7**
Navasota, *U.S.A.* **113 K6**
Navassa I., *W. Indies* **121 C5**
Nävekvarn, *Sweden* **11 F10**
Naver →, *U.K.* **13 C4**
Navia, *Spain* **36 B4**
Navia →, *Spain* **36 B4**
Navia de Suarna, *Spain* **36 C3**
Navibandar, *India* **68 J3**
Navidad, *Chile* **126 C1**
Naviraí, *Brazil* **127 A5**
Navlakhi, *India* **68 H4**
Navlya, *Russia* **33 F8**
Năvodari, *Romania* **29 F13**
Navoi = Nawoiy, *Uzbekistan* **52 E7**
Navojoa, *Mexico* **118 B3**
Navolato, *Mexico* **118 C3**
Návpaktos, *Greece* **46 C3**
Návplion, *Greece* **46 D4**
Navrongo, *Ghana* **83 C4**
Navsari, *India* **66 J8**
Nawa Kot, *Pakistan* **68 E4**
Nawab Khan, *Pakistan* **68 D3**
Nawabganj, *Ut. P., India* **69 F9**
Nawabganj, *Ut. P., India* **69 E8**
Nawabshah, *Pakistan* **68 F3**
Nawada, *India* **69 G11**
Nawakot, *Nepal* **69 F11**
Nawalgarh, *India* **68 F6**
Nawanshahr, *India* **69 C6**
Nawar, Dasht-i-, *Afghan.* **68 C3**
Nawi, *Sudan* **80 D3**
Nawoiy, *Uzbekistan* **52 E7**
Naxçıvan, *Azerbaijan* **70 B5**
Naxçıvan □, *Azerbaijan* **52 F5**
Náxos, *Greece* **47 D7**
Nay, *France* **20 E3**
Nay, Mui, *Vietnam* **62 B3**
Nāy Band, *Būshehr, Iran* **71 E7**
Nāy Band, *Khorāsān, Iran* **71 C8**
Nayakhan, *Russia* **53 C16**
Nayarit □, *Mexico* **118 C4**
Nayé, *Senegal* **82 C2**
Nayong, *China* **58 D5**
Nayoro, *Japan* **54 B11**
Nayyāl, W. →, *Si. Arabia* **70 D3**
Nazaré, *Brazil* **125 F11**
Nazaré, *Portugal* **37 F1**
Nazareth = Nazerat, *Israel* **74 C4**
Nazareth, *U.S.A.* **117 F9**
Nazas, *Mexico* **118 B4**
Nazas →, *Mexico* **118 B4**
Nazca, *Peru* **124 F4**
Naze, The, *U.K.* **15 F9**
Nazerat, *Israel* **74 C4**
Nāzīk, *Iran* **70 B5**
Nazilli, *Turkey* **47 D10**
Nazko, *Canada* **102 C4**
Nazko →, *Canada* **102 C4**
Nazret, *Ethiopia* **81 F4**
Nazwa, *Oman* **75 C6**
Nchanga, *Zambia* **87 E2**
Ncheu, *Malawi* **87 E3**
Ndala, *Tanzania* **86 C3**
Ndalatando, *Angola* **84 F2**
Ndali, *Benin* **83 D5**
Ndareda, *Tanzania* **86 C4**
Ndélé, *C.A.R.* **84 C4**
Ndiael ⌓, *Senegal* **82 B1**
Ndikinimeki, *Cameroon* **83 E7**
N'Dioum, *Senegal* **82 B2**
Ndjamena, *Chad* **79 F8**
Ndola, *Zambia* **87 E2**
Ndoto Mts., *Kenya* **86 B4**
Nduguti, *Tanzania* **86 C3**
Ndumu ⌓, *S. Africa* **89 D5**
Néa Alikarnassós, *Greece* **47 F7**
Néa Ankhíalos, *Greece* **46 B4**
Néa Epídhavros, *Greece* **46 D5**
Néa Flippiás, *Greece* **46 B2**
Néa Ionia, *Greece* **46 B4**
Néa Kallikrátia, *Greece* **44 F7**
Néa Mákri, *Greece* **46 C5**
Néa Moudhaniá, *Greece* **44 F7**
Néa Péramos, *Attikí, Greece* **46 C5**
Néa Péramos, *Kavála, Greece* **45 F8**
Néa Víssi, *Greece* **45 E10**
Néa Zíkhna, *Greece* **44 E7**
Neagh, Lough, *U.K.* **12 B5**
Neah Bay, *U.S.A.* **110 B2**
Neale, L., *Australia* **92 D5**
Neales, The →, *Australia* **95 D2**
Neamţ □, *Romania* **29 C11**
Neápolis, *Kozáni, Greece* **44 F5**
Neápolis, *Kríti, Greece* **49 D7**
Neápolis, *Lakonía, Greece* **46 E5**
Near Is., *U.S.A.* **100 C1**
Neath, *U.K.* **15 F4**
Neath Port Talbot □, *U.K.* **15 F4**
Nebbou, *Burkina Faso* **83 C4**
Nebelat el Hagana, *Sudan* **81 E2**
Nebine Cr. →, *Australia* **95 D4**
Nebitdag, *Turkmenistan* **52 F6**
Nebo, *Australia* **94 C4**
Nebolchy, *Russia* **32 C7**
Nebraska □, *U.S.A.* **112 E5**
Nebraska City, *U.S.A.* **112 E7**
Nébrodi, Monti, *Italy* **43 E7**
Necedah, *U.S.A.* **112 C9**
Nechako →, *Canada* **102 C4**
Neches →, *U.S.A.* **113 L8**
Nechisar △, *Ethiopia* **81 F4**
Neckar →, *Germany* **25 F4**
Neckartal-Odenwald ⌓, *Germany* **25 F5**
Necochea, *Argentina* **126 D4**
Neda, *Spain* **36 B2**
Nedelino, *Bulgaria* **45 E9**
Nedelišće, *Croatia* **41 B13**
Nédha →, *Greece* **46 D3**
Nedoboyivtsi, *Ukraine* **29 B11**
Needles, *Canada* **102 D5**
Needles, *U.S.A.* **111 L12**
Needles, The, *U.K.* **15 G6**
Ñeembucú □, *Paraguay* **126 B4**
Neemuch = Nimach, *India* **68 G6**
Neenah, *U.S.A.* **114 C1**
Neepawa, *Canada* **103 C9**
Neftçala, *Azerbaijan* **71 B6**
Neftegorsk, *Russia* **35 H4**
Neftekumsk, *Russia* **35 H7**
Nefyn, *U.K.* **14 E3**
Négala, *Mali* **82 C3**
Negapatam = Nagappattinam, *India* **66 P11**
Negara, *Indonesia* **63 J17**
Negaunee, *U.S.A.* **114 B2**
Negele, *Ethiopia* **81 F4**
Negev Desert = Hanegev, *Israel* **74 E4**
Negoiul, Vf., *Romania* **29 E9**
Negombo, *Sri Lanka* **66 R11**
Negotin, *Serbia & M.* **44 B6**
Negotino, *Macedonia* **44 E6**
Negra, Peña, *Spain* **36 C4**
Negra, Pta., *Peru* **124 E2**
Negrais, C. = Maudin Sun, *Burma* **67 M19**
Negreşti, *Romania* **29 D12**
Negreşti-Oaş, *Romania* **29 C8**
Negril, *Jamaica* **120 a**
Negro →, *Argentina* **128 E4**
Negro →, *Brazil* **124 D7**
Negro →, *Uruguay* **127 C4**
Negros, *Phil.* **61 G5**
Negru Vodă, *Romania* **29 G13**
Neguac, *Canada* **105 C6**
Nehalem →, *U.S.A.* **110 E3**
Nehāvand, *Iran* **71 C6**
Nehbandān, *Iran* **71 D9**
Nehoiu, *Romania* **29 E11**
Nei Monggol Zizhiqu □, *China* **56 D7**
Neijiang, *China* **58 C5**
Neillsville, *U.S.A.* **112 C9**
Neilton, *U.S.A.* **108 C2**
Neiqiu, *China* **56 F8**
Neiva, *Colombia* **124 C3**
Neixiang, *China* **56 H6**
Nejanilini L., *Canada* **103 B9**
Nejd = Najd, *Si. Arabia* **75 B3**
Nejo, *Ethiopia* **81 F4**
Nekā, *Iran* **71 B7**
Nekemte, *Ethiopia* **81 F4**
Nêkheb, *Egypt* **80 B3**
Neksø, *Denmark* **11 J9**
Nelas, *Portugal* **36 E3**
Nelia, *Australia* **94 C3**
Nelidovo, *Russia* **32 D7**
Neligh, *U.S.A.* **112 D5**
Nelkan, *Russia* **53 D14**
Nellore, *India* **66 M11**
Nelson, *Canada* **102 D5**
Nelson, *N.Z.* **91 J4**
Nelson, *U.K.* **14 D5**
Nelson, *Ariz., U.S.A.* **109 J7**
Nelson, *Nev., U.S.A.* **111 K12**
Nelson →, *Canada* **103 C9**
Nelson, C., *Australia* **95 F3**
Nelson, Estrecho, *Chile* **128 G2**
Nelson Forks, *Canada* **102 B4**
Nelson House, *Canada* **103 B9**
Nelson L., *Canada* **103 B8**
Nelson Lakes △, *N.Z.* **91 J4**
Nelspoort, *S. Africa* **88 E3**
Nelspruit, *S. Africa* **89 D5**
Néma, *Mauritania* **82 B3**
Neman = Nemunas →, *Lithuania* **9 J19**
Neman, *Russia* **9 J20**
Neméa, *Greece* **46 D4**
Nemeiben L., *Canada* **103 B7**
Nemërçkë, Mal, *Albania* **44 F4**
Nemira, Vf., *Romania* **29 D11**
Nemiscau, *Canada* **104 B4**
Nemiscau, L., *Canada* **104 B4**
Nemours, *France* **19 D9**
Nemšová, *Slovak Rep.* **27 C11**
Nemunas →, *Lithuania* **9 J19**
Nemuro, *Japan* **54 C12**
Nemuro-Kaikyō, *Japan* **54 C12**
Nemyriv, *Ukraine* **31 H10**
Nen Jiang →, *China* **57 B13**
Nenagh, *Ireland* **12 D3**
Nenasi, *Malaysia* **65 L4**
Nene →, *U.K.* **15 E8**
Nénita, *Greece* **47 C8**
Nenjiang, *China* **60 B7**
Neno, *Malawi* **87 F3**
Neodesha, *U.S.A.* **113 G7**
Neokhórion, *Aitolía kai Akarnanía, Greece* **46 C3**
Neokhórion, *Árta, Greece* **46 B2**
Néon Karlovásion, *Greece* **47 D8**
Néon Petrítsi, *Greece* **44 E7**
Neosho, *U.S.A.* **113 G7**
Neosho →, *U.S.A.* **113 H7**
Nepal ■, *Asia* **69 F11**
Nepalganj, *Nepal* **69 E9**
Nepalganj Road, *India* **69 E9**
Nephi, *U.S.A.* **108 G8**
Nephin, *Ireland* **12 B2**
Nepi, *Italy* **41 F9**
Nepomuk, *Czech Rep.* **26 B6**
Neptune, *U.S.A.* **117 F10**
Nera →, *Italy* **41 F9**
Nera →, *Romania* **28 F6**
Nérac, *France* **20 D4**
Nerang, *Australia* **95 D5**
Neratovice, *Czech Rep.* **26 A7**
Nerchinsk, *Russia* **53 D12**
Nereju, *Romania* **29 E11**
Nerekhta, *Russia* **32 D11**
Neresnytsya, *Ukraine* **29 B8**
Néret, L., *Canada* **105 B5**
Neretvanski Kanal, *Croatia* **41 E14**
Neringa, *Lithuania* **9 J19**
Neris →, *Lithuania* **9 J21**
Nerja, *Spain* **37 J7**
Nerl →, *Russia* **32 D11**
Nerpio, *Spain* **39 G2**
Nerva, *Spain* **37 H4**
Nervi, *Italy* **40 D6**
Neryungri, *Russia* **53 D13**
Nescopeck, *U.S.A.* **117 E8**
Nesebŭr, *Bulgaria* **45 D11**
Ness, L., *U.K.* **13 D4**
Ness City, *U.S.A.* **112 F5**
Nesterov, *Russia* **30 D9**
Nesterov, *Ukraine* **33 G2**
Nestórion, *Greece* **44 F5**
Néstos →, *Greece* **45 E8**
Nesvady, *Slovak Rep.* **27 D11**
Nesvizh = Nyasvizh, *Belarus* **33 F4**
Netanya, *Israel* **74 C3**
Netarhat, *India* **69 H11**
Nete →, *Belgium* **17 C4**
Netherdale, *Australia* **94 K6**
Netherlands ■, *Europe* **17 C5**
Netherlands Antilles ⊠, *W. Indies* **124 A5**
Neto →, *Italy* **43 C10**
Netrang, *India* **68 J5**
Nettancourt, *France* **19 D11**
Nettetal, *Germany* **24 D2**
Nettilling L., *Canada* **101 B12**
Nettuno, *Italy* **42 A5**
Netzahualcoyotl, Presa, *Mexico* **119 D6**
Neu-Isenburg, *Germany* **25 E4**
Neu-Ulm, *Germany* **25 G6**
Neubrandenburg, *Germany* **24 B9**
Neubukow, *Germany* **24 A7**
Neuburg, *Germany* **25 G7**
Neuchâtel, *Switz.* **25 J2**
Neuchâtel □, *Switz.* **25 J2**
Neuchâtel, Lac de, *Switz.* **25 J2**
Neudau, *Austria* **26 D9**
Neuenhagen, *Germany* **24 C9**
Neuenhaus, *Germany* **24 C2**
Neuf-Brisach, *France* **19 D14**
Neufahrn, *Bayern, Germany* **25 G8**
Neufahrn, *Bayern, Germany* **25 G7**
Neufchâteau, *Belgium* **17 E5**
Neufchâteau, *France* **19 D12**
Neufchâtel-en-Bray, *France* **18 C8**
Neufchâtel-sur-Aisne, *France* **19 C11**
Neuhaus, *Germany* **24 B6**
Neuillé-Pont-Pierre, *France* **18 E7**
Neuilly-St-Front, *France* **19 C10**
Neukalen, *Germany* **24 B8**
Neumarkt, *Germany* **25 F7**
Neumünster, *Germany* **24 A5**
Neung-sur-Beuvron, *France* **19 E8**
Neunkirchen, *Austria* **26 D9**
Neunkirchen, *Germany* **25 F3**
Neuquén, *Argentina* **128 D3**
Neuquén □, *Argentina* **126 D2**
Neuruppin, *Germany* **24 C8**
Neusäss, *Germany* **25 G6**
Neuse →, *U.S.A.* **115 H7**
Neusiedl, *Austria* **27 D9**
Neusiedler See, *Austria* **27 D9**
Neusiedler See-Seewinkel △, *Austria* **27 D9**
Neuss, *Germany* **24 D2**
Neussargues-Moissac, *France* **20 C7**
Neustadt, *Bayern, Germany* **25 F8**
Neustadt, *Bayern, Germany* **25 G7**
Neustadt, *Bayern, Germany* **25 F6**
Neustadt, *Bayern, Germany* **25 E7**
Neustadt, *Brandenburg, Germany* **24 C8**
Neustadt, *Hessen, Germany* **24 E5**
Neustadt, *Niedersachsen, Germany* **24 C5**
Neustadt, *Rhld-Pfz., Germany* **25 F4**
Neustadt, *Sachsen, Germany* **24 D10**
Neustadt, *Schleswig-Holstein, Germany* **24 A6**
Neustadt, *Thüringen, Germany* **24 E7**
Neustrelitz, *Germany* **24 B9**
Neuvic, *France* **20 C6**
Neuville-sur-Saône, *France* **21 C8**
Neuvy-le-Roi, *France* **18 E7**
Neuvy-St-Sépulchre, *France* **19 F8**
Neuvy-sur-Barangeon, *France* **19 E9**
Neuwerk, *Germany* **24 B4**
Neuwied, *Germany* **24 E3**
Neva →, *Russia* **32 C6**
Nevada, *Iowa, U.S.A.* **112 D8**
Nevada, *Mo., U.S.A.* **113 G7**
Nevada □, *U.S.A.* **108 G5**
Nevada City, *U.S.A.* **110 F6**
Nevado, Cerro, *Argentina* **126 D2**
Nevado de Colima = Volcán de Colima △, *Mexico* **118 D4**
Nevado de Tres Cruces △, *Chile* **126 B2**
Nevel, *Russia* **32 D5**
Nevers, *France* **19 F10**
Nevertire, *Australia* **95 E4**
Nevesinje, *Bos.-H.* **44 C2**
Neville, *Canada* **103 D7**
Nevinnomyssk, *Russia* **35 H6**
Nevis, *St. Kitts & Nevis* **121 C7**
Nevrokop = Gotse Delchev, *Bulgaria* **44 E7**
Nevşehir, *Turkey* **70 B2**
Nevskoye, *Russia* **30 D9**
New →, *U.S.A.* **114 F5**
New Aiyansh, *Canada* **102 B3**
New Albany, *Ind., U.S.A.* **114 F3**
New Albany, *Miss., U.S.A.* **113 H10**
New Albany, *Pa., U.S.A.* **117 E8**
New Amsterdam, *Guyana* **124 B7**
New Angledool, *Australia* **95 D4**
New Baltimore, *U.S.A.* **116 D2**
New Bedford, *U.S.A.* **117 E14**
New Berlin, *N.Y., U.S.A.* **117 D9**
New Berlin, *Pa., U.S.A.* **116 F8**
New Bern, *U.S.A.* **115 H7**
New Bethlehem, *U.S.A.* **116 F5**
New Bloomfield, *U.S.A.* **116 F7**
New Boston, *U.S.A.* **113 J7**
New Braunfels, *U.S.A.* **113 L5**
New Brighton, *N.Z.* **91 K4**
New Brighton, *U.S.A.* **116 F4**
New Britain, *Papua N. G.* **96 H7**
New Britain, *U.S.A.* **117 E12**
New Brunswick, *U.S.A.* **117 F10**
New Brunswick □, *Canada* **105 C6**
New Bussa, *Nigeria* **83 D5**
New Caledonia ⊠, *Pac. Oc.* **96 K8**
New Castile = Castilla-La Mancha □, *Spain* **6 H5**
New Castle, *Ind., U.S.A.* **114 F3**
New Castle, *Pa., U.S.A.* **116 F4**
New City, *U.S.A.* **117 E11**
New Concord, *U.S.A.* **116 G3**
New Cumberland, *U.S.A.* **116 F4**
New Cuyama, *U.S.A.* **111 L7**
New Delhi, *India* **68 E7**
New Denver, *Canada* **102 D5**
New Don Pedro Reservoir, *U.S.A.* **110 H6**
New England, *U.S.A.* **107 B12**
New England, *N. Dak., U.S.A.* **112 B3**
New England Ra., *Australia* **95 E5**
New Forest, *U.K.* **15 G6**
New Galloway, *U.K.* **13 F4**
New Glasgow, *Canada* **105 C7**
New Guinea, *Oceania* **96 H5**
New Hamburg, *Canada* **116 C4**
New Hampshire □, *U.S.A.* **117 C13**
New Hampton, *U.S.A.* **112 D8**
New Hanover, *S. Africa* **89 D5**
New Hartford, *U.S.A.* **117 C9**
New Haven, *Conn., U.S.A.* **117 E12**
New Haven, *Mich., U.S.A.* **116 D2**
New Hazelton, *Canada* **102 B3**
New Hebrides = Vanuatu ■, *Pac. Oc.* **96 J8**
New Holland, *U.S.A.* **117 F8**
New Iberia, *U.S.A.* **113 K9**
New Ireland, *Papua N. G.* **96 H7**
New Jersey □, *U.S.A.* **114 E8**
New Kensington, *U.S.A.* **116 F5**
New Lexington, *U.S.A.* **114 F4**
New Liskeard, *Canada* **104 C4**
New London, *Conn., U.S.A.* **117 E12**
New London, *Ohio, U.S.A.* **116 E2**
New London, *Wis., U.S.A.* **112 C10**
New Madrid, *U.S.A.* **113 G10**
New Martinsville, *U.S.A.* **114 F5**
New Meadows, *U.S.A.* **108 D5**
New Melones L., *U.S.A.* **110 H6**
New Mexico □, *U.S.A.* **109 J10**
New Milford, *Conn., U.S.A.* **117 E11**
New Milford, *Pa., U.S.A.* **117 E9**
New Norcia, *Australia* **93 F2**
New Norfolk, *Australia* **95 G4**
New Orleans, *U.S.A.* **113 L9**
New Philadelphia, *U.S.A.* **116 F3**
New Plymouth, *N.Z.* **91 H5**
New Plymouth, *U.S.A.* **108 E5**
New Port Richey, *U.S.A.* **115 L4**
New Providence, *Bahamas* **120 A4**
New Quay, *U.K.* **15 E3**
New Radnor, *U.K.* **15 E4**
New Richmond, *Canada* **105 C6**
New Richmond, *U.S.A.* **112 C8**
New River Gorge △, *U.S.A.* **114 G5**
New Roads, *U.S.A.* **113 K9**
New Rochelle, *U.S.A.* **117 F11**
New Rockford, *U.S.A.* **112 B5**
New Romney, *U.K.* **15 G8**
New Ross, *Ireland* **12 D5**
New Salem, *U.S.A.* **112 B4**
New Scone = Scone, *U.K.* **13 E5**
New Siberian I. = Novaya Sibir, Ostrov, *Russia* **53 B16**
New Siberian Is. = Novosibirskiye Ostrova, *Russia* **53 B15**
New Smyrna Beach, *U.S.A.* **115 L5**
New South Wales □, *Australia* **95 E4**
New Tecumseth, *Canada* **116 B5**
New Town, *U.S.A.* **112 B3**
New Tredegar, *U.K.* **15 F4**
New Ulm, *U.S.A.* **112 C7**
New Waterford, *Canada* **105 C7**
New-Wes-Valley, *Canada* **105 C9**
New Westminster, *Canada* **110 A4**
New York, *U.S.A.* **117 F11**
New York □, *U.S.A.* **117 D9**
New York J.F. Kennedy International ✈ (JFK), *U.S.A.* **117 F11**
New York Mts., *U.S.A.* **109 J6**
New Zealand ■, *Oceania* **91 J6**
Newaj →, *India* **68 G7**
Newala, *Tanzania* **87 E4**
Newark, *Del., U.S.A.* **114 F8**
Newark, *N.J., U.S.A.* **117 F10**
Newark, *N.Y., U.S.A.* **116 C7**
Newark, *Ohio, U.S.A.* **116 F2**
Newark International ✈ (EWR), *U.S.A.* **117 F10**
Newark-on-Trent, *U.K.* **14 D7**
Newark Valley, *U.S.A.* **117 D8**
Newberg, *U.S.A.* **108 D2**
Newberry, *Mich., U.S.A.* **114 B3**
Newberry, *S.C., U.S.A.* **115 H5**
Newberry ⌓, *U.S.A.* **108 E2**
Newberry Springs, *U.S.A.* **111 L10**
Newboro L., *Canada* **117 B8**
Newbridge = Droichead Nua, *Ireland* **12 C5**
Newburgh, *Canada* **116 B8**
Newburgh, *U.S.A.* **117 E10**
Newbury, *U.K.* **15 F6**
Newbury, *N.H., U.S.A.* **117 B12**
Newbury, *Vt., U.S.A.* **117 B12**
Newburyport, *U.S.A.* **115 D10**
Newcastle, *Australia* **95 E5**
Newcastle, *N.B., Canada* **105 C6**
Newcastle, *Ont., Canada* **104 D4**
Newcastle, *S. Africa* **89 D4**
Newcastle, *U.K.* **12 B6**
Newcastle, *Calif., U.S.A.* **110 G5**
Newcastle, *Wyo., U.S.A.* **112 D2**
Newcastle Emlyn, *U.K.* **15 E3**
Newcastle Ra., *Australia* **92 C5**
Newcastle-under-Lyme, *U.K.* **14 D5**
Newcastle-upon-Tyne, *U.K.* **14 C6**
Newcastle Waters, *Australia* **94 B1**
Newcastle West, *Ireland* **12 D2**
Newcomb, *U.S.A.* **117 C10**
Newcomerstown, *U.S.A.* **116 F3**
Newdegate, *Australia* **93 F2**
Newell, *Australia* **94 B4**
Newell, *U.S.A.* **112 C3**
Newfane, *U.S.A.* **116 C6**
Newfield, *U.S.A.* **117 D8**
Newfound L., *U.S.A.* **117 C13**
Newfoundland, *Canada* **105 C8**
Newfoundland, *U.S.A.* **117 E9**
Newfoundland & Labrador □, *Canada* **105 B8**
Newhall, *U.S.A.* **111 L8**
Newhaven, *U.K.* **15 G8**
Newkirk, *U.S.A.* **113 G6**
Newlyn, *U.K.* **15 G2**
Newman, *Australia* **92 D2**
Newman, *U.S.A.* **110 H5**
Newmarket, *Canada* **116 B5**
Newmarket, *Ireland* **12 D2**
Newmarket, *U.K.* **15 E8**
Newmarket, *U.S.A.* **117 C14**
Newnan, *U.S.A.* **115 J3**
Newport, *Ireland* **12 C2**
Newport, *I. of W., U.K.* **15 G6**
Newport, *Newp., U.K.* **15 F5**
Newport, *Ark., U.S.A.* **113 H9**
Newport, *Ky., U.S.A.* **114 F3**
Newport, *N.H., U.S.A.* **117 C12**
Newport, *N.Y., U.S.A.* **117 C9**
Newport, *Oreg., U.S.A.* **108 D1**
Newport, *Pa., U.S.A.* **116 F7**
Newport, *R.I., U.S.A.* **117 E13**
Newport, *Tenn., U.S.A.* **115 H4**
Newport, *Vt., U.S.A.* **117 B12**
Newport, *Wash., U.S.A.* **108 B5**
Newport □, *U.K.* **15 F4**
Newport Beach, *U.S.A.* **111 M9**
Newport News, *U.S.A.* **114 G7**
Newport Pagnell, *U.K.* **15 E7**
Newquay, *U.K.* **15 G2**
Newry, *U.K.* **12 B5**
Newton, *Ill., U.S.A.* **112 F10**
Newton, *Iowa, U.S.A.* **112 E8**
Newton, *Kans., U.S.A.* **113 F6**
Newton, *Mass., U.S.A.* **117 D13**
Newton, *Miss., U.S.A.* **113 J10**
Newton, *N.C., U.S.A.* **115 H5**
Newton, *N.J., U.S.A.* **117 E10**
Newton, *Tex., U.S.A.* **113 K8**
Newton Abbot, *U.K.* **15 G4**
Newton Aycliffe, *U.K.* **14 C6**
Newton Falls, *U.S.A.* **116 E4**
Newton Stewart, *U.K.* **13 G4**
Newtonmore, *U.K.* **13 D4**
Newtown, *U.K.* **15 E4**
Newtownabbey, *U.K.* **12 B6**
Newtownards, *U.K.* **12 B6**
Newtownbarry = Bunclody, *Ireland* **12 D5**
Newtownstewart, *U.K.* **12 B4**
Newville, *U.S.A.* **116 F7**
Nexon, *France* **20 C5**
Neya, *Russia* **34 A6**
Neyrīz, *Iran* **71 D7**
Neyshābūr, *Iran* **71 B8**
Nezhin = Nizhyn, *Ukraine* **33 G6**
Nezperce, *U.S.A.* **108 C5**
Nezvysko, *Ukraine* **29 B10**
Ngabang, *Indonesia* **62 D3**
Ngabordamlu, Tanjung, *Indonesia* **63 F8**
N'Gage, *Angola* **84 F3**
Ngala, *Nigeria* **83 C7**
Ngambé, *Centre, Cameroon* **83 D7**
Ngambé, *Littoral, Cameroon* **83 E7**
Ngami Depression, *Botswana* **88 C3**
Ngamo, *Zimbabwe* **87 F2**
Ngangala, *Sudan* **81 G3**
Nganglong Kangri, *China* **67 C12**
Ngao, *Thailand* **64 C2**
Ngaoundéré, *Cameroon* **84 C2**
Ngapara, *N.Z.* **91 L3**
Ngara, *Tanzania* **86 C3**
Ngawi, *Indonesia* **63 G14**
Nghia Lo, *Vietnam* **58 G5**
Ngoboli, *Sudan* **81 G3**
Ngoma, *Malawi* **87 E3**
Ngomahura, *Zimbabwe* **87 G3**
Ngomba, *Tanzania* **87 D3**
Ngop, *Sudan* **81 F3**
Ngoring Hu, *China* **60 C4**
Ngorkou, *Mali* **82 B4**
Ngorongoro, *Tanzania* **86 C4**
Ngorongoro ⌓, *Tanzania* **86 C4**
Ngozi, *Burundi* **86 C2**
Ngudu, *Tanzania* **86 C3**
Nguigmi, *Niger* **79 F8**
Nguila, *Cameroon* **83 E7**
Nguiu, *Australia* **92 B5**
Ngukurr, *Australia* **94 A1**
Ngunga, *Tanzania* **86 C3**
Nguru, *Nigeria* **83 C7**
Nguru Mts., *Tanzania* **86 D4**

Ngusi, *Malawi* 87 E3
Nguyen Binh, *Vietnam* 58 F5
Nha Trang, *Vietnam* 65 F7
Nhacoongo, *Mozam.* 89 C6
Nhamaabué, *Mozam.* 87 F4
Nhamundá →, *Brazil* 125 D7
Nhangulaze, L., *Mozam.* 89 C5
Nhill, *Australia* 95 F3
Nho Quan, *Vietnam* 58 G5
Nhulunbuy, *Australia* 94 A2
Nia-nia, *Dem. Rep. of the Congo* 86 B2
Niafounké, *Mali* 82 B4
Niagara Falls, *Canada* 116 C5
Niagara Falls, *U.S.A.* 116 C6
Niagara-on-the-Lake, *Canada* 116 C5
Niah, *Malaysia* 62 D4
Niamey, *Niger* 83 C5
Niandan-Koro, *Guinea* 82 C3
Nianforando, *Guinea* 82 D2
Niangara, *Dem. Rep. of the Congo* 86 B2
Niangbo, *Ivory C.* 82 D3
Niangoloko, *Burkina Faso* 82 C4
Niantic, *U.S.A.* 117 E12
Niaro, *Sudan* 81 E3
Nias, *Indonesia* 62 D1
Niassa ⌓, *Mozam.* 87 E4
Niassa □, *Mozam.* 87 E4
Nibāk, *Si. Arabia* 71 E7
Nibe, *Denmark* 11 H3
Nicaragua ■, *Cent. Amer.* 120 D2
Nicaragua, L. de, *Nic.* 120 D2
Nicastro, *Italy* 43 D9
Nice, *France* 21 E11
Nice ✕ (NCE), *France* 21 E11
Niceville, *U.S.A.* 115 K2
Nichicun, L., *Canada* 105 B5
Nichinan, *Japan* 55 J5
Nicholas Channel, *W. Indies* 120 B3
Nicholasville, *U.S.A.* 114 G3
Nichols, *U.S.A.* 117 D8
Nicholson, *Australia* 92 C4
Nicholson, *U.S.A.* 117 E9
Nicholson →, *Australia* 94 B2
Nicholson L., *Canada* 103 A8
Nicholson Ra., *Australia* 93 E2
Nicholville, *U.S.A.* 117 B10
Nicobar Is., *Ind. Oc.* 50 J13
Nicola, *Canada* 102 C4
Nicolls Town, *Bahamas* 120 A4
Nicopolis, *Greece* 46 B2
Nicosia, *Cyprus* 49 D12
Nicosia, *Italy* 43 E7
Nicótera, *Italy* 43 D8
Nicoya, *Costa Rica* 120 D2
Nicoya, G. de, *Costa Rica* 120 E3
Nicoya, Pen. de, *Costa Rica* 120 E2
Nida, *Lithuania* 30 C8
Nidd →, *U.K.* 14 D6
Nidda, *Germany* 25 E5
Nidda →, *Germany* 25 E4
Nidwalden □, *Switz.* 25 J4
Nidzica, *Poland* 31 E7
Niebüll, *Germany* 24 A4
Nied →, *Germany* 19 C13
Niederaula, *Germany* 24 E5
Niederbayern □, *Germany* 25 G8
Niederbronn-les-Bains, *France* 19 D14
Niedere Tauern, *Austria* 26 D7
Niederlausitz, *Germany* 24 D9
Niederösterreich □, *Austria* 26 C8
Niedersachsen □, *Germany* 24 C4
Niedersächsisches Wattenmeer △, *Germany* 24 B3
Niekerkshoop, *S. Africa* 88 D3
Niellé, *Ivory C.* 82 C3
Niemba, *Dem. Rep. of the Congo* 86 D2
Niemen = Nemunas →, *Lithuania* 9 J19
Niemodlin, *Poland* 31 H4
Nienburg, *Germany* 24 C5
Niepołomice, *Poland* 31 H7
Niers →, *Germany* 24 D1
Niesky, *Germany* 24 D10
Nieszawa, *Poland* 31 F5
Nieu Bethesda, *S. Africa* 88 E3
Nieuw Amsterdam, *Suriname* 125 B7
Nieuw Nickerie, *Suriname* 125 B7
Nieuwoudtville, *S. Africa* 88 E2
Nieuwpoort, *Belgium* 17 C2
Nieves, Pico de las, *Canary Is.* 48 G4
Nièvre □, *France* 19 E10
Niga, *Mali* 82 C3
Niğde, *Turkey* 70 B2
Nigel, *S. Africa* 89 D4
Niger □, *Nigeria* 83 D6
Niger ■, *W. Afr.* 83 B7
Niger →, *W. Afr.* 83 D6
Niger Delta, *Africa* 83 E6
Nigeria ■, *W. Afr.* 83 D6
Nighasin, *India* 69 E9
Nightcaps, *N.Z.* 91 L2
Nigrita, *Greece* 44 F7
Nii-Jima, *Japan* 55 G9
Niigata, *Japan* 54 F9
Niigata □, *Japan* 55 F9
Niihama, *Japan* 55 H6
Niihau, *U.S.A.* 106 H14
Niimi, *Japan* 55 G6
Niitsu, *Japan* 54 F9
Nijar, *Spain* 39 J2
Nijil, *Jordan* 74 E4
Nijkerk, *Neths.* 17 B5
Nijmegen, *Neths.* 17 C5
Nijverdal, *Neths.* 17 B6
Nīk Pey, *Iran* 71 B6
Nike, *Nigeria* 83 D6
Nikiniki, *Indonesia* 63 F6
Nikísiani, *Greece* 45 F8
Nikítas, *Greece* 44 F7
Nikki, *Benin* 83 D5
Nikkō, *Japan* 55 F9
Nikkō △, *Japan* 55 F9
Nikolayev = Mykolayiv, *Ukraine* 33 J7
Nikolayevsk, *Russia* 34 E7
Nikolayevsk-na-Amur, *Russia* 53 D15
Nikolsk, *Russia* 34 D8
Nikolskoye, *Russia* 53 D17
Nikopol, *Bulgaria* 45 C8
Nikopol, *Ukraine* 33 J8
Niksar, *Turkey* 72 B7
Nīkshahr, *Iran* 71 E9
Nikšić, *Serbia & M.* 44 D2
Nîl, Nahr en →, *Africa* 80 H7
Nîl el Abyad →, *Sudan* 81 D3
Nîl el Azraq →, *Sudan* 81 D3
Nila, *Indonesia* 63 F7
Niland, *U.S.A.* 111 M11
Nile = Nîl, Nahr en →, *Africa* 80 H7
Nile Delta, *Egypt* 80 H7
Niles, *Mich., U.S.A.* 114 E2
Niles, *Ohio, U.S.A.* 116 E4
Nilüfer →, *Turkey* 45 F12
Nim Ka Thana, *India* 68 F6
Nimach, *India* 68 G6
Nimbahera, *India* 68 G6
Nîmes, *France* 21 E8
Nimfaíon, Ákra = Pínnes, Ákra, *Greece* 45 F8
Nimmitabel, *Australia* 95 F4
Nimule, *Sudan* 81 G3
Nimule △, *Sudan* 81 G3
Nin, *Croatia* 41 D12
Nīnawá, *Iraq* 70 B4
Nīnawá □, *Iraq* 70 B4
Nindigully, *Australia* 95 D4
Nineveh = Nīnawá, *Iraq* 70 B4
Ning Xian, *China* 56 G4
Ningaloo ⌓, *Australia* 92 D1
Ning'an, *China* 57 B15
Ningbo, *China* 59 C13
Ningcheng, *China* 57 D10
Ningde, *China* 59 D12
Ningdu, *China* 59 D10
Ninggang, *China* 59 D9
Ningguo, *China* 59 B12
Ninghai, *China* 59 C13
Ninghua, *China* 59 D11
Ningi, *Nigeria* 83 C6
Ningjin, *China* 56 F8
Ningjing Shan, *China* 58 C2
Ninglang, *China* 58 D3
Ningling, *China* 56 G8
Ningming, *China* 58 F6
Ningnan, *China* 58 D4
Ningpo = Ningbo, *China* 59 C13
Ningqiang, *China* 56 H4
Ningshan, *China* 56 H5
Ningsia Hui A.R. = Ningxia Huizu Zizhiqu □, *China* 56 F4
Ningwu, *China* 56 E7
Ningxia Huizu Zizhiqu □, *China* 56 F4
Ningxiang, *China* 59 C9
Ningyang, *China* 56 G9
Ningyuan, *China* 59 E8
Ninh Binh, *Vietnam* 58 G5
Ninh Giang, *Vietnam* 64 B6
Ninh Hoa, *Vietnam* 64 F7
Ninh Ma, *Vietnam* 64 F7
Nini-Suhien △, *Ghana* 82 D4
Ninove, *Belgium* 17 D4
Nioaque, *Brazil* 127 A4
Niobrara, *U.S.A.* 112 D6
Niobrara →, *U.S.A.* 112 D6
Niokolo-Koba △, *Senegal* 82 C2
Niono, *Mali* 82 C3
Nionsamoridougou, *Guinea* 82 D3
Nioro du Rip, *Senegal* 82 C1
Nioro du Sahel, *Mali* 82 B3
Niort, *France* 20 B3
Nipawin, *Canada* 103 C8
Nipfjället, *Sweden* 10 C6
Nipigon, *Canada* 104 C2
Nipigon, L., *Canada* 104 C2
Nipishish L., *Canada* 105 B7
Nipissing, L., *Canada* 104 C4
Nipomo, *U.S.A.* 111 K6
Nipton, *U.S.A.* 111 K11
Niquelândia, *Brazil* 125 F9
Nīr, *Iran* 70 B5
Nirasaki, *Japan* 55 G9
Nirmal, *India* 66 K11
Nirmali, *India* 69 F12
Niš, *Serbia & M.* 44 C5
Nisa, *Portugal* 37 F3
Nisāb, *Si. Arabia* 70 D5
Nişāb, *Yemen* 75 E4
Nišava →, *Serbia & M.* 44 C5
Niscemi, *Italy* 43 E7
Nishinomiya, *Japan* 55 G7
Nishino'omote, *Japan* 55 J5
Nishiwaki, *Japan* 55 G7
Nísíros, *Greece* 47 E9
Niška Banja, *Serbia & M.* 44 C6
Niskibi →, *Canada* 104 A2
Nisko, *Poland* 31 H9
Nisporeni, *Moldova* 29 C13
Nisqually →, *U.S.A.* 110 C4
Nissáki, *Greece* 49 A3
Nissan →, *Sweden* 11 H6
Nissum Bredning, *Denmark* 11 H2
Nissum Fjord, *Denmark* 11 H2
Nistru = Dnister →, *Europe* 33 J6
Nisutlin →, *Canada* 102 A2
Nitchequon, *Canada* 105 B5
Niterói, *Brazil* 127 A7
Nith →, *Canada* 116 C4
Nith →, *U.K.* 13 F5
Nitmiluk △, *Australia* 92 B5
Nitra, *Slovak Rep.* 27 C11
Nitra →, *Slovak Rep.* 27 D11
Nitriansky □, *Slovak Rep.* 27 C11
Nittenau, *Germany* 25 F8
Niuafo'ou, *Tonga* 91 B11
Niue, *Cook Is.* 97 J11
Niulan Jiang →, *China* 58 D4
Niut, *Indonesia* 62 D4
Niutou Shan, *China* 59 C13
Niuzhuang, *China* 57 D12
Nivala, *Finland* 8 E21
Nivelles, *Belgium* 17 D4
Nivernais, *France* 19 E10
Niwas, *India* 69 H9
Nixon, *U.S.A.* 113 L6
Nizamabad, *India* 66 K11
Nizamghat, *India* 67 E19
Nizhne Kolymsk, *Russia* 53 C17
Nizhneangarsk, *Russia* 53 D11
Nizhnegorskiy = Nyzhnohirskyy, *Ukraine* 33 K8
Nizhnekamsk, *Russia* 34 C10
Nizhneudinsk, *Russia* 53 D10
Nizhnevartovsk, *Russia* 52 C8
Nizhniy Chir, *Russia* 35 F6
Nizhniy Lomov, *Russia* 34 D6
Nizhniy Novgorod, *Russia* 34 B7
Nizhniy Tagil, *Russia* 52 D6
Nizhyn, *Ukraine* 33 G6
Nizina Mazowiecka, *Poland* 31 F8
Nizip, *Turkey* 70 B3
Nízké Tatry, *Slovak Rep.* 27 C12
Nízké Tatry △, *Slovak Rep.* 27 C12
Nízký Jeseník, *Czech Rep.* 27 B10
Nizza Monferrato, *Italy* 40 D5
Njakwa, *Malawi* 87 E3
Njanji, *Zambia* 87 E3
Njegoš, *Serbia & M.* 44 D2
Njinjo, *Tanzania* 87 D4
Njombe, *Tanzania* 87 D3
Njombe →, *Tanzania* 86 D4
Njurundabommen, *Sweden* 10 B11
Nkambe, *Cameroon* 83 D7
Nkana, *Zambia* 87 E2
Nkandla, *S. Africa* 89 D5
Nkawkaw, *Ghana* 83 D4
Nkayi, *Zimbabwe* 87 F2
Nkhotakota, *Malawi* 87 E3
Nkhotakota ⌓, *Malawi* 87 E3
Nkongsamba, *Cameroon* 83 E6
Nkurenkuru, *Namibia* 88 B2
Nkwanta, *Ghana* 82 D4
Nmai →, *Burma* 58 F2
Noakhali = Maijdi, *Bangla.* 67 H17
Nobel, *Canada* 116 A4
Nobeoka, *Japan* 55 H5
Noblejas, *Spain* 36 F7
Noblesville, *U.S.A.* 114 E3
Noboribetsu, *Japan* 54 C10
Noce →, *Italy* 40 B8
Nocera Inferiore, *Italy* 43 B7
Nocera Umbra, *Italy* 41 E9
Noci, *Italy* 43 B10
Nocona, *U.S.A.* 113 J6
Nocrich, *Romania* 29 E9
Noda, *Japan* 55 G9
Nogales, *Mexico* 118 A2
Nogales, *U.S.A.* 109 L8
Nogaro, *France* 20 E3
Nogat →, *Poland* 30 D6
Nōgata, *Japan* 55 H5
Nogent, *France* 19 D12
Nogent-le-Rotrou, *France* 18 D7
Nogent-sur-Seine, *France* 19 D10
Noggerup, *Australia* 93 F2
Noginsk, *Moskva, Russia* 32 E10
Noginsk, *Tunguska, Russia* 53 C10
Nogoa →, *Australia* 94 C4
Nogoyá, *Argentina* 126 C4
Nógrád □, *Hungary* 28 C4
Noguera Pallaresa →, *Spain* 38 D5
Noguera Ribagorzana →, *Spain* 38 D5
Nohar, *India* 68 E6
Nohfelden, *Germany* 25 F3
Nohta, *India* 69 H8
Noia, *Spain* 36 C2
Noire, Montagne, *France* 20 E6
Noires, Mts., *France* 18 D3
Noirétable, *France* 20 C7
Noirmoutier, Î. de, *France* 18 F4
Noirmoutier-en-l'Île, *France* 18 F4
Nojane, *Botswana* 88 C3
Nojima-Zaki, *Japan* 55 G9
Nok Kundi, *Pakistan* 66 E3
Nok Ta Phao, Ko, *Thailand* 65 b
Nokaneng, *Botswana* 88 B3
Nokia, *Finland* 9 F20
Nokomis, *Canada* 103 C8
Nokomis L., *Canada* 103 B8
Nola, *C.A.R.* 84 D3
Nola, *Italy* 43 B7
Nolay, *France* 19 F11
Noli, C. di, *Italy* 40 D5
Nolinsk, *Russia* 34 B9
Noma Omuramba →, *Namibia* 88 B3
Nombre de Dios, *Panama* 120 E4
Nome, *U.S.A.* 100 B3
Nomo-Zaki, *Japan* 55 H4
Nonacho L., *Canada* 103 A7
Nonancourt, *France* 18 D8
Nonda, *Australia* 94 C3
None, *Italy* 40 D4
Nong Chang, *Thailand* 64 E2
Nong Het, *Laos* 64 C4
Nong Khai, *Thailand* 64 D4
Nong'an, *China* 57 B13
Nongoma, *S. Africa* 89 D5
Nongsa, *Indonesia* 65 d
Nonoava, *Mexico* 118 B3
Nonoava →, *Mexico* 118 B3
Nonthaburi, *Thailand* 64 F3
Nontron, *France* 20 C4
Nonza, *France* 21 F13
Noonamah, *Australia* 92 B5
Noondie, L., *Australia* 93 E2
Noord Brabant □, *Neths.* 17 C5
Noord Holland □, *Neths.* 17 B4
Noordbeveland, *Neths.* 17 C3
Noordoostpolder, *Neths.* 17 B5
Noordwijk, *Neths.* 17 B4
Noosa Heads, *Australia* 95 D5
Nootka I., *Canada* 102 D3
Nopiming ⌓, *Canada* 103 C9
Nora, *Eritrea* 81 D5
Nora, *Sweden* 10 E9
Noralee, *Canada* 102 C3
Noranda = Rouyn-Noranda, *Canada* 104 C4
Norberg, *Sweden* 10 D9
Nórcia, *Italy* 41 F10
Norco, *U.S.A.* 111 M9
Nord □, *France* 19 B10
Nord-Kivu □, *Dem. Rep. of the Congo* 86 C2
Nord-Ostsee-Kanal, *Germany* 24 A5
Nord-Pas-de-Calais □, *France* 19 B9
Nordaustlandet, *Svalbard* 4 B9
Nordborg, *Denmark* 11 J3
Nordby, *Denmark* 11 J2
Norddeich, *Germany* 24 B3
Nordegg, *Canada* 102 C5
Norden, *Germany* 24 B3
Nordenham, *Germany* 24 B4
Norderney, *Germany* 24 B3
Norderstedt, *Germany* 24 B6
Nordfjord, *Norway* 9 F11
Nordfriesische Inseln, *Germany* 24 A4
Nordhausen, *Germany* 24 D6
Nordhorn, *Germany* 24 C3
Norðoyar, *Færoe Is.* 8 E9
Nordinge-Nol, *Sweden* 11 G6
Nordingrå, *Sweden* 10 B12
Nordjyllands Amtskommune □, *Denmark* 11 G4
Nordkapp, *Norway* 8 A21
Nordkapp, *Svalbard* 4 A9
Nordkinnhalvøya, *Norway* 8 A22
Nördlicher Teutoburger Wald-Wiehengebirge ⌓, *Germany* 24 C4
Nördlingen, *Germany* 25 G6
Nordrhein-Westfalen □, *Germany* 24 D3
Nordstrand, *Germany* 24 A4
Nordvik, *Russia* 53 B12
Nore →, *Ireland* 12 D4
Norfolk, *Canada* 116 D4
Norfolk, *Nebr., U.S.A.* 112 D6
Norfolk, *Va., U.S.A.* 114 G7
Norfolk □, *U.K.* 15 E8
Norfolk I., *Pac. Oc.* 96 K8
Norfork L., *U.S.A.* 113 G8
Norilsk, *Russia* 53 C9
Norma, Mt., *Australia* 94 C3
Normal, *U.S.A.* 112 E10
Norman, *U.S.A.* 113 H6
Norman →, *Australia* 94 B3
Norman Wells, *Canada* 100 B7
Normanby →, *Australia* 94 A3
Normandie-Maine ⌓, *France* 18 D6
Normandin, *Canada* 104 C5
Normanhurst, Mt., *Australia* 93 E3
Normanton, *Australia* 94 B3
Normétal, *Canada* 104 C4
Norquay, *Canada* 103 C8
Norquinco, *Argentina* 128 E2
Norra Dellen, *Sweden* 10 C10
Norra Kvill △, *Sweden* 11 G9
Norra Ulvön, *Sweden* 10 A12
Norrahammar, *Sweden* 11 G8
Norrbottens län □, *Sweden* 8 C19
Nørre Åby, *Denmark* 11 J3
Nørre Alslev, *Denmark* 11 K5
Nørresundby, *Denmark* 11 G3
Norrhult-Klavreström, *Sweden* 11 G9
Norris Point, *Canada* 105 C8
Norristown, *U.S.A.* 117 F9
Norrköping, *Sweden* 11 F10
Norrland, *Sweden* 9 E16
Norrsundet, *Sweden* 10 D11
Norrtälje, *Sweden* 10 E12
Norseman, *Australia* 93 F3
Norsk, *Russia* 53 D14
Norte, Pta. del, *Canary Is.* 48 G2
Norte, Serra do, *Brazil* 124 F7
North, C., *Canada* 105 C7
North Adams, *U.S.A.* 117 D11
North America 98 F10
North Arm, *Canada* 102 A5
North Atlantic Ocean, *Atl. Oc.* 2 C7
North Augusta, *U.S.A.* 115 J5
North Ayrshire □, *U.K.* 13 F4
North Bass I., *U.S.A.* 116 E2
North Battleford, *Canada* 103 C7
North Bay, *Canada* 104 C4
North Belcher Is., *Canada* 104 A4
North Bend, *Oreg., U.S.A.* 108 E1
North Bend, *Pa., U.S.A.* 116 E7
North Bend, *Wash., U.S.A.* 110 C5
North Bennington, *U.S.A.* 117 D11
North Berwick, *U.K.* 13 E6
North Berwick, *U.S.A.* 117 C14
North C., *Canada* 105 C7
North C., *N.Z.* 91 F4
North Canadian →, *U.S.A.* 113 H7
North Canton, *U.S.A.* 116 F3
North Cape = Nordkapp, *Norway* 8 A21
North Cape = Nordkapp, *Svalbard* 4 A9
North Caribou L., *Canada* 104 B1
North Carolina □, *U.S.A.* 115 H6
North Cascades △, *U.S.A.* 108 B3
North Channel, *Canada* 104 C3
North Channel, *U.K.* 13 F3
North Charleston, *U.S.A.* 115 J6
North Chicago, *U.S.A.* 114 D2
North Creek, *U.S.A.* 117 C11
North Dakota □, *U.S.A.* 112 B5
North Downs, *U.K.* 15 F8
North East, *U.S.A.* 116 D5
North East Frontier Agency = Arunachal Pradesh □, *India* 67 F19
North East Lincolnshire □, *U.K.* 14 D7
North Eastern □, *Kenya* 86 B5
North Esk →, *U.K.* 13 E6
North European Plain, *Europe* 6 E10
North Foreland, *U.K.* 15 F9
North Fork, *U.S.A.* 110 H7
North Fork American →, *U.S.A.* 110 G5
North Fork Feather →, *U.S.A.* 110 F5
North Fork Grand →, *U.S.A.* 112 C3
North Fork Red →, *U.S.A.* 113 H5
North Frisian Is. = Nordfriesische Inseln, *Germany* 24 A4
North Gower, *Canada* 117 A9
North Hd., *Australia* 93 F1
North Henik L., *Canada* 103 A9
North Highlands, *U.S.A.* 110 G5
North Horr, *Kenya* 86 B4
North I., *Kenya* 86 B4
North I., *N.Z.* 91 H5
North Kingsville, *U.S.A.* 116 E4
North Kitui ⌓, *Kenya* 86 C4
North Knife →, *Canada* 103 B10
North Koel →, *India* 69 G10
North Korea ■, *Asia* 57 E14
North Lakhimpur, *India* 67 F19
North Lanarkshire □, *U.K.* 13 F5
North Las Vegas, *U.S.A.* 111 J11
North Lincolnshire □, *U.K.* 14 D7
North Little Rock, *U.S.A.* 113 H8
North Loup →, *U.S.A.* 112 E5
North Luangwa △, *Zambia* 87 E3
North Magnetic Pole, *Canada* 4 A2
North Minch, *U.K.* 13 C3
North Moose L., *Canada* 103 C8
North Moose L., *Man., Canada* 103 C8
North Myrtle Beach, *U.S.A.* 115 J6
North Nahanni →, *Canada* 102 A4
North Olmsted, *U.S.A.* 116 E3
North Ossetia □, *Russia* 35 J7
North Pagai, I. = Pagai Utara, Pulau, *Indonesia* 62 E2
North Palisade, *U.S.A.* 110 H8
North Platte, *U.S.A.* 112 E4
North Platte →, *U.S.A.* 112 E4
North Pole, *Arctic* 4 A
North Portal, *Canada* 103 D8
North Powder, *U.S.A.* 108 D5
North Pt., *Barbados* 121 g
North Pt., *Trin. & Tob.* 125 J16
North Pt., *U.S.A.* 116 A1
North Rhine Westphalia = Nordrhein-Westfalen □, *Germany* 24 D3
North River, *Canada* 105 B8
North Ronaldsay, *U.K.* 13 B6
North Saskatchewan →, *Canada* 103 C7
North Sea, *Europe* 16
North Seal →, *Canada* 103 B9
North Somerset □, *U.K.* 15 F5
North Sporades = Vóriai Sporádhes, *Greece* 46 B5
North Sydney, *Canada* 105 C7
North Syracuse, *U.S.A.* 117 C8
North Taranaki Bight, *N.Z.* 91 H5
North Thompson →, *Canada* 102 C4
North Tonawanda, *U.S.A.* 116 C6
North Troy, *U.S.A.* 117 B12
North Truchas Pk., *U.S.A.* 109 J11
North Twin I., *Canada* 104 B4
North Tyne →, *U.K.* 14 B5
North Uist, *U.K.* 13 D1
North Vancouver, *Canada* 102 D4
North Vernon, *U.S.A.* 114 F3
North Wabasca L., *Canada* 102 B6
North Walsham, *U.K.* 14 E9
North West = Severo-Zapadnyy □, *Russia* 52 C4
North-West □, *S. Africa* 88 D4
North West C., *Australia* 92 D1
North West Christmas I. Ridge, *Pac. Oc.* 97 G11
North West Frontier □, *Pakistan* 68 C4
North West Highlands, *U.K.* 13 D4
North West River, *Canada* 105 B7
North Western □, *Zambia* 87 E2
North Wildwood, *U.S.A.* 114 F8
North York Moors, *U.K.* 14 C7
North York Moors △, *U.K.* 14 C7
North Yorkshire □, *U.K.* 14 C6
Northallerton, *U.K.* 14 C6
Northam, *Australia* 93 F2
Northam, *S. Africa* 88 C4
Northampton, *Australia* 93 E1
Northampton, *U.K.* 15 E7
Northampton, *Mass., U.S.A.* 117 D12
Northampton, *Pa., U.S.A.* 117 F9
Northamptonshire □, *U.K.* 15 E7
Northbridge, *U.S.A.* 117 D13
Northcliffe, *Australia* 93 F2
Northeast Providence Chan., *W. Indies* 120 A4
Northeim, *Germany* 24 D6
Northern = Limpopo □, *S. Africa* 89 C4
Northern □, *Ghana* 83 D4
Northern □, *Malawi* 87 E3
Northern □, *S. Leone* 82 D2
Northern □, *Zambia* 87 E3
Northern Areas □, *Pakistan* 69 A5
Northern Cape □, *S. Africa* 88 D3
Northern Circars, *India* 67 L13
Northern Indian L., *Canada* 103 B9
Northern Ireland □, *U.K.* 12 B5
Northern Light L., *Canada* 104 C1
Northern Marianas ☑, *Pac. Oc.* 96 F6
Northern Mid-Atlantic Ridge, *Atl. Oc.* 4 D6
Northern Province □, *S. Africa* 89 C4
Northern Range, *Trin. & Tob.* 125 K15
Northern Territory □, *Australia* 92 D5
Northfield, *Minn., U.S.A.* 112 C8
Northfield, *Vt., U.S.A.* 117 B12
Northland □, *N.Z.* 91 F4
Northome, *U.S.A.* 112 B7

Northport, *Ala., U.S.A.* 115 J2
Northport, *Wash., U.S.A.* 108 B5
Northumberland □, *U.K.* 14 B6
Northumberland, C., *Australia* 95 F3
Northumberland Is., *Australia* 94 C4
Northumberland Str., *Canada* 105 C7
Northville, *U.S.A.* 117 C10
Northwest Providence Channel, *W. Indies* 120 A4
Northwest Territories □, *Canada* 100 B9
Northwich, *U.K.* 14 D5
Northwood, *Iowa, U.S.A.* 112 D8
Northwood, *N. Dak., U.S.A.* 112 B6
Norton, *U.S.A.* 112 F5
Norton, *Zimbabwe* 87 F3
Norton Sd., *U.S.A.* 100 B3
Nortorf, *Germany* 24 A5
Norwalk, *Calif., U.S.A.* 111 M8
Norwalk, *Conn., U.S.A.* 117 E11
Norwalk, *Iowa, U.S.A.* 112 E8
Norwalk, *Ohio, U.S.A.* 116 E2
Norway, *Maine, U.S.A.* 115 C10
Norway, *Mich., U.S.A.* 114 C2
Norway ■, *Europe* 8 E14
Norway House, *Canada* 103 C9
Norwegian Sea, *Atl. Oc.* 7 B6
Norwich, *Canada* 116 D4
Norwich, *U.K.* 15 E9
Norwich, *Conn., U.S.A.* 117 E12
Norwich, *N.Y., U.S.A.* 117 D9
Norwood, *Canada* 116 B7
Norwood, *U.S.A.* 117 B10
Noshiro, *Japan* 54 D10
Nosivka, *Ukraine* 33 G6
Nosovka = Nosivka, *Ukraine* 33 G6
Noşratābād, *Iran* 71 D8
Noss Hd., *U.K.* 13 C5
Nossebro, *Sweden* 11 F6
Nossob →, *S. Africa* 88 D3
Nossombougou, *Mali* 82 C3
Nosy Barren, *Madag.* 85 H8
Nosy Be, *Madag.* 85 G9
Nosy Boraha, *Madag.* 89 B8
Nosy Lava, *Madag.* 89 A8
Nosy Varika, *Madag.* 89 C8
Noteć →, *Poland* 31 F2
Notikewin →, *Canada* 102 B5
Notio Aigaio = Notios Aiyaíon □ 47 E7
Notios Aiyaíon □ 47 E7
Notios Evvoïkos Kólpos, *Greece* 46 C5
Noto, *Italy* 43 F8
Noto, G. di, *Italy* 43 F8
Notodden, *Norway* 9 G13
Notre Dame B., *Canada* 105 C8
Notre-Dame-de-Koartac = Quaqtaq, *Canada* 101 B13
Notre-Dame-des-Bois, *Canada* 117 A13
Notre-Dame-d'Ivugivic = Ivujivik, *Canada* 101 B12
Notre-Dame-du-Nord, *Canada* 104 C4
Notsé, *Togo* 83 D5
Nottawasaga B., *Canada* 116 B4
Nottaway →, *Canada* 104 B4
Nottingham, *U.K.* 14 E6
Nottingham, City of □, *U.K.* 14 E6
Nottingham I., *Canada* 101 B12
Nottinghamshire □, *U.K.* 14 D6
Nottoway →, *U.S.A.* 114 G7
Notwane →, *Botswana* 88 C4
Nouâdhibou, *Mauritania* 78 D2
Nouâdhibou, Ras, *Mauritania* 78 D2
Nouakchott, *Mauritania* 82 B1
Nouâmghâr, *Mauritania* 82 B1
Nouméa, *N. Cal.* 96 K8
Nouna, *Burkina Faso* 82 C4
Noupoort, *S. Africa* 88 E3
Nouveau Comptoir = Wemindji, *Canada* 104 B4
Nouvelle-Amsterdam, Î., *Ind. Oc.* 3 F13
Nouvelle-Calédonie = New Caledonia ⧄, *Pac. Oc.* 96 K8
Nouzonville, *France* 19 C11
Nová Baňa, *Slovak Rep.* 27 C11
Nová Bystřice, *Czech Rep.* 26 B8
Nova Casa Nova, *Brazil* 125 E10
Nova Esperança, *Brazil* 127 A5
Nova Friburgo, *Brazil* 127 A7
Nova Gorica, *Slovenia* 41 C10
Nova Gradiška, *Croatia* 28 E2
Nova Iguaçu, *Brazil* 127 A7
Nova Iorque, *Brazil* 125 E10
Nova Kakhovka, *Ukraine* 33 J7
Nova Lamego, *Guinea-Biss.* 82 C2
Nova Lima, *Brazil* 127 A7
Nova Lusitânia, *Mozam.* 87 F3
Nova Mambone, *Mozam.* 89 C6
Nova Odesa, *Ukraine* 33 J6
Nová Paka, *Czech Rep.* 26 A8
Nova Pavova, *Serbia & M.* 28 F5
Nova Scotia □, *Canada* 105 C7
Nova Siri, *Italy* 43 B9
Nova Sofala, *Mozam.* 89 C5
Nova Ushytsya, *Ukraine* 29 B12
Nova Varoš, *Serbia & M.* 44 C3
Nova Venécia, *Brazil* 125 G10
Nova Zagora, *Bulgaria* 45 D10
Novaci, *Macedonia* 44 E5
Novaci, *Romania* 29 E8
Novaféltria, *Italy* 41 E9
Novannenskiy = Novoannenskiy, *Russia* 34 E6
Novar, *Canada* 116 A5
Novara, *Italy* 40 C5
Novato, *U.S.A.* 110 G4
Novaya Kakhovka = Nova Kakhovka, *Ukraine* 33 J7
Novaya Kazanka, *Kazakhstan* 35 F9
Novaya Ladoga, *Russia* 32 B7
Novaya Lyalya, *Russia* 52 D7
Novaya Sibir, Ostrov, *Russia* 53 B16
Novaya Zemlya, *Russia* 52 B6
Nové Město, *Slovak Rep.* 27 C10
Nové Město na Moravě, *Czech Rep.* 26 B9
Nové Město nad Metují, *Czech Rep.* 27 A9
Nové Zámky, *Slovak Rep.* 27 C11
Novelda, *Spain* 39 G4
Novellara, *Italy* 40 D7
Noventa Vicentina, *Italy* 41 C8
Novgorod, *Russia* 32 C6
Novgorod-Severskiy = Novhorod-Siverskyy, *Ukraine* 33 G7
Novhorod-Siverskyy, *Ukraine* 33 G7
Novi Bečej, *Serbia & M.* 28 E5
Novi Iskar, *Bulgaria* 44 D7
Novi Kneževac, *Serbia & M.* 28 D5
Novi Lígure, *Italy* 40 D5
Novi Pazar, *Bulgaria* 45 C11
Novi Pazar, *Serbia & M.* 44 C4
Novi Sad, *Serbia & M.* 28 E4
Novi Slankamen, *Serbia & M.* 28 E5
Novi Travnik, *Bos.-H.* 28 F2
Novi Vinodolski, *Croatia* 41 C11
Novigrad, *Istra, Croatia* 41 C10
Novigrad, *Zadar, Croatia* 41 D12
Novigradsko More, *Croatia* 41 D12
Novo Hamburgo, *Brazil* 127 B5
Novo Ivanivka, *Ukraine* 29 E14
Novo Mesto, *Slovenia* 41 C12
Novo Miloševo, *Serbia & M.* 28 E5
Novo Remanso, *Brazil* 125 E10
Novoaleksandrovsk, *Russia* 35 H5
Novoaleksandrovskaya = Novoaleksandrovsk, *Russia* 35 H5
Novoaltaysk, *Russia* 52 D9
Novoannenskiy, *Russia* 34 E6
Novoazovsk, *Ukraine* 33 J10
Novocheboksarsk, *Russia* 34 B8
Novocherkassk, *Russia* 35 G5
Novodevichye, *Russia* 34 D9
Novogrudok = Navahrudak, *Belarus* 32 F3
Novohrad-Volynskyy, *Ukraine* 33 G4
Novokachalinsk, *Russia* 54 B6
Novokhopersk, *Russia* 34 E5
Novokuybyshevsk, *Russia* 34 D9
Novokuznetsk, *Russia* 52 D9
Novomirgorod, *Ukraine* 33 H6
Novomoskovsk, *Russia* 32 E10
Novomoskovsk, *Ukraine* 33 H8
Novopolotsk = Navapolatsk, *Belarus* 32 E5
Novorossiysk, *Russia* 33 K9
Novorybnoye, *Russia* 53 B11
Novorzhev, *Russia* 32 D5
Novosej, *Albania* 44 E4
Novoselytsya, *Ukraine* 29 B11
Novoshakhtinsk, *Russia* 33 J10
Novosibirsk, *Russia* 52 D9
Novosibirskiye Ostrova, *Russia* 53 B15
Novosil, *Russia* 33 F9
Novosokolniki, *Russia* 32 D6
Novotitarovskaya, *Russia* 35 H4
Novotroitsk, *Russia* 52 D6
Novoukrayinka, *Ukraine* 33 H6
Novouljanovsk, *Russia* 34 C9
Novouzensk, *Russia* 34 E9
Novovolynsk, *Ukraine* 31 H11
Novovoronezhskiy, *Russia* 33 G10
Novoyavoriske, *Ukraine* 31 J10
Novozybkov, *Russia* 33 F6
Novska, *Croatia* 41 C14
Novy Urengoy, *Russia* 52 C8
Nový Bor, *Czech Rep.* 26 A7
Novy Bug = Novyy Buh, *Ukraine* 33 J7
Nový Bydžov, *Czech Rep.* 26 A8
Novy Dvor, *Belarus* 31 F11
Nowy Dwór Mazowiecki, *Poland* 31 F7
Nový Jičín, *Czech Rep.* 27 B11
Novyy Afon, *Georgia* 35 J5
Novyy Buh, *Ukraine* 33 J7
Novyy Oskol, *Russia* 33 G9
Novyy Port, *Russia* 52 C8
Now Shahr, *Iran* 71 B6
Nowa Deba, *Poland* 31 H8
Nowa Ruda, *Poland* 31 H3
Nowa Sarzyna, *Poland* 31 H9
Nowa Sól, *Poland* 31 G2
Nowata, *U.S.A.* 113 G7
Nowbarān, *Iran* 71 C6
Nowe, *Poland* 30 E5
Nowe Miasteczko, *Poland* 31 G2
Nowe Miasto, *Poland* 31 G7
Nowe Miasto Lubawskie, *Poland* 30 E6
Nowe Skalmierzyce, *Poland* 31 G4
Nowe Warpno, *Poland* 30 E1
Nowghāb, *Iran* 71 C8
Nowgong, *Assam, India* 67 F18
Nowgong, *Mad. P., India* 69 G8
Nowogard, *Poland* 30 E2
Nowogród, *Poland* 31 E8
Nowogród Bobrzanski, *Poland* 31 G2
Nowogrodziec, *Poland* 31 G2
Nowra, *Australia* 95 E5
Nowshera, *Pakistan* 66 C8
Nowy Dwór Gdański, *Poland* 30 D6
Nowy Sącz, *Poland* 31 J7
Nowy Staw, *Poland* 30 D6
Nowy Targ, *Poland* 31 J7
Nowy Tomyśl, *Poland* 31 F3
Nowy Wiśnicz, *Poland* 31 J7
Noxen, *U.S.A.* 117 E8
Noxon, *U.S.A.* 108 C6
Noyabr'sk, *Russia* 52 C8
Noyant, *France* 18 E7
Noyers, *France* 19 E10
Noyon, *France* 19 C9
Noyon, *Mongolia* 56 C2
Nozay, *France* 18 E5
Nqutu, *S. Africa* 89 D5
Nsanje, *Malawi* 87 F4
Nsawam, *Ghana* 83 D4
Nsomba, *Zambia* 87 E2
Nsukka, *Nigeria* 83 D6
Ntui, *Cameroon* 83 E7
Nu Jiang →, *China* 58 E2
Nu Shan, *China* 58 E2
Nuba Mts. = Nubah, Jibalan, *Sudan* 81 E3
Nubah, Jibalan, *Sudan* 81 E3
Nubia, *Africa* 76 D7
Nubian Desert = Nûbîya, Es Sahrâ en, *Sudan* 80 C3
Nûbîya, Es Sahrâ en, *Sudan* 80 C3
Nubledo, *Spain* 36 B5
Nuboai, *Indonesia* 63 E9
Nubra →, *India* 69 B7
Nucet, *Romania* 28 D7
Nueces →, *U.S.A.* 113 M6
Nueltin L., *Canada* 103 A9
Nueva Carteya, *Spain* 37 H6
Nueva Gerona, *Cuba* 120 B3
Nueva Palmira, *Uruguay* 126 C4
Nueva Rosita, *Mexico* 118 B4
Nueva San Salvador, *El Salv.* 120 D2
Nueva Tabarca, *Spain* 39 G4
Nuéve de Julio, *Argentina* 126 D3
Nuevitas, *Cuba* 120 B4
Nuevo, G., *Argentina* 128 E4
Nuevo Casas Grandes, *Mexico* 118 A3
Nuevo Guerrero, *Mexico* 119 B5
Nuevo Laredo, *Mexico* 119 B5
Nuevo León □, *Mexico* 118 C5
Nuevo Rocafuerte, *Ecuador* 124 D3
Nugget Pt., *N.Z.* 91 M2
Nugrus, Gebel, *Egypt* 80 C3
Nuhaka, *N.Z.* 91 H6
Nuits-St-Georges, *France* 19 E11
Nukey Bluff, *Australia* 95 E2
Nukhayb, *Iraq* 70 C4
Nukheila, *Sudan* 80 D2
Nuku'alofa, *Tonga* 91 E12
Nukus, *Uzbekistan* 52 E6
Nules, *Spain* 38 F4
Nullagine, *Australia* 92 D3
Nullagine →, *Australia* 92 D3
Nullarbor, *Australia* 93 F5
Nullarbor △, *Australia* 93 F2
Nullarbor Plain, *Australia* 93 F4
Numalla, L., *Australia* 95 D3
Numan, *Nigeria* 83 D7
Numata, *Japan* 55 F9
Numatinna →, *Sudan* 81 F2
Numaykoos Lake ⌓, *Canada* 103 B9
Numazu, *Japan* 55 G9
Numbulwar, *Australia* 94 A2
Numfoor, *Indonesia* 63 E8
Numurkah, *Australia* 95 F4
Nunaksaluk I., *Canada* 105 A7
Nunap Isua, *Greenland* 101 C15
Nunavut □, *Canada* 101 D8
Nunda, *U.S.A.* 116 D7
Nuneaton, *U.K.* 15 E6
Nungarin, *Australia* 93 F2
Nungo, *Mozam.* 87 E4
Nungwe, *Tanzania* 86 C3
Nunivak I., *U.S.A.* 100 B3
Nunkun, *India* 69 C7
Nùoro, *Italy* 42 B2
Nūrābād, *Iran* 71 E8
Nure →, *Italy* 40 C6
Nuremberg = Nürnberg, *Germany* 25 F7
Nuri, *Mexico* 118 B3
Nuri, *Sudan* 80 D3
Nuriootpa, *Australia* 95 E2
Nuristān □, *Afghan.* 66 B7
Nurlat, *Russia* 34 C10
Nurmes, *Finland* 8 E23
Nürnberg, *Germany* 25 F7
Nurpur, *Pakistan* 68 D4
Nurra, La, *Italy* 42 B1
Nurran, L. = Terewah, L., *Australia* 95 D4
Nurrari Lakes, *Australia* 93 E5
Nurri, *Italy* 42 C2
Nürtingen, *Germany* 25 G5
Nurzec →, *Poland* 31 F9
Nus, *Italy* 40 C4
Nusa Barung, *Indonesia* 63 H15
Nusa Dua, *Indonesia* 63 K18
Nusa Kambangan, *Indonesia* 63 G13
Nusa Tenggara Barat □, *Indonesia* 62 F5
Nusa Tenggara Timur □, *Indonesia* 63 F6
Nusaybin, *Turkey* 73 D9
Nushki, *Pakistan* 68 E2
Nuuk, *Greenland* 101 B14
Nuwakot, *Nepal* 69 E10
Nuweiba', *Egypt* 70 D2
Nuwerus, *S. Africa* 88 E2
Nuweveldberge, *S. Africa* 88 E3
Nuyts, C., *Australia* 93 F5
Nuyts, Pt., *Australia* 93 G2
Nuyts Arch., *Australia* 95 E1
Nxai Pan △, *Botswana* 88 B3
Nxau-Nxau, *Botswana* 88 B3
Nyaake, *Liberia* 82 E3
Nyabing, *Australia* 93 F2
Nyack, *U.S.A.* 117 E11
Nyagan, *Russia* 52 C7
Nyahanga, *Tanzania* 86 C3
Nyahua, *Tanzania* 86 D3
Nyahururu, *Kenya* 86 B4
Nyainqentanglha Shan, *China* 60 C4
Nyakanazi, *Tanzania* 86 C3
Nyakrom, *Ghana* 83 D4
Nyâlâ, *Sudan* 81 E1
Nyamandhlovu, *Zimbabwe* 87 F2
Nyambiti, *Tanzania* 86 C3
Nyamlell, *Sudan* 81 F2
Nyamwaga, *Tanzania* 86 C3
Nyandekwa, *Tanzania* 86 C3
Nyanding →, *Sudan* 81 F3
Nyandoma, *Russia* 32 B11
Nyanga △, *Zimbabwe* 87 F3
Nyangana, *Namibia* 88 B3
Nyanguge, *Tanzania* 86 C3
Nyankpala, *Ghana* 83 D4
Nyanza, *Rwanda* 86 C2
Nyanza □, *Kenya* 86 C3
Nyanza-Lac, *Burundi* 86 C2
Nyaponges, *Sudan* 81 F3
Nyasa, L., *Africa* 87 E3
Nyasvizh, *Belarus* 33 F4
Nyazura, *Zimbabwe* 87 F3
Nyazwidzi →, *Zimbabwe* 87 G3
Nyborg, *Denmark* 11 J4
Nybro, *Sweden* 11 H9
Nyda, *Russia* 52 C8
Nyeri, *Kenya* 86 C4
Nyerol, *Sudan* 81 F3
Nyhammar, *Sweden* 10 D8
Nyika △, *Malawi* 87 E3
Nyinahin, *Ghana* 82 D4
Nyíradony, *Hungary* 28 C6
Nyírbátor, *Hungary* 28 C7
Nyíregyháza, *Hungary* 28 C6
Nykarleby = Uusikaarlepyy, *Finland* 8 E20
Nykøbing, *Storstrøm, Denmark* 11 K5
Nykøbing, *Vestsjælland, Denmark* 11 J5
Nykøbing, *Viborg, Denmark* 11 H2
Nyköping, *Sweden* 11 F11
Nykroppa, *Sweden* 10 E8
Nykvarn, *Sweden* 10 E11
Nyland, *Sweden* 10 A11
Nylstroom = Modimolle, *S. Africa* 89 C4
Nymagee, *Australia* 95 E4
Nymboida △, *Australia* 95 D5
Nymburk, *Czech Rep.* 26 A8
Nynäshamn, *Sweden* 11 F11
Nyngan, *Australia* 95 E4
Nyoma Rap, *India* 69 C8
Nyoman = Nemunas →, *Lithuania* 9 J19
Nyon, *Switz.* 25 J2
Nyong →, *Cameroon* 83 E6
Nyons, *France* 21 D9
Nyou, *Burkina Faso* 83 C4
Nýrsko, *Czech Rep.* 26 B6
Nysa, *Poland* 31 H4
Nysa →, *Europe* 24 C10
Nysa Kłodzka →, *Poland* 31 H4
Nysäter, *Sweden* 10 E6
Nyslott = Savonlinna, *Finland* 32 B5
Nyssa, *U.S.A.* 108 E5
Nystad = Uusikaupunki, *Finland* 9 F19
Nysted, *Denmark* 11 K5
Nyunzu, *Dem. Rep. of the Congo* 86 D2
Nyurba, *Russia* 53 C12
Nyzhankovychi, *Ukraine* 31 J9
Nyzhnohirskyy, *Ukraine* 33 K8
Nyzhny Vorota, *Ukraine* 29 B8
Nzébéla, *Guinea* 82 D3
Nzega, *Tanzania* 86 C3
Nzérékoré, *Guinea* 82 D3
Nzeto, *Angola* 84 F2
Nzilo, Chutes de, *Dem. Rep. of the Congo* 87 E2
N'zo ⌓, *Ivory C.* 82 D3
N'zo →, *Ivory C.* 82 D3
Nzubuka, *Tanzania* 86 C3

O

O Barco, *Spain* 36 C4
O Carballiño, *Spain* 36 C2
O Corgo, *Spain* 36 C3
O Pino, *Spain* 36 C2
O Porriño, *Spain* 36 C2
Ō-Shima, *Japan* 55 G9
Oa, Mull of, *U.K.* 13 F2
Oacoma, *U.S.A.* 112 D5
Oahe, L., *U.S.A.* 112 C4
Oahe Dam, *U.S.A.* 112 C4
Oahu, *U.S.A.* 106 H16
Oak Harbor, *U.S.A.* 110 B4
Oak Hill, *U.S.A.* 114 G5
Oak Ridge, *U.S.A.* 115 G3
Oak View, *U.S.A.* 111 L7
Oakan-Dake, *Japan* 54 C12
Oakdale, *Calif., U.S.A.* 110 H6
Oakdale, *La., U.S.A.* 113 K8
Oakes, *U.S.A.* 112 B5
Oakesdale, *U.S.A.* 108 C5
Oakey, *Australia* 95 D5
Oakfield, *U.S.A.* 116 C6
Oakham, *U.K.* 15 E7
Oakhurst, *U.S.A.* 110 H7
Oakland, *U.S.A.* 110 H4
Oakley, *Idaho, U.S.A.* 108 E7
Oakley, *Kans., U.S.A.* 112 F4
Oakover →, *Australia* 92 D3
Oakridge, *U.S.A.* 108 E2
Oakville, *Canada* 116 C5
Oakville, *U.S.A.* 110 D3
Oamaru, *N.Z.* 91 L3
Oancea, *Romania* 29 E12
Oasi Faunistica di Vendicari ⌓, *Italy* 43 F8
Oasis, *Calif., U.S.A.* 111 M10
Oasis, *Nev., U.S.A.* 110 H9
Oates Land, *Antarctica* 5 C11
Oatlands, *Australia* 95 G4
Oatman, *U.S.A.* 111 K12
Oaxaca, *Mexico* 119 D5
Oaxaca □, *Mexico* 119 D5
Ob →, *Russia* 52 C7
Oba, *Canada* 104 C3
Obala, *Cameroon* 83 E7
Obama, *Japan* 55 G7
Oban, *Nigeria* 83 D6
Oban, *U.K.* 13 E3
Obbia, *Somali Rep.* 75 F4
Obera, *Argentina* 127 B4
Oberammergau, *Germany* 25 H7
Oberasbach, *Germany* 25 F6
Oberbayern □, *Germany* 25 G7
Oberdrauburg, *Austria* 26 E5
Obere Donau ⌓, *Germany* 25 G5
Oberer Bayerischer Wald ⌓, *Germany* 25 F8
Oberfranken □, *Germany* 25 E7
Oberhausen, *Germany* 24 D2
Oberkirch, *Germany* 25 G4
Oberlausitz, *Germany* 24 D10
Oberlin, *Kans., U.S.A.* 112 F4
Oberlin, *La., U.S.A.* 113 K8
Oberlin, *Ohio, U.S.A.* 116 E2
Obernai, *France* 19 D14
Oberndorf, *Germany* 25 G4
Oberon, *Australia* 95 E4
Oberösterreich □, *Austria* 26 C7
Oberpfalz □, *Germany* 25 F8
Oberpfälzer Wald, *Germany* 25 F8
Oberpfälzer Wald ⌓, *Germany* 25 F8
Oberstdorf, *Germany* 25 H6
Obertyn, *Ukraine* 29 B10
Oberursel, *Germany* 25 E4
Oberwart, *Austria* 27 D9
Obi, *Indonesia* 63 E7
Obiaruku, *Nigeria* 83 D6
Óbidos, *Brazil* 125 D7
Óbidos, *Portugal* 37 F1
Obihiro, *Japan* 54 C11
Obilatu, *Indonesia* 63 E7
Obilnoye, *Russia* 35 G7
Obing, *Germany* 25 G8
Objat, *France* 20 C5
Obluchye, *Russia* 53 E14
Obninsk, *Russia* 32 E9
Obo, *C.A.R.* 86 A2
Oboa, Mt., *Uganda* 86 B3
Obock, *Djibouti* 81 E5
Obodivka, *Ukraine* 29 B14
Oborniki, *Poland* 31 F3
Oborniki Śląskie, *Poland* 31 G3
Oboyan, *Russia* 33 G9
Obozerskaya = Obozerskiy, *Russia* 52 C5
Obozerskiy, *Russia* 52 C5
Obrenovac, *Serbia & M.* 44 B4
Obrovac, *Croatia* 41 D12
Obruk, *Turkey* 72 C5
Obrzycko, *Poland* 31 F3
Observatory Inlet, *Canada* 102 B3
Obshchi Syrt, *Russia* 6 E16
Obskaya Guba, *Russia* 52 C8
Obuasi, *Ghana* 83 D4
Obubra, *Nigeria* 83 D6
Obudu, *Nigeria* 83 D6
Obwalden □, *Switz.* 25 J4
Obzor, *Bulgaria* 45 D11
Ocala, *U.S.A.* 115 L4
Ocampo, *Chihuahua, Mexico* 118 B3
Ocampo, *Tamaulipas, Mexico* 119 C5
Ocaña, *Spain* 36 F7
Ocanomowoc, *U.S.A.* 112 D10
Occidental, Cordillera, *Colombia* 124 C3
Occidental, Grand Erg, *Algeria* 78 B6
Ocean City, *Md., U.S.A.* 114 F8
Ocean City, *N.J., U.S.A.* 114 F8
Ocean City, *Wash., U.S.A.* 110 C2
Ocean Falls, *Canada* 102 C3
Ocean I. = Banaba, *Kiribati* 96 H8
Ocean Park, *U.S.A.* 110 D2
Oceano, *U.S.A.* 111 K6
Oceanport, *U.S.A.* 117 F10
Oceanside, *U.S.A.* 111 M9
Ochagavía, *Spain* 38 C3
Ochakiv, *Ukraine* 33 J6
Ochamchira, *Georgia* 35 J5
Ochil Hills, *U.K.* 13 E5
Ocho Rios, *Jamaica* 120 a
Ochsenfurt, *Germany* 25 F6
Ochsenhausen, *Germany* 25 G5
Ocilla, *U.S.A.* 115 K4
Ockelbo, *Sweden* 10 D10
Ocmulgee →, *U.S.A.* 115 K4
Ocna Mureş, *Romania* 29 D8
Ocna Sibiului, *Romania* 29 E9
Ocnele Mari, *Romania* 29 E9
Ocniţa, *Moldova* 29 B12
Oconee →, *U.S.A.* 115 K4
Oconto, *U.S.A.* 114 C2
Oconto Falls, *U.S.A.* 114 C1
Ocosingo, *Mexico* 119 D6
Ocotal, *Nic.* 120 D2
Ocotlán, *Mexico* 118 C4
Ocotlán de Morelos, *Mexico* 119 D5
Ocreza →, *Portugal* 37 F3
Öcsa, *Hungary* 28 C4
Octeville, *France* 18 C5
Oda, *Ghana* 83 D4
Oda, *Japan* 55 G6
Oda, J., *Sudan* 80 C4
Ódáðahraun, *Iceland* 8 D5
Ödåkra, *Sweden* 11 H6
Odate, *Japan* 54 D10
Odawara, *Japan* 55 G9
Odda, *Norway* 9 F12
Odder, *Denmark* 11 J4
Odei →, *Canada* 103 B9
Odemira, *Portugal* 37 H2
Ödemiş, *Turkey* 47 C9
Odendaalsrus, *S. Africa* 88 D4
Odensbacken, *Sweden* 10 E9
Odense, *Denmark* 11 J4
Odenwald = Neckartal-Odenwald ⌓, *Germany* 25 F5
Odenwald, *Germany* 25 F5
Oder →, *Europe* 24 B10
Oder-Havel Kanal, *Germany* 24 C10
Oderzo, *Italy* 41 C9

Odesa, *Ukraine* 33 J6
Ödeshög, *Sweden* 11 F8
Odessa = Odesa, *Ukraine* 33 J6
Odessa, *Canada* 117 B8
Odessa, *Tex., U.S.A.* 113 K3
Odessa, *Wash., U.S.A.* 108 C4
Odiakwe, *Botswana* 88 C4
Odiel →, *Spain* 37 H4
Odienné, *Ivory C.* 82 D3
Odintsovo, *Russia* 32 E9
Odiongan, *Phil.* 61 E4
Odobeşti, *Romania* 29 E12
Odolanów, *Poland* 31 G4
O'Donnell, *U.S.A.* 113 J4
Odorheiu Secuiesc, *Romania* 29 D10
Odoyevo, *Russia* 32 F9
Odra = Oder →, *Europe* 24 B10
Odra →, *Spain* 36 C6
Odžaci, *Serbia & M.* 28 E4
Odžak, *Bos.-H.* 28 E3
Odzi, *Zimbabwe* 89 B5
Odzi →, *Zimbabwe* 89 B5
Oebisfelde, *Germany* 24 C6
Oeiras, *Brazil* 125 E10
Oeiras, *Portugal* 37 G1
Oelrichs, *U.S.A.* 112 D3
Oelsnitz, *Germany* 25 E8
Oelwein, *U.S.A.* 112 D9
Oenpelli, *Australia* 92 B5
Oetz, *Austria* 26 D3
Of, *Turkey* 73 B9
Ofanto →, *Italy* 43 A9
Offa, *Nigeria* 83 D5
Offaly □, *Ireland* 12 C4
Offenbach, *Germany* 25 E4
Offenburg, *Germany* 25 G3
Officer, The →, *Australia* 93 E5
Offida, *Italy* 41 F10
Ofidhousa, *Greece* 47 E8
Ofotfjorden, *Norway* 8 B17
Ōfunato, *Japan* 54 E10
Oga, *Japan* 54 E9
Oga-Hantō, *Japan* 54 E9
Ogaden, *Ethiopia* 75 F3
Ōgaki, *Japan* 55 G8
Ogallala, *U.S.A.* 112 E4
Ogasawara Gunto, *Pac. Oc.* 96 E6
Ogbomosho, *Nigeria* 83 D5
Ogden, *U.S.A.* 108 F7
Ogdensburg, *U.S.A.* 117 B9
Ogeechee →, *U.S.A.* 115 K5
Ogilby, *U.S.A.* 111 N12
Oglio →, *Italy* 40 C7
Oglio Nord ⌓, *Italy* 40 C6
Oglio Sud ⌓, *Italy* 40 C7
Ogmore, *Australia* 94 C4
Ognon →, *France* 19 E12
Ogoja, *Nigeria* 83 D6
Ogoki, *Canada* 104 B2
Ogoki →, *Canada* 104 B2
Ogoki L., *Canada* 104 B2
Ogoki Res., *Canada* 104 B2
Ogooué →, *Gabon* 84 E1
Ogosta →, *Bulgaria* 44 C7
Ogowe = Ogooué →, *Gabon* 84 E1
Ogr = Sharafa, *Sudan* 81 E2
Ograźden, *Macedonia* 44 E6
Ogre, *Latvia* 9 H21
Ogrein, *Sudan* 80 D3
Ogulin, *Croatia* 41 C12
Ogun □, *Nigeria* 83 D5
Ogurchinskiy, Ostrov, *Turkmenistan* 71 B7
Oguta, *Nigeria* 83 D6
Ogwashi-Uku, *Nigeria* 83 D6
Ogwe, *Nigeria* 83 E6
Ohai, *N.Z.* 91 L2
Ohakune, *N.Z.* 91 H5
Ohata, *Japan* 54 D10
Ohau, L., *N.Z.* 91 L2
Ohio □, *U.S.A.* 116 F2
Ohio →, *U.S.A.* 114 G1
Ohře →, *Czech Rep.* 26 A7
Ohre →, *Germany* 24 C7
Ohrid, *Macedonia* 44 E4
Ohridsko Jezero, *Macedonia* 44 E4
Ohrigstad, *S. Africa* 89 C5
Öhringen, *Germany* 25 F5
Oi Qu, *China* 58 C2
Oiapoque, *Brazil* 125
Oikou, *China* 57 E9
Oil City, *U.S.A.* 116 E5
Oil Springs, *Canada* 116 D2
Oildale, *U.S.A.* 111 K7
Oinousa, *Greece* 47 C8
Oise □, *France* 19 C9
Oise →, *France* 19 C9
Oiseaux du Djoudj △, *Senegal* 82 B1
Oistins, *Barbados* 121 g
Oistins B., *Barbados* 121 g
Ōita, *Japan* 55 H5
Ōita □, *Japan* 55 H5
Oiticica, *Brazil* 125 E10
Ojacaliente, *Mexico* 118 C4
Ojai, *U.S.A.* 111 L7
Ojcowski △, *Poland* 31 H6
Ojinaga, *Mexico* 118 B4
Ojiya, *Japan* 55 F9
Ojo de Liebre ⌓, *Mexico* 118 B2
Ojos del Salado, Cerro, *Argentina* 126 B2
Oka →, *Russia* 34 B7
Okaba, *Indonesia* 63 F9
Okahandja, *Namibia* 88 C2
Okanagan L., *Canada* 102 D5
Okanogan, *U.S.A.* 108 B4
Okanogan →, *U.S.A.* 108 B4
Okány, *Hungary* 28 D6
Okapi △, *Dem. Rep. of the Congo* 86 B2
Okaputa, *Namibia* 88 C2
Okara, *Pakistan* 68 D5
Okaukuejo, *Namibia* 88 B2
Okavango Delta, *Botswana* 88 B3
Okavango Swamp = Okavango Delta, *Botswana* 88 B3
Okaya, *Japan* 55 F9
Okayama, *Japan* 55 G6
Okayama □, *Japan* 55 G6
Okazaki, *Japan* 55 G8
Oke-Iho, *Nigeria* 83 D5
Okęcie, Warszawa ✕ (WAW), *Poland* 31 F7
Okeechobee, *U.S.A.* 115 M5
Okeechobee, L., *U.S.A.* 115 M5
Okefenokee ⌓, *U.S.A.* 115 K4
Okefenokee Swamp, *U.S.A.* 115 K4
Okehampton, *U.K.* 15 G4
Okene, *Nigeria* 83 D6
Oker →, *Germany* 24 C6
Okha, *India* 68 H3
Okha, *Russia* 53 D15
Ókhi Óros, *Greece* 46 C6
Okhotsk, *Russia* 53 D15
Okhotsk, Sea of, *Asia* 53 D15
Okhotskiy Perevoz, *Russia* 53 C14
Okhtyrka, *Ukraine* 33 G8
Oki-Shotō, *Japan* 55 F6
Okiep, *S. Africa* 88 D2
Okigwi, *Nigeria* 83 D6
Okija, *Nigeria* 83 D6
Okinawa □, *Japan* 55 L4
Okinawa-Guntō, *Japan* 55 L4
Okinawa-Jima, *Japan* 55 L4
Okino-erabu-Shima, *Japan* 55 L4
Okitipupa, *Nigeria* 83 D5
Oklahoma □, *U.S.A.* 113 H6
Oklahoma City, *U.S.A.* 113 H6
Okmulgee, *U.S.A.* 113 H7
Oknitsa = Ocniţa, *Moldova* 29 B12
Oko, W. →, *Sudan* 80 C4
Okolo, *Uganda* 86 B3
Okolona, *U.S.A.* 113 J10
Okombahe, *Namibia* 88 C2
Okonek, *Poland* 30 E3
Okotoks, *Canada* 102 C6
Okrika, *Nigeria* 83 E6
Oksibil, *Indonesia* 63 E10
Oktabrsk = Oktyabrsk, *Kazakhstan* 52 E6
Oktyabrsk, *Kazakhstan* 52 E6
Oktyabrsk, *Russia* 34 D9
Oktyabrskiy = Aktsyabrski, *Belarus* 33 F5
Oktyabrskiy, *Russia* 35 G5
Oktyabrskoy Revolyutsii, Ostrov, *Russia* 53 B10
Oktyabrskoye = Zhovtneve, *Ukraine* 33 J7
Okulovka, *Russia* 32 C7
Okuru, *N.Z.* 91 K2
Okushiri-Tō, *Japan* 54 C9
Okuta, *Nigeria* 83 D5
Okwa →, *Botswana* 88 C3
Ola, *U.S.A.* 113 H8
Ólafsfjörður, *Iceland* 8 C4
Ólafsvík, *Iceland* 8 D2
Olaine, *Latvia* 30 B10
Olancha, *U.S.A.* 111 J8
Olancha Pk., *U.S.A.* 111 J8
Olanchito, *Honduras* 120 C2
Öland, *Sweden* 11 H10
Ölands norra udde, *Sweden* 11 G11
Ölands södra udde, *Sweden* 11 H10
Olargues, *France* 20 E6
Olary, *Australia* 95 E3
Olascoaga, *Argentina* 126 D3
Olathe, *U.S.A.* 112 F7
Olavarría, *Argentina* 126 D3
Oława, *Poland* 31 H4
Olbernhau, *Germany* 24 E9
Ólbia, *Italy* 42 B2
Ólbia, G. di, *Italy* 42 B2
Olching, *Germany* 25 G7
Olcott, *U.S.A.* 116 C6
Old Bahama Chan. = Bahama, Canal Viejo de, *W. Indies* 120 B4
Old Baldy Pk. = San Antonio, Mt., *U.S.A.* 111 L9
Old Castile = Castilla y Leon □, *Spain* 36 D6
Old Crow, *Canada* 100 B6
Old Dale, *U.S.A.* 111 L11
Old Forge, *N.Y., U.S.A.* 117 C10
Old Forge, *Pa., U.S.A.* 117 E9
Old Perlican, *Canada* 105 C9
Old Shinyanga, *Tanzania* 86 C3
Old Speck Mt., *U.S.A.* 117 B14
Old Town, *U.S.A.* 115 C11
Old Washington, *U.S.A.* 116 F3
Old Wives L., *Canada* 103 C7
Oldbury, *U.K.* 15 F5
Oldcastle, *Ireland* 12 C4
Oldeani, *Tanzania* 86 C4
Oldenburg, *Niedersachsen, Germany* 24 B4
Oldenburg, *Schleswig-Holstein, Germany* 24 A6
Oldenzaal, *Neths.* 17 B6
Oldham, *U.K.* 14 D5
Oldman →, *Canada* 102 D6
Oldmeldrum, *U.K.* 13 D6
Olds, *Canada* 102 C6
Olduvai Gorge, *Tanzania* 86 C4
Oldziyt, *Mongolia* 56 B5
Olean, *U.S.A.* 116 D6
Olecko, *Poland* 30 D9
Oléggio, *Italy* 40 C5
Oleiros, *Portugal* 36 F3
Oleiros, *Spain* 36 B2
Olekma →, *Russia* 53 C13
Olekminsk, *Russia* 53 C13
Oleksandriya, *Kirovohrad, Ukraine* 33 H7
Oleksandriya, *Rivne, Ukraine* 33 G4
Oleksandrovka, *Ukraine* 33 H7
Olema, *U.S.A.* 110 G4
Olenek, *Russia* 53 C12
Olenek →, *Russia* 53 B13
Olenino, *Russia* 32 D7
Oléron, Î. d', *France* 20 C2
Olesk, *Ukraine* 31 G11
Oleśnica, *Poland* 31 G4
Olesno, *Poland* 31 H5
Olevsk, *Ukraine* 33 G4
Olga, *Russia* 53 E14
Olga, L., *Canada* 104 C4
Olga, Mt., *Australia* 93 E5
Ølgod, *Denmark* 11 J2
Olhão, *Portugal* 37 H3
Olhopil, *Ukraine* 29 B14
Olhovatka, *Russia* 30 D9
Olib, *Croatia* 41 D11
Oliena, *Italy* 42 B2
Oliete, *Spain* 38 D4
Olifants = Elefantes →, *Africa* 89 C5
Olifants →, *Namibia* 88 C2
Olifantshoek, *S. Africa* 88 D3
Ólimbos, *Greece* 47 F9
Ólimbos, Óros, *Greece* 44 F6
Olímpia, *Brazil* 127 A6
Olimpos-Beydaglari △, *Turkey* 47 E12
Olinda, *Brazil* 125 E12
Olite, *Spain* 38 C3
Oliva, *Argentina* 126 C3
Oliva, *Spain* 39 G4
Oliva, Punta del, *Spain* 36 B5
Oliva de la Frontera, *Spain* 37 G4
Olivares, *Spain* 38 F2
Olivehurst, *U.S.A.* 110 F5
Oliveira de Azeméis, *Portugal* 36 E2
Oliveira do Douro, *Portugal* 36 D2
Olivenza, *Spain* 37 G3
Oliver, *Canada* 102 D5
Oliver L., *Canada* 103 B8
Olivet, *France* 19 E8
Olkhovka, *Russia* 34 F7
Olkusz, *Poland* 31 H6
Ollagüe, *Chile* 126 A2
Olmedo, *Spain* 36 D6
Olmeto, *France* 21 G12
Olney, *Ill., U.S.A.* 114 F1
Olney, *Tex., U.S.A.* 113 J5
Olofström, *Sweden* 11 H8
Oloma, *Cameroon* 83 E7
Olomane →, *Canada* 105 B7
Olomouc, *Czech Rep.* 27 B10
Olomoucký □, *Czech Rep.* 27 B10
Olonets, *Russia* 32 B7
Olongapo, *Phil.* 61 D4
Olonne-sur-Mer, *France* 20 B2
Oloron, Gave d' →, *France* 20 E2
Oloron-Ste-Marie, *France* 20 E3
Olot, *Spain* 38 C7
Olovo, *Bos.-H.* 28 F3
Olovyannaya, *Russia* 53 D12
Oloy →, *Russia* 53 C16
Olsberg, *Germany* 24 D4
Olshammar, *Sweden* 11 F8
Olshanka, *Ukraine* 33 H6
Olshany, *Ukraine* 33 G8
Olsztyn, *Poland* 30 E7
Olsztynek, *Poland* 30 E7
Olt □, *Romania* 29 F9
Olt →, *Romania* 29 G9
Olten, *Switz.* 25 H3
Olteniţa, *Romania* 29 F11
Olton, *U.S.A.* 113 H3
Oltu, *Turkey* 73 B9
Oluanpi, *Taiwan* 59 G13
Olula del Rio, *Spain* 39 H2
Olur, *Turkey* 73 B10
Olutanga, *Phil.* 61 H5
Olvega, *Spain* 38 D2
Olvera, *Spain* 37 J5
Olymbos, *Cyprus* 49 D12
Olympia, *Greece* 46 D3
Olympia, *U.S.A.* 110 D4
Olympic △, *U.S.A.* 110 C3
Olympic Dam, *Australia* 95 E2
Olympic Mts., *U.S.A.* 110 C3
Olympus, *Cyprus* 49 E11
Olympus, Mt. = Ólimbos, Óros, *Greece* 44 F6
Olympus, Mt. = Uludağ, *Turkey* 45 F13
Olympus, Mt., *U.S.A.* 110 C3
Olyphant, *U.S.A.* 117 E9
Om →, *Russia* 52 D8
Om Hajer, *Eritrea* 81 E4
Om Koi, *Thailand* 64 D2
Ōma, *Japan* 54 D10
Ōmachi, *Japan* 55 F8
Omae-Zaki, *Japan* 55 G9
Ōmagari, *Japan* 54 E10
Omagh, *U.K.* 12 B4
Omagh □, *U.K.* 12 B4
Omaha, *U.S.A.* 112 E7
Omak, *U.S.A.* 108 B4
Omalos, *Greece* 49 D5
Oman ■, *Asia* 75 C6
Oman, G. of, *Asia* 71 E8
Omaruru, *Namibia* 88 C2
Omaruru →, *Namibia* 88 C1
Omate, *Peru* 124 G4
Ombai, Selat, *Indonesia* 63 F6
Omboué, *Gabon* 84 E1
Ombrone →, *Italy* 40 F8
Omdurmân, *Sudan* 81 D3
Omegna, *Italy* 40 C5
Omemee, *Canada* 116 B6
Omeonga, *Dem. Rep. of the Congo* 86 C1
Ometepe, I. de, *Nic.* 120 D2
Ometepec, *Mexico* 119 D5
Ominato, *Japan* 54 D10
Omineca →, *Canada* 102 B4
Omiš, *Croatia* 41 E13
Omišalj, *Croatia* 41 C11
Omitara, *Namibia* 88 C2
Ōmiya, *Japan* 55 G9
Omme Å →, *Denmark* 11 J2
Ommen, *Neths.* 17 B6
Ömnögovĭ □, *Mongolia* 56 C3
Omo △, *Ethiopia* 81 F4
Omo →, *Ethiopia* 81 F4
Omo Valley, *Ethiopia* 81 F4
Omodeo, L., *Italy* 42 B1
Omodhos, *Cyprus* 49 E11
Omoko, *Nigeria* 83 D6
Omolon →, *Russia* 53 C16
Omono-Gawa →, *Japan* 54 E10
Omsk, *Russia* 52 D8
Omsukchan, *Russia* 53 C16
Ōmu, *Japan* 54 B11
Omul, Vf., *Romania* 29 E10
Omulew →, *Poland* 31 E8
Ōmura, *Japan* 55 H4
Omuramba Omatako →, *Namibia* 88 B2
Omuramba Ovambo →, *Namibia* 88 B2
Omurtag, *Bulgaria* 45 C10
Ōmuta, *Japan* 55 H5
Oña, *Spain* 36 C7
Onaga, *U.S.A.* 112 F6
Onalaska, *U.S.A.* 112 D9
Onancock, *U.S.A.* 114 G8
Onang, *Indonesia* 63 E5
Onaping L., *Canada* 104 C3
Oñati, *Spain* 38 B2
Onavas, *Mexico* 118 B3
Onawa, *U.S.A.* 112 D6
Oncócua, *Angola* 88 B1
Onda, *Spain* 38 F4
Ondaejin, *N. Korea* 57 D15
Ondangwa, *Namibia* 88 B2
Ondarroa, *Spain* 38 B2
Ondava →, *Slovak Rep.* 27 C14
Ondjiva, *Angola* 88 B2
Ondo, *Nigeria* 83 D5
Ondo □, *Nigeria* 83 D6
Öndörshil, *Mongolia* 56 B5
Öndverðarnes, *Iceland* 8 D1
One Tree, *Australia* 95 E3
Onega, *Russia* 52 C4
Onega →, *Russia* 6 C13
Onega, L. = Onezhskoye Ozero, *Russia* 32 B8
Oneida, *U.S.A.* 117 C9
Oneida L., *U.S.A.* 117 C9
O'Neill, *U.S.A.* 112 D5
Onekotan, Ostrov, *Russia* 53 E16
Onema, *Dem. Rep. of the Congo* 86 C1
Oneonta, *U.S.A.* 117 D9
Oneşti, *Romania* 29 D11
Onezhskoye Ozero, *Russia* 32 B8
Ongarue, *N.Z.* 91 H5
Ongers →, *S. Africa* 88 E3
Ongerup, *Australia* 93 F2
Ongjin, *N. Korea* 57 F13
Ongkharak, *Thailand* 64 E3
Ongniud Qi, *China* 57 C10
Ongoka, *Dem. Rep. of the Congo* 86 C2
Ongole, *India* 66 M12
Ongon = Havirga, *Mongolia* 56 B7
Oni, *Georgia* 35 J6
Onida, *U.S.A.* 112 C4
Onilahy →, *Madag.* 89 C7
Onitsha, *Nigeria* 83 D6
Onoda, *Japan* 55 G5
Onpyŏng-ni, *S. Korea* 57 H14
Ons, I. de, *Spain* 36 C2
Onsala, *Sweden* 11 G6
Onslow, *Australia* 92 D2
Onslow B., *U.S.A.* 115 H7
Ontake-San, *Japan* 55 G8
Ontario, *Calif., U.S.A.* 111 L9
Ontario, *Oreg., U.S.A.* 108 D5
Ontario □, *Canada* 104 B2
Ontario, L., *N. Amer.* 116 C7
Ontinyent, *Spain* 39 G4
Ontonagon, *U.S.A.* 112 B10
Ontur, *Spain* 39 G3
Onyx, *U.S.A.* 111 K8
Oodnadatta, *Australia* 95 D2
Ooldea, *Australia* 93 F5
Oombulgurri, *Australia* 92 C4
Oorindi, *Australia* 94 C3
Oost-Vlaanderen □, *Belgium* 17 C3
Oostende, *Belgium* 17 C2
Oosterhout, *Neths.* 17 C4
Oosterschelde →, *Neths.* 17 C4
Oosterwolde, *Neths.* 17 B6
Ootacamund = Udagamandalam, *India* 66 P10
Ootsa L., *Canada* 102 C3
Op Luang △, *Thailand* 64 C2
Opaka, *Bulgaria* 45 C10
Opala, *Dem. Rep. of the Congo* 86 C1
Opalenica, *Poland* 31 F3
Opan, *Bulgaria* 45 D9
Opanake, *Sri Lanka* 66 R12
Opasatika, *Canada* 104 C3
Opasquia ⌓, *Canada* 104 B1
Opatija, *Croatia* 41 C11
Opatów, *Poland* 31 H8
Opava, *Czech Rep.* 27 B10
Opelika, *U.S.A.* 115 J3
Opelousas, *U.S.A.* 113 K8
Opémisca, L., *Canada* 104 C5
Opheim, *U.S.A.* 108 B10
Ophthalmia Ra., *Australia* 92 D2
Opi, *Nigeria* 83 D6
Opinaca →, *Canada* 104 B4
Opinaca, Rés., *Canada* 104 B4
Opinnagau →, *Canada* 104 B3
Opiscotéo, L., *Canada* 105 B6
Opobo, *Nigeria* 83 E6
Opochka, *Russia* 32 D5
Opoczno, *Poland* 31 G7
Opol, *Phil.* 61 G6
Opole, *Poland* 31 H4
Opole Lubelskie, *Poland* 31 G8
Opolskie □, *Poland* 31 H5
Oponono L., *Namibia* 88 B2
Oporto = Porto, *Portugal* 36 D2
Opotiki, *N.Z.* 91 H6
Opp, *U.S.A.* 115 K2
Oppdal, *Norway* 9 E13
Óppido Mamertina, *Italy* 43 D8
Opportunity, *U.S.A.* 108 C5
Oprişor, *Romania* 28 F8
Oprtalj, *Croatia* 41 C10
Opua, *N.Z.* 91 F5
Opunake, *N.Z.* 91 H4
Opuwo, *Namibia* 88 B1
Opuzen, *Croatia* 41 E14
Ora, *Cyprus* 49 E12
Oracle, *U.S.A.* 109 K8
Oradea, *Romania* 28 C6
Öræfajökull, *Iceland* 8 D5
Orahovac, *Serbia & M.* 44 D4
Orahovica, *Croatia* 28 E2
Orai, *India* 69 G8
Oraison, *France* 21 E9
Oral = Zhayyq →, *Kazakhstan* 52 E6
Oral, *Kazakhstan* 34 E10
Oran, *Algeria* 78 A5
Orange, *Australia* 95 E4
Orange, *France* 21 D8
Orange, *Calif., U.S.A.* 111 M9
Orange, *Mass., U.S.A.* 117 D12
Orange, *Tex., U.S.A.* 113 K8
Orange, *Va., U.S.A.* 114 F6
Orange →, *S. Africa* 88 D2
Orange, C., *Brazil* 125 C8
Orange Cove, *U.S.A.* 110 J7
Orange Free State = Free State □, *S. Africa* 88 D4
Orange Grove, *U.S.A.* 113 M6
Orange Walk, *Belize* 119 D7
Orangeburg, *U.S.A.* 115 J5
Orangeville, *Canada* 116 C4
Orango, *Guinea-Biss.* 82 C1
Orani, *Phil.* 61 D4
Oranienburg, *Germany* 24 C9
Oranje = Orange →, *S. Africa* 88 D2
Oranjemund, *Namibia* 88 D2
Oranjerivier, *S. Africa* 88 D3
Oranjestad, *Aruba* 121 D5
Orapa, *Botswana* 85 J5
Orarak, *Sudan* 81 F3
Oras, *Phil.* 61 E6
Orašje, *Bos.-H.* 28 E3
Orăştie, *Romania* 29 E8
Orava →, *Slovak Rep.* 27 B12
Orava, Vodna nádrž, *Slovak Rep.* 27 B12
Oraviţa, *Romania* 28 E6
Orb →, *France* 20 E7
Orba →, *Italy* 40 D5
Ørbæk, *Denmark* 11 J4
Orbe, *Switz.* 25 J2
Orbec, *France* 18 C7
Orbetello, *Italy* 41 F8
Órbigo →, *Spain* 36 C5
Orbisonia, *U.S.A.* 116 F7
Orbost, *Australia* 95 F4
Örbyhus, *Sweden* 10 D11
Orcadas, *Antarctica* 5 C18
Orcas I., *U.S.A.* 110 B4
Orce, *Spain* 39 H2
Orce →, *Spain* 39 H2
Orchard City, *U.S.A.* 109 G10
Orchies, *France* 19 B10
Orchila, I., *Venezuela* 121 D6
Orchilla, Pta., *Canary Is.* 48 G1
Órcia →, *Italy* 41 F8
Orco →, *Italy* 40 C4
Orcutt, *U.S.A.* 111 L6
Ord, *U.S.A.* 112 E5
Ord →, *Australia* 92 C4
Ord, Mt., *Australia* 92 C4
Ordenes = Ordes, *Spain* 36 B2
Orderville, *U.S.A.* 109 H7
Ordes, *Spain* 36 B2
Ordesa y Monte Perido △, *Spain* 38 C4
Ording = St-Peter-Ording, *Germany* 24 A4
Ordos = Mu Us Shamo, *China* 56 E5
Ordu, *Turkey* 72 B7
Ordubad, *Azerbaijan* 73 C12
Orduña, *Álava, Spain* 38 C2
Orduña, *Granada, Spain* 37 H7
Ordway, *U.S.A.* 112 F3
Ordzhonikidze, *Ukraine* 33 J8
Ore, *Dem. Rep. of the Congo* 86 B2
Ore Mts. = Erzgebirge, *Germany* 24 E8
Orebić, *Croatia* 41 F14
Örebro, *Sweden* 10 E9
Örebro län □, *Sweden* 10 E8
Orecchiella ⌓, *Italy* 40 D7
Oregon, *U.S.A.* 112 D10
Oregon □, *U.S.A.* 108 E3
Oregon City, *U.S.A.* 110 E4
Oregon Dunes ⌓, *U.S.A.* 108 E1
Öregrund, *Sweden* 10 D12
Öregrundsgrepen, *Sweden* 10 D12
Orekhov = Orikhiv, *Ukraine* 33 J8
Orekhovo-Zuyevo, *Russia* 32 E10
Orel, *Russia* 33 F9
Orel →, *Ukraine* 33 H8
Orellana, *Spain* 37 F5
Orellana, Canal de, *Spain* 37 F5
Orellana, Embalse de, *Spain* 37 F5
Orem, *U.S.A.* 108 F8
Ören, *Turkey* 47 D9
Orenburg, *Russia* 52 D6
Örencik, *Turkey* 47 B11
Orense = Ourense, *Spain* 36 C3
Orense □, *Spain* 36 C3
Orepuki, *N.Z.* 91 M1
Orestiás, *Greece* 45 E10
Orestos Pereyra, *Mexico* 118 B3

Øresund, *Europe* 11 J6
Orford Ness, *U.K.* 15 E9
Organ Pipe Cactus ⌂, *U.S.A.* 109 K7
Organos, Pta. de los, *Canary Is.* 48 F2
Organyà, *Spain* 38 C6
Orgaz, *Spain* 37 F7
Orgeyev = Orhei, *Moldova* 29 C13
Orhaneli, *Turkey* 45 G12
Orhaneli →, *Turkey* 45 G12
Orhangazi, *Turkey* 45 F13
Orhei, *Moldova* 29 C13
Orhon Gol →, *Mongolia* 60 A5
Ória, *Italy* 43 B10
Oriental, Cordillera, *Colombia* 124 B4
Oriental, Grand Erg, *Algeria* 78 B7
Orientale □, *Dem. Rep. of the Congo* 86 B2
Oriente, *Argentina* 126 D3
Orihuela, *Spain* 39 G4
Orihuela del Tremedal, *Spain* 38 E3
Orikhiv, *Ukraine* 33 J8
Orikum, *Albania* 44 F3
Orillia, *Canada* 116 B5
Orinoco →, *Venezuela* 124 B6
Orion, *Canada* 103 D6
Oriskany, *U.S.A.* 117 C9
Orissa □, *India* 67 K14
Orissaare, *Estonia* 9 G20
Oristano, *Italy* 42 C1
Oristano, G. di, *Italy* 42 C1
Orizaba, *Mexico* 119 D5
Orizaba, Pico de, *Mexico* 119 D5
Orizare, *Bulgaria* 45 D11
Orjen, *Bos.-H.* 44 D2
Orjiva, *Spain* 37 J7
Orkanger, *Norway* 8 E13
Örkelljunga, *Sweden* 11 H7
Örken, *Sweden* 11 G9
Örkény, *Hungary* 28 C4
Orkla →, *Norway* 8 E13
Orkney, *S. Africa* 88 D4
Orkney □, *U.K.* 13 B5
Orkney Is., *U.K.* 13 B6
Orland, *U.S.A.* 110 F4
Orlando, *U.S.A.* 115 L5
Orlando, C. d', *Italy* 43 D7
Orléanais, *France* 19 E9
Orléans, *France* 19 E8
Orleans, *U.S.A.* 117 B12
Orléans, Î. d', *Canada* 105 C5
Orlice →, *Czech Rep.* 26 A8
Orlivka, *Ukraine* 29 E13
Orlov, *Slovak Rep.* 27 B13
Orlov Gay, *Russia* 34 E9
Orlová, *Czech Rep.* 27 B11
Orlovat, *Serbia & M.* 28 E5
Orly, Paris ✈ (ORY), *France* 19 D9
Ormara, *Pakistan* 66 G4
Ormea, *Italy* 40 D4
Ormília, *Greece* 44 F7
Ormoc, *Phil.* 61 F6
Ormond, *N.Z.* 91 H6
Ormond Beach, *U.S.A.* 115 L5
Ormož, *Slovenia* 41 B13
Ormskirk, *U.K.* 14 D5
Ormstown, *Canada* 117 A11
Ornans, *France* 19 E13
Orne □, *France* 18 D7
Orne →, *France* 18 C6
Orneta, *Poland* 30 D7
Ornö, *Sweden* 10 E12
Örnsköldsvik, *Sweden* 10 A12
Oro, *N. Korea* 57 D14
Oro →, *Mexico* 118 B3
Oro Grande, *U.S.A.* 111 L9
Oro Valley, *U.S.A.* 109 K8
Orobie, Alpi, *Italy* 40 B6
Orobie Bergamasche ⌂, *Italy* 40 C6
Orobie Valtellinesi ⌂, *Italy* 40 B6
Orocué, *Colombia* 124 C4
Orodara, *Burkina Faso* 82 C4
Orodo, *Nigeria* 83 D6
Orofino, *U.S.A.* 108 C5
Orol Dengizi = Aral Sea, *Asia* 52 E7
Oromiya □, *Ethiopia* 81 F5
Oromocto, *Canada* 105 C6
Oron, *Nigeria* 83 E6
Orono, *Canada* 116 C6
Orono, *U.S.A.* 115 C11
Oronsay, *U.K.* 13 E2
Oropesa, *Spain* 36 F5
Oroquieta, *Phil.* 61 G5
Orosei, *Italy* 42 B2
Orosei, G. di, *Italy* 42 B2
Orosháza, *Hungary* 28 D5
Oroszlány, *Hungary* 28 C3
Orotukan, *Russia* 53 C16
Oroville, *Calif., U.S.A.* 110 F5
Oroville, *Wash., U.S.A.* 108 B4
Oroville, L., *U.S.A.* 110 F5
Orrefors, *Sweden* 11 H9
Orroroo, *Australia* 95 E2
Orrviken, *Sweden* 10 A8
Orrville, *U.S.A.* 116 F3
Orsa, *Sweden* 10 C8
Orsara di Púglia, *Italy* 43 A8
Orsasjön, *Sweden* 10 C8
Orsha, *Belarus* 32 E6
Örsjö, *Sweden* 11 H9
Orsk, *Russia* 52 D6
Orşova, *Romania* 28 F7
Ørsted, *Denmark* 11 H4
Örsundsbro, *Sweden* 10 E11
Orta, L. d', *Italy* 40 C5
Orta Nova, *Italy* 43 A8
Ortaca, *Turkey* 47 E10
Ortakent, *Turkey* 47 D9
Ortaklar, *Turkey* 47 D9
Ortaköy, *Çorum, Turkey* 72 B6
Ortaköy, *Niğde, Turkey* 72 C6
Orte, *Italy* 41 F9
Ortegal, C., *Spain* 36 B3
Orthez, *France* 20 E3
Ortigueira, *Spain* 36 B3
Orting, *U.S.A.* 110 C4
Ortisei, *Italy* 41 B8
Ortles, *Italy* 40 B7
Ortón →, *Bolivia* 124 F5
Ortona, *Italy* 41 F11
Ortonville, *U.S.A.* 112 C6
Orūmīyeh, *Iran* 70 B5
Orūmīyeh, Daryācheh-ye, *Iran* 70 B5
Orune, *Italy* 42 B2
Oruro, *Bolivia* 124 G5
Orust, *Sweden* 11 F5
Oruzgān □, *Afghan.* 66 C5
Orvault, *France* 18 E5
Orvieto, *Italy* 41 F9
Orwell, *N.Y., U.S.A.* 117 C9
Orwell, *Ohio, U.S.A.* 116 E4
Orwell →, *U.K.* 15 F9
Orwigsburg, *U.S.A.* 117 F8
Oryakhovo, *Bulgaria* 44 C7
Orynyn, *Ukraine* 29 B11
Orzinuovi, *Italy* 40 C6
Orzyc →, *Poland* 31 F8
Orzysz, *Poland* 30 E8
Osa →, *Poland* 30 E5
Osa, Pen. de, *Costa Rica* 120 E3
Osage, *U.S.A.* 112 D8
Osage →, *U.S.A.* 112 F9
Osage City, *U.S.A.* 112 F7
Ōsaka, *Japan* 55 G7
Osan, *S. Korea* 57 F14
Osawatomie, *U.S.A.* 112 F7
Osborne, *U.S.A.* 112 F5
Osby, *Sweden* 11 H7
Osceola, *Ark., U.S.A.* 113 H10
Osceola, *Iowa, U.S.A.* 112 E8
Oschatz, *Germany* 24 D9
Oschersleben, *Germany* 24 C7
Óschiri, *Italy* 42 B2
Oscoda, *U.S.A.* 116 B1
Osečina, *Serbia & M.* 44 B3
Ösel = Saaremaa, *Estonia* 9 G20
Osery, *Russia* 32 E10
Osgoode, *Canada* 117 A9
Osh, *Kyrgyzstan* 52 E8
Oshakati, *Namibia* 85 H3
Oshawa, *Canada* 116 C6
Oshigambo, *Namibia* 88 B2
Oshkosh, *Nebr., U.S.A.* 112 E3
Oshkosh, *Wis., U.S.A.* 112 C10
Oshmyany = Ashmyany, *Belarus* 9 J21
Oshnovīyeh, *Iran* 70 B5
Oshogbo, *Nigeria* 83 D5
Oshtorīnān, *Iran* 71 C6
Oshwe, *Dem. Rep. of the Congo* 84 E3
Osi, *Nigeria* 83 D6
Osieczna, *Poland* 31 G3
Osijek, *Croatia* 28 E3
Ósilo, *Italy* 42 B1
Ósimo, *Italy* 41 E10
Osintorf, *Belarus* 32 E6
Osipovichi = Asipovichy, *Belarus* 32 F5
Osiyan, *India* 68 F5
Osizweni, *S. Africa* 89 D5
Oskaloosa, *U.S.A.* 112 E8
Oskarshamn, *Sweden* 11 G10
Oskarström, *Sweden* 11 H6
Oskélanéo, *Canada* 104 C4
Öskemen, *Kazakhstan* 52 E9
Oskol →, *Ukraine* 33 H9
Oslo, *Norway* 9 G14
Oslob, *Phil.* 61 G5
Oslofjorden, *Norway* 9 G14
Osmanabad, *India* 66 K10
Osmancık, *Turkey* 72 B6
Osmaniye, *Turkey* 70 B3
Osmanlı, *Turkey* 45 E10
Ösmo, *Sweden* 10 F11
Osnabrück, *Germany* 24 C4
Ośno Lubuskie, *Poland* 31 F1
Osoblaha, *Czech Rep.* 27 A10
Osogovska Planina, *Macedonia* 44 D6
Osor, *Italy* 41 D11
Osorio, *Brazil* 127 B5
Osorno, *Chile* 128 E2
Osorno, *Spain* 36 C6
Osoyoos, *Canada* 102 D5
Osøyro, *Norway* 9 F11
Ospika →, *Canada* 102 B4
Osprey Reef, *Australia* 94 A4
Oss, *Neths.* 17 C5
Ossa, Mt., *Australia* 95 G4
Óssa, Óros, *Greece* 46 B4
Ossa de Montiel, *Spain* 39 G2
Ossabaw I., *U.S.A.* 115 K5
Osse →, *France* 20 D4
Osse →, *Nigeria* 83 D6
Ossi, *Italy* 42 B1
Ossining, *U.S.A.* 117 E11
Ossipee, *U.S.A.* 117 C13
Ossokmanuan L., *Canada* 105 B7
Ossora, *Russia* 53 D17
Ostashkov, *Russia* 32 D7
Östavall, *Sweden* 10 B9
Oste →, *Germany* 24 B5
Ostend = Oostende, *Belgium* 17 C2
Oster, *Ukraine* 33 G6
Österbotten = Pohjanmaa, *Finland* 8 E20
Osterburg, *Germany* 24 C7
Osterburg, *U.S.A.* 116 F6
Osterburken, *Germany* 25 F5
Österbybruk, *Sweden* 10 D11
Österbymo, *Sweden* 11 G9
Österdalälven, *Sweden* 10 C7
Østerdalen, *Norway* 9 F14
Österfärnebo, *Sweden* 10 D10
Österforse, *Sweden* 10 A11
Östergötlands län □, *Sweden* 11 F9
Osterholz-Scharmbeck, *Germany* 24 B4
Østerild, *Denmark* 11 G2
Östermyra = Seinäjoki, *Finland* 9 E20
Osterode, *Germany* 24 D6
Östersund, *Sweden* 10 A8
Östervåla, *Sweden* 10 D11
Ostfriesische Inseln, *Germany* 24 B3
Ostfriesland, *Germany* 24 B3
Östhammar, *Sweden* 10 D12
Óstia, Lido di, *Italy* 41 G9
Ostíglia, *Italy* 41 C8
Östmark, *Sweden* 10 D6
Östra Husby, *Sweden* 11 F10
Ostrava, *Czech Rep.* 27 B11
Ostravský □, *Czech Rep.* 27 B10
Ostróda, *Poland* 30 E6
Ostrogozhsk, *Russia* 33 G10
Ostroh, *Ukraine* 33 G4
Ostrołęka, *Poland* 31 E8
Ostrov, *Bulgaria* 45 C8
Ostrov, *Czech Rep.* 26 A5
Ostrov, *Romania* 29 F12
Ostrov, *Russia* 32 D5
Ostrów Lubelski, *Poland* 31 G9
Ostrów Mazowiecka, *Poland* 31 F8
Ostrów Wielkopolski, *Poland* 31 G4
Ostrowiec-Świętokrzyski, *Poland* 31 H8
Ostrožac, *Bos.-H.* 28 G2
Ostrzeszów, *Poland* 31 G4
Ostseebad Kühlungsborn, *Germany* 24 A7
Osttirol □, *Austria* 26 E5
Ostuni, *Italy* 43 B10
Osum →, *Albania* 44 F4
Osŭm →, *Bulgaria* 45 C8
Ōsumi-Kaikyō, *Japan* 55 J5
Ōsumi-Shotō, *Japan* 55 J5
Osun □, *Nigeria* 83 D5
Osuna, *Spain* 37 H5
Oswegatchie →, *U.S.A.* 117 B9
Oswego, *U.S.A.* 117 C8
Oswego →, *U.S.A.* 117 C8
Oswestry, *U.K.* 14 E4
Oświęcim, *Poland* 31 H6
Otaci, *Moldova* 29 B12
Otago □, *N.Z.* 91 L2
Otago Harbour, *N.Z.* 91 L3
Otaheite B., *Trin. & Tob.* 125 K15
Ōtake, *Japan* 55 G6
Otaki, *N.Z.* 91 J5
Otaru, *Japan* 54 C10
Otaru-Wan = Ishikari-Wan, *Japan* 54 C10
Otava →, *Czech Rep.* 26 B7
Otavalo, *Ecuador* 124 C3
Otavi, *Namibia* 88 B2
Otchinjau, *Angola* 88 B1
Otelec, *Romania* 28 E5
Otelnuk, L., *Canada* 105 A6
Oţelu Roşu, *Romania* 28 E7
Otero de Rey = Outeiro de Rei, *Spain* 36 B3
Othello, *U.S.A.* 108 C4
Othonoí, *Greece* 46 B1
Óthris, Óros, *Greece* 46 B4
Oti ⌂, *Togo* 83 C5
Otjiwarongo, *Namibia* 88 C2
Otmuchów, *Poland* 31 H4
Otočac, *Croatia* 41 D12
Otoineppu, *Japan* 54 B11
Otok, *Croatia* 41 E13
Otopeni, Bucureşti ✈ (OTP), *Romania* 45 B10
Otorohanga, *N.Z.* 91 H5
Otoskwin →, *Canada* 104 B2
Otra →, *Norway* 9 G13
Otradnyy, *Russia* 34 D10
Otranto, *Italy* 43 B11
Otranto, C. d', *Italy* 43 B11
Otranto, Str. of, *Italy* 43 B11
Otrokovice, *Czech Rep.* 27 B10
Otse, *S. Africa* 88 D4
Ōtsu, *Japan* 55 G7
Ōtsuki, *Japan* 55 G9
Ottawa = Outaouais →, *Canada* 104 C5
Ottawa, *Canada* 117 A9
Ottawa, *Ill., U.S.A.* 112 E10
Ottawa, *Kans., U.S.A.* 112 F7
Ottawa Is., *Canada* 101 C11
Ottélé, *Cameroon* 83 E7
Ottensheim, *Austria* 26 C7
Otter Cr. →, *U.S.A.* 117 B11
Otter L., *Canada* 103 B8
Otterndorf, *Germany* 24 B4
Otterup, *Denmark* 11 J4
Otterville, *Canada* 116 D4
Ottery St. Mary, *U.K.* 15 G4
Otto Beit Bridge, *Zimbabwe* 87 F2
Ottosdal, *S. Africa* 88 D4
Ottumwa, *U.S.A.* 112 E8
Otu, *Nigeria* 83 D5
Otukpa, *Nigeria* 83 D6
Oturkpo, *Nigeria* 83 D6
Otway, B., *Chile* 128 G2
Otway, C., *Australia* 95 F3
Otwock, *Poland* 31 F8
Otyniya, *Ukraine* 29 B9
Ötztaler Ache →, *Austria* 26 D3
Ötztaler Alpen, *Austria* 26 E3
Ou →, *Laos* 64 B4
Ou Neua, *Laos* 58 F3
Ou-Sammyaku, *Japan* 54 E10
Ouachita →, *U.S.A.* 113 K9
Ouachita, L., *U.S.A.* 113 H8
Ouachita Mts., *U.S.A.* 113 H7
Ouagadougou, *Burkina Faso* 83 C4
Ouahigouya, *Burkina Faso* 82 C4
Ouahran = Oran, *Algeria* 78 A5
Oualâta, *Mauritania* 82 B3
Ouallam, *Niger* 83 C5
Ouallene, *Algeria* 78 D6
Ouargaye, *Burkina Faso* 83 C5
Ouargla, *Algeria* 78 B7
Ouarkoye, *Burkina Faso* 82 C4
Ouarzazate, *Morocco* 78 B4
Ouassouas, *Mali* 83 B5
Ouatagouna, *Mali* 83 B5
Oubangi →, *Dem. Rep. of the Congo* 84 E3
Ouche →, *France* 19 E12
Ouddorp, *Neths.* 17 C3
Oude Rijn →, *Neths.* 17 B4
Oudeïka, *Mali* 83 B4
Oudenaarde, *Belgium* 17 D3
Oudon →, *France* 18 E6
Oudtshoorn, *S. Africa* 88 E3
Ouellé, *Ivory C.* 82 D4
Ouémé →, *Benin* 83 D5
Ouessa, *Burkina Faso* 82 C4
Ouessant, Î. d', *France* 18 D1
Ouesso, *Congo* 84 D3
Ouest, Pte. de l', *Canada* 105 C7
Ouezzane, *Morocco* 78 B4
Ougarou, *Burkina Faso* 83 C5
Oughterard, *Ireland* 12 C2
Ouidah, *Benin* 83 D5
Ouidi, *Niger* 83 C7
Ouistreham, *France* 18 C6
Oujda, *Morocco* 78 B5
Oujeft, *Mauritania* 82 A2
Oulainen, *Finland* 8 D21
Ould Yenjé, *Mauritania* 82 B2
Oullins, *France* 21 C8
Oulu, *Finland* 8 D21
Oulujärvi, *Finland* 8 D22
Oulujoki →, *Finland* 8 D21
Oulx, *Italy* 40 C3
Oum Chalouba, *Chad* 79 E10
Oum Hadjer, *Chad* 79 F9
Oumé, *Ivory C.* 82 D3
Ounasjoki →, *Finland* 8 C21
Ounguati, *Namibia* 88 C2
Ounianga Sérir, *Chad* 79 E10
Our →, *Lux.* 17 E6
Ouranópolis, *Greece* 44 F7
Ourârene, *Niger* 83 B6
Ouray, *U.S.A.* 109 G10
Ourcq →, *France* 19 C10
Ourense, *Spain* 36 C3
Ouricuri, *Brazil* 125 E10
Ourinhos, *Brazil* 127 A6
Ourique, *Portugal* 37 H2
Ouro Fino, *Brazil* 127 A6
Ouro-Ndia, *Mali* 82 B4
Ouro Prêto, *Brazil* 127 A7
Ouro Sogui, *Senegal* 82 B2
Oursi, *Burkina Faso* 83 C4
Ourthe →, *Belgium* 17 D5
Ouse →, *E. Susx., U.K.* 15 G8
Ouse →, *N. Yorks., U.K.* 14 D7
Oust, *France* 20 F5
Oust →, *France* 18 E4
Outamba-Kilimi △, *S. Leone* 82 D2
Outaouais →, *Canada* 104 C5
Outardes →, *Canada* 105 C6
Outeiro de Rei, *Spain* 36 B3
Outer Hebrides, *U.K.* 13 D1
Outes = Serra de Outes, *Spain* 36 C2
Outjo, *Namibia* 88 C2
Outlook, *Canada* 103 C7
Outokumpu, *Finland* 8 E23
Outreau, *France* 19 B8
Ouvèze →, *France* 21 E8
Ouyen, *Australia* 95 F3
Ouzouer-le-Marché, *France* 19 E8
Ovada, *Italy* 40 D5
Ovalau, *Fiji* 91 C8
Ovalle, *Chile* 126 C1
Ovamboland, *Namibia* 88 B2
Ovar, *Portugal* 36 E2
Overath, *Germany* 24 E3
Overflakkee, *Neths.* 17 C4
Overijssel □, *Neths.* 17 B6
Overland Park, *U.S.A.* 112 F7
Overton, *U.S.A.* 111 J12
Övertorneå, *Sweden* 8 C20
Överum, *Sweden* 11 F10
Ovid, *U.S.A.* 117 D8
Ovidiopol, *Ukraine* 33 J6
Ovidiu, *Romania* 29 F13
Oviedo, *Spain* 36 B5
Oviksfjällen, *Sweden* 10 A7
Oviši, *Latvia* 9 H19
Ovoot, *Mongolia* 56 B7
Övör Hangay □, *Mongolia* 56 B2
Ovoro, *Nigeria* 83 D6
Øvre Årdal, *Norway* 9 F12
Övre Fryken, *Sweden* 10 E7
Ovruch, *Ukraine* 33 G5
Owaka, *N.Z.* 91 M2
Owambo = Ovamboland, *Namibia* 88 B2
Owasco L., *U.S.A.* 117 D8
Owase, *Japan* 55 G8
Owatonna, *U.S.A.* 112 C8
Owbeh, *Afghan.* 66 B3
Owego, *U.S.A.* 117 D8
Owen Falls Dam, *Uganda* 86 B3
Owen Sound, *Canada* 116 B4
Owens →, *U.S.A.* 110 J9
Owens L., *U.S.A.* 111 J9
Owensboro, *U.S.A.* 114 G2
Owerri, *Nigeria* 83 D6
Owl →, *Canada* 103 B10
Owo, *Nigeria* 83 D6
Owosso, *U.S.A.* 114 D3
Owyhee, *U.S.A.* 108 F5
Owyhee →, *U.S.A.* 108 E5
Owyhee, L., *U.S.A.* 108 E5
Ox Mts. = Slieve Gamph, *Ireland* 12 B3
Öxarfjörður, *Iceland* 8 C5
Oxbow, *Canada* 103 D8
Oxelösund, *Sweden* 11 F11
Oxford, *N.Z.* 91 K4
Oxford, *U.K.* 15 F6
Oxford, *Mass., U.S.A.* 117 D13
Oxford, *Miss., U.S.A.* 113 H10
Oxford, *N.C., U.S.A.* 115 G6
Oxford, *N.Y., U.S.A.* 117 D9
Oxford, *Ohio, U.S.A.* 114 F3
Oxford L., *Canada* 103 C9
Oxfordshire □, *U.K.* 15 F6
Oxía Nisís, *Greece* 46 C3
Oxie, *Sweden* 11 J7
Oxílithos, *Greece* 46 C6
Oxnard, *U.S.A.* 111 L7
Oxsjövålen, *Sweden* 10 B7
Oxus = Amudarya →, *Uzbekistan* 52 E6
Oya, *Malaysia* 62 D4
Oyama, *Japan* 55 F9
Oyambre ⌂, *Spain* 36 B6
Oyem, *Gabon* 84 D2
Oyen, *Canada* 103 C6
Oykel →, *U.K.* 13 D4
Oymyakon, *Russia* 53 C15
Oyo, *Nigeria* 83 D5
Oyo □, *Nigeria* 83 D5
Oyonnax, *France* 19 F12
Oyster Bay, *U.S.A.* 117 F11
Ōyübari, *Japan* 54 C11
Özalp, *Turkey* 73 C10
Ozamiz, *Phil.* 61 G5
Ozark, *Ala., U.S.A.* 115 K3
Ozark, *Ark., U.S.A.* 113 H8
Ozark, *Mo., U.S.A.* 113 G8
Ozark Plateau, *U.S.A.* 113 G9
Ozarks, L. of the, *U.S.A.* 112 F8
Ożarów, *Poland* 31 H8
Ózd, *Hungary* 28 B5
Ozernoye, *Russia* 34 E10
Ozero Svityaz, *Ukraine* 31 G10
Ozersk, *Russia* 30 D8
Ozette L., *U.S.A.* 110 B2
Ozieri, *Italy* 42 B2
Ozimek, *Poland* 31 H5
Ozinki, *Russia* 34 E9
Ozona, *U.S.A.* 113 K4
Ozorków, *Poland* 31 G6
Ozren, *Bos.-H.* 28 G3
Ozuluama, *Mexico* 119 C5
Ozun, *Romania* 29 E10
Ozurgeti, *Georgia* 35 K5

P

Pa, *Burkina Faso* 82 C4
Pa-an, *Burma* 67 L20
Pa Mong Dam, *Thailand* 64 D4
Pa Sak →, *Thailand* 62 B2
Paamiut, *Greenland* 101 B15
Paar →, *Germany* 25 G7
Paarl, *S. Africa* 88 E2
Pab Hills, *Pakistan* 68 F2
Pabbay, *U.K.* 13 D1
Pabianice, *Poland* 31 G6
Pabna, *Bangla.* 67 G16
Pabo, *Uganda* 86 B3
Pacaja →, *Brazil* 125 D8
Pacaraima, Sa., *S. Amer.* 124 C6
Pacasmayo, *Peru* 124 E3
Paceco, *Italy* 42 E5
Pachhar, *India* 68 G7
Pachino, *Italy* 43 F8
Pachitea →, *Peru* 124 E4
Pachmarhi, *India* 69 H8
Pachpadra, *India* 66 G8
Pachuca, *Mexico* 119 C5
Pacific, *Canada* 102 C3
Pacific-Antarctic Ridge, *Pac. Oc.* 97 M16
Pacific Grove, *U.S.A.* 110 J5
Pacific Ocean 97 G14
Pacific Rim △, *Canada* 102 D4
Pacifica, *U.S.A.* 110 H4
Pacitan, *Indonesia* 63 H14
Packwood, *U.S.A.* 110 D5
Pacov, *Czech Rep.* 26 B8
Pacy-sur-Eure, *France* 18 C8
Padaido, Kepulauan, *Indonesia* 63 E9
Padang, *Indonesia* 62 E2
Padang Endau, *Malaysia* 65 L4
Padangpanjang, *Indonesia* 62 E2
Padangsidempuan, *Indonesia* 62 D1
Padborg, *Denmark* 11 K3
Paddle Prairie, *Canada* 102 B5
Paddockwood, *Canada* 103 C7
Paderborn, *Germany* 24 D4
Padeş, Vf., *Romania* 28 E7
Padina, *Romania* 29 F12
Padma, *India* 69 G11
Pádova, *Italy* 41 C8
Padra, *India* 68 H5
Padrauna, *India* 69 F10
Padre I., *U.S.A.* 113 M6
Padre Island ⌂, *U.S.A.* 113 M6
Padrón, *Spain* 36 C2
Padstow, *U.K.* 15 G3
Padua = Pádova, *Italy* 41 C8
Paducah, *Ky., U.S.A.* 114 G1
Paducah, *Tex., U.S.A.* 113 H4
Padul, *Spain* 37 H7
Paengnyŏng-do, *S. Korea* 57 F13
Paeroa, *N.Z.* 91 G5
Paesana, *Italy* 40 D4
Pafúri, *Mozam.* 89 C5
Pag, *Croatia* 41 D12
Paga, *Ghana* 83 C4
Pagadian, *Phil.* 61 H5
Pagai Selatan, Pulau, *Indonesia* 62 E2
Pagai Utara, Pulau, *Indonesia* 62 E2
Pagalu = Annobón, *Atl. Oc.* 77 G4
Pagara, *India* 69 G9
Pagastikós Kólpos, *Greece* 46 B5
Pagatan, *Indonesia* 62 E5
Page, *U.S.A.* 109 H8
Pagėgiai, *Lithuania* 30 C8

Pago Pago, *Amer. Samoa* 91 B13
Pagosa Springs, *U.S.A.* 109 H10
Pagwa River, *Canada* 104 B2
Pahala, *U.S.A.* 106 J17
Pahang →, *Malaysia* 65 L4
Pahiatua, *N.Z.* 91 J5
Pahokee, *U.S.A.* 115 M5
Pahrump, *U.S.A.* 111 J11
Pahute Mesa, *U.S.A.* 110 H10
Pai, *Thailand* 64 C2
Paicines, *U.S.A.* 110 J5
Paide, *Estonia* 9 G21
Paignton, *U.K.* 15 G4
Paiho, *Taiwan* 59 F13
Päijänne, *Finland* 9 F21
Pailani, *India* 69 G9
Pailin, *Cambodia* 64 F4
Paimpol, *France* 18 D3
Painan, *Indonesia* 62 E2
Painesville, *U.S.A.* 116 E3
Paint Hills = Wemindji, *Canada* 104 B4
Paint L., *Canada* 103 B9
Painted Desert, *U.S.A.* 109 J8
Paintsville, *U.S.A.* 114 G4
País Vasco □, *Spain* 38 C2
Paisley, *Canada* 116 B3
Paisley, *U.K.* 13 F4
Paisley, *U.S.A.* 108 E3
Paita, *Peru* 124 E2
Paiva →, *Portugal* 36 D2
Paizhou, *China* 59 B9
Pajares, *Spain* 36 B5
Pajares, Puerto de, *Spain* 36 C5
Pajęczno, *Poland* 31 G5
Pak Lay, *Laos* 64 C3
Pak Phanang, *Thailand* 65 H3
Pak Sane, *Laos* 64 C4
Pak Song, *Laos* 64 E6
Pak Suong, *Laos* 58 H4
Pakaur, *India* 69 G12
Pakenham, *Canada* 117 A8
Pákhnes, *Greece* 49 D6
Pakhuis, *S. Africa* 88 E2
Pakistan ■, *Asia* 68 E4
Pakkading, *Laos* 64 C4
Paklenica △, *Croatia* 41 D12
Pakokku, *Burma* 67 J19
Pakość, *Poland* 31 F5
Pakowki L., *Canada* 103 D6
Pakpattan, *Pakistan* 68 D5
Pakrac, *Croatia* 28 E2
Pakruojis, *Lithuania* 30 C10
Paks, *Hungary* 28 D3
Paktīā □, *Afghan.* 66 C6
Paktīkā □, *Afghan.* 66 C6
Pakwach, *Uganda* 86 B3
Pakxe, *Laos* 64 E5
Pal Lahara, *India* 69 J11
Pala, *Chad* 79 G9
Pala, *Dem. Rep. of the Congo* 86 D2
Pala, *U.S.A.* 111 M9
Palabek, *Uganda* 86 B3
Palacios, *U.S.A.* 113 L6
Palafrugell, *Spain* 38 D8
Palagiano, *Italy* 43 B10
Palagonia, *Italy* 43 E7
Palagruža, *Croatia* 41 F13
Palaiókastron, *Greece* 49 D8
Palaiokhóra, *Greece* 49 D5
Pálairos, *Greece* 46 C2
Palaiseau, *France* 19 D9
Palam, *India* 66 K10
Palamás, *Greece* 46 B4
Palamòs, *Spain* 38 D8
Palampur, *India* 68 C7
Palamut, *Turkey* 47 C9
Palana, *Australia* 95 F4
Palana, *Russia* 53 D16
Palanan, *Phil.* 61 C5
Palanan Pt., *Phil.* 61 C5
Palandri, *Pakistan* 69 C5
Palanga, *Lithuania* 9 J19
Palangkaraya, *Indonesia* 62 E4
Palani Hills, *India* 66 P10
Palanpur, *India* 68 G5
Palapye, *Botswana* 88 C4
Palas, *Pakistan* 69 B5
Palas de Rei, *Spain* 36 C3
Palashi, *India* 69 H13
Palasponga, *India* 69 J11
Palatka, *Russia* 53 C16
Palatka, *U.S.A.* 115 L5
Palau, *Italy* 42 A2
Palau ■, *Pac. Oc.* 96 G5
Palauk, *Burma* 64 F2
Palawan, *Phil.* 61 G3
Palayankottai, *India* 66 Q10
Palazzo, Pte., *France* 21 F12
Palazzo San Gervásio, *Italy* 43 B8
Palazzolo Acréide, *Italy* 43 E7
Paldiski, *Estonia* 9 G21
Pale, *Bos.-H.* 28 G3
Paleleh, *Indonesia* 63 D6
Palembang, *Indonesia* 62 E2
Palencia, *Spain* 36 C6
Palencia □, *Spain* 36 C6
Palenque, *Mexico* 119 D6
Paleokastrítsa, *Greece* 49 A3
Paleometokho, *Cyprus* 49 D12
Palermo, *Italy* 42 D6
Palermo, *U.S.A.* 108 G3
Palermo ✕ (PMO), *Italy* 42 D6
Palestina, *Chile* 128 A3
Palestine, *Asia* 74 D4
Palestine, *U.S.A.* 113 K7
Palestrina, *Italy* 41 G9
Paletwa, *Burma* 67 J18
Palghat, *India* 66 P10
Palgrave, Mt., *Australia* 92 D2
Pali, *India* 68 G5
Palikir, *Micronesia* 96 G7
Palinuro, *Italy* 43 B8
Palinuro, C., *Italy* 43 B8
Palioúrion, Ákra, *Greece* 44 G7
Palisades Reservoir, *U.S.A.* 108 E8
Paliseul, *Belgium* 17 E5
Palitana, *India* 68 J4
Palizada, *Mexico* 119 D6
Palk Bay, *Asia* 66 Q11
Palk Strait, *Asia* 66 Q11
Palkānah, *Iraq* 70 C5
Palkot, *India* 69 H11
Pallanza = Verbánia, *Italy* 40 C5
Pallarenda, *Australia* 94 B4
Pallasovka, *Russia* 34 E8
Pallës, Bishti i, *Albania* 44 E3
Pallinup →, *Australia* 93 F2
Pallisa, *Uganda* 86 B3
Pallu, *India* 68 E6
Palm Bay, *U.S.A.* 115 L5
Palm Beach, *U.S.A.* 115 M6
Palm Coast, *U.S.A.* 115 L5
Palm Desert, *U.S.A.* 111 M10
Palm Is., *Australia* 94 B4
Palm Springs, *U.S.A.* 111 M10
Palma, *Mozam.* 87 E5
Palma, B. de, *Spain* 48 B9
Palma de Mallorca, *Spain* 48 B9
Palma de Mallorca ✕ (PMI), *Spain* 39 F7
Palma del Río, *Spain* 37 H5
Palma di Montechiaro, *Italy* 42 E6
Palma Soriano, *Cuba* 120 B4
Palmares, *Brazil* 125 E11
Palmarola, *Italy* 42 B5
Palmas, *Brazil* 127 B5
Palmas, C., *Liberia* 82 E3
Pálmas, G. di, *Italy* 42 D1
Palmdale, *U.S.A.* 111 L8
Palmeira das Missões, *Brazil* 127 B5
Palmeira dos Índios, *Brazil* 125 E11
Palmela, *Portugal* 37 G2
Palmer, *Antarctica* 5 C17
Palmer, *U.S.A.* 100 B5
Palmer →, *Australia* 94 B3
Palmer Arch., *Antarctica* 5 C17
Palmer Lake, *U.S.A.* 112 F2
Palmer Land, *Antarctica* 5 D18
Palmerston, *Australia* 92 B5
Palmerston, *Canada* 116 C4
Palmerston, *N.Z.* 91 L3
Palmerston North, *N.Z.* 91 J5
Palmerton, *U.S.A.* 117 F9
Palmetto, *U.S.A.* 115 M4
Palmi, *Italy* 43 D8
Palmira, *Argentina* 126 C2
Palmira, *Colombia* 124 C3
Palmyra = Tudmur, *Syria* 70 C3
Palmyra, *Mo., U.S.A.* 112 F9
Palmyra, *N.J., U.S.A.* 117 F9
Palmyra, *N.Y., U.S.A.* 116 C7
Palmyra, *Pa., U.S.A.* 117 F8
Palmyra Is., *Pac. Oc.* 97 G11
Palo Alto, *U.S.A.* 110 H4
Palo Seco, *Trin. & Tob.* 125 K15
Palo Verde, *U.S.A.* 111 M12
Palo Verde △, *Costa Rica* 120 D2
Paloich, *Sudan* 81 E3
Palomar Mt., *U.S.A.* 111 M10
Palompon, *Phil.* 61 F6
Palopo, *Indonesia* 63 E6
Palos, C. de, *Spain* 39 H4
Palos de la Frontera, *Spain* 37 H4
Palos Verdes, *U.S.A.* 111 M8
Palos Verdes, Pt., *U.S.A.* 111 M8
Pålsboda, *Sweden* 10 E9
Palu, *Indonesia* 63 E5
Palu, *Turkey* 70 B3
Paluke, *Liberia* 82 D3
Paluzza, *Italy* 41 B10
Palwal, *India* 68 E7
Pama, *Burkina Faso* 83 C5
Pama ⌓, *Burkina Faso* 83 C5
Pamanukan, *Indonesia* 63 G12
Pamekasan, *Indonesia* 63 G15
Pamenang, *Indonesia* 63 J19
Pamiers, *France* 20 E5
Pamir, *Tajikistan* 52 F8
Pamlico →, *U.S.A.* 115 H7
Pamlico Sd., *U.S.A.* 115 H8
Pampa, *U.S.A.* 113 H4
Pampa de las Salinas, *Argentina* 126 C2
Pampanua, *Indonesia* 63 E6
Pampas, *Argentina* 126 D3
Pampas, *Peru* 124 F4
Pamphylia, *Turkey* 72 D4
Pamplona, *Colombia* 124 B4
Pamplona, *Spain* 38 C3
Pampoenpoort, *S. Africa* 88 E3
Pamukçu, *Turkey* 47 B9
Pamukkale, *Turkey* 47 D11
Pan de Azúcar △, *Chile* 126 B1
Pan Xian, *China* 58 E5
Pana, *U.S.A.* 112 F10
Panabo, *Phil.* 61 H6
Panaca, *U.S.A.* 109 H6
Panagyurishte, *Bulgaria* 45 D8
Panaitan, *Indonesia* 63 G11
Panaji, *India* 66 M8
Panamá, *Panama* 120 E4
Panama ■, *Cent. Amer.* 120 E4
Panamá, G. de, *Panama* 120 E4
Panama Canal, *Panama* 120 E4
Panama City, *U.S.A.* 115 K3
Panamint Range, *U.S.A.* 111 J9
Panamint Springs, *U.S.A.* 111 J9
Panão, *Peru* 124 E3
Panaon I., *Phil.* 61 F6
Panare, *Thailand* 65 J3
Panarea, *Italy* 43 D8
Panaro →, *Italy* 41 D8
Panay, *Phil.* 61 F5
Panay, G., *Phil.* 63 B6
Pančevo, *Serbia & M.* 28 F5
Panch'iao, *Taiwan* 59 E13
Panciu, *Romania* 29 E12
Pancorbo, Desfiladero, *Spain* 36 C7
Pâncota, *Romania* 28 D6
Panda, *Mozam.* 89 C5
Pandan, *Malaysia* 65 d
Pandan, *Antique, Phil.* 61 F5
Pandan, *Catanduanes, Phil.* 61 D6
Pandan, Selat, *Singapore* 65 d
Pandan Tampoi = Tampoi, *Malaysia* 65 d
Pandegelang, *Indonesia* 63 G12
Pandhana, *India* 68 J7
Pandharpur, *India* 66 L9
Pando, *Uruguay* 127 C4
Pando, L. = Hope, L., *Australia* 95 D2
Pandokrátor, *Greece* 49 A3
Pandora, *Costa Rica* 120 E3
Pandrup, *Denmark* 11 G3
Panevéggio-Pale di San Martino ⌓, *Italy* 41 B8
Panevėžys, *Lithuania* 9 J21
Panfilov, *Kazakhstan* 52 E8
Panfilovo, *Russia* 34 E6
Pang-Long, *Burma* 67 H21
Pang Sida △, *Thailand* 64 E4
Pang-Yang, *Burma* 67 H21
Panga, *Dem. Rep. of the Congo* 86 B2
Pangaíon Óros, *Greece* 45 F8
Pangalanes, Canal des = Ampangalana, Lakandranon', *Madag.* 89 C8
Pangani, *Tanzania* 86 D4
Pangani →, *Tanzania* 86 D4
Pangfou = Bengbu, *China* 57 H9
Pangil, *Dem. Rep. of the Congo* 86 C2
Pangkah, Tanjung, *Indonesia* 63 G15
Pangkajene, *Indonesia* 63 E5
Pangkalanbrandan, *Indonesia* 62 D1
Pangkalanbuun, *Indonesia* 62 E4
Pangkalpinang, *Indonesia* 62 E3
Pangnirtung, *Canada* 101 B13
Pangong Tso, *India* 68 B8
Panguitch, *U.S.A.* 109 H7
Pangutaran Group, *Phil.* 61 H4
Panhandle, *U.S.A.* 113 H4
Pani Mines, *India* 68 H5
Pania-Mutombo, *Dem. Rep. of the Congo* 86 D1
Panikota I., *India* 68 J4
Panipat, *India* 68 E7
Panjal Range = Pir Panjal Range, *India* 68 C7
Panjang, Hon, *Vietnam* 65 H4
Panjgur, *Pakistan* 66 F4
Panjim = Panaji, *India* 66 M8
Panjin, *China* 57 D12
Panjinad Barrage, *Pakistan* 66 E7
Panjnad →, *Pakistan* 68 E4
Panjwai, *Afghan.* 68 D1
Pankshin, *Nigeria* 83 D6
Panmunjŏm, *N. Korea* 57 F14
Panna, *India* 69 G9
Panna Hills, *India* 69 G9
Pannawonica, *Australia* 92 D2
Pannga, Tanjung, *Indonesia* 63 K19
Pannirtuuq = Pangnirtung, *Canada* 101 B13
Pano Akil, *Pakistan* 68 F3
Pano Lefkara, *Cyprus* 49 E12
Pano Panayia, *Cyprus* 49 E11
Panorama, *Brazil* 127 A5
Pánormon, *Greece* 49 D6
Pansemal, *India* 68 J6
Panshan = Panjin, *China* 57 D12
Panshi, *China* 57 C14
Pantanal, *Brazil* 124 H7
Pantanos de Centla ⌓, *Mexico* 119 D6
Pantar, *Indonesia* 63 F6
Pante Macassar, *E. Timor* 63 F6
Pante Makasar = Pante Macassar, *E. Timor* 63 F6
Pantelleria, *Italy* 42 F4
Pantón, *Spain* 36 C3
Pánuco, *Mexico* 119 C5
Panyam, *Nigeria* 83 D6
Panyu, *China* 59 F9
Panzhihua, *China* 58 D3
Páola, *Italy* 43 C9
Paola, *Malta* 49 D2
Paola, *U.S.A.* 112 F7
Paonia, *U.S.A.* 109 G10
Paoting = Baoding, *China* 56 E8
Paot'ou = Baotou, *China* 56 D6
Paoua, *C.A.R.* 84 C3
Pápa, *Hungary* 28 C2
Papa Stour, *U.K.* 13 A7
Papa Westray, *U.K.* 13 B6
Papagayo →, *Mexico* 119 D5
Papagayo, G. de, *Costa Rica* 120 D2
Papakura, *N.Z.* 91 G5
Papantla, *Mexico* 119 C5
Papar, *Malaysia* 62 C5
Paparoa △, *N.Z.* 91 K3
Pápas, Ákra, *Greece* 46 C3
Papeete, *Tahiti* 97 J13
Papenburg, *Germany* 24 B3
Paphlagonia, *Turkey* 72 B5
Paphos, *Cyprus* 49 E11
Papigochic →, *Mexico* 118 B3
Paposo, *Chile* 126 B1
Papoutsa, *Cyprus* 49 E12
Papua □, *Indonesia* 63 E9
Papua New Guinea ■, *Oceania* 96 H6
Papudo, *Chile* 126 C1
Papuk, *Croatia* 28 E2
Papun, *Burma* 67 K20
Papunya, *Australia* 92 D5
Pará = Belém, *Brazil* 125 D9
Pará □, *Brazil* 125 D8
Paraburdoo, *Australia* 92 D2
Paracale, *Phil.* 61 D5
Paracatu, *Brazil* 125 G9
Paracel Is., *S. China Sea* 62 A4
Parachilna, *Australia* 95 E2
Parachinar, *Pakistan* 68 C4
Paraćin, *Serbia & M.* 44 C5
Paradas, *Spain* 37 H5
Paradela, *Spain* 36 C3
Paradhísi, *Greece* 49 C10
Paradip, *India* 67 J15
Paradise, *Calif., U.S.A.* 110 F5
Paradise, *Nev., U.S.A.* 111 J11
Paradise →, *Canada* 105 B8
Paradise Hill, *Canada* 103 C7
Paradise River, *Canada* 105 B8
Paradise Valley, *U.S.A.* 108 F5
Parado, *Indonesia* 63 F5
Paragould, *U.S.A.* 113 G9
Paragua →, *Venezuela* 124 B6
Paraguaçu →, *Brazil* 125 F11
Paraguaçu Paulista, *Brazil* 127 A5
Paraguaná, Pen. de, *Venezuela* 124 A5
Paraguarí, *Paraguay* 126 B4
Paraguarí □, *Paraguay* 126 B4
Paraguay ■, *S. Amer.* 126 A4
Paraguay →, *Paraguay* 126 B4
Paraíba = João Pessoa, *Brazil* 125 E12
Paraíba □, *Brazil* 125 E11
Paraíba do Sul →, *Brazil* 127 A7
Parainen, *Finland* 9 F20
Paraiso, *Mexico* 119 D6
Parak, *Iran* 71 E7
Parakhino Paddubye, *Russia* 32 C7
Parakou, *Benin* 83 D5
Paralimni, *Cyprus* 49 D12
Parálion-Astrous, *Greece* 46 D4
Paramaribo, *Suriname* 125 B7
Paramithiá, *Greece* 46 B2
Páramos del Batallón y La Negra △, *Venezuela* 121 E5
Paramushir, Ostrov, *Russia* 53 D16
Paran →, *Israel* 74 E4
Paraná, *Argentina* 126 C3
Paraná, *Brazil* 125 F9
Paraná □, *Brazil* 127 A5
Paraná →, *Argentina* 126 C4
Paranaguá, *Brazil* 127 B6
Paranaíba, *Brazil* 125 G8
Paranaíba →, *Brazil* 125 H8
Paranapanema →, *Brazil* 127 A5
Paranapiacaba, Serra do, *Brazil* 127 A6
Paranas, *Phil.* 61 F6
Paranavaí, *Brazil* 127 A5
Parang, *Maguindanao, Phil.* 63 C6
Parang, *Sulu, Phil.* 61 J4
Parângul Mare, Vf., *Romania* 29 E8
Paraparaumu, *N.Z.* 91 J5
Parapóla, *Greece* 46 E5
Paraspóri, Ákra, *Greece* 47 F9
Paray-le-Monial, *France* 19 F11
Parbati →, *Mad. P., India* 68 G7
Parbati →, *Raj., India* 68 F7
Parbhani, *India* 66 K10
Parchim, *Germany* 24 B7
Parczew, *Poland* 31 G9
Pardes Hanna-Karkur, *Israel* 74 C3
Pardilla, *Spain* 36 D7
Pardo →, *Bahia, Brazil* 125 G11
Pardo →, *Mato Grosso, Brazil* 127 A5
Pardubice, *Czech Rep.* 26 A8
Pardubický □, *Czech Rep.* 26 B8
Pare, *Indonesia* 63 G15
Pare Mts., *Tanzania* 86 C4
Parecis, Serra dos, *Brazil* 124 F7
Paredes de Nava, *Spain* 36 C6
Paren, *Russia* 53 C17
Parent, *Canada* 104 C5
Parent, L., *Canada* 104 C4
Parentis-en-Born, *France* 20 D2
Parepare, *Indonesia* 63 E5
Parfino, *Russia* 32 D6
Párga, *Greece* 46 B2
Pargas = Parainen, *Finland* 9 F20
Pargo, Pta. do, *Madeira* 48 D2
Paria, G. de, *Venezuela* 125 K14
Pariaguán, *Venezuela* 124 B6
Paricutín, Cerro, *Mexico* 118 D4
Parigi, *Indonesia* 63 E6
Parika, *Guyana* 124 B7
Parikkala, *Finland* 32 B5
Parima, Serra, *Brazil* 124 C6
Parinari, *Peru* 124 D4
Pariñas, Pta., *S. Amer.* 122 D2
Parincea, *Romania* 29 D12
Parintins, *Brazil* 125 D7
Pariparit Kyun, *Burma* 67 M18
Paris, *Canada* 116 C4
Paris, *France* 19 D9
Paris, *Idaho, U.S.A.* 108 E8
Paris, *Ky., U.S.A.* 114 F3
Paris, *Tenn., U.S.A.* 115 G1
Paris, *Tex., U.S.A.* 113 J7
Paris, Ville de □, *France* 19 D9
Paris Charles de Gaulle ✕ (CDG), *France* 19 D9
Paris Orly ✕ (ORY), *France* 19 D9
Parish, *U.S.A.* 117 C8
Parishville, *U.S.A.* 117 B10
Park, *U.S.A.* 110 B4
Park City, *U.S.A.* 113 G6
Park Falls, *U.S.A.* 112 C9
Park Head, *Canada* 116 B3
Park Hills, *U.S.A.* 113 G9
Park Range, *U.S.A.* 108 G10
Park Rapids, *U.S.A.* 112 B7
Park River, *U.S.A.* 112 A6
Park Rynie, *S. Africa* 89 E5
Parkā Bandar, *Iran* 71 E8
Parkano, *Finland* 9 E20
Parker, *Ariz., U.S.A.* 111 L12
Parker, *Pa., U.S.A.* 116 E5
Parker Dam, *U.S.A.* 111 L12
Parkersburg, *U.S.A.* 114 F5
Parkes, *Australia* 95 E4
Parkfield, *U.S.A.* 110 K6
Parkhill, *Canada* 116 C3
Parkland, *U.S.A.* 110 C4
Parkston, *U.S.A.* 112 D6
Parksville, *Canada* 102 D4
Parla, *Spain* 36 E7
Pârliţa, *Moldova* 29 C12
Parma, *Italy* 40 D7
Parma, *Idaho, U.S.A.* 108 E5
Parma, *Ohio, U.S.A.* 116 E3
Parma →, *Italy* 40 D7
Paranaguá, *Brazil* 125 F10
Parnaíba, *Brazil* 125 D10
Parnaíba →, *Brazil* 125 D10
Parnassós, *Greece* 46 C4
Párnis, *Greece* 46 C5
Párnitha △, *Greece* 46 C5
Párnon Óros, *Greece* 46 D4
Pärnu, *Estonia* 9 G21
Paroo →, *Australia* 95 E3
Páros, *Greece* 47 D7
Parowan, *U.S.A.* 109 H7
Parpaillon, *France* 21 D10
Parral, *Chile* 126 D1
Parras, *Mexico* 118 B4
Parrett →, *U.K.* 15 F4
Parris I., *U.S.A.* 115 J5
Parrsboro, *Canada* 105 C7
Parry I., *Canada* 116 A4
Parry Is., *Canada* 98 B8
Parry Sound, *Canada* 116 A5
Parsberg, *Germany* 25 F7
Parsęta →, *Poland* 30 D2
Parsnip →, *Canada* 102 B4
Parsons, *U.S.A.* 113 G7
Parsons Ra., *Australia* 94 A2
Partanna, *Italy* 42 E5
Partenio ⌓, *Italy* 43 B7
Parthenay, *France* 18 F6
Partinico, *Italy* 42 D6
Partizánske, *Slovak Rep.* 27 C11
Partridge I., *Canada* 104 A2
Paru →, *Brazil* 125 D8
Parvān □, *Afghan.* 66 B6
Parvatipuram, *India* 67 K13
Parvatsar, *India* 68 F6
Påryd, *Sweden* 11 H9
Parys, *S. Africa* 88 D4
Pas, Pta. des, *Spain* 48 C7
Pas-de-Calais □, *France* 19 B9
Pasada, *Spain* 36 B5
Pasadena, *Canada* 105 C8
Pasadena, *Calif., U.S.A.* 111 L8
Pasadena, *Tex., U.S.A.* 113 L7
Pasaje →, *Argentina* 126 B3
Paşalimanı, *Turkey* 45 F11
Pasar, *Indonesia* 63 J17
Pasay, *Phil.* 61 D4
Pascagoula, *U.S.A.* 113 K10
Pascagoula →, *U.S.A.* 113 K10
Paşcani, *Romania* 29 C11
Pasco, *U.S.A.* 108 C4
Pasco, Cerro de, *Peru* 124 F3
Pasco I., *Australia* 92 D2
Pascoag, *U.S.A.* 117 E13
Pascua, I. de, *Chile* 97 K17
Pasewalk, *Germany* 24 B9
Pasfield L., *Canada* 103 B7
Pasha →, *Russia* 32 B7
Pasinler, *Turkey* 73 C9
Pasir Mas, *Malaysia* 65 J4
Pasir Panjang, *Singapore* 65 d
Pasir Putih, *Malaysia* 65 K4
Pasirian, *Indonesia* 63 H15
Pasirkuning, *Indonesia* 62 E2
Påskallavik, *Sweden* 11 G10
Paskūh, *Iran* 71 E9
Pasłęk, *Poland* 30 D6
Pasłęka →, *Poland* 30 D6
Pasley, C., *Australia* 93 F3
Pašman, *Croatia* 41 E12
Pasni, *Pakistan* 66 G3
Paso Cantinela, *Mexico* 111 N11
Paso de Indios, *Argentina* 128 E3
Paso de los Libres, *Argentina* 126 B4
Paso de los Toros, *Uruguay* 126 C4
Paso Robles, *U.S.A.* 109 J3
Paspébiac, *Canada* 105 C6
Pasrur, *Pakistan* 68 C6
Passage West, *Ireland* 12 E3
Passaic, *U.S.A.* 117 F10
Passau, *Germany* 25 G9
Passero, C., *Italy* 43 F8
Passo Fundo, *Brazil* 127 B5
Passos, *Brazil* 125 H9
Passow, *Germany* 24 B10
Passy, *France* 21 C10
Pastavy, *Belarus* 9 J22
Pastaza →, *Peru* 124 D3
Pasto, *Colombia* 124 C3
Pastrana, *Spain* 38 E2
Pasuruan, *Indonesia* 63 G15
Pasym, *Poland* 30 E7
Pásztó, *Hungary* 28 C4
Patagonia, *Argentina* 128 F3
Patagonia, *U.S.A.* 109 L8
Patambar, *Iran* 71 D9
Patan = Lalitapur, *Nepal* 69 F11
Patan, *Gujarat, India* 66 H8
Patan, *Maharashtra, India* 68 H5
Patani, *Indonesia* 63 D7
Pătârlagele, *Romania* 29 E11
Pataudi, *India* 68 E7
Patchewollock, *Australia* 95 F3
Patchogue, *U.S.A.* 117 F11
Pate, *Kenya* 86 C5
Patea, *N.Z.* 91 H5
Pategi, *Nigeria* 83 D6
Patensie, *S. Africa* 88 E3
Paterna, *Spain* 39 F4
Paternion, *Austria* 26 E6

Paternò, *Italy* 43 E7
Pateros, *U.S.A.* 108 B4
Paterson, *U.S.A.* 117 F10
Paterson Ra., *Australia* 92 D3
Pathankot, *India* 68 C6
Pathein = Bassein, *Burma* 67 L19
Pathfinder Reservoir, *U.S.A.* 108 E10
Pathiu, *Thailand* 65 G2
Pathum Thani, *Thailand* 64 E3
Pati, *Indonesia* 63 G14
Patía →, *Colombia* 124 C3
Patiala, *Punjab, India* 68 D7
Patiala, *Ut. P., India* 69 F8
Patine Kouka, *Senegal* 82 C2
Patitírion, *Greece* 46 B5
Patkai Bum, *India* 67 F19
Pátmos, *Greece* 47 D8
Patna, *India* 69 G11
Patnos, *Turkey* 73 C10
Pato Branco, *Brazil* 127 B5
Patong, Ao, *Thailand* 65 a
Patonga, *Uganda* 86 B3
Patos, *Albania* 44 F3
Patos, *Brazil* 125 E11
Patos, L. dos, *Brazil* 127 C5
Patos, Río de los →, *Argentina* 126 C2
Patos de Minas, *Brazil* 125 G9
Patquía, *Argentina* 126 C2
Pátrai, *Greece* 46 C3
Pátraikós Kólpos, *Greece* 46 C3
Patras = Pátrai, *Greece* 46 C3
Patrocínio, *Brazil* 125 G9
Pattada, *Italy* 42 B2
Pattani, *Thailand* 65 J3
Pattaya, *Thailand* 62 B2
Patten, *U.S.A.* 115 C11
Patterson, *Calif., U.S.A.* 110 H5
Patterson, *La., U.S.A.* 113 L9
Patterson, Mt., *U.S.A.* 110 G7
Patti, *Punjab, India* 68 D6
Patti, *Ut. P., India* 69 G10
Patti, *Italy* 43 D7
Pattoki, *Pakistan* 68 D5
Patton, *U.S.A.* 116 F6
Patuakhali, *Bangla.* 67 H17
Patuanak, *Canada* 103 B7
Patuca △, *Honduras* 120 D2
Patuca →, *Honduras* 120 C3
Patuca, Punta, *Honduras* 120 C3
Pătulele, *Romania* 28 F7
Pátzcuaro, *Mexico* 118 D4
Pau, *France* 20 E3
Pau, Gave de →, *France* 20 E2
Pauillac, *France* 20 C3
Pauk, *Burma* 67 J19
Paul I., *Canada* 105 A7
Paul Smiths, *U.S.A.* 117 B10
Paulatuk, *Canada* 100 B7
Paulhan, *France* 20 E7
Paulistana, *Brazil* 125 E10
Paulo Afonso, *Brazil* 125 E11
Paulpietersburg, *S. Africa* 89 D5
Pauls Valley, *U.S.A.* 113 H6
Pauma Valley, *U.S.A.* 111 M10
Pauri, *India* 69 D8
Pāveh, *Iran* 70 C5
Pavelets, *Russia* 32 F10
Pavia, *Italy* 40 C6
Pavilion, *U.S.A.* 116 D6
Pavilly, *France* 18 C7
Pāvilosta, *Latvia* 9 H19
Pavlikeni, *Bulgaria* 45 C9
Pavlodar, *Kazakhstan* 52 D8
Pavlograd = Pavlohrad, *Ukraine* 33 H8
Pavlohrad, *Ukraine* 33 H8
Pavlovo, *Russia* 34 C6
Pavlovsk, *Russia* 34 E5
Pavlovskaya, *Russia* 35 G4
Pavlovskiy-Posad, *Russia* 32 E10
Pavullo nel Frignano, *Italy* 40 D7
Pawai, Pulau, *Singapore* 65 d
Pawayan, *India* 69 E9
Pawhuska, *U.S.A.* 113 G6
Pawling, *U.S.A.* 117 E11
Pawnee, *U.S.A.* 113 G6
Pawnee City, *U.S.A.* 112 E6
Pawtucket, *U.S.A.* 117 E13
Paximádhia, *Greece* 49 E6
Paxoí, *Greece* 46 B2
Paxton, *Ill., U.S.A.* 114 E1
Paxton, *Nebr., U.S.A.* 112 E4
Payakumbuh, *Indonesia* 62 E2
Payerne, *Switz.* 25 J2
Payette, *U.S.A.* 108 D5
Paymogo, *Spain* 37 H3
Payne Bay = Kangirsuk, *Canada* 101 B13
Payne L., *Canada* 101 C12
Paynes Find, *Australia* 93 E2
Paynesville, *Liberia* 82 D2
Paynesville, *U.S.A.* 112 C7
Pays de la Loire □, *France* 18 E6
Paysandú, *Uruguay* 126 C4
Payson, *U.S.A.* 109 J8
Paz →, *Guatemala* 120 D1
Paz, B. de la, *Mexico* 118 C2
Pāzanān, *Iran* 71 D6
Pazar, *Turkey* 73 B9
Pazarcık, *Turkey* 72 D7
Pazardzhik, *Bulgaria* 45 D8
Pazarköy, *Turkey* 47 B9
Pazarlar, *Turkey* 47 C11
Pazaryeri, *Turkey* 47 B11
Pazaryolu, *Turkey* 73 B9
Pazin, *Croatia* 41 C10
Pčinja →, *Macedonia* 44 E5
Pe Ell, *U.S.A.* 110 D3
Peabody, *U.S.A.* 117 D14
Peace →, *Canada* 102 B6
Peace Point, *Canada* 102 B6
Peace River, *Canada* 102 B5
Peach Springs, *U.S.A.* 109 J7
Peachland, *Canada* 102 D5
Peachtree City, *U.S.A.* 115 J3
Peak, The = Kinder Scout, *U.K.* 14 D6
Peak Charles △, *Australia* 93 F3
Peak District △, *U.K.* 14 D6
Peak Hill, *N.S.W., Australia* 95 E4
Peak Hill, *W. Austral., Australia* 93 E2
Peak Ra., *Australia* 94 C4
Peake Cr. →, *Australia* 95 D2
Peal de Becerro, *Spain* 37 H7
Peale, Mt., *U.S.A.* 109 G9
Pearblossom, *U.S.A.* 111 L9
Pearl →, *U.S.A.* 113 K10
Pearl City, *U.S.A.* 106 H16
Pearl Harbor, *U.S.A.* 106 H16
Pearl River = Zhu Jiang →, *China* 59 F9
Pearl River, *U.S.A.* 117 E10
Pearsall, *U.S.A.* 113 L5
Peary Land, *Greenland* 4 A6
Pease →, *U.S.A.* 113 H5
Peawanuck, *Canada* 101 C11
Pebane, *Mozam.* 87 F4
Pebas, *Peru* 124 D4
Pebble Beach, *U.S.A.* 110 J5
Peć, *Serbia & M.* 44 D4
Pécciolі, *Italy* 40 E7
Pechea, *Romania* 29 E12
Pechenga, *Russia* 52 C4
Pechenizhyn, *Ukraine* 29 B9
Pechiguera, Pta., *Canary Is.* 48 F6
Pechnezhskoye Vdkhr., *Ukraine* 33 G9
Pechora, *Russia* 52 C6
Pechora →, *Russia* 52 C6
Pechorskaya Guba, *Russia* 52 C6
Pechory, *Russia* 9 H22
Pecica, *Romania* 28 D6
Pecka, *Serbia & M.* 44 B3
Pécora, C., *Italy* 42 C1
Pecos, *U.S.A.* 113 K3
Pecos →, *U.S.A.* 113 L3
Pécs, *Hungary* 28 D3
Pedder, L., *Australia* 95 G4
Peddie, *S. Africa* 89 E4
Pedernales, *Dom. Rep.* 121 C5
Pedieos →, *Cyprus* 49 D12
Pedirka, *Australia* 95 D2
Pedra Azul, *Brazil* 125 G10
Pedreguer, *Spain* 39 G5
Pedreiras, *Brazil* 125 D10
Pedro Afonso, *Brazil* 125 E9
Pedro Cays, *Jamaica* 120 C4
Pedro de Valdivia, *Chile* 126 A2
Pedro Juan Caballero, *Paraguay* 127 A4
Pedro Muñoz, *Spain* 37 F8
Pedrógão Grande, *Portugal* 36 F2
Pee Dee →, *U.S.A.* 115 J6
Peebinga, *Australia* 95 E3
Peebles, *U.K.* 13 F5
Peekskill, *U.S.A.* 117 E11
Peel, *I. of Man* 14 C3
Peel →, *Australia* 95 E5
Peel →, *Canada* 100 B6
Peel Sd., *Canada* 100 A10
Peene →, *Germany* 24 A9
Peera Peera Poolanna L., *Australia* 95 D2
Peerless Lake, *Canada* 102 B6
Peers, *Canada* 102 C5
Pegasus Bay, *N.Z.* 91 K4
Peggau, *Austria* 26 D8
Pegnitz, *Germany* 25 F7
Pegnitz →, *Germany* 25 F6
Pego, *Spain* 39 G4
Pegu, *Burma* 67 L20
Pegu Yoma, *Burma* 67 K20
Pehčevo, *Macedonia* 44 E6
Pehlivanköy, *Turkey* 45 E10
Pehuajó, *Argentina* 126 D3
Pei Xian = Pizhou, *China* 56 G9
Peine, *Chile* 126 A2
Peine, *Germany* 24 C6
Peip'ing = Beijing, *China* 56 E9
Peipus, L. = Chudskoye, Ozero, *Russia* 9 G22
Peissenberg, *Germany* 25 H7
Peitz, *Germany* 24 D10
Peixe, *Brazil* 125 F9
Peixe →, *Brazil* 125 H8
Pek →, *Serbia & M.* 44 B5
Pekalongan, *Indonesia* 63 G13
Pekan, *Malaysia* 65 L4
Pekan Nenas, *Malaysia* 65 d
Pekanbaru, *Indonesia* 62 D2
Pekang, *Taiwan* 59 F13
Pekin, *U.S.A.* 112 E10
Peking = Beijing, *China* 56 E9
Pekutatan, *Indonesia* 63 J17
Péla, *Guinea* 82 D3
Pelabuhan Klang, *Malaysia* 65 L3
Pelabuhan Ratu, Teluk, *Indonesia* 63 G12
Pelabuhanratu, *Indonesia* 63 G12
Pélagos, *Greece* 46 B6
Pelaihari, *Indonesia* 62 E4
Pelat, Mt., *France* 21 D10
Pełczyce, *Poland* 31 E2
Peleaga, Vf., *Romania* 28 E7
Pelée, Mt., *Martinique* 120 c
Pelee, Pt., *Canada* 104 D3
Pelee I., *Canada* 116 E2
Pelekech, *Kenya* 86 B4
Peleng, *Indonesia* 63 E6
Pelentong, *Malaysia* 65 d
Pélézi, *Ivory C.* 82 D3
Pelhřimov, *Czech Rep.* 26 B8
Pelican, *U.S.A.* 102 B1
Pelican L., *Canada* 103 C8
Pelican Narrows, *Canada* 103 B8
Pelister △, *Macedonia* 44 F5
Pelješac, *Croatia* 41 F14
Pelkosenniemi, *Finland* 8 C22
Pella, *Greece* 44 F6
Pella, *S. Africa* 88 D2
Pella, *U.S.A.* 112 E8
Pélla □, *Greece* 44 F6
Pello, *Finland* 8 C21
Pellworm, *Germany* 24 A4
Pelly →, *Canada* 100 B6
Pelly Bay, *Canada* 101 B11
Peloponnese = Pelopónnisos □, *Greece* 46 D4
Pelopónnisos □, *Greece* 46 D4
Peloritani, Monti, *Italy* 43 D8
Pelorus Sd., *N.Z.* 91 J4
Pelotas, *Brazil* 127 C5
Pelotas →, *Brazil* 127 B5
Pelovo, *Bulgaria* 45 C8
Pelplin, *Poland* 30 E5
Pelvoux, Massif du, *France* 21 D10
Pemalang, *Indonesia* 63 G13
Pemanggil, Pulau, *Malaysia* 65 L5
Pematangsiantar, *Indonesia* 62 D1
Pemba, *Mozam.* 87 E5
Pemba, *Zambia* 87 F2
Pemba Channel, *Tanzania* 86 D4
Pemba I., *Tanzania* 86 D4
Pemberton, *Australia* 93 F2
Pemberton, *Canada* 102 C4
Pembina, *U.S.A.* 112 A6
Pembroke, *Canada* 104 C4
Pembroke, *U.K.* 15 F3
Pembrokeshire □, *U.K.* 15 F3
Pembrokeshire Coast △, *U.K.* 15 F2
Pen-y-Ghent, *U.K.* 14 C5
Peña, Sierra de la, *Spain* 38 C4
Peña de Francia, Sierra de la, *Spain* 36 E4
Penafiel, *Portugal* 36 D2
Peñafiel, *Spain* 36 D6
Peñaflor, *Spain* 37 H5
Penal, *Trin. & Tob.* 125 K15
Peñalara, *Spain* 36 E7
Penamacôr, *Portugal* 36 E3
Penang = Pinang, *Malaysia* 65 c
Penápolis, *Brazil* 127 A6
Peñaranda de Bracamonte, *Spain* 36 E5
Peñarroya, *Spain* 38 E4
Peñarroya-Pueblonuevo, *Spain* 37 G5
Penarth, *U.K.* 15 F4
Peñas, C. de, *Spain* 36 B5
Penas, G. de, *Chile* 128 F2
Peñas de San Pedro, *Spain* 39 G3
Peñas del Chache, *Canary Is.* 48 E6
Peñausende, *Spain* 36 D5
Pench'i = Benxi, *China* 57 D12
Pend Oreille →, *U.S.A.* 108 B5
Pend Oreille, L., *U.S.A.* 108 C5
Pendálofon, *Greece* 44 F5
Pendembu, *Eastern, S. Leone* 82 D2
Pendembu, *Northern, S. Leone* 82 D2
Pender B., *Australia* 92 C3
Pendik, *Turkey* 45 F13
Pendjari →, *Benin* 83 C5
Pendjari △, *Benin* 83 C5
Pendleton, *U.S.A.* 108 D4
Pendra, *India* 69 H9
Peneda-Gerês △, *Portugal* 36 D2
Penedo, *Brazil* 125 F11
Penelokan, *Indonesia* 63 J18
Penetanguishene, *Canada* 116 B5
Penfield, *U.S.A.* 116 E6
Pengalengan, *Indonesia* 63 G12
Penge, *Kasai-Or., Dem. Rep. of the Congo* 86 D1
Penge, *Sud-Kivu, Dem. Rep. of the Congo* 86 C2
P'enghu Ch'üntou, *Taiwan* 59 F12
Penglai, *China* 57 F11
Pengshan, *China* 58 B4
Pengshui, *China* 58 C7
Penguin, *Australia* 95 G4
Pengxi, *China* 58 B5
Pengze, *China* 59 C11
Penhalonga, *Zimbabwe* 87 F3
Peniche, *Portugal* 37 F1
Penicuik, *U.K.* 13 F5
Penida, Nusa, *Indonesia* 63 K18
Peninnes, Alpes = Pennine, Alpi, *Alps* 25 J3
Peninsular Malaysia □, *Malaysia* 65 L4
Peñíscola, *Spain* 38 E5
Penitente, Serra do, *Brazil* 125 E9
Penkridge, *U.K.* 14 E5
Penmarch, *France* 18 E2
Penmarch, Pte. de, *France* 18 E2
Penn Hills, *U.S.A.* 116 F5
Penn Yan, *U.S.A.* 116 D7
Penna, Punta della, *Italy* 41 F11
Pennant, *Canada* 103 C7
Penne, *Italy* 41 F10
Penner →, *India* 66 M12
Pennine, Alpi, *Alps* 25 J3
Pennines, *U.K.* 14 C5
Pennington, *U.S.A.* 110 F5
Pennington →, *Nigeria* 83 E6
Pennino, Mte., *Italy* 41 E9
Pennsburg, *U.S.A.* 117 F9
Pennsylvania □, *U.S.A.* 114 E7
Penny, *Canada* 102 C4
Peno, *Russia* 32 D7
Penobscot →, *U.S.A.* 115 C11
Penobscot B., *U.S.A.* 115 C11
Penola, *Australia* 95 F3
Penong, *Australia* 93 F5
Penonomé, *Panama* 120 E3
Penrith, *Australia* 95 E5
Penrith, *U.K.* 14 C5
Penryn, *U.K.* 15 G2
Pensacola, *U.S.A.* 115 K2
Pensacola Mts., *Antarctica* 5 E1
Pense, *Canada* 103 C8
Penshurst, *Australia* 95 F3
Penticton, *Canada* 102 D5
Pentland, *Australia* 94 C4
Pentland Firth, *U.K.* 13 C5
Pentland Hills, *U.K.* 13 F5
Pentland Hills ⌓, *U.K.* 13 F5
Penza, *Russia* 34 D7
Penzance, *U.K.* 15 G2
Penzberg, *Germany* 25 H7
Penzhino, *Russia* 53 C17
Penzhinskaya Guba, *Russia* 53 C17
Penzhou, *China* 58 B4
Penzlin, *Germany* 24 B9
Peoria, *Ariz., U.S.A.* 109 K7
Peoria, *Ill., U.S.A.* 112 E10
Pepacton Reservoir, *U.S.A.* 117 D10
Pepani →, *S. Africa* 88 D3
Pepel, *S. Leone* 82 D2
Peqin, *Albania* 44 E3
Pera Hd., *Australia* 94 A3
Perabumulih, *Indonesia* 62 E2
Perak →, *Malaysia* 65 K3
Perakhóra, *Greece* 46 C4
Perales de Alfambra, *Spain* 38 E4
Perales del Puerto, *Spain* 36 E4
Pérama, *Kérkira, Greece* 49 A3
Pérama, *Kríti, Greece* 49 D6
Perancak, *Indonesia* 63 J17
Peräpohjola, *Finland* 8 C22
Perast, *Serbia & M.* 44 D2
Percé, *Canada* 105 C7
Perche, *France* 18 D8
Perche ⌓, *France* 18 D7
Perchtoldsdorf, *Austria* 27 C9
Percival Lakes, *Australia* 92 D4
Percy, *France* 18 D5
Percy Is., *Australia* 94 C5
Perdido, Mte., *Spain* 38 C5
Perdu, Mt. = Perdido, Mte., *Spain* 38 C5
Perechyn, *Ukraine* 28 B7
Perehinske, *Ukraine* 29 B9
Pereira, *Colombia* 124 C3
Perelazovskiy, *Russia* 35 F6
Perenjori, *Australia* 93 E2
Peresecina, *Moldova* 29 C13
Pereslavl-Zalesskiy, *Russia* 32 D10
Peretu, *Romania* 29 F10
Pereyaslav-Khmelnytskyy, *Ukraine* 33 G6
Pereyma, *Ukraine* 29 B14
Pérez, I., *Mexico* 119 C7
Perg, *Austria* 26 C7
Pergamino, *Argentina* 126 C3
Pergau →, *Malaysia* 65 K3
Pérgine Valsugana, *Italy* 41 B8
Pérgola, *Italy* 41 E9
Perham, *U.S.A.* 112 B7
Perhentian, Kepulauan, *Malaysia* 65 K4
Periam, *Romania* 28 D5
Péribonka →, *Canada* 105 C5
Péribonka, L., *Canada* 105 B5
Perico, *Argentina* 126 A2
Pericos, *Mexico* 118 B3
Périers, *France* 18 C5
Périgord, *France* 20 D4
Périgord-Limousin ⌓, *France* 20 C4
Périgueux, *France* 20 C4
Perijá △, *Venezuela* 121 E5
Perijá, Sierra de, *Colombia* 124 B4
Peristéra, *Greece* 46 B5
Peristerona →, *Cyprus* 49 D12
Perito Moreno, *Argentina* 128 F2
Perivol = Dragovishtitsa, *Bulgaria* 44 D6
Perkasie, *U.S.A.* 117 F9
Perković, *Croatia* 41 E13
Perlas, Arch. de las, *Panama* 120 E4
Perlas, Punta de, *Nic.* 120 D3
Perleberg, *Germany* 24 B7
Perlez, *Serbia & M.* 28 E5
Perm, *Russia* 52 D6
Përmet, *Albania* 44 F4
Pernambuco = Recife, *Brazil* 125 E12
Pernambuco □, *Brazil* 125 E11
Pernatty Lagoon, *Australia* 95 E2
Pernik, *Bulgaria* 44 D7
Peron Is., *Australia* 92 B5
Peron Pen., *Australia* 93 E1
Péronne, *France* 19 C9
Perosa Argentina, *Italy* 40 D4
Perow, *Canada* 102 C3
Perpignan, *France* 20 F6
Perris, *U.S.A.* 111 M9
Perros-Guirec, *France* 18 D3
Perry, *Fla., U.S.A.* 115 K4
Perry, *Ga., U.S.A.* 115 J4
Perry, *Iowa, U.S.A.* 112 E7
Perry, *Okla., U.S.A.* 113 G6
Perryton, *U.S.A.* 113 G4
Perryville, *U.S.A.* 113 G10
Persan, *France* 19 C9
Persberg, *Sweden* 10 E8
Perşembe, *Turkey* 72 B7
Persepolis, *Iran* 71 D7
Pershotravensk, *Ukraine* 33 G4
Persia = Iran ■, *Asia* 71 C7
Persian Gulf, *Asia* 71 E6
Perstorp, *Sweden* 11 H7
Pertek, *Turkey* 73 C8
Perth, *Australia* 93 F2
Perth, *Canada* 117 B8
Perth, *U.K.* 13 E5
Perth & Kinross □, *U.K.* 13 E5
Perth Amboy, *U.S.A.* 117 F10
Perth-Andover, *Canada* 105 C6
Pertuis, *France* 21 E9
Pertusato, C., *France* 21 G13
Peru, *Ind., U.S.A.* 114 E2
Peru, *N.Y., U.S.A.* 117 B11
Peru ■, *S. Amer.* 124 D4
Peru Basin, *Pac. Oc.* 97 J18
Peru-Chile Trench, *Pac. Oc.* 124 G3
Perúgia, *Italy* 41 E9
Perušić, *Croatia* 41 D12
Pervomaysk, *Russia* 34 C6
Pervomaysk, *Ukraine* 33 H6
Pervouralsk, *Russia* 52 D6
Pésaro, *Italy* 41 E9
Pescadores = P'enghu Ch'üntou, *Taiwan* 59 F12
Pescara, *Italy* 41 F11
Pescara →, *Italy* 41 F11
Peschanokopskoye, *Russia* 35 G5
Péscia, *Italy* 40 E7
Pescina, *Italy* 41 F10
Peshawar, *Pakistan* 68 B4
Peshkopi, *Albania* 44 E4
Peshtera, *Bulgaria* 45 D8
Peshtigo, *U.S.A.* 114 C2
Peski, *Russia* 34 E6
Pêso da Régua, *Portugal* 36 D3
Pesqueira, *Brazil* 125 E11
Pessac, *France* 20 D3
Pest □, *Hungary* 28 C4
Pestovo, *Russia* 32 C8
Pestravka, *Russia* 34 D9
Péta, *Greece* 46 B3
Petah Tiqwa, *Israel* 74 C3
Petalídhion, *Greece* 46 E3
Petaling Jaya, *Malaysia* 65 L3
Petaloudhes, *Greece* 49 C10
Petaluma, *U.S.A.* 110 G4
Pétange, *Lux.* 17 E5
Petaro, *Pakistan* 68 G3
Petatlán, *Mexico* 118 D4
Petauke, *Zambia* 87 E3
Petawawa, *Canada* 104 C4
Petén Itzá, L., *Guatemala* 120 C2
Peter I., *Br. Virgin Is.* 121 e
Peter I.s Øy, *Antarctica* 5 C16
Peter Pond L., *Canada* 103 B7
Peterbell, *Canada* 104 C3
Peterborough, *Australia* 95 E2
Peterborough, *Canada* 116 B6
Peterborough, *U.K.* 15 E7
Peterborough, *U.S.A.* 117 D13
Peterborough □, *U.K.* 15 E7
Peterculter, *U.K.* 13 D6
Peterhead, *U.K.* 13 D7
Peterlee, *U.K.* 14 C6
Petermann Ranges, *Australia* 92 E5
Petersburg, *Alaska, U.S.A.* 100 C6
Petersburg, *Pa., U.S.A.* 116 F6
Petersburg, *Va., U.S.A.* 114 G7
Petersburg, *W. Va., U.S.A.* 114 F6
Petersfield, *U.K.* 15 F7
Petershagen, *Germany* 24 C4
Petília Policastro, *Italy* 43 C9
Petit-Canal, *Guadeloupe* 120 b
Petit Goâve, *Haiti* 121 C5
Petit Jardin, *Canada* 105 C8
Petit Lac Manicouagan, *Canada* 105 B6
Petit-Mécatina →, *Canada* 105 B8
Petit-Mécatina, Î. du, *Canada* 105 B8
Petit Piton, *St. Lucia* 121 f
Petit-Saguenay, *Canada* 105 C5
Petit Saint Bernard, Col du, *Italy* 21 C10
Petitcodiac, *Canada* 105 C6
Petite Terre, Îles de la, *Guadeloupe* 120 b
Petitot →, *Canada* 102 A4
Petitsikapau L., *Canada* 105 B6
Petlad, *India* 68 H5
Peto, *Mexico* 119 C7
Petone, *N.Z.* 91 J5
Petorca, *Chile* 126 C1
Petoskey, *U.S.A.* 114 C3
Petra, *Jordan* 74 E4
Petra, *Spain* 48 B10
Petra, Ostrova, *Russia* 4 B13
Petra Velikogo, Zaliv, *Russia* 54 C6
Petrel = Petrer, *Spain* 39 G4
Petrella, Monte, *Italy* 42 A6
Petrer, *Spain* 39 G4
Petreto-Bicchisano, *France* 21 G12
Petrich, *Bulgaria* 44 E7
Petrified Forest △, *U.S.A.* 109 J9
Petrijanec, *Croatia* 41 B13
Petrikov = Pyetrikaw, *Belarus* 33 F5
Petrila, *Romania* 29 E8
Petrinja, *Croatia* 41 C13
Petrodvorets, *Russia* 32 C5
Petrolândia, *Brazil* 125 E11
Petrolia, *Canada* 116 D2
Petrolina, *Brazil* 125 E10
Petropavl, *Kazakhstan* 52 D7
Petropavlovsk = Petropavl, *Kazakhstan* 52 D7
Petropavlovsk-Kamchatskiy, *Russia* 53 D16
Petropavlovskiy = Akhtubinsk, *Russia* 35 F8
Petrópolis, *Brazil* 127 A7
Petroşani, *Romania* 29 E8
Petrova Gora, *Croatia* 41 C12
Petrovac, *Serbia & M.* 44 D2
Petrovac, *Serbia & M.* 44 B5
Petrovaradin, *Serbia & M.* 28 E4
Petrovsk, *Russia* 34 D7
Petrovsk-Zabaykalskiy, *Russia* 53 D11
Petrovskaya, *Russia* 33 K9
Petrozavodsk, *Russia* 32 B8
Petrus Steyn, *S. Africa* 89 D4
Petrusburg, *S. Africa* 88 D4
Petzeck, *Austria* 26 E5
Peumo, *Chile* 126 C1
Peureulak, *Indonesia* 62 D1
Pevek, *Russia* 53 C18
Peveragno, *Italy* 40 D4
Peyrehorade, *France* 20 E2
Peyruis, *France* 21 D9
Pézenas, *France* 20 E7
Pezinok, *Slovak Rep.* 27 C10
Pfaffenhofen, *Germany* 25 G7

Pfälzerwald ⌂, *Germany* 25 F5
Pfarrkirchen, *Germany* 25 G8
Pfeffenhausen, *Germany* 25 G7
Pforzheim, *Germany* 25 G4
Pfullendorf, *Germany* 25 H5
Pfungstadt, *Germany* 25 F4
Pha Taem △, *Thailand* 64 E5
Phagwara, *India* 66 D9
Phaistós, *Greece* 49 D6
Phala, *Botswana* 88 C4
Phalera = Phulera, *India* 68 F6
Phalodi, *India* 68 F5
Phalsbourg, *France* 19 D14
Phaluai, Ko, *Thailand* 65 b
Phan, *Thailand* 64 C2
Phan Rang, *Vietnam* 65 G7
Phan Ri = Hoa Da, *Vietnam* 65 G7
Phan Thiet, *Vietnam* 65 G7
Phanae, *Greece* 47 C7
Phanat Nikhom, *Thailand* 64 F3
Phangan, Ko, *Thailand* 65 H3
Phangnga, *Thailand* 65 H2
Phangnga, Ao, *Thailand* 65 a
Phanom Sarakham, *Thailand* 64 F3
Phaphund, *India* 69 F8
Pharenda, *India* 69 F10
Pharr, *U.S.A.* 113 M5
Phatthalung, *Thailand* 65 J3
Phayao, *Thailand* 64 C2
Phelps, *U.S.A.* 116 D7
Phelps L., *Canada* 103 B8
Phenix City, *U.S.A.* 115 J3
Phet Buri, *Thailand* 64 F2
Phetchabun, *Thailand* 64 D3
Phetchabun, Thiu Khao, *Thailand* 64 E3
Phetchaburi = Phet Buri, *Thailand* 64 F2
Phi Phi, Ko, *Thailand* 65 J2
Phiafay, *Laos* 64 E6
Phibun Mangsahan, *Thailand* 64 E5
Phichai, *Thailand* 64 D3
Phichit, *Thailand* 64 D3
Philadelphia, *Miss., U.S.A.* 113 J10
Philadelphia, *N.Y., U.S.A.* 117 B9
Philadelphia, *Pa., U.S.A.* 117 G9
Philip, *U.S.A.* 112 C4
Philippeville, *Belgium* 17 D4
Philippi, *Greece* 45 E8
Philippi, *U.S.A.* 114 F5
Philippi L., *Australia* 94 C2
Philippine Sea, *Pac. Oc.* 50 H16
Philippines ■, *Asia* 61 F5
Philippolis, *S. Africa* 88 E4
Philippopolis = Plovdiv, *Bulgaria* 45 D8
Philipsburg, *Canada* 117 A11
Philipsburg, *Mont., U.S.A.* 108 C7
Philipsburg, *Pa., U.S.A.* 116 F6
Philipstown = Daingean, *Ireland* 12 C4
Philipstown, *S. Africa* 88 E3
Phillip I., *Australia* 95 F4
Phillips, *U.S.A.* 112 C9
Phillipsburg, *Kans., U.S.A.* 112 F5
Phillipsburg, *N.J., U.S.A.* 117 F9
Philmont, *U.S.A.* 117 D11
Philomath, *U.S.A.* 108 D2
Phimai, *Thailand* 64 E4
Phitsanulok, *Thailand* 64 D3
Phnom Dangrek, *Thailand* 62 B2
Phnom Penh, *Cambodia* 65 G5
Phnum Penh = Phnom Penh, *Cambodia* 65 G5
Phoenicia, *U.S.A.* 117 D10
Phoenix, *Ariz., U.S.A.* 109 K7
Phoenix, *N.Y., U.S.A.* 117 C8
Phoenix Is., *Kiribati* 96 H10
Phoenixville, *U.S.A.* 117 F9
Phon, *Thailand* 64 E4
Phon Tiou, *Laos* 64 D5
Phong →, *Thailand* 64 D4
Phong Saly, *Laos* 58 G4
Phong Tho, *Vietnam* 64 A4
Phonhong, *Laos* 64 C4
Phonum, *Thailand* 65 H2
Phosphate Hill, *Australia* 94 C2
Photharam, *Thailand* 64 F2
Phra Nakhon Si Ayutthaya, *Thailand* 64 E3
Phra Thong, Ko, *Thailand* 65 H2
Phrae, *Thailand* 64 C3
Phrom Phiram, *Thailand* 64 D3
Phrygia, *Turkey* 72 C4
Phu Chong-Na Yoi △, *Thailand* 64 E5
Phu Dien, *Vietnam* 64 C5
Phu Hin Rang Kla △, *Thailand* 64 D3
Phu Kradung △, *Thailand* 64 D3
Phu Loi, *Laos* 64 B4
Phu Luang △, *Thailand* 64 D3
Phu Ly, *Vietnam* 58 G5
Phu Phan △, *Thailand* 64 D4
Phu Quoc, Dao, *Vietnam* 65 G4
Phu Tho, *Vietnam* 58 G5
Phuc Yen, *Vietnam* 58 G5
Phuket, *Thailand* 65 a
Phuket, Ko, *Thailand* 65 a
Phul, *India* 68 D6
Phulad, *India* 68 G5
Phulchari, *Bangla.* 69 G13
Phulera, *India* 68 F6
Phulpur, *India* 69 G10
Phun Phin, *Thailand* 65 H2
Piacenza, *Italy* 40 C6
Piai, Tanjung, *Malaysia* 65 d
Pian Cr. →, *Australia* 95 E4
Pian-Upe ⌂, *Uganda* 86 B3
Piana, *France* 21 F12
Pianella, *Italy* 41 F11
Pianosa, *Puglia, Italy* 41 F12
Pianosa, *Toscana, Italy* 40 F7
Piapot, *Canada* 103 D7
Pias, *Portugal* 37 G3
Piaseczno, *Poland* 31 F8
Piaski, *Poland* 31 G9
Piastów, *Poland* 31 F7
Piatra, *Romania* 29 G10
Piatra Craiului △, *Romania* 29 E10
Piatra Neamţ, *Romania* 29 D11
Piatra Olt, *Romania* 29 F9
Piauí □, *Brazil* 125 E10
Piauí →, *Brazil* 125 E10
Piave →, *Italy* 41 C9
Piazza Ármerina, *Italy* 43 E7
Pibor →, *Sudan* 81 F3
Pibor Post, *Sudan* 81 F3
Picardie □, *France* 19 C10
Picardie, Plaine de, *France* 19 C9
Picardy = Picardie □, *France* 19 C10
Picayune, *U.S.A.* 113 K10
Picerno, *Italy* 43 B8
Pichhor, *India* 69 G8
Pichilemu, *Chile* 126 C1
Pichor, *India* 68 G8
Pickerel L., *Canada* 104 C1
Pickering, *U.K.* 14 C7
Pickering, Vale of, *U.K.* 14 C7
Pickle Lake, *Canada* 104 B1
Pickwick L., *U.S.A.* 115 H1
Pico Bonito △, *Honduras* 120 C2
Pico Truncado, *Argentina* 128 F3
Picos, *Brazil* 125 E10
Picos de Europa △, *Spain* 36 B6
Picton, *Australia* 95 E5
Picton, *Canada* 116 B7
Picton, *N.Z.* 91 J5
Pictou, *Canada* 105 C7
Picture Butte, *Canada* 102 D6
Pictured Rocks ⌂, *U.S.A.* 114 B2
Picún Leufú, *Argentina* 128 D3
Pidbuzh, *Ukraine* 31 J10
Pidurutalagala, *Sri Lanka* 66 R12
Piechowice, *Poland* 31 H2
Piedimonte Matese, *Italy* 43 A7
Piedmont = Piemonte □, *Italy* 40 D5
Piedmont, *Ala., U.S.A.* 115 J3
Piedmont, *S.C., U.S.A.* 107 D10
Piedra →, *Spain* 38 D3
Piedrabuena, *Spain* 37 G6
Piedrahita, *Spain* 36 E5
Piedralaves, *Spain* 36 E6
Piedras Blancas, *Spain* 36 B5
Piedras Negras, *Mexico* 118 B4
Piekary Śląskie, *Poland* 31 H5
Pieksämäki, *Finland* 9 E22
Piemonte □, *Italy* 40 D5
Pienaarsrivier, *S. Africa* 89 D4
Pieniężno, *Poland* 30 D7
Pieninský △, *Europe* 27 B13
Pieńsk, *Poland* 31 G2
Piercefield, *U.S.A.* 117 B10
Pierceland, *Canada* 103 C7
Piería □, *Greece* 44 F6
Pierpont, *U.S.A.* 116 E4
Pierre, *U.S.A.* 112 C4
Pierre-Buffière, *France* 20 C5
Pierre-de-Bresse, *France* 19 F12
Pierrefontaine-les-Varans, *France* 19 E13
Pierrefort, *France* 20 D6
Pierrelatte, *France* 21 D8
Pierreville, *Trin. & Tob.* 125 K16
Piešťany, *Slovak Rep.* 27 C10
Piesting →, *Austria* 27 C9
Pieszyce, *Poland* 31 H3
Piet Retief, *S. Africa* 89 D5
Pietarsaari, *Finland* 8 E20
Pietermaritzburg, *S. Africa* 89 D5
Pietersburg = Polokwane, *S. Africa* 89 C4
Pietragalla, *Italy* 43 B8
Pietrasanta, *Italy* 40 E7
Pietroşiţa, *Romania* 29 E10
Pietrosul, Vf., *Maramureş, Romania* 29 C9
Pietrosul, Vf., *Suceava, Romania* 29 C10
Pieve di Cadore, *Italy* 41 B9
Pieve di Teco, *Italy* 40 D4
Pievepélago, *Italy* 40 D7
Pigadhítsa, *Greece* 44 G5
Pigeon L., *Canada* 116 B6
Piggott, *U.S.A.* 113 G9
Pigna, *Italy* 40 E4
Pigüe, *Argentina* 126 D3
Pihani, *India* 69 F9
Pihlajavesi, *Finland* 9 F23
Pijijiapan, *Mexico* 119 D6
Pikalevo, *Russia* 32 C8
Pikangikum Berens, *Canada* 103 C10
Pikes Peak, *U.S.A.* 112 F2
Piketberg, *S. Africa* 88 E2
Pikeville, *U.S.A.* 114 G4
Pikou, *China* 57 E12
Pikwitonei, *Canada* 103 B9
Piła, *Poland* 31 E3
Pila, *Spain* 39 G3
Pilaía, *Greece* 44 F6
Pilanesberg △, *S. Africa* 88 D4
Pilani, *India* 68 E6
Pilar, *Paraguay* 126 B4
Pilar de la Horadada, *Spain* 39 H4
Pilat ⌂, *France* 21 C8
Pilawa, *Poland* 31 G8
Pilaya →, *Bolivia* 124 H6
Pilbara, *Australia* 92 D2
Pilcomayo →, *Paraguay* 126 B4
Pilgrim's Rest, *S. Africa* 89 C5
Pilgrimstad, *Sweden* 10 B9
Píli, *Greece* 47 E9
Pilibhit, *India* 69 E8
Pilica →, *Poland* 31 G8
Pilion, *Greece* 46 B5
Pilis, *Hungary* 28 C4
Pilisvörösvár, *Hungary* 28 C3
Pilkhawa, *India* 68 E7
Pilliga, *Australia* 95 E4
Pílos, *Greece* 46 E3
Pilot Mound, *Canada* 103 D9
Pilot Point, *U.S.A.* 113 J6
Pilot Rock, *U.S.A.* 108 D4
Pilštanj, *Slovenia* 41 B12
Piltene, *Latvia* 30 A8
Pilzno, *Poland* 31 J8
Pima, *U.S.A.* 109 K9
Pimba, *Australia* 95 E2
Pimenta Bueno, *Brazil* 124 F6
Pimentel, *Peru* 124 E3
Pina de Ebro, *Spain* 38 D4
Pinamalayan, *Phil.* 61 E4
Pinang, *Malaysia* 65 c
Pinar, C. des, *Spain* 48 B10
Pinar del Río, *Cuba* 120 B3
Pınarbaşı, *Çanakkale, Turkey* 47 B8
Pınarbaşı, *Kayseri, Turkey* 72 C7
Pınarhisar, *Turkey* 45 E11
Pinatubo, Mt., *Phil.* 61 D3
Pincehely, *Hungary* 28 D3
Pinchang, *China* 58 B6
Pincher Creek, *Canada* 102 D6
Pinchi L., *Canada* 102 C4
Pinckneyville, *U.S.A.* 112 F10
Pińczów, *Poland* 31 H7
Pindar, *Australia* 93 E2
Pindi Gheb, *Pakistan* 68 C5
Pindiga, *Nigeria* 83 D7
Pindos △, *Greece* 46 B3
Pindos Óros, *Greece* 46 B3
Pindus Mts. = Pindos Óros, *Greece* 46 B3
Pine →, *B.C., Canada* 102 B4
Pine →, *Sask., Canada* 103 B7
Pine, C., *Canada* 105 C9
Pine Bluff, *U.S.A.* 113 H9
Pine Bluffs, *U.S.A.* 112 E2
Pine City, *U.S.A.* 112 C8
Pine Cr. →, *U.S.A.* 116 E7
Pine Creek, *Australia* 92 B5
Pine Falls, *Canada* 103 C9
Pine Flat Res., *U.S.A.* 110 J7
Pine Grove, *U.S.A.* 117 F8
Pine Pass, *Canada* 102 B4
Pine Point, *Canada* 102 A6
Pine Ridge, *U.S.A.* 112 D3
Pine River, *Canada* 103 C8
Pine River, *U.S.A.* 112 B7
Pine Valley, *U.S.A.* 111 N10
Pinecrest, *U.S.A.* 110 G6
Pineda de Mar, *Spain* 38 D7
Pinedale, *Calif., U.S.A.* 110 J7
Pinedale, *Wyo., U.S.A.* 108 E9
Pinega →, *Russia* 52 C5
Pinehill, *Australia* 94 C4
Pinehouse L., *Canada* 103 B7
Pineimuta →, *Canada* 104 B1
Pinerolo, *Italy* 40 D4
Pineto, *Italy* 41 F11
Pinetop, *U.S.A.* 109 J9
Pinetown, *S. Africa* 89 D5
Pineville, *U.S.A.* 113 K8
Piney, *France* 19 D11
Ping →, *Thailand* 64 E3
Pingaring, *Australia* 93 F2
Pingba, *China* 58 D6
Pingbian, *China* 58 F4
Pingchuan, *China* 58 D3
Pingding, *China* 56 F7
Pingdingshan, *China* 56 H7
Pingdong, *Taiwan* 59 F13
Pingdu, *China* 57 F10
Pingelly, *Australia* 93 F2
Pingguo, *China* 58 F6
Pinghe, *China* 59 E11
Pinghu, *China* 59 B13
Pingjiang, *China* 59 C9
Pingle, *China* 59 E8
Pingli, *China* 58 A7
Pingliang, *China* 56 G4
Pinglu, *China* 56 E7
Pingluo, *China* 56 E4
Pingnan, *Fujian, China* 59 D12
Pingnan, *Guangxi Zhuangzu, China* 59 F8
Pingquan, *China* 57 D10
Pingrup, *Australia* 93 F2
Pingshan, *China* 58 C5
Pingtan, *China* 59 E12
Pingtang, *China* 58 E6
P'ingtung, *Taiwan* 59 F13
Pingwu, *China* 56 H3
Pingxiang, *Guangxi Zhuangzu, China* 58 F6
Pingxiang, *Jiangxi, China* 59 D9
Pingyao, *China* 56 F7
Pingyi, *China* 57 G9
Pingyin, *China* 56 F9
Pingyuan, *Guangdong, China* 59 E10
Pingyuan, *Shandong, China* 56 F9
Pingyuanjie, *China* 58 F4
Pinhal, *Brazil* 127 A6
Pinhal Novo, *Portugal* 37 G2
Pinheiro, *Brazil* 125 D9
Pinheiro Machado, *Brazil* 127 C5
Pinhel, *Portugal* 36 E3
Pini, *Indonesia* 62 D1
Piniós →, *Ilía, Greece* 46 D3
Piniós →, *Trikkala, Greece* 46 B4
Pinjarra, *Australia* 93 F2
Pink Mountain, *Canada* 102 B4
Pinkafeld, *Austria* 27 D9
Pinnacles, *U.S.A.* 110 J5
Pinnacles ⌂, *U.S.A.* 110 J5
Pinnaroo, *Australia* 95 F3
Pinneberg, *Germany* 24 B5
Pínnes, Ákra, *Greece* 45 F8
Pinon Hills, *U.S.A.* 111 L9
Pinos, *Mexico* 118 C4
Pinos, Mt., *U.S.A.* 111 L7
Pinos Pt., *U.S.A.* 109 H3
Pinos Puente, *Spain* 37 H7
Pinotepa Nacional, *Mexico* 119 D5
Pinrang, *Indonesia* 63 E5
Pins, Pte. aux, *Canada* 116 D3
Pinsk, *Belarus* 33 F4
Pintados, *Chile* 124 H5
Pinyang, *China* 59 D13
Pinyug, *Russia* 52 C5
Pioche, *U.S.A.* 109 H6
Piombino, *Italy* 40 F7
Piombino, Canale di, *Italy* 40 F7
Pioner, Ostrov, *Russia* 53 B10
Pionerskiy, *Russia* 30 D7
Pionki, *Poland* 31 G8
Piorini, L., *Brazil* 124 D6
Piotrków Trybunalski, *Poland* 31 G6
Piove di Sacco, *Italy* 41 C9
Pīp, *Iran* 71 E9
Pipar, *India* 68 F5
Pipar Road, *India* 68 F5
Piparia, *Mad. P., India* 68 H8
Piparia, *Mad. P., India* 68 J7
Pipéri, *Greece* 46 B6
Pipestone, *U.S.A.* 112 D6
Pipestone →, *Canada* 104 B2
Pipestone Cr. →, *Canada* 103 D8
Piplan, *Pakistan* 68 C4
Piploda, *India* 68 H6
Pipmuacan, Rés., *Canada* 105 C5
Pippingarra, *Australia* 92 D2
Pipriac, *France* 18 E5
Piqua, *U.S.A.* 114 E3
Piquiri →, *Brazil* 127 A5
Pir Panjal Range, *India* 68 C7
Pīr Sohrāb, *Iran* 71 E9
Pira, *Benin* 83 D5
Piracicaba, *Brazil* 127 A6
Piracuruca, *Brazil* 125 D10
Piræus = Piraiévs, *Greece* 46 D5
Piraiévs, *Greece* 46 D5
Pirajuí, *Brazil* 127 A6
Piram I., *India* 68 J5
Piran, *Slovenia* 41 C10
Pirané, *Argentina* 126 B4
Pirano = Piran, *Slovenia* 41 C10
Pirapora, *Brazil* 125 G10
Pirawa, *India* 68 G7
Pirdop, *Bulgaria* 45 D8
Pírgos, *Ilía, Greece* 46 D3
Pírgos, *Kríti, Greece* 47 F7
Pirgovo, *Bulgaria* 45 C9
Piribebuy, *Paraguay* 126 B4
Pirimapun, *Indonesia* 63 F9
Pirin △, *Bulgaria* 44 E7
Pirin Planina, *Bulgaria* 44 E7
Píríneos = Pyrénées, *Europe* 20 F4
Piripiri, *Brazil* 125 D10
Pirmasens, *Germany* 25 F3
Pirna, *Germany* 24 E9
Pirot, *Serbia & M.* 44 C6
Piru, *Indonesia* 63 E7
Piru, *U.S.A.* 111 L8
Piryatin = Pyryatyn, *Ukraine* 33 G7
Piryí, *Greece* 47 C7
Pisa, *Italy* 40 E7
Pisa →, *Poland* 31 E8
Pisa, Firenze ✕ (PSA), *Italy* 40 E7
Pisagne, *Italy* 40 C7
Pisagua, *Chile* 124 G4
Pisarovina, *Croatia* 41 C12
Pisco, *Peru* 124 F3
Piscu, *Romania* 29 E12
Písek, *Czech Rep.* 26 B7
Pishan, *China* 60 C2
Pishcha, *Ukraine* 31 G10
Pishchanka, *Ukraine* 29 B13
Pīshīn, *Iran* 71 E9
Pishin, *Pakistan* 68 D2
Pishin Lora →, *Pakistan* 68 E1
Pisidia, *Turkey* 72 D4
Pising, *Indonesia* 63 F6
Pismo Beach, *U.S.A.* 111 K6
Piso, L., *Liberia* 82 D2
Pissila, *Burkina Faso* 83 C4
Pissis, Cerro, *Argentina* 126 B2
Pissos, *France* 20 D3
Pissouri, *Cyprus* 49 E11
Pisticci, *Italy* 43 B9
Pistóia, *Italy* 40 E7
Pistol B., *Canada* 103 A10
Pisuerga →, *Spain* 36 D6
Pisz, *Poland* 30 E8
Pit →, *U.S.A.* 108 F2
Pita, *Guinea* 82 C2
Pitarpunga, L., *Australia* 95 E3
Pitcairn I., *Pac. Oc.* 97 K14
Pitch L., *Trin. & Tob.* 125 K15
Piteå, *Sweden* 8 D19
Piteälven →, *Sweden* 8 D19
Piterka, *Russia* 34 E8
Piteşti, *Romania* 29 F9
Pithapuram, *India* 67 L13
Pithara, *Australia* 93 F2
Píthion, *Greece* 45 E10
Pithiviers, *France* 19 D9
Pithoragarh, *India* 69 E9
Pithoro, *Pakistan* 68 G3
Pitigliano, *Italy* 41 F8
Pitkyaranta, *Russia* 32 B6
Pitlochry, *U.K.* 13 E5
Pitsilia, *Cyprus* 49 E12
Pitt I., *Canada* 102 C3
Pittsburg, *Calif., U.S.A.* 110 G5
Pittsburg, *Kans., U.S.A.* 113 G7
Pittsburg, *Tex., U.S.A.* 113 J7
Pittsburgh, *U.S.A.* 116 F5
Pittsfield, *Ill., U.S.A.* 112 F9
Pittsfield, *Maine, U.S.A.* 115 C11
Pittsfield, *Mass., U.S.A.* 117 D11
Pittsfield, *N.H., U.S.A.* 117 C13
Pittston, *U.S.A.* 117 E9
Pittsworth, *Australia* 95 D5
Pituri →, *Australia* 94 C2
Piura, *Peru* 124 E2
Piva →, *Serbia & M.* 44 C2
Piwniczna, *Poland* 31 J7
Pixley, *U.S.A.* 110 K7
Piyai, *Greece* 46 B3
Pizarra, *Spain* 37 J6
Pizhou, *China* 56 G9
Pizzo, *Italy* 43 D9
Placentia, *Canada* 105 C9
Placentia B., *Canada* 105 C9
Placer, *Masbate, Phil.* 61 F5
Placer, *Surigao N., Phil.* 61 G6
Placerville, *U.S.A.* 110 G6
Placetas, *Cuba* 120 B4
Plačkovica, *Macedonia* 44 E6
Plainfield, *N.J., U.S.A.* 117 F10
Plainfield, *Ohio, U.S.A.* 116 F3
Plainfield, *Vt., U.S.A.* 117 B12
Plains, *Mont., U.S.A.* 108 C6
Plains, *Tex., U.S.A.* 113 J3
Plainview, *Nebr., U.S.A.* 112 D6
Plainview, *Tex., U.S.A.* 113 H4
Plainwell, *U.S.A.* 114 D3
Plaisance, *France* 20 E4
Plaistow, *U.S.A.* 117 D13
Pláka, *Greece* 47 B7
Pláka, Ákra, *Greece* 49 D8
Plakenska Planina, *Macedonia* 44 E5
Planá, *Czech Rep.* 26 B5
Plana Cays, *Bahamas* 121 B5
Planada, *U.S.A.* 110 H6
Plancoët, *France* 18 D4
Plandište, *Serbia & M.* 28 E6
Plano, *U.S.A.* 113 J6
Plant City, *U.S.A.* 115 M4
Plaquemine, *U.S.A.* 113 K9
Plasencia, *Spain* 36 E4
Plaški, *Croatia* 41 C12
Plaster City, *U.S.A.* 111 N11
Plaster Rock, *Canada* 105 C6
Plastun, *Russia* 54 B8
Plasy, *Czech Rep.* 26 B6
Plata, Río de la, *S. Amer.* 126 C4
Plátani →, *Italy* 42 E6
Plátanos, *Greece* 49 D5
Plateau □, *Nigeria* 83 D6
Platí, Ákra, *Greece* 45 F8
Platte, *U.S.A.* 112 D5
Platte →, *Mo., U.S.A.* 112 F7
Platte →, *Nebr., U.S.A.* 112 E7
Platteville, *U.S.A.* 112 D9
Plattling, *Germany* 25 G8
Plattsburgh, *U.S.A.* 117 B11
Plattsmouth, *U.S.A.* 112 E7
Plau, *Germany* 24 B8
Plauen, *Germany* 24 E8
Plauer See, *Germany* 24 B8
Plav, *Serbia & M.* 44 D3
Plavinas, *Latvia* 9 H21
Plavnica, *Serbia & M.* 44 D3
Plavno, *Croatia* 41 D13
Plavsk, *Russia* 32 F9
Playa Blanca, *Canary Is.* 48 F6
Playa Blanca Sur, *Canary Is.* 48 F6
Playa de las Americas, *Canary Is.* 48 F3
Playa de Mogán, *Canary Is.* 48 G4
Playa del Inglés, *Canary Is.* 48 G4
Playa Esmerelda, *Canary Is.* 48 F5
Playgreen L., *Canada* 103 C9
Pleasant Bay, *Canada* 105 C7
Pleasant Hill, *U.S.A.* 110 H4
Pleasant Mount, *U.S.A.* 117 E9
Pleasanton, *Calif., U.S.A.* 110 H5
Pleasanton, *Tex., U.S.A.* 113 L5
Pleasantville, *N.J., U.S.A.* 114 F8
Pleasantville, *Pa., U.S.A.* 116 E5
Pléaux, *France* 20 C6
Plei Ku, *Vietnam* 64 F7
Plélan-le-Grand, *France* 18 D4
Pléneuf-Val-André, *France* 18 D4
Pleniţa, *Romania* 29 F8
Plenty →, *Australia* 94 C2
Plenty, B. of, *N.Z.* 91 G6
Plentywood, *U.S.A.* 112 A2
Plérin, *France* 18 D4
Plessisville, *Canada* 105 C5
Plestin-les-Grèves, *France* 18 D3
Pleszew, *Poland* 31 G4
Pleternica, *Croatia* 28 E2
Plétipi, L., *Canada* 105 B5
Pleven, *Bulgaria* 45 C8
Plevlja, *Serbia & M.* 44 C3
Plevna, *Canada* 116 B8
Plitvička Jezera △, *Croatia* 41 D12
Plješevica, *Croatia* 41 D12
Ploaghe, *Italy* 42 B1
Ploče, *Croatia* 41 E14
Płock, *Poland* 31 F6
Plöckenpass, *Italy* 41 B9
Plöckenstein, *Germany* 25 G9
Ploemeur, *France* 18 E3
Ploërmel, *France* 18 E4
Ploieşti, *Romania* 29 F11
Plomárion, *Greece* 47 C8
Plombières-les-Bains, *France* 19 E13
Plomin, *Croatia* 41 C11
Plön, *Germany* 24 A6
Plonge, Lac la, *Canada* 103 B7
Płońsk, *Poland* 31 F7
Plopeni, *Romania* 29 E10
Plopişului, Munţii, *Romania* 28 C7
Płoty, *Poland* 30 E2
Plouaret, *France* 18 D3
Plouay, *France* 18 E3
Ploučnice →, *Czech Rep.* 26 A7
Ploudalmézeau, *France* 18 D2
Plouescat, *France* 18 D2
Plougasnou, *France* 18 D3
Plougastel-Daoulas, *France* 18 D2

Plouguerneau, *France* 18 D2
Plouha, *France* 18 D4
Plouhinec, *France* 18 E2
Plovdiv, *Bulgaria* 45 D8
Plovdiv □, *Bulgaria* 45 D8
Plum, *U.S.A.* 116 F5
Plum I., *U.S.A.* 117 E12
Plumas, *U.S.A.* 110 F7
Plummer, *U.S.A.* 108 C5
Plumtree, *Zimbabwe* 87 G2
Plungė, *Lithuania* 9 J19
Pluvigner, *France* 18 E3
Plymouth, *Trin. & Tob.* 125 J16
Plymouth, *U.K.* 15 G3
Plymouth, *Calif., U.S.A.* 110 G6
Plymouth, *Ind., U.S.A.* 114 E2
Plymouth, *Mass., U.S.A.* 117 E14
Plymouth, *N.C., U.S.A.* 115 H7
Plymouth, *N.H., U.S.A.* 117 C13
Plymouth, *Pa., U.S.A.* 117 E9
Plymouth, *Wis., U.S.A.* 114 D2
Plympton-Wyoming, *Canada* 116 D2
Plynlimon = Pumlumon Fawr, *U.K.* 15 E4
Plyusa, *Russia* 32 C5
Plyusa →, *Russia* 32 C5
Plzeň, *Czech Rep.* 26 B6
Plzeňský □, *Czech Rep.* 26 B6
Pniewy, *Poland* 31 F3
Pô, *Burkina Faso* 83 C4
Pô △, *Burkina Faso* 83 C4
Po →, *Italy* 41 D9
Po, Foci del, *Italy* 41 D9
Po Hai = Bo Hai, *China* 57 E10
Pobé, *Benin* 83 D5
Pobé, *Burkina Faso* 83 C4
Pobeda, *Russia* 53 C15
Pobedy, Pik, *Kyrgyzstan* 52 E8
Pobiedziska, *Poland* 31 F4
Pobla de Segur, *Spain* 38 C5
Pobladura del Valle, *Spain* 36 C5
Pobra de Trives, *Spain* 36 C3
Pocahontas, *Ark., U.S.A.* 113 G9
Pocahontas, *Iowa, U.S.A.* 112 D7
Pocatello, *U.S.A.* 108 E7
Počátky, *Czech Rep.* 26 B8
Pochep, *Russia* 33 F7
Pochinki, *Russia* 34 C7
Pochinok, *Russia* 32 E7
Pöchlarn, *Austria* 26 C8
Pochutla, *Mexico* 119 D5
Pocito Casas, *Mexico* 118 B2
Pocking, *Germany* 25 G9
Pocomoke City, *U.S.A.* 114 F8
Poços de Caldas, *Brazil* 127 A6
Podbořany, *Czech Rep.* 26 A6
Poddębice, *Poland* 31 G5
Poděbrady, *Czech Rep.* 26 A8
Podensac, *France* 20 D3
Podenzano, *Italy* 40 D6
Podgorač, *Croatia* 28 E3
Podgorica, *Serbia & M.* 44 D3
Podgorie, *Albania* 44 F4
Podilska Vysochyna, *Ukraine* 29 B13
Podkarpackie □, *Poland* 31 H9
Podkova, *Bulgaria* 45 E9
Podlapača, *Croatia* 41 D12
Podlaskie □, *Poland* 31 E10
Podoleni, *Romania* 29 D11
Podolínec, *Slovak Rep.* 27 B13
Podolsk, *Russia* 32 E9
Podor, *Senegal* 82 B1
Podporozhye, *Russia* 32 B8
Podu Iloaiei, *Romania* 29 C12
Podu Turcului, *Romania* 29 D12
Podujevo, *Serbia & M.* 44 D5
Podyjí △, *Czech Rep.* 26 C8
Poel, *Germany* 24 B6
Pofadder, *S. Africa* 88 D2
Poggiardo, *Italy* 43 B11
Poggibonsi, *Italy* 40 E8
Póggio Mirteto, *Italy* 41 F9
Pogoanele, *Romania* 29 F12
Pogorzela, *Poland* 31 G4
Pogradec, *Albania* 44 F4
Pogranichnyy, *Russia* 54 B5
Poh, *Indonesia* 63 E6
P'ohang, *S. Korea* 57 F15
Pohjanmaa, *Finland* 8 E20
Pohnpei, *Micronesia* 96 G7
Pohorelá, *Slovak Rep.* 27 C13
Pohořelice, *Czech Rep.* 27 C9
Pohorje, *Slovenia* 41 B12
Pohri, *India* 68 G6
Poiana Mare, *Romania* 28 G8
Poiana Ruscăi, Munţii, *Romania* 28 E7
Poiana Stampei, *Romania* 29 C10
Poinsett, C., *Antarctica* 5 C8
Point Arena, *U.S.A.* 110 G3
Point Baker, *U.S.A.* 102 B2
Point Edward, *Canada* 104 D3
Point Fortin, *Trin. & Tob.* 125 K15
Point Hope, *U.S.A.* 100 B3
Point L., *Canada* 100 B8
Point Lisas, *Trin. & Tob.* 125 K15
Point Pedro, *Sri Lanka* 66 Q12
Point Pelee △, *Canada* 116 E2
Point Pleasant, *N.J., U.S.A.* 117 F10
Point Pleasant, *W. Va., U.S.A.* 114 F4
Point Reyes ⌓, *U.S.A.* 110 G2
Pointe-à-Pitre, *Guadeloupe* 120 b
Pointe-au-Pic = La Malbaie, *Canada* 105 C5
Pointe-Claire, *Canada* 117 A11
Pointe-Gatineau, *Canada* 117 A9
Pointe-Noire, *Congo* 84 E2
Pointe Noire, *Guadeloupe* 120 b
Poio, *Spain* 36 C2
Poirino, *Italy* 40 D4
Poisonbush Ra., *Australia* 92 D3
Poissonnier Pt., *Australia* 92 C2
Poitiers, *France* 18 F7
Poitou, *France* 20 B3
Poitou-Charentes □, *France* 20 B4
Poix-de-Picardie, *France* 19 C8
Poix-Terron, *France* 19 C11
Pojoaque, *U.S.A.* 109 J11
Pokaran, *India* 66 F7
Pokataroo, *Australia* 95 D4
Pokhara, *Nepal* 69 E10
Pokhvistnevo, *Russia* 34 D11
Poko, *Dem. Rep. of the Congo* 86 B2
Poko, *Sudan* 81 F3
Pokrov, *Russia* 32 E10
Pokrovsk, *Russia* 53 C13
Pokrovskoye, *Russia* 33 J10
Pola = Pula, *Croatia* 41 D10
Pola, *Russia* 32 D7
Pola de Allande, *Spain* 36 B4
Pola de Lena, *Spain* 36 B5
Pola de Siero, *Spain* 36 B5
Pola de Somiedo, *Spain* 36 B4
Polacca, *U.S.A.* 109 J8
Polan, *Iran* 71 E9
Pol'ana, *Slovak Rep.* 27 C12
Poland ■, *Europe* 31 G3
Polanica-Zdrój, *Poland* 31 H3
Połaniec, *Poland* 31 H8
Polanów, *Poland* 30 D3
Polar Bear ⌓, *Canada* 104 A2
Polatlı, *Turkey* 72 C5
Polatsk, *Belarus* 32 E5
Polcura, *Chile* 126 D1
Połczyn-Zdrój, *Poland* 30 E3
Poleski △, *Poland* 31 G10
Polessk, *Russia* 9 J19
Polesye = Pripet Marshes, *Europe* 33 F5
Polgar, *Hungary* 28 C6
Pŏlgyo-ri, *S. Korea* 57 G14
Poli, *Cameroon* 83 C7
Políaigos, *Greece* 46 E6
Policastro, G. di, *Italy* 43 C8
Police, *Poland* 30 E1
Polička, *Czech Rep.* 27 B9
Policoro, *Italy* 43 B9
Polignano a Mare, *Italy* 43 A9
Poligny, *France* 19 F12
Políkhnitas, *Greece* 47 B8
Polillo Is., *Phil.* 61 D4
Polillo Strait, *Phil.* 61 D4
Polis, *Cyprus* 49 D11
Polístena, *Italy* 43 D9
Políyiros, *Greece* 44 F7
Polk, *U.S.A.* 116 E5
Polkowice, *Poland* 31 G3
Polla, *Italy* 43 B8
Pollachi, *India* 66 P10
Pollença, *Spain* 48 B10
Pollença, B. de, *Spain* 48 B10
Póllica, *Italy* 43 B8
Pollino △, *Italy* 43 C9
Pollino, Mte., *Italy* 43 C9
Polna, *Russia* 32 C5
Polnovat, *Russia* 52 C7
Pology, *Ukraine* 33 J9
Polokwane, *S. Africa* 89 C4
Polonne, *Ukraine* 33 G4
Polonnoye = Polonne, *Ukraine* 33 G4
Polski Trŭmbesh, *Bulgaria* 45 C9
Polsko Kosovo, *Bulgaria* 45 C9
Polson, *U.S.A.* 108 C6
Poltár, *Slovak Rep.* 27 C12
Poltava, *Ukraine* 33 H8
Põltsamaa, *Estonia* 9 G21
Polunochnoye, *Russia* 52 C7
Põlva, *Estonia* 9 G22
Polyana, *Ukraine* 28 B7
Polynesia, *Pac. Oc.* 97 F11
Polynésie française = French Polynesia ⊠, *Pac. Oc.* 97 K13
Pomarance, *Italy* 40 E7
Pomaro, *Mexico* 118 D4
Pombal, *Portugal* 36 F2
Pómbia, *Greece* 49 E6
Pomene, *Mozam.* 89 C6
Pomeroy, *Ohio, U.S.A.* 114 F4
Pomeroy, *Wash., U.S.A.* 108 C5
Pomézia, *Italy* 42 A5
Pomichna, *Ukraine* 33 H6
Pomona, *Australia* 95 D5
Pomona, *U.S.A.* 111 L9
Pomorie, *Bulgaria* 45 D11
Pomorskie □, *Poland* 30 D5
Pomorskie, Pojezierze, *Poland* 30 E3
Pomos, *Cyprus* 49 D11
Pomos, C., *Cyprus* 49 D11
Pompano Beach, *U.S.A.* 115 M5
Pompei, *Italy* 43 B7
Pompey, *France* 19 D13
Pompeys Pillar, *U.S.A.* 108 D10
Pompeys Pillar ⌓, *U.S.A.* 108 D10
Pompton Lakes, *U.S.A.* 117 F10
Ponape = Pohnpei, *Micronesia* 96 G7
Ponask L., *Canada* 104 B1
Ponca, *U.S.A.* 112 D6
Ponca City, *U.S.A.* 113 G6
Ponce, *Puerto Rico* 121 d
Ponchatoula, *U.S.A.* 113 K9
Poncheville, L., *Canada* 104 B4
Pond, *U.S.A.* 111 K7
Pond Inlet, *Canada* 101 A12
Pondicherry, *India* 66 P11
Ponds, I. of, *Canada* 105 B8
Ponferrada, *Spain* 36 C4
Pongo, Wadi →, *Sudan* 81 F2
Poniatowa, *Poland* 31 G9
Poniec, *Poland* 31 G3
Ponikva, *Slovenia* 41 B12
Ponnani, *India* 66 P9
Ponoka, *Canada* 102 C6
Ponorogo, *Indonesia* 63 G14
Pons = Ponts, *Spain* 38 D6
Pons, *France* 20 C3
Ponsul →, *Portugal* 36 F3
Pont-à-Mousson, *France* 19 D13
Pont-Audemer, *France* 18 C7
Pont-Aven, *France* 18 E3
Pont Canavese, *Italy* 40 C4
Pont-d'Ain, *France* 19 F12
Pont-de-Roide, *France* 19 E13
Pont-de-Salars, *France* 20 D6
Pont-de-Vaux, *France* 19 F11
Pont-de-Veyle, *France* 19 F11
Pont-du-Château, *France* 19 G10
Pont-l'Abbé, *France* 18 E2
Pont-l'Évêque, *France* 18 C7
Pont-St-Esprit, *France* 21 D8
Pont-St-Martin, *Italy* 40 C4
Pont-Ste-Maxence, *France* 19 C9
Pont-sur-Yonne, *France* 19 D10
Ponta do Sol, *Madeira* 48 D2
Ponta Grossa, *Brazil* 127 B5
Ponta Pora, *Brazil* 127 A4
Pontacq, *France* 20 E3
Pontailler-sur-Saône, *France* 19 E12
Pontarlier, *France* 19 F13
Pontassieve, *Italy* 41 E8
Pontaumur, *France* 20 C6
Pontcharra, *France* 21 C10
Pontchartrain L., *U.S.A.* 113 K10
Pontchâteau, *France* 18 E4
Ponte da Barca, *Portugal* 36 D2
Ponte de Sor, *Portugal* 37 F2
Ponte dell'Ólio, *Italy* 40 D6
Ponte di Legno, *Italy* 40 B7
Ponte do Lima, *Portugal* 36 D2
Ponte do Pungué, *Mozam.* 87 F3
Ponte-Leccia, *France* 21 F13
Ponte nelle Alpi, *Italy* 41 B9
Ponte Nova, *Brazil* 127 A7
Ponteareas, *Spain* 36 C2
Pontebba, *Italy* 41 B10
Ponteceso, *Spain* 36 B2
Pontecorvo, *Italy* 42 A6
Pontedeume, *Spain* 36 B2
Ponteix, *Canada* 103 D7
Pontevedra, *Spain* 36 C2
Pontevedra □, *Spain* 36 C2
Pontevedra, R. de →, *Spain* 36 C2
Pontevico, *Italy* 40 C7
Pontiac, *Ill., U.S.A.* 112 E10
Pontiac, *Mich., U.S.A.* 114 D4
Pontian Kechil, *Malaysia* 65 d
Pontianak, *Indonesia* 62 E3
Pontine Is. = Ponziane, Ísole, *Italy* 42 B5
Pontine Mts. = Kuzey Anadolu Dağları, *Turkey* 72 B7
Pontínia, *Italy* 42 A6
Pontivy, *France* 18 D4
Pontoise, *France* 19 C9
Ponton →, *Canada* 102 B5
Pontorson, *France* 18 D5
Pontrémoli, *Italy* 40 D6
Pontrieux, *France* 18 D3
Ponts, *Spain* 38 D6
Pontypool, *Canada* 116 B6
Pontypool, *U.K.* 15 F4
Ponza, *Italy* 42 B5
Ponziane, Ísole, *Italy* 42 B5
Poochera, *Australia* 95 E1
Poole, *U.K.* 15 G6
Poole □, *U.K.* 15 G6
Poona = Pune, *India* 66 K8
Pooncarie, *Australia* 95 E3
Poopelloe L., *Australia* 95 E3
Poopó, L. de, *Bolivia* 124 G5
Popayán, *Colombia* 124 C3
Poperinge, *Belgium* 17 D2
Popilta L., *Australia* 95 E3
Popina, *Bulgaria* 45 B10
Popio L., *Australia* 95 E3
Poplar, *U.S.A.* 112 A2
Poplar →, *Canada* 103 C9
Poplar Bluff, *U.S.A.* 113 G9
Poplarville, *U.S.A.* 113 K10
Popocatépetl, Volcán, *Mexico* 119 D5
Popokabaka, *Dem. Rep. of the Congo* 84 F3
Pópoli, *Italy* 41 F10
Popovača, *Croatia* 41 C13
Popovo, *Bulgaria* 45 C10
Poppberg, *Germany* 25 F7
Poppi, *Italy* 41 E8
Poprad, *Slovak Rep.* 27 B13
Poprad →, *Slovak Rep.* 27 B13
Porali →, *Pakistan* 68 G2
Porbandar, *India* 68 J3
Porcher I., *Canada* 102 C2
Porcuna, *Spain* 37 H6
Porcupine →, *Canada* 103 B8
Porcupine →, *U.S.A.* 100 B5
Porcupine Gorge △, *Australia* 94 C3
Pordenone, *Italy* 41 C9
Pordim, *Bulgaria* 45 C8
Poreč, *Croatia* 41 C10
Poretskoye, *Russia* 34 C8
Pori, *Finland* 9 F19
Porí, *Greece* 46 F5
Porkhov, *Russia* 32 D5
Porlamar, *Venezuela* 124 A6
Porlezza, *Italy* 40 B6
Porma →, *Spain* 36 C5
Pornic, *France* 18 E4
Poronaysk, *Russia* 53 E15
Póros, *Greece* 46 D5
Poroshiri-Dake, *Japan* 54 C11
Poroszló, *Hungary* 28 C5
Poroto Mts., *Tanzania* 87 D3
Porpoise B., *Antarctica* 5 C9
Porquerolles, Î. de, *France* 21 F10
Porrentruy, *Switz.* 25 H3
Porreres, *Spain* 48 B10
Porsangen, *Norway* 8 A21
Porsgrunn, *Norway* 9 G13
Port Alberni, *Canada* 102 D4
Port Alfred, *S. Africa* 88 E4
Port Alice, *Canada* 102 C3
Port Allegany, *U.S.A.* 116 E6
Port Allen, *U.S.A.* 113 K9
Port Alma, *Australia* 94 C5
Port Angeles, *U.S.A.* 110 B3
Port Antonio, *Jamaica* 120 a
Port Aransas, *U.S.A.* 113 M6
Port Arthur, *Australia* 95 G4
Port Arthur, *U.S.A.* 113 L8
Port au Choix, *Canada* 105 B8
Port au Port B., *Canada* 105 C8
Port-au-Prince, *Haiti* 121 C5
Port Augusta, *Australia* 95 E2
Port Austin, *U.S.A.* 116 B2
Port Bell, *Uganda* 86 B3
Port Bergé Vaovao, *Madag.* 89 B8
Port Blandford, *Canada* 105 C9
Port-Bouët, *Ivory C.* 82 D4
Port Bradshaw, *Australia* 94 A2
Port Broughton, *Australia* 95 E2
Port Burwell, *Canada* 116 D4
Port Canning, *India* 69 H13
Port-Cartier, *Canada* 105 B6
Port Chalmers, *N.Z.* 91 L3
Port Charlotte, *U.S.A.* 115 M4
Port Chester, *U.S.A.* 117 F11
Port Clements, *Canada* 102 C2
Port Clinton, *U.S.A.* 114 E4
Port Colborne, *Canada* 116 D5
Port Coquitlam, *Canada* 102 D4
Port Credit, *Canada* 116 C5
Port-Cros △, *France* 21 F10
Port Curtis, *Australia* 94 C5
Port d'Alcúdia, *Spain* 48 B10
Port Dalhousie, *Canada* 116 C5
Port d'Andratx, *Spain* 48 B9
Port Darwin, *Australia* 92 B5
Port Darwin, *Falk. Is.* 128 G5
Port Davey, *Australia* 95 G4
Port-de-Bouc, *France* 21 E8
Port-de-Paix, *Haiti* 121 C5
Port de Pollença, *Spain* 48 B10
Port de Sóller, *Spain* 48 B9
Port Dickson, *Malaysia* 65 L3
Port Douglas, *Australia* 94 B4
Port Dover, *Canada* 116 D4
Port Edward, *Canada* 102 C2
Port Elgin, *Canada* 116 B3
Port Elizabeth, *S. Africa* 88 E4
Port Ellen, *U.K.* 13 F2
Port-en-Bessin-Huppain, *France* 18 C6
Port Erin, *I. of Man* 14 C3
Port Essington, *Australia* 92 B5
Port Ewen, *U.S.A.* 117 E11
Port Fairy, *Australia* 95 F3
Port Fouâd = Bûr Fuad, *Egypt* 80 H8
Port Gamble, *U.S.A.* 110 C4
Port-Gentil, *Gabon* 84 E1
Port Germein, *Australia* 95 E2
Port Gibson, *U.S.A.* 113 K9
Port Glasgow, *U.K.* 13 F4
Port Harcourt, *Nigeria* 83 E6
Port Hardy, *Canada* 102 C3
Port Harrison = Inukjuak, *Canada* 101 C12
Port Hawkesbury, *Canada* 105 C7
Port Hedland, *Australia* 92 D2
Port Henry, *U.S.A.* 117 B11
Port Hood, *Canada* 105 C7
Port Hope, *Canada* 116 C6
Port Hope, *U.S.A.* 116 C2
Port Hope Simpson, *Canada* 105 B8
Port Hueneme, *U.S.A.* 111 L7
Port Huron, *U.S.A.* 116 D2
Port Iliç, *Azerbaijan* 73 C13
Port Jefferson, *U.S.A.* 117 F11
Port Jervis, *U.S.A.* 117 E10
Port-Joinville, *France* 18 F4
Port Katon, *Russia* 33 J10
Port Kelang = Pelabuhan Klang, *Malaysia* 65 L3
Port Kenny, *Australia* 95 E1
Port-la-Nouvelle, *France* 20 E7
Port Lairge = Waterford, *Ireland* 12 D4
Port Laoise, *Ireland* 12 C4
Port Lavaca, *U.S.A.* 113 L6
Port Leyden, *U.S.A.* 117 C9
Port Lincoln, *Australia* 95 E2
Port Loko, *S. Leone* 82 D2
Port Louis, *France* 18 E3
Port-Louis, *Guadeloupe* 120 b
Port Louis, *Mauritius* 77 H9
Port MacDonnell, *Australia* 95 F3
Port McNeill, *Canada* 102 C3
Port Macquarie, *Australia* 95 E5
Port Maria, *Jamaica* 120 a
Port Matilda, *U.S.A.* 116 F6
Port Mellon, *Canada* 102 D4
Port-Menier, *Canada* 105 C7
Port Moody, *Canada* 110 A4
Port Morant, *Jamaica* 120 a
Port Moresby, *Papua N. G.* 96 H6
Port Musgrave, *Australia* 94 A3
Port-Navalo, *France* 18 E4
Port Neches, *U.S.A.* 113 L8
Port Nolloth, *S. Africa* 88 D2
Port Nouveau-Québec = Kangiqsualujjuaq, *Canada* 101 C13
Port of Spain, *Trin. & Tob.* 121 D7
Port Orange, *U.S.A.* 115 L5
Port Orchard, *U.S.A.* 110 C4
Port Orford, *U.S.A.* 108 E1
Port Pegasus, *N.Z.* 91 M1
Port Perry, *Canada* 116 B6
Port Phillip B., *Australia* 95 F3
Port Pirie, *Australia* 95 E2
Port Renfrew, *Canada* 102 D4
Port Roper, *Australia* 94 A2
Port Rowan, *Canada* 116 D4
Port Safaga = Bûr Safâga, *Egypt* 70 E2
Port Said = Bûr Sa'îd, *Egypt* 80 H8
Port St. Joe, *U.S.A.* 115 L3
Port St. Johns = Umzimvubu, *S. Africa* 89 E4
Port-St-Louis-du-Rhône, *France* 21 E8
Port St. Lucie, *U.S.A.* 115 M5
Port-Ste-Marie, *France* 20 D4
Port Sanilac, *U.S.A.* 116 C2
Port Severn, *Canada* 116 B5
Port Shepstone, *S. Africa* 89 E5
Port Simpson, *Canada* 102 C2
Port Stanley = Stanley, *Falk. Is.* 128 G5
Port Stanley, *Canada* 116 D3
Port Sudan = Bûr Sûdân, *Sudan* 80 D4
Port Sulphur, *U.S.A.* 113 L10
Port-sur-Saône, *France* 19 E13
Port Talbot, *U.K.* 15 F4
Port Taufiq = Bûr Taufiq, *Egypt* 80 J8
Port Townsend, *U.S.A.* 110 B4
Port-Vendres, *France* 20 F7
Port Vila, *Vanuatu* 96 J8
Port Wakefield, *Australia* 95 E2
Port Washington, *U.S.A.* 114 D2
Portadown, *U.K.* 12 B5
Portaferry, *U.K.* 12 B6
Portage, *Pa., U.S.A.* 116 F6
Portage, *Wis., U.S.A.* 112 D10
Portage la Prairie, *Canada* 103 D9
Portageville, *U.S.A.* 113 G10
Portalegre, *Portugal* 37 F3
Portalegre □, *Portugal* 37 F3
Portales, *U.S.A.* 113 H3
Portarlington, *Ireland* 12 C4
Portbou, *Spain* 38 C8
Portel, *Portugal* 37 G3
Portela, Lisboa ✈ (LIS), *Portugal* 37 G1
Porter L., *N.W.T., Canada* 103 A7
Porter L., *Sask., Canada* 103 B7
Porterville, *S. Africa* 88 E2
Porterville, *U.S.A.* 110 J8
Portes-lès-Valence, *France* 21 D8
Porthcawl, *U.K.* 15 F4
Porthill, *U.S.A.* 108 B5
Porthmadog, *U.K.* 14 E3
Portile de Fier, *Europe* 28 F7
Portimão, *Portugal* 37 H2
Portishead, *U.K.* 15 F5
Portiţei, Gura, *Romania* 29 F14
Portknockie, *U.K.* 13 D6
Portland, *N.S.W., Australia* 95 E5
Portland, *Vic., Australia* 95 F3
Portland, *Canada* 117 B8
Portland, *Conn., U.S.A.* 117 E12
Portland, *Maine, U.S.A.* 101 D12
Portland, *Mich., U.S.A.* 114 D3
Portland, *Oreg., U.S.A.* 110 E4
Portland, *Pa., U.S.A.* 117 F9
Portland, *Tex., U.S.A.* 113 M6
Portland ✈ (PDX), *U.S.A.* 110 E4
Portland, I. of, *U.K.* 15 G5
Portland B., *Australia* 95 F3
Portland Bight, *Jamaica* 120 a
Portland Bill, *U.K.* 15 G5
Portland Canal, *U.S.A.* 102 B2
Portland Pt., *Jamaica* 120 a
Portmadoc = Porthmadog, *U.K.* 14 E3
Portmore, *Jamaica* 120 a
Porto, *France* 21 F12
Porto, *Portugal* 36 D2
Porto □, *Portugal* 36 D2
Porto, G. de, *France* 21 F12
Pôrto Alegre, *Brazil* 127 C5
Porto Azzurro, *Italy* 40 F7
Porto Cristo, *Spain* 48 B10
Pôrto de Móz, *Brazil* 125 D8
Porto Empédocle, *Italy* 42 E6
Pôrto Esperança, *Brazil* 124 G7
Pôrto Franco, *Brazil* 125 E9
Pôrto Lágos, *Greece* 45 E9
Pôrto Mendes, *Brazil* 127 A5
Porto Moniz, *Madeira* 48 D2
Pôrto Murtinho, *Brazil* 124 H7
Pôrto Nacional, *Brazil* 125 F9
Porto-Novo, *Benin* 83 D5
Porto Petro, *Spain* 48 B10
Porto San Giórgio, *Italy* 41 E10
Porto Sant' Elpídio, *Italy* 41 E10
Porto Santo, I. de, *Madeira* 78 B2
Porto Santo Stéfano, *Italy* 40 F8
Pôrto São José, *Brazil* 127 A5
Pôrto Seguro, *Brazil* 125 G11
Porto Tolle, *Italy* 41 D9
Porto Tórres, *Italy* 42 B1
Pôrto União, *Brazil* 127 B5
Pôrto Válter, *Brazil* 124 E4
Porto-Vecchio, *France* 21 G13
Pôrto Velho, *Brazil* 124 E6
Portobelo, *Panama* 120 E4
Portoferráio, *Italy* 40 F7
Portogruaro, *Italy* 41 C9
Portola, *U.S.A.* 110 F6
Portomaggiore, *Italy* 41 D8
Portoscuso, *Italy* 42 C1
Portovénere, *Italy* 40 D6
Portoviejo, *Ecuador* 124 D2
Portpatrick, *U.K.* 13 G3
Portree, *U.K.* 13 D2
Portrush, *U.K.* 12 A5
Portsmouth, *Dominica* 121 C7
Portsmouth, *U.K.* 15 G6
Portsmouth, *N.H., U.S.A.* 115 D10
Portsmouth, *Ohio, U.S.A.* 114 F4
Portsmouth, *R.I., U.S.A.* 117 E13
Portsmouth, *Va., U.S.A.* 114 G7
Portsmouth □, *U.K.* 15 G6
Portsoy, *U.K.* 13 D6
Portstewart, *U.K.* 12 A5
Porttipahdan tekojärvi, *Finland* 8 B22
Portugal ■, *Europe* 36 F3
Portugalete, *Spain* 38 B1

Portumna, *Ireland* 12 C3
Portville, *U.S.A.* 116 D6
Porvenir, *Chile* 128 G2
Porvoo, *Finland* 9 F21
Porzuna, *Spain* 37 F6
Posada, *Italy* 42 B2
Posada →, *Italy* 42 B2
Posadas, *Argentina* 127 B4
Posadas, *Spain* 37 H5
Poschiavo, *Switz.* 25 J6
Posets, *Spain* 38 C5
Posht-e Badam, *Iran* 71 C7
Posídhion, Ákra, *Greece* 44 G7
Posidium, *Greece* 47 F9
Poso, *Indonesia* 63 E6
Posong, *S. Korea* 57 G14
Posse, *Brazil* 125 F9
Possession I., *Antarctica* 5 D11
Pössneck, *Germany* 24 E7
Possum Kingdom L., *U.S.A.* 113 J5
Post, *U.S.A.* 113 J4
Post Falls, *U.S.A.* 108 C5
Postavy = Pastavy, *Belarus* 9 J22
Poste-de-la-Baleine = Kuujjuarapik, *Canada* 104 A4
Postmasburg, *S. Africa* 88 D3
Postojna, *Slovenia* 41 C11
Poston, *U.S.A.* 111 M12
Postville, *Canada* 105 B8
Potamós, *Andikíthira, Greece* 46 F5
Potamós, *Kíthira, Greece* 46 E4
Potchefstroom, *S. Africa* 88 D4
Potcoava, *Romania* 29 F9
Poteau, *U.S.A.* 113 H7
Poteet, *U.S.A.* 113 L5
Potenza, *Italy* 43 B8
Potenza →, *Italy* 41 E10
Potenza Picena, *Italy* 41 E10
Poteriteri, L., *N.Z.* 91 M1
Potgietersrus = Mokopane, *S. Africa* 89 C4
Poti, *Georgia* 35 J5
Potiskum, *Nigeria* 83 C7
Potlogi, *Romania* 29 F10
Potomac →, *U.S.A.* 114 G7
Potosí, *Bolivia* 124 G5
Potosi Mt., *U.S.A.* 111 K11
Pototan, *Phil.* 61 F5
Potrerillos, *Chile* 126 B2
Potsdam, *Germany* 24 C9
Potsdam, *U.S.A.* 117 B10
Pottenstein, *Germany* 25 F7
Pottersville, *U.S.A.* 117 C11
Pottstown, *U.S.A.* 117 F9
Pottsville, *U.S.A.* 117 F8
Pottuvil, *Sri Lanka* 66 R12
P'otzu, *Taiwan* 59 F13
Pouancé, *France* 18 E5
Pouce Coupé, *Canada* 102 B4
Poughkeepsie, *U.S.A.* 117 E11
Pouilly-sur-Loire, *France* 19 E9
Poulaphouca Res., *Ireland* 12 C5
Poulsbo, *U.S.A.* 110 C4
Poultney, *U.S.A.* 117 C11
Poulton-le-Fylde, *U.K.* 14 D5
Pouso Alegre, *Brazil* 127 A6
Pout, *Senegal* 82 C1
Pouthisat, *Cambodia* 64 F4
Pouzauges, *France* 18 F6
Pova de Santa Iria, *Portugal* 37 G1
Považská Bystrica, *Slovak Rep.* 27 B11
Poverty B., *N.Z.* 91 H7
Povlen, *Serbia & M.* 44 B3
Póvoa de Lanhosa, *Portugal* 36 D2
Póvoa de Varzim, *Portugal* 36 D2
Povorino, *Russia* 34 E6
Povungnituk = Puvirnituq, *Canada* 101 B12
Powassan, *Canada* 104 C4
Poway, *U.S.A.* 111 N9
Powder →, *U.S.A.* 112 B2
Powder River, *U.S.A.* 108 E10
Powell, *U.S.A.* 108 D9
Powell, L., *U.S.A.* 109 H8
Powell River, *Canada* 102 D4
Powers, *U.S.A.* 114 C2
Powys □, *U.K.* 15 E4
Poyang Hu, *China* 59 C11
Poyarkovo, *Russia* 53 E13
Poysdorf, *Austria* 27 C9
Poza de la Sal, *Spain* 36 C7
Poza Rica, *Mexico* 119 C5
Pozanti, *Turkey* 72 D6
Požarevac, *Serbia & M.* 44 B5
Pozazal, Puerto, *Spain* 36 C6
Požega, *Croatia* 28 E2
Požega, *Serbia & M.* 44 C4
Poznań, *Poland* 31 F3
Poznań ✕ (POZ), *Poland* 31 F3
Pozo, *U.S.A.* 111 K6
Pozo Alcón, *Spain* 37 H8
Pozo Almonte, *Chile* 124 H5
Pozo Colorado, *Paraguay* 126 A4
Pozoblanco, *Spain* 37 G6
Pozzallo, *Italy* 43 F7
Pozzomaggiore, *Italy* 42 B1
Pozzuoli, *Italy* 43 B7
Pra →, *Ghana* 83 D4
Prabuty, *Poland* 30 E6
Prača, *Bos.-H.* 28 G3
Prachatice, *Czech Rep.* 26 B6
Prachin Buri, *Thailand* 64 E3
Prachuap Khiri Khan, *Thailand* 65 G2
Pradelles, *France* 20 D7
Prades, *France* 20 F6
Prado, *Brazil* 125 G11
Prado del Rey, *Spain* 37 J5
Præstø, *Denmark* 11 J6
Pragersko, *Slovenia* 41 B12
Prague = Praha, *Czech Rep.* 26 A7
Praha, *Czech Rep.* 26 A7
Praha ✕ (PRG), *Czech Rep.* 26 A7
Prahecq, *France* 20 B3
Prahova □, *Romania* 29 E10
Prahova →, *Romania* 29 F10
Prahovo, *Serbia & M.* 44 B6
Praia, *C. Verde Is.* 77 E1
Práia a Mare, *Italy* 43 C8
Praid, *Romania* 29 D10
Prainha, *Amazonas, Brazil* 124 E6
Prainha, *Pará, Brazil* 125 D8
Prairie, *Australia* 94 C3
Prairie City, *U.S.A.* 108 D4
Prairie Dog Town Fork →, *U.S.A.* 113 H5
Prairie du Chien, *U.S.A.* 112 D9
Prairies, L. of the, *Canada* 103 C8
Pramánda, *Greece* 46 B3
Prampram, *Ghana* 83 D5
Pran Buri, *Thailand* 64 F2
Prang, *Ghana* 83 D4
Prapat, *Indonesia* 62 D1
Prasonísi, Ákra, *Greece* 49 D9
Prästmon, *Sweden* 10 A11
Praszka, *Poland* 31 G5
Prata, *Brazil* 125 G9
Pratabpur, *India* 69 H10
Pratapgarh, *Raj., India* 68 G6
Pratapgarh, *Ut. P., India* 69 G9
Pratas Is. = Dongsha Dao, *China* 59 G11
Prato, *Italy* 40 E8
Prátola Peligna, *Italy* 41 F10
Prats-de-Mollo-la-Preste, *France* 20 F6
Pratt, *U.S.A.* 113 G5
Prattville, *U.S.A.* 115 J2
Pravdinsk, *Russia* 30 D8
Pravdinsk, *Russia* 34 B6
Pravets, *Bulgaria* 44 D7
Pravia, *Spain* 36 B4
Praya, *Indonesia* 62 F5
Pré-en-Pail, *France* 18 D6
Precipice △, *Australia* 95 D5
Precordillera, *Argentina* 126 C2
Predáppio, *Italy* 41 D8
Predazzo, *Italy* 41 B8
Predeal, *Romania* 29 E10
Predejane, *Serbia & M.* 44 D6
Preeceville, *Canada* 103 C8
Preetz, *Germany* 24 A6
Pregolya →, *Russia* 30 D7
Pregrada, *Croatia* 41 B12
Preiļi, *Latvia* 9 H22
Preko, *Croatia* 41 D12
Prelog, *Croatia* 41 B13
Prémery, *France* 19 E10
Premià de Mar, *Spain* 38 D7
Premont, *U.S.A.* 113 M5
Premuda, *Croatia* 41 D11
Prentice, *U.S.A.* 112 C9
Prenzlau, *Germany* 24 B9
Preobrazheniye, *Russia* 54 C6
Preparis North Channel, *Ind. Oc.* 67 M18
Preparis South Channel, *Ind. Oc.* 67 M18
Přerov, *Czech Rep.* 27 B10
Prescott, *Canada* 117 B9
Prescott, *Ariz., U.S.A.* 109 J7
Prescott, *Ark., U.S.A.* 113 J8
Prescott Valley, *U.S.A.* 109 J7
Preservation Inlet, *N.Z.* 91 M1
Preševo, *Serbia & M.* 44 D5
Presho, *U.S.A.* 112 D4
Presicce, *Italy* 43 C11
Presidencia de la Plaza, *Argentina* 126 B4
Presidencia Roque Saenz Peña, *Argentina* 126 B3
Presidente Epitácio, *Brazil* 125 H8
Presidente Hayes □, *Paraguay* 126 A4
Presidente Prudente, *Brazil* 127 A5
Presidio, *Mexico* 118 B4
Presidio, *U.S.A.* 113 L2
Preslav, *Bulgaria* 45 C10
Preslavska Planina, *Bulgaria* 45 C10
Prešov, *Slovak Rep.* 27 B14
Prešovský □, *Slovak Rep.* 27 B13
Prespa, *Bulgaria* 45 E8
Préspa △, *Greece* 44 F5
Prespa, L. = Prespansko Jezero, *Macedonia* 44 F5
Prespansko Jezero, *Macedonia* 44 F5
Presque I., *U.S.A.* 116 D4
Presque Isle, *U.S.A.* 115 B12
Prestatyn, *U.K.* 14 D4
Prestea, *Ghana* 82 D4
Presteigne, *U.K.* 15 E5
Přeštice, *Czech Rep.* 26 B6
Preston, *Canada* 116 C4
Preston, *U.K.* 14 D5
Preston, *Idaho, U.S.A.* 108 E8
Preston, *Minn., U.S.A.* 112 D8
Preston, C., *Australia* 92 D2
Prestonburg, *U.S.A.* 114 G4
Prestwick, *U.K.* 13 F4
Pretoria, *S. Africa* 89 D4
Preuilly-sur-Claise, *France* 18 F7
Préveza, *Greece* 46 C2
Préveza □, *Greece* 46 B2
Prey Veng, *Cambodia* 65 G5
Priazovskoye, *Ukraine* 33 J8
Pribilof Is., *U.S.A.* 100 C2
Priboj, *Serbia & M.* 44 C3
Příbram, *Czech Rep.* 26 B7
Price, *U.S.A.* 108 G8
Price I., *Canada* 102 C3
Prichard, *U.S.A.* 115 K1
Priego, *Spain* 38 E2
Priego de Córdoba, *Spain* 37 H6
Priekule, *Latvia* 9 H19
Priekule, *Lithuania* 30 C8
Prien, *Germany* 25 H8
Prienai, *Lithuania* 9 J20
Prieska, *S. Africa* 88 D3
Priest L., *U.S.A.* 108 B5
Priest River, *U.S.A.* 108 B5
Priest Valley, *U.S.A.* 110 J6
Prievidza, *Slovak Rep.* 27 C11
Prignitz, *Germany* 24 B7
Prijedor, *Bos.-H.* 41 D13
Prijepolje, *Serbia & M.* 44 C3
Prikaspiyskaya Nizmennost = Caspian Depression, *Eurasia* 35 G9
Prikro, *Ivory C.* 82 D4
Prikubanskaya Nizmennost, *Russia* 35 H4
Prilep, *Macedonia* 44 E5
Priluki = Pryluky, *Ukraine* 33 G7
Prime Seal I., *Australia* 95 G4
Primorsk, *Russia* 30 D6
Primorsk, *Russia* 32 B5
Primorsko, *Bulgaria* 45 D11
Primorsko-Akhtarsk, *Russia* 33 J10
Primorskoye, *Ukraine* 33 J9
Primrose L., *Canada* 103 C7
Prince Albert, *Canada* 103 C7
Prince Albert, *S. Africa* 88 E3
Prince Albert △, *Canada* 103 C7
Prince Albert Mts., *Antarctica* 5 D11
Prince Albert Pen., *Canada* 100 A8
Prince Albert Sd., *Canada* 100 A8
Prince Alfred, C., *Canada* 4 B1
Prince Charles I., *Canada* 101 B12
Prince Charles Mts., *Antarctica* 5 D6
Prince Edward I. □, *Canada* 105 C7
Prince Edward Is., *Ind. Oc.* 3 G11
Prince Edward Pt., *Canada* 116 C8
Prince George, *Canada* 102 C4
Prince of Wales, C., *U.S.A.* 98 C3
Prince of Wales I., *Australia* 94 A3
Prince of Wales I., *Canada* 100 A10
Prince of Wales I., *U.S.A.* 100 C6
Prince Patrick I., *Canada* 4 B2
Prince Regent Inlet, *Canada* 4 B3
Prince Rupert, *Canada* 102 C2
Princes Town, *Trin. & Tob.* 125 K15
Princess Charlotte B., *Australia* 94 A3
Princess May Ranges, *Australia* 92 C4
Princess Royal I., *Canada* 102 C3
Princeton, *Canada* 102 D4
Princeton, *Calif., U.S.A.* 110 F4
Princeton, *Ill., U.S.A.* 112 E10
Princeton, *Ind., U.S.A.* 114 F2
Princeton, *Ky., U.S.A.* 114 G2
Princeton, *Mo., U.S.A.* 112 E8
Princeton, *N.J., U.S.A.* 117 F10
Princeton, *W. Va., U.S.A.* 114 G5
Príncipe, I. de, *Atl. Oc.* 76 F4
Principe da Beira, *Brazil* 124 F6
Prineville, *U.S.A.* 108 D3
Prins Harald Kyst, *Antarctica* 5 D4
Prinsesse Astrid Kyst, *Antarctica* 5 D3
Prinsesse Ragnhild Kyst, *Antarctica* 5 D4
Prinzapolca, *Nic.* 120 D3
Prior, C., *Spain* 36 B2
Priozersk, *Russia* 32 B6
Pripet = Prypyat →, *Europe* 33 G6
Pripet Marshes, *Europe* 33 F5
Pripyat Marshes = Pripet Marshes, *Europe* 33 F5
Pripyats = Prypyat →, *Europe* 33 G6
Prislop, Pasul, *Romania* 29 C9
Pristen, *Russia* 33 G9
Priština, *Serbia & M.* 44 D5
Pritzwalk, *Germany* 24 B8
Privas, *France* 21 D8
Priverno, *Italy* 42 A6
Privolzhsk, *Russia* 34 B5
Privolzhskaya Vozvyshennost, *Russia* 34 E7
Privolzhskiy, *Russia* 34 E8
Privolzhskiy □, *Russia* 34 B10
Privolzhye, *Russia* 34 D9
Priyutnoye, *Russia* 35 G6
Prizren, *Serbia & M.* 44 D4
Prizzi, *Italy* 42 E6
Prnjavor, *Bos.-H.* 28 F2
Probolinggo, *Indonesia* 63 G15
Prochowice, *Poland* 31 G3
Proctor, *U.S.A.* 117 C11
Proddatur, *India* 66 M11
Prodhromos, *Cyprus* 49 E11
Proença-a-Nova, *Portugal* 36 F3
Profítis Ilías, *Greece* 49 C9
Profondeville, *Belgium* 17 D4
Progreso, *Coahuila, Mexico* 118 B4
Progreso, *Yucatán, Mexico* 119 C7
Prokhladnyy, *Russia* 35 J7
Prokletije, *Albania* 44 D3
Prokopyevsk, *Russia* 52 D9
Prokuplje, *Serbia & M.* 44 C5
Proletarsk, *Russia* 35 G5
Proletarskaya = Proletarsk, *Russia* 35 G5
Prome, *Burma* 67 K19
Prophet →, *Canada* 102 B4
Prophet River, *Canada* 102 B4
Propriá, *Brazil* 125 F11
Propriano, *France* 21 G12
Proserpine, *Australia* 94 J6
Prosna →, *Poland* 31 F4
Prospect, *U.S.A.* 117 C9
Prosser, *U.S.A.* 108 C4
Prostějov, *Czech Rep.* 27 B10
Prostki, *Poland* 30 E9
Proston, *Australia* 95 D5
Proszowice, *Poland* 31 H7
Próti, *Greece* 46 D3
Provadiya, *Bulgaria* 45 C11
Provence, *France* 21 E9
Provence-Alpes-Côte d'Azur □, *France* 21 D10
Providence, *Ky., U.S.A.* 114 G2
Providence, *R.I., U.S.A.* 117 E13
Providence Bay, *Canada* 104 C3
Providence Mts., *U.S.A.* 111 K11
Providencia, I. de, *Colombia* 120 D3
Provideniya, *Russia* 53 C19
Provins, *France* 19 D10
Provo, *U.S.A.* 108 F8
Provost, *Canada* 103 C6
Prozor, *Bos.-H.* 28 G2
Prrenjas, *Albania* 44 E4
Prudhoe Bay, *U.S.A.* 100 A5
Prudhoe I., *Australia* 94 C4
Prud'homme, *Canada* 103 C7
Prudnik, *Poland* 31 H4
Prüm, *Germany* 25 E2
Prundu, *Romania* 29 F11
Pruszcz Gdański, *Poland* 30 D5
Pruszków, *Poland* 31 F7
Prut →, *Romania* 29 E13
Pruzhany, *Belarus* 33 F3
Prvič, *Croatia* 41 D11
Prydz B., *Antarctica* 5 C6
Pryluky, *Ukraine* 33 G7
Pryor, *U.S.A.* 113 G7
Prypyat →, *Europe* 33 G6
Przasnysz, *Poland* 31 E7
Przedbórz, *Poland* 31 G6
Przedecz, *Poland* 31 F5
Przemków, *Poland* 31 G2
Przemyśl, *Poland* 31 J9
Przeworsk, *Poland* 31 H9
Przewóz, *Poland* 31 G1
Przhevalsk = Karakol, *Kyrgyzstan* 52 E8
Przysucha, *Poland* 31 G7
Psakhná, *Greece* 46 C5
Psará, *Greece* 47 C7
Psathoúra, *Greece* 46 B6
Psel →, *Ukraine* 33 H7
Pserimos, *Greece* 47 E9
Psíra, *Greece* 49 D7
Pskov, *Russia* 32 D5
Pskovskoye, Ozero, *Russia* 32 D5
Psunj, *Croatia* 28 E2
Pteleón, *Greece* 46 B4
Ptich = Ptsich →, *Belarus* 33 F5
Ptolemaís, *Greece* 44 F5
Ptsich →, *Belarus* 33 F5
Ptuj, *Slovenia* 41 B12
Ptujska Gora, *Slovenia* 41 B12
Pu Xian, *China* 56 F6
Pua, *Thailand* 64 C3
Puán, *Argentina* 126 D3
Pu'an, *China* 58 E5
Puan, *S. Korea* 57 G14
Pubei, *China* 58 F7
Pucallpa, *Peru* 124 E4
Pucheng, *China* 59 D12
Pucheni, *Romania* 29 E10
Puchheim, *Germany* 25 G7
Púchov, *Slovak Rep.* 27 B11
Pucioasa, *Romania* 29 E10
Pučišća, *Croatia* 41 E13
Puck, *Poland* 30 D5
Pucka, Zatoka, *Poland* 30 D5
Puçol, *Spain* 39 F4
Pudasjärvi, *Finland* 8 D22
Puding, *China* 58 D5
Pudozh, *Russia* 32 B9
Puduchcheri = Pondicherry, *India* 66 P11
Pudukkottai, *India* 66 P11
Puebla, *Mexico* 119 D5
Puebla □, *Mexico* 119 D5
Puebla de Alcocer, *Spain* 37 G5
Puebla de Don Fadrique, *Spain* 39 H2
Puebla de Don Rodrigo, *Spain* 37 F6
Puebla de Guzmán, *Spain* 37 H3
Puebla de la Calzada, *Spain* 37 G4
Puebla de Sanabria, *Spain* 36 C4
Puebla de Trives = Pobra de Trives, *Spain* 36 C3
Pueblo, *U.S.A.* 112 F2
Pueblo Hundido, *Chile* 126 B1
Puelches, *Argentina* 126 D2
Puelén, *Argentina* 126 D2
Puente Alto, *Chile* 126 C1
Puente-Genil, *Spain* 37 H6
Puente la Reina, *Spain* 38 C3
Puenteareas = Ponteareas, *Spain* 36 C2
Puentedeume = Pontedeume, *Spain* 36 B2
Puentes de Garcia Rodriguez = As Pontes de García Rodríguez, *Spain* 36 B3
Pu'er, *China* 58 F3
Puerca, Pta., *Puerto Rico* 121 d
Puerco →, *U.S.A.* 109 J10
Puerto Aisén, *Chile* 128 F2
Puerto Ángel, *Mexico* 119 D5
Puerto Arista, *Mexico* 119 D6
Puerto Armuelles, *Panama* 120 E3
Puerto Ayacucho, *Venezuela* 124 B5
Puerto Barrios, *Guatemala* 120 C2
Puerto Bermejo, *Argentina* 126 B4
Puerto Bermúdez, *Peru* 124 F4
Puerto Bolívar, *Ecuador* 124 D3
Puerto Cabello, *Venezuela* 124 A5
Puerto Cabezas, *Nic.* 120 D3
Puerto Cabo Gracias á Dios, *Nic.* 120 D3
Puerto Carreño, *Colombia* 124 B5
Puerto Castilla, *Honduras* 120 C2
Puerto Chicama, *Peru* 124 E3
Puerto Coig, *Argentina* 128 G3
Puerto Cortés, *Costa Rica* 120 E3
Puerto Cortés, *Honduras* 120 C2
Puerto Cumarebo, *Venezuela* 124 A5
Puerto de Alcudia = Port d'Alcúdia, *Spain* 48 B10
Puerto de Cabrera, *Spain* 48 B9
Puerto de Gran Tarajal, *Canary Is.* 48 F5
Puerto de la Cruz, *Canary Is.* 48 F3
Puerto de los Angeles ⌓, *Mexico* 118 C3
Puerto de Mazarrón, *Spain* 39 H3
Puerto de Pozo Negro, *Canary Is.* 48 F6
Puerto de Sóller = Port de Sóller, *Spain* 48 B9
Puerto de Somosierra, *Spain* 36 D7
Puerto del Carmen, *Canary Is.* 48 F6
Puerto del Rosario, *Canary Is.* 48 F6
Puerto Deseado, *Argentina* 128 F3
Puerto Escondido, *Mexico* 119 D5
Puerto Heath, *Bolivia* 124 F5
Puerto Inírida, *Colombia* 124 C5
Puerto Juárez, *Mexico* 119 C7
Puerto La Cruz, *Venezuela* 124 A6
Puerto Leguízamo, *Colombia* 124 D4
Puerto Limón, *Colombia* 124 C4
Puerto Lobos, *Argentina* 128 E3
Puerto Lumbreras, *Spain* 39 H3
Puerto Madryn, *Argentina* 128 E3
Puerto Maldonado, *Peru* 124 F5
Puerto Manatí, *Cuba* 120 B4
Puerto Montt, *Chile* 128 E2
Puerto Morazán, *Nic.* 120 D2
Puerto Morelos, *Mexico* 119 C7
Puerto Natales, *Chile* 128 G2
Puerto Padre, *Cuba* 120 B4
Puerto Páez, *Venezuela* 124 B5
Puerto Peñasco, *Mexico* 118 A2
Puerto Pinasco, *Paraguay* 126 A4
Puerto Plata, *Dom. Rep.* 121 C5
Puerto Pollensa = Port de Pollença, *Spain* 48 B10
Puerto Princesa, *Phil.* 61 G3
Puerto Quepos, *Costa Rica* 120 E3
Puerto Real, *Spain* 37 J4
Puerto Rico, *Canary Is.* 48 G4
Puerto Rico ⊠, *W. Indies* 121 d
Puerto Rico Trench, *Atl. Oc.* 121 C6
Puerto San Julián, *Argentina* 128 F3
Puerto Sastre, *Paraguay* 126 A4
Puerto Serrano, *Spain* 37 J5
Puerto Suárez, *Bolivia* 124 G7
Puerto Vallarta, *Mexico* 118 C3
Puerto Wilches, *Colombia* 124 B4
Puertollano, *Spain* 37 G6
Pueyrredón, L., *Argentina* 128 F2
Púez Odle ⌓, *Italy* 41 B8
Puffin I., *Ireland* 12 E1
Pugachev, *Russia* 34 D9
Pugal, *India* 68 E5
Puge, *China* 58 D4
Puge, *Tanzania* 86 C3
Puget Sound, *U.S.A.* 108 C2
Puget-Théniers, *France* 21 E10
Púglia □, *Italy* 43 A9
Pugŏdong, *N. Korea* 57 C16
Pugu, *Tanzania* 86 D4
Pūgūnzī, *Iran* 71 E8
Pui, *Romania* 28 E8
Puieşti, *Romania* 29 D12
Puig Major, *Spain* 48 B9
Puigcerdà, *Spain* 38 C6
Puigmal, *Spain* 38 C7
Puigpunyent, *Spain* 48 B9
Puijiang, *China* 58 B4
Puisaye, Collines de la, *France* 19 E10
Puiseaux, *France* 19 D9
Pujehun, *S. Leone* 82 D2
Pujiang, *China* 59 C12
Pujols, *France* 20 D3
Pujon-chŏsuji, *N. Korea* 57 D14
Pukaki, L., *N.Z.* 91 L3
Pukapuka, *Cook Is.* 97 J11
Pukaskwa △, *Canada* 104 C2
Pukatawagan, *Canada* 103 B8
Pukchin, *N. Korea* 57 D13
Pukch'ŏng, *N. Korea* 57 D15
Pukë, *Albania* 44 D3
Pukekohe, *N.Z.* 91 G5
Pukhrayan, *India* 69 F8
Pukou, *China* 59 A12
Pula, *Croatia* 41 D10
Pula, *Italy* 42 C1
Pulacayo, *Bolivia* 124 H5
Pulai, *Malaysia* 65 d
Pulandian, *China* 57 E11
Pularumpi, *Australia* 92 B5
Pulaski, *N.Y., U.S.A.* 117 C8
Pulaski, *Tenn., U.S.A.* 115 H2
Pulaski, *Va., U.S.A.* 114 G5
Pulau →, *Indonesia* 63 F9
Puławy, *Poland* 31 G8
Pulga, *U.S.A.* 110 F5
Pulicat L., *India* 66 N12
Pullman, *U.S.A.* 108 C5
Pulog, Mt., *Phil.* 61 C4
Pułtusk, *Poland* 31 F8
Pülümür, *Turkey* 73 C8
Pumlumon Fawr, *U.K.* 15 E4
Puná, I., *Ecuador* 124 D2
Punakaiki, *N.Z.* 91 K3
Punakha, *Bhutan* 67 F16
Punasar, *India* 68 F5
Punata, *Bolivia* 124 G5
Punch, *India* 69 C6
Punch →, *Pakistan* 68 C5
Punda Maria, *S. Africa* 89 C5
Pune, *India* 66 K8
P'ungsan, *N. Korea* 57 D15
Pungue, Ponte de, *Mozam.* 87 F3
Puning, *China* 59 F11
Punjab □, *India* 68 D7
Punjab □, *Pakistan* 68 E6
Puno, *Peru* 124 G4
Punpun →, *India* 69 G11
Punta, Cerro de, *Puerto Rico* 121 d
Punta Alta, *Argentina* 128 D4
Punta Arenas, *Chile* 128 G2
Punta de Díaz, *Chile* 126 B1
Punta del Hidalgo, *Canary Is.* 48 F3
Punta Gorda, *Belize* 119 D7
Punta Gorda, *U.S.A.* 115 M5
Punta Prieta, *Mexico* 118 B2
Punta Prima, *Spain* 48 B11

Punta Umbria, *Spain* 37 **H4**
Puntarenas, *Costa Rica* 120 **E3**
Punto Fijo, *Venezuela* 124 **A4**
Punxsatawney, *U.S.A.* 116 **F6**
Pupuan, *Indonesia* 63 **J18**
Puqi, *China* 59 **C9**
Puquio, *Peru* 124 **F4**
Pur →, *Russia* 52 **C8**
Puracé, Vol., *Colombia* 124 **C3**
Puračić, *Bos.-H.* 28 **F3**
Puralia = Puruliya, *India* 69 **H12**
Puranpur, *India* 69 **E9**
Purbeck, Isle of, *U.K.* 15 **G5**
Purcell, *U.S.A.* 113 **H6**
Purcell Mts., *Canada* 102 **D5**
Puri, *India* 67 **K14**
Purmerend, *Neths.* 17 **B4**
Purnia, *India* 69 **G12**
Purnululu △, *Australia* 92 **C4**
Pursat = Pouthisat, *Cambodia* 64 **F4**
Purukcahu, *Indonesia* 62 **E4**
Puruliya, *India* 69 **H12**
Purus →, *Brazil* 124 **D6**
Puruvesi, *Finland* 32 **B5**
Purvis, *U.S.A.* 113 **K10**
Pŭrvomay, *Bulgaria* 45 **D9**
Purwa, *India* 69 **F9**
Purwakarta, *Indonesia* 63 **G12**
Purwo, Tanjung, *Indonesia* 63 **K18**
Purwodadi, *Indonesia* 63 **G14**
Purwokerto, *Indonesia* 63 **G13**
Puryŏng, *N. Korea* 57 **C15**
Pusa, *India* 69 **G11**
Pusan, *S. Korea* 57 **G15**
Pushkin, *Russia* 32 **C6**
Pushkino, *Moskva, Russia* 32 **D9**
Pushkino, *Saratov, Russia* 34 **E8**
Püspökladány, *Hungary* 28 **C6**
Pustoshka, *Russia* 32 **D5**
Puszczykowo, *Poland* 31 **F3**
Putahow L., *Canada* 103 **B8**
Putao, *Burma* 67 **F20**
Putaruru, *N.Z.* 91 **H5**
Putbus, *Germany* 24 **A9**
Putian, *China* 59 **E12**
Putignano, *Italy* 43 **B10**
Puting, Tanjung, *Indonesia* 62 **E4**
Putlitz, *Germany* 24 **B8**
Putna, *Romania* 29 **C10**
Putna →, *Romania* 29 **E12**
Putnam, *U.S.A.* 117 **E13**
Putnok, *Hungary* 28 **B5**
Putorana, Gory, *Russia* 53 **C10**
Putrajaya, *Malaysia* 65 **L3**
Puttalam, *Sri Lanka* 66 **Q11**
Puttgarden, *Germany* 24 **A7**
Püttlingen, *Germany* 25 **F2**
Putumayo →, *S. Amer.* 124 **D5**
Putuo, *China* 59 **C14**
Putussibau, *Indonesia* 62 **D4**
Putyla, *Ukraine* 29 **B10**
Puvirnituq, *Canada* 101 **B12**
Puy-de-Dôme, *France* 20 **C6**
Puy-de-Dôme □, *France* 20 **C7**
Puy-l'Évêque, *France* 20 **D5**
Puyallup, *U.S.A.* 110 **C4**
Puyang, *China* 56 **G8**
Puylaurens, *France* 20 **E6**
Pūzeh Rīg, *Iran* 71 **E8**
Puzhaykove, *Ukraine* 29 **B14**
Pwani □, *Tanzania* 86 **D4**
Pweto, *Dem. Rep. of the Congo* 87 **D2**
Pwllheli, *U.K.* 14 **E3**
Pyana →, *Russia* 34 **C8**
Pyapon, *Burma* 67 **L19**
Pyasina →, *Russia* 53 **B9**
Pyatigorsk, *Russia* 35 **H6**
Pyatykhatky, *Ukraine* 33 **H7**
Pydna, *Greece* 44 **F6**
Pyè = Prome, *Burma* 67 **K19**
Pyetrikaw, *Belarus* 33 **F5**
Pyhäjoki, *Finland* 8 **D21**
Pyinmana, *Burma* 67 **K20**
Pyla, C., *Cyprus* 49 **E12**
Pymatuning Reservoir, *U.S.A.* 116 **E4**
Pyŏktong, *N. Korea* 57 **D13**
Pyŏnggang, *N. Korea* 57 **E14**
P'yŏngt'aek, *S. Korea* 57 **F14**
P'yŏngyang, *N. Korea* 57 **E13**
Pyote, *U.S.A.* 113 **K3**
Pyramid L., *U.S.A.* 108 **G4**
Pyramid Pk., *U.S.A.* 111 **J10**
Pyramids, *Egypt* 80 **J7**
Pyrénées, *Europe* 20 **F4**
Pyrénées △, *France* 20 **F3**
Pyrénées-Atlantiques □, *France* 20 **E3**
Pyrénées-Orientales □, *France* 20 **F6**
Pyryatyn, *Ukraine* 33 **G7**
Pyrzyce, *Poland* 31 **E1**
Pyskowice, *Poland* 31 **H5**
Pytalovo, *Russia* 32 **D4**
Pyu, *Burma* 67 **K20**
Pyzdry, *Poland* 31 **F4**

Q

Qaanaaq, *Greenland* 4 **B4**
Qabirri →, *Azerbaijan* 35 **K8**
Qachasnek, *S. Africa* 89 **E4**
Qa'el Jafr, *Jordan* 74 **E5**
Qa'emābād, *Iran* 71 **D9**
Qā'emshahr, *Iran* 71 **B7**
Qagan Nur, *China* 56 **C8**
Qahar Youyi Zhongqi, *China* 56 **D7**
Qahremānshahr = Bākhtarān, *Iran* 70 **C5**
Qaidam Pendi, *China* 60 **C4**
Qajarīyeh, *Iran* 71 **D6**
Qala, Ras il, *Malta* 49 **C1**
Qala-i-Jadid = Spīn Būldak, *Afghan.* 68 **D2**
Qala Point = Qala, Ras il, *Malta* 49 **C1**
Qala Viala, *Pakistan* 68 **D2**
Qala Yangi, *Afghan.* 68 **B2**
Qal'at al Akhḍar, *Si. Arabia* 70 **E3**
Qal'at Dīzah, *Iraq* 70 **B5**
Qal'at Şāliḥ, *Iraq* 70 **D5**
Qal'at Sukkar, *Iraq* 70 **D5**
Qalyûb, *Egypt* 80 **H7**
Qamani'tuaq = Baker Lake, *Canada* 100 **B10**
Qamdo, *China* 58 **B1**
Qamruddin Karez, *Pakistan* 68 **D3**
Qandahār, *Afghan.* 66 **D4**
Qandahār □, *Afghan.* 66 **D4**
Qapān, *Iran* 71 **B7**
Qapshaghay, *Kazakhstan* 52 **E8**
Qaqortoq, *Greenland* 101 **B6**
Qâra, *Egypt* 80 **B2**
Qara Qash →, *China* 69 **B8**
Qarabutaq, *Kazakhstan* 52 **E7**
Qaraçala, *Azerbaijan* 35 **L9**
Qaraghandy, *Kazakhstan* 52 **E8**
Qaraghayly, *Kazakhstan* 52 **E8**
Qārah, *Si. Arabia* 70 **D4**
Qarataū, *Kazakhstan* 52 **E8**
Qarataū, *Kazakhstan* 52 **E7**
Qardho = Gardo, *Somali Rep.* 75 **F4**
Qardud, *Sudan* 81 **E2**
Qareh →, *Iran* 70 **B5**
Qareh Tekān, *Iran* 71 **B6**
Qarqan He →, *China* 60 **C3**
Qarqaraly, *Kazakhstan* 52 **E8**
Qarrasa, *Sudan* 81 **E3**
Qarshi, *Uzbekistan* 52 **F7**
Qartabā, *Lebanon* 74 **A4**
Qaryat al Gharab, *Iraq* 70 **D5**
Qaryat al 'Ulyā, *Si. Arabia* 70 **E5**
Qasr 'Amra, *Jordan* 70 **D3**
Qaşr-e Qand, *Iran* 71 **E9**
Qasr Farâfra, *Egypt* 80 **B2**
Qatanā, *Syria* 74 **B5**
Qatar ■, *Asia* 71 **E6**
Qatlīsh, *Iran* 71 **B8**
Qattâra, *Egypt* 80 **A2**
Qattâra, Munkhafed el, *Egypt* 80 **B2**
Qattâra Depression = Qattâra, Munkhafed el, *Egypt* 80 **B2**
Qawām al Ḩamzah = Al Ḩamzah, *Iraq* 70 **D5**
Qāyen, *Iran* 71 **C8**
Qazaqstan = Kazakhstan ■, *Asia* 52 **E7**
Qazimämmäd, *Azerbaijan* 35 **K9**
Qazvin, *Iran* 71 **B6**
Qazvin □, *Iran* 71 **B6**
Qeissan, *Sudan* 81 **E3**
Qena, *Egypt* 80 **B3**
Qena, W. →, *Egypt* 80 **B3**
Qeqertarsuaq, *Greenland* 101 **B5**
Qeqertarsuaq, *Greenland* 101 **B14**
Qeshlāq, *Iran* 70 **C5**
Qeshm, *Iran* 71 **E8**
Qeys, *Iran* 71 **E7**
Qezel Owzen →, *Iran* 71 **B6**
Qezi'ot, *Israel* 74 **E3**
Qi Xian, *China* 56 **G8**
Qian Gorlos, *China* 57 **B13**
Qian Xian, *China* 56 **G5**
Qiancheng, *China* 58 **D7**
Qianjiang, *Guangxi Zhuangzu, China* 58 **F7**
Qianjiang, *Hubei, China* 59 **B9**
Qianjiang, *Sichuan, China* 58 **C7**
Qianshan, *China* 59 **B11**
Qianwei, *China* 58 **C4**
Qianxi, *China* 58 **D6**
Qianyang, *Hunan, China* 59 **D8**
Qianyang, *Shaanxi, China* 56 **G4**
Qianyang, *Zhejiang, China* 59 **B12**
Qiaojia, *China* 58 **D4**
Qichun, *China* 59 **B10**
Qidong, *Hunan, China* 59 **D9**
Qidong, *Jiangsu, China* 59 **B13**
Qijiang, *China* 58 **C6**
Qikiqtarjuaq, *Canada* 101 **B13**
Qila Safed, *Pakistan* 66 **E2**
Qila Saifullāh, *Pakistan* 68 **D3**
Qilian Shan, *China* 60 **C4**
Qimen, *China* 59 **C11**
Qin He →, *China* 56 **G7**
Qin Jiang →, *Guangxi Zhuangzu, China* 58 **F7**
Qin Jiang →, *Jiangxi, China* 59 **D10**
Qin Ling = Qinling Shandi, *China* 56 **H5**
Qin'an, *China* 56 **G3**
Qing Xian, *China* 56 **E9**
Qingcheng, *China* 57 **F9**
Qingdao, *China* 57 **F11**
Qingfeng, *China* 56 **G8**
Qinghai □, *China* 60 **C4**
Qinghai Hu, *China* 60 **C5**
Qinghecheng, *China* 57 **D13**
Qinghemen, *China* 57 **D11**
Qingjian, *China* 56 **F6**
Qingjiang = Huaiyin, *China* 57 **H10**
Qingliu, *China* 59 **D11**
Qinglong, *China* 58 **E5**
Qingping, *China* 58 **D6**
Qingpu, *China* 59 **B13**
Qingshui, *China* 56 **G4**
Qingshuihe, *China* 56 **E6**
Qingtian, *China* 59 **C13**
Qingtongxia Shuiku, *China* 56 **F3**
Qingxi, *China* 58 **D7**
Qingxu, *China* 56 **F7**
Qingyang, *Anhui, China* 59 **B11**
Qingyang, *Gansu, China* 56 **F4**
Qingyi Jiang →, *China* 58 **C4**
Qingyuan, *Guangdong, China* 59 **F9**
Qingyuan, *Liaoning, China* 57 **C13**
Qingyuan, *Zhejiang, China* 59 **D12**
Qingyun, *China* 57 **F9**
Qingzhen, *China* 58 **D6**
Qinhuangdao, *China* 57 **E10**
Qinling Shandi, *China* 56 **H5**
Qinshui, *China* 56 **G7**
Qinyang = Jiyuan, *China* 56 **G7**
Qinyuan, *China* 56 **F7**
Qinzhou, *China* 58 **G7**
Qionghai, *China* 64 **C8**
Qionglai, *China* 58 **B4**
Qionglai Shan, *China* 58 **B4**
Qiongzhou Haixia, *China* 64 **B8**
Qiqihar, *China* 53 **E13**
Qiraîya, W. →, *Egypt* 74 **E3**
Qiryat Ata, *Israel* 74 **C4**
Qiryat Gat, *Israel* 74 **D3**
Qiryat Mal'akhi, *Israel* 74 **D3**
Qiryat Shemona, *Israel* 74 **B4**
Qiryat Yam, *Israel* 74 **C4**
Qishan, *China* 56 **G4**
Qitai, *China* 60 **B3**
Qiubei, *China* 58 **E5**
Qixia, *China* 57 **F11**
Qiyang, *China* 59 **D8**
Qızılağac Körfäzi, *Azerbaijan* 71 **B6**
Qojūr, *Iran* 70 **B5**
Qom, *Iran* 71 **C6**
Qom □, *Iran* 71 **C6**
Qomolangma Feng = Everest, Mt., *Nepal* 69 **E12**
Qomsheh, *Iran* 71 **D6**
Qoraqalpoghistan □, *Uzbekistan* 52 **E6**
Qorveh, *Iran* 73 **E12**
Qostanay, *Kazakhstan* 52 **D7**
Qoţūr, *Iran* 73 **C11**
Qu Jiang →, *China* 58 **B6**
Qu Xian, *China* 58 **B6**
Quabbin Reservoir, *U.S.A.* 117 **D12**
Quairading, *Australia* 93 **F2**
Quakenbrück, *Germany* 24 **C3**
Quakertown, *U.S.A.* 117 **F9**
Qualicum Beach, *Canada* 102 **D4**
Quambatook, *Australia* 95 **F3**
Quambone, *Australia* 95 **E4**
Quamby, *Australia* 94 **C3**
Quan Long = Ca Mau, *Vietnam* 65 **H5**
Quanah, *U.S.A.* 113 **H5**
Quang Ngai, *Vietnam* 64 **E7**
Quang Tri, *Vietnam* 64 **D6**
Quang Yen, *Vietnam* 58 **G6**
Quannan, *China* 59 **E10**
Quantock Hills, *U.K.* 15 **F4**
Quanzhou, *Fujian, China* 59 **E12**
Quanzhou, *Guangxi Zhuangzu, China* 59 **E8**
Qu'Appelle, *Canada* 103 **C8**
Quaqtaq, *Canada* 101 **B13**
Quaraí, *Brazil* 126 **C4**
Quarré-les-Tombes, *France* 19 **E11**
Quarteira, *Portugal* 37 **H2**
Quartu Sant'Élena, *Italy* 42 **C2**
Quartzsite, *U.S.A.* 111 **M12**
Quatsino Sd., *Canada* 102 **C3**
Quba, *Azerbaijan* 35 **K9**
Qūchān, *Iran* 71 **B8**
Queanbeyan, *Australia* 95 **F4**
Québec, *Canada* 105 **C5**
Québec □, *Canada* 105 **C6**
Quebrada del Condorito △, *Argentina* 126 **C3**
Quedlinburg, *Germany* 24 **D7**
Queen Alexandra Ra., *Antarctica* 5 **E11**
Queen Charlotte City, *Canada* 102 **C2**
Queen Charlotte Is., *Canada* 102 **C2**
Queen Charlotte Sd., *Canada* 102 **C3**
Queen Charlotte Strait, *Canada* 102 **C3**
Queen Elizabeth ⌓, *U.K.* 13 **E4**
Queen Elizabeth △, *Uganda* 86 **C3**
Queen Elizabeth Is., *Canada* 98 **B10**
Queen Mary Land, *Antarctica* 5 **D7**
Queen Maud G., *Canada* 100 **B9**
Queen Maud Land = Dronning Maud Land, *Antarctica* 5 **D3**
Queen Maud Mts., *Antarctica* 5 **E13**
Queens Chan., *Australia* 92 **C4**
Queenscliff, *Australia* 95 **F3**
Queensland □, *Australia* 94 **C3**
Queenstown, *Australia* 95 **G4**
Queenstown, *N.Z.* 91 **L2**
Queenstown, *Singapore* 65 **d**
Queenstown, *S. Africa* 88 **E4**
Queets, *U.S.A.* 110 **C2**
Queguay Grande →, *Uruguay* 126 **C4**
Queimadas, *Brazil* 125 **F11**
Quelimane, *Mozam.* 87 **F4**
Quellón, *Chile* 128 **E2**
Quelpart = Cheju do, *S. Korea* 57 **H14**
Queluz, *Portugal* 37 **G1**
Quemado, *N. Mex., U.S.A.* 109 **J9**
Quemado, *Tex., U.S.A.* 113 **L4**
Quemoy = Chinmen, *Taiwan* 59 **E13**
Quemú-Quemú, *Argentina* 126 **D3**
Quequén, *Argentina* 126 **D4**
Querétaro, *Mexico* 118 **C4**
Querétaro □, *Mexico* 118 **C5**
Querfurt, *Germany* 24 **D7**
Quérigut, *France* 20 **F6**
Querqueville, *France* 18 **C5**
Quesada, *Spain* 37 **H7**
Queshan, *China* 56 **H8**
Quesnel, *Canada* 102 **C4**
Quesnel →, *Canada* 102 **C4**
Quesnel L., *Canada* 102 **C4**
Questa, *U.S.A.* 109 **H11**
Questembert, *France* 18 **E4**
Quetico ⌓, *Canada* 104 **C1**
Quetta, *Pakistan* 68 **D2**
Queyras ⌓, *France* 21 **D10**
Quezaltenango, *Guatemala* 120 **D1**
Quezon City, *Phil.* 61 **D4**
Qufār, *Si. Arabia* 70 **E4**
Qui Nhon, *Vietnam* 64 **F7**
Quibaxe, *Angola* 84 **F2**
Quibdo, *Colombia* 124 **B3**
Quiberon, *France* 18 **E3**
Quiberon, Presqu'île de, *France* 18 **E3**
Quickborn, *Germany* 24 **B5**
Quiet L., *Canada* 102 **A2**
Quiindy, *Paraguay* 126 **B4**
Quila, *Mexico* 118 **C3**
Quilán, C., *Chile* 128 **E2**
Quilcene, *U.S.A.* 110 **C4**
Quilimarí, *Chile* 126 **C1**
Quilino, *Argentina* 126 **C3**
Quill Lakes, *Canada* 103 **C8**
Quillabamba, *Peru* 124 **F4**
Quillagua, *Chile* 126 **A2**
Quillaicillo, *Chile* 126 **C1**
Quillan, *France* 20 **F6**
Quillota, *Chile* 126 **C1**
Quilmes, *Argentina* 126 **C4**
Quilon, *India* 66 **Q10**
Quilpie, *Australia* 95 **D3**
Quilpué, *Chile* 126 **C1**
Quilua, *Mozam.* 87 **F4**
Quimilí, *Argentina* 126 **B3**
Quimper, *France* 18 **E2**
Quimperlé, *France* 18 **E3**
Quinault →, *U.S.A.* 110 **C2**
Quincy, *Calif., U.S.A.* 110 **F6**
Quincy, *Fla., U.S.A.* 115 **K3**
Quincy, *Ill., U.S.A.* 112 **F9**
Quincy, *Mass., U.S.A.* 117 **D14**
Quincy, *Wash., U.S.A.* 108 **C4**
Quines, *Argentina* 126 **C2**
Quinga, *Mozam.* 87 **F5**
Quingey, *France* 19 **E12**
Quintana de la Serena, *Spain* 37 **G5**
Quintana Roo □, *Mexico* 119 **D7**
Quintanar de la Orden, *Spain* 37 **F7**
Quintanar de la Sierra, *Spain* 38 **D2**
Quintanar del Rey, *Spain* 39 **F3**
Quinte West, *Canada* 116 **B7**
Quintero, *Chile* 126 **C1**
Quintin, *France* 18 **D4**
Quinto, *Spain* 38 **D4**
Quípar →, *Spain* 39 **G3**
Quirihue, *Chile* 126 **D1**
Quirindi, *Australia* 95 **E5**
Quirinópolis, *Brazil* 125 **G8**
Quiroga, *Spain* 36 **C3**
Quissac, *France* 21 **E8**
Quissanga, *Mozam.* 87 **E5**
Quissico, *Mozam.* 89 **C5**
Quitilipi, *Argentina* 126 **B3**
Quitman, *U.S.A.* 115 **K4**
Quito, *Ecuador* 124 **D3**
Quixadá, *Brazil* 125 **D11**
Quixaxe, *Mozam.* 87 **F5**
Qujing, *China* 58 **E4**
Qulan, *Kazakhstan* 52 **E8**
Qul'ân, Jazâ'ir, *Egypt* 70 **E2**
Qumbu, *S. Africa* 89 **E4**
Quneitra, *Syria* 74 **B4**
Qŭnghirot, *Uzbekistan* 52 **E6**
Qu'nyido, *China* 58 **B2**
Quoin I., *Australia* 92 **B4**
Quoin Pt., *S. Africa* 88 **E2**
Quorn, *Australia* 95 **E2**
Qŭqon, *Uzbekistan* 52 **E8**
Qurein, *Sudan* 81 **E3**
Qurnat as Sawdā', *Lebanon* 74 **A5**
Qûs, *Egypt* 80 **B3**
Qusar, *Azerbaijan* 35 **K9**
Quşaybā', *Si. Arabia* 70 **E4**
Qusaybah, *Iraq* 70 **C4**
Quseir, *Egypt* 70 **E2**
Qūshchī, *Iran* 70 **B5**
Quthing, *Lesotho* 89 **E4**
Qūţīābād, *Iran* 71 **C6**
Quwo, *China* 56 **G6**
Quyang, *China* 56 **E8**
Quynh Nhai, *Vietnam* 64 **B4**
Quyon, *Canada* 117 **A8**
Quzhou, *China* 59 **C12**
Quzi, *China* 56 **F4**
Qvareli, *Georgia* 35 **K7**
Qyzylorda, *Kazakhstan* 52 **E7**

R

Ra, Ko, *Thailand* 65 **H2**
Raab, *Austria* 26 **C6**
Raahe, *Finland* 8 **D21**
Raalte, *Neths.* 17 **B6**
Raasay, *U.K.* 13 **D2**
Raasay, Sd. of, *U.K.* 13 **D2**
Rab, *Croatia* 41 **D11**
Raba, *Indonesia* 63 **F5**
Rába →, *Hungary* 28 **C2**
Raba →, *Poland* 31 **H7**
Rabaçal →, *Portugal* 36 **D3**
Rabah, *Nigeria* 83 **C6**
Rabai, *Kenya* 86 **C4**
Rabak, *Sudan* 81 **E3**
Rabastens, *France* 20 **E5**
Rabastens-de-Bigorre, *France* 20 **E4**
Rabat = Victoria, *Malta* 49 **C1**
Rabat, *Malta* 49 **D1**
Rabat, *Morocco* 78 **B4**
Rabaul, *Papua N. G.* 96 **H7**
Rābigh, *Si. Arabia* 75 **C2**
Rabka, *Poland* 31 **J6**
Râbniţa, *Moldova* 29 **C14**
Rābor, *Iran* 71 **D8**
Rača, *Serbia & M.* 44 **B4**
Răcăciuni, *Romania* 29 **D11**
Răcăşdia, *Romania* 28 **F6**
Racconigi, *Italy* 40 **D4**
Race, C., *Canada* 105 **C9**
Rach Gia, *Vietnam* 65 **G5**
Rachid, *Mauritania* 82 **B2**
Raciąż, *Poland* 31 **F7**
Racibórz, *Poland* 31 **H5**
Racichy, *Belarus* 30 **E10**
Racine, *U.S.A.* 114 **D2**
Rackerby, *U.S.A.* 110 **F5**
Radama, Nosy, *Madag.* 89 **A8**
Radama, Saikanosy, *Madag.* 89 **A8**
Radan, *Serbia & M.* 44 **D5**
Rădăuţi, *Romania* 29 **C10**
Rădăuţi-Prut, *Romania* 29 **B11**
Radbuza →, *Czech Rep.* 26 **B6**
Radcliff, *U.S.A.* 114 **G3**
Radeberg, *Germany* 24 **D9**
Radebeul, *Germany* 24 **D9**
Radeče, *Slovenia* 41 **B12**
Radekhiv, *Ukraine* 33 **G3**
Radekhov = Radekhiv, *Ukraine* 33 **G3**
Radenthein, *Austria* 26 **E6**
Radew →, *Poland* 30 **D2**
Radford, *U.S.A.* 114 **G5**
Radhanpur, *India* 68 **H4**
Radhwa, Jabal, *Si. Arabia* 70 **E3**
Radika →, *Macedonia* 44 **E4**
Radisson, *Qué., Canada* 104 **B4**
Radisson, *Sask., Canada* 103 **C7**
Radium Hot Springs, *Canada* 102 **C5**
Radlje ob Dravi, *Slovenia* 41 **B12**
Radnevo, *Bulgaria* 45 **D9**
Radnice, *Czech Rep.* 26 **B6**
Radnor Forest, *U.K.* 15 **E4**
Radolfzell, *Germany* 25 **H4**
Radom, *Poland* 31 **G8**
Radomir, *Bulgaria* 44 **D6**
Radomka →, *Poland* 31 **G8**
Radomsko, *Poland* 31 **G6**
Radomyshl, *Ukraine* 33 **G5**
Radomyśl Wielki, *Poland* 31 **H8**
Radoszyce, *Poland* 31 **G7**
Radoviš, *Macedonia* 44 **E6**
Radovljica, *Slovenia* 41 **B11**
Radstadt, *Austria* 26 **D6**
Radstock, C., *Australia* 95 **E1**
Răducăneni, *Romania* 29 **D12**
Raduša, *Macedonia* 44 **D5**
Radvanichy, *Belarus* 31 **F11**
Radviliškis, *Lithuania* 9 **J20**
Radville, *Canada* 103 **D8**
Raḍwá, J., *Si. Arabia* 80 **C4**
Radymno, *Poland* 31 **J9**
Radzanów, *Poland* 31 **F7**
Radziejów, *Poland* 31 **F5**
Radzyń Chełmiński, *Poland* 30 **E5**
Radzyń Podlaski, *Poland* 31 **G9**
Rae, *Canada* 102 **A5**
Rae Bareli, *India* 69 **F9**
Rae Isthmus, *Canada* 101 **B11**
Raeren, *Belgium* 17 **D6**
Raeside, L., *Australia* 93 **E3**
Raetihi, *N.Z.* 91 **H5**
Rafaela, *Argentina* 126 **C3**
Rafah, *Gaza Strip* 74 **D3**
Rafai, *C.A.R.* 86 **B1**
Raffadali, *Italy* 42 **E6**
Raffili, *Sudan* 81 **F2**
Rafḩā, *Si. Arabia* 70 **D4**
Rafsanjān, *Iran* 71 **D8**
Raft Pt., *Australia* 92 **C3**
Râgâ, *Sudan* 81 **F2**
Raga →, *Sudan* 81 **F2**
Ragachow, *Belarus* 33 **F6**
Ragag, *Sudan* 81 **E1**
Ragama, *Sri Lanka* 66 **R11**
Ragged, Mt., *Australia* 93 **F3**
Ragged Pt., *Barbados* 121 **g**
Raghunathpalli, *India* 69 **H11**
Raghunathpur, *India* 69 **H12**
Raglan, *N.Z.* 91 **G5**
Ragusa, *Italy* 43 **F7**
Raha, *Indonesia* 63 **E6**
Rahad, Nahr ed →, *Sudan* 81 **E3**
Rahaeng = Tak, *Thailand* 64 **D2**
Rahatgarh, *India* 69 **H8**
Rahden, *Germany* 24 **C4**
Raheita, *Eritrea* 81 **E5**
Rahimyar Khan, *Pakistan* 68 **E4**
Rāhjerd, *Iran* 71 **C6**
Rahole ⌓, *Kenya* 86 **B4**
Rahon, *India* 68 **D7**
Raichur, *India* 66 **L10**
Raiganj, *India* 69 **G13**
Raigarh, *India* 67 **J13**
Raijua, *Indonesia* 63 **F6**
Raikot, *India* 68 **D6**
Railton, *Australia* 95 **G4**
Rainbow Bridge ⌓, *U.S.A.* 109 **H8**
Rainbow Lake, *Canada* 102 **B5**
Rainier, *U.S.A.* 110 **D4**
Rainier, Mt., *U.S.A.* 110 **D5**
Rainy L., *Canada* 103 **D10**
Rainy River, *Canada* 103 **D10**
Raippaluoto, *Finland* 8 **E19**
Raipur, *India* 67 **J12**
Ra'is, *Si. Arabia* 80 **C4**
Raisen, *India* 68 **H8**
Raisio, *Finland* 9 **F20**
Raj Nandgaon, *India* 67 **J12**
Raj Nilgiri, *India* 69 **J12**
Raja, Ujung, *Indonesia* 62 **D1**
Raja Ampat, Kepulauan, *Indonesia* 63 **E7**
Rajahmundry, *India* 67 **L12**
Rajang →, *Malaysia* 62 **D4**
Rajanpur, *Pakistan* 68 **E4**
Rajapalaiyam, *India* 66 **Q10**
Rajasthan □, *India* 68 **F5**
Rajasthan Canal = Indira Gandhi Canal, *India* 68 **F5**

Rajauri, India 69 C6
Rajgarh, Mad. P., India 68 G7
Rajgarh, Raj., India 68 F7
Rajgarh, Raj., India 68 E6
Rajgir, India 69 G11
Rajgród, Poland 30 E9
Rajkot, India 68 H4
Rajmahal Hills, India 69 G12
Rajpipla, India 66 J8
Rajpur, India 68 H6
Rajpura, India 68 D7
Rajshahi, Bangla. 67 G16
Rajshahi □, Bangla. 69 G13
Rajula, India 68 J4
Rakaia, N.Z. 91 K4
Rakaia →, N.Z. 91 K4
Rakan, Ra's, Qatar 71 E6
Rakaposhi, Pakistan 69 A6
Rakata, Pulau, Indonesia 62 F3
Rakhiv, Ukraine 29 B9
Rakhni, Pakistan 68 D3
Rakhni →, Pakistan 68 E3
Rakhny-Lisovi, Ukraine 29 B13
Rakitnoye, Russia 54 B7
Rakitovo, Bulgaria 45 E8
Rakiura △, N.Z. 91 M1
Rakoniewice, Poland 31 F3
Rakops, Botswana 88 C3
Rakovica, Croatia 41 D12
Rakovník, Czech Rep. 26 A6
Rakovski, Bulgaria 45 D8
Rakvere, Estonia 9 G22
Raleigh, U.S.A. 115 H6
Ralja, Serbia & M. 44 B4
Ralls, U.S.A. 113 J4
Ralston, U.S.A. 116 E8
Ram →, Canada 102 A4
Rām Allāh, West Bank 74 D4
Rama, Nic. 120 D3
Ramacca, Italy 43 E7
Ramakona, India 69 J8
Ramales de la Victoria, Spain 36 B7
Rāmallāh = Rām Allāh, West Bank 74 D4
Raman, Thailand 65 J3
Ramanathapuram, India 66 Q11
Ramanetaka, B. de, Madag. 89 A8
Ramanujganj, India 69 H10
Ramat Gan, Israel 74 C3
Ramatlhabama, S. Africa 88 D4
Ramban, India 69 C6
Rambervillers, France 19 D13
Rambipuji, Indonesia 63 H15
Rambouillet, France 19 D8
Rame Hd., Australia 95 F4
Ramechhap, Nepal 69 F12
Ramenskoye, Russia 32 E10
Ramganga →, India 69 F8
Ramgarh, Jharkhand, India 69 H11
Ramgarh, Raj., India 68 F6
Ramgarh, Raj., India 68 F4
Rāmhormoz, Iran 71 D6
Ramīān, Iran 71 B7
Ramingining, Australia 94 A2
Ramla, Israel 74 D3
Ramlu, Eritrea 81 E5
Ramm = Rum, Jordan 74 F4
Ramm, Jabal, Jordan 74 F4
Râmna →, Romania 29 E12
Ramnad = Ramanathapuram, India 66 Q11
Ramnagar, Jammu & Kashmir, India 69 C6
Ramnagar, Uttaranchal, India 69 E8
Ramnäs, Sweden 10 E10
Râmnicu Sărat, Romania 29 E12
Râmnicu Vâlcea, Romania 29 E9
Ramon, Russia 33 G10
Ramona, U.S.A. 111 M10
Ramonville-St-Agne, France 20 E5
Ramore, Canada 104 C3
Ramos →, Nigeria 83 D6
Ramotswa, Botswana 88 C4
Rampur, H.P., India 68 D7
Rampur, Mad. P., India 68 H5
Rampur, Ut. P., India 69 E8
Rampur Hat, India 69 G12
Rampura, India 68 G6
Ramrama Tola, India 69 J8
Ramree I., Burma 67 K19
Rāmsar, Iran 71 B6
Ramsey, I. of Man 14 C3
Ramsey, U.S.A. 117 E10
Ramsey L., Canada 104 C3
Ramsgate, U.K. 15 F9
Ramsjö, Sweden 10 B9
Ramstein, Germany 25 F3
Ramtek, India 66 J11
Ramvik, Sweden 10 B11
Rana Pratap Sagar Dam, India 68 G6
Ranaghat, India 69 H13
Ranahu, Pakistan 68 G3
Ranau, Malaysia 62 C5
Rancagua, Chile 126 C1
Rance →, France 18 D5
Rancheria →, Canada 102 A3
Ranchester, U.S.A. 108 D10
Ranchi, India 69 H11
Rancho Cucamonga, U.S.A. 111 L9
Randalstown, U.K. 12 B5
Randan, France 19 F10
Randazzo, Italy 43 E7
Randers, Denmark 11 H4
Randers Fjord, Denmark 11 H4
Randfontein, S. Africa 89 D4
Randle, U.S.A. 110 D5
Randolph, Mass., U.S.A. 117 D13
Randolph, N.Y., U.S.A. 116 D6
Randolph, Utah, U.S.A. 108 F8
Randolph, Vt., U.S.A. 117 C12
Randsburg, U.S.A. 111 K9
Råneälven →, Sweden 8 D20
Rangae, Thailand 65 J3
Rangaunu B., N.Z. 91 F4
Rangeley, U.S.A. 117 B14
Rangeley L., U.S.A. 117 B14
Rangely, U.S.A. 108 F9
Ranger, U.S.A. 113 J5
Rangia, India 67 F17
Rangiora, N.Z. 91 K4
Rangitaiki →, N.Z. 91 G6
Rangitata →, N.Z. 91 K3
Rangitoto ke te tonga = D'Urville I., N.Z. 91 J4
Rangkasbitung, Indonesia 63 G12
Rangon →, Burma 67 L20
Rangoon, Burma 67 L20
Rangpur, Bangla. 67 G16
Rangsit, Thailand 64 F3
Ranibennur, India 66 M9
Raniganj, Ut. P., India 69 F9
Raniganj, W. Bengal, India 67 H15
Ranikhet, India 69 E8
Raniwara, India 66 G8
Rāniyah, Iraq 70 B5
Ranka, India 69 H10
Ranken →, Australia 94 C2
Rankin, U.S.A. 113 K4
Rankin Inlet, Canada 100 B10
Rankins Springs, Australia 95 E4
Rankweil, Austria 26 D2
Rannoch, L., U.K. 13 E4
Rannoch Moor, U.K. 13 E4
Ranobe, Helodranon' i, Madag. 89 C7
Ranohira, Madag. 89 C8
Ranomafana, Toamasina, Madag. 89 B8
Ranomafana, Toliara, Madag. 89 C8
Ranomafana △, Madag. 89 C8
Ranomena, Madag. 89 C8
Ranong, Thailand 65 H2
Ranotsara Nord, Madag. 89 C8
Rānsa, Iran 71 C6
Ransiki, Indonesia 63 E8
Rantabe, Madag. 89 B8
Rantauprapat, Indonesia 62 D1
Rantemario, Indonesia 63 E5
Rantoul, U.S.A. 114 E1
Ranum, Denmark 11 H3
Ranyah, W. →, Si. Arabia 80 C5
Raon l'Étape, France 19 D13
Raoping, China 59 F11
Raoyang, China 56 E8
Rap, Ko, Thailand 65 b
Rapa, French Polynesia 97 K13
Rapa Nui = Pascua, I. de, Chile 97 K17
Rapallo, Italy 40 D6
Rapar, India 68 H4
Rāpch, Iran 71 E8
Raper, C., Canada 101 B13
Rapid City, U.S.A. 112 D3
Rapid River, U.S.A. 114 C2
Rapla, Estonia 9 G21
Rapti →, India 69 F10
Rapu Rapu I., Phil. 61 E6
Raqaba ez Zarqa →, Sudan 81 F2
Raquette →, U.S.A. 117 B10
Raquette Lake, U.S.A. 117 C10
Rarotonga, Cook Is. 97 K12
Ra's al 'Ayn, Syria 70 B4
Ra's al Khaymah, U.A.E. 71 E7
Râs el Mâ, Mali 82 B4
Râs Ghârib, Egypt 80 B3
Râs Mallap, Egypt 80 B3
Râs Muhammad △, Egypt 80 B3
Rasca, Pta. de la, Canary Is. 48 G3
Răşcani, Moldova 29 C12
Raseiniai, Lithuania 9 J20
Rashad, Sudan 81 E3
Rashîd, Egypt 80 H7
Rashîd, Masabb, Egypt 80 H7
Rashmi, India 68 G6
Rasht, Iran 71 B6
Rasi Salai, Thailand 64 E5
Raška, Serbia & M. 44 C4
Râsnov, Romania 29 E10
Rason L., Australia 93 E3
Raşova, Romania 29 F12
Rasovo, Bulgaria 44 C7
Rasra, India 69 G10
Rasskazovo, Russia 34 D5
Rast, Romania 29 G8
Rastatt, Germany 25 G4
Rastede, Germany 24 B4
Răstoliţa, Romania 29 D9
Rasul, Pakistan 68 C5
Raszków, Poland 31 G4
Rat Buri, Thailand 64 F2
Rat Islands, U.S.A. 100 C1
Rat L., Canada 103 B9
Rätan, Sweden 10 B8
Ratangarh, India 68 E6
Raţāwī, Iraq 70 D5
Rath, India 69 G8
Rath Luirc, Ireland 12 D3
Rathdrum, Ireland 12 D5
Rathenow, Germany 24 C8
Rathkeale, Ireland 12 D3
Rathlin I., U.K. 12 A5
Rathmelton, Ireland 12 A4
Ratibor = Racibórz, Poland 31 H5
Rätikon, Austria 26 D2
Ratingen, Germany 24 D2
Ratlam, India 68 H6
Ratnagiri, India 66 L8
Ratodero, Pakistan 68 F3
Raton, U.S.A. 113 G2
Rattaphum, Thailand 65 J3
Ratten, Austria 26 D8
Rattray Hd., U.K. 13 D7
Rättvik, Sweden 10 D9
Ratz, Mt., Canada 102 B2
Ratzeburg, Germany 24 B6
Raub, Malaysia 65 L3
Rauch, Argentina 126 D4
Raudales de Malpaso, Mexico 119 D6
Raufarhöfn, Iceland 8 C6
Raufoss, Norway 9 F14
Raukumara Ra., N.Z. 91 H6
Rauma, Finland 9 F19
Raumo = Rauma, Finland 9 F19
Raung, Gunung, Indonesia 63 J17
Raurkela, India 69 H11
Rausu-Dake, Japan 54 B12
Răut →, Moldova 29 C14
Rava-Ruska, Ukraine 31 H10
Rava Russkaya = Rava-Ruska, Ukraine 31 H10
Ravalli, U.S.A. 108 C6
Ravānsar, Iran 70 C5
Ravanusa, Italy 42 E6
Rāvar, Iran 71 D8
Ravena, U.S.A. 117 D11
Ravenna, Italy 41 D9
Ravenna, Nebr., U.S.A. 112 E5
Ravenna, Ohio, U.S.A. 116 E3
Ravensburg, Germany 25 H5
Ravenshoe, Australia 94 B4
Ravensthorpe, Australia 93 F3
Ravenswood, Australia 94 C4
Ravenswood, U.S.A. 114 F5
Ravi →, Pakistan 68 D4
Ravna Gora, Croatia 41 C11
Ravna Reka, Serbia & M. 44 B5
Ravne na Koroškem, Slovenia 41 B11
Rawa Mazowiecka, Poland 31 G7
Rawalpindi, Pakistan 68 C5
Rawāndūz, Iraq 70 B5
Rawang, Malaysia 65 L3
Rawene, N.Z. 91 F4
Rawicz, Poland 31 G3
Rawka →, Poland 31 F7
Rawlinna, Australia 93 F4
Rawlins, U.S.A. 108 F10
Rawlinson Ra., Australia 93 D4
Rawson, Argentina 128 E3
Raxaul, India 69 F11
Ray, U.S.A. 112 A3
Ray, C., Canada 105 C8
Raya Ring, Ko, Thailand 65 a
Rayadurg, India 66 M10
Rayagada, India 67 K13
Raychikhinsk, Russia 53 E13
Rāyen, Iran 71 D8
Rayleigh, U.K. 15 F8
Raymond, Canada 102 D6
Raymond, Calif., U.S.A. 110 H7
Raymond, N.H., U.S.A. 117 C13
Raymond, Wash., U.S.A. 110 D3
Raymondville, U.S.A. 113 M6
Raymore, Canada 103 C8
Rayón, Mexico 118 B2
Rayong, Thailand 64 F3
Rayville, U.S.A. 113 J9
Raz, Pte. du, France 18 D2
Razan, Iran 71 C6
Ražana, Serbia & M. 44 B3
Ražanj, Serbia & M. 44 C5
Razāzah, Buḩayrat ar, Iraq 70 C4
Razazah, L. = Razāzah, Buḩayrat ar, Iraq 70 C4
Razdelna, Bulgaria 45 C11
Razdel'naya = Rozdilna, Ukraine 29 D15
Razdolnoye, Russia 54 C5
Razdolnoye, Ukraine 33 K7
Razeh, Iran 71 C6
Razgrad, Bulgaria 45 C10
Razim, Lacul, Romania 29 F14
Razlog, Bulgaria 44 E7
Razmak, Pakistan 68 C3
Ré, Î. de, France 20 B2
Reading, U.K. 15 F7
Reading, U.S.A. 117 F9
Reading □, U.K. 15 F7
Realicó, Argentina 126 D3
Réalmont, France 20 E6
Ream, Cambodia 65 G4
Reata, Mexico 118 B4
Reay Forest, U.K. 13 C4
Rebais, France 19 D10
Rebi, Indonesia 63 F8
Rebiana, Libya 79 D10
Rebiana, Sahrā', Libya 79 D10
Rebun-Tō, Japan 54 B10
Recanati, Italy 41 E10
Recaş, Romania 28 E6
Recco, Italy 40 D6
Recherche, Arch. of the, Australia 93 F3
Rechna Doab, Pakistan 68 D5
Rechytsa, Belarus 33 F6
Recife, Brazil 125 E12
Recklinghausen, Germany 17 C7
Reconquista, Argentina 126 B4
Recreo, Argentina 126 B2
Recz, Poland 31 E2
Red →, La., U.S.A. 113 K9
Red →, N. Dak., U.S.A. 100 C10
Red Bank, U.S.A. 117 F10
Red Bay, Canada 105 B8
Red Bluff, U.S.A. 108 F2
Red Bluff L., U.S.A. 113 K3
Red Cliffs, Australia 95 E3
Red Cloud, U.S.A. 112 E5
Red Creek, U.S.A. 117 C8
Red Deer, Canada 102 C6
Red Deer →, Alta., Canada 103 C7
Red Deer →, Man., Canada 103 C8
Red Deer L., Canada 103 C8
Red Hook, U.S.A. 117 E11
Red Indian L., Canada 105 C8
Red L., Canada 103 C10
Red Lake, Canada 103 C10
Red Lake Falls, U.S.A. 112 B6
Red Lake Road, Canada 103 C10
Red Lodge, U.S.A. 108 D9
Red Mountain, U.S.A. 111 K9
Red Oak, U.S.A. 112 E7
Red Rock, Canada 104 C2
Red Rock, L., U.S.A. 112 E8
Red Rocks Pt., Australia 93 F4
Red Sea, Asia 75 C2
Red Slate Mt., U.S.A. 110 H8
Red Sucker L., Canada 104 B1
Red Tower Pass = Turnu Roşu, P., Romania 29 E9
Red Wing, U.S.A. 112 C8
Reda, Poland 30 D5
Redang, Malaysia 65 K4
Redange, Lux. 17 E5
Redcar, U.K. 14 C6
Redcar & Cleveland □, U.K. 14 C7
Redcliff, Canada 103 C6
Redcliffe, Australia 95 D5
Redcliffe, Mt., Australia 93 E3
Reddersburg, S. Africa 88 D4
Redding, U.S.A. 108 F2
Redditch, U.K. 15 E6
Redfield, U.S.A. 112 C5
Redford, U.S.A. 117 B11
Redhead, Trin. & Tob. 125 K16
Redkino, Russia 32 D9
Redlands, U.S.A. 111 M9
Redmond, Oreg., U.S.A. 108 D3
Redmond, Wash., U.S.A. 110 C4
Redon, France 18 E4
Redonda, Antigua & B. 121 C7
Redondela, Spain 36 C2
Redondo, Portugal 37 G3
Redondo Beach, U.S.A. 111 M8
Redruth, U.K. 15 G2
Redvers, Canada 103 D8
Redwater, Canada 102 C6
Redwood, U.S.A. 117 B9
Redwood △, U.S.A. 108 F1
Redwood City, U.S.A. 110 H4
Redwood Falls, U.S.A. 112 C7
Ree, L., Ireland 12 C3
Reed, L., Canada 103 C8
Reed City, U.S.A. 114 D3
Reedley, U.S.A. 110 J7
Reedsburg, U.S.A. 112 D9
Reedsport, U.S.A. 108 E1
Reedsville, U.S.A. 116 F7
Reefton, N.Z. 91 K3
Rees, Germany 24 D2
Reese →, U.S.A. 108 F5
Refahiye, Turkey 73 C8
Reftele, Sweden 11 G7
Refugio, U.S.A. 113 L6
Rega →, Poland 30 D2
Regalbuto, Italy 43 E7
Regen, Germany 25 G9
Regen →, Germany 25 F8
Regensburg, Germany 25 F8
Regenstauf, Germany 25 F8
Reggâne = Zaouiet Reggâne, Algeria 78 C6
Reggello, Italy 41 E8
Réggio di Calábria, Italy 43 D8
Réggio nell'Emília, Italy 40 D7
Reghin, Romania 29 D9
Regina, Canada 103 C8
Regina Beach, Canada 103 C8
Registro, Brazil 127 A6
Reguengos de Monsaraz, Portugal 37 G3
Rehar →, India 69 H10
Rehli, India 69 H8
Rehoboth, Namibia 88 C2
Rehovot, Israel 74 D3
Reichenbach, Germany 24 E8
Reid, Australia 93 F4
Reidsville, U.S.A. 115 G6
Reigate, U.K. 15 F7
Reillo, Spain 38 F3
Reims, France 19 C11
Reina Adelaida, Arch., Chile 128 G2
Reina Sofia, Tenerife ✗ (TFS), Canary Is. 48 F3
Reinbek, Germany 24 B6
Reindeer →, Canada 103 B8
Reindeer I., Canada 103 C9
Reindeer L., Canada 103 B8
Reinga, C., N.Z. 91 F4
Reinosa, Spain 36 B6
Reitz, S. Africa 89 D4
Reivilo, S. Africa 88 D3
Rejaf, Sudan 81 G3
Rejmyre, Sweden 11 F9
Rejowiec Fabryczny, Poland 31 G10
Reka →, Slovenia 41 C11
Rekovac, Serbia & M. 44 C5
Reliance, Canada 103 A7
Rémalard, France 18 D7
Remarkable, Mt., Australia 95 E2
Rembang, Indonesia 63 G14
Remedios, Panama 120 E3
Remeshk, Iran 71 E8
Remetea, Romania 29 D10
Remich, Lux. 17 E6
Remiremont, France 19 D13
Remo, Ethiopia 81 F5
Remontnoye, Russia 35 G6
Remoulins, France 21 E8
Remscheid, Germany 17 C7
Ren Xian, China 56 F8
Rendang, Indonesia 63 J18
Rende, Italy 43 C9
Rendína, Greece 46 B3
Rendsburg, Germany 24 A5
Renfrew, Canada 117 A8
Renfrewshire □, U.K. 13 F4
Rengat, Indonesia 62 E2
Rengo, Chile 126 C1
Renhua, China 59 E9
Renhuai, China 58 D6
Reni, Ukraine 29 E13
Renk, Sudan 81 E3
Renmark, Australia 95 E3
Rennell Sd., Canada 102 C2
Renner Springs, Australia 94 B1
Rennes, France 18 D5
Rennie L., Canada 103 A7
Reno, U.S.A. 110 F7
Reno →, Italy 41 D9
Renovo, U.S.A. 116 E7
Renqiu, China 56 E9
Rens, Denmark 11 K3
Renshou, China 58 C5
Rensselaer, Ind., U.S.A. 114 E2
Rensselaer, N.Y., U.S.A. 117 D11
Rentería, Spain 38 B3
Renton, U.S.A. 110 C4
Réo, Burkina Faso 82 C4
Reocín, Spain 36 B6
Reotipur, India 69 G10
Répcelak, Hungary 28 C2
Republic, Mo., U.S.A. 113 G8
Republic, Wash., U.S.A. 108 B4
Republican →, U.S.A. 112 F6
Repulse B., Australia 94 J6
Repulse Bay, Canada 101 B11
Requena, Peru 124 E4
Requena, Spain 39 F3
Réquista, France 20 D6
Reşadiye = Datça, Turkey 47 E9
Reşadiye, Turkey 72 B7
Reşadiye Yarımadası, Turkey 47 E9
Resavica, Serbia & M. 44 B5
Resen, Macedonia 44 E5
Reserve, U.S.A. 109 K9
Resht = Rasht, Iran 71 B6
Resistencia, Argentina 126 B4
Reşiţa, Romania 28 E6
Resko, Poland 30 E2
Reso = Raisio, Finland 9 F20
Resolution I., Canada 101 B13
Resolution I., N.Z. 91 L1
Ressano Garcia, Mozam. 89 D5
Reston, Canada 103 D8
Reszel, Poland 30 D8
Retalhuleu, Guatemala 120 D1
Retenue, L. de, Dem. Rep. of the Congo 87 E2
Retezat △, Romania 28 E7
Retezat, Munţii, Romania 28 E8
Retford, U.K. 14 D7
Rethel, France 19 C11
Rethem, Germany 24 C5
Réthímnon, Greece 49 D6
Réthímnon □, Greece 49 D6
Reti, Pakistan 68 E3
Retiche, Alpi, Switz. 25 J6
Retiers, France 18 E5
Retortillo, Spain 36 E4
Retournac, France 21 C8
Rétság, Hungary 28 C4
Réunion ⊠, Ind. Oc. 77 J9
Reus, Spain 38 D6
Reuterstadt Stavenhagen, Germany 24 B8
Reutlingen, Germany 25 G5
Reutte, Austria 26 D3
Reval = Tallinn, Estonia 9 G21
Revel, France 20 E6
Revelganj, India 69 G11
Revelstoke, Canada 102 C5
Reventazón, Peru 124 E2
Revigny-sur-Ornain, France 19 D11
Revillagigedo, Is. de, Pac. Oc. 118 D2
Revin, France 19 C11
Revúca, Slovak Rep. 27 C13
Revuè →, Mozam. 87 F3
Rewa, India 69 G9
Rewari, India 68 E7
Rexburg, U.S.A. 108 E8
Rey, Iran 71 C6
Rey, I. del, Panama 120 E4
Rey Malabo, Eq. Guin. 83 E6
Reyðarfjörður, Iceland 8 D6
Reyes, Pt., U.S.A. 110 H3
Reyhanlı, Turkey 72 D7
Reykjahlið, Iceland 8 D5
Reykjanes, Iceland 8 E2
Reykjavík, Iceland 8 D3
Reynolds Ra., Australia 92 D5
Reynoldsville, U.S.A. 116 E6
Reynosa, Mexico 119 B5
Rēzekne, Latvia 9 H22
Rezina, Moldova 29 C13
Rezovo, Bulgaria 45 D12
Rezvān, Iran 71 E8
Rgotina, Serbia & M. 44 B6
Rhamnus, Greece 46 C6
Rhayader, U.K. 15 E4
Rheda-Wiedenbrück, Germany 24 D4
Rhede, Germany 24 D2
Rhein →, Europe 17 C6
Rhein-Main-Donau-Kanal, Germany 25 F7
Rhein-Ruhr, Düsseldorf ✗ (DUS), Germany 24 D2
Rhein-Taunus ⌂, Germany 25 E4
Rhein-Westerwald ⌂, Germany 24 E3
Rheinbach, Germany 24 E2
Rheine, Germany 24 C3
Rheinfelden, Germany 25 H3
Rheinhessen-Pfalz □, Germany 25 F3
Rheinland-Pfalz □, Germany 25 E2
Rheinsberg, Germany 24 B8
Rhin = Rhein →, Europe 17 C6
Rhine = Rhein →, Europe 17 C6
Rhinebeck, U.S.A. 117 E11
Rhineland-Palatinate = Rheinland-Pfalz □, Germany 25 E2
Rhinelander, U.S.A. 112 C10
Rhinns Pt., U.K. 13 F2

Rhino Camp, *Uganda* 86 B3
Rhir, Cap, *Morocco* 78 B4
Rho, *Italy* 40 C6
Rhode Island □, *U.S.A.* 117 E13
Rhodes = Ródhos, *Greece* 49 C10
Rhodope Mts. = Rhodopi Planina, *Bulgaria* 45 E8
Rhodopi Planina, *Bulgaria* 45 E8
Rhön, *Germany* 24 E5
Rhondda, *U.K.* 15 F4
Rhondda Cynon Taff □, *U.K.* 15 F4
Rhône □, *France* 21 C8
Rhône →, *France* 21 E8
Rhône-Alpes □, *France* 21 C9
Rhum, *U.K.* 13 E2
Rhyl, *U.K.* 14 D4
Ri-Aba, *Eq. Guin.* 83 E6
Ria Formosa ⌓, *Portugal* 37 H3
Riachão, *Brazil* 125 E9
Riangnom, *Sudan* 81 F3
Riaño, *Spain* 36 C6
Rians, *France* 21 E9
Riansáres →, *Spain* 37 F7
Riasi, *India* 69 C6
Riau □, *Indonesia* 62 D2
Riau, Kepulauan, *Indonesia* 62 D2
Riau Arch. = Riau, Kepulauan, *Indonesia* 62 D2
Riaza, *Spain* 36 D7
Riaza →, *Spain* 36 D7
Riba de Saelices, *Spain* 38 E2
Riba-Roja de Turia, *Spain* 39 F4
Ribadavia, *Spain* 36 C2
Ribadeo, *Spain* 36 B3
Ribadesella, *Spain* 36 B5
Ribado, *Nigeria* 83 D7
Ribao, *Cameroon* 83 D7
Ribas = Ribes de Freser, *Spain* 38 C7
Ribas do Rio Pardo, *Brazil* 125 H8
Ribauè, *Mozam.* 87 E4
Ribble →, *U.K.* 14 D5
Ribe, *Denmark* 11 J2
Ribe Amtskommune □, *Denmark* 11 J2
Ribeauvillé, *France* 19 D14
Ribécourt-Dreslincourt, *France* 19 C9
Ribeira = Santa Uxía, *Spain* 36 C2
Ribeira Brava, *Madeira* 48 D2
Ribeirão Prêto, *Brazil* 127 A6
Ribemont, *France* 19 C10
Ribera, *Italy* 42 E6
Ribérac, *France* 20 C4
Riberalta, *Bolivia* 124 F5
Ribes de Freser, *Spain* 38 C7
Ribnica, *Slovenia* 41 C11
Ribnitz-Damgarten, *Germany* 24 A8
Ričany, *Czech Rep.* 26 B7
Riccarton, *N.Z.* 91 K4
Ríccia, *Italy* 43 A7
Riccione, *Italy* 41 E9
Rice, *U.S.A.* 111 L12
Rice L., *Canada* 116 B6
Rice Lake, *U.S.A.* 112 C9
Rich, C., *Canada* 116 B4
Richard Toll, *Senegal* 82 B1
Richards Bay, *S. Africa* 89 D5
Richardson →, *Canada* 103 B6
Richardson Lakes, *U.S.A.* 114 C10
Richardson Springs, *U.S.A.* 110 F5
Riche, C., *Australia* 93 F2
Richelieu, *France* 18 E7
Richey, *U.S.A.* 112 B2
Richfield, *U.S.A.* 109 G8
Richfield Springs, *U.S.A.* 117 D10
Richford, *U.S.A.* 117 B12
Richibucto, *Canada* 105 C7
Richland, *Ga., U.S.A.* 115 J3
Richland, *Wash., U.S.A.* 108 C4
Richland Center, *U.S.A.* 112 D9
Richlands, *U.S.A.* 114 G5
Richmond, *Australia* 94 C3
Richmond, *N.Z.* 91 J4
Richmond, *U.K.* 14 C6
Richmond, *Calif., U.S.A.* 110 H4
Richmond, *Ind., U.S.A.* 114 F3
Richmond, *Ky., U.S.A.* 114 G3
Richmond, *Mich., U.S.A.* 116 D2
Richmond, *Mo., U.S.A.* 112 F8
Richmond, *Tex., U.S.A.* 113 L7
Richmond, *Utah, U.S.A.* 108 F8
Richmond, *Va., U.S.A.* 114 G7
Richmond, *Vt., U.S.A.* 117 B12
Richmond Hill, *Canada* 116 C5
Richmond Ra., *Australia* 95 D5
Richtersveld △, *S. Africa* 88 D2
Richwood, *U.S.A.* 114 F5
Ricla, *Spain* 38 D3
Ridder = Leninogorsk, *Kazakhstan* 52 D9
Riddlesburg, *U.S.A.* 116 F6
Ridgecrest, *U.S.A.* 111 K9
Ridgefield, *Conn., U.S.A.* 117 E11
Ridgefield, *Wash., U.S.A.* 110 E4
Ridgeland, *U.S.A.* 115 J5
Ridgetown, *Canada* 116 D3
Ridgewood, *U.S.A.* 117 F10
Ridgway, *U.S.A.* 116 E6
Riding Mountain △, *Canada* 103 C9
Ridley, Mt., *Australia* 93 F3
Riebeek-Oos, *S. Africa* 88 E4
Ried, *Austria* 26 C6
Riedlingen, *Germany* 25 G5
Riedstadt, *Germany* 25 F4
Rienza →, *Italy* 41 B8
Riesa, *Germany* 24 D9
Riesi, *Italy* 43 E7
Riet →, *S. Africa* 88 D3
Rietavas, *Lithuania* 30 C8
Rietbron, *S. Africa* 88 E3
Rietfontein, *Namibia* 88 C3
Rieti, *Italy* 41 F9
Rieupeyroux, *France* 20 D6
Riez, *France* 21 E10
Rif = Er Rif, *Morocco* 78 A5
Riffe L., *U.S.A.* 110 D4
Rifle, *U.S.A.* 108 G10
Rift Valley, *Africa* 76 G7
Rift Valley □, *Kenya* 86 B4
Rīga, *Latvia* 9 H21
Rīga ✕ (RIX), *Latvia* 30 B10
Riga, G. of, *Latvia* 9 H20
Rigacikun, *Nigeria* 83 C6
Rīgān, *Iran* 71 D8
Rīgas Jūras Līcis = Riga, G. of, *Latvia* 9 H20
Rigaud, *Canada* 117 A10
Rigby, *U.S.A.* 108 E8
Rīgestān, *Afghan.* 66 D4
Riggins, *U.S.A.* 108 D5
Rignac, *France* 20 D6
Rigolet, *Canada* 105 B8
Rihand Dam, *India* 69 G10
Riihimäki, *Finland* 9 F21
Riiser-Larsen-halvøya, *Antarctica* 5 C4
Rijau, *Nigeria* 83 C6
Rijeka, *Croatia* 41 C11
Rijeka Crnojevića, *Serbia & M.* 44 D3
Rijssen, *Neths.* 17 B6
Rika →, *Ukraine* 29 B8
Rike, *Ethiopia* 81 E4
Rikuchū-Kaigan △, *Japan* 54 E11
Rikuzentakada, *Japan* 54 E10
Rila, *Bulgaria* 44 D7
Rila Planina, *Bulgaria* 44 D7
Riley, *U.S.A.* 108 E4
Rima →, *Nigeria* 83 C6
Rimah, Wadi ar →, *Si. Arabia* 70 E4
Rimau, Pulau, *Malaysia* 65 c
Rimavská Sobota, *Slovak Rep.* 27 C13
Rimbey, *Canada* 102 C6
Rimbo, *Sweden* 10 E12
Rimersburg, *U.S.A.* 116 E5
Rimforsa, *Sweden* 11 F9
Rimi, *Nigeria* 83 C6
Rímini, *Italy* 41 D9
Rimouski, *Canada* 105 C6
Rimrock, *U.S.A.* 110 D5
Rinca, *Indonesia* 63 F5
Rincón de la Victoria, *Spain* 37 J6
Rincón de Romos, *Mexico* 118 C4
Rinconada, *Argentina* 126 A2
Rind →, *India* 69 G9
Ringarum, *Sweden* 11 F10
Ringas, *India* 68 F6
Ringe, *Denmark* 11 J4
Ringim, *Nigeria* 83 C6
Ringkøbing, *Denmark* 11 H2
Ringkøbing Amtskommune □, *Denmark* 11 H2
Ringkøbing Fjord, *Denmark* 11 H2
Ringsjön, *Sweden* 11 J7
Ringsted, *Denmark* 11 J5
Ringvassøy, *Norway* 8 B18
Ringwood, *U.S.A.* 117 E10
Rinía, *Greece* 47 D7
Rinjani, *Indonesia* 62 F5
Rinteln, *Germany* 24 C5
Río, Punta del, *Spain* 39 J2
Rio Branco, *Brazil* 124 E5
Río Branco, *Uruguay* 127 C5
Río Bravo ⌓, *N. Amer.* 118 B4
Río Bravo del Norte →, *Mexico* 119 B5
Rio Brilhante, *Brazil* 127 A5
Rio Claro, *Brazil* 127 A6
Rio Claro, *Trin. & Tob.* 121 D7
Río Colorado, *Argentina* 128 D4
Río Cuarto, *Argentina* 126 C3
Rio das Pedras, *Mozam.* 89 C6
Rio de Janeiro, *Brazil* 127 A7
Rio de Janeiro □, *Brazil* 127 A7
Rio do Sul, *Brazil* 127 B6
Río Dulce △, *Guatemala* 120 C2
Río Gallegos, *Argentina* 128 G3
Río Grande, *Argentina* 128 G3
Rio Grande, *Brazil* 127 C5
Río Grande, *Mexico* 118 C4
Río Grande, *Nic.* 120 D3
Rio Grande, *Puerto Rico* 121 d
Rio Grande, *U.S.A.* 113 N6
Rio Grande City, *U.S.A.* 113 M5
Río Grande de Santiago →, *Mexico* 118 C3
Rio Grande do Norte □, *Brazil* 125 E11
Rio Grande do Sul □, *Brazil* 127 C5
Río Hato, *Panama* 120 E3
Río Lagartos, *Mexico* 119 C7
Rio Largo, *Brazil* 125 E11
Rio Maior, *Portugal* 37 F2
Rio Marina, *Italy* 40 F7
Río Mulatos, *Bolivia* 124 G5
Río Muni □, *Eq. Guin.* 84 D2
Rio Negro, *Brazil* 127 B6
Rio Pardo, *Brazil* 127 C5
Río Pilcomayo △, *Argentina* 126 B4
Río Platano ⌓, *Honduras* 120 C3
Rio Rancho, *U.S.A.* 109 J10
Río Segundo, *Argentina* 126 C3
Río Tercero, *Argentina* 126 C3
Rio Tinto, *Portugal* 36 D2
Rio Verde, *Brazil* 125 G8
Río Verde, *Mexico* 119 C5
Rio Vista, *U.S.A.* 110 G5
Ríobamba, *Ecuador* 124 D3
Ríohacha, *Colombia* 124 A4
Riom, *France* 20 C7
Riom-ès-Montagnes, *France* 20 C6
Rion-des-Landes, *France* 20 E3
Rionero in Vúlture, *Italy* 43 B8
Rioni →, *Georgia* 35 J5
Riós, *Spain* 36 D3
Ríosucio, *Colombia* 124 B3
Riou L., *Canada* 103 B7
Rioz, *France* 19 E13
Ripatransone, *Italy* 41 F10
Ripley, *Canada* 116 B3
Ripley, *Calif., U.S.A.* 111 M12
Ripley, *N.Y., U.S.A.* 116 D5
Ripley, *Tenn., U.S.A.* 113 H10
Ripley, *W. Va., U.S.A.* 114 F5
Ripoll, *Spain* 38 C7
Ripon, *U.K.* 14 C6
Ripon, *Calif., U.S.A.* 110 H5
Ripon, *Wis., U.S.A.* 114 D1
Riposto, *Italy* 43 E8
Risan, *Serbia & M.* 44 D2
Riscle, *France* 20 E3
Rishā', W. ar →, *Si. Arabia* 70 E5
Rishiri-Rebun-Sarobetsu △, *Japan* 54 B10
Rishiri-Tō, *Japan* 54 B10
Rishon le Ẕiyyon, *Israel* 74 D3
Risle →, *France* 18 C7
Risnjak △, *Croatia* 41 C11
Rison, *U.S.A.* 113 J8
Risør, *Norway* 9 G13
Rita Blanca Cr. →, *U.S.A.* 113 H3
Riti, *Nigeria* 83 D6
Ritter, Mt., *U.S.A.* 110 H7
Rittman, *U.S.A.* 116 F3
Ritzville, *U.S.A.* 108 C4
Riva del Garda, *Italy* 40 C7
Riva Lígure, *Italy* 40 E4
Rivadavia, *Buenos Aires, Argentina* 126 D3
Rivadavia, *Mendoza, Argentina* 126 C2
Rivadavia, *Salta, Argentina* 126 A3
Rivadavia, *Chile* 126 B1
Rivarolo Canavese, *Italy* 40 C4
Rivas, *Nic.* 120 D2
Rive-de-Gier, *France* 21 C8
River Cess, *Liberia* 82 D3
River Jordan, *Canada* 110 B2
Rivera, *Argentina* 126 D3
Rivera, *Uruguay* 127 C4
Riverbank, *U.S.A.* 110 H6
Riverdale, *U.S.A.* 110 J7
Riverhead, *U.S.A.* 117 F12
Riverhurst, *Canada* 103 C7
Rivers, *Canada* 103 C8
Rivers □, *Nigeria* 83 E6
Rivers Inlet, *Canada* 102 C3
Riversdale, *S. Africa* 88 E3
Riverside, *U.S.A.* 111 M9
Riverton, *Australia* 95 E2
Riverton, *Canada* 103 C9
Riverton, *N.Z.* 91 M2
Riverton, *U.S.A.* 108 E9
Riverton Heights, *U.S.A.* 110 C4
Rives, *France* 21 C9
Rivesaltes, *France* 20 F6
Riviera, *U.S.A.* 111 K12
Riviera di Levante, *Italy* 40 D6
Riviera di Ponente, *Italy* 40 D5
Rivière-au-Renard, *Canada* 105 C7
Rivière-du-Loup, *Canada* 105 C6
Rivière-Pentecôte, *Canada* 105 C6
Rivière-Pilote, *Martinique* 120 c
Rivière St-Paul, *Canada* 105 B8
Rivière-Salée, *Martinique* 120 c
Rivne, *Ukraine* 29 D14
Rivne, *Ukraine* 33 G4
Rívoli, *Italy* 40 C4
Rivoli B., *Australia* 95 F3
Rixheim, *France* 19 E14
Riyadh = Ar Riyāḍ, *Si. Arabia* 70 E5
Rize, *Turkey* 73 B9
Rizhao, *China* 57 G10
Rizokarpaso, *Cyprus* 49 D13
Rizzuto, C., *Italy* 43 D10
Rjukan, *Norway* 9 G13
Ro, *Greece* 47 E11
Roa, *Spain* 36 D7
Road Town, *Br. Virgin Is.* 121 e
Roan Plateau, *U.S.A.* 108 G9
Roanne, *France* 19 F11
Roanoke, *Ala., U.S.A.* 115 J3
Roanoke, *Va., U.S.A.* 114 G6
Roanoke →, *U.S.A.* 115 H7
Roanoke I., *U.S.A.* 115 H8
Roanoke Rapids, *U.S.A.* 115 G7
Roatán, *Honduras* 120 C2
Robāt Sang, *Iran* 71 C8
Robāṭkarīm, *Iran* 71 C6
Robāṭkarīm □, *Iran* 71 B6
Robbins I., *Australia* 95 G4
Róbbio, *Italy* 40 C5
Robe →, *Australia* 92 D2
Röbel, *Germany* 24 B8
Robert Lee, *U.S.A.* 113 K4
Robertsdale, *U.S.A.* 116 F6
Robertsganj, *India* 69 G10
Robertson, *S. Africa* 88 E2
Robertson I., *Antarctica* 5 C18
Robertson Ra., *Australia* 92 D3
Robertsport, *Liberia* 82 D2
Robertstown, *Australia* 95 E2
Roberval, *Canada* 105 C5
Robeson Chan., *N. Amer.* 4 A4
Robesonia, *U.S.A.* 117 F8
Robi, *Ethiopia* 81 F4
Robinson, *U.S.A.* 114 F2
Robinson →, *Australia* 94 B2
Robinson Ra., *Australia* 93 E2
Robinvale, *Australia* 95 E3
Robledo, *Spain* 39 G2
Roblin, *Canada* 103 C8
Roboré, *Bolivia* 124 G7
Robson, *Canada* 102 D5
Robson, Mt., *Canada* 102 C5
Robstown, *U.S.A.* 113 M6
Roca, C. da, *Portugal* 37 G1
Roca Partida, I., *Mexico* 118 D2
Rocamadour, *France* 20 D5
Rocas, I., *Brazil* 125 D12
Rocca San Casciano, *Italy* 41 D8
Roccadáspide, *Italy* 43 B8
Roccastrada, *Italy* 41 F8
Roccella Iónica, *Italy* 43 D9
Rocha, *Uruguay* 127 C5
Rochdale, *U.K.* 14 D5
Rochechouart, *France* 20 C4
Rochefort, *Belgium* 17 D5
Rochefort, *France* 20 C3
Rochefort-en-Terre, *France* 18 E4
Rochelle, *U.S.A.* 112 E10
Rocher River, *Canada* 102 A6
Rocheservière, *France* 18 F5
Rochester, *U.K.* 15 F8
Rochester, *Ind., U.S.A.* 114 E2
Rochester, *Minn., U.S.A.* 112 C8
Rochester, *N.H., U.S.A.* 117 C14
Rochester, *N.Y., U.S.A.* 116 C7
Rociu, *Romania* 29 F10
Rock →, *Canada* 102 A3
Rock Creek, *U.S.A.* 116 E4
Rock Falls, *U.S.A.* 112 E10
Rock Hill, *U.S.A.* 115 H5
Rock Island, *U.S.A.* 112 E9
Rock Rapids, *U.S.A.* 112 D6
Rock Sound, *Bahamas* 120 B4
Rock Springs, *Mont., U.S.A.* 108 C10
Rock Springs, *Wyo., U.S.A.* 108 F9
Rock Valley, *U.S.A.* 112 D6
Rockall, *Atl. Oc.* 6 D3
Rockdale, *Tex., U.S.A.* 113 K6
Rockdale, *Wash., U.S.A.* 110 C5
Rockeby = Mungkan Kandju △, *Australia* 94 A3
Rockefeller Plateau, *Antarctica* 5 E14
Rockford, *U.S.A.* 112 D10
Rockglen, *Canada* 103 D7
Rockhampton, *Australia* 94 C5
Rockingham, *Australia* 93 F2
Rockingham, *U.S.A.* 115 H6
Rockingham B., *Australia* 94 B4
Rocklake, *U.S.A.* 112 A5
Rockland, *Canada* 117 A9
Rockland, *Idaho, U.S.A.* 108 E7
Rockland, *Maine, U.S.A.* 115 C11
Rockland, *Mich., U.S.A.* 112 B10
Rocklin, *U.S.A.* 110 G5
Rockly B., *Trin. & Tob.* 125 J16
Rockmart, *U.S.A.* 115 H3
Rockport, *Mass., U.S.A.* 117 D14
Rockport, *Mo., U.S.A.* 112 E7
Rockport, *Tex., U.S.A.* 113 L6
Rocksprings, *U.S.A.* 113 K4
Rockville, *Conn., U.S.A.* 117 E12
Rockville, *Md., U.S.A.* 114 F7
Rockwall, *U.S.A.* 113 J6
Rockwell City, *U.S.A.* 112 D7
Rockwood, *Canada* 116 C4
Rockwood, *Maine, U.S.A.* 115 C11
Rockwood, *Tenn., U.S.A.* 115 H3
Rocky Ford, *U.S.A.* 112 F3
Rocky Gully, *Australia* 93 F2
Rocky Harbour, *Canada* 105 C8
Rocky Island L., *Canada* 104 C3
Rocky Lane, *Canada* 102 B5
Rocky Mount, *U.S.A.* 115 H7
Rocky Mountain △, *U.S.A.* 108 F11
Rocky Mountain House, *Canada* 102 C6
Rocky Mts., *N. Amer.* 108 G10
Rocky Point, *Namibia* 88 B2
Rocroi, *France* 19 C11
Rod, *Pakistan* 66 E3
Rødby, *Denmark* 11 K5
Rødbyhavn, *Denmark* 11 K5
Roddickton, *Canada* 105 B8
Rødding, *Denmark* 11 J3
Rödeby, *Sweden* 11 H9
Rødekro, *Denmark* 11 J3
Rodenkirchen, *Germany* 24 B4
Rodez, *France* 20 D6
Rodholívas, *Greece* 44 F7
Rodhópi □, *Greece* 45 E9
Rodhopoú, *Greece* 49 D5
Ródhos, *Greece* 49 C10
Ródhos ✕ (RHO), *Greece* 47 E10
Rodi Gargánico, *Italy* 41 G12
Rodna, *Romania* 29 C9
Rodnei, Munţii, *Romania* 29 C9
Rodney, *Canada* 116 D3
Rodney, C., *N.Z.* 91 G5
Rodniki, *Russia* 34 B5
Rodonit, Kepi i, *Albania* 44 E3
Rodriguez, *Ind. Oc.* 3 E13
Roe →, *U.K.* 12 A5
Roebling, *U.S.A.* 117 F10
Roebourne, *Australia* 92 D2
Roebuck B., *Australia* 92 C3
Roermond, *Neths.* 17 C6
Roes Welcome Sd., *Canada* 101 B11
Roeselare, *Belgium* 17 D3
Rogachev = Ragachow, *Belarus* 33 F6
Rogačica, *Serbia & M.* 44 B3
Rogagua, L., *Bolivia* 124 F5
Rogaška Slatina, *Slovenia* 41 B12
Rogatec, *Slovenia* 41 B12
Rogatica, *Bos.-H.* 28 G4
Rogatyn, *Ukraine* 33 H3
Rogdhia, *Greece* 49 D7
Rogers, *U.S.A.* 113 G7
Rogers City, *U.S.A.* 114 C4
Rogersville, *Canada* 105 C6
Roggan →, *Canada* 104 B4
Roggan L., *Canada* 104 B4
Roggeveldberge, *S. Africa* 88 E3
Roggiano Gravina, *Italy* 43 C9
Rogliano, *France* 21 F13
Rogliano, *Italy* 43 C9
Rogoaguado, L., *Bolivia* 124 F5
Rogojampi, *Indonesia* 63 J17
Rogoźno, *Poland* 31 F3
Rogue →, *U.S.A.* 108 E1
Rohan, *France* 18 D4
Róhda, *Greece* 49 A3
Rohnert Park, *U.S.A.* 110 G4
Rohri, *Pakistan* 68 F3
Rohri Canal, *Pakistan* 68 F3
Rohtak, *India* 68 E7
Roi Et, *Thailand* 64 D4
Roja, *Latvia* 9 H20
Rojas, *Argentina* 126 C3
Rojişte, *Romania* 29 F8
Rojo, C., *Mexico* 119 C5
Rokan →, *Indonesia* 62 D2
Rokel →, *S. Leone* 82 D2
Rokiškis, *Lithuania* 9 J21
Rokitno, *Russia* 33 G8
Rokycany, *Czech Rep.* 26 B6
Rolândia, *Brazil* 127 A5
Rolla, *U.S.A.* 113 G9
Rolleston, *Australia* 94 C4
Rollingstone, *Australia* 94 B4
Rom, *Sudan* 81 F3
Roma, *Australia* 95 D4
Roma, *Italy* 41 G9
Roma, *Sweden* 11 G12
Roma, *U.S.A.* 113 M5
Roma Fiumicino ✕ (FCO), *Italy* 41 G9
Romain C., *U.S.A.* 115 J6
Romaine, *Canada* 105 B7
Romaine →, *Canada* 105 B7
Roman, *Bulgaria* 44 C7
Roman, *Romania* 29 D11
Roman-Kosh, Gora, *Ukraine* 33 K8
Romanche →, *France* 21 C9
Romang, *Indonesia* 63 F7
Români, *Egypt* 74 E1
Romania ■, *Europe* 29 D10
Romanija, *Bos.-H.* 28 G3
Romano, Cayo, *Cuba* 120 B4
Romans-sur-Isère, *France* 21 C9
Romanshorn, *Switz.* 25 H5
Rombari, *Sudan* 81 G3
Romblon, *Phil.* 61 E5
Rome = Roma, *Italy* 41 G9
Rome, *Ga., U.S.A.* 115 H3
Rome, *N.Y., U.S.A.* 117 C9
Rome, *Pa., U.S.A.* 117 E8
Rometta, *Italy* 43 D8
Romilly-sur-Seine, *France* 19 D10
Romney, *U.S.A.* 114 F6
Romney Marsh, *U.K.* 15 F8
Romny, *Ukraine* 33 G7
Rømø, *Denmark* 11 J2
Romodan, *Ukraine* 33 G7
Romodanovo, *Russia* 34 C7
Romont, *Switz.* 25 J2
Romorantin-Lanthenay, *France* 19 E8
Romsdalen, *Norway* 9 E12
Romsey, *U.K.* 15 G6
Ron, *Vietnam* 64 D6
Rona, *U.K.* 13 D3
Ronan, *U.S.A.* 108 C6
Roncador, Cayos, *Colombia* 120 D3
Roncador, Serra do, *Brazil* 125 F8
Ronciglione, *Italy* 41 F9
Ronco →, *Italy* 41 D9
Ronda, *Spain* 37 J5
Ronda, Serranía de, *Spain* 37 J5
Rondane, *Norway* 9 F13
Rondônia □, *Brazil* 124 F6
Rondonópolis, *Brazil* 125 G8
Rong, Koh, *Cambodia* 65 G4
Rong Jiang →, *China* 58 E7
Rong Xian, *Guangxi Zhuangzu, China* 59 F8
Rong Xian, *Sichuan, China* 58 C5
Rong'an, *China* 58 E7
Rongchang, *China* 58 C5
Ronge, L. la, *Canada* 103 B7
Rongjiang, *China* 58 E7
Rongshui, *China* 58 E7
Rønne, *Denmark* 11 J8
Ronne Ice Shelf, *Antarctica* 5 D18
Ronneby, *Sweden* 11 H9
Ronnebyån →, *Sweden* 11 H9
Rönneshytta, *Sweden* 11 F9
Ronsard, C., *Australia* 93 D1
Ronse, *Belgium* 17 D3
Roodepoort, *S. Africa* 89 D4
Roof Butte, *U.S.A.* 109 H9
Rooiboklaagte →, *Namibia* 88 C3
Roorkee, *India* 68 E7
Roosendaal, *Neths.* 17 C4
Roosevelt, *U.S.A.* 108 F8
Roosevelt →, *Brazil* 124 E6
Roosevelt, Mt., *Canada* 102 B3
Roosevelt I., *Antarctica* 5 D12
Ropczyce, *Poland* 31 H8
Roper →, *Australia* 94 A2
Roper Bar, *Australia* 94 A1
Roque Pérez, *Argentina* 126 D4
Roquefort, *France* 20 D3
Roquemaure, *France* 21 D8
Roquetas de Mar, *Spain* 39 J2
Roquetes, *Spain* 38 E5
Roquevaire, *France* 21 E9
Roraima □, *Brazil* 124 C6
Roraima, Mt., *Venezuela* 124 B6
Røros, *Norway* 9 E14
Rorschach, *Switz.* 25 H5
Rosa, *Zambia* 87 D3
Rosa, L., *Bahamas* 121 B5
Rosa, Monte, *Europe* 40 C4
Rosal de la Frontera, *Spain* 37 H3
Rosalia, *U.S.A.* 108 C5
Rosamond, *U.S.A.* 111 L8
Rosans, *France* 21 D9
Rosario, *Argentina* 126 C3
Rosário, *Brazil* 125 D10
Rosario, *Baja Calif., Mexico* 118 B1
Rosario, *Sinaloa, Mexico* 118 C3
Rosario, *Paraguay* 126 A4

Rosario de la Frontera, *Argentina* 126 B3
Rosario de Lerma, *Argentina* 126 A2
Rosario del Tala, *Argentina* 126 C4
Rosário do Sul, *Brazil* 127 C5
Rosarito, *Mexico* 111 N9
Rosarno, *Italy* 43 D8
Rosas = Roses, *Spain* 38 C8
Roscoe, *U.S.A.* 117 E10
Roscoff, *France* 18 D3
Roscommon, *Ireland* 12 C3
Roscommon □, *Ireland* 12 C3
Roscrea, *Ireland* 12 D4
Rose →, *Australia* 94 A2
Rose Blanche-Harbour Le Cou, *Canada* 105 C8
Rose Pt., *Canada* 102 C2
Rose Valley, *Canada* 103 C8
Roseau, *Dominica* 121 C7
Roseau, *U.S.A.* 112 A7
Rosebery, *Australia* 95 G4
Rosebud, *S. Dak., U.S.A.* 112 D4
Rosebud, *Tex., U.S.A.* 113 K6
Roseburg, *U.S.A.* 108 E2
Rosedale, *U.S.A.* 113 J9
Rosehearty, *U.K.* 13 D6
Roseland, *U.S.A.* 110 G4
Rosemary, *Canada* 102 C6
Rosenberg, *U.S.A.* 113 L7
Rosendaël, *France* 19 A9
Rosenheim, *Germany* 25 H8
Roses, *Spain* 38 C8
Roses, G. de, *Spain* 38 C8
Roseto degli Abruzzi, *Italy* 41 F11
Rosetown, *Canada* 103 C7
Rosetta = Rashîd, *Egypt* 80 H7
Roseville, *Calif., U.S.A.* 110 G5
Roseville, *Mich., U.S.A.* 116 D2
Rosewood, *Australia* 95 D5
Roshkhvār, *Iran* 71 C8
Rosières-en-Santerre, *France* 19 C9
Rosignano Maríttimo, *Italy* 40 E7
Rosignol, *Guyana* 124 B7
Roşiori de Vede, *Romania* 29 F10
Rositsa, *Bulgaria* 45 C11
Rositsa →, *Bulgaria* 45 C9
Roskilde, *Denmark* 11 J6
Roskilde Amtskommune □, *Denmark* 11 J6
Roskovec, *Albania* 44 F3
Roslavl, *Russia* 32 F7
Rosmaninhal, *Portugal* 36 F3
Rosmead, *S. Africa* 88 E4
Røsnæs, *Denmark* 11 J4
Rosolini, *Italy* 43 F7
Rosporden, *France* 18 E3
Ross, *Australia* 95 G4
Ross, *N.Z.* 91 K3
Ross Béthio, *Mauritania* 82 B1
Ross Dependency, *Antarctica* 5 D12
Ross I., *Antarctica* 5 D11
Ross Ice Shelf, *Antarctica* 5 E12
Ross L., *U.S.A.* 108 B3
Ross-on-Wye, *U.K.* 15 F5
Ross River, *Australia* 94 C1
Ross River, *Canada* 102 A2
Ross Sea, *Antarctica* 5 D11
Rossall Pt., *U.K.* 14 D4
Rossan Pt., *Ireland* 12 B3
Rossano, *Italy* 43 C9
Rossburn, *Canada* 103 C8
Rosseau, *Canada* 116 A5
Rosseau, L., *Canada* 116 A5
Rosses, The, *Ireland* 12 A3
Rossignol, L., *Canada* 104 B5
Rossignol L., *Canada* 105 D6
Rossland, *Canada* 102 D5
Rosslare, *Ireland* 12 D5
Rosslare Harbour, *Ireland* 12 D5
Rosslau, *Germany* 24 D8
Rosso, *Mauritania* 82 B1
Rosso, C., *France* 21 F12
Rossosh, *Russia* 33 G10
Røssvatnet, *Norway* 8 D16
Røst, *Norway* 8 C15
Rosthern, *Canada* 103 C7
Rostock, *Germany* 24 A8
Rostov, *Don, Russia* 33 J10
Rostov, *Yaroslavl, Russia* 32 D10
Rostrenen, *France* 18 D3
Roswell, *Ga., U.S.A.* 115 H3
Roswell, *N. Mex., U.S.A.* 113 J2
Rota, *Spain* 37 J4
Rotan, *U.S.A.* 113 J4
Rotenburg, *Hessen, Germany* 24 E5
Rotenburg, *Niedersachsen, Germany* 24 B5
Roth, *Germany* 25 F7
Rothaargebirge, *Germany* 24 D4
Rothaargebirge ⌓, *Germany* 24 E4
Rothenburg ob der Tauber, *Germany* 25 F6
Rother →, *U.K.* 15 G8
Rothera, *Antarctica* 5 C17
Rotherham, *U.K.* 14 D6
Rothes, *U.K.* 13 D5
Rothesay, *Canada* 105 C6
Rothesay, *U.K.* 13 F3
Roti, *Indonesia* 63 F6
Rotja, Pta., *Spain* 39 G6
Roto, *Australia* 95 E4
Rotondo, Mte., *France* 21 F13
Rotoroa, L., *N.Z.* 91 J4
Rotorua, *N.Z.* 91 H6
Rotorua, L., *N.Z.* 91 H6
Rott →, *Germany* 25 G9
Rottenburg, *Germany* 25 G4
Rottenmann, *Austria* 26 D7
Rotterdam, *Neths.* 17 C4
Rotterdam, *U.S.A.* 117 D10
Rottne, *Sweden* 11 G8
Rottnest I., *Australia* 93 F2
Rottumeroog, *Neths.* 17 A6
Rottweil, *Germany* 25 G4
Rotuma, *Fiji* 96 J9
Roubaix, *France* 19 B10
Roudnice nad Labem, *Czech Rep.* 26 A7
Rouen, *France* 18 C8
Rouergue, *France* 20 D5
Rouillac, *France* 20 C3
Rouleau, *Canada* 103 C8
Round Mountain, *U.S.A.* 108 G5
Round Mt., *Australia* 95 E5
Round Rock, *U.S.A.* 113 K6
Roundup, *U.S.A.* 108 C9
Rousay, *U.K.* 13 B5
Rouses Point, *U.S.A.* 117 B11
Rouseville, *U.S.A.* 116 E5
Roussillon, *Isère, France* 21 C8
Roussillon, *Pyrénées-Or., France* 20 F6
Rouxville, *S. Africa* 88 E4
Rouyn-Noranda, *Canada* 104 C4
Rovaniemi, *Finland* 8 C21
Rovato, *Italy* 40 C7
Rovenki, *Ukraine* 33 H10
Rovereto, *Italy* 40 C8
Rovigo, *Italy* 41 C8
Rovinj, *Croatia* 41 C10
Rovno = Rivne, *Ukraine* 33 G4
Rovnoye, *Russia* 34 E8
Rovuma = Ruvuma →, *Tanzania* 87 E5
Row'ān, *Iran* 71 C6
Rowena, *Australia* 95 D4
Rowley Shoals, *Australia* 92 C2
Roxa, *Guinea-Biss.* 82 C1
Roxas, *Capiz, Phil.* 61 F5
Roxas, *Isabela, Phil.* 61 C4
Roxas, *Mind. Or., Phil.* 61 E4
Roxboro, *U.S.A.* 115 G6
Roxborough, *Trin. & Tob.* 125 J16
Roxburgh, *N.Z.* 91 L2
Roxbury, *U.S.A.* 116 F7
Roxen, *Sweden* 11 F9
Roy, *Mont., U.S.A.* 108 C9
Roy, *N. Mex., U.S.A.* 113 H2
Roy, *Utah, U.S.A.* 108 F7
Royal Canal, *Ireland* 12 C4
Royal Leamington Spa, *U.K.* 15 E6
Royal Natal △, *S. Africa* 89 D4
Royal Tunbridge Wells, *U.K.* 15 F8
Royale, Isle, *U.S.A.* 112 B10
Royan, *France* 20 C2
Roye, *France* 19 C9
Royston, *U.K.* 15 E7
Rožaj, *Serbia & M.* 44 D4
Różan, *Poland* 31 F8
Rozay-en-Brie, *France* 19 D9
Rozdilna, *Ukraine* 29 D15
Rozhnyativ, *Ukraine* 29 B9
Rozhyshche, *Ukraine* 33 G3
Rožmitál pod Třemšínem, *Czech Rep.* 26 B6
Rožňava, *Slovak Rep.* 27 C13
Rozogi, *Poland* 30 E8
Rozoy-sur-Serre, *France* 19 C11
Roztoczański △, *Poland* 31 H10
Rozzano, *Italy* 40 C6
Rrëshen, *Albania* 44 E3
Rrogozhine, *Albania* 44 E3
Rtanj, *Serbia & M.* 44 C5
Rtishchevo, *Russia* 34 D6
Rúa = A Rúa, *Spain* 36 C3
Ruacaná, *Namibia* 88 B1
Ruaha △, *Tanzania* 86 D3
Ruahine Ra., *N.Z.* 91 H6
Ruapehu, *N.Z.* 91 H5
Ruapuke I., *N.Z.* 91 M2
Ruâq, W. →, *Egypt* 74 F2
Rub' al Khālī, *Si. Arabia* 75 D4
Rubeho Mts., *Tanzania* 86 D4
Rubezhnoye = Rubizhne, *Ukraine* 33 H10
Rubh a' Mhail, *U.K.* 13 F2
Rubha Hunish, *U.K.* 13 D2
Rubha Robhanais = Lewis, Butt of, *U.K.* 13 C2
Rubi, *Spain* 38 D7
Rubicon →, *U.S.A.* 110 G5
Rubicone →, *Italy* 41 D9
Rubik, *Albania* 44 E3
Rubino, *Ivory C.* 82 D4
Rubio, *Venezuela* 124 B4
Rubizhne, *Ukraine* 33 H10
Rubondo △, *Tanzania* 86 C3
Rubtsovsk, *Russia* 52 D9
Ruby L., *U.S.A.* 108 F6
Ruby Mts., *U.S.A.* 108 F6
Rubyvale, *Australia* 94 C4
Rucheng, *China* 59 E9
Ruciane-Nida, *Poland* 30 E8
Rūd Sar, *Iran* 71 B6
Ruda, *Sweden* 11 G10
Ruda Śląska, *Poland* 31 H5
Rudall, *Australia* 95 E2
Rudall →, *Australia* 92 D3
Rudall River △, *Australia* 92 D3
Rüdersdorf, *Germany* 24 C9
Rudewa, *Tanzania* 87 E3
Rudkøbing, *Denmark* 11 K4
Rudky, *Ukraine* 31 J10
Rudna, *Poland* 31 G3
Rudnik, *Bulgaria* 45 D11
Rudnik, *Poland* 31 H9
Rudnik, *Serbia & M.* 44 B4
Rudnya, *Russia* 32 E6
Rudnytsa, *Ukraine* 29 B13
Rudnyy, *Kazakhstan* 52 D7
Rudo, *Bos.-H.* 28 G4
Rudolfa, Ostrov, *Russia* 52 A6
Rudolstadt, *Germany* 24 E7
Rudong, *China* 59 A13
Rudozem, *Bulgaria* 45 E8
Rudyard, *U.S.A.* 114 B3
Rue, *France* 19 B8
Ruenya →, *Africa* 87 F3
Rufa'a, *Sudan* 81 E3
Rufiji →, *Tanzania* 86 D4
Rufino, *Argentina* 126 C3
Rufisque, *Senegal* 82 C1
Rufling Pt., *Br. Virgin Is.* 121 e
Rufunsa, *Zambia* 87 F2
Rugao, *China* 59 A13
Rugby, *U.K.* 15 E6
Rugby, *U.S.A.* 112 A5
Rügen, *Germany* 24 A9
Rügen ⌓, *Germany* 24 A9
Rugles, *France* 18 D7
Ruhengeri, *Rwanda* 86 C2
Ruhla, *Germany* 24 E6
Ruhland, *Germany* 24 D9
Ruhnu, *Estonia* 9 H20
Ruhr →, *Germany* 24 D2
Ruhuhu →, *Tanzania* 87 E3
Rui'an, *China* 59 D13
Ruichang, *China* 59 C10
Ruidoso, *U.S.A.* 109 K11
Ruijin, *China* 59 E10
Ruili, *China* 58 E1
Ruivo, Pico, *Madeira* 48 D3
Ruj, *Bulgaria* 44 D6
Rujen, *Macedonia* 44 D6
Rujm Tal'at al Jamā'ah, *Jordan* 74 E4
Ruk, *Pakistan* 68 F3
Rukhla, *Pakistan* 68 C4
Ruki →, *Dem. Rep. of the Congo* 84 E3
Rukwa □, *Tanzania* 86 D3
Rukwa, L., *Tanzania* 86 D3
Rulhieres, C., *Australia* 92 B4
Rum = Rhum, *U.K.* 13 E2
Rum, *Jordan* 74 F4
Rum Cay, *Bahamas* 121 B5
Rum Jungle, *Australia* 92 B5
Ruma, *Serbia & M.* 28 E4
Ruma △, *Kenya* 86 C3
Rumāḥ, *Si. Arabia* 70 E5
Rumania = Romania ■, *Europe* 29 D10
Rumaylah, *Iraq* 70 D5
Rumbêk, *Sudan* 81 F2
Rumburk, *Czech Rep.* 26 A7
Rumford, *U.S.A.* 115 C10
Rumia, *Poland* 30 D5
Rumilly, *France* 21 C9
Rumoi, *Japan* 54 C10
Rumonge, *Burundi* 86 C2
Rumson, *U.S.A.* 117 F11
Rumuruti, *Kenya* 86 B4
Runan, *China* 56 H8
Runanga, *N.Z.* 91 K3
Runaway, C., *N.Z.* 91 G6
Runaway Bay, *Jamaica* 120 a
Runcorn, *U.K.* 14 D5
Rundu, *Namibia* 88 B2
Rungwa, *Tanzania* 86 D3
Rungwa ⌓, *Tanzania* 86 D3
Rungwa →, *Tanzania* 86 D3
Rungwe, *Tanzania* 87 D3
Rungwe, Mt., *Tanzania* 84 F6
Runka, *Nigeria* 83 C6
Runn, *Sweden* 10 D9
Runton Ra., *Australia* 92 D3
Ruokolahti, *Finland* 32 B5
Ruoqiang, *China* 60 C3
Rupa, *India* 67 F18
Rupar, *India* 68 D7
Rupat, *Indonesia* 62 D2
Rupea, *Romania* 29 D10
Rupen →, *India* 68 H4
Rupert, *U.S.A.* 108 E7
Rupert →, *Canada* 104 B4
Rupert B., *Canada* 104 B4
Rupert House = Waskaganish, *Canada* 104 B4
Rupsa, *India* 69 J12
Rur →, *Germany* 24 D1
Rurrenabaque, *Bolivia* 124 F5
Rus →, *Spain* 39 F2
Rusambo, *Zimbabwe* 87 F3
Rusape, *Zimbabwe* 87 F3
Ruschuk = Ruse, *Bulgaria* 45 C9
Ruse, *Bulgaria* 45 C9
Ruse □, *Bulgaria* 45 C10
Rusenski Lom △, *Bulgaria* 44 C7
Ruşeţu, *Romania* 29 F12
Rush, *Ireland* 12 C5
Rushan, *China* 57 F11
Rushden, *U.K.* 15 E7
Rushmore, Mt., *U.S.A.* 112 D3
Rushville, *Ill., U.S.A.* 112 E9
Rushville, *Ind., U.S.A.* 114 F3
Rushville, *Nebr., U.S.A.* 112 D3
Russas, *Brazil* 125 D11
Russell, *Canada* 103 C8
Russell, *Kans., U.S.A.* 112 F5
Russell, *N.Y., U.S.A.* 117 B9
Russell, *Pa., U.S.A.* 116 E5
Russell Cave ⌓, *U.S.A.* 115 H3
Russell L., *Man., Canada* 103 B8
Russell L., *N.W.T., Canada* 102 A5
Russellkonda, *India* 67 K14
Russellville, *Ala., U.S.A.* 115 H2
Russellville, *Ark., U.S.A.* 113 H8
Russellville, *Ky., U.S.A.* 115 G2
Rüsselsheim, *Germany* 25 F4
Russi, *Italy* 41 D9
Russia ■, *Eurasia* 53 C11
Russian →, *U.S.A.* 110 G3
Russkoye Ustie, *Russia* 4 B15
Rust, *Austria* 27 D9
Rustam, *Pakistan* 68 B5
Rustam Shahr, *Pakistan* 68 F2
Rustavi, *Georgia* 35 K7
Rustenburg, *S. Africa* 88 D4
Ruston, *U.S.A.* 113 J8
Rutana, *Burundi* 86 C3
Rute, *Spain* 37 H6
Ruteng, *Indonesia* 63 F6
Ruth, *U.S.A.* 116 C2
Rutherford, *U.S.A.* 110 G4
Rutland, *U.S.A.* 117 C12
Rutland □, *U.K.* 15 E7
Rutland Water, *U.K.* 15 E7
Rutledge →, *Canada* 103 A6
Rutledge L., *Canada* 103 A6
Rutqa, W. →, *Syria* 73 E9
Rutshuru, *Dem. Rep. of the Congo* 86 C2
Ruvo di Púglia, *Italy* 43 A9
Ruvu, *Tanzania* 86 D4
Ruvu →, *Tanzania* 86 D4
Ruvuba △, *Burundi* 86 C2
Ruvuma □, *Tanzania* 87 E4
Ruvuma →, *Tanzania* 87 E5
Ruwais, *U.A.E.* 71 E7
Ruwenzori, *Africa* 86 B2
Ruwenzori △, *Uganda* 86 B2
Ruya →, *Zimbabwe* 89 B5
Ruyigi, *Burundi* 86 C3
Ruyuan, *China* 59 E9
Ruzayevka, *Russia* 34 C7
Rŭzhevo Konare, *Bulgaria* 45 D8
Ružomberok, *Slovak Rep.* 27 B12
Ruzyne, Praha ✕ (PRG), *Czech Rep.* 26 A7
Rwanda ■, *Africa* 86 C3
Ryakhovo, *Bulgaria* 45 C10
Ryan, L., *U.K.* 13 G3
Ryazan, *Russia* 32 E10
Ryazhsk, *Russia* 32 F11
Rybache = Rybachye, *Kazakhstan* 52 E9
Rybachiy, *Russia* 30 C7
Rybachye, *Kazakhstan* 52 E9
Rybinsk, *Russia* 32 C10
Rybinskoye Vdkhr., *Russia* 32 C10
Rybnik, *Poland* 31 H5
Rybnitsa = Râbniţa, *Moldova* 29 C14
Rybnoye, *Russia* 32 E10
Rychnov nad Kněžnou, *Czech Rep.* 27 A9
Rychwał, *Poland* 31 F5
Rycroft, *Canada* 102 B5
Ryd, *Sweden* 11 H8
Rydaholm, *Sweden* 11 H8
Ryde, *U.K.* 15 G6
Ryderwood, *U.S.A.* 110 D3
Rydzyna, *Poland* 31 G3
Rye, *U.K.* 15 G8
Rye →, *U.K.* 14 C7
Rye Bay, *U.K.* 15 G8
Rye Patch Reservoir, *U.S.A.* 108 F4
Ryegate, *U.S.A.* 108 C9
Ryki, *Poland* 31 G8
Ryley, *Canada* 102 C6
Rylsk, *Russia* 33 G8
Rylstone, *Australia* 95 E4
Rymanów, *Poland* 31 J8
Ryn, *Poland* 30 E8
Ryn Peski, *Kazakhstan* 35 G9
Ryōtsu, *Japan* 54 E9
Rypin, *Poland* 31 E6
Ryssby, *Sweden* 11 H8
Rysy, *Europe* 27 B13
Ryūgasaki, *Japan* 55 G10
Ryūkyū Is. = Ryūkyū-rettō, *Japan* 55 M3
Ryūkyū-rettō, *Japan* 55 M3
Rzepin, *Poland* 31 F1
Rzeszów, *Poland* 31 H8
Rzhev, *Russia* 32 D8

S

Sa, *Thailand* 64 C3
Sa Canal, *Spain* 48 C7
Sa Conillera, *Spain* 48 C7
Sa Dec, *Vietnam* 65 G5
Sa Dragonera, *Spain* 48 B9
Sa Mesquida, *Spain* 48 B11
Sa Pobla, *Spain* 38 F8
Sa Savina, *Spain* 48 C7
Sa'ādatābād, *Fārs, Iran* 71 D7
Sa'ādatābād, *Hormozgān, Iran* 71 D7
Sa'ādatābād, *Kermān, Iran* 71 D7
Saale →, *Germany* 24 D7
Saaler Bodden, *Germany* 24 A8
Saalfeld, *Germany* 24 E7
Saalfelden, *Austria* 26 D5
Saane →, *Switz.* 25 H3
Saanich, *Canada* 110 B3
Saar →, *Europe* 17 E6
Saar-Hunsrück ⌓, *Germany* 25 F2
Saarbrücken, *Germany* 25 F2
Saarburg, *Germany* 25 F2
Saaremaa, *Estonia* 9 G20
Saarijärvi, *Finland* 9 E21
Saariselkä, *Finland* 8 B23
Saarland □, *Germany* 25 F2
Saarlouis, *Germany* 25 F2
Sab 'Ābar, *Syria* 70 C3
Saba, *W. Indies* 121 C7
Šabac, *Serbia & M.* 44 B3
Sabadell, *Spain* 38 D7
Sabah □, *Malaysia* 62 C5
Sabak Bernam, *Malaysia* 65 L3
Sabalān, Kūhhā-ye, *Iran* 70 B5
Sabalana, Kepulauan, *Indonesia* 63 F5
Sábana de la Mar, *Dom. Rep.* 121 C6
Sábanalarga, *Colombia* 124 A4
Sabang, *Indonesia* 62 C1
Săbăoani, *Romania* 29 C11
Sabará, *Brazil* 125 G10
Sabarmati →, *India* 68 H5
Sabattis, *U.S.A.* 117 B10
Sabáudia, *Italy* 42 A6
Saberania, *Indonesia* 63 E9
Sabhah, *Libya* 79 C8
Sabi →, *India* 68 E7
Sabidana, J., *Sudan* 80 D4
Sabie, *S. Africa* 89 D5
Sabinal, *Mexico* 118 A3
Sabinal, *U.S.A.* 113 L5
Sabiñánigo, *Spain* 38 C4
Sabinar, Punta del, *Spain* 39 J2
Sabinas, *Mexico* 118 B4
Sabinas →, *Mexico* 118 B4
Sabinas Hidalgo, *Mexico* 118 B4
Sabine →, *U.S.A.* 113 L8
Sabine L., *U.S.A.* 113 L8
Sabine Pass, *U.S.A.* 113 L8
Sabinov, *Slovak Rep.* 27 B14
Sabinsville, *U.S.A.* 116 E7
Sabirabad, *Azerbaijan* 35 K9
Sablayan, *Phil.* 61 E4
Sable, *Canada* 105 A6
Sable, C., *Canada* 105 D6
Sable, C., *U.S.A.* 107 E10
Sable I., *Canada* 105 D8
Sablé-sur-Sarthe, *France* 18 E6
Sabonkafi, *Niger* 83 C6
Sabor →, *Portugal* 36 D3
Sabou, *Burkina Faso* 82 C4
Sabres, *France* 20 D3
Sabrina Coast, *Antarctica* 5 C9
Sabugal, *Portugal* 36 E3
Sabulubbek, *Indonesia* 62 E1
Sabuncu, *Turkey* 47 B12
Sabzevār, *Iran* 71 B8
Sabzvārān, *Iran* 71 D8
Sac City, *U.S.A.* 112 D7
Sacedón, *Spain* 38 E2
Săcele, *Romania* 29 E10
Sachigo →, *Canada* 104 A2
Sachigo, L., *Canada* 104 B1
Sachkhere, *Georgia* 35 J6
Sachsen □, *Germany* 24 E9
Sachsen-Anhalt □, *Germany* 24 D7
Sächsische Schweiz △, *Germany* 24 E10
Sacile, *Italy* 41 C9
Sackets Harbor, *U.S.A.* 117 C8
Sackville, *Canada* 105 C7
Saco, *Maine, U.S.A.* 115 D10
Saco, *Mont., U.S.A.* 108 B10
Sacramento, *U.S.A.* 110 G5
Sacramento →, *U.S.A.* 110 G5
Sacramento Mts., *U.S.A.* 109 K11
Sacramento Valley, *U.S.A.* 110 G5
Sacratif, C., *Spain* 37 J7
Săcueni, *Romania* 28 C7
Sada, *Spain* 36 B2
Sada-Misaki, *Japan* 55 H6
Sádaba, *Spain* 38 C3
Sadabad, *India* 68 F8
Sadani, *Tanzania* 86 D4
Sadao, *Thailand* 65 J3
Sadd el Aali, *Egypt* 80 C3
Saddle Mt., *U.S.A.* 110 E3
Sade, *Nigeria* 83 C7
Sadimi, *Dem. Rep. of the Congo* 87 D1
Sadiola, *Mali* 82 C2
Sa'dīyah, Hawr as, *Iraq* 73 F12
Sado, *Japan* 54 F9
Sado →, *Portugal* 37 G2
Sadon, *Burma* 67 G20
Sadon, *Russia* 35 J6
Sadovoye, *Russia* 35 G7
Sadra, *India* 68 H5
Sadri, *India* 68 G5
Sæby, *Denmark* 11 G4
Saegertown, *U.S.A.* 116 E4
Saelices, *Spain* 38 F2
Safaalan, *Turkey* 45 E12
Safaga, *Egypt* 80 B3
Şafājah, *Si. Arabia* 70 E3
Šafárikovo = Tornal'a, *Slovak Rep.* 27 C13
Säffle, *Sweden* 10 E6
Safford, *U.S.A.* 109 K9
Saffron Walden, *U.K.* 15 E8
Safi, *Morocco* 78 B4
Şafīābād, *Iran* 71 B8
Safīd Dasht, *Iran* 71 C6
Safīd Kūh, *Afghan.* 66 B3
Safīd Rūd →, *Iran* 71 B6
Safipur, *India* 69 F9
Safonovo, *Russia* 32 E7
Safranbolu, *Turkey* 72 B5
Saft Rashîn, *Egypt* 80 J7
Şafwān, *Iraq* 70 D5
Sag Harbor, *U.S.A.* 117 F12
Saga, *Japan* 55 H5
Saga □, *Japan* 55 H5
Sagae, *Japan* 54 E10
Sagala, *Mali* 82 C3
Sagamartha = Everest, Mt., *Nepal* 69 E12
Sagamore, *U.S.A.* 116 F5
Sagar, *Karnataka, India* 66 M9
Sagar, *Mad. P., India* 69 H8
Sagara, L., *Tanzania* 86 D3
Sagay, *Phil.* 61 F5
Saginaw, *U.S.A.* 114 D4
Saginaw →, *U.S.A.* 114 D4
Saginaw B., *U.S.A.* 114 D4
Sagleipie, *Liberia* 82 D3
Saglouc = Salluit, *Canada* 101 B12
Sagŏ-ri, *S. Korea* 57 G14
Sagone, *France* 21 F12
Sagone, G. de, *France* 21 F12
Sagres, *Portugal* 37 J2
Sagua la Grande, *Cuba* 120 B3
Saguache, *U.S.A.* 109 G10
Saguaro △, *U.S.A.* 109 K8
Saguenay →, *Canada* 105 C5
Sagunt, *Spain* 38 F4
Sagunto = Sagunt, *Spain* 38 F4
Sagwara, *India* 68 H6
Sahaba, *Sudan* 80 D3

Sahagún, *Spain* 36 C5
Saḩam al Jawlān, *Syria* 74 C4
Sahamandrevo, *Madag.* 89 C8
Sahand, Kūh-e, *Iran* 70 B5
Sahara, *Africa* 78 D6
Saharan Atlas = Saharien, Atlas, *Algeria* 78 B6
Saharanpur, *India* 68 E7
Saharien, Atlas, *Algeria* 78 B6
Saharsa, *India* 69 G12
Sahasinaka, *Madag.* 89 C8
Sahaswan, *India* 69 E8
Sahel, *Africa* 78 E5
Sahel, Canal du, *Mali* 82 C3
Sahibganj, *India* 69 G12
Sāḩilīyah, *Iraq* 70 C4
Sahiwal, *Pakistan* 68 D5
Saḩneh, *Iran* 70 C5
Sahrawi = Western Sahara ■, *Africa* 78 D3
Sahuaripa, *Mexico* 118 B3
Sahuarita, *U.S.A.* 109 L8
Sahuayo, *Mexico* 118 C4
Šahy, *Slovak Rep.* 27 C11
Sai →, *India* 69 G10
Sai Buri, *Thailand* 65 J3
Sa'id Bundas, *Sudan* 79 G10
Sa'īdābād = Sīrjān, *Iran* 71 D7
Sa'īdābād, *Iran* 71 B7
Sa'īdīyeh, *Iran* 71 B6
Saidpur, *Bangla.* 67 G16
Saidpur, *India* 69 G10
Saidu, *Pakistan* 69 B5
Saignes, *France* 20 C6
Saigon = Thanh Pho Ho Chi Minh, *Vietnam* 65 G6
Saijō, *Japan* 55 H6
Saikai △, *Japan* 55 H4
Saikanosy Masoala, *Madag.* 89 B9
Saikhoa Ghat, *India* 67 F19
Saiki, *Japan* 55 H5
Sailana, *India* 68 H6
Saillans, *France* 21 D9
Sailolof, *Indonesia* 63 E8
Saimaa, *Finland* 9 F23
Saimbeyli, *Turkey* 72 D7
Saimen = Saimaa, *Finland* 9 F23
Şa'in Dezh, *Iran* 70 B5
St. Abb's Head, *U.K.* 13 F6
St-Affrique, *France* 20 E6
St-Agrève, *France* 21 C8
St-Aignan, *France* 18 E8
St. Alban's, *Canada* 105 C8
St. Albans, *U.K.* 15 F7
St. Albans, *Vt., U.S.A.* 117 B11
St. Albans, *W. Va., U.S.A.* 114 F5
St. Alban's Head, *U.K.* 15 G5
St. Albert, *Canada* 102 C6
St-Amand-en-Puisaye, *France* 19 E10
St-Amand-les-Eaux, *France* 19 B10
St-Amand-Montrond, *France* 19 F9
St-Amarin, *France* 19 E14
St-Amour, *France* 19 F12
St-André-de-Cubzac, *France* 20 D3
St-André-les-Alpes, *France* 21 E10
St. Andrew's, *Canada* 105 C8
St. Andrews, *U.K.* 13 E6
St-Anicet, *Canada* 117 A10
St. Anns B., *Canada* 105 C7
St. Ann's Bay, *Jamaica* 120 a
St. Anthony, *Canada* 105 B8
St. Anthony, *U.S.A.* 108 E8
St-Antoine, *Canada* 105 C7
St-Antonin-Noble-Val, *France* 20 D5
St. Arnaud, *Australia* 95 F3
St-Astier, *France* 20 C4
St-Aubin-du-Cormier, *France* 18 D5
St-Augustin, *Canada* 105 B8
St-Augustin →, *Canada* 105 B8
St. Augustine, *U.S.A.* 115 L5
St-Aulaye, *France* 20 C4
St. Austell, *U.K.* 15 G3
St-Avold, *France* 19 C13
St. Barbe, *Canada* 105 B8
St-Barthélemy, *W. Indies* 121 C7
St-Béat, *France* 20 F4
St. Bees Hd., *U.K.* 14 C4
St. Bees I., *Australia* 94 J7
St-Benoît-du-Sault, *France* 20 B5
St-Bonnet-en-Champsaur, *France* 21 D10
St-Brevin-les-Pins, *France* 18 E4
St-Brice-en-Coglès, *France* 18 D5
St. Bride's, *Canada* 105 C9
St. Brides B., *U.K.* 15 F2
St-Brieuc, *France* 18 D4
St-Calais, *France* 18 E7
St-Cast-le-Guildo, *France* 18 D4
St. Catharines, *Canada* 116 C5
St. Catherines I., *U.S.A.* 115 K5
St. Catherine's Pt., *U.K.* 15 G6
St-Céré, *France* 20 D5
St-Cergue, *Switz.* 25 J2
St-Cernin, *France* 20 C6
St-Chamond, *France* 21 C8
St. Charles, *Ill., U.S.A.* 114 E1
St. Charles, *Mo., U.S.A.* 112 F9
St. Charles, *Va., U.S.A.* 114 F7
St-Chély-d'Apcher, *France* 20 D7
St-Chinian, *France* 20 E6
St. Christopher-Nevis = St. Kitts & Nevis ■, *W. Indies* 121 C7
St-Ciers-sur-Gironde, *France* 20 C3
St. Clair, *Mich., U.S.A.* 116 D2
St. Clair, *Pa., U.S.A.* 117 F8
St. Clair →, *U.S.A.* 116 D2
St. Clair, L., *Canada* 104 D3
St. Clair, L., *U.S.A.* 116 D2
St. Clairsville, *U.S.A.* 116 F4
St-Claud, *France* 20 C4
St. Claude, *Canada* 103 D9
St-Claude, *France* 19 F12
St. Clears, *U.K.* 15 F3
St-Clet, *Canada* 117 A10
St. Cloud, *Fla., U.S.A.* 115 L5
St. Cloud, *Minn., U.S.A.* 112 C7
St. Cricq, C., *Australia* 93 E1
St. Croix, *U.S. Virgin Is.* 121 C7
St. Croix →, *U.S.A.* 112 C8
St. Croix Falls, *U.S.A.* 112 C8
St-Cyprien, *France* 20 F7
St-Cyr-sur-Mer, *France* 21 E9
St. David's, *Canada* 105 C8
St. David's, *U.K.* 15 F2
St. David's Head, *U.K.* 15 F2
St-Denis, *France* 19 D9
St-Dié, *France* 19 D13
St-Dizier, *France* 19 D11
St-Égrève, *France* 21 C9
St. Elias, Mt., *U.S.A.* 100 B5
St. Elias Mts., *N. Amer.* 102 A1
St-Eloy-les-Mines, *France* 19 F9
St-Émilion, *France* 20 D3
St-Étienne, *France* 21 C8
St-Étienne-de-Tinée, *France* 21 D10
St-Étienne-du-Rouvray, *France* 18 C8
St. Eugène, *Canada* 117 A10
St. Eustatius, *W. Indies* 121 C7
St-Exupery, Lyon ✕ (LYS), *France* 21 C9
St-Fargeau, *France* 19 E10
St-Félicien, *Canada* 104 C5
St-Florent, *France* 21 F13
St-Florent, G. de, *France* 21 F13
St-Florent-sur-Cher, *France* 19 F9
St-Florentin, *France* 19 E10
St-Flour, *France* 20 C7
St. Francis, *U.S.A.* 112 F4
St. Francis →, *U.S.A.* 113 H9
St. Francis, C., *S. Africa* 88 E3
St. Francisville, *U.S.A.* 113 K9
St-François, L., *Canada* 117 A10
St-Fulgent, *France* 18 F5
St-Gabriel, *Canada* 104 C5
St. Gallen = Sankt Gallen, *Switz.* 25 H5
St-Galmier, *France* 19 G11
St-Gaudens, *France* 20 E4
St-Gaultier, *France* 18 F8
St-Gengoux-le-National, *France* 19 F11
St-Geniez-d'Olt, *France* 20 D6
St. George, *Australia* 95 D4
St. George, *Canada* 105 C6
St. George, *S.C., U.S.A.* 115 J5
St. George, *Utah, U.S.A.* 109 H7
St. George, C., *Canada* 105 C8
St. George, C., *U.S.A.* 115 L3
St. George Ra., *Australia* 92 C4
St. George's, *Canada* 105 C8
St-Georges, *Canada* 105 C5
St. George's, *Grenada* 121 D7
St. George's B., *Canada* 105 C8
St. Georges Basin, *N.S.W., Australia* 95 F5
St. Georges Basin, *W. Austral., Australia* 92 C4
St. George's Channel, *Europe* 12 E6
St. Georges Hd., *Australia* 95 F5
St-Georges-lès-Baillargeaux, *France* 20 B4
St-Germain-de-Calberte, *France* 20 D7
St-Germain-en-Laye, *France* 19 D9
St-Germain-Lembron, *France* 20 C7
St-Gervais-d'Auvergne, *France* 19 F9
St-Gervais-les-Bains, *France* 21 C10
St-Gildas, Pte. de, *France* 18 E4
St-Gilles, *France* 21 E8
St-Girons, *Ariège, France* 20 F5
St-Girons, *Landes, France* 20 E2
St. Gotthard P. = San Gottardo, P. del, *Switz.* 25 J4
St. Helena, *Atl. Oc.* 76 H3
St. Helena, *U.S.A.* 108 G2
St. Helena, Mt., *U.S.A.* 110 G4
St. Helena B., *S. Africa* 88 E2
St. Helens, *Australia* 95 G4
St. Helens, *U.K.* 14 D5
St. Helens, *U.S.A.* 110 E4
St. Helens, Mt., *U.S.A.* 110 D4
St. Helier, *U.K.* 15 H5
St-Herblain, *France* 18 E5
St-Hilaire-du-Harcouët, *France* 18 D5
St-Hippolyte, *France* 19 E13
St-Hippolyte-du-Fort, *France* 20 E7
St-Honoré-les-Bains, *France* 19 F10
St-Hubert, *Belgium* 17 D5
St-Hyacinthe, *Canada* 104 C5
St. Ignace, *U.S.A.* 114 C3
St. Ignace I., *Canada* 104 C2
St. Ignatius, *U.S.A.* 108 C6
St-Imier, *Switz.* 25 H2
St. Ives, *Cambs., U.K.* 15 E7
St. Ives, *Corn., U.K.* 15 G2
St-James, *France* 18 D5
St. James, *U.S.A.* 112 D7
St-Jean →, *Canada* 105 B7
St-Jean, L., *Canada* 105 C5
St-Jean-d'Angély, *France* 20 C3
St-Jean-de-Braye, *France* 19 E8
St-Jean-de-Luz, *France* 20 E2
St-Jean-de-Maurienne, *France* 21 C10
St-Jean-de-Monts, *France* 18 F4
St-Jean-du-Gard, *France* 20 D7
St-Jean-en-Royans, *France* 21 C9
St-Jean-Pied-de-Port, *France* 20 E2
St-Jean-Port-Joli, *Canada* 105 C5
St-Jean-sur-Richelieu, *Canada* 117 A11
St-Jérôme, *Canada* 104 C5
St. John, *Canada* 105 C6
St. John, *U.S.A.* 113 G5
St. John →, *Liberia* 82 D2
St. John →, *U.S.A.* 115 C12
St. John, C., *Canada* 105 C8
St. John I., *U.S. Virgin Is.* 121 e
St. John's, *Antigua & B.* 121 C7
St. John's, *Canada* 105 C9
St. Johns, *Ariz., U.S.A.* 109 J9
St. Johns, *Mich., U.S.A.* 114 D3
St. Johns →, *U.S.A.* 115 K5
St. John's Pt., *Ireland* 12 B3
St. Johnsbury, *U.S.A.* 117 B12
St. Johnsville, *U.S.A.* 117 D10
St-Joseph, *Martinique* 120 c
St. Joseph, *La., U.S.A.* 113 K9
St. Joseph, *Mo., U.S.A.* 112 F7
St. Joseph →, *U.S.A.* 114 D2
St. Joseph, I., *Canada* 104 C3
St. Joseph, L., *Canada* 104 B1
St-Jovite, *Canada* 104 C5
St-Juéry, *France* 20 E6
St-Julien-Chapteuil, *France* 21 C8
St-Julien-de-Vouvantes, *France* 18 E5
St-Julien-en-Genevois, *France* 19 F13
St-Junien, *France* 20 C4
St-Just-en-Chaussée, *France* 19 C9
St-Just-en-Chevalet, *France* 20 C7
St. Kitts & Nevis ■, *W. Indies* 121 C7
St. Laurent, *Canada* 103 C9
St-Laurent-de-la-Salanque, *France* 20 F6
St-Laurent-du-Pont, *France* 21 C9
St-Laurent-en-Grandvaux, *France* 19 F12
St-Laurent-Médoc, *France* 20 C3
St. Lawrence, *Australia* 94 C4
St. Lawrence, *Canada* 105 C8
St. Lawrence →, *Canada* 105 C6
St. Lawrence, Gulf of, *Canada* 105 C7
St. Lawrence I., *U.S.A.* 100 B3
St. Lawrence Islands △, *Canada* 117 B9
St. Leonard, *Canada* 105 C6
St-Léonard-de-Noblat, *France* 20 C5
St. Lewis →, *Canada* 105 B8
St-Lô, *France* 18 C5
St-Louis, *France* 19 E14
St-Louis, *Guadeloupe* 120 b
St. Louis, *Senegal* 82 B1
St. Louis, *U.S.A.* 112 F9
St. Louis →, *U.S.A.* 112 B8
St-Loup-sur-Semouse, *France* 19 E13
St. Lucia ■, *W. Indies* 121 f
St. Lucia, L., *S. Africa* 89 D5
St. Lucia Channel, *W. Indies* 121 D7
St. Maarten ⊠, *W. Indies* 121 C7
St. Magnus B., *U.K.* 13 A7
St-Maixent-l'École, *France* 20 B3
St-Malo, *France* 18 D4
St-Malo, G. de, *France* 18 D4
St-Mandrier-sur-Mer, *France* 21 E9
St-Marc, *Haiti* 121 C5
St-Marcellin, *France* 21 C9
St-Marcouf, Îs., *France* 18 C5
St. Maries, *U.S.A.* 108 C5
St-Martin ⊠, *W. Indies* 121 C7
St-Martin, C., *Martinique* 120 c
St. Martin, L., *Canada* 103 C9
St-Martin-de-Crau, *France* 21 E8
St-Martin-de-Ré, *France* 20 B2
St-Martin-d'Hères, *France* 21 C9
St-Martin-Vésubie, *France* 21 D11
St. Martins, *Barbados* 121 g
St-Martory, *France* 20 E4
St. Mary Pk., *Australia* 95 E2
St. Marys, *Australia* 95 G4
St. Marys, *Canada* 116 C3
St. Mary's, *Corn., U.K.* 15 H1
St. Mary's, *Orkney, U.K.* 13 C6
St. Marys, *Ga., U.S.A.* 115 K5
St. Marys, *Pa., U.S.A.* 116 E6
St. Mary's, C., *Canada* 105 C9
St. Mary's B., *Canada* 105 C9
St. Marys Bay, *Canada* 105 D6
St-Mathieu, Pte., *France* 18 D2
St. Matthew I., *U.S.A.* 100 B2
St-Maurice →, *Canada* 104 C5
St. Mawes, *U.K.* 15 G2
St-Maximin-la-Ste-Baume, *France* 21 E9
St-Médard-en-Jalles, *France* 20 D3
St-Méen-le-Grand, *France* 18 D4
St-Mihiel, *France* 19 D12
St. Moritz, *Switz.* 25 J5
St-Nazaire, *France* 18 E4
St. Neots, *U.K.* 15 E7
St-Nicolas-de-Port, *France* 19 D13
St-Niklaas, *Belgium* 17 C4
St-Omer, *France* 19 B9
St-Palais-sur-Mer, *France* 20 C2
St-Pamphile, *Canada* 105 C6
St-Pardoux-la-Rivière, *France* 20 C4
St-Pascal, *Canada* 105 C6
St. Paul, *Canada* 102 C6
St-Paul, *France* 21 D10
St. Paul, *Minn., U.S.A.* 112 C8
St. Paul, *Nebr., U.S.A.* 112 E5
St-Paul →, *Canada* 105 B8
St. Paul →, *Liberia* 82 D2
St. Paul, I., *Ind. Oc.* 3 F13
St-Paul-de-Fenouillet, *France* 20 F6
St. Paul I., *Canada* 105 C7
St-Paul-lès-Dax, *France* 20 E2
St-Péray, *France* 21 D8
St. Peter, *U.S.A.* 112 C8
St. Peter-Ording, *Germany* 24 A4
St. Peter Port, *U.K.* 15 H5
St. Peters, *N.S., Canada* 105 C7
St. Peters, *P.E.I., Canada* 105 C7
St. Petersburg = Sankt-Peterburg, *Russia* 32 C6
St. Petersburg, *U.S.A.* 115 M4
St-Philbert-de-Grand-Lieu, *France* 18 E5
St-Pie, *Canada* 117 A12
St-Pierre, *Martinique* 120 c
St-Pierre, *St-P. & M.* 105 C8
St-Pierre, L., *Canada* 104 C5
St-Pierre-d'Oléron, *France* 20 C2
St-Pierre-en-Port, *France* 18 C7
St-Pierre-et-Miquelon ⊠, *N. Amer.* 105 C8
St-Pierre-le-Moûtier, *France* 19 F10
St-Pierre-sur-Dives, *France* 18 C6
St-Pol-de-Léon, *France* 18 D3
St-Pol-sur-Mer, *France* 19 A9
St-Pol-sur-Ternoise, *France* 19 B9
St-Pons, *France* 20 E6
St-Pourçain-sur-Sioule, *France* 19 F10
St-Priest, *France* 21 C8
St-Quay-Portrieux, *France* 18 D4
St-Quentin, *Canada* 105 C6
St-Quentin, *France* 19 C10
St-Rambert-d'Albon, *France* 21 C8
St-Raphaël, *France* 21 E10
St. Regis, *U.S.A.* 108 C6
St-Renan, *France* 18 D2
St-Saëns, *France* 18 C8
St-Savin, *France* 20 B4
St-Savinien, *France* 20 C3
St. Sebastien, Tanjon' i, *Madag.* 89 A8
St-Seine-l'Abbaye, *France* 19 E11
St-Sernin-sur-Rance, *France* 20 E6
St-Sever, *France* 20 E3
St-Siméon, *Canada* 105 C6
St. Simons I., *U.S.A.* 115 K5
St. Simons Island, *U.S.A.* 115 K5
St. Stephen, *Canada* 105 C6
St-Sulpice, *France* 20 E5
St-Sulpice-Laurière, *France* 20 B5
St-Sulpice-les-Feuilles, *France* 20 B5
St-Syprien = St-Cyprien, *France* 20 F7
St-Thégonnec, *France* 18 D3
St. Thomas, *Canada* 116 D3
St. Thomas I., *U.S. Virgin Is.* 121 e
St-Tite, *Canada* 104 C5
St-Tropez, *France* 21 E10
St-Troud = St. Truiden, *Belgium* 17 D5
St. Truiden, *Belgium* 17 D5
St-Vaast-la-Hougue, *France* 18 C5
St-Valery-en-Caux, *France* 18 C7
St-Valéry-sur-Somme, *France* 19 B8
St-Vallier, *France* 19 F11
St-Vallier-de-Thiey, *France* 21 E10
St-Varent, *France* 18 F6
St-Vaury, *France* 20 B5
St. Vincent, *Italy* 40 C4
St. Vincent, G., *Australia* 95 F2
St. Vincent & the Grenadines ■, *W. Indies* 121 D7
St-Vincent-de-Tyrosse, *France* 20 E2
St. Vincent Passage, *W. Indies* 121 D7
St-Vith, *Belgium* 17 D6
St-Vivien-de-Médoc, *France* 20 C2
St. Walburg, *Canada* 103 C7
St-Yrieix-la-Perche, *France* 20 C5
Ste-Adresse, *France* 18 C7
Ste-Agathe-des-Monts, *Canada* 104 C5
Ste-Anne, *Guadeloupe* 120 b
Ste-Anne, L., *Canada* 105 B6
Ste-Anne-des-Monts-Tourelle, *Canada* 105 C6
Ste-Croix, *Switz.* 25 J2
Ste-Enimie, *France* 20 D7
Ste-Foy-la-Grande, *France* 20 D4
Ste. Genevieve, *U.S.A.* 112 G9
Ste-Hermine, *France* 20 B2
Ste-Livrade-sur-Lot, *France* 20 D4
Ste-Marguerite →, *Canada* 105 B6
Ste-Marie, *Canada* 105 C5
Ste-Marie, *Martinique* 120 c
Ste-Marie-aux-Mines, *France* 19 D14
Ste-Maure-de-Touraine, *France* 18 E7
Ste-Maxime, *France* 21 E10
Ste-Menehould, *France* 19 C11
Ste-Mère-Église, *France* 18 C5
Ste-Rose, *Guadeloupe* 120 b
Ste. Rose du Lac, *Canada* 103 C9
Ste-Savine, *France* 19 D11
Ste-Sigolène, *France* 21 C8
Saintes, *France* 20 C3
Saintes, Îs. des, *Guadeloupe* 120 b
Stes-Maries-de-la-Mer, *France* 21 E8
Saintfield, *U.K.* 12 B6
Saintonge, *France* 20 C3
Saipan, *Pac. Oc.* 96 F6
Sairang, *India* 67 H18
Sairecábur, Cerro, *Bolivia* 126 A2
Saitama □, *Japan* 55 F9
Saiteli = Kadınhanı, *Turkey* 72 C5
Saiţi, *Moldova* 29 D14
Saiyid, *Pakistan* 68 C5
Saja-Besaya ⌓, *Spain* 36 B6
Sajama, *Bolivia* 124 G5
Sajan, *Serbia & M.* 28 E5
Sajó →, *Hungary* 28 C6
Sajószentpéter, *Hungary* 28 B5
Sajum, *India* 69 C8
Sak →, *S. Africa* 88 E3
Sakaba, *Nigeria* 83 C6
Sakai, *Japan* 55 G7
Sakaide, *Japan* 55 G6
Sakaiminato, *Japan* 55 G6
Sakākah, *Si. Arabia* 70 D4
Sakakawea, L., *U.S.A.* 112 B4
Sakami →, *Canada* 104 B4
Sakami, L., *Canada* 104 B4
Sâkâne, 'Erg i-n, *Mali* 83 A4
Sakania, *Dem. Rep. of the Congo* 87 E2
Sakaraha, *Madag.* 89 C7
Sakarya, *Turkey* 72 B4
Sakarya →, *Turkey* 72 B4
Sakashima-Guntō, *Japan* 55 M2
Sakassou, *Ivory C.* 82 D3
Sakata, *Japan* 54 E9
Sakchu, *N. Korea* 57 D13
Sakeny →, *Madag.* 89 C8
Sakété, *Benin* 83 D5
Sakha □, *Russia* 53 C13
Sakhalin, *Russia* 53 D15
Sakhalinskiy Zaliv, *Russia* 53 D15
Şaki, *Azerbaijan* 35 K8
Šakiai, *Lithuania* 9 J20
Sakon Nakhon, *Thailand* 64 D5
Sakrand, *Pakistan* 68 F3
Sakri, *India* 69 F12
Sakrivier, *S. Africa* 88 E3
Sakskøbing, *Denmark* 11 K5
Sakti, *India* 69 H10
Sakuma, *Japan* 55 G8
Sakurai, *Japan* 55 G7
Saky, *Ukraine* 33 K7
Sal →, *Russia* 35 G5
Sala, *Eritrea* 81 D4
Šal'a, *Slovak Rep.* 27 C10
Sala, *Sweden* 10 E10
Sala →, *Eritrea* 81 D4
Sala Consilina, *Italy* 43 B8
Sala-y-Gómez, *Pac. Oc.* 97 K17
Salaberry-de-Valleyfield, *Canada* 117 A10
Salacgrīva, *Latvia* 30 A11
Salada, L., *Mexico* 109 K6
Saladas, *Argentina* 126 B4
Saladillo, *Argentina* 126 D4
Salado →, *Buenos Aires, Argentina* 126 D4
Salado →, *La Pampa, Argentina* 128 D3
Salado →, *Santa Fe, Argentina* 126 C3
Salado →, *Mexico* 113 M5
Salaga, *Ghana* 83 D4
Sālah, *Syria* 74 C5
Şalāḩ ad Dīn □, *Iraq* 70 C4
Sălaj □, *Romania* 28 C8
Sálakhos, *Greece* 49 C9
Salala, *Liberia* 82 D2
Salala, *Sudan* 80 C4
Salālah, *Oman* 75 D5
Salamanca, *Chile* 126 C1
Salamanca, *Spain* 36 E5
Salamanca, *U.S.A.* 116 D6
Salamanca □, *Spain* 36 E5
Salāmatābād, *Iran* 70 C5
Salamis, *Cyprus* 49 D12
Salamís, *Greece* 46 D5
Salar de Atacama, *Chile* 126 A2
Salar de Uyuni, *Bolivia* 124 H5
Sălard, *Romania* 28 C7
Salas, *Spain* 36 B4
Salas de los Infantes, *Spain* 36 C7
Salatiga, *Indonesia* 63 G14
Salaverry, *Peru* 124 E3
Salawati, *Indonesia* 63 E8
Salaya, *India* 68 H3
Salayar, *Indonesia* 63 F6
Salazar →, *Spain* 38 C3
Salbris, *France* 19 E9
Salcia, *Romania* 29 G9
Sălciua, *Romania* 29 D8
Salcombe, *U.K.* 15 G4
Saldaña, *Spain* 36 C6
Saldanha, *S. Africa* 88 E2
Saldanha B., *S. Africa* 88 E2
Saldus, *Latvia* 9 H20
Saldus □, *Latvia* 30 B9
Sale, *Australia* 95 F4
Sale, *Italy* 40 D5
Salé, *Morocco* 78 B4
Sale, *U.K.* 14 D5
Salekhard, *Russia* 52 C7
Salem, *India* 66 P11
Salem, *Ill., U.S.A.* 114 F1
Salem, *Ind., U.S.A.* 114 F2
Salem, *Mass., U.S.A.* 117 D14
Salem, *Mo., U.S.A.* 113 G9
Salem, *N.H., U.S.A.* 117 D13
Salem, *N.J., U.S.A.* 114 F8
Salem, *N.Y., U.S.A.* 117 C11
Salem, *Ohio, U.S.A.* 116 F4
Salem, *Oreg., U.S.A.* 108 D2
Salem, *S. Dak., U.S.A.* 112 D6
Salem, *Va., U.S.A.* 114 G5
Salemi, *Italy* 42 E5
Sälen, *Sweden* 10 C7
Salernes, *France* 21 E10
Salerno, *Italy* 43 B7
Salerno, G. di, *Italy* 43 B7
Salford, *U.K.* 14 D5
Salgir →, *Ukraine* 33 K8
Salgótarján, *Hungary* 28 B4
Salgueiro, *Brazil* 125 E11
Salibabu, *Indonesia* 63 D7
Salibea = Salybia, *Trin. & Tob.* 125 K15
Salida, *U.S.A.* 106 C5
Salies-de-Béarn, *France* 20 E3
Salihli, *Turkey* 72 C3
Salihorsk, *Belarus* 33 F4
Salima, *Malawi* 85 G6
Salina, *Italy* 43 D7
Salina, *Kans., U.S.A.* 112 F6
Salina, *Utah, U.S.A.* 109 G8
Salina Cruz, *Mexico* 119 D5
Salina di Margherita di Savoia ⌓, *Italy* 43 A9
Salinas, *Brazil* 125 G10
Salinas, *Chile* 126 A2
Salinas, *Ecuador* 124 D2
Salinas, *U.S.A.* 110 J5
Salinas →, *Guatemala* 119 D6
Salinas →, *U.S.A.* 110 J5
Salinas, B. de, *Nic.* 120 D2
Salinas, Pampa de las, *Argentina* 126 C2
Salinas Ambargasta, *Argentina* 126 B3
Salinas de Hidalgo, *Mexico* 118 C4
Salinas Grandes, *Argentina* 126 C3
Salinas Pueblo Missions ⌓, *U.S.A.* 109 J10
Saline →, *Ark., U.S.A.* 113 J8
Saline →, *Kans., U.S.A.* 112 F6
Saline di Trapani e Paceco ⌓, *Italy* 42 E5
Salines, C. de ses, *Spain* 48 B10
Salinópolis, *Brazil* 125 D9

Salins-les-Bains, *France* 19 F12
Salir, *Portugal* 37 H2
Salisbury, *U.K.* 15 F6
Salisbury, *Md., U.S.A.* 114 F8
Salisbury, *N.C., U.S.A.* 115 H5
Salisbury I., *Canada* 101 B12
Salisbury Plain, *U.K.* 15 F6
Săliște, *Romania* 29 E8
Salka, *Nigeria* 83 C5
Şalkhad, *Syria* 74 C5
Salkove, *Ukraine* 29 B14
Salla, *Finland* 8 C23
Sallanches, *France* 21 C10
Sallent, *Spain* 38 D6
Salles, *France* 20 D3
Salles-Curan, *France* 20 D6
Salling, *Denmark* 11 H2
Salliq = Coral Harbour, *Canada* 101 B11
Sallisaw, *U.S.A.* 113 H7
Sallom Junction, *Sudan* 80 D4
Salluit, *Canada* 101 B12
Salmās, *Iran* 70 B5
Salmerón, *Spain* 38 E2
Salmo, *Canada* 102 D5
Salmon, *U.S.A.* 108 D7
Salmon →, *Canada* 102 C4
Salmon →, *U.S.A.* 108 D5
Salmon Arm, *Canada* 102 C5
Salmon Gums, *Australia* 93 F3
Salmon River Mts., *U.S.A.* 108 D6
Salo, *Finland* 9 F20
Salò, *Italy* 40 C7
Salobreña, *Spain* 37 J7
Salome, *U.S.A.* 111 M13
Salon, *India* 69 F9
Salon-de-Provence, *France* 21 E9
Salonica = Thessaloníki, *Greece* 44 F6
Salonta, *Romania* 28 D6
Salor →, *Spain* 37 F3
Salou, *Spain* 38 D6
Salou, C. de, *Spain* 38 D6
Saloum →, *Senegal* 82 C1
Salpausselkä, *Finland* 9 F22
Salsacate, *Argentina* 126 C2
Salses, *France* 20 F6
Salsk, *Russia* 35 G5
Salso →, *Italy* 42 E6
Salsomaggiore Terme, *Italy* 40 D6
Salt, *Spain* 38 D7
Salt →, *Canada* 102 B6
Salt →, *U.S.A.* 109 K7
Salt L., The, *Australia* 95 E3
Salt Lake City, *U.S.A.* 108 F8
Salt Range, *Pakistan* 68 C5
Salta, *Argentina* 126 A2
Salta □, *Argentina* 126 A2
Saltara, *Italy* 41 E9
Saltash, *U.K.* 15 G3
Saltburn by the Sea, *U.K.* 14 C7
Saltcoats, *U.K.* 13 F4
Saltee Is., *Ireland* 12 D5
Saltfjellet, *Norway* 8 C16
Saltfjorden, *Norway* 8 C16
Saltholm, *Denmark* 11 J6
Saltillo, *Mexico* 118 B4
Salto, *Argentina* 126 C3
Salto, *Uruguay* 126 C4
Salto del Guaíra, *Paraguay* 127 A5
Salton City, *U.S.A.* 111 M11
Salton Sea, *U.S.A.* 111 M11
Saltpond, *Ghana* 83 D4
Saltsburg, *U.S.A.* 116 F5
Saltsjöbaden, *Sweden* 10 E12
Saluda →, *U.S.A.* 115 J5
Salûm, *Egypt* 80 A2
Salûm, Khâlig el, *Egypt* 80 A2
Salur, *India* 67 K13
Saluzzo, *Italy* 40 D4
Salvador, *Brazil* 125 F11
Salvador, *Canada* 103 C7
Salvador, El ■, *Cent. Amer.* 120 D2
Salvador, L., *U.S.A.* 113 L9
Salvaterra de Magos, *Portugal* 37 F2
Sálvora, I. de, *Spain* 36 C2
Salween →, *Burma* 67 L20
Salyan, *Azerbaijan* 52 F5
Salybia, *Trin. & Tob.* 125 K15
Salza →, *Austria* 26 D7
Salzach →, *Austria* 26 C5
Salzburg, *Austria* 26 D6
Salzburg □, *Austria* 26 D6
Salzgitter, *Germany* 24 C6
Salzkotten, *Germany* 24 D4
Salzwedel, *Germany* 24 C7
Sam, *India* 68 F4
Sam Neua, *Laos* 58 G5
Sam Ngao, *Thailand* 64 D2
Sam Rayburn Reservoir, *U.S.A.* 113 K7
Sam Son, *Vietnam* 64 C5
Sam Teu, *Laos* 64 C5
Sama de Langreo = Langreo, *Spain* 36 B5
Samagaltay, *Russia* 53 D10
Samales Group, *Phil.* 61 J4
Samâlût, *Egypt* 80 B3
Samana, *India* 68 D7
Samana Cay, *Bahamas* 121 B5
Samandağı, *Turkey* 72 D6
Samandıra, *Turkey* 45 F13
Samanga, *Tanzania* 87 D4
Samangān □, *Afghan.* 66 B5
Samangwa, *Dem. Rep. of the Congo* 86 C1
Samani, *Japan* 54 C11
Samanli Dağları, *Turkey* 45 F13
Samar, *Phil.* 61 F6
Samara, *Russia* 34 D10
Samara →, *Russia* 34 D10
Samara →, *Ukraine* 33 H8
Samaria = Shōmrōn, *West Bank* 74 C4
Samariá, *Greece* 49 D5
Samaria △, *Greece* 46 F5
Samarinda, *Indonesia* 62 E5
Samarkand = Samarqand, *Uzbekistan* 52 F7
Samarqand, *Uzbekistan* 52 F7
Sāmarrā', *Iraq* 70 C4
Samastipur, *India* 69 G11
Şamaxi, *Azerbaijan* 35 K9
Samba, *Dem. Rep. of the Congo* 86 C2
Samba, *India* 69 C6
Sambalpur, *India* 67 J14
Sambar, Tanjung, *Indonesia* 62 E4
Sambas, *Indonesia* 62 D3
Sambava, *Madag.* 89 A9
Sambawizi, *Zimbabwe* 87 F2
Sambhal, *India* 69 E8
Sambhar, *India* 68 F6
Sambhar L., *India* 68 F6
Sambiase, *Italy* 43 D9
Sambir, *Ukraine* 31 J10
Sambor, *Cambodia* 64 F6
Samborombón, B., *Argentina* 126 D4
Sambuca di Sicília, *Italy* 42 E6
Samburu ⌓, *Kenya* 86 B4
Samch'ŏk, *S. Korea* 57 F15
Samch'onp'o, *S. Korea* 57 G15
Same, *Tanzania* 86 C4
Samer, *France* 19 B8
Samfya, *Zambia* 87 E2
Sámi, *Greece* 46 C2
Şämkir, *Azerbaijan* 35 K8
Şamlı, *Turkey* 47 B9
Samnah, *Si. Arabia* 70 E3
Samo Alto, *Chile* 126 C1
Samoa ■, *Pac. Oc.* 91 B13
Samoan Is., *Pac. Oc.* 91 A13
Samobor, *Croatia* 41 C12
Samoëns, *France* 19 F13
Samokov, *Bulgaria* 44 D7
Šamorín, *Slovak Rep.* 27 C10
Samorogouan, *Burkina Faso* 82 C4
Sámos, *Greece* 47 D8
Samoš, *Serbia & M.* 28 E5
Samos, *Spain* 36 C3
Sámos □, *Greece* 47 D8
Samothráki = Mathráki, *Greece* 49 A3
Samothráki, *Greece* 45 F9
Samoylovka, *Russia* 34 E6
Sampa, *Ghana* 82 D4
Sampacho, *Argentina* 126 C3
Sampalan, *Indonesia* 63 K18
Sampang, *Indonesia* 63 G15
Samper de Calanda, *Spain* 38 D4
Sampéyre, *Italy* 40 D4
Sampit, *Indonesia* 62 E4
Sampit, Teluk, *Indonesia* 62 E4
Samrong, *Cambodia* 64 E4
Samrong, *Thailand* 64 E3
Samsø, *Denmark* 11 J4
Samsø Bælt, *Denmark* 11 J4
Samsun, *Turkey* 72 B7
Samtredia, *Georgia* 35 J6
Samui, Ko, *Thailand* 65 b
Samur →, *Russia* 35 K9
Samurskiy Khrebet, *Russia* 35 K8
Samusole, *Dem. Rep. of the Congo* 87 E1
Samut Prakan, *Thailand* 64 F3
Samut Songkhram →, *Thailand* 62 B1
Samwari, *Pakistan* 68 E2
San, *Mali* 82 C4
San →, *Cambodia* 64 F5
San →, *Poland* 31 H8
San Adrián, *Spain* 38 C3
San Adrián, C. de, *Spain* 36 B2
San Agustin, C., *Phil.* 61 H7
San Agustín de Valle Fértil, *Argentina* 126 C2
San Ambrosio, *Pac. Oc.* 97 K20
San Andreas, *U.S.A.* 110 G6
San Andres, *Phil.* 61 E6
San Andrés, I. de, *Caribbean* 120 D3
San Andrês del Rabanedo, *Spain* 36 C5
San Andres Mts., *U.S.A.* 109 K10
San Andrés Tuxtla, *Mexico* 119 D5
San Angelo, *U.S.A.* 113 K4
San Anselmo, *U.S.A.* 110 H4
San Antonio, *Belize* 119 D7
San Antonio, *Chile* 126 C1
San Antonio, *Phil.* 61 D4
San Antonio, *N. Mex., U.S.A.* 109 K10
San Antonio, *Tex., U.S.A.* 113 L5
San Antonio →, *U.S.A.* 113 L6
San Antonio, C., *Argentina* 126 D4
San Antonio, C. de, *Cuba* 120 B3
San Antonio, C. de, *Spain* 39 G5
San Antonio, Mt., *U.S.A.* 111 L9
San Antonio de los Baños, *Cuba* 120 B3
San Antonio de los Cobres, *Argentina* 126 A2
San Antonio Oeste, *Argentina* 128 E4
San Arcángelo, *Italy* 43 B9
San Ardo, *U.S.A.* 110 J6
San Augustín, *Canary Is.* 48 G4
San Augustine, *U.S.A.* 113 K7
San Bartolomé, *Canary Is.* 48 F6
San Bartolomé de Tirajana, *Canary Is.* 48 G4
San Bartolomeo in Galdo, *Italy* 43 A8
San Benedetto del Tronto, *Italy* 41 F10
San Benedetto Po, *Italy* 40 C7
San Benedicto, I., *Mexico* 118 D2
San Benito, *U.S.A.* 113 M6
San Benito →, *U.S.A.* 110 J5
San Benito Mt., *U.S.A.* 110 J6
San Bernardino, *U.S.A.* 111 L9
San Bernardino Mts., *U.S.A.* 111 L10
San Bernardino Str., *Phil.* 61 E6
San Bernardo, *Chile* 126 C1
San Bernardo, I. de, *Colombia* 124 B3
San Blas, *Mexico* 118 B3
San Blas, Arch. de, *Panama* 120 E4
San Blas, C., *U.S.A.* 115 L3
San Bonifacio, *Italy* 41 C8
San Borja, *Bolivia* 124 F5
San Buenaventura = Ventura, *U.S.A.* 111 L7
San Buenaventura, *Mexico* 118 B4
San Carlos = Sant Carles, *Spain* 48 B8
San Carlos, *Argentina* 126 C2
San Carlos, *Chile* 126 D1
San Carlos, *Baja Calif. S., Mexico* 118 C2
San Carlos, *Coahuila, Mexico* 118 B4
San Carlos, *Nic.* 120 D3
San Carlos, *Neg. Occ., Phil.* 61 F5
San Carlos, *Pangasinan, Phil.* 61 D4
San Carlos, *Uruguay* 127 C5
San Carlos, *U.S.A.* 109 K8
San Carlos, *Venezuela* 124 B5
San Carlos de Bariloche, *Argentina* 128 E2
San Carlos de Bolívar, *Argentina* 128 D4
San Carlos de la Rápita = Sant Carles de la Ràpita, *Spain* 38 E5
San Carlos del Zulia, *Venezuela* 124 B4
San Carlos L., *U.S.A.* 109 K8
San Cataldo, *Italy* 42 E6
San Celoni = Sant Celoni, *Spain* 38 D7
San Clemente, *Chile* 126 D1
San Clemente, *Spain* 39 F2
San Clemente, *U.S.A.* 111 M9
San Clemente I., *U.S.A.* 111 N8
San Cristóbal = Es Migjorn Gran, *Spain* 48 B11
San Cristóbal, *Argentina* 126 C3
San Cristóbal, *Dom. Rep.* 121 C5
San Cristóbal, *Venezuela* 124 B4
San Cristóbal de la Casas, *Mexico* 119 D6
San Damiano d'Asti, *Italy* 40 D5
San Daniele del Friuli, *Italy* 41 B10
San Diego, *Calif., U.S.A.* 111 N9
San Diego, *Tex., U.S.A.* 113 M5
San Diego, C., *Argentina* 128 G3
San Diego de la Unión, *Mexico* 118 C4
San Diego International ✕ (SAN), *U.S.A.* 111 N9
San Dimitri, Ras, *Malta* 49 C1
San Dimitri Point = San Dimitri, Ras, *Malta* 49 C1
San Donà di Piave, *Italy* 41 C9
San Estanislao, *Paraguay* 126 A4
San Esteban de Gormaz, *Spain* 38 D1
San Felice Circeo, *Italy* 42 A6
San Felice sul Panaro, *Italy* 41 D8
San Felipe, *Chile* 126 C1
San Felipe, *Mexico* 118 A2
San Felipe, *Venezuela* 124 A5
San Felipe →, *U.S.A.* 111 M11
San Félix, *Chile* 126 B1
San Félix, *Pac. Oc.* 97 K20
San Fernando = Sant Ferran, *Spain* 48 C7
San Fernando, *Chile* 126 C1
San Fernando, *Baja Calif., Mexico* 118 B1
San Fernando, *Tamaulipas, Mexico* 119 C5
San Fernando, *La Union, Phil.* 61 C4
San Fernando, *Pampanga, Phil.* 61 D4
San Fernando, *Spain* 37 J4
San Fernando, *Trin. & Tob.* 121 D7
San Fernando, *U.S.A.* 111 L8
San Fernando de Apure, *Venezuela* 124 B5
San Fernando de Atabapo, *Venezuela* 124 C5
San Fernando di Púglia, *Italy* 43 A9
San Francisco, *Argentina* 126 C3
San Francisco, *U.S.A.* 110 H4
San Francisco →, *U.S.A.* 109 K9
San Francisco, C. de, *Colombia* 122 C3
San Francisco, Paso de, *S. Amer.* 126 B2
San Francisco de Macorís, *Dom. Rep.* 121 C5
San Francisco del Monte de Oro, *Argentina* 126 C2
San Francisco del Oro, *Mexico* 118 B3
San Francisco International ✕ (SFO), *U.S.A.* 110 H4
San Francisco Javier = Sant Francesc de Formentera, *Spain* 48 C7
San Fratello, *Italy* 43 D7
San Gabriel, *Chile* 126 C1
San Gabriel Mts., *U.S.A.* 111 L9
San Gavino Monreale, *Italy* 42 C1
San German, *Puerto Rico* 121 d
San Gimignano, *Italy* 40 E8
San Giórgio di Nogaro, *Italy* 41 C10
San Giórgio Iónico, *Italy* 43 B10
San Giovanni Bianco, *Italy* 40 C6
San Giovanni in Fiore, *Italy* 43 C9
San Giovanni in Persiceto, *Italy* 41 D8
San Giovanni Rotondo, *Italy* 41 G12
San Giovanni Valdarno, *Italy* 41 E8
San Giuliano Terme, *Italy* 40 E7
San Gorgonio Mt., *U.S.A.* 111 L10
San Gottardo, P. del, *Switz.* 25 J4
San Gregorio, *Uruguay* 127 C4
San Gregorio, *U.S.A.* 110 H4
San Guiseppe Jato, *Italy* 42 E6
San Ignacio, *Belize* 119 D7
San Ignacio, *Bolivia* 124 G6
San Ignacio, *Mexico* 118 B2
San Ignacio, *Paraguay* 120 C2
San Ignacio ⌓, *Mexico* 118 B2
San Ignacio, L., *Mexico* 118 B2
San Ildefonso, C., *Phil.* 61 C5
San Isidro, *Argentina* 126 C4
San Isidro, *Phil.* 61 H7
San Jacinto, *U.S.A.* 111 M10
San Jaime = Sant Jaume, *Spain* 48 B11
San Javier, *Misiones, Argentina* 127 B4
San Javier, *Santa Fe, Argentina* 126 C4
San Javier, *Bolivia* 124 G6
San Javier, *Chile* 126 D1
San Javier, *Spain* 39 H4
San Jeronimo Taviche, *Mexico* 119 D5
San Joaquin, *U.S.A.* 110 J6
San Joaquin →, *U.S.A.* 110 G5
San Joaquin Valley, *U.S.A.* 110 J6
San Jon, *U.S.A.* 113 H3
San Jordi = Sant Jordi, *Spain* 48 B9
San Jorge, *Argentina* 126 C3
San Jorge, B. de, *Mexico* 118 A2
San Jorge, G., *Argentina* 128 F3
San José = San Josep, *Spain* 48 C7
San José, *Costa Rica* 120 E3
San José, *Guatemala* 120 D1
San José, *Mexico* 118 C2
San Jose, *Mind. Occ., Phil.* 61 E4
San Jose, *Nueva Ecija, Phil.* 61 D4
San Jose, *U.S.A.* 110 H5
San Jose →, *U.S.A.* 109 J10
San Jose de Buenavista, *Phil.* 63 B6
San José de Chiquitos, *Bolivia* 124 G6
San José de Feliciano, *Argentina* 126 C4
San José de Jáchal, *Argentina* 126 C2
San José de Mayo, *Uruguay* 126 C4
San José del Cabo, *Mexico* 118 C3
San José del Guaviare, *Colombia* 124 C4
San Josep, *Spain* 48 C7
San Juan, *Argentina* 126 C2
San Juan, *Mexico* 118 C4
San Juan, *Phil.* 61 F6
San Juan, *Puerto Rico* 121 d
San Juan, *Trin. & Tob.* 125 K15
San Juan □, *Argentina* 126 C2
San Juan →, *Argentina* 126 C2
San Juan →, *Nic.* 120 D3
San Juan →, *U.S.A.* 109 H8
San Juan Bautista = Sant Joan Baptista, *Spain* 48 B8
San Juan Bautista, *Paraguay* 126 B4
San Juan Bautista, *U.S.A.* 110 J5
San Juan Bautista Valle Nacional, *Mexico* 119 D5
San Juan Capistrano, *U.S.A.* 111 M9
San Juan Cr. →, *U.S.A.* 110 J5
San Juan de Alicante, *Spain* 39 G4
San Juan de Guadalupe, *Mexico* 118 C4
San Juan de la Costa, *Mexico* 118 C2
San Juan de los Morros, *Venezuela* 124 B5
San Juan del Norte, *Nic.* 120 D3
San Juan del Norte, B. de, *Nic.* 120 D3
San Juan del Río, *Mexico* 119 C5
San Juan del Sur, *Nic.* 120 D2
San Juan I., *U.S.A.* 110 B3
San Juan Island △, *U.S.A.* 110 B4
San Juan Mts., *U.S.A.* 109 H10
San Just, Sierra de, *Spain* 38 E4
San Justo, *Argentina* 126 C3
San Kamphaeng, *Thailand* 64 C2
San Lázaro, C., *Mexico* 118 C2
San Lázaro, Sa., *Mexico* 118 C3
San Leandro, *U.S.A.* 110 H4
San Leonardo de Yagüe, *Spain* 38 D1
San Lorenzo = Sant Llorenç des Cardassar, *Spain* 48 B10
San Lorenzo, *Argentina* 126 C3
San Lorenzo, *Ecuador* 124 C3
San Lorenzo, *Paraguay* 126 B4
San Lorenzo →, *Mexico* 118 C3
San Lorenzo, I., *Mexico* 118 B2
San Lorenzo, Mte., *Argentina* 128 F2
San Lorenzo de la Parrilla, *Spain* 38 F2
San Lorenzo de Morunys = Sant Llorenç de Morunys, *Spain* 38 C6
San Lucas, *Bolivia* 124 H5
San Lucas, *Baja Calif. S., Mexico* 118 C3
San Lucas, *Baja Calif. S., Mexico* 118 B2
San Lucas, *U.S.A.* 110 J5
San Lucas, C., *Mexico* 118 C3
San Lúcido, *Italy* 43 C9
San Luis, *Argentina* 126 C2
San Luis, *Cuba* 120 B3
San Luis, *Guatemala* 120 C2
San Luis, *Ariz., U.S.A.* 109 K6
San Luis, *Colo., U.S.A.* 109 H11
San Luis □, *Argentina* 126 C2
San Luis, I., *Mexico* 118 B2
San Luis, Sierra de, *Argentina* 126 C2
San Luis de la Paz, *Mexico* 118 C4
San Luis Obispo, *U.S.A.* 111 K6
San Luis Potosí, *Mexico* 118 C4
San Luis Potosí □, *Mexico* 118 C4
San Luis Reservoir, *U.S.A.* 110 H5
San Luis Río Colorado, *Mexico* 118 A2
San Manuel, *U.S.A.* 109 K8
San Marco, C., *Italy* 42 C1
San Marco Argentano, *Italy* 43 C9
San Marco in Lámis, *Italy* 41 G12
San Marcos, *Guatemala* 120 D1
San Marcos, *Mexico* 118 B2
San Marcos, *Calif., U.S.A.* 111 M9
San Marcos, *Tex., U.S.A.* 113 L6
San Marino, *San Marino* 41 E9
San Marino ■, *Europe* 41 E9
San Martín, *Antarctica* 5 C17
San Martín, *Argentina* 126 C2
San Martín →, *Bolivia* 124 F6
San Martín, L., *Argentina* 128 F2
San Martín de la Vega, *Spain* 36 E7
San Martín de los Andes, *Argentina* 128 E2
San Martín de Valdeiglesias, *Spain* 36 E6
San Mateo = Sant Mateu, *Baleares, Spain* 48 B7
San Mateo = Sant Mateu, *Valencia, Spain* 38 E5
San Mateo, *Phil.* 61 C4
San Mateo, *U.S.A.* 110 H4
San Matías, *Bolivia* 124 G7
San Matías, G., *Argentina* 128 E4
San Miguel = Sant Miguel, *Spain* 48 B7
San Miguel, *El Salv.* 120 D2
San Miguel, *Panama* 120 E4
San Miguel, *U.S.A.* 110 K6
San Miguel →, *Bolivia* 124 F6
San Miguel de Tucumán, *Argentina* 126 B2
San Miguel del Monte, *Argentina* 126 D4
San Miguel I., *U.S.A.* 111 L6
San Miniato, *Italy* 40 E7
San Nicolás, *Canary Is.* 48 G4
San Nicolas, *Phil.* 61 B4
San Nicolás de los Arroyas, *Argentina* 126 C3
San Nicolas I., *U.S.A.* 111 M7
San Onofre, *U.S.A.* 111 M9
San Pablo, *Bolivia* 126 A2
San Pablo, *Phil.* 61 D4
San Pablo, *U.S.A.* 110 H4
San Páolo di Civitate, *Italy* 41 G12
San Pedro, *Buenos Aires, Argentina* 126 C4
San Pedro, *Misiones, Argentina* 127 B5
San Pedro, *Chile* 126 C1
San Pédro, *Ivory C.* 82 E3
San Pedro, *Mexico* 118 C2
San Pedro □, *Paraguay* 126 A4
San Pedro →, *Chihuahua, Mexico* 118 B3
San Pedro →, *Nayarit, Mexico* 118 C3
San Pedro →, *U.S.A.* 109 K8
San Pedro, Pta., *Chile* 126 B1
San Pedro, Sierra de, *Spain* 37 F4
San Pedro Channel, *U.S.A.* 111 M8
San Pedro de Atacama, *Chile* 126 A2
San Pedro de Jujuy, *Argentina* 126 A3
San Pedro de las Colonias, *Mexico* 118 B4
San Pedro de Macorís, *Dom. Rep.* 121 C6
San Pedro del Norte, *Nic.* 120 D3
San Pedro del Paraná, *Paraguay* 126 B4
San Pedro del Pinatar, *Spain* 39 H4
San Pedro Mártir △, *Mexico* 118 A1
San Pedro Mártir, Sierra, *Mexico* 118 A1
San Pedro Mixtepec, *Mexico* 119 D5
San Pedro Ocampo = Melchor Ocampo, *Mexico* 118 C4
San Pedro Sula, *Honduras* 120 C2
San Pietro, *Italy* 42 C1
San Pietro Vernótico, *Italy* 43 B11
San Quintín, *Mexico* 118 A1
San Rafael, *Argentina* 126 C2
San Rafael, *Calif., U.S.A.* 110 H4
San Rafael, *N. Mex., U.S.A.* 109 J10
San Rafael Mt., *U.S.A.* 111 L7
San Rafael Mts., *U.S.A.* 111 L7
San Ramón de la Nueva Orán, *Argentina* 126 A3
San Remo, *Italy* 40 E4
San Roque, *Argentina* 126 B4
San Roque, *Spain* 37 J5
San Rosendo, *Chile* 126 D1
San Saba, *U.S.A.* 113 K5
San Salvador, *El Salv.* 120 D2
San Salvador, *Spain* 48 B10
San Salvador de Jujuy, *Argentina* 126 A3
San Salvador I., *Bahamas* 121 B5
San Salvo, *Italy* 41 F11
San Sebastián = Donostia-San Sebastián, *Spain* 38 B3
San Sebastián, *Argentina* 128 G3
San Sebastian, *Puerto Rico* 121 d
San Sebastián de la Gomera, *Canary Is.* 48 F2
San Serra = Son Serra, *Spain* 48 B10
San Serverino Marche, *Italy* 41 E10
San Severo, *Italy* 41 G12
San Simeon, *U.S.A.* 110 K5
San Simon, *U.S.A.* 109 K9
San Stéfano di Cadore, *Italy* 41 B9
San Stino di Livenza, *Italy* 41 C9
San Telmo = Sant Telm, *Spain* 48 B9
San Telmo, *Mexico* 118 A1
San Tiburcio, *Mexico* 118 C4
San Valentin, Mte., *Chile* 128 F2
San Vicente de Alcántara, *Spain* 37 F3
San Vicente de la Barquera, *Spain* 36 B6
San Vincente del Raspeig, *Spain* 39 G4
San Vincenzo, *Italy* 40 E7
San Vito, *Costa Rica* 120 E3
San Vito, *Italy* 42 C2
San Vito, C., *Italy* 42 D5
San Vito al Tagliamento, *Italy* 41 C9
San Vito Chietino, *Italy* 41 F11
San Vito dei Normanni, *Italy* 43 B10
Sana', *Yemen* 75 D3
Sana →, *Bos.-H.* 41 C13
Sanaba, *Burkina Faso* 82 C4
Şanāfīr, *Si. Arabia* 80 B3
Sanaga →, *Cameroon* 83 E6
Sanaloa, Presa, *Mexico* 118 C3
Sanana, *Indonesia* 63 E7
Sanand, *India* 68 H5
Sanandaj, *Iran* 70 C5
Sanandita, *Bolivia* 126 A3
Sanary-sur-Mer, *France* 21 E9
Sanawad, *India* 68 H7
Sancellas = Sencelles, *Spain* 48 B9
Sancergues, *France* 19 E9
Sancerre, *France* 19 E9
Sancerrois, Collines du, *France* 19 E9
Sancha He →, *China* 58 D6
Sanchahe, *China* 57 B14
Sánchez, *Dom. Rep.* 121 C6
Sanchor, *India* 68 G4
Sancoins, *France* 19 F9
Sancti Spíritus, *Cuba* 120 B4
Sancy, Puy de, *France* 20 C6
Sand →, *S. Africa* 89 C5
Sand Hills, *U.S.A.* 112 D4
Sand Lakes ⌓, *Canada* 103 B9
Sand Springs, *U.S.A.* 113 G6

Sanda, *Japan* 55 G7
Sandakan, *Malaysia* 62 C5
Sandan = Sambor, *Cambodia* 64 F6
Sandanski, *Bulgaria* 44 E7
Sandaré, *Mali* 82 C2
Sandared, *Sweden* 11 G6
Sandarne, *Sweden* 10 C11
Sanday, *U.K.* 13 B6
Sandefjord, *Norway* 9 G14
Sanders, *U.S.A.* 109 J9
Sanderson, *U.S.A.* 113 K3
Sandersville, *U.S.A.* 115 J4
Sandfire Roadhouse, *Australia* 92 C3
Sandfly L., *Canada* 103 B7
Sandfontein, *Namibia* 88 C2
Sandhammaren, C., *Sweden* 11 J8
Sandheads, The, *India* 69 J13
Sandía, *Peru* 124 F5
Sandıklı, *Turkey* 47 C12
Sandila, *India* 69 F9
Sandnes, *Norway* 9 G11
Sandnessjøen, *Norway* 8 C15
Sandoa, *Dem. Rep. of the Congo* 84 F4
Sandomierz, *Poland* 31 H8
Sândominic, *Romania* 29 D10
Sandover →, *Australia* 94 C2
Sandoway, *Burma* 67 K19
Sandoy, *Færoe Is.* 8 F9
Sandpoint, *U.S.A.* 108 B5
Sandray, *U.K.* 13 E1
Sandringham, *U.K.* 14 E8
Sandstone, *Australia* 93 E2
Sandu, *China* 58 E6
Sandusky, *Mich., U.S.A.* 116 C2
Sandusky, *Ohio, U.S.A.* 116 E2
Sandvig, *Sweden* 11 J8
Sandviken, *Sweden* 10 D10
Sandwich, C., *Australia* 94 B4
Sandwich B., *Canada* 105 B8
Sandwich B., *Namibia* 88 C1
Sandy, *Oreg., U.S.A.* 110 E4
Sandy, *Pa., U.S.A.* 116 E6
Sandy, *Utah, U.S.A.* 108 F8
Sandy Bay, *Canada* 103 B8
Sandy Bight, *Australia* 93 F3
Sandy C., *Queens., Australia* 94 C5
Sandy C., *Tas., Australia* 95 G3
Sandy Cay, *Bahamas* 121 B4
Sandy Cr. →, *U.S.A.* 108 F9
Sandy L., *Canada* 104 B1
Sandy Lake, *Canada* 104 B1
Sandy Valley, *U.S.A.* 111 K11
Sånfjällets △, *Sweden* 10 B7
Sanford, *Fla., U.S.A.* 115 L5
Sanford, *Maine, U.S.A.* 115 D10
Sanford, *N.C., U.S.A.* 115 H6
Sanford →, *Australia* 93 E2
Sanford, Mt., *U.S.A.* 100 B5
Sang-i-Masha, *Afghan.* 68 C2
Sanga, *Mozam.* 87 E4
Sanga →, *Congo* 84 E3
Sangamner, *India* 66 K9
Sanganeb Atoll △, *Sudan* 80 D4
Sangar, *Afghan.* 68 C1
Sangar, *Russia* 53 C13
Sangar Sarai, *Afghan.* 68 B4
Sangaredi, *Guinea* 82 C2
Sangarh →, *Pakistan* 68 D4
Sangasso, *Mali* 82 C3
Sangatte, *France* 19 B8
Sangay, *Ecuador* 124 D3
Sange, *Dem. Rep. of the Congo* 86 D2
Sangeang, *Indonesia* 63 F5
Sângeorz-Băi, *Romania* 29 C9
Sanger, *U.S.A.* 110 J7
Sângera, *Moldova* 29 D13
Sangerhausen, *Germany* 24 D7
Sanggan He →, *China* 56 E9
Sanggau, *Indonesia* 62 D4
Sanghar, *Pakistan* 68 F3
Sangihe, Kepulauan, *Indonesia* 63 D7
Sangihe, Pulau, *Indonesia* 63 D7
Sangju, *S. Korea* 57 F15
Sangkapura, *Indonesia* 62 F4
Sangkhla, *Thailand* 64 E2
Sangkulirang, *Indonesia* 62 D5
Sangla, *Pakistan* 68 D5
Sangli, *India* 66 L9
Sangmélima, *Cameroon* 83 E7
Sangod, *India* 68 G7
Sangre de Cristo Mts., *U.S.A.* 113 G2
Sangre Grande, *Trin. & Tob.* 125 K15
Sangro →, *Italy* 41 F11
Sangrur, *India* 68 D6
Sangudo, *Canada* 102 C6
Sangue →, *Brazil* 124 F7
Sangüesa, *Spain* 38 C3
Sanguinaires, Îs., *France* 21 G12
Sangzhi, *China* 59 C8
Sanhala, *Ivory C.* 82 C3
Sanibel, *U.S.A.* 115 M4
Sanikiluaq, *Canada* 101 C12
Sanin-Kaigan △, *Japan* 55 G7
Sanirajak, *Canada* 101 B11
Sanjawi, *Pakistan* 68 D3
Sanje, *Uganda* 86 C3
Sanjiang, *China* 58 E7
Sanjo, *Japan* 54 F9
Sankh →, *India* 69 H11
Sankt Andrä, *Austria* 26 E7
Sankt Augustin, *Germany* 24 E3
Sankt Blasien, *Germany* 25 H4
Sankt Gallen, *Switz.* 25 H5
Sankt Gallen □, *Switz.* 25 H5
Sankt Goar, *Germany* 25 E3
Sankt Ingbert, *Germany* 25 F3
Sankt Johann im Pongau, *Austria* 26 D6
Sankt Johann in Tirol, *Austria* 26 D5
Sankt Michel = Mikkeli, *Finland* 9 F22
Sankt-Peterburg, *Russia* 32 C6
Sankt Pölten, *Austria* 26 C8
Sankt Ulrich = Ortisei, *Italy* 41 B8
Sankt Valentin, *Austria* 26 C7
Sankt Veit an der Glan, *Austria* 26 E7
Sankt Wendel, *Germany* 25 F3
Sankt Wolfgang, *Austria* 26 D6
Sankuru →, *Dem. Rep. of the Congo* 84 E4
Sanliurfa, *Turkey* 70 B3
Sanlúcar de Barrameda, *Spain* 37 J4
Sanluri, *Italy* 42 C1
Sânmartin, *Romania* 29 D10
Sanmen, *China* 59 C13
Sanmenxia, *China* 56 G6
Sanming, *China* 59 D11
Sannaspos, *S. Africa* 88 D4
Sannicandro Gargánico, *Italy* 41 G12
Sânnicolau Mare, *Romania* 28 D5
Sannieshof, *S. Africa* 88 D4
Sannīn, J., *Lebanon* 74 B4
Sanniquellie, *Liberia* 82 D3
Sannûr, W. →, *Egypt* 80 B3
Sanoe, *Antarctica* 5 D2
Sanok, *Poland* 31 J9
Sanquhar, *U.K.* 13 F5
Sans Souci, *Trin. & Tob.* 125 K16
Sansanding, *Mali* 82 C3
Sansepolcro, *Italy* 41 E9
Sansha, *China* 59 D13
Sanshui, *China* 59 F9
Sanski Most, *Bos.-H.* 41 D13
Sansui, *China* 58 D7
Sant Antoni Abat, *Spain* 48 C7
Sant Boi de Llobregat, *Spain* 38 D7
Sant Carles, *Spain* 48 B8
Sant Carles de la Ràpita, *Spain* 38 E5
Sant Celoni, *Spain* 38 D7
Sant Feliu de Guíxols, *Spain* 38 D8
Sant Feliu de Llobregat, *Spain* 38 D7
Sant Ferran, *Spain* 48 C7
Sant Francesc de Formentera, *Spain* 48 C7
Sant Jaume, *Spain* 48 B11
Sant Joan Baptista, *Spain* 48 B8
Sant Jordi, *Ibiza, Spain* 48 C7
Sant Jordi, *Mallorca, Spain* 48 B9
Sant Jordi, G. de, *Spain* 38 E6
Sant Llorenç de Morunys, *Spain* 38 C6
Sant Llorenç del Munt y l'Obac ⌓, *Spain* 38 D3
Sant Llorenç des Cardassar, *Spain* 48 B10
Sant Mateu, *Baleares, Spain* 48 B7
Sant Mateu, *Valencia, Spain* 38 E5
Sant Miguel, *Spain* 48 B7
Sant Telm, *Spain* 48 B9
Sant' Ágata Militello, *Italy* 43 D7
Santa Agnés, *Spain* 48 B7
Santa Ana, *Bolivia* 124 F5
Santa Ana, *El Salv.* 120 D2
Santa Ana, *Mexico* 118 A2
Santa Ana, *U.S.A.* 111 M9
Sant' Ángelo Lodigiano, *Italy* 40 C6
Sant' Antíoco, *Italy* 42 C1
Santa Bárbara, *Chile* 126 D1
Santa Barbara, *Honduras* 120 D2
Santa Bárbara, *Mexico* 118 B3
Santa Bárbara, *Spain* 38 E5
Santa Barbara, *U.S.A.* 111 L7
Santa Bárbara, Mt., *Spain* 39 H2
Santa Barbara Channel, *U.S.A.* 111 L7
Santa Barbara I., *U.S.A.* 111 M7
Santa Catalina, Gulf of, *U.S.A.* 111 N9
Santa Catalina, I., *Mexico* 118 B2
Santa Catalina I., *U.S.A.* 111 M8
Santa Catarina □, *Brazil* 127 B6
Santa Catarina, I. de, *Brazil* 127 B6
Santa Caterina di Pittinuri, *Italy* 42 B1
Santa Caterina Villarmosa, *Italy* 43 E7
Santa Cecília, *Brazil* 127 B5
Santa Clara, *Cuba* 120 B4
Santa Clara, *Calif., U.S.A.* 110 H5
Santa Clara, *Utah, U.S.A.* 109 H7
Santa Clara, El Golfo de, *Mexico* 118 A2
Santa Clara de Olimar, *Uruguay* 127 C5
Santa Clarita, *U.S.A.* 111 L8
Santa Clotilde, *Peru* 124 D4
Santa Coloma de Farners, *Spain* 38 D7
Santa Coloma de Gramenet, *Spain* 38 D7
Santa Comba, *Spain* 36 B2
Santa Croce Camerina, *Italy* 43 F7
Santa Croce di Magliano, *Italy* 41 G11
Santa Cruz, *Argentina* 128 G3
Santa Cruz, *Bolivia* 124 G6
Santa Cruz, *Chile* 126 C1
Santa Cruz, *Costa Rica* 120 D2
Santa Cruz, *Madeira* 48 D3
Santa Cruz, *Phil.* 61 D4
Santa Cruz, *U.S.A.* 110 J4
Santa Cruz →, *Argentina* 128 G3
Santa Cruz de la Palma, *Canary Is.* 48 F2
Santa Cruz de la Palma ✕ (SPC), *Canary Is.* 48 F2
Santa Cruz de Mudela, *Spain* 37 G7
Santa Cruz de Tenerife, *Canary Is.* 48 F3
Santa Cruz del Norte, *Cuba* 120 B3
Santa Cruz del Retamar, *Spain* 36 E6
Santa Cruz del Sur, *Cuba* 120 B4
Santa Cruz do Rio Pardo, *Brazil* 127 A6
Santa Cruz do Sul, *Brazil* 127 B5
Santa Cruz I., *U.S.A.* 111 M7
Santa Cruz Is., *Solomon Is.* 96 J8
Santa Cruz Mts., *Jamaica* 120 a
Santa Domingo, Cay, *Bahamas* 120 B4
Sant' Egídio alla Vibrata, *Italy* 41 F10
Santa Elena, *Argentina* 126 C4
Santa Elena, C., *Costa Rica* 120 D2
Sant' Eufémia, G. di, *Italy* 43 D9
Santa Eulàlia des Riu, *Spain* 48 C8
Santa Fe, *Argentina* 126 C3
Santa Fe, *Spain* 37 H7
Santa Fe, *U.S.A.* 109 J11
Santa Fé □, *Argentina* 126 C3
Santa Fé do Sul, *Brazil* 125 H8
Santa Filomena, *Brazil* 125 E9
Santa Fiora, *Italy* 41 F8
Santa Gertrudis, *Spain* 48 C7
Santa Giustina, *Italy* 41 B9
Santa Inês, *Brazil* 125 F11
Santa Inés, *Spain* 37 G5
Santa Inés, I., *Chile* 128 G2
Santa Isabel, *Argentina* 126 D2
Santa Isabel, Pico, *Eq. Guin.* 83 E6
Santa Isabel do Morro, *Brazil* 125 F8
Santa Lucía, *Corrientes, Argentina* 126 B4
Santa Lucía, *San Juan, Argentina* 126 C2
Santa Lucía, *Spain* 39 H4
Santa Lucia, *Uruguay* 126 C4
Santa Lucia Range, *U.S.A.* 110 K5
Santa Magdalena, I., *Mexico* 118 C2
Santa Margarita, *Argentina* 126 D3
Santa Margarita, *Spain* 48 B10
Santa Margarita, *U.S.A.* 110 K6
Santa Margarita →, *U.S.A.* 111 M9
Santa Margarita, I., *Mexico* 118 C2
Santa Margherita, *Italy* 42 D1
Santa Margherita Ligure, *Italy* 40 D6
Santa María, *Argentina* 126 B2
Santa Maria, *Brazil* 127 B5
Santa Maria, *Phil.* 61 C4
Santa Maria, *U.S.A.* 111 L6
Santa María →, *Mexico* 118 A3
Santa María, B. de, *Mexico* 118 B3
Santa Maria, C. de, *Portugal* 37 J3
Santa Maria Cápua Vétere, *Italy* 43 A7
Santa Maria da Feira, *Portugal* 36 E2
Santa Maria da Vitória, *Brazil* 125 F10
Santa Maria del Camí, *Spain* 48 B9
Santa Maria di Léuca, C., *Italy* 43 C11
Santa María la Real de Nieva, *Spain* 36 D6
Santa Marinella, *Italy* 41 F8
Santa Marta, *Colombia* 124 A4
Santa Marta, Sierra Nevada de, *Colombia* 124 A4
Santa Marta de Tormes, *Spain* 36 E5
Santa Marta Grande, C., *Brazil* 127 B6
Santa Marta Ortigueira, Ría de, *Spain* 36 B3
Santa Maura = Levkás, *Greece* 46 C2
Santa Monica, *U.S.A.* 111 M8
Santa Monica Mts. ⌓, *U.S.A.* 111 L8
Santa Olalla, *Huelva, Spain* 37 H4
Santa Olalla, *Toledo, Spain* 36 E6
Santa Paula, *U.S.A.* 111 L7
Santa Pola, *Spain* 39 G4
Santa Ponça, *Spain* 48 B9
Santa Rita, *U.S.A.* 109 K10
Santa Rosa, *La Pampa, Argentina* 126 D3
Santa Rosa, *San Luis, Argentina* 126 C2
Santa Rosa, *Brazil* 127 B5
Santa Rosa, *Calif., U.S.A.* 110 G4
Santa Rosa, *N. Mex., U.S.A.* 113 H2
Santa Rosa and San Jacinto Mts. ⌓, *U.S.A.* 111 M10
Santa Rosa de Copán, *Honduras* 120 D2
Santa Rosa de Río Primero, *Argentina* 126 C3
Santa Rosa del Sara, *Bolivia* 124 G6
Santa Rosa I., *Calif., U.S.A.* 111 M6
Santa Rosa I., *Fla., U.S.A.* 115 K2
Santa Rosa Range, *U.S.A.* 108 F5
Santa Rosalía, *Mexico* 118 B2
Santa Sylvina, *Argentina* 126 B3
Santa Tecla = Nueva San Salvador, *El Salv.* 120 D2
Santa Teresa, *Argentina* 126 C3
Santa Teresa, *Australia* 94 C1
Santa Teresa, *Mexico* 119 B5
Santa Teresa △, *Uruguay* 127 C5
Santa Teresa di Riva, *Italy* 43 E8
Santa Teresa Gallura, *Italy* 42 A2
Santa Uxía, *Spain* 36 C2
Santa Vitória do Palmar, *Brazil* 127 C5
Santa Ynez →, *U.S.A.* 111 L6
Santa Ynez Mts., *U.S.A.* 111 L6
Santa Ysabel, *U.S.A.* 111 M10
Santadi, *Italy* 42 C1
Santaella, *Spain* 37 H6
Santai, *China* 58 B5
Santana, *Madeira* 48 D3
Sântana, *Romania* 28 D6
Santana, Coxilha de, *Brazil* 127 C4
Santana do Livramento, *Brazil* 127 C4
Santander, *Spain* 36 B7
Santander Jiménez, *Mexico* 119 C5
Santanilla, Is., *Honduras* 120 C3
Santanyí, *Spain* 48 B10
Santaquin, *U.S.A.* 108 G8
Santarcángelo di Romagna, *Italy* 41 D9
Santarém, *Brazil* 125 D8
Santarém, *Portugal* 37 F2
Santarém □, *Portugal* 37 F2
Santaren Channel, *W. Indies* 120 B4
Santee, *U.S.A.* 111 N10
Santee →, *U.S.A.* 115 J6
Santéramo in Colle, *Italy* 43 B9
Santerno →, *Italy* 41 D8
Santhià, *Italy* 40 C5
Santi-Quaranta = Sarandë, *Albania* 44 G3
Santiago, *Brazil* 127 B5
Santiago, *Canary Is.* 48 F2
Santiago, *Chile* 126 C1
Santiago, *Panama* 120 E3
Santiago, *Phil.* 61 C4
Santiago □, *Chile* 126 C1
Santiago →, *Mexico* 98 G9
Santiago →, *Peru* 124 D3
Santiago, Punta de, *Eq. Guin.* 83 E6
Santiago de Compostela, *Spain* 36 C2
Santiago de Cuba, *Cuba* 120 C4
Santiago de los Cabelleros, *Dom. Rep.* 121 C5
Santiago del Estero, *Argentina* 126 B3
Santiago del Estero □, *Argentina* 126 B3
Santiago del Teide, *Canary Is.* 48 F3
Santiago do Cacém, *Portugal* 37 G2
Santiago Ixcuintla, *Mexico* 118 C3
Santiago Papasquiaro, *Mexico* 118 C3
Santiaguillo, L. de, *Mexico* 118 C4
Santiguila, *Mali* 82 C3
Santillana, *Spain* 36 B6
Santisteban del Puerto, *Spain* 37 G7
Santo Amaro, *Brazil* 125 F11
Santo Anastácio, *Brazil* 127 A5
Santo André, *Brazil* 127 A6
Santo Ângelo, *Brazil* 127 B5
Santo Antônio do Içá, *Brazil* 124 D5
Santo Antônio do Leverger, *Brazil* 125 G7
Santo Domingo, *Dom. Rep.* 121 C6
Santo Domingo, *Baja Calif., Mexico* 118 A1
Santo Domingo, *Baja Calif. S., Mexico* 118 B2
Santo Domingo, *Nic.* 120 D3
Santo Domingo de la Calzada, *Spain* 38 C2
Santo Domingo de los Colorados, *Ecuador* 124 D3
Santo Domingo Pueblo, *U.S.A.* 109 J10
Santo Stéfano di Camastro, *Italy* 43 D7
Santo Tirso, *Portugal* 36 D2
Santo Tomás, *Mexico* 118 A1
Santo Tomás, *Peru* 124 F4
Santo Tomé, *Argentina* 127 B4
Santo Tomé de Guayana = Ciudad Guayana, *Venezuela* 124 B6
Santomera, *Spain* 39 G3
Santoña, *Spain* 36 B7
Santoríni = Thíra, *Greece* 47 E7
Santos, *Brazil* 127 A6
Santos, Sierra de los, *Spain* 37 G5
Santos Dumont, *Brazil* 127 A7
Sanur, *Indonesia* 63 K18
Sanwer, *India* 68 H6
Sanxenxo, *Spain* 36 C2
Sanyuan, *China* 56 G5
São Bartolomeu de Messines, *Portugal* 37 H2
São Bernardo do Campo, *Brazil* 127 A6
São Borja, *Brazil* 127 B4
São Brás de Alportel, *Portugal* 37 H3
São Carlos, *Brazil* 127 A6
São Cristóvão, *Brazil* 125 F11
São Domingos, *Brazil* 125 F9
São Domingos, *Guinea-Biss.* 82 C1
São Francisco, *Brazil* 125 G10
São Francisco →, *Brazil* 125 F11
São Francisco do Sul, *Brazil* 127 B6
São Gabriel, *Brazil* 127 C5
São Gonçalo, *Brazil* 127 A7
Sao Hill, *Tanzania* 87 D4
São João, *Guinea-Biss.* 82 C1
São João da Boa Vista, *Brazil* 127 A6
São João da Madeira, *Portugal* 36 E2
São João da Pesqueira, *Portugal* 36 D3
São João del Rei, *Brazil* 127 A7
São João do Araguaia, *Brazil* 125 E9
São João do Piauí, *Brazil* 125 E10
São Joaquim, *Brazil* 127 B6
São Joaquim △, *Brazil* 127 B6
São Jorge, Pta. de, *Madeira* 48 D3
São José, *Brazil* 127 B5
São José do Norte, *Brazil* 127 C5
São José do Rio Prêto, *Brazil* 127 A6
São José dos Campos, *Brazil* 127 A6
São Leopoldo, *Brazil* 127 B5
São Lourenço, *Brazil* 127 A6
São Lourenço →, *Brazil* 125 G7
São Lourenço, Pta. de, *Madeira* 48 D3
São Lourenço do Sul, *Brazil* 127 C5
São Luís, *Brazil* 125 D10
São Luís Gonzaga, *Brazil* 127 B5
São Marcos →, *Brazil* 125 G9
São Marcos, B. de, *Brazil* 125 D10
São Martinho da Cortiça, *Portugal* 36 E2
São Mateus, *Brazil* 125 G11
São Mateus do Sul, *Brazil* 127 B5
São Miguel do Oeste, *Brazil* 127 B5
São Paulo, *Brazil* 127 A6
São Paulo □, *Brazil* 127 A6
São Paulo, I., *Atl. Oc.* 2 D8
São Paulo de Olivença, *Brazil* 124 D5
São Pedro do Sul, *Portugal* 36 E2
São Roque, *Madeira* 48 D3
São Roque, C. de, *Brazil* 125 E11
São Sebastião, I. de, *Brazil* 127 A6
São Sebastião do Paraíso, *Brazil* 127 A6
São Teotónio, *Portugal* 37 H2
São Tomé, *São Tomé & Príncipe* 76 F4
São Tomé, C. de, *Brazil* 127 A7
São Tomé & Príncipe ■, *Africa* 77 F4
São Vicente, *Brazil* 127 A6
São Vicente, *Madeira* 48 D2
São Vicente, C. de, *Portugal* 37 H1
Saona, I., *Dom. Rep.* 121 C6
Saône →, *France* 19 G11
Saône-et-Loire □, *France* 19 F11
Saonek, *Indonesia* 63 E8
Sápai, *Greece* 45 E9
Sapam, Ao, *Thailand* 65 a
Sapanca, *Turkey* 72 B4
Saparua, *Indonesia* 63 E7
Sapele, *Nigeria* 83 D6
Sapelo I., *U.S.A.* 115 K5
Şaphane, *Turkey* 47 B11
Sapi ⌓, *Zimbabwe* 87 F2
Sapiéntza, *Greece* 46 E3
Sapo △, *Liberia* 82 D3
Sapone, *Burkina Faso* 83 C4
Saposoa, *Peru* 124 E3
Sapotskina, *Belarus* 30 E10
Sapouy, *Burkina Faso* 83 C4
Sapozhok, *Russia* 34 D5
Sapphire, *Australia* 94 C4
Sappho, *U.S.A.* 110 B2
Sapporo, *Japan* 54 C10
Sapri, *Italy* 43 B8
Sapulpa, *U.S.A.* 113 H6
Saqqez, *Iran* 70 B5
Sar Dasht, *Āzarbāyjān-e Gharbī, Iran* 73 D11
Sar Dasht, *Khuzestān, Iran* 71 C6
Sar-e Pol □, *Afghan.* 66 B4
Sar Gachīneh = Yāsūj, *Iran* 71 D6
Sar Planina, *Macedonia* 44 E4
Sara, *Burkina Faso* 82 C4
Sara, *Phil.* 61 F5
Šara △, *Serbia & M.* 44 D5
Sara Buri = Saraburi, *Thailand* 64 E3
Sarāb, *Iran* 70 B5
Sarabadi, *Iraq* 70 C5
Saraburi, *Thailand* 64 E3
Saradiya, *India* 68 J4
Saraféré, *Mali* 82 B4
Saragossa = Zaragoza, *Spain* 38 D4
Saraguro, *Ecuador* 124 D3
Sarai Naurang, *Pakistan* 68 C4
Saraikela, *India* 69 H11
Saraiu, *Romania* 29 F13
Sarajevo, *Bos.-H.* 28 G3
Sarakhs, *Turkmenistan* 71 B9
Saran, Gunung, *Indonesia* 62 E4
Saranac L., *U.S.A.* 117 B10
Saranac Lake, *U.S.A.* 117 B10
Saranda, *Tanzania* 86 D3
Sarandë, *Albania* 44 G3
Sarandí del Yi, *Uruguay* 127 C4
Sarandí Grande, *Uruguay* 126 C4
Sarangani B., *Phil.* 61 J6
Sarangani Is., *Phil.* 61 J6
Sarangarh, *India* 67 J13
Saransk, *Russia* 34 C7
Sarapul, *Russia* 52 D6
Sarasota, *U.S.A.* 115 M4
Sarata, *Ukraine* 29 D14
Sarata →, *Ukraine* 29 E14
Saratoga, *Calif., U.S.A.* 110 H4
Saratoga, *Wyo., U.S.A.* 108 F10
Saratoga △, *U.S.A.* 117 D11
Saratoga Springs, *U.S.A.* 117 C11
Saratok, *Malaysia* 62 D4
Saratov, *Russia* 34 E7
Sarāvān, *Iran* 71 E9
Saravane, *Laos* 64 E6
Sarawak □, *Malaysia* 62 D4
Saray, *Tekirdağ, Turkey* 45 E11
Saray, *Van, Turkey* 73 C11
Saraya, *Guinea* 82 C2
Saraya, *Senegal* 82 C2
Saraycık, *Turkey* 47 B11
Sarayköy, *Turkey* 47 D10
Saraylar, *Turkey* 45 F11
Sarayönü, *Turkey* 72 C5
Sarbāz, *Iran* 71 E9
Sarbīsheh, *Iran* 71 C8
Sárbogárd, *Hungary* 28 D3
Sarca →, *Italy* 40 C7
Sarcelles, *France* 19 D9
Sarda →, *India* 67 F12
Sardarshahr, *India* 68 E6
Sardegna □, *Italy* 42 B1
Sardhana, *India* 68 E7
Sardina, Pta., *Canary Is.* 48 F4
Sardinia = Sardegna □, *Italy* 42 B1
Sardis, *Turkey* 47 C10
Sārdūīyeh = Dar Mazār, *Iran* 71 D8
Saren, *Indonesia* 63 J18
S'Arenal, *Spain* 48 B9
Sarentino, *Italy* 41 B8
Saréyamou, *Mali* 82 B4
Sargasso Sea, *Atl. Oc.* 97 D20
Sargodha, *Pakistan* 68 C5
Sarh, *Chad* 79 G9
Sarhala, *Ivory C.* 82 D3
Sārī, *Iran* 71 B7
Sari d'Orcino, *France* 21 F12
Sária, *Greece* 47 F9
Saria, *India* 69 J10
Sariab, *Pakistan* 68 D2
Sarıbeyler, *Turkey* 47 B9
Sarıgöl, *Turkey* 72 C3
Sarikamiş, *Turkey* 73 B10
Sarıkaya, *Turkey* 72 C6
Sarikei, *Malaysia* 62 D4
Sarıköy, *Turkey* 45 F11
Sarila, *India* 69 G8
Sarina, *Australia* 94 C4
Sariñena, *Spain* 38 D4
Sarita, *U.S.A.* 113 M6
Sariwŏn, *N. Korea* 57 E13
Sariyar Barajı, *Turkey* 72 B4
Sarıyer, *Turkey* 45 E13
Sarju →, *India* 69 F9
Sark, *U.K.* 15 H5
Sarkad, *Hungary* 28 D6
Sarkari Tala, *India* 68 F4
Şarkışla, *Turkey* 72 C7
Şarköy, *Turkey* 45 F11
Sarlat-la-Canéda, *France* 20 D5
Sărmăşag, *Romania* 28 C7
Sărmaşu, *Romania* 29 D9
Sarmi, *Indonesia* 63 E9
Sarmiento, *Argentina* 128 F3
Sarmizegetusa, *Romania* 28 E7
Särna, *Sweden* 10 C7
Sarnano, *Italy* 41 E10
Sarnen, *Switz.* 25 J4
Sarnia, *Canada* 116 D2
Sarno, *Italy* 43 B7

Sarnthein = Sarentino, *Italy* 41 B8
Särö, *Sweden* 11 G5
Sarolangun, *Indonesia* 62 E2
Saronikós Kólpos, *Greece* 46 D5
Saronno, *Italy* 40 C6
Saros Körfezi, *Turkey* 45 F10
Sárospatak, *Hungary* 28 B6
Sarpsborg, *Norway* 9 G14
Sarracín, *Spain* 36 C7
Sarralbe, *France* 19 D14
Sarre = Saar →, *Europe* 17 E6
Sarre, *Italy* 40 C4
Sarre-Union, *France* 19 D14
Sarrebourg, *France* 19 D14
Sarreguemines, *France* 19 C14
Sarria, *Spain* 36 C3
Sarrión, *Spain* 38 E4
Sarro, *Mali* 82 C3
Sarstedt, *Germany* 24 C5
Sartène, *France* 21 G12
Sarthe □, *France* 18 D7
Sarthe →, *France* 18 E6
Sartilly, *France* 18 D5
Saruhanlı, *Turkey* 47 C9
Săruleşti, *Romania* 29 F11
Saruna →, *Pakistan* 68 F2
Sárvár, *Hungary* 28 C1
Sarvar, *India* 68 F6
Sarvestān, *Iran* 71 D7
Särvfjället, *Sweden* 10 B7
Sárviz →, *Hungary* 28 D3
Sary-Tash, *Kyrgyzstan* 52 F8
Sarych, Mys, *Ukraine* 33 K7
Saryshagan, *Kazakhstan* 52 E8
Sarzana, *Italy* 40 D6
Sarzeau, *France* 18 E4
Sasan Gir, *India* 68 J4
Sasaram, *India* 69 G11
Sasebo, *Japan* 55 H4
Saser, *India* 69 B7
Saskatchewan □, *Canada* 103 C7
Saskatchewan →, *Canada* 103 C8
Saskatoon, *Canada* 103 C7
Saskylakh, *Russia* 53 B12
Saslaya △, *Nic.* 120 D2
Sasolburg, *S. Africa* 89 D4
Sasovo, *Russia* 34 C5
Sassandra, *Ivory C.* 82 E3
Sassandra →, *Ivory C.* 82 E3
Sássari, *Italy* 42 B1
Sassnitz, *Germany* 24 A9
Sasso Marconi, *Italy* 41 D8
Sassocorvaro, *Italy* 41 E9
Sassoferrato, *Italy* 41 E9
Sasstown, *Liberia* 82 E3
Sassuolo, *Italy* 40 D7
Sástago, *Spain* 38 D4
Sasyk, Ozero, *Ukraine* 29 E14
Sata-Misaki, *Japan* 55 J5
Satadougou, *Mali* 82 C2
Satakunda = Satakunta, *Finland* 9 F20
Satakunta, *Finland* 9 F20
Satama-Soukoura, *Ivory C.* 82 D4
Satara, *India* 66 L8
Satara, *S. Africa* 89 C5
Satbarwa, *India* 69 H11
Såtenäs, *Sweden* 11 F6
Säter, *Sweden* 10 D9
Satevó, *Mexico* 118 B3
Satilla →, *U.S.A.* 115 K5
Satmala Hills, *India* 66 J9
Satna, *India* 69 G9
Šator, *Bos.-H.* 41 D13
Sátoraljaújhely, *Hungary* 28 B6
Satpura Ra., *India* 66 J10
Satrup, *Germany* 24 A5
Satsuna-Shotō, *Japan* 55 K5
Sattahip, *Thailand* 64 F3
Satu Mare, *Romania* 28 C7
Satu Mare □, *Romania* 28 C8
Satui, *Indonesia* 62 E5
Satun, *Thailand* 65 J3
Saturnina →, *Brazil* 124 F7
Sauce, *Argentina* 126 C4
Sauceda, *Mexico* 118 B4
Saucillo, *Mexico* 118 B3
Sauda, *Norway* 9 G12
Sauðarkrókur, *Iceland* 8 D4
Saudi Arabia ■, *Asia* 70 B3
Saugeen →, *Canada* 116 B3
Saugerties, *U.S.A.* 117 D11
Saugues, *France* 20 D7
Saugus, *U.S.A.* 111 L8
Saujon, *France* 20 C3
Sauk Centre, *U.S.A.* 112 C7
Sauk Rapids, *U.S.A.* 112 C7
Saulgau, *Germany* 25 G5
Saulieu, *France* 19 E11
Sault, *France* 21 D9
Sault Ste. Marie, *Canada* 104 C3
Sault Ste. Marie, *U.S.A.* 101 D11
Saumlaki, *Indonesia* 63 F8
Saumur, *France* 18 E6
Saunders, C., *N.Z.* 91 L3
Saunders I., *Antarctica* 5 B1
Saunders Point, *Australia* 93 E4
Sauri, *Nigeria* 83 C6
Saurimo, *Angola* 84 F4
Sausalito, *U.S.A.* 110 H4
Sauveterre-de-Béarn, *France* 20 E3
Sauzé-Vaussais, *France* 20 B4
Savá, *Honduras* 120 C2
Sava, *Italy* 43 B10
Sava →, *Serbia & M.* 28 F5
Savage, *U.S.A.* 112 B2
Savage I. = Niue, *Cook Is.* 97 J11
Savage River, *Australia* 95 G4
Savai'i, *Samoa* 91 A12
Savalou, *Benin* 83 D5
Savane, *Mozam.* 87 F4
Savanna, *U.S.A.* 112 D9
Savanna-la-Mar, *Jamaica* 120 a
Savannah, *Ga., U.S.A.* 115 J5
Savannah, *Mo., U.S.A.* 112 F7
Savannah, *Tenn., U.S.A.* 115 H1
Savannah →, *U.S.A.* 115 J5
Savannakhet, *Laos* 64 D5
Savant L., *Canada* 104 B1
Savant Lake, *Canada* 104 B1
Săvârşin, *Romania* 28 D7
Savaştepe, *Turkey* 47 B9
Savé, *Benin* 83 D5
Save →, *France* 20 E5
Save →, *Mozam.* 89 C5
Sāveh, *Iran* 71 C6
Savelugu, *Ghana* 83 D4
Savenay, *France* 18 E5
Săveni, *Romania* 29 C11
Saverdun, *France* 20 E5
Saverne, *France* 19 D14
Savigliano, *Italy* 40 D4
Savigny-sur-Braye, *France* 18 E7
Sávio →, *Italy* 41 D9
Šavnik, *Serbia & M.* 44 D3
Savo, *Finland* 8 E22
Savoie □, *France* 21 C10
Savolax = Savo, *Finland* 8 E22
Savona, *Italy* 40 D5
Savona, *U.S.A.* 116 D7
Savonlinna, *Finland* 32 B5
Savoy = Savoie □, *France* 21 C10
Şavşat, *Turkey* 73 B10
Sävsjö, *Sweden* 11 G8
Savur, *Turkey* 70 B4
Sawahlunto, *Indonesia* 62 E2
Sawai, *Indonesia* 63 E7
Sawai Madhopur, *India* 68 G7
Sawang Daen Din, *Thailand* 64 D4
Sawankhalok, *Thailand* 64 D2
Sawara, *Japan* 55 G10
Sawatch Range, *U.S.A.* 109 G10
Sawel Mt., *U.K.* 12 B4
Sawi, *Thailand* 65 G2
Sawla, *Ghana* 82 D4
Sawmills, *Zimbabwe* 87 F2
Sawtooth ⌂, *U.S.A.* 108 D6
Sawtooth Range, *U.S.A.* 108 E6
Sawu, *Indonesia* 63 F6
Sawu Sea, *Indonesia* 63 F6
Saxby →, *Australia* 94 B3
Saxmundham, *U.K.* 15 E9
Saxony = Sachsen □, *Germany* 24 E9
Saxony, Lower = Niedersachsen □, *Germany* 24 C4
Saxton, *U.S.A.* 116 F6
Say, *Mali* 82 C4
Say, *Niger* 83 C5
Saya, *Nigeria* 83 D5
Sayabec, *Canada* 105 C6
Sayaboury, *Laos* 64 C3
Sayán, *Peru* 124 F3
Sayan, Vostochnyy, *Russia* 53 D10
Sayan, Zapadnyy, *Russia* 53 D10
Saydā, *Lebanon* 74 B4
Sayhandulaan = Oldziyt, *Mongolia* 56 B5
Sayhūt, *Yemen* 75 D5
Saykhin, *Kazakhstan* 35 F8
Saylac = Zeila, *Somali Rep.* 75 E3
Saynshand, *Mongolia* 60 B6
Sayre, *Okla., U.S.A.* 113 H5
Sayre, *Pa., U.S.A.* 117 E8
Sayreville, *U.S.A.* 117 F10
Sayula, *Mexico* 118 D4
Sayward, *Canada* 102 C3
Sazanit, *Albania* 44 F3
Sázava →, *Czech Rep.* 26 B7
Sazin, *Pakistan* 69 B5
Sazlika →, *Bulgaria* 45 E9
Scaër, *France* 18 D3
Scafell Pike, *U.K.* 14 C4
Scalea, *Italy* 43 C8
Scalloway, *U.K.* 13 A7
Scalpay, *U.K.* 13 D3
Scandia, *Canada* 102 C6
Scandiano, *Italy* 40 D7
Scandicci, *Italy* 41 E8
Scandinavia, *Europe* 8 E16
Scansano, *Italy* 41 F8
Scapa Flow, *U.K.* 13 C5
Scappoose, *U.S.A.* 110 E4
Scarámia, Capo, *Italy* 43 F7
Scarba, *U.K.* 13 E3
Scarborough, *Trin. & Tob.* 121 D7
Scarborough, *U.K.* 14 C7
Scariff I., *Ireland* 12 E1
Scarp, *U.K.* 13 C1
Scarpe-Escaut ⌂, *France* 19 B10
Scebeli, Wabi →, *Somali Rep.* 75 G3
Šćedro, *Croatia* 41 E13
Schaal See, *Germany* 24 B6
Schaalsee ⌂, *Germany* 24 B6
Schaffhausen, *Switz.* 25 H4
Schagen, *Neths.* 17 B4
Schaghticoke, *U.S.A.* 117 D11
Schärding, *Austria* 26 C6
Scharhörn, *Germany* 24 B4
Scheessel, *Germany* 24 B5
Schefferville, *Canada* 105 B6
Scheibbs, *Austria* 26 C8
Schelde →, *Belgium* 17 C4
Schell Creek Ra., *U.S.A.* 108 G6
Schellsburg, *U.S.A.* 116 F6
Schenectady, *U.S.A.* 117 D11
Schenevus, *U.S.A.* 117 D10
Scherfede, *Germany* 24 D5
Schesslitz, *Germany* 25 F7
Schiedam, *Neths.* 17 C4
Schiermonnikoog, *Neths.* 17 A6
Schiltigheim, *France* 19 D14
Schio, *Italy* 41 C8
Schiphol, Amsterdam ✕ (AMS), *Neths.* 17 B4
Schladming, *Austria* 26 D6
Schlanders = Silandro, *Italy* 40 B7
Schlei →, *Germany* 24 A5
Schleiden, *Germany* 24 E2
Schleiz, *Germany* 24 E7
Schleswig, *Germany* 24 A5
Schleswig-Holstein □, *Germany* 24 A5
Schlüchtern, *Germany* 25 E5
Schmalkalden, *Germany* 24 E6
Schmölln, *Germany* 24 E8
Schneeberg, *Austria* 26 D8
Schneeberg, *Germany* 24 E8
Schneverdingen, *Germany* 24 B5
Schœlcher, *Martinique* 120 c
Schoharie, *U.S.A.* 117 D10
Schoharie Cr. →, *U.S.A.* 117 D10
Scholls, *U.S.A.* 110 E4
Schönberg, *Mecklenburg-Vorpommern, Germany* 24 B6
Schönberg, *Schleswig-Holstein, Germany* 24 A6
Schönbuch ⌂, *Germany* 25 G5
Schönebeck, *Germany* 24 C7
Schongau, *Germany* 25 H6
Schöningen, *Germany* 24 C6
Schopfheim, *Germany* 25 H3
Schorndorf, *Germany* 25 G5
Schortens, *Germany* 24 B3
Schouten I., *Australia* 95 G4
Schouten Is. = Supiori, *Indonesia* 63 E9
Schouwen, *Neths.* 17 C3
Schramberg, *Germany* 25 G4
Schrankogel, *Austria* 26 D4
Schreiber, *Canada* 104 C2
Schrems, *Austria* 26 C8
Schrobenhausen, *Germany* 25 G7
Schroffenstein, *Namibia* 88 D2
Schroon Lake, *U.S.A.* 117 C11
Schruns, *Austria* 26 D2
Schuler, *Canada* 103 C6
Schumacher, *Canada* 104 C3
Schurz, *U.S.A.* 108 G4
Schuyler, *U.S.A.* 112 E6
Schuylerville, *U.S.A.* 117 C11
Schuylkill →, *U.S.A.* 117 G9
Schuylkill Haven, *U.S.A.* 117 F8
Schwabach, *Germany* 25 F7
Schwaben □, *Germany* 25 G6
Schwäbisch-Fränkischer Wald ⌂, *Germany* 25 G5
Schwäbisch Gmünd, *Germany* 25 G5
Schwäbisch Hall, *Germany* 25 F5
Schwäbische Alb, *Germany* 25 G5
Schwabmünchen, *Germany* 25 G6
Schwalmstadt, *Germany* 24 E5
Schwandorf, *Germany* 25 F8
Schwaner, Pegunungan, *Indonesia* 62 E4
Schwanewede, *Germany* 24 B4
Schwarmstedt, *Germany* 24 C5
Schwarze Elster →, *Germany* 24 D8
Schwarzenberg, *Germany* 24 E8
Schwarzrand, *Namibia* 88 D2
Schwarzwald, *Germany* 25 G4
Schwaz, *Austria* 26 D4
Schwechat, *Austria* 27 C9
Schwechat, Wien ✕ (VIA), *Austria* 27 C9
Schwedt, *Germany* 24 B10
Schweinfurt, *Germany* 25 E6
Schweizer-Reneke, *S. Africa* 88 D4
Schwenningen = Villingen-Schwenningen, *Germany* 25 G4
Schwerin, *Germany* 24 B7
Schweriner See, *Germany* 24 B7
Schwetzingen, *Germany* 25 F4
Schwyz, *Switz.* 25 H4
Schwyz □, *Switz.* 25 H4
Sciacca, *Italy* 42 E6
Scicli, *Italy* 43 F7
Sciliar ⌂, *Italy* 41 B8
Scilla, *Italy* 43 D8
Scilly, Isles of, *U.K.* 15 H1
Ścinawa, *Poland* 31 G3
Scione, *Greece* 44 G7
Scioto →, *U.S.A.* 114 F4
Scituate, *U.S.A.* 117 D14
Scobey, *U.S.A.* 112 A2
Scone, *Australia* 95 E5
Scone, *U.K.* 13 E5
Scordia, *Italy* 43 E7
Scoresbysund = Ittoqqortoormiit, *Greenland* 4 B6
Scorniceşti, *Romania* 29 F9
Scotia, *Calif., U.S.A.* 108 F1
Scotia, *N.Y., U.S.A.* 117 D11
Scotia Sea, *Antarctica* 5 B18
Scotland, *Canada* 116 C4
Scotland □, *U.K.* 13 E5
Scott, *Antarctica* 5 D11
Scott, C., *Australia* 92 B4
Scott City, *U.S.A.* 112 F4
Scott Glacier, *Antarctica* 5 C8
Scott I., *Antarctica* 5 C11
Scott Is., *Canada* 102 C3
Scott L., *Canada* 103 B7
Scott Reef, *Australia* 92 B3
Scottburgh, *S. Africa* 89 E5
Scottdale, *U.S.A.* 116 F5
Scottish Borders □, *U.K.* 13 F6
Scottsbluff, *U.S.A.* 112 E3
Scottsboro, *U.S.A.* 115 H3
Scottsburg, *U.S.A.* 114 F3
Scottsdale, *Australia* 95 G4
Scottsdale, *U.S.A.* 109 K7
Scottsville, *Ky., U.S.A.* 115 G2
Scottsville, *N.Y., U.S.A.* 116 C7
Scottville, *U.S.A.* 114 D2
Scranton, *U.S.A.* 117 E9
Scugog, L., *Canada* 116 B6
Sculeni, *Moldova* 29 C12
Scunthorpe, *U.K.* 14 D7
Scuol Schuls, *Switz.* 25 J6
Scutari = Shkodër, *Albania* 44 D3
Scutari = Üsküdar, *Turkey* 45 F13
Seabrook, L., *Australia* 93 F2
Seaford, *U.K.* 15 G8
Seaford, *U.S.A.* 114 F8
Seaforth, *Australia* 94 J6
Seaforth, *Canada* 116 C3
Seaforth, L., *U.K.* 13 D2
Seagraves, *U.S.A.* 113 J3
Seaham, *U.K.* 14 C6
Seal →, *Canada* 103 B10
Seal L., *Canada* 105 B7
Sealy, *U.S.A.* 113 L6
Searchlight, *U.S.A.* 111 K12
Searcy, *U.S.A.* 113 H9
Searles L., *U.S.A.* 111 K9
Seascale, *U.K.* 14 C4
Seaside, *Calif., U.S.A.* 110 J5
Seaside, *Oreg., U.S.A.* 110 E3
Seaspray, *Australia* 95 F4
Seattle, *U.S.A.* 110 C4
Seattle-Tacoma International ✕ (SEA), *U.S.A.* 110 C4
Seaview Ra., *Australia* 94 B4
Sebago L., *U.S.A.* 117 C14
Sebago Lake, *U.S.A.* 117 C14
Sebastián Vizcaíno, B., *Mexico* 118 B2
Sebastopol = Sevastopol, *Ukraine* 33 K7
Sebastopol, *U.S.A.* 110 G4
Sebba, *Burkina Faso* 83 C5
Sebderat, *Eritrea* 81 D4
Sébékoro, *Mali* 82 C3
Seben, *Turkey* 72 B4
Sebeş, *Romania* 29 E8
Sebeşului, Munţii, *Romania* 29 E8
Sebewaing, *U.S.A.* 114 D4
Sebezh, *Russia* 32 D5
Sebha = Sabhah, *Libya* 79 C8
Sébi, *Mali* 82 B4
Şebinkarahisar, *Turkey* 73 B8
Sebiş, *Romania* 28 D7
Sebnitz, *Germany* 24 E10
Sebring, *Fla., U.S.A.* 115 M5
Sebring, *Ohio, U.S.A.* 116 F3
Sebringville, *Canada* 116 C3
Sebta = Ceuta, *N. Afr.* 78 A4
Sebuku, *Indonesia* 62 E5
Sebuku, Teluk, *Malaysia* 62 D5
Sečanj, *Serbia & M.* 28 E5
Secchia →, *Italy* 40 C8
Sechelt, *Canada* 102 D4
Sechura, Desierto de, *Peru* 124 E2
Seclin, *France* 19 B10
Secondigny, *France* 18 F6
Sečovce, *Slovak Rep.* 27 C14
Secretary I., *N.Z.* 91 L1
Secunderabad, *India* 66 L11
Security-Widefield, *U.S.A.* 112 F2
Sedalia, *U.S.A.* 112 F8
Sedan, *France* 19 C11
Sedan, *U.S.A.* 113 G6
Sedano, *Spain* 36 C7
Sedbergh, *U.K.* 14 C5
Seddon, *N.Z.* 91 J5
Seddonville, *N.Z.* 91 J4
Sedé Boqér, *Israel* 74 E3
Sedeh, *Fārs, Iran* 71 D7
Sedeh, *Khorāsān, Iran* 71 C8
Séderon, *France* 21 D9
Sederot, *Israel* 74 D3
Sédhiou, *Senegal* 82 C1
Sedico, *Italy* 41 B9
Sedlčany, *Czech Rep.* 26 B7
Sedley, *Canada* 103 C8
Sedona, *U.S.A.* 109 J8
Sedova, Pik, *Russia* 52 B6
Sedro Woolley, *U.S.A.* 110 B4
Šeduva, *Lithuania* 30 C10
Sędziszów, *Poland* 31 H7
Sędziszów Małapolski, *Poland* 31 H8
Seebad Ahlbeck, *Germany* 24 B10
Seefeld in Tirol, *Austria* 26 D4
Seehausen, *Germany* 24 C7
Seeheim, *Namibia* 88 D2
Seeheim-Jugenheim, *Germany* 25 F4
Seeis, *Namibia* 88 C2
Seekoei →, *S. Africa* 88 E4
Seeley's Bay, *Canada* 117 B8
Seelow, *Germany* 24 C10
Sées, *France* 18 D7
Seesen, *Germany* 24 D6
Seevetal, *Germany* 24 B6
Seewinkel = Neusiedler See-Seewinkel △, *Austria* 27 D9
Sefadu, *S. Leone* 82 D2
Seferihisar, *Turkey* 47 C8
Séfeto, *Mali* 82 C3
Sefwi Bekwai, *Ghana* 82 D4
Segamat, *Malaysia* 65 L4
Şegarcea, *Romania* 29 F8
Ségbana, *Benin* 83 C5
Segbwema, *S. Leone* 82 D2
Seget, *Indonesia* 63 E8
Segonzac, *France* 20 C3
Segorbe, *Spain* 38 F4
Ségou, *Mali* 82 C3
Segovia = Coco →, *Cent. Amer.* 120 D3
Segovia, *Spain* 36 E6
Segovia □, *Spain* 36 E6
Segré, *France* 18 E6
Segre →, *Spain* 38 D5
Séguéla, *Ivory C.* 82 D3
Séguénéga, *Burkina Faso* 83 C4
Seguin, *U.S.A.* 113 L6
Segundo →, *Argentina* 126 C3
Segura →, *Spain* 39 G4
Segura, Sierra de, *Spain* 39 G2
Seh Konj, Kūh-e, *Iran* 71 D8
Seh Qal'eh, *Iran* 71 C8
Sehitwa, *Botswana* 88 C3
Sehlabathebe △, *Lesotho* 89 D4
Sehore, *India* 68 H7
Sehwan, *Pakistan* 68 F2
Şeica Mare, *Romania* 29 D9
Seil, *U.K.* 13 E3
Seiland, *Norway* 8 A20
Seilhac, *France* 20 C5
Seiling, *U.S.A.* 113 G5
Seille →, *Moselle, France* 19 C13
Seille →, *Saône-et-Loire, France* 19 F11
Sein, Î. de, *France* 18 D2
Seinäjoki, *Finland* 9 E20
Seine →, *France* 18 C7
Seine, B. de la, *France* 18 C6
Seine-et-Marne □, *France* 19 D10
Seine-Maritime □, *France* 18 C7
Seine-St-Denis □, *France* 19 D9
Seini, *Romania* 29 C8
Seirijai, *Lithuania* 30 D10
Seistan = Sīstān, *Asia* 71 D9
Seistan, Daryācheh-ye = Sīstān, Daryācheh-ye, *Iran* 71 D9
Sejerø, *Denmark* 11 J5
Sejerø Bugt, *Denmark* 11 J5
Sejny, *Poland* 30 D10
Seka, *Ethiopia* 81 F4
Sekayu, *Indonesia* 62 E2
Seke, *Tanzania* 86 C3
Sekenke, *Tanzania* 86 C3
Seki, *Turkey* 47 E11
Sekondi-Takoradi, *Ghana* 82 E4
Sekota, *Ethiopia* 81 E4
Seksna, *Russia* 32 C10
Sekudai, *Malaysia* 65 d
Sekuma, *Botswana* 88 C3
Selah, *U.S.A.* 108 C3
Selama, *Malaysia* 65 K3
Selárgius, *Italy* 42 C2
Selaru, *Indonesia* 63 F8
Selatan, Selat, *Malaysia* 65 c
Selb, *Germany* 25 E8
Selby, *U.K.* 14 D6
Selby, *U.S.A.* 112 C4
Selca, *Croatia* 41 E13
Selçuk, *Turkey* 47 D9
Selden, *U.S.A.* 112 F4
Sele →, *Italy* 43 B7
Selebi-Pikwe, *Botswana* 89 C4
Selemdzha →, *Russia* 53 D13
Selendi, *Manisa, Turkey* 47 C10
Selendi, *Manisa, Turkey* 47 C9
Selenga = Selenge Mörön →, *Asia* 60 A5
Selenge Mörön →, *Asia* 60 A5
Selenicë, *Albania* 44 F3
Selenter See, *Germany* 24 A6
Sélestat, *France* 19 D14
Seletan, Tanjung, *Indonesia* 62 E4
Selevac, *Serbia & M.* 44 B4
Sélibabi, *Mauritania* 82 B2
Seliger, Ozero, *Russia* 32 D7
Seligman, *U.S.A.* 109 J7
Şelim, *Turkey* 73 B10
Selîma, El Wâhât el, *Sudan* 80 C2
Selimiye, *Turkey* 47 D9
Selinda Spillway →, *Botswana* 88 B3
Selinoús, *Greece* 46 D3
Selinsgrove, *U.S.A.* 116 F8
Selizharovo, *Russia* 32 D7
Selkirk, *Canada* 103 C9
Selkirk, *U.K.* 13 F6
Selkirk I. = Horse I., *Canada* 103 C9
Selkirk Mts., *Canada* 100 C8
Sellafield, *U.K.* 14 C4
Sellama, *Sudan* 81 E2
Selliá, *Greece* 49 D6
Sellières, *France* 19 F12
Sells, *U.S.A.* 109 L8
Sellye, *Hungary* 28 E2
Selma, *Ala., U.S.A.* 115 J2
Selma, *Calif., U.S.A.* 110 J7
Selma, *N.C., U.S.A.* 115 H6
Selmer, *U.S.A.* 115 H1
Selongey, *France* 19 E12
Selous ⌂, *Tanzania* 87 D4
Selowandoma Falls, *Zimbabwe* 87 G3
Selpele, *Indonesia* 63 E8
Selsey Bill, *U.K.* 15 G7
Seltso, *Russia* 32 F8
Seltz, *France* 19 D15
Selu, *Indonesia* 63 F8
Sélune →, *France* 18 D5
Selva = La Selva del Camp, *Spain* 38 D6
Selva, *Argentina* 126 B3
Selva Lancandona = Montes Azules ⌂, *Mexico* 119 D6
Selvas, *Brazil* 124 E5
Selwyn L., *Canada* 103 B8
Selwyn Mts., *Canada* 100 B6
Selwyn Ra., *Australia* 94 C3
Selyatyn, *Ukraine* 29 C10
Seman →, *Albania* 44 F3
Semarang, *Indonesia* 63 G14
Sembabule, *Uganda* 86 C3
Sembawang, *Singapore* 65 d
Sembung, *Indonesia* 63 J18
Şemdinli, *Turkey* 73 D11
Sémé, *Senegal* 82 B2
Semeih, *Sudan* 81 E3
Semenanjung Blambangan, *Indonesia* 63 K17
Semenov, *Russia* 34 B7
Semenovka, *Chernihiv, Ukraine* 33 F7
Semenovka, *Kremenchuk, Ukraine* 33 H7
Semeru, *Indonesia* 63 H15
Semey, *Kazakhstan* 52 D9
Semikarakorskiy, *Russia* 35 G5
Semiluki, *Russia* 33 G10
Seminoe Reservoir, *U.S.A.* 108 F10

Seminole, *Okla., U.S.A.* 113 H6
Seminole, *Tex., U.S.A.* 113 J3
Seminole Draw →, *U.S.A.* 113 J3
Semipalatinsk = Semey, *Kazakhstan* 52 D9
Semirara Is., *Phil.* 61 F4
Semitau, *Indonesia* 62 D4
Semiyarka, *Kazakhstan* 52 D8
Semiyarskoye = Semiyarka, *Kazakhstan* 52 D8
Semmering P., *Austria* 26 D8
Semnān, *Iran* 71 C7
Semnān □, *Iran* 71 C7
Semporna, *Malaysia* 63 D5
Semuda, *Indonesia* 62 E4
Semur-en-Auxois, *France* 19 E11
Sen →, *Cambodia* 62 B3
Senā, *Iran* 71 D6
Sena, *Mozam.* 87 F4
Sena Madureira, *Brazil* 124 E5
Senador Pompeu, *Brazil* 125 E11
Senaki, *Georgia* 35 J6
Senang, Pulau, *Singapore* 65 d
Senanga, *Zambia* 85 H4
Senatobia, *U.S.A.* 113 H10
Sencelles, *Spain* 48 B9
Sendafa, *Ethiopia* 81 F4
Sendai, *Kagoshima, Japan* 55 J5
Sendai, *Miyagi, Japan* 54 E10
Sendai-Wan, *Japan* 54 E10
Senden, *Bayern, Germany* 25 G6
Senden, *Nordrhein-Westfalen, Germany* 24 D3
Sendhwa, *India* 68 J6
Sene →, *Ghana* 83 D4
Senec, *Slovak Rep.* 27 C10
Seneca, *U.S.A.* 115 H4
Seneca Falls, *U.S.A.* 117 D8
Seneca L., *U.S.A.* 116 D8
Senecaville L., *U.S.A.* 116 G3
Senegal ■, *W. Afr.* 82 C2
Sénégal →, *W. Afr.* 82 B1
Senegambia, *Africa* 76 E2
Senekal, *S. Africa* 89 D4
Senftenberg, *Germany* 24 D10
Senga Hill, *Zambia* 87 D3
Senge Khambab = Indus →, *Pakistan* 68 G2
Sengiley, *Russia* 34 D9
Sengua →, *Zimbabwe* 87 F2
Senhor-do-Bonfim, *Brazil* 125 F10
Senica, *Slovak Rep.* 27 C10
Senigállia, *Italy* 41 E10
Senio →, *Italy* 41 D9
Senirkent, *Turkey* 47 C12
Senise, *Italy* 43 B9
Senj, *Croatia* 41 D11
Senja, *Norway* 8 B17
Senkaku-Shotō, *Japan* 55 L1
Senkuang, *Indonesia* 65 d
Senlis, *France* 19 C9
Senmonorom, *Cambodia* 64 F6
Sennâr, *Sudan* 81 E3
Sennar □, *Sudan* 81 E3
Senneterre, *Canada* 104 C4
Senno, *Belarus* 32 E5
Sénnori, *Italy* 42 B1
Seno, *Laos* 64 D5
Senonches, *France* 18 D8
Senorbì, *Italy* 42 C2
Senožeče, *Slovenia* 41 C11
Sens, *France* 19 D10
Senta, *Serbia & M.* 28 E5
Sentani, *Indonesia* 63 E10
Sentery = Lubao, *Dem. Rep. of the Congo* 86 D2
Sentinel, *U.S.A.* 109 K7
Šentjur, *Slovenia* 41 B12
Sentosa, *Singapore* 65 d
Senya Beraku, *Ghana* 83 D4
Seo de Urgel = La Seu d'Urgell, *Spain* 38 C6
Seohara, *India* 69 E8
Seonath →, *India* 69 J10
Seondha, *India* 69 F8
Seoni, *India* 69 H8
Seoni Malwa, *India* 68 H8
Seoul = Sŏul, *S. Korea* 57 F14
Sepīdān, *Iran* 71 D7
Sepo-ri, *N. Korea* 57 E14
Sępólno Krajeńskie, *Poland* 30 E4
Sepone, *Laos* 64 D6
Sępopol, *Poland* 30 D8
Sept-Îles, *Canada* 105 B6
Septemvri, *Bulgaria* 45 D8
Sepúlveda, *Spain* 36 D7
Sequeros, *Spain* 36 E4
Sequim, *U.S.A.* 110 B3
Sequoia △, *U.S.A.* 110 J8
Serafimovich, *Russia* 34 F6
Seraing, *Belgium* 17 D5
Serakhis →, *Cyprus* 49 D11
Seram, *Indonesia* 63 E7
Seram Sea, *Indonesia* 63 E7
Seranantsara, *Madag.* 89 B8
Serang, *Indonesia* 63 G12
Serangoon, *Singapore* 65 d
Serasan, *Indonesia* 62 D3
Seravezza, *Italy* 40 E7
Şerbettar, *Turkey* 45 E10
Serbia □, *Serbia & M.* 44 C5
Serbia & Montenegro ■, *Europe* 44 C4
Şercaia, *Romania* 29 E10
Serdo, *Ethiopia* 81 E5
Serdobsk, *Russia* 34 D7
Sered', *Slovak Rep.* 27 C10
Seredka, *Russia* 32 C5
Serednye, *Ukraine* 29
Şereflikoçhisar, *Turkey* 72 C5
Seregno, *Italy* 40 C6
Seremban, *Malaysia* 65 L3
Serengeti △, *Tanzania* 86 C3
Serengeti Plain, *Tanzania* 86 C4
Serenje, *Zambia* 87 E3
Seret →, *Ukraine* 29 B10
Sereth = Siret →, *Romania* 29 E12
Sergach, *Russia* 34 C7
Sergen, *Turkey* 45 E11
Sergino, *Russia* 52 C7
Sergipe □, *Brazil* 125 F11
Sergiyev Posad, *Russia* 32 D10
Seria, *Brunei* 62 D4
Serian, *Malaysia* 62 D4
Seriate, *Italy* 40 C6
Seribu, Kepulauan, *Indonesia* 62 F3
Sérifontaine, *France* 19 C8
Sérifos, *Greece* 46 D6
Sérignan, *France* 20 E7
Sérigny →, *Canada* 105 A6
Serik, *Turkey* 72 D4
Seringapatam Reef, *Australia* 92 B3
Serinhisar, *Turkey* 47 D11
Seririt, *Indonesia* 63 J17
Sermaize-les-Bains, *France* 19 D11
Sermata, *Indonesia* 63 F7
Sermersuaq, *Greenland* 4 B4
Sérmide, *Italy* 41 D8
Sernovodsk, *Russia* 34 D10
Sernur, *Russia* 34 B9
Serock, *Poland* 31 F8
Serón, *Spain* 39 H2
Serós, *Spain* 38 D5
Serov, *Russia* 52 D7
Serowe, *Botswana* 88 C4
Serpa, *Portugal* 37 H3
Serpeddí, Punta, *Italy* 42 C2
Serpentara, *Italy* 42 C2
Serpentine Lakes, *Australia* 93 E4
Serpent's Mouth = Sierpe, Bocas de la, *Venezuela* 125 L15
Serpis →, *Spain* 39 G4
Serpneve, *Ukraine* 29 D14
Serpukhov, *Russia* 32 E9
Serra da Estrela ⌓, *Portugal* 36 E3
Serra de Outes, *Spain* 36 C2
Serra do Navio, *Brazil* 125 C8
Serra San Bruno, *Italy* 43 D9
Serradilla, *Spain* 36 F4
Sérrai, *Greece* 44 E7
Sérrai □, *Greece* 44 E7
Serramanna, *Italy* 42 C1
Serranía San Luís △, *Paraguay* 126 A4
Serras d'Aire e Candeeiros ⌓, *Portugal* 37 F2
Serravalle Scrívia, *Italy* 40 D5
Serre-Ponçon, L. de, *France* 21 D10
Serres, *France* 21 D9
Serrezuela, *Argentina* 126 C2
Serrinha, *Brazil* 125 F11
Sersale, *Italy* 43 C9
Sertã, *Portugal* 36 F2
Sertanópolis, *Brazil* 127 A5
Sêrtar, *China* 58 A3
Serua, *Indonesia* 63 F8
Serui, *Indonesia* 63 E9
Serule, *Botswana* 88 C4
Sérvia, *Greece* 44 F6
Serzedelo, *Portugal* 36 D2
Ses Salines, *Spain* 48 B10
Sese Is., *Uganda* 86 C3
Sesepe, *Indonesia* 63 E7
Sesfontein, *Namibia* 88 B1
Sesheke, *Zambia* 88 B3
Sésia →, *Italy* 40 C5
Sesimbra, *Portugal* 37 G1
S'Espalmador, *Spain* 48 C7
S'Espardell, *Spain* 48 C7
Sessa Aurunca, *Italy* 42 A6
S'Estanyol, *Spain* 48 B9
Sestao, *Spain* 38 B2
Sesto Calende, *Italy* 40 C5
Sesto San Giovanni, *Italy* 40 C6
Sestri Levante, *Italy* 40 D6
Sestriere, *Italy* 40 D3
Sestroretsk, *Russia* 32 B6
Sestrunj, *Croatia* 41 D11
Sestu, *Italy* 42 C2
Setana, *Japan* 54 C9
Sète, *France* 20 E7
Sete Lagôas, *Brazil* 125 G10
Sétif, *Algeria* 78 A7
Seto, *Japan* 55 G8
Setonaikai, *Japan* 55 G6
Setonaikai △, *Japan* 55 G6
Settat, *Morocco* 78 B4
Séttimo Torinese, *Italy* 40 C4
Setting L., *Canada* 103 C9
Settle, *U.K.* 14 C5
Settlement Pt., *Bahamas* 115 M6
Settlers, *S. Africa* 89 C4
Setúbal, *Portugal* 37 G2
Setúbal □, *Portugal* 37 G2
Setúbal, B. de, *Portugal* 37 G2
Seugne →, *France* 20 C3
Seul, Lac, *Canada* 104 B1
Seurre, *France* 19 F12
Sevan, *Armenia* 35 K7
Sevan, Ozero = Sevana Lich, *Armenia* 35 K7
Sevana Lich, *Armenia* 35 K7
Sevastopol, *Ukraine* 33 K7
Seven Sisters, *Canada* 102 C3
Sever →, *Spain* 37 F3
Sévérac-le-Château, *France* 20 D7
Severn →, *Canada* 104 A2
Severn →, *U.K.* 15 F5
Severn L., *Canada* 104 B1
Severnaya Zemlya, *Russia* 53 B10
Severo-Kurilsk, *Russia* 53 D16
Severo-Yeniseyskiy, *Russia* 53 C10
Severo-Zapadnyy □, *Russia* 52 C4
Severočeský □, *Czech Rep.* 26 A7
Severodonetsk = Syeverodonetsk, *Ukraine* 33 H10
Severodvinsk, *Russia* 52 C4
Severomoravský □, *Czech Rep.* 27 B10
Sevier, *U.S.A.* 109 G7
Sevier →, *U.S.A.* 109 G7
Sevier Desert, *U.S.A.* 108 G7
Sevier L., *U.S.A.* 108 G7
Sevilla, *Spain* 37 H5
Sevilla □, *Spain* 37 H5
Seville = Sevilla, *Spain* 37 H5
Sevlievo, *Bulgaria* 45 C9
Sevnica, *Slovenia* 41 B12
Sèvre-Nantaise →, *France* 18 E5
Sèvre-Niortaise →, *France* 20 B3
Sevsk, *Russia* 33 F8
Sewa →, *S. Leone* 82 D2
Sewani, *India* 68 E6
Seward, *Alaska, U.S.A.* 100 B5
Seward, *Nebr., U.S.A.* 112 E6
Seward, *Pa., U.S.A.* 116 F5
Seward Peninsula, *U.S.A.* 100 B3
Sewell, *Chile* 126 C1
Sewer, *Indonesia* 63 F8
Sewickley, *U.S.A.* 116 F4
Sexsmith, *Canada* 102 B5
Seychelles ■, *Ind. Oc.* 50 K9
Seyðisfjörður, *Iceland* 8 D6
Seydişehir, *Turkey* 72 D4
Seydvān, *Iran* 70 B5
Seyhan →, *Turkey* 70 B2
Seyhan Barajı, *Turkey* 72 D6
Seyitgazi, *Turkey* 47 B12
Seyitömer, *Turkey* 47 B11
Seym →, *Ukraine* 33 G7
Seymen, *Turkey* 45 E11
Seymour, *Australia* 95 F4
Seymour, *S. Africa* 89 E4
Seymour, *Conn., U.S.A.* 117 E11
Seymour, *Ind., U.S.A.* 114 F3
Seymour, *Tex., U.S.A.* 113 J5
Seyne, *France* 21 D10
Seyssel, *France* 21 C9
Sežana, *Slovenia* 41 C10
Sézanne, *France* 19 D10
Sezze, *Italy* 42 A6
Sfântu Gheorghe, *Covasna, Romania* 29 E10
Sfântu Gheorghe, *Tulcea, Romania* 29 F14
Sfântu Gheorghe, Braţul →, *Romania* 29 F14
Sfax, *Tunisia* 79 B8
Sha Xi →, *China* 59 D12
Sha Xian, *China* 59 D11
Shaanxi □, *China* 56 G5
Shaba = Katanga □, *Dem. Rep. of the Congo* 86 D2
Shaba ⌓, *Kenya* 86 B4
Shaballe = Scebeli, Wabi →, *Somali Rep.* 75 G3
Shabla, *Bulgaria* 45 C12
Shabogamo L., *Canada* 105 B6
Shabunda, *Dem. Rep. of the Congo* 86 C2
Shache, *China* 60 C2
Shackleton Ice Shelf, *Antarctica* 5 C8
Shackleton Inlet, *Antarctica* 5 E11
Shādegān, *Iran* 71 D6
Shadi, *China* 59 D10
Shadi, *India* 69 C7
Shadrinsk, *Russia* 52 D7
Shadyside, *U.S.A.* 116 G4
Shaffa, *Nigeria* 83 C7
Shafter, *U.S.A.* 111 K7
Shaftesbury, *U.K.* 15 F5
Shagamu, *Nigeria* 83 D5
Shagram, *Pakistan* 69 A5
Shah Alizai, *Pakistan* 68 E2
Shah Bunder, *Pakistan* 68 G2
Shahabad, *Punjab, India* 68 D7
Shahabad, *Raj., India* 68 G7
Shahabad, *Ut. P., India* 69 F8
Shahadpur, *Pakistan* 68 G3
Shahba, *Syria* 74 C5
Shahdād, *Iran* 71 D8
Shahdād, Namakzār-e, *Iran* 71 D8
Shahdadkot, *Pakistan* 68 F2
Shahdol, *India* 69 H9
Shahe, *China* 56 F8
Shahganj, *India* 69 F10
Shahgarh, *India* 66 F6
Shahjahanpur, *India* 69 F8
Shahpur, *India* 68 H7
Shahpur, *Baluchistan, Pakistan* 68 E3
Shahpur, *Punjab, Pakistan* 68 C5
Shahpur Chakar, *Pakistan* 68 F3
Shahpura, *Mad. P., India* 69 H9
Shahpura, *Raj., India* 68 G6
Shahr-e Bābak, *Iran* 71 D7
Shahr-e Kord, *Iran* 71 C6
Shāhrakht, *Iran* 71 C9
Shahrig, *Pakistan* 68 D2
Shahukou, *China* 56 D7
Shaikhabad, *Afghan.* 68 B3
Shajapur, *India* 68 H7
Shakargarh, *Pakistan* 68 C6
Shakawe, *Botswana* 88 B3
Shaker Heights, *U.S.A.* 116 E3
Shakhty, *Russia* 35 G5
Shakhunya, *Russia* 34 B8
Shaki, *Nigeria* 83 D5
Shākir, *Egypt* 80 B3
Shaksam Valley, *Asia* 69 A7
Shala, L., *Ethiopia* 81 F4
Shali, *Russia* 35 J7
Shallow Lake, *Canada* 116 B3
Shalqar, *Kazakhstan* 52 E6
Shalskiy, *Russia* 32 B8
Shaluli Shan, *China* 58 B2
Shām, *Iran* 71 E8
Shām, Bādiyat ash, *Asia* 70 C3
Shamâl Bahr el Ghazal □, *Sudan* 81 F2
Shamâl Dârfûr □, *Sudan* 81 E2
Shamâl Kordofân □, *Sudan* 81 E3
Shamâl Sînî □, *Egypt* 74 E2
Shamattawa, *Canada* 104 A1
Shamattawa →, *Canada* 104 A2
Shambe, *Sudan* 81 F3
Shambe △, *Sudan* 81 F3
Shambu, *Ethiopia* 81 F4
Shamīl, *Iran* 71 E8
Shamkhor = Şämkir, *Azerbaijan* 35 K8
Shāmkūh, *Iran* 71 C8
Shamli, *India* 68 E7
Shammar, Jabal, *Si. Arabia* 70 E4
Shamo = Gobi, *Asia* 56 C6
Shamo, L., *Ethiopia* 81 F4
Shamokin, *U.S.A.* 117 F8
Shamrock, *U.S.A.* 113 H4
Shamva, *Zimbabwe* 87 F3
Shan □, *Burma* 67 J21
Shan Xian, *China* 56 G9
Shanan →, *Ethiopia* 81 F5
Shanchengzhen, *China* 57 C13
Shāndak, *Iran* 71 D9
Shandon, *U.S.A.* 110 K6
Shandong □, *China* 57 G10
Shandong Bandao, *China* 57 F11
Shang Xian = Shangzhou, *China* 56 H5
Shanga, *Nigeria* 78 F6
Shangalowe, *Dem. Rep. of the Congo* 87 E2
Shangani, *Zimbabwe* 89 B4
Shangani →, *Zimbabwe* 87 F2
Shangbancheng, *China* 57 D10
Shangcheng, *China* 59 B10
Shangchuan Dao, *China* 59 G9
Shangdu, *China* 56 D7
Shanggao, *China* 59 C10
Shanghai, *China* 59 B13
Shanghai Shi □, *China* 59 B13
Shanghang, *China* 59 E11
Shanghe, *China* 57 F9
Shanglin, *China* 58 F7
Shangnan, *China* 56 H6
Shangqiu, *China* 56 G8
Shangrao, *China* 59 C11
Shangshui, *China* 60 C6
Shangsi, *China* 58 F6
Shangyou, *China* 59 E10
Shangyu, *China* 59 B13
Shangzhi, *China* 57 B14
Shangzhou, *China* 56 H5
Shanhetun, *China* 57 B14
Shani, *Nigeria* 83 C7
Shanklin, *U.K.* 15 G6
Shannon, *N.Z.* 91 J5
Shannon △, *Australia* 93 F2
Shannon →, *Ireland* 12 D2
Shannon, Mouth of the, *Ireland* 12 D2
Shannon Airport, *Ireland* 12 D3
Shansi = Shanxi □, *China* 56 F7
Shantar, Ostrov Bolshoy, *Russia* 53 D14
Shantipur, *India* 69 H13
Shantou, *China* 59 F11
Shantung = Shandong □, *China* 57 G10
Shanwei, *China* 59 F10
Shanxi □, *China* 56 F7
Shanyang, *China* 56 H5
Shanyin, *China* 56 E7
Shaodong, *China* 59 D8
Shaoguan, *China* 59 E9
Shaoshan, *China* 59 D9
Shaowu, *China* 59 D11
Shaoxing, *China* 59 C13
Shaoyang, *Hunan, China* 59 D8
Shaoyang, *Hunan, China* 59 D8
Shap, *U.K.* 14 C5
Shapinsay, *U.K.* 13 B6
Shaqq el Gi'eifer →, *Sudan* 81 D2
Shaqra', *Si. Arabia* 70 E5
Shaqrā', *Yemen* 75 E4
Sharafa, *Sudan* 81 E2
Sharafkhāneh, *Iran* 70 B5
Sharashova, *Belarus* 31 F11
Sharbot Lake, *Canada* 117 B8
Sharhorod, *Ukraine* 29 B13
Shari, *Japan* 54 C12
Sharjah = Ash Shāriqah, *U.A.E.* 71 E7
Shark B., *Australia* 93 E1
Shark Bay ⌓, *Australia* 93 F2
Sharm el Sheikh, *Egypt* 80 B3
Sharon, *Mass., U.S.A.* 117 D13
Sharon, *Pa., U.S.A.* 116 E4
Sharon Springs, *Kans., U.S.A.* 112 F4
Sharon Springs, *N.Y., U.S.A.* 117 D10
Sharp Pt., *Australia* 94 A3
Sharpe L., *Canada* 104 B1
Sharpsville, *U.S.A.* 116 E4
Sharq el Istiwa'iya □, *Sudan* 81 G3
Sharya, *Russia* 34 A7
Shasha, *Ethiopia* 81 F4
Shashemene, *Ethiopia* 81 F4
Shashi, *Botswana* 89 C4
Shashi, *China* 59 B9
Shashi →, *Africa* 87 G2
Shasta, Mt., *U.S.A.* 108 F2
Shasta L., *U.S.A.* 108 F2
Shatawi, *Sudan* 81 E3
Shatsk, *Russia* 34 C5
Shatsk, *Ukraine* 31 G10
Shatskyi ⌓, *Ukraine* 31 G10
Shatt al Arab, *Asia* 71 D6
Shatura, *Russia* 32 E10
Shaumyani = Shulaveri, *Georgia* 35 K7
Shaunavon, *Canada* 103 D7
Shaver L., *U.S.A.* 110 H7
Shaw →, *Australia* 92 D2
Shaw I., *Australia* 94 J7
Shawanaga, *Canada* 116 A4
Shawangunk Mts., *U.S.A.* 117 E10
Shawano, *U.S.A.* 114 C1
Shawinigan, *Canada* 104 C5
Shawnee, *U.S.A.* 113 H6
Shay Gap, *Australia* 92 D3
Shayang, *China* 59 B9
Shaybārā, *Si. Arabia* 70 E3
Shayib el Banat, Gebel, *Egypt* 80 B3
Shaykh, J. ash, *Lebanon* 74 B4
Shaykh Miskīn, *Syria* 74 C5
Shaykh Sa'īd, *Iraq* 70 C5
Shchekino, *Russia* 32 E9
Shchigry, *Russia* 33 G9
Shchors, *Ukraine* 33 G6
Shchuchinsk, *Kazakhstan* 52 D8
She Xian, *Anhui, China* 59 C12
She Xian, *Hebei, China* 56 F7
Shebekino, *Russia* 33 G9
Shebele = Scebeli, Wabi →, *Somali Rep.* 75 G3
Sheboygan, *U.S.A.* 114 D2
Shebshi Mts., *Nigeria* 83 D7
Shediac, *Canada* 105 C7
Sheelin, L., *Ireland* 12 C4
Sheep Haven, *Ireland* 12 A4
Sheerness, *U.K.* 15 F8
Sheet Harbour, *Canada* 105 D7
Sheffield, *U.K.* 14 D6
Sheffield, *Ala., U.S.A.* 115 H2
Sheffield, *Mass., U.S.A.* 117 D11
Sheffield, *Pa., U.S.A.* 116 E5
Shehojele, *Ethiopia* 81 E4
Shehong, *China* 58 B5
Sheikh Idris, *Sudan* 81 E3
Sheikhpura, *India* 69 G11
Shek Hasan, *Ethiopia* 81 E4
Shekhupura, *Pakistan* 68 D5
Sheki = Şaki, *Azerbaijan* 35 K8
Shelburne, *N.S., Canada* 105 D6
Shelburne, *Ont., Canada* 116 B4
Shelburne, *U.S.A.* 117 B11
Shelburne B., *Australia* 94 A3
Shelburne Falls, *U.S.A.* 117 D12
Shelby, *Mich., U.S.A.* 114 D2
Shelby, *Miss., U.S.A.* 113 J9
Shelby, *Mont., U.S.A.* 108 B8
Shelby, *N.C., U.S.A.* 115 H5
Shelby, *Ohio, U.S.A.* 116 F2
Shelbyville, *Ill., U.S.A.* 112 F10
Shelbyville, *Ind., U.S.A.* 114 F3
Shelbyville, *Ky., U.S.A.* 114 F3
Shelbyville, *Tenn., U.S.A.* 115 H2
Sheldon, *U.S.A.* 112 D7
Sheldrake, *Canada* 105 B7
Shelengo, Khawr →, *Sudan* 81 E2
Shelikhova, Zaliv, *Russia* 53 D16
Shell Lakes, *Australia* 93 E4
Shellbrook, *Canada* 103 C7
Shellharbour, *Australia* 95 E5
Shelon →, *Russia* 32 C6
Shelter I, *U.S.A.* 117 E12
Shelton, *Conn., U.S.A.* 117 E11
Shelton, *Wash., U.S.A.* 110 C3
Shemakha = Şamaxi, *Azerbaijan* 35 K9
Shëmri, *Albania* 44 D4
Shemsi, *Sudan* 80 D2
Shen Xian, *China* 56 F8
Shenandoah, *Iowa, U.S.A.* 112 E7
Shenandoah, *Pa., U.S.A.* 117 F8
Shenandoah, *Va., U.S.A.* 114 F6
Shenandoah △, *U.S.A.* 114 F6
Shenandoah →, *U.S.A.* 114 F7
Shenchi, *China* 56 E7
Shendam, *Nigeria* 83 D6
Shendī, *Sudan* 81 D3
Shenge, *S. Leone* 82 D2
Shengfang, *China* 56 E9
Shëngjergj, *Albania* 44 E4
Shëngjin, *Albania* 44 E3
Shengzhou, *China* 59 C13
Shenjingzi, *China* 57 B13
Shenmu, *China* 56 E6
Shennongjia, *China* 59 B8
Shenqiu, *China* 56 H8
Shensi = Shaanxi □, *China* 56 G5
Shenyang, *China* 57 D12
Shenzhen, *China* 59 F10
Sheo, *India* 68 F4
Sheopur Kalan, *India* 66 G10
Shepetivka, *Ukraine* 33 G4
Shepetovka = Shepetivka, *Ukraine* 33 G4
Shepparton, *Australia* 95 F4
Sheppey, I. of, *U.K.* 15 F8
Shepton Mallet, *U.K.* 15 F5
Sheqi, *China* 56 H7
Sher Qila, *Pakistan* 69 A6
Sherab, *Sudan* 81 E1
Sherborne, *U.K.* 15 G5
Sherbro →, *S. Leone* 82 D2
Sherbro I., *S. Leone* 82 D2
Sherbrooke, *N.S., Canada* 105 C7
Sherbrooke, *Qué., Canada* 117 A13
Sherburne, *U.S.A.* 117 D9
Shereik, *Sudan* 80 D3
Shergarh, *India* 68 F5
Sherghati, *India* 69 G11
Sheridan, *Ark., U.S.A.* 113 H8
Sheridan, *Wyo., U.S.A.* 108 D10
Sheringham, *U.K.* 14 E9
Sherkin I., *Ireland* 12 E2
Sherkot, *India* 69 E8
Sherman, *U.S.A.* 113 J6
Sherpur, *India* 69 G10
Sherridon, *Canada* 103 B8
Sherwood Forest, *U.K.* 14 D6
Sherwood Park, *Canada* 102 C6
Sheslay →, *Canada* 102 B2
Shethanei L., *Canada* 103 B9
Shetland □, *U.K.* 13 A7
Shetland Is., *U.K.* 13 A7
Shetrunji →, *India* 68 J5

Shevchenkovo, *Ukraine* 29 E14
Shewa, *Ethiopia* 81 F4
Shewa Gimira, *Ethiopia* 81 F4
Sheyenne →, *U.S.A.* 112 B6
Shibām, *Yemen* 75 D4
Shibata, *Japan* 54 F9
Shibecha, *Japan* 54 C12
Shibetsu, *Japan* 54 B11
Shibîn el Kôm, *Egypt* 80 H7
Shibîn el Qanâtir, *Egypt* 80 H7
Shibing, *China* 58 D7
Shibogama L., *Canada* 104 B2
Shibushi, *Japan* 55 J5
Shicheng, *China* 59 D11
Shickshinny, *U.S.A.* 117 E8
Shickshock Mts. = Chic-Chocs, Mts., *Canada* 105 C6
Shidao, *China* 57 F12
Shidian, *China* 58 E2
Shido, *Japan* 55 G7
Shiel, L., *U.K.* 13 E3
Shield, C., *Australia* 94 A2
Shīeli, *Kazakhstan* 52 E7
Shifang, *China* 58 B5
Shiga □, *Japan* 55 G8
Shigu, *China* 58 D2
Shiguaigou, *China* 56 D6
Shihchiachuangi = Shijiazhuang, *China* 56 E8
Shihezi, *China* 60 B3
Shijak, *Albania* 44 E3
Shijiazhuang, *China* 56 E8
Shijiu Hu, *China* 59 B12
Shikarpur, *India* 68 E8
Shikarpur, *Pakistan* 68 F3
Shikohabad, *India* 69 F8
Shikoku □, *Japan* 55 H6
Shikoku-Sanchi, *Japan* 55 H6
Shikotsu-Ko, *Japan* 54 C10
Shikotsu-Tōya △, *Japan* 54 C10
Shiliguri, *India* 67 F16
Shilka, *Russia* 53 D12
Shilka →, *Russia* 53 D13
Shillelagh, *Ireland* 12 D5
Shillington, *U.S.A.* 117 F9
Shillong, *India* 67 G17
Shilo, *West Bank* 74 C4
Shilong, *China* 59 F9
Shilou, *China* 56 F6
Shilovo, *Russia* 34 C5
Shimabara, *Japan* 55 H5
Shimada, *Japan* 55 G9
Shimane □, *Japan* 55 G6
Shimanovsk, *Russia* 53 D13
Shimba Hills ⌓, *Kenya* 86 C4
Shimen, *China* 59 C8
Shimenjie, *China* 59 C11
Shimian, *China* 58 C4
Shimizu, *Japan* 55 G9
Shimodate, *Japan* 55 F9
Shimoga, *India* 66 N9
Shimoni, *Kenya* 86 C4
Shimonoseki, *Japan* 55 H5
Shimpuru Rapids, *Namibia* 88 B2
Shimsk, *Russia* 32 C6
Shin, L., *U.K.* 13 C4
Shinan, *China* 58 F7
Shinano-Gawa →, *Japan* 55 F9
Shinās, *Oman* 71 E8
Shīndand, *Afghan.* 66 C3
Shinglehouse, *U.S.A.* 116 E6
Shingū, *Japan* 55 H7
Shingwidzi, *S. Africa* 89 C5
Shinjō, *Japan* 54 E10
Shinkafe, *Nigeria* 83 C6
Shinshār, *Syria* 74 A5
Shinyanga, *Tanzania* 86 C3
Shinyanga □, *Tanzania* 86 C3
Shio-no-Misaki, *Japan* 55 H7
Shiogama, *Japan* 54 E10
Shiojiri, *Japan* 55 F8
Shipchenski Prokhod, *Bulgaria* 45 D9
Shiping, *China* 58 F4
Shippagan, *Canada* 105 C7
Shippensburg, *U.S.A.* 116 F7
Shippenville, *U.S.A.* 116 E5
Shiprock, *U.S.A.* 109 H9
Shiqian, *China* 58 D7
Shiqma, N. →, *Israel* 74 D3
Shiquan, *China* 56 H5
Shiquan He = Indus →, *Pakistan* 68 G2
Shīr Kūh, *Iran* 71 D7
Shiragami-Misaki, *Japan* 54 D10
Shirakawa, *Fukushima, Japan* 55 F10
Shirakawa, *Gifu, Japan* 55 F8
Shirane-San, *Gumma, Japan* 55 F9
Shirane-San, *Yamanashi, Japan* 55 G9
Shiraoi, *Japan* 54 C10
Shīrāz, *Iran* 71 D7
Shirbīn, *Egypt* 80 H7
Shire →, *Africa* 87 F4
Shiretoko-Misaki, *Japan* 54 B12
Shirinab →, *Pakistan* 68 D2
Shiriya-Zaki, *Japan* 54 D10
Shiroishi, *Japan* 54 F10
Shīrvān, *Iran* 71 B8
Shirwa, L. = Chilwa, L., *Malawi* 87 F4
Shishi, *China* 59 E12
Shishou, *China* 59 C9
Shitai, *China* 59 B11
Shivpuri, *India* 68 G7
Shixian, *China* 57 C15
Shixing, *China* 59 E10
Shiyan, *China* 59 A8
Shiyata, *Egypt* 80 B2
Shizhu, *China* 58 C7
Shizong, *China* 58 E5
Shizuishan, *China* 56 E4
Shizuoka, *Japan* 55 G9
Shizuoka □, *Japan* 55 G9
Shklov = Shklow, *Belarus* 32 E6
Shklow, *Belarus* 32 E6
Shkodër, *Albania* 44 D3
Shkumbini →, *Albania* 44 E3
Shmidta, Ostrov, *Russia* 53 A10
Shō-Gawa →, *Japan* 55 F8
Shoal L., *Canada* 103 D9
Shoal Lake, *Canada* 103 C8
Shōdo-Shima, *Japan* 55 G7
Sholapur = Solapur, *India* 66 L9
Shōmrōn, *West Bank* 74 C4
Shoreham by Sea, *U.K.* 15 G7
Shori →, *Pakistan* 68 E3
Shorkot Road, *Pakistan* 68 D5
Shoshone, *Calif., U.S.A.* 111 K10
Shoshone, *Idaho, U.S.A.* 108 E6
Shoshone L., *U.S.A.* 108 D8
Shoshone Mts., *U.S.A.* 108 G5
Shoshong, *Botswana* 88 C4
Shoshoni, *U.S.A.* 108 E9
Shostka, *Ukraine* 33 G7
Shou Xian, *China* 59 A11
Shouchang, *China* 59 C12
Shouguang, *China* 57 F10
Shouning, *China* 59 D12
Shouyang, *China* 56 F7
Show Low, *U.S.A.* 109 J9
Shpola, *Ukraine* 33 H6
Shpykiv, *Ukraine* 29 B13
Shreveport, *U.S.A.* 113 J8
Shrewsbury, *U.K.* 15 E5
Shri Mohangarh, *India* 68 F4
Shrirampur, *India* 69 H13
Shropshire □, *U.K.* 15 E5
Shū, *Kazakhstan* 52 E8
Shū →, *Kazakhstan* 50 E10
Shuangbai, *China* 58 E3
Shuangcheng, *China* 57 B14
Shuangfeng, *China* 59 D9
Shuanggou, *China* 57 G9
Shuangjiang, *China* 58 F2
Shuangliao, *China* 57 C12
Shuangshanzi, *China* 57 D10
Shuangyang, *China* 57 C13
Shuangyashan, *China* 60 B8
Shubra el Kheima, *Egypt* 80 H7
Shubra Khit, *Egypt* 80 H7
Shucheng, *China* 59 B11
Shugozero, *Russia* 32 C8
Shuguri Falls, *Tanzania* 87 D4
Shuiji, *China* 59 D12
Shuiye, *China* 56 F8
Shujalpur, *India* 68 H7
Shukpa Kunzang, *India* 69 B8
Shulan, *China* 57 B14
Shulaveri, *Georgia* 35 K7
Shule, *China* 60 C2
Shumagin Is., *U.S.A.* 100 C4
Shumen, *Bulgaria* 45 C10
Shumerlya, *Russia* 34 C8
Shumikha, *Russia* 52 D7
Shunchang, *China* 59 D11
Shunde, *China* 59 F9
Shungay, *Kazakhstan* 35 F8
Shuo Xian = Shuozhou, *China* 56 E7
Shuozhou, *China* 56 E7
Shūr →, *Fārs, Iran* 71 D7
Shūr →, *Kermān, Iran* 71 D8
Shūr →, *Yazd, Iran* 71 D7
Shūr Āb, *Iran* 71 C6
Shūr Gaz, *Iran* 71 D8
Shūrāb, *Iran* 71 C8
Shūrjestān, *Iran* 71 D7
Shurugwi, *Zimbabwe* 87 F3
Shūsf, *Iran* 71 D9
Shūsh, *Iran* 73 F13
Shūshtar, *Iran* 71 D6
Shuswap L., *Canada* 102 C5
Shuya, *Russia* 34 B5
Shuyang, *China* 57 G10
Shūzū, *Iran* 71 D7
Shwebo, *Burma* 67 H19
Shwegu, *Burma* 67 G20
Shweli →, *Burma* 67 H20
Shymkent, *Kazakhstan* 52 E7
Shyok, *India* 69 B8
Shyok →, *Pakistan* 69 B6
Shyroke, *Ukraine* 28 B8
Shyroke, *Ukraine* 29 E15
Si Chon, *Thailand* 65 H2
Si Kiang = Xi Jiang →, *China* 59 F9
Si Lanna △, *Thailand* 64 C2
Si-ngan = Xi'an, *China* 56 G5
Si Prachan, *Thailand* 64 E3
Si Racha, *Thailand* 64 F3
Si Xian, *China* 57 H9
Siachen Glacier, *Asia* 69 B7
Siahaf →, *Pakistan* 68 E3
Siahan Range, *Pakistan* 66 F4
Siaksriindrapura, *Indonesia* 62 D2
Sialkot, *Pakistan* 68 C6
Siam = Thailand ■, *Asia* 64 E4
Sian = Xi'an, *China* 56 G5
Sian Ka'an ⌓, *Mexico* 119 D7
Sianów, *Poland* 30 D3
Siantan, *Indonesia* 62 D3
Sīāreh, *Iran* 71 D9
Siargao I., *Phil.* 61 G7
Siari, *Pakistan* 69 B7
Siasi, *Phil.* 63 C6
Siasi I., *Phil.* 61 J4
Siátista, *Greece* 44 F5
Siau, *Indonesia* 63 D7
Šiauliai, *Lithuania* 9 J20
Šiauliai □, *Lithuania* 30 C10
Siazan = Siyäzän, *Azerbaijan* 35 K9
Sibâi, Gebel el, *Egypt* 70 E2
Sibang, *Indonesia* 63 K18
Sibayi, L., *S. Africa* 89 D5
Sibdu, *Sudan* 81 E2
Šibenik, *Croatia* 41 E12
Siberia = Sibirskiy □, *Russia* 53 D10
Siberia, *Russia* 50 C13
Siberut, *Indonesia* 62 E1
Sibi, *Pakistan* 68 E2
Sibil = Oksibil, *Indonesia* 63 E10
Sibiloi △, *Kenya* 86 B4
Sibirskiy □, *Russia* 53 D10
Sibiti, *Congo* 84 E2
Sibiu, *Romania* 29 E9
Sibiu □, *Romania* 29 E9
Sibley, *U.S.A.* 112 D7
Sibolga, *Indonesia* 62 D1
Sibsagar, *India* 67 F19
Sibu, *Malaysia* 62 D4
Sibuco, *Phil.* 61 H5
Sibuguey B., *Phil.* 61 H5
Sibut, *C.A.R.* 84 C3
Sibutu, *Phil.* 63 D5
Sibutu Group, *Phil.* 61 J3
Sibutu Passage, *E. Indies* 63 D5
Sibuyan I., *Phil.* 61 E5
Sibuyan Sea, *Phil.* 61 E5
Sic, *Romania* 29 D8
Sicamous, *Canada* 102 C5
Siccus →, *Australia* 95 E2
Sichuan □, *China* 58 B5
Sichuan Pendi, *China* 58 B5
Sicilia, *Italy* 43 E7
Sicily = Sicilia, *Italy* 43 E7
Sicily, Str. of 42 E4
Sicuani, *Peru* 124 F4
Šid, *Serbia & M.* 28 E4
Sidamo, *Ethiopia* 81 G4
Sidaouet, *Niger* 83 B6
Sidári, *Greece* 49 A3
Siddhapur, *India* 68 H5
Siddipet, *India* 66 K11
Sidensjö, *Sweden* 10 A12
Sidéradougou, *Burkina Faso* 82 C4
Siderno, *Italy* 43 D9
Sidhauli, *India* 69 F9
Sídheros, Ákra, *Greece* 49 D8
Sidhi, *India* 69 G9
Sidhirókastron, *Greece* 44 E7
Sîdi Abd el Rahmân, *Egypt* 80 A2
Sîdi Barrâni, *Egypt* 80 A2
Sidi-bel-Abbès, *Algeria* 78 A5
Sîdi Haneish, *Egypt* 80 A2
Sidi Ifni, *Morocco* 78 C3
Sidi Omar, *Egypt* 80 A1
Sidlaw Hills, *U.K.* 13 E5
Sidley, Mt., *Antarctica* 5 D14
Sidmouth, *U.K.* 15 G4
Sidmouth, C., *Australia* 94 A3
Sidney, *Canada* 102 D4
Sidney, *Mont., U.S.A.* 112 B2
Sidney, *N.Y., U.S.A.* 117 D9
Sidney, *Nebr., U.S.A.* 112 E3
Sidney, *Ohio, U.S.A.* 114 E3
Sidney Lanier, L., *U.S.A.* 115 H4
Sido, *Mali* 82 C3
Sidoarjo, *Indonesia* 63 G15
Sidon = Saydā, *Lebanon* 74 B4
Sidra, G. of = Surt, Khalīj, *Libya* 79 B9
Siedlce, *Poland* 31 F9
Sieg →, *Germany* 24 E3
Siegburg, *Germany* 24 E3
Siegen, *Germany* 24 E4
Siem Pang, *Cambodia* 64 E6
Siem Reap = Siemreab, *Cambodia* 64 F4
Siemiatycze, *Poland* 31 F9
Siemreab, *Cambodia* 64 F4
Siena, *Italy* 41 E8
Sieniawa, *Poland* 31 H9
Sieradz, *Poland* 31 G5
Sieraków, *Poland* 31 F3
Sierck-les-Bains, *France* 19 C13
Sierning, *Austria* 26 C7
Sierpc, *Poland* 31 F6
Sierpe, Bocas de la, *Venezuela* 125 L15
Sierra Blanca, *U.S.A.* 109 L11
Sierra Blanca Peak, *U.S.A.* 109 K11
Sierra City, *U.S.A.* 110 F6
Sierra Colorada, *Argentina* 128 E3
Sierra de Aracena y Picas de Aroche ⌓, *Spain* 37 H4
Sierra de Bahoruco △, *Dom. Rep.* 121 C5
Sierra de Baza ⌓, *Spain* 39 H2
Sierra de Castril ⌓, *Spain* 39 H2
Sierra de España ⌓, *Spain* 39 H3
Sierra de Grazalema ⌓, *Spain* 37 J5
Sierra de Gredos ⌓, *Spain* 36 E5
Sierra de Hornachuelos ⌓, *Spain* 37 H5
Sierra de Huétor ⌓, *Spain* 37 H7
Sierra de La Culata △, *Venezuela* 121 E5
Sierra de Lancandón △, *Guatemala* 120 C1
Sierra de las Nieves ⌓, *Spain* 37 J6
Sierra de las Quijadas △, *Argentina* 126 C2
Sierra de María-Los Vélez ⌓, *Spain* 39 H2
Sierra de San Luis △, *Venezuela* 121 D6
Sierra de Yeguas, *Spain* 37 H6
Sierra del São Mamede ⌓, *Portugal* 37 F3
Sierra Gorda, *Chile* 126 A2
Sierra Leone ■, *W. Afr.* 82 D2
Sierra Madre, *Mexico* 119 D6
Sierra Mágina ⌓, *Spain* 37 H7
Sierra Mojada, *Mexico* 118 B4
Sierra Nevada, *Spain* 37 H7
Sierra Nevada, *U.S.A.* 110 H8
Sierra Nevada ⌓, *Spain* 37 H7
Sierra Nevada △, *Venezuela* 121 E5
Sierra Nevada de Santa Marta △, *Colombia* 121 D5
Sierra Norte de Seville ⌓, *Spain* 37 H5
Sierra Subbéticas ⌓, *Spain* 37 H6
Sierra Vista, *U.S.A.* 109 L8
Sierras de Cardeña y Montoro ⌓, *Spain* 37 G6
Sierras de Cazorla, Segura y las Villas ⌓, *Spain* 39 J2
Sierraville, *U.S.A.* 110 F6
Sierre, *Switz.* 25 J3
Sifani, *Ethiopia* 81 E5
Sifié, *Ivory C.* 82 D3
Sífnos, *Greece* 46 E6
Sifton, *Canada* 103 C8
Sifton Pass, *Canada* 102 B3
Sigean, *France* 20 E6
Sighetu-Marmaţiei, *Romania* 29 C8
Sighişoara, *Romania* 29 D9
Sigli, *Indonesia* 62 C1
Siglufjörður, *Iceland* 8 C4
Sigmaringen, *Germany* 25 G5
Signa, *Italy* 40 E8
Signakhi = Tsnori, *Georgia* 35 K7
Signal, *U.S.A.* 111 L13
Signal de Botrang, *Belgium* 17 D6
Signal Pk., *U.S.A.* 111 M12
Signy I., *Antarctica* 5 C18
Signy-l'Abbaye, *France* 19 C11
Sigsig, *Ecuador* 124 D3
Sigüenza, *Spain* 38 D2
Siguiri, *Guinea* 82 C3
Sigulda, *Latvia* 9 H21
Sihora, *India* 69 H9
Sihui, *China* 59 F9
Siikajoki →, *Finland* 8 D21
Siilinjärvi, *Finland* 8 E22
Siirt, *Turkey* 73 D9
Sijarira Ra. = Chizarira, *Zimbabwe* 87 F2
Sika, *India* 68 H3
Sikani Chief →, *Canada* 102 B4
Sikao, *Thailand* 65 J2
Sikar, *India* 68 F6
Sikasso, *Mali* 82 C3
Sikeston, *U.S.A.* 113 G10
Sikhote Alin, Khrebet, *Russia* 53 E14
Sikhote Alin Ra. = Sikhote Alin, Khrebet, *Russia* 53 E14
Sikiá, *Greece* 44 F7
Síkinos, *Greece* 47 E7
Sikkim □, *India* 67 F16
Siklós, *Hungary* 28 E3
Sil →, *Spain* 36 C3
Silacayoapan, *Mexico* 119 D5
Šilalė, *Lithuania* 30 C9
Silandro, *Italy* 40 B7
Silawad, *India* 68 J6
Silay, *Phil.* 61 F5
Silba, *Croatia* 41 D11
Silchar, *India* 67 G18
Şile, *Turkey* 45 E13
Siler City, *U.S.A.* 115 H6
Silgarhi Doti, *Nepal* 69 E9
Silghat, *India* 67 F18
Sili, *Burkina Faso* 82 C4
Silifke, *Turkey* 70 B2
Siliguri = Shiliguri, *India* 67 F16
Siling Co, *China* 60 C3
Silistea Nouă, *Romania* 29 F10
Silistra, *Bulgaria* 45 B11
Silivri, *Turkey* 45 E12
Siljan, *Sweden* 10 D8
Siljansnäs, *Sweden* 10 D8
Silkeborg, *Denmark* 11 H3
Silkwood, *Australia* 94 B4
Silla, *Spain* 39 F4
Sillajhuay, Cordillera, *Chile* 124 G5
Sillamäe, *Estonia* 9 G22
Sillé-le-Guillaume, *France* 18 D6
Silleda, *Spain* 36 C2
Silloth, *U.K.* 14 C4
Sílo, *Greece* 45 E9
Siloam Springs, *U.S.A.* 113 G7
Silopi, *Turkey* 73 D10
Silsbee, *U.S.A.* 113 K7
Siluko, *Nigeria* 83 D6
Šilutė, *Lithuania* 9 J19
Silvan, *Turkey* 73 C9
Silvani, *India* 69 H8
Silver City, *U.S.A.* 109 K9
Silver Cr. →, *U.S.A.* 108 E4
Silver Creek, *U.S.A.* 116 D5
Silver L., *U.S.A.* 110 G6
Silver Lake, *Calif., U.S.A.* 111 K10
Silver Lake, *Oreg., U.S.A.* 108 E3
Silverdalen, *Sweden* 11 G9
Silverton, *Colo., U.S.A.* 109 H10
Silverton, *Tex., U.S.A.* 113 H4
Silves, *Portugal* 37 H2
Silvi Marina, *Italy* 41 F11
Silvies →, *U.S.A.* 108 E4
Silvrettahorn, *Switz.* 40 B7
Silwa Bahari, *Egypt* 80 C3
Silz, *Austria* 26 D3
Simaltala, *India* 69 G12
Simanggang = Bandar Sri Aman, *Malaysia* 62 D4
Simao, *China* 58 F3
Simard, L., *Canada* 104 C4
Şimareh →, *Iran* 73 F12
Simav, *Turkey* 47 B10
Simav →, *Turkey* 45 F12
Simav Dağları, *Turkey* 47 B10
Simba, *Tanzania* 86 C4
Simbach, *Germany* 25 G9
Simbirsk, *Russia* 34 C9
Simbo, *Tanzania* 86 C2
Simcoe, *Canada* 116 D4
Simcoe, L., *Canada* 116 B5
Simdega, *India* 69 H11
Simeonovgrad, *Bulgaria* 45 D9
Simeria, *Romania* 28 E8
Simeto →, *Italy* 43 E8
Simeulue, *Indonesia* 62 D1
Simferopol, *Ukraine* 33 K8
Sími, *Greece* 47 E9
Simi Valley, *U.S.A.* 111 L8
Simien Mts. △, *Ethiopia* 81 E4
Simikot, *Nepal* 69 E9
Simitli, *Bulgaria* 44 E7
Simla, *India* 68 D7
Simlångsdalen, *Sweden* 11 H7
Şimleu-Silvaniei, *Romania* 28 C7
Simmern, *Germany* 25 F3
Simmie, *Canada* 103 D7
Simmler, *U.S.A.* 111 K7
Simnas, *Lithuania* 30 D10
Simo älv = Simojoki →, *Finland* 8 D21
Simojoki →, *Finland* 8 D21
Simojovel, *Mexico* 119 D6
Simonette →, *Canada* 102 B5
Simonstown, *S. Africa* 88 E2
Simontornya, *Hungary* 28 D3
Simpang Empat, *Malaysia* 65 c
Simplonpass, *Switz.* 25 J4
Simplontunnel, *Switz.* 25 J4
Simpson Desert, *Australia* 94 D2
Simpson Desert △, *Australia* 94 C2
Simpson Pen., *Canada* 101 B11
Simpungdong, *N. Korea* 57 D15
Simrishamn, *Sweden* 11 J8
Simsbury, *U.S.A.* 117 E12
Simushir, Ostrov, *Russia* 53 E16
Sin Cowe I., *S. China Sea* 62 C4
Sinabang, *Indonesia* 62 D1
Sinadogo, *Somali Rep.* 75 F4
Sinai = Es Sînâ', *Egypt* 74 F3
Sinai, Mt. = Mûsa, Gebel, *Egypt* 70 D2
Sinai Peninsula, *Egypt* 50 G7
Sinaia, *Romania* 29 E10
Sinaloa □, *Mexico* 118 C3
Sinaloa de Leyva, *Mexico* 118 B3
Sinalunga, *Italy* 41 E8
Sinan, *China* 58 D7
Sinandrei, *Romania* 28 E6
Sinarádhes, *Greece* 49 A3
Sincan, *Turkey* 72 B5
Sincanlı, *Turkey* 47 C12
Sincelejo, *Colombia* 124 B3
Sinch'ang, *N. Korea* 57 D15
Sinchang-ni, *N. Korea* 57 E14
Sinclair, *U.S.A.* 108 F10
Sinclair Mills, *Canada* 102 C4
Sinclair's B., *U.K.* 13 C5
Sinclairville, *U.S.A.* 116 D5
Sincorá, Serra do, *Brazil* 125 F10
Sind, *Pakistan* 68 G3
Sind □, *Pakistan* 68 G3
Sind →, *Jammu & Kashmir, India* 69 B6
Sind →, *Mad. P., India* 69 F8
Sind Sagar Doab, *Pakistan* 68 D4
Sindal, *Denmark* 11 G4
Sindangan, *Phil.* 61 G5
Sindangbarang, *Indonesia* 63 G12
Sinde, *Zambia* 87 F2
Sindelfingen, *Germany* 25 G4
Sindh = Sind □, *Pakistan* 68 G3
Sındırgı, *Turkey* 47 B10
Sindou, *Burkina Faso* 82 C3
Sindri, *India* 69 H12
Sine →, *Senegal* 82 C1
Sinegorskiy, *Russia* 35 G5
Sinekli, *Turkey* 45 E12
Sinelnikovo = Synelnykove, *Ukraine* 33 H8
Sinendé, *Benin* 83 C5
Sines, *Portugal* 37 H2
Sines, C. de, *Portugal* 37 H2
Sineu, *Spain* 48 B10
Sinfra, *Ivory C.* 82 D3
Sing Buri, *Thailand* 64 E3
Singa, *Sudan* 81 E3
Singapore ■, *Asia* 65 d
Singapore, Straits of, *Asia* 65 d
Singapore Changi ✈ (SIN), *Singapore* 65 M4
Singaraja, *Indonesia* 63 J18
Singen, *Germany* 25 H4
Singida, *Tanzania* 86 C3
Singida □, *Tanzania* 86 D3
Singitikós Kólpos, *Greece* 44 F7
Singkaling Hkamti, *Burma* 67 G19
Singkang, *Indonesia* 63 E6
Singkawang, *Indonesia* 62 D3
Singkep, *Indonesia* 62 E2
Singleton, *Australia* 95 E5
Singleton, Mt., *N. Terr., Australia* 92 D5
Singleton, Mt., *W. Austral., Australia* 93 E2
Singö, *Sweden* 10 D12
Singoli, *India* 68 G6
Singora = Songkhla, *Thailand* 65 J3
Singosan, *N. Korea* 57 E14
Sinhung, *N. Korea* 57 D14
Siniátsikon, Óros, *Greece* 44 F5
Siniscóla, *Italy* 42 B2
Sinj, *Croatia* 41 E13
Sinjai, *Indonesia* 63 F6
Sinjajevina, *Serbia & M.* 44 D3
Sinjār, *Iraq* 70 B4
Sinkat, *Sudan* 80 D4
Sinkiang Uighur = Xinjiang Uygur Zizhiqu □, *China* 60 B3
Sinmak, *N. Korea* 57 E14
Sinnai, *Italy* 42 C2
Sinnamary, *Fr. Guiana* 125 B8
Sinni →, *Italy* 43 B9
Sinnuris, *Egypt* 80 J7
Sinoie, Lacul, *Romania* 29 F13
Sinop, *Turkey* 72 A6
Sinor, *India* 68 J5
Sinp'o, *N. Korea* 57 E15
Sinsheim, *Germany* 25 F4
Sinsk, *Russia* 53 C13
Sintang, *Indonesia* 62 D4
Sinton, *U.S.A.* 113 L6
Sintra, *Portugal* 37 G1
Sintra-Cascais ⌓, *Portugal* 37 G1

Sinŭiju, *N. Korea* 57 D13
Sinyukha →, *Ukraine* 33 H6
Sinzig, *Germany* 24 E3
Sio →, *Hungary* 28 D3
Siocon, *Phil.* 61 H5
Siófok, *Hungary* 28 D3
Sion, *Switz.* 25 J3
Sion Mills, *U.K.* 12 B4
Sioux City, *U.S.A.* 112 D6
Sioux Falls, *U.S.A.* 112 D6
Sioux Lookout, *Canada* 104 B1
Sioux Narrows, *Canada* 103 D10
Sipalay, *Phil.* 61 G5
Šipan, *Croatia* 44 D1
Siparia, *Trin. & Tob.* 125 K15
Sipil Daği △, *Turkey* 47 C9
Siping, *China* 57 C13
Sipiwesk L., *Canada* 103 B9
Siple, *Antarctica* 5 D7
Šipovo, *Bos.-H.* 28 F2
Sipra →, *India* 68 H6
Sipura, *Indonesia* 62 E1
Siquia →, *Nic.* 120 D3
Siquijor, *Phil.* 61 G5
Siquirres, *Costa Rica* 120 D3
Şīr Abu Nu'ayr, *U.A.E.* 71 E7
Şīr Banī Yās, *U.A.E.* 71 E7
Sir Edward Pellew Group, *Australia* 94 B2
Sir Graham Moore Is., *Australia* 92 B4
Sir James MacBrien, Mt., *Canada* 100 B7
Sira →, *Norway* 9 G12
Siracusa, *Italy* 43 E8
Sirajganj, *Bangla.* 69 G13
Sirakoro, *Mali* 82 C3
Şiran, *Turkey* 73 B8
Sirasso, *Ivory C.* 82 D3
Sirathu, *India* 69 G9
Sīrdān, *Iran* 71 B6
Sirdaryo = Syrdarya →, *Kazakhstan* 52 E7
Sire, *Ethiopia* 81 F4
Siren, *U.S.A.* 112 C8
Sirente-Velino ⌓, *Italy* 41 F10
Sirer, *Spain* 48 C7
Siret, *Romania* 29 C11
Siret →, *Romania* 29 E12
Sirghāyā, *Syria* 74 B5
Şiria, *Romania* 28 D6
Sirinath △, *Thailand* 65 a
Sirino, Mte., *Italy* 43 B8
Sīrjān, *Iran* 71 D7
Sirmaur, *India* 69 G9
Sírna, *Greece* 47 E8
Şirnak, *Turkey* 73 D10
Sirohi, *India* 68 G5
Sironj, *India* 68 G7
Síros, *Greece* 46 D6
Sirretta Pk., *U.S.A.* 111 K8
Sīrrī, *Iran* 71 E7
Sirsa, *India* 68 E6
Sirsa →, *India* 69 F8
Siruela, *Spain* 37 G5
Sisak, *Croatia* 41 C13
Sisaket, *Thailand* 64 E5
Sisante, *Spain* 39 F2
Sisargas, Is., *Spain* 36 B2
Sishen, *S. Africa* 88 D3
Sishui, *Henan, China* 56 G7
Sishui, *Shandong, China* 57 G9
Sisipuk L., *Canada* 103 B8
Sisophon, *Cambodia* 64 F4
Sisseton, *U.S.A.* 112 C6
Sissonne, *France* 19 C10
Sīstān, *Asia* 71 D9
Sīstān, Daryācheh-ye, *Iran* 71 D9
Sīstān va Balūchestān □, *Iran* 71 E9
Sisteron, *France* 21 D9
Sisters, *U.S.A.* 108 D3
Siswa Bazar, *India* 69 F10
Sitakili, *Mali* 82 C2
Sitamarhi, *India* 69 F11
Sitampiky, *Madag.* 89 B8
Sitapur, *India* 69 F9
Siteki, *Swaziland* 89 D5
Sitges, *Spain* 38 D6
Sithoniá, *Greece* 44 F7
Sitía, *Greece* 49 D8
Sitka, *U.S.A.* 102 B1
Sitoti, *Botswana* 88 C3
Sitra, *Egypt* 80 B2
Sittang Myit →, *Burma* 67 L20
Sittard, *Neths.* 17 C5
Sittensen, *Germany* 24 B5
Sittingbourne, *U.K.* 15 F8
Sittona, *Eritrea* 81 E4
Sittoung = Sittang Myit →, *Burma* 67 L20
Sittwe, *Burma* 67 J18
Situbondo, *Indonesia* 63 G16
Siuna, *Nic.* 120 D3
Siuri, *India* 69 H12
Siutghiol, Lacul, *Romania* 29 F13
Sīvand, *Iran* 71 D7
Sivas, *Turkey* 70 B3
Sivaslı, *Turkey* 47 C11
Siverek, *Turkey* 70 B3
Sivrihisar, *Turkey* 72 C4
Sīwa, *Egypt* 80 B2
Sīwa, El Wâhât es, *Egypt* 80 B2
Siwa Oasis = Sīwa, El Wâhât es, *Egypt* 80 B2
Siwalik Range, *Nepal* 69 F10
Siwan, *India* 69 F11
Siwana, *India* 68 G5
Six Cross Roads, *Barbados* 121 g
Sixmilebridge, *Ireland* 12 D3
Sixth Cataract, *Sudan* 81 D3
Siyâl, Jazâ'ir, *Egypt* 80 C4
Siyäzän, *Azerbaijan* 35 K9
Siziwang Qi, *China* 56 D6
Sjælland, *Denmark* 11 J5
Sjællands Odde, *Denmark* 11 J5
Sjenica, *Serbia & M.* 44 C3
Sjöbo, *Sweden* 11 J7
Sjötofta, *Sweden* 11 G7
Sjötorp, *Sweden* 11 F8
Sjumen = Shumen, *Bulgaria* 45 C10
Sjuntorp, *Sweden* 11 F6
Skadarsko Jezero, *Serbia & M.* 44 D3
Skadovsk, *Ukraine* 33 J7
Skælskør, *Denmark* 11 J5
Skærbæk, *Denmark* 11 J2
Skaftafell, *Iceland* 8 D5
Skagafjörður, *Iceland* 8 D4
Skagastølstindane, *Norway* 9 F12
Skagaströnd, *Iceland* 8 D3
Skagen, *Denmark* 11 G4
Skagern, *Sweden* 10 E8
Skagerrak, *Denmark* 11 G2
Skagit →, *U.S.A.* 110 B4
Skagway, *U.S.A.* 100 C6
Skala-Podilska, *Ukraine* 29 B11
Skala Podolskaya = Skala-Podilska, *Ukraine* 29 B11
Skalat, *Ukraine* 33 H3
Skalbmierz, *Poland* 31 H7
Skälderviken, *Sweden* 11 H6
Skalica, *Slovak Rep.* 27 C10
Skallingen, *Denmark* 11 J2
Skalni Dol = Kamenyak, *Bulgaria* 45 C10
Skanderborg, *Denmark* 11 H3
Skåne, *Sweden* 11 J7
Skåne län □, *Sweden* 11 H7
Skaneateles, *U.S.A.* 117 D8
Skaneateles L., *U.S.A.* 117 D8
Skänninge, *Sweden* 11 F9
Skanör med Falsterbo, *Sweden* 11 J6
Skantzoúra, *Greece* 46 B6
Skara, *Sweden* 11 F7
Skärblacka, *Sweden* 11 F9
Skardu, *Pakistan* 69 B6
Skåre, *Sweden* 10 E7
Skärhamn, *Sweden* 11 G5
Skarszewy, *Poland* 30 D5
Skaryszew, *Poland* 31 G8
Skarżysko-Kamienna, *Poland* 31 G7
Skattkärr, *Sweden* 10 E7
Skattungbyn, *Sweden* 10 C8
Skawina, *Poland* 31 J6
Skebobruk, *Sweden* 10 E12
Skeena →, *Canada* 102 C2
Skeena Mts., *Canada* 102 B3
Skegness, *U.K.* 14 D8
Skeldon, *Guyana* 124 B7
Skeleton Coast, *Namibia* 85 H2
Skeleton Coast ⌓, *Namibia* 88 C1
Skellefteå, *Sweden* 8 D19
Skellefteälven →, *Sweden* 8 D19
Skelleftehamn, *Sweden* 8 D19
Skender Vakuf, *Bos.-H.* 28 F2
Skerries, The, *U.K.* 14 D3
Skhidnytsya, *Ukraine* 31 J10
Skhíza, *Greece* 46 E3
Skhoinoúsa, *Greece* 47 E7
Ski, *Norway* 9 G14
Skíathos, *Greece* 46 B5
Skibbereen, *Ireland* 12 E2
Skiddaw, *U.K.* 14 C4
Skidegate, *Canada* 102 C2
Skídhra, *Greece* 44 F6
Skien, *Norway* 9 G13
Skierniewice, *Poland* 31 G7
Skikda, *Algeria* 78 A7
Skillingaryd, *Sweden* 11 G8
Skillinge, *Sweden* 11 J8
Skilloura, *Cyprus* 49 D12
Skinári, Ákra, *Greece* 46 D2
Skinnskatteberg, *Sweden* 10 E9
Skipton, *U.K.* 14 D5
Skiring, C., *Senegal* 82 C1
Skirmish Pt., *Australia* 94 A1
Skiropoúla, *Greece* 46 C6
Skíros, *Greece* 46 C6
Skivarp, *Sweden* 11 J7
Skive, *Denmark* 11 H3
Skjálfandafljót →, *Iceland* 8 D5
Skjálfandi, *Iceland* 8 C5
Skjern, *Denmark* 11 J2
Skoczów, *Poland* 31 J5
Škofja Loka, *Slovenia* 41 B11
Skoghall, *Sweden* 10 E7
Skogstorp, *Sweden* 10 E10
Skoki, *Poland* 31 F4
Skole, *Ukraine* 33 H2
Skópelos, *Greece* 46 B5
Skopí, *Greece* 49 D8
Skopin, *Russia* 32 F10
Skopje, *Macedonia* 44 D5
Skopje ✕ (SKP), *Macedonia* 44 E5
Skórcz, *Poland* 30 E5
Skørping, *Denmark* 11 H3
Skövde, *Sweden* 11 F7
Skovorodino, *Russia* 53 D13
Skowhegan, *U.S.A.* 115 C11
Skradin, *Croatia* 41 E12
Skrea, *Sweden* 11 H6
Skrunda, *Latvia* 30 B9
Skrwa →, *Poland* 31 F6
Skuleskogen △, *Sweden* 10 A12
Skull, *Ireland* 12 E2
Skultorp, *Sweden* 11 F7
Skultuna, *Sweden* 10 E10
Skunk →, *U.S.A.* 112 E9
Skuodas, *Lithuania* 9 H19
Skurup, *Sweden* 11 J7
Skutskär, *Sweden* 10 D11
Skvyra, *Ukraine* 33 H5
Skwierzyna, *Poland* 31 F2
Skye, *U.K.* 13 D2
Skykomish, *U.S.A.* 108 C3
Skyros = Skíros, *Greece* 46 C6
Skyttorp, *Sweden* 10 D11
Slade Pt., *Australia* 94 K7
Slættaratindur, *Færoe Is.* 8 E9
Slagelse, *Denmark* 11 J5
Slamet, *Indonesia* 63 G13
Slaney →, *Ireland* 12 D5
Slangberge, *S. Africa* 88 E3
Slănic, *Romania* 29 E10
Slano, *Croatia* 44 D1
Slantsy, *Russia* 32 C5
Slaný, *Czech Rep.* 26 A7
Śląskie □, *Poland* 31 H6
Slätbaken, *Sweden* 11 F10
Slate Is., *Canada* 104 C2
Slatina, *Croatia* 28 E2
Slatina, *Romania* 29 F9
Slatina Timiş, *Romania* 28 E7
Slatington, *U.S.A.* 117 F9
Slaton, *U.S.A.* 113 J4
Slave →, *Canada* 102 A6
Slave Coast, *W. Afr.* 83 D5
Slave Lake, *Canada* 102 B6
Slave Pt., *Canada* 102 A5
Slavgorod, *Russia* 52 D8
Slavinja, *Serbia & M.* 44 C6
Slavkov u Brna, *Czech Rep.* 27 B9
Slavkovský Les ⌓, *Czech Rep.* 26 A5
Slavonija, *Europe* 28 E2
Slavonski Brod, *Croatia* 28 E3
Slavsk, *Russia* 30 C8
Slavska, *Ukraine* 29 B8
Slavskoye, *Russia* 30 D7
Slavuta, *Ukraine* 33 G4
Slavyanka, *Russia* 54 C5
Slavyanovo, *Bulgaria* 45 C8
Slavyansk = Slovyansk, *Ukraine* 33 H9
Slavyansk-na-Kubani, *Russia* 33 K10
Sława, *Poland* 31 G3
Slawharad, *Belarus* 32 F6
Sławno, *Poland* 30 D3
Sławoborze, *Poland* 30 E2
Sleaford, *U.K.* 14 D7
Sleaford B., *Australia* 95 E2
Sleat, Sd. of, *U.K.* 13 D3
Sleeper Is., *Canada* 101 C11
Sleeping Bear Dunes ⌓, *U.S.A.* 114 C2
Sleepy Eye, *U.S.A.* 112 C7
Slemon L., *Canada* 102 A5
Ślesin, *Poland* 31 F5
Slide Mt., *U.S.A.* 117 E10
Slidell, *U.S.A.* 113 K10
Sliema, *Malta* 49 D2
Slieve Aughty, *Ireland* 12 C3
Slieve Bloom, *Ireland* 12 C4
Slieve Donard, *U.K.* 12 B6
Slieve Gamph, *Ireland* 12 B3
Slieve Gullion, *U.K.* 12 B5
Slieve League, *Ireland* 12 B3
Slieve Mish, *Ireland* 12 D2
Slievenamon, *Ireland* 12 D4
Sligeach = Sligo, *Ireland* 12 B3
Sligo, *Ireland* 12 B3
Sligo, *U.S.A.* 116 E5
Sligo □, *Ireland* 12 B3
Sligo B., *Ireland* 12 B3
Slippery Rock, *U.S.A.* 116 E4
Slite, *Sweden* 11 G12
Slīteres ⌓, *Latvia* 30 A9
Sliven, *Bulgaria* 45 D10
Slivnitsa, *Bulgaria* 44 D7
Sljeme, *Croatia* 41 C12
Sloan, *U.S.A.* 111 K11
Sloansville, *U.S.A.* 117 D10
Slobidka, *Ukraine* 29 C14
Slobozia, *Moldova* 29 D14
Slobozia, *Argeş, Romania* 29 F10
Slobozia, *Ialomiţa, Romania* 29 F12
Slocan, *Canada* 102 D5
Słomniki, *Poland* 31 H7
Slonim, *Belarus* 33 F3
Slough, *U.K.* 15 F7
Slough □, *U.K.* 15 F7
Sloughhouse, *U.S.A.* 110 G5
Slovak Rep. ■, *Europe* 27 C13
Slovakia = Slovak Rep. ■, *Europe* 27 C13
Slovakian Ore Mts. = Slovenské Rudohorie, *Slovak Rep.* 27 C12
Slovenia ■, *Europe* 41 C11
Slovenija = Slovenia ■, *Europe* 41 C11
Slovenj Gradec, *Slovenia* 41 B12
Slovenska Bistrica, *Slovenia* 41 B12
Slovenské Konjice, *Slovenia* 41 B12
Slovenské Rudohorie, *Slovak Rep.* 27 C12
Slovenský Raj △, *Slovak Rep.* 27 C13
Slovyansk, *Ukraine* 33 H9
Słowiński △, *Poland* 30 D4
Słubice, *Poland* 31 F1
Sluch →, *Ukraine* 33 G4
Sluis, *Neths.* 17 C3
Slŭnchev Bryag, *Bulgaria* 45 D11
Slunj, *Croatia* 41 C12
Słupca, *Poland* 31 F4
Słupia →, *Poland* 30 D3
Słupsk, *Poland* 30 D4
Slurry, *S. Africa* 88 D4
Slutsk, *Belarus* 33 F4
Slyne Hd., *Ireland* 12 C1
Slyudyanka, *Russia* 53 D11
Småland, *Sweden* 11 G9
Smålandsfarvandet, *Denmark* 11 J5
Smålandsstenar, *Sweden* 11 G7
Smalltree L., *Canada* 103 A8
Smallwood Res., *Canada* 105 B7
Smarhon, *Belarus* 32 E4
Smarje, *Slovenia* 41 B12
Smartt Syndicate Dam, *S. Africa* 88 E3
Smartville, *U.S.A.* 110 F5
Smeaton, *Canada* 103 C8
Smedby, *Sweden* 11 H10
Smederevo, *Serbia & M.* 44 B4
Smederevska Palanka, *Serbia & M.* 44 B4
Smedjebacken, *Sweden* 10 D9
Smela = Smila, *Ukraine* 33 H6
Smerwick Harbour, *Ireland* 12 D1
Smethport, *U.S.A.* 116 E6
Smidovich, *Russia* 53 E14
Śmigiel, *Poland* 31 F3
Smila, *Ukraine* 33 H6
Smilyan, *Bulgaria* 45 E8
Smith, *Canada* 102 B6
Smith Center, *U.S.A.* 112 F5
Smith River ⌓, *U.S.A.* 108 F2
Smith Sd., *N. Amer.* 4 B4
Smithburne →, *Australia* 94 B3
Smithers, *Canada* 102 C3
Smithfield, *S. Africa* 89 E4
Smithfield, *N.C., U.S.A.* 115 H6
Smithfield, *Utah, U.S.A.* 108 F8
Smiths Falls, *Canada* 117 B9
Smithton, *Australia* 95 G4
Smithville, *Canada* 116 C5
Smithville, *U.S.A.* 113 K6
Smoky →, *Canada* 102 B5
Smoky Bay, *Australia* 95 E1
Smoky Hill →, *U.S.A.* 112 F6
Smoky Hills, *U.S.A.* 112 F5
Smoky Lake, *Canada* 102 C6
Smøla, *Norway* 8 E13
Smolensk, *Russia* 32 E7
Smolikas, Óros, *Greece* 44 F4
Smolník, *Slovak Rep.* 27 C13
Smolyan, *Bulgaria* 45 E8
Smooth Rock Falls, *Canada* 104 C3
Smoothstone L., *Canada* 103 C7
Smorgon = Smarhon, *Belarus* 32 E4
Smotrych, *Ukraine* 29 B11
Smotrych → 29 B11
Smulţi, *Romania* 29 E12
Smyadovo, *Bulgaria* 45 C11
Smygehamn, *Sweden* 11 J7
Smyrna = İzmir, *Turkey* 47 C9
Smyrna, *U.S.A.* 114 F8
Snæfell, *Iceland* 8 D6
Snaefell, *I. of Man* 14 C3
Snæfellsjökull, *Iceland* 8 D2
Snake →, *U.S.A.* 108 C4
Snake I., *Australia* 95 F4
Snake Range, *U.S.A.* 108 G6
Snake River Plain, *U.S.A.* 108 E7
Snasahögarna, *Sweden* 10 A6
Snåsavatnet, *Norway* 8 D14
Snedsted, *Denmark* 11 H2
Sneek, *Neths.* 17 A5
Sneeuberge, *S. Africa* 88 E3
Snejbjerg, *Denmark* 11 H2
Snelling, *U.S.A.* 110 H6
Snezhnoye, *Ukraine* 33 J10
Snežnik, *Slovenia* 41 C11
Śniadowo, *Poland* 31 E8
Śniardwy, Jezioro, *Poland* 30 E8
Śnieżka, *Europe* 26 A8
Snigirevka = Snihurivka, *Ukraine* 33 J7
Snihurivka, *Ukraine* 33 J7
Snina, *Slovak Rep.* 27 C15
Snizort, L., *U.K.* 13 D2
Snøhetta, *Norway* 9 E13
Snohomish, *U.S.A.* 110 C4
Snoul, *Cambodia* 65 F6
Snow Hill, *U.S.A.* 114 F8
Snow Lake, *Canada* 103 C8
Snow Mt., *Calif., U.S.A.* 110 F4
Snow Mt., *Maine, U.S.A.* 117 A14
Snow Shoe, *U.S.A.* 116 E7
Snowbird L., *Canada* 103 A8
Snowdon, *U.K.* 14 D3
Snowdonia △, *U.K.* 14 D4
Snowdrift = Łutselk'e, *Canada* 103 A6
Snowdrift →, *Canada* 103 A6
Snowflake, *U.S.A.* 109 J8
Snowshoe Pk., *U.S.A.* 108 B6
Snowtown, *Australia* 95 E2
Snowville, *U.S.A.* 108 F7
Snowy →, *Australia* 95 F4
Snowy Mt., *U.S.A.* 117 C10
Snowy Mts., *Australia* 95 F4
Snug Corner, *Bahamas* 121 B5
Snyatyn, *Ukraine* 29 B10
Snyder, *Okla., U.S.A.* 113 H5
Snyder, *Tex., U.S.A.* 113 J4
Soahanina, *Madag.* 89 B7
Soalala, *Madag.* 89 B8
Soaloka, *Madag.* 89 B8
Soamanonga, *Madag.* 89 C7
Soan →, *Pakistan* 68 C4
Soanierana-Ivongo, *Madag.* 89 B8
Soanindraniny, *Madag.* 89 B8
Şoarş, *Romania* 29 E9
Soavina, *Madag.* 89 C8
Soavinandriana, *Madag.* 89 B8
Sob →, *Ukraine* 29 B14
Soba, *Nigeria* 83 C6
Sobat, Nahr →, *Sudan* 81 F3
Soběslav, *Czech Rep.* 26 B7
Sobhapur, *India* 68 H8
Sobinka, *Russia* 32 E11
Sobótka, *Poland* 31 H3
Sobra, *Croatia* 41 F14
Sobradinho, Reprêsa de, *Brazil* 125 E10
Sobral, *Brazil* 125 D10
Sobrance, *Slovak Rep.* 27 C15
Sobreira Formosa, *Portugal* 36 F3
Soc Giang, *Vietnam* 58 F6
Soc Trang, *Vietnam* 65 H5
Soča →, *Europe* 26 E6
Socastee, *U.S.A.* 115 J6
Sochaczew, *Poland* 31 F7
Soch'e = Shache, *China* 60 C2
Sochi, *Russia* 35 J4
Société, Is. de la, *French Polynesia* 97 J12
Society Is. = Société, Is. de la, *French Polynesia* 97 J12
Socompa, Portezuelo de, *Chile* 126 A2
Socorro, *N. Mex., U.S.A.* 109 J10
Socorro, *Tex., U.S.A.* 109 L10
Socorro, I., *Mexico* 118 D2
Socotra, *Yemen* 75 E5
Socovos, *Spain* 39 G3
Socuéllamos, *Spain* 39 F2
Soda L., *U.S.A.* 109 J5
Soda Plains, *India* 69 B8
Soda Springs, *U.S.A.* 108 E8
Sodankylä, *Finland* 8 C22
Soddy-Daisy, *U.S.A.* 115 H3
Söderala, *Sweden* 10 C10
Söderåsen △, *Sweden* 11 H7
Söderbärke, *Sweden* 10 D9
Söderfors, *Sweden* 10 D11
Söderhamn, *Sweden* 10 C11
Söderköping, *Sweden* 11 F10
Södermanland, *Sweden* 9 G17
Södermanlands län □, *Sweden* 10 E10
Södertälje, *Sweden* 10 E11
Sodiri, *Sudan* 81 E2
Sodo, *Ethiopia* 81 F4
Södra Dellen, *Sweden* 10 C10
Södra Finnskoga, *Sweden* 10 D6
Södra Sandby, *Sweden* 11 J7
Södra Ulvön, *Sweden* 10 B12
Södra Vi, *Sweden* 11 G9
Sodražica, *Slovenia* 41 C11
Sodus, *U.S.A.* 116 C7
Sodwana Bay △, *S. Africa* 89 D5
Soekmekaar, *S. Africa* 89 C4
Soest, *Germany* 24 D4
Soest, *Neths.* 17 B5
Sofádhes, *Greece* 46 B4
Sofala □, *Mozam.* 89 B5
Sofara, *Mali* 82 C4
Sofia = Sofiya, *Bulgaria* 44 D7
Sofia →, *Madag.* 89 B8
Sofievka, *Ukraine* 33 H7
Sofikón, *Greece* 46 D5
Sofiya, *Bulgaria* 44 D7
Sofiya □, *Bulgaria* 44 D7
Sofiya ✕ (SOF), *Bulgaria* 44 D7
Sōfu-Gan, *Japan* 55 K10
Sogakofe, *Ghana* 83 D5
Sogamoso, *Colombia* 124 B4
Sogār, *Iran* 71 E8
Sögel, *Germany* 24 C3
Sogndalsfjøra, *Norway* 9 F12
Søgne, *Norway* 9 G12
Sognefjorden, *Norway* 9 F11
Söğüt, *Bilecik, Turkey* 47 A12
Söğüt, *Burdur, Turkey* 47 D11
Söğüt Dağı, *Turkey* 47 D11
Söğütköy, *Turkey* 47 E10
Sŏgwipo, *S. Korea* 57 H14
Soh, *Iran* 71 C6
Sohâg, *Egypt* 80 B3
Sohagpur, *India* 68 H8
Sŏhori, *N. Korea* 57 D15
Soignies, *Belgium* 17 D4
Soin, *Burkina Faso* 82 C4
Soira, *Eritrea* 81 E4
Soissons, *France* 19 C10
Sōja, *Japan* 55 G6
Sojat, *India* 68 G5
Sok →, *Russia* 34 D10
Sokal, *Ukraine* 33 G3
Söke, *Turkey* 47 D9
Sokelo, *Dem. Rep. of the Congo* 87 D1
Sokhós, *Greece* 44 F7
Sokhumi, *Georgia* 35 J5
Soko Banja, *Serbia & M.* 44 C5
Sokodé, *Togo* 83 D5
Sokol, *Russia* 32 C11
Sokolac, *Bos.-H.* 28 G3
Sokółka, *Poland* 30 E10
Sokolo, *Ségou, Mali* 82 C3
Sokolo, *Sikasso, Mali* 82 C3
Sokolov, *Czech Rep.* 26 A5
Sokołów Małpolski, *Poland* 31 H9
Sokołów Podlaski, *Poland* 31 F9
Sokoły, *Poland* 31 F9
Sokoto, *Nigeria* 83 C6
Sokoto □, *Nigeria* 83 C6
Sokoto →, *Nigeria* 83 C5
Sokyrnytsya, *Ukraine* 29 B8
Sokyryany, *Ukraine* 29 B12
Sol Iletsk, *Russia* 52 D6
Sola →, *Poland* 31 H6
Solai, *Kenya* 86 B4
Solan, *India* 68 D7
Solander I., *N.Z.* 91 M1
Solano, *Phil.* 61 C4
Solapur, *India* 66 L9
Solca, *Romania* 29 C10
Solda Gölü, *Turkey* 47 D11
Soldăneşti, *Moldova* 29 C13
Soldeu, *Andorra* 38 C6
Soldotna, *U.S.A.* 100 B4
Soléa, *Cyprus* 49 D12
Solec Kujawski, *Poland* 31 E5
Soledad, *Colombia* 124 A4
Soledad, *U.S.A.* 110 J5
Soledad, *Venezuela* 124 B6
Solent, The, *U.K.* 15 G6
Solenzara, *France* 21 G13
Solesmes, *France* 19 B10
Solfonn, *Norway* 9 F12
Solhan, *Turkey* 70 B4
Soligorsk = Salihorsk, *Belarus* 33 F4
Solihull, *U.K.* 15 E6
Solikamsk, *Russia* 52 D6
Solila, *Madag.* 89 C8
Solimões = Amazonas →, *S. Amer.* 125 D9
Solin, *Croatia* 41 E13
Solingen, *Germany* 24 D3
Sollebrunn, *Sweden* 11 F6
Sollefteå, *Sweden* 10 A11

Sollentuna, *Sweden* 10 E11
Sóller, *Spain* 48 B9
Sollerön, *Sweden* 10 D8
Solling, *Germany* 24 D5
Solling-Vogler ⌂, *Germany* 24 D5
Solnechnogorsk, *Russia* 32 D9
Solo →, *Indonesia* 63 G15
Solofra, *Italy* 43 B7
Sologne, *France* 19 E8
Solok, *Indonesia* 62 E2
Sololá, *Guatemala* 120 D1
Solomon, N. Fork →, *U.S.A.* 112 F5
Solomon, S. Fork →, *U.S.A.* 112 F5
Solomon Is. ■, *Pac. Oc.* 96 H7
Solon, *China* 60 B7
Solon Springs, *U.S.A.* 112 B9
Solor, *Indonesia* 63 F6
Solotcha, *Russia* 32 E10
Solothurn, *Switz.* 25 H3
Solothurn □, *Switz.* 25 H3
Solotvyn, *Ukraine* 29 B9
Solsona, *Spain* 38 C6
Solt, *Hungary* 28 D4
Šolta, *Croatia* 41 E13
Solṭānābād, *Khorāsān, Iran* 71 C8
Solṭānābād, *Khorāsān, Iran* 71 B8
Soltau, *Germany* 24 C5
Soltsy, *Russia* 32 C6
Solunska Glava, *Macedonia* 44 E5
Solvang, *U.S.A.* 111 L6
Solvay, *U.S.A.* 117 C8
Sölvesborg, *Sweden* 11 H8
Solway Firth, *U.K.* 14 C4
Solwezi, *Zambia* 87 E2
Sōma, *Japan* 54 F10
Soma, *Turkey* 47 B9
Somabhula, *Zimbabwe* 89 B4
Somali Pen., *Africa* 76 F8
Somali Rep. ■, *Africa* 75 F4
Somalia = Somali Rep. ■, *Africa* 75 F4
Sombernon, *France* 19 E11
Sombor, *Serbia & M.* 28 E4
Sombra, *Canada* 116 D2
Sombrerete, *Mexico* 118 C4
Sombrero, *Anguilla* 121 C7
Şomcuta Mare, *Romania* 29 C8
Somdari, *India* 68 G5
Someido ⌂, *Spain* 36 B4
Somers, *U.S.A.* 108 B6
Somerset, *Ky., U.S.A.* 114 G3
Somerset, *Mass., U.S.A.* 117 E13
Somerset, *Pa., U.S.A.* 116 F5
Somerset □, *U.K.* 15 F5
Somerset East, *S. Africa* 88 E4
Somerset I., *Canada* 100 A10
Somerset West, *S. Africa* 88 E2
Somersworth, *U.S.A.* 117 C14
Somerton, *U.S.A.* 109 K6
Somerville, *U.S.A.* 117 F10
Someş →, *Romania* 28 C7
Someşul Mare →, *Romania* 29 C8
Somme □, *France* 19 C9
Somme →, *France* 19 B8
Somme, B. de la, *France* 18 B8
Sommen, *Jönköping, Sweden* 11 F8
Sommen, *Östergötland, Sweden* 11 F9
Sommepy-Tahure, *France* 19 C11
Sömmerda, *Germany* 24 D7
Sommesous, *France* 19 D11
Sommières, *France* 21 E8
Somnath, *India* 68 J4
Somogy □, *Hungary* 28 D2
Somogyszob, *Hungary* 28 D2
Somoto, *Nic.* 120 D2
Sompolno, *Poland* 31 F5
Somport, Puerto de, *Spain* 38 C4
Son →, *India* 69 G11
Son Ha, *Vietnam* 64 E7
Son Hoa, *Vietnam* 64 F7
Son La, *Vietnam* 58 G4
Son Serra, *Spain* 48 B10
Son Servera, *Spain* 38 F8
Son Tay, *Vietnam* 58 G5
Soná, *Panama* 120 E3
Sonamarg, *India* 69 B6
Sonamukhi, *India* 69 H12
Sonar →, *India* 69 G8
Sŏnch'ŏn, *N. Korea* 57 E13
Sondags →, *S. Africa* 88 E4
Sóndalo, *Italy* 40 B7
Sondar, *India* 69 C6
Sønder Felding, *Denmark* 11 J2
Sønder Omme, *Denmark* 11 J2
Sønderborg, *Denmark* 11 K3
Sønderjyllands Amtskommune □, *Denmark* 11 J3
Sondershausen, *Germany* 24 D6
Sóndrio, *Italy* 40 B6
Sone, *Mozam.* 87 F3
Sonepur, *India* 67 J13
Song, *Nigeria* 83 D7
Song, *Thailand* 64 C3
Song Cau, *Vietnam* 64 F7
Song Xian, *China* 56 G7
Songan, *Indonesia* 63 J18
Songch'ŏn, *N. Korea* 57 E14
Songea, *Tanzania* 87 E4
Songeons, *France* 19 C8
Songhua Hu, *China* 57 C14
Songhua Jiang →, *China* 60 B8
Songimvelo ⌂, *S. Africa* 89 D5
Songjiang, *China* 59 B13
Songjin, *N. Korea* 57 D15
Songjŏng-ni, *S. Korea* 57 G14
Songkan, *China* 58 C6
Songkhla, *Thailand* 65 J3
Songming, *China* 58 E4
Songnim, *N. Korea* 57 E13
Songo, *Mozam.* 85 H6
Songo, *Sudan* 79 G10
Songpan, *China* 58 A4
Songtao, *China* 58 C7
Songwe, *Dem. Rep. of the Congo* 86 C2
Songwe →, *Africa* 87 D3
Songxi, *China* 59 D12
Songzi, *China* 59 B8
Sonhat, *India* 69 H10
Sonid Youqi, *China* 56 C7
Sonipat, *India* 68 E7
Sonkach, *India* 68 H7
Sonkovo, *Russia* 32 D9
Sonmiani, *Pakistan* 68 G2
Sonmiani B., *Pakistan* 68 G2
Sonnino, *Italy* 42 A6
Sono →, *Brazil* 125 E9
Sonoma, *U.S.A.* 110 G4
Sonora, *Calif., U.S.A.* 110 H6
Sonora, *Tex., U.S.A.* 113 K4
Sonora □, *Mexico* 118 B2
Sonora →, *Mexico* 118 B2
Sonoran Desert, *U.S.A.* 111 L12
Sonoyta, *Mexico* 118 A2
Sonqor, *Iran* 73 E12
Sŏnsan, *S. Korea* 57 F15
Sonseca, *Spain* 37 F7
Sonsonate, *El Salv.* 120 D2
Sonstorp, *Sweden* 11 F9
Sonthofen, *Germany* 25 H6
Soochow = Suzhou, *China* 59 B13
Sooke, *Canada* 110 B3
Sop Hao, *Laos* 58 G5
Sop Prap, *Thailand* 64 D2
Sopelana, *Spain* 38 B2
Sopi, *Indonesia* 63 D7
Sopo, Nahr →, *Sudan* 81 F2
Sopot, *Bulgaria* 45 D8
Sopot, *Poland* 30 D5
Sopot, *Serbia & M.* 44 B4
Sopotnica, *Macedonia* 44 E5
Sopron, *Hungary* 28 C1
Sopur, *India* 69 B6
Sør-Rondane, *Antarctica* 5 D4
Sora, *Italy* 41 G10
Sorah, *Pakistan* 68 F3
Söråker, *Sweden* 10 B11
Sorano, *Italy* 41 F8
Soraon, *India* 69 G9
Sorbas, *Spain* 39 H2
Sörbygden, *Sweden* 10 B10
Sore, *France* 20 D3
Sorel-Tracy, *Canada* 104 C5
Soresina, *Italy* 40 C6
Sörforsa, *Sweden* 10 C10
Sórgono, *Italy* 42 B2
Sorgues, *France* 21 D8
Sorgun, *Turkey* 72 C6
Soria, *Spain* 38 D2
Soria □, *Spain* 38 D2
Soriano, *Uruguay* 126 C4
Soriano nel Cimino, *Italy* 41 F9
Sorkh, Kuh-e, *Iran* 71 C8
Sorø, *Denmark* 11 J5
Soro, *Guinea* 82 C3
Soroca, *Moldova* 29 B13
Sorocaba, *Brazil* 127 A6
Soroki = Soroca, *Moldova* 29 B13
Sorong, *Indonesia* 63 E8
Soroní, *Greece* 49 C10
Soroti, *Uganda* 86 B3
Sørøya, *Norway* 8 A20
Sørøysundet, *Norway* 8 A20
Sorraia →, *Portugal* 37 G2
Sorrell, *Australia* 95 G4
Sorrento, *Italy* 43 B7
Sorsele, *Sweden* 8 D17
Sörsjön, *Sweden* 10 C7
Sorso, *Italy* 42 B1
Sorsogon, *Phil.* 61 E6
Sortavala, *Russia* 32 B6
Sortino, *Italy* 43 E8
Sortland, *Norway* 8 B16
Sorvizhi, *Russia* 34 B9
Sos del Rey Católico, *Spain* 38 C3
Sŏsan, *S. Korea* 57 F14
Soscumica, L., *Canada* 104 B4
Sösdala, *Sweden* 11 H7
Sosna →, *Russia* 33 F10
Sosnovka, *Kirov, Russia* 34 B10
Sosnovka, *Tambov, Russia* 34 D5
Sosnovyy Bor, *Russia* 32 C5
Sosnowiec, *Poland* 31 H6
Sospel, *France* 21 E11
Sossus Vlei, *Namibia* 88 C2
Šoštanj, *Slovenia* 41 B12
Sŏsura, *N. Korea* 57 C16
Sot →, *India* 69 F8
Sotkamo, *Finland* 8 D23
Soto del Barco, *Spain* 36 B4
Soto la Marina →, *Mexico* 119 C5
Soto y Amío, *Spain* 36 C5
Sotrondio, *Spain* 36 B5
Sotuta, *Mexico* 119 C7
Souanké, *Congo* 84 D2
Soubré, *Ivory C.* 82 D3
Souderton, *U.S.A.* 117 F9
Soúdha, *Greece* 49 D6
Soúdhas, Kólpos, *Greece* 49 D6
Souflíon, *Greece* 45 E10
Soufrière, *Guadeloupe* 120 b
Soufrière, *St. Lucia* 121 f
Soufrière Bay, *Dominica* 121 f
Souillac, *France* 20 D5
Souilly, *France* 19 C12
Soukhouma, *Laos* 64 E5
Sŏul, *S. Korea* 57 F14
Soulac-sur-Mer, *France* 20 C2
Soulougou, *Burkina Faso* 83 C5
Soultz-sous-Forêts, *France* 19 D14
Sound, The = Øresund, *Europe* 11 J6
Sound, The, *U.K.* 15 G3
Soúnion, Ákra, *Greece* 46 D6
Sources, Mt. aux, *Lesotho* 89 D4
Soure, *Brazil* 125 D9
Soure, *Portugal* 36 E2
Souris, *Man., Canada* 103 D8
Souris, *P.E.I., Canada* 105 C7
Souris →, *Canada* 112 A5
Sourou →, *Africa* 82 C4
Soúrpi, *Greece* 46 B4
Sousa, *Brazil* 125 E11
Sousel, *Portugal* 37 G3
Sousse, *Tunisia* 79 A8
Soustons, *France* 20 E2
Sout →, *S. Africa* 88 E2
South Africa ■, *Africa* 88 E3
South America 122 E5
South Atlantic Ocean 2 F8
South Aulatsivik I., *Canada* 105 A7
South Australia □, *Australia* 95 E2
South Ayrshire □, *U.K.* 13 F4
South Baldy, *U.S.A.* 109 J10
South Bass I., *U.S.A.* 116 E2
South Bend, *Ind., U.S.A.* 114 E2
South Bend, *Wash., U.S.A.* 110 D3
South Boston, *U.S.A.* 115 G6
South Branch, *Canada* 105 C8
South Brook, *Canada* 105 C8
South Carolina □, *U.S.A.* 115 J5
South Charleston, *U.S.A.* 114 F5
South China Sea, *Asia* 62 C4
South Cumberland Is. △, *Australia* 94 J7
South Dakota □, *U.S.A.* 112 C5
South Deerfield, *U.S.A.* 117 D12
South Downs, *U.K.* 15 G7
South East C., *Australia* 95 G4
South-East Indian Rise, *Ind. Oc.* 5 B10
South East Is., *Australia* 93 F3
South Esk →, *U.K.* 13 E6
South Foreland, *U.K.* 15 F9
South Fork American →, *U.S.A.* 110 G5
South Fork Feather →, *U.S.A.* 110 F5
South Fork Grand →, *U.S.A.* 112 C3
South Fork Republican →, *U.S.A.* 112 E4
South Georgia, *Antarctica* 128 G9
South Gloucestershire □, *U.K.* 15 F5
South Hadley, *U.S.A.* 117 D12
South Haven, *U.S.A.* 114 D2
South Henik L., *Canada* 103 A9
South Honshu Ridge, *Pac. Oc.* 96 E6
South Horr, *Kenya* 86 B4
South I., *Kenya* 86 B4
South I., *N.Z.* 91 L3
South Indian Lake, *Canada* 103 B9
South Invercargill, *N.Z.* 91 M2
South Island △, *Kenya* 86 B4
South Kitui ⌂, *Kenya* 86 C4
South Knife →, *Canada* 103 B10
South Koel →, *India* 69 H11
South Korea ■, *Asia* 57 G15
South Lake Tahoe, *U.S.A.* 110 G6
South Lanarkshire □, *U.K.* 13 F5
South Loup →, *U.S.A.* 112 E5
South Luangwa △, *Zambia* 87 E3
South Magnetic Pole, *Antarctica* 5 C9
South Milwaukee, *U.S.A.* 114 D2
South Molton, *U.K.* 15 F4
South Moose L., *Canada* 103 C8
South Nahanni →, *Canada* 102 A4
South Nation →, *Canada* 117 A9
South Natuna Is. = Natuna Selatan, Kepulauan, *Indonesia* 62 D3
South Negril Pt., *Jamaica* 120 a
South Orkney Is., *Antarctica* 5 C18
South Ossetia □, *Georgia* 35 J7
South Pagai, I. = Pagai Selatan, Pulau, *Indonesia* 62 E2
South Paris, *U.S.A.* 117 B14
South Pittsburg, *U.S.A.* 115 H3
South Platte →, *U.S.A.* 112 E4
South Pole, *Antarctica* 5 E
South Porcupine, *Canada* 104 C3
South Portland, *U.S.A.* 115 D10
South Pt., *Barbados* 121 g
South Pt., *U.S.A.* 116 B1
South River, *Canada* 104 C4
South River, *U.S.A.* 117 F10
South Ronaldsay, *U.K.* 13 C6
South Sandwich Is., *Antarctica* 5 B1
South Saskatchewan →, *Canada* 103 C7
South Seal →, *Canada* 103 B9
South Shetland Is., *Antarctica* 5 C18
South Shields, *U.K.* 14 C6
South Sioux City, *U.S.A.* 112 D6
South Taranaki Bight, *N.Z.* 91 H5
South Thompson →, *Canada* 102 C4
South Twin I., *Canada* 104 B4
South Tyne →, *U.K.* 14 C5
South Uist, *U.K.* 13 D1
South West C., *Australia* 95 G4
South West C., *N.Z.* 91 M1
South Williamsport, *U.S.A.* 116 E8
South Yorkshire □, *U.K.* 14 D6
Southampton, *Canada* 116 B3
Southampton, *U.K.* 15 G6
Southampton, *U.S.A.* 117 F12
Southampton □, *U.K.* 15 G6
Southampton I., *Canada* 101 B11
Southaven, *U.S.A.* 113 H9
Southbank, *Canada* 102 C3
Southbridge, *N.Z.* 91 K4
Southbridge, *U.S.A.* 117 D12
Southeast Pacific Basin, *Pac. Oc.* 5 C15
Southend, *Canada* 103 B8
Southend-on-Sea, *U.K.* 15 F8
Southend-on-Sea □, *U.K.* 15 F8
Southern = Janub △, *Sudan* 81 F2
Southern = Yedebub Biheroch Bihereseboch na Hizboch □, *Ethiopia* 81 F4
Southern = Yuzhnyy □, *Russia* 35 H5
Southern □, *Malawi* 87 F4
Southern □, *S. Leone* 82 D2
Southern □, *Zambia* 87 F2
Southern Alps, *N.Z.* 91 K3
Southern Cross, *Australia* 93 F2
Southern Indian L., *Canada* 103 B9
Southern Ocean, *Antarctica* 5 C6
Southern Pines, *U.S.A.* 115 H6
Southern Uplands, *U.K.* 13 F5
Southington, *U.S.A.* 117 E12
Southland □, *N.Z.* 91 L1
Southold, *U.S.A.* 117 E12
Southport, *Australia* 95 D5
Southport, *U.K.* 14 D4
Southport, *Fla., U.S.A.* 115 K3
Southport, *N.Y., U.S.A.* 116 D8
Southwest △, *Australia* 95 G4
Southwestern Pacific Basin, *Pac. Oc.* 5 A12
Southwold, *U.K.* 15 E9
Southwood △, *Australia* 95 D5
Soutpansberg, *S. Africa* 89 C4
Souvigny, *France* 19 F10
Sovata, *Romania* 29 D10
Soverato, *Italy* 43 D9
Sovetsk, *Kaliningrad, Russia* 9 J19
Sovetsk, *Kirov, Russia* 34 B9
Sovetskaya Gavan = Vanino, *Russia* 53 E15
Sovicille, *Italy* 41 E8
Soweto, *S. Africa* 89 D4
Sōya-Kaikyō = La Perouse Str., *Asia* 54 B11
Sōya-Misaki, *Japan* 54 B10
Soyaux, *France* 20 C4
Sozh →, *Belarus* 33 F6
Sozopol, *Bulgaria* 45 D11
Spa, *Belgium* 17 D5
Spain ■, *Europe* 7 H5
Spalding, *Australia* 95 E2
Spalding, *U.K.* 14 E7
Spangler, *U.S.A.* 116 F6
Spanish, *Canada* 104 C3
Spanish Fork, *U.S.A.* 108 F8
Spanish Town, *Br. Virgin Is.* 121 e
Spanish Town, *Jamaica* 120 a
Sparks, *U.S.A.* 110 F7
Sparreholm, *Sweden* 10 E10
Sparta = Spárti, *Greece* 46 D4
Sparta, *Mich., U.S.A.* 114 D3
Sparta, *N.J., U.S.A.* 117 E10
Sparta, *Wis., U.S.A.* 112 D9
Spartanburg, *U.S.A.* 115 H5
Spartansburg, *U.S.A.* 116 E5
Spárti, *Greece* 46 D4
Spartivento, C., *Calabria, Italy* 43 E9
Spartivento, C., *Sard., Italy* 42 D1
Sparwood, *Canada* 102 D6
Spas-Demensk, *Russia* 32 E7
Spas-Klepiki, *Russia* 32 E11
Spassk Dalniy, *Russia* 53 E14
Spassk-Ryazanskiy, *Russia* 32 E11
Spátha, Ákra, *Greece* 49 D5
Spatsizi →, *Canada* 102 B3
Spatsizi Plateau Wilderness ⌂, *Canada* 102 B3
Spean →, *U.K.* 13 E4
Spearfish, *U.S.A.* 112 C3
Spearman, *U.S.A.* 113 G4
Speculator, *U.S.A.* 117 C10
Speia, *Moldova* 29 D14
Speightstown, *Barbados* 121 g
Speke Gulf, *Tanzania* 86 C3
Spello, *Italy* 41 F9
Spence Bay = Taloyoak, *Canada* 100 B10
Spencer, *Idaho, U.S.A.* 108 D7
Spencer, *Iowa, U.S.A.* 112 D7
Spencer, *N.Y., U.S.A.* 117 D8
Spencer, *Nebr., U.S.A.* 112 D5
Spencer, C., *Australia* 95 F2
Spencer B., *Namibia* 88 D1
Spencer G., *Australia* 95 E2
Spencerville, *Canada* 117 B9
Spences Bridge, *Canada* 102 C4
Spennymoor, *U.K.* 14 C6
Spenser Mts., *N.Z.* 91 K4
Spentrup, *Denmark* 11 H4
Sperkhiós →, *Greece* 46 C4
Sperrin Mts., *U.K.* 12 B5
Spessart, *Germany* 25 F5
Spétsai, *Greece* 46 D5
Spey →, *U.K.* 13 D5
Speyer, *Germany* 25 F4
Spezand, *Pakistan* 68 E2
Spezzano Albanese, *Italy* 43 C9
Spiekeroog, *Germany* 24 B3
Spiez, *Switz.* 25 J3
Spíli, *Greece* 49 D6
Spilimbergo, *Italy* 41 B9
Spīn Būldak, *Afghan.* 68 D2
Spinalónga, *Greece* 49 D7
Spinazzola, *Italy* 43 B9
Spineni, *Romania* 29 F9
Spirit Lake, *U.S.A.* 110 D4
Spirit River, *Canada* 102 B5
Spiritwood, *Canada* 103 C7
Spišská Nová Ves, *Slovak Rep.* 27 C13
Spišské Podhradie, *Slovak Rep.* 27 B13
Spital, *Austria* 26 D7
Spithead, *U.K.* 15 G6
Spittal an der Drau, *Austria* 26 E6
Spitzbergen = Svalbard, *Arctic* 51 B5
Spjelkavik, *Norway* 9 E12
Split, *Croatia* 41 E13
Split ✈ (SPU), *Croatia* 41 E13
Split L., *Canada* 103 B9
Split Lake, *Canada* 103 B9
Splitski Kanal, *Croatia* 41 E13
Splügenpass, *Switz.* 25 J5
Spofford, *U.S.A.* 113 L4
Spokane, *U.S.A.* 108 C5
Spoleto, *Italy* 41 F9
Spooner, *U.S.A.* 112 C9
Sporyy Navolok, Mys, *Russia* 52 B7
Sprague, *U.S.A.* 108 C5
Spratly I., *S. China Sea* 62 C4
Spratly Is., *S. China Sea* 62 C4
Spray, *U.S.A.* 108 D4
Spreča →, *Bos.-H.* 28 F3
Spree →, *Germany* 24 C9
Spreewald, *Germany* 24 D9
Spremberg, *Germany* 24 D10
Sprengisandur, *Iceland* 8 D5
Spring City, *U.S.A.* 117 F9
Spring Creek, *U.S.A.* 108 F6
Spring Garden, *U.S.A.* 110 F6
Spring Hall, *Barbados* 121 g
Spring Hill, *U.S.A.* 115 L4
Spring Mts., *U.S.A.* 109 H6
Spring Valley, *U.S.A.* 111 N10
Springbok, *S. Africa* 88 D2
Springboro, *U.S.A.* 116 E4
Springdale, *Canada* 105 C8
Springdale, *U.S.A.* 113 G7
Springe, *Germany* 24 C5
Springer, *U.S.A.* 113 G2
Springerville, *U.S.A.* 109 J9
Springfield, *Canada* 116 D4
Springfield, *N.Z.* 91 K3
Springfield, *Colo., U.S.A.* 113 G3
Springfield, *Ill., U.S.A.* 112 F10
Springfield, *Mass., U.S.A.* 117 D12
Springfield, *Mo., U.S.A.* 113 G8
Springfield, *Ohio, U.S.A.* 114 F4
Springfield, *Oreg., U.S.A.* 108 D2
Springfield, *Tenn., U.S.A.* 115 G2
Springfield, *Vt., U.S.A.* 117 C12
Springfontein, *S. Africa* 88 E4
Springhill, *Canada* 105 C7
Springhill, *U.S.A.* 113 J8
Springhouse, *Canada* 102 C4
Springs, *S. Africa* 89 D4
Springsure, *Australia* 94 C4
Springvale, *U.S.A.* 117 C14
Springville, *Calif., U.S.A.* 110 J8
Springville, *N.Y., U.S.A.* 116 D6
Springville, *Utah, U.S.A.* 108 F8
Springwater, *U.S.A.* 116 D7
Spruce-Creek, *U.S.A.* 116 F6
Spruce Knob-Seneca Rocks ⌂, *U.S.A.* 114 F6
Spruce Mt., *U.S.A.* 117 B12
Spur, *U.S.A.* 113 J4
Spurn Hd., *U.K.* 14 D8
Spuž, *Serbia & M.* 44 D3
Spuzzum, *Canada* 102 D4
Squam L., *U.S.A.* 117 C13
Squamish, *Canada* 102 D4
Square Islands, *Canada* 105 B8
Squillace, G. di, *Italy* 43 D9
Squinzano, *Italy* 43 B11
Squires, Mt., *Australia* 93 E4
Srbac, *Bos.-H.* 28 E2
Srbica, *Serbia & M.* 44 D4
Srbija = Serbia □, *Serbia & M.* 44 C5
Srbobran, *Serbia & M.* 28 E4
Sre Ambel, *Cambodia* 65 G4
Sre Khtum, *Cambodia* 65 F6
Sre Umbell = Sre Ambel, *Cambodia* 65 G4
Srebrenica, *Bos.-H.* 28 F4
Sredinny Ra. = Sredinnyy Khrebet, *Russia* 53 D16
Sredinnyy Khrebet, *Russia* 53 D16
Središče, *Slovenia* 41 B13
Sredna Gora, *Bulgaria* 45 D8
Srednekolymsk, *Russia* 53 C16
Sredni Rodopi, *Bulgaria* 45 E8
Srednogorie, *Bulgaria* 45 D8
Śrem, *Poland* 31 F4
Sremska Mitrovica, *Serbia & M.* 28 F4
Sremski Karlovci, *Serbia & M.* 28 E4
Srepok →, *Cambodia* 64 F6
Sretensk, *Russia* 53 D12
Sri Lanka ■, *Asia* 66 R12
Srikakulam, *India* 67 K13
Srinagar, *India* 69 B6
Srinagarind Res., *Thailand* 64 E2
Środa Śląska, *Poland* 31 G3
Środa Wielkopolski, *Poland* 31 F4
Srono, *Indonesia* 63 J17
Srpska Crnja, *Serbia & M.* 28 E5
Srpski Itebej, *Serbia & M.* 28 E5
Staaten →, *Australia* 94 B3
Staaten River △, *Australia* 94 B3
Staberhuk, *Germany* 24 A7
Stade, *Germany* 24 B5
Stadskanaal, *Neths.* 17 A6
Stadtallendorf, *Germany* 24 E5
Stadthagen, *Germany* 24 C5
Stadtlohn, *Germany* 24 D2
Stadtroda, *Germany* 24 E7
Staffa, *U.K.* 13 E2
Staffanstorp, *Sweden* 11 J7
Stafford, *U.K.* 14 E5
Stafford, *U.S.A.* 113 G5
Stafford Springs, *U.S.A.* 117 E12
Staffordshire □, *U.K.* 14 E5
Stagnone, *Italy* 42 E5
Stagnone di Marsala ⌂, *Italy* 42 E5
Staines, *U.K.* 15 F7
Stainz, *Austria* 26 E8
Stakhanov, *Ukraine* 33 H10
Stalać, *Serbia & M.* 44 C5
Stalis, *Greece* 49 D7
Stallarholmen, *Sweden* 10 E11
Ställdalen, *Sweden* 10 E8
Stalowa Wola, *Poland* 31 H9
Stalybridge, *U.K.* 14 D5
Stamford, *Australia* 94 C3
Stamford, *U.K.* 15 E7
Stamford, *Conn., U.S.A.* 117 E11
Stamford, *N.Y., U.S.A.* 117 D10

Stamford, *Tex., U.S.A.* 113 J5
Stampriet, *Namibia* 88 C2
Stamps, *U.S.A.* 113 J8
Stančevo = Kalipetrovo, *Bulgaria* 45 B11
Standerton, *S. Africa* 89 D4
Standish, *U.S.A.* 114 D4
Stanford, *S. Africa* 88 E2
Stanford, *U.S.A.* 108 C8
Stånga, *Sweden* 11 G12
Stanger, *S. Africa* 89 D5
Stängselåsen = Salpausselkä, *Finland* 9 F22
Stanišić, *Serbia & M.* 28 E4
Stanislaus →, *U.S.A.* 110 H5
Stanisławów, *Poland* 31 F8
Stanley, *Australia* 95 G4
Stanley, *Falk. Is.* 128 G5
Stanley, *U.K.* 14 C6
Stanley, *Idaho, U.S.A.* 108 D6
Stanley, *N. Dak., U.S.A.* 112 A3
Stanley, *N.Y., U.S.A.* 116 D7
Stanley Mission, *Canada* 103 B8
Stanovoy Khrebet, *Russia* 53 D13
Stanovoy Ra. = Stanovoy Khrebet, *Russia* 53 D13
Stansmore Ra., *Australia* 92 D4
Stansted, London ✈ (STN), *U.K.* 15 F8
Stanthorpe, *Australia* 95 D5
Stanton, *U.S.A.* 113 J4
Stanwood, *U.S.A.* 110 B4
Staples, *U.S.A.* 112 B7
Stąporków, *Poland* 31 G7
Star City, *Canada* 103 C8
Star Lake, *U.S.A.* 117 B9
Stará L'ubovňa, *Slovak Rep.* 27 B13
Stara Moravica, *Serbia & M.* 28 E4
Stara Pazova, *Serbia & M.* 28 F5
Stara Planina, *Bulgaria* 44 C7
Stara Sil, *Ukraine* 31 J9
Stará Turá, *Slovak Rep.* 27 C10
Stara Ushytsya, *Ukraine* 29 B12
Stara Zagora, *Bulgaria* 45 D9
Starachowice, *Poland* 31 G8
Staraya Russa, *Russia* 32 D6
Starbuck I., *Kiribati* 97 H12
Starchiojd, *Romania* 29 E11
Starcke △, *Australia* 94 A4
Stargard Szczeciński, *Poland* 30 E2
Stari Bar, *Serbia & M.* 44 D3
Stari Trg, *Slovenia* 41 C12
Staritsa, *Russia* 32 D8
Starke, *U.S.A.* 115 L4
Starnberg, *Germany* 25 H7
Starnberger See, *Germany* 25 H7
Starobilsk, *Ukraine* 33 H10
Starodub, *Russia* 33 F7
Starogard Gdański, *Poland* 30 E5
Starokonstantinov = Starokonstyantyniv, *Ukraine* 33 H4
Starokonstyantyniv, *Ukraine* 33 H4
Starokozache, *Ukraine* 29 D14
Starominskaya, *Russia* 33 J10
Staroshcherbinovskaya, *Russia* 33 J10
Start Pt., *U.K.* 15 G4
Stary Sącz, *Poland* 31 J7
Staryy Biryuzyak, *Russia* 35 H8
Staryy Chartoriysk, *Ukraine* 33 G3
Staryy Krym, *Ukraine* 33 K8
Staryy Oskol, *Russia* 33 G9
Staryy Sambir, *Ukraine* 31 J9
Stassfurt, *Germany* 24 D7
Staszów, *Poland* 31 H8
State College, *U.S.A.* 116 F7
Stateline, *U.S.A.* 110 G7
Staten, I. = Estados, I. de Los, *Argentina* 128 G4
Staten I., *U.S.A.* 117 F10
Statesboro, *U.S.A.* 115 J5
Statesville, *U.S.A.* 115 H5
Statia = St. Eustatius, *W. Indies* 121 C7
Stauffer, *U.S.A.* 111 L7
Staunton, *Ill., U.S.A.* 112 F10
Staunton, *Va., U.S.A.* 114 F6
Stavanger, *Norway* 9 G11
Staveley, *N.Z.* 91 K3
Stavelot, *Belgium* 17 D5
Stavern, *Norway* 9 G14
Stavoren, *Neths.* 17 B5
Stavropol, *Russia* 35 H6
Stavros, *Cyprus* 49 D11
Stavrós, *Greece* 49 D6
Stavrós, Ákra, *Greece* 49 D6
Stavroúpolis, *Greece* 45 E8
Stawell, *Australia* 95 F3
Stawell →, *Australia* 94 C3
Stawiski, *Poland* 30 E9
Stawiszyn, *Poland* 31 G5
Stayner, *Canada* 116 B4
Stayton, *U.S.A.* 108 D2
Steamboat Springs, *U.S.A.* 108 F10
Steblevë, *Albania* 44 E4
Steele, *U.S.A.* 112 B5
Steelton, *U.S.A.* 116 F8
Steen River, *Canada* 102 B5
Steens Mt., *U.S.A.* 108 E4
Steenwijk, *Neths.* 17 B6
Steep Pt., *Australia* 93 E1
Steep Rock, *Canada* 103 C9
Ştefan Vodă, *Moldova* 29 D14
Ştefăneşti, *Romania* 29 C12
Stefanie △, *Ethiopia* 81 G4
Stefanie L. = Chew Bahir, *Ethiopia* 81 G4
Stefansson Bay, *Antarctica* 5 C5
Stege, *Denmark* 11 K6
Ştei, *Romania* 28 D7
Steiermark □, *Austria* 26 D8
Steigerwald, *Germany* 25 F6
Steigerwald ⌓, *Germany* 25 F6
Steilacoom, *U.S.A.* 110 C4
Steilrandberge, *Namibia* 88 B1
Steinbach, *Canada* 103 D9
Steinfurt, *Germany* 24 C3
Steinhausen, *Namibia* 88 C2
Steinheim, *Germany* 24 D5
Steinhuder Meer, *Germany* 24 C5
Steinhuder Meer ⌓, *Germany* 24 C5
Steinkjer, *Norway* 8 D14
Steinkopf, *S. Africa* 88 D2
Steinwald ⌓, *Germany* 25 F8
Stellarton, *Canada* 105 C7
Stellenbosch, *S. Africa* 88 E2
Stelvio, Paso dello, *Italy* 40 B7
Stenay, *France* 19 C12
Stendal, *Germany* 24 C7
Stende, *Latvia* 30 A9
Stenhamra, *Sweden* 10 E11
Stenshuvud △, *Sweden* 11 J8
Stenstorp, *Sweden* 11 F7
Stenungsund, *Sweden* 11 F5
Steornabhaigh = Stornoway, *U.K.* 13 C2
Stepanakert = Xankändi, *Azerbaijan* 70 B5
Stepanavan, *Armenia* 35 K7
Stephens Creek, *Australia* 95 E3
Stephens I., *Canada* 102 C2
Stephens L., *Canada* 103 B9
Stephenville, *Canada* 105 C8
Stephenville, *U.S.A.* 113 J5
Stepnica, *Poland* 30 E1
Steppe, *Asia* 50 D9
Stereá Ellas □, *Greece* 46 C4
Sterkstroom, *S. Africa* 88 E4
Sterling, *Colo., U.S.A.* 112 E3
Sterling, *Ill., U.S.A.* 112 E10
Sterling, *Kans., U.S.A.* 112 F5
Sterling City, *U.S.A.* 113 K4
Sterling Heights, *U.S.A.* 114 D4
Sterling Run, *U.S.A.* 116 E6
Sterlitamak, *Russia* 52 D6
Šternberk, *Czech Rep.* 27 B10
Stérnes, *Greece* 49 D6
Sterzing = Vipiteno, *Italy* 41 B8
Stettin = Szczecin, *Poland* 30 E1
Stettiner Haff, *Germany* 24 B10
Stettler, *Canada* 102 C6
Steubenville, *U.S.A.* 116 F4
Stevenage, *U.K.* 15 F7
Stevens Point, *U.S.A.* 112 C10
Stevenson, *U.S.A.* 110 E5
Stevenson, The →, *Australia* 95 D2
Stevenson L., *Canada* 103 C9
Stevensville, *U.S.A.* 108 C6
Stevns Klint, *Denmark* 11 J6
Stewart, *Canada* 102 B3
Stewart, *U.S.A.* 110 F7
Stewart →, *Canada* 100 B6
Stewart, C., *Australia* 94 A1
Stewart, I., *Chile* 128 G2
Stewart I., *N.Z.* 91 M1
Stewarts Point, *U.S.A.* 110 G3
Stewartville, *U.S.A.* 112 D8
Stewiacke, *Canada* 105 C7
Steynsburg, *S. Africa* 88 E4
Steyr, *Austria* 26 C7
Steyr →, *Austria* 26 C7
Steytlerville, *S. Africa* 88 E3
Stia, *Italy* 41 E8
Stigler, *U.S.A.* 113 H7
Stigliano, *Italy* 43 B9
Stigtomta, *Sweden* 11 F10
Stikine →, *Canada* 102 B2
Stilfontein, *S. Africa* 88 D4
Stilís, *Greece* 46 C4
Stillwater, *N.Z.* 91 K3
Stillwater, *Minn., U.S.A.* 112 C8
Stillwater, *N.Y., U.S.A.* 117 D11
Stillwater, *Okla., U.S.A.* 113 G6
Stillwater Range, *U.S.A.* 108 G4
Stillwater Reservoir, *U.S.A.* 117 C9
Stilo, Pta., *Italy* 43 D9
Stilwell, *U.S.A.* 113 H7
Stînga Nistrului □, *Moldova* 29 C14
Štip, *Macedonia* 44 E6
Stíra, *Greece* 46 C6
Stirling, *Canada* 116 B7
Stirling, *U.K.* 13 E5
Stirling □, *U.K.* 13 E4
Stirling Ra., *Australia* 93 F2
Stirling Range △, *Australia* 93 F2
Stittsville, *Canada* 117 A9
Stjernøya, *Norway* 8 A20
Stjørdalshalsen, *Norway* 8 E14
Stockach, *Germany* 25 H5
Stockaryd, *Sweden* 11 G8
Stockerau, *Austria* 27 C9
Stockholm, *Sweden* 10 E12
Stockholm Arlanda ✈ (ARN), *Sweden* 10 E11
Stockholms län □, *Sweden* 10 E12
Stockport, *U.K.* 14 D5
Stocksbridge, *U.K.* 14 D6
Stockton, *Calif., U.S.A.* 110 H5
Stockton, *Kans., U.S.A.* 112 F5
Stockton, *Mo., U.S.A.* 113 G8
Stockton-on-Tees, *U.K.* 14 C6
Stockton-on-Tees □, *U.K.* 14 C6
Stockton Plateau, *U.S.A.* 113 K3
Stoczek Łukowski, *Poland* 31 G8
Stöde, *Sweden* 10 B10
Stoeng Treng, *Cambodia* 64 F5
Stoer, Pt. of, *U.K.* 13 C3
Stogovo, *Macedonia* 44 E4
Stoholm, *Denmark* 11 H3
Stoke-on-Trent, *U.K.* 14 D5
Stoke-on-Trent □, *U.K.* 14 D5
Stokes △, *Australia* 93 E2
Stokes Pt., *Australia* 95 G3
Stokes Ra., *Australia* 92 C5
Stokksnes, *Iceland* 8 D6
Stokmarknes, *Norway* 8 B16
Stolac, *Bos.-H.* 44 C1
Stolberg, *Germany* 24 E2
Stolbovoy, Ostrov, *Russia* 53 B14
Stolbtsy = Stowbtsy, *Belarus* 32 F4
Stolin, *Belarus* 33 G4
Stöllet, *Sweden* 10 D7
Stolnici, *Romania* 29 F9
Stomíon, *Greece* 49 D5
Ston, *Croatia* 41 F14
Stone, *U.K.* 14 E5
Stoneboro, *U.S.A.* 116 E4
Stonehaven, *U.K.* 13 E6
Stonehenge, *Australia* 94 C3
Stonehenge, *U.K.* 15 F6
Stonewall, *Canada* 103 C9
Stony L., *Man., Canada* 103 B9
Stony L., *Ont., Canada* 116 B6
Stony Point, *U.S.A.* 117 E11
Stony Pt., *U.S.A.* 117 C8
Stony Rapids, *Canada* 103 B7
Stony Tunguska = Tunguska, Podkamennaya →, *Russia* 53 C10
Stonyford, *U.S.A.* 110 F4
Stopnica, *Poland* 31 H7
Storå, *Sweden* 10 E9
Storå →, *Denmark* 11 H2
Stora Gla, *Sweden* 10 E6
Stora Le, *Sweden* 10 E5
Stora Lulevatten, *Sweden* 8 C18
Storavan, *Sweden* 8 D18
Stord, *Norway* 9 G11
Store Bælt, *Denmark* 11 J4
Store Heddinge, *Denmark* 11 J6
Store Mosse △, *Sweden* 11 G7
Storebro, *Sweden* 11 G9
Storfors, *Sweden* 10 E8
Storlien, *Sweden* 10 A6
Storm B., *Australia* 95 G4
Storm Lake, *U.S.A.* 112 D7
Stormberge, *S. Africa* 88 E4
Stormsrivier, *S. Africa* 88 E3
Stornoway, *U.K.* 13 C2
Storo, *Italy* 40 C7
Storozhinets = Storozhynets, *Ukraine* 29 B10
Storozhynets, *Ukraine* 29 B10
Storrs, *U.S.A.* 117 E12
Storsjön, *Gävleborg, Sweden* 10 D10
Storsjön, *Jämtland, Sweden* 10 B7
Storsjön, *Jämtland, Sweden* 10 A8
Storstrøms Amtskommune □, *Denmark* 11 J5
Storuman, *Sweden* 8 D17
Storuman, *Sweden* 8 D17
Storvätteshågna, *Sweden* 10 B6
Storvik, *Sweden* 10 D10
Storvreta, *Sweden* 10 E11
Stouffville, *Canada* 116 C5
Stoughton, *Canada* 103 D8
Stour →, *Dorset, U.K.* 15 G6
Stour →, *Kent, U.K.* 15 F9
Stour →, *Suffolk, U.K.* 15 F9
Stourbridge, *U.K.* 15 E5
Stout L., *Canada* 103 C10
Stove Pipe Wells Village, *U.S.A.* 111 J9
Støvring, *Denmark* 11 H3
Stow, *U.S.A.* 116 E3
Stowbtsy, *Belarus* 32 F4
Stowmarket, *U.K.* 15 E9
Strabane, *U.K.* 12 B4
Stracin, *Macedonia* 44 D6
Stradella, *Italy* 40 C6
Strahan, *Australia* 95 G4
Strajitsa, *Bulgaria* 45 C9
Strakonice, *Czech Rep.* 26 B6
Straldzha, *Bulgaria* 45 D10
Stralsund, *Germany* 24 A9
Strand, *S. Africa* 88 E2
Stranda, *Møre og Romsdal, Norway* 9 E12
Stranda, *Nord-Trøndelag, Norway* 8 E14
Strandby, *Denmark* 11 G4
Strangford L., *U.K.* 12 B6
Strängnäs, *Sweden* 10 E11
Stranraer, *U.K.* 13 G3
Strasbourg, *Canada* 103 C8
Strasbourg, *France* 19 D14
Strasburg, *Germany* 24 B9
Străşeni, *Moldova* 29 C13
Stråssa, *Sweden* 10 E9
Stratford, *Canada* 116 C4
Stratford, *N.Z.* 91 H5
Stratford, *Calif., U.S.A.* 110 J7
Stratford, *Conn., U.S.A.* 117 E11
Stratford, *Tex., U.S.A.* 113 G3
Stratford-upon-Avon, *U.K.* 15 E6
Strath Spey, *U.K.* 13 D5
Strathalbyn, *Australia* 95 F2
Strathaven, *U.K.* 13 F4
Strathcona ⌓, *Canada* 102 D3
Strathmore, *Canada* 102 C6
Strathmore, *U.K.* 13 E5
Strathmore, *U.S.A.* 110 J7
Strathnaver, *Canada* 102 C4
Strathpeffer, *U.K.* 13 D4
Strathroy, *Canada* 116 D3
Strathy Pt., *U.K.* 13 C4
Strattanville, *U.S.A.* 116 E5
Stratton, *U.S.A.* 117 A14
Stratton Mt., *U.S.A.* 117 C12
Straubing, *Germany* 25 G8
Straumnes, *Iceland* 8 C2
Strausberg, *Germany* 24 C9
Strawberry →, *U.S.A.* 108 F8
Strážnice, *Czech Rep.* 27 C10
Streaky B., *Australia* 95 E1
Streaky Bay, *Australia* 95 E1
Streator, *U.S.A.* 112 E10
Středočeský □, *Czech Rep.* 26 B7
Streetsboro, *U.S.A.* 116 E3
Streetsville, *Canada* 116 C5
Strehaia, *Romania* 29 F8
Strelcha, *Bulgaria* 45 D8
Strelka, *Russia* 53 D10
Streng →, *Cambodia* 64 F4
Stresa, *Italy* 40 C5
Streymoy, *Færoe Is.* 8 E9
Strezhevoy, *Russia* 52 C8
Stříbro, *Czech Rep.* 26 A6
Strilky, *Ukraine* 31 J9
Strimón →, *Greece* 44 F7
Strimonikós Kólpos, *Greece* 44 F7
Strofádhes, *Greece* 46 D3
Stroma, *U.K.* 13 C5
Stromberg-Heuchelberg ⌓, *Germany* 25 F4
Strómboli, *Italy* 43 D8
Stromeferry, *U.K.* 13 D3
Stromness, *U.K.* 13 C5
Strömsbruk, *Sweden* 10 C11
Stromsburg, *U.S.A.* 112 E6
Strömsnäsbruk, *Sweden* 11 H7
Strömstad, *Sweden* 11 F5
Strömsund, *Sweden* 8 E16
Strongilí, *Greece* 47 E11
Strongoli, *Italy* 43 C10
Strongsville, *U.S.A.* 116 E3
Stronie Śląskie, *Poland* 31 H3
Stronsay, *U.K.* 13 B6
Stropkov, *Slovak Rep.* 27 B14
Stroud, *U.K.* 15 F5
Stroud Road, *Australia* 95 E5
Stroudsburg, *U.S.A.* 117 F9
Stroumbi, *Cyprus* 49 E11
Struer, *Denmark* 11 H2
Struga, *Macedonia* 44 E4
Strugi Krasnyye, *Russia* 32 C5
Strumica, *Macedonia* 44 E6
Strumica →, *Europe* 44 E7
Strumok, *Ukraine* 29 E14
Struthers, *Canada* 104 C2
Struthers, *U.S.A.* 116 E4
Stryama, *Bulgaria* 45 D8
Stryker, *U.S.A.* 108 B6
Stryków, *Poland* 31 G6
Stryy, *Ukraine* 33 H2
Strzegom, *Poland* 31 H3
Strzelce Krajeńskie, *Poland* 31 F2
Strzelce Opolskie, *Poland* 31 H5
Strzelecki Cr. →, *Australia* 95 D2
Strzelin, *Poland* 31 H4
Strzelno, *Poland* 31 F5
Strzybnica, *Poland* 31 H5
Strzyżów, *Poland* 31 J8
Stuart, *Fla., U.S.A.* 115 M5
Stuart, *Nebr., U.S.A.* 112 D5
Stuart →, *Canada* 102 C4
Stuart Bluff Ra., *Australia* 92 D5
Stuart L., *Canada* 102 C4
Stuart Ra., *Australia* 95 D1
Stubbekøbing, *Denmark* 11 K6
Stuben, *Austria* 26 D3
Studen Kladenets, Yazovir, *Bulgaria* 45 E9
Studenka, *Czech Rep.* 27 B11
Stugun, *Sweden* 10 A9
Stuhr, *Germany* 24 B4
Stull L., *Canada* 104 B1
Stung Treng = Stoeng Treng, *Cambodia* 64 F5
Stupart →, *Canada* 104 A1
Stupava, *Slovak Rep.* 27 C10
Stupino, *Russia* 32 E10
Sturgeon B., *Canada* 103 C9
Sturgeon Bay, *U.S.A.* 114 C2
Sturgeon Falls, *Canada* 104 C4
Sturgeon L., *Alta., Canada* 102 B5
Sturgeon L., *Ont., Canada* 104 C1
Sturgeon L., *Ont., Canada* 116 B6
Sturgis, *Canada* 103 C8
Sturgis, *Mich., U.S.A.* 114 E3
Sturgis, *S. Dak., U.S.A.* 112 C3
Sturkö, *Sweden* 11 H9
Štúrovo, *Slovak Rep.* 27 D11
Sturt △, *Australia* 95 D3
Sturt Cr. →, *Australia* 92 C4
Sturt Stony Desert, *Australia* 95 D3
Stutterheim, *S. Africa* 88 E4
Stuttgart, *Germany* 25 G5
Stuttgart, *U.S.A.* 113 H9
Stuttgart Echterdingen ✈ (STR), *Germany* 25 G5
Stuyvesant, *U.S.A.* 117 D11
Stykkishólmur, *Iceland* 8 D2
Styria = Steiermark □, *Austria* 26 D8
Styrsö, *Sweden* 11 G5
Su Xian = Suzhou, *China* 56 H9
Suakin, *Sudan* 80 D4
Suan, *N. Korea* 57 E14
Suaqui, *Mexico* 118 B3
Suar, *India* 69 E8
Subang, *Indonesia* 63 G12
Subansiri →, *India* 67 F18
Subarnarekha →, *India* 69 H12
Subayhah, *Si. Arabia* 70 D3
Subcetate, *Romania* 28 E8
Subi, *Indonesia* 62 D3
Subiaco, *Italy* 41 G10
Subotica, *Serbia & M.* 28 D4
Suca, *Ethiopia* 81 F4
Suceava, *Romania* 29 C11
Suceava □, *Romania* 29 C10
Suceava →, *Romania* 29 C11
Sucha-Beskidzka, *Poland* 31 J6
Suchań, *Poland* 31 E2
Suchan, *Russia* 54 C6
Suchedniów, *Poland* 31 G7
Suchitoto, *El Salv.* 120 D2
Suchou = Suzhou, *China* 59 B13
Süchow = Xuzhou, *China* 57 G9
Suchowola, *Poland* 30 E10
Suck →, *Ireland* 12 C3
Sucre, *Bolivia* 124 G5
Sućuraj, *Croatia* 41 E14
Sucuriú →, *Brazil* 125 H8
Sud, Pte. du, *Canada* 105 C7
Sud-Kivu □, *Dem. Rep. of the Congo* 86 C2
Sud-Ouest, Pte., *Canada* 105 C7
Suda →, *Russia* 32 C9
Sudak, *Ukraine* 33 K8
Sudan, *U.S.A.* 113 H3
Sudan ■, *Africa* 81 E3
Sudbury, *Canada* 104 C3
Sudbury, *U.K.* 15 E8
Sûdd, *Sudan* 81 F3
Sudeifel = Deutsch-Luxemburgischer ⌓, *Germany* 25 F2
Süderbrarup, *Germany* 24 A5
Süderlügum, *Germany* 24 A4
Süderoogsand, *Germany* 24 A4
Sudeten Mts. = Sudety, *Europe* 27 A9
Sudety, *Europe* 27 A9
Südheide ⌓, *Germany* 24 C6
Suðuroy, *Færoe Is.* 8 F9
Sudi, *Tanzania* 87 E4
Sudirman, Pegunungan, *Indonesia* 63 E9
Sudiţi, *Romania* 29 F12
Sudogda, *Russia* 34 C5
Sudong, Pulau, *Singapore* 65 d
Sudova Vyshnya, *Ukraine* 31 J10
Sudr, *Egypt* 80 B3
Sudzha, *Russia* 33 G8
Sue →, *Sudan* 81 F2
Sueca, *Spain* 39 F4
Suedinenie, *Bulgaria* 45 D8
Suemez I., *U.S.A.* 102 B2
Suez = El Suweis, *Egypt* 80 J8
Suez, G. of = Suweis, Khalîg el, *Egypt* 80 J8
Suez Canal = Suweis, Qanâ es, *Egypt* 80 H8
Suffield, *Canada* 102 C6
Suffolk, *U.S.A.* 114 G7
Suffolk □, *U.K.* 15 E9
Şugag, *Romania* 29 E8
Sugargrove, *U.S.A.* 116 E5
Sugarive →, *India* 69 F12
Suğla Gölü, *Turkey* 72 D5
Sugluk = Salluit, *Canada* 101 B12
Suhaia, Lacul, *Romania* 29 G10
Şuḩār, *Oman* 71 E8
Sühbaatar □, *Mongolia* 56 B8
Suhl, *Germany* 24 E6
Şuhut, *Turkey* 47 C12
Sui, *Pakistan* 68 E3
Sui Xian, *China* 56 G8
Šuica, *Bos.-H.* 28 G2
Suichang, *China* 59 C12
Suichuan, *China* 59 D10
Suide, *China* 56 F6
Suifenhe, *China* 57 B16
Suihua, *China* 60 B7
Suijiang, *China* 58 C4
Suining, *Hunan, China* 59 D8
Suining, *Jiangsu, China* 57 H9
Suining, *Sichuan, China* 58 B5
Suiping, *China* 56 H7
Suippes, *France* 19 C11
Suir →, *Ireland* 12 D4
Suisun City, *U.S.A.* 110 G4
Suixi, *China* 59 G8
Suiyang, *Guizhou, China* 58 D6
Suiyang, *Heilongjiang, China* 57 B16
Suizhong, *China* 57 D11
Suizhou, *China* 59 B9
Sujangarh, *India* 68 F6
Sukabumi, *Indonesia* 63 G12
Sukadana, *Indonesia* 62 E3
Sukagawa, *Japan* 55 F10
Sukaraja, *Indonesia* 62 E4
Sukawati, *Indonesia* 63 K18
Sukch'ŏn, *N. Korea* 57 E13
Sukhindol, *Bulgaria* 45 C9
Sukhinichi, *Russia* 32 E8
Sukhona →, *Russia* 52 D4
Sukhothai, *Thailand* 64 D2
Sukhumi = Sokhumi, *Georgia* 35 J5
Sukkur, *Pakistan* 68 F3
Sukkur Barrage, *Pakistan* 68 F3
Sukovo, *Serbia & M.* 44 C6
Sukri →, *India* 68 G4
Sukumo, *Japan* 55 H6
Sukunka →, *Canada* 102 B4
Sula →, *Ukraine* 33 H7
Sula, Kepulauan, *Indonesia* 63 E7
Sulaco →, *Honduras* 120 C2
Sulaiman Range, *Pakistan* 68 D3
Sulak →, *Russia* 35 J8
Sūlār, *Iran* 71 D6
Sulawesi, *Indonesia* 63 E6
Sulawesi Sea = Celebes Sea, *Indonesia* 63 D6
Sulawesi Selatan □, *Indonesia* 63 E6
Sulawesi Tengah □, *Indonesia* 63 E6
Sulawesi Tenggara □, *Indonesia* 63 E6
Sulawesi Utara □, *Indonesia* 63 D6
Sulechów, *Poland* 31 F2
Sulęcin, *Poland* 31 F2
Sulejów, *Poland* 31 G6
Sulejówek, *Poland* 31 F8
Süleymanlı, *Turkey* 47 C9
Sulima, *S. Leone* 82 D2
Sulina, *Romania* 29 E14
Sulina, Braţul →, *Romania* 29 E14
Sulingen, *Germany* 24 C4
Suliţa, *Romania* 29 C11
Sulitjelma, *Norway* 8 C17
Sułkowice, *Poland* 31 J6
Sullana, *Peru* 124 D2
Süller, *Turkey* 47 C11
Sullivan, *Ill., U.S.A.* 112 F10

Sullivan, *Ind., U.S.A.* 114 F2
Sullivan, *Mo., U.S.A.* 112 F9
Sullivan Bay, *Canada* 102 C3
Sullivan I. = Lanbi Kyun, *Burma* 65 G2
Sullom Voe, *U.K.* 13 A7
Sully-sur-Loire, *France* 19 E9
Sulmierzyce, *Poland* 31 G4
Sulmona, *Italy* 41 F10
Süloğlu, *Turkey* 45 E10
Sulphur, *La., U.S.A.* 113 K8
Sulphur, *Okla., U.S.A.* 113 H6
Sulphur Pt., *Canada* 102 A6
Sulphur Springs, *U.S.A.* 113 J7
Sultan, *Canada* 104 C3
Sultan, *U.S.A.* 110 C5
Sultan Dağları, *Turkey* 72 C4
Sultanhisar, *Turkey* 47 D10
Sultaniça, *Turkey* 45 F10
Sultaniye, *Turkey* 45 F12
Sultanpur, *Mad. P., India* 68 H8
Sultanpur, *Punjab, India* 68 D6
Sultanpur, *Ut. P., India* 69 F10
Sulu Arch., *Phil.* 61 J4
Sulu Sea, *E. Indies* 61 G4
Sülüklü, *Turkey* 72 C5
Sululta, *Ethiopia* 81 F4
Suluova, *Turkey* 72 B6
Suluq, *Libya* 79 B10
Sulzbach, *Germany* 25 F3
Sulzbach-Rosenberg, *Germany* 25 F7
Sulzberger Ice Shelf, *Antarctica* 5 E13
Sumalata, *Indonesia* 63 D6
Sumampa, *Argentina* 126 B3
Sumatera, *Indonesia* 62 D2
Sumatera Barat □, *Indonesia* 62 E2
Sumatera Utara □, *Indonesia* 62 D1
Sumatra = Sumatera, *Indonesia* 62 D2
Šumava △, *Czech Rep.* 26 C6
Sumba, *Indonesia* 63 F5
Sumba, Selat, *Indonesia* 63 F5
Sumbawa, *Indonesia* 62 F5
Sumbawa Besar, *Indonesia* 62 F5
Sumbawanga □, *Tanzania* 84 F6
Sumbe, *Angola* 84 G2
Sumbu △, *Zambia* 87 D3
Sumburgh Hd., *U.K.* 13 B7
Sumdeo, *India* 69 D8
Sumdo, *China* 69 B8
Sumedang, *Indonesia* 63 G12
Sümeg, *Hungary* 28 D2
Sumeih, *Sudan* 81 F2
Šumen = Shumen, *Bulgaria* 45 C10
Sumenep, *Indonesia* 63 G15
Sumgait = Sumqayıt, *Azerbaijan* 35 K9
Summer L., *U.S.A.* 108 E3
Summerland, *Canada* 102 D5
Summerside, *Canada* 105 C7
Summersville, *U.S.A.* 114 F5
Summerville, *Ga., U.S.A.* 115 H3
Summerville, *S.C., U.S.A.* 115 J5
Summit Lake, *Canada* 102 C4
Summit Peak, *U.S.A.* 109 H10
Sumner, *Iowa, U.S.A.* 112 D8
Sumner, *Wash., U.S.A.* 110 C4
Sumoto, *Japan* 55 G7
Šumperk, *Czech Rep.* 27 B9
Sumqayıt, *Azerbaijan* 35 K9
Sumter, *U.S.A.* 115 J5
Sumy, *Ukraine* 33 G8
Sun City, *S. Africa* 88 D4
Sun City, *Ariz., U.S.A.* 109 K7
Sun City, *Calif., U.S.A.* 111 M9
Sun City Center, *U.S.A.* 115 M4
Sun Lakes, *U.S.A.* 109 K8
Sun Valley, *U.S.A.* 108 E6
Sunagawa, *Japan* 54 C10
Sunan, *N. Korea* 57 E13
Sunart, L., *U.K.* 13 E3
Sunburst, *U.S.A.* 108 B8
Sunbury, *Australia* 95 F3
Sunbury, *U.S.A.* 117 F8
Sunchales, *Argentina* 126 C3
Suncho Corral, *Argentina* 126 B3
Sunch'ŏn, *S. Korea* 57 G14
Suncook, *U.S.A.* 117 C13
Sunda, Selat, *Indonesia* 62 F3
Sunda Is., *Indonesia* 96 H2
Sunda Str. = Sunda, Selat, *Indonesia* 62 F3
Sundance, *Canada* 103 B10
Sundance, *U.S.A.* 112 C2
Sundar Nagar, *India* 68 D7
Sundarbans, *Asia* 67 J16
Sundargarh, *India* 67 H14
Sundays = Sondags →, *S. Africa* 88 E4
Sunderland, *Canada* 116 B5
Sunderland, *U.K.* 14 C6
Sundown △, *Australia* 95 D5
Sundre, *Canada* 102 C6
Sunds, *Denmark* 11 H3
Sundsvall, *Sweden* 10 B11
Sundsvallsbukten, *Sweden* 10 B11
Sung Hei, *Vietnam* 65 G6
Sungai Acheh, *Malaysia* 65 c
Sungai Kolok, *Thailand* 65 J3
Sungai Lembing, *Malaysia* 65 L4
Sungai Petani, *Malaysia* 65 K3
Sungaigerong, *Indonesia* 62 E2
Sungailiat, *Indonesia* 62 E3
Sungaipenuh, *Indonesia* 62 E2
Sungari = Songhua Jiang →, *China* 60 B8
Sunghua Chiang = Songhua Jiang →, *China* 60 B8
Sungikai, *Sudan* 81 E2
Sungurlu, *Turkey* 72 B6
Sunja, *Croatia* 41 C13
Sunland Park, *U.S.A.* 109 L10
Sunnansjö, *Sweden* 10 D8
Sunndalsøra, *Norway* 9 E13
Sunne, *Sweden* 10 E7
Sunnemo, *Sweden* 10 E7
Sunnyside, *U.S.A.* 108 C3
Sunnyvale, *U.S.A.* 110 H4
Suntar, *Russia* 53 C12
Sunyani, *Ghana* 82 D4
Suomenselkä, *Finland* 8 E21
Suomussalmi, *Finland* 8 D23
Suoyarvi, *Russia* 32 A7
Supai, *U.S.A.* 109 H7
Supaul, *India* 69 F12
Superior, *Ariz., U.S.A.* 109 K8
Superior, *Mont., U.S.A.* 108 C6
Superior, *Nebr., U.S.A.* 112 E5
Superior, *Wis., U.S.A.* 112 B8
Superior, L., *N. Amer.* 104 C2
Supetar, *Croatia* 41 E13
Suphan Buri, *Thailand* 64 E3
Suphan Dağı, *Turkey* 70 B4
Supiori, *Indonesia* 63 E9
Supraśl, *Poland* 31 E10
Supraśl →, *Poland* 31 E9
Supung Shuiku, *China* 57 D13
Sūq Suwayq, *Si. Arabia* 70 E3
Suqian, *China* 57 H10
Suqutra = Socotra, *Yemen* 75 E5
Sūr, *Lebanon* 74 B4
Şūr, *Oman* 75 C6
Sur, Pt., *U.S.A.* 110 J5
Sura →, *Russia* 34 C8
Surab, *Pakistan* 68 E2
Surabaja = Surabaya, *Indonesia* 63 G15
Surabaya, *Indonesia* 63 G15
Surahammar, *Sweden* 10 E10
Suraia, *Romania* 29 E12
Surakarta, *Indonesia* 63 G14
Surakhany, *Azerbaijan* 35 K10
Šurany, *Slovak Rep.* 27 C11
Surat, *Australia* 95 D4
Surat, *India* 66 J8
Surat Thani, *Thailand* 65 H2
Suratgarh, *India* 68 E5
Suraż, *Poland* 31 F9
Surazh, *Belarus* 32 E6
Surazh, *Russia* 33 F7
Surduc, *Romania* 29 C8
Surduc Pasul, *Romania* 29 E8
Surdulica, *Serbia & M.* 44 D6
Surendranagar, *India* 68 H4
Surf, *U.S.A.* 111 L6
Surfers Paradise, *Australia* 95 D5
Surgères, *France* 20 B3
Surgut, *Russia* 52 C8
Sùria, *Spain* 38 D6
Suriapet, *India* 66 L11
Surigao, *Phil.* 61 G6
Surigao Strait, *Phil.* 61 F6
Surin, *Thailand* 64 E4
Surin Nua, Ko, *Thailand* 65 H1
Surinam = Suriname ■, *S. Amer.* 125 C7
Suriname ■, *S. Amer.* 125 C7
Suriname →, *Suriname* 125 B7
Sürmaq, *Iran* 71 D7
Sürmene, *Turkey* 73 B9
Surovikino, *Russia* 35 F6
Surrey, *Canada* 110 A4
Surrey □, *U.K.* 15 F7
Sursand, *India* 69 F11
Sursar →, *India* 69 F12
Sursee, *Switz.* 25 H4
Sursk, *Russia* 34 D7
Surskoye, *Russia* 34 C8
Surt, *Libya* 79 B9
Surt, Khalīj, *Libya* 79 B9
Surtanahu, *Pakistan* 68 F4
Surte, *Sweden* 11 G6
Surtsey, *Iceland* 8 E3
Sürüç, *Turkey* 73 D8
Suruga-Wan, *Japan* 55 G9
Susa, *Italy* 40 C4
Suså →, *Denmark* 11 J5
Sušac, *Croatia* 41 F13
Susak, *Croatia* 41 D11
Susaki, *Japan* 55 H6
Süsangerd, *Iran* 71 D6
Susanville, *U.S.A.* 108 F3
Susch, *Switz.* 25 J6
Suşehri, *Turkey* 73 B8
Sušice, *Czech Rep.* 26 B6
Susleni, *Moldova* 29 C13
Susner, *India* 68 H7
Susong, *China* 59 B11
Susquehanna, *U.S.A.* 117 E9
Susquehanna →, *U.S.A.* 117 G8
Susques, *Argentina* 126 A2
Sussex, *Canada* 105 C6
Sussex, *U.S.A.* 117 E10
Sussex, E. □, *U.K.* 15 G8
Sussex, W. □, *U.K.* 15 G7
Sustut →, *Canada* 102 B3
Susuman, *Russia* 53 C15
Susunu, *Indonesia* 63 E8
Susurluk, *Turkey* 47 B10
Susuz, *Turkey* 73 B10
Susz, *Poland* 30 E6
Sütçüler, *Turkey* 72 D4
Şuţeşti, *Romania* 29 E12
Sutherland, *S. Africa* 88 E3
Sutherland, *U.K.* 13 C4
Sutherland, *U.S.A.* 112 E4
Sutherland Falls, *N.Z.* 91 L1
Sutherlin, *U.S.A.* 108 E2
Suthri, *India* 68 H3
Sutjeska △, *Bos.-H.* 28 G3
Sutlej →, *Pakistan* 68 E4
Sutter, *U.S.A.* 110 F5
Sutter Creek, *U.S.A.* 110 G6
Sutton, *Canada* 117 A12
Sutton, *Nebr., U.S.A.* 112 E6
Sutton, *W. Va., U.S.A.* 114 F5
Sutton →, *Canada* 104 A3
Sutton Coldfield, *U.K.* 15 E6
Sutton in Ashfield, *U.K.* 14 D6
Sutton L., *Canada* 104 B3
Suttor →, *Australia* 94 C4
Suttsu, *Japan* 54 C10
Suva, *Fiji* 91 D8
Suva Gora, *Macedonia* 44 E5
Suva Planina, *Serbia & M.* 44 C6
Suva Reka, *Serbia & M.* 44 D4
Suvorov, *Russia* 32 E9
Suvorov Is. = Suwarrow Is., *Cook Is.* 97 J11
Suvorove, *Ukraine* 29 E13
Suvorovo, *Bulgaria* 45 C11
Suwałki, *Poland* 30 D9
Suwana, *Indonesia* 63 K18
Suwannaphum, *Thailand* 64 E4
Suwannee →, *U.S.A.* 115 L4
Suwanose-Jima, *Japan* 55 K4
Suwarrow Is., *Cook Is.* 97 J11
Suwayq aş Şuqban, *Iraq* 70 D5
Suweis, Khalîg el, *Egypt* 80 J8
Suweis, Qanâ es, *Egypt* 80 H8
Suwŏn, *S. Korea* 57 F14
Suzdal, *Russia* 32 D11
Suzhou, *Anhui, China* 56 H9
Suzhou, *Jiangsu, China* 59 B13
Suzu, *Japan* 55 F8
Suzu-Misaki, *Japan* 55 F8
Suzuka, *Japan* 55 G8
Suzzara, *Italy* 40 D7
Svalbard, *Arctic* 51 B5
Svalbard Radio = Longyearbyen, *Svalbard* 4 B8
Svalöv, *Sweden* 11 J7
Svalyava, *Ukraine* 28 B7
Svaneke, *Denmark* 11 J9
Svängsta, *Sweden* 11 H8
Svanskog, *Sweden* 10 E6
Svappavaara, *Sweden* 8 C19
Svärdsjö, *Sweden* 10 D9
Svartå, *Sweden* 10 E8
Svartisen, *Norway* 8 C15
Svartvik, *Sweden* 10 B11
Svatove, *Ukraine* 33 H10
Svatovo = Svatove, *Ukraine* 33 H10
Svay Chek, *Cambodia* 64 F4
Svay Rieng, *Cambodia* 65 G5
Svealand □, *Sweden* 10 D9
Svedala, *Sweden* 11 J7
Sveg, *Sweden* 10 B8
Svendborg, *Denmark* 11 J4
Svenljunga, *Sweden* 11 G7
Svenstavik, *Sweden* 10 B8
Svenstrup, *Denmark* 11 H3
Sverdlovsk, *Ukraine* 33 H10
Sverdrup Is., *Canada* 98 B10
Svetac, *Croatia* 41 E12
Sveti Nikola, Prokhad, *Europe* 44 C6
Sveti Nikole, *Macedonia* 44 E5
Sveti Rok, *Croatia* 41 D12
Svetlaya, *Russia* 54 A9
Svetlogorsk = Svyetlahorsk, *Belarus* 33 F5
Svetlogorsk, *Russia* 30 D7
Svetlograd, *Russia* 35 H6
Svetlovodsk = Svitlovodsk, *Ukraine* 33 H7
Svetlyy, *Russia* 30 D7
Svidník, *Slovak Rep.* 27 B14
Svilaja Planina, *Croatia* 41 E13
Svilajnac, *Serbia & M.* 44 B5
Svilengrad, *Bulgaria* 45 E10
Svir →, *Russia* 32 B7
Sviritsa, *Russia* 32 B7
Svishtov, *Bulgaria* 45 C9
Svislach, *Belarus* 31 E11
Svitava →, *Czech Rep.* 27 B9
Svitavy, *Czech Rep.* 27 B9
Svitlovodsk, *Ukraine* 33 H7
Svobodnyy, *Russia* 53 D13
Svoge, *Bulgaria* 44 D7
Svolvær, *Norway* 8 B16
Svratka →, *Czech Rep.* 27 B9
Svrljig, *Serbia & M.* 44 C6
Svyetlahorsk, *Belarus* 33 F5
Swabian Alps = Schwäbische Alb, *Germany* 25 G5
Swaffham, *U.K.* 15 E8
Swainsboro, *U.S.A.* 115 J4
Swakop →, *Namibia* 88 C2
Swakopmund, *Namibia* 88 C1
Swale →, *U.K.* 14 C6
Swan →, *Australia* 93 F2
Swan →, *Canada* 103 C8
Swan Hill, *Australia* 95 F3
Swan Hills, *Canada* 102 C5
Swan Is. = Santanilla, Is., *Honduras* 120 C3
Swan L., *Canada* 103 C8
Swan Peak, *U.S.A.* 108 C7
Swan Ra., *U.S.A.* 108 C7
Swan River, *Canada* 103 C8
Swanage, *U.K.* 15 G6
Swansea, *Australia* 95 G4
Swansea, *Canada* 116 C5
Swansea, *U.K.* 15 F4
Swansea □, *U.K.* 15 F3
Swar →, *Pakistan* 69 B5
Swartberge, *S. Africa* 88 E3
Swartmodder, *S. Africa* 88 D3
Swartnossob →, *Namibia* 88 C2
Swartruggens, *S. Africa* 88 D4
Swarzędz, *Poland* 31 F4
Swastika, *Canada* 104 C3
Swatow = Shantou, *China* 59 F11
Swaziland ■, *Africa* 89 D5
Sweden ■, *Europe* 9 G16
Swedru, *Ghana* 83 D4
Sweet Home, *U.S.A.* 108 D2
Sweetgrass, *U.S.A.* 108 B8
Sweetwater, *Nev., U.S.A.* 110 G7
Sweetwater, *Tenn., U.S.A.* 115 H3
Sweetwater, *Tex., U.S.A.* 113 J4
Sweetwater →, *U.S.A.* 108 E10
Swellendam, *S. Africa* 88 E3
Swider →, *Poland* 31 F8
Świdnica, *Poland* 31 H3
Świdnik, *Poland* 31 G9
Świdwin, *Poland* 30 E2
Świebodzice, *Poland* 31 H3
Świebodzin, *Poland* 31 F2
Świecie, *Poland* 30 E5
Swierzawa, *Poland* 31 G2
Świętokrzyski △, *Poland* 31 H7
Świętokrzyskie □, *Poland* 31 H7
Świętokrzyskie, Góry, *Poland* 31 H7
Swift Current, *Canada* 103 C7
Swift Current →, *Canada* 103 C7
Swilly, L., *Ireland* 12 A4
Swindon, *U.K.* 15 F6
Swindon □, *U.K.* 15 F6
Swinemünde = Świnoujście, *Poland* 30 E1
Swinford, *Ireland* 12 C3
Świnoujście, *Poland* 30 E1
Switzerland ■, *Europe* 25 J4
Swords, *Ireland* 12 C5
Swoyerville, *U.S.A.* 117 E9
Syasstroy, *Russia* 32 B7
Sychevka, *Russia* 32 E8
Syców, *Poland* 31 G4
Sydenham →, *Canada* 116 D2
Sydney, *Australia* 95 E5
Sydney, *Canada* 105 C7
Sydney L., *Canada* 103 C10
Sydney Mines, *Canada* 105 C7
Sydprøven = Alluitsup Paa, *Greenland* 101 B15
Sydra, G. of = Surt, Khalīj, *Libya* 79 B9
Syeverodonetsk, *Ukraine* 33 H10
Syke, *Germany* 24 C4
Sykesville, *U.S.A.* 116 E6
Syktyvkar, *Russia* 52 C6
Sylacauga, *U.S.A.* 115 J2
Sylarna, *Sweden* 8 E15
Sylhet, *Bangla.* 67 G17
Sylhet □, *Bangla.* 67 G17
Sylt, *Germany* 24 A4
Sylvan Beach, *U.S.A.* 117 C9
Sylvan Lake, *Canada* 102 C6
Sylvania, *U.S.A.* 115 J5
Sylvester, *U.S.A.* 115 K4
Sym, *Russia* 52 C9
Symón, *Mexico* 118 C4
Synelnykove, *Ukraine* 33 H8
Synevyr △, *Ukraine* 29 B8
Synevyrska Polyana, *Ukraine* 29 B8
Synnott Ra., *Australia* 92 C4
Synyak, *Ukraine* 28 B7
Syowa, *Antarctica* 5 C5
Syracuse, *Kans., U.S.A.* 113 G4
Syracuse, *N.Y., U.S.A.* 117 C8
Syracuse, *Nebr., U.S.A.* 112 E6
Syrdarya →, *Kazakhstan* 52 E7
Syria ■, *Asia* 70 C3
Syrian Desert = Shām, Bādiyat ash, *Asia* 70 C3
Sysslebäck, *Sweden* 10 D6
Syzran, *Russia* 34 D9
Szabolcs-Szatmár-Bereg □, *Hungary* 28 B6
Szadek, *Poland* 31 G5
Szamocin, *Poland* 31 E4
Szamos →, *Hungary* 28 B7
Szamotuły, *Poland* 31 F3
Száraz →, *Hungary* 28 D6
Szarvas, *Hungary* 28 D5
Százhalombatta, *Hungary* 28 C3
Szczawnica, *Poland* 31 J7
Szczebrzeszyn, *Poland* 31 H9
Szczecin, *Poland* 30 E1
Szczecinek, *Poland* 30 E3
Szczeciński, Zalew = Stettiner Haff, *Germany* 24 B10
Szczekociny, *Poland* 31 H6
Szczucin, *Poland* 31 H8
Szczuczyn, *Poland* 30 E9
Szczyrk, *Poland* 31 J6
Szczytna, *Poland* 31 H3
Szczytno, *Poland* 30 E7
Szechuan Basin = Sichuan Pendi, *China* 58 B5
Szechwan = Sichuan □, *China* 58 B5
Szécsény, *Hungary* 28 B4
Szeged, *Hungary* 28 D5
Szeghalom, *Hungary* 28 C6
Székesfehérvár, *Hungary* 28 C3
Szekszárd, *Hungary* 28 D3
Szendrő, *Hungary* 28 B5
Szentendre, *Hungary* 28 C4
Szentes, *Hungary* 28 D5
Szentgotthárd, *Hungary* 28 D1
Szentlőrinc, *Hungary* 28 D3
Szerencs, *Hungary* 28 B6
Szigetszentmiklós, *Hungary* 28 C4
Szigetvár, *Hungary* 28 D2
Szikszó, *Hungary* 28 B5
Szklarska Poreba, *Poland* 31 H2
Szkwa →, *Poland* 31 E8
Szlichtyngowa, *Poland* 31 G3
Szob, *Hungary* 28 C3
Szolnok, *Hungary* 28 C5
Szombathely, *Hungary* 28 C1
Szprotawa, *Poland* 31 G2
Sztum, *Poland* 30 E6
Sztutowo, *Poland* 30 D6
Szubin, *Poland* 31 E4
Szydłowiec, *Poland* 31 G7
Szypliszki, *Poland* 30 D10

T

Ta Khli Khok, *Thailand* 64 E3
Ta Lai, *Vietnam* 65 G6
Tab, *Hungary* 28 D3
Tabacal, *Argentina* 126 A3
Tabaco, *Phil.* 61 E5
Tabagné, *Ivory C.* 82 D4
Ţābah, *Si. Arabia* 70 E4
Tabanan, *Indonesia* 63 K18
Tabankort, *Niger* 83 B5
Ţabas, *Khorāsān, Iran* 71 C9
Ţabas, *Khorāsān, Iran* 71 C8
Tabasará, Serranía de, *Panama* 120 E3
Tabasco □, *Mexico* 119 D6
Tabāsīn, *Iran* 71 D8
Tabatinga, Serra da, *Brazil* 125 F10
Taber, *Canada* 102 D6
Taberg, *Sweden* 11 G8
Taberg, *U.S.A.* 117 C9
Tabla, *Niger* 83 C5
Tablas de Daimiel △, *Spain* 37 F7
Tablas I., *Phil.* 61 E5
Tablas Strait, *Phil.* 61 E4
Table B., *Canada* 105 B8
Table B., *S. Africa* 88 E2
Table Mt., *S. Africa* 88 E2
Table Rock L., *U.S.A.* 113 G8
Tabletop, Mt., *Australia* 94 C4
Tábor, *Czech Rep.* 26 B7
Tabora, *Tanzania* 86 D3
Tabora □, *Tanzania* 86 D3
Tabou, *Ivory C.* 82 E3
Tabrīz, *Iran* 70 B5
Tabuaeran, *Kiribati* 97 G12
Tabuenca, *Spain* 38 D3
Tabūk, *Si. Arabia* 70 D3
Taburno-Camposauro ⌓, *Italy* 43 A7
Täby, *Sweden* 10 E12
Tacámbaro de Codallos, *Mexico* 118 D4
Tacheng, *China* 60 B3
Tach'i, *Taiwan* 59 E13
Tachia, *Taiwan* 59 E13
Tach'ing Shan = Daqing Shan, *China* 56 D6
Tachov, *Czech Rep.* 26 B5
Tácina →, *Italy* 43 D9
Tacloban, *Phil.* 61 F6
Tacna, *Peru* 124 G4
Tacoma, *U.S.A.* 110 C4
Tacuarembó, *Uruguay* 127 C4
Tademaït, Plateau du, *Algeria* 78 C6
Tadio, L., *Ivory C.* 82 D3
Tadjoura, *Djibouti* 81 E5
Tadjoura, Golfe de, *Djibouti* 81 E5
Tadmor, *N.Z.* 91 J4
Tadoule L., *Canada* 103 B9
Tadoussac, *Canada* 105 C6
Tadrés ⌓, *Niger* 83 B6
Tadzhikistan = Tajikistan ■, *Asia* 52 F8
Taechŏn-ni, *S. Korea* 57 F14
Taegu, *S. Korea* 57 G15
Taegwan, *N. Korea* 57 D13
Taejŏn, *S. Korea* 57 F14
Taen, Ko, *Thailand* 65 b
Tafalla, *Spain* 38 C3
Tafar, *Sudan* 81 F2
Tafelbaai = Table B., *S. Africa* 88 E2
Tafermaar, *Indonesia* 63 F8
Tafí Viejo, *Argentina* 126 B2
Tafīhān, *Iran* 71 D7
Tafiré, *Ivory C.* 82 D3
Tafo, *Ghana* 83 D4
Tafresh, *Iran* 71 C6
Taft, *Iran* 71 D7
Taft, *Phil.* 61 F6
Taft, *U.S.A.* 111 K7
Taftān, Kūh-e, *Iran* 71 D9
Taga Dzong, *Bhutan* 67 F16
Taganrog, *Russia* 33 J10
Taganrogskiy Zaliv, *Russia* 33 J10
Tagânt, *Mauritania* 82 B2
Tagatay, *Phil.* 61 D4
Tagbilaran, *Phil.* 61 G5
Tággia, *Italy* 40 E4
Tagish, *Canada* 102 A2
Tagish L., *Canada* 102 A2
Tagliacozzo, *Italy* 41 F10
Tagliamento →, *Italy* 41 C10
Táglio di Po, *Italy* 41 D9
Tago, *Phil.* 61 G7
Tagomago, *Spain* 48 B8
Tagourāret, *Mauritania* 82 B3
Taguatinga, *Brazil* 125 F10
Tagudin, *Phil.* 61 C4
Tagum, *Phil.* 61 H6
Tagus = Tejo →, *Europe* 37 F2
Tahakopa, *N.Z.* 91 M2
Tahan, Gunung, *Malaysia* 65 K4
Tahat, *Algeria* 78 D7
Tāherī, *Iran* 71 E7
Tahiti, *French Polynesia* 97 J13
Tahlequah, *U.S.A.* 113 H7
Tahoe, L., *U.S.A.* 110 G6
Tahoe City, *U.S.A.* 110 F6
Tahoka, *U.S.A.* 113 J4
Taholah, *U.S.A.* 110 C2
Tahoua, *Niger* 83 C6
Tahrūd, *Iran* 71 D8
Tahsis, *Canada* 102 D3
Tahta, *Egypt* 80 B3
Tahtaköprü, *Turkey* 45 G13
Tahtalı Dağları, *Turkey* 72 C7
Tahulandang, *Indonesia* 63 D7
Tahuna, *Indonesia* 63 D7
Taï, *Ivory C.* 82 D3
Taï △, *Ivory C.* 82 D3
Tai Hu, *China* 59 B12
Tai Rom Yen △, *Thailand* 65 H2

Tai Shan, *China* 57 F9
Tai'an, *China* 57 F9
Taibei = T'aipei, *Taiwan* 59 E13
Taibique, *Canary Is.* 48 G2
Taibus Qi, *China* 56 D8
Taicang, *China* 59 B13
T'aichung, *Taiwan* 59 E13
Taieri →, *N.Z.* 91 M3
Taigu, *China* 56 F7
Taihang Shan, *China* 56 G7
Taihape, *N.Z.* 91 H5
Taihe, *Anhui, China* 56 H8
Taihe, *Jiangxi, China* 59 D10
Taihu, *China* 59 B11
Taijiang, *China* 58 D7
Taikang, *China* 56 G8
Tailem Bend, *Australia* 95 F2
Tailfingen, *Germany* 25 G5
Tailuko, *Taiwan* 59 E13
Taimyr Peninsula = Taymyr, Poluostrov, *Russia* 53 B11
Tain, *U.K.* 13 D4
T'ainan, *Taiwan* 59 F13
Taínaron, Ákra, *Greece* 46 E4
Taining, *China* 59 D11
T'aipei, *Taiwan* 59 E13
Taiping, *China* 59 B12
Taiping, *Malaysia* 65 K3
Taipingzhen, *China* 56 H6
Tairbeart = Tarbert, *U.K.* 13 D2
Taishan, *China* 59 F9
Taishun, *China* 59 D12
Taita Hills, *Kenya* 86 C4
Taitao, Pen. de, *Chile* 128 F2
T'aitung, *Taiwan* 59 F13
Taivalkoski, *Finland* 8 D23
Taiwan ■, *Asia* 59 F13
Taiwan Strait, *Asia* 59 E12
Taixing, *China* 59 A13
Taiyara, *Sudan* 81 E3
Taïyetos Óros, *Greece* 46 D4
Taiyiba, *Israel* 74 C4
Taiyuan, *China* 56 F7
Taizhong = T'aichung, *Taiwan* 59 E13
Taizhou, *China* 59 A12
Taizhou Liedao, *China* 59 C13
Ta'izz, *Yemen* 75 E3
Tājābād, *Iran* 71 D7
Tajikistan ■, *Asia* 52 F8
Tajima, *Japan* 55 F9
Tajo = Tejo →, *Europe* 37 F2
Tajrīsh, *Iran* 71 C6
Tak, *Thailand* 64 D2
Takāb, *Iran* 70 B5
Takachiho, *Japan* 55 H5
Takachu, *Botswana* 88 C3
Takada, *Japan* 55 F9
Takahagi, *Japan* 55 F10
Takaka, *N.Z.* 91 J4
Takamatsu, *Japan* 55 G7
Takaoka, *Japan* 55 F8
Takapuna, *N.Z.* 91 G5
Takasaki, *Japan* 55 F9
Takatsuki, *Japan* 55 G7
Takaungu, *Kenya* 86 C4
Takayama, *Japan* 55 F8
Take-Shima, *Japan* 55 J5
Takefu, *Japan* 55 G8
Takengon, *Indonesia* 62 D1
Takeo, *Japan* 55 H5
Tåkern, *Sweden* 11 F8
Takeshima = Tok-do, *Asia* 55 F5
Tākestān, *Iran* 71 C6
Taketa, *Japan* 55 H5
Takev, *Cambodia* 65 G5
Takh, *India* 69 C7
Takht-Sulaiman, *Pakistan* 68 D3
Takikawa, *Japan* 54 C10
Takla L., *Canada* 102 B3
Takla Landing, *Canada* 102 B3
Takla Makan = Taklamakan Shamo, *China* 60 C3
Taklamakan Shamo, *China* 60 C3
Taku →, *Canada* 102 B2
Takua Thung, *Thailand* 65 a
Takum, *Nigeria* 83 D6
Tal Halāl, *Iran* 71 D7
Tala, *Uruguay* 127 C4
Talachyn, *Belarus* 32 E5
Talacogan, *Phil.* 61 G6
Talagang, *Pakistan* 68 C5
Talagante, *Chile* 126 C1
Talak, *Niger* 83 B6
Talamanca, Cordillera de, *Cent. Amer.* 120 E3
Talant, *France* 19 E11
Talara, *Peru* 124 D2
Talas, *Kyrgyzstan* 52 E8
Talas, *Turkey* 72 C6
Talâta, *Egypt* 74 E1
Talata Mafara, *Nigeria* 83 C6
Talaud, Kepulauan, *Indonesia* 63 D7
Talaud Is. = Talaud, Kepulauan, *Indonesia* 63 D7
Talavera de la Reina, *Spain* 36 F6
Talavera la Real, *Spain* 37 G4
Talayan, *Phil.* 61 H6
Talayuela, *Spain* 36 F5
Talbandh, *India* 69 H12
Talbert, Sillon de, *France* 18 D3
Talbot, C., *Australia* 92 B4
Talbragar →, *Australia* 95 E4
Talca, *Chile* 126 D1
Talcahuano, *Chile* 126 D1
Talcher, *India* 67 J14
Talcho, *Niger* 83 C5
Taldy Kurgan = Taldyqorghan, *Kazakhstan* 52 E8
Taldyqorghan, *Kazakhstan* 52 E8
Tālesh, *Iran* 71 B6
Tālesh, Kūhhā-ye, *Iran* 71 B6
Talguharai, *Sudan* 80 D4
Tali Post, *Sudan* 81 F3
Taliabu, *Indonesia* 63 E6
Talibon, *Phil.* 63 B6
Talibong, Ko, *Thailand* 65 J2
Talihina, *U.S.A.* 113 H7
Talisayan, *Phil.* 61 G6
Taliwang, *Indonesia* 62 F5
Tall 'Afar, *Iraq* 70 B4
Tall Kalakh, *Syria* 74 A5
Talla, *Egypt* 80 B3
Talladega, *U.S.A.* 115 J2
Tallahassee, *U.S.A.* 115 K3
Tallangatta, *Australia* 95 F4
Tallard, *France* 21 D10
Tällberg, *Sweden* 10 D9
Tallering Pk., *Australia* 93 E2
Talli, *Pakistan* 68 E3
Tallinn, *Estonia* 9 G21
Tallmadge, *U.S.A.* 116 E3
Tallulah, *U.S.A.* 113 J9
Tălmaciu, *Romania* 29 E9
Talmont-St-Hilaire, *France* 20 B2
Talne, *Ukraine* 33 H6
Talnoye = Talne, *Ukraine* 33 H6
Talodi, *Sudan* 81 E3
Talovaya, *Russia* 34 E5
Taloyoak, *Canada* 100 B10
Talpa de Allende, *Mexico* 118 C4
Talparo, *Trin. & Tob.* 125 K15
Talsi, *Latvia* 9 H20
Talsi □, *Latvia* 30 A9
Taltal, *Chile* 126 B1
Taltson →, *Canada* 102 A6
Talwood, *Australia* 95 D4
Talyawalka Cr. →, *Australia* 95 E3
Tam Ky, *Vietnam* 64 E7
Tam Quan, *Vietnam* 64 E7
Tama, *U.S.A.* 112 E8
Tama ⌂, *Ethiopia* 81 F4
Tamale, *Ghana* 83 D4
Taman, *Russia* 33 K9
Taman Negara △, *Malaysia* 65 K4
Tamani, *Mali* 82 C3
Tamano, *Japan* 55 G6
Tamanrasset, *Algeria* 78 D7
Tamaqua, *U.S.A.* 117 F9
Tamar →, *U.K.* 15 G3
Tamarinda, *Spain* 48 B10
Tamarite de Litera, *Spain* 38 D5
Tamashima, *Japan* 55 G6
Tamási, *Hungary* 28 D3
Tamaské, *Niger* 83 C6
Tamaulipas □, *Mexico* 119 C5
Tamaulipas, Sierra de, *Mexico* 119 C5
Tamazula, *Mexico* 118 C3
Tamazunchale, *Mexico* 119 C5
Tamba-Dabatou, *Guinea* 82 C2
Tambacounda, *Senegal* 82 C2
Tambelan, Kepulauan, *Indonesia* 62 D3
Tambellup, *Australia* 93 F2
Tambo, *Australia* 94 C4
Tambo de Mora, *Peru* 124 F3
Tambohorano, *Madag.* 89 B7
Tambora, *Indonesia* 62 F5
Tambov, *Russia* 34 D5
Tambre →, *Spain* 36 C2
Tambuku, *Indonesia* 63 G15
Tamburâ, *Sudan* 81 F2
Tâmchekket, *Mauritania* 82 B2
Tâmega →, *Portugal* 36 D2
Tamenglong, *India* 67 G18
Tamgué, Massif du, *Guinea* 82 C2
Tamiahua, L. de, *Mexico* 119 C5
Tamil Nadu □, *India* 66 P10
Tamis →, *Serbia & M.* 28 F5
Tamluk, *India* 69 H12
Tammerfors = Tampere, *Finland* 9 F20
Tammisaari, *Finland* 9 F20
Tämnaren, *Sweden* 10 D11
Tamo Abu, Pegunungan, *Malaysia* 62 D5
Tampa, *U.S.A.* 115 M4
Tampa, Tanjung, *Indonesia* 63 K19
Tampa B., *U.S.A.* 115 M4
Tampere, *Finland* 9 F20
Tampico, *Mexico* 119 C5
Tampin, *Malaysia* 65 L4
Tampoi, *Malaysia* 65 d
Tamsweg, *Austria* 26 D6
Tamu, *Burma* 67 G19
Tamuja →, *Spain* 37 F4
Tamworth, *Australia* 95 E5
Tamworth, *Canada* 116 B8
Tamworth, *U.K.* 15 E6
Tamyang, *S. Korea* 57 G14
Tan An, *Vietnam* 65 G6
Tan Chau, *Vietnam* 65 G5
Tan-Tan, *Morocco* 78 C3
Tana →, *Kenya* 86 C5
Tana →, *Norway* 8 A23
Tana, L., *Ethiopia* 81 E4
Tana River Primate ⌂, *Kenya* 86 C5
Tanabe, *Japan* 55 H7
Tanafjorden, *Norway* 8 A23
Tanahbala, *Indonesia* 62 E1
Tanahgrogot, *Indonesia* 62 E5
Tanahjampea, *Indonesia* 63 F6
Tanahmasa, *Indonesia* 62 E1
Tanahmerah, *Indonesia* 63 F10
Tanakpur, *India* 69 E9
Tanakura, *Japan* 55 F10
Tanami, *Australia* 92 C4
Tanami Desert, *Australia* 92 C5
Tanana →, *U.S.A.* 100 B4
Tananarive = Antananarivo, *Madag.* 89 B8
Tánaro →, *Italy* 40 D5
Tancheng, *China* 57 G10
Tanch'ŏn, *N. Korea* 57 D15
Tanda, *Ut. P., India* 69 F10
Tanda, *Ut. P., India* 69 E8
Tanda, *Ivory C.* 82 D4
Tandag, *Phil.* 61 G7
Tandaia, *Tanzania* 87 D3
Tăndărei, *Romania* 29 F12
Tandaué, *Angola* 88 B2
Tandil, *Argentina* 126 D4
Tandil, Sa. del, *Argentina* 126 D4
Tandlianwala, *Pakistan* 68 D5
Tando Adam, *Pakistan* 68 G3
Tando Allahyar, *Pakistan* 68 G3
Tando Bago, *Pakistan* 68 G3
Tando Mohommed Khan, *Pakistan* 68 G3
Tandou L., *Australia* 95 E3
Tandragee, *U.K.* 12 B5
Tandsjöborg, *Sweden* 10 C8
Tane-ga-Shima, *Japan* 55 J5
Taneatua, *N.Z.* 91 H6
Tanen Tong Dan = Dawna Ra., *Burma* 64 D2
Tanew →, *Poland* 31 H9
Tanezrouft, *Algeria* 78 D6
Tang, Koh, *Cambodia* 65 G4
Tang, Ra's-e, *Iran* 71 E8
Tang Krasang, *Cambodia* 64 F5
Tanga, *Tanzania* 86 D4
Tanga □, *Tanzania* 86 D4
Tanganyika, L., *Africa* 86 D3
Tangaza, *Nigeria* 83 C5
Tanger, *Morocco* 78 A4
Tangerang, *Indonesia* 63 G12
Tangerhütte, *Germany* 24 C7
Tangermünde, *Germany* 24 C7
Tanggu, *China* 57 E9
Tanggula Shan, *China* 60 C4
Tanghe, *China* 56 H7
Tanghla Range = Tanggula Shan, *China* 60 C4
Tangier = Tanger, *Morocco* 78 A4
Tangorin, *Australia* 94 C3
Tangorombohitr'i Makay, *Madag.* 89 C8
Tangshan, *China* 57 E10
Tangtou, *China* 57 G10
Tanguiéta, *Benin* 83 C5
Tangxi, *China* 59 C12
Tangyan He →, *China* 58 C7
Tanimbar, Kepulauan, *Indonesia* 63 F8
Tanimbar Is. = Tanimbar, Kepulauan, *Indonesia* 63 F8
Taninthari = Tenasserim, *Burma* 65 F2
Tanjay, *Phil.* 61 G5
Tanjong Malim, *Malaysia* 65 L3
Tanjong Pelepas, *Malaysia* 65 d
Tanjore = Thanjavur, *India* 66 P11
Tanjung, *Indonesia* 63 J19
Tanjung, *Phil.* 62 E5
Tanjung Tokong, *Malaysia* 65 c
Tanjungbalai, *Indonesia* 62 D1
Tanjungbatu, *Indonesia* 62 D5
Tanjungkarang Telukbetung, *Indonesia* 62 F3
Tanjungpandan, *Indonesia* 62 E3
Tanjungpinang, *Indonesia* 62 D2
Tanjungredeb, *Indonesia* 62 D5
Tanjungselor, *Indonesia* 62 D5
Tank, *Pakistan* 68 C4
Tankhala, *India* 68 J5
Tankwa-Karoo △, *S. Africa* 88 E2
Tännäs, *Sweden* 10 B6
Tannersville, *U.S.A.* 117 E9
Tannis Bugt, *Denmark* 11 G4
Tannu-Ola, *Russia* 53 D10
Tannum Sands, *Australia* 94 C5
Tano →, *Ghana* 82 D4
Tanon Str., *Phil.* 61 F5
Tanout, *Niger* 83 C6
Tanshui, *Taiwan* 59 E13
Tansilla, *Burkina Faso* 82 C4
Tanta, *Egypt* 80 H7
Tantoyuca, *Mexico* 119 C5
Tantung = Dandong, *China* 57 D13
Tanumshede, *Sweden* 11 F5
Tanunda, *Australia* 95 E2
Tanus, *France* 20 D6
Tanzania ■, *Africa* 86 D3
Tanzilla →, *Canada* 102 B2
Tao, Ko, *Thailand* 65 G2
Tao'an = Taonan, *China* 57 B12
Tao'er He →, *China* 57 B13
Taohua Dao, *China* 59 C14
Taolanaro, *Madag.* 89 D8
Taole, *China* 56 E4
Taonan, *China* 57 B12
Taormina, *Italy* 43 E8
Taos, *U.S.A.* 109 H11
Taoudenni, *Mali* 78 D5
Taoyuan, *China* 59 C8
T'aoyüan, *Taiwan* 59 E13
Tapa, *Estonia* 9 G21
Tapa Shan = Daba Shan, *China* 58 B7
Tapachula, *Mexico* 119 E6
Tapah, *Malaysia* 65 K3
Tapajós →, *Brazil* 125 D8
Tapaktuan, *Indonesia* 62 D1
Tapanahoni →, *Suriname* 125 C8
Tapanui, *N.Z.* 91 L2
Tapauá →, *Brazil* 124 E6
Tapes, *Brazil* 127 C5
Tapeta, *Liberia* 82 D3
Taphan Hin, *Thailand* 64 D3
Tapi →, *India* 66 J8
Tapia de Casariego, *Spain* 36 B4
Tapirapecó, Serra, *Venezuela* 124 C6
Tapo-Capara △, *Venezuela* 121 E5
Tapolca, *Hungary* 28 D2
Tapuae-o-Uenuku, *N.Z.* 91 K4
Tapul Group, *Phil.* 61 J4
Tapurucuará, *Brazil* 124 D5
Ţaqţaq, *Iraq* 70 C5
Taquara, *Brazil* 127 B5
Taquari →, *Brazil* 124 G7
Tara, *Australia* 95 D5
Tara, *Canada* 116 B3
Tara, *Russia* 52 D8
Tara, *Zambia* 87 F2
Tara △, *Serbia & M.* 44 C3
Tara →, *Serbia & M.* 44 C2
Taraba □, *Nigeria* 83 D7
Taraba →, *Nigeria* 83 D7
Tarābulus, *Lebanon* 74 A4
Tarābulus, *Libya* 79 B8
Taraclia, *Taraclia, Moldova* 29 E13
Taraclia, *Tighina, Moldova* 29 D14
Taradehi, *India* 69 H8
Tarajalejo, *Canary Is.* 48 F5
Tarakan, *Indonesia* 62 D5
Tarakit, Mt., *Kenya* 86 B4
Tarama-Jima, *Japan* 55 M2
Taran, Mys, *Russia* 9 J18
Taranagar, *India* 68 E6
Taranaki □, *N.Z.* 91 H5
Taranaki, Mt., *N.Z.* 91 H5
Tarancón, *Spain* 38 E1
Tarangire △, *Tanzania* 86 C4
Taransay, *U.K.* 13 D1
Táranto, *Italy* 43 B10
Táranto, G. di, *Italy* 43 B10
Tarapacá, *Colombia* 124 D5
Tarapacá □, *Chile* 126 A2
Tarapoto, *Peru* 124 E3
Tarare, *France* 21 C8
Tararua Ra., *N.Z.* 91 J5
Tarascon, *France* 21 E8
Tarascon-sur-Ariège, *France* 20 F5
Tarashcha, *Ukraine* 33 H6
Tarauacá, *Brazil* 124 E4
Tarauacá →, *Brazil* 124 E5
Taravo →, *France* 21 G12
Tarawa, *Kiribati* 96 G9
Tarawera, *N.Z.* 91 H6
Tarawera, L., *N.Z.* 91 H6
Taraz, *Kazakhstan* 52 E8
Tarazona, *Spain* 38 D3
Tarazona de la Mancha, *Spain* 39 F3
Tarbagatay, Khrebet, *Kazakhstan* 52 E9
Tarbat Ness, *U.K.* 13 D5
Tarbela Dam, *Pakistan* 68 B5
Tarbert, *Arg. & Bute, U.K.* 13 F3
Tarbert, *W. Isles, U.K.* 13 D2
Tarbes, *France* 20 E4
Tarboro, *U.S.A.* 115 H7
Tarcău, Munţii, *Romania* 29 D11
Tarcento, *Italy* 41 B10
Tarcoola, *Australia* 95 E1
Tarcoon, *Australia* 95 E4
Tardets-Sorholus, *France* 20 E3
Tardoire →, *France* 20 C4
Taree, *Australia* 95 E5
Tarfa, W. el →, *Egypt* 80 B3
Tarfaya, *Morocco* 78 C3
Târgovişte, *Romania* 29 F10
Târgu Bujor, *Romania* 29 E12
Târgu Cărbuneşti, *Romania* 29 F8
Târgu Frumos, *Romania* 29 C12
Târgu-Jiu, *Romania* 29 E8
Târgu Lăpuş, *Romania* 29 C8
Târgu Mureş, *Romania* 29 D9
Târgu Neamţ, *Romania* 29 C11
Târgu Ocna, *Romania* 29 D11
Târgu Secuiesc, *Romania* 29 E11
Târguşor, *Romania* 29 F13
Tărhăus, Vf., *Romania* 29 D11
Ţarif, *U.A.E.* 71 E7
Tarifa, *Spain* 37 J5
Tarija, *Bolivia* 126 A3
Tarija □, *Bolivia* 126 A3
Tariku →, *Indonesia* 63 E9
Tarim Basin = Tarim Pendi, *China* 60 C3
Tarim He →, *China* 60 C3
Tarim Pendi, *China* 60 C3
Taritatu →, *Indonesia* 63 E9
Tarka →, *S. Africa* 88 E4
Tarkastad, *S. Africa* 88 E4
Tarkhankut, Mys, *Ukraine* 33 K7
Tarko Sale, *Russia* 52 C8
Tarkwa, *Ghana* 82 D4
Tarlac, *Phil.* 61 D4
Tarm, *Denmark* 11 J2
Tarma, *Peru* 124 F3
Tarn □, *France* 20 E6
Tarn →, *France* 20 D5
Tarn-et-Garonne □, *France* 20 D5
Tarna →, *Hungary* 28 C4
Târnava Mare →, *Romania* 29 D8
Târnava Mică →, *Romania* 29 D8
Târnăveni, *Romania* 29 D9
Tarnica, *Poland* 31 J9
Tarnobrzeg, *Poland* 31 H8
Tarnogród, *Poland* 31 H9
Tarnos, *France* 20 E2
Târnova, *Moldova* 29 B12
Târnova, *Romania* 28 E6
Tarnów, *Poland* 31 H8
Tarnowskie Góry, *Poland* 31 H5
Tärnsjö, *Sweden* 10 D10
Táro →, *Italy* 40 C7
Ţārom, *Iran* 71 D7
Taroom, *Australia* 95 D4
Taroudannt, *Morocco* 78 B4
Tarp, *Germany* 24 A5
Tarpon Springs, *U.S.A.* 115 L4
Tarquínia, *Italy* 41 F8
Tarragona, *Spain* 38 D6
Tarragona □, *Spain* 38 D6
Tarraleah, *Australia* 95 G4
Tarrasa = Terrassa, *Spain* 38 D7
Tàrrega, *Spain* 38 D6
Tarrytown, *U.S.A.* 117 E11
Tårs, *Denmark* 11 G4
Tarshiha = Me'ona, *Israel* 74 B4
Tarsus, *Turkey* 70 B2
Tartagal, *Argentina* 126 A3
Tärtär, *Azerbaijan* 35 K8
Tärtär →, *Azerbaijan* 35 K8
Tartas, *France* 20 E3
Tartu, *Estonia* 9 G22
Ţarţūs, *Syria* 70 C2
Tarumizu, *Japan* 55 J5
Tarussa, *Russia* 32 E9
Tarutao = Ko Tarutao △, *Thailand* 65 J2
Tarutao, Ko, *Thailand* 65 J2
Tarutung, *Indonesia* 62 D1
Tarutyne, *Ukraine* 29 D14
Tarvísio, *Italy* 41 B10
Taseko →, *Canada* 102 C4
Tash-Kömür, *Kyrgyzstan* 52 E8
Tash-Kumyr = Tash-Kömür, *Kyrgyzstan* 52 E8
Tashauz = Dashhowuz, *Turkmenistan* 52 E6
Tashi Chho Dzong = Thimphu, *Bhutan* 67 F16
Ţashk, Daryācheh-ye, *Iran* 71 D7
Tashkent = Toshkent, *Uzbekistan* 52 E7
Tashtagol, *Russia* 52 D9
Tasiilaq, *Greenland* 4 C6
Tasikmalaya, *Indonesia* 63 G13
Tåsinge, *Denmark* 11 J4
Tåsjön, *Sweden* 8 D16
Taskan, *Russia* 53 C16
Tasker, *Niger* 83 C7
Taşköprü, *Turkey* 72 B6
Taşlâc, *Moldova* 29 C14
Tasman B., *N.Z.* 91 J4
Tasman Mts., *N.Z.* 91 J4
Tasman Pen., *Australia* 95 G4
Tasman Plateau, *S. Ocean* 5 A10
Tasman Sea, *Pac. Oc.* 96 L8
Tasmania □, *Australia* 95 G4
Tăşnad, *Romania* 28 C7
Tassili n'Ajjer, *Algeria* 78 C7
Tassili Tin-Rerhoh, *Algeria* 83 A5
Tata, *Hungary* 28 C3
Tatabánya, *Hungary* 28 C3
Tatahouine, *Tunisia* 79 B8
Tataouine, *Tunisia* 79 B8
Tatar Republic = Tatarstan □, *Russia* 34 C10
Tatarbunary, *Ukraine* 29 E14
Tatarsk, *Russia* 52 D8
Tatarstan □, *Russia* 34 C10
Tateyama, *Japan* 55 G9
Tathlina L., *Canada* 102 A5
Tathra, *Australia* 95 F4
Tatinnai L., *Canada* 103 A9
Tatla L., *Canada* 102 C4
Tatlısu, *Turkey* 45 F11
Tatnam, C., *Canada* 103 B10
Tatra = Tatry, *Slovak Rep.* 27 B13
Tatranský △, *Slovak Rep.* 27 B13
Tatry, *Slovak Rep.* 27 B13
Tatshenshini →, *Canada* 102 B1
Tatsuno, *Japan* 55 G7
Tatta, *Pakistan* 68 G2
Tatuī, *Brazil* 127 A6
Tatum, *U.S.A.* 113 J3
Tat'ung = Datong, *China* 56 D7
Tatvan, *Turkey* 70 B4
Taubaté, *Brazil* 127 A6
Tauberbischofsheim, *Germany* 25 F5
Taucha, *Germany* 24 D8
Tauern-tunnel, *Austria* 26 D6
Taufikia, *Sudan* 81 F3
Taulé, *France* 18 D3
Taumarunui, *N.Z.* 91 H5
Taumaturgo, *Brazil* 124 E4
Taung, *S. Africa* 88 D3
Taungdwingyi, *Burma* 67 J19
Taunggyi, *Burma* 67 J20
Taungup, *Burma* 67 K19
Taungup Taunggya, *Burma* 67 K18
Taunsa, *Pakistan* 68 D4
Taunsa Barrage, *Pakistan* 68 D4
Taunton, *U.K.* 15 F4
Taunton, *U.S.A.* 117 E13
Taunus, *Germany* 25 E4
Taupo, *N.Z.* 91 H6
Taupo, L., *N.Z.* 91 H5
Tauragė, *Lithuania* 9 J20
Tauragė □, *Lithuania* 30 C9
Tauranga, *N.Z.* 91 G6
Tauranga Harb., *N.Z.* 91 G6
Taureau, Rés., *Canada* 104 C5
Taurianova, *Italy* 43 D9
Taurus Mts. = Toros Dağları, *Turkey* 70 B2
Tauste, *Spain* 38 D3
Tauz = Tovuz, *Azerbaijan* 35 K7
Tavas, *Turkey* 47 D11
Tavastehus = Hämeenlinna, *Finland* 9 F21
Tavda, *Russia* 52 D7
Tavda →, *Russia* 52 D7
Tavernes de la Valldigna, *Spain* 39 F4
Taveta, *Tanzania* 86 C4
Taveuni, *Fiji* 91 C9
Taviano, *Italy* 43 C11
Tavignano →, *France* 21 F13
Tavira, *Portugal* 37 H3
Tavistock, *Canada* 116 C4
Tavistock, *U.K.* 15 G3
Tavolara, *Italy* 42 B2
Távora →, *Portugal* 36 D3
Tavoy, *Burma* 64 E2
Tavşanlı, *Turkey* 47 B11
Taw →, *U.K.* 15 F3
Tawa →, *India* 68 H8
Tawas City, *U.S.A.* 114 C4
Tawau, *Malaysia* 62 D5
Taweisha, *Sudan* 81 E2

Tawitawi, *Phil.* 63 B6
Tawu, *Taiwan* 59 F13
Taxco de Alarcón, *Mexico* 119 D5
Taxila, *Pakistan* 68 C5
Tay ⌓, *U.K.* 13 E5
Tay →, *U.K.* 13 E5
Tay, Firth of, *U.K.* 13 E5
Tay, L., *Australia* 93 F3
Tay, L., *U.K.* 13 E4
Tay Ninh, *Vietnam* 65 G6
Tayabamba, *Peru* 124 E3
Tayabas Bay, *Phil.* 61 E4
Taylakova, *Russia* 52 D8
Taylakovy = Taylakova, *Russia* 52 D8
Taylor, *Canada* 102 B4
Taylor, *Nebr., U.S.A.* 112 E5
Taylor, *Pa., U.S.A.* 117 E9
Taylor, *Tex., U.S.A.* 113 K6
Taylor, Mt., *U.S.A.* 109 J10
Taylorville, *U.S.A.* 112 F10
Taymā, *Si. Arabia* 70 E3
Taymyr, Oz., *Russia* 53 B11
Taymyr, Poluostrov, *Russia* 53 B11
Tayport, *U.K.* 13 E6
Tayrona △, *Colombia* 121 D5
Tayshet, *Russia* 53 D10
Taytay, *Phil.* 61 F3
Tāyyebād, *Iran* 71 C9
Tāyyebād □, *Iran* 71 C9
Taz →, *Russia* 52 C8
Taza, *Morocco* 78 B5
Tāza Khurmātū, *Iraq* 70 C5
Tazawa-Ko, *Japan* 54 E10
Tazin, *Canada* 103 B7
Tazin L., *Canada* 103 B7
Tazovskiy, *Russia* 52 C8
Tbilisi, *Georgia* 35 K7
Tchad = Chad ■, *Africa* 79 F8
Tchad, L., *Chad* 79 F8
Tchaourou, *Benin* 83 D5
Tch'eng-tou = Chengdu, *China* 58 B5
Tchentlo L., *Canada* 102 B4
Tchetti, *Benin* 83 D5
Tchibanga, *Gabon* 84 E2
Tchien, *Liberia* 82 D3
Tchin Tabaraden, *Niger* 83 B6
Tch'ong-k'ing = Chongqing, *China* 58 C6
Tczew, *Poland* 30 D5
Te Anau, L., *N.Z.* 91 L1
Te Aroha, *N.Z.* 91 G5
Te Awamutu, *N.Z.* 91 H5
Te Ika a Maui = North I., *N.Z.* 91 H5
Te Kuiti, *N.Z.* 91 H5
Te-n-Dghâmcha, Sebkhet, *Mauritania* 82 B1
Te Puke, *N.Z.* 91 G6
Te Waewae B., *N.Z.* 91 M1
Te Wai Pounamu = South I., *N.Z.* 91 L3
Teaca, *Romania* 29 D9
Teague, *U.S.A.* 113 K6
Teano, *Italy* 43 A7
Teapa, *Mexico* 119 D6
Teba, *Spain* 37 J6
Tebakang, *Malaysia* 62 D4
Teberda, *Russia* 35 J5
Teberu, *Malaysia* 65 d
Tébessa, *Algeria* 78 A7
Tebicuary →, *Paraguay* 126 B4
Tebingtinggi, *Riau, Indonesia* 62 E2
Tebingtinggi, *Sumatera Utara, Indonesia* 62 D1
Tebulos, *Georgia* 35 J7
Tecate, *Mexico* 111 N10
Tecer Dağları, *Turkey* 72 C7
Tech →, *France* 20 F7
Techiman, *Ghana* 82 D4
Techirghiol, *Romania* 29 F13
Tecka, *Argentina* 128 E2
Tecomán, *Mexico* 118 D4
Tecopa, *U.S.A.* 111 K10
Tecoripa, *Mexico* 118 B3
Tecuala, *Mexico* 118 C3
Tecuci, *Romania* 29 E12
Tecumseh, *Canada* 116 D2
Tecumseh, *Mich., U.S.A.* 114 D4
Tecumseh, *Okla., U.S.A.* 113 H6
Tedzhen = Tejen, *Turkmenistan* 52 F7
Tees →, *U.K.* 14 C6
Tees B., *U.K.* 14 C6
Teeswater, *Canada* 116 C3
Tefé, *Brazil* 124 D6
Tefenni, *Turkey* 47 D11
Tegal, *Indonesia* 63 G13
Tegallalang, *Indonesia* 63 J18
Tegalsari, *Indonesia* 63 J17
Tegel, Berlin ✕ (TXL), *Germany* 24 C9
Tegernsee, *Germany* 25 H7
Teggiano, *Italy* 43 B8
Tegid, L. = Bala, L., *U.K.* 14 E4
Tegina, *Nigeria* 83 C6
Tegucigalpa, *Honduras* 120 D2
Teguidda i-n-Tessoum, *Niger* 83 B6
Tehachapi, *U.S.A.* 111 K8
Tehachapi Mts., *U.S.A.* 111 L8
Tehamiyam, *Sudan* 80 D4
Teheran = Tehrān, *Iran* 71 C6
Tehilla, *Sudan* 80 D4
Téhini, *Ivory C.* 82 D4
Tehoru, *Indonesia* 63 E7
Tehrān, *Iran* 71 C6
Tehran □, *Iran* 71 C6
Tehri, *India* 69 D8
Tehuacán, *Mexico* 119 D5
Tehuantepec, *Mexico* 119 D5
Tehuantepec, G. de, *Mexico* 119 D5
Tehuantepec, Istmo de, *Mexico* 119 D6
Teide, Pico de, *Canary Is.* 48 F3
Teifi →, *U.K.* 15 E3
Teign →, *U.K.* 15 G4
Teignmouth, *U.K.* 15 G4
Teiuş, *Romania* 29 D8
Teixeira Pinto, *Guinea-Biss.* 82 C1
Tejakula, *Indonesia* 63 J18
Tejam, *India* 69 E9
Tejen, *Turkmenistan* 52 F7
Tejen →, *Turkmenistan* 71 B9
Tejo →, *Europe* 37 F2
Tejon Pass, *U.S.A.* 111 L8
Tekamah, *U.S.A.* 112 E6
Tekapo, L., *N.Z.* 91 K3
Tekax, *Mexico* 119 C7
Teke, *Turkey* 45 E13
Tekeli, *Kazakhstan* 52 E8
Tekeze →, *Ethiopia* 81 E4
Tekija, *Serbia & M.* 44 B6
Tekirdağ, *Turkey* 45 F11
Tekirdağ □, *Turkey* 45 E11
Tekirova, *Turkey* 47 E12
Tekkali, *India* 67 K14
Tekke, *Turkey* 72 B7
Tekman, *Turkey* 73 C9
Tekoa, *U.S.A.* 108 C5
Tekong Besar, Pulau, *Singapore* 65 d
Tel Aviv ✕ (TLV), *Israel* 74 C3
Tel Aviv-Yafo, *Israel* 74 C3
Tel Lakhish, *Israel* 74 D3
Tel Megiddo, *Israel* 74 C4
Tela, *Honduras* 120 C2
Telanaipura = Jambi, *Indonesia* 62 E2
Telašćica ⌓, *Croatia* 41 E12
Telavi, *Georgia* 35 J7
Telč, *Czech Rep.* 26 B8
Telciu, *Romania* 29 C9
Telde, *Canary Is.* 48 G4
Telegraph Creek, *Canada* 102 B2
Telekhany = Tsyelyakhany, *Belarus* 33 F3
Telemark, *Norway* 9 G12
Telén, *Argentina* 126 D2
Teleneşti, *Moldova* 29 C13
Teleng, *Iran* 71 E9
Teleño, *Spain* 36 C4
Teleorman □, *Romania* 29 G10
Teleorman →, *Romania* 29 G10
Teles Pires →, *Brazil* 124 E7
Telescope Pk., *U.S.A.* 111 J9
Teletaye, *Mali* 83 B5
Telfer Mine, *Australia* 92 C3
Telford, *U.K.* 15 E5
Telford and Wrekin □, *U.K.* 14 E5
Telfs, *Austria* 26 D4
Télimélé, *Guinea* 82 C2
Teljo, J., *Sudan* 81 E2
Telkwa, *Canada* 102 C3
Tell City, *U.S.A.* 114 G2
Tellicherry, *India* 66 P9
Telluride, *U.S.A.* 109 H10
Teloloapán, *Mexico* 119 D5
Telpos Iz, *Russia* 6 C17
Telsen, *Argentina* 128 E3
Telšiai, *Lithuania* 9 H20
Telšiai □, *Lithuania* 30 C9
Teltow, *Germany* 24 C9
Teluk Anson = Teluk Intan, *Malaysia* 65 K3
Teluk Bahang, *Malaysia* 65 c
Teluk Betung = Tanjungkarang Telukbetung, *Indonesia* 62 F3
Teluk Intan, *Malaysia* 65 K3
Teluk Kumbar, *Malaysia* 65 c
Telukbutun, *Indonesia* 62 D3
Telukdalem, *Indonesia* 62 D1
Tema, *Ghana* 83 D5
Temax, *Mexico* 119 C7
Temba, *S. Africa* 89 D4
Tembagapura, *Indonesia* 63 E9
Tembe, *Dem. Rep. of the Congo* 86 C2
Tembe ⌓, *S. Africa* 89 D5
Tembleque, *Spain* 36 F7
Temblor Range, *U.S.A.* 111 K7
Teme →, *U.K.* 15 E5
Temecula, *U.S.A.* 111 M9
Temerloh, *Malaysia* 62 D2
Teminabuan, *Indonesia* 63 E8
Temir, *Kazakhstan* 52 E6
Temirtau, *Kazakhstan* 52 D8
Temirtau, *Russia* 52 D9
Témiscamie →, *Canada* 105 B5
Témiscaming, *Canada* 104 C4
Témiscamingue, L., *Canada* 104 C4
Temnikov, *Russia* 34 C6
Temo →, *Italy* 42 B1
Temosachic, *Mexico* 118 B3
Tempe, *U.S.A.* 109 K8
Témpio Pausânia, *Italy* 42 B2
Tempiute, *U.S.A.* 110 H11
Temple, *U.S.A.* 113 K6
Temple B., *Australia* 94 A3
Templemore, *Ireland* 12 D4
Templeton, *U.S.A.* 110 K6
Templeton →, *Australia* 94 C2
Templin, *Germany* 24 B9
Tempoal, *Mexico* 119 C5
Temryuk, *Russia* 33 K9
Temska →, *Serbia & M.* 44 C6
Temuco, *Chile* 128 D2
Temuka, *N.Z.* 91 L3
Tenabo, *Mexico* 119 C6
Tenaha, *U.S.A.* 113 K7
Tenakee Springs, *U.S.A.* 102 B1
Tenali, *India* 67 L12
Tenancingo, *Mexico* 119 D5
Tenango, *Mexico* 119 D5
Tenasserim, *Burma* 65 F2
Tenasserim □, *Burma* 64 F2
Tenby, *U.K.* 15 F3
Tenda, Colle di, *France* 21 D11
Tendaho, *Ethiopia* 81 E5
Tende, *France* 21 D11
Tendelti, *Sudan* 81 E3
Tendrovskaya Kosa, *Ukraine* 33 J6
Tendukhera, *India* 69 H8
Teneguía, Volcanes de, *Canary Is.* 48 F2
Teneida, *Egypt* 80 B2
Tenenkou, *Mali* 82 C4
Ténéré, *Niger* 83 B7
Tenerife, *Canary Is.* 48 F3
Tenerife, Pico, *Canary Is.* 48 G1
Tenerife Norte ✕ (TFN), *Canary Is.* 48 F3
Tenerife Sur ✕ (TFS), *Canary Is.* 48 F3
Teng Xian, *Guangxi Zhuangzu, China* 59 F8
Teng Xian, *Shandong, China* 57 G9
Tengah, Kepulauan, *Indonesia* 62 F5
Tengchong, *China* 58 E2
Tengchowfu = Penglai, *China* 57 F11
Tenggarong, *Indonesia* 62 E5
Tenggol, Pulau, *Malaysia* 65 K4
Tengiz, Ozero, *Kazakhstan* 52 D7
Tenhult, *Sweden* 11 G8
Teniente Enciso △, *Paraguay* 126 A3
Teniente Rodolfo Marsh, *Antarctica* 5 C18
Tenino, *U.S.A.* 110 D4
Tenkasi, *India* 66 Q10
Tenke, *Katanga, Dem. Rep. of the Congo* 87 E2
Tenke, *Katanga, Dem. Rep. of the Congo* 87 E2
Tenkodogo, *Burkina Faso* 83 C4
Tenna →, *Italy* 41 E10
Tennant Creek, *Australia* 94 B1
Tennessee □, *U.S.A.* 115 H2
Tennessee →, *U.S.A.* 114 G1
Teno, Pta. de, *Canary Is.* 48 F3
Tenom, *Malaysia* 62 C5
Tenosique, *Mexico* 119 D6
Tenryū-Gawa →, *Japan* 55 G8
Tenterden, *U.K.* 15 F8
Tenterfield, *Australia* 95 D5
Teo, *Spain* 36 C2
Teófilo Otoni, *Brazil* 125 G10
Tepa, *Indonesia* 63 F7
Tepalcatepec →, *Mexico* 118 D4
Tepecik, *Bursa, Turkey* 45 F12
Tepecik, *Kütahya, Turkey* 47 B11
Tepehuanes, *Mexico* 118 B3
Tepelenë, *Albania* 44 F4
Tepetongo, *Mexico* 118 C4
Tepic, *Mexico* 118 C4
Teplá, *Czech Rep.* 26 B5
Teplice, *Czech Rep.* 26 A6
Teplyk, *Ukraine* 29 B14
Tepoca, C., *Mexico* 118 A2
Tequila, *Mexico* 118 C4
Ter →, *Spain* 38 C8
Ter Apel, *Neths.* 17 B7
Téra, *Niger* 83 C5
Tera →, *Spain* 36 D5
Teraina, *Kiribati* 97 G11
Terakeka, *Sudan* 81 F3
Téramo, *Italy* 41 F10
Terang, *Australia* 95 F3
Terang, Teluk, *Indonesia* 63 K19
Terazit, Massif de, *Niger* 83 A6
Tercan, *Turkey* 73 C9
Tercero →, *Argentina* 126 C3
Terebovlya, *Ukraine* 33 H3
Teregova, *Romania* 28 E7
Tereida, *Sudan* 81 E3
Terek →, *Russia* 35 J8
Terepaima △, *Venezuela* 121 E6
Tereshka →, *Russia* 34 E8
Teresina, *Brazil* 125 E10
Terespol, *Poland* 31 F10
Teresva, *Ukraine* 29 B8
Terewah, L., *Australia* 95 D4
Terges →, *Portugal* 37 H3
Tergnier, *France* 19 C10
Teridgerie Cr. →, *Australia* 95 E4
Terlizzi, *Italy* 43 A9
Terme, *Turkey* 72 B7
Termez = Termiz, *Uzbekistan* 52 F7
Términi Imerese, *Italy* 42 E6
Términos, L. de, *Mexico* 119 D6
Termiz, *Uzbekistan* 52 F7
Térmoli, *Italy* 41 F12
Ternate, *Indonesia* 63 D7
Terneuzen, *Neths.* 17 C3
Terney, *Russia* 53 E14
Terni, *Italy* 41 F9
Ternitz, *Austria* 26 D9
Ternivka, *Ukraine* 29 B14
Ternopil, *Ukraine* 33 H3
Ternopol = Ternopil, *Ukraine* 33 H3
Terowie, *Australia* 95 E2
Terpní, *Greece* 44 F7
Terra Bella, *U.S.A.* 111 K7
Terra Nova △, *Canada* 105 C9
Terrace, *Canada* 102 C3
Terrace Bay, *Canada* 104 C2
Terracina, *Italy* 42 A6
Terralba, *Italy* 42 C1
Terrasini, *Italy* 42 D6
Terrassa, *Spain* 38 D7
Terrasson-la-Villedieu, *France* 20 C5
Terre Haute, *U.S.A.* 114 F2
Terrebonne B., *U.S.A.* 113 L9
Terrell, *U.S.A.* 113 J6
Terrenceville, *Canada* 105 C9
Terry, *U.S.A.* 112 B2
Terryville, *U.S.A.* 117 E11
Terschelling, *Neths.* 17 A5
Tersko-Kumskiy Kanal, *Russia* 35 H7
Tertenía, *Italy* 42 C2
Terter = Tärtär →, *Azerbaijan* 35 K8
Teruel, *Spain* 38 E3
Teruel □, *Spain* 38 E4
Tervel, *Bulgaria* 45 C11
Tervola, *Finland* 8 C21
Teryaweyna L., *Australia* 95 E3
Tešanj, *Bos.-H.* 28 F3
Teseney, *Eritrea* 81 D4
Tesha →, *Russia* 34 C6
Teshio, *Japan* 54 B10
Teshio-Gawa →, *Japan* 54 B10
Tešica, *Serbia & M.* 44 C5
Tesiyn Gol →, *Mongolia* 60 A4
Teslić, *Bos.-H.* 28 F2
Teslin, *Canada* 102 A2
Teslin →, *Canada* 102 A2
Teslin L., *Canada* 102 A2
Tessalit, *Mali* 83 A5
Tessaoua, *Niger* 83 C6
Tessin, *Germany* 24 A8
Tessit, *Mali* 83 B5
Test →, *U.K.* 15 G6
Testa del Gargano, *Italy* 41 G13
Testigos, Is. Las, *Venezuela* 121 D7
Tét, *Hungary* 28 C2
Têt →, *France* 20 F7
Tetachuck L., *Canada* 102 C3
Tetas, Pta., *Chile* 126 A1
Tete, *Mozam.* 87 F3
Tete □, *Mozam.* 87 F3
Teterev →, *Ukraine* 33 G6
Teterow, *Germany* 24 B8
Teteven, *Bulgaria* 45 D8
Tethul →, *Canada* 102 A6
Tetiyev, *Ukraine* 33 H5
Teton →, *U.S.A.* 108 C8
Tétouan, *Morocco* 78 A4
Tetovo, *Macedonia* 44 D4
Tetyushi, *Russia* 34 C9
Teuco →, *Argentina* 126 B3
Teulada, *Italy* 42 D1
Teulon, *Canada* 103 C9
Teun, *Indonesia* 63 F7
Teutoburger Wald, *Germany* 24 C4
Tevere ⌓, *Italy* 41 F9
Tevere →, *Italy* 41 G9
Teverya, *Israel* 74 C4
Teviot →, *U.K.* 13 F6
Tewantin, *Australia* 95 D5
Tewkesbury, *U.K.* 15 F5
Texada I., *Canada* 102 D4
Texarkana, *Ark., U.S.A.* 113 J8
Texarkana, *Tex., U.S.A.* 113 J7
Texas, *Australia* 95 D5
Texas □, *U.S.A.* 113 K5
Texas City, *U.S.A.* 113 L7
Texel, *Neths.* 17 A4
Texline, *U.S.A.* 113 G3
Texoma, L., *U.S.A.* 113 J6
Teykovo, *Russia* 32 D11
Teza →, *Russia* 34 B5
Tezin, *Afghan.* 68 B3
Teziutlán, *Mexico* 119 D5
Tezpur, *India* 67 F18
Tezzeron L., *Canada* 102 C4
Tha-anne →, *Canada* 103 A10
Tha Deua, *Laos* 64 D4
Tha Deua, *Laos* 64 C3
Tha Pla, *Thailand* 64 D3
Tha Rua, *Thailand* 64 E3
Tha Sala, *Thailand* 65 H2
Tha Song Yang, *Thailand* 64 D1
Thaba Putsoa, *Lesotho* 89 D4
Thabana Ntlenyana, *Lesotho* 89 D4
Thabazimbi, *S. Africa* 89 C4
Thādiq, *Si. Arabia* 70 E5
Thai Binh, *Vietnam* 58 G6
Thai Muang, *Thailand* 65 H2
Thai Nguyen, *Vietnam* 58 G5
Thailand ■, *Asia* 64 E4
Thailand, G. of, *Asia* 65 G3
Thakhek, *Laos* 64 D5
Thal, *Pakistan* 68 C4
Thal Desert, *Pakistan* 68 D4
Thala La = Hkakabo Razi, *Burma* 67 E20
Thalabarivat, *Cambodia* 64 F5
Thallon, *Australia* 95 D4
Thalu, Ko, *Thailand* 65 b
Thalwil, *Switz.* 25 H4
Thames, *N.Z.* 91 G5
Thames →, *Canada* 116 D2
Thames →, *U.K.* 15 F8
Thames →, *U.S.A.* 117 E12
Thames Estuary, *U.K.* 15 F8
Thamesford, *Canada* 116 C4
Thamesville, *Canada* 116 D3
Than, *India* 68 H4
Than Uyen, *Vietnam* 64 B4
Thana Gazi, *India* 68 F7
Thandla, *India* 68 H6
Thane, *India* 66 K8
Thanesar, *India* 68 D7
Thanet, I. of, *U.K.* 15 F9
Thangool, *Australia* 94 C5
Thanh Hoa, *Vietnam* 64 C5
Thanh Hung, *Vietnam* 65 H5
Thanh Pho Ho Chi Minh, *Vietnam* 65 G6
Thanh Thuy, *Vietnam* 64 A5
Thanjavur, *India* 66 P11
Thann, *France* 19 E14
Thano Bula Khan, *Pakistan* 68 G2
Thaolinta L., *Canada* 103 A9
Thaon-les-Vosges, *France* 19 D13
Thap Lan △, *Thailand* 64 E4
Thap Sakae, *Thailand* 65 G2
Thap Than, *Thailand* 64 E2
Thar Desert, *India* 68 F5
Tharad, *India* 68 G4
Thargomindah, *Australia* 95 D3
Tharrawaddy, *Burma* 67 L19
Tharthār, Buḩayrat ath, *Iraq* 70 C4
Tharthar, L. = Tharthār, Buḩayrat ath, *Iraq* 70 C4
Tharthār, W. ath →, *Iraq* 70 C4
Thasopoúla, *Greece* 45 F8
Thásos, *Greece* 45 F8
That Khe, *Vietnam* 58 F6
Thatcher, *Ariz., U.S.A.* 109 K9
Thatcher, *Colo., U.S.A.* 113 G2
Thaton, *Burma* 67 L20
Thau, Bassin de, *France* 20 E7
Thaungdut, *Burma* 67 G19
Thayer, *U.S.A.* 113 G9
Thayetmyo, *Burma* 67 K19
Thazi, *Burma* 67 J20
The Bight, *Bahamas* 121 B4
The Crane, *Barbados* 121 g
The Dalles, *U.S.A.* 108 D3
The Great Divide = Great Dividing Ra., *Australia* 94 C4
The Hague = 's-Gravenhage, *Neths.* 17 B4
The Pas, *Canada* 103 C8
The Range, *Zimbabwe* 87 F3
The Rock, *Australia* 95 F4
The Settlement, *Br. Virgin Is.* 121 e
The Woodlands, *U.S.A.* 113 K7
Thebes = Thívai, *Greece* 46 C5
Thebes, *Egypt* 80 B3
Thedford, *U.S.A.* 112 E4
Theebine, *Australia* 95 D5
Thekulthili L., *Canada* 103 A7
Thelon →, *Canada* 103 A8
Thénezay, *France* 18 F6
Thenon, *France* 20 C5
Theodore, *Australia* 94 C5
Theodore, *Canada* 103 C8
Theodore, *U.S.A.* 115 K1
Theodore Roosevelt △, *U.S.A.* 112 B3
Theodore Roosevelt L., *U.S.A.* 109 K8
Thepha, *Thailand* 65 J3
Thérain →, *France* 19 C9
Theresa, *U.S.A.* 117 B9
Thermaïkós Kólpos, *Greece* 44 F6
Thermí, *Greece* 47 B8
Thermopolis, *U.S.A.* 108 E9
Thermopylae P., *Greece* 46 C4
Thesprotía □, *Greece* 46 B2
Thessalía □, *Greece* 46 B4
Thessalon, *Canada* 104 C3
Thessaloníki, *Greece* 44 F6
Thessaloníki □, *Greece* 44 F7
Thessaloníki ✕ (SKG), *Greece* 44 F7
Thessaloníki, Gulf of = Thermaïkós Kólpos, *Greece* 44 F6
Thessaly = Thessalía □, *Greece* 46 B4
Thetford, *U.K.* 15 E8
Thetford Mines, *Canada* 105 C5
Theun →, *Laos* 64 C5
Theunissen, *S. Africa* 88 D4
Thevenard, *Australia* 95 E1
Thiámis →, *Greece* 46 B2
Thiberville, *France* 18 C7
Thibodaux, *U.S.A.* 113 L9
Thicket Portage, *Canada* 103 B9
Thief River Falls, *U.S.A.* 112 A6
Thiel Mts., *Antarctica* 5 E16
Thiene, *Italy* 41 C8
Thiérache, *France* 19 C10
Thiers, *France* 20 C7
Thiès, *Senegal* 82 C1
Thiesi, *Italy* 42 B1
Thiet, *Sudan* 81 F2
Thika, *Kenya* 86 C4
Thikombia, *Fiji* 91 B9
Thille-Boubacar, *Senegal* 82 B1
Thimphu, *Bhutan* 67 F16
Þingvallavatn, *Iceland* 8 D3
Thionville, *France* 19 C13
Thíra, *Greece* 47 E7
Thirasía, *Greece* 47 E7
Third Cataract, *Sudan* 80 D3
Thirsk, *U.K.* 14 C6
Thiruvananthapuram = Trivandrum, *India* 66 Q10
Thisted, *Denmark* 11 H2
Thistle I., *Australia* 95 F2
Thívai, *Greece* 46 C5
Thiviers, *France* 20 C4
Thizy, *France* 19 F11
Þjórsá →, *Iceland* 8 E3
Thlewiaza →, *Canada* 103 A10
Tho Vinh, *Vietnam* 64 C5
Thoa →, *Canada* 103 A7
Thoen, *Thailand* 64 D2
Thoeng, *Thailand* 64 C3
Thohoyandou, *S. Africa* 85 J6
Tholdi, *Pakistan* 69 B7
Thomas, *U.S.A.* 113 H5
Thomas, L., *Australia* 95 D2
Thomaston, *U.S.A.* 115 J3
Thomasville, *Ala., U.S.A.* 115 K2
Thomasville, *Ga., U.S.A.* 115 K4
Thomasville, *N.C., U.S.A.* 115 H5
Thompson, *Canada* 103 B9
Thompson, *U.S.A.* 117 E9
Thompson →, *Canada* 102 C4
Thompson →, *U.S.A.* 112 F8
Thompson Falls, *U.S.A.* 108 C6
Thompson Pk., *U.S.A.* 108 F2
Thompson Springs, *U.S.A.* 109 G9
Thompsontown, *U.S.A.* 116 F7
Thomson, *U.S.A.* 115 J4
Thomson →, *Australia* 94 C3
Thônes, *France* 21 C10
Thong Yang, *Thailand* 65 b
Thonon-les-Bains, *France* 19 F13
Thorez, *Ukraine* 33 H10
Þórisvatn, *Iceland* 8 D4
Thornaby on Tees, *U.K.* 14 C6
Thornbury, *Canada* 116 B4
Thorne, *U.K.* 14 D7
Thornhill, *Canada* 102 C3
Thorold, *Canada* 116 C5
Þórshöfn, *Iceland* 8 C6
Thouarcé, *France* 18 E6
Thouars, *France* 18 F6

Thouet →, France 18 E6
Thouin, C., Australia 92 D2
Thousand Oaks, U.S.A. 111 L8
Thrace, Turkey 45 F10
Thrakikón Pélagos, Greece 45 F8
Three Forks, U.S.A. 108 D8
Three Gorges Dam, China 59 B8
Three Hills, Canada 102 C6
Three Hummock I., Australia 95 G3
Three Pagodas Pass, Asia 64 E2
Three Points, C., Ghana 82 E4
Three Rivers, Calif., U.S.A. 110 J8
Three Rivers, Tex., U.S.A. 113 L5
Three Sisters, U.S.A. 108 D3
Three Springs, Australia 93 E2
Throssell, L., Australia 93 E3
Throssell Ra., Australia 92 D3
Thrushton △, Australia 95 D4
Thuan Hoa, Vietnam 65 H5
Thubun Lakes, Canada 103 A6
Thueyts, France 21 D8
Thuin, Belgium 17 D4
Thuir, France 20 F6
Thule = Qaanaaq, Greenland 4 B4
Thule Air Base = Uummannaq, Greenland 4 B5
Thun, Switz. 25 J3
Thunder B., U.S.A. 116 B1
Thunder Bay, Canada 104 C2
Thunersee, Switz. 25 J3
Thung Salaeng Luang △, Thailand 64 D3
Thung Song, Thailand 65 H2
Thunkar, Bhutan 67 F17
Thuong Tra, Vietnam 64 D6
Thur →, Switz. 25 H5
Thurgau □, Switz. 25 H5
Thüringen □, Germany 24 D6
Thüringer Wald, Germany 24 E6
Thurles, Ireland 12 D4
Thurn P., Austria 26 D5
Thurrock □, U.K. 15 F8
Thursday I., Australia 94 A3
Thurso, Canada 104 C4
Thurso, U.K. 13 C5
Thurso →, U.K. 13 C5
Thurston I., Antarctica 5 D16
Thury-Harcourt, France 18 D6
Thutade L., Canada 102 B3
Thy, Denmark 11 H2
Thyborøn, Denmark 11 H2
Thyolo, Malawi 87 F4
Ti-n-Amzi →, Niger 83 B5
Ti-n-Barraouene, O. →, Africa 83 B5
Ti-n-Zaouatene, Algeria 83 B5
Ti Tree, Australia 94 C1
Tiadiaye, Senegal 82 C1
Tian Shan, Asia 60 B3
Tianchang, China 59 A12
Tiandeng, China 58 F6
Tiandong, China 58 F6
Tian'e, China 58 E6
Tianhe, China 58 E7
Tianjin, China 57 E9
Tiankoura, Burkina Faso 82 C4
Tianlin, China 58 E6
Tianmen, China 59 B9
Tianquan, China 58 B4
Tianshui, China 56 G3
Tiantai, China 59 C13
Tianyang, China 58 F6
Tianyar, Indonesia 63 J18
Tianzhen, China 56 D8
Tianzhu, China 58 D7
Tianzhuangtai, China 57 D12
Tiaret, Algeria 78 A6
Tiassalé, Ivory C. 82 D4
Tibagi, Brazil 127 A5
Tibagi →, Brazil 127 A5
Tibati, Cameroon 83 D7
Tibe, Ethiopia 81 F4
Tiber = Tevere →, Italy 41 G9
Tiberias = Teverya, Israel 74 C4
Tiberias, L. = Yam Kinneret, Israel 74 C4
Tibesti, Chad 79 D9
Tibet = Xizang Zizhiqu □, China 60 C3
Tibet, Plateau of, Asia 50 F12
Tibiao, Phil. 61 F5
Tibiri, Niger 83 C6
Ţibleş, Vf., Romania 29 C9
Ţibleşului, Munţii, Romania 29 C9
Tibnī, Syria 70 C3
Tibooburra, Australia 95 D3
Tibro, Sweden 11 F8
Tiburón, I., Mexico 118 B2
Ticao I., Phil. 61 E5
Tîchît, Mauritania 82 B3
Ticho, Ethiopia 81 F4
Ticino □, Switz. 25 J4
Ticino →, Italy 25 K5
Ticleni, Romania 29 F8
Ticonderoga, U.S.A. 117 C11
Ticul, Mexico 119 C7
Tidaholm, Sweden 11 F7
Tidan, Sweden 11 F8
Tiddim, Burma 67 H18
Tidioute, U.S.A. 116 E5
Tidjikja, Mauritania 82 B2
Tidore, Indonesia 63 D7
Tiébissou, Ivory C. 82 D3
Tiel, Neths. 17 C5
Tiel, Senegal 82 C1
Tieling, China 57 C12
Tielt, Belgium 17 C3
Tien Shan = Tian Shan, Asia 60 B3
Tien-tsin = Tianjin, China 57 E9
Tien Yen, Vietnam 64 B6
T'ienching = Tianjin, China 57 E9
Tienen, Belgium 17 D4
Tiénigbé, Ivory C. 82 D3
Tientsin = Tianjin, China 57 E9
Tieri, Australia 94 C4
Tierp, Sweden 10 D11
Tierra Amarilla, Chile 126 B1
Tierra Amarilla, U.S.A. 109 H10
Tierra Colorada, Mexico 119 D5
Tierra de Barros, Spain 37 G4
Tierra de Campos, Spain 36 C6
Tierra del Fuego, I. Gr. de, Argentina 128 G3
Tiétar →, Spain 36 F4
Tieté →, Brazil 127 A5
Tiffin, U.S.A. 114 E4
Tifton, U.S.A. 115 K4
Tifu, Indonesia 63 E7
Tighina, Moldova 29 D14
Tigil, Russia 53 D16
Tignish, Canada 105 C7
Tigray □, Ethiopia 81 E4
Tigre →, Peru 124 D4
Tigre →, Venezuela 124 B6
Tigris = Dijlah, Nahr →, Asia 70 D5
Tigveni, Romania 29 E9
Tigyaing, Burma 67 H20
Tîh, Gebel el, Egypt 80 B3
Tijara, India 68 F7
Tijuana, Mexico 111 N9
Tikal, Guatemala 120 C2
Tikal △, Guatemala 120 C2
Tikamgarh, India 69 G8
Tikaré, Burkina Faso 83 C4
Tikhoretsk, Russia 35 H5
Tikhvin, Russia 32 C7
Tikiraqjuaq = Whale Cove, Canada 103 A10
Tiko, Cameroon 83 E6
Tikrīt, Iraq 70 C4
Tiksi, Russia 53 B13
Tilamuta, Indonesia 63 D6
Tilburg, Neths. 17 C5
Tilbury, Canada 116 D2
Tilbury, U.K. 15 F8
Tilcara, Argentina 126 A2
Tilden, U.S.A. 112 D6
Tilemses, Niger 83 B5
Tilemsi, Vallée du, Mali 83 B5
Tilhar, India 69 F8
Tilichiki, Russia 53 C17
Tílissos, Greece 49 D7
Till →, U.K. 14 B5
Tillabéri, Niger 83 C5
Tillamook, U.S.A. 108 D2
Tillberga, Sweden 10 E10
Tillia, Niger 83 B5
Tillsonburg, Canada 116 D4
Tillyeria, Cyprus 49 D11
Tilogne, Senegal 82 B2
Tílos, Greece 47 E9
Tilpa, Australia 95 E3
Tilt →, U.K. 13 E5
Tilton, U.S.A. 117 C13
Tiltonsville, U.S.A. 116 F4
Tim, Denmark 11 H2
Timagami, L., Canada 104 C3
Timanfaya △, Canary Is. 48 F6
Timaru, N.Z. 91 L3
Timashevo, Russia 34 D10
Timashevsk, Russia 35 H4
Timau, Kenya 86 B4
Timbákion, Greece 49 D6
Timbedgha, Mauritania 82 B3
Timber Creek, Australia 92 C5
Timber Lake, U.S.A. 112 C4
Timber Mt., U.S.A. 110 H10
Timbo, Guinea 82 C2
Timbo, Liberia 82 D3
Timbuktu = Tombouctou, Mali 82 B4
Timeiaouine, Algeria 83 A5
Timétrine, Mts., Mali 83 B4
Timfi Óros, Greece 46 B2
Timfristós, Óros, Greece 46 C3
Timi, Cyprus 49 E11
Tîmia, Niger 83 B6
Timimoun, Algeria 78 C6
Timirist, Râs, Mauritania 82 B1
Timiş = Tamis →, Serbia & M. 28 F5
Timiş □, Romania 28 E6
Timiskaming, L. = Témiscamingue, L., Canada 104 C4
Timişoara, Romania 28 E6
Timmersdala, Sweden 11 F7
Timmins, Canada 104 C3
Timok →, Serbia & M. 44 B6
Timor, Asia 63 F7
Timor Leste = East Timor ■, Asia 63 F7
Timor Sea, Ind. Oc. 92 B4
Timrå, Sweden 10 B11
Tin Can Bay, Australia 95 D5
Tin Ethisane, Mali 83 B4
Tin Gornai, Mali 83 B4
Tin Mt., U.S.A. 110 J9
Tina →, S. Africa 89 E4
Tîna, Khalîg el, Egypt 80 A3
Tinaca Pt., Phil. 61 J6
Tinajo, Canary Is. 48 E6
Tinca, Romania 28 D6
Tindal, Australia 92 B5
Tindouf, Algeria 78 C4
Tinée →, France 21 E11
Tineo, Spain 36 B4
Tinfunque △, Paraguay 126 A3
Ting Jiang →, China 59 E11
Tinggi, Pulau, Malaysia 65 L5
Tinglev, Denmark 11 K3
Tingo Maria, Peru 124 E3
Tingrela, Ivory C. 82 C3
Tingsryd, Sweden 11 H9
Tingstäde, Sweden 11 G12
Tinh Bien, Vietnam 65 G5
Tinnevelly = Tirunelveli, India 66 Q10
Tinogasta, Argentina 126 B2
Tínos, Greece 47 D7
Tiñoso, C., Spain 39 H3
Tinpahar, India 69 G12
Tintina, Argentina 126 B3
Tintinara, Australia 95 F3
Tintioulé, Guinea 82 C3
Tinto →, Spain 37 H4
Tioga, N. Dak., U.S.A. 112 A3
Tioga, Pa., U.S.A. 116 E7
Tioman, Pulau, Malaysia 65 L5
Tione di Trento, Italy 40 B7
Tionesta, U.S.A. 116 E5
Tior, Sudan 81 F3
Tipongpani, India 67 F19
Tipperary, Ireland 12 D3
Tipperary □, Ireland 12 D4
Tipton, Calif., U.S.A. 110 J7
Tipton, Iowa, U.S.A. 112 E9
Tipton Mt., U.S.A. 111 K12
Tiptonville, U.S.A. 113 G10
Tīrān, Iran 71 C6
Tīrān, Si. Arabia 80 B3
Tiranë, Albania 44 E3
Tiranë ✕ (TIA), Albania 43 A12
Tirano, Italy 40 B7
Tiraspol, Moldova 29 D14
Tirdout, Mali 83 B4
Tire, Turkey 47 C9
Tirebolu, Turkey 73 B8
Tiree, U.K. 13 E2
Tiree, Passage of, U.K. 13 E2
Tîrgovişte = Târgovişte, Romania 29 F10
Tîrgu-Jiu = Târgu-Jiu, Romania 29 E8
Tîrgu Mureş = Târgu Mureş, Romania 29 D9
Tirich Mir, Pakistan 66 A7
Tiriolo, Italy 43 D9
Tiriro, Guinea 82 C3
Tiritiri o te Moana = Southern Alps, N.Z. 91 K3
Tírnavos, Greece 46 B4
Tirodi, India 66 J11
Tirol □, Austria 26 D3
Tirschenreuth, Germany 25 F8
Tirso →, Italy 42 C1
Tirstrup, Denmark 11 H4
Tiruchchirappalli, India 66 P11
Tirunelveli, India 66 Q10
Tirupati, India 66 N11
Tiruppur, India 66 P10
Tiruvannamalai, India 66 N11
Tisa, India 68 C7
Tisa →, Serbia & M. 28 E5
Tisdale, Canada 103 C8
Tishomingo, U.S.A. 113 H6
Tisjön, Sweden 10 D7
Tisnaren, Sweden 11 F9
Tišnov, Czech Rep. 27 B9
Tisovec, Slovak Rep. 27 C12
Tisza = Tisa →, Serbia & M. 28 E5
Tiszaföldvár, Hungary 28 D5
Tiszafüred, Hungary 28 C5
Tiszalök, Hungary 28 B6
Tiszavasvári, Hungary 28 C6
Tit-Ary, Russia 53 B13
Titaguas, Spain 38 F3
Titao, Burkina Faso 83 C4
Titel, Serbia & M. 28 E5
Tithwal, Pakistan 69 B5
Titicaca, L., S. Amer. 124 G5
Titisee, Germany 25 H4
Titiwa, Nigeria 83 C7
Tito, Italy 43 B8
Titova Korenica, Croatia 41 D12
Titu, Romania 29 F10
Titule, Dem. Rep. of the Congo 86 B2
Titusville, Fla., U.S.A. 115 L5
Titusville, Pa., U.S.A. 116 E5
Tivaouane, Senegal 82 C1
Tivat, Serbia & M. 44 D2
Tivedens △, Sweden 11 F8
Tiverton, U.K. 15 G4
Tívoli, Italy 41 G9
Tiyo, Eritrea 81 E5
Tizi-Ouzou, Algeria 78 A6
Tizimín, Mexico 119 C7
Tjæreborg, Denmark 11 J2
Tjällmo, Sweden 11 F9
Tjeggelvas, Sweden 8 C17
Tjieggelvas = Tjeggelvas, Sweden 8 C17
Tjirebon = Cirebon, Indonesia 63 G13
Tjluring, Indonesia 63 J17
Tjörn, Sweden 11 F5
Tkibuli = Tqibuli, Georgia 35 J6
Tkvarcheli = Tqvarcheli, Georgia 35 J5
Tlacotalpan, Mexico 119 D5
Tlahualilo, Mexico 118 B4
Tlaquepaque, Mexico 118 C4
Tlaxcala, Mexico 119 D5
Tlaxcala □, Mexico 119 D5
Tlaxiaco, Mexico 119 D5
Tlemcen, Algeria 78 B5
Tlumach, Ukraine 29 B10
Tłuszcz, Poland 31 F8
Tlyarata, Russia 35 J8
To Bong, Vietnam 64 F7
Toa Payoh, Singapore 65 d
Toad →, Canada 102 B4
Toad River, Canada 102 B3
Toamasina, Madag. 89 B8
Toamasina □, Madag. 89 B8
Toay, Argentina 126 D3
Toba, China 58 B1
Toba, Japan 55 G8
Toba, Danau, Indonesia 62 D1
Toba Kakar, Pakistan 68 D3
Toba Tek Singh, Pakistan 68 D5
Tobago, Trin. & Tob. 121 D7
Tobarra, Spain 39 G3
Tobelo, Indonesia 63 D7
Tobermory, Canada 116 A3
Tobermory, U.K. 13 E2
Tobi, Pac. Oc. 63 D8
Tobin, U.S.A. 110 F5
Tobin, L., Australia 92 D4
Tobin L., Canada 103 C8
Toblach = Dobbiaco, Italy 41 B9
Toboali, Indonesia 62 E3
Tobol →, Russia 52 D7
Toboli, Indonesia 63 E6
Tobolsk, Russia 52 D7
Tobor, Senegal 82 C1
Tobruk = Tubruq, Libya 79 B10
Tobyhanna, U.S.A. 117 E9
Tobyl = Tobol →, Russia 52 D7
Tocantinópolis, Brazil 125 E9
Tocantins □, Brazil 125 F9
Tocantins →, Brazil 125 D9
Toccoa, U.S.A. 115 H4
Toce →, Italy 40 C5
Tochi →, Pakistan 68 C4
Tochigi, Japan 55 F9
Tochigi □, Japan 55 F9
Tocina, Spain 37 H5
Töcksfors, Sweden 10 E5
Toco, Trin. & Tob. 125 K16
Toconao, Chile 126 A2
Tocopilla, Chile 126 A1
Tocumwal, Australia 95 F4
Tocuyo →, Venezuela 124 A5
Todd →, Australia 94 C2
Todeli, Indonesia 63 E6
Todenyang, Kenya 86 B4
Todgarh, India 68 G5
Todi, Italy 41 F9
Todos os Santos, B. de, Brazil 125 F11
Todos Santos, Mexico 118 C2
Todtnau, Germany 25 H3
Toe Hd., U.K. 13 D1
Toecé, Burkina Faso 83 C4
Tofield, Canada 102 C6
Tofino, Canada 102 D3
Töfsingdalens △, Sweden 10 B6
Tofua, Tonga 91 D11
Tōgane, Japan 55 G10
Togba, Mauritania 82 B2
Togian, Kepulauan, Indonesia 63 E6
Togliatti, Russia 34 D9
Togo ■, W. Afr. 83 D5
Togtoh, China 56 D6
Tohma →, Turkey 72 C7
Tōhoku □, Japan 54 E10
Töhöm, Mongolia 56 B5
Toinya, Sudan 81 F2
Toiyabe Range, U.S.A. 108 G5
Tojikiston = Tajikistan ■, Asia 52 F8
Tojo, Indonesia 63 E6
Tōjō, Japan 55 G6
Tok, U.S.A. 100 B5
Tok-do, Asia 55 F5
Tokachi-Dake, Japan 54 C11
Tokachi-Gawa →, Japan 54 C11
Tokaj, Hungary 28 B6
Tokala, Indonesia 63 E6
Tōkamachi, Japan 55 F9
Tokanui, N.Z. 91 M2
Tokar, Sudan 80 D4
Tokara-Rettō, Japan 55 K4
Tokarahi, N.Z. 91 L3
Tokashiki-Shima, Japan 55 L3
Tokat, Turkey 72 B7
Tŏkch'ŏn, N. Korea 57 E14
Tokeland, U.S.A. 110 D3
Tokelau Is., Pac. Oc. 96 H10
Tokmak, Kyrgyzstan 52 E8
Tokmak, Ukraine 33 J8
Toko Ra., Australia 94 C2
Tokoro-Gawa →, Japan 54 B12
Tokuno-Shima, Japan 55 L4
Tokushima, Japan 55 G7
Tokushima □, Japan 55 H7
Tokuyama, Japan 55 G5
Tōkyō, Japan 55 G9
Tolaga Bay, N.Z. 91 H7
Tolbukhin = Dobrich, Bulgaria 45 C11
Toledo, Brazil 127 A5
Toledo, Spain 36 F6
Toledo, Ohio, U.S.A. 114 E4
Toledo, Oreg., U.S.A. 108 D2
Toledo, Wash., U.S.A. 108 C2
Toledo, Montes de, Spain 37 F6
Toledo Bend Reservoir, U.S.A. 113 K8
Tolentino, Italy 41 E10
Tolfa, Italy 41 F8
Tolga, Australia 94 B4
Toliara, Madag. 89 C7
Toliara □, Madag. 89 C8
Tolima, Colombia 124 C3
Tolitoli, Indonesia 63 D6
Tolkmicko, Poland 30 D6
Tollarp, Sweden 11 J7
Tollensesee, Germany 24 B9
Tollhouse, U.S.A. 110 H7
Tolmachevo, Russia 32 C5
Tolmezzo, Italy 41 B10
Tolmin, Slovenia 41 B10
Tolna, Hungary 28 D3
Tolna □, Hungary 28 D3
Tolo, Teluk, Indonesia 63 E6
Tolochin = Talachyn, Belarus 32 E5
Tolosa, Spain 38 B2
Tolox, Spain 37 J6
Toluca, Mexico 119 D5
Tom Burke, S. Africa 89 C4
Tom Price, Australia 92 D2
Toma, Burkina Faso 82 C4
Tomah, U.S.A. 112 D9
Tomahawk, U.S.A. 112 C10
Tomai, Moldova 29 D13
Tomakomai, Japan 54 C10
Tomales, U.S.A. 110 G4
Tomales B., U.S.A. 110 G3
Tomar, Portugal 37 F2
Tómaros, Óros, Greece 46 B2
Tomarza, Turkey 72 C6
Tomashevka, Belarus 31 G10
Tomashpil, Ukraine 29 B13
Tomaszów Lubelski, Poland 31 H10
Tomaszów Mazowiecki, Poland 31 G7
Tomatlán, Mexico 118 D3
Tombadonkéa, Guinea 82 C2
Tombador, Serra do, Brazil 124 F7
Tombe, Sudan 81 F3
Tombigbee →, U.S.A. 115 K2
Tombouctou, Mali 82 B4
Tombstone, U.S.A. 109 L8
Tombua, Angola 88 B1
Tomé, Chile 126 D1
Tomelilla, Sweden 11 J7
Tomelloso, Spain 37 F7
Tomini, Indonesia 63 D6
Tomini, Teluk, Indonesia 63 E6
Tominian, Mali 82 C4
Tomiño, Spain 36 D2
Tomintoul, U.K. 13 D5
Tomislavgrad, Bos.-H. 28 G2
Tomkinson Ranges, Australia 93 E4
Tommot, Russia 53 D13
Tomnop Ta Suos, Cambodia 65 G5
Tomo →, Colombia 124 B5
Toms Place, U.S.A. 110 H8
Toms River, U.S.A. 117 G10
Tomsk, Russia 52 D9
Tomtabacken, Sweden 11 G8
Tona, Spain 38 D7
Tonalá, Mexico 119 D6
Tonale, Passo del, Italy 40 B7
Tonantins, Brazil 124 D5
Tonasket, U.S.A. 108 B4
Tonawanda, U.S.A. 116 D6
Tonb, Iran 71 E7
Tonbridge, U.K. 15 F8
Tondano, Indonesia 63 D6
Tondela, Portugal 36 E2
Tønder, Denmark 11 K2
Tondi Kiwindi, Niger 83 C5
Tondibi, Mali 83 B4
Tondoro, Namibia 88 B2
Tone →, Australia 93 F2
Tone-Gawa →, Japan 55 F9
Tonekābon, Iran 71 B6
Tong Xian, China 56 E9
Tongâ, Sudan 81 F3
Tonga ■, Pac. Oc. 91 D11
Tonga Trench, Pac. Oc. 96 J10
Tongaat, S. Africa 89 D5
Tong'an, China 59 E12
Tongareva, Cook Is. 97 H12
Tongariro △, N.Z. 91 H5
Tongatapu Group, Tonga 91 E12
Tongbai, China 59 A9
Tongcheng, Anhui, China 59 B11
Tongcheng, Hubei, China 59 C9
Tongchŏn-ni, N. Korea 57 E14
Tongchuan, China 56 G5
Tongdao, China 58 D7
Tongeren, Belgium 17 D5
Tonggu, China 59 C10
Tongguan, China 56 G6
Tonghae, S. Korea 57 F15
Tonghai, China 58 E4
Tonghua, China 57 D13
Tongjiang, China 58 B6
Tongjosŏn Man, N. Korea 57 E15
Tongking, G. of = Tonkin, G. of, Asia 60 E5
Tongliang, China 58 C6
Tongliao, China 57 C12
Tongling, China 59 B11
Tonglu, China 59 C12
Tongnae, S. Korea 57 G15
Tongnan = Anyue, China 58 B5
Tongobory, Madag. 89 C7
Tongoy, Chile 126 C1
Tongren, China 58 D7
Tongres = Tongeren, Belgium 17 D5
Tongsa Dzong, Bhutan 67 F17
Tongue, U.K. 13 C4
Tongue →, U.S.A. 112 B2
Tongwei, China 56 G3
Tongxiang, China 59 B13
Tongxin, China 56 F3
Tongyang, N. Korea 57 E14
Tongyu, China 57 B12
Tongzi, China 58 C6
Tonj, Sudan 81 F2
Tonj →, Sudan 81 F2
Tonk, India 68 F6
Tonkawa, U.S.A. 113 G6
Tonkin = Bac Phan, Vietnam 64 B5
Tonkin, G. of, Asia 60 E5
Tonle Sap, Cambodia 64 F4
Tonnay-Charente, France 20 C3
Tonneins, France 20 D4
Tonnerre, France 19 E10
Tönning, Germany 24 A4
Tono, Japan 54 E10
Tonopah, U.S.A. 109 G5
Tonosí, Panama 120 E3
Tons →, Haryana, India 68 D7
Tons →, Ut. P., India 69 F10
Tønsberg, Norway 9 G14
Tonto ⌂, U.S.A. 109 K8
Tonya, Turkey 73 B8
Toobanna, Australia 94 B4
Toodyay, Australia 93 F2
Tooele, U.S.A. 108 F7
Toompine, Australia 95 D3
Toora, Australia 95 F4
Toora-Khem, Russia 53 D10
Toowoomba, Australia 95 D5
Top Springs, Australia 92 C5
Topalu, Romania 29 F13

Topaz, *U.S.A.* 110 G7
Topeka, *U.S.A.* 112 F7
Topl'a →, *Slovak Rep.* 27 C14
Topley, *Canada* 102 C3
Toplica →, *Serbia & M.* 44 C5
Toplița, *Romania* 29 D10
Topocalma, Pta., *Chile* 126 C1
Topock, *U.S.A.* 111 L12
Topola, *Serbia & M.* 44 B4
Topolčani, *Macedonia* 44 E5
Topol'čany, *Slovak Rep.* 27 C11
Topolnitsa →, *Bulgaria* 45 D8
Topolobampo, *Mexico* 118 B3
Topoloveni, *Romania* 29 F10
Topolovgrad, *Bulgaria* 45 D10
Topolvățu Mare, *Romania* 28 E6
Toppenish, *U.S.A.* 108 C3
Topraisar, *Romania* 29 F13
Topusko, *Croatia* 41 C12
Torà, *Spain* 38 D6
Tora Kit, *Sudan* 81 E3
Toraka Vestale, *Madag.* 89 B7
Torata, *Peru* 124 G4
Torbalı, *Turkey* 47 C9
Torbat-e Heydārīyeh, *Iran* 71 C8
Torbat-e Jām, *Iran* 71 C9
Torbay, *Canada* 105 C9
Torbay ☐, *U.K.* 15 G4
Torbjörntorp, *Sweden* 11 F7
Tordesillas, *Spain* 36 D6
Töreboda, *Sweden* 11 F8
Torekov, *Sweden* 11 H6
Torellò, *Spain* 38 C7
Toreno, *Spain* 36 C4
Torfaen ☐, *U.K.* 15 F4
Torgau, *Germany* 24 D8
Torgelow, *Germany* 24 B10
Torhamn, *Sweden* 11 H9
Torhout, *Belgium* 17 C3
Torhovytsya, *Ukraine* 29 B10
Tori, *Ethiopia* 81 F3
Tori-Shima, *Japan* 55 J10
Torigni-sur-Vire, *France* 18 C6
Torija, *Spain* 38 E1
Torin, *Mexico* 118 B2
Torino, *Italy* 40 C4
Torit, *Sudan* 81 G3
Torkamān, *Iran* 70 B5
Torkovichi, *Russia* 32 C6
Tormac, *Romania* 28 E6
Tormes →, *Spain* 36 D4
Tornado Mt., *Canada* 102 D6
Tornal'a, *Slovak Rep.* 27 C13
Torneå = Tornio, *Finland* 8 D21
Torneälven →, *Europe* 8 D21
Torneträsk, *Sweden* 8 B18
Tornio, *Finland* 8 D21
Tornionjoki = Torneälven →, *Europe* 8 D21
Tornquist, *Argentina* 126 D3
Toro, *Baleares, Spain* 48 B11
Toro, *Zamora, Spain* 36 D5
Torö, *Sweden* 11 F11
Toro ⌓, *Uganda* 86 C3
Toro, Cerro del, *Chile* 126 B2
Toro Pk., *U.S.A.* 111 M10
Törökszentmiklós, *Hungary* 28 C5
Toroníios Kólpos, *Greece* 44 F7
Toronto, *Canada* 116 C5
Toronto, *U.S.A.* 116 F4
Toronto Lester B. Pearson International ✕ (YYZ), *Canada* 116 C5
Toropets, *Russia* 32 D6
Tororo, *Uganda* 86 B3
Toros Dağları, *Turkey* 70 B2
Torpa, *India* 69 H11
Torquay, *U.K.* 15 G4
Torquemada, *Spain* 36 C6
Torrance, *U.S.A.* 111 M8
Torrão, *Portugal* 37 G2
Torre Annunziata, *Italy* 43 B7
Torre de Moncorvo, *Portugal* 36 D3
Torre del Campo, *Spain* 37 H7
Torre del Greco, *Italy* 43 B7
Torre del Mar, *Spain* 37 J6
Torre-Pacheco, *Spain* 39 H4
Torre Péllice, *Italy* 40 D4
Torreblanca, *Spain* 38 E5
Torrecampo, *Spain* 37 G6
Torrecilla en Cameros, *Spain* 38 C2
Torredembarra, *Spain* 38 D6
Torredonjimeno, *Spain* 37 H7
Torrejón de Ardoz, *Spain* 36 E7
Torrejoncillo, *Spain* 36 F4
Torrelaguna, *Spain* 36 E7
Torrelavega, *Spain* 36 B6
Torremaggiore, *Italy* 41 G12
Torremolinos, *Spain* 37 J6
Torrens, L., *Australia* 95 E2
Torrens Cr. →, *Australia* 94 C4
Torrens Creek, *Australia* 94 C4
Torrent, *Spain* 39 F4
Torrenueva, *Spain* 37 G7
Torreón, *Mexico* 118 B4
Torreperogil, *Spain* 37 G7
Torres, *Brazil* 127 B5
Torres, *Mexico* 118 B2
Torres Novas, *Portugal* 37 F2
Torres Strait, *Australia* 96 H6
Torres Vedras, *Portugal* 37 F1
Torrevieja, *Spain* 39 H4
Torrey, *U.S.A.* 109 G8
Torridge →, *U.K.* 15 G3
Torridon, L., *U.K.* 13 D3
Torrijos, *Spain* 36 F6
Tørring, *Denmark* 11 J3
Torrington, *Conn., U.S.A.* 117 E11
Torrington, *Wyo., U.S.A.* 112 D2
Torroella de Montgrì, *Spain* 38 C8
Torrox, *Spain* 37 J7
Torsås, *Sweden* 11 H9
Torsby, *Sweden* 10 D6
Torshälla, *Sweden* 10 E10
Tórshavn, *Færoe Is.* 8 E9
Torslanda, *Sweden* 11 G5
Torsö, *Sweden* 11 F7
Tortola, *Br. Virgin Is.* 121 e
Tórtoles de Esgueva, *Spain* 36 D6
Tortolì, *Italy* 42 C2
Tortona, *Italy* 40 D5
Tortorici, *Italy* 43 D7
Tortosa, *Spain* 38 E5
Tortosa, C., *Spain* 38 E5
Tortosendo, *Portugal* 36 E3
Tortue, I. de la, *Haiti* 121 B5
Tortuguero △, *Costa Rica* 120 D3
Tortum, *Turkey* 73 B9
Ţorūd, *Iran* 71 C7
Torul, *Turkey* 73 B8
Toruń, *Poland* 31 E5
Torun, *Ukraine* 29 B8
Tory I., *Ireland* 12 A3
Torysa →, *Slovak Rep.* 27 C14
Torzhok, *Russia* 32 D8
Torzym, *Poland* 31 F2
Tosa, *Japan* 55 H6
Tosa-Shimizu, *Japan* 55 H6
Tosa-Wan, *Japan* 55 H6
Toscana ☐, *Italy* 40 E8
Toscano, Arcipelago, *Italy* 40 F7
Toshkent, *Uzbekistan* 52 E7
Tosno, *Russia* 32 C6
Tossa de Mar, *Spain* 38 D7
Tösse, *Sweden* 11 F6
Tostado, *Argentina* 126 B3
Tostedt, *Germany* 24 B5
Tostón, Pta. de, *Canary Is.* 48 F5
Tosu, *Japan* 55 H5
Tosya, *Turkey* 72 B6
Toszek, *Poland* 31 H5
Totana, *Spain* 39 H3
Totebo, *Sweden* 11 G10
Toteng, *Botswana* 88 C3
Tôtes, *France* 18 C8
Tótkomlós, *Hungary* 28 D5
Totma, *Russia* 52 C5
Totnes, *U.K.* 15 G4
Totness, *Suriname* 125 B7
Toto, *Nigeria* 83 D6
Totonicapán, *Guatemala* 120 D1
Totten Glacier, *Antarctica* 5 C8
Tottenham, *Australia* 95 E4
Tottenham, *Canada* 116 B5
Tottori, *Japan* 55 G7
Tottori ☐, *Japan* 55 G7
Touaret, *Niger* 83 A6
Touba, *Ivory C.* 82 D3
Touba, *Senegal* 82 C1
Toubkal, Djebel, *Morocco* 78 B4
Toucy, *France* 19 E10
Tougan, *Burkina Faso* 82 C4
Touggourt, *Algeria* 78 B7
Tougouri, *Burkina Faso* 83 C4
Tougué, *Guinea* 82 C2
Toukoto, *Mali* 82 C3
Toul, *France* 19 D12
Toulepleu, *Ivory C.* 82 D3
Toulon, *France* 21 E9
Toulouse, *France* 20 E5
Toulouse Blagnac ✕ (TLS), *France* 20 E5
Toummo, *Niger* 79 D8
Toumodi, *Ivory C.* 82 D3
Tounan, *Taiwan* 59 F13
Toungo, *Nigeria* 83 D7
Toungoo, *Burma* 67 K20
Touques →, *France* 18 C7
Touraine, *France* 18 E7
Tourcoing, *France* 19 B10
Touriñán, C., *Spain* 36 B1
Tournai, *Belgium* 17 D3
Tournan-en-Brie, *France* 19 D9
Tournay, *France* 20 E4
Tournon-St-Martin, *France* 18 F7
Tournon-sur-Rhône, *France* 21 C8
Tournus, *France* 19 F11
Tours, *France* 18 E7
Toussora, Mt., *C.A.R.* 84 C4
Touws →, *S. Africa* 88 E3
Touwsrivier, *S. Africa* 88 E3
Tovarkovskiy, *Russia* 32 F10
Tovste, *Ukraine* 29 B10
Tovuz, *Azerbaijan* 35 K7
Towada, *Japan* 54 D10
Towada-Hachimantai △, *Japan* 54 D10
Towada-Ko, *Japan* 54 D10
Towanda, *U.S.A.* 117 E8
Towang, *India* 67 F17
Tower, *U.S.A.* 112 B8
Towerhill Cr. →, *Australia* 94 C3
Towner, *U.S.A.* 112 A4
Townsend, *U.S.A.* 108 C8
Townshend I., *Australia* 94 C5
Townsville, *Australia* 94 B4
Towraghondi, *Afghan.* 66 B3
Towson, *U.S.A.* 114 F7
Towuti, Danau, *Indonesia* 63 E6
Toya-Ko, *Japan* 54 C10
Toyama, *Japan* 55 F8
Toyama ☐, *Japan* 55 F8
Toyama-Wan, *Japan* 55 F8
Toyapakeh, *Indonesia* 63 K18
Toyohashi, *Japan* 55 G8
Toyokawa, *Japan* 55 G8
Toyonaka, *Japan* 55 G7
Toyooka, *Japan* 55 G7
Toyota, *Japan* 55 G8
Tozeur, *Tunisia* 78 B7
Tozkhurmato, *Iraq* 70 C5
Tqibuli, *Georgia* 35 J6
Tqvarcheli, *Georgia* 35 J5
Trá Li = Tralee, *Ireland* 12 D2
Tra On, *Vietnam* 65 H5
Trabancos →, *Spain* 36 D5
Traben-Trarbach, *Germany* 25 F3
Trabzon, *Turkey* 73 B8
Tracadie-Sheila, *Canada* 105 C7
Tracy, *Calif., U.S.A.* 110 H5
Tracy, *Minn., U.S.A.* 112 C7
Tradate, *Italy* 40 C5
Trade Town, *Liberia* 82 D3
Trafalgar, C., *Spain* 37 J4
Traian, *Brăila, Romania* 29 E12
Traian, *Tulcea, Romania* 29 E13
Trail, *Canada* 102 D5
Trainor L., *Canada* 102 A4
Trákhonas, *Cyprus* 49 D12
Tralee, *Ireland* 12 D2
Tralee B., *Ireland* 12 D2
Tramore, *Ireland* 12 D4
Tramore B., *Ireland* 12 D4
Tran Ninh, Cao Nguyen, *Laos* 64 C4
Tranås, *Sweden* 11 F8
Tranbjerg, *Denmark* 11 H4
Trancas, *Argentina* 126 B2
Trancoso, *Portugal* 36 E3
Tranebjerg, *Denmark* 11 J4
Tranemo, *Sweden* 11 G7
Trang, *Thailand* 65 J2
Trangahy, *Madag.* 89 B7
Trangan, *Indonesia* 63 F8
Trangie, *Australia* 95 E4
Trångsviken, *Sweden* 10 A7
Trani, *Italy* 43 A9
Tranoroa, *Madag.* 89 C8
Tranqueras, *Uruguay* 127 C4
Transantarctic Mts., *Antarctica* 5 E12
Transilvania, *Romania* 29 D9
Transilvanian Alps = Carpații Meridionali, *Romania* 29 E9
Transnistria = Stînga Nistrului ☐, *Moldova* 29 C14
Transtrand, *Sweden* 10 C7
Transtrandsfjällen, *Sweden* 10 C6
Transylvania = Transilvania, *Romania* 29 D9
Trápani, *Italy* 42 D5
Trapper Pk., *U.S.A.* 108 D6
Traralgon, *Australia* 95 F4
Trarza, *Mauritania* 82 B2
Trasacco, *Italy* 41 G10
Trăscău, Munții, *Romania* 29 D8
Trasimeno, L., *Italy* 41 E9
Träslövsläge, *Sweden* 11 G6
Trasvase Tajo-Segura, Canal de, *Spain* 38 E2
Trat, *Thailand* 65 F4
Tratani →, *Pakistan* 68 E3
Traun, *Austria* 26 C7
Traunreut, *Germany* 25 H8
Traunsee, *Austria* 26 D6
Traunstein, *Germany* 25 H8
Traveller's L., *Australia* 95 E3
Travemünde, *Germany* 24 B6
Travers, Mt., *N.Z.* 91 K4
Traverse City, *U.S.A.* 114 C3
Travis, L., *U.S.A.* 113 K5
Travnik, *Bos.-H.* 28 F2
Trbovlje, *Slovenia* 41 B12
Trébbia →, *Italy* 40 C6
Trebel →, *Germany* 24 B9
Trébeurden, *France* 18 D3
Trebević △, *Bos.-H.* 28 G3
Třebíč, *Czech Rep.* 26 B8
Trebinje, *Bos.-H.* 44 D2
Trebisacce, *Italy* 43 C9
Trebišnjica →, *Bos.-H.* 44 D2
Trebišov, *Slovak Rep.* 27 C14
Trebižat →, *Bos.-H.* 41 E14
Trebnje, *Slovenia* 41 C12
Třeboň, *Czech Rep.* 26 B7
Trebonne, *Australia* 94 B4
Třeboňsko ⌓, *Czech Rep.* 26 B7
Trebujena, *Spain* 37 J4
Trecate, *Italy* 40 C5
Tregaron, *U.K.* 15 E4
Tregnago, *Italy* 41 C8
Tregrosse Is., *Australia* 94 B5
Tréguier, *France* 18 D3
Trégunc, *France* 18 E3
Treherne, *Canada* 103 D9
Tréia, *Italy* 41 E10
Treignac, *France* 20 C5
Treinta y Tres, *Uruguay* 127 C5
Treis-karden, *Germany* 25 E3
Treklyano, *Bulgaria* 44 D6
Trelawney, *Zimbabwe* 89 B5
Trélazé, *France* 18 E6
Trelew, *Argentina* 128 E3
Trélissac, *France* 20 C4
Trelleborg, *Sweden* 11 J7
Tremadog Bay, *U.K.* 14 E3
Trémiti, *Italy* 41 F12
Tremonton, *U.S.A.* 108 F7
Tremp, *Spain* 38 C5
Trenche →, *Canada* 104 C5
Trenčiansky ☐, *Slovak Rep.* 27 C11
Trenčín, *Slovak Rep.* 27 C11
Trenggalek, *Indonesia* 63 H14
Trenque Lauquen, *Argentina* 126 D3
Trent →, *Canada* 116 B7
Trent →, *U.K.* 14 D7
Trentino-Alto Adige ☐, *Italy* 41 B8
Trento, *Italy* 40 B8
Trenton = Quinte West, *Canada* 116 B7
Trenton, *Mo., U.S.A.* 112 E8
Trenton, *N.J., U.S.A.* 117 F10
Trenton, *Nebr., U.S.A.* 112 E4
Trepassey, *Canada* 105 C9
Trepuzzi, *Italy* 43 B11
Tres Arroyos, *Argentina* 126 D3
Três Corações, *Brazil* 127 A6
Três Lagoas, *Brazil* 125 H8
Tres Lomas, *Argentina* 126 D3
Tres Marías, Islas, *Mexico* 118 C3
Tres Montes, C., *Chile* 128 F1
Tres Pinos, *U.S.A.* 110 J5
Três Pontas, *Brazil* 127 A6
Tres Puentes, *Chile* 126 B1
Tres Puntas, C., *Argentina* 128 F3
Três Rios, *Brazil* 127 A7
Tres Valles, *Mexico* 119 D5
Tresco, *U.K.* 15 H1
Treska →, *Macedonia* 44 E5
Treskavica, *Bos.-H.* 28 G3
Trespaderne, *Spain* 36 C7
Tresticklan △, *Sweden* 11 F5
Trets, *France* 21 E9
Treuchtlingen, *Germany* 25 G6
Treuenbrietzen, *Germany* 24 C8
Trevi, *Italy* 41 F9
Trevíglio, *Italy* 40 C6
Trevínca, Peña, *Spain* 36 C4
Treviso, *Italy* 41 C9
Trévoux, *France* 21 C8
Trgovište, *Serbia & M.* 44 D6
Triabunna, *Australia* 95 G4
Triánda, *Greece* 49 C10
Triangle, *Zimbabwe* 89 C5
Triaucourt-en-Argonne, *France* 19 D12
Tribal Areas ☐, *Pakistan* 68 C4
Tribsees, *Germany* 24 A8
Tribulation, C., *Australia* 94 B4
Tribune, *U.S.A.* 112 F4
Tricárico, *Italy* 43 B9
Tricase, *Italy* 43 C11
Trichinopoly = Tiruchchirappalli, *India* 66 P11
Trichur, *India* 66 P10
Trida, *Australia* 95 E4
Trier, *Germany* 25 F2
Trieste, *Italy* 41 C10
Trieste, G. di, *Italy* 41 C10
Trieux →, *France* 18 D3
Triggiano, *Italy* 43 A9
Triglav, *Slovenia* 41 B10
Triglavski △, *Slovenia* 41 B10
Trigno →, *Italy* 41 F11
Trigueros, *Spain* 37 H4
Tríkeri, *Greece* 46 B5
Trikhonis, Límni, *Greece* 46 C3
Tríkkala, *Greece* 46 B3
Tríkkala ☐, *Greece* 46 B3
Trikomo, *Cyprus* 49 D12
Trikora, Puncak, *Indonesia* 63 E9
Trilj, *Croatia* 41 E13
Trillo, *Spain* 38 E2
Trim, *Ireland* 12 C5
Trincomalee, *Sri Lanka* 66 Q12
Trindade, *Brazil* 125 G9
Trindade, I., *Atl. Oc.* 2 F8
Třinec, *Czech Rep.* 27 B11
Trinidad, *Bolivia* 124 F6
Trinidad, *Cuba* 120 B4
Trinidad, *Trin. & Tob.* 121 D7
Trinidad, *Uruguay* 126 C4
Trinidad, *U.S.A.* 113 G2
Trinidad →, *Mexico* 119 D5
Trinidad & Tobago ■, *W. Indies* 121 D7
Trinitápoli, *Italy* 43 A9
Trinity, *Canada* 105 C9
Trinity, *U.S.A.* 113 K7
Trinity →, *Calif., U.S.A.* 108 F2
Trinity →, *Tex., U.S.A.* 113 L7
Trinity B., *Canada* 105 C9
Trinity Hills, *Trin. & Tob.* 125 K15
Trinity Is., *U.S.A.* 100 C4
Trinity Range, *U.S.A.* 108 F4
Trinkitat, *Sudan* 80 D4
Trino, *Italy* 40 C5
Trinway, *U.S.A.* 116 F2
Trionto, C., *Italy* 43 C9
Triora, *Italy* 40 D4
Tripoli = Tarābulus, *Lebanon* 74 A4
Tripoli = Tarābulus, *Libya* 79 B8
Trípolis, *Greece* 46 D4
Tripolitania, *N. Afr.* 79 B8
Tripura ☐, *India* 67 H18
Tripylos, *Cyprus* 49 E11
Trischen, *Germany* 24 A4
Tristan da Cunha, *Atl. Oc.* 77 K2
Trisul, *India* 69 D8
Trivandrum, *India* 66 Q10
Trivento, *Italy* 41 G11
Trnava, *Slovak Rep.* 27 C10
Trnavský ☐, *Slovak Rep.* 27 C10
Troarn, *France* 18 C6
Trochu, *Canada* 102 C6
Trodely I., *Canada* 104 B4
Troezen, *Greece* 46 D5
Trogir, *Croatia* 41 E13
Troglav, *Croatia* 41 E13
Tróia, *Italy* 43 A8
Troilus, L., *Canada* 104 B5
Troina, *Italy* 43 E7
Trois-Pistoles, *Canada* 105 C6
Trois-Rivières, *Canada* 104 C5
Trois-Rivières, *Guadeloupe* 120 b
Troisdorf, *Germany* 24 E3
Troitsk, *Russia* 52 D7
Troitsko Pechorsk, *Russia* 52 C6
Troitskoye, *Russia* 35 G7
Trölladyngja, *Iceland* 8 D5
Trollhättan, *Sweden* 11 F6
Trollheimen, *Norway* 8 E13
Trombetas →, *Brazil* 125 D7
Tromsø, *Norway* 8 B18
Trona, *U.S.A.* 111 K9
Tronador, Mte., *Argentina* 128 E2
Trøndelag, *Norway* 8 D14
Trondheim, *Norway* 8 E14
Trondheimsfjorden, *Norway* 8 E14
Trönninge, *Sweden* 11 H6
Tronto →, *Italy* 41 F10
Troodos, *Cyprus* 49 E11
Troon, *U.K.* 13 F4
Tropea, *Italy* 43 D8
Tropic, *U.S.A.* 109 H7
Tropojë, *Albania* 44 D4
Trosa, *Sweden* 11 F11
Trostan, *U.K.* 12 A5
Trostberg, *Germany* 25 G8
Trostyanets, *Ukraine* 29 B14
Trostyanets, *Ukraine* 33 G8
Trou Gras Pt., *St. Lucia* 121 f
Trout →, *Canada* 102 A5
Trout L., *N.W.T., Canada* 102 A4
Trout L., *Ont., Canada* 103 C10
Trout Lake, *Canada* 102 B6
Trout Lake, *U.S.A.* 110 E5
Trout River, *Canada* 105 C8
Trout Run, *U.S.A.* 116 E7
Trouville-sur-Mer, *France* 18 C7
Trowbridge, *U.K.* 15 F5
Troy, *Turkey* 47 B8
Troy, *Ala., U.S.A.* 115 K3
Troy, *Kans., U.S.A.* 112 F7
Troy, *Mo., U.S.A.* 112 F9
Troy, *Mont., U.S.A.* 108 B6
Troy, *N.Y., U.S.A.* 117 D11
Troy, *Ohio, U.S.A.* 114 E3
Troy, *Pa., U.S.A.* 117 E8
Troyan, *Bulgaria* 45 D8
Troyes, *France* 19 D11
Trpanj, *Croatia* 41 E14
Trstenik, *Serbia & M.* 44 C5
Trubchevsk, *Russia* 33 F7
Truchas Peak, *U.S.A.* 113 H2
Trucial States = United Arab Emirates ■, *Asia* 71 F7
Truckee, *U.S.A.* 110 F6
Trudfront, *Russia* 35 H8
Trudovoye, *Russia* 54 C6
Trujillo, *Honduras* 120 C2
Trujillo, *Peru* 124 E3
Trujillo, *Spain* 37 F5
Trujillo, *U.S.A.* 113 H2
Trujillo, *Venezuela* 124 B4
Truk, *Micronesia* 96 G7
Trumann, *U.S.A.* 113 H9
Trumansburg, *U.S.A.* 117 D8
Trumbull, Mt., *U.S.A.* 109 H7
Trŭn, *Bulgaria* 44 D6
Trun, *France* 18 D7
Trundle, *Australia* 95 E4
Trung-Phan = Annam, *Vietnam* 64 E7
Truro, *Canada* 105 C7
Truro, *U.K.* 15 G2
Truskavets, *Ukraine* 33 H2
Trŭstenik, *Bulgaria* 45 C8
Trustrup, *Denmark* 11 H4
Trutch, *Canada* 102 B4
Truth or Consequences, *U.S.A.* 109 K10
Trutnov, *Czech Rep.* 26 A8
Truxton, *U.S.A.* 117 D8
Truyère →, *France* 20 D6
Tryavna, *Bulgaria* 45 D9
Tryonville, *U.S.A.* 116 E5
Trzcianka, *Poland* 31 E3
Trzciel, *Poland* 31 F2
Trzcińsko Zdrój, *Poland* 31 F1
Trzebiatów, *Poland* 30 D2
Trzebiez, *Poland* 30 E1
Trzebnica, *Poland* 31 G4
Trzemeszno, *Poland* 31 F4
Tržič, *Slovenia* 41 B11
Tsagan Aman, *Russia* 35 G8
Tsamandás, *Greece* 46 B2
Tsandi, *Namibia* 88 B1
Tsaratanana, *Madag.* 89 B8
Tsaratanana ⌓, *Madag.* 89 A8
Tsaratanana, Mt. de = Maromokotro, *Madag.* 89 A8
Tsarevo, *Bulgaria* 45 D9
Tsaritsáni, *Greece* 46 B4
Tsau, *Botswana* 88 C3
Tsavo East △, *Kenya* 86 C4
Tsavo West △, *Kenya* 86 C4
Tsebrykove, *Ukraine* 33 J6
Tsentralnyy ☐, *Russia* 34 D4
Tses, *Namibia* 88 D2
Tsetserleg, *Mongolia* 60 B5
Tsévié, *Togo* 83 D5
Tshabong, *Botswana* 88 D3
Tshane, *Botswana* 88 C3
Tshela, *Dem. Rep. of the Congo* 84 E2
Tshesebe, *Botswana* 89 C4
Tshibeke, *Dem. Rep. of the Congo* 86 C2
Tshibinda, *Dem. Rep. of the Congo* 86 C2
Tshikapa, *Dem. Rep. of the Congo* 84 F4
Tshilenge, *Dem. Rep. of the Congo* 86 D1
Tshinsenda, *Dem. Rep. of the Congo* 87 E2
Tshofa, *Dem. Rep. of the Congo* 86 D2
Tshwane, *Botswana* 88 C3
Tsigara, *Botswana* 88 C4
Tsihombe, *Madag.* 89 D8
Tsiigehtchic, *Canada* 100 B6
Tsimlyansk, *Russia* 35 G6
Tsimlyansk Res. = Tsimlyanskoye Vdkhr., *Russia* 35 F6
Tsimlyanskoye Vdkhr., *Russia* 35 F6
Tsinan = Jinan, *China* 56 F9
Tsineng, *S. Africa* 88 D3
Tsínga, *Greece* 45 E8
Tsinghai = Qinghai ☐, *China* 60 C4
Tsingtao = Qingdao, *China* 57 F11
Tsingy de Bemaraha ⌓, *Madag.* 89 B8
Tsingy de Namoraka ⌓, *Madag.* 89 B8
Tsinjoarivo, *Madag.* 89 B8
Tsinjomitondraka, *Madag.* 89 B8
Tsiroanomandidy, *Madag.* 89 B8
Tsiteli-Tsqaro, *Georgia* 35 K8

Tsitondroina, *Madag.* 89 **C8**
Tsitsikamma △, *S. Africa* 88 **E3**
Tsivilsk, *Russia* 34 **C8**
Tsivory, *Madag.* 89 **C8**
Tskhinvali, *Georgia* 35 **J7**
Tsna →, *Russia* 34 **C6**
Tsnori, *Georgia* 35 **K7**
Tso Moriri, L., *India* 69 **C8**
Tsobis, *Namibia* 88 **B2**
Tsodilo Hill, *Botswana* 88 **B3**
Tsogttsetsiy = Baruunsuu, *Mongolia* 56 **C3**
Tsolo, *S. Africa* 89 **E4**
Tsomo, *S. Africa* 89 **E4**
Tsu, *Japan* 55 **G8**
Tsu L., *Canada* 102 **A6**
Tsuchiura, *Japan* 55 **F10**
Tsuen Wan, *China* 59 **F10**
Tsugaru-Kaikyō, *Japan* 54 **D10**
Tsumeb, *Namibia* 88 **B2**
Tsumis, *Namibia* 88 **C2**
Tsuruga, *Japan* 55 **G8**
Tsurugi-San, *Japan* 55 **H7**
Tsuruoka, *Japan* 54 **E9**
Tsushima, *Gifu, Japan* 55 **G8**
Tsushima, *Nagasaki, Japan* 55 **G4**
Tsuyama, *Japan* 55 **G7**
Tsvetkovo, *Ukraine* 33 **H6**
Tsyelyakhany, *Belarus* 33 **F3**
Tua →, *Portugal* 36 **D3**
Tual, *Indonesia* 63 **F8**
Tuam, *Ireland* 12 **C3**
Tuamotu Arch. = Tuamotu Is., *French Polynesia* 97 **J13**
Tuamotu Is., *French Polynesia* 97 **J13**
Tuamotu Ridge, *Pac. Oc.* 97 **K14**
Tuanfeng, *China* 59 **B10**
Tuanxi, *China* 58 **D6**
Tuao, *Phil.* 61 **C4**
Tuapse, *Russia* 35 **H4**
Tuas, *Singapore* 65 **d**
Tuatapere, *N.Z.* 91 **M1**
Tuba City, *U.S.A.* 109 **H8**
Tuban, *Indonesia* 63 **G15**
Tubani, *Botswana* 88 **C3**
Tubarão, *Brazil* 127 **B6**
Tūbās, *West Bank* 74 **C4**
Tubas →, *Namibia* 88 **C2**
Tübingen, *Germany* 25 **G5**
Tubruq, *Libya* 79 **B10**
Tubuai Is., *French Polynesia* 97 **K13**
Tuc Trung, *Vietnam* 65 **G6**
Tucacas, *Venezuela* 124 **A5**
T'uch'ang, *Taiwan* 59 **E13**
Tuchodi →, *Canada* 102 **B4**
Tuchola, *Poland* 30 **E4**
Tuchów, *Poland* 31 **J8**
Tuckanarra, *Australia* 93 **E2**
Tucson, *U.S.A.* 109 **K8**
Tucumán □, *Argentina* 126 **B2**
Tucumcari, *U.S.A.* 113 **H3**
Tucupita, *Venezuela* 124 **B6**
Tucuruí, *Brazil* 125 **D9**
Tucuruí, Reprêsa de, *Brazil* 125 **D9**
Tuczno, *Poland* 31 **E3**
Tudela, *Spain* 38 **C3**
Tudmur, *Syria* 70 **C3**
Tudor, L., *Canada* 105 **A6**
Tudora, *Romania* 29 **C11**
Tuella →, *Portugal* 36 **D3**
Tugela →, *S. Africa* 89 **D5**
Tuguegarao, *Phil.* 61 **C4**
Tugur, *Russia* 53 **D14**
Tui, *Spain* 36 **C2**
Tuineje, *Canary Is.* 48 **F5**
Tukangbesi, Kepulauan, *Indonesia* 63 **F6**
Tukarak I., *Canada* 104 **A4**
Tukayyid, *Iraq* 70 **D5**
Tûkh, *Egypt* 80 **H7**
Tukhlya, *Ukraine* 29 **B8**
Tukkae, Ao, *Thailand* 65 **a**
Tukobo, *Ghana* 82 **D4**
Tuktoyaktuk, *Canada* 100 **B6**
Tukums, *Latvia* 9 **H20**
Tukums □, *Latvia* 30 **B10**
Tukuyu, *Tanzania* 87 **D3**
Tula, *Hidalgo, Mexico* 119 **C5**
Tula, *Tamaulipas, Mexico* 119 **C5**
Tula, *Nigeria* 83 **D7**
Tula, *Russia* 32 **E9**
Tulancingo, *Mexico* 119 **C5**
Tulare, *Serbia & M.* 44 **D5**
Tulare, *U.S.A.* 110 **J7**
Tulare Lake Bed, *U.S.A.* 110 **K7**
Tularosa, *U.S.A.* 109 **K10**
Tulbagh, *S. Africa* 88 **E2**
Tulcán, *Ecuador* 124 **C3**
Tulcea, *Romania* 29 **E13**
Tulcea □, *Romania* 29 **E13**
Tulchyn, *Ukraine* 29 **B13**
Tūleh, *Iran* 71 **C7**
Tulemalu L., *Canada* 103 **A9**
Tulgheş, *Romania* 29 **D10**
Tuli, *Zimbabwe* 87 **G2**
Tulia, *U.S.A.* 113 **H4**
Tuliszków, *Poland* 31 **F5**
Tulita, *Canada* 100 **B7**
Ţūlkarm, *West Bank* 74 **C4**
Tulla, *Ireland* 12 **D3**
Tullahoma, *U.S.A.* 115 **H2**
Tullamore, *Australia* 95 **E4**
Tullamore, *Ireland* 12 **C4**
Tulle, *France* 20 **C5**
Tulln, *Austria* 26 **C9**
Tullow, *Ireland* 12 **D5**
Tullus, *Sudan* 81 **E1**
Tully, *Australia* 94 **B4**
Tully, *U.S.A.* 117 **D8**
Tulnici, *Romania* 29 **E11**
Tulovo, *Bulgaria* 45 **D9**
Tulsa, *U.S.A.* 113 **G7**
Tulsequah, *Canada* 102 **B2**
Tulu Milki, *Ethiopia* 81 **F4**
Tulu Welel, *Ethiopia* 81 **F3**
Tulua, *Colombia* 124 **C3**
Tulucești, *Romania* 29 **E13**
Tulun, *Russia* 53 **D11**
Tulungagung, *Indonesia* 63 **H14**
Tuma, *Russia* 32 **E11**
Tuma →, *Nic.* 120 **D3**
Tumacacori ⌓, *U.S.A.* 109 **L8**
Tumaco, *Colombia* 124 **C3**
Tumatumari, *Guyana* 124 **B7**
Tumba, *Sweden* 10 **E11**
Tumba, L., *Dem. Rep. of the Congo* 84 **E3**
Tumbarumba, *Australia* 95 **F4**
Tumbaya, *Argentina* 126 **A2**
Tumbes, *Peru* 124 **D2**
Tumbur, *Sudan* 81 **G3**
Tumbwe, *Dem. Rep. of the Congo* 87 **E2**
Tumby Bay, *Australia* 95 **E2**
Tumd Youqi, *China* 56 **D6**
Tumen, *China* 57 **C15**
Tumen Jiang →, *China* 57 **C16**
Tumeremo, *Venezuela* 124 **B6**
Tumkur, *India* 66 **N10**
Tump, *Pakistan* 66 **F3**
Tumpat, *Malaysia* 65 **J4**
Tumu, *Ghana* 82 **C4**
Tumucumaque, Serra, *Brazil* 125 **C8**
Tumut, *Australia* 95 **F4**
Tumwater, *U.S.A.* 110 **C4**
Tuna, *India* 68 **H4**
Tunadal, *Sweden* 10 **B11**
Tunapuna, *Trin. & Tob.* 125 **K15**
Tunas de Zaza, *Cuba* 120 **B4**
Tunbridge Wells = Royal Tunbridge Wells, *U.K.* 15 **F8**
Tunçbilek, *Turkey* 47 **B11**
Tunceli, *Turkey* 73 **C8**
Tuncurry, *Australia* 95 **E5**
Tundla, *India* 68 **F8**
Tundubai, *Sudan* 80 **D2**
Tunduru, *Tanzania* 87 **E4**
Tundzha →, *Bulgaria* 45 **E10**
Tungabhadra →, *India* 66 **M11**
Tungaru, *Sudan* 81 **E3**
Tungla, *Nic.* 120 **D3**
Tungsha Tao = Dongsha Dao, *China* 59 **G11**
Tungshih, *Taiwan* 59 **E13**
Tungsten, *Canada* 102 **A3**
Tunguska, Nizhnyaya →, *Russia* 53 **C9**
Tunguska, Podkamennaya →, *Russia* 53 **C10**
Tunica, *U.S.A.* 113 **H9**
Tunis, *Tunisia* 78 **A7**
Tunis ✕ (TUN), *Tunisia* 42 **F3**
Tunisia ■, *Africa* 78 **B6**
Tunja, *Colombia* 124 **B4**
Tunkhannock, *U.S.A.* 117 **E9**
Tunliu, *China* 56 **F7**
Tunnel Creek △, *Australia* 92 **C4**
Tunnsjøen, *Norway* 8 **D15**
Tunø, *Denmark* 11 **J4**
Tunungayualok I., *Canada* 105 **A7**
Tunuyán, *Argentina* 126 **C2**
Tunuyán →, *Argentina* 126 **C2**
Tuo Jiang →, *China* 58 **C5**
Tuolumne, *U.S.A.* 110 **H6**
Tuolumne →, *U.S.A.* 110 **H5**
Tūp Āghāj, *Iran* 70 **B5**
Tupã, *Brazil* 127 **A5**
Tupelo, *U.S.A.* 115 **H1**
Tupik, *Russia* 32 **E7**
Tupinambaranas, *Brazil* 124 **D7**
Tupiza, *Bolivia* 126 **A2**
Tupižnica, *Serbia & M.* 44 **C6**
Tupman, *U.S.A.* 111 **K7**
Tupper, *Canada* 102 **B4**
Tupper Lake, *U.S.A.* 117 **B10**
Tupungato, Cerro, *S. Amer.* 126 **C2**
Tuquan, *China* 57 **B11**
Túquerres, *Colombia* 124 **C3**
Tura, *Russia* 53 **C11**
Turabah, *Ḥā'il, Si. Arabia* 70 **D4**
Turabah, *Makkah, Si. Arabia* 80 **C5**
Tūrān, *Iran* 71 **C8**
Turan, *Russia* 53 **D10**
Ţurayf, *Si. Arabia* 70 **D3**
Turbacz, *Poland* 31 **J7**
Turbe, *Bos.-H.* 28 **F2**
Turčianske Teplice, *Slovak Rep.* 27 **C11**
Turcoaia, *Romania* 29 **E13**
Turda, *Romania* 29 **D8**
Turek, *Poland* 31 **F5**
Turen, *Venezuela* 124 **B5**
Turfan = Turpan, *China* 60 **B3**
Turfan Basin = Turpan Hami, *China* 50 **E12**
Turfan Depression = Turpan Hami, *China* 50 **E12**
Turgeon →, *Canada* 104 **C4**
Tŭrgovishte, *Bulgaria* 45 **C10**
Turgut, *Turkey* 47 **D10**
Turgutlu, *Turkey* 47 **C9**
Turgwe →, *Zimbabwe* 89 **C5**
Turhal, *Turkey* 72 **B7**
Turia →, *Spain* 39 **F4**
Turiaçu, *Brazil* 125 **D9**
Turiaçu →, *Brazil* 125 **D9**
Turiec →, *Slovak Rep.* 27 **B11**
Turin = Torino, *Italy* 40 **C4**
Turka, *Ukraine* 31 **J10**
Turkana, L., *Africa* 86 **B4**
Türkeli, *Turkey* 45 **F11**
Turkestan = Türkistan, *Kazakhstan* 52 **E7**
Túrkeve, *Hungary* 28 **C5**
Turkey ■, *Eurasia* 72 **C7**
Turkey Creek, *Australia* 92 **C4**
Turki, *Russia* 34 **D6**
Türkistan, *Kazakhstan* 52 **E7**
Türkmenbashi, *Turkmenistan* 52 **E6**
Turkmenistan ■, *Asia* 52 **F6**
Türkmenli, *Turkey* 47 **B8**
Türkoğlu, *Turkey* 72 **D7**
Turks & Caicos Is. ☒, *W. Indies* 121 **B5**
Turks Island Passage, *W. Indies* 121 **B5**
Turku, *Finland* 9 **F20**
Turkwel →, *Kenya* 86 **B4**
Turlock, *U.S.A.* 110 **H6**
Turnagain →, *Canada* 102 **B3**
Turnagain, C., *N.Z.* 91 **J6**
Turneffe Is., *Belize* 119 **D7**
Turner, *U.S.A.* 108 **B9**
Turner Pt., *Australia* 94 **A1**
Turner Valley, *Canada* 102 **C6**
Turners Falls, *U.S.A.* 117 **D12**
Turnhout, *Belgium* 17 **C4**
Türnitz, *Austria* 26 **D8**
Turnor L., *Canada* 103 **B7**
Turnov, *Czech Rep.* 26 **A8**
Tŭrnovo = Veliko Tŭrnovo, *Bulgaria* 45 **C9**
Turnu Măgurele, *Romania* 29 **G9**
Turnu Roşu, P., *Romania* 29 **E9**
Turobin, *Poland* 31 **H9**
Turpan, *China* 60 **B3**
Turpan Hami, *China* 50 **E12**
Turrës, Kala e, *Albania* 44 **E3**
Turriff, *U.K.* 13 **D6**
Tursāq, *Iraq* 70 **C5**
Tursi, *Italy* 43 **B9**
Turtle Head I., *Australia* 94 **A3**
Turtle Is., *S. Leone* 82 **D2**
Turtle L., *Canada* 103 **C7**
Turtle Lake, *U.S.A.* 112 **B4**
Turtleford, *Canada* 103 **C7**
Turuépano △, *Venezuela* 121 **D7**
Turukhansk, *Russia* 53 **C9**
Turzovka, *Slovak Rep.* 27 **B11**
Tuscaloosa, *U.S.A.* 115 **J2**
Tuscánia, *Italy* 41 **F8**
Tuscany = Toscana □, *Italy* 40 **E8**
Tuscarawas →, *U.S.A.* 116 **F3**
Tuscarora Mt., *U.S.A.* 116 **F7**
Tuscola, *Ill., U.S.A.* 114 **F1**
Tuscola, *Tex., U.S.A.* 113 **J5**
Tuscumbia, *U.S.A.* 115 **H2**
Tuskegee, *U.S.A.* 115 **J3**
Tustin, *U.S.A.* 111 **M9**
Tuszyn, *Poland* 31 **G6**
Tutak, *Turkey* 73 **C10**
Tutayev, *Russia* 32 **D10**
Tuticorin, *India* 66 **Q11**
Tutin, *Serbia & M.* 44 **D4**
Tutóia, *Brazil* 125 **D10**
Tutong, *Brunei* 62 **D4**
Tutova →, *Romania* 29 **D12**
Tutrakan, *Bulgaria* 45 **B10**
Tuttle Creek L., *U.S.A.* 112 **F6**
Tuttlingen, *Germany* 25 **H4**
Tutuala, *E. Timor* 63 **F7**
Tutuila, *Amer. Samoa* 91 **B13**
Tutume, *Botswana* 85 **J5**
Tutun, *Egypt* 80 **J7**
Tututepec, *Mexico* 119 **D5**
Tuva □, *Russia* 53 **D10**
Tuvalu ■, *Pac. Oc.* 96 **H9**
Tuxer Alpen, *Austria* 26 **D4**
Tuxpan, *Mexico* 119 **C5**
Tuxtla Gutiérrez, *Mexico* 119 **D6**
Tuy = Tui, *Spain* 36 **C2**
Tuy An, *Vietnam* 64 **F7**
Tuy Duc, *Vietnam* 65 **F6**
Tuy Hoa, *Vietnam* 64 **F7**
Tuy Phong, *Vietnam* 65 **G7**
Tuya L., *Canada* 102 **B2**
Tuyen Hoa, *Vietnam* 64 **D6**
Tuyen Quang, *Vietnam* 58 **G5**
Tūysarkān, *Iran* 71 **C6**
Tuz Gölü, *Turkey* 72 **C5**
Ţūz Khurmātū = Tozkhurmato, *Iraq* 70 **C5**
Tuzi, *Serbia & M.* 44 **D3**
Tuzigoot ⌓, *U.S.A.* 109 **J7**
Tuzla, *Bos.-H.* 28 **F3**
Tuzlov →, *Russia* 33 **J10**
Tuzluca, *Turkey* 73 **B10**
Tuzly 29 **E15**
Tvååker, *Sweden* 11 **G6**
Tvardiţa, *Moldova* 29 **D13**
Tver, *Russia* 32 **D8**
Tvrdošin, *Slovak Rep.* 27 **B12**
Tvrdošovce, *Slovak Rep.* 27 **C11**
Tvŭrditsa, *Bulgaria* 45 **D9**
Twain, *U.S.A.* 110 **E5**
Twain Harte, *U.S.A.* 110 **G6**
Twardogóra, *Poland* 31 **G4**
Tweed, *Canada* 116 **B7**
Tweed →, *U.K.* 13 **F6**
Tweed Heads, *Australia* 95 **D5**
Tweedsmuir ⌓, *Canada* 102 **C3**
Twentynine Palms, *U.S.A.* 111 **L10**
Twillingate, *Canada* 105 **C9**
Twin Bridges, *U.S.A.* 108 **D7**
Twin Falls, *Canada* 105 **B7**
Twin Falls, *U.S.A.* 108 **E6**
Twin Valley, *U.S.A.* 112 **B6**
Twinsburg, *U.S.A.* 116 **E3**
Twistringen, *Germany* 24 **C4**
Twitchell Reservoir, *U.S.A.* 111 **L6**
Two Harbors, *U.S.A.* 112 **B9**
Two Hills, *Canada* 102 **C6**
Two Rivers, *U.S.A.* 114 **C2**
Two Rocks, *Australia* 93 **F2**
Twofold B., *Australia* 95 **F4**
Tyachiv, *Ukraine* 33 **H2**
Tychy, *Poland* 31 **H5**
Tyczyn, *Poland* 31 **J9**
Tykocin, *Poland* 31 **E9**
Tyler, *Minn., U.S.A.* 112 **C6**
Tyler, *Tex., U.S.A.* 113 **J7**
Tyligul →, *Ukraine* 33 **J6**
Tymanivka, *Ukraine* 29 **B13**
Týn nad Vltavou, *Czech Rep.* 26 **B7**
Tynda, *Russia* 53 **D13**
Tyndall, *U.S.A.* 112 **D6**
Tyne →, *U.K.* 14 **C6**
Tyne & Wear □, *U.K.* 14 **B6**
Týnec nad Sázavou, *Czech Rep.* 26 **B7**
Tynemouth, *U.K.* 14 **B6**
Tyre = Sūr, *Lebanon* 74 **B4**
Tyresta △, *Sweden* 10 **E12**
Tyrifjorden, *Norway* 9 **F14**
Tyringe, *Sweden* 11 **H7**
Tyrnyauz, *Russia* 35 **J6**
Tyrol = Tirol □, *Austria* 26 **D3**
Tyrone, *U.S.A.* 116 **F6**
Tyrone □, *U.K.* 12 **B4**
Tyrrell →, *Australia* 95 **F3**
Tyrrell, L., *Australia* 95 **F3**
Tyrrell L., *Canada* 103 **A7**
Tyrrhenian Sea, *Medit. S.* 6 **G8**
Tysfjorden, *Norway* 8 **B17**
Tysmenytsya, *Ukraine* 29 **B9**
Tystberga, *Sweden* 11 **F11**
Tytuvėnai, *Lithuania* 30 **C10**
Tyub Karagan, Mys, *Kazakhstan* 35 **H10**
Tyuleni, Ostrova, *Kazakhstan* 35 **H10**
Tyuleniy, *Russia* 35 **H8**
Tyuleniy, Mys, *Azerbaijan* 35 **K10**
Tyumen, *Russia* 52 **D7**
Tywi →, *U.K.* 15 **F3**
Tywyn, *U.K.* 15 **E3**
Tzaneen, *S. Africa* 89 **C5**
Tzermiádhes, *Greece* 49 **D7**
Tzoumérka, Óros, *Greece* 46 **B3**
Tzukong = Zigong, *China* 58 **C5**

U

U Taphao, *Thailand* 64 **F3**
U.S.A. = United States of America ■, *N. Amer.* 106 **C7**
U.S. Virgin Is. ☒, *W. Indies* 121 **e**
Uatumã →, *Brazil* 124 **D7**
Uaupés, *Brazil* 124 **D5**
Uaupés →, *Brazil* 124 **C5**
Uaxactún, *Guatemala* 120 **C2**
Ub, *Serbia & M.* 44 **B4**
Ubá, *Brazil* 127 **A7**
Uba, *Nigeria* 83 **C7**
Ubaitaba, *Brazil* 125 **F11**
Ubangi = Oubangi →, *Dem. Rep. of the Congo* 84 **E3**
Ubauro, *Pakistan* 68 **E3**
Ubaye →, *France* 21 **D10**
Ubayyiḍ, W. al →, *Iraq* 70 **C4**
Ube, *Japan* 55 **H5**
Úbeda, *Spain* 37 **G7**
Uberaba, *Brazil* 125 **G9**
Uberlândia, *Brazil* 125 **G9**
Überlingen, *Germany* 25 **H5**
Ubiaja, *Nigeria* 83 **D6**
Ubin, Pulau, *Singapore* 65 **d**
Ubolratna Res., *Thailand* 64 **D4**
Ubombo, *S. Africa* 89 **D5**
Ubon Ratchathani, *Thailand* 64 **E5**
Ubondo, *Dem. Rep. of the Congo* 86 **C2**
Ubort →, *Belarus* 33 **F5**
Ubrique, *Spain* 37 **J5**
Ubud, *Indonesia* 63 **J18**
Ubundu, *Dem. Rep. of the Congo* 86 **C2**
Ucayali →, *Peru* 124 **D4**
Uchab, *Namibia* 88 **B2**
Uchiura-Wan, *Japan* 54 **C10**
Uchquduq, *Uzbekistan* 52 **E7**
Uchte, *Germany* 24 **C4**
Uchur →, *Russia* 53 **D14**
Uckermark, *Germany* 24 **B9**
Ucluelet, *Canada* 102 **D3**
Uda →, *Russia* 53 **D14**
Udagamandalam, *India* 66 **P10**
Udainagar, *India* 68 **H7**
Udaipur, *India* 68 **G5**
Udaipur Garhi, *Nepal* 69 **F12**
Udala, *India* 69 **J12**
Udbina, *Croatia* 41 **D12**
Uddeholm, *Sweden* 10 **D7**
Uddevalla, *Sweden* 11 **F5**
Uddjaure, *Sweden* 8 **D17**
Uden, *Neths.* 17 **C5**
Udgir, *India* 66 **K10**
Udhampur, *India* 69 **C6**
Udi, *Nigeria* 83 **D6**
Údine, *Italy* 41 **B10**
Udmurtia □, *Russia* 52 **D6**
Udon Thani, *Thailand* 64 **D4**
Udupi, *India* 66 **N9**
Udvoy Balkan, *Bulgaria* 45 **D10**
Udzungwa △, *Tanzania* 86 **D4**
Udzungwa Range, *Tanzania* 87 **D4**
Ueckermünde, *Germany* 24 **B10**
Ueda, *Japan* 55 **F9**
Uedineniya, Os., *Russia* 4 **B12**
Uele →, *Dem. Rep. of the Congo* 84 **D4**
Uelen, *Russia* 53 **C19**
Uelzen, *Germany* 24 **C6**
Uetersen, *Germany* 24 **B5**
Uetze, *Germany* 24 **C6**
Ufa, *Russia* 52 **D6**
Uffenheim, *Germany* 25 **F6**
Ugab →, *Namibia* 88 **C1**
Ugalla →, *Tanzania* 86 **D3**
Ugalla River ⌓, *Tanzania* 86 **D3**
Uganda ■, *Africa* 86 **B3**
Ugento, *Italy* 43 **C11**
Ugep, *Nigeria* 83 **D6**
Ughelli, *Nigeria* 83 **D6**
Ugie, *S. Africa* 89 **E4**
Ugíjar, *Spain* 37 **J7**
Ugine, *France* 21 **C10**
Uglegorsk, *Russia* 53 **E15**
Uglich, *Russia* 32 **D10**
Ugljan, *Croatia* 41 **D12**
Ugljane, *Croatia* 41 **E13**
Ugra →, *Russia* 32 **E9**
Ugŭrchin, *Bulgaria* 45 **C8**
Uh →, *Slovak Rep.* 27 **C15**
Uherské Hradiště, *Czech Rep.* 27 **B10**
Uherský Brod, *Czech Rep.* 27 **B10**
Úhlava →, *Czech Rep.* 26 **B6**
Uhlenhorst, *Namibia* 88 **C2**
Uhniv, *Ukraine* 31 **H10**
Uhrichsville, *U.S.A.* 116 **F3**
Uibhist a Deas = South Uist, *U.K.* 13 **D1**
Uibhist a Tuath = North Uist, *U.K.* 13 **D1**
Uig, *U.K.* 13 **D2**
Uíge, *Angola* 84 **F2**
Uijŏngbu, *S. Korea* 57 **F14**
Ŭiju, *N. Korea* 57 **D13**
Uinta Mts., *U.S.A.* 108 **F8**
Uis, *Namibia* 88 **C1**
Uitenhage, *S. Africa* 88 **E4**
Uithuizen, *Neths.* 17 **A6**
Ujazd, *Poland* 31 **H5**
Újfehértó, *Hungary* 28 **C6**
Ujh →, *India* 68 **C6**
Ujhani, *India* 69 **F8**
Uji-guntō, *Japan* 55 **J4**
Ujjain, *India* 68 **H6**
Ujście, *Poland* 31 **E3**
Újszász, *Hungary* 28 **C5**
Ujung Pandang, *Indonesia* 63 **F5**
Uka, *Russia* 53 **D17**
Ukara I., *Tanzania* 86 **C3**
Uke-Shima, *Japan* 55 **K4**
Ukerewe I., *Tanzania* 86 **C3**
Ukholovo, *Russia* 34 **D5**
Ukhrul, *India* 67 **G19**
Ukhta, *Russia* 52 **C6**
Ukiah, *U.S.A.* 110 **F3**
Ukmergė, *Lithuania* 9 **J21**
Ukraine ■, *Europe* 33 **H7**
Ukwi, *Botswana* 88 **C3**
Ulaan-Uul, *Mongolia* 56 **B6**
Ulaanbaatar, *Mongolia* 53 **E11**
Ulaangom, *Mongolia* 60 **A4**
Ulaanjirem, *Mongolia* 56 **B3**
Ulamba, *Dem. Rep. of the Congo* 87 **D1**
Ulan Bator = Ulaanbaatar, *Mongolia* 53 **E11**
Ulan Erge, *Russia* 35 **G7**
Ulan Khol, *Russia* 35 **H8**
Ulan Ude, *Russia* 53 **D11**
Ulanów, *Poland* 31 **H9**
Ulaş, *Sivas, Turkey* 72 **C7**
Ulaş, *Tekirdağ, Turkey* 45 **E11**
Ulaya, *Morogoro, Tanzania* 86 **D4**
Ulaya, *Tabora, Tanzania* 86 **C3**
Ulcinj, *Serbia & M.* 44 **E3**
Ulco, *S. Africa* 88 **D3**
Ule älv = Oulujoki →, *Finland* 8 **D21**
Ule träsk = Oulujärvi, *Finland* 8 **D22**
Uleåborg = Oulu, *Finland* 8 **D21**
Ulefoss, *Norway* 9 **G13**
Ulëz, *Albania* 44 **E3**
Ulfborg, *Denmark* 11 **H2**
Ulhasnagar, *India* 66 **K8**
Uliastay, *Mongolia* 60 **B4**
Uljma, *Serbia & M.* 28 **E6**
Ulla →, *Spain* 36 **C2**
Ulladulla, *Australia* 95 **F5**
Ullapool, *U.K.* 13 **D3**
Ullared, *Sweden* 11 **G6**
Ulldecona, *Spain* 38 **E5**
Ullswater, *U.K.* 14 **C5**
Ullŭng-do, *S. Korea* 55 **F5**
Ulm, *Germany* 25 **G5**
Ulmarra, *Australia* 95 **D5**
Ulmeni, *Buzău, Romania* 29 **E11**
Ulmeni, *Maramureş, Romania* 29 **C8**
Ulonguè, *Mozam.* 87 **E3**
Ulricehamn, *Sweden* 11 **G7**
Ulrika, *Sweden* 11 **F9**
Ulsan, *S. Korea* 57 **G15**
Ulsta, *U.K.* 13 **A7**
Ulster □, *U.K.* 12 **B5**
Ulstrem, *Bulgaria* 45 **D10**
Ulubat Gölü, *Turkey* 45 **F12**
Ulubey, *Turkey* 47 **C11**
Uluborlu, *Turkey* 47 **C12**
Uluçinar, *Turkey* 72 **D6**
Uludağ, *Turkey* 45 **F13**
Uludağ △, *Turkey* 45 **F13**
Uludere, *Turkey* 73 **D10**
Uluguru Mts., *Tanzania* 86 **D4**
Ulukışla, *Turkey* 72 **D6**
Ulungur He →, *China* 60 **B3**
Uluru = Ayers Rock, *Australia* 93 **E5**
Uluru-Kata Tjuta △, *Australia* 93 **E5**
Ulutau, *Kazakhstan* 52 **E7**
Uluwatu, *Indonesia* 63 **K18**
Ulva, *U.K.* 13 **E2**
Ulverston, *U.K.* 14 **C4**
Ulverstone, *Australia* 95 **G4**
Ulya, *Russia* 53 **D15**
Ulyanovo, *Russia* 30 **D9**
Ulyanovsk = Simbirsk, *Russia* 34 **C9**
Ulyasutay = Uliastay, *Mongolia* 60 **B4**
Ulysses, *U.S.A.* 113 **G4**
Umag, *Croatia* 41 **C10**
Umala, *Bolivia* 124 **G5**
Uman, *Ukraine* 33 **H6**
Umaria, *India* 67 **H12**
Umarkot, *Pakistan* 66 **G6**
Umarpada, *India* 68 **J5**

Umatilla, *U.S.A.* 108 **D4**
Umbagog L., *U.S.A.* 117 **B13**
Umbakumba, *Australia* 94 **A2**
Umbértide, *Italy* 41 **E9**
Umbrella Mts., *N.Z.* 91 **L2**
Umbria □, *Italy* 41 **F9**
Umeå, *Sweden* 8 **E19**
Umeälven →, *Sweden* 8 **E19**
Umera, *Indonesia* 63 **E7**
Umfolozi ⌓, *S. Africa* 89 **D5**
Umfuli →, *Zimbabwe* 87 **F2**
Umfurudzi ⌓, *Zimbabwe* 87 **F3**
Umgusa, *Zimbabwe* 87 **F2**
Umim Urūmah, *Si. Arabia* 80 **B4**
Umka, *Serbia & M.* 44 **B4**
Umkomaas, *S. Africa* 89 **E5**
Umlazi, *S. Africa* 85 **L6**
Umm ad Daraj, J., *Jordan* 74 **C4**
Umm al Qaywayn, *U.A.E.* 71 **E7**
Umm al Qittayn, *Jordan* 74 **C5**
Umm Arda, *Sudan* 81 **D3**
Umm Bāb, *Qatar* 71 **E6**
Umm Badr, *Sudan* 81 **E2**
Umm Baiyud, *Sudan* 81 **E3**
Umm Bel, *Sudan* 81 **E2**
Umm Birkah, *Si. Arabia* 80 **B4**
Umm Boim, *Sudan* 81 **E2**
Umm Dam, *Sudan* 81 **E3**
Umm Debi, *Sudan* 81 **E3**
Umm Dubban, *Sudan* 81 **D3**
Umm Durman = Omdurmân, *Sudan* 81 **D3**
Umm el Fahm, *Israel* 74 **C4**
Umm Gafala, *Sudan* 81 **E2**
Umm Gimala, *Sudan* 81 **E2**
Umm Inderaba, *Sudan* 80 **D3**
Umm Keddada, *Sudan* 81 **E2**
Umm Koweika, *Sudan* 81 **E3**
Umm Lajj, *Si. Arabia* 70 **E3**
Umm Merwa, *Sudan* 80 **D3**
Umm Qantur, *Sudan* 81 **E3**
Umm Qurein, *Sudan* 81 **F2**
Umm Ruwaba, *Sudan* 81 **E3**
Umm Saiyala, *Sudan* 81 **E3**
Umm Shanqa, *Sudan* 81 **E2**
Umm Shutur, *Sudan* 81 **F3**
Umm Sidr, *Sudan* 81 **E2**
Umm Zehetir, *Egypt* 80 **J8**
Umnak I., *U.S.A.* 100 **C3**
Umniati →, *Zimbabwe* 87 **F2**
Umpqua →, *U.S.A.* 108 **E1**
Umreth, *India* 68 **H5**
Umtata, *S. Africa* 89 **E4**
Umuahia, *Nigeria* 83 **D6**
Umuarama, *Brazil* 127 **A5**
Umurbey, *Turkey* 45 **F10**
Umvukwe Ra., *Zimbabwe* 87 **F3**
Umzimvubu, *S. Africa* 89 **E4**
Umzingwane →, *Zimbabwe* 87 **G2**
Umzinto, *S. Africa* 89 **E5**
Una, *India* 68 **J4**
Una →, *Bos.-H.* 41 **D13**
Unac →, *Bos.-H.* 41 **D13**
Unadilla, *U.S.A.* 117 **D9**
Unalakleet, *U.S.A.* 100 **B3**
Unalaska, *U.S.A.* 100 **C3**
Unalaska I., *U.S.A.* 100 **C3**
'Unayzah, *Si. Arabia* 70 **E4**
'Unayzah, J., *Asia* 70 **C3**
Uncastillo, *Spain* 38 **C3**
Uncía, *Bolivia* 124 **G5**
Uncompahgre Peak, *U.S.A.* 109 **G10**
Uncompahgre Plateau, *U.S.A.* 109 **G9**
Undara Volcanic △, *Australia* 94 **B3**
Unden, *Sweden* 11 **F8**
Underbool, *Australia* 95 **F3**
Undersaker, *Sweden* 10 **A7**
Unecha, *Russia* 33 **F7**
Ungarie, *Australia* 95 **E4**
Ungarra, *Australia* 95 **E2**
Ungava, Pén. d', *Canada* 101 **C12**
Ungava B., *Canada* 101 **C13**
Ungeny = Ungheni, *Moldova* 29 **C12**
Unggi, *N. Korea* 57 **C16**
Ungheni, *Moldova* 29 **C12**
Unguala →, *Ethiopia* 81 **F5**
Ungwana B., *Kenya* 86 **C5**
Ungwatiri, *Sudan* 81 **D4**
Uni, *Russia* 34 **B10**
União da Vitória, *Brazil* 127 **B5**
Uničov, *Czech Rep.* 27 **B10**
Uniejów, *Poland* 31 **G5**
Unije, *Croatia* 41 **D11**
Unimak I., *U.S.A.* 100 **C3**
Union, *Miss., U.S.A.* 113 **J10**
Union, *Mo., U.S.A.* 112 **F9**
Union, *S.C., U.S.A.* 115 **H5**
Union City, *Calif., U.S.A.* 110 **H4**
Union City, *N.J., U.S.A.* 117 **F10**
Union City, *Pa., U.S.A.* 116 **E5**
Union City, *Tenn., U.S.A.* 113 **G10**
Union Gap, *U.S.A.* 108 **C3**
Union Springs, *U.S.A.* 115 **J3**
Uniondale, *S. Africa* 88 **E3**
Uniontown, *U.S.A.* 114 **F6**
Unionville, *U.S.A.* 112 **E8**
Unirea, *Romania* 29 **F12**
United Arab Emirates ■, *Asia* 71 **F7**
United Kingdom ■, *Europe* 7 **E5**
United States of America ■, *N. Amer.* 106 **C7**
Unity, *Canada* 103 **C7**
Universales, Mtes., *Spain* 38 **E3**
University Park, *U.S.A.* 109 **K10**
Unjha, *India* 68 **H5**
Unna, *Germany* 24 **D3**
Unnao, *India* 69 **F9**
Uno, Ilha, *Guinea-Biss.* 82 **C1**
Unsengedsi →, *Zimbabwe* 87 **F3**
Unst, *U.K.* 13 **A8**
Unstrut →, *Germany* 24 **D7**
Unterfranken □, *Germany* 25 **F5**
Unterschleissheim, *Germany* 25 **G7**
Unuk →, *Canada* 102 **B2**
Ünye, *Turkey* 72 **B7**
Unzen-Amakusa △, *Japan* 55 **H5**
Unzha, *Russia* 34 **A7**
Unzha →, *Russia* 34 **B6**
Uozu, *Japan* 55 **F8**
Upata, *Venezuela* 124 **B6**
Upemba △, *Dem. Rep. of the Congo* 87 **D2**
Upemba, L., *Dem. Rep. of the Congo* 87 **D2**
Upernavik, *Greenland* 4 **B5**
Upington, *S. Africa* 88 **D3**
Upleta, *India* 68 **J4**
'Upolu, *Samoa* 91 **A13**
Upper □, *Ghana* 83 **C4**
Upper Alkali L., *U.S.A.* 108 **F3**
Upper Arrow L., *Canada* 102 **C5**
Upper Foster L., *Canada* 103 **B7**
Upper Hutt, *N.Z.* 91 **J5**
Upper Klamath L., *U.S.A.* 108 **E3**
Upper Lake, *U.S.A.* 110 **F4**
Upper Manzanilla, *Trin. & Tob.* 125 **K15**
Upper Missouri River Breaks ⌓, *U.S.A.* 108 **C9**
Upper Musquodoboit, *Canada* 105 **C7**
Upper Red L., *U.S.A.* 112 **A7**
Upper Sandusky, *U.S.A.* 114 **E4**
Upper Volta = Burkina Faso ■, *Africa* 82 **C4**
Upphärad, *Sweden* 11 **F6**
Uppland, *Sweden* 10 **D12**
Upplands-Väsby, *Sweden* 10 **E11**
Uppsala, *Sweden* 10 **E11**
Uppsala län □, *Sweden* 10 **D11**
Upshi, *India* 69 **C7**
Upstart, C., *Australia* 94 **B4**
Upton, *U.S.A.* 112 **C2**
Uqsuqtuuq = Gjoa Haven, *Canada* 100 **B10**
Ur, *Iraq* 70 **D5**
Urad Qianqi, *China* 56 **D5**
Urakawa, *Japan* 54 **C11**
Ural = Uralskiy □, *Russia* 52 **C7**
Ural = Zhayyq →, *Kazakhstan* 52 **E6**
Ural, *Australia* 95 **E4**
Ural Mts. = Uralskie Gory, *Eurasia* 52 **D6**
Uralla, *Australia* 95 **E5**
Uralsk = Oral, *Kazakhstan* 34 **E10**
Uralskie Gory, *Eurasia* 52 **D6**
Uralskiy □, *Russia* 52 **C7**
Urambo, *Tanzania* 86 **D3**
Urandangi, *Australia* 94 **C2**
Uranium City, *Canada* 103 **B7**
Uraricoera →, *Brazil* 124 **C6**
Urawa, *Japan* 55 **G9**
Uray, *Russia* 52 **C7**
'Uray'irah, *Si. Arabia* 71 **E6**
Urbana, *Ill., U.S.A.* 114 **E1**
Urbana, *Ohio, U.S.A.* 114 **E4**
Urbánia, *Italy* 41 **E9**
Urbel →, *Spain* 36 **C7**
Urbino, *Italy* 41 **E9**
Urbión, Picos de, *Spain* 38 **C2**
Urcos, *Peru* 124 **F4**
Urdinarrain, *Argentina* 126 **C4**
Urdos, *France* 20 **F3**
Urdzhar, *Kazakhstan* 52 **E9**
Ure →, *U.K.* 14 **C6**
Uren, *Russia* 34 **B7**
Ures, *Mexico* 118 **B2**
Urewera △, *N.Z.* 91 **H6**
Urfa = Sanliurfa, *Turkey* 70 **B3**
Urganch, *Uzbekistan* 52 **E7**
Urgench = Urganch, *Uzbekistan* 52 **E7**
Ürgüp, *Turkey* 70 **B2**
Uri, *India* 69 **B6**
Uri □, *Switz.* 25 **J4**
Uribia, *Colombia* 124 **A4**
Uricani, *Romania* 28 **E8**
Uriondo, *Bolivia* 126 **A3**
Urique, *Mexico* 118 **B3**
Urique →, *Mexico* 118 **B3**
Urk, *Neths.* 17 **B5**
Urkiola ⌓, *Spain* 38 **B3**
Urla, *Turkey* 47 **C8**
Urlați, *Romania* 29 **F11**
Urmia = Orūmīyeh, *Iran* 70 **B5**
Uroševac, *Serbia & M.* 44 **D5**
Uroyan, Montanas de, *Puerto Rico* 121 **d**
Urshult, *Sweden* 11 **H8**
Uruaçu, *Brazil* 125 **F9**
Uruapan, *Mexico* 118 **D4**
Urubamba →, *Peru* 124 **F4**
Uruçara, *Brazil* 124 **D7**
Uruçuí, *Brazil* 125 **E10**
Uruguai →, *Brazil* 127 **B5**
Uruguaiana, *Brazil* 126 **B4**
Uruguay ■, *S. Amer.* 126 **C4**
Uruguay →, *S. Amer.* 126 **C4**
Urumchi = Ürümqi, *China* 52 **E9**
Ürümqi, *China* 52 **E9**
Urup →, *Russia* 35 **H5**
Urup, Ostrov, *Russia* 53 **E16**
Uryupinsk, *Russia* 34 **E5**
Urzhum, *Russia* 34 **B9**
Urziceni, *Romania* 29 **F11**
Usa →, *Russia* 52 **C6**
Uşak, *Turkey* 47 **C11**
Uşak □, *Turkey* 47 **C11**
Usakos, *Namibia* 88 **C2**
Ušće, *Serbia & M.* 44 **C4**
Usedom, *Germany* 24 **B10**
Usedom ⌓, *Germany* 24 **B10**
Useless Loop, *Australia* 93 **E1**
'Usfān, *Si. Arabia* 80 **C4**
Ush-Tobe, *Kazakhstan* 52 **E8**
Ushakova, Ostrov, *Russia* 4 **A12**
Ushakovo, *Russia* 30 **D7**
Ushant = Ouessant, Î. d', *France* 18 **D1**
Ushashi, *Tanzania* 86 **C3**
Ushat, *Sudan* 81 **F2**
'Ushayrah, *Si. Arabia* 80 **C5**
Ushibuka, *Japan* 55 **H5**
Ushuaia, *Argentina* 128 **G3**
Ushumun, *Russia* 53 **D13**
Ushytsya →, *Ukraine* 29 **B12**
Usk, *Canada* 102 **C3**
Usk →, *U.K.* 15 **F5**
Uska, *India* 69 **F10**
Üsküdar, *Turkey* 45 **F13**
Uslar, *Germany* 24 **D5**
Usman, *Russia* 33 **F10**
Usoke, *Tanzania* 86 **D3**
Usolye Sibirskoye, *Russia* 53 **D11**
Usoro, *Nigeria* 83 **D6**
Uspallata, P. de, *Argentina* 126 **C2**
Uspenskiy, *Kazakhstan* 52 **E8**
Ussel, *France* 20 **C6**
Usson-du-Poitou, *France* 20 **B4**
Ussuri →, *Asia* 54 **A7**
Ussuriysk, *Russia* 53 **E14**
Ussurka, *Russia* 54 **B6**
Ust-Bolsheretsk, *Russia* 53 **D16**
Ust-Buzulukskaya, *Russia* 34 **E6**
Ust-Chaun, *Russia* 53 **C18**
Ust-Chorna, *Ukraine* 29 **B8**
Ust-Donetskiy, *Russia* 35 **G5**
Ust-Ilimsk, *Russia* 53 **D11**
Ust-Ishim, *Russia* 52 **D8**
Ust-Kamchatsk, *Russia* 53 **D17**
Ust-Kamenogorsk = Öskemen, *Kazakhstan* 52 **E9**
Ust-Khayryuzovo, *Russia* 53 **D16**
Ust-Kut, *Russia* 53 **D11**
Ust-Kuyga, *Russia* 53 **B14**
Ust-Labinsk, *Russia* 35 **H4**
Ust-Luga, *Russia* 32 **C5**
Ust-Maya, *Russia* 53 **C14**
Ust-Mil, *Russia* 53 **D14**
Ust-Nera, *Russia* 53 **C15**
Ust-Nyukzha, *Russia* 53 **D13**
Ust-Olenek, *Russia* 53 **B12**
Ust-Omchug, *Russia* 53 **C15**
Ust-Port, *Russia* 52 **C9**
Ust-Tsilma, *Russia* 52 **C6**
Ust Urt = Ustyurt Plateau, *Asia* 52 **E6**
Ustaritz, *France* 20 **E2**
Ustecký □, *Czech Rep.* 26 **A7**
Uster, *Switz.* 25 **H4**
Ústí nad Labem, *Czech Rep.* 26 **A7**
Ústí nad Orlicí, *Czech Rep.* 27 **B9**
Ústica, *Italy* 42 **D6**
Ustinov = Izhevsk, *Russia* 52 **D6**
Ustka, *Poland* 30 **D3**
Ustroń, *Poland* 31 **J5**
Ustrzyki Dolne, *Poland* 31 **J9**
Ustyluh, *Ukraine* 31 **H11**
Ustyurt Plateau, *Asia* 52 **E6**
Ustyuzhna, *Russia* 32 **C9**
Usu, *China* 60 **B3**
Usuki, *Japan* 55 **H5**
Usulután, *El Salv.* 120 **D2**
Usumacinta →, *Mexico* 119 **D6**
Usumbura = Bujumbura, *Burundi* 86 **C2**
Usure, *Tanzania* 86 **C3**
Usutuo →, *Mozam.* 89 **D5**
Uta, *Indonesia* 63 **E9**
Utah □, *U.S.A.* 108 **G8**
Utah L., *U.S.A.* 108 **F8**
Utansjö, *Sweden* 10 **B11**
Utara, Selat, *Malaysia* 65 **c**
Utarni, *India* 68 **F4**
Utatlan, *Guatemala* 120 **C1**
Ute Creek →, *U.S.A.* 113 **H3**
Utebo, *Spain* 38 **D3**
Utena, *Lithuania* 9 **J21**
Utete, *Tanzania* 86 **D4**
Uthai Thani, *Thailand* 64 **E3**
Uthal, *Pakistan* 68 **G2**
Utiariti, *Brazil* 124 **F7**
Utica, *N.Y., U.S.A.* 117 **C9**
Utica, *Ohio, U.S.A.* 116 **F2**
Utiel, *Spain* 39 **F3**
Utikuma L., *Canada* 102 **B5**
Utö, *Sweden* 10 **F12**
Utopia, *Australia* 94 **C1**
Utraula, *India* 69 **F10**
Utrecht, *Neths.* 17 **B5**
Utrecht, *S. Africa* 89 **D5**
Utrecht □, *Neths.* 17 **B5**
Utrera, *Spain* 37 **H5**
Utsjoki →, *Finland* 8 **B22**
Utsunomiya, *Japan* 55 **F9**
Uttar Pradesh □, *India* 69 **F9**
Uttaradit, *Thailand* 64 **D3**
Uttaranchal □, *India* 69 **D8**
Uttoxeter, *U.K.* 14 **E6**
Utuado, *Puerto Rico* 121 **d**
Uummannaq, *Greenland* 4 **B4**
Uummannaq, *Greenland* 4 **B5**
Uummannarsuaq = Nunap Isua, *Greenland* 101 **C15**
Uusikaarlepyy, *Finland* 8 **E20**
Uusikaupunki, *Finland* 9 **F19**
Uva, *Russia* 34 **B11**
Uvac →, *Serbia & M.* 44 **C3**
Uvalde, *U.S.A.* 113 **L5**
Uvarovo, *Russia* 34 **E6**
Uvat, *Russia* 52 **D7**
Uvinza, *Tanzania* 86 **D3**
Uvira, *Dem. Rep. of the Congo* 86 **C2**
Uvs Nuur, *Mongolia* 60 **A4**
'Uwairidh, Ḥarrat al, *Si. Arabia* 70 **E3**
Uwajima, *Japan* 55 **H6**
Uwanda ⌓, *Tanzania* 86 **D3**
Uweinat, Jebel, *Sudan* 80 **C1**
Uxbridge, *Canada* 116 **B5**
Uxin Qi, *China* 56 **E5**
Uxmal, *Mexico* 119 **C7**
Üydzin, *Mongolia* 56 **B4**
Uyo, *Nigeria* 83 **D6**
Üyüklü Tepe, *Turkey* 47 **D9**
Uyûn Mûsa, *Egypt* 74 **F1**
Uyuni, *Bolivia* 124 **H5**
Uzbekistan ■, *Asia* 52 **E7**
Uzen, Bolshoi →, *Kazakhstan* 35 **F9**
Uzen, Mal →, *Kazakhstan* 35 **F9**
Uzerche, *France* 20 **C5**
Uzès, *France* 21 **D8**
Uzh →, *Ukraine* 33 **G6**
Uzhgorod = Uzhhorod, *Ukraine* 28 **B7**
Uzhhorod, *Ukraine* 28 **B7**
Uzhok, *Ukraine* 28 **B7**
Užice, *Serbia & M.* 44 **C3**
Uzlovaya, *Russia* 32 **F10**
Üzümlü, *Turkey* 47 **E11**
Uzunköprü, *Turkey* 45 **E10**
Uzunkuyu, *Turkey* 47 **C8**

V

Vaal →, *S. Africa* 88 **D3**
Vaal Dam, *S. Africa* 89 **D4**
Vaalbos △, *S. Africa* 88 **D3**
Vaalwater, *S. Africa* 89 **C4**
Vaasa, *Finland* 8 **E19**
Vabre, *France* 20 **E6**
Vác, *Hungary* 28 **C4**
Vacaria, *Brazil* 127 **B5**
Vacaville, *U.S.A.* 110 **G5**
Vaccarès, Étang de, *France* 21 **E8**
Vach = Vakh →, *Russia* 52 **C8**
Vache, Î. à, *Haiti* 121 **C5**
Väckelsång, *Sweden* 11 **H8**
Väddö, *Sweden* 10 **D12**
Väderstad, *Sweden* 11 **F8**
Vadnagar, *India* 68 **H5**
Vado Lígure, *Italy* 40 **D5**
Vadodara, *India* 68 **H5**
Vadsø, *Norway* 8 **A23**
Vadstena, *Sweden* 11 **F8**
Vaduz, *Liech.* 25 **H5**
Værøy, *Norway* 8 **C15**
Vágar, *Færoe Is.* 8 **E9**
Vaggeryd, *Sweden* 11 **G8**
Vagney, *France* 19 **D13**
Vagnhärad, *Sweden* 11 **F11**
Vagos, *Portugal* 36 **E2**
Vågsfjorden, *Norway* 8 **B17**
Váh →, *Slovak Rep.* 27 **D11**
Vahsel B., *Antarctica* 5 **D1**
Váhtjer = Gällivare, *Sweden* 8 **C19**
Vaï, *Greece* 49 **D8**
Vaigach, *Russia* 52 **B6**
Vaiges, *France* 18 **D6**
Vaihingen, *Germany* 25 **G4**
Vail, *U.S.A.* 106 **C5**
Vailly-sur-Aisne, *France* 19 **C10**
Vaisali →, *India* 69 **F8**
Vaison-la-Romaine, *France* 21 **D9**
Vakarel, *Bulgaria* 44 **D7**
Vakfikebir, *Turkey* 73 **B8**
Vakh →, *Russia* 52 **C8**
Vakhtan, *Russia* 34 **B8**
Vál, *Hungary* 28 **C3**
Val-de-Marne □, *France* 19 **D9**
Val-d'Isère, *France* 21 **C10**
Val-d'Oise □, *France* 19 **C9**
Val-d'Or, *Canada* 104 **C4**
Val Grande △, *Italy* 40 **B5**
Val Marie, *Canada* 103 **D7**
Val Thorens, *France* 21 **C10**
Valaam, *Russia* 32 **B6**
Valadares, *Portugal* 36 **D2**
Valahia, *Romania* 29 **F9**
Valais □, *Switz.* 25 **J3**
Valais, Alpes du, *Switz.* 25 **J3**
Valandovo, *Macedonia* 44 **E6**
Valašské Meziříčí, *Czech Rep.* 27 **B10**
Valáxa, *Greece* 46 **C6**
Vålberg, *Sweden* 10 **E7**
Valbo, *Sweden* 10 **D10**
Valbondione, *Italy* 40 **B7**
Vâlcani, *Romania* 28 **D5**
Vâlcea □, *Romania* 29 **F9**
Valcheta, *Argentina* 128 **E3**
Valdagno, *Italy* 41 **C8**
Valdahon, *France* 19 **E13**
Valdai Hills = Valdayskaya Vozvyshennost, *Russia* 32 **D7**
Valday, *Russia* 32 **D7**
Valdayskaya Vozvyshennost, *Russia* 32 **D7**
Valdeazogues →, *Spain* 37 **G6**
Valdecañas, Embalse de, *Spain* 36 **F5**
Valdemarsvik, *Sweden* 11 **F10**
Valdemoro, *Spain* 36 **E7**
Valdepeñas, *Spain* 37 **G7**
Valderaduey →, *Spain* 36 **D5**
Valdérice, *Italy* 42 **D5**
Valderrobres, *Spain* 38 **E5**
Valdés, Pen., *Argentina* 128 **E4**
Valdez, *U.S.A.* 100 **B5**
Valdivia, *Chile* 128 **D2**
Valdobbiádene, *Italy* 41 **C8**
Valdosta, *U.S.A.* 115 **K4**
Valdoviño, *Spain* 36 **B2**
Valdres, *Norway* 9 **F13**
Vale, *Georgia* 35 **K6**
Vale, *U.S.A.* 108 **E5**
Vale of Glamorgan □, *U.K.* 15 **F4**
Valea lui Mihai, *Romania* 28 **C7**
Valea Mărului, *Romania* 29 **E12**
Valemount, *Canada* 102 **C5**
Valença, *Brazil* 125 **F11**
Valença, *Portugal* 36 **C2**
Valença do Piauí, *Brazil* 125 **E10**
Valençay, *France* 19 **E8**
Valence, *France* 21 **D8**
Valence d'Agen, *France* 20 **D4**
Valencia, *Spain* 39 **F4**
Valencia, *Trin. & Tob.* 125 **K15**
Valencia, *U.S.A.* 109 **J10**
Valencia, *Venezuela* 124 **A5**
Valencia □, *Spain* 39 **F4**
Valencia ✈ (VLC), *Spain* 39 **F4**
Valencia, G. de, *Spain* 39 **F5**
Valencia de Alcántara, *Spain* 37 **F3**
Valencia de Don Juan, *Spain* 36 **C5**
Valencia I., *Ireland* 12 **E1**
Valenciennes, *France* 19 **B10**
Văleni, *Romania* 29 **F9**
Vălenii de Munte, *Romania* 29 **E11**
Valensole, *France* 21 **E9**
Valentigney, *France* 19 **E13**
Valentim, Sa. do, *Brazil* 125 **E10**
Valentin, *Russia* 54 **C7**
Valentine, *U.S.A.* 113 **K2**
Valenza, *Italy* 40 **C5**
Valera, *Venezuela* 124 **B4**
Valga, *Estonia* 9 **H22**
Valguarnera Caropepe, *Italy* 43 **E7**
Valier, *U.S.A.* 108 **B7**
Valinco, G. de, *France* 21 **G12**
Valjevo, *Serbia & M.* 44 **B3**
Valka, *Latvia* 9 **H21**
Valkeakoski, *Finland* 9 **F20**
Valkenswaard, *Neths.* 17 **C5**
Vall de Uxó = La Vall d'Uixó, *Spain* 38 **F4**
Valla, *Sweden* 10 **E10**
Valladolid, *Mexico* 119 **C7**
Valladolid, *Spain* 36 **D6**
Valladolid □, *Spain* 36 **D6**
Vallata, *Italy* 43 **A8**
Valldemossa, *Spain* 48 **B9**
Valle d'Aosta □, *Italy* 40 **C4**
Valle de Arán, *Spain* 38 **C5**
Valle de la Pascua, *Venezuela* 124 **B5**
Valle de las Palmas, *Mexico* 111 **N10**
Valle de Santiago, *Mexico* 118 **C4**
Valle de Suchil, *Mexico* 118 **C4**
Valle de Zaragoza, *Mexico* 118 **B3**
Valle del Ticino ⌓, *Italy* 40 **C6**
Valle Fértil, Sierra del, *Argentina* 126 **C2**
Valle Gran Rey, *Canary Is.* 48 **F2**
Valle Hermoso, *Mexico* 119 **B5**
Valledupar, *Colombia* 124 **A4**
Vallehermoso, *Canary Is.* 48 **F2**
Vallejo, *U.S.A.* 110 **G4**
Vallenar, *Chile* 126 **B1**
Vallentuna, *Sweden* 10 **E12**
Valleraugue, *France* 20 **D7**
Vallet, *France* 18 **E5**
Valletta, *Malta* 49 **D2**
Valley Center, *U.S.A.* 111 **M9**
Valley City, *U.S.A.* 112 **B6**
Valley Falls, *Oreg., U.S.A.* 108 **E3**
Valley Falls, *R.I., U.S.A.* 117 **E13**
Valley of the Kings, *Egypt* 80 **B3**
Valley Springs, *U.S.A.* 110 **G6**
Valley View, *U.S.A.* 117 **F8**
Valley Wells, *U.S.A.* 111 **K11**
Valleyview, *Canada* 102 **B5**
Valli di Comácchio, *Italy* 41 **D9**
Vallimanca, Arroyo, *Argentina* 126 **D4**
Vallo della Lucánia, *Italy* 43 **B8**
Vallon-Pont-d'Arc, *France* 21 **D8**
Vallorbe, *Switz.* 25 **J2**
Valls, *Spain* 38 **D6**
Valmaseda = Balmaseda, *Spain* 38 **B1**
Valmiera, *Latvia* 9 **H21**
Valnera, *Spain* 36 **B7**
Valognes, *France* 18 **C5**
Valona = Vlorë, *Albania* 44 **F3**
Valongo, *Portugal* 36 **D2**
Valozhyn, *Belarus* 32 **E4**
Valpaços, *Portugal* 36 **D3**
Valparaíso, *Chile* 126 **C1**
Valparaíso, *Mexico* 118 **C4**
Valparaiso, *U.S.A.* 114 **E2**
Valparaíso □, *Chile* 126 **C1**
Valpovo, *Croatia* 28 **E3**
Valréas, *France* 21 **D9**
Vals, *Switz.* 25 **J5**
Vals →, *S. Africa* 88 **D4**
Vals, Tanjung, *Indonesia* 63 **F9**
Vals-les-Bains, *France* 21 **D8**
Valsad, *India* 66 **J8**
Valtellina, *Italy* 40 **B6**
Valuyki, *Russia* 33 **G10**
Valverde, *Canary Is.* 48 **G2**
Valverde del Camino, *Spain* 37 **H4**
Valverde del Fresno, *Spain* 36 **E4**
Vama, *Romania* 29 **C10**
Vamdrup, *Denmark* 11 **J3**
Våmhus, *Sweden* 10 **C8**
Vammala, *Finland* 9 **F20**
Vámos, *Greece* 49 **D6**
Van, *Turkey* 70 **B4**
Van, L. = Van Gölü, *Turkey* 70 **B4**
Van Alstyne, *U.S.A.* 113 **J6**
Van Blommestein Meer, *Suriname* 125 **C7**
Van Buren, *Canada* 105 **C6**
Van Buren, *Ark., U.S.A.* 113 **H7**
Van Buren, *Maine, U.S.A.* 115 **B11**
Van Buren, *Mo., U.S.A.* 113 **G9**
Van Canh, *Vietnam* 64 **F7**
Van Diemen, C., *N. Terr., Australia* 92 **B5**
Van Diemen, C., *Queens., Australia* 94 **B2**
Van Diemen G., *Australia* 92 **B5**
Van Gölü, *Turkey* 70 **B4**
Van Horn, *U.S.A.* 113 **K2**

Van Ninh, Vietnam 64 F7
Van Rees, Pegunungan, Indonesia 63 E9
Van Wert, U.S.A. 114 E3
Van Yen, Vietnam 58 G5
Vanadzor, Armenia 35 K7
Vanavara, Russia 53 C11
Vancouver, Canada 102 D4
Vancouver, U.S.A. 110 E4
Vancouver, C., Australia 93 G2
Vancouver I., Canada 102 D3
Vancouver International ✈ (YVR), U.S.A. 110 A3
Vanda = Vantaa, Finland 9 F21
Vandalia, Ill., U.S.A. 112 F10
Vandalia, Mo., U.S.A. 112 F9
Vandenburg, U.S.A. 111 L6
Vanderbijlpark, S. Africa 89 D4
Vandergrift, U.S.A. 116 F5
Vanderhoof, Canada 102 C4
Vanderkloof Dam, S. Africa 88 E3
Vanderlin I., Australia 94 B2
Vänern, Sweden 11 F7
Vänersborg, Sweden 11 F6
Vang Vieng, Laos 64 C4
Vanga, Kenya 86 C4
Vangaindrano, Madag. 89 C8
Vanguard, Canada 103 D7
Vanino, Russia 53 E15
Vânju Mare, Romania 28 F7
Vanna, Norway 8 A18
Vännäs, Sweden 8 E18
Vannes, France 18 E4
Vanoise, Massif de la, France 21 C10
Vanrhynsdorp, S. Africa 88 E2
Vansbro, Sweden 10 D8
Vansittart B., Australia 92 B4
Vantaa, Finland 9 F21
Vanua Balavu, Fiji 91 C9
Vanua Levu, Fiji 91 C8
Vanuatu ■, Pac. Oc. 96 J8
Vanwyksvlei, S. Africa 88 E3
Vanzylsrus, S. Africa 88 D3
Vapnyarka, Ukraine 29 B13
Var □, France 21 E10
Var →, France 21 E11
Vara, Sweden 11 F6
Varades, France 18 E5
Varáita →, Italy 40 D4
Varallo, Italy 40 C5
Varāmīn, Iran 71 C6
Varāmīn □, Iran 71 B6
Varanasi, India 69 G10
Varangerfjorden, Norway 8 A23
Varangerhalvøya, Norway 8 A23
Varano, Lago di, Italy 41 G12
Varaždin, Croatia 41 B13
Varazze, Italy 40 D5
Varberg, Sweden 11 G6
Vardak □, Afghan. 66 B6
Vardar = Axiós →, Greece 44 F6
Varde, Denmark 11 J2
Varde Å →, Denmark 11 J2
Vardø, Norway 8 A24
Varel, Germany 24 B4
Varella, Mui, Vietnam 64 F7
Varėna, Lithuania 9 J21
Varennes-sur-Allier, France 19 F10
Varennes-Vauzelles, France 19 E10
Vareš, Bos.-H. 28 F3
Varese, Italy 40 C5
Vârfurile, Romania 28 D7
Vårgårda, Sweden 11 F6
Varginha, Brazil 127 A6
Vargön, Sweden 11 F6
Varillas, Chile 126 A1
Varkaus, Finland 9 E22
Värmdölandet, Sweden 10 E12
Värmeln, Sweden 10 E6
Värmlands län □, Sweden 10 E6
Värmlandsbro, Sweden 10 E7
Varna, Bulgaria 45 C11
Varna □, Bulgaria 45 C11
Värnamo, Sweden 11 G8
Varnsdorf, Czech Rep. 26 A7
Várpalota, Hungary 28 C3
Vars, Canada 117 A9
Vars, France 21 D10
Varto, Turkey 73 C9
Varvarin, Serbia & M. 44 C5
Varysburg, U.S.A. 116 D6
Varzaneh, Iran 71 C7
Varzi, Italy 40 D6
Varzo, Italy 40 B5
Varzy, France 19 E10
Vas □, Hungary 28 C1
Vasa = Vaasa, Finland 8 E19
Vasa Barris →, Brazil 125 F11
Vásárosnamény, Hungary 28 B7
Vascão →, Portugal 37 H3
Vaşcău, Romania 28 D7
Vascongadas = País Vasco □, Spain 38 C2
Vashkivtsi, Ukraine 29 B10
Vasht = Khāsh, Iran 66 E2
Vasilevichi, Belarus 33 F5
Vasilikón, Greece 46 C5
Vasilkov = Vasylkiv, Ukraine 33 G6
Vaslui, Romania 29 D12
Vaslui □, Romania 29 D12
Väsman, Sweden 10 D9
Vassar, Canada 103 D9
Vassar, U.S.A. 114 D4
Västerås, Sweden 10 E10
Västerbotten, Sweden 8 D18
Västerdalälven →, Sweden 10 D8
Västergötland, Sweden 11 F7
Västerhaninge, Sweden 10 E12
Västervik, Sweden 11 G10
Västmanland, Sweden 9 G16
Västmanlands län □, Sweden 10 E10
Vasto, Italy 41 F11
Västra Götalands Län □, Sweden 11 F6
Vasvár, Hungary 28 C1
Vasylivka, Ukraine 29 E13
Vasylkiv, Ukraine 33 G6
Vatan, France 19 E8
Vatersay, U.K. 13 E1
Váthia, Greece 46 E4
Vatican City ■, Europe 41 G9
Vaticano, C., Italy 43 D8
Vatili, Cyprus 49 D12
Vatin, Serbia & M. 28 E6
Vatnajökull, Iceland 8 D5
Vatoa, Fiji 91 D9
Vatólakkos, Greece 49 D5
Vatoloha, Madag. 89 B8
Vatomandry, Madag. 89 B8
Vatra-Dornei, Romania 29 C10
Vatrak →, India 68 H5
Vättern, Sweden 11 F8
Vaucluse □, France 21 E9
Vaucouleurs, France 19 D12
Vaud □, Switz. 25 J2
Vaudreuil-Dorion, Canada 117 A10
Vaughn, Mont., U.S.A. 108 C8
Vaughn, N. Mex., U.S.A. 109 J11
Vaujours L., Canada 104 A5
Vaupés = Uaupés →, Brazil 124 C5
Vaupés □, Colombia 124 C4
Vauvert, France 21 E8
Vauxhall, Canada 102 C6
Vav, India 68 G4
Vavatenina, Madag. 89 B8
Vava'u, Tonga 91 D12
Vavoua, Ivory C. 82 D3
Vawkavysk, Belarus 33 F3
Vaxholm, Sweden 10 E12
Växjö, Sweden 11 H8
Våxtorp, Sweden 11 H7
Vaygach, Ostrov, Russia 52 C6
Váyia, Greece 46 C5
Váyia, Ákra, Greece 49 C10
Veaikevárri = Svappavaara, Sweden 8 C19
Vechelde, Germany 24 C6
Vechta, Germany 24 C4
Vechte →, Neths. 17 B6
Vecsés, Hungary 28 C4
Veddige, Sweden 11 G6
Vedea →, Romania 29 G10
Vedia, Argentina 126 C3
Vedrette di Ries-Aurina ⌓, Italy 41 B9
Vedum, Sweden 11 F7
Veendam, Neths. 17 A6
Veenendaal, Neths. 17 B5
Vefsna →, Norway 8 D15
Vega, Norway 8 D14
Vega, U.S.A. 113 H3
Vega Baja, Puerto Rico 121 d
Vegadeo, Spain 36 B3
Vegorrítis, Límni, Greece 44 F5
Vegreville, Canada 102 C6
Veinge, Sweden 11 H7
Veisiejai, Lithuania 30 D10
Vejbystrand, Sweden 11 H6
Vejen, Denmark 11 J3
Vejer de la Frontera, Spain 37 J5
Vejle, Denmark 11 J3
Vejle Amtskommune □, Denmark 11 J3
Vejle Fjord, Denmark 11 J3
Vela Luka, Croatia 41 F13
Velas, C., Costa Rica 120 D2
Velasco, Sierra de, Argentina 126 B2
Velay, Mts. du, France 20 D7
Velbert, Germany 24 D3
Veldhoven, Neths. 17 C5
Velddrif, S. Africa 88 E2
Velebit ⌓, Croatia 41 D12
Velebit Planina, Croatia 41 D12
Velebitski Kanal, Croatia 41 D11
Veleka →, Bulgaria 45 D11
Velencei-tó, Hungary 28 C3
Velenje, Slovenia 41 B12
Veles, Macedonia 44 E5
Velestínon, Greece 46 B4
Vélez-Málaga, Spain 37 J6
Vélez Rubio, Spain 39 H2
Velhas →, Brazil 125 G10
Velika, Croatia 28 E2
Velika Gorica, Croatia 41 C13
Velika Kapela, Croatia 41 C12
Velika Kladuša, Bos.-H. 41 C12
Velika Kruša, Serbia & M. 44 D4
Velika Morava →, Serbia & M. 44 B5
Velika Plana, Serbia & M. 44 B5
Velikaya →, Russia 32 D5
Velikaya Kema, Russia 54 B8
Velikaya Lepetikha, Ukraine 33 J7
Veliké Kapušany, Slovak Rep. 27 C15
Velike Lašče, Slovenia 41 C11
Veliki Jastrebac, Serbia & M. 44 C5
Veliki Kanal, Serbia & M. 28 E4
Veliki Popović, Serbia & M. 44 B5
Velikiye Luki, Russia 32 D6
Veliko Gradište, Serbia & M. 44 B5
Veliko Tŭrnovo, Bulgaria 45 C9
Velikonda Range, India 66 M11
Vélingara, Kolda, Senegal 82 C2
Vélingara, Louga, Senegal 82 B2
Velingrad, Bulgaria 44 D7
Velino, Mte., Italy 41 F10
Velizh, Russia 32 E6
Velké Karlovice, Czech Rep. 27 B11
Velké Meziříčí, Czech Rep. 26 B9
Vel'ký Javorník, Slovak Rep. 27 B11
Vel'ký Krtíš, Slovak Rep. 27 C12
Vel'ký Meder, Slovak Rep. 27 D10
Vel'ký Tribeč, Slovak Rep. 27 C11
Velletri, Italy 42 A5
Vellinge, Sweden 11 J6
Vellmar, Germany 24 D5
Vellore, India 66 N11
Velsk, Russia 32 B11
Velten, Germany 24 C9
Veluwezoom △, Neths. 17 B6
Velva, U.S.A. 112 A4
Velvendós, Greece 44 F6
Velyka Mykhaylivka, Ukraine 29 C14
Velyki Luchky, Ukraine 28 B7
Velykyy Bereznyy, Ukraine 28 B7
Velykyy Bychkiv, Ukraine 29 C9
Vemb, Denmark 11 H2
Vemdalen, Sweden 10 B7
Ven, Sweden 11 J6
Venaco, France 21 F13
Venado Tuerto, Argentina 126 C3
Venafro, Italy 43 A7
Venarey-les-Laumes, France 19 E11
Venaría, Italy 40 C4
Venčane, Serbia & M. 44 B4
Vence, France 21 E11
Vendas Novas, Portugal 37 G2
Vendée □, France 18 F5
Vendée →, France 18 F5
Vendéen, Bocage, France 20 B2
Vendeuvre-sur-Barse, France 19 D11
Vendôme, France 18 E8
Vendrell = El Vendrell, Spain 38 D6
Vendsyssel, Denmark 11 G4
Vendychany, Ukraine 29 B12
Venelles, France 21 E9
Véneta, L., Italy 41 C9
Véneto □, Italy 41 C9
Venev, Russia 32 E10
Venézia, Italy 41 C9
Venézia, G. di, Italy 41 C10
Venezuela ■, S. Amer. 124 B5
Venezuela, G. de, Venezuela 124 A4
Vengurla, India 66 M8
Venice = Venézia, Italy 41 C9
Venice, U.S.A. 115 M4
Vénissieux, France 21 C8
Venjansjön, Sweden 10 D8
Venkatapuram, India 67 K12
Venlo, Neths. 17 C6
Vennesla, Norway 9 G12
Venosa, Italy 43 B8
Venray, Neths. 17 C6
Venta, Lithuania 30 B9
Venta →, Latvia 30 A8
Venta de Baños, Spain 36 D6
Venta de Cardeña = Cardeña, Spain 37 G6
Ventana, Punta de la, Mexico 118 C3
Ventana, Sa. de la, Argentina 126 D3
Ventersburg, S. Africa 88 D4
Venterstad, S. Africa 88 E4
Ventimíglia, Italy 40 E4
Ventnor, U.K. 15 G6
Ventoténe, Italy 42 B6
Ventoux, Mt., France 21 D9
Ventspils, Latvia 9 H19
Ventspils □, Latvia 30 A8
Ventuarí →, Venezuela 124 C5
Ventucopa, U.S.A. 111 L7
Ventura, U.S.A. 111 L7
Venus B., Australia 95 F4
Vera, Argentina 126 B3
Vera, Spain 39 H3
Veracruz, Mexico 119 D5
Veracruz □, Mexico 119 D5
Veraval, India 68 J4
Verbánia, Italy 40 C5
Verbicaro, Italy 43 C8
Verbier, Switz. 25 J3
Vercelli, Italy 40 C5
Verchovchevo, Ukraine 33 H8
Vercors ⌓, France 21 D9
Verdalsøra, Norway 8 E14
Verde →, Argentina 128 E3
Verde →, Goiás, Brazil 125 G8
Verde →, Mato Grosso do Sul, Brazil 125 H8
Verde →, Chihuahua, Mexico 118 B3
Verde →, Oaxaca, Mexico 119 D5
Verde →, Veracruz, Mexico 118 C4
Verde →, Paraguay 126 A4
Verde →, U.S.A. 106 D4
Verde, Cay, Bahamas 120 B4
Verde Island Pass, Phil. 61 E4
Verden, Germany 24 C5
Verdhikoúsa, Greece 46 B3
Verdi, U.S.A. 110 F7
Verdon ⌓, France 21 E10
Verdon →, France 21 E9
Verdun, France 19 C12
Verdun-sur-le-Doubs, France 19 F12
Vereeniging, S. Africa 89 D4
Verga, C., Guinea 82 C2
Vergara, Uruguay 127 C5
Vergato, Italy 40 D8
Vergemont Cr. →, Australia 94 C3
Vergennes, U.S.A. 117 B11
Vergt, France 20 C4
Verín, Spain 36 D3
Verkhnedvinsk = Vyerkhnyadzvinsk, Belarus 32 E4
Verkhnevilyuysk, Russia 53 C13
Verkhniy Baskunchak, Russia 35 F8
Verkhovye, Russia 33 F9
Verkhovyna, Ukraine 29 B9
Verkhoyansk, Russia 53 C14
Verkhoyansk Ra. = Verkhoyanskiy Khrebet, Russia 53 C13
Verkhoyanskiy Khrebet, Russia 53 C13
Vermenton, France 19 E10
Vermilion, Canada 103 C6
Vermilion, U.S.A. 116 E2
Vermilion →, Canada 103 C6
Vermilion, B., U.S.A. 113 L9
Vermilion Bay, Canada 103 D10
Vermilion L., U.S.A. 112 B8
Vermillion, U.S.A. 112 D6
Vermillion →, Canada 104 C5
Vermont □, U.S.A. 117 C12
Vermosh, Albania 44 D3
Vernadsky, Antarctica 5 C17
Vernal, U.S.A. 108 F9
Vernalis, U.S.A. 110 H5
Vernazza, Italy 40 D6
Verner, Canada 104 C3
Verneuil-sur-Avre, France 18 D7
Verneukpan, S. Africa 88 E3
Vernier, Switz. 25 J2
Vérnio, Italy 40 D8
Vernon, Canada 102 C5
Vernon, France 18 C8
Vernon, U.S.A. 113 H5
Vernonia, U.S.A. 110 E3
Vernouillet, France 18 D8
Vero Beach, U.S.A. 115 M5
Véroia, Greece 44 F6
Véroli, Italy 41 G10
Verona, Canada 117 B8
Verona, Italy 40 C7
Verona, U.S.A. 112 D10
Verrès, Italy 40 C4
Versailles, France 19 D9
Versmold, Germany 24 C4
Vert, C., Senegal 82 C1
Vertou, France 18 E5
Vertus, France 19 D11
Verulam, S. Africa 89 D5
Verviers, Belgium 17 D5
Vervins, France 19 C10
Veržej, Slovenia 41 B13
Verzy, France 19 C11
Vescovato, France 21 F13
Veselí nad Lužnicí, Czech Rep. 26 B7
Veselie, Bulgaria 45 D11
Veselovskoye Vdkhr., Russia 35 G5
Veshenskaya, Russia 34 F5
Vesle →, France 19 C10
Vesoul, France 19 E13
Vessigebro, Sweden 11 H6
Vesterålen, Norway 8 B16
Vestfjorden, Norway 8 C15
Vestmannaeyjar, Iceland 8 E3
Vestsjællands Amtskommune □, Denmark 11 J5
Vestspitsbergen, Svalbard 4 B8
Vestvågøy, Norway 8 B15
Vesuvio, Italy 43 B7
Vesuvius, Mt. = Vesuvio, Italy 43 B7
Vesyegonsk, Russia 32 C9
Veszprém, Hungary 28 C2
Veszprém □, Hungary 28 C2
Vésztő, Hungary 28 D6
Vetlanda, Sweden 11 G9
Vetluga, Russia 34 B7
Vetlugu →, Russia 34 B8
Vetluzhskiy, Kostroma, Russia 34 A7
Vetluzhskiy, Nizhniy Novgorod, Russia 34 B7
Vetovo, Bulgaria 45 C10
Vetralla, Italy 41 F9
Vetren, Bulgaria 45 D8
Vettore, Mte., Italy 41 F10
Veurne, Belgium 17 C2
Veveno →, Sudan 81 F3
Vevey, Switz. 25 J2
Vévi, Greece 44 F5
Veynes, France 21 D9
Veys, Iran 71 D6
Vézelay, France 19 E10
Vézelise, France 19 D13
Vézère →, France 20 D4
Vezhen, Bulgaria 45 D8
Vezirköprü, Turkey 72 B6
Vezzani, France 21 F13
Vi Thanh, Vietnam 65 H5
Viacha, Bolivia 124 G5
Viadana, Italy 40 D7
Viamão, Brazil 127 C5
Viana, Brazil 125 D10
Viana, Spain 38 C2
Viana do Alentejo, Portugal 37 G3
Viana do Bolo, Spain 36 C3
Viana do Castelo, Portugal 36 D2
Viana do Castelo □, Portugal 36 D2
Vianden, Lux. 17 E6
Viangchan = Vientiane, Laos 64 D4
Vianópolis, Brazil 125 G9
Viar →, Spain 37 H5
Viaréggio, Italy 40 E7
Viaur →, France 20 D5
Vibble, Sweden 11 G12
Vibo Valéntia, Italy 43 D9
Viborg, Denmark 11 H3
Viborg Amtskommune □, Denmark 11 H3
Vibraye, France 18 D7
Vic, Spain 38 D7
Vic, Étang de, France 20 E7
Vic-en-Bigorre, France 20 E4
Vic-Fezensac, France 20 E4
Vic-le-Comte, France 19 G10
Vic-sur-Cère, France 20 D6
Vícar, Spain 39 J2
Vicenza, Italy 41 C8
Vich = Vic, Spain 38 D7
Vichada →, Colombia 124 C5
Vichuga, Russia 34 B5
Vichy, France 19 F10
Vicksburg, Ariz., U.S.A. 111 M13
Vicksburg, Miss., U.S.A. 113 J9
Vico, France 21 F12
Vico, L. di, Italy 41 F9
Vico del Gargano, Italy 41 G12
Vicovu de Sus, Romania 29 C10
Victor, India 68 J4
Victor, U.S.A. 116 D7
Victor Harbor, Australia 95 F2
Victoria, Argentina 126 C3
Victoria, Canada 102 D4
Victoria, Chile 128 D2
Victoria, Guinea 82 C2
Victoria, Malta 49 C1
Victoria, Phil. 61 D4
Victoria, Romania 29 E9
Victoria, Kans., U.S.A. 112 F5
Victoria, Tex., U.S.A. 113 L6
Victoria □, Australia 95 F3
Victoria →, Australia 92 C4
Victoria, Grand L., Canada 104 C4
Victoria, L., Africa 86 C3
Victoria, L., Australia 95 E3
Victoria, Mt., Burma 67 J18
Victoria Beach, Canada 103 C9
Victoria de Durango = Durango, Mexico 118 C4
Victoria de las Tunas, Cuba 120 B4
Victoria Falls, Zimbabwe 87 F2
Victoria Harbour, Canada 116 B5
Victoria I., Canada 100 A8
Victoria L., Canada 105 C8
Victoria Ld., Antarctica 5 D11
Victoria Nile →, Uganda 86 B3
Victoria River, Australia 92 C5
Victoria Str., Canada 100 B9
Victoria West, S. Africa 88 E3
Victorias, Phil. 61 F5
Victoriaville, Canada 105 C5
Victorica, Argentina 126 D2
Victorville, U.S.A. 111 L9
Vicuña, Chile 126 C1
Vicuña Mackenna, Argentina 126 C3
Vidal, U.S.A. 111 L12
Vidal Junction, U.S.A. 111 L12
Vidalia, U.S.A. 115 J4
Vidamlya, Belarus 31 F10
Vidauban, France 21 E10
Videbæk, Denmark 11 H2
Videle, Romania 29 F10
Vídho, Greece 49 A3
Vidigueira, Portugal 37 G3
Vidin, Bulgaria 44 C6
Vidio, C., Spain 36 B4
Vidisha, India 68 H7
Vidra, Romania 29 E11
Viduša, Bos.-H. 44 D2
Vidzy, Belarus 9 J22
Viechtach, Germany 25 F8
Viedma, Argentina 128 E4
Viedma, L., Argentina 128 F2
Vieira do Minho, Portugal 36 D2
Vielha, Spain 38 C5
Viella = Vielha, Spain 38 C5
Vielsalm, Belgium 17 D5
Vienenburg, Germany 24 D6
Vieng Pou Kha, Laos 58 G3
Vienna = Wien, Austria 27 C9
Vienna, Ill., U.S.A. 113 G10
Vienna, Mo., U.S.A. 112 F9
Vienne, France 21 C8
Vienne □, France 20 B4
Vienne →, France 18 E7
Vientiane, Laos 64 D4
Vientos, Paso de los, Caribbean 121 C5
Vieques, Isla de, Puerto Rico 121 d
Vierge Pt., St. Lucia 121 f
Viernheim, Germany 25 F4
Viersen, Germany 24 D2
Vierwaldstättersee, Switz. 25 J4
Vierzon, France 19 E9
Vieste, Italy 41 G13
Vietnam ■, Asia 64 C6
Vieux-Boucau-les-Bains, France 20 E2
Vieux Fort, St. Lucia 121 f
Vif, France 21 C9
Vigan, Phil. 61 C4
Vigévano, Italy 40 C5
Vigia, Brazil 125 D9
Vigía Chico, Mexico 119 D7
Víglas, Ákra, Greece 49 D9
Vignemalle, France 20 F3
Vigneulles-lès-Hattonchâtel, France 19 D12
Vignola, Italy 40 D8
Vigo, Spain 36 C2
Vigo, Ría de, Spain 36 C2
Vigsø Bugt, Denmark 11 G2
Vihiers, France 18 E6
Vihowa, Pakistan 68 D4
Vihowa →, Pakistan 68 D4
Vijayawada, India 67 L12
Vijosë →, Albania 44 F3
Vík, Iceland 8 E4
Vika, Sweden 10 D8
Vikarbyn, Sweden 10 D9
Vikeke = Viqueque, E. Timor 63 F7
Viken, Skåne, Sweden 11 H6
Viken, Västra Götaland, Sweden 11 F8
Viking, Canada 102 C6
Vikmanshyttan, Sweden 10 D9
Vikna, Norway 8 D14
Vikos-Aoos △, Greece 46 B2
Vila da Maganja, Mozam. 87 F4
Vila de Rei, Portugal 36 F2
Vila do Bispo, Portugal 37 H2
Vila do Conde, Portugal 36 D2
Vila Franca de Xira, Portugal 37 G2
Vila Gamito, Mozam. 87 E3
Vila Gomes da Costa, Mozam. 89 C5
Vila Machado, Mozam. 87 F3
Vila Mouzinho, Mozam. 87 E3
Vila Nova de Famalicão, Portugal 36 D2
Vila Nova de Fos Côa, Portugal 36 D3
Vila Nova de Gaia, Portugal 36 D2
Vila Nova de Ourém, Portugal 36 F2
Vila Pouca de Aguiar, Portugal 36 D3
Vila Real, Portugal 36 D3
Vila Real □, Portugal 36 D3
Vila-real de los Infantes, Spain 38 F4
Vila Real de Santo António, Portugal 37 H3
Vila Vasco da Gama, Mozam. 87 E3
Vila Velha, Brazil 127 A7

Vila Viçosa, *Portugal* **37 G3**
Vilafranca del Maestrat, *Spain* .. **38 E4**
Vilafranca del Penedès, *Spain* ... **38 D6**
Vilagarcía de Arousa, *Spain* **36 C2**
Vilaine →, *France* **18 E4**
Vilanandro, Tanjona, *Madag.* ... **89 B7**
Vilanculos, *Mozam.* **89 C6**
Vilanova de Castelló, *Spain* **39 F4**
Vilanova i la Geltrú, *Spain* **38 D6**
Vilar Formosa, *Portugal* **36 E4**
Vilaseca, *Spain* **38 D6**
Vilaseca-Salou = Vilaseca, *Spain* **38 D6**
Vilbjerg, *Denmark* **11 H2**
Vilcheka, Zemlya, *Russia* **4 A11**
Vilches, *Spain* **37 G7**
Vileyka, *Belarus* **32 E4**
Vilhelmina, *Sweden* **8 D17**
Vilhena, *Brazil* **124 F6**
Viliya = Neris →, *Lithuania* **9 J21**
Viljandi, *Estonia* **9 G21**
Vilkaviškis, *Lithuania* **30 D10**
Vilkija, *Lithuania* **30 C10**
Vilkitskogo, Proliv, *Russia* **53 B11**
Vilkovo = Vylkove, *Ukraine* **29 E14**
Villa Abecia, *Bolivia* **126 A2**
Villa Ahumada, *Mexico* **118 A3**
Villa Ana, *Argentina* **126 B4**
Villa Ángela, *Argentina* **126 B3**
Villa Bella, *Bolivia* **124 F5**
Villa Cañás, *Argentina* **126 C3**
Villa Colón, *Argentina* **126 C2**
Villa Constitución, *Argentina* ... **126 C3**
Villa de María, *Argentina* **126 B3**
Villa del Rio, *Spain* **37 H6**
Villa Dolores, *Argentina* **126 C2**
Villa Frontera, *Mexico* **118 B4**
Villa Guillermina, *Argentina* **126 B4**
Villa Hayes, *Paraguay* **126 B4**
Villa Iris, *Argentina* **126 D3**
Villa Juárez, *Mexico* **118 B4**
Villa María, *Argentina* **126 C3**
Villa Mazán, *Argentina* **126 B2**
Villa Minozzo, *Italy* **40 D7**
Villa Montes, *Bolivia* **126 A3**
Villa Ocampo, *Argentina* **126 B4**
Villa Ocampo, *Mexico* **118 B3**
Villa Ojo de Agua, *Argentina* ... **126 B3**
Villa San Giovanni, *Italy* **43 D8**
Villa San José, *Argentina* **126 C4**
Villa San Martín, *Argentina* **126 B3**
Villa Santina, *Italy* **41 B9**
Villa Unión, *Mexico* **118 C3**
Villablino, *Spain* **36 C4**
Villacarlos, *Spain* **48 B11**
Villacarriedo, *Spain* **36 B7**
Villacarrillo, *Spain* **37 G7**
Villacastín, *Spain* **36 E6**
Villach, *Austria* **26 E6**
Villacidro, *Italy* **42 C1**
Villada, *Spain* **36 C6**
Villadiego, *Spain* **36 C6**
Villadóssola, *Italy* **40 B5**
Villafeliche, *Spain* **38 D3**
Villafranca, *Spain* **38 C3**
Villafranca de los Barros, *Spain* . **37 G4**
Villafranca de los Caballeros, *Baleares, Spain* **48 B10**
Villafranca de los Caballeros, *Toledo, Spain* **37 F7**
Villafranca del Cid = Vilafranca del Maestrat, *Spain* **38 E4**
Villafranca del Panadés = Vilafranca del Penedès, *Spain* . **38 D6**
Villafranca di Verona, *Italy* **40 C7**
Villafranca Tirrena, *Italy* **43 D8**
Villagrán, *Mexico* **119 C5**
Villaguay, *Argentina* **126 C4**
Villaharta, *Spain* **37 G6**
Villahermosa, *Mexico* **119 D6**
Villahermosa, *Spain* **39 G2**
Villaines-la-Juhel, *France* **18 D6**
Villajoyosa, *Spain* **39 G4**
Villalba, *Spain* **36 B3**
Villalba de Guardo, *Spain* **36 C6**
Villalón de Campos, *Spain* **36 C5**
Villalpando, *Spain* **36 D5**
Villaluenga, *Spain* **36 E7**
Villamanán, *Spain* **36 C5**
Villamartín, *Spain* **37 J5**
Villamayor de Santiago, *Spain* .. **38 F2**
Villamblard, *France* **20 C4**
Villanova Monteleone, *Italy* **42 B1**
Villanueva, *U.S.A.* **113 H2**
Villanueva de Castellón = Vilanova de Castelló, *Spain* .. **39 F4**
Villanueva de Córdoba, *Spain* .. **37 G6**
Villanueva de la Fuente, *Spain* .. **39 G2**
Villanueva de la Serena, *Spain* .. **37 G5**
Villanueva de la Sierra, *Spain* .. **36 E4**
Villanueva de los Castillejos, *Spain* **37 H3**
Villanueva de los Infantes, *Spain* **37 G7**
Villanueva del Arzobispo, *Spain* **39 G2**
Villanueva del Fresno, *Spain* ... **37 G3**
Villanueva y Geltrú = Vilanova i la Geltrú, *Spain* **38 D6**
Villaputzu, *Italy* **42 C2**
Villaquilambre, *Spain* **36 C5**
Villar del Arzobispo, *Spain* **38 F4**
Villar del Rey, *Spain* **37 F4**
Villard-de-Lans, *France* **21 C9**
Villarramiel, *Spain* **36 C6**
Villarreal = Vila-real de los Infantes, *Spain* **38 F4**
Villarrica, *Chile* **128 D2**
Villarrica, *Paraguay* **126 B4**
Villarrobledo, *Spain* **39 F2**
Villarroya de la Sierra, *Spain* ... **38 D3**
Villarrubia de los Ojos, *Spain* ... **37 F7**
Villars-les-Dombes, *France* **19 F12**
Villasayas, *Spain* **38 D2**
Villaseca de los Gamitos = Villaseco de los Gamitos, *Spain* **36 D4**
Villaseco de los Gamitos, *Spain* . **36 D4**
Villasimíus, *Italy* **42 C2**
Villastar, *Spain* **38 E3**
Villatobas, *Spain* **36 F7**
Villavicencio, *Argentina* **126 C2**
Villavicencio, *Colombia* **124 C4**
Villaviciosa, *Spain* **36 B5**
Villazón, *Bolivia* **126 A2**
Ville-Marie, *Canada* **104 C4**
Ville Platte, *U.S.A.* **113 K8**
Villedieu-les-Poêles, *France* **18 D5**
Villefort, *France* **20 D7**
Villefranche-de-Lauragais, *France* **20 E5**
Villefranche-de-Rouergue, *France* **20 D6**
Villefranche-du-Périgord, *France* **20 D5**
Villefranche-sur-Saône, *France* . **21 C8**
Villel, *Spain* **38 E3**
Villemur-sur-Tarn, *France* **20 E5**
Villena, *Spain* **39 G4**
Villenauxe-la-Grande, *France* ... **19 D10**
Villenave-d'Ornon, *France* **20 D3**
Villeneuve-d'Ascq, *France* **19 B10**
Villeneuve-l'Archevêque, *France* **19 D10**
Villeneuve-lès-Avignon, *France* . **21 E8**
Villeneuve-sur-Allier, *France* ... **19 F10**
Villeneuve-sur-Lot, *France* **20 D4**
Villeneuve-sur-Yonne, *France* .. **19 D10**
Villeréal, *France* **20 D4**
Villers-Bocage, *France* **18 C6**
Villers-Cotterêts, *France* **19 C10**
Villers-sur-Mer, *France* **18 C6**
Villersexel, *France* **19 E13**
Villerupt, *France* **19 C12**
Villeurbanne, *France* **21 C8**
Villiers, *S. Africa* **89 D4**
Villingen-Schwenningen, *Germany* **25 G4**
Villmanstrand = Lappeenranta, *Finland* **9 F23**
Vilna, *Canada* **102 C6**
Vilnius, *Lithuania* **9 J21**
Vils, *Austria* **26 D3**
Vils →, *Bayern, Germany* **25 G9**
Vils →, *Bayern, Germany* **25 F7**
Vilsbiburg, *Germany* **25 G8**
Vilshofen, *Germany* **25 G9**
Vilusi, *Serbia & M.* **44 D2**
Vilvoorde, *Belgium* **17 D4**
Vilyuy →, *Russia* **53 C13**
Vilyuysk, *Russia* **53 C13**
Vimianzo, *Spain* **36 B1**
Vimioso, *Portugal* **36 D4**
Vimmerby, *Sweden* **11 G9**
Vimoutiers, *France* **18 D7**
Vimperk, *Czech Rep.* **26 B6**
Viña del Mar, *Chile* **126 C1**
Vinarós, *Spain* **38 E5**
Vincennes, *U.S.A.* **114 F2**
Vincent, *U.S.A.* **111 L8**
Vinchina, *Argentina* **126 B2**
Vindelälven →, *Sweden* **8 E18**
Vindeln, *Sweden* **8 D18**
Vinderup, *Denmark* **11 H2**
Vindhya Ra., *India* **68 H7**
Vineland, *U.S.A.* **114 F8**
Vineuil, *France* **18**
Vinga, *Romania* **28 D6**
Vingåker, *Sweden* **10 E9**
Vinh, *Vietnam* **64 C5**
Vinh Linh, *Vietnam* **64 D6**
Vinh Long, *Vietnam* **65 G5**
Vinh Yen, *Vietnam* **58 G5**
Vinhais, *Portugal* **36 D3**
Vinica, *Croatia* **41 B13**
Vinica, *Macedonia* **44 E6**
Vinica, *Slovenia* **41 C12**
Vinita, *U.S.A.* **113 G7**
Vinkovci, *Croatia* **28 E3**
Vinnitsa = Vinnytsya, *Ukraine* .. **33 H5**
Vinnytsya, *Ukraine* **33 H5**
Vinslöv, *Sweden* **11 H7**
Vinson Massif, *Antarctica* **5 D16**
Vintjärn, *Sweden* **10 D10**
Vinton, *Calif., U.S.A.* **110 F6**
Vinton, *Iowa, U.S.A.* **112 D8**
Vinton, *La., U.S.A.* **113 K8**
Vinţu de Jos, *Romania* **29 D8**
Viöl, *Germany* **24 A5**
Vipava, *Slovenia* **41 C10**
Vipiteno, *Italy* **41 B8**
Viqueque, *E. Timor* **63 F7**
Vir, *Croatia* **41 D12**
Virac, *Phil.* **61 E6**
Virachey, *Cambodia* **64 F6**
Virachey △, *Cambodia* **64 E6**
Virago Sd., *Canada* **102 C2**
Viramgam, *India* **68 H5**
Viranşehir, *Turkey* **70 B3**
Virawah, *Pakistan* **68 G4**
Virbalis, *Lithuania* **30 D9**
Virden, *Canada* **103 D8**
Vire, *France* **18 D6**
Vire →, *France* **18 C5**
Vírgenes, C., *Argentina* **128 G3**
Virgin →, *U.S.A.* **109 H6**
Virgin Gorda, *Br. Virgin Is.* .... **121 e**
Virgin Is. (British) ☑, *W. Indies* .. **121 e**
Virgin Is. (U.S.) ☑, *W. Indies* ... **121 e**
Virgin Islands △, *U.S. Virgin Is.* . **121 C7**
Virginia, *S. Africa* **88 D4**
Virginia, *U.S.A.* **112 B8**
Virginia □, *U.S.A.* **114 G7**
Virginia Beach, *U.S.A.* **114 G8**
Virginia City, *Mont., U.S.A.* ... **108 D8**
Virginia City, *Nev., U.S.A.* **110 F7**
Virginia Falls, *Canada* **102 A3**
Virginiatown, *Canada* **104 C4**
Virje, *Croatia* **41 B13**
Viroqua, *U.S.A.* **112 D9**
Virovitica, *Croatia* **28 E2**
Virpazar, *Serbia & M.* **44 D3**
Virpur, *India* **68 J4**
Virserum, *Sweden* **11 G9**
Virton, *Belgium* **17 E5**
Virudunagar, *India* **66 Q10**
Virunga △, *Dem. Rep. of the Congo* **86 B2**
Vis, *Croatia* **41 E13**
Visalia, *U.S.A.* **110 J7**
Visayan Sea, *Phil.* **61 F5**
Visby, *Sweden* **11 G12**
Viscount Melville Sd., *Canada* .. **98 B9**
Visé, *Belgium* **17 D5**
Višegrad, *Bos.-H.* **28 G4**
Viseu, *Brazil* **125 D9**
Viseu, *Portugal* **36 E3**
Viseu □, *Portugal* **36 E3**
Vişeu de Sus, *Romania* **29 C9**
Vishakhapatnam, *India* **67 L13**
Vişina, *Romania* **29 G9**
Vişineşti, *Moldova* **29 D13**
Visingsö, *Sweden* **11 F8**
Viskafors, *Sweden* **11 G6**
Viskan →, *Sweden* **11 G6**
Viški Kanal, *Croatia* **41 E13**
Vislanda, *Sweden* **11 H8**
Visnagar, *India* **68 H5**
Višnja Gora, *Slovenia* **41 C11**
Viso, Mte., *Italy* **40 D4**
Viso del Marqués, *Spain* **37 G7**
Visoko, *Bos.-H.* **28 G3**
Visokoi I., *Antarctica* **5 B1**
Visp, *Switz.* **25 J3**
Vissefjärda, *Sweden* **11 H9**
Visselhövede, *Germany* **24 C5**
Vissenbjerg, *Denmark* **11 J4**
Vista, *U.S.A.* **111 M9**
Vistonikos, Ormos = Vistonís, Límni, *Greece* **45 E9**
Vistonís, Límni, *Greece* **45 E9**
Vistula = Wisła →, *Poland* **30 D5**
Vit →, *Bulgaria* **45 C8**
Vitanje, *Slovenia* **41 B12**
Vitebsk = Vitsyebsk, *Belarus* ... **32 E6**
Viterbo, *Italy* **41 F9**
Vitez, *Bos.-H.* **28 F2**
Viti Levu, *Fiji* **91 C7**
Vitigudino, *Spain* **36 D4**
Vitim, *Russia* **53 D12**
Vitim →, *Russia* **53 D12**
Vitina, *Bos.-H.* **41 E14**
Vitina, *Greece* **46 D4**
Vítkov, *Czech Rep.* **27 B10**
Vitória, *Brazil* **125 H10**
Vitória da Conquista, *Brazil* ... **125 F10**
Vitória de São Antão, *Brazil* ... **125 E11**
Vitoria-Gasteiz, *Spain* **38 C2**
Vitosha △, *Bulgaria* **44 D7**
Vitré, *France* **18 D5**
Vitry-le-François, *France* **19 D11**
Vitry-sur-Seine, *France* **19 D9**
Vitsand, *Sweden* **10 D7**
Vitsi, Óros, *Greece* **44 F5**
Vitsyebsk, *Belarus* **32 E6**
Vittaryd, *Sweden* **11 H7**
Vitteaux, *France* **19 E11**
Vittel, *France* **19 D12**
Vittória, *Italy* **43 F7**
Vittório Véneto, *Italy* **41 C9**
Vittsjö, *Sweden* **11 H7**
Viveiro, *Spain* **36 B3**
Vivian, *U.S.A.* **113 J8**
Viviers, *France* **21 D8**
Vivonne, *France* **20 B4**
Vizcaíno, Desierto de, *Mexico* .. **118 B2**
Vizcaíno, Sierra, *Mexico* **118 B2**
Vizcaya □, *Spain* **38 B2**
Vize, *Turkey* **45 E11**
Vizianagaram, *India* **67 K13**
Vizille, *France* **21 C9**
Viziňada, *Croatia* **41 C10**
Viziru, *Romania* **29 E12**
Vizzini, *Italy* **43 E7**
Vlaardingen, *Neths.* **17 C4**
Vlădeasa, Vf., *Romania* **28 D7**
Vladičin Han, *Serbia & M.* **44 D6**
Vladikavkaz, *Russia* **35 J7**
Vladimir, *Russia* **32 D11**
Vladimir Volynskiy = Volodymyr-Volynskyy, *Ukraine* **33 G3**
Vladimirci, *Serbia & M.* **44 B3**
Vladimirovac, *Serbia & M.* **28 E5**
Vladimirovka, *Russia* **35 F8**
Vladimirovo, *Bulgaria* **44 C7**
Vladimirovka, *Kazakhstan* **34 E10**
Vladislavovka, *Ukraine* **33 K8**
Vladivostok, *Russia* **53 E14**
Vlăhiţa, *Romania* **29 D10**
Vlakhiótis, *Greece* **46 E4**
Vlasenica, *Bos.-H.* **28 F3**
Vlašić, *Bos.-H.* **28 F2**
Vlašim, *Czech Rep.* **26 B7**
Vlasinsko Jezero, *Serbia & M.* .. **44 D6**
Vlasotince, *Serbia & M.* **44 D6**
Vlieland, *Neths.* **17 A4**
Vlissingen, *Neths.* **17 C3**
Vlorë, *Albania* **44 F3**
Vlorës, Gjiri i, *Albania* **44 F3**
Vltava →, *Czech Rep.* **26 A7**
Vo Dat, *Vietnam* **65 G6**
Vobarno, *Italy* **40 C7**
Voćin, *Croatia* **28 E2**
Vöcklabruck, *Austria* **26 C6**
Vodice, *Croatia* **41 E12**
Vodňany, *Czech Rep.* **26 B7**
Vodnjan, *Croatia* **41 D10**
Voe, *U.K.* **13 A7**
Vogel Pk., *Nigeria* **83 D7**
Vogelkop = Doberai, Jazirah, *Indonesia* **63 E8**
Vogelsberg, *Germany* **24 E5**
Voghera, *Italy* **40 D6**
Vohibinany, *Madag.* **89 B8**
Vohilava, *Madag.* **89 C8**
Vohimarina = Iharana, *Madag.* .. **89 A9**
Vohimena, Tanjon' i, *Madag.* ... **89 D8**
Vohipeno, *Madag.* **89 C8**
Voi, *Kenya* **86 C4**
Void-Vacon, *France* **19 D12**
Voineşti, *Iaşi, Romania* **29 C12**
Voineşti, *Prahova, Romania* ... **29 E10**
Voïotía □, *Greece* **46 C5**
Voiron, *France* **21 C9**
Voisey B., *Canada* **105 A7**
Voitsberg, *Austria* **26 D8**
Vojens, *Denmark* **11 J3**
Vojmsjön, *Sweden* **8 D17**
Vojnić, *Croatia* **41 C12**
Vojnik, *Italy* **41 B12**
Vojvodina □, *Serbia & M.* **28 E5**
Vokhtoga, *Russia* **32 C11**
Volary, *Czech Rep.* **26 C6**
Volborg, *U.S.A.* **112 C2**
Volcán de Colima △, *Mexico* ... **118 D4**
Volcano Is. = Kazan-Rettō, *Pac. Oc.* **96 E6**
Volcans △, *Rwanda* **86 C2**
Volcans d'Auvergne ⌓, *France* .. **20 C6**
Volchansk = Vovchansk, *Ukraine* **33 G9**
Volchya →, *Ukraine* **33 H8**
Volda, *Norway* **9 E12**
Volga = Privolzhskiy □, *Russia* .. **34 B10**
Volga, *Russia* **32 C10**
Volga →, *Russia* **35 G9**
Volga Hts. = Privolzhskaya Vozvyshennost, *Russia* **34 E7**
Volgo-Baltiyskiy Kanal, *Russia* . **32 B9**
Volgo-Donskoy Kanal, *Russia* .. **35 F7**
Volgodonsk, *Russia* **35 G6**
Volgograd, *Russia* **35 F7**
Volgogradskoye Vdkhr., *Russia* . **34 E8**
Volgorechensk, *Russia* **34 B5**
Volímai, *Greece* **46 D2**
Volintiri, *Moldova* **29 D14**
Volissós, *Greece* **47 C7**
Volkach, *Germany* **25 F6**
Völkermarkt, *Austria* **26 E7**
Volkhov, *Russia* **32 C7**
Volkhov →, *Russia* **32 B7**
Völklingen, *Germany* **25 F2**
Volkovysk = Vawkavysk, *Belarus* **33 F3**
Volksrust, *S. Africa* **89 D4**
Volnansk, *Ukraine* **33 H8**
Volnovakha, *Ukraine* **33 J9**
Volochanka, *Russia* **53 B10**
Volodarsk, *Russia* **34 B6**
Volodymyr-Volynskyy, *Ukraine* . **33 G3**
Vologda, *Russia* **32 C10**
Volokolamsk, *Russia* **32 D8**
Volokonovka, *Russia* **33 G9**
Vólos, *Greece* **46 B4**
Volosovo, *Russia* **32 C5**
Volovets, *Ukraine* **29 B8**
Volovo, *Russia* **32 F10**
Volozhin = Valozhyn, *Belarus* .. **32 E4**
Volsk, *Russia* **34 D8**
Volta □, *Ghana* **83 D5**
Volta →, *Ghana* **83 D5**
Volta, L., *Ghana* **83 D5**
Volta Blanche = White Volta →, *Ghana* **83 D4**
Volta Redonda, *Brazil* **127 A7**
Voltaire, C., *Australia* **92 B4**
Volterra, *Italy* **40 E7**
Voltri, *Italy* **40 D5**
Volturno →, *Italy* **42 A6**
Vólvi, L., *Greece* **44 F7**
Volyně, *Czech Rep.* **26 B6**
Volzhsk, *Russia* **34 C9**
Volzhskiy, *Russia* **35 F7**
Vondrozo, *Madag.* **89 C8**
Vónitsa, *Greece* **46 C2**
Vopnafjörður, *Iceland* **8 D6**
Vorarlberg □, *Austria* **26 D2**
Vóras Óros, *Greece* **44 F5**
Vorbasse, *Denmark* **11 J3**
Vorchdorf, *Austria* **26 C6**
Vorderrhein →, *Switz.* **25 J5**
Vordingborg, *Denmark* **11 J5**
Vorë, *Albania* **44 E3**
Voreio Aigaio = Vórios Aiyaíon □, *Greece* **47 C7**
Voreppe, *France* **21 C9**
Vóriai Sporádhes, *Greece* **46 B5**
Vórios Aiyaíon □, *Greece* **47 C7**
Vórios Evvoïkos Kólpos, *Greece* **46 C5**
Vorkuta, *Russia* **52 C7**
Vormsi, *Estonia* **9 G20**
Vóroi, *Greece* **46 F6**
Vorona →, *Russia* **34 E6**
Voronezh, *Russia* **33 G10**
Voronezh, *Ukraine* **33 G7**
Voronezh →, *Russia* **33 G10**
Vorontsovo-Aleksandrovskoye = Zelenokumsk, *Russia* **35 H6**
Vorpommersche Boddenlandschaft △, *Germany* **24 A8**
Vorskla →, *Ukraine* **33 H8**
Vörts Järv, *Estonia* **9 G22**
Võru, *Estonia* **9 H22**
Vosges, *France* **19 D14**
Vosges □, *France* **19 D13**
Vosges du Nord ⌓, *France* **19 D14**
Voskopojë, *Albania* **44 F4**
Voskresensk, *Russia* **32 E10**
Voskresenskoye, *Russia* **34 B7**
Voss, *Norway* **9 F12**
Vostok, *Antarctica* **5 D8**
Vostok I., *Kiribati* **97 J12**
Votice, *Czech Rep.* **26 B7**
Votsuri-Shima, *Japan* **55 M1**
Vouga →, *Portugal* **36 E2**
Vouillé, *France* **18 F7**
Voúxa, Ákra, *Greece* **49 D5**
Vouzela, *Portugal* **36 E2**
Vouziers, *France* **19 C11**
Vovchansk, *Ukraine* **33 G9**
Vowchyn, *Belarus* **31 F10**
Voyageurs △, *U.S.A.* **112 A8**
Vozhe, Ozero, *Russia* **32 B10**
Vozhega, *Russia* **32 B11**
Voznesensk, *Ukraine* **33 J6**
Voznesenye, *Russia* **32 B8**
Vrå, *Denmark* **11 G3**
Vráble, *Slovak Rep.* **27 C11**
Vraćevšnica, *Serbia & M.* **44 B4**
Vrakhnéïka, *Greece* **46 C3**
Vrancea □, *Romania* **29 E11**
Vrancei, Munţii, *Romania* **29 E11**
Vrangelya, Ostrov, *Russia* **53 B19**
Vranica, *Bos.-H.* **28 G2**
Vranje, *Serbia & M.* **44 D5**
Vranjska Banja, *Serbia & M.* ... **44 D6**
Vranov nad Topl'ou, *Slovak Rep.* **27 C14**
Vransko, *Slovenia* **41 B11**
Vransko Jezero, *Croatia* **41 E12**
Vrapčište, *Macedonia* **44 E4**
Vratsa, *Bulgaria* **44 C7**
Vrbas, *Serbia & M.* **28 E4**
Vrbas →, *Bos.-H.* **28 E2**
Vrbnik, *Croatia* **41 C11**
Vrbovec, *Croatia* **41 C13**
Vrbovsko, *Croatia* **41 C12**
Vrchlabí, *Czech Rep.* **26 A8**
Vrede, *S. Africa* **89 D4**
Vredefort, *S. Africa* **88 D4**
Vreden, *Germany* **24 C2**
Vredenburg, *S. Africa* **88 E2**
Vredendal, *S. Africa* **88 E2**
Vretstorp, *Sweden* **10 E8**
Vrgorac, *Croatia* **41 E14**
Vrhnika, *Slovenia* **41 C11**
Vrîdi, *Ivory C.* **82 D4**
Vrigstad, *Sweden* **11 G8**
Vrindavan, *India* **68 F7**
Vríses, *Greece* **49 D6**
Vrnograč, *Bos.-H.* **41 C12**
Vrondádhes, *Greece* **47 C8**
Vrpolje, *Croatia* **28 E3**
Vršac, *Serbia & M.* **28 E6**
Vrsacki Kanal, *Serbia & M.* ... **28 E5**
Vrútky, *Slovak Rep.* **27 B11**
Vryburg, *S. Africa* **88 D3**
Vryheid, *S. Africa* **89 D5**
Vsetín, *Czech Rep.* **27 B11**
Vu Liet, *Vietnam* **64 C5**
Vŭcha →, *Bulgaria* **45 D8**
Vučitrn, *Serbia & M.* **44 D4**
Vukovar, *Croatia* **28 E3**
Vulcan, *Canada* **102 C6**
Vulcan, *Romania* **29 E8**
Vulcaneşti, *Moldova* **29 E13**
Vulcano, *Italy* **43 D7**
Vŭlchedruma, *Bulgaria* **44 C7**
Vulkaneshty = Vulcaneşti, *Moldova* **29 E13**
Vunduzi →, *Mozam.* **87 F3**
Vung Tau, *Vietnam* **65 G6**
Vŭrbitsa, *Bulgaria* **45 D10**
Vurshets, *Bulgaria* **44 C7**
Vutcani, *Romania* **29 D12**
Vuya, *Sudan* **81 F2**
Vuzlove, *Ukraine* **28 B7**
Vwaza ⌓, *Malawi* **87 E3**
Vyartsilya, *Russia* **32 A6**
Vyatka = Kirov, *Russia* **52 D5**
Vyatka →, *Russia* **34 C10**
Vyatskiye Polyany, *Russia* ... **34 B10**
Vyazemskiy, *Russia* **53 E14**
Vyazma, *Russia* **32 E8**
Vyazniki, *Russia* **34 B6**
Vyborg, *Russia* **32 B5**
Vychegda →, *Russia* **52 C5**
Vychodné Beskydy, *Europe* ... **27 B15**
Vyerkhnyadzvinsk, *Belarus* ... **32 E4**
Vyhoda, *Ukraine* **29 B8**
Vyksa, *Russia* **34 C6**
Vylkove, *Ukraine* **29 E14**
Vylok, *Ukraine* **28 B7**
Vynohradiv, *Ukraine* **29 B8**
Vyrnwy, L., *U.K.* **14 E4**
Vyshkiv, *Ukraine* **29 B8**
Vyshkove, *Ukraine* **29 B8**
Vyshniy Volochek, *Russia* ... **32 D8**
Vyshzha = imeni 26 Bakinskikh Komissarov, *Turkmenistan* ... **71 B7**
Vyškov, *Czech Rep.* **27 B9**
Vysokaye, *Belarus* **31 F10**
Vysoké Mýto, *Czech Rep.* ... **27 B9**
Vysokovsk, *Russia* **32 D9**
Vyšší Brod, *Czech Rep.* **26 C7**
Vytegra, *Russia* **32 B9**
Vyzhnytsya, *Ukraine* **29 B10**
Vyzhnytsya ⌓, *Ukraine* **29 B10**

W

W du Benin △, *Benin* **83 C5**
W du Burkina Faso △, *Burkina Faso* **83 C4**
W du Niger △, *Niger* **83 C5**
W.A.C. Bennett Dam, *Canada* .. **102 B4**
Wa, *Ghana* **82 C4**
Waal →, *Neths.* **17 C5**
Waalwijk, *Neths.* **17 C5**
Waat, *Sudan* **81 F3**
Wabakimi △, *Canada* **104 B2**
Wabana, *Canada* **105 C9**
Wabasca →, *Canada* **102 B5**
Wabasca-Desmarais, *Canada* .. **102 B6**
Wabash, *U.S.A.* **114 E3**
Wabash →, *U.S.A.* **114 G1**

Wabi →, *Ethiopia* 81 F5
Wabigoon L., *Canada* 103 D10
Wabowden, *Canada* 103 C9
Wąbrzeźno, *Poland* 31 E5
Wabu Hu, *China* 59 A11
Wabuk Pt., *Canada* 104 A2
Wabush, *Canada* 105 B6
Wąchock, *Poland* 31 G8
Wächtersbach, *Germany* 25 E5
Waco, *U.S.A.* 113 K6
Waconichi, L., *Canada* 104 B5
Wad Ban Naqa, *Sudan* 81 D3
Wad Banda, *Sudan* 81 E2
Wad el Haddad, *Sudan* 81 E3
Wad en Nau, *Sudan* 81 E3
Wad Hamid, *Sudan* 81 D3
Wad Medanî, *Sudan* 81 E3
Wad Thana, *Pakistan* 68 F2
Wadai, *Africa* 76 E5
Wadayama, *Japan* 55 G7
Waddeneilanden, *Neths.* 17 A5
Waddenzee, *Neths.* 17 A5
Waddi, Chappal, *Nigeria* 83 D7
Waddington, *U.S.A.* 117 B9
Waddington, Mt., *Canada* 102 C3
Waddy Pt., *Australia* 95 C5
Wadebridge, *U.K.* 15 G3
Wadena, *Canada* 103 C8
Wadena, *U.S.A.* 112 B7
Wädenswil, *Switz.* 25 H4
Wadern, *Germany* 25 F2
Wadeye, *Australia* 92 B4
Wadhams, *Canada* 102 C3
Wādī as Sīr, *Jordan* 74 D4
Wadi Gemâl, *Egypt* 80 C4
Wadi Halfa, *Sudan* 80 C3
Wadi Rum △, *Jordan* 74 F4
Wadian, *China* 59 A9
Wadlew, *Poland* 31 G6
Wadowice, *Poland* 31 J6
Wadsworth, *Nev., U.S.A.* 108 G4
Wadsworth, *Ohio, U.S.A.* 116 E3
Waegwan, *S. Korea* 57 G15
Wafangdian, *China* 57 E11
Wafrah, *Si. Arabia* 70 D5
Wageningen, *Neths.* 17 C5
Wager B., *Canada* 101 B11
Wagga Wagga, *Australia* 95 F4
Waghete, *Indonesia* 63 E9
Wagin, *Australia* 93 F2
Wagner, *U.S.A.* 112 D5
Wagon Mound, *U.S.A.* 113 G2
Wagoner, *U.S.A.* 113 H7
Wągrowiec, *Poland* 31 F4
Wah, *Pakistan* 68 C5
Wahai, *Indonesia* 63 E7
Wahiawa, *U.S.A.* 106 H15
Wâḥid, *Egypt* 74 E1
Wahnai, *Afghan.* 68 C1
Wahni, *Ethiopia* 81 E4
Wahoo, *U.S.A.* 112 E6
Wahpeton, *U.S.A.* 112 B6
Waiau →, *N.Z.* 91 K4
Waibeem, *Indonesia* 63 E8
Waiblingen, *Germany* 25 G5
Waidhofen an der Thaya, *Austria* 26 C8
Waidhofen an der Ybbs, *Austria* 26 D7
Waigeo, *Indonesia* 63 E8
Waihi, *N.Z.* 91 G5
Waihou →, *N.Z.* 91 G5
Waika, *Dem. Rep. of the Congo* 86 C2
Waikabubak, *Indonesia* 63 F5
Waikaremoana, L., *N.Z.* 91 H6
Waikari, *N.Z.* 91 K4
Waikato →, *N.Z.* 91 G5
Waikerie, *Australia* 95 E3
Waikokopu, *N.Z.* 91 H6
Waikouaiti, *N.Z.* 91 L3
Wailuku, *U.S.A.* 106 H16
Waimakariri →, *N.Z.* 91 K4
Waimate, *N.Z.* 91 L3
Wainganga →, *India* 66 K11
Waingapu, *Indonesia* 63 F6
Waini →, *Guyana* 124 B7
Wainwright, *Canada* 103 C6
Waiouru, *N.Z.* 91 H5
Waipara, *N.Z.* 91 K4
Waipawa, *N.Z.* 91 H6
Waipiro, *N.Z.* 91 H7
Waipoua Forest, *N.Z.* 91 F4
Waipu, *N.Z.* 91 F5
Waipukurau, *N.Z.* 91 J6
Wairakei, *N.Z.* 91 H6
Wairarapa, L., *N.Z.* 91 J5
Wairoa, *N.Z.* 91 H6
Waitaki →, *N.Z.* 91 L3
Waitangi, *N.Z.* 91 F5
Waitara, *N.Z.* 91 H5
Waitomo Caves, *N.Z.* 91 H5
Waitsburg, *U.S.A.* 108 C5
Waiuku, *N.Z.* 91 G5
Wajima, *Japan* 55 F8
Wajir, *Kenya* 86 B5
Waka, *Ethiopia* 81 F4
Wakasa, *Japan* 55 G7
Wakasa-Wan, *Japan* 55 G7
Wakatipu, L., *N.Z.* 91 L2
Wakaw, *Canada* 103 C7
Wakayama, *Japan* 55 G7
Wakayama □, *Japan* 55 H7
Wake Forest, *U.S.A.* 115 H6
Wake I., *Pac. Oc.* 96 F8
WaKeeney, *U.S.A.* 112 F5
Wakefield, *Jamaica* 120 a
Wakefield, *N.Z.* 91 J4
Wakefield, *U.K.* 14 D6
Wakefield, *Mass., U.S.A.* 117 D13
Wakefield, *Mich., U.S.A.* 112 B10
Wakkanai, *Japan* 54 B10
Wakkerstroom, *S. Africa* 89 D5
Wakool, *Australia* 95 F3
Wakool →, *Australia* 95 F3
Wakre, *Indonesia* 63 E8
Wakuach, L., *Canada* 105 A6
Walamba, *Zambia* 87 E2
Wałbrzych, *Poland* 31 H3
Walbury Hill, *U.K.* 15 F6
Walcha, *Australia* 95 E5
Walcheren, *Neths.* 17 C3
Walcott, *U.S.A.* 108 F10
Wałcz, *Poland* 31 E3
Waldbröl, *Germany* 24 E3
Waldburg Ra., *Australia* 93 D2
Waldeck, *Germany* 24 D5
Walden, *Colo., U.S.A.* 108 F10
Walden, *N.Y., U.S.A.* 117 E10
Waldkirch, *Germany* 25 G3
Waldkirchen, *Germany* 25 G9
Waldkraiburg, *Germany* 25 G8
Waldport, *U.S.A.* 108 D1
Waldron, *U.S.A.* 113 H7
Waldviertel, *Austria* 26 C8
Walebing, *Australia* 93 F2
Walembele, *Ghana* 82 C4
Walensee, *Switz.* 25 H5
Wales □, *U.K.* 15 E3
Walewale, *Ghana* 83 C4
Walgett, *Australia* 95 E4
Walgreen Coast, *Antarctica* 5 D15
Walker, *U.S.A.* 112 B7
Walker, L., *Canada* 105 B6
Walker L., *Canada* 103 C9
Walker L., *U.S.A.* 108 G4
Walkerston, *Australia* 94 K7
Walkerton, *Canada* 116 B3
Wall, *U.S.A.* 112 D3
Walla Walla, *U.S.A.* 108 C4
Wallace, *Idaho, U.S.A.* 108 C6
Wallace, *N.C., U.S.A.* 115 H7
Wallaceburg, *Canada* 116 D2
Wallachia = Valahia, *Romania* 29 F9
Wallal, *Australia* 95 D4
Wallam Cr. →, *Australia* 95 D4
Wallambin, L., *Australia* 93 F2
Wallangarra, *Australia* 95 D5
Wallaroo, *Australia* 95 E2
Walldürn, *Germany* 25 F5
Wallenhorst, *Germany* 24 C4
Wallenpaupack, L., *U.S.A.* 117 E9
Wallingford, *U.S.A.* 117 E12
Wallis & Futuna, Is., *Pac. Oc.* 96 J10
Wallowa, *U.S.A.* 108 D5
Wallowa Mts., *U.S.A.* 108 D5
Walls, *U.K.* 13 A7
Walls of Jerusalem △, *Australia* 95 G4
Wallula, *U.S.A.* 108 C4
Wallumbilla, *Australia* 95 D4
Walmsley, L., *Canada* 103 A7
Walney, I. of, *U.K.* 14 C4
Walnut Canyon ⌓, *U.S.A.* 109 J8
Walnut Creek, *U.S.A.* 110 H4
Walnut Ridge, *U.S.A.* 113 G9
Walpole, *Australia* 93 F2
Walpole, *U.S.A.* 117 D13
Wals, *Austria* 26 D5
Walsall, *U.K.* 15 E6
Walsenburg, *U.S.A.* 113 G2
Walsh, *U.S.A.* 113 G3
Walsh →, *Australia* 94 B3
Walsrode, *Germany* 24 C5
Walterboro, *U.S.A.* 115 J5
Walters, *U.S.A.* 113 H5
Waltershausen, *Germany* 24 E6
Waltham, *U.S.A.* 117 D13
Waltman, *U.S.A.* 108 E10
Walton, *U.S.A.* 117 D9
Walton-on-the-Naze, *U.K.* 15 F9
Walvis Bay, *Namibia* 88 C1
Walvisbaai = Walvis Bay, *Namibia* 88 C1
Wamba, *Dem. Rep. of the Congo* 86 B2
Wamba, *Kenya* 86 B4
Wamba, *Nigeria* 83 D6
Wamego, *U.S.A.* 112 F6
Wamena, *Indonesia* 63 E9
Wamsutter, *U.S.A.* 108 F9
Wamulan, *Indonesia* 63 E7
Wan Xian, *China* 56 E8
Wana, *Pakistan* 68 C3
Wanaaring, *Australia* 95 D3
Wanaka, *N.Z.* 91 L2
Wanaka, L., *N.Z.* 91 L2
Wan'an, *China* 59 D10
Wanapitei L., *Canada* 104 C3
Wandel Sea = McKinley Sea, *Arctic* 4 A7
Wandérama, *Ivory C.* 82 D4
Wanderer, *Zimbabwe* 87 F3
Wandhari, *Pakistan* 68 F2
Wanding, *China* 58 E2
Wandoan, *Australia* 95 D4
Wanfu, *China* 57 D12
Wang →, *Thailand* 64 D2
Wang Kai, *Sudan* 81 F2
Wang Noi, *Thailand* 64 E3
Wang Saphung, *Thailand* 64 D3
Wang Thong, *Thailand* 64 D3
Wanga, *Dem. Rep. of the Congo* 86 B2
Wangal, *Indonesia* 63 F8
Wanganella, *Australia* 95 F3
Wanganui, *N.Z.* 91 H5
Wangaratta, *Australia* 95 F4
Wangary, *Australia* 95 E2
Wangcang, *China* 58 A6
Wangcheng, *China* 59 C9
Wangdu, *China* 56 E8
Wangen, *Germany* 25 H5
Wangerooge, *Germany* 24 B3
Wangiwangi, *Indonesia* 63 F6
Wangjiang, *China* 59 B11
Wangmo, *China* 58 E6
Wangolodougou, *Ivory C.* 82 D3
Wangqing, *China* 57 C15
Wankaner, *India* 68 H4
Wanless, *Canada* 103 C8
Wanneroo, *Australia* 93 F2
Wannian, *China* 59 C11
Wanning, *China* 64 C8
Wanon Niwat, *Thailand* 64 D4
Wanquan, *China* 56 D8
Wanrong, *China* 56 G6
Wanshan, *China* 58 D7
Wanshengchang, *China* 58 C6
Wantage, *U.K.* 15 F6
Wanxian, *China* 58 B7
Wanyuan, *China* 58 A7
Wanzai, *China* 59 C10
Wapakoneta, *U.S.A.* 114 E3
Wapato, *U.S.A.* 108 C3
Wapawekka L., *Canada* 103 C8
Wapikopa L., *Canada* 104 B2
Wapiti →, *Canada* 102 B5
Wappingers Falls, *U.S.A.* 117 E11
Wapsipinicon →, *U.S.A.* 112 E9
Wapusk △, *Canada* 103 B10
Warab □, *Sudan* 81 F2
Warangal, *India* 66 L11
Waraseoni, *India* 69 J9
Waratah, *Australia* 95 G4
Waratah B., *Australia* 95 F4
Warburg, *Germany* 24 D5
Warburton, *Vic., Australia* 95 F4
Warburton, *W. Austral., Australia* 93 E4
Warburton, The →, *Australia* 95 D2
Warburton Ra., *Australia* 93 E4
Ward, *N.Z.* 91 J5
Ward →, *Australia* 95 D4
Ward Mt., *U.S.A.* 110 H8
Warden, *S. Africa* 89 D4
Wardha, *India* 66 J11
Wardha →, *India* 66 K11
Ware, *Canada* 102 B3
Ware, *U.K.* 15 F8
Ware, *U.S.A.* 117 D12
Waregem, *Belgium* 17 D3
Wareham, *U.S.A.* 117 E14
Waremme, *Belgium* 17 D5
Waren, *Germany* 24 B8
Warendorf, *Germany* 24 D4
Warialda, *Australia* 95 D5
Wariap, *Indonesia* 63 E8
Warin Chamrap, *Thailand* 64 E5
Warka, *Poland* 31 G8
Warkopi, *Indonesia* 63 E8
Warm Springs, *U.S.A.* 109 G5
Warman, *Canada* 103 C7
Warmbad = Bela Bela, *S. Africa* 89 C4
Warmbad, *Namibia* 88 D2
Warmińsko-Mazurskie □, *Poland* 30 D8
Warminster, *U.K.* 15 F5
Warminster, *U.S.A.* 117 F9
Warnemünde, *Germany* 24 A8
Warner Mts., *U.S.A.* 108 F3
Warner Robins, *U.S.A.* 115 J4
Warnow →, *Germany* 24 A8
Waroona, *Australia* 93 F2
Warracknabeal, *Australia* 95 F3
Warragul, *Australia* 95 F4
Warrego →, *Australia* 95 E4
Warrego Ra., *Australia* 94 C4
Warren, *Australia* 95 E4
Warren, *Ark., U.S.A.* 113 J8
Warren, *Mich., U.S.A.* 114 D4
Warren, *Minn., U.S.A.* 112 A6
Warren, *Ohio, U.S.A.* 116 E4
Warren, *Pa., U.S.A.* 116 E5
Warrenpoint, *U.K.* 12 B5
Warrensburg, *Mo., U.S.A.* 112 F8
Warrensburg, *N.Y., U.S.A.* 117 C11
Warrenton, *S. Africa* 88 D3
Warrenton, *U.S.A.* 110 D3
Warri, *Nigeria* 83 D6
Warrina, *Australia* 95 D2
Warrington, *U.K.* 14 D5
Warrington, *U.S.A.* 115 K2
Warrington □, *U.K.* 14 D5
Warrnambool, *Australia* 95 F3
Warroad, *U.S.A.* 112 A7
Warruwi, *Australia* 94 A1
Warsa, *Indonesia* 63 E9
Warsak Dam, *Pakistan* 68 B4
Warsaw = Warszawa, *Poland* 31 F8
Warsaw, *Ind., U.S.A.* 114 E3
Warsaw, *N.Y., U.S.A.* 116 D6
Warsaw, *Ohio, U.S.A.* 116 F3
Warstein, *Germany* 24 D4
Warszawa, *Poland* 31 F8
Warszawa ✕ (WAW), *Poland* 31 F7
Warta, *Poland* 31 G5
Warta →, *Poland* 31 F1
Warthe = Warta →, *Poland* 31 F1
Waru, *Indonesia* 63 E8
Warwick, *Australia* 95 D5
Warwick, *U.K.* 15 E6
Warwick, *N.Y., U.S.A.* 117 E10
Warwick, *R.I., U.S.A.* 117 E13
Warwickshire □, *U.K.* 15 E6
Wasaga Beach, *Canada* 116 B4
Wasagaming, *Canada* 103 C9
Wasatch Ra., *U.S.A.* 108 F8
Wasbank, *S. Africa* 89 D5
Wasco, *Calif., U.S.A.* 111 K7
Wasco, *Oreg., U.S.A.* 108 D3
Wase, *Nigeria* 83 D6
Waseca, *U.S.A.* 112 C8
Wasekamio L., *Canada* 103 B7
Wash, The, *U.K.* 14 E8
Washago, *Canada* 116 B5
Washburn, *N. Dak., U.S.A.* 112 B4
Washburn, *Wis., U.S.A.* 112 B9
Washim, *India* 66 J10
Washington, *U.K.* 14 C6
Washington, *D.C., U.S.A.* 114 F7
Washington, *Ga., U.S.A.* 115 J4
Washington, *Ind., U.S.A.* 114 F2
Washington, *Iowa, U.S.A.* 112 E9
Washington, *Mo., U.S.A.* 112 F9
Washington, *N.C., U.S.A.* 115 H7
Washington, *N.J., U.S.A.* 117 F10
Washington, *Pa., U.S.A.* 116 F4
Washington, *Utah, U.S.A.* 109 H7
Washington □, *U.S.A.* 108 C3
Washington, Mt., *U.S.A.* 117 B13
Washington Court House, *U.S.A.* 114 F4
Washington I., *U.S.A.* 114 C2
Washougal, *U.S.A.* 110 E4
Washpool △, *Australia* 95 D5
Wasian, *Indonesia* 63 E8
Wasilków, *Poland* 31 E10
Wasilla, *U.S.A.* 100 B5
Wasior, *Indonesia* 63 E8
Wāsiț □, *Iraq* 70 C5
Waskaganish, *Canada* 104 B4
Waskaiowaka, L., *Canada* 103 B9
Waskesiu Lake, *Canada* 103 C7
Wasserburg, *Germany* 25 G8
Wasserkuppe, *Germany* 24 E5
Wassy, *France* 19 D11
Waswanipi, *Canada* 104 C4
Waswanipi, L., *Canada* 104 C4
Watampone, *Indonesia* 63 E6
Watamu, *Kenya* 86 C5
Watarrka △, *Australia* 92 D5
Water Park Pt., *Australia* 94 C5
Water Valley, *U.S.A.* 113 H10
Waterberg Plateau ⌓, *Namibia* 88 C2
Waterberge, *S. Africa* 89 C4
Waterbury, *Conn., U.S.A.* 117 E11
Waterbury, *Vt., U.S.A.* 117 B12
Waterbury L., *Canada* 103 B8
Waterdown, *Canada* 116 C5
Waterford, *Canada* 116 D4
Waterford, *Ireland* 12 D4
Waterford, *Calif., U.S.A.* 110 H6
Waterford, *Pa., U.S.A.* 116 E5
Waterford □, *Ireland* 12 D4
Waterford Harbour, *Ireland* 12 D5
Waterhen L., *Canada* 103 C9
Waterloo, *Belgium* 17 D4
Waterloo, *Ont., Canada* 116 C4
Waterloo, *Qué., Canada* 117 A12
Waterloo, *S. Leone* 82 D2
Waterloo, *Ill., U.S.A.* 112 F9
Waterloo, *Iowa, U.S.A.* 112 D8
Waterloo, *N.Y., U.S.A.* 116 D8
Watersmeet, *U.S.A.* 112 B10
Waterton Lakes △, *Canada* 102 D6
Watertown, *Conn., U.S.A.* 117 E11
Watertown, *N.Y., U.S.A.* 117 C9
Watertown, *S. Dak., U.S.A.* 112 C6
Watertown, *Wis., U.S.A.* 112 D10
Waterval-Boven, *S. Africa* 89 D5
Waterville, *Canada* 117 A13
Waterville, *Maine, U.S.A.* 115 C11
Waterville, *N.Y., U.S.A.* 117 D9
Waterville, *Pa., U.S.A.* 116 E7
Waterville, *Wash., U.S.A.* 108 C3
Watervliet, *U.S.A.* 117 D11
Wates, *Indonesia* 63 G14
Watford, *Canada* 116 D3
Watford, *U.K.* 15 F7
Watford City, *U.S.A.* 112 B3
Wathaman →, *Canada* 103 B8
Wathaman L., *Canada* 103 B8
Watheroo, *Australia* 93 F2
Watheroo △, *Australia* 93 F2
Wating, *China* 56 G4
Watkins Glen, *U.S.A.* 116 D8
Watling I. = San Salvador I., *Bahamas* 121 B5
Watonga, *U.S.A.* 113 H5
Watrous, *Canada* 103 C7
Watrous, *U.S.A.* 113 H2
Watsa, *Dem. Rep. of the Congo* 86 B2
Watseka, *U.S.A.* 114 E2
Watson, *Australia* 93 F5
Watson, *Canada* 103 C8
Watson Lake, *Canada* 102 A3
Watsontown, *U.S.A.* 116 E8
Watsonville, *U.S.A.* 110 J5
Wattiwarriganna Cr. →, *Australia* 95 D2
Wattwil, *Switz.* 25 H5
Watuata = Batuata, *Indonesia* 63 F6
Watubela, Kepulauan, *Indonesia* 63 E8
Watubela Is. = Watubela, Kepulauan, *Indonesia* 63 E8
Wau = Wâw, *Sudan* 81 F2
Waubamik, *Canada* 116 A4
Waubay, *U.S.A.* 112 C6
Wauchope, *N.S.W., Australia* 95 E5
Wauchope, *N. Terr., Australia* 94 C1
Wauchula, *U.S.A.* 115 M5
Waukarlycarly, L., *Australia* 92 D3
Waukegan, *U.S.A.* 114 D2
Waukesha, *U.S.A.* 114 D1
Waukon, *U.S.A.* 112 D9
Waupaca, *U.S.A.* 112 C10
Waupun, *U.S.A.* 112 D10
Waurika, *U.S.A.* 113 H6
Wausau, *U.S.A.* 112 C10
Wautoma, *U.S.A.* 112 C10
Wauwatosa, *U.S.A.* 114 D2
Waveney →, *U.K.* 15 E9
Waverley, *N.Z.* 91 H5
Waverly, *Iowa, U.S.A.* 112 D8
Waverly, *N.Y., U.S.A.* 117 E8
Wavre, *Belgium* 17 D4
Wâw, *Sudan* 81 F2
Wāw al Kabīr, *Libya* 79 C9
Wawa, *Canada* 104 C3
Wawa, *Nigeria* 83 D5
Wawa, *Sudan* 80 C3
Wawanesa, *Canada* 103 D9
Wawona, *U.S.A.* 110 H7
Waxahachie, *U.S.A.* 113 J6
Way, L., *Australia* 93 E3
Waycross, *U.S.A.* 115 K4
Wayi, *Sudan* 81 F3
Wayland, *U.S.A.* 116 D7
Wayne, *Nebr., U.S.A.* 112 D6
Wayne, *W. Va., U.S.A.* 114 F4
Waynesboro, *Ga., U.S.A.* 115 J4
Waynesboro, *Miss., U.S.A.* 115 K1
Waynesboro, *Pa., U.S.A.* 114 F7
Waynesboro, *Va., U.S.A.* 114 F6
Waynesburg, *U.S.A.* 114 F5
Waynesville, *U.S.A.* 115 H4
Waynoka, *U.S.A.* 113 G5
Wazirabad, *Pakistan* 68 C6
Wda →, *Poland* 30 E5
We, *Indonesia* 62 C1
Weald, The, *U.K.* 15 F8
Wear →, *U.K.* 14 C6
Weatherford, *Okla., U.S.A.* 113 H5
Weatherford, *Tex., U.S.A.* 113 J6
Weaverville, *U.S.A.* 108 F2
Webb City, *U.S.A.* 113 G7
Webequie, *Canada* 104 B2
Webo = Nyaake, *Liberia* 82 E3
Webster, *Mass., U.S.A.* 117 D13
Webster, *N.Y., U.S.A.* 116 C7
Webster, *S. Dak., U.S.A.* 112 C6
Webster City, *U.S.A.* 112 D8
Webster Springs, *U.S.A.* 114 F5
Weda, *Indonesia* 63 D7
Weda, Teluk, *Indonesia* 63 D7
Weddell I., *Falk. Is.* 128 G4
Weddell Sea, *Antarctica* 5 D1
Wedderburn, *Australia* 95 F3
Wedel, *Germany* 24 B5
Wedemark, *Germany* 24 C5
Wedgeport, *Canada* 105 D6
Wedza, *Zimbabwe* 87 F3
Wee Waa, *Australia* 95 E4
Weed, *U.S.A.* 108 F2
Weed Heights, *U.S.A.* 110 G7
Weedsport, *U.S.A.* 117 C8
Weedville, *U.S.A.* 116 E6
Weenen, *S. Africa* 89 D5
Weener, *Germany* 24 B3
Weert, *Neths.* 17 C5
Węgierska-Górka, *Poland* 31 J6
Węgliniec, *Poland* 31 G2
Węgorzewo, *Poland* 30 D8
Węgorzyno, *Poland* 30 E2
Węgrów, *Poland* 31 F9
Wehda □, *Sudan* 81 F3
Wei He →, *Hebei, China* 56 F8
Wei He →, *Shaanxi, China* 56 G6
Weichang, *China* 57 D9
Weichuan, *China* 56 G7
Weida, *Germany* 24 E8
Weiden, *Germany* 25 F8
Weifang, *China* 57 F10
Weihai, *China* 57 F12
Weil, *Germany* 25 H3
Weilburg, *Germany* 24 E4
Weilheim, *Germany* 25 H7
Weimar, *Germany* 24 E7
Weinan, *China* 56 G5
Weingarten, *Germany* 25 F4
Weinheim, *Germany* 25 F4
Weining, *China* 58 D5
Weipa, *Australia* 94 A3
Weir →, *Australia* 95 D4
Weir →, *Canada* 103 B10
Weir River, *Canada* 103 B10
Weirton, *U.S.A.* 116 F4
Weiser, *U.S.A.* 108 D5
Weishan, *Shandong, China* 57 G9
Weishan, *Yunnan, China* 58 E3
Weissenburg, *Germany* 25 F6
Weissenfels, *Germany* 24 D7
Weisswasser, *Germany* 24 D10
Wéitra, *Austria* 26 C7
Weixi, *China* 58 D2
Weixin, *China* 58 D5
Weiyuan, *China* 56 G3
Weiz, *Austria* 26 D8
Weizhou Dao, *China* 58 G7
Wejherowo, *Poland* 30 D5
Wekusko L., *Canada* 103 C9
Welch, *U.S.A.* 114 G5
Weldya, *Ethiopia* 81 E4
Welega, *Ethiopia* 81 F3
Welford △, *Australia* 94 D3
Welkite, *Ethiopia* 81 F4
Welkom, *S. Africa* 88 D4
Welland, *Canada* 116 D5
Welland →, *U.K.* 15 E7
Wellesley Is., *Australia* 94 B2
Wellingborough, *U.K.* 15 E7
Wellington, *Australia* 95 E4
Wellington, *Canada* 116 C7
Wellington, *N.Z.* 91 J5
Wellington, *S. Africa* 88 E2
Wellington, *Somst., U.K.* 15 G4
Wellington, *Telford & Wrekin, U.K.* 15 E5
Wellington, *Colo., U.S.A.* 112 E2
Wellington, *Kans., U.S.A.* 113 G6
Wellington, *Nev., U.S.A.* 110 G7
Wellington, *Ohio, U.S.A.* 116 E2
Wellington, *Tex., U.S.A.* 113 H4
Wellington, I., *Chile* 128 F2
Wellington, L., *Australia* 95 F4
Wells, *U.K.* 15 F5
Wells, *Maine, U.S.A.* 117 C14
Wells, *N.Y., U.S.A.* 117 C10
Wells, *Nev., U.S.A.* 108 F6
Wells, L., *Australia* 93 E3
Wells, Mt., *Australia* 92 C4
Wells Gray ⌓, *Canada* 102 C4
Wells-next-the-Sea, *U.K.* 14 E8
Wells River, *U.S.A.* 117 B12
Wellsboro, *U.S.A.* 116 E7
Wellsburg, *U.S.A.* 116 F4
Wellsville, *N.Y., U.S.A.* 116 D7
Wellsville, *Ohio, U.S.A.* 116 F4
Wellsville, *Utah, U.S.A.* 108 F8

Wellton, *U.S.A.* 109 **K6**
Welmel, Wabi →, *Ethiopia* 81 **F5**
Welo, *Ethiopia* 81 **E4**
Wels, *Austria* 26 **C7**
Welshpool, *U.K.* 15 **E4**
Welwyn Garden City, *U.K.* 15 **F7**
Wem, *U.K.* 14 **E5**
Wembere →, *Tanzania* 86 **C3**
Wemindji, *Canada* 104 **B4**
Wen Xian, *China* 56 **G7**
Wenatchee, *U.S.A.* 108 **C3**
Wenchang, *China* 64 **C8**
Wencheng, *China* 59 **D13**
Wenchi, *Ghana* 82 **D4**
Wenchow = Wenzhou, *China* 59 **D13**
Wenchuan, *China* 58 **B4**
Wenden, *U.S.A.* 111 **M13**
Wendeng, *China* 57 **F12**
Wendesi, *Indonesia* 63 **E8**
Wendo, *Ethiopia* 81 **F4**
Wendover, *U.S.A.* 108 **F6**
Weng'an, *China* 58 **D6**
Wengcheng, *China* 59 **E9**
Wengyuan, *China* 59 **E10**
Wenjiang, *China* 58 **B4**
Wenling, *China* 59 **C13**
Wenlock →, *Australia* 94 **A3**
Wenshan, *China* 58 **F5**
Wenshang, *China* 56 **G9**
Wenshui, *China* 56 **F7**
Wensleydale, *U.K.* 14 **C6**
Wensu, *China* 60 **B3**
Wensum →, *U.K.* 14 **E8**
Wentworth, *Australia* 95 **E3**
Wentzel L., *Canada* 102 **B6**
Wenut, *Indonesia* 63 **E8**
Wenxi, *China* 56 **G6**
Wenxian, *China* 56 **H3**
Wenzhou, *China* 59 **D13**
Weott, *U.S.A.* 108 **F2**
Wepener, *S. Africa* 88 **D4**
Werda, *Botswana* 88 **D3**
Werdau, *Germany* 24 **E8**
Werder, *Germany* 24 **C8**
Werdohl, *Germany* 24 **D3**
Wereilu, *Ethiopia* 81 **E4**
Weri, *Indonesia* 63 **E8**
Werneck, *Germany* 25 **F6**
Wernigerode, *Germany* 24 **D6**
Werra →, *Germany* 24 **D5**
Werrimull, *Australia* 95 **E3**
Werris Creek, *Australia* 95 **E5**
Wertach →, *Germany* 25 **G6**
Wertheim, *Germany* 25 **F5**
Wertingen, *Germany* 25 **G6**
Wesel, *Germany* 24 **D2**
Weser →, *Germany* 24 **B4**
Weser-Ems □, *Germany* 24 **C3**
Weserbergland, *Germany* 24 **C5**
Weserbergland Schaumburg Hameln ⌂, *Germany* 24 **C5**
Wesiri, *Indonesia* 63 **F7**
Weslemkoon L., *Canada* 116 **A7**
Wesleyville, *U.S.A.* 116 **D4**
Wessel, C., *Australia* 94 **A2**
Wessel Is., *Australia* 94 **A2**
Wesselburen, *Germany* 24 **A4**
Wessington Springs, *U.S.A.* 112 **C5**
West, *U.S.A.* 113 **K6**
West →, *U.S.A.* 117 **D12**
West Antarctica, *Antarctica* 5 **D15**
West Baines →, *Australia* 92 **C4**
West Bank ◪, *Asia* 74 **C4**
West Bend, *U.S.A.* 114 **D1**
West Bengal □, *India* 69 **H13**
West Berkshire □, *U.K.* 15 **F6**
West Beskids = Západné Beskydy, *Europe* 27 **B12**
West Branch, *U.S.A.* 114 **C3**
West Branch Susquehanna →, *U.S.A.* 117 **F8**
West Bromwich, *U.K.* 15 **E6**
West Burra, *U.K.* 13 **A7**
West Canada Cr. →, *U.S.A.* 117 **C10**
West Cape Howe, *Australia* 93 **G2**
West Chazy, *U.S.A.* 117 **B11**
West Chester, *U.S.A.* 117 **G9**
West Coast ⌂, *Namibia* 88 **C1**
West Coast △, *S. Africa* 88 **E2**
West Columbia, *U.S.A.* 113 **L7**
West Covina, *U.S.A.* 111 **L9**
West Des Moines, *U.S.A.* 112 **E8**
West Dunbartonshire □, *U.K.* 13 **F4**
West End, *Bahamas* 120 **A4**
West Falkland, *Falk. Is.* 128 **G5**
West Fargo, *U.S.A.* 112 **B6**
West Farmington, *U.S.A.* 116 **E4**
West Fjord = Vestfjorden, *Norway* 8 **C15**
West Fork Trinity →, *U.S.A.* 113 **J6**
West Frankfort, *U.S.A.* 112 **G10**
West Hartford, *U.S.A.* 117 **E12**
West Haven, *U.S.A.* 117 **E12**
West Hazleton, *U.S.A.* 117 **F9**
West Helena, *U.S.A.* 113 **H9**
West Hurley, *U.S.A.* 117 **E10**
West Ice Shelf, *Antarctica* 5 **C7**
West Indies, *Cent. Amer.* 121 **D7**
West Jordan, *U.S.A.* 108 **F8**
West Lorne, *Canada* 116 **D3**
West Lothian □, *U.K.* 13 **F5**
West Lunga →, *Zambia* 87 **E1**
West MacDonnell △, *Australia* 92 **D5**
West Memphis, *U.S.A.* 113 **H9**
West Midlands □, *U.K.* 15 **E6**
West Mifflin, *U.S.A.* 116 **F5**
West Milton, *U.S.A.* 116 **E8**
West Monroe, *U.S.A.* 113 **J8**
West Newton, *U.S.A.* 116 **F5**
West Nicholson, *Zimbabwe* 87 **G2**
West Palm Beach, *U.S.A.* 115 **M5**
West Plains, *U.S.A.* 113 **G9**
West Point, *N.Y., U.S.A.* 117 **E11**
West Point, *Nebr., U.S.A.* 112 **E6**
West Point, *Va., U.S.A.* 114 **G7**
West Pt. = Ouest, Pte. de l', *Canada* 105 **C7**
West Pt., *Australia* 95 **F2**
West Road →, *Canada* 102 **C4**
West Rutland, *U.S.A.* 117 **C11**
West Schelde = Westerschelde →, *Neths.* 17 **C3**
West Seneca, *U.S.A.* 116 **D6**
West Siberian Plain, *Russia* 50 **C11**
West Sussex □, *U.K.* 15 **G7**
West-Terschelling, *Neths.* 17 **A5**
West Valley City, *U.S.A.* 108 **F8**
West Virginia □, *U.S.A.* 114 **F5**
West-Vlaanderen □, *Belgium* 17 **D2**
West Walker →, *U.S.A.* 110 **G7**
West Wyalong, *Australia* 95 **E4**
West Yellowstone, *U.S.A.* 108 **D8**
West Yorkshire □, *U.K.* 14 **D6**
Westall, Pt., *Australia* 95 **E1**
Westbrook, *U.S.A.* 115 **D10**
Westbury, *Australia* 95 **G4**
Westby, *U.S.A.* 112 **A2**
Westend, *U.S.A.* 111 **K9**
Westerland, *Germany* 9 **J13**
Westerly, *U.S.A.* 117 **E13**
Western □, *Ghana* 82 **D4**
Western □, *Kenya* 86 **B3**
Western □, *S. Leone* 82 **D2**
Western □, *Zambia* 87 **F1**
Western Australia □, *Australia* 93 **E2**
Western Cape □, *S. Africa* 88 **E3**
Western Dvina = Daugava →, *Latvia* 9 **H21**
Western Ghats, *India* 66 **N9**
Western Isles □, *U.K.* 13 **D1**
Western Sahara ■, *Africa* 78 **D3**
Western Samoa = Samoa ■, *Pac. Oc.* 91 **B13**
Westernport, *U.S.A.* 114 **F6**
Westerschelde →, *Neths.* 17 **C3**
Westerstede, *Germany* 24 **B3**
Westerwald, *Germany* 24 **E3**
Westfield, *Mass., U.S.A.* 117 **D12**
Westfield, *N.Y., U.S.A.* 116 **D5**
Westfield, *Pa., U.S.A.* 116 **E7**
Westhill, *U.K.* 13 **D6**
Westhope, *U.S.A.* 112 **A4**
Westland △, *N.Z.* 91 **K2**
Westland Bight, *N.Z.* 91 **K3**
Westlock, *Canada* 102 **C6**
Westmar, *Australia* 95 **D4**
Westmeath □, *Ireland* 12 **C4**
Westminster, *U.S.A.* 114 **F7**
Westmont, *U.S.A.* 116 **F6**
Westmoreland, *Barbados* 121 **g**
Westmorland, *U.S.A.* 111 **M11**
Weston, *Oreg., U.S.A.* 108 **D4**
Weston, *W. Va., U.S.A.* 114 **F5**
Weston I., *Canada* 104 **B4**
Weston-super-Mare, *U.K.* 15 **F5**
Westover, *U.S.A.* 116 **F6**
Westport, *Canada* 117 **B8**
Westport, *Ireland* 12 **C2**
Westport, *N.Z.* 91 **J3**
Westport, *N.Y., U.S.A.* 117 **B11**
Westport, *Oreg., U.S.A.* 110 **D3**
Westport, *Wash., U.S.A.* 110 **D2**
Westray, *Canada* 103 **C8**
Westray, *U.K.* 13 **B5**
Westree, *Canada* 104 **C3**
Westville, *U.S.A.* 110 **F6**
Westwood, *U.S.A.* 108 **F3**
Wetar, *Indonesia* 63 **F7**
Wetaskiwin, *Canada* 102 **C6**
Wete, *Tanzania* 84 **F7**
Wetherby, *U.K.* 14 **D6**
Wethersfield, *U.S.A.* 117 **E12**
Wetteren, *Belgium* 17 **D3**
Wetzlar, *Germany* 24 **E4**
Wewoka, *U.S.A.* 113 **H6**
Wexford, *Ireland* 12 **D5**
Wexford □, *Ireland* 12 **D5**
Wexford Harbour, *Ireland* 12 **D5**
Weyburn, *Canada* 103 **D8**
Weyer Markt, *Austria* 26 **D7**
Weyhe, *Germany* 24 **C4**
Weyib →, *Ethiopia* 81 **F5**
Weymouth, *Canada* 105 **D6**
Weymouth, *U.K.* 15 **G5**
Weymouth, *U.S.A.* 117 **D14**
Weymouth, C., *Australia* 94 **A3**
Wha Ti, *Canada* 100 **B8**
Whakaari = White I., *N.Z.* 91 **G6**
Whakatane, *N.Z.* 91 **G6**
Whale →, *Canada* 105 **A6**
Whale Cove, *Canada* 103 **A10**
Whales, B. of, *Antarctica* 5 **D12**
Whalsay, *U.K.* 13 **A8**
Whangamata, *N.Z.* 91 **G5**
Whangamomona, *N.Z.* 91 **H5**
Whanganui △, *N.Z.* 91 **H5**
Whangarei, *N.Z.* 91 **F5**
Whangarei Harb., *N.Z.* 91 **F5**
Wharfe →, *U.K.* 14 **D6**
Wharfedale, *U.K.* 14 **C5**
Wharton, *N.J., U.S.A.* 117 **F10**
Wharton, *Pa., U.S.A.* 116 **E6**
Wharton, *Tex., U.S.A.* 113 **L6**
Wheatland, *Calif., U.S.A.* 110 **F5**
Wheatland, *Wyo., U.S.A.* 112 **D2**
Wheatley, *Canada* 116 **D2**
Wheaton, *Md., U.S.A.* 114 **F7**
Wheaton, *Minn., U.S.A.* 112 **C6**
Wheelbarrow Pk., *U.S.A.* 110 **H10**
Wheeler, *Oreg., U.S.A.* 108 **D2**
Wheeler, *Tex., U.S.A.* 113 **H4**
Wheeler →, *Canada* 105 **A6**
Wheeler L., *U.S.A.* 115 **H2**
Wheeler Pk., *N. Mex., U.S.A.* 109 **H11**
Wheeler Pk., *Nev., U.S.A.* 109 **G6**
Wheeler Ridge, *U.S.A.* 111 **L8**
Wheeling, *U.S.A.* 116 **F4**
Whernside, *U.K.* 14 **C5**
Whiskey Jack L., *Canada* 103 **B8**
Whiskeytown-Shasta-Trinity ⌂, *U.S.A.* 108 **F2**
Whistleduck Cr. →, *Australia* 94 **C2**
Whistler, *Canada* 102 **C4**
Whitby, *Canada* 116 **C6**
Whitby, *U.K.* 14 **C7**
White →, *Ark., U.S.A.* 113 **J9**
White →, *Ind., U.S.A.* 114 **F2**
White →, *S. Dak., U.S.A.* 112 **D5**
White →, *Tex., U.S.A.* 113 **J4**
White →, *Utah, U.S.A.* 108 **F9**
White →, *Vt., U.S.A.* 117 **C12**
White →, *Wash., U.S.A.* 110 **C4**
White, L., *Australia* 92 **D4**
White B., *Canada* 105 **C8**
White Bird, *U.S.A.* 108 **D5**
White Butte, *U.S.A.* 112 **B3**
White City, *U.S.A.* 108 **E2**
White Cliffs, *Australia* 95 **E3**
White Hall, *U.S.A.* 112 **F9**
White Haven, *U.S.A.* 117 **E9**
White Horse, Vale of, *U.K.* 15 **F6**
White I., *N.Z.* 91 **G6**
White L., *Canada* 117 **A8**
White L., *U.S.A.* 113 **L8**
White Mountain Peak, *U.S.A.* 109 **G4**
White Mts., *Calif., U.S.A.* 110 **H8**
White Mts., *N.H., U.S.A.* 117 **B13**
White Mts. △, *Australia* 94 **C4**
White Nile = Nîl el Abyad →, *Sudan* 81 **D3**
White Nile Dam = Khazzān Jabal al Awliyā, *Sudan* 81 **D3**
White Otter L., *Canada* 104 **C1**
White Pass, *U.S.A.* 110 **D5**
White Plains, *U.S.A.* 117 **E11**
White River, *Canada* 104 **C2**
White River, *S. Africa* 89 **D5**
White River, *U.S.A.* 112 **D4**
White Rock, *Canada* 110 **A4**
White Russia = Belarus ■, *Europe* 32 **F4**
White Sands ⌂, *U.S.A.* 109 **K10**
White Sea = Beloye More, *Russia* 52 **C4**
White Sulphur Springs, *Mont., U.S.A.* 108 **C8**
White Sulphur Springs, *W. Va., U.S.A.* 114 **G5**
White Swan, *U.S.A.* 110 **D6**
White Volta →, *Ghana* 83 **D4**
Whitecliffs, *N.Z.* 91 **K3**
Whitecourt, *Canada* 102 **C5**
Whiteface Mt., *U.S.A.* 117 **B11**
Whitefield, *U.S.A.* 117 **B13**
Whitefish, *U.S.A.* 108 **B6**
Whitefish L., *Canada* 103 **A7**
Whitefish Point, *U.S.A.* 114 **B3**
Whitegull, L. = Goélands, L. aux, *Canada* 105 **A7**
Whitehall, *Mich., U.S.A.* 114 **D2**
Whitehall, *Mont., U.S.A.* 108 **D7**
Whitehall, *N.Y., U.S.A.* 117 **C11**
Whitehall, *Wis., U.S.A.* 112 **C9**
Whitehaven, *U.K.* 14 **C4**
Whitehorse, *Canada* 102 **A1**
Whitemark, *Australia* 95 **G4**
Whiteplains, *Liberia* 82 **D2**
Whiteriver, *U.S.A.* 109 **K9**
Whitesand →, *Canada* 102 **A5**
Whitesands, *S. Africa* 88 **E3**
Whitesboro, *N.Y., U.S.A.* 117 **C9**
Whitesboro, *Tex., U.S.A.* 113 **J6**
Whiteshell ⌂, *Canada* 103 **D9**
Whitesville, *U.S.A.* 116 **D7**
Whiteville, *U.S.A.* 115 **H6**
Whitewater, *U.S.A.* 114 **D1**
Whitewater Baldy, *U.S.A.* 109 **K9**
Whitewater L., *Canada* 104 **B2**
Whitewood, *Australia* 94 **C3**
Whitewood, *Canada* 103 **C8**
Whithorn, *U.K.* 13 **G4**
Whitianga, *N.Z.* 91 **G5**
Whitman, *U.S.A.* 117 **D14**
Whitney, *Canada* 116 **A6**
Whitney, Mt., *U.S.A.* 110 **J8**
Whitney Point, *U.S.A.* 117 **D9**
Whitstable, *U.K.* 15 **F9**
Whitsunday I., *Australia* 94 **J7**
Whitsunday Islands △, *Australia* 94 **J7**
Whitsunday Passage, *Australia* 94 **J6**
Whittier, *U.S.A.* 111 **M8**
Whittlesea, *Australia* 95 **F4**
Wholdaia L., *Canada* 103 **A8**
Whyalla, *Australia* 95 **E2**
Wiang Kosai △, *Thailand* 64 **D2**
Wiarton, *Canada* 116 **B3**
Wiawso, *Ghana* 82 **D4**
Wiay, *U.K.* 13 **D1**
Wiązów, *Poland* 31 **H4**
Wibaux, *U.S.A.* 112 **B2**
Wichian Buri, *Thailand* 64 **E3**
Wichita, *U.S.A.* 113 **G6**
Wichita Falls, *U.S.A.* 113 **J5**
Wick, *U.K.* 13 **C5**
Wicked Pt., *Canada* 116 **C7**
Wickenburg, *U.S.A.* 109 **K7**
Wickepin, *Australia* 93 **F2**
Wickham, *Australia* 92 **D2**
Wickham, C., *Australia* 95 **F3**
Wickliffe, *U.S.A.* 116 **E3**
Wicklow, *Ireland* 12 **D5**
Wicklow □, *Ireland* 12 **D5**
Wicklow Hd., *Ireland* 12 **D6**
Wicklow Mts., *Ireland* 12 **C5**
Wicklow Mts. △, *Ireland* 12 **C5**
Widawa, *Poland* 31 **G5**
Widawka →, *Poland* 31 **G5**
Widgeegoara Cr. →, *Australia* 95 **D4**
Widgiemooltha, *Australia* 93 **F3**
Widnes, *U.K.* 14 **D5**
Więcbork, *Poland* 31 **E4**
Wiehengebirge = Nördlicher Teutoburger Wald-Wiehengebirge ⌂, *Germany* 24 **C4**
Wiehl, *Germany* 24 **E3**
Wiek, *Germany* 24 **A9**
Wielbark, *Poland* 30 **E7**
Wieleń, *Poland* 31 **F3**
Wielichowo, *Poland* 31 **F3**
Wieliczka, *Poland* 31 **J7**
Wielkopolski △, *Poland* 31 **F3**
Wielkopolskie □, *Poland* 31 **F4**
Wieluń, *Poland* 31 **G5**
Wien, *Austria* 27 **C9**
Wien ✈ (VIA), *Austria* 27 **C9**
Wiener Neustadt, *Austria* 27 **D9**
Wieprz →, *Poland* 31 **G8**
Wieprza →, *Poland* 30 **D3**
Wieruszów, *Poland* 31 **G5**
Wiesbaden, *Germany* 25 **E4**
Wiesental, *Germany* 25 **F4**
Wiesloch, *Germany* 25 **F4**
Wiesmoor, *Germany* 24 **B3**
Wieżyca, *Poland* 30 **D5**
Wigan, *U.K.* 14 **D5**
Wiggins, *Colo., U.S.A.* 112 **E2**
Wiggins, *Miss., U.S.A.* 113 **K10**
Wight, I. of □, *U.K.* 15 **G6**
Wigierski △, *Poland* 30 **D10**
Wigry, Jezioro, *Poland* 30 **D10**
Wigston, *U.K.* 15 **E6**
Wigton, *U.K.* 14 **C4**
Wigtown, *U.K.* 13 **G4**
Wigtown B., *U.K.* 13 **G4**
Wil, *Switz.* 25 **H5**
Wilamowice, *Poland* 31 **J6**
Wilber, *U.S.A.* 112 **E6**
Wilberforce, *Canada* 116 **A6**
Wilberforce, C., *Australia* 94 **A2**
Wilburton, *U.S.A.* 113 **H7**
Wilcannia, *Australia* 95 **E3**
Wilcox, *U.S.A.* 116 **E6**
Wildbad, *Germany* 25 **G4**
Wildeshausen, *Germany* 24 **C4**
Wildeshauser Geest ⌂, *Germany* 24 **C4**
Wildon, *Austria* 26 **E8**
Wildrose, *U.S.A.* 111 **J9**
Wildspitze, *Austria* 26 **E3**
Wilga →, *Poland* 31 **G8**
Wilge →, *S. Africa* 89 **D4**
Wilhelm II Coast, *Antarctica* 5 **C7**
Wilhelmsburg, *Austria* 26 **C8**
Wilhelmshaven, *Germany* 24 **B4**
Wilhelmstal, *Namibia* 88 **C2**
Wilkes-Barre, *U.S.A.* 117 **E9**
Wilkes Land, *Antarctica* 5 **D9**
Wilkie, *Canada* 103 **C7**
Wilkinsburg, *U.S.A.* 116 **F5**
Wilkinson Lakes, *Australia* 93 **E5**
Willandra Creek →, *Australia* 95 **E4**
Willapa B., *U.S.A.* 108 **C2**
Willapa Hills, *U.S.A.* 110 **D3**
Willard, *N.Y., U.S.A.* 116 **D8**
Willard, *Ohio, U.S.A.* 116 **E2**
Willcox, *U.S.A.* 109 **K9**
Willemstad, *Neth. Ant.* 121 **D6**
Willet, *U.S.A.* 117 **D9**
William →, *Canada* 103 **B7**
William 'Bill' Dannely Res., *U.S.A.* 115 **J2**
William Creek, *Australia* 95 **D2**
Williams, *Australia* 93 **F2**
Williams, *Ariz., U.S.A.* 109 **J7**
Williams, *Calif., U.S.A.* 110 **F4**
Williams Harbour, *Canada* 105 **B8**
Williams Lake, *Canada* 102 **C4**
Williamsburg, *Ky., U.S.A.* 115 **G3**
Williamsburg, *Pa., U.S.A.* 116 **F6**
Williamsburg, *Va., U.S.A.* 114 **G7**
Williamson, *N.Y., U.S.A.* 116 **C7**
Williamson, *W. Va., U.S.A.* 114 **G4**
Williamsport, *U.S.A.* 116 **E7**
Williamston, *U.S.A.* 115 **H7**
Williamstown, *Australia* 95 **F3**
Williamstown, *Ky., U.S.A.* 114 **F3**
Williamstown, *Mass., U.S.A.* 117 **D11**
Williamstown, *N.Y., U.S.A.* 117 **C9**
Willimantic, *U.S.A.* 117 **E12**
Willingboro, *U.S.A.* 114 **E8**
Williston, *S. Africa* 88 **E3**
Williston, *Fla., U.S.A.* 115 **L4**
Williston, *N. Dak., U.S.A.* 112 **A3**
Williston L., *Canada* 102 **B4**
Willits, *U.S.A.* 108 **G2**
Willmar, *U.S.A.* 112 **C7**
Willmore Wilderness ⌂, *Canada* 102 **C5**
Willoughby, *U.S.A.* 116 **E3**
Willow Bunch, *Canada* 103 **D7**
Willow L., *Canada* 102 **A5**
Willow Wall, The, *China* 57 **C12**
Willowick, *U.S.A.* 116 **E3**
Willowlake →, *Canada* 102 **A4**
Willowmore, *S. Africa* 88 **E3**
Willows, *U.S.A.* 110 **F4**
Willowvale = Gatyana, *S. Africa* 89 **E4**
Wills, L., *Australia* 92 **D4**
Wills Cr. →, *Australia* 94 **C3**
Willsboro, *U.S.A.* 117 **B11**
Willunga, *Australia* 95 **F2**
Wilmette, *U.S.A.* 114 **D2**
Wilmington, *Australia* 95 **E2**
Wilmington, *Del., U.S.A.* 114 **F8**
Wilmington, *N.C., U.S.A.* 115 **H7**
Wilmington, *Ohio, U.S.A.* 114 **F4**
Wilmington, *Vt., U.S.A.* 117 **D12**
Wilmslow, *U.K.* 14 **D5**
Wilpena Cr. →, *Australia* 95 **E2**
Wilsall, *U.S.A.* 108 **D8**
Wilson, *N.C., U.S.A.* 115 **H7**
Wilson, *N.Y., U.S.A.* 116 **C6**
Wilson, *Pa., U.S.A.* 117 **F9**
Wilson →, *Australia* 92 **C4**
Wilson Bluff, *Australia* 93 **F4**
Wilson Inlet, *Australia* 93 **G2**
Wilsons Promontory, *Australia* 95 **F4**
Wilster, *Germany* 24 **B5**
Wilton, *U.S.A.* 112 **B4**
Wilton →, *Australia* 94 **A1**
Wiltshire □, *U.K.* 15 **F6**
Wiltz, *Lux.* 17 **E5**
Wiluna, *Australia* 93 **E3**
Wimborne Minster, *U.K.* 15 **G6**
Wimereux, *France* 19 **B8**
Wimmera →, *Australia* 95 **F3**
Winam G., *Kenya* 86 **C3**
Winburg, *S. Africa* 88 **D4**
Winchendon, *U.S.A.* 117 **D12**
Winchester, *U.K.* 15 **F6**
Winchester, *Conn., U.S.A.* 117 **E11**
Winchester, *Idaho, U.S.A.* 108 **C5**
Winchester, *Ind., U.S.A.* 114 **E3**
Winchester, *Ky., U.S.A.* 114 **G3**
Winchester, *N.H., U.S.A.* 117 **D12**
Winchester, *Nev., U.S.A.* 111 **J11**
Winchester, *Tenn., U.S.A.* 115 **H2**
Winchester, *Va., U.S.A.* 114 **F6**
Wind →, *U.S.A.* 108 **E9**
Wind Cave △, *U.S.A.* 112 **D3**
Wind River Range, *U.S.A.* 108 **E9**
Windau = Ventspils, *Latvia* 9 **H19**
Windber, *U.S.A.* 116 **F6**
Winder, *U.S.A.* 115 **J4**
Windermere, *U.K.* 14 **C5**
Windhoek, *Namibia* 88 **C2**
Windischgarsten, *Austria* 26 **D7**
Windom, *U.S.A.* 112 **D7**
Windorah, *Australia* 94 **D3**
Window Rock, *U.S.A.* 109 **J9**
Windrush →, *U.K.* 15 **F6**
Windsor, *Australia* 95 **E5**
Windsor, *N.S., Canada* 105 **D7**
Windsor, *Ont., Canada* 116 **D2**
Windsor, *U.K.* 15 **F7**
Windsor, *Colo., U.S.A.* 112 **E2**
Windsor, *Conn., U.S.A.* 117 **E12**
Windsor, *Mo., U.S.A.* 112 **F8**
Windsor, *N.Y., U.S.A.* 117 **D9**
Windsor, *Vt., U.S.A.* 117 **C12**
Windsor & Maidenhead □, *U.K.* 15 **F7**
Windsorton, *S. Africa* 88 **D3**
Windward Is., *W. Indies* 121 **D7**
Windward Passage = Vientos, Paso de los, *Caribbean* 121 **C5**
Winefred L., *Canada* 103 **B6**
Winejok, *Sudan* 81 **F2**
Winfield, *U.S.A.* 113 **G6**
Wingate Mts., *Australia* 92 **B5**
Wingham, *Australia* 95 **E5**
Wingham, *Canada* 116 **C3**
Winisk, *Canada* 104 **A2**
Winisk →, *Canada* 104 **A2**
Winisk L., *Canada* 104 **B2**
Wink, *U.S.A.* 113 **K3**
Winkler, *Canada* 103 **D9**
Winklern, *Austria* 26 **E5**
Winlock, *U.S.A.* 110 **D4**
Winneba, *Ghana* 83 **D4**
Winnebago, L., *U.S.A.* 114 **D1**
Winnecke Cr. →, *Australia* 92 **C5**
Winnemucca, *U.S.A.* 108 **F5**
Winnemucca L., *U.S.A.* 108 **F4**
Winnett, *U.S.A.* 108 **C9**
Winnfield, *U.S.A.* 113 **K8**
Winnibigoshish, L., *U.S.A.* 112 **B7**
Winnipeg, *Canada* 103 **D9**
Winnipeg →, *Canada* 103 **C9**
Winnipeg, L., *Canada* 103 **C9**
Winnipeg Beach, *Canada* 103 **C9**
Winnipegosis, *Canada* 103 **C9**
Winnipegosis L., *Canada* 103 **C9**
Winnipesaukee, L., *U.S.A.* 117 **C13**
Winnisquam L., *U.S.A.* 117 **C13**
Winnsboro, *La., U.S.A.* 113 **J9**
Winnsboro, *S.C., U.S.A.* 115 **H5**
Winnsboro, *Tex., U.S.A.* 113 **J7**
Winokapau, L., *Canada* 105 **B7**
Winona, *Minn., U.S.A.* 112 **C9**
Winona, *Miss., U.S.A.* 113 **J10**
Winooski, *U.S.A.* 117 **B11**
Winooski →, *U.S.A.* 117 **B11**
Winschoten, *Neths.* 17 **A7**
Winsen, *Germany* 24 **B6**
Winsford, *U.K.* 14 **D5**
Winslow, *Ariz., U.S.A.* 109 **J8**
Winslow, *Wash., U.S.A.* 110 **C4**
Winsted, *U.S.A.* 117 **E11**
Winston-Salem, *U.S.A.* 115 **G5**
Winter Garden, *U.S.A.* 115 **L5**
Winter Haven, *U.S.A.* 115 **M5**
Winter Park, *U.S.A.* 115 **L5**
Winterberg, *Germany* 24 **D4**
Winterhaven, *U.S.A.* 111 **N12**
Winters, *U.S.A.* 110 **G5**
Wintersville, *U.S.A.* 116 **F4**
Winterswijk, *Neths.* 17 **C6**
Winterthur, *Switz.* 25 **H4**
Winthrop, *U.S.A.* 108 **B3**
Winton, *Australia* 94 **C3**
Winton, *N.Z.* 91 **M2**
Wipper →, *Germany* 24 **D7**
Wirrulla, *Australia* 95 **E1**
Wisbech, *U.K.* 15 **E8**
Wisconsin □, *U.S.A.* 112 **C10**
Wisconsin →, *U.S.A.* 112 **D9**
Wisconsin Rapids, *U.S.A.* 112 **C10**
Wisdom, *U.S.A.* 108 **D7**
Wishaw, *U.K.* 13 **F5**
Wishek, *U.S.A.* 112 **B5**
Wisła, *Poland* 31 **J5**
Wisła →, *Poland* 30 **D5**
Wisłok →, *Poland* 31 **H9**

Wisłoka →, Poland 31 H8
Wismar, Germany 24 B7
Wisner, U.S.A. 112 E6
Wissant, France 19 B8
Wissembourg, France 19 C14
Wisznice, Poland 31 G10
Witbank, S. Africa 89 D4
Witdraai, S. Africa 88 D3
Witham, U.K. 15 F8
Witham →, U.K. 14 E7
Withernsea, U.K. 14 D8
Witjira △, Australia 95 D2
Witkowo, Poland 31 F4
Witney, U.K. 15 F6
Witnica, Poland 31 F1
Witnossob →, Namibia 88 D3
Wittdün, Germany 24 A4
Witten, Germany 24 D3
Wittenberge, Germany 24 B7
Wittenburg, Germany 24 B7
Wittenheim, France 19 E14
Wittenoom, Australia 92 D2
Wittingen, Germany 24 C6
Wittlich, Germany 25 F2
Wittmund, Germany 24 B3
Wittow, Germany 24 A9
Wittstock, Germany 24 B8
Witvlei, Namibia 88 C2
Witzenhausen, Germany 24 D5
Wkra →, Poland 31 F7
Władysławowo, Poland 30 D5
Wleń, Poland 31 G2
Wlingi, Indonesia 63 H15
Włocławek, Poland 31 F6
Włodawa, Poland 31 G10
Włoszczowa, Poland 31 H6
Woburn, U.S.A. 117 D13
Wodian, China 56 H7
Wodonga = Albury-Wodonga, Australia 95 F4
Wodzisław Śląski, Poland 31 H5
Wœrth, France 19 D14
Woinbogoin, China 58 A2
Woippy, France 19 C13
Wojcieszów, Poland 31 H2
Wokam, Indonesia 63 F8
Woking, U.K. 15 F7
Wokingham, U.K. 15 F7
Wokingham □, U.K. 15 F7
Wolbrom, Poland 31 H6
Wołczyn, Poland 31 G5
Woldegk, Germany 24 B9
Wolf →, Canada 102 A2
Wolf Creek, U.S.A. 108 C7
Wolf L., Canada 102 A2
Wolf Point, U.S.A. 112 A2
Wolfe I., Canada 117 B8
Wolfeboro, U.S.A. 117 C13
Wolfen, Germany 24 D8
Wolfenbüttel, Germany 24 C6
Wolfratshausen, Germany 25 H7
Wolfsberg, Austria 26 E7
Wolfsburg, Germany 24 C6
Wolgast, Germany 24 A9
Wolhusen, Switz. 25 H4
Wolin, Poland 30 E1
Woliński △, Poland 30 E1
Wollaston, Is., Chile 128 H3
Wollaston L., Canada 103 B8
Wollaston Lake, Canada 103 B8
Wollaston Pen., Canada 100 B8
Wollongong, Australia 95 E5
Wolmaransstad, S. Africa 88 D4
Wolmirstedt, Germany 24 C7
Wołomin, Poland 31 F8
Wołów, Poland 31 G3
Wolseley, S. Africa 88 E2
Wolsey, U.S.A. 112 C5
Wolstenholme, C., Canada 98 C12
Wolsztyn, Poland 31 F3
Wolvega, Neths. 17 B6
Wolverhampton, U.K. 15 E5
Wondai, Australia 95 D5
Wongalarroo L., Australia 95 E3
Wongan Hills, Australia 93 F2
Wŏnju, S. Korea 57 F14
Wonosari, Indonesia 63 G14
Wonosobo, Indonesia 63 G13
Wonowon, Canada 102 B4
Wŏnsan, N. Korea 57 E14
Wonthaggi, Australia 95 F4
Wood Buffalo △, Canada 102 B6
Wood Is., Australia 92 C3
Wood L., Canada 103 B8
Woodah I., Australia 94 A2
Woodbourne, U.S.A. 117 E10
Woodbridge, Canada 116 C5
Woodbridge, U.K. 15 E9
Woodburn, U.S.A. 108 D2
Woodenbong, Australia 95 D5
Woodend, Australia 95 F3
Woodford, Australia 95 D5
Woodfords, U.S.A. 110 G7
Woodlake, U.S.A. 110 J7
Woodland, Calif., U.S.A. 110 G5
Woodland, Maine, U.S.A. 115 C12
Woodland, Pa., U.S.A. 116 F6
Woodland, Wash., U.S.A. 110 E4
Woodland Caribou ⌓, Canada 103 C10
Woodlands, Singapore 65 d
Woodridge, Canada 103 D9
Woodroffe, Mt., Australia 93 E5
Woods, L., Australia 94 B1
Woods, L. of the, Canada 103 D10
Woodstock, Australia 94 B4
Woodstock, N.B., Canada 105 C6
Woodstock, Ont., Canada 116 C4
Woodstock, U.K. 15 F6
Woodstock, Ill., U.S.A. 112 D10
Woodstock, Vt., U.S.A. 117 C12
Woodsville, U.S.A. 117 B13
Woodville, N.Z. 91 J5
Woodville, Miss., U.S.A. 113 K9
Woodville, Tex., U.S.A. 113 K7
Woodward, U.S.A. 113 G5
Woody, U.S.A. 111 K8
Woody →, Canada 103 C8
Woolacombe, U.K. 15 F3
Woolamai, C., Australia 95 F4
Wooler, U.K. 14 B5
Woolgoolga, Australia 95 E5
Woomera, Australia 95 E2
Woonsocket, R.I., U.S.A. 117 E13
Woonsocket, S. Dak., U.S.A. 112 C5
Wooramel →, Australia 93 E1
Wooramel Roadhouse, Australia 93 E1
Wooster, U.S.A. 116 F3
Worcester, S. Africa 88 E2
Worcester, U.K. 15 E5
Worcester, Mass., U.S.A. 117 D13
Worcester, N.Y., U.S.A. 117 D10
Worcestershire □, U.K. 15 E5
Wörgl, Austria 26 D5
Workington, U.K. 14 C4
Worksop, U.K. 14 D6
Workum, Neths. 17 B5
Worland, U.S.A. 108 D10
Wormhout, France 19 B9
Worms, Germany 25 F4
Worsley, Canada 102 B5
Wörth, Germany 25 F8
Wortham, U.S.A. 113 K6
Wörther See, Austria 26 E7
Worthing, Barbados 121 g
Worthing, U.K. 15 G7
Worthington, Minn., U.S.A. 112 D7
Worthington, Pa., U.S.A. 116 F5
Wosi, Indonesia 63 E7
Wou-han = Wuhan, China 59 B10
Wousi = Wuxi, China 59 B13
Wowoni, Indonesia 63 E6
Wrangel I. = Vrangelya, Ostrov, Russia 53 B19
Wrangell, U.S.A. 102 B2
Wrangell Mts., U.S.A. 100 B5
Wrath, C., U.K. 13 C3
Wray, U.S.A. 112 E3
Wrekin, The, U.K. 15 E5
Wrens, U.S.A. 115 J4
Wrexham, U.K. 14 D4
Wrexham □, U.K. 14 D5
Wriezen, Germany 24 C10
Wright = Paranas, Phil. 61 F6
Wright, U.S.A. 112 D2
Wright Pt., Canada 116 C3
Wrightson, Mt., U.S.A. 109 L8
Wrightwood, U.S.A. 111 L9
Wrigley, Canada 100 B7
Wrocław, Poland 31 G4
Wronki, Poland 31 F3
Września, Poland 31 F4
Wschowa, Poland 31 G3
Wu Jiang →, China 58 C6
Wu'an, China 56 F8
Wubin, Australia 93 F2
Wubu, China 56 F6
Wuchang, China 57 B14
Wucheng, China 56 F9
Wuchuan, Guangdong, China 59 G8
Wuchuan, Guizhou, China 58 C7
Wuchuan, Nei Monggol Zizhiqu, China 56 D6
Wudi, China 57 F9
Wuding, China 58 E4
Wuding He →, China 56 F6
Wudinna, Australia 95 E2
Wudu, China 56 H3
Wufeng, China 59 B8
Wugang, China 59 D8
Wugong Shan, China 59 D9
Wuhan, China 59 B10
Wuhe, China 57 H9
Wuhsi = Wuxi, China 59 B13
Wuhu, China 59 B12
Wujiang, China 59 B13
Wukari, Nigeria 83 D6
Wulajie, China 57 B14
Wulanbulang, China 56 D6
Wular L., India 69 B6
Wulehe, Ghana 83 D5
Wulian, China 57 G10
Wuliang Shan, China 58 E3
Wuliaru, Indonesia 63 F8
Wuling Shan, China 58 C7
Wulong, China 58 C6
Wulumuchi = Ürümqi, China 52 E9
Wum, Cameroon 83 D7
Wuming, China 58 F7
Wun Rog, Sudan 81 F2
Wuning, China 59 C10
Wunnummin L., Canada 104 B2
Wunsiedel, Germany 25 E8
Wunstorf, Germany 24 C5
Wuntho, Burma 67 H19
Wupatki ⌓, U.S.A. 109 J8
Wuping, China 59 E11
Wuppertal, Germany 24 D3
Wuppertal, S. Africa 88 E2
Wuqing, China 57 E9
Wurtsboro, U.S.A. 117 E10
Würzburg, Germany 25 F5
Wurzen, Germany 24 D8
Wushan, China 56 G3
Wushishi, Nigeria 83 D6
Wusuli Jiang = Ussuri →, Asia 54 A7
Wutach →, Germany 25 H4
Wutai, China 56 E7
Wuting = Huimin, China 57 F9
Wutong, China 59 E8
Wutonghaolai, China 57 C11
Wutongqiao, China 58 C4
Wuwei, Anhui, China 59 B11
Wuwei, Gansu, China 60 C5
Wuxi, Jiangsu, China 59 B13
Wuxi, Sichuan, China 58 B7
Wuxiang, China 56 F7
Wuxuan, China 58 F7
Wuxue, China 59 C10
Wuyang, China 56 H7
Wuyi, Hebei, China 56 F8
Wuyi, Zhejiang, China 59 C12
Wuyi Shan, China 59 D11
Wuyishan, China 59 D12
Wuyo, Nigeria 83 C7
Wuyuan, Jiangxi, China 59 C11
Wuyuan, Nei Monggol Zizhiqu, China 56 D5
Wuzhai, China 56 E6
Wuzhi Shan, China 64 C7
Wuzhong, China 56 E4
Wuzhou, China 59 F8
Wyaaba Cr. →, Australia 94 B3
Wyalkatchem, Australia 93 F2
Wyalusing, U.S.A. 117 E8
Wyandotte, U.S.A. 114 D4
Wyandra, Australia 95 D4
Wyangala, L., Australia 95 E4
Wyara, L., Australia 95 D3
Wycheproof, Australia 95 F3
Wye →, U.K. 15 F5
Wyemandoo, Australia 93 E2
Wyk, Germany 24 A4
Wymondham, U.K. 15 E9
Wymore, U.S.A. 112 E6
Wyndham, Australia 92 C4
Wyndham, N.Z. 91 M2
Wynne, U.S.A. 113 H9
Wynyard, Australia 95 G4
Wynyard, Canada 103 C8
Wyola L., Australia 93 E5
Wyoming = Plympton-Wyoming, Canada 116 D2
Wyoming □, U.S.A. 108 E10
Wyomissing, U.S.A. 117 F9
Wyong, Australia 95 E5
Wyrzysk, Poland 31 E4
Wyśmierzyce, Poland 31 G7
Wysoka, Poland 31 E4
Wysokie, Poland 31 H9
Wysokie Mazowieckie, Poland 31 F9
Wyszków, Poland 31 F8
Wyszogród, Poland 31 F7
Wytheville, U.S.A. 114 G5
Wyżyna Małopolska, Poland 31 H7

X

Xaafuun, Somali Rep. 75 E5
Xaçmaz, Azerbaijan 35 K9
Xai-Xai, Mozam. 89 D5
Xainza, China 60 C3
Xalapa, Mexico 119 D5
Xangongo, Angola 88 B2
Xankändi, Azerbaijan 70 B5
Xanlar, Azerbaijan 35 K8
Xanten, Germany 24 D2
Xánthi, Greece 45 E8
Xánthi □, Greece 45 E8
Xanthos, Turkey 47 E11
Xanxerê, Brazil 127 B5
Xapuri, Brazil 124 F5
Xar Moron He →, China 57 C11
Xarrë, Albania 44 G4
Xátiva, Spain 39 G4
Xau, L., Botswana 88 C3
Xavantina, Brazil 127 A5
Xenia, U.S.A. 114 F4
Xeropotamos →, Cyprus 49 E11
Xertigny, France 19 D13
Xhora, S. Africa 89 E4
Xhumo, Botswana 88 C3
Xi Jiang →, China 59 F9
Xi Xian, Henan, China 59 A10
Xi Xian, Shanxi, China 56 F6
Xia Xian, China 56 G6
Xiachengzi, China 57 B16
Xiachuan Dao, China 59 G9
Xiaguan, China 60 D5
Xiajiang, China 59 D10
Xiajin, China 56 F9
Xiamen, China 59 E12
Xi'an, China 56 G5
Xian Xian, China 56 E9
Xianfeng, China 58 C7
Xiang Jiang →, China 59 C9
Xiangcheng, Henan, China 56 H8
Xiangcheng, Henan, China 56 H7
Xiangcheng, Sichuan, China 58 C2
Xiangdu, China 58 F6
Xiangfan, China 59 A9
Xianggang = Hong Kong □, China 59 F10
Xianghuang Qi, China 56 C7
Xiangning, China 56 G6
Xiangquan, China 56 F7
Xiangquan He = Sutlej →, Pakistan 68 E4
Xiangshan, China 59 C13
Xiangshui, China 57 G10
Xiangtan, China 59 D9
Xiangxiang, China 59 D9
Xiangyin, China 59 C9
Xiangyun, China 58 E3
Xiangzhou, China 58 F7
Xianju, China 59 C13
Xianning, China 59 C10
Xianshui He →, China 58 B3
Xiantao, China 59 B9
Xianyang, China 56 G5
Xianyou, China 59 E12
Xiao Hinggan Ling, China 60 B7
Xiao Xian, China 56 G9
Xiaofeng, China 59 B12
Xiaogan, China 59 B9
Xiaojin, China 58 B4
Xiaolan, China 59 F9
Xiaoshan, China 59 B13
Xiaoyi, China 56 F6
Xiapu, China 59 D12
Xiawa, China 57 C11
Xiayi, China 56 G9
Xichang, China 58 D4
Xichong, China 58 B5
Xichou, China 58 E5
Xichuan, China 56 H6
Xide, China 58 C4
Xiemahe, China 59 B8
Xieng Khouang, Laos 64 C4
Xifei He →, China 56 H9
Xifeng, Gansu, China 56 G4
Xifeng, Guizhou, China 58 D6
Xifeng, Liaoning, China 57 C13
Xifengzhen = Xifeng, China 56 G4
Xigazê, China 60 D3
Xihe, China 56 G3
Xihua, China 56 H8
Xilagani, Greece 45 F9
Xiliao He →, China 57 C12
Xilin, China 58 E5
Xilókastron, Greece 46 C4
Ximana, Mozam. 87 F3
Xime, Guinea-Biss. 82 C2
Ximeng, China 58 F2
Xin Jiang →, China 59 C11
Xin Xian = Xinzhou, China 56 E7
Xinavane, Mozam. 89 D5
Xinbin, China 57 D13
Xincai, China 59 A10
Xinchang, China 59 C13
Xincheng, Guangxi Zhuangzu, China 58 E7
Xincheng, Jiangxi, China 59 D10
Xindu, China 58 B5
Xinfeng, Guangdong, China 59 E10
Xinfeng, Jiangxi, China 59 D11
Xinfeng, Jiangxi, China 59 E10
Xinfengjiang Skuiku, China 59 F10
Xing Xian, China 56 E6
Xing'an, Guangxi Zhuangzu, China 59 E8
Xingan, Jiangxi, China 59 D10
Xingcheng, China 57 D11
Xingguo, China 59 D10
Xinghe, China 56 D7
Xinghua, China 57 H10
Xinghua Wan, China 59 E12
Xinglong, China 57 D9
Xingning, China 59 E10
Xingping, China 56 G5
Xingren, China 58 E5
Xingshan, China 59 B8
Xingtai, China 56 F8
Xingu →, Brazil 125 D8
Xingwen, China 58 C5
Xingyang, China 56 G7
Xinhe, China 56 F8
Xinhua, China 59 D8
Xinhuang, China 58 D7
Xinhui, China 59 F9
Xining, China 60 C5
Xinjian, China 59 C10
Xinjiang, China 56 G6
Xinjiang Uygur Zizhiqu □, China 60 B3
Xinjie, China 58 D3
Xinjin = Pulandian, China 57 E11
Xinjin, China 58 B4
Xinkai He →, China 57 C12
Xinle, China 56 E8
Xinlitun, China 57 D12
Xinlong, China 58 B3
Xinmin, China 57 D12
Xinning, China 59 D8
Xinping, China 58 E3
Xinshao, China 59 D8
Xintai, China 57 G9
Xintian, China 59 E9
Xinxian, China 59 B10
Xinxiang, China 56 G7
Xinxing, China 59 F9
Xinyang, China 59 A10
Xinye, China 59 A9
Xinyi, China 59 F8
Xinyu, China 59 D10
Xinzhan, China 57 C14
Xinzheng, China 56 G7
Xinzhou, Hubei, China 59 B10
Xinzhou, Shanxi, China 56 E7
Xinzo de Limia, Spain 36 C3
Xiongyuecheng, China 57 D12
Xiping, Henan, China 56 H8
Xiping, Henan, China 56 H6
Xiping, Zhejiang, China 59 C12
Xique-Xique, Brazil 125 F10
Xisha Qundao = Paracel Is., S. China Sea 62 A4
Xishui, Guizhou, China 58 C6
Xishui, Hubei, China 59 B10
Xitole, Guinea-Biss. 82 C2
Xiu Shui →, China 59 C10
Xiuning, China 59 C12
Xiuren, China 59 E8
Xiushan, China 58 C7
Xiushui, China 59 C10
Xiuwen, China 58 D6
Xiuyan, China 57 D12
Xixabangma Feng, China 67 E14
Xixia, China 56 H6
Xixiang, China 56 H4
Xiyang, China 56 F7
Xizang Zizhiqu □, China 60 C3
Xlendi, Malta 49 C1
Xochob, Mexico 119 D7
Xu Jiang →, China 59 D11
Xuan Loc, Vietnam 65 G6
Xuan'en, China 58 C7
Xuanhan, China 58 B6
Xuanhua, China 56 D8
Xuanwei, China 58 C5
Xuanzhou, China 59 B12
Xuchang, China 56 G7
Xudat, Azerbaijan 35 K9
Xuefeng Shan, China 59 D8
Xuejiaping, China 59 B8
Xun Jiang →, China 59 F8
Xun Xian, China 56 G8
Xundian, China 58 E4
Xunwu, China 59 E10
Xunyang, China 56 H5
Xunyi, China 56 G5
Xupu, China 59 D8
Xúquer →, Spain 39 F4
Xushui, China 56 E8
Xuwen, China 59 G8
Xuyen Moc, Vietnam 65 G6
Xuyong, China 58 C5
Xuzhou, China 57 G9
Xylophagou, Cyprus 49 E12

Y

Ya Xian, China 64 C7
Yaamba, Australia 94 C5
Ya'an, China 58 C4
Yaapeet, Australia 95 F3
Yabassi, Cameroon 83 E6
Yabelo, Ethiopia 81 G4
Yabelo ⌓, Ethiopia 81 F4
Yablanitsa, Bulgaria 45 C8
Yablonovy Ra. = Yablonovyy Khrebet, Russia 53 D12
Yablonovyy Khrebet, Russia 53 D12
Yabluniv, Ukraine 29 B9
Yablunytsya, Ukraine 29 B9
Yabrai Shan, China 56 E2
Yabrūd, Syria 74 B5
Yabucoa, Puerto Rico 121 d
Yacambú △, Venezuela 121 E6
Yacheng, China 64 C7
Yacuiba, Bolivia 126 A3
Yacuma →, Bolivia 124 F5
Yadgir, India 66 L10
Yadkin →, U.S.A. 115 H5
Yadrin, Russia 34 C8
Yaeyama-Rettō, Japan 55 M1
Yagaba, Ghana 83 C4
Yağcılar, Turkey 47 B10
Yagodnoye, Russia 53 C15
Yahila, Dem. Rep. of the Congo 86 B1
Yahk, Canada 102 D5
Yahotyn, Ukraine 33 G6
Yahuma, Dem. Rep. of the Congo 84 D4
Yahyalı, Turkey 72 C6
Yaita, Japan 55 F9
Yaiza, Canary Is. 48 F6
Yajiang, China 58 B3
Yajua, Nigeria 83 C7
Yakima, U.S.A. 108 C3
Yakima →, U.S.A. 108 C3
Yako, Burkina Faso 82 C4
Yakobi I., U.S.A. 102 B1
Yakoruda, Bulgaria 44 D7
Yakovlevka, Russia 54 B6
Yaku-Shima, Japan 55 J5
Yakumo, Japan 54 C10
Yakutat, U.S.A. 100 C6
Yakutia = Sakha □, Russia 53 C13
Yakutsk, Russia 53 C13
Yala, Thailand 65 J3
Yalboroo, Australia 94 J6
Yale, U.S.A. 116 C2
Yalgoo, Australia 93 E2
Yalgorup △, Australia 93 D2
Yalinga, C.A.R. 84 C4
Yalkubul, Punta, Mexico 119 C7
Yalleroi, Australia 94 C4
Yalobusha →, U.S.A. 113 J9
Yalong Jiang →, China 58 D3
Yalova, Turkey 45 F13
Yalpuh, Ozero, Ukraine 29 E13
Yalta, Ukraine 33 K8
Yalu Jiang →, China 57 E13
Yalvaç, Turkey 72 C4
Yam Ha Melah = Dead Sea, Asia 74 D4
Yam Kinneret, Israel 74 C4
Yamada, Japan 55 H5
Yamagata, Japan 54 E10
Yamagata □, Japan 54 E10
Yamaguchi, Japan 55 G5
Yamaguchi □, Japan 55 G5
Yamal, Poluostrov, Russia 52 B8
Yamal Pen. = Yamal, Poluostrov, Russia 52 B8
Yamanashi □, Japan 55 G9
Yamanie Falls △, Australia 94 B4
Yamba, Australia 95 D5
Yambarran Ra., Australia 92 C5
Yambéring, Guinea 82 C2
Yâmbiô, Sudan 81 G2
Yambol, Bulgaria 45 D10
Yamdena, Indonesia 63 F8
Yame, Japan 55 H5
Yamethin, Burma 67 J20
Yamma-Yamma, L., Australia 95 D3
Yamoussoukro, Ivory C. 82 D3
Yampa →, U.S.A. 108 F9
Yampi Sd., Australia 92 C3
Yampil, Moldova 33 H5
Yampol = Yampil, Moldova 33 H5
Yamrat, Nigeria 83 C6
Yamrukchal = Botev, Bulgaria 45 D8
Yamuna →, India 69 G9
Yamunanagar, India 68 D7

Yamzho Yumco, *China* 60 D4
Yan, *Nigeria* 83 C7
Yana →, *Russia* 53 B14
Yanagawa, *Japan* 55 H5
Yanai, *Japan* 55 H6
Yan'an, *China* 56 F5
Yanbian, *China* 58 D3
Yanbu 'al Baḥr, *Si. Arabia* 70 F3
Yanchang, *China* 56 F6
Yancheng, *Henan, China* 56 H8
Yancheng, *Jiangsu, China* 57 H11
Yanchep Beach, *Australia* 93 F2
Yanchi, *China* 56 F4
Yanchuan, *China* 56 F6
Yanco Cr. →, *Australia* 95 F4
Yandicoogina, *Australia* 92 D2
Yandoon, *Burma* 67 L19
Yanfeng, *China* 58 E3
Yanfolila, *Mali* 82 C3
Yang Xian, *China* 56 H4
Yang-Yang, *Senegal* 82 B1
Yangambi, *Dem. Rep. of the Congo* 86 B1
Yangbi, *China* 58 E2
Yangcheng, *China* 56 G7
Yangch'ü = Taiyuan, *China* 56 F7
Yangchun, *China* 59 F8
Yanggao, *China* 56 D7
Yanggu, *China* 56 F8
Yangjiang, *China* 59 G8
Yangliuqing, *China* 57 E9
Yangon = Rangoon, *Burma* 67 L20
Yangping, *China* 59 B8
Yangpingguan, *China* 56 H4
Yangquan, *China* 56 F7
Yangshan, *China* 59 E9
Yangshuo, *China* 59 E8
Yangtse = Chang Jiang →, *China* 59 B13
Yangtze Kiang = Chang Jiang →, *China* 59 B13
Yangudi Rassa △, *Ethiopia* 81 E5
Yangxin, *China* 59 C10
Yangyang, *S. Korea* 57 E15
Yangyuan, *China* 56 D8
Yangzhong, *China* 59 A12
Yangzhou, *China* 59 A12
Yanhe, *China* 58 C7
Yanji, *China* 57 C15
Yanjin, *China* 58 C5
Yanjing, *China* 58 C2
Yankari △, *Nigeria* 83 D7
Yankton, *U.S.A.* 112 D6
Yanonge, *Dem. Rep. of the Congo* 86 B1
Yanqi, *China* 60 B3
Yanqing, *China* 56 D8
Yanshan, *Hebei, China* 57 E9
Yanshan, *Jiangxi, China* 59 C11
Yanshan, *Yunnan, China* 58 F5
Yanshou, *China* 57 B15
Yantabulla, *Australia* 95 D4
Yantai, *China* 57 F11
Yantarnyy, *Russia* 30 D6
Yanting, *China* 58 B5
Yantra →, *Bulgaria* 45 C9
Yanwa, *China* 58 D2
Yanyuan, *China* 58 D3
Yanzhou, *China* 56 G9
Yao Noi, Ko, *Thailand* 65 a
Yao Xian, *China* 56 G5
Yao Yai, Ko, *Thailand* 65 a
Yao'an, *China* 58 E3
Yaodu, *China* 58 A5
Yaoundé, *Cameroon* 83 E7
Yaowan, *China* 57 G10
Yap, *Pac. Oc.* 96 G5
Yapen, *Indonesia* 63 E9
Yapen, Selat, *Indonesia* 63 E9
Yapero, *Indonesia* 63 E9
Yappar →, *Australia* 94 B3
Yaqui →, *Mexico* 118 B2
Yar-Sale, *Russia* 52 C8
Yaraka, *Australia* 94 C3
Yaransk, *Russia* 34 B8
Yarbasan, *Turkey* 47 C10
Yardımcı Burnu, *Turkey* 47 E12
Yare →, *U.K.* 15 E9
Yaremcha, *Ukraine* 29 B9
Yarensk, *Russia* 52 C5
Yarfa, *Si. Arabia* 80 C4
Yarí →, *Colombia* 124 D4
Yarkand = Shache, *China* 60 C2
Yarker, *Canada* 117 B8
Yarkhun →, *Pakistan* 69 A5
Yarlung Ziangbo Jiang = Brahmaputra →, *Asia* 69 H13
Yarmouth, *Canada* 105 D6
Yarmūk →, *Syria* 74 C4
Yaroslavl, *Russia* 32 D10
Yarqa, W. →, *Egypt* 74 F2
Yarra Yarra Lakes, *Australia* 93 E2
Yarram, *Australia* 95 F4
Yarraman, *Australia* 95 D5
Yarras, *Australia* 95 E5
Yartsevo, *Sib., Russia* 53 C10
Yartsevo, *Smolensk, Russia* 32 E7
Yarumal, *Colombia* 124 B3
Yasawa Group, *Fiji* 91 C7
Yaselda, *Belarus* 33 F4
Yasen, *Ukraine* 29 B9
Yashi, *Nigeria* 83 C6
Yashikera, *Nigeria* 83 D5
Yashkul, *Russia* 35 G7
Yasin, *Pakistan* 69 A5
Yasinovataya, *Ukraine* 33 H9
Yasinski, L., *Canada* 104 B4
Yasinya, *Ukraine* 29 B9
Yasothon, *Thailand* 64 E5
Yass, *Australia* 95 E4
Yāsūj, *Iran* 71 D6
Yatağan, *Turkey* 47 D10
Yatakala, *Niger* 83 C5
Yates Center, *U.S.A.* 113 G7
Yathkyed L., *Canada* 103 A9
Yatsushiro, *Japan* 55 H5
Yatta Plateau, *Kenya* 86 C4
Yauco, *Puerto Rico* 121 d
Yavari →, *Peru* 124 D4
Yávaros, *Mexico* 118 B3
Yavatmal, *India* 66 J11
Yavne, *Israel* 74 D3
Yavoriv, *Ukraine* 31 J10
Yavorov = Yavoriv, *Ukraine* 31 J10
Yavuzeli, *Turkey* 72 D7
Yawatahama, *Japan* 55 H6
Yawri B., *S. Leone* 82 D2
Yaxi, *China* 58 D6
Yazd, *Iran* 71 D7
Yazd □, *Iran* 71 D7
Yazd-e Khvāst, *Iran* 71 D7
Yazıköy, *Turkey* 47 E9
Yazman, *Pakistan* 68 E4
Yazoo →, *U.S.A.* 113 J9
Yazoo City, *U.S.A.* 113 J9
Ybbs, *Austria* 26 C8
Ybycuí △, *Paraguay* 126 B4
Ybytyruzú △, *Paraguay* 127 B4
Yding Skovhøj, *Denmark* 11 J3
Ye, *Burma* 64 E1
Ye Xian, *China* 56 H7
Yebyu, *Burma* 64 E2
Yechŏn, *S. Korea* 57 F15
Yecla, *Spain* 39 G3
Yécora, *Mexico* 118 B3
Yedebub Biheroch Bihereseboch na Hizboch □, *Ethiopia* 81 F4
Yedintsy = Edineţ, *Moldova* 29 B12
Yedseram →, *Nigeria* 83 C7
Yefremov, *Russia* 32 F10
Yeghegnadzor, *Armenia* 73 C11
Yegorlyk →, *Russia* 35 G5
Yegorlykskaya, *Russia* 35 G5
Yegoryevsk, *Russia* 32 E10
Yegros, *Paraguay* 126 B4
Yehbuah, *Indonesia* 63 J17
Yehuda, Midbar, *Israel* 74 D4
Yei, *Sudan* 81 G3
Yei, Nahr →, *Sudan* 81 F3
Yejmiadzin, *Armenia* 35 K7
Yekaterinburg, *Russia* 52 D7
Yelabuga, *Russia* 34 C11
Yelan, *Russia* 34 E6
Yelarbon, *Australia* 95 D5
Yelatma, *Russia* 34 C5
Yelets, *Russia* 33 F10
Yélimané, *Mali* 82 B2
Yelizavetgrad = Kirovohrad, *Ukraine* 33 H7
Yell, *U.K.* 13 A7
Yell Sd., *U.K.* 13 A7
Yellow Sea, *China* 57 G12
Yellowhead Pass, *Canada* 102 C5
Yellowknife, *Canada* 102 A6
Yellowknife →, *Canada* 102 A6
Yellowstone △, *U.S.A.* 108 D9
Yellowstone →, *U.S.A.* 112 B3
Yellowstone L., *U.S.A.* 108 D8
Yelnya, *Russia* 32 E7
Yelsk, *Belarus* 33 G5
Yelwa, *Nigeria* 83 C5
Yemen ■, *Asia* 75 E3
Yen Bai, *Vietnam* 58 G5
Yenagoa, *Nigeria* 83 E6
Yenakiyeve, *Ukraine* 33 H10
Yenakiyevo = Yenakiyeve, *Ukraine* 33 H10
Yenangyaung, *Burma* 67 J19
Yenbo = Yanbu 'al Baḥr, *Si. Arabia* 70 F3
Yenda, *Australia* 95 E4
Yende Millimou, *Guinea* 82 D2
Yendéré, *Burkina Faso* 82 C4
Yendi, *Ghana* 83 D4
Yéni, *Niger* 83 C5
Yenice, *Ankara, Turkey* 72 C5
Yenice, *Aydın, Turkey* 47 D10
Yenice, *Çanakkale, Turkey* 47 B9
Yenice, *Edirne, Turkey* 45 F10
Yenice →, *Turkey* 72 D6
Yenifoça, *Turkey* 47 C8
Yenihisar, *Turkey* 47 D9
Yeniköy, *Bursa, Turkey* 45 F13
Yeniköy, *Çanakkale, Turkey* 47 B8
Yeniköy, *Kütahya, Turkey* 47 C11
Yenipazar, *Turkey* 47 D10
Yenisaía, *Greece* 45 E8
Yenişehir, *Turkey* 45 F13
Yenisey →, *Russia* 52 B9
Yeniseysk, *Russia* 53 D10
Yeniseyskiy Zaliv, *Russia* 52 B9
Yennádhi, *Greece* 49 C9
Yenne, *France* 21 C9
Yenotayevka, *Russia* 35 G8
Yenyuka, *Russia* 53 D13
Yeo →, *U.K.* 15 G5
Yeo, L., *Australia* 93 E3
Yeo I., *Canada* 116 A3
Yeola, *India* 66 J9
Yeoryioúpolis, *Greece* 49 D6
Yeovil, *U.K.* 15 G5
Yepes, *Spain* 36 F7
Yeppoon, *Australia* 94 C5
Yeráki, *Greece* 46 D4
Yerbent, *Turkmenistan* 52 F6
Yerbogachen, *Russia* 53 C11
Yerevan, *Armenia* 35 K7
Yerington, *U.S.A.* 108 G4
Yerkesik, *Turkey* 47 D10
Yerköy, *Turkey* 72 C6
Yermak, *Kazakhstan* 52 D8
Yermo, *U.S.A.* 111 L10
Yerólakkos, *Cyprus* 49 D12
Yeropol, *Russia* 53 C17
Yeropótamos →, *Greece* 49 D6
Yeroskipos, *Cyprus* 49 E11
Yershov, *Russia* 34 E9
Yerushalayim = Jerusalem, *Israel* 74 D4
Yerville, *France* 18 C7
Yes Tor, *U.K.* 15 G4
Yesan, *S. Korea* 57 F14
Yeşilhisar, *Turkey* 72 C6
Yeşilırmak →, *Turkey* 72 B7
Yeşilkent, *Turkey* 72 D7
Yeşilköy, *Turkey* 45 F12
Yeşilova, *Turkey* 47 D11
Yeşilyurt, *Manisa, Turkey* 47 C10
Yeşilyurt, *Muğla, Turkey* 47 D10
Yesnogorsk, *Russia* 32 E9
Yeso, *U.S.A.* 113 H2
Yessentuki, *Russia* 35 H6
Yessey, *Russia* 53 C11
Yeste, *Spain* 39 G2
Yetman, *Australia* 95 D5
Yeu, Î. d', *France* 18 F4
Yevlakh = Yevlax, *Azerbaijan* 35 K8
Yevlax, *Azerbaijan* 35 K8
Yevpatoriya, *Ukraine* 33 K7
Yeya →, *Russia* 33 J10
Yeysk, *Russia* 33 J10
Yezd = Yazd, *Iran* 71 D7
Yezerishche, *Belarus* 32 E5
Yhati, *Paraguay* 126 B4
Yhú, *Paraguay* 127 B4
Yi →, *Uruguay* 126 C4
Yi 'Allaq, G., *Egypt* 74 E2
Yi He →, *China* 57 G10
Yi Xian, *Anhui, China* 59 C11
Yi Xian, *Hebei, China* 56 E8
Yi Xian, *Liaoning, China* 57 D11
Yialí, *Greece* 47 E9
Yialiás →, *Cyprus* 49 D12
Yi'allaq, G., *Egypt* 80 A3
Yialousa, *Cyprus* 49 D13
Yiáltra, *Greece* 46 C4
Yianisádhes, *Greece* 49 D8
Yiannitsa, *Greece* 44 F6
Yibin, *China* 58 C5
Yichang, *China* 59 B8
Yicheng, *Henan, China* 59 B9
Yicheng, *Shanxi, China* 56 G6
Yichuan, *China* 56 F6
Yichun, *Heilongjiang, China* 60 B7
Yichun, *Jiangxi, China* 59 D10
Yidu, *China* 57 F10
Yidun, *China* 58 B2
Yifag, *Ethiopia* 81 E4
Yifeng, *China* 59 C10
Yihuang, *China* 59 D11
Yijun, *China* 56 G5
Yıldız Dağları, *Turkey* 45 E11
Yıldızeli, *Turkey* 72 C7
Yiliang, *Yunnan, China* 58 D5
Yiliang, *Yunnan, China* 58 E4
Yilong, *China* 58 B6
Yimen, *China* 58 E4
Yimianpo, *China* 57 B15
Yinchuan, *China* 56 E4
Yindarlgooda, L., *Australia* 93 F3
Ying He →, *China* 56 H9
Ying Xian, *China* 56 E7
Yingcheng, *China* 59 B9
Yingde, *China* 59 E9
Yingjiang, *China* 58 E1
Yingjing, *China* 58 C4
Yingkou, *China* 57 D12
Yingshan, *Henan, China* 59 B9
Yingshan, *Hubei, China* 59 B10
Yingshan, *Sichuan, China* 58 B6
Yingshang, *China* 59 A11
Yingtan, *China* 59 C11
Yining, *China* 52 E9
Yinjiang, *China* 58 C7
Yinmabin, *Burma* 67 H19
Yiofiros →, *Greece* 49 D7
Yioúra, *Nótios Aiyaíon, Greece* 46 D6
Yioúra, *Thessalía, Greece* 46 B6
Yipinglang, *China* 58 E3
Yirba Muda, *Ethiopia* 81 F4
Yirga Alem, *Ethiopia* 81 F4
Yirol, *Sudan* 81 F3
Yirrkala, *Australia* 94 A2
Yishan, *China* 58 E7
Yishui, *China* 57 G10
Yishun, *Singapore* 65 d
Yíthion, *Greece* 46 E4
Yitong, *China* 57 C13
Yiwu, *China* 59 C13
Yixing, *China* 59 B12
Yiyang, *Henan, China* 56 G7
Yiyang, *Hunan, China* 59 C9
Yiyang, *Jiangxi, China* 59 C11
Yizhang, *China* 59 E9
Yizheng, *China* 59 A12
Yli-Kitka, *Finland* 8 C23
Ylitornio, *Finland* 8 C20
Ylivieska, *Finland* 8 D21
Yngaren, *Sweden* 11 F10
Yoakum, *U.S.A.* 113 L6
Yob ⌂, *Eritrea* 81 D4
Yobe □, *Nigeria* 83 C7
Yog Pt., *Phil.* 63 B6
Yogan, *Togo* 83 D5
Yoğuntaş, *Turkey* 45 E11
Yogyakarta, *Indonesia* 63 G14
Yogyakarta □, *Indonesia* 63 G14
Yoho △, *Canada* 102 C5
Yojoa, L. de, *Honduras* 120 D2
Yŏju, *S. Korea* 57 F14
Yok Don △, *Vietnam* 64 F6
Yokadouma, *Cameroon* 84 D2
Yokkaichi, *Japan* 55 G8
Yoko, *Cameroon* 83 D7
Yokohama, *Japan* 55 G9
Yokosuka, *Japan* 55 G9
Yokote, *Japan* 54 E10
Yola, *Nigeria* 83 D7
Yolaina, Cordillera de, *Nic.* 120 D3
Yoloten, *Turkmenistan* 71 B9
Yom →, *Thailand* 62 A2
Yonago, *Japan* 55 G6
Yonaguni-Jima, *Japan* 55 M1
Yŏnan, *N. Korea* 57 F14
Yonezawa, *Japan* 54 F10
Yong Peng, *Malaysia* 65 L4
Yong Sata, *Thailand* 65 J2
Yongamp'o, *N. Korea* 57 E13
Yong'an, *China* 59 E11
Yongcheng, *China* 56 H9
Yŏngch'ŏn, *S. Korea* 57 G15
Yongchuan, *China* 58 C5
Yongchun, *China* 59 E12
Yongde, *China* 58 E2
Yongdeng, *China* 56 F2
Yongding, *China* 59 E11
Yŏngdŏk, *S. Korea* 57 F15
Yŏngdŭngpo, *S. Korea* 57 F14
Yongfeng, *China* 59 D10
Yongfu, *China* 58 E7
Yonghe, *China* 56 F6
Yŏnghŭng, *N. Korea* 57 E14
Yongji, *China* 56 G6
Yongjia, *China* 59 C13
Yŏngju, *S. Korea* 57 F15
Yongkang, *Yunnan, China* 58 E2
Yongkang, *Zhejiang, China* 59 C13
Yongnian, *China* 56 F8
Yongning, *Guangxi Zhuangzu, China* 58 F7
Yongning, *Ningxia Huizu, China* 56 E4
Yongping, *China* 58 E2
Yongqing, *China* 56 E9
Yongren, *China* 58 D3
Yongshan, *China* 58 C4
Yongsheng, *China* 58 D3
Yongshun, *China* 58 C7
Yongtai, *China* 59 E12
Yŏngwŏl, *S. Korea* 57 F15
Yongxin = Jinggangshan, *China* 59 D10
Yongxing, *China* 59 D9
Yongxiu, *China* 59 C10
Yongzhou, *China* 59 D8
Yonibana, *S. Leone* 82 D2
Yonkers, *U.S.A.* 117 F11
Yonne □, *France* 19 E10
Yonne →, *France* 19 D9
York, *Australia* 93 F2
York, *U.K.* 14 D6
York, *Ala., U.S.A.* 113 J10
York, *Nebr., U.S.A.* 112 E6
York, *Pa., U.S.A.* 114 F7
York, C., *Australia* 94 A3
York, City of □, *U.K.* 14 D6
York, Kap, *Greenland* 4 B4
York, Vale of, *U.K.* 14 C6
York Haven, *U.S.A.* 116 F8
York Sd., *Australia* 92 C4
Yorke Pen., *Australia* 95 E2
Yorkshire Dales △, *U.K.* 14 C5
Yorkshire Wolds, *U.K.* 14 C7
Yorkton, *Canada* 103 C8
Yorkville, *U.S.A.* 110 G3
Yoro, *Honduras* 120 C2
Yoron-Jima, *Japan* 55 L4
Yorosso, *Mali* 82 C4
Yos Sudarso, Pulau = Dolak, Pulau, *Indonesia* 63 F9
Yosemite △, *U.S.A.* 110 H7
Yosemite Village, *U.S.A.* 110 H7
Yoshino-Kumano △, *Japan* 55 H8
Yoshkar Ola, *Russia* 34 B8
Yŏsu, *S. Korea* 57 G14
Yotvata, *Israel* 74 F4
You Jiang →, *China* 58 F6
You Xian, *China* 59 D9
Youbou, *Canada* 110 B2
Youghal, *Ireland* 12 E4
Youghal B., *Ireland* 12 E4
Youkounkoun, *Guinea* 82 C2
Young, *Australia* 95 E4
Young, *Canada* 103 C7
Young, *Uruguay* 126 C4
Younghusband, L., *Australia* 95 E2
Younghusband Pen., *Australia* 95 F2
Youngstown, *Canada* 103 C6
Youngstown, *N.Y., U.S.A.* 116 C5
Youngstown, *Ohio, U.S.A.* 116 E4
Youngsville, *U.S.A.* 116 E5
Youngwood, *U.S.A.* 116 F5
Youxi, *China* 59 D12
Youyang, *China* 58 C7
Youyu, *China* 56 D7
Yozgat, *Turkey* 72 C6
Ypacaraí △, *Paraguay* 126 B4
Ypané →, *Paraguay* 126 A4
Yport, *France* 18 C7
Ypres = Ieper, *Belgium* 17 D2
Yreka, *U.S.A.* 108 F2
Yssingeaux, *France* 21 C8
Ystad, *Sweden* 11 J7
Ysyk-Köl, *Kyrgyzstan* 52 E8
Ythan →, *U.K.* 13 D7
Ytterhogdal, *Sweden* 10 B8
Ytyk-Kyuyel, *Russia* 53 C14
Yu Jiang →, *China* 58 F7
Yu Shan, *Taiwan* 59 F13
Yu Xian = Yuzhou, *China* 56 G7
Yu Xian, *Hebei, China* 56 E8
Yu Xian, *Shanxi, China* 56 E7
Yuan Jiang →, *Hunan, China* 59 C8
Yuan Jiang →, *Yunnan, China* 58 F4
Yuan'an, *China* 59 B8
Yuanjiang, *Hunan, China* 59 C9
Yuanjiang, *Yunnan, China* 58 F4
Yüanli, *Taiwan* 59 E13
Yüanlin, *Taiwan* 59 F13
Yuanling, *China* 59 C8
Yuanmou, *China* 58 E3
Yuanqu, *China* 56 G6
Yuanyang, *Henan, China* 56 G7
Yuanyang, *Yunnan, China* 58 F4
Yuba →, *U.S.A.* 110 F5
Yuba City, *U.S.A.* 110 F5
Yūbari, *Japan* 54 C10
Yubdo, *Ethiopia* 81 F4
Yūbetsu, *Japan* 54 B11
Yubo, *Sudan* 81 F2
Yucatán □, *Mexico* 119 C7
Yucatán, Canal de, *Caribbean* 120 B2
Yucatán, Península de, *Mexico* 98 H11
Yucatan Basin, *Cent. Amer.* 98 H11
Yucatan Channel = Yucatán, Canal de, *Caribbean* 120 B2
Yucca, *U.S.A.* 111 L12
Yucca Valley, *U.S.A.* 111 L10
Yucheng, *China* 56 F9
Yuci, *China* 56 F7
Yudu, *China* 59 E10
Yuechi, *China* 58 B6
Yuendumu, *Australia* 92 D5
Yueqing, *China* 59 C13
Yueqing Wan, *China* 59 D13
Yuexi, *Anhui, China* 59 B11
Yuexi, *Sichuan, China* 58 C4
Yueyang, *China* 59 C9
Yugan, *China* 59 C11
Yugoslavia = Serbia & Montenegro ■, *Europe* 44 C4
Yuhuan, *China* 59 C13
Yuhuan Dao, *China* 59 C13
Yujiang, *China* 59 C11
Yukhnov, *Russia* 32 E8
Yukon →, *U.S.A.* 100 B3
Yukon Territory □, *Canada* 100 B6
Yüksekova, *Turkey* 73 D11
Yukta, *Russia* 53 C11
Yukuhashi, *Japan* 55 H5
Yulara, *Australia* 93 E5
Yule →, *Australia* 92 D2
Yuleba, *Australia* 95 D4
Yuli, *Nigeria* 83 D7
Yuli, *Taiwan* 59 F13
Yulin, *Guangxi Zhuangzu, China* 59 F8
Yülin, *Hainan, China* 65 C7
Yulin, *Shaanxi, China* 56 E5
Yuma, *Ariz., U.S.A.* 111 N12
Yuma, *Colo., U.S.A.* 112 E3
Yuma, B. de, *Dom. Rep.* 121 C6
Yumbe, *Uganda* 86 B3
Yumbi, *Dem. Rep. of the Congo* 86 C2
Yumen, *China* 60 C4
Yumurtalık, *Turkey* 72 D6
Yun Gui Gaoyuan, *China* 58 E3
Yun Ho →, *China* 57 E9
Yun Ling, *China* 58 D2
Yun Xian, *Hubei, China* 59 A8
Yun Xian, *Yunnan, China* 58 E3
Yuna, *Australia* 93 E2
Yunak, *Turkey* 72 C4
Yunan, *China* 59 F8
Yuncheng, *Henan, China* 56 G8
Yuncheng, *Shanxi, China* 56 G6
Yunfu, *China* 59 F9
Yungas, *Bolivia* 124 G5
Yungay, *Chile* 126 D1
Yunhe, *China* 59 C12
Yunkai Dashan, *China* 59 F8
Yunlin, *Taiwan* 59 F13
Yunlong, *China* 58 E2
Yunmeng, *China* 59 B9
Yunnan □, *China* 58 E4
Yunquera de Henares, *Spain* 38 E1
Yunt Dağı, *Turkey* 47 C9
Yunta, *Australia* 95 E2
Yunxi, *China* 56 H6
Yunxiao, *China* 59 F11
Yuping, *China* 58 D7
Yupyongdong, *N. Korea* 57 D15
Yuqing, *China* 58 D6
Yuraygir △, *Australia* 95 D5
Yurga, *Russia* 52 D9
Yurimaguas, *Peru* 124 E3
Yurkiyka, *Ukraine* 29 B13
Yurubí △, *Venezuela* 121 D6
Yuryev-Polskiy, *Russia* 32 D10
Yuryevets, *Russia* 34 B6
Yuscarán, *Honduras* 120 D2
Yûsef, Bahr →, *Egypt* 80 B3
Yushan, *China* 59 C12
Yushanzhen, *China* 58 C7
Yushe, *China* 56 F7
Yushu, *Jilin, China* 57 B14
Yushu, *Qinghai, China* 60 C4
Yusufeli, *Turkey* 73 B9
Yutai, *China* 56 G9
Yutian, *China* 57 E9
Yuxarı Qarabağ = Nagorno-Karabakh □, *Azerbaijan* 70 B5
Yuxi, *China* 58 E4
Yuyao, *China* 59 B13
Yuzawa, *Japan* 54 E10
Yuzha, *Russia* 34 B6
Yuzhno-Sakhalinsk, *Russia* 53 E15
Yuzhnyy □, *Russia* 35 H5
Yuzhou, *China* 56 G7
Yvelines □, *France* 19 D8
Yverdon-les-Bains, *Switz.* 25 J2
Yvetot, *France* 18 C7
Yzeure, *France* 19 F10

Z

Zaanstad, *Neths.* 17 B4
Zāb al Kabīr →, *Iraq* 70 C4
Zāb aş Şaghīr →, *Iraq* 70 C4
Žabalj, *Serbia & M.* 28 E5
Žabari, *Serbia & M.* 44 B5
Zabarjad, *Egypt* 80 C4

Zabaykalsk, Russia 53 E12
Zabki, Poland 31 F8
Ząbkowice Śląskie, Poland 31 H3
Žabljak, Serbia & M. 44 C3
Zabłudów, Poland 31 F9
Žabno, Poland 31 H7
Zābol, Iran 71 D9
Zābol □, Afghan. 66 D5
Zābolī, Iran 71 E9
Zabolotiv, Ukraine 29 B10
Zabolottya, Ukraine 31 G11
Zabré, Burkina Faso 83 C4
Zábřeh, Czech Rep. 27 B9
Zabrze, Poland 31 H5
Zabuzhzhya, Ukraine 31 G10
Zabzuga, Ghana 83 D5
Zacapa, Guatemala 120 D2
Zacapu, Mexico 118 D4
Zacatecas, Mexico 118 C4
Zacatecas □, Mexico 118 C4
Zacatecoluca, El Salv. 120 D2
Zachary, U.S.A. 113 K9
Zachodnio-Pomorskie □, Poland 30 E2
Zacoalco, Mexico 118 C4
Zacualtipán, Mexico 119 C5
Zadar, Croatia 41 D12
Zadawa, Nigeria 83 C7
Zadetkyi Kyun, Burma 65 G2
Zadonsk, Russia 33 F10
Zafarqand, Iran 71 C7
Zafora, Greece 47 E8
Zafra, Spain 37 G4
Żagań, Poland 31 G2
Zagaoua, Chad 79 E10
Žagarė, Lithuania 30 B10
Zagazig, Egypt 80 H7
Zāgheh, Iran 71 C6
Zaglivérion, Greece 44 F7
Zagnanado, Benin 83 D5
Zagorá, Greece 46 B5
Zagorje, Slovenia 41 B11
Zagórów, Poland 31 F4
Zagórz, Poland 31 J9
Zagreb, Croatia 41 C12
Zagreb ✈ (ZAG), Croatia 41 C13
Zāgros, Kūhhā-ye, Iran 71 C6
Zagros Mts. = Zāgros, Kūhhā-ye, Iran 71 C6
Žagubica, Serbia & M. 44 B5
Zaguinaso, Ivory C. 82 C3
Zagyva →, Hungary 28 C5
Zahamena ⌓, Madag. 89 B8
Zāhedān, Fārs, Iran 71 D7
Zāhedān, Sīstān va Balūchestān, Iran 71 D9
Zahlah, Lebanon 74 B4
Zahna, Germany 24 D8
Záhony, Hungary 28 B7
Zainsk, Russia 34 C11
Zaïre = Congo →, Africa 84 F2
Zaječar, Serbia & M. 44 C6
Zaka, Zimbabwe 89 C5
Zakamensk, Russia 53 D11
Zakarpatska □, Ukraine 29 B8
Zakataly = Zaqatala, Azerbaijan 35 K8
Zakháro, Greece 46 D3
Zakhodnaya Dzvina = Daugava →, Latvia 9 H21
Zākhū, Iraq 70 B4
Zákinthos, Greece 46 D2
Zákinthos □, Greece 46 D2
Zakopane, Poland 31 J6
Zakroczym, Poland 31 F7
Zákros, Greece 49 D8
Zala, Ethiopia 81 F4
Zala □, Hungary 28 D1
Zala →, Hungary 28 D2
Zalaegerszeg, Hungary 28 D1
Zalakomár, Hungary 28 D2
Zalalövő, Hungary 28 D1
Zalamea de la Serena, Spain 37 G5
Zalamea la Real, Spain 37 H4
Zalău, Romania 28 C8
Žalec, Slovenia 41 B12
Zaleshchiki = Zalishchyky, Ukraine 29 B10
Zalesye, Russia 30 D8
Zalew Wiślany, Poland 30 D6
Zalewo, Poland 30 E6
Zalingei, Sudan 79 F10
Zalishchyky, Ukraine 29 B10
Zama L., Canada 102 B5
Zambeke, Dem. Rep. of the Congo 86 B2
Zambeze →, Africa 87 F4
Zambezi = Zambeze →, Africa 87 F4
Zambezi, Zambia 85 G4
Zambezi △, Zimbabwe 87 F2
Zambezia □, Mozam. 87 F4
Zambia ■, Africa 87 F2
Zamboanga, Phil. 61 H5
Zambrów, Poland 31 F9
Zametchino, Russia 34 D6
Zamfara □, Nigeria 83 C6
Zamfara →, Nigeria 83 C5
Zamora, Mexico 118 D4
Zamora, Spain 36 D5
Zamora □, Spain 36 D5
Zamość, Poland 31 H10
Zamtang, China 58 A3
Zan, Ghana 83 D4
Záncara →, Spain 39 F1
Zandvoort, Neths. 17 B4
Zanesville, U.S.A. 116 G2
Zangābād, Iran 70 B5
Zangue →, Mozam. 87 F4
Zanjān, Iran 71 B6
Zanjān □, Iran 71 B6
Zanjān →, Iran 71 B6
Zannone, Italy 42 B6
Zante = Zákinthos, Greece 46 D2
Zanthus, Australia 93 F3
Zanzibar, Tanzania 86 D4
Zaouiet El-Kala = Bordj Omar Driss, Algeria 78 C7
Zaouiet Reggâne, Algeria 78 C6
Zaoyang, China 59 A9
Zaozhuang, China 57 G9
Zap Suyu = Zāb al Kabīr →, Iraq 70 C4
Zapadna Morava →, Serbia & M. 44 C5
Zapadnaya Dvina = Daugava →, Latvia 9 H21
Zapadnaya Dvina, Russia 32 D7
Západné Beskydy, Europe 27 B12
Zapadni Rodopi, Bulgaria 44 E7
Západočeský □, Czech Rep. 26 B6
Zapala, Argentina 128 D2
Zapaleri, Cerro, Bolivia 126 A2
Zapata, U.S.A. 113 M5
Zapatón →, Spain 37 F4
Zaporizhzhya, Ukraine 33 J8
Zaporozhye = Zaporizhzhya, Ukraine 33 J8
Zaqatala, Azerbaijan 35 K8
Zara, Turkey 70 B3
Zaragoza, Coahuila, Mexico 118 B4
Zaragoza, Nuevo León, Mexico 119 C5
Zaragoza, Spain 38 D4
Zaragoza □, Spain 38 D4
Zarand, Kermān, Iran 71 D8
Zarand, Markazī, Iran 71 C6
Zărandului, Munţii, Romania 28 D7
Zaranj, Afghan. 66 D2
Zarasai, Lithuania 9 J22
Zárate, Argentina 126 C4
Zarautz, Spain 38 B2
Zaraysk, Russia 32 E10
Zard, Kūh-e, Iran 71 C6
Zāreh, Iran 71 C6
Zari, Nigeria 83 C7
Zaria, Nigeria 83 C6
Żarki, Poland 31 H6
Zárkon, Greece 46 B4
Zarneh, Iran 70 C5
Zărneşti, Romania 29 E10
Zarós, Greece 49 D6
Żarów, Poland 31 H3
Zarqā', Nahr az →, Jordan 74 C4
Zarrīn, Iran 71 C7
Zaruma, Ecuador 124 D3
Żary, Poland 31 G2
Zarza de Granadilla, Spain 36 E4
Zarzis, Tunisia 79 B8
Zas, Spain 36 B2
Zaskar →, India 69 B7
Zaskar Mts., India 69 C7
Zastavna, Ukraine 29 B10
Zastron, S. Africa 88 E4
Žatec, Czech Rep. 26 A6
Zaterechnyy, Russia 35 H7
Zator, Poland 31 J6
Zatyshshya, Ukraine 29 C14
Zavala, Bos.-H. 44 D1
Zavāreh, Iran 71 C7
Zave, Zimbabwe 89 B5
Zavetnoye, Russia 35 G6
Zavidovići, Bos.-H. 28 F3
Zavitinsk, Russia 53 D13
Zavodovski, I., Antarctica 5 B1
Zavolzhsk, Russia 34 B6
Zavolzhye, Russia 34 B6
Zawadzkie, Poland 31 H5
Zawichost, Poland 31 H8
Zawidów, Poland 31 G2
Zawiercie, Poland 31 H6
Zāwiyat al Bayḍā = Al Bayḍā, Libya 79 B10
Zâwyet Shammas, Egypt 80 A2
Zâwyet Um el Rakham, Egypt 80 A2
Zâwyet Ungeîla, Egypt 80 A2
Zāyā, Iraq 70 C5
Zāyandeh →, Iran 71 C7
Zaysan, Kazakhstan 52 E9
Zaysan, Oz., Kazakhstan 52 E9
Zayü, China 58 C1
Zazafotsy, Madag. 89 C8
Zázrivá, Slovak Rep. 27 B12
Zbarazh, Ukraine 33 H3
Zbąszyń, Poland 31 F2
Zbąszynek, Poland 31 F2
Zblewo, Poland 30 E5
Zbruch → 29 B11
Žďár nad Sázavou, Czech Rep. 26 B8
Zdolbuniv, Ukraine 33 G4
Ždrelo, Serbia & M. 44 B5
Zduńska Wola, Poland 31 G5
Zduny, Poland 31 G4
Zeballos, Canada 102 D3
Zebediela, S. Africa 89 C4
Zebila, Ghana 83 C4
Zeebrugge, Belgium 17 C3
Zeehan, Australia 95 G4
Zeeland □, Neths. 17 C3
Zeerust, S. Africa 88 D4
Zefat, Israel 74 C4
Zege, Ethiopia 81 E4
Zeggerene, Iracher, Mali 83 B5
Zégoua, Mali 82 C3
Zehdenick, Germany 24 C9
Zeil, Mt., Australia 92 D5
Zeila, Somali Rep. 75 E3
Zeist, Neths. 17 B5
Zeitz, Germany 24 D8
Żelechów, Poland 31 G8
Zelena, Ukraine 29 B9
Zelengora, Bos.-H. 44 C2
Zelenodolsk, Russia 34 C9
Zelenogorsk, Russia 32 B5
Zelenograd, Russia 32 D9
Zelenogradsk, Russia 9 J19
Zelenokumsk, Russia 35 H6
Železná Ruda, Czech Rep. 26 B6
Železnik, Serbia & M. 44 B4
Zelienople, U.S.A. 116 F4
Želiezovce, Slovak Rep. 27 C11
Zelina, Croatia 41 C13
Zell, Baden-W., Germany 25 H3
Zell, Rhld-Pfz., Germany 25 E3
Zell am See, Austria 26 D5
Zella-Mehlis, Germany 24 E6
Zelów, Poland 31 G6
Zeltweg, Austria 26 D7
Žemaitijos △, Lithuania 30 B8
Zémio, C.A.R. 86 A2
Zempléni-hegység, Hungary 28 B6
Zemplínska šírava, Slovak Rep. 27 C15
Zempoala, Mexico 119 D5
Zemun, Serbia & M. 44 B4
Zengbé, Cameroon 83 D7
Zengcheng, China 59 F9
Zenica, Bos.-H. 28 F2
Žepče, Bos.-H. 28 F3
Zeraf, Bahr ez →, Sudan 81 F3
Zerbst, Germany 24 D8
Żerków, Poland 31 F4
Zermatt, Switz. 25 J3
Zernez, Switz. 25 J6
Zernograd, Russia 35 G5
Zerqan, Albania 44 E4
Zestaponi, Georgia 35 J6
Zetel, Germany 24 B3
Zeulenroda, Germany 24 E7
Zeven, Germany 24 B5
Zevenaar, Neths. 17 C6
Zévio, Italy 40 C8
Zeya, Russia 53 D13
Zeya →, Russia 53 D13
Zeytinbaği, Turkey 45 F12
Zeytindağ, Turkey 47 C9
Zghartā, Lebanon 74 A4
Zgierz, Poland 31 G6
Zgorzelec, Poland 31 G2
Zguriţa, Moldova 29 B13
Zhabinka, Belarus 31 F11
Zhabokrych, Ukraine 29 B13
Zhailma, Kazakhstan 52 D7
Zhambyl = Taraz, Kazakhstan 52 E8
Zhangaly, Kazakhstan 35 G10
Zhangaqazaly, Kazakhstan 52 E7
Zhangbei, China 56 D8
Zhangguangcai Ling, China 57 B15
Zhangjiakou, China 56 D8
Zhangping, China 59 E11
Zhangpu, China 59 E11
Zhangshu, China 59 C10
Zhangwu, China 57 C12
Zhangye, China 60 C5
Zhangzhou, China 59 E11
Zhanhua, China 57 F10
Zhanjiang, China 59 G8
Zhannetty, Ostrov, Russia 53 B16
Zhanyi, China 58 E4
Zhanyu, China 57 B12
Zhao Xian, China 56 F8
Zhao'an, China 59 F11
Zhaocheng, China 56 F6
Zhaojue, China 58 C4
Zhaoping, China 59 E8
Zhaoqing, China 59 F9
Zhaotong, China 58 D4
Zhaoyuan, Heilongjiang, China 57 B13
Zhaoyuan, Shandong, China 57 F11
Zharkovskiy, Russia 32 E7
Zhashkiv, Ukraine 33 H6
Zhashui, China 56 H5
Zhayyq →, Kazakhstan 52 E6
Zhdanov = Mariupol, Ukraine 33 J9
Zhecheng, China 56 G8
Zhegao, China 59 B11
Zhejiang □, China 59 C13
Zheleznodorozhnyy, Russia 30 D8
Zheleznogorsk, Russia 33 F8
Zheleznogorsk-Ilimskiy, Russia 53 D11
Zheltyye Vody = Zhovti Vody, Ukraine 33 H7
Zhen'an, China 56 H5
Zhenba, China 58 A6
Zhenfeng, China 58 E5
Zheng'an, China 58 C6
Zhengding, China 56 E8
Zhenghe, China 59 D12
Zhengyang, China 59 A10
Zhengyangguan, China 59 A11
Zhengzhou, China 56 G7
Zhenhai, China 59 C13
Zhenjiang, China 59 A12
Zhenkang, China 58 F2
Zhenlai, China 57 B12
Zhenning, China 58 D5
Zhenping, Henan, China 56 H7
Zhenping, Shaanxi, China 58 B7
Zhenxiong, China 58 D5
Zhenyuan, Gansu, China 56 G4
Zhenyuan, Guizhou, China 58 D7
Zherdevka, Russia 34 E5
Zherebkove, Ukraine 29 C14
Zherong, China 59 D12
Zhetiqara, Kazakhstan 52 D7
Zhezqazghan, Kazakhstan 52 E7
Zhicheng, China 59 B8
Zhidan, China 56 F5
Zhigansk, Russia 53 C13
Zhigulevsk, Russia 34 D9
Zhijiang, Hubei, China 59 B8
Zhijiang, Hunan, China 58 D7
Zhijin, China 58 D5
Zhilinda, Russia 53 C12
Zhilino, Russia 30 D8
Zhirnovsk, Russia 34 E7
Zhitomir = Zhytomyr, Ukraine 33 G5
Zhizdra, Russia 32 F8
Zhlobin, Belarus 33 F6
Zhmerinka = Zhmerynka, Ukraine 33 H5
Zhmerynka, Ukraine 33 H5
Zhob, Pakistan 68 D3
Zhob →, Pakistan 68 C3
Zhodino = Zhodzina, Belarus 32 E5
Zhodzina, Belarus 32 E5
Zhokhova, Ostrov, Russia 53 B16
Zhongdian, China 58 D2
Zhongdong, China 58 F6
Zhongdu, China 58 E7
Zhongning, China 56 F3
Zhongshan, Antarctica 5 C6
Zhongshan, Guangdong, China 59 F9
Zhongshan, Guangxi Zhuangzu, China 59 E8
Zhongtiao Shan, China 56 G6
Zhongwei, China 56 F3
Zhongxiang, China 59 B9
Zhongyang, China 56 F6
Zhorany, Ukraine 31 G10
Zhoucun, China 57 F9
Zhouning, China 59 D12
Zhoushan, China 59 B14
Zhoushan Dao, China 59 C14
Zhouzhi, China 56 G5
Zhovti Vody, Ukraine 33 H7
Zhovtneve, Ukraine 31 H11
Zhovtneve, Ukraine 33 J7
Zhovtnevoye = Zhovtneve, Ukraine 33 J7
Zhu Jiang →, China 59 F9
Zhuanghe, China 57 E12
Zhucheng, China 57 G10
Zhugqu, China 56 H3
Zhuhai, China 59 F9
Zhuji, China 59 C13
Zhukovka, Russia 32 F7
Zhumadian, China 56 H8
Zhuo Xian = Zhuozhou, China 56 E8
Zhuolu, China 56 D8
Zhuozhou, China 56 E8
Zhuozi, China 56 D7
Zhushan, China 59 A8
Zhuxi, China 58 A7
Zhuzhou, China 59 D9
Zhvanets, Ukraine 29 B11
Zhytomyr, Ukraine 33 G5
Zi Shui →, China 59 C9
Žiar nad Hronom, Slovak Rep. 27 C11
Zīārān, Iran 71 B6
Ziarat, Pakistan 68 D2
Zibo, China 57 F10
Zichang, China 56 F5
Zidarovo, Bulgaria 45 D11
Zidi = Wandhari, Pakistan 68 F2
Ziębice, Poland 31 H4
Zielona Góra, Poland 31 G2
Zierikzee, Neths. 17 C3
Ziesar, Germany 24 C8
Zifta, Egypt 80 H7
Zigey, Chad 79 F9
Zigong, China 58 C5
Ziguinchor, Senegal 82 C1
Zihuatanejo, Mexico 118 D4
Zijin, China 59 F10
Zile, Turkey 72 B6
Žilina, Slovak Rep. 27 B11
Žilinský □, Slovak Rep. 27 B12
Zillah, Libya 79 C9
Zillertaler Alpen, Austria 26 D4
Zima, Russia 53 D11
Zimapán, Mexico 119 C5
Zimba, Zambia 87 F2
Zimbabwe, Zimbabwe 87 G3
Zimbabwe ■, Africa 87 F3
Zimi, S. Leone 82 D2
Zimnicea, Romania 29 G10
Zimovniki, Russia 35 G6
Zinave △, Mozam. 89 C5
Zinder, Niger 83 C6
Zinga, Tanzania 87 D4
Zingaro ⌓, Italy 42 D5
Zingst, Germany 24 A8
Ziniaré, Burkina Faso 83 C4
Zinnowitz, Germany 24 A9
Zion △, U.S.A. 109 H7
Zirbitzkogel, Austria 26 D7
Zirc, Hungary 28 C2
Žiri, Slovenia 41 B11
Žirje, Croatia 41 E12
Zirl, Austria 26 D4
Zirndorf, Germany 25 F6
Ziros, Greece 49 D8
Zirreh, Gowd-e, Afghan. 66 E3
Zisterdorf, Austria 27 C9
Zitácuaro, Mexico 118 D4
Žitava →, Slovak Rep. 27 C11
Žitište, Serbia & M. 28 E5
Zitong, China 58 B5
Zítsa, Greece 46 B2
Zittau, Germany 24 E10
Zitundo, Mozam. 89 D5
Živinice, Bos.-H. 28 F3
Ziwa Maghariba = Kagera □, Tanzania 86 C3
Ziway, L., Ethiopia 81 F4
Zixi, China 59 D11
Zixing, China 59 E9
Ziyang, Shaanxi, China 56 H5
Ziyang, Sichuan, China 58 B5
Ziyuan, China 59 D8
Ziyun, China 58 E6
Zizhong, China 58 C5
Zlarin, Croatia 41 E12
Zlatar, Croatia 41 B13
Zlatar, Serbia & M. 44 C3
Zlataritsa, Bulgaria 45 C9
Zlaté Moravce, Slovak Rep. 27 C11
Zlatibor, Serbia & M. 44 C3
Zlatitsa, Bulgaria 45 D8
Zlatna, Romania 29 D8
Zlatna Panega, Bulgaria 45 C8
Zlatni Pyasŭtsi, Bulgaria 45 C12
Zlatograd, Bulgaria 45 E9
Zlatoust, Russia 52 D6
Zletovo, Macedonia 44 E6
Zlín, Czech Rep. 27 B10
Zlínský □, Czech Rep. 27 B10
Złocieniec, Poland 30 E3
Złoczew, Poland 31 G5
Zlot, Serbia & M. 44 B5
Złotoryja, Poland 31 G2
Złotów, Poland 30 E4
Zmeinogorsk, Kazakhstan 52 D9
Żmigród, Poland 31 G3
Zmiyev, Ukraine 33 H9
Znamenka = Znamyanka, Ukraine 33 H7
Znamensk, Russia 30 D8
Znamyanka, Ukraine 33 H7
Żnin, Poland 31 F4
Znojmo, Czech Rep. 26 C9
Zobeyrī, Iran 70 C5
Zobia, Dem. Rep. of the Congo 86 B2
Zoetermeer, Neths. 17 B4
Zogang, China 58 C1
Zogno, Italy 40 C6
Zogqên, China 58 A2
Zolochev = Zolochiv, Ukraine 33 H3
Zolochiv, Ukraine 33 H3
Zolotonosha, Ukraine 33 H7
Zolotyy Potik, Ukraine 29 B10
Zomba, Malawi 87 F4
Zongo, Dem. Rep. of the Congo 84 D3
Zonguldak, Turkey 72 B4
Zongyang, China 59 B11
Zonqor Pt., Malta 49 D2
Zonza, France 21 G13
Zorgo, Burkina Faso 83 C4
Zorita, Spain 37 F5
Zorleni, Romania 29 D12
Zornitsa, Bulgaria 45 D10
Zorritos, Peru 124 D2
Żory, Poland 31 H5
Zorzor, Liberia 82 D3
Zossen, Germany 24 C9
Zou Xiang, China 56 G9
Zouan-Hounien, Ivory C. 82 D3
Zouar, Chad 79 D9
Zouérate = Zouîrât, Mauritania 78 D3
Zouîrât, Mauritania 78 D3
Zourika, Niger 83 B6
Zourma, Burkina Faso 83 C4
Zoutkamp, Neths. 17 A6
Zrenjanin, Serbia & M. 28 E5
Zuarungu, Ghana 83 C4
Zuba, Nigeria 83 D6
Zubayr, Yemen 81 D5
Zubtsov, Russia 32 D8
Zuénoula, Ivory C. 82 D3
Zuera, Spain 38 D4
Zufār, Oman 75 D5
Zug □, Switz. 25 H4
Zugdidi, Georgia 35 J5
Zugersee, Switz. 25 H4
Zugspitze, Germany 25 H6
Zuid-Holland □, Neths. 17 C4
Zuidbeveland, Neths. 17 C3
Zuidhorn, Neths. 17 A6
Zújar, Spain 37 H8
Zújar →, Spain 37 G5
Żukowo, Poland 30 D5
Zula, Eritrea 81 D4
Zülpich, Germany 24 E2
Zumaia, Spain 38 B2
Zumárraga, Spain 38 B2
Zumbo, Mozam. 87 F3
Zummo, Nigeria 83 D7
Zumpango, Mexico 119 D5
Zungeru, Nigeria 83 D6
Zunhua, China 57 D9
Zuni, U.S.A. 109 J9
Zunyi, China 58 D6
Zuo Jiang →, China 58 F6
Zuozhou, China 58 F6
Županja, Croatia 28 E3
Žur, Serbia & M. 44 D4
Zurbātiyah, Iraq 70 C5
Zürich, Switz. 25 H4
Zürich □, Switz. 25 H4
Zürichsee, Switz. 25 H4
Żuromin, Poland 31 E6
Žut, Croatia 41 E12
Zutphen, Neths. 17 B6
Zuurberg △, S. Africa 88 E4
Zuwārah, Libya 79 B8
Zūzan, Iran 71 C8
Žužemberk, Slovenia 41 C11
Zvenigorodka = Zvenyhorodka, Ukraine 33 H6
Zvenyhorodka, Ukraine 33 H6
Zverinogolovskoye, Russia 52 D7
Zvezdets, Bulgaria 45 D11
Zvishavane, Zimbabwe 87 G3
Zvolen, Slovak Rep. 27 C12
Zvonce, Serbia & M. 44 D6
Zvornik, Bos.-H. 28 F4
Zwedru = Tchien, Liberia 82 D3
Zweibrücken, Germany 25 F3
Zwelitsha, S. Africa 85 L5
Zwenkau, Germany 24 D8
Zwettl, Austria 26 C8
Zwickau, Germany 24 E8
Zwierzyniec, Poland 31 H9
Zwiesel, Germany 25 F9
Zwoleń, Poland 31 G8
Zwolle, Neths. 17 B6
Zwolle, U.S.A. 113 K8
Zychlin, Poland 31 F6
Zyrardów, Poland 31 F7
Zyryan, Kazakhstan 52 E9
Zyryanka, Russia 53 C16
Zyryanovsk = Zyryan, Kazakhstan 52 E9
Żywiec, Poland 31 J6
Zyyi, Cyprus 49 E12

KEY TO EUROPEAN MAP PAGES

Large scale maps
(>1:2 500 000)

Medium scale maps
(1:2 800 000 – 1:9 900 000)

Small scale maps
(<1:10 000 000)

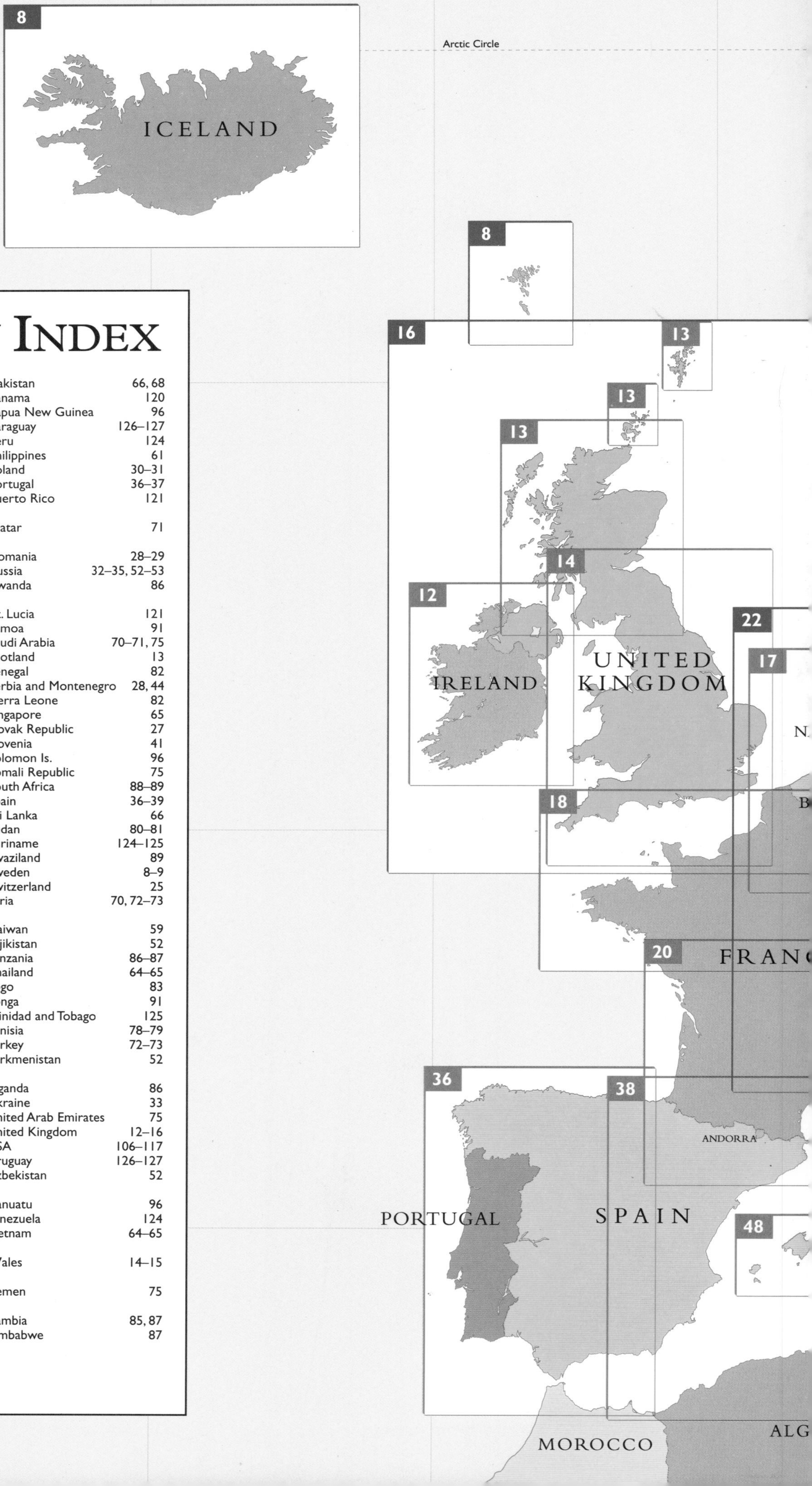

World Country Index

Afghanistan 66
Albania 44
Algeria 78
Angola 84–85
Argentina 126, 128
Armenia 73
Australia 92–95
Austria 26–27
Azerbaijan 73

Bahamas 120–121
Bahrain 71
Bangladesh 67
Barbados 121
Belarus 32–33
Belgium 17
Belize 120
Benin 83
Bhutan 67
Bolivia 124
Bosnia-Herzegovina 41, 44
Botswana 88
Brazil 124–125, 127
Brunei 62
Bulgaria 44–45
Burkina Faso 82–83
Burma (Myanmar) 67
Burundi 86

Cambodia 64–65
Canary Is. 48
Cameroon 83, 84
Canada 100–105
Central African Republic 84
Chad 79
Chile 126–127, 128
China 56–60
Colombia 124
Congo 84
Congo, Dem. Rep. of the 84–85, 86–87
Costa Rica 120
Croatia 41
Cuba 120–121
Cyprus 49
Czech Republic 26–27

Denmark 11
Djibouti 81
Dominican Republic 121

East Timor 63
Ecuador 124
Egypt 80
El Salvador 120
England 14–15
Equatorial Guinea 84
Eritrea 80–81
Estonia 32
Ethiopia 75, 81

Fiji 91
Finland 8–9
France 18–21
French Guiana 125

Gabon 84
Gambia 82
Georgia 35
Germany 24–25
Ghana 82–83
Greece 44–47
Greenland 4
Guadeloupe 120
Guatemala 120
Guinea 82
Guinea-Bissau 82
Guyana 124

Haiti 121
Honduras 120
Hungary 28

Iceland 8
India 66–69
Indonesia 62–63
Iran 70–71, 73
Iraq 70–71, 73
Irish Republic 12
Israel 74
Italy 40–43
Ivory Coast 82

Jamaica 120
Japan 54–55
Jordan 74

Kazakhstan 52
Kenya 86
Korea, North 57
Korea, South 57
Kuwait 70–71
Kyrgyzstan 52

Laos 64
Latvia 32
Lebanon 74
Lesotho 89
Liberia 82
Libya 79
Lithuania 32
Luxembourg 17

Macedonia 44
Madagascar 89
Malawi 87
Malaysia 62–63, 65
Mali 78, 82–83
Malta 49
Martinique 120
Mauritania 78, 82
Mexico 118–119
Moldova 29
Mongolia 60
Morocco 78
Mozambique 87, 89

Namibia 88
Nepal 69
Netherlands 17
New Zealand 91
Nicaragua 120
Niger 78–79, 83
Nigeria 83
Northern Ireland 12
Norway 8–9

Oman 75

Pakistan 66, 68
Panama 120
Papua New Guinea 96
Paraguay 126–127
Peru 124
Philippines 61
Poland 30–31
Portugal 36–37
Puerto Rico 121

Qatar 71

Romania 28–29
Russia 32–35, 52–53
Rwanda 86

St. Lucia 121
Samoa 91
Saudi Arabia 70–71, 75
Scotland 13
Senegal 82
Serbia and Montenegro 28, 44
Sierra Leone 82
Singapore 65
Slovak Republic 27
Slovenia 41
Solomon Is. 96
Somali Republic 75
South Africa 88–89
Spain 36–39
Sri Lanka 66
Sudan 80–81
Suriname 124–125
Swaziland 89
Sweden 8–9
Switzerland 25
Syria 70, 72–73

Taiwan 59
Tajikistan 52
Tanzania 86–87
Thailand 64–65
Togo 83
Tonga 91
Trinidad and Tobago 125
Tunisia 78–79
Turkey 72–73
Turkmenistan 52

Uganda 86
Ukraine 33
United Arab Emirates 75
United Kingdom 12–16
USA 106–117
Uruguay 126–127
Uzbekistan 52

Vanuatu 96
Venezuela 124
Vietnam 64–65

Wales 14–15

Yemen 75

Zambia 85, 87
Zimbabwe 87